Dictionary of Jesus and the Gospels

Editors:

Joel B. Green

Scot McKnight

Consulting Editor:

I. Howard Marshall

InterVarsity Press

DOWNERS GROVE, ILLINOIS 60515
LEICESTER, ENGLAND

InterVarsity Press
P.O. Box 1400, Downers Grove, IL 60515, USA
38 De Montfort Street, Leicester LE1 7GP, England

© 1992 by InterVarsity Christian Fellowship of the U.S.A.

All rights reserved. No part of this publication may be reproduced, stored in a retrieval system or transmitted in any form or by any means, electronic, mechanical, photocopying, recording or otherwise, without the prior permission of InterVarsity Press.

InterVarsity Press, U.S.A., is the book-publishing division of InterVarsity Christian Fellowship, a student movement active on campus at hundreds of universities, colleges and schools of nursing in the United States of America, and a member movement of the International Fellowship of Evangelical Students. For information about local and regional activities, write Public Relations Dept., InterVarsity Christian Fellowship, 6400 Schroeder Rd., P.O. Box 7895, Madison, WI 53707-7895.

Inter-Varsity Press, England, is the book-publishing division of the Universities and Colleges Christian Fellowship (formerly the Inter-Varsity Fellowship), a student movement linking Christian Unions in universities and colleges throughout the United Kingdom and the Republic of Ireland, and a member movement of the International Fellowship of Evangelical Students. For information about local and national activities write to UCCF, 38 De Montfort Street, Leicester LE1 7GP.

All Scripture quotations, unless otherwise indicated, are the authors' own translations. Those identified NIV are taken from the Holy Bible, New International Version, © 1973, 1978, 1984, by the International Bible Society, and used by permission of Zondervan Bible Publishers. All rights reserved. Those identified RSV are from the Revised Standard Version of the Bible, copyright 1946, 1952, 1971 by the Division of Christian Education of the National Council of the Churches of Christ in the U.S.A., and used by permission. Those identified NRSV are from the New Revised Standard Version of the Bible, copyright 1989 by the Division of Christian Education of the National Council of the Churches of Christ in the U.S.A., and used by permission.

ISBN 0-8308-1777-8
UK ISBN 0-85110-646-3

Printed in the United States of America. ∞

Library of Congress Cataloging-in-Publication Data

Dictionary of Jesus and the Gospels/editors, Joel B. Green, Scot
  McKnight; consulting editor, I. Howard Marshall.
    p.   cm.
  Includes bibliographical references and index.
  ISBN 0-8308-1777-8
  1. Bible. N.T. Gospels—Criticism, interpretation, etc.—
Dictionaries. I. Green, Joel B., 1956-   II. McKnight, Scot.
III. Marshall, I. Howard.
BS2555.2.D53   1992
226'.03—dc20   91-32382
                                CIP

British Library Cataloguing in Publication Data

A catalogue record for this book is available from the British Library.

19	18	17	15	14	13	12	11	10	9	8	7	6
06	05	04	03	02	01	00	99	98				

InterVarsity Press

Executive Director
Kenneth DeRuiter

Editorial Staff

Editorial Director
Andrew T. Le Peau

Reference Book Editor and Project Editor
Daniel G. Reid, Ph.D.

Managing Editor
James Hoover

Editorial Assistants
Dorothy Bowman, Kathleen Carlson,
Gloria Duncan, Rhonda Skinner
Cynthia Bunch, Cynthia Reid

Proofreader
Robin Sheffield

Production Staff

Production Manager
Nancy Fox

Production Coordinator
Deborah Keiser

Design
Kathy Lay Burrows

Design Assistant
Amy Munroe

Typesetters
Marjorie Sire, Gail Munroe

Programming Consultant
Richard E. Ecker

Contents

Preface

We live in the Age of Information. This is no less true today for students of the New Testament who are inundated with a virtual flood of research on Jesus and the Gospels. How can those in professional ministry, leaders in local churches and other Christian organizations, seminarians, even academic scholars, stay abreast of fresh studies of Jesus and the Gospels?

In the last thirty years new methodologies and approaches have been championed, some becoming commonplace. Older viewpoints have been transformed, some overturned, others confirmed. Unfortunately, while these new studies have helped us appreciate better the perspectives of the Gospel Evangelists and brought into sharper relief the challenge of the life and message of Jesus, they have also grown more numerous and technical. How can the fruit of vital study of Jesus and the Gospels in recent years reach the front lines of ministry and life together in our communities of faith?

At the same time, New Testament scholarship informed by classical Christian faith has more and more entered the discourse on Jesus and the Gospels. A growing body of evangelical scholars have begun engaging the academic community in stimulating ways. Regrettably, while the general populace on both sides of the Atlantic have been exposed to the sensationalism of such projects as the Jesus Seminar and *Jesus: The Evidence,* no major undertaking has made available to the larger church the representative scholarship of students of Jesus and the Gospels which is both critically responsible and theologically evangelical.

The *Dictionary of Jesus and the Gospels* has been prepared to meet such needs as these. For students it provides introductory discussions and comprehensive surveys. For pastors and teachers it provides reliable and readable information. For theologians and biblical scholars it provides up-to-date reviews.

Because of its narrow focus on Jesus and the Gospels, the *Dictionary* consists of fewer entries than other one-volume dictionaries. In selecting topics it was decided that subjects that would be handled adequately in a one-volume Bible dictionary would not be included in the *Dictionary of Jesus and the Gospels.* The goal was to provide greater depth of coverage and concentration than would normally be available.

Articles in the *Dictionary of Jesus and the Gospels* treat questions arising from the Gospels themselves, longstanding traditions of interpretation of Jesus and the Gospels, significant background issues, and the range of methodological approaches used in Gospels study today. These essays concentrate on Jesus and the Gospels, limiting their discussions to the needs of those who study, teach and expound the Gospels. To be both evangelical and critical at the same time has been the object of the *Dictionary*. Its contributors, all representative of contemporary evangelicalism, have attempted to portray a range of interpretive alternatives in their discussions as well as to be faithful to the Gospels as Scripture.

We pray that the *Dictionary of Jesus and the Gospels* will be found useful to those preparing for and engaged in Christian ministry in all its forms—from the small group to the lecture hall, from the marketplace to the seminary, from the local church to the department of religious studies, and beyond.

Joel B. Green
Scot McKnight
I. Howard Marshall

How to Use This Dictionary

Abbreviations
Comprehensive tables of abbreviations for general matters as well as for scholarly, biblical and ancient literature may be found on pages xiii-xxi.

Authorship of Articles
The authors of articles are indicated by their first initials and last name at the end of each article. A full list of contributors may be found on pages xxiii-xxv, in alphabetical order of last name.

Bibliographies
A bibliography has been appended to each article. The bibliographies include works cited in the articles and other significant related works. All bibliographical entries are listed in alphabetical order by the author's last name.

Full bibliographical information has been supplied whenever possible. Abbreviations used in the bibliographies appear in the tables of abbreviations.

Bibliographies for each of the four Gospels include a special listing of commentaries on the respective Gospel.

Cross-references
The *Dictionary* has been extensively cross-referenced in order to aid readers in making the most of material appearing throughout the volume. Four types of cross-referencing will be found:

1. One-line entries appearing in alphabetical order throughout the *Dictionary* direct readers to articles where a topic is discussed:

Abba. *See* God; Prayer; Son of God.

2. An asterisk after a single word in the body of an article, typically at its first occurrence, indicates that an article by that title appears in the *Dictionary*. For example, "Christ"* directs the reader to an article entitled **Christ.**

3. A cross-reference appearing within parentheses in the body of an article also directs the reader to an article by that title. For example, "(*see* Kingdom of God)" directs the reader to an article entitled **Kingdom of God.** Such cross-references are used either to prevent the confusion an asterisk might introduce (i.e.,

"kingdom of God*" could refer to either an article on "God" or "Kingdom of God") or to direct the reader's attention to an article of related interest.

4. Cross-references have been appended to the end of articles, immediately preceding the bibliography, to direct readers to articles significantly related to the subject:

See also SON OF DAVID; SON OF GOD; SON OF MAN.

Indexes

Since most of the *Dictionary* articles cover broad topics in some depth, the subject index is intended to assist readers in finding relevant information on narrower topics that might, for instance, appear in a standard Bible dictionary. For example, while there is no article entitled "Adam," the subject index will direct the reader to pages where Adam is discussed in the articles on "Genealogy," "Temptation of Jesus" and "Typology."

Similarly, an index of Gospel citations is provided to assist readers in gaining access to information related to various topics.

Finally, an index of the articles in the dictionary allows readers to quickly review the breadth of topics covered and select the ones most apt to serve their interests or needs.

Transliteration

Hebrew and Greek words have been transliterated according to a system set out on page xxii. Greek verbs appear in their lexical form (rather than infinitive) in order to assist those with little or no knowledge of the language in using other reference works.

Abbreviations

General Abbreviations

κτλ	καὶ τὰ λοιπά, and the remainder	MT	Masoretic Text (of the Old Testament)
2d ed.	second edition	n.d.	no date
3d ed.	third edition	n.s.	new series
A	Codex Alexandrinus	NT	New Testament
B	Codex Vaticanus	o.s.	old series
C	Codex Ephraemi Syri	OT	Old Testament
c.	circa, about (with dates); column	p. or pp.	page or pages
cent.	century	*pace*	with due respect to, but differing from
cf.	*confer*, compare	par.	parallel passage in another/other Gospel(s)
chap(s).	chapter(s)		
D	Codex Bezae	passim	throughout
DSS	Dead Sea Scrolls	pl.	plural
e.g.	*exempli gratia,* for example	Q	Quelle ("sayings" source for Synoptic Gospels)
ed.	edition; editor(s), edited by		
esp.	especially	repr.	reprint
ET	English translation	rev.	revised
EVV	English versions of the Bible	sy	Syriac
Gk	Greek	Tg.	Targum
Heb	Hebrew	v. or vv.	verse or verses
i.e.	*id est,* that is	vol.	volume
km.	kilometer	x	times (2 x = two times, etc.)
LXX	Septuagint	§ or §§	section or paragraph number(s) (usually indicating Loeb Classical Library numbering system for Josephus)
mg.	margin		
MS or MSS	manuscript or manuscripts		

Translations of the Bible

ASV	American Standard Version (1901)	NEB	New English Bible
AV	Authorized Version (= KJV)	NIV	New International Version
JB	Jerusalem Bible	NRSV	New Revised Standard Version
KJV	King James Version (= AV)	REB	Revised English Bible
NASB	New American Standard Bible	RV	Revised Version (1881-85)

Books of the Bible

Old Testament	Job	Mic	1-2 Cor
Gen	Ps	Nahum	Gal
Ex	Prov	Hab	Eph
Lev	Eccles	Zeph	Phil
Num	Song	Hag	Col
Deut	Is	Zech	1-2 Thess
Josh	Jer	Mal	1-2 Tim
Judg	Lam		Tit
Ruth	Ezek	New Testament	Philem
1-2 Sam	Dan	Mt	Heb
1-2 Kings	Hos	Mk	Jas
1-2 Chron	Joel	Lk	1-2 Pet
Ezra	Amos	Jn	1-2-3 Jn
Neh	Obad	Acts	Jude
Esther	Jon	Rom	Rev

The Apocrypha and Septuagint

1-2-3-4 Kgdms	1-2-3-4 Kingdoms	1-2-3-4 Macc	1-2-3-4 Maccabees
Add Esth	Additions to Esther	Pr Azar	Prayer of Azariah
Bar	Baruch	Pr Man	Prayer of Manasseh
Bel	Bel and the Dragon	Sir	Sirach (or Ecclesiasticus)
1-2 Esdr	1-2 Esdras	Sus	Susanna
4 Ezra	4 Ezra	Tob	Tobit
Jdt	Judith	Wis	Wisdom of Solomon
Ep Jer	Epistle of Jeremiah		

The Old Testament Pseudepigrapha

Adam and Eve	Life of Adam and Eve	Pss. Sol.	Psalms of Solomon
Ahiq.	Ahiqar	Pseud.-Phoc.	Pseudo-Phocylides
Apoc. Abr.	Apocalypse of Abraham	Sib. Or.	Sibylline Oracles
2-3 Apoc. Bar.	Syriac, Greek Apocalypse of Baruch	T. 12 Patr.	Testament of the Twelve Patriarchs
Asc. Isa.	Ascension of Isaiah	T. Reub.	Testament of Reuben
Apoc. Mos.	Apocalypse of Moses	T. Sim.	Testament of Simeon
As. Mos.	Assumption of Moses (or Testament of Moses)	T. Levi	Testament of Levi
Apoc. Elijah	Apocalypse of Elijah	T. Judah	Testament of Judah
Apoc. Zeph.	Apocalypse of Zephaniah	T. Iss.	Testament of Issachar
Bib. Ant.	Biblical Antiquities of Pseudo-Philo	T. Zeb.	Testament of Zebulon
1-2-3 Enoch	Ethiopic, Slavonic, Hebrew Enoch	T. Dan.	Testament of Dan
Ep. Arist.	Epistle of Aristeas	T. Naph.	Testament of Naphthali
Ep. Diognetus	Epistle to Diognetus	T. Gad.	Testament of Gad
Jos. and As.	Joseph and Asenath	T. Asher	Testament of Asher
Jub.	Jubilees	T. Jos.	Testament of Joseph
Liv. Proph.	The Lives of the Prophets (followed by prophet abbreviated)	T. Benj	Testament of Benjamin
		T. Abr.	Testament of Abraham
		T. Job	Testament of Job
Mart. Isa.	Martyrdom of Isaiah	T. Mos.	Testament of Moses (or Assumption of Moses)
Odes Sol.	Odes of Solomon		

Early Christian Literature

Acts Pil.	Acts of Pilate		Gos. Naass.	Gospel of the Naassenes
Augustine			Gos. Pet.	Gospel of Peter
Civ. D.	De Civitate Dei		Gos. Thom.	Gospel of Thomas
Conf.	Confessiones		Hippolytus	
De cons.	De consensu evangelistarum		Apos. Trad.	Apostolic Tradition
Hom.	Homilia		Ignatius	
Quaest. Evan.	Quaestiones Evangeliorum		Eph.	Letter to the Ephesians
Barn.	Barnabas		Magn.	Letter to the Magnesians
Chrysostom			Phld.	Letter to the Philadelphians
Hom. Mt.	Homilies on Matthew		Pol.	Letter to Polycarp
Regno	De Regno		Rom.	Letter to the Romans
Clement of Alexandria			Smyrn.	Letter to the Smyrneans
Paed.	Paedagogus		Trall.	Letter to the Trallians
Clement of Rome			Irenaeus	
1-2 Clem.	1-2 Clement		Haer.	Adversus haereses
Cyprian			Jerome	
Ep.	Epistulae		Ep.	Epistulae
Cyril of Jerusalem			Vir.	De Viris Illustribus
Cat.	Catechesis		Justin Martyr	
Did.	Didache		Apol. I, II	Apology I, II
Diogn.	Epistle to Diognetus		Dial. Tryph.	Dialogus cum Tryphone Judaeo
Epiphanius			Mart. Pol.	Martyrdom of Polycarp
Haer.	Haereses		Origen	
Eusebius			Comm. Joh.	In Johannem Commentarius
Hist. Eccl.	Historia Ecclesiastica		Comm. Mt.	In Matthaeum Commentarius
Dem. Ev.	Demonstratio Evangelica		Contra Celsum	Contra Celsum
In Ps.	Commentary on the Psalms		Polycarp	
Praep. Ev.	Praeparatio Evangelica		Phil.	Letter to the Philippians
Gospels:			Tertullian	
Gos. Bar.	Gospel of Bartholomew		De praesc.	De praescriptione haereticorum
Gos. Eb.	Gospel of the Ebionites		Marc.	Adversus Marcionem
Gos. Eg.	Gospel of the Egyptians		De car.	De carne Christi
Gos. Heb.	Gospel of the Hebrews			

Classical and Hellenistic Writers and Sources

Aeschylus			Dio Chrysostom	
Suppl	Supplices		De Homero	De Homero et Socrate
Appian			Disc.	Discourses
Mith. W.	Mithridatic Wars		Diodorus	
Civ. W.	The Civil Wars		Bib. Hist.	Bibliotheca Historica
Aristotle			Diogenes Laertius	
Cael.	De Caelo		Vit.	Vitae
Pol.	Politica		Epictetus	
Corp. Herm.	Corpus Hermeticum		Disc.	Discourses
Demosthenes			Diss.	Dissertationes
Lacrit.	Against Lacritus		Galen	
Dio Cassius			De Placitis	De Placitis Hippocratis et Platonis
Epit.	Roman History		Isocrates	
Hist.	Roman History		Panath.	Panathenaicus

Josephus		
Ant.	*Antiquities of the Jews*	
J.W.	*Jewish Wars*	
Life	*Life of Flavius Josephus*	
Ag. Ap.	*Against Apion*	
Justinian		
Digest	*Digest of Roman Law*	
Livy		
Epit.	*Epitomae*	
Hist.	*History of Rome*	
Lucian of Samosata		
Philops.	*Philopseudes*	
Philo		
Cher.	*De Cherubim*	
Decal.	*De Decalogo*	
Det. Pot. Ins.	*Quod Deterius Potiori Insidiari Soleat*	
Deus Imm.	*Quod Deus Sit Immutabilis*	
Flacc.	*In Flaccum*	
Fug.	*De Fuga et Inventione*	
Gig.	*De Gigantibus*	
Jos.	*De Josepho*	
Leg. All.	*Legum Allegoriae*	
Leg. Gai.	*Legatio ad Gaium*	
Migr. Abr.	*De Migratione Abrahami*	
Mut. Nom.	*De Mutatione Nominum*	
Op. Mund.	*De Opificio Mundi*	
Poster. C.	*De Posteritate Caini*	
Praem. Poen.	*De Praemiis et Poenis*	
Quaest. in Ex.	*Quaestiones in Exodum*	
Quaest. in Gen.	*Quaestiones in Genesin*	
Rer. Div. Her.	*Quis Rerum Divinarum Heres sit*	
Sacr.	*De Sacrificiis Abelis et Caini*	
Som.	*De Somnis*	
Spec. Leg.	*De Specialibus Legibus*	
Vit. Mos.	*De Vita Mosis*	

Philostratus		
Vit. Ap.	*Vita Apollonii*	
Pindar		
Isth.	*Isthmia*	
Plato		
Crat.	*Cratylus*	
Leg.	*Leges*	
Soph.	*Sophista*	
Symp.	*Symposion*	
Pliny (the elder)		
Nat. Hist.	*Naturalis Historia*	
Plutarch		
Anton.	*De Antonio*	
Rom.	*Quaestiones Romanae*	
Mor.	*Moralia*	
Non Posse Suav.	*Non Posse Suaviter Vivi Secundum Epicuram*	
Pomp.	*De Pompeio*	
Ser. Num. Pun.	*De iis qui sero a numine puniuntur*	
Polybius		
Hist.	*Histories*	
Quintilian		
Inst. orat.	*Institutio oratoria*	
Suetonius		
Claudius	*from* The Twelve Caesars	
Domitian	*from* The Twelve Caesars	
Nero	*from* The Twelve Caesars	
Tiberius	*from* The Twelve Caesars	
Vespasian	*from* The Twelve Caesars	
Tacitus		
Ann.	*Annales ab excessu divi Augusti*	
Hist.	*Historiae*	
Xenophon		
Mem.	*Memorabilia Socratis*	

Dead Sea Scrolls and Related Texts

CD	Cairo (Genizah text of the) *Damascus (Document/Rule)*
P	Pesher (commentary)
Q	Qumran
1Q, 3Q, 4Q etc.	Numbered caves of Qumran yielding written material (e.g., 1Q = Qumran Cave 1); followed by abbreviation or number of document
1QapGen	*Genesis Apocryphon* from Qumran Cave 1
1QH	*Hôdāyôt* or *Thanksgiving Hymns* from Qumran Cave 1

1QIsa^{a,b}	First or second copy of Isaiah from Qumran Cave 1
1QM	*Milḥāmāh* or *War Scroll* from Qumran Cave 1
1QpHab	*Pesher on Habakkuk* from Qumran Cave 1
1QS	*Serek hayyahad* or *Rule of the Community, Manual of Discipline* from Qumran Cave 1
1QSa	Appendix A, *Messianic Rule,* to 1QS from Qumran Cave 1
1QSb	Appendix B, *Rule of Benediction,* to 1QS from Qumran Cave 1

3Q15	*Copper Scroll* from Qumran Cave 3	4QMMT	*Miqsat Ma'aseh Torah* (unpublished) from Qumran Cave 4
4Q139	Ordinances or commentaries on biblical laws from Qumran Cave 4	4QPBless	Patriarchal Blessing from Qumran Cave 4
4Q169	Pesher on Nahum from Qumran Cave 4	4QPhyl	Phylacteries from Qumran Cave 4
4Q171	Pesher on Psalms from Qumran Cave 4	4QPrNab	*Prayer of Nabonidus* from Qumran Cave 4
4Q176	*Tanhumim* or *Consolations* from Qumran Cave 4	4QPsDan A*ª*	Pseudo-Danielic Writings from Qumran Cave 4
4Q186	(see 4QMess ar)	4QPssJosh	*Psalms of Joshua* from Qumran Cave 4
4Q246	(see 4QPs DanA*ª*)	4QShirShabb	*Songs of Sabbath Sacrifice* or *Angelic Liturgy* from Qumran Cave 4
4Q504	*Words of the Luminaries* from Qumran Cave 4	4QTestim	*Testimonia* text from Qumran Cave 4
4Q513-14	Ordinances or commentaries on biblical laws from Qumran Cave 4	4QtgJob	*Targum of Job* from Qumran Cave 4
4QCryptic	Magical text from Qumran Cave 4	4QtgLev	*Targum of Leviticus* from Qumran Cave 4
4QEn Giants*ª⁻ᵉ*	*1 Enoch* fragments from Book of Giants from Qumran Cave 4	4QZodiac	Magical text (unpublished) from Qumran Cave 4
4QEn	*1 Enoch* fragments from Qumran Cave 4	5Q15	*New Jerusalem* from Qumran Cave 5
4QEnastr*ª⁻ᵍ*	1 Enoch fragments from Astronomical Book from Qumran Cave 4	11QMelch	*Melchizedek* from Qumran Cave 11
4QFlor	*Florilegium* or *Eschatological Midrashim* from Qumran Cave 4	11QpaleoLev	Copy of Leviticus in paleo-Hebrew script from Qumran Cave 11
4QMess ar	Aramaic "Messianic" text from Qumran Cave 4	11QPs*ª*	*Psalms Scroll* from Qumran Cave 11
		11QTemple	*Temple Scroll* from Qumran Cave 11
		11QtgJob	*Targum of Job* from Qumran Cave 11

Targumic Material

Tg. Onq.	*Targum Onqelos*	*Tg. Neof.*	*Targum Neofiti I*
Tg. Neb.	*Targum of the Prophets*	*Tg. Ps.-J.*	*Targum Pseudo-Jonathan*
Tg. Ket.	*Targum of the Writings*	*Tg. Yer. I*	*Targum Yerušalmi I*
Frg. Tg.	*Fragmentary Targum*	*Tg. Yer. II*	*Targum Yerušalmi II*
Sam. Tg.	*Samaritan Targum*	*Yem. Tg.*	*Yemenite Targum*
Tg. Isa	*Targum of Isaiah*	*Tg. Esth I, II*	*First or Second Targum of Esther*

Order and Tractates in the Mishna, Tosepta and Talmud Same-named tractates in the Mishna, Tosepta, Babylonian Talmud and Jerusalem Talmud are distinguished by *m.*, *t.*, *b.* and *y.* respectively.

'Abot	*'Abot*	B. Bat.	*Baba Batra*
'Arak.	*'Arakin*	Bek.	*Bekorot*
'Abod. Zar.	*'Aboda Zara*	Ber.	*Berakot*

Beṣa	*Beṣa* (= *Yom Ṭob*)	*Nez.*	*Neziqin*
Bik.	*Bikkurim*	*Nid.*	*Niddah*
B. Meṣ.	*Baba Meṣi'a*	*Ohol.*	*Oholot*
B. Qam.	*Baba Qamma*	*'Or.*	*'Orla*
Dem.	*Demai*	*Para*	*Para*
'Erub.	*'Erubin*	*Pe'a*	*Pe'a*
'Ed.	*'Eduyyot*	*Pesaḥ.*	*Pesaḥim*
Giṭ.	*Giṭṭin*	*Qinnim*	*Qinnim*
Ḥag.	*Ḥagiga*	*Qidd.*	*Qidduśin*
Ḥal.	*Ḥalla*	*Qod.*	*Qodaśin*
Hor.	*Horayot*	*Roš Haš.*	*Roš Haššana*
Ḥul.	*Ḥullin*	*Sanh.*	*Sanhedrin*
Kelim	*Kelim*	*Šabb.*	*Šabbat*
Ker.	*Keritot*	*Šeb.*	*Šebi'it*
Ketub.	*Ketubot*	*Šebu.*	*Šebu'ot*
Kil.	*Kil'ayim*	*Šeqal.*	*Šeqalim*
Ma'aś.	*Ma'aśerot*	*Soṭa*	*Soṭa*
Mak.	*Makkot*	*Sukk.*	*Sukka*
Makš.	*Makširin* (= *Mašqin*)	*Ta'an.*	*Ta'anit*
Meg.	*Megilla*	*Tamid*	*Tamid*
Me'il.	*Me'ila*	*Tem.*	*Temura*
Menaḥ.	*Menaḥot*	*Ter.*	*Terumot*
Mid.	*Middot*	*Ṭohar.*	*Ṭoharot*
Miqw.	*Miqwa'ot*	*Ṭ. Yom*	*Ṭebul Yom*
Mo'ed	*Mo'ed*	*'Uq.*	*'Uqṣin*
Mo'ed Qaṭ.	*Mo'ed Qaṭan*	*Yad.*	*Yadayim*
Ma'aś. Š.	*Ma'aśer Šeni*	*Yebam.*	*Yebamot*
Našim	*Našim*	*Yoma*	*Yoma* (= *Kippurim*)
Nazir	*Nazir*	*Zabim*	*Zabim*
Ned.	*Nedarim*	*Zebaḥ.*	*Zebaḥim*
Neg.	*Nega'im*	*Zer.*	*Zera'im*

Other Rabbinic Works

'Abot R. Nat.	*'Abot de Rabbi Nathan*
'Ag. Ber.	*'Aggadat Berešit*
Bab.	*Babylonian*
Bar.	*Baraita*
Der. Er. Rab.	*Derek Ereṣ Rabba*
Der. Er. Zuṭ.	*Derek Ereṣ Zuṭ*
Gem.	*Gemara*
Kalla	*Kalla*
Mek.	*Mekilta*
Midr.	*Midraš* (cited with abbreviation for biblical book; but *Midr. Qoh.* = *Midraš Qohelet*)
Pal.	*Palestinian*
Pesiq. R.	*Pesiqta Rabbati*
Pesiq. Rab Kah.	*Pesiqta de Rab Kahana*
Pirqe R. El.	*Pirqe Rabbi Eliezer*
Rab.	*Rabbah* (following abbreviation for biblical book: *Gen. Rab.* = *Genesis Rabbah*)
Ṣem.	*Ṣemaḥot*
Sipra	*Sipra*
Sipre	*Sipre*
Sop.	*Soperim*
S. 'Olam Rab.	*Seder 'Olam Rabbah*
Talm.	*Talmud*
Yal.	*Yalquṭ*

Periodicals, Reference Works and Serials

AB	Anchor Bible		CCWJCW	Cambridge Commentaries on Writings of the Jewish and Christian World 200 B.C. to A.D. 200
ABQ	*American Baptist Quarterly*			
AGJU	Arbeiten zur Geschichte des antiken Judentums und des Urchristentums		*CD*	*Church Dogmatics*, Karl Barth
AGSU	Arbeiten zur Geschichte des Spätjudentums und Urchristentums		CG	Nag Hammadi Gnostic Codices
			CGTC	Cambridge Greek Testament Commentary
AJBI	*Annual of the Japanese Biblical Institute*			
AJT	*American Journal of Theology*		*CII*	*Corpus inscriptionum iudaicarum*, J. B. Frey (1936-1952)
ALGHJ	Arbeiten zur Literatur und Geschichte des hellenistischen Judentums			
			CNT	Commentaire du Nouveau Testament
ALUOS	*Annual of Leeds University Oriental Society*		CRINT	Compendia rerum iudaicarum ad novum testamentum
AnBib	Analecta Biblica			
ANRW	Aufstieg und Niedergang der römischen Welt		*CT*	*Christianity Today*
			DJD	Discoveries in the Judaean Desert
ASNU	Acta seminarii neotestamentici upsaliensis		*DRev*	*Downside Review*
			EB	Études bibliques
ATANT	Abhandlungen zur Theologie des Alten und Neuen Testaments		EBC	The Expositor's Bible Commentary
			EBT	*Encyclopedia of Biblical Theology*
ATLABibS	American Theological Library Association Bibliography Series		*EDNT*	*Exegetical Dictionary of the New Testament*
			EKK	Evangelisch-katholischer Kommentar zum Neuen Testament
AusBR	*Australian Biblical Review*			
ATR	*Anglican Theological Review*		*ELS*	*Enchiridion Locorum Sanctorum. Documenta S. Evangelii Loca Respicientia*
BAGD	W. Bauer, W. F. Arndt, F. W. Gingrich and F. W. Danker, *Greek-English Lexicon of the New Testament and Other Early Christian Literature*			
			EvQ	*Evangelical Quarterly*
			ExpT	*Expository Times*
			FB	Facet Books
BBB	Bonner biblische Beiträge		FIRA	Fontes Iuris Romani Antejustiniani
BCJ	Brown Classics in Judaica		FJ	The Foundation of Judaism
BDB	F. Brown, S. R. Driver and C. A. Briggs, *Hebrew and English Lexicon of the Old Testament*		*GBL*	*Das Grosse Bibellexikon*
			GNS	Good News Studies
			GNTE	Guides to New Testament Exegesis
BG	Berlin Gnostic Codex		*GTJ*	*Grace Theological Journal*
BGU	Ägyptische Urkunden aus den Museen zu Berlin: Griech. Urkunden I-VIII (1895-1933)		*HBD*	*Harper's Bible Dictionary*
			Herm	Hermeneia
			HeyJ	*Heythrop Journal*
Bib	*Biblica*		HNT	Handbuch zum Neuen Testament
BibO	Biblica et orientalia		HNTC	Harper's New Testament Commentaries
BibRes	*Biblical Research*		HSS	Harvard Semitic Studies
BibS(F)	Biblische Studien (Freiburg, 1895-)		HTKNT	Herders theologischer Kommentar zum Neuen Testament
BibS(N)	Biblische Studien (Neukirchen, 1951-)			
BMI	The Bible and Its Modern Interpreters		*HZ*	*Historische Zeitschrift*
BRev	*Bible Review*		*IBS*	*Irish Biblical Studies*
BSac	*Bibliotheca Sacra*		ICC	International Critical Commentary
BT	*The Bible Translator*		*IDB*	*Interpreter's Dictionary of the Bible*
BJRL	*Bulletin of the John Rylands University Library of Manchester*		*IDBSup*	*Interpreter's Dictionary of the Bible, Supplementary Volume*
BJS	Brown Judaic Studies		*IEJ*	*Israel Exploration Journal*
BTB	*Biblical Theology Bulletin*		*Int*	*Interpretation*
BZ	*Biblische Zeitschrift*		IntC	Interpretation Commentaries
BZNW	Beihefte zur *Zeitschrift für die Neutestamentliche Wissenschaft*		IRT	Issues in Religion and Theology
			ISBE	*International Standard Bible Encyclopedia* (rev. ed.)
CBQ	*Catholic Biblical Quarterly*			

JAOS	Journal of the American Oriental Society	PG	Patrologia graeca, ed. J. P. Migne
JBL	Journal of Biblical Literature	PRS	Perspectives in Religious Studies
JCSR	Journal of Comparative Sociology and Religion	PTMS	Pittsburgh Theological Monograph Series
JETS	Journal of the Evangelical Theological Society	PTR	Princeton Theological Review
		RAC	Reallexikon für Antike und Christentum
JR	Journal of Religion	RB	Revue biblique
JRE	Journal of Religious Ethics	RE	Real-Encyklopädie der klassischen Altertumswissenschaft, Pauly-Wissowa
JRS	Journal of Roman Studies		
JSJ	Journal for the Study of Judaism in the Persian, Hellenistic and Roman Period	RelSRev	Religious Studies Review
		RevQ	Revue de Qumrân
JSNT	Journal for the Study of the New Testament	RHPR	Revue d'histoire et de philosophie religieuses
JSNTSup	Journal for the Study of the New Testament Supplement Series	RST	Regensburger Studien zur Theologie
		SAJ	Studies in Ancient Judaism
JSOT	Journal for the Study of the Old Testament	SANT	Studien zum Alten und Neuen Testament
JSOTSup	Journal for the Study of the Old Testament Supplement Series	SBEC	Studies in the Bible and Early Christianity
JSPSup	Journal for the Study of the Pseudepigrapha and Related Literature Supplement Series	SBLASP	Society of Biblical Literature Abstracts and Seminar Papers
JTS	Journal of Theological Studies	SBLDS	SBL Dissertation Series
JTSA	Journal of Theology for South Africa	SBLMS	SBL Monograph Series
KNT	Kommentar zum Neuen Testament	SBLSBS	SBL Sources for Biblical Study
LAE	Light from the Ancient East, A. Deissmann	SBT	Studies in Biblical Theology
		ScrHier	Scripta hierosolymitana
LSJ	Liddell-Scott-Jones, Greek-English Lexicon	SCJ	Studies in Christianity and Judaism
		SE	Studia Evangelica
MBTh	Münsterische Beiträge zur Theologie	SEA	Svensk Exegetisk Årsbok
MeyerK	H. A. W. Meyer, Kritisch-exegetischer Kommentar über das Neue Testament	SEG	Supplementum Epigraphicum Graecum (Leiden, 1923-)
MNTC	Moffatt New Testament Commentary	SIG³	Sylloge Inscriptionum Graecarum (3d ed.; Leipzig, 1915-24)
MPAT	A Manual of Palestinian Aramaic Texts		
NA²⁶	Nestle-Aland, Novum Testamentum Graece, 26th ed.	SJ	Studia Judaica
		SJLA	Studies in Judaism in Late Antiquity
NAC	The New American Commentary	SNTSMS	Society for New Testament Studies Monograph Series
NCB	New Century Bible		
NewDocs	New Documents Illustrating Early Christianity	SJT	Scottish Journal of Theology
		Str-B	H. Strack and P. Billerbeck, Kommentar zum Neuen Testament
NIBC	New International Biblical Commentary		
NICNT	The New International Commentary on the New Testament	StudLit	Studia Liturgica
		TD	Theology Digest
NIDNTT	New International Dictionary of New Testament Theology	TDNT	Theological Dictionary of the New Testament
NovT	Novum Testamentum	TDGR	Translated Documents of Greece and Rome, ed. R. K. Sherk
NovTSup	Supplement to Novum Testamentum		
NRT	La nouvelle revue théologique	THKNT	Theologische Handkommentar zum Neuen Testament
NTD	Das Neue Testament Deutsch	TI	Theological Inquiries
NTOA	Novum Testamentum et Orbis Antiquus	TJ	Trinity Journal
		TLZ	Theologische Literaturzeitung
NTS	New Testament Studies	TNTC	Tyndale New Testament Commentary
PC	Proclamation Commentaries	TPINTC	Trinity Press International New Testament Commentaries
PEQ	Palestine Exploration Quarterly		

TS	*Theological Studies*	UBSGNT	United Bible Societies Greek New Testament
TSAJ	Texte und Studien zum Antiken Judentum		
		VoxEv	*Vox Evangelica*
TSFBul	*Theological Students Fellowship Bulletin*	VT	*Vetus Testamentum*
TToday	*Theology Today*	WBC	Word Biblical Commentary
TWOT	*Theological Wordbook of the Old Testament*	WEC	Wycliffe Exegetical Commentary
TynB	*Tyndale Bulletin*	WUNT	Wissenschaftliche Untersuchungen zum Neuen Testament
TZ	*Theologische Zeitschrift*		

Transliteration

Hebrew

Consonants

א = ʾ

ב = b

ב = ḇ

ג = g

ג = ḡ

ד = d

ד = ḏ

ה = h

ו = w

ז = z

ח = ḥ

ט = ṭ

י = y

כ = k

כ = ḵ

ל = l

מ = m

נ = n

ס = s

ע = ʿ

פ = p

פ = p̄

צ = ṣ

ק = q

ר = r

שׂ = ś

שׁ = š

ת = t

ת = ṯ

Long Vowels

(ה), = â

י.. = ê

י. = î

ו = ô

ו = û

, = ā

.. = ē

. = ō

Short Vowels

_ = a

˯ = e

. = i

, = o

˰ = u

_ɪ = ᵃ

˯ɪ = ᵉ

ɪ = ᵉ

˯ɪ = ᵒ

Greek

A = A

α = a

B = B

β = b

Γ = G

γ = g

Δ = D

δ = d

E = E

ε = e

Z = Z

ζ = z

H = Ē

η = ē

Θ = Th

θ = th

I = I

ι = i

K = K

κ = k

Λ = L

λ = l

M = M

μ = m

N = N

ν = n

Ξ = X

ξ - x

O = O

o = o

Π = P

π = p

P = R

ρ = r

Σ = S

σ/ς = s

T = T

τ = t

Y = Y

υ = y

Φ = Ph

φ = ph

X = Ch

χ = ch

Ψ = Ps

ψ = ps

Ω = Ō

ω = ō

ʿP, ῥ = rh

ʿ = h

γξ = nx

γγ = ng

αυ = au

ευ = eu

ου = ou

υι = ui

List of Contributors

Allison, Dale C., Jr., Ph.D. Research Fellow, Friends University, Wichita, Kansas, USA.

Banks, Robert, Ph.D. Homer L. Goddard Professor of the Ministry of the Laity, Fuller Theological Seminary, Pasadena, California, USA.

Bartchy, S. Scott, Ph.D. Adjunct Associate Professor, Department of History, University of California, Los Angeles, California, USA.

Barton, Stephen C., M.A. Lecturer in New Testament, Department of Theology, University of Durham, Durham, U.K.

Bauckham, Richard J., Ph.D. Reader in the History of Christian Thought. University of Manchester, Manchester, U.K.

Bauer, David R., Ph.D. Associate Professor of Biblical Studies, Asbury Theological Seminary, Wilmore, Kentucky, USA.

Bayer, Hans F., Ph.D. Dozent in New Testament Exegesis and Department Head in New Testament, German Theological Seminary, Giessen, Germany.

Beasley-Murray, G. R., Ph.D., D.D. Senior Professor of New Testament Interpretation, The Southern Baptist Theological Seminary, Louisville, Kentucky, USA.

Black, David Alan, D.Theol. Scholar in Residence, The Lockman Foundation, La Habra, California, USA.

Blackburn, Barry L., Ph.D. Professor of New Testament, Atlanta Christian College, East Point, Georgia, USA.

Blomberg, Craig L., Ph.D. Associate Professor of New Testament, Denver Seminary, Denver, Colorado, USA.

Bock, Darrell L., Ph.D. Associate Professor of New Testament Studies, Dallas Theological Seminary, Dallas, Texas, USA.

Brown, Colin, Ph.D. Professor of Systematic Theology and Associate Dean of the Center for Advanced Theological Studies, Fuller Theological Seminary, Pasadena, California, USA.

Broyles, Craig C., Ph.D. Assistant Professor of Religious Studies, Trinity Western University, Langley, British Columbia, Canada.

Bruce, F. F., D.D. Late Rylands Professor of Biblical Criticism and Exegesis, University of Manchester, Manchester, U.K.

Burge, Gary M., Ph.D. Karl A. Olsson Professor of Religion and Chair, Department of Biblical and Theological Studies, North Park College, Chicago, Illinois, USA.

Burnett, Fred W., Ph.D. Professor of New Testament and Coordinator of Classical Studies, Anderson College, Anderson, Indiana, USA.

Calvert, Nancy L., M.Div. Ph.D. Candidate, University of Sheffield, Sheffield, U.K., and Visiting Instructor, Wheaton College, Wheaton, Illinois, USA.

Caragounis, Chrys C., D.Theol. Associate Professor, University of Lund, Sweden.

Chilton, Bruce, Ph.D. Bernard Iddings Bell Professor of Religion, Bard College, Annandale-on-Hudson, New York, USA.

Corley, Bruce, Th.D. Professor of New Testament and Dean, School of Theology, Southwestern Baptist Theological Seminary, Fort Worth, Texas, USA.

Corley, Kathleen E., M.A., Ph.D. (Cand.). Sioux Falls College, Sioux Falls, South Dakota, USA.

Crump, David M., Ph.D. Pastor, Immanuel Christian Reformed Church, Salt Lake City, Utah, USA.

Danker, Frederick William, Ph.D. Professor Emeritus of Biblical Theology, Lutheran School of Theology at Chicago, Chicago, Illinois, USA.

Davids, Peter H., Ph.D. Scholar in Residence, Langley Vineyard Christian Fellowship, Langley, British Columbia, Canada.

Davidson, Maxwell J., Ph.D. Lecturer in Systematic Theology, Baptist Theological College of Western Australia, Perth, Western Australia, Australia.

Dockery, David S., Ph.D. General Editor, Broadman Press, Nashville, Tennessee, USA.

Dunn, James D. G., D.D. Lightfoot Professor of Divinity, University of Durham, Durham, U.K.

Edwards, Ruth B., Ph.D. Senior Lecturer in New Testament, University of Aberdeen, Aberdeen, U.K.

Ellingworth, Paul, Ph.D. Translation Consultant, United Bible Societies, Aberdeen, U.K.

Elliott, Mark A., Th.M. Ph.D. Candidate, University of Aberdeen, Aberdeen, U.K.

Evans, Craig A., Ph.D. Professor of Biblical Studies, Trinity Western University, Langley, British Columbia, Canada.

Farris, Stephen C., Ph.D. Professor of Preaching and Worship, Knox College, Toronto School of Theology, Toronto, Ontario, Canada.

Fee, Gordon D., Ph.D, Professor of New Testament, Regent College, Vancouver, British Columbia, Canada.

France, R. T., Ph.D. Principal, Wycliffe Hall, Oxford, U.K.

Garland, David E., Ph.D. Professor of New Testament Interpretation, The Southern Baptist Theological Seminary, Louisville, Kentucky, USA.

Geddert, Timothy J., Ph.D. Assistant Professor of New Testament, Mennonite Brethren Biblical Seminary, Fresno, California, USA.

Giles, Kevin N., Th.D. Rector, St. Matthew's Church, Marryatville, South Australia, Australia.

Green, Joel B., Ph.D. Academic Dean and Associate Professor of New Testament, New College Berkeley, Berkeley, California, USA.

Greidanus, Sidney, Th.D. Associate Professor of Preaching and Worship, Calvin Theological Seminary, Grand Rapids, Michigan, USA.

Guelich, Robert A., D.Theol. Late Professor of New Testament, Fuller

Theological Seminary, Pasadena, California, USA.

Hawthorne, Gerald F., Ph.D. Professor of Greek, Wheaton College, Wheaton, Illinois, USA.

Heard, Warren J., Jr., Ph.D. Assistant Professor of Counseling Psychology and New Testament, Trinity Evangelical Divinity School, Deerfield, Illinois, USA.

Hearon, Holly E., D. Min. Ph.D. Candidate, Graduate Theological Union, Berkeley, California, USA.

Herzog, William R., II, Ph.D. Dean of the Faculty and Professor of New Testament Interpretation, Colgate Rochester Divinity School/Bexley Hall/Crozer Theological Seminary, Rochester, New York, USA.

Hoehner, Harold W., Ph.D. Professor of New Testament Studies, Dallas Theological Seminary, Dallas, Texas, USA.

Howard, Carol D. C., M.Div. Th.D. Candidate, Harvard Divinity School, Cambridge, Massachusetts, USA.

Huffman, Douglas S., M.A. New Testament Teaching Fellow/Ph.D Student. Trinity Evangelical Divinity School, Deerfield, Illinois, USA.

Hurst, Lincoln D., Ph.D. Associate Professor of Religion, University of California, Davis, California, USA.

Hurtado, Larry W., Ph.D. Professor of Religion and Director of the Institute for the Humanities, University of Manitoba, Winnipeg, Manitoba, Canada.

Johnson, David H., Ph.D. (Cand.). Instructor, Providence Theological Seminary, Otterburne, Manitoba, Canada.

Kruse, Colin G., Ph.D. Senior Lecturer in New Testament, Ridley College, University of Melbourne, Melbourne, Victoria, Australia.

Kynes, William L., Ph.D. Pastor, National Evangelical Free Church, Annandale, Virginia, USA.

Levison, John R., Ph.D. Assistant Professor of Biblical Studies, North Park College, Chicago, Illinois, USA.

Liefeld, Walter L., Ph.D. Distinguished Professor of New Testament, Trinity Evangelical Divinity School, Deerfield, Illinois, USA.

Losie, Lynn A., Ph.D. Associate Professor of Religion, Azusa Pacific University, Azusa, California, USA.

Lunde, Jonathan M., Th.M. Ph.D. Candidate, Trinity Evangelical Divinity School, Deerfield, Illinois, USA.

McKnight, Edgar V., Ph.D. William R. Kenan, Jr. Professor of Religion, Furman University, Greenville, South Carolina, USA.

McKnight, Scot, Ph.D. Assistant Professor of New Testament, Trinity Evangelical Divinity School, Deerfield, Illinois, USA.

Marshall, I. Howard, Ph.D. Professor of New Testament Exegesis, University of Aberdeen, Aberdeen, U.K.

Martin, Clarice J., Ph.D. Assistant Professor of New Testament, Princeton Theological Seminary, Princeton, New Jersey, USA.

Michaels, J. Ramsey, Th.D. Professor of Religious Studies, Southwest Missouri State University, Springfield, Missouri, USA.

Moo, Douglas J., Ph.D. Professor of New Testament, Trinity Evangelical Divinity School, Deerfield, Illinois, USA.

Morris, Leon, Ph.D. Principal Emeritus, Ridley College, Melbourne, Australia.

Mulholland, M. Robert, Jr., Th.D. Vice President and Professor of New Testament, Asbury Theological Seminary, Wilmore, Kentucky, USA.

Osborne, Grant R., Ph.D. Professor of New Testament, Trinity Evangelical Divinity School, Deerfield, Illinois, USA.

Page, Sydney H. T., Ph.D. Academic Vice President and Professor of New Testament, Edmonton Baptist Seminary, Edmonton, Alberta, Canada.

Painter, John, Ph.D. Reader in Religious Studies, La Trobe University, Melbourne, Australia.

Paschal, R. Wade, Jr., Ph.D. Director, Beeson International Center for Biblical Preaching and Pastoral Leadership, Asbury Theological Seminary, Wilmore, Kentucky, USA.

Riesner, Rainer, D. Theol. Habil Privatdozent für Neuen Testament, Evangelisch-Theologische Fakultät, Universität Tübingen, Tübingen, Germany.

Schmidt, Thomas E., Ph.D. Associate Professor of New Testament, Westmont College, Santa Barbara, California, USA.

Scholer, David M., Th.D. Distinguished Professor of New Testament and Early Church History, North Park College and Theological Seminary, Chicago, Illinois, USA.

Scott, J. Julius, Jr., Ph.D. Professor of Biblical and Historical Studies,

Wheaton College Graduate School, Wheaton, Illinois, USA.

Shirbroun, G. Franklin, Ph.D. Professor of New Testament, The Episcopal School of Theology at Claremont, Claremont, California, USA.

Shogren, Gary S., Ph.D. Assistant Professor of New Testament, Biblical Theological Seminary, Hatfield, Pennsylvania, USA.

Sloan, Robert B., D.Theol. Associate Professor of Religion, Baylor University, Waco, Texas, USA.

Smith, Robert H., Th.D. Professor of New Testament, Pacific Lutheran Theological Seminary/Graduate Theological Union, Berkeley, California, USA.

Snodgrass, Klyne R., Ph.D. Dean of the Faculty and Paul W. Brandel Professor of New Testament Studies, North Park Theological Seminary, Chicago, Illinois, USA.

Stanton, Graham N., Ph.D. Professor of New Testament Studies, King's College, University of London, London, U.K.

Stein, Robert H., Ph.D. Professor of New Testament, Bethel Theological Seminary, St. Paul, Minnesota, USA.

Thompson, Marianne Meye, Ph.D. Associate Professor of New Testament, Fuller Theological Seminary, Pasadena, California, USA.

Travis, Stephen H., Ph.D. Vice-Principal, St. John's College, Nottingham, U.K.

Trites, Allison A., Ph.D. The John Payzant Distinguished Professor of Biblical Studies, Acadia Divinity College, Acadia University, Wolfville, Nova Scotia, Canada.

Turner, Max, Ph.D. Director of Research and Lecturer in New Testament, London Bible College, Middlesex, U.K.

Twelftree, Graham H., Ph.D. Minister, Hope Valley Uniting Church, Adelaide, South Australia, Australia.

Watson, Duane F., Ph.D. Assistant Professor of New Testament and Greek, Malone College, Canton, Ohio, USA.

Weatherly, Jon A., Ph.D. Associate Professor of Biblical Studies, Cincinnati Bible College and Seminary, Cincinnati, Ohio, USA.

Westerholm, Stephen, Th.D. Assistant Professor of Biblical Studies, McMaster University, Hamilton, Ontario, Canada.

Whitacre, Rodney A., Ph.D. Associate

Professor of Biblical Studies, Trinity Episcopal School for Ministry, Ambridge, Pennsylvania, USA.

Wilkins, Michael J., Ph.D. Department Chair and Professor of New Testament Language and Literature, Talbot School of Theology, Biola University, La Mirada, California, USA.

Williams, David John, Ph.D. Vice Principal, Ridley College, University of Melbourne, Melbourne, Victoria, Australia.

Williamson, H. G. M., D.D. Reader in Hebrew and Aramaic, University of Cambridge, Cambridge, U.K.

Wise, Michael O., Ph.D. Associate Professor of Aramaic, Department of Near Eastern Languages and Civilizations, University of Chicago, Chicago, Illinois, USA.

Witherington, Ben, III, Ph.D. Associate Professor of Biblical and Wesleyan Studies, Ashland Theological Seminary, Ashland, Ohio, USA.

Yamauchi, Edwin M., Ph.D. Professor of History, Miami University, Oxford, Ohio, USA.

TRANSLATOR

Robert W. Yarbrough, Ph.D. Assistant Professor of New Testament, Wheaton College, Wheaton, Illinois, USA: Archeology and Geography; Galilee; Teacher.

ABBA. *See* GOD; PRAYER; SON OF GOD.

ABIATHAR

The high priest (*see* Priest, Priesthood) who, according to Jesus, gave David and his men the Bread of the Presence which only priests were allowed to eat (Mk 2:25-26). This reference is extremely problematical since 1 Samuel 21:1-6 indicates that Ahimelech gave the bread to David. Matthew (12:4) and Luke (6:4) remove reference to Abiathar, and several manuscripts of Mark omit the reference (D, W, 1009, 1546, it, Syr) although none, interestingly, substitutes Ahimelech for Abiathar. The possible solutions to the problem are few: (1) the phrase *epi Abiathar archiereōs* ("when Abiathar was high priest") has been misunderstood; (2) the author of Mark misrepresented Jesus; (3) Jesus was mistaken; (4) the OT references are faulty.

The first option (Wenham, Lane) suggests the phrase is a general reference to the section in 1 Samuel where Abiathar plays a significant role, similar to the usage in Mark 12:26 by which Jesus specifies a particular portion of Moses'* writings with the phrase *epi tou batou* ("about the bush"). But this explanation has been effectively rejected (Lagrange, Rogers) as contrary to the attested usage of such a phrase and not parallel to 12:26.

The second option sees 2:25-26 as a later addition to the account (Hultgren, Klostermann). But it has been argued that this explanation disregards the literary integrity of the passage as a whole (Taylor).

The argument that Jesus was mistaken pointedly raises theological issues regarding the authority of Jesus and the Gospels. But another explanation, a variation on (4), may provide a satisfactory solution to the problem. In 1—2 Samuel, 1 Kings and 1 Chronicles, two different traditions appear. The major tradition presents Abiathar, son of Ahimelech, who gave the bread to David, as priest under David prior to David's kingship and co-priest with Zadok under David's reign (1 Sam 21:1-9; 22:9-16, 20-22; 23:6-9; 30:7; 2 Sam 15:24-36; 17:15; 19:11; 20:25; 1 Kings 1:7-25; 2:26-27; 4:4; 1 Chron 15:11). The minor tradition, usually dismissed as an error, presents Ahimelech, son of Abiathar, as co-priest with Zadok during David's reign (2 Sam 8:17; 1 Chron 18:16; 24:3-31).

The existence of two traditions, rather than an error, is supported by the presence of the minor tradition in the material of the major at 2 Samuel 8:17, and especially by the presence of the major tradition in the material of the minor at 1 Chronicles 15:11. The latter is noteworthy in that the Chronicler, in an otherwise verbatim reproduction of 2 Samuel 8:15-18 (par. 1 Chron 18:14-17), retains Ahimelech son of Abiathar as priest with Zadok but changes the role of David's sons from priests (*kōhᵃnîm* in 2 Sam 8:18) to chiefs (*hāri'šōnîm* in 1 Chron 18:17). Such a concern for accuracy regarding the priesthood would seem to require a reversal of Abiathar and Ahimelech to agree with the rest of Samuel and Kings, unless the Chronicler knew a tradition which preserved the order of Ahimelech as son of Abiathar. The Chronicler appears not to have been interested in materials prior to the Davidic kingship, retaining only the death of Saul as the historical prelude to David's reign (1 Chron 10). Thus the Chronicler provides no information on the period of David's flight from Saul during which the Ahimelech/Abiathar account occurs. The Chronicler's strong reliance on the minor tradition, however, implies that Abiathar would have been the priest who gave David the bread rather than Ahimelech.

While the evidence is inconclusive and susceptible to various interpretations, it is possible to view the presence of Abiathar in Mark 2:25-26 not as a mistake of Jesus or Mark but as reflecting Jesus' and/or Mark's acquaintance with the minor tradition which reversed the roles of Abiathar and Ahimelech. Whatever the case, until the dual traditions within the OT are resolved, there remains scriptural evidence for the reliability of Mark 2:25-26.

See also GOSPELS (HISTORICAL RELIABILITY); OLD TESTAMENT IN THE GOSPELS.

BIBLIOGRAPHY. R. W. Corney, "Abiathar," *IDB* 1.6-7;

A. J. Hultgren, "The Formation of the Sabbath Peri-
cope in Mark 2:23-28," *JBL* 91 (1972) 38-43; E. Kloster-
mann, *Das Markus-Evangelium* (HNT 3; Tübingen:
J. C. B. Mohr, 1936); M.-J. Lagrange, *Évangile selon
Saint Marc* (Paris: Librairie LeCoffre, 1966); W. L.
Lane, *The Gospel According to Mark* (NICNT; Grand
Rapids: Eerdmans, 1974); A. D. Rogers, "Mark 2:26,"
JTS (n.s.) 2 (1951) 44-45; V. Taylor, *The Gospel According
to St. Mark* (2d ed.; New York: St. Martin's Press, 1966);
J. W. Wenham, "Mark 2:26," *JTS* (n.s.) 1 (1950) 156.

M. R. Mulholland

ABIDING

As a common translation of the Greek verb *menein*, "to
abide" has rich theological associations in the Fourth
Gospel where 40 of the 112 NT occurrences of the
verb occur (it appears another 26 times in the Epistles
of John). It is used to communicate the enduring
character of Christ,* and more importantly, when
used with the preposition "in" and a personal object,
it points to the relationship of mutual indwelling of
the Father, the Son (*see* Son of God) and the believer.

1. Abiding As a Quality of Character.

In the Greek OT *menein*, when used in a theological
sense, most commonly speaks of the abiding character
of God.* In contrast to the transitory nature of all
things human, God remains, he endures, he is
immutable. In the NT period this was considered to
be a trait of the Messiah also, as evidenced by the
crowds in John's Gospel who say, "We have heard
from the Law* that the Christ abides forever" (12:34).
And John would have us know that Jesus is the Son
who abides forever (8:35), who gives food that abides
unto eternal life (6:27), and who enables one to
produce fruit that abides (15:16).

In addition, in the first use of the verb in the
Gospel, the Evangelist relates that John the Baptist (*see*
John the Baptist) saw the Holy Spirit (*see* Holy Spirit)
coming down from heaven* as a dove and remaining
(*emeinen*) on Jesus (1:32). This was no momentary
experience of the Spirit, perhaps like that of the
judges or prophets,* but an enduring reality in Jesus'
life.

2. Abiding in Relationship.

Of greater interest is the use in John's Gospel of the
phrase "to abide in" with a personal object to express
the relationship of Jesus to the Father and both to
believers. The priority must be given to Jesus' mutual
indwelling with the Father: "Don't you believe that I am
in the Father and the Father is in me? The words that
I speak to you are not from myself, but the Father who

abides in me does his work" (14:10). This is a dynamic
relationship which energizes the ministry of Jesus. Out
of this personal union come his words and his works
which manifest the character of God. "Do not believe
me unless I do what my Father does. But if I do it, even
though you do not believe me, believe the miracles, that
you may learn and understand that the Father is in me,
and I in the Father" (10:37-38 NIV).

The Son obeys the Father and imitates the Father
(5:19-20; 14:31), but the Father imparts his life to the
Son ("I live because of the Father," 6:57; also 5:26),
and together they share this common life and are
united in love (3:35; 5:20; 14:31; 15:10; 17:21-23). This
relationship between the Father and the Son becomes
the model and source of the relationship between
Jesus and his disciples.*

Jesus called men and women into this relationship
of mutual indwelling using the most graphic imagery:
"He who eats my flesh and drinks my blood abides in
me and I in him" (6:56). Just as the Father has loved
Jesus, so Jesus has loved his disciples, and they are to
abide in his love (15:9). Just as Jesus has remained in
his Father's love by obeying his commands (*see* Commandment), so the disciples are to abide in Jesus' love
by obeying his commands (15:10). And as they abide
in him, Jesus will convey his life to them, even as a
vine* gives life to its branches (15:4-6). His life will
manifest itself in their lives as they bear fruit, even as
his works were the work of his Father. Apart from him
the disciples can do nothing, just as Jesus could do
nothing apart from the Father (5:19, 30).

Jesus mediates to his disciples the relationship he
enjoys with his heavenly Father. "Just as the living
Father sent me and I live because of the Father, so the
one who feeds on me will live because of me" (6:57
NIV). The one who loves Jesus will be loved by the
Father, and together the Father and the Son will make
their abode (*monē*—a cognate of *menein*) with him
(14:23). "I have given them the glory* that you gave
me, that they may be one as we are one: I in them and
you in me" (17:22-23). This is the perfect unity that
results from the mutual indwelling of the Father, the
Son and the believers.

"Abiding in Christ" assumes the most intimate
union possible. The identification of Jesus with the
true vine (15:1), a symbol of Israel* (cf. Hos 10:1; Jer
2:21; Ps 80:9-12, 15-16; Is 5:7), in which the disciples
are to abide, suggests a corporate dimension to his
person that has important christological implications.

This union with Christ, however, must not be confused with ideas of the Hellenistic mystery cults (*see*
Hellenism), some of which taught a loss of individuality or a pantheistic absorption of the believer into

the being of the divine. The teaching of the Fourth Gospel maintains throughout a moral dimension that assumes individual responsibility. It is a relationship that always begins with the divine initiative, but which calls for a human response: "Abide in me . . . abide in my word . . . abide in my love" (15:4, 7, 9).

BIBLIOGRAPHY. M. L. Appold, *The Oneness Motif in the Fourth Gospel: Motif Analysis and Exegetical Probe into the Theology of John* (WUNT 2.1: Tübingen: J. C. B. Mohr [Paul Siebeck], 1976); C. K. Barrett, *The Gospel according to St. John* (2d ed.; New York: Macmillan, 1978); G. R. Beasley-Murray, *John* (WBC 36; Waco, TX: Word, 1987); R. Borig, *Der wahre Weinstock: Untersuchungen zu Jo 15,1-10* (SANT 16: Munich: Kösel-Verlag, 1967); R. E. Brown, *The Gospel According to John (XIII-XXI)* (AB 29A; Garden City, NY: Doubleday, 1970); C. H. Dodd, *The Interpretation of the Fourth Gospel* (Cambridge: University Press, 1953); F. Hauck, "μένω κτλ," *TDNT* IV.574-76; K. Munzer, "Remain," *NIDNTT* 3.223-26; R. Schnackenberg, *The Gospel According to St. John* (3 vols.; New York: Crossroad, 1982) vol. III.

W. L. Kynes

ABOMINATION OF DESOLATION. *See* APOCALYPTIC TEACHING.

ABRAHAM

1. Abraham in the OT and Early Jewish Literature
2. Abraham in the Synoptic Gospels
3. Abraham in the Gospel According to John

1. Abraham in the OT and Early Jewish Literature. The patriarchs became increasingly important to the Jewish people after they returned from their exile in Babylon. Abraham was one of these important figures whose stature is reflected in extra-biblical Jewish literature and in the NT.

1.1. Abraham in the OT. Later accounts of Abraham are based on the stories of the patriarch found in the OT. The depiction of the life of Abraham is found in Genesis, from his inclusion in the genealogy* of his father, Terah (11:27), to his death and burial (25:7-10). The major events in Abraham's life are his leaving his father and birthplace (12:1), his sojourns in Egypt and Gerar (12:10-20; 20:1-18), his battle with the kings (14:1-16), his meeting with Melchizedek (14:17-20), God's covenant with him (15:7-21; 17:2, 4), his union with Hagar and the birth of Ishmael (16:1-15), God's commandment of circumcision for Abraham and his descendants (17:9-14), the promise of the birth of Isaac (17:15-21), the birth of Isaac (21:1-7), the offering of Isaac (22:1-19) and the death and burial of Sarah (23:1-20).

Four primary themes are found in the Genesis account: the promises from God that Abraham would have many descendants (12:2; 13:16; 15:5; 17:2, 4; 22:17) and land (12:7; 13:14-15; 15:7), the obedience of Abraham (12:1-4; 17:1; 22:16-18) and the subsequent blessing of all nations through Abraham (12:3; 22:18).

Within the OT Abraham functions in three primary ways. First, he is the *father of the Jewish people* (Gen 25:19; 26:15, 24; 28:13; 32:9; 48:15-16; Ex 3:6; Deut 1:8; 6:10; 9:5; 30:20; Josh 24:3; 1 Chron 1:27-28, 34; 16:13; Ps 105:6; Is 41:8; Jer 33:26; Mic 7:20). Second, he is the *original source of blessing for the Jewish people* (Gen 26:3-5, 24; 28:4; 35:12; 50:24; Ex 2:24; 6:3-8; 32:13; 33:1; Num 32:11; Deut 1:8; 6:10; 9:5, 27; 29:13; 30:20; 34:4; 2 Kings 13:23; 1 Chron 16:15-16; 2 Chron 20:7; Neh 9:7-8; Ps 105:7-11, 42; Is 51:2; Mic 7:20). Third, his name is used to identify the God of the Jewish people as "the *God of Abraham*" (Gen 28:13; 31:42, 53; 32:9; Ex 3:6, 15-16; 4:5; 1 Kings 18:36; 1 Chron 29:18; 2 Chron 30:6; Ps 47:9).

Abraham functions in three more noteworthy ways. His obedience to God and his laws (Gen 26:4-5; see also Neh 9:7-8) was the basis for the blessing of his descendants. God's compassion toward the Jewish people is sometimes invoked on the basis of his covenant with Abraham (Deut 9:27; 2 Kings 13:23; Mic 7:18-20). Finally, God brings Abraham out of the midst of idolatry (Josh 24:2-3).

1.2. Abraham in Early Jewish Literature. The authors of Jewish literature from 200 B.C. to A.D. 200 used many of the same themes found in the OT accounts in accordance with their particular situations. Josephus* and Philo portray Abraham as one who assimilates pagan, particularly Hellenistic (*see* Hellenism), culture (e.g., Josephus *Ant.* 1.154-157, 161, 166-168; Philo *Abr.* 88 and *Quis her.* 88). In other texts Abraham is one who isolates himself from Gentile* influence (*Jub.* 22:16, *Bib. Ant.* 6.4). The authors of these texts have not only apologetic motives, as in the case of Diaspora authors Philo and Josephus, but didactic motives as well. The Jews are permitted or instructed to live in their respective situations in the same way that Abraham is portrayed as living in a particular situation at a particular time.

Four major themes are found in these texts. First, the stress on Abraham as a tenacious monotheist, often portrayed as the first, is prevalent in texts from Palestine and the Diaspora from 200 B.C. to A.D. 200 (*Jub.* 11:16-17; 12:1-5, 16-21; 20:6-9; Pseudo-Philo *Bib. Ant.* 6.4; Josephus *Ant.* 1.154-157; Philo *Abr.* 68-71, 88; *Praem.* 27, 57-58; *Virt.* 212-216; *Ebr.* 107-110; *Apoc. Ab.* 1—8). Second, God establishes a covenant with Abraham through which his descendants are blessed (*Jub.* 15:9-10; Pseudo-Philo *Bib. Ant.* 7.4; 1 QapGen 21.8-14; *m. B. Qam.* 8.6; *m. B. Meṣ.* 7.1) and are shown compassion (Pseudo-Philo *Bib. Ant.* 30.7; *Pss. Sol.* 9:8-11; *T. Levi* 15:4; *As. Mos.* 3:8-9). However, often one must obey the stipulations of the covenant to remain within it (*Jub.* 15:26-27). Eventually other nations would be blessed as well (Sir 44:21). Third, Abraham's character is extolled. He is righteous (*T. Ab.* 1:1A), hospitable (*T. Ab.* 1:1-3A; Philo *Abr.* 107-110; Josephus *Ant.* 1.196) and virtuous (Josephus *Ant.* 1.154, 165, 256; Philo *Abr.* 68, 269; *Quis her.* 88; *Mig.* 166-167). He is faithful (Sir 44:20; 1 Macc 2:52; *Jub.* 17:17-18), he loves God (*Jub.* 17:18) and is even called the friend of God (CD 3.2-4). Josephus maintains that Abraham and his seed are rewarded because of his virtue and piety (*Ant.* 1.234). Fourth, Abraham lived according to the Mosaic Law* (*Jub.* 15:1-2; 16:20; Sir 44:20; *m. Qidd.* 4:14) or the natural/philosophical law (Philo *Abr.* 3-6). Abraham is alive (4 Macc 7:19; 16:25; *T. Levi* 18:14; *T. Jud.* 25:1; *T. Benj.* 10:6) and praises those who die for keeping the Law (4 Macc 13:13-18). Abraham established the covenant by being circumcised (Sir 44:20). Additionally, Abraham is noted for his powers of intercession (*T. Ab.* 18:10-11A) and his ascension to the heavens* where he receives revelation (Pseudo-Philo *Bib. Ant.* 18.5; *T. Ab.* 10—14; *Apoc. Ab.* 15:4-30; 4 Ezra 3:14-15).

2. Abraham in the Synoptic Gospels.

Abraham is mentioned in all of the Synoptic Gospels (Mt 1:1-2, 17; 3:9; 8:11; 22:32; Mk 12:26; Lk 1:55, 73; 3:8, 34; 13:16, 28; 16:22-30; 19:9; 20:37).

2.1. Abraham Tradition Common to All Three Synoptics. Abraham is mentioned only once in Mark (12:26), and then within the context of the Sadducees' question regarding the marital status in the resurrection of the woman who had married seven brothers consecutively (12:18-27; see also Mt 22:23-33; Lk 20:27-40). The Sadducees, who did not believe in the resurrection (Mk 12:18; Mt 22:23; Lk 20:27), present the idea of the resurrection as an absurdity within the context of present human relationships.

In both Mark and Matthew, Jesus gives the Sadducees a twofold answer since they know neither the "Scriptures nor the power of God" (Mk 12:24; Mt 22:29). By the power of God, those who have risen from the dead are like angels and do not marry. Thus, marriage is made obsolete. Secondly, Jesus uses God's identification of himself to Moses at the burning bush (Ex 3:6) as proof that God is the God of the living, not of the dead. After all, God can only be God of those who are alive. God is faithful to his promises to the patriarchs to be their God (in the case of Abraham,

see Gen 17:7) and, subsequently, to his covenant people as well. The account in Luke divides the modes of life into present and future ages (Lk 20:34-35), adding "for all live to him" (Lk 20:38). The author of 4 Maccabees similarly portrays the patriarchs as those who "do not die to God, but live in (or 'to') God" (4 Macc 7:19; 16:25).

2.2. Abraham Traditions Common to Matthew and Luke.

2.2.1. The Genealogies. Although both Matthew and Luke include Abraham in their genealogies* (Mt 1:1-2, 17; Lk 3:34), he is more significant in Matthew. The Evangelist introduces the Gospel with "the book of the genealogy of Jesus Christ, the son of David (*see* Son of David), the son of Abraham" (1:1). The transition to the genealogy is simple since it begins with Abraham "the father of Isaac" (1:2; see also 1 Chron 1:34). Abraham is mentioned a third time in chapter one (1:17) where the Evangelist outlines turning points in Israelite history as being fourteen generations from Abraham to David, fourteen generations from David to the Babylonian exile and fourteen generations from the exile to the Christ.*

It is important that Jesus is the son of Abraham for three major reasons: (1) It means that Jesus is a Jew, a physical descendant of Abraham; (2) although the title "son of Abraham" was not messianic (Davies/Allison, 158), in order for the Messiah to transmit the blessings begun with Abraham to his people, he had to be a descendant of Abraham; (3) Abraham was the originator of Israelite history while Jesus appears to be its culminator (Mt 1:17).

Although Luke's genealogy only mentions Abraham (Lk 3:34), it is still significant that Jesus is a "son of Abraham" since as such he is a Jew and a channel of blessing to the people of God. In Luke, Jesus' genealogy, traced back to Adam and God, may reflect the theme of extension of salvation* to the Gentiles, since it envisages his relationship to all humankind as God's Son (*see* Son of God; Fitzmyer, I:190).

2.2.2. Children of Abraham from Stone (Mt 3:9; Lk 3:8). Both Evangelists mention Abraham within the larger context of the ministry of John the Baptist* at the Jordan River (Mt 3:1-17; Lk 3:1-9; see Jn 8:33, 39). John warns those coming to him for baptism* (Pharisees* and Sadducees in Mt 3:7; a "multitude" in Lk 3:7) that they can rely no longer on their ethnic privilege as descendants of Abraham to guarantee them protection from the wrath of God. God can raise up "children"* (Mt 3:9; Lk 3:8) of Abraham from stone (See Is 51:1-2; Pseudo-Philo *Bib. Ant.* 23.4-5; Gen 17:17; 18:10-14). The genealogical tree of Abraham (Is 11:1; see Wallace-Hadrill) is even in danger of destruction. It is not Abrahamic descent that will save them from the wrath of God, but conduct which is "consonant with an inner reform of life" (Fitzmyer, I:468; see also Jn 8:39 and below).

2.2.3. Abraham at the Eschatological Banquet (Mt 8:10-11; Lk 13:28-29). Both Matthew and Luke speak of the eschatological banquet (*see* Table Fellowship) at which Abraham, Isaac and Jacob will preside (Luke adds "all the prophets" in 13:28). It is common in Jewish tradition that Abraham, Isaac and Jacob are found together with the righteous (*see* Justice, Righteousness; see Ward, 176; cf. 4 Macc 13:17; *T. Levi* 18:14; *T. Judah* 25:1; *T. Benj.* 10:6. See also Acts 3:13; 7:32 for occurrences of the threesome). The Matthean account occurs at the conclusion of the story of the Gentile centurion (Mt 8:1-13; see Lk 7:1-10), whose faith is unrivalled even by the Jews (Mt 8:10). In Luke the eschatological banquet scene is inserted within the parable of the narrow door (Lk 13:22-30). Both contexts, however, depict the inclusion of the Gentiles at the eschatological banquet in the kingdom of God* (Mt 8:11; Lk 13:29; see Ps 107:3; Is 49:12) and the exclusion of certain Jews (Mt 8:12; Lk 13:27-28). In these accounts Abraham is primarily an eschatological figure, although in Matthew as well as in Luke the Evangelist is establishing a "connection and continuity between the history of Abraham and the events of which he himself is writing" (Dahl, 140). The portrayal of Abraham as a heavenly figure is certainly not unique (see above, 1.2.), nor is his reputation for hospitality, even to Gentiles (see above, 1.2.; *T. Ab Rec. A* 1:1-2).

2.3. References to Abraham Particular to Luke.

2.3.1. The Hymns. Luke is unique in his inclusion of hymns within his infancy narrative. Luke may have used outside source material in the composition of these hymns. However, to "admit such sources does not mean that Luke has not reworked them, in his own style" (Fitzmyer, I:309). Two of these hymns refer to Abraham (Lk 1:46-55, 67-79). The *Magnificat* is the hymn of Mary (*see* Mary's Song) as she rejoices in anticipation of the birth of Jesus (see also 1 Sam 2:1-10). The theme of the hymn is that God helps his people in the present as he helped them in the past. Historically, he has destroyed the powerful and rich (*see* Rich and Poor); he has helped the oppressed and the poor (Ex 2:24). God continues to help the poor and oppressed in the present time (Lk 1:47-48). This assistance is based on God's faithfulness to the descendants (literally "seed"; see also Acts 3:25; 7:1-5) of Abraham because of his promises to him (see 1. above; Mic. 7:20). Abraham himself was without land or descendants until he was blessed by God (Gen 17:7-

8; 18:18; 22:17-18). Mary's experience "is not an isolated incident but rather part of the merciful remembrance of God who wants to fulfill his promises of salvation" (Zorrilla, 233). Successive generations will also experience the compassion of God (1:48).

The *Benedictus* is a prophecy given by Zechariah (*see* Zechariah's Song) concerning his son, John. John will prepare the way before the Lord (Lk 1:76) who will bring salvation to his people (Lk 1:68-69). This salvation, the purpose of which is to enable persons to serve God without fear from enemies (Lk 1:71, 73), is based on the mercy promised to the Jewish ancestors for which the covenant (or oath, Gen 22:16-17; 26:3) sworn to Abraham (Lk 1:72-73; Ps 105:7-11) is the foundation. Dahl (146-147) sees the messianic redemption as described in terms "reminiscent of the deliverance from Egypt, and seen as the fulfillment of God's oath to Abraham" (Ps 106:10; Gen 15:13-14; Acts 7:2-8, 17).

2.3.2. A Daughter of Abraham. The "bent" woman who is healed on the Sabbath (Lk 13:10-17) is called a "daughter of Abraham" (13:16). This is the only use of the expression "daughter of Abraham" in the Greek Bible. In Luke only Jews are called children of Abraham (Dahl, 151). In the pericope the Sabbath* and the synagogue* "segregate this needy woman from divine help" (Green, 649). Jesus recognizes that as a child of Abraham she is one to whom salvation was promised (Lk 1:46-55; see 2.3.1. above). God's faithfulness to the descendants of Abraham continues because of his promises to the patriarch. This is seen especially in the case of the excluded and the outcast. The daughter of Abraham who is excluded by the religious structure is healed (see 2.3.2. above). Zacchaeus, the outcast son of Abraham, has salvation extended to him. Luke's special concern for the oppressed is noticeable when the rich man, though he is a child of Abraham, is not allowed to join Lazarus in Abraham's bosom (see 2.3.3. below) because of his lack of compassion toward Lazarus while they both were alive. Thus, those thought to be excluded from the chosen are included, while those thought to be chosen are excluded.

The healing of the bent woman is a sign of salvation happening as fulfilled by the ministry of Jesus, the "lord of the Sabbath" (Lk 6:5). Notably, she is healed on the Sabbath, a day commemorating the Israelites' liberation from bondage (Deut 5:15; see Lk 13:16), and it is on this day that the woman's bondage is removed. By rebuking the disease, Jesus is also rebuking Satan (13:16; see also Green, 653; *see* Demon, Devil, Satan). She may be one of those who is included in the eschatological banquet presided over by

Abraham and his descendants (Lk 13:28-30; see 2.2.3. above).

2.3.3. Abraham's Bosom. The heavenly Abraham (see 1.2. above) is included within this pericope which condemns the rich man and exalts the poor man Lazarus. (For analyses of similar folk tales, see Fitzmyer, 2:1126). After his death Lazarus is carried by angels* to "Abraham's bosom." "Abraham's bosom" is not a synonym for Paradise, although this passage reflects the tradition in which Abraham is thought to be in heaven (see 1.2. above). The poor man enjoys close fellowship with Abraham (Marshall, 636), perhaps reminiscent of the intimacy between Abraham and Jacob in Jubilees 23:1-3 (see also Lk 13:29). The rich man has died and resides in Hades, separated from Abraham by a great chasm (Lk 16:26; cf. *1 Enoch* 22). The rich man cries out to Abraham, calling him "Father" (Lk 16:24, 27, 30) and demanding assistance from Lazarus. Abraham answers him, calling him "child" (Lk 16:25). The rich man's status as a child of Abraham does not bring him relief. Father Abraham himself refuses to assist him (Lk 16:25-26; for Abraham as judge, see *T. Ab.* 10:6-16A). Abraham will not even send Lazarus to the rich man's family to warn them because they already have the Law of Moses (Lk 16:31). Luke is stressing that salvation involves a "reaction of faith" (Fitzmyer, 2:1129) which the rich man did not have. He was thus condemned, although he was a Jew. Abraham is also appropriate in this pericope because, unlike the rich man, he was often portrayed as having followed the Law (see 1.2. above), which was not burdensome (Philo *Abr.* 5; Deut 30:11-14).

2.3.4. Zacchaeus As Son of Abraham. Zacchaeus is a rich, chief tax collector for the Romans (Lk 19:2; *see* Taxes), and as such he is a sinner* (Lk 6:24), especially in the eyes of the Jews (Lk 18:9-14; 19:7; see also Loewe, 321-23). Upon interacting with Jesus, Zacchaeus repents (Lk 19:8; see Lev 6:1-7; cf. the story of the rich ruler, Lk 18:18-25). Salvation is extended to Zacchaeus, the "son of Abraham" who once was lost, by Jesus who "came to seek and to save the lost" (Lk 19:10; Ezek 34:16). Zacchaeus is again a true son of Abraham who, like other outcast Jews, has received the fulfillment of the promises to Abraham in the ministry of Jesus (Gen 17:7; see 2.3.2. above; Dahl, 149-54).

3. Abraham in the Gospel According to John.

The name of Abraham, while occurring nowhere else in the Johannine writings, is found ten times in John 8:31-59. Throughout the account Jesus points out that although the questioning Jews are descendants of

Abraham in a physical sense (Jn 8:37), they deny it by their actions (Brown, 357). First, they are not like Abraham because they strive to kill Jesus, a messenger of God (Jn 8:40, 42; Gen 18:1-15; perhaps Jn 8:35 refers to Eliezer and Isaac, the house slave and the son; see Gen 15:2; 17:19). Second, while Abraham was known for his exemplary character (see 1.2. above), Jesus' opponents are said to be children of the devil, whose desires they fulfill (8:44). Third, Jesus' opponents are unlike Abraham because they do not recognize that Jesus is God (Jn 8:58-59; for Abraham as the first monotheist, see 1.2. above). Other references to Abraham in the chapter concern the death of Abraham (Gen 25:8, which lacks a testament; see *T. Ab.* which provides an explanation for this lack) and Abraham's rejoicing to see Jesus' day (Jn 8:56).

Just how Abraham saw Jesus' day goes unexplained. Brown refers to *Jubilees* 16:17-19: "Abraham was told that it was through Isaac that the holy people of God would be descendant, and that both Abraham and Sarah rejoiced at the news" (Brown, 360; see Gen 17:17; 21:6). Perhaps the Evangelist is referring to the Genesis account in the knowledge that Jesus would come from this holy people. Another explanation might be that Abraham was given a revelation of the future like the one in *Apocalypse of Abraham* which mentions God's "chosen one" (31:1). Abraham had special knowledge of God (see 1.2. above, especially so in the works of Philo; see Jn 8:32) which, in terms of contemporary Jewish thought, meant that he escaped idolatry (*Ap. Ab.* 6—8; *Jub.* 12) and the consequent slavery to sin (*Jub.* 20:6-10). This portrayal of Abraham certainly fits the theme of freedom (8:32) and slavery (8:34-35) in John 8.

See also MOSES.

BIBLIOGRAPHY. R. E. Brown, *The Gospel according to John (I-XII)* (AB 29A; Garden City, NY: Doubleday, 1985); N. A. Dahl, "The Story of Abraham in Luke-Acts," in *Studies in Luke-Acts: Essays Presented in Honor of Paul Schubert,* ed. L. E. Keck and J. L. Martyn (Nashville: Abingdon, 1966) 139-58; W. D. Davies and D. C. Allison, Jr., *The Gospel according to Saint Matthew* (vol. 1) (ICC; Edinburgh: T & T Clark, 1988); J. A. Fitzmyer, *The Gospel according to Luke* (AB 28A, 28B; Garden City, NY: Doubleday, 1981, 1985); J. B. Green, "Jesus and a Daughter of Abraham (Luke 13:10-17): Test Case for a Lucan Perspective on Jesus' Miracles," *CBQ* 51 (1989) 643-54; M. D. Hamm, "Freeing of the Bent Woman and the Restoration of Israel: Luke 13:10-17 as Narrative Theology," *JSNT* 31 (1987) 23-44; W. P. Loewe, "Towards an Interpretation of Lk 19:1-10," *CBQ* 36 (1974) 321-331; I. H. Marshall, *Commentary on Luke* (NIGTC; Grand Rapids: Eerdmans, 1978);

D. S. Wallace-Hadrill, "A Suggested Exegesis of Matthew iii. 9, 10 (= Luke iii. 8, 9)," *ExpT* 62 (1950-51) 349; R. B. Ward, "Abraham Traditions in Early Christianity," in *Studies on the Testament of Abraham,* ed. G. W. E. Nickelsburg, Jr. (SCS 6; Missoula: Scholars Press, 1976) 173-184; C. H. Zorrilla, "The Magnificat: Song of Justice," in *Conflict and Context: Hermeneutics in the Americas,* ed. M. L. Branson and C. R. Padilla (Grand Rapids: Eerdmans, 1986) 220-37.

N. L. Calvert

ADULTERY. *See* DIVORCE.

AMEN

Amen is used one hundred times in the Gospels—thirty-one times by Matthew, thirteen times by Mark, six times by Luke and twenty-five times (always doubled, "amen, amen") by John. The word is simply a transliteration of the Greek word *amēn,* which in turn is a transliteration of the Hebrew *'āmēn,* a word derived from a verb that means "confirm, support, establish, verify." Yet in no English version, except those based on the *Textus Receptus* (cf. KJV and NKJV and only at Mt 6:13; 28:20; Mk 16:20; Lk 24:53; Jn 21:25) does it appear as "amen." Rather it is always translated as "verily," "truly," "solemnly" or is not translated at all other than in a way to give emphasis to what is being said: "Believe me," "I tell you this," "Remember this" and so on.

In the OT "amen" was used most frequently as the response of an individual or the congregation to corroborate or affirm a word spoken by another—a prayer* that was made (1 Chron 16:36), a curse that was pronounced (Deut 27:14-26) or a doxology that was sung to God* (Ps 41:13; 72:19; cf. 3 Macc 7:23). "Amen" was the acknowledgement of the validity of the word spoken, of its binding nature. As a consequence "amen" meant something like "Yes, I (we) fully agree" or "Yes, this is true" or "May it most certainly be as you say!" Sometimes it appears in a doubled form, "amen, amen" (Num 5:22; Neh 8:6), apparently to make the response especially emphatic. This doubled response-form is the only form found to date in the literature from Qumran (cf. 1QS 1:20; 2:10, 18). Only very occasionally is "amen" found at the beginning of a saying (1 Kings 1:36; Jer 28:6), and never is it used by people to confirm or validate their own words. The NT, exclusive of the Gospels, uses "amen" in a way similar to that of the OT—such as being placed at the end of a doxology (Rom 1:25), used as the response of the people to a prayer (1 Cor 14:16), employed as an emphatic "Yes" to God (2 Cor 1:20).

In the Gospels, however, the situation is quite different. "Amen" is never found at the *end* of a saying as a response of the people but only at the beginning of a saying. It is always the *first* word of the formulaic expression "Amen, I say to you," and it is always and only spoken by Jesus, apparently to emphasize the significance of the words he was about to speak. No other person—apostle* or prophet*—of the early church* felt at liberty to follow his example by making use of this very formula (but cf. 1 Cor 7:12).

It is difficult to classify the sayings of Jesus introduced by "Amen, I say to you." Some of them are sayings about the kingdom of heaven/kingdom of God* (e.g., Mt 13:17; 18:3) and about entering the kingdom (Mk 10:15; Jn 3:3-5). Some are sayings about the eschaton (Mt 10:23; 16:28 par. Mk 9:1; 25:40, 45). Some are sayings that challenge the Judaism* of Jesus' day, or better, its exaggeration (Mt 6:2, 5, 16; 8:10), but many cannot be classified so easily. Nevertheless, the "amen"-sayings of Jesus are weighty utterances. They affirm such things as the importance of reconciliation (Mt 5:26), of giving freely (Mt 10:42), of faith* (Mt 17:20; Jn 5:24), of joy* over the lost being found (Mt 18:13), of humility and openness to God versus arrogant independence from him (Mt 21:31) and of not attributing good to evil origins (Mk 3:28). Interestingly, however, not every statement of Jesus is introduced in this emphatic way. Many of his significant sayings have no introductory formula whatsoever (e.g., Mk 10:45).

Scholars have observed: (1) that as yet no exact Hebrew equivalent of the expression "Amen I say to you" has turned up, (2) that it is found in all the Gospels and (3) that it appears in all strata of the Gospel tradition. These facts suggest, then, that "here we have the creation of a new expression by Jesus" (Jeremias, 36), "an authentic reminiscence" of Jesus' own words (Brown, 84). Surely this is so. This new expression was intended by Jesus not so much to direct attention to his divinity as to his authority* to speak for God as *the* messenger of God. Although not precisely identical, the closest analogy to his "Amen, I say to you" is the formula so frequently used by those who spoke the words of God in the OT—"Thus says the Lord"—that expression of the prophets by which they made clear that their words were God's. To be sure, Jesus was more than a prophet, but there is a sense in which he stood in that same tradition (*see* Prophet) as one filled with the Holy Spirit* (Lk 4:1). With the words "Amen, I say to you," Jesus certainly went beyond the OT prophets because he, unlike them, had been given the Spirit without measure (Jn 3:34). Like them, however, he was in essence saying the same thing but in a higher key: "You must listen to what I have to say, because the words that I speak are not mine; they are the very words of God!" (Jn 3:34).

Although the expression "Amen, I say to you" did indeed originate with Jesus and was used frequently by him to give expression to his unique authority, it may also be true that, aware of this, the Gospel writers added this formula to other of Jesus' remarks to make them especially emphatic. This inference may be drawn from noting that there are places in Mark where an important saying of Jesus is introduced with the formula "Amen, I say to you," but where Matthew and Luke, who have identical or similar sayings, either omit the formula altogether (Mt 12:39; 16:4; Lk 11:29b with Mk 8:12; Mt 19:29 with Mk 10:29; Lk 17:6 with Mk 11:23), or modify it in some way such as "For this reason I say to you" (Mt 12:31 with Mk 3:28), "But I say to you" (Mt 26:29 with Mk 14:25). "But I say to you truly (*alēthōs*, Lk 9:27 with Mk 9:1), "Truly (*alēthōs*) I say to you" (Lk 21:3 with Mk 12:43), "For I say to you" (Lk 22:18 with Mk 14:25), or simply "I say to you" (Lk 22:34 with Mk 14:30). Furthermore, in the Lukan parallels to Matthew, although "amen" always appears in Matthew, it never does in Luke—either there is no formula whatsoever (Mt 5:18 par. Lk 16:17; Mt 18:13 cf. Lk 15:5) or "I say to you" shows up without the prepositioned "amen" (Mt 5:26 par. Lk 12:59; Mt 8:10 par. Lk 7:9; Mt 10:15 cf. Lk 10:12; Mt 11:11 par. Lk 7:28; Mt 13:17 par. Lk 10:24), or it is replaced by "Yes (*nai*), I say to you" (Mt 23:36 par. Lk 11:51), "Truly (*alēthōs*), I say to you" (Mt 24:47 par. Lk 12:44). In any case, it is clear that each instance of the "Amen, I say to you" formula was intended to underscore the authority of Jesus to speak for God, and to emphasize the importance of his words.

See also PROPHETS AND PROPHECY.

BIBLIOGRAPHY. H. Bietenhard, "Amen," *NIDNTT* 1.97-99; R. E. Brown, *The Gospel according to John,* vol. 1 (AB 29; Garden City, NY: Doubleday, 1966); J. A. Fitzmyer, *The Gospel according to Luke,* vol. 1 (AB 28; Garden City, NY: Doubleday, 1981) 536-37; J. Jeremias, *New Testament Theology* (London: SCM, 1971) 35-36; H. Schlier, "ἀμήν," *TDNT* I.335-38.

G. F. Hawthorne

ANGELS

According to the Gospels, angels are spirit beings who serve God,* particularly in connection with Jesus' work of proclaiming and establishing the kingdom of God. They are important in passages dealing with certain significant events in Jesus' life and work, including his birth,* the temptations* in the wilder-

ness, the coming of the Son of man* and the eschatological judgment,* and the resurrection.* While first-century Jewish thought regarded revelation as a major role for angels, the Gospels make this function prominent only in the birth and resurrection narratives. These events at the beginning and end of the Gospels mark the coming of the Son to dwell on earth and his return to heaven.*

1. Terminology and General Jewish Background
2. The Nature of Angels
3. The Angel of the Lord
4. The Synoptic Gospels
5. The Gospel of John
6. Conclusion

1. Terminology and General Jewish Background.
In the NT "angel" translates the Greek word *angelos.* In classical Greek an *angelos* was a messenger who represented the one sending him and who enjoyed the protection of the gods. In the OT *mal'ak* was used for both human messengers (e.g., Gen 32:3; Is 33:7) and angels (e.g., Gen 21:17; Ps 103:20). The LXX translators used *angelos* for *mal'ak* when they understood it to refer to angels. Likewise, they used *angelos* to render a few other expressions for angels, such as "sons of God" (e.g., Job 1:6). In the Gospels *angelos* occurs fifty-four times; in five instances it refers to human messengers (Mt 11:10; Mk 1:2; Lk 7:24, 27; 9:52), and the remaining occurrences refer to angels.

In the OT world view angels are spirits created by God and subordinate to him. They worship him as members of his court (Dan 7:10) and serve him by intervening in human affairs, bringing divine messages (Gen 22:11-12), protecting and aiding his people (1 Kings 19:5; Ps 91:11) and smiting their enemies (2 Kings 19:35). Particularly important is the one called the Angel of the Lord (see below). Compared with the OT, intertestamental Jewish literature such as *1 Enoch, Jubilees* and the writings of the Qumran community, evidence a wide proliferation of ideas about angels. Nevertheless, the essential elements of the beliefs we encounter in the Gospels are already present in the OT. It is unnecessary to seek elsewhere, such as in Greek mystery religions, for the origins of NT beliefs concerning angels.

2. The Nature of Angels.
The Gospels only incidentally provide information on the nature of angels, and not from any speculative interest. Angels belong to the structure of reality and are mentioned in matter-of-fact language, as when Jesus answered the Sadducees'* objection to the idea of resurrection (Mt 22:30; Lk 20:34-36). The fact that

angels belong to God clearly indicates their subordination to him (Lk 12:8-9; Jn 1:51). They also belong to Jesus, the eschatological Son of man (Mt 13:41). On the other hand, the devil's angels are destined with him for eternal fire (Mt 25:41; *see* Demon, Devil, Satan; Heaven and Hell). The Gospels offer no prehistory of these angels, though the notion of angelic sin was developed in Jewish writings (e.g., *1 Enoch* 6—9; *2 Apoc. Bar.* 56:12-14) and is reflected in the NT (2 Pet 2:4; Jude 6). The fact that their ultimate fate is in God's hands presupposes his sovereignty over them and the devil. Angels can dwell in heaven (Mt 18:10; Mk 12:25) and move freely between heaven and earth (Mt 28:2; Lk 2:13; Jn 1:51). Those who watch over "little ones" enjoy access to God (Mt 18:10). They are holy (Lk 9:26) and can be associated with God's glory* in visible form (Lk 2:9; cf. 24:4), though this is a derived glory, arising from their close association with God (cf. Lk 9:26). Their numbers are very great (Mt 26:53; Lk 2:13; cf. Dan 7:10).

No speculation is entertained about their appearance, although they can present themselves in human form (as in the case of the "two men" seen at Jesus' tomb, Lk 24:4) and converse with people (Lk 1:13-20; 24:5-7). Since angels never die, they do not need to marry and reproduce (Mt 22:30; Lk 20:36). They are never said in the Gospels to possess wings.

Gabriel, whose name means "God is strong" or "man of God," is the only angel named in the Gospels (Lk 1:19, 26). He stands in God's presence (Lk 1:19; cf. *1 Enoch* 9:1; *Jub.* 2:18; 1QH 6:13; *T. Levi* 3:5, 7), which means, in the imagery of a royal court, that he is God's personal servant. It was Gabriel who appeared as a man to Daniel, interpreting a vision and giving insight (Dan 8:15-26; 9:21-27). The only other angel named in the Bible is Michael (Dan 10:13, 21; Jude 9; Rev 12:7), though various non-canonical Jewish writings name many angels. Gabriel features in several lists of leading angels or archangels, the earliest of which include four names (*1 Enoch* 9:1; 1QM 9:14-16), while others enumerate seven (*1 Enoch* 20; cf. *Tob.* 12:15; Rev 8:2). In their angelology the Gospels show marked restraint, not engaging in speculation about angels. Their focus is on Jesus himself.

3. The Angel of the Lord.

In the OT the phrase "the Angel of the Lord" occurs some sixty times. This angel is a special servant of Yahweh who helps accomplish God's will among his people. Thus he appeared to Moses* at the burning bush (Ex 3:2), opposed Balaam (Num 22:22-35) and encouraged Gideon (Judg 6:11-16). He is said to have caused death among Israel's* enemies (2 Kings 19:35) and in Israel itself (1 Chron 21:14-15), though he usually comes to the aid of God's people (Ex 14:19; Judg 2:1; 1 Kings 19:7; Ps 34:7). Often this angel cannot be distinguished from Yahweh himself (e.g., Gen 16:11, cf. Gen 16:13; Judg 6:12, cf. Judg 6:14). According to the Gospels an "angel of the Lord" appeared to Zechariah, announcing the birth of John the Baptist* (Lk 1:11). He also told Joseph of Jesus' conception by the Holy Spirit* (Mt 1:20, 24), announced Jesus' birth to the shepherds (Lk 2:9-12) and rolled back the stone at his tomb (Mt 28:2). From the linguistic data of the LXX and the NT, it is not clear whether or not these occasions involved the Angel of the Lord as described in the OT. However, general similarities between the Gospel nativity narratives and certain OT passages which mention the Angel of the Lord suggest that the angel in the nativity accounts is to be identified with the Angel of the Lord of the OT.

4. The Synoptic Gospels.

Angels play a special role in four major events during the life and ministry of Jesus as recorded in the Synoptic Gospels.

4.1. The Birth Narratives of Jesus. The angel Gabriel announced to Zechariah the imminent birth of John the Baptist, stating that John would prepare the way for what God was about to do (Lk 1:11-20). Bringing divine revelation was considered a primary function of angels in OT times (e.g., Gen 31:11-13; Dan 10:13-14; Zech 2:3-5), as it was in the intertestamental period (e.g., *1 Enoch* 10; 93:2; 4 Ezra 4:1-4). In particular, the Angel of the Lord announced the forthcoming births of Ishmael (Gen 16:11) and Samson (Judg 13:3-5). Gabriel also revealed to Mary that she would bear the Son of God through the Holy Spirit (Lk 1:26-38). Joseph learned from an angel in a dream of Mary's pregnancy and that the child would be named "Jesus" (Mt 1:18-25; cf. Lk 2:21). Within the context of the biblical tradition it was appropriate that an event of such salvific importance should be announced by heavenly messengers.

Luke tells us that an angel told the shepherds of Jesus' birth (Lk 2:8-12), and they, like Mary and Zechariah, were reassured by him in the midst of their fear (Lk 2:9-10; cf. Lk 1:12-13, 29-30). This angel was accompanied by brightness marking the activity of God (cf. Lk 9:34). A "multitude of the heavenly host" (Lk 2:13 RSV; cf. 1 Kings 22:19; 1QH 3:22) then appeared, praising God. Evidently, these angels are to be understood as heavenly attendants in God's royal entourage rather than as a celestial army (cf. 1QH 3:35; 1QM 12:7-8).

Matthew relates the role of angels in protecting Jesus during his early years. An angel of the Lord warns Joseph in a dream, telling him to flee to Egypt because of Herod the Great (Mt 2:13; *see* Herodian Dynasty). The return journey was also in obedience to angelic revelation in a dream (Mt 2:19-21), and it was presumably an angel who spoke to Joseph in the dream that led him to settle in Galilee (Mt 2:22-23).

4.2. The Temptations of Jesus. Jesus was tempted by Satan at the threshold of his messianic ministry. At one point the devil quoted Psalm 91:11-12 (Mt 4:6; Lk 4:10-11), urging Jesus to throw himself from the pinnacle of the Temple and trust that God's angels would protect him. While such a spectacle might have appeared capable of vindicating his messianic status, Jesus rejected the devil's suggestion, perceiving that it would have constituted an attempt to force God's intervention on his behalf (Deut 6:16; Mt 4:7; Lk 4:12). Angels ministered to Jesus at the conclusion of his temptations (Mt 4:11; Mk 1:13; cf. Heb 1:14). Specifically, this may mean that they provided food (cf. Elijah, 1 Kings 19:5-8). If so, God's care of the Messiah* who is faithful to his office would be contrasted with Satan's proposal that he obtain food and angelic intervention illegitimately. According to Luke 22:43 Jesus was also strengthened by an angel in Gethsemane.* While scholars are uncertain whether or not this verse was part of the original text, the idea that angels might strengthen the servants of God is well documented, as in the Qumran War Scroll (1 QM 12:7-9; 17:5-8) and the account of the Maccabean resistance (2 Macc 10:29-30).

4.3. The Coming of the Son of Man and the Final Judgment. Jesus taught that he would come to earth again as the Son of man "in clouds with great power and glory" (Mk 13:26; cf. 14:62) and accompanied by angels, to execute judgment* (Mt 16:27; Mk 8:38; cf. Lk 9:26). Such allusions derive from Daniel 7, with its figure "like a son of man" who is presented before God and given an everlasting kingdom (Dan 7:13-14). God is depicted as sitting in judgment, attended by innumerable angels (Dan 7:9-10).

The idea that angels will serve God in relation to the final judgment is important in Jewish apocalyptic* eschatology* of the intertestamental period. They function as a kind of heavenly police force, arresting offenders, presenting evidence and executing punishment. In Jesus' teaching the end of the age will see angels separating the righteous from the wicked (Mt 13:36-42; *see* Sinner; Justice, Righteousness). Angels will be dispatched to gather God's people from all over the earth (Mt 24:31; Mk 13:27; cf. *1 Enoch* 100:4),

and they will be with the Son of man when he sits in judgment (Mt 25:31). They will also assist in inflicting punishment on evildoers (Mt 13:41-42, 49-50; cf. *1 Enoch* 90:20-26; CD 2:5-7). When Jesus taught that those who acknowledged him and his teaching would ultimately be acknowledged before God's angels at his coming, the angels were being cast in the role of hearing evidence in the heavenly courtroom (cf. *1 Enoch* 99:3). Those ashamed of him will be denied before the heavenly court (Mk 8:38; Lk 9:26; 12:8-9). Matthew 10:32-33, however, places this acknowledgement and denial before the Father, without any mention of angels. But this does not imply that for Luke (12:8) "the angels of God" is a periphrasis designating God himself, for the word "God" is still used. Moreover, in Luke 9:26, a saying set in a similar scene of eschatological judgment, both God and angels are mentioned.

4.4. The Resurrection Narratives. In all four Gospels (Jn 20:11-13 is discussed below) angels announce Jesus' resurrection. In the Matthean account, an angel rolled back the stone at Jesus' tomb (again, probably the Angel of the Lord, Mt 28:2), and reassured and instructed the women who had gone there (Mt 28:5-7). In Luke "two men" appear in similarly dazzling dress (Lk 24:4-7; cf. 24:23), while Mark 16:5 has "a young man" in white (cf. 2 Macc 3:26, 33-34). At this critical point in the gospel story angels intervene, bringing divine revelation and encouraging and instructing Jesus' followers. Similarly, angels were integral to the events surrounding the Savior's birth. We might best understand the mediation of angels at both his birth and resurrection as marking the unique meeting of heaven and earth in these events.

4.5 Angels and the Welfare of Humans. Angels have various functions in relation to God's people. "Little ones" (perhaps childlike believers rather than children as such) have guardian angels who dwell in God's presence (Mt 18:10; *see* Child, Children). The language is drawn from the context of a royal court and concerns access to the king. Angels with such access to God are particularly important in Jewish thought, being called "angels of the Presence" (*Jub.* 1:27; T. Levi. 3:4-8; 1QH 6:13; 1QSb 4:26). Since the "little ones" are served by such angels who actually look on God's face—a privilege not normally belonging even to the angels closely associated with God's throne (*1 Enoch* 14:21)—it is clear that God has great concern for them.

Elsewhere, angels are said to be linked with God's people as a nation (Dan 12:1), with individual churches (Rev 1:20), with the worshiping community at Qumran (1QSa 2:8-9) and with pious individuals (1QH 5:20-22). Jesus could speak of joy* in the presence of God's angels (either the joy of angels or joy shared by God and angels) when a sinner repents, a further indication of the angels' alignment with the purposes of God (Lk 15:10; cf. 15:7). In a manner unparalleled in Jewish writings prior to the second century A.D., Jesus speaks of angels carrying Lazarus to a place of bliss at death (Lk 16:22).

As we have already noted, Jesus received angelic assistance following his temptation in the wilderness (Mt 4:11; Mk 1:13). At the close of his ministry, in the midst of his arrest in Gethsemane, he professed to have at his disposal more than twelve legions of angels (Mt 26:53). The implied military* function of these angels is reminiscent of the Qumran sectarians' anticipation that angels would fight for them in the eschatological war (1QM 7:6; 13:10). Yet Jesus chose the way of suffering and death to fulfill his mission (see Death of Jesus).

5. The Gospel of John.

Compared with the Synoptics, there are relatively few references to angels in the Gospel of John and no mention of them in relation to a final judgment. This is understandable in the light of John's realized eschatology.* There are only three (or perhaps four) passages to consider.

John's Gospel reflects popular beliefs regarding angels in at least one instance. The idea that angels bring divine revelation is reflected in the crowd's interpretation of the divine voice from heaven (Jn 12:29). While some identify it as thunder, others perceive it to be the voice of an angel. John 5:4 (though unlikely to have been part of the original text) accords with a then-popular notion that unusual phenomena were attributable to angels. Here the healing properties of the pool at Bethesda are ascribed to the stirring of the waters by an angel of the Lord.

Early in the Fourth Gospel Jesus tells Nathanael he will "see heaven opened, and God's angels ascending and descending on the Son of man" (Jn 1:51). The allusion is to the patriarch Jacob's vision of a ladder on which angels ascended and descended, linking heaven and earth (Gen 28:10-17). Jesus appears to be telling Nathanael in a figurative way that once again God would reveal himself from heaven to the pious on earth, and that this revelation would directly involve Jesus as the Son of man (cf. Jn 1:14, 18; 3:13).

Finally, on resurrection morning Mary Magdalene looks into the tomb and finds two angels in white seated where Jesus' body had lain (Jn 20:11-12).

Apparently they were not present immediately prior to this, when Peter and his companion had gone inside (Jn 20:3-8).

6. Conclusion.

The Gospels present angels as exercising functions similar to what we may observe in the OT and intertestamental Jewish writings. These include mediating heavenly revelation, aiding the pious and assisting in the final judgment. However, unlike the OT and other Jewish writings, the angelology of the Gospels is, like the Gospels as a whole, essentially christocentric. The functions of angels relate directly to the life and ministry of Jesus. Specifically, angels mediate direct revelation from God only at two moments: Jesus' birth and his resurrection. In the interim, he himself is the pre-eminent disclosure of God.

See also APOCALYPTIC; BIRTH OF JESUS; DEMON, DEVIL, SATAN; JUDGMENT; RESURRECTION; SON OF MAN; TEMPTATION OF JESUS.

BIBLIOGRAPHY. K. Barth, Church Dogmatics (Edinburgh: T. & T. Clark, 1956) III.3.369-531; R. E. Brown, The Birth of the Messiah: A Commentary on the Infancy Narratives in Matthew and Luke (Garden City, NY: Doubleday, 1977); P. J. Budd, "Angel, Messenger, Gabriel, Michael," NIDNTT 1.101-105; T. H. Gaster, "Angel," IDB 1.128-34; W. Grundmann, G. von Rad and G. Kittel, "ἄγγελος κτλ," TDNT I.74-87; H. B. Kuhn, "The Angelology of the Non-Canonical Jewish Apocalypses," JBL 67 (1948) 217-32; I. H. Marshall, The Gospel of Luke: A Commentary on the Greek Text (NIGTC; Grand Rapids: Eerdmans, 1978); L. Morris, The Gospel according to John (Grand Rapids: Eerdmans, 1971); J. Michl, "Angel," EBT 1.20-28; Y. Yadin, The Scroll of the War of the Sons of Light against the Sons of Darkness (Oxford: University Press, 1962) 229-42.

M. J. Davidson

ANOINTING

1. Usage in the Gospels
2. The Anointing of Jesus

1. Usage in the Gospels.

Acts of anointing are described in the Gospels in the contexts of fasting* (Mt 6:17), healing* (Mk 6:13; Lk 10:34; Jn 9:6, 11), burial (Mk 16:1; Mt 26:12; see Burial of Jesus) and honoring guests (Lk 7:46). Each context reflects a well-established custom (for healing, cf. Is 1:6; burial, cf. Lk 23:56; Jn 19:39). Honoring guests by anointing them was a custom associated with wealth (cf. Amos 6:6; Mic 6:15). In the case of fasting, Jesus breaks with tradition by instructing those fasting to assume a festive appearance to draw attention away from their act of piety (cf. 2 Sam 12:20-23; Jdt 10:3; 16:7).

The verb most frequently employed for "anointing" is *aleiphō*. It refers to the external act of anointing and appears in a variety of contexts (Mt 6:17; Mk 6:13; 16:1; Lk 7:38, 46; Jn 11:2; 12:3). *Chriō*, from which we derive "Christ,"* or "the anointed one," appears only once in the Gospels, of Jesus' anointing by the Holy Spirit (Lk 4:18; Is 61:1 LXX; *see* Holy Spirit). Even though *epichriō*, "to smear," shares a root word with "*chriō*," it suggests no messianic nuance; it is associated with healing in John 9:6, 11.

2. The Anointing of Jesus.

2.1. The Four Gospels. Each Evangelist records the anointing of Jesus, though their emphases differ.

2.1.1. Mark. Mark 14:3-9, appearing at the outset of Mark's passion narrative, helps link that narrative to the rest of the Gospel by presenting the woman's act and Jesus' death as integral to the gospel (*euangelion*; cf. Mk 1:1, 14-15; 8:35; 10:29; 14:9; *see* Gospel [Good News]). Some have seen in this episode a royal anointing, noting how in Mark Jesus goes to his death as the Messiah (Mk 14:61; 15:2, 9, 12, 18, 26, 32). Jesus' interpretive words, however, employ the rare word *myrizō* ("to anoint"—never used in the LXX for a royal anointing) and explicitly designate her act as an anointing for burial.

This story portrays the anonymous woman* as a genuine disciple.* First, she is contrasted with the Jewish leadership and "one of the Twelve," Judas (Mk 14:1-2, 10-11). Second, because she recognizes Jesus' impending departure, even her use of this oil, worth almost a year's wage for a day laborer, is "a beautiful thing." Jesus' words—"You will always have the poor" (v. 7)—have sometimes been read as fatalistic: poverty is inevitable (*see* Rich and Poor). This is unfortunate since Jesus thus alludes to Deuteronomy 15:11, which calls on God's people to assist the poor. Her act of love* toward Jesus now takes precedence over those acts of piety which must continue after his departure (cf. Mk 2:19-20). Finally, though Jesus' other followers cannot understand his predictions of death (e.g., Mk 8:31-33), she recognizes that the cross lies in his path.

2.1.2. Matthew. Matthew 26:6-13 marks a turning point in Matthew's Gospel with the beginning of the passion narrative. Following on the fourth and final prediction of Jesus' death (Mt 26:2; *see* Predictions of Jesus' Passion and Resurrection), which alone omits reference to the resurrection* (cf. Mt 16:21; 17:22-23; 20:18-19), it focuses attention on Jesus' impending crucifixion. Yet Matthew ties the anointing to the

resurrection by declaring that the one whom "you do not always have" (Mt 26:11) is raised to be "with you always" (Mt 28:20; cf. 1:23).

The anonymous woman who anoints Jesus fulfills for Matthew the role of a true witness in the midst of false witnesses (religious leaders; cf. Mt 23:2-3; 26:59) and inconstant witnesses (disciples; cf. Mt 16:22; 26:14, 56, 75). In anointing Jesus for burial the woman witnesses not only to Jesus' death (cf. Mt 28:1; the women do not come to embalm the body), but also to his kingship (cf. Mt 2:2; 16:28; 19:28; 21:5; 25:31; also Mt 2:11, the oils used in ritual anointing) and messiahship (Mt 1:22; 2:4; 26:28). The disciples, like the legalistic Pharisees* of Matthew's Gospel, see only the waste of the ointment and chastise her. Jesus responds by calling what she has done a "good work," pleasing to God (cf. Mt 5:16), and proclaiming that what she has done will be told in all the world.

2.1.3. Luke. Luke 7:36-50 places Jesus' anointing during his Galilean* ministry. Rather than focusing on Jesus' burial, this story enlarges upon the affirmations made of Jesus in Luke 7:33-35: one who enjoys a festive meal, a friend of sinners,* and Wisdom* recognized by her children. Luke narrates a surprising and complex interplay of social interactions: Simon—Jesus' host, a Pharisee with religious insight, concerned with cleanliness—fails to act as a host or recognize Jesus' significance, and shows no concern for cleanliness (*see* Clean and Unclean); a sinful woman (a prostitute*?) embraces forgiveness,* functions as Jesus' host (Lk 7:44), and performs a generous act of love; and Jesus, friend of sinners, nevertheless extends grace to Simon by sharing his table, then, contrary to Simon's opinion, he exercises prophetic insight into Simon's thoughts.

Sharing center stage with Jesus is this woman, who washes Jesus' feet with her tears and anoints them (rather than his head—cf. Ps 23:5) with valuable oil. A recipient of forgiveness, she responds spontaneously and graciously to Jesus, recognizing in him God's redemption (Lk 1:68; 7:29-30; 19:44).

2.1.4. John. John 12:1-8 marks the beginning of John's passion narrative. Set in Bethany, where Lazarus* was raised (Jn 11), the narrative is thus rooted in Jesus' proclamation, "I am the resurrection and the life" (Jn 11:25). It is shadowed by the Sanhedrin's* plot against Jesus, a direct consequence of his having raised Lazarus. John differs from the other Gospels by identifying the woman who anoints Jesus as Mary of Bethany (cf. Jn 11:2). Some confusion surrounds why Mary anoints Jesus' feet (cf. Jn 11:32), then immediately wipes away the expensive oil with her hair. Since the woman is not designated a "sinner," as in Luke, her action seems inappropriate. Some have suggested that Mary anoints Jesus' feet as if preparing his body for burial. This, then, would be a prophetic anointing, since it is Nicodemus, not Mary, who later brings spices to anoint Jesus' body (Jn 19:39-40). Another interpretation links the anointing of Jesus' feet with the washing of the disciples' feet by Jesus (Sabbe). In this context Mary's act of anointing exemplifies the attitude of service and devotion to which Jesus will call the disciples (Jn 13:12-15). Mary's action and attitude stand in stark contrast to that of Judas, highlighting her role as a true disciple.

2.2. Tradition History. In spite of these differences, these four stories are remarkably similar with respect to form (i.e., setting, the woman and the ointment, the reaction, Jesus' response) and detail (Green, 106-8). Two details are especially noteworthy. First is the major agreement of Luke and John against Matthew and Mark regarding the object of the woman's attention (feet versus head). Second, there are verbal agreements between Mark and John: the type and cost of the ointment (Mk 14:3, 5; Jn 12:3, 5); Jesus' command, "Leave her alone!" (Mk 14:6; Jn 12:7); and the contrast between the poor (whom you will always have) and Jesus (whom you will not always have) (Mk 14:7; Jn 12:8; cf. Mt 26:11). This suggests that Mark/Matthew represents one form of the tradition, Luke another, with John's story a conflation of the two (*see* Tradition Criticism). Some have argued on this basis that John knew and used the Synoptics as sources, but then John's redactional activity becomes inexplicable (*see* Synoptics and John). It is more likely that John had his own source which already reflected a cross-fertilization between the traditions behind the Synoptics. Whether the Synoptics represent two separate incidents in Jesus' ministry—the one centering on the penitent woman interrupting a meal at a Pharisee's house in Galilee (Luke), the other a pre-burial anointing in Bethany (Mark-Matthew)—continues to be debated.

See also BURIAL OF JESUS; DEATH OF JESUS.

BIBLIOGRAPHY. J. B. Green, *The Death of Jesus: Tradition and Interpretation in the Passion Narrative* (WUNT 2:33; Tübingen: J. C. B. Mohr [Paul Siebeck], 1988); F. J. Matera, *Passion Narratives and Gospel Theologies: Interpreting the Synoptics through Their Passion Stories* (TI; New York/Mahwah: Paulist, 1986); R. Pesch, "Die Salbung Jesu im Bethanien (Mk 14,3-9). Eine Studie zur Passionsgeschichte," in *Orientierung an Jesus. Zur Theologie der Synoptiker: Für Josef Schmid*, ed. P. Hoffmann (Freiburg: Herder, 1973) 267-85; M. Sabbe, "The Footwashing in Jn 13 and Its Relation to the Synoptic Gospels," *ETL* 58 (1982) 279-308; D. Senior, *The Passion of Jesus in the Gospel of Mark* (Wilmington, DE: Michael Glazier, 1984); R. F Thiemann, "The Unnamed Woman at Bethany," *Today* 44 (1987) 179-88.

J. B. Green and H. E. Hearon

ANTIPAS. *See* HERODIAN DYNASTY.

ANTI-SEMITISM

The term *anti-Semitism* refers to prejudice, hostility or hatred directed against the Jewish people. The question of whether the Gospels* are anti-Semitic is complicated by the conflicting definitions given to the term. A variety of details in the Gospels have been alleged to demonstrate the Gospel writers' hostility to the Jews. These details reflect the conflict between the early Christian communities and non-Christian Jews as well as the conflict between Jesus and his contemporaries. However, other details indicate that the Gospels censure or condemn only those Jews who rejected Jesus and the gospel (*see* Gospel [Good News]).

1. Definitions
2. Alleged Anti-Semitism in the Gospels

1. Definitions.
Anti-Semitism is defined in different ways, some more restrictive than others. Most narrowly defined, it refers to the hostility toward the Jews based on nineteenth-century theories of racial superiority. Used more broadly, anti-Semitism refers to any attitude of prejudice or hostility directed at the Jewish people as such. In this sense it is often distinguished from "anti-Judaism," which refers to criticism of Jewish religious beliefs or practices. In its widest application, however, anti-Semitism is used to refer to both hostility toward Jews and denial of the validity of Judaism* as a religion.

The issue of whether the Gospels contain anti-Semitic material is decided in part by the way anti-Semitism is defined. If it refers only to attitudes based on nineteenth-century racial theories, then the first-century Gospels cannot be anti-Semitic. If it is used in the broadest sense to include negation of Judaism as a religion, then the question is more complex. None of the Gospels allows ongoing validity to Judaism apart from belief in Jesus as the Messiah (*see* Christ). But they present such belief not as the replacement of Judaism but as its fulfillment. The status of Judaism is thereby markedly redefined, but its legitimacy is not denied. Furthermore, religious controversy between Christians and Jews may have nothing to do with hostility to the Jews as a people. Condemnation of some Jews on religious grounds is fundamentally different from prejudice against all Jews on racial grounds. The Hebrew Scriptures themselves provide examples of such religious condemnation within Jewish circles. A proper evaluation of the Gospels' attitude toward the Jews must consider not only their denunciation of Jewish rejection of Jesus but also their affirmation of Jewish belief in Jesus and their ongoing concern for evangelism among the Jews. These factors indicate that the Gospel writers regarded the Jews as no different from non-Jews in their need for positive response to the gospel.

Furthermore, the anti-Semitic use of material from the Gospels must be distinguished from anti-Semitism in the Gospels themselves. Various texts of the Gospels have been understood in ways that contributed to anti-Semitic attitudes, but such interpretation, even if it is common, may not necessarily reflect the intentions of the Evangelists. Like all texts, allegedly anti-Semitic passages must be interpreted within their historical and theological contexts. Ancient rhetorical conventions were considerably different from modern ones; ideological opponents were routinely condemned in venomous terms. Language which sounds violent to modern ears is often relatively temperate by the standards of the first century.

2. Alleged Anti-Semitism in the Gospels.

Various details of all four Gospels have been understood to indicate that the Evangelists were hostile to the Jews in some respect. Some of the more prominent are examined under the headings below.

2.1. Generalizing Language. The Gospels use certain expressions which have been understood as anti-Jewish stereotypes. But the way the expressions are used suggests otherwise.

2.1.1. This Generation. All the Synoptics include sayings of Jesus in which "this generation" is denounced as unbelieving and subject to judgment.* Though it is recognized that the phrase could have been used by Jesus in intra-Jewish controversy, certain redactional features, such as the apparently unfavorable comparison with Gentiles* (Mt 12:39-42; Lk 11:29-32; cf Mk 8:12), are taken to indicate anti-Semitism on the part of the Evangelists.

However, Josephus'* use of *generation* illustrates the way a Jewish writer of the first century could use the term with reference only to one segment of the generation. On three occasions he uses it to refer not to the entire Jewish nation but to the Zealot faction which resisted the Romans in the siege of Jerusalem (*J.W.* 5.442-43, 566; 6.408; *see* Revolutionary Movements). The Synoptists use the expression in much the same way, implicitly limiting it to unbelievers. For

example, in the context preceding the denunciation of this generation in Matthew 12:39-42, the Jewish crowd's positive response is contrasted with the Pharisees'* unbelief (12:23-24). Luke notes a similar division among Jesus' Jewish contemporaries (Lk 7:29-30) immediately before a denunciation of this generation (7:31-35). The statements reflect the sharp conflict between Jesus and his opponents, but their setting indicates that Jews are not condemned en masse.

2.1.2. The Jews. Likewise, the use of "the Jews" for the opponents of Jesus has been taken as an indication of hostility toward all Jews. This usage is frequent in John, but it is also found once in Matthew (Mt 28:15) and several times in Luke's second volume (e.g., Acts 9:23; 12:3; 13:45; 17:5; 22:30; 26:2).

Again, however, Josephus' usage is pertinent. Frequently he designates those Jews who fought against Rome* simply as "the Jews," even in contexts where they are distinguished from other Jews who had no part in the rebellion (e.g., *J.W.* 2.466; 5.109-10; 6.71-79, 251-53). The limitation of the term is implicit in the context.

There are similar indications that John did not intend to characterize all Jews as unbelievers with his use of "the Jews" for Jesus' opponents. On some occasions the expression "the Jews" alternates with more specific terms for Jesus' opponents such as "rulers" or "chief priests and Pharisees" (Jn 7:1, 13, 26, 32, 45-49; 8:13, 48, 57; 9:13, 15-16, 18; *see* Priest and Priesthood). Likewise, Jewish persons may be distinguished in the narrative from the group called "the Jews" (5:15; 7:11-13; 9:22). "The Jews" can even be divided among those who accept Jesus' claims and those who reject them (10:19-21; cf Acts 14:1-5). John affirms that Jesus was a Jew (Jn 4:9) and that "salvation comes from the Jews" (4:22). Some scholars have taken these different uses as indications of various levels of redaction with different degrees of anti-Jewish hostility. However, Josephus' usage shows that "the Jews" could be used by a single author with various tacit restrictions in different contexts. John's Jews thus need not characterize all Jews as Jesus' opponents; it is implicitly limited to the antagonistic leaders.

Nevertheless, the question remains as to why John called Jesus' opponents "the Jews" so often. He could and did employ more specific terms, such as "rulers," "Pharisees" and "chief priests." The answer probably lies in John's application of the traditions about Jesus to the situation Christians faced when he wrote. John's church appears to have been in conflict with non-Christian Jews. His interest in the expulsion of

Christian Jews from the synagogue (9:22; 12:42; 16:2) suggests that such was the experience of some in his circle. By designating Jesus' opponents as "the Jews," John could make a subtle connection between them and the Jews who opposed Christians at the time that he wrote. But John clearly did not intend to represent all Jews as unbelievers; those expelled from the synagogue* for their belief in Jesus were themselves Jews. John's use of "the Jews" thus indicates an intense theological conflict between Christians and non-Christian Jews, but it does not indicate that the writer regarded all Jews as evil and unbelieving.

2.2. Denunciation and Pronouncement of Judgment. Various texts of all four Gospels have been alleged to condemn all Jews, sometimes with a contrasting pronouncement of blessing on the Gentiles. However, several details of these texts indicate that the Evangelists understood the statements to extend only to those Jews who rejected Jesus. Only some of the more notorious examples can be treated here, but similar observations can be made concerning other texts.

2.2.1. The Parable of the Wicked Tenants. This parable* (Mt 21:33-46; Mk 12:1-12; Lk 20:9-19) has been taken to imply that the privileges of Israel are transferred to the Gentiles (Mt 21:41, 43; Mk 12:9; Lk 20:16). But all the Evangelists specify the leaders, in contrast to the crowds, as the ones against whom the parable was spoken (Mt 21:45-46; Mk 12:12; Lk 20:19), thus suggesting their loss of leadership among God's people.

Matthew 21:43 appears to signify more: a withdrawal of Israel's elect status as a nation. However, the singular *ethnei* ("nation") instead of the plural *ethnesin* ("Gentiles") implies a transfer of the kingdom not to the Gentiles as such but to another nation, namely, the church, which Matthew understands as composed of both Jews and Gentiles. The text reflects the intense controversy between those who accept Jesus as Messiah and those who reject such a claim, but its denial of Jewish religious prerogatives does not imply a condemnation of Jews as such. For Matthew, belief in Jesus, not ethnicity, determines elect status.

2.2.2. The Denunciation of the Pharisees. All the Synoptics present Jesus' discourse against the scribes and Pharisees, though Matthew's version is the most extensive (Mt 23:1-36; Mk 12:38-40 [scribes only]; Lk 11:39-52; 20:45-47). Because the Pharisees are understood by modern Jews to be the founders of post-Temple Judaism, this discourse is taken as a particularly sharp attack on the Jews. Matthew is especially seen as waging a bitter, personal attack on his Jewish contemporaries who, under the leadership of the Pharisees, have cast Christians out of the synagogues.

Again, several other elements of the text deserve notice. In all the Synoptics the denunciation of the Pharisees follows the crucial question about the Messiah (Mt 22:42; Mk 12:35; Lk 20:41). The discourse thus reflects not a mere personal conflict but the crucial issue in the Gospels: response to Jesus. The contrast between the Pharisees and "teachers of the Law*" and "the Christ" as teacher (Mt 23:8-11) implies not a condemnation of all Jews but an appeal to the Jewish masses to follow Jesus instead of the leaders who reject him (cf. Mt 15:12-14; 16:6, 12). The harshness of the denunciation has parallels in the criticism of outsiders in the Qumran literature (e.g., 1QS 4:9-14; *see* Dead Sea Scrolls) and in Matthew's own condemnation of believers whose lives are inconsistent (7:21-23). Thus, Matthew's Jesus does not condemn the Pharisees because they are Jewish. The condemnation springs in part from their rivalry for the allegiance of the Jewish people. Finally, though, the Pharisees are condemned because in Matthew's view their rejection of Jesus disqualifies them from the status they claim for themselves.

2.2.3. The Jerusalem Oracles. Jesus' oracles of judgment against Jerusalem (Mt 23:37-39; Lk 13:34-35; 19:11 44) have been understood as the Evangelists' interpretation of the destruction of Jerusalem (*see* Destruction of Jerusalem) as the condemnation of the Jews. But again the judgment appears to be confined to those who reject Jesus.

Luke particularly stresses the role of Jerusalem as the city that kills Jesus (e.g., Lk 9:31, 51). But for Luke Jerusalem does not function as a figure for the Jewish nation as a whole; rather, Luke distinguishes Jerusalem from the rest of Israel* (Lk 13:31-35; cf Acts 13:27). Further, Luke does not insist that all Jerusalemites opposed Jesus or that their judgment is irrevocable: the "daughters of Jerusalem" are sympathetic to Jesus in the Lukan passion narrative (23:27-30; *see* Passion Narrative), and in Acts the Jerusalemites are offered forgiveness* (2:22-24, 38, 40; 3:13-20).

In Jesus' apocalyptic discourse (*see* Apocalyptic Teaching) Matthew and Luke deliver different versions of Jesus' instructions to flee at the approach of disaster (Mt 24:15-16; Lk 21:20). If the reference is to the destruction of Jerusalem, then the text implies that faithful disciples* of Jesus are found in Jerusalem and escape the fate that befalls the rest of the city. Moreover, Luke indicates that the redemption of Jesus' Jerusalemite audience will follow the city's destruction (21:28; cf 20:45; 21:37-38; 24:21). Because of its rejection of Jesus, the city is condemned with harsh language, but that condemnation does not preclude the salvation* of some.

2.2.4. "Your Father the Devil." The assertion "You are from your father, the devil" (Jn 8:44) has been repeatedly employed to malign the Jewish people. However, it is doubtful that John intended it so. The statement is severe, but it is set in the midst of bitter controversy: Jesus' opponents deny the legitimacy of his birth (8:41), claim he is not a real Jew and judge him demon-possessed (8:48; *see* Demon, Devil, Satan). In the framework of Johannine dualism and according to the rhetorical conventions of the day, such harsh accusations call forth a harsh response. But there is little to indicate that John condemns all Jews as diabolical. The belief of some Jews is noted earlier in the episode (8:30), and these are challenged to ongoing discipleship* (8:31). Indeed, John may intend the controversy which follows as a struggle between Jesus and his opponents for the loyalty of these believers. In that struggle both sides employ pointed language characteristic of such controversies in the ancient world, but the Christians' condemnation of their opponents is based on their response to Jesus, not their ethnicity as such.

2.3. Responsibility for the Crucifixion. All the Gospels indicate that the Jewish leaders initiated the plot to kill Jesus and that Pilate's attempt to release Jesus was met with the Jewish crowd's demand for his death (*see* Death of Jesus). This version of the events has been widely understood as reflecting a tendency to exonerate the Romans and implicate the Jews. Again, however, the evidence requires a more balanced assessment.

2.3.1. Pilate's Role. Pilate's (*see* Pontius Pilate) capitulation to the crowd's demand is not presented by the Evangelists in a positive light (*see* Trial of Jesus). All the Synoptics include references to Gentiles in Jesus' predictions of the passion (Mt 20:19; Mk 10:33; Lk 18:32; *see* Predictions of Jesus' Passion and Resurrection), and Pilate is presumably numbered among them. In Matthew, Pilate yields to the crowd despite the warning of his wife's dream (27:19). His washing of his hands is an empty gesture (27:24); he can no more evade his responsibility than could Judas (*see* Judas Iscariot) or the high priests (27:3-7). In Luke, Pilate pronounces Jesus' innocence three times (23:4, 15, 22). However, this serves to emphasize Jesus' innocence (cf 23:41, 47; Acts 3:13; 13:28), not to exonerate Pilate, who in Acts is numbered among those who gather against the Lord's Anointed (Acts 4:25-28). In Mark, Pilate's resistance to the crowd's demand is minimal. In John, he is cynical and self-serving (18:35, 38; 19:8). Thus, no consistent exoneration of Pilate can be traced in any of the Gospels.

2.3.2. The Jewish Crowds. Both Matthew and Luke refer to the crowd which demands Jesus' death as *laos* ("people"; Mt 27:25; Lk 23:13; *see* People, Crowd). This term is used in the LXX and NT to refer especially to the nation of Israel. Hence, some have understood Matthew and Luke to indicate that the entire Jewish nation is implicated in the demand for Jesus' death.

It is not clear, however, that this is the case. Elsewhere in Luke's Jerusalem narrative, *laos* is used not to signify all Israel but to indicate the common people as distinguished from the Temple* hierarchy (e.g., 19:48; 20:6, 19; 21:38; 22:2). That distinction appears to be the reason for its use in the trial scene. In 23:13 the *laos* is a group distinct from the high priests and leaders. That Luke does not understand this *laos* to include all Israel is explicitly indicated in Acts 13:27-28, where only "the residents of Jerusalem and their leaders" are specified as those responsible for Jesus' death.

Matthew's phrase "all the people" probably reflects an established use of the phrase in the context of execution. Deuteronomy 13:9 (MT and LXX: 13:10) and 17:7 indicate the responsibility of "all the people" to stone a condemned person; the Mishnah (*m. Sanh.* 6:4) indicates that such stoning is the responsibility of "all Israelites." Matthew may have been directly influenced by Jeremiah 26:8-9, 15, where "all the people" demand Jeremiah's death and thereby bring innocent blood on themselves. In all these cases phrases similar to Matthew's indicate the unanimity of the crowd; clearly none of these texts envisages all Israelites as calling for or taking part in an execution. It therefore appears likely that Matthew's phrase also implies the crowd's unanimity. Furthermore, the phrase is comparable to other Matthean expressions which are widely understood to be hyperbolic (3:5-6; 24:9). Thus, this language should not be pressed so that the entire nation is gathered before Pilate to condemn Jesus.

The so-called blood curse (Mt 27:25) must be understood in this light. Matthew may understand "our children" to refer to the generation which experiences the destruction of Jerusalem in A.D. 70, particularly if he is influenced by Jeremiah 26. The statement highlights Jewish rejection of Jesus, connecting the rejection at the passion with that of the subsequent generation. But in making that connection Matthew does not suggest that the entire nation definitively and permanently rejects Jesus. The implication that unbelieving Jews forfeit their place among the people of God (cf. Mt 21:43) reflects the exclusivism of messianic belief, but not hostility to Jews as such.

2.3.3. The Identity of the Crucifiers. Luke 23:25-26 and John 19:16-18 have been understood as implying that

Jews, not Romans, performed the act of crucifying Jesus. In both cases the interpretation depends on identifying the antecedent of "they" with the Jews in the preceding context. But other factors indicate that Luke and John did not intend to place full responsibility for Jesus' execution at the feet of the Jewish leaders. Crucifixion was regularly carried out by Romans throughout the empire; the charges against Jesus were political in nature, especially as evidenced by the inscription on the cross; and Pilate not only pronounced the death sentence but also had jurisdiction over Jesus' body (see Burial of Jesus). Thus, while responsibility for Jesus' crucifixion is never completely deferred from the Jewish leadership, neither are the Romans fully exonerated in the Lukan and Johannine accounts. Moreover, both Gospels distinguish the soldiers (stratiōtai) from Jewish figures in the crucifixion account (Lk 23:35-37; Jn 19:31-32). John earlier mentions a speira ("cohort"; 18:3, 12) that participates in Jesus' arrest, a term usually referring to Roman soldiers. Luke elsewhere mentions Jewish soldiers, but these he calls stratēgoi and strateuomenoi, not stratiōtai, which he reserves elsewhere for Romans. Likewise, the Lukan centurion (23:47) bears a Roman military title. In both Luke and John, Pilate's "turning over" of Jesus to his Jewish opponents stresses the role of certain Jews in instigating the crucifixion. But neither Evangelist implies that anyone other than Roman soldiers were the actual executioners. Jewish involvement is stressed, but Rome is not exonerated.

See also GENTILES; ISRAEL; PEOPLE, CROWD.

BIBLIOGRAPHY. J. Ashton, "The Identity and Function of the Ioudaioi in the Fourth Gospel," NovT 27 (1985) 40-75; C. A. Evans, "Is Luke's View of the Jewish Rejection of Jesus Anti-Semitic?" in Reimaging the Death of the Lukan Jesus, ed. D. D. Sylva (Athenäum Monografien: Theologie; Bd. 73; Bonner Biblische Beiträge; Frankfurt am Main: Anton Hain, 1990) 29-56, 174-183; J. G. Gager, The Origins of Anti-Semitism: Attitudes toward Judaism in Pagan and Christian Antiquity (New York: Oxford University, 1983); D. A. Hagner, The Jewish Reclamation of Jesus (Grand Rapids: Zondervan, 1984); J. Isaac, The Teaching of Contempt: Christian Roots of Anti-Semitism (New York: McGraw-Hill, 1965); L. T. Johnson, "The New Testament's Anti-Jewish Slander and the Conventions of Ancient Polemic," JBL 108 (1989) 419-41; P. Richardson and D. Granskou, eds., Anti-Judaism in Early Christianity (SCJ 2; Waterloo, Ontario: Wilfrid Laurier University, 1986); R. R. Ruether, Faith and Fratricide: The Theological Roots of Anti-Semitism (New York: Seabury, 1974); J. T. Sanders, The Jews in Luke-Acts (London: SCM, 1987); S. Sandmel, Anti-Semitism in the New Testament? (Philadelphia: Fortress, 1978); J. N. Sevenster, The Roots of Pagan Anti-Semitism in the Ancient World (NovTSup 41; Leiden: Brill, 1975); J. A. Weatherly, "The Jews in Luke-Acts," TynB 40 (1989) 107-17.

J. A. Weatherly

APHORISM. See CHREIA/APHORISM.

APOCALYPTIC

The adjective is used in at least three different ways: to refer to a type of literature (apocalypse), a kind of eschatology* (apocalyptic eschatology) and an historical movement (apocalypticism). The NT contains only one apocalypse (Revelation), but Jesus and first-century Christians borrowed much from Jewish apocalyptic eschatology, and many scholars would consider early Christianity itself an apocalyptic movement, or place it within the broader current of Jewish apocalypticism.

1. Apocalypse
2. Apocalyptic Eschatology
3. Apocalypticism

1. Apocalypse.

Because the ancients did not consistently use apokalypsis (the Greek word means simply "revelation") to designate works that belong to the genre, any list of apocalypses must be our own, just as any definition must be a modern construct.

1.1. Definition. K. Koch took six features to be characteristic: long discourse cycles, forecasts of spiritual turmoil, paraenetic discourses, pseudonymity, mythical images rich in symbolism and composite character (evidenced by breaks, contradictions and other signs of long literary development). There is, however, a certain lack of precision in all this, and it is better to accept the definition, at once more comprehensive yet more exact, proposed by the Society of Biblical Literature Genres Project:

> "Apocalypse" is a genre of revelatory literature with a narrative framework, in which a revelation is mediated by an otherworldly being to a human recipient, disclosing a transcendent reality which is both temporal, insofar as it envisages eschatological salvation, and spatial insofar as it involves another, supernatural world. (Collins 1979, 9)

This definition embraces a large number of old Jewish, early Christian, Gnostic, Greek, Latin and Persian books, all of which evaluate the present and offer consolation and encouragement by focusing on a symbolic universe whose center is a transcendent order or a better future.

1.2. Jewish Apocalypses. For the purposes of NT

study, the Jewish apocalypses composed between 250 B.C. (certain Aramaic portions of *1 Enoch* found in the Dead Sea Scrolls* appear to be that early) and A.D. 150 are most important. Many apocalypses have been lost and are known only by name. Of those extant, there are perhaps fifteen (some have uncertain dates), written first in Hebrew, Aramaic and Greek but preserved (by Christians) in translations in numerous languages. These may be divided into two groups, those that recount an otherworldly journey and those that do not. To the former belong *1 Enoch* 1—36, 37—71 (the Similitudes), 72—82 (the Heavenly Luminaries); *Testament of Levi* 2—5; *Testament of Abraham* 10—15; the *Apocalypse of Abraham; 3 Apocalypse of Baruch;* the *Apocalypse of Zephaniah;* and *2 Enoch.* To the latter group belong *1 Enoch* 83—90 (the Animal Apocalypse); 93 + 91:12-17 (the Apocalypse of Weeks); Daniel 7—12; *Jubilees* 23; *4 Ezra;* and *2 Apocalypse of Baruch.*

Apocalypses in the second group revolve around an historical crisis. They also contain historical reviews which divide history into distinct periods. This is not true of the members of the first group, with the exception of the *Apocalypse of Abraham* (which, being from the second century A.D., is not an early apocalypse). Thus, as J. J. Collins has summarized:

> . . . it would seem that there are two strands of tradition in the Jewish apocalypses, one of which is characterized by visions, with an interest in the development of history, while the other is marked by other-worldly journeys with a stronger interest in cosmological speculation. (Collins 1984, 5)

1.3. Common Features. The ancient Jewish apocalypses share several significant features. All draw heavily on OT phraseology, themes and motifs. All are filled with mysterious revelations, heavenly secrets, obscure symbolism and esoteric wisdom. All reflect alienation from the world as it is. All are also pseudonymous, so that in each case the purported author, who is the recipient of revelation, is always a great hero from the sacred past (Enoch, Abraham,* Ezra, etc.). Finally, most of the apocalypses wrestle with the problem of evil and most anticipate evil's eschatological undoing; but it is wrong to imagine that all of them are primarily concerned with eschatological matters.

1.4. Mark 13. Along with its Synoptic parallels (Mt 24; Lk 21), Mark 13 has often been dubbed a "little apocalypse" *(see* Apocalyptic Teaching). It does undeniably share certain important features of the genre. It belongs, however, to an anonymous, not pseudonymous, work. More importantly, its revelations are not attributed to a heavenly intermediary.

The earthly Jesus himself uncovers the future. There are in addition no allegories and no involved symbolism. If therefore the definition given above (1.1.) is accepted, one must hesitate to classify Mark 13 as an apocalypse. Still, like so many Jewish examples of the testament genre, it is very closely related.

2. Apocalyptic Eschatology.
This phrase may be employed in more than one sense.

2.1. Definition. "Apocalyptic eschatology" could designate the eschatological teachings distinctive of or common to the Jewish apocalypses *(see* Eschatology). This, however, would severely limit the term, for there are apocalypses with very little eschatological material (e.g., *2 Enoch*). For this and other reasons it is best to give "apocalyptic eschatology" the more common and broader meaning: it refers to that cluster of themes and expectations which developed, often in association with belief in a near end, in the altered circumstances of the post-exilic period *(see* Judaism). Characteristic features include emphasis on eschatological signs; expectation of a cosmic cataclysm; belief in a temporally near, other-worldly kingdom; concern for universal human history; and interest in heavenly redeemer figures, such as Melchizedek in the Dead Sea Scrolls or the hidden Son of man in *1 Enoch.*

2.2. Origins. For G. von Rad, Jewish apocalyptic eschatology grew out of the wisdom* tradition (301-308). Other scholars have supposed it was begotten by Persian, Egyptian or Hellenistic influence, while additional factors such as cosmogonic myths and priestly interest in the heavenly temple have also received attention. But most, while not discounting other factors, have looked to OT prophecy as the major source. As P. Hanson has written, "apocalyptic eschatology is the mode assumed by the prophetic tradition once it had been transferred to a new and radically altered setting in the post-exilic community." This position is justified, despite the problems created by the dearth of material from the fourth and third centuries B.C. and our consequent inability to trace the historical development. OT passages such as Isaiah 24—27 (eschatological prophecies mixed with semi-mythological conceptions); Ezekiel 40—48 (tour/vision of a new or ideal Jerusalem); and Zechariah 1—8 (visions clarified by an angelic interpreter) show us prophetic eschatology beginning to grow into apocalyptic eschatology.

2.3. Jesus and the Gospels. Although he wrote no apocalypse, many have thought that Jesus was a proponent of apocalyptic eschatology. He, however, rejected sign-seeking (Mk 8:11-13; Lk 17:20-21) and explicitly disavowed knowledge of the date of the end (Mk 13:32). He also, with his proclamation of the presence of the kingdom (Mk 2:18-22; Lk 11:20), broke through the pessimistic tendency to draw a hard and fast distinction between the present evil age and the coming good age. And he directed attention away from a mythological, other-worldly redeemer to his own historical person (see Messiah; Son of Man). Furthermore, there is no evidence that Jesus had studied any of the apocalypses that have come down to us; at least he never cites or alludes to such, and their direct influence cannot be traced in his teaching.

These facts entail that one can scarcely, without further ado, turn Jesus and those who recorded his teaching into advocates of apocalyptic eschatology. At the same time, Jesus taught the resurrection* of the dead (Mk 12:18-27) and looked for a transcendent kingdom of God* (Mt 25:31-46). He referred to the eschatological downfall of Satan* (Mk 3:20-27; Lk 10:18) and, probably with Daniel 7 in mind, spoke of the Son of man* coming on the clouds of heaven. In addition, he anticipated eschatological tribulation (Lk 12:49-53) and warned of a final judgment* (Mt 11:20-24). All this is characteristic of apocalyptic eschatology, and thus its influence on Jesus cannot be denied.

Taking into account all the facts, the conclusion is this: while Jesus adopted much of the language and teaching of apocalyptic eschatology, he simultaneously revised certain of its elements and consciously rejected others. (Recall that in many areas Jesus was critical of contemporary thinking.) The relationship of Jesus' eschatological teaching to apocalyptic eschatology is analogous to the relationship between prophecy and apocalyptic: despite close, genetic connections, the two are not the same thing.

3. Apocalypticism.

As with "apocalypse" and "apocalyptic eschatology," "apocalypticism," which concerns the social-historical rather than the literary-theological, is also ambiguous.

3.1. Definition. "Apocalypticism" may be taken to designate something like a millenarian movement, that is, an historical movement, usually short-lived, which is marked by energy and enthusiasm and dominated by the hope that a new order of reality will soon overthrow the existing social order. The so-called cargo cults illustrate the phenomenon. Some would consider early Christianity just such an apocalyptic movement, which raises the prospect of applying to it certain models developed from the sociological study of millenarian movements (Gager). More commonly, however, NT scholars use apocalypticism to refer to a movement within post-exilic Judaism.*

Stimulated by instability and religious crisis (as during the time of Antiochus IV Epiphanes), its members—among whom were the authors of the apocalypses—lived in the symbolic universe of apocalyptic eschatology. The extent and importance of the movement has been variously estimated, some thinking of it as marginal, others as mainstream.

3.2. The Jesus Movement. What was early Christianity's relationship to this so-called movement? According to E. Käsemann, "apocalyptic was the mother of all Christian theology" (102). While exaggerated, there is truth in this statement. The influence of apocalyptic eschatology on significant portions of the NT is clear (see the examples from the Gospels in section 2.3.). Moreover, such texts as Luke 19:11 and Acts 1:6 show that the early church* had in its midst people who hoped that the eschatological climax would come in the near future. It would seem, then, that one might set the Jesus movement within the Jewish apocalyptic movement. And yet the NT contains much of importance which has no parallel in the literary remains of Jewish apocalypticism (including the Gospel genre [see Gospel (Genre)] and a concentration on immediately past salvific events). Further, even when Revelation—which comes not from the early community but from the end of the first century—is included, "a whole range of speculative interests" closely linked with the apocalyptic movement—such as uranography, cosmography, meteorology—"is missing from the New Testament" (M. Stone). The relationship of the early community to apocalypticism is then one of significant continuity beside significant discontinuity.

The circumstance may be illustrated further by reference to the doctrine of the resurrection. The expectation is found in Daniel 7—12; *1 Enoch* 37-71; 83-90; 4 Ezra and *2 Apocalypse of Baruch,* and it was accepted by the Pharisees,* whose origins lie within the apocalyptic movement. The importance of the idea in the NT seemingly shows the church's close ties with apocalypticism. But that is not the whole story. The NT does not just look forward to the general resurrection. It also proclaims, as past event, that Jesus, the crucified Messiah, has already risen from the dead and that the general resurrection has commenced (see Eschatology; Heaven and Hell).

Once more, then, the character of early Christianity is ambiguous. On the one hand the centrality of the resurrection firmly associated the church with Jewish apocalypticism. On the other, does not the announcement of the Messiah's resurrection before the day of judgment, with all its attendant implications, make for something truly new? Of course one may object that an historical phenomenon should be classified on the basis of shared characteristics, not peculiarities. But perhaps an analogy may help here. It is true that Aristotle was a member of Plato's school, just as Origen was a member of the catechetical school at Alexandria. Still, each thinker inherited a tradition only to remake it and hand the world something new. Hence, to characterize either Aristotle or Origen primarily in terms of his predecessors is constrictive and so misleading. In the same way one runs the risk of historical distortion by simply setting the early Jesus movement, whether pre- or post-Easter, squarely within the Jewish apocalyptic movement. For although Jesus and the first Christians drew from Jewish apocalypticism ideas and inspiration as well as followers, from the outset they passed beyond their nurture and went their own way.

See also APOCALYPTIC TEACHING; ESCHATOLOGY; KINGDOM OF GOD.

BIBLIOGRAPHY. J. J. Collins, *The Apocalyptic Imagination* (New York: Crossroad, 1984); idem, ed., *Apocalypse: The Morphology of a Genre. Semeia 14* (Missoula: Society of Biblical Literature, 1979); J. G. Gager, *Kingdom and Community* (Englewood Cliffs: Prentice-Hall, 1975); P. Hanson, *The Dawn of Apocalyptic* (rev. ed.; Philadelphia: Fortress, 1979); D. Hellholm, ed., *Apocalypticism in the Mediterranean World and the Near East* (Tübingen: Mohr-Siebeck, 1983); E. Käsemann, "The Beginnings of Christian Theology," in *New Testament Questions of Today* (Philadelphia: Fortress, 1969) 82-107; K. Koch, *The Rediscovery of Apocalyptic* (SBT 2/22; London: SPCK, 1972); C. Rowland, *The Open Heaven* (New York: Crossroad, 1982); D. S. Russell, *The Method and Message of Jewish Apocalyptic* (London: SCM, 1964); M. E. Stone, *Scriptures, Sects and Visions* (Philadelphia: Fortress, 1980); G. von Rad, *Old Testament Theology* (2 vols.; New York: Harper & Row, 1965), vol. 1.

D. C. Allison, Jr.

APOCALYPTIC TEACHING

"Apocalyptic" (from the Gk *apokalypsis,* meaning "revelation") refers to a historical movement, a type of literature and to the cluster of theological themes associated with them (*see* Apocalyptic). Apocalyptic is dominated by an eschatological dualism. This may be summed up as a perspective which views the present age as under the power of evil until the Day of the Lord when God will save the elect, judge the wicked and inaugurate the future age of righteousness.* Apocalypticists were often determinists, believing God's will determines everything. The result was often a passiveness or even a pessimism regarding the present age. Hope found its object in the future alone. Using a distinctive literary type (frequently character-

ized by visions, symbols, pseudonymity, etc.) apocalypses were written to encourage the saints to keep faith despite the trials of the present age.

Some New Testament interpreters (e.g., Käsemann) have viewed apocalyptic as the controlling center or nurturing parent of Christianity. Others have treated it as Christianity's embarrassment. Scholarly views range broadly. Jesus is judged by some to have been fanatically apocalyptic and by others to have been free of such corruptions. Each Gospel writer in turn is judged by some scholars to have increased, and by others to have decreased, the apocalyptic elements in their received Gospel traditions.

Several critical questions call for answers. Was Jesus an apocalyptic seer predicting an early end to the present world order, or was he opposed to apocalyptic speculation? Did the Gospel writers faithfully preserve the emphasis of Jesus? Do the Gospels use apocalyptic as a literary genre? How should so-called apocalyptic texts (like Mk 13) be interpreted? What significance does apocalypticism have for interpreting Jesus and the Gospels? What significance does it have for the contemporary Christian? This article will respond briefly to those questions.

1. Jesus and Apocalypticism
2. The So-Called Apocalyptic Discourse (Mk 13)
3. The Abomination of Desolation
4. Jesus' Teaching about the Coming Kingdom
5. The Four Gospels
6. The Significance of Apocalypticism for Today

1. Jesus and Apocalypticism.

During the nineteenth century biblical scholars attempted to defend Jesus against the charge that he was an apocalyptic dreamer who wrongly predicted an early and cataclysmic end to the existing world order. Some defended Jesus by claiming that Jesus did not intend to predict literal future events for the world, but was speaking spiritually. The apocalyptic predictions, it was argued, all had been spiritually fulfilled.

Others defended Jesus by charging the early church and the Gospel writers with error. One view is that chapters like Mark 13 did not derive from anything Jesus really said. Rather, an early Jewish apocalypse was taken up by the Gospel writers and erroneously credited to Jesus. This "little apocalypse" theory, first advanced by T. Colani, has been defended by an array of scholars ever since.

Many nineteenth-century scholars portrayed Jesus as a gentle teacher who taught the nearness of God. Unfortunately, they lamented, Jesus has been misrepresented in the Gospels as a fanatical preacher of coming judgment.*

At the turn of the century J. Weiss and A. Schweitzer overturned that consensus by reconstructing a historical Jesus who was thoroughly apocalyptic in outlook, indeed more so than those who had preserved the traditions about him. Under this new reckoning, Jesus believed that the expected divine intervention which would inaugurate the new age would occur at some time during his ministry. His expectations were disappointed more than once, and he finally went to his death imagining that by so doing he would surely spur God to act. The early church was left with the challenge of giving Jesus a more respectable image, covering up his errors and presenting his teaching in a way which served the needs of a community that knew the end (and the kingdom of God*) had not come as predicted, but that still believed it would come soon.

This view in its various forms, generally known as "consistent eschatology," has been influential during the twentieth century (see Eschatology). Some, like R. Bultmann, have been unconcerned with defending Jesus' apocalyptic perspective or even attempting to reconstruct a portrait of the historical Jesus.* Bultmann's famous program of demythologizing the NT did not attempt to strip Jesus of his mythological trappings (as did many nineteenth-century interpreters), but to reinterpret those mythical elements in terms of their existential meaning (see Myth). Understood from this perspective, the mythology inherent in Jesus' apocalyptic teaching was a means of addressing men and women with the need to be open to God's future—a future near at hand for each individual. Other scholars, such as R. H. Hiers, do not find it troubling to think of Jesus as someone who had mistaken expectations and made inaccurate predictions.

Not all twentieth-century interpreters have been persuaded that Jesus was an apocalyptic preacher who predicted an imminent end to the world. C. H. Dodd and others have insisted on a realized eschatology, maintaining that Jesus fulfilled OT prophetic hopes and preached a kingdom which was inaugurated in his own ministry. Those passages which suggested a future fulfillment were either intended to be interpreted in this light or were the creation of the early church. Both consistent and realized eschatology seem problematic. Many conservative scholars such as G. E. Ladd, E. E. Ellis and I. H. Marshall have adopted a compromise position first defended by W. G. Kümmel. The kingdom is paradoxically "present" and "still to come." Jesus' mission was to inaugurate the kingdom, but he taught that it would be consummated at a future coming.

The Gospel writers faithfully preserve this paradoxical position. They use apocalyptic imagery to report and interpret events in Jesus' earthly life (e.g., Mt 27:51-53; 28:2-4), and they also use apocalyptic imagery to refer to events predicted for the future (God's final act of judgment and salvation* at the coming of the Son of man; cf. Mt 25:31-46; Mk 13:24-27).

This already/not yet approach may be open to the charge that it is very convenient (unfalsifiable and therefore indefensible, some would say), but unless some such paradoxical interpretation is adopted, neither Jesus' view nor any of the Gospel writers' views can be understood adequately.

2. The So-Called Apocalyptic Discourse (Mk 13).

Mark 13 opens with a conversation between Jesus and his disciples* over the Jerusalem Temple. The disciples admire its beauty; Jesus predicts its destruction (see Destruction of Jerusalem); the disciples then inquire about the timing of that event and the "sign" when "all these things" will be fulfilled. A long discourse by Jesus follows, in which are predicted a series of woes (see Blessing and Woe), political disturbances, persecution of believers, an "abomination of desolation" (see below), a time of unprecedented distress and finally the coming of the Son of man.* Interspersed with these are calls for discernment, faithful discipleship,* courageous testimony, endurance and vigilance in the face of deceivers. The last ten verses of the chapter contain two parables* (28-29, 34-36), renewed calls to "watch" (33, 37) and some hotly debated statements about the timing of "these things" (30-32).

What is the source of this enigmatic chapter? Is it a Jewish apocalyptic tract (as Colani's "little apocalypse theory" advocated)? Is the chapter a composite of authentic sayings of Jesus, ethical instruction from the early church and possibly prophetic words by early Christian prophets* (as most modern critical scholars argue)? Or is it Mark's abbreviation of a longer well-preserved "pre-Synoptic eschatological discourse" that goes back to Jesus himself (as Wenham has recently argued)?

If the problems involved in tracing the sources of this chapter are complicated, those involved in interpreting this chapter are legion. The chapter provokes the following questions, to name only a few:

1. What relationship was predicted between the destruction of the Temple* and the coming of the Son of man? Were both events predicted to happen within a generation (cf. v. 30)?

2. What is/are the requested "sign(s)"? Is the "abomination of desolation" (v. 14) the sign that the Temple's destruction is imminent? Or is the Temple's

destruction the sign that the coming of the Son of man is imminent? Is there perhaps a "baffling multiplicity of signs," as C. E. B. Cranfield has put it? Is it possible that Jesus did not intend to give any signs at all?

3. Is apocalyptic calculation encouraged or discouraged? Does the discourse map out an apocalyptic timetable, or is verse 32 ("no one knows") the real answer to the disciples' question?

Mark 13:30 says that "all these things" will happen within the present generation (genea). If genea refers to Jesus' contemporaries, and if "all these things" includes the return of the Son of man, then the prediction was an error. Some have denied that genea must refer to Jesus' contemporaries. Others deny that "all these things" necessarily includes the return of the Son of man (Geddert). The text suggests that it includes all the events related to the destruction of the Temple (cf. 13:4, 23). But exactly what all those things include is never made explicitly clear.

Mark 13:32 denies that anyone (even Jesus) knows when the final day of eschatological fulfillment will take place. It would seem to follow that neither Jesus nor Mark knew whether or not the final Day of the Lord would take place at the time of the Temple's destruction. The self-confessed ignorance of Jesus and Mark on this point is an adequate explanation for the ambiguity of 13:30 and many other verses in the chapter.

Modern interpreters often seem intent on proving one of the following two options: (1) Mark 13 teaches that the destruction of the Temple (and accompanying events) will lead directly to the final intervention of God or (2) Mark 13 teaches that the final eschatological events are *not* to be connected to the historical events predicted in this chapter. These two irreconcilable options have found nearly equal numbers of supporters.

However, if 13:32 is the controlling presupposition for Mark 13, it would seem to follow that the decision modern interpreters are trying to make is one that both Jesus and Mark refused to make. If Jesus did not know when the end would come, it is unlikely that he would claim to know whether or not history would go on after the crisis surrounding the Temple's destruction.

Mark 13:30 does not indicate what is included in "all these things" which must happen within one generation. The phrase is likely drawn from the disciples' question in 13:4. What no one could know was whether or not the final return of the Son of man was one of "all these things." What seems to be indicated by 13:30 is that the Temple's destruction *and its accompanying events* were predicted to occur within a generation of Jesus. What is left indeterminate is whether

the final return of the Son of man would be one of those accompanying events. It might be; it might not be. Jesus did not know; Mark did not know; readers are urged not to be misled by those who think they know (13:5-6, 21-22). The readers' responsibility is to allow their ignorance of this timing to become a motivation for faithful discipleship and service (13:32-37).

Mark was not, as some have argued, a careless redactor who hopelessly confused his readers by juxtaposing contradictory and irreconcilable positions in this one discourse. Rather he was a Gospel writer who claimed to know no more about the timing of the end than Jesus knew, and who presented a discourse that works out for the disciples the implications of the fact that the end could come at any time.

The calls for discernment and understanding (vv. 5, 14), the ambiguous statements (e.g., v. 13: is it about the end of one's life, the end of the crisis, the end of the age?), the cryptic reference to an "abomination of desolation" standing "where it should not" (v. 14), the warnings against deception (vv. 5, 22), the ambiguities of the parable of the fig tree (vv. 28-29), the uncertain references in verse 30—all these help to preserve both the ambiguity and the discipleship challenge of Mark 13.

Prior to the Temple's destruction, the chapter was intended to warn and encourage believers as they prepared for and responded to the tumultuous events Jesus was predicting; these events, after all, might be the final events of world history. After the Temple's destruction, if history should go on (as we now know it has), it calls believers to be equally discerning and alert: the predicted preliminaries have happened; the end could come at any time.

Mark 13, therefore, does not teach either the conjunction or the disjunction of the two great events predicted (the destruction of the Temple and the end of the age). It rather teaches that the relationship between them is unknowable (though of course the uncertainty disappeared when the first event came and the second did not follow immediately after).

What then is/are the sign(s) about which the disciples asked (v. 4)? On the one hand, everything that happens can function as a sign; that is, a sign of God's sovereign control of history and his care for his faithful people. If events turn out as Jesus predicted, then clearly God is in control.

But, on the other hand, if the disciples wanted signs that would help them predict the timing of the end, no such signs were supplied. In fact not a single event predicted in the chapter is called a sign. The word itself (sēmeion) does not appear at all in Jesus' answer, except in verse 22 where the disciples are warned against sign-givers. The disciples are told that various events are *not* to be considered evidences that the end has come (e.g., 13:7), and other events are called (only) the beginning of the travails (13:8).

If Jesus did not endorse sign-seeking, he certainly did call for another sort of watching. The first word of Jesus' discourse is "watch" (*blepete*, v. 5—a word that regularly means "be discerning" in Mark's Gospel, cf. 4:12; 8:18). The last word of the discourse is another word for "watch" (*grēgoreite*, v. 37—a word that means "be alert and faithful," cf. 14:34, 37-38).

The overall message of Mark 13 seems to be that since no one knows when the end will come, vigilance is required at every moment. Trials will test faithfulness, but the disciple must serve and if necessary suffer "to the end" (13:13). Sign-seeking and apocalyptic calculation are not endorsed.

Mark probably wrote shortly before or during the Roman-Jewish War (A.D. 66-70) that resulted in the Temple's destruction by the Romans. As it turns out, the Son of man did not return at that time. Those who heeded Jesus' call to flee (13:14) were saved. Others experienced the judgment Jesus predicted for those who rejected him (cf. 12:9). These events serve, as do so many events in the OT, to point toward the final judgment and the salvation that is yet to come at a future unknown date.

Is Mark 13 an "apocalyptic discourse"? It is in the sense that it clearly reflects a view of history/eschatology in which a present age of crisis and persecution will give way to a future age in which God exercises judgment on his enemies and vindicates and rewards his elect. Moreover, it contains eschatological predictions and warns the elect of impending deceptions and disasters. One of the typical patterns of apocalyptic literature is reflected in the structure of the chapter—the beginning of woes (v. 8b), a time of great tribulation (v. 19) and a cosmic upheaval in which God intervenes (vv. 24-27).

But in other ways Mark 13 is very unlike "apocalyptic literature." Its concern is not with timetables and calculations. It reports no other-worldly journeys. It contains no visions of the abode of the dead, the divine courtroom or the heavenly throne room. In contrast with typical apocalypses, it insists that the timing of the end is unknown to the angels, indeed even to the revealer of the discourse (13:32). The discipleship teaching of Mark 13 (reflected in the numerous imperatives, e.g., vv. 5, 9, 11, 23, 33) and its apparent anti-sign-seeking message, set it apart from typical apocalypses. It is Jesus' farewell discourse offering hope and calling for faithfulness. It has the same function today for Christians who know that the end did not come with the crisis of A.D. 70 but who look forward to the fulfillment of the promise of 13:26-27.

3. The Abomination of Desolation.

The "abomination of desolation," or "desolating sacrilege" (*to bdelugma tēs erēmōseōs*), is a phrase that derives from Daniel 9:27; 11:31; 12:11 and 1 Maccabees 1:54-64. In 1 Maccabees the phrase clearly refers to the historical event of Antiochus IV erecting a pagan altar in the Jerusalem Temple. That "abomination" was an important factor leading to the Maccabean revolt and the overthrow of Israel's Syrian overlords in 164 B.C.

The prophecy in Daniel appears to point toward the same event. However, as a prophetic word, it may well have further future fulfillments. It was apparently understood that way by Jews who applied it to a crisis in A.D. 40 when the emperor Caligula intended to set up a statue of himself in the Temple. It was certainly taken by Jesus and the Gospel writers as a prophecy pointing to a future fulfillment.

Both Mark and Matthew report Jesus' prediction of a future appearance of "the abomination of desolation" (cf. Mk 13:14; Mt 24:15). Luke interprets the prophecy as a prediction of the surrounding of Jerusalem by the armies of Rome (Lk 21:20; cf. Mk 13:14-23).

Many scholars (especially German) interpret the prophecy in terms of an antichrist figure not necessarily connected with the events of the Jewish war in A.D. 66-70. That seems to be how Paul appropriated the concept in 2 Thessalonians 2:4, where he refers to one who "exalts himself . . . so that he takes his seat in the sanctuary of God, proclaiming himself to be God" (if in fact this stems from the same prophecy).

Both Mark and Matthew, after including Jesus' prediction of the "abomination of desolation," add the words "let the reader understand" (cf. Mk 13:14; Mt 24:15). The authors are alerting their readers to this reapplication of the Daniel prophecy and calling on them to discern how and when it is fulfilled. Perhaps it was for political reasons that the predictions were shrouded in symbolic language.

The prophecy concerning the "abomination of desolation" was fulfilled when the Jerusalem Temple was desecrated and destroyed in A.D. 70. This does not, however, rule out the possibility of another fulfillment in the future.

4. Jesus' Teaching about the Coming Kingdom.

If Mark 13 were the only source from which to discern Jesus' relationship to apocalyptic, we would perhaps conclude that his concerns (e.g., discipleship) diverged considerably from typical apocalypticists, while his expectations for the future were very similar to theirs.

But alongside Jesus' futuristic expectation must be placed his teaching about the present reality of the kingdom of God (e.g., Mt 11:12; 12:28; Mk 10:14; Lk 11:20; 17:20-21). Texts such as these either state or imply that in some sense the kingdom has already come, the expected turning of the ages was already taking place within the ministry of Jesus. Because the Gospels portray the kingdom as both a future hope and a present reality, they preserve, but also weaken, the dualistic future-oriented perspective of apocalyptic. On this point, however, scholars are not in full agreement, perhaps because the Gospel writers were less concerned to eliminate paradoxes than modern scholars often seem to be.

The early church interpreted the life, death* and resurrection* of Jesus, and also the coming of the Spirit,* using OT texts which explicitly or implicitly refer to the "last days" (see esp. Acts 2:17; see Old Testament in the Gospels). The earliest Christians were under the conviction that even though the old age had still not ended, the new age had already dawned. It was as though the two ages of Jewish apocalyptic eschatology had overlapped. Or to put it another way, it was as though the fulfillment was split into two parts. In one sense the expectations were already fulfilled; in another they were yet to be fulfilled (Acts 2:38-40). There is no better explanation for earliest Christians viewing matters in this way than that Jesus had taught them to do so.

It may in fact have been one of the unique contributions of Jesus that he took key themes from OT prophecy (calls to covenant faithfulness, divine disclosure of the meaning and significance of historical events, anticipations of God's work in history to bring about his purposes) and some of the key themes of intertestamental apocalyptic (the concept of two ages, predictions of final judgment and vindication, divine visitations by an exalted Son of man, revelations granted to special seers), saw himself as the fulfiller of both, and fused them into the concept of a kingdom which was already and not yet present. Luke 17:20-37, for example, gives evidence of both aspects in Jesus' concept of the kingdom.

Some modern interpreters are reluctant to admit that this complex, paradoxical view of eschatology could possibly have been in the mind of the Gospel writers, let alone Jesus. Jesus' own views are often thought to have been much simpler (though there is little agreement on which half of the paradox might be authentic). The Gospel writers are thought to have carelessly mixed Jesus' real views with very different views that they or their predecessors in the early church held. Contemporary interpreters who credit Jesus and the Gospel writers with the paradoxical scheme outlined above are accused of making a desperate attempt to salvage a badly confused set of teachings. The burden of proof, however, must surely be on those scholars who would seek to interpret away either the realized or the futurist side of Jesus' teaching (see Beasley-Murray).

The question remains how literally Jesus and the Gospel writers intended their apocalyptic predictions to be understood. G. B. Caird's study of biblical language cautions against assuming that a literal fulfillment was always intended. Jesus and the Gospel writers often incorporated symbolism and imagery into their depictions. They clearly expected a real future return of the Son of man to judge and save (e.g., Mt 25:31-46), but many of the picturesque (or horrific) ways of describing that coming were intended to evoke OT descriptions of the coming of God, not to predict future rearrangements of the heavenly bodies or other phenomena (cf. Mk 13:24-25 par.). There is need for neither embarrassment nor demythologizing if the real intentions of Jesus and the Gospel writers are carefully discerned.

We conclude that Jesus shared some, but only some, of the views of first-century Jewish apocalypticists. He taught that his own coming already had planted the seeds of that kingdom, that his ministry evidenced the powerful advancing of that kingdom, indeed that the time of fulfillment had arrived (e.g., Lk 11:20). But he also taught that there would be a future Day of the Lord (e.g., Lk 21:34-36) that would bring the old order to an end and fully establish God's final kingdom. This paradoxical "already" but "not yet" has implications for many of the key themes addressed by apocalyptic writers.

Jesus taught that the Evil One was still in control of this present world, but that in some sense he was already defeated. Jesus taught that with his own coming, judgment on the world had come, but that nevertheless a future judgment was to be expected (Jn 12:31; 16:11). He taught that final vindication for his followers would be in eternity, but that even in this life they would also be well compensated for any sacrifices they were being asked to make (Mk 10:29-30). He taught that final salvation was still awaited (Mt 24:13), yet that salvation was already available to those who followed him (Lk 19:9).

5. The Four Gospels.

Each Gospel writer faithfully preserves the "already/

not yet" perspective of Jesus. There are, nevertheless, discernible differences in emphasis between the four Gospels.

5.1. Mark. Mark's perspective is that futuristic prophecy and calls for discipleship are inseparably bound together. This is set forth by attaching apocalyptic promises to calls for discipleship (cf. 8:31—9:1; 10:17-31) and by utilizing discipleship teaching in apocalyptic contexts (as noted above). The ultimate expression of discipleship in Mark is the passion of Jesus (*see* Death of Jesus). Mark's record of Jesus' last night (14:17—15:1; *see* Gethsemane) seems to be structured around the four watches of the night listed in 13:35. In each scene Jesus models faithful watching while those around him fail. Mark thereby defines for disciples what it means to watch in the end times (Geddert).

5.2. Matthew. Matthew's so-called apocalyptic discourse (Mt 24) closely parallels that of Mark, though it appears to heighten apocalyptic expectation by citing at least one sign (24:30). The parables that follow (24:43-44, 45-51; 25:1-13, 14-30, 31-46) reveal an emphasis on discipleship that is just as strong as Mark's.

A difference may be observed, however, in the way in which Matthew ties apocalyptic themes to discipleship. Mark characteristically holds out the promise of eschatological blessing for those who obediently follow (e.g., 10:28); Matthew characteristically holds out the threat of eschatological woe for those who are disobedient or refuse to accept Jesus (cf. 24:51; 25:30, 41). The ethical teaching of the Sermon on the Mount* and other Matthean texts are regularly tied to the need for "greater righteousness" in preparation for coming judgment (as shown by G. Bornkamm).

The instant of Jesus' death is linked to the tearing of the Temple curtain, an earthquake, the splitting of rocks, and the resurrection and appearance of ancient holy ones (cf. 27:51-53). The resurrection occasions another earthquake, a brightly shining angel who rolls away the stone, and the terror of those who observe (cf. 28:2-4). Such apocalyptic motifs reveal that for Matthew, Jesus' death and resurrection are unique, apocalyptically significant events. They inaugurate the new epoch of fulfillment and world mission (Mt 28:18-20).

5.3. Luke. Luke is unique as the only Gospel writer who also wrote about the life of the early church (i.e., Acts). For Luke "history" is of paramount importance; it is the arena in which God acts. Some (H. Conzelmann) have even argued that Luke "de-apocalypticized" the Gospel by historicizing the traditions and pushing future expectations far into the distance.

It is probably true that Luke uses fewer apocalyptic images than Matthew in conveying the significance of Jesus' death and resurrection. But it is not true that the future return of the Son of man is a minor emphasis in Luke and Acts. Luke includes various apocalyptic-type passages as well as two lengthy discourses on the end: the so-called Q* Apocalypse (17:20-37); and 21:5-36, which is substantially parallel to the discourses of Mark 13 and Matthew 24.

The Luke 17 material clearly betrays both a realized (v. 21) and a futurist (v. 24) perspective. In chapter 21 Luke, more so than the other evangelists, seems to distinguish between the historical events surrounding the fall of the Temple (21:8-9, 12-24) and the eschatological events that will take place at a later time (21:10-11, 25-36).

H. Conzelmann underestimated Luke's interest in futurist eschatology. A. J. Mattill, in responding to Conzelmann, seems to have underestimated the realized elements. The kingdom is portrayed in Luke as already and not yet, just as it is in the other Gospels, even though differences in emphasis can be detected (cf. the commentaries on Luke by E. E. Ellis, I. H. Marshall and others).

5.4. John. John is unique among the evangelists in his portrayal of Jesus' eschatology. The realized aspects are highlighted, often by taking apocalyptic themes and attaching them to the events of Jesus' life, and especially to his death. For example, during Jesus' ministry judgment is already being experienced by those who reject Jesus (cf. 3:18) and resurrection by those who believe (cf. 5:24-25). Judgment on the world and Satan's defeat occur when Jesus is rejected and "lifted up" (12:27-33).

Some have argued that futurist eschatology disappears from John. After all, the major apocalyptic themes are already exhausted in characterizing the significance of Jesus' life and death. However, futuristic eschatology is not absent from John (cf. 21:22). Part of the literary method of John's Gospel involves symbolism and ambiguity. Often in John, statements have a literal meaning and a symbolic or spiritual meaning (e.g., 2:19). When John uses apocalyptic themes, he often has one eye on the historical events of Jesus' life and death, and another on the final eschatological events for which Jesus is preparing. It is John's way of presenting the already/not yet paradox.

The method of presentation in John is unique among the Gospels. John's ambiguity (more properly, polyvalence) suggests a profound theology of eschatological fulfillment. The resurrected and exalted Lord, present to believers through the indwelling Spirit (cf. Jn 20:22), mediates the blessings of the eschaton. Yet futuristic eschatology is not thereby eliminated (cf. Burge; *contra* Bultmann). The emphasis may shift, but John's apocalyptic eschatology is not irreconcilable with that of the historical Jesus and the Synoptic writers.

6. The Significance of Apocalypticism for Today.

There is much in Jewish (and some post-biblical Christian) apocalyptic literature which is inconsistent with the gospel of Jesus Christ. Feverish calculations as to when the end will come, desperate waiting for divine intervention, maledictions against enemies—all these contribute to the negative image that apocalyptic has in some circles.

Yet there is much in apocalyptic which is at the heart of the gospel. Trust in God's sovereignty, a future-oriented hope, a recognition that material earthly existence is not the only reality and the anticipation of a future resurrection to judgment and/or salvation—these are apocalyptic themes which are integral to biblical eschatology. They begin in the OT and are carried forward by Jesus and the NT writers.

The early church did not introduce apocalypticism into the teachings of Jesus, nor was there any need to excise it from those teachings. Like Jesus, each Gospel writer portrayed (albeit with distinct emphases) that the main themes of OT prophecy (e.g., confidence in God's faithfulness, calls for obedience) can be combined with many key themes of Jewish apocalyptic (e.g., expectation of divine intervention in future judgment and salvation). Indeed they must be combined in our own understanding if we are to grasp the significance of Jesus' teaching.

Yet Jesus did more than teach a particular eschatology. He himself was the Seer commissioned to impart to his followers God's revelation *(apokalypsis)*. He presented himself as the appointed Savior and Judge, the authoritative Son of man. With his own life, death and resurrection he inaugurated the kingdom. At his Second Coming he himself will consummate it.

The central teachings of the Gospels can be ascertained even while experts continue to debate the merits and shortcomings of apocalypticism. At points those main teachings coincide with first-century apocalypticism; at other points they diverge from it.

The NT teaches, as did apocalyptic writers, that history is moving inexorably toward a *telos*, a goal which will not be reached fully by historical processes. This goal-oriented view of history does not, however, diminish the significance of the present age (as it did for some apocalyptic writers). On the contrary, this present age is most significant as Christians proclaim and live out the good news that brings about transfor-

mation in the lives of individuals and in the world. Such faithful service during the master's absence will elicit God's "well done" when the final reckoning takes place (cf. Mt 25:23).

It is consistent with the message of Jesus and the Gospels to maintain a lively interest in futuristic prophecy. Jesus called his followers to "watch" in the interim time of waiting for God's final consummation. "Watching," however, does not mean calculating timetables and matching newspaper events with the symbols of biblical apocalyptic. Jesus' followers should not claim to know more about the timing of "that Day" than Jesus himself did (cf. Mk 13:32). "Watching" means being on guard against deception and being faithful in times of testing. The primary purpose of futuristic prophecy is to build hope, to motivate proclamation and service, and to promote faithful discipleship.

Christians can learn from apocalyptic. When injustice, loss or persecution threaten to drown out their confidence in God's sovereignty, the apocalyptic perspective invites them to lift their gaze from this world to a new heaven and earth. The kingdom is not yet. At the same time, Christians must never allow apocalyptic to lead to apathy in the face of global problems, or silence in a world that needs to hear the proclamation of the good news. The kingdom is already.

See also APOCALYPTIC; DESTRUCTION OF JERUSALEM; ESCHATOLOGY; JUDGMENT; KINGDOM OF GOD; SON OF MAN.

BIBLIOGRAPHY. D. C. Allison, *The End of the Ages Has Come* (Philadelphia: Fortress, 1985); G. R. Beasley-Murray, *Jesus and the Future* (London: Macmillan, 1954); idem, *Jesus and the Kingdom of God* (Grand Rapids: Eerdmans, 1986); G. M. Burge, *The Anointed Community: The Holy Spirit in the Johannine Tradition* (Grand Rapids: Eerdmans, 1987); G. B. Caird, *The Language and Imagery of the Bible* (Philadelphia: Westminster, 1980); E. E. Ellis, "Present and Future in the Eschatology of Luke," *NTS* 12 (1965-66) 27-41; D. Ford, *The Abomination of Desolation in Biblical Eschatology* (Washington, D.C.: University Press of America, 1979); T. J. Geddert, *Watchwords: Mark 13 in Markan Eschatology* (JSNTSS 26; Sheffield: JSOT, 1989); R. H. Hiers, *Jesus and the Future* (Atlanta: John Knox, 1981); E. Käsemann, "The Beginnings of Christian Theology," in *New Testament Questions of Today* (Philadelphia: Fortress, 1969) 82-107; W. G. Kümmel, *Promise and Fulfilment* (London: SCM, 1961); G. E. Ladd, *The Presence of the Future* (Grand Rapids: Eerdmans, 1974); J. Marcus and M. L. Soards, *Apocalyptic and the New Testament* (Sheffield: JSOT, 1989); I. H. Marshall, "Is Apocalyptic the Mother of Christian Theology?" in

Tradition and Interpretation in the New Testament, ed. G. F. Hawthorne and O. Betz (Grand Rapids: Eerdmans, 1987) 33-42 and in *Jesus the Saviour* (Downers Grove: InterVarsity, 1990) 57-69; A. J. Mattill, *Luke and the Last Things* (Dillsboro, N.C.: Western North Carolina Press, 1979); A. L. Moore, *The Parousia in the New Testament* (Leiden: E. J. Brill, 1966); A. Schweitzer, *The Quest of the Historical Jesus* (New York: Macmillan, 1906); J. Weiss, *Jesus' Proclamation of the Kingdom of God* (Philadelphia: Fortress, 1971); D. Wenham, *The Rediscovery of Jesus' Eschatological Discourse* (Sheffield: JSOT, 1984).   T. J. Geddert

APOCRYPHAL GOSPELS. *See* GOSPELS (APOCRYPHAL).

APOSTLE

The term "apostle" (*apostolos*) is used in the Gospels to designate the twelve disciples* called and sent out by Jesus to preach the Gospel (*see* Gospel [Good News]) of the kingdom (*see* Kingdom of God) and demonstrate its presence by performing signs and wonders (*see* Miracles). The term is not applied to Jesus himself in the Gospels, nevertheless there is good reason to believe that he thought of himself as the apostle of God,* sent into the world* to proclaim and inaugurate the kingdom of God. There is also good reason to believe that the origin of the Christian apostolate is to be traced back to Jesus, in particular to his sending of the Twelve on their Galilean (*see* Galilee) mission, and that the notion of apostleship betrays certain affinities with the Jewish institution of the *šāliaḥ* ("envoy"). This in turn enables us to understand better the nature of the Christian apostolate.

1. Terminology
2. The Origin of the Idea of Apostleship
3. Jesus, Apostle of God
4. The Apostleship of Jesus' Disciples
5. Nuances in the Evangelists' Understanding of the Apostolate

1. Terminology.

In addition to the word *apostolos,* two other terms are significant for our understanding of apostleship in the Gospels. First there is the cognate verb *apostellō* ("to send"), which is used in all four Gospels. The second is the verb *pempō* ("to send"), used synonymously in John's Gospel. The use of these terms in non-biblical sources has been documented often (see e.g., Rengstorf) and need only be noted here in the broadest outline.

1.1. Apostolos. In classical Greek *apostolos* was used in an impersonal way, for example, in reference to the dispatch of a fleet (or an army) and then in reference to the fleet (or army) itself. There are a couple of isolated places where *apostolos* is used personally; however, it is noteworthy that in these cases the idea of being an authorized agent is quite secondary; it is simply the quality of having been sent that is primary. *Apostolos* is found only once in the LXX (3 Kings 14:6 par. 1 Kings 14:6 ET), which is quite surprising because the OT contains many references to messengers sent from God. In the papyri the term is used in an impersonal way (e.g., to designate an invoice accompanying a shipment of corn). Josephus* uses *apostolos* twice, and in one of these cases it refers to Jewish emissaries who came to Rome* to petition Caesar for the liberty to live according to their own laws. This comes closer to the use of *apostolos* in the Gospels, but clearly still falls somewhat short of it. The use of *apostolos* in the Gospels, and indeed its primary usage throughout the NT to designate someone who is sent (by Christ*) to convey a message from God, is then virtually unique in ancient literature.

1.2. Apostellō and Pempō. In secular Greek the verbs *apostellō* and *pempō* are used of the sending of persons and things. There is, however, a discernible difference in the usage of the two terms. *Pempō* is used where mere sending is involved, whereas *apostellō* is used to denote sending of persons with a commission and in some cases to denote a divine sending and authorization.

In the LXX the verb *apostellō* is used more than 709 times, and almost always as a translation equivalent for the Hebrew verb *šālaḥ* ("to send"). *Šālaḥ* denotes for the most part the idea of being sent with a commission, either by another human agent or by God. *Pempō* is used much less, and only five times to translate *šālaḥ*. Josephus uses both terms, sometimes as synonyms (where a mere sending is involved), but he chooses *apostellō* when he wants to convey the idea of being sent with a commission.

In the NT (with the exception of John's Gospel), it may be said that *pempō* is used where the simple idea of sending is conveyed, and *apostellō* when something of a commission is involved. In John's Gospel, however, the two terms are used interchangeably.

2. The Origin of the Idea of Apostleship.

The term *apostolos* occurs infrequently outside the NT, and this stands in marked contrast to the frequency of its use within the NT. It is found, for example, only once in the LXX, whereas it occurs seventy-nine times in the NT. How can we account for this? Where did this Christian use of *apostolos* originate?

2.1. The Traditional View. Both Mark 3:14 and Luke

6:13 affirm that Jesus chose twelve disciples "whom he also named apostles," thus tracing the naming of the Twelve as apostles back to Jesus himself. This might seem to settle the issue for many. Those who trace the idea of the Christian apostolate back to Jesus recognize, of course, that Jesus himself probably did not use the Greek term *apostolos*. He would have used, most likely, either the Aramaic (*šᵉlîḥā'*) or the Hebrew (*šālîaḥ*) equivalent. Those espousing this view argue that *apostolos* in our Gospels must be understood in terms of the Jewish institution of the *šālîaḥ* ("envoy"), an idea with which Jesus would have been well acquainted and had applied to his understanding of his relationship with his disciples.

The institution of the *šālîaḥ* is well documented in rabbinic writings (cf. e.g., *m. Ber.* 5:5; *see* Rabbinic Traditions and Writings) where it refers to someone who has been authorized to carry out certain functions on behalf of another. The adage "a man's envoy is as himself" occurs frequently in the rabbinic literature, and it underlines both the representative character of the *šālîaḥ* and that he carries the full authority* of his principal. It is suggested, then, that it was in terms of this institution that Jesus understood his relationship to his disciples and that it is his use of this idea that lies behind the use of *apostolos* in the Gospels.

2.2. Difficulties with the Traditional View. The traditional view is not as strong as it first seems, for two reasons. First, better manuscripts omit the words "whom he also named apostles" from Mark 3:14. That leaves Luke 6:13 as the lone testimony to the naming of the Twelve as apostles by Jesus. Luke's text may be based on a weakly attested variant of Mark, and the inclusion of this clause in Mark in some manuscripts may be due to a scribal gloss.

If we set Mark 3:14 and Luke 6:13 to one side, then all we are left with in the Gospels are: (1) a number of texts where the Twelve are spoken of by the Evangelists as apostles (Mt 10:2; Mk 6:30; Lk 9:10; 17:5; 22:14; 24:10); (2) one saying of Jesus in Luke 11:49 ("Therefore also the Wisdom* of God said, 'I will send to them prophets and apostles, and they will kill and persecute some of them' ") which does include a reference to apostles, but this is omitted in the parallel saying of Jesus in Matthew 23:34; and (3) one Johannine saying of Jesus ("Truly, truly, I say to you, a servant is not greater than his master; nor is one sent *[apostolos]* greater than the one who sent him" [13:16]), which is clearly not a statement related primarily to the Christian apostolate.

Second, while the institution of the *šālîaḥ* ("envoy") is well documented in rabbinic literature, its docu-

mentation cannot be dated earlier than the second century A.D. There is no known use of the nominal form *šālîaḥ* before that time. The upshot of this is that it is very difficult to sustain the view that the use of the word *apostolos* in the Gospels demonstrates either that the origin of the Christian apostolate can be traced back to Jesus, or that Jesus understood it in terms of the Jewish institution of the *šālîaḥ*. This has prompted some scholars to seek alternative ways to explain the origin of the Christian apostolate.

2.3. Alternative Views. One factor which seems to point to a possible alternative explanation for the origin of the apostolate is the rather uneven distribution of the word *apostolos* within the NT as a whole. Of the seventy-nine occurrences in the NT, sixty-eight are found in Luke-Acts and the Pauline corpus—documents which are particularly related to the early Christian mission. This has prompted a number of scholars (e.g., W. Schmithals) to argue that the idea of the Christian apostolate originated, not in the time of Jesus' mission, but in the early period of the church's* post-Easter mission.

This view needs to be taken seriously. The major Pauline letters are among the earliest NT documents, and were almost certainly written before any of the Gospels. Therefore the emergence of the Christian idea of apostle, at a literary level at least, must be traced to these. It is, therefore, theoretically possible that the idea of the Christian apostolate originated in the early period of the Christian mission, then found literary expression in the major Pauline letters, and later on was used by the evangelists when they wrote their accounts of Jesus' calling and commissioning of his disciples.

Another view is that the concept originated in a Jewish or a Jewish-Christian Gnosticism native in Syria. As Antioch (in Syria) is thought to be the homeland of the church's mission, it is argued that the concept could have been easily borrowed and appropriated into the thinking of the early Christian mission there. However, this last suggestion has not generally commended itself to scholars, not least because the documents to which appeal is made in support of the existence of pre-Christian Gnosticism do not date from the pre-Christian period. Many scholars, therefore, favor the view that the concept of the apostolate arose from within the Church's own missionary experience.

2.4. Return to (a Modified) Traditional View. In more recent times a growing number of scholars have been willing to trace the origin of the Christian apostolate back to the period of Jesus. However, those who do so are reluctant to tie it too closely to the institution of *šālîaḥ* ("envoy") documented in rabbinic writings, as did the earlier proponents of this view. Attention is now focussed instead on the *šālaḥ/apostellō* sending terminology occurring in both the OT and the NT.

The more recent approach begins appropriately with the earliest literary references to the Christian apostolate, that is, those in the letters of Paul. In these letters Paul speaks of himself frequently as an apostle (*apostolos*) of Jesus Christ, and of Christ's having sent (*apostellō*) him with a commission to proclaim the gospel to the Gentiles.* *Apostolos/apostellō* in Paul's letters, then, bears the same basic meaning as the *šālaḥ/apostellō* terminology in the OT, that of a person being sent with a commission.

Turning to the Gospels, we find that while the use of the noun *apostolos* is quite meager, that of the verb *apostellō* (and in the case of John's Gospel the use of the verb *pempō* as well) is quite substantial. Each of the four Gospels uses *apostellō* many times, including what we might call technical uses in which the idea of being sent with a commission is involved. In each of the Gospels these technical uses occur in both narrative statements made by the Evangelist, and in sayings of Jesus which the Evangelist includes in his narrative. These technical uses, like those found in the Pauline letters, correspond with the use of the *šālaḥ/apostellō* sending terminology in the OT to denote the sending of a person with a commission (see 1.2. above). Thus it seems clear that the Christian notion of the apostolate has definite links with the OT notion of sending with a commission (and this in turn corresponds with the role of the Jewish *šālîaḥ* as it is documented in the rabbinic literature).

However, the question remains: Can we trace the forging of this link back to Jesus, and was he therefore the one who provided the church with its understanding of the apostolate? Theoretically, of course, this link could have been forged in the period of the early Christian mission, and once forged the resulting notion of the apostolate could have been used anachronistically by the Evangelists in their Gospel accounts of Jesus' ministry. Is there any way to reach a responsible decision as to which of these alternatives is to be preferred?

2.5. Jesus and the Christian Apostolate. The case for tracing the idea of the Christian apostolate back to Jesus himself would gain cogency if it could be shown that there are authentic sayings of Jesus in the Gospels (especially in the Synoptics) in which the technical use of *apostellō* mentioned above may be found. In fact there are a number of such sayings whose authenticity can be argued quite strongly on critical grounds. They include both sayings in which Jesus speaks of his having been sent by the Father, and sayings in which he speaks about his own sending of the Twelve/Seventy.

Examples of sayings relating to Jesus himself include Matthew 15:24 in which he says to the Canaanite woman, "I was *sent* only to the lost sheep* of the house of Israel,*" and Luke 4:18 where Jesus cites Isaiah 61:1 saying: "The Spirit of the Lord is upon me, because he has anointed me to preach the Gospel to the poor. He has *sent* me to proclaim release to the captives."

One example of the sayings which relate to Jesus' disciples having been sent by him is Luke 22:35, where Jesus asks them, "When I *sent* you out without purse or bag or sandals did you lack anything?" In addition there is a series of sayings in which Jesus comments that those who receive his disciples receive him, and those who receive him receive the One who sent him (Mt 10:40/Lk 10:16; Mk 9:37/Lk 9:48/Mt 18:5).

It can be argued strongly on critical grounds that all these sayings rest on authentic Jesus tradition. For example, Matthew's retention of 15:24 with its exclusivist note ("only to the lost sheep of the house of Israel"), despite the embarrassment it may have caused in a church already involved in Gentile mission in the pre-Pauline era (cf. Acts 10:1-48; 11:20-24), strongly supports its dominical character. The reliability of the tradition behind Luke 4:18, with its citation from Isaiah 61:1, is underlined by the fact that allusion is made to Isaiah 61:1 in other sayings of Jesus (Lk 6:20/Mt 5:3-6 and Mt 11:2-6/Lk 7:18-23) which bear the hallmarks of authenticity. In the case of Luke 22:35 it can be argued that the whole pericope in which it is found (Lk 22:35-38), with its advice to take up the sword, is not the sort of saying the church would want to put on the lips of Jesus while at the same time trying to keep the remembrance of him free from any association with the Zealots (*see* Revolutionary Movements). (For a fuller discussion of the case for the authenticity of the tradition underlying these sayings and others mentioned above, see Kruse 13-29.)

Because there are strong arguments in favor of the authenticity of these sayings, there is also a strong case for claiming that the idea of the Christian apostolate originated with Jesus and that he understood it in a way similar to that reflected in the use of *šālaḥ/apostellō* terminology in the OT. This in turn means that Jesus' understanding of the apostolate has close affinities with that of the function of the *šālîaḥ* reflected in the rabbinic writings.

We can now turn our attention from arguments *that*

the idea of the Christian apostolate originated with Jesus and seek to understand *what*, according to the Gospels, that apostolate entailed. We begin with a discussion of Jesus' own apostolic consciousness.

3. Jesus, Apostle of God.

The term *apostolos* is only once applied to Jesus in the NT (Heb 3:1), it being nowhere used of him in the Gospels. However, there are a number of sayings of Jesus in the Synoptic Gospels in which he betrays a consciousness of having been sent by God (Mt 15:24; Lk 4:18; Mt 10:40; Mk 9:37; Lk 9:48; 10:16). The Gospel of John attributes to Jesus some thirty-nine statements to the effect that he has been sent by God, including statements using both *apostellō* and *pempō* (cf. e.g., 5:30, 36, 38; 6:29, 57; 7:16, 29; 8:16, 42; 10:36).

3.1. The Source of Jesus' Apostolic Consciousness. It appears from the Gospels that the primary aspect of Jesus' consciousness was that of his filial relationship with the Father (cf. e.g., the boy Jesus' reply to his parents in Lk 2:49: "Did you not know that I must be in my Father's house?"), and that he had been sent by the Father to carry out his mission (cf. Lk 4:43: "I must preach the kingdom of God to the other cities also; for I was sent for this purpose"). This consciousness of having been sent by God is stressed heavily by the Fourth Evangelist. A secondary aspect of Jesus' apostolic consciousness is that of having been endowed with the Spirit (*see* Holy Spirit) to carry out the commission which the Father had given him. Each of the Gospels tells how Jesus was endowed with the Spirit at his baptism.* On a number of occasions Jesus appeals to this endowment as evidence that he is the one sent by God to bring in the time of fulfillment spoken of in the OT. For example, in Luke 4:16-21 Jesus cites the prophecy of Isaiah 61:1-2 claiming that this prophecy has now been fulfilled. In Matthew 12:28 he replies to those who assert that he exorcises by the power of Beelzebul by saying, "If by the Spirit of God I cast out demons, then the kingdom of God has come upon you."

It seems, then, that Jesus' own apostolic consciousness was rooted in his sense of unique filial relationship with the Father (*see* Abba; Son of God) and of having been commissioned by him to inaugurate the time of fulfillment. The activity of the Spirit in his ministry was something to which he called the attention of others so that they might come to recognize that he was sent by God, rather than being the evidence by which he himself was convinced of his calling.

3.2. The Scope of Jesus' Apostolate. One feature of Jesus' own apostleship which is rather striking is its limited scope. According to Matthew 15:24 ("I was sent only to the lost sheep of the house of Israel"), Jesus understood his mission to be limited to the Jewish people, and this is reflected in the fact that the Synoptic Gospels never depict him deliberately setting out to evangelize non-Jews. He was sent to announce the coming of the kingdom of God among the Jewish towns of Galilee* and Judea (Mk 1:35-39/Lk 4:42-43). Even the remarkable ministry in Samaria (*see* Samaritan), recounted in John 4, is not presented as something which Jesus set out deliberately to undertake (as was the case with the ministry in Jewish towns).

3.3. A Prophetic and Prophecy-Fulfilling Apostolate. Jesus' mission was prophetic insofar as he, like other great prophets (*see* Prophet, Prophecy) before him, proclaimed the coming of the kingdom of God (Mk 1:14-15/Mt 4:17). However, it went beyond anything that the prophets did in that he was sent not only to proclaim the kingdom, but actually to inaugurate it as well. Accordingly, Luke tells us that Jesus understood the great prophecy of Isaiah 61:1-2 as being fulfilled in his mission (Lk 4:16-21; cf. Lk 6:20/Mt 5:3-6; Mt 11:2-6/Lk 7:18-23).

3.4. Jesus' Apostolate and the Kingdom. What did it mean in practice for Jesus to inaugurate the kingdom? Jesus' statement "the kingdom of God is drawing near" really means that God himself is drawing near. And what did God do when he drew near in the person and mission of Jesus? He began his work of bringing in a new era. He called a nation to repentance, he sat at table (*see* Table Fellowship) with tax collectors (*see* Taxes), sinners,* Pharisees* and others; he lifted the heavy burden of religious tradition from the shoulders of the people of the land and liberated those who suffered from disease and demonic oppression. But above all he drew near to forgive the sins (*see* Forgiveness of Sins) of all who heeded the call to repentance, and to enter into a restored relationship with them.

But there was also a dark and mysterious side to what God was doing when he drew near in the person and mission of Jesus. The kingdom had not only to be proclaimed and inaugurated. A way had to be opened whereby sinful men and women could participate in it. The crucial part of Jesus' mission was the giving of his life as a ransom for many (Mk 10:45; *see* Ransom Saying); the pouring out of his blood for the remission of sins (Mt 26:28; Mk 14:23-24; Lk 22:20). It was to achieve this, above all, that Jesus was sent as apostle of God.

4. The Apostleship of Jesus' Disciples.

Each of the Synoptic Gospels recounts how Jesus

called the Twelve and sent them out on a Galilean mission. Some doubts have been raised about the historicity of such a mission, but there are compelling reasons to reject such objections. Not least among these is the existence of a reference to that mission in the saying of Jesus in Luke 22:35: "When I sent you out without purse or bag or sandals, did you lack anything?" (cf. 2.5. above). Leaving aside, then, the question of historicity, we may explore the mission traditions of the Gospels to discover what they reveal of the nature of the apostleship of the Twelve.

4.1. The Mission of the Twelve. Mark 3:13-14 reads: "And he went up on the mountain,* and called to him those whom he wished; and they came to him. And he appointed Twelve, whom he also named apostles, so that they might be with him, and so that he might send them to preach." Mark emphasizes that the mission and apostolate of the Twelve originates in the call of Jesus. The purpose for which they were called is clearly spelled out: "so that (*hina*) they might be with him, and so that (*hina*) he might send them to preach." There are two parts to the call and the second was intimately related to the first.

The first part (to be with him) involved travelling up and down the country with him, sharing food and accommodation with him, experiencing the same acceptance and rejection which he encountered, and observing and sometimes participating in the ministry which he was carrying out. The second part (being sent out to preach) was dependent on the first (being with him) for, as we shall see, their preaching ministry was essentially an extension of his. Mark 6:7-13; Matthew 10:1-42; and Luke 9:1-6 present Jesus' charge to the Twelve.

There are a number of significant points of comparison between their mission and the mission of Jesus himself. First, Jesus, who said that he had not been sent except to the lost sheep of the house of Israel (Mt 15:24), insisted that the same limitations apply to the mission of the Twelve: "Do not go into the way of the Gentiles, and do not enter a Samaritan town, but go rather to the lost sheep of the house of Israel" (Mt 10:5-6). Second, the thrust of their mission was to be the same. They were to proclaim that the kingdom of heaven was at hand, and its presence was to be demonstrated by mighty works (Mt 10:7-8). Third, and possibly most important of all, Jesus maintained that the reception his disciples were accorded by the people would be regarded as the reception the people wished to accord to himself, and to the Father who had sent him (Mt 10:40).

All of this has important significance for our understanding of the mission of the Twelve and of the nature of apostleship itself. That the limitations applying to their mission, its essential thrust and the significance of the people's response to it all closely parallel the essential features of Jesus' own mission suggest strongly that their mission was in fact an extension of his. This in turn suggests that the *apostellō* sending terminology which, as we have seen, is used by Jesus in the Synoptic Gospels (and John), reflects an understanding of the relationship existing between himself and his disciples in terms of the institution of the *šālîaḥ*. His disciples were commissioned to act as his representatives, under his authority, proclaiming his message and exercising his power. In the case of Jesus' disciples, then, the words of the rabbinic adage "a man's envoy is as himself" truly apply.

4.2. The Mission of the Seventy. Each of the Synoptic Gospels recounts a Galilean mission of the Twelve, but Luke alone recounts a mission of the Seventy. There are problems surrounding the latter. First, there is the question of whether the text of Luke 10:1 (and 10:17) should read "seventy" or "seventy-two." Both readings are found in the manuscripts and the witnesses seem evenly divided. Other considerations, such as the symbolism of the Seventy(-two), have produced no scholarly consensus about the original reading.

Second, material found in the Markan (6:7-13) and Matthean (10:1-42) charges to the Twelve appears in part in the Lukan charge to the Twelve (9:1-6) and in part in the Lukan charge to the Seventy (10:1-16). Assuming, as most scholars still do, that Mark was written first, and that Matthew and Luke made use of some form of Mark as well as a sayings source (Q*) in the composition of their Gospels, it seems that Matthew used his Markan material plus the Q mission-sayings when composing his charge to the Twelve, while Luke used the same sources to compose two charges—that to the Twelve and that to the Seventy (*see* Synoptic Problem).

Third, when Luke depicts Jesus referring back to the mission of the Twelve (22:35), reference is made to material included in the charge to the Seventy. From this it may be inferred that Luke was not trying to reproduce verbatim different charges to different people, but rather providing an account of the sort of thing which Jesus would have said to two different groups.

In light of all this, the question is asked whether the mission of the Seventy has any basis in history or if it should simply be regarded as a literary creation of the Evangelist. It has been suggested, for instance, that Luke invented the story to prefigure the wider mission of the church to the Gentiles. Thus, it is urged, just as the mission of the Twelve speaks of a mission to the tribes of Israel, so the mission of the Seventy speaks of the mission to the nations of the world. (Gen 10 contains a list of nations comprising seventy names in the MT, and seventy-two in the LXX.) Another suggestion is that Luke invented the mission of the Seventy to deal with the tension between the church's tradition concerning the mission of the Twelve and its recognition of the mission of a far wider group of witnesses.

However, there are other ways of explaining the phenomena. First, it is theoretically possible that Luke regarded the existence of mission material in his two sources (Mark and Q) as evidence for two different missions, and he used those sources to compose two mission charges. Second, and more likely, Luke was the recipient of reliable tradition about the two historic missions, and in composing his Gospel he used the mission material from his two sources to provide an account of the sort of thing Jesus would have said in sending out the two groups.

4.3. Post-Easter Mission of Jesus' Disciples. While the mission accounts of the Synoptic Gospels (there is none in John) relate to activity in the pre-Easter period, there appear to be allusions in the charges to a later and wider mission of the disciples in the post-Easter period. For example, the saying "Behold, I am sending you out as sheep/lambs in the midst of wolves" (Mt 10:16/Lk 10:3) does not in some ways fit well with the disciples' actual Galilean mission experience (cf. e.g., Lk 10:17-20). They appear to have been halcyon days. This has led some to suggest that this saying (and others which foreshadow great difficulties and persecution for the missionary band) is a tradition which emanated from the post-Easter period when the church was actually experiencing persecution. However, it is not necessary to draw that conclusion. Jesus would have been well aware of the mounting tension created by his mission and would have been able to foresee the opposition which he would increasingly experience, and which would culminate in his death in Jerusalem. It would have required no great insight or prophetic foreknowledge on Jesus' part to see that his followers would experience similar persecution at a later time.

All this suggests that the material now found together in the mission charges may include not only the sayings which related directly to the pre-Easter Galilean mission but also sayings of Jesus foreshadowing the post-Easter mission of his followers. Then they would encounter the same hostile opposition which he himself encountered toward the end of his ministry. This in turn lends support to the view that the apostolic role of the Twelve in the post-Easter period was at least anticipated by the historical Jesus.

Such a post-Easter mission is, of course, assumed in the post-resurrection commission sayings which are found in one form or another in each of the four Gospels (but in Mark in the longer ending only) and Acts. In both Matthew and Luke, Jesus (re)commissions the Twelve (less Judas Iscariot*), this time to make disciples of all nations (Mt 28:18-20) and to proclaim repentance and remission of sins in his name to all nations (Lk 24:44-49). This reflects the Evangelists' belief that the Jesus who called and commissioned the Twelve for the limited Galilean mission recommissioned the same men (less Judas) to be apostles of the worldwide mission. It also shows that the early church understood that the restrictions applying to Jesus' mission, and which were also applied by him to the Galilean mission of the Twelve, were now deliberately lifted, and a mission to Samaritans* and Gentiles,* as well as Jews, was actually enjoined.

5. Nuances in the Evangelists' Understanding of the Apostolate.

Each of the four Evangelists portrays the apostolate in his own way. Some things are common to all or most of the Evangelists, but others receive distinctive emphasis in one or other of the Evangelists alone.

5.1. Common Elements. Common to all the Evangelists is the firm belief that membership in the apostolate is a matter of choice on the part of Christ; there are no volunteers. Each of the Synoptic Gospels make this plain by showing how Jesus took the initiative in specifically calling certain people to follow him (Mt 4:18-22; 9:9; Mk 1:16-20; 2:14; Lk 5:1-11, 27-28). And when it came to the appointment of the Twelve, again Jesus called those whom he desired (Mt 10:1-4; Mk 3:13-19; Lk 6:12-16). While the Gospel of John does not include an account of the appointment of the Twelve, it refers to them as such several times (6:67, 70-71; 20:24) and also stresses that membership in the apostolate is a matter of Christ's choice (6:70; 13:18; 15:16, 19).

All the Synoptic Evangelists indicate that the appointment of the Twelve was (initially at least) for a Galilean mission in which they would carry on in Jesus' name the same sort of activity in which he himself was involved (Mt 10:5-8; Mk 6:7-13; Lk 9:1-6).

5.2. Different Elements. While all four Gospels (and Acts) contain a post-resurrection commission by Christ, these reveal different aspects and/or understandings of the apostolate.

5.2.1. Matthew. In Matthew Jesus says to the eleven: "All authority in heaven and on earth has been given to me. Therefore go and make disciples of all nations, baptizing them in the name of the Father and of the Son and of the Holy Spirit, teaching them to observe all that I have commanded you; and behold, I am with you always (lit. all the days), to the close of the age" (28:18-20). The fourfold use of the word "all" is our clue to Matthew's emphasis on the nature of the apostolic task: It rests on the authority of the risen Christ ("all authority . . . has been given to me. Go therefore . . ."), its scope is to encompass "all the nations," its content is teaching "all that I have commanded you" and its promise is "Behold, I am with you always, to the close of the age."

5.2.2. Mark. In Mark the commission-saying is found only in the longer ending, and there is considerable doubt whether this should be regarded as an authentic part of the Gospel (*see* Mark, Gospel of). The saying runs: "Go into all the world and preach the Gospel to the whole creation. He who believes and is baptized will be saved but he who does not believe will be condemned" (16:15-16). The stress here is on the universal nature of the apostolic commission and on the serious implications of people's response to the apostolic message.

5.2.3. Luke. In Luke's Gospel the commission-saying reads: "Thus it is written, that the Christ should suffer and rise from the dead on the third day, and that repentance and forgiveness of sins should be preached in his name to all nations, beginning from Jerusalem. You are witnesses of these things. And behold, I send the promise of my Father upon you; but stay in the city, until you are clothed with power from on high" (24:46-49). Once again the universal scope of the apostolic commission is stressed ("to all nations"). In addition, Luke stresses that the role of the apostolate is to bear witness* to the death and resurrection of Jesus Christ and to call for repentance and offer forgiveness in his name.

This notion of the apostolic task as witness is developed further in Acts, where the apostles are told they are to be Christ's "witnesses in Jerusalem and in all Judea and Samaria and to the end of the earth" (1:8). What this witness involves is spelled out in the account of Matthias' appointment to succeed Judas Iscariot: "So one of the men who have accompanied us all the time that the Lord Jesus went in and out among us, beginning from the baptism of John until the day when he was taken up from us—one of these men must become with us a witness to his resurrection" (1:21-22).

Finally, there is in the Lukan commission-saying an emphasis on the empowering (by the Spirit) which the apostles were to receive to carry out their task (this also is further developed in Acts).

5.2.4. John. In John's Gospel Jesus appears to his disciples after his resurrection and says to them, "Peace be with you. As the Father has sent me, even so I send you" (20:21). The wording of the commission here implies that the apostolic task involved an extension of the ministry of Jesus himself. In the verses which follow (22-23) Jesus breathed on his disciples and said, "Receive the Holy Spirit. If you forgive the sins of any, they are forgiven them; if you retain the sins of any, they are retained." This both elucidates how their mission can be said to be an extension of his (because of the Holy Spirit bestowed) and something of what that means (the forgiving and retaining of sins—presumably by preaching the Gospel and informing people of the consequences of receiving or rejecting it, just as Jesus had done).

See also DISCIPLE; GENTILES.

BIBLIOGRAPHY. F. Agnew, "On the Origin of the Term Apostolos," *CBQ* 38 (1976) 49-53; idem, "The Origin of the NT Apostle-Concept: A Review of Research," *JBL* 105 (1986) 75-96; C. K. Barrett, *The Signs of an Apostle* (London: Epworth, 1970); K. Giles, *Patterns of Ministry Among the First Christians* (Melbourne: Collins Dove, 1989); R. W. Herron, "The Origin of the New Testament Apostolate," *WTJ* 45 (1983) 101-31; J. Jeremias, *Jesus' Promise to the Nations* (Philadelphia: Fortress, 1982); J. A. Kirk, "Apostleship since Rengstorf: Towards a Synthesis," *NTS* 21 (1974-75) 249-64; C. G. Kruse, *New Testament Models for Ministry: Jesus and Paul* (Nashville: Nelson, 1984); J. B. Lightfoot, "The Name and Office of an Apostle," in *Saint Paul's Epistle to the Galatians* (Grand Rapids: Zondervan, reprint 1953) 92-101; K. H. Rengstorf, "ἀπόστολος," *TDNT* I.407-47; W. Schmithals, *The Office of Apostle in the Early Church* (Nashville: Abingdon, 1969); R. Schnackenburg, "Apostles before and during Paul's Time," in *Apostolic History and the Gospel,* eds. W. W. Gasque and R. P. Martin (Grand Rapids: Eerdmans, 1970) 287-303.

C. G. Kruse

ARAMAIC. *See* LANGUAGES OF PALESTINE; TARGUMS.

ARCHEOLOGY AND GEOGRAPHY

We begin with a short discussion of the actual or presupposed geographical data, most of which are contained in the Gospels. Special attention will be devoted to the question of whether the results of archeological investigations can shed light on NT and early church traditions referring to details of locale. In conclusion we will consider what theological significance can be attributed to geographic factors, and whether these factors furnish any grounds for drawing conclusions about the historical reliability (*see* Gospels [Historical Reliability]) and the origin of the Gospels.

1. The Infancy Narratives
2. Areas of John the Baptist's Activity
3. The Public Ministry of Jesus in Galilee
4. Withdrawal Areas around Galilee
5. The Journeys to Jerusalem
6. Jerusalem
7. Historical and Theological Significance

1. The Infancy Narratives.

1.1. The Birthplace of John the Baptist. To visit Elizabeth, Mary went "into the hill country [*oreinē*], to a city of Judah" (Lk 1:39). The Greek word describes the district around Jerusalem (Pliny *Nat. Hist.* 5.14). A literary tradition that can be traced back to the sixth century identifies the birthplace with En-Kerem (Arabic *Ain Karim*), seven kilometers west of Jerusalem (*ELS* 44ff.). Remains of two fourth-century churches indicate, however, that the tradition stretches back to a still-earlier time (*GBL* II.776). The identification of this site with the priestly city of Juttah (Josh 15:55; 21:16) ten kilometers south of Hebron is ruled out on philological grounds alone (*see* John the Baptist).

1.2. Bethlehem. According to Matthew 2:1 and Luke 2:4 Jesus was born in Bethlehem (Gk *Bēthleem*), the native city of the house of David (*see* Birth of Jesus). It has often been argued that this is nothing more than a deduction from the prophecy of Micah 5:2, and that Jesus actually hailed from Nazareth. Against this is the fact that Bethlehem as Jesus' birthplace appears in two traditions that are totally different from each other. When John 7:42 is taken as indicating that the Fourth Evangelist knew nothing of Jesus' birth in the city of David, the intentional ambiguity found throughout John's Gospel is being misunderstood. That Joseph set out for Bethlehem because of a tax census (Lk 2:1-4) is explicable only if he had land holdings there—indeed, it is probable that it was his place of residence (cf. Mt 2:11, 22-23). This is not necessarily contradicted by Luke's presentation, since *katalyma* (Lk 2:7) need not refer to a guest house but far more commonly denotes a large room. Worth mention only as a curiosity is the occasional claim that Jesus' birthplace was the Bethlehem that lay eleven kilometers northwest of Nazareth (J. Klausner, *Jesus of Nazareth*, 1952, 315-16).

A somewhat independent reference to Jesus' origin in the city of David is the early Christian geographical tradition, not derivable from the Gospels, placing Jesus' birth in a cave in Bethlehem (*GBL* I.196-97). The present Church of the Nativity, lying at the west edge of the hill that marked the old city, was erected over a large rock cave, some 12 x 3 meters in size. This cavern is one of several that were located near houses and served as stalls or for the storage of supplies (cf. Lk 11:33) in the first century. Already at the beginning of the second century, the local tradition was so well established that Hadrian (in c. A.D. 135) made the cave into a sanctuary to Adonis in order to eliminate veneration of it by Jewish Christians (*ELS* 83ff.). According to Jerome the "manger" (*phatnē*) of Luke 2:7 was still visible in his time and consisted of a rock groove with plain clay walls (*ELS* 91) in a side cave some 3 x 3 meters in size (*GBL* II.847). Due to the marble paneling and rebuilding, today it is very difficult to envision the original appearance of this grotto.

1.3. The Shepherd Fields. Based on Genesis 35:21 and Micah 4:8, some Jews expected the Messiah to appear at a place called the "shepherd's tower" (Heb *migdal-ēder*) east of Bethlehem (*GBL* II.977-78). Luke 2:8 may envision the shepherds at this site. From the fourth century at the latest, the shepherd fields were sought east of Bethlehem at the village of Beth Sahur (*ELS* 90ff.). Excavations in this area have brought to light a small shepherd settlement dating to the first century (*GBL* I.197).

1.4. Rachel's Tomb. Already in NT times, this tomb near Bethlehem was venerated based on Genesis 35:19. This is probably the same site as the present one at the junction that leads to Jerusalem (*GBL* I.197). There may have been a connection between the tradition surrounding this tomb and Matthew 2:16-18.

1.5. The Tomb of Herod the Great. Matthew 2:19 mentions the death of the Jewish king. Originally, he had foreseen a family burial site a little north of the modern Damascus gate in Jerusalem in a rotunda modeled after Augustus' mausoleum in Rome. Herod was transferred, however, to the Herodium, his refuge located southwest of Bethlehem on a hill partially constructed from rubble (Josephus *J.W.* 1.33.8 §673). For a long time his grave was suspected to lie in the main tower, but today it is rather thought to be at the base of the fortress (*GBL* II.813; *see* Herodian Dynasty).

2. Areas of John the Baptist's Activity.

2.1. The Desert John Inhabited. As the parallels to Jesus' birth narratives show, the Baptist was already "in the desert" as a small child (Lk 1:80). Some researchers have suspected that John was brought up in the Qumran community, since the Essenes adopted youths and instructed them in their doctrine (Josephus *J.W.* 2.8.2 §120; cf. 1QH 9:35-36). The local Christian traditions regarding the desert frequented by the Baptist are of late origin and contradictory (*ELS* 62ff.). Even if John was in contact with the Essenes during his youth, after his prophetic calling from God he turned away from their exclusivist teachings to preach repentance to the populace at large (*see* Mountain and Wilderness).

2.2. The Baptism of Jesus. According to Matthew 3:13-17 Jesus was baptized (*see* Baptism) at the Jordan River where it forms the eastern border (cf. Mk 1:4-5) of the desert of Judea (Mt 3:1). This points to the area between the mouth of the Wadi Farah and the site where the Jordan enters the Dead Sea. Already in the third century Origen (*Comm. Joh.* 6.104) knew a local tradition about the heights of Jericho on the east bank of the river. This tradition connected the site with the name Bethabara (probably a ford). Subsequently, the Byzantine tradition without exception transferred Jesus' baptismal site to this location, more precisely to the Wadi el-Charrar (*ELS* 171ff.). This may result from a local Jewish tradition, quite independent of Christian tradition, that located Elijah's* ascension (2 Kings 2:5-14) in this very area (*GBL* I.193). It is quite possible that John chose this baptismal site deliberately in order to hint that he was the eschatological Elijah (cf. Mt 11:14; 17:11-13; Mk 9:12-13; Lk 1:17).

2.3. The Mountain of the Temptation. While a symbolic understanding would also be possible (Mt 4:8; cf. Lk 4:5 [(*see* Temptation of Jesus)]), it appears that early Byzantine tradition regarded this mountain to have been the Dschebel Qarantal northwest of Jericho, on which the Hasmonean fortress of Dok lay (*ELS* 189-90). Perhaps the Jerusalem Talmud polemicizes against such a veneration (*y. 'Abod. Zar.* 39c). According to the Qumran *Copper Scroll* it seems possible that there was an Essene hideaway there (3Q15 7:11-13). Local Christian tradition preserves, perhaps, the memory that Jesus withdrew (Mk 1:12-13 par.) in a similar manner to the peaceful solitude of this deserted place (*GBL* II.659).

2.4. Aenon and Salim. John also baptized at another site, by a sizable spring Aenon (Heb *'ynôn;* Gk *Ainôn*) in the vicinity of Salim (Gk *Saleim;* Jn 3:23). Baptizing in the Jordan could have been hazardous during high water, but its tributaries were considered as waters of the Jordan (*GBL* I.64). Because of the travel route presupposed by the Fourth Evangelist (cf. Jn 3:22; 4:1-6), modern researchers have tried to identify Salim with Ain Farah twelve kilometers northwest of Sichem.

The early Byzantine tradition (*ELS* 214ff.), however, places the site twelve kilometers southeast of Scythopolis (Beth-shan), where the lush springs of Ed-Der arise near Tel Shech Salim (*GBL* III.1318). In favor of the Baptist's having chosen this site is the fact that Elisha's birthplace, Abel-Mehola, where Elijah made him his disciple (1 Kings 19:15-21), was not far distant. The *Copper Scroll* suggests (3Q15 12:6-7) that an Essene group that practiced baptism settled in this area (*DJD* IV.262). Early Christian pilgrims were shown the palace of Melchizedek near Salim, a feature which may point to a tradition formed by this Essene group (cf. 11QMelch) in competition with Jerusalem. Since the area lay in the jurisdiction of Scythopolis, a city of the Decapolis, the Baptist was safe here from persecution by Herod Antipas.

2.5. Bethany beyond the Jordan. At this place (*topos*) east of the Jordan (Jn 1:28: *en Bēthania peran tou Iordanou*), a delegation from Jerusalem interrogated John the Baptist regarding who he claimed to be (Jn 1:19-28). At Bethany Jesus called his first personal followers from among the Baptist's adherents (Jn 1:35-51; cf. Acts 1:21-22). There he tarried, obviously to avoid harassment, shortly before the passion. In so doing he gained still more followers from among John's ranks (Jn 10:40-42). In the third century Origen found no place by this name on the east bank of the Jordan. He therefore opted for the reading *Bēthabara* that appears in a few texts (*Comm. Joh.* 4.204). The oldest manuscripts ($\mathfrak{P}^{66}$, $\mathfrak{P}^{75}$), however, support *Bēthania,* and the transition from John 10:40-42 to 11:1-2 shows that the Evangelist was aware of how similar Bethany (on the far side of the Jordan) and Bethany (near Jerusalem) sounded (Jn 11:1, 18). The distances presupposed in John 1—2 and 10—11 speak in favor of a location nearer Galilee* than Judea. In recent time various more precise attempts to pin down the location have not succeeded (*GBL* I.193-94).

One explanation that clarifies much holds Bethany to have been the district of *Batanaea* (Gk *Batanaia*), the Bashan of the OT, which is designated in the LXX as *peran tou Iordanou* (Num 32:32-33; Deut 3:8; 4:47). A Greek transliteration of *Bēthania* would not be surprising given the surfeit of various spellings in the targums* and rabbinic literature (*see* Rabbinic Traditions and Writings). *Batanaea* belonged to the tetrarchy of the tolerant Herod Philip (Josephus *Ant.* 18.106-7) and thus furnished Jesus a safe refuge. This attempted explanation does not necessarily conflict with Jesus' baptism at the south end of the Jordan valley, since his baptism is only presupposed in John 1:32-34, not depicted. John 1:35-51 is parallel to the calling of the first disciples* recorded in the Synoptics

(Mk 1:16-20 par.) in the vicinity of the Sea of Galilee. Locating Bethany in the north of the Holy Land would fit in well with this. In this northerly setting (Hermon area, "Damascus") certain groups with Essene ties appear to have expected the onset of the eschaton (*see* Galilee). Occasionally the appearance of the eschatological Elijah was also looked for in the north (cf. 1 Kings 19:15; *SDtn* 41 [79b]). That could explain why John began baptizing here (Jn 10:40). Perhaps John 10:16 and 11:52 refer to a mission Jesus had among such Jewish fringe groups. If one accepts a connection between the Mandaeans and the Baptist's followers, then the role played in the Mandaean writings (*GBL* II.648) by the river Yarmuk on the Batanaean border is interesting. Luke 3:3 also presupposes that the Baptist's impact was felt throughout the entire Jordan area.

2.6. Death and Burial. The site of the Baptist's execution is not given in the Gospels, but Josephus cites the fortress Machaerus east of the Dead Sea (*Ant.* 18.119). Mark 6:22-25 may preserve a recollection of this site when it speaks of separate celebrations for men and women on Herod Antipas' birthday. At Machaerus two large dining halls (*triclinia*) have been excavated. Rapid communication (cf. Mt 11:2-3 par.) between the fortress and other parts of the country was facilitated by a very well-constructed access road (*GBL* II.905-6).

Since no later than the fourth century, the Baptist's burial site was presumed to be in Samaria (Jerome *Ep.* 43.13; 108.13). This location, independent of the Gospels (cf. Mk 6:29), is probably correct. The grave site, uncovered under churches of the twelfth and fourth centuries, reflects a first-century Jewish arrangement. It is obvious that prior to this the grave of Elijah was venerated at the same spot. The choice of this site by John's disciples could have been entirely deliberate since their master's life so closely followed Elijah traditions. In view of the Baptist's ministry in Aenon near Salim, the existence of John's followers in Samaria is not surprising.

3. The Public Ministry of Jesus in Galilee.

3.1. Nazareth. Since Nazareth (Gk *Nazaret*) is not mentioned in the OT, in the Apocrypha or in rabbinic literature, some during the last century disputed its existence in NT times. In addition to an inscription mentioning it as a settlement for priests in the third to fourth century, excavations of recent years have removed every doubt (*GBL* II.1031-37). The name is sometimes derived from the Aramaic *nāṣᵉraṭ*, "lookout," "watchtower." Against this, however, speaks its setting in a fertile high valley. Matthew 2:23 connects

the messianic branch (Heb *nēṣer*) of Isaiah 11:1 with the name Nazareth (*see* Nazarene). Perhaps members of the house of David from Babylon or the area around Damascus resettled the area in late Hellenistic times and gave it a consciously messianic name (cf. Julius Africanus [Eusebius *Hist. Eccl.* 1.7.6-12]; *GBL* II.801-2).

Remains dating from NT times consist especially of cisterns and silos hewn from rock, along with tombs. As it expanded, Nazareth may have grown to a settlement of some 200 persons. It is unfounded to imagine it as remote for two reasons. First, it was only an hour's walk from the district capital of old Galilee, Sepphoris, with its theater built during the reign of Herod the Great (*GBL* III.1429). Second, it lay near one of the most important trade routes of the Roman Empire, the road from Egypt to Damascus. If the so-called Nazareth inscription actually comes from there (*GBL* II.1037), then Greek was a common language among the populace.

The connection between Jesus and Nazareth, the birthplace of his mother, Mary (Lk 1:26), is verified in such various Gospel traditions (e.g., Mk 1:9; Lk 2:39; 4:16; Mt 2:23; 4:13; Jn 1:45-46) that it is disputed only by outsiders. After an obviously successful expulsion from his family proper (Lk 4:16-30; cf. Mk 3:21, 31-35; 6:4), Jesus switched his residence to Capernaum (Mt 4:16; cf. Jn 2:12). As yet no sure signs of what is likely to have been the quite modest synagogue* presupposed by the Gospels (Mk 6:1-2 par.) have been found. The precipice (*ophryos*) of the hill on which Nazareth was built, and from which some attempted to hurl Jesus (Lk 4:29), has been confirmed archeologically on the west side of the present-day Church of the Annunciation. When Matthew (Mt 2:23) and Luke (Lk 1:26 and elsewhere) call Nazareth a city (*polis*), it may be due to their sources containing the ambiguous Hebrew expression *'îr*, which may mean either city or village. Under the Church of the Annunciation lie the remains of a fifth-century Byzantine basilica and a still older, obviously Jewish, worship structure. A fragmentary inscription containing Luke 1:28 indicates that already in pre-Byzantine times there was common knowledge of the annunciation to Mary in this area. Remains of another Byzantine structure, along with a house from NT times, lie under the convent of the Dames de Nazareth. Byzantine pilgrims probably sought Joseph's house here. An old Jewish-Christian baptistry is located under Joseph's Church.

3.2. Cana. To distinguish this Cana (Gk *Kana*) from the Kanah southeast of Tyre (Josh 19:28), John calls it "Cana in Galilee" (Jn 2:1, 12; 4:46; 21:2). Jesus did two miracles* and obviously had relatives there. The place visited by pilgrims today, Kafr Kennā, six kilometers north of Nazareth, was not regarded as the NT Cana until the seventeenth century and is based on a local, philologically impossible identification of names. Most researchers identify it rather with the site of the ruins at Khirbeth Qânâ, twelve kilometers north of Nazareth, which was a burgeoning settlement especially in the first six centuries A.D. Ancient pilgrim reports (*ELS* 206f.) can also be related to this location. Cana was a strategically vital center on the Roman road from Ptolemais (Akko) on the Mediterranean to Magdala on the Sea of Galilee (Josephus *Life* 16 §86). As yet there have not been systematic excavations, so it is presently impossible to investigate archeologically the frequently alleged connection between John 2:1-12 and the cult of Dionysius. Against the existence of such a cult, however, stands the fact that Cana was, at least after the Bar-Kokhba revolt (A.D. 132-135), a settlement of Jewish priests (*GBL* II.751-53). John 2:12 indicates an awareness that one "descended" from Cana to Capernaum.

3.3. Nain. The site Nain (Gk *Nain*) has occasionally been identified with a [N]ain in Judaea (Josephus *J.W.* 4.511). Textually, however, this is uncertain. The place Josephus mentions may be the Ain of Joshua 15:32 and 19:7, near Hebron. According to the context of Luke 7:1-11, Nain should be sought in the Galilee region (*GBL* II.1022-23). Early Byzantine tradition points unwaveringly to the present-day Arabic village Nein, eight kilometers southeast of Nazareth (*ELS* 341ff.). During NT times this probably belonged to the Galilean portion of the plain of Jezreel. Nazareth was hardly a city *(polis)*; the city gate mentioned in Luke 7:11-12 could have been no more than the outlet of a street. Excavations have not yet been possible, however. Five kilometers north of Nazareth lies Shunem, where Elisha raised a youth from the dead (2 Kings 4:18-37). The parallel resurrection story about Elijah (1 Kings 17:17-24) could have affected the formulation of Luke 7:11-12, but the witnesses of Jesus' miracle themselves saw a connection with Elijah (cf. Lk 7:18).

3.4. The Sea of Gennesaret. An essential portion of Jesus' ministry was concentrated on the shore of the Sea of Gennesaret (Gk *Gennēsaret*). Matthew and Mark call it the "Sea of Galilee" (Mt 4:18; Mk 1:16 and elsewhere) or simply the "sea" (Mt 8:24; Mk 4:39 and elsewhere). Since the Hebrew *yām* can mean either the high seas or an inland sea, this mode of expression shows the connection of both Evangelists with ancient Palestinian tradition. Luke, in contrast, chose the proper Greek literary designation *limnē* (Lk 5:1-2 and elsewhere). The name "Sea of Tiberias" (Jn 21:1;

cf. 6:1) is not necessarily an anachronism in the first century (cf. Josephus *J.W.* 3.3.5 §57; 4.8.2 §§456-57). The "twenty-five or thirty stadia" (five-six kilometers) of John 6:19 probably depicts (accurately) the middle of the northern portion of the sea, with the entire body of water measuring about twenty-one kilometers (thirteen miles) north to south and thirteen kilometers (eight miles) at its widest point.

Occasionally reports that mention the sea preserve clear examples of local color. Due to the elevation well below sea level (212 meters), temperatures that permit sleeping outdoors are common (cf. Mk 8:2). The low-lying setting results in sudden violent downdrafts and storms (cf. Mt 8:24; Mk 4:37; Lk 8:23; Jn 6:18). Especially notorious is a wind that blows from the east (cf. Mt 14:22-24; Mk 6:45-48), which arises mostly when the seasons are changing, e.g., around Passover (cf. Mk 6:39; Jn 6:4). Most notably, the Gospels on the whole present the sea's fishing industry in an expert fashion (M. Nun, *New Testament Fishery*, 1989). An outstanding example of boat travel on the sea is furnished by two recent finds dating to NT times: a boat mosaic from Magdala, and a derelict boat raised from beneath the water near Nof Ginnosar (*GBL* III.1371-72).

3.5. Tiberias. Herod Antipas established Tiberias (Gk *Tiberias*) c. A.D. 17-18 in the vicinity of the OT Hammath (Josh 19:35) as the new regional capital of Galilee. He named it after his patron Tiberius. It is striking that the Gospels make no mention of Jesus' ministry in Tiberias. Many pious Jews considered the city to be unclean (Josephus *Ant.* 18.2.3 §38), but that would hardly have deterred Jesus. In addition not everyone shared this view, as the strong support enjoyed by the nationalist-religious revolutionary Zealots (*see* Revolutionary Movements) in Tiberias proves (Josephus *Life* 9 §§32-42; 17-20 §§87-101; 53-64 §§271-335). Furthermore, the assumption that Jesus avoided Hellenized cities is untenable, because Magdala, Jericho and, not least, Jerusalem all belonged in that category. Jesus at least had devotees in Tiberias (cf. Jn 6:23), among whom may have been the wife of the Herodian steward Chuza (Lk 8:3). Presumably the reason that Jesus made no public foray into Tiberias lies in the danger posed by Herod Antipas (cf. Lk 13:31-33). The Jerusalem Talmud presupposes a Jewish Christian church in Tiberias (*y. Sanh.* 25d), presumably at about the end of the first century. Of the synagogues discovered to date, one may date back as far as the second or third centuries A.D. (*GBL* III. 1554-56).

3.6. Magdala. This strongly Hellenized site lay five kilometers northeast of Tiberias. Because of its important dried-fish industry, its Greek name was Taricheia (Josephus *Life* 72 §§403-4). Excavations have uncovered a small synagogue from NT times. They also confirm the urban character of Magdala (*GBL* II.909-10). The rabbis criticized the immorality of its inhabitants (Str-B I.1047), but most of them sided with the Jews in the revolt against Rome (Josephus *Life* 29 §142). Magdala receives direct mention only in a few late manuscripts at Matthew 15:39 and Mark 8:10. The places mentioned in the original text (see 3.8. below), however, are not scribal slips for Magdala; they rather refer to a region lying further to the north. One of Jesus' most loyal followers, Mary Magdalene (Mt 27:55-56; 28:1 par.), hailed from Magdala; the second portion of her name may give a clue that Jesus ministered there.

3.7. Gennesaret. The NT site, in contrast to the OT city of Chinnereth (Josh 19:35), is located south of (not at) Tell el'Oreimeh, on the northeastern edge of the exceedingly fertile (Josephus *J.W.* 3.10.8 §§516-21) plain of Gennesaret. It is not entirely clear whether the Gospels refer to the site (cf. Mt 14:34) or the plain (cf. Mk 6:53-56). The late Byzantine text-form at Matthew 14:34 (*eis tēn gēn Gennēsaret*) provides the first unambiguous reference to it as an area.

3.8. Dalmanutha/Magadan. Except at Mark 8:10 Dalmanutha (Gk *Dalmanoutha*) is not attested as a site where Jesus went ashore. The parallel (Mt 15:39) speaks of "the region of Magadan." The rest of the narrative (Mt 16:1-4; Mk 8:11-13) seems to indicate a place on the west shore of the Sea of Galilee. It has been proposed that Mark understood "Dalmanutha," which in Aramaic could mean "area of his [Jesus'] stay," as a specific place name (*GBL* I.247-48). Some derive Magadan (Gk *Magadan*) from *may-gad*, "water of (the Canaanite god of springs) Gad"; this would fit in well with the abundant springs of Tabgha two kilometers southwest of Capernaum. Josephus calls them the "spring of Capernaum" (*J.W.* 3.10.8 §517), and Byzantine sources speak of the seven springs (Gk *Heptapēgon*, from which the garbled Arabic *Eṭ-Ṭābghah* is derived). This appears to have been, in fact, one of Jesus' preferred locations for ministry, one at which he was able to reach large crowds (*GBL* 2.767). The important trade route from Caesarea Maritima to Damascus bordered the Sea of Galilee at this point, and there was sufficient drinking water available. As early as the end of the fourth century, the Christian pilgrim Egeria found here three firmly grounded local traditions (*ELS* 281-82): the Sermon on the Mount (*see* Sermon on the Mount), the feeding of the five thousand, and the post-resurrection appearance of Jesus related in John 21. These

traditions deserve to be taken seriously because there was a continuous Jewish-Christian presence in Capernaum from NT times until the fourth century, providing a means by which the traditions could be passed along.

3.9. The Sermon on the Mount. In the fourth century Egeria found the place of remembrance for Matthew 5—7 to be a cave—not uncommon for Jewish-Christian memorial sites—which can only have been the so-called cave of Job 200 meters east of the Church of the Miraculous Feeding (or Multiplied Loaves) (*GBL* II.767). The "level field" (Gk *topos pedinos*) mentioned in Luke 6:17 below a hill (Lk 6:12; cf. Mt 5:1) bears identification with the level stretches, large enough to hold several thousand, lying above this cave. Not until later did the local tradition (influenced by Mt 5:1) shift the scene further up the hill. In favor of a location in Tabgha are: (1) the mention of Capernaum (Lk 7:1; cf. Mt 8:5) following directly after the Sermon on the Plain and (2) the fact that here is one of the few places where the hills extend right down to the seashore (*see* Sermon on the Mount).

3.10. First and Second Miraculous Feeding. The Jewish Christians thought of the first feeding (Mt 14:13-21 par.) as taking place at an exposed rock at the edge of a small, fertile plain in Tabgha. The pilgrim Egeria found that the rock had been incorporated into a church building, serving as the altar, as it is today. Since the area was uninhabited in NT times, one could speak of a "lonely place" (Mt 14:13; Mk 6:32). Now it appears, nevertheless, that John presupposes that the feeding of the five thousand took place on the eastern shore (cf. Jn 6:1, 17, 22-24). The original text has multiple variants at this point, however, and John can just as easily be understood to assume a location on the western shore (R. E. Brown, *The Gospel of John*, 1971, I.231-59). Luke 9:10 also can be understood to say that the feeding took place not in but on the way to Bethsaida. Perhaps behind Luke 9:12 (*episitismos*, "food," "something to eat") stands a Hebrew wordplay (*bêt ṣēdâ*, "house of food"). The view that the feeding of the four thousand is not simply a doublet may be upheld by topographical considerations: Matthew 15:31 presupposes the presence of Gentiles,* and Mark 7:31 appears to have the Decapolis in mind. Late Byzantine traditions (*ELS* 278-79) actually transfer the second feeding to the area of Kursi (see 4.1. below) on the eastern shore (*GBL* I.442).

3.11. Jesus' Appearance by the Sea. Egeria located the encounter between the resurrected Jesus and his disciples* (Jn 21) in Tabgha at some rock stairsteps still visible today (cf. Jn 21:9). A small church had been erected in the immediate vicinity already in the fourth century. The beach of Tabgha was an especially good fishing area, since the water of the warm springs and the vegetation they carry attract many fish, especially at night (cf. Jn 21:3). Another indication of fishermen's fondness for this site is a small, ancient boat harbor (*GBL* II.767).

3.12. Capernaum. This site (Gk *Kapharnaoum*) is mentioned by Josephus (*J.W.* 3.10.8 §517; *Life* 72 §403) and became Jesus' place of residence for a time at the beginning of his public Galilean ministry (Mt 4:13-17; 9:1; cf. Jn 2:12). Excavations of recent years establish beyond any doubt that Capernaum is to be identified with the site of the ruins at Tel-ḥûm (*GBL* II.764-68), which was still famous as recently as the seventeenth century (*ELS* 296ff.). The large village of some 1500 residents consisted of individual living quarters containing large families. Beneath an octagonal fifth-century Byzantine church and a fourth-century Jewish-Christian house synagogue, the remains of a private house were uncovered. It had, as early as the second half of the first century, served as an assembly hall for religious meetings. Inscriptions and the reports of early Christian travelers (*ELS* 299) make it possible to identify the building as Peter's house (cf. Mt 9:27-31; Mk 1:29; 2:1; 3:20; 9:33). Remains from synagogues of the third and first centuries A.D. (Lk 7:5; cf. Mk 1:21-29) have been found beneath the celebrated white limestone synagogue that dates to the end of the fourth century. The tradition reflected in Mark 1:29-39, which probably goes back to Peter, is characterized by notable local color: the synagogue lay not far (Mk 1:29) from the house of Peter's large family (Mk 1:29-30), at the door of which there really was an open area (Mk 1:33). Mark 2:4 (otherwise Lk 5:19) presupposes correctly a building method utilizing clay roofs.

Apparently separated by vacant land from the Jewish village, a small Roman-style settlement stood at the present site of Greek Orthodox property. One can easily envision the residence of the Gentile centurion (cf. Lk 7:6). An imperial road passed nearby. The toll booth (Gk *telōnion*, Mk 2:14) manned by Matthew Levi may have demanded heavy taxes from fishermen rather than road tolls. Halfway between Capernaum and Tabgha lies a small inlet whose acoustic qualities may have served well as Jesus preached at water's edge (Lk 5:1-3). Capernaum was not destroyed in either of the two Jewish revolts. It was gradually deserted, beginning in the tenth century. Jesus' pronouncement of woe (Mt 11:20-24; Lk 10:13-15; *see* Blessing and Woe) has Capernaum's eschatological fate in view; it says nothing about a temporal destruction.

3.13. Chorazin. Although no story from Chorazin (Gk *Chorazin*) has been preserved, Jesus' pronouncement of judgment* (Mt 11:20-24; Lk 10:12-15) indicates an extensive ministry there. Excavations have so far found vestiges of a Jewish village dating from the second to fourth century A.D., but as yet hardly any evidence from NT times.

3.14. Bethsaida. The Jewish village of Bethsaida (Gk *Bēthsaida*) was declared a *polis* by the tetrarch Herod Philip and named Julias, probably not after the daughter of Augustus, Julias (Josephus *Ant.* 18.2.1 §28), but rather after Augustus' wife Livia-Julia, sometime after A.D. 30. So it may be not without significance for the age of the Gospel traditions that they use only the old Jewish name. The city lay on the east bank of the Jordan, not far from where it flows into the Sea of Galilee in the district of Gaulanitis (Josephus *J.W.* 3.10.7 §515). Recent excavations on the mound of ruins called et-Tell have uncovered extensive remains of houses dating from NT times. Some have contained fishing gear. This establishes the location of the city. West of where the Jordan flowed in former times, right at the edge of the sea, lies the small site of the ruins of El-Aradsch. Presumably it was already settled in NT times. It contains the remains of a Byzantine synagogue or church.

It is not easy to decide which of the two sites should be connected with the longer ministry of Jesus in this area (Mt 11:21; Lk 10:13; cf. Lk 9:10). The healing* of the blind man outside the village *(kōmē)* of Bethsaida (Mk 8:22-26) may favor the El-Aradsch location. John gives as the birthplace of several disciples, "Bethsaida in Galilee," and he calls it a *polis* (Jn 1:44; 12:21). Josephus also calls the rebel leader Judas, who hailed from near Gamla in Gaulinitis, "the Galilean" (*Ant.* 17.13.1 §341; *J.W.* 2.8.1 §118). The references in John, therefore, can relate to the Julian city. A semitically influenced, loose usage of *polis* is, however, also a possibility. In this case El-Aradsch is a viable choice; it fell to Antipas after the death of Herod the Great and thus became part of the political region of Galilee.

3.15. The Mountain in Galilee. According to Matthew 28:16 an important appearance of the resurrected Jesus took place "on the [definite article] mountain in Galilee." An identification with Mount Tabor, which was apparently uninhabited in Jesus' day, goes back to Theodosius early in the sixth century (*ELS* 321). The same identification may, however, be presupposed also in the fourth century by Eusebius (*In Ps* 88:13) and Epiphanius of Salamis (*GBL* III.1517-19). Mount Tabor ranks among the mountains possessing eschatological significance in rabbinic literature (Str-B IV/2.930-31).

4. Withdrawal Areas around Galilee.

4.1. The Land of the Gerasenes. According to Mark 5:1-20, Jesus healed a demon-possessed (*see* Demon, Devil, Satan) Gentile man here, an area on the east shore of the Sea of Galilee. Mark could hardly have had in mind the far distant Decapolis city of Gerasa; he rather makes use of a Semitic designation, "land of the foreigners" (Heb *gērûšîm;* Gk *Gerasēnoi*), as the name for an entire region (*GBL* I.442-43). The city of the Decapolis presupposed in Mark 5:14, 20, must be Hippos. The "country of the Gadarenes" (*chōra tōn Gadarēnōn*) of Matthew 8:28-34 is found to bear the name for the regional capital, Gadara. If the reading "country of the Gergesenes" in Luke 8:26-39 is original, this perhaps reflects the Semitic name for Hippos (*Gergesa*). Or it may refer to the Girgasites, who, according to Deuteronomy 3:14 and Joshua 12:5 (LXX), settled in this area. A local tradition that has received some archeological support locates the miracle at El-Kursi.

4.2. Tyre and Sidon. Upper Galilee bordered on the territory of the Gentile city Tyre (Gk *Tyros*). When threatened, Jesus found this to be a natural place to withdraw (Mt 15:21; Mk 7:24). Mark 7:24-30 mirrors quite authentically the ethnic tensions that obtained in the border area between Tyre and Galilee (Theissen, 63-84).

4.3. The Decapolis. Another nearby place of refuge (Mk 7:31, Gk *Dekapoleōs*) for Jesus was that area lying east of the Jordan comprised of Hellenistic-Gentile cities loosely linked by various alliances and political associations (*GBL* I.263-64). A Jewish minority lived there as well (cf. Mt 4:25).

4.4. Caesarea Philippi. Matthew 16:13 and Mark 8:27 use this name (*Kaisareias tēs Philippou*), not the later name Neronias, for the capital city of Herod Philip, whose tolerance was well known and in whose jurisdiction Jesus could accordingly feel himself to be secure. In this region around Hermon, Jewish groups expected the arrival of the age to come (*GBL* I.225-26). It may therefore be no accident that Jesus chose this site to elicit from Peter, who expressed the sentiments of the entire band of disciples,* a confession of his messiahship (Mt 16:13-20 par.; *see* Christ).

4.5. The Mount of Transfiguration. The geographical context favors identifying this with Hermon (*GBL* II.562-63) rather than Tabor (*GBL* III.1517-19). In favor of this are the words of Matthew 17:1 and Mark 9:2, "a very high mountain" (*horos hypsēlos*), which is reminiscent of Testament of Levi 2:5 (cf. Deut 4:48 MT; 4Q213:16-17) with its clear reference to Hermon. This conclusion appears to receive additional support from the most ancient local tradition (Eusebius

In Ps 88:13; *see* Transfiguration).

5. The Journeys to Jerusalem.

5.1. The Journey through Samaria. Luke 9:51-56 accurately depicts the tensions between Samaritans* and Jewish pilgrims bound for Jerusalem (Josephus *J.W.* 2.12.3 §§232-33). Luke 17:11 presents difficulties, for it asserts that Jesus passed *dia meson Samareias kai Galilaias* to Jerusalem (I. H. Marshall, *Commentary on Luke,* 1978, 650). It is preferable to think of Jesus passing through the Samaritan-Galilee border area (cf. Lk 17:12-19); the notion that he journeyed first through Samaria and then through Galilee is highly unlikely.

5.2. Sychar and Jacob's Well. There was no doubt in the local tradition of the early church that Jacob's well was to be located one-half kilometer southeast of OT Shechem (*ELS* 219ff.). This permits confirmation of John's outstanding knowledge of that locale, as borne out in John 4:4-42 (*GBL* III.1503-5). There is an artificial (Jn 4:11, *phrear*), very deep (Jn 4:11) well at the junction of important roads (cf. Jn 4:3-4, 6) near the traditional site of Joseph's tomb (cf. Jn 4:5) which Samaritans considered sacred. By "woman of Samaria" (Jn 4:7) is not meant an inhabitant of the ancient imperial city of Israel, which had generally been called Sebaste since Herod the Great, but rather an adherent to Samaritan religious views and practices. Her home was in Sychar (Gk *Sychar,* Jn 4:5, 8, 28), which is to be identified with Askar at the foot of Ebal some 1.5 kilometers away. At that time it was probably the major Samaritan settlement. The holy mountain of the Samaritans (cf. Jn 4:20) was Gerazim. Recent excavations make it clear that the Samaritan sanctuary at Jesus' time, already in ruins, stood not at Tell er-Ras on the slope of Mt. Gerazim, but on top of this mountain, where later a Byzantine church was erected.

5.3. Ephraim. Jesus withdrew to this location (Gk *Ephraim*) before the passion. It is to be identified with Ophrah in the territory of Benjamin (Josh 18:23) and the modern Arabic Christian village Et-Taiyibeh (formerly Afra) some thirty kilometers north of Jerusalem (*GBL* I.322). Here, "near the wilderness," as John 11:54 rightly notes, a group must have existed among which Jesus did not feel threatened.

5.4. Jericho. In Jesus' day the OT Jericho (Gk *Ierichō*) was only a deserted heap of rubble. To the south, at the mouth of the Wadi Qilt, Herod the Great had constructed his winter residence, whose opulence is attested by excavations (*GBL* II.659). The chief tax collector Zacchaeus belonged to the upper class of this Hellenistic city (*see* Hellenism). Priests dwelled there too (cf. Lk 10:30-31), however, as spacious burial accommodations indicate. According to Luke 18:35-43 Jesus healed a blind man as he entered Jericho on the way to Jerusalem; Mark 10:46-52 (cf. Mt 20:29-34) has it that the healing took place as Jesus left. Some suggest that Luke speaks of the NT site, Mark and Matthew the Jericho site of the OT. But if the local tradition of Byzantine vintage is correct (Jerome, *Ep.* 108.12), the healing occurred (as Matthew and Mark have it) as Jesus exited the Herodian city.

5.5. Bethphage and Bethany. The setting of Bethany (Gk *Bēthania),* whose distance from Jerusalem is correctly given in John 11:18 as fifteen stadia (c. 3 kilometers) from Jerusalem, has been ascertained by modern excavations (*GBL* I.193). Inscriptions in a one-time Jewish receptacle for ritual washing suggest that there was a Jewish Christian presence well into Byzantine times. The local tradition that touts a tomb in the area as belonging to Lazarus (cf. Jn 11:1-44) may, therefore, be reliable. The home of the obviously unmarried siblings Lazarus, Mary and Martha (Jn 11:1) furnished a secure place for Jesus to stay (Mt 21:17; Mk 11:11; cf. Lk 21:27), even in the last days. Perhaps Bethany was one of the three sites east of Jerusalem to which the Qumran Temple Scroll assigned lepers (11QMiqd 46:16-18; cf. Mt 26:6; Mk 14:3; *see* Leprosy). The Evangelists locate Bethany, just as they do Bethphage (Gk *Bēthphagē;* which rabbinic sources place on the outer fringe of Jerusalem; Str-B I.839-40), in the vicinity of the Mount of Olives (Mt 21; Mk 11:1; Lk 19:29). Even if the precise location of Bethphage still remains unknown, its placement before Bethany (Mk 11:1; Lk 19:29) as one approaches Jerusalem from the Roman road out of Jericho (*GBL* I.196) is correct.

6. Jerusalem.

6.1. The Temple. The Lukan birth narrative underscores the significance of the Temple* for devout Jews of NT times. Zechariah learned of the birth of his son John through an angel's appearance at the altar of incense (Lk 1:8-20; *see* Zechariah's Song). The newly born Jesus was presented in the Temple by his parents, and godly Jews uttered prophecies about him on that occasion (Lk 2:22-38). Jesus' family made an annual pilgrimage from Galilee to Jerusalem (Lk 2:41-51); Jesus himself frequently joined the great pilgrim bands that journeyed to the holy city (Jn 2:13; 5:1; 7:2-13; Mk 11:1-19 par.; *see* Feasts). The pillared colonnades that surrounded the Temple were the location of Jesus' teaching (Jn 7:28-39; Mk 11:27—13:37 par.). "The portico of Solomon" (Jn 10:23) on the Temple's east side (Josephus *Ant.* 20.10.7 §221; *J.W.* 5.5.1 §185) receives special mention. Some archeologists hold

that it actually stands atop a wall of Solomon's Temple (*GBL* II.510). Excavations conducted thus far (*GBL* III.1536-41) show that there was ample reason for the excited reactions of Jesus' disciples (Mk 13:1) and Josephus (*Ant* 15.11.4 §411-425) over the structure's size and splendor.

The Temple was the basis for the political and economic might of the Sadduceans (*see* Judaism). Through the Temple cleansing (*see* Temple Cleansing), a symbolic action meant to send a clear message, Jesus did away with the bloody sacrifice of animals and established the Temple as the eschatological house of prayer* for all peoples (Mk 11:15-18 par.; Jn 2:13-22). The cleansing may have taken place in the royal portico on the Temple's south side (*GBL* II.668-69). At the end of his ministry Jesus even foretold the destruction of the sanctuary (Mk 13:1-2). That gave ultimate impetus to the strategy of the Sadducees, who could marshall a host of Jerusalem Temple loyalists against Jesus (Mk 14:57-60 par.). At a Feast of Tabernacles Jesus had proclaimed himself as the spring welling up in the eschatological Temple (Jn 7:37-39) and described himself (Jn 2:18-22; cf. Mt 12:6) as well as the redeemed community he founded (cf. 2 Sam 7:12-16; 4QFlor 1:2-13) as the new, spiritual Temple.

6.2. Bethesda. John 5:2 is to be translated, "There is in Jerusalem by the Sheep Pool the [site] with five porticoes called in Hebrew [i.e., Aramaic] Bethesda" (*GBL* I.194-95). A location north of the Temple square for this (twin-) pool (cf. Sir 50:3), whose name has been passed along (Jn 5:2) in a rich variety of variant forms (*Bēthesda, Bēthzatha, Bēthsaida* [House of Fish— i.e., baptismal symbol?]), is consistently attested both by ancient reports from Christian pilgrims (*ELS* 460ff.) and by modern excavations. The five *stoai* (not necessarily porticoes with pillars) were probably located on the four sides and along the dividing wall of the two pools. How the waters came to be disturbed (Jn 5:7) is as yet uncertain. Baths on the east side point to a Jewish healing sanctuary; the Roman emperor Hadrian converted them into a pagan shrine to Serapis. The text-critically secondary verses of John 5:3b-4 also indicate a Jewish sanctuary; they may preserve a local legend current in Jerusalem. The legends about Solomon in the Jewish apocryphal *Testament of Solomon* may likewise have a connection with Bethesda. On the basis of a reference in the *Copper Scroll* (3Q15 11:11-14), a shrine with connections to the Essenes or Therapeutae is possible.

6.3. Siloam. In NT times the mouth of the Siloam channel, whose source was the spring at Gihon, was itself regarded as a spring (Josephus *J.W.* 5.4.1-2 §§140-45). The pool of Siloam (Gk *Silōam,* Jn 9:7, 11), whose waters flowed from the same source, is identifiable based on reports from ancient Christian travelers (*ELS* 467ff.) and recent archeological finds (*GBL* III.1444-46). The rabbis regarded its water, which during the Feast of Tabernacles was poured out in the Temple to celebrate end-time expectations (Str-B II.774-780; cf. Jn 7:3-4), as ceremonially cleansing (*see* Clean and Unclean) and physically therapeutic. Based on references on the *Copper Scroll* (3Q15 10:15-16) it is possible that the Essenes also regarded Siloam as a sacred site. Hadrian made an overt attempt to supplant a Jewish sanctuary with a Nymphaeum. Although Jesus sent the blind man to wash in Siloam (Jn 9:1-7), he was clearly the healing agent. Tracing the name Siloam to the Hebrew *šālaḥ*, "sent" (Jn 9:7), may reflect a pre-Christian tradition (*Vit. Proph.* 13). In conjunction with the messianic conception of shiloh in Genesis 49:10 (cf. 4QPatr 2:4) it may refer to Jesus' own being sent as Messiah. Perhaps the "tower of Siloam" (Lk 13:4) should be identified with the circular tower somewhat northeast of the pool dating from the second century B.C.

6.4. The Hall in Which the Last Supper Took Place.
Jesus celebrated the last Passover meal with his disciples in an "upper room" (Gk *anagaion;* Mk 14:15; Lk 22:12; *see* Last Supper). In Luke's presentation this room is to be identified with the first gathering place of the earliest Jerusalem believers. Luke uses the expression *to hyperōon* (Acts 1:13; cf. 9:37, 39; 20:8), which denotes a hall for religious worship* (*GBL* II.1075-77). The definite article shows that Luke was aware of a tradition about this location; the tradition was subsequently passed on without a break into Byzantine times (*ELS* 473ff.). Remains of a synagogue erected by Jewish Christians between A.D. 73 and 135 on the site of the upper room can still be seen on the hill, known today as Zion, in the southwest section of Old Jerusalem at the so-called tomb of David. Josephus' allusion to the "gate of the Essenes" (*J.W.* 5.4.2 §145) and modern excavations justify the assumption that a quarter containing members of this sect was located nearby. This strengthens the view of those scholars who maintain that Jesus celebrated the Passover in A.D. 30 according to the Essene solar calendar on Tuesday evening (E. Ruckstuhl).

6.5. Gethsemane.
The description of the Evangelists alone (Mt 26:36; Mk 14:32; cf. Jn 18:1-2 [ford of the brook Kidron]) rules out any doubt regarding the general location of the Garden of Gethsemane (*see* Gethsemane) on the west slope of the Mount of Olives. The name (Hebrew/Aramaic *gaṭ š*^e*mānî [m])* suggests an olive garden with an oil press. Such an installation (*GBL* I.460-61) is actually located in a cave

(cf. Jn 18:4) in an area (*ELS* 533ff.) probably already known to pre-Byzantine tradition (Origen, *PG* 13.740). The local circumstances would have permitted Jesus to take flight over the Mount of Olives and into the desert right up to the last minute. Luke 22:41 may indicate that memorial sites were shown in Gethsemane already in the days of the Evangelists.

6.6. The Palace of the High Priest.
This palace, in which the proceedings against Jesus (*see* Trial of Jesus) took place (Mt 26:58; Mk 14:54; cf. Lk 22:54), stood on the hill west of the city according to Josephus (*J.W.* 2.426). Late and secondary is the local tradition associated with the Armenian Church of the Redeemer, which lies only forty meters north of the site of the Last Supper (*ELS* 566ff.). Reports of early Byzantine pilgrims (*ELS* 562ff.), which have some archeological support, point to the area of the Church of St. Peter in Gallicantu (*GBL* III.1109-10). This location on the west edge of modern Mount Zion poses no problems for the authenticity of the local tradition about the room where the Last Supper was held. The impressive tiered street passing nearby, dating to NT times and leading toward the area of Jerusalem inhabited by Essenes, was divided by mounds to preserve ritual purity despite use by persons of different grades of purity (cf. *Ep. Arist.* 106). The Sanhedrin's* official convening site was at that time probably outside the Temple near the modern square in front of the Wailing Wall.

6.7. The Praetorium.
The official residence of the Roman prefect (*praitōrion*), where Jesus' hearing before Pilate took place (Mt 27:27; Mk 15:16; Jn 18:28, 33; 19:9), is today identified by many researchers with the new palace constructed beginning in 20 B.C. (Josephus *J.W.* 5.4.3-4 §§156-183) by Herod the Great. Its location was in west Jerusalem, south of the modern citadel (*GBL* III.1221-22). Its existence is presupposed in the story of the Magi (Mt 2:1-12). There is, however, no local tradition of any kind in support of this. The tradition for the Fortress of Antonia on the northwest corner of the Temple square is very late and decisively contradicted by archeological investigations at the convent of the Sisters of Zion (*GBL* I.68). The most ancient reports from Christian travelers (*ELS* 583ff.), finally made intelligible by recent excavations, refer to an area on the west slope of the Tyropoeon valley opposite the southwest corner of the Temple (*GBL* III.1223-24). This is where Josephus (*Ant.* 20.8.11 §§189-92; *J.W.* 6.7.1 §358), probably with some archeological support, locates the Hasmonean royal palace. Gabbatha (Jn 19:13) could refer to the rock cliff, still visible today, opposite the Wailing Wall (*GBL* I.398). The Greek

name *lithostrōtos* that occurs in the same context (Jn 19:13) may refer to a paved square in front of the Praetorium. Such a location for the Praetorium would also fit well with Mark's account, according to which the crowd (presumably from the Temple) "came up" (Mk 15:8).

6.8. Hakeldama. This piece of ground received its popular Aramaic name "field of blood" (Acts 1:19; Gk *Hakeldamach*) in connection with Jesus' betrayer, Judas (*see* Judas Iscariot), either because of his violent death (Acts 1:18-19) or due to the innocent nature of Jesus' shed blood (Mt 27:4). The potter's field cited in Mt 27:7-10 probably lay at the end of the Hinnom valley (cf. Jer 19:1-2). Christian tradition since at least the fourth century (*ELS* 575ff.) is almost unanimous in placing Hakeldama here on the grounds of the Onophrius cloister (*GBL* II.508-9).

6.9. The Hinnom Valley. Various Jewish groups associated this valley, which wrapped around the old city of Jerusalem on the west and south, with the expected eschatological judgment* (*GBL* II.578-79). In Jesus' own usage the Aramaic *gêt-hennā* (Gk *geenna;* Mt 5:22, 29-30 and elsewhere) likewise became a concept for the place of end-time punishment.

6.10. Golgotha. The garden tomb north of the Damascus Gate at the alleged hill of Golgotha is a fantasy of the nineteenth century, excluded by the archeological data. Recent investigations (*GBL* I.480-82) show rather that the site of the Church of the Holy Sepulchre actually lay a bit outside the city wall (cf. Mt 28:11; Jn 19:17-42) in the vicinity of a gate (Heb 13:12; cf. Josephus *J.W.* 5.4.2 §146 [*Gennath-* (i.e., garden) gate]) and a busy street (Mt 27:39). Remains have also been found of the temple of Aphrodite, which Hadrian in A.D. 135 erected to displace a Jewish-Christian worship site (*ELS* 619ff.). Golgotha was a rock formation that took shape as a result of quarrying activity. It rose as high as twelve meters and owed its Aramaic name *gûlgultā'* (Gk *Golgotha*), "the skull" (Lk 23:33; cf. Mt 27:33; Mk 15:22; Jn 19:17), to its shape. All four Gospels betray unusual knowledge of local details in connection with Jesus' burial (*see* Burial of Jesus). Mark 16:5 presupposes that the ledge on which Jesus' body was placed lay on the right side of the rock burial chamber; this detail is corroborated by the tomb under the dome of the Church of the Holy Sepulchre, which is regarded as genuine for several good reasons (*GBL* I.178). Matthew 27:60; Luke 23:53 and John 19:41 all seem to agree also on the unfinished condition of this tomb. In addition John's Gospel is aware that Golgotha lay very near the city (Jn 19:20) and that Jesus' tomb was in the immediate vicinity (Jn 19:42) of a garden (Jn 19:41). This has all been confirmed by the archeological data. Archeology gives us some insight into the gruesome details of crucifixion, regarded in NT times as the most fearsome form of execution (*GBL* II.840-42; *see* Death of Jesus).

6.11. Emmaus. Alleged locations of Emmaus (Gk *Emmaous*) near Kiriat Jearim and El-Qubeibeh are late and secondary (*ELS* 714ff.). Local tradition utterly fails to support the suggestion of Moza; in Josephus (*J.W.* 7.6.6 §217) the original name of the place (after sifting variants through textual criticism) is not *Ammaous* but *Amassa* or *Amosa*. The best solution is to follow the manuscripts that place Emmaus 160 stadia from Jerusalem (Lk 24:13) and to identify it, as pre-Byzantine tradition probably did (*ELS* 706ff.), with Emmaus-Nicopolis (today the destroyed Arab village '*Amwâs*) twenty-three kilometers west of Jerusalem. There one also finds the warm springs which one would expect, given the name Emmaus (Heb *ḥāmmaṭ*, "hot spring"). The reading "sixty stadia" in other manuscripts probably arose through a scribal omission. A journey to Emmaus and back on foot on the same day as the resurrection (Lk 24:33-34) does not appear to have been an impossible feat in that day and culture. The designation of Emmaus as "village" (Lk 24:13: *kōmē*) is not surprising in view of its destruction in 4 B.C. (Josephus *J.W.* 2.4.3 §§60-63) and similar references found in other contemporary sources (*GBL* I.313-14).

6.12. The Mount of Olives. Because Zechariah 14:4-5 expected the intervention of God in the eschatological battle with the Gentile nations to take place on the Mount of Olives (Gk *ho oros tōn elaiōn*), many Jewish end-time expectations were associated with it (Str-B I.840-842). Thus it was that the Egyptian false prophet (Acts 21:38) wished to launch the eschatological assault on Jerusalem from there (Josephus *J.W.* 2.13.5 §§261-63). Jesus and his disciples often visited the Mount of Olives (Lk 21:37; cf. Jn 8:1), an area that was still within the jurisdiction of the nearby city. There is absolutely no justification for the assumption that "Galilee" in Mark 14:28; 16:7 (par.) refers to a resting place for Galilean pilgrims on the Mount of Olives (*GBL* 2.1088-91). Jesus' messianic triumphal entry (*see* Triumphal Entry) began there, which could have been misunderstood by the political authorities (Mk 11:1-11 par.). Luke 19:37 betrays special geographic awareness in speaking about "the descent of the Mount of Olives," down which the Roman road steeply led. Here Jesus announced the destruction of the city (Lk 19:41-44; *see* Destruction of Jerusalem), as he also made it a place for apocalyptic instruction (Mt 24:3; Mk 13:3; cf. Acts 1:6-7; *see* Apocalyptic Teaching). From no later than the second century (*Acts of John* 97) a cave on the heights of the Mount of Olives was venerated (*ELS* 384ff.). Constantine ordered a basilica to be built over it. Perhaps this preserves an authentic recollection of one of Jesus' distinctive teaching sites. Since at least the fourth century the location of Jesus' ascension has been sought immediately nearby (Eusebius *Dem. Ev.* 4.18); Luke's statements such as "on the Mount of Olives" (Acts 1:12) and "out to (*pros*) Bethany" (Lk 24:50) comport with this. The visible return of the resurrected (*see* Resurrection) Christ to the Mount of Olives is announced in Acts 1:11.

7. Historical and Theological Significance.

7.1. John the Baptist. The Baptist began his ministry in the northern portion of the Holy Land, where some of the Jews expected the coming of the eschatological Elijah (Mal 3:1; cf. Mk 1:2-8; see 2.5. above). Both of his other known baptismal sites were associated with Elijah traditions (see 2.2., 2.4. above). His followers buried John at the traditional site of Elijah's tomb (see 2.6. above). This cannot all be happenstance. It rather shows how in Jewish thought certain areas had significance for the expectation of OT fulfillment. Put another way, John's choice of a specific place for a symbolic action could call attention to a certain claim about his mission, in this case that he was the end-time prophet (*see* Prophets and Prophecy) in the tradition of Elijah.

7.2. The Gospels in General. The Synoptics, probably for purely catechetical reasons, offer a simplified picture of the geographic framework of Jesus' ministry: (1) baptism and temptation (*see* Temptation of Jesus) in the lower Jordan valley (Mk 1:1-13 par.); (2) ministry in Galilee (Mk 1:14—9:50), at the end interrupted increasingly by short stays on the other side of the Galilean border (Mk 7:24-31; 8:27-30 par.); (3) journey to Jerusalem (Mk 10:1-52); (4) brief sojourn in the holy city (Mk 11—16 par.). As isolated allusions in the Synoptics also show (Mt 23:37; Lk 4:44; 13:6-9 and elsewhere), John's presentation, which portrays about a three-year ministry with frequent trips between Galilee and Jerusalem (Jn 2:13; 6:4; 12:1), deserves preference historically. The Fourth Gospel's description is also not exhaustive, however, for it seems intentionally (cf. Jn 21:25) to restrict itself to mentioning very little when it comes to the ministry in Galilee and surrounding areas. The geographic schema of the Synoptics has relative historical justification of its own, however: the concrete place-names that appear in the Gospel tradition point to a clear concentration of Jesus' ministry in Galilee and Jerusalem.

Three historical questions must be kept constantly in mind regarding what the geographical information

says: (1) about the framework of Jesus' ministry; (2) about the local color of the pre-Gospel traditions and (3) about the local knowledge of the Evangelists themselves. The question of the eventual theological significance of geographic factors is associated with these prior questions.

7.3. Jesus. For his family, as for Jesus himself (Jn 7:41-42), his birth in Bethlehem was an indication of his Davidic-messianic ministry (*see* Son of David). The name of his later residence, Nazareth, kept the memory of the prophecy in Isaiah 11:1 alive (3.1. above). From the heights around Nazareth he viewed a panorama of OT salvation* history. It may be no accident that Jesus drew parallels between his own fate and that of Jonah (Mt 12:39-41 par.; 16:4; *see* Sign of Jonah), whose grave was thought by early Jewish tradition to be the only grave of a prophet in Galilee (Gath-Hefer in the immediate vicinity of Nazareth; *GBL* I.411). The choice of preaching sites like the springs of Tabgha (3.8. above) and the Jerusalem Temple also had practical reasons: here Jesus could reach great masses of persons, both from Jerusalem and from the Diaspora. The initial concentration of his own proclamation as well as that of the disciples he sent out (Mt 10:5-6) remains, however, striking. Especially deserving of explanation is the emphasis placed by Jesus' pronouncements of judgment (Mt 11:20-24 par) on Chorazin, Bethsaida and Capernaum, all lying near each other on the northwest shore of the Sea of Galilee. It was likely not first of all the Evangelist Matthew (Mt 4:12-16), but rather Jesus himself, who saw this concentration on the southern portion of Naphtali, bordering Zebulun, as a symbolic action in fulfillment of Isaiah 9:1-2 (MT 8:23—9:1).

The phase in which Jesus resided in Capernaum (3.12. above) should probably be distinguished from a time during which withdrawal to areas outside of Galilee became necessary (see 4. above) because of increasingly threatening circumstances. To this second phase belong *logia* that speak of Jesus' homelessness (Mt 8:20 par.). It is hardly accidental that it was precisely in the Mount Hermon area, to which at least a few Jewish groups attached special eschatological expectations, that Jesus, on the occasion of Peter's confession and the Transfiguration, divulged his messiahship (see 4.4., 4.5. above).

There is another reason why Jesus evaded persecution in the north: his death in Jerusalem had deep theological significance (Mk 10:33-34 par.; Lk 13:33; Lk 13:34-35 par.). Here he would identify with Israel's prophets, martyred in Jerusalem (cf. Lk 13:24); and offer his life as an atoning sacrifice, thus terminating the validity of the Temple and its cult. Jerusalem remained, however, even in Jesus' proclamation the focal point of the eschatological pilgrimage of all the nations to the one true God (Mt 8:11-12 par.). When after his resurrection* Jesus expressed the desire to meet his disciples in Galilee again (Mk 14:28; 16:7 par.), he was saying that their earlier mission that started there would be renewed. In the same way the resurrected Christ revealed himself at Tabgha (see 3.11. above), which had been a center of his earthly ministry. A manifestation that was decisive for revealing his mission took place on Tabor, a place rich with end-time associations (see 3.15. above). Jesus departed from his disciples on the Mount of Olives, which in both OT and Jewish expectation is specially related to the eschaton (see 6.12. above).

7.4. Mark. Contrary to a widely held notion, the geographical knowledge of the Second Evangelist does not rule out his Palestinian origin. One can, nevertheless, detect a certain difference. While Mark does not seem to know his way around Galilee very well (see 3.8., 4.1. above), he offers a number of more specific allusions in regard to Jerusalem (see 5.5., 6.1., 6.7., 6.10. above). That agrees fully with the traditional identification of the Evangelist with John Mark of Jerusalem (Acts 12:12). Especially detailed knowledge of Galilee and the north appear in traditions which one can easily envision as Petrine in origin (see 3.4., 3.12., 3.14., 4.4. above).

Much has been made of the theological significance of geographical information in Mark's Gospel. Already in pre-Markan tradition a connection was probably seen between the two miraculous feedings (both stress the isolated [erēmos topos] or desolate [erēmia] nature of the location) and the miraculous feeding of Israel in the wilderness (Mk 6:31.; 8:4 par.). This connection was probably intended by Jesus himself (cf. allusions to manna and wilderness in Jn 6:26-59). Perhaps Mark wished to anchor the Gentile* mission in Jesus' ministry with his especially expansive description (Mk 5:1-20) of Jesus' first journey into Gentile territory (see 5.1. above). The stilling of the storm (Mk 4:35-41) that precedes Mk 5:1-20 may intend to draw a parallel between Jesus' ministry and the mission of the prophet Jonah (cf. Jon 1:4-17). It is likewise possible, in view of its close connection with Mark 7:1-23 (clean and unclean) and Mark 7:24-30 (healing of a Gentile woman*), that the location of the second miraculous feeding (Mk 8:1-10; cf. 7:31) in the Gentile Decapolis (see 3.10., 4.3. above) looks ahead to the table fellowship between Jewish and Gentile Christians. The journey from the north to Jerusalem is a prototype for the life of the disciples as they follow Jesus. This is underscored by the repetition of the motif of the "Way" (Mk 8:27; 9:33-34; 10:52).

7.5. Matthew. Corresponding to the scribal characteristics that the first Gospel bears, one encounters geographical information most of all in connection with the fulfillment of OT promises: the birth of Jesus (see 1.2. above) in Bethlehem (Mt 2:1-8; cf. Mic 5:1), the flight to Egypt (Mt 2:13-15; cf. Hos 11:1), Rachel's tomb (see 1.4. above) near Bethlehem (Mt 2:16-18; cf. Jer 31:15), life in Nazareth (Mt 2:22-23; cf. Is 11:1), concentration of the areas belonging to the tribes of Zebulun and Naphtali (Mt 4:12-16; cf. Is 9:1-2 [MT 8:23—9:1]), the procurement of the potter's field or field of blood (Mt 27:5-10; cf. Jer 32:9). The location of Jesus' first great (ethical) discourse on "the mountain" (Mt 5:1) awakens remembrances of the giving of the Law* through Moses* on Sinai. Gadara (see 4.1. above) forms the border of the land of Israel in the rabbinic outlook (Mt 8:28; cf. Str-B I.490). The coupling of the cities of Tyre and Sidon (Mt 15:21) is reminiscent of the OT and indicates that the Evangelist saw Jesus' stay in this Gentile region as paradigmatic. Calling the northern Transjordan "Judea on the other side of the Jordan" (Mt 19:1) is probably due to Joshua 19:34. Even if it holds true for Matthew that the area of Jesus' proper mission is restricted to the purely Jewish districts of Galilee and Jerusalem (Mt 10:5-6), he nevertheless emphasizes how many followers Jesus had from other areas (Mt 4:25) containing Jewish majorities (Judea) or minorities (Decapolis and Transjordan).

The First Gospel's geographical information comports with a Palestinian provenance. It is most specific regarding Jerusalem and its surroundings (see 5.5., 6.8., 6.10. above), as well as the area of Capernaum (see 3.8., 3.9., 3.12., 3.15. above). The roles played in Matthew by Capernaum as the "city of Jesus" (cf. Mt 9:1) and the house in which Jesus sometimes lived (see 3.12. above) are striking (Mt 9:27-31; 13:1; cf. Mt 4:13). In comparison to John, however, Matthew's geographical references are fewer and less explicit than one would expect from a Gospel that tradition attributes to an eyewitness. The unique emphasis on Jesus' preaching becoming known as far as Syria (Mt 4:24) fits with other indicators that point to the First Gospel's final redaction in this locale.

7.6. Luke. The Third Evangelist may well owe his sometimes interesting geographical information on Galilee and its environs entirely to tradition (see 3.1., 3.3., 3.9., 3.10., 4.1., 5.1. above). He hardly had any closer knowledge of Galilee, since he would otherwise not have referred to Nazareth (3.1.) and Nain (3.3.) as cities (poleis). Still more peculiar are a few references, more specific than one might expect, to local features of Jerusalem and its surroundings (see 1.1., 1.2., 1.3., 6.1., 6.4., 6.5., 6.10., 6.12. above). The precise knowledge in the Synoptics of the distance between Jerusalem and Emmaus is unique (see 6.11. above). An unforced explanation is possible by recognizing that the author of Luke's two-part work had visited the holy city himself according to the events related in one of the "we" sections of Acts (21:15-18). The geographical references in Acts, especially concerning the area between Jerusalem and Caesarea Maritima, strengthen the view that its author was a travel companion of Paul.

Any possible deeper significance for geographical references may lie at the level of the tradition (see 1.3., 3.3., 3.10. above). The Evangelist who wrote for learned Greeks could hardly assume that his readers would have knowledge of OT-prophetic geography. A precise reference such as the one concerning Emmaus betrays rather an historical interest. Nevertheless, for Luke the anchoring of Christian teaching in the reliably transmitted story of Jesus was also theologically relevant (cf. Lk 1:1-4).

7.7. John. Compared to the other three Gospels, John offers by far the most references to places. Often the references are quite specific. His knowledge is sound in whatever areas he describes, whether Galilee (see 3.2., 3.4., 3.5., 3.14 above) and the north (see 2.4., 2.5. above), Samaria (see 5.2. above) or Jerusalem (see 6.1., 6.2., 6.3., 6.5., 6.7., 6.10. above) and its surroundings (see 5.3., 5.5. above). The only meaningful explanation for this is that the Evangelist, or at the least the disciple who vouched for the tradition (Jn 21:24), was a native of Palestine, though not necessarily of Jerusalem.

Just as John gave a more comprehensive picture of the temporal duration of Jesus' appearance, he also depicts more fully its geographical scope. According to the Fourth Evangelist Jesus also ministered in areas like Batanaea (see 2.5. above) and Samaria (see 5.2. above) where Jewish fringe groups lived. Contact with them appears to have brought on him the opprobrious designation of "Samaritan" (Jn 8:48). It is striking that Jesus often ministered at sacred sites like Jacob's well (see 5.2. above), Bethesda (6.2.), Siloam (6.3.) and of course the Jerusalem Temple (see 6.1.). This was to fulfill the expectations associated with them, to surpass those expectations, and thereby to render them superfluous. In the presence of Gerazim, and in view of the Jerusalem Temple, the supersession of all Jewish sanctuaries through worship of Jesus "in spirit and truth" becomes an explicit theme (Jn 4:20-24).

In John's Gospel Jesus' ministry concentrates so strongly on Jerusalem that one can raise the question

whether the stereotyped talk of "the Jews" (*hoi Ioudaioi*) does not also strike a resounding geographical note (making "the Jews" equivalent to "Judeans"; *GBL* II.736). With the name *Bethany* John linked geographically the inbreaking of salvation in the north with its fulfillment in the south (see 2.5. above). In connection with Siloam he can make christological use of Jewish interpretation of a place name's meaning (6.3.). It is hardly accidental that the most secure anchoring of Jesus' ministry in time and space comes to the fore in the work of the Evangelist who places special emphasis on the Incarnation (Jn 1:14).

See also GALILEE; MOUNTAIN AND WILDERNESS; TEMPLE.

BIBLIOGRAPHY. D. Baldi, *Enchiridion Locorum Sanctorum* (3d ed.; Jerusalem: Franciscan, 1982); G. Dalman, *Sacred Sites and Ways: Studies in the Topography of the Gospels* (New York: Macmillan, 1935); W. D. Davies, *The Gospel and the Land* (Berkeley: University of California, 1974); M. Hengel, "Luke the Historian and the Geography of Palestine in the Acts of the Apostles," in *Between Jesus and Paul* (Philadelphia: Fortress, 1983) 97-128; C. Kopp, *The Holy Places of the Gospels* (Edinburgh/London: Nelson, n.d.); G. Kroll, *Auf den Spuren Jesu* (11th ed.; Leipzig: St. Benno, 1990); R. H. Lightfoot, *Locality and Doctrine in the Gospels* (London: Hodder and Stoughton, 1938); B. Pixner, *Wege des Messias und Stätten der Urkirche* (Giessen: Brunnen, 1991); R. Riesner, "Bethany beyond the Jordan," *TynB* 38 (1987) 29-63; idem, "Galiläa," *GBL* I.406-7; idem, "Jerusalem," *GBL* II.661-77; idem, "Judäa," *GBL* II.735-36; J. A. T. Robinson, *The Priority of John* (Yorktown Heights, NY: Meyer-Stone, 1987); E. Ruckstuhl, *Chronology of the Last Days of Jesus* (New York: Desclee, 1965); W. Sanday, *Sacred Sites of the Gospels* (Oxford: Clarendon, 1903); B. E. Schein, *Following the Way* (Minneapolis: Augsburg, 1980); G. Theissen, *Lokalkolorit und Zeitgeschichte in den Evangelien* (NTOA 8; Freiburg: Universitätsverlag, 1989).

R. Riesner

ARETALOGY. *See* DIVINE MAN/THEIOS ANER.

ARREST OF JESUS. *See* TRIAL OF JESUS.

ASCENSION

The present, ascended status of Jesus is a foundational aspect of the apostolic faith, well attested in the NT writings. Usually, Jesus' exaltation in heaven* is thought of as the counterpart of his resurrection.* Only Luke provides a narrative in which the ascension of Jesus into heaven is described as an event in space and time, subsequent to the resurrection. Ascension theology is determinative for much of Luke's thought.

1. The Ascension in the NT.

The ascension is spoken of in various ways in the NT.

1.1. Ascended Status. Most of the references speak simply of Jesus' ascended status. They do not mention how he came to be in heaven. Behind the comments about Jesus now "sitting at the right hand of God" stands Psalm 110:1, the most quoted OT text in the NT. Mark roots the exegetical use of the psalm in the teaching of Jesus (Mk 12:35-37; 14:62). In the earliest NT affirmations about Jesus' exaltation, preserved in two pre-Pauline hymns, his reign in heaven is the direct sequel to his death; the resurrection is not mentioned (Phil 2:8-11; 1 Tim 3:16). In other places it is simply accepted that Jesus' present home is in heaven. Thus, in Paul's earliest letter the Thessalonians are said to be awaiting God's* "Son from heaven whom he raised from the dead" (1 Thess 1:10; cf. 4:16). Similarly, in the book of Revelation the present reign of Christ in heaven is taken for granted (Rev 1:12-18; 3:21; 6:1-7; 7:17).

In the Synoptic tradition the sayings about the coming of the Son of man (*see* Son of Man) on the clouds of heaven imply an exalted heavenly reign prior to the Parousia (*see* Eschatology), but again the texts say nothing about how Jesus came to be in heaven (Mt 16:27; 24:30; 26:64; Mk 8:38; 13:26; Lk 21:27; 22:69).

1.2. Movement toward Heaven. A second category of texts alludes to the ascension understood as a movement upward to heaven, but they do not describe how it occurred. In some of these passages the word *ascension* or its equivalent is used (e.g., Rom 10:6-8; Eph 4:7-11); in others the specific terms are missing (e.g., Heb 4:14; 6:19-20; 9:24; 1 Pet 3:22). Johannine thought basically follows this pattern. For John, Jesus is he who comes down from heaven (Jn 3:17, 31; 6:38; 8:23; 13:3; 16:28) and then later returns to his Father in heaven (Jn 3:13; 13:1-3; 16:5; 16:28). On three occasions the ascent of the Son is specifically described as "ascending" (*anabainō:* Jn 3:13; 6:62; 20:17), but more commonly it is spoken of as a "journey" (*poreuomai:* Jn 14:2, 13, 28; 16:7, 28) or as "going" to the Father (*hypagō:* Jn 7:33; 8:14, 21; 13:33; 14:4; 16:5, 10, 17). In John 20:17, where the resurrected Jesus speaks to Mary, it is implied that the ascension takes place sometime after the resurrection: "Do not hold me, for I have not yet ascended (*anabainō*) to the Father."

Along with these references we should associate John's teaching on the glorification of the Son of man. Three times John speaks of the Son of man being "lifted up" (*hypsoō:* Jn 3:14; 8:28; 12:32-34). This expression bears in mind the cross, but only in so far as it is one step in the process which leads to glorification (*see* Glory). For John the passion (*see* Passion Narrative), death (*see* Death of Jesus), resurrection and ascension of Jesus is "the hour" of his glorification. As this "hour" approaches Jesus prays, "Now Father, glorify (*doxazō*) me in your own presence with the glory which I had with you before the world was made" (Jn 17:5; cf. Jn 7:39; 12:16, 23; 13:31-32). Only when the Son is glorified is the Holy Spirit (*see* Holy Spirit), the Paraclete, given to the disciples* (Jn 7:39; 16:7).

1.3. Visible Event. Luke alone describes the ascension as an event visible in space and time (Lk 24:50-51; Acts 1:9-11). In the Acts passage he dates the ascension forty days after the resurrection. This has led some scholars (e.g., Lohfink, Franklin) to conclude that Luke is attempting to give a new understanding of the exaltation. He wants his readers to believe that the exaltation took place forty days after the resurrection. Jesus ascended into heaven only when the resurrection appearances were concluded. Other scholars (e.g., Fitzmyer, Maile) reject this view, arguing that the two ascension narratives in Luke-Acts are departure scenes rather than interpretations of the exaltation.

2. Pre-Christian Ascension Traditions.

One of the major contributions of Lohfink's important study of the ascension in Luke-Acts is his full and detailed survey of similar traditions in Greco-Roman and Jewish literature. He demonstrates that there was a widespread belief in antiquity that a divine person, or a special agent of God (or the gods), could be taken up into heaven.

In the Greco-Roman world two forms of ascension story can be distinguished: (1) The journey of the soul to heaven and (2) an actual translation, or rapture. In Judaism various forms of ascension are described. These include: (1) A journey to heaven to receive revelations and a subsequent return to earth (e.g., *T. Abr.* 7:19—8:3); (2) the taking up of the soul after death (e.g., *T. Abr.* 14:6-7); (3) the rapture, or translation, of a living person who is taken up to heaven never to return (e.g., Enoch, Elijah,* Ezra and Baruch); and (4) the return to heaven of God or a messenger from God at the end of an earthly appearance (e.g., Gen 17:22; *Jub.* 32:20 and esp. Tob. 12:20-22; *see* Apocalyptic).

Lohfink notes certain parallels between the Greco-Roman ascension stories and the Lukan narratives, such as the mention of a mountain, a cloud and the worship of those present, but he finds few linguistic connections. The parallels are much closer with the Jewish ascension stories of Enoch, Elijah, Ezra, Baruch and Moses.* Luke's use of many of the terms in the LXX account of Elijah's rapture (2 Kings = 4 Kgdms 2:9-13) in his ascension narratives is striking.

But to find close parallels with the well-known Jewish raptures, notably that of Elijah, does not say all that needs to be said about the possible background for Luke's ascension narratives. The impact of other literary forms must also be considered. There are parallels with commissioning narratives in the OT and in the NT, especially Matthew 28:16-20, with OT departure scenes following a farewell address (*see* Farewell Discourse), and in regard to Luke 24:50-51 with Sirach 50:20-22 (see Parsons, 52-58).

3. The Two Lukan Accounts of the Ascension.

Luke 24:50-51 gives a brief account of the ascension in which Jesus is said to have led the eleven out to Bethany, blessed them and "then parted from them and was carried up (*anepherō*) into heaven." In Acts 1:9-11 there is a longer account in which Luke dates the ascension forty days after the resurrection. He says that while the disciples "were looking on," Jesus "was lifted up and a cloud took him out of their sight." Two angelic figures appeared and said, "Men of Galilee, why do you stand looking into heaven? This Jesus, who was taken up from you into heaven, will come in the same way as you saw him go into heaven."

Various explanations of these differences have been given. These include the following: (1) Acts 1:9-11 is a later interpolation; (2) the two accounts reflect two different traditions about the ascension which Luke took over intact; (3) the two accounts refer to two different events: the first to Jesus' ascension immediately following his resurrection, and the second to the end of his bodily appearances forty days later; (4) the two accounts are but one of several examples where Luke gives duplicate accounts of one event, giving different details to make differing theological points.

Interpolation theories or appeals to lost sources find virtually no scholarly support today. They lack concrete evidence and better explanations are available. The suggestion that Luke 24:50-51 alludes to Jesus' exaltation immediately following his resurrection and not to his subsequent departure is supported

by the shorter reading of Luke 24:51 which omits the words, "and he was carried up into heaven," but the longer reading has the stronger textual support, including 𝔓⁷⁵. Positive evidence that Luke in 24:50-51 is speaking of Jesus' bodily ascension at a point of time after the resurrection is indicated by Acts 1:2, where Luke says that in his first book he dealt with everything Jesus did until he ascended (*anelēmphthē*). As Luke uses the same Greek term in the departure scene in Acts 1:11, it is to be assumed the same matter is in mind. The many overlapping details in Luke's two accounts of Jesus' final departure also support the view that they are describing one event. Both passages mention the eleven, the world mission, the need to stay in Jerusalem until the Holy Spirit is given, the role of the apostles as witnesses, the ascent of Jesus into heaven and the return of the eleven to Jerusalem. Many key terms also are found in both texts.

The differences are explained by the differing literary locations of the two narratives, one at the end of the Gospel, the other at the beginning of Acts, and by the differing theological points Luke wanted to make in each case. In the Gospel the ascension is for Luke a fitting conclusion to the whole drama of Jesus' life. It is the goal of his earthly ministry (Lk 9:51). As he departs he gives a farewell blessing to the eleven. In Acts 1:9-11 the ascension sets the scene for all that follows. Jesus commissions the Twelve for their mission, promises them the Holy Spirit, and ascends on high to reign as the living Lord* of the church* until his return in like manner.

4. Resurrection and Exaltation.

If Luke wanted the church to understand that the exaltation of Jesus took place forty days after the resurrection, rather than as the immediate sequel to the resurrection, we would expect he would have consistently, or at least usually, kept these two phenomena apart. But this is not the case. Along with other NT writers Luke can speak either of the exaltation as the immediate sequel to the cross, without mentioning the resurrection, or of the resurrection and ascension as two steps in the one movement.

Luke 22:69 is important. In Luke's version of Jesus' reply to the Jewish leaders at his trial (*see* Trial of Jesus) the words "you will see . . ." and "coming with the clouds of heaven" are omitted (cf. Mk 14:62). Only the heavenly session of the Son of man is mentioned, and this is said to be "from now on." Here the exaltation and heavenly session of Jesus are the immediate sequel to his death. Again in Luke 24:26 the risen Jesus connects his suffering on the cross with his entry into glory. No intermediate stage is envisaged. In

Acts 2:32-36 the death, resurrection, exaltation and heavenly session are intimately related. It is because God raised and exalted Jesus that he is now proclaimed as both Lord and Christ.* In this Lukan sermon, appeal is made to Psalm 16:10 (Acts 2:31) where an allusion to the resurrection of the Messiah is seen. As David did not rise from the grave, it is argued, the text must refer to Jesus. In underlining that Psalm 16:10 points to Jesus, Luke says, "David did not ascend (anebē) into the heavens" (Acts 2:34)—it was Jesus who ascended. Luke does not indicate when this ascent took place, but a chronological separation between the resurrection and the ascension—presumably in this context understood as the exaltation—does not seem to be envisaged.

The other references to the resurrection in the speeches of Acts also allow for no intermediate stage between the resurrection and exaltation (cf. Acts 3:15-16; 4:10; 5:30-32; 10:40-43; 13:31-37). It seems best to conclude therefore that Luke, along with the rest of the NT writers, thought that the exaltation followed the resurrection. Luke's special contribution was the addition of a departure scene which in Acts 1:3 he dates forty days after the resurrection.

5. Redaction or Composition?

Even if it is accepted that Luke 24:50-51 and Acts 1:9-11 are to be understood as farewell or departure scenes, the question still remains, did Luke construct them on the basis of received tradition or did he freely create them? Because the hand of Luke is so heavily imposed on the material, this question is not easily resolved.

Lohfink gives a carefully reasoned case for Lukan composition. He maintains that what Luke received from the tradition was a recognition scene (Lk 24:36-43) and a commissioning scene (Lk 24:44-49) which have other Gospel parallels (e.g., Mt 28:16-20; Jn 20:19-23; etc.) and to these he added the departure/rapture scene which is unique to his writings. Besides the fact that only Luke recounts the departure of Jesus, Lohfink notes that Luke elsewhere adds departure scenes for angels* or other heavenly beings (Lk 1:38; 2:15; 9:33; 24:31; Acts 10:7; 12:10) and that the vocabulary, style and theology of Luke 24:50-51 and Acts 1:9-11 are characteristically Lukan. Thus he concludes that Luke created the ascension narratives, modeling them on Jewish rapture stories, especially that of Elijah.

If it was Luke's intent to interpret the exaltation as an event forty days after the resurrection, then Luke's addition of these departure scenes is of tremendous theological significance. It is evidence for a Lukan reinterpretation of an earlier understanding of the exaltation. But if, as it has been argued, Luke viewed the resurrection and the exaltation as two sides of one event, the addition of the departure scenes is less significant. They only add an account of the final parting of Jesus from his disciples. Nevertheless, their origins still remain an issue.

Evidence which leads other scholars to argue for pre-Lukan tradition as the basis for Luke's ascension narratives is of a cumulative nature. In seeking to pinpoint traditional material, the mention of the quite specific location, Bethany (Lk 24:50), has often been noted and several scholars have found traces of pre-Lukan ascension tradition in Acts 1:9 (see Parsons 61, 140-44). Furthermore, a number of early extra-canonical texts also describe Jesus' final departure, and although most of these can be discounted as being dependent on Luke, Parsons argues that Mark 16:19 and Barnabas 15:9 are probably independent witnesses (Parsons, 144-48).

John's Gospel does not recount a departure scene, but the Evangelist quite clearly allows for a separation between the resurrection and the final departure of Jesus to the Father (Jn 20:17). Finally, it is to be noted that along with Luke, Paul chronologically limits the period in which the risen Jesus appeared in bodily form (1 Cor 15:8).

Whether or not the specific forty-day period for resurrection appearances (Acts 1:3) should be taken literally is uncertain. Elsewhere, Luke describes this interval unspecifically as "many days" (Acts 13:31). Possibly he rounded off the days of appearances, bringing them up to the number forty, which was a well-known sacred, round number. Or he may have begun with Pentecost—the feast of the fiftieth day after Passover—and then came back to the first suitable period prior to that. The only other place Luke mentions forty days is in reference to the period of fasting and temptation Jesus endured before he began his ministry (Lk 4:2). One suggestion is that Luke introduced the forty-day period of resurrection appearances in which Jesus taught the apostles* about the kingdom of God (Acts 1:3; see Kingdom of God) as a counterpart to the forty days Jesus spent in preparation before he began his ministry. In the final period of forty days Jesus prepared the apostles for their ministry.

6. Luke's Ascension Theology.

Although we have argued that Luke distinguishes between the exaltation following the resurrection and the departure following the appearances, these two events are closely related in Luke's theology. The departure of Jesus into heaven highlights his heavenly reign, completes his earthly ministry and, together with the outpouring of the Holy Spirit, inaugurates "the last days." In important ways the ascension/departure narrative is formulative for Luke's christology, pneumatology, soteriology, ecclesiology, eschatology and missiology.

It is because Jesus now reigns in heaven that he is confessed as Lord and Christ (Acts 2:36). In the resurrection he is exalted to sit at the right hand of God (Acts 2:33), and the departure scene confirms this. The fourfold repetition of the phrase "into heaven" in Acts 1:1-11, and the same phrase in the longer reading of Luke 24:51, makes it clear as to where Jesus belongs. The ascension is the visible and concrete expression of Jesus' exalted status.

Only after his resurrection appearances are completed and Jesus has departed to reign in heaven can the Holy Spirit be given (Acts 2:33). The Spirit is none other than the presence of Jesus (Acts 16:7), albeit in another form. Some speak of the period after Jesus' departure into heaven as "the age of the church," but Luke would seem to suggest that it would be best described as "the age of the Spirit."

Luke does not develop the idea that Jesus died on the cross to pay the penalty for sin, even though this thought appears in Luke 22:19-20 and Acts 20:28. Instead, Luke thinks more of Jesus entering glory through his suffering (Lk 24:26, 46; Acts 3:18; 17:3; 26:23) and from his throne on high granting forgiveness* and the Holy Spirit (Acts 2:38) to those who repent (cf. Lk 13:3; 15:7; 24:7; Acts 2:38; 3:19; 5:30-31; 8:22; see Repentance).

Those who respond to the proclamation of Jesus as the crucified but now exalted Messiah become members of the restored or true Israel,* but those who do not listen are cut off from the people of God (Acts 3:23). Usually the word church is used by Luke simply to refer to a local community of Christians, but in Acts 20:28 he calls the restored Israel "the church of God."

The gathering of true Israel, which includes believing Gentiles,* is to take place between the departure of Jesus and his return. The angelic figures who appear as Jesus ascends announce that "this Jesus, who was taken up from you into heaven, will come in the same way as you saw him go into heaven" (Acts 1:11). Having given prominence to the future return of Jesus, Luke says very little else on this matter. His gaze is so captured from this point on with the wonder of the age after Pentecost, in which Christ is the ascended Lord of the church, that he places the main emphasis on realized eschatology.

The mission to proclaim Jesus as the crucified

Messiah who now reigns in heaven is given first to the apostles (Acts 1:8) and then taken up by all believers. This mission is sustained and directed by the ascended Lord of the church, mainly through the activity of the Holy Spirit (e.g., Acts 4:29-31; 13:1-3; 16:6-10).

In summary, the NT uses ascension terminology of both Jesus' exaltation following his resurrection and of his final departure into heaven following his resurrection appearances. These two matters are nevertheless intimately related for they both bear testimony to one fundamental tenet of the apostolic faith, namely the transcendent reign of Christ as Lord. See also GLORY; HEAVEN AND HELL; RESURRECTION; SON OF GOD; SON OF MAN.

BIBLIOGRAPHY. J. G. Davies, He Ascended into Heaven: A Study in the History of a Doctrine (London: Lutterworth, 1958); J. A. Fitzmyer, "The Ascension of Christ and Pentecost," TS 45 (1984) 409-40; E. Franklin, Christ the Lord (Philadelphia: Westminster, 1975); J. B. Green, " 'The Message of Salvation' in Luke-Acts," Ex Auditu 5 (1989) 21-23; D. M. Hay, Glory at the Right Hand: Psalm 110 in Early Christianity (Nashville: Abingdon, 1973); G. Lohfink, Die Himmelfahrt Jesu: Untersuchungen zu den Himmelfahrts—und Erhöhungstexten bei Lukas (Munich: Kosel, 1971); J. F. Maile, "The Ascension in Luke-Acts," TynB 37 (1986) 29-59; G. C. Nicholson, Death As Departure: The Johannine Descent-Ascent Schema (SBLDS 63; Chico, CA: Scholars, 1983); M. C. Parsons, The Departure of Jesus in Luke-Acts (JSOTSup 21; Sheffield: Academic, 1987); A. M. Ramsey, "What was the Ascension?" in History and Chronology in the New Testament (London: SPCK, 1965) 135-44; P. A. van Stempvoort, "The Interpretation of the Ascension in Luke-Acts," NTS 5 (1959) 30-42.

K. Giles

ATONEMENT. See DEATH OF JESUS; LAST SUPPER; RANSOM SAYING.

AUTHENTICITY. See FORM CRITICISM; GOSPELS (HISTORICAL RELIABILITY); TRADITION CRITICISM.

AUTHORITY AND POWER

Authority is the right to effect control over objects, individuals or events. While human authority may be delegated, God's* authority arises from himself alone. Power, meanwhile, is the ability to bring about what one desires. In the Gospels God reveals his authority and power in the person of Jesus.

1. Terminology and Background
2. Authority and Power in the Person of Jesus
3. The Emphases of the Gospel Writers

1. Terminology and Background.

In the NT the usual term for "authority" is *exousia* (Matthew 10 x, Mark 10 x, Luke 16 x, John 8 x). The OT attributes the word *exousia* to God only rarely, in passages such Daniel 4:34 (4:31 LXX). *Dynamis* is the common NT expression for "power" (Matthew 12 x, Mark 10 x, Luke 15 x, John 0 x). In the LXX it is used of God most often in the Psalms; but in general other terms for power and authority, such as *dynasteia* and *ischys*, dominate the vocabulary of the Greek OT.

Whereas the nations linked their gods with forces of nature, Yahweh is worshipped as the one true God, who created the cosmos and rules it as king (Ps 66:7). He may delegate authority to the human race (Ps 8:5-6), to his special people (Ps 68:35), to kings (1 Chron 22:10), or to Satan (Job 1:12). In Daniel's vision, God gives authority over every nation to "one like a son of man" (Dan 7:14, 27). God's power to save is typified in the Exodus (Ex 15:6, Deut 3:24) and in the hoped-for New Exodus (Ezek 36:22-38; cf. Sir 36:1-11).

In the NT God continues to stand in stark contrast to the gods of the Gentiles.* Their power is conceded to be finite and their authority circumscribed by Fate, but the true God may act freely (Mt 19:26). This explains why "The Power" may stand for God's name, as it does in Matthew 26:64 and parallels. He holds the power of life* and death and eternal punishment (Mt 10:28; *see* Judgment). Thus, when the Sadducees deny the doctrine of the resurrection,* they are doubting the power of God (Mk 12:24). He gives authority as he chooses— to Satan (Lk 4:6) and to earthly rulers (Jn 19:10-11).

2. Authority and Power in the Person of Jesus.

2.1. Jesus Anointed by God. The coming Messiah (*see* Christ) was to be anointed with the powerful Spirit of God (Is 9:6-7; cf. *Pss. Sol.* 17:22-25; *see* Holy Spirit), and Jesus inaugurates his ministry by claiming to be that anointed one (Lk 4:16-21). It is in the work of Christ that the kingdom of God (*see* Kingdom of God) advances with power. Later, when the imprisoned John the Baptist (*see* John the Baptist) seeks confirmation of Jesus' messianic identity, Jesus adduces his miraculous deeds as evidence (Lk 7:22-23 par.).

2.2. Jesus' Powerful Deeds: Healings, Miracles, Exorcisms. The Talmud records some minor miracles from the Second Temple Period, but Jesus' power was unrivalled. His mastery over disease is epitomized in the healing* of the paralytic in Capernaum (Mk 2:1-12 par.). Jesus begins by declaring the man's sins forgiven, an apparent act of blasphemy. He then heals the man in order to demonstrate that "the Son of man" has authority on earth to forgive sins (*see* Forgiveness of Sins).

Jesus' power over nature is exemplified in the miracle* of stilling the storm; the disciples ponder the identity of a man who can command the wind and the waves (Mk 4:41 par.). Likewise, he can raise the dead. In the Synoptic Gospels he gives life to Jairus' daughter (Mk 5:21-43 par.) and to the young man of Nain (Lk 7:11-17); in John 11:38-44 he raises Lazarus.*

The history-of-religions school attempted to define the Jesus of the Gospels as a Hellenistic *theios anēr*, or "divine man" (*see* Divine Man). Reconstructed from scant historical evidence, this figure was defined as a man associated with the gods; the supernatural substance at his control could be passed on to others for healing. The healing of the woman with the hemorrhage is typically cited as a parallel to the divine man. Jesus' healing power seems at first glance to be a miraculous substance: She touches his garment and is healed, and Jesus feels the power leaving him (Mk 5:27-32 par.). But any hint of magic evaporates when Jesus concludes that the woman's faith led to her cure. The *theios anēr* viewpoint also disregards the monotheistic and basically Jewish matrix of the Gospels: Jesus is presented as the unique Son of God, whose deeds manifest the coming of God's reign in fulfillment of biblical prophecy (*see* Old Testament in the Gospels).

The Jews practiced elaborate rites of exorcism (see Tob 6:7-8; Josephus *Ant.* 8.2.5 §§45-47; cf. Mt 12:27 par.), but Jesus is able to silence demons and cast them out with a terse command (Mk 1:21-28 par.; *see* Demon, Devil, Satan). In Matthew 12:28 and Luke 11:20 he points out that the destruction of the devil by God's Spirit (Luke "finger of God") is a sign of the advancing kingdom. But in fact the Jews, in accordance with Deuteronomy 13:1-5, would not let exorcisms or miracles act as the definitive proof of Jesus' identity. How could this man be of God when he consistently ignored the Sabbath* customs (Mk 2:24; 3:2 and par.; Jn 7:23; 9:16, 31, 33) and refused to grant them an incontrovertible sign from heaven* (Mk 8:11-12)?

Thus left with a paradox, the Jewish leaders construe Jesus' power in a variety of ways, sometimes by arguing that a miracle has not taken place (Jn 9:8-9, 18-19), at other times by simply rejecting Jesus out of hand (Jn 11:45-53). A darker explanation of his power is that he can manipulate demons with the permission of Beelzebul (Mt 12:24 par.; cf. Jn 7:20; 10:21). The Talmud, too, accuses Jesus of being a sorcerer who learned the black arts in Egypt (e.g., *b. Sanh.* 43a). The same charge was raised in the second century A.D. by the Jew Trypho (Justin *Dial. Tryph.* 69.7) and by the Greek Celsus (Origen *Contra Celsum* 1.6), a viewpoint updated for the twentieth century by writers such as

M. Smith. But the absence of incantations and elixirs from Jesus' swift and potent exorcisms leaves no room for this ancient theory.

In the end the Jewish leaders fulfil Jesus' prediction that his own people would not benefit from his powerful deeds (Lk 4:24-27).

2.3. Jesus' Authoritative Teaching. Jesus' message is critically important both in its divine authority and in its function within the last judgment (*see* Teacher). He claims that his words will never pass away (Mk 13:31 par.; cf. Is 40:8; Ps 119:89). To escape disaster one must heed his gospel* (e.g., Jn 12:48-50; Mk 8:38).

"He teaches with authority and not as the scribes," so exclaims the crowd (Mk 1:22 par. *see* People, Crowd). D. Daube conjectures that the crowd is merely distinguishing Jesus from lower-level clerical scribes,* and favorably comparing him with ordained rabbis. But Daube mistakenly assumes that the Hebrew *rešût* underlies this use of *exousia,* a necessary proof if "authority" is to bear the technical meaning of "ordination." In fact, the context shows that Jesus' authority puts him above any class of scribe. Scribal authority arose from the learned interpretation of Torah and the citation of earlier rabbis. At the same time, the Qumran sectarians (*see* Dead Sea Scrolls) practiced an allegorical midrash* to discover the hidden message of the OT. Jesus, by contrast, is unschooled in scribal hermeneutics (cf. Jn 7:15-18); he nevertheless boldly prefaces his teaching with "Amen"* and entertains no alternatives to his gospel. His claim to be an authority greater than Jonah or Solomon (Mt 12:41-42 par.) comes at a time when prophets* were thought to be extinct (cf. 1 Macc 9:27). Indeed, the Transfiguration* account, with its vision of Moses* and Elijah,* reaches its climax in the Father's command to hear Jesus (Mk 9:7 par.). It is worth noting that many scholars today are concentrating on the authority of Jesus within its sociological context (*see* Sociological Approaches to the Gospels).

Jesus claims the authority to forgive sins, but he also pronounces judgment, first on Galilean cities (Mt 11:20-24 par.), then on Jerusalem (Mt 23:37-39 par.). The Son of man (*see* Son of Man) is the eschatological judge in Matthew 16:27; 25:31-46. According to Mark 10:40, however, Jesus does not have the authority to assign the seats on his right and left in the kingdom.

One of Jesus' final actions is to cleanse the Jerusalem Temple.* When the scribes demand to know the source of his authority (Mk 11:27-33 par.), he presses them on their opinion of John the Baptist. He leaves them with the implication that he and John, in contrast with the scribes, were authorized and sent by God.

On several occasions, Jesus states that the Son of

man possesses unusual authority. At the Parousia the Son of man will appear in power and glory* (Mk 13:26 par.). But in the present the Son of man can, for example, forgive sins (Mk 2:10 par.). Jewish literature does not picture the Messiah or the Son of man as exercising this right. While some commentators believe that Jesus is claiming that any human being can forgive sins, the Jews' remark about blasphemy in this context strongly suggests that Jesus was asserting that authority for himself. Similarly, in the controversy over gleaning on the Sabbath (Mk 2:27-28 par.), Jesus declares that "the Son of man is lord even of the Sabbath." His statement can hardly be synonymous with "the Sabbath was made for humans" (Mk 2:27 only), as if to say that all people can be flexible in their Sabbath observance (*see* Sabbath). Jesus is demonstrating his personal authority to interpret God's Law.*

2.4. Delegated to the Disciples. John the Baptist preached that Jesus would baptize people with the Holy Spirit (Mk 1:8 par.). But even while he is on earth he enables his disciples* to duplicate his deeds: to preach and to do powerful acts in his name, such as exorcism, healing and raising the dead (Mk 3:14-15; 6:7, 13; 16:17-18; Mt 10:1, 7-8; Lk 9:1-2; 10:1-12, 17; but see Mt 7:21-23; 24:5). Later on, in Mark 9:38-41 and parallels, the disciples wish to suppress an outsider who is casting out demons in Jesus' name, but Jesus prevents them (contrast with Acts 19:11-17; and note the fourth-century use of Jesus' name by non-Christians in *PGM* IV.3019-20).

Christ also gives his followers the authority of "binding and loosing," which seems to be the power to proclaim the forgiveness or the retaining of people's sins (Mt 18:18; cf. Jn 20:22-23). The disciples are further authorized to pronounce symbolic judgment on those who reject their message (Mk 6:11 par.).

Even though Jesus' followers will do works to surpass his own (Jn 14:12), he emphasizes: "Nevertheless, do not rejoice at this, that the spirits submit to you, but rejoice that your names are written in heaven" (Lk 10:20 NRSV). In the age to come the disciples who remain faithful will be rewarded with more authority (Lk 22:28-30).

2.5. Power in Humility and Submission to the Cross. As the Servant of the Lord (*see* Servant of Yahweh), Jesus rejects the exploitive power of the world* and the devil, and lives in submission to God (cf. Mt 12:15-21). Even while he invites people to follow him absolutely, he does not force them against their will (Lk 18:18-25).

Matthew and Luke also record that Satan tempts Jesus with the lure of power and authority; the test lies in his demand that Jesus worship* him (*see* Temptation of Jesus). Jesus resists this temptation to grab earthly power at the cost of disobedience. It follows that he later rejects the option of insurrection when the crowd wishes to make him king (Jn 6:15). His final entry to Jerusalem is not in regal splendor, but in humility (Mt 21:1-5).

In recent study fresh attention has been given to the powerlessness of Jesus against the forces that oppressed and executed him. In this way Jesus identifies himself with the poor and afflicted and condemns the corrupt power structures. We may wish, however, to emphasize several safeguards in order to maintain the original balance of the Evangelists. First, Jesus' divine authority is not merely freedom to act (so Anderson), but also the ability to exercise control over objects, individuals and events. Second, his powerlessness in the passion accounts is due not to his inability to take control of the situation (esp. Mt 26:53), but rather to his solidarity with the will of God (*see* Gethsemane). Third, God powerfully vindicates Jesus for his obedient suffering; the cross cannot be separated from the power of Jesus' resurrection.

3. The Emphases of the Gospel Writers.
Although Mark portrays Jesus as a teacher (e.g., Mk 1:21; 4:1-2; 10:1; 11:18), he stresses the authority of Jesus rather than the content of his message. The Son of God (*see* Son of God) exorcises demons with a word and heals with a touch or by an act of will (Mk 1:40-41; 3:9-10). But his conflict with the scribes also includes their concerns over the content of his message, and he is finally condemned as a blasphemer (Mk 14:64).

The content of Jesus' message receives more attention in Matthew and Luke than in Mark. It is not in the Capernaum synagogue,* but after the Sermon on the Mount (*see* Sermon on the Mount) that the crowd marvels at Jesus' authority (Mt 7:28-29). While affirming the validity of the OT (Mt 5:17-19), Jesus explores its deeper meaning against the reasoning of the scribes (Mt 5:21-48). He reiterates the formula "You have heard that it was said . . . but I say" (*see* Law). The exaltation of Jesus means that all authority has been granted him. Jesus will always be present with his followers as they carry his teaching to every nation (Mt 28:18-20; *see* Gentiles).

Luke refers to authority and power more than do Matthew and Mark, and for him power is the operation of the Holy Spirit. Mary is therefore told that the Spirit of God and the power of the Most High have been active in the conception of Jesus (Lk 1:35; *see* Birth of Jesus). Later, Jesus is anointed with God's Spirit (Lk 3:21-22); he returns to Galilee in his power (Lk 4:14); he announces that the Spirit is upon him

(Lk 4:18-19); and he has the power of the Lord* for healing (Lk 5:17). The disciples too are promised power from heaven (24:49).

In the Fourth Gospel Jesus has authority because he is the Son of the Father (Jn 5:19-20). He may work on the Sabbath because his Father in heaven does the same (Jn 5:17-18). The Father has placed all things into the hands of the Son (Jn 3:35; 17:2), including all judgment (Jn 5:22, 27). That the Messiah or the Son of man would participate in the judgment was not unknown in Judaism* (see *1 Enoch* 45:3; 4 Ezra 2:42-48). But Jesus goes further and claims that the Son will raise the dead for judgment (Jn 5:21, 25, 28-29; 6:39-40). In fact, he himself is the resurrection and the life (Jn 11:25). In Jewish theology the power of resurrection was reserved strictly for God (note a singular exception in *b. Sanh.* 113a). Besides raising Lazarus, Jesus has the authority to lay down his own life and to take it up again (Jn 10:17-18; cf. 2:19-22).

Despite the absence of exorcism accounts in John's Gospel, the authority of Satan's kingdom also comes into sharp relief. Jesus is said to have overcome both the world (Jn 16:33) and its "prince" (Jn 12:31).

In conclusion, the Evangelists perceive divine authority and power as the mighty revelation of God in Christ in order to advance his kingdom. When the disciples display God's power, they do so not in their own right but in the name of Jesus. Jesus' authority and power, emerging as fresh revelations of the Messiah's true identity, have provided a foundation for the church's christology.

See also COMMANDMENT; DEMONS, DEVIL, SATAN; ETHICS OF JESUS; HEALING; KINGDOM OF GOD; TEACHER.

BIBLIOGRAPHY. H. Anderson, "Jesus: Aspects of the Question of His Authority," in *The Social World of Formative Christianity and Judaism: Essays in Tribute to Howard Clark Kee*, ed. J. Neusner et al. (Philadelphia: Fortress, 1988); G. R. Beasley-Murray, *Jesus and the Kingdom of God* (Grand Rapids: Eerdmans, 1986); D. Bossman, "Authority: The New Testament and First-Century Judaism in Cultural Perspective," in *Theology and Authority: Maintaining a Tradition of Tension*, ed. R. Penaskovic (Peabody, MA: Hendrickson, 1987) 1-13; D. Daube, "*Exousia* in Mark 1, 22 and 27," *JTS* 39 (1938) 45-59; J. Dawsey, "Jesus and the Language of Authority," in *Theology and Authority: Maintaining a Tradition of Tension*, ed. R. Penaskovic (Peabody, MA: Hendrickson, 1987) 14-23; W. Foerster, "ἔξεστιν κτλ," *TDNT* II.560-75; W. Grundmann, "δύναμαι κτλ," *TDNT* II.284-317; J. D. Kingsbury, "The Religious Authorities in the Gospel of Mark," *NTS* 36 (1990) 42-65; D. A. Lee-Pollard, "Powerlessness as Power: A Key Emphasis in the Gospel of Mark," *SJT*

40 (1987) 173-88; C. H. Powell, *The Biblical Concept of Power* (London: Epworth, 1963); D. Senior, " 'With Swords and Clubs . . .'—The Setting of Mark's Community and His Critique of Abusive Power," *BTB* 17 (1987) 10-20; M. Smith, *Jesus the Magician* (San Francisco: Harper & Row, 1978).

G. S. Shogren

B

BABYLONIAN TALMUD. *See* RABBINIC TRADITIONS AND WRITINGS.

BANQUET. *See* TABLE FELLOWSHIP.

BAPTISM

Baptism is associated with a general group of practices related to washing. In addition to the common terms for baptism (*baptō, baptizō, baptisma, baptismos, baptistēs*), one must also be aware of terms associated with the act of complete or partial washings (*louō, niptō*). Here we will survey the common terminology associated with baptism, the background and context of NT baptism and the practice of baptism associated with the ministries of John the Baptist (*see* John the Baptist) and Jesus.

1. Terminology
2. Background and Context
3. The Baptism of John
4. The Baptism of Jesus

1. Terminology.
Of the five different words found in the NT that are built on the root *bap-*, two are verbs and three are nouns. The basic form is the Greek verb *baptō*, occurring three times (Lk 16:24; Jn 13:26; Rev 19:13) with the literal meaning "to dip" or "to dye." On the other hand the intensive form, *baptizō*, which occurs seventy-seven times, is used always or almost always in the cultic sense of Jewish washings (e.g., Mk 7:4), the baptism of John (e.g., Mk 1:4), the baptism that Jesus and/or his disciples performed during his public ministry (e.g., Jn 3:22, 26) and baptism with/in the Holy Spirit and fire (e.g., Mt 3:11, 14). In the latter usage the term takes on a metaphorical meaning that may be understood in terms of Judaism's eschatological imagery of a stream, deluge or flood of fire that would purge the righteous and destroy the wicked (*see* Holy Spirit).

The noun form, *baptisma*, is not found outside the NT and is only found in the singular. The term implies not only the external act of baptism, but also

denotes the inner meaning and force of the act. Baptism may then be appropriately employed for Spirit baptism as well as water baptism.

2. Background and Context.
2.1. World Religions. Baptism is not a distinctive or uniquely Christian idea. The practice of baptism is widespread. Examples include the Hindu rituals in the Ganges River, the purification ritual in the Babylonian cult of Enki, and the Egyptian practices of purifying newborn children and the symbolic revivification rites performed on the dead. *Baptizō* and related terms were used to define ritual practices in early Cretan religion, Thracian religion, Eleusinian mystery religions and in several gnostic groups and cults.

Common elements are associated with these widespread baptismal practices. Except when used metaphorically, baptism is always associated with water. Baptism is performed in connection with the removal of guilt, cleansing and the granting of a new start. Christian baptism shares these common traits and contexts; it also has specific historical contexts and theological significance that give it a distinctive Christian meaning. The context for John's baptism and Christian baptism is informed by the OT, Judaism* and the practices of the Qumran community (*see* Dead Sea Scrolls).

2.2. Jewish Practices. Followers of John or Jesus who participated in the baptismal rite, whether Jew or Gentile,* would not have found this practice totally unfamiliar. Water is the element naturally used for cleansing the body, and its symbolic use entered into almost every religious practice, and none more completely than Jewish practices. The purification rituals of Judaism stressed cleanliness and worthiness to serve the Lord (Lev 13—17; Num 19). The ritual of washing was similar to baptism in its purifying implications (Mk 7:4; Heb 9:20; *see* Clean and Unclean). In Psalm 51:2, 7 the psalmist asked for divine cleansing. Especially significant is Isaiah 4:4, which calls for a washing away of sins by the "spirit of burning," an adumbration of the theme taken up by John in his baptism.

In addition to these OT examples, Jews had a counterpart of the Christian practice in their proselyte rituals. It is not certain when Jewish proselyte baptism began, some arguing that it began at the same time as the Christian rite (McKnight) and others that it preceded the Christian rite (Beasley-Murray). The account of Naaman the leper (2 Kings 5), which is possibly a purification washing, is similar to later proselyte baptism. Much later (by the third century A.D.), it became accepted that male Jewish proselytes were to be baptized in the presence of witnesses seven days after circumcision. In later traditions Judaism required three things of converts to Judaism: (1) circumcision, (2) baptism or ritual bath, and (3) the offering of sacrifice. These rituals of circumcision and washing were most likely preceded by catechetical instruction. The Talmud refers to a baptized proselyte as a newborn child (b. Yeban, 2). Yet for Judaism the decisive turn from heathenism took place in circumcision (see McKnight). The baptism or ritual bath prepared the newly made Jew to offer a sacrifice as the initial act of worship.

Conversion from heathenism to Judaism was viewed as an entry into life from the dead, and this was the source for the Christian doctrine of the new life* of a convert to Christ. It should be noted, however, that in Judaism the concept is only secondarily associated with proselyte baptism, and it shows up only in later traditions. The distinctive Christian understanding of baptism in terms of dying and rising is based on the convert's relationship to Christ who died and rose from the dead (Beasley-Murray, *NIDNTT* 1.144-45).

3. The Baptism of John.

Just as John was the forerunner of Jesus, so his baptism was the forerunner of Christian baptism. Yet the background of John's baptism remains fiercely debated. The cultural and religious context at the time of Jesus require that a number of factors be considered.

3.1. Jewish Proselyte Baptism As Antecedent to John's Baptism. It is natural to seek a prototype for John's baptism within Judaism of the first century. But determining the relationship between Jewish practices and understandings of baptism or lustration and those of John or the early church is fraught with difficulties.

In its most-developed form Jewish proselyte baptism was an initiatory rite performed only once upon the Gentile convert, as was John's baptism and Christian baptism. In line with OT lustrations, Jewish proselyte baptism served to cleanse the convert from moral and cultic impurity. John's baptism for the remission of

sins reflects a similar concept. J. Jeremias has argued that *Testament of Levi* 14:6 supports a pre-Christian Jewish proselyte baptism. The passage, which he dates in the late second-century B.C., reads "with harlots and adulteresses you shall be joined, and the daughters of the Gentiles you shall take as wives, purifying them with unlawful purifications" *(katharizontes autas katharismō paranomō)*. He contends that the terminology, theology, catechetical instruction and performance of the rite by Christians resembles the Jewish performance of the rite (see Jeremias, 29-40; Daube, 106-8).

There is, however, no clear evidence prior to A.D. 70 that proselytes underwent baptism as a requirement of conversion (see McKnight). This has been argued forcefully, in spite of the continued citation of texts like *Sibylline Oracles* (4.165) and Epictetus (*Diss.* 2.9.19). In addition, the following arguments can be made against the idea that Jewish proselyte baptism served as the primary antecedent for John's baptism or Christian baptism. There is no mention of proselyte baptism in the OT, Philo or Josephus. Passages such as *Testament of Levi* 14:6 remain ambiguous or inconclusive at best. It is therefore doubtful that proselyte baptism existed, at least as a clearly analogous rite, in John's time.

A. Oepke points out that Jewish baptism was political and ritualistic, whereas John's baptism was ethical and eschatological (similar to Ps 51:7; Is 1:15-16; 4:4; Jer 2:22; 4:14; Ezek 36:25; Zech 13:1). Grammatically, there is an important distinction to be observed. The NT uses active and passive (primarily) forms of *baptō* and *baptizō*, while texts referring to Jewish proselyte baptism primarily employ middle or reflexive forms (Oepke, 530-35). Thus, what was self-administered in Judaism was seen more as an act of God* (and surrender to him) in early Christianity.

It is especially significant that John's baptism was received by Jews rather than Gentiles. John demanded moral repentance* and cleansing for the Pharisees.* Jewish proselyte baptism, of course, served as an initiation rite for Gentiles, but Jews, since they were already the people of God, did not need the rite. If John's baptism was developed from Jewish proselyte practices, he transformed it significantly.

3.2. Qumran Washings As Antecedents of John's Baptism. A better alternative for the background of John's baptism can be found in the lustrations practiced by the Qumran community. Numerous studies have been made of the relationship between the baptism of John and the lustrations spoken of in the *Manual of Discipline* (1QS 3.4-9; 6:14-23; see Badia). Such a relationship can be maintained without accepting suggestions such as John's full-fledged membership in an Essene community located in the area surrounding the Jordan River.

The Qumran community operated outside the Temple* cult and viewed the priests* as evil and impure. Thus, its only available rituals were the baths and lustrations described in the OT. John's practice of baptism, integrated with his call to repentance and renewal, complements this situation nicely. The Qumran community maintained a strong orientation toward eschatological fulfillment (see Eschatology), seeing itself, in light of Isaiah 40:3, as preparers of the way. John's message was dually focused around the call to repentance, and eschatological expectation and preparation (Mt 3:2; Mk 1:4, 7, 8; Jn 1:23).

Similarly, the Qumran community recognized the inability of the washings to cleanse a person apart from true repentance. John's preaching and baptism also created this tension (Mt 3:7-9). Like the sectarians of Qumran, John did not envision the water purifying apart from repentance (Mt 3:11; Lk 3:7). John's baptismal practices align themselves better with lustrations of Qumran than with Jewish proselyte baptism. On the other hand, we must not lose sight of the major distinction between John and Qumran: whereas the Qumran community's rite was self administered and practiced daily (or frequently), and is thus best classified as "ritual lustrations," John's baptism was a one-time, initiation rite.

3.3. The Significance of John's Baptism.
We must not necessarily conclude that John was seeking to convert people into a messianic community. Rather, John was concerned with bringing about a messianic consciousness within the parameters of genuine repentance. John's call for a one-time baptism for those who had been born as Jews was unprecedented. He insisted that one's ancestry was not adequate to guarantee one's relationship with God. That new commitment was solemnized in baptism. There is no evidence that John permitted those who became followers of Jesus to be rebaptized.

The Gospel writers emphasize the points of linkage between Jesus' inauguration of his messianic rule and John's preaching and baptism. It would be mistaken to understand John's baptism as completely analogous to early Christian baptism, though the Gospel writers do not care to distinguish between John's baptism and early Christian baptism. Early Christian baptism was an obvious initiatory rite into the church, though it retained an emphasis on moral purity and cleansing (Acts 2:38). John operated within the perspective of OT expectations for righteousness (see Justice, Righteousness) and, apparently, with a framework analo-

gous to that of Qumran where baptism was regarded as both a means of accomplishing the necessary cleansing and as a sign of repentance. Though there are obvious connections between John and the early church, we must cautiously suggest a dependent relationship. In fact, though baptism was not a part of Jesus' ministry, Jesus initially allowed his disciples* to continue the practice (Jn 3:22), though he later seems to have discontinued the rite (Jn 4:1-3). John's ministry looked forward, expecting the coming kingdom (see Kingdom of God), while Jesus' ministry celebrates the kingdom's inauguration in the present.

4. The Baptism of Jesus.
4.1. Jesus' Baptism by John. The baptism of Jesus at the hands of John the Baptist is explained in some detail in Matthew 3:13-17, briefly recounted in Mark 1:9-11, mentioned in Luke 3:21-22, and implied in John 1:29-34. All four accounts directly link with baptism the anointing of Jesus with the Spirit and the declaration of his sonship (see Son of God). It is this anointing that inaugurates the ministry of Jesus which will be characterized by the power of the Spirit of the new age (Mt 12:18; 28; Lk 4:18; 11:20; Acts 10:38).

What was the relevance of John's baptism to Jesus? Did Jesus need to repent? Matthew alone tells us that John tried to deter Jesus from being baptized, ostensively because baptism implies that a person has sin of which they must repent. John seems to recognize his own sinfulness in comparison with Jesus and notes that their roles should be reversed—Jesus should be baptizing John. Jesus' reply seems to acknowledge the logic of John's argument, but he nevertheless requests baptism for a different reason.

Theologically, the baptism of Jesus identifies Jesus as the messianic servant who stands in solidarity with his people. As their representative he came "to fulfill all righteousness" (Mt 3:15). *Righteousness* in Matthew's Gospel refers to those who are upright and law-abiding, obedient and faithful to God's commandments (see Przybylski). Matthew has portrayed Jesus fulfilling specific prophecies as well as more general biblical themes. Now he fulfills the moral demands of God's will. In so doing, Jesus identifies and sanctions John's ministry as divinely ordained and his message as one to be heeded.

Jesus began his ministry with the same demand for repentance, affirming John's baptizing work. Yet one important difference must be observed. Jesus was to baptize with fire and the Spirit (Mt 3:11; Lk 3:16). The relationship between water baptism and Spirit baptism came to have greater significance in the Epistles and Acts, but its importance in the Gospel account conclusively shows that Jesus never thought of baptism as merely a mechanical act.

4.2. The Baptism with Which Jesus Is Baptized. When the sons of Zebedee asked Jesus to sit at his side, one on the left and the other on the right (Mk 10:35-37), a question apparently stemming from their mother (cf. Mt 20:20-21), Jesus referred them to his own drinking of a bitter cup and his own baptism, each of which alludes to some kind of physical distress (*see* Predictions of Jesus' Passion and Resurrection). Jesus states that the sons of Zebedee would experience such—but he still had no right to assign seats in the kingdom. The meaning of this metaphorical use of *baptism* appears to be "painful destiny," in this case death or martyrdom. According to the grammar, while verse 38 implies that the brothers cannot share in the same fate as Jesus (since the death of Jesus is a unique moment of God's judgment), verse 39 backs up and concedes that they, too, may die for their association with Jesus (cf. Mk 8:34-38). At the same time, the Lukan form of the saying (Lk 12:50) suggests that the "baptism" also includes the persecution that led up to the death of Jesus and interprets it as an eschatological tribulation.

4.3. Jesus' Command to Baptize. Matthew 28:19 clearly joins baptism with teaching as partners in the process of making disciples. "Make disciples" is the mandate of the risen Christ (*see* Resurrection). "Baptizing and teaching" are the two procedures associated with the accomplishment of that mandate. Thus Matthew's commission, not unlike baptism in the Fourth Gospel (Jn 3:22-24), joins baptism with discipleship.*

But the resurrection command has a fuller meaning. It is a commitment to ("in the name" is literally "into the name," implying entrance into an allegiance) the Father, the Son and the Holy Spirit (all three of whom were involved in the event of Jesus' own baptism in Mt 3:16-17). Matthew wants his readers to know that Jesus has taken his place along with the Father and the Spirit as the object of the disciples' worship* and commitment. Matthew's unique use of the trinitarian formula summarizes in the more formal language of the community the essence of what Jesus had taught his disciples about God,* instruction that had implied a unique relationship between Jesus and the Spirit with the Father.

See also GENTILES; HOLY SPIRIT; JOHN THE BAPTIST; REPENTANCE.

BIBLIOGRAPHY. R. E. Averbeck, "The Focus of Baptism in the New Testament," *GTJ* 1 (1980) 265-301; L. F. Badia, *The Qumran Baptism and John the Baptist's Baptism* (Lanham, MD: University Press of America, 1980); G. R. Beasley-Murray, *Baptism in the New Testament* (Grand Rapids: Eerdmans, 1962); G. R. Beasley-Murray and R. T. Beckwith, "Baptism," *NIDNTT* 1.143-61; C. L. Blomberg, *Matthew* (NAC; Nashville: Broadman, 1992); D. Daube, *The New Testament and Rabbinic Judaism* (London: Athlone, 1956); J. D. G. Dunn, *Baptism in the Holy Spirit* (Philadelphia: Westminster, 1970); J. Jeremias, *Infant Baptism in the First Four Centuries* (Philadelphia: Westminster, 1962); S. McKnight, *A Light among the Gentiles* (Minneapolis: Fortress, 1991); A. Oepke, "βάπτω κτλ," *TDNT* I.529-46; B. Przybylski, *Righteousness in Matthew and His World of Thought* (SNTSMS 41; Cambridge: University Press, 1980).   D. S. Dockery

BARTHOLOMEW. *See* DISCIPLES.

BEATITUDES. *See* BLESSING AND WOE; SERMON ON THE MOUNT.

BEELZEBUL. *See* DEMON, DEVIL, SATAN.

BELOVED DISCIPLE. *See* DISCIPLES; JOHN, GOSPEL OF

BENEDICTUS. See ZECHARIAH'S SONG.

BENEFACTOR

A desire for lasting memory penetrated much of Greco-Roman culture. States capitalized on this interest by urging wealthy citizens to serve administratively at their own expense, while assuming the expenses of certain public works and a variety of cultural programs. This combination of personal desire and political objectives is documented in thousands of inscriptions in which the virtues and the contributions of honorands are celebrated, and often with a formulaic uniformity that spans Periclean Athens and some current Hellenic expression.

1. The Terminology of the Benefactor
2. Benefactor in the Gospels

1. The Terminology of Benefactor.
Numerous terms are used to express the concept of a civic-oriented person, who is first of all understood, expressly or tacitly, to be a man or woman of *aretē*, that is, one marked by characteristics and deeds of superior excellence. Warriors were especially qualified for such distinction in Homer's world, and a common synonym in his epics is the term *aguthos,* which identifies goodness with social status and bravery (*Iliad* 21.273-283).

After Homer, Hellenes developed elaborate ceremonies in honor of athletes (*see* Pindar's odes), heads of state and other contributors to the public welfare. Philosophers encouraged progressive democratization of excellence by emphasizing a variety of moral virtues in definition of model citizenry. The verb *euergeteō* ("render beneficent service") and the cognate noun *euergetēs* ("benefactor") appear frequently in honorary documents and in the Septuagint, but numerous other expressions, such as *dikaiosynē* (uprightness; *see* Justice, Righteousness), *eusebeia* (piety) and *sōtēria* (healing,* deliverance; *see* Salvation) were used in recognition of exceptional merit in public circles and private clubs and associations. It is important, therefore, to recognize that the English term "benefactor," as used in this article, does not translate any single Greek term, but embraces the general Greco-Roman perception of beneficent deities and exceptionally fine persons.

2. Benefactor in the Gospels.

2.1. Deity as Model of Beneficence. Of primary significance is the importance attached to the divine as model for human character and performance. According to Greek thinkers (e.g., Xenophon, *Memorabilia* 4.3.2-14), generous concern for humanity is God's primary characteristic. Such thoughtful disposition marks a deity as *agathos*. For Greco-Roman publics much of the point of the story of the man who addressed Jesus as "good teacher" (Lk 18:18 par. Mk 10:17) relates to this perception. God is the point of departure for proper understanding of goodness. The commandments relate to desirable civic qualities and the instruction "Sell and give to the poor" urges the inquirer to share God's reputation for generosity. The culminating directive connotes that Jesus himself is to be classified as a person of extraordinary merit and himself the gift of a generous God. Similarly, divine generosity is the model for a disciple's* approach to people in need (Lk 6:35 [cf. Mt 7:11]; 8:1-3).

2.2. Salvation. As testimonies to the beneficent power of Isis and Asclepius attest, Greco-Romans prized salvation,* ranging from security of the state to healing of bodily ailments. Luke, most Hellenic of the Evangelists, especially features words of the *sōtēr-* family, thereby portraying Jesus as a benefactor who is at the same time the supreme benefaction of God. Supporting this thematic perspective is Luke's use of the term *euergetēs* at Luke 22:25. Jesus is critical of those who claim such reputation without corresponding production. In accordance with Mediterranean ideals, he emphasizes service* (v. 27), and in keeping with the prediction made in 1:32 cites his own dedication to the ideal. His disciples in turn are invited to practice the Hellenic-type invitation to imitate their benefactor,

Jesus the Great. According to Acts 4:9, some of them finally learned their lesson. In economical wordplay, Luke further reveals the category in which Jesus is to be understood by declaring in Luke 23:33 that he was crucified between two *kakourgoi* (malefactors). On a similar note, the application of studies in cultural anthropology to the interpretation of biblical texts, especially Luke-Acts, reveals the rich diversity in the reciprocity systems of the Mediterranean world. Well known is the patron-client relationship critiqued in a number of Luke's pericopae (e.g., 6:32-36; cf. Moxnes).

2.3. Words and Deeds. A frequent rhetorical ploy in descriptions of eminent figures is the use of the word-deed pair. The greatest of leaders and benefactors are those who are noted for both. Thucydides, for example, highlights the political acumen of Pericles with an oratorical masterpiece. Luke (24:19) notes that Jesus was a prophet effective in "deed and word" (so also Moses,* but with the terms reversed, Acts 7:22). This thematic note in Luke's two-volume work sheds further light on the rationale for escalating emphasis on the words and deeds of Jesus in the Gospel tradition.

All the Evangelists are agreed on the importance of the death* of Jesus as God's own demonstration of beneficence and as Jesus' contribution to the salvation of humanity. Mark (10:45) and Matthew (20:28) interpret the death of Jesus as an instrument of "ransom" (*see* Ransom Saying) and cite a centurion's verdict on the superstar status of the crucified one (Mk 15:39; cf. Mt 27:54).

In John's Gospel the death of Jesus is perceived as an hour of glory* (12:20-33) and described in terms of widespread outreach (12:32), a common motif in honorary documents. It is God who glorifies Jesus but, in place of a centurion's verdict, John uses the inscription of a prefect to proclaim the death of Jesus as the performance of an exceptional person.

Luke's variation of the tradition also found in Mark and Matthew conforms to his own Hellenic outlook. The centurion affirms that Jesus was an "upright" person (Lk 23:47). This verdict comes immediately after the statement that the officer had observed the piety of Jesus (v. 46). By thus linking piety and uprightness, two principal characteristics of exceptional people, Luke dramatically confirms Jesus as the Great Benefactor. So had Caesar Augustus been described (*Res Gestae* 34). The fact that Luke does not, as in Mark and Matthew, interpret the crucifixion as an instrument of salvation is in further keeping with his Hellenic stress. As Supreme Benefactor, God displays good will by resurrecting Jesus and offering both Jews and Gentiles* an opportunity to repent* and enjoy renewed relations with God by recognizing

Jesus as the ultimate display of divine beneficence (Acts 2—4).

All the Evangelists cite miracles* to emphasize the beneficent performance of Jesus and to offer a dynamic context for understanding the climactic beneficence of God in connection with the death and resurrection* of Jesus. In turn the second element of the deed-word pair is supplied in Jesus' numerous speeches and sayings. Through this combination, especially nuanced in Luke's Gospel, Hellenically oriented publics would further appreciate what sympathetic Jewish auditors and readers might readily conclude through acquaintance with their Scriptures: Jesus is the Great Benefactor, the unique gift of the Supreme Benefactor.

See also HELLENISM.

BIBLIOGRAPHY. F. Danker, *Benefactor: Epigraphic Study of a Graeco-Roman and New Testament Semantic Field* (St. Louis: Clayton Publishing House, 1982); idem, *Proclamation Commentaries: Luke* (2d ed., Philadelphia: Fortress, 1987); J. Elliott, "Patronage and Clientism in Early Christian Society," *Forum* 3/4 (1987) 39-48; O. Jessen and J. Oehler, *"Euergetēs,"* in Pauly-Wissowa RE (1909) 6.978-81; B. Malina, *The New Testament World: Insights from Cultural Anthropology* (Atlanta: John Knox, 1981); H. Moxnes, *The Economy of the Kingdom: Social Conflict and Economic Relations in Luke's Gospel* (Philadelphia: Fortress, 1988); H. Willrich, *"Euergetis,"* in Pauly-Wissowa RE (1909) 6.981-82.

F. W. Danker

BETHLEHEM. *See* ARCHEOLOGY AND GEOGRAPHY; BIRTH OF JESUS.

BETRAYAL OF JESUS. *See* JUDAS ISCARIOT.

BIRTH OF JESUS

The examination of the birth of Jesus requires an extensive study of various aspects of the birth narratives found in Matthew 1—2 and Luke 1—2.

1. Genre and Sources of the Birth Narratives
2. Theological and Redactional Emphases in Matthew 1—2 and Luke 1—2
3. Use of OT Prophecy in the Birth Narratives
4. Genealogies in Matthew and Luke
5. The Date of Jesus' Birth
6. The Location of Jesus' Birth
7. The Virginal Conception
8. The Magi and the Shepherds
9. Canonical Information about Jesus' Childhood

1. Genre and Sources of the Birth Narratives.

The question of the genre of the birth narratives is still being debated, and opinions vary as to whether these stories are more like pagan birth legends or like Jewish infancy narratives, with most scholars now persuaded that they are closer to the latter than the former.

1.1. The Issue of Midrash. The attempt to see the birth narratives in light of Jewish literary practices has been taken a step further by those who view these stories as being essentially midrashic in character (Gundry 1982; Brown 1977). Midrash,* or midrash pesher, by definition is an imaginative interpretation or expansion based on some OT text, usually in an attempt to show how particular OT material has contemporary relevance (Laurentin). Given this definition it is easy to see how Matthew's treatment of the OT in his formulaic quotations might be cited as examples of midrashic exegesis. But what the First Evangelist does with his OT quotes and how he handles his narrative material are not one and the same thing (*see* Old Testament in the Gospels).

Midrash is a hermeneutical technique, *not* in itself a literary genre. It could also be argued that we have examples of imaginative haggadah in the birth narratives (cf. Hendrickx who calls Mt 1—2 a "haggadic midrash," though it might be better to say midrashic haggadah). A haggadic tale, like a legend, generally develops over a much longer period of time than the few decades that exist between the time of Jesus and the final form of the Gospels. Even as late as the 80-90s there were still some eyewitnesses to the Gospel events, and Luke claims to have relied at least in part on their testimony. It is agreed by most scholars that: (1) no extra-biblical materials provide such precise parallels with the birth narrative material that they can definitely be affirmed as the source(s) of the Gospel material; and (2) that both Matthew and Luke used sources for their birth narratives.

1.2. The Issue of Historical Tradition. To a great degree, how one evaluates the birth narratives is determined by one's presuppositions about the proper starting place for evaluating this material. For instance, if one assumes that both Matthew and Luke received an historical tradition or traditions (*see* Tradition Criticism) about the circumstances surrounding Jesus' birth and then took that source material, wrote it up in their own manner so as to highlight the theological points they wanted to make, and especially in the case of Matthew wrote it up so as to draw out potential links with the OT, it is possible to come to a plausible explanation of the character of this material. On this explanation real historical substance is posited for the birth narratives, with the Evangelists engaging in some creative editing and rewording of these historical sources according to their respective purposes and according to the conventions of ancient history-writing.

Certainly in light of Luke's prologue (1:1-4) one would naturally expect that this Evangelist was not only using sources, but sources he felt were historically credible to which he contributed his own editing, expansions and corrections (*see* Redaction Criticism). On the other hand, it is possible to assume that at most the authors only present us with some historical fragments in the midst of a largely fictional account, and that the point of the narratives is primarily theological not historical. Thus, it has been argued, the authors should not be faulted for not presenting straightforward history. If one starts with this assumption it is possible to come to the conclusions found in works such as R. H. Gundry's commentary on Matthew or R. E. Brown's impressive study *The Birth of the Messiah.*

No approach is free from problems, but special difficulties attend those who begin with the assumption of the *essential* non-historicity of the birth narrative material. First, it means that one must treat the birth narrative material as substantially different *in character* from the rest of the Gospel tradition, a great deal of which can be plausibly argued to have a basis in historical events in Jesus' life. In short, it requires that we see the birth stories as some sort of separate entities, perhaps even of a different genre from the rest of the Gospel material. There are, however, various indications that the birth narratives should not be separated from the rest of their respective Gospels. For instance, the thematic and theological unity of Luke 1—2 with the rest of Luke's Gospel has been demonstrated (Minear). Various of Luke's major themes are given their first airing in the birth narratives.

Second, the problem of supernatural phenomena is not unique to the birth narrative material, and unless one objects to the possibility of miracles* a priori, the supernatural occurrences recorded in the birth narratives present no greater obstacles to the case for historicity than do the supernatural events recorded elsewhere in the Gospels. Indeed, one may say that especially in the case of Luke 1—2 the birth narratives are in some ways less miraculous in character than some of the miracle narratives having to do with the ministry of Jesus.

Third, there is evidence in both Matthew 1—2 and Luke 1—2 that we are not dealing with free compositions. The fact that Luke 1—2 abounds in Hebraisms in contrast to the classical Greek prologue in Luke 1:1-4 speaks for the use of a Semitic narrative source(s) of

considerable proportions at least up to Luke 2:40 (Farris; *see* Languages of Palestine). Further, the way Matthew sometimes awkwardly works his formula citations into his narrative suggests he was working with one or several narrative sources to which he has added OT quotations.

Fourth, there are various details in these narratives that are theologically irrelevant and suggest an historical source (e.g., the name of Anna's father). In other cases they go against the grain of the Evangelist's purpose (e.g., Luke tries to cast John the Baptist* and his parents in the shadow of Jesus and Mary to a certain extent, yet he has Mary go visit Elizabeth who is the first to utter Spirit-inspired words). This is more true of Luke 1—2 than Matthew 1—2, but even in the latter birth narrative we find some anomalies that suggest something other than free creation (e.g., Mt 1:23 says Jesus will be called Immanuel, but no one does so).

All of this suggests that to assume we must choose between either theology or history in this material is to accept a false dichotomy. What we likely have is material of historical substance that has been theologically interpreted so as to bring out its greater significance. Theological history-writing, not historicized theology, might well describe what we find here and throughout the Gospels. Both historical material and theological redaction can be found throughout the Gospels (*see* Gospels [Historical Reliability]).

It is true that the stories surrounding the birth of Jesus record some events in which only one or two people were involved. In such cases this would mean that ultimately if these traditions have historical kernels, they must finally go back to either Mary or Joseph (Laurentin). The assumption of a testimony of the Holy Family, widely held in the church until the twentieth century, can neither be proved nor disproved by the historical critical study of the text. If there was such a testimony or testimonies which circulated not as a whole but in parts, perhaps grouped according to source, it would explain how the Gospel writers had access to such essentially private data as Mary's or Joseph's testimony of their encounters with or dreams about the supernatural. This might also explain why Matthew's Gospel seems to present Joseph's side of the story, while Luke's Gospel presents Mary's. It might suggest that Matthew and Luke had access to only one part of the birth traditions (Feuillet, McHugh).

2. Theological and Redactional Emphases in Matthew 1—2 and Luke 1—2.

Since the major theological and redactional thrusts of

the birth narratives have been amply presented by Brown, we will highlight only some of the more prominent motifs. It is true that in terms of *dramatis personae*, the birth narratives do not focus on Jesus but on those who have contact with the child or his parent(s). Thus, an examination of how the Evangelists portray some of the major figures in these birth stories should tell us a great deal about the authors' emphases and tendencies.

2.1. Matthew. Though the First Evangelist does mention Mary in the genealogy,* it is Joseph and his dreams* that link together the various narratives in Matthew 1—2 (cf. 1:18-25; 2:13; 2:19-23). By contrast, Mary is the linking figure in Luke 1—2 (cf. 1:26-38, 39-56; 2:5-7; 2:19, 34, 39, 48, 51).

The First Evangelist focuses on Joseph's reaction to the divine intervention in Mary's life, and in particular he shows how Joseph is repeatedly led by dreams to do God's* will. It is no accident that, apart from Jesus, only Joseph is called "son of David"* in these stories. He is seen as the typical patriarch who will guide and protect Mary and Jesus as God directs. It is Joseph who is presented to the Evangelist's audience as a model disciple and son of Israel.* He is obedient to the heavenly dreams, but he is also called a righteous (*see* Justice, Righteousness) man (1:19), that is, one who upholds the Law.* Thus, in 1:18-19 he is depicted as caught between the holy Law of God and his love for Mary (McHugh). The intention of the Evangelist is to paint a picture of a devout Jewish man who is willing to give up what was often perceived to be a Jewish father's greatest privilege—siring his first-born son—in order to obey God's will (1:24).

It is possible that this special attention given Joseph is due either to the concern of the author to demonstrate how Jesus became legally a son of David and/or is part of the attempt to show the respectability of Jesus' origins. In this presentation Mary is not only submissive to Joseph's leading, but also completely silent. Thus, it may be that the author reaffirms the traditional Jewish roles of male headship and female subordination, perhaps because he had a Jewish-Christian audience.

The interlude involving the Magi and King Herod (*see* Herodian Dynasty) presents two contrasts: (1) between the spiritually obtuse and those searching; and (2) between the vulnerable babe born King of the Jews who is protected by God, and Herod the oriental tyrant who is protective of his throne but in the end is unable to keep it (2:19). The way these stories are interwoven is by a theological or christological structuring of the material. Thus, Matthew 1 will answer the questions Who and How (Jesus' identity as

son of David and how he came by it), while the second chapter will focus on locales—the "Where" of Jesus' birth and the "Whence" of his destiny (Stendahl, Brown). He is born in Bethlehem, but he is called out of the land of bondage and sent to Israel to begin to call it back to its true destiny. There is more focus on christology proper (Who Jesus is) than on how he became such.

2.2. Luke. The Lukan birth narratives are more complex for several reasons. There is more narrative material and significant characters in the narration. There is also considerably more interest in presenting a connected narrative reflecting on the human drama, in particular the joys and anxieties wrapped up in childbearing. There are two major paeans of praise (1:46-55, 67-79; *see* Mary's Song; Zechariah's Song) and also the shorter *Nunc Dimittis* (2:29-32; *see* Simeon's Song) which help to structure this material. Note that there is no genealogy in the birth or infancy narratives proper.

Luke's birth narratives are in many respects the feminine counterpart to those found in Matthew 1—2, which is not surprising since a full one-third of the uniquely Lukan material in this Gospel is about women (Witherington, 1988). In Luke 1—2 it is Elizabeth and Mary, not Zechariah and Joseph, who are the first to hear of Christ's coming. It is these women who are praised and blessed, and they first sing and prophesy about the Christ child (*see* Women).

It is especially in the speech material that we hear one of Luke's major themes: Jesus' coming means God's liberation for the poor and oppressed amongst Israel (1:54, 68-69; *see* Rich and Poor), but also light* for the Gentiles* (2:32). These songs have been characterized as a reflection of the piety of Jewish *ʿanāwîm* or "poor." But to a large extent this is also how various of the key figures in Luke 1—2 are portrayed—Elizabeth, Mary, Simeon, Anna. All these characters are seen as devout but poor Jews longing for the salvation* God had long since promised them. It appears, however, that Mary is portrayed as more than just a devout Jewess, for she is open to God's new action through her and her son to a degree not true of the others—she alone is said to ponder the implications of all these events. As such, she may be seen as a model disciple. More certainly, Mary is seen as the type of an OT prophetess (cf. 1:46-55), and she represents Israel who willingly obeys God's bidding despite the personal cost. She is God's servant.

The theme of male-female role reversal comes into play in the presentation of Elizabeth and Zechariah. Elizabeth, not Zechariah, is seen as the person of true and full faith, and she gives her child the name the angel indicates (1:60). It is precisely at the point when Zechariah agrees with the action of Elizabeth that he is freed from his dumbness and is able to praise God.

In a sense we also see this reversal in the story of Anna and Simeon. Simeon is content to die, having seen the arrival of the Coming One, but Anna is invigorated to new roles—going forth to testify that redemption and liberation have come in this child (2:36-38). While Anna and Simeon are both old and both representatives of the old order of Jewish piety and of the yearnings of Israel for Messiah (see Christ), their contrasting reactions to seeing Jesus are striking. Note also how Luke frames his infancy narrative with a man and a woman who are connected with the Temple* (1:5-25; 2:22-40). Hence Luke indicates how Jesus affects the very heart of Israel—Jerusalem and the Temple—a theme he will return to near the end of the story.

Luke stresses that it is the women especially who react with exuberance at the coming of their liberator. Recent feminist analysis of Matthew 1—2 and Luke 1—2 has stressed, however, that the new roles of women or new portrayal of women in these stories is nonetheless contained in an essentially patriarchal package which highlights and even celebrates women's distinctively feminine role of childbearing (Anderson). On the other hand, a recent feminist interpretation of Luke 2:41-52 argues that the stress on the Fatherhood of God undermines male dominance by devaluing patriarchal institutions and human fatherhood (Fiorenza; see Liberation Hermeneutics). This conclusion may be doubted and certainly could not be argued on the basis of Matthew 1—2. There it is essential to the author's argument that Joseph be established as legally Jesus' father so he may be counted as a son of David, a theme not absent in Luke (cf. 1:69; 2:11; 3:31).

More play is given to the matter of the virginal conception in Luke 1—2 than in Matthew 1—2, but in both cases it is the fact of the coming of Messiah, not the how, that is stressed. One must not underestimate either the Jewish flavor of both birth narratives or the skill with which the Evangelists have integrated their source material into moving and meaningful presentations about the good news that is and has come in Jesus. The shape of their presentations strikingly differs—even when they use many of the same elements. This in itself demonstrates that the First and Third Evangelists were not rigid editors of their sources, but creative shapers of their material who used their sources to highlight their own theological emphases and successfully integrated this material into the larger schemas of their respective Gospels (cf. Minear, Schubert).

3. Use of OT Prophecy in the Birth Narratives

No other section of the Gospels is so clearly linked to OT prophecy as is Matthew 1—2. This is true not merely because these two chapters bear so many quotations or allusions to the OT, but also because their author uses scriptural language in his narrative and discourses. The very structure of the five pericopes in Matthew 1—2 seems to be determined largely by five formula quotations, which are frequently the focus of scholarly attention (France). Nevertheless, it is the incidents in the story which have led to the collection and structuring of these quotations in their present form (see Old Testament in the Gospels).

Nowhere is it more evident that the story has led the author to an appropriate Scriptural prophecy to relate to it (rather than the Scripture engendering the story itself) than at the close of the birth narrative where we find the problematic but ostensible OT quote "He will be called a Nazarene" (2:23; see Nazarene). The way the author uses these quotes may reflect the midrash* pesher technique, but this is a very different matter than the suggestion that the author's very narrative is an exercise in creative midrash on the OT (Gundry, 1982). Matthew's text for the story is not primarily the OT but a collection of traditions about Jesus' birth which he has reshaped and retold in the light of OT prophecy. The effect of concluding narrative sections by recalling prophecies is that the prophecies seem almost like afterthoughts brought in to confirm information already given in the narrative. In fact, the function of the quotes is to confirm that some rather unusual twists in the story were all along part of God's plan for the coming Messiah.

Notice too that Matthew's narrative action turns on responses to dreams or visions, or to external sources of guidance such as the star. History is shown to reflect a divine schema, or at least God's repeated intervention by various means (words or actions) corrects the course of historical actions or prevents them from going awry. The reshaping of tradition must not be underestimated, but at the same time neither should the author's use of historical sources. France is right to query what fulfillment of the OT might mean to the First Evangelist if in fact he knew that his story was created out of the OT text itself.

Of course the argument could be pushed back one step further, and it could be maintained that the sources the Evangelist received were ahistorical to begin with, a fact he did not comprehend. Two important factors argue against this suggestion. First, various key ideas in these stories are shared in common by Luke and Matthew, such as the betrothed couple Mary and Joseph, the virginal conception, the

Davidic descent of Joseph, the birth in Bethlehem during Herod the Great's reign, the angelic revelation of the name "Jesus" and Jesus' upbringing in Nazareth. These ideas are shared in common *even though* there is even more material in Matthew 1—2/Luke 1—2 that is not shared in common, and this shows that our authors are not likely to have borrowed from each other. Second, the character of the narrative (not the quotations) in Matthew 1—2 and also in Luke 1—2 is not dramatically different from that of the narratives in the rest of these two Gospels, and few would doubt that there are historical sources which lie behind at least some of the ministry material.

One must also recognize, however, that traditions about the birth of Moses, and particularly those found in the Palestinian Targums (*see* Targum), may have affected the way Matthew words his narrative and presents Jesus (Bourke), just as it is likely that various sorts of OT prophetic material have affected the presentation in the Lukan birth narratives (cf. Mal 3:1-3; Dan 9).

Apart from the songs in Luke 1—2, the influence of the OT is less immediately apparent in the Lukan birth narratives than is the case with Matthew 1—2. Nevertheless, it may be reflected in (1) the Septuagintalisms in Luke 1—2 (i.e., use of the language of the Greek OT, especially in the Annunciation to Mary); (2) the focus on women and the importance to them of the birth of a son to whom divine promises are attached (cf. the OT stories about Sarah, Hannah and others); (3) the importance of the naming of the child and the significance of the name given; and (4) the stress on the miraculous means by which conception was announced and then took place, thus emphasizing fulfillment of the divine word.

The first of the Matthean formula quotations and the most important for our purposes is the citation of Isaiah 7:14 at Matthew 1:23. The following observations are crucial.

First, the pre-Christian interpretation of Isaiah 7:14 seems to have seen its fulfillment in Hezekiah, the son and successor of Ahaz. Apparently, there is no evidence that any early Jew saw this as a prophecy about Messiah, much less a prophecy about a virginal conception. The Targums do tend to interpret Isaiah 9:5-6 messianically, but it is not clear that they view Isaiah 7:14 in a similar light.

Second, the Hebrew term *'almâh* which is used in Isaiah 7:14 (MT) refers to a young woman of marriageable age. Though the idea of virginity is probably implicit in the term, this is not a technical term for *virgo intacta*. The Hebrew *b'tûlâ* comes nearer to being such a term (Wenham).

Third, the term *'almâh* is never used in the OT of a married woman, but does refer to a sexually mature woman. There are no texts in the OT where *'almâh* clearly means one who is sexually active, but it is possible that Song of Solomon 6:8 (cf. Prov 30:19) implies this. It would appear then that *'almâh* normally, if not always, implies a virgin, though the term does not focus on that attribute.

Fourth, several of the Greek translations of the OT (i.e., Aq, Sym, Theod) translate *'almâh* with *neanis;* however, the LXX clearly translates it with *parthenos.* It is probably correct to say that if *'almâh* did not normally have overtones of virginity, it is difficult if not impossible to see why the translators of the LXX used *parthenos* as the Greek equivalent.

Fifth, the Hebrew texts speak of "the young woman," so the prophet has some particular person in view.

Sixth, the Greek term *parthenos* seems to mean or strongly imply one who is a virgin, but this may not always be the case. In the LXX of Genesis 34:3, Dinah is called a *parthenos* even though the story is about her being seduced by Shechem. It should be noted, however, that after the rape Dinah is called a *paidiskē* (34:4). This text then *may* imply that *parthenos* sometimes has a meaning broader than "virgin" (cf. Gen 24:16, 43, 57 MT and LXX), and it is clear that it can be virtually equivalent to *'almâh* on occasion (Gen 24:43). It may be debated whether in some rare cases *parthenos* may even mean something *other* than a virgin (cf. Dodd, Carmignac). One must conclude that Matthew did not deduce the idea of a virginal conception from the Isaianic prophecy, though given a prior belief in such an idea, this text became an appropriate vehicle to express the idea in prophetic language.

Space does not allow a further treatment of all the formula quotations in Matthew 1—2 (cf. Gundry), but mention should be made of the citation of Micah 5:2 in Matthew 2:6. It is a curious fact that while it is Matthew who cites this text, he never refers to the shepherd tradition that Luke records, nor does he make anything of Jesus being a shepherd figure like David.

The Third Evangelist offers us no formula quotations comparable to what we find in Matthew, and when he does cite the OT in Luke 1—2, it is both brief and enigmatic (cf. 2:23-24 citing Ex 13:2, 12, 15 and Lev 12:8). On the other hand, various of the speeches/songs in Luke 1—2 are redolent with OT language and are written in the spirit of OT prophecy (cf. Lk 1:46-55, 67-79; 2:29-32). In general, however, Luke's narrative is not structured on the basis of OT citations or allusions, nor does it stress the issue of fulfilled prophecy in the manner of Matthew 1—2.

4. Genealogies in Matthew and Luke.

Over the past twenty years scholars have spent a great deal of energy trying to unravel the mysteries of Jesus' two very different genealogies (*see* Genealogy). Since at least the time of Annius of Viterbo in A.D. 1490 it has been traditional to assume that Matthew's genealogy traces Jesus' lineage through Joseph (his legal genealogy), whereas Luke's genealogy traces his lineage through Mary (his natural genealogy).

This conjecture finds some support from the fact that the Matthean birth narrative focuses more on the role of Joseph than of Mary, while Luke's narrative makes Mary the more central figure in the drama. It also comports with the ancient conjecture that Joseph is ultimately the source of much of the Matthean birth narratives, while Mary is the source for most of Luke's material. The theory that Luke presents Jesus' lineage through Mary requires not only that one take the phrase "as was supposed of Joseph" (*hōs enomizeto*, 3:23a) as a parenthetical remark, but even more awkwardly it requires that the author use the word "son" (*huios*, 3:23b) to mean both son and grandson in the same breath, and leave out any mention of Mary's name!

Another theory which has gained some currency in recent debate is the view that Matthew presents the royal or legal genealogy, whereas Luke presents David's actual physical descendants. In view of the fact that there were ancient king lists that would only trace the line of succession, and selectively at that, this conjecture is not impossible, but unfortunately there is no way either to prove or disprove this theory. R. P. Nettlehorst has revived the theory that we have two genealogies from Joseph's side of the family, but he reverses one part of the usual conjecture and maintains that Luke traces the line through Joseph's father while Matthew traces the line through Joseph's maternal grandfather. None of these theories are free of difficulties. Since we do not have enough information to settle the issue, we can only show which conjectures are more or less probable.

4.1. Comparisons and Contrasts. One cannot help but be impressed with the notable differences in the two genealogies, differences which suggest they were deliberately schematized to serve rather different purposes in their respective Gospels. If so, then it may be counter-productive to treat them in the same manner as one would modern genealogies or try to reconcile the one genealogy with the other.

Some noteworthy differences may be listed. In Matthew (1) the genealogy introduces the Gospel, and in particular the birth narratives, and traces the line down from Abraham through Joseph to Jesus, using the term "begot" (*egennēsen*); (2) there is an artificial division of the names into three groups of fourteen; (3) there is a notable insertion of several women and possibly some brothers; (4) there is omission of various names; (5) there is an awkward circumlocution at the end of the genealogy reflecting the author's belief in a virginal conception.

By contrast Luke's genealogy (1) follows the baptism* and introduces the ministry of Jesus and thus, properly speaking, is not part of the birth narratives; (2) repeatedly uses the phrase "the son of" without any verbs, and traces the line from Jesus up to Adam and God; (3) begins with a circumlocution indicating the author's knowledge that Jesus was not really Joseph's son, and in fact omits the article before Joseph's name (which might place Joseph's name outside the actual list); (4) inserts a *Rhēsa* and an extra *Kainan* into the genealogical list (cf. Gen 10:24; 11:12; and 1 Chron 1:24).

On the surface it would appear that Matthew's genealogy is trying to show Jesus as a true Israelite, and in particular of Davidic descent, while Luke is trying to show that Jesus is truly a human being. This might account for some of the differences in form and content between the genealogies we encounter. In both genealogies, however, the primary point is to say or explain something to the audience about Jesus and his character, not so much about his ancestors (Witherington, 1988).

4.2. Theological Purposes. Several features of the Matthean genealogy call for special attention. The Matthean genealogy should be seen in light of the pericope that follows (1:18-25). Taken together this material focuses on Jesus as both son of David (*see* Son of David) and son of God (*see* Son of God), themes which are developed elsewhere. Matthew 1:18-25 is probably meant to explain the genealogy and in particular how Jesus could be born of Mary, but not of Joseph, and yet still be in the Davidic line (Stendahl). This means that the genealogy and the pericope that follows it assume, and to some extent attempt to explain, the virginal conception. There seems to be a recognition of the difficulties involved in the nature of Jesus' irregular origins and thus this material may be seen as an attempt at apologetics in light of Matthew's acceptance of the virginal conception. This in part explains the anomaly of including several women* in the genealogy, for it was unusual to list women in a genealogy *unless* the father was unknown, or when sons from one patriarch came from his union with different wives, or if the women were related to or were famous figures (as here).

Matthew's genealogy mentions not only Mary but four other women as well. Various theories have been advanced to explain the presence of women—in particular Tamar, Rahab, Ruth and Bathsheba—in the genealogy of Jesus.

First, it has been conjectured that the author is trying to identify Jesus with Gentiles and sinners, but it is not clear that all these women fit into one or both of these categories.

Second, possibly these women were subjects of controversy in the Jewish debate about Messiah. This is difficult, if not impossible, to prove for all four of these women; and in any case some of the data used to make such a case is later than the NT period.

Third, maybe the author mentions these four women because he wants to show how not only Jesus but other Davidic kings had irregularities in their past and yet were God's anointed ones. The problem with this conjecture is that it would seem not to illuminate and exonerate the Christian stories about Jesus' origins, but cast them and the stories about Jesus' ancestors under the same cloud of suspicion.

Finally, it has been urged that the point of these four women being mentioned is that they were vehicles of God's messianic plan *despite* their irregular unions. This view is perhaps the least inadequate (Johnson). Thus, it appears our author wishes by this genealogy to call attention to Mary as an instrument of God's messianic plan (and the source of Jesus' humanity) and to show Jesus' indebtedness to women as well as men for his Davidic ancestry.

By contrast Luke's genealogy attempts to place Jesus in the broader context of humanity in general rather than Judaism in particular. This is only natural since Luke is writing for a Gentile audience and wishes to show that Jesus is for them as well. It is worth noting, however, that Jesus is presented as the ideal human who not only is one with all humanity but also grows in wisdom* and stature and is to be seen as the model of how a person should relate to God, others, temptation* and other aspects of discipleship.* It is possible that Jesus is being portrayed by Luke as the new Adam, the initiator of a new race of human beings, the difference being that this Adam—unlike the first—is an obedient son of God. Perhaps more importantly, Luke probably added the words "son of God" at the end of a Jewish list he acquired, for it was not Jewish practice to call someone son of God in a genealogy. There is then stress not only on Jesus' full humanity (a son of Adam) but also on his origins ultimately being from God (a son of God).

It will be seen that both in the case of Matthew and Luke these genealogies serve primarily theological and christological purposes and only secondarily historical ones. Our authors were not concerned to present detailed or exhaustive lists of Jesus' actual ancestors, but only to highlight some aspects of his heritage which would best illuminate for their respective audiences Jesus' significance and nature.

5. The Date of Jesus' Birth.
The reckoning of time in antiquity went through a variety of changes until Julius Caesar, on the basis of the Egyptian solar calendar, standardized a 365-day year with an extra day inserted on leap years. Both the church and the Western world followed this method of reckoning time until the reforms of Pope Gregory XIII promulgated on February 24, 1582. Since that time the Gregorian calendar has been followed.

In A.D. 525, when Pope John I asked a Scythian monk named Dionysius to prepare a standard calendar for the Western Church that would be reckoned from the birthdate of Christ, Dionysius relied both on the Julian calendar and on available information about the date of the founding of the city of Rome to compute the birthdate of Christ. In Dionysius' calendar, A.D. 1 was set at 754 A.U.C. (*anno urbis conditae*, i.e., from the founding of the city of Rome), with Jesus' birthday being set as 25 December 753 A.U.C. Unfortunately, Dionysius miscalculated the birth of Jesus, for the Gospels state that Jesus was born during the reign of Herod the Great, who died before the turn of the era (estimates range from about 4 to 1 B.C.). Thus, historically, we come up with the anomaly of Jesus being born several years B.C.

Several key factors in the Gospels provide help in determining more precisely the birthdate of Jesus (*see* Chronology): (1) the date of Herod's death; (2) possibly the date of the census of Quirinius which Luke uses as a synchronism (Lk 2:1-2); (3) possibly the date Luke assigns to the beginning of the Baptist's ministry (Lk 3:1) coupled with the reference to Jesus' approximate age (Lk 3:23); and (4) possibly the astral phenomenon the Magi are said to have seen *if* that phenomenon was the result of a natural occurrence (e.g., a conjunction of planets).

5.1. Herod's Death. In order to reckon the date of Herod the Great's death, evidence that is primarily literary and numismatic must be considered. Josephus tells us that Herod the Great was proclaimed King of Judea by the Romans when Calvinus and Pollio were proconsuls, or in late 40 B.C. (*Ant.* 14.381-85; *J.W.* 1.282-85; Tacitus *Hist.* 5.9). He then adds that Herod (*see* Herodian Dynasty) reigned for thirty-seven years from the time of that proclamation (*Ant.* 17.191; *J.W.*

1.665.). There is considerable debate as to whether Josephus was reckoning according to solar years, or following the accession-year chronology (Herod did not gain possession of his domain until 37 B.C.). There is also the question of whether or not he was counting inclusively, that is, reckoning partial years as whole years.

Most scholars are still persuaded by the work of E. Schürer (cf. Bernegger, Hoehner) that Josephus is correct about the time of Herod's accession and the length of his reign. This would place the death of Herod at about 3 B.C. However, Josephus also tells us that an eclipse of the moon occurred shortly before Herod's death (*Ant.* 17.167), and in view of the fact that this is the only time Josephus mentions this sort of phenomenon, it is improbable that he fabricated this piece of information. There were no such eclipses in 3 B.C., but there was one on March 12/13, 4 B.C. He also informs us that Passover was celebrated shortly after Herod's death (*Ant.* 17.213; *J.W.* 2.10). In 4 B.C. the first day of Passover would have been April 11. Thus, it is likely Herod died between March 12 and April 11, 4 B.C. and presumably the discrepancy of one year is accounted for by inclusive reckoning of regnal years. This means that Jesus was born sometime before March of 4 B.C.

The numismatic evidence is complex, but we do know that Herod's first coin was dated "Year 3." This coin was minted perhaps shortly after his final capture of Jerusalem in 37 B.C., thus backdating his reign to the time in 40 B.C. when the Romans proclaimed him to be ruler of Judea (cf. Edmonds). This evidence also places Herod's death at about 3 B.C., but here again the question of inclusive reckoning of years arises, which would seem to allow the possibility of 4 B.C.

5.2. Census under Quirinius. For those who believe that the Gospels are accurate historical records of Jesus' life, one of the most difficult problems in the NT is the census Luke presents in 2:1-2. First, there is no evidence for an empire-wide census being taken during the time of Augustus, and we might expect that such a mammoth undertaking would have been mentioned by one or another of the ancient historians who recorded the period.

Second, Quirinius was sent by Augustus to be governor of Syria (and Judea) in A.D. 6 (not 6 B.C.) and thereafter did take a notable census for the empire. Josephus tells us he visited Judea in 6-7 A.D. to assess the property of the Jews in preparation for the registering and taxing of that property (*Ant.* 18.1.1-2.). There is no evidence that he was governor of the region twice or that he undertook a census of the region twice. It has been suggested that Luke may

have confused Quirinius with P. Quintilius Varus who was legate of Syria during the period 6-3 B.C. Against this is the fact that Luke was apparently knowledgeable about Latin names and would have known a *cognomen* (Quirinius) from a mere *nomen* (Quintilius).

Third, a Roman census would not have required Jews to travel to their ancestral home for registration. In any case, is it probable that the Romans would undertake such a census in a client state that already had its own ruler (Herod)?

In response to these problems various answers have been given. In the first place, if there was a census that affected Judea during the reign of Herod the Great, it would probably proceed along the lines of a Jewish census, not a Roman one. In that case it is plausible that Jews would return to their ancestral homes and that both adults would go (especially if Mary was also of Davidic descent). Second, elsewhere Luke manifests a knowledge of the later census by Quirinius which prompted the revolt of Judas the Galilean in A.D. 6-7 (Acts 5:37). Is it likely that he would have confused this census, which he knew to be a later one, with one during the reign of Herod?

Third, it is not certain that Luke in 2:1 means that Augustus took one enormous census of the whole empire. The language is general and may mean no more than that the various parts of the empire were subject to various censuses during the time of Augustus. What the Greek in fact says is that Caesar decreed that "all of the Roman world be enrolled" (Thorley). Both the present tense of *apographō* ("to enroll") and the use of *pas* ("all") suggest that Luke means that Caesar decreed that the enrollment, which had previously been going on in some parts of the empire, should now be extended to all parts, including client states. The Roman historian A. N. Sherwin-White states, "A census or taxation-assessment of the whole provincial empire . . . was certainly accomplished for the first time in history under Augustus" (168-69).

Fourth, there is some evidence of a census of Judea under Saturninus between 9-6 B.C. (cf. Tertullian *Adv. Marc.* 4.19). We also know that Quirinius undertook more than one census during his governorship, and that he did not scruple to enroll a basically autonomous group such as the Apameans.

Fifth, Luke's precise wording in 2:2 is curious, and could mean either that he is referring to the *first* or *former* census that was taken under Quirinius' rule of Syria (which would perhaps imply that this was an earlier census than the one mentioned in Acts 5:37), or it is grammatically possible that *prōtē* means something like "prior to" or "before" in which case Luke is speaking of a census undertaken by someone else *prior* to the [more famous or infamous] census under Quirinius which led to Jewish revolt. Such a comparative use of *prōte* is not unprecedented, but grammatically there are problems with such a view.

Thus it is more probable that Luke is referring to a census under Quirinius that took place prior to the famous one in A.D. 6-7. If so, we have no clear record outside Luke of such an action by Quirinius, though it is not impossible that it took place. Herod's power was on the wane at the time of Jesus' birth, and a census in preparation for the change of power could well have been forced on Herod since he had fallen into some disfavor with Augustus near the end of his life. We know also that Quirinius had been made consul in 12 B.C. and a person of his rank serving in the East frequently had far-reaching authority and duties. It is thus not improbable that, acting as Caesar's agent, he had Herod take a census. It is also possible he was governor more than once in Syria, though the possibility also remains that Luke may be identifying him by his later and, to his audience, more familiar office. It is less likely that Luke means that Quirinius started a census in 6 B.C. and finished it in 6-7 A.D., for he says that this was the first census the governor took (distinguishing it from some later one). The upshot of all this is that Luke's reference to the census does not suggest a different date for Jesus' birth than does the Matthean evidence.

5.3. John the Baptist.

Luke also tells us that John the Baptist* began his ministry during the fifteenth year of Tiberius' reign. Since Augustus died in the summer of A.D. 14 and Tiberius assumed the throne later that year, this would place John's ministry about A.D. 29, though possibly it might be reckoned as early as A.D. 27 (Hoehner). It is uncertain how long it was after John began his ministry that Jesus began his, but both the Lukan narrative (Lk 3) as well as Mark 1:14 suggest that John's ministry came first. Luke then tells us that Jesus was about thirty years old when he began his ministry. The Greek word *hōsei* indicates an approximation or round number which would allow for a few years on either side.

If Jesus did begin his ministry by working with or at the same time as the Baptist, as the Johannine tradition suggests (cf. Jn 3:22-30), and if rabbinic tradition is correct in saying that Jesus was age 33-34 when he began his ministry (*b. Sanh.* 106b), Jesus' ministry may have begun as early as A.D. 29, if not shortly before then. This would mean that Jesus was born about 4 B.C. or perhaps a bit earlier. Both Luke 1 and independently Matthew 2 are in agreement in placing the birth of Jesus during the reign of Herod, and Luke informs us John was also born under that reign.

5.4. Astral Phenomenon.

Those scholars who have insisted that the astral phenomenon should be primary in determining the date of Jesus' birth have had to deal with a multitude of problems. First of all, it is not clear that the First Evangelist intends some sort of purely natural phenomenon. In Matthew 2 it says both that the Magi saw the star at its rising, which presumably is what led them to Jerusalem (whether from the east or west is not clear), and then at 2:9 we are told that when they left Jerusalem "the star . . . went ahead of them until it stopped over the place where the child was." The text seems to suggest that the "star" led them not merely to Bethlehem (and why would they need such leading just for the six-mile trek from Jerusalem to Bethlehem?) but to the precise location of Jesus. This hardly sounds like a normal astral phenomenon, and certainly not one that could be identified with either a conjunction of planets or a comet.

Kepler long ago rejected the theory that it was a conjunction of planets, though there was a notable conjunction of Jupiter and Saturn in 7 B.C. in the constellation Pisces, and it is also true that both the Berlin Star Table and the Sippar Star Almanac indicate great interest and close study of planetary movements during 7 B.C. and afterwards (Brown). Modern astronomers have stressed that the conjunction of Jupiter and Saturn in question was not close enough to appear to be a single star (Boa and Proctor). E. L. Martin's careful and detailed study argues for the year of Herod's death as 1 B.C. and the star being the conjunction of Venus and Jupiter seen from August 12, 3 B.C. onward. He further urges that the Magi did not come to honor Jesus until fifteen months after his birth (on December 25, 2 B.C.) and that at that time Jupiter had stopped over Bethlehem in the meridian position in the constellation of the Virgin. There are, however, many assumptions made in these calculations, and most scholars would reject such a late date for Herod's death (but cf. Thorley). Another theory appeals to the appearance of Halley's comet, which took place in the region in 12 B.C.—a date too early to be correlated with Jesus' birth.

Kepler's own theory that the Magi witnessed a supernova or the birth of a new star is possible, especially since Chinese astronomers did record such a nova for 5/4 B.C. (France). It is interesting that some early Christians thought that only a supernatural explanation of the "star" would suffice, for in the Arabic Infancy Gospel 7 the star is identified with an angel.

In short, it is doubtful that natural astral phenomena can help us pinpoint the time of Jesus's birth. There are various imponderables about the story of the Magi that make calculations almost impossible (e.g., how long after Jesus' birth did the Magi come and honor him?). Most scholars who consider the story of the Magi historically possible would stress that there seems to have been an interval, perhaps over a year, between the time of the birth and the coming of the Magi. Taking all the evidence together it appears that Jesus was born in or before 4 B.C.

In regard to the day of Jesus' birth, as early as Hippolytus (A.D. 165-235) it was said to be December 25, a date also set by John Chrysostom (A.D. 345-407) whose arguments prevailed in the Eastern Church. There is nothing improbable about a mid-winter birth. Luke 2:8 tells us that the shepherds' flocks were kept outside when Jesus was born. This detail might favor a date between March and November when such animals would normally be outside. But the Mishnah (*m. šeqal.* 7.4) suggests that sheep around Bethlehem might also be outside during the winter months (Hoehner). Therefore, though there is no certainty, it appears that Jesus was born somewhere between 4-6 B.C., perhaps in mid-winter. Both the traditional Western date for Christmas (Dec. 25) and the date observed by the Armenian Church (Jan. 6) are equally possible. The biblical and extra-biblical historical evidence is simply not specific enough to point decisively to either traditional date. The celebration of the nativity is attested in Rome as early as A.D. 336 and this celebration also involved recognizing January 6 as Epiphany, the day the Magi visited Jesus.

6. The Location of Jesus' Birth.

Both the First and Third Gospels, probably based on independent sources, inform us that Jesus was born in Bethlehem, the City of David. While it is possible that this location was chosen by the Evangelists because of the prophecy found in Micah 5:2, only the First Evangelist makes anything of this connection, and it is only he that makes very much of Jesus being *a* or *the* son of David in his Gospel. It is likely that the reference to Bethlehem, at least in the case of Luke's Gospel, is historical in character. It is also worth pointing out that even in the First Gospel, it appears that the quotations, such as that found in Matthew 2:6, have been worked by the Evangelist into his source material, in which case it is likely on the basis of Matthew 2:1a that the reference to Bethlehem existed in the source used by the First Evangelist (France). In short, the source material led the Evangelist to use the Micah quotation, not vice versa.

The question of the specific location of Jesus' birth is an intriguing one. Matthew 2:11 mentions that the Magi found Jesus in a house (*oikos*), but this may have

transpired some time after the birth itself and in a different location. Later Christian tradition unfortunately has tended to amalgamate the visit of the Shepherds and the Magi, locating both at the site of Jesus' birth. In reality, Matthew says nothing about shepherds and Luke nothing about Magi, and only the former are connected with a scene involving a manger.

Luke 2:7 should be seen in light of the larger context of Luke 2:4-7, which does *not* suggest that Mary went into labor immediately or even shortly after she and Joseph arrived in Bethlehem. To the contrary, we are told that "while they were there" (not upon arrival) the days were fulfilled and Mary went into labor. This implies that they had been in Bethlehem for some unspecified amount of time prior to Mary going into labor. Thus the familiar image of Mary and Joseph arriving in Bethlehem and being unable to find a place to stay on the night of arrival probably has no basis in the text itself (Bailey).

A second crucial point is how one translates *kataluma* in Luke 2:7. The word can mean guest room, house or inn. It can be doubted whether there would have been an inn in Bethlehem in Jesus' day since it was not on any major road, and inns normally were to be found only on major roads, especially the Roman ones (but cf. Jer 41:17, which does not refer to a place *in* Bethlehem). Furthermore, when Luke wants to speak of a commercial inn he uses *pandocheion;* 10:34 refers to an establishment found on the major road between Jerusalem and Jericho. Also, when Luke uses the word *kataluma* in his Gospel (22:11 and par.; cf. 1 Kings 1:18), it clearly does not mean an inn but a guest room. It is also worth pointing out that the Arabic and Syriac versions of the NT have never translated *kataluma* as inn.

It becomes more likely that by *kataluma* Luke means either house or guest room, and the latter translation must have the edge precisely because in the vast majority of ancient Near-Eastern peasant homes for which we have archaeological and literary evidence, the manger was *within* the home, not in some separate barn. The animals as well as the family slept within one large enclosed space that was divided so that usually the animals would be on a lower level, and the family would sleep on a raised dais (Bailey). In this particular case, we should probably envision Mary and Joseph staying in the home of relatives or friends, a home which was crowded due to the census being taken, a home where Luke tells us there was no longer any room in "*the* guest room" (noting the definite article before the noun). Consequently, Mary gave birth to her child perhaps in the family room and placed the baby in the stone manger. This means that a good deal of the popular conception of this scene has no basis in the text. In particular, the idea of Mary and Joseph being cast out from civilized accommodations and taking up temporary residence in a barn is probably based on a misunderstanding of the text.

There is also a tradition cited in the second century A.D. by Justin Martyr that Joseph and Mary, being unable to find accommodations in Bethlehem, took up quarters in a cave near the village (*Dial. Tryph.* 79). This is a plausible conjecture, and in fact various peasants did make their homes in caves during the time of Jesus. But Luke suggests neither that the Holy Family took up residence outside the city, nor that they were in a cave (and Luke would hardly have spoken of a cave with a guest room).

7. The Virginal Conception.
Even in the twentieth century the virginal conception is still the subject of a debate which shows no signs of abating (Cranfield, Bostock, Benson). What is at issue is a virginal conception, not a virgin birth, and so the technically correct term will be used in this section (Brown, 1973).

In our discussion of the genre of the birth narratives we noted that any comparison of Matthew 1—2 and Luke 1—2 to pagan divine birth stories leads to the conclusion that the Gospel stories cannot be explained simply on the basis of such comparisons. This is particularly the case in regard to the matter of the virginal conception, for what we find in Matthew and Luke is not the story of some sort of sacred marriage (*hieros gamos*) or a divine being descending to earth and, in the guise of a man, mating with a human woman, but rather the story of a miraculous conception without aid of any man, divine or otherwise. The Gospel story is rather about how Mary conceived without any form of intercourse through the agency of the Holy Spirit.* As such this story is without precedent either in Jewish or pagan literature, even including the OT (Machen).

It is doubtful that the idea of a virginal conception was part of Jewish messianic expectations in or before the era when the Gospels were written (McHugh). While it may be that Jewish infancy narratives influenced the Evangelists in some respects, they did not derive the idea of the virginal conception from those sources (*see* Miracle and Miracle Stories).

7.1. The Issue of Historicity. There are also serious problems for those who maintain that the virginal conception is a theological idea without basis in historical fact. It is difficult if not impossible to explain why Christians would create so many problems for themselves and invite the charge of Jesus' illegitimate birth by promulgating such an idea if it had no historical basis. The reality of the charge of illegitimacy was well known in the time of Origen, but it may have existed even in the time the Gospels were written (cf. Jn 8:41; Mk 6:3; Stauffer). It is also evident that both Luke and the First Evangelist felt under some constraint to refer to the virginal conception, even to the point of awkwardly alluding to the concept in their genealogies.

One must also explain why this idea was accepted so widely by Christians in the early second century. Ignatius of Antioch is very matter-of-fact about the idea (*Smyrn.* 1:1). While it might be argued that at least in the case of Matthew he derived the idea from Isaiah 7:14, even this is unlikely. As we have already pointed out, neither the Hebrew '*almâh* nor the Greek *parthenos* are simply technical terms for a *virgo intacta*, though certainly the terms may imply or even point to virginity in some cases. The point is that even in the LXX version of Isaiah 7:14 the text itself would not lead one to come up with such an idea, for it would normally be understood to mean that a young woman of marriageable age, who had previously never had a child, would conceive and give birth.

Furthermore, it is not certain that the virginal conception is known only to the First and Third Evangelists. Even if that were true, we would have *two* likely independent witnesses to the idea. That Paul uses *ginomai* rather than *gennaō* in Romans 1:3 may reflect a knowledge of the virginal conception, as may several other Pauline texts (Gal 4:4; Phil 2:7; cf. Cranfield). It is also possible that John 1:13 and 6:41-42 reflect a knowledge of this idea. Perhaps more plausible is the conjecture that Mark 6:3 reflects a knowledge that Jesus was not physically the son of Joseph. Although calling a person a son of his mother is not without some precedent in the Bible (cf. 1 Chron 2:16), it is quite unusual and in a patriarchal culture may well have had a pejorative thrust (Russell, Stauffer). Whether or not this material outside the First and Third Gospels reflects a knowledge of the virginal conception, few would dispute that we do have such an idea in both Matthew and Luke (but cf. Bostock).

7.1.1. Matthew. Matthew 1:18-25 may be seen in part as an explanation of Matthew's genealogical statement about Jesus' birth through Mary in Matthew 1:16. But Matthew 1:18 immediately confronts us with an exegetical difficulty. In the phrase *prin ē sunelthein* we find an expression of a limitation. The question is, does the phrase, which literally says "before they came together," mean "before they had marital union," or "before they married and cohabited." The former would imply that Mary and Joseph consummated their marriage after the birth of Jesus; the latter translation does not necessarily connote sexual sharing.

Under normal circumstances in a Jewish setting it is difficult to imagine a Jew or Jewish Christian separating the idea of marriage and its physical consummation, but many scholars, mostly Catholic, will contend that we are not dealing with a normal state of affairs (Laurentin). The point of this verse, however, is to make clear that Joseph could in no way have been responsible for siring Jesus. Jesus is the result of God's creative act in Mary alone. It is interesting that the First Evangelist is only interested in Joseph's conduct until the birth, so that it may be seen that Jesus was born of a virgin as prophecy foretold.

More crucial for our purposes is Matthew 1:25. The textual problem at this point is not major. Only Codex Bobiensis and the Sinaitic Syriac omit the key clause, *ouk eginōsken autēn heōs ou*, probably because certain scribes thought this clause might imply that Mary had other children by Joseph, or at least had sexual relations with him after the birth of Jesus. The verb "to know" is in the imperfect and thus implies the duration of time Joseph did not have sexual relations with Mary. The stress is on what was the case prior to the birth of Jesus, but the phrase "he used not to" or "he was not knowing her until" at least *implies* that the previously abstained from action later took place. Neither the grammatical nor lexical evidence supports the attempts to take *heōs* to mean something like "while" or "without" in the case of Matthew 1:25, when it precedes an aorist indicative verb and follows an imperfect. The translation "while" is only possible with a verb in the subjunctive. The meaning of *heōs* without *ou* is not relevant here. Thus Mary's virginity *ante partum* is affirmed here, but her virginity *post partum* is likely ruled out.

The mention of Jesus' brothers and sisters (e.g., Mk 6:3), who are never called by the Greek word for cousins, would also militate against the possibility of a perpetual virginity. But this idea must in no way be confused with the concept of the virginal conception. Nor should the later Catholic idea of the immaculate conception of Mary by her mother, of which the Gospels know nothing, be confused with the virginal conception by Mary. The First Evangelist simply affirms the virginal conception as a result of the action of the Holy Spirit in Mary but does not go into any detail about the nature of this miracle in the same way Luke does.

7.1.2. Luke. The crux of the Lukan story is found in 1:34-35, but it must be kept in mind that Luke has already told us at 1:27 that Mary was a virgin. Scholars have generally distinguished Mary's "how" question from the "how" question of Zechariah in 1:18. The latter seems to reflect doubt on Zechariah's part, while the former seems to be a request by Mary for explanation as to how the promised event will transpire. It is also true that "how" questions are characteristic of biblical annunciation stories and there is no doubt that our author has shaped this story in light of OT precedents. It is rarely disputed that *ginoskō* has a sexual connotation here, but the question is how to interpret the present tense—whether as "I have not known before now," "I do not know at present" or "I do not intend to know" (eternal present).

The problems with the theory that Mary here takes a vow to virginity are as follows: (1) Luke portrays Mary as reflecting the normal Jewish mindset concerning marriage and children (1:48); (2) Mary has *already* entered the process of Jewish marriage; (3) Jewish views of virginity in the relevant period do not support the idea that Jewish women who were engaged might take a vow to virginity; and (4) Luke's audience could hardly have understood our text to mean this without additional information.

One should probably understand Mary's words to mean that she wondered how this conception would transpire in the immediate present or near future since she was still in the betrothal period and had not yet had sexual relations with Joseph. The response of the angel explains that Mary will conceive through the agency of the Holy Spirit. The second verb in verse 35—*episkiazō*—likely has the meaning of "to overshadow" in the sense of protecting, especially if there is an allusion here to the Shekinah glory cloud of God's divine presence (Lk 9:34). This latter verb is not likely a reference to divine impregnation, but rather divine protection during the encounter with the Holy Spirit which results in conception. It may be that Luke intends for us to see here the beginning of the eschatological reversal of the curse on Eve (Gen 3:16). In any case, one or both of these verbs refer to the virginal conception.

There is nothing in the narrative that follows Luke 1:34-35 to suggest that Mary had anything other than a normal pregnancy and delivery. Indeed, the story in 2:22-40 about the trip to the Temple so that Mary could perform the ceremony of purification in fulfillment of the Law (Lev 12:8) suggests that Luke thought Mary had a normal delivery and required ritual cleansing. Luke tells us a bit more than Matthew about the process that resulted in the virginal conception, but basically both writers maintain a discrete silence about the details. They affirm the virginal conception and alter their respective genealogies accordingly (Lk 1:23; Mt 1:16), but they are mainly concerned with the *fact* that Messiah has come and the significance of the event. Only secondarily do they show interest in *how* his coming was made possible. Furthermore, neither Evangelist ever directly refers to the matter again once the story of the ministry begins. When all is said and done, it is easier to explain the Gospel evidence on the assumption that the virginal conception was an historical event that the Gospel writers tried to explain, rather than to assume it was a theologoumenon.

7.2. The Meaning of the Event. The significance of this event should not be minimized. It indicates not merely that Jesus was God's Son through the Holy Spirit (Brown, 1973), but that Jesus was a unique person who was the product of both the divine and the human in a manner unlike any others before or since. To be sure, our two authors do not try to address the relationship of a virginal conception to the doctrine of the incarnation of a pre-existent Son, but it may be that the author of John 1 later saw that the two concepts were connected (cf. Jn 1:13).

In terms of its theological significance, the virginal conception explains *how* the incarnation transpired, though Matthew and Luke do not speak of the event in terms of the incarnation of a pre-existent being (Fuller). Later theological reflection was also to see in the virginal conception the explanation of how Jesus could be born with a human nature not tainted with original sin. The doctrine of the virginal conception also stresses that Jesus was fully human, participating in the whole human life cycle from womb to tomb.

But perhaps most significantly of all, this concept conveys the fact that Jesus is a miraculous gift to humanity, not initially the product of any normal human activity or process. He is a gift that comes ultimately from God, but comes through Mary in a way that allows one to say that Jesus' origins are both human and divine. It is clear that if Jesus had indeed been illegitimate, it would hardly have been possible for Luke with any personal integrity to present Jesus' conception as a greater miracle than that of John the Baptist's (contra Hellwig), nor for Matthew to see in Jesus' conception something so holy that a righteous man like Joseph could be persuaded to accept it and accept Jesus as his legal son and thus as a son of David.

Both narratives collapse without the assumption of a virginal conception. Furthermore, the arguments of both Evangelists about the theological significance of

Jesus' origins are predicated on the assumption by both writers of the historical reality of the virginal conception. Otherwise there would be no need for the sort of apologetics and adjustments of genealogies that we find in these narratives.

8. The Magi and the Shepherds.
Though Christian tradition and art have frequently depicted both shepherds* and Magi visiting the newborn Jesus simultaneously, they are never associated or mentioned in the same breath within the Gospels. Luke betrays no hint of knowing about the Magi, nor does the First Evangelist ever mention shepherds. We may deduce from this that the stories about these different participants came from separate sources.

8.1. The Magi. The traditions about the Magi as we find them in Matthew do not refer to kings, but rather to astrologers and/or wise men, and the text says nothing about there being three of them, nor are they named. The term Magi comes to us by way of the Latin (the plural of *Magus*) but ultimately goes back to the Greek *magos* and refers to a magician, sorcerer or one wise in interpreting the stars and/or dreams (hence the translation "wise men"). In ancient Media and Persia these Magi were often associated with the priestly caste, and it has often been assumed in Christian tradition that these men came from Persia to find the Christ.

Other conjectures about the Magi's origins have included various parts of Arabia, and it has even been speculated that they might have come from Asia Minor. This conjecture is based on the phrase "we saw his star in the east" (Mt 2:2); Magi in Persia would presumably have seen his star in the *west* (Marsh-Edwards). Against the conjecture that the Wise Men came from Asia Minor it seems probable that *en tē anatolē* of Matthew 2:2 means "at its rising" not "in the east," and 2:1 says specifically these Magi are from the east.

The historicity of the Magi has been frequently challenged, and it has been said that their story was composed out of such OT texts as Psalm 72:10-11, Isaiah 60:1-11 and the visit of the Queen of Sheba bearing gifts from Arabia for Solomon. It has even been suggested that the whole story is a midrash on 1 Kings 10. These conjectures in most cases originated because it has been thought that the story in itself was highly improbable. What Persian wise man would come to honor the birth of a Jewish peasant?

But these objections overlook the well-documented intense interest by ancient astrologers in Persia and elsewhere in the connection between astral phenomena and political events and the fact that in A.D. 66 the eastern astrologer Tiridates and other Magi visited Rome (cf. Dio Cassius 63.7; Suetonius, *Nero* 13). It was also widely believed during this era that stars heralded the birth of human beings destined for greatness (Brown, 1977), and in fact both Suetonius and Tacitus tell us that at the turn of the era there was an expectation of a world-ruler who would come from Judea (Suetonius, *Vesp.* 4; Tacitus, *Ann.* 5.13). Furthermore, the gifts brought by the Magi are regularly mentioned in ancient sources as valuable products of Arabia and other eastern countries. There is nothing inherently improbable about the story itself, though doubtless the First Evangelist has shaped his source material to bring out the points he wishes to stress.

Finally, the view that the story is a midrash on various OT texts fails to explain certain salient features in the text. Psalm 72:10-11 and Isaiah 60:1-11 are about kings, not Magi, even if later Christian tradition wrongly identified the Magi as kings, and 1 Kings 10 is about a singular queen, not about stargazers. As we noted in our discussion of genre, midrash is not a very apt description of Matthew's narrative material even after he has edited his sources, but it may be useful to describe how he handles his Scriptural quotations and fits them into his source material (France).

The point of including the story about the Wise Men in Matthew's Gospel is probably to show how wise men, even Gentile wise men, sought Jesus out, while a Jewish king who should have known the OT prophecies neither personally sought out nor properly honored the new son of David. Indeed, this story may be part of Matthew's larger agenda of showing how Jesus' own people largely rejected him.

8.2. The Shepherds. Due to their trade, the shepherds would have been viewed as unclean peasants in various Jewish circles. They present fewer historical difficulties to the interpreter than do the Magi. In Luke's schema they represent the sort of simple and marginalized people for whom the birth of a liberating Messiah would be good news indeed (Lk 1:52; 4:18). Historically there is nothing improbable about finding shepherds in the vicinity of Bethlehem. Though it could be argued that Luke has created this scene out of such OT texts as 1 Samuel 16—17, this seems unlikely because there is no attempt here to portray Jesus as some sort of Davidic shepherd. He is seen rather as the world savior whom even the humble poor recognize. The suggestion that Luke created this scene bearing in mind the Tower of the Flock (mentioned in Gen 35:21 and Mic 4:8) and later traditions associating the coming of Messiah with that Tower is also unlikely.

9. Canonical Information about Jesus' Childhood.

Though later apocryphal documents like the *Infancy Gospel of Thomas* have a good deal to say about the so-called hidden years of Jesus, these documents amount to little more than pious fiction and are generally recognized to be of little or no historical worth (*see* Gospels [Apocryphal]). In the Gospels themselves there is only one story about what Jesus was like between infancy and adulthood—Luke 2:41-52.

This story has historical value not least because it appears to reflect badly on Jesus' parents, that is, they do not adequately understand him (2:50). In view of the increasingly reverential portrait Christians painted of the Holy Family, it is unlikely that Luke invented this material. In particular, Mary, who is portrayed as a potential disciple in Luke 1—2, is shown to lack full understanding of Jesus and his actions (Luke 1:29, 34; 2:33), though like a good disciple she is reflecting on what she does not understand (2:50-51). Neither here nor earlier does Luke paint an idealized picture of Mary; he shows both her faith and her lack of understanding. These and other factors lead one to doubt that this story should be viewed as essentially legendary in character.

In terms of literary form, this is a pronouncement story (McHugh), and given that it has a less Semitic style and in fact has thirteen Lukanisms, it appears to have come from a different source than Luke's other birth narrative material. It may be that Luke composed this story himself on the basis of oral material. The story has no miraculous content which might raise historical difficulties, and a trip to the Temple by a young man shortly before he came of age was customary as part of a Jewish father's obligation to acquaint his son with his religious duties. Nor is there anything improbable about Jesus' family traveling some distance from Jerusalem and expecting Jesus to be amongst the other pilgrims, some of whom would likely have been relatives or fellow residents from Nazareth or the surrounding area. It was customary for Galileans to go up to Jerusalem in rather large parties during the high feast days, not least because of concerns about safety along the roads (Lk 10:30). The story in itself has marks of authenticity since it is about Jesus beginning to disengage from parental authority and following the will of his heavenly Father alone, a motif we find in other authentic Gospel material (Witherington, 1984). It may even be that in 2:19 and 51 Luke is indicating his source for this information (Brown, 1977).

Here as elsewhere in Luke 1—2, Mary is in the foreground and Joseph in the background. Luke 2:41-52 is in some respects rather like John 2:1-12 because the story ends by Jesus doing what Mary wants, without verbally indicating that he would do so. The tensions between the claims of physical and spiritual allegiance are evident when Mary speaks of Jesus' father (Joseph) and Jesus replies in terms of his actual Father (God).

Jesus is portrayed as a sort of child prodigy here, but Luke also wishes to indicate that Jesus grew and matured like other children (2:52). He grew intellectually (wisdom), physically (stature) and spiritually (the grace of God). From this singular story we may gather that Jesus' childhood was in many respects like that of other children of devout parents—it was a period of growth, development and learning. In particular, it was a period of learning about one's faith, and as a youth a time for sorting out God's will from his parents' wishes. Absent in this story are any traces of Jesus the child miracle-worker, which the authors of the apocryphal Gospels liked to stress. Instead, the one truly remarkable aspect about Jesus in this story is what he knows of God, both of his Word and of his will—a knowledge that astounded both teachers and parents.

See also CHRONOLOGY; GENEALOGY; MARY'S SONG; SIMEON'S SONG; ZECHARIAH'S SONG.

BIBLIOGRAPHY. J. C. Anderson, "Mary's Difference: Gender and Patriarchy in the Birth Narratives," *JR* 67 (1987) 183-202; K. E. Bailey, "The Manger and the Inn: The Cultural Background of Luke 2:7," *TheolRev* 2 (2, 1979) 33-44; G. P. Benson, "Virgin Birth, Virgin Conception," *ExpT* 98 (1987) 139-140; P. M. Bernegger, "Affirmation of Herod's Death in 4 B.C.," *JTS* n.s. 34 (1983) 526-31; K. Boa and W. Proctor, *The Return of the Star of Bethlehem* (Garden City, NY: Doubleday, 1980); G. Bostock, "Divine Birth, Human Conception," *ExpT* 98 (1987) 331-33; idem, "Virgin Birth or Human Conception?" *ExpT* 97 (1986) 260-63; M. M. Bourke, "The Literary Genus of Matthew 1—2," *CBQ* 22 (1960) 160-75; R. E. Brown, *The Virginal Conception and Bodily Resurrection of Jesus* (New York: Paulist, 1973); R. E. Brown, *The Birth of the Messiah* (London: Geoffrey Chapman, 1977); R. E. Brown, "Gospel Infancy Narrative Research from 1976 to 1986: Part I (Matthew)," *CBQ* 48 (1986) 468-83, and "Part II (Luke)," *CBQ* 48 (1986) 660-73; R. E. Brown et al., eds., *Mary in the New Testament* (Philadelphia: Fortress, 1978); J. Carmignac, "The Meaning of *Parthenos* in Luke 1.24: A Reply to C. H. Dodd," *BT* 28 (3, 1977) 324-330; C. E. B. Cranfield, "Some Reflections on the Subject of the Virgin Birth," *SJT* 41 (1988) 177-89; C. H. Dodd, "New Testament Translation Problems I," *BibTrans* 27 (1976) 301-11; O. Edmonds, "Herodian Chronology," *PEQ* (1982) 29-42; S. C. Farris, "On Discerning Semitic Sources in Luke 1-2," in *Gospel Perspectives 2: Studies of History and Tradition in the Four Gospels,* ed. R. T. France and D. Wenham (Sheffield: JSOT, 1981) 201-37; A. Feuillet, *Jesus and His Mother according to the Lukan Infancy Narratives* (Still River, MA: St. Bede's, 1984); E. S. Fiorenza, "Luke 2:41-52," *Int* 36 (1982) 399-403; R. T. France, "Scripture, Tradition and History in the Infancy Narratives of Matthew," in *Gospel Perspectives, 2: Studies of History and Tradition in the Four Gospels,* ed. R. T. France and D. Wenham (Sheffield: JSOT, 1981) 201-37; ller, "The Conception/Birth of Jesus as a Christological Moment," *JSNT* 1 (1978) 37-52; R. H. Gundry, *Matthew: A Commentary on His Literary and Theological Art* (Grand Rapids: Eerdmans, 1982); idem, *The Use of the Old Testament in St. Matthew's Gospel* (NovTSup 18; Leiden: E. J. Brill, 1967); M. K. Helwig, "The Dogmatic Implications of the Birth of the Messiah," *Emmanuel* 84 (1978) 21-24; H. Hendrickx, *The Infancy Narratives* (London: Geoffrey Chapman, 1984); H. W. Hoehner, *Chronological Aspects of the Life of Christ* (Grand Rapids: Zondervan, 1977); M. D. Johnson, *The Purpose of the Biblical Genealogies, with Special Reference to the Setting of the Genealogies of Jesus* (SNTSMS 8; Cambridge: University Press, 1969); R. Laurentin, *The Truth of Christmas Beyond the Myths* (Petersham, MA: St. Bede's, 1986); J. G. Machen, *The Virgin Birth of Christ* (Grand Rapids: Baker, 1930); J. McHugh, *The Mother of Jesus in the New Testament* (London: Darton, Longman & Todd, 1975); E. L. Martin, *The Birth of Christ Recalculated,* (2d ed. Pasadena: Foundation for Biblical Research, 1980); P. Minear, "Luke's Use of the Birth Stories," in *Studies in Luke-Acts,* ed. L. E. Keck and J. L. Martyn (London: S.P.C.K., 1968) 111-30; R. P. Nettlehorst, "The Genealogy of Jesus," *JETS* 31 (1988) 169-172; J. K. Russell, " 'The Son of Mary' (Mark vi.3)," *ExpT* 60 (1948-49) 195; J. Schaberg, *The Illegitimacy of Jesus* (SanFrancisco: Harper and Row, 1985); A. N. Sherwin-White, *Roman Society and Roman Law in the New Testament* (Grand Rapids: Baker, rpr. 1978); E. Stauffer, "Jeschu Ben Mirjam: Kontroversgeschichtliche Ammerkungen en Mk. 6.3," in *Neotestamentica et Semitica: Studies in Honour of Matthew Black,* ed. E. E. Ellis and M. Wilcox (Edinburgh: T. & T. Clark, 1969) 119-128; K. Stendahl, "*Quis et Unde?* An Analysis of Mt 1-2," in *Judentum Urchristentum Kirche, Festschrift fur Joachim Jeremias,* ed. W. Eltester (ZNW Beihefte 26; Berlin: Alfred Topelmann, 1960) 94-105; J. Thorley, "When Was Jesus Born?" *Greece and Rome* n.s. 28 (1981) 81-89; G. J. Wenham, "Betulah, 'A Girl of Marriageable Age,' " *VT* 22 (1972) 326-48; B. Witherington, *Women in the Ministry of Jesus* (SNTSMS 51; Cambridge: University Press, 1984); idem, *Women in the Earliest Churches* (SNTSMS 59; Cambridge: University Press, 1988).

B. Witherington III

BLASPHEMY

In both the Old and New Testaments blasphemy is, at its root, a word or act detracting from the power and glory* of God.*

1. Background
2. Blasphemy Against the Holy Spirit
3. Jesus Accused of Blasphemy

1. Background.

The Greek noun *blasphēmia* may be derived from *phēmē* (a "saying") and a shortened form of *blaptō* ("injure") or *blax* ("stupid") or *ballō* ("throw" or "strike") or *blabos* ("harm").

1.1. Greek Usage. In Greek literature "to blaspheme" meant to speak ill or abusively rather than to speak well of someone (*euphēmeō*, Philo *Migr. Abr.* 117; *euphēmia*, Josephus *Ant.* 16.2.1 §14; 17.8.4 §200; 2 Cor 6:8). This meaning is also found in (e.g.) 2 Maccabees (10:34; 12:14), Philo (*Spec. Leg.* 4:197), Josephus (*Life* §232) as well as in the NT (Acts 13:34; 18:6; Rom 14:16; 1 Cor 10:30; Tit 3:2; 1 Pet 4:4). Someone can be said to blaspheme against an idol or false god (Diodorus 2.21.7; Philo *Spec. Leg.* 1.53; Josephus *Ant.* 4.8.10 §207; Acts 19:37). Blasphemy is also associated with "bad language" (2 Macc 12:14) or insulting a person (Mt 12:32) as shown by the synonyms *oneidizō* ("revile," Mt 27:44 par. Mk 15:32 and Lk 23:39) and *loidoreō* ("to abuse," Jn 9:28; Acts 23:4; Josephus *J.W.* 2.14.8 §302).

1.2. Old Testament. In the canonical OT and Apocrypha blasphemy referred to contemptuous or dishonoring speech or actions against God through denying his ability (2 Kings 19:4, 6, 22; Ps 74:18; Is 37:6), oppressing his people (Is 52:5), gloating over their downfall (Ezek 35:12), killing Israelites (Tob 1:18 [S]), speaking directly against God (Dan 3:29), paying homage to an idol (Is 66:3; contrast Bel 9) or insulting his followers (2 Macc 12:14) or the Temple (1 Macc 7:38). However, the key passage is Leviticus 24:15-16: "Whoever curses God shall bear the sin. One who blasphemes the name of the Lord shall be put to death" (NRSV, cf. Lev 24:11; Ex 20:7).

1.3. Philo and Josephus. Originally the two sentences of Leviticus 24:15-16 probably had identical meanings. But Philo, taking them separately, understood the first to be the lesser offense of cursing a false god, the penalty of death being reserved for naming the Name of the God of Israel (*Vit. Mos.* 2.203-5; also Josephus *Ag. Ap.* 2.34 §237; *Ant.* 4.207). On the greater offense Josephus says: "Let him that blasphemeth God be stoned, then hung for a day, and buried ignominiously and in obscurity" (*Ant.* 4.8.6 §202; cf. Deut 21:22-23). On the actual nature of the offense of blasphemy,

Philo says that if anyone "even ventures to utter his name unreasonably, let him suffer the penalty of death" (*Vit. Mos.* 2.206). In turn Philo seems to understand the unreasonable utterance of the holy name of God to be treating it as a mere expletive (*Vit. Mos.* 2.208).

1.4. Rabbinic Judaism. For the rabbis there were also two sins referred to in Leviticus 24:15-16. They understood the first sentence to mean that for cursing God the only sentence necessary was excommunication, for God would exact the penalty (*b. Ker.* 7b). From its interpretation of the second sentence the Mishnah gives us the only rabbinic definition of blasphemy, and it is similar to that of Philo's: "The blasphemer is not culpable unless he pronounces the Name itself" (*m. Sanh.* 7:5).

2. Blasphemy Against the Holy Spirit.

All three Synoptic Gospels record the twin sayings of Jesus that whoever blasphemes or speaks against the Son of man (Mark has "sons of men [i.e., people] will be forgiven"; *see* Son of Man) will be forgiven (*see* Forgiveness), but that the person who blasphemes against the Holy Spirit (*see* Holy Spirit) will never be forgiven (Mt 12:31-32 par. Mk 3:28-29 and Lk 12:10; cf. *Did.* 11.7; *Gos. Thom.* 44; *Gos. Bar.* 5:2). These sayings have caused much scholarly debate and anguish among Christians. The Aramaic original of the first saying was probably a broad statement saying that all sins and blasphemies on the part of or against persons (*bar ᵉnāšāʾ*, a generic or collective term) will be forgiven, except blasphemy against the Holy Spirit. By translating the generic singular of the Aramaic with the plurals "the sons of men," Mark means that all people will be forgiven all sins and blasphemies—except blasphemies against the Holy Spirit (Mk 3:28-29). The Q* tradition, probably best represented by Luke 12:10, took the saying to refer to blaspheming against the Son of man, or Jesus, being forgiven. Matthew 12:31-32 is a conflation of Q* and Mark.

The origin of these sayings has been discussed at length. The "Amen, I say to you" sayings (*see* Amen), such as this one, have been thought to have arisen either from Hellenistic Christian prophets* within the context of worship* or from a Jewish apocalyptic* milieu. However, it is yet to be shown how this unparalleled formula came to be attributed exclusively to Jesus. Indeed, the use of *amēn* in the Gospels is without parallel. In Jewish literature (e.g., Num 5:22; Deut 27:15; Neh 5:13; *y. Soṭa* 18b; *b. Šebu.* 36a) and the remainder of the NT (Rom 1:25; 9:5; 11:36; 15:33; 16:27; 1 Cor 14:16; 16:24; Gal 1:5; Rev 5:14; 7:12; 22:20) it was a response formula assenting to someone else's blessing,* curse, oath,* word or prayer* (though see *T. Abr.* 8:7). Occasionally it was added to one's own prayer as a concluding hope (Tob 8:8; *m. Ta'an.* 4:8). However, in all the strata of traditions in the Gospels it is used exclusively to introduce and confirm Jesus' own words. This factor, along with the retention of "amen" in its Semitic form, the unusual Semitism of the phrase "the sons of men," the accompanying sayings associating Jesus' ministry with sinners, and the unprecedented scope of forgiveness, indicates the authenticity of the saying about all sins and blasphemies being forgiven.

The second saying, that of blasphemy against the Holy Spirit, appears to contradict the previous saying. However this is an established OT idiom (Gen 2:16-17; Ex 12:10) and is also found elsewhere in the NT (Mt 15:24-32; 25:29; Mk 2:17; 9:37; Jn 1:11-12; 7:16). In this way the gravity of the sin that is excepted is emphasized. In light of the harshness and severity of the saying, its authenticity can hardly be doubted.

2.1. The Unforgivable Sin. There has been a great deal of discussion regarding the nature of the unforgivable sin. For Jesus the ambiguous statement, as reconstructed above, would have meant that an attack on him was pardonable, perhaps because the public mystery of his true mission and identity could mean that it was done innocently (cf. Acts 3:17). However, an attack on the Spirit of God working in him was beyond forgiveness. That would be detracting from the power (*see* Authority and Power) and majesty of God. In turn, the saying shows that Jesus was conscious of unprecedented spiritual power at work through himself, which he considered to be self-evidently of God.

For Mark the two sayings meant that all sins are forgivable except blasphemy against the Holy Spirit. That is, to have seen the power of his ministry, as in his exorcisms (*see* Demon, Devil, Satan), and then to say that Jesus had an unclean spirit was an attack on the Holy Spirit. The Spirit's work was thereby attributed not to God but to Satan (Mk 3:22; cf. Is 5:20). There can be no greater sin.

Matthew has a similar perspective, but by deleting the reference to Jesus' contemporaries (Mk 3:30) he makes the sayings more obviously applicable to the early church. Thus for Matthew it may have been forgivable not to recognize the identity of Jesus (cf. 21:32), but there was no excuse for the Christian who did not recognize the work of the Spirit. That would amount to apostasy.

In Luke the saying appears in the context of teaching about the followers of Jesus being called on to defend themselves and their ministries (Lk 12:8-12).

To blaspheme against the Holy Spirit would be to deny God and the work of his Spirit in their lives, especially his ability to support them in trying times. In Acts 5:1-5 Luke gives an example of an unpardonable sin against the Holy Spirit.

3. Jesus Accused of Blasphemy.
All the Gospels agree that Jesus claimed or admitted equality with God—or claimed to be the Son of God (*see* Son of God)—and that this was considered by the Jews to be blasphemous and worthy of the death penalty (Mt 26:63-66; Mk 14:61-65; Lk 22:66-71; Jn 10:31-39; 19:7).

3.1. Blasphemy and God's Prerogative to Forgive. In Mark 2:5 Jesus is reported as saying, "My son, your sins are forgiven" (par. Mt 9:3 and Lk 5:21). This passive expression would probably have been understood as an attempt to avoid pronouncing God's name: "God forgives you." The ambiguity of the statement "your sins are forgiven," which is consistent with Jesus' self-disclosure, could mean that Jesus was merely providing the man with assurance (cf. Mt 9:2, *tharsei,* "take heart"), reporting to the man the forgiveness God was offering him (cf. 2 Sam 12:13). However, the Aramaic expression reflected in the present indicative passive, "they are forgiven" (*aphientai*) means, "your sins are at this moment forgiven." Indeed, the scribes are said to interpret the saying as Jesus himself offering forgiveness: "Can it be that this fellow thus blasphemes? Who can forgive sins but God?" (Mk 2:7 par. Mt 9:3 and Lk 5:21). In turn Jesus affirms that he was forgiving sins; that is, he did what the scribes considered to be the prerogative of God (Mk 2:10 par. Mt 9:6 and Lk 5:24).

As was seen above, in Jesus' time there was a wide understanding of the nature of blasphemy. On the one hand, according to the narrow rabbinic definition of blasphemy, Jesus would not be guilty before the Law. In the Qumran document known as the Prayer of Nabonidus (4QPrNab), an exorcist is said to pardon the sin of a sick person. On the other hand, a more general definition of blasphemy known to Philo (*Vit. Mos.* 2.206) would indicate that those who observed Jesus may have thought he had encroached on the prerogative of God. Furthermore, there is a strand of tradition in the OT (Ex 34:6-7; Ps 103:3; 130:4; Is 43:25; 44:22; Dan 9:9), as well as in the Dead Sea Scrolls (1QS 2:9; CD 3:18; 20:34), in which God is clearly the one who forgives. Not even the Messiah (*see* Christ) was expected to forgive sins, only to be the means whereby God would forgive in the eschaton (Is 53; Jer 31; cf. *Tg. Is* 53:4-6). The offense, then, was the diminishing of God's majesty and honor by usurping a role considered to be uniquely his alone.

3.2. *Jesus Made Himself to be Equal with God.* In John's Gospel there are passages where statements by Jesus are said to provoke the Jews to accuse him of blasphemy or even attempt to carry out the death penalty for blasphemy.

3.2.1. John 5:16-18 provides the conclusion to the story of Jesus healing* a lame man at the Bethzatha pool and contains two accusations. The first is that "because he does these things" (*hoti tauta epoiei*) on the Sabbath* (cf. Jn 9:14; 20:30) the Jews persecute Jesus. The second accusation, of making himself equal to God, arises out of Jesus' response to the first accusation. Jesus' claim to be able to work on the Sabbath is based on his claiming the same right as his Father to work continually, including on the Sabbath (2 Macc 9:12; *Ep. Arist.* 210; Philo *Leg. All.* 1.5-6; *Cher.* 87-88; *Corp. Herm.* 11.5, 14; *Exod. Rab.* 30:6; *Gen. Rab.* 11:10). The Jews find fault in this not only because he claimed God to be his own Father (*patera idion*) but in claiming his capacity for common activity with God he also claimed to be equal with God. As in Mark 2:7 (see 3.1. above) the blasphemous act was in usurping the uniqueness or prerogative of God.

3.2.2. In John 8:58 Jesus says, "Before Abraham* was born (*genesthai*), I am (*egō eimi*)." In John's Gospel *egō eimi* represents the name of God. So John portrays the Jews attempting to carry out the death sentence for blasphemy as set out in Leviticus 24:16. The historicity of this claim by Jesus has been brought into serious question by some NT scholars. Nevertheless, John is probably correct in indicating that, prior to trying him for blasphemy before the Sanhedrin,* the Jewish authorities perceived evidence of blasphemy in Jesus' activity and his view of himself.

3.2.3. John 10:33 is the first time the official charge of blasphemy occurs in the Fourth Gospel. It would not be blasphemous for someone to describe Jesus as divine. According to Scripture God's anointed would be called God's Son (2 Sam 7:14; 1 Chron 17:13). What would be blasphemous, according to John, is Jesus himself claiming this divine status for himself; the blasphemy of self-deification. Jesus answers the charge by quoting from Psalm 82:6, thereby showing that it is not blasphemous to refer to people like judges as "gods" through whom the Word of God came. Jesus also says that as he has been given this status (*hagiazein*) and sent into the world by the Father, it cannot be blasphemous for him to say "I am the Son of God" (10:36). The Jews are not satisfied. Perhaps they feel his answer is beside the point since Jesus is claiming to be more than a son of God in a reduced sense, for John says that they attempted to arrest Jesus (Jn 10:39). Although they were initially unsuccessful, they eventually took him to trial (Jn 19:7).

3.3. *Jesus Tried for Blasphemy.* Matthew and Mark agree that the charge of blasphemy was involved in the trial of Jesus (Mt 26:57-75 par. Mk 14:53-72; cf. Lk 22:54-71; *see* Trial of Jesus). Jesus is asked if he is the Messiah (*su ei ho Christos;* Mt 26:63 par. Mk 14:61 and Lk 22:67). Jesus' two-part answer provokes the charge of blasphemy. In Mark the first part of Jesus' reply was probably "I am" (*egō eimi,* 14:62, cf. Codex Koridethianus [Θ]; Mt 26:63). The fact that Jesus took on a messianic title or identity which only God could bestow and confirm by his blessing may, in itself, have been considered blasphemous (cf. Jn 19:7; Acts 5:34-39). This may have caused Matthew to place the responsibility for the direct answer back on the high priest by having Jesus say, "You have said so" (Mt 26:64), and for Luke to have Jesus evade the answer. In turn both Matthew and Luke have Jesus say, in effect, that God will confirm his messiahship. The second part of Jesus' reply is about the Son of man being seated at the right hand of Power (Lk 22:69; cf. Ps 110:1), and is generally agreed to belong to the reliable traditions about Jesus. In its original Jewish setting this saying was probably meant to emphasize God's approval. This would have compounded the earlier blasphemous act of taking on a messianic title. In Matthew and Mark Jesus' answer concludes with an allusion to Daniel 7:13 which reinforces Jesus' claims of a unique relationship with God. As related in the Mishnah, the appropriate response for the high priest having heard blasphemy is to tear his clothes (cf. *m. Sanh.* 7:5).

See also HOLY SPIRIT; "I AM" SAYINGS; SON OF GOD; SON OF MAN; TRIAL OF JESUS.

BIBLIOGRAPHY. E. Bammel, ed., *The Trial of Jesus* (SBT, 2d ser., 13; 2d ed.; London: SCM, 1971); J. Blinzler, *The Trial of Jesus* (3d ed.; Cork: Mercier, 1961); M. E. Boring, "The Unforgiveable Sin Logion Mark III 28-29/ Matt XII 31-32/Luke XII 10," *NovT* 18 (1976) 258-79; D. R. Catchpole, *The Trial of Jesus* (SPB 18; Leiden: E. J. Brill, 1971); J. D. G. Dunn, *Jesus and the Spirit* (Philadelphia: Westminster, 1979); O. E. Evans, "The Unforgivable Sin," *ExpT* 68 (1957) 240-44; D. Juel, *Messiah and Temple* (SBLDS 31; Missoula, MT: Scholars, 1977); O. Linton, "The Trial of Jesus and the Interpretation of Psalm CX," *NTS* 7 (1960-61) 265-62; E. Lövestam, *Spiritus Blasphemia* (Lund; Gleerup, 1968); Str-B I.1006-20.   G. H. Twelftree

BLESSING AND WOE

The Gospels frequently present "blessing" and "woe"

as opposites. But whereas "blessing" indicates a state of happiness or joy associated with the eschatological new day occasioned by the presence and activity of Jesus, "woe" may be used more broadly. A woe may express either sorrow or pity, or a malediction or judgment pronounced on particular individuals or communities for their sins. A woe, like a blessing, may have eschatological connotations.

1. Blessing
2. Woe

1. Blessing.

1.1. Blessings in the Greek World. The word *blessed* (Gk *makarios;* synonyms *olbios,* "fortunate"; *eutychēs,* "blessed with good fortune"; *eudaimon,* "blessed with a good spirit") was a familiar ascription in the Greek world. It was used of the gods who were not subject to earthly frailties or misfortunes and did not have to toil. It was used of persons who were judged in some way to share the privileged state of the gods. It was ascribed to the dead who had transcended the griefs of this mortal life (Plato *Leg.* XII.947d); to the rich, who were presumed to be free from care; and to the wise (Menander *Frag.* 114K: "Blessed is the man who has both mind and money for he employs the latter for what he should"). The Greek blessings reveal what was valued and what was thought to make for earthly happiness: a lovely bride, excellent children, moral rectitude, wisdom, wealth, honor and fame.

1.2. Blessings in the OT. The OT contains forty-five beatitudes, twenty-six of which appear in the Psalms. In the LXX *makarios* regularly translates the Hebrew *'ašrê,* which means, "Oh the happiness of the one." The OT blessing (or makarism) ascribes happiness to a person or group because of certain praiseworthy religious behaviors or attitudes. They are to be congratulated because they are in the enviable position of having divine approval. Those who are blessed are those who have God* as Lord (Ps 144:15), who fear God (Ps 112:1-3; 128:1-4; Prov 84:12), who trust in God (Ps 84:12), who dwell or take refuge in God (Ps 2:12; 84:4) and who prudently obey God (Ps 119:1-2; Prov 8:32-34; Is 56:2) or heed the counsels of the wise (Sir 50:28). They are judged to be fortunate because it is assumed that God rewards trust in him with worldly well-being. The blessed have a quiver full of sons as heirs (Ps 127:3-5; 112:1-3), a full life and a good wife (Ps 128:1-4; Sir 26:1), prosperity and honor (Ps 1:1-2; 84:12; Job 29:10-11) and live under the protection of God (Ps 41:2; Sir 34:15). The blessing in this literature displays a distinctly hortatory tone because it implies that if one wishes to join the ranks of the happy, one should emulate their virtuous conduct or attitudes.

The connection of the blessing with any eschatological (*see* Eschatology) hope is rare in the Hebrew Bible, but it does appear (Is 30:18; Dan 12:12). The blessings in non-canonical literature, however, reflect a significant change of focus from how to be happy in this life to how to be happy in the life to come (Tob 13:14-16; *Pss. Sol.* 4:23; 6:1; 17:44; 18:6; *1 Enoch* 58:2; 81:4; 82:4; *2 Enoch* 42:6-14; 52:1-16, see also Lk 1:45; Jas 1:12; Rev 14:13; 19:9; 20:6). The blessings are completely future-oriented, and no promise is held out for well-being in this life. It assumes that happiness is to be found only in the sphere of God in the life to come and cannot be found in external circumstances of this present evil age. Therefore, blessedness has become an eschatological concept. It was something that would come in the future with the arrival of the day of salvation and the end of history. Because those who are blessed are usually those in distress, the emphasis is on consolation of the faithful in their present situation of despair rather than on moral exhortation.

1.3. Blessings in Jesus' Ministry. *Makarios* appears fifty times in the NT, forty-four of which are beatitudes. Thirteen occur in Matthew; fifteen in Luke; and two in John. The beatitudes normally consist of *makarios/ object/hoti* clause giving the reason for the ascription. Matthew's Sermon on the Mount (*see* Sermon on the Mount) and Luke's Sermon on the Plain contain a series of beatitudes with *makarios* repeated, something that does not occur in the OT. It is widely accepted, however, that the key for understanding the NT beatitudes lies not in their form but in their context and content.

Jesus' blessings exhibit some distinctive characteristics. First, the state of blessedness is related to the joy* that is occasioned by the presence and activity of Jesus. He ascribes happiness to the poor (*see* Rich and Poor), hungry, weeping and hated, not because these persons have accomplished anything themselves, but because Jesus' presence signifies the inauguration of the kingdom of God (*see* Kingdom of God) and a new reality for them. Jesus' ministry and divine blessing are integrally related. Consequently, he ascribes happiness to those who are not scandalized by the manifestation of the kingdom in his ministry but respond to him with faith* (Mt 11:16; see Jn 20:29). He pronounces Peter blessed because Peter is open to God's revelation of Jesus' identity—a revelation that eludes flesh and blood (Mt 16:17).

Second, since blessings had become associated with the end time (see Lk 14:15; Rev 19:9; 20:6), Jesus directly pronouncing his listeners as blessed implies that the new day is at hand. Sirach looked back to a golden past and considered those blessed who saw Elijah* (Sir. 48:11). The author of the *Psalms of Solomon* looked forward to a magnificent future and ascribed blessedness to those who would be born in the days of the Messiah (*see* Christ) and see the good fortune of Israel and the good things of the Lord (*Pss. Sol.* 17:44; 18:6). In the Gospels Jesus declares that Elijah has already come in John the Baptist (*see* John the Baptist) and hints that the Messiah is in their midst. Therefore, the long-awaited blessings of the future age are perceived to have broken into the present. Jesus directly addresses his disciples* as blessed because they are able to see and hear what the prophets* and the righteous longed to see (Mt 13:16-17; Lk 10:23-24).

Third, as announcements of congratulations, many of the beatitudes are paradoxical, particularly when compared to the practical wisdom* expressed in Greek and OT blessings. The poor, the mourners, the meek, the hungry and the persecuted would not be esteemed as happy by those who prize only earthly well-being; they would be placed in the category of the unfortunate and miserable. By contrast, Jesus announces, "Happy are the unhappy for God will make them happy." Their deliverance is not yet, but they should be fully conscious of divine blessing and favor. Appearances to the contrary, congratulations are in order because Jesus' presence fulfills all meaningful desires for happiness. This condition has nothing to do with the pursuit of happiness or with fortunate external circumstances. It has to do with openness to the gracious activity of God to save his people. As with the prophetic/apocalyptic* blessings, Jesus' ascription of blessing to the poor, the hungry, the weeping and the hated (Lk 6:20-22) provides encouragement for the faithful in times of distress. They can be confident that God will vindicate them.

Fourth, one might also contend that the blessings have the capacity to establish a new existence for the hearer (the connection with Is 61 is noteworthy). They bring forth what they declare.

1.4. The Beatitudes in Luke and Matthew. The series of beatitudes in Luke and Matthew display some noticeable differences. Luke's Beatitudes seem to apply to socioeconomic conditions: the poor, the hungry, the weeping; and they are addressed directly in the second person. Matthew's Beatitudes are considered by some to be more spiritualized or ethicized. Those blessed are the poor *in spirit* (the meek), the ones hungering and thirsting *for righteousness,* the merciful, the pure in heart, and the peacemakers; and they are addressed indirectly in the third person. The Lukan Beatitudes are combined with

woes, and this combination emphasizes that a reversal of circumstances will come about: the hungry will become satisfied; the filled will become hungry. No reversal of conditions is implied in Matthew. The merciful will not cease being merciful, the pure in heart will not become less pure when they see God and the peacemakers will not become any less peacemakers. Therefore, the Matthean Beatitudes are said by Dodd, for example, to depict "types of character that have God's approval." This fact suggests that, like the Wisdom blessings, the Matthean Beatitudes are primarily hortatory.

Some scholars regard the Matthean Beatitudes to be entrance requirements for the kingdom instead of eschatological blessings. The Beatitudes have been changed into examples of the God-ordained higher righteousness (*see* Justice, Righteousness) required of disciples. In this sense, the beatitude becomes an implicit imperative, and the blessings are conditional. If one is pure in heart, then one will be blessed.

One cannot ignore the fact that some of Jesus' pronouncements of blessing elsewhere in the Gospels do set up ethical conditions for blessing. For example, only those who hear and keep the Word of God are blessed (Lk 11:28; Jn 13:17). Only those servants who are found watching and doing (Lk 12:37-38, 43; Mt 24:46) and only those who are compassionate toward the poor and the outcast (Lk 14:14; see Mt 25:34) are blessed. These other conditional blessings might support interpreting the Matthean Beatitudes as conditional entrance requirements.

It is argued against this view that the Beatitudes in Matthew need to be seen in the context of Jesus' healing ministry that precedes them (Mt 4:23—5:2). Davies and Allison contend also that the series of beatitudes are separated structurally from the main corpus of imperatives in the rest of the sermon because ". . . its function is to put grace before imperative, greeting before confrontation, blessing before demand . . ." (440). Only after the comforting words of congratulation in Matthew 5:3-12, pointing to the priority of God's gracious activity, are the hearers then confronted with the charge of greater responsibilities and tasks. One should also note that being persecuted can hardly be an entrance requirement since this is not something that one can attain on one's own and is no virtue in and of itself. The persecuted are proclaimed blessed because Jesus' presence signifies the invasion of a new reality that transcends the troubles of this age. Koch is correct in his conclusion that the poor in spirit, those who mourn, the meek and those who hunger and thirst for righteousness portray different aspects of one attitude toward the world nearing its close—an attitude of lasting patience and hope. To such as these belongs the promise of the supreme blessing of the kingdom of Heaven.

2. Woe.

2.1. Woes in the OT. The OT contains a variety of woe interjections (*hôy, 'ôy; 'y*) ranging in tone from an exclamation (Is 1:24; Jer 47:6) to a mourning cry (1 Kings 13:30; Jer 22:18) to an expression of pity (Is 1:4), to an imprecation denoting extreme hostility (Is 33:1; Hab 2:6-19). The LXX translates the woes indiscriminately as *ouai, o* and *oimmoi*. As blessing it might be classified as a wisdom-type ascription; the woe is a prophetic-type ascription. It is the converse of the beatitude. Unlike the beatitude, woes in the OT can be found occurring in a series (Is 5:8-22; Hab 2:6-19). Most of the woes introduce an announcement of doom looming on the horizon for the people; the coming disaster is clearly implied in the woe. The prophets become increasingly bitter in their indictments of the spiritual obduracy of the people and particularly that of the leaders of the people (Zech 11:17). These woes not only warn of imminent calamity, they announce that God's vengeance will befall the subject. In keeping with this development the series of woes found in *1 Enoch* 93—103 are almost equivalent to curses.

2.2. Woes in the Gospels. In the Gospels the woe can be construed as an expression of sorrow and pity—"Alas!"—or as a malediction akin to a curse. When Jesus utters a woe for the world because of the inevitability of temptations to sin (Mt 18:7), it is essentially a lament and a warning. This woe does not threaten or call down destruction on the world but mourns over the inexorable consequences of sin (*see* Sinners). Those who succumb to temptation will inevitably find themselves in dire straits. It is quite a different matter for the one causing others to stumble; this woe serves as a stern warning. Those who lead others to sin are in danger of fiery Gehenna (Mt 18:9; *see* Heaven and Hell). The woe over women who are pregnant at the time of the great tribulation laments the fact that when the cataclysm comes they will be able to flee only with difficulty (Mt 24:19; Mk 13:17; Lk 21:23). Jesus also utters a woe concerning the one who betrays the Son of man (*see* Son of Man); it would have been better for him not to have been born (Mt 26:24; Mk 14:21; Lk 22:22). Again, this woe is an expression of deep sorrow as well as a warning to the one who by his treachery would cut himself off from the kingdom of God.

The woes Jesus pronounces against the Galilean cities of Chorazin and Bethsaida are not laments but maledictions. These cities stubbornly refused to respond to his mighty works, and consequently Jesus proclaims that the infamous cities of Tyre and Sidon will be better off in the judgment* than they (Mt 11:21-22; Lk 10:13-14). Formally, the two kinds of woe differ. The malediction consists of *ouai*, the dative case of the second person pronoun and the name of those addressed. The woes expressing "Alas!" are general and conditional. Anyone who might fall into the circumstances described is lamented. The woes pronouncing judgment are directed at specific individuals for specific evil behavior. The Galilean cities and the scribes* and Pharisees* (Mt 23:13-32; Pharisees and lawyers in Lk 11:42-44, 46-53) are condemned for particular behavior and attitudes which are identified by a *hoti* clause specifying the reason for the denunciation. The immediate context also pertains to the day of judgment (Mt 11:22, 24; 23:32, 38-39). The woe condemns particular persons for their sin and announces that they will be judged for their sins. If one views Jesus' ascribing people blessed as in some way an eschatological pronouncement, and if one considers the woe to be a counterpart to blessing, the woe of judgment might be seen as eschatological as well.

In Matthew 23:13-32 the scribes and Pharisees are proleptically judged for shutting the kingdom of heaven off to others (Mt 23:13), turning converts into double sons of hell (Mt 23:15), teaching falsely (Mt 23:16-24), neglecting the weightier matters of the Law* (Mt 23:25-26), hypocrisy (Mt 23:27-28; *see* Hypocrite) and a murderous spirit (Mt 23:32). The parallel in Luke 11:42-54 also includes woes on the Pharisees for seeking the first seats in the synagogues* (Lk 11:43) and woes on the lawyers for binding heavy burdens on others (Lk 11:46).

In Luke's Sermon on the Plain a series of woes immediately follow the Beatitudes. Woes can be found linked to blessings in the OT (Is 1:4-5; Eccl 10:16-17; Tob 13:12, 14; *1 Enoch* 5:7; 99:2; *2 Enoch* 52; see the blessings connected with curses in Deut 27:15—28:19). These woes in Luke predict a reversal of fortunes as the rich, the well-fed, the laughing and the well-spoken-of will in God's future know only hunger and sadness. Implicit in this denunciation is a condemnation of their self-assurance that derives from a false sense of earthly well-being.

See also HYPOCRITE; JUDGMENT; SERMON ON THE MOUNT.

BIBLIOGRAPHY. I. Broer, *Die Seligpreisungen der Bergpredigt* (BBB 61; Bonn: Peter Harnstein, 1986); W. D. Davies and D. Allison, *A Critical and Exegetical Commentary on the Gospel according to Matthew* (ICC; Edinburgh: T. & T. Clark, 1988) vol. 1; C. H. Dodd, "The Beatitudes: A Form-Critical Study," in *More New Testament*

Studies (Grand Rapids: Eerdmans, 1968) 1-10; D. E. Garland, *The Intention of Matthew 23* (NovT 52; Leiden: E. J. Brill, 1979); R. Guelich, "The Matthean Beatitudes: 'Entrance Requirements' or Eschatological Beatitudes?" *JBL* 95 (1976) 415-434; F. Hauck, "μακάριος κτλ," in *TDNT* IV.362; K. Koch, *The Growth of the Biblical Tradition* (New York: Charles Scribner's Sons, 1969); T. Y. Mullins, "Ascription As a Literary Form," *NTS* 19 (1973) 194-205; G. Strecker, "Die Makarismen der Bergpredigt," *NTS* 17 (1971) 255-75.

D. E. Garland

BLINDNESS AND DEAFNESS

The Gospels, like elsewhere in biblical literature, frequently use the words *blindness, deafness, eye* and *ear* in a figurative sense, conveying more than the activity of the body's sense organs. God* is made known through words and deeds. To see and hear God's revelation fully requires not only physical sensation but spiritual sensitivity. It requires a personal response of understanding and commitment. Therefore, blindness and deafness can describe the inability to comprehend the spiritual truth inherent within material sights or words. This condition of hardness of heart may be due to religious or moral impairment, or due to God's intention.

Salvation* is frequently associated with sight in Jewish and Christian literature (Ex 14:13; 2 Chron 20:17; Ps 50:23; 91:16; 119:123; Is 40:5; 42:16-17; 59:11; 1QS 11:2-3; CD 20:34; *T. Gad.* 5:7; 2 Clem 1:6-7; 9:2). The formula of the frequently quoted *Shema* emphasizes the equally important role of hearing in revelation: "Hear, O Israel, the Lord our God, the Lord is one" (Deut 6:4). It is a call to discern and obey the will of God. In contrast to God who both "sees" and "hears" (Ex 2:24; 3:7, 9; 12:13; Deut 5:28; Is 37:17; Zech 7:11-13), idols are "blind" and "deaf" (Deut 4:28), as are those who worship them (Ps 115:5-6). The OT prophets chasten the Hebrew people for having eyes and ears, and yet not seeing or hearing (Is 6:9-10; 43:8; Jer 5:21; Ezek 12:2). Responsibility for such spiritual blindness and deafness is sometimes said to be borne by God (Deut 29:4; Is 6:9-10) but, on the other hand, can be traced to the person's own obduracy. Yet God can overcome this hardness of heart (Is 29:18; 35:4-5; 42:6-7, 16; 61:1; *see* Hardness of Heart).

1. Blindness.

The theme of blindness and sight is significant in Mark's theology, particularly with respect to the disciples.* Mark never calls the disciples "blind," but throughout the Gospel he portrays them as spiritually dull (Mk 4:13, 35-41; 6:52; 7:18; 8:1-10, 14-21, 31-33; 9:1-13, 19, 32; 10:10, 13, 23-32, 35-45). The blindness of the disciples is illustrated by two stories of healings* of the blind. Mark strategically places these stories before and after a major section in which Jesus predicts his suffering and relates it to the nature of true discipleship* (Mk 8:27—10:45).

The healing of the blind man of Bethsaida which is found only in Mark (8:22-26) is a two-part healing (the only one of its type in the NT) that typifies the gradual growth in spiritual sight of the disciples. It is preceded by the second story of Jesus miraculously feeding thousands, after which the disciples still do not understand. (Jesus quotes Is 6:9-10 [or Jer 5:21]; cf. Mk 4:12.) It is immediately followed by (and symbolically tied to) Peter's confession of Jesus as the Christ (Mk 8:27-30), a confession at best incomplete because it refuses to accept the idea of suffering (Mk 8:31-38).

The story forming the end bracket around Mark 8:27—10:45 is the restoring of sight to Bartimaeus (Mk 10:46-52), a story that might better be classified as a calling of a disciple rather than as a miracle story (*see* Miracles, Miracle Stories). Thus, the section of teaching on the necessity of the true disciple to accept and participate in Jesus' suffering closes with Bartimaeus, a prototypical disciple, whose "faith has healed/saved (*sōzō*) him" (Mk 10:52). Bartimaeus follows Jesus "in the way," which is the way to the cross. The passion journey to Jerusalem then begins immediately with chapter 11. For Mark salvation is vision. But the vision can only be complete after the crucifixion when the disciples understand the significance of the cross and accept its implications. Until then they are blind.

In John's Gospel verbs of seeing are important and are often employed in conjunction with "believing" (Jn 4:29, 39-42; 9:7, 35-38; 20:8, 29) even in the words of Jesus (6:36; 12:44-46; 14:9-10). John uses five different verbs to express the act of seeing, each of which may carry a slightly different meaning but does not consistently translate a special type of sight.

John records fewer miracles than the Synoptic writers and makes more use of the symbolic possibilities behind miracles. There is only one story of a blind healing in the Gospel of John (Jn 9), but it is a long and carefully crafted portrayal of spiritual blindness. As the drama unfolds, the man born blind recovers not only physical sight but spiritual insight. Three times the man claims not to know who Jesus is (Jn 9:12, 25, 36), but his insight expands progressively, as is shown by the titles he uses of Jesus. First, he calls him a "man" (Jn 9:11), then a "prophet"* (Jn 9:17),

"Messiah" (Jn 9:22; *see* Christ), a "man from God" (Jn 9:31-33) and finally "Son of man"* (Jn 9:35) and "Lord"* (Jn 9:38).

The Pharisees*/Jews, on the other hand, who do not believe the man or Jesus, claim three times (Jn 9:16, 24, 29) to know who Jesus is, yet they are depicted as growing in blindness until they finally indict themselves: "What, are we blind, too?" (Jn 9:40). The physical blindness of the man born blind is not due to sin, says Jesus (Jn 9:3), but the spiritual blindness of the Pharisees/Jews does incur guilt (Jn 9:41). Jesus can describe his mission in terms of bringing sight: "For judgment I have come into this world that those who do not see might see and those who see might become blind" (Jn 9:39). John is critical of faith that is based solely on seeing a miracle or "sign" (Jn 2:23-25; 3:2-3; 4:45-48; 6:26; 7:37). The highest form of faith* is that which does not see and yet believes (Jn 20:29).

In John 9 the theme of sight is interwoven with that of light* (Jn 9:5, 39). The absence of light is another potential cause of blindness. John uses the symbol of light and its opposition to darkness throughout the Gospel (Jn 1:4-13; 3:19-21; 8:12; 9:5; 11:9-10; 12:35-36, 44-46). Jesus is the light of the world, but many people refuse to see and thus choose to walk in darkness: "I have come as light into the world that whoever believes in me may not remain in darkness" (Jn 12:46). For John, as for Mark, seeing is a metaphor for faith or salvation.

Matthew and Luke do not make as much clear symbolic use of Jesus' healings of the blind, although such miracles are undoubtedly understood to point beyond the physical dimension. Both Evangelists see Jesus' healing of the blind and deaf as part of the messianic expectation (Mt 11:1-4 par. Lk 7:18-23; Lk 4:16-21). Luke makes use of the OT theme of blindness/deafness as hardness of heart. Spiritual understanding may be hidden from the eyes (Lk 9:45; 18:34; 19:42; 24:16), but at the end of the Gospel the risen Jesus opens the eyes and minds of the disciples (Lk 24:31, 45) to understand the Scriptures. Luke, unlike John and Mark, emphasizes literal seeing of Jesus' miracles as the proper beginning of faith.

Matthew's most significant figurative use of the term *blind* is in his vilification of the scribes* and Pharisees (Mt 15:14 and Mt 23) for misconstruing the Law* and true righteousness (*see* Justice, Righteousness). *Blind* is used with *hypocrite* as an indication of the ethical disposition of the Jewish leaders. Other sayings in the Synoptic Gospels also indicate that the eye is involved in moral matters (Mt 5:29 and 18:9 par. Mk 9:47; Mt 6: 22-23 par. Lk 11:34-36; Mt 7:3-5 par. Lk 6:41-42; Mt 20:15, literally translated: "Is your eye evil because I am good?"). Only the pure in heart see God (Mt 5:8).

2. Deafness.

Hearing as a spiritual activity is emphasized in the Synoptic Gospels by means of the parable* of the sower and its interpretation (Mk 4; Mt 13; Lk 8). The parable of the sower is the key to all parables. All three Synoptic writers use Isaiah 6:9-10 to explain why Jesus' teaching was not accepted (Mt 13:14-15; Mk 4:10-12; Lk 8:10; cf. Acts 28:26-27). John uses the same OT text with respect to signs rather than parables (Jn 12:40). The efficacy of the parables depends on the nature of the hearers. Jesus often calls upon his hearers to listen carefully: "The one who has ears to hear, let them hear" (Mt 11:15; 13:9, 43 par. Mk 4:9, 23 and Lk 8:8) and other similar injunctions (Mt 15:10; Mk 4:24; 7:14; Lk 6:27; 9:44). Matthew and Luke (following Q*) record the parable of those who hear and do Jesus' words. They are like a house built on a rock. And Luke's Jesus blesses the one who obeys God's word over the one who gave him birth (Lk 11:28).

There is no mention of deafness in John's Gospel, but there are people who do not hear. Verbs of hearing are important and, like verbs of seeing, are often coupled with the idea of "believing" and "living" (Jn 5:24-25; 8:47; 10:27; 12:47; 14:24; 15:3; 18:37). For John, Jesus is the incarnate *Logos.** The term *logos* has a range of meaning but can be used in a special sense as revelation of eternal truth to be accepted, a command to be obeyed. Human beings are created by the Logos, meaning that they have the potential to respond to God's word, but in fact they often fail to do so—they are deaf. The word, like the light, has life-giving power (Jn 6:63). Jesus not only speaks the words of life, he is the Word.

See also HARDNESS OF HEART; LIGHT.

BIBLIOGRAPHY. P. J. Achtemeier, " 'And He Followed Him': Miracles and Discipleship in Mark 10:46-52," *Semeia* 11 (1978) 115-45; R. E. Brown, *The Gospel according to John* (AB 29a; Garden City, NJ: Doubleday, 1966); 501-3, 525-32; C. A. Evans, "The Function of Isaiah 6:9-10 in Mark and John," *NovT* 24 (1982) 124-138; D. E. Garland, *The Intention of Matthew 23* (Leiden: E. J. Brill, 1979); E. S. Johnson, Jr., "Mark 8:22-26: The Blind Man from Bethsaida," *NTS* 25 (1979) 370-383; idem, "Mark 10:46-52: Blind Bartimaeus," *CBQ* 40 (1978) 191-204; W. Michaelis, "ὁράω κτλ," *TDNT* V.315-82; J. Painter, "John 9 and the Interpretation of the Fourth Gospel," *JSNT* 28 (1986) 31-61; G. L. Phillips, "Faith and Vision in the Fourth Gospel," in *Studies in the Fourth Gospel*, ed. F. L. Cross (London: Mowbray, 1957) 83-96.

C. D. C. Howard

BREAD

In biblical times bread was the staple food, a synonym for food itself and even the symbol for that which in any way might sustain physical life* (Deut 8:3). Paradoxically, the ordinariness of bread is the basis of its extraordinary importance in the Gospels. There was little change in the way it was made down to the time of Jesus. Bread was made from the flour of ground wheat or barley. The flour was mixed with salt and water and the dough baked in an oven or on a metal griddle in a leavened or unleavened state. The loaves were of varying shapes and sizes, sometimes flat and round or in the shape of a modern rectangular loaf. The barley loaves (Jn 6:9) were of a lesser quality and were the food of the poor.

1. Terminology
2. The Markan Material and Its Redaction
3. The Q Material
4. Luke's Special Material
5. The Johannine Material

1. Terminology.

Bread is denoted by a single Hebrew word (*leḥem*) and Greek equivalent (*artos*). *Artos* is used twenty-one times each in Mark and Matthew, fifteen times in Luke, twenty-four times in John and ninety-seven times in the NT. Because *artos* can mean food generally we note also the use of *trophē* four times in Matthew, once in Luke and John and sixteen times in the NT; *brōma* once each in Matthew and Mark, twice in Luke, once in John and seventeen times in the NT; and *brōsis* twice in Matthew, four times in John and eleven times in the NT. Certain other words are associated with *artos* in particular contexts. The showbread (shew-bread), *hoi artoi tēs protheseōs*, is mentioned in Mark 2:26 (par. Mt 12:4 and Lk 6:4) and in Hebrews 9:2. Twelve loaves of unleavened bread made from fine flour were placed on a table in the holy place arranged in two rows. They were a perpetual offering, replaced each Sabbath* when the old loaves were eaten by the priests.* Jesus refers to David who, when he and those with him were hungry, entered the Temple* and ate the showbread which only the priests should eat, thereby illustrating that necessity takes precedence over Sabbath law on the assumption that Sabbath law is of the same order as laws pertaining to the disposal of the showbread (Mk 2:23-28; *see* Abiathar).

The Feast* of the Unleavened Bread (*azuma*) is mentioned in Mark 14:1 (par. Lk 22:1) and Mark 14:12 (par. Mt 26:17 and Lk 22:7). The Passover, the first of the seven days of the Feast of Unleavened Bread, falls on the fifteenth day of the month Nisan. *Azuma* was

originally an agricultural festival celebrating the beginning of the harvest. Because of the Exodus it was combined with Passover. Unleavened bread then signified the bread made and eaten in haste. Luke 22:1 states the relation of Passover and *azuma* imprecisely as if one were the name of the other. In the Synoptics the approach of Passover heralds the passion of Jesus. Unleavened bread was used in ritual because leaven was viewed as a form of corruption inappropriate for holy use.

Manna is not strictly bread. From the time of Josephus* (*Ant.* 3.1.6) it has seemed certain that the manna provided for the people of Israel during the Exodus was the sap sucked by a scale insect from the tamarisk during the rainy season and dropped in small balls on the ground. This manna sustained the Israelites in the desert and was called "bread from heaven" (Ps 78:24; Jn 6:31, 49, 58) because it was viewed as the gift of divine providence where no natural food was to be found. What was at first intended to indicate simply the divine provision of food came to signify a new kind of bread, heavenly bread.

2. The Markan Material and Its Redaction.

From Mark comes the reference to the showbread (Mk 2:26 par. Mt 12:4 and Lk 6:4). Mark alone mentions the press of the crowd (*see* People, Crowd) so that Jesus and his disciples were not able to eat bread (Mk 3:20), perhaps omitted by Matthew and Luke because it says that Jesus (amongst others) *was not able* to eat bread. At the sending out of the Twelve Jesus lists what they were not to take. In Mark 6:8 and Luke 9:3 bread is listed. Matthew 10:9-10 does not mention bread, though the exclusion of it is implied by Jesus' words, "laborers deserve their keep." Matthew correctly interpreted one element of the reasoning underlying the commission in Mark but omits the sense of travelling light because of the urgency of the task.

Mention of bread occurs in the feeding of the 5,000 (Mk 6:37, 38, 41, 44; Mt 14:17, 19; Lk 9:13, 16; Jn 6:5, 7, 9, 11, 13) and the feeding of the 4,000 with the ensuing discussion about the leaven of the Pharisees* (Mk 8:4, 5, 6, 14, 16, 17, 19; Mt 15:33, 34, 36; 16:5, 7, 8, 9, 10). Neither Luke nor John refers to this second feeding, though John's account shares characteristics with both stories in Mark and some aspects of the accounts in Matthew and Luke. All Gospels mention the five loaves, but only John specifies that they were barley loaves, perhaps revealing that the boy who donated his own meal was poor. John accentuates the extent of the miracle* by taking Mark's estimate of 200 denarii of bread (Mk 6:37) and having Philip say that such an amount would not be sufficient.

After the feeding the Gospels (except Luke) describe the miraculous sea crossing. Only in Mark (Mk 6:52) does the narrator (Markan redaction) subsequently comment that the disciples did not understand about the bread. According to Matthew and Mark in feeding the 4,000 Jesus made use of seven loaves. Matthew (Mt 16:5-10) follows Mark (Mk 8:14-19) with the discussion of the leaven of the Pharisees in which Jesus recalls the feedings with five and seven loaves and shows that the disciples* do not understand. Matthew alone takes this opportunity (Mt 16:11-12) to show (through Jesus' explanation) that Jesus was not speaking about bread but the teaching of the Pharisees and Sadducees, and the disciples did subsequently come to understand. Thus Matthew softens Mark's critical picture of the disciples at this point.

Mark 7:2, 5 and Matthew 15:2 record the question of the Pharisees to Jesus concerning his disciples eating bread (food) with unclean (unwashed; see Clean and Unclean) hands in contravention of the tradition of the elders. Jesus says that they have elevated tradition above the commandment* of God,* keeping the tradition but breaking the commandment. In Mark 7:14-23 Jesus denies that what is eaten defiles a person and the narrator concludes, "Thus he declared all foods (brōmata) clean" (Mk 7:19). Mark does not use artos (although it can mean food) because he wants to emphasize the inclusion of foods considered unclean. Matthew does not use this saying. Instead he returns to the issue which introduced the discussion and has Jesus conclude "but to eat with unwashed hands does not defile a person" (Mt 15:20). The treatment suggests that Matthew has not abandoned the dietary laws as Mark has, and that the whole discussion was irrelevant to Luke. This reveals something of the life setting (Sitz im Leben) of each Evangelist.

Luke also omits the story of the Syrophoenician woman (Mk 7:24-30 par. Mt 15:21-28). In response to the woman's request that he should heal her daughter Jesus replied, "It is not fitting to take the children's bread and to give it to dogs" (Mk 7:27 par. Mt 15:26). Restoring life through healing* (exorcism) is made comparable to the gift of bread. In Mark Jesus introduces this saying with the words "Allow the children first (prōton) to be satisfied," implying there will be a time for others. This is missing from Matthew, who makes the healing of the woman's daughter exceptional by having Jesus stress, "O woman, great is your faith" (Mt 15:28). Luke omitted this story, perhaps because it was not appealing to Gentile readers.

At the final supper (see Last Supper) with his disciples Jesus took bread, spoke the words of blessing, broke the bread and gave it to the disciples (Mk 14:22 par. Mt 26:26 and Lk 22:19). The same order of events occurs in the stories of the feedings (Mk 6:41 par. Mt 14:19 and Lk 9:16 and Jn 6:11; Mk 8:6 par. Mt 15:36) suggesting a eucharistic interpretation of the feeding stories. But the pattern of taking bread, giving thanks, breaking the bread and distributing it to the guests did not originate at the Last Supper. Rather, Jesus followed customary Jewish practice attested in the early rabbinic period (see Table Fellowship). As the acting head of the house Jesus took the bread and pronounced the blessing, "Blessed art thou, Lord our God, King of the universe, who brings forth bread from the earth." We are reminded that the grain harvest in Israel was precarious, depending on the rain, dependent on God. The verb used to denote the blessing* is either eulogeō (Mk 6:41 par. Mt 15:35 and Lk 9:16; Mk 14:22 par. Mt 26:26; Lk 24:30) or eucharisteō (Mk 8:6 par. Mt 15:36; Lk 22:19; Jn 6:11), which are used here without difference of meaning. What distinguishes the Last Supper from the feeding stories are the words which identified the bread with Jesus' body and the wine* with his blood (Mk 14:22-24).

3. The Q Material.

Mark narrates the story of the temptations of Jesus (see Temptation of Jesus) but does not describe them. In Matthew and Luke (see Q) the second and third temptations are in a different order, but the first temptation concerns turning stones to bread. This ordering of bread first highlights its importance. The words of the tempter (see Demon, Devil, Satan) vary slightly in Matthew (Mt 4:3) and Luke (Lk 4:3), but the messianic character of the temptation is indicated by the introductory words, "If you are son of God . . ." (see Son of God). It was expected that the Messiah (see Christ) would provide bread, just as Moses* had provided manna (see Barrett, 288-89 for references). Later, Jesus did provide bread for the crowds that followed him. Here the temptation was to provide bread to satisfy his own physical need. The temptation was to elevate bread to the order of a first priority and make the provision of bread a characteristic of his messiahship. That Jesus refused to do this shows a different set of priorities. In both Matthew 4:4 and Luke 4:4 Jesus used the words of Deuteronomy 8:3, "one does not live by bread alone," though only Matthew continues, "but by every word proceeding from the mouth of God." Luke presupposes these words, so he is unlikely to have omitted them and we may suppose that they were added by Matthew. There was more to life than sheer physical survival; life is more than food (Mt 6:25 par. Lk 12:23). Alternatively, by using bread as a symbol for what sustains spiritual/eternal life, a similar point is made (Jn 6:27).

Recognition that there is more to life than bread did not lead to the devaluation of bread. In the prayer* Jesus taught his disciples bread is not the first order of priority. This is reserved for the will of God. Bread came next, "Give us today our daily bread" (Mt 6:11 par. Lk 11:3), even before the petition for forgiveness.* Because the word translated "daily" (*epiousios*) is unknown elsewhere in the NT, LXX and secular Greek until a single and uncertain use in a fifth century A.D. papyrus, the *linguistic* basis for the translation is uncertain. On the basis of a similar expression (*epiousia hēmera*) in Acts 7:26, it is argued that the meaning is "bread for tomorrow." J. Jeremias understands it in terms of the tomorrow of eschatological (*see* Eschatology) fulfillment when Jesus and his disciples will banquet in the kingdom of God (Mt 26:29; Lk 22:30; *see* Kingdom of God). But the use of this expression in Proverbs 27:1 shows that the meaning can be the coming day which, from the perspective of the morning, is today. Certainly Matthew did not interpret *arton . . . epiousion* as bread for tomorrow, given the fact that in Matthew 6:34 Jesus says, "Do not be anxious for tomorrow. . . ." But this saying does not come from Q and cannot be used to settle the question of the meaning of *arton . . . epiousion* there. Origen's suggestion that the phrase should be understood as if it were written *epi tēn ousian*, only shows that it was an unusual expression for which he sought a congenial meaning, "the bread necessary for existence." The daily prayer for daily bread is assumed by K. G. Kuhn, who argues that the otherwise unknown expression brings out the underlying Aramaic meaning. While this argument is not essential, it fits well with the view that the prayer is consistent with the rules regarding the gathering of the manna sufficient only for daily needs. If this is correct, Matthew 6:34 fits well with the petition in the prayer.

Continuing the theme of petition is the saying of Matthew 7:9 (par. Lk 11:11): "Which one among you if his son asks bread of him shall give him a stone?" The question presupposes that no father would do such a thing. No less can be expected of God (Mt 7:11 par. Lk 11:13). In a context where Matthew and Luke have the same material in the same order and wording there is strong textual evidence for some differences between Matthew 7:9 and Luke 11:11. Very likely the original text of Luke did not mention bread. Luke might have made this change because he had already used the request for bread in 11:5.

4. Luke's Special Material.
Luke records the parable* of the friend who comes at midnight requesting three loaves of bread (Lk 11:5). Even if the householder is unwilling to be disturbed for the sake of a friend, he will respond to need and persistence, thus illustrating the theme of persistence in prayer. Luke 14:1 tells that Jesus was going to "eat bread" on the Sabbath with a ruler who was a Pharisee. "To eat bread" is an idiom for "to have a meal." The same is true in Luke's parable of the great banquet where Jesus pronounced a blessing on those who would "eat bread in the kingdom of God" (Lk 14:15). In the parable where the lost son acknowledged that his father's hired servants "had bread enough and to spare" (Lk 15:17), bread has the general sense of food.

Finally, Luke alone describes the meeting of the risen Jesus with two disciples on the road to Emmaus. At the end of the day Jesus joined the disciples for a meal, and they recognized him when he took the bread, gave thanks, broke it and gave it to them (Lk 24:30). Later it is said that "he was made known to them in the breaking of bread" (Lk 24:35). These actions in themselves are characteristically Jewish, but Luke intends the reader to perceive in them a reflection of the Last Supper leading to the recognition of Jesus.

5. The Johannine Material.
John also narrates the feeding of the five thousand with the five loaves and two fishes. John extends this episode by having the crowd follow Jesus the next day, seeking and finding him. The dialog between Jesus and the crowd leads to a monolog in which Jesus addressed first the Jews, then the mass of disciples and finally the Twelve. The traditional material is developed in terms of the quest for the Messiah. The crowd followed Jesus into the desert because they sought him as a messianic deliverer. The giving of bread in the desert was taken as confirmation, but Jesus' withdrawal demonstrated his rejection of the quest to make him king (Jn 6:14-15). The next day the crowd came again seeking and finding him in a way that at first suggests a successful quest (Jn 6:22, 25-26). Jesus now turned the discussion to the bread which gives eternal life (*see* Life), the bread which God gives, the bread from heaven (6:23, 26, 31, 32, 33, 34, 35, 41, 48, 50, 51, 58). *Artos* is used of food and is interchanged with *brōsis* (6:27, 55; not *brōma* as in Jn 4:34) because of the phrase "food and drink" (*brōsis* and *posis*) in 6:51-58 where Jesus confronts the Jews with the scandal of his death in terms of his body and blood.

The discussion has turned from the quest for the Messiah to the quest for life, eternal life. This involved the contrast between ordinary physical life which is sustained by loaves of bread, and eternal life understood as a new quality and purpose of life and a life beyond death which is sustained by Jesus, not the Law of Moses.* In this discussion the *manna* is called the bread from heaven by the crowd for whom it has become a symbol for the Law (6:31, 49, 58 and see Borgen). When Jesus identified himself as the bread of life he claimed that he, rather than the Law, was the source of eternal life. This argument reflects the conflict with the synagogue* which led to the stress on the necessity of eating the true bread (Jesus' body) and drinking his blood, the true drink. Through the use of bread as a symbol John has focussed first on the saving efficacy of belief in Jesus and then drawn out the saving efficacy of his death (*see* Death of Jesus). Only those who come to believe in him and his saving death find the fulfillment of their quest for life.

John also depicts the meal Jesus shared with his disciples on the night that he was betrayed. In the place of the institution of the Last Supper he describes the washing of the disciples' feet as an acted parable of the service Jesus performs for them. At the supper Jesus spoke of Judas* (who was to betray him) quoting Psalm 41:9, "The one who eats my bread lifted up his heel against me" (Jn 13:18) and drawing attention to the betrayal as an act of treachery.

In the context of the final meal (Jn 21:9-13) Jesus provided bread and fish. The disciples, at Jesus' direction, made a catch of fish, but when they arrived ashore Jesus already had bread and fish prepared for breakfast. It may be that the reader is intended to recall the bread and fish of John 6, "Jesus took the bread and gave it to them, and likewise the fish." Only the reference to giving thanks is missing, but the disciples already knew that it was the Lord (Jn 21:7, 12). This feeding story confirms that the disciples' quest for life has been fulfilled. Bread and fish, not bread and wine, constitute this meal of fulfillment in the quest for life. In Johannine terms water is the comparable drink to symbolize the satisfaction of the thirst for life (Jn 4:13-15; 7:37-39).

See also LIFE; TABLE FELLOWSHIP; WATER; WINE.

BIBLIOGRAPHY. C. K. Barrett, *The Gospel according to St. John* (2d ed.; London: SPCK, 1978); J. Behm, "ἄρτος," *TDNT* I.477-78; P. Borgen, *Bread from Heaven: On the Midrashic Exposition of the Manna Pericopae in the Homilies of Philo and the Gospel of John* (Leiden: E. J. Brill, 1965); R. Bultmann, *The Gospel according to John* (Philadelphia: Westminster, 1971) 218-37; W. Foerster, "ἐπιούσιος," *TDNT* II.590-99; J. Jeremias, *The Prayers of Jesus* (London: SCM, 1967); K. G. Kuhn, *Achtzehngebet und Vaterunser und der Reim* (WUNT 1; Tübingen: J. C. B. Mohr, 1950); R. Meyer, "μάννα," *TDNT* IV.462-66; J. Painter, "Tradition and Interpretation in John 6," *NTS* 35 (1989) 421-50; idem, "Quest Stories in John 1-4" *JSNT* 44 (1991) 33-70.

J. Painter

BRIDE, BRIDEGROOM

The word *bride* (Gk *nymphē*) occurs three times in the Gospels, or four if the variant reading of Matthew 25:1 is accepted, and *bridegroom* (Gk *nymphios*) occurs eleven times. Both words occur elsewhere in the NT only in Revelation; *nymphē* four times (Rev 18:23; 21:2, 9; 22:17) and *nymphios* once (Rev 18:23). Allowing for parallels in the Gospels and the occurrence of both words in the one pericope, the actual number of passages in which the words occur is five, of which only four call for any comment. The fifth is a passing reference to the bridegroom in John 2:9 (see below).

In Matthew 10:35 and its parallel in Luke 12:53, Jesus speaks of the divisive effect that his coming will have on human society and on families in particular, such that a father will be divided against his son and a son against his father, etc. In this context *nymphē* is set over against *penthera*, "mother-in-law" and clearly has the sense of "daughter-in-law." This reflects the distinctively Jewish use of the word. Generally, from Homeric times, *nymphē* simply meant "bride" or "young wife" and *nymphios*, correspondingly, "bridegroom" or "young husband." But in Jewish use from the time of LXX the words acquired the additional meaning "daughter-in-law" and "son-in-law" respectively (e.g., *nymphē* LXX Gen 11:31; 38:11, 13, 16, 24; 1 Kings 4:19; *nymphios* LXX Judges 15:6; 2 Esdras 23:28). This extension of meaning was brought about by Semitic usage, for the Hebrew *kalāh* (Aram *kalthā'*) means both bride and (predominantly) daughter-in-law and the Hebrew *ḥātān* (Aram *ḥatnā'*) both bridegroom and son-in-law (*see* Languages of Palestine).

1. Rejoicing at the Bridegroom's Voice.
2. The Arrival of the Bridegroom.
3. Joy in the Presence of the Bridegroom.

1. Rejoicing at the Bridegroom's Voice.

The only other unquestioned occurrence of *nymphē* (but see below) is in material attributed to John the Baptist* in John 3:29: "He who has the bride is the bridegroom; the friend of the bridegroom (*ho philos tou nymphiou*), who stands and hears him, rejoices greatly at the bridegroom's voice; therefore this joy of mine is now full." John was expressing his own perception of how he stood in relation to Jesus, whom he had identified as the Christ.* The latter was the central figure in God's saving work (cf. Jn 1:29), as the bridegroom is central to a wedding. John's own role, like the friend of the bridegroom, was ancillary and meaningless without the other (cf. Jn 1:23). Nevertheless, if the wedding metaphor can be pressed, that role was an important one.

At a Jewish wedding the bridegroom was attended by his friends, whom Jesus in his parable* described as "the sons of the bridechamber" (RSV "wedding guests," Mk 2:19 par. Mt 9:15; Lk 5:34), and by one friend in particular, "the friend of the bridegroom," the best man (the expression "best man" actually occurs in Judg 14:20). The friend of the bridegroom had an important role which he sometimes performed before the wedding in the betrothal (cf. 2 Cor 11:2; in *Exod Rab.* 46.1 on 34:1 the marriage agreement, drawn up at the betrothal, was committed into the hands of the best man) and certainly at the wedding. On the eve of that day (Mt 25:1-13, though unsupported elsewhere, indicates it was after sunset, hence the need for the lights) the two bridal parties assembled, the bridegroom's under the direction of the friend of the bridegroom who acted throughout as master of ceremonies. Thus attended, the bridegroom fetched his betrothed from her father's house where she was waiting with her bridal party. They then proceeded together to the house, usually the bridegroom's, where the wedding feast was to be held, the bride on her arrival retiring to her own chamber.

The next day was marked by celebration and toward the end of that day a meal, in the course of which the marriage was contracted. The celebration might continue after this for a week or more (cf. Judg 14:12; Tob 8:20 and Jn 2:1-11 for the strain this must sometimes have put on the family's resources), but on that night the couple retired together to the bridal chamber to consummate their marriage, superintended by the friend of the bridegroom. Hence "the bridegroom's voice" of John 3:29 is probably the call of the bridegroom for the best man to collect the *signum virginitatis* (blood-stained cloth, a sign of the woman's virginity), a practice reflecting the provision of Deuteronomy 22:13-21 (cf. Mt 1:19 for Joseph's refusal to act according to this law). We have, then, in John 3:29 a metaphor drawn from a common incident from the life of that time to express the Baptist's unselfish joy in the coming of Jesus and the latter's ascendancy over him.

But is there more to it than that and does the metaphor merge into allegory? That is, should we see here a deliberate identification of Jesus with the bridegroom and regard "bridegroom" as effectively a title of Jesus? In recording this incident this is probably how the Evangelist understood it, with the

church as the bride of Christ according to the Christian development reflected in 2 Corinthians 11:2 and Ephesians 5.25 and the passages from Revelation cited above. But (assuming that we have here an authentic tradition) we should not suppose that the Baptist had gone so far down this track as these later writers. On the other hand, he could hardly have been unaware that in the OT Israel* is regarded as the bride of God (Is 54:5; 62:4-5; Jer 2:2; 3:20; Ezek 16:8; Hos 2:19-20; see Stauffer, 654 for the development of this idea in later Judaism). It is difficult, then, to avoid the conclusion that this not only suggested to him the metaphor, but that it became for him a means of testifying "that God himself was in Christ betrothing his bride to himself afresh" (Murray). Nowhere else, either in the OT or in the later literature to the time of Jesus, is the Messiah represented as the bridegroom (see Jeremias, 1101-1102). If the Baptist did so, it would be a mark of his originality, and Jesus' own use of the imagery may have been influenced by him.

2. The Arrival of the Bridegroom.

Matthew 25:1-13, the parable of the ten virgins, reflects the ritual of the marriage eve as outlined above. At what precise point in that ritual the story comes in depends on which reading of the text is preferred. The better-attested reading has the bridesmaids going out simply "to meet the bridegroom," but some reputable texts add ". . . and the bride." The latter would imply that the ten had gone from the bridegroom's house or that of his parents to meet the couple, the former that they had gone from the bride's house to meet the bridegroom who had come with his attendants to fetch her. In terms of the logic of the imagery, the shorter reading makes the best sense, as the bridesmaids are more likely to have been with the bride and to have gone out from her to meet the bridegroom than to have been waiting somewhere else for them both. The shorter reading is also consistent with the absence of any mention of the bride in the remainder of the parable (cf. vv. 5-6). However, the longer text has been defended on the grounds that the words "and the bride" were probably omitted by a copyist because they were felt to be incompatible with the widely held view that Christ, the bridegroom, would come to fetch his bride, the church, and not make his entry with her. But it is doubtful whether a copyist would have been so sensitive to the logic of the allegory. The shorter text should be accepted.

It is still a question whether Jesus intended the parable as an allegory of the bridegroom. Many argue that he did not. Thus Jeremias identifies a number of editorial additions, most notably verse 13, which he believes has been borrowed from Mark 13:35 and changes the focus of the parable. It is not about maintaining a watch—all ten of the virgins slept!—but about being prepared. It is not, then, primarily concerned with the Parousia, but with the present. Jeremias concludes, "that Matthew 25:1-13 is not an allegory of the heavenly bridegroom, but that Jesus was telling a story about an actual wedding, or rather what immediately preceded the beginning of an actual wedding feast" as an illustration of the importance of the present (the time in which to prepare) "in view of the imminent eschatological crisis" (Jeremias, 1963, 42).

There is some force in this argument. Unquestionably the focus of the parable is on being prepared. But, for all that, we should not be in too great a hurry to dismiss verse 13 as redactional or the possibility that in making his point Jesus also intended his hearers to identify the crisis with his own coming as the heavenly bridegroom. We have already noticed that the OT and later Judaism* provided a background to this idea, as indeed did other teaching of Jesus when he represented the kingdom of God* as a marriage feast and in one instance specifically as the marriage feast of the king's son (Mt 22:1-10). In short, there appears to be no compelling argument that Jesus did not think of himself as the bridegroom and good reason to think that he did.

3. Joy in the Presence of the Bridegroom.
So also with the parable in Mark 2:19-20 (par. Mt 9:15; Lk 5:34-35). To the accusing question why his disciples* did not fast (see Fasting), Jesus replied with the counter-question "Can the wedding guests fast while the bridegroom is with them? As long as they have the bridegroom with them, they cannot fast." On the assumption that Jesus would not have confessed his messiahship in this way at this time, the second clause has been interpreted as simply a paraphrase for "the wedding," in which case the counter-question is a genuine metaphor and perhaps even a secular proverb: "Can one weep at a wedding?" to which the implied answer is no! So then, the disciples could not be expected to fast now that the kingdom of God had come.

On this understanding, the choice of metaphor is due simply to the common comparison of the kingdom with a wedding, and it is only a metaphor. But this means that the following verse must be dismissed as a gloss, for there can be no question that the reference in verse 20 is to Jesus as the bridegroom and

to his passion (see Death of Jesus): "The day will come," he declared, "when the bridegroom is taken away from them, and then they will fast in that day." It is better, however, to accept this verse as authentic, recognizing that a good case can be made for Jesus' having been aware of what lay before him and that from time to time he did make veiled allusions to his passion (see Predictions of Jesus' Passion and Resurrection). Furthermore, there is the likelihood that he did identify himself with the bridegroom and that, to that extent, these parables were allegorical, although the full development of the allegory with the church as the bride of Christ had to await a later day.

BIBLIOGRAPHY. H. Daniel-Rops, *Daily Life in Palestine* (London: George Weidenfeld and Nicholson, 1962); J. Jeremias, "νύμφη, νυμφίος," *TDNT* IV.1099-1106; idem, *The Parables of Jesus* (New York: Scribner's, 1963); I. H. Marshall, *Eschatology and the Parables* (London: Theological Students' Fellowship, 1973); J. O. F. Murray, *Jesus According to John* (London: Longmans, 1936); E. Stauffer, "γαμέω, γάμος," *TDNT* I.648-57; V. Taylor, *The Names of Jesus* (London: Macmillan, 1962).   D. J. Williams

BURIAL OF JESUS
The burial of Jesus, an integral component of the earliest kerygma (cf. 1 Cor 15:3-5; Acts 13:26-31), is narrated in all four canonical Gospels (Mt 27:57-61; Mk 15:42-47; Lk 23:50-56; Jn 19:38-42) and in the apocryphal *Gospel of Peter* 6:23-24 (see Gospels [Apocryphal]). Whether a primitive passion narrative (see Passion Narrative) included a burial account (Pesch) or such an account was appended to the passion story when it was joined to resurrection* and appearance stories (Green, 311-13) is debated. What is clear is that in its present forms, the burial story serves a transitional function—confirming the death of Jesus (see especially Mk 15:44-45; Jn 19:33) and preparing for the empty-tomb episode and resurrection* announcement.

1. Funerary Customs in Antiquity
2. The Growth of the Tradition
3. The Burial Site

1. Funerary Customs in Antiquity.
In order to ascertain more fully the significance of the reports of Jesus' burial in our Gospels it is necessary to set those accounts in historical context. In this case two streams of tradition have particular relevance— Roman and Jewish—and, given the character of Jesus' demise, it is especially important that we reflect on attitudes toward the burial of executed criminals.

1.1. Roman Funerary Practice. Funerary rites appropriate to persons of the Roman Empire were determined by one's status in society. For most persons, including both the poor and ordinary people of some means, the corpse was prepared for a period of lying-in-state by washing and anointing* (cf. Acts 9:37). From 400 B.C. into the first century A.D. cremation followed, though inhumation increased in popularity after the turn of the era to become the common practice in the second century A.D. For all persons burial was the norm, even if in extraordinary circumstances it might consist only of the perfunctory throwing of a little soil on the deceased. Indeed, it was thought that ". . . to leave a corpse unburied had unpleasant repercussions on the fate of the departed soul" (Toynbee, 43).

Against this backdrop the Roman habit of refusing burial to executed criminals is all the more significant. Speaking of the decision of Pomponius Labeo to commit suicide rather than face trial (A.D. mid-30s), Tacitus notes that a person legally condemned forfeited his estate and was debarred from burial (*Ann.* 6.29). Victims of crucifixion remained on their crosses as a matter of course, left to carrion birds as a continuing deterrent against crimes against the state. On the other hand, Philo reports cases, particularly on the eve of festive occasions, when the crucified were removed and given to their relatives for burial (*Flacc.* 10.83-84).

1.2. Jewish Funerary Practice. The value of proper interment in Jewish tradition is witnessed in many quarters. It is implicit in the prominence given reports of burial in the OT narratives (e.g., Gen 23; 49:29-33; 50:25-26). To be refused burial, to be left exposed as refuse for birds and beasts—this fate is understood as a divine curse (e.g., Deut 28:26; Jer 8:1-2; 16:1-4; Ezek 29:5). Furthermore, Josephus observes that among his people the obligation to share is realized in part by not leaving a corpse unburied (*Ag. Ap.* 2.29 §211; cf. Tob 1:16—2:10).

In contrast to the Romans the Jewish custom of burying all the dead included extending funerary rites to the executed, even those sentenced to crucifixion, apparently in response to Deuteronomy 21:22-23: "When someone is convicted of a crime punishable by death and is executed, and you hang him on a tree, his corpse must not remain all night upon the tree; you shall bury him that same day, for anyone hung on a tree is under God's curse" (NRSV; cf. Josephus, *J.W.* 3.8.5 §377; 4.5.2. §317). However, funeral rites extended to criminals were qualitatively different from normal practice. Criminals, as Josephus* puts it with reference to Achan (Josh 7:25-26), were given the ignominious burial proper to the condemned (*Ant.*

5.1.14 §44; cf. 4.8.6 §202). In practical terms this meant (at least) that executed criminals were denied burial in their family tombs (e.g., 1 Kings 13:21-22; Jer 26:23)

L. Y. Rahmani has gathered evidence, which he dates to the period prior to A.D. 70, that after the flesh of the executed had wasted away the bones were gathered and buried in the family tomb (cf. *m. Sanh.* 6:5-6; *t. Sanh.* 9:8). His dating of the practice in the first half of the first century A.D. is consistent with the discovery of the bones of one Jehoḥanan, a victim of crucifixion from the same period, in an ossuary at Giv'at ha-Mivtar. He had been twice buried.

In fact, the practice of both primary and secondary burial in this period is well attested (Rahmani; Meyers; Hachlili) and can be set within the context of what little we know of first-century Jewish burial customs. When death occurred the eyes of the deceased were closed, the mouth bound up, the corpse washed (cf. *Gos. Pet.* 6:24) and anointed (*m. Sanh.* 13:5)—perhaps both at the place of death (cf. Jn 19:40) or at the home of the deceased and again at the tomb (cf. Mk 16:1). The warm climate dictated a speedy burial, with the use of spices necessary to counter the stench of decomposition. For the same reason the body might be laid on sand or salt. The deceased were buried in their own clothes or in specially prepared wraps (cf. Mk 15:46; Jn 19:40; *Gos. Pet.* 6:24). Coffins were used in some cases (cf. Lk 7:14), though it is unclear whether their usage was normal in Jerusalem. When the body was in place, the tomb was closed off by a large rock (the *gôlēl*), held in place by a smaller stone (the *dôp̄eq*). After a twelve-month period of decomposition, the bones were collected and placed in an ossuary. The purpose of this secondary burial seems to have been both psycho-social and theological: to help complete the work of mourning by extending that work to twelve months; and to assure the sinlessness of the deceased by means of the expiation accorded the process of decomposition (Rahmani; Meyers, 91-92).

Of course it was this concern for expiation that was primary in the burial rites of the executed. In the Talmud we read of the criminal: "Both death and [shameful] burial [in the criminals' graveyard] are necessary [for forgiveness]. R. Adda b. Ahabah objected: They observe no mourning rites, but grieved for him, for grief is borne only in the heart. But should you think that having been [shamefully] buried, he attains forgiveness, they should observe mourning rites! The decay of the flesh too is necessary [for forgiveness]" (*b. Sanh.* 47a-47b; cf. also *t. Sanh.* 9:9; *y. Sanh.* 6:12). The expiatory effects of decomposition were not restricted to criminals however (*m. Mo'ed Qaṭ.* 1:5; *y. Mo'ed Qaṭ.* 1:5; Meyers, 81-82).

1.3. Summary. The few details related by the Evangelists vis-a-vis the pre-burial treatment of Jesus' body are fully consonant with known practices. Two immediate questions arise, however. Although both Roman and Jewish practices allow for Jesus' burial (the former more by concession), one would expect in his case ignominious treatment; is this the case, according to our accounts? Moreover, since Joseph is not depicted as a relative of Jesus, his interest in the body is suspect. Not surprisingly, in the development of the narrative tradition of Jesus' burial these two issues have been paramount.

2. The Growth of the Tradition.

2.1. Joseph of Arimathea. Although other tradition-historical questions are present (on historical and traditional issues in general, see Blinzler; Broer), the two primary tendencies requiring elucidation are related to the identity of Joseph and the relative honor paid Jesus by the sort of burial he received. As for Joseph, two streams of interpretation are easily discerned. The first has Joseph as a foe, one of the Jews, carrying out the last act of the crime against Jesus. Though Joseph himself is never named as Jesus' enemy, the notion that Jesus' burial was an act of his enemies is embedded in Acts 13:29—"When [the people of Jerusalem and their rulers] had carried out all that was written about him, they took him down from the tree and laid him in a tomb"—and is also attested in John 19:31 (in tension with 19:38) and later in the *Gospel of Peter* 6:21; *Epistula Apostolorum* 9a; and Lactantius, *Divinae Institutiones* 4.19.

On the other hand, both Matthew 27:57 ("one discipled by Jesus") and John 19:38 ("who was a disciple of Jesus") portray him in more intimate terms. Throughout Matthew's Gospel a clear distinction is made between Jesus' followers and his detractors, and Matthew's portrayal of Joseph is of a piece with this larger theme. Discipleship* is a major motif of the burial and resurrection narratives (see *matheteuō* ["to learn as a disciple"]—27:57; 28:19; *mathētēs* ["disciple"]—27:64; 28:7-8, 13, 16), and Joseph's gracious actions on Jesus' behalf mark him as a disciple. Joseph and Nicodemus appear as secret disciples in John, and it may be that John has presented them thus by way of representing further those who believed but refused to confess their faith publicly "for they loved human praise more than the praise of God" (12:42-43). On the other hand, their actions would have been initiated at no little risk to themselves; Jesus had been executed as an insurrectionist and they might easily have been implicated in treason as well (cf. *Ṣem.* 2.11; *see* Revolutionary Movements). It seems most likely, then, that

Jesus' death provided for them the impetus for this more public identification with the Messiah (*see* Christ).

Mark and Luke are ordinarily taken to provide additional evidence for Joseph's close relationship to Jesus as his disciple,* but the evidence here is more ambiguous than is commonly recognized. It is true that the Second Evangelist describes Joseph as one who was awaiting the kingdom of God (*see* Kingdom of God), but the notation in 12:34 that a friendly scribe* was only "not far from the kingdom" leaves open Joseph's claim to discipleship in Mark. His identification as a member of the Sanhedrin* (note the use of *symboulion* ["assemble together"] in 15:1 to describe the action of the Sanhedrin, and the parallel use of *bouleutēs* ["assembly"] in 15:43 to designate the same body) would not suggest his intimacy with Jesus. Indeed, the antagonistic role of the Sanhedrin in the passion story drives to the opposite conclusion. In the end one is left with the conclusion that Joseph undertook his act of service in Mark as an expression of his piety as a Jew, his response to the longstanding Jewish insistence that no corpse be left unburied.

In the same way Luke makes no effort explicitly to identify Joseph as a disciple of Jesus. Like Pilate (*see* Pontius Pilate), Joseph is exculpated from responsibility for Jesus' execution (23:51). He is further characterized as an exemplary person, representing OT faith at its best—righteous (*see* Justice, Righteousness) like Zechariah, Elizabeth and Simeon (1:6; 2:25), awaiting the kingdom like Simeon and Anna (2:25, 38). As a rule, Jewish leaders in Luke-Acts are cast as opponents of Jesus and the early community. Joseph is an exception, but not the only one (cf. 8:41-56; 13:31; Acts 5:33-39; 6:7; 15:5).

It is also noteworthy that in all canonical versions of the burial Joseph does not appear to act in concert with the women disciples who witness his work. This fact throws further doubt on whether Joseph was understood to be Jesus' disciple in the earliest tradition.

Joseph, then, was an enigmatic figure, and the tradition has grappled with the question of how to make Joseph's actions understandable to a Christian readership. In the light of the available evidence it seems probable that, historically, his actions were motivated by his response to the Law. As Brown perceives, it is further likely that his service to Jesus was later remembered as ". . . an honor rendered by one who came to believe that Jesus was the fulfillment of the law" (Brown, 245).

2.2. What Sort of Burial? How could Messiah Jesus receive anything but an honorable, indeed royal, burial? This is a second pressing question shaping the tradition-historical development of the burial account. We have reason to believe from an historical viewpoint that his burial must have been lackluster. It is clear nonetheless that the later Evangelists were unwilling to leave unchanged the rather simple burial story as reported in Mark. Thus Matthew has added to his Markan source that the linen in which Jesus' body was wrapped was clean, the tomb in which he was buried new (27:59-60). Similarly, Luke reports that it was "a tomb wherein no one had yet been laid" (23:53). Both Evangelists thereby underscore the special honor paid Jesus. John, however, far outdistances Matthew and Luke, portraying Jesus' burial as that of a king. Since his arrest Jesus has been presented with greatness and honor, and this theme is continued by the enormous quantity of sweet-smelling spices brought by Nicodemus (cf. 2 Chron 16:14; Josephus, *Ant.* 17.8.1 §199; *Ṣem.* 8:6), his honorable burial according to Jewish custom and the use of a new tomb. Just as the character of Joseph undergoes metamorphosis in the tradition, so the honor shown Jesus by the nature of his burial grows.

2.3. Other Emphases of the Synoptic Evangelists. Matthew alone reports that Joseph is both a disciple and rich (*see* Rich and Poor). This might seem an oxymoron (cf. 19:21-26), but Matthew appears to be identifying Joseph as a wealthy person exemplary for his willingness to risk himself in costly identification with Jesus. Some see here a further allusion to Jesus' identification as the Isaianic Servant (*see* Servant of Yahweh), who was "assigned a grave . . . with the rich" (Is 53:9). Matthew is also unique in including an account of the setting of the guard at the tomb (27:62-66), presumably to refute allegations that Jesus' body had been stolen by his followers (cf. *Gos. Pet.* 8:28—11:49; Craig).

Mark's account continues the major theme of discipleship failure for which his Gospel is noted. In this case the disciples are contrasted with both the faithful women and the disciples of John. The presence of the women is emphasized by their repeated introduction (15:40, 47; 16:1). Their role in the story is clarified by their designation as those who followed and served Jesus (15:41)—the very qualities that mark authentic discipleship (9:35; 10:43). They witness Jesus' death, burial and empty tomb; the apostles,* on the other hand, are conspicuous by their absence. The passion of John the Baptist* (6:14-29) transparently anticipates and parallels that of Jesus (cf. Green, 151). The striking similarities, many of which are linguistic, serve to throw into stark relief one glaring dissimilarity—namely, John's disciples take his body and bury it, but Jesus' disciples are nowhere to be seen.

Interestingly, Luke drops any reference to the approaching of Sabbath* at the outset of his story (cf. Mk 15:42). Moreover, he neglects any mention of the purchase of burial materials (cf. Mk 15:46). And he adds the statement "On the sabbath day they rested, according to the commandments" (23:56). Luke thus avoids any suggestion that Joseph or the women engaged in Sabbath-breaking. As at Jesus' birth, so at his burial, the Law is fulfilled (2:21-24).

3. The Burial Site.
The precise location of Jesus' tomb has been the focus of a longstanding debate, with two sites finding most support today. First, on the ground floor of the Church of the Holy Sepulchre in Jerusalem the traditional tomb is enclosed by a shrine first built in Constantinian times. So much of the hillside surrounding the tomb has been removed by early masons and pilgrims, however, that very little remains of this site. In the nineteenth century a second site was put forward, now known as Gordon's Calvary, located to the north of the present Old City of Jerusalem. Here one gains a good picture of the sort of tomb Jesus would have been buried in: a forecourt before a cave, the mouth of which could be covered by a large, disk-shaped stone set in a groove cut in the rock beneath it; following this is the entrance to the burial chamber, a stone step and central pit tall enough to allow one to stand erect in the chamber, with stone benches carved into the bedrock on three sides of the chamber for interment (Smith). On the testimony of the Fourth Gospel it is presumed that Jesus would have been buried in a garden in close proximity to Golgotha (Jn 19:41), and this has encouraged support of Gordon's site, situated as it is in a well-tended garden. Other archaeological evidence has cast doubt on this site, however, while reaffirming the correctness of the traditional site of the Holy Sepulchre.

See also ARCHEOLOGY AND GEOGRAPHY; DEATH OF JESUS.

BIBLIOGRAPHY. J. Blinzler, "Die Grablegung Jesu in historischer Sicht," in *Resurrexit: Actes du Symposium International sur la Résurrection de Jésus,* ed. E. Dhanis, S.J. (Vatican City: Libreria Editrice Vaticana, 1974) 56-102; I. Broer, *Die Urgemeinde und das Grab Jesu: Eine Analyse der Grablegungsgeschichte im Neuen Testament* (SANT 31; Munich: Kösel, 1972); R. E. Brown, "The Burial of Jesus (Mark 15:42-47)," *CBQ* 50 (1988) 233-45; W. L. Craig, "The Guard at the Tomb," *NTS* 30 (1984) 273-81; J. B. Green, *The Death of Jesus: Tradition and Interpretation in the Passion Narrative* (WUNT 2:33; Tübingen: J.C.B. Mohr [Paul Siebeck], 1988); R. Hachlili, "A Second Temple Period Jewish Necropolis in Jericho," *BA* 43 (4, 1980) 235-40; E. M. Meyers, *Jewish*

Ossuaries: Reburial and Rebirth. Secondary Burials in Their Ancient Near Eastern Setting (BibO 24; Rome: Biblical Institute, 1971); R. Pesch, "Der Schluss der vormarkinische Passionsgeschichte und des Markusevangeliums: Mk 15,42-16,8," in *L'Évangile selon Marc: Tradition et Rédaction,* ed. M. Sabbe (Leuven: Leuven University, 1974) 365-409; L. Y. Rahmani, "Ancient Jerusalem's Funerary Customs and Tombs," *BA* 44 (1981) 171-77, 229-35; 45 (1982) 43-53, 109-119; R. H. Smith, "Holy Sepulchre, Church of the," *IDBSup* 413-15; J. M. C. Toynbee, *Death and Burial in the Roman World* (London: Thames and Hudson, 1971).

J. B. Green

C

CAESAR AUGUSTUS. *See* BIRTH OF JESUS; CHRONOLOGY; ROME; TAXES.

CAIAPHAS. *See* TRIAL OF JESUS.

CANON

In a Christian context the canon is the list of those writings which are acknowledged by the church* as documents of the divine revelation. More generally the word has come to mean the list of writings comprised in the sacred scriptures of any religious body. The Greek word *kanōn* ("rule") was probably borrowed from the Phoenician equivalent of Hebrew *qāneh* ("reed," "rod"). From its primary sense, "rod," it came to be used of a measuring rod or rule, and then of the series of graduated marks on a measuring rod, indicating units of length. From the sense of "series" was derived the meaning "list." The use of the word to denote the list of biblical books is first attested in Athanasius (A.D. 367). Before that, "canon" had already been used in the church for the "rule" of faith, the standard by which the adequacy or inadequacy of statements of Christian belief was assessed.

Strictly speaking, one should use the term canon only with reference to a closed list of authoritative writings, "to which nothing may be added and from which nothing may be taken away" (a recurring expression) but one may speak of an incipient canon or a canon in process of formation.

1. The OT Canon in the Gospels
2. Gospel Origins
3. The Fourfold Gospel
4. The Gospels in the Second Century
5. The Gospels in the NT Canon
6. Canon Criticism

1. The OT Canon in the Gospels.

While the relation of the Gospels to the NT canon is of paramount importance, the Gospels themselves bear witness to an already existing canon of Holy Scripture. All four of them not only presuppose the divine authority of the OT writings but claim that those writings were uniquely "fulfilled" in the gospel events (*see* Old Testament in the Gospels; Typology).

Mark begins by telling how John the Baptist* came "as it is written in the prophet Isaiah" (Mk 1:2) and describes toward the end how Jesus submitted to his captors with the words: "Let the Scriptures be fulfilled" (Mk 14:49). Matthew, who generally reproduces Mark's emphasis in this regard, adds his own introductory formula twelve times: "that it might be fulfilled which was spoken by the Lord through the prophet" (Mt 1:22, etc., with variations). Luke's nativity narrative (*see* Birth of Jesus) is full of OT echoes, and in his resurrection* account he tells how Jesus reminded the twelve disciples* of his earlier insistence "that everything must be fulfilled which was written concerning me in the Law,* the Prophets and the Psalms," special emphasis being laid on the necessity "that the Christ should suffer and on the third day rise from the dead, and that repentance* and forgiveness* of sins should be proclaimed in his name to all the nations . . ." (Lk 24:44-48). John remarks repeatedly that Jesus' fulfillment of OT prophecy was not really understood by his disciples until after his resurrection; he tells moreover how Jesus on the cross ensured that every last prophecy of his passion* should be fulfilled (Jn 19:28-30).

The OT writings are referred to as "the Scriptures," sometimes as "the Law and the Prophets" (Mt 22:40) or "Moses* and the Prophets" (Lk 16:29), once as "the Law, the Prophets and the Psalms" (Lk 24:44). This last formula, whether it comes from Luke or from Jesus, could denote the traditional threefold division of the Hebrew Bible (the Psalms standing for the "Writings" as a whole, at the head of which they stand), but it need not.

In the traditional division of the Hebrew Bible (Law, Prophets, Writings), the Law comprised the five books of Moses; the Prophets comprised the Former Prophets (Joshua, Judges, Samuel, Kings) and the Latter Prophets (Isaiah, Jeremiah, Ezekiel and the Twelve so-called Minor Prophets); the Writings comprised Psalms, Proverbs, Job, followed by the Song

93

of Songs, Ruth, Lamentations, Ecclesiastes, Esther (a group designated the five *Megilloth,* or "scrolls"), and lastly Daniel, Ezra-Nehemiah, Chronicles. This arrangement yielded a total of twenty-four books.

In the last decade of the first century, Josephus* followed a different arrangement and achieved a total of twenty-two books (corresponding to the number of letters in the Hebrew alphabet). He probably reckoned Ruth as an appendix to Judges and Lamentations as an appendix to Jeremiah (*Ag. Ap.* 1.38-41).

What were the limits of "the Scriptures" acknowledged by Jesus and his disciples? That they included the Law and the Prophets (both former and latter) is clear. They also included the Psalms and some at least of the other Writings. Daniel is referred to in Matthew 24:15 as "Daniel the prophet" (as he is also in the Qumran text 4QFlor 2.3).

Whether or not the corpus of Hebrew Scripture had been formally "closed" by Jesus' time cannot be proved, and it is not of prime importance to the student of the Gospels. One piece of evidence suggests that the Bible known to Jesus ended, as the Hebrew Bible traditionally does, with Chronicles. This is his reference to the roll of martyrs as beginning with Abel, whose murder is related in Genesis 4:8, and ending with Zechariah, who is most probably Zechariah the son of Jehoiada, stoned to death in the Temple court according to 2 Chronicles 24:24. This saying occurs in both Luke 11:50-51, and Matthew 23:35—even if Matthew calls Zechariah "the son of Berechiah" (cf. Zech 1:1)—so it is earlier than either of these Gospels, being assignable to the Q* material. There is no good reason to doubt that it is an authentic utterance of Jesus, whatever its implications may be for the limits of the canon in his day.

There is no clear evidence in the Gospels of a work outside the Hebrew Bible as we know it being quoted as authoritative. In Luke 11:49 the quotation introduced by the words "Therefore thus says the Wisdom of God" has been thought to come from a wisdom or apocalyptic writing, but its source must remain a matter of speculation. It is possible that the wording of Matthew may here and there (e.g., Mt 19:28; 24:31) reflect that of the *Parables of Enoch* (*1 Enoch* 37-71); but there is no evidence that Jesus himself knew any of the Enoch literature, and it is totally improbable that he was in any way indebted to it.

2. Gospel Origins.

The Christian church started off, then, with a body of sacred writings, known to us as the canon of the OT. But these sacred writings, vested with supreme author-

ity in the primitive church, were the Scriptures as interpreted and fulfilled by Jesus. It avails nothing to possess a sacred book if one cannot understand it. But the early Christians believed that the key to its understanding had been put into their hands: they could understand it as people of an earlier generation could not. Even the prophets, they held, did not immediately comprehend their own oracles: they "searched and enquired" in their endeavor to ascertain "what person or time was indicated by the Spirit of Christ within them when he testified in advance about the sufferings which lay in store for Christ and the glories that were to follow these things" (1 Pet 1:10, 11). But those who lived in the age of fulfillment had no need to "search and enquire," for they knew: the person was Jesus; the time was now.

The key could not be inferior in authority to the lock which it fitted: the record of Jesus' records and deeds stood from the beginning on the same level as the record of God's mighty acts of earlier days and of his speaking through the prophets. Indeed, Jesus and the message of life proclaimed in his name were found to be the sum and substance of the OT revelation.

So long as eyewitnesses remained alive to bear witness to what they had seen and heard, the need for a written record of their testimony was perhaps not greatly felt; but as the first Christian generation came to an end the first Gospel* writings began to appear and soon circulated among the churches. Our canonical Gospels* probably belong to the period c. A.D. 65-100. At first each of them will have had a limited circulation in its own locality. Mark's Gospel may well have been produced in Rome* for the strengthening of Christians there, who were in a state of shock after the suddenness and ferocity of the Neronian persecution. But not long after its appearance in Rome a copy appears to have been taken to Alexandria and gladly accepted by the church of that city (this possibly lies behind the tradition which associates John Mark with the inception of Alexandrian Christianity). In Antioch, at the end of the first Christian century and beginning of the second, Matthew seems to have been known as "the gospel": This is indicated by references in Ignatius and the *Didache.*

But with free communication among the churches, those in one area soon became aware of Gospel writings cherished by churches elsewhere, and they found their store of knowledge enriched as they read those others in addition to the one they originally knew. So, probably quite early in the second century, the fourfold Gospel began to circulate among the churches in place of a single Gospel writing.

3. The Fourfold Gospel.

Why should there be a fourfold Gospel and not a single one? The fact was that (in the providence of God, a Christian might say) there were four Gospel writings in circulation early in the second century, each of them acknowledged by its readers as carrying apostolic authority (which need not imply apostolic authorship) and no one of them (certainly not Marcion's edition of Luke; see 4.1) worthy to be preferred over the others by the churches. The Gospel writings which explicitly (and falsely) claim apostolic authorship did not begin to appear until after mid-century (see Gospels [Apocryphal]). The idea of a unified Gospel writing might have seemed superficially attractive, but when such a work was produced (see 4.2) its inadequacies were apparent. The circulation of the fourfold Gospel was evidently facilitated by the early Christian adoption of the codex form of book in preference to the scroll. It would not have been convenient to have the fourfold Gospel written on one scroll, but it could easily be accommodated in a single codex. It is not certain that Papias, bishop of Hierapolis in Phrygia early in the second century, knew a Gospel collection. He certainly knew three of the canonical Gospels, and it may be purely accidental that his knowledge of all four is not now attested. According to fragments of his work preserved by Eusebius (*Hist. Eccl.* 3.39.15, 16), he claims the authority of one whom he calls "the elder" for the statement that Mark wrote down what he remembered of Peter's preaching, and adds (possibly, but not explicitly, on the same authority) that Matthew compiled the oracles of the Lord "in the Hebrew speech" and that everyone translated his work as best he could. According to the so-called anti-Marcionite prolog to the Fourth Gospel, he said that John produced his Gospel "while still in the body."

The fourfold Gospel, in fact, is one of two Christian collections which began to circulate among the churches in the first half of the second century, the other being the corpus of Pauline letters. When the four Gospel writings were collected into the fourfold Gospel, the original sequel to the Gospel of Luke, the Acts of the Apostles, was detached from that Gospel and left to embark on a career of its own. But a key role was soon found for it. So long as the fourfold Gospel and the Pauline collection circulated separately, one can hardly speak of a canon, even in embryo. The bringing together of the two collections into one was facilitated by the existence of Acts, the hinge which joined the two. The fourfold Gospel and the Pauline corpus, without Acts, resembled, in A. Harnack's words, "an edifice of two wings without the central structure, and therefore incomplete and uninhabitable" (*History of Dogma* II [1896] 48, n. 2). But Acts provided the central structure of an edifice which now took on the shape of the canon as we have received it.

4. The Gospels in the Second Century.

4.1. Marcion. The first Christian canon of which we have definite knowledge was Marcion's edition of the Greek NT, published at Rome about A.D. 144. Marcion, who came from Sinope in Asia Minor, repudiated the authority of the OT for the church and presented his disciples with a corpus of Holy Scripture comprising two divisions—The Gospel and The Apostle. The latter was an edition of ten letters of Paul (the nine to churches and one to Philemon); the former was an edition of the Gospel of Luke, expurgated in conformity with Marcion's theological presuppositions.

Marcion may have preferred Luke's record because of that evangelist's traditional association with Paul. Paul, in Marcion's eyes, was the only faithful apostle of Jesus. He knew other Gospels than Luke, but rejected them because they were ascribed, directly or indirectly, to members of the Twelve who (he maintained) allowed the pure gospel of Christ to be adulterated with Jewish ideas. In editing Luke's Gospel he carefully removed material which acknowledged the authority of the OT or suggested that Jesus and his message bore any relation to what had gone before. Jesus, the heavenly revealer of the previously unknown Father, appeared without earthly antecedents; he was not the Jewish Messiah* foretold by the OT prophets. Marcion's Gospel accordingly began with Luke 3:1a and went on immediately to Luke 4:31: "In the fifteenth year of Tiberius Caesar Jesus came down to Capernaum"— down directly from heaven, that is to say.

Marcion on principle excluded the narrative of Jesus' birth and boyhood (Lk 1:26-56; 2:1-52) and his genealogy* (Lk 3:23-37), for Jesus had no human descent. He excluded all reference to John the Baptist's birth and ministry, with the baptism* of Jesus (Lk 1:5-25, 57-60; 3:2-22), for Jesus could have had no forerunner; he excluded the Temptation* narrative (Lk 4:1-12) because, apart from anything else, Jesus is represented there as appealing to the authority of the OT, and the same reason provided sufficient ground for excluding Jesus' preaching at Nazareth, in which he claims to fulfill an OT prophecy (Lk 4:16-30). Also excluded were the words "The old is good" (Lk 5:39), which might imply some approval of the OT order, the reference to Jesus' family (Lk 8:19), and the description of Zacchaeus as a son of Abraham* (Lk 19:9).

But contemporaries of Marcion freely acknowledged other Gospels than Luke's. Of one of these contemporaries, Valentinus (founder of a leading gnostic school), Tertullian remarked half a century later that, while Marcion nullified Holy Scripture by excising what did not meet with his approval, Valentinus nullified it by misinterpretation, although he seemed to use the entire New Testament (Tertullian, *De praescr.*, 38). This testimony is largely confirmed by the earliest Valentinian writings, which cite Matthew and John as authoritative in addition to Luke.

4.2. Catholic Reaction. The promulgation of Marcion's canon stimulated ecclesiastical authorities in Rome and elsewhere to define the NT canon more specifically. Justin Martyr (c. 160) wrote a treatise, *Against Marcion,* which unfortunately has not survived. In his surviving works he speaks of the "memoirs of Peter," possibly the Gospel of Mark (*Dial. Tryph.* 106.3), and of the "memoirs of the apostles" which, he says, were called "gospels" and were read in church along with the compositions of the prophets (*Apol.I,* 66.3; 67.3).

Justin's disciple Tatian (c. 170) produced a new edition of the fourfold Gospel by unstitching the sections of its four component parts and then rearranging them so as to form one continuous narrative. This edition, the *Diatessaron* ("harmony of four"), proved very popular, especially in Tatian's native Assyria, where the Syriac-speaking church was most unwilling to abandon it at the beginning of the fifth century in favor of a new Syriac version of the four separate Gospels. The Gospel of John provided the framework into which Tatian fitted the contents of the other three. Even if here and there Tatian amplified his narrative with material from a fifth document (such as the *Gospel according to the Hebrews*), his *Diatessaron* bears clear enough witness to the distinctive authority of the four "canonical" Gospels.

The most important reply to Marcion was made by Tertullian in his five-volume *Adversus Marcionem* (*Against Marcion,* c. 207), our principal source of information about Marcion's canon, factual if vituperative. By the time Tertullian wrote, the general shape of the catholic canon (or, as he preferred to call it, the *instrumentum*) was complete.

The catholic response to Marcion presented a canon comprising four Gospel writings, not one only, and thirteen Pauline epistles, not ten only, with epistles by other "apostolic men" and the Revelation of John, while Acts served as the hinge joining the fourfold Gospel to the other writings. Two witnesses

to this catholic canon toward the end of the second century are Irenaeus and the Muratorian list. Irenaeus (c. 180) gives no list of NT books, but it is plain from his extant works that he recognized and appealed to the four Gospels, Acts, the Pauline epistles, some General Epistles and Revelation—in fact, to twenty-two out of the twenty-seven books of our NT.

His remarks on the Gospels are of special interest. He reproduces the account of their origin which he had received:

> Matthew published among the Hebrews a gospel in writing also in their own speech, while Peter and Paul were preaching the gospel and founding the church in Rome. After their departure Mark in his turn, Peter's disciple and interpreter, delivered to us in writing the content of Peter's preaching. Luke also, the follower of Paul, set down in a book the gospel preached by him [Paul]. Then John, the Lord's disciple who leaned back on his bosom, published his gospel while he was living at Ephesus in Asia. (*Haer.* 3.1.1, quoted by Eusebius, *Hist. Eccl.* 5.8.2-4)

That is what Irenaeus received by tradition, but he adds an original argument to show that there must be four Gospels, but no more:

> As there are four quarters of the world in which we live, and four universal winds, and as the church is dispersed over all the earth, and the Gospel is the pillar and base of the church, so it is natural that it should have four pillars, breathing immortality from every quarter and kindling human life anew. Clearly therefore the Word, . . . having been made manifest to the human race, has given us the gospel in fourfold form, but held together by one Spirit." (*Haer.* 3.11.8)

Either by the time of Irenaeus the fourfold shape of the Gospel was as much taken for granted in the Catholic church as the four winds of heaven, or Irenaeus is at pains to exclude the idea that there were other Gospel writings equally worthy of acceptance as authoritative.

Then, having referred to the divine Word in OT terms as "enthroned on the cherubim" (cf. 1 Sam 4:4; Ps 80.1), Irenaeus recalls that the cherubim, as described in Ezekiel 1:10; 10:14 (cf. the variation in Rev 4:7), had four faces apiece—the faces of a lion, an ox (or calf), a human being and an eagle—and relates the four Gospels to these four faces, John to the eagle, Luke to the ox, Matthew to the human being and Mark to the lion, pointing respectively to Christ's royalty and deity, to his sacrifice, to his humanity and to his endowment with the Spirit of prophecy.

The Muratorian list (so called after L. A. Muratori, who discovered and published it in 1740) is a list of writings acknowledged apparently in the Roman church toward the end of the second century. It comprises practically the same NT books as those attested by Irenaeus, with the addition of Jude and the strange omission of 1 Peter. It is defective at the beginning, but since its first complete sentence names Luke as "the third book of the gospel" and "John, one of the disciples," is said to have written "the fourth Gospel," it is a reasonable inference that Matthew and Mark were listed as the first and second.

Its account of the origins of the Gospels has no historical value but it indicates how questions about their authority were being answered at the time. As for the third Gospel:

> After the ascension of Christ, Luke the physician, whom Paul had taken along as a legal expert, wrote [the record] down in his own name in accordance with [Paul's] opinion. He himself, however, never saw the Lord in the flesh and therefore, as far as he could follow [the source of events], began to tell it from the nativity of John.

This last remark may suggest an anti-Marcionite emphasis, since Marcion omitted all reference to John the Baptist from his edition of the Gospel. For the rest, an attempt is made to claim for Luke's record the apostolic authority of Paul. A Roman governor had on his provincial staff a legal expert (*iuris studiosus*, the term used here), who drafted official documents "in the name" and "in accordance with the opinion" of his superior; so Luke (it is implied) composed his record in his own name but in accordance with Paul's opinion.

The Muratorian account of the Fourth Gospel has this to say:

> Encouraged by his fellow-disciples and bishops, John said, "Fast along with me three days from today, and whatever may be revealed to each, let us relate it to one another." The same night it was revealed to Andrew, one of the apostles, that John in his own name should write everything down, and that they should all revise it. Therefore, although the various books of the Gospel begin in different ways, it makes no difference to the faith of believers, since in them all everything has been declared by one primary Spirit, concerning our Lord's nativity, passion and resurrection, his association with his disciples and his twofold advent—the first in humility, when he was despised, which is past; his second resplendent, in royal power, his coming again. It is no wonder, then, that John should so constantly present the

several details in his letters also, saying of himself, "What we have seen with our eyes and heard with our ears and our hands have handled, these things have we written." For in this way he claims to be not only a spectator but a hearer, and also a writer in order of the wonderful facts about our Lord.

The tale about John's fellow-disciples may reflect a tradition that others in addition to John were involved in the publication of his Gospel; compare the attestation at the end of the Gospel (probably by members of the Johannine community): "we know that his testimony is true" (Jn 21:24). The insistence that all four of the Gospels maintain the same traditional faith may betray an awareness of some who were unhappy about the Fourth Gospel because of its differences from the other three. The emphasis on the eyewitness testimony of this Gospel is confirmed by the assurance in 1 John 1:1 that the Johannine teaching is based on firsthand experience

At the end of the Muratorian list any writings proceeding from "the Asian founder of the Cataphrygians" are rejected, along with other heretical works. The Cataphrygians are the Montanists, founded by Montanus around A.D. 155. They claimed that the gift of prophecy had been revived among them, and that their inspired utterances should be equally venerated with the sacred Scriptures. Their contention that the Paraclete promises of John 14—16 (*see* Holy Spirit) had been fulfilled by the rise of their movement caused some of their orthodox opponents to look skeptically on the Fourth Gospel. Outstanding among these was Gaius, a learned Roman churchman (c. 180), whose arguments against the apostolic authority of this Gospel were taken seriously enough for Hippolytus to publish a refutation of them a generation later.

5. The Gospels in the NT Canon.

5.1. Canonical and Uncanonical Gospels. Contemporary with Irenaeus and the compiler of the Muratorian list was Clement of Alexandria. Clement shows a degree of tolerance toward uncanonical gospels and other writings not readily matched among orthodox Christian fathers, but he sets the four canonical Gospels on a plane by themselves. According to the "elders" he says:

> The first Gospels to be written were those with genealogies [Matthew and Luke]. The Gospel according to Mark took shape as follows: Peter had publicly proclaimed the word at Rome and told forth the gospel by the Spirit. Then those present, many in number, besought Mark, as one who had accompanied Peter for a long time and remem-

bered what he had said, to make a written record of what he had said. Mark did this, and communicated his Gospel to those who made the request of him. When Peter came to know of it, he neither vigorously forbade it nor advocated it. Last of all John (according to the tradition), aware that the "bodily" facts had been set forth in the [other] Gospels, yielded to the exhortation of his friends and, divinely carried along by the Spirit, composed a "spiritual" Gospel. (quoted by Eusebius, *Hist. Eccl.* 6.14.5-7)

Clement had received the fourfold Gospel and accepted its contents as especially authoritative, but he had no objection to citing other gospels when he thought fit. He knew, for example, that the *Gospel according to the Egyptians* was not one of "the four Gospels that have been handed down to us," but he quoted it at least four times (see Gospels [Apocryphal]).

The *Gospel according to the Egyptians* was apparently popular among the Gentile Christians of Alexandria, as the *Gospel according to the Hebrews* was among the Jewish Christians. The latter bore some relation to Matthew's Gospel, but included some uncanonical material; the former had more of a gnostic emphasis.

Most of the so-called apocryphal Gospels belong to the period when the distinctiveness of the fourfold Gospel was becoming increasingly recognized. One of the earliest, the *Gospel of Thomas,* is a compilation of 114 sayings ascribed to Jesus, issued in Greek around 120. Fragments from its Greek text were included among the first Oxyrhynchus papyri to be published. The complete text of a fourth-century Coptic version was found among the Nag Hammadi papyri about 1945.

Some apocryphal Gospels were designed to supply details about the life and activities of Jesus which the canonical four did not give. This is particularly so with the so-called Infancy Gospels—the *Protevangelium of James,* for example, which relates Mary's conception, birth and upbringing and goes on to tell how she gave birth to Jesus; and the *Infancy Gospel of Thomas,* which tells of Jesus' boyhood, portraying him as a juvenile prodigy.

These and other Gospels lay explicit claim to the authority of an apostle or other close associate of Jesus (unlike the canonical Gospels, which are strictly anonymous works). The *Gospel of Peter* is extant in its passion narrative, which gives a docetic account of Jesus' crucifixion; it was current in parts of Syria at the end of the second century. The *Gospel of Nicodemus* (also known as the *Acts of Pilate*) narrates Jesus' trial, death and resurrection, and in particular his "harrowing of hell."

Other Gospels expound various forms of gnosticism, such as the *Gospel of Philip* and the *Apocryphon of John,* which record revelations said to have been given by the risen Jesus. An Egyptian gnostic work of the mid-third century, *Pistis Sophia* ("Faith Wisdom"), tells how Jesus continued to live with his disciples for eleven or twelve years after his resurrection and imparted to them much teaching about salvation, mostly in reply to questions asked—especially by Mary Magdalene.

5.2. Alexandrian Fathers. Origen, the greatest Christian scholar of his age, had no objection to the *Gospel according to the Hebrews,* but listed the *Gospel according to the Egyptians,* together with other gnosticizing Gospels and Acts, among the "false" books. He acknowledged the four canonical Gospels, the Acts of the Apostles, the Pauline epistles and Hebrews, 1 Peter, 1 John and Revelation as "undisputed" books.

The fourfold Gospel, in Origen's view, is to be received as the first fruits of all the Scriptures; for it the Law of Moses and the rest of the OT prepared the way. "For it was after the fruits of the prophets who prophesied until the Lord Jesus that the perfect Word blossomed." Even Acts and the epistles are not on the same level of inspiration as the Gospels. And if the Gospels are the first fruits of all Scripture, John is the first fruits of the four Gospels (*Comm. Joh.,* 1.4-6).

The authority of John's Gospel was stressed also by Origen's disciple Dionysius, who was bishop of Alexandria from 247/8 until 265. He concluded on stylistic grounds that the Gospel and the Revelation of John could not have come from the same author. Therefore, since Revelation was written by another John, a holy and inspired man indeed, such a non-apostolic writing could not be accorded the same degree of authority as the apostolic Gospel.

Athanasius, bishop of Alexandria 328-373, is the first writer to list as "canonical" (his own word) exactly the twenty-seven books of the NT as we know it. He gives the four Gospels pride of place at the head of his list (issued in 367). There are some books not in the canon which, he says, are helpful for the instruction of recent converts, but there are others, written by heretics and falsely claiming ancient authority, which should be totally ignored.

The order in which Athanasius lists the Gospels (Matthew-Mark-Luke-John) is at least as early as Irenaeus and (it appears) the Muratorian canon. It may be based on what was believed to be the chronological order of their composition; it has been for centuries the traditional order. Clement of Alexandria, as has been said, gives the order Matthew-Luke-Mark-John. The Old Latin witnesses prefer the order

Matthew-John-Luke-Mark (giving priority to the two which bear apostolic names). Occasionally the order John-Matthew-Luke-Mark appears (John coming first perhaps because of its opening words "In the beginning").

6. Canon Criticism.

Canon criticism, or canonical criticism, is not a variety of criticism of the same order as form criticism* or redaction criticism.* It denotes that approach to the books of the Bible which treats them not as individual documents but as components of the completed corpus of Holy Scripture. One important aspect of this approach is more aptly called canonical exegesis. Canonical exegesis endeavors to determine what a given passage means not only in the immediate context of its date, authorship and setting but in the wider context of the canon in which it was ultimately incorporated. This is a valid exegetical quest, but it presupposes the completion of the canonizing process.

Since the Christian canon comprises OT and NT together, it is necessary to consider the approach to the OT in the Gospels, the relation of each of the four Gospels to the fourfold Gospel, and the relation of the Gospels to the NT and to the whole Bible.

6.1. The OT in the Gospels. The books of the OT are treated in the Gospels as one literary corpus. Within this corpus individual authors may be identified—Moses as the giver of the Law (Mk 10:3-4; Jn 5:45-47; etc.) and, among other writers, Isaiah and David especially (Mk 1:2; 12:35-37; etc.). Jeremiah and Daniel are cited by name in Matthew (see Mt 2:17; 24:15). The story of Jonah (*see* Sign of Jonah) is referred to (Mt 12:39-41, etc.), but the book which bears his name is not mentioned. Whether individual authors are named or not, however, they share the same divine authority, for all of them spoke by the Spirit (Mk 12:36; Lk 4:18), and the substance of their ministry was the coming Savior: Jesus is the one "of whom Moses in the law and also the prophets wrote" (Jn 1:45).

It is difficult to distinguish in this regard the teaching of Jesus from the evangelists' application, but for the present purpose it makes little practical difference. Sometimes the identity of the OT writer is relevant to the application: It is of the essence of the argument in Mark 12:35-37, for example, that Psalm 110:1 should have been spoken by David himself. In the same way, the recognition of Moses as the lawgiver is common ground in those debates between Jesus and the scribes* in the Fourth Gospel where they claim to be exponents, even disciples, of Moses

and charge Jesus with breaking the law that Moses gave.

But it is only rarely that the OT author's identity is so important: what matters is that the voice of God is heard in those writings. It was not an issue of great moment that a prophecy from Malachi should be attributed to Isaiah in Mark 1:2 or one from Zechariah to Jeremiah in Matthew 27:9-10 (in both places the quotations were probably taken from "testimony" collections in which texts from a variety of OT writers were linked together under one rubric); what was really of moment was that the words were those of the Spirit of prophecy.

6.2. The Gospels and the Fourfold Gospel. Mark intends his readers to bear in mind that the one to whom the words and deeds in his record of Jesus' ministry are ascribed is the Son of God,* although this "messianic secret" (*see* Messiah) is not publicly proclaimed until the centurion declares it at the moment of Jesus' death (Mk 15:39; *see* Death of Jesus). The reader of the Fourth Gospel is not allowed to forget that the words and deeds which it records are those of the incarnate Word (*see* Logos). But in canonical criticism, where the fourfold Gospel is the context of each individual Gospel passage, the christological insights of Mark and John (as well as of Matthew and Luke) may control the understanding of any one of those passages.

Traditionally, the predominant control has been exercised by the Johannine christology. Calvin said that he was accustomed to treat the Gospel of John as the key which unlocked the meaning of the other three (*Commentary on John*, 1553, Introduction). So too William Temple could say of the evangelists' witness to Christ: "Let the Synoptists repeat for us as closely as they can the very words He spoke; but let St. John tune our ears to hear them" (*Readings in St. John's Gospel* [London: Macmillan, 1939], xxxii). Calvin and Temple were in effect practicing canonical criticism: To them the fourfold Gospel was a canonical entity, of which each part could best be understood in the light of the others, and especially in the light of the final component.

This canonical approach requires that each Gospel be treated first as a composition in its own right; it cannot be effectively undertaken until the literary interrelationships of the four have been explored. It could not be undertaken with a "harmony" of the Gospels in which the individuality of the several evangelists was submerged. Such a "harmony" is not a canonical document. At all costs the study of the Gospels must not provide any ground for Harnack's complaint that the canonizing process "works like whitewash; it hides the original colours and obliterates all the contours" (*The Origin of the New Testament*, 141).

A canonical approach which can "do justice to the integrity of the fourfold Gospel corpus" without infringing the canons of historical or literary criticism is recommended by B. S. Childs in a chapter entitled "A Canonical Harmony of the Gospels" (*The New Testament as Canon*, 157-209). Such an approach, if thoroughly developed, can enrich our understanding of the aim and achievement of each Evangelist in relation to the consentient testimony not only of the fourfold Gospel but of all Sacred Scripture to Jesus as Son of God and Savior of the world.

See also GOSPELS (APOCRYPHAL); JOHN, GOSPEL OF; LUKE, GOSPEL OF; MARK, GOSPEL OF; MATTHEW, GOSPEL OF; SYNOPTIC PROBLEM; TEXTUAL CRITICISM; TRADITION CRITICISM.

BIBLIOGRAPHY. J. Barr, *Holy Scripture: Canon, Authority, Criticism* (Philadelphia: Westminster, 1983); R. T. Beckwith, *The Old Testament Canon of the New Testament Church* (Grand Rapids: Eerdmans, 1985); F. F. Bruce, *The Canon of Scripture* (Downers Grove, IL: InterVarsity, 1988); H. von Campenhausen, *The Formation of the Christian Bible* (London: A. & C. Black, 1972); B. S. Childs, *The New Testament as Canon: An Introduction* (Philadelphia: Fortress, 1984); A. A. T. Ehrhardt, "The Gospels in the Muratorian Fragment," in *The Framework of the New Testament Stories* (Manchester: University Press, 1964) 11-36; W. R. Farmer, *Jesus and the Gospel: Tradition, Scripture, and Canon* (Philadelphia: Fortress, 1982); R. T. France, *Jesus and the Old Testament* (London: Tyndale, 1971); H. Y. Gamble, *The New Testament Canon: Its Making and Meaning* (Philadelphia: Fortress, 1985); A. von Harnack, *The Origin of the New Testament* (London: Williams & Norgate, 1925); E. Hennecke, *New Testament Apocrypha*, ed. W. Schneemelcher, Eng. trans. ed. R. McL. Wilson, I: *Gospels and Related Writings* (Philadelphia: Westminster, 1963); L. M. McDonald, *The Formation of the Christian Biblical Canon* (Nashville: Abingdon, 1988); B. M. Metzger, *The Canon of the New Testament* (Oxford: University Press, 1987); C. F. D. Moule, *The Birth of the New Testament* (3d ed.; London: A. & C. Black, 1981); E. H. Pagels, *The Gnostic Gospels* (New York: Random House, 1979); W. Sanday, *The Gospels in the Second Century* (London: Macmillan, 1876).   F. F. Bruce

CENSUS. *See* BIRTH OF JESUS.

CENTURION. *See* MILITARY.

CHILD, CHILDREN

"And those who ate were about five thousand, not counting women and children" (Mt 14:21; cf. 15:38). The additional mention of the women and children in Matthew's version of the miraculous feedings certainly has the effect of augmenting the scope of the miracle.* It expresses also the Evangelist's conviction that women and children belong to the people of God* and are recipients of the divine grace revealed in Jesus. At the same time, however, it is important to note that their mention presupposes a patriarchal social structure in which the male household head held precedence and the identity and roles of women and children were defined in relation to him.

So we ought not to come to the Gospels expecting too much of what they might have to say about the child and children. (1) Like the Bible as a whole, the Gospels are products of their time and (patriarchal) social setting. (2) Again, like the Bible as a whole, the Gospels were written by male adults for male adults and their dependents, who included children. This helps to explain why much of the biblical (and Gospel) material on children in relation to morality has to do with the obligation upon children of obedience to their parents, in accordance with the fifth commandment. Elsewhere, as we shall see, the child and children are used in metaphorical ways to express what is incumbent, religiously and spiritually, upon adults. (3) The discovery of childhood as a recognized developmental stage of importance in its own right is a modern phenomenon, as P. Ariès (1962) and others have shown. And Robert Raikes' Sunday schools for children were not begun in England until the late-eighteenth century. In other words, the modern, Western fascination with children and the modern sentimentalizing of childhood ought not to be read back into the Gospels.

1. Jesus
2. The Gospels

1. Jesus.

1.1. Jesus As a Child. It is worth pointing out that two of the four canonical Gospels have no material whatsoever on Jesus as a child. For Mark and John it is Jesus' adult public ministry, culminating in his death* and resurrection,* which constitutes "the gospel" (and, for John, Jesus' incarnation). And in none of the Gospels does the adult Jesus refer directly to his own childhood in his teaching. Matthew and Luke contain birth and infancy narratives, and in Luke 2:41-51 there is a story about "the boy (*ho pais*) Jesus" at the age of twelve attending the Passover with his parents in Jerusalem and revealing in the Temple* signs of his great wisdom.* On strictly critical grounds, however, it is impossible to establish the historical value of this material (Brown; see Gospels [Historical Reliability]). Many scholars today would argue that this tradition may be more influenced by post-Easter faith than by historical incident, bearing witness that Jesus, the son of Mary and Joseph, was also the Son of God (cf. Mt 1:18-23; Lk 1:30-35; 3:23-38; see Birth of Jesus).

Yet the Gospel stories stand in contrast with those which come to us from the mid-second century onwards—the (apocryphal) stories about Jesus' "hidden years" prior to his baptism (see Gospels [Apocryphal]). The earliest and most important of these are the so-called *Protevangelium of James* and the *Infancy Gospel of Thomas*. These stories are pious fictions produced, in the absence of controlling canonical tradition, for the purpose of satisfying curiosity and defending christological dogma. As O. Cullmann puts it: "The further away in time we get from the roots, the more unrestrained becomes the application to Jesus of what is recounted about the birth and infancy of sons of the gods and children of supernatural origin" (366).

1.2. Jesus and Children. There are several noteworthy Gospel traditions relevant to the study of Jesus' attitude to children, with Mark 9:33-37 and 10:13-16 (and pars.) being particularly noteworthy. These have received attention in the commentaries and in the works of, among others, S. Légasse (1969), G. Krause (1973) and H.-R. Weber (1979). Useful too are historical studies of the position of children in Judaism* and in the Greco-Roman world of the first century, among which those of W. Barclay (1959), R. de Vaux (1961), A. Oepke (1967), B. Rawson (1986) and T. Wiedemann (1989) are important.

It is necessary, however, to approach these famous texts about children with certain prior observations in mind. First, it is worth noting that Jesus himself did not marry and had no children of his own. Like Paul after him, and contrary to the prevailing social expectations of the time, Jesus understood his vocation as requiring the renunciation of marital and family* ties (Mt 19:11-12; cf. 1 Cor 7:7). Second, Jesus called on his disciples to subordinate their own familial obligations for his sake. This included obligations to children: "If anyone comes to me and does not hate his own father and mother and wife and children (*ta tekna*) and brothers and sisters . . . he cannot be my disciple" (Lk 14:26 par. Mt 10:37; cf. Mk 10:29-30). Third, Jesus warned his disciples* of serious enmities between parents and their children on his account (Mk 13:12 par. Mt 10:21 and Lk 21:16). Fourth, Jesus is nowhere depicted as a teacher of children, except in so far as they were present in the crowds of men and women who thronged to hear him. Children at play provide the stuff of one of Jesus' parables* (Mt 11:16-19 par. Lk 7:31-35), but the parable itself is addressed to adults. Finally, and more generally, children *per se* were not at the heart of Jesus' priorities. What was central was the prophetic summons of Israel* to repentance and a renewed obedience to the will of God in view of the imminent coming of God. As part of this, children are expected to obey their parents in accordance with the commandments* (e.g., Mk 7:9-13; 10:19). Similarly, the numerous accounts of the miraculous healing of children (e.g., the healing* of Jairus' twelve-year-old daughter in Mk 5:21-43) are expressions of the power and character of God's coming rule already at work through Jesus (see Miracles, Miracle Stories).

Commentators agree that the sayings of Jesus about children have a complex tradition history. The tendency of the tradition is to develop the metaphorical potential of the child for teaching about Christian discipleship.* As H.-R. Weber says, "Already Mark, Matthew and Luke seem to have been more interested in what a child symbolizes than in Jesus' attitude to actual children" (49). But it may be that Weber is looking for something which is not there, and that for Jesus, as well as for the Evangelists, it was the child as metaphor which was most important in his teaching. Nonetheless, several findings are highly probable.

1.2.1. The Kingdom Belongs to Such As These. Jesus held that children have a share in the kingdom of God (see Kingdom of God). The saying of Jesus in verse 14 of Mark 10:13-14, 16 makes this clear. In this episode Jesus countermands the disciples, welcomes the children and, as a sign of blessing (reminiscent, perhaps, of the blessing of Ephraim and Manasseh by Jacob in Gen 48; see Blessing and Woe), lays his hands upon them. We would be surprised to discover otherwise concerning the attitude of Jesus. The covenantal religion of Israel embraced children. The teaching of the rabbis did likewise (cf. Str-B, 1.786). And the Essenes augmented their ranks by adopting male children (Josephus *J.W.* 2.120).

1.2.2. Receiving the Kingdom As a Child. Jesus taught that the kingdom of God was to be received "as a child (*hōs paidion*)" (Mk 10:15 par. Mt 18:3 and Lk 18:17; cf. Jn 3:3, 5). Here, in a surprising and powerful simile, Jesus makes the child the model for receiving or entering the kingdom. Many suggestions have been made as to precisely how the child is a model (e.g., Best, 1986, 94-97). For Matthew it meant humility (18:4). But the very quality of the saying as metaphor suggests that a variety of meanings is possible and legitimate. Nevertheless, it is most unlikely that the

Gnostic interpretation in terms of sexual innocence, in *Gospel of Thomas* 22 (cf. 37), bears any resemblance to the understanding of Jesus.

1.2.3. Welcoming Little Children. Jesus placed special importance on receiving with kindness and hospitality the least important members of society: children (*see* Mercy). This seems to be the sense underlying the heavily reworked tradition of Mark 9:33-37 and parallels. According to Best, "The so-called *shaliach* principle is employed here to suggest that Jesus is encountered and helped when the child, who is the least of all humans, is encountered and helped" (1981, 80).

2. The Gospels.

Study of the history of the Gospel tradition shows that the stories and sayings about children were very important for the first followers of Jesus in their various attempts to work out what it meant to be God's new covenant people in the period after Jesus' death and resurrection. Invariably, the child becomes a metaphor of discipleship, a way of talking about God and the shared life of faith* in the light of Christ.

2.1. The Gospel of Matthew. The material on children in Matthew is understood best in relation to the Evangelist's emphasis on God as the heavenly Father, on Jesus as the Son of God (*see* Son of God) and on believers as both children of God and brothers and sisters of one another. It relates also to the priority in Matthean ethics of the virtue of humility as the basis for life together as the people of God (*see* Ethics of Jesus).

The birth and infancy narratives (Mt 1—2) are a good case in point. Here in 1:18-25 Jesus is portrayed as the divinely begotten Son (*huios*). But he is also the vulnerable child (*paidion*) who, with his equally vulnerable mother (2:11, 13-14, 20-21), is threatened from the beginning by the (Jewish) powers-that-be, and watched over by his heavenly Father working through angelic intermediaries (*see* Angels). So the coming of Jesus the Son is in weakness and humility, the very qualities which mark him out as the true king of Israel (cf. 2:2, 6, 8, 11) and which subsequently form the center of his teaching (e.g., 5:3-12; 11:29) and lifestyle (cf. 21:5).

In that teaching the figure of the child is prominent. First, it expresses a doctrine of revelation and election. The Father and the Son are made known to the least likely, to "babes" (*nēpioi*, 11:25-26); those, that is, who recognize their weakness and utter dependence upon divine grace and accept the invitation of Jesus as the Wisdom* of God (11:27-29). Second, it expresses a requirement of membership in the

kingdom of God: radical humility (18:1-4; cf. 5:3-5). Third, it provides a way of talking about pastoral care in the Christian community (18:5-14): the leaders of the church* are to avoid at all costs (antinomian) teaching or behavior which would lead the "little ones" (*mikroi*) to stray from the narrow path of righteousness (*see* Justice, Righteousness). Fourth, it expresses a concern for persecuted followers of Christ and, in particular, early Christian missionaries. This seems to be the sense of the reference to "these little ones" in 10:42, as also of the reference to "the least (*elachistoi*) of these my brethren" in 25:40 (cf. 25:45).

When Jesus comes to the Temple after his triumphal entry into Jerusalem (*see* Triumphal Entry), it is not surprising, therefore, that those who rejoice at the arrival in Zion of the Son of David (*see* Son of David) are children (*paidia*, 21:15; cf. the reference to *nēpioi* and *thēlazontes* in 21:16 = Ps 8:3 LXX). It is they who represent God's new covenant people and inherit the kingdom of God.

2.2. The Gospel of Mark. In contrast with Matthew the theology of Mark is less anthropomorphic and the Gospel of Mark is less explicitly ecclesiological and ethical in its orientation. The picture of God as the loving heavenly Father who cares for his Son and for his children on earth as they are obedient to him is much more muted in Mark. Prominent instead is an emphasis on the sovereignty and transcendence of God, the mystery of the divine purpose especially in relation to suffering, and the imperative of faith and watchfulness in the midst of darkness (e.g., Mk 4; 13). Nevertheless, God is depicted as Father and Jesus as the Son (e.g., 1:11; 9:7; 13:32; 14:36; 15:39), while those who do God's will are identified as the spiritual family of Jesus (3:35).

It is significant that the main teaching about children in Mark's Gospel (i.e., 9:33-37; 10:13-16) comes in the central section, 8:27—10:45, where the focus is on the nature of discipleship of the Christ who is to be crucified and raised. Here the child is a metaphor of discipleship (cf. 10:24b), and this is appropriate in a Gospel which emphasizes so strongly that divine power is revealed in weakness and that true greatness lies in becoming last of all for Jesus' sake (e.g., 8:34-35; 12:41-44). It is hardly coincidental that Mark has two stories in which Jesus heals children (5:21-43; 9:14-29), and that both take the form of a raising from death in response to the power of Jesus. For Mark death and resurrection constitute "the way (*hodos*)" of Jesus himself and of all who would follow him.

In 9:33-37, as Best (1981) points out, several sayings have been brought together and placed at the head of a longer block of teaching of the disciples "in the house" (9:33-50). In this context the Jesus of Mark seems to be saying that true greatness is shown in being a servant of all (*see* Service), even to the point of being able to welcome unimportant outsiders—a child (9:36-37), an anonymous exorcist (9:38-41)—into the fellowship.

The material in 10:13-16 is also part of a larger block of tradition relevant to Christian discipleship (10:1-31), dealing successively with marriage and divorce* (10:2-12), children (10:13-16) and property (10:17-31). The second section clearly affirms the legitimate place of children in the Christian fellowship. As with the anonymous exorcist, they are not to be "forbidden" (cf. *kōluein* in 9:39 and 10:14). Rather, Jesus welcomes them in the most demonstrative way by "taking them in his arms" (cf. *enkalizesthai* in 9:36 and 10:16) and blessing them. Particularly important for Mark, though, is the saying in 10:15 where childlike receiving is a metaphor of faith (cf. Légasse, 189ff.; and, for a Jungian interpretation, see Via, 128-133). The possible import of the tradition for Christian liturgical practice, and for infant baptism in particular, seems not to have been a concern of this Evangelist (so Best 1986, 92-94, contra Jeremias, 48ff.).

2.3. The Gospel of Luke. Traditions about children play an important part in expressing what Luke believed about God, the good news of salvation* and how to live the life of Christian faith. These traditions are suggestive of a Christian community ethos which, in partial contrast to the Markan ethos, is more optimistic and world-affirming.

First, the stories of the two miraculous births (Lk 1—2) show that the God of biblical faith is at work again bringing salvation to his people. In a dramatic and powerful narrative, the birth of sons to Elizabeth and Mary is a new beginning in salvation history and the fulfillment of God's covenant promise. Hence, their arrival is marked by prophetic and angelic witness, miraculous signs and outbursts of joy. Even the unborn infant (*brephos*) John leaps for joy at the coming of Mary (1:41, 44), the one who is to give birth to the Son of God (1:32, 35).

Second, the stories of Jesus' presentation at the Temple (2:22-40) and his pilgrimage to the Temple as a boy of twelve (2:41-51) fulfill an important apologetic function, showing that even as a child Jesus revealed those divine qualities which marked him out as the fulfillment of Israel's hopes and as the savior of the world (2:40, 52). The latter episode not only highlights Jesus' divine sonship (2:49), but also its potential cost for Jesus' natural kin (2:48-50; cf. 14:26-27).

Third, children in Luke exemplify the Evangelist's emphasis on the gracious mercy of God toward the poor, the weak and the marginal (*see* Rich and Poor). Witness the birth of a son to a barren woman (1:7, 25) and to a lowly "handmaiden" (*doulē*, 1:48); the revelation of the babe (*brephos*) to shepherds* from the countryside (2:8-14); the identification of the children (*tekna*) of Wisdom as including tax* collectors and sinners* (9:34-35; cf. 9:29-30); the miraculous healing of a man's "only (*monogenēs*, so Luke) son," which moves everyone to wonder at "the majesty of God" (9:37-43); and the parable of the two sons (15:11-32).

Finally, Luke's theology of divine grace toward the poor has an ethical and social corollary (see Beck). It is noteworthy that in Luke's version of the tradition about true greatness (9:46-48), Jesus identifies closely with the child (*paidion*) by putting him "by his side" and, in a more concrete way than in Mark and Matthew, says that, "Whoever receives this child (*touto to paidion*) . . . receives me." Similarly, in Luke's redaction of Mark 10:13-16 it is not children (*paidia*) but "even infants (*kai ta brephē*)" who are brought to Jesus and whom he calls (18:15-17). God's mercy toward the weak is conveyed in Jesus' mercy toward the weak also, and this is the example which disciples of Jesus are to follow (cf. 22:26).

2.4. The Fourth Gospel. Even more than in the Synoptics, child-related material in John is almost entirely metaphorical. It is also distinctly scarce, as the word-statistics in H.-R. Weber's study (56) show. Missing is the Q* parable about the children playing. Missing, likewise, are the stories of Jesus blessing the children and teaching his disciples to "receive" children and to become "like a child." There are no birth or infancy narratives. Stories of children being healed by Jesus are reduced to one (Jn 4:46-54).

This is not to suggest that the Fourth Evangelist deliberately omits material about children, only that his principal concerns lie elsewhere and that his conceptual framework is distinctive. So, for instance, John's interest is more in Jesus' revelatory discourses in Samaria and Judea than in his public ministry among the people (including the children) of Galilee.* Again, the teaching of the Johannine Jesus is predominantly about himself rather than about entry into the kingdom of God or the ethics of the kingdom of God, where (from a Synoptic viewpoint) sayings about children are particularly important.

Oepke (653) makes the important observation that in the Fourth Gospel a consistent linguistic distinction is maintained between Jesus as the Son of God (*ho huios tou theou*) and believers as the children of God (*ta tekna tou theou*) (as in Jn 1:12; 11:52; cf. 1 Jn 3:1-2, 10; 5:2). The strong Pauline eschatological and ecclesiological doctrine that sonship is something which believers share with Christ (e.g., Gal 4:6-7; Rom 8:14-17, 23, 29; 9:4) is absent. This reflects the fact that the central (and highly polemical) focus of this Gospel is christological: Jesus is the unique Son who comes from the Father to reveal his glory* to the world.

So believers are "children of God." This has several connotations, as M. de Jonge shows also. First, God is the source of their life (1:12-13; 3:3-16). Second, and conversely, believers belong no longer to the devil nor to those (including "the Jews") whose father he is (8:39-47; cf. 1 Jn 3:4-12). Third, salvation is universal, available to all who are born anew/from above (1:12-13; 3:4-16; *see* New Birth). Fourth, the believer's relationship with the Father is mediated by the Son and dependent upon obedience to the Son (14:6-17). Interestingly, Jesus does not teach his disciples to pray "Our Father. . . ." Instead he says, "Whatever you ask in my name, I will do it . . ." (14:13). Fifth, God's children are to love one another (13:33-35, noting *teknia* at v. 33). So there is a horizontal dimension to being a child of God which, though rather muted in John's Gospel, comes strongly to the fore in the distinctly ecclesiological concerns of the Epistles (e.g., 1 Jn 2:1, 12-13, 18; 3:1-2, 7, 10).

See also FAMILY; SON OF GOD; WOMEN.

BIBLIOGRAPHY. P. Ariès, *Centuries of Childhood* (London: Jonathan Cape, 1962); W. Barclay, *Educational Ideals in the Ancient World* (Grand Rapids: Baker, 1974); B. E. Beck, *Christian Character in the Gospel of Luke* (London: Epworth, 1989); E. Best, *Following Jesus* (Sheffield: JSOT, 1981); idem, *Disciples and Discipleship* (Edinburgh: T. & T. Clark, 1986); R. E. Brown, *The Birth of the Messiah* (Garden City, NY: Doubleday, 1977); O. Cullmann, "Infancy Gospels," in *New Testament Apocrypha*, ed. E. Hennecke and W. Schneemelcher (2 vols.; Philadelphia: Westminster, 1964-67) I.363-417; M. de Jonge, *Jesus, Stranger from Heaven and Son of God* (Missoula: Scholars, 1977); R. de Vaux, *Ancient Israel* (2 vols.; New York: McGraw-Hill, 1965); J. Jeremias, *Infant Baptism in the First Four Centuries* (London: SCM, 1960); G. Krause, *Die Kinder im Evangelium* (Stuttgart/Göttingen: Klotz, 1973); S. Légasse, *Jésus et L'Enfant* (Paris: Gabalda, 1969); A. Oepke, "παῖς κτλ," *TDNT* V.636-54; B. Rawson, ed., *The Family in Ancient Rome* (New York: Cornell University, 1986); D. O. Via, Jr., *The Ethics of Mark's Gospel in the Middle of Time* (Philadelphia: Fortress, 1985); H.-R. Weber, *Jesus and the Children* (Geneva: WCC, 1979); T. Wiedemann, *Adults and Children in the Roman Empire* (London: Routledge, 1989).   S. C. Barton

CHILDHOOD OF JESUS. *See* BIRTH OF JESUS.

CHREIA/APHORISM

A *chreia* (pl. *chreiai*) is "a saying or act that is well-aimed or apt, expressed concisely, attributed to a person, and regarded as useful for living" (Hock-O'Neil, 26). Chreiai originated in the Socratic and Cynic philosophical circles (fourth century B.C.) to express the wit of philosophers, kings and military commanders. Chreiai were common to both oral and written expression in the Greco-Roman world and were often placed in written collections. An example of a chreia is: "Diogenes the philosopher, on being asked by someone how he could become famous, responded: 'By worrying as little as possible about fame' " (Hock-O'Neil, 85). The Gospels contain numerous chreiai of Jesus and the early Church, and thus a knowledge of chreiai is important for interpreting the Gospels.

The chreia was the basis of one of the many types of rhetorical exercises described in the *Progymnasmata*, the rhetorical textbooks written from the first through the fifth centuries A.D. In the educational system of the Roman Empire these were the curricula for post-secondary education and preparation for rhetorical instruction and public life. The *Progymnasmata* give us most of our information about the chreia and include those of Aelius Theon of Alexandria (first century), Hermogenes (third century) and Aphthonius (fourth century). When discussing chreiai in the New Testament, the *Progymnasmata* of Theon is generally used. His *Progymnasmata* is the oldest surviving handbook, contains the most elaborate discussion and is roughly contemporary with the books of the New Testament (mid to late first century A.D.).

1. Classification
2. Manner of Presentation
3. Manipulation and Use of the Chreia
4. Literary Distinctions
5. Chreiai and the Gospels

1. Classification.

In Theon chreiai are classified in the three broad categories of *sayings, action* and *mixed*. Of these three categories, the *action* chreia is rare and consists of active or passive action in either the situation prompting the action or the response to the situation. The *mixed* chreia contains both speech and action, either in the situation prompting the speech or action, or the response to the situation or both: "And he [Jesus] entered the Temple* and began to drive out those who sold, saying to them, 'It is written, "My house shall be a house of prayer*"; but you have made it a den of robbers' " (Lk 19:45-46 RSV).

The *sayings* chreia may be broken down into three types: *statement, response* and *double*. The *statement* type usually begins with a finite verb in a formula like "he said" or "he used to say." It can be subdivided again into those with or without a specified situation mentioned as having prompted the saying. An example of a *statement*-sayings chreia with a situation mentioned is: "Now after John was arrested, Jesus came into Galilee,* preaching the gospel* of God,* and saying, 'The time is fulfilled, and the kingdom of God* is at hand; repent,* and believe in the gospel' " (Mk 1:14-15 RSV).

The *response*-sayings chreia usually begins with a participle in a formula like "on seeing" or "on being asked." It is of four kinds, all of which are preceded by a speech or reference to a speech in the situation. A question in the situation is involved in three of the four kinds. The question may require only a yes or no answer, more information than a yes or no answer or an explanation in addition to the answer to the question (usually beginning with "for" [*gar*] or "because" [*hoti*]). In the fourth kind a remark rather than a question is the situation for a simple response (usually beginning with "to the one who" [*pros ton*]). An example of a response-sayings chreia needing more information than a yes or no answer is: "And the multitudes asked him [John the Baptist*], 'What then shall we do?' And he answered them, 'He who has two coats, let him share with him who has none; and he who has food, let him do likewise" (Lk 3:10-11 RSV).

In the *double* chreia, each of two sayings could stand independently. Usually the latter rebuts the former, as in: "Then Jesus came from Galilee to the Jordan to John, to be baptized by him. John would have prevented him, saying, 'I need to be baptized by you, and do you come to me?' [chreia 1]. But Jesus answered him, 'Let it be so now; for thus it is fitting for us to fulfil all righteousness.*' Then he consented" [chreia 2] (Mt 3:13-15 RSV).

2. Manner of Presentation.

Chreia can also be described by their manner of presentation or the formal features of the saying itself. They may be presented as a wish, a maxim, an explanation, a double entendre, a syllogism, an enthymeme (an incomplete syllogism); they may be presented symbolically, figuratively, with wit, with an example, with change of subject or in a combination of any of these. An example of a chreia as a maxim is John 4:43-44: "After the two days he [Jesus] departed to Galilee. For Jesus himself testified that a prophet* has no honor in his own country" (Jn 4:43-44 RSV). A chreia with wit is: "Then Peter came up and said to him, 'Lord, how often shall my brother sin

against me, and I forgive him. As many as seven times?' Jesus said to him, 'I do not say to you seven times, but seventy times seven' " (Mt 18:21-22 RSV).

3. Manipulation and Use of the Chreia.

The chreiai and their elaboration were the building blocks of the argumentation, or at times the entire content, of oral and written expression. In the *Progymnasmata*, the meaning of the saying or action in the chreia could be worked out (*ergasia*) as a training exercise in rhetorical composition. According to Theon there were eight topics for the working out of a chreia: recitation (in the same or similar words), inflection (in all the numbers and cases of the language), commentary (append a positive statement), objection (append a negative statement which is the antithesis of the previous positive statement), expansion (recite with greater length), condensation (put in a more concise form), refutation (cite as impossible or false) and/or confirmation (with an argument) (Hock-O'Neil, 95-107).

The *Progymnasmata* of Hermogenes includes an elaboration *(ergasia)* exercise for the chreia in eight topics which treat the chreia as a thesis to be supported: praise of the author, the chreia, rationale, statement from the opposite, analogy, example, citation of an authority (or judgment) and exhortation (Hock-O'Neil, 177). These topics correspond to the standard elements of both an individual argument and the outline of the ancient speech as a whole. This basic outline was used from the first century B.C. onwards. In the Gospels the sayings, actions and situations of chreiai are often expanded with elements of these exercises. For example, Mark 10:13-16 presents an elaborated chreia, found in a more condensed form in Matthew 19:13-15.

4. Literary Distinctions.

The chreia can be a saying or an action, is attributed to a specific person and gives personal or collective wisdom which may or may not be useful for daily living. It needs to be distinguished from other literary forms in the Gospels, especially the maxim, aphorism and pronouncement story. The *maxim (gnōmē)* is always a saying, is not attributed to a specific person and always gives collective wisdom useful for daily living. A maxim attributed to a person becomes a chreia. An *aphorism* is a succinct and pointed statement of a principle, or general truth. It is always a saying, is attributed to a specific person and may or may not give collective wisdom useful for daily living. The aphorism may be the sayings component of a chreia, such as "It is easier for a camel to go through the eye of a needle than for a rich man to enter the kingdom of God" (Mk 10:25 RSV). A *pronouncement story* is a brief narrative ending with a pronouncement by someone in response to a saying or observation. A chreia and a pronouncement story are often the same, the latter being an expanded version of the former.

5. Chreiai and the Gospels.
As our discussion has indicated, chreiai in concise as well as expanded versions are the literary forms of the sayings and actions of Jesus used in the composition of the Gospels. Scholarship has been aware of the chreiai, but only recently has it utilized knowledge of them to analyze the internal rhetoric of the Gospels. This was partly due to Dibelius's assumption that the content and construction of the chreiai differed from the Gospel tradition; an understanding reached with a restrictive conception of chreiai that was ignorant of schemes for the manipulation and elaboration of chreiai. The inaccessibility of the texts of the *Progymnasmata*, only recently made widely available, has also hindered the study of the Gospels in light of the chreiai and contributed to this major weakness in form criticism.*

The works of Plutarch and Diogenes Laertius show that chreiai were expanded for use in biographies. The Gospels share many features of ancient biography and, not unexpectedly, a portion of the Gospels and pronouncement stories can be explained as expanded chreiai (*see* Gospel [Genre]).

Knowledge of chreiai helps us better to understand the formation, transmission and development of the traditions underlying the Gospels. It also provides new explanations of the composition of the units of the Gospels. From a study of chreiai in the Gospels it can be concluded that the Gospel writers were familiar with the chreia form and able to use the progymnasmatic techniques of their composition as taught by rhetoricians. Collections of the chreiai of Jesus and others were available to them, but whether they were in an oral or written form—or both—is uncertain.

See also FORM CRITICISM; RHETORICAL CRITICISM.

BIBLIOGRAPHY. G. W. Buchanan, *Jesus: The King and His Kingdom* (Macon, GA: Mercer University Press, 1984); J. R. Butts, "The Chreia in the Synoptic Gospels," *BTB* 16 (1986) 132-38; J. D. Crossan, *In Fragments: The Aphorisms of Jesus* (New York: Harper and Row, 1983); M. Dibelius, *From Tradition to Gospel* (New York: Charles Scribner's Sons, 1935) 152-64; R. F. Hock and E. N. O'Neil (trans. and ed.), *The Chreia in Ancient Rhetoric:* Vol. I. *The Progymnasmata* (Texts and Translations 27; Graeco-Roman Religion Series 9; Atlanta: Scholars, 1986); B. L. Mack, "Anecdotes and Arguments: The Chreia in Antiquity and Early Christianity" (Occasional Papers of the Institute of Antiquity and Christianity 10; Claremont: Institute for Antiquity and Christianity, 1987); B. L. Mack and V. K. Robbins, *Patterns of Persuasion in the Gospels* (FF; Sonoma, CA: Polebridge, 1989); V. K. Robbins, "The Chreia," in *Greco-Roman Literature and the New Testament,* ed. D. E. Aune (SBLSBS 21; Atlanta: Scholars, 1988) 1-23; J. G. Williams, *Those Who Ponder Proverbs: Aphoristic Thinking and Biblical Literature* (Sheffield: Almond, 1981). D. F. Watson

CHRIST

The Greek word translated "christ" (*christos*) appears 531 times in the NT (Nestle-Aland 26th ed.), and "Christ" is one of the most familiar terms by which Jesus is known, both in the NT and in subsequent Christian tradition. All the canonical Gospels (*see* Canon) apply the term to Jesus, but each has its own interesting variation in the way Jesus is presented as "Christ." The use of "Christ" in the Gospels reflects both the Jewish origins (*see* Judaism) of Christianity and the distinctive modifications of Jewish tradition that characterize early Christian faith. For all the Evangelists Jesus is "the Christ," the Messiah of Israel's* hope. But they also reflect the conviction that Jesus is also the Son of God* and bears a significance that suggests divinity or is at least divine-like. Moreover, Jesus' crucifixion is presented as a decisive aspect of his messianic work, although there seems to have been no Jewish precedent for seeing Messiah's work as involving his own violent death (*see* Death of Jesus).

In order to deal with the use of the term in the canonical Gospels, we must address related questions as well, especially the background of the term and the associated eschatological expectations of ancient Judaism, as well as the use of the term "Christ" in early Christianity prior to the Gospels.

1. Derivation, Meaning and Background
2. NT Usage Outside the Gospels
3. "Christ" in the Four Gospels
4. Conclusion

1. Derivation, Meaning and Background.
The term "christ" is an anglicized form of the Greek word *christos*, originally an adjective meaning "anointed (with ointment or oil)" from the verb *chriō* (to anoint or smear with oil or ointment). *Christos* had no special religious significance in Greek culture prior to the influence of ancient Jewish and Christian usage (on the history of the term, see Grundmann et al.). In ancient Greek-speaking Jewish and Christian circles

christos translates the Hebrew term *māšîaḥ* (about forty-five times in the LXX), which likewise means "anointed (with oil)" but carries a special significance owing to the Israelite practice of anointing with oil a person installed in a special office, such as king or priest (e.g., 1 Sam 9:15-16; 10:1, Saul; 16:3, 12-13, David; Ex 28:41, Aaron and his sons; 1 Chron 29:22, Zadok and Solomon). In such settings the anointing signified that the person was commissioned and approved (by God and the people) for the special office or task. The term *māšîaḥ* is especially significant in some OT passages in connection with the Israelite king (e.g., 1 Sam 24:6; 2 Sam 1:14; cf. Ps 2:2), where the term seems to be a royal title ("the Lord's anointed," etc.) and it appears that the religious connotation is emphasized.

In postexilic OT texts one finds the hope for a renewed (Davidic) monarchy, often pictured with grandiose dimensions and qualities (e.g., Hag 2:20-23; Zech 9:9-10; 12:7—13:1). Out of this hope, but probably not until sometime in the Hellenistic period (after 331 B.C.), Jews came to use *māšîaḥ* (and the Greek equivalent, *christos)* as a designation for a future agent ("messiah") to be sent by God, usually to restore Israel's independence and righteousness.* Recent research suggests, however, that ancient Jewish eschatological expectations of deliverance and sanctification of the elect did not always include the explicit or prominent anticipation of a "messiah," and there seems to have been some variation in the ways "messiah" figures were pictured (e.g., Neusner-Green-Frerichs, de Jonge).

In the Qumran texts, for example (150 B.C.—A.D. 70; *see* Dead Sea Scrolls), we find what appears to be an expectation of two "anointed" figures (e.g., 1QS 9:10-11; CD 12:22-23) who would preside over the elect in the future: a "messiah of Israel" (probably a royal figure) and a "messiah of Aaron" (a priestly figure). For the Qumran community, the latter figure was apparently seen as outranking the royal "messiah" (see S. Talmon in Neusner-Green-Frerichs). In the *Psalms of Solomon* (late first century B.C.), however, hope for the restoration of Israel is tied to God's raising up a descendant of David as "the Lord's anointed one" (*christos kyriou*, 17:32; 18:7), and the messianism here is of a purely royal variety. *1 Enoch* conveys still another image, in which the messianic figure ("the elect one," "the son of man") is pictured in quite exalted terms in heavenly glory and seems to be identified as Enoch (cf. Gen 5:21-24). It is not entirely clear whether this is another type of messianism or if royal/messianic imagery has been appropriated here to describe another type of exalted figure connected with hopes for eschatological salvation.*

We cannot discuss further here the details of pre-Christian Jewish eschatological hopes and the diversity of messianic expectations. It must be emphasized, however, that in the Jewish texts the expectations and speculations about messiah(s) are tied to and overshadowed by other aspirations, such as freedom of the Jewish people from Gentile* domination, and/or the triumph of a particular religious vision of the divine will (e.g., at Qumran), and/or a more general longing for God's kingdom or triumph over unrighteousness and injustice. That is, Jewish hope for messiah(s) was never the center of religious concern for its own sake, but functioned as part of the attempt to project God's eschatological triumph and the realization of aspirations connected with God's triumph. This contrasts with the way the person of Jesus quickly became central and vital in early Christian devotion.

In the NT something like the royal messianism of the *Psalms of Solomon* seems to be the Jewish messianic expectation most often alluded to and presupposed in relating Jesus to the Jewish religious background. This suggests that the idea of a divinely appointed royal agent who would deliver and purify the nation may have been reasonably well known in Jewish circles (e.g., Acts 2:30-36), though it is not so clear how widely embraced such a hope was.

2. NT Usage Outside the Gospels.

It is worth noting the distribution of the term *christos* in the NT. Of the 531 occurrences of the term, 383 are in the Pauline corpus, and 270 of these are in the seven letters whose authorship is virtually undisputed today (Rom, 1 Cor, 2 Cor, Gal, Phil, 1 Thess, Philem). In some other NT writings, likewise, use of *christos* is quite frequent for their size: 1 Peter (22); 1 John (8); Jude (6). But in some larger writings the term is not comparatively frequent: Heb (12); Rev (7). Given their size, the Gospels (especially the Synoptics) do not use *christos* very frequently: Matthew (16); Mark (7); Luke (12, plus 25 occurrences in Acts); John (19).

This quick glimpse of the distribution of *christos* in the NT shows three things. First, the variation in the frequency of the term may indicate differences in the importance attached to it by the different NT authors. However, the differing subject matter and purposes of the individual authors may also have accounted for the frequency variation. Second, the heavy concentration of occurrences of *christos* in Paul's letters (the earliest NT writings) suggests that the term very early became an important part of the vocabulary of Christian faith. Third, the strikingly small share of the total NT occurrences of *christos* in the Gospels, and the variation among the Gospels in the number of uses of *christos*, make it appropriate to question the meaning and role of the term in these specific writings. Before we discuss in detail the Gospels' use of *christos*, however, it will be helpful to comment further on the Christian use of *christos* prior to the Gospels.

2.1. Pre-Gospel Use. The Gospels are commonly dated approximately A.D. 65-100, several decades after the beginning of the Christian movement. For tracing the use of *christos* in the earlier decades, our most important evidence is found in the undisputed letters of Paul, which are generally dated approximately A.D. 50-60, and constitute the earliest surviving Christian writings. Several important studies of Paul's use of *christos* are available (e.g., Kramer, Dahl, Hengel), and we cannot discuss all the issues addressed in these studies. It is necessary here only to review some matters relevant to the use of *christos* in the Gospels.

First, we may compare Paul's use of *christos* with his use of other key christological titles in these writings. Occurrences of *christos* in the seven undisputed letters constitute fifty-one per cent of the total NT occurrences of the term (seventy-two per cent of occurrences are in the writings attributed to Paul in the NT). We might compare the distribution of *kyrios* ("Lord"): 719 occurrences in the NT, 189 (twenty-six per cent) in the undisputed Pauline letters; and the distribution of "Son/Son of God/his Son": 105 occurrences in the NT, fifteen times (fourteen per cent) in these Pauline letters. Two things relevant to *christos* are evident: (1) *christos* is by far Paul's favorite of early Christian titles for Jesus; (2) on the basis of the early date of Paul's letters, we may conclude that in the earliest years of the Christian movement *christos* quickly became a prominent Christian title for Jesus.

Close examination of *christos* in Paul's letters, however, shows that he uses the term almost as a name, or as part of the name for Jesus, and not characteristically as a title. Thus, for example, in Paul *christos* usually appears in the following formulae: "Christ Jesus," "Jesus Christ," "the Lord Jesus Christ" and sometimes simply "Christ." This has led some to ask whether or how well Paul connected the term *christos* to an understanding of Jesus as "messiah," and to what degree *christos* was for Paul, like a name, simply a way of referring to Jesus. In answering this question, several factors are important.

First, it is clear that *christos* was not immediately meaningful as a religious term to ancient Gentiles unfamiliar with Jewish messianic expectations. For example, evidence indicates that *christos* was often understood by pagans to be the name *chrestos* ("useful"), a common Greek name, especially for slaves (e.g., Suetonius, *Claudius* 25.4). This being so, it is

worth asking how easily Paul's Gentile converts would have understood or appreciated a presentation of Jesus as the Messiah.

Second, however, it is likely that Paul, as a Jew familiar with his ancestral tradition (Gal 1:13-14), knew the significance of *christos* in connection with Jewish messianic expectations. In all likelihood, the term *christos* began to be used with reference to Jesus among Jewish Christians even before Paul's apostolic mission. *Christos* must have been appropriated by Jewish Christians from Greek-speaking Jewish circles where it functioned as the translation for *mašiaḥ*. Otherwise, it is impossible to account for the emergence of *christos* as a title for Jesus. Paul's frequent and easy use of the term reflects a well-established Christian usage and is strong evidence that *christos* was a part of the religious vocabulary of Christian groups within the very first few years (A.D. 30-50).

Third, although in Paul's letters *christos* functions syntactically more characteristically as a quasi-name for Jesus than a title (as in "the Christ"), it appears that the term retains in Paul something of its messianic connotation. This is so not only in explicit passages such as Romans 9:5, with its reference to Jesus as "the Christ" (*ho christos*), but also in the wider pattern of Paul's usage. As Kramer has shown, Paul characteristically uses *christos* (either alone or in connection with "Jesus") in passages that refer to Jesus' death and resurrection* (e.g., 1 Cor 15; Rom 3:23; 5:6-7; Gal 3:13), and it is likely that these passages reflect Paul's familiarity with and emphasis on the early Christian conviction that Jesus' crucifixion was part of his mission as the "Messiah." (Hahn's view, 161-62, that the earliest Christian affirmation of Jesus as Messiah was exclusively in connection with the hope of his eschatological return does not do justice to this close connection between the term *christos* and Jesus' death and resurrection in Paul, the earliest evidence of Christian usage we possess.)

Thus, although Paul's letters do not seem to emphasize or make explicit the messianic connotation of the term "Christ," they provide evidence that the term derived from circles of Jewish Christians where this connotation was emphasized and that the proclamation of Jesus as Messiah was a part of the earliest faith of Christianity. Paul's use of *christos* almost as a name for Jesus has been taken by some scholars as suggesting that among his Gentile converts the term's association with Jewish messianic expectations was not emphasized. But, as the Gospels demonstrate, the claim that Jesus is the Messiah remained a part of early Christian faith well after the Christian movement grew beyond its initial stage as a sect of ancient

Judaism. As will be shown in the next sections, although early Christians modified the connotation of the term *christos* in light of Jesus' death and their experience of his resurrected glory, the term retained something of its sense as designating Jesus as the "Messiah," the divinely designated agent of salvation.

2.2. Use of "Christos" in Other NT Writings. In the many occurrences of *christos* in the writings in the Pauline corpus whose authorship is disputed or widely doubted among scholars (often called "deutero-Pauline" letters: Eph, Col, 2 Thess, 1 Tim, 2 Tim, Titus), the usage is basically like that found in the undisputed Pauline letters. However, the use of the term in NT writings outside the Pauline corpus and the Gospels is relevant to understanding the background for the use of *christos* in the Gospels. For example, 1 Peter uses the term twenty-two times, often in connection with the theme of suffering—both of Christ and/or of Christians: the OT prophets predicted Christ's sufferings (1:11); Christ's redemptive suffering is mentioned several times (e.g., 2:21; 3:18; 4:1; 5:1); and Christians share in Christ's sufferings (4:13). This connection between the term *christos* and suffering probably reflects the early Christian emphasis mentioned earlier Jesus' crucifixion was a messianic event. It also shows how the idea of Jesus the suffering Messiah was used to inspire Christians to endure sufferings in his name.

In Revelation, along with more formulaic uses of *christos* ("Jesus Christ," e.g., 1:1-2, 5), there are interesting passages where the term is used as a title, "messiah" (e.g., 11:15 "our Lord and his Christ"; 12:10 "the authority of his Christ"). These passages portray the eschatological triumph of God in terms drawn from Jewish messianic expectation and thus confirm the continuing awareness in Christian circles of the late first century A.D. that "Christ" is a messianic designation.

Likewise, in 1 John 2:22 and 5:1, the confession that Jesus is "the Christ" reflects the messianic claim. But this same document shows the emergence of distinctively Christian doctrinal disputes about the reality or importance of Jesus' human nature (e.g., 4:2, "Jesus Christ has come in the flesh"), and the author coins the term "antichrist" to describe those whose christology he finds seriously inadequate (2:22). In 1 John we see again how *christos* can function both to designate Jesus in messianic terms and also almost as a name for Jesus.

This brief survey of uses of *christos* in NT writings other than the Gospels gives us a general understanding of the first-century Christian background of the term that is presupposed as familiar to the readers of the Gospels. With this background in mind, we are now able to discuss in comparatively greater detail how the individual Evangelists use the term in their stories of Jesus.

3. "Christ" in the Four Gospels.

As we have indicated already, each Evangelist applies *christos* to Jesus, but does so with particular nuances and emphases. We shall therefore discuss their usage individually; and, accepting commonly held scholarly opinion, we shall deal with the Evangelists in their probable chronological order (*see* Synoptic Problem).

Modern scholarly investigation of NT christology has expended a great deal of effort in analyzing the use of christological titles in the Gospels and in the other NT writings (e.g., Hahn). In spite of this, certain disagreements remain in contemporary discussions, making a survey such as this a difficult enterprise. To some degree conclusions about one particular title, such as *christos*, are connected with conclusions about the Evangelists' use of the other titles, and this will be reflected in the following discussion.

3.1. Mark. The earliest of the canonical Gospels, Mark, shows the complexity of applying the term *christos* to Jesus. In varying ways this complexity characterizes all four Evangelists.

From the opening words in 1:1, the author indicates familiarity and acceptance of the term as applied to Jesus ("the gospel of Jesus Christ"), and at various other points the author uses the term as a way of referring to Jesus. For example, in 9:41 a reward is promised to anyone who gives a cup of water to Jesus' disciples "because you are Christ's" (cf. Mt 10:42).

The warning in 13:21-22 about the coming times of crisis when some will say, "Look, here is the Christ!," and the caution about "false Christs" implicitly show that for Mark the title belongs properly to Jesus alone, whose coming with glory will need no such announcement (13:26-27). *Christos* is used as a title here, and this passage insists that the only genuine fulfillment of the messianic hopes—falsely appropriated by deceivers—will be Jesus' appearance as "the Son of Man* coming in clouds with great glory." The warning about deceivers probably reflects a conflict between early Christian claims about Jesus as Messiah and other messianic hopes circulating among Jewish groups. (Cf. 13:6, which refers to deceivers who claim "I am he!" The variation in some manuscripts, "I am the Christ," is probably a scribal harmonization with the form of the saying in Mt 24:5. Scholars debate whether the significance of "I am he" is a messianic claim or a claim to divinity alluding to God's self-description; see the discussion of 14:61-62 below.)

In several other passages, however, *christos* is used with a certain reserve or subtlety that has generated scholarly debate over Mark's intent. Perhaps the most familiar of these is 8:29-30, where Peter acclaims Jesus as "the Christ" (*ho christos*) and is immediately ordered by Jesus "to tell no one about him" (cf. Mt 16:16-20; Lk 9:20-21). Believing that Jesus did not see himself as the Messiah, some scholars have suggested that Jesus' original response to Peter's acclamation was the rebuke "Get behind me, Satan!" in 8:33, and that Jesus rejected the messianic appellation altogether. In this view, Mark recast the incident, introducing the command to secrecy (8:30) and making Jesus' rebuke apply to Peter's rejection of Jesus' sufferings (8:31-33). There are, then, two issues: Jesus' own attitude toward the appellation "messiah" and Mark's treatment of the messiah/*christos* term here. The latter question is the primary concern before us, but a few comments about the authenticity of the Markan scene are relevant as well.

The speculative attempt to reconstruct the original dialog between Peter and Jesus as described above is probably ill-conceived. There is little basis for regarding Jesus' command to silence in 8:30 as Markan invention while holding Jesus' rebuke of Peter in 8:33 as authentically from Jesus. On the one hand, both function quite well as redactional elements (*see* Redaction Criticism) in the scene, and both can be explained as deriving from Mark's editorial purpose (Lk 9:20-22 does not include Jesus' rebuke of Peter). On the other hand, both statements can equally well be attributed to Jesus. If Jesus did predict his own rejection and death (not so unlikely in view of the ancient Jewish tradition of Israel's rejection of prophets and the martyrdom of John the Baptist* with whom Jesus associated himself), Peter's negative response is thoroughly understandable, as is Jesus' rebuke of Peter in 8:33 (*see* Predictions of Jesus' Passion and Resurrection). And the notion that Jesus could not possibly have seen himself in messianic terms rests to some degree on the assumption that "messiah" carried a single meaning, having to do with a Davidic, royal figure with military intentions. With such a figure, it is widely thought, Jesus cannot be compared and he could not have thought of himself in this fashion. But the diversity evident in ancient Jewish messianic speculations (e.g., Smith, Neusner-Green-Frerichs, de Jonge) suggests that Jesus may have rejected this or that form of messianic speculation while understanding his mission in the light of his own definition of messiahship. Therefore, Jesus could have ordered silence about the use of the

Messiah/Christ title among his disciples because the term did not itself communicate clearly his own vision of his task and was subject to what he considered severe misunderstandings. In light of this, the command to silence in 8:30 can be as plausibly authentic a saying as Jesus' rebuke of Peter in 8:33.

Debates about what Jesus himself may or may not have felt about the term "messiah" (*christos*) are thus more complicated than even some scholars recognize. Determining Mark's intention is comparatively easier, though still not without problems. In view of Mark's use of *christos* in the passages examined already, we must conclude that Mark intends Peter's acclamation of Jesus as "Christ" to be taken at least in some sense positively. Jesus' command in 8:30 is to say nothing about him to others; it is not a rejection of the term *christos* outright. Yet 8:30-33 indicates a reserve about the term, and the reason seems to be that none of the pre-Christian definitions of *christos* prepare one to understand Jesus' mission, as is shown by Peter's reaction to Jesus' prediction of his suffering. Thus 8:29-33 hints that the term *christos* achieves its proper meaning as a title for Jesus in light of his divinely mandated sufferings (the divine necessity indicated by the "must suffer" of 8:31). That is, this passage suggests that Jesus is the Christ, but cannot be so identified apart from an appreciation of his crucifixion as central to his messianic task.

The appearance of the title "Christ" in 8:27-30 must also be seen in the light of the overall narrative of Mark. At various points earlier in Mark others have asked about Jesus (1:27; 2:7; 4:41; 6:2-3) or have offered identifications of him (1:24; 3:22; 5:7; 6:14-16). In 8:27-30, however, Jesus himself poses the question of his identity and demands a response from the Twelve, which has the effect of making explicit the simmering question of his true significance. Consequently, 8:27-30 is a turning-point in Mark. Jesus' question is to be dealt with in light of the preceding narratives of his ministry, and gathers up all that has gone before it in Mark. Structurally his question also anticipates the question of the priest in 14:61, which is the climax of the Jewish trial and rejection of Jesus (*see* Trial of Jesus). In the latter episode Jesus is asked about his identity, and the messianic acclamation of Peter is also affirmed by Jesus himself.

In 14:61-62 the chief priest asks Jesus, "Are you the Christ, the son of the Blessed One?" Jesus responds affirmatively, "I am" (*egō eimi*), and then predicts his own vindication at God's "right hand." The Markan form of Jesus' reply is more emphatic than the parallels (cf. Mt 26:64; Lk 22:70, the variants in some Markan manuscripts are probably scribal harmonizations with these parallels). The "I am," a possible allusion to the self-descriptive language of God in the OT (e.g., Is 43:10, 13), may also have been intended by Mark to hint at Jesus' transcendent significance.

This is made even more likely by the allusion here to the glorification of the "son of man" in Daniel 7:13-14. Jesus' full reply to the priest's question asserts that, though he does not seem to fit some messianic expectations (such as the royal-Davidic model mentioned in 12:35), he is rightfully *christos* and his status will be vindicated directly in glorious dimensions. Contrary to the views of some earlier scholars, the phrase "the son of man" (v. 62) is not a title for a well-known figure in Jewish eschatological speculation (see, e.g., Casey) and was not intended by Mark as a preferred title in place of *christos* (see esp. Kingsbury, 1983). For Mark, Jesus is the Christ (Messiah), the Son of God (*see* Son of God), and the allusion to the Danielic scene of divine triumph serves to make it clear that "the son of man," rejected by the Jewish leaders, will in fact be vindicated as *christos* and divine Son in heavenly glory (*see* Son of Man).

Another much-discussed passage is 12:35-37 (cf. Mt 22:41-45; Lk 20:41-44). Jesus' question about how the Christ can be the Son of David* is of course not a theoretical question. The reader is expected to understand that the question really (albeit somewhat obliquely) has to do with Jesus' true identity and significance. And the point of 12:35-37 is to indicate the inadequacy of "Son of David" as the category for understanding who the Christ is, for David calls him "Lord" (Gk *kyrios;* Heb. *'ǎdōnāy*), suggesting that the Christ is far superior to David. That is, David is not an adequate model for the work or person of the Christ. Here again, *christos* is implicitly accepted as a title for Jesus, but one popular understanding of the term (attributed to "the scribes," v. 35) is found inadequate. In light of the places where God addresses Jesus as the divine Son (1:11; 9:7), as well as other indications of Jesus' divine-like significance in Mark (e.g., stilling the storm in 4:35-41, esp. the disciples' awe-filled question in v. 41), the reader is expected to see that Jesus "the Christ" is far greater than the commonly accepted notions of the Messiah.

The final occurrence of *christos* in Mark is in 15:32, where observers of Jesus' crucifixion mockingly address him as "the Christ, the king of Israel." This is one of many examples of Markan irony (especially frequent in the passion account), and is one of several places where the question of whether Jesus is the king of Israel or king of the Jews appears in the narrative of the trial and crucifixion (cf. 15:2, 9, 12, 18-20, 26; see Juel). The Markan irony in the mockery of Jesus

as "the Christ" in 15:32 is that, contrary to the mockers, Jesus is "the Christ, the king of Israel," though his ultimate vindication lies by way of his crucifixion and apparent failure. The pagan form of the mockery, in the title attached to the cross ("The King of the Jews"), gives the charge for which Jesus was executed, but is also an ironic truth: Jesus really is the rightful "king," rejected both by pagan and Jewish leaders.

It is interesting to note the distribution of uses of *christos* in Mark. The occurrences of *christos* are concentrated in the second half of the book, where the shadow of Jesus' coming death looms over the narrative. After the opening words in 1:1, *christos* does not appear in Mark until 8:29-30, in a complex of material that combines Jesus' explicit question about his significance with the first prediction of his sufferings (the variants in 1:34 are probably scribal harmonizations with Lk 4:41). Thereafter, aside from 9:41, *christos* appears in the material describing Jesus' final confrontation with Jewish authorities in Jerusalem, which culminates in his execution. The true stature of "the Christ" is the one teasing question Jesus asks in a list of questions debated in 11:27—12:40. Jesus' discourse about the future (13:5-37) includes the prominent reference to "false Christs," who are to be distinguished from the true Christ, Jesus. In the Jewish trial the question whether Jesus is the Christ culminates the interrogation. And in the crucifixion account the mocking acclamation of Jesus as "the Christ" is the final ironic indignity heaped upon Jesus by his tormentors. Mark uses *christos* sparingly, but every occurrence is significant.

Thus, although Mark affirms other christological titles for Jesus (especially important is "Son of God" and its variations in 1:1, 11, 24, 34; 3:11-12; 5:7; 9:7; 15:39; see, e.g., Kingsbury, 1983), *christos* too is an important term in Mark's acclamation of Jesus. The cluster of uses of *christos* in the accounts of Jesus' final conflict with the Jewish religious establishment, their rejection of him and his execution at the hands of the Roman ruler reflects two things: (1) the close link in early Christian proclamation and in Mark between the term *christos* and Jesus' death, and (2) the recognition that the Christian identification of Jesus as *christos* involves a claim with special reference to Jewish religious hopes and beliefs.

Mark insists that *christos* receives its true meaning as a title for Jesus only in light of Jesus himself, his divinely ordained suffering and his transcendent significance as "Son of God." And Mark shows that the identification of Jesus as *christos* involves a claim that challenged the Jewish religious leadership, both for its handling of Jesus in his own ministry and for its continued negative response to the early Christian proclamation about Jesus.

The clustering of uses of *christos* in the final chapters of the story of Jesus is found also in Matthew and Luke, as we shall see. Thus, Mark was either influential in this matter and/or with the other Synoptics reflected the association of *christos* with references to Jesus' death. But unlike the other Evangelists, Mark's use of *christos* is almost entirely confined to the passion material, making the association of the term with the death of Jesus more emphatic.

3.2. Matthew. With some ninety per cent of Mark appearing also in Matthew, it is not surprising that a considerable number of the Markan uses of *christos* reappear in Matthew. But there are also noteworthy distinctives in Matthew's use of the term, including his pattern of usage.

First, there is a cluster of occurrences of *christos* early in the book. The opening words of Matthew (1:1) refer to "Jesus Christ, the son of David, the son of Abraham." This illustrates the Judaic flavor of Matthew's account and prefigures the way Matthew will connect Jesus to the history and religious hopes of Israel in the material that follows. The Judaic quality of Matthew's presentation of Jesus is evident also in 1:16, which concludes Jesus' genealogy by referring to him simply as "the Christ." The connection between Jesus and Israel is illustrated in 1:17, which portrays Israel's history in three stages, culminating with "the Christ."

Matthew's emphasis on the royal connotations of the term "Christ" is indicated in 2:1-4, where the Magi ask about the birth of the "king of the Jews" and Herod responds by inquiring about OT prophecies of the birthplace of "the Christ."

But following this cluster of occurrences, *christos* does not appear in Matthew until 11:2, where the imprisoned Baptist hears of "the deeds of the Christ," the works of Jesus (cf. Lk 7:18). This phrase may refer retrospectively to the entire preceding narrative of Jesus' ministry (Mt 1—10). If so, it gives an explicitly messianic coloring to the whole.

Matthew's affirmation of the *christos* title is also evident in the next occurrence of the term in 16:16, where Peter acclaims Jesus as "the Christ, the Son of the living God." This forms Matthew's parallel to Mark 8:29. The second part of the acclamation both expands Mark's simpler form and makes each of the two titles interpret the other. That is, "Son of the living God" underscores Jesus' exalted status, and "the Christ" emphasizes that this divine Son fulfills all

messianic hopes. Matthew 16:20 retains from Mark 8:30 Jesus' command to secrecy, but the order to silence concerning the *christos* title is more explicit in Matthew than in Mark. As in Mark, there is a cluster of occurrences of *christos* in the chapters concerning Jesus' final days in Jerusalem. Matthew 22:41-45 presents the question about the Christ as Son of David (discussed above), and like Mark makes the question the climax of a series of debates between Jesus and his critics. But in a saying unique to Matthew (23:10), the disciples are told that their true "master" (*kathēgetēs*) is "the Christ." This reflects Matthew's emphasis that "the Christ" is the authoritative teacher of the community, a theme most evident in the large blocks of teaching material in this Gospel (chaps. 5—7, 10, 13, 18, 23—25).

The remaining occurrences in Matthew appear in passages paralleled in Mark. But the Matthean form of the passages generally make more explicit the theme of Jesus' messianic status. In 24:5 the deceivers' false claim, which conflicts with Jesus' rightful status, is directly messianic; "I am the Christ" (cf. 24:23; Mk 13:6, "I am"). In 26:63-64 the priest's question as to whether Jesus claims to be "the Christ, the Son of God" is introduced with a solemn adjuration; and though Jesus' response appears less direct ("You have said so"), it is to be taken as a positive reply. This is confirmed in 26:68 by the distinctively Matthean form of the taunt by Jesus' tormentors, "Prophesy to us, you Christ!" (cf. Mk 14:65; Lk 22:64). And finally, in a uniquely Matthean wording, Pilate twice asks what the Jews wish him to do with "Jesus who is called Christ" (27:17, 23), making the question of Jesus' messiahship quite explicit.

It is clear that *christos* is a major christological title for Matthew. In comparison with Mark, the title seems more prominent and important an item of religious vocabulary in Matthew. "Christ" appears in Matthew over twice as many times as in Mark and in passages where the term is lacking in the Markan parallel. Further, there is a more explicit connection between *christos* and Israel in Matthew, a feature particularly evident in the nativity account. Like Mark, however, Matthew has a cluster of occurrences in the material describing Jesus' final conflict with the Jewish leaders and his execution. And, like Mark, for Matthew it is Jesus who defines the term "Christ/Messiah" rather than it being defined by others. Jewish expectations about Messiah are not adequate for considering Jesus' messianic claims. Thus, Jesus the Christ is "Son of the living God," and his rejection and crucifixion form an important part of his messianic mission, both of these claims constituting significant modifications of pre-

Christian messianic speculation.

3.3. Luke. In considering the use of *christos* in Luke, we must also take account of the second volume of the author's work, the Acts of the Apostles, which we shall briefly examine first (see also Fitzmyer, 197-200).

3.3.1. Usage in Acts. A little over half (thirteen) of the twenty-five occurrences of *christos* in Acts are in formulaic references to Jesus: "Jesus Christ" (2:38; 3:6; 4:10; 8:12; 9:34; 10:36, 48; 16:18), "Christ Jesus" (18:5; 24:24), "the Lord Jesus Christ" (11:17; 15:26; 28:31). Aside from 4:26, where *christos* appears in a quotation from Psalm 2:2, the other eleven occurrences are in descriptions of Christians attempting to persuade Jews that Jesus is "the Christ," that is, they attempt to present Jesus as the fulfillment of messianic hopes. In these cases, the term is used as a title and obviously derives its meaning from the context of Jewish expectations of a messiah. Some of the Acts passages reflect the attempt to deal with Jesus' sufferings as the fulfillment of OT texts interpreted as messianic prophecies (2:31; 3:18; 17:3; 26:23). Other passages describe a more general claim that Jesus is the Messiah (2:36; 3:20; 5:42; 8:5; 9:22; 18:28).

Acts claims to present the preaching of the earliest decades of Christianity. This, plus the peculiar wording of some passages in Acts, has led some scholars to argue that from this book we can reconstruct early forms of Christian faith in the book that are distinguishable from more mature forms in other NT writings. Sometimes these suggestions focus on 2:36, where God is said to have "made him [Jesus] both Lord and Christ," or on 3:20, which describes Jesus as "the Christ appointed for you [Israel]." In the former passage, it is suggested, we may have a remnant of an early adoptionist type of christology in which Jesus is seen as being appointed Messiah at his resurrection. In the latter passage some have found a remnant of the view of Jesus as a kind of Messiah-designate, who will exercise his office only in the future when he is sent to preside in the eschatological restoration of Israel. Scholars proposing these suggestions believe that we may be able to see traces of the development and change in the earliest Christian understanding of Jesus as Messiah.

The author of Acts certainly did not embrace either of the forms of christology just described. Luke's birth narrative (Luke 1—2), for example, shows that the author regarded Jesus as Messiah from the time of his miraculous conception onward (*see* Birth of Jesus). And it is questionable that he would have incorporated christological views in tension with his own in his account of early Christianity without indicating that they were deficient. This does not settle fully the question of the original meaning of the statements, but it suggests that the author of Acts did not understand the statements the way some modern scholars have.

In fact, nothing in either passage conveys the christological views some attribute to them. The titles "Lord and Christ" (*kyrios* and *christos*) in Acts 2:36 represent quite an exalted view of Jesus, and the passage simply asserts that Jesus holds such an exalted status by God's will. Nothing demands the conclusion that Jesus was made Messiah only at his baptism or resurrection. It is anachronistic to read an adoptionist christology into this passage. Similarly, 3:20 simply urges that, in spite of its rejection of Jesus, Israel may yet partake in the fulfillment of messianic hopes by recognizing in Jesus its only true Messiah. We certainly have here a reflection of the eschatological orientation of early Christian faith, which included the conviction that Jesus the Messiah would be vindicated on a grand scale in a future triumph of God's purposes. But, again, nothing in Acts 3:20 requires the conclusion that it preserves traces of a purely futurist understanding of Jesus' messiahship. The passages can be read as reflecting some sort of adoptionist or purely futurist messianism only by first presuming what must first be demonstrated—that such views must have characterized the earliest Christian circles. But our constructions of early christologies must surely rest on more than presumptions.

In sum, the use of *christos* in Acts reflects three characteristics: (1) "Christ" is part of the common namelike designation of Jesus in early Christian circles; (2) the term was also used as a title when the author wished to make explicit the claim that Jesus was the fulfillment of Israel's hopes for God's redemption; (3) the author shows special concern to insist that Jesus' crucifixion was predicted in the OT and does not disqualify Jesus from being Messiah (*see* Death of Jesus; Typology).

3.3.2. Usage in the Gospel. The frequent use of *christos* as a title in Acts is to be set alongside the consistent use of the term in this way in all twelve occurrences in Luke's Gospel. The one possible exception is 2:11, where the angel announces the birth of "a Savior, who is Christ the Lord" [*christos kyrios*]. But even here it is probable that the author uses the term as a title, "the Christ, the Lord" (cf. Acts 2:36; assuming that the variant attested in some versions, "the Lord's Christ" [*christos kyriou*], is not the original reading).

Certainly in all other occurrences of *christos* in Luke the term is used as a title (Messiah) and Jesus is explicitly connected with ancient Jewish messianic hopes. This connection is evident in 2:26, where we are introduced to Simeon, who awaited the "consolation of Israel" and had been promised by God that he would live to see "the Lord's Christ" (*see* Simeon's Song). Likewise, in 3:15 the Baptist is asked if he is "the Christ," and replies by contrasting himself with the "mightier" one coming after him. In 4:41 the demons'* knowledge of Jesus has to do explicitly with his messianic status: "they knew that he [Jesus] was the Christ" (cf. Mk 1:34). Thereafter, *christos* does not appear until 9:20 in Peter's acclamation of Jesus as "The Christ of God," a more Judaic-sounding acclamation than the versions in Matthew 16:16 and Mark 8:29. (Note also the Jewish mockery of Jesus in Luke 23:35.)

As with the other Synoptics, Luke also presents a clustering of occurrences of *christos* in the material describing Jesus' final days of conflict in Jerusalem. There is Jesus' question about Messiah being thought of as David's son (20:41), an issue we have dealt with earlier in our discussion of Mark. Unlike Matthew and Mark, in Luke 21:8 Jesus' prediction of deceivers does not explicitly mention false messiahs, but refers only to those who will say, "I am he!" In the Jewish trial, however, the priest demands simply whether Jesus claims to be "the Christ" (22:67), and the following question, "Are you the Son of God, then?" (22:70) should also be taken as an inquiry about Jesus' messianic claim. Jesus' response, "You say that I am," seems less direct than the Markan version (14:62), but is no doubt to be taken as an affirmation. As we have seen, Luke clearly presents Jesus as Messiah. This emphasis is further borne out in the Lukan version of the charges against Jesus before Pilate in 23:2, which includes the statement that Jesus claimed to be "Christ a king." Luke thereby links the Jewish and Roman trials as considerations of Jesus' messiahship. For, in spite of Pilate's statement that he found Jesus innocent of any of the charges against him (23:13-16, 22), the mockery by both Jews and Romans (23:35-37) and the inscription on the cross (23:38) make Jesus' execution a rejection of his messianic claim.

The final Lukan affirmations of Jesus' messiahship appear in 24:26-27 and 44-47, where the risen Jesus identifies himself as "the Christ," whose sufferings and subsequent glory are predicted in the OT. At the same time, these passages also show that Jesus' messianic status involves a significant departure from more familiar Jewish messianic expectations, especially in light of his crucifixion. Even Jesus' disciples are pictured as ill-prepared for his execution ("O foolish men, and slow of heart to believe," 24:25), and the risen Jesus must "open their minds" to read the OT

so as to see that all was predicted (24:27, 45).

Thus, as with the other Synoptics, in Luke the claim that Jesus is "Christ" is not simply an identification of him with Jewish expectations but is a redefinition of the meaning of messiahship. And this redefinition is based almost entirely on the story of Jesus, producing a distinctively Christian notion of "the Christ." Luke emphasizes the sufferings of "the Christ" as the divinely predicted completion and core of his earthly work, issuing in the proclamation of forgiveness to Israel and the world (24:47) recounted in Acts (e.g., 1:8).

Like Matthew, Luke emphatically links Jesus with the OT and Israel. This is reflected in the pattern of occurrences of *christos* in both Gospels. Both Matthew and Luke have important occurrences in their nativity narratives as well as the cluster of occurrences in their final chapters, and both nativity accounts make Jesus' birth the fulfillment of Israelite hopes. To be sure, both Matthew and Luke also make Jesus' messiahship a crisis for Israel, and portray the Jewish rejection of Jesus as a failure to embrace Israel's true king. Modern scholarship has given much attention to the critique of the Jews in these Gospels. In light of the way Christian societies have treated Jews over the centuries, this critique has an uncomfortable ring to it. But the strongly negative portrayal of Jewish opponents of Jesus in the Gospels did not arise from simple maliciousness. It reflects how deeply important to early Christians was the conviction that Jesus was "the Christ," the Messiah understood to have been promised by God in the OT and pictured in various ways (inaccurately, in the eyes of early Christians) in ancient Jewish tradition. For the Christians whose faith is reflected in the Gospels, Jesus was certainly much more than the Messiah of any Jewish expectation, but they never surrendered the claim that Jesus was also the true Messiah.

3.4. John. The profound redefinition of messiahship in early Christianity and the tension with Jewish messianic traditions is nowhere more evident than in John. Of the nineteen occurrences of *christos* in John, only two are formulaic ("Jesus Christ," 1:17; 17:3). In all other occurrences *christos* is used as a title and Jewish messianic expectations are either mentioned or alluded to. Although there is much more to the christology of John than the claim that Jesus is the Messiah, the comparatively greater frequency of *christos* in John and the emphatic way the term functions in the narrative make it clear that Jesus' messiahship is a major feature of the author's faith.

Perhaps most important for assessing the significance of *christos* in John is 20:31, where the author explicitly gives his purpose as seeking to promote belief that "Jesus is the Christ the Son of God." On the one hand, the acclamation of Jesus as "the Christ" forms a central part of the author's own summary of Christian faith, one of the two titles the author chooses here to portray Jesus. On the other hand, "the Christ" is also "the Son of God," and John regards Jesus' divine sonship as the key christological category, involving the understanding of Jesus as pre-existent and sharing richly in divine glory (e.g., 17:1-5). Thus, 20:31 reflects the claims that Jesus is the Messiah and that this Messiah is much more exalted than Jewish messianic speculations characteristically allowed. Though these claims are also reflected in varying ways in the other canonical Gospels, in John they are asserted with particular force.

Much more than the other Evangelists, John uses Jewish messianic speculations as a foil for the presentation of Jesus. In 1:19-28 he introduces us to Jewish speculations, where Jewish authorities interrogate the Baptist as to whether he claims to be "the Christ," Elijah* or "the prophet"*—and to each he answers negatively. The Baptist acclaims Jesus as "the Lamb of God"* (1:29, 35) and "the Son of God" (1:34), but these titles must be read in connection with 3:25-30, where the Baptist again denies that he himself is "the Christ" and applies the title to Jesus. The author presents the Baptist as a true witness to Jesus, and the Baptist's acclamations refer both to Jesus' divine sonship and his messianic status.

The implied messianism in the Baptist's acclamation of Jesus is confirmed in the narratives reporting the responses to Jesus by, among others, the followers of the Baptist. In 1:41 Andrew refers to Jesus as "the Messiah" (*messias*), and this transliterated Aramaic term is translated by the author as *christos*. In 1:45 Philip describes Jesus as the one predicted in "the law and also the prophets." That the Messiah is in mind is confirmed shortly in the guileless Nathaniel's acclamation of Jesus as "the Son of God . . . the King of Israel" (1:49). As Jesus' response to Nathaniel suggests (1:50-51), these disciples do not realize the fullness of Jesus' person and status, but John intends us to see that their acclamations of Jesus in messianic categories are correct as far as they go.

In 7:25-44 Jewish messianic speculations are played off against the messianic identity of Jesus. The crowd wonders if the authorities secretly think that Jesus is "the Christ" (7:26), but some find difficulty reconciling this interpretation of Jesus with a tradition that "when the Christ appears, no one will know where he comes from" (7:27, a messianic tradition not otherwise clearly attested). In 7:31 there is an allusion to the

Messiah as one who performs signs, and Jesus' signs are taken by some as suggesting Jesus' messiahship. A little later we read (7:40-44) that while some conclude that Jesus is "the Christ," others have difficulty reconciling Jesus' Galilean background with traditions that Messiah will come from Bethlehem and be a descendant of David.

Again, in 12:34 the crowd refers to a tradition that "the Christ remains forever" and questions how this can be reconciled with Jesus' prediction that he will be "lifted up." And the Samaritan* woman alludes to a tradition that Messiah "will show us all things" (4:25), finding in Jesus' uncanny knowledge of her life a suggestion that he may be "the Christ" (4:29).

The accuracy of John's references to Jewish messianic traditions is an interesting question that cannot detain us here. Some of these traditions are not otherwise clearly attested, but recent research suggests that John includes some material of Palestinian provenance and these references to Jewish messianic traditions may be more valuable than some have recognized (see, e.g., M. de Jonge, 1972/73).

More germane to the present discussion is the question of what the author's point is in these passages. In brief, it seems that John is utilizing irony in the passages where the Jews cannot reconcile Jesus and their messianic traditions. The Jews unwittingly show that they do not properly understand their own traditions and/or do not really know enough about Jesus whom they think they know and can dismiss so easily. Thus, in light of passages such as 1:1-18 and 6:41-45, the reader sees that the Jews do not really know where Jesus comes from (heaven) and that Jesus does fulfill the tradition about Messiah's origin being unknown. Similarly, in 12:34 the Son of man who is to be "lifted up" does also "remain forever," for he has come down from heaven and ascends back to heavenly glory with God, thus fulfilling the messianic tradition invoked here. We are probably to take 7:40-42 as ironic also—John expects his readers to know the Christian tradition that Jesus was born in Bethlehem and so fulfills what "the Scripture said" about the birthplace of the Messiah.

The interplay between Jewish messianism and the early Christian redefinition is also evidenced in 10:22-39. Here "the Jews" ask Jesus directly if he claims to be "the Christ" (10:34), and Jesus' response is an indirect affirmation (10:25-39). But Jesus also quickly employs the Father/Son language to describe his status, and its offensiveness to the Jews (10:33, 39) shows that it is intended to connote much more than a simple identification of Jesus as the Messiah of Jewish expectation. In this incident the Jews' problem is not their difficulty fitting what they know of Jesus into some specific messianic tradition, but an inability to accept the claim that Jesus the Messiah is the Son of God who shares in divinity with the Father (10:37-38).

Other passages confirm that *christos* is an important christological title in John and that the author wishes to present Jesus as the true Messiah. In 9:22 it is the confession of Jesus as "the Christ" that leads to synagogue expulsion, a passage commonly thought today to reflect the christological controversies between the Johannine Christians and the Jewish authorities of their own day. In a manner unique among the Gospel writers, John twice links the term *christos* explicitly with the Semitic term "Messiah" (*messias*, 1:41; 4:25). The Fourth Evangelist considers Jewish definitions of the Messiah inadequate, but he does not surrender the basic category in portraying Jesus.

Within the Lazarus episode, structurally important as the seventh and climactic "sign" in John, Martha's acclamation of Jesus as "the Christ, the Son of God" (11:27) both affirms Jesus' preceding self-description as "the resurrection and the life" and corresponds to the Evangelist's own description of the proper Christian confession in 20:31.

The tension between Jewish messianic traditions and the Johannine understanding of Jesus has led some scholars to suggest that *christos* was not such a major christological title for John (e.g., Maloney). Certainly, the Johannine view of Jesus as "the Son (of God)" is the key to the author's christology and the controlling motif in his presentation of Jesus. It is as "the Son" that Jesus' true transcendent significance is best disclosed. But John does not consider *christos* an inadequate title. Rather, he considers Jewish messianic speculations inadequate for a proper understanding of who Messiah is, and he regards the Jewish authorities as incapable of accepting the proper definition of Messiah and the divine Son. John does not reject *christos* as a christological title in favor of others, such as "Son of man" or "Son of God." He demands the recognition that Jesus, the divine Son and the Son of man, is "the Christ." He reflects a redefinition of "the Christ" category in light of Jesus' divine significance, and prefers the combination of "Christ" and "Son of God" as the way of confessing Jesus properly.

For John, Jesus is more than the messianic king of Israel, but he is the messianic king, albeit of such a transcendent stature as not imagined by "the Jews." This view of Jesus as Messiah is precisely why the author so sharply criticizes the Jewish authorities for

rejecting Jesus. Jesus flees the crowd's attempt to make him king "by force" (6:15) after the bread miracle; but this should not be taken as a total rejection of the royal-messianic office, for other passages show that John affirms Jesus as the true king. For example, at Jesus' last entry into Jerusalem, the crowd greets Jesus as "the King of Israel" (12:13). In this event John sees the fulfillment of Zechariah 9:9, with its prediction of Zion's king coming to the city (12:14-16). Thus, however shallow the crowd's understanding as they acclaim Jesus king, the Evangelist sees the royal title as proper to Jesus.

The intertwining of the author's views of Jesus as royal Messiah and as transcendent Son of God appears also in the passion narrative.* In 18:33-38 Pilate asks Jesus if he claims to be "king of the Jews," the Roman interpretation of the messianic claim. Jesus' response comprises a rejection of ordinary earthly kingship but an affirmation of his higher kingship and a consequent mission to "bear witness to the truth" of God. Subsequently, the author continues to weave together the theme of Jesus' kingship and his divine sonship. Several times Jesus is referred to contemptuously by the Romans as "king" (18:39; 19:3, 14-15), and in 19:19-22 the kingship theme is emphasized in the uniquely Johannine account of Pilate's (*see* Pontius Pilate) refusal to remove the title on the cross. The charges against Jesus in John are a combination of the messianic and transcendent aspects of his christology. In 19:12 "the Jews" accuse Jesus of making himself a king against Caesar, but in 19:7 Jesus is accused of blasphemy for making himself "the Son of God." Though the Jewish and Roman opponents of Jesus are ignorant of the ironic truth of their mockeries and charges, the reader of John is to see the greater truth of Jesus' divine sonship and royal status.

Unlike the Synoptic Gospels, where *christos* is almost entirely confined to the passion and nativity accounts (Mt and Lk), in John *christos* appears throughout the whole book, suggesting the title's importance for the Fourth Gospel. Uniquely, John makes it clear that the Baptist is not Messiah and has the Baptist endorse Jesus as Messiah. John is also unique in having Jesus' first disciples acclaim him in a variety of messianic terms. Jesus is recognized as Messiah by the Samaritan woman, and at several points John portrays the inability of "the Jews" to recognize Jesus' messiahship. All these data make it evident that the author believes Jesus to be the true Messiah and considers Jesus' messianic significance an important feature of Christian faith.

John does not play off one christological title

against another. He uses an abundance of honorific titles—many more than the other Evangelists—to describe Jesus (e.g., the several "I am" formulas; *see* "I Am" Sayings). "Son of man" is not a preferred alternative to "Christ" (contra Maloney). The Son of man, who has actually come down from heaven, is "the Christ, the Son of God"—this is the heart of John's faith.

4. Conclusion.

Modern scholarship has been criticized justly for depending too heavily on studies of the NT christological titles in its attempt to determine the nature of NT christology. No treatment of any or all the titles can disclose fully the christological faith of the NT writers. But titles such as "Christ" are significant indications of the faith of authors such as the four Evangelists. In all four Gospels, "Christ" is an important way of referring to Jesus. One can say that "Christ" is for the Evangelists an essential christological term. But they all show an awareness that early Christian faith involved both an appropriation and a major adaptation of the significance of the term as applied to Jesus.

In varying ways two major modifications of the Messiah category are reflected in the Gospels: (1) The crucifixion of Jesus was both a major obstacle to Jewish acceptance of Jesus as Messiah, requiring justification from the OT, and also the event that demanded of the early Christian circles a reformulation of the nature of the Messiah and his work; and (2) the early Christian conviction about the transcendent significance or nature of Jesus makes the Messiah much more exalted in nature and more centrally important for religious life than Jewish tradition was characteristically prepared to grant. (It would be anachronistic to read back into the Gospels the details of the "two nature" christology of later centuries. But only a shallow reading of the Gospels can fail to note the exalted, even transcendent, role and qualities attributed to Jesus in differing ways by each of the Evangelists.)

In the modifications of the Messiah category and the dogged insistence on retaining "Christ" as a title for Jesus in the four Gospels, we see something of the essence of early Christian faith, a religious movement that emerged initially as a distinctive development of the pre-Christian biblical tradition. In this development Jesus became "the Christ" for all nations and not just for Israel. But the Gospels show that early Christians tied their confession of Jesus as "the Christ" to the biblical heritage and to Israel's hopes for a redeemer. However much "Christ" became part of the name-formula for referring to Jesus, for the Evangelists the term retained a connection with ancient visions of God's decisive eschatological intervention on behalf of his people. For the Evangelists the Jewish rejection of Jesus was their rejection of Israel's Messiah.

As perhaps no other christological title, the Evangelists' use of "Christ" shows the Jewish roots of Christian faith and the innovation this faith represented.

See also SERVANT OF YAHWEH; SON OF DAVID; SON OF GOD; SON OF MAN.

BIBLIOGRAPHY: M. Casey, *Son of Man* (London: SPCK, 1979); O. Cullmann, *The Christology of the New Testament* (rev. ed.; Philadelphia: Westminster, 1963); N. Dahl, *The Crucified Messiah and Other Essays* (Minneapolis: Augsburg, 1974) 37-47; M. de Jonge, "The Use of the Word 'Anointed' in the Time of Jesus," *NovT* 8 (1966) 132-48; idem, "Jewish Expectations about the 'Messiah' according to the Fourth Gospel," *NTS* 19 (1972/73) 246-70; idem, "The Use of *ho christos* in the Passion Narratives," in *Jesus aux origines de la christologie*, ed. J. Dupont (Leuven: Leuven Univ., 1975) 169-92; idem, *Christology in Context* (Philadelphia: Westminster, 1988); J. Fitzmyer, *The Gospel According to Luke I-IX* (AB; Garden City: Doubleday, 1981) 192-219; W. Grundmann et al., "χρίω κτλ," *TDNT* 9.493-580; F. Hahn, *The Titles of Jesus in Christology* (New York: World, 1969); M. Hengel, *Between Jesus and Paul* (London: SCM, 1983) 65-77; D. Jones, "The Title *christos* in Luke-Acts," *CBQ* 32 (1970) 69-76; D. Juel, *Messiah and Temple* (SBLDS 31; Missoula: Scholars, 1977); J. D. Kingsbury, *Matthew: Structure, Christology, Kingdom* (Philadelphia: Fortress, 1975); idem, *The Christology of Mark's Gospel* (Philadelphia: Fortress, 1983); W. Kramer, *Christ, Lord, Son of God* (SBT 50; London: SCM, 1966); F. Maloney, "The Fourth Gospel's Presentation of Jesus as 'the Christ' and J. A. T. Robinson's Redating," *Downside Review* 95 (1977) 239-53; C. F. D. Moule, "The Christology of Acts," in *Studies in Luke-Acts*, ed. L. E. Keck and J. L. Martyn (New York: Abingdon, 1966) 159-85; J. Neusner, W. S. Green, E. Frerichs, *Judaisms and Their Messiahs at the Turn of the Christian Era* (Cambridge: University Press, 1987); K. Rengstorf, "χρίστος" *NIDNTT* 2.334-43; R. Schnackenburg, "Die Messiasfrage im Johannesevangelium," in *Neutestamentliche Aufsätze*, ed. J. Blinzler, O. Kuss, F. Mussner (Regensburg: Pustet, 1963) 240-64; S. S. Smalley, "The Christology of Acts Again," in *Christ and Spirit in the New Testament*, ed. B. Lindars and S. S. Smalley (Cambridge: Cambridge University, 1973) 79-94; M. Smith, "What Is Implied by the Variety of Messianic Figures?," *JBL* 78 (1959) 66-72. L. W. Hurtado

CHRISTOLOGY. *See* CHRIST; LOGOS; SON OF DAVID; SON OF GOD; SON OF MAN; WISDOM.

CHRONOLOGY

A chronology of Jesus' life gives a framework of his ministry.

1. Birth of Jesus
2. Commencement of Jesus' Ministry
3. Duration of Jesus' Ministry
4. Death of Jesus
5. Summary

1. Birth of Jesus.

The early Christians were not as concerned with the date as they were with the fact of Jesus' birth (*see* Birth of Jesus). Both the year and time of year can only be approximately determined.

1.1. Year of Jesus' Birth. In attempting to pinpoint the year of his birth, one must look at it in relationship to Herod's death and the census of Quirinius.

1.1.1. Herod the Great's Death As the Terminus ad Quem. According to Matthew 2:1 and Luke 1:5 Jesus' birth came before Herod's death (*see* Herodian Dynasty). According to Josephus an eclipse of the moon occurred shortly before Herod's death (*Ant.* 17.6.4 §167). This is the only eclipse mentioned by Josephus,* and this occurred on March 12/13, 4 B.C. After Herod's death Josephus mentions that the Passover (*see* Feasts) was celebrated, the first day of which would have occurred on April 11, 4 B.C. Hence, Herod's death would have occurred between March 12 and April 11, and thus Jesus' birth would have been no later than March/April 4 B.C.

1.1.2. Census of Quirinius as the Terminus a Quo. According to Luke 2:1-5 the census of Quirinius was taken just before Jesus' birth and hence Jesus could not have been born before the census. The date of this census is difficult to pinpoint. Although no Roman historian specifically mentions this census, there were periodic censuses. Furthermore, Luke was not confusing this with the one held in A.D. 6 because that was just after the deposition of Herod's son Archelaus, whereas the context of the birth narrative of Jesus was in the days of Herod the Great. Trying to synchronize Quirinius's governorship of Syria with the time just before Herod's death proves difficult. Some suggest that he was governor not only in A.D. 6, but also from 11/10 to 8/7 B.C. Others suggest that this census took place before Quirinius was governor in A.D. 6/7, and some think that Quirinius had been proconsul of Syria and Cilicia during the last years of Herod the Great under the legates Saturninus and Varus. Regardless of what construct one may propose,

it is not improbable that Quirinius was involved with a census during the last years of Nero. Toward the end of his reign Herod fell out of favor with Rome* (c. 8/7 B.C.). This was followed by his sons engaging in an intense struggle for the throne at a time when Herod was extremely ill. All of these factors would allow for the Roman government to take a census in his land in order to assess the situation before his death. Although it is difficult to pinpoint the exact year of the census, it was probably sometime between 6 and 4 B.C.

1.1.3. Star of the Magi. Some think that Jesus' birth must have occurred around 6 B.C. because Herod killed children up to two years of age (Mt 2:16) and that the star of the magi (Mt 2:2) can be identified with the confluence of planets at approximately 7 or 6 B.C. However, it is difficult to identify the star of the magi in this way because there was also a conjunction of the planets in 5 and 4 B.C. Also, the description that the star "stood over where the child was" in Bethlehem seems not to indicate a natural confluence of planets but a supernatural phenomenon. Furthermore, the account of Herod killing male children up to two years old in an effort to assure the death of Jesus was characteristic of Herod's paranoia regarding a successor to his throne. It is conceivable that Herod and the magi thought that Jesus had been born when the magi first saw the star in the East, possibly a year or two before their audience with Herod. Although the appearance of the star does not give additional evidence for chronology, it is reasonable to see the magi's discussion with Herod as occurring toward the end of his life, possibly 5 or 4 B.C.

1.2. Date of Jesus' Birth. The traditional date of Christ's birth for the Western Church has been December 25, while the Eastern Church has observed a January 6 date. The account of shepherds attending their flocks during the night (Lk 2:8) does not make a midwinter date improbable.

1.3. Conclusion. With the census of Quirinius having occurred sometime during the period 6-4 B.C., and Herod's death having occurred in the spring of 4 B.C., it seems likely that Jesus was born in December 5 B.C. or January 4 B.C.

2. Commencement of Jesus' Ministry.

Except for the account of Jesus' visit to the Temple* when he was twelve years old (Lk 2:41-51), the Gospels do not provide chronological data until the beginning of his ministry.

2.1. Commencement of John the Baptist's Ministry. Luke 3:1-3 specifically states that John the Baptist's (*see* John the Baptist) ministry began in the fifteenth year of

Tiberius. Although there has been debate about how this is to be reckoned, the most natural way to calculate it would be on the basis of either the Julian calendar used by Rome, making it the fifteenth year from January 1 to December 31, A.D. 29, or to reckon it from the beginning of Tiberius' reign (the normal Roman method), which would place it during the period August 19, A.D. 28 to August 18, A.D. 29. Using either one of these calendars, the fifteenth year of Tiberius would have occurred sometime between August 19, A.D. 28 and December 31, A.D. 29. Hence, John the Baptist's ministry began sometime during this period.

2.2. Commencement of Jesus' Ministry. The Gospels give the impression that not long after the beginning of John the Baptist's ministry, Jesus was baptized and began his ministry. If Jesus were born in the winter of 5/4 B.C. and baptized in the summer or autumn of A.D. 29, he would have been around thirty-two years of age, with his thirty-third birthday approaching in December, 29 or January, 30. This fits well with Luke's statement that Jesus was about (*hōsei*) thirty years of age when he began his ministry (3:23).

2.3. First Passover of Jesus' Ministry. The first recorded visit of Jesus to Jerusalem after his baptism* is found in John 2:13—3:21. John records that on that occasion the Jews spoke of the Herodian Temple having been constructed forty-six years ago (Jn 2:20). Josephus states that Temple construction began in Herod's eighteenth year (Josephus *Ant.* 15.11.1 §380), which coincides with the arrival of Augustus in Syria (Josephus *Ant.* 15.10.3 §354), and according to Dio Cassius this occurred in the spring or summer of 20 B.C. (Dio Cassius 54.7.4-6). Herod's eighteenth year would have been from Nisan 1, 20 B.C. to Nisan 1, 19 B.C. There were two stages in building the Temple: the first was the inner sanctuary, called the *naos*, located within the priests' court. This sanctuary was completed by the priests (*see* Priest and Priesthood) in one year and six months (Josephus *Ant.* 15.11.6 §421). The second stage included the whole Temple area, including the three courts, and was called the *hieron*. This was not completed until A.D. 63. This distinction is maintained by Josephus and the NT writers. In discussing the Temple with Jesus, the Jews were referring to the *naos* as having stood for forty-six years. If the construction of the *naos* began in 20/19 B.C. and was completed in one and a half years (i.e., in 18/17 B.C.), forty-six years would bring the date to the year A.D. 29/30. Consequently, Jesus' first Passover was the spring of A.D. 30.

2.4. Conclusion. The fifteenth year of Tiberius, A.D. 28-29, marked the commencement of John the Bap-

tist's ministry. If John began his ministry in the early part of A.D. 29 and Jesus was baptized in the summer or autumn of that same year, he would have been thirty-two-years old. Jesus' first Passover in A.D. 30 would have been four to nine months after he began his ministry, which was forty-six years after the *naos* was completed. Therefore, Jesus began his ministry sometime in the summer or autumn of A.D. 29.

3. Duration of Jesus' Ministry.

Facts relating to the length of Jesus' ministry are gathered primarily from John. John mentions three Passovers (Jn 2:13; 6:4; 11:55). However, there needs to be an additional year of his ministry between the Passovers of John 2:13 and 6:4. The Passover of 6:4 took place around the time Jesus fed the five thousand, the only miracle mentioned in all four Gospels. Previous to this feeding miracle* the Synoptic Gospels mention the disciples plucking grain in Galilee* (Mt 12:1; Mk 2:23; Lk 6:1), and this must have taken place after the Passover of John 2:13. The reason for this is that the Passover of John 2:13 occurred shortly after Jesus' baptism and the locale of his ministry was in Judea, whereas the plucking of the grain occurred a considerable time after Jesus' baptism and the locale of his ministry was in Galilee. Therefore, the plucking of the grain would fit well around the Passover between the Passovers recorded in John 2:13 and 6:4.

John provides two other indications of time that would indicate an additional year between these two Passovers. First, after the Passover of John 2:13 Jesus ministered in Judea and then went to Samaria. There he mentioned that there were four months until harvest (Jn 4:35), which would mean the following January/February. While some would read this as a proverbial statement, it seems best to take this as a literal chronological reference. The second time-note is in John 5:1 where there is mention of another feast. Although not specified, some interpreters understand it to be another Passover, although it more likely refers to the Feast of Tabernacles. These two time-notes would substantiate that there was another Passover between those of John 2:13 and 6:4. This would make a total of four Passovers during Jesus' public ministry, and hence his ministry would have been 3½ to 3¾ years in length.

4. Death of Jesus.

In determining the date of the death of Jesus (*see* Death of Jesus), it is necessary to discuss the day, as well as the year, of his death.

4.1. Day of Jesus' Death. In discussing the date of Jesus' death, we need to determine the day of the week and the day of the Jewish month.

4.1.1. Day of the Week. Traditionally, Jesus is thought to have died on the Friday of passion week. In Matthew 12:40 Jesus says: "For as Jonah was three days and three nights in the belly of the whale; so shall the Son of man be three days and three nights in the heart of the earth." From this evidence some conclude Jesus could not have died on Friday; Jesus may have died on Wednesday or Thursday, thus allowing for three days and three nights. However, when one recognizes that the Jews reckoned a part of a day as a whole day, Jesus' death on Friday does not present a real problem. Furthermore, the NT repeatedly refers to Jesus' resurrection as having occurred on the third day (not the fourth day; e.g., Mt 16:21; 17:23; Lk 9:22; 18:33; Acts 10:40; 1 Cor 15:4). Moreover, the Gospels specifically mention the day before the Sabbath* (Friday) as the day of his death (Mt 27:62; Mk 15:42; Lk 23:54; Jn 19:14, 31, 42). Therefore, both scripturally and traditionally, it seems best to accept Friday as the day of Jesus' death. The passion week can be charted as follows:

4.1.2. Day of the Month. All the Gospels state that Jesus ate the Last Supper* the day before his crucifixion (Mt 26:20; Mk 14:17; Lk 22:14; Jn 13:2; cf. also 1 Cor 11:23). The Synoptic Gospels (Mt 26:17; Mk 14:12; Lk 22:7-8) portray the Last Supper as the Passover meal celebrated on Thursday evening Nisan 14, with Jesus crucified the following day, namely, Friday Nisan 15. On the other hand, John states that the Jews who took Jesus to the praetorium did not enter it "in order that they might not be defiled but might eat the Passover" (Jn 18:28) and that Jesus' trial was on the "day of preparation for the Passover" and not after eating the Passover (Jn 19:14). This means that Jesus' Last Supper (which occurred on Thursday night, Nisan 13) was not a Passover and that Jesus was tried and crucified on Friday, Nisan 14, just before the Jews ate their Passover.

Several theories have been proposed in the attempt to reconcile the Synoptics and John. Some think that the Last Supper was not a Passover meal but a meal the night before the Passover (Jn 13:1, 29). However, the Synoptics explicitly state that the Last Supper was

Day	Event	Scripture
Saturday	Arrived at Bethany	Jn 12:1
Sunday	Crowd came to see Jesus	Jn 12:9-11
Monday	Triumphal Entry	Mt 21:1-9; Mk 11:1-10; Lk 19:28-44
Tuesday	Cursed Fig Tree	Mt 21:18-19; Mk 11:12-14
	Cleansed Temple	Mt 21:12-13; Mk 11:15-17; Lk 19:45-46
Wednesday	Fig Tree Withered	Mt 21:20-22; Mk 11:20-26
	Temple Controversy	Mt 21:23—23:39; Mk 11:27—12:44; Lk 20:1—21:4
	Olivet Discourse	Mt 24:1—25:46; Mk 13:1-37; Lk 21:5-36
Thursday	Last Supper	Mt 26:20-30; Mk 14:17-26; Lk 22:14-30
	Betrayed and Arrested	Mt 26:47-56; Mk 14:43-52; Lk 22:47-53; Jn 18:2-12
	Tried by Annas and Caiaphas	Mt 26:57-75; Mk 14:53-72; Lk 22:54-65; Jn 18:13-27
Friday	Tried by Sanhedrin	Mt 27:1; Mk 15:1; Lk 22:66
	Tried by Pilate, Herod	Mt 27:2-30; Mk 15:2-19; Lk 23:1-25; Jn 18:28—19:16
	Crucified and Buried	Mt 27:31-60; Mk 15:20-46; Lk 23:26-54; Jn 19:16-42
Saturday	Dead in Tomb	
Sunday	Resurrected	Mt 28:1-15; Mk 16:1-8; Lk 24:1-35

a Passover (Mt 26:2, 17-19; Mk 14:1, 12, 14, 16; Lk 22:1, 7-8, 13, 15). In trying to harmonize the accounts some have proposed that Jesus and his disciples* had a private Passover. However, the Passover lamb had to be slaughtered within the Temple precincts and the priests would not have allowed the slaughter of the Paschal lamb for a private Passover. Others think that they celebrated it according to the Qumran calendar, but there is no evidence that Jesus and his disciples followed the Qumran calendar. Some think it was celebrated on two consecutive days because it would have been impossible to slay all the Passover lambs on one day. Finally, it may be that different calendars were in use during the period. On the one hand, the Synoptic Gospels followed the method of the Galileans and the Pharisees.* By this reckoning the day was measured from sunrise to sunrise, with Jesus and his disciples having their Paschal lamb slaughtered in the late afternoon of Thursday, Nisan 14, and eating the Passover with unleavened bread later that evening. On the other hand, John's Gospel followed the method of the Judeans in reckoning the day from sunset to sunset. Thus, the Judean Jews had the Paschal lamb slaughtered in the late afternoon of Friday Nisan 14, and ate the Passover with the unleavened bread that night, which by then had become Nisan 15. Thus, Jesus had eaten the Passover meal when his enemies, who had not yet celebrated the Passover, arrested him.

4.2. Year of Jesus' Death. The year of Jesus' death can be narrowed by several considerations.

4.2.1. Officials of the Trial. The three officials involved in the trial were Caiaphas the high priest (Mt 26:3, 57; Jn 11:49-53; 18:13-14), who began his office in A.D. 18 and was deposed at the Passover of A.D. 37 (Josephus *Ant.* 18.2.2 §35; 4.3 §90-95); Pilate (*see* Pontius Pilate), prefect of Judea (Mt 27:2-26; Mk 15:1-15; Lk 23:1-25; Jn 18:28—19:16; Acts 3:13; 4:27; 13:28; 1 Tim 6:13) from A.D. 26 to 36 (Josephus *Ant.* 18.4.2 §89); and Herod Antipas, tetrarch of Galilee and Perea (Lk 23:6-12) from 4 B.C. until A.D. 39 (Josephus *Ant.* 18.7.1-2 §§240-56; 19.8.2 §351). Thus Jesus' trial must have occurred between A.D. 26 and 36.

4.2.2. Contributions of Astronomy. Having concluded that Jesus' death occurred on Friday Nisan 14, and sometime between A.D. 26 and 36, astronomical evidence narrows the possibilities to A.D. 27, 30, 33 and 36. Of these dates, A.D. 27 is the least likely astronomically, and it has been debated whether Nisan 14 fell on a Friday in A.D. 30. The A.D. 33 date presents the least problem astronomically.

4.2.3. Ministry of Christ. Having discussed the

ministry of Jesus, it is safe to eliminate A.D. 27 and 36 because neither fits within the framework of his ministry. The year A.D. 30 is accepted by many, but it presents real difficulty if one accepts the commencement of John the Baptist's ministry occurring in the fifteenth year of Tiberius, A.D. 29 (Lk 3:1-3), for this would mean that Jesus' ministry could not have lasted more than one year. Again A.D. 33 seems to fit the evidence best.

4.2.4. Confirmation of History. Pilate is portrayed by his contemporary Philo (*Leg. Gai.* 301-2) and later by Josephus (*Ant.* 18.3.1. §§55-59; *J.W.* 2.9.2-4 §§167-77) as one who was greedy, inflexible and cruel, and who resorted to robbery and oppression, a portrait not out of keeping with Luke 13:1. However, during Jesus' trial, Pilate is seen as one who was readily submissive to the pressures of the religious leaders who were demanding that Jesus be handed over to them.

How can such a change be explained? It must be understood that Pilate was probably appointed by Sejanus, a trusted friend of Tiberius as well as the prefect of the Praetorian Guard. A dedicated anti-Semite, Sejanus wanted to exterminate the Jewish race (Philo *Flacc.* 1; *Leg. Gai.* 159-61). When Pilate made trouble for the Jews in Palestine, Sejanus accepted his actions and did not report it to Tiberius. However, when Sejanus was deposed and executed by Tiberius on October 18, A.D. 31, Pilate no longer had protection in Rome. In fact, it is most likely that Herod Antipas reported his causing a riot, probably at the Feast of Tabernacles in A.D. 32 (Philo *Leg. Gai.* 299-305). In light of this precedent we can understand why, when in the midst of a trial it was witnessed that Jesus stirred up trouble in Judea and Galilee (Lk 23:5), Pilate was eager to allow Herod Antipas to try Jesus (Lk 23:6-12).

In this context a trial date of A.D. 33 makes good sense for three reasons: (1) Pilate, on hearing that Jesus caused trouble in Galilee, handed Jesus over to Herod Antipas. Though this was not required by Roman law, it would have been calculated to avoid a further report from Herod to the emperor. (2) The lack of progression in the trial account of Luke 23:6-12 makes sense if Herod Antipas did not want to make a judgment that Pilate might use against him. (3) Luke 23:12 states that Pilate and Herod Antipas were friends from that day onward, which would be inaccurate if the crucifixion were in A.D. 30 because they were clearly at odds with each other in A.D. 32. Hence, a date of A.D. 33 best fits the historical evidence.

4.3. Conclusion. Having discussed the day of the week and month as well as the year of his death, we conclude that the evidence points to Jesus' dying on Friday Nisan 14/April 3, A.D. 33.

5. Summary.

The birth, life and death of Jesus can be charted as follows:

Jesus' Birth	Winter 5/4 B.C.
Herod the Great's Death	March/April 4 B.C.
Commencement of the Baptist's Ministry	A.D. 29
Commencement of Jesus' Ministry	Summer/Autumn A.D. 29
Jesus' First Passover (Jn 2:13)	April 7, A.D. 30
Jesus' Second Passover	April 25, A.D. 31
Jesus at Feast of Tabernacles (Jn 5:1)	October 21-28, A.D. 31
Jesus' Third Passover (Jn 6:4)	April 13/14, A.D. 32
Jesus at Feast of Tabernacles (Jn 7:2, 10)	September 10-17, A.D. 32
Jesus at Feast of Dedication (Jn 10:22-39)	December 18, A.D. 32
Jesus' Death	Friday, April 3, A.D. 33
Jesus' Resurrection	Sunday, April 5, A.D. 33
Jesus' Ascension (Acts 1)	Thursday, May 14, A.D. 33
Day of Pentecost (Acts 2)	Sunday, May 24, A.D. 33

BIBLIOGRAPHY. W. R. Armstrong and J. Finegan, "Chronology of the NT," in *ISBE* 1.686-93; R. T. Beckwith, "St. Luke, the Date of Christmas and the Priestly Courses at Qumran," *RQ* 33 (1977) 73-94; J. Finegan, *Handbook of Biblical Chronology* (Princeton: Princeton University, 1964); R. T. France, "Chronological Aspects of 'Gospel Harmony,' " *VoxEv* 16 (1986) 33-59; H. W. Hoehner, *The Chronological Aspects of the Life of Christ* (Grand Rapids: Zondervan, 1977); A. Jaubert, *The Date of the Last Supper* (New York: Alba, 1965); J. Jeremias, *The Eucharistic Words of Jesus* (3d ed.; New York: Scribners, 1966); I. H. Marshall, *Last Supper and Lord's Supper* (Grand Rapids: Eerdmans, 1980); G. Ogg, *The Chronology of the Public Ministry of Jesus* (Cambridge: University Press, 1940); E. Ruckstuhl, *Chronology of the Last Days of Jesus* (New York: Desclee, 1965). H. W. Hoehner

CHURCH

The mission of Jesus was concerned with the creation of a community which formed the basis of the church that developed after Easter and Pentecost.

1. The Problem
2. The Kingdom of God and Community
3. The *ekklēsia* Sayings
4. Jesus and the Structures of the Church
5. Continuity between the Church and Jesus

1. The Problem.

The four Gospels were produced in Christian communities by persons who believed that the existence of these groups was the proper consequence of the coming of Jesus. Inevitably they reflect to some extent the nature, life and interests of the churches in which they were produced. The actual word "church" (Gk *ekklēsia*) is found in Matthew 16:18 and 18:17. The latter passage describes a procedure to be followed if a person's "brother" sins against him; if the matter cannot be settled privately or by a small group, it is to be brought before "the church," and we may presume that this practice was followed in communities known to Matthew. In the former passage Jesus promises that he will build his church "on this rock [Gk *petra*]," having previously said to Peter: "You are Peter [Gk *petros*, 'rock']." These, however, are the only two uses of the term in all four Gospels, and this infrequency of usage, combined with a suspicion that the texts may indeed represent primarily the theology and practice of groups known to Matthew, has caused doubts whether these sayings attributed to Jesus truly represent his words or even his mind.

Some scholars would go even further and deny that Jesus intended the church. They are not suggesting that Jesus thought purely in individualistic terms. Rather their position is determined by an understanding of his teaching which holds that his mind was dominated by the imminent end of the world and the coming of the kingdom of God*—a "thorough-going" eschatology* which affected the entirety of his thinking and, in particular, left no time for the development of an organized community. Thus C. K. Barrett suggests that "beyond the time of suffering he envisaged no period of continuing history, in which a Church organized in this world might find a place, but an apocalyptic act of vindication" (p. 87; *see* Apocalyptic Teaching). To be sure, events proved Jesus to be wrong: "Jesus foretold the kingdom, and it was the Church that came" (A. Loisy, quoted by Barrett, p. 68) sums up crisply what happened according to this view. Such a denial that Jesus expected the church does not rest merely on a critical examination of two texts but on a total interpretation of the eschatology of Jesus.

A less radical view is presented by E. Schweizer, who allows that Jesus called disciples but claims that he did nothing to create a group distinguishable from the rest of the world. Schweizer here takes a remarkably existentialist view of the mission of Jesus, a view that seems to be shaped by his genuine concern to warn against thinking that belonging to a particular group can insulate a person from a real meeting with Jesus.

2. The Kingdom of God and Community.

Two factors may lead us to see things differently. The first is that a different interpretation of the eschatology of Jesus is possible and indeed preferable and is widely held. Jesus, it can be claimed, saw the fulfillment of the hope of the coming of the kingdom of God happening during his ministry and looked forward to its future consummation at an unspecified point in the future. If this point be granted, then a different understanding becomes possible. The second factor is that the original question may have been wrongly put, or at least wrongly focussed. It is more appropriate to ask what intention Jesus may have had with respect to community.

2.1. Community. The concept of the kingdom of God implies a community. While it has been emphasized almost *ad nauseam* that the primary concept is that of the sovereignty or kingship or actual rule of God and not of a territory ruled by a king, it must be also emphasized that kingship cannot be exercised in the abstract but only over a people. The concept of the kingship of God implies both the existence of a group of people who own him as king and the establishment of a realm of people within which his gracious power is manifested. Past scholarship rightly reacted against the tendency to identify the kingdom of God with the empirical, visible church (and above all to identify the rule of God with the exercise of authority by church leaders), but this reaction has obscured the fact that there is a community of people who own God as king (however imperfectly they may obey him) and in whom his gracious power is at work.

2.2. Israel. Jesus' message was directed toward Israel* and was concerned with the renewal of Israel, i.e., of the people of God. The goal was the renewal of the people as a community and not simply the repentance of individuals, although the path to the former lay through the latter. This point has been emphasized by B. F. Meyer. Jesus used imagery which spoke of Israel as a vineyard which needed new tenants to care for it. He prophesied doom in collective terms for those who did not respond to his message. He expressed concern for the lost sheep* of the house of Israel and might almost have been suspected of a concern for Israel to the exclusion of the Gentiles.* His concern is expressed for people in that they are "daughters of Abraham" or "sons of Abraham" (Lk 13:16; 19:9; *see* Abraham).

An important text (Mt 19:28/Lk 22:29-30) promises that the Twelve (*see* Disciples) will sit on thrones judging the twelve tribes of Israel (*see* Judgment). This text, which seems particularly time-bound to modern readers, probably refers to the Twelve sharing in

judgment on the unbelieving people of Israel in association with Jesus rather than to some kind of rule over a reconstituted ethnic Israel. The language is symbolical, but the symbolism points to some kind of community which corresponds to the twelve tribes of Israel. Jesus is saying in the strongest way possible that the old Israel is coming under judgment, and that the judgment will be in the hands of those who have been called by him as his close disciples. The implication is that there will be what we may call a new Israel.

2.3. Discipleship. Jesus called people to be his disciples. Here we have to make a distinction between the group of the Twelve who were specially called to be associated with him in his mission (and who came to be known as apostles) and the much wider group who did not in every case travel from place to place with him. Some of the sayings about discipleship* may be particularly directed to the former group, but nevertheless the concept of "following Jesus" is part of the message addressed to all who sought eternal life or a place in the kingdom of God.

2.4. Communal Images. It is, then, not surprising that various communal images are found in the teaching of Jesus. The disciples form the "little flock" (Lk 12:32). They are likened to a "city" (Mt 5:14), to a planted field (Mt 13:24; 15:13) or to a group of wedding guests (Mk 2:19). In an important saying Jesus speaks of his disciples as members of his family* (Mk 3:34-35) and he both regards their relationship to him as somehow replacing his normal kinship relationships and also requires them to have a love for him greater than for their kin (Mk 10:29-30). Within this grouping the disciples are to regard themselves as brothers (Mt 23:8).

3. The *Ekklēsia* Sayings.

In the light of this argument it becomes credible that Jesus did speak of the disciples as constituting an *ekklēsia*. This term could be the translation-equivalent of more than one Hebrew or Aramaic word (*see* Languages of Palestine). It can refer to a local group of pious people, equivalent to a "synagogue"* (a synagogue is first of all a group of people and only secondarily the place where they meet).

3.1. Matthew 18:17. The saying in Matthew 18:17 can be taken in this way. It could admittedly make sense in the lifetime of Jesus as an isolated saying regarding discipline within a Jewish community (notice how Jesus assumes that his hearers offer sacrifices at the Temple, Mt 5:23-24). In this setting it would not be surprising for pious Jews to regard recalcitrant brothers "like a Gentile or tax-collector."

However, Matthew certainly thought that Jesus was

addressing disciples, for the pericope goes on to assume the hearers meet together "in my name" (Mt 18:20), which is precisely what "church" signifies. The saying presupposes that the disciples constitute such a group, which implies some kind of organization, and to which there is no other reference in the teaching of Jesus. Nothing anywhere else indicates that he organized his disciples (whether the Twelve or a wider group) in this kind of way.

Further, this is an extraordinary statement on the lips of Jesus in view of his positive attitude to tax-collectors (cf. Mk 2:15-17). It is not surprising that many commentators would regard this pericope as a creation of the early church and as reflecting a narrowly Jewish-Christian church with an exclusive attitude toward Gentiles and tax-collectors (see Taxes).

One difficulty with this view is that elsewhere Matthew shows the same positive attitude to tax-collectors as we find in the other Gospels (Mt 9:10-11; 11:19; 21:31-32). Clearly the saying refers to some kind of breaking off of relations with the unrepentant offender, and the problem is simply whether Jesus or his followers (who knew his attitude to tax-collectors and sinners*) could have used this form of expression to make the point. The solution may be that Jesus is deliberately using shocking language: so dreadful is it that within the community of disciples a person should persist in sin that his fellow-disciples should treat him just as the Jews treated tax-collectors and sinners. This interpretation frees Matthew from an almost unbelievable inconsistency. Jesus' language is startling and liable to misinterpretation—as it often has been.

The reference to the *ekklēsia* still remains strange. However, if Jesus expected persecution for his followers, he may well have foreseen their exclusion from the synagogues and their consequent organization into their own groups. Matthew's readers would have had no difficulty with the saying since they would assume that Jesus was speaking prophetically of the local church and they would read it in the light of the previous use of the term in Matthew 16.

3.2. Matthew 16:18. This passage creates less difficulty. It has been shown that the language used here corresponds to that used at Qumran where God appointed the Teacher of Righteousness to build for himself a congregation (*ēdâ*) (4QpPs37.III:16; see Dead Sea Scrolls). Several factors are significant for understanding this passage.

First, Jesus creates a (new) "congregation" which is evidently a special group within Judaism.* This fits in with the self-consciousness of the Qumran community who saw themselves in the same way. Second,

whereas at Qumran God creates a congregation for himself, Jesus speaks of building "my congregation," thus apparently himself taking the place of God. More precisely, Jesus speaks as the Messiah (see Christ) and "my congregation" means "the congregation of me, the Messiah." Such a community may be seen in the concept of the "remnant" in the Old Testament and especially in the "saints of the Most High" who are represented by the Son of Man* as their leader.

Third, the congregation is built on "this rock," which is generally taken to refer to Peter who has just been mentioned. The fact that the saying uses the feminine form *petra* is attributed to the fact that the masculine form *petros* signifies a "[lump of] stone" rather than a large expanse of rock which might serve as a foundation for a building. On this view it is Peter—as the one to whom God has revealed that Jesus is the Messiah and who confesses him as such—upon whom the congregation is built. However, it has been argued by C. Caragounis that the two Greek words do not necessarily refer to the same entity, that the Aramaic word underlying *petra* is not necessarily that which underlies *petros* and that the focus of the passage suggests that the foundation of the church is the content of Peter's confession that Jesus is the Messiah.

Finally, that Jesus is speaking on a cosmic scale is apparent from the references to the opposition from the "gates of Hades" and to the keys of the kingdom of God. This is the divinely instituted community of the end time against which the full force of evil is pitted.

All this material shows that Jesus proclaimed the rule of God and urged people to return to God in repentance and obedience, that he called them to be his own disciples and to constitute the *ekklēsia* of the Messiah, that he saw them as the children* of God called to live together as brothers and sisters. It may surely be affirmed that here we have the essence of the church.

4. Jesus and the Structures of the Church.
The argument so far is based on the classical presentation by R. N. Flew. He detected five elements in the mission of Jesus which encapsulate the idea of the church: (1) the disciples as the nucleus of the new Israel; (2) the ethical teaching (see Ethics of Jesus) given to them and the power of the Spirit*; (3) the conception of Messiahship and the consequent allegiance; (4) the message as constitutive of a community; (5) the mission of the new community.

Each of these elements can be traced as part of the constitution of the church after Easter and leave no doubt that we are justified in thinking of the church as part of the purpose of Jesus. But to what extent did Jesus prepare for or anticipate other features of the church as it later developed?

4.1. The place of the Twelve. The Twelve appear primarily as Jesus' companions and colleagues in his mission. Some kind of authority is given to them in Matthew 16 and 18. The promises made to Peter are repeated to all of the disciples in Matthew 18. They will make decisions which will be ratified by God. They will be able to act in concert in prayer* and see their prayers answered. In this situation some kind of leadership is envisaged. But the horizon is limited to their lifetime, and nothing is said about leadership in the future except in the eschatological symbolism of Matthew 19:28 (par. Luke 22:29-30).

4.2. Baptism. The question of baptism* as an initiation rite does not arise in the Synoptic Gospels. When it is discussed in John it is as an expression of repentance and a type of Spirit-baptism rather than as entry to a community, although the latter need not be excluded. According to John the disciples practiced baptism during the lifetime of Jesus.

4.3. Lord's Supper. The Lord's Supper is established by Jesus as a memorial to him which is to be continued by his followers, but no instructions are given regarding the details of how it is to be conducted or by whom (see Last Supper).

5. Continuity between the Church and Jesus.
According to Luke, soon after the resurrection* the disciples met together and engaged in: teaching by the apostles, fellowship, breaking of bread and prayers (Acts 2:42-47). All four of these items have their roots in the lifetime of Jesus.

First, the position of the apostles is that of those who teach on Jesus' behalf. The accounts of the calling and mission of the Twelve and the Seventy(-two) indicate that Jesus taught them and prepared them for mission (see Gentiles). The Gospels generally indicate that Jesus gave special teaching to the disciples over against his general teaching to the crowds. Second, the concept and practice of fellowship may reflect the common life of the inner group of disciples of Jesus. The concept of brotherhood within the community is reflected in Matthew 23:8. Third, the practice of the breaking of bread is linked to the common meals of the disciples with Jesus and to the Last Supper. Fourth, the prayers of the post-resurrection community reflect the example and instruction of Jesus to them.

To these items we may add a fifth, the ongoing mission which continues the public teaching of Jesus

with its challenge to Israel to repent (see Repentance). Thus there is significant continuity between Jesus and the church.

See also ESCHATOLOGY; ISRAEL; KINGDOM OF GOD.

BIBLIOGRAPHY. C. K. Barrett, *Jesus and the Gospel Tradition* (London: SPCK, 1967); C. C. Caragounis, *Peter and the Rock* (Berlin: De Gruyter, 1990); R. N. Flew, *Jesus and His Church* (2d ed.; London: Epworth, 1943); L. Goppelt, *Theology of the New Testament* (Grand Rapids: Eerdmans, 1981), Vol. I; D. Guthrie, *New Testament Theology* (Downers Grove, IL: InterVarsity, 1981); J. Jeremias, *New Testament Theology* (New York: Scribners, 1971); I. H. Marshall, "New Wine in Old Wine-Skins: V. The Biblical Use of the Word 'Ekklēsia,' " *ExpTim* 84 (1972-73) 359-64; B. F. Meyer, *The Aims of Jesus* (London: SCM, 1979); E. Schweizer, *Church Order in the New Testament* (London: SCM, 1961). I. H. Marshall

CITIES OF PALESTINE. *See* ARCHEOLOGY AND GEOGRAPHY.

CLEAN AND UNCLEAN
Distinctions between what is to be considered ritually clean and unclean are established in Pentateuchal Law.* With some sources of uncleanness, contact is prohibited; with others, procedures for cleansing from incurred defilement are laid down. While observance of the fundamental rules was routine among pious Jews of the Second Temple Period, certain religious groups were in part characterized by particular and expanded interpretations, and meticulous observance, of the relevant laws. In the Gospels the indifference shown by Jesus and his disciples* on matters of ritual purity provokes queries from Pharisees.* Conversely, Jesus perceives the Pharisees as showing an exaggerated concern for ritual purity while neglecting the more fundamental demands of ethics* and piety.

    1. The Laws of Ritual Purity
    2. The Practice of Ritual Purity
    3. Ritual Purity in the Gospels
    4. Conclusion

1. The Laws of Ritual Purity.
Pentateuchal Law prohibits the Israelites from incurring certain kinds of uncleanness. Transgression of these laws would make impossible Yahweh's continued presence in the midst of his people (cf. Lev 15:31) and would result in the pollution of the land (Num 35:33; Deut 21:23) and the expulsion of its people (Lev 18:24-30; 20:22). The language of defilement is used indiscriminately in matters ranging from

sexual morality to rules of diet. Thus the apodictic law of Leviticus 18 forbids sexual intercourse with certain near relatives, with women during their menstrual periods, with the wife of another, with members of the same sex and with beasts. Such acts are said to bring defilement to the perpetrators and even to the land, if the guilty are not isolated from the rest of the people. Similarly, according to Leviticus 19:31 consulting a medium or wizard brings defilement and must be avoided. Children are not to be offered "to Molech," lest Yahweh's sanctuary be defiled (20:1-3; cf. 18:21). Leviticus 11 forbids the Israelites to eat meat declared "unclean" (cf. also Deut 14): To do so would defile a people intended to be holy as Yahweh their God* is holy (11:44-45). Blood is not to be eaten (7:27; 17:10-14). Moreover, priests* are governed by special laws of purity which must not be transgressed (Lev 21—22) lest the sanctuary be profaned (21:12, 23; cf. 22:2, 32).

In all these cases defilement can and must simply be avoided. Other texts, however, describe types of uncleanness—often involving accidental or even unavoidable defilement—together with procedures for cleansing. Thus, while Leviticus 11 prohibits both eating and touching the carcasses of unclean animals (11:8, 11), for the latter act procedures of cleansing are set forth (11:24-25, 27-28). Contact with or eating from the carcass of a permitted animal results in uncleanness which can be cleansed (11:39-40). A woman* at the time of menstruation and after the birth of a child is unclean for a period; rites of purification are prescribed (Lev 12; 15:19-24). The same applies to those with particular skin conditions (Lev 13:1—14:32), those who experience various bodily emissions (Lev 15), and those in contact or present in the same tent with a corpse (Num 19:11-19).

Varying degrees of severity accompany the different types of defilement. This is reflected not simply in the different lengths of the period before cleansing is possible and the different rites prescribed for the cleansing, but also in the fact that some types of incurred uncleanness, but not others, may be transmitted further. Contact with an animal carcass renders one unclean, but the uncleanness simply passes with the coming of evening (Lev 11:24, 27). Those who carry such a carcass must wash their garments, but they too become clean in the evening (11:25, 28). A period of purification lasting forty days is prescribed for a woman who gives birth to a son; for a daughter the period is eighty days (Lev 12). More complicated rites of cleansing are prescribed for those whose defiling skin conditions have healed (Lev 14:1-32). In the case of those experiencing various discharges

from the body, the uncleanness spreads to those who touch them and even to those who touch a bed or chair on which the affected party has sat (Lev 15:4-12, 20-24, 26-27).

As noted, certain types of food were not to be eaten (Lev 11; Deut 14). Permitted foods can, however, be made unclean through contact with a source of defilement; also susceptible are household utensils (Lev 11:32-38; 15:12; Num 19:15).

These laws are stated without explanation. Rules to assist in the classification of animals as clean or unclean are indeed given (Lev 11:3, 9, 20-21, etc.), but no reason why, for example, those beasts which do not "chew the cud" or "part the hoof" should be considered unclean. The absence of indications in the text has left the field open for speculation, and many types of rationale have been proposed: hygienic, allegorical (i.e., the forbidden creatures represent particular vices) and cultic (i.e., animals significant in foreign cultic practices are to be avoided) among others. In addition to the lack of textual support, it should be noted that none of these explanations covers all cases.

A more comprehensive solution is attempted by M. Douglas. The laws of purity cannot be understood apart from the commandment to be holy with which they are associated (e.g., Lev 11:44). Holiness implies wholeness and completeness, freedom from physical deformity (e.g., Lev 21:17-21) and bodily discharge (Lev 15), and adherence to right order (hence the laws of sexual morality and condemnation of such confusions of creation's order as are mentioned in Lev 18:23; 19:19). Underlying the declaration of some animals as clean and others as unclean, Douglas believes, is the understanding that some creatures conform to their place in the created order while others do not (e.g., eels live in the water but, contrary to the norm for such creatures, do not swim; the norm for four-legged creatures of the earth is that they hop, jump or walk, not fly). The latter are declared unclean.

Whether or not Douglas has correctly uncovered the rationale behind particulars of the purity laws is of lesser significance. Jews of our period conformed to the laws because they were commanded by Yahweh, not because they agreed upon or even perceived a rationale behind them. But Douglas is undoubtedly correct in seeing the requirement of holiness as the context within which the laws of purity have their place.

Yahweh chose to live in the midst of his people. His presence brings them glory* and protection but also threatens and imperils them: Yahweh is a consuming fire (Deut 4:24), and those among whom he lives risk his wrath when they transgress his will. A number of stories illustrate the theme; the provoking wrongs are both ritual and moral (Lev 10:1-3; Num 11:1-3, 33; 16:31-35, 41-50; 21:4-9; 25:1-9; 2 Sam 6:6-8; etc.). What is unclean is an abomination to Yahweh and will not be tolerated. Thus it is incumbent upon the priests to teach the people the distinction between the clean and the unclean (Lev 10:10-11), and incumbent upon the people to observe the distinction and to purify themselves of whatever defilements they may incur. The unclean are not to be permitted in the courtyard of the sanctuary (Lev 12:4; 2 Chron 23:19; 26:21; cf. Lev 15:31; Num 19:13, 20). Indeed, the opening chapters of Numbers present a detailed scheme for the camp of the Israelite tribes in the wilderness which reflects these notions of purity. In the center is Yahweh's sanctuary. In the circle next to the tabernacle are the priests (3:38) and the Levite clans (1:53), that is, those who have been sanctified by Yahweh to serve in his sanctuary (3:5-10). Then, in a circle further removed from the tabernacle, lie the camps of the lay tribes of Israelites (Num 2). The unclean are banished outside the camp to prevent its defilement (Num 5:1-3; cf. also Deut 23:9-14).

2. The Practice of Ritual Purity.

The vision of purity which so dominates parts of the Pentateuch is much less evident in the remainder of the OT. Occasional references probably indicate that observance of certain basic rules could normally be assumed (e.g., 1 Sam 20:26; 2 Sam 11:4); and the sense that foreign lands were unclean, and that to die outside Israel would therefore be a loss, was probably general (cf. 1 Sam 26:19-20; Hos 9:3; Amos 7:17). On the other hand, the historical books of the so-called Deuteronomistic history (Joshua—2 Kings), while explaining the disasters that befell the people of Israel and Judah for their unfaithfulness to Yahweh, do not include violations of purity laws among the wrongs, and even countenance without comment the presence of foreign mercenaries in the courtyard of Yahweh's Temple* (2 Kings 11:4-12; the parallel version in 2 Chron 23:1-11 reflects the postexilic sensitivity to the need for purity). Prophets like Amos, Hosea, Isaiah and Jeremiah find fault on many counts with their contemporaries: idolatry and pride, immorality and deceit, abuses of justice and oppression of the needy. . . . But observance of purity laws figures neither in their vision of what should have been in their own day nor in that of what will be in the future when wrongs are set right. The language of "uncleanness," when used, generally relates to moral issues (e.g., Is 1:15-16, 18; 4:4; 6:5; Jer 3:2; 13:27). It is in the book of Ezekiel

the priest that concerns for ritual purity become more apparent, particularly in the visions of what the sanctuary and community would be like after the exile (Ezek 40—48). Pre-exilic laxity is denounced; hereafter, the sanctity of the Temple is to be strictly preserved (44:5-9, 23, 25-27; 45:3-5; etc.).

Otherwise it is largely in postexilic literature that issues of ritual purity play a significant role. Chronicles, in retelling the stories of Samuel-Kings, often betrays a sensitivity lacking in the earlier accounts to the need to keep the sanctuary and its environs free from incursions by foreigners and Israelites who are ritually impure (cf. e.g., 2 Chron 8:11 and 1 Kings 9:24; 2 Chron 23:19 and 2 Kings 11:18; 2 Chron 24:8 and 2 Kings 12:9; 2 Chron 26:16-21 and 2 Kings 15:5; and see 2 Chron 30:17-19). Texts from Ezra (2:62-63; 6:20-21), Nehemiah (7:64-65; 12:30, 45; 13:4-9, 22, 30), Daniel (1:8), Haggai (2:10-14) and Zechariah (14:20-21) may be cited as illustrations of a growing perception of the need to observe standards of ritual purity. Telling too are passages in apocryphal books like Tobit (1:10-12; 2:9), Judith (11:12-15; 12:2, 19) and the additions to Esther (14:15-17).

At the turn of the era observance of the fundamental requirements was normal among Jews. Jews were known throughout the ancient world for their refusal to eat pork and other unclean foods (cf. Acts 10:14). As a rule Jews would not eat with Gentiles* (cf. Acts 10:28; 11:3; Gal 2:12-13). Lepers (see Leprosy) were isolated from the community (cf. Lk 17:12). Mothers of newborn children observed the prescribed rites of purification (cf. Lk 2:22). Josephus* relates that Herod was hard-pressed to find Jews who would reside on the defiled soil of Tiberias (Ant. 18.2.3 §§36-38). John's Gospel indicates that Jews took into account the need for purification when travelling to Jerusalem to keep a feast* (11:55; cf. Josephus J.W. 1.11.6 §229; Acts 21:24-27) and notes that water* for purification was available at a wedding feast (2:6).

It was particularly among sectarian groups, however, that observance of purity laws was rigorous and consistent. The Essenes, as described by Josephus, were careful to eat their meals in a state of ritual purity. They immersed (J.W. 2.8.5 §129) before eating food prepared by priests (i.e., to guarantee its purity, Ant. 18.1.5 §22) which was reserved for full members of the party (J.W. 2.8.7 §139); members swore an oath not to eat the food of non-members (J.W. 2.8.8 §143). The same concern is evident in the Dead Sea Scrolls (see Dead Sea Scrolls). Members of the Qumran sect could not eat or drink anything belonging to nonmembers (1QS 5:16). Nonmembers were forbidden to "enter the water (i.e., of purification) in order to touch the purity (i.e., the pure food) of the holy men" (1QS 5:13). Partaking of the pure food (1QS 6:16-17) and drink (1QS 6:20-21) of the community was not immediately permitted those who decided to join the sect, but was reserved for those at a more advanced stage of initiation.

These requirements go beyond biblical Law, where ritual purity was not prescribed for the eating of ordinary meals (cf. Lev 14:46-47; Deut 12:15, 22; 15:22). But Scripture does require purity of priests consuming dedicated foods (Lev 22:3-9) as well as of lay Israelites eating their portion of peace offerings (Lev 7:19-21). It was by extension of these laws (perhaps with an eye to the declaration that all Israel is a "kingdom of priests," Ex 19:6) that sectarians ate ordinary meals in a state of purity.

Rabbinic texts speak of "associates" who made a similar commitment (t. Dem. 2:2). Many scholars identify the "associates" with the Pharisees known to us from Josephus and the NT. The evidence for this claim, however, falls short of proof. Nonetheless, it is clear from the importance placed on issues of ritual purity in rabbinic texts relating to the pre-70 period, from a number of Gospel texts, and from Josephus's insistence that the Pharisees were the most scrupulous of the parties in their observance of the ancestral laws, that Pharisees too were meticulous in their interpretation and observance of purity regulations. A few details will be noted in the discussion of Gospel texts.

3. Ritual Purity in the Gospels.

3.1. The Gospel of Mark. If the details of a couple incidents in the Gospel be pressed, Jesus incurred ritual defilement, according to OT laws, though the Gospel texts themselves do not mention it. According to Mark 5:27 he was touched by a woman with a "flow of blood." Such a touch, by the laws of Leviticus 15:25-30, conveyed uncleanness. A still more severe defilement was conveyed, by the laws of Numbers 19, when Jesus entered a house in which a dead body was present (Mk 5:39-40; cf. Num 19:14) and when he touched a corpse (Mk 5:41; cf. Num 19:11). On the other hand, it is likely that "Simon the leper," in whose house Jesus ate, according to Mark 14:3, was now cured of the skin condition which still served to identify him. Given the observance of basic requirements of purity among Jews of the period, it is hard to conceive a leper entertaining guests in his house during the time of his uncleanness.

The significance of such incidents should not be exaggerated. As we have noted, many kinds of defilement could scarcely be avoided; incurring them did not involve any defiance of biblical Law, provided that

steps were taken for purification in cases where these were prescribed. And indeed, according to Mark 1:44, Jesus once told a cured leper to carry out the prescribed rites, though the reason for the observance ("as a witness to them") is ambiguous. Possibly the witness is to Jesus' faithful observance of the Law; more likely is the notion that the demonstration of divine power seen in the healing of the leper serves as a witness against those who refuse to heed Jesus.

According to Mark 2:15-17 Jesus ate with "tax collectors and sinners" (see Taxes; Sinner) and was criticized by the scribes* of the Pharisees for doing so (see Table Fellowship). Was ritual purity the issue? "Tax collectors and (notorious) sinners" were hardly among those specially observant of purity regulations. Hence those who were committed to eating ordinary food in a state of ritual purity would not themselves eat in such company. It certainly follows that Jesus for his part had not made that kind of commitment, and it is quite conceivable that those for whom rigorous maintenance of purity was an ideal would fault him for failing to do so. But the force of the passage suggests that something more basic was at issue. Jesus is, after all, not being criticized for eating with ordinary people who failed to observe special standards of purity. The point of the charge is that he is associating with notorious sinners, those living in open defiance of the basic laws of Judaism,* those whom the righteous avoided so as not to appear to condone, or be affected by, their behavior (cf. Ps 1:1; Prov 28:7; m. 'Abot 1:7; etc.). Suitably, Jesus' reply addresses this latter issue, not questions of purity. To be sure, his companions are sinners; but, just as it is the sick to whom the physician must attend, so sinners may appropriately be sought out for the message of God's kingdom (Mk 2:17; see Kingdom of God).

Purity clearly is the issue in Mark 7:1-23. According to verses 1-5, Pharisees and scribes observe that some of Jesus' disciples eat with unwashed hands and (after a parenthesis in which the Evangelist explains Jewish concerns for purity to his readers) ask Jesus why his followers do not adhere to "the tradition of the elders"* in this matter. Jesus replies first by attacking those who keep this "human tradition" and set aside God's word in the process (7:6-13), then by addressing the issue of ritual purity in a general maxim (7:15). Finally, the maxim is explained in private to the disciples (7:17-23).

The early history of Jewish handwashing at mealtimes is largely unknown. The presence of the pericope in Mark's (and Matthew's) Gospel can only be explained on the assumption that some Jews at least had adopted the custom in the pre-70 period. And in fact this seems to have been the case with the "associates" (*t. Dem.* 2:11). Moreover, *Tosepta Demai* 2:10 indicates that some non-associates followed the practices of the associates in private. This, as Alon suggests, might especially apply to so simple a matter as handwashing. Indeed, it is more likely that a widespread custom (perhaps introduced into Palestine by Hellenistic influence) was in time assimilated into, and adopted as part of, Pharisaic purity regulations than that popular observance followed a decree from the sages. Note that John 2:6 also appears to assume that handwashing before meals was customary among Jews.

According to Mark 7:3, 5 such handwashing was required by the "tradition of the elders." Its neglect is thus seen as a violation, not of scriptural Law, but of the extrabiblical tradition programmatically adopted by the Pharisees (Josephus *Ant.* 13.10.6 §297). That such handwashing was a part of the Pharisaic tradition in the time of Jesus cannot be confirmed from other sources (unless, as many assume, the regulations governing the associates were a part of that tradition); but it is at least not inconsistent with what we do know.

For handwashing to be required as a purification ritual before each meal, hands must be both regarded as susceptible to defilement not affecting the rest of the body (otherwise the washing of hands only would serve no purpose) and routinely assumed to be so defiled. The former condition could readily be derived from texts like Leviticus 15:11; and rabbinic tradition (*see* Rabbinic Traditions and Writings) does assume the uncleanness of hands (because they are "fidgety," i.e., liable to touch what is unclean) and dates the declaration of their uncleanness to Hillel and Shammai (*b. Šabb.* 14b). On the other hand, according to the careful distinctions worked out in rabbinic texts, the degree of uncleanness normally affecting hands (second degree, *m. Yad.* 3:1) is not sufficient to defile ordinary food. Such distinctions may not have been fully worked out in the pre-70 period. In any case, the attempt to preserve ritual cleanness in the eating of ordinary food was probably understood as an extension of the laws governing the eating of dedicated foods: Meals in the home were treated as though they were sacred meals in the Temple. Mark 7 indicates that there were Jews in pre-70 Palestine who washed their hands before eating as a part of this larger endeavor. It also indicates that Jesus and his disciples were not among them.

Such handwashing was done, according to Mark 7:3, either with a "handful" of water or by pouring water over "cupped" hands: The Greek term *pygmē* is ambiguous. Mark 7:4 speaks of other purificatory rites. A cleansing by immersion after returning from the market is not known in rabbinic literature, though the preconditions for such a view to be held by a scrupulous Jew are found in Torah. The purification of 7:4a may, however, refer again to the hands. The cleansing of vessels (7:4b) will be considered below.

In Mark's account the question asked Jesus is met with a broad attack, in two parts, on the Pharisaic tradition as a whole. First, Isaiah 29:13 is cited as condemning such adherence to the "human precepts." Second, an example is given by which adherence to the tradition results in the violation of a fundamental command of the Word of God (7:9-13). The replies are suitable enough in the context, since the question of handwashing does indeed raise the issue of the validity of extrabiblical tradition. They do not, however, relate directly to ritual purity.

Mark 7:15 does relate directly, though its force may be differently construed. On the face of it the saying denies that eating can render one unclean. So fundamental a claim would undercut the issue of handwashing by declaring pointless the whole enterprise of ritual purity. Not just Pharisaic tradition, but biblical laws on the subject as well would be set aside. Those who think this interpretation self-evident must either deny the origin of the saying with Jesus or explain why the early church (with exceptions like Paul; cf. Rom 14:14) missed the point and debated the issue. On the other hand, the statement need not mean more than that moral impurity is a more serious matter and one more worthy of careful attention than ritual impurity. (See, e.g., Mk 9:37; Mt 10:20; Jn 12:44; Acts 5:4, where apparent denials of one claim in order to affirm another in fact mean "not so much" the former "as" the latter.) On such an understanding the maxim leaves open the issue whether laws of ritual purity have any point, but it does bring into question the priorities of those who rigorously pursue them. Such an emphasis is consistent with the precedence assigned throughout the Jesus tradition to ethical and humanitarian concerns over matters of religious observance.

In Mark 7:18-23 the maxim is interpreted. An indifferent attitude toward matters of ritual purity is justified by noting that what enters the body leaves it as well—without entering the "heart." The "heart" is seen as the source of true (moral) uncleanness. A parenthesis at the end of verse 19 ("pronouncing all foods clean"), presumably added by the Evangelist, understands the discussion to mean that all foods may be eaten.

In sum, Mark's Gospel does not share the vision

which inspired the pursuit of ritual purity. For Mark's Gentile readers Jewish purity concerns are foreign (7:3-4) and irrelevant, representing in part a human tradition which has come to displace fundamental aspects of the divine will, and in part divine commands belonging to an old order now set aside with the dawning of the new age.

3.2. The Gospel of Matthew. In Matthew's Gospel Jesus does not do away with OT laws (see 5:17-19), though he does reinterpret them (5:21-48), declare that all the Law and the Prophets "depend on" the love commandments* (22:37-40), and insist that God is more concerned with justice (*see* Justice, Righteousness), mercy* and faith* (the "weightier matters of the Law") than with the meticulous observance of ritual demands (23:23; cf. 9:13; 12:7). Suitably, then, Matthew's Gospel (15:1-20) contains a parallel to the handwashing dispute in Mark, with its maxim declaring that moral uncleanness rather than ritual truly matters. But the implication that all foods are clean (Mk 7:19) is not drawn, and only scribal regulations are explicitly set aside (15:20).

In the series of woes pronounced against the scribes and Pharisees, their purification of vessels is addressed (23:25-26). Several OT texts speak of the possibility of household vessels becoming unclean and prescribe procedures for their cleansing (Lev 11:32-38; 15:12; Num 19:15, 18). It is not surprising, then, that Pharisees were concerned with the cleanness of vessels. Indeed, rabbinic texts provide some evidence that, for assessments of ritual cleanness, a distinction was made between the outside and the inside of a vessel (perhaps based on the reference to a vessel's "inside" in Lev 11:33) in the period before 70 (e.g., *Sipra* to Lev 11:33). According to the Jerusalem Talmud (*y. Ber.* 8:2), Shammaites believed that an uncleanness which affected the outside of a vessel could contaminate the inside, whereas Hillelites denied this.

The Shammaite position, which would require attention to be paid to the cleanness of the outside of a vessel, is perhaps assumed in the charge of Matthew 23:25-26: Pharisees cleanse the outside of vessels, the insides of which are full of extortion and greed. The latter claim could mean that the vessels contain what has been gained by extortion and greed. More likely, the "inside" of the vessel is used metaphorically for the scribes and Pharisees themselves, who are perceived as sinful in their hearts for all their concern for the cleanness of cups. On this understanding, the metaphor continues in verse 26, and the point is that if the Pharisees would see that their hearts were clean, they would not need to concern themselves with

external (ritual) purity. The pointlessness of observing laws of ritual purity without practicing moral righteousness is thus a crucial theme in Matthew, though it is not suggested that regulations of purity are simply to be abandoned.

3.3. The Gospel of Luke. For Luke it is important that the parents of Jesus observed the Mosaic Law (2:22-24, 27; cf. 1:6), and he relates that they went to Jerusalem to observe the rites connected with a mother's purification after the birth of a child (2:22; cf. Lev 12; only the mother needed to be purified, though Luke, on the most probable reading, speaks loosely of "their purification"). The sacrifice mentioned in Luke 2:24 is that for the purification of a mother who is poor (Lev 12:8), though the preceding verses actually combine with purification the notion of the child's dedication (2:22; cf. 1 Sam 1:24-28) and the redemption of the firstborn son (2:23; cf. Ex 13:2; 34:19-20; Num 18:15-16).

Luke has no direct parallel to the Markan handwashing controversy. On the other hand, according to Luke 11:37-38 Jesus' own failure to wash (presumably his hands, though Booth thinks an immersion is intended) before a meal provoked the wonder of his Pharisaic host. Jesus' reply in 11:39-41 appears to be a variant of the saying in Matthew 23:25-26. In Luke's version the Pharisees themselves (rather than the vessels) are said to be full of rapacity and evil. Verse 40 has no parallel in Matthew and is capable of quite different meanings: "Did not he (God) who made the outside (i.e., material things or perhaps the human body) make the inside (i.e., the heart) as well (i.e., ought not one to be at least as concerned for the purity of the latter as the former)?" or (less likely), "The one who has dealt with (i.e., cleansed) the outside has not (thereby) dealt with (cleansed) the inside." Luke 11:41, like Matthew 23:26, tells the Pharisees that by pursuing something other than laws of ritual purity, they would in fact find all things "clean." In Luke they are directed to give alms.

3.4. The Gospel of John. Ritual purity is not an issue in John (though see 3:25). The purification of pilgrims before a festival in Jerusalem is noted in 11:55. Doubtless John sees the changing of water (set aside for rites of purification) into wine by Jesus as symbolic of the transition from the old age to the new (2:1-11). And Johannine irony is present in the note that those attempting to secure the execution of God's Son carefully avoided incurring ritual defilement (18:28).

4. Conclusion.

The vision of a people submissive to God's rule and fit for his presence was central to much Second

Temple Jewish piety. Adherence to laws of ritual purity must be seen in this context. It must not be assumed either that such adherence marked a merely external conformity to a code or that it necessarily displaced moral and ethical concerns. The Qumran texts provide an eloquent and contemporary witness to the compatibility of ritual and moral scruples (e.g., 1QS 3:4-12), and the evident intention of various groups to extend the laws of ritual purity designed for the Temple to the Jewish home speaks for a profound longing for the divine presence and a lively sense that only the pure might experience it. It is a vision inspired by the laws of the Pentateuch and implemented by an expanded observance of its terms.

On the other hand, in Jesus' vision of Israel's calling and responsibility, the rigorous pursuit of ritual purity had no evident place. His mealtime association with disreputable people is among the best-attested aspects of his public career. Explicit statements to that effect are supported by a number of sayings and parables* intended to defend such activity (Mk 2:14-17; Mt 11:19; 21:28-32; Lk 15:1-32; 19:1-10), and the language of Matthew 11:19 was hardly the invention of the early church. As we have noted, the attacks on Jesus' association with sinners are not based on considerations of purity. Nonetheless, it is self-evident that no one eating meals in such company could share the vision of those dedicated to preserving ritual purity at their meals.

Moreover, the explicit statements on the issue of purity attributed to Jesus must substantially represent his position, cohering as they do not only with each other but also with sayings regarding Sabbath observance (Mk 2:25-28; 3:4; Mt 12:11-12; etc.), meticulous tithing (Mt 23:23) and the bringing of gifts to the Temple (Mt 5:23-24). Time and again the Jesus of the Gospels accuses his contemporaries of expressing their piety in religious observances like these while neglecting "weightier" moral and humanitarian concerns which alone truly matter. To this positive evidence must be added the absence within the Jesus tradition of any suggestion that Jesus' followers (largely drawn from among less-observant Jews) should adopt and adhere to an interpretation of the biblical laws of ritual purity. Unlike the Pharisees (and others), Jesus did not see Israel's task as the accurate interpretation and careful implementation of all aspects of biblical Law.

Much of this is reminiscent of the pre-exilic prophets. There too we find attacks on contemporary expressions of religiosity as mere covers for social abuses. Indeed, the same ambiguity arises in the prophetic denunciations of sacrifices and offerings,

festivals and songs as in Jesus' denunciation of tithing and purity practices. While the words at times suggest that the cultic and ritual aspects of religion have no place whatever in a world of ideal piety, the point is rather the condemnation of wrongs than the advocacy of a religion without cult (cf. Amos 5:21-26; Is 1:10-17; Jer 7:21-24; etc.). Still, no more than Jesus does Amos or Hosea, Isaiah or Jeremiah see a contemporary need for new interpretation or expanded observance of ritual requirements. Such matters will care for themselves when justice and mercy find adequate expression.

The negative role played by laws of purity in the Gospels is thus in part the result of an attack (like that in the pre-exilic prophets) on religiosity combined with perceived abuses. But to this must be added Jesus' conviction that a new age had dawned, that God was intervening in a new way for the salvation* of his people and the establishment of his rule. In a sense the coming of the kingdom represented the culmination of earlier sacred history ("the Law and the Prophets") and the fulfillment of hopes and promises there expressed. At the same time the "new wine*" could not be contained in "old wineskins" (Mk 2:22), aspects of the old piety were now out of season (e.g., Mk 2:19) and the proclamation of the kingdom, which must be brought without encumbrances to "sinners" and "righteous" alike, demanded from both a response of commitment and faith. Jesus' deliberate overriding of purity concerns is both explained in part by the thrust of his message and is part of the explanation why that message found little response among those with a different vision.

See also JUDAISM; LAW; PHARISEES; RABBINIC TRADITIONS AND WRITINGS; SINNERS; TABLE FELLOWSHIP.

BIBLIOGRAPHY. G. Alon, *Jews, Judaism and the Classical World* (Jerusalem: Magnes, 1977); R. P. Booth, *Jesus and the Laws of Purity* (Sheffield: JSOT, 1986); M. Borg, *Conflict, Holiness and Politics in the Teachings of Jesus* (New York/Toronto: Mellen, 1984); G. W. Buchanan, "The Role of Purity in the Structure of the Essene Sect," *RevQ* 4 (1963-64) 397-406; A. Büchler, "The Law of Purification in Mark vii. 1-23," *ExpT* 21 (1909-10) 34-40; C. Carlston, "The Things that Defile (Mark VII. 14) and the Law in Matthew and Mark," *NTS* 15 (1968-69) 75-96; M. Douglas, *Purity and Danger* (London: Routledge and Kegan Paul, 1966); idem, "Deciphering a Meal," in *Implicit Meanings* (London: Routledge and Kegan Paul, 1975) 249-75; H. Maccoby, "The Washing of Cups," *JSNT* 14 (1982) 3-15; N. J. McEleney, "Authenticating Criteria and Mark 7.1-23," *CBQ* 34 (1972) 431-60; J. Neusner, "The Fellowship (*ḥavurah*) in the Second Jewish Commonwealth," *HTR* 53 (1960)

125-42; idem, " 'First Cleanse the Inside.' The 'Halak-hic' Background of a Controversy-Saying," *NTS* 22 (1975-76) 486-95; idem, *The Idea of Purity in Ancient Israel* (Leiden: Brill, 1973); H. Räisänen, "Jesus and the Food Laws. Reflections on Mark 7.15," *JSNT* 16 (1982) 79-100; E. P. Sanders, *Jesus and Judaism* (London: SCM, 1985); S. Westerholm, *Jesus and Scribal Authority* (Lund: CWK Gleerup, 1978).

S. Westerholm

CLEANSING OF THE TEMPLE. *See* TEMPLE; TEMPLE CLEANSING.

COMFORTER. *See* HOLY SPIRIT.

COMMANDMENT

In all four Gospels the unmistakable basis of the ethical teaching of Jesus is "the commandment" or "the commandments" of God.* In this respect, Jesus in the Gospels is no different from any other Jewish teacher.* The question for the student of the Gospels is, What did Jesus mean by "the commandments?" Did he mean all the commands of God recorded in the Hebrew Bible, or was he referring more specifically to the Ten Commandments, or Decalog (Ex 20:1-17; Deut 5:6-16), or to his own twofold command to love* God and neighbor (Mt 22:34-40 par. Mk 12:28-34 and Lk 10:25-28), or to his own ethical* teaching in general (*see* Ethics of Jesus)?

These questions can be answered only from a careful survey of the New Testament terminology for "commandment" and from the evidence of each Gospel.

    1. Terminology
    2. Commandment in the Synoptic Gospels and Jesus
    3. Commandment in the Gospel of John

1. Terminology.

The dominant Greek word in the NT for "command," in the sense of a commandment from God, is *entolē*, with sixty-seven occurrences. Of these, all but three (Lk 15:29; Col 4:10; Tit 1:14) refer specifically to divine commandments. In this respect the NT follows the terminology of the LXX, where *entolē* is used 245 times. Approximately 160 of these render the Hebrew *miṣwâ*, ordinarily translated as "command" or "commandment" in English. Forty-two other instances of *entolē* in the LXX have no Hebrew equivalent because they are in the apocryphal books, and about forty render various other Hebrew words such as *piqqudim*, "directions" or "orders"; *dābār*, "word"; *ḥōq*, "rule" or "prescription"; *ḥuqqâ*, "statute"; and *tôrâ*, "teaching" or "law."

2. Commandment in the Synoptic Gospels and Jesus.

There are sixteen occurrences of *entolē* in the synoptic Gospels: six in Matthew, six in Mark and four in Luke. Eleven are found in just three passages: (1) the debate over ritual defilement (Mk 7:1-23 par. Mt 15:1-20, specifically Mk 7:8-13 and Mt 15:3-6); (2) the question of a rich man to Jesus (Mk 10:17-22 par. Mt 19:16-22 par. Lk 18:18-23; cf. Lk 10:25-28); (3) the question about the "first," or "great," commandment (Mk 12:28-34 par. Mt 22:34-40; cf. Lk 10:25-28).

Of the five remaining instances, three are incidental (Lk 1:6; 15:29; 23:56), while two (Mk 10:5 and Mt 5:19) require separate treatment. Luke 1:6 refers very generally to Zechariah and Elizabeth "walking in all the commandments and ordinances of the Lord blameless" (all quotations within article are from RSV unless otherwise noted). This reference contributes to the larger Lukan schema in which the lasting value of the Mosaic Law* is upheld. Luke 23:56 mentions explicitly the keeping of the Sabbath* as "according to the commandment," while Luke 15:29 mentions the "commands" of a human father to his son in the context of a parable* (only by treating the parable as an allegory is it possible to see in it a reference to the commandments of God). Mark 10:5 will be treated as a postscript to Mark 7:8-13, while Matthew 5:19 will be discussed last.

2.1. The Debate over Ritual Defilement. According to Mark, Jesus responds to the Pharisees'* criticism that his disciples* do not wash before eating by contrasting "the commandment of God" with "your tradition" (Mk 7:8-9). He then illustrates "the commandment of God" with a reference to "honor your father and your mother" from the Decalog (Ex 20:12; Deut 5:16) and its corollary in Exodus 21:17, "He who speaks evil of father or mother, let him surely die." This is introduced as something that "Moses* said" (7:10). As Mark sees it, what "Moses said" is also "the commandment of God," which is the same as "the word of God" (7:13). Though Jesus does not explicitly refer here to the commandment or word of God as something written, he does firmly deny that the oral tradition of the Pharisees handed down from the elders* (cf. *M. Pirqe 'Abot* 1.1) is faithful to it.

Later in his Gospel Mark views the authority of Moses somewhat differently. When asked about divorce, Jesus inquires in return, "What did Moses command you?" (Mk 10:3). The Pharisees reply, "Moses allowed a man to write a certificate of divorce* and to put his wife away." Then Jesus says, "For your hardness of heart he wrote you this commandment" (10:5; *see* Hardness of Heart). The verb "command" (*entellō*) and the noun "commandment" (*entolē*) are used here for what was in fact a concession and not a command. Jesus then subordinates the "commandment" of Moses to the provision of God at creation that "a man shall leave his father and mother and be joined to his wife, and the two shall become one" (Mk 10:7-8; cf. Gen 2:24). In this instance the word of Moses is no longer viewed as "the commandment of God," for the coming of Jesus has introduced a new era with new possibilities for faithfulness.

Matthew's account of the debate is much the same as Mark's except that Jesus' answer to the Pharisees mocks the form of their own charge against his disciples (Mt 15:2-3: "Why do your disciples transgress the traditions of the elders? . . . *And* why do *you transgress* the commandment of God for the sake of your traditions?") and in place of the expression "For Moses said" (Mk 7:3) Matthew substitutes "For God said" (Mt 15:4 NIV). Thus he avoids equating Moses's words with the words of God. Luke lacks the exchange altogether.

2.2. The Question of the Rich Man. In Mark the inquirer is simply "someone" or "a man" (Mk 10:17). He is a "rich man" because in the course of the story it comes out that he "had great possessions" (10:22). When he asks Jesus, "Good Teacher, what must I do to inherit eternal life?" (10:17), Jesus replies, as any Jewish teacher might, "Why do you call me good? No one is good but God alone. You know the commandments" (10:18-19a). Jesus then lists six commandments from the Decalog: " 'Do not kill, Do not commit adultery, Do not steal, Do not bear false witness, Do not defraud, Honor your father and your mother' " (10:19b; cf. Ex 20:12-16; Deut 5:16-20).

The only one of these commandments not explicit in the Decalog is "Do not defraud," and Mark's choice of this expression—implicit either in "Do not steal" or in the concluding, unexpressed command not to "covet"—may have been dictated by the awareness that the questioner was in fact a man of wealth (cf. 10:22). "Honor your father and your mother" has been shifted to the end, possibly for emphasis (cf. the emphasis given it in Mk 7:10; also Eph 6:2) and to anticipate the man's response that he has obeyed these commandments "from my youth" (10:20). The first three commandments have been omitted, perhaps because they are implicit in the phrase "God alone" in Mark 10:18, while Jesus' position on the Sabbath commandment is already on record in Mark 2:27-28. Not content merely to repeat the Decalog, Jesus in Mark's Gospel selects from it and—at least to a limited degree—interprets it.

The rich man complies with the request to drop the adjective "good" in addressing Jesus. "Teacher," he says, "all these I have observed from my youth" (10:20). His obedience to the commandments is almost, but not quite, enough. Mark comments that Jesus "loved" the man for his obedience—that is, he showed him love, probably with an embrace—but Jesus continued, "You lack one thing; go, sell what you have, and give to the poor, and you will have treasure in heaven. And come follow me." Those who seriously undertake to follow Jesus can do so only by divesting themselves of the baggage of material possessions and "traveling light." To them is promised eternal life, here called "treasure in heaven" in contrast to the material possessions they had given up. Ironically, it is an invitation, not a command, that finally drives the rich man away (Mk 10:22).

Luke follows Mark rather closely, supplying only the additional information that the man is a "ruler" or magistrate of some kind. Matthew's modifications in the story, though small, are more substantial. Instead of "Good Teacher, what must I do to inherit eternal life?" (Mk 10:17; cf. Lk 18:18), the man asks, "Teacher, what good deed must I do to inherit eternal life? (Mt 19:16). Jesus' answer, accordingly, is also different: "Why do you ask me about what is good?" (Mt 19:17). Matthew avoids Mark's implication that Jesus does not want to be called "good." "One there is who is good," Jesus continues. "If you would enter life, keep the commandments" (19:17). He pauses and the rich man asks him, "Which?" Jesus enumerates "the commandments" in the same way as in Mark, except that he omits "Do not defraud" and substitutes another not found explicitly in the Decalog, "You shall love your neighbor as yourself" (Mt 19:19). Instead of interpreting "You shall not covet" as "Do not defraud," Jesus in Matthew states the last commandment positively. "You shall not covet your neighbor's house; you shall not covet your neighbor's wife . . . or anything that is your neighbor's" (Ex 20:17; cf. Deut 5:21) has become simply "Love your neighbor as yourself" (cf. Lev 19:18). With this he anticipates the second of two "great commandments" in Matthew 22:39.

Mark's rich man, though not a "ruler," has become a rich "young man" in Matthew (19:20), and Matthew furthers this impression by omitting the phrase "from my youth" (Mk 10:20; cf. Lk 18:21). Matthew also omits (this time with Luke) the reference in Mark to a show of affection on Jesus' part (Mk 10:21). Finally, the terminology of "lacking" something is attributed in Matthew to the young man himself. Instead of being told, "One thing you lack" (Mk 10:21; cf. Lk 18:22), the young man asks Jesus, "What do I still lack?" (Mt 19:20). Jesus replies, "If you would be perfect, go, sell what you possess and give to the poor, and you will have treasure in heaven; and come, follow me" (19:21). The condition laid down is the same as in the other two Gospels except that to Matthew it is the condition for being "perfect," or "complete" (cf. Mt 5:48), not simply for inheriting eternal life.*

2.3. The Question about the "First," or "Great," Commandment. According to Mark, a scribe* asked Jesus, "Which commandment is the first of all?" (Mk 12:28). For once Jesus makes no reference to any specific commandment of the Decalog. Instead, he answers with a quotation of the Jewish confession known as the Shema, based on Deuteronomy 6:4-5: "Hear, O Israel: The Lord our God, the Lord is one; and you shall love the Lord your God with all your heart, and with all your soul, and with all your mind, and with all your strength" (Mk 12:29-30). Then, significantly, he answers another question that has not been asked. Combining Deuteronomy 6:4-5 with Leviticus 19:18b, he adds, "The second is this, 'You shall love your neighbor as yourself.' There is no other commandment greater than these" (12:31).

The scribe had asked for one "first" commandment, but in reply Jesus gave him two. The implication is that love for God and love for one's neighbor cannot be separated. The scribe accepts the reformulation of his question and immediately echoes what Jesus had just said: To love God with all one's heart and understanding and strength and to love one's neighbor as oneself is "much more than whole burnt offerings and sacrifices" (Mk 12:3, 33). Because the scribe has "answered wisely," Jesus tells him, "You are not far from the kingdom of God" (12:34a; *see* Kingdom of God). But how far is "not far"? Neither Jesus nor Mark explicitly answers that question. Just as in Mark 10:21, obedience to the commandments is almost—but not quite—sufficient for salvation. Despite Jesus' warm commendation of the inquiring scribe, Mark concludes with the remark that "after that no one dared to ask him any question" (12:34b), and in the verses that immediately follow, Jesus' critique of the scribes continues (Mk 12:35-37, 38-40).

In Matthew, the questioner is a "lawyer" rather than a "scribe"; he is further identified as a Pharisee, and he asks Jesus the question "to test him" (Mt 22:34-35). "Teacher," he asks, "which is the great commandment in the law?" (22:36). The answer is much the same as in Mark except that the first part of the Shema, "Hear O Israel: The Lord our God, the Lord is one" (Mk 12:29; cf. Deut 6:4), is omitted, and the "great and first commandment" is stated more briefly: "You shall love the Lord your God with all your soul and with all your mind" (22:37-38). Jesus adds that "a second is like it,

You shall love your neighbor as yourself" (22:39). As in Mark, one commandment is asked for, and Jesus gives two: "On these two commandments depend all the law and the prophets" (22:40). Nothing is said in Matthew about the questioner's response, nor does Jesus tell him he is "not far from the kingdom of God." Moreover, the series of adversarial questions from Jewish religious leaders does not end here, as in Mark, but only after one more exchange (Mt 22:46).

In Luke there is no mention of "commandments" or any question of which is the first or greatest. Instead, a lawyer asks Jesus the same question the rich ruler will ask later: "Teacher, what shall I do to inherit eternal life?" (Lk 10:25). Unlike the ruler, he asks this only "to put him to the test" (cf. the lawyer in Mt 22:35). "What is written in the law?" Jesus asks in return, "How do you read?" (10:26). The lawyer himself mentions love for God and neighbor, but without calling these "commandments" or identifying them as "first" and "second" (10:27). Jesus commends him for this answer, even though Luke comments negatively on his motives in asking, "Who is my neighbor?" (10:29). Jesus' parable of the merciful Samaritan (10:30-37) demonstrates that the "neighbor" is none other than the enemy. The "first," or "great commandment" (though these words are never used) turns out to be the love of enemies. Jesus has already made this clear in Luke 6:27-36, while in Matthew 5:43-48 it is also love for enemies that makes a disciple "perfect as your heavenly Father is perfect" (5:48; cf. 19:21).

2.4. The "Least" of the Commandments. Throughout the Synoptic tradition Jesus combines a profound respect for the ancient commandments of the Law (especially the Decalog) with new and radical words of his own that are never called "commandments." Yet these words of Jesus focus or reinterpret the commandments of the Law. For this reason it is difficult to be sure what is meant in Matthew 5:19, where it is not a question of the "greatest" but of the "least" of the commandments.

Jesus warns his disciples that "whoever relaxes one of the least of these commandments and teaches men so, shall be called least in the kingdom of heaven; but he who does them and teaches them shall be called great in the kingdom of heaven." By "these commandments" does he mean the commandments "in the law," as in Matthew 22:36, or does he mean his own commands, presumably those that will follow almost immediately in the Sermon on the Mount* (i.e., Mt 5:21-48 and chapters 6—7)? The latter are never called "commandments" in Matthew (or in any of the Gospels). The closest Matthew comes to referring to

Jesus' teachings as "commandments" (*entolai*) is at the very end of his Gospel, where after his resurrection* Jesus tells the disciples to teach the Gentiles* to obey "all that I have commanded you" (28:20; Gk, *panta hosa eneteilamēn humin*).

Although it is possible that Matthew is presupposing already in 5:19 the post-resurrection notion of teaching the "commandments" of Jesus, the context does not support it. Jesus has just spoken of "the Law and the Prophets" (5:17) or simply "the Law" (5:18), both with reference to the Hebrew Scriptures. Therefore the phrase "these commandments" in the next verse probably refers to the commandments of Scripture. The "least of these" is equivalent to "any of these" (cf. the "least of these my brethren" in Mt 25:40, 45) and might appear to stand in a long Jewish tradition that resisted all distinctions between major and minor commandments in the Law (see e.g., *Pirqe 'Abot* 4.2, "Run to fulfill the lightest duty even as the weightiest"; also James 2:10; see 2. above).

Yet this appearance is deceptive, for Matthew intends just the opposite. Later in his Gospel, Jesus will say, "On these two commandments [i.e., love for God and love for neighbor] depend all the law and the prophets" (22:40). It is precisely by obeying the two great commandments that a person obeys all the commandments, even the "least" (cf. the so-called Golden Rule of Mt 7:12: "So whatever you wish that men would do to you, do so to them; for this is the law and the prophets").

2.5. The Historical Jesus. How much of this material goes back to Jesus? In view of the tendency in the Christian church to identify Jesus with God and the commandments of God with Jesus' commandments, it is likely that for Jesus himself "the commandments" referred consistently to the commands of God in the Hebrew Scriptures, just as they did for most Jewish teachers. The Gospel writers would have had no reason to read this emphasis back into the teaching of Jesus. Yet the Synoptics also testify that Jesus did not hesitate to select, summarize or combine these ancient commands in order to undermine the prevailing interpretations and rationalizations of his time. Their unanimous testimony cannot be easily discounted.

Throughout the Synoptic tradition, wherever Jesus speaks of commandments, there is always the hint of "something more" that is needed to make a person righteous before God, whether it is loving an enemy or selling one's possessions to give to the poor. Only Luke tells the story of the servant who comes in from working in the field and is given no rest, but is told to prepare supper for the master. Yet this story is the unspoken presupposition of all Jesus' teaching: "So

you also, when you have done all that is commanded you [*panta ta diatachthenta*], say, 'We are unworthy servants; we have only done what was our duty' " (Lk 17:10).

3. Commandment in the Gospel of John.
Of the ten occurrences of the noun *entolē* in John's Gospel, four refer to a "command" (Jn 10:18; 12:49-50) or "commands" (Jn 15:10b) given to Jesus by God the Father (cf. the use of the verb *entellomai* in 14:31). Five occurrences refer to a "command" (Jn 13:34; 15:12) or "commands" (Jn 14:15, 21; 15:10a) given by Jesus to his disciples (cf. the use of the verb in 15:14, 17). One occurrence refers to "orders" given by the Pharisees to inform them of Jesus' whereabouts (Jn 11:57). Nowhere in John is *entolē* used to refer to the "commandments" of the Hebrew Scriptures (the verb *entellomai* is so used only in John 8:5, a passage not originally a part of John's Gospel). The contrast in the use of "commandment" between the Synoptics and John could hardly be more striking.

The point of departure for "the commandments" in John's Gospel is not the Decalog, but the sending of Jesus the Son into the world: "For this reason the Father loves me, because I lay down my life, that I may take it again. No one takes it from me, but I lay it down of my own accord. I have power [*exousia*] to lay it down, and I have power to take it again; this charge [*entolē*, "commandment"] I have received from my Father" (Jn 10:17, 18b). At the end of his public ministry Jesus concludes, "For I have not spoken on my own. . . . the Father who sent me has himself given me commandment what to say and what to speak. And I know that his commandment is eternal life. What I say, therefore, I say as the Father has bidden me" (Jn 12:49-50; cf. 15:10).

In the latter half of John's Gospel, the emphasis shifts to the commands given by Jesus to his disciples: "A new commandment I give to you, that you love one another; even as I have loved you, that you also love one another" (Jn 13:34; cf. 15:12, 17). "Love of neighbor" or "love of enemy" in the Synoptic tradition has given way in the Gospel of John to love of "one another" in the sense of brother or sister in the community of faith (cf. 1 Jn 4:20—5:3). Love for God with "all the heart, soul, mind and strength" has given way to love for Jesus.

In his farewell discourse* Jesus himself takes the place that belonged to God in the "first" or "great" commandment in the Synoptic tradition: "If you love me, you will keep my commandments" (Jn 14:15); "He who has my commandments and keeps them, he it is who loves me" (14:21); "If you keep my commandments, you will abide in my love, just as I have kept my Father's commandments and abide in his love" (15:10). Because of the charge or "commandment" he himself has received from God, Jesus in John's Gospel takes the place of God in the piety and practice of Christians. The "commandments" are no longer simply the ancient commandments of God, but "my commandments," the commands of Jesus himself: "You are my friends if you do what I command you" (15:14); "This I command you, that you love one another" (15:17).

John takes up where the Synoptics leave off. After his resurrection in Matthew, Jesus told the disciples, "All authority *[exousia]* in heaven and on earth has been given to me. Go, therefore, and make disciples of all nations . . . teaching them to observe all that I have commanded you; and lo, I am with you always, to the close of the age" (Mt 28:18-20). The "commandments" in the Gospel of John are seen from this same post-resurrection standpoint, as Jesus tells his followers again and again (in different words) to "observe all that I have commanded you."

See also ETHICS OF JESUS; JUSTICE, RIGHTEOUSNESS; LAW; LOVE.

BIBLIOGRAPHY. R. H. Fuller, "The Double Commandment of Love: A Test Case for Authenticity," in *Essays on the Love Commandment*, ed. R. H. Fuller (Philadelphia: Fortress, 1978); idem, "The Decalogue in the New Testament," *Int* 43 (1989) 243-55; V. P. Furnish, *The Love Command in the New Testament* (Nashville: Abingdon, 1972); J. L. Houlden, *Ethics in the New Testament* (New York: Oxford, 1977); P. Perkins, *Love Commands in the New Testament* (New York: Paulist, 1982); K. H. Schelkle, *Theology of the New Testament: III. Morality* (Collegeville, MN: Liturgical Press, 1970) 113-36; G. Schrenk, "ἐντέλλομαι, ἐντολή," *TDNT* II.544-56.   J. R. Michaels

CONFLICT, CONFLICT STORIES. *See* DEATH OF JESUS; DEMON, DEVIL, SATAN; DISCIPLES; FORM CRITICISM; PHARISEES.

COSMOS. *See* WORLD.

CRITERIA OF AUTHENTICITY. *See* FORM CRITICISM; GOSPELS (HISTORICAL RELIABILITY); TRADITION CRITICISM.

CROSS. *See* DEATH OF JESUS.

CROWD. *See* PEOPLE, CROWD.

CRUCIFIXION. *See* DEATH OF JESUS; TRIAL OF JESUS.

CUP. *See* LAST SUPPER; PREDICTIONS OF JESUS' PASSION AND RESURRECTION; WINE.

D

DAVID. *See* SON OF DAVID.

DAY OF THE LORD. *See* ESCHATOLOGY.

DEAD SEA SCROLLS

In 1947 a Bedouin shepherd, following a stray into a cave along the shores of the Dead Sea, chanced upon the first of a group of ancient manuscripts which have revolutionized biblical studies and the study of ancient Judaism.* The seven major scrolls which emerged from that cave were only the beginning. Following their discovery, Bedouin and scholars competed to explore the caves of the region in hopes of new manuscript discoveries. Eventually, a total of eleven caves yielded literary texts, now known as the Dead Sea Scrolls (DSS). Approximately 800 separate manuscripts, many very fragmentary, came to light in the course of these explorations. The nearby site of Qumran, hitherto regarded as an ancient fortress, was also excavated during five campaigns between 1951-56, and scholars came to believe that the site was connected to the caves and the scrolls.

Publication of the discoveries was at first comparatively rapid by scholarly standards. Six of the seven scrolls from the first discovery, now known as Cave 1, were completely published within seven years. The sixth, the *Genesis Apocryphon,* appeared in a partial edition in 1956. The great bulk of the discoveries were early consigned to an international editorial team consisting of six scholars from Europe and the United States. This team succeeded in publishing substantial portions of the DSS in a series of volumes, *Discoveries in the Judaean Desert (of Jordan* appears on some volumes). Five such volumes appeared in the decade spanning the late 1950s to the late 1960s. Since that time, however, even with occasional preliminary editions, the rate of publication has slowed substantially. Volume six of the series appeared in 1977, volume seven in 1982, and volume eight bears a publication date of 1989. At the present time, estimates of the percentage of the material which remains unpublished range between forty and sixty per cent. The reasons for the nonpublication of so much vital material after forty years are various, some of them legitimate (the fragmentary nature of many of the scrolls, death of original team members, the demands of academic responsibilities) and some suggesting scandalous scholarly conduct. Recent plans are to have an expanded group of approximately twenty-five scholars publish the remaining material by the year 2000. The discussion which follows is obviously limited by this situation, and it is necessary at the outset to recognize the tentative nature of the analysis which follows in light of unknown possible correlations among the unpublished texts.

1. Description of Contents
2. Interpretation of the Finds
3. The Dead Sea Scrolls and the Gospels

1. Description of Contents.

1.1. Biblical Materials. The biblical scrolls recovered from the caves number several hundred; 122 come from Cave 4 alone. These scrolls include copies of every book of the Hebrew Bible with the exception of the book of Esther. The most frequently attested books are Genesis, Exodus, Deuteronomy, Isaiah and Psalms—this last book numbering some thirty copies.

The biblical scrolls from Qumran have had a tremendous impact on the study of the Hebrew Bible, both with regard to textual criticism and with regard to what was once known as higher criticism. Their importance for textual criticism is obvious when one considers that prior to their discovery the oldest manuscripts of the Hebrew Bible dated from the tenth century. Thus the DSS lifted the curtain to a period over a millennium earlier in the formation of the text.

With regard to matters of criticism, perhaps a discussion of the manuscript known as 11QPs[a] can serve as a typical example of the rich applications the scrolls make possible. It contains forty-one of the biblical psalms as well as apocryphal psalms 151, 154 and 155. It also contains three previously unknown psalms, a portion of Ecclesiasticus chapter 51, and a ten-line supplement enumerating the total of David's writings (3,600). The date of the composition of the three unknown psalms is disputed by scholars, but is probably the late Persian or early Hellenistic period. The text of Ecclesiasticus 51 differs markedly from that previously known from the Septuagint and other early versions. Its presence in a collection of psalmic material attributed entirely to David is intriguing. The attribution is a premier example of the tendency in Second Temple Judaism to ascribe poetic writings of unknown authorship to David. Also it appears to confirm the long-held suspicion that Jesus ben Sira did not write that portion of Ecclesiasticus.

But this manuscript of the book of Psalms raises much broader issues as well. The order of the psalms in 11QPs^a is substantially different from the order in the Masoretic Text. At least once (Ps 145) it evidences a different form of the canonical psalm. Certain groupings of psalms, such as the Songs of Ascent and the Passover Hallel—viewed as units by the Masoretic Text—appear scattered throughout the Qumran text. In addition to 11QPs^a, several other non-Masoretic psalters have turned up among the DSS, as have other copies of the above-mentioned apocryphal psalms. These facts suggest that the Psalter as we know it was perhaps only one variant in use among the Jews at the time of Jesus. Taken together with other similar evidence, this scroll may indicate that the third division of the canon, the Writings, was still in flux at the time.

1.2. Non-Biblical Materials. The vast majority of manuscripts from the caves near Qumran are non-biblical texts. Many of these works were entirely unknown prior to the discoveries; others were known to scholars only by name or through reference in ancient literature. Since the diversity of the scrolls does not lend itself to a single classificatory scheme, what follows is organized according to these broad categories: major (i.e., lengthy) texts, interpretive texts, apocryphal and pseudepigraphic texts, liturgical texts and so-called magical texts.

1.2.1. Major Texts.

Damascus Covenant. This work, also known as the *Zadokite Fragments,* came to light even before the discovery of the Qumran texts. S. Schechter discovered two fragmentary exemplars of it in the Cairo genizah at the end of the nineteenth century. Fragments of it have subsequently turned up among the DSS, being found in Caves 4, 5 and 6. The documents which Schechter found consist of three fragments, representing two versions or recensions, which he designated A and B. The two fragments of A correspond to two very different portions of the document—called respectively the Admonition and the

Laws. Basically, the Admonition encompasses so-called historical summaries and the establishment of a new covenant community, while the Laws consist of halakic regulations for a communal life lived out in "camps." Of particular interest are the mentions of a "Teacher of Righteousness," a "Spouter of Lies" and an "Interpreter of the Law," along with the messiah(s) of Israel and Aaron.

The Discipline Scroll. A document that is often compared with the *Damascus Covenant,* particularly in terms of halakah (*h^alākâ,* lit., "the way," meaning a guide for living; *see* Rabbinic Traditions and Writings), is the *Discipline Scroll* (1QS, also known as the *Manual of Discipline*). The *Discipline Scroll* is an enigmatic text whose present form is the result of a process of editing and redaction, such that distinct literary units can be isolated. The text presents a number of difficulties since we lack the historical and sociological context to understand many of the references. In addition to this, the paleography and the rough Hebrew syntax combine to make very different translations possible. Emendations have been widely proposed—for example, the standard study by P. Wernberg-Møller proposes 63 emendations.

In addition to the principal text, two so-called appendices have been discovered. The first, known as the *Messianic Rule* (1QS^a), is two columns long and deals with the "last days." Its actual connection with the principal text is unclear, for although it apparently originally belonged to the same scroll from Cave 1, it was written by another scribe* and differs both in concept and terminology. It discusses the education of children* raised in the community, the stages of progression within the community according to age and ability, and procedures for the communal meal presided over by priests* and the "messiah of Israel." The second appendix has been called the *Rule of Benediction* (1QS^b) and is very poorly preserved. It consists of several blessings pronounced by the *maśkîl* ("wise leader") over the community, the priests and the prince. Like the *Messianic Rule* it has a definite eschatological setting.

The War Scroll. This scroll consists of nineteen badly deteriorated columns. It was originally somewhat longer, although there is no way to gauge just how much longer. It seems to have been intended as a manual to guide the "Sons of Light" in the final eschatological war, in which they would face, and eventually vanquish, the "Sons of Darkness." Nevertheless, the text is essentially a theological, not a military, composition.

Among the topics it treats are: preliminary preparations for the war; rules for the sounding and inscrip-

The Dead Sea Scrolls
A listing of some significant texts with their abbreviations

CD	Cairo (Genizah text of the) *Damascus (Document/Rule)*

Qumran Cave 1

1QapGen	*Genesis Apocryphon*
1QH	*Hôdāyôt* or *Thanksgiving Hymns*
1QIsaa,b	First or second copy of Isaiah
1QM	*Milḥāmāh* or *War Scroll*
1QpHab	*Pesher on Habakkuk*
1QS	*Serek hayyaḥad* or *Rule of the Community, Manual of Discipline*
1QSa	Appendix A, *Messianic Rule*, to 1QS
1QSb	Appendix B, *Rule of Benediction*, to 1QS

Qumran Cave 3

3Q15	*Copper Scroll*

Qumran Cave 4

4QCryptic	Magical text
4QEna-g	*1 Enoch* fragments
4QEnastra-g	*1 Enoch* fragments from Astronomical Book
4QEn Giantsa-e	*1 Enoch* fragments from Book of Giants
4QFlor	*Florilegium* or *Eschatological Midrashim*
4QMess ar	Aramaic "Messianic" text
4QMMT	*Miqsat Ma'aseh Torah* (unpublished)
4QPhyl	Phylacteries
4QPrNab	*Prayer of Nabonidus*
4QPsDan Aa	Pseudo-Danielic Writings
4QPssJosh	*Psalms of Joshua*
4QShirShabb	*Songs of Sabbath Sacrifice* or *Angelic Liturgy*
4QTestim	*Testimonia* text
4QtgLev	*Targum of Leviticus*
4QtgJob	*Targum of Job*
4QZodiac	Magical text (unpublished)
4Q139	Ordinances or commentaries on biblical laws
4Q169	Pesher on Nahum
4Q171	Pesher on Psalms
4Q176	*Tanhumim* or *Consolations*
4Q186	(see 4QMess ar)
4Q246	(see 4QPsDan Aa)
4Q504	*Words of the Luminaries*
4Q513-14	Ordinances or commentaries on biblical laws

Qumran Cave 5

5Q15	*New Jerusalem*

Qumran Cave 11

11QMelch	*Melchizedek*
11QpaleoLev	Copy of Leviticus in paleo-Hebrew script
11QPsa	*Psalms Scroll*
11QTemple	*Temple Scroll*
11QtgJob	*Targum of Job*
11QTorah	(alternative designation for *Temple Scroll*)

tion of trumpets used to guide the course of the battle; the dimensions and inscriptions of shields and standards used; the battle array, including who may and may not participate in the conflict; the role of the priests and Levites; and the ebb and flow of the final battle against the *Kittim* (probably the Romans).

The weapons and tactics which the scroll describes suggest Roman, rather than Greek, military strategy, thus enabling the dating of the text to be narrowed to the later decades of the first century B.C. Literary analysis further suggests that the text as we now have it is considerably expanded and reworked, perhaps utilizing as its kernel a work based on Daniel 11:40—12:3. This literary hypothesis of expansion is supported by the discovery of fragments of six exemplars of this work in Cave 4. These fragments provide evidence of various recensions of portions of the War Scroll, some differing rather markedly from the manuscript from cave 1.

The Hymns. The composition known as the *Hymns*, or 1Q *Hôdāyôt*, consists of eighteen partial columns and sixty-six numbered fragments, as published in the *editio princeps*. Subsequently, two additional fragments have been identified. The fact that none of the columns is complete has led to differing divisions of the text and, consequently, differing reckonings as to the number of hymns it contains. The situation is further complicated by five manuscripts from Cave 4; these fill in lacunae in the manuscript from cave 1 but also show the order of hymns to have been variable. The copies of the text date from the first century A.D.

All the hymns or psalms begin "I thank thee, Lord" or "Blessed art thou, O Lord," and many thus fit the type known to form-critics as psalms of individual thanksgiving. Deviations from the biblical models, however, are sufficient to make the genre of these compositions a moot point in scholarship on the DSS. Also debated is the identity of the author(s), and whether this question can legitimately be asked of the texts. Bound up with this matter is the question of what function the writings served within the community that produced or employed them. Another interesting aspect of the hymns is their midway position between the psalmic literature of the Hebrew Bible and that of later Judaism, including the NT.

The Temple Scroll. The most recently published of the major DSS is known as the *Temple Scroll* (11QTemple; also 11QTorah). Sixty-seven columns, in varying degrees of fragmentation, are comprised by the nineteen parchment sheets. The scroll is twenty-eight feet when unwound—making it the longest of the DSS. A study of the writing indicates that two scribes labored to produce this copy. The scroll is an amal-

gam of biblical and extrabiblical ordinances and descriptions concerned with a temple,* its services and its festivals (*see* Feasts). After a lost beginning, the first well-preserved columns describe the temple building with its key installations. From there the text proceeds to detail various festivals, sacrifices and procedures, the temple courtyards and laws of impurity (*see* Clean and Unclean), finishing with nonsequential extracts from the Deuteronomic Code (Deut 12—26). Among the most striking literary features of the scroll is its change of biblical quotations attributed to Moses from third to first person. This has the effect of making Moses seem to be at once the author and addressee of the text. In addition, scriptural portions may be conflated, emended or glossed.

The New Jerusalem Text. A text that is related to the *Temple Scroll*, although not major, may conveniently be brought into the discussion here. This is the Aramaic text known as the *New Jerusalem*, attested by copies from Caves 1, 2, 4, 5 and 11. The text comprises a vision in which the author ("Ezekiel"?) is shown various buildings, streets and gates; in each case measurements both in cubits and reeds are provided. The description is very schematic, and many measurements are unrealistically large. Evidently inspired by Ezekiel 48:16-17, the city described is approximately 18 x 13 miles in size.

The Copper Scroll. Perhaps no DSS has occasioned greater difficulties in reading and interpretation than the *Copper Scroll*. This is the only text inscribed on copper, and unlike all but a few it was written in early Mishnaic Hebrew rather than in archaizing Late Biblical Hebrew (*see* Languages of Palestine).

Basically, the twelve columns consist of a series of topographic descriptions or toponyms, often followed by the instruction to dig a specified depth. Then follows a specified weight or amount of money, precious vessels or the like. At first glance the amounts seem incredible. Various interpretations of this document about buried treasure include Milik's thesis that it represents a "folk-loristic treasure trove" that is not to be attributed to the Qumran community. In this view it was only coincidentally found, along with the materials of that group in Cave 3, being removed somewhat from the other deposits of that cave. This suggests two independent deposits; the Copper Scroll belonged to the second, around A.D. 100. This position has gained significant support. Others believe the contents described in the scroll are of an actual treasure, probably associated with the Jerusalem Temple—but even those who agree on this point dispute the text's dating. Apart from the problem of the scroll's origin, there are major problems in merely reading the letters of the error-filled document. However deciphered, it also seems to contain many new Hebrew terms and unknown toponyms. The Copper Scroll occupies a central position in the question of who wrote the Dead Sea Scrolls.

1.2.2. Interpretive Texts.

Pesharim. Among the most fascinating of the Hebrew texts discovered in the caves are those known as the pesharim (*pĕšārîm,* pl. of *pēšer,* meaning "solution" or "interpretation"). These are usually grouped into two categories—thematic and continuous. Thematic pesharim consist of selected portions of the Hebrew Bible with interpretive comments, and are organized around a central theme or idea. In contrast, continuous pesharim comment verse by verse on a portion of the Hebrew Bible, usually the prophets, but sometimes so-called prophetic psalms. At least fifteen, perhaps eighteen, texts belonging to this latter category have been identified.

Continuous pesharim purport to be mysterious explications of divine truth from Scripture, a truth revealed only to the author and his group. These commentaries are unconcerned with the literal sense of the text, instead using metaphor, paronomasia and development of key words or phrases to unmask the hidden significance of a given biblical portion. The most complete of these pesharim is the commentary on Habakkuk. This pesher preserves thirteen almost-complete columns, providing the text of Habakkuk along with commentary.

Also relatively complete is the pesher known as 4Q171, which preserves the text of Psalms 37:7-40; 45:1-2 and possibly 60:8-9. Psalm 37 is a psalm of personal tribulation, offering the righteous hope in spite of the evident prosperity of the wicked. The author of the pesher has interpreted the psalm in terms of his community's enemies and eschatological justification.

From a historical vantage point the pesher on Nahum, 4Q169, may be the most important of the pesharim. The author, though mixing historical and eschatological descriptions, mentions a "Demetrius, King of Greece," and refers to a Jewish ruler who crucified great numbers of his opponents. References to these persons and events are preserved in the writings of Josephus,* leading some scholars to identify Demetrius as Demetrius III Eucaerus (95-88 B.C.) and the Jewish ruler as Alexander Jannaeus (103-76 B.C.). Other fragmentary pesher commentaries are known on Micah, Zephaniah, Isaiah and certain Psalms.

Of the thematic pesharim, none has aroused more profound interest than the text known as 11Q *Melchizedek.* Fourteen fragments preserve the remains of three columns. This manuscript comments on isolated OT texts, in particular Leviticus 25:9-10, 13; Deuteronomy 15:2; and Isaiah 61:1. The events connected with these biblical texts are portrayed as taking place in "the end of days," which is further identified as the "tenth Jubilee." According to the text Melchizedek will free those who belong to his "inheritance" and (if suggested restorations are followed) "atone for their iniquities." He will further exact God's vengeance upon Belial and those of his "lot." The text presents a conception of Melchizedek that is approximately contemporary with that of Hebrews 7, connecting him with divine judgment, a day of atonement and a primary role among God's angels. Also of interest is Melchizedek's possible identification with the archangel Michael, which would represent a combination of OT figures and motifs in a single person reminiscent of the way Jesus is characterized by the NT.

Three additional thematic pesharim are important. The first of these is known as 4Q *Ordinances.* This pesher is halakic and quite revealing in terms of biblical interpretation. The author interprets Exodus 30:11-16 (the traditional basis for the annual Temple tax required of all male Jews) as referring only to a onetime payment. Leviticus 25:39-46, which prohibits the purchase of fellow Israelites as slaves, is here understood to ban also the sale of a Jew to Gentiles.*

The second thematic pesher is 4Q *Florilegium.* Here four large fragments have been joined to form two columns, leaving twenty-three extra, unjoined sections. The author combines quotations from 2 Samuel 7:10-14; Exodus 15:17-18; Amos 9:11; Psalm 1:1; Isaiah 8:11; Ezekiel 37:23 (uncertain) and Psalm 2:1 with interpretative comments. All of these verses are related to the "end of days," when God will order that a new "temple of Adam" be built. Therein men will perform sacrifices and the "deeds of the Torah," free from outside harassment or impurity. Prominent in the text are references to the "Shoot of David" and the "Interpreter of the Law," terms familiar from other Qumran texts.

The third thematic pesher, 4Q *Testimonia,* has (perhaps falsely) furnished many scholars with the basic substance of Qumran messianic expectation. The text is a catena of quotations from Deuteronomy 5:28-29; 18:18-19; Numbers 24:15-17; Deuteronomy 33:8-11; Joshua 6:26 and an extrabiblical literary work known as 4Q *Psalms of Joshua.* These are arranged in the body of the text into four groups, each set off by a scribal device. One reason this text is important is because it furnishes explicit evidence for the existence, long posited, of *testimonia* or *florilegia* (collections of proof-texts) in pre-Christian Judaism.

Targumim. To date there are three Aramaic targumim (*targûmîm,* plural of *targûm,* meaning "translation" or "interpretation"; *see* Targums) among the DSS. Of these by far the longest and most complete is the targum to Job from Cave 11. The significance of this text is considerable, since it represents the only incontestably pre-Christian targum of any appreciable length. The surviving text includes portions of chapters 17 through 42, with the last six chapters the least damaged. On the whole, despite slight additions, subtractions and dislocations, the Hebrew text on which the scroll was based seems to have been essentially the Masoretic Text. Even the supposedly disordered third cycle of debates (22:1—31:40) and the Hymn to Wisdom (28:1—28:28, often regarded as an interpolation), are here and in the same problematic order as in the Masoretic Text. The most radical divergence from the Hebrew text, probably reflecting a different original, occurs after 42:8-11: verses 12 through 17 are missing and were evidently never a part of the targum.

The other two targumim are extremely fragmentary. The first contains an Aramaic translation of Leviticus 16:12-15, 18-21, and it is not certain that these fragments were part of a targum at all. It is equally conceivable that they may have come from a liturgical work which quoted these verses. If, nevertheless, they do represent portions of a targum, then we have for the first time a pre-Christian targum to a book of the Pentateuch. The translation of the Hebrew is literal (unexpanded). Finally, 4Q157 preserves only portions of Job 3:5-9 and 4:16—5:4, reflecting a text virtually identical to the Masoretic Text.

1.2.3. Apocryphal and Pseudepigraphic Texts. Included among the DSS are manuscripts of nonbiblical books that were known before the discoveries at the caves and which are part of the Pseudepigrapha. Apocryphal books attested at Qumran include Tobit and Ecclesiasticus (also known as Sirach). Pseudepigraphic works include the *Testament of Levi* (in Aramaic), a portion of the *Testament of Naphtali* (in Hebrew), *Enoch* and *Jubilees. Jubilees* seems to have been popular, to judge by the fourteen or fifteen manuscripts thus far identified. Portions have been discovered in Caves 2, 3, 4 and 11. Not surprisingly, previously unknown texts that can now be classified as pseudepigraphic were also unearthed. Among these are the *Psalms of Joshua* mentioned above and a Daniel cycle.

Enoch. In 1976 Milik published his long-awaited book on the fragments of Enoch, which were discovered in Cave 4. The book contains most (but not all) of the Aramaic texts forming parts of different sec-

tions from 1 Enoch. Thus it includes seven fragmentary manuscripts (4Q En^{a-g}) that preserve among them parts of the Book of Watchers, the Book of Dreams and the Epistle of Enoch. Also included in the book are four other manuscripts (4Q Enastr^{a-d}) that point to a vastly expanded recension of what is known in *1 Enoch* as the Astronomical Book. Additionally, portions of a literature clearly related to *1 Enoch,* but previously unknown, are included under the title Book of Giants (4Q En Giants^{a-e}). Significant by its absence from the Qumran fragments is the so-called Book of Parables, which uses the term "son of man," an important self-designation of Jesus (*see* Son of Man).

Genesis Apocryphon. One of the pseudepigraphic texts that surfaced among the DSS was the otherwise unknown *Genesis Apocryphon.* Dated around the turn of the eras, it presents the patriarchs of Genesis telling their own stories. In so doing it is closely dependent on the biblical stories, with frequent expansions derived from unknown midrashic sources. Columns 1 through 5 originally concerned the birth of Noah; 6 through 17 dealt with the flood and the postdiluvian division of the earth among Noah's sons; 18 through 22, where the text breaks off, spoke of Abram according to Genesis 11 through 15.

Most scholars regard the *Genesis Apocryphon* as a midrashic composition, while recognizing features more akin to the known targumim. It is thus related to intertestamental works, such as *Jubilees,* which are often called "rewritten Bible." The primary importance of the text lies perhaps in its language. As one of the longest Aramaic texts from Qumran, it is of special significance in the effort to recover the form of Palestinian Aramaic used at the time of Jesus. The language is of a form transitional between the book of Daniel and the targumim, antedating as well the materials from the Wadi Murabbaʿat, Wadi Seiyal and Wadi Ḥabra.

Prayer of Nabonidus. Fragments of an Aramaic pseudepigraphon known as the *Prayer of Nabonidus* were found in Cave 4. The fragments make up two incomplete columns, including the beginning of column 1. As the name suggests, the text is ostensibly a prayer delivered by the last king of Babylon, Nabonidus. It tells the story of the king's seven-year period of illness—a time when he prayed to "the gods of silver and gold" for a cure. At length a Jewish "exorcist" delivered him, and in gratitude the king wrote this prayer. The parallels with the fourth chapter of Daniel and the story of Nebuchadnezzar's madness are patent, leading many scholars to conclude that in this text we have remnants of the popular traditions from which the Aramaic portions of Daniel were derived. Such literature had the twofold purpose of warning the Jews not to turn to paganism and of preaching to the Gentiles about the folly of idol worship.

The Daniel Cycle. The prayer of Nabonidus is evidently just one part of a Daniel cycle, a group that apparently included at least five additional works. Three of these (pseudo-Daniel a, b and c) seem to contain an apocalyptic overview of Jewish history, narrated by Daniel. The fourth, yet unpublished, work is a recounting of a dream in which four trees (or their "angels") speak to the author. Each tree represents a kingdom (compare Dan 2 and 7), the first of which is identified as Babylon and the second as Persia. Depending on its date, this work (known in two exemplars) could have a bearing on the interpretation (or history of interpretation) of the fourth kingdom mentioned in Daniel 2 and 7. Another text from this Daniel cycle is known as 4Q Ps DanA^a (4Q243; also designated 4Q246). This fragmentary but striking work preserves the phrases "son of God" and "son of the Most High," as well as phraseology reminiscent of Luke 1:32 and 1:35 (*see* Son of God).

Words of Moses. The *Words of Moses* seems to be a sort of apocryphon to Deuteronomy. God speaks to Moses, who in turn relays the commands to the people, evidently via Eleazar and Joshua. At one point the text requires the appointment of officials (perhaps priests) "to clarify . . . all these words of the Torah." Another example of haggadic explanation occurs in the third column (3:8-10), where the date of the Day of Atonement is explained by reason that "your fathers were wandering in the desert until the tenth day of the month."

Book of Mysteries. Another tantalizing pseudepigraphon is the *Book of Mysteries.* Of the thirteen remaining fragments, only the first is complete enough to comprehend. This fragment contains two poetic distichs, cast as oracles, while the rhetorical, rather eloquent, prose that follows each distich provides "signs" by which the truth of the oracles is to be proved. Of particular interest is the appearance in the text (unfortunately in broken context) of the phrase *razê peša'.* This phrase is probably the Hebrew equivalent of the Greek *mystērion tēs anomias* ("mystery of lawlessness") of 2 Thessalonians 2:7.

1.2.4. Liturgical Texts. Among the texts from Qumran many are liturgical (*see* Worship). One of the most interesting of these is known as the *Angelic Liturgy.* The composition is partially preserved in six manuscripts from Cave 4, as well as in fragments from Cave 11 and Masada. The author describes heaven as a complicated temple consisting of seven sanctuaries

attended by seven chief prince-priests, their deputies and seven angelic priesthoods. Also included are the praise offerings that the angels* offer up on the Sabbath.* Altogether the work comprised thirteen compositions, one for each of the first thirteen Sabbaths of the year. The text is of importance for the study of angelology (*see* Angels), Second Temple liturgical song and the investigation of early Jewish mysticism. A striking phrase in the first hymn states that the angelic priests, by their heavenly cultus, "atone for those who turn from sin." It is possible to interpret this statement to imply that the earthly temple cultus is really not essential; here then is an important witness to a conception of Judaism that is not temple-centered (at least in a physical sense). Such ideas, of course, are the starting point both for Christianity and rabbinic Judaism.

An equally noteworthy liturgical opus is known as the *Words of the Luminaries.* Fragmentary remaining instructions show that the compositions contained in this manuscript were intended for use on given days of the week. The mood of these compositions is with one exception penitential; hence they may appropriately be classed *taḥᵃnûnîm* (confessional prayers reflecting such biblical passages as Dan 9:4-19). The instructions evidence that these *taḥᵃnûnîm* were used liturgically, as in later Judaism. The single evident exception to the somber tone of the *Words of the Luminaries* is a composition written for the Sabbath. This prayer* is appropriately full of praise rather than contrition.

Among many that might be singled out, two further liturgically oriented works can be mentioned here. One is 4Q Lamentations. The text is comprised of five fragments, the order of which is still uncertain. As the name implies, it is a lament or series of laments over the city of Jerusalem, whose imagery is achieved chiefly by allusion to Lamentations, Isaiah and Jeremiah. It is possible that the work was occasioned by a destruction of Jerusalem that happened at the time of Antiochus IV Epiphanes (compare 1 Macc 1:29-32). Alternatively, it may be merely a poetic reminiscence of the famous razing by the forces of Nebuchadnezzar in 586 B.C. The second text contains vocabulary strikingly similar to that of the *Rule of Benediction,* and is known as 11Q *Berachot.* Its four fragments speak of blessings upon the "congregation" in eschatological terms borrowed from the prophets.

Another group of documents from Qumran that are in a broad sense related to liturgy and worship are the phylacteries. A number of these have surfaced from Caves 1, 4, 5, 8 and an unidentified cave. These phylacteries (which are head *tᵉpillîn*) are instructive not only regarding the content of the portions of

Scripture contained and their order but also have noteworthy textual variants. Four t͑ᵉpillin were discovered in their capsules. This fortune enabled scholars to investigate several technical points that are treated extensively in rabbinic literature—such matters as the shape of the capsule, the nature of the leather for scriptural portions and the type of thread with which the capsules are tied.

The order of the scriptural portions in the t͑ᵉpillin has been a matter of heated discussion in the history of Judaism. In the early medieval period the most famous controversy on this subject occurred between Rashi and Rabbenu Tam. The Qumran t͑ᵉpillin are not strictly in the order for which either man argued. The fact that some t͑ᵉpillin (arm t͑ᵉpillin from Cave 8 are arranged according to Rashi's system, while others from the approximately contemporary finds at Murabbaʻat accord with the position of Rabbenu Tam, suggests that both systems were used concurrently in first-century Palestine.

The contents of the t͑ᵉpillin published so far often add additional scriptural verses to the classical portion, but the added verses differ among the various examples. No clear rationale has been adduced to explain these additions. Noteworthy perhaps is that 1Q13, 4Qa and XQPhyl3 all contain the Decalog (Deut 5:1-21), which is not included in rabbinic phylacteries. Thus the phylacteries from Qumran raise many questions about the halakah governing their production at this point in the history of Judaism.

1.2.5. "Magical" Documents. The breadth of material included among the DSS is demonstrated by a group of documents which might be categorized as magical. One zodiac from Cave 4 is known to exist (4Q Zodiac) but has not been published. It may be identical with an unpublished brontologion (predicting events using thunder), which comprises two fragmentary columns. Somewhat more can be said about the document known as 4Q Cryptic. This is an encoded series of horoscopes in which the author used a mixture of alphabets and wrote from left to right, the opposite of the usual direction for Hebrew. The text describes three people in reference to their astrological birth signs; this in turn is related to their physical and spiritual qualities. There are terminological parallels with the *Manual of Discipline.* Such texts indicate that astrological ideas had been assimilated very early and quite deeply by the Jews, in spite of the clear connection they apparently had with idolatry for the authors of the Hebrew Bible (for example, Is 47:13-14; Jer 10:1-3). This type of interest was more typical of popular Jewish religion in this period than has often been realized.

Another zodiacal document, known as 4QMess ar, has been called a messianic horoscope. This very poorly preserved text contains the Aramaic phrase *bḥyr ʾlh'*, the equivalent of the Greek phrase *ho eklektos tou theou* (the elect of God) witnessed by some manuscripts of John 1:34. It is not certain, however, that this phrase is intended in a messianic sense. It occurs as part of a description of an unborn child, who is ascribed wisdom and precocious intellect. He is also to have a long life, and the success of his plans is assured by his position as the "elect of God." The description of the child is clearly influenced by biblical descriptions of Solomon, and the text has no clear astronomical terminology. It might therefore better be considered an example of physiognomic literature, of which there are many Greco-Roman examples. It may actually describe the birth of Noah (compare *1 Enoch* 106).

2. Interpretation of the Finds.
The majority of scholars identify the DSS as the products of an ancient Jewish sect known as the Essenes. For this identification they rely on a combination of external and internal evidence. The external evidence consists of a passage from Pliny the Elder and the archeology of the site of Qumran. In the course of a travelog Pliny describes the Essenes as living along the shores of the Dead Sea somewhere north of En Gedi. This description could fit Qumran. Archeology further indicates that the site was in use at approximately the time the ancient source describes. Structures found at Qumran have been identified as functional for such a community, and include what have been understood to be a potter's shop and communal dining hall. Three inkwells and other materials construed as evidence of scribal activity suggest to many scholars that the scrolls found in the nearby caves had their origins in a reputed scriptorium on the site.

Internal evidence consists of a comparison between passages describing the Essenes in Philo and Josephus and the contents of texts such as 1QS and CD. All agree in describing or presupposing a communal organization. Similarities include novitiate periods, communal regulations, strict observance of the Sabbath vis à vis rabbinic law, and certain legal positions such as the transmission of ritual impurity by oil.

But there are significant difficulties involved with the identification of the DSS as the products of an Essene community living at Qumran. Many of these problems have been pointed out by N. Golb in postulating his "Jerusalem hypothesis." The source upon which Pliny relies, for example, postdates the First

Revolt. Therefore, it presumably describes a community living on the shores of the Dead Sea after A.D. 70, while archeology suggests that use of Qumran (except by the Romans) ceased before that. The agreements between the classical sources' descriptions of Essene life and certain DSS texts are balanced, if not outweighed, by significant disagreements. And the vast majority of the DSS have no obvious relation to those descriptions at all, whether to agree or to disagree. Many have no obvious relation to one another—not what one would expect if they are all the products of a small sectarian community. Further, hundreds of different hands can be identified among the texts. This fact implies a multiplicity of scribes, of course, and even more striking, very few of the scribes so far identified copied out more than one text. How can these data be explained other than to posit an origin for the majority of the texts elsewhere than at Qumran?

An equally disturbing problem for the hypothesis of an Essene scriptorium (the identification of which has always been problematic, given the lack of ancient parallels) at Qumran is the lack of autographic and documentary texts among the scrolls. The scrolls include only one contract, if that, which is anomalous in comparison with what both other Judean manuscript discoveries and common sense would have predicted. And only one of the scrolls is an original—the hundreds of others are all scribal copies. The one autograph, the *Copper Scroll*, points back to Jerusalem by its list of treasures and its toponyms. It is thus not unreasonable, in light of the problems with the Essene hypothesis, to suggest a Jerusalem origin for all or most of the DSS. If such a view is correct, then the potential significance of the scrolls for an understanding of Judaism at the time of Jesus, and of the Gospels as products of that milieu, increases by orders of magnitude. For on this interpretation, the DSS represent the product of a wider portion of society than the Essene hypothesis stipulates. The question of how much wider remains a problem to be determined by literary analysis and must, of course, await the publication of the remaining texts before it can receive a definitive answer.

Although the Jerusalem hypothesis is not yet widely accepted, more and more scholars are coming to realize that a substantial proportion of the DSS are not sectarian products. One recent estimate, by a scholar familiar with all the unpublished materials, suggests that only twenty per cent are thus closely related. It would seem, then, that the explanatory power of the Essene hypothesis is weakening as more and more of the evidence comes to light. Indeed, recent discussion

of an unpublished halakic letter, 4QMMT, has attributed it to the Sadducean sect; by any reckoning, the Essene orthodoxy is beginning to break up. What will replace it remains to be seen, of course, but a reasonable optimism would expect a more nuanced and historically satisfying understanding of the scrolls. The result for students of the NT will be the need for a great deal of re-evaluation. Indeed, much NT scholarship already lags behind the new developments in scrolls studies rather badly, relying on the outdated analyses written in the first two decades of Qumran research.

3. The Dead Sea Scrolls and the Gospels.

As stated, NT scholarship in relation to the DSS is best described as outdated. For example, no book is more often quoted in this regard than the volume edited by K. Stendahl in 1957, *The Scrolls and the New Testament.* It is paradigmatic that, rather than produce a new series of essays on relations between Qumran studies and the NT, the book simply continues to be reprinted. Similarly, the two-volume work by H. Braun, *Qumran und das Neue Testament,* is now outdated. Both these works still contain useful material, but it is necessary to use them very cautiously, because so much has happened in DSS studies since they were written.

An illustration of the potential for new understandings may be found in the letter alluded to above, the unpublished 4QMMT. Though it is unpublished, underground copies circulate widely, and it has been described in print more than once. The letter (if such it is—neither opening nor closing formulae are preserved) discusses a series of about twenty legal topics upon which the text's authors and the Temple authorities disagree. In this fact alone its significance for NT studies is enormous, for until now we really had no factual statement about what was going on in the Temple of Jesus' day (some scholars do date the text to the Maccabean period, but such an early dating is highly problematic because of the letter's language and contents). Josephus's descriptions of the Temple cultus are difficult to use with confidence, because he apparently often describes things the way they ought to have been (as he understood the relevant OT texts) rather than the way they really were. This fact becomes apparent when comparing the theoretical descriptions of his *Antiquities* with the historical narratives of his *War and Vita;* not infrequently they disagree. The Tannaitic legal discussions are likewise often idealizing (*see* Rabbinic Traditions and Writings). With MMT we can discover what was really happening, at least with regard to the topics upon which it touches. For example, the authors oppose allowing offerings by Gentiles. It will be recalled that the First Revolt with Rome was partly fueled by just such sentiments, as Eleazar bar Ananias seized control of the Temple and refused to allow any more sacrifices on behalf of Gentiles.

Another insight from MMT consists in the manner of its halakic argument. Repeatedly its authors precede their legal positions with the phrases '^a*naḥnû ḥōšᵉḇîm*, '^a*naḥnû 'ōmrîm*, "we believe, we say." The formal identity with Matthew's depiction of Jesus' legal arguments in the Sermon on the Mount ("You have heard . . . but *I say*") is patent (*see* Sermon on the Mount). Presumably, therefore, Matthew has preserved a common first-century rhetorical structure heretofore unparalleled in early Jewish materials.

Moving to more general considerations, perhaps the most interesting relationship between the Gospels and the NT concerns their principal personage. The Gospels focus, of course, on Jesus of Nazareth; correspondingly, a small group of the DSS focus on an enigmatic figure known as the Teacher of Righteousness (*môrēh haṣṣedeq*). The parallels are particularly striking in comparing the Matthean portrait of Jesus with the Teacher, for in both cases the men are depicted as a new Moses.* The Teacher is viewed both before and after his arrival—that is to say, there existed a group which anticipated the arrival of a Mosaic figure who would deliver a new Law when he came. At a certain point in time, a man emerged from the group who claimed to be this new Moses. Not all of the group received him, and the community split over the issue of his leadership. We possess the texts which describe the predicted figure and, also, later texts written after his arrival. The Teacher of Righteousness did indeed present the requisite new Law— the Temple Scroll. It was expected that the eschaton would dawn at this point, and when it did not, considerable reinterpretation was necessary. This situation also appears in our texts. Little is clear as to the continued existence of the group as years passed and the expected irruption of eschatological times still delayed. The texts do describe the death of the Teacher, but this may have been an expected event prior to the end, since Moses also died before entering the promised land.

Present scholarly consensus places the appearance of the Teacher in the mid- to late-second century B.C. He apparently had a conflict with the nascent Hasmonean hegemony, perhaps represented by Jonathan Maccabee (161-143 B.C.). The last historical event to which the scrolls refer is the conquest of Jerusalem by Ptolemy in 63 B.C. This is a rather curious situation

if the Essene hypothesis is correct, for that theory as usually presented requires that the group continued for 125 years beyond Ptolemy—125 years of silence. In this context one should note R. Eisenman's dating of the pertinent texts to the first century A.D.

Many other points of contact between the Gospels and the DSS, both conceptual and linguistic, will have been evident in the preceding discussion. A true assessment of the relationship must await full publication of the scrolls.

See also JUDAISM.

BIBLIOGRAPHY. J. M. Allegro, *Qumrân Cave 4: I (4Q158-4Q186)* (DJD 5; Oxford: Clarendon, 1968); N. Avigad and Y. Yadin, *A Genesis Apocryphon: A Scroll from the Wilderness of Judaea* (Jerusalem: Magnes Press and Heikhal Ha-Sefer, 1956); M. Baillet, J. T. Milik and R. de Vaux, *Les "Petites Grottes" de Qumrân: Exploration de la falaise, les grottes 2Q, 3Q, 5Q, 6Q, 7Q à 10Q, le rouleau de cuivre* (DJD 3; Oxford: Clarendon, 1962); M. Baillet, *Qumrân Grotte 4: III (4Q482-4Q520)* (DJD 7; Oxford: Clarendon, 1982); D. Barthélemy and J. T. Milik, *Qumran Cave I* (DJD 1; Oxford: Clarendon, 1955); F. M. Cross et al., *Scrolls from Qumrân Cave I: The Great Isaiah Scroll, the Order of the Community, the Pesher to Habakkuk* (Jerusalem: Albright Institute and Shrine of the Book, 1972); F. M. Cross, *The Ancient Library of Qumran and Modern Biblical Studies* (rev. ed.; New York: Doubleday, 1961); R. Eisenman, *Maccabees, Zadokites, Christians and Qumran* (Leiden: Brill, 1983); N. Golb, "Who Hid the Dead Sea Scrolls?" *BA* 48 (1985) 68-82; J. T. Milik, *The Books of Enoch* (Oxford: Clarendon, 1976); C. Newsom, *Songs of the Sabbath Sacrifice: A Critical Edition* (HSS 27; Atlanta: Scholars Press, 1985); J. P. van der Ploeg and A. S. van der Woude, *Le targum de Job de la grotte XI de Qumran* (Leiden: Brill, 1971); C. Rabin, *The Zadokite Documents* (2d ed.; Oxford: Clarendon, 1958); J. A. Sanders, *The Psalms Scroll from Qumran Cave 11* (DJD 4; Oxford: Clarendon, 1965); E. Schuller, *Non-Canonical Psalms from Qumran: A Pseudepigraphic Collection* (HSS 28; Atlanta: Scholars, 1986); E. Tov, *The Greek Minor Prophets Scroll from Naḥal ḥever (8ḥevXIIgr): The Seiyâl Collection, I* (DJD 8; Oxford: Clarendon, 1989); M. O. Wise, *A Critical Study of the Temple Scroll from Qumran Cave 11* (Chicago: Oriental Institute, 1990); Y. Yadin, *The Temple Scroll* (3 vols. plus supplementary plates; Jerusalem: Israel Exploration Society, 1983). M. O. Wise

DEAFNESS. *See* BLINDNESS AND DEAFNESS; HARDNESS OF HEART.

DEATH OF JESUS

The crucifixion of Jesus under Pontius Pilate* is

among the most historically certain and theologically pregnant events of Jesus' life.

1. Crucifixion in the Ancient World.

In spite of its cruelty as a form of punishment, crucifixion was practiced throughout the ancient world. It was employed as a method of execution (or, in some cases, impalement after death) among the Persians, Indians, Assyrians and others, and later among the Greeks and Romans. Some evidence suggests crucifixion was used as a mode of execution by Jews before the time of Herod the Great (Josephus, *J.W.* 1.4.6 §§97-98; *Ant.* 13.14.2 §§379-383; 11QTemple 64:6-13).

1.1. Crucifixion: A Cruel Practice. Among the torturous penalties noted in the literature of antiquity, crucifixion was particularly heinous. The act itself damaged no vital organs, nor did it result in excessive bleeding. Hence, death came slowly, sometimes after several days, through shock or a painful process of asphyxiation as the muscles used in breathing suffered increasing fatigue. Often, as a further disgrace, the person was denied burial and the body was left on the cross to serve as carrion for the birds or to rot.

Crucifixion was quintessentially a public affair. Naked and affixed to a stake, cross or tree, the victim was subjected to savage ridicule by frequent passersby, while the general populace was given a grim reminder of the fate of those who assert themselves against the authority of the state.

Descriptions of the act of crucifixion are rare in the extant literature of antiquity. This is not due to the infrequency of the practice, but rather to literary-aesthetic considerations. Members of the cultured literary elite were hesitant to dwell long on this horrific, brutal act. Indeed, even the passion narratives (*see* Passion Narrative) of our Gospels, which Hengel regards as the most detailed descriptions of their kind (Hengel 1977, 25), are remarkably brief in their recounting of the actual act of crucifixion. Eschewing all details, they simply report, "They crucified him" (Mt 27:35; Mk 15:25; Lk 23:33; Jn 19:18).

Even where we find descriptions it is obvious that no standard form of crucifixion was uniformly practiced. In fact, the accounts are not always clear even on whether the crucifixion took place before or after the victim's death. Nor is it evident in each case whether the victim was bound or nailed to the stake, or whether a crossbeam was always used. In the Roman world, however, the form of crucifixion was apparently more uniform: it included a flogging beforehand, and victims often carried the crossbeam to the place of crucifixion, where they were nailed or bound to the cross with arms extended, raised up, and perhaps seated on a sedicula, or small wooden peg (Hengel 1977, 22-32).

On the other hand, even in the Roman world the procedure was subject to variation, depending on the whims of the executioners. For example, in his eyewitness account of the Roman siege of Jerusalem, Josephus* observes how hundreds of Jewish prisoners were "scourged and subjected to torture of every description . . . , and then crucified opposite the city walls." Hoping that the gruesome sight might induce the Jews to surrender the city, Titus, the Roman commander, gave his soldiers freedom to continue the crucifixions as they pleased. "The soldiers out of rage and hatred amused themselves by nailing their prisoners in different positions . . . ." (Josephus, *J.W.* 5.11.1 §§449-451).

Archeological evidence related to the practice of crucifixion in first-century Palestine is even more sparse. In 1968 an ossuary was discovered in a buried cave at Giv'at ha-Mivtar in northern Jerusalem. It contained the bones of an adult male who had died by crucifixion during the period between the onset of the first century A.D. and the mid-60s. Initial study of the skeletal remains indicated that a nail had been driven through each of his forearms, and his heel bones had been pierced by a single iron nail. The latter nail was found still embedded in what investigators took to be the heel bones of both feet. Wood fragments found at both ends of the nail indicated that the nail first passed through a small wooden plaque, then through the victim's feet, and then into a vertical, olivewood beam. Apparently as a *coup de grâce*, his shins had been broken intentionally.

Zias and Sekeles recently re-evaluated the skeletal remains of the ossuary, together with related photographs, casts and radiographs. On this basis they proposed a number of amendments to earlier findings. Most importantly, they determined that the still-intact iron nail had passed from the right side to the left of the right heel bone (*calcaneum*) only. A different picture of the crucified man results, for on this reconstruction the feet were not anchored with one nail, but the victim apparently straddled the upright beam. Moreover, finding no clear evidence of traumatic injury to the bones of the forearm or hands, they propose the victim was tied to the crossbeam, not nailed. Finally, they questioned whether the bones of the lower limbs had been broken prior to death.

Although this discovery adds archeological evidence to literary descriptions of crucifixion, it is nevertheless clear that the paucity of direct anthropological evidence of this nature restricts the certainty one might attach to its interpretation.

1.2. Crucifixion: A Military and Political Punishment. As a rule, Roman citizens were spared from this form of execution though, in extreme occasions (e.g., high treason) death by crucifixion might be imposed. More generally among the Romans, crucifixion was a penalty reserved for those of lower status—namely, dangerous criminals, slaves and the populace of foreign provinces. Among these peoples crucifixion served as a means of asserting Roman authority and maintaining law and order. Thus, in the province of Judea, it proved to be a generally effective weapon against resistance to Roman occupation (*see* Rome).

1.3. Crucifixion: Interpretive Stigma. In his important survey of the treatment of crucifixion in ancient literature, Hengel queries whether, outside early Christianity, death by crucifixion was ever interpreted in a positive manner. Within the Gentile world, he finds in Stoicism the use of crucifixion as a metaphor ". . . for the suffering from which the wise man can free himself only by death, which delivers the soul from the body to which it is tied" (Hengel 1977, 88; cf. pp. 64-68). However, beyond this the cruelty of the cross seems to have forbidden any positive interpretation or metaphorical use of death by crucifixion.

If this was true for the Gentile world, it was even more so for the Jewish. Inasmuch as the use of crucifixion by the Romans as a deterrent against Jewish nationalism was widespread, we might have anticipated that the cross would come to serve as a symbol for martyrdom. However, in addition to the humiliation and brutality associated with this form of execution, for Jews an additional, profoundly religious, obstacle existed.

Already by the time of the first century A.D., the victim of crucifixion was understood in terms of Deuteronomy 21:22-23—specifically, "anyone who is hung on a tree is under the curse of God." In its own context, this passage refers to the public display of the corpse of an executed criminal. But the NT gives evidence that this meaning was expanded considerably within the early church to include persons who had been crucified. This is seen in the verbal allusions to Deuteronomy 21:22-23 (e.g., Acts 5:30; 13:29; 1 Pet 2:24) and Paul's explicit citation of Deuteronomy

21:23 in Galatians 3:13. Apart from and prior to Christianity, evidence from the Qumran literature (4QpNah 3—4.1.7-8; 11QTemple 64:6-13) as well as from the writings of the first-century Alexandrian Jew Philo (*Spec. Leg.* 3.152; *Post C.* 61; *Somn.* 2.213) attests that victims of crucifixion could be understood this way within Judaism.* Thus, the cross could not be interpreted positively as a symbol of the Jewish resistance.

2. The Crucifixion of Jesus.

The crucifixion of Jesus of Nazareth under Pontius Pilate is well attested in Christian and non-Christian sources (*see* Jesus in Non-Christian Sources). It is reported in the four canonical Gospels in the midst of remarkably full passion accounts, and referred to as an historical event throughout the NT (especially in Paul). The Latin historian Tacitus mentions Jesus' death in *The Annals*: "Christus . . . had undergone the death penalty in the reign of Tiberius, by sentence of the procurator Pontius Pilate" (15.44). In a text whose authenticity is under suspicion, Josephus recalls that Pilate condemned Jesus to be crucified (Josephus, *Ant.* 18.3.3 §§63-64). For these and other reasons, the historicity of the death of Jesus on the cross is beyond doubt (Green 1988, 1). However, numerous problems revolve around (1) our ability to date the crucifixion, (2) the historicity of some details recorded in the crucifixion accounts themselves and (3) the interpretation of Jesus' death by Jesus and his first followers.

2.1. The Date of Jesus' Crucifixion. All four Gospels narrate the execution of Jesus on a Friday—that is, on the day before the Sabbath* (Mt 27:57, 62; Mk 15:42; Lk 23:54; Jn 19:31, 42). The major chronological issue, therefore (*see* Chronology), revolves around the relation of this Friday to Passover (*see* Feasts). Assuming the Jewish reckoning of the day from sunset to sunset, the Passover feast would have been eaten on the evening of 15 Nisan. The Synoptic Gospels (e.g., Mk 14:12-16) recount the Last Supper* as a Passover meal on Thursday evening, 15 Nisan. Hence, in their reckoning the day of Jesus' arrest, trial* and death was 15 Nisan, the day of Passover. John's Gospel, on the other hand, dates the death of Jesus on 14 Nisan, the day of preparation for Passover (13:1-4; 18:28; 19:14, 31).

If we take these conclusions to the relevant astronomical data and assume Jesus was crucified around A.D. 30, we come up with the following options: According to the Johannine reckoning, Jesus was executed on April 3, A.D. 33 or April 7, A.D. 30; according to the Synoptic reckoning, A.D. 27 and 34 would be the probable years. Should we adopt the

Johannine reckoning or the Synoptic?

Three avenues for solving this dilemma have been proposed. Some scholars argue that the Synoptics have preserved the correct chronology,* and that John has revised the tradition in order to portray Jesus more fully as the Passover Lamb (*see* Lamb of God). It is true that John has a theological concern of this nature (cf. 1:29, 36; 18:28; 19:14, 31, 36-37); however, recent redaction-critical study (*see* Redaction Criticism) has determined the high probability that the Johannine chronology actually came to him in his passion tradition (Dauer, 133-136, 140-142). Others have argued that the Synoptic account is tendentious, resulting from Mark's creative attempt to portray the Last Supper as a Passover meal. This argument fails to consider the tightly integrated character of the Passover elements in the Synoptic tradition, as well as the degree to which even John's narrative of the Last Supper is paschal in character (Green 1988, 113-116).

Third, many have attempted to harmonize the Synoptic and Johannine chronologies. Two of these theories are particularly noteworthy. First, some have championed the view that Galileans (like Jesus and his disciples) and Pharisees* reckoned the day from sunrise to sunrise, unlike the Judeans and Sadducees who reckoned the day from sunset to sunset. Hence, the Passover meal (Last Supper) was celebrated on Thursday evening 14 Nisan by Jesus, his disciples and other Galileans. The Judeans shared the Passover meal on Friday evening 15 Nisan. Others have found more plausible the theory that the Passover was celebrated on two different days in the year of the crucifixion, due to the disparity between the Pharisaic and Sadducean calendars. Both views require two consecutive days of Passover sacrifices, a possibility for which we have no clear evidence. At the same time, we can imagine this being allowed in order to maintain peace among the different groups within first-century Judaism. (See the review in Marshall, 57-75, 184-185.)

In the end, we are left with the conclusion that Jesus was crucified on 14 Nisan—that is, April 7 A.D. 30 or April 3, A.D. 33. The later date is corroborated by Pilate's need to appease the Jews in order to be "Caesar's friend" (Jn 19:12) and his new friendship with Herod (cf. Lk 23:12)—both of which are best understood in connection with Pilate's changing policies toward the Jews after A.D. 32 (Hoehner, 71-114; *see* Chronology). However, a date in A.D. 33 raises other problems inasmuch as it compresses the available time for the subsequent Christian movement and the Pauline mission.

2.2. The Crucifixion Accounts. Like the rest of the passion story, the crucifixion of Jesus is not recounted merely to chronicle what happened. This event, Jesus' execution on a cross, was of such a scandalous nature that it cried out for interpretation and legitimization. The result is a tightly woven tapestry combining both elements—event and interpretation—with the latter largely dependent on references to the OT (*see* Old Testament in the Gospels). Thus, Jesus' garments are divided (Ps 22:18), he is crucified with two criminals (Is 53:12), he is mocked (Ps 22:7; 70:3) and taunted (Ps 42:10), he is offered wine* (Ps 69:21; Prov 31:6), he cries out from the cross (Ps 22:1; 31:5), he is acclaimed as God's Son (cf. Wis 2, 4—5) or as the Righteous One (Is 53:11), and is thus vindicated after maltreatment (Is 52:13-15; 53:10-12). The crucifixion narratives demonstrate in story form that Christ* died "according to the Scriptures" (*see* Old Testament in the Gospels).

Some scholars continue the now outdated practice of trying to peel back the layers of theological interpretation in order to arrive at the story's historical kernel. Reported events, however, by virtue of their being reported, are always interpreted events. Hence, although the task of determining the historical plausibility of these narrated events remains an important one, attempts to sunder theology from history are misguided.

2.2.1. Crucifixion Traditions. Most scholars assume that Matthew's only narrative source for the crucifixion was Mark. In all likelihood, the Fourth Evangelist used his own, non-Markan source (Dauer; Green 1988, 105-134). In the past commentators largely worked with the hypothesis that Luke's account was for the most part also independent of the Markan narrative (e.g., Taylor). More recently, however, greater emphasis has been placed on Luke's creative shaping of the Markan story (e.g., Matera, 150-220; Neyrey).

Several lines of evidence point to Luke's use of early, non-Markan tradition for his account of Jesus' crucifixion, however, though scholars disagree on the nature of that traditional material (Green 1988, 86-101). First, Luke includes significant material not found in Mark which, under close literary analysis, does not appear to have come from Luke's creative pen. This material includes Jesus' warning to Jerusalem in 23:27-31, Jesus' intercessory prayer* from the cross in 23:34a, Jesus' interaction with the crucified criminals in 23:39-43, and Luke's description of the repentance of the multitudes (*see* People, Crowd) in 23:48.

Second, in some cases Luke narrates actions also reported in Mark, but in ways sufficiently different so as to suggest his use of alternative traditional material.

One example of this phenomenon appears in the use of Psalm 22:7 in the record of the mockery of Jesus by the passers-by. Interestingly, Mark 15:29-30 betrays the influence of the latter half of Psalm 22:7 ("shaking their heads"), while Luke 23:35 has been influenced by the first half of Psalm 22:7 ("seeing . . . they mocked"). This suggests the significance of Psalm 22:7 in the early passion tradition, and indicates that this tradition came to Mark and Luke independently. Other noteworthy examples include the reports of Jesus' last words from the cross (see below) and the confession of the centurion.

Third, some aspects of the Lukan narrative that depart from Mark are paralleled in other sources. Thus, for example, the reaction of the crowds in Luke 23:48 is similar to that found in Gos. Pet. 7:25 ("Then the Jews* and the elders* and the priests,* perceiving what great evil they had done to themselves, began to lament and to say, 'Woe on our sins, the judgment and the end of Israel* is drawn nigh.' "). Finally, the linguistic and syntactic deviations from Mark's account in Luke are not easily explained on the basis of Luke's creativity alone.

Evidence of this character has suggested to some that Luke knew a second, connected passion narrative; to others that he was familiar with a series of disparate non-Markan traditions, whether oral or written. It is plausible that three roughly parallel early crucifixion accounts are represented in our canonical Gospels. This speaks in favor of the antiquity of the tradition, which may have been a part of a larger, early passion narrative.

2.2.2. History and Interpretation in the Crucifixion.

Turning to the accounts themselves, we see that they all agree in having Jesus led away to the place of crucifixion. The mention of the name of Simon of Cyrene serves no theological purpose, though his being drafted to carry the cross is reminiscent of Jesus' words about discipleship* ("taking up the cross," Mk 8:34). Simon is missing altogether from the Johannine narrative, probably as a result of John's overall attempt to indicate how, even in his passion, Jesus is master of his own fate. Others, however, see in Jesus' carrying "his *own* cross" (Jn 19:17) a reference to the *Akedah*—that is, the attempt by John to develop a parallel between Jesus' passion and the binding of Isaac (see Gen 22:6, where the wood was placed on Isaac by his father).

A number of other aspects of Jesus' crucifixion deserve brief discussion.

The Location of Golgotha All of the Gospels mention that Golgotha was the place of Jesus' execution. Matthew, Mark and John translate the Aramaic *gûlgaltâ* (Hebrew, *gulgôlāt*) as "Place of the Skull." Luke, who avoids Aramaic place names, has "Skull," a more accurate translation. Many attempts have been made to explain the meaning of this place reference: A hill in the shape of a skull? A rocky mound on which no vegetation could grow?

The precise location of Golgotha is disputed, though our knowledge of crucifixion in the Roman world and the Gospel accounts themselves suggest its location outside the walls of Jerusalem (Jn 19:20; cf. Heb 13:12) in a public place, perhaps near a busy road (e.g., Mk 15:29, 40). According to John 19:41, the site of Jesus' crucifixion was in close proximity to his borrowed tomb.

Strong circumstantial evidence supports the location of Golgotha in the area on which now stands the Church of the Holy Sepulchre, located within the Old City of Jerusalem. According to archeological findings in the 1960s, interpreted in tandem with Josephus's description of the city's fortifications, this site would have been well outside the city walls. Before the expansion of the city it was a quarry into which a number of tombs had been cut.

Before modern investigators realized the more narrow perimeter of the city walls as it was in the first third of the first century A.D., they focused their searches on the area to the north of the Old City. There they located a rocky hill whose stony face appeared to resemble a skull. Kenyon notes that the present shape of the hill is due largely to subsequent quarrying, however.

Jesus' Prayer. Only Luke records that, following his crucifixion, Jesus prayed on behalf of those responsible for his death (23:34). This prayer is missing from a number of important manuscripts, presumably because some later copyists were uncomfortable with this portrait of Jesus extending mercy to his Jewish opponents (*see* Textual Criticism). The major themes of the prayer—forgiveness* and ignorance—are important in Luke-Acts (cf. Lk 1:77; 7:47-50; Acts 2:38; 3:17; 5:31; 10:43; 13:27, 38; 14:16); furthermore, its presence is important to the structure of the passion story, which narrates a saying of Jesus in each major section. Some scholars regard the prayer as having been created by Luke on the basis of the similar request of Stephen in Acts 7:60. But why should Stephen provide the model for Jesus, and not vice versa? Moreover, Jesus' request for the exoneration of his persecutors accords well with what we otherwise know of Jesus' teaching on one's attitude to hostility (e.g., Mt 5:44; *see* Love; see further, Lohse, 129-130).

The Division of Jesus' Clothing. The evangelists agree in their narration of the division of Jesus' clothing among the soldiers. Some evidence suggests this distribution of the victim's clothing happened as a matter of course in antiquity, but the language of Psalm 22:18 has clearly influenced the way this event has been reported.

The Inscription on the Cross. The inscription on the cross is reported by all the Gospels with remarkable consistency, each noting that it was as "The King of the Jews" that Jesus was executed. Historically, this notice would have marked Jesus as a messianic pretender to the throne. No doubt Jesus' first followers saw in this charge an ironic proclamation of the true identity of Jesus, and this has been further emphasized in the Johannine elaboration of this report (19:19-22).

In the past it was common to assert that an inscription of this kind was normally affixed to the cross in a Roman crucifixion. Recent re-examination of the available evidence reveals the opposite. Prior to their execution condemned persons might be required to display publicly the charge under which they had been sentenced to death, but the inscription reported by the Gospels is without parallel. For this reason the historical veracity of this measure should not be questioned. As Harvey has observed: "The first historians of Jesus' death can therefore have been under no compulsion to invent [such a notice]" (Harvey, 13).

The Mocking. Mark, Matthew and Luke agree that the Jewish leaders mocked Jesus on the cross, though Luke goes on to add that the soldiers joined in the derision (cf. Mk 15:16-20). In short, they insist, if Jesus were who he said he was, he would not be in this shameful, awful predicament. The historicity of the general contours of this account is almost certain for three reasons. First, it is consistent with what we know of Roman custom, which locates the act of crucifixion in the public arena precisely in order to foster this sort of derision. Second, it dovetails well with what we know of attitudes toward death in late Judaism, as suggested by a text like Psalm 22:7-8 or Wisdom 2:18, 20. Those who have a special relationship with God will not undergo shameful death. Third, the content of the mockery parodies the charges leading to Jesus' execution.

Jesus' Last Words. A more difficult issue is raised by Jesus' last words on the cross, reported variously as follows:

Mark 15:34, citing Psalm 22:1: "My God, my God, why have you forsaken me?"

Luke 23:46, citing Psalm 31:5: "Father, into your hands I commit my spirit."

John 19:30: "It is finished."

The case for the historicity of the Markan version (followed by Mt 27:46) is strongest, though a number of modern interpreters argue that the quotation of Psalm 22:1 in Mark 15:34 is Mark's way of providing the content of the wordless shout in Mark 15:37. Aside from the fact that this would require Mark's narration of only one cry instead of two, the most prominent obstacle to this thesis is the offensiveness of Psalm 22:1 on the lips of Jesus. This is also the strongest argument favoring its authenticity. Assuming Luke had Mark's Gospel as a source for Jesus' passion, he clearly bypassed this cry of dereliction in his account. Also, in some manuscripts of Mark 15:34, "forsaken" has been replaced by "reproached," with the result that the force of the psalmic citation has been weakened dramatically. These provide literary evidence for the offensiveness of this citation in the early church.

Some have suggested that the use of Psalm 22:1 here was intended to call to mind the vindication of the Righteous One, promised in the psalm when read as a whole. In first-century Judaism, was the citation of the opening of a psalm designed to recall the psalm in its entirety? Evidence for this phenomenon is very late. We are left with the starkness of Jesus' cry from the cross, a starkness that speaks pointedly for its historicity. Who would invent for Jesus so scandalous an outburst?

What, then, of the quotation of Psalm 31:5 in the Lukan account? Has Luke simply substituted one psalmic citation for another? Three lines of evidence converge to suggest that Luke is not independently responsible for the use of Psalm 31:5 in this context (Green 1988, 97-98). First, we see an interesting coincidence of language when moving from Luke 23:46 to the way in which both Matthew and John report Jesus' death. Luke, in the words of the psalm, reports that Jesus "commits his spirit," while Matthew 27:50 records that Jesus "yielded up his spirit" and John 19:30 has it that Jesus "delivered up his spirit." Luke is the only writer who actually cites Psalm 31:5 here, but these parallels suggest the common use of a very old tradition rooted in the psalm.

Second, even though Luke elsewhere consistently employs the Greek Old Testament (LXX), here his citation is drawn from the Hebrew text (MT). Luke, who gives no indication that he knew Hebrew, seems to have borrowed this material from a source which had already translated the Hebrew text into Greek (*see* Languages of Palestine).

Finally, some scholars have suggested that the allusions to Psalm 31:5 in Acts 7:59 and 1 Peter 4:19 indicate the general use of the psalm in dangerous settings. It may even have been used as an evening benediction in late Judaism. This speaks to the appropriateness of Psalm 31:5 in the final moments of Jesus' passion, and leaves open the possibility of the saying's authenticity.

2.3. Jesus' Crucifixion as Interpretive Problem. "The chief priests and our rulers delivered him up to the death sentence. They crucified him, but we had hoped he was about to redeem Israel" (Lk 24:20-21). By not explicitly identifying the "they" responsible for the crucifixion in this text, Luke continues his strategy of exonerating the Roman authorities while inculpating the Jewish leadership. The dashed hopes of Jesus' followers are the real point at issue here, however. With these words, Cleopas and his friend voice their shock and discouragement over Jesus' death. They also strike at the root of the interpretive problem raised by a crucified Messiah (*see* Christ).

It is true that Christian apologetic found in Isaiah 52:13—53:12 a prophecy of the suffering Messiah (e.g., Acts 3:13-18; 1 Pet 2:21-24; see later, Athanasius, "On the Incarnation"). But first-century Jewish messianic expectation focused pre-eminently on a royal, glorious Son of David.* The Isaianic passage never mentions the Messiah, and late Judaism did not turn to this passage to fill in its portrait of the expected deliverer (*see* Servant of Yahweh).

If the notion of a "suffering Messiah" runs counter to what we know of messianic speculation in the first century, how much more an oxymoron a "crucified Messiah" must have seemed. After all, according to current interpretation of Deuteronomy 21:22-23, a victim of crucifixion was cursed of God. Yet, the "Messiah" is literally "God's Anointed." Clearly, the cross of Christ presented a conspicuous enigma—it cried out for reinterpretation.

Some regard the resurrection* of Jesus as the crucial key to overturning the ignominy of the cross. Its role in authenticating Jesus' mission *in spite of the cross* should not be downplayed. At the same time, we would be gravely mistaken were we to assume the cross of Christ carried no significance apart from the resurrection. In fact, one might better say that the resurrection authenticated the mission and message of Jesus, *including the message of his death on a cross*. As we shall see, the Gospels present the cross as the culmination of his mission (cf., e.g., Mk 10:45; Lk 24:25-27; Jn 12:23-28). At this point, it will be worthwhile to reflect briefly on two closely related questions—namely, how Jesus understood his death and how it was interpreted by the earliest churches.

Combining his own creative reflection on the development of atonement theology in earliest Christianity with his synthesis of traditional scholarship on the subject, Hengel has argued that the interpretation of Jesus' death as a vicarious, atoning sacrifice stems from Jesus' own understanding of his death. His point of departure is the Pauline material and pre-Pauline traditions that ensure that the interpretation of Jesus' death as saving event can be traced back at least as far back as the earliest Greek-speaking Christian communities (e.g., Rom 4:25; 1 Cor 15:3-5; Gal 2:20-21).

Pushing further, Hengel insists that, in order to understand the crucifixion of Jesus as the execution of the Messiah, Jewish Christians would have had to attribute to that death overwhelmingly positive significance. The interpretive categories offered by major currents of modern scholarship, Jesus as "righteous sufferer" and "prophet-martyr," are rejected by Hengel as inadequate for this purpose. The only satisfactory answer is that the first disciples, too, understood Jesus' death as an atoning sacrifice.

Pushing still further, Hengel traces this interpretation back to the ransom saying* and Jesus' words at the Last Supper (Mk 10:45; 14:24). Thus, Jesus anticipated his death and understood himself in his death as fulfilling the role of the Suffering Servant of the Lord (Is 52:13—53:12). Hengel concludes, "It was not primarily their own theological reflections, but above all the interpretive sayings of Jesus at the Last Supper which showed them how to understand his death properly" (Hengel 1981, 73; cf. Lohse).

Against this reconstruction, some will take issue with Hengel's acceptance of the authenticity of the ransom sayings attributed to Jesus in Mark 10:45 and 14:24. At the same time, it is worth noting that a growing number of scholars are admitting the probability that Jesus anticipated his execution by Roman authorities. He could scarcely have done otherwise given the content of his message (see below). To admit this, however, is to admit its corollary—namely, the probability that Jesus reflected on the relation of his mission and his death. For example, why did Jesus inquire of his disciples, "Who do you say that I am?" (Mt 16:13-26; Mk 8:27-38; Lk 9:18-26)? Did his interest lie solely in soliciting from them a confession of his identity? Understood in its context, Jesus' inquiry and subsequent teaching on the suffering of the Son of man* can be taken only as his attempt to relate in the most intimate way his execution and mission. Jesus thus regarded his imminent death as somehow integral to his mission, to bring redemption to Israel and the nations (*see* Gentiles; see Meyer, 216-219).

A more pressing concern to be raised against Hengel's study is its claim to have recovered *the one, earliest* interpretation of Jesus' death. He is not alone in this pitfall, however. In spite of the rich variety of imagery employed in the NT for coming to terms with Jesus' death, the history of reflection on the cross is littered with attempts to discern its significance in narrow terms. In reality, just as the crucifixion of Jesus is the most historically certain of the events of Jesus' life, it is also the most widely interpreted.

Another perspective on Jesus' death with a claim to having been rooted in Jesus' own understanding has been outlined by Allison. He undertakes an interesting survey of the expectation of a final, great tribulation in Jewish literature. From this he is able to show that the notion of a great tribulation was often associated with the coming of the eschatological era of salvation, but not according to any fixed model. Working backward from the passion accounts of our Gospels, he discovers that Jesus' death marked the beginning of the fulfillment of eschatological expectation, that the death of Jesus belongs to the messianic woes that mark the birth of the new era.

This crisis-oriented interpretation is suggested by several events of the passion—including darkness at noon (Mk 15:33), the rending of the Temple curtain (Mk 15:38) and the resurrection of the holy ones (Mt 27:51-53). Allison also sifts through the Gospels to discover evidence that Jesus himself understood his ministry in terms of the eschatological distress (e.g., Mt 11:12-13; Lk 12:49-53). Accordingly, ". . . Jesus foresaw for himself suffering, death, and vindication in the eschatological drama, which he took to be already unfolding" (Allison, 142). In short, Jesus' death and resurrection marked the dawning of the great Day of the Lord (see Eschatology).

These are only two more focused interpretations of Jesus' execution that lay good claim to having arisen out of Jesus' own understanding of his mission and death. Even more fundamental than these is the overarching reality that Jesus' suffering and death were recognized and proclaimed for their centrality to God's redemptive plan. The enigma of a crucified Messiah begged for interpretation. Taking their cues from Jesus' own understanding, those first disciples saw in the cross the fulfillment of God's purpose.

3. Why Was Jesus Crucified?

For the most recent chapter in the quest of the historical Jesus (see Historical Jesus) a central question is, Why was Jesus crucified? Of course, on one level this query is answered easily enough. Historical data outside the Gospels points clearly to the reality that, in a Roman province like Judea, an execution of this kind could be carried out only under the orders of the Roman procurator. Moreover, as we have seen, crucifixion was used in the Roman provinces above all as a deterrent against sedition. By inference, then, we might conclude that Jesus was crucified under Pontius Pilate as an insurrectionist. This inference is supported by the Gospels themselves, for there the issue put before Pilate is clearly one of sedition.

In the only explicit record of the charges brought against Jesus, Luke 23:2, 5 reads, "We have found this man subverting our nation, opposing the payment of taxes to Caesar, and saying of himself that he is the Christ. . . . He stirs up the people throughout Judea by his teaching . . . ." Pilate's question to Jesus, reported in all four Gospels, is equally unambiguous in its political edge: "Are you the king of the Jews?" (Mt 27:11; Mk 15:2; Lk 23:3; Jn 18:33). Finally, Jesus is executed alongside two insurrectionists, and the inscription on the cross declares this to have been his crime as well.

Jesus, then, was executed for sedition. But rather than answering our initial question, this conclusion only sharpens it. We are left puzzled by the possible nexus between what we know of Jesus' life and the rationale for this death sentence. "The portrait of Jesus, as it is presented to us not only in the gospels but throughout the New Testament, is utterly irreconcilable with this explanation of his death" (Harvey, 14; see pp. 11-35; Sanders, 294-318).

Indeed, at his arrest Jesus protests that he is not leading a rebellion against the state (Mt 26:55; Mk 14:48; Lk 22:52). Moreover, Jesus' followers were not rounded up and summarily executed, as one would have expected had Jesus been leading an insurrectionist movement (cf., e.g., Josephus Ant. 20.5.1—20.8.10 §§97-188; J.W. §§2.12.3—2.14.1 §§232-272). Furthermore, after Jesus' death his disciples were allowed to form a community in Jerusalem, an unthinkable development had they been known as a seditious party. Finally, had Jesus taught political resistance against Rome, we might imagine that his followers would have involved themselves in aggressive opposition against the state subsequent to his death. We are left, therefore, with a most enigmatic set of circumstances.

One scholar who has taken this problem seriously is E. P. Sanders. He tries to solve this puzzle with special reference to Jesus' physical demonstration against the Temple (Mt 21:12-13; Mk 11:15-17; Lk 19:45-46). This act, Sanders insists, was not intended as a cleansing of the Temple, but as a portent of its destruction (see Temple Cleansing; Destruction of Jerusalem). This, he argues, was Jesus' last public act, after which was put in motion the decisive plot against his life. Set within the context of Jesus' proclamation of the kingdom of God* and his capacity to excite the hopes of the people, this act against the Temple was sufficient to bring Jesus to the attention of the Romans as a political threat. He was executed, then, at the behest of the Jewish leadership as a dangerous man, but not as an actual leader of an insurgent party.

Although plausible in its own way, Sanders's reconstruction of the rationale for Jesus' execution overlooks important aspects of the Gospel accounts. He is simply unable to come to terms with the role of the Jewish leaders in the process of Jesus' passion. In fact, his hypothesis leaves little room at all for the contribution of the Jews to this action, since, in his mind, the Jesus-Jewish (Pharisaic) conflict recorded in the Gospels is anachronistic. Moreover, his attempt to discount the material recorded in the Gospels which intervenes between the Temple action and the onset of the passion story fails to convince. Although we can believe the Temple action was a significant causal factor in Jesus' arrest and condemnation, it seems unlikely that it was the immediate cause.

Harvey, on the other hand, argues that the Jewish leaders did hand Jesus over to Roman authority, but only after their failure to cope effectively with this Jew whom they regarded as a threat to general peace and security. In this regard, Harvey is drawn to the Lukan account, according to which Jesus was not found guilty or condemned as deserving death by the Jewish leaders (Lk 22:66-71; Acts 13:27-28; cf. Jn 18:19-23). Harvey therefore concludes that the Sanhedrin* held an informal hearing, the purpose of which was to decide whether, and on what grounds, to hand Jesus over to Pilate. What is lacking from Harvey's account is any discussion of why the Sanhedrin might have regarded Jesus as a threat (see Trial of Jesus).

A hint in this direction is provided by John 11:45-53. Here the Sanhedrin, meeting informally, initiates a plot against Jesus because they fear reprisals from Rome: "If we allow Jesus to go on like this, everyone will believe in him and the Romans will come and destroy both our Temple and our nation" (Jn 11:48). In fact, in the decades before the Jewish War Palestine was the scene of repeated liberation movements, and Rome's repeated response was to kill both the leaders of such movements and their followers (see Revolutionary Movements).

At this point, Sanders is certainly correct: Jesus would have posed no immediate threat had it not been for his following. At the same time, we need not follow Sanders in aborting completely the record of Jesus-Jewish hostility recorded in the Gospels. First-century Judaism was marked by conflict—both inter-

nally, among the various forms of Judaism existing at the time, and externally, with Rome. Jesus' mission, construed in broad terms as the restoration of Israel in the context of the coming of God's universal rule, must have posed a threat within the social and power matrix of first-century Judaism. No less, of course, Jesus' proclamation of the eschatological kingdom would have posed a political threat to those most supportive of the present order, including the Roman authorities themselves. Even though Jesus presented no threat of a violent, military takeover, his message of liberation and his growing popularity nevertheless made him a dangerous political risk (see Liberation Hermeneutics; Sociological Analysis of the Gospels). This threat, heightened by Jesus' activity subsequent to his arrival in Jerusalem for Passover, led to his execution.

4. The Death of Jesus in the Gospel of Matthew

Any treatment of Jesus' death in the First Gospel must move beyond the boundaries of Matthew's passion narrative. Regardless of the tradition-history (see Tradition Criticism) of the passion story, it is now carefully integrated into the Gospel as a whole. We will discuss Matthew's portrayal of Jesus' death under four headings: (1) the rejection of Jesus and the gospel, (2) the death of Jesus and Matthew's christology, (3) the way of the cross and (4) the death of Jesus and the new era of salvation.

4.1. The Rejection of Jesus and the Gospel. Matthew's tragic account of Israel's rejection of God's Messiah provides the central drama of his Gospel. This theme reaches its climax in 27:25, where the Jews accept full responsibility for Jesus' execution: "His blood be on us and our children!" Its roots lie deep in Matthew's narrative of Jesus' life and ministry, and can be traced back to the story of Herod and the Magi from the East (see Birth of Jesus).

Matthew 2:1-12 is framed in such a way as to spotlight the character of the various responses to the birth of Jesus. The importance of this story and the reactions it describes lies in its position as the first story wherein the birth of Jesus is made public, and in the reader's awareness of Jesus' identity as "Immanuel," the one who would save his people from their sins (1:21-23). How would Herod, king of the Jews, respond to the news of the birth of this king of the Jews?

Having discovered the place of Messiah's birth, the Magi go to Bethlehem to worship him. Herod, however, and with him the chief priests and teachers of the Law,* knew the town of the Messiah's birth but did not go to welcome him or pay him homage. Quite the contrary, Herod's troubled spirit gives way to malice, and he orders the deaths of the male children in the area of Bethlehem. Against Herod's plans for Jesus' premature death, God repeatedly intervenes to protect the child (2:12-13, 22). But the die is cast; Jesus' rejection and violent death are clearly foreshadowed.

Although with the onset of Jesus' mission the crowds respond favorably to his message (e.g., 7:28-29), contained in that message are portents of the coming crisis: "Blessed are those who are persecuted for the sake of righteousness" (5:10; cf. 5:44). No doubt for Matthew, Jesus, who was committed to the way of righteousness, was the ultimate exemplar of these words. Jesus did not seek death, but he recognized that a life of righteousness* was a life lived contrary to the conventions of his world. Only persecution could result.

The seemingly inevitable change in attitude toward Jesus is prefigured by the introduction of John the Baptist* in 11:1-19. Jesus compares his own fate with that of the imprisoned John: just as they rejected John, so will they reject Jesus. This motif is consummated in 14:1-12, where Matthew narrates the decapitation of John. The parallels between the executions of John and Jesus are striking. In each story, the plot against the protagonist is forestalled by his popularity (14:3-5; 21:45-46; 26:3-5). Both indicate that the Roman ruler in each case was reluctant to carry out the execution, but gave in to external pressure (14:9-10; 27:11-26). After his death disciples of John came, took his body, and buried it (14:12); likewise, after Jesus' death a disciple of Jesus came, took his body and buried it (27:57-60). These verbal and conceptual similarities mark the execution of John as an anticipatory allusion to the similar fate of Jesus.

Between the introduction of John in 11:1 and his reappearance in 14:1 lie additional portraitures of hostility and rejection. In 12:1-13 a conflict arises between Jesus and the Pharisees over appropriate behavior on the Sabbath. This leads to the first mention of a Jewish plot against Jesus in 12:14. Additional records of conflict follow: in 12:24-32 where Jesus is accused by the Pharisees of casting out demons* by Beelzebub; in 12:38-42 where the Pharisees and teachers of the Law, compared to an evil and adulterous generation, ask for a miraculous sign; and in 13:53-58 where Jesus is rejected even by his own townspeople.

In the midst of this section marked by hostility and the anticipation of Israel's final rejection of Jesus, Matthew introduces a counterpoint: Jesus is the Spirit-anointed Servant chosen by God (12:17-21, citing Is 42:1-4). If he is rejected by Israel, it is as a result of his obedience to his divine mission. During Jesus' public ministry the Pharisees and teachers of the Law appear routinely as his opponents. With the opening of the passion narrative in 26:1-5, the chief priests (see Priests and Priesthood) and the elders assume this role. They, in turn, enter into a contract with one of Jesus' disciples (26:14-16), then incite the crowds against Jesus. Finally, this progressive circle of hostility reaches its climax: they "all" (pas) call for his death (27:25).

Thus, the cross casts its shadow across the entirety of Matthew's Gospel. Its cruel reality is present by way of anticipation and threat in the motifs of hostility and rejection. Jesus' death is Israel's ultimate rejection of God's Messiah.

4.2. The Death of Jesus and Matthew's Christology. Matthew's christological interests are manifest already in his introduction of Jesus as Messiah, Son of David and Son of Abraham (see Abraham) in 1:1. The subsequent record of Jesus' genealogy* (1:2-18) accentuates his identity as the Messiah.

Also evident early on, and of central importance to Matthew's christology, is his portrayal of Jesus' solidarity with God's people and God's purpose. As the genealogical record shows, Jesus' coming is rooted deeply in the history of God's dealings with Israel (1:1-18). The story of Jesus' birth, with its parallels to Israel's past, adds to this theme. He is born in the midst of hostility, forced into exile and brought out of Egypt into the land of Israel (2:1-23). Matthew's employment of OT quotations to signify Jesus as the consummation of OT promise (e.g., 1:22-23; 2:15-18) also fits into this scheme, rooting Jesus solidly in the history of Israel and divine promise (see Old Testament in the Gospels; Typology). Jesus' mission thus reveals God's will and is inexorably intertwined with the pain and hope of Israel.

Jesus was crucified as a messianic pretender, but this would not have kept Matthew's readers from perceiving a deeper significance in the repeated recital of this charge (26:63; 27:11, 17, 22, 27-31, 37). Unwittingly and ironically, the high priest, Pilate and the soldiers all proclaim the true identity of Jesus. Yet, for this interpretive twist to occur, titles like "Messiah" and "king of the Jews" must have been filled with new content, for somehow, in this context, they must be correlated with the death of Jesus.

Not surprisingly, then, "Christ" is interpreted alongside other christological images in the passion story. Chief among these are "Son of God" and "Servant." The association of Christ and Son of God in the passion account is clearest in the request of the high priest, "Tell us if you are the Christ, the Son of

God" (26:63). Also pertinent is the mockery of Jesus on the cross, where Son of God and King of the Jews are set in apposition (27:40, 42-43). The crucial question, then, concerns what significance we should attach to this usage. For the first clue to this riddle, we turn to the Gethsemane* episode, for here Jesus addresses God in prayer as "my Father" (26:39, 42; see Abba). This prayer is above all an act of submission to God. As Son of God, Jesus responds to the will of God with complete, unreserved obedience.

Likewise, in the arrest scene Jesus makes reference to "my Father" (26:53). In this context Jesus' authority* as God's Son occupies center stage, but he does not exercise this power (see Authority and Power) as a means of escape. To have done so would have been to depart from his own teaching (5:44) and from God's will (26:54, 56).

A similar motif appears in the Son of God reference in 27:40. In their mockery of Jesus, the passers-by say, "Come down from the cross, if you are the Son of God," and in doing so model the form of the temptations presented Jesus by the devil in 4:3, 6: "If you are the Son of God . . . ." The inference in each case is that, as the Son of God, Jesus could do what his tempters request of him. To do so, however, would be to deny the character of obedience to God inherent in his sonship (see Temptation of Jesus).

In short, to refer to Jesus as Son of God is to speak pointedly of his fidelity to his mission, of his total obedience to God. This motif is also highlighted by Matthew's portrayal of Jesus as Servant in the passion account. The repeated references to Jesus' silence (26:63; 27:14) and innocence (27:4, 18-19, 23-24) indicate Jesus' passion is the fulfillment of his role as God's Servant in ways that underscore his faithfulness to the divine mission (cf. Is 53:7, 11).

On the other hand, with the Servant motif Matthew expands the theological field of his portrayal of the passion. This is evident in Jesus' interpretive words at the Last Supper, where terminology such as "on behalf of" and "poured out for many" are reminiscent of the work of the Servant in Isaiah 52:13—53:12. These sayings interpret Jesus' death as efficacious, thus showing how Jesus would "save his people from their sins" (1:21). And this helps us appreciate the significance of the taunt in 27:42: "He saved others, but he cannot save himself!" Jesus' mission is salvific, but he can open the way of salvation only by the sacrifice of his life (cf. 16:25).

Commentators have often noted the heightened christology of Matthew's passion account when compared with Mark's. At the outset, Jesus announces his imminent execution (26:1-2). He declares the

arrival of the appointed time (26:18). He prophecies his betrayal *and* identifies his betrayer (26:21, 25). He opens the way for Judas (see Judas Iscariot) to perform his act of betrayal (26:50). He declares his capacity to escape his fate miraculously (26:53). Jesus is presented as one who has power and is in control of the events of his passion. And this is where Matthew's christological portrait comes into focus. Jesus does not exercise his power as Messiah, Son of God to escape from death, but not because he lacks royal status or authority. Rather, Jesus exercises that power in unexpected ways; in obedience to God and in pouring out his life for others.

The story of Jesus' death in Matthew is thus the story of his fidelity to God, his faithfulness to his mission and his willing solidarity with the pain and hope of his people.

4.3. The Way of the Cross. The degree to which the cross is understood by Matthew as the ultimate expression of Jesus' mission is nowhere better seen than in the series of passion predictions in 16:21-27; 17:22-23 and 20:17-28. In these Jesus characterizes his mission as a journey to Jerusalem, and thus to Golgotha.

The first is framed by Peter's confession of Jesus as "the Christ, the Son of the Living God" (16:16) and Peter's rebuke of Jesus following his announcement of imminent suffering. Clearly, Jesus' self-understanding, embracing the "divine must" *(dei)* of his passion, departs from more common messianic expectations, even among his disciples. Jesus, however, is convinced that suffering lies at the heart of his mission as Christ, Son of God, and even extends this definition to his view of discipleship. Like him, Jesus' disciples are faced with the challenge to lose their lives.

Even though Jesus' disciples have "little faith" (e.g., 14:31; 17:20), they are unable to comprehend the way of the cross. After the second passion prediction* they are "filled with grief" (17:23). And in the context of the third they seem to miss Jesus' whole point by concerning themselves with positions of eminence and authority. In the passion story itself their failure is sealed by their fearful abandonment of Jesus at his arrest (26:56). Their faithless behavior is accentuated by the actions of less well-known characters. The woman who anoints Jesus at Bethany (26:6-13), Joseph of Arimathea (27:57-60) and the faithful women at the cross and tomb (27:55-56, 61)—these are examples of persons in the passion narrative who are set in bold relief by their authentic responses to the good news (see Gospel).

For apprehending the way of the cross, the importance of the final passion prediction cannot be overestimated. Here Jesus' ministry of service and redemption is cast in the language of sacrificial death· ". . . the Son of Man did not come to be served but to serve and to give his life a ransom for many" (20:28; *see* Ransom Saying). With this terminology, building on Matthew's earlier presentation of Jesus as the Suffering Servant (cf. 8:17; 12:17-21), the cross is set squarely at the center of Jesus' life and work.

4.4. The Death of Jesus and the New Era of Salvation. Israel's rejection of Jesus and his message does not signify the end of the story for Matthew. Even in his predictions of suffering and death, Jesus' eyes focus also on resurrection (16:21; 17:23; 20:19). Likewise, his interpretive words at the Last Supper, so centered on his passion, anticipate his future in the kingdom of God (26:29). And in 26:32 he predicts his resurrection and future role in reconstituting the scattered band of disciples. Even without turning to the resurrection narrative itself, in the tearing of the Temple curtain, the earthquake and the confession by the centurion, we have testimony of Jesus' vindication in spite of his rejection by Israel (27:51-54).

With mention of the centurion's confession, we open a further arena of discussion. In both subtle and transparent ways, Matthew proclaims the passing of the kingdom of God from Israel to "a people who will produce its fruit" (21:43). In his mind this reorientation of the kingdom is related directly to the crisis of rejection, Israel's delivering the Messiah over to be crucified. For example, we may observe the shift in Jesus' role as savior. In 1:21, "he will save *his* people from their sins," but in 26:28 his blood "is poured out for *many* (i.e., "all") for the forgiveness of sins." The time of Israel's ultimate rejection of Jesus is a time of death, but death leads to life, a new era of salvation for "the nations" (28:18-20).

The newness of this era is marked in a different way by the interpretive sayings of Jesus at the Last Supper. By his use of the words "covenant" and "forgiveness of sins" in the same breath (26:28), Jesus interprets his mission against the backdrop of Jeremiah 31:31-34. "The time is coming," Jeremiah proclaims, when the Lord will make a "new covenant." That time has come, according to Jesus. In his death he inaugurates the new order of salvation.

Here again is evidence that for Jesus death was no unexpected event unrelated to his life and work. In his death Jesus' obedience to God is manifest, and in this the cross is comprehended as the heart of his mission to open the way of salvation to all.

5. The Death of Jesus in the Gospel of Mark.
The oft-cited judgment of a century ago that Mark's Gospel is a passion narrative with an extended introduction highlights the prominence of Jesus' death for Mark. It fails, however, to come to terms with the theological and literary nexus between Jesus' life and death. In fact, Mark represents Jesus' ministry as a relentless progression of events whose climax is Golgotha. In the cross Jesus is revealed as the Son of God who obtains salvation for the new community of faith—a community called to follow him in sacrificial discipleship.

5.1. The Death of Jesus and Mark's Christology. Who is Jesus? This query constitutes an important leitmotif for the Second Gospel. Although we are informed at the outset that Jesus is Messiah and Son of God (1:1-15), the characters of Mark's account do not share this insight (e.g., 5:41) and, in any case, we are well into the narrative before it becomes clear what these christological titles mean. Mark wants to instruct his audience about the true nature of Jesus, and he does so by means of a narrative oriented around the cross.

Anticipatory allusions to Jesus' passion dot the landscape of the Gospel of Mark, demonstrating the intimate relation between Jesus' identity and his suffering. Already in 2:19-20 Jesus intimates his sudden, unexpected, puzzling death. Elsewhere, religious and political authorities plot his death (3:6; 11:18; 12:12), and Jesus himself prophetically announces his rejection and death (8:31; 9:12, 31; 10:32-34, 38-39, 45). As in Matthew's parallel (see above, 4.1.), so in Mark 6:14-29 the story of John's passion prefigures Jesus' suffering and death.

The link between Jesus' death and his identity is nowhere better seen than in the crucifixion account itself, for Mark understands the moment of Jesus' death as the moment of divine revelation. Only in his death can Jesus be fully appreciated. This is the significance of the confession of the centurion, the only human throughout the Gospel to recognize Jesus as God's Son (15:39). In the crucifixion story Mark expressly notes that it is only as the centurion sees Jesus' dying breath that he makes his confession. That is, in the cross Jesus is recognized rightly as the Son of God. In the body of the Gospel God acclaims Jesus as God's Son at the inauguration of his mission at his baptism* (1:9-11) and in the brief revelation of Jesus' glory at the Transfiguration* (9:2-8). The relationship between these three events in Jesus' career emphasizes the centrality of Jesus' death to the mission for which he was ordained by God.

This understanding, focused on Jesus' status as Son of God, is paralleled in Mark's portrait of Jesus, Son of man. Indeed, it is precisely as Son of man that Jesus will suffer rejection and death (e.g., 8:31; 14:21). As

Son of man, Jesus' divine mission is consummated as he gives his life in service to humanity as a ransom for many (10:45). As Son of man, he also anticipates his vindication and glory* (e.g., 8:38; 14:62).

What is the significance of the crucified Son of God for Mark? Of the aforementioned anticipatory references, the most consequential for interpreting the meaning of Jesus' death are the three passion predictions* (8:31; 9:31; 10:32-34) and the ransom saying* (10:45). These underscore the centrality of the cross to God's redemptive plan, Jesus' obedience in taking up the cross (cf. 14:32-49) and so place Jesus' crucifixion at the heart of his divine mission. This interpretation is manifest not only in the "divine must" theme of the predictions (dei), but also in the later, repeated association of passion events with OT promise. The cross of Christ brings to consummation God's revealed will, as in 14:21 where we should probably not think of any one text or set of texts but of OT promise as a whole. On the other hand, specific OT texts are fulfilled in Jesus' passion (e.g., Zech 13:7, cited in Mk 14:27). More prominent are the numerous ways in which Jesus is presented typologically as the Suffering Servant and Suffering Righteous One (see Servant of Yahweh; Typology).

How Jesus' death functions as the center of God's redemptive plan comes to light in two Markan texts: 10:45 and 14:24. The significance of the former is indicated by its position at the close of the central section of Mark's Gospel, 8:22—10:52, just before the triumphal entry.* In this section, which boldly outlines the correlation between the way of the Christ and that of his disciples, the ransom-saying is hardly ancillary to Mark's message, as some have argued. The latter text serves as the climax of the Last Supper scene. In both cases Jesus' death is interpreted as salvific. In this ultimate act of service, Jesus lays down his life as an atoning sacrifice for the salvation of humanity. The irony of the scene of mockery at the cross may be understood along these lines: It is by refusing to save himself that he is able to save others (15:31; cf. 8:35).

The irony of Mark's passion story is even more pervasive, extending through the appearance of Jesus before the Sanhedrin (e.g., even as Jesus is being mocked as a false prophet, his prophecy concerning Peter's denial is fulfilled [14:65-72]) and on to the crucifixion account. Paramount in this regard is the sixfold use of "king" with reference to Jesus (15:2, 9, 12, 18, 26, 32) combined with the threefold mockery of Jesus on the cross (15:29-32). Condemned as a pretender to the throne, Jesus ironically does have royal status, but not as one might have anticipated. His obedience to the divine mission expressed preeminently in the cross—this is a portent of his royal status that will be evident to all following his vindication and coming as the glorious Son of man.

5.2. The Way of the Cross. Golgotha is not only the ultimate expression of the Christ's mission for Mark. For disciples, too, there is a *via dolorosa*, a way of the cross.

5.2.1. "Take up the Cross." Mark 8:22—10:52 renders transparent the meeting of christology and discipleship around the cross. This section is framed by two healing* miracles.* The first (8:22-26) serves as a parable*: The disciples understand Jesus only vaguely; they need a fuller, sharper vision of Christ's identity. Heretofore they have become cognizant of his power, his victory over evil forces of all kinds. Though Peter confesses him as Christ, he is unprepared for subsequent talk of suffering and death (8:27-33). Yet for Jesus messiahship can be understood fully only within the matrix of the suffering Son of man. What is more, according to Jesus, if the way of the Christ is the way of suffering, so is the way of discipleship (8:34).

Prior to the second healing story (10:46-52), Jesus for the third time (10:32-45) announces his upcoming passion: Jesus and his disciples are on the way (hodos) to Jerusalem, the place of betrayal and death. Apparently still believing that "Christ" signifies "glorious king," James and John express their desire for seats of honor in the coming kingdom. Jesus redirects their thoughts to suffering and calamity, intimating that they would share his fate. Discipleship signifies a service best exemplified in the death of Jesus. Interestingly, like the healing account in 8:22-26, the subsequent story of Bartimaeus can be read as a parable. Faithful, persistent Bartimaeus, first found sitting by the way (hodos), having been healed by Jesus, now sees clearly and follows Jesus on the way (hodos). The invitation to follow Jesus is an invitation to take the way of the cross.

5.2.2. The Suffering of the Community. This motif is continued and deepened in the relationship Mark draws between the suffering of the community (Mark 13) and the suffering of the Messiah (Mark 14—15). The signs of tribulation are paralleled in Jesus' passion as follows:

13:2	Destruction of the Temple	14:58; 15:38
13:9, 11-12	"delivered up"	14:10-11, 18, passim
13:12-13	Betrayal	14:10, 21, 43
13:24	Darkness	15:33
13:26	Son of man: Tribulation, Parousia	14:62

13:32-33	The "Hour"	14:32-42
13:5, 9, 23, 33, 35, 37	Eschatological Watching	14:34, 37-38
13:25	provides the chronology for	14:17—15:1
13:36	"Come," "Find," "Sleep"	14:37, 40

On a literary level, these parallels tie together the fate of Jesus and his disciples; they are of profound theological importance too. On the one hand, they signify that the suffering of the disciples is a participation in the suffering of the Christ. On the other, they indicate the cosmic ramifications of this suffering. The cross of Christ is the turning point in history, the birthing of a new age, the coming of the kingdom of God into the world. This gives added gravity to the sufferings of Jesus' disciples. Like him, they will suffer rejection. Indeed, Mark's intended audience seems already to have found itself in a situation of persecution. This juxtaposition of images in Mark 13—15 affirms that their suffering, too, is a part of the divine plan; that their pain is a part of the process by which the kingdom of God is breaking into the world.

5.2.3. Discipleship Failure and the New Community. Mark's Gospel repeatedly intimates the failure of the hardhearted disciples (6:52) to understand the significance of Jesus' mission. Their failure reaches its acme in 14:50-52 where they abandon Jesus to the arresting party in Gethsemane. It is true that Jesus anticipates their rehabilitation (14:27-28), but the intervening narrative provides unexpected tableaus of faithfulness. In a deliberate contrast with the actions of the Jewish leaders and Judas ("one of the Twelve"!), the anonymous woman anoints Jesus for burial (14:1-11). Simon of Cyrene becomes a model disciple who "takes up the cross" (15:21; cf. 8:34), and a group of women disciples stand by faithfully at Jesus' death (15:40-41).

Even more important for their role in Mark's theology of Jesus' passion are the rending of the Temple veil (15:38) and the confession of the centurion. Together, these narrated events reveal Jesus' identity, as we have seen, but they also speak to the theme of discipleship. The first, drawing on the Temple material found earlier in the Second Gospel, demonstrates that Jesus is the Messiah who destroys the Temple and reconstitutes it as the community of the faithful. The importance of the latter in this context lies in the fact that it is precisely a Gentile centurion who makes the confession of Jesus as Son of God. A more emphatic word about the *universal* implications of Jesus' death could hardly be found.

6. The Death of Jesus in the Gospel of Luke.
The Third Evangelist leaves his readers in no doubt as to the centrality of Jesus' death for his Gospel. He sets the stage for Jesus' passion above all by highlighting his narrative of Jesus' life as a tale of conflict. In addition, throughout Luke-Acts he sounds the cadence: "the Christ must suffer!" What is less transparent is the meaning of Jesus' death for Luke.

6.1. The Rejection of the Messiah. Luke characterizes Jesus' life as a story of conflict and rejection—ominously predicted by Simeon (2:34-35; *see* Simeon's Song), paradigmatically represented by Jesus' opposition at Nazareth (4:16-30), tragically fulfilled in Pilate's handing Jesus over to the will of the chief priests and Jewish public (23:25). On one level this portrait is nothing more than what one would have expected. For Luke, Jesus is a prophet* (cf. e.g., 4:24; 7:16, 39; 24:19; Acts 3:17-26; 7:37), and rejection and death are the lot of all the prophets (cf. Neh 9:26; Lk 4:24; 6:23; 11:47-51; 13:33-34; Acts 7:52). In Luke, Jesus the prophet attracted opposition especially by his concern for a brand of justice* at odds with that practiced by the religious leadership and by his concomitant openness to outcasts through table fellowship* (Karris). In the Gospel of Luke, Jesus' primary opponents appear to be the religious leadership in Jerusalem, and among them the chief priests are singled out for special development. Contrasting with their malevolence is the relatively benign political leadership. In each of the canonical Gospels we find that the major share of blame for the death of Jesus is attributed to the Jews (especially the Jewish leaders) rather than to the Romans. This is especially clear in Luke's Gospel, where Jesus' innocence is declared by Pilate three times and confirmed by Herod (23:4, 14-15, 22).

The Lukan motif of conflict is not limited to Jesus' interaction with the human characters of the Gospel, however. The divine anointing of Jesus for his mission is set within the immediate context of temptation by the devil (3:21—4:13), and the subsequent narrative demonstrates the continual cosmic dimensions of opposition against Jesus (e.g., 13:10-17). With the onset of the passion story, supernatural conflict moves again to center court: Satan enters Judas (22:3; cf. 22:31) and Jesus' struggle on the Mount of Olives as throughout his mission is colored in eschatological, cosmic hues (22:53; cf. *peirasmos*, "struggle," in 4:13; 8:13; 22:28, 40, 46).

Against this backdrop it is surely significant that Luke does not set the disciples over against Jesus as they are in the other Synoptics. Although Judas does betray Jesus, he does so under the power of Satan (22:3; *see* Demon, Devil). Likewise, Peter's denial is related to Satan's influence (22:31-34). In recounting

Jesus' arrest, Luke is conspicuously silent about the disciples, with the result that their fate is left open; they do not abandon Jesus, as in Matthew and Mark. Indeed, the disciples are "with" Jesus in a way not paralleled in the other Synoptic Gospels (22:28). This has important repercussions for our reading of the link between Jesus' crucifixion and discipleship, a theme to which we will return shortly.

6.2. "The Christ Must Suffer!" It is true that Luke inherited from Mark an emphasis on the necessity of Jesus' passion (e.g., Mk 8:31). On the other hand, in Luke Jesus evinces a purposefulness about the cross that is without parallel in the Synoptic Gospels. Not only does he "set his face to go up to Jerusalem" (9:51), the place of rejection and death (18:31-32), but also, with the onset of his passion, he exercises a surprising prescience regarding the details of his betrayal, arrest and death. More so than in the other Synoptics, here Jesus is in control of the events of his passion.

When Jesus foretells his suffering and rejection, he notes their necessity in salvation-historical terms (*dei*). This characterization is continued even after the passion account by means of showing how the crucified Jesus could be the Messiah of God. "Was it not necessary for the Christ to suffer these things and to enter into his glory?" (Lk 24:25-27). Phrases of this kind appear again and again in Luke-Acts.

Students of Luke-Acts have long been aware of the gravity of the *that* of Jesus' death for Luke. Noting that the weight of Luke's theological interest falls on Jesus' resurrection and exaltation, however, they have puzzled over the meaning of the cross. In what way is the death of Jesus crucial to God's redemptive purpose? On this theological problem Luke has seemed less than clear. Indeed, according to many interpreters, to the question Why did Jesus have to die? Luke seems only to answer, Because God willed it!

6.2.1. The Death of Jesus and Lukan Soteriology. In the past many commentators have assumed Luke attributed to Jesus' death the salvific meaning found elsewhere in the NT. Thus Luke, like the other NT writers, affirmed that "Jesus died for our sins." More recent scholarship has reacted against this reading, insisting that Luke must be read on his own terms and not within the theological categories of the Pauline theology of the cross. Accordingly, students of Luke have pointed out that: (1) Luke neglects to recount the ransom logion in his parallel to Mark 10:41-45 (Lk 22:24-27); (2) the sermons in Acts do not draw a direct line between the cross and forgiveness* of sins; and (3) material in Luke-Acts borrowed from Isaiah

52:13—53:12 fails to mention the vicarious, atoning significance of the Servant's death (e.g., Lk 22:37; Acts 8:32-33; *see* Servant of Yahweh).

Of course, the eucharistic words of Jesus (22:19-20) do root human salvation in the death of Jesus (*see* Last Supper). However, noting their absence in some textual witnesses, a number of scholars have postulated that they were missing from Luke's original text (cf. RSV [some editions], NEB). Others, who accept their originality to the Lukan narrative, are nevertheless impressed with how non-Lukan these verses appear linguistically. As in Acts 20:28 (the only other passage in the Lukan corpus that clearly bases human salvation in the death of Jesus), Luke appears to be repeating ancient terminology without making its theology his own.

A conclusion of this sort is confirmed by those passages in which Luke makes transparent his understanding of the means of salvation. In Acts 2:33; 5:30-31 and 10:43 we discern Luke's concern to show that the means of salvation is the exaltation of Jesus. Of these three passages, 5:30-31 is of particular interest for two reasons. First, it is here that the logic is most clear: as a result of his exaltation Jesus is enthroned as Prince and Savior and in these capacities is able to offer salvation. Second, this text underscores again the necessity of Jesus' death for salvation history.

Clearly the death of Jesus has positive significance for Luke, but just as clearly that significance is not centered on an interpretation of the cross as a vicarious sacrifice. How then might this significance be understood?

6.2.2. The Death of Jesus: A Martyrdom? The interpretation of Jesus' death as a martyrdom has enjoyed widespread support in this century (see Beck). This view exploits the connections between the Lukan passion and the literature of martyrdom in late Judaism. Common themes include the presence of supernatural conflict and divine help, the innocence and endurance of the victim and the portrait of the martyr's death as exemplary for the faithful.

Although this interpretation attributes positive significance to the death of Jesus in Luke and makes good on a number of important aspects of the Lukan portrayal, it has come under serious scrutiny in recent years. First, it has been questioned how far Luke actually anticipated Jesus' disciples would be asked to follow in Jesus' steps. Thus, the call to take up the cross (Mk 8:34) has become in Luke a call to a lifestyle marked by the cross ("day by day," 9:23), not a reference to impending persecution. Second, a number of details integral to martyr tales are missing from Luke, most notably the horrific detail in descriptions of the means of death. Moreover, in Luke, Jesus, unlike the martyrs of Jewish literature, appears as one who struggles with the prospect of death (Lk 22:39-46). Third, as has become clear from continued study of the religious background of the first century, the themes of the martyrological literature are not in every case unique to that corpus. Thus, one might postulate that Luke and the literature of martyrdom drew from a common world of thought. Finally, it has become evident that the notion of Jesus as martyr fails to do justice to the richness of Luke's mural of Jesus' passion. Although it may be one among other Lukan concerns, by itself it falls short as a summary of Luke's theology of Jesus' death.

6.3. From the Suffering Righteous One to the Suffering Servant. Other students of Luke have noted the repeated evidences of Jesus' innocence in Luke 23 and the many parallels between Jesus and the Suffering Righteous One in the Psalms and Book of Wisdom. On this basis they have postulated for Luke an interpretation of Jesus' passion as the suffering and death of God's Righteous Sufferer who goes to his death in spite of his innocence but is subsequently vindicated by God. This view makes sense of the innocence motif in the passion story, dovetails well with the "contrast formulae" in the speeches in Acts (e.g., "you put Jesus to death, but God raised him from the dead," 2:23-24) and demonstrates in Jesus' life how God overturns injustice—an important theme in Luke-Acts.

At the same time, it is clear that even this interpretation is insufficient to grasp the heart of Luke's understanding of Jesus' death, for it fails to explain the *divine necessity* of the cross in salvation-historical terms. A more successful interpretive model focuses on the Suffering Servant of Isaiah, which is a clearer embodiment of the OT Righteous Sufferer (Green, 1990).

That Luke is interested more pointedly in the Suffering Servant is manifest in the passion story itself, and elsewhere in his two-part work. In the passion story (1) Jesus cites Isaiah 53:12 as a general allusion to his suffering and death, thus communicating that in his passion he fulfills the role of the Suffering Servant; (2) Jesus is repeatedly declared innocent and acclaimed by the centurion as a "righteous man," an allusion to Isaiah 53:11 (cf. the conjunction of *dikaios* ["righteous"] and Jesus' suffering in Acts 3:13-14, where Jesus' passion is described in words borrowed from Is 52:13—53:12); (3) Jesus refuses to speak in his own self-defense (23:9; Is 53:7); and (4) in his mockery, Jesus is called "the Chosen One," a designation for God's Servant (23:35; Is 42:1).

Outside the passion story, numerous references to Jesus' role as the Servant appear, the most explicit in the citation of Isaiah 53:7-8 in Acts 8:32-33 and the prophetic reference to Jesus' mission by Simeon in words borrowed from Isaiah 49:6 (2:32).

The significance of the identification of Jesus' passion as that of the Suffering Servant for Luke is threefold. First, it indicates how Luke can emphasize the salvation-historical necessity of the cross *and* spotlight Jesus' exaltation or vindication as the salvific event. The Isaianic portrayal of the Suffering Servant holds together these twin motifs, particularly in Isaiah 53:11, where, following his suffering, God's Righteous One will justify many. In other words, Luke's characterization of Jesus as the Servant indicates the necessity of his death and the salvific import of his vindication.

Second, Luke's emphasis on the Servant provides a framework for drawing out the universal implications of Jesus' mission. That Jesus would be "a light for revelation to the Gentiles" was predicted by Simeon (2:32; Is 49:6), so it is noteworthy that at Jesus' death he was acclaimed as the Righteous One by a Gentile. However, the importance of Jesus' death is not only for the Gentile, but also for the Jew (e.g., 23:34, 48) and the criminal (23:43). That is, in Jesus' death one finds the culmination of a life lived for others, including outsiders (*see* Gentiles).

Third, by portraying Jesus' career, and especially his death and exaltation, as that of the Suffering Servant, Luke demonstrates in the ultimate manner his understanding of the way of salvation. Already in the lives of Elizabeth and Zechariah, Luke shows that God's salvation comes through a pattern of reversal (Lk 1). For Luke the inbreaking of the kingdom of God marks a transposition of roles as the God who is faithful vindicates the faithful. The career of Jesus illustrates this theme of reversal for he is the innocent Servant who suffers unto death but is raised up and designated Prince and Savior. By putting aside thoughts of self-glorification and obediently adopting the role of the servant (cf. 12:37; 22:25-27), Jesus embodies the righteousness, humiliation and lowliness of the Servant. The cross is the consequence, but God overturned this humiliation, vindicating his Servant, exalting him and in so doing opened the way of repentance and forgiveness. For Luke this is the way of salvation, and this is the way of discipleship.

7. The Death of Jesus in the Gospel of John

Until relatively recent years, students of the Fourth Gospel downplayed the importance of the passion for John's presentation of Jesus. Some even posited a theological chasm between chapters 17 and 18 of John, suggesting that Jesus' trial and execution had no place in the portrayal of the glorious Jesus found elsewhere in the Fourth Gospel. Happily, this view has begun to fall into disfavor among Johannine scholars, as studies have (1) recognized the numerous allusions to the passion in the earlier sections of the Gospel (cf. 2:12-22; 3:14) and the fact that eight chapters of the Gospel are related to the passion (12—19), and (2) begun to demonstrate anew the integration of the cross into the totality of John's christology. We will discuss the meaning of Jesus' death for John first by mentioning two subsidiary themes—the sovereignty of Jesus in the passion account and Jesus' death as sacrifice—then by noting how the cross relates to the journey of the Son of God from incarnation* to exaltation.

7.1. Jesus, Sovereign King. When turning from the Synoptic versions to the Johannine account of Jesus' suffering and death, one is immediately struck with the majesty of Jesus in John. He has long known his betrayer (6:70) and actually sets in motion the act of betrayal (13:27). In the arrest scene it is neither Judas nor the arresting party that is in charge, but Jesus himself, revealing himself as the "I Am" (*egō eimi*) and negotiating the release of his disciples (18:1-11) (*see* I Am Sayings). In his hearing before Pilate he is presented as king and even takes the role of judge (18:28—19:16). Requiring no assistance, he bears his own cross (19:17). He cares for his mother from the cross (19:25-27) and, before the soldiers can perform the *coup de grâce*, breaking his legs to speed his death, he dies of his own accord (19:20-33).

In this manner John demonstrates the truth of Jesus' words, "No one takes my life from me, but I lay it down of my own volition" (10:18). Clearly John is concerned to relate Jesus' passion to his larger representation of Jesus' glorious sojourn on earth (cf. Jn 1:14b) as a self-giving act.

7.2. Jesus' Death: Life for the World. Though it is not the linchpin for John's understanding of the death of Jesus, the sacrificial significance of the cross is nevertheless important to his Gospel. This motif initially appears in 1:29, 36, where the forgiveness of sins is related to the appellation "Lamb of God." Though Lamb of God is capable of other nuances as well, it is at least associated with the theological world of the Passover lamb (*see* Lamb of God). This is suggested not only by the atonement theology resident in 1:29, but also by John's clear attempts to portray Jesus' death as a Passover sacrifice in the passion story. In this regard the following details may be noted: the time of Jesus' death coincided with the time of the paschal sacrifice (Jn 19:14; cf. 18:28); the hysop and basin are present at the cross (19:29; Ex 12:22); *seeing* the blood flow from the side of Jesus is emphasized (19:35; Ex 12:13); and the soldiers do not break Jesus' legs (19:31-37; Ex 12:46). This emphasis on Passover is probably related to the extended discourse on Jesus as the bread* of life (6:25-59): Whoever partakes of Jesus' flesh and blood will have life.*

Similarly, John 3:16 links the Incarnation of God's Son to the offer of life. The language of atonement found more pervasively in Paul also has a place in the Johannine narrative. Thus, *hyper* ("on behalf of") is used in John to underscore the redemptive nature of the cross in 6:51; 10:11, 15; 11:50-52; 18:14. Finally, John understands the footwashing at Jesus' final meal with his disciples not only as a demonstration of exemplary behavior, but also as a symbol of Jesus' salvific death (13:8-11).

7.3. Crucifixion and Exaltation. In terms of the integration of Jesus' death with the Johannine christology as a whole, the most pervasive motif is that of "raising up" or "exaltation." This, we are repeatedly informed, is the fate of Jesus the Son of man (3:14-15; 8:28; 12:32-33). Clearly, this "being lifted up" (*hypsoō*, 3:14; 8:28; 12:32) has a double meaning. On the one hand, it is associated in John's schema with the terminology of glorification (*see* Glory). On the other, in 8:28 we read that the Jews will be the agents of Jesus' "lifting up," and in 12:32-33 John notes that "lifting up" is a metaphor for the way Jesus will be put to death (cf. 18:32).

John therefore sees some intimate connection between Jesus' crucifixion and his exaltation, and this suggests that Jesus' death must be set within the larger Johannine portrait of Jesus' earthly career. For the Fourth Evangelist, the life of the Son of God is best understood as a journey: He comes from his pre-existent state in heaven,* dwells among women and men, then returns to heaven. He who descended from glory must ascend to glory (e.g., 3:13, 31; 6:38; 8:23; 13:1-3).

How is his passion related to this christological movement? It is the means by which he returns to the Father. That is, John overcomes the scandal of the cross by interpreting it in terms of Jesus' exaltation. This reading is encouraged by the fact that in those places where the reference to the "lifting up" of Jesus is clearest—3:14; 8:28; 12:32-34—John has developed the larger theme of the Son's journey from and return to God. In this way the cross is interpreted by the journey motif as the means by which the Son of man left the world below to return to the world above (Nicholson).

What is more, Jesus' death, understood as a lifting up (3:14), appears as the ultimate expression of love, the gift of God (3:16). Indeed, Jesus' own love for his followers reaches its acme in his sacrificial service and death (13:1; 15:13).

See also BURIAL OF JESUS; GETHSEMANE; PASSION NARRATIVE; PREDICTIONS OF JESUS' PASSION AND RESURRECTION; RANSOM SAYING.

BIBLIOGRAPHY. D. C. Allison, Jr., *The End of the Ages Has Come: An Early Interpretation of the Passion and Resurrection of Jesus* (Philadelphia: Fortress, 1985); B. E. Beck, " *'Imitatio Christi'* and the Lucan Passion Narrative," in *Suffering and Martyrdom in the New Testament: Studies Presented to G.M. Styler by the Cambridge New Testament Seminar,* ed. W. Horbury and B. McNeil (Cambridge: University Press, 1981) 28-47; A. Dauer, *Die Passionsgeschichte im Johannesevangelium: Eine traditionsgeschichtliche und theologische Untersuchung zu John 18,1-19,30* (München: Kösel, 1972); J. B. Green, "The Death of Jesus, God's Servant," in *Reimaging the Death of the Lukan Jesus,* ed. D. Sylva (BBB 73; Frankfurt-am-Main: Anton Hain, 1990) 1-28, 170-173; idem, *The Death of Jesus: Tradition and Interpretation in the Passion Narrative* (WUNT 2:33; Tübingen: J.C.B. Mohr [Paul Siebeck], 1988); A. E. Harvey, *Jesus and the Constraints of History* (Philadelphia: Westminster, 1982); M. Hengel, *The Atonement: The Origins of the Doctrine in the New Testament* (Philadelphia: Fortress, 1981); idem, *Crucifixion in the Ancient World and the Folly of the Message of the Cross* (London: SCM, 1977); H. W. Hoehner, *Chronological Aspects of the Life of Christ* (Grand Rapids: Zondervan, 1977); D. Juel, *Messiah and Temple: The Trial of Jesus in the Gospel of Mark* (SBLDS 31; Missoula, MT: Scholars, 1977); R. J. Karris, O.F.M., *Luke: Artist and Theologian. Luke's Passion Narrative as Literature* (TI; New York: Paulist, 1985); K. M. Kenyon, *The Bible and Recent Archaeology,* rev. ed. by P. R. S. Moorey (Atlanta: John Knox, 1987); J. Kodell, O.S.B., "Luke's Theology of the Death of Jesus," in *Sin, Salvation, and the Spirit,* ed. D. Durken, O.S.B. (Collegeville, MN: Liturgical, 1979) 221-230; B. Lindars, "The Passion in the Fourth Gospel," in *God's Christ and His People: Studies in Honour of Nils Alstrup Dahl,* ed. J. Jervell and W. A. Meeks (Oslo: Universitetsferlaget, 1977) 71-86; E. Lohse, *Märtyrer und Gottesknecht: Untersuchungen zur urchristlichen Verkündigung vom Sühntod Jesu Christi,* (2d ed.; Göttingen: Vandenhoek & Ruprecht, 1963); I. H. Marshall, *Last Supper and Lord's Supper* (Grand Rapids,: Eerdmans, 1980); F. J. Matera, *Passion Narratives and Gospel Theologies: Interpreting the Synoptics through Their Passion Stories* (TI; New York/Mahwah: Paulist, 1986); B. F. Meyer, *The Aims of Jesus* (London: SCM, 1979); J. Neyrey, S.J., *The Passion according to Luke: A Redaction Study of Luke's Soteriology* (TI; New York/Mahwah: Paulist, 1986); G. C. Nicholson, *Death as Departure: The Johannine Descent-Ascent Schema* (SBLDS 63; Chico, CA: Scholars, 1983); E. P. Sanders, *Jesus and Judaism* (London: SCM, 1985); D. Senior, *The Passion Narrative according to Matthew: A Redactional Study* (Leuven: Leuven University, 1975); idem, *The Passion of Jesus in the Gospel of Luke* (Wilmington, DE: Michael Glazier, 1989); idem, *The Passion of Jesus in the Gospel of Mark* (Wilmington, DE: Michael Glazier, 1984); idem, *The Passion of Jesus in the Gospel of Matthew* (Wilmington, Delaware: Michael Glazier, 1985); V. Taylor, *The Passion Narrative of St. Luke: A Critical and Historical Investigation* (SNTSMS 19; Cambridge: University Press, 1982); J. B. Tyson, *The Death of Jesus in Luke-Acts* (Columbia, South Carolina: University of South Carolina, 1986); H.-R. Weber, *The Cross: Tradition and Interpretation* (London: S.P.C.K., 1979); J. Zias and E. Sekeles, "The Crucified Man from Giv'at ha-Mivtar: A Reappraisal," *IEJ* 35 (1985) 22-27.

J. B. Green

DEBTOR. *See* SINNER.

DEFILEMENT. *See* CLEAN AND UNCLEAN.

DEMON, DEVIL, SATAN

For Jesus and the Gospel writers the Devil, or Satan, is the chief enemy of Jesus and the establishing of the kingdom of God.* In his ministry, especially in his exorcisms, Jesus engages in the first stage of the defeat of Satan in casting out his evil minions. Jesus' complete defeat of the Devil and his demons is expected in the eschaton.

1. Background
2. Terminology
3. Exorcism in the NT World
4. Jesus and the Demonic
5. Emphases of the Gospel Writers

1. Background.

Israel's* confidence in the sovereignty of Yahweh was not conducive to the development of a consistent demonology. In the OT the satyrs, or "hairy ones" (Lev 17:7; 2 Chron 11:15; Is 13:21; 34:14); the *śēdîm* (Deut 32:17; Ps 106:37); the horse leech or vampire (Prov 30:15); Azazel (Lev 16:8, 10, 26; cf. *1 Enoch* 10:8) and Lilith (RSV = night hag, Is 34:14), a demon cited in Akkadian sources, thought to be found in desolate places with the unclean owl and kite, may all have been understood to be evil spiritual beings. Both good and evil spiritual beings were from and under the control of Yahweh (1 Kings 22:21-23 [par. 2 Chron

18:20-23]; 1 Sam 16:14-23).

It was probably due to Persian influence that Jews began to speculate on the origin of demons (*Jub.* 2:2; 4:22; *1 Enoch* 6:1—7:6; cf. *m. 'Abot* 5:6), and the belief developed that evil spiritual beings were more independent of God than those who performed positive functions for him (Job 1—2). The Essenes at Qumran believed that everyone was ruled either by the Prince of Light* or the Angel* of Darkness whom God had created. But this dualism was only secondary in that, in the first place, it was God who created both these spirits and designed humans to live under them (1QS 3:13—4:26).

In Greek thought the word *daimonion* was used in a variety of ways: for a deity (Philo *Vit. Mos.* 1.276), a lesser deity (Plutarch *Rom.* 51), a divine power or unknown supernatural force (Josephus *J.W.* 1.69), the human element in touch with the divine (Galen *De Placitis* 5.6.4) and an intermediary between humans and the gods (*Corp. Herm.* XVI.18). Josephus,* for example, made no arbitrary distinction between good and evil demons: a demon could give good fortune as well as cause death (*Ant.* 16.76; *J.W.* 1.556). It was the activities of a demon that determined its nature (*Ant.* 13.415; 16.210; *J.W.* 1.628). When a demon overtook a person and caused sickness or frenzy and was life-threatening, it was thought necessary to expel it (*J.W.* 7.185). The demons were popularly thought to be the spirits of the dead (*J.W.* 1.599, 607; 6.47; Lucian *Philops.* 29; Pliny *Nat. Hist.* 18.118).

2. Terminology.

The Gospels use a variety of terms, often interchangeable, for the Devil and evil spirits.

2.1. Devil. The Greeks used *diabolos* for a slanderer (Xenophon *Agesilaus* 11.5), and the LXX used it to translate *śāṭān* ("adversary") in the sense of accusing people and attempting to separate them from God (1 Chron 21:1; Job 1:6—2:7; Ps 108:6 [LXX]; Zech 3:1-2). In the Gospels he is portrayed as the adversary of Jesus (Mt 4:1-11; par. Lk 4:1-13), the enemy of his work (Mt 13:39) and the chief of the demons (Mt 25:41). Mark does not use the term. John uses it at 6:70; 8:44 and 13:2. In Matthew and Luke *Devil* is used interchangeably with *Satan* (cf. Mt 4:1, 5, 8, 11 and 4:10; Mk 4:15 and Lk 8:12).

2.2. Satan. The English transliteration of the Greek *satanas* (Mk 1:13; Lk 22:3), in turn, is a transliteration of the Hebrew *śāṭān* (see 2.1. above and 11QPsᵃ 19:15). In the intertestamental literature the name occurs in the form *maśṭēmāh* (1QM 13:4, 11; *Jub.* 10:8). In the Gospels it is used as a synonym for the Devil (cf. Mt 4:1, 10; Lk 13:16), the arch-demon (Mk 3:23, 26 [par.

Mt 12:26; Lk 11:18]; cf. Lk 10:18) and, notably on one occasion, in the sense of a testing adversary (Lk 22:31; cf. Job 1) as well as in the sense of attempting to separate people from God (Mk 4:15; 8:33 [par. Mt 16:23]).

2.3. Beelzebul. In the NT *beelzeboul* (*beezeboul*, in some manuscripts, represents an assimilation of *l* to the *z*) occurs only in Matthew 10:25; 12:24 (par. Mk 3:22; Lk 11:15); Matthew 12:27 (par. Lk 11:18, 19). The Vulgate and Syriac versions have attempted to explain the term by correcting it to *beelzebub*, the god of Ekron (2 Kings 1:2-3, 6, 16; Josephus *Ant.* 19.9). However, perhaps coined on the spot by Jesus' critics, the term is probably derived from the Hebrew words *ba'al* ("lord," Hos 2:18), used mostly of local manifestations of the Canaanite fertility god who was the chief adversary of the Israelite religion (1 Kings 18:16-40), and *zᵉbul* ("exalted dwelling," 1 Kings 8:13). The meaning "lord of heaven" for the prince of demons (Mt 12:24) would have been well understood as a euphemism for Satan in light of the LXX substituting "demons" for "idols" in Psalm 96:5 [95:5].

2.4. The Evil One. As a name for the Devil *ho ponēros* occurs in Matthew 5:37 (possibly Mt 6:13 [par. Lk 11:4]); Matthew 13:19, 38 and John 17:15 (cf. Eph 6:16; 2 Thess 3:3; 1 John 2:13-14; 3:12; 5:18-19). The other titles for the Devil in the Gospels are "the Tempter" (*ho peirazōn*, Mt 4:3), "Prince of Demons" (*ho archōn tōn daimoniōn*, Mt 9:34; 12:24 [par. Mk 3:22; Lk 11:15]), "the Enemy" (*ho echthros*, Mt 13:39; Lk 10:19) and "Ruler of this World" (*ho archōn tou kosmou toutou*, Jn 16:11; cf. 12:31; 14:30).

2.5. Demons. The word is also used only once in the LXX, in some manuscripts, at Isaiah 65:11 to translate the Hebrew *gad*, the god of fortune of the Syrians. Only at Matthew 8:31 is *daimōn* used in the NT for an evil spirit. Otherwise, *daimonion* is used in the Gospels: eleven times in Matthew, thirteen in Mark, twenty-three in Luke and six in John.

2.6. Spirits. In line with the development of the use of *pneuma* for either good or bad spiritual beings, the Synoptic writers use the word not only of the Holy Spirit* but, with the qualifications of *ponēros* ("evil," Mt 12:45 [par. Lk 11:26, *ponēroteros*]; Lk 7:21; 8:2; cf. 1QapGen 20:16-17) and *akathartos* ("unclean," Mk 6:7 [par. Mt 10:1]), for demons (Mk 1:23 [par. Lk 4:33]; Mk 1:26 [par. Lk 4:35]; Mk 3:11 [par. Lk 4:41; 6:18]; Mk 5:2 [par. Mt 8:28; Lk 8:27]; Mk 5:13 [par. Lk 8:33]; Mk 7:25 [par. Mt 15:22]).

2.7. Legion. The word *legiōn* (Diodorus *Siculus* 26.5), meaning "many," was borrowed from the Latin *legio* (Plutarch *Rom.* 13.1; *Otho* 12.3) and is used in the NT only of the number of angels at Jesus' disposal (Mt

26:53) and in the story of the Gadarene demoniac (Mk 5:9 [par. Lk 8:30]) where it suggests a multiform demon.

2.8. Demon Possession. In the OT there is the belief that evil spiritual beings can torment people (1 Sam 16:14-23) so that protection from their harm was sought (Ps 91). The Dead Sea Scrolls retell the story of Abraham, saying that during the night the Most High God sent a spirit to scourge Pharaoh and all his household (1QapGen 20). Josephus believed that people could be possessed or "overtaken" (*lambanomenos*) by demons causing frenzy (*J.W.* 3.485; 7.120, 389), suffocation and strangling (*Ant.* 6.166). Philo believed that invisible living beings hovered in the air, and that evil spirits among them could be breathed in, or might take over, fill or descend into a person, causing disastrous pestilences (Philo *Gig.* 6-31).

In harmony with beliefs of that day, the Gospels depict demons causing convulsions, loud screaming, a change of voice or character, chaotic and unpredictable behavior, preternatural strength and an indifference to pain. Notably, a disturbance is caused by and in the sufferer when confronted by Jesus (Mk 1:21-28; 5:1-20; 7:24-30; 9:14-29 and par.). Also, the demon-possessed were considered to have special insight into the identity of Jesus (Mk 1:24; 3:11; cf. Acts 16:17).

3. Exorcism in the NT World.

At the time of Jesus and the writing of the Gospels the destructive work of demons in human life was combatted in a number of ways. One way is illustrated in the Magical Papyri (*PGM* V.99-171), the story of Eleazar (Josephus *Ant.* 8.46-49), the Jewish exorcists of Matthew 12:27 (par. Lk 11:19), the so-called strange exorcist (Mk 9:38-39 [par. Lk 9:49-50]), the sons of Sceva (Acts 19:11-20) and the rabbinic material (*Pesiq. R.* 40b) where exorcism was thought to be successful because of what was said and done by the exorcist. However, while Apollonius of Tyana (Philostratus *Vit. Ap.* 4.20) and rabbis Simeon and Ḥanina ben Dosa (*b. Pesaḥ.* 112b) attained legendary status, and stories of them contain legendary details, they were historical figures of the period who were thought to be successful because of who they were. In the case of the rabbis their charismatic presence was seen to arise out of a special relationship with God (*b. Pesaḥ.* 112b). Between these two extremes of understanding and methods of exorcism, the retelling of the story of Abraham in *Genesis Apocryphon* 20 shows that an exorcism could be regarded successful because of the personal force of the healer as well as what he said or did.

In the mendicant priests and soothsayers of Plato's

Republic (364B-365A), the sons of Sceva, the sorcerers known to Celsus (Origen *Contra Cels.* 1.68), Apollonius of Tyana and particularly the Cynics (Diogenes Laertius *Vit.* 6.101; Lucian *Peregrinus* 10-11), we can see that the peripatetic philosopher-healer would have been a familiar sight in the time of Jesus and the Evangelists.

4. Jesus and the Demonic.

Despite the relative importance of exorcism to Jesus and the Gospel writers, there are only four longer exorcism stories of Jesus in the Gospels (Mk 1:21-28; 5:1-20; 7:24-30; 9:14-29), a very brief report of an exorcism (Mt 9:32-34 and 12:22 [par. Lk 11:14]) and a number of references and sayings on Jesus' dealing with the demons (Mk 1:32-34, 39; 3:7-12 and parallels; cf. Acts 10:38).

4.1. The Demoniacs. The four stories of Jesus dealing with the demons and demoniacs show that such people might sometimes, but not always, have been socially rootless, perhaps driven to the margins of society by their behavior or the economic situation in Palestine. Nevertheless, Jesus can be seen dealing with a range of people, not just the disadvantaged or the wealthy.

The story of the demoniac with an unclean spirit in the Capernaum synagogue* (Mk 1:21-28) portrays a man in the mainstream of Jewish society and participating in the religious life of his community. The chaotic and unpredictable character of the demoniac could mean that at times the man showed no adverse symptoms of his condition. Or it may have been thought the demon only revealed itself when confronted by a spiritual enemy.

Also, the epileptic boy appears to have remained with his family and to have been sufficiently controllable for him to accompany his father to see the disciples* of Jesus (Mk 9:14-29). The Syrophoenician woman's demonized daughter also remained in a family situation (Mk 7:24-30). However, the woman did not bring her daughter out of the home. Perhaps the girl was a danger to the public, or too sick to move or terrified of leaving home. The woman, being Hellenized, may have been from the leading stratum of society and found her daughter's sickness an embarrassment, for the demon-possessed were the focus of ridicule (cf. Philo *Flacc.* 36, 40). And, if being cared for at home is sign of wealth, we perhaps have here, as in the story of the epileptic boy, some evidence that these families may have had some financial means above the average.

The story of the Gadarene demoniac reveals a different picture (Mk 5:1-20). The man lived on the margins of society among the tombs, perhaps living in burial caves (see Num 19:11, 16; 11QTemple 48:11-13; 49:5-21; 50:3-8 and *Acts of Andrew* 6). To be "unclean" meant he would have been thought to be rejected by God (cf. *m. Kelim;* Is 35:8), unable to enter the Temple or participate in worship or religious meals. That there had been an unsuccessful attempt to restrain the Gadarene demoniac (Mk 5:3-4) shows that chaining was one way violent demoniacs were dealt with.

4.2. Was Jesus an Exorcist? Although the view is occasionally advanced that Jesus was not an exorcist, or that it was an insignificant aspect of his ministry, there is ample evidence that he had a reputation for being extremely successful in expelling evil spirits from people. First, the exorcism stories associated with Jesus in the Gospels (see 4.1. above), which recent research has shown belong to the bedrock of reliable data about the historical Jesus, are the most compelling evidence of Jesus being an exorcist.

Second, there are sayings of and about Jesus that presume his ministry of exorcism and which are also generally regarded to belong to the bedrock of historical material: the charge that Jesus cast out demons by Beelzebul (Mk 3:22 [par. Mt 9:34 and 12:24; Lk 11:15]); the saying that Jesus exorcised by the Spirit or finger of God (Mt 12:28 [par. Lk 11:20]) and the parable of the strong man, which is a picture of exorcism (Mk 3:27 [par. Mt 12:29; Lk 11:21-22]; cf. *Gos. Thom.* 35). It is difficult to be certain of the origin of Jesus' warning to Herod in which exorcism is mentioned: "Go tell that fox, 'Behold, I cast out demons and perform cures today and tomorrow, and the third day I finish my course . . .' " (Lk 13:32). But it is likely to be authentic, for it is difficult to see why such a situation and saying should be constructed.

Third, in the NT era the names of exorcists with high reputations were used by other exorcists in their healing* incantations (Pseudo-Philo [LAB] 60; Josephus *Ant.* 8.46-49). The NT carries a number of reports of this happening in relation to Jesus, showing that he had a high reputation as an exorcist. There is the pericope about the strange exorcist using the name of Jesus (Mk 9:38; par. Lk 9:49) and the seventy disciples are said to return with the report: "Lord, even the demons are subject to us in your name!" (Lk 10:17). Then, in Acts 16:18 Paul is depicted as using the name of Jesus Christ to perform an exorcism.

Fourth, there is evidence outside the NT that Jesus cast out demons. For example, the Magical Papyri have the now-famous incantation intended for use by exorcists: "I adjure you by the god of the Hebrews, Jesu, . . ." (*PGM* IV.3019-3020). Also, in that the use of Jesus' name for healing was censured by the Jews, we

probably have further evidence that Jesus was at least considered a powerful healer by them (*t. ḥul.* 2:22-23; *y. Šabb.* 14.4.14d; *y. 'Abod. Zar.* 2:2.40d-41a; *b. 'Abod. Zar.* 27b).

4.3. Jesus' Methods of Dealing with the Demons. From the Gospel records it is clear that Jesus showed no interest in the demonic apart from his battle against the Devil and his minions.

4.3.1. Familiar Techniques. In dealing with the demons, historical investigation shows that Jesus' technique involved a number of features. First, there was an initial dramatic confrontation between Jesus and the demon(iac). For example, in Mark 1:23 the man screams out when he meets Jesus in the Capernaum synagogue so that it is suddenly obvious that he is a demoniac (cf. Mk 5:6-7; 7:25; 9:20). The historical reliability of this feature in the story is all but assured by the existence of this feature in other literature (Philostratus *Vit. Ap.* 4.20) and the Gospel writers show no consistent use of it.

In two stories the demon(iac)s speak in their initial confrontation with Jesus: "What have we to do with you, Jesus of Nazareth? Have you come to destroy us? I know who you are, the Holy One of God!" (Mk 1:24) and "What have I to do with you, Jesus, son of the Most High God? I adjure you by God not to torment me" (Mk 5:7). This material is probably historically reliable, for it is unlikely that those responsible for transmitting the Gospel traditions would create the idea of the demons declaring Jesus' messiahship. The parallels to the question "What have I (or we) to do with you" (Judg 11:12; 1 Kings 17:18; 2 Sam 16:5-14; Josephus *Ant.* 7.265; Philo *Deus Imm.* 138) show that the demons are seeking to defend themselves against Jesus. Parallels found outside the Gospels to the demons saying they know who Jesus is, show they are seeking to gain control over a spiritual enemy (Acts 19:15; *PGM* VIII.6-7, 13). The knowledge the demons have of Jesus may be supernatural or it may indicate— as the names used for Jesus suggest—he was recognized to be an exorcist in the Jewish tradition where healers such as Jesus often relied on God as a source of power-authority. So, in turn, the demons attempted to disarm Jesus by exposing his allegiance and special relationship with God (Ps 106:16; Sir 45:6; *b. Pes.* 112b). To say "I adjure (*horkizō*) you by God . . ." was a way of attempting to bind or put a curse upon a person and thus compel them to do or say something (Josh 6:26; 1 Kings 22:16; 2 Chron 18:15; Mt 26:63; *PGM* IV.3019).

Second, the stories in the Gospels show Jesus using a number of formulae to expel the demons. In Mark 1:25 Jesus says to the demon "Be quiet . . ." (*phimoō*).

This command is not so much for silence, but, in view of its use in the period as an incantational restriction, Jesus is seeking to bind the demon (*P. Oslo* 1.161-162). In three stories Jesus is reported as saying: "Come out of [him]" (Mk 1:25; 5:8; 9:25). This command is the basic method found in common to all kinds of exorcists we know in the NT period (Lucian *Philops.* 11 and 16; Philostratus *Vit. Ap.* 4.20; *PGM* IV.1243-1249). In Mark 5:9 Jesus asks the demon "What is your name?" This verse suggests that Jesus had already commanded the demon to come out of the man, but in response the demon had tried to fend off Jesus' attack by using a formula to bind (*horkizō*) Jesus (see 4.3.2. below). So, apparently being initially unsuccessful (cf. Mk 8:22-26), Jesus uses another way of overcoming the demon by asking its name, thereby disarming it (cf. *PGM* IV.3037-3079). In this category, the importance of an exorcist knowing the name of the demon (cf. Philostratus *Vit. Ap.* 4.20), comes Jesus' request in Mark 9:21-22 for the history of the lad's illness. Some ancient exorcists had difficulty in getting demons to speak (*PGM* IV.3039-3041). Jesus seems to have experienced no such difficulty (Mk 1:23-25; 5:5-7). In Mark 9:25 Jesus commands the demon not to return to the person (cf. Mt 12:43-45; par. Luke 11:24-26). The idea of demons returning to people is extremely old and well documented in the NT period (Josephus *Ant.* 8.46-49; Philostratus *Vit. Ap.* 4.20; *PGM* IV.1254, 3024-3025). In the face of Jesus' attempt to cast them out, the demons plead for leniency in the story of the Gadarene demoniac (Mk 5:10-12; cf. *1 Enoch* 12—14; *Jub.* 10). The request not to be sent out of the area coincides with the contemporary notion that demons were especially associated with particular regions (cf. Tob 8:3).

Third, Jesus is reported as transferring demons from a person to some pigs (Mk 5:13). It is sometimes said that the pigs episode was the proof offered by Jesus for the success of his exorcism. However, against this view it is to be noted that the demons were probably thought to have been transferred from the man to the pigs and then to the sea. Also, it was sometimes thought appropriate to transfer the demons from the sufferer to some object like a pebble, a piece of wood, a pot or some water in order to effect a cure. These objects, thought to contain the demons, were thrown away or destroyed to effect and perhaps signify the demon's departure from the situation. Further, the proof of the cure in the story in Mark 5 is not the destruction of the pigs but the people seeing the cured man "sitting there, clothed and in his right mind" (5:15). Thus, rather than as a proof of cure, the pigs episode was probably understood as an integral part of the cure.

Fourth, on one occasion Jesus is said to perform an exorcism from a distance (Mk 7:24-30). There is nothing in the pericope that necessitates a healing from a distance—the daughter could have accompanied the woman, perhaps on a stretcher (cf. Mk 2:3; 9:14-29). Nor are the elements of the story which make it an exorcism from a distance generally thought to be the product of Christian redaction. On the other hand, there are other stories of this kind from the same milieu as the Gospels (Philostratus *Vit. Ap.* 3.38; *b. Ber.* 34b). No literary links are to be found between these and the Jesus story, but they do both have in common the motif of healing at a distance. We can be reasonably confident then that Jesus, like other exorcists of his period, was known as an exorcist able to heal from a distance.

Fifth, violence is involved in the reports of Jesus' dealings with the demons. The drowning of the pigs in Mark 5:11-13 is perhaps the best example. In Mark 1:26 the demon is said to convulse the man, and in Mark 9:26 the demon also apparently convulses the boy and leaves him as dead. Two reasons indicate that this aspect of the reports of Jesus' exorcisms is most probably historically reliable. On the one hand, there are stories outside the NT showing similar violence, yet they are sufficiently different to show that there is no dependence on them by the NT writers (Josephus *Ant.* 8.49; Philostratus *Vit. Ap.* 4.20). On the other hand, Mark shows no consistent use of, nor interest in, this violence.

4.3.2. Unfamiliar Techniques. Alongside these aspects of Jesus' exorcisms, which were common to other exorcists of the period, there were other features of his technique less familiar to his observers.

First, when Jesus expelled demons he did not use mechanical devices. A feature common to many other exorcists' technique was the aid of some apparatus, device or feature of speech. In Tobit 8:3 incense is burned to expel the demon; in *Jubilees* 10:10 and 12 medicines are used; in the *Genesis Apocryphon* 20 Abraham lays hands on the Pharaoh; Eleazar uses a finger ring and bowl of water (Josephus *Ant.* 8.46-49); David is said to use music (Josephus *Ant.* 6.166); in the Babylonian Talmud amulets, palm tree prickles, wood chips, ashes, pitch, cumin, dog's hair and thread are used; Lucian tells of the use of iron rings and the Magical Papyri tells of exorcists using amulets, olive branches, marjoram and special sounds.

All this seems extremely remote from: "Be bound, and come out of him" (Mk 1:25) or "You dumb and deaf spirit, I command you, come out of him, and never enter him again" (Mk 9:25). The only thing near a mechanical aid was the use of the herd of pigs.

However, the pigs were not used to exorcise the demons but to provide a habitat for the expelled demons. In this simple, unaided word of command to the demons Jesus was operating in a way similar to some of the rabbis (*b. Me'il.* 17b) and Apollonius of Tyana (Philostratus *Vit. Ap.* 4.20).

Second, unlike even some of the Jewish holy men, Jesus is not reported as praying (*see* Prayer) when he performed an exorcism. Even though Ḥanina ben Dosa did not use incantations he, like the Abraham of the Qumran Scrolls, prayed to remove the demon (*b. Ber.* 34b; cf. *b. Ta'an.* 24b; 1QapGen 20). Thus, like Apollonius (Philostratus *Vit. Ap.* 4.20) and some of the rabbis (*b. Me'il.* 17b), rather than praying Jesus is said to use simple, recognizable formulae, relying on his own resources to defeat the offending demons.

Third, and related to the previous point, Jesus did not invoke any power-authority. One frequent source of power-authority was a powerful name (cf. *PGM* IV.3019). The name of Solomon is often used and, in Acts 19:13, the sons of Sceva try using Jesus' name, as does the strange exorcist (Mk 9:38-39; par. Luke 9:49-50). In the light of Matthew 12:28 (par. Lk 11:20), where Jesus declares his source of power-authority to be the Spirit (Luke has "finger") of God, we might expect that in dealing with the demons Jesus would call on the Spirit (or "finger") of God. But he does not. Like some of the rabbis (*b. Me'il.* 17b) and Apollonius (Philostratus *Vit. Ap.* 4.20), Jesus appeared to rely on his own charismatic personal force to subdue and expel the demons.

Fourth, an element of contemporary exorcistic technique that Jesus did not use was the command *horkizō* (Aramaic, *shb'*). In the context of dealing with demons, *horkizō* meant "to charge," "adjure" or "bind" someone by another being, usually a superior power, in order to carry out the wishes of the exorcist (Mk 5:7; Acts 19:13; cf. 1 Thess 5:27). Jesus apparently neither acknowledged the use of a source of power-authority nor used the accompanying command *horkizō*. Instead, Jesus says 'I' (*egō*, Aramaic, *'ǎnā'*) command you . . ." (Mk 9:25).

The emphatic *egō* is relatively infrequent on the lips of Jesus in the Synoptic Gospels, and it is not consistently used in the words of Jesus to the demons (only at Mk 9:25). This suggests that the early church is not responsible for it in Mark 9:25. There is no known use of *egō* in contemporary incantations of adjuration by an exorcist and so it is probable that its use by Jesus is significant in understanding him as an exorcist. That is, along with no direct declaration of his source of power-authority being the Holy Spirit, and the use of *egō*, Jesus deliberately drew attention to himself and

his own resources in his ability to expel demons. Nevertheless, although Jesus believed that he was operating out of his own resources, at the same time he believed that it was God who was to be seen as operative in his activity.

4.4. Jesus' Understanding of His Exorcisms. Although his reply to John the Baptist* (Mt 11:2-6) does not allow the conclusion that the exorcism of demons was the key to Jesus' ministry, it was at least one of the most important aspects of his ministry (Mt 12:28 [par. Lk 11:20]).

It is in the collection of sayings usually called the Beelzebul Controversy that we discover most about how Jesus understood his exorcisms (Mk 3:22-27 [par. Mt 9:32-34 and 12:22-30; Lk 11:14-23]). In turn, the probably authentic saying "If by the Spirit (Luke has "finger") of God that I cast out demons then the kingdom of God has come upon you" tells us most about Jesus' understanding of his exorcisms. With due regard for the difficulty of establishing the exact nuance of what Jesus may have said, taking account of the emphatic "I," which is most likely a reflection of the Aramaic, this verse shows that Jesus believed that where the Spirit was operating in him there was the coming of the kingdom of God (see 4.3.2. above; *see* Kingdom of God).

For Jesus his ministry of exorcism was not preparatory to the kingdom, nor a sign of the kingdom nor an indication that the kingdom had arrived, nor even an illustration of the kingdom, but actually the kingdom of God itself in operation.

The parable* of the strong man (Mt 12:29 [par. Mk 3:27; Lk 11:21-22]) shows that Jesus believed that in his exorcisms he was binding Satan in order to plunder his property—those hitherto held by Satan. In pre-Christian literature there is the expectation that the Messiah (*see* Christ) would do battle with Satan, but Jesus is the first to make a specific connection between the relatively ordinary events of exorcism and the defeat of Satan, between exorcism and eschatology. However, there are sayings which assume the continuing existence of Satan and his final defeat in the final judgment and are generally agreed to contain significant traces of authentic Jesus tradition (e.g., Mt 13:24-30). This tension is resolved in the light of Isaiah 24:21-22 and *1 Enoch* 10:4-6 where the defeat of Satan or evil is expected to take place in two stages. Thus, Jesus probably believed that his exorcisms were the first stage of the binding of Satan and the final defeat would take place in the final judgment (Mt 13:30).

5. Emphases of the Gospel Writers.

The Synoptic Evangelists share similar views on the

Devil and demons and Jesus' dealings with them. The Fourth Gospel has a unique contribution to make on this theme.

5.1. The Gospel of Matthew. There is a variety of names used for the Devil in Matthew (see 1. above). The "Devil," his most common name (4:1, 5, 8, 11; 13:39; 25:41), used interchangeably with "Satan" (4:10; 12:26; 16:23) and at the head of an army of evil demons (12:24; 25:41), is the archenemy of God and the ministry of Jesus. In 4:13 the term "the Tempter" (*ho peirazos;* also in 1 Thess 3:5) conveys the idea of the Devil putting Jesus to the test.

Matthew's view of Jesus as an exorcist is distinctive among the Synoptic Evangelists. Most notable is Matthew's playing down the role of exorcism in Jesus' ministry. Thus, Matthew leaves out Mark's programmatic story of the demoniac in the synagogue (Mk 1:21-28) and does not include an exorcism story until 8:24-34. Yet, for Matthew, Jesus' dealing with demons is important in revealing the significance of Jesus. The passage 12:22-30 (cf. 9:32-34) gathers up much of what Matthew says elsewhere on the topic. In this pericope Matthew has introduced the idea that the demoniac was blind (cf. 9:32-34; Lk 11:14) to highlight the messianic significance of Jesus' exorcisms (Is 42:7, 16; 29:18 [32:3]; 35:5; 42:18-20; 43:8; 61:1 [LXX]). The crowd is said to perceive this, for the people respond: "Can this be the Son of David?"

Following the brief exorcism story is the Pharisees' accusation that Jesus was empowered by the Prince of Demons (12:24), which is answered in part in the parable of the strong man (12:29). This parable shows that Matthew believed that in his exorcisms Jesus engaged in the first part of Satan's defeat. The explanation of the parable of the wheat and the weeds (13:36-43) shows that he also believed that Jesus would be involved in the second and final stage of the defeat of Satan (cf. 8:29). The eschatological significance of Jesus' exorcisms is spelled out in the well-known saying "But if I in the Spirit of God cast out demons, then has come upon you the kingdom of God" (12:28). This significance given to the exorcisms is also seen in the way Matthew retells the exorcism stories. That is, Matthew removes the idea of a demon binding or putting a supernatural restriction on Jesus (*horkizō,* 8:29; par. Mk 5:7). The earliest manuscripts have very little punctuation, so in 8:29 Matthew may have intended the demoniacs to declare rather than ask: "You have come here to torment us before the time." In "come" (*erchomai*) Matthew is probably alluding to the coming of God's kingdom and his anointed messenger (6:10; 16:28). In saying that the torment is "before time" (*pro kairou*)—that is, before the final

judgment*— Matthew is saying that in Jesus the eschatological torture of the demons has already begun. The powerful status of Jesus is also seen in this story where the dialog between Jesus and the demoniac is reduced so that all that remains is the simple authoritative command "Go"—the only time Matthew mentions Jesus' words to demons.

From Matthew's perspective the Son of God (*see* Son of God) does not need to use complicated techniques. And in the healing of the epileptic boy Jesus suffers no ignorance of the patient's history (7:17-18) and is instantly and completely successful (17:18; cf. Mk 9:24-27). In the story of the healing of the Canaanite woman's daughter, the woman kneels or worships (*proskuneō*) Jesus and initially addresses him: "Have mercy on me, O Lord, Son of David." She goes on to address Jesus as "Lord" three times (15:21-28; Mk 7:24-30). In short, for Matthew Jesus' successful dealings with the demons reveal Jesus to be the Son of David or of God (*see* Son of David).

5.2. The Gospel of Mark. Mark uses the word *Satan* for the Devil. Satan's key function is to deflect Jesus from his mission, as in the Temptation story (1:13) and through Peter's rebuke, which Mark identifies with Satan speaking (8:33). If Mark intends the sower (4:3, 14) to be Jesus then, again, Satan is depicted as destroying the work of Jesus through taking away the word planted in people (4:15). As in the other Synoptic Gospels, Satan is the archdemon, also called Beelzebul, whose minions, or himself directly, possess people (3:22-27).

Mark uses the word *demon* thirteen times and *unclean spirit* eleven times, and sometimes synonymously (cf. 3:22, 30; 7:25-26). "Demons" are only mentioned in the context of exorcism (1:34, 39; 3:15). They cause people to convulse and cry out (1:26), to have preternatural strength, to injure themselves (5:3-5), they throw people down, cause foaming at the mouth, grinding of the teeth (9:18) and provoke people to destroy themselves (9:22). Demons are able to enter animals as well (5:11-13).

One of the questions addressed in Mark's Gospel is the identity of Jesus (1:27; 2:7; 4:41; 6:1-6, 14-16, 49-50, 54; 8:27-28). Mark asserts from the beginning (1:1), and has God confirm (1:11), that Jesus is the Son of God. Then, throughout the first part of his story, Mark shows the human characters ignorant of Jesus' true identity. Yet through the cries of the demons, Mark is able to remind his readers who Jesus is (1:24-25, 34; 3:11-12; 5:7).

From Mark's perspective the importance of Jesus' dealing with the demons can be gauged by noting that one of Jesus' first public acts is an exorcism. And of his thirteen healing stories the largest single category is that of exorcism (1:21-28; 5:1-20; 7:24-30; 9:14-29). Then Mark heightens the importance of Jesus' exorcisms through the summaries of Jesus' ministry (1:32-34; 3:11-12).

Mark portrays Jesus using techniques that would have been familiar to his readers from their knowledge of other exorcists. Jesus "rebukes" (*epitimaō*, 1:25; 3:12; 9:25), "muzzles" (*phimoō*, 1:25-26) and "commands" (*epitassō*, 9:25) that demons never enter a person again. Jesus uses the supposed power in a name to gain ascendancy over a demon (5:9), transfers demons from one habitat to another (5:12-13) and exorcises from a distance (7:24-29). In confronting the demons Jesus is empowered by the Spirit and is doing battle against Satan (3:22-30). Through the exorcisms (1:24, 27) and confrontations with the demons (1:34; 3:11-12, 23-27; 5:7) and the demonic (4:41) the Jesus of Mark is shown to be the Son of God (3:11; 5:7).

5.3. The Gospel of Luke. The name *Devil* in Luke is not used of the false accuser of the pre-Christian Greek literature but is used interchangeably with *Satan*. In Luke 11:15-19 *Beelzebul* is used of the archevil demon standing in opposition to the mission of Jesus.

As in Matthew the Devil first appears in the Temptation story (4:1-13). In Luke the passage ends by saying that the Devil "left him for awhile" (4:13). The reader, therefore, expects the enemy of Jesus to reappear in Luke's story. Indeed, contrary to Conzelmann's view, Jesus' ministry is far from Satan-free in Luke. Luke often depicts Jesus contending with evil spiritual beings throughout his ministry (4:33-37; 6:18; 7:21; 8:2, 26-39; 9:37-43; 11:14; 13:11, 32). In these encounters Luke believed that Jesus was dealing with Satan (11:14-23; 13:11, 16; cf. 10:17-18). Like Mark, Luke depicts Satan or the Devil as attempting to destroy the work of Jesus, but Luke more clearly shows the Devil as the enemy of the early church too (Lk 8:11-12; Acts 6:7; 13:5).

The most direct attack by Satan on Jesus since the Temptation comes when Satan enters into Judas so that Judas goes away to betray Jesus (22:3-4). Luke extends Satan's attack to demand the disciples' surrender (Lk 22:31-32; cf. 2 Sam 15:20-21; Job 1:6-12). In this episode Luke expresses his view that the power of Satan is limited in contrast to the authority of Jesus' prayer for his followers. Satan is able to "shake in a sieve" (*siniazō*) but not totally destroy Peter and the disciples.

In the story of the return of the seventy (-two) disciples Luke relates a vision of Jesus which can be translated: "I have been seeing Satan falling like lightning from heaven" (10:18). Luke is emphasizing that the eschatological expectation of Satan's downfall was already taking place, that it was an ongoing process and linked to the exorcistic ministry of the church. In the Beelzebul pericope Luke has already associated exorcism and the destruction of Satan.

Unlike the Fourth Gospel, the cross is not associated with the defeat of Satan, though the crucifixion is a battle with Satan (Luke 22:53; *see* Death of Jesus). The stories of demonic activity in Acts show that Luke did not believe that Satan had been finally defeated in the Temptation, in his exorcisms, or in the death and resurrection* of Jesus. It would seem that Luke maintained the view of Jesus (see 4.4. above) that the ministry of Jesus was the first stage in the defeat of Satan, the final stage to be in the eschaton (cf. 8:31).

Although the first three healing stories in Luke picture Jesus dealing with demons (4:31-37, 38-41), he broadens Mark's view of the early stages of the ministry of Jesus to emphasize his healing and teaching (4:18). Jesus' exorcisms reveal him as "the Son of God" and Messiah (4:41; 9:35, 37) and are performed in the power of the Spirit, for in the early part of Luke Jesus' sonship is linked with the coming of the Spirit (1:35; 3:22; 4:3, 9; cf. 4:18 and 31-37). This connection between being empowered by the Spirit, healing—particularly exorcism—and christology is obviously important to Luke for he draws attention to it in a summary of Jesus' ministry in Acts 10:38 (cf. Lk 4:43).

Unlike Mark, Luke sustains the impression that exorcism remained an important and integral part of Jesus' ministry (cf. 7:21 and Mt 11:4; Lk 13:32). In Acts 10:36-39 Luke gives his description of the importance and place of exorcism in Jesus' ministry showing that Jesus was an exorcist because of the Holy Spirit; in other words, that God was with him and that exorcism was the work of God.

Thus, in retelling the exorcism stories, Luke heightens the ability and authority* of Jesus. For example, in the healing of the demoniac in the synagogue the demon does not cry out after Jesus' command of submission (Mk 1:26; par. Lk 4:35). In the healing of the epileptic boy Jesus asks no questions; he lacks no knowledge (Lk 9:37-43; cf. Mk 9:16, 21). In Mark this healing seems to be in two stages—the demon leaves the boy as dead so that he has to be raised—but in Luke Jesus is immediately successful (9:42). Luke faithfully reflects the tradition he receives from Mark and does not question that Jesus, with few variations, used the same techniques as his contemporaries.

In 4:39 Luke says Jesus "stood over" Simon's

mother-in-law (cf. Mk 1:31). The practice of an exorcist standing over the patient has its roots in ancient Babylonian healings, and in the NT period it is directly paralleled in the Magical Papyri (e.g., *PGM* IV.745, 1229, 2735) where the focus of attention in healing was often directed toward the head. This story, in which he says the woman had a spirit of infirmity and was bound by Satan, blurs the distinction between healing in general and exorcism and, in effect, gives all sickness a demonic and cosmic dimension; in all healing God's adversary is being subdued.

5.4. The Gospel of John. In the Synoptic Gospels Jesus is accused of being in league with the Devil (Mt 12:22-30; par. Mk 3:20-27; Lk 11:14-23). In John's Gospel Jesus faces the less serious charge of being possessed by a demon (7:20). Nevertheless, for Jesus to be possessed meant that he was thought to be mad (10:20-21) and a Samaritan (8:48-49, 52), in that he was putting forth heretical or unacceptable and unbelievable opinions (cf. Justin *Apol.* 26.1-5; Origen *Contra Cels* 6.11).

As in the Synoptic Gospels, the Devil is portrayed as attempting to destroy Jesus and his mission. Judas the betrayer is called a devil (6:70), and Satan is said to direct and enter Judas (13:2, 27). As in the Qumran literature (see 1. above), people are depicted as children belonging either to God or the Devil. In 8:44 the Devil is contrasted with Jesus. The Devil is said to control his "children" (cf. 1 Jn 3:8), to be a murderer from the beginning (cf. Wis 2:24; contrast the "Word" in Jn 1), to contain no truth and to be the father of lies. In the death and resurrection, or "hour" (12:23-36) of Jesus, the Devil, or Ruler of this World, is judged and brought down (12:31; 14:30; 16:11). However, the Devil remains sufficiently powerful for Jesus to pray that his followers would be kept from *tou ponērou* ("the evil," 17:15), probably meaning the Evil One (cf. 1 Jn 2:13, 14; 3:12; 5:18, 19) until the judgment on the last day (12:48).

The Fourth Gospel (as well as the epistles and Apocalypse of John) says nothing about exorcism or of Jesus being an exorcist. In light of the evidence that Jesus was an exorcist (see 4.2. above), it does not seem reasonable to suggest that the author(s) of the Johannine material knew nothing of the tradition that Jesus was an exorcist. Rather, the Johannine literature probably suppresses or ignores this tradition. Can this be explained?

It has been thought that John was embarrassed about portraying Jesus as a man of this time, using healing techniques of his contemporaries. However, this cannot be the case, for John is happy to include other techniques familiar to other healers: healing from a distance (4:46-54) and the use of spittle (9:1-7).

Rather, a number of aspects of Johannine theology have probably contributed to the suppression of Jesus' association with exorcism. First is the Johannine notion of the function of Jesus' miracles (*see* Miracles and Miracle Stories). The end of an earlier edition of the Gospel than we now have spelled out the Johannine understanding of the role of the miracles of Jesus as follows: "Jesus did many other signs in the presence of the disciples, which are not written in this book; but these are written that you may believe that Jesus is the Christ, the Son of God, and that believing you may have life in his name" (20:30-31). In other words, for John the miracles are considered so to reveal the identity of Jesus that the readers would conclude that he was the Christ. So not only did John choose spectacular miracles, but miracles which were thought to be the work of God, like the turning of water into wine. By contrast, to associate Jesus with the relatively common healing of exorcism performed by many other healers would have appeared banal.

A second factor which may have contributed to the Johannine material not mentioning Jesus being an exorcist may be linked with the playing down of the theme of the kingdom of God. In the Synoptic Gospels exorcism and the kingdom of God are so closely associated that for John to exclude one probably meant that he felt obliged to exclude the other.

Third, in the Synoptic Gospels the defeat of Satan is linked with Jesus' exorcisms. In John the defeat of Satan is linked with the cross (Jn 14:30; 16:11). This shift in Johannine theology probably carried with it the need to remove reference to exorcisms, which other Christians had associated with the defeat of Satan. Probably for these reasons the Johannine material omits the tradition that Jesus was an exorcist. *See also* HEALING; TEMPTATION.

BIBLIOGRAPHY. F. C. Conybeare, "The Demonology of the Old Testament," *JQR* 8 (1896) 576-608; 9 (1897) 59-114, 444-70, 581-602; P. L. Day, *An Adversary in Heaven: Satan in the Hebrew Bible* (Atlanta: Scholars Press, 1988); J. D. G. Dunn and G. H. Twelftree, "Demon-Possession and Exorcism in the New Testament," *Churchman* 94 (1980) 210-25; S. Eitrem, *Some Notes on the Demonology in the New Testament* (2d ed.; Osloae: A. W. Brøgger, 1966); S. R. Garrett, *The Demise of the Devil: Magic and the Demonic in Luke's Writings* (Minneapolis: Augsburg Fortress, 1989); L. Gaston, "Beelzebul," *TZ* 18 (1962) 247-55; J. B. Green, "Jesus and the Daughter of Abraham (Luke 13:10-17): Test Case for a Lukan Perspective on the Miracles of Jesus," *CBQ* 51 (1989) 643-54; R. H. Hiers, "Satan,

Demons, and the Kingdom of God," *SJT* 27 (1974) 35-47; P. W. Hollenbach, "Jesus, Demoniacs, and Public Authorities: A Socio-Historical Study," *JAAR* 49 (1981) 567-88; J. M. Hull, *Hellenistic Magic and the Synoptic Tradition* (London: SCM, 1974); E. Langton, *Essentials of Demonology* (London: Epworth, 1949); idem, *Good and Evil Spirits: A Study of the Jewish and Christian Doctrine* (London: SPCK, 1942); T. Ling, *The Significance of Satan* (London: SPCK, 1961); E. C. B. MacLaurin, "Beelzeboul," *NovT* 20 (1978) 156-60; J. B. Russell, *The Devil: Perspectives of Evil from Antiquity to Primitive Christianity* (London and Ithaca: Cornell University, 1977); idem, *Satan: The Early Christian Tradition* (Ithaca: Cornell University, 1981); H. Schlier, *Principalities and Powers in the New Testament* (Frieburg: Herder; Edinburgh and London: Nelson; 1961); J. Z. Smith, "Towards Interpreting Demonic Powers in Hellenistic and Roman Antiquity," *ANRW* II.16.1 (1978) 425-439; G. H. Twelftree, *Christ Triumphant: Exorcism Then and Now* (London: Hodder and Stoughton, 1985); G. H. Twelftree, *"EI DE . . . EGŌ EKBALLŌ TA DAIMONIA . . .," in Gospel Perspectives 6: The Miracles of Jesus*, ed. D. Wenham and C. Blomberg (Sheffield: JSOT, 1986) 361-400.

G. H. Twelftree

DEMYTHOLOGIZING. *See* MYTH.

DESERT. *See* MOUNTAIN AND WILDERNESS.

DESTRUCTION OF JERUSALEM

1. The Jewish War
2. The Destruction of Jerusalem
3. The Gospels and the Destruction of Jerusalem

1. The Jewish War.

The destruction of Jerusalem in A.D. 70 brought to a climax a war between the Romans (*see* Rome) and the Jews of Palestine. The war has become known as the Jewish War following the lead of the first-century Jewish historian Flavius Josephus (*see* Josephus), who referred to his seven-volume history of events leading up to the fall of Jerusalem as *peri tou Ioudaikou polemou* ("concerning the Jewish War," *Life* 74 §412).

1.1. Events Precipitating the War. After many years of tension under Roman rule, several crucial events directly led to the outbreak of the war. On the one hand, the policies and cruelty of the Roman procurator Florus (A.D. 64-66) set the stage for the war (Josephus *Ant.* 20.11.1 §257; Tacitus *Hist.* 5.10.1). First, he antagonized the Jews by siding with the Greeks (*see* Hellenism) in several incidents during 66 in a long-standing, civil-rights conflict between the Jews and

Greeks of Caesarea. Then in the summer of 66 he took seventeen talents from the sacrosanct Temple* treasury to allay governmental expenses (Josephus *J.W.* 2.14.6 §293) and compounded the offense by having Roman troops sack part of the city, scourge and crucify prisoners in reaction to the resulting public protest (*J.W.* 2.14.6-8 §§296-308). When he later moved two cohorts (c. 1200 men) to Jerusalem, crowds prevented them from reaching the Roman garrison at the Antonia in a confrontation that resulted in a stampede that left many dead (*J.W.* 2.15.5 §§325-28).

On the other hand, in response to Florus's activities the Jews laid the "foundation for the war" by stopping sacrifices for Gentiles* and thus the twice-daily sacrifices for the emperor's welfare (*J.W.* 2.17.2 §409). This was an act of rebellion. The sacrifices represented a special concession from the Romans to the Jews in lieu of their participating in the rituals of emperor worship (*J.W.* 2.17.3 §§415-16). Florus's activities in Jerusalem gave rise to a group of insurgents in Jerusalem (*see* Revolutionary Movements) who captured the Antonia and massacred the Roman garrison there in August of 66. Later, they attacked Herod's palace and the camp of Florus's cohort, and massacred the Roman forces after they had agreed to surrender in exchange for safe passage (*J.W.* 2.17.7-8 §§430-40). With the Roman fortress of Masada having already fallen to a rebel force (*J.W.* 2.17.2 §408), the revolt spread to other attacks against the Romans and the taking of the Herodian fortresses of Cypros near Jericho and Machaeros in Perea (*J.W.* 2.18.6 §§484-86).

1.2. The Course of the War. After the Jews' successful attack and massacre of the Roman forces in Jerusalem, the capture of the surrounding fortresses in early fall of 66 and the outbreaks of violence in Caesarea, the Decapolis and Syrian cities (*J.W.* 2.18.1-5 §§457-80), it was time for Rome's intervention. Cestius Gallus, the Syrian legate, assembled an army of 30,000 and moved on the province on Rome's behalf. He took control of Galilee* with little resistance (*J.W.* 2.18.11 §§510-12) and then marched on Jerusalem, eventually making his camp a mile to the north on Mt. Scopus in November of 66 (*J.W.* 2.19.4 §§527-28). Though victory was in his grasp, Cestius, for some inexplicable reason, abandoned the siege after about a week (*J.W.* 2.19.6-7 §§538-40). Withdrawing his forces in retreat, he suffered nearly 5,000 casualties and the loss of valuable military supplies to the Jews (*J.W.* 2.19.7-9 §§540-55).

During the winter months of 66/67 the Jews made preparation for the inevitable attack by Rome in the spring by setting up a revolutionary government throughout the province. The peace party led by the high priests, having greater influence on the populace than the rebel leaders, initially took control and selected the ex-high priest Ananus as commander of the forces (*J.W.* 2.20.3 §§562-64). The revolutionary government divided the territory into six districts (Idumea, Perea, Jericho, western Judea, northeastern Judea, Galilee) and set up military governors to establish civil administration and prepare for war (*J.W.* 2.20.3-4 §§562-68). Josephus was made the military governor of Galilee (*J.W.* 2.20.4 §568; *Life* 7 §29). Many distinguished inhabitants, however, took the occasion to leave Jerusalem as if it were a "sinking ship" (*J.W.* 2.20.1 §556).

In the spring of 67 the Roman general Vespasian, sent by Nero, and his son Titus arrived with an army of nearly 60,000 men (*J.W.* 3.4.2 §69). Using friendly Sepphoris as a base in Galilee, Vespasian encountered little resistance in that district except from the fortified places where most of the resistance had moved. His first sustained opposition came from the hilltop fortress Jotapata under Josephus' command. After a seven-week siege it fell in July 67 (*J.W.* 3.7.5-31 §§150-288; 3.7.33-36 §§316-39). Josephus surrendered and was taken prisoner (*J.W.* 3.8.8 §392; cf. 4.10.7 §§622-29). Then the Roman forces took the port of Joppa (*J.W.* 3.9.7-8 §§445-61) in late July to protect the supply routes, Tiberias in August (*J.W.* 3.9.2-4 §§414-31), Tarichaeae in September (*J.W.* 3.10.1-5 §§462-502), the fortress of Gamala in October after a four-week siege (*J.W.* 4.1.3-7 §§11-53; 4.1.9-10 §§62-83) and finally Gischala. There the rebel leader John of Gischala escaped for Jerusalem with his band of followers (*J.W.* 4.2.1-5 §§84-120). Having subdued the district of Galilee, Vespasian set up garrisons throughout the area during the winter months to maintain control.

Military activities resumed in the spring of 68. In March Vespasian took the district of Perea, except for the fortress Machaeros, when the wealthy surrendered the capital, Gadara (*J.W.* 4.8.3 §413). He then moved through western Judea with little resistance and took Idumea (*J.W.* 4.8.2 §§443-48). Jericho capitulated on his arrival in June (*J.W.* 4.8.1-2 §§450-51), leaving him with control of almost all the province of Judea. He then set up strategic military camps to prepare for the attack on Jerusalem (*J.W.* 4.9.1 §§486-90).

The actual siege of Jerusalem, however, was delayed for nearly two years. First came the news of Nero's death in June 68. Since a military command terminated with the death of the emperor who had given it, Vespasian waited for word from the new emperor

(*J.W.* 4.9.2 §§497-98). But no word came out of the ensuing political turmoil in Rome, with Galba's accession and assassination in January 69, then Otho's accession and assassination in April 69, followed by Vitellius' struggle for power. In June of 69, still having received no official word, Vespasian resumed military action on his own and consolidated his gains in Judea, only to break off the activities in July when he was proclaimed emperor by the Roman forces in the East (*J.W.* 4.10.4, 6 §601, §§616-20). After consolidating his strength in the East in the spring of 70 he left Alexandria, Egypt, for Rome and placed Titus in charge of taking Jerusalem (*J.W.* 4.11.5 §658).

2. The Destruction of Jerusalem.

Josephus, our primary source of information about the war, describes the isolation, surrounding, siege and fall of Jerusalem in *The Jewish War* books 4—6. It is a period of political turmoil in Rome, a change of Roman command in Judea and a disastrous civil war among the Jews within the walls of Jerusalem. The city eventually fell to the Romans but more as a result of Jewish self-destruction than Roman military power.

2.1. Civil War. The city was torn by internal power struggles almost from the beginning of the war. On the one hand, the political forces were divided between extremists and moderates, a war party and a peace party. On the other hand, the extremists themselves were divided not only from the moderates but among themselves.

Initially, after the successful rout of Cestius, the moderates had gained control of Jerusalem under the leadership of the ex-high priest Ananus. By the end of 67, however, the war party led by Eleazar son of Simon, who had distinguished himself in the attack on the retreating Cestius, and a group around him which Josephus called the "Zealots" (*J.W.* 2.8.13 §§160-61), gained strength from numerous other extremists and brigands who had moved to Jerusalem after Vespasian's invasion of Galilee (*J.W.* 4.3.3 §§135-36).

Joined by these extremist forces Eleazar and his band began terrorizing the moderates and attacking the authority of the high priests (*J.W.* 4.3.4-6 §§138-50). They seized the Temple and replaced the high priest with a priest chosen by lot (*J.W.* 4.3.6 §§147-50). Ananus, supported by a public aroused by the sacrilege, regained the outer courts and pinned Eleazar and the Zealots inside (*J.W.* 4.3.11-12 §§193-207). The Zealots, however, were encouraged by John of Gischala, who had come to Jerusalem after being routed from Gischala by Titus (*J.W.* 4.2.4 §106; 4.3.1-3 §§121-28, §§135-37) and was supposedly on the side of Ananus and the moderates, to seek help from the

Idumeans (*J.W.* 4.4.1 §§224-32). Eventually, a large Idumean force entered the city under cover of a severe storm (*J.W.* 4.4.6-7 §§288-304), linked up with the Zealots by retaking the outer courts and killing the ex-high priest Ananus (*J.W.* 4.5.1-2 §§305-17). The Zealots then went on such a brutal rampage, attacking supporters of the moderates, that the majority of the Idumean force broke with Eleazar and returned home. Others went over to John of Gischala and his band (*J.W.* 4.5§5-6.1 §§345-65). The extremists had gained control of the city.

Chronology of Events Leading to the Destruction of Jerusalem

66 August	Jewish insurgents capture Antonia; Cestius, Syrian legate, attacks Jerusalem and retreats.
67 Spring-Fall	Roman army under Vespasian subdues Galilee.
67-68 Winter	Zealot party formed under Eleazar controls Jerusalem.
68 Spring	Vespasian subdues Judea.
June	Nero's death and ensuing turmoil in leadership delays siege of Jerusalem.
69 Spring	Turmoil within Jerusalem with three parties vying for power.
June	Vespasian resumes campaign.
July	Vespasian proclaimed emperor and departs.
70 Spring	Command given to Titus, Vespasian's son.
May	Titus breaches Agrippa's wall.
August	Titus takes and burns the Temple.
September	Jerusalem sacked and burned.

The Zealots under Eleazar, however, soon split with John of Gischala because of his desire for absolute power (*J.W.* 4.7.1 §§389-90; 5.1.2 §§5-8). In the spring of 69 these two rival groups were joined by a third led by Simon bar Giora from Gerasa. Simon had first moved to Masada after losing his command in northeastern Judea in 67 (*J.W.* 4.9.3 §§503-8). When he learned about Ananus' death, he gathered a force from the refugees of the Zealot's brutal campaign in Jerusalem, along with some Idumeans, and pitched camp outside Jerusalem (*J.W.* 4.9.8 §§538-44). From

there he was admitted into the city by the remainder of the moderates and a populace wearied of the brutality of John and the Zealots (*J.W.* 4.9.11 §§573-76).

In the struggle that followed Simon became the "master of Jerusalem" (*J.W.* 4.9.12 §577), with an army of nearly 15,000 that controlled most of the city. John occupied the outer courts of the Temple and part of the Lower City of Jerusalem with 6,000 men. The Zealots held the inner Temple with 2400 (*J.W.* 5.6.1 §§248-51). During Titus' siege of Jerusalem in the spring of 70, John used the opening of the Temple during the Passover to storm the inner courts and force the Zealots to join him against Simon (*J.W.* 5.3.1 §§98-105). Only as Titus was about to breach the walls did he reluctantly agree to recognize and work with Simon in defense of the city (*J.W.* 5.7.4 §§278-79). Meanwhile, the civil war had not only cost unity and hundreds of lives, but the vital stores of grain had been destroyed by fire during the internal conflict (*J.W.* 5.1.4-5 §§22-28). According to Josephus, the ensuing famine alone cost over 600,000 lives (*J.W.* 5.13.7 §569).

2.2. The Fall of Jerusalem. In the spring of 70 Titus took command of the Roman forces. During Passover of 70 he moved his troops closer to the city walls and began his assault from the north. In May he breached Agrippa's wall after nearly two weeks of attack (*J.W.* 5.6.4—7.2 §§275-302).

When the Jewish resistance appeared to slow the preparations for the siege of the second north wall and the Antonia, Titus threw up a four-mile circumvallation around the city with troops stationed at posts along the wall to prevent provisions from reaching the famine-starved inhabitants (*J.W.* 5.12.2 §§502-11). On more than one occasion Josephus noted the impossibility of escape from the city, a condition that existed even prior to the building of the Roman wall around it (*J.W.* 4.9.1 §490). Attempted escape from the city meant death either from the rebels on the inside or from the Romans on the outside (*J.W.* 4.9.10 §§564-65; 5.13.4 §551; 6.6.2 §323).

In July Titus broke through the second north wall and the Antonia, and moved his forces into position to attack the north and west Temple fortifications. He managed to get control of the outer courts on the ninth of August and took the inner courts on the tenth, plundering the Temple, setting it on fire and slaughtering thousands (*J.W.* 6.4.7—5.2 §§260-85). John's troops, who had held the Temple and the Lower City, escaped to the Upper City (*J.W.* 6.5.1 §277). In celebration the Romans desecrated the Jewish sanctuary by offering a sacrifice to their standards in the outer court (*J.W.* 6.6.1 §316).

In September Titus ordered the burning and sacking of the city (*J.W.* 6.6.3 §354). After taking the Lower City, his forces took the Upper City, breaching it in less than a day and gaining control of Herod's palace and towers (*J.W.* 6.8.4 §§392-99). John, who along with Simon had escaped into underground passages, eventually surrendered (*J.W.* 6.9.5 §433). Simon was captured attempting to tunnel his way out (*J.W.* 7.2.1 §§26-33). Titus then had the Temple and city walls razed "to the ground," except for Herod's three towers and a part of the west wall, which he left standing to show the "character and strength" of the city (*J.W.* 6.9.1 §413; 7.1.1 §§1-4). Since it was too late in the year to sail to Rome, he waited until the spring to return with his spoils from the Temple and nearly 100,000 prisoners, including Simon and John, to join Vespasian in a triumphal march in Rome in 71 (*J.W.* 7.5.3-6 §§121-57).

The fall and destruction of Jerusalem effectively ended the Jewish War. The only resistance remained in the fortresses of Herodian, Machaeros and Masada. Their reductions followed in 71-73, with Masada, commanded by Eleazar son of Jair (*J.W.* 7.8.1 §253), the last to fall (*J.W.* 7.8.5—9.2 §§304-406).

3. The Gospels and the Destruction of Jerusalem.

Apart from the mention of the destruction of a city in the parable of the great supper in Matthew 22:7 (frequently taken as an allusion to the destruction of Jerusalem) and the lament over Jerusalem in Matthew 23:37-38 (par. Lk 13:34-35), only Luke directly alludes to a siege of the city. The lament of Matthew 23:37-38 and its parallel in Luke 13:34-35 speak generally of a coming abandonment and desolation of her "house" in the language of Jeremiah 12:7 and 22:5. By contrast, Luke 19:43-44, with the reference to a siege and surrounding of Jerusalem, comes closest to the actual events described by Josephus (19:43-44; cf. *J.W.* 5.6.2 §262; 5.11.4 §466; 5.12.2 §§508-11), while Luke 21:20 (cf. Mk 13:14) identifies the city's approaching "desolation" (cf. Dan 12:11 LXX) with the surrounding of the city by troops (cf. *J.W.* 5.11.6 §§486-90). The frequent reference to Jerusalem's destruction corresponds to the prominent role of Jerusalem for Luke-Acts.

All four Gospels have Jesus making reference to a future destruction of the Temple (Mt 24:2; Mk 13:2; Lk 21:6; cf. Mt 26:61; Mk 14:38; Jn 2:19), an event that of necessity would seem to assume the fall of Jerusalem. Furthermore, the warning against the "abomination of desolation" in the Olivet Discourse (Mk 13:14; cf. Dan 12:11) has often been interpreted as referring to the Roman desecrating presence in one form or another in the Temple during the war.

Despite those who would attribute these references to the influence of hindsight, nothing in either of the references to the fate of Jerusalem or the Temple corresponds so closely to the events as to necessitate the sayings being created in the light of the events of 66—70. Luke's description of the siege and razing of Jerusalem (19:43-44; 21:20) reflects the normal strategy for taking a fortified city in the ancient world (e.g., Jer 6:3, 6). Neither reference contains any distinctive feature of the destruction of Jerusalem such as the barricading of the city with a four-mile wall, the disastrous civil war and famine from within, or the fall of the Temple. Some elements actually conflict with the information given by Josephus. For example, the Roman presence and wall leaves the warning against entering and the summons to flee the city (21:20) without a historical reference point. Furthermore, the Roman presence in the Temple could hardly have represented the "abomination of desolation" (Mk 13:14). Rome breached the Temple at the climax of the war, a fact that again makes the call for those in Judea to flee anachronistic: by that time they had been conquered and under control of Roman forces for nearly two years. The frequent use of OT prophetic imagery in these passages indicates that these sayings were prophecies of impending judgment. The events of 70 may have given poignancy to Luke's sayings in 19:43-44 and 21:20, but the underlying prophecy of the coming destruction of Jerusalem and the Temple ultimately have their roots in Jesus' ministry.

See also APOCALYPTIC TEACHING; REVOLUTIONARY MOVEMENTS; TEMPLE.

BIBLIOGRAPHY. M. Aberbach, *The Roman-Jewish War (66-70 A.D.): Its Origins and Consequences* (London: R. Golub, 1966); P. Bilde, "The Causes of the Jewish War according to Josephus," *JSJ* 10 (1979) 179-202; S. G. F. Brandon, *The Fall of Jerusalem and the Christian Church* (London: SPCK, 1951); C. H. Dodd, "The Fall of Jerusalem and the 'Abomination of Desolation,' " *JRS* 37 (1947) 47-54; L. Gaston, *No Stone on Another: Studies in the Significance of the Fall of Jerusalem in the Synoptic Gospels* (SNTMS 23; Leiden: E. J. Brill, 1970); M. Goodman, "The First Jewish Revolt: Social Conflict and the Problem of Debt," *JJS* 33 (1982) 417-27; M. Hengel, *Die Zeloten* (Leiden: E. J. Brill, 1976); R. A. Horsley, "Banditry and the Revolt against Rome AD 66-70," *CBQ* 43 (1981) 409-32; B. Reicke, "Synoptic Prophecies on the Destruction of Jerusalem," in *Studies in New Testament and Early Christian Literature: Essays in Honor of A. P. Wikgren*, ed. D. E. Aune (*SNT*

33; Leiden: E. J. Brill, 1972) 121-34; D. M. Rhoads, *Israel in Revolution 6-74 C.E.* (Philadelphia: Fortress, 1976); E. M. Smallwood, *The Jews under Roman Rule: From Pompey to Diocletian: A Study in Political Relations* (SJLA 20; Leiden: E. J. Brill, 1981).

R. A. Guelich

DEVIL. *See* DEMON, DEVIL, SATAN.

DIASPORA. *See* GENTILES; HELLENISM.

DISCIPLES

The first-century Greco-Roman world displayed a variety of religious, philosophical and political leaders, each of whom had followers committed to their cause, teaching and beliefs. While several different terms designated these followers, *disciple* was one of the most commonly used. It also became the most commonly used term to designate the followers of Jesus, to the extent that in Jesus' so-called Great Commission the objective of the world-wide mission was to "make disciples" of all nations (Mt 28:19; *see* Gentiles).

    1. Terminology and Concept
    2. Disciples of Jesus
    3. The Twelve
    4. The Early Church

1. Terminology and Concept.

The English word *disciple* normally designates a "follower," "adherent" or "student" of a great master, religious leader or teacher.* *Disciple* is the word used most commonly to translate the Greek word *mathētēs* and the Hebrew words *talmîd* and *limmûd*.

1.1. OT Background. Disciple terminology is strikingly scarce in the OT, but other evidence points to master-disciple relationships within the national life of Israel.* The single occurrence of *talmîd* in the OT (*mathētēs* does not occur in the LXX) indicates a student or apprentice in musical instruction (1 Chron 25:8). The prophet Isaiah refers to the group gathered around him as "my disciples" (Is 8:16; *limmûday*), and their relationship is characterized by an educational process accentuating speaking and listening (Is 50:4; *limmûdim*). The term *limmûdim* was used to specify the "disciples" of Yahweh (Is 54:13), indicating that *limmûdim* could be disciples of both Yahweh and a human master.

In spite of the relative absence of disciple terminology and explicit teaching on discipleship, the nature of the prophetic ministry (the prophets associated with Samuel, 1 Sam 19:20-24; the sons of the prophets associated with Elisha, 2 Kings 4:1, 38; 9:1), the writing

prophets (Jeremiah and Baruch, Jer 36:32), the scribes (Ezra, Ezra 7:6, 11) and the wisdom tradition (Prov 22:17; 25:1; wise counselors, Jer 18:18) provide compelling evidence for the existence of master-disciple relationships within the social structure of Israel. Each of these institutions was involved in the process of communicating the revelation of Yahweh (prophecy,* law,* wisdom*) and the suggested intimacy of the relationship indicates mutual support in the task of revealing the word of the Lord to the nation.

1.2. Greek-Speaking World. In the earliest classical Greek literature, *mathētēs* was used in three ways: in a general sense (in morphological relation to the verb *manthanein,* "to learn") of "learner" (Isocrates *Panath.* 16.7); with a technical sense of "adherent" to a great teacher, teaching or master (Xenophon *Mem.* 1.6.3.4); and with a more restricted sense of an "institutional pupil" of the Sophists (Demosthenes *Lacrit.* 35.41.7). Socrates (and those opposed to the Sophists) resisted using *mathētēs* for his followers in order to avoid Sophistic misassociations (Plato *Soph.* 233.B.6-C.6), but he used the term freely to refer to "learners" (Plato *Crat.* 428.B.4) and "adherents" (Plato *Symp.* 197.B.1) where there was no danger of misunderstanding. In the Hellenistic (*see* Hellenism) period at the time of Jesus *mathētēs* continued to be used with general connotations of a "learner" (Diodorus *Bib. Hist.* 23.2.1.13, 26), but it was used more regularly to refer to an "adherent" (Dio Chrysostom *Regno* 1.38.6). The type of adherence was determined by the master, ranging from being the follower of a great thinker and master of the past like Socrates (Dio Chrysostom *De Homero.* 1.2), to being the pupil of a philosopher like Pythagoras (Diodorus *Bib. Hist.* 12. 20. 1. 3), to being the devotee of a religious master like Epicurus (Plutarch *Non Posse Suav.* 1100.A.6).

1.3. Judaism at the Time of Jesus. Within Judaism* of the first century several different types of individuals were called "disciples," using the essentially equivalent terms *mathētēs* and *talmîd.* The terms designated adherents or followers who were committed to a recognized leader, teacher or movement; relationships running the spectrum from philosophical (Philo *Sacr.* 7.4; 64.10; 79.10) to technical (rabbinical scribes; *m. 'Abot* 1:1; *b. Šabb.* 31a) to sectarian (Pharisees* in Josephus, *Ant.* 13.289; 15.3, 370) to revolutionary (Zealot-like nationalists in *Midr. Šir Haširim Zûta; see* Revolutionary Movements). Apart from the disciples of Jesus, the Gospels present us with "disciples of the Pharisees" (Mt 22:15-16; Mk 2:18) who possibly belonged to one of the academic institutions; "disciples of John the Baptist" (Mk 2:18), the courageous men and women who had left the status quo of Jewish society to follow the eschatological prophet John the Baptist*; and the "disciples of Moses" (Jn 9:24-29), who were Jews focused on their privileged position as those to whom God had revealed himself through Moses.*

2. Disciples of Jesus.
2.1. First Followers. From the beginning of his public ministry, Jesus had followers. His first followers, according to the Johannine tradition, were originally disciples of John the Baptist. Since the Baptist's ministry prepared the way for Jesus, it is natural that some of John's disciples would make the transition to following Jesus. The first followers were Andrew and another unnamed disciple (likely the apostle John). Andrew, convinced that Jesus was the Messiah (*see* Christ), brought his brother, Simon Peter, to Jesus. Philip, another person from the same hometown as Andrew and Peter, was next called by Jesus, and he in turn brought Nathanael to Jesus (cf. Jn 1:35-49). These first followers were likely the "disciples" (2:2) who next traveled with Jesus to the wedding celebration at Cana, experienced the first miraculous sign and believed in Jesus.

This early movement to follow Jesus gained momentum as the news of Jesus traveled through social relationships in a relatively localized area. Since Jesus focused his ministry in the Galilee* region, the early disciples were drawn from an existing network of relatives (e.g., the brothers: Andrew and Simon Peter; John and James), business partners (e.g., Peter and Andrew were partners in the fishing industry with James and John, Lk 5:10), neighbors and acquaintances (most of the twelve disciples were from Capernaum and Bethsaida).

The Jesus movement accelerated rapidly. In the early stages of his ministry a great company of disciples attached themselves to Jesus (Lk 6:17; 10:1; Jn 6:60). Jesus appealed to the multitude of people and a groundswell of followers came after him to become his disciples. But the early company of disciples was apparently a mixed sort. In John's Gospel there is a unique record of disciples who had followed Jesus for some period of time, but after a discourse by Jesus which they found particularly hard to accept (cf. Jn 6:60), John writes, "As a result of this many of his disciples were going away to the things they left behind, and were no longer walking with him" (Jn 6:66). The expressions "going away to the things left behind" and "no longer walking with him" mark the return of these disciples to their old lives before they had begun to follow Jesus. In John's usage the expressions indicate that these disciples were

following Jesus because he was an exciting new miracle worker* and teacher (cf. Jn 2:23-25). They had made some kind of a commitment to Jesus, but when his teaching did not conform to their expectations they left him. They were only loosely attached to the movement.

2.2. The Disciples and the Crowds. Two groups were in attendance for much of Jesus' ministry: the disciples and the "crowds," or "multitudes" (*hoi ochloi; see* People, Crowd). The disciples were those who obeyed Jesus' call to follow him. The crowds were those to whom Jesus continued to offer a call. The crowds were basically a neutral though curious group who were not attached in any serious way to Jesus. Although they followed Jesus (Mt 4:25), the crowds did not exhibit the twin prerequisites of discipleship*: paying the cost and committing themselves to the cause. They followed only in a physical sense, never in the truest sense of devoting themselves to following Jesus. They were the people of Israel of Jesus' day who were the object of Jesus' evangelistic ministry. They flocked to him for healing* (Mt 15:29-31) and teaching (Mt 5:28-29), but could not understand (Mt 13:10-17) because they were not true believers. At different times they were either positively or negatively oriented toward him. They were amazed at his teaching (Mt 7:28; 21:9-10) and shouted "Hosanna!" at his entry into Jerusalem, but at other times laughed at him (Mt 9:23-25), came to arrest him (Mt 26:47), were led astray by the chief priests (*see* Priest, Priesthood) and elders* (Mt 27:20) and in the end accepted responsibility for his death (Mt 27:24; *see* Death of Jesus).

The objective of Jesus' ministry among the crowd was to make them disciples. As he taught and preached to them, individuals were moved to faith and began to serve Jesus as Lord (Mt 8:18-21; 17:14-15; 19:16-22). Out of this neutral group referred to as the "crowd" came both disciples and opponents of Jesus. Making disciples from among the crowd was the object of Jesus' ministry in Israel (Mt 9:35-38), and the worldwide commission he gave to his disciples before he ascended was for them to make disciples of the nations (Mt 28:18).

2.3. The Twelve Disciples and Other Disciples. The four Evangelists witness that in the midst of the ebb and flow of the popularity of the Jesus movement, a core of twelve disciples were called by Jesus. Modern scholarship is widely agreed that Matthew and Mark (at least from Mk 3:13 par. Mt 10:1) generally identify the terms *disciple* and *the Twelve* with one another (e.g., Meye, Luz), though not to the extent of implying that the term "disciple" should be limited to the Twelve (contra Strecker). Mark gives evidence of disciples outside the circle of the Twelve (Hengel), and Matthew specifically speaks of them (Mt 8:19, 21) and alludes to a wider circle of disciples (Mt 10:24-25, 42), even acknowledging through the verb *mathēteuō* the discipleship of Joseph of Arimathea (Mt 27:57; Przybylski, 109; *see* Burial of Jesus). Matthew and Mark have literary and theological purposes for generally identifying the disciples and the Twelve, but they are in agreement with Luke and John who more clearly speak of other disciples of Jesus. Luke seems to indicate that Jesus chose the Twelve from among a much larger number of disciples (cf. Lk 6:13, 17).

"Following Jesus" is a technical expression for going after him as his disciple. Some disciples physically followed Jesus in his itinerant ministry (e.g., the Twelve), while a wider group of disciples followed Jesus in a more figurative sense (e.g., Joseph of Arimathea, Jn 19:38). Following Jesus meant togetherness with him while traveling on the Way, but that following could be manifested in either a physical or figurative sense. The difference between the Twelve and the broader group of disciples is the role to which they were called. The Twelve were called to be co-workers with Jesus, and leaving all to follow Jesus was a necessary sacrifice in order to join with him in the proclamation of the kingdom (cf. Mt 10:1-15) and train for their future role in the church* (cf. Mt 19:23-30).

2.4. The Women Who Followed Jesus. The Gospels and Acts give prominent place to various women who were disciples of Jesus. These women were part of the wider group of disciples around Jesus, but some of them physically accompanied Jesus during his itinerancy. Luke tells of a preaching tour through Galilee during which Jesus and the Twelve "with him" were accompanied by several women who had been healed by Jesus and were now contributing to the support of Jesus and the Twelve (Lk 8:1-3). While parallels can be found for women* supporting rabbis* and their disciples out of their own money, property or foodstuffs, the wording in Luke 8 indicates that these women were themselves disciples of Jesus (e.g., "with him" [*syn autō*] expresses discipleship in Luke's Gospel and seems in this case to apply to the women; cf. Lk 8:38; 9:18; 22:56). Women disciples of a great master was an unusual occurrence in Palestine of the first century, as even the early disciples' reaction to Jesus' interaction with the Samaritan* woman reveals (Jn 4:27), yet these women exhibited the twin characteristics of Jesus' disciples—they had paid the cost and were committed to him. This same group of women followed Jesus up to Jerusalem, attended the crucifixion and were the first ones to arrive at the empty tomb (Lk 23:49, 55; 24:9; *see* Resurrection).

Later, in the book of Acts, we find many women who had significant roles in the early church. Luke uses the feminine form of the word for disciple (*mathētria*, Acts 9:36) in a casual way, so indicating that women believers were commonly called "disciples."

3. The Twelve.

The four Gospels unanimously testify to the core of Twelve who were called by Jesus into a special relationship with him. Although the Twelve are disciples, examples of what it means to be a believer in Jesus, they also are designated as "apostles."* In the introduction to the list of the Twelve, Luke states that Jesus "called his disciples to him, and chose twelve of them, whom he also named apostles" (Lk 6:13). This is a clue to the role of the Twelve: not only are they Jesus' disciples (committed followers), but they are also in training to be his apostles (commissioned representatives). Although Acts and the Pauline letters evidence more specific uses of the term "apostle," both "apostle" and "disciple" are applied to the Twelve in the Gospels. As "disciples" the Twelve are set aside as the examples of what Jesus accomplishes in his followers; as apostles the Twelve are set aside as the leaders within the new movement to come, the church.* (See Discipleship).

The chart on page 179 lists the Twelve as they are found in the Synoptic Gospels and Acts.

The Twelve displayed a remarkable diversity in background, including businessmen (Peter, Andrew, James and John), a tax collector (Matthew; *see* Taxes), and a zealous revolutionary (Simon the Zealot).

Within the Twelve is a recognizable division of groups of four. The first name of each of the groups remains the same in all of the lists (the first, fifth and ninth place is occupied, respectively, by Peter, Philip and James of Alphaeus). The order of the names within the groups varies, except for the first name. The sequence of the groups is the same in each list. This grouping suggests that the Twelve were organized into smaller units, each with a leader.

The first group is composed of those two pairs of brothers who were the first called—Peter, Andrew, James and John (Mt 4:18-22 par.), commonly called the "inner circle." This inner circle accompanied Jesus on special occasions such as the healing of Jairus' daughter (Mk 5:37 par.) and the Transfiguration* (Mk 9:2 par.); they were the audience of the Olivet Discourse (Mk 13:3; *see* Apocalyptic Teaching) and were with Jesus during his agony in the Garden of Gethsemane* (Mt 26:37 par.).

The Twelve are normally mentioned as a group,

The Twelve as they are found in the Synoptic Gospels and Acts.

Matthew 10:2-4	Mark 3:16-19	Luke 6:13-16	Acts 1:13
Simon, called Peter, first	*Simon, named Peter*	*Simon, named Peter*	*Peter*
Andrew, brother of Peter	James son of Zebedee	Andrew, brother of Peter	John
James son of Zebedee	John, brother of James	James	James
John, brother of James	Andrew	John	Andrew
Philip	*Philip*	*Philip*	*Philip*
Bartholomew	Bartholomew	Bartholomew	Thomas
Thomas	Matthew	Matthew	Bartholomew
Matthew the tax collector	Thomas	Thomas	Matthew
James son of Alphaeus	*James son of Alphaeus*	*James son of Alphaeus*	*James son of Alphaeus*
Thaddaeus (or Lebbaeus)	Thaddaeus	Simon, called the Zealot	Simon the Zealot
Simon the Cananean	Simon the Cananean	Judas son of James	Judas son of James
Judas Iscariot the betrayer	Judas Iscariot the betrayer	Judas Iscariot the betrayer	

with only occasional focus on individuals. Peter is the most familiar of the apostles to NT readers, with his name mentioned 210 times in the NT. The name of Paul is mentioned 162 times. The combined appearances of the names of all the other apostles totals only 142 times. Not much is known about the individual lives of the Twelve except what can be gathered from the scant biblical data and from some statements of the early church fathers.

3.1. Simon Peter. Simon, later called Peter, was a native of Galilee, where he grew up making his living as a fisherman along with his father and his brother, Andrew. After being called to follow Jesus, Peter soon became the most prominent of the disciples. Peter occurs first in all of the lists, indicating his place of leadership within the Twelve. In the Gospels he regularly functions as the spokesman for the Twelve (e.g., Mt 14:28; 15:15; 18:21; 26:35, 40; Mk 8:29; 9:5; 10:28; Jn 6:68), and during the days of the early church Peter fulfilled Jesus' prediction that he would play a foundational role as the rock of the church and holder of the keys of the kingdom of heaven (Mt 16:17-19; cf. Acts 1:8; 2:14-41; 8:14-25; 10:34-48). Peter is called "first" (e.g., Mt 10:2) in the sense that he was first among equals (*primus inter pares*) as the leader of the Twelve. (*See* Discipleship.)

3.2. Andrew. Andrew is best known as the brother of Simon Peter. Originally a disciple of John the Baptist, Andrew is the first follower of Jesus to be identified by name. He immediately went to tell his brother Peter about Jesus (cf. Jn. 1:35-42). Later he and Peter left their fishing business to follow Jesus in his earthly ministry, and he became part of the inner circle around Jesus (Mk 1:16 and par.; 1:29; 13:3). It was Andrew who brought to Jesus the boy with the loaves and fishes in John's account of the feeding of the five thousand (Jn 6:8: *see* Miracles and Miracle Stories), and, again in John, Andrew with Philip brought the inquisitive Greeks to Jesus (Jn 12:22).

3.3. James and John (Sons of Zebedee). James and John, the sons of Zebedee, were also from Bethsaida. They were from a family of some wealth (*see* Rich and Poor) and influence, probably derived from a profitable fishing trade (cf. Mk 1:20; Lk 5:10; Jn 18:15). They were called "the sons of thunder" (Mk 3:17), quite likely because of their fiery temperament (Mk 9:38-41; Lk 9:51-54), which may explain their aggressive ambition (Mk 10:35-45; as well as their mother's, Mt 20:20-21). James and John, along with Peter and Andrew (all fishing partners, cf. Lk 5:10), were called to follow Jesus in his earthly ministry (Mk 1:19-20 par.) and became part of the inner circle around Jesus. James is distinguished as the first apostolic martyr, a victim of the sword during the persecution undertaken by Herod Agrippa I (Acts 12:2).

An unnamed disciple of Jesus, known as "one of the

disciples, whom Jesus loved," is referred to only in John's Gospel (Jn 13:23; 19:26-27; 20:2; 21:7, 20; 21:4 [possibly 1:40, 18:15 and 19:35]), and is also said to be connected with the authorship of the Fourth Gospel (Jn 21:20-24). Proposals for the identity of the beloved disciple include: (1) he was not a real person but a symbolic figure; (2) Lazarus; (3) John Mark; (4) an unknown Jerusalem disciple of Jesus connected with the high priest; (5) the apostle John, the son of Zebedee; (6) disciples of the apostle John; and (7) an unnamed woman disciple of Jesus. Notwithstanding vigorous scholarly support for the competing proposals, the internal evidence from the Fourth Gospel (particularly those disciples close to Jesus in the scenes in which he appears), plus the external evidence from early church fathers such as Irenaeus (*Haer.* III.1.1) and Polycrates (cited in Eusebius *Hist. Eccl.* III.31.3; also V.24.2-3) weigh most heavily in favor of the apostle John, the son of Zebedee, as being the "beloved disciple."

"The Beloved Disciple" is the only one of the Twelve recorded to have witnessed the crucifixion, along with several women disciples. After the crucifixion he took Jesus' mother into his own home (Jn 19:25-27). He was the first of the Twelve to see the empty tomb and was one of the early leaders of the church, one of those recognized by Paul as a "pillar of the church" (Gal 2:9).

3.4. Philip. Philip was also from Bethsaida. He appears to have been a disciple of John the Baptist before Jesus called him (Jn 1:43-44). Philip and Andrew often occur together in the listings of the Twelve (Mk 3:18; Acts 1:13—the only two Greek names) and in the rare incidents in which they are mentioned by name (Jn 6:8; 12:22). In John he is depicted as having a clear understanding of OT expectations concerning Messiah as well as a missionary heart (Jn 1:43-46; 12:21-22), yet he also exhibited defective spiritual insight (Jn 6:5-7; 14:7-9).

3.5. Bartholomew. Bartholomew appears in all four lists of the twelve disciples, but he is otherwise unmentioned in the NT. From the ninth century onward Bartholomew has been frequently identified with Nathanael. This is based on the conjecture that Nathanael's surname was Bartholomew, so that his full name would have been Nathanael Bar-Tholami. Since the Synoptic Gospels never mention Nathanael, while John never mentions Bartholomew, the juxtaposition of the names Philip and Bartholomew in the Synoptic lists of the Twelve (not in the list in Acts) suggests the close relationship between Philip and Nathanael depicted in John 1:43-51. All of Nathanael's companions are apostles (Jn 1:35-51), he appears as a

member of a group of apostles (Jn 21:1-2) and Christ's promise to him suggests an apostolic function (Jn 1:50-1).

If the identification of Bartholomew with Nathanael is correct, Philip brought Bartholomew (Nathanael), a native of Cana of Galilee (Jn 21:2), to acknowledge Jesus as the Messiah (Jn 1:45-46). A true Israelite, without guile, Nathanael gave a profound declaration of the messianic identity of Jesus. Jesus, in turn, stated that Nathanael would see even greater demonstrations of messianism (Jn 1:47-51).

If the identification of Bartholomew with Nathanael is incorrect, then we have no other NT information about Bartholomew other than the four lists.

3.6. Thomas. Thomas the "twin" (*didymus;* Jn 11:16; 20:24; 21:2), known popularly as "doubting Thomas" because of his misgivings concerning Jesus' resurrection (Jn 20:24) and his imperception of Jesus' destiny (Jn 14:5), is otherwise portrayed in the Gospels as a strong figure. His courage stands out when he urges the other disciples to travel with Jesus to Judea so that they might die with him (Jn 11:16). His faithfulness is revealed when he gathers with some of the other disciples in Galilee after the resurrection (Jn 21:2), and his spiritual insight is demonstrated in his confession of Jesus as Lord* and God* (Jn 20:28), one of the most profound declarations of Jesus' deity in the NT.

3.7. Matthew. Matthew, while employed as a tax collector, was called to follow Jesus (Mt 9:9). When recounting the call Mark and Luke refer to him as Levi, suggesting that this tax collector had two names, Matthew Levi, originating either from birth or from the time of his conversion. His tax collector's booth was probably located on one of the main trade highways near Capernaum, where he collected tolls for Herod Antipas from the commercial traffic traveling through this area (*see* Taxes). After his call Matthew immediately followed Jesus and arranged a banquet for him at his home (*see* Table Fellowship), to which were invited a large crowd of tax collectors and sinners* (Lk 5:29-30). Little else is known of Matthew Levi, except for the widely attested tradition from the second century on that he was the author of the Gospel according to Matthew (*see* Matthew, Gospel According to).

3.8. James (Son of Alphaeus). Apart from his name appearing in the four NT lists, James the son of Alphaeus is otherwise unmentioned. He is usually identified with "James the younger," the son of Mary and the brother of Joses (Mk 15:40; cf. Mt 27:56). If so, the designation "younger or less" (Gk *ho mikros*) distinguishes him from James the brother of Jesus and

James the son of Zebedee, referring to his younger age, smaller stature or lesser renown. His mother, Mary, was in attendance at the crucifixion and the discovery of the empty tomb (Mt 27:56; Mk 15:40; 16:1; Lk 24:10).

3.9. Thaddaeus/Judas of James. Thaddaeus (some texts have Lebbaeus, or conflations) is mentioned in the third group of disciples by Matthew (Mt 10:3) and Mark (Mk 3:18), while Luke refers to "Judas the son of James" (lit. Judas of James) in his two lists (Lk 6:16; Acts 1:13). The uniformity of the rest of the names from list to list assures us that these names refer to the same person. Judas is probably the given name and Thaddaeus is a nickname or place name. The NT records only one incident about this person: his question to Jesus during the message to the disciples after the Last Supper* (Jn 14:22).

3.10. Simon the Zealot. In addition to Simon Peter there was a disciple known as Simon the Cananaean (Mt 10:4; Mk 3:18; a Greek transliteration of the Aramaic word for "zeal" or "zealot" [qan'ānā']) or Simon the Zealot (Lk 6:15; Acts 1:13). The expression indicates that this Simon was a zealous nationalist prior to his call to follow Jesus, and may indicate some of his ongoing temperament. Later, the term *zealot* was used to designate the religiously motivated Jewish revolutionaries who were active in guerilla-type warfare in the period leading up to A.D. 70 and the destruction of Jerusalem (*see* Revolutionary Movements).

3.11. Judas Iscariot. "Iscariot" most likely identifies this Judas's place of origin, especially since his father is described as "Simon Iscariot" (Jn 6:71; 13:2, 26). Judas Iscariot* was the treasurer for the apostolic band (Jn 12:4-6; 13:29). Since this office was not usually given to one known to be greedy and irresponsible, we may assume that he displayed positive characteristics recognizable by the others. However, John tells us that during his time as treasurer Judas had become a thief, pilfering from the treasury funds (Jn 12:6).

The event for which Judas is best known is his betrayal of Jesus. Both Luke and John portray him as under the direction of Satan (Lk 22:3; Jn 13:2; *see* Demon, Devil, Satan). His greed, which prompted him to steal (Jn 12:4-6), may have motivated him to betray Jesus for the paltry amount of thirty pieces of silver, possibly only a partial payment of the agreed-on sum (Mt 26:14-6; Mk 14:10-11; Lk 22:3-6). The treacherous act which took place at the Last Supper apparently came as a surprise to all except Jesus (Mt 26:20-25; Mk 14:17-21). Securing a band of soldiers from the chief priests and Pharisees (Jn 18:3), Judas led them to where Jesus was alone with the disciples in the Garden of Gethsemane, away from the crowds, and kissed Jesus to identify him for the soldiers (Mt 26:47-56; Mk 14:43-52; Lk 22:47-53; Jn 18:2-12).

When Jesus was officially condemned to death, Judas was filled with remorse and returned the pieces of silver to the priests, who used the blood money to purchase a burial plot for strangers. Then Judas went and committed suicide (cf. Mt 27:3-10; Acts 1:18-19). After Jesus' ascension Judas was replaced in the circle of the Twelve by Matthias, about whom nothing else is known (Acts 1:26).

4. The Early Church.

The term *mathētēs* is used regularly in Luke-Acts to designate the person who has placed his faith in Jesus Christ. In Luke 6:13, 17 reference is made to a great multitude of disciples. These disciples of Jesus were convinced believers in Jesus' messiahship and are set in contrast with the "great throng of people" (v. 17) who could be termed "the curious." This can be compared with Luke's usage of *mathētēs* in Acts, where he speaks of the multitude of believers (Acts 4:32) and the multitude of "disciples" (Acts 6:2). In Luke's writings the expressions "those who believe" and "the disciples" signify the same group of people (cf. Acts 6:7; 9:26; 11:26; 14:21-22). As Acts records, by the time of the early church the term *disciple* had become synonymous with the true believer—all those who confessed Jesus as Messiah—or, as they were first called at Antioch, "Christians" (*Christianoi*, Acts 11:26). *See also* APOSTLE; DISCIPLESHIP; JUDAS ISCARIOT.

BIBLIOGRAPHY. E. Best, *Disciples and Discipleship: Studies in the Gospel According to Mark* (Edinburgh: T. & T. Clark, 1986); H. D. Betz, *Nachfolge und Nachahmung Jesu Christi im Neuen Testament* (BHT 37; Tübingen: J. C. B. Mohr [Paul Siebeck], 1967); M. Hengel, *The Charismatic Leader and His Followers* (New York: Crossroad, 1981); U. Luz, "The Disciples in the Gospel, according to Matthew," in *The Interpretation of Matthew* (IRT 3; Philadelphia: Fortress, 1983); R. Meye, *Jesus and the Twelve: Discipleship and Revelation in Mark's Gospel* (Grand Rapids: Eerdmans, 1968); B. Przybylski, *Righteousness in Matthew and His World of Thought* (SNTSMS 41; Cambridge: University Press, 1980); K. H. Rengstorf, " μαθητής," *TDNT* IV.415-61; E. P. Sanders, *Jesus and Judaism* (Philadelphia: Fortress, 1985); F. Segovia, ed., *Discipleship in the New Testament* (Philadelphia: Fortress, 1985); G. Strecker, *Der Weg der Gerechtigkeit. Untersuchungen zur Theologie des Matthäus* (FRLANT 87; 2d rev. ed; Göttingen: Vandenhoeck & Ruprecht, 1971); G. Theissen, *Sociology of Early Palestinian Christianity* (Philadelphia: Fortress, 1978); J. J.

Vincent, *Disciple and Lord: The Historical and Theological Significance of Discipleship in the Synoptic Gospels* (Sheffield: Academy, 1976); M. J. Wilkins, *The Concept of Disciple in Matthew's Gospel: As Reflected in the Use of the Term Μαθητής* (NovTSup 59; Leiden: E. J. Brill, 1988); B. Witherington, *Women in the Ministry of Jesus: A Study of Jesus' Attitude toward Women and Their Roles as Reflected in His Earthly Ministry* (SNTSMS 51; Cambridge: University Press, 1984).

M. J. Wilkins

DISCIPLESHIP

The scene of disciples* following Jesus around during his earthly ministry dominates the Gospel* panorama. That vision of discipleship demands our attention, both on an historical as well as a personal level. Discipleship can be narrowly understood in terms of the historical master-disciple relationship (*see* Disciples). It can also be understood more broadly as Christian experience, and what that way of life entails. To understand fully the Gospel portrait of discipleship, one must keep in view (1) the moment within the ministry of Jesus in which the challenge of discipleship is given to and lived out by the disciples, and (2) the moment within the church's* life when the would-be disciple is tested.

Our purpose is first to study the four Gospel records of Jesus and his disciples in order to appreciate the unique perspective of discipleship intended by each evangelist for his community. Then the Gospel records will be viewed together in order to gain the broadest perspective of Jesus' form of discipleship. In this way the view of Jesus and his historical disciples will be clarified, and the call of discipleship to the church heard more distinctly.

1. The Emphases of the Gospel Writers
2. Jesus' Form of Discipleship

1. The Emphases of the Gospel Writers.

1.1. Matthew: Examples with a Commission. Matthew views the disciples of Jesus from alternating perspectives. At times he specifies that the disciples are with Jesus, while parallel passages in Mark and Luke do not (9:19). In other instances he excludes them from those who are accompanying Jesus while the Synoptic parallels portray them as present (12:15). At times Matthew purposely projects a very positive picture of the disciples by including the term "disciples" when it is absent in the parallels (12:49), but at other times he includes the term in such a way that the disciples are singled out for negative associations not specified in the parallels (26:56). At times Matthew omits reference to the disciples sharing guilt with Peter (16:23), yet on

other occasions they are specified as sharing in his guilt (14:31). At times it appears that Matthew purposely carries forward the traditional association of the disciples with the apostolic title "the Twelve" (10:1), but on other occasions he implies a wider circle of disciples (8:21; 27:57).

1.1.1. Understanding Jesus' Teaching. Matthew has arranged his disciple material to accentuate Jesus as the effective teacher* of his disciples. Each of the major discourses is primarily directed to the disciples (5:1; 10:1; 13:10, 36; 18:1; 23:1; 24:1-3), and teaching segments are often transformed into explicit discipleship-teaching pericopae by including the term "disciple" (8:21, 23; 9:27; 10:42; 12:49; 13:10; 15:23; 16:5; 17:6; 17:10; 18:1; 19:10; 21:20; 24:3; 26:8, 40, 45). On at least three occasions the teaching of Jesus leads to an explicit statement that the disciples understand (16:12; 17:13; 13:52), whereas Mark says that the disciples do not understand (cf. Mk 6:52; 8:21; 9:10, 32). Some scholars take this contrast between the understanding of the disciples in Matthew and the lack of understanding in Mark to mean that Matthew has idealized the disciples by omitting or toning down anything derogatory about them. On the contrary, although he does not focus on the disciples' failure (e.g., 8:25; 13:16; 14:23), Matthew explicitly tells of their deficient faith* (14:31; 16:8, 22-23; 17:20) and does in fact present negative aspects of the disciples (e.g., 26:8, 56). Instead of idealizing, the theme of the disciples' understanding accentuates Jesus' teaching and his role as an effective teacher.

1.1.2. Examples of Christian Existence. Matthew has not intended the disciples to be an idealistic paradigm. He shows both positive and negative traits. The positive aspect, which is especially present in the discipleship teachings, shows what will happen to true disciples who fully obey and follow Jesus. The negative traits show what can happen to disciples who do not identify with Jesus in his obedience to the will of the Father (e.g., they stumble, 16:23; flee, 26:56; fall asleep, 26:40, 45; and act in brash boldness, 26:35). Portrayed both positively and negatively (15:23; 16:5-12; 17:6-7; 16:19; 19:13-15), the disciples become examples of imperfect followers of Jesus who are taught and who advance to understanding and solidarity with Jesus. And, as an example for Matthew's church, they provide a very practical and realistic display of what it means to be called a disciple (28:16, 18).

1.1.3. With Jesus or against Him. Three groups—Jesus' disciples, the crowds (*see* People, Crowd) and the Jewish leaders—provide a background for Matthew's story of Jesus. The Jewish leaders are the antagonists, the ones responsible for Jesus' crucifixion (*see* Death of Jesus). The crowds are a basically neutral group who are the object of Jesus' ministry of preaching, teaching and healing,* but as a group they do not exercise faith in him. Although some scholars suggest that the disciples are pictured in relationship to the crowds as true versus false believers in the church, or idealized believers who rise above the masses in the church, or the priestly class in the church serving the lay people, Matthew pictures the disciples as Jesus' true followers, true believers and the crowds as the mass of people who are the object of Jesus' saving ministry. Jesus' objective amidst the crowd is to make them disciples. The sign of faith is their departure from the crowd and calling Jesus "Lord" (8:18-21; 17:14-5; 19:16-22).

From Matthew's perspective the disciples are "with" Jesus, the Jewish leaders are "against" Jesus and the crowds must make a decision to be either with him or against him (cf. 12:30; Mk 9:40; Lk 9:50—the saying in Matthew is more restrictive). At first the crowds are amazed at Jesus' teaching (7:28-29) and miracles* (9:8), and receive Jesus' compassionate attention (9:35-38; 14:13-14), apparently siding with Jesus. But they increasingly demonstrate hardness of heart (cf. 13:2-3; 10-17; 34-36; see Hardness of Heart), until at the end the Jewish leaders persuade the crowds to ask for the death of Jesus (27:15-25). Only the disciples are "with" Jesus as his followers after the resurrection.*

The crowds of Israel* had their opportunity to become disciples during Jesus' earthly mission (9:35—10:15; 14:14-19; 15:29-36). After his resurrection Jesus sends the disciples to the larger crowd, the nations, to make disciples of them (28:16-20; see Gentile).

1.1.4. Simon Peter. Since the disciples function in Matthew's Gospel as an example—both positive and negative—of what it means to be a disciple, the portrait of Simon Peter in Matthew's Gospel provides a personalized example of discipleship for Matthew's church. The focus in Matthew is on Jesus who calls, instructs and sends out disciples to make more of what he has made them to be. But Matthew presents the disciples as a nameless, faceless, collective unity. Peter stands out in sharp relief against this backdrop of anonymity, being the only named disciple to become the focus of special attention. He functions as an example much like the disciples do as a group. In his strengths and in his weaknesses he can be an example to Matthew's church; so Matthew accentuates the truly human element in Peter. The church would find much in common with Peter's typically human characteristics. In his likeness to ordinary believers with their highs and lows, he provides a means for instructing the church in the path of discipleship.

Peter likewise serves this function for the leaders of Matthew's church. In his success and failure as a leader, Peter provides an instructive case study for the leadership of Matthew's church. In several instances the questions and responses Peter voices to Jesus on behalf of the disciples were issues that still spoke to the church of Matthew's day (e.g., 15:15; 17:24-25; 18:21). As Jesus instructs Peter, instruction is provided for the church. The focus is on Jesus, who promised to Peter, "I will build my church" and who had called him, corrected him and instructed him. As Jesus worked with and through Peter, so he would with the church.

1.1.5. A Manual on Discipleship. Matthew's Gospel is, at least in part, a manual on discipleship. In the process of handing on his tradition concerning the disciples, Matthew exalts Jesus as the supreme Lord* and teacher of the historical disciples and the post-resurrection community. Although the disciples are susceptible to incomprehension (as in Mark), Matthew emphasizes that Jesus' teaching brings understanding. A number of factors point to Matthew's intention to provide in his Gospel resources for discipleship: (1) the major discourses are directed at least in part to the disciples; (2) most of the sayings directed to the disciples are in fact teaching on discipleship; (3) the disciples are portrayed in a positive yet realistic light; and (4) the disciples are called, trained and commissioned to carry out their climactic mandate to "make disciples" (28:19). The goal of the believer's life of faith is made clear, and the disciple is outfitted to make more disciples.

1.2. Mark: Servants of the Redemptive Servant.

1.2.1. Conflicting Profiles. Because Mark reveals such conflicting profiles of the disciples, Mark's portrait of them is perhaps the most ambiguous among the Gospel accounts. On the one hand, the disciples receive a positive portrayal when they are introduced as being specially selected and commissioned with authority* by Jesus (1:16-20; 3:13-19) to hear the secrets of the kingdom (4:10-12; see Kingdom of God) and to promote his ministry (3:14-15; 6:7-13, 35). Empowered by Jesus for ministry in Israel, the disciples do as Jesus does: they preach, heal and exorcise demons (see Demon, Devil, Satan). On the other hand, the disciples are painted in unflattering colors when, despite their enlightenment by God and empowerment by Jesus, they are shown to be uncomprehending. They do not understand Jesus' parabolic teaching (4:13; 7:17-18; see Parable), do not grasp Jesus' true identity as the Son of God (see Son of God) who calms the seas (4:35-41; 6:45-52) and do not perceive Jesus' potential to feed the multitudes miraculously (6:34-44;

8:1-10). More critically, the disciples do not truly comprehend the nature of Jesus' ministry or teaching (8:14-21), which in essence involves the way to the cross (8:31-33; 9:30-32) through servanthood (10:32-45; *see* Service). This incomprehension eventually leads Judas to betray him (14:43-46), the disciples to forsake him (14:50) and Peter to deny him (14:54, 66-72).

What does Mark intend in portraying the disciple in this manner? Some understand Mark's motives to be polemical (e.g., J. Tyson; T. J. Weeden; E. Trocmé, W. H. Kelber): the disciples are literary figures who represent a faction of the church against which the Evangelist engages in polemic. The incomprehension of the disciples is evidence that they are opposed to Jesus and his program. Mark's church is to recognize the failings of the disciples and be warned of their opponents within the church. But a more nuanced line of interpretation recognizes Mark's intent to be pastoral (e.g., R. Meye, E. Best, E. Focant, F. Matera): The evangelist employs the obtuseness of the disciples to instruct his community about the meaning of authentic discipleship. Although Mark has the highest regard for the disciples, he uses their failures to instruct his community. Thus Mark deals with a fact of history: during Jesus' earthly life the disciples did not completely understand him. Mark uses the historical disciples to show his readers how difficult it is to grasp the mystery of Jesus and the cross. Those passages which stress the incomprehension of the disciples instruct Mark's church about the necessity of "thinking God's thoughts rather than human thoughts" (e.g., 8:33). The resurrection scene provides fulfillment of Jesus' predictions (9:9; 14:28) and obligates the reader to project a reconciliation of the disciples and Peter with Jesus, since they will see him in Galilee* just as he told them (16:7). The summons to Galilee provides the assurance that Peter and the disciples, in spite of denying and forsaking Jesus, have not been rejected by the risen Lord.

1.2.2. Servanthood. Mark introduces his Gospel as "the beginning of the gospel of Jesus Christ, the Son of God." Through the development of his plot Mark contrasts two fundamentally opposing points of view concerning his Gospel (*see* Gospel [Good News]) message: "thinking the things of God" and "thinking the things of humankind" (cf. 8:33). The disciples' response to Jesus is a major portion of the plot. The disciples had been specially called to follow Jesus and respond to him as the one effectively proclaiming the "gospel of God." They were given the mystery of the kingdom; they experienced in their own lives God's redeeming activity. Privy to special instruction, they were even empowered to act in Jesus' name to preach the gospel, to heal, to exorcise and to teach. Yet they misunderstood. They became confused and afraid. When adversity set in, the disciples reflected little faith and much hardness of heart. This confusion ate away at their fundamental perception of who Jesus was, as well as the implications of Jesus' identity for the life of discipleship (Guelich).

Although Jesus has come as God's promised, Spirit-anointed, royal Son to herald and inaugurate the kingdom, Mark writes to correct those who would look to the glory of the final consummation of the kingdom instead of its vulnerable beginnings. The kingdom is here in hidden fashion, and Jesus the Messiah (*see* Christ), Son of God (1:1), must be understood in terms of suffering and the cross (8:31-33; 9:30-32; 10:32-34; *see* Predictions of Jesus' Death and Resurrection). The pivotal pronouncement of servanthood in Mark 10:45 (*see* Ransom Saying) declares the essence of Jesus' ministry. By comprehending this, the disciples will comprehend the essence of discipleship as servanthood, including their motivation, position, ambition, expectations and example (note the crucial placement of the servanthood passages at 9:33-37 and 10:35-45, within the larger discipleship section of 8:27—10:45). The disciple who is privileged to be a member of Jesus' kingdom is a servant, which means thinking God's thoughts (8:31-33), pursuing the life of the cross (8:34-38) through the message (9:1-8) and example of Jesus (9:9-32) and, hence, rejecting status (9:33-37), exclusivism (9:38—10:16) and the treasures of this world (10:17-31). The disciples in Mark's Gospel are privileged members of the kingdom of God, and their incomprehension comes from their worldly expectations. Discipleship instruction directs them to think God's way, the way of suffering and the cross through servanthood.

1.3. Luke: Followers on the Costly Way.

1.3.1. Lukan Distinctives. Detecting the Lukan understanding of discipleship requires taking into consideration literary usage in both the Gospel and Acts, as well as comparing Luke's Gospel with the other Synoptics.

In Acts *disciple* (6:1-2, 7; 9:10, 26; 11:26; 14:21-22; 15:10; 16:1) is used as a synonym for believers in Christ (cf. "believers," 4:32; "disciples," 6:2). Disciples were all those who confessed Jesus as Messiah. The term is employed as a synonym for "Christians" (11:26; 26:28), "saints" (9:13, 32, 41) and "Nazarenes" (24:5). The usage in Luke's Gospel foreshadows that in Acts (Lk 6:13; 8:9; 9:54; 10:23; 11:1; 14:26; 19:37, 39). The great multitude of disciples in Luke 6:13, 17 is distinguished from the "great throng of people"

(6:17). In contrast with the crowds, who could be termed "the curious," the disciples were convinced believers in Jesus.

The picture of the disciples in Luke's Gospel bears many similarities to those found in Matthew and Mark, but differences occur as well. The most notable differences are: (1) the accounts of the calling of Jesus' first followers (5:1-11; Mk 2:16-18; Mt 4:18-22); (2) mention of a large number of disciples never encountered in Matthew or Mark (6:13, 17, 19; 19:37-39); (3) Jesus sending out not only the Twelve (cf. 9:1-6; Mk 6:6-13; Mt 10:5-15) but also Seventy(-two) others (10:1-16); (4) the scandal of Peter's denials being somewhat tempered by Jesus' prayer for Peter and the hint of his future role of strengthening the other disciples (22:31-32); (5) omission of the devastating statement that all the disciples left Jesus and fled at the betrayal scene at Gethsemane* (cf. 22:53-54; Mt 26:56; Mk 14:50); and (6) his inclusion of a statement about "all those knowing" Jesus being with the women* from Galilee at the crucifixion (*pantes hoi gnōstoi*, masculine plural; 23:49; Mt 27:55-56; Mk 15:40-1).

1.3.2. Followers on the Way. Following Jesus is synonymous with discipleship, but Luke depicts the phenomenon in a unique manner: the disciples of Jesus are followers on the Way. Luke's geographical perspective, with Jerusalem at the center, concentrates on Jesus as he journeys the road to Jerusalem for the passion (9:51; *see* Passion Narrative) with the disciples traveling along with him (9:57). For Luke, salvation itself is "the way" (*hē hodos*), a pattern of life revealed by God. This idea of salvation* as a "way" leads in time to calling the Christian community "the Way" (Acts 9:2; 19:9, 23; 22:4; 24:14, 22), an early designation or title for the organized community of disciples, which eventually is known as "the church." From the Lukan perspective, disciples must enter into and stride along that Way in the footsteps of their Master.

1.3.3. Entrance to the Way. Both in his Gospel and the Acts Luke emphasizes that entrance into the Way of salvation and discipleship is found through faith alone (7:50; 8:48; 17:19; cf. Acts 10:43; 13:38-39; 16:31). More so than the other Evangelists, Luke stresses that true faith is characterized by "counting the cost," both positively and negatively, of what the life of discipleship entails. To count the cost negatively means to recognize that one enters into the life of discipleship through detachment from all other allegiances and through giving total allegiance to Jesus as Master. A key passage is Luke 14:25-33, where Jesus addresses the crowds about the conditions of entrance into discipleship. The crowds have not yet begun to follow Jesus and, before they make a commitment, Jesus tells them that they must count the cost. Nothing else may pre-empt the disciple's focus of allegiance on Jesus: neither family* (14:26), nor wealth (12:13-21; 16:10-13, 14-16, 19-31; *see* Rich and Poor), nor one's own life* (14:26) nor anything at all (14:33). Entrance into the way of discipleship means entering the narrow gate to salvation (13:22-30) to follow after Jesus alone (14:27; 9:23).

To count the cost positively means to recognize that love for God—undivided loyalty to him—is at the center of faith. A key passage is Luke 10:25-37, where a lawyer came to Jesus asking about obtaining eternal life. The lawyer rightly understood that to obtain eternal life one's heart, soul, mind and strength must be focused on loving God, and that the practical demonstration of love* for God is loving one's neighbor as oneself. Counting the cost in the positive sense means to recognize that love for God and neighbor is the evidence that one has made unqualified commitment to Jesus and his Way.

1.3.4. Traveling along the Way. Discipleship begins upon entering the Way of salvation; it advances as one travels along the Way. Luke specifies that self-denial, taking up the cross and following Jesus not only characterizes entrance into the Way but life on the Way. With the addition of "each day" to the cross-bearing proclamation, the Lukan Jesus calls for daily self-denial, daily bearing one's cross and daily following in the footsteps of the Master (cf. 9:23; Mk 8:34). Life on the Way involves being doers of the Word (11:27-28), because not all who are walking on the Way truly belong to the Way. Public statements of commitment must be judged by the fruit of one's life (6:43-49; 19:11-27). That fruit consists, at least in part, in loving and doing good to others (6:17-36), proper stewardship of material possessions (6:35; 8:3), servanthood (22:24-30), prayer* (10:2; 11:1; 18:1-8) and testimony to the Way (9:1-6; 10:1-12, 17-20; 12:8-12; 14:23-24; 24:44-49).

Luke accents the cost of following Jesus on the Way. When understood within the context of their first century social and religious setting, these demands allow us to see that Jesus was calling for a distinct form of discipleship. Becoming Jesus' disciple was not a vocational change, nor a political attachment, nor even a new stirring of God; it was being faced with the eternal decision of whether one would follow Jesus as the Way to eternal life. Any other attachment, whether familial or religious or economic, was substituting another god for Jesus. Entrance to the Way and life on the Way are both had through following Jesus in discipleship.

1.4. John: Believers Marked by Jesus.

1.4.1. Recognition and Belief. Recent scholarly investigations into the meaning and nature of discipleship from the Johannine perspective have employed a variety of methodologies. But there is a general agreement concerning three fundamental aspects of discipleship within the Johannine community (cf. Segovia).

(1) The central characteristic of the disciple is belief or acceptance of Jesus' claims vis-a-vis the Father. The disciples, particularly the Twelve (6:67, 70; 13:18; 15:16, 19; cf. 6:64, 66), are characteristically those who from the beginning recognize, acclaim and believe Jesus for who he truly is (1:41, 45, 49; 6:69; 13:13; 20:28-31; 21:7, 12; cf. 20:31). In John's Gospel "Jesus' disciples" appear for the first time at the beginning of Jesus' public ministry, the wedding at Cana (2:2). After the first of Jesus' signs and the manifestation of his glory* the disciples believed in him. This kind of belief somehow differs in quality from the belief of others who observe his miraculous signs in Jerusalem. Jesus regards their belief as deficient and does not entrust himself to them (2:23-25).

(2) Belief is portrayed as necessitating and undergoing a process of gradual understanding and perception. The disciples' lack complete understanding of "the hour" of Jesus' ministry (2:21-22; 4:27, 33; 6:60; 9:2; 10:6; 11:8, 11-15; 12:16; 13:36; 14:5, 8, 22; 16:17-18), but through Jesus' ministry and teaching (6:67-71; 9:2-7; 11:5-45), the resurrection appearances (20:8-10, 17-18, 19-21) and the reception of the Spirit* (20:19-23), the disciples finally comprehend Jesus' full status as the Son of God.

(3) A sustained and deliberate contrast is drawn between believers and unbelievers, between disciples and non-disciples. The non-disciple, the unbeliever, is a part of the unbelieving "world."* Although by definition the category "world" includes anyone who rejects Jesus' claims, in the Johannine narrative (and Farewell Discourse*) it becomes practically synonymous with that of "the Jews" and thus gives rise to a very specific contrast between the believing disciples and the unbelieving Jews (1:10-11; 3:19; 7:4, 7; 8:23; 12:31; 14:17, 19, 22, 27, 30-31; 18:36).

1.4.2. Deficient Belief. Among those who observed Jesus' signs and heard his teaching were those who responded with deficient belief. A festival crowd at the beginning of Jesus' ministry observed the signs he performed and believed in him. Yet Jesus would not entrust himself to them (2:23-25), recognizing in them a failure to believe fully. After a discourse which many of his disciples found particularly hard to accept (6:60), Jesus condemned the disciples for their unbelief (6:64). John then writes, "As a result of this many of his disciples were going away to the things

they left behind, and were no longer walking with him" (6:66). These disciples apparently were following Jesus because he was an exciting new miracle-worker and teacher and, as in John 2:23-25, Jesus recognized the deficiency of their belief. They had made some kind of a commitment to Jesus, but when his teaching did not conform to their expectations, they left him.

1.4.3. Marks of Belief. Once this group of Jesus' disciples turns away, Simon Peter steps forward to give a clear statement of what it means for the Twelve to follow Jesus: "Lord, to whom shall we go? You have the words of eternal life. We believe and know that you are the Holy One of God" (6:68-69). From this point on in John's Gospel the word *disciple* is used only of those who profess to believe on Jesus for eternal life (*see* Life). To truly believe is to pass beyond mere curiosity and to become convinced of the truth of Jesus' words for the meaning and purpose of life. Further, John records three sayings of Jesus which test the reality of the belief of the disciples, three marks of belief which will result in the observable life of a disciple. Inner belief will cause such a radical change that the external life will bear evidence of that belief.

The first mark of the true disciple is "abiding in Jesus' word." Although certain Jews believed in Jesus, the ensuing context indicates the nature of their belief: they needed to be set free from sin (cf. 8:32 with 8:33-36), they were seeking to kill him (8:37), their father was the Devil (8:2-44), they were not of God (8:47) and they tried to stone Jesus (8:59). These Jews had deficient faith similar to those encountered in John 2:23-25. True discipleship, true belief, will be evidenced by abiding in Jesus' words. This means passing beyond mere curiosity and becoming convinced of the truth of Jesus' words for the meaning and purpose of life (cf. 6:66-69). The evidence of true belief is seen in disciples who cling to Jesus' word as the truth for every area of life. True disciples are freed through Jesus' liberating word from bondage to sin.

Love for each other, as Jesus has loved them, is the second identifying mark of the true disciple-believer (13:34-35). The love of disciples for each other shows that they are Jesus' disciples and do not belong to the world of humanity. Since the contrast is between the world and disciples, all disciples are included. Love is not proof of superior commitment; love of other disciples is evidence that one is a believer.

The third mark of the disciple is a life that bears fruit. Jesus states, "This is to my Father's glory, that you bear much fruit, showing yourselves to be my disciples" (15:8). The true believer-disciple will bear fruit because true life is in the branch (*see* Vine). The unbeliever will not bear fruit, because branches which have no life cannot bear fruit. Eventually non-fruitbearing branches will be broken off and cast into the fire (15:6)—a picture consistent with other portrayals of the final destiny of unbelievers (*see* Judgment).

2. Jesus' Form of Discipleship.

Jesus' ministry of calling, training and sending out disciples stands as a captivating historical phenomenon. While there have been numerous recent attempts at classifying his ministry according to other types of social/religious movements of the first century (e.g., as a wandering charismatic, Zealot brigand, Cynic philosopher, Qumran/Essene separatist, Jewish rabbi,* apocalyptic* scribe,* Israelite prophet* figure) which have probably revealed some authentic parallel characteristics, Jesus' particular form of discipleship still defies classification. Nonetheless, looking back on the Evangelists' portraits of discipleship, some points become clear.

2.1. Called by Jesus.

2.1.1. Responding to the Call to Life. Although discipleship was a voluntary matter with other types of master-disciple relationships of the first century, with Jesus the initiative lay with his call (Mk 1:17; 2:14; Mt 4:19; 9:9; cf. Lk 5:10-11, 27-28) and his choice (Jn 15:16) of those who would be his disciples. The response to the call involves recognition and belief in Jesus' identity (Jn 2:11; 6:68-69), obedience to his summons (Mk 1:18, 20) and counting the cost of full allegiance to him (Lk 14:25-28; Mt 19:23-30). His calling is the beginning of something new. It means losing one's old life (Mk 8:34-37; Lk 9:23-25) and finding new life in the family of God through obeying the will of the Father (Mt 12:46-50).

2.1.2. The Group of Disciples. We should distinguish between the disciples in a narrow sense—especially those Twelve who literally followed Jesus around—and a broader group of adherents and sympathizers. The latter was comprised of, among others, the common masses of people (Lk 6:13), a variety of men and women (Lk 8:2-3; 23:49, 55; 24:13, 18, 33), tax collectors (Lk 19:1-10), scribes (Mt 8:18-21) and religious leaders (Jn 19:38-42; Mt 27:57). The term "disciple" designates one as a believer in Jesus; all true believers are disciples (cf. Acts 4:32 with 6:2). The Twelve were distinguished from the larger group by referring to them as "apostles" (Lk 6:13). The Twelve were both *disciples* by virtue of being believers and *apostles* because they were commissioned leaders (Mt 10:1-2).

2.1.3. Counting the Cost. In Jesus' lifetime the call to be a disciple meant to count the cost of allegiance to

Jesus; but this took various forms. The Twelve were called to leave all—including family, profession and property—and follow Jesus in his itinerant ministry. This was their training for their future role in the community (cf. Mt 19:23-30). Apparently others besides the Twelve were also called to this itinerancy (cf. Jn 6:66; Lk 8:2-3; 23:49, 55). But, while all disciples were called to count the cost of their allegiance (Lk 14:25-33; Mt 8:18-22), leaving everything and following Jesus around was not intended for all (e.g., Mk 5:18-19). Nicodemus and Joseph of Arimathea apparently became followers of Jesus sometime during his ministry (cf. Jn 3:1-14; 19:38-42), yet they presumably remained within the religious establishment and retained their wealth. When demonstration of their faith and allegiance to Jesus was required, they came forward to claim the body of Jesus (Mt 27:57-60; *see* Burial of Jesus).

2.1.4. Jesus Breaks through Religious Barriers. Unlike some of the sectarians within Judaism,* Jesus broke through the barriers which separated the clean from the unclean (*see* Clean and Unclean), the obedient from the sinful. He summoned the fisherman as well as the tax collector (*see* Taxes) and, in the opinion of some, even a zealous revolutionary (*see* Revolutionary Movements). A decisive factor is that Jesus called to himself those who, in the eyes of sectarians, did not seem to enjoy the necessary qualifications for fellowship with him (Mt 9:9-13; Mk 2:13-17). In calling the despised to himself, in sitting down to a meal with tax collectors (*see* Table Fellowship), Jesus demonstrates that they have been adopted into fellowship with God.

2.2. Following Jesus.

2.2.1. Attachment to Jesus. During Jesus' earthly ministry the disciple was to "follow" Jesus, an allegiance to his person which is regarded as the decisive act, whether it is a literal or figurative attachment. Jewish disciples would follow their master around, often literally imitating him. The goal of Jewish disciples was someday to become masters, or rabbis, themselves and to have their own disciples who would follow them. But Jesus' disciples were to remain disciples of their Master and teacher and to follow him only (cf. Mt 23:1-12). By the time of the Evangelists, the word "disciple" (*mathētēs*), although still carrying connotations of "learner," generally meant "adherent." Even though it is probable that Jesus' disciples memorized much of his teaching and passed it on as the tradition of the church, the disciples were committed more to his person than to his teaching. Following Jesus means togetherness with him and service to him while traveling on the Way.

2.2.2. Continuing to Count the Cost. Even as entrance

to the Way of following Jesus required the would-be disciple to count the cost, so traveling on the Way requires disciples to count the cost (Mk 8:34). The disciples must daily deny themselves, take up the cross and follow Jesus (Lk 9:23). It is possible for one not to be a true part of the Way while externally traveling with Jesus (e.g., Judas). Therefore, the challenge is directed not only to the crowd but also to the disciples (cf. Mk 8:34—9:1; Mt 10:37-39; 16:24-26; Lk 9:23-27).

2.2.3. Becoming Like Jesus. Jesus declared that to be a disciple is to become like the Master (Mt 10:24-25; Lk 6:40). Becoming like Jesus includes going out with the same message, ministry and compassion (Mt 10:5-15), practicing the same religious and social traditions (Mk 2:18-22; Mt 12:1-8), belonging to the same family of obedience (Mt 12:46-49); exercising the same servanthood (Mk 10:42-45, par. Mt 20:26-28; Jn 13:12-17), experiencing the same suffering (Mt 10:16-25; Mk 10:38-39).

2.2.4. Growing in Discipleship. The Evangelists unanimously testify to the imperfections of the disciples, both of the larger group and of the Twelve. At the same time they testify to the growth of the disciples. The Evangelists give a realistic portrayal of good and bad traits in the disciples, yet they also show how Jesus taught them (Mk 4:10-12), corrected them (Mt 16:5-12), admonished them (Mt 17:19-20), supported them (Lk 22:31-34), comforted them (Jn 20:19-22) and restored them (Jn 21:15-19). In turn the disciples could become examples of what Jesus desires to do for the church (Mt 28:19-20). H. Kvalbein correctly declares that "it is basically wrong to think of the 'disciples' as models for some special or 'higher quality' Christians among other Christians." All of those who truly believed were called disciples in Jesus' day, and they are examples of how every Christian today should grow in discipleship.

2.3. Commissioned by Jesus. Through the Great Commission of Matthew 28:16-20 Jesus focuses his followers on the ongoing importance of discipleship through the ages.

2.3.1. Make Disciples. Jesus committed his earthly ministry to "making disciples" within Israel (cf. Jn 4:1), and he commissioned his disciples to "make disciples" among the nations (Mt 28:16-20; *see* Gentiles). The obvious meaning of "making disciples" is to proclaim the gospel message among those who have not yet received forgiveness of sins (Lk 24:46-47; Jn 20:21; *see* Forgiveness of Sins). The command finds remarkable verbal fulfillment in the activities of the early church (e.g., Acts 14:21), where disciples went from Jerusalem to Judea, to Samaria (*see* Samaritans), to the ends of the earth proclaiming the message of Jesus and making disciples. In the early church to believe in the gospel message was to become a disciple (cf. Acts 4:32 with 6:2). The injunction of the Great Commission is given at least to the eleven remaining disciples (cf. Mt 28:16), but in their own role as disciples they are paradigms for all disciples. As Jesus addresses the disciples and commands them to "make disciples of all the nations," Jesus is telling them to continue the work he began with them.

2.3.2. Baptizing and Teaching Disciples to Obey. The imperative (*mathēteusate*) implies both the call to discipleship and the process of becoming a disciple. Even as men and women are called from among the nations to start life as a disciple, they must in turn "follow" the Lord through baptism* and through obedience to Jesus' teaching. The participles "baptizing" (*baptizontes*) and "teaching" (*didaskontes*) describe activities through which the new disciple grows in discipleship. Growth in discipleship includes both identification with Jesus' death and resurrection (baptism) and obedience to all that Jesus had commanded the disciples in his earthly ministry (teaching).

2.3.3. Jesus with His Disciples. Jesus concludes the commission with the crucial element of discipleship: the presence of the Master ("And surely I am with you always, to the very end of the age," Mt 28:20). As the new disciple is baptized and taught to observe all that Jesus commanded, Jesus is present. Both those obeying the command and those responding are comforted by the awareness that the risen Jesus will continue to fashion all his disciples. The Master is always present for his disciples to follow.

See also APOSTLE; DISCIPLES; SERMON ON THE MOUNT.

BIBLIOGRAPHY. E. Best, *Disciples and Discipleship* (Edinburgh: T. & T. Clark, 1986); R. E. Brown, *The Community of the Beloved Disciple* (Mahwah, NJ: Paulist, 1979); J. A. Fitzmyer, *Luke the Theologian* (Mahwah, NJ: Paulist, 1989); C. Focant, "L'Incompréhension des Disciples dans le deuxième Evangile," *RB* 82 (1985) 161-85; R. A. Guelich, *Mark 1—8:26* (WBC 34A; Dallas: Word, 1989); P. D. Hanson, *The People Called* (San Francisco: Harper & Row, 1986); M. Hengel, *The Charismatic Leader and His Followers* (New York: Crossroad, 1981); R. A. Horsley, *Sociology and the Jesus Movement* (New York: Crossroad, 1989); W. H. Kelber, *Mark's Story of Jesus* (Philadelphia: Fortress, 1979); H. Kvalbein, " 'Go therefore and make disciples . . .': The Concept of Discipleship in the New Testament," *Themelios* 13 (1988) 48-53; U. Luz, "The Disciples in the Gospel according to Matthew," *The Interpretation of Matthew* (IRT 3; Philadelphia: Fortress, 1983); F. J. Matera, *What Are They Saying about Mark* (New York:

Paulist, 1987); B. L. Melbourne, *Slow To Understand* (Lanham, MD: University Press of America, 1988); R. P. Meye, *Jesus and the Twelve* (Grand Rapids: Eerdmans, 1968); K. H. Rengstorf, "μαθητής," *TDNT* IV:415-61; E. Schweizer, *Lordship and Discipleship* (SBT 28; London: SCM, 1960); F. F. Segovia, ed., *Discipleship in the New Testament* (Philadelphia: Fortress, 1985); E. Trocmé, *The Formation of the Gospel according to Mark* (Philadelphia: Westminster, 1975); J. Tyson, "The Blindness of the Disciples in Mark," in *The Messianic Secret*, ed. C. Tuckett (IRT 1; Philadelphia: Fortress, 1983); J. J. Vincent, *Disciple and Lord* (Sheffield: Academic, 1976); T. J. Weeden, Sr., *Mark—Traditions in Conflict* (Philadelphia: Fortress, 1971); M. J. Wilkins, *Following the Master: A Biblical Theology of Discipleship* (Grand Rapids: Zondervan, forthcoming; idem, *The Concept of Disciple in Matthew's Gospel* (NovT Sup 59; Leiden: E. J. Brill, 1988).

M. J. Wilkins

DIVINE MAN/*THEIOS ANĒR*

In NT scholarship the term *Divine Man*, or its Greek form *Theios Anēr*, designates an alleged type of religio-philosophical hero, legendary or historical, which was more or less indigenous to Greece or at least Hellenism and whose representatives were characterized by moral virtue, wisdom and/or miraculous power so that they were held to be divine. As commonly used, the term excludes the traditional Greek gods (except Asclepius, who was believed to have lived a human-like existence on earth before his death and apotheosis). Rather, it encompasses figures who in spite of their divinity were still regarded as humans.

1. History-of-Religions and Form-Critical Research
2. Scholarly Developments of the *Theios Anēr* Concept
3. The Ongoing Application of the *Theios Anēr* in Gospel Criticism
4. Critique

1. History-of-Religions and Form-Critical Research.
The roots of the *Theios Anēr* as an analytical concept lie in the history-of-religions school of the early twentieth century. To explain the successful spread of various eastern cults in the Hellenistic* era, R. Reitzenstein appealed to itinerant prophets whose characteristics of holiness, wisdom, miracle-working power and superhuman status bound them together as a type: the *Theios Anthrōpos* (Divine Human). The result of such studies was that early Christianity was firmly situated in its larger cultural and religious matrix (*see* Hellenism).

The early form critics (*see* Form Criticism) used the

Theios Anēr to elucidate the origin and christology of the Gospel miracle stories (*see* Miracles and Miracle Stories). They argued that most of the miracle stories were formulated, if not created outright, by Gentile Christians in order to magnify and win converts for Jesus, the superior *Theios Anēr*. (Although the expression *Theios Anēr* does not occur in the Gospels, or for that matter in the NT, the title *Son of God* was viewed as its equivalent.) From the beginning of the application of the *Theios Anēr* type to Gospel—and particularly Synoptic—studies, the implications for the historicity of the miracle stories have been very negative.

Aside from the problem generally posed by the so-called nature miracles, it has been frequently maintained that the historicity of most of these accounts is quite doubtful. Not only were they formulated by Gentile Christians removed by time and probably distance from the ministry of Jesus and the life of the earliest Jewish church in Jerusalem, but these same Christians were also under pressure to make Jesus successful in competition with Hellenistic, pagan religious heroes.

In many ways the account of the origin and *Sitz im Leben* (life setting) of the miracle stories offered by the form-critical school was difficult to contradict. Scholars of comparative religion (e.g., L. Bieler) continued to document parallels between the Jesus portrayed in the miracle stories (and in certain other Gospel traditions recounting miraculous events, e.g., birth,* baptism,* transfiguration,* passion and resurrection* narratives) and various divine-human miracle workers of repute in the Hellenistic world, such as Asclepius, Pythagoras and Apollonius of Tyana. Such parallels include types of miraculous actions (e.g., exorcisms,* healings,* raisings from the dead, control of the elements) and motifs appearing in the stories (e.g., ridicule of the miracle worker; a patient's previous unsuccessful attempts to find a cure; miracle performed by touch, words, and/or spittle; and immediate occurrence of the miracle).

In addition, one could show a definite similarity in the form or structure between the Gospel stories and those with so-called Divine Men as their subjects. Repeatedly these stories are constituted by three principal elements: (1) a description of the distress or problem that the miracle worker will rectify, (2) a description of the miracle-producing action and (3) a conclusion, which at least confirms the miracle worker's success.

2. Scholarly Developments of the *Theios Anēr* Concept.
Twentieth-century scholars who have found the *Theios Anēr* to be a useful analytic category have offered

several proposals for its relevance to understanding the Gospels.

2.1. The Hellenistic-Jewish Milieu. Early on, for example, scholars pointed to Diaspora or Hellenistic Judaism as the cultural/religious medium through which the *Theios Anēr* type came to influence the early church's presentation of Jesus. Hellenistic-Jewish Christians, so the argument runs, found it natural to portray Jesus as a *Theios Anēr* in their attempt to defend and advance their new faith, since previously they had used precisely the same strategy in their efforts to promote OT heroes, especially Moses. This hypothesis, however, was carefully reviewed by C. Holladay, who analyzed three representatives of Hellenistic Judaism—Josephus, Philo and Artapanus—in order to observe how these authors presented Jewish heroes in their apologetic and propagandistic efforts. He concluded that, at least in the sources he studied, there is no evidence that in order to glorify Judaism* or win converts Hellenized Jews tended to divinize their heroes or to amplify their thaumaturgical activities. Holladay's work has forced a major reassessment of the theory that the *Theios Anēr* concept was mediated to early Christianity via Hellenistic Judaism, and in fact has resulted in dampened enthusiasm for *Theios Anēr* as an interpretative tool.

2.2. Pre-Canonical Miracle Collections. On another front, there has been significant interest in the question of whether the Gospels made use of written or at least more or less fixed oral collections of miracle stories, and if so whether their christological orientation is appropriately described as *Theios Anēr*. It is frequently held that behind the Fourth Gospel lies a written collection of Jesus' signs, frequently referred to as the Semeia Source, which originally ended with John 20:30-31 (*see* John, Gospel of). Partially influenced by this hypothesis, others have suggested that one or more similar collections were incorporated into the earliest Synoptic Gospel, Mark. In the U.S.A., at any rate, scholars have tended to single out the miracles of 4:35—6:44; 6:45—8:10 as having been derived from two rather parallel (both begin with a sea miracle and end with a feeding miracle) collections of Jesus' miracles.

Those who find the arguments for such pre-canonical miracle collections cogent frequently describe them as expressive of a *Theios Anēr* christology. Moreover, some even suggest that the circles in which these miracle collections were developed and committed to writing possessed a theological outlook uninformed or at least uninterested in what came to be the heart of the gospel message: Jesus Christ, crucified as an expiatory sacrifice inaugurating a new covenant and

raised and exalted to heaven by God, who thus vindicated him and inaugurated the first stage of the resurrection of the dead. G. Corrington has gone so far as to argue that the Markan linkage between Jesus' miracles and his authority*/status as Son of man*/Messiah* (particularly in Mk 2:1-12) represents a secondary development. In the miracle catenae at Mark's disposal, the miracles simply aimed to document the divine power possessed by Jesus, in other words, that he was a *Theios Anēr*.

However, this entire line of approach is marred by precarious speculation and unproven assumptions. Various Gospel scholars remain skeptical of the possibility of isolating fixed miracle collections behind Mark, and the diversity of results among those who have attempted to isolate these collections erodes confidence in the enterprise. Moreover, even if Mark utilized such collections, (1) it requires a blind leap to conclude that those who first formulated and used them had no use for the saving value of Jesus' death and the eschatological significance of his resurrection, and (2) precise determination of the extent of Markan redactional activity will remain problematic since the miracle stories (and versions of them) that Mark heard and/or read remain inaccessible to us.

2.3. Aretalogy and Gospel Genre. The *Theios Anēr* concept has also figured in the debate over the genre of the Gospels. Some have claimed that this genre, far from being unique, can be described as the aretalogy of a *Theios Anēr*, a genre with representatives predating Mark. Early on, the Greek word *aretalogia* referred to a rendition of a god's virtues, mighty deeds and miracles. Eventually, it is argued, the term was broadened to encompass a similar recounting of a *Theios Anēr*'s wonders. In the modern era, however, a few scholars have applied the term to include such glorifying biographical works as Philo's *Life of Moses* and Philostratus's *Life of Apollonius of Tyana*. Such "aretalogies," so the theory goes, demonstrate the literary model adopted by the Gospels, which seek to promote their *Theios Anēr*, Jesus. This view, however, has failed to gain substantial support because the extant "Lives" (1) are not called aretalogies and (2) vary rather considerably among themselves in form, content and function (*see* Gospel [Genre]).

2.4. Markan Christology. Up until about thirty years ago, those who employed the *Theios Anēr* as an analytic tool in Gospel studies believed that the Evangelists essentially *synthesized* the portrait of Jesus as a *Theios Anēr* found in the miracle traditions with the perspective found in the sayings source Q and the passion and resurrection narratives (*see* Passion Narratives). However, T. Weeden, anticipated by others, argued that Mark was actually a polemic against interlopers in the Markan community who brought with them a *Theios Anēr* christology and the traditions which expressed it, principally the miracle stories. According to Weeden, such stories, which of course figure prominently in the first half of Mark, only *appear* to promote a *Theios Anēr* interpretation of Jesus: "The *theios-anēr* position is set up only to be discredited by Jesus once the disciples confess to that position" (164). Now the way was clear to compare Mark with Paul, who himself, according to the prior research of D. Georgi, had done battle with earlier proponents of a *Theios Anēr* christology at Corinth (see especially 2 Cor 10—13).

Initially, Weeden's work engendered considerable support, particularly in North America. But by the early 1980s J. D. Kingsbury was able to chronicle a growing disenchantment with it. Increasing doubt about the viability of the *Theios Anēr* concept and its relationship to the Son of God* title, a growing tendency in Gospel studies to give priority to literary criticism* rather than tradition-critical (*see* Tradition Criticism) or history-of-religions considerations, and the sheer mass of miracles present in Mark (including several in the second half) have converged to undermine Weeden's thesis (*see* Mark, Gospel of).

3. The Ongoing Application of *Theios Anēr* in Gospel Criticism.

In spite of these trends, the *Theios Anēr* continues to live in Gospel studies, as the contributions by H. D. Betz and Corrington show. In broad outline they are in agreement: *Theios Anēr* is a valid and useful category and well describes the christological orientation of certain pre-canonical traditions, especially the miracle stories. Mark made use of many such traditions, but critically reinterpreted them by means of the messianic secret, the passion narrative, the historicizing of the Jesus materials, an emphasis on eschatology (Betz) and/or by transforming the miracles into proofs of Jesus' authority as Son of man/Messiah (Corrington). Matthew has likewise critically adapted these *Theios Anēr* materials, primarily by stressing that Jesus' miracles fulfilled the OT prophecies (*see* Old Testament in the Gospels; Typology). On the other hand, Luke's christological outlook is very similar—if not identical—to the collection of miracle stories and traditions employed by Mark (and John). In John the miracles become "signs" of the epiphany of the Logos* in Jesus.

4. Critique.

However, such continuing employment of the *Theios Anēr* as a typical Hellenistic figure during the NT era ought to be reconsidered. Among so-called divine-human miracle workers of repute in the Hellenistic era, there was an extreme amount of diversity. Their divinity was expressed in a wide variety of (sometimes conflicting) ways, although the terms *Theios Anēr* and/or *huios theou* ("Son of God") were very rarely applied to them. Equally diverse were the kinds of miracles they purportedly performed and the social roles they played (kings, seers, shamans, hero physicians). D. Tiede and, even more so, E. Gallagher have demonstrated the diversity of criteria according to which these figures were judged to be divine. In the face of the precious little homogeneity that exists among the motley assortment of figures to whom Hellenistic sources attribute both divinity and miraculous power, and in view of a rich tradition of miracle-working in Jewish tradition (Moses,* Elijah,* Elisha, the Josephan "sign prophets," etc.; *see* Revolutionary Movements), the so-called *Theios Anēr* type hardly seems to offer a useful tool for evaluating christological trends in either pre-canonical or canonical traditions.

Aside from the question of whether it is desirable to continue speaking of a *Theios Anēr* type, it certainly is legitimate to ask whether the Gospel miracle traditions, in their christology, their themes and motifs, and/or their structure, have been influenced by Hellenistic ideas and concepts (1) which were associated, rarely or frequently, with miracle workers (gods or divine humans) and (2) which would have been alien to the culture and possibly to the religious sensibilities of the early Jewish church. While one might expect a certain amount of assimilation to occur, the evidence makes it very difficult to conclude confidently that this has happened in any given case.

In light of the tendency of Palestinian Judaism to assimilate exalted biblical, eschatological and/or angelic figures to God (e.g., Moses, Melchizedek, Yahoel) and in light of Christ's heavenly status in early Christianity, we can hardly deny the christology of the miracle stories to the early Aramaic-speaking church. In addition, Palestinian-Jewish parallels—or at least closely related conceptions—exist for all of the themes and motifs that have been dubbed "Hellenistic." Finally, the "miracle story form" is not an arbitrary pattern indigenous to Hellenistic culture but naturally results when one recites, in logico-chronological fashion, a miracle of salvation* or deliverance. Not only can one find examples in the OT (e.g., 2 Kings 6:1-7), but one can also demonstrate that such narratives would have performed valuable functions among the earliest believers (*inter alia* they glorify and authenticate Jesus' divine authority and messianic status). All of this strongly militates against a confident relegation of much of the Gospel miracle tradition to a secondary or tertiary stage of development.

See also DEMON, DEVIL, SATAN; HEALING; MIRACLES AND MIRACLE STORIES; PROPHETS AND PROPHECY.

BIBLIOGRAPHY. L. Bieler, *THEIOS ANĒR* (2 vols.; Vienna: O. Höfels, 1935-36); H. D. Betz, "Gottmensch II," *RAC* 12:234-312 (partially based on "Jesus as Divine Man," in *Jesus and the Historian*, ed. F. Trotter [Philadelphia: Westminster, 1968] 114-33); B. Blackburn, Theios Anēr *and the Markan Miracle Traditions* (WUNT 2.40; Tübingen: J. C. B. Mohr, 1991); G. Corrington, *The "Divine Man"* (New York: Peter Lang, 1986); E. Gallagher, *Divine Man or Magician?* (SBLDS 64; Chico: Scholars, 1982); D. Georgi, *The Opponents of Paul in Second Corinthians* (Philadelphia: Fortress, 1986); C. Holladay, Theios Anēr *in Hellenistic-Judaism* (SBLDS 40; Missoula: Scholars, 1977); J. D. Kingsbury, *The Christology of Mark's Gospel* (Philadelphia: Fortress, 1983); R. Reitzenstein, *Hellenistic Mystery-Religions* (PTMS 15; Pittsburg: Pickwick, 1978); D. Tiede, *The Charismatic Figure As Miracle Worker* (SBLDS 1; Missoula: SBL, 1972); T. Weeden, Sr., *Mark—Traditions in Conflict* (Philadelphia: Fortress, 1971).

B. L. Blackburn

DIVORCE

1. The Sources
2. A Summary of Various Interpretations
3. Defining the Terms
4. The History of Jesus' Divorce Teachings
5. Conclusion

1. The Sources.

Within the NT there are five important passages which deal with Jesus' teaching on divorce: Matthew 5:32; 19:3-9; Mark 10:2-12; Luke 16:18 and 1 Corinthians 7:10-15. These five passages fall into three groups.

1.1. Matthew 5:32 and Luke 16:18. These two passages resemble each other in being isolated sayings lacking a specific historical setting and context in the life of Jesus. Their content is also similar. Both have two parts. The first states that the man who divorces his wife and marries another commits adultery (Luke) or causes his wife to commit adultery (Matthew), and the second states that whoever marries a divorced woman commits adultery. The major difference between these two accounts is Matthew's famous "except on the ground of unchastity" clause.

1.2. Matthew 19:3-9 and Mark 10:2-12. These two passages also resemble each other and both appear in the same place in the narrative of Jesus' life. Their content and wording are also quite similar. Both state

that a man who divorces his wife and marries another commits adultery. The main differences between them is that Matthew once again has an exception clause—"except for unchastity," and Mark has "and if she divorces her husband and marries another, she commits adultery" (Mk 10:12).

1.3. 1 Corinthians 7:10-15. The earliest of these five passages is 1 Corinthians 7:10-15. Here Paul introduces Jesus' saying on divorce in 7:10 by the words, "To the married I give charge, not I but the Lord. . . ." In so doing Paul makes clear that the command which follows comes from the Lord; it is an utterance spoken by the Lord Jesus during his earthly ministry. Jesus said that a wife should not "separate herself" from her husband and that a husband should not "send away" his wife. The difference in these two terms should not be pressed. Both mean to "divorce," but they describe this from two different perspectives. This saying in 7:10-11 resembles the Markan saying in that it envisions the possibility of a wife divorcing her husband. Paul, however, parenthetically tempers the ideal of marriage with the possibility of a separation without remarriage. To Jesus' saying Paul adds an additional apostolic command in 7:12-15 which entertains a new situation in which an unbelieving spouse leaves the believing partner. Paul urges the believer to continue the marriage if the unbelieving partner consents, but if the unbeliever desires to separate—that is, to divorce—then so be it. The believer is not "bound." Thus Paul adds to the ideal of continued marriage the realization that the believer really cannot do anything if his or her unbelieving mate chooses to divorce.

As might be expected there are a number of textual variants associated with these texts. The majority seek to make one saying conform more exactly to another. Some variants involve changes, such as making the first part of Matthew 5:32 into a conditional clause in order to match the latter part of the verse. Others seek to make the two exception clauses in Matthew 5:32 (*parektos logou porneias*) and 19:9 (*mē epi porneia*) identical. In general, however, no substantive issue of interpretation is affected by these variants.

2. A Summary of Various Interpretations.

In discussing the various interpretations concerning Jesus' teaching on divorce, one must not lose sight of the great unanimity that exists in this area. All exegetes agree that Jesus saw divorce as a tragedy. Any divorce denotes a failure of the divine purpose, for those God joined together in marriage should not be separated. Thus there is no so-called good divorce, and the discussion that follows must be understood in this light.

2.1. Divorce in the Case of Unchastity Is Permitted, but Not Remarriage. This was the view of the majority of the early church fathers. Exegetical support is found in the placement of the exception clause in Matthew 19:9. "Except for unchastity" is interpreted as modifying only the verb "divorces" and not the verb "marries." Thus the text is interpreted, "Whoever divorces his wife except for unchastity commits adultery and the one who remarries [without exception] commits adultery." The purpose of the exception clause is not to permit remarriage in cases of unchastity but simply to say that in such a situation, divorce, in the sense of separation from bed and board, is not adultery. (This idea of divorce as separation only, once thought of as unknown in Judaism, may be alluded to in the Dead Sea Scrolls,* for in 11QTemple 56:17-19; 57:17-19 and CD 4:20-21 polygamy and remarriage after divorce appear to be forbidden.) Divorce is permissible in cases of unchastity, but not remarriage. Matthew 19:9 is therefore understood as making two separate propositions involving two different persons: (1) The person who divorces, except for unchastity, commits adultery; (2) the person who remarries always commits adultery. Matthew 5:32 is interpreted similarly.

There are several problems with this interpretation. One is that the parallels in Mark 10:9 and Luke 16:18 envision one person rather than two—"whoever divorces . . . and remarries . . . commits adultery." If Matthew 19:9 truly refers to two different persons, one would expect a plural verb "they commit adultery" rather than "he commits adultery." Elsewhere when the Evangelist seeks to designate two separate people in such a sentence, he demonstrates this by repeating the relative clause (cf. Mt 5:22, "whoever insults . . . and whoever says . . ."; 20:26-27, "whoever would be . . . and whoever would be . . ."). If Matthew wanted to express this view, he could easily have written "whoever divorces . . . commits adultery, and whoever remarries . . . commits adultery" or at least "whoever divorces . . . and whoever remarries [they not he] commit adultery."

It should also be noted that according to this interpretation the man who divorces his wife, except for unchastity, commits adultery. Yet how can a divorce except for unchastity be considered adultery? One can argue such a divorce is wrong, forbidden, sinful, evil, etc. But how is it adultery? How can divorce, understood in this interpretation as separation of bed and board, be adultery? Unless divorce assumes remarriage, it is difficult to perceive how divorce is adultery, for barring a radical redefinition, adultery involves some kind of sexual union. (Even in Mt 5:28 adultery is still connected with "lust.") On the other hand, to assume that divorce involves remarriage refutes this interpretation which requires that divorce must be understood as separation apart from remarriage.

Another problem with this view is that the word *divorce* is understood in two different ways. In 19:9 it refers to separation alone. Yet in 19:3 and 8 divorce is understood in the sense that the Pharisees* understood this term, and they clearly believed that divorce included the right to remarry, for divorce was usually performed by saying "You are free to marry any man" (*Giṭ.* ix.3). This is assumed in Mark 10:11-12 where "divorce and remarry" are paired, and in 10:9 where "put asunder," which is a synonym for divorce, is defined in 10:11-12 as divorcing and remarrying. This is also assumed in Deuteronomy 24:1-4 where the remarrying of the divorced person is discussed. Divorce without remarriage is, of course, possible, but in the setting of the NT it is more hypothetical than actual. Remarriage is assumed. Thus, it is only reasonable to assume that "divorce" in Matthew 19:9 should be understood in a similar way as in 19:3 and 8: "putting away with the right to remarry." If Jesus and/or Matthew wanted to indicate a use of this term different from that assumed by the questioners about divorce, they would have had to indicate this clearly. This they did not do.

2.2. Divorce and Remarriage Are Permitted in Cases of Unchastity and Desertion. This interpretation is associated with Erasmus and is the view of the Protestant Reformers. Many evangelicals hold this view today. According to this interpretation both divorce and remarriage are permissible in the case of unchastity. Support is found in the context of the Jewish audiences of Jesus and Matthew, because for them divorce meant not only separation from a wife but the right to remarriage. For the Pharisees divorce was assumed to include the right of remarriage. If Jesus or Matthew excluded the right to remarry from divorce and if they sought to communicate this to their audiences, they would have had to make this clear. Since they did not do so, we must assume that they understood the term *divorce* in the same way their audiences did.

Paul also seems to support this view in 1 Corinthians 7:12-15 where he may be giving a second exception. Paul states that when a believer is deserted by an unbelieving partner, the believer "is not bound" (7:15). Is Paul referring here to being bound in marriage, that the believer is no longer bound to the deserting partner but is now free to remarry? Or is he referring to no longer being bound to seek to maintain the marriage (7:12-14)? In 1 Corinthians 7:39 Paul states that a wife is "bound" to her husband as long as he lives, but if he dies she is free to marry in the

Lord. Although the word *bound* used here is not identical with that used in 7:15, they are related. The subject being discussed is also the same—remarriage. In Romans 7:3 Paul also says that when a husband dies the wife is "free" to remarry. In light of the fact that similar terms are used in 1 Corinthians 7:39 and Romans 7:3 with regard to the right to remarry, it is probable that not being "bound" in the case of desertion by an unbeliever means being free to remarry. Understood in this way, Paul then teaches that remarriage is permissible when a believer is deserted by his or her unbelieving mate.

The major difficulty with this interpretation is the fact that the parallel accounts in Mark and Luke lack an exception clause. While it is logically correct to say that Mark and Luke by omitting the exception clause do not preclude it, the simple reading of Mark and/or Luke gives the impression that no divorce or remarriage is possible. However, if Jesus is using exaggerated language here to emphasize his point against a hostile audience (see 4.1. below), his omission of any qualification may be understandable.

2.3. Divorce of Unlawful Marriages Is Permitted. In this interpretation "unchastity" is understood to refer to some marital flaw which in essence nullifies the marriage. One such view sees unchastity as referring to incestuous marriage, such as that described in Leviticus 18:6-18; 20:17 and Deuteronomy 27:22 (cf. also 11QTemple 57:11-19; CD 4:20; 5:8-11). NT support is seen in 1 Corinthians 5:1 where unchastity is used to describe the incestuous relationship of a man living with his stepmother. The unchastity of Acts 15:20, 29; 21:25 is also frequently interpreted as referring to an illicit marital union involving incest. A similar interpretation sees unchastity as referring to premarital unfaithfulness by the wife during the engagement period as described in Deuteronomy 22:20-21. In this case, as in an incestuous marriage, no true marriage has taken place. What occurs is not so much a divorce as an annulment. In both these instances unchastity is understood as annulling a non-marriage. Thus there is no compromising of Jesus' absolute forbidding of divorce, for no true marriage relationship is being ended.

One other variation of this interpretation sees unchastity as involving intermarriage between a Jew and a Gentile,* such as is prohibited in Deuteronomy 7:1-5. This relationship is seen as a form of fornication in Jubilees 30:7, 10, and especially 30:11. Paul's teaching in 1 Corinthians 7:12-15, however, would argue against such an interpretation, for there the believer is told not to separate from his or her unbelieving mate if the mate is willing to continue the relationship.

The main problem with this view involves interpreting unchastity as meaning incest or premarital infidelity. As we shall see in the next section, unchastity (i.e., *porneia*) has too broad a range of meaning to be interpreted so narrowly. It may indeed include these narrow meanings, but it cannot be restricted to them.

2.4. Unchastity Is Not an Exception. This unusual interpretation is called "the preteritive view." According to this view the exception clause is not to be interpreted as an exception at all. It is to be interpreted "completely apart from the question of unchastity" rather than "except in the case of unchastity." In other words, Jesus is maintaining that all divorce and remarriage is adultery and that he simply does not want to discuss the case of unchastity. It is irrelevant to the issue. Thus the term *except* is understood as prescinding adultery from consideration. According to this view the Matthean exceptions are not exceptions at all, so that Matthew holds the same view on divorce as found in Mark and Luke. The result is a harmonization of all four Gospel accounts.

Grammatically, however, this is a very difficult interpretation to defend. The "except" (*mē epi*) found in Matthew 19:9 usually means "except for" and separates something from a larger entity. The natural way of interpreting *mē epi* is "X is . . . except in the case of Y." Thus, the most natural way of interpreting Matthew 19:9 is "divorce and remarriage (X) is adultery except in the case of unchastity (Y)." It is most unnatural to interpret *mē epi* in the preteritive sense, and no one would favor such an interpretation if exegetical rather than harmonistic considerations were the primary concern.

2.5. Matthew Has Interpreted Jesus' Saying by Means of an Exception Clause. This interpretation sees Matthew's exception clauses as exegetical additions which the Evangelist has appended to Jesus' divorce sayings. In so doing he has taken Jesus' original teaching beyond what Jesus actually said for the sake of applying them to the situation of his audience. This traditio-historical approach (*see* Tradition History) to the exception clauses can be viewed from various perspectives. For some, Matthew is seen as having corrupted the original teaching of Jesus in order to make it more palatable for his readers.

On the other hand, Matthew can also be seen as an inspired interpreter of Jesus who possessed the mind of Christ.* According to this understanding, Matthew, led by the Spirit (Jn 16:13, 15), has interpreted Jesus' words and shown that Mark 10:11-12 and Luke 16:18 are overstatements addressed to a hostile audience and that Jesus did not intend in a single sentence to establish a law which would cover every conceivable situation. This view receives support from 1 Corinthians 7:15 if this verse is interpreted as giving another exception.

The strength of this view is that it deals forthrightly with the grammar and recognizes the exception clauses as real exceptions not mentioned in Mark, Luke and 1 Corinthians. It is less prone to those harmonistic attempts which do violence to the text and claim that the exception clauses are not real exceptions. The weakness of this view is that it either sees Matthew as contradicting Jesus' teaching or it sees in Jesus' teaching an overstatement in which universal language is used to teach a non-universal truth (see 4.1. below).

3. Defining the Terms.

In seeking to understand Jesus' teaching on divorce, the interpretation of the two exception clauses plays a pivotal role. Yet, as already seen in the previous section, unanimity is lacking as to exactly what the terms *unchastity* and *except* mean. Along with this there is confusion as to what the term *divorce* means. Without an accurate understanding of these terms, a correct interpretation of the divorce saying is impossible.

It is clear from its use in the NT and the Septuagint that "unchastity," or *porneia*, can refer to a number of unlawful sexual acts. It can refer to incest (1 Cor 5:1; and possibly Acts 15:20, 29; 21:25); adultery (in Jer 3:9 adultery and *porneia* appear in synonymous parallelism); prostitution (Mt 21:31-32; Lk 15:30; 1 Cor 6:13-18); sexual immorality in general (Mk 7:21-22/Mt 15:19; 1 Cor 6:9-11; 7:2); and even as a metaphor for idolatry (Rev 17:1-5, 15-16). It has been pointed out that *porneia* cannot be equated with "adultery" because there is a separate Greek word for adultery—*moicheia*—and because in Mark 7:21-22/Matthew 15:19; 1 Corinthians 6:9 and Hebrews 13:4 *porneia* is distinguished from *moicheia*. But while there is a distinction between the two words, it is one of specificity. *Moicheia* is a specific term and means adultery; *porneia* is a much more inclusive term and means any unlawful sexual act. These terms are not synonyms, but *porneia* includes *moicheia*. In other words "adultery" is a subspecies of "unchastity" which, unless qualified, refers to sexual immorality in general.

Because "unchastity" in Matthew 5:32 and 19:9 is unqualified, it cannot be limited to incest, sexual unfaithfulness during the engagement period or even adultery. It refers to any and all unlawful sexual activity. Unless qualified, Matthew's audience would have interpreted this term broadly as "sexual immorality" and included not only adultery, incest, premarital infidelity, but also homosexuality (Lev 18:22), bestiality (Lev 18:23) and any other sexual conduct condemned in the OT.

It has been objected that since adultery was punishable by stoning, unchastity as a cause for divorce could not refer to adultery because stoning the guilty parties to death would make divorce superfluous. Yet, although the OT and the rabbinic materials (*see* Rabbinic Traditions and Writings) speak of putting an adulterer to death, the degree to which this was literally carried out is uncertain. The historicity of the narrative materials which speak of this possibility, such as Susanna and the non-canonical John 7:53—8:11, is open to question. It appears that whereas in theory adulterers were to be put to death by stoning (or burning), in practice other penalties were frequently imposed (cf. Prov 6:33-35; Hos 2:3, 10; Ezek 16:37-39; 23:29). Thus Joseph sought not Mary's stoning but divorce, when he thought her guilty of adultery (Mt 1:19; cf. also *Soṭa* 4.3).

Attempts to interpret "except" in Matthew 19:9 in a preteritive manner have already been described (see 2.4. above). With an absence of any exegetical grounds for choosing this rare and unusual interpretation, this attempt must be rejected. "Except" must be understood as excluding one group from the general statement "whoever divorces his wife and marries another commits adultery." That group consists of those who divorce and remarry in light of the unchastity of their original partner.

The final term which must be defined is *divorce*. Does divorce assume the right to remarry or does it assume only the right to put away one's wife and be separate—a separation from bed and board? That divorce can be conceived of without subsequent remarriage is clear. One is not obligated to remarry upon divorce. The expression "divorce and remarry" in all four Gospel accounts indicates this. Yet whereas divorce and remarriage are separate activities, did the common understanding of the term *divorce* assume the right to remarry? This question, based upon evidence from rabbinic literature, is to be answered in the affirmative.

The essential part of a Jewish bill of divorce consisted of the words "You are free to marry any man" (*Giṭ* 9.3). This is clearly Matthew's understanding in 5:32, for how does divorcing a woman make (not "stigmatize") her an adulteress? It is because "divorce" assumes that the divorced woman will exercise her right to remarry. Thus, whereas remarriage was not a necessary part of a divorce, the right to remarry was. Jesus could, of course, have redefined "divorce" and excluded the right to remarry. But because his audience had asked him about the right to divorce and remarry, if he wished to convey a different meaning of divorce which excludes the right to remarry, he would have had to make this clear to his audience. This is especially true in that he is trying in Mark 10:2-12 and parallels to clarify a pharisaic misinterpretation. Since he did redefine the meaning of divorce, we must assume that he meant by "divorce" what his audience meant. (Note how in 1 Cor 7:11 Paul defines what he means by separation in 1 Cor 7:10.) As a result, although the later church distinction between divorce with the right to remarry and divorce in the sense of separation may not have been unknown in Judaism,* this was not the normal way Jesus' (or Matthew's) audience thought. "Divorce" therefore in our texts should be understood as assuming the right to remarry.

4. The History of Jesus' Divorce Teachings.

4.1. The **Ipsissima Verba** *of Jesus.* In seeking to reconstruct exactly what Jesus said concerning divorce, we are fortunate in having multiple sources: Mark 10:2-12/Matthew 19:3-9; Luke 16:18/Matthew 5:32 and 1 Corinthians 7:10-11. There is no need to question the general setting of Jesus' divorce saying in Mark 10:2-12/Matthew 19:3-9, for this fits well the debate among the Pharisees concerning the grounds for divorce. Whereas the school of Shammai limited divorce to unchastity (or at least indecent conduct) because of their interpretation of Deuteronomy 24:1, the school of Hillel was much more liberal and permitted divorce even for burning the husband's supper. Rabbi Akiba went even further and permitted divorce if a husband found a more attractive woman (*Giṭ.* 9.10). Thus the question "Is it lawful to divorce one's wife?" (Mk 10:2) fits well the situation of Jesus' day. It is quite likely that the question was a hostile one as well (Mk 10:2, "tested him"). There is also no reason to doubt that Deuteronomy 24:1, which was the center of the rabbinic discussion, was alluded to or that Jesus referred to Genesis 1:27 and 2:24.

Concerning the actual saying itself, the exception clause is best understood as a Matthean interpretative addition to help show his Jewish-Christian readers that Jesus was not seeking in his divorce statement "to abolish the Law*" (Mt 5:17). Neither Mark, Luke nor Paul mention it. Thus we have three separate sources (Mark, Q,* Paul) which witness to Jesus' teaching on divorce and yet lack an exception clause. Also, the more difficult nature of their form of Jesus' teaching argues in favor of the exception clause being secondary. Why would Mark, Luke and Paul choose to omit it?

The original form of Jesus' saying was probably "Whoever divorces his wife and marries another commits adultery." If we omit the exception clause, we find this in Mark 10:10b, Luke 16:18a and Matthew 19:9a. Paul states this in a different form in 1 Corinthians 7:11b when he says "the husband should not divorce his wife." Matthew 5:32a, which assumes that the divorced woman will remarry, is a logical implication of this, but its authenticity is doubtful. The expression "against her" in Mark 10:11 is most probably an interpretative comment by the Evangelist.

The authenticity of Mark 10:12, "and if she divorces her husband and marries another, she commits adultery," is usually denied because it supposedly reflects a Greco-Roman milieu where women could divorce their husbands, whereas Jewish wives could not. Therefore, Jesus could not have uttered this saying. It is now evident that Jewish women were at certain times and places able to divorce their husbands, although this was rare. Josephus* reflects the practice of mainstream Judaism when he states, ". . . it is (only) the man who is permitted . . . to do this [divorce] . . ." (*Ant.* 15.7.10 §259). More important, however, is the fact that according to Mark 6:17-18 the most famous marriage in Galilee* was the marriage of Herod Antipas and Herodias, who had divorced her husband, Philip (*see* Herodian Dynasty). Thus, according to this passage and its parallels, there existed in Galilee a glaring example of a woman who divorced her husband, and in fact John the Baptist (*see* John the Baptist) lost his life because he said to Herod "It is not lawful to have your brother's wife" (Mk 6:18). This indicates that Jesus could have taught concerning a woman divorcing her husband. (Some difficulties exist between the Synoptic accounts and Josephus *Ant.* 18.5.1-2 §§109-119.) The fact that Paul alludes to this possibility in his quotation of Jesus' divorce saying (1 Cor 7:10) lends support to the case for its authenticity. Its omission in the Lukan and Matthean parallels, on the other hand, weakens the case. Absolute certainty as to the authenticity or inauthenticity of Mark 10:12 is unwarranted, but, all things considered, it is more likely that it is an interpretative comment which brings out a legitimate consequence of Jesus' teaching.

It is not impossible that Jesus uttered Matthew 5:32b/Luke 16:18b, "and he who marries a divorced woman commits adultery," for Jesus could very well have uttered several variant sayings on divorce at different times and places in his ministry. Yet if every variant saying on divorce is assumed to be a different saying of Jesus, we shall have at least six different authentic sayings of Jesus: Mark 10:11/Luke 16:18a; Matthew 19:9; 1 Corinthians 7:11b; Mark 10:12/

1 Corinthians 7:10b; Matthew 5:32a and Matthew 5:32b/Luke 16:18b. It seems much more likely that some of these sayings, such as Matthew 5:32a and Matthew 5:32b/Luke 16:18b are interpretations—apostolic and therefore authoritative interpretations—of Jesus' teaching on divorce. All appear to be legitimate implications of Jesus' teaching on divorce.

The authenticity of Jesus' teaching on divorce in Mark 10:10b/Luke 16:18a/Matthew 19:9a is supported not only by the multiple attestation of Mark, Q and Paul in 1 Corinthians 7:11b but by the criterion of coherence, for this divorce saying fits well other sayings in which Jesus heightens or overrides an OT teaching (*see* Old Testament in the Gospels). It also fits other passages in which Jesus is asked a hostile question by his audience (cf. Mk 11:27-33; 12:13-17, 18-27). In addition, this teaching may also fit in part the criterion of dissimilarity, for Jesus' teaching on divorce conflicts sharply with normal Jewish practice as typified by Hillel and even Shammai. (How familiar Jesus' audience was with the Qumran community's teaching on this subject is hard to assess.)

Having established that Jesus taught that divorce and remarriage were adultery, we must now proceed to interpret these words. Most interpretations have treated Jesus' words as if they were the objective, referential language of jurisprudence seeking to convey a legal precept. Yet Mark 10:2 indicates that the question was asked in a hostile setting. Thus Jesus' words are perhaps better interpreted as expressive or commissive language which contain an emotive quality. Much of Jesus' teaching was uttered in such a context, and it is not surprising that his answers frequently contain hyperbole and overstatement (cf. Mt 5:23-24, 29-30, 34-36, 40; Mk 7:15). Thus Jesus, in his great concern to show that divorce destroys God's purpose in marriage and in light of the loose attitude of his audience toward divorce, expressed the will of God without exception. "God hates divorce! All divorce is wrong!" (cf. Mal 2:16a). The very question of the Pharisees, "When is divorce permissible?" witnesses to a decidedly wrong focus. This may at times be a legitimate question, and later Matthew and Paul would deal with that question, but in this particular instance Jesus used emotive and exaggerated language to emphasize the divine ideal and purpose in marriage.

4.2. The Markan Contribution. The main contribution of Mark to Jesus' teaching involves his development of its universal implications. He does this by the addition of "against her" in 10:11 but above all by his repeating of the divorce saying from the perspective of the woman in 10:12.

4.3. The Matthean Contribution. In both 5:32 and 19:9 Matthew has added an exception clause to Jesus' teaching which permits both divorce and remarriage in instances of unchastity. In so doing he reveals that he does not interpret Jesus' teaching as conflicting with the Law (Mt 5:17) or as an attempt to set down a legal principle to cover all circumstances. Like Paul, he believes that as an authoritative spokesman for his Lord he can help bring out the meaning of Jesus' teaching with regard to the specific case of unchastity. Does Matthew teach that divorce is mandatory in the case of unchastity? There may be an allusion to this in Matthew 1:19 where "being a just man" is best interpreted as a causal participial phrase explaining why Joseph was going to divorce Mary (*see* Birth of Jesus). The rabbinic literature seems to require divorce in such instances (cf. *Soṭa* 5.1). Yet the OT example of Hosea, the lack of any clear command in the NT and the great emphasis on forgiving one another (*see* Forgiveness of Sins), argues strongly against any interpretation which would make divorce mandatory in cases of adultery.

The placement of Jesus' teaching concerning being a eunuch for the kingdom of heaven (Mt 19:10-12) is frequently seen as the Evangelist's interpretation of the preceding teaching on divorce. Thus, being a eunuch for the kingdom of heaven means that divorced believers cannot remarry and must become as eunuchs. Has Matthew placed 19:10-12 at this point because he sees it as supporting an absolute prohibition of remarriage? There are several reasons to question this interpretation. For one, we have already concluded that, according to the general norms of language, Matthew 19:9 and 5:32 permit divorce and remarriage in the case of unchastity. Second, verse 12 concludes with the understanding that not everyone is "able to receive this," and in verse 11 Jesus states that "not everyone can receive this precept, but only those to whom it is given." It is difficult to assume that "those to whom it is given" refers to any and all Christians in contrast to unbelievers. This teaching looks more like gospel advice concerning marriage than a mandatory requirement that divorced believers not remarry. Simply being a divorced believer does not enable one to receive this precept. It is better therefore to understand "this word" in 9:11 as referring to the saying in 19:10 concerning marriage in general rather than to the sayings in 19:4-9 concerning divorce and remarriage and in 19:10 concerning marriage. The placement of 19:10-12 after 19:3-9 is best seen as due to topical considerations—that is, they both deal with marriage—rather than due to a specific attempt to interpret 19:3-9 by means of 19:10-12.

4.4. The Lukan Contribution. Due to the brevity of the divorce saying in Luke and its traditional nature it is difficult to find within it any uniquely Lukan emphasis. Some attempts have been made to arrive at a Lukan emphasis by means of the context in which this saying is placed. Is the Evangelist trying to demonstrate the abiding validity of the Law (16:16)? Is this teaching directed by Luke against the Pharisees because of their love of money (16:14)? Has Luke simply listed it with other pharisaic vices (16:14-17)? At this time it is difficult to single out a particular Lukan contribution with regard to the divorce saying.

4.5. The Pauline Contribution. In 1 Corinthians 7:12-15 Paul introduces an issue concerning divorce that does not surface elsewhere. He explicitly states in 7:12 that what follows is not a teaching of the historical Jesus ("I say, not the Lord"), although he believes that what he says is equally authoritative. Paul gives an exception to Jesus' teaching in 7:15 which allows for remarriage in the case of desertion by an unbelieving partner. In such cases the deserted believer is "not bound." This most probably means "free to remarry." This interpretation fits well with Paul's general view that "because of the temptation to immorality, each man should have his own wife and each woman her own husband" (7:2). A deserted wife or husband still faces this same problem. If "it is better to marry than to be aflame with passion" (7:9), and if "not all men [and women] can receive this precept [of being a eunuch with respect to marriage], but only those to whom it is given" (Mt 19:11), how do these words help a deserted man or woman if they cannot remarry? Being free to remarry—"not being bound"—resolves this problem.

5. Conclusion.

The particular interpretation of Jesus' teaching on divorce and the history of its tradition suggested above is not without its own difficulty. Its strongest point is that it takes the two exception clauses in Matthew and 1 Corinthians seriously. It requires that we see Jesus' statement on divorce as containing elements of exaggeration for effect. This does not in any sense mean that one can multiply ad infinitum other exceptions which permit divorce and remarriage. On the other hand, it does raise the question of whether there may be other exceptions. Nevertheless, if Jesus used exaggeration in his divorce saying, this means that in his thinking God's hatred of divorce was so great that he could only express his conviction on this subject by means of exaggerated language. Rather than lessening the importance of Jesus' teaching on this subject, exaggerated language heightens it. The evil of divorce is so great that Jesus could only express himself on this subject by means of exaggeration.

In light of this, it is difficult to counsel a Christian that divorce is an option for them. Clearly the burden of proof weighs heavily on anyone considering divorce, for God hates divorce. Divorce is never good, for it witnesses to a failure of the divine purpose. Yet there may be occasions when divorce is the lesser evil. According to the interpretation given above, it is permissible (not mandatory) in the case of sexual infidelity and desertion. Such an action, however, should be considered as drastic as when a surgeon must amputate a limb or cut out a cancer intertwined with one's vital organs. Are there other possible occasions when divorce is a lesser evil? From the standpoint of the Gospels such a question must be asked fearfully, knowing God's hatred for divorce and the fact that one shall one day need to justify any such action before him. But as an example, one might consider the case of a wife who suffers great physical abuse from her husband and is eventually murdered by him. Would divorce have been a lesser evil?

One particular problem that this interpretation faces is found in Matthew 5:32b/Luke 16:18b: "whoever marries a divorced woman commits adultery." In Luke this is a very difficult saying, for it appears to punish the innocent party—the wife who has been divorced by her husband. Furthermore, in the socioeconomic environment of Jesus' day, what was a woman* to do? Remarriage seems a far more desirable alternative than various other options. The Matthean version is not as difficult to interpret, for here the woman who has been divorced appears to be the woman divorced in the earlier part of the verse for unchastity. Defining marriage to an adulteress as adultery is not difficult. Luke, however, gives the impression that the divorced woman is innocent and wronged. The sin seems to lie with the man who divorced her. It may be, however, that the whole issue of determining who is innocent is irrelevant because Jesus was simply seeking to emphasize the wrongness of all divorce.

See also ETHICS OF JESUS; LAW; WOMEN.

BIBLIOGRAPHY. D. J. Atkinson, *To Have and To Hold* (London: Collins, 1979); H. Baltensweiler, *Die Ehe im Neuen Testament* (Zürich: Zwingli, 1967); J. P. Bonsirven, *Le Divorce dans le Nouveau Testament* (Paris: Desclee, 1948); D. R. Catchpole, "The Synoptic Divorce Material as a Traditio-Historical Problem," *BJRL* 57 (1975) 92-127; J. Dupont, *Mariage et divorce dans l'Evangile* (Bruges: de Brouwer, 1959); J. A. Fitzmyer, "The Matthean Divorce Texts and Some New Palestinian Evidence," *TS* 37 (1976) 197-226; W. A. Heth and

G. J. Wenham, *Jesus and Divorce* (Nashville: Nelson, 1984); A. Isaksson, *Marriage and Ministry in the New Temple* (Lund: Gleerup, 1965); W. F. Luck, *Divorce and Remarriage* (San Francisco: Harper & Row, 1987); F. J. Mahoney, "Matthew 19, 3-12 and Celibacy. A Redactional and Form Critical Study," *JSNT* 2 (1979) 42-60; J. Murray, *Divorce* (Philadelphia: Orthodox Presbyterian Church, 1953); V. N. Olsen, *The New Testament Logia on Divorce* (Tübingen: J. C. B. Mohr, 1971); D. W. Shaner, *A Christian View of Divorce According to the Teachings of the New Testament* (Leiden: Brill, 1969); R. H. Stein, "Is It Lawful for a Man to Divorce His Wife?" *JETS* 22 (1979) 115-22.   R. H. Stein

DOMINICAL SAYINGS. *See* FORM CRITICISM; GOSPELS (HISTORICAL RELIABILITY); TRADITION CRITICISM.

DREAMS

A sequence of thoughts or images occurring during sleep. Dreams have been the subject of intense interest and critical reflection from time immemorial. Modern concepts of dreams are indebted to Sigmund Freud (1856-1939), who established the basic principles which guide modern dream research. Scripture, however, nowhere reflects an interest in the psychoanalysis of dreams.

The major references to dreams in the Bible, including the Gospels, are those instances in which dreams functioned as vehicles of divine revelation. These references appear in three major clusters: the early patriarchal period (Gen 20—41), the life of Daniel (Dan 1—7), and the infancy narrative of Matthew's Gospel (Mt 1—2; *see* Birth of Jesus). As it was commonly held in the ancient world, the Jews believed that God communicated his will through dreams (Num 12:6: "I [the LORD] speak to him in dreams" [NIV]).

The references to dreams in the Gospels are limited to the six occurrences in Matthew. Significantly, each occurrence concerns the person of Jesus. Through dreams Mary's conception was explained to Joseph (1:20); the wise men were warned not to return to Herod* (2:12); Joseph was told to flee with his family to Egypt (2:13); Joseph was warned against settling in Judea (2:22); and Pontius Pilate's* wife was convicted on Jesus' account (27:19). That all of these accounts are from the hand of the Evangelist is suggested by the use of the stereotypical phrase *kat' onar*, "in a dream," occurring in each of these passages.

These dreams recorded in Matthew are of two basic subtypes. The dreams of the infancy narrative were given for guidance and were clearly supernatural,

while the source of the dream of Pilate's wife is less clear; it may point to disturbed mental activity, or it may have been a supernatural sign of Jesus' righteousness.* In Matthew, however, the dream of Pilate's wife plays no less important a role than those of Joseph and the wise men. The concerns are essentially the same in both subtypes: questions of destiny, security, personal well-being, etc. Hence, the dream of Pilate's wife serves to reinforce with the others the basic Matthean theme that Jesus is God's chosen one. The very fact that we should be given a glimpse of her emotional torment, a torment so severe that she felt it necessary to interrupt her husband while he was sitting "on the judge's seat" (27:19), clearly reinforces Matthew's stress on Jesus' innocence and the treachery of his opposition.

The details of the dreams in the infancy narrative follow a relatively meaningful sequence. One can argue that these details play an important part in the purpose of Matthew to show the divine care exercised in the life of Jesus. First there was God's directive that Joseph take Mary as his wife and thus establish a home with a father and mother in which Jesus would be protected from the charge of illegitimacy (1:19-23). This is followed by a dream in which the wise men who worshiped Jesus as "king" are instructed to return to their country, without first reporting back to Herod (2:12). There can be little doubt that Matthew intends thereby to show God's particular provision for the infant Jesus in the face of life-threatening danger.

This theme of divine protection extends to the third nativity dream, recorded in 2:13. In commanding the holy family to seek refuge from Herod in a Roman province of some one million Jews, God takes sovereign action to preserve the infant from the massacre in Bethlehem and (potentially) in other towns of Judea. In addition, it was the function of this dream to make possible the fulfillment of Hosea 11:1, cited in Matthew 2:15: "Out of Egypt I called my son" (NIV). In Matthew's chronicling of the events surrounding the nativity of Jesus, there can be little doubt that this prediction-fulfillment motif anticipates the opposition to Jesus throughout his life, culminating in his death in Jerusalem under the eyes of another Herod (*see* Old Testament in the Gospels).

The final two revelatory dreams, recounted in 2:19-23, continue the theme of divine preservation. Joseph is informed that the enemies of Jesus are dead and that he is to return "to the land of Israel" (2:20). But since Joseph was probably intent on raising the child in Bethlehem, the city of David, he was guided by a fifth and final dream to settle instead in despised Galilee.* Once again, Scripture is fulfilled: By settling the family in Galilee Joseph ensures that Jesus will be called (pejoratively) "a Nazarene"* (2:23).

From Matthew's perspective, then, Jesus, the new-born child of Mary, is himself the King of the Jews. Accordingly, asserts Matthew, through dreams God intervenes in human history to make known his divine purposes for this child and to protect him.

A final issue is raised by the fact that an "angel* of the Lord" is mentioned in connection with four of the five dreams in the infancy narrative (1:20, 24; 2:13, 19). It is not clear whether we are to think merely of angels or more specifically of a manifestation of Yahweh. The lack of precise data with regard to the identity of this figure has given rise to various conclusions. Without question the angel of the Lord is to be identified in some way with God, yet he appears to be distinguished from God. Perhaps the best view is to see the angel of the Lord as a self-manifestation of Yahweh in a form that would communicate his presence and concern to those to whom he appeared.

See also ANGELS; APOCALYPTIC.

BIBLIOGRAPHY. M. M. Bourke, "The Literary Genre of Matthew 1-2," *CBQ* 22 (1960) 160-75; P. J. Budd, "Dream," *NIDNTT* 1.511-13; D. A. Carson, "Matthew," *EBC* 8.75-95; A. Oepke, "ὄναρ," *TDNT* V.220-38; W. Richter, "Traum und Traumbedeutung im Alten Testament," *BZ* 7 (1963) 202-19; J. H. Stek, "Dream," *ISBE* 1.991-92.   D. A. Black

DRUNKENNESS. *See* WINE.

E

EARTH. *See* WORLD.

EATING AND DRINKING. *See* TABLE FELLOWSHIP.

ELDER

Originally the Hebrew *zāqēn* meant a "bearded one," or older member of a family, and the term is used frequently in the Bible for those who are older in years. However, the term *elder* most frequently refers to the ruling head of the family or clan. In Jesus' day these were predominantly the aristocratic leaders of the Jewish patrician families. They served in local village councils and alongside the Pharisees* and Sadducees in the Sanhedrin,* the great council of the Jews in Jerusalem.

1. OT Background
2. Post-Exilic and Intertestamental Developments
3. The Judaism of Jesus' Day
4. The Emphases of the Evangelists

1. OT Background
The institutional office of elder derived from the earliest history of the nation when families and clans controlled the politics of the Hebrews. As heads of the major families the elders naturally became the leaders of the clans and formed councils to lead the tribes. Yet there was no instance when they were the sole authority, for they always represented the people under the leadership of divinely appointed leaders such as Moses (Ex 3:16, 18; 18:12). At Sinai "seventy of the elders of Israel" were convened to ratify the covenant (Ex 24:1, 9), an event celebrated by later Jews as constituting also the divine commission of the office of elder. In Numbers 11:16-17, 24-25, which was clearly an anointing ceremony, we read of the Spirit being placed on them and their prophesying. Henceforth they shared Moses' burdens and assisted him in his office.

Deuteronomy speaks of the legal responsibilities of the elders: the local administration of justice (Deut 19:11-13), functioning as civil judges at the city gates

which were the ancient courtrooms (Deut 22:15; 25:7), and adjudicating in family squabbles (Deut 21:18-21; 22:13-21). After the settlement in Canaan the elders became a ruling class with not only judicial but political and military powers (1 Sam 4:3; 8:4-9). During the monarchy their authority was lessened by the creation of a centralized government with its civil service. But the elders as local rulers still exercised considerable influence and acted as buffers against dictatorial tendencies on the part of the monarchy. Saul sought their favor (1 Sam 15:30), and both David (2 Sam 3:17; 5:3) and Rehoboam (1 Kings 12:6-8) turned to the elders when seeking the throne. There was always tension between the elders and the king, since their spheres of authority overlapped; but the elders still adjudicated both legal and religious matters among the people.

2. Post-Exilic and Intertestamental Developments.
During the exile both the monarchy and the tribal structure of Israel collapsed, and the elders gained even more authority than before. In exilic communities (Jer 29:1) and in Palestine (Ezek 8:1; 14:1) elders were quite prominent. Yet there was a difference, for now it was not clans or tribes but individual families that had risen to leadership. During the post-exilic period these families became an aristocracy, and their elders wielded great influence. In Ezra 5:9; 6:6-15 they were the primary instigators of the rebuilding of the Temple, and both Darius and the Persian governor Tattenai worked with them. Town elders continued to exercise power (cf. Ezra 10:14; cf. the "family heads" of 10:16), and Nehemiah had many running battles with these "nobles and officials" (Neh 5:7; 7:5), but it was the aristocratic family which increasingly gained the upper hand.

During the intertestamental period these family heads and elders slowly took control of the apparatus of state and began meeting as a council to rule the nation, becoming the precursor of the Sanhedrin. It may be that the earliest form was the "company" of twelve chieftains mentioned in Ezra 2:2 and Nehemiah 7:7, possibly representing symbolically the twelve tribes. Under Hellenistic rule this council, called the *Gerousia,* had wide-ranging powers, since the Greeks allowed their subject peoples to govern their own internal affairs. At some point there came to be seventy (or seventy-one if one counts the high priest) members (cf. *m. Sanh.* 1:6, Josephus *J.W.* 2.18.6 §482), and the council consisted of elders and aristocratic priests, with the high priest at the head (*see* Priest, Priesthood). During the reign of the Hasmoneans, however, the makeup of the Gerousia was altered again. Their powers were reduced due to the monarchic tendencies of the rulers, and there was a growing influx of scribal (Pharisaic) leaders, with the result that the power structure was divided into nobility (elders and priests) and lay (scribes) factions. This continued into the NT period.

Two further restrictions of the Sanhedrin's (and therefore the elder's) authority occurred in the fifty years prior to Jesus. Under the Roman governor Gabinius (57-55 B.C.) Palestine was divided into five *synedria,* and for ten years the Sanhedrin had jurisdiction over only the three in Judea, approximately a third of its former territory. The old lines of authority were reinstated under Hyrcanus II (47 B.C.), but that too was short-lived, for Herod the Great began his reign by executing forty-five members of the Sanhedrin who had supported Antigonus (Josephus *Ant.* 15.1.2 §6) and forcing the nobility to submit. During this time, however, the elders continued to serve as heads of influential families and as community leaders. Moreover, the "council of elders" represented the nation in its dealings with the Greeks and Romans and also performed judicial functions at home. At Qumran there was no apparent office, but elders as the heads of families were second in order to the priests in both judicial and halachic authority, and a council of twelve lay and three priestly members ruled the community (*see* Dead Sea Scrolls).

3. The Judaism of Jesus' Day.
In the first century the *presbyteroi* ("elders") primarily served a community function. Their duties are described in the Mishnaic tractate *Sanhedrin,* although the extent to which it depicts pre-A.D. 70 Judaism is greatly debated (*see* Rabbinic Traditions and Writings). Both in Judea and in diasporate communities there appear to have been a council of seven elders which functioned primarily at the civic level and an executive committee of three *archontes* ("rulers")—the head of the synagogue, the minister of the congregation and the collector of alms- which functioned mainly at the synagogue level (cf. Judith 6:15-17; 7:9-10).

However, there was no clear distinction between civic and religious life in Jewish communities, and the two groups together controlled the daily life of the Jewish people. In cosmopolitan cities with a mixed population and special synagogues (e.g., Rome), there may have been separate councils of elders for synagogue and community; but in the average Jewish community the same group of elders ruled over both civic and synagogue affairs, and often the *archontes* were chosen from among the elders.

The *presbyteroi* exercised full jurisdiction over civic as well as religious life. They decided what type of disciplinary action was appropriate, whether flogging or—most serious of all—the ban or excommunication. While the elders did not control synagogue worship (that was under the jurisdiction of the *archontes*), they did take the seats of honor and officially enforced the Law. They also administered both village and synagogue affairs, making decisions in a wide variety of situations. Often the president of the synagogue was an elder, and the office went beyond the hereditary leaders of the noble families to encompass elected lay leaders of the community (probably chosen annually).

Corresponding to the local councils was the supreme Gerousia, or Sanhedrin, in Jerusalem. There the term *elder* was used generally to describe all the members (cf. the *presbyterion,* or "council of the elders," in Lk 22:66; Acts 22:5) or specifically to refer to the lay leaders that constituted the third and least influential group (with the Sadducees and Pharisees) in the Sanhedrin, the lay nobility. A third use of the term denotes the scribes as interpreters of the Law (cf. the "tradition of the elders" in Mk 7:3, 5 and pars.). This latter use became predominant in the post-A.D. 70 period, when it was used for the scribal scholars who developed the tannaitic tradition.

4. The Emphases of the Evangelists.
Presbyteros as a title in the Gospels occurs only in the passion predictions (*see* Predictions and Jesus Passion and Resurrection) and in the passion narratives themselves (*see* Passion Narrative). It always (apart from Lk 7:3, in which the "elders" of a synagogue attest to the piety of a centurion) refers to the lay members of the Sanhedrin and in every case except the first passion prediction (Mk 8:31 and pars., where it may stress their juridical function) occurs after mention of the "chief priests." This is probably due to the greater influence of the priestly members in the Sanhedrin.

Mark retains the complete list of "chief priests, elders, scribes" which constituted the Sanhedrin, with this order in Mk 14:53 and 15:1 (so linking the elders with the priestly faction, the normal political alignment) but with the "scribes" named before the elders in Mk 11:27 and 14:43 (probably due to the greater political influence of the scribes in the first century).

Matthew, in spite of his greater interest in the Sanhedrin's involvement in the passion events (eleven references in contrast with five in Mark, three in Luke and none in John), usually omits mentioning the "scribes" (cf. Mt 21:23 par. Mk 11:27; 26:3; Mt 26:47 par. Mk 14:43; Mt 27:1 par. Mk 15:1; Mt 27:3, 12, 20; and 28:12; though he includes them in Mt 16:21; Mt 26:57 par. Mk 14:53; Mt 27:41) perhaps in order to depict the elders more generally as representatives of the nation as a whole (note *presbyteroi tou laou* ["elders of the people"] in Mt 21:23; 26:3, 47; 27:1).

Luke retains the complete list in Luke 9:22 (par. Mk 8:31); and 20:1 (par. Mk 11:27) but in Luke 22:66 (par. Mk 15:1) replaces the list with "the council of the elders of the people" (cf. Acts 22:5). Luke's interest is not so much in the distinct groups as in the leaders of Israel* as a whole.

John shows no interest in the elders and mentions only the "chief priests and Pharisees" (Jn 18:3; cf. "chief priests and officers" in Jn 19:6). Elsewhere, he uses only the plural "they" for the Sanhedrin (cf. Jn 18:28-31) or refers even more generally to "the Jews" (Jn 18:38; 19:14).

See also JUDAISM; PHARISEE; SANHEDRIN; SCRIBE; SYNAGOGUE.

BIBLIOGRAPHY. G. Bornkamm, "πρέσβυς κτλ," *TDNT* VI.651-83; M. Brauch, "Elder," *Baker Encyclopedia of the Bible*, ed. W. A. Elwell (2 vols.; Grand Rapids: Baker, 1988) 1.679-81; L. Coenan, "Bishop, Presbyter, Elder," *NIDNTT* 1.195-97; G. H. Davies, "Elder in the Old Testament," *IDB* 2.72-73; E. Ferguson, *Backgrounds of Early Christianity* (Grand Rapids: Eerdmans, 1987); A. E. Harvey, "Elders," *JTS* n.s. 25 (1974) 318-32; B. Reicke, "The Constitution of the Primitive Church in the Light of Jewish Documents," in *The Scrolls and the NT*, ed. K. Stendahl (New York: Harper and Brothers, 1957); S. Safrai, "Jewish Self-Government," in *The Jewish People in the First Century*, ed. S. Safrai and M. Stern (Philadelphia: Fortress, 1974) 377-419; E. Schürer, *The History of the Jewish People in the Age of Jesus Christ (175 B.C.-A.D. 135)*, rev. and ed. G. Vermes and F. Millar (3 vols.; Edinburgh: T. & T. Clark, 1973-79) II, par. 23, 27; E. Schweizer, *Church Order in the New Testament* (London: SCM, 1961); M. H. Shepherd, "Elder in the NT," *IDB* 2.73-75.

G. R. Osborne

ELIJAH AND ELISHA

Elijah and Elisha were two great prophets (*see* Proph-

ets and Prophecy) of Israel.* The memory of their ministries and miraculous activity led to the expectation that the period of the end would bring a rebirth of their divinely inspired labor. Each of these figures can be examined with reference to the OT, Judaism and the NT. In particular, Elijah is portrayed as a witness, as one whose pattern of ministry is repeated, and as one who returns.

1. Elijah.

1.1. Elijah in the OT. Elijah was a major prophetic figure in Israel during the ninth century B.C. (1 Kings 17—19; 21:17-29; 2 Kings 1:2-16; 2:1-12). He is best remembered for his call to reform at Mt. Carmel, his miraculous work and his rapture to heaven.* In Malachi 4:5-6 (MT 3:23-24) the prophet promises Elijah's return to reconcile fathers and sons before the Day of the Lord. This promise of Elijah's return also alludes to Malachi 3:1 and the messenger who goes before the Lord. This aspect of Malachi's prophecy influenced both Judaism and the Gospels.

1.2. Elijah in Ancient Judaism. Elijah appears in many texts of ancient Judaism* as a great figure who will return. In Sirach (48:1-12) he is called a prophet-like-fire, whose word flamed like a torch, and he is expected to return to allay divine wrath, to reconcile father and son, and to restore Jacob (48:1, 10). *1 Enoch* 89:52 (cf. 90:31) figuratively refers to Elijah as a spared sheep. 1 Maccabees 2:58 notes his zeal for the Law and that he was taken up alive to heaven. In addition, the prophet to come mentioned in 1 Maccabees 4:46 and 14:41 may refer to Elijah. Josephus,* in his re-telling of the history of the Jewish people, summarizes Elijah's career (*Ant.* 8.13.1-8 §§316-62). And 4 Ezra (6:26; cf. 7:109) speaks of the apocalyptic* return of the men who were taken up to heaven without tasting death (e.g., Enoch, Moses [in Jewish tradition] and Elijah). The Mishnah tractate *'Edduyot* (8:7) declares Elijah's future role as a judge who settles disputes and declares which families are clean. In *Soṭah* (9:15) he is responsible for the resurrection of the dead. So in Judaism the return of Elijah signals the arrival of the time of fulfillment, calls the people to reconciliation and brings judgment* (cf. also *As. Mos.* 2:14; perhaps 1QS 9:11; *m. B. Meṣ* 1:8; 3:4).

Recent scholarship has debated whether ancient Judaism conceived of the return of Elijah prior to the coming of Messiah (*see* Christ). M. Faierstein argues that such a concept did not exist and the old scholarly consensus to the contrary must be abandoned. One text that clearly makes such a connection is *Targum Pseudo-Jonathan* (Deut 30:4), but the date of this tradition is difficult to establish and may post-date the

Judaism of Jesus' time. A talmudic text (*'Erub.* 43a-b) also makes this connection, but it is considered too late to be of value (third century A.D.).

D. Allison has argued that the presence within Judaism of an association between the coming of Elijah and the coming of Messiah would best explain the question in Mark 9:11, "Why do the teachers of the Law* say that Elijah must come first?" If this were a Christian development, how did it come to be attributed to the scribes*? Indeed, the problem of Elijah coming first seems to pose a real difficulty arising from the environment of the disciples* or the early church. Allison also regards the Talmudic evidence as significant in showing that such a view was circulating in Judaism, despite the fact, one might add, that Christians had identified this figure with John the Baptist (*see* John the Baptist). Allison's most important point is that the logic of Jewish eschatology* demands a connection between the coming of Elijah and the coming of Messiah. If one believed that the Messiah's coming would be associated with the arrival of the Day of the Lord (as is witnessed within first-century Judaism), it would follow that Malachi's prophecy of Elijah appearing before the last days would be read as an event preceding the coming of Messiah.

J. Fitzmyer (1985), in defending Faierstein, regards Mark 9:9-11 as a non-messianic text. But in doing so he argues that "Son of man" (*see* Son of Man) is not a messianic title. The disciples are not asking why Elijah must precede the Messiah, but why he must precede the "rising from the dead" or "the rising of the Son of man from the dead." However, while the title "Son of man" is distinct from "Messiah," the function of the two figures is sufficiently related that Fitzmyer's distinction is not decisive. Fitzmyer also challenges the appeal to the Talmud, questioning whether the evidence is even derived from the third century A.D. (*see* Rabbinic Traditions and Writings) and is clearly Palestinian in origin (the possibility remaining that it is fourth-fifth century and Babylonian in origin). This challenge passes by the force of Allison's argument, which notes the presence of a tradition within at least a sector of Judaism, which persisted despite its use in Christian apologetic. Fitzmyer also rejects Allison's appeal to logic in his ordering of first-century eschatological belief. Though he acknowledges that "some first-century Jews did believe in the coming of Messiahs" (e.g., 1QS 9:1; *T. Levi* 18:1-9; *T. Jud.* 24:1-6), Fitzmyer argues that none of these texts explicitly links Messiah's coming to the Day of the Lord. But it may be argued that a Messiah who comes and exercises decisive judgment with the Lord is bringing that Day, even if the exact

phrase is not used (*Pss. Sol.* 17—18; 1QM 19:2-8; 4Q161-64). In sum, though the evidence is not as overwhelming as many have assumed, the probability remains that at least some within early Judaism understood the coming of Elijah as an event preceding the arrival of Messiah.

1.3. Elijah in the NT. Elijah is the fourth most frequently cited OT figure in the NT (Moses, eighty times; Abraham, seventy-three times; David, fifty-nine times; Elijah, twenty-nine times). All but two of these references are in the Gospels (Rom 11:2; Jas 5:17). Only two of these citations are in John (1:21, 25). The remaining twenty-five references within the Synoptics are widely distributed, though most appear in at least two of the Synoptics. One text is unique to Matthew (11:14). Two are unique to Luke (1:17; 4:25-26). Some passages are shared by all of the Synoptics (Mt 16:14 par. Mk 8:28 and Lk 9:19; Mt 17:3-4, 10-12 par. Mk 9:4-5, 11-13 and Lk 9:30, 33). Some material is shared by Mark and Matthew (Mk 15:35-36 par. Mt 27:47, 49) and one passage by Mark and Luke (Mk 6:15 par. Lk 9:8). Allusions to Malachi also appear (Mk 1:2-3; Mt 10:11; Lk 7:27), as do references to a ministry of fire (Mt 3:11; Lk 9:54; 12:49), recalling Elijah's ministry of judgment at Mt. Carmel (1 Kings 18) and his calling fire down on the messengers of King Ahaziah (2 Kings 1).

1.4. The Three Emphases of the NT. The Elijah passages divide into three emphases: the witness, the figure "like Elijah" and the hope of a coming Elijah. The first two emphases are in all three Synoptics, while the last is limited to Matthew and Mark.

1.4.1. The Witness. All three Synoptics depict Elijah as a witness at the Transfiguration* (Mt 17; Mk 9; Lk 9) where he appears with Moses* and speaks with Jesus. The mountain (*see* Mountain and Wilderness) setting suggests a revelatory moment, as does the heavenly endorsement of Jesus as the "prophet to be heard," the prophet-like-Moses (Deut 18:15, 18). Elijah appears to represent the time of Jewish hope as a witness to this event (Liefeld). Luke alone speaks of their conversation as being about Jesus' exodus (9:31, *tēn exodon autou*), his death (*see* Death of Jesus) and resurrection* in Jerusalem.

1.4.2. "Like Elijah." Numerous passages speak of the figure "like Elijah." Several texts speak of John the Baptist in this light, either by appealing to the imagery of Malachi 3:1 (Mk 1:2-3; Mt 10:11; Lk 7:27), by Jesus' remarks (Mt 11:14; 17:10-13 par.) or by angelic proclamation (Lk 1:17). The Fourth Gospel (Jn 1:21, 27) notes John's explicit denial that he is this figure. This evidence led J. A. T. Robinson to argue that the association of Elijah with John was the work of Jesus and the church, while John saw Jesus as Elijah, not Messiah. But the popular view that Jesus is Elijah (Mt 16:14 par.) is clearly meant to be understood as speculation, not something from John. John's hesitation to accept the Elijah identification may well be a result of his recognizing that Elijah was yet to come; he did not wish to be perceived as the final manifestation of Elijah hope (Mt 17:10-12; cf. Rev 11:3). Luke's unique and careful wording of John coming in "the spirit" of Elijah might suggest the same conclusion (1:17). If John is an Elijah-like figure, his testimony as a forerunner and his baptism of Jesus is a form of divine attestation to be placed alongside the voice from heaven. Jesus' ministry also led to his being associated with Elijah. He explicitly compares his ministry to the period of Elijah in Luke 4:25-26. The people think he might be Elijah, and this view reaches the ears of Herod (Mk 6:15; Lk 9:8). This is popular speculation brought about by Jesus' miracles (*see* Miracles and Miracle Stories). However, the prophetic picture of Jesus preferred by the early church was the portrait of the prophet-like-Moses (Acts 3:12-26). Jesus' ministry is not that of Elijah, though Jesus' miracles, involving a variety of people and races, bear resemblance to those of the prophet. One other connection exists between Elijah and Jesus. At the cross, Jesus cries out in the language of Psalm 22, but those listening to him think he is calling on Elijah for help (Mt 27:47, 49; Mk 15:35-36). In this instance Elijah is portrayed as one who comes to the aid of the pious.

1.4.3. Future Elijah. The hope of a future Elijah seems to be reflected in Matthew 17:10-11 and Mark 9:11-12. The difficulty lies in the fact that Jesus responds to the issue of scribal belief that Elijah must come first by commenting that Elijah has already come in John. Is Jesus saying John completely fulfills the expectation of Elijah? Or is Jesus saying that Elijah is a type which appears now in John and will reappear again before the Day of the Lord? This "already/not yet" tension is common in the NT and may very well lie behind this saying of Jesus (Wink). In short, Elijah is a prophet whose presence suggests the end time, whether in his return at the end or in the ministry of John the Baptist.

1.5. The So-Called Double Elijah Theme and the Lukan Portrait of Jesus and Elijah. Fitzmyer has argued that Luke has a "double Elijah" motif. Jesus denies that he is Elijah and applies the ascription to John the Baptist, even though the Baptist thinks that Jesus is Elijah. The theme of denial reappears when Jesus rejects a ministry of judgment (Lk 9:54-56). On the other hand, Luke implicitly compares Jesus' ministry to that of Elijah (Lk 4:25-27; 7:16; 9:8, 19, 62). However, Luke

3:16 and 7:19 refer to Jesus as "the one to come," thereby depicting Jesus as messianic, not prophetic (cf. "one to come" in Lk 13:35 and 19:38). So John is not portrayed as expecting Jesus to be Elijah. In addition, Luke 7:16; 9:8 and 9:19 are confessions by the people, which are later shown to be inadequate (Lk 9:18-20). The parallel between Jesus' call to discipleship*—utilizing the imagery of putting hand to plow and not looking back (Lk 9:62)—and prophetic calls to allegiance is not surprising, given the prophetic character of Jesus' ministry.

In sum, the prophetic character of Jesus' ministry does allow comparisons to the great prophet Elijah, even though the two are not identified. Jesus' prophetic activity signals the presence of the eschaton, but he is not Elijah, the prophet of the eschaton, since Jesus is not the forerunner but "the one to come." For Luke the messenger of Malachi 3 is only John the Baptist and does not include Jesus (Lk 1:17; 7:27; contra Fitzmyer). Jesus parallels Elijah only in his eschatological activity.

Another suggested point of Elijah typology* is the call to rain down fire from heaven (Lk 9:54; cf. 2 Kings 1:10, 12, 14). Taken together with the reference to Jesus' being "received up" (Lk 9:51; cf. 2 Kings 2:9, 10, 11), these features are said to suggest an Elijah typology (Evans). Yet a third link is the refusal by Jesus to allow the newly called disciple to bid his family goodbye before setting out on the path of discipleship, an act distinctly unlike Elijah's permission for Elisha to tell his family* farewell (Lk 9:62; 1 Kings 19:20). Evans argues that by introducing this motif and omitting the material found in Mark 1:6 and 9:9-13, Luke begins his travel section (9:51—19:44) by framing his portrayal of Jesus as the "new Elijah." But it may be argued that Jesus' refusal to bring down fire from heaven (9:51-56) severs the connection, while the parallel of being "taken up to heaven" (Lk 9:51) only reflects that Jesus is specially blessed in his reception. None of these allusions require the conclusion that Jesus is identified as the "new Elijah." The refusal to allow the disciple to bid farewell to his family shows the greater urgency of the era of Jesus. Jesus is not Elijah; he is more than Elijah. Luke's typology is one of "times" not "persons." There is allusion to Elijah's ministry in Luke, but it serves to cast Jesus' ministry in relief against the background of the great prophet of old. The time of salvation* has come, and it is a time which demands response.

2. Elisha.

2.1. Elisha in the OT and Ancient Judaism. Next to Elijah, Elisha stands as a second great prophet of the ninth century. 1 Kings 19:15-21 relates his call, but most of his ministry is recounted in 2 Kings 2—13. He is seen as Elijah's protégé, having been called by him and seen Elijah's rapture by a chariot of fire. Elisha's ministry involved not only prophetic declaration, but miraculous activity extending to raising the Shunamite's son from the dead (2 Kings 4:18-37, a miracle paralleling that of Elijah in 1 Kings 17:17-24), multiplying loaves (2 Kings 4:42-44) and healing Naaman of leprosy* (2 Kings 5:1-27).

There is only one brief intertestamental reference to Elisha, and it summarizes his career (Sir 48:12-14). It notes his presence at Elijah's departure, the inability of rulers to subdue him and his performance of miraculous deeds.

2.2. Elisha in the NT. In the one direct Gospel reference to Elisha, he is mentioned with Elijah as sharing a period of miraculous ministry—a time like that of Jesus (Lk 4:27). Jesus mentions the Naaman incident, which pictures a ministry to Gentiles* in a period of Israelite rejection, as a warning not to reject him as Israel had rejected Elisha (and Elijah).

Numerous events in Jesus' ministry bear similarity with the prophetic activity of Elisha. Jesus' ministry was introduced by a predecessor. He ministered in Galilee* and Samaria, a ministry that included a concern for the poor (*see* Rich and Poor) and outcast. Most of all, his miracles are similar to Elisha's. Jesus heals (*see* Healing) ten lepers (Lk 17:11, 19), multiplies the loaves (Mt 14:13-21 par.; Mt 15:29-39; Jn 6:1-15) and raises a widow's only son (Lk 7:11-17, where Luke's language actually recalls Elijah's healing in 1 Kings 17:23). These connections show Jesus functioning at a level equal to and surpassing one of the most powerful of the OT prophets.

One final connection between Jesus and Elisha is the description of the call to the four disciples (Mt 4:18-22 par.). The description of the disciples immediately leaving their nets to follow him recalls the narrative of Elisha's call in 1 Kings 19:19-21, since it is similar in form. These called disciples pick up the mantle of Jesus, just as Elisha had done with the mantle of Elijah.

See also JOHN THE BAPTIST; TRANSFIGURATION; TYPOLOGY.
BIBLIOGRAPHY. D. Allison, "Elijah Must Come First," *JBL* 103 (1984) 256-58; C. F. Evans, "The Central Section of St. Luke's Gospel," in *Studies in the Gospels: Essays in Memory of R. H. Lightfoot* (Oxford: Blackwell, 1957) 37-53; M. Faierstein, "Why Do the Scribes Say That Elijah Must Come First?" *JBL* 100 (1981) 75-86; J. Fitzmyer, *The Gospel according to Luke I-IX* (AB 28; Garden City, NY: Doubleday, 1981); idem, *Luke the Theologian* (London: Geoffrey Chapman, 1989); idem,

"More about Elijah Coming First," *JBL* 104 (1985) 295-96; J. Jeremias, "Ἠλ(ε)ίας," *TDNT* II.928-41; J. Klausner, *The Messianic Idea in Israel* (New York: Macmillan, 1955) 451-57; W. Liefeld, "Theological Motifs in the Transfiguration Narrative," in *New Dimensions in New Testament Study,* ed. R. Longenecker and M. Tenney (Grand Rapids: Zondervan, 1974) 171-74; J. A. T. Robinson, "Elijah, John, and Jesus," *NTS* 4 (1958) 263-81; J. Stek, "Elijah," *ISBE* 2.64-68; idem, "Elisha," *ISBE* 2.70-72; Str-B IV.764-98; W. Wink, *John the Baptist in Gospel Tradition* (SNTSMS 7; Cambridge: University Press, 1968). D. L. Bock

EMPEROR (ROMAN). *See* ROME.

ESCHATOLOGY
The word refers to teaching about the last things, specifically to history's consummation and the events directly associated with it. Characteristic of the Gospels is the note of eschatological fulfillment and the focus of eschatological hope in the person of Jesus. Perhaps the pre-eminent contribution of modern NT scholarship has been the demonstration that eschatology lies at the heart of Jesus' message and indeed at the heart of all the NT.

1. The Message of Jesus
2. The Gospel Writers
3. Contemporary Interpretation

1. The Message of Jesus.
Against the once popular view of the kingdom of God as an evolving society, J. Weiss and A. Schweitzer argued around the turn of the century that Jesus expected history's near end. On their view, Jesus was a preacher of repentance* in the face of impending judgment.* Largely in response to this picture of Jesus as a mistaken apocalyptic visionary, C. H. Dodd developed his theory of "realized eschatology." According to Dodd, Jesus believed that the prophecies of the OT had already met fulfillment, that the "Day of the Lord" had arrived. Most contemporary scholars now think of Weiss and Schweitzer on the one hand and of Dodd on the other as representing two extremes, between which a third position commends itself. Jesus did believe that the kingdom of God had, in some sense, already come. At the same time he spoke of eschatological events still to occur. The phrase "already and not yet" is now a commonplace of scholarship (*see* Kingdom of God).

1.1. The Future. Jesus' future expectations were drawn first from the well of OT and Jewish tradition. He anticipated the resurrection* of the dead (Mk 12:18-27) and a great judgment (Lk 10:13-15; 11:31-32).

He thought in terms of rewards for the righteous (Lk 6:20-23) and recompense for the wicked (Lk 6:46-49). He expected the end to be heralded by trouble for the saints (Lk 12:49-53) and, perhaps, by upheavals in nature (Mk 13:24-25). Exactly how Jesus imagined the coming aeon—whether as an earthly, millennial kingdom, or as an old-world-made-new, or as a completely new world—is unclear.

Jesus' major contribution to eschatology was christological. He made response to himself a criterion for judgment (Lk 12:8-9). He also probably identified his own fate with that of the Son of man* in Daniel 7 and conceived of himself as the messianic Son of David.* The fact that he chose twelve disciples*—a symbol of the restoration of the twelve tribes of Israel*—and stood above that group as its leader itself implies that he thought of himself as Israel's king.

1.2. The Present. Jesus did not relegate God's reign to the future. He explicitly announced its presence (Lk 11:20) and indirectly indicated its arrival by speaking of the defeat of Satan (Lk 10:18; 11:22), a secret presence (Mk 4:11-12, 26-29), new wine* (Mk 2:22), and a joy* opposed to fasting* (Mk 2:18-20). Although controversial, it is probable that Luke 17:20-21, in which the kingdom is "in your midst," refers to Jesus himself. His presence meant the presence of the kingdom.

1.3. The Relationship between Present and Future. Traditionally Christians have thought that the OT prophesies two messianic advents and that Jesus fulfilled certain OT prophecies at his first coming and will fulfill others at his second coming. But the distinction between two advents cannot be found in the OT and is foreign to Jewish eschatology. It is not likely that Jesus thought in terms of or spoke about two messianic advents. More probably the end time was for him constituted by a sequence of events, some of which had already occurred. The formulation "eschatology in the process of realization" (Jeremias, 230) is apt. The Messiah (*see* Christ) had appeared. Many prophecies had been fulfilled (Lk 17:18-23). But there had not been fulfillment without remainder. Much was left to unfold, particularly the Son of man's eschatological suffering and vindication (Mk 9:31).

1.4. When? According to the modern consensus, Jesus thought the eschatological judgment to be near. Recent attempts to deny this do not persuade. It must nonetheless be emphasized that Jesus rejected the type of chronological speculation found in some of the apocalypses (Lk 17:20-21) and plainly confessed his ignorance of the end's date (Mk 13:32). Further, Mark 13:20 (possibly dominical) and Luke 13:6-9 (probably dominical) assume that the day or hour of

the consummation is not set in concrete, that its arrival is partly contingent upon divine grace and human response. In addition, Luke 10:13-15 and other texts reflect bitter disappointment over Jewish failure. How such disappointment affected Jesus' eschatological convictions we do not know; but the general failure of Israel to welcome the Messiah (something unforeseen by the tradition) cannot but have made for second thoughts about what the future held. Jesus' expectations were probably more contingent and indeterminate than many have supposed (*see* Apocalyptic Teaching; Destruction of Jerusalem).

2. The Gospel Writers.
All four Gospels reflect the "already and not yet" pattern, but Matthew's eschatology is more realized than Mark's, and John's even more so. Luke's views are much harder to characterize.

2.1. Mark. The author of Mark, like Jesus before him, thought of eschatology as in the process of realization. For him, however, Jesus had suffered, died and risen, and this meant that the eschatological tribulation and the general resurrection had already commenced.

2.1.1. The Future. What Mark expected is found primarily in Mark 13. Here we have a Christian version of what is found so often in Jewish pictures of the end (*see* Apocalyptic). There will be a time of trial and difficulty. False prophets will arise (13:5-6). There will be wars, earthquakes and famines (13:7-8). The faithful will suffer (13:9-13). Palestine will be afflicted with dangers (13:14-23). The heavens will show great signs (13:24-25). And then God's eschatological agent (Jesus) will appear (13:26-27).

2.1.2. The Past. Jesus inaugurated the time of eschatological fulfillment (1:14-15). Especially noteworthy are the significant correlations between Mark 13 (about the end of the age) and Mark 14—15 (about the end of Jesus). Compare 15:33 (darkness at the crucifixion) with 13:24 (darkness at the end); 15:38 (the Temple veil torn) with 13:2 (the Temple will be destroyed); 14:34, 37 (Jesus tells his disciples to "watch" then comes [*erchetai*] and finds [*heuriskei*] them sleeping [*katheudontas*]) with 13:35-36 ("watch lest the master come [*elthōn*] and find [*heurē*] you sleeping" [*katheudontas*]); 14:10, 18, 21, 41 (Jesus is "delivered up") with 13:9 (the disciples will be "delivered up"); 14:53-65 (Jesus appears before a council of Jewish elders) with 13:9 (the disciples will appear before Jewish councils); 14:65 (Jesus is beaten) with 13:9 (the disciples will be beaten); 15:1-15 (Jesus before Pilate) with 13:9 (the disciples will stand before governors and kings). The meaning of these and other parallels, as well as of those between Mark 13 and Zechariah 9—14 (a little apocalypse) is plain: Jesus' end belongs to the eschatological drama (*see* Death of Jesus).

2.1.3. The Present. If the end began with the end of Jesus, then the period between the crucifixion and the Parousia must be eschatological time. The present (characterized by Mk 13:5-13) is conceptualized as the tribulation attendant upon the new age. That is, the sufferings of Jesus and of his church together constitute the labor pains after which the new world comes.

2.1.4. When? Mark 9:1 ("some standing here will not taste death before they see that the kingdom of God has come with power") may be taken to imply that Mark expected things to wind up shortly. But many scholars refer 9:1 to the Transfiguration* or the resurrection* or (less plausibly) to the destruction of Jerusalem in A.D. 70 (*see* Destruction of Jerusalem). Apart from 9:1 it seems probable that, given his view of the present, Mark did not reckon with history going on for any great period of time (cf. 13:30). Yet 13:32 means that no certainty surrounded the issue.

2.2. Matthew. Matthew's views on eschatology are very close to Mark's.

2.2.1. The Future. Almost everything that can be said about Mark's expectations holds equally for Matthew (if one does not follow the few who have thought Mt 24 to be a realized apocalypse fulfilled in A.D. 70). The one outstanding difference is a concentration on Jesus' role as the Son of man in the final judgment (13:41; 16:28; 25:31; etc.). Also, if *krinontes* in 19:28 means "ruling," the verse implies the eschatological salvation* of Israel (an idea not clearly present in Mark).

2.2.2. The Past. The emphasis on realized eschatology can be seen from two facts in particular. First, Matthew sprinkled his narrative with so-called formula quotations (1:23; 2:15, 18; etc.). These constantly remind readers that Jesus fulfilled the eschatological hopes and messianic expectations of Judaism.* Secondly, 27:51b-53 (unique to Matthew) recounts that Jesus was not the only one to rise from the dead: so did many saints. Thus the Messiah's vindication cannot be viewed in isolation. Rather, Jesus' resurrection inaugurated the general resurrection. Compare the pre-Pauline confession in Romans 3:3-4, which literally proclaims that Jesus was designated Son of God* by "(the) resurrection of the dead" (the Greek is the technical term for the general resurrection).

2.2.3. The Present. In Matthew, as in Mark, the present is eschatological time. Note especially that certain end-time prophecies of Mark 13 have been transferred to Matthew 10, with the result that the

Christian mission draws to itself the language of eschatological tribulation. Also indicative of Matthew's outlook is the key promise of the Messiah's perpetual supporting presence (1:23; 18:20; 28:20). This brings to realization a Jewish eschatological expectation: God would be "with" his people especially in the latter days (Zech 8:23; Jub. 1:17, 26; etc.). So the present is simultaneously the age of tribulation and the age of the kingdom's presence—precisely the view of Jesus.

2.2.4. When? There is no indication that Matthew held the consummation to be imminent. But his constant dwelling on eschatology and his conception of the present imply that he expected the end to come sooner rather than later.

2.3. Luke. Luke's convictions—which must be reconstructed with the help of both Luke and Acts— are not easily determined. One fact, however, has seemed clear to many: Luke was especially conscious of the expanding interval of time between the first and second advents.

2.3.1. The Future. Luke believed that Jesus would return in the same way that he left (Acts 1:11), and that this event would open that day on which God judges the world by Jesus Christ (Acts 17:31). The Third Evangelist also believed in the general resurrection (Lk 20:27-40; Acts 24:15), but exactly how he envisaged the coming "times of refreshing" and "the restitution of all things" (Acts 3:19-21) is disputed.

2.3.2. The Past. Luke did not carry forward the connection between Jesus' end and the eschaton. Perhaps he shied away from some aspects of realized eschatology because it also characterized groups he perceived as heretical (proto-Gnostics?). Alternatively, many have urged that his perspective was due to a conception of salvation-history. H. Conzelmann claimed that in Luke-Acts history is divided into three stages: the period of Israel, the period of Jesus, the period of the church.* On this scheme the Jesus event, despite its fulfillment of OT prophecies, belongs to the past and is not properly eschatological. Several recent studies, however, have questioned Conzelmann and denied that Luke drove a wedge between history and eschatology. The issue demands further investigation.

2.3.3. The Present. "Eschatology in the process of realization" does not so obviously characterize Luke, and according to Conzelmann the time of the church is the time before the end, not part of the end. Present and future have been compartmentalized (cf. the "before all this" of 21:12). It is just possible, however, that Luke recognized the eschatological content of such texts as Luke 1:32-33; 2:38; and Acts 2:17-21 and equated the church age with the inaugurated messianic kingdom (cf. 1 Cor 15:20-28).

2.3.4. When? Some have thought Luke held no near expectation, others that he thought the end very near. The disagreement is created by the existence in Luke-Acts of two different groups of texts. In one the end appears at hand (e.g., Lk 3:9; 18:7-8; 21:31-32), in the other there is an awareness of the delay of the Parousia (e.g., Lk 12:45; 19:11). Rather than dismissing one group in favor of the other it seems best to take Acts 1:7 ("It is not for you to know times or seasons") seriously and surmise that Luke thought the time of the end an open question.

2.4. John. One of the distinctive features of the Fourth Gospel is its great emphasis on realized eschatology.

2.4.1. The Future. Very little is said about the eschatological future. There is a yet outstanding "last day" (6:39), which will feature the resurrection (5:28-29; 6:39-40); but other specifics are lacking. Also, there is no hint at all as to when the last day will arrive.

2.4.2. The Past. John, like Mark and Matthew, associated the end of Jesus with end-time themes. In his gospel the death of Jesus is "the judgment of this world" (12:31). The crucifixion brings about the casting out of the devil (16:11; *see* Demon, Devil) and is associated with the destruction of "the son of perdition" (17:12; cf. 2 Thess 2:3). Moreover, in John the Son of man already has authority* (5:27; cf. Dan 7:13-14), already judges (9:35-39; 12:30-34) and is already lifted up and exalted (3:14). One is tempted to say that in John, Jesus himself is the eschaton, its real content. When Jesus came, the end came.

2.4.3. The Present. In Johannine thought eternal life* (6:47), living water* (4:14), bread* from heaven* (6:25-34), divine sonship (1:12) and even the resurrection (5:25)—all things traditionally associated with the eschaton—may be experienced now. Although there is in all this more continuity with the other Gospels than often assumed, the constant emphasis on the realization of eschatological hopes dominates the Fourth Gospel. C. H. Dodd exaggerated only a little when he wrote of John: "All that the church hoped for in the second coming of Christ is already given in its present experience of Christ through the Spirit" (Dodd, 121).

3. Contemporary Interpretation.

The theological problems posed by eschatology are numerous and complex. Was Jesus wrong in his imminent expectation? Should eschatological language be translated into existentialist categories? Can Christians, after 2,000 years, still look forward to the Parousia? Adequate answers must take into account at least four considerations. First, the gospel prophecies were never intended to be understood with unimaginative literalness. Just as it is misguided to mine Genesis for scientific data about the physical universe, so too is it wrong to turn the similes and metaphors of NT eschatology into information about future cosmological states.

Second, if it is the end which determines the meaning of what has gone before, then those preoccupied with the meaning of history and human existence must be preoccupied with history's conclusion and its relationship to the present. This explains the focus of the gospels. To grasp the significance of the here and now requires that vision be pulled from the present and cast toward the future. Third, salvation-history is not a predetermined scheme. It is rather a dynamic relationship between God and his people. The Lord of the Gospels can shorten the interim period (Mk 13:20) or lengthen it (Lk 13:6-9). His grace means that history is open and that there can be no eschatological timetable. True prophecy accordingly does not so much depict the future as isolate one possible course of events, one which can be communicated either as a warning which may or may not be heeded, or as a promise whose conditions may or may not be met.

Finally, the heart of eschatology is not when or what but who, not a schedule or a plan but a person. The Gospels move us to contemplate the future not by giving us a blueprint but by relating all to Jesus, Messiah and Son of man.

See also APOCALYPTIC; APOCALYPTIC TEACHING; JUDGMENT.
BIBLIOGRAPHY. D. C. Allison, Jr., *The End of the Ages Has Come* (Philadelphia: Fortress, 1985); G. R. Beasley-Murray, *Jesus and the Kingdom of God* (Grand Rapids: Eerdmans, 1986); H. Conzelmann, *The Theology of St. Luke* (London: Faber and Faber, 1960); C. H. Dodd, *The Apostolic Preaching and Its Developments* (New York: Willett, Clark, 1937); E. E. Ellis, *Eschatology in Luke* (FBBS 30; Philadelphia: Fortress, 1972); J. Jeremias, *The Parables of Jesus* (2d rev. ed.; New York: Charles Scribner's Sons, 1972); A. J. Mattill, Jr., *Luke and the Last Things* (Dillsboro: Western North Carolina, 1979); N. Perrin, *Jesus and the Language of the Kingdom* (Philadelphia: Fortress, 1976); J. A. T. Robinson, *Jesus and His Coming* (2d ed.; Philadelphia: Westminster, 1979); W. Willis, ed., *The Kingdom of God in 20th Century Interpretation* (Peabody, MA: Hendrickson, 1987).

D. C. Allison, Jr.

ESSENES. *See* DEAD SEA SCROLLS; JUDAISM.

ETERNAL LIFE. *See* JOHN, GOSPEL OF; LIFE.

ETHICS OF JESUS

Biblical thought may generally be divided into two categories: theology and ethics. Theology is the attempt to understand God and his dealings with this world, while ethics is the human conduct which flows from that understanding. In Judaism* ethics was originally identified with the Law,* which was a gracious guide to the nation whose heart was to be in harmony with the God who was both its Father and king. In time, however, ethics degenerated for many into a preoccupation with outward acts, with no necessary corresponding inner loyalty to God. In Jesus' teaching we see a return to the radical belief in God as Father and king, a belief which for him pervades all areas of human life—social, intellectual, spiritual and moral. Other topics, such as eschatology,* rewards, punishments (see Heaven and Hell) and the Law itself, must be understood in the light of that central conviction.

1. Ethics, Eschatology and the Kingdom
2. Ethics and the Presence of the Kingdom
3. Ethics and Rewards
4. Ethics and the Law
5. Conclusion

1. Ethics, Eschatology and the Kingdom.

The relationship of ethics to the topics of eschatology and the kingdom of God (see Kingdom of God) is one of the most convoluted and confusing chapters in modern Gospel study. Much discussion has centered on the meaning and role of the so-called eschatological sections of the Gospels (see Apocalyptic Teaching; Eschatology) and their relationship to Jesus' proclamation of the kingdom. The modern discussion, unfortunately, has bogged down almost from the beginning as the result of three critical misunderstandings.

The first misunderstanding has been to go back to the usage of the OT or of the first-century Aramaic language (see Languages of Palestine), and from these backgrounds to try to fix limits on what the phrase "the kingdom of God" could have meant for Jesus. But Jesus spent a great deal of time explaining what he meant by the kingdom, and if so, it follows that he did not mean what his contemporaries meant by it.

The second misunderstanding, closely related to the first, is to attempt to make, as G. Dalman has done, a subtle distinction between the kingdom as "reign" rather than "realm." That it could not be both is hardly evident from Jesus' teaching. Even in English the word *kingdom* does service for both, and certainly few kings have ever exercised kingship without also having a realm over which to exercise it. We shall find

ourselves in some difficulty if, when we hear Jesus talk of entering the kingdom of God, there is no realm into which his followers can enter. Few would believe that Jesus invited men and women to enter into the kingship of God—to share his sovereignty with him. What he invited was entry into that sphere of territory where God's kingly rule would be operating over them (see Church).

The third misunderstanding has been to ask whether the kingdom is present or future. Again, Jesus' teaching does not yield to such reductive reasoning. For him the kingdom is past, present and future.

1.1. The Modern Debate. The modern debate concerning the interrelationship of ethics, eschatology and the kingdom began in 1906 with A. Schweitzer's epochal work *The Quest of the Historical Jesus.* Schweitzer, having effectively dismissed all previous attempts to reconstruct the life of Jesus, then produced his own attempt, which was even more implausible than the ones he had rejected. Showing a complete disregard for critical method, Schweitzer declared that Jesus expected the coming of a "Son of man," other than himself, during his own ministry or during the mission of the Twelve, and that when that hope failed to materialize, he changed course and brought about his own crucifixion in order to force God's hand (see Historical Jesus).

While this reconstruction was to win few enthusiasts, it had an unfortunate aftermath. What Schweitzer had erected was a colossal blunder—the "end-of-the-world Jesus"—which has, despite the arguments of critics from C. H. Dodd onward, weighed heavy on the ground of NT study. And perhaps what is most disturbing is that all that was needed to bring down the structure was the wrecking ball of accurate description.

But lack of exegetical accuracy was not the only difficulty with Schweitzer's theory. Another was its failure to accommodate ethical teaching to the question of eschatology. Having insisted with J. Weiss that eschatology was the indispensable framework for the interpretation of NT teaching, he was then faced with the ethical teaching of the Gospels, which he declared to be an "interim ethic" (*Interimsethik*)—an ethic of impractical idealism which could never have been designed for a long period. It was possible for Jesus to talk in this way only because he believed that the interval between his preaching and the end of the world was so short that he could afford to be impractical. That view of the ethics of Jesus was soon met not only with blanket incredulity but substantial arguments to the contrary. In the ethical teaching of Jesus (as in the ethics of the whole NT), the sanctions for the teaching are only in very rare cases the expectation of a future crisis. The reasons are nearly always based on what God has done, on the character of God himself, on the character of Jesus or on the nature of the Christian revelation. They are certainly *not* based on any final crisis.

Another writer to deal extensively with the question of the kingdom and eschatology was R. Bultmann. Reacting to Schweitzer, Bultmann observed that a teacher who believed that the end of the world was close would hardly have devoted so much of his time to arguments about the Jewish Law and how one should live in this world. Bultmann's answer was to understand both eschatology and ethics existentially; while it cannot be denied that Jesus had an apocalyptic* belief in the near end of the world, modern men and women who reject such primitive thinking can still see in the eschatological announcement and ethical demand the critical moment when they confront God.* Bultmann's approach has been heavily criticized, even by his own pupils. In addition to replacing a first-century Jewish framework with a modern philosophical one, his position was fatally stricken by an uncritical acceptance of the notion that first-century people accepted with naive literalness their images of God and the universe. It is now recognized that figures such as Jesus and Paul were as aware of the metaphorical nature of their language as are sophisticated moderns like Bultmann (*see* Myth).

Yet another major contributor to the debate was C. H. Dodd. According to Dodd's influential *The Parables of the Kingdom* (1941), Jesus proclaimed that the kingdom had arrived fully in his preaching, and that all future elements were realized in the present (hence, "realized eschatology"). Statements about the future were actually symbols for the present. Dodd's denuding of the kingdom of all futurity prompted a quick reaction, with some critics accusing him of being a Platonist. Dodd subsequently revised his views so as to account for future kingdom references in Jesus' teaching.

Other writers have proposed varying solutions to the problem of how present and future cohere in the teaching of Jesus. W. G. Kümmel suggested that Jesus understood the kingdom as the ultimate end of history, but that it was present in a proleptic manner in his own life and work. J. Jeremias produced a view almost indistinguishable from Dodd's, while G. E. Ladd tried to maintain an equal balance between present and future. On the whole most recent writers have viewed Jesus' eschatology as lying somewhere between thoroughgoing (e.g., Schweitzer) and realized (e.g., Dodd), with each element variously weighted.

2. Ethics and the Presence of the Kingdom.

As noted above, any attempt to limit the kingdom in Jesus' teaching to either present or future is to be rejected. Both elements are present in the Gospels— although, as we shall see, the present aspects far outweigh the future as the backdrop for Jesus' ethical pronouncements.

Those passages which indicate that the kingdom of God is in some sense still to come are, of course, not difficult to trace. Mark occasionally uses "the kingdom of God" to refer to that eternal life* beyond the grave which is the goal of the process (9:47; 14:25). In another sense Jesus is a king who has not yet entered his royal status (10:37), whose coronation occurs only when the places on his right and his left are occupied by those to whom they have been assigned (15:17, 27). Luke's version of the Lord's Prayer (*see* Prayer) contains the phrase "your kingdom come" (Lk 11:2)— although Matthew adds the gloss, "your will be done on earth, as it is in heaven" (6:10), which shows that for him God's reign is active on earth so long as there are human agents to do his will. In Mark 14:25 (par. Mt 26:29 and Lk 22:18) Jesus says, "I will no more drink of the fruit of the vine* until I drink it new in the kingdom of God," while Matthew 7:21-22 and 25:34 depict the kingdom as the final reward of the righteous (for other future references, cf., e.g., Mt 16:28; Mk 10:30; Lk 18:30).

But by far the overall tenor of Jesus' teaching supports Dodd's contention that for Jesus the kingdom was already substantially present. There are in fact eight possible ways to understand the kingdom in the ministry of Jesus, all of which, in various ways, illuminate Dodd's emphasis on the presence of the kingdom.

2.1. The Kingdom Is Present As the Fulfillment of Prophecy. Here the primary text is Mark 1:15: "The time has come, the kingdom of God has drawn near (*engiken*), repent and believe the Gospel." What is most significant in this passage is that the first two verbs are in the perfect (i.e., past) tense. Mark could well have used the present "the time *is* coming, the kingdom *is* drawing near." Something appears *to have happened* for Jesus to speak in this way. The verb *engiken*, furthermore, while it is related to the adjective *engus*, "near," must in Mark 1:15 mean "has arrived." For the Hebrews the expressions "draw near" or "bring near" were simply idiomatic expressions for "arrive" or "put." The former usage is well known from Lamentations 4:18 (LXX): there *engiken ho kairos hēmōn, eplērōthēsan hai hēmerai hēmōn, parestin ho kairos hēmōn* means "our end *drew near*, our days were numbered, for our end *had come*." "Draw near" (*engiken*) and

"have come" (*parestin*) are synonymous expressions (cf. also Ezek 7:3-12 LXX). The latter usage appears also in (e.g.) Leviticus 2:8, where to bring a sacrifice "near" to the altar means to place it upon the altar—not to drop it halfway between the altar and the Tabernacle entrance.

Two other points in regard to Mark 1:15 need to be noted. First, "The time has fully come." What time? Clearly the time proclaimed in OT prophecy. Second, "Repent and believe the gospel." But what is the gospel? Clearly it is an announcement (*see* Gospel [Good News]). The word *euangelion* is often translated as "good news"; but regularly in the LXX it means, simply, "news" (Heb *b'śôrâ*). And any Jew who believed that at the end of time God would bring in an eschatological kingdom would have found little "news" in being told that this was still true and that nothing had subsequently altered the picture. If Jesus is proclaiming news, it is because he has something *new* to say.

The one context in the OT where we find the term *euangelion* frequently in use is in the prophecies of Isaiah 40—66. To the prophet "the good news" is the proclamation "Behold your God." And when we come to Isaiah 52:7—"How lovely on the mountain are the feet of the herald who comes to proclaim the prosperity and bring good news"—we find a news of deliverance which calls to Zion, "Your God reigns" (52:8). In Isaiah 40—66 the good news is that God has arrived; he has come upon the scene of history to make his presence felt. Above all, *he has come to assert his kingly power:* "Your God has taken up the power of government and is reigning over his world." And if we can accept this as the character of the Isaian prophecy, it would be perverse to argue that Jesus was echoing the prophecy in his declaration without also insisting that he was proclaiming, "Your God is here; your God reigns."

But what could such kingly power mean in the time of Jesus? It is seldom considered that this question might equally have been asked in 545 B.C. At that time outward appearances hardly justified the idea that God's primal reign of justice* had already begun. Jerusalem was in ruins, its leaders were in exile, and most were reluctant to return to Palestine to rebuild a ruined city. The prophet was idealizing, proclaiming that the sovereign reign of God is a reality even in these depressing circumstances, inviting Israel* to respond and be ready to receive their God. And if a prophet can do that five-and-a-half centuries before Jesus, there is no reason why Jesus should not have proclaimed also that in this hostile, unrepentant and beleaguered world, the kingdom of God has become a present reality.

2.2. The Kingdom Is Present As a Divine Power Breaking in upon the Kingdom of Satan and Overthrowing the Power of Satan in the World. This point is made with special clarity in Jesus' response to the claim that he drives out demons by the authority of Beelzebul (*see* Demon, Devil, Satan): "If I by the finger of God cast out demons, the kingdom of God has come upon you" (Lk 11:20; Mt 12:28). What is most interesting about this inbreaking is that it is not conditional upon belief. In Luke's version of the proclamation of the missionaries to the cities of Galilee,* the message is "the kingdom of God has arrived . . ." (*ēngiken . . . he basileia tou theou,* Lk 10:9). Elsewhere (Lk 16:16), the kingdom is being proclaimed (*euangelizetai,* present tense) and people are taking it by force (*biazetai,* present tense). We are clearly dealing with an explosion of activity which cannot be easily defined or categorized, but which is impacting the current state of affairs.

2.3. The Kingdom Is Present As a Small Beginning with Great Potential. In the three parables* of growth (the mustard seed, the seed growing secretly, and the leaven, Mk 4:26-32; Mt 13:33; Lk 17:31), the kingdom has arrived, but in small, unexpected ways. It is like the mustard seed: One may not think much of it at the moment, but it has immense potential. It is like a little leaven which is put into the loaf and causes it to expand. It is like a seed which is put into the soil and produces its fruit. The kingdom is here. Do you find it hard to believe? Wait for the results. Do not be downhearted, nor take much notice of circumstances which appear to belie this gospel announcement. What is small now will have considerable results later. Under this heading we might also add (although with some tentativeness) the mysterious saying of Mark 9:1: "There are some standing by who will not taste death until they see the kingdom having come with power."

The parables of growth entitle us to draw distinctions between the coming of the kingdom, the kingdom arriving as a present reality and its future coming with power (*see* Authority and Power). It is, of course, extremely difficult to determine what Jesus intended by the "kingdom coming with power"—and what Mark thought he intended. But one meaning which may be ruled out in both instances is the Parousia. Our concern here, however, is the contrast between the coming of the kingdom incognito and its open coming with power in the future.

2.4. The Kingdom Is Present As an Opportunity Requiring Resolute Action. Here the parables of the pearl and of the treasure in the field (Mt 13:44-46) are especially noteworthy. In the second, as is so often the case in the parables of Jesus, we are not to ask niggling questions about the morality of the transaction. As with the parable of the unjust steward (Lk 16:1-9), the point of comparison is the need for resolute and determined action in the face of a crisis. Here is an opportunity which will not occur again; it is an opportunity to be grasped, even at the sacrifice of all else.

2.5. The Kingdom Is Present As a Call to Responsibility and Labor. In the parable of the two sons (Mt 21:28-31) a man says to one son, "Go, work in the vineyard," to which the son responds yes—but does not go. The other son is asked the same thing, and says no—but goes. "Which did the will of his father?" The appended comment from Jesus is, "Yes, and prostitutes* and tax* collectors are going into the kingdom ahead of you Pharisees." Here, the willing but disobedient son of the parable is applicable to the Pharisees. Unlike them, prostitutes and tax collectors are already entering the kingdom (*see* Sinner).

2.6. The Kingdom Is Present As a Way of Life Which Demands Total Obedience to God and Complete Self-Sacrifice. This theme appears in Matthew 5:26-33; Mark 8:34-37 and Mark 10:17-23. In the latter passage the hearer fails to follow Jesus and Jesus' response is, "How hard it is for the rich to enter the kingdom of God!" Following Jesus and entering the kingdom are equated. In Luke 9:57-62 (par. Mt 8:18-22) the three claimants to discipleship* each want to be included among Jesus' disciples. Again, when Jesus says that the last one is not fit for the kingdom, the natural implication is that being a disciple* of Jesus and entering the kingdom are different ways of describing the same thing. One could possibly hold that the kingdom is the transcendent, everlasting kingdom for which one qualifies by being a disciple here on earth. But this would not be the natural way of taking the words. Those who become disciples of Jesus enter the service of the kingdom, and only those who are prepared to undergo drastic sacrifice are fit for the kingdom.

Luke 12:31-32 is the end of a passage which in very similar words is recorded by Matthew in the Sermon on the Mount (Mt 6:34; *see* Sermon on the Mount). Luke's version, "But seek his kingdom and these things shall be added to you," is especially intriguing. What does he mean by "seeking his kingdom"? Is this a lifelong quest which ends only at death or at the Parousia? Or is it following Jesus in such a way that the present claims of the kingdom are put above all others? This passage raises the same question as the previous one. There are proper things which ought to be done, but in any ethical scheme there must also be a hierarchy of values, with following Jesus/entering the kingdom taking priority over all other claims.

2.7. The Kingdom Is Present As a Call to New Life and

Service. In Jesus' teaching the *paidion* sayings (Mk 10:13-16 par. Mt 19:13-15 and Lk 18:15-17; Matt 18:3), which stress the necessity of being like a child (*see* Child, Children), must be taken in tandem with the servant sayings (Lk 22:26; Mk 10:43 par. Mt 20:26; see Chilton and McDonald)—the most obvious point of contact being the Greek root *pais*, which may mean either "child" or "servant." Yet the comparison moves beyond mere lexical likeness. Children embody a lack of self-consciousness and a newness of life, with their only point of reference being trust in the parent. Servants are likewise single-minded; they are concerned solely with serving the master. For Jesus the call of the kingdom is a call to newness and a job to be done, not a summons to spiritual self-awareness or an introverted search for salvation.*

2.8. The Kingdom Is Present Not Only As a Challenge to Individuals But As a Challenge to the Nation. In Luke 12:32 we read, "Fear not, little flock; it is your Father's good pleasure to give you the kingdom." We will miss the national character of this saying (as well as that of the complementary passage in Mk 6:34 where Jesus observes that "the people were like sheep without a shepherd") if we are unfamiliar with the OT picture of the nation as a flock and the king as the shepherd (*see* Shepherd, Sheep). The classic text is Ezekiel 34, where the shepherds of Israel (the national leaders) are abandoning the flock. God answers, "I will be shepherd of my flock, I will make them lie down, I will seek the lost, I will bring back the strayed . . . and I will set up over them one shepherd, my servant David" (34:15-27). It is the anointed king who is the shepherd of the flock. When Jesus addresses his disciples in this manner his language cannot but carry messianic and national overtones.

That much of Jesus' teaching is a political challenge to the nation of Israel* is central to an accurate appreciation of his ethical teaching (Caird, Borg). In this regard the common distinction between "personal" and "social" in the ethics of Jesus is somewhat misleading. Israel had always been intended to be a community of "the one and the many," in which what affects the smallest member affects the whole—and vice versa. Social and personal dimensions could never ultimately be separated, and it is only a divorce of Jesus from his Jewish context which enables such a distinction to continue to flourish.

Recent opinion which stresses the role of politics in Jesus' disputes with the Pharisees point out that both sides of the debate were asking the same question: "What does it mean for Israel to be the holy nation of God?" For centuries the Jews had been preoccupied with questions concerning their national destiny as the chosen people, and especially with their undeserved suffering at the hands of the Gentile* empires. But when God would bring his kingdom of justice and peace* to earth, the tables would be turned, and Israel would reign over all.

Jesus does not challenge the close connection between Israel's destiny and its election, but for him God's sovereignty is the primary consideration. If God were truly their king they would know that they had been chosen not as vessels of vengeance but as a beacon light, pointing the way of salvation for all. Suffering and service,* not nationalism and pride, was to constitute their corporate life, a role Jesus acted out in his own experience and which he encouraged in his friends. In his understanding even paying taxes* to Caesar (Mk 12:17; Mt 22:21; Lk 20:25) was not incompatible with giving a full and uncompromising obedience to God.

Herein has lain yet another mistake in interpreting the ethical teaching of Jesus. His comment regarding paying taxes to Caesar has been used by some (e.g., Martin Luther) to establish a complex theory that God has set up two realms, the divine and the secular, each with its own clearly defined aegis. Jesus' point was not intended to be put to this use. Far from establishing any elaborate theology, Jesus was answering a simple question of ethics. How far must I go in this world in trying to live with my enemies? The implications of his teaching can, of course, be drawn out and applied to a later age, but this should not be allowed to replace its original and sublimely simple meaning: insofar as it does not conflict with your duty to God, do all you can to live at peace with your adversaries (cf. also Mt 5:41, where "the extra mile" probably refers to the right of a Roman soldier to impress a Jewish native to carry his pack for a limited distance).

Ultimately, then, Jesus is confronting the Jews with a challenge: first let them learn what it means for God to rule over them; then perhaps they will know what place they will have in God's ultimate plan for the earth.

3. Ethics and Rewards.
In the light of what we have said above, the presence of the kingdom in Jesus' teaching may now be regarded as a datum from which other features of that teaching may be construed. And one of the most frequently discussed issues arising from Jesus' statements about the kingdom concerns the role of rewards and punishments. Both themes are well attested in the teaching of Jesus (for rewards cf., e.g., Mt 6:4, 6, 18; 16:27; for punishment cf., e.g., Mt 5:22, 29, 30; 7:19; 10:28; 13:49-50; 18:6; 25:30). To students of

ethics both elements have always appeared as a difficulty; to do things out of a fear of punishment or hope of reward is not regarded as the highest of ethical motivations (see Heaven and Hell).

To this it must be admitted that there is an element of pragmatism in the ethical teaching of Jesus: "By their fruits you shall know them" (Mt 7:20 par. Lk 6:44). He judges by results, which was very different from the religion of most Pharisees.* They obeyed the Law not because it was sensible or reasonable or leads to desirable consequences, but simply because *it was commanded*. It was sheer, naked obedience. The rabbis could then take the view that all of the commandments are equal, since each gives equal opportunity to obey the will of God.

Jesus, on the other hand, distinguished between the Law's weightier and lesser matters (see Law). Sometimes it has been charged that his teaching on reward has the effect of making ethics prudential—it is nothing more than enlightened self-interest. To do good for the sake of gain is mercenary, even if that gain is spiritual.

What significance, then, do the elements of judgment and reward have in the teaching of Jesus. This question may be treated under seven heads:

3.1. Jesus Distinguished between Two Types of Reward. "Do not announce your good deeds with a flourish of trumpets. Those who do already have their reward" (*apechousin ton misthon*, Mt 6:2). The Greek verb *apechō* was the word ordinarily used on a receipt, meaning "paid in full." Hence, for Jesus outward acts do, of themselves, carry a certain recompense (here, worldly recognition). But there is a deeper, more satisfying type of reward which Jesus advocates, and this reflects his pervasive distinction between that which is arbitrary and that which is proper. Arbitrary rewards have nothing to do with the nature of the activity being rewarded (e.g., "practice the piano two hours a day and you will get a new bicycle"); proper rewards are intrinsic to the activity itself (e.g., "practice the piano two hours a day and one day you will be able to play Mozart"). For Jesus the joys of the kingdom are the result of being a certain kind of person.

3.2. Jesus Encouraged Disinterested Goodness. Some deeds are to be done out of the uncalculating goodness of the heart. "If one in authority makes you go one mile, go with him two" (Mt 5:41). "When you are having guests for lunch or supper, do not invite your friends, your brothers or other relations, or your rich neighbors; they will only ask you back again, and so you will be repaid. But when you give a party, ask the poor, the crippled, the lame and the blind. That is the way to find happiness, because they have no means of repaying you" (Lk 14:12-14 REB). Disinterested goodness does not expect to be repaid. It is true that Luke has Jesus add, "You will be repaid on that day when the good rise from the dead" (Lk 14:14 REB), but there are no grounds for understanding this to mean anything extrinsic to the activity. We might paraphrase Jesus as saying: "If you do good out of the uncalculating goodness of your heart, then in the resurrection* you will have the reward of being confirmed as the sort of person who enjoys doing good out of the uncalculating goodness of your heart."

3.3. Acts Are the Fruit of Character. This is more radical than anything we have yet encountered. Those who have a legal religion are told what to do; and the Pharisees on the whole believed that ethics consisted mainly in taking the Law and doing what it says. According to Jesus, if you are the wrong sort of person you cannot do what you are told. First make the tree good, then the acts will follow (Mt 7:16-20). Good is the fruit which grows spontaneously on the tree of good character, an emphasis that profoundly deepens the quality of human ethics by insisting that it has to do not with acts but with what one is.

What one is determines what one does—a theory opposed not only to Pharisaism but also to classical Greek ethics, especially those of Aristotle. According to Aristotle, habit is the product of constantly doing the right thing; if one does it long enough, it becomes habitual, and one ends up being good. Aristotle and the Pharisees could agree that goodness is achieved by doing right until it becomes a habit. Jesus declares this to be impossible; only a good tree can produce good fruit (a point to be elaborated later by Paul in Rom 7:4-6 and Gal 5:22-23). Jesus looked for people who would not merely do good but be good, who enjoy goodness and for whom goodness is its own reward. This ethical point has a profound theological element within it, as appears in the parable of the sheep and the goats (Mt 25:32-34). The reward for good conduct is the invitation "enter into the joy* of your Lord." The ultimate reward is being the kind of person who can enjoy God. The true end of human beings is to glorify God and enjoy him forever, an idea which would then raise for Jesus' hearers a question: are they the sort of people who would enjoy God?

3.4. Good Acts Issuing from Good Character Is the Kind of Ethic Contained in the Beatitudes. Jesus' repeated words "Blessed are those . . ." suggest that the proper end of men and women is bliss. The Beatitudes (Mt 5:3-12; Lk 6:20-26) describe in a variety of ways how eternal bliss can be anticipated here and

now by living the life of the kingdom (*see* Sermon on the Mount). "Blessed are the poor in spirit" (Mt 5:3; cf. Lk 6:20, "Blessed are you poor"). Some of the verb tenses are future, but it is clear that this bliss is to be anticipated in the present.

With that Aristotle certainly would have agreed. In the tenth book of *Ethics* he sums up ethical obligation with the phrase "as far as possible here and now to live the life of heaven." But in the Beatitudes Jesus has turned normal human ethics upside down. The whole of Aristotle's ten books of *Ethics* is concerned with the nature of happiness; the true end of men and women is to be happy. As we have just seen, Jesus does not disagree with this. But of what does true happiness consist? "Wealth, joy, satisfaction and popularity" are the usual worldly answers. Jesus, however, addresses those for whom such temporal prizes have failed to satisfy. Wealth? "Blessed are you poor." Joy? "Blessed are you who mourn." Satisfaction? "Blessed are you who are hungry." Popularity? "Blessed are you when people hate you" (Lk 6:20-22). And if Jesus pronounces his benediction on these antitheses of worldly goals, it is because it is precisely the poor, the mourning, the hungry and the persecuted who are most open to receive the better gifts of God.

The above point is most easily grasped in the beatitude about the hungry (Lk 6:21; Mt 5:6). When is it blessed to be hungry? Just before dinner. Why is it blessed to be hungry? Because Jesus comes to announce the messianic banquet (*see* Table Fellowship). It is ready, and blessed are those who are hungry for it, who come to it with the most need for its unimaginable bounty. Undeterred by the bogus satisfactions of the present age, they are those who hunger for the banquet which only God has to offer.

3.5. Jesus Repudiated Any Idea of Moral Contract. Here the principal witness is Matthew's parable of the laborers in the vineyard (Mt 20:1-16). Some work the full day, others work only one hour. And when the owner pays them all the same day's wage, he meets the expected complaint by saying, "You contracted with me for one denarius, and I paid you the contract money; so what are you grumbling about?" The modern answer, of course, would be "differential." But the point of the parable is that God does not operate according to contracts. He pays men and women what they need, not what they have earned. So also the parable of Luke 17:7-10: Is the master grateful to the servant for carrying out orders? If one reckons in terms of duty done, then duty to God is unlimited; no matter how far one goes, enough has never been done. But the intention of this is not to load the human psyche with an impossible task, only to explode the notion that God deals with people in such a way. There is no such thing as a moral contract.

It follows that the Sermon on the Mount, and the Beatitudes in particular, must not be regarded as new Law but as descriptive of life in the kingdom. So also in Mark 10:17-27, the story of the rich man who wanted to enter the kingdom of God. "What must I do to inherit eternal life?" he asks. The first thing he learns is that this is not the right question. If it is a matter of doing, it will mean unlimited demands. The disciples wonder, "Who then can be saved?" If the privileged cannot, what hope have the underprivileged? Jesus does not respond, "Oh, how easy it is for the underprivileged!" Rather, he says that with humans it is impossible, but not with God. With God all things are possible. Jesus thus undermines the whole contract system under which the man was operating.

The rewards that Jesus offers are open precisely to those who recognize that they cannot earn them, a point made most forcibly by the parable of the Pharisee and the publican (Lk 18:9-14). If obedience is possible, it is only because it is God's gift. Jesus requires unlimited obedience, but he also says, "Fear not, little flock, it is your Father's good pleasure to give you the kingdom" (Lk 12:32). It is for this reason that Jesus constantly emphasizes the calling of the downtrodden. They are the ones to whom he offers the free gift of God. For Jesus the ethical requirements of the Gospel are possible not because men and women are capable of doing them. They are possible because with God all things are possible.

3.6. For Jesus, God Is the Ultimate Reward. In Luke 10 we find a number of judgments* pronounced on the cities of Galilee, and while these statements probably refer to imminent historical crises (Caird, Borg), they carry an implication for the theme in general. The last judgment means confronting God. Jesus' ethical principles are determined by his extraordinary affirmation that life, here and hereafter, is to be lived in the presence of God. It is from that central claim that all the statements about reward issue; God himself is the ultimate reward. For those who disregard the gospel of the kingdom, whose selfish horizons are bounded completely by this world, the presence of God would be far more terrifying than anything to be found in the lake of fire. But for those who practice the presence of God in this life, the vision of God in the next (Mt 5:8) is the final and fitting conclusion to their journey.

3.7. The Law of the Kingdom Is the Law of Love, and Those Who Love Reap the Reward of Being Like the Father of Love. The great commandment, "You shall love* your neighbor as yourself" (Lev 19:18), is repeated by Jesus as the sum total of the Law (Mk 12:28-31 par. Mt 22:34-40 and Lk 10:25-29; cf. Rom 13:10), but he weds it to Deuteronomy 6:4 ("You shall love the Lord your God with all your heart and all your soul and all your mind," Mt 22:37; Mk 12:30). This double command stands at the head of Jesus' ethical teaching as its quintessence. The uniting of the two commandments prevents love in Jesus' teaching from being misunderstood as a simple humanistic desire directed blindly at others, or a narcissistic preoccupation with oneself. For Jesus love of others and of oneself is possible only if one first loves the God of Israel with all one's being.

The so-called Golden Rule (Mt 7:12; Lk 6:31) is found in other religions and philosophies, albeit in a negative form. The Rabbi Hillel, for example, said, "What you do not wish done to you, do not to others; this is the Law, and all the rest is commentary." Inaction, on the other hand, is regarded by most ethicists as an unacceptable standard. It is hardly comparable with an ethic of unlimited concern and action on behalf of others. G. B. Caird has put it as follows: "The Pharisees, in their passionate devotion to the Law, attempted to make it applicable to every vicissitude of daily life; and their method was to spell out in detail the exact reference of its terms, so as to define the precise limits of their liability. The question 'who is my neighbor?' is a request for definition; and the answer of Jesus frustrates the lawyer's desire to define his liability (Lk 10:29). . . . The righteousness which exceeds that of the Pharisees demands a positive commitment to the well-being of others; it is an ethic of unlimited liability" (Caird 1985, 24).

Luke's version, "You must be merciful" (6:36; *see* Mercy), is amplified by Matthew into the form "You must be perfect" (5:48). A great deal of commentary has been expended on Matthew's interpretation, which is often portrayed as an impossible ideal. In the OT, however, to be perfect is a human virtue indicating total loyalty (compare the "purity of heart" of Mt 5:8, which S. Kierkegaard once defined as "to will one thing"). Mercy, on the other hand, is the very nature of the God of Israel.

The law of non-retaliation (Mt 5:38-42) appears to be a reversal of the *lex talionis* of Exodus 21:24 ("an eye for an eye, a tooth for a tooth"), Leviticus 24:20 and Deuteronomy 19:21, and thus has implications for Jesus' view of the Law (see 4. below). Some commentators, furthermore, have pointed out that to refuse to resist evil, even to encourage it (implied by turning the other cheek, inviting another blow), has often seemed unrealistic, if not outright immoral (cf. Dungen). On this two things may be said:

First, "love" in Jesus' command does not mean that

Christians should have the same feeling for a Nero or a Hitler that they have for their family or friends. What Jesus requires is the unnatural act of putting others first, an act which will not be frustrated even by the abuse and hatred of an antagonist. This is the very nature of God. He does not return evil for evil (Mt 5:43-45; Lk 6:27-31); he expects no compensation (Mt 5:46-48; Lk 6:32-36); he does not prematurely condemn (Mt 7:1-5; Lk 6:37-38; cf. 1 Cor 13:4-7). Those, on the other hand, who harbor hatred in their hearts are guilty in God's eyes of murder (Mt 5:21-26), a precept the world cannot accept. While those who retaliate think that they have heroically resisted aggression, in fact they have made a complete surrender to evil. "Where before there was one under the control of evil, now there are two. Evil propagates by contagion. It can be contained and defeated only when hatred, insult and injury are absorbed and neutralized by love" (Caird 1968, 104).

Second, "turn the other cheek" is almost certainly an aphorism (*see* Chreia/Aphorism). Aphorisms are a common feature of human speech, and at times they are mutually contradictory (e.g., "Penny wise, pound foolish"; "look after the pennies, and the pounds will take care of themselves"). Such sayings are true of a certain person or situation. Elsewhere, Jesus implies that it is legitimate to resist evil. Rather than accepting the teaching of the Pharisees, for instance, he repudiates them for the wrongs they have committed against the people of the land (Lk 11; Mt 23). When struck on the cheek at his trial (Jn 18:22-23; *see* Trial of Jesus), Jesus is not seen to accept the affront quietly or to encourage another blow, but protests against its injustice. In Matthew 18:15-17 wrongs committed within the church are to be confronted and resolved, with the possible punishment of excommunication. It would seem that there are some instances in the Gospels where it is right and proper to remonstrate with an evildoer rather than let evil go unchecked.

4. Ethics and the Law.

Granted that this is the tone of Jesus' ethical teaching, what then becomes of the Law? It is sometimes said that Jesus intended to found a new Torah, or at least that Matthew held this view of Jesus' teaching. In fact both impressions are false. The evidence that for Matthew Jesus is a new lawgiver is limited mainly to the arrangement of his teaching in five lengthy discourses, the first of which is given on a mountain, and the six so-called antitheses of Matthew 5:21-48. But over against these must be set other passages, particularly Matthew 5:17-20, which few will question enshrines Matthew's view of the Law and ethics (*see*

Matthew, Gospel of).

The debate concerns whether, and to what extent, Matthew 5:17-20 represents Jesus' view. Much depends on the interpretation of almost every word of every sentence. What is meant, for instance, by "fulfilling" the Law or by possessing a "righteousness beyond that of the Scribes* and Pharisees," or by keeping "the least of these commandments*"? Such things could, of course, mean "to obey," to keep the Law in its entirety. But this would make Jesus a martinet, a legalist par excellence. This reading is ruled out entirely both by the overall impression of Jesus' life and by Matthew's intention in his succeeding chapters to depict Jesus as setting aside parts of the Law (at least the ritual parts concerning cleanness and uncleanness), and introducing drastic modifications of other parts. Or, on the other hand, "fulfilling the Law" could indicate a penetration into the depths of the intention of the Law, fulfilling its spirit rather than the details of its outward acts (see 4.7. below).

The great objection to the latter interpretation remains the "jot" (*iota*) and "tittle" (*keraia*) of verse 18. On the surface this appears to indicate a meticulous and literalistic legalism. But such an idea contradicts the manner in which Jesus behaves in the rest of the Gospels. There he is often attacked by the Pharisees precisely because he is *not* a legalist. One way out of the dilemma is to claim that Matthew 5:17-20 is Matthew's teaching, not that of Jesus. But this is unlikely insofar as we find the same tension preserved in Luke. In Luke 16:16-18 are three verses wedged between two Lukan parables commonly attributed to the Q* source (*see* Synoptic Problem), but which make an odd sequence. But it does not take long to see the connecting link: all three concern the Law. The first (v. 16) affirms that the Law has passed away, the second (v. 17) that the Law can never pass away, while the third (v. 18) demands a radical obedience which even the Pharisees did not require. Thus by most canons of Gospel criticism these Lukan verses provide some justification for thinking that Matthew 5:17-20 is not peculiarly Matthean. The only sense in which they can be seen as such is that Matthew may have found them isolated in his source and put them together in his own interesting juxtaposition. But there is no longer any reason to doubt that Matthew could here be representing the viewpoint of Jesus.

Another passage which undermines the conception that Matthew represents Jesus as a new lawgiver is Matthew 23:2-3. Here the denunciation of the Pharisees opens with a sanction of Moses' teaching. "The Scribes and Pharisees sit upon the seat of Moses.* Everything they tell you to do, do and observe. But do not do according to their works, for they say and do not do." But considering once again that in the Gospels Jesus spends much of his time engaging in debate with the Pharisees precisely over their respective interpretations of the Law, this instruction seems odd at the very least.

We are therefore faced all the way through with a mystery, a paradoxical nature of Jesus' teaching. Part of the explanation may lie in the nature of the Jewish Law. In addition to being the religious charter of the nation, the Torah was the civil and criminal code, and the Pharisees were its lawyers. In this case Matthew 5:20; 23:2-3 and Luke 16:17 probably raise the same questions as does Paul's advice in Romans 13:1-4: The civil powers are ordained by God; therefore, accept their authority.

If, then, there are indications that Jesus was in fact not a new lawgiver, what could he have been doing? The easiest way to understand his approach is to recognize that he is drawing a number of subtle distinctions. We may begin with his treatment of the Sabbath.*

4.1. The Sabbath. There is little doubt that the breaking of the Sabbath by Jesus was one of the principal sources of friction with the Pharisees. In justice, however, it is important to realize what the Sabbath meant to them. The Sabbath was the outward symbol of the covenant with Israel (Ex 31:12-17). In the Diaspora the Sabbath was the primary bulwark against the assimilation of the Jews into the culture and religion of pagan society, and any threat to the Sabbath was a threat to the very existence of Israel. The Pharisees therefore had a legitimate cause for which they were fighting.

In light of this it comes as a surprise that in the Gospels Jesus is seen to break the Sabbath deliberately, an act which undermines both Pharisaic and Mishnaic concerns. The Pharisees in particular were zealous to obey all 613 commandments in their everyday life, and, unlike the backward-looking and conservative Sadducees, they were progressive in their earnest desire to understand what the Law means.

This desire is especially seen in the Pharisaic concern with defining "work." In the Mishnah, for example, work is broken down into thirty-nine different activities (*see* Rabbinic Traditions and Writings). This in turn gave rise to some very important disputes, such as whether a doctor may work on the Sabbath. Doctors, it was decided, could work on the Sabbath if death were imminent, but in other cases they must desist (cf. Mk 1:32, where the people waited until the end of the Sabbath at sunset before presenting the sick to Jesus for healing*).

Jesus apparently had no such reservations. The Gospels relate four accounts in which he invited the wrath of the Pharisees by healing on the Sabbath, and in none of the four cases can the sick person be said to be in any immediate danger. One had a withered hand (Mk 3:1-6); two were paralytics, one for eighteen years (Lk 13:10-17), the other for thirty-eight (Jn 5:2-18); and one had dropsy (Lk 14:1-6). The Pharisee's claim that in each case the cure could have been delayed one more day seems justified. And yet in all four cases Jesus goes on the offensive, choosing the Sabbath as the right day for such merciful interventions.

The gravamen of the Pharisees' complaint was that Jesus was setting himself above the Sabbath, and therefore changing the Law of Moses. Jesus' answer to this charge is found in his comment after he healed the woman who had been paralyzed: "Was it not necessary that this woman, a daughter of Abraham* whom Satan has bound for eighteen years, be loosed from this bond on the Sabbath day?" (Lk 13:16). In Mark's three passion predictions (Mk 8:31; 9:31; 10:32-34) the important word *dei,* "it is necessary," is used to denote a divine necessity for Jesus' death laid down for him in Scripture. There was also a divine necessity for healing on the Sabbath, insofar as the Sabbath was divinely ordained to be for Israel a foretaste of the kingdom of God. By healing those bound by the kingdom of Satan, Jesus had enabled the kingdom of God to break in upon human life (Lk 11:20; Mk 3:27). Thus, since the Sabbath was a foretaste of the kingdom, there was no better day for him to perform his acts of mercy. Since the kingdom had arrived, the Son of man (*see* Son of Man) was Lord* of the Sabbath (Mk 2:28).

When Jesus' disciples pluck ears of grain on the Sabbath (Mk 2:23-28), it therefore comes as no surprise that Jesus should appeal to David's example in 1 Samuel 21:1-6, with the added comment that "the Sabbath was made for humankind, not humankind for the Sabbath" (Mk 2:27). This indicates something which for Jesus the Pharisees had missed—the humanitarian purpose of the Sabbath in Deuteronomy. To interpret it in an antihumanitarian fashion is to misinterpret it. Matthew 12:5-7 makes the same case. If the kingdom has arrived, all this activity is justified. The Pharisees, of course, do not accept that the kingdom has arrived. Here it would appear that the author of Hebrews has faithfully represented Jesus' teaching by seeing the Sabbath as a shadow of that rest which remains for the people of God when they enter the kingdom (cf. Heb 4). The followers of Jesus live in a constant Sabbath rest insofar as they live in the kingdom. They are the weary and heavy-laden who have found rest (Mt 11:28).

4.2. Divorce. Another example of Jesus' approach to the Law was his treatment of divorce.* But any discussion of this issue will be complicated if one compares Mark and Matthew on the subject. We cannot here elaborate the problem, except to say that there are good grounds for assuming that Mark is right to say that Jesus did not allow divorce among his followers on any pretext, and that something has gone wrong in our extant version of Matthew, in which *mē epi porneia* indicates an exception (Mt 19:9; cf. Mk 10:2-12; see Banks, Guelich, Mohrlang).

The occasion of Jesus' teaching was a question about the interpretation of the Mosaic Law found in Deuteronomy 24:1-2, where a man is allowed to divorce his wife if some "unseemly thing" (Heb *erwaṭ dābār*) is found in her. On the basis of this law the conservative followers of Rabbi Shammai permitted divorce only for proven adultery, the liberal followers of Rabbi Hillel allowed it if the husband disliked his wife's cooking, and Rabbi Akiba allowed it even if a man would see a woman more beautiful than his wife.

Jesus' response to all of this is that divorce was allowed by Moses—but only because of the hardness of the human heart. It was never the will of God, only permitted. Rather than abolishing the Law, Jesus moves to another passage, Genesis 2—a weightier passage than Deuteronomy. Genesis 2 was Torah as much as Deuteronomy 24. But it reveals God's intention not merely as Lawgiver but as Creator. There is a law of God built into creation—lifelong fidelity—to which Deuteronomy is but an afterthought. If Jesus goes on to say that remarriage after divorce is adultery, it would not represent for him new legislation. Where there is hardness of heart, divorce is inevitable and lawful. But where the kingdom has been preached, where men and women have accepted the invitation to enter the kingdom, putting themselves under God's kingly reign, it now becomes possible to deal with hardness of heart (*see* Hardness of Heart); it is now possible to attain to the purposes of the Creator. In the kingdom divorce is not so much forbidden as it is unnecessary. There is now another way of dealing with it.

4.3. Tithing Mint and Herb. Jesus' concentration on "the weightier matters" of the Law is also seen in one of his "woes" to the Pharisees recorded in Matthew 23:23 (par. Lk 11:42). The Pharisees "pay tithes on mint and dill and herb, but have no care for the weightier matters of the Law, justice and the love of God. These you should have done, without neglecting the others." For the Jews who paid agricultural tithes,

some produce fell into the category of the uncertain. Should one tithe on garden vegetables such as lettuce? Maybe. Parsley and mint? Probably not, but pay the tithe anyhow; you might be inadvertently breaking the Law. Herein is illustrated the Pharisaic principle of "putting a hedge around the Law"—not to protect it, but to provide a margin of safety. Whatever one thinks is right to do, go a little bit further. Any commandment is an opportunity to show one's obedience. The more trivial the commandment, the more disinterested and altruistic the obedience. For Jesus this kind of scrupulous observance of pettifogging possibilities will only lead in the end to a neglect of the cardinal principles. It is psychologically inevitable that such concerns concentrate on the manageable—the visual, perceptible things—to the neglect of "the weightier matters."

4.4. Other Legal Matters: Oaths, Murder. So far we have seen no evidence of Jesus rescinding the Law. In Matthew and Luke it is clear that a superficial obedience to the Decalog is in view, and that this is not radical obedience to the purposes of God. Such radical obedience is the righteousness (*see* Justice, Righteousness) which exceeds that of the Scribes and Pharisees (Mt 5:20). How extreme Jesus is on this point is further seen from a study of the other antitheses. The one which best illustrates the change he is introducing is the third, on perjury (Mt 5:33-37).

Here all swearing is forbidden (*see* Oaths, Swearing) with the stunning conclusion, "Let your speech be Yes, Yes, No, No; anything more than this comes from the evil one" (Mt 5:37). If this seems more than a little inhibiting, it is because we miss the point. What Jesus meant is clearly seen in the only parallel to this logion in the NT, James 5:12. There the form is "let your Yes be Yes, and your No, No." A yes must always mean yes; a no must always mean no. The reason an oath is said to come from the Devil is the implication which lies behind it. If one is not on oath, he or she is free to tell lies. Jesus therefore demands an honesty so radical, so universal, that one's word is always true, whether on oath or not.

The taking of oaths then becomes not merely irrelevant but dangerous; it undermines the demand for radical honesty. That kind of going behind the letter to the intention appears to form the gravamen of Jesus' complaint. Rather than going too far, the Pharisees *did not go far enough.* The same point is made in the commandment* against murder (Mt 5:21-26). Such a law is to be kept by a fundamental attitude of the heart which would make it impossible even to *think* of murdering. Behind overt action lies character and motive. One can pass a law against murder and then enforce it. But one cannot pass a law against being a murderous person. Law by its very nature can deal only with activities. It can, of course, take account of intention. Today some countries have a law against "loitering with intent." But first one must at least loiter. Jesus has in fact moved out of the realm of law to ethics proper. Ethics has a debt beyond the reach of law.

This is hardly to claim that Jesus was not interested in actions. There are a number of recorded sayings, particularly the one with which the Sermon on the Mount ends (Mt 7:24-27)—the saying of the two houses—in which doing is important. As much as any Pharisee, Jesus requires that ethical principles of character should find their way into action. But at the same time, for him actions are not enough.

We are now in a position to summarize Jesus' teaching about the Law in four propositions: (1) There are weightier matters to the Law; (2) one needs to penetrate behind the Law's letter to its original divine intention; (3) one needs to penetrate behind action to character; and (4) it is possible to take this view of the Law because the kingdom has arrived.

4.5. The Role of the Heart. In Mark 10:43-44 (par. Mt 20:25-27) Jesus says, "Among you, whoever wants to be great must be your servant, and whoever wants to be first must be the slave of all" (REB). This text can be generalized as one of the major headings of the ethical teaching of Jesus. Among whom? Among you who have entered the kingdom. The ethical teaching of Jesus is the way of the kingdom. His teaching is not to be interpreted prescriptively as commandments to be obeyed as the Jews obeyed the Decalog. For Jesus ethics are primarily *descriptive;* they illustrate how men and women will behave in the kingdom. "If you enter the kingdom, this is what you will be taking on—a higher standard of ethical observance than can ever be enforced by law." The reference to the heart (Mk 7:18-23 par. Mt 15:17-20) is especially noteworthy: "It is not what goes in that defiles . . . it is what comes out; for from within, from the heart, comes evil thoughts, fornications, thefts, murders, adulteries and so forth." Mark adds, in effect, that by saying this Jesus abrogated the whole Levitical Law regarding cleanness (*see* Clean and Unclean) and uncleanness (Mk 7:19; cf. Acts 10:10-16). Whatever else Jesus may complete and confirm, he does not keep that part of the Law. It is the heart which is the source of evil, and it is the heart which must be changed, with behavior following spontaneously.

And where for Jesus does the Law and his own example fit into all of this? The tree is known by its fruit (Mt 7:17-20; Lk 6:43-45). Behavior flows from the heart, and if the heart is changed, then with the Law

of the OT and the example of Jesus as a guide, men and women can find their way to the practical application of their obedience to the law of love and to the radical demands of the God who is king.

4.6. The Final Split with the Pharisees. Such an interpretation of the Law was bound to bring Jesus and the Pharisees to a final parting of the ways. Here it is wiser to follow Luke's version of the vitriolic "woes" (11:37-52; *see* Blessing and Woe), which have undergone less editing than Matthew's (23:13-36). For Jesus the Pharisees concentrate on minutiae to the neglect of the weightier matters (Lk 11:42). They are like unmarked graves which men and women walk over without being aware of the contamination they incur (Lk 11:44 par. Mt 23:27)—a comment showing Jesus' deep sense of irony.

The Pharisees attacked Jesus for not avoiding the company of contaminating people; Jesus turns the Pharisees on their heads by telling the crowds, "Beware of the leaven of the Pharisees" (Mk 11:15). Leaven here is a symbol for silent, pervasive, spreading evil. For Jesus the Pharisees were superficial environmentalists: concerned with all kinds of outward pollution, they contain a deeper, more insidious, more virulent form of contamination—that contamination which comes from contact with those who think they know everything about God and his will but do not understand him in the slightest. Self-regarding and apprehensive, the Pharisees fear that the holiness of Israel will be contaminated by what it touches. To Jesus the holiness of God is capable of looking after itself; it is an outgoing power, reaching all who need help. It is incapable of being contaminated, except by selfishness.

But if the Pharisees and Jesus could not close ranks on this crucial point, it was also because they had vastly different conceptions of God. To the Pharisees God was a lawgiver who approves of, and rewards, those who keep his Law. To Jesus he was the heavenly Father who loves even his erring children and whose sovereign grace is a dynamic, redemptive force let loose into the world to restore and redeem. Those who took the Pharisaic view of God were relatively few, because in order to please such a deity one would have to be a professional; obeying 613 commandments is a full-time job. How is the layperson to carry such a weight? The Pharisees "load them with intolerable burdens and will not lift a finger to ease the load" (Lk 11:46). For Jesus the Law is the gift of a gracious God, and to interpret it as an intolerable burden is wholly to misunderstand the God from whom it comes. If ordinary men and women break down under the strain of obedience to the Law, then there must be something seriously wrong with that reading of the will of God.

4.7. Fulfilling the Law. If what we have said above constitutes Jesus' approach to the Law, how then can it be said that Jesus fulfills it? Returning to Matthew 5:17, it is probable that the word *fulfill* here "includes not only an element of discontinuity (that which has now been realized *transcends* the Law) but an element of continuity as well (that which transcends the Law is nevertheless something to which the Law itself *points forward*" (Banks). Putting it another way, to say that the teaching of Jesus fulfills the Law is to say that his teaching "fills the Law full"—with new meaning.

5. Conclusion.

The ethical teaching of Jesus may now be summarized under five points.

5.1. The Presence of the Kingdom. On the question of Jesus' expectation of the future, Schweitzer was radically mistaken. But modified forms of his thesis are still with us. Too much attention continues to be paid to the notion that for Jesus the kingdom was focused primarily on some event or events subsequent to the initial proclamation recorded in Mark 1:15. Those who hold this view, of course, will always find deep embarrassment in fitting ethics into their scheme; but that has not stopped them from futurizing the kingdom, even at the expense of robbing Jesus' ethics of their ultimate basis. Jesus, on the other hand, taught that entry into the kingdom was synonymous with entering the life of discipleship—of submitting to the demands of the God who is king. His ethics are dominated by the central burning conviction that God's rule is now actively present in the affairs of individuals, kings and nations.

5.2. The Priority of Character. For Jesus ethics are to some extent realistic and pragmatic. Those who freely receive God's gifts must (1) show them in outward acts, and (2) pass them on to others, lest they become stagnant and die. But ethics are also the fruit of character, a claim which many of the Pharisees, with their exclusive emphasis on outward acts, could not accept. The rewards which Jesus promises are not extrinsic to human character, but point to the building up of a personality which would ultimately be at home in the presence of God.

5.3. The Rediscovered Spirit of the Law. The Law of Israel was understood by Jesus as a gracious provision, given not only by a sovereign king but by a loving Father. To obey his Law meant to be in conformity with the purposes which are built into creation. Jesus, like Paul after him, understood that a rigid obedience to the Law, because of corrupting influences (selfish-

ness, nationalism, pride), had failed to achieve God's primal purposes. Therefore, those who would obey God's will and respond to his love must go behind the letter, back to the Law's original intention.

5.4. The Redefined People of God. What we call the gospel of Jesus was not in the first instance a new religion. It was a call to the nation of Israel, asking it to believe that God's power is always breathtakingly fresh, always ready to break into their history, always an outgoing and transforming power reaching into the lives of those who need help. But in order to receive that power they must also accept a radically different interpretation of what it meant for them to be the chosen people. Going back to the prophecies of Isaiah 40—66, he reminded them of God's kingly reign. Rather than privilege, they had been chosen for responsibility; rather than authority and glory,* they had been chosen for service and suffering; that through them God's kingly power might reach out into the world, overthrowing the forces of evil.

It is in this context that some of Jesus' most powerful ethical statements are to be understood, particularly those which concern love. Rather than hating their national enemies and exulting in their ruin, the Jews were to love them and ask God for their well-being. Instead of avoiding their corrupting contamination, they were to become their friends. And, in perhaps the most uncomfortable statement of all, they were to content themselves with the benevolent administration of Rome. To make friends with Caesar did not mean that they could not also give to God a full and uncompromising obedience.

5.5. The Personal and Communal Dynamic. Finally, too much distinction has been made between the personal and the social in the ethics of Jesus. For him ethics were surely personal, insofar as they flow from each individual's relationship to God. But ethics must also be incorporated into the community of God. If the majority of God's people had not responded to the challenge, Jesus would work through a remnant, as God had done so often in Israel's history. Through Jesus—and subsequently through his followers, whether Jew or Gentile—God's promise to the nations would be fulfilled. The community Jesus founded may be understood truly as a "church," but only if that term is seen as a community of men and women in whom Jesus is personally present, who put one another before themselves and through whom God's redemptive power can reach out into the world, driving out evil and drawing all into a body of individuals who are willing to put themselves under his kingly sovereignty and fatherly love.

See also COMMANDMENT; DISCIPLESHIP; DIVORCE; FAMILY;

FASTING; FORGIVENESS OF SINS; HYPOCRITE; JUDGMENT; KINGDOM OF GOD; LAW; MERCY; OATHS AND SWEARING; PEACE; RICH AND POOR; SWEARING; SABBATH; SERMON ON THE MOUNT; SINNER; TAXES.

BIBLIOGRAPHY. N. Anderson, *The Teaching of Jesus* (Downers Grove, IL: InterVarsity, 1983) 79-148; R. Banks, *Jesus and the Law in the Synoptic Tradition* (SNTSMS 28; Cambridge: University Press, 1975); M. J. Borg, *Conflict, Holiness and Politics in the Teachings of Jesus* (New York: Edwin Mellen, 1984); idem, "An Orthodoxy Reconsidered: The 'End-of-the-World Jesus,' " in *The Glory of Christ in the New Testament: Studies in Christology in Memory of George Bradford Caird*, ed. L. D. Hurst and N. T. Wright (Oxford: Clarendon, 1987) 207-17; G. B. Caird, *The Gospel of St. Luke* (London: A. & C. Black, 1968); idem, *Jesus and the Jewish Nation* (The University of London: Athlone, 1965); idem, *New Testament Theology*, ed. and completed by L. D. Hurst (Oxford: Clarendon, 1992; an abbreviated and revised treatment of this dictionary article by L. D. Hurst is found in chap. 9 of this work); idem, "Perfection and Grace," in *Duty and Delight: Routley Remembered*, ed. C. R. Young et al. (Carol Stream, IL: Litton, 1985); B. D. Chilton and J. I. H. McDonald, *Jesus and the Ethics of the Kingdom* (London: SPCK, 1987); B. D. Chilton, *God in Strength: Jesus' Announcement of the Kingdom* (Sheffield: JSOT, 1987); idem, ed., *The Kingdom of God in the Teaching of Jesus* (IRT 5; Philadelphia: Fortress, 1984); G. Dalman, *The Words of Jesus* (Edinburgh: T. & T. Clark, 1902); C. H. Dodd, *The Parables of the Kingdom* (London, Nisbet, 1941); D. L. Dungen, "Jesus and Violence," in *Jesus, the Gospels, and the Church: Essays in Honor of William A. Farmer*, ed. E. P. Sanders (Macon, GA: Mercer University, 1987) 135-62; R. H. Fuller, ed., *Essays on the Love Commandment* (Philadelphia: Fortress, 1978); V. P. Furnish, *The Love Command in the New Testament* (Nashville: Abingdon, 1972); R. Guelich, *The Sermon on the Mount: A Foundation for Understanding* (Waco, TX: Word, 1982); D. Guthrie, *New Testament Theology* (Downers Grove, IL: InterVarsity, 1981) 896-910; A. E. Harvey, *Strenuous Commands: The Ethic of Jesus* (Philadelphia: Trinity, 1990); R. Hiers, *Jesus and Ethics: Four Interpretations* (Philadelphia: Westminster, 1968); J. L. Houlden, *Ethics and the New Testament* (Baltimore: Penguin, 1973); J. Jeremias, *The Parables of Jesus* (3d ed.; New York: Scribner's, 1972); W. G. Kümmel, *Promise and Fulfilment* (London: SCM, 1961); G. E. Ladd, *The Presence of the Future* (Grand Rapids: Eerdmans, 1974); G. Lohfink, *Jesus and Community: The Social Dimension of Christian Faith* (Philadelphia: Fortress, 1984); T. W. Manson, *Ethics and the Gospel* (London: SCM, 1960); idem, *The Servant Messiah* (Cambridge: University Press, 1953); idem, *The Teaching of Jesus* (Cambridge: University Press, 1935); R. Mohrlang, *Matthew and Paul on Ethics* (SNTSMS 48; Cambridge: University Press, 1983); E. P. Sanders, *Jesus and Judaism* (Philadelphia: Fortress, 1985); W. Schrage, *The Ethics of the New Testament* (Philadelphia: Fortress, 1988); A. N. Wilder, *Eschatology and Ethics in the Teaching of Jesus* (New York: Harper, 1950).
L. D. Hurst

EUCHARIST. *See* LAST SUPPER.

EVIL SPIRIT. *See* DEMON, DEVIL, SATAN.

EXALTATION. *See* ASCENSION OF JESUS; DEATH OF JESUS; GLORY.

EXORCISM. *See* DEMON, DEVIL, SATAN.

F

FAITH

The language of faith ("believe," "trust," "faithful," "reliable," etc.) is essential to human relationships in general, but gains its special biblical connotations from the interaction of God* with humanity, his reliability and our response of trust in him.

1. Faith in the Synoptic Gospels
2. Faith in the Gospel of John

1. Faith in the Synoptic Gospels.

1.1. The Synoptic Tradition in General. By comparison with Paul's letters or the Gospel of John the Synoptic Gospels make relatively little use of the terminology of faith, and their uses of such language do not usually carry the same weight of theological connotation. The most prominent use is in connection with Jesus' miracles,* which are typically performed in response to the faith either of the sufferer (Mk 5:34; 10:52) or, more frequently, of those who request Jesus' aid on behalf of another (Mk 2:5; 9:23-24; Mt 8:10, 13; 15:28). Conversely, absence of faith hinders Jesus' miraculous activity (Mk 6:5-6)—though Mark warns us against too tight a connection between faith and healing* by commenting that even in this situation of unbelief Jesus "laid his hands on a few sick people and healed them." *Faith* in such contexts focuses on a practical trust in the power of Jesus to meet physical need (or, in the case of exorcisms, to bring spiritual deliverance). It is exemplified in the centurion, who recognizes in Jesus a functional authority (*see* Authority and Power) akin to that of an army officer (Mt 8:8-10). Thus it is not Jesus himself who exercises faith, but those who come to him for help. The correlative to the faith of the suppliant is the authority of Jesus.

Jesus performs miracles in response to faith; his disciples,* by contrast, should be able to achieve similarly miraculous results by the exercise of faith (Mk 11:22-24; Mt 17:19-21). Where Jesus' disciples prove powerless, the cause is traced to "unbelief" (Mk 9:19), or "little faith" (Mt 17:20—see below). But while Jesus responds to faith rather than exercising it himself, it may be significant that Mark describes this miracle-working faith of the disciples as faith in God rather than faith in Jesus (Mk 11:22). The key to the exercise of such faith is not its quantity, but the God to whom it is directed; thus Jesus rejects the notion that faith needs to be "increased" to be effective— even the smallest faith ("like a mustard seed") will see spectacular results (Lk 17:5-6; Mt 17:20).

In the Synoptic tradition the noun *pistis* ("faith") is used almost exclusively in relation to miracles (see, however, Lk 18:8; 22:32, where it refers rather to the loyalty of disciples). The verb *pisteuō* ("I believe"), however, while it too occurs prominently in such contexts, is used also without reference to miracles or to physical need, to describe the proper response to the preaching of the gospel* by Jesus (Mk 1:15; Lk 8:12-13) and indeed also to the preaching of John the Baptist* (Mk 11:31; Mt 21:25, 32). Thus "to believe" becomes almost a synonym for "to be a disciple," and this discipleship* is further spelled out in Matthew 18:6 as believing in (*eis*) Jesus. This verse (and its parallel in Mark 9:42, if the longer reading be accepted) is the only place in the Synoptic tradition where "believing in Jesus" is explicitly mentioned as the basis of a new relationship with God (though see the mocking use of *pisteuō ep' auton* ["believe in him"] in Mt 27:42), but such language is a natural sequel to the use of the language of faith both for the practical recognition of Jesus' supernatural authority and also for the appropriate response to the gospel which he came to proclaim.

1.2. Mark. Mark does not offer a focus on faith which is clearly distinctive from the general Synoptic perspective set out in the previous section. It should be noted, however, that it is only in Mark that Jesus' programmatic announcement of the arrival of the time of fulfillment includes the call to "believe" as well as to "repent." Mark 1:15 is a structurally prominent verse and must be understood as setting out what Mark regards as the main focus of Jesus' Galilean ministry. The call of John the Baptist to repentance* (1:4) is expanded by Jesus into the classic Christian call to conversion, "repent and believe in the gospel."

Believing is thus marked out by its link with *metanoia* ("repentance") as more than either a practical dependence or an intellectual credence. It is a life-changing commitment, the beginning of a new relationship with God.

1.3. Matthew. While Mark refers occasionally to the "unbelief" (*apistia*) of those who observed Jesus' ministry (Mk 6:6; 9:19, 24; cf. Mt 13:58), in Matthew it is the disciples themselves who are accused of "little faith" (*oligopistia*: Mt 6:30; 8:26; 14:31; 16:8; 17:20; cf. Lk 12:28). While "little faith" may sound less serious than "unbelief," in Matthew 17:20 it is contrasted with faith even as small as a mustard seed, which can achieve the results which are closed to *oligopistia*. Practically speaking, therefore, *oligopistia* amounts to no faith at all; even if the persons concerned are technically "believers," their faith has no value in terms of practical reliance on God. In each use of the language of *oligopistia* in Matthew the reference is to the need for practical trust in the power of God to provide for the necessities of life, to heal or to deliver from physical danger. To fail in such practical trust is, even in disciples, a mark of an "unbelieving generation" (17:17).

Nonetheless, it is faith which is the essential basis of belonging to the people of God. Matthew's special concern with this question comes into sharp focus in 8:10-13, where the exemplary faith of the Gentile centurion, matched by "no one in Israel," provides the context for Jesus' vision of many coming from east and west to share in the Jewish messianic banquet, while the "sons of the kingdom" themselves are excluded. Participation in the blessings of salvation* is no longer to be on the basis of race, but of a new principle which allows non-Jews (*see* Gentiles) to sit with the Jewish patriarchs, but at the same time offers no guarantee of salvation for those who were born Jews (*see* Israel). And that principle is faith, a faith which has in the case of the centurion expressed itself in a remarkable recognition of the unique authority of Jesus.

A similar connotation appears in the story of the Canaanite woman (15:21-28), where an explicit raising of the question of the Jews' exclusive right to the blessings brought by the Messiah leads to Jesus' declaration to this representative of the Jews' traditional enemy, "Great is your faith; your request is granted." Faith produces a new order in which the first are last and the last first. It will be the tax collectors and prostitutes rather than the Jewish religious authorities who go into the kingdom* of God, because it was they who believed God's message through John the Baptist and so found "the way of righteousness" (21:32; *see*

Justice, Righteousness). Faith is not just the key to Jesus' miraculous work, it is also the way into the kingdom of God.

1.4. Luke. If in Matthew there is a tendency to use the terminology of faith more in relation to spiritual salvation, this tendency is more pronounced in Luke. The familiar pronouncement "Your faith has saved you," which occurs as the climax of several healing stories in each of the Synoptics, occurs also in Luke 7:50 with reference not to physical healing but to the forgiveness* of sins. The link between faith and salvation (in a non-physical sense) is explicit in Luke 8:12, where the devil's (*see* Demon, Devil) aim is to prevent people from "believing and being saved." In Luke 12:46 the judgment* on the unfaithful servant is to be cut in two and given a place "with the unbelievers," which thus appears to be a synonym for the spiritually lost. Such uses of the terminology of faith prepare the way for the prominent use in Acts of "to believe" as a regular term for becoming and continuing as a disciple.

Faith (or faithfulness—the decision as to which term best represents *pistis* is sometimes difficult) is therefore a distinctive characteristic of the true people of God. At the beginning of Luke's Gospel we see two contrasting examples of response to the promise of a miraculous birth: Zechariah "did not believe" (1:20), but Mary "believed that what the Lord had spoken to her would be fulfilled" (1:45). As such she is congratulated (*makaria*) as a paradigm of faith, which for her involves not only intellectual acceptance of God's surprising announcement, but the personal commitment to be herself the means of its fulfillment, with all the upheaval that must involve. It is faith, in something like the same sense, that the Son of man* hopes to find on earth at his coming—the persistent faithfulness of the people of God. And it is such faith that Peter is in danger of losing under the pressure of the events of Jesus' passion (22:32; *see* Passion Narrative). Faith involves the loyalty of God's people to his will even when such loyalty is costly.

2. Faith in the Gospel of John.

It is well known that the noun *pistis* does not occur in John's Gospel, while the verb *pisteuō* occurs nearly 100 times. The reason for this linguistic trait is a matter of speculation. It has been attributed to an increasing use of *pistis* to designate the body of Christian doctrine, whereas John's interest is rather in the *relationship* expressed by the verbal form or to the use of *pistis* in the context of a Pauline faith/works dichotomy, which is "not a live controversy for John" (Painter). At any rate, the verb expresses a vital component in

John's understanding of salvation. It summarizes what God requires of his people: "This is the work of God, that you should believe in the one whom he has sent" (6:28-29). And it is used in 21:31 to describe John's main purpose in writing, "that you may believe that Jesus is the Son of God, and that through believing you may have life in his name."

John's usage is distinctive. While he does sometimes use the verb in the normal way, with the simple dative of the person or thing believed, he generally uses one of three other constructions.

(1) The intellectual content of the verb is expressed twelve times by *pisteuō* with *hoti*, "believe that . . ." All these uses (except 9:18) refer to christological conviction, believing that Jesus is the Messiah (*see* Christ), the Son of God,* has come from God, etc.

(2) In no less than thirty-six cases John uses *pisteuō eis* (literally, "believe into"), and once *pisteuō en* ("believe in"). This usage is known only in Christian writings, and in the rest of the NT it occurs only ten times (three of which are in 1 John), so it may fairly be regarded as John's special contribution to Christian language. All these uses except two refer to belief "into Jesus," or (in 1:12; 2:23; 3:18) "into the name of Jesus"; the two exceptions are references to belief in God (12:44; 14:1), but in each case this is combined directly with belief in Jesus.

(3) In thirty cases *pisteuō* is used absolutely, with no explicit indication of the object of belief. Often these uses follow closely on references to believing "into Jesus" (e.g., 3:18; 4:39, 41; 6:40, 47; 9:35-38), so that the meaning is not in doubt. In the context of John's overall usage of the verb it can apparently be used absolutely as a shorthand expression for Christian commitment.

Not only is John's linguistic usage distinctive, but the subject-matter of his language about faith is remarkably single-minded. While a few of his uses of *pisteuō* with the dative refer to God, to Scripture (or Moses*) or to a word spoken, in the vast majority of cases where an object is expressed it is the person of Jesus himself who is the object of faith. This is in striking contrast with the Synoptic usage noted above, where only one passage explicitly mentions believing in Jesus. While faith in the Synoptics is primarily faith in God and is directed principally toward the experience of miraculous power, in John it is faith in Jesus, and its focus is not on miracles and on the meeting of physical need, but on the establishment of a relationship which results in eternal life.

There is, however, a connection between miracles and faith in John. By his first miracle at Cana Jesus "revealed his glory and his disciples believed in him" (2:11; cf 2:23; 4:53). But it is that way round—faith results from the miracle, not vice versa. And even this connection is of limited value—a faith based *solely* on miracles is superficial and inadequate (2:23-25; 4:48; 6:26-29). Faith which is based on Jesus' "works" is apparently legitimate, but inferior to a faith which needs no such prop (14:10-11; 20:29).

It is interesting to note that John, who stresses so much Jesus' dependence on the Father, does not use the language of faith in this connection. As in the Synoptics, Jesus is not spoken of as believing in God; he is the object, not the subject, of faith.

Believing is the appropriate response to revelation. John's Gospel presents a series of "testimonies" *(martyria)* to the truth* *(alētheia)* about Jesus, beginning with the testimony of John the Baptist ("that all might believe through him," 1:7), and including the testimony of other human witnesses, of Scripture, of the words and works of Jesus himself, of the Paraclete (*see* Holy Spirit) and ultimately of the Father (*see* Witness). In adducing this impressive range of witnesses to the truth which has been revealed in Jesus, John aims to lead his readers to the faith which is the only appropriate response to such revelation. If in Jesus, the Word (*see* Logos) incarnate, "truth" has now become visible in the world* (1:14), the only response must be to believe in that truth, and that means to believe in Jesus, and so to find life through his name.

Such "believing" is closely related to "knowing." If to believe is the key to eternal life (3:16 etc.), so also is "to know" (17:3). "Believing" and "knowing" appear as virtual synonyms in 6:69. There is no trace in John of the modern dichotomy between faith and knowledge.

Believing therefore plays a central role in the whole system of John's theology of salvation. It is a response to revelation, and it results in knowledge of the truth. But since that revelation has come to us in a person, who is himself the truth, neither faith nor knowledge can be understood in primarily intellectual terms. The object of believing can only be the person of Jesus himself. John's special expression "believe into" is well adapted to convey this central theme of his theology, which, while the terms used are different, is closely related to Paul's language about the incorporation of believers "into" the body of Christ, so that they are "in Christ." John's equally striking language about "abiding in" Jesus reinforces the same idea.

See also Forgiveness of Sins; Repentance.

Bibliography. R. Bultmann and A. Weiser, "πιστεύω κτλ," *TDNT* VI.174-228; C. H. Dodd, *The Interpretation of the Fourth Gospel* (Cambridge: University Press, 1953) 179-86; D. Guthrie, *New Testament Theology* (Downers

Grove, IL: InterVarsity, 1981) 573-84; W. F. Howard, *Christianity according to St. John* (London: Duckworth, 1943) 151-73; O. Michel, "Faith," *NIDNTT* 1.593-606; J. Painter, *John: Witness and Theologian* (2d ed.; London: SPCK, 1979) 71-85; idem, "Eschatological Faith in the Gospel of John," in *Reconciliation and Hope*, ed. R. Banks (Grand Rapids: Eerdmans, 1974) 36-52.

R. T. France

FAMILY

The evidence of the NT as a whole suggests that household relations were a subject of major concern in early Christianity. This is because following Jesus, or conversion to the Christian way, was as much a social matter as a personal one. In a culture where individual identity was defined in terms primarily of the household group to which the individual belonged (see Malina), it was inevitable that allegiance to Jesus as "Lord" *(Kyrios)* would have an effect on family ties and family life. Often the conversion of whole households would occur, and the first Christians developed rules for the right ordering of family life and the exercise of hospitality. Worship* and fellowship normally took place in the homes of local Christian leaders, and the patriarchal authority relations of the household tended to become the model for the roles and relations of church members.

On the other hand, conversion and Christian belonging also threatened the family. The charismatic freedom of early Christian worship, itself the expression of the believers' quite-novel self-understanding as all now children of God through Christ,* seems to have generated anxieties about the potential subversion of normal gender roles and household relations. Sometimes the conversion of one partner in a marriage* (more often the wife) precipitated marital conflict and even divorce (see 1 Cor 7:10-16; *see* Marriage and Divorce). Some converts apparently adopted an ascetic lifestyle and rejected sexual relations and marital ties altogether. For others the call to itinerant missionary activity necessitated the radical subordination of family ties for the sake of Christ and the gospel.* There is also specific evidence of the persecution of believers by members of their own families. So Christian belonging was not necessarily conducive to strong family ties and a happy family life.

All four Gospels contain material pertinent to the theme of family ties. Very often talk about family ties provides an idiom for saying important things about christology, ecclesiology and the life of faith.*

1. The Gospel of Mark
2. The Gospel of Matthew
3. Luke-Acts
4. The Fourth Gospel

1. The Gospel of Mark.

This Gospel is predominantly pessimistic about family ties. The way of Jesus is the way of rejection, suffering and death*; a pattern to be the expectation of followers of Jesus as well (Mk 4:17; 8:34-35; 9:49; 10:30; 13:9-13). This somber mood deeply affects the material on the family. Jesus' relations with his own family are cast in a uniformly negative light. Mark provides no genealogies* or birth narratives, unlike Matthew and Luke (*see* Birth of Jesus); nor any stories of Jesus' youth at home.

In Mark, Jesus consistently acts independently of his natural kin, and he lives in what appears to be his own (or Peter's?*) house in Capernaum (cf. Mk 1:29; 2:1, 15; 3:19; 9:33). Instead of the company of his family, Jesus chooses that of the Twelve (Mk 3:13-19); and when his mother and brothers come asking for him, he deliberately distances himself from them and identifies his true family as "whoever does the will of God" (Mk 3:31-35). Significantly, the final mention of Jesus' family is cast in negative terms too, an episode which revolves around the saying of Jesus, "A prophet is not without honor, except in his own country, and among his own kin, and in his own house" (Mk 6:1-6a). Jesus' kinsfolk play no further part in the Gospel story. They are not rehabilitated at the end. In contrast with the Fourth Gospel, the Jesus of Mark has no special relationship with his mother, and she appears not to be present at the cross (Mk 15:40-41; cf. Jn 19:25-27; *see* Death of Jesus).

The material in Mark on discipleship* and family ties is consistent with the portrayal of Jesus' own family ties. Those summoned to share the mission of Jesus leave their occupations and families (Mk 1:16-20; 10:28-30) and become dependent on the hospitality of others (Mk 6:10-11). The response of their kinsfolk is likely to be hostile: note the somber redactional qualifier "with persecutions" *(meta diōgmōn)* in Mark 10:30 and the explicit warning of kinship-sponsored incrimination and persecution in Mark 13:12-13.

This is not to say that Mark is anti-family. There is much evidence to the contrary: (1) foremost is Jesus' prohibition of divorce and remarriage (Mk 10:2-12); (2) Jesus affirms the obligations of the fifth commandment (Mk 7:9-13); (3) Jesus repeatedly and positively receives children (Mk 9:36-37; 10:13-16; *see* Child, Children); (4) Jesus uses familial terminology to describe those who do God's will (Mk 3:34b, 35); (5) Jesus promises an alternative household and family ties ("one hundredfold") to replace those the missionary disciple has left behind; (6) there are numerous accounts of healing* miracles* involving the restoration of members of a family (Mk 1:30-31; cf. 5:21-43; 7:24-30; 9:14-29).

T. J. Weeden and others have sought to explain the negative portrayal of Jesus' family as part of a polemic by the Evangelist and his community against the leaders (including James, the Lord's brother) of the Jerusalem Church. Other explanations are more persuasive, however. (1) It is very likely that the Markan account preserves accurate historical reminiscence of tension and misunderstanding between the charismatic leader Jesus and his natural kin. (2) In terms of the shape of Mark's narrative, Jesus' rejection by his family in the first half of the story anticipates his rejection by his people as a whole in the climactic second half. (3) Theologically, Mark's deep ambivalence about ties of natural kinship expresses his conviction that there is a new criterion for membership in the people of God: faith in Jesus the Son of God,* not birth or adoption into the Jewish *ethnos*. (4) Sociologically, as H. C. Kee has shown, the family-ties material conveys the anguish and conflict accompanying membership of the Marcan community, as well as the continuing importance of the household both for its corporate life and for mission.

2. The Gospel of Matthew.

A central concern of Matthew's Gospel is to express what it means to be the people of God in the light of the coming of the Son of God. Theology, christology and ethics are linked together closely, and material about the family or the use of the idiom of household ties is strikingly prevalent. For Matthew, God is preeminently the heavenly Father who is "with us" graciously in the person of Jesus who is his Son. Matthew's story tells of the coming of the Son to call God's sons and daughters in Israel* to repentance because the heavenly kingdom is near (*see* Kingdom of God). With divine authority* Jesus teaches the true and demanding will of God for his people and chooses a group of disciples (*mathētai*) to be the nucleus of a renewed nation. The rejection and crucifixion* of Jesus by Israel precipitates a mission to the Gentiles* and the reconstituting of the people of God as the church* (*ekklēsia*). The material on the family in Matthew is intelligible only against this theological backdrop.

First, there is a strong emphasis on spiritual kinship. Jesus displaces Israel as God's true Son, because Jesus teaches and does the Father's will. The remnant in and beyond Israel who obey and follow Jesus become children of God who call God "our Father" (Mt 6:9; *see* Abba). They also become Jesus' true family (Mt 12:46-50), and the relationship they share with each other in the church (*ekklēsia*) is characterized most often as a kinship (e.g., Mt 23:8) or as a household (see M. H. Crosby) where God is Father and the followers of Jesus are God's children (Mt 18:1-4; 23:9).

Second, it is implied strongly that following Jesus and belonging to God's household involves itinerant mission work for some at least (see E. Schweizer; *see* Apostle). This takes priority over ties of natural kinship and the responsibilities of family life (Mt 8:18-27; 10:21-23, 24-25, 34-39). No doubt the pain and conflict this brings are understood by Matthew as part of the cost of choosing the "narrow gate" and "hard way" which leads to life (Mt 7:13-14).

On the other hand, it is true also that the privilege of belonging to God's household brings with it obligations in the realm of family life as part of obedience to the commandments* of God's Son. These include the demand of restraint and control in sexual relations, the prohibition of divorce and the duty of filial piety (Mt 5:27-30, 31-32; 19:3-9, 19). Unique to Matthew is the saying of Jesus which commends celibacy "for the sake of the kingdom of heaven" (Mt 19:12); but this is quite consistent with the strong emphasis in Matthew on the self-denial, discipline and single-mindedness required of followers of Jesus (e.g., Mt 6:24) and exemplified by Jesus himself.

So the material on the family in Matthew contributes significantly to the Evangelist's concern to provide an authoritative basis in the story of Jesus for the formation and development of a new household of faith, a people separate from Israel and shaping its own understanding of life together as children of the heavenly Father.

3. Luke-Acts.

The theology of Luke's two volumes is dominated by a salvation-history perspective according to which God's plan of salvation began with Israel, was fulfilled in the coming of Jesus and was being brought to fruition in the gathering of Gentiles into the people of God in the church. The material about the family very clearly expresses this theology, along with its implications for the life of faith.

The continuity of salvation history—linking Israel, Jesus and the church—is reflected in the positive portrayal of Jesus' own family. This is quite at odds with the picture in Mark, as some scholars have shown (see Brown et al., and Fitzmyer). Mary, for example, is given more prominence in Luke's writings than in any other NT document (*see* Birth of Jesus). At the beginning of the story she is the specially favored woman in Israel chosen by God to give birth to his Son, the Davidic Messiah (Lk 1:26-35; *see* Son of David), and she is the one who proclaims, in the words of the *Magnificat*, the Lukan gospel of good news to the poor (Lk 1:46-55; *see* Mary's Song). Together with Joseph she is a witness to the miraculous events and revelatory utterances attending both the birth of Jesus and his presentation at the Temple.* Her bold witness, transparent piety, quiet faith, obedience to Torah and ready acceptance of the will of God make her a model of the true Israelite and the true disciple. This explains her remarkable presence, at the beginning of Luke's second volume, in the upper room (Acts 1:14). Her presence and witness are a guarantee of the salvific continuity between Israel, Jesus and the Church.

It is noteworthy that the brothers of Jesus are also in the upper room. Unlike the Fourth Gospel (Jn 7:5), they are not depicted as unbelievers. More clearly than in Mark and Matthew, Jesus' mother and his brothers are affirmed as "those who hear the word of God and do it" (cf. Lk 8:19-21 with Mk 3:31-35 and Mt 12:46-50). Nor are they included among those of Jesus' own country (*patris*) who refuse to acknowledge him (cf. Lk 4:24 with Mk 6:4 and Mt 13:57). It appears that Luke is kinder than the other Evangelists to those who surround Jesus. This may be motivated by his desire to present Jesus' brothers, James especially, as leaders of the Jerusalem church (e.g., Acts 15:13) and as witnesses to the truth about him in the period after his ascension.*

Material about family and household life is central also to what the Evangelist wants to say about the life of faith. This may be summarized under two points. First, discipleship to Jesus is a very costly affair. Luke accentuates the radical detachment which is required: from possessions, from family ties and even from one's own spouse (e.g., Lk 9:57-62; 12:51-53; 14:15-24, 25-35; 18:18-30). This compliments Luke's great emphasis on the importance of both conversion in response to the preaching of the "good news" and mission to all nations (Lk 24:47; Acts 1:8), for mission is the means of bringing God's new people into existence.

Second, belonging to God's new people involves household-based expressions of solidarity. As J. Koenig has shown, stories and teaching about households, hospitality and table fellowship* may be found throughout Luke-Acts. He thinks that Luke is trying to foster "cooperative house church mission." P. Esler suggests that the focus on table fellowship is intended primarily to legitimate the development of a common life shared by Jews and Gentiles. Most important,

though, is the recognition that for Luke the family and household are not ends in themselves. This corresponds with the force of the boy Jesus' reply to his anxious parents in the Temple: "Did you not know that I must be in my Father's house (*en tois tou patros mou*)?" (Lk 2:49 RSV).

4. The Fourth Gospel.

Central to the message of this Gospel is the revelation of Jesus as the Son of God and savior of the world. His coming into the world provokes division, however. Some believe in him, both from within and without Israel. Others, most poignantly those often referred to as "the Jews" or "the Pharisees,"* reject him. The underlying irony of the whole Gospel is that those who should have believed in him do not, and those who seem unlikely recipients of revelation believe. The principal aim of the Gospel is to confirm believers in their faith (Jn 20:30-31) and to provide a basis in the story of Jesus for developing their own identity and life together as God's people.

The family-related material has to be understood against this background. It expresses both the division which Jesus causes and the identity of the elect. Most important for John is the affirmation of Jesus as the Son of God. This establishes his closeness to God who is the Father and his unique authority to reveal the way to the Father (Jn 1:18; 5:17-30; 14:6-7). Whoever "receives" Jesus the Son becomes a child of God (Jn 1:12-13; cf. the use of *orphanos* ["orphan"] in 14:18); and this is a matter not of physical birth into the family of the Jewish people, but of spiritual birth "from above" (*anōthen*, Jn 3:3, 7). Consequently, Samaritans* and Greeks (*see* Hellenism) can now belong to the people of God, as well as Jews (Jn 4:4-42; 12:20-26). In fact the true descendants of "our father Abraham" are redefined radically, not as his descendants by blood, but as those who acknowledge Jesus, the pre-existent I Am.* Conversely, those who refuse to believe are redefined in a most polemical way as children of the devil (Jn 8:31-59; *see* Demon, Devil, Satan).

It is striking that John, unlike Matthew, is sparing in his use of the language of kinship to describe relations between those who are God's children. This may be related to the so-called Johannine individualism and to his distinctive emphasis on the vertical relations between believers and the Son—they are his "friends" or "little children"—and between the Son and the Father. Only after the resurrection* does Jesus refer to the disciples as his "brothers" (Jn 20:17); and from then on, as the Johannine Epistles show, "brother" (*adelphos*) becomes an important ecclesiological term (Jn 21:23; 1 Jn 2:9-11; 3:10-17). Perhaps its later use, along with much other familial terminology, was intended to counter the Johannine community's schismatic tendencies (see Segovia).

The portrayal of the mother of Jesus deserves special mention. As in Luke-Acts, she is interpreted in a positive light. Only this Gospel has the story of the wedding at Cana (Jn 2:1-11) and the episode at the foot of the cross (Jn 19:26-27). Strikingly, these two stories bracket the whole narrative of Jesus' ministry. Never referred to by her personal name, Jesus' mother functions as a representative figure: "Woman" (Jn 2:4; 19:26). According to R. F. Collins, she "symbolizes the one who faithfully awaits the messianic times" and, at the cross, is accepted into the community of salvation, the new family of the church.

As in the Synoptics, the Fourth Gospel represents as well an attempt to deal with the adverse implications of discipleship for family ties. J. L. Martyn has shown how in John 9 the story of the man born blind expresses something of the cost of discipleship in John's own day: expulsion from the synagogue* community and rifts between parents and their children (Jn 9:18-23). This parallels Jesus' relations with his brothers. Not only are they distinguished from the disciples (Jn 2:11-12), but the final editorial comment on them in the Gospel is that "his brothers did not believe in him" (Jn 7:5). Their unbelief is representative of the unbelief of "the Jews" and of Jerusalem and Judea as a whole. The prolog puts it in a nutshell: "He came to his own home (ta idia), and his own people (hoi idioi) received him not" (Jn 1:11 RSV).

It is very likely, as W. A. Meeks and others have argued, that this christological statement in John 1:11 has a sociological correlate. Just as the Johannine Jesus is a stranger to the world, to the Jews and even to his own family, likewise the Johannine community is radically estranged from the wider society, from the society of the synagogue and from the society of its members' families. The Fourth Gospel's unique emphasis on Jesus as the only way to the Father (Jn 14:6) is the expression of a group developing an alternative society based on the tie of belief in Jesus rather than on ties of natural kinship.

See also CHILDREN.

BIBLIOGRAPHY. R. E. Brown et al., *Mary in the New Testament* (Philadelphia: Fortress; New York: Paulist, 1978); R. F. Collins, "The Representative Figures of the Fourth Gospel—II," *Downside Review* 94 (1976) 118-132; M. H. Crosby, *House of Disciples* (New York: Orbis, 1988); P. F. Esler, *Community and Gospel in Luke-Acts* (SNTSMS 57; Cambridge: University Press, 1987); J. A. Fitzmyer, *Luke the Theologian* (London: Geoffrey Chapman, 1989); H. C. Kee, *Community of the New Age* (London: SCM, 1977); J. Koenig, *New Testament Hospitality* (Philadelphia: Fortress, 1985); B. J. Malina, *The New Testament World: Insights from Cultural Anthropology* (Atlanta: John Knox, 1981); J. L. Martyn, *History and Theology in the Fourth Gospel* (rev. ed., Nashville: Abingdon, 1979); W. A. Meeks, "The Son of Man in Johannine Sectarianism," in *The Interpretation of John*, ed. J. Ashton (Philadelphia: Fortress, 1986) 141-173; E. Schweizer, "Matthew's Church," in *The Interpretation of Matthew*, ed. G. N. Stanton (Philadelphia: Fortress, 1983) 129-155; F. F. Segovia, *Love Relationships in the Johannine Tradition* (SBLDS 58; Chico: Scholars Press, 1982); T. J. Weeden, *Mark: Traditions in Conflict* (Philadelphia: Fortress, 1971).

S. C. Barton

FAREWELL DISCOURSE

1. The Literary Form
2. The Lukan Farewell Discourse (Lk 22:21-38)
3. The Johannine Farewell Discourse (Jn 13—17)

1. The Literary Form.

1.1. Development and Structure of the Form. The farewell discourse is a literary form known in classical, biblical and pseudepigraphical material (*see* Form Criticism). The form exists as a part of larger works and as independent pieces of literature generally called "testaments." The story of the death of Socrates in Plato's *Phaedo* and his final discussion with his students became the model for death scenes in classical literature (Stauffer, c. 29; Kurz, 253-54). In biblical literature we can find similar addresses attributed to Jacob (Gen 48—49), Moses* (Deut 31—34), Joshua (Josh 23—24) and David (1 Chron 28—29). In the NT we can see this form in Luke 22, John 13—17 and Acts 20:17-38.

The popularity of the genre in biblical and extra-biblical literature is easy to understand. The farewell scene of the great leader gave the writer an opportunity to summarize the achievements and teachings of that person, developing an apology for the life of the person if needed and applying the lessons of the person's life to the problems facing future generations. The origin of the genre is almost certainly in wisdom* literature: the teaching of the father to the sons (Cortés, 67). The purpose of the farewell discourse is always to teach and to instruct. Sometimes the structure may take on an apologetic function, but even here the purpose is to draw distinctions between the teaching of the father figure and the problems at hand in the community. Apocalyptic* visions are easily incorporated into the structure as a more dramatic means of warning and instructing the community. In the context of the impending death of the father or father figure, these teachings are given added gravity and significance as the summing up of the life and purpose of the figure.

The typical structure of a farewell discourse can be summarized:

Reference to approaching death
Gathering of family or disciples
Review of the figure's life
Exhortation
Predictions or prophecies
Blessings, final prayer or final warnings
Death and burial

The order of these items is not inflexible. Structural parts may be repeated or completely omitted (see von Nordheim, II.85-89). Frequently, but not always, the figure will commission his sons/disciples to carry on his work or will name a successor (see *Adam and Eve* 50:1; *2 Apoc. Bar.* 45:1-2; *1 Enoch* 82:1-2; 4 Ezra 14:26, 46).

1.2. Purpose of the Form. The power of the form lies in its ability to focus the exhortation or teaching the author desires to give to the community. The life of the departing person serves both as a model to the community and as a legitimizing figure for the teaching. The context of the last or departing words of a respected person gives added moral power to these teachings. For the NT writers the form was especially pertinent since there was already a definite historical tradition of the Last Supper (*see* Last Supper). It is not surprising that Luke and John use the form to organize the final teachings of Jesus and stress the points of that teaching relevant to their Gospels (*see* Redaction Criticism).

2. The Lukan Farewell Discourse (Lk 22:21-38).

2.1. Structure and Composition. The Lukan form of the Last Supper is very different from its Synoptic counterparts. Compared to the other Synoptic accounts, the Lukan account appears to be a composite of traditions. Viewed as a farewell discourse the material follows a recognizable pattern:

Prediction of death (22:21-23)
Exhortation to disciples (22:24-26)
Review of life (22:27)
Promises/prophecies (22:28-30)
Warnings (22:31-34)
Final warning (22:35-38)

It is difficult to know how much of this structure was created by Luke or whether it existed in some form in his sources (Marshall, 808). E. Bammel has suggested

that 22:28-30 form the conclusion of Q. The content of these verses suggests that Q was itself a testamentary document (Bammel, 46-50). Therefore, the concept of a testament of Jesus may have been suggested to Luke by his sources. But it is hard to imagine that Luke is not guided by the farewell discourse structure as he handles the traditions he is using. The ties between Luke and Mark in these verses are those common to the Last Supper tradition: the naming of the betrayer (Lk 22:21-23 par. Mk 14:18-21; *see* Judas Iscariot) and the prediction of Peter's denial (Lk 22:31-34 par. Mk 14:26-31). But even these common traditions seem to be reshaped by the farewell discourse context: the prediction of the betrayal now forms the announcement of Jesus' coming death (*see* Death of Jesus) and is followed by an exhortation to the disciples.* Similarly, the prediction of Peter's denial is now tied to a future role for Peter in which he will serve as the one who turns and strengthens the faith of the community and so carry on the ministry of Jesus (22:32). The basic principle for composition seems to be the farewell discourse form.

2.2. Jesus As the Departing Master. The role of Jesus in this passage is typical of a farewell discourse. On the one hand he is the example, both of the servant whom the disciples are to emulate (22:27) and the persecuted whose trial the disciples may share (22:35-37). There is also an implicit apologetic note in this material. Jesus' prayer* for Peter shows that he knows and anticipates the failure of the disciples at the time of the crucifixion (22:31-32; cf. Jn 16:32-33) and that he has minimized the effect of this crisis through his prayer and his appointment of Peter as one who will turn and strengthen others after his denial (22:32). In short the scattering of the disciples in the face of persecution does not reflect on Jesus or his ministry but is part of the drama of salvation.*

2.3. The Commissioning of the Disciples. The form of farewell discourse is further evident in the various commissions given the disciples. This is specifically visible in the Q* saying of Luke 22:29. The commission given to Jesus by the Father (*see* God) is turned over to the disciples: Just as the Father has assigned a kingdom (*see* Kingdom of God) to Jesus, so also Jesus has assigned a kingdom to the disciples. In particular they can anticipate sharing in the judgment and authority of the kingdom. As the disciples have shared in Jesus' trials (v. 28), they will share in the authority* of the kingdom. It is significant that the word describing this transfer is *diatithemai*, which can be translated, "to make a covenant, a bequest or to assign." Marshall argues that since God is the subject of the verb here, the idea cannot be "to make a bequest" (Marshall,

816), but in fact the "*kagō . . . kathōs*" ("and I . . . just as") structure of the saying emphasizes that what the Father has given the Son (*see* Son of God) is now being turned over to the disciples. The transfer nature of this promise is intentional. The disciples are being recognized as heirs of the promise of the kingdom and of the authority inherent in that kingdom (E. Bammel, 46-47).

What comes before and after this statement serves to modify and define this commission. That which is given to the disciples in the first instance does not represent a transfer of authority (22:25-27) but a transfer of mission, the essence of which is service. Although the disciples will sit on the twelve thrones executing judgment, their fitness for that task is predicated on taking up the humble attitude of a servant. The exhortation of verses 24-27 is necessarily placed before 28-30. Sharing in the exaltation of Jesus requires first sharing in his humility.

Similarly, after the promise of 22:28-30 we find two sobering reminders of the task yet to be done. First is the reminder that the disciples will fail before they succeed. The scattering of the disciples at the crucifixion is viewed by Matthew and Mark as a fulfillment of Scripture (Mt 26:30-35; Mk 14:26-31; cf Jn 16:32; *see* Old Testament in the Gospels). Two themes are unique to Luke: the suggestion that Jesus' prayer helps them endure this trial and the task that Jesus assigns Peter (22:32). Peter, despite his failure, is implicitly singled out for special leadership. Again, the emphasis is not so much on transfer of authority as on mission. Peter is to care for the disciples much as Jesus has. This anticipates Peter's role in Acts where he will be the leader of the early church, but not the sole possessor of Jesus' authority.

Finally, Jesus anticipates the ongoing mission of the disciples. Luke 22:35-38 functions as a final warning to the community. Looking back to the success of their mission recorded in Luke 10, Jesus warns that the future will be different (22:35-38). In their earlier mission all their needs were met without carrying purses or extra clothing; now they will have to go prepared for struggle. This is not a sign of their personal failure; it was anticipated in Scripture (22:37 quoting Is 53:12). These verses implicitly explain what Jesus meant in 22:28, "You are those who have continued with me in my trials." The glory* of the kingdom is preceded by the struggle. But the disciples, not understanding what Jesus is saying, produce two swords as if Jesus is calling them to battle (cf. Jn 16:29-33).

As a farewell discourse Luke 22:21-38 accomplishes several tasks. It interprets Jesus' ministry as one of service and defends it as one ordained by God* in Scripture. The disciples are promised a triumphant role in the future kingdom of God. However, before this hope is realized they must carry on Jesus' ministry of service—even in the midst of trials. The discourse both warns and exhorts the reader, and the message is legitimized through the role and example of Jesus.

3. The Johannine Farewell Discourse (Jn 13—17).
3.1. Composition and Redaction. The structure of the Johannine farewell discourse is more apparent than that of Luke's Gospel. The section begins with the announcement of Jesus' coming death and departure, "When Jesus knew that his hour had come to depart out of this world to the Father, having loved his own who were in the world, he loved them to the end" (Jn 13:1). The problem in the Johannine material arises in 14:31 where Jesus says, "Rise let us go hence." This is followed by another large block of discourse material in John 15—17, finally followed by the departure of the disciples and Jesus in 18:1.

Various solutions to this problem have been offered. R. Bultmann rearranged the chapters so that 14:31 would connect with 18:1 at the end of the discourse. He further reorganized the sections of the discourse into what he argued is a more understandable format (Bultmann, 460-61). The problem with such a solution is providing a satisfactory explanation for how this order was ever disturbed. What Bultmann does show, however, is the close theological connection between the earlier and later portions of the discourse, especially in the case of John 17.

A second suggestion is that chapters 15—17 represent a second farewell discourse appended to the first by a later writer with different concerns. J. Becker argues that these later chapters concentrate on ecclesiology, whereas John 14 focuses on christology. Similarly, the negative connotations of "world"* in John 15 and the emphasis on "remaining" (*see* Abiding) rather than being "in Christ" in these chapters suggests the concerns of the author of 1 John rather than the author of the Gospel. The chief problem with this argument is that it overstates the differences between chapters 14 and 15—17. For example, there are ecclesiological concerns in chapter 14 (especially in terms of the disciples' future work, 14:12-14; the commands to obey, 14:21, 23; and the role of the Spirit, 14:15-18, 26). In all of these chapters Jesus is placed as the mediator between the Father and the believers (cf. 14:12-24; 15:1-18; 16:4-15; 17:6-19).

The distinctiveness of John 15—17 lies in its greater emphasis on the hatred and opposition in the world.

John 14 argues that Jesus has been the obedient servant of the Father (14:9-11) who has revealed the Father to his disciples (14:1-6). The disciples are now called to obedience to continue his work (14:12-24). John 15—17 places greater stress on the hatred of the world (15:18-25; 17:14-16), the distress the disciples must suffer (16:16-33) and the need for the church to endure (15:1-10).

In addition the stress on the role of the Spirit (*see* Holy Spirit) changes somewhat in 16:5-15, emphasizing the Spirit's role in challenging the sin of the world. This contrasts with John 14 where the Spirit reminds the disciples of Jesus' words and provides the ongoing presence of Jesus in believers (14:15-17, 26). It is thus possible to see John 15—17 as an expansion of the farewell discourse which takes up the challenge of increased hostility facing the church (Painter).

The question remains: Are we dealing with one or more than one writer here? R. Brown, among many scholars, seems to argue for a plurality of authors. But a strong case can be made that the same author is at work throughout. In most cases the change in historical context serves to explain the differences between the two parts of the discourse. John 17 in particular is so close to John 14 in terms of the themes of the mutual indwelling of the Father in the Son and the Son in the disciples that it is difficult to imagine that the same writer is not at work.

3.2. The Problem of Jesus' Departure. Given the unity of composition and authorship in John 13—17, it is not difficult to trace the structure of the Johannine farewell discourse. Much of the material forms a review of Jesus' life, performing both an apologetic and hortatory function. Jesus is the faithful servant of God who glorifies God (13:32), has done the work of his Father (14:10-12), obeyed the Father (14:31), loved the disciples (15:9) and revealed all things to them (15:15). Most of these themes are repeated in John 17 (17:4, 6, 8, 12, 14, 18, 22). Jesus is portrayed in these chapters as the faithful servant of God who has been obedient in all things and is justified by God in his glorification. The note of apology is obvious. Jesus' ministry is justified by his absolute obedience to the Father. At the same time Jesus is being held up as an example to the disciples. As he is obedient, so must they obey (14:15-23; 17:6-17).

3.3. Instructions and Warnings. The instructions to the disciples are few and simple: they are to keep the commandments or words of Jesus (14:15, 21, 23; 15:14); believe in the mutual indwelling of Father and Son (14:11); remain in the vine (15:1-7, 9); bear fruit (15:8) and love one another (13:34-35; 15:12, 17). In all these instances, except the commandment* to

faith,* they are following the sacrificial model of Jesus who is the obedient servant of God (Jn 15:12-17; *see* Servant of Yahweh).

With the commandments come certain promises. First is the promise that Jesus will return (14:2-3; 16:16-17, 19-20, 22). Jesus' departure is not the final word. The disciples will share a future with him in the mansions of the Father (14:2-4) and enjoy the presence of the love* and glory of the Father (17:22, 24-25). In the meantime the disciples are promised that they will do the works of Jesus and even greater works than his (14:12). They can do these works because they are promised that the Father will hear and answer the prayers of the disciples (14:13-14; 15:7, 16; 16:23-24) and will dwell in them through the Holy Spirit (14:16-17, 21, 23, 26; 15:26; 16:7-15).

There is also a note of warning in these discourses, especially in the expansion of 15—17. There is a warning of persecution (15:18-21; 16:2-4; 17:14). This will bring a time of sorrow (16:6, 20-22). But for those that endure, this sorrow will turn to joy (16:22).

3.4. The Successors to the Mission of Jesus. There is a sense in these discourses that Jesus is turning over his ministry and commission to the disciples. This is evident in 14:12 where the promise is given that the disciples will do "greater works" than Jesus; in 15:12 where Jesus tells the disciples that he has "chosen" them so that they might bear fruit; and in 15:18-25 where the disciples are told that they will be hated as Jesus was hated. This theme is seen even more clearly in John 17 where the disciples receive everything that the Father has given the Son: the name (17:6), the words (17:8) and the glory (17:22). Jesus in his prayer specifically commissions the disciples to carry on his ministry, sending them as he was sent (17:18-19) and looking forward to those who will believe in their words as they have believed in his (17:20-26).

The Johannine farewell discourse summarizes the message of the gospel for the faithful community. The discourse serves an apologetic function defending the exalted christology of the community. These discourses also exhort the community to remain unmoved in this faith, practicing love for fellow believers and continuing in the power of the Holy Spirit to do the work that Jesus has given them. The form of the farewell discourse provides an efficient means of focusing the christological and ecclesiological issues in a way that meets the changing needs of the Johannine church.

See also LAST SUPPER; PASSION NARRATIVE; SERVICE..

BIBLIOGRAPHY. E. Bammel, "Das Ende von Q," in *Verborum Veritas: Festschrift für Gustav Stählin zum 70. Geburtstag,* ed. O. Böcher and K. Haacker (Wuppertal:

Theologische-Verlag Rolf Brockhaus, 1970) 39-50; J. Becker, "Die Abschiedsreden Jesu im Johannes-evangelium," *ZNW* 61 (1970) 215-246; idem, "Aufbau, Schichtung und theologiegeschichtliche Stellung des Gebetes in Johannes 17," *ZNW* 60 (1969) 56-83; R. Brown, *The Community of the Beloved Disciple* (New York: Paulist, 1979); R. Bultmann, *The Gospel of John* (Oxford: Basil Blackwell, 1971); E. Cortés, *Los Discursos de Adiós de Gen 49 à Jn 13-17. Pistas para la historia de un género literario en la antigua literatura judia* (Barcelona: Editorial Herder, 1976); W. S. Kurz, "Luke 22:14-28 and Greco-Roman and Biblical Farewell Addresses," *JBL* 104 (1985) 251-68; I. H. Marshall, *The Gospel of Luke: A Commentary on the Greek Text* (NIGTC; Grand Rapids: Eerdmans, 1978); E. von Nordheim, *Die Lehre der Alten. I: Das Testament als Literaturgattung im Judentum der hellenistisch-römischen Zeit; II: Das Testament als Literaturgattung im Alten Testament und im alten vorderen Orient* (ALGHJ 18; Leiden: E. J. Brill, 1980, 1985); J. Painter, "The Farewell Discourses and the History of Johannine Christianity," *NTS* 27 (1981) 525-43; E. Stauffer, "Abschiedsreden," *RAC* 1.c.29-35.

R. W. Paschal, Jr.

FASTING

Fasting is a tangible expression or direct corollary of one's relationship with God rather than a religious discipline. Though he does not prohibit it, Jesus views his own presence at the dawn of the age of salvation* as rendering fasting generally inappropriate.

1. Fasting among the Jews
2. Fasting in the Gospels
3. Fasting in the Early Church

1. Fasting among the Jews.

1.1. In the OT. Jewish meals were never purely physical or social occasions. In addition to accompanying worship,* festivals* and covenant-making, meals embodied central aspects of such activities. Therefore, abstaining from eating and drinking, that is fasting, also generally possessed a religious significance. Occasionally fasting was unavoidable due to lack of food (Ex 34:28; 1 Kings 19:8; Mt 15:32 par. Mk 8:3; 2 Cor 6:5), though mostly it was a byproduct of divine obedience or calling. More often abstinence was personally or corporately chosen because it expressed some deep loss, as in the case of David after the deaths of Saul and Jonathan (2 Sam 1:12; cf. 2 Sam 3:35; 1 Kings 21:27; Neh 1:4; Ps 35:13; 69:10; Joel 1:13-15; 2:12-15), or some significant hope, such as Israel in preparation for war against the Philistines (1 Sam 7:6; 2 Sam 12:16-23; Judg 20:26; 2 Chron 20:3). It was a natural accompaniment of or preparation for com-

municating with God (Deut 9:9; Dan 9:3) or, in the case of the Day of Atonement, a sign of repentance prescribed by God (Lev 16:29-31; 23:27-29; Num 29:7). It was also considered to be a religious practice that might be appropriate for those outside Israel (Jn 3:5).

After the exile the number of prescribed (Ezra 8:21; Zech 8:19; cf. 2 Kings 25:1, 3-4, 8-9, 25) and perhaps even unprescribed fasts (e.g., Neh 9:1; Esth 4:1-3, 16-17; Dan 9:2-3) seems to have increased. The emphasis was often on the joyfulness of these occasions. Where appropriate, personal distress is also poignantly described (Ps 109:24). Prophetic protests against the hypocritical character of some fasting occur at points (Jer 14:12; Zech 7:5), and in some cases these lead to an equation or redefinition of fasting in terms of such actions as feeding the hungry and combating injustice (Is 58:4-7).

1.2. In Judaism. Fasting continued to have significance in the intertestamental writings and, of particular importance for the Gospels, among various first-century religious groups (*see* Judaism). Though all observed the three major fasts (i.e., Day of Atonement, New Year and, according to Strack-Billerbeck, 4:77-114, a fast covering prior calamities), differences between such groups expressed themselves partly in varied practices concerning the partaking of or abstaining from food. Sadducees seem to have associated themselves with the Temple* and, therefore, with the traditional fasts. The Qumran community (*see* Dead Sea Scrolls) also observed the Day of Atonement (1QpHab 11:7). The Pharisees* developed additional fasts, apparently twice a week (Lk 18:12; *Did* 8.1; and more generally, *Pss. Sol.* 3:8).

The Gospels give us glimpses of fasting among pious individuals such as Anna the prophetess (Lk 2:37). They also contrast the practice of ascetic groups, such as the disciples of John the Baptist* who were known to fast frequently (Lk 5:33), and Pharisees with the practice of Jesus' followers (Mt 9:14; Mk 2:18).

2. Fasting in the Gospels.

2.1. Jesus and His Disciples' Fasting. When queried about his disciples' practice, Jesus first quotes what is likely a proverbial saying about the inappropriateness of wedding guests fasting while the bridegroom (*see* Bride, Bridegroom) is in their company (cf. *Gos. Thom.* 104) or the wedding festival is in progress. Taking up a common symbol for the age of salvation, a wedding celebration, and identifying himself with the bridegroom, though probably not messianically, he explains that fasting will only come into consideration when he is removed from them (Mk 2:19-20 and pars).

The authenticity of this saying has been challenged

233

on the grounds that Jesus would not have spoken allegorically in this fashion, nor would he have predicted his future suffering so early in his ministry or ultimately commend the practice of fasting. However, in an adjacent passage Jesus follows a proverbial saying or scriptural illustration with a direct reference to himself (Mk 2:17). When compared with the more detailed and later predictions of his death (*see* Predictions of Jesus' Passion and Resurrection), the allusion here is quite general (see Mk 8:31 et al.). And he does not prescribe fasting in the future so much as contrast the present fellowship and joy of the age of salvation being initiated with the future sadness associated with his forceful removal from his disciples (cf. especially the reference to "mourning" rather than "fasting" in Mt 9:15, and more generally cf. Jn 16:16-20). The two parables which follow contrast sharply the conduct of Jesus' disciples with that of John's disciples and the Pharisees (Mk 2:21-22).

2.2. Jesus and Fasting in General. Despite the saying of Mark 2:19-20, elsewhere Jesus appears to take for granted that some fasting will continue during his ministry (Mt 6:16-18). In the Sermon on the Mount* he criticizes its ostentatious display. Contrary to the practice of hypocrites,* genuine fasting should be conducted toward God alone and disguised toward others by a joyful, even lavish, appearance. Jesus' reference to fasting here should not be interpreted as an injunction to fast. It is more a recognition of its congruity with prayer* (Mt 6:5-15) and simplicity (Mt 6:19-34) in the lifestyle of his Jewish disciples.*

2.3. Jesus' Own Experience of Fasting. Several times Jesus is described as going without food and drink. He does so during his sojourn in the wilderness (*see* Mountain and Wilderness) prior to his temptations (Mt 4:2 and par.; *see* Temptation of Jesus) when he rises early to pray in a solitary location (Mk 1:35) and as a result of his ministering to those in need (Mk 8:31). On one occasion he declared to his disciples that he had "food" to eat of which they were ignorant, so referring to his fulfillment of his Father's purpose (Jn 4:31-34). Such passages suggest that for Jesus fasting was often a corollary of other activities to which he gave a high priority—spiritual struggle, prayer and evangelism. He does not take up fasting as a discipline in its own right.

There is no evidence that he fasted regularly during the time of his public ministry. His concern that he and his disciples gain sufficient sustenance after extending themselves for other's sake (Mk 2:23) and that people coming to hear him who had missed out on a meal be properly fed (Mk 8:1-13) are also revealing. So too are his associating hospitality with a

person's embracing the good news of the kingdom (Lk 19:5-8; *see* Kingdom of God) and with both his and his disciple's anticipation of the quality of life in the kingdom itself (Lk 22:14-18; *see* Table Fellowship).

3. Fasting in the Early Church.
In line with the secondary place accorded fasting by Jesus, the Apostolic Fathers fail to cite any saying or action of Jesus as a justification of fasting as a religious discipline. Though other references to fasting occur on Jesus' lips (Mk 9:29; Mt 17:21), textual critics are now satisfied that this is due to an early gloss. Such additions also exist outside the gospels and indicate the importance of fasting among some early Christians (Acts 10:30; 1 Cor 7:5). Even so, with the New Testament epistles there is no reference to fasting among Gentile Christians, not even in passages where ascetic practices are mentioned (e.g., Col 2:15-22). However, Jewish Christians, Paul among them, when enduring physical deprivation (e.g., 2 Cor 6:5; 11:27) or engaging in specific prayer (e.g. Acts 13:3; 14:23) seem to have engaged in fasting as it is found in the Old Testament.

See also JUSTICE, RIGHTEOUSNESS; PRAYER.

BIBLIOGRAPHY. I. Abrahams, *Studies in Pharisaism and the Gospels* (2 vols.; Cambridge: University Press, 1917-24) I.121-28; J. Behm "νῆστις κτλ," *TDNT* IV.924-35; J. G. Cremer, *Die Fastenaussage Jesu* (Bonn: Hanstein, 1965); A. Feuillet, "La Controverse sur la Jeûne," *NRT* 90 (1968) 113-36; 252-77; B. J. Malina, *Christian Origins and Cultural Anthropology: Practical Models for Biblical Interpretation* (Atlanta: John Knox, 1986); G. E. Moore, *Judaism in the First Centuries of the Christian Era: The Age of the Tannaim* (3 vols.; Cambridge, MA: Harvard, 1927); K. Schaeffer, " . . . und dann werden sie fasten, an jenem Tage (Mk 2, 20 und Parallelen)," in *Synoptische Studien: Festschrift A. Wikenhauser* (Munich: Karl Zink, 1953) 124-27; J. F. Wimmer, *Fasting in the New Testament: A Study in Biblical Theology* (New York: Paulist, 1982); J. Zeisler, "The Removal of the Bridegroom: A Note on Mk II, 18-22 and Parallels," *NTS* 19 (1972-73) 190-94.   R. Banks

FATHER. *See* GOD.

FAVORABLE YEAR OF THE LORD. *See* JUBILEE.

FEASTS
The Gospels present Jesus' parents (Lk 2:41) and the adult Jesus (esp. John's Gospel) as Jews who participate in the Jewish feasts. To a limited degree these observances provide the narrative framework for

Gospel stories, and in the case of the Last Supper (*see* Last Supper) the significance of the festival of the Passover provides the interpretive context for understanding Jesus' mission. As the Evangelists assume a basic familiarity with Jewish festival observance, this article will focus primarily on their development and observance within Judaism.*

1. Terminology
2. Feasts in the OT
3. Feasts in Intertestamental Judaism
4. Feasts in the Gospels

1. Terminology.

The biblical terms meaning "feast" are Greek *heortē*, Hebrew *môʿēd*, and (with an originally more restricted meaning) Hebrew *ḥaḡ*. *Heortē* is an old Greek word, attested as early as Homer. It means both "festival" and "feast," and appears over twenty-five times in the NT, mostly in the Gospels. Often another word or phrase appears to define specifically which feast is meant, for example: *pascha*, "Passover"; *skēnopēgia*, "Tabernacles"; or *azymos*, "Unleavened Bread." But it is not uncommon for *heortē* to appear without further definition. In these cases it is necessary to rely on the context to determine which of the several festivals is intended, and it is not always possible to reach a certain conclusion.

The Hebrew term *môʿēd* had a rather broad meaning already within the OT. Its etymology connects *môʿēd* to a fixed place or a fixed time, and by extension to an assembly at a fixed place or time. But the term occurs in the summarizing Numbers 29:39, a passage that begins by discussing daily sacrifices, Sabbath* offerings and new moons. Accordingly, it does not refer only to feasts, though it can be used for them. The word which does apply only to feasts, and specifically to the annual pilgrimage festivals, is *ḥaḡ*. Its etymology is disputed, but whatever the original denotation, within the OT *ḥaḡ* refers only to Passover, Weeks (Pentecost) and Tabernacles. In the postbiblical period, however, the two Semitic words came to be more or less interchangeable. Indeed, *ḥaḡ* came to designate the new moon and even the festivals of heretics. Thus not much should be made of a particular author's choice of terms in most postbiblical texts.

2. Feasts in the OT.

2.1. Source Texts. The OT was, of course, the source for most elements of festival observance in the time of Jesus. But it includes several different religious calendars. These appear to derive from different geographical regions on the one hand, and from different historical periods on the other. Since scholarship has yet to reach a consensus on which of these explanations may apply to which list, the following discussion makes no particular claims regarding source or date; it simply considers the various accounts in a convenient order.

The shortest calendar is that of Exodus 23:14-17. It refers to three *ḥaggîm:* That of the unleavened bread, that of the harvest, and that of the ingathering. It commands the men of Israel to appear three times per year before the Lord, but makes no stipulation as to where they must go to make that appearance. A second religious calendar within Exodus appears at 34:18-23. Here the number of *ḥaggîm* is the same, but their names are slightly different. Many scholars see it as significant that these two festal calendars mention the Feast of Unleavened Bread but say nothing of the Passover. In this view, the connection of Passover and Unleavened Bread in Exodus 12 becomes a secondary historical development.

The calendar of Deuteronomy 16:1-17 is again essentially the same, but it adds in verses 2, 11, 15 and 16 that the men are to appear "at the place which he will choose." Unlike the calendars of Exodus, then, this calendar suggests a centralized cultus. Also, here Passover and Unleavened Bread are linked. In both the calendars of Exodus and in that of Deuteronomy, which were based on an autumnal new year, no fixed dates for the festivals occur. In the different regions of Israel the agricultural cycle was somewhat different, of course, and therefore it is probable that this natural cycle was at first the only regulator of originally agricultural feasts.

With the calendar of Leviticus 23, however, precise dates now appear. Another change is the institution (if such it is) of a vernal new year. While the names of the months previously described were, where given, Canaanite, they now accord with the Babylonian calendar. The implication is that while the previous calendars antedated the Babylonian captivity, Leviticus 23 constitutes later material. But the literary complexion of this chapter of Leviticus is difficult, and at least some of the portions seem to be pre-exilic. In addition, the Levitical calendar is much fuller than those already described; it includes the Sabbath, the Feast of the First Sheaf, the Feast of the First Day of the Seventh Month (originally a new year festival?) and the Day of Atonement. Clearly, not all of these additions arose late in the history of Israel; Leviticus 23 adds them to the festivals of the "earlier" calendars in part because it is not concerned only with the *ḥaggîm*.

It is possible to see yet another list of feast days in Ezekiel 45:18-25. This text, describing the restoration

Table 1. A Comparison of Festival Calendars

TS 13-29	Num 28-29	Lev 23	Deut 16	Ezek 45
The Tamid 13:8-16	Tamid 28:3-8			
Sabbath Offering 13:17—14:?	Sabbath 28:9-10	Sabbath 23:3		
New Moon 14:?—14:8	New Moon 28:11-16			
New Year of First Month 14:9—15:?				New Year 45:18-20
Millu'im 15:13—17:5				
Pesaḥ 17:6-9	Pesaḥ 28:16	Pesaḥ 23:5	Pesaḥ 16:1-5	Pesaḥ 45:21-24
Unleavened Bread 17:10-16	Unleavened Bread 28:17-25	Unleavened Bread 23:6-8		
Lacuna? 18:?-18:?				
Omer/First Fruits of Barley 18:?-10		Omer 23:10-14		
Weeks 18:10—19:9	Weeks 28:26-31	Weeks 23:15-22	Weeks 16:9-12	
First Fruits Wine 19:11—21:10				
First Fruits Oil 21:12—23:2				
Wood Festival 23:3—25:2				
New Year of Seventh Month 25:2—25:10	New Year 29:1-6	New Year 23:24-25		
Day of Atonement 25:10—27:10	Atonement 29:7-11	Atonement 23:27-32		Atonement 45:25
Tabernacles 27:10—29:2	Tabernacles 29:12-34	Tabernacles 23:34-36, 39-43	Tabernacles 16:13-17	
Eighth Day Assembly 29:2	Assembly 29:35-39	Assembly 23:36		

hopes of the exilic prophet, lists two atoning festivals, one for each half of the year. On the first day of the first month (the vernal new year), the people are to offer a sacrifice for their sins, and again on the seventh of that month. The two ceremonies together accomplish the cleansing or expiation of the Temple.* At the beginning of the seventh month, and for the seven following days, another atoning procedure is to take place. The only other festival occasion singled out is the Passover, set for the fourteenth of the first month and here denominated a *ḥaḡ*.

The final festival calendar occurs in Numbers 28—29, often regarded as a sort of commentary on the cycle prescribed by Leviticus. The basic difference between the calendars of Leviticus and Numbers consists in the sacrificial details that the latter provides. Where the occasions are the same, the sacrifices that Numbers 28—29 requires do not agree with those of Ezekiel.

The table on page 236 summarizes several of the more detailed OT calendars alongside that of the intertestamental "new Torah" known as the Temple Scroll (TS; to be discussed below).

2.2. The Three Great Feasts. The pilgrimage times of Passover (with Unleavened Bread), Weeks and Tabernacles were the major landmarks of the religious year in Israel.

By the time of the NT, Passover (*pesaḥ*) had become the pinnacle occasion, but it had not always been so. A long period of development, often difficult to trace, lies behind the NT reality. In addition to the information that can be extracted from the various religious calendars, liturgical and historical texts contain precious additional facts for tracing such development. Also of great significance are two ostraca and a papyrus text, the "Passover Papyrus," from Elephantine (where lived a group of Jewish mercenaries from c. 600-380 B.C.). These brief allusions aside, nothing more will be said about the problem of historical development within the OT period; but it must be borne in mind that all through the periods of this discussion, practices were not always uniform among celebrants of the major feasts. Thus, even for the NT period one must be leery of relying on a single textual tradition (e.g., the Mishnah or Josephus) as evidence for actual practice.

The Passover was celebrated at the full moon of the first month of a vernal new year. On the tenth day each family chose a year-old lamb. At twilight on the fourteenth day they killed this unblemished animal and spread its blood on the lintel and door posts. The meat was roasted and eaten on the same night, with any remains burnt thereafter. The bones of the lamb were to remain unbroken. Along with the meat, the family was to eat unleavened bread and bitter herbs, all the while dressed for a hasty departure as commemoration of the Exodus from Egypt. On the next day began the Festival of Unleavened Bread, which continued for seven days. From the fifteenth to the twenty-first no leaven was consumed. The first and last days of Unleavened Bread were days of rest and of worship.

Weeks (*šābûʿôṯ*), the second great feast of the year, was a harvest festival which originally commemorated the wheat harvest specifically. It fell seven weeks after the cutting of the first barley and cereal grains. Starting from the day after the Sabbath on which the first sheaf was presented to Yahweh (at least according to one understanding of the passage in Lev 23), seven complete weeks were counted. One thus arrived at a total of fifty days, whence the Greek name for the feast, Pentecost (*pentēkostē*, lit. "fiftieth" [day]). In the ceremony the people offered two loaves made out of the new flour. The loaves were to be leavened—the only instance of such a ritual prescription in the OT. Apparently, the point of the leavened offering was to establish an antithetical connection with the earlier Unleavened Bread.

The third great feast of the religious calendar was the Feast of Tabernacles (also known in the English versions as Booths). The underlying Hebrew is *sukkôṯ*, the reference being to the temporary "huts" which were the hallmark of this festival. It is also known as "the feast of Yahweh" (Lev 23:39), and was the most important and best attended of the pilgrimages to the sanctuary. In recognition of this importance, both within the OT (Ezek 45:25) and in postbiblical Hebrew and Aramaic it was sometimes called simply "the feast." This feast also underwent some interesting historical development; that of the postbiblical period will occupy us at some length below. The essence of the biblical prescriptions by the early postexilic period required a pilgrimage to Jerusalem, where a feast was kept for seven days. The people were to live in huts to recall that Israel lived in huts after the Exodus from Egypt. Like Weeks, this festival was originally a harvest festival, particularly connected with the produce of the threshing floor and the olive and winepresses. And it was an occasion for great rejoicing. During the NT period community leaders danced in the Temple courtyards, singing and wielding lighted torches.

3. Feasts in Intertestamental Judaism.
By the second century B.C. if not earlier, the biblical prescriptions for the feasts were regarded as estab-

lished. That is to say, we have no evidence that communities of Jews felt free to disregard any of the relevant passages, and if differences between the biblical calendars were perceived (differences which were originally a result of geographic and temporal distance, as noted above) they were harmonized. Thus the basic biblical prescriptions for a given festival's observance were not at issue. Nevertheless, the intertestamental period was not one of uniform festival procedures, a point that is important to recall when reading the Gospels. The reasons for this lack of uniformity were many, but for the present purposes we shall be concerned with three: (1) lack of agreement on the proper calendar; (2) disagreements about the proper interpretation of the biblical texts; and (3) continued development, adding to the biblical prescriptions extrabiblical elements.

It was only with the discovery of the Dead Sea Scrolls (*see* Dead Sea Scrolls) that scholars came to appreciate the centrality of disagreement about the proper calendar. Books such as Jubilees had already alerted them to the fact that such disagreements existed, and hints of such were also found in rabbinic literature. But the scrolls brought home with a special force just what might be the implications of such divisions among Jewry. For if there were no agreement on the calendar, neither could there be agreement on when the biblical festivals should be celebrated. And if the people should celebrate a festival on the wrong day, had they not actually failed to celebrate the festival at all? At stake were basic issues of adherence to Scripture.

Many of the Dead Sea Scrolls (but not all) presuppose or advocate a solar calendar of 364 days. Significant evidence indicates that the solar calendar was a very early development in Israel, indeed perhaps the original calendar. For example, it seems to underlie the patriarchal journeys of Genesis. It has been well argued (by Jaubert and others) that the solar calendar regulated religious life in the early postexilic years, and further that it was only in the early second century B.C. that its nemesis, the lunar or lunisolar calendar, came to predominate. Perhaps one can see this pivotal change reflected in Daniel 7:25 (speaking of Antiochus IV), "he will plan to alter times and law." If this view is correct, then the lunar calendar was a progressive move while the solar calendar represented the older, conservative position. Even among themselves, advocates of the solar calendar were divided (cf. esp. *1 Enoch* 82:5-6): some held that the year should consist of 360 days, some of 364 and others of 365—the variations depending on whether and how one intercalated. Of course, with each dif-

ferent scheme the varieties of festival practice proliferated.

Under the 364-day scheme the festivals did not "wander" as they did in other systems. Every year they would always fall on the same day. In each set of three months, one intercalary day was added, and the serial days aligned with fixed days of the week, as illustrated in Table 2:

Table 2. The 364 Day Calendar

Months	1, 4, 7, 10	2, 5, 8, 11	3, 6, 9, 12
Wednesday	1, 8, 15, 22, 29	6, 13, 20, 27	4, 11, 18, 25
Thursday	2, 9, 16, 23, 30	7, 14, 21, 28	5, 12, 19, 26
Friday	3, 10, 17, 24, 1	8, 15, 22, 29	6, 13, 20, 27
Saturday	4, 11, 18, 25, 2	9, 16, 23, 30	7, 14, 21, 28
Sunday	5, 12, 19, 26, 3	10, 17, 24, 1	8, 15, 22, 29
Monday	6, 13, 20, 27, 4	11, 18, 25, 2	9, 16, 23, 30
Tuesday	7, 14, 21, 28, 5	12, 19, 26, 3	10, 17, 24, 31

The lunar or lunisolar calendars required much more attention to intercalation. Rabbinic Judaism's system (apparently already in force among many Jews during the intertestamental period) relied on observation of the new moon to decide when months began and ended, and whether a given year should have an extra month added (necessary seven times in every nineteen years).

Groups among the Jews who observed these different calendars would not celebrate the festivals at the same time and might even have been unable to participate together in the cultus—provided, of course, that these differences were not merely theoretical. Some scholars believe that the solar calendar was never practiced and that its various versions represent no more than idealized positions held by certain groups. Perhaps that is correct in certain instances; the Temple Scroll calendar may be an example of one such idealized program. (Not only does this Qumran text stipulate a 364-day calendar, but operating by analogy it adds otherwise-unknown pilgrimage festivals to the biblical requirements.)

Yet it is hard to believe that the radically different perspectives on proper festival observance never burst the bounds of theoretical discussion. And there is evidence that such in fact did happen. For example, Josephus* records that the Sicarii of Masada conducted a raid on En Gedi during Unleavened Bread at one point during the First Revolt (Josephus *J.W.* 4.7.2 §§402-4). Such a raid on the part of fastidious observers of the Law* (as archeology has shown the Sicarii to be) seems unlikely in the extreme, unless they actually observed a ritual calendar different from that of the inhabitants of En Gedi. For the raiders the day of the attack evidently did not fall during the period of the feast.

Thus, different views on the proper calendar meant that festival observance could differ profoundly among various groups of Second Temple Jews. A second factor leading to diverse observances of the festivals was disagreement about just what the biblical texts required. A brief look at problems involved with the Feast of Tabernacles can serve as a representative example here.

Leviticus 23:40 requires of those celebrating Tabernacles that "you shall take up for yourselves on the first day *p^{c}rî 'eṣ hādār kappōt t^{e}mārîm wa'^{a}nap 'eṣ 'ābōt w^{c}ar^{c}bê nāḥal* and you shall rejoice before Yahweh your God." The NASB renders the words left untranslated as "the foliage of beautiful trees, palm branches and boughs of leafy trees and willows of the brook"; but not all intertestamental Jews would have agreed with this interpretation of the phrase.

Later, rabbinic Judaism saw here a reference to four different elements, known as the "four kinds." This understanding is reflected already in Targum Onqelos, which renders the portion "fruits of the tree: citrons and palm branches and myrtle branches and willows of the brook." The much earlier book of *Jubilees*, however, understands Leviticus rather differently. In chapter 16 of that book, Abraham is said to observe the very first Feast of Tabernacles at Beersheba. As part of his observance, he took "branches of leaves and willow from the stream . . . branches of palm trees and fruit of good trees" (*Jub.* 16:30-31). Thus, the author of *Jubilees* understood at least one and perhaps two of the elements of the "four kinds" differently from rabbinic Judaism. The "citron" is conspicuous by its absence, being replaced by "fruit of good trees" (= the Hebrew *p^{c}rî 'eṣ hādār*). And apart from this difference other elements of Abraham's celebration are likewise distinct from later practice.

Still other views existed in the intertestamental years. For example, 2 Maccabees 10:5-7 describes the "festival of purification" which attended the sanctification of the Temple by the men of Judas Maccabees in 164 B.C. This festival was modeled on the Feast of Tabernacles and later became known as Hanukkah.

What is particularly interesting is that 2 Maccabees 10:7 states that the Jews celebrated "holding wreathed wands and branches bearing ripe fruit and palm fronds" (trans. by Goldstein). As Goldstein comments, "The Greek words here certainly do not fit the practices of [later] Jews . . . and there is some difficulty even in fitting them to the biblical texts bearing on Tabernacles." Without entering into the technicalities behind his translation (which is perhaps open to question), it is clear that the epitomist of 2 Maccabees, Jonathan of Cyrene (or his source), held a view of Leviticus 23:40 which accords neither with *Jubilees* nor with rabbinic exegesis. Which understanding was held by which group of Jews and when are questions which we simply cannot yet answer with any precision.

With regard to the third source of division on festival observance, the growth of extrabiblical customs, Tabernacles can continue to serve as an example. To return to *Jubilees* 16 for a moment: the author comments on the proper observance that "it is ordained forever that . . . they should place crowns on their heads" (*Jub.* 16:30). Such a commandment does not exist in the Bible. In fact, this "eternal ordinance" is a borrowing from Greek festal customs, although it was probably so well established in Israel by the time of *Jubilees* that its author—who preaches strenuously against certain Greek customs—was ignorant of its origins. The author's stress on its eternal verity makes it clear that not everyone in Israel accepted the wearing of crowns as a proper observance of Tabernacles.

Another such borrowed custom played a significant role in the history of the intertestamental period. During one Feast of Tabernacles Alexander Jannaeus (ruled 103-76 B.C.) offered sacrifice in his role as high priest (*see* Priest, Priesthood). The custom was to pour an oblation of water following the sacrifice, but the Pharisees* and Sadducees disagreed on where the liquid should be directed: The Pharisees held that it should be poured on the altar, while their opponents required the water to be poured out on the ground. Jannaeus poured the water on the ground. The people gathered at the festival, being persuaded by the Pharisaic ruling, were enraged and began to pelt the priest-king with their citrons. Thereupon Jannaeus ordered his mercenary soldiers to fall upon the crowd and 6,000 Jews perished (see Josephus *Ant.* 13.13.5 §§372-73; *J.W.* 1.88, and cf. *b. Sukk.* 48b). Ironically, the custom of pouring out an oblation, however directed, is not a biblical one and once again derives apparently from the Greeks. Thus, in attempting to understand the significance of Gospel references to feasts (especially with regard to fine details), one should be aware of the diversity of observance which characterized the Judaism of Jesus' day.

4. Feasts in the Gospels.

Prominent though they were in Jewish religious life, the three major feasts and the customs involved with their observance play a relatively limited role in the Gospels. Seldom do the narratives presume more than a basic familiarity with Jewish festival belief and practice. The one major exception to this generalization is the Passover as it figures in the narratives describing the Last Supper. As has been repeatedly argued, numerous details in all four Gospels point to a setting within the context of the observance of Passover by Jesus and his disciples* (cf., e.g., Jeremias, Marshall); indeed, it is this setting that helps provide the immediate context for understanding Jesus' actions and words (see Last Supper). Outside the Gospels the comparison between Jesus and the paschal lamb is so pervasive (e.g., 1 Cor 5:7; 1 Pet 1:19; Rev 5:6, 9, 12; see Lamb of God) that it almost certainly derives from Jesus and his celebration of the Last Supper.

Particularly with the Gospel of John, knowledge of the calendar of Jewish festivals helps determine the chronology of Jesus' mission. Thus, for example, John narrates three Passover festivals (Jn 2:23; 6:4; 11:55), giving rise to the traditional notion of a three-year public ministry for Jesus. John's concern is not strictly chronological, however. Thus, his mention of the approaching Passover in John 6:4 is one piece of the larger Exodus typology within his account of the feeding miracle (see Miracles, Miracle Stories), with its emphasis on provision of food, manna in the wilderness and the designation of Jesus as the eschatological prophet* ("like Moses," Deut 18:15-18).

More difficult is the chronology* of the passion week as it relates to Passover observance. This is not the problem of the apparent identification of the Feast of Unleavened Bread and the Passover in Luke 23:1, which reflects the virtual inseparability of these two festivals in current practice. Rather, as is transparent from a comparative reading of the Gospels, the Synoptics seem to have a different chronology of the events of Jesus' final week than one finds in John. Thus the evening during which the Last Supper is celebrated and the time of Jesus' crucifixion—both in relation to the sacrifice of the Passover lambs—are in question. Jaubert has attempted to solve this problem with recourse to John's use of a different calendar than the Synopticists, but her position has won few adherents (see Death of Jesus; Chronology).

Otherwise, the Feast of Passover provides the narrative framework for stories about Jesus. A group of

Passover pilgrims may be involved in Jesus' feeding of the multitudes (Mk 6:32-44 and par.; 8:1-21 and par.). One of the three pilgrimage feasts, probably Passover, forms the backdrop for Pilate's violence against Galilean visitors (Lk 13:1-3). Within the context of Luke's concern with portraying the exemplary piety of those involved with Jesus' birth and childhood (e.g., Lk 2:22-24, 25, 27, 36-37, 39; see Birth of Jesus), Jesus' pilgrimage to Jerusalem with his parents ("as was their custom") for the festival of Passover, further illustrates their righteousness (see Justice, Righteousness) before God. The presence of thousands of pilgrims in Jerusalem at Passover also explains the large crowds at Jesus' entry into Jerusalem (see People, Crowd; Triumphal Entry) and at his hearing before Pilate (see Pontius Pilate; Trial of Jesus), the presence of Roman officials at Jerusalem at this time (rather than in Caesarea, Pilate's normal residence), and, perhaps, the recognition of the threat Jesus posed by his prophetic action in the Temple. (To be branded a troublemaker from Galilee and to have the appearance of a large following was to be recognized as a threat to the state. See Temple Cleansing; Death of Jesus.)

The Gospels make no specific reference to the Feast of Weeks, or Pentecost. In the NT the term *pentēkostē* occurs only in 1 Corinthians 16:8; Acts 20:16; and Acts 2:1. This latter usage comes in connection with Luke's account of the outpouring of the Holy Spirit (see Holy Spirit) and the birth of the church.* These events apparently took place at the first Pentecost following the crucifixion. Hence, although not occurring within the Gospels themselves, these events are closely linked to the context of the Gospels. As Lohse has noted, the connection has the effect of tying the Jewish festival calendar into the weave of promise and fulfillment, and thus of salvation history.

The term for the Feast of Tabernacles, *skēnopēgia*, occurs only twice in the NT, in John 5:1 (textual variant) and 7:2. The narrative units that together comprise John 7 are dramatically oriented around the feast, so that in verses 1-9 the feast is near, in verses 10-13 Jesus goes up to the festival, in verses 14-36 he is teaching during the festival week, and verses 37-52 narrate what occurred on the last day of the festival. Thus, in John's narrative the Feast of Tabernacles becomes the backdrop for Jesus' self-revelation as the one who brings salvation, drawing on the festival images of outpoured water* (Jn 7:37-38) and light* (cf. Jn 8:12).

The Fourth Evangelist sometimes qualifies his mention of Passover with the phrase "of the Jews" (Jn 2:13; 6:4; 11:55). On this basis some scholars (e.g., Jeremias) have reasoned that he thus distinguishes between the

Jewish Passover and a separate, Christian Passover memorializing Jesus' passion. John's usage elsewhere, however—(e.g.) "Jewish purification rites" (Jn 2:6), "Jewish festival" (Jn 5:1) and "Jewish feast of Tabernacles" (Jn 7:2)—suggests that John is only setting Judaism in general over against Jesus and the Jesus movement.

See also CHRONOLOGY; LAST SUPPER; DEATH OF JESUS.

BIBLIOGRAPHY. J. Goldstein, II Maccabees (AB 41A; Garden City, NY: Doubleday, 1983); A. Jaubert, "Le calendrier des Jubilés et de la secte de Qumran: ses origines bibliques," VT 3 (1955) 250-64; idem, The Date of the Last Supper (Staten Island, NY: Alba House, 1965); J. Jeremias, "πάσχα," TDNT V.896-904; idem, The Eucharistic Words of Jesus (2d ed.; New York: Scribners, 1966); E. Lohse, "πεντηκοστή," TDNT VI.44-53; I. H. Marshall, Last Supper and Lord's Supper (Grand Rapids: Eerdmans, 1980); W. Michaelis, "σκηνή κτλ," TDNT VII.368-94; S. Talmon, "The Calendar Reckoning of the Sect from the Judaean Desert," ScrHier 4 (1957) 162-199; R. de Vaux, Ancient Israel 2: Religious Institutions (New York: McGraw-Hill, 1965). M. O. Wise

FEEDING MIRACLES. See BREAD; TABLE FELLOWSHIP.

FESTIVALS. See FEASTS.

FLAVIUS JOSEPHUS. See JOSEPHUS.

FLOCK. See SHEPHERD, SHEEP.

FOOTWASHING. See SERVICE.

FORGIVENESS OF SINS

The Greek verb aphiēmi ("forgive"), together with its cognate noun aphesis, is the most frequently used term for forgiveness in the Gospels. The verb has a wide range of meanings, including those of letting people go or dismissing them (e.g., Mk 4:36), divorcing a wife (1 Cor 7:11-13), or leaving a person (Lk 10:30) or a place (Jn 4:3). Forgiveness can also be expressed as remitting (apolyō), pardoning (charizomai) or forgiving (aphiēmi) a debt.

1. Forgiveness in the OT.

In the OT, although there are examples of one human being forgiving another (Gen 50:17; Ex 10:17; 1 Sam 15:25; 25:28; Prov 17:9), the majority of references to the forgiveness of sins have God* as subject. It belongs to his nature that he is "a God forgiving iniquity and transgression and sin" (Ex 34:7; cf. Num 14:18-20; Neh 9:17; Ps 130:4; Mic 7:18: Dan 9:9). The OT thus contains many prayers* for God's forgiveness both of individuals (e.g., 2 Kings 5:18; Ps 25:11) and especially of his people Israel* (e.g., 1 Kings 8:30-50; 2 Chron 6:21-39; Ps 79:9). In the psalms the distinction between prayers for individual and corporate forgiveness cannot be drawn sharply, since what were originally prayers of individuals came to be used in corporate worship.*

Yet the OT never represents forgiveness as automatic: It flows from the sovereign freedom of the living God. Thus, although God's forgiveness may be integrated into legal provisions and so be expected in certain situations, especially where sacrifice is involved (Lev 4:20-35; Num 15:25-28), God may on occasions refuse to forgive (Ex 23:21; Deut 29:20; Josh 24:19; 2 Kings 24:4; Is 22:14; Lam 3:42; Hos 1:6; cf. Jer 5:7); a prophet may even pray that God will not forgive his adversaries (Is 2:9; Jer 18:23), and Job asks God in perplexity, "Why do you not pardon my transgression?" (7:21).

2. Forgiveness in the Gospels.

2.1. The Son of Man's Power to Forgive Sins. In both OT and NT God's forgiveness is often referred to in reverent passive expressions. "Blessed is he whose transgression is forgiven" (Ps 32:1) is clarified by the following verse: "Blessed is the man to whom the Lord imputes no iniquity" (cf. Deut 21:8; Is 6:7; 33:24; 40:2). Such texts are a clue to the understanding of the Synoptic story of the healing of the lame man (Mk 2:1-12 par.). The scribes' indignation ("Who has the power [dynatai] to forgive sins but one, [that is,] God?" v. 7, cf. Lk 5:21), is caused by Jesus' statement "Your sins are forgiven" (v. 5 par., cf. v. 9 par.). Their anger is aroused not because forgiveness of one human being by another was unknown, but because, as the scribes* rightly perceived, the passive formula implied a claim to make performative statements in God's name. If such a statement had not been capable of validation in action ("take up your bed and walk," v. 11), it would indeed have been blasphemous. Jesus' statement that he heals the lame man "in order that you may know that the Son of man has authority [exousia] to forgive sins on earth" (v. 10) makes the claim virtually explicit. On one level, the story is full of dramatic irony; on another, it has profound christological significance.

Though less developed, Luke's story of the woman* at the house of Simon the Pharisee* (7:36-50) has some of the same features. Simon's assumption that Jesus claimed to be a prophet but was "not really" one (v. 39) and the guests' unanswered question "Who is this, who even forgives sins?" (v. 49) would have added meaning for early readers of the Gospel. For them Jesus was more than a prophet,* and they were urgently searching for themselves by what names he might most worthily be called.

Closely related to forgiveness are those passages which speak of the remission of a debt. The ideas of remission and forgiveness are especially close in the story of the two debtors (Mt 18:23-35). There, as Jesus' final comment makes explicit, the remission of a debt is a parable* of forgiveness in the kingdom of heaven. In the eschatological community inaugurated by Jesus, God's rule has already been established in a newly effective way. Luke 7:41-43 is similar, though a different Greek verb, *charizomai,* "give freely, remit, pardon," is used. Also in the Lord's Prayer, where Luke 11:4 has "forgive us our sins," Matthew 6:12 has "forgive us our debts," sins being thought of as (metaphorically) incurring indebtedness to God.

2.2. Forgiveness and Community.
Such passages illustrate a further principle: God's forgiveness cannot be effectively received except by those who are ready to forgive others. This is given special emphasis in Matthew's version of the Lord's Prayer by being made the subject of a unique comment: "If you do not forgive others, then your Father will not forgive the wrongs you have done" (6:15). The same thought is expressed positively in the previous verse, and in different words in Luke 6:37. There is even a scale of gratitude: the greater the forgiveness, the greater the love* (Lk 7:47).

Jesus' teaching is thus addressed to a community based on the giving and receiving of forgiveness, from which those who refuse to forgive their enemies exclude themselves. Conversely, forgiveness is related to repentance* (Lk 24:47) and faith* in God (Mk 2:5 par.) and may be considered as the removal of barriers to reconciliation. Forgiveness thus remains, as in the OT, divine initiative, but it extends (by implication through Jesus) to the messianic community as a whole, whose members consider one another as brothers and sisters, and as such are to forgive one another without limit (Mt 18:22; cf. Lk 17:3-4). The process is continued when the risen Jesus endows his disciples* with the Holy Spirit* and confers on them as his envoys the power both to forgive sins and to withhold forgiveness (Jn 20:23). The reference here is certainly to discipline within the believing community, not to the refusal to forgive personal wrongs. Jesus' earlier statements about "binding and loosing" to Peter (Mt 16:19) and to the disciples (Mt 18:18) are similar, but probably refer more generally to decisions about what is to be permitted and prohibited within the community rather

than to forgiveness alone. In the NT, as in the OT, the forgiveness of sins is not automatic.

2.3. The Unforgivable Sin.
This truth is given its most absolute expression in Jesus' saying about the "eternal sin" against the Holy Spirit (Mk 3:28-29 par.), which God (implied) will never forgive. This sin is not defined, and the contrast with forgivable blasphemies* is unclear, since these may be either blasphemies against God or slanders against other human beings. The best clue to the meaning of the saying is probably in Mark's final comment: "[Jesus said this] because they said, 'He has an unclean spirit' " (v. 30). Those who witness Jesus' mighty acts, yet attribute his power to Beelzebul, are calling good evil and so excluding themselves from the sphere in which God is acknowledged as king.

2.4. Forgiveness and the Post-Resurrection Community.
Other Gospel sayings, while doubtless rooted in the ministry of the historical Jesus, also point toward the concerns and developing institutions of the primitive church. That church celebrates no animal sacrifices, so there is no exact parallel in the Gospels to the OT link between sacrifice and forgiveness. Yet in Matthew's account of the Last Supper,* the blood of the new covenant is said to be "poured out for many for the forgiveness of sins" (26:28), probably a correct interpretation of Mark's simple "for many" (14:24), since forgiveness was an essential aspect of the new covenant predicted by Jeremiah (31:34; *see* Ransom Saying). Similarly, at the beginning of the Gospel John's (*see* John the Baptist) baptism* is said in identical language to be "for the forgiveness of sins" (Mk 1:4; Lk 3:3; cf. Lk 1:77), a phrase used also in the setting of a post-resurrection meal (Lk 24:47) and linked soon after with Christian baptism (Acts 2:38).

The exact relation between the sacraments on the one hand and forgiveness on the other is not spelled out in the Gospels. But the language implies that the purpose and/or the effect of baptism and the Lord's Supper is to claim from God, on the grounds of his promise, forgiveness of the participants' sins. Yet although God's forgiveness becomes effective under his rule and within the believing community, the community itself, and thus the offer of forgiveness, are without bounds. The message of "repentance toward [many manuscripts have 'and'] forgiveness of sins" is to be preached "to all the nations beginning from Jerusalem" (Lk 24:47).

The theme of forgiveness is strongly implied in two Gospel passages from which the language of forgiveness is absent. In John 8:3-11 (not originally part of John's Gospel but bearing all the marks of historical authenticity), Jesus' refusal to condemn the woman taken in adultery is reminiscent of the collocation "judge not . . . condemn not . . . forgive" in Luke 6:37. In the parable* of the prodigal son (Lk 15:11-32), the father is not to be allegorized as an image of God, yet the meeting of the father's acceptance and the son's sorrow (vv. 20-21) represents at a deeper level the divine initiative in the forgiveness of sins and the appropriate response of believing repentance.

The Gospel writers, while reflecting the concerns of the post-resurrection communities to which they belonged and for which they wrote, are generally faithful to the historical perspective of the events they record (*see* Gospels [Historical Reliability]). In particular, their accounts are not distorted by dependence on Pauline and other theological reflection (doubtless increasingly influential during the period of the Gospels' composition) about the relation between the death of Christ (*see* Death of Jesus) and the salvation* of which God's forgiveness is an essential aspect. Yet it may be said that the common roots of that reflection may be found in the Gospel records, especially— though not exclusively—in the simple, not yet formulaic, statements that Christ's blood was shed "for you" (Lk 22:20) and "for many" (*hyper pollōn*, Mt 14:24; *peri pollōn*, Mt 26:28) "for the forgiveness of sins."

See also FAITH; REPENTANCE; SINNERS.

BIBLIOGRAPHY. F. Büchsel et al., "ἵλεως κτλ," *TDNT* III.300-23; R. Bultmann, "ἀφίημι κτλ," *TDNT* I.509-12; H. Conzelmann, "χάρις κτλ," *TDNT* IX.372-402; R. G. Crawford, "A Parable of the Atonement," *EvQ* 57 (1985) 247-267; D. J. Doughty, "The Authority of the Son of Man (Mk 2:1-3:6)," *ZNW* 74 (1983) 161-181; K. Kertelge, "Die Vollmacht des Menschensohnes zur Sündenvergebung (Mk 2, 10)" in *Orientierung an Jesus: Festschrift für Josef Schmid*, ed. P. Koffmann et al. (Freiburg im Breisgau: Herder, 1973) 205-13; A. Oepke, "λούω κτλ," *TDNT* IV.295-307; V. Taylor, *Forgiveness and Reconciliation* (2d ed., London: Macmillan, 1946). P. Ellingworth

FORM CRITICISM

This method of analysis focuses on the individual, self-contained units of material into which the Gospels may be subdivided. It identifies the different "forms" or subgenres of literature which appear, and it attempts to describe the ways in which these forms developed during the period of time in which they were passed along by word of mouth prior to the writing of the Gospels themselves.

1. The Method
2. Critique
3. Alternatives
4. Criteria of Authenticity

1. The Method.

1.1. Origins. At the beginning of the twentieth century, scholars such as H. Gunkel and J. Wellhausen had already developed form criticism for many portions of the OT. In NT studies source criticism still captured the attention of most. By 1920, however, a trio of German scholars was busily researching the oral pre-history of the Gospels. K. L. Schmidt, M. Dibelius and most notably R. Bultmann pioneered the form criticism of the NT. English-speaking circles were at first relatively skeptical of this new discipline, but by the 1930s and 1940s in Great Britain, V. Taylor and R. H. Lightfoot were cautiously appropriating and advocating many form-critical principles in their work.

The earliest form critics based their study on several foundational presuppositions. All agreed that the teachings of Jesus and the narratives about his life which comprise the Gospels were transmitted orally over a considerable period of time before they were ever written down. They believed that these units of material for the most part circulated independently of one another. They affirmed that the closest parallels to the transmission of the gospel tradition could be found in the oral, folk literature of other ancient, European cultures (ranging as far afield as Iceland and Yugoslavia). They concluded that comparison with these parallels made it highly likely that the final form in which the Gospels appeared could not be trusted to supply a reliable account of what Jesus actually said and did. Rather one had to work backward and remove various accretions and embellishments which had crept into the tradition and so try to recover the original, pure forms. These forms, they believed, were originally short, streamlined and unadorned, and very Jewish in style and milieu.

1.2. Objectives. The original form-critical agenda included three main tasks: classifying the individual pericopes (self-contained units of teaching or narrative) according to form, assigning each form to a *Sitz im Leben* ("life-situation") in the early church and reconstructing the history of the tradition (*see* Tradition Criticism).

1.2.1. Analysis of Forms. No universally agreed-upon list of forms exists. At least six major categories appear quite frequently. The first four focus primarily on Jesus' teachings; the last two on the narrative material.

(1) *Individual logia, or sayings.* These include wisdom or proverbial sayings (e.g., Mt 8:20), prophetic (*see* Prophets, Prophecy) and apocalyptic* utterances (e.g., Lk 12:54-56), legal sayings and church rules (e.g., Mk 7:6-8), including what are often called "sentences of holy law" (e.g., Mt 18:15-17) and "I-sayings" (e.g., Mt 12:27-28), in which Jesus reveals something about his

own identity or mission.

(2) *Pronouncement stories.* These have also been called apophthegms and paradigms. They are short stories about an action of Jesus whose primary purpose is to lead up to a climactic pronouncement on a given topic (e.g., Mk 2:13-17; 3:31-35; 12:13-17). They are related to the Hellenistic chreiai*—pithy summaries of the actions and teachings of a great figure designed to epitomize some important attribute of that individual. Though given only scant attention in most traditional form criticism, chreia studies have proliferated in recent years. Many pronouncement stories are also conflict or controversy stories, pitting Jesus against his opponents on a crucial topic which divided them.

(3) *Parables.** These are short, metaphorical narratives, usually fictitious, designed to reveal some aspect of the kingdom of God.* Form critics have regularly subdivided them into similitudes (explicit, present-tense comparisons—e.g., Mk 4:30-32), parables proper (past-tense stories—e.g., Mt 25:1-13) and example-stories (narratives built on metonymy rather than metaphor—e.g., Lk 12:16-21). In this century parables have usually been sharply distinguished from allegory, but this distinction is coming under increasing attack.

(4) *Speeches.* These are longer, connected utterances of Jesus, usually believed to have been constructed out of shorter forms which once circulated independently of each other (e.g., Mt 5—7; Mk 4:1-34; 13:5-37). Speeches may in turn be subdivided into various other categories (e.g., farewell addresses [Jn 14—17] or symposia [Luke 14:1-24]; *see* Farewell Discourse).

(5) *Miracle* Stories.* These are narratives of the supernatural deeds of Jesus. They divide into two main categories—healing* miracles and nature miracles. These may then be subdivided into categories such as reanimations (Lk 7:11-17) or exorcisms (Mk 5:1-20) and rescue miracles (Mk 4:35-41) or gift miracles (Jn 2:1-11).

(6) *Other Historical Narratives.* Many of these have often been labeled legends or myths,* partly because of their content (associating Jesus with God* in some way) and partly because not all of each narrative is believed to be historically trustworthy (e.g., Lk 2:1-20; Mt 4:1-11; Mk 16:1-8).

1.2.2. Use in the Early Church. The form critic next tries to determine in which contexts in the life of the early Christian community each of these forms would have been most valued. For example, it is widely accepted that pronouncement stories would have been most used in popular preaching. Miracle stories were probably most significant in Christian apologetic

against Greco-Roman beliefs in other divine men (*see* Divine Man) or primeval heroes. Legends, it is often maintained, were created primarily out of a desire to glorify and exalt Jesus. Sentences of holy law were probably most relevant in settling church disputes. Parables may well have been transmitted during times of popular storytelling. Many forms are not readily associated with just one *Sitz im Leben,* and most critics agree that this objective is the most speculative of the three.

1.2.3. Writing the Tradition-History. Finally, each form is studied in light of what kinds of changes it most likely underwent during the transmission of the oral tradition. For example, it is usually affirmed that the bulk of the parables was well preserved, but introductions and conclusions were commonly altered as they were applied to new contexts. The pronouncement stories carefully preserved the pronouncements (comparable to the punch line of a joke), but the historical trappings in which they were encased might be altered greatly. Legends usually formed around a historical kernel which was then significantly embellished. Prophetic sayings (and various other forms) were often first spoken by early Christian prophets in the name of the risen Lord and later read back onto the lips of the earthly Jesus (*see* Prophet, Prophecy).

Form critics also believe that various tendencies of the developing tradition were widely applicable, irrespective of the given form of a pericope. Most of these can be summarized under what Bultmann termed "the law of increasing distinctness": stories became longer, incidental details were added, nameless characters were identified and place names were included. Additional dialog, interpretation, expansion and contemporization all appeared. Reapplication from a Palestinian-Jewish to a Hellenistic-Jewish and eventually to a Hellenistic-Gentile context also greatly transformed the form and content of much of the tradition.

2. Critique.

From the outset of the discipline there were conservative scholars who questioned many of the form critics' conclusions. But for a majority of scholars representing a wide spectrum of theological traditions, form criticism became the single most important modern tool for Gospel analysis. In the 1950s redaction criticism* developed, which has in many ways superseded form criticism during the last thirty years. But most redaction critics, like Gospel scholars specializing in other disciplines, have presupposed most of the methodology and conclusions of form criticism even when they have devoted much of their attention to other questions. In recent years, however, many NT scholars are utilizing forms of literary criticism which point to the carefully wrought unity of the Gospel narratives and calling into question many of the older axioms of traditio-historical development. Each of the three main objectives on the form-critical agenda therefore deserves careful evaluation.

2.1. Analysis of Forms.

2.1.1. Aids to Interpretation. Form criticism can provide guidelines to interpreting individual pericopes. This objective is probably the most significant and manageable of the three. The Gospels are not monolithic narratives; each section cannot be treated like every other. Interpretation is genre-bound, that is, there are often distinct hermeneutical rules for distinct literary forms. Recognizing that the emphasis in a pronouncement story is on the pronouncement helps the interpreter to avoid stressing peripheral details. For example, the focus of Mark 3:31-35 is not on Jesus' apparent neglect of his family but on his embracing his followers as part of his family. This approach also reveals how often Jesus' pronouncements focused on the radical newness of the kingdom *vis-à-vis* the prevailing forms of Judaism* of the day (e.g., Mk 2:23-28).

Recent form criticism of the miracle stories has demonstrated how they usually focus on christology and the kingdom—demonstrating who Jesus was and what was the nature of the new society he envisioned. Thus the cursing of the fig tree (Mk 11:12-14, 20-25) was no petulant outburst, nor even primarily a lesson about faith, but a symbolic demonstration of God's impending judgment* on Israel* (comparable to the cleansing of the Temple around which Mark sandwiches this miracle-story—see vv. 15-19; *see* Temple Cleansing). So too Jesus' walking on the water (Mk 6:45-52) was neither a convenient way to get across the lake nor an arbitrary demonstration of his gravity-defying power but a revelation of himself as the Lord of the wind and waves (cf. Ps 107:23-32) and the very "I am" (Yahweh) of Exodus 3:14 (*see* "I Am" Sayings).

Parable research has probably benefitted the most from form criticism. Only about half of the passages in the Gospels usually called parables are specifically labeled as such by the Evangelists. Sometimes those which are not so labeled are treated differently. For example, the story of the rich man and Lazarus (Lk 16:19-31) has often been viewed as a true story, or at least as giving an accurate description of the afterlife. In light of the structural parallels between this passage and many which are explicitly labeled parallels, both of these views are doubtful. One dare not derive

doctrine from the details of a parable unless it can be corroborated by less metaphorical teachings elsewhere in Scripture.

2.1.2. Keys to Gospel Outlines. Classification of the Gospel pericopes by form also enables one to discern the types of structures and outlines which the four Evangelists used. Sometimes they arrange material in chronological order, sometimes in topical order. In several instances they seem to have grouped a series of like forms together. Thus Mark 2:1—3:6 collects together a group of pronouncement stories; 4:35—6:6a comprises a collection of miracles (as does most of Mt 8—9); and Matthew 13:1-52 is made up primarily of parable (as is most of Luke 14—16).

2.1.3. Ambiguities. Many passages, however, do not easily fall into one of the primary form-critical categories. Many seem to mix together several forms. For example, Mark 2:1-12 shares features of both a healing miracle and a pronouncement story. Early form critics usually assumed that mixed forms had undergone more complex development and that their historical kernel was therefore less recoverable. But in the ancient world students of rhetoric (*see* Rhetorical Criticism) regularly claimed that mixed forms were aesthetically pleasing (e.g., Quintillian *Inst. Orat.* 8.6.4.9), so it is likely that many such forms appeared right at the start of the Gospel tradition. Other form-critical categories seem to combine form and content. An example-story is largely indistinguishable from a parable in form; so too a myth and a historical narrative. Interpretive presuppositions unrelated to pure literary form seem to have influenced several of the form critics' classifications.

2.2. Use in the Early Church. In principle the attempt to assign a *Sitz im Leben* to each form is well motivated and potentially helpful. If one can discern how the early church used a certain aspect of the Gospel tradition, one may better understand in what contexts today it may be most useful. Occasionally comparative data permit reasonable inferences; Paul's knowledge of Jesus' "words of institution" (1 Cor 11:23-25) suggests that part or all of the story of the Last Supper* (Lk 22:13-38) may have been read or recited during celebrations of the Eucharist, much as it often is today. But in most cases such reconstructions are highly speculative because they are based on what other ancient cultures did in settings that are not always closely parallel to the rise of Christianity.

2.3. Writing the Tradition-History. This objective has perhaps been the focus of the greatest amount of scholarly energy, but it is also laden with the most pitfalls. Most scholars have recognized some of these pitfalls, but few have appreciated their cumulative effect in casting serious doubt on all hypotheses of the development of the tradition which assume that primitive forms underwent substantial modification prior to their inclusion in the written texts of the Gospels.

2.3.1. Tendencies of the Tradition. Several considerations challenge the widely held notion that stories of what Jesus did and said would have been significantly distorted during the period of oral tradition (see section 1.2.3.).

(1) Probably little more than twenty years elapsed between the events described and the first written accounts (c. A.D. 30-50). Eyewitnesses of Jesus' ministry, including hostile ones, could easily have refuted and discredited Christian claims during this period if those claims had been in any way mistaken.

(2) From the outset Jesus' disciples may well have kept private, written notes along the lines of those kept by other rabbis and disciples (see Schürmann). And the fact that they were sent out to preach about Jesus and his message during his lifetime (Mk 6:7-13; Lk 10:1-16) suggests that they would have begun to preserve the tradition early on.

(3) The so-called law of increasing distinctness is extremely misleading. Detailed analyses of the oral traditions of the cultures closest in time and space to ancient Israel, coupled with a comprehensive comparison of Mark with Matthew and Luke, later apocryphal traditions, sayings in the church fathers and textual variants show that no consistent patterns of lengthening or abbreviation prevail (see Sanders). If anything, a slight tendency toward decreasing distinctness occurs with longer forms such as parables, miracle stories and other historical narratives.

Several additional "tendencies" of the tradition prove equally suspect. The various Gospel pericopes probably did not circulate in as much isolation from one another as has often been assumed. For example, the OT, intertestamental literature and rabbinic material demonstrate that parables and other stories often concluded with aphoristic generalizations. These may well have been part of Jesus' teaching from the outset rather than free-floating sayings which were attached at a later date. Some of the speeches in the Gospels may be compilations of shorter teachings from discrete settings, but most ancient historians and biographers tended to digest and excerpt longer wholes in writing their speeches and narratives. The same may well have occurred for passages like the Sermon on the Mount* or the Olivet Discourse (*see* Apocalyptic Teaching; see Wenham).

2.3.2. The Delay of the Parousia. Many of the additions to the Gospel tradition postulated by form critics reflect ongoing concerns for church life and behavior. It is often assumed that the earliest *kerygma* ("proclamation") had no interest in ethical mandates, establishment of church order or teachings about an extended interval between Christ's first and second comings. Form critics usually so stress Jesus' teaching about his imminent return that any details which point to the delay of the Parousia are assumed to be secondary additions to the tradition.

But it is not at all clear that Jesus' teaching was so one-sided or that the early church would have had to modify the tradition in any substantial way as it became increasingly apparent that Christ was not returning as quickly as some might have hoped. After all, the Jews had heard for centuries during the prophetic era that "the Day of the Lord" was "at hand" (e.g., Joel 2:1; Obad 15; Hab 2:3), and yet they had come to grips with the fact that "soon" in God's timing often does not correspond to human expectation. Psalm 90:4 became an influential text both in rabbinic Judaism (cf. *2 Apoc. Bar.* 48:12-13; *Pirqe R. El.* 28) and in early Christianity (2 Pet 3:8-9; see Bauckham).

2.3.3. Early Christian Prophecy. The view that the early church failed to distinguish sayings of early Christian prophets from teachings of the historical Jesus (*see* Historical Jesus; see Boring) must almost certainly be laid to rest (Aune). The evidence on which this hypothesis was originally based was meager enough; more careful, recent studies have shown that it is virtually non-existent.

The closest parallels come from the practices of certain Greco-Roman prophets speaking in the name of mythological gods, especially at oracles or temples of healing. The only NT example which records words of the ascended Lord* spoken directly to his people appears in a context (Rev 2:1-3:22) where he is clearly distinguished from the earthly Jesus. The only examples in the NT of the words of Christian prophets (Acts 11:28; 21:10-11) clearly attribute the Lord's message to a human speaker—Agabus. And in 1 Corinthians 14:29 Paul makes it clear that no prophecy could be accepted that did not conform to the previously revealed Word of God, so even if some sayings crept into the tradition from certain prophets, they would not likely have distorted the original gospel message as is often alleged. The lack of sayings attributed to Jesus on topics of later church controversy (e.g., circumcision or speaking in tongues) further supports the view that Christian prophecy was not confused with the teachings of the historical Jesus.

3. Alternatives.

The lasting legacy of form criticism has been its

concern for studying the period of the oral transmission of the Gospel tradition, even if many of its conclusions about that period should be rejected. But two recent schools of thought have proposed alternative models of oral transmission that prove more promising. Each maintains that the early church would have preserved the various units of tradition more carefully than classic form criticism granted. A third approach abandons virtually all attempts to analyze the oral tradition.

3.1. The Guarded Tradition Hypothesis. In the late 1950s and early 1960s two Swedish scholars, H. Riesenfeld and B. Gerhardsson, proposed that Jesus had his disciples memorize his most significant teachings and even certain narratives about what he did. Other ancient Jewish rabbis followed these practices, and memories were cultivated so as to produce prodigious feats of recall—such as memorizing the entire Hebrew Bible. The twelve disciples were viewed as an authoritative circle of leadership which carefully safeguarded the traditions. Paul seems to point to the existence of such a guarded tradition when he speaks of passing on what had been delivered to him (e.g., 1 Cor 11:23; 15:3).

Reaction to this approach was at first largely negative. Other scholars pointed out that Jesus was not simply an ordinary rabbi, that the rabbinic evidence was from later than the first century, that there was scant evidence in the Gospels themselves of any concern to preserve Jesus' teaching and that the numerous differences among Gospel parallels precluded any significant amount of memorization. More recently, however, R. Riesner has advanced the discussion further. In a wide-ranging study of educational practices common to first-century Israel and its neighbors, he concludes that at least six additional arguments support the view that Jesus' followers would have carefully preserved accurate information about him without necessarily memorizing it word-for-word:

(1) Jesus' words were received as being on a par with those of the prophets, which are among the portions of the OT usually held to be the most historically reliable. (2) Expectations about the Messiah included seeing him as a teacher of wisdom,* whose words should be safeguarded. (3) Over ninety per cent of Jesus' sayings are couched in quasi-poetic form which would have been easy to remember. (4) Like other rabbis, Jesus seems to have encouraged the practice of memorization before meditation or application (e.g., Mk 9:10; 13:28; Lk 11:1). (5) Mandatory elementary education for boys until about the age of twelve (such as Jesus' disciples would have received) almost exclusively involved rote memorization. (6) Almost all teachers in both Greco-Roman and Jewish circles gathered disciples around them to perpetuate their teachings and lifestyle, so however different Jesus was from the rabbis in other ways, he probably resembled them in this respect (*see* Teacher).

3.2. Flexible Transmission within Fixed Limits. A second alternative to classic form criticism offers a less conservative paradigm for the transmission of the tradition than the memorization hypothesis. Recent studies of oral folklore and sacred history in pre-literate cultures, especially by the anthropologist A. Lord, have shown that epic stories of up to 100,000 words in length were often memorized by specially designated storytellers or folk singers. The plot, characters, main events and a sizable number of the details remained constant every time the stories were retold or sung. Members of the community were sufficiently familiar with them to correct the singer if he erred in any crucial way. Yet anywhere from ten to forty per cent of the precise wording could vary from one performance to the next, quite like the variation found in the Synoptic Gospels. Lord has suggested that much of these Gospel narratives may reflect the product of a succession of oral performances of the stories they recount. Studies of the Jewish targums* (Aramaic paraphrases of OT texts with explanatory elaborations) from the first centuries of the Common Era suggest that something similar to what Lord has envisioned was practiced in Jewish circles. As a result a growing number of Gospel specialists are adopting more and more of the methods of this newest alternative to form criticism.

W. Kelber has applied Lord's studies to the Gospels and has emphasized the disjunction between orality and literacy. Before traditions are written down in a fixed form, there is no single identifiable, canonical form of any tradition. Each oral performance is somewhat different and not necessarily any further from or closer to the words of the original speaker. It is therefore impossible to recover the earliest form of a Gospel pericope; at best one can speak of an "originating structure." Kelber also pits the written Gospels against the earlier, unwritten forms as the product of a segment of the Christian community which was challenging the authority of the apostles as the guardians of the oral tradition. He sees the textuality of the Gospels as creating a more rigid, fixed way of telling the story of Jesus than was permitted by oral tradition. Although traces of orality still appear in the Gospels, especially Mark, the value of classic form criticism is greatly diminished for this approach.

Yet it appears that in several respects this line of interpretation has relied on too one-sided an appropriation of cultural anthropology. Other studies show that the disjunction between orality and literacy need not be as marked or that cultures may prefer written or unwritten forms for various ideological reasons unrelated to accuracy of preservation. What is more, oral traditions continued to circulate alongside the written texts until at least the mid-second century and were sometimes even preferred by early Christians as more trustworthy. And a more careful investigation of the written traditions of the Gospels (especially variants among manuscripts, canonical parallels and second-century quotations of the Gospels) shows that Kelber has also exaggerated the rigidity of textuality. Study of the oral pre-history of the Gospel traditions therefore remains a crucial prelude to understanding their canonical forms.

3.3. Rhetorical Analysis. K. Berger has recently compiled the most comprehensive treatment of Gospel forms since Bultmann (and goes beyond him by analyzing texts found in all parts of the NT). Unlike most of his predecessors, Berger limits himself almost entirely to classifying forms and identifying their function, believing the reconstruction of any oral pre-history to be beyond the reach of modern scholars, given the limited data available to them. Against W. Schmithals he agrees that there often was a period of oral transmission, and with many conservatives he believes that many traditions were reasonably well preserved. But he affirms that it is usually not possible to move from what is probably true about a group of texts in general to what is likely for any individual passage or form. Berger therefore rejects the comparative-religions approach which seeks analogies in other oral traditions of antiquity. Instead, he focuses exclusively on parallel forms and genres in written texts from the ancient Jewish and Greco-Roman worlds.

Berger's volume falls into four sections. The last three follow, in turn, the three categories of rhetoric most commonly discussed by ancient philosophers: deliberative (or exhortational), epideictic (laudatory or condemnatory) and juridical (or apologetic). The first main section discusses forms which could function in more than one of these three kinds of rhetoric. They include analogical and metaphorical texts, simple statements, speeches, chreia and apophthegms and argumentation.

Under deliberative genres Berger deals with virtue and vice lists, community rules, paraenesis (exhortation), domestic codes, beatitudes, warnings, proverbs and related forms.

As examples of epideictic rhetoric he considers various kinds of lists and catalogs meant to praise or blame, acclamations and doxologies, narrative commentary, reports of martyrdom, symbolic actions, travel narratives, summary statements, miracle stories, hymns and prayers, proclamations, apocalyptic, etiologies, liturgy, encomium, dialog and so on.

As examples of judicial rhetoric Berger examines sayings on holiness or impurity, verdicts and criticisms, eyewitness reports, accusations and apologies.

Berger's use of the ancient threefold division of rhetoric has been widely adopted in recent NT genre criticism, especially of the epistles. Its value for assessing the function of a written text as a whole is undisputed. Its application in analyzing subgenres or forms which are the products of oral tradition (as particularly found in the Gospels) is less clear. Significantly, Berger's first section, which studies forms used in more than one kind of rhetoric, focuses much more on the Gospels than do his other three sections. Here his discussions read much like a summary of the state of the art of more traditional form criticism. Nor is it obvious that the study of the pre-history of Gospel forms should be so totally abandoned. Granted that one must proceed with great caution in an area this susceptible to speculation, the recent alternatives to classic form criticism discussed above suggest that progress can be made in the study of the oral transmission of the Gospel traditions. How this is accomplished for individual passages or forms comprises the next topic of discussion.

4. Criteria of Authenticity.

For many form critics their most significant task has been to assess the authenticity of the discrete units of Gospel tradition. For some, more authority attaches to those portions which reflect Jesus' *ipsissima verba* (very own words) or *ipsissima vox* (very own voice) than to less carefully preserved forms. For others, historical reliability and theological value are entirely separate issues. Either way, numerous criteria have been developed to help form critics sift the more authentic from the less authentic.

4.1. The Individual Criteria. Four principal criteria have been almost universally accepted. (1) The criterion of dissimilarity states that any teaching or action of Jesus which distinguishes him both from the Judaism of his day and from the early Christian church may be accepted as authentic. (2) The criterion of multiple attestation places more confidence in those details which are found in more than one Gospel source (e.g., Mk, Q,* M,* L,* Jn) or in more than one form. (3) The criterion of Palestinian environment or language more readily accepts that which is very Semitic in style or background. (4) The criterion of coherence includes texts which fit well with material already authenticated by one of the other three criteria.

4.2. Critique. A distinction must be made between the positive and negative use of these criteria. Most form critics have assumed that material which could not be authenticated by one of these means must therefore be inauthentic. But this does not follow. The dissimilarity criterion can demonstrate only what is distinctive about Jesus; what he shared with his contemporaries will by definition fail the test. Multiple attestation does increase the confidence one can place in a tradition, but singly attested material may prove equally genuine. The intermingling of Semitic and Hellenistic (*see* Hellenism) cultures in the first century makes the third criterion very difficult to apply; it is hard to maintain that a Semitic form or style could not have been created in early Christianity or that Jesus could not have utilized Greco-Roman concepts and forms of speech (*see* Languages of Palestine). Coherence is a very subjective concept. Presumably all of the Gospel material cohered in the minds of the Evangelists; how is any modern scholar to say that apparent inconsistencies are sharp enough to call into question the truthfulness of the accounts?

Beyond these specific criticisms, a major presupposition behind the use of the criteria of authenticity must be called into question. The entire undertaking is usually predicated on the assumption that the Gospel traditions are inherently suspect unless good reasons can be advanced for accepting them. Actually, there are excellent reasons for believing large segments of the Gospels to be historically reliable (totally apart from any presuppositions about the inspiration of Scripture), so that a more positive approach must be adopted (*see* Gospels [Historical Reliability]). The burden of proof must rest with the skeptic who would doubt any portion of the Gospels (see Goetz and Blomberg). Instead of utilizing criteria of authenticity, one ought to assume authenticity and then ask if there are good reasons for denying it (e.g., irreconcilably contradictory accounts). Problems should then be examined one by one and judgments rendered.

4.3. Application. Nevertheless, even for those who adopt a stance of methodical doubt, the criteria may be used to authenticate many key themes and aspects of the Gospel tradition (though it is usually not recognized to what extent this is true). Jesus' parables are widely held to be authentic; almost no early Christians used the form, while rabbinic parallels almost entirely elucidated Scripture rather than revealing the in-breaking kingdom of God. Key teachings about the kingdom, especially those in which Jesus makes plain that it has arrived (e.g., Mt 12:28) or those which balance present and future hope (e.g., Mk 8:34-38) are similarly distinctive. Other items which pass the dissimilarity test include Jesus' compassion for the outcasts of society, his frequent conflicts with the Jewish authorities over the interpretation of the Law,* especially the Sabbath* regulations, and his stringent demands for discipleship* (e.g., Mt 8:21-22; Lk 14:26; Mk 10:21).

Another major section of Gospel pericopes includes Jesus' teachings about the Son of man.* This term was rarely used in Judaism and never appears on the lips of any other NT speaker except Stephen (Acts 7:56). Although it is widely debated, the background for the title is most likely Daniel 7:13, and it probably should be taken as messianic. But it was ambiguous enough that Jesus could invest it with his own meaning and not risk the nationalistic misinterpretations of his role that more widely used titles like Messiah might have invoked. Jesus' intimate relationship with his Father is another feature of the Gospels widely accepted as authentic. But by the criterion of coherence it is only a small step from this to the use of the title Son of God* as equally authentic (texts like Mt 11:27 may form the bridge).

Illustrations could be multiplied. The significance of most of Jesus' miracles closely ties in with his authentic kingdom teachings. Jesus' predictions about establishing his church* (Mt 16:18; 18:17), widely believed to be inauthentic, in fact can be authenticated by a criterion of "necessary explanation." Some kind of promises of this nature must have formed the foundation for Peter's remarkable recovery from his denial to his leadership of the church at Pentecost. R. Latourelle has maintained that the application of the various criteria can eventually lead to the authentication of Jesus' baptism,* temptation,* Transfiguration,* call to repentance,* Beatitudes, passion,* crucifixion and resurrection,* commissioning of the apostles* and numerous other details in addition to all of those already mentioned. R. Gruenler has shown that even if one accepts only a handful of Jesus' sayings as authentic (as in the largely skeptical studies of N. Perrin), the uniquely authoritative and self-referential claims implied enable one by the criterion of coherence to validate large numbers of more explicitly christological texts.

See also GOSPELS (HISTORICAL RELIABILITY); LITERARY CRITICISM; REDACTION CRITICISM; SYNOPTIC PROBLEM; RHETORICAL CRITICISM; TRADITION CRITICISM.

BIBLIOGRAPHY. D. E. Aune, *Prophecy in Early Christianity and the Ancient Mediterranean World* (Grand Rapids: Eerdmans, 1983); R. Bauckham, "The Delay of the

Parousia," *TynB* 31 (1980) 3-36; K. Berger, *Formgeschichte des Neuen Testaments* (Heidelberg: Quelle und Meyer, 1984); C. L. Blomberg, *Interpreting the Parables* (Downers Grove: InterVarsity, 1989); M. E. Boring, *Sayings of the Risen Jesus* (Cambridge: University Press, 1982); R. Bultmann, *The History of the Synoptic Tradition* (Oxford: Blackwell, 1963); M. Dibelius, *From Tradition to Gospel* (Cambridge: J. Clarke, 1934); B. Gerhardsson, *Memory and Manuscript* (Lund: Gleerup, 1961); S. C. Goetz and C. L. Blomberg, "The Burden of Proof," *JSNT* 11 (1981) 39-63; R. G. Gruenler, *New Approaches to Jesus and the Gospels* (Grand Rapids: Baker, 1982); A. J. Hultgren, *Jesus and His Adversaries* (Minneapolis: Augsburg, 1979); W. Kelber, *The Oral and the Written Gospel* (Philadelphia: Fortress, 1983); R. Latourelle, *Finding Jesus through the Gospels* (New York: Alba, 1979); E. V. McKnight, *What Is Form Criticism?* (Philadelphia: Fortress, 1969); R. Riesner, *Jesus als Lehrer* (Tübingen: Mohr, 1981); E. P. Sanders, *The Tendencies of the Synoptic Tradition* (Cambridge: University Press, 1969); H. Schürmann, "Die vorösterlichen Anfänge der Logientradition," in *Der historische Jesus und der kerygmatische Christus*, ed. H. Ristow and K. Matthiae (Berlin: Evangelische Verlagsanstalt, 1960) 342-70; V. Taylor, *The Formation of the Gospel Tradition* (London: Macmillan, 1933); G. Theissen, *The Miracle Stories of the Early Christian Tradition* (Edinburgh: T. & T. Clark, 1983); D. Wenham, *The Rediscovery of Jesus' Eschatological Discourse* (Sheffield: JSOT, 1984).

C. L. Blomberg

FOURTH PHILOSOPHY. *See* REVOLUTIONARY MOVEMENTS.

FREEDOM

The Gospels contain few explicit references to freedom. *Eleutheria* (freedom) does not appear in the Gospels, *eleutheros* ("free") appears only three times (Mt 17:26; Jn 8:33, 36) and *eleutheroō* ("set free") appears only twice (Jn 8:32, 36). Thus, most of what the Gospels say about freedom must be inferred from the appearance of the subject in other terms.

Freedom in the Gospels does not refer to the kinds of political and social freedom which so readily occur to modern minds: the freedom of personal self-actualization, the human right to liberty or freedom from social oppression of whatever type. The interest of the Gospel writers lies elsewhere: in the religious and moral freedom Jesus offers to those who follow him. Whether this freedom also results in social or political freedom is an issue debated today but only indirectly addressed in the Gospels. They reflect a highly stratified society which perceived goods as

limited (*see* Poverty and Riches). Increasing one's own goods meant necessarily decreasing the goods of another, something considered dishonorable. It was honorable simply to maintain what one had been given (see Malina). Still, Jesus' own freedom and teachings have profound implications for the freedom of his followers.

To whatever extent the Gospel writers may have been influenced by other ways of thinking about freedom, the freedom they describe is neither the political freedom of individuals or states which was of primary interest to the Greeks, nor the inner philosophical freedom of the Stoics who abandoned themselves to circumstances, nor the freedom which the devout Jew found through observance of the Law, nor the freedom of separation from the material world found in much of gnostic thought.

1. The Freedom of Jesus.
The Gospels simply assume, but do not discuss, the freedom of God. They speak more clearly about the freedom of Jesus which may be suggestively characterized as follows:

Jesus is independent of all parties and groups in Judaism* in his day and free with regard to Jewish traditions (e.g., Sabbath* observance) and many social and religious conventions (e.g., relationships with lepers,* a Samaritan,* women* and sinners*). In other words, Jesus is free to associate with any and all who heed his message, just as God loves* both sinner and saint. "This is why Jesus is the paradigm of freedom from the ideological use of 'God' to sanction either the status quo or efforts to remodel it on the basis of our grievances" (Keck, 79).

Jesus is free to reinterpret the Law* of Moses, as illustrated in his familiar words "But I say to you" (*see* Commandment). He enjoys the freedom of authority given him by the Father, such as his authority to judge others and to have life* in himself to give to whom he wills (Jn 5:21-29). Thus he is free to lay down his life or to take it again (Jn 10:17-18).

Jesus' freedom, however, does not mean independence. He is sent by the Father and only does what the Father wills (Jn 6:38). His freedom is based on the oneness with the Father established by the Father's loving gift (Jn 17). In turn, Jesus' freedom is a model for the freedom of his followers who gain their freedom through their relationship to him (Jn 8:36).

2. The Freedom of Jesus' Disciples.
According to the Gospels humans are both free and not free. The call to repentance and discipleship implies the freedom to respond. Moreover, John's

Gospel suggests that persons choose to come, or not to come, to the light* (3:20-21; cf. 5:40). On the other hand, humans are in bondage to sin (cf. Jn 8:34; Lk 4:18) and death else they would not need the gift of life. Often this bondage is characterized in other ways, such as blindness* (Jn 9) and physical affliction (Lk 13:10-12).

2.1. The Synoptics. From the Synoptics we may draw several general observations regarding the freedom of Jesus' disciples.

Although freedom was not a topic in Jesus' teaching, he "articulated (by word and deed) the impingement of God's kingdom in such a way that what occurred can be called liberation" (Keck, 77-78). In John's Gospel a similar articulation occurs in terms of (eternal) life, light and truth* (cf. Jn 8:31-32). In the Synoptics liberation is dramatically realized and illustrated in Jesus' exorcism of demons* and his healings.* These events demonstrate that this freedom is not divisible between body and spirit.

The Gospels' understanding of liberation was shaped by apocalyptic* and implies several things (Keck, 80): (1) freedom is not the result of one's own efforts, but is an event of God's grace; (2) liberation does not happen without a struggle; (3) in the present age no one is wholly free; (4) freedom in the present is proleptic and finite; and (5) grounding freedom in the dialectic of "already" and the "not yet" emancipates us from idolatrous expectations of the relative freedoms which can be won through human struggle (*see* Eschatology).

As R. Pesch has observed, "Jesus urged freedom on his listeners in provocative words" (Pesch, 58). This is exemplified in Jesus words: "Whoever would save one's life will lose it" (Mk 8:35); "Do not be anxious about your life, what you shall eat . . ." (Lk 12:22-23); "Love your enemies, do good to those who hate you . . ." (Lk 6:27-28).

Freedom is also the subject of many of Jesus' parables* (Pesch, 59). The parable of the soils demonstrates a relaxed attitude in the face of clear failure (Mk 4:3-8). The parables of seed growing mysteriously of its own accord (Mk 4:26-29) or of a barely visible mustard seed growing into a huge shrub (Mk 4:30-32) show an unworried confidence in the power of the kingdom of God. These are expressions of the freedom of the reign of God (*see* Kingdom of God).

2.2. John's Gospel. John's Gospel (especially 8:31-36) throws a distinctive light on the freedom Jesus offers. For John real freedom comes through knowing the truth, that is, Jesus, the revelation of God (8:31-32, 36). It can be expressed in other symbols and metaphors, such as light which dispels darkness or blindness (Jn

9) and life which frees from death (Jn 11). A gift from Jesus, freedom depends on a continuing relationship with him (8:31). "The disciple will never be free from him without at the same time losing all freedom" (Käsemann, 145).

As with all expressions of salvation* found in the Fourth Gospel, here too the emphasis is on the present experience of freedom. This freedom is rejected by those who (falsely) think they are free already but who are really slaves of sin (8:33-35). Yet the freedom Jesus offers is freedom from sin and death (11:26; 5:24). In turn, Jesus' gift of freedom creates communities of "friends" (*philoi*, in contrast to *douloi*, "slaves") of Jesus (15:14-15).

This freedom is not independence from God or Jesus or others who are free. Freedom is only for those who remain in Jesus' word (8:31) and keep his commandments which he has from the Father (15:14), that is, those who love one another (15:12-17). As Keck observes, ". . . the real measure of the freedom which Jesus confers is the capacity to love, for the degree to which one loves another is the degree to which one is freed from self-protection and self-aggrandizement" (82). It is the Holy Spirit,* who guides them into all truth, that is instrumental in securing the freedom of believers (16:12-15).

See also LIBERATION HERMENEUTICS; LIFE; LIGHT; SALVATION.

BIBLIOGRAPHY. J. Blunck, "Freedom," *NIDNTT* 1.715-21; C. H. Dodd, "Behind a Johannine Dialogue [John 8: 31-58]," in *More New Testament Studies* (Manchester: University Press, 1968) 41-57; E. Käsemann, *Jesus Means Freedom* (London: SCM, 1969); L. Keck, "The Son Who Creates Freedom," in *Jesus Christ and Human Freedom*, ed. E. Schillebeeckx and Bas van Iersel (New York: Herder and Herder, 1974) 71-82; B. Malina, "Freedom: A Theological Inquiry into the Dimensions of a Symbol," *BTB* 8 (1978) 62-76; idem, *The New Testament World: Insights from Cultural Anthropology* (Atlanta: John Knox, 1981); R. Pesch, "Jesus, a Free Man," in *Jesus Christ and Human Freedom*, ed. E. Schillebeeckx and Bas van Iersel (New York: Herder and Herder, 1974) 56-70; H. Schlier, "ἐλεύθερος κτλ," *TDNT* II.487-502.

G. F. Shirbroun

FRUIT OF THE VINE. *See* VINE, FRUIT OF THE VINE.

FULFILLMENT. *See* LAW; OLD TESTAMENT IN THE GOSPELS; TYPOLOGY

G

GALILEE

1. History and Geography
2. Society and Religion
3. Jesus and Galilee

1. History and Geography.

Originally, the Hebrew name *haggālîl* probably denoted the region around Kadesh northwest of Lake Hula (Josh 21:32; 1 Chron 6:61). Later it referred to the entire region belonging to the tribe of Naphtali, including the eastern portion of Asher and the northern portion of Zebulun and Issachar. The demise of the Northern Kingdom, Israel (722/721 B.C.), brought destruction to the Jewish population and the immigration of pagan foreigners (2 Kings 17:6; Tob 1:2); thus the name "region of the Gentiles" (*gālîl haggôyîm*) came into use (Is 8:23). During the Maccabean Revolt many of the remaining Jews were evacuated (1 Macc 5:23). The Hasmonean king Aristobulus I conquered Galilee (by now it bore the Greek name *Galilaia*) in 104/103 B.C., bringing it once more under Jewish domination. He forced the Gentile population to convert to Judaism* (Josephus *Ant.* 13.11.3 §§318-19). Under Herod the Great (40-4 B.C.) and his son Herod Antipas, who ruled until A.D. 39, Galilee enjoyed prosperous times (*see* Herodian Dynasty). After the short reign of Herod Agrippa I (A.D. 41-44) it came under direct Roman rule (*see* Rome). The failure of the procurators led to the growth of the Zealots, a nationalistic, revolutionary movement (*see* Revolutionary Movements). Finally, the Jewish War broke out (A.D. 66), which was over in Galilee by A.D. 68. Not until after the fall of Jerusalem (A.D. 70; *see* Destruction of Jerusalem) did Galilee (Tiberias) become the center of rabbinic learning (*see* Rabbinic Traditions and Writings).

At the time of Jesus the borders of Galilee ran as follows (Josephus *J.W.* 3.3.1 §§35-39): the southern boundary was the north edge of the Plain of Esdraelon. The eastern boundary was the Jordan River from as far north as Lake Hula southward through the Sea of Galilee. The northern boundary was Gischala (probably the place of origin of Paul's parents; see Jerome *Vir.* III.5). The western boundary was Cabul. These borders bounded a territory about forty kilometers in diameter. Any location could be reached in no more than two days' journey. Geographically, Galilee may be divided into three different areas. Lower Galilee in the south consists of a hilly region with occasional plains. Upper Galilee in the north rises to an elevation of 1200 meters; in NT times it was heavily forested and partially impassable. The Jordan Valley and the Sea of Galilee lie c. 200 meters below sea level. Fertile soil, relatively abundant precipitation and a mild climate furnish good conditions for agriculture.

2. Society and Religion.

In Jesus' time Galilee was an intensively worked export area for wheat and olives, but also for wine. The fishing activity on the Sea of Galilee and the dried fish industry in the town of Magdala were of special significance (Josephus *J.W.* 2.21.4-5 §§608-10; 3.9.7 §§443-45). According to Josephus,* therefore, Galilee was a rich and heavily populated land (*J.W.* 3.3.2 §§42-43; *Vit.* 63 §325). The population may be placed at between two and three hundred thousand. Wealth was, however, very unevenly distributed. To be sure, alongside the rich upper class there was a somewhat-larger middle class than was common in ancient times. But the majority of the population was lower-class (tenant farmers, day laborers). In addition to religiously grounded rejection of the Roman ruling class, social need kindled a mood finding expression in revolutionary activity, especially from the second half of the A.D. 40s onward. The inflexibility and fearlessness of the Galileans was proverbial (Josephus *J.W.* 3.3.2 §41).

In NT times Jews comprised the vast majority of the Galilean population. The view that the area was at that time half-pagan is a modern scientific myth. Josephus refers repeatedly to the piety of the Galileans and their loyalty to the Torah (Malinowski). NT references to the large numbers of synagogues in Galilee confirm this (Mt 4:23; 9:35; Mk 1:39; Lk 4:14-15). These references are supported by archeological findings (*GBL* III.1507-12). Nevertheless, in addition to the native Aramaic there was very widespread knowledge of Greek; this is already evident from names like Andrew and Philip among Jesus' disciples* (*see* Languages of Palestine). Inhabitants of Jerusalem regarded Galilee as a backward locale (cf. Acts 2:7), peculiar first of all because of its dialect (Mt 26:73), in which laryngeal sounds were swallowed. Pharisaism (*see* Pharisee) attracted its adherents mostly from the middle class of the larger Galilean towns. As conservative country folk, however, most Galileans prior to A.D. 70 had reservations about the innovations of the pharisaical Halakah. Occasional disparaging remarks from rabbis indicate that the dislike was mutual (*y. Šabb.* 15d).

3. Jesus and Galilee.
Prior to his public ministry Jesus lived in Nazareth, located in Lower Galilee (Mt 2:22-23; 4:12-13; 13:54; Mk 6:1; Lk 4:16). He devoted the first portion of his activity to Galilee (Mt 4:23; Mk 1:14, 39; Lk 4:15-16), especially to the areas of Chorazin, Bethsaida and Capernaum on the northwest bank of the Sea of Galilee (Mt 11:21-24; Lk 10:13-15). Matthew was probably not the first to see in this the fulfillment of the OT prophecy of Isaiah 8:23—9:1 (Mt 4:12-17: Jesus himself performed by this kind of geographical concentration a kind of sign as a covert reference to his messianic claim; *see* Old Testament in the Gospels). Some Jewish circles expected the inbreaking of the end times to take place in the northern reaches of the promised land (Riesner *TynB,* 1987). Even if John's Gospel is reliable in reporting Jesus' pilgrimages to Jerusalem, the schematic outline of the Synoptics (first Galilee, then Jerusalem) is justified in locating Jesus' original emphasis in Galilee. Jesus' parables* also testify to an intensive Galilean ministry, for they generally reflect the specific conditions of rural Galilee, as J. Jeremias' work on the parables has effectively demonstrated. Since immediately after the first Easter early Christianity spread primarily into Hellenized cities, this is a remarkable indicator of the reliability of the Synoptic tradition.

After a time of preaching the gospel, Jesus had to recognize that a thoroughgoing conversion of the Galileans was not taking place. He therefore pronounced divine judgment on the chief centers of his Galilean ministry (Mt 11:21-24 par.). The logion found in Luke 13:1-3 belongs here too; it cannot serve as proof that *Galilean* was another term for *Zealot* in NT times. After this so-called Galilean crisis, and also due to the growing danger posed by the petty king Herod

Antipas (Mt 14:13; cf. Lk 13:31-33), Jesus withdrew with his most loyal disciples into regions outside Galilee's borders. These included the "hills of Tyre" (Mk 7:24) and the Decapolis (Mk 7:31), or Gaulanitis (Mk 8:27). This withdrawal results in tensions which reflect a situation that can be traced back to Hasmonean times and the relations between Galileans and the Gentiles of surrounding areas (Mk 7:24-30; cf. Mk 5:1-20). This is a clear indication that authentic local color is in evidence (Theissen). Both Matthew (Mt 28:16-20) and John (Jn 21) know of appearances of the resurrected (*see* Resurrection) Jesus in Galilee, and Mark must presuppose the same (Mk 14:28; 16:7). So Jewish-Christian churches may have formed in Galilee immediately after the first Easter (Acts 9:31; cf. Str-B I.159-60).

See also ARCHEOLOGY AND GEOGRAPHY.

BIBLIOGRAPHY. A. Alt, *Kleine Schriften* II (4th ed.; Munich: C. Kaiser, 1978) 361-455; W. Bösen, *Galiläa* (Stuttgart: KBW, 1985); G. Dalman, *The Words of Jesus* (Edinburgh: T. & T. Clark, 1902); S. Freyne, *Galilee from Alexander the Great to Hadrian* (Wilmington: M. Glazier, 1980); idem, *Galilee, Jesus, and the Gospels: Literary Approaches and Historical Investigations* (Philadelphia: Fortress, 1988); M. Hengel, *Die Zeloten* (2d ed.; Leiden: E. J. Brill, 1976); G. Kroll, *Auf den Spuren Jesu* (11th ed.; Leipzig: St. Benno, 1990); W. S. LaSor, "Galilee," *ISBE* 2.386-91; F. X. Malinowski, "Torah Tendencies in Galilean Judaism according to Flavius Josephus with Gospel Comparisons," *BTB* 10 (1980) 30-36; W. H. Mare, "Galilee," *The New International Dictionary of Biblical Archaeology,* ed. E. M. Blaicklock and R. K. Harrison (Grand Rapids: Zondervan, 1986) 202-3; E. M. Meyers, *The Cultural Setting of Galilee,* ANRW II 19/1 (1979) 686-702; B. Pixner, *Wege des Messias und Stätten der Urkirche* (Giessen: Grunnen, 1991); R. Riesner, "Galiläa," *GBL* (1987) 1.406-7; idem, "Bethany beyond the Jordan," *TynB* 38 (1987) 29-63; idem, *Jesus als Lehrer* (3d ed.; WUNT II/7; Tübingen: J. C. B. Mohr, 1988) 206-10; G. Theissen, *Lokalkolorit und Zeitgeschichte in den Evangelien* (NTOA 8; Göttingen: Vandenhoeck & Ruprecht, 1989) 63-84.

R. Riesner

GEHENNA. *See* HEAVEN AND HELL.

GENEALOGY
A genealogy is the record of a person's ancestral descent. While the word itself is not found in the Gospels (cf. 1 Tim 1:4; Tit 3:9; Heb 7:6), the only extended examples of genealogies in the NT are in Matthew and Luke and trace the ancestry of Jesus.

As Matthew's and Luke's infancy narratives differ

from each other, so do their genealogies: each has a different structure, (somewhat) different contents and different purposes, and each is located in a different place in their respective Gospels.

1. Matthew's Genealogy (Mt 1:1-17)
2. Luke's Genealogy (Lk 3:23-38)
3. A Comparison of the Genealogies

1. Matthew's Genealogy (Mt 1:1-17).

1.1. Structure and Placement. Matthew begins his Gospel with a genealogy of Jesus. The title of the genealogy in Matthew 1:1 (which some have argued to be the title of the whole Gospel) hints at its overall structure, naming "Jesus Christ, son of David, son of Abraham." The Greek *biblos geneseōs* (cf. Gen 2:4; 5:1 LXX) is literally "book of genesis" or "birth record." Matthew uses the same word (*genesis*) in Matthew 1:18, seeming to indicate that 1:18-25 is a closer look at the last portion of the genealogy. Similar to many OT genealogies, the cognate verb *gennaō* ("to beget," "to be the father of") occurs throughout the list. Matthew also uses the related noun *genea* ("generation") in his unique summary statement (Mt 1:17). This summary statement, forming a bracket (*inclusio*) with the genealogy's "title" (Mt 1:1), recaps its structure, naming Abraham,* David (*see* Son of David) and Christ.*

1.1.1. Three Fourteens. The most notable structural characteristic is pointed out by Matthew himself in 1:17: the names in the list are gathered into three groups of fourteen, with significant historical events placed at their junctures. Some have explained this structure as a mnemonic device, based on the number fourteen since it represents the numeric value of David's name in Hebrew (d = 4, v = 6, d = 4). Others see only Matthew's desire to make the list symmetrical with the fourteen names from Abraham to David. Some further explain the symmetry as having apocalyptic* significance: history is in order and the time of the Messiah has come.

Matthew's desire for symmetry is seen clearly by the fact that he has omitted the names of four Davidic kings from his second grouping: between Joram and Uzziah (Azariah) in Matthew 1:8 come Ahaziah, Jehoash (alias Joash) and Amaziah (1 Chron 3:11-12; 2 Kings 8:16—15:7), and between Josiah and Jeconiah (alias Jehoiachin) in Matthew 1:11 comes Eliakim (alias Jehoiakim, 1 Chron 3:15-16). It was not at all uncommon to drop names from a genealogical table (cf. e.g., Ezra 7:1-5; 1 Chron 6:3-15). The term *son* may refer to a grandson or a descendant even further removed (e.g., Mt 1:1), and the *all* of Matthew 1:17 is simply a reference to all of the names Matthew mentions, not a statement that his list is all-inclusive.

For Matthew's omission of four Davidic kings to be simply the result of error seems unlikely. Perhaps the best explanation for these selective omissions is that they were all cursed (note the curse of Ahab's family [1 Kings 21:21] extended to the house of Joram to the third or fourth generation [Ex 20:5 et al; cf. 2 Chron 22:7-9; 24:22-24; 25:14-28]; the curse of Jehoiakim [Jer 36:30]; Jeconiah (alias Coniah) was also recipient of such a curse [Jer 22:28-30] but may be included since he appears at a key point in history).

A close counting of Matthew's three groups, however, reveals the third to contain only thirteen sons (including Jesus), an apparent contradiction with Matthew 1:17. Some suggest that Jehoiakim, the omitted father of Jeconiah, is to be assumed; but such an assumption has no basis and, if accepted, would simply make the second group number fifteen, since Matthew is quite clear that Jeconiah—"at the Babylonian deportation"—is the dividing point between groups two and three (Mt 1:11-12). Some suggest placing Jeconiah first in group three and counting David twice—as fourteenth in group one and first in group two—since he is mentioned twice in Matthew 1:6. But if David is to be so counted, there is no reason not to double-count Jeconiah who is also mentioned twice (Mt 1:11-12). This would again result in fifteen sons in the second group.

Perhaps the solution lies in Matthew's departure from the normal "begat" formula at 1:16. There he uses the passive (*egennēthē*) rather than the active form of the verb with reference to Mary (*ex hēs*, "by whom"). Jesus is born of Mary (*see* Birth of Jesus) and, thus, Mary should be counted as one of the (now) fourteen names in group three. Mary is only one of five women in Matthew's genealogy; why should she alone be counted as a separate "generation"? Simply put, the other women shared with their husbands in the procreation of descendants and Matthew counts them and their husbands each as one generation. In the case of Mary and Joseph, however, Joseph clearly had no part in the biological procreation of Jesus; only Mary did. While Joseph is mentioned only as Mary's husband (cf. discussion of textual variants in commentaries), he is still counted since he did indeed serve as Jesus' earthly father. To the objection that Mary and Joseph were really of the same generation comes the simple response that, by his obvious omissions elsewhere, we know Matthew is not concerned with counting all the actual generations.

1.1.2. Other Details. Not only does Matthew omit names in the structuring of his genealogy, he also makes some unusual additions. Specifically, he mentions a brother, Zerah, two other sets of brothers and five women. Along with Judah, the phrase "and his brothers" occurs in Matthew 1:2, perhaps because it was customary to speak of all twelve patriarchs together or because descendants from all twelve tribes were Israelites and would have an equal interest in the Messiah. Zerah may be mentioned because he and Perez were twins and their birth story testifies of God's* reordering of the usual selection of heirs (Gen 38:27-30). Matthew 1:11 uses "and his brothers" again, this time with Jeconiah, perhaps to signal the end of the monarchy and its father-to-son succession of kings.

1.2. Purpose. Recent studies indicate that only rarely do ancient Semitic genealogies intend to preserve strict biological ancestry; rather, genealogies can serve a number of purposes (even simultaneously), such as: to show identity and duty, to demonstrate credentials for power and property, to structure history and to indicate one's character. The value of genealogies in the post-exilic Israelite society is illustrated in Ezra 2:62; 8:1 and Nehemiah 7:5. The omission of certain names in a list does not necessarily make the genealogy inaccurate nor deter it from accomplishing its purpose. Matthew's genealogy structures (Israelite) history in a memorable fashion and rehearses royal Davidic lineage leading up to the birth of Jesus. Beginning his account of Jesus' life with a genealogy is similar to the OT accounts of Noah and Abraham, which are both prefaced with genealogies (Gen 5:1-32 and 11:10-32, respectively).

1.2.1. "Son of David". Matthew's Gospel proclaims Jesus as king and from the beginning sets out to show that Jesus is heir to David's throne. Matthew seems preoccupied with David, mentioning him five times in 1:1-17 (seventeen times total in Matthew; note the titular use of "Son of David" in Mt 9:27; 12:23; 15:22; 20:30-31; 21:9, 15; cf. 22:42). Furthermore, Matthew adds the descriptive phrase "the king" only to David's name in 1:6, even though every name in the second group served in that capacity. The three parts of Matthew's genealogy can be viewed in terms of the house of David: the first group being its origin and rise to power, the second group being its decay and downfall, the third group being its quiet restoration by the promised "Son of David." The "king" theme is obvious in Matthew's infancy narrative in 2:1-12 (see Nolan).

Jesus was the fulfillment of the messianic expectation of Israel, and Matthew's genealogy presents his ancestral credentials. Indeed, in reporting the genealogy of "Jesus Christ," Matthew makes the title "Messiah" (Greek: *christos; see* Christ) part of Jesus' name (Mt 1:1).

1.2.2. Why the Five Women? Another unique feature of Matthew's genealogy is his inclusion of five women*: Tamar (Mt 1:3), Rahab (Mt 1:5), Ruth (Mt 1:5), [Bathsheba] the wife of Uriah (Mt 1:6) and Mary (Mt 1:16). The presence of women's names is taken by some as evidence that Matthew constructed the genealogy rather than reproduce it wholesale from his (OT and/or public) sources. Although not common, the appearance of women in genealogical tables was not unknown (e.g., Gen 22:20-24; 25:1-6; 36:1-14; 1 Chron 2:3-4, 18-20, 46-47; 3:1-9). It appears, however, that the women in Matthew's record do something more than specify clans or tribes by distinguishing children of wives from those of concubines. Several theories have developed for the purpose of the women in Matthew's genealogy. Mary's place in Matthew's list has been discussed above, and it seems likely that the other four women are to be taken as somehow foreshadowing Mary's unique role.

Jerome proposed that the four OT women were mentioned because they were regarded as terrible sinners so as to presage Jesus' role as savior. Such proposals are unlikely, however, for while Tamar was a seductress, Rahab a prostitute,* and Uriah's wife an adulteress, it is not at all convincing that Ruth was promiscuous. Ironically, rabbinic references to these women are often complimentary. Furthermore, Mary, the fifth woman in the list, does not fit into the same category (cf. Lk 1:28-30).

Luther held that Matthew included the four OT women because they were foreigners so as to show that Jesus, the Jewish Messiah, had ties to Gentiles as well. Tamar was an Aramean (*Jub.* 41:1), Rahab was a Canaanite (Josh 2:1-14), Ruth was a Moabite (Ruth 1:4) and Bathsheba—not directly called a foreigner (and perhaps for this reason not directly named)—was "the wife of Uriah" who was a Hittite (2 Sam 11:3). While somewhat promising—and perhaps a partial motive for Matthew—this theory seems insufficient, again because it does not include Mary, who was not a foreigner. Furthermore, it appears that early Judaism may well have accepted the four OT women as honored proselytes (Rahab and Ruth, *Sipre* Num 78; Rahab, *y Ber.* 2.7, *b. Meg.* 14b, *b. Zebaḥ.* 116b; Tamar, *b. Meg.* 10b, *b. Soṭa* 10a, cf. Gen. *Rab.* 85.11-12, *b. 'Abod. Zar.* 36b; Bathsheba, cf. *b. Sanh.* 107a; but see Ruth *Rab.* 8.1).

R. E. Brown recently put forth a plausible two-part explanation for the women in Matthew's genealogy. Each had something odd or extraordinary—even scandalous—about her union with her male partner, and each played an important role in God's plan (some by their own initiative and often at great personal risk). Tamar took scandalous initiative in playing a harlot with Judah, and yet God chose the offspring of that union to bring about the line of David. Rahab, although a harlot, played an important role in the conquest of the promised land (Josh 2:1-21; Heb 11:31; Jas 2:25). Ruth, a forbidden Moabite (Deut 23:3), was married to Boaz at her risky initiative (to Boaz's surprise), and their marriage eventuated the Davidic line (Ruth 3:6-14; 4:13-17). Uriah's wife (Bathsheba) had an adulterous affair with King David and yet, using her initiative, God saw to it that her son, Solomon, became heir to the throne (1 Kings 1:11-31). Even post-biblical Judaism saw the work of the Holy Spirit (see Holy Spirit) in these unusual unions. Divine intervention was certainly part of other marriages represented in Matthew's genealogy (e.g., overcoming the barrenness of Sarah, Rebekah and Rachel), but since those unions were relatively without scandal, they are not mentioned. The four OT women Matthew does mention are those who best foreshadow Mary's role as an "unwed mother" whom God uses in his divine plan. Thus, Matthew may well have included the OT women in his genealogy in order to head off criticism or slander regarding the unique circumstances in which Jesus was born. By their inclusion he is reminding his reader that God often works in unusual ways and through unlikely persons.

Somewhat similar to Brown, A.-J. Levine incorporates the central ideas of the first two theories into a new theory. Levine observes that each of the four OT women, while socioeconomically and religiously powerless, manifests faith when the men in their respective stories do not. Levine argues that the rest of the Gospel of Matthew continues contrasting the privileged, the elite and the leaders with the excluded, the despised and the poor (see Rich and Poor). Levine herself notes that Mary does not fit the pattern established by the four OT women. In Matthew, unlike his OT counterparts, Joseph is the one who acts in faith.* In this theory Mary and Joseph are contrasted with the examples of previous generations. The only textual evidence for such contrast, however, is the verb change in 1:16, and that applies only to Mary (see above).

M. D. Johnson has suggested another—perhaps more simple—purpose for the women in Matthew's genealogy. The four OT women had been the subject of controversy in Jewish circles concerned with messianic ancestry. By the end of the first century B.C. they were actually glorified in the Pharisaic (see Pharisees) tradition expecting a Davidic Messiah. Perhaps Matthew mentions them to show that, in every respect, Jesus fulfills the Pharisaic expectations

for the Messiah. This proposal fits with Matthew's ubiquitous theme of scriptural fulfillment and his argument against the Jewish leaders for their rejection of Jesus.

2. Luke's Genealogy (Lk 3:23-38).

2.1. Structure and Placement. Luke locates his genealogy of Jesus just after the account of Jesus' baptism and just before his temptation (see Temptation of Jesus) and public ministry. This placement resembles the genealogy of the tribes of Israel and of Moses* in Exodus 6:14-25. Unlike Matthew, Luke uses "the [son] of" formula (cf. 1 Chron 3:10-24; 6:16-30; Ezra 7:1-5; in Luke, however, the word *huios*, "son," occurs only once at the beginning and is assumed in the rest of the list). He also provides an unstructured, uninterrupted list of seventy-seven names (not counting Jesus), and traces Jesus' ancestry backward in time from Jesus through David through Abraham to "Adam, son of God" (see Ezra 7:1-5). Not only is Luke's list longer than Matthew's, it also contains more names where the two lists overlap: from Abraham to Jesus Matthew includes forty-two names and Luke fifty-six. While Matthew has several uncommon insertions throughout his list (e.g., women, brothers, etc.), Luke makes only one parenthetical remark at the beginning of his list about Jesus "being the son (as was supposed) of Joseph" (*ōn huios, hōs enomizeto, Iōsēph*, Lk 3:23; note also the article is missing before Joseph). Other than these few unique features, Luke's genealogy lacks the many peculiarities of Matthew's list and is a simple, linear genealogy.

2.2. Purpose. The very different structure and placement of Luke's genealogy from that of Matthew suggest different purposes as well. While Luke seems similarly concerned to show Jesus to be a descendant of David (Lk 1:27, 36, 69; 2:4; 3:31; 18:38-39; Acts 2:22-32; 13:22-23), he traces the messianic line through David's son Nathan instead of through Solomon.

2.2.1. "Son of Adam, Son of God." Even though no other known biblical or Jewish genealogy culminates in the naming of God, this is not to be used alone as an argument for Jesus' divinity any more than it is for the divinity of Joseph and the others in the list. It is noteworthy, however, that Luke traces Jesus' sonship all the way back to God immediately after his record of the voice from heaven declaring Jesus, "my beloved Son . . ." (Lk 3:22). Likewise, after the genealogy Luke records the temptation of Jesus during which the devil asks Jesus if he is the Son of God (Lk 4:3, 9; see Son of God). Interestingly, the only voices in Luke to declare Jesus to be the Son of God are angelic (Lk 1:32, 35; see Angels), demonic (Lk 4:41; 8:28; see

OT Genealogies	Matthew 1:1-17	Luke 3:23-28	OT Genealogies	Matthew 1:1-17	Luke 3:23-28
[God]		God	Jehoshaphat	Jehoshaphat	Eliakim
Adam		Adam	Joram	Joram	Jonam
Seth		Seth	Ahaziah		Joseph
Enosh		Enos	Joash		Judah
Kenan		Kenan	Amaziah		Simeon
Mahalalel		Mahalalel	Azariah	Uzziah (= Azariah)	Levi
Jared		Jared	Jotham	Jotham	Matthat
Enoch		Enoch	Ahaz	Ahaz	Jorim
Methuselah		Methuselah	Hezekiah	Hezekiah	Eliezer
Lamech		Lamech	Manasseh	Manasseh	Joshua
Noah		Noah	Amon	Amon	Er
Shem		Shem	Josiah	Josiah	Elmadam
Arpachshad		Arphaxad	Jehoiakim		Cosam
		Cainan	Jeconiah	Jeconiah	Addi
Shela		Shela	Pedaiah		Melchi
Eber		Heber	(the brother		Neri
Peleg		Peleg	of Shealtiel)	Shealtiel	Shealtiel
Reu		Reu	Zerubbabel	Zerubbabel	Zerubbabel
Serug		Serug			Rhesa
Nahor		Nahor		Abiud	Joanan
Terah		Terah			Joda
Abram	Abraham	Abraham		Eliakim	Josech
Isaac	Isaac	Isaac			Semein
Israel	Jacob	Jacob		Azor	Mattathias
Judah	Judah	Judah			Maath
Perez	Perez	Perez		Zadok	Naggai
Hezron	Hezron	Hezron			Hesli
Ram	Ram (*Aram*)	Ram (*Arni*)		Achim	Nahum
		Admin			Amos
Amminadab	Amminadab	Amminadab		Eliud	Mattathias
Nahshon	Nahshon	Nahshon			Joseph
Salma	Salmon	Salmon		Eleazar	Jannai
Boaz	Boaz	Boaz			Melchi
Obed	Obed	Obed		Matthan	Levi
Jesse	Jesse	Jesse			Matthat
David	David	David	Jacob		Heli
Solomon	Solomon	Nathan	Joseph	Joseph	Joseph
Rehoboam	Rehoboam	Mattatha	[Mary]		
Abijah	Abijah	Menna	Jesus		Jesus
Asa	Asa	Melea			

Demon, Devil, Satan), Satan's (Lk 4:3, 9) and God's (Lk 3:22; 9:35; cf. 22:70; Acts 9:20). While Jesus as the Son of God is more than a human ascription in Luke, his genealogy seems to underscore Jesus' humanity and his ancestral credentials as God's selected agent.

2.2.2. Universal Ministry. What is clear in Luke-Acts is that the Evangelist saw all peoples—Jews and Gentiles*—as invited into a relationship with God through Jesus. The Jews were the vehicle by which God brought the savior of all humanity into the world. Luke's point is not that all of humanity will be saved, but that salvation* is equally offered to all of humanity. By placing this all-inclusive genealogy at the beginning of Jesus' ministry, Luke indicates that the benefits of Jesus' ministry will be available to all (Lk 24:46-47; Acts 1:8; 13:46-48; 26:23; 28:28).

3. A Comparison of the Genealogies.

Many of the differences between the two NT genealogies have been noted above. This section is devoted to a more pictorial comparison of the genealogies, with their potential OT sources, and then a discussion of plausible solutions for apparent discrepancies between the two NT accounts.

3.1. The OT and the Two NT Genealogies. Both Matthew's and Luke's genealogies contain several variations in the spelling of names. These come from variations in the practice of translation (and/or transliteration) of the names from Hebrew to Greek, Greek to English, and Hebrew to English, as well as possible scribal errors and corrections. Some have tried to explain Matthew's rendering of kings Asa and Amon as Asaph (Mt 1:8) and Amos (Mt 1:10), respectively, as an attempt to bring a heritage of wisdom and prophecy to Jesus. It seems best to understand the Shealtiel and Zerubbabel of Luke's record not to be the same as those of Matthew's and the parallel OT records since all the names around them from David to Joseph in Luke's list are of different people (descendants of Nathan rather than Solomon). Levirate law is the best way to understand the unique attribution of Zerubbabel to Shealtiel's brother, Pedaiah, in the MT of 1 Chronicles 3:19 (cf. Ezra 3:2, 8; 5:2; Neh 12:1; Hag 1:1, 12, 14; 2:2, 23). Admin (*Admin*) in Luke 3:33 is often judged a corruption and duplication of Amminadab (*Aminadab*), but the acceptable practice of omission of names from genealogies must be remembered (likewise for Luke's "extra" mention of Cainan [*Kainam*] in Lk 3:36; cf. 3:37). Aram (*Aram*) in Matthew 1:4 and Arni (*Arni*) in Luke 3:33 are both taken to be variations of Ram in 1 Chronicles 2:9-10 (*rām* in MT; LXX has both *Aram* and *Ram;* Ruth 4:19 LXX has *Arann*). In table 1 the English spellings are those used in the NASB. The OT genealogies referenced are found in 1 Chronicles 1:1-28 (and Gen 5; 11:10-26); 2:1-15 (and Ruth 4:18-22) and 3:1-17.

3.2. Plausible Solutions to Discrepancies. Why do Matthew and Luke's genealogies differ from one another after David? Up to that point, the lists generally agree with the OT records. No biblical records exist, however, of the names between Zerubbabel and Joseph (nine in Matthew; eighteen in Luke), and, if granted that Luke's Shealtiel and Zerubbabel are different from those in Matthew's, no biblical record exists for the names after Nathan in Luke's list. These portions are problematic; but with this divergence after David, it becomes quite clear that Luke and Matthew are doing two different tasks. Four basic solutions have developed.

Julius Africanus (A.D. 170-245) proposed that both lists give Jesus' legal descent through Joseph: Matthew giving Joseph's natural lineage and Luke giving Joseph's legal lineage (cf. Eusebius *Hist. Eccl.* 1.7). Africanus explains that Jacob and Eli (alias Heli) were uterine brothers (born of the same mother by different fathers). When Eli died childless, Jacob took the widow as wife to raise up a child in the dead brother's name in accordance with levirate law (Deut 25:5-10). Thus, Joseph was Jacob's natural son (Matthew), but the legal heir to Eli (Luke). Some feel this solution asks for too many happy coincidences.

Several modern scholars also hold that both lists give Jesus' legal descent, reversing the roles of the genealogies in Africanus' solution: Matthew providing Joseph's legal lineage and Luke providing Joseph's

natural lineage. This solution struggles, however, against the more natural understanding of Matthew's "begat" formula as indicating a blood relationship between Jacob and Joseph (Mt 1:16).

Annius of Viterbo (c. A.D. 1490), followed by Martin Luther and many today, understand Matthew as giving Joseph's ancestry and Luke as giving Mary's. It suggests that Mary was the brother-less heir to Eli whose estate would then go to Mary's husband. Luke 3:23 is understood as saying, "Jesus, being the descendant (as it was supposed, through Joseph) of Heli." If this were the case, however, it is strange that Luke mentions Joseph instead of Mary, since he everywhere else focuses on Mary in his infancy narrative (Matthew focuses on Joseph). Note also that Luke has some concern to show Joseph to be of Davidic descent (Lk 1:27; 2:4). The Talmudic references to a Miriam, the daughter of "Eli" (*'ly bslym, y. ḥag.* 2.77d and *y. Sanh.* 6.23c) are most likely not references to Mary the mother of Jesus since R. Eleazar b. Jose, who claims to have witnessed this Miriam's torture, lived during the second century A.D.

Tertullian (*De car.* 20) and a few modern scholars have suggested that Matthew gives Mary's ancestry and Luke gives Joseph's. Such a solution again strains the natural understanding of Matthew's "begat" formula. Although H. A. Blair has proposed that the text of Matthew 1:16 be amended to read "Jacob begat Joseph, and Joseph begat Mary, of whom was born Jesus who is called the Christ," there is no textual evidence for such a reading.

While Matthew and Luke each have somewhat different purposes for a genealogy of Jesus, both affirm the virginal conception explicitly in their infancy narratives and implicitly in the genealogies as well. A final solution to the intricate issues involved in comparing the two lists may never be found, but enough is known to show that the apparent discrepancies are not insoluble. The most important things to learn from these genealogies are not the names of Jesus' grandfathers (Jacob or Eli or both), but that he is the messianic king by God's providential working (Matthew) and that he is God's agent, offering all the world salvation (Luke).

See also BIRTH OF JESUS; LUKE, GOSPEL OF; MATTHEW, GOSPEL OF; SON OF DAVID; SON OF GOD; WOMEN.

BIBLIOGRAPHY. R. E. Brown, *The Birth of the Messiah* (Garden City, NY: Doubleday, 1977); W. D. Davies, *The Setting of the Sermon on the Mount* (Cambridge: University Press, 1964); R. T. Hood, "The Genealogies of Jesus," in *Early Christian Origins*, ed. A. Wikgren (Chicago: Quadrangle, 1961) 1-15; M. D. Johnson, *The Purpose of Biblical Genealogies* (SNTSMS 8; 2d ed;

Cambridge: University Press, 1988); A.-J. Levine, *The Social and Ethnic Dimensions of Matthean Social History* (Lewiston, NY: Edwin Mellen, 1988); B. M. Nolan, *The Royal Son of God: The Christology of Matthew 1-2 in Its Gospel Setting* (OBO 23; Göttingen: Vandenhoeck & Ruprecht, 1979); R. L. Overstreet, "Difficulties of New Testament Genealogies," *GTJ* 2 (1981) 303-26; R. R. Wilson, "The Old Testament Genealogies in Recent Research," *JBL* 94 (1975) 169-89.

D. S. Huffman

GENEROSITY. *See* BENEFACTOR.

GENTILES

The Christian church* is largely Gentile, in spite of the facts that its origins are in a Jew (Jesus Christ), its first leaders were all Jews (the apostles*), and it grew out of Jewish soil (Palestine). Furthermore, the Gentile nature of the church is even more remarkable in light of the fact that Jesus, so far as we know, never intentionally entered Gentile lands for the sake of recruitment and evangelism though his practice is consistent with Paul's Gentile mission (see Scobie). Jesus' hesitations here are further enhanced by some early Christian scruples about ministering to Gentiles (cf. Acts 1-15). The Gentile nature of the church, then, requires historical explanation.

1. Judaism and the Gentiles
2. Jesus and the Gentiles
3. Mark and the Gentiles
4. Matthew and the Gentiles
5. Luke and the Gentiles
6. John and the Gentiles

1. Judaism and the Gentiles.
Scholars have often pointed to active, even aggressive, missionary activity on the part of Jews prior to Jesus and Paul as the impetus for the church becoming Gentile in orientation (but see McKnight). The relationship of Jews to Gentiles, however, was sensitive and at times volatile. On the one hand, there is abundant evidence that Jews *integrated themselves* into the way of the Gentiles so that Jewish religious ideas would be more comfortable in Gentile lands. Thus, Judaism* of the Second Temple period is known for (1) its emphasis on monotheistic universalism (that God* is truly one and God of all; cf. Sir. 13:15; 18:13; Philo *Decal.* 64); (2) its friendliness to Gentiles (Philo *Flacc.* 94); (3) its apparent permission to Gentiles to participate at various levels (e.g., synagogue* attendance) in Judaism (Josephus *J.W.* 2.412-16); (4) its participation in Hellenistic* education (Philo *Vit. Mos.* 1.23-24; Josephus *Ant.* 15.373; *J.W.* 1.602); and (5) its continual

intermarriage (Josephus *Ant.* 2:91-92). At times this assimilation resulted in overt apostasy (Philo *Spec. Leg.* 1:56-7; *Vit. Mos.* 2.193-208; Josephus *Ag. Ap.* 1:180).

Alongside this evidence of integration to Gentile ways, there exists evidence of *resistance* to Gentile ways. We observe (1) that Jews were intent on separation from Gentiles and paganism because of the Gentile sinfulness (e.g., in exclusive table fellowship* customs; *Ep. Arist.* 139, 151, 277; CD 11:15; 12:6, 9; see Esler, 73-86); (2) that they prohibited Gentile participation in the Temple* worship* (Josephus *J.W.* 1.152, 354); (3) that they exhorted Jews not to marry Gentiles (Ezra; Neh; Tob 1:9; 3:10; *T. Levi* 9:10; 14:6); (4) that they revolted violently when religious reforms were imposed on them (1 Macc); and (5) that the Gentiles would one day be judged and punished by God (Sir 36:1-17; *1 Enoch* 48:7-10; 63:1-12; 4 Ezra 7:37-9).

In spite of these negative comments, a persistent feature of Judaism is a positive attitude toward a true proselyte who would forsake paganism and become a Jew, both spiritually and nationally. A notable aspect of Jewish attitudes toward proselytism is that there would be a massive conversion of Gentiles on the Last Day (Tob 13:11; Sir 36:11-7; *1 Enoch* 48:4; *T. Simeon* 7:2; *Sib. Or.* 5:493-500; *2 Bar* 68:5). And this conversion is frequently portrayed in terms of Gentiles flocking to Zion at the last day, not in terms of Jewish missionaries reaching out to Gentiles (cf. Is 19:23; Zech 8:21; Jer 3:17). But it is not the case, as much of recent scholarship has demonstrated, that Judaism as a whole can be categorized as a missionary movement (see McKnight).

2. Jesus and the Gentiles.
Jesus' relationship to and teachings about Gentiles comprises several main lines of thinking. Although Jesus adopted the typical Jewish stance that Gentiles were sinners,* he certainly distanced himself from the normal view that Gentiles were doomed to punishment. Furthermore, Jesus evidently knew that his mission was essentially directed toward the Jews and that after his death (*see* Death of Jesus) and vindication a worldwide mission to the Gentiles would take place. However, such a position did not exclude exceptional Gentiles from experiencing the salvation* of the kingdom (*see* Kingdom of God) prior to that future.

2.1. Scholarship. Scholars disagree on the authenticity of many sayings of Jesus that deal with the Gentiles. In general, critical scholars who do not believe that Jesus Christ was raised from among the dead also do not believe he commanded a worldwide Gentile mission as reflected in Matthew 28:16-20. Many scholars argue that the negative aspersions made by

Jesus and the prohibition of mission to the Gentiles (e.g., Mt 18:17) are authentic and that the positive encounters are, at least in part, the product of early Christian imagination. Others argue that although Jesus was consistently particularistic in viewpoint (ministering to Jews alone), his message naturally was unfolded by the early church into a panoramic vision of Gentile inclusion—but Jesus did not unfold this message himself (Harnack, Bertholet, Goguel). A further development of this view is that Jesus, though he did not have a universal thrust to his ministry, had a vision of the future that included Gentile participation in God's kingdom (with differing nuances, Jeremias, Hahn, Hengel, Senior, Wilson, Scobie). A final view, the one expounded briefly below, is that Jesus' mission was limited to Israel* (during his life), but his intention was to use this particularistic concentration to launch a universal program of Gentile participation, whether at the end of history or immediately after the passion (with differing nuances, Sundkler, Bosch, Manson, Caird).

However difficult it is to synthesize coherently all the Gospel evidence regarding Jesus and the Gentiles, it must be said that "the Gentile factor" is a consistent aspect of the ministry and teaching of Jesus. Gentiles appear in various forms of Jesus' teachings and they come to him at different periods in his ministry and for different reasons. Since the OT predicts a large-scale Gentile participation in God's promises, and since Jesus announces the inaugural fulfillment of those promises in himself, it is reasonable to conclude that the Gentiles were a (even if small) factor in Jesus' kingdom ministry and teachings. It is reasonable to argue that Jesus' particularistic ministry was universalistic in thrust. Jesus inherited the notion of Gentiles streaming to Zion to worship on the holy mountain (as by centripetal force) and, after his resurrection, commanded his followers to move outward from Jerusalem to the nations for their salvation (as by centrifugal force).

2.2. Gentile Sinners. As a Jew, Jesus recognized that Gentiles were sinners: they greet only their friends (Mt 5:47), pursue material things (Mt 6:32), think God will answer long prayers* (Mt 6:7) and use power to their own advantage (Mk 10:42). On the clear difference between Jews and Gentiles, Jesus and the earliest Christians were agreed: Gentiles were sinners (Gal 2:15; Eph 2:12). This is not to say that Jews could not be sinners; rather, it was a given fact that Gentiles were sinners, and it was the exception when Jews were called "sinners."

2.3. Jesus' Hesitations. This conventional understanding of Gentiles has also been used to explain Jesus' direct prohibition of missionary work among Gentiles: "Go nowhere among the Gentiles, and enter no town of the Samaritans, but go rather to the lost sheep of the house of Israel" (Mt 10:5-6 RSV; *see* Shepherd and Sheep). At other times Jesus seemed hesitant to minister to Gentiles. At first Jesus attempted to put off the Syro-Phonoecian woman* (Mk 7:27; Mt 15:26), and he seemed to have misgivings about entering the Gentile centurion's home to heal his servant/son (Mt 8:7). Quite possibly the enigmatic saying of Jesus, "Do not give dogs what is holy" (Mt 7:6), ought to be understood as a similar prohibition against evangelizing the Gentiles. However, this hesitation to minister to Gentiles seems to be anchored in other ideas.

2.4. The Elimination of Vengeance. In contrast to much of Judaism at the time, Jesus' message eliminated the expectation of judgment* and vengeance on the Gentiles. In his inaugural sermon in Nazareth, Jesus stated that he was fulfilling the predictions of Isaiah 58 and 61 (*see* Jubilee). But Jesus stopped quoting Isaiah just prior to the prediction of "the day of the vengeance of our God" (Is 61:2). When John and James asked Jesus to pray for God's judgment to come down immediately on the Samaritan* villages that rejected Jesus, Jesus rebuked them and went on with his ministry (Lk 9:51-56). When Jesus described his ministry to John the Baptist's* disciples, he did so in the terms of the glorious deeds to be accomplished in the kingdom as described by Isaiah 35 and 61 (Lk 7:18-23). But in each of these passages the element of vengeance appears, yet Jesus omitted that element in his use of each passage. When the Roman military force put a Galilean to death, Jesus did not vow retaliation; he exhorted the Israelites to repent (Lk 13:1-5). For Jesus, God's vengeance is on sinners for sin, not on Gentiles for being Gentiles (Lk 18:7). Jesus' message was one of mercy and grace to the Gentiles and thereby stood in contrast with a prevailing expectation of Judaism.

2.5. Ministry to Gentiles. Even if Jesus aligned himself with Jewish castigations of Gentiles as sinners and even if he prohibited Gentile missions, Jesus attracted great numbers of Gentiles (Mk 3:7-12; Mt 15:29-31). Furthermore, he ministered to them and preached the Gospel to them (Mk 5:1-20; 7:24-30; Mt 8:5-13 par. Lk 7:1-10; Jn 4:1-42; 12:20-22). His distance from them is to be explained on a religious basis: He castigates sinners (both Gentiles and Jews) and invites all to repent, whether Jew or Gentile.

Jesus' encounters with Gentiles are instructive for understanding Jesus' relationship with Gentiles. Gentiles approached Jesus; he did not go out of his way to find them. Thus, the Gerasene demoniac (*see* Demon, Devil, Satan) came to Jesus (Mk 5:2), the centurion sought Jesus out (Mt 8:5; Lk 7:2-7), the Syro-Phonoecian woman searched for Jesus (Mk 7:25) and the Greeks asked to meet with Jesus (Jn 12:20-22). Only once does Jesus initiate a conversation with a non-Jew, the Samaritan woman (Jn 4:1-42). It is clear that Jesus did not initiate the Gentile mission by his own behavior. Jesus' ministry reflected the theme of the Gentiles coming to Israel for salvation (see McKnight). He focussed his efforts on the Jewish nation and its obligation to receive the Messiah (*see* Christ) of the final days. His emphasis on the Jews, however, did not exclude Gentile participation in the kingdom during his ministry. However, Gentile participation was nonetheless an exception and not the rule.

2.6. The Gentile Future. At several junctures in his ministry Jesus taught that many Gentiles would enter the kingdom of God and be accepted on equal footing with the Jews. For Jesus the present is the time of the Jews; the future is the time of the Gentiles. Though Jesus did not himself begin that mission to the Gentiles, he revealed that the future was wrapped-up with such a concern (Mk 13:10; 14:9; Jn 10:16). Jesus' followers would evangelize the nations as the light of the world (Mt 5:13-16; 24:14). In several parables Jesus alluded to Gentile participation in the kingdom of God (Mk 4:30-32; Mt 22:1-14; 25:31-46; Lk 11:29-32). Jesus seems to have predicted that many Gentiles would flock to Jerusalem and sit in fellowship with the patriarchs (Mt 8:11-12); on the other hand, some scholars argue that for Jesus this prediction concerned only diaspora Jews and not Gentiles (see Allison). In fact the Temple, Jesus says, "will be called a house of prayer for the nations" (Mk 11:17).

The instrument in the future salvation of the Gentiles is the preaching of the gospel* (of the kingdom) by the followers of Jesus, the church (Mk 13:10; 14:9). Jesus predicted that the end would not occur until the message of the kingdom was heard in the Gentile world (Mt 24:14). The lifestyle of the disciples would accompany this proclamation of the Gospel and exhort Gentiles to give glory* to God (Mt 5:13-16; Jn 17:18, 21). If the number seventy-two (or seventy) was chosen by Jesus because it symbolizes the number of Gentile nations (Gen 10; *1 Enoch* 89:59-67), then the mission of the Seventy-Two (or Seventy) might prefigure the Gentile mission (*see* Apostle). And the last words of Jesus, according to Matthew, were those commissioning the disciples of Jesus to make disciples throughout the entire world (Mt 28:16-20).

The future salvation of Gentiles stands in bold contrast to the future judgment on Israelites for rejecting God's Messiah. John the Baptist warned the Jews of this (Lk 3:7-10) and Jesus developed the same theme (Lk 13:28-30; Mt 21:33-46; Jn 8:31-47). The smoke and ashes of Jerusalem in A.D. 70 (*see* Destruction of Jerusalem) memorialized the judgment of God on unbelieving Judaism for its rejection of God's salvation (Mk 13; Lk 21; Mt 23:1—25:46).

Though each Evangelist passes on many of the traditions about Jesus, the relative role the Gentiles play in any particular Gospel is woven into the fabric of that Evangelist's theology. Whereas the Gentiles do not become a major theme in Mark, where they do appear, their role is related to Mark's major ideas (christology, ecclesiology and evangelism). Both Matthew and Luke lay emphasis on the salvation-historical role of the Gentiles. John's emphasis is the universal implications of Jesus as the savior. It is accurate to state that none of the Evangelists has a theology of the Gentiles.

3. Mark and the Gentiles.

For Mark the Gospel of Jesus Christ, God's Son, is not and cannot be understood until Jesus is comprehended as the crucified Messiah who, through that humiliation, brings salvation to humans. Interestingly, in Mark the first and only human to confess Jesus as God's Son after the crucifixion is a Gentile centurion (Mk 15:39).

Jesus' first priority is to the Jews; then the Gentiles can hear the gospel (7:27). Consequently, the new community of the followers of Jesus includes Gentiles who do and will respond to the gospel about God's Son in faith* (7:24-30; 13:9; 14:10). Accordingly, though many Jews will be excluded for unbelief (4:12; 6:1-6; 7:1-23; 11:12-19; 12:9; 15:11-15), Gentiles will be brought into God's fellowship because of faith (11:17; 12:1-12). Mark 14:28 and 16:7 may indicate the replacement of Galilee for Jerusalem as the locus of God's activity, though more probably a resurrection* appearance is in mind.

Occasionally Mark's literary designs seem to indicate an interest in the Gentiles. What Jesus does to Jews, he also does to Gentiles. As Jesus exorcises among the Jews (1:21-28), so he also exorcises among the Gentiles (5:1-20); as Jews believe, so also do Gentiles (5:18-20; 7:29-30); as the Jews see a feeding miracle* (6:30-44), so also the Gentiles see a similar revelation (8:1-13). Mark also betrays a Gentile (and liberating) concern when he states that food laws are not an end in themselves (7:19).

4. Matthew and the Gentiles.

Matthew both begins and ends his Gospel on a

Gentile note (1:1, Abraham* as the father of many nations; 1:1-17, the inclusion of several Gentile women; 28:16-20, the commissioning of the disciples* to go to the Gentiles). One of the major themes of Matthew's Gospel concerns the universal implications of the Gospel of the kingdom of heaven. Many stories and sayings about Gentiles are found only in Matthew (e.g., 1:1-17; 2:1-12; 6:7-8; 12:15-21; 22:1-14; 25:31-46).

4.1. The Kingdom and Universalism. The idea of the kingdom of God shows up in Matthew's emphasis on Gentile participation in the kingdom. Since God is King and ruler of all, and his Messiah is King of the Jews (2:2; 4:8-10, 12-16), those who submit to his reign are subjects of the kingdom of God. Some of these subjects are Gentiles (2:1-12; 12:15-21; 28:16-20).

4.2. Gentiles and Israel. The covenantal privilege of the Jews is forfeited through their rejection of the Messiah and, as a consequence, the church, which includes Gentiles, replaces Israel as God's people. Matthew brings these two notions to the fore: the rejection of Messiah by the Jews and salvation going to the Gentiles.

Jesus' priority is to offer the kingdom of God and its blessings to the Jews (10:5-6; 15:21-28), but he warns of judgment at hand if he is rejected (8:11-12; 10:13-15; 11:20-24). And he is rejected (9:1-17; 11:7-19; 12:1-14, 22-45). Consequently, Jesus predicts the destruction of Jerusalem as a judgment on unbelieving Judaism (23:1—25:46). But according to Matthew this idea of replacement has its precursor in Jewish history, throughout which Gentiles have come to the God of Israel for salvation (1:1-17; 12:38-42). Nationalism ends with Jesus (5:43-47; 17:24-27; 22:15-22). The final judgment then includes all nations and all are brought to the same bar of judgment to face the same requirements (25:31-46).

4.3. The Gentile Future and Salvation-History. During this time of ministry, Jesus also predicts a conversion of the Gentiles and their participation in the kingdom (5:13-16; 8:11-12; 10:18; 13:24-30, 36-43; 13:31-32; 21:33-46; 22:1-14; 24:9-14, 29-31; 26:6-13; 28:16-20). Unlike Mark, Matthew seems to make some clear distinctions between periods of history (cf. 21:33-46; 22:14): (1) the time of the Jewish privilege (Abraham to Jesus' mission, with a probationary extension until the destruction of Jerusalem); (2) the time of Gentile reception (after the passion of Jesus and especially after the destruction of Jerusalem); and (3) the time of consummation (*see* Matthew, Gospel of).

In this scheme there is an overlap between the time of the Jews and the time of the Gentiles. Gentiles begin to come to faith before and during Jesus' ministry and especially after his death through world evangel-

ization. And the Jews continue to hear about the kingdom of God for a generation after the passion. But with the coming of the destruction of Jerusalem, the time of the Jews seems all but over and the driving emphasis after A.D. 70 is the mission to the Gentiles.

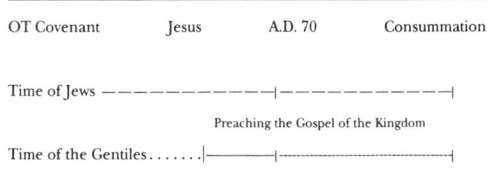

During the time of the Jews, Gentiles do come to faith and enter the kingdom, but only in an exceptional, anticipatory manner (2:1-12; 8:5-13; 15:21-28; 27:54). After the resurrection of Jesus the major focus of preaching shifts from an exclusive concern with the Jews, and after the destruction, preaching to the Gentiles becomes dominant (5:13-16; 8:11-12; 10:18; 21:33-46; 22:1-14; 24:9-14, 29-31; 26:6-13). Accordingly, Matthew places the universal mission of the church at the climax of his Gospel (28:16-20).

5. Luke and the Gentiles.

Along with Matthew, Luke emphasizes universal salvation, in part because it was his intention to write about the growth of the church throughout the Roman* Empire. Although some scholars have argued that Luke's Gospel is a Gospel of universalism to the extent that Luke generates the view that the Gentile mission began during Jesus' life, this seems to overstate the evidence. Indeed, S. G. Wilson contends that Luke does not have "any consistent theology of the Gentiles" (239). Consequently, though Luke does show traces of universalism, it is not a dominating theme in his Gospel. While the evidence for Luke's view of the Gentiles is essentially the same as that of Mark and Matthew, contemporary scholarship is actively debating the significance of the Gentiles in Luke-Acts (e.g., Esler; Marshall, 231-34).

Luke, like Matthew, begins and ends both of his works with an emphasis on the universal implications of the Gospel (Lk 1:48; 1:79; 2:14, 30-32; 3:6; 24:47; Acts 1:8; 28:28).

For Luke the inauguration of the kingdom of God in Jesus brings in its wake the salvation of persons throughout the entire world. Luke seems to operate with three periods of salvation history: (1) the time of Israel and promise; (2) the time of Jesus and the inauguration of salvation (the time of fulfillment); and (3) the time of the church and the worldwide proclamation of salvation. Even if one disagrees that this simple threefold breakdown of salvation-history accurately represents Luke, Gentile salvation seems to belong predominantly (but not exclusively) to the time of the church and hence it is described in some detail in Luke's second volume, the Acts of the Apostles.

5.1. The Time of Fulfillment in the Savior. The births of John the Baptist and Jesus inaugurate the fulfillment of the promises given to Israel. In turning many of the children of Israel to the Lord, John preaches the good news of salvation (1:16-17, 68, 73, 77). The angel, Mary and others see the same purposes fulfilled in God's salvific work in Jesus (1:32-33, 54-55; 2:25, 34, 38; 19:9). But the salvation that comes in Jesus is not readily accepted by Israel (2:34; 3:8; 13:6-9; 16:19-31; 19:41-48), and so the time of fulfillment also ushers in salvation for the Gentiles (2:32; 20:9-19). A distinctive emphasis of Luke is that the salvation that extends to the Gentiles is the fulfillment of God's eternal will expressed originally to Israel.

Furthermore, in contact with this line of promise and fulfillment is the occasional connection Luke makes between the Gentiles and the Holy Spirit.* Simeon's predictions about the Messiah being a light to the Gentiles are inspired by the Holy Spirit (2:27, 32), and Jesus' announcement in the synagogue at Nazareth associates the Holy Spirit (4:18) with Gentiles (4:26-27). Finally, the mission charge given by Jesus to the disciples to evangelize the world is made possible by the power of God's Spirit (24:44-49).

The actual mission to the Gentiles is the result of the commands given by the risen Lord. Whether seen in the final words of Jesus prior to his ascension* (24:44-49) or in the various commands throughout Acts (Acts 1:8; 9:15-16; 22:6-11, 17-21; 26:12-23), the impetus for the Gentile mission is provided according to Luke by the words of the risen Lord.

5.2. The Future Salvation of the Gentiles. For Luke, as for Matthew, the salvation of the Gentiles belongs to the time after Jesus' passion and vindication. There remains here, as seen in Mark, Matthew and Paul, the priority of Israel (1:16, 68; Acts 3:26; 13:46). Though Simeon predicts that the little Jewish boy will be the Messiah of Israel and a source of great division within Israel, he also prophesies that this Messiah will be "a light of revelation to the Gentiles" (2:32), a ministry that does not take place until the time of the church (Acts). The number of those from among the Gentiles who are saved reverses Jewish expectations: while Jews are not permitted entry into eternal fellowship with God, the Gentiles are (13:28-29). In parabolic form Jesus predicts a Gentile mission that follows the rejection of the Messiah by Israel (14:15-24). After his

resurrection Jesus exhorts his disciples to preach repentance and forgiveness (*see* Forgiveness of Sins) in his name to all nations, beginning from Jerusalem (24:47-48; Acts 1:8).

Having emphasized the future salvation of the Gentiles, Luke knows of some exceptions, notably the centurion of Capernaum (7:1-10), the demoniac (8:26-39) and some Samaritans (17:16; cf. 10:33). Luke, more than Matthew and Mark, seems to tone down the presence of the ministry of Jesus in non-Jewish territory (cf. Luke's omission of the tradition found in Mk 6:45; 7:24-31; 8:27). Evidently, Luke is trying to show more clearly that the salvation of the Gentiles is not something that gets underway during the time of Jesus. As some have observed, this may be part of Luke's understanding of the geographical plan for the growth of the church (Acts 1:8).

Having emphasized rejection by many Jews and the consequent turning to the Gentiles, Luke speaks also of a temporal limitation to Gentile salvation. According to Luke 21:24 Jerusalem will be sacked by Gentiles and "trodden down by the Gentiles, until the times of the Gentiles are fulfilled." This suggests either that (1) the city will be dominated for only a limited time and that during this period Gentiles will be converted to the Messiah (cf. Dan 8:13-14; 12:5-13; Mk 13:20; Rom 11:25-27) or that (2) the mission to the Gentiles will run its predestined course, and God will then turn once more to work with the nation of Israel.

5.3. The Laudable Piety of Gentiles. A notable feature in Luke-Acts is the piety of the Gentiles and the unacceptable. This theme begins in the OT (4:16-30) and continues through the time of Jesus and the church. A comparison of Luke's account of the centurion with Matthew's, a story evidently derived from Q,* reveals several distinctive Lukan emphases. In particular, Luke dramatizes the piety of the centurion. The elders* who are sent by the centurion to obtain mercy from Jesus state that the centurion "is worthy to have you do this for him, for he loves our nation, and he built us our synagogue" (7:4-5). Luke describes the centurion Cornelius in similar terms (Acts 10:2, 22; cf. also 8:27). All of this is part of Luke's favorable description of those unacceptable by Jewish standards (4:18; 5:27; 7:11-17, 36-50; 15:11-32; 19:2-10).

6. John and the Gentiles.

Though John's treatment of the Gentiles is essentially consistent with that of the Synoptics, his overall theology is markedly different. It is this theology that gives different emphases to his presentation of the Gentiles and the theme of universalism. If the emphasis of the Synoptics is along the plane of salvation-history, whereby the Gentiles occupy a time subsequent to Jesus' passion and resurrection, the emphasis in John is on the present time as a time of Jesus' revelation to the world. It is not that John does not contain a salvation-historical perspective (12:20-23); rather, his emphasis is elsewhere.

6.1. Jesus, the Savior of the World. A major emphasis of John is that Jesus is the "light* of the world,"* an idea that both coheres with the Synoptic tradition and yet gives it fuller interpretation. For John the term "world" can denote the world of the universe (in contrast to the heavenly world, 1:9; 3:17), the world of human beings (12:19) and the world that stands in sin and either remains opposed to the revelation of truth* in Jesus Christ or believes in the Son for eternal life (1:10-12; 7:7; 15:18-19; 17:1-26). This latter sense is in mind where Jesus is described as savior. Accordingly, God loves the world (3:16) and sends his Son to be the savior of the world (3:17; 4:42; 6:33, 51; 11:27; 12:20-23) as well as its judge (9:39). Thus, the Word is "the light of all people" (1:4; cf. also 1:9; 3:17-21; 11:9; 12:46-47) who has come into this world from the Father to reveal the Father and divine truth to those who believe (16:28; 17:18; 18:37). Jesus is the Lamb of God (*see* Lamb of God) who bears the sins of the world (1:29; 11:51-52). And Jesus' sacrifice is beneficial for believing Jews as well (11:49-51; 18:14).

In another set of contrasts, Jesus is the light of the world (8:12; 9:5) who brings the light of revelation to a world of darkness (3:16-21; 12:33-36). Jesus also is portrayed as the Good Shepherd (*see* Shepherd and Sheep) who has a flock that is larger than Israel (10:11, 16) or as the bread* of God that comes down from heaven to give life to the world (6:33, 51).

John's description of Jesus as the savior of the world is distinctive. Though it remains consistent with the universal implications of Jesus' ministry in the Synoptics, it is nonetheless more christologically focused. If the Synoptics emphasize the universal dimensions of God's kingdom inaugurated in Jesus, John emphasizes that Jesus Christ, the Word (*see* Logos) from the Father, is the light of the world who brings salvation to that world through his death (12:20-23). Thus John is completely consistent with the Synoptic tradition in showing that the Gentile mission does not belong to the earthly life of Jesus; rather, the mission to the Gentiles is future (12:20-23; 16:8-10; 17:18, 20-23; 20:21-23).

6.2. The Gentile Mission and the Holy Spirit. Like Luke (24:48-49; Acts 1:8), John connects the Gentile mission with the Holy Spirit. Thus when the Holy Spirit (the Paraclete; *see* Holy Spirit) comes, he will convince the world of sin, righteousness and judgment (16:8-10; *see*

Justice, Righteousness). After his resurrection Jesus imparts his peace,* commissions the disciples and breathes the Holy Spirit on them (20:21-23; cf. 15:26-27). And yet this mission is the mission of Jesus (17:18; 20:21). These texts show the integral connection between the mission of Jesus, the Holy Spirit and the disciples' mission to the world (Burge).

6.3. The Gentiles, the Jews and Faith. An unremitting evaluation of the Jews as unbelieving punctuates John's Gospel (e.g., 1:11; 2:13-22; 4:19-26; 12:37-43), a theme generated by the opposition the Jews maintain toward Jesus (e.g., 5:16, 18, 39-47; 7:1-5, 25-36). The consequence of Jewish rejection of Jesus is judgment (3:18; 5:25-30; 12:48). In effect a secondary consequence of rejection is that eternal life is granted to the Gentiles (12:19). In John's Gospel salvation is by faith and this salvation is granted to anyone who believes, whether Jew or Gentile (3:36; 4:39; 8:24). Thus Jewish unbelief amounts to a turning to the Gentiles (8:31-59; 10:16). Though the Gentile mission is still future, John's presentation of the necessity of faith and the unbelief of the Jews places all people on the same level. The effect is a presentation of Jesus as the savior of the world.

6.4. Gentile Encounters. The first Gentile Jesus encounters in John's Gospel is the Samaritan woman. She learns that Jesus, the living water, brings a spiritual salvation that is acquired by faith. Moreover, even though this salvation is from the Jews (4:1-42), it breaks down racial and religious boundaries. Immediately following his encounter with the Samaritan woman, Jesus heals an official's son (4:46-54). If this is a variant report of the centurion's servant found in Matthew 8:5-12 and Luke 7:1-10, then the official is a Gentile. The Johannine Jesus' only other encounter with Gentiles is with the Greeks (12:20-22). As if to highlight the interest of the Greeks as a sign that the eschatological day of salvation for Gentiles has arrived, Jesus says, "The hour has come for the Son of man to be glorified" (12:23).

See also ANTI-SEMITISM; JUDAISM.

BIBLIOGRAPHY. D. C. Allison, Jr., "Who Will Come from East and West? Observations on Matt. 8:11-12; Luke 13:28-29," *IBS* 11 (1989) 158-70; A. Bertholet, *Die Stellung der Israeliten und der Juden zu den Fremden* (Freiburg/Leipzig: J. C. B. Mohr, 1896); D. Bosch, *Die Heidenmission in der Zukunftsschau Jesu: Eine Untersuchung zur Eschatologie der synoptischen Evangelien* (ATANT 36; Zürich: Zwingli, 1959); G. Burge, *The Anointed Community: The Holy Spirit in the Johannine Tradition* (Grand Rapids: Eerdmans, 1987); G. B. Caird, *Jesus and the Jewish Nation* (London: Athlone, 1965); P. F. Esler, *Community and Gospel in Luke-Acts:*

The Social and Political Motivations of Lucan Theology (SNTSMS 57; Cambridge: University Press, 1987); M. Coguel, "Jésus et les origines de l'universalisme chrétien," *RHPR* 12 (1932) 193-211; F. Hahn, *Mission in the New Testament* (SBT 47; London: SCM, 1981); A. von Harnack, *The Mission and Expansion of Christianity in the First Three Centuries* (2 vols.; London: Williams and Norgate, 1904-5); M. Hengel, "The Origins of the Christian Mission," in *Between Jesus and Paul: Studies in the Earliest History of Christianity* (Philadelphia: Fortress, 1983) 48-64; J. Jeremias, *Jesus' Promise to the Nations* (SBT 24; London: SCM, 1958); T. W. Manson, *Only to the House of Israel? Jesus and the Non-Jew* (Philadelphia: Fortress, [1954] 1964); I. H. Marshall, *Luke: Historian and Theologian* (2d ed.; Grand Rapids: Zondervan, 1989); S. McKnight, *A Light among the Gentiles: Jewish Missionary Activity in the Second Temple Period* (Minneapolis: Fortress, 1991); R. F. O' Toole, *The Unity of Luke's Theology: An Analysis of Luke-Acts* (GNS 9; Wilmington, DE: Michael Glazier, 1984); C. H. H. Scobie, "Jesus or Paul? The Origin of the Universal Mission of the Christian Church," in *From Jesus to Paul: Studies in Honour of Francis Wright Beare*, ed. P. Richardson and J. C. Hurd (Waterloo, Ont.: Wilfred Laurier University, 1984) 47-60; D. Senior and C. Stuhlmueller, *The Biblical Foundations for Mission* (Maryknoll, N.Y.: Orbis, 1983); B. Sundkler, "Jésus et les païens," *RHPR* 16 (1936) 462-99; R. Walker, *Die Heilsgeschichte im ersten Evangelium* (FRLANT 91; Göttingen: Vandenhoeck & Ruprecht, 1967); S. Wilson, *The Gentiles and the Gentile Mission in Luke-Acts* (SNTSMS 23; Cambridge: University Press, 1973). S. McKnight

GEOGRAPHY. See Archeology and Geography.

GETHSEMANE

According to the Gospels of Matthew and Mark, the site where Jesus prayed in lonely anguish before his arrest (Mt 26:36; Mk 14:32). The word is a transliteration of the Hebrew/Aramaic *gaṭ šᵉmenè*, "oil press," presumably used here to refer to an olive grove on the slope of the Mount of Olives (Mt 26:30; Mk 14:26). John 18:1 speaks of a garden across the Kidron Valley from the city of Jerusalem. Luke places the incident on the Mount of Olives. All refer to the same general location. According to the Synoptic Gospels, it was here, immediately following his vigil, that Jesus was publicly betrayed by Judas* and arrested.

1. Gethsemane in the Gospels of Matthew and Mark
2. The Mount of Olives in the Gospel of Luke
3. The Gethsemane Tradition in the Gospel of John and in the Epistle to the Hebrews
4. The Historicity of the Gethsemane Tradition

1. Gethsemane in the Gospels of Matthew and Mark.

Because the First and Second Evangelists present the Gethsemane episode in similar ways, Matthew 26:36-46 and Mark 14:32-42 will be treated together. Matthew's sole dependence on the Second Gospel for this story is widely assumed.

Over the past seventy years, the prehistory of the Markan version of the Gethsemane story has been subjected to extravagant analyses (see Feldmeier, 65-140; Holleran, 107-45). Many scholars, struck by the duplication of almost every detail in the Markan story, have been persuaded that two primitive sources underlie Mark 14:32-42 (e.g., Barbour, Holleran, Stanley). On the other hand, the thesis that the Markan story constitutes a very old, pre-Markan traditional unit has recently found new support, though some have come to regard the scene as a Markan creation almost in its entirety. The debate has led to little by way of a critical consensus. However, the number of independent witnesses to this tradition (see below) suggests a complex tradition-history (*see* Tradition Criticism).

Central to Matthew's and Mark's accounts is the concrete unfolding of the divine plan anticipated in the earlier passion predictions (*see* Predictions of Jesus' Passion and Resurrection). Although human agents are involved in these fateful events (e.g., Judas Iscariot, Pontius Pilate,* the Jewish leaders), God is the primary actor. This interpretation comes to the fore above all in the portrait of Jesus' prayer* as a process of discerning and submitting to God's will. It is also present in the reference to the "cup," signifying divine judgment (cf. Mk 10:38-39 par. Mt 20:22-23; Mk 14:27 par. Mt 26:31; Ps 75:8; Is 51:17, 22; Jer 25:15-38; Ezek 23:31-34); and to the "hour," signifying God's appointed time for Jesus' passion.

Related to this theme, though also emphasizing Jesus' obedience, is the conjunction of Mark's Son of man* and Son of God* christologies in this pericope. "Son of man" has been central to Mark's presentation of Jesus' anticipated suffering (8:31; 9:12, 31; 10:33-34): "the Son of man *will be* delivered up." Now, "the Son of man *is* delivered up into the hands of sinners" (14:41). Jesus' status as Son of God was affirmed by the Evangelist in 1:1, then proclaimed by God at Jesus' baptism* (1:10-11) and Transfiguration* (9:7). In addressing his prayer to "*Abba,** Father" (14:36), Jesus acknowledges his intimate, Father-Son relationship with God. Significantly, this affirmation comes to the fore in the face of suffering and death. Hence, "Son of God" must be understood in Mark against the backdrop of the "must" (*dei*) of the suffering of the Son of man. It is as God's obedient Son that Jesus, Son of man, embraces death, God's will (*see* Death of Jesus).

Closely related to the theme of Jesus' obedience is that of discipleship* failure. Throughout the Second Gospel, the disciples* have demonstrated their incapacity to grasp the identity of Jesus and the implications of God's redemptive plan (e.g., 8:32; 9:32; 10:32). Now, as Jesus struggles with God's will, the disciples evidence their continued lack of understanding by their inability to stay awake (and by their subsequent abandonment, 14:50-52).

Jesus' acknowledged intimacy with God ("*Abba,*" 14:36) highlights a further, central theme, one which gives clearer definition to the intended meaning of the "cup" in 14:36. As Feldmeier has seen, Gethsemane functions as the crisis in the passion narrative, indeed in the life of the Son of God. Here, for the first time, Jesus experiences the silence of God, a divine estrangement that comes to expression finally in Jesus' cry of derelliction from the cross (15:34). Gethsemane, then, does not so much demonstrate Jesus' anguish in the face of death as his fear of being abandoned by God. The humanity of Jesus could hardly be emphasized more acutely.

Noting Matthew's wording of Jesus' command to his disciples in 26:36, "Sit here *(autou)*, while I go yonder and pray," some interpreters raise the possibility that Matthew is consciously alluding to the story of Abraham* and Isaac (cf. Gen 22:5). There, in a story widely regarded for its portrait of profound faith, the servants of Abraham are given similar instructions. With this allusion Jesus' faith in the midst of his anguish is emphasized all the more.

Both Mark and Matthew underscore the paraenetic value of Jesus' words and actions in this scene. In his prayer Jesus exemplifies the appropriate response to eschatological crisis. Jesus' command "Watch!" recalls the content of his final discourse in both Gospels. In Matthew's Gospel disciples are to keep watch—like the owner of the house (24:42-44) and the wise maidens (25:13). In Mark the connection is even more accentuated (cf. 13:5, 9, 23, 33-37), especially by the following highly suggestive verbal parallels:

13:36: *elthōn . . . heurē . . . katheudontas*
(coming . . . he finds . . . sleeping)
14:37: *erchetai . . . heuriskei . . . katheudontas*
(he comes . . . he finds . . . sleeping)
14:40: *elthōn . . . heuren . . . katheudontas*
(coming . . . he found . . . sleeping)

Clearly, the passion of Jesus is the eschatological turning-point in redemptive history. At the same time,

disciples, having been found sleeping at this moment, are encouraged by this story "to stay on guard" in anticipation of the final, eschatological woes (*see* Apocalyptic Teaching; Eschatology).

Finally, we may observe that Jesus' prayer in both Gospels contains allusions that contribute to its interpretation. Thus, the Markan version suggests conceptual borrowing from selected psalmic laments—such as Psalms 42:9-11; 55:4-8; 61:1-3. Matthew 26:37 actually recasts Mark 14:33 (substituting *lypeō* [sorrowful] for Mark's *ekthambeō* [greatly disturbed]) to achieve a more direct reference to Psalm 42:5. For both evangelists the result is a typological portrait of Jesus as the Suffering Righteous One. Matthew's rendition evidences an allusion of another sort, presenting Jesus' prayer in terms that closely parallel the Lord's Prayer (cf. 6:10; 26:42; *see* Prayer). In this way Jesus proves himself a living example of his own teaching.

2. The Mount of Olives in the Gospel of Luke.

Before discussing the significance of Luke 22:39-46 for the Third Gospel, we must address some important text- and source-critical questions (*see* Textual Criticism; Synoptic Problem).

2.1. The Originality of Luke 22:43-44. The presence or absence of these two verses is crucial to an interpretation of the scene as a whole. The textual evidence is ambiguous, though it is clear that the omission of these verses from so many and diverse witnesses (e.g., P[69] [apparently], P[5], א [first corrector], A, B, T, W) could not have been accidental. Some modern interpreters (see Fitzmyer, 1443-4; RSV) exclude these verses, noting their uniqueness within the Synoptic tradition, judging them as inappropriate to their context and suggesting they were added later for the purpose of Christian instruction. Others, however, observe the impressive Lukan character of these verses, which speaks for their originality to the Third Gospel. In addition to (1) the inclusion of characteristic Lukan vocabulary (Green 1988, 56-57), one may also observe (2) the Lukan emphasis on the appearance of an angel* (e.g., 1:11, 26; 2:13, 15; Acts 5:19; 7:30; 8:26; 10:3; 12:7), (3) Luke's interest in simile ("his sweat was like drops of blood," v. 44; cf. e.g., 3:22; 10:18; 11:44; 22:31) and (4) Luke's fondness for physical manifestations (like sweat) accompanying extramundane events (e.g., 1:20; 3:22; Acts 2:2-3; 9:18). These data, along with the fact that the presence of these verses is of a piece with Luke's interpretation of this scene as a whole, point clearly to the originality of 22:43-44.

Moreover, it is not difficult to imagine a rationale

for the early exclusion of these verses in the manuscript tradition. The portrait of Jesus contained therein—human, agonizing, needful, requiring angelic support—would have been problematic to some (cf. *Gos. Nic.* 20; Green 1988, 56). Accordingly, they may have been dropped for doctrinal reasons. There is thus good reason for taking these verses as original to Luke.

2.2. The Source-Critical Question. In writing this story, was Luke dependent only on the Markan parallel (Mk 14:26, 32-42) or did he draw on additional material? In recent years, the tendency has been to highlight Luke's creative use of his Markan source and so to downplay Luke's use of non-Markan tradition (whether oral or written). (On this scene, see Fitzmyer, 1436-9: Luke's story is "a stark abridgment of the Marcan account.") In fact, much of the Lukan account of Jesus' prayer of anguish can be explained with reference to Luke's creative use of Mark.

Four lines of evidence suggest a general conclusion of this sort is overly simplistic, however. First, Luke's linguistic and syntactical deviations from Mark are not easily explicable with reference only to Luke's creative hand. Second, Luke's deletion of Mark 14:33-34 from his account is most easily explained by Luke's aversion to doublets—that is, by his decision to incorporate the record of Jesus' anguish in verses 43-44 instead of, rather than in addition to, the similar Markan material. Third, in verse 42 Luke reports the content of Jesus' prayer with language from the Lord's Prayer as found in Matthew 6:10: "not my will but your will be done." This language is missing from Luke's version of the Lord's Prayer (11:2-4) and has no parallel in Mark. Finally, the presence of verses 43-44 (no parallel in Mark) speaks for Luke's use of non-Markan tradition. Thus, while in all probability Luke was dependent on the Markan account, he appears to have also had access to a second, roughly parallel tradition (see Green 1988, 53-8; Holleran, 170-98; Taylor, 69-72).

2.3. The Significance of This Scene for Luke. Primary to Luke's understanding of this scene is the role of Jesus as a model for his disciples. This motif comes onto the stage initially with the use of *akoloutheō*, a term suggestive of "following as a disciple," in verse 39. Structurally, the scene is bracketed by the phrases "Pray that you may not enter into temptation" (v. 40) and "Rise and pray that you might not enter into temptation" (v. 46). As Jesus prays, they are to pray; as he rises, so should they (vv. 45-46). Thus, for Luke this story has a paraenetic edge: the way to stand the test—intense, submissive prayer—is exemplified by Jesus. This theme is not unique to this passage in Luke's passion account; elsewhere we find the disciples "with" Jesus (22:24-30; 23:26-27, 49) in a way not found in Mark (cf. 14:50-52, for which Luke offers no parallel).

Also of profound importance to Luke's scene is the way in which every aspect of the story is subordinated to the divine necessity of Jesus' suffering and his unreserved submission to the will of God. This emphasis is accomplished by Luke's economy of style, namely the brevity with which he presents the scene. The mention of only one time of prayer (compare the threefold pattern in Mt and Mk) highlights Jesus' firm resolve to be obedient to God. Indeed, just as Jesus' instructions to the disciples frame this story, so his communion with God (agonizing prayer and reception of divine aid) stands as its centerpoint. Again, these motifs are found throughout Luke's narrative (on the necessity [*dei*] of Jesus' death, see, e.g., 22:19-20, 22, 37; 24:26; on his acceptance of his fate, see, e.g., 22:15-18; 23:27-31, 46).

Luke is also interested in portraying this scene as a cosmic battle. This is evident in his use of *peirasmos* in verses 40 and 46, a term denoting struggle with Satan (cf. 4:13; 8:13); and in his reference to angelic assistance. In fact, Jesus' passion as a whole is marked by supernatural conflict (e.g., 22:3, 28, 31, 53), though the present scene clearly constitutes the critical point in this struggle.

More generally, a number of interpreters have understood Luke's presentation of this episode as a central element of Luke's portrayal of Jesus' passion as a martyrdom (see Barbour). The case for this interpretation is strengthened by the observation that martyr-tales regularly present their martyrs as exemplary figures. On the other hand, Luke's portrait of Jesus in agonizing prayer not only lacks parallels in the martyrological literature, where death is happily embraced, but stands in clear tension with that literature.

Another reading of this story proposes that Luke is especially concerned to further his portrait of Jesus as the Isaianic Servant of the Lord (Green 1986). According to this view, the necessity of Jesus' suffering, his having been chosen for this fate, his willing obedience and his reception of strengthening aid through a divine messenger are to be read against their background in the Isaianic Servant texts (especially Is 41:10; 42:1, 6; 49:5; 50:5-9; 52:13—53:12). That is, Luke's portrayal of Jesus in prayer on the Mount of Olives demonstrates that it was to fulfill his role as Servant of the Lord that Jesus had to suffer.

3. The Gethsemane Tradition in the Gospel of John and in Hebrews.
The Fourth Evangelist narrates no Gethsemane

episode as such, but he manifests his knowledge of this tradition. In 18:1-2 he places Jesus and his disciples in a garden on the far side of the Kidron Valley, and in 18:11 Jesus makes reference to the "cup" given him by God, a cup he must drink. Both details are paralleled in the Synoptic Gethsemane tradition. Furthermore, John 17:1-18 portrays Jesus praying immediately before his arrest.

More significant in this context, however, is the prayer of Jesus in 12:27-29. The prayer itself, "Father, save me from this hour" (v. 27), has been variously punctuated—as a hypothetical question (RSV, NIV) or as a petition (NEB). Given the note of anguish in verse 27a (see Ps 6:3-4; 42:6; Mk 14:34), Jesus' experience of turmoil is evident either way. Here, a number of important Johannine motifs converge: Jesus' obedience to his mission and thus to God; the "hour" as the time of Jesus' death, the climax of the work for which the Son was sent; and the transparent interpretation of Jesus' death as glorification and exaltation (cf. 12:23, 32; *see* Death of Jesus; Glory).

In his attempt to demonstrate Christ's qualifications for the high priesthood, the author of Hebrews utilizes material reminiscent of the Gethsemane tradition. This connection is suggested generally by the observation that the Gethsemane story is the only account in our canonical Gospels that comes close to this portrayal of Jesus praying with "strong crying and tears to the one who was able to save him." In addition, we may observe (1) the connection between Luke 22:43-44; John 12:27-29; and Hebrews 5:7: he prayed and was heard; (2) that John 12:27 and Hebrews 5:7 each speak of God's saving Jesus; and (3) that both Luke 22:44 and Hebrews 5:7 mention his tears. Clearly, Hebrews 5:7 represents a very early Christian reflection on the Gethsemane story.

4. The Historicity of the Gethsemane Tradition.
Many have doubted the historicity of the story of Jesus' struggle in prayer in Gethsemane, citing as primary evidence the impossibility of obtaining eyewitness testimony from sleeping disciples. On this basis, some have gone on to suggest a derivation from martyrological literature, while others hold that the scene originated in early reflection on the OT (especially Ps 22:20; 31:9-10, 22; 42:5-6, 11; 43:5; 69:1-2). As previously noted (2.3), this scene actually stands in contrast to the martyr-tales, whose protagonists gladly go to their deaths. The role of the OT in providing language and imagery for theological interpretation of the story should not be downplayed, but no convincing argument has been put forth to

support the notion that the psalms actually gave birth to this tradition (Barbour; Dunn, 18-19).

Given the number of independent testimonies to this episode (Matthew-Mark, Luke, John, Hebrews), the antiquity of the Gethsemane tradition is beyond question. Its fundamental historicity is supported by additional data. First, the story underscores so profoundly the weakness of Jesus that it is unlikely to have been created out of nothing. Second, like the subsequent departure of the disciples recorded in Matthew and Mark, the scandalous failure of the disciples in this scene is unlikely to have originated in the earliest tradition. On the other hand, some have argued that the sleeping of the disciples more likely serves theological interests than Jesus' prayer, for it highlights the clarity of Jesus' understanding of his task over against the disciples' persistent dullness. This line of argumentation supports even more the historicity of Jesus' prayer of anguish. Finally, we may note the appearance of "Abba" in Mark 14:36, the use of which takes us "back to the very speech and language of Jesus himself" (Dunn, 20).

See also DEATH OF JESUS; PASSION NARRATIVE; TRIAL OF JESUS.

BIBLIOGRAPHY. R. S. Barbour, "Gethsemane in the Tradition of the Passion," *NTS* 16 (1969-70) 231-51; J. D. G. Dunn, *Jesus and the Spirit: A Study of the Religious and Charismatic Experience of Jesus and the First Christians as Reflected in the New Testament* (Philadelphia: Westminster, 1975); R. Feldmeier, *Die Krisis des Gottessohnes: Die Gethsemaneerzählung als Schlüssel der Markuspassion* (WUNT 2:21; Tübingen: J.C.B. Mohr [Paul Siebeck], 1987); J. A. Fitzmyer, S.J., *The Gospel according to Luke*, vol. 2 (AB 28A; Garden City, NY: Doubleday, 1985); J. B. Green, *The Death of Jesus: Tradition and Interpretation in the Passion Narrative* (WUNT 2:33; Tübingen: J.C.B. Mohr [Paul Siebeck], 1988); idem, "Jesus on the Mount of Olives (Luke 22:39-46): Tradition and Theology," *JSNT* 26 (1986) 29-48; J. W. Holleran, *The Synoptic Gethsemane: A Critical Study* (Rome: Gregorian University, 1973); D. Senior, C.P., *The Passion of Jesus in the Gospel of Matthew* (Wilmington, DE: Michael Glazier, 1985); D. M. Stanley, S.J., *Jesus in Gethsemane: The Early Church Reflects on the Suffering of Jesus* (New York/Ramsey: Paulist, 1980); V. Taylor, *The Passion Narrative of St. Luke: A Critical and Historical Investigation* (SNTSMS 19; Cambridge: University Press, 1982).

J. B. Green

GLORY

The Gospels' use of "glory" (Gk *doxa, doxazein*) presupposes the specialized theological background of the OT. Few concepts in antiquity were more important than honor, distinction, esteem and glory. The classical word *doxa* originally meant "opinion" (derived from *dokeō*), or a well-informed reputation or renown. Related closely to *timē* ("honor"), it referred to a distinguished quality that was readily evident in a person.

1. Old Testament Background
2. Synoptic Gospels
3. John

1. Old Testament Background.

The LXX literally gave a technical meaning to *doxa*. Here *doxa* came to mean honor intended for God,* or the majesty and eminence which radiated from God's own being. This use of glory originated from the Hebrew concept of *kābôd*. God himself could not be seen, but his radiance—as that of a fire or light— could be apprehended (Ex 16:7; Deut 5:24). His *kābôd* was the visible manifestation of his power. Thus his glory was apparent at the Tabernacle (Ex 40:34) and later within Solomon's Temple (1 Kings 8:11). This presence was the special privilege of Israel,* but it could be lost such as when the sons of Eli lost the ark to the Philistines in 1 Samuel 4. "Ichabod" (1 Sam 4:21-22), the name of Eli's new grandson, means "no glory." God's *kābôd* had departed. To enjoy the presence of God was to enjoy his glory. In the last days the glory of Yahweh would come to earth visibly and convert the Gentiles (Ezek 39:21). It is for this reason that Simeon in Luke 2:29-32 offers his hymn of praise and consolation: he had witnessed the arrival of this glory (*see* Simeon's Song). In Christ the glory of God was apparent in Israel once more.

2. Synoptic Gospels.

The Gospel writers follow the use of the LXX when they employ *doxa*. There is initially a mundane or routine use describing the grandeur of some earthly thing, such as the kingdom of the world* (Mt 4:8; Lk 4:5-6) or Solomon's splendor (Mt 6:29; Lk 12:27). Here the meaning approximates time or honor. Similarly people may seek to "glorify" one another (Mt 6:2; Lk 14:10; Jn 5:44; 8:50; 12:43; etc.), but this too refers to honor or giving regard. This is likely the meaning of Lk 4:15: Jesus is given high honor by all in Galilee.*

But a second use is by far more prominent. Consistent with the OT, *doxa* also describes God or the things of God. The glory of the Lord appears again and again in the birth narratives (Lk 2:9, 14, 32; *see* Birth of Jesus) and in the Transfiguration* account (Lk 9:31-32), suggesting that it is God himself at work in the coming of Christ. Appropriately, people are directed to give God glory or praise (Mt 9:8; 15:31; Mk 2:12; Lk 2:20; 5:25-26; 7:16; 13:13; 17:5; 18:43; 23:47; etc.). This merely echoes so much of the literature of the OT (*kābôd*, Ps 22:23; 50:15; Is 66:5).

The more significant theological development is the way the Synoptic Gospels portray the glory of Jesus Christ. Since Christ is associated with God it is natural for him to reflect God's glory. However, this is not clearly indicated for Christ's earthly ministry. The Synoptics consistently speak of the glory of Christ in future eschatological language. The request of James and John in Mark 10:37 is instructive. Here Christ's glory will be possessed in heaven following his death—and this is what the brothers seek to enjoy. Matthew curiously alters Christ's "glory" to "kingdom" in his parallel story (Mt 20:21) in order to construct what seems to be the primary theological force of *doxa*. The glory of Christ will appear only when the Son of man* returns at the end of the age (Mt 16:27; 19:28; 24:30; 25:31; Mk 8:38; 10:37; 13:26; Lk 9:26; 21:27). Luke 24:26 explains that the divine glory of Christ had to await the threshold of death ("Was it not necessary that the Christ should suffer these things and enter into his glory?" cf. Acts 2:32-33; 3:13). Then, having assumed a glorious position with God the Father, Christ would return emanating this glory (*see* Apocalyptic Teaching; Eschatology).

The only exception to this Synoptic pattern is Luke's Transfiguration account (9:28-36). Luke develops the parallels to the Exodus story of Mt. Sinai (*see* Mountain and Wilderness) beyond Mark when he adds that Moses* and Elijah* appeared in glory (9:31). The *kābôd* of Yahweh was present. But in addition, Jesus also is seen "in his glory" (9:32). For Luke, Jesus' eschatological glory was not just future, but could be assumed under unique circumstances during his life on earth.

3. John.

This brings us to what is by all accounts a most unexpected development in the Fourth Gospel. Glory is never associated with any futurist Son of man saying. John vigorously advances the theme into the earthly ministry of Jesus. He employs the *doxa/doxazein* word-group forty-one times (compared with Mt eleven times, Mk four times, Lk twenty-two times). The OT notion of the glory of God still persists (5:44; 7:18; 9:24; 11:4, 40; 12:43; etc.), but the primary focus is on the glory of Christ. We are told that Christ dwelt in glory before the Incarnation* (12:41; 17:5, 24), and that during his earthly career this glory was still visible (1:14; 8:54; 11:4; 13:32; 17:1, 5, 10, 22). The Synoptic description has Jesus' glory still veiled, but the Johannine christology makes it primary: "We have beheld his glory" (1:14); "It is my father who glorifies me" (8:54).

This is consonant with the view offered elsewhere in the NT, where the divinity of the Son of God* is inseparable from his glory (1 Cor 2:8; 2 Cor 4:4; Eph 3:16; Heb 1:3; Jas 2:1). When the NT writers reached the conclusion that Christ was eternally one with God, it was left to John to sketch these results into the Messiah's earthly life. Jesus Christ was showing *doxa* when he revealed the Father through his work. This is especially true for his signs (2:11). But this is also true of Christ's death (*see* Death of Jesus) which is one more revelation of this glory. In John crucifixion is described as glorification (7:39; 12:16, 23; 13:31; cf. 21:19). It is not just a transport to a realm of glory (as in the Synoptics). It is an unveiling, a fresh radiating of God showing himself once more at work.

This interest in the present glory of the Johannine Christ helps us interpret the Fourth Gospel's repeated use of the term "light."* Since glory is pictured as a radiant quality, light and glory often appear together in the OT (see Is 60:1-3; 58:8 LXX) and in Hellenistic religion (*see* Hellenism). John employs "light" (*phōs*) twenty-three times (triple that of any other Gospel) to express the Hebraic thought that in bringing God's glory, so too Christ ushers a divine light into the world (1:4-9; 3:19; 8:12; 12:46).

See also ESCHATOLOGY; DEATH OF JESUS; LIGHT; TRANSFIGURATION.

BIBLIOGRAPHY. S. Aalen, "Glory," *NIDNTT* 2.44-52; R. E. Brown, *The Gospel according to John, I-XII* (AB; Garden City, NY: Doubleday, 1966) 503-4; G. B. Caird, "The Glory of God in the Fourth Gospel," *NTS* 15 (1968-69) 265-77; G. H. Davies, "Glory," *IDB* 2.401-3; C. H. Dodd, *Interpretation of the Fourth Gospel* (Cambridge: University Press, 1953) 201-13; E. F. Harrison, "Glory," *ISBE* 2.477-83; D. Hill, "The Request of the Zebedee Sons and the Johannine *DOXA* Theme," *NTS* 13 (1966-67) 281-85; G. Von Rad, "δοκέω κτλ," *TDNT* II.232-55. G. M. Burge

GNOSTIC GOSPELS. *See* CANON; GOSPELS (APOCRYPHAL).

GOD

In the canonical Gospels, "God" (*theos*) is the traditional deity of ancient Israel referred to in the OT; and, as everywhere in the NT, the exclusivist monotheism of ancient Jewish piety, which involves a rejection of all other deities, is the religious orientation adapted to early Christian devotion to Jesus. In the Gospels God is the ultimate authority* and the ultimate good. The Gospels are narratives about Jesus, but his whole significance rests on the claim that God is the source of Jesus' authority, the one whose kingdom (*see* Kingdom of God) he truly proclaims. That is, though the Gospels are undeniably christological narratives, they are also deeply God-centered. Their whole thrust is that the one whose story they narrate represents God's new overture of revelation, fulfillment and salvation.* In this they agree; but there are also interesting differences in emphasis among the Evangelists in the ways they refer to God, which reflect their varying purposes, situations and destinations (*see* Redaction Criticism), and may also indicate theological development across the decades that separate them from one another. Also, the Gospels allow us with some confidence to describe important features of Jesus' own experience of, and teaching about, God. Jesus' own special sense of God as his Father, to whom he was called to respond as God's obedient Son, probably formed a central feature of Jesus' mission and is reflected in the Gospels.

1. God in the Gospels: General Matters
2. God in the Individual Gospels
3. God in Jesus' Experience and Ministry

1. God in the Gospels: General Matters.
Understandably, scholarly study of the Gospels has tended to focus on their presentation of Jesus. But though the Gospels are narratives of Jesus' ministry and are explicitly concerned with presenting his significance (*see* Gospel [Genre]), they are on a deeper level dominated by God, whom Jesus proclaims and represents as Son (*see* Son of God) and Christ.* The Gospels affirm as valid the OT witness to the unique God of Israel.* Thus, for example, God is the creator who instituted marriage (Mt 19:4-6) and gave divine commandments* through Moses (Mk 7:5-13). But the Evangelists also proffer new information about God's purposes, which are now advanced significantly and definitively in Jesus; and so the Gospels are theological narratives.

1.1. Terminology. (Exact figures for the frequency of the following terms dealt with may vary, depending upon decisions about textual variants and in some cases on the interpretation of particular passages; but the basic patterns of comparative frequencies are not affected.) In addition to the actual term "God" (*theos*), which is used frequently in each Gospel (48 times in Mark, 51 in Matthew, 122 in Luke, 73 in John), the term "Lord"* (*kyrios*) is used with reference to God numerous times as well (9 times in Mark, 18 in Matthew, 37 in Luke, 5 in John; the term is also used frequently with reference to Jesus, e.g., Mt 7:21; 8:2;

15:22; Mk 11:3). Many of the uses of *kyrios* for God are in citations of the OT and in expressions derived from the OT (e.g., "angel* of the Lord"), and in these passages the term functions as the Greek translation of the Hebrew OT name for God, Yahweh. For example, twenty-five of the uses of *kyrios* for God in Luke are in the first two chapters, where the phrasing is so heavily influenced by the OT.

The third frequently used term for God is "Father" (*patēr*), doubtless the most familiar term for God in Christian tradition and also perhaps the most theologically significant title for God in the NT. Unlike the other terms for God already mentioned—without exception in the Synoptics, and with only a few exceptions in John—"Father" as a title for God appears only in the sayings attributed to Jesus (the Johannine exceptions are in editorial remarks by the Evangelist in 1:14, 18, a saying of Philip in 14:8 and the crowd's claim in 8:41).

But it must be noted that this usage is very unevenly distributed in the Gospels: 4 instances in Mark, 44 in Matthew, 15 in Luke, and 109 in John. An even more remarkable variation appears if one considers only the occurrences of the absolute form, "the Father": once in Mark, twice in Matthew, three times in Luke, seventy-three times in John. Jeremias (1967, 29-35) pointed to such figures as indications of "a growing tendency to introduce the title 'Father' for God into the sayings of Jesus" in the early church (e.g., cf. Mk 3:35 par. Mt 12:50; Mk 14:25 par. Mt 26:29; Mk 10:40 par. Mt 20:23); and he cogently argued that the Gospel of John was particularly reflective of, and influential in, the title "*the* Father" becoming "the name of God in Christendom."

In addition to John's considerably more frequent use of the absolute form "the Father," we should observe another interesting distinguishing feature in John's use of "Father" for God. In the Synoptics the divine title "Father" is restricted to Jesus' prayers* and his sayings addressed to followers and to audiences made up of followers and the crowds. When speaking to others (e.g., Jewish religious leaders, Satan), Jesus uses *theos* or *kyrios*. In John, however, Jesus refers to God as "Father" in sayings addressed to an assortment of characters: (e.g.) the Samaritan* woman* (4:21-23) and hostile critics (e.g., 5:17-47; 6:25-58; 8:12-30, 34-38). Indeed, in John, Jesus' reference to God as his "Father" often functions as the occasion for offense to be taken by critics. That is, "Father," which in the Synoptics denotes the situation of Jesus and his disciples* ("your Father") before God, takes on a sharpened *christological* function in John as a sometimes polemical term intended primarily to express

the exalted status of Jesus. In keeping with this, in the Johannine writings only Jesus is "son" (*huios*) of God; Jesus' followers are called God's "children" (*tekna*), a term lacking the connotation of special rights and status implied by "son."

In addition to "God," "Lord" and "Father," there are also indirect forms of speech used to refer to God. There is Jesus' demand of the Jerusalem priests* whether the baptism* ministry of John was "from Heaven*" (Mk 11:30 par. Mt 21:25 and Lk 20:4), the high priest's reference to God as "the Blessed" in the interrogation of Jesus (Mk 14:61; cf. Mt 26:63) and Jesus' reference to God as "the Power" in his reply (Mk 14:62 par. Mt 26:64; cf. Lk 22:69). The several uses of "Most High" in Luke (1:32, 35, 76; 6:35) are to be included as well, though this particular expression is directly indebted to OT usage (e.g., Dan 4:17, 24-25). All these reverential circumlocutions reflect the profound reverence for God characteristic of the Jewish background of Jesus and the early Christian movement.

Moreover, in those passages where certain events "must" (*dei*) take place to advance or fulfill the redemptive plan, God is to be understood as the one whose purposes make the events necessary (e.g., Mk 8:31; 9:11; 13:7, 10). There are also a number of occurrences of what has been called the divine passive, where actions are described in passive verb forms with no subject explicitly mentioned but where God is to be understood as the subject of the verbs (e.g., Mk 3:28, "all sins will be forgiven [by God]"; Mt 7:1-2, 7). Still another type of indirect reference to God is found in all three Synoptic accounts of Jesus' baptism, where the divine acclamation of Jesus is attributed simply to "a voice from heaven" (Mk 1:11 par. Mt 3:17 and Lk 3:22). Likewise, the Transfiguration* accounts attribute the divine acknowledgement of Jesus to "a voice from the cloud" (Mk 9:7 par. Mt 17:5 and Lk 9:35). In both scenes the context requires God to be understood as the one who speaks.

1.2. God's Role. In all the Gospels God is the enveloping presence, the overarching character in the narratives, who, though often referred to by others and only occasionally named as acting directly within the stories, gives the accounts, the characters and actions their whole significance (*see* Literary Criticism). The entire Gospel narratives in fact consist in the portrayal of God's purpose, and all characters and events in the narratives receive their evaluation and meaning in the light of their relationship to this divine purpose.

Several major examples of Gospel characters will suffice to illustrate this. The Baptist (*see* John the

Baptist) is the forerunner of Jesus the Christ, but this in turn depends on the claim that the Baptist was sent by God (e.g., Jn 1:6; Mk 11:27-33). The crowds acclaim Jesus because they see in him some manifestation of what they believe to be God's saving purposes (e.g., Mk 2:12; 11:8-10). It is those who do the will of God who are Jesus' true family, his followers (Mk 3:35 par. Mt 12:50 and Lk 8:21). The Sadducees (*see* Judaism) oppose Jesus because they are blind to God's power and purposes (Mk 12:24 par. Mt 22:29). Indeed, the ultimate theological irony of the Gospel stories is that the rejection of Jesus by the Jewish religious leaders constitutes the rejection of God's Son, the divinely appointed Christ. They accuse Jesus of blasphemy* (Mk 14:64 par. Mt 26:65 and Lk 22:71) but are themselves guilty of opposing God in the name of God.

Even the significance of Jesus, the explicitly central character in the Gospels, wholly has to do with his relationship to God. Jesus' message announces and interprets the kingdom of God (e.g., Mk 1:14-15, and the parables in Mk 4 par. Mt 13). The demons (*see* Demon, Devil, Satan) acclaim Jesus in various expressions that all denote his status before God (e.g., "the Holy One of God," Mk 1:24 par. Lk 4:34; "Son of God," Mk 3:11 par. Lk 4:41; Mk 5:7 par. Mt 8:29 and Lk 8:28). Jesus surely claims authority, but either implicitly (e.g., Mk 2:10) or explicitly (e.g., Jn 3:35; 5:19-23; 12:49) indicates that this authority is from God and is intended to promote God's purpose and glory.* In all the Gospels Jesus is the Messiah (Christ), and is often referred to in royal terms (e.g., Mt 21:1-11; *see* Christ). But this must be set in the context of Jesus' proclamation of the kingdom of God, which makes God as "king" one of the most pervasive, though often implicit, images in the Gospels. Thus, God is the high king whom Jesus the Messiah represents in a unique way as a kind of vice-gerent.

Even in John, where we have the most explicitly exalted view of Christ's person presented, everything rests on the claim that Jesus has come from God (e.g., 5:43; 6:57; 8:18; 9:33), Jesus' glorification depends upon God's act (e.g., 17:1). Jesus' exaltation is completed by ascending to God (13:1-3; 14:28), and the claim that Jesus is "the way, the truth, and the life" has to do with the special access he provides to God (14:6).

God is not often directly mentioned as actor in Gospel scenes, but those where God is the actor are of major significance for the larger narratives. The Synoptic scenes of Jesus' baptism and Transfiguration are crucial and function to confirm authoritatively for the readers Jesus' significance as God's Son. In both these scenes, uniquely in the Synoptics, God's voice sounds clearly above the din of conflicting views

about Jesus that come from other characters in the narratives. In other words God functions as the ultimate authority and his acclamations of Jesus are (in literary-critical terms) the reliable voice in the narratives by which all other voices are to be judged. Likewise, in the crucifixion scenes (*see* Death of Jesus) God's rending of the Temple veil (an important example of the divine passive verb form mentioned earlier, Mk 15:38 par. Mt 27:51 and Lk 23:45) functions as divine confirmation of Jesus' significance and of the negative view to be taken of the Temple* leadership who have rejected Jesus.

In John there are no baptismal and Transfiguration acclamations by God. The only time God's voice sounds is in 12:28, giving assurance to Jesus (and the readers) that God will "glorify [God's] name" through Jesus. John emphasizes, however, that Jesus' "works," including the "signs" which figure so prominently, are to be seen as acts of God which confirm Jesus' significance (5:36; cf. 3:2). For example, in the climactic sign, the raising of Lazarus,* Jesus' prayer in 11:41-42 explicitly makes the miracle a divine answer to Jesus' appeal. Through these deeds and through the Scriptures, "the Father has borne witness" to Jesus, making Jesus' status hang entirely on God.

2. God in the Individual Gospels.
The individual Evangelists employ terminology and references to God in varying ways that reflect something of their individual literary purposes and style and that may also reflect their respective situations in the history of first-century Christianity.

2.1. Mark. In light of the commonly accepted view that Mark is the earliest Gospel (*see* Synoptic Problem), the references to God in this narrative are especially important historically (see Donahue). Of particular interest are the four references to God as "Father" (always in sayings of Jesus: 8:38; 11:25; 13:32; 14:36). In Mark 8:38 Jesus warns that "the Son of man" (*see* Son of Man) will be manifested "in the glory of his Father," stating implicitly Mark's christological affirmation which permeates the whole of his Gospel: Jesus, the Son of man of present lowly circumstance, is the Son of God.

The expression "your Father . . . who is in heaven" in Mark 11:25 may give a glimpse of the background to Matthew's familiar way of referring to God (unless one accepts Sparks's proposal that Mk 11:25 is not an original part of Mark).

In Mark 13:32 two things should be noted. First, Jesus, "the Son," does not know the time of the end; only God, "the Father," knows (reflecting a subordination of Jesus to God that Luke appears to have softened by omitting the statement from his form of the eschatological discourse in Lk 21). Second, this statement gives us the earliest Gospel use of the absolute forms "the Father" and "the Son" found elsewhere in the Synoptics only in Jesus' much-studied exclamation in Matthew 11:25-27 and its parallel in Luke 10:21-22, but frequent in John.

Finally, Mark 14:36 is unique in the Gospels in attributing to Jesus use of the term *abba,* used elsewhere in the NT only by Paul in references to early Christian prayer (Rom 8:15; Gal 4:6). It is remarkable that Mark (like Paul) in addressing Greek-speaking (and largely Gentile*) readers used this Aramaic expression alongside the Greek term for "father" *(patēr).* Writing for Christians acquainted with *abba* as a loan-word associated with prayer (as Paul's references indicate), Mark probably intended his readers to see in Jesus' Gethsemane* prayer both a precedent for their own submission to God and a reminder that the basis of their filial relationship to God lay in Jesus' own.

The role of God in the Synoptics as the ultimate reliable voice who confirms Jesus' status as Son of God is especially important in Mark (as Kingsbury has shown), where the question of Jesus' transcendent identity is such an important matter about which the human characters are obtuse, and various voices (e.g., disciples, crowds, Herod,* religious leaders, demons) all make conflicting and inadequate attempts to label Jesus. In an expression unique in the Gospels, Mark 1:14 has Jesus preaching "the gospel* of God" (a phrase found elsewhere in the NT only in Paul; e.g., Rom 1:1; 15:16), which reflects a theocentric emphasis in Mark's presentation of Jesus' message. And Donahue's examination of Jesus' replies to questions in Mark 12 shows that Jesus' teaching here is "theistic rather than explicitly christological" (581), presenting God as the one to whom true allegiance belongs (above what Caesar may claim, 12:13-17), the life-giving deity who will raise the dead and vindicate those who trust in him (12:18-27), and the one God to be loved wholly, whose service is the basis for all other duty (12:28-34). This theistic emphasis is also implicit in Jesus' reply to the demand that he identify his authority (11:27-33), for the readers know that Heaven sent the Baptist to prepare the way for Jesus and that Jesus' authority comes from God also.

2.2. Matthew. Among the Synoptics Matthew uses "Father" for God by far the most frequently (44 times), and is the only Synoptic "which refers to God as *patēr* nearly as often as it uses *theos*" (Mowery, 24). As the term appears only on the lips of Jesus, it is not found in Matthew until Jesus begins his teaching ministry in chapter five. The majority of instances of the divine title "Father" (mainly in the forms "your/our heavenly Father," e.g., 5:16, 45; 6:1, 9) in Matthew are in passages where Jesus gives directions and assurances about various duties and situations of discipleship (e.g., seventeen instances in the Sermon on the Mount). Matthew sometimes replaced *theos* in Markan material with references to God as "Father" (Mt 12:50 par. Mk 3:35; Mt 26:29 par. Mk 14:25). And in the Q* material comparison of Matthew's version of sayings with Luke's suggests that Matthew (or his tradition?) has a special fondness for the paternal image of God (cf. e.g., Mt 5:45 par. Lk 6:35; Mt 6:26 par. Lk 12:24; Mt 10:29-32 par. Lk 12:6-8).

Matthew is noted for the large amount of Jesus' teachings about God it contains, in which Jesus memorably emphasizes God's all-seeing, all-knowing faithfulness. Some of this material is unique to Matthew, such as 6:1-8 ("your Father" will reward genuine piety, will hear modest prayer* "in secret" and "knows what you need before you ask him"); and other teaching material is paralleled in Luke (Q material), such as 6:25-34 and its parallel Luke 12:22-32 (God who feeds the birds and "clothes the grass of the field" will provide all you need), and 7:7-11 and its parallel Luke 11:9-13 (approach "your heavenly Father" confidently, for God is much more ready to give "good things" to his own than are earthly fathers). As Donahue observed, Matthew presents a very " 'human' and immediate picture of God" (567).

Both Matthew and Luke are structurally distinguished from Mark by a nativity account (*see* Birth of Jesus) in which God is directly active. In both cases God's actions are described in language influenced by the OT narratives of his works. In Matthew, Mary is "with child of the Holy Spirit" (of God), and an "angel of the Lord" directs Joseph at each major turning point.

2.3. Luke. In Luke there is not the same emphasis on God as "Father" characteristic of Matthew. Far and away, Luke prefers the term *theos* (122 times, not counting Acts). Four additional features of Luke's treatment of God are prominent. First, as shown by Luke's unique two-volume literary structure, which involves an account of the early church attached to his story of Jesus, Luke emphasizes that the events he narrates form the divine plan and purpose. That is, Luke particularly portrays God as the architect of the redemptive plan whose unfolding Luke narrates. Luke's interest in divine purpose is reflected in his more frequent use of the term *dei* as an expression of divine necessity (about 27x in Luke-Acts, 14x in Luke alone; cf. 4 in Matthew, 5x in Mark, 9x in John). Luke's notion of divine necessity, however, is not the same as determinism, but dynamically incorporates human volitional cooperation, such as in Luke 4:43, where Jesus declares that he "must" proclaim God's kingdom in the other cities of Galilee* (see also 2:49; 13:33; 22:37; and Cosgrove, esp. 180-82).

Second, Luke is noted for the strong emphasis he places on God's miraculous works throughout Luke-Acts. From the nativity account onward, God acts powerfully to advance his purposes (see, e.g., the poetic exclamations in Lk 1:46-55, 68-79). Some have anachronistically characterized Luke's interest in miracles* as reflecting a theology of glory rather than the cross, but this judgment of Luke through the categories of Protestant polemics of the sixteenth century hardly constitutes proper historical-critical method. Luke's purposes in narrating God's mighty works were to assure readers that God is genuinely in charge of the world* and to provide examples of divine attestation of the Christian message, rather than to provide a theology of the Christian life (and much less to satisfy later critics of particular dogmatic orientations).

A third major feature of Luke's treatment of God is Luke's strong doxological interest. More emphatically than in the other Gospels, in Luke, "God is the one who is to be praised and glorified" (Donahue, 568). Some dozen times in the Gospel alone, Luke has people giving glory to God (e.g., 2:14, 20; 5:25-26; 7:16; 13:13; 17:15; 18:43). In Mark 15:39 the centurion speaks of Jesus, but the Luke 23:47 parallel has him glorify God; and the Gospel ends with the disciples praising God (24:53).

Fourth, as reflected, for example, in the uniquely Lukan parables* in chapter fifteen, the God of Luke's Gospel is emphatically merciful and eager to forgive and redeem. The songs of the birth narratives celebrate the sending of the Christ as God's mercy upon those who wait for his redemption (e.g., 1:50, 54, 68-72). The God who orders all things, therefore, does so to accomplish his merciful intentions. In Luke divine providence orders all things in the service of divine mercy.*

2.4. John. We have already noted John's considerably more frequent use of *patēr* as a title for God (109 times, more than twice the number for any other Evangelist), and have observed that in John the title plays a polemical role not associated with the term in the other Gospels. This polemical connotation is particularly clear in 5:18, where Jesus' reference to God as "his own Father" is one of the reasons "the Jews" seek to kill Jesus. In John, more emphatically than in any other Gospel, one cannot honor God without honoring "the Son" (e.g., 3:35-36; 5:22-23; 6:28-29).

This is because John emphasizes the transcendence of God more than the other Evangelists (e.g., 1:18; 6:46). For John the invisible God can now be understood and approached only through the one whom God has sent to declare him, Jesus "the Son" (e.g., 1:18; 14:6-9). This emphasis on God's invisible and transcendent nature makes John resemble other Greco-Roman era Jewish writers, such as Philo of Alexandria (see, e.g., Hagner). But unlike Philo and other ancient Jewish writers who emphasize God's transcendence to criticize pagan religious traditions and to avoid crude anthropomorphism, John underscores God's transcendence and invisibility to undercut competing claims to know the true God from Jews who reject Christ.

When John refers to God's works, it is most often to associate Christ with them. Like God, the *Logos** was "in the beginning" (1:1-2), and God's creation was through the *Logos* (1:3). God, the judge of all who will reward the righteous (*see* Justice, Righteousness) with resurrection* life, has now given to the Son to share in the judgment* and to "give life to whom he will" (5:21-22, 26-29).

Yet this strikingly exalted view of Christ is combined with an equally definite subordination of "the Son" to "the Father." The Son's prominence arises from the Father having given "all things" into the Son's hands (3:35). Believers can come to Christ only as God grants them the ability to respond (6:65). Repeatedly, the exalted Son expresses his subordination and service to the Father, credits the Son's message as given to him by the Father, makes the Son's aim the glory of God and leaves it to God to bring the Son glory (e.g., 5:19; 6:37-40; 8:28-29, 38, 42, 49-50, 54; 10:25, 29-30, 37-38).

Alleging a fundamental incompatibility between them, Sundberg claimed that John combined an older subordinationist christology with a body of "disjunctive" material expressing a newer view, a "binitarian theology rather than christology" in which "the Son is a god like the Father is God" (37). But one suspects that such comments reflect more an inability to grasp Johannine christological sophistication than any actual conflict in the christology of John. There is no indication whatsoever that the Fourth Evangelist noticed any tension between the subordinationist theme and his exalted view of Christ as one with the Father; the author repeatedly and effortlessly expresses both notions within the same or closely adjacent statements (e.g., 10:29-30).

The two passages where Jewish offense is taken at

Christ associating himself improperly with God, which Sundberg offers as evidence of a new Johannine christology (5:18; 10:30-33), are not an entirely new feature in the Gospels; there are earlier echoes of the charge of blasphemous christology in Mark (14:64) and Matthew (26:65). Even more importantly, in John the two accusations of what amounts to di-theism are put on the lips of the Jewish opponents of Jesus (and of the Johannine community), who are consistently portrayed by John as failing to understand the truth and as distorting the divine revelation. To be sure, Thomas' exclamation to the risen Christ, "My Lord and my God!" (20:28), represents an escalation of christological rhetoric distinctive in the Gospels, an escalation that probably resulted from, as much as it may have contributed to, Jewish rejection of Christian devotion to Christ. But the veneration of Christ in divine categories reflected in Thomas' exclamation can be traced back far earlier than the Gospel of John to the earliest levels of Christian tradition in the NT (see, e.g., Hurtado).

There is in John no clumsy introduction of a new di-theism in which Christ is a second god. The accusations in 5:19 and 10:30 that portray Jesus as a second god are the complaints of hostile Jewish outsiders who distort the sophisticated monotheism of the Johannine community. John portrays a remarkable balancing of the convictions that Christ is uniquely associated with God and is also the obedient Son who is glorified by the one transcendent God precisely because the Son contentedly subordinates himself to God and seeks God's glory.

3. God in Jesus' Experience and Ministry.

The Gospels reflect, and themselves exemplify, adaptations of Jesus tradition to the needs and circumstances of various first-century churches, and one cannot use the Gospels simplistically to describe Jesus' own teachings (see Gospels [Historical Reliability]). Still less do the Gospels provide us an unmediated access to Jesus' own religious experience. Nevertheless, there is good reason for confidence in making certain basic claims about Jesus' references to God and perhaps even about Jesus' own religious life. Two major features strongly attested in the Jesus tradition are especially worth noting: (1) Jesus refers to God as his Father, particularly in prayer, and (2) Jesus encourages his followers to use similar language and to relate to God as their Father as well.

Although details of his discussion have been challenged effectively (see, e.g., Barr), Jeremias' investigations into the tradition of Jesus' references to God as Father have proven generally persuasive about several main matters (1967; 1971, 61-67; see also Bauckham, Dunn, Fitzmyer). First, Jesus referred to God in a highly personal way (e.g., "my Father") and, especially in prayer, characteristically used the Aramaic term 'abbā' to address God. Second, 'abbā' constituted an unusual (perhaps unique) form of direct address to God for Jesus' day. Third, Jesus' use of this unusual and rather intimate form for addressing God in prayer suggests strongly that Jesus' religious life was characterized by relating to God in a very intense and personalized way that is not fully paralleled even in other examples of very devout spirituality in the ancient Jewish setting. "Jesus seems to have thought of himself as God's son in a distinctive sense" (Dunn, 38).

This special sense of sonship to God likely provided the experiential impetus of Jesus' mission. The Synoptic baptismal narratives (Mk 1:9-11 par. Mt 3:13-17 and Lk 3:21-22), though stylized and adapted to the didactic needs of first-century churches, are intended to reflect an authentic feature of Jesus' religious experience: the divine acclamation of Jesus as "son" in a special sense, which also entailed the corollary of a special (and representative?) responsibility and mission. The dominant category in Jesus' religious life was probably not messiahship but sonship to God, and from this "his other basic convictions about himself and his mission arose" (Dunn, 39).

If Jesus did believe he had a special relationship with God which was a major part of the basis for his own mission, it is all the more striking that the early Christian tradition so strongly indicates that Jesus also encouraged his followers to relate to God as "Father" in quite an intimate manner. The earliest evidence for this is technically indirect but quite early and strong. In addition to the Gospel tradition about Jesus teaching his disciples to address God as "Father," even earlier and more striking are Paul's references in Galatians 4:6 and Romans 8:15 to Greek-speaking Christian use of abba (along with the normal Greek term for "father," patēr) to address God in prayer (probably in corporate worship settings). These latter passages show that the practice was sufficiently well established already before the time of these letters (50-60 A.D.) as to need no introduction. And these remarkable references indicate that 'abbā' was taken over as a loan-word from Aramaic-speaking churches and used in Greek-speaking (heavily Gentile) Christian churches, doubtless on account of the term's strong religious and sentimental connotations. Given that 'abbā' was a highly unusual form for addressing God in prayer in first-century Aramaic, some powerful influence must be posited for the practice becoming sufficiently regularized to have been influential even beyond Aramaic-speaking Christian groups. The only cogent suggestion is that Jesus' own use of *'abbā'* in prayer and his encouragement to his followers to do the same constitute the powerful originating influence required.

This makes Jesus' understanding of his relationship with God all the more remarkable. The God of Jesus' religious experience was "Father" in an unusually intense manner that involved a powerful sense of personal and special mission. And the mission to which God called Jesus apparently included extending an unusually intimate relationship to God as "Father" among those who accepted Jesus' proclamation of God's kingdom. Whatever the partial analogies offered (e.g., by Vermes) for Jesus' own intimacy with God among ancient Jewish holy men, there is no parallel for Jesus' sense that God called him to become the pioneer and catalyst for a special filial relationship to God to be enjoyed by his disciples.

See also CHRIST; HOLY SPIRIT; "I AM" SAYINGS; KINGDOM OF GOD; LOGOS; LORD; PRAYER; SON OF GOD; WISDOM; WORSHIP.

BIBLIOGRAPHY. J. Barr, "*Abba* Isn't Daddy," *JTS* 39 (1988) 28-47; C. K. Barrett, " 'The Father is greater than I' (Jo. 14:28): Subordinationist Christology in the New Testament," in *Neues Testament und Kirche,* ed. J. Gnilka (Freiburg: Herder, 1974) 144-59; R. Bauckham, "The Sonship of the Historical Jesus in Christology," *SJT* 31 (1978) 245-60; C. H. Cosgrove, "The Divine *Dei* in Luke-Acts," *NovT* 26 (1984) 168-90; J. R. Donahue, "A Neglected Factor in the Theology of Mark," *JBL* 101 (1982) 563-94; J. D. G. Dunn, *Jesus and the Spirit* (Philadelphia: Westminster, 1975); J. A. Fitzmyer, "Abba and Jesus' Relation to God," in *À cause de l'Évangile: Mélanges offerts à Dom Jacques Dupont,* ed. R. Gantoy (Paris: Cerf, 1985) 16-38; D. A. Hagner, "The Vision of God in Philo and John: A Comparative Study," *JETS* 14 (1971) 81-94; L. W. Hurtado, *One God, One Lord: Early Christian Devotion and Ancient Jewish Monotheism* (Philadelphia: Fortress, 1988); J. Jeremias, *The Prayers of Jesus* (SBT 6; London: SCM, 1967); idem, *New Testament Theology: The Proclamation of Jesus* (New York: Scribner's, 1971); J. D. Kingsbury, *The Christology of Mark's Gospel* (Philadelphia: Fortress, 1983); R. L. Mowery, "God, Lord and Father: The Theology of the Gospel of Matthew," *BibRes* 33 (1988) 24-36; H. F. D. Sparks, "The Doctrine of the Divine Fatherhood in the Gospels," in *Studies in the Gospels,* ed. D. E. Nineham (Oxford: Blackwell, 1967) 241-62; A. C. Sundberg, "Christology in the Fourth Gospel," *BibRes* 21 (1976) 29-37; G. Vermes, *Jesus the Jew* (London: Collins, 1973).

L. W. Hurtado

GOLDEN RULE. *See* SERMON ON THE MOUNT.

GOLGOTHA. *See* DEATH OF JESUS.

GOOD. *See* ETHICS OF JESUS.

GOOD NEWS. *See* GOSPEL (GOOD NEWS); JUBILEE.

GOOD SAMARITAN. *See* PARABLE; SAMARITANS.

GOSPEL (GENRE)

Discussion of the literary genre of the NT Gospels involves two basic issues: (1) the literary nature of the canonical Gospels as continuous prose narratives of Jesus' ministry and their relationship to other early Christian writings; (2) the relationship of the Gospels to their Greco-Roman literary setting. There are two practical purposes served in this discussion: (1) a better understanding of the place of the Gospels in the literary history of early Christianity and the Greco-Roman world; (2) a more intelligent interpretation of the Gospels as their features are illuminated by comparison with their literary background.

Until the 1970s there was practically a consensus that the Gospels constituted a unique literary genre in the Greco-Roman world, and that any apparent analogies with other early Christian writings or from the wider Greco-Roman literary setting were irrelevant. This consensus has been challenged, however, and various scholars have argued that the Gospels are related to one or more types of Greco-Roman literature, most often biographical writings.

It is likely that both sides in the debate have a legitimate point. On the one hand, the Gospels share various characteristics of one or more types of Greco-Roman literature and in light of this can be likened to certain literary genres of that period. Moreover, we should expect that the NT authors would have been influenced by general literary conventions and practices of their day. Yet the NT Gospels also exhibit a certain uniqueness and thus form at least a partially distinctive category or subgenre. That is, the Evangelists, though influenced by their literary environment, seem to have produced works whose origin and characteristics are to be understood most directly in terms of the early Christian groups for which the Gospels were written.

1. Definition and Significance of Genre
2. The Scholarly Debate
3. The Genre of the Gospels
4. Conclusion

1. Definition and Significance of Genre.

A literary genre is a category or type of literature, such as biography or novel. Literary genres are not universal and static categories but have developed and changed over time, and genres popular in one age or culture may not be found in another. Even if a genre, such as biography, appears in more than one period or culture, the specific characteristics of the genre will often vary significantly in the different settings.

In seeking to determine a writing's genre, therefore, we must work with the genres and literary conventions relevant to the era of the writing. Thus, for example, the question of the genre(s) of the Gospels must be addressed by examining their characteristics in comparison with the types of literature current in the Greco-Roman setting (or at least accessible to the authors). Genres are to be thought of in terms of clusters of characteristics or traits. The analysis of a work's relation to literary genres should involve comparison of all the characteristics of the relevant genres and of the work in question. Emphasis on isolated characteristics of a work can produce misleading conclusions. A writing can be associated with a particular genre only to the degree that all the characteristics of the writing can be understood adequately in terms of the features of the genre.

The sorts of characteristics and factors to be considered in trying to determine a writing's genre include the following: formal features (e.g., structure, style, motifs, devices), author's intention, compositional process, setting of author, setting of intended use, and contents. Every reader brings expectations to a writing that shape the reading process and affect how the writing is understood. Acquaintance with the genre of a writing allows one's understanding of a writing to be guided in light of the features and intentions that characterize the genre. If an author sets out to write in accordance with the conventions and features of a particular genre, it may be comparatively easy to identify the genre of the writing.

But sometimes things are not so easy. For example, if an author adapts a genre to achieve a purpose not ordinarily associated with that genre, or if an author simply does not follow very methodically the full conventions of a given genre, it may be much more difficult to categorize the writing. In any case, identifying a writing's genre requires informed judgment that must be based on familiarity with the writing and its literary and social context.

2. The Scholarly Debate.

The question of the genre of the Gospels is basically a modern issue, characteristic of the modern histori-

cal investigation of the NT. Our cultural and chronological distance from the first-century setting and our modern desire to overcome this distance through accurate knowledge of the past fuel the attempt to analyze the Gospels in their literary context. It is interesting to note that the discussion of this topic has been related to wider developments in Gospel studies.

2.1. The Earlier Consensus. In 1915 C. W. Votaw argued that the Gospels can be likened to the popular biographical literature of the Greco-Roman era. But in 1923, in reply to Votaw, K. L. Schmidt argued influentially that the Gospels are a unique type of early Christian writing, not explainable by reference to any other type of literature of the ancient world. This position became the standard view among NT scholars, virtually unchallenged until recent decades.

Schmidt's case reflected in part the distinction made earlier by F. Overbeck, in which the NT was portrayed as relatively unsophisticated in comparison to the more polished literature of the classical authors and the Christian writings of the late second century and thereafter. Also, Schmidt reflected the approach of early form criticism,* which tended to view the Gospels basically as collections of the Jesus traditions of early Christian communities and minimized the role of the Evangelists as authors. Moreover, form critics emphasized that the impetus for the Gospels was not literary but kerygmatic (from the Gk *kerygma,* "proclamation"). That is, form criticism emphasized that the Gospels embody the early Christian proclamation of the significance of Jesus and were written exclusively to serve this proclamation.

2.2. The Re-Opening of the Question. By the 1970s there was a renewed investigation of the relationship of the Gospels to Greco-Roman literature. This re-examination of the previous consensus seems to have arisen in part from developments in Gospel studies (in the 1950s and subsequently) that balanced the form-critical view of the Gospels as collections of tradition with emphasis on the role of the Evangelists as effective editors of the tradition (redaction criticism*) and/or as authors who significantly determined the nature of their narratives of Jesus (recent literary criticism* of the Gospels). Although some early contributions to the renewed question of the genre of the Gospels posited a classification of them as "aretalogies" (purported narratives of divine men* in antiquity), this category has not proven viable for a variety of reasons (e.g., see Kee), including the lack of evidence for such a literary genre so defined in antiquity.

Scholars who now propose links between the Gospels and Greco-Roman literature focus on one of three genres: biography, history or novel. The modern discussion has also raised the question of whether the Gospels belong to one genre collectively or must be classified individually in different genres. Most of those who have addressed the genre of the Gospels, however, have tended to emphasize possible connections with the genre of Greco-Roman popular biography.

3. The Genre of the Gospels.

Proper consideration of the genre of the Gospels involves a variety of factors, and the variations among the four canonical accounts make it wise to treat them individually.

3.1. Basic Factors. There are, of course, formal features of the Gospels that must be considered. The Gospels are all narratives about Jesus that include examples of his deeds and sayings in a loose chronological framework that concentrates on the period between the beginning of his ministry and his death/resurrection. They are not impartial accounts; they all enthusiastically endorse Jesus and are quite negative in their treatment of any opposition to Jesus. In the case of Matthew and Luke, there are birth accounts attached that seem likewise intended to show dramatically the significance of Jesus (*see* Birth of Jesus).

The narrative mode of the canonical Gospels and their general shape as accounts of Jesus' ministry and death/resurrection set them apart from the surviving apocryphal Gospels (*see* Gospels [Apocryphal]). The latter form an assortment of writings about Jesus that include revelation/sayings collections (e.g., *Gospel of Thomas*), fanciful narratives of Jesus' childhood (the several so-called Infancy Gospels), and other writings that may be likened a bit more to the canonical Gospels but are also shaped by different religious interests (e.g., *Gospel of Peter*). The distinctive form of the Gospels in comparison with other early Christian literature justifies viewing them as a group or subgroup unto themselves in the literary history of early Christianity.

Though they exhibit distinguishing features as continuous narratives concerned with Jesus' ministry, the canonical Gospels can be likened to genres of Greco-Roman literature, particularly popular biography of that era (see, e.g., Aune 1987, 17-76). Indeed, in some cases there are specific formal features of a Gospel that directly reflect literary practices of the ancient setting (e.g., Luke's preface in 1:1-4 and the prefaces to Greco-Roman literary works).

In addition to the narrative form of the Gospels, however, we should consider their contents. Here also, the Gospels can be likened to other examples of

Greco-Roman biographical writings that promote a particular hero (see, e.g., Talbert, "Biographies"; and Tiede). But the NT Gospels also diverge from general Greco-Roman literary culture. For example, though the Gospels may often reflect Greco-Roman themes, values and literary motifs (e.g., Luke's presentation of Jesus' death as heroic martyrdom, the motif of important teaching and events set at meal scenes, or the motif of the teacher and his disciples), more fundamentally the Evangelists invoke the OT (e.g., the many allusions and citations) and specifically early Christian beliefs in their presentation of Jesus (e.g., Jesus as "Christ"). These distinguishing features did not render their narratives more meaningful or harmonious with the literary and cultural tastes of the Greco-Roman world, and this indicates that the Evangelists were by no means simply patterning their narratives after genres of contemporary literature. Likewise, if we take into account the compositional process that probably lies behind the Gospels, there are general similarities with some types of Greco-Roman writings but also significant differences.

The Gospel writers did not invent the idea of narrating Jesus' ministry. We must surely grant some (in some places considerable) authorial contribution to the finished products. But, both in many features of their form and in most of their contents (or all, depending on one's critical opinion), the Gospels reflect the Jesus tradition of Christian groups. That is, the immediate setting that shaped the work of the Evangelists was not the literary activities of the larger Greco-Roman era but the religious and social activities, needs and questions of early Christianity.

In the case of accounts of some figures associated with particular philosophical traditions (e.g., Socrates, Pythagoras), there may have been bodies of tradition about these individuals that were carried along in the groups that revered their memory. This would provide a general similarity to the Gospels' relationship to the Jesus tradition. Nevertheless, there appears to be no direct analogy to the rather considerable Jesus tradition available to the Evangelists, the massive preoccupation with proclaiming and teaching about Jesus, and the rather exclusive claims made on his behalf in the early Christian movement.

The popularity of biographical writings in the Greco-Roman era may have conditioned the Evangelists to find the writing of their books about Jesus a worthy task. But the major reason biography-like accounts of Jesus appeared is that the early Christian message from the first was focussed on Jesus as the personal vehicle of revelation and redemption (see, e.g., Stanton). The impetus, basic contents and general narrative complexion of the Gospels reflect primarily the Jesus-centered proclamation of early Christianity.

That the Gospels do not explicitly name their authors is evidence of their highly traditional nature. Contrary to the frequent literary practice of the Greco-Roman era, the Gospels do not convey their author's identities (the present superscriptions were added after the Gospels began to be circulated, probably when they were circulated as a fourfold collection). With the exception of Luke-Acts, the Gospels do not have such common literary devices as prefaces either. These things suggest that in general the Evangelists did not see themselves primarily as authors writing for a general audience, but more likely as "servants [hyperetai] of the word" (Lk 1:2).

Furthermore, the intended and characteristic use of the Gospels is somewhat distinctive. As indicated already, the Evangelists did not write for the general public but for the Christian groups with which they were associated. Suggestions that the Gospels were composed to fit some fixed lectionary schedule have been judged implausible. But the Gospels were apparently intended for corporate reading and teaching within Christian groups and quickly found a role in their liturgical activities. Although some Greco-Roman biographical writings may have been intended primarily for followers of a particular philosophical tradition, the close association of the Gospels with early Christian worship and proclamation suggests that we should see them as church documents with a certain biographical character rather than as biographies with a religious tone.

Furthermore, in Greco-Roman biography the central figure is glorified in terms of values that do not really derive from the figure or rest on his authority. Instead, the biographer shows the main character to be a model who embodies the virtues (sometimes the vices) already recognized by the writer and expected readers. The biographer seeks to show the essence of the main figure by recounting incidents and sayings that display and prove his character.

Although the Evangelists portray Jesus in ways that seem intended to dispose the Christian readers to find encouragement and inspiration to live as his followers, we can hardly say that the Gospels focus on the essence of Jesus' character or emphasize Jesus primarily as a model of particular virtues. In fact, they supply surprisingly little about Jesus' personality or character. The Evangelists were mainly concerned to show Jesus' significance in the divine purpose, not his virtues. Thus, in emphasis and aim, as in several other respects, the Gospels exhibit distinctive features that do not derive from Greco-Roman literary genres.

3.2. Mark. Commonly regarded today as the earliest of the NT Gospels and the major narrative source of Matthew and Luke, it is important to try to understand the features of Mark and the forces that shaped this influential narrative. Matthew and Luke are called "Synoptic" Gospels because of their strong resemblance to Mark, making the question of the genre of Mark at least partially relevant for these other two Gospels as well (*see* Synoptic Problem).

It has long been recognized that Mark and the other Synoptics are composed of traditions about Jesus that circulated in the early churches and that can be classified into broad types of Jesus material (e.g., parables,* miracle* stories, chreia* or pronouncement stories, passion narratives,* etc.). These all exhibit in various ways rhetorical features of popular-level oral narratives as these were adapted in the proclamation and life of early Christianity. In the general narrative style of Mark as well, there is evidence of the continuing impact of oral narration. This indicates that the Gospels are not simply literary works, but are constructed in close connection with the teaching and preaching activities of early Christianity.

Some have noted that the plot or shape of Mark's story of Jesus reflects the general structure of Greek tragedy (introduction, rising action, climax/crisis, falling action, catastrophe, denouement), and a few have suggested that the Evangelist was influenced directly by this form of literature (e.g., Bilezikian, Standaert). But most scholars (e.g., Aune 1987, 48-49) believe that the resemblances are to a large extent coincidental, and that Mark's plot reflects the broad narrative structure of pre-Markan Jesus tradition in which Jesus' ministry, death and resurrection were portrayed in terms of a general structure found in widespread literature of a variety of ancient cultures: a righteous person undergoes opposition, persecution and vindication. This judgment seems correct, for not only Matthew and Luke but also John's Gospel (which is not usually thought to have been directly dependent on the Synoptics) reflect essentially this basic plot (*see* Synoptics and John).

Some features of Mark (and of Matthew and Luke as well) are characteristic of ancient biography (e.g., anecdotal narrative style, absence of character growth), but there are no indications that the author was consciously shaping his work in the light of any literary precedents or patterns. If we ask, however, how the Evangelist came to compose a written narrative of Jesus in the form he did, it may be that very general literary influences can be included in the answer.

Surely the primary reasons Mark took pen in hand were the perceived needs of the Christians for whom he wrote, and the immediate influences on him stemmed from the religious circles in which the writer worked. But it may well be that the developing popularity of biography as a literary vehicle in the Greco-Roman era (see, e.g., Cox, Momigliano) helped make it seem logical or appropriate to the author to produce the first book narrating Jesus' ministry, though it is difficult to say whether such general influence was perceived consciously by the author. That is, the relevance of the genre of Greco-Roman biography for a historical explanation of Mark may be less in terms of direct or specific similarities and influence and more in terms of the general climate that contributed to the author's decision to serve Christ and Christians through his pioneering written work.

3.3. Matthew and Luke. In comparison with Mark, both Matthew and Luke reflect a somewhat higher literary level and exhibit more features that can be compared with characteristics of Greco-Roman biographical literature. Aune refers to Matthew and Luke as early stages of the "literaturization," the more direct appropriation of literary tastes, that went on in early Christianity in the first few centuries.

In addition to their birth accounts, additional features such as the genealogies* and post-resurrection appearance/vindication scenes, make Matthew and Luke seem closer to ancient biographies of figures described as sons of gods or divine. Also, both Matthew and Luke have a more refined Greek style in comparison to Mark. In short, Matthew and Luke allow more scope for positing influence of the Greco-Roman literary environment. Nevertheless, like Mark, Matthew and Luke seem to have taken their major stimuli from, and had their primary connections with, the religious life of early Christianity. And the Christian matrix of these works has produced a profound adaptation of whatever Greco-Roman literary influences we can detect.

In Matthew, for example, Jesus is presented largely in terms of ideas, values and issues that stem from the OT and the Jewish and early Christian setting. The genealogy links Jesus with great figures of the OT and with the history of Israel. Like other subjects of Greco-Roman biography, Jesus is presented in Matthew as the great teacher. But in Matthew Jesus' teaching is presented thoroughly in terms of the vocabulary and motifs of the Jewish and early Christian background, which are often noticeably different from those of the general literary culture. For example, the citation of numerous OT prophecies as fulfilled by Jesus proba-

bly reflects the narrative style of OT historical books (esp. 1 Sam—2 Kings), which likewise make fulfillment of the words of prophets a major device in their accounts.

Shuler has offered a definition of Matthew as a type of laudatory biography he calls "encomium biography," but this proposal is inadequate for several reasons. All ancient biographies were either laudatory and sought the same basic objectives as the rhetorical category of speeches called encomium or (occasionally) were condemnatory and critical. Shuler's category is not recognized in ancient sources and is too vague and broad to be of use. And Shuler is surely wide of the mark when he refers to Matthew as an attempt to relate the Evangelist's message "to the society in which he lived." The many indications that the Evangelist presumed an acceptance of the OT as Scripture and Christian beliefs and vocabulary as normative show that Matthew was written as an in-house document for the encouragement and edification of fellow Christians, not for the general public.

It is with Luke that scholars usually find the closest analogies to Greco-Roman literature. The author is believed to have drawn upon Mark as his major narrative source, but the use of a formal preface (Lk 1:1-4; cf. Acts 1:1) and chronologies (Lk 2:1-2; 3:1-2) are only two more obvious indications that this Evangelist consciously drew upon literary conventions of his time as well in composing his account. The scholarly attempt to categorize Luke in terms of a particular genre, however, has not resulted in agreement on what genre is preferable.

A major difficulty in reaching agreement is that one must take into account the second part of the Evangelist's work, the Acts of the Apostles. Talbert has proposed that the combined work, Luke-Acts, is an integral work and represents a particular type of biography designed to show the valid succession of a tradition, in this case the tradition of Jesus in the ministry of the apostles featured in Acts. Others who agree that the genre of Luke must be decided in light of Acts have argued (e.g., Aune) that the two-volume work is an example of Greco-Roman historiography, in this case a history of the Christian message that begins with Jesus and continues on through to the Pauline Gentile mission.

Praeder, however, analyzed Luke-Acts as a Christian adaptation of the Greco-Roman genre of novel. Indeed, she regards all four canonical Gospels similarly, though she grants that their contents, setting and intended uses require that they be taken as forming a separate sub-genre within the genre of "the ancient novel." Still others (e.g., Pervo) see as misguided the attempt to categorize Luke by reference to Acts, and have urged that there is no reason why Luke and Acts cannot be linked to different genres. Pervo regards Acts as most closely related to the Greco-Roman genre of novel, but seems to consider Luke an example of popular biography.

In view of these disagreements among scholars with special competence in Greco-Roman literature, perhaps the wisest course is to recognize the limitations inherent in approaching the Gospels, even Luke with its clear appropriation of Greco-Roman literary devices and techniques, in terms of Greco-Roman literary genres alone. To be sure, the author of Luke seems to have had direct acquaintance with formal literary conventions of the Greco-Roman era and both unconsciously and consciously drew on them in producing Luke-Acts. But the same author also shows a rich familiarity with, and the influence of, other aspects of his more immediate background in early Christian circles, as shown in his linguistic style (which is much influenced by the LXX) and in various motifs drawn from the OT.

Also, in view of the fluidity in Greco-Roman literary genres and the influences of genres on one another, it is wise to be cautious about invoking a specific literary genre as the key to Luke (or Luke-Acts) on the basis of selected features of the work. For example, Greco-Roman historiography seems not to have conformed strictly to the standards espoused by the ancients who tried to define the literary genre. Popular historiography incorporated narrative features (such as fictional embroidering of events and dialogs) associated also with novels. Likewise, what may be termed historical novels affected a style like popular historiography. Biography too was not a tightly defined genre. Authors wishing to portray a great person had a variety of literary styles and approaches they could adapt.

In summary, Luke's appropriation of particular features of Greco-Roman literary practice can be demonstrated and our grasp of the literary texture of Luke-Acts has been enhanced as a result. In spite of the scholarly disagreement mentioned, given the author's expressed intention (Lk 1:1-4) and taking Luke-Acts as a work of unified intention, the closest broad genre with which to compare Luke-Acts is probably Greco-Roman historiography. But Luke-Acts is a historical account with a sizable biographical component (Luke) and a certain amount of authorial freedom exercised in portraying dramatic scenes; and the whole was governed primarily by the ethos and needs of the Christians for whom the Evangelist wrote.

3.4. John. Not nearly as much scholarly effort has been spent on John's relationship to Greco-Roman literature. Talbert has classified John (with Mk) as an innovative example of a biography intended to correct a misunderstanding of the central character. But Talbert's categories are his own rather than those recognized by ancient writers, and his view of John as advocating a corrective christology is not widely shared.

Most scholars tend to see John as written mainly to consolidate a particular Christian community's tradition and to guide the community in the aftermath of a bitter conflict with Jewish synagogue authorities. John is both broadly similar to the Synoptics and quite distinctive in features of contents, style and arrangement. In place of a birth account and genealogy, 1:1-14 makes Jesus' birth the personal, historical manifestation of the divine Word (*logos**). In place of the parables and pronouncement stories, there are extensive dialogs (e.g., 3:1-21; 4:4-26) and discourses (esp. chaps. 14—16) in which Jesus delivers teachings. The dialog was a well-established literary motif in Greco-Roman literature.

The narrative order exhibits differences from the Synoptics also (e.g., the Temple incident in chap. 2), and the overall arrangement is distinctive (e.g., linkage of Jesus' movements with Jewish feasts) as is the vocabulary (e.g., "signs," "eternal life"). Nevertheless, John is much more easily compared with the other canonical Gospels than with any other type of ancient literature, non-Christian or Christian.

There are also interesting similarities between John and the Synoptic accounts in particular incidents such as the feeding account. The similarities show that common features were shared by different streams of the Jesus tradition. John seems to show also that the idea of a written narrative of Jesus' ministry suggested itself to more than one Christian independently in the latter decades of the first century. And it is likely that common factors, such as the general situation of the Christian movement at that time, plus, perhaps, the general literary climate, helped make the composition of a written account of Jesus' ministry seem an appropriate service to provide.

4. Conclusion.

Although there are numerous differences among them, the four canonical Gospels exhibit a basically similar type of Jesus literature: (1) connected narratives of his ministry, death and resurrection; (2) composed out of the Jesus tradition; (3) reflecting and serving early Christian proclamation; (4) intended for Christian readers and presupposing their beliefs and vocabulary. Their general formal characteristics and/or the beliefs they affirm set them apart from other early Christian literature, canonical and non-canonical, in varying ways and degrees. They thereby constitute a distinctive group of writings within early Christianity.

Similarities to other Greco-Roman narrative genres such as biography reflect the cultural setting in which the Gospels were written. The Greco-Roman genres provide partially analogous writings that help us understand better some particular features of the Gospels, and may certainly help us see the literary expectations and categories through which non-Christian readers in particular may have viewed the Gospels. It is likely that the Evangelists consciously and, perhaps more often, unconsciously reflected features of Greco-Roman popular literature.

The Gospels are not fully explainable, however, simply in terms of the Greco-Roman literary setting or by linking them with literary genres of that era. The impetus for the Gospels derives from the religious complexion and needs of early Christianity; and their contents, presuppositions, major themes and literary texture are all heavily influenced by their immediate religious setting as well. In very general terms, the Gospels can be likened to other examples of Greco-Roman popular biography, but they also form a distinctive group within that broad body of ancient writings.

See also GOSPELS (APOCRYPHAL).

BIBLIOGRAPHY. D. E. Aune, *The New Testament in Its Literary Environment* (Philadelphia: Westminster, 1987); idem, ed., *Greco-Roman Literature and the New Testament* (Atlanta: Scholars, 1988); G. G. Bilezikian, *The Liberated Gospel: A Comparison of the Gospel of Mark and Greek Tragedy* (Grand Rapids: Baker, 1977); P. Cox, *Biography in Late Antiquity* (Berkeley: University of California, 1983); R. Guelich, "The Gospel Genre," in *The Gospel and the Gospels*, ed. P. Stuhlmacher (Grand Rapids: Eerdmans, 1991) 173-208; R. N. Gundry, "Recent Investigations into the Literary Genre 'Gospel,' " in *New Dimensions in New Testament Study*, ed. R. N. Longenecker and M. C. Tenney (Grand Rapids: Zondervan, 1974) 97-114; H. C. Kee, "Aretalogies, Hellenistic 'Lives,' and the Sources of Mark," in *Colloquy 12*, The Center for Hermeneutical Studies in Hellenistic and Modern Culture, ed. W. Wuellner (Berkeley, 1975); A. Momigliano, *The Development of Greek Biography* (Cambridge, MA: Harvard University, 1971); F. Overbeck, "Über die Anfänge der patristichen Literatur," *HZ* 12 (1882) 417-72; R. I. Pervo, *Profit with Delight: The Literary Genre of the Acts of the Apostles* (Philadelphia: Fortress, 1987); S. M. Praeder, "Luke-Acts and the Ancient Novel," in *SBLSAP* (1981) 269-92; K. L. Schmidt, "Die Stellung der Evangelien in der allgemeinen Literaturgeschichte," in *Eucharisterion*, ed. H. Schmidt (Göttingen: Vandenhoeck & Ruprecht, 1923) 50-134; P. L. Shuler, *A Genre for the Gospels* (Philadelphia: Fortress, 1982); B. Standaert, *L'Evangile selon Marc: Composition et genre littéraire* (Brugge: Sint-Andriesabdijj, 1978); G. N. Stanton, *Jesus of Nazareth in New Testament Preaching* (SNTSMS 27; Cambridge: Cambridge University, 1974); C. H. Talbert, *What Is a Gospel?* (Philadelphia: Fortress, 1977); idem, "Biographies of Philosophers and Rulers as Instruments of Religious Propaganda in Mediterranean Antiquity," in *ANRW* 2. 16/2:1619-1651; D. L. Tiede, "Religious Propaganda and the Gospel Literature of the Early Christian Mission," in *ANRW* 2. 25/2:1705-29; C. W. Votaw, *The Gospels and Contemporary Biographies in the Greco-Roman World* (Philadelphia: Fortress, 1970; reprint from *AJT* 19 [1915], 45-73, 217-49).

L. W. Hurtado

GOSPEL (GOOD NEWS)

Gospel, or "good news," designates Jesus' message of the appearance of God's* kingdom (*see* Kingdom of God), a message entailing liberty for those held captive to any form of affliction and demonstrated most dramatically in acts of healing.* In some instances the term encompasses the whole story of the life, death* and resurrection* of Jesus.

1. Terminology, Distribution and Origins
2. Luke
3. Matthew and Mark

1. Terminology, Distribution and Origins.
Matthew (4 x) and Mark (8 x, including Mk 16:15) use the noun form *euangelion* (the message of "good news"), which is usually the object of the verb *kēryssō* ("to preach"). Luke (10 x) makes exclusive use of the verb form *euangelizō* (the activity of "preaching good news"), except in Luke 7:22, a citation from Isaiah 61:1 (par. Mt 11:5). Neither term appears in John. The general usage of these terms appears to be consistent with their etymology: the *eu-* prefix meaning "well, good" and *angellō*, meaning "to proclaim news."

Each Evangelist uses these terms in a distinctive manner. In six of the eight instances of *gospel* in Mark (including Mk 16:15) it appears as a Markan expansion (Mk 1:1, 14-15; 8:35; 10:29; 16:15) which is not followed by either Matthew or Luke. Mark uses the term absolutely (i.e., without qualification), except in Mark 1:1 ("of Jesus Christ") and 1:14 ("of God," i.e., the kingdom of God; see Mk 1:15). Matthew, on the other hand, where he parallels Mark either omits *gospel* (Mt 4:17 par. Mk 1:14-15; Mt 16:25 par. Mk 8:35), replaces it with another term (Mt 19:29 par. Mk 10:29) or in the two cases where he does include it he specifies it ("this gospel of the kingdom," Mt 24:14 par. Mk 13:10; "this gospel," Mt 26:13 par. Mk 14:9). Two other occurrences in Matthew are formulaic summary statements preceding extended teachings of Jesus (Mt 4:23 introduces the Sermon on the Mount [*see* Sermon on the Mount]); Mt 9:35 the commission of the Twelve). Here too Matthew qualifies "gospel" with "of the kingdom." According to W. Marxsen (123-24) these summary statements (not paralleled in Mark) are composed of Markan terminology, but one should note that Matthew 9:35 finds a parallel in Luke 8:1, where the verbal form (*euangelizō*) appears. The remaining occurrence in Matthew is also paralleled in Luke (Mt 11:5 par. Lk 7:22). Here the verbal form is used by both Evangelists as they present Jesus' citation of Isaiah 61:1 in answer to John the Baptist's (*see* John the Baptist) question from prison.

Except for the two Matthean parallels just noted, all occurrences of the term in Luke, who uses the verb, are unique to that Gospel. Luke's use of the verbal form has no correlation with Mark's use of the noun form. In parallel passages where Luke uses the verbal form (4:43; 8:1; 9:6; 20:1), the other Synoptics use *kēryssō* (Mt 9:35; Mk 1:38; 6:12) or *didaskō* (Mt 21:23; Mk 6:6). In instances where Luke does have a parallel to a Markan passage using "gospel," Luke omits any reference to "gospel" (4:15; 9:25; 18:29).

Since each Evangelist engages a distinctive use of *euangelion* and *euangelizō*, the terms themselves may well be traceable to the redactional level. In his Gospel Luke uses the verbal form exclusively and reserves the use of the noun until Acts, where it is used of the apostolic preaching (Peter in Acts 15:7; Paul in Acts 20:24). It will be argued below that the appearance of the verb in Luke's Gospel stems from its use in Isaiah 40—66, especially Isaiah 61:1. Only Luke records Jesus' reading and self-application of Isaiah 61:1 at the synagogue* in Nazareth.

The origins of the singular noun form *to euangelion*, appearing in Mark and Matthew, are not traceable directly to the LXX. The LXX uses only the plural *ta euangelia* for "the reward for good news" and the feminine *hē euangelia* for "good news" and does not use either term in a religious sense (Friedrich, 725). *Euangelion* was used in the Roman imperial cult and applied to the emperor, who was thought to be divine, in the oral proclamations of his birth, his coming of age and especially of his accession to the throne (Friedrich, 724-25). While the singular noun form does have this Roman usage, it will be shown that the

background of the term in Mark and Matthew is thoroughly rooted in the OT. The appearance of *euangelion* probably stems from Mark since there are no indications that it was present in any pre-Markan traditions (see Marxsen, 117-25).

The reader of the Gospels must be wary of reading a post-Easter definition into the Evangelists' use of the term *gospel* (such as is found in Pauline writings, 1 Cor 15:1-4; Rom 1:2-4). In the Synoptics it is found in the mouth of Jesus at the beginning of his ministry: "The time is fulfilled, and the kingdom of God is at hand; repent, and believe in the gospel" (Mk 1:14-15; cf. Mt 4:17, 23; Lk 4:18, 43). They use the term to designate Jesus' message without prior definition, implying that it was a term known to their audience.

2. Luke.

The term *gospel* shows an affinity to Jesus' association with John the Baptist. Angels* use the term to announce the births of both John (Lk 1:19) and Jesus (Lk 2:10; *see* Birth of Jesus). Luke describes John's ministry as "preaching good news" (Lk 3:18), and once he is imprisoned Jesus himself begins to "preach good news" (Lk 4:14-21, 43). Later, when John from prison asks Jesus if he is "the one to come," Jesus responds affirmatively by saying that "the poor have the good news preached to them" (Lk 7:22). Finally, when addressing the Pharisees,* Jesus says that from the time of John the Baptist "the good news of the kingdom of God is being preached" (Lk 16:16).

We should also note the affinity between these appearances of the term *gospel* and Isaiah 40—66. This affinity may imply that both John and Jesus in part derived their understanding of their ministries from Isaiah 40—66, much of which announces the restoration of Jews in Babylonian captivity back to their homeland. Luke describes John the Baptist's ministry by a citation from Isaiah 40:3-5: He is the "voice of one calling in the desert" (*see* Mountain and Wilderness) to "prepare the way for the Lord" and the appearance of his "salvation"* (Lk 3:4-6).

Luke 4:16-21 clarifies what Jesus' audiences in the Third Gospel would have understood by the term *gospel*. Luke appears to have transposed this story, which in Mark 6:1-6 and Matthew 13:53-58 occurs toward the end of Jesus' Galilean ministry, intentionally placing it near the beginning of his Gospel. In fact Luke 4:14-15 with verse 23 implies that Jesus went to Capernaum and performed miracles* there before going to Nazareth. Luke makes this scene in Nazareth (Lk 4:14-43) his counterpart to Mark 1:14-15. Note, for example, how Luke's "Today this Scripture has been fulfilled . . ." (Lk 4:21) corresponds to Mark's "The time is fulfilled" (Mk 1:15). Luke's setting the story at the beginning of Jesus' ministry draws the reader's attention to its programmatic significance.

After John's imprisonment (3:20) Jesus goes to Galilee* and to the synagogue of his own hometown of Nazareth (Lk 4:16). There he reads from Isaiah 61:1-2a (LXX, with an insertion from Is 58:6, "to send the oppressed away in liberty"), which proclaims liberation from Babylonian captivity (see, e.g., Is 61:3-4). By declaring that "today this scripture is fulfilled in your hearing" (Lk 4:21) Jesus identifies himself with the one upon whom the Spirit (see Holy Spirit) of the Lord* rests "to *preach good news (euangelisasthai)*." "To preach good news" is twice paralleled by another verb of speaking, "to proclaim" (*kēryxai*, Lk 4:18, 19): The content of this good news is thus associated with proclaiming "liberty" (*aphesis*), "recovery of sight" and "the favorable year of the Lord."

The recipients of these four messages and of the action of "sending away in liberty" are the helpless and afflicted: "the poor" (*see* Rich and Poor), "the captives," "the blind" (*see* Blindness and Deafness) and "the oppressed." Of the five messages/actions on behalf of the helpless, Luke will single out the preaching of good news as the summary characterization of Jesus' ministry (Lk 4:43; 8:1; 9:6; 20:1). In this respect the other four simply unpack the significance of "preaching good news." In Luke 4 the task that appears most strongly associated with "preaching good news" is that of healing, which is suggested in the phrase "recovery of sight to the blind." After this reading Jesus is aware that his audience will demand such acts of healing, but he notes that both Elijah and Elisha (*see* Elijah and Elisha) had performed healings for outsiders, not for those of their homeland (Lk 4:23-27). (Elijah was sent to a widow near Sidon, whose son he cured, and the only leper that Elisha healed was Naaman the Syrian, 1 Kings 17:17-24; 2 Kings 5.)

Jesus is met with a twofold response. After he claimed to be the herald preaching the good news that the favorable year of the Lord has arrived, "all spoke well of him" (Lk 4:22). But after he specified that "the poor" to whom this good news was addressed may well be outsiders and not those of the in-group, namely those of his own hometown/land, they "were furious" (Lk 4:28). Thus in Jesus' view the recipients of this "good news" are to be the helpless in general—their "worthiness" is not to be determined by their religious standing or national allegiance. It is this understanding of the "good news" that leads to Jesus' rejection (see Sanders).

Behind the "good news" of Isaiah 61 may be the metaphor of the "year of Jubilee" (Lev 25) in which

debts were forgiven, slaves set free and lands restored to the original families (*see* Jubilee). The original significance of such an allusion would be obvious for the captives in Babylon: They would be set free and restored to their homeland. In the Hebrew Masoretic Text the phrase "to proclaim liberty (*dᵉrôr*) to captives" uses a technical term for this "year of Jubilee" (Lev 25:10; Jer 34:8, 15, 17; cf. Ezek 46:17). The LXX translates this and another Hebrew technical term associated with the year of Jubilee (*yôbēl*, esp. in Lev 25) with the Greek *aphesis*.

The possibility of an allusion to the year of Jubilee is increased in the Lukan context of Jesus' two modifications of the Isaiah reading. First, he inserts a phrase from Isaiah 58:6 (LXX) between Isaiah 61:1 and 2. This phrase also contains the term *aphesis* (though it is here used to translate a different Hebrew word associated with setting slaves free), thus drawing further attention to this "liberty" of Jubilee. Second, Jesus breaks off the quote in the middle of Isaiah 61:2, thus omitting the other object of the verb "proclaim"—"the day of vengeance of our God." Jesus, by suddenly closing off the reading, draws his listeners' attention to his proclamation of "the year of the Lord's favor."

If Isaiah 61 alludes to the year of Jubilee and if this is Jesus' interpretation of the passage, he is not alone. The Qumran text 11QMelch 1-4, 9 explicitly makes this connection. The year of Jubilee described in Leviticus 25:13 as applied to the "last days" is seen to refer to the liberation of the captives and to the "year of favor" mentioned in Isaiah 61:1-2.

In Luke 4:43 Jesus describes his own ministry in Galilee, which includes the incident in Nazareth, as "preaching the good news of *the kingdom of God*" (*basileia tou theou*, note also Lk 16:16). The connection between "good news" and God's kingly rule is also evident in Isaiah 40—66. In two key passages from these chapters a "herald of good news" (*euangelizomenos*) announces that the Lord is returning to Jerusalem as a victorious warrior-king (Is 40:9-10; 52:7). These instances are consistent with earlier OT usage of "good news" (MT, *bśr* and cognates; LXX, *euangel-* and cognates), where it most often refers to messages of military victory (e.g., 2 Sam 4:10; 18:19-28, 31; Ps 68:11-12; Nahum 1:15). In Isaiah 52:7 the herald's message is "Your God reigns!" (LXX, "will reign," *basileusei;* cf. Ps 96:2, 10). In Isaiah 40:9-10 the message is "Behold, your God! Behold . . . his arm rules. . . ." But in the Targum* the message of the "herald of good news" is identical in both passages: "The kingdom of your God is revealed." 11QMelch 15-19 explicitly equates the "herald who proclaims . . . 'Your God has now claimed his kingdom' " in Isaiah 52:7

with "the one anointed with the Spirit" in Isaiah 61:1. As the herald of good news proclaims "peace" in Isaiah 52:7, so he, as "the one anointed," "comforts all who mourn" in Isaiah 61:2. Furthermore, we should note evidence that in Palestinian Judaism,* both before and after the time of Jesus, there was the expectation of a herald of good news who would come and announce the revelation of God as king, along with his salvation and peace* (Friedrich, 715-16).

Luke 7:22 (par. Mt 11:5) also refers to Isaiah 61:1 with the words "the poor have good news preached to them." Jesus uses the phrase, along with another phrase from Isaiah 61:1, "the blind receive their sight," in responding to the Baptist's question whether or not he is "the coming one" (*ho erchomenos*, Lk 7:19-20). This designation is so general it may not point to any single eschatological figure mentioned in the OT (see, e.g., Ps 118:26; Dan 7:13; 9:26; Mal 3:1; Gen 49:10; Hab 2:3). Coming from John the Baptist, this expression has most direct reference to his earlier claim that "he who is mightier than I *is coming*" (*erchetai*, Lk 3:16). The people's question to which the Baptist's claim responds may imply that this "coming one" is "the Christ*" (Lk 3:15). But his further description of this personage (Lk 3:16-17) appears to be derived from the Elijah-messenger foretold in Malachi 3:1-2; 4:1, 5 (*erchetai* in 3:1), one who announces a fiery purge. Jesus' reply to John in Luke 7:22, however, presents a personage foretold in Isaiah, one who heralds liberty for captives. Jesus' point, therefore, is to answer yes to the Baptist's question but also to specify "the coming one" as one who is preaching good news, not fiery judgment.* (In this light Jesus' comment in Lk 7:23 makes clear sense.) Again we should observe the close connection made between the preaching of the gospel and healing, both in Isaiah 61:1 and in this Lukan passage (see Lk 7:21). We should also note that in his answer to John, Jesus refers to other OT passages—all from Isaiah (Is 29:18; 35:5-6; 26:19).

Each of the above occurrences of the term "to announce the gospel" appears in connection with the pairing of Jesus and John the Baptist and with an echo of Isaiah 40—66. Subsequent appearances of the term in Luke do not add any nuances or overtones to the term; it is used simply as a designation for Jesus' message (Lk 8:1; 9:6; 20:1). Like Luke 4:43, Luke 8:1 specifies the "good news" as "of the kingdom of God." Luke 9:6 collocates the term with Jesus' acts of healing, a feature we have already observed.

3. Matthew and Mark.
As in Luke, Matthew and Mark describe the role of John the Baptist by citing Isaiah 40:3 (Mt 3:3; Mk 1:3; Lk 3:4-6); all three Synoptics record that once John was imprisoned (Mt 4:12; Mk 1:14; Lk 3:20) Jesus began to preach the "gospel," and each collocates this with "the kingdom (of God)" (Mt 4:23; Mk 1:14-15; Lk 4:43).

In Jesus' eschatological discourse both Mark and Matthew record Jesus' saying that the gospel must be preached to all nations (Mt 24:14; Mk 13:10). After the woman anoints Jesus at the house of Simon the leper, Jesus says that she will be remembered wherever the gospel is preached (Mt 26:13; Mk 14:9). In each passage Matthew specifies it as *"this [touto] gospel."* Both of these pericopes refer to the preaching of the gospel that will take place in the missionary activity which will follow Jesus' death and resurrection. Hence the term here may embrace more than Jesus' message of the kingdom and include the whole story of Jesus—his death and resurrection in particular (note esp. Mt 26:12-13).

3.1. Mark. Mark 1:14-15 presents four features which are also prominent in Isaiah 40—66: The term *gospel*, the anticipation of a period of time, the kingdom of God and the need for repentance* (*metanoeō*). In Isaiah 61 the servant, in addition to "preaching good news," is to "proclaim the favorable year of the Lord" (note also Dan 7:22). In Isaiah 40:9 and 52:7 a "herald of good news" announces the advent of God's kingdom (esp. clear in the Aramaic Targum). Isaiah 59:20 affirms the message of the herald in Isaiah 40:9 and 52:7-10—"The redeemer will come to Zion" (the herald in 52:9 announces that Zion's king has "redeemed Jerusalem")—but adds this crucial qualification, "to those who *repent* (LXX, *apostrephō*) of their sins." It is possible that there is more import in this Markan use of *gospel* than this Isaianic background. R. P. Martin, following W. Marxsen, argues that "Mark's record is written from the vantage-point of all that his ministry accomplished as a past fact" and thus the term *gospel* here would include "its full Christian content" (Martin, 27).

In Mark's so-called title (Mk 1:1), "the *gospel* of Jesus Christ" does not denote a "Gospel" (i.e., a generic designation for the book) but "good news" (i.e., the message or story about to be told). The genitive ("of") is probably both subjective and objective: Jesus proclaims the gospel and it proclaims his story. Mark is thus the first to transform *gospel* from what was exclusively oral proclamation (in both Roman and early Christian usage) to written proclamation. (Even in Mk 1:1-2 one must note the close association between the term *gospel* and the prophecies of Is 40—66.)

In Mark 8:35 and 10:29, where Jesus promises

reward for those who forsake worldly relationships and goods for his sake, Mark uniquely adds the phrase "and the gospel's (sake)." In the longer ending of Mark this version of the Great Commission uses the term explicitly: "Go into all the world and preach the gospel . . ." (Mk 16:15). Since the next verse makes clear that the listener's destiny is determined by his or her response to this "gospel," the term appears to include the message of the death and resurrection of Jesus.

3.2. Matthew. As we have seen, Matthew always specifies the noun *gospel* with "of the kingdom," except in 26:13 where the demonstrative "this" associates it closely with Jesus' death. Matthew 4:23 and 9:35 (par. Lk 8:1) are summaries of Jesus' ministry. They use identical formulae and both associate his preaching of the gospel with healing. Matthew parallels Luke in recording Jesus' response to the Baptist's question (Mt 11:2-6), where the verb form appears in the citation from Isaiah 61:1. Matthew, however, draws a closer connection between "the coming one" of the Baptist's question (Mt 11:3) and Jesus as "the Christ" (Mt 11:2).

In conclusion, it would appear that neither Jesus nor the Evangelists coined the term *gospel* (at least the verb form), but that Jesus' audience had a prior understanding of that term. Since the usage and associations of the term in the Synoptics coincide with those in Isaiah, it is likely that the meaning of *gospel* has its roots in this message of restoration and healing for the helpless. The preaching of the "good news" is collocated with the kingdom in both the Synoptics (Mk 1:14-15; Mt 4:23; 9:35; Lk 4:43; 8:1; 16:16) and in Isaiah (Is 40:9-10; 52:7) and so also with healing in both the Synoptics (Mt 4:23; 9:35; 11:5; Lk 7:22; 9:6) and in Isaiah (Is 61:1; 26:19; 29:18; 35:5-6).

See also GOSPEL (GENRE); JUBILEE; KINGDOM OF GOD.

BIBLIOGRAPHY. G. Friedrich, "εὐαγγελίζομαι," *TDNT* II:707-37; R. A. Guelich, *Mark 1-8:26* (WBC 34A; Dallas: Word, 1989) 13-14; R. Martin, *Mark: Evangelist and Theologian* (Grand Rapids: Zondervan, 1972) 17-28; W. Marxsen, *Mark the Evangelist* (Nashville: Abingdon, 1969) 117-50; J. A. Sanders, "From Isaiah 61 to Luke 4," in *Christianity, Judaism, and other Greco-Roman Cults*, ed. J. Neusner (Leiden: Brill, 1975) 75-106.   C. C. Broyles

GOSPELS (APOCRYPHAL)

The writing of Gospels did not end with the production of the Gospels which became canonical or even with the fixing of the canon* of four canonical Gospels. Many other Gospels continued to be written for many centuries. Most of these do not resemble the canonical Gospels in genre (*see* Gospels [Genre]). For the purpose of this article a Gospel must be defined as a work which recounts all or part of Jesus' earthly life and teaching (including his appearances on earth between the resurrection* and the ascension*). This definition excludes some works which were called Gospels, such as the *Gospel of Truth*, the *Gospel of Philip*, the Coptic *Gospel of the Egyptians* and the *Gospel of Eve*. There is no space here even to mention a large number of late apocryphal Gospels. Most attention will be given to those Gospels most relevant to the study of Jesus and the canonical Gospels. (It should also be noted that many extracanonical traditions about the life and teaching of Jesus, some of great importance for the study of the canonical Gospels, are not found in Gospels as such, but in other early Christian literature.)

1. Gospel of Thomas
2. Gospel of Peter
3. Papyrus Fragments of Unknown Gospels
4. Jewish Christian Gospels
5. Gospel of the Egyptians
6. Secret Gospel of Mark
7. Birth and Infancy Gospels
8. Gospel of Nicodemus
9. Post-Resurrection Revelations

1. Gospel of Thomas.

The Coptic version of the *Gospel of Thomas* was discovered in 1945 among the Nag Hammadi codices. Since then it has received more scholarly attention than any other extracanonical Gospel, mainly because of the claim that it preserves early Gospel traditions independently of the canonical Gospels. Certainly, it is more important for the study of Jesus and the canonical Gospels than any other extracanonical Gospel of which we have a complete text. As well as the Coptic version of the whole *Gospel of Thomas*, there are three fragments in Greek, which were discovered among the Oxyrhynchus papyri and published in 1897 and 1904 (P. Oxy. 1, 654, 655), but not recognized as fragments of the *Gospel of Thomas* until the Coptic version became known. Though there are significant differences between the Greek fragments (which are from three distinct copies of the work) and the Coptic text, they are recognizably from the same work, which must therefore have existed in at least two redactions. The original language was probably Greek, though some have argued for a Semitic original.

The earliest of the Greek fragments (P. Oxy. 1) was written no later than A.D. 200 and provides the only firm *terminus ad quem* for the writing of the Gospel. Hippolytus, writing between 222 and 235, provides the earliest reference to it by name. The Gospel has been dated as early as A.D. 50-70 and as late as the end of the second century. But since parallels to its more explicitly Gnostic concepts and terminology date from the second century, it is probably no older than the end of the first century. The attribution of the Gospel to "Didymus Judas Thomas" (prologue) shows that it derives from the East Syrian Christian tradition, centered on Edessa. It was only in this tradition (from which come also the *Book of Thomas* and the *Acts of Thomas*) that the apostle Thomas was known as Judas Thomas and regarded as a kind of spiritual twin-brother of Jesus. Thomas was thought (perhaps correctly) to have been in some sense responsible for the founding of the church in this area, and it is probable that the oral Gospel traditions of this church were transmitted under the name of Thomas and that the *Gospel of Thomas* drew on these oral traditions. Its points of contact with other literature from this area and especially its probable use by the *Acts of Thomas* (end of second or early third century) confirms this hypothesis.

The *Gospel of Thomas* is a collection of sayings of Jesus, numbered as 114 sayings (*logia*) by modern scholars. There are no narratives and only minimal narrative contexts provided for a few sayings (22, 60, 100), though the latter are important for showing that *Thomas* does not, like most of the Gnostic Gospels (see 9. below), have a post-resurrection setting. As a sayings collection, the Gospel has often been compared with the hypothetical Gospel source Q* and with the many ancient collections of sayings of the wise. The genre is consistent with the theology of *Thomas*, which presents Jesus as a revealer of the secret wisdom by which the elect may recognize their true spiritual identity and recover their heavenly origin. Some scholars deny that Thomas is properly Gnostic and locate it rather in the tradition of Jewish Wisdom theology or in the encratite tradition characteristic of East Syrian Christianity. But although there are real contacts with both these traditions, some of the sayings most distinctive of *Thomas* express a distinctively Gnostic theology (e.g., 18, 29, 50, 83-84).

It seems that the tradition of the sayings of Jesus on which *Thomas* drew was Jewish Christian in origin (see especially saying 12 on James the Just) but had developed in a gnosticizing direction. Some sayings of clearly Gnostic origin had entered the tradition and the editor of *Thomas* selected from the tradition sayings which were compatible with his own Gnostic theology. The apostle Thomas has become the authority for an esoteric interpretation of the tradition of the sayings of Jesus (cf. 1, 13).

The majority of the sayings in the *Gospel of Thomas* have parallels in the Synoptic Gospels (including the triple tradition, the Q material, and matter peculiar to Mt and to Lk; *see* Synoptic Problem; M; L), but whether *Thomas* is dependent on the canonical Gospels is still debated. Arguments for dependence try to show both that Thomas reflects the specifically Matthean and Lukan redactions of Gospel traditions and that its differences from the Synoptics can be explained as deliberate redactional changes expressing a Gnostic interpretation. But neither of these points has been conclusively established. On the other hand, it is striking that the order of the sayings in *Thomas* almost never corresponds to that of the Synoptics, while the association of sayings by catchword connections—one of the few reasons that can be discerned for the order in *Thomas*—is characteristic of oral tradition. It has been argued on form-critical grounds that *Thomas* sometimes preserves sayings, especially parables, in a more primitive form than the Synoptics. Finally, it should be noticed that since a significant number of the sayings in *Thomas* which do not have parallels in the canonical Gospels are also attested in other extracanonical sources, it is impossible to argue that the canonical Gospels were the only source of Gospel traditions used by *Thomas*. It follows that even if the editor of *Thomas* knew the canonical Gospels, a parallel to them need not derive from them.

The most probable opinion is that *Thomas* is dependent on a tradition substantially independent of the canonical Gospels, though influence from the canonical Gospels cannot be ruled out—whether during the oral transmission of the tradition, or at the stage of editing or at the stage of translation into Coptic. *Thomas* can therefore provide useful evidence for the study of the origins and development of the traditions behind the canonical Gospels, provided that due allowance is made for its greater distance (both theologically and probably chronologically) from the historical Jesus. It is even quite possible that a few of the sayings in *Thomas* which have no parallels in the canonical Gospels (such as the parables in 97 and 98) are authentic sayings of Jesus.

2. Gospel of Peter.
A substantial fragment of the *Gospel of Peter*, in a manuscript of the eighth or ninth century A.D., was discovered in 1887 at Akhmim in Egypt. It contains a narrative which begins at the end of the trial* of Jesus, includes the crucifixion (*see* Death of Jesus), burial* and resurrection* of Jesus, and breaks off in the course of a story which must have described a resurrection appearance to a group of the disciples.* The

words "I, Simon Peter" (14:60) identify the text as part of the Gospel attributed to Peter to which some writers of the early church refer. We have only two other indications of the rest of its contents. The Syriac *Didascalia* (early third century), which used the *Gospel of Peter*, refers briefly (ch. 21) to the resurrection appearance in the house of Levi which must have followed the end of the Akhmim fragment. According to Origen (Comm. Mt. 10.17), the *Gospel of Peter* supplied evidence that the brothers of the Lord were sons of Joseph by his first marriage. This may indicate that the Gospel began with a birth narrative. In addition to the Akhmim fragment, there are two tiny fragments of another Greek manuscript (P. Oxy. 2949) of the late second or early third century. The differences between one of these and the Akhmim text suggest that the latter cannot be relied on to preserve the text of the original Gospel very accurately.

The quite probable use of the *Gospel of Peter* by Justin and very probable use of it by Melito of Sardis suggest that it must date from before the middle of the second century. At the end of the second century, Bishop Serapion of Antioch heard of a dispute over its use in the church of Rhossus. When he discovered it was being used to support docetic heresy and that a few passages in it were suspect from this point of view, he disallowed its use (Eusebius, *Hist. Eccl.* 6.12). Recent scholarship has come to the conclusion that, on the evidence of the Akhmim fragment, the Gospel itself cannot be considered docetic, though there are phrases which docetists could interpret in their support. This conclusion is confirmed by its probable use by Justin, Melito and the Syriac *Didascalia*, which suggests that it was quite widely accepted in orthodox circles.

The Gospel is distinguished, in the text we have, by its interest in the fulfillment of prophecy in the passion narrative,* its strongly anti-Jewish bias (*see* Anti-Semitism), which emphasizes the sole responsibility of the Jews for the death of Jesus, its heightening of the miraculous, and its apologetic interest in supplying evidence for the resurrection. Distinctive features include Herod's participation in the trial of Jesus and ordering of the crucifixion to be carried out by Jews, and the account (which has a close parallel in *Ascension of Isaiah* 3:16-17) of the exit of the risen Christ from the tomb, escorted by angels.*

The Gospel's relationship to the canonical Gospels is disputed. There are parallels to all four canonical Gospels, but remarkably few verbal parallels. Some scholars have thought the *Gospel of Peter* completely independent of the canonical Gospels; most have thought it dependent on all four. J. D. Crossan has

recently argued that although sections dependent on the canonical Gospels have been secondarily added to the text, the greater part of the Akhmim text is not only independent of the canonical Gospels, but actually a source used by all four canonical Gospels.

A more plausible view needs to build on the following three observations: (1) The major parallels are with special Matthean material (M) and with Markan material; (2) Close verbal parallels are largely limited to the passages parallel to Markan material, which are closer to the text of Mark itself than to Matthew's redaction of Mark; (3) If Markan and M passages are distinguished, both in Matthew and in the *Gospel of Peter*, it can be seen that connections between Markan and M passages are quite differently made in Matthew and the *Gospel of Peter* respectively. It seems then that the *Gospel of Peter* drew primarily on Mark's Gospel and on Matthew's special source, independently of Matthew's Gospel. Whereas Matthew gave priority to the Markan narrative and augmented it from his special source, the *Gospel of Peter* gave priority to the narrative of M and augmented it from Mark. M was probably the oral tradition of the church of Antioch and its neighboring churches, which acquired written form in the *Gospel of Peter* no doubt some decades after Matthew had used it. On this view, the *Gospel of Peter* would be valuable evidence for the study of Matthew's use of his sources.

3. Papyrus Fragments of Unknown Gospels.
Among the papyrus fragments of extracanonical Gospels there are some which cannot be identified as belonging to any known Gospel. The following are the most important:

3.1. P. Oxy. 840. This fourth- or fifth-century manuscript contains the conclusion of a discourse by Jesus, followed by a visit to the Temple in which Jesus engages in a discussion about ritual purification (*see* Clean and Unclean) with a Pharisaic chief priest named Levi. Some scholars have defended the historicity of the account.

3.2. P. Egerton 2. This manuscript, dating from around A.D. 150, is one of the two earliest Christian manuscripts extant, along with the fragment of the Gospel of John in 𝔓⁵². It contains fragments of four pericopes. The first gives the conclusion of a controversy between Jesus and the Jewish leaders, in which Jesus has been accused of breaking the Law and at the conclusion of which he escapes an attempt to stone him. There is close verbal relationship with several parts of John's Gospel. The second pericope concerns the healing of a leper, the third contains a version of the question about the tribute money, and the fourth contains an otherwise unknown miracle story. The second and third resemble Synoptic material.

The relationship of this unknown Gospel to the canonical Gospels is disputed. Some have argued that it is entirely independent of all four, shares common tradition with them or was even a source used by Mark and John. If this were accepted, the distinctively Johannine material in the first pericope would be very important for the study of the sources of John's Gospel. But it seems at least equally possible that this unknown Gospel draws on oral tradition which had been substantially influenced by the canonical Gospels.

3.3. Oxy P. 1224. The legible parts of this fourth-century manuscript contain parallels to three Synoptic sayings of Jesus and one otherwise unknown saying whose authenticity was defended by J. Jeremias. It could be from an early Gospel independent of the Synoptics, but is too brief for any firm conclusions.

3.4. Fayyum Fragment. This third-century fragment parallels Mark 14:27, 29-30 with some variation. It is too brief for its relationship to Mark to be ascertainable.

3.5. Strasbourg Coptic Fragment. Unlike the preceding fragments, which are all in Greek, this fifth- or sixth-century fragment is in Coptic. "We, the apostles" are the speakers, but this phrase could be consistent with attribution to a particular apostle (cf. *Gos. Pet.* 14:59). The contents are a prayer* of Jesus, a conversation with the disciples and a revelation of his glory* to them, all in the context of bidding them farewell, most probably before the passion but possibly before the ascension. There are close contacts with both Synoptic and Johannine material, on which this unknown Gospel is probably dependent.

4. Jewish Christian Gospels.

The Gospels used by specifically Jewish Christian groups in the early church—whether, like the Ebionites, they were heretical in the eyes of the Catholic Church, or, like the Nazarenes, they were orthodox but separate from the predominantly Gentile Catholic Church—have unfortunately survived only in quotations by the Fathers, along with some untrustworthy evidence from the Middle Ages. The titles which the Fathers use for these Gospels and the manner in which they refer to them leave it very unclear how many such Gospels there were and from which the surviving quotations come. Recent scholarly consensus distinguishes three, all of which seem to have resembled the Synoptic Gospels in genre:

4.1. Gospel of the Hebrews. The most recent investigation by A. F. J. Klijn assigns seven quotations to this

Gospel. These show no sign of dependence on the canonical Gospels. One saying also appears in the *Gospel of Thomas* (2). Otherwise the traditions are quite distinctive to this Gospel, including the account of the risen Christ's appearance to his brother James the Just, who was highly revered in Jewish Christian tradition. The Gospel was written in Greek before the middle of the second century. It may well have originated in Egypt, where its title would have designated it the Gospel of the Greek-speaking Jewish Christian community and distinguished it from the *Gospel of the Egyptians* (see 5. below) used by the Gentile Christian community in Egypt.

4.2. Gospel of the Nazarenes. Klijn assigns twenty-two quotations definitely to this Gospel, but many of these are indications of points where a few words differed from the text of Matthew's Gospel. Others are more substantial additions to or variations from the text of Matthew. The Gospel was evidently a free translation (in targumic style; *see* Targums) of Matthew into Aramaic or Syriac. The view of Jerome and others that it was actually the Semitic original from which our Greek Matthew was translated cannot be maintained. In Jerome's time it was used by the Nazarene community in Beroea in Syria, and may have originated among them in the second century.

4.3. Gospel of the Ebionites. Epiphanius preserves seven quotations of this Gospel, which was composed in Greek and based on all three Synoptic Gospels. Taking Matthew as its principal authority, it drew on Mark and Luke in order to combine the three in a harmonized narrative. It is thus an example of the apparently rather common second-century tendency to produce harmonies of the various Gospel texts, of which Tatian's *Diatessaron* is the most famous example.

Ebionite theology is evident in the quotations. Since the Ebionites rejected the virginal conception and held an adoptionist christology, the Gospel began with the baptism* of Jesus. The Ebionite prohibition on eating meat and their opposition to the Temple* cult are also reflected.

5. Gospel of the Egyptians.

This Gospel appears to have been the one predominantly used by Gentile Christians in Egypt until it was superseded by the canonical Gospels in orthodox circles. Unfortunately, little is known of it. The only clear information comes from Clement of Alexandria, who refers to a conversation it contained between Jesus and Salome (a woman disciple of Jesus who is prominent in apocryphal, especially Gnostic, Gospel traditions). This contained sayings, also known from the *Gospel of Thomas* (22, 37; cf. also 2 Clem. 12:1-2), about the rejection of sexuality, which reflect an encratite view of salvation as the restoration of the original condition of humanity without sexual differentiation. Whether the Gospel was not merely encratite but Gnostic is unknown. The Sethian Gnostic work from Nag Hammadi, which is also known as the *Gospel of the Egyptians* (CG III, 2 and IV, 2), is a quite different work.

6. Secret Gospel of Mark.

M. Smith discovered in 1958 (but did not publish until 1973) a previously unknown letter of Clement of Alexandria in an eighteenth-century copy. The majority of scholars have provisionally accepted Smith's case for the authenticity of the letter, though not all rule out the possibilities that it is an ancient pseudepigraphon (in which case its witness to the *Secret Gospel of Mark* could still be of value) or a modern forgery.

Clement claims to know three versions of Mark's Gospel: (1) the Gospel used publicly in the church (our canonical Mark), which Mark wrote first; (2) the *Secret Gospel*, which Mark wrote later, in Alexandria, by adding to his earlier text certain secret traditions which are revealed only to initiates; (3) the version used by the Carpocratian Gnostics, who have made their own additions to the *Secret Gospel*. Clement gives no more than two words of the material peculiar to (3), but quotes the two passages which the *Secret Gospel* adds to the public Gospel. After Mark 10:34, the *Secret Gospel* had a story set in Bethany, which is clearly related to the Johannine account of the raising of Lazarus, but told in Markan rather than Johannine language. Six days after Jesus raised the young man (who is anonymous in the *Secret Gospel*) from the dead, he came to Jesus at night, wearing only a linen cloth, and Jesus taught him the mystery of the kingdom of God.* The reference must be to some kind of initiation, most likely involving baptism. The *Secret Gospel's* second addition to Mark occurs in 10:46: it is an oddly brief reference to Jesus' refusal to receive the young man's sister and his mother and Salome.

Smith argued that the additional material is so characteristically Markan that it must derive from the same body of tradition as canonical Mark. Some have argued that canonical Mark is a later, expurgated version of the *Secret Gospel*. Others regard the material in the *Secret Gospel* as late interpolations, deliberately imitative of Markan style and content. So far the evidence remains peculiarly puzzling.

7. Birth and Infancy Gospels.

From the second century onwards, interest in the

family background and early life of Jesus produced many works devoted solely to this theme. Two second-century works on this theme proved extraordinarily popular for many centuries, and all later Gospels of this kind were indebted to one or both of them.

7.1. Protevangelium of James. This tells of the miraculous birth of Mary to her childless parents, Joachim and Anna, who dedicate her to the Temple where she lives until entrusted to Joseph. The story from the annunciation to the massacre of the innocents (concluding with the martyrdom of Zechariah, the father of John the Baptist,* at that time) makes free use of the narratives of both Matthew and Luke, laying special emphasis on the virginity of Mary. The birth of Jesus in a cave is miraculous, preserving Mary's virginal state. Her perpetual virginity is implied, since the brothers of Jesus are considered sons of Joseph by a previous marriage. The work is attributed to one of them, James, though he does not appear in the narrative. The main purpose of the work is clearly the glorification of the figure of Mary as a pure virgin, though an apologetic defense of her virginity against Jewish anti-Christian polemic may also have influenced the traditions it contains. It has been called midrashic (according to the loose use of that term in some NT scholarship; *see* Midrash) because of its creative use of OT texts in developing the narrative. It probably originated in second-century Syria, where its ideas about the virginity of Mary can be paralleled from other texts.

7.2. Infancy Gospel of Thomas. This work consists solely of a series of stories of miracles performed by the child Jesus up to his twelfth year. For example, Jesus makes sparrows out of clay and brings them to life (a story which later found its way into the Qur'an). He heals the injured, raises the dead, curses his enemies so that they die, proves superior in knowledge to all his schoolteachers. The general effect is to manifest his superhuman nature to all who encounter him.

In its original form the work must date from the second century, but from the extant texts in many versions it is very difficult to establish the original text.

7.3. Later Gospels. The Coptic *History of Joseph* does for Joseph what the *Protevangelium of James* did for Mary. The Latin *Infancy Gospel of Matthew* (often called Pseudo-Matthew) transmitted much of the content of the *Protevangelium of James* and the *Infancy Gospel of Thomas,* along with further legends of its own, to the medieval West. The Latin *Infancy Gospel* published by M. R. James is important for one of its sources, otherwise unknown, which must be of early origin. Many other late birth and infancy Gospels in many languages are extant.

8. Gospel of Nicodemus.

This title is given to a work combining two distinct parts: the *Acts of Pilate* and the *Descensus ad Inferos* (descent to Hades). The *Acts of Pilate* is an account of the trial and crucifixion of Jesus, and of an investigation by the Sanhedrin which receives evidence of the resurrection of Jesus. The work is notable for its anti-Jewish and apologetic tendencies. *Descensus ad Inferos* is the fullest account from the early church of Christ's activity in the realm of the dead between his death and his resurrection: his victory over the powers of Hades and his liberation of Adam and the righteous dead. The *Gospel of Nicodemus* in its present form is generally assigned to the fifth century, but undoubtedly draws on earlier sources.

9. Post-Resurrection Revelations.

Those who wished to amplify the known teaching of Jesus or to trace to Jesus secret revelations handed down in esoteric tradition found the most suitable literary vehicle to be an account of Jesus teaching his disciples in the period between his resurrection and ascension. Often such accounts take the form of a dialog in which Jesus is questioned by his disciples about subjects left unclear by his teaching before his death. Gospels of this kind sometimes draw on traditions of the sayings of Jesus, in order to interpret and develop them further, but often the contents are unrelated to Gospel traditions. Though the apocalyptic discourse of Jesus in the Synoptics (Mt 24 par.) was sometimes a model for such works, their genre is often as close to that of the apocalypses as to other kinds of Gospel (and so several of these works are entitled Apocalypses).

Though this kind of Gospel proved especially useful to and popular among Gnostics, it did not originate with and was not confined to Gnostics. Orthodox examples from the early second century are the *Apocalypse of Peter* and the *Epistle of the Apostles*, both significant for the Gospel traditions they contain, the latter for the way in which it seems to draw on the canonical Gospels, including John, within a continuing oral tradition. The Freer Logion (added to Mk 16:14 in one manuscript) is not a complete work, but illustrates the second-century tendency to ascribe additional revelations to the risen Christ. Later non-Gnostic works of this type, from the third century or later, are the *Questions of Bartholomew*, the Syriac *Testament of our Lord*, and the Ethiopic *Testament of Our Lord in Galilee*. Gnostic works of this type include the *Apocryphon of James* (CG I, 2), the *Book of Thomas* (CG II, 7), the *Sophia of Jesus Christ* (CG III, 4 and BG 8502, 3), the *Dialogue of the Saviour* (CG III, 5), the *First Apocalypse of James* (CG V, 3), the Coptic *Apocalypse of Peter* (CG VII, 3), the *Gospel of Mary* (BG 8502, 1), the *Pistis Sophia* and the *Books of Jeu*.

See also GOSPEL (GENRE); JESUS IN NON-CHRISTIAN SOURCES.

BIBLIOGRAPHY. R. E. Brown, "The *Gospel of Peter* and Canonical Gospel Priority," *NTS* 33 (1987) 321-343; J. H. Charlesworth and J. R. Mueller, *The New Testament Apocrypha and Pseudepigrapha: A Guide to Publications* (ATLA Bibliography Series 17; Metuchen, NJ, and London: American Theological Library Association and Scarecrow Press, 1987); J. D. Crossan, *Four Other Gospels* (Minneapolis: Winston, 1985); idem, *The Cross That Spoke* (San Francisco: Harper and Row, 1988); F. T. Fallon and R. Cameron, "The Gospel of Thomas: A Forschungsbericht and Analysis," *ANRW* 2.25/6: 4195-4251; S. Gero, "Apocryphal Gospels: A Survey of Textual and Literary Problems," *ANRW* 2.25/5: 3969-96; E. Hennecke et al., eds., *New Testament Apocrypha* (London: SCM Press, 1963), vol. 1; G. Howard, "The Gospel of the Ebionites," *ANRW* 2.25/5: 4034-53; A. F. J. Klijn, "Das Hebräer- und das Nazoräerevangelium," *ANRW* 2.25/5: 3997-4033; H. Koester, *Ancient Christian Gospels: Their History and Development* (Philadelphia: Trinity Press International, 1990); P. Perkins, *The Gnostic Dialogue* (New York: Paulist, 1980); D. R. Schwartz, "Viewing the Holy Utensils (P. Ox. V, 840)," *NTS* 32 (1986) 153-59; M. Smith, "Clement of Alexandria and Secret Mark: The Score at the End of the First Decade," *HTR* 75 (1982) 449-461; C. Tuckett, *Nag Hammadi and the Gospel Tradition* (Edinburgh: T. & T. Clark, 1986); D. Wenham, ed., *Gospel Perspectives 5: The Jesus Tradition Outside the Gospels* (Sheffield: JSOT, 1985): D. F. Wright, "Papyrus Egerton 2 (the *Unknown Gospel*)—Part of the *Gospel of Peter?*," *Second Century* 5 (1985-86) 129-150.   R. J. Bauckham

GOSPELS (HISTORICAL RELIABILITY)

Different scholars come to widely divergent conclusions when they assess the historical reliability of the Gospels. About the only point on which virtually all are agreed is that the Gospels were written primarily for theological rather than historical purposes. In other words, Matthew, Mark, Luke and John above all wanted to commend their understanding of the person and work of Jesus to their first-century audiences. But most scholars also recognize that in order for the four Evangelists' representations of Jesus to be convincing, they had to match the course of events in his life. How much of a match is required and how much is actually present are questions which are both vigorously debated. This essay is written from the conviction that a fair assessment of the evidence supports a high degree of historicity. It must be stressed, however, that the Gospels have to be evaluated according to the historiographical canons of their day and not anachronistically compared with modern conceptions of what is and is not so-called reliable history.

1. External Evidence
2. Internal Evidence
3. Philosophical Considerations

1. External Evidence.

1.1. The Text of the Gospels. Non-Christian religions often allege that the Gospels as they now appear cannot be trusted because the text has been greatly corrupted. This allegation has virtually no evidence to support it. There are 2,328 manuscripts and manuscript fragments surviving from the earliest centuries of the Christian church and representing all portions of the Gospels. The earliest fragment of any portion of the NT currently in existence is the John Rylands papyrus fragment (𝔓⁵²) of John 18:31-33, 37-38, which probably dates to c. A.D. 125 or within about thirty years of the original composition of the Fourth Gospel. Twenty-one papyri containing major sections of one or more Gospels can be dated to the third and fourth centuries, while five virtually complete NTs survive from the fourth and fifth centuries. Compared with the numbers and ages of manuscripts which have survived for most other ancient documents, including many believed to contain reliable accounts of historical events, this evidence is overwhelming.

As a result, textual critics (*see* Textual Criticism) have been able to reconstruct a highly reliable prototype of what the original Gospel writers undoubtedly wrote. Estimates suggest that from ninety-seven to ninety-nine per cent of the original text is securely recoverable. More than fifty-four per cent of all of the verses in the Gospels are entirely free of textual variants, and the vast majority of those which remain have no bearing on questions of historicity. Modern editions of the Greek NT (Nestle-Aland; UBS) print the textual variants which have any significant effect on meaning, and most modern English translations use footnotes to alert readers to the most disputed texts (e.g., Mt 6:13b; Mk 16:9-20; Jn 7:53-8:11).

1.2. Archeology. Archeology* has not played nearly as major a role in Gospel studies as it has for many other sections of Scripture. Occasionally the existence of previously unattested places or people has been demonstrated. For example, only in 1888 did the site

of the pool of Bethesda become known (Jn 5:2), and excavations demonstrated that it contained five porticoes as described by John. So too, in 1961 the first reference in Roman sources to "Pontius Pilate,* Prefect of Judea" was discovered in an inscription in Caesarea Maritimis. But for the most part, the type of information which the Gospels contain—narratives of actions and teachings of Jesus—do not lend themselves to archeological corroboration or contradiction. Since no one was able to tape-record them, there are no physical traces by which one can test the trustworthiness of the Gospel record.

1.3. Written Testimony Outside the Gospels. Virtually all biblical scholars acknowledge that there is enough information from ancient non-Christian sources to give lie to the myth (still, however, widely believed in popular circles and by some scholars in other fields— see esp. G. A. Wells) which claims that Jesus never existed. Most also recognize that only a paucity of the testimony of the Gospels can be corroborated by a comparison with other materials. Given that Jesus was not perceived by non-Christians as a significant political or military leader, this is not surprising. Ancient historians had little reason to consider that centuries later he would prove significant; even as the founder of a religious movement, he had little impact during his lifetime (*see* Jesus in Non-Christian Sources).

1.3.1. Greco-Roman Testimony. The third-century writer Julius Africanus cites a first-century Greek historian, Thallus, who referred to the darkness that occurred at the time of the crucifixion (*see* Death of Jesus). Early in the second century the Roman legate Pliny the Younger wrote that Christians met regularly and sang hymns to Christ "as if to a god" (*Epp.* 10:96.7), in a way that suggested he realized that Jesus had been a human but doubted that he was a god. About the same time the Roman historian Tacitus clearly referred to "Christ who had been executed by sentence of the procurator Pontius Pilate in the reign of Tiberius" (*Ann.* 15:44). Tacitus' Roman contemporary Suetonius speaks in one passage of "Chrestus" as the one at whose instigation a riot involving Jews and Christians in Rome broke out (*Claudius* 25:4)—probably a garbled reference to Christ as the founder of Christianity.

1.3.2. Jewish Testimony. Jewish literature from the first centuries of the Christian era contains additional references to Jesus. Some have been censored, so once there were probably even more than now remain. A famous passage in the Talmud speaks of Jesus as "the Nazarene" who "practiced magic and led Israel astray" (*b. Sanh.* 107b). This reference is particularly interesting because it seems to admit that Jesus worked miracles, even though its interpretation of them differs from Christian belief. In several places Jesus is called the son of "Pandera"; the second-century Christian writer Origen explained that the Jews believed that Jesus was the child of Mary by an adulterous relationship with a Roman soldier by that name (*Contra Celsum* 1:32). The name and legend could well have come from a corruption of the Greek word *parthenos* for "virgin" and thus provide indirect though corrupt testimony to the Gospels' claim that Jesus was not the natural child of Joseph but was virgin-conceived (*see* Birth of Jesus). Again in the Talmud (*b. Sanh.* 43a) Jesus is said to have been hanged on the eve of the Passover. This text also teaches that "Jesus had five disciples, Mattha, Naqai, Nezer, Buni and Todah," possible references to Matthew, Nicodemus, an anonymous Nazarene, John and Thaddeus.

The most interesting of all of the Jewish testimonies to Jesus is the account in Josephus* (*Ant.* 18.63-64). Here one learns that Jesus was a wise man who wrought surprising feats, taught many, gathered a large following and was crucified by Pilate. Extant copies of Josephus' writings also affirm that Jesus was the Messiah and that he was raised from the dead. Because Josephus was not a Christian, few people believe that he actually wrote these words; they may well have been added by scribes in later Christian circles which preserved his work. But the rest of his statements fit his style elsewhere and are most likely authentic. Josephus also offers independent corroboration of the ministry of John the Baptist* (18:117) and of James, the brother of Jesus (20:200).

1.3.3. Other Christian Testimony. Outside the New Testament various apocryphal Gospels present additional teachings and deeds of Christ (*see* Gospels [Apocryphal]). Some of these are clearly legendary attempts to fill in the "gaps" in the Gospel record—stories of Jesus the child prodigy (e.g., the *Infancy Gospel of Thomas* and the *Protevangelium of James)* or additional details concerning his trial, death, descent into hell and resurrection* (e.g., the *Gospel of Nicodemus* and the *Gospel of Peter).* Many emanate from Gnostic circles and purport to reveal secret teachings of Christ, often spoken after his resurrection in private conversation with the disciples (e.g., the *Apocryphon of John* and the *Dialogue of the Savior).* Two of these contain some sayings attributed to Jesus and often believed to be authentic, or at least as trustworthy as parts of the canonical Gospels (the Coptic *Gospel of Thomas* and the *Apocryphon of James).* But none of these extra-canonical writings can be shown to date from before the mid-second century, so that

the trustworthiness of the NT Gospels, which date from the first century, is in no way impugned. Though widely disputed, those documents from the Gnostic library at Nag Hammadi (esp. the Coptic *Gospel of Thomas)* which contain teachings of Jesus most closely paralleled in the NT are precisely those which are most clearly dependent on and inferior to the Synoptic Gospels (see Blomberg in France & Wenham, vol. 5; Tuckett).

It has often been observed how little the Acts, epistles and Revelation reflect any awareness of the Gospel tradition. Only rarely is a teaching of Jesus quoted (but see Acts 20:35; 1 Cor 7:10; 9:14; 11:23-25; 1 Tim 5:18). Nevertheless, the epistles are filled with numerous allusions to Jesus' teaching (e.g., Rom 12:14; 12:17; 13:8-9; 14:10; 16:9; 1 Thess 2:14-16; 5:2), which suggests that such awareness was much more widespread than a superficial survey of Scripture discloses (see Stanton). The book of James contains allusions to the Sermon on the Mount* in nearly every paragraph, while Acts reflects the basic outline of Mark in several of the longer speeches which summarize the gospel as preached by Peter and Paul (and in 10:36-41 and 13:24-25 even more specific details are included).

1.4. Authorship. Many people have tried to assess the historicity of the Gospels in light of their authorship. It is often assumed that if the traditional ascriptions are correct, then these writers would have reflected firsthand eyewitness testimony in the case of Matthew and John, and secondhand in the case of Luke (cf. Lk 1:1-4). If the ascriptions are incorrect, as most modern scholars believe, then it is often assumed that the Gospels' historicity is impugned. But in fact eyewitnesses can err, accidentally or deliberately, while secondary sources can preserve accurate information reliably transmitted to them. For these reasons, the value of the debate over authorship for questions of historicity has probably been exaggerated.

Strictly speaking, the four Gospels are anonymous documents. The titles were added later, probably early in the second century when the texts were first gathered together as four versions of the one gospel. But the virtually unanimous early-Christian testimony which associates them with Matthew, Mark, Luke and John (see e.g., Eusebius, *Hist. Eccl.* 3:39.4, 16; Irenaeus, *Haer.* 3:1.1-2) should be treated very seriously. And even scholars who see the Gospels as written by anonymous Christians almost always date them within the first century. This is certainly well within a time period that would have permitted accurate information about the life and times of Jesus to have been preserved, even if it in no way guarantees such preservation.

1.5. Sources. An author, however close in time to the events he or she describes, is nevertheless only as reliable as his or her sources. The most common reconstruction of the literary interrelationship of the Synoptic Gospels has Matthew and Luke depending on at least two written sources—Mark and Q* (a hypothetical document accounting for material Matthew and Luke have in common which is not found in Mark; see Synoptic Problem). Q is usually dated to the 50s and Mark is assumed to have utilized source material at least that old. With Christ's crucifixion no earlier than A.D. 30, the time gap between events and written accounts is reduced to about twenty years, a far cry from the centuries that were usually necessary for supernatural legends to attach themselves to other historical characters from antiquity (see Stein).

1.6. Oral Tradition. Any time lag between events and their recording allows for potential distortion. Despite all of the external evidence so far cited, many scholars doubt the reliability of the Gospels because they doubt either the ability or the interest of early Christians to have preserved accurately the story of Jesus' ministry as they passed it along by word of mouth. A number of factors, however, supports the likelihood that the Gospel tradition was carefully preserved.

(1) Jesus was perceived by his followers as one who proclaimed God's* Word in a way which demanded careful retelling. (2) Over ninety per cent of his teachings has poetic elements which would have made them easy to memorize. (3) The almost universal method of education in antiquity, and especially in Israel, was rote memorization, which enabled people accurately to recount quantities of material far greater than all of the Gospels put together. (4) Oral storytelling often permitted a wide range of freedom in selecting and describing details but required fixed points of a narrative to be preserved unchanged. (5) Written notes and a kind of shorthand were often privately kept by rabbis* and their disciples, despite a publicly stated preference for oral tradition. (6) The lack of teachings ascribed to Jesus about later church controversies (e.g., circumcision, speaking in tongues) suggests that the disciples did not freely invent material and read it back onto the lips of Jesus. (7) The degree to which Jesus emphasized his imminent return, that is, to the exclusion of envisioning the establishment of an ongoing community of followers, has been exaggerated (*see* Church). Hence, the claim that the disciples would have had no interest in preserving the Gospel tradition until the second generation of Christianity is doubtful (*see* Form Criticism).

2. Internal Evidence.

2.1. The Intentions of the Evangelists. Gospel studies have often introduced a false dichotomy between history and theology. One group of scholars seeks to harmonize all of the data of the four Gospels in order to create a composite, comprehensive life of Christ which blurs the unique emphases of each Gospel in its own right. Another group so emphasizes the theological distinctives of each individual Evangelist that it rejects the possibility of constructing any kind of plausible harmony. The two clearest statements in the Gospels about their authors' own intentions suggest that history and theology both played important roles (Lk 1:1-4; Jn 20:31). In fact, it is often precisely when one recognizes the theological emphases of a particular Gospel that one can understand why it differs from the others and can see those differences as complementary rather than contradictory.

Various studies of the Gospel genre (*see* Gospel [Genre]) have linked Matthew, Mark, Luke and John with apocalyptic,* aretalogy (a Greco-Roman story of a "divine man"*), tragedy or comedy, midrash* (a Jewish form of interpretive re-writing of authoritative narrative) or parable,* while many have viewed the Gospel as a new genre invented by Mark. But probably the best approach sees important parallels with the more historically reliable Jewish and Greco-Roman biographies and histories (see esp. Aune).

Ancient biographers and historians did not feel constrained to write from detached and so-called objective viewpoints. They did not give equal treatment to all periods of an individual's life. They felt free to write in topical as well as chronological sequence. They were highly selective in the material they included, choosing that which reinforced the morals they wished to inculcate. In an era which knew neither quotation marks nor plagiarism, speakers' words were abbreviated, explained, paraphrased and contemporized in whatever ways individual authors deemed beneficial for their audiences. All of these features occur in the Gospels, and none of them detracts from the Evangelists' integrity. At the same time, little if any material was recorded solely out of historical interest; interpreters must recognize theological motives as central to each text.

2.2. A Comparison of the Synoptics.

2.2.1. Agreement. The most striking feature one notices in comparing Matthew, Mark and Luke is their similarity. Approximately ninety-one per cent (c. 601 out of 661 verses) of Mark's information reappears in Matthew or Luke, and usually in both. An additional 235 verses appear in some form in both Matthew and

Luke but not in Mark. Approximately sixty-eight per cent of the self-contained units of narrative common to Mark and either Matthew or Luke appear in the same sequence in each. Given the wealth of detail which could have been told about Jesus, the fact that these three Evangelists chose to follow such similar outlines (and almost certainly to borrow from one another in some kind of literary interrelationship) suggests that a relatively fixed manner of telling the gospel originated at an early date in the life of the church. This common *kerygma* ("proclamation") clearly enhances the case for the Gospels' historical reliability.

2.2.2. Disagreement. Nevertheless, numerous differences among the Synoptics appear whenever parallel accounts are laid side-by-side. For many critics these differences are of such a nature and number that no amount of external evidence can convince them of the Gospels' trustworthiness. On the other hand, most of the differences are so minor that it seems unfair to refer to them as contradictions. Historians and biographers regularly add, omit or reword stories and portions of stories without necessarily falsifying them. At the same time, there are a handful of more glaring discrepancies which puzzle all readers. But plausible solutions have been suggested for all of them; fair-minded scholars must at least consider credible harmonizations before dismissing the whole process as impossible. In many instances it is precisely when one understands the varying theological concerns of the different Evangelists that one can appreciate how apparently discrepant accounts are in fact complementary rather than contradictory (see Blomberg in Carson and Woodbridge). The following survey offers a representative sampling of seven major types of problems which appear, a few of the most famous illustrations of those problems and some possible solutions.

(1) The theologies of the Evangelists may seem to conflict. Mark portrays the disciples as without understanding following Jesus' walking on the water (Mk 6:52); Matthew has them worship* him as the Son of God* (Mt 14:33). In Mark, after stilling the storm, Jesus berates the disciples for their lack of faith* (Mk 4:40); in Matthew he concedes that they have "a little faith" (Mt 8:26). Both tendencies are credible in light of the disciples' mixture of faith and disbelief elsewhere and each fits into distinctive emphases of the Gospels in which they appear.

(2) One Evangelist may seem to correct his source. In Mark, Jesus' reply to the so-called rich young ruler seems to deny his goodness (Mk 10:18); Matthew rewords the comment so that Jesus merely inquires, "Why do you ask me about the good?" (Mt 19:17). Matthew is not contradicting Mark but trying to avoid a misinterpretation of him. Similarly, Luke reports Jesus as telling his followers to hate their parents (Lk 14:26); Matthew explains that this means they must love* God much more than family* (Mt 10:37).

(3) Events may appear in contradictory orders in different Gospels. Luke places Jesus' rejection in Nazareth at the beginning of his Galilean ministry (Lk 4:16-30); Mark locates it much later (Mk 6:1-6). Usually, it is best not to assume chronology* unless it is explicitly indicated. Luke has topically relocated this story at the front of his Gospel to show the type of rejection Jesus would receive from his native people throughout his ministry. In the same way, Luke reverses the order of the second and third temptations* of Christ to build toward a climax with Jesus in the Temple in Jerusalem (Lk 4:1-13; cf. Mt 4:1-11). Both of these are key themes throughout his work.

(4) A passage may be so abbreviated that it seems to contradict a fuller parallel. Mark has Jairus and his companions come to Jesus twice, once to tell him of his daughter's illness and once to say that she has died (Mk 5:21-43). Matthew so compresses the account that Jairus comes only once and tells Jesus right at the outset of the story that his daughter is dead (Mt 9:18-26). This type of literary abridgment was common in antiquity and not perceived as misleading or in error (cf. Lucian, *How to Write History*, 56). Similar telescoping appears in Matthew's account of the withered fig tree (Mt 21:18-22; cf. Mk 11:12-14, 20-21) and in Luke's account of Jesus' trial before the Sanhedrin,* if Luke is not in fact using a different tradition altogether, rather than Mark (Lk 22:66-71; cf. Mk 14:53—15:1).

(5) Sayings of Jesus may appear in different contexts. The Sermon on the Mount* (Mt 5—7) and the Olivet Discourse (Mt 24—25) gather together teachings which are scattered all around the Gospel of Luke. Some of these may simply reflect Jesus' repeated utterances; others no doubt reflect the common practice of creating composite speeches. Again, no one questioned the integrity of ancient historians when they utilized a device that modern readers often find artificial. Yet again, both sermons may be excerpts of a much longer original.

(6) A unique event may be told twice in apparently contradictory ways. Many see the feedings of the 5,000 and the 4,000 (Mk 6:32-44; 8:1-10) or the two anointings of Jesus (Lk 7:36-50; Mk 14:3-9) as doublets of the same events. In each case, these are probably better viewed as separate incidents.

(7) Names and numbers may appear to contradict each other. In Matthew Jesus heals two blind men

along the Jericho road (Mt 20:30); in Mark he heals one (Mk 10:46). The latter does not exclude the former. In Mark Jesus exorcises a demoniac in the region near Gerasa (Mk 5:1); in Matthew it occurs in Gadara (Mt 8:28). The former is probably a city; the latter, a province.

2.3. The Synoptics and John. The Fourth Gospel stands out as distinct from the Synoptics in at least five principal ways (*see* Synoptics and John). (1) Most of John's material is unparalleled in Matthew, Mark and Luke, and only rarely does a passage common to the first three Gospels reappear in John. (2) John seems to have a much higher christology; only in his Gospel do explicit equations of Jesus with God ever appear (e.g., Jn 1:1; 10:30; 20:28). (3) The chronologies of John and the Synoptics are difficult to harmonize. Especially noteworthy are John's references to Jewish festivals (*see* Feasts), which indicate Jesus had at least a three-year ministry traveling back and forth between Judea and Galilee* (in the Synoptics Jesus seems to visit Jerusalem for the first time the week before his death) and to the day of his crucifixion (apparently on Passover rather than the day after as in the Synoptics). (4) Other historical anachronisms seem to abound, most notably the reference to Jewish excommunication of Christians from the synagogues (Jn 9:22). (5) John's writing style differs markedly from that of the Synoptics; Jesus' language is indistinguishable from John's and Christ speaks in lengthy discourses rather than pithy aphorisms. As a result, even scholars who grant a substantial measure of historical reliability to the Synoptics usually view John as having so overlaid his material with theological interpretation that the Fourth Gospel has become largely worthless for the reconstruction of the historical Jesus.

On the other hand, major themes of John include the revelation of truth* (see esp. 19:35), the incarnation* of the Logos* in space and time (1:14) and the inspiration of the apostles* by the Holy Spirit* to enable them to remember what Jesus did and said (14:26; 15:26). John would undermine his own theological emphases if his historical information were in error. He must be given an opportunity to be viewed as reliable before he is assumed to be untrustworthy.

Each of the five distinctives noted above must be set in a proper context. (1) Information is no less reliable for not being multiply attested. John probably wrote either to supplement the Synoptics or in independence from them; either way he was not likely to repeat much of their material (21:25). (2) The Synoptics certainly know of Jesus' divine status even if it is not emphasized (Mt 1:18; Lk 1:35; Mk 14:62), while John also underlines Jesus' subordination to the Father (Jn

14:28). The christologies differ but they do not contradict each other. (3) The Synoptics do not preclude a three-year ministry or additional visits to Jerusalem. The evidence suggesting Jesus' crucifixion on Passover in John (esp. 13:1; 18:28; 19:14, 31) is better taken as referring to the week-long Passover festival rather than just the first day of that feast. (4) Closer analysis dispels allegations of anachronism. The reference to putting Jesus' disciples out of the synagogue* does not refer to practice outside of Jerusalem nor to any formal ban on Christians as occurred toward the end of the first century. (5) Historical accuracy does not require exact quotation, merely faithful paraphrase. John's extended discourses may reflect homiletical development of the teachings of Jesus, shorter parallels to which may usually be found in the Synoptics (cf. e.g., Jn 3:3 with Mk 10:15). They also often represent private teaching for the disciples, whereas the Synoptics tend to focus more on his public ministry. There is no doubt that history and theology are interwoven in more complex fashion in John, but once it is recognized that he is utilizing a more dramatic genre (see esp. Michaels), a good case can be made for the historical trustworthiness of the Fourth Gospel within the conventions of its genre (see Robinson).

3. Philosophical Considerations.

3.1. Miracles and the Supernatural. For many readers the historicity of the Gospels is called into question simply because they are filled with miracle stories about the supernatural deeds of Christ. Disbelief in the miracles usually stems from any one of three different objections. (1) Philosophers of science often allege that modern science has proved the impossibility of the supernatural. (2) Philosophers of history often argue that the evidence in favor of a miracle can never outweigh the evidence against it, so that a rational person may never conclude that testimony in behalf of a supernatural event is reliable. Unless someone has personally experienced the same kind of miracle, there is always a more likely explanation for someone else's claim that one has occurred. (3) Philosophers of religion often compare the miracle stories in the Gospels with those in other ancient religious and philosophical traditions and believe that all are equally suspect.

In fact, none of these claims can withstand close scrutiny. First, the proper domain of science is the realm of the repeatable, predictable and verifiable. Miracles by definition are non-repeatable events. If there is a theistic God such as the Judeo-Christian tradition has affirmed, miracles are a natural corollary of his existence. Whether or not such a God exists cannot be determined by science. Second, personal experience is not a reliable criterion for determining truth. By that criterion evidence against the existence of ice would always demand that a primitive person in a tropical climate disbelieve it. Third, the testimony on behalf of other ancient miracles is usually not as strong, as consistent or as religiously significant as it is in the Gospels. Nevertheless, there is no reason to deny altogether the possibility of the miraculous in certain other ancient settings.

For many philosophers and theologians, the issue of the Gospels' credibility rests ultimately with the accounts of Jesus' resurrection.* Several alternatives have been put forward to explain the origin of belief in the risen Lord. Those which have largely been abandoned in scholarly circles include the views that (1) Jesus never really died on the cross but later revived; (2) his body was stolen; (3) the women went to the wrong tomb and found it empty; and (4) mass hallucination.

More common is some form of the view that the disciples' belief in the abiding significance of Jesus' message and goals convinced them that he was still alive spiritually and that this belief eventually became transformed, in Jewish categories, into the idea of a bodily resurrection. Had the Gospel begun in Hellenistic circles and later been transformed by Judaism, this view might be credible. But the direction of development was precisely the reverse. From the very outset belief in an empty tomb, and therefore a raised body, formed part of the Gospel tradition (see esp. 1 Cor 15:3-7), and in Jewish circles mere immortality of the soul was seldom affirmed. As long as one rejects a priori antisupernatural prejudices, the evidence may be seen to support a bodily resurrection of Jesus. All the proposed alternatives are even more incredible (see Ladd).

3.2 The Burden of Proof. Notwithstanding all of the evidence in favor of the general trustworthiness of the Gospels, many critics find little they can confidently endorse because they adopt a skeptical stance on the issue of the burden of proof. That is to say, they assume that each portion of the Gospels is suspect, and reverse that verdict only when overwhelming evidence points to historical reliability. But this method inverts standard procedures of historical investigation; it applies more rigorous criteria to the biblical material than students of ancient history ever apply elsewhere.

Once a historian has proved reliable where verifiable, once apparent errors or contradictions receive plausible solutions, the appropriate approach is to give that writer the benefit of the doubt in areas where

verification is not possible (cf. Goetz and Blomberg). Neither external nor internal testimony can prove the accuracy of most of the details of the Gospels; the necessary comparative data simply are lacking. But the coherence and consistency of material which cannot be tested with that which can be tested goes a long way toward inspiring confidence in the remaining portions of the texts.

See also FORM CRITICISM; REDACTION CRITICISM; SYNOPTICS AND JOHN; SYNOPTIC PROBLEM; TRADITION CRITICISM.

BIBLIOGRAPHY. K. Aland and B. Aland, *The Text of the New Testament* (Grand Rapids: Eerdmans, 1987); D. E. Aune, *The New Testament in Its Literary Environment* (Philadelphia: Westminster, 1987); C. L. Blomberg, *The Historical Reliability of the Gospels* (Downers Grove: InterVarsity, 1987); D. A. Carson and J. D. Woodbridge, eds., *Hermeneutics, Authority and Canon* (Grand Rapids: Zondervan, 1983); J. D. G. Dunn, *The Evidence for Jesus* (Philadelphia: Westminster, 1985); R. T. France, *The Evidence for Jesus* (Downers Grove: InterVarsity, 1986); R. T. France, D. Wenham and C. Blomberg, eds. *Gospel Perspectives* (6 vols.; Sheffield: JSOT, 1980-86); S. C. Goetz and C. L. Blomberg, "The Burden of Proof," *JSNT* 11 (1981) 39-63; G. R. Habermas, *Ancient Evidence for the Life of Jesus* (Nashville: Nelson, 1984); G. E. Ladd, *I Believe in the Resurrection of Jesus* (Grand Rapids: Eerdmans, 1975); R. Latourelle, *Finding Jesus through the Gospels* (New York: Alba, 1979); idem, *The Miracles of Jesus and the Theology of Miracles* (New York: Paulist, 1988); I. H. Marshall, *I Believe in the Historical Jesus* (Grand Rapids: Eerdmans, 1977); J. R. Michaels, *Servant and Son* (Atlanta: John Knox, 1981); R. Riesner, *Jesus als Lehrer* (Tübingen: Mohr, 1981); J. A. T. Robinson, *The Priority of John* (London: SCM, 1985); G. N. Stanton, *Jesus of Nazareth in New Testament Preaching* (Cambridge: University Press, 1974); R. H. Stein, *The Synoptic Problem* (Grand Rapids: Baker, 1987); C. M. Tuckett, *Nag Hammadi and the Gospel Tradition* (Edinburgh: T. & T. Clark, 1986); idem, "Thomas and the Synoptics," *NovT* 30 (1988) 132-57; G. A. Wells, *The Historical Evidence for Jesus* (New York: Prometheus, 1982).

C. L. Blomberg

GREAT COMMANDMENT. *See* COMMANDMENT.

GREAT COMMISSION. *See* APOSTLE; GENTILES; RESURRECTION.

GRIESBACH HYPOTHESIS. *See* SYNOPTIC PROBLEM.

H

HADES. *See* HEAVEN AND HELL.

HARDNESS OF HEART

The well-known OT idea of spiritual obduracy or moral insensitivity (often referred to as "hardness of heart") occurs in Jesus' teaching and in editorial comments in the Gospels, especially in Mark and John. In these latter writings the concept makes an especially important theological contribution.

1. OT Background
2. The Synoptic Gospels
3. The Gospel of John
4. Jesus

1. OT Background.

According to OT usage the heart is the seat of understanding, moral affection and will (Deut 6:5). A soft heart is receptive to the divine will; a hard heart is not. Pharaoh is the classic OT example of hardness of heart. Despite the many plagues brought against him through Moses,* Pharaoh (or God) "hardened his heart" (Ex 4:21; 7:3; 8:15, 32; 9:12, 34-35; 10:20, 27; 11:10) and refused to allow the Israelites to leave Egypt. God also hardened the heart of Sihon, king of Heshbon (Deut 2:30), who fought against Israel* and was defeated (Num 21:21-31).

Other figures of speech are used to express the idea of obduracy: "blind eyes," "deaf ears," "stiff neck" and "stubborn shoulder." These figures are frequently used in reference to Israel (Deut 29:2-4; Is 6:9-10; 29:9-10; 63:17; Jer 5:21-23; Ezek 11:19; 12:1-3). Sometimes God sends a lying spirit to deceive Israel or its leaders (Judg 9:23; 1 Sam 16:14; 18:10; 19:9; 2 Sam 17:14; 1 Kings 12:15). This tradition is also part of the obduracy idea.

As in the case of Pharaoh, Israel sometimes hardens itself and at other times is hardened by God. Isaiah 6:9-10, quoted in all four Gospels, is perhaps the most significant obduracy passage. According to the MT and Targum,* God commands the prophet to "make the heart of this people fat." The LXX, however, gives the text a different nuance: "for the

heart of this people has become fat." This difference is significant in the NT.

2. The Synoptic Gospels.

2.1. Mark. The theme of obduracy occurs in four passages in the Gospel of Mark. In 3:5 Pharisees* opposed to Jesus are described as having "hardness of heart." In 4:12 Jesus paraphrases Is 6:9-10, applying the passage to "outsiders" (i.e., non-disciples). In 6:52 and 8:17-21 even the disciples* of Jesus are described as having hardened hearts, unseeing eyes and deaf ears. Only two of the passages, 4:12 and 8:17-21, are presented as sayings of Jesus.

The interpretation of the first text has been vigorously debated, with the first word, the conjunction *hina*, at the center of the discussion. It has been variously translated "who," "with the result that," "in order that (it be fulfilled)" or "because." These suggestions, however, do not do justice to the syntax of the saying as a whole or to its wider context in Mark. It is better to understand *hina* in its normal final sense "in order that," as several scholars recently have come to recognize. That is, according to Mark, Jesus tells parables in order that outsiders (i.e., non-disciples) will not understand, repent* or be forgiven (*see* Forgiveness of Sins). Mark's citation is thus basically true to the thrust of the Isaianic passage as it is found in the MT and Targum.

In Mark 8:17-21 Jesus applies the language of obduracy to the disciples themselves. Many interpreters believe that these passages reflect the Evangelist's interest in the secrecy theme, a theme which may have been an early attempt to explain why Jesus' messianic status was not understood, by the disciples or by anyone else, before the resurrection* (See Christ; Gospel of Mark).

2.2. Matthew. The First Gospel shows little interest in the Markan obduracy theme. The Evangelist omits reference to the disciples' obdurate condition (cf. Mt 14:25-33 with Mk 6:48-52; Mt 16:5-12 with Mk 8:17-21). He also omits reference to the Pharisees' "hardness of heart" (cf. Mt 12:13 with Mk 3:5), although Jesus does inveigh against the scribes* and Pharisees, calling them "hypocrites," "fools" and "blind guides" (Mt 23:13-36). Even though Matthew retains Mark's paraphrase of Isaiah 6:9-10 (Mt 13:13), he introduces the text with the conjunction *hoti* ("because"), not *hina* ("in order that") as in Mark. He then augments his Markan source with a verbatim quotation of the LXX version of Isaiah 6:9-10 (Mt 13:14-15), a version which suggests, contrary to the MT and Targum, that obduracy is not a condition brought on by God. Matthew's understanding of obduracy may be summed up in two points: (1) The disciples of Jesus on occasion may have suffered temporary lapses of faith, but they were never spiritually obdurate or opposed to Jesus; (2) Jesus' teaching did not promote obduracy, it only encountered it.

2.3. Luke. The Third Gospel also appears to reject Mark's obduracy theme. Although the Evangelist retains Mark's *hina* clause, "in order that seeing they may not see . . ." (Lk 8:10), he omits the second clause ("lest they repent and it be forgiven them"). As the Lukan context makes clear, the point is that Jesus' parables may hinder non-disciples from understanding the "secrets" of the kingdom, but they do not prevent repentance and forgiveness. Failure to respond is in part due to the Devil (*see* Demons, Devil, Satan), who wishes to snatch away Jesus' word, "lest [people] believe and be saved" (Lk 8:12). Like Matthew, Luke does not portray the disciples as obdurate, only as "slow of heart" until the event of Easter and the opening of their minds to understand the Scriptures (Lk 24:25, 45-47).

3. The Gospel of John.

The hardness-of-heart idea in the Fourth Gospel has a function somewhat similar to that in Mark. Alluding to OT obduracy language (perhaps to Is 6:9 itself), Jesus says that he "came into the world in order that [*hina*] those who do not see may see and those who see may become blind" (Jn 9:39). The lack of belief in Jesus, despite his many signs, is said to have fulfilled Scripture (Jn 12:37-38, where Is 53:1 is cited) and is apparently God's will: "For this reason they could not believe, because again spoke Isaiah, 'He has blinded their eyes and hardened their heart . . .' " (Jn 12:39-40, paraphrasing Is 6:10). These passages constitute an important part of a larger theme of mystery and misunderstanding that pervades the Fourth Gospel (2:19-21; 3:1-15; 6:60-66; 8:27; 14:9). The Jewish response of unbelief in Jesus' ministry of signs (*semeia*) recalls what Moses said to Israel: "You have seen all that the Lord did before your eyes in the land of Egypt . . . the signs [LXX: *semeia*], and those great wonders; but to this day the Lord has not given you a mind to understand, or eyes to see, or ears to hear" (Deut 29:2-4 RSV).

4. Jesus.

Did Jesus himself make use of the language and theology of obduracy? Although some scholars in the past have questioned the authenticity of Mark 4:11-12, a saying attributed to Jesus, it is likely that it does reflect something that Jesus said. But it is probable that the saying originally applied to the whole of Jesus' ministry, not to the parables only. Furthermore, it is possible that Jesus compared himself to the prophet Isaiah whose message had also fallen on deaf ears and alluded to Isaiah 6:9-10 as a way of explaining why so many of his contemporaries had failed to perceive the true significance of his ministry. People did not understand Jesus because their eyes could not see and their ears could not hear. The undiscerning and unbelieving response, therefore, was not evidence that Jesus' ministry was a failure; it was an important witness to the continuity of the biblical witness against Israel's hardness of heart.

BIBLIOGRAPHY. F. Eakin, "Spiritual Obduracy and Parable Purpose," in *The Use of the Old Testament in the New and Other Essays*, ed. J. Efird (Durham: Duke University, 1972) 87-107; C. A. Evans, "Obduracy and the Lord's Servant: Some Observations on the Use of the Old Testament in the Fourth Gospel," in *Early Jewish and Christian Exegesis*, ed. C. A. Evans and W. F. Stinespring (Homage 10; Atlanta: Scholars, 1987) 221-36; idem, *To See and Not Perceive: Isaiah 6.9-10 in Early Jewish and Christian Interpretation* (JSOTSup 64; Sheffield: JSOT, 1989); J. Marcus, "Mark 4:10-12 and Marcan Epistemology," *JBL* 103 (1984) 557-74; K. L. Schmidt and M. A. Schmidt, "παχύνω κτλ," *TDNT* 5.1022-31.   C. A. Evans

HEALING

According to all four canonical Gospels, Jesus devoted a substantial portion of his ministry to performing miracles* of healing for a wide variety of people. These miracles sometimes occurred in response to faith* and sometimes to instill faith. They demonstrated Jesus' compassion and his concern to break down social barriers. They challenged the Jewish Sabbath* Laws and exposed Israel's* faithlessness. Above all, they supported his teaching that the kingdom of God* was arriving with his ministry and that he himself was God's unique Son (*see* Abba; Son of God).

1. Classification
2. Meaning
3. Emphases of the Gospel Writers

4. Authenticity

5. Sociology

6. Significance for Today

1. Classification.

Three major kinds of healing miracles occur in the Gospels. Each requires slightly different interpretation, and some scholars would evaluate the historical reliability* of the various categories differently as well.

1.1. Exorcisms. Frequently, Jesus casts one or more demons out of individuals who have been possessed by them (*see* Demon, Devil). The demons regularly demonstrate that they know who Jesus is, even when most or all of the human onlookers do not (e.g., Mk 1:24; 5:7). They use this knowledge to try to gain mastery over Jesus, since knowledge of one's adversary's name was a key component in exorcisms of that day. But in every instance they fail. Jesus proves his superiority over Satan.

The Gospel accounts differ from many other exorcism stories of antiquity in the immediacy of the exorcisms, the lack of a struggle or extreme violence by the demons and the lack of magical paraphernalia customarily used by the exorcist. Many modern scholars have assumed that what ancient people believed to be demon-possession was simply some severe psychological or physical affliction which today would be treated by medicine or therapy. But the Gospels themselves distinguish between the two (e.g., Mt 10:1; Mk 3:10-11), and contemporary experiences of possession and exorcism which science has been unable to explain are too numerous to support this reductionist approach.

1.2. Physical Healings. Jesus regularly helped blind people to see (e.g., Mt 9:27-31; Mk 8:22-26), the deaf to hear (e.g., Mt 11:5; Mk 7:32-37) and the lame to walk (e.g., Jn 5:1-15). He cleansed lepers (e.g., Lk 5:12-16; 17:11-19), cured fevers (e.g., Mk 1:29-31; Jn 4:43-53), stopped a hemorrhage (Mk 5:24-34), restored a withered hand (Mk 3:1-6), replaced a cut-off ear (Lk 22:51) and healed a wide variety of unspecified illnesses. He healed with a word (e.g., Mt 8:16), without praying to God or invoking his name (except in one instance when he specifically declares that it is for the crowd's benefit—Jn 11:41-42) and sometimes at a long distance from the one who was sick (e.g., Mt 8:5-13). On two occasions he used indirect means and two stages in the healing (Mk 8:22-26; Jn 9:1-7), but normally the cures were instantaneous and unmediated.

Many scholars are willing to grant that people were genuinely healed after their encounters with Jesus, but they attribute the healing to a psychosomatic power of suggestion. The Gospels, however, are clear that Jesus' healings were genuinely supernatural events. H. C. Kee has helpfully delineated the differences in ancient thought concerning medicine (building on the foundation of natural order), miracle (based on belief in divine intervention), and magic (manipulating mysterious forces for personal benefit). Kee demonstrates that Jesus' healings normally belong to the second of these three categories.

1.3 Resurrections. The Gospels report that on three occasions Jesus brought back to life an individual who had recently died (Mk 5:35-43; Lk 7:11-17; Jn 11:1-44). In the first two the death seems just to have occurred within a matter of hours; in the case of Lazarus four days have passed (Jn 11:39). Some writers prefer to speak of these as resuscitations or reanimations to distinguish them from the resurrection* of Jesus and from the coming resurrection of all believers which is a restoration to life without death ever again intruding. But inasmuch as these terms suggest a non-miraculous procedure, they do not correspond to what the Gospels describe. For critics who are inclined to disbelieve the miraculous, the resurrections are the most incredible of all of Jesus' healing miracles. Ultimately their credibility depends on the evidence for the resurrection of Jesus. If the latter is admitted, then the former, temporary resurrections follow as a natural corollary, a foretaste of the future, permanent resurrection of all God's people.

2. Meaning.

2.1. Teaching about Faith. Sometimes Jesus heals an individual in response to that person's faith. Both Jairus' daughter and the woman with the hemorrhage are explicitly declared to be healed as a result of their faith or of the faith of their loved ones (Mk 5:34, 36). Sometimes lack of faith prevents Jesus from healing, as at his hometown of Nazareth (Mt 13:58). Jesus similarly explains that his disciples were unable to exorcise a demon-possessed epileptic because of their lack of faith (Mt 17:20). Many Christians deduce from accounts like these that if a person could only generate enough faith, healing would always occur. But this does not follow. There is a balancing theme which pervades the Gospels as well. Frequently, healings occur where there is little or no faith in order to try to instill belief in Jesus as the Son of God. All of the healings in John have this as one purpose (Jn 20:31); sometimes it is pre-eminent (Jn 4:53-54). After Peter's mother-in-law is cured of her fever, she serves Jesus (Mt 8:15). Jesus upbraids several of the cities in which he has worked miracles because they did not repent (Mt 11:20-24). So it is clear that miracles may be designed to produce faith where there is none;

once that faith has developed, healings may be less necessary (cf. Jesus' attitude to those who demanded signs to support their faith, Jn 4:48; 20:29).

2.2. Jesus' Compassion. Although it seems a natural inference that one of Jesus' main motives for healing would be his compassion for the sick, the Gospels state this explicitly only on rare occasions (e.g., Mt 14:14; 20:34). If compassion were a dominant motive, then presumably all sick people in his day (or in any other day) would have been healed, and this was patently not the case (cf. Jn 5:3-5 in which Jesus singles out only one of the many disabled people lying near the Bethesda pool). Jesus undoubtedly had compassion for all the sick, but the broader testimony of Scripture is that God's power may be demonstrated at least as dramatically through people's suffering as through their health. (In the Gospels the classic example is the passion and crucifixion of Christ; authentic discipleship also embraced the way of the cross [cf. Mk 8:31-35].)

2.3. Breaking Down Social Barriers. Frequently Jesus heals in such a way as to incur the anger of the Jewish leaders. He does not have to touch the leper to cleanse him, but does so deliberately to show that he is unconcerned with the ritual taboos that separated classes of people (Mk 1:41; *see* Clean and Unclean). He sends ten lepers (*see* Leprosy) to the priest* for their cures to be confirmed, but only a Samaritan* returns to give thanks; Jesus declares that one clean, leaving open the question of what happened to the other nine (Lk 17:11-19). The point is that the despised, outcast Samaritan is the hero; the social barriers Judaism* had erected are being destroyed. Jesus praises a Syro-Phoenician woman for her faith and heals her daughter, demonstrating that his saving power is not to be limited to Israel* (Mk 7:24-30; *see* Gentiles). In each of these instances Jesus is preparing the way for the establishment of a broadly inclusive religious movement not bounded by barriers of race, sex or nationality.

2.4. Challenging Israel's Law and Exposing the Nation's Faithlessness. Closely related to the previous category are those examples of Jesus breaking the Sabbath laws (e.g., Mk 3:1-6; Lk 13:10-17; 14:1-6). He does not have to heal on the Sabbath; not one of the maladies he cures on that day is said to be life-threatening. But he shows that the restrictions regularly attached to Jewish Sabbath law were of human rather than divine origin. He praises the Roman centurion for a quality of faith superior to that which he has found anywhere in Israel and predicts that many Gentiles will replace many Jews in God's kingdom (Mt 8:10-11). He laments the wickedness of the generation of Israelites in which he lives as contributing to the inability of his disciples* to effect an exorcism (Mt 17:17). This is not a critique by a reformer but a condemnation by one who is in the process of inaugurating a new age in redemptive history, in which the laws of the Mosaic covenant cannot carry over unchanged (*see* Law).

2.5. Teaching about Sin. Two healings recorded in John juxtapose opposite perspectives on the relationship between sickness and sin.* After healing the man who had been an invalid for thirty-eight years, Jesus tells him, "Stop sinning or something worse may happen to you" (Jn 5:14). Here Jesus presumes the common Jewish view that illness was a punishment for sin. But later, when his disciples ask him why a certain man had been born blind, he denies that it had anything to do with the sin of either that man or his parents (Jn 9:3). Instead, it was to manifest God's glory. Thus, sometimes healings undo a punishment for sin; other times there is no relation between health and obedience, or between sin and sickness, beyond the general observation that all evil came into the world through original sin.

2.6. Signs of the Kingdom and of the Messiah. The Gospels nowhere distinguish between the meaning of Jesus' miracles of healing and other kinds of miracles. When one studies all of the miracles of the Gospels, it becomes clear that their predominant purpose is to demonstrate the inauguration of the kingdom of God in the person and work of Jesus the Messiah (cf. esp. Betz and Grimm, Wenham and Blomberg; *see* Christ). But an analysis of the healing miracles alone makes this point evident.

Several passages in the Gospels give an explicit rationale for Jesus' healings. Jesus declares that his exorcisms prove that the "kingdom of God has come upon you" (Mt 12:28). He sends the messengers from John the Baptist* back to their imprisoned leader to tell him that the healing of the blind, lame, deaf and lepers (*see* Leprosy) and the resurrections from the dead answer John's question about whether or not Jesus was "the one to come" (Mt 11:4-6). He heals the paralytic who was lowered through the roof, so demonstrating that the Son of Man* has authority* to forgive sins (*see* Forgiveness of Sins), a prerogative reserved for God alone (Mk 2:10-11). Giving sight to the blind leads to Jesus' claim to be "the light* of the world" (Jn 9:5) just as raising Lazarus reinforces his pronouncement that he is "the resurrection and the life" (Mt 11:25). Numerous summary statements throughout the Gospel link his healing with his preaching as the two major foci of his ministry (e.g., Mt 4:23; 9:35; 21:14), summed up under the call to repentance "for the kingdom of God is near" (Mk 1:15).

In addition to these specific statements, several healing miracles point to the arrival of the messianic age more indirectly. When Jesus heals a deaf-mute, Mark describes the man as one who could "hardly talk" (Mk 7:32), an expression found in the LXX only in Isaiah 35:6, in which the prophet is describing the wonders of the age to come, including the fact that the "mute tongue" will "shout for joy." The resurrection of the widow of Nain's son (Lk 7:11-17) strikingly resembles Elisha's raising the son of the Shunammite woman (2 Kings 4:8-37), especially since Nain was located on approximately the same site as ancient Shunem. Even the crowds pick up on the resemblance as they marvel at the "great prophet" (Lk 7:16) who has arisen among them (probably implying the ultimate, eschatological prophet, fulfilling Deut 18:18). The nature of Jesus' messianic mission is clarified, in ways not particularly pleasing to his followers, when he heals Malchus' ear which Peter has cut off (Jn 18:10-11). His will be the way of the cross, not resisting the suffering which God has ordained for him.

3. Emphases of the Gospel Writers.

3.1. Mark. Of all the Evangelists, Mark devotes the largest percentage of his Gospel to the miracles and healings of Jesus (approx. thirty-one per cent). For Mark they demonstrate the establishment of God's reign and the need for repentance (6:7-12). Mark focuses on the power of Jesus and on his dramatic confrontations with the forces of Satan. Jesus conquers disease, demons and death (5:1-43). Mark stresses the immediacy of the miracles (1:29, 42; 2:8). His stories of Jesus' exorcisms contain more demonstrations of combat and violence than is common elsewhere in the Gospels (1:25; 5:6-13). Jesus discloses his emotions and even his anger at the work of the devil (3:5; 9:19).

As throughout his Gospel, Mark stresses what has come to be called the "messianic secret" (*see* Christ; Mark, Gospel of). Repeatedly, after various healings, Jesus commands those healed not to tell others who he is or what has happened (e.g., 1:34; 3:12; 5:43; 7:36). There have been numerous explanations of this motif. The most popular in critical circles is that associated with W. Wrede: Jesus never claimed to be the Messiah but later was confessed as such by his followers. To account for the silence of the earlier tradition, they alleged that Jesus at first forbade them to tell others of his messianic works and words. Many scholars have backed away from parts of Wrede's hypothesis and affirmed a core of genuinely messianic Jesus material, but most agree that Mark has substantially embellished and emphasized this theme,

along with the motifs of misunderstanding and secrecy. More convincing are two less radical explanations: (1) Jesus recognized that most of his contemporaries were looking for a political Messiah which did not correspond to his mission (see esp. Jn 6:15); and (2) Only after his suffering, death and resurrection could the nature of his messianic ministry be fully understood (see esp. Mk 9:9).

On two occasions Mark deliberately contrasts the unbelief of both the disciples and the crowds with Jesus' ability to heal and the belief generated in those healed (8:14-21, 22-26; 9:1-13, 14-32). Yet at the same time the disciples are commissioned and empowered to carry out healings identical to those Jesus himself performed (6:7-12). Mark further uses healings to frame his first main section of stories about Jesus' controversies with the Jewish leaders (2:1-12; 3:1-6), and elsewhere sees healing as a kind of teaching itself (1:27). His is also the only Gospel to refer to the use of anointing oil in conjunction with healing (6:13).

Mark's emphasis on Jesus' miracles has often been linked with a divine man* christology—a portrayal of Jesus in terms of other Hellenistic wonder-workers of his day. But Jesus' exasperation with those who demanded of him signs as they did of others (8:11-13) and his warning against false prophets who would perform miracles (13:21-23) call this interpretation into question. Other scholars have suggested that Mark was trying to counter a divine man christology by emphasizing Jesus' suffering and servanthood. But surely then he would not have needed to include nearly as many miracles as he did. Better than either of these approaches is one which sees Mark's purposes as more pastoral than polemical. Mark expected miracles, especially healings, to continue to occur in the church of his day (9:28-29), hence the emphasis on signs and wonders in 1:1—8:26. But Mark's church is also undergoing suffering and persecution, frequently without supernatural alleviation. So it needs to learn to follow Jesus on the way to the cross (8:34), hence the emphasis on humility and servanthood in 8:27—16:7 (see Best).

3.2. Matthew. Matthew's largest group of healing miracles occurs in chapters 8—9. Here Matthew presents Jesus as one mighty in deed, while sharply focusing on his sovereignty and authority. Matthew regularly abbreviates the healing stories, eliminating distracting detail and dialog in order to focus more exclusively on christology (e.g., 8:28-34; 9:1-8). At times this compression or telescoping of narrative is so drastic as to border on contradiction with his sources (9:18-26; cf. Mk 5:21-43). For Matthew, Jesus is the promised Jewish Messiah, the Son of David,* and several of those whom Jesus heals confess him as such (9:27-31; 20:29-34). Several who are healed further acknowledge him as Lord* (8:2; 15:22; 17:15). The healings fulfill OT Scripture (11:4-5; cf. Is 61:1; 35:6), especially those connected with Isaiah's Suffering Servant (8:17; cf. Is 53:4; see Servant of Yahweh). Twice Matthew depicts Jesus as healing two blind men (9:27-31; 20:29-34), where the parallel accounts mention only one. Perhaps Matthew is concerned to apply the Deuteronomic criterion that a matter is confirmed by the testimony of two or more witnesses (Deut 19:15).

Matthew's Gospel is at one and the same time the most particularist and the most universalist. He includes statements in conjunction with his healings and those of his disciples which reserve their miracle-working power for Israel (10:5-6; 15:24). In reserving his healing ministry for the crowds who are not yet his disciples, he can be seen as presenting himself as the healer of Israel, where the nation's leaders have failed (see Gerhardsson). Yet, upon seeing the Canaanite woman's faith, he is persuaded to heal her daughter (15:28). The best resolution of this apparent tension is to recognize Matthew's view of salvation history. God's call for repentance comes to the Jews first, but after they have had a chance to respond it must go forth into all the world.

In his summary statements of key stages of Jesus' ministry, Matthew regularly refers to the role of Jesus' healing with distinctive emphasis (e.g., 4:23-24; 9:35). These summaries consistently juxtapose Jesus' healing with his preaching and teaching to give both aspects of his ministry equal weight. Matthew's larger outline mirrors this balance (cf. chaps. 5—7 with 8—9). Similarly, Matthew diminishes the miraculous and heightens the controversy in a series of healing stories so as to give both elements equal attention (e.g., 9:1-8; 12:1-14). So too, healing as well as teaching leads to Jesus' rejection, arrest and crucifixion (21:10-17, 23-27; 26:57-66).

But after the resurrection the Great Commission does not repeat Jesus' earlier commands to the disciples to heal the sick as they evangelize (28:18-20; cf. 10:7-8). Arguably, Matthew expects his community to continue to experience both physical and spiritual salvation in Jesus. But he does not expect them to be able to reproduce such miracles with the frequency that the twelve disciples once did (see Heil).

3.3. Luke. Luke's Gospel is most concerned with Jesus' true humanity and his compassion for the outcasts of society. Only in Luke does Jesus cleanse the Samaritan leper (17:11-19). He is also most interested in portraying Jesus as Savior (see Salvation) of the world* (2:11). Part of the holistic salvation which Jesus brings includes physical healing. Jesus' programmatic manifesto of liberation (see Jubilee) combines preaching good news (see Gospel [Good News]) to the poor (see Rich and Poor) with providing sight for the blind (4:18). The same combination recurs later (7:21-22) in a Q* passage which Luke has redacted to stress the role of healings in testifying to Jesus as the promised "coming one."

In Luke's Gospel the lines are more blurred between healing and exorcism. Disease and demon-possession may both be attributed to Satan (5:35 and 39 employ the identical word for a "rebuke"), and a crippled woman's malady is ascribed to a "spirit" of infirmity (13:11-12)—an expression otherwise unparalleled in the NT. At the same time, the demons regularly recognize Jesus as the Son of God (4:41; 8:28) who is victorious over them. Occasionally, Jesus' ability to heal and vanquish demons borders on the magical—e.g., power goes out from a mere touch of his robe (8:44). Yet Luke makes it clear that it is faith and not magic which saves (8:48). In fact, many writers believe that it is Luke, of the four Evangelists, who makes most clear the possibility of miracles serving as a basis of faith (cf. esp. Achtemeier). Despite the influential view of H. Conzelmann to the contrary, it is obvious that Luke does not envision the interval between Jesus' temptation and Gethsemane as a "Satan-free" period. Rather, Luke pictures Jesus embroiled in an eschatological battle with Satan, whose powers he is decisively vanquishing as he ushers in the age of the new covenant (see esp. 10:17-18).

Luke does not portray the Jews in so uncompromising terms as does Matthew. He is more concerned with the worthiness of the Gentiles than with the faithlessness of Israel (7:1-10; cf. Mt 8:5-13). But while he uses different texts and typologies (see Typology), most notably parallels with Elijah and Elisha (e.g., 7:1-28) to depict Jesus as the eschatological prophet (7:16), he is equally concerned to portray Jesus as the fulfillment of Jewish hopes (4:16-21; 24:44). In fact he is most interested in tracing Jesus' journey to Jerusalem and his ministry under the shadow of the cross (9:51). His healings and other miracles are but a prelude to suffering which has been ordained by the Scriptures (13:32). Thus like Mark and Matthew, Luke expects that healings will continue in the apostolic age and beyond (see section 6.1.), but he recognizes their limited value in creating faith (16:31) and subordinates them to conversion and salvation in importance (10:20).

3.4. John. John offers the most contrast in his view of Jesus' healings. For him they are pre-eminently signs designed to bring people to faith in Jesus as the

Messiah and Son of God (4:54). Many commentators find this in flat contradiction with the Synoptic accounts, which portray Jesus as refusing to work miracles in response to the demand for a sign (Mt 12:38-42; Mk 8:11-13). But there is an important difference. Neither in John nor in the Synoptics will Jesus produce a sign on demand, especially when the request comes from one who is skeptical of Jesus' power or hostile to his preaching (cf. Jn 6:30-59). God's power cannot be commanded by human whim, and Jesus will not coerce anyone to believe. Even his own family members coming to him with legitimate requests cannot dictate what he will do. He may grant their requests but only at the precise time he chooses (2:3-7; 7:3-10).

At the same time, fair-minded assessment of Jesus' powers should elicit a confession of faith (20:31). Yet John recognizes this will not always occur. Even as he is the Evangelist most concerned to appropriate the apologetic value of Jesus' miracles, he is also the one who consistently praises those who do not need such crutches for their faith (4:48; 20:29). With maturity comes less dependence on the miraculous. So too, when healings plant the seeds of belief, they must grow into a deeper faith which better understands who Jesus is (9:35-38).

For John healings are not only signs but works (5:36). They show that the miracles are not independent actions but part of God's total activity, or "work," in Jesus (4:34; 5:17). The signs inevitably lead to explanatory discourses which invest them with symbolic and christological significance. Healing the blind man and raising Lazarus reinforce Jesus' claims to be the light* of the world (9:5) and the resurrection and the life (11:25). These two healings demonstrate God's glory* (11:40; 9:3), a key motif throughout John's Gospel. Healings in John further provoke controversies with the Jews* as polemical as those found in Matthew (9:13-41)—including disputes over Sabbath laws (5:16-47)—and issuing in death threats (11:45-57; 12:10-11). But ultimately these debates focus more on the christological questions; many of the Jewish leaders reject Jesus' claims, but many others are more favorably impressed (9:16; 11:45).

Overall there are fewer miracles in John than in any of the Synoptics, and only a handful of healings, none of which is an exorcism. But those which are presented are given more explicitly theological interpretation, in keeping with John's more generally complex interplay of history and theology. Fundamentally, they function as signs of God's glory and a testimony (*see* Witness) of the Father to the Son through the works which he enables him to perform (see Fortna).

4. Authenticity.

4.1. Challenges.
In the modern western world many people do not believe in the miraculous healings of the Gospels because they think that science has disproved the possibility of miracles. Biblical miracles, however, by definition involve a supernatural God; if such a God exists, it is only logical to conceive of him as occasionally choosing to transcend the laws of medicine and physics which normally govern the universe. Even today, after fervent prayer or the involvement of faith healers, many people recover from illness in ways which physicians cannot explain.

Other skeptics argue on philosophical grounds that the evidence or testimony for a miraculous healing could never outweigh the evidence in favor of some naturalistic explanation. But it is not obvious why this should be so; such logic actually requires excluding a much larger category of unusual events which human experience has nevertheless proved real (see Brown).

Still other critics argue on historical grounds that the picture of Jesus as healer must be understood as the vestige of a primitive world view which permitted many ancient teachers and leaders to have miracles ascribed to them. Unless one is prepared to accept the equally good testimony of other ancient writers to the thaumaturgic powers of various rabbis (e.g., Hanina ben Dosa and Honi the Rain-maker), Greek philosophers and divine men (e.g., Apollonius of Tyana and Asclepius; *see* Divine Man), and occasionally even a Roman emperor (e.g., Vespasian), one has no reason for believing the Gospels. This argument holds up to a point; there may well be other genuinely supernatural miracles in many periods of world history. God may well use unbelievers to serve his purposes, and the devil certainly employs counterfeit signs to serve his (see Richards). There may be extra-canonical, non-Christian accounts of healings which are true, but for the most part it is inaccurate to say that numerous other accounts have as much evidence in support of them as do the Gospel healings. And A. E. Harvey's helpful survey of miracle stories in ancient Jewish and Greco-Roman sources demonstrates just how unique the Gospel accounts are both in style and significance.

4.2. Corroboration.
Once antisupernatural bias is removed, the Gospel healing miracles actually satisfy the various historical criteria of authenticity quite well. There is good external evidence supporting them. Other portions of the New Testament refer back to Christ's wonder-working powers (e.g., Acts 10:38; 1 Cor 15:4-8; Heb 2:4), and apocryphal Christian texts, while fancifully embellishing the accounts of Jesus' ministry, nevertheless bear indirect testimony to his power to heal by focusing so much attention on this aspect of

his career (see esp. the *Infancy Gospel of Thomas* and the *Acts of Pilate*). Non-Christian Jewish sources also recognize that Jesus was a healer. Both Josephus (*Ant.* 18:63-64) and the Talmud (*b. Sanh.* 107b) refer to his extraordinary powers, although the latter source attributes them to a demonic rather than a divine origin.

Internal evidence proves even more supportive. The miracles pass the dissimilarity test (*see* Form Criticism); although earlier Jews and later Christians apparently healed some people miraculously, with prayer* to God and invocation of the name of Christ regularly featured in their attempts. While individual parallels can be identified for specific Gospel healings (cf. esp. Lk 7:11-17 with Philostratus *The Life of Apollonius of Tyana* 4.45), the overall directness, authority, simplicity and restraint of the accounts of Jesus' healings are unique.

The healings satisfy the criterion of multiple attestation (*see* Form Criticism); they recur in all layers or sources of the Gospel tradition (Mark, John, Q,* M* and L*), and references to them appear in multiple forms as well (summary statements [e.g., Mk 3:7-12], dialogs [e.g., Mt. 11:1-6], controversy stories [e.g., Mk 2:1-12] as well as the numerous narrative accounts of the healings themselves).

They correspond to the Palestinian environment of the early first century; features like the use of spittle (Jn 9:6; Mk 8:23) in a therapeutic context, or the types of illnesses prevalent, all fit in well with the times and customs. Even as specific a detail as the description of the pool of Bethesda near the Sheep Gate having five porticoes (Jn 5:2), where Jesus healed a long-term invalid, has been corroborated by archeology.

Most importantly, the meaning of the healings, as already noted, is closely bound up with Jesus' teaching about the presence of the kingdom of God. They thereby satisfy the criterion of coherence, fitting well with that body of sayings of Jesus most commonly held to be authentic.

5. Sociology.

A major new development in the past decade of NT scholarship centers on sociological analysis. Jesus' healings, no less than other portions of the Gospels, have been scrutinized not so much from a historical perspective, asking "What really happened?" as from a social-scientific perspective, asking "How did the stories of these events function in first-century society?" The work of H. C. Kee and G. Theissen has proved seminal here. They compare the Gospel accounts with stories of healings in other Greco-Roman contexts (e.g., of Isis or Asklepios) which were not necessarily ever viewed as entirely historical.

Rather, the stories of healings functioned symbolically to affirm meaning, order and integration of reality in a world filled with conflict and suffering. Similarly, the Gospel healings should be viewed as symbolic accounts which affirm, from a primarily rural, poor and uncultured perspective, the possibility of rescue, salvation and redemption in this life in a world of rapidly overturning geographical, economic and cultural norms.

The sociological method offers important insights into the function of miracle stories in the early Christian world. It is less clear that this method stands as strictly opposed to traditional historical methods as it alleges. The Gospel accounts remain tied to history in a way not entirely identical to various Greco-Roman parallels. If substantial portions of the Evangelist's narratives, including stories of the miraculous, did not occur as described, the claims of Christianity to be built on a unique space-time incarnation of God would be undermined. But granted that Jesus did perform miracles, sociology can prove very beneficial in explaining why people continued to talk and write about them.

6. Significance for Today.

The question of whether or not people living after NT times can expect miraculous healing has often polarized Christianity. At one end of the spectrum many argue that the miracles are unique and not to be repeated following the close of the apostolic age. Others expect them to be common in every age for those filled with the Holy Spirit* and sufficient faith. In fact, the data of the NT supports neither of these extremes. Evidence reinforces both the claim that miraculous healings will appear in almost every age of church history and the observation that such healings will still be more the exception than the norm (see Sabourin).

6.1. Evidence for Continuation. As he sent them out to minister in the cities of Israel, Jesus commanded his disciples to carry on exactly the same kind of healing ministry which he had been performing, and he gave them the power to execute his commands (Mt 10:1-10). Some of the injunctions he gave the disciples on these early missions were later rescinded (Lk 22:35-38), but not the command to heal.

The book of Acts includes close parallels between the types of healings wrought by Christ and those performed by the disciples, proving that the crucifixion, resurrection and coming of the Holy Spirit at Pentecost did not alter the disciples' ability or need to effect miraculous cures. They are able to heal the lame (Acts 3:1-10; 14:8-10), to cast out demons (16:16-18;

5:16) and to raise the dead (9:36-41; probably 20:7-12). The almost magical powers attached to Christ's robe reappear in conjunction with Peter's shadow (5:15) and Paul's handkerchiefs (19:11-12). The wording of the account of Peter's healing of Aeneas (9:32-35) and of the resurrection of Dorcas (9:36-41) so closely parallels the wording of similar stories in the Gospels (Lk 5:17-26; 8:49-56) that Luke almost certainly was trying to make clear that the apostles* had received exactly the same healing power which Jesus himself had. Nor is this power limited to apostles. For example, Luke describes the deacons Stephen and Philip as equally endowed with the ability to work signs and wonders (Acts 6:8; 8:13).

6.2. Evidence of Exceptionality. Though some would argue that there is healing in the atonement (Mt 8:17), clearly no one receives full physical healing until the life to come, since all die. There is good evidence, therefore, that supernatural, physical healing should be viewed as the exception rather than the rule in this life. Healings, like other miracles, are not uniformly spread throughout the pages of Scripture or periods of church history. They tend to be clustered around the initial stages of key advances in the knowledge of God's Word and will—Moses with Pharaoh, Elijah and Elisha, Jesus and the next two centuries of church history, and sporadically throughout the Christian era until a substantial outpouring of the Holy Spirit has once again made healings well known in the twentieth century.

On the pages of the Gospels there is no indication that Jesus healed all or even a majority of the sick people in his day. He warns against those who would work counterfeit signs and wonders in his name (Mt 7:21-23), especially as the last days unfold (Mt 24:5). He refuses to work signs on demand and warns against an inappropriate dependence on the spectacular (Mt 12:38-42; Jn 4:48; 20:29). Even the most well-authenticated signs do not necessarily prove their divine origin (Mt 9:32-33; 12:22-24); Christian faith should therefore be based on a more solid foundation.

Some of the devil's strongest temptations involved his encouraging Christ to rely on his miraculous power to avoid the way of suffering and the road to the cross (Lk 4:1-12; *see* Temptation of Jesus). Gethsemane* is the most powerful testimony in all of Scripture to the divinely ordained necessity of not always receiving protection from suffering (Lk 22:39-46). In his epistles Paul echoes this theology (esp. 2 Cor 4:7-18; 6:3-10). Not all receive or benefit from gifts of healing, and Paul personally and agonizingly learns the lesson that God's grace is sufficient for him and that God's power is made

perfect in Paul's weakness (2 Cor 12:8).

6.3. Conclusion.
Miraculous healings can and do occur today. They are perhaps most prevalent in areas into which the kingdom of God is advancing for the first time, or for the first time in a long while. Exorcisms tend to occur most in conjunction with the preaching of the gospel in lands and areas in which Satan has long held sway and in which Christianity has not flourished. To the extent that Western societies continue to become more paganized, one may expect a continued revival of healings and exorcisms there as well. As Christian individuals and congregations mature, it may well be that the need for such miracles, as a testimony to a non-Christian culture of the truth and power of the gospel, will diminish. But Christians of all theological persuasions must scrupulously avoid dictating to God what he must do or what he cannot do. Ultimately, God's Spirit blows where it wills, and no one can unerringly predict where his gifts of healing will break out (see Smedes).

See also DEMON, DEVIL, SATAN.

BIBLIOGRAPHY. P. J. Achtemeier, "The Lukan Perspective on the Miracles of Jesus: A Preliminary Sketch," in *Perspectives in Luke-Acts,* ed. C. H. Talbert (Danville, IL: AABPR, 1978) 153-67; E. Best, "The Miracles in Mark," *RevExp* 75 (1978) 539-54; O. Betz and W. Grimm, *Wesen und Wirklichkeit der Wunder Jesu* (Frankfurt a. M.: P. Lang, 1977); C. Brown, *Miracles and the Critical Mind* (Grand Rapids: Eerdmans, 1984); R. T. Fortna, *The Fourth Gospel and Its Predecessor* (Philadelphia: Fortress, 1988); B. Gerhardsson, *The Mighty Acts of Jesus according to Matthew* (Lund: Gleerup, 1979); J. B. Green, "Jesus and a Daughter of Abraham (Luke 13:10-17): Test Case for a Lucan Perspective on Jesus' Miracles," *CBQ* 51 (1989) 643-54; A. E. Harvey, *Jesus and the Constraints of History* (Philadelphia: Westminster, 1982); J. P. Heil, "Significant Aspects of the Healing Miracles in Matthew," *CBQ* 41 (1979) 274-87; H. C. Kee, *Miracle in the Early Christian World* (New Haven: Yale, 1983); idem, *Medicine, Miracle and Magic in New Testament Times* (Cambridge: University Press, 1986); R. Latourelle, *The Miracles of Jesus and the Theology of Miracles* (New York: Paulist, 1988); J. Richards, *Deliver Us from Evil* (London: Darton, Longman & Todd, 1974); L. Sabourin, *The Divine Miracles Discussed and Defended* (Rome: Catholic Book Agency, 1977); L. B. Smedes, ed., *Ministry and the Miraculous* (Pasadena: Fuller Theological Seminary, 1987); G. Theissen, *Miracle Stories of the Early Christian Tradition* (Edinburgh: T. & T. Clark, 1983); H. van der Loos, *The Miracles of Jesus* (Leiden: Brill,

1965); D. Wenham and C. Blomberg, eds., *Gospel Perspectives 6: The Miracles of Jesus* (Sheffield: JSOT, 1986).

C. L. Blomberg

HEART. *See* ETHICS OF JESUS; HARDNESS OF HEART.

HEAVEN AND HELL

Beyond the common reference to the physical "sky," the Gospels use *heaven* to refer both to the abode of God,* as well as to the place of eternal habitation for those who obey God and follow Jesus. The Gospels use the concept of *hell* to refer to the place of punishment for those who reject God, Jesus and the prophets.*

1. Heaven
2. Hell

1. Heaven.

1.1. Heaven in the OT. The most common words for *heaven* in the OT are the Hebrew *šāmayîm* or the Aramaic *šᵉmayîn*. Given the large number of occurrences, only predominant usages can be addressed here (see Traub).

On the most mundane level, *šāmayîm/šᵉmayîn* are used to refer simply to the physical "sky" or "air" above the earth (Gen 1:8; Ps 104:2). Used in this way, it refers to one of the creations of God (Gen 1:1; Ps 33:6; Amos 9:6) which therefore ought not to be worshiped (Jer 44:17-23; Is 47:13-14). Given God's dominion over it (Deut 4:39; 10:14), it is understood to be the source from which he sends the various physical phenomena which affect the earth (e.g., Gen 8:2; Ex 9:23; Deut 33:13; Josh 10:11; Job 38:29, 37; Ps 147:8; Is 55:10; Jer 49:36). It is also the place where God has set the multiple heavenly lights and bodies (Gen 1:14; Job 9:9; 38:31). Though it can represent lasting duration (Ps 89:29; Deut 11:21), it too is subject to judgment* and destruction (2 Sam 22:8; Is 51:6; Job 14:12). It will, however, be recreated (Is 65:17; 66:22).

Alongside this conception is the OT belief that heaven is the habitation of God (1 Kings 8:30; Ps 14:2; Is 63:15) and of angels* (Gen 28:12; 1 Kings 22:19; cf. Is 6:2-3). Heaven either contains God's throne (Ps 103:19; 1 Kings 22:19) or functions as the throne itself (Is 66:1). It cannot, however, contain him (1 Kings 8:27). Given this close association, he is referred to as the "God of heaven" (Gen 24:3; 2 Chron 36:23; Ezra 1:2; Neh 1:4), who hears from his lofty abode both to judge the ungodly (Gen 19:24; 1 Kings 8:32) and to help his people (Ps 102:19-20 [MT 102:20-21]; 113:5-9; 1 Kings 8:30-52). Heaven, therefore, is the source of many blessings* (Gen 49:25; Deut 33:13; 1 Kings 8:35). Since God is understood to be "above," he is sought

there in prayer, often with upstretched hands (Ex 9:29; 1 Kings 8:22).

Finally, the tendency to use *heaven* as a substitute for the name of God begins in the OT. In Daniel 4:26 [MT 4:23] Daniel announces to Nebuchadnezzar that the purpose of the Lord's judgment on him is to convince him that "heaven" rules. Clearly, this is a circumlocution for the divine name, a tendency that is hinted at elsewhere in the OT (e.g., Ps 73:9; Job 20:27; Dan 12:7) and further developed in the subsequent literature.

1.2. Heaven in the LXX. The LXX translators used the Greek *ouranos/ouranoi* to render the Hebrew *šāmayîm* and the Aramaic *šᵉmayîn* (cf. 1 Kgdms 2:10; 2 Kgdms 22:10; Is 44:23; Hab 3:3), subsuming all of the connotations which the latter words entail. In only a few instances do the translators add *ouranos*, mainly to achieve greater vividness and concreteness, as well as to emphasize the linkage between God and heaven (see Traub). Most importantly, through the LXX the plural *ouranoi* ("heavens") comes into the Greek usage, leading to its frequent use in the NT.

1.3. Heaven in Other Jewish Literature. Subsequent Jewish literature draws heavily on these diverse portrayals of heaven, developing them far beyond the detail found in the OT. Frequently, the physical aspects of heaven are discussed, as the human author is given a cosmic tour to observe its secrets (e.g., *T. Levi* 2:6—3:8; *1 Enoch* 17:2—18:14; 43:1-4; 72:1—80:8). At the end of the age these will be involved in the catastrophic and apocalyptic* events that transpire (e.g., 4 Ezra 5:4-5; *T. Levi* 4:1; *1 Enoch* 1:4; 80:2-7; *Sib. Or.* 3:75-90).

Under the influence of such OT phrases as "heaven of heavens" and "heaven and heaven of heavens" (Deut 10:14; 1 Kings 8:27; 2 Chron 2:6 [MT 2:5]; 6:18), the belief in multiple layers of heaven developed (e.g., *T. Levi* 2:6—3:8; *b. Roš Haš.* 24b; *b. Sanh.* 110a). At the uppermost height is God's throne (*T. Levi* 3:4; 5:1), surrounded by angels (*T. Levi* 3:1-8; *1 Enoch* 51:4; 61:10-11). *Paradise*, usually identified as the Garden of Eden, was believed to be preserved with God in heaven. It would ultimately be opened to the righteous in the next age so that they might eat of the Tree of Life (*T. Levi* 18:10-11; cf. also *2 Apoc. Bar.* 4:3-7). In 4 Ezra 7:36-38 the author presents "paradise" as a place of "delight and rest" opposite the pit of "hell." This may provide evidence of a tradition similar to which Jesus draws upon in Luke 16:19-31.

In addition to the belief in the destruction and recreation of heaven (*1 Enoch* 72:1; 91:16; *Sib. Or.* 3:75-90; *b. 'Abod. Zar.* 17a), the notion of a "transfiguration" of the old heaven is also present (*Jub.* 1:29; *1 Enoch*

45:4; *T. Levi* 18:1-14). Rather than eternity in heaven, the reward for the righteous usually is a life of bliss on a cleansed or recreated earth (cf. *2 Apoc. Bar.* 73:1—74:3; *1 Enoch* 25:3-7; 45:4-5; 51:3-5; *Apoc. Abr.* 29:17-21; cf. 4 Ezra 7:119-124; but cf. Josephus *Ant.* 18. §14; *J.W.* 2. §163; 3. §§374-75).

The tendency to use *heaven* as a circumlocution for the divine name is most evident in the rabbinic writings (e.g., *b. 'Abod. Zar.* 18a; *b. Sanh.* 15b; 17a). Typical are such phrases as "the kingdom of heaven" (*m. Ber.* 2:2; *b. Ḥag.* 5b), "the fear of heaven" (*m. 'Abot* 1:3; *b. Ber.* 33b), "the sake of heaven" (*m. 'Abot* 4:11) and the "name of heaven" (*m. 'Abot* 4:4; *b. Ḥag.* 16a).

1.4. Heaven in the Gospels. Much of the use of "heaven" in the Gospels mirrors this literary milieu. Moreover, the use of the concept of heaven is broader than merely the use of the word *ouranos*.

1.4.1. The Message of John the Baptist. Given the limited amount of John's preaching in the Gospels (*see* John the Baptist), only a few allusions to John's use of the concept of heaven are preserved. One such allusion occurs in Matthew 3:12 and its parallel Luke 3:17, where he describes the ministry of the "mightier" one who would follow him. John declares that he will "clear his threshing floor" and "gather his wheat into (his) granary." Since the eschaton was about to dawn, the great and final separation between the wicked and the righteous was soon to transpire. Accordingly, the "granary" appears to function as a metaphor for heaven, to which those whom the "coming one" finds righteous will be taken (cf. Mt 13:30, 40-43). In John 1:32, the Baptist bears witness to the anointing of Jesus by the Spirit of God, who descended from heaven in the appearance of a dove (*see* Holy Spirit). Finally, John uses "heaven" as a circumlocution for the divine name in John 3:27.

1.4.2. The Teaching of Jesus in the Gospels. Jesus speaks of heaven in several ways. As in the OT, he employs *ouranos* to refer simply to the sky or the air. For instance, heaven is the domain of the birds (Mt 6:26; 8:20 par. Lk 9:58; Mk 4:32 par. Mt 13:32 and Lk 13:19) as well as the abode of the clouds (Mk 14:62 par. Mt 26:64). It bears portents of coming weather (Lk 12:56; Mt 16:2-3), and it will be the theater of future catastrophic events (Mk 13:25-26 par. Mt 24:29-30 and Lk 21:26-27). When used in this sense, it is included in the created order under God's sovereign dominion (Mt 11:25 par. Lk 10:21). Unlike the Law and Jesus' teachings, it may not endure forever (Mt 5:18 par. Lk 16:17; Mk 13:31 par. Mt 24:35 and Lk 21:33).

More significantly, heaven is the abode of God (e.g., Mt 5:16; 6:1; 7:21; 10:32), from which also the Spirit (Jn 15:26) and the Son (Jn 3:13; 6:33, 38) are sent. It

is also the place to which Jesus ascended (Lk 24:51). It is not surprising, therefore, that the will of God is done perfectly in heaven (Mt 6:10). The angels, too, are said to inhabit heaven (Mk 12:25 par. Mt 22:30; Mk 13:32 par. Mt 24:36; Mt 18:10; 28:2; Lk 2:15; Jn 1:51).

By metonymy, heaven is also used by Jesus as a circumlocution for the divine name. One evidence of this tendency is shown in his query to the religious leaders regarding John's baptism*; either it came from humans or from heaven (Mk 11:30 par. Mt 21:25 and Lk 20:4). Likewise, the repentant prodigal confesses that he has sinned both against his father and against heaven (Lk 15:18, 21).

Finally, Jesus refers to heaven as the place of future bliss for the righteous (Mt 13:43; *see* Justice, Righteousness) who follow him. Those who are persecuted because they are Jesus' disciples* are instructed to rejoice because they have a "great reward" in heaven (Mt 5:12 par. Lk 6:23). Similarly, those who give sacrificially to the needy will gain an incorruptible "treasure" (Mt 6:20 par. Lk 12:33; cf. Mk 10:21 par. Mt 19:21 and Lk 18:22). Jesus' disciples are promised a "room" in his "Father's house" where they will be with Jesus (Jn 14:2-3). Accordingly, the image of the banquet is employed to portray heaven as a place of joy* and celebration (cf. Mt 8:11 par. Lk 13:28-29; Mt 25:10; 22:1-10 par. Lk 14:16-24; 22:29-30; cf. also Mk 14:25 par. Mt 26:29 and Lk 22:16). In contrast to the suffering of gehenna, it is characterized as "life"* (Mk 9:43, 45 par. Mt 18:8-9). Moreover, it is understood to be eternal (e.g., Mk 10:30 par. Mt 19:29 and Lk 18:30; Jn 3:16, 36; 5:24; et passim; Mt 25:46; Lk 16:9). Those who enter the kingdom of God (*see* Kingdom of God) will gain this eternal life (Mk 10:17-25 par. Mt 19:16-24 and Lk 18:18-25). Far from being a place of inactivity, Jesus implies that heaven will involve further responsibility for its inhabitants (Mt 25:21, 23 par. Lk 19:17, 19; Mt 24:47 par. Lk 12:44).

Though no explicit discussion is given regarding when heaven begins, most sayings portray the "end of the age" (Mt 13:30, 40-43; Mk 10:30 par. Luke 18:30) or the Son of man's (*see* Son of Man) return (Mt 25:10, 31-34; 24:46-47 par. Lk 12:43-44; Mt 25:19 par. Lk 19:15) as the inaugural event of the consummated kingdom (Mt 8:11 par. Lk 7:29; Mk 14:25 par. Mt 26:29 and Lk 22:16, 18). Both the parable of Lazarus (Lk 16:19-31) and the saying to the thief on the cross (Lk 23:43), however, imply an immediate transfer to heaven of the righteous at death.

It is difficult to know precisely the referent in Jesus' use of the term *paradise* in Luke 23:43. Given its use in the LXX and especially in related Jewish literature, it is likely that it refers generically to heaven (e.g.,

4 Ezra 7:36-38), or specifically to the Garden of Eden which has been preserved by God in heaven for the future enjoyment of the righteous (e.g., *T. Levi* 18:10-11; *2 Apoc. Bar.* 4:3-7; cf. Gen 2:8-9; 13:10; Is 51:3). Fitzmyer has argued rather convincingly, however, that *paradise* in Luke 23:43 should be understood as a way of describing Jesus' "entrance into his glory" after death, implying a heavenly existence (Lk 24:26; cf. Acts 2:33; 5:31). In either case, the adverb *today* suggests that Jesus' and the thief's enjoyment of heaven would begin immediately subsequent to death.

1.4.3. The Emphases of the Gospel Writers. Matthew alone employs the phrase "kingdom of heaven" in place of "kingdom of God." Though some have tried to make a distinction in the referents of the two phrases, the presence of numerous parallels nullifies this claim (e.g., Mt 5:3 par. Lk 6:20; Mt 8:11 par. Lk 13:29; Mt 11:11 par. Lk 7:28; Mt 13:11 par. Mk 4:11 and Lk 8:10; Mt 13:31 par. Mk 4:30 and Lk 13:18; Mt 19:14 par. Mk 10:14 and Lk 18:16). This tendency to use *heaven* is evidenced elsewhere when speaking of the Father. Repeatedly, Matthew identifies God as the "Father in heaven" or the "heavenly Father" where parallel passages do not (e.g., Mt 6:9 par. Lk 11:2; Mt 6:26, 32 par. Lk 12:24, 30; Mt 10:32-33 par. Lk 12:8-9; Mt 12:50 par. Mk 3:35). This makes it likely that some of the unparalleled occurrences of this phrase are redactional as well (e.g., Mt 5:16; 6:1; 15:13; 16:17; 18:10, 14, 19, 35; 23:9; *see* Redaction Criticism).

Whereas the Synoptists utilize the images of some kind of reward in heaven, the kingdom of God (heaven) or various parabolic portrayals (*see* Parables) of celebration and joy to speak of heaven, John opts mainly for the notion of "eternal life" (e.g., Jn 3:16, 36; 4:14; 5:24; 6:27 et passim, but cf. Jn 3:3, 5). Additionally, while the Synoptists portray heaven as future, John's Jesus asserts that believers who have been given a new birth by God (Jn 3:3, 5) have this "life" now (Jn 5:24; 3:36). The resurrection* is still an important event, but not so that eternal life can begin. Rather it seals the believer in this "life," eternally (Jn 11:25-26; 5:24-25; see Thompson). Then those believers will be given a room in the Father's "house" so that they might be with Jesus (Jn 14:2-3).

2. Hell.

References to *hell* in the Gospels draw on a rich and varied background, the historical development of which is complicated and elusive. Beginning with the OT, the concept progresses through ever-increasing stages of detail and description. In addition to hades and gehenna, the Gospels employ several other images to speak of hell. Given this diverse background, the Gospel presentation is neither uniform nor tidy. Rather, the reader is left with more general notions of the concept.

2.1. Sheol/Hades.

2.1.1. Sheol in the OT. Any discussion of the background of hell in the Gospels must begin with a discussion of the problematic use of šᵊ'ōl, frequently rendered *sheol* in English translation. Though its precise meaning in any given instance may be difficult to ascertain, it is evident that it refers in some way to the place of the dead. A problem arises, however, when it is discovered that both the righteous (cf. Gen 37:35; Is 38:10; Ps 30:3, 9) and the unrighteous (cf. Num 16:30, 33) go there. This led the early church to teach that the OT saints went to an upper level of sheol, from which Christ* delivered them. This doctrine rests on tenuous exegetical support at best, and it is better to understand sheol as originally referring simply to the grave (cf. Is 14:11; Job 17:13-16; Ps 30:3 [MT 30:4], 9; 88:3-5 [MT 88:4-6]; Prov 7:27) and/or death (cf. Hos 13:14; Hab 2:5; Is 28:15, 18; 38:18; Song 8:6; Ps 49:14 [MT 49:15]; 89:48 [MT 89:49]; 116:3; Prov 5:5; 1 Kings 2:6, 9). Gradually, however, it began to take on the specialized connotations of a realm of the dead (cf. Is 14:9-10; Job 26:5-6), moving closer to the notions surrounding the concept of hell. This would then explain its character as the universal lot of humankind (Eccles 9:10), as well as the place reserved for the wicked (cf. Ps 9:17 [MT 9:18]; 31:17 [MT 31:18]; 49:13-14).

When described, its location is almost always in a downward direction (cf. Ps 55:15 [MT 55:16]; 86:13; Prov 9:18; 15:24; Is 14:15; Jon 2:2 [MT 2:3]), functioning as the extreme opposite of the heights of heaven (Job 11:8; Ps 139:8; Amos 9:2). It is portrayed as a place of "darkness" (Job 17:13) and "dust" (Job 17:16), and the place where the worm feasts (Job 17:14; 24:19-20; Is 14:11). Its inhabitants are reduced to silence (Ps 6:5 [MT 6:6]; 31:17 [MT 31:18]; Is 38:18). The general belief is that once one passes through its portals (Is 38:10), there will be no return (e.g., Job 7:9-10; Is 38:10, 18). Some notions of future hope for the righteous do exist (Hos 13:14; Ps 16:10; 49:15 [MT 49:16]; Job 14:13; 1 Sam 2:6). Many of these themes will be picked up by the subsequent literature, including the NT.

2.1.2. Hades in the LXX and Apocrypha. The Greek *hadēs* is employed by the LXX translators to render the Hebrew sheol, obviously including all of the related connotations. Additionally, *hadēs* translates such words as "darkness" (Job 38:17), "silence" (cf. Ps 94:17 [LXX 93:17]), "death" (Prov 14:12; 16:25; Is 28:15) and "the pit" (Is 38:18; 14:19).

The apocryphal literature largely reflects OT usage, indicating that the location of hades is in the depths (cf. Sir 21:10; 51:5-6). Once through its "gates" (cf. Wis 16:13; 3 Macc 5:51; 6:31), however, this literature allows more hope of return than indicated in the OT (cf. Wis 16:13; Sir 48:5; Tob 13:2; but cf. also Wis 2:1). Not surprisingly, it is used often simply to signify death (cf. Sir 9:12; 14:12; 3 Macc 4:8; 5:42, 51; 6:31) or the grave (Tob 3:10), where the inhabitants reside in silence (Sir 17:27; 41:4).

2.1.3. Hades in Other Jewish Literature. Subsequent Jewish literature picks up and further develops many of the themes already seen in the OT and apocryphal literature. Accordingly, some passages evidence the belief that hades is the universal destiny of humankind (*Pseudo-Phoc.* 112-15), while the notion that it is a place of punishment reserved for the wicked is also represented (*Apoc. Zeph.* 10:3-14). Furthermore, hades is sometimes thought of as a temporary place of residence until the resurrection (cf. *Sib. Or.* 2:227-30; 4 Ezra 4:42; but cf. *Pseudo-Phoc.* 112-15; *b. Yebam.* 17a [*š ˀōl*]).

2.2. Gehenna. An even more common name for hell in the Gospels is *geenna.* It too has roots in the OT, and then is developed in subsequent literature.

2.2.1. Gehenna in the OT. Behind the word *gehenna,* as it frequently appears in English translation, stands the Greek *geenna,* which is a transliteration of the Aramaic *gēhinnām.* The Aramaic is itself derived from the Hebrew *gē hinnōm* (Josh 15:8; 18:16) and *gē ben hinnōm* (Josh 15:8; see Jeremias), which refer to a valley located on the south slope of Jerusalem (Josh 15:8; 18:16), literally, the "Valley of (the son of) Hinnom." It gained its infamous notoriety during the reigns of Ahaz and Manasseh, both of whom burned sacrifices there to Molech, even to the point of sacrificing their own sons in the fire (cf. 2 Chron 28:3; 33:6; 2 Kings 16:3). This elicited prophetic condemnations on the valley, identifying it as the scene of future carnage and desolation resulting from God's judgment (Jer 7:30-33; 19:1-13; 32:34-35; cf. also Is 31:9; 66:24; 2 Kings 23:10; Lev 18:21).

2.2.2. Gehenna in Other Jewish Literature. Throughout much of the subsequent Jewish literature, it is evident that *geenna* came to be equated with the place of God's final judgment of the wicked. Like sheol, it is located in the depths of the earth (*Sib. Or.* 4:184-86), and descriptions include "fire," "darkness" and "gnashing of teeth" (cf. *Apoc. Abr.* 15:6; *Sib. Or.* 1:100-103; 2:292-310). There is also the implication that this punishment is an eternal one (*Sib. Or.* 2:292-310; Josephus *Ant.* 18.14; *J.W.* 2.163; 3.374-75).

In the rabbinic literature, gehenna appears frequently. It is one of the seven things created prior to the creation of the world (*b. Pesaḥ.* 54a). In at least one place, gehenna is equated with sheol (*b. B. Bat.* 79a; cf. *b. ʿErub.* 19a). Many will be spared from it, including those who fear God (*b. Yebam.* 102b), those who follow the Torah in obedience and good deeds (*b. Šabb.* 118a; *b. Giṭ.* 7a; *b. B. Bat.* 10a; *b. Ḥag.* 27a), and those who are especially unfortunate in this life (*b. ʿErub.* 41b). Solely a place of retribution, gehenna is reserved for the wicked (*b. ʿErub.* 19a; *b. Yebam.* 63b; *b. Ḥag.* 15a; cf. also *b. B. Bat.* 74a; *b. Šabb.* 104a), including those guilty of a variety of sinful acts: idolatry (*b. Taʿan.* 5a), immorality (*b. Qidd.* 40a; *b. Soṭa* 4b), arrogance (*m. ʾAbot* 5:19; *b. B. Bat.* 78b; *b. ʿAbod. Zar.* 18b), flattery and foolish speech (*b. Soṭa* 41b; *b. Šabb.* 33a), a lack of compassion on the poor (*b. Beṣa* 32b; *see* Rich and Poor) and listening too much to women* (*m. ʾAbot* 1:5; *b. B. Meṣ.* 59a). With its entrance in the Valley of Hinnom (*b. Sukk.* 32b), it is believed to contain various levels (*b. Soṭa* 10b). Though generally its fiery torments (*b. Šabb.* 39a; *b. B. Bat.* 84a) are believed to be limited in duration (*m. ʿEd.* 2:10; *b. Šabb.* 33b; *b. Roš Haš.* 16b-17a), the thoroughly wicked do not reascend from it (*b. B. Meṣ.* 58b; *b. Roš Haš.* 16b-17a).

2.3. Hell in the Gospels. In speaking of hell, the Gospels do not confine themselves to its specific names. Actually, the word *hadēs* only occurs there four times (Mt 16:18; 11:23 par. Lk 10:15; Lk 16:23), and *geenna* eleven times (Mk 9:43, 45, 47; Mt 5:22, 29-30; 10:28; 18:9; 23:15, 33; Lk 12:5). To complement these the Gospels employ images which are present in other Jewish literature of the period. Two of the most common are "darkness" (cf. *1 Enoch* 103:7; 1QS 4:11-14) and "fire" (cf. Is 66:24; Deut 32:22; 4 Ezra 7:36, 61; *2 Apoc. Bar.* 44:15; *1 Enoch* 10:13; 91:9; 108:3; 4 Macc 9:9; 12:12; 1QS 2:5-9; 1QM 3:29-36; cf. also Mal 4:1 [MT 3:19]; Ezek 38:22; Gen 19:24; Amos 1:4; Jer 43:12; Hos 8:14). Throughout, the Gospels preserve the distinction between *hell* and *death* or the *grave* (cf. Lk 12:5; 16:22).

2.3.1. The Message of John the Baptist. Convinced as he was that the end of the age was near, the Baptist proclaimed that the mission of the Messiah would be characterized both by the salvation of the righteous and the eschatological (*see* Eschatology) judgment of the wicked. To describe the latter, he employed the common image of "fire," asserting that the "unfruitful" (Mt 3:10 par. Lk 3:9) and the "chaff" (Mt 3:12 par. Lk 3:17) would soon be gathered and "burned" by the "coming one."

2.3.2. The Teaching of Jesus in the Gospels. Throughout the teachings of Jesus, the concept of hell is used consistently to refer to the place of punishment and suffering prepared for the devil (*see* Demon, Devil, Satan) and his angels (Mt 25:41; Lk 8:31), as well as for those people who reject God. Accordingly, those who reject Jesus (Mt 11:20-24 par. Lk 10:12-15; cf. also Mt 8:8-12 par. Lk 7:6-9 with 13:28-29; Mt 22:1-14; 25:41-46) and the prophets (Mt 23:31-33; Lk 16:29-31) reap it as their reward. In addition, those guilty of hypocrisy (Mt 23:15, 33; *see* Hypocrite), hateful language and intent (Mt 5:22), unfaithfulness (Mt 24:45-51 par. Lk 12:41-46), unrepentance (Mt 5:29-30; 18:8-9 par. Mk 9:43-47; *see* Repentance) and disobedience (Mt 5:22; 7:19; 13:40, 42, 50; 25:30; Jn 15:6) are liable to its judgment. Predictably, its location is understood by Jesus to be in the depths, the very opposite of the heights of heaven (cf. Mt 11:23 par. Lk 10:15).

There is, however, no explicit distinction in Jesus' teachings between hades and gehenna (contra Jeremias; see also Boyd). He does emphasize that individuals sent to the latter will be in the body (cf. Mt 5:29-30; 10:28; 18:8-9; Mk 9:43-47; cf. also Lk 12:4-5). But he implies the same of the rich man in hades (Lk 16:23-24). Life does continue on the earth while the rich man is in hades (Lk 16:27-31), suggesting that the judgment is yet in the future. However, both gehenna and hades are used in reference to the future judgment (cf. Mt 11:23 par. Lk 10:15; Mt 5:22; 23:33). Therefore, any explicit distinction must rely on other NT passages, which may or may not reflect Jesus' intention here (e.g., Rev 20:13-14; cf. *2 Apoc. Bar.* 21:23; *1 Enoch* 51:1-2; *Sib. Or.* 2:227-30; *4 Ezra* 4:42). Given the fluidity with which these concepts are used in the antecedent and related literature (e.g., *b. B. Bat.* 79a; *Apoc. Zeph.* 10:3-14), it should not be surprising to find the same in Jesus' use.

Finally, it seems that Jesus taught that hell would involve an eternal, conscious punishment. Probably the clearest indication of this is in Matthew 25:46, where the lots of the two groups are contrasted by means of the adjective *eternal* (i.e., "eternal life" as opposed to "eternal punishment"). Additionally, such images as the "undying worm" (Mk 9:48; cf. Is 66:24), the "fire that is not put out" (Mk 9:48; Mt 25:41) and the emotive picture of "weeping and gnashing of teeth" (Mt 8:12 par. Lk 13:28; Mt 13:42, 50; 22:13; 24:51; 25:30; cf. *Sib. Or.* 2:305) all contribute to this perspective (cf. also *1 Enoch* 22:11-13; *T. Gad* 7:5; *T. Benj.* 7:5). However, the use of the verb *destroy* (*apollumi;* Mt 10:28), and the frequent image of "burning" has been understood by some to imply annihilation (e.g., Mt 7:19; 13:40, 42, 50; Jn 15:6; cf. *4 Ezra* 7:61; *1 Enoch* 10:13-14; 38:3-6; 90:26-7; 91:9; 108:3; see McKnight).

2.3.3. The Emphases of the Gospel Writers. Luke includes two unique references to hell. In Luke 8:31 he alone explicitly identifies the "abyss" as the place feared by the demons possessing the Gerasene man (cf. Mk 5:10; Mt 8:29; cf. also *2 Apoc. Bar.* 59:5; *1 Enoch* 10:4; 18:11; 54:5; 88:1; 90:24-27; *Jub.* 5:6).

Luke is also alone in recording the parable of the rich man and Lazarus* (Lk 16:19-31). It remains unclear whether or not Jesus used this story to describe the actual situation beyond the grave. There is substantial evidence of the prior existence of similar traditions elsewhere in Judaism,* raising the question of Jesus' purpose in using it (see Grobel; cf. Hock; cf. also *1 Enoch* 22; *4 Ezra* 7:36). If Jesus did make use of existing tradition, his point may have been the distinctive feature of his parable—the impossibility of a resurrection to convince the "brothers" to listen to the prophets—rather than to describe eschatological conditions. Regardless, hades is explicitly reserved for the wicked, while Lazarus is sent to a place of comfort. Typical of Luke's emphasis elsewhere, Lazarus is an example of the poor and the downtrodden who are shown favor by God (cf. Lk 4:18; 6:20; 7:22; 14:13, 21).

Matthew's Gospel presents the greatest concentration of references to hell. This is not surprising, given Matthew's tendency to draw extensively on apocalyptic imagery. Matthew alone preserves the statement that hades will not prevail against his "assembly" (*ekklēsia,* Mt 16:18; *see* Church). He also records three unique references to gehenna. In Matthew 5:22 the one guilty of hateful language against another will be liable to the "gehenna of fire." The two other references appear in Jesus' condemnation of the scribes* and Pharisees.* In Matthew 23:15 their proselytizing activity is said to result in the making of "son[s] of gehenna." Then in Matthew 23:33 their complicity in the deaths of the prophets puts them in dire danger of gehenna's judgment.

Matthew includes additional references in parabolic settings, making pronounced use of the apocalyptic image of "fire." In Matthew 13:40, 42 the angels gather the "weeds" at the "end of the age" and burn them with fire. The same fate befalls the "bad fish" in Matthew 13:50 and the accursed "on the left" at the great judgment of the nations in Matthew 25:41-46 (cf. also Mt 7:19). Finally, Matthew repeatedly describes the lot of the wicked with the emotive phrase "weeping and gnashing of teeth." Except for one parallel (Mt 8:12 par. Lk 13:28), Matthew alone includes the phrase five times (cf. Mt 13:42, 50; 22:13; 24:51; 25:30).

See also Angels; Apocalyptic; Demon, Devil, Satan; Eschatology; Judgment; Life; Resurrection.

BIBLIOGRAPHY. W. Boyd, "Gehenna—According to J. Jeremias," in *Studia Biblica 1978: II. Papers on the*

Gospels, ed. E. Livingstone (Sheffield: JSOT, 1980) 9-12; J. Fitzmyer, *Luke the Theologian: Aspects of His Teaching* (New York: Paulist, 1989) 203-33; K. Grobel, ". . . Whose Name Is Neves," *NTS* 10 (1963-64) 373-82; R. Harris, *"šᵉ'ōl," TWOT* 2.2303-4; R. Hock, "Lazarus and Micyllus: Greco-Roman Backgrounds to Luke 16:19-31," *JBL* 106 (1987) 447-63; J. Jeremias, "γέεννα," *TDNT* I.657-58; idem, *"ᾅδης," TDNT* I.146-49; S. McKnight, "Eternal Consequences or Eternal Consciousness?" in *Through No Fault of Their Own?: The Fate of Those Who Have Never Heard,* eds. W. V. Crockett and J. G. Sigountos (Grand Rapids: Baker 1991); M. Thompson, "Eternal Life in the Gospel of John," *Ex Auditu* 5 (1989) 35-55; H. Traub and G. von Rad, *"οὐρανός," TDNT* V.497-543.   J. Lunde

HEBREW (NATIONALITY). *See* ISRAEL.

HELL. *See* HEAVEN AND HELL.

HELLENISM
1. Definition and Use of the Term
2. Historical and Cultural Background
3. Hellenism and Judaism
4. Hellenism and the Gospels

1. Definition and Use of the Term.
"Hellenism" derives from the Greek verb *hellēnizō,* meaning "to speak Greek," and hence "to make Greek" and "to act in a Greek way." Today it is used in two broad senses: (1) Greek civilization in general, especially the high culture and humane spirit of classical Greece and (2) the culture of a wide area of the Mediterranean and Near East which came under strong Greek influence in the Hellenistic period after the death of Alexander the Great. This influence included the use of the Greek language in its *koinē* form (*see* Languages of Palestine). It continued during and after the Roman conquest of the area.

The word *Hellenism* nowhere occurs in the Gospels (it is used in 2 Macc 4:13 of the peak of Hellenization, i.e., the adoption of pagan ways, in Palestine under Antiochus IV). But closely related terms appear—with various meanings: (1) In Mark 7:26 *Hellēnis,* literally "Greek woman," is used of the Syro-Phoenician woman whose daughter Jesus heals. Here it seems to mean a Greek-speaking pagan from the region of the Hellenized cities of Tyre and Sidon. (2) In John 7:35 the Jews ask whether Jesus intends to go to the Diaspora to teach the "Greeks" (*Hellēnes*). The term probably means again pagans of Greek culture rather than Greek-speaking Jews or proselytes. (3) In John 12:20, however, the "Greeks" who seek Jesus are almost certainly proselytes,

pagan converts to Judaism,* at Jerusalem for the festival (*see* Feasts). They too were probably Greek-speakers. (4) In John 19:20 the notice on the cross is written in Hebrew (= Aramaic?), Latin and Greek. Here the term *Hellēnisti* is used unambiguously of the Greek language. Thus in the Gospels the term *Greek* applies to both language and culture (including religion).

2. Historical and Cultural Background.
2.1. Early Greece. The roots of Greek civilization and the first documentary evidence for the Greek language go back to the Bronze Age, when princes of the Mycenaean palace culture kept records in the so-called Linear B script, fostered the arts and traded widely in the Near East. This early culture was followed by a dark age of illiteracy and comparative poverty. But some arts were kept alive. A continuing tradition of oral poetry culminated magnificently in the epic poems of Homer, whose *Iliad* and *Odyssey* were to have a profound influence on Greek religion and education down to the Hellenistic Age and beyond. By Homer's time (c. eighth century B.C.) trade had been reopened with the East, writing had been re-introduced in the form of the Phoenician alphabet (adapted to Greek needs), and a wave of overseas colonization had begun.

2.2. Classical Greece. The Geometric Age (c. 900-700 B.C.) was followed by the Archaic Age (c. 700-480 B.C.) and the great Classical Age (480-323 B.C.). At this time Greece consisted of many small, independent city-states known as *poleis* (sing. *polis*), with a common language (Greek) and religion, but speaking their own dialects (e.g., Attic at Athens, Laconian at Sparta) and having their own local religious cults and distinctive styles in sculpture, vase painting and other arts. During the Archaic Age many of these communities were governed by autocratic rulers, or "tyrants" (*tyrannoi*); but "tyranny" gave way to oligarchy (rule by a few) or to democracy, as at fifth-century Athens, where all free, male citizens had a vote and shared directly in government. The Classical Period was the golden age of Greek literature and art, when Aeschylus, Sophocles and Euripides composed their tragedies, when the historians Herodotus and Thucydides wrote. It was the age of the great philosophers Socrates, Plato and Aristotle; of orators like Demosthenes; of sculptors like Pheidias; and of the building of fine temples, such as the Temple of Zeus at Olympia and the Parthenon at Athens. But it was also a period of interstate rivalry and sometimes war. Having united to defeat the Persian invaders (490-479 B.C.), the Greeks were themselves torn apart in the Peloponnesian War (431-404 B.C.) between Athens and Sparta.

2.3. Alexander the Great. The fourth century saw the

rise of a new power on the northern fringes of the Greek world in the kingdom of Macedon. The Macedonians were of related stock to the rest of the Greeks but were not regarded by them as full Hellenes. Their dialect was quite distinctive, and they retained a monarchy long after other Greek states had moved on to other forms of government. But their rulers were anxious to be considered Greeks. They established relations with Athens, competing as early as c. 500 B.C. in the Olympic Games (open only to Hellenes). Perdiccas II (king c. 450-413 B.C.) established a new capital at Pella, and invited distinguished Greek artists and poets to his court. Philip II (king 359-336 B.C.) went further, invading Greece and defeating the Athenians at Chaeronea, effectively putting an end to the independent Greek city-states. Philip was succeeded by his son, Alexander, a man of great intelligence, courage, chivalry and military skill, who in his youth had been tutored by Aristotle. His invasion and conquest of Asia Minor, Phoenicia, Palestine, Egypt and Babylonia became legendary (cf. 1 Macc 1—4). He died in 323 B.C. at the age of thirty-three. He had taken his army as far as India. He had destroyed the old Persian Empire, founded cities (such as Alexandria in Egypt), and opened up new ways for Greek and "barbarian" to live together.

2.4. The Hellenistic Age.

2.4.1. Cosmopolitanism. Alexander's empire was too vast to hold together long. It was soon divided into three parts, ruled by powerful dynasties—the Antigonids in Macedon, the Seleucids in Syria and the Ptolemies in Egypt. But the effects of his conquests were far-reaching, causing the spread of the Greek language and of a Hellenizing culture throughout the Near East. The old independent Greek city-states, with their dialects, distinctive styles and distrust of barbarians had now gone for good. They were replaced by a cosmopolitan culture involving peoples of many different ethnic origins, using what was basically Attic Greek for their *lingua franca*.

2.4.2. Art and Literature. The Hellenistic Age is sometimes disparaged as decadent compared with Classical Greece. It needs to be stressed that artistically it was a period of creativity, when sculptors and painters maintained a high peak of technical skill. The old idealism of Classical art gave place to a vigorous realism in which subjects such as old age, poverty and pain were portrayed as well as moving representations of physical beauty. In architecture attention was paid to town planning and dramatic effect; civic amenities such as stoas and theaters were constructed on a grand scale; new art forms, such as mosaic, were developed. In literature it was an age of

erudition rather than originality, as can be seen typically in the poems of Callimachus and Aratus, and in the Homeric scholarship which flourished at Alexandria. But there were also authors of charm and elegance, like the epic poet Apollonius Rhodius, the pastoral poet Theocritus and the novelist Chariton. Among historians Polybius was outstanding, among writers of biography (a popular new literary genre) Plutarch.

2.4.3. Science and Philosophy. In medicine, science and engineering there were spectacular advances, as shown by the work of men like Galen and Archimedes. In philosophy the chief feature was the development of different "schools" such as the Academics, following in the tradition of Plato, and the Peripatetics, following that of Aristotle, the Stoics and Epicureans. While also studying and developing logic and physics, such philosophers were deeply concerned with ethics, especially the nature of virtue and the proper conduct for an individual.

The Stoics stressed the importance of living in harmony with nature (*physis*). They believed in divine Providence, allegorizing many of the old tales of the gods and postulating a *logos*, or divine "reason," which permeated the world.

The Epicureans are famous today for their early atomic theory and the view that everything has material causes. They taught that the gods took no interest in human affairs and that pleasure (*hēdonē*) and calm detachment (*ataraxia*) are the key to virtuous living. (They understood these ideals in a lofty way rather than in terms of sensual pleasure or an easy life.)

There were also Cynics, who cherished personal freedom, despised material possessions and practiced a simple, ascetic life. They never had an organized school like the other philosophers, and in the later Hellenistic Age many became wandering preachers and beggars.

2.4.4. Religion. The Hellenistic Age saw simultaneously a decline among intellectuals of belief in the old Homeric gods and a growth, especially among the uneducated, of magical practices and exotic new cults, often of an emotional nature, the product of Greek contact with the so-called mystery religions of the East. These cults included those of Isis and Serapis (from Egypt), of Cybele, the "Great Mother," and of Attis (from Phrygia). Ancient Greek nature cults, such as the Eleusinian and Dionysiac mysteries, were also revitalized. This was an age of syncretism, when the gods of one people were assimilated to those of another: Greek gods were identified with their Roman and oriental counterparts, taking on new traits as they did so (e.g., Zeus Hypsistos and Dionysos Sabazios). There also developed in the Hellenistic East a ruler-cult, in which living kings were given divine honors. In Rome the early emperors were regarded as divine only after their death, but in many parts of the Empire they were worshiped during their lifetime.

2.4.5. The Rise of Rome. The Hellenistic Age was a time of almost constant jockeying for power. The town of Pergamon, originally part of the Seleucid kingdom, asserted its independence and, under its powerful Attalid dynasty, came to dominate Hellenized Asia Minor. In 201 B.C. it joined with Rhodes to call in Roman aid against Macedon, giving the Romans a pretext for intervening in Greek affairs. Extended and beautified by an ambitious building program, it became an artistic and literary center with a library rivaling that of Alexandria. In 133 B.C. its last king, Attalus III, bequeathed his kingdom to Rome.

Under Ptolemaic rule Palestine was subject to gradual and peaceful Hellenization for around a hundred years. Then in 198 B.C. the conquest of Palestine (and Phoenicia) by the Seleucid king Antiochus III led to a much more rapid and violent phase of Hellenization, notably under Antiochus IV Epiphanes. He built a Greek gymnasium at Jerusalem and shocked Jews to the core by setting up an altar to Zeus Olympios in the Temple* itself. His forced imposition of Greek customs, and persecution of those who remained loyal to the Jewish faith, led to the Maccabean Revolt and a period of Jewish independence under the Hasmonean rulers. But even in this period more subtle Hellenization continued, as can be seen in the use of Greek names by rulers like Alexander Janneus (103-76 B.C.) and in their Greek coin types (some of which used the Greek title of *basileus*, or king). A dispute over the succession led eventually to Rome being called in, and to the conquest of Palestine and Syria by Pompey, whose entry into the Holy of Holies in the Jerusalem Temple (63 B.C.) was another dreadful act of sacrilege for the Jews (*see* Rome).

2.4.6. Economic and Social Life. Conditions varied in the different Hellenistic kingdoms. The ancient economy was basically agrarian, and the Hellenistic Age saw many improvements to methods of agriculture, especially in Egypt, where farming and related industries were under royal control. There were state monopolies in oil, textiles (except wool) and papyrus, the paper of the ancient world. The tax system was highly organized, and administration was bureaucratic. Foreign residents—notably Greeks—had more privileges than native Egyptians.

In the Seleucid Empire the economic system was less unified: taxation was farmed out to tax collectors, who bid for franchises—a system which continued in Roman times. Direct taxes were usually levied only on non-citizens, but citizens paid indirect taxes* like customs and sales taxes. Much use was made of slave labor, the number of slaves increasing in the Hellenistic period through war, piracy and kidnapping. In the crafts and professions it was an age of specialization; trade guilds and other voluntary associations were important (see Koester; Walbank).

Social divisions ran deep. Most privileged were the kings, their families and "friends"; then came the higher administrators, followed by wealthy independent citizens such as merchants; below that were craftsmen and artisans, peasant farmers and petty employees of the bureaucracy; below that, slaves. Women took their social class from their husbands: not many professions were open to them, and most were kept busy with domestic pursuits and home industries. They had few legal rights and, apart from members of the privileged upper classes, limited education and social life.

3. Hellenism and Judaism.

3.1. The Diaspora. By the time of Jesus many Jews lived outside Palestine in the Diaspora (Dispersion), especially in large cities such as Alexandria, Antioch and Rome. Under Roman rule they were exempt from taking part in the state cult and from military* service. They sought to uphold Jewish monotheism and ethical standards, and to keep the Sabbath* and food laws. Lacking access to the Temple cult, they focused worship* and religious education on the synagogue.* Some managed to get to Jerusalem for festivals. But inevitably there was assimilation to the Hellenistic environment, particularly where there was intermarriage. Greek was the first language for most Diaspora Jews, the language in which they read and studied their Scriptures. Many were educated in Greek philosophy, rhetoric and literature, and a lively Jewish literature in Greek grew up, including such typical literary forms as history, tragedy, epic and romance. Philo and others sought to reconcile Platonic and Stoic philosophy with the Jewish faith. Writings like Wisdom and 4 Maccabees also reveal extensive Greek influence. At a popular level Hellenistic ideas of Fate, Fortune, astrology and magic were adopted.

3.2. Hellenized Judaism in Palestine. In the past the Hellenized Judaism of the Diaspora has often been contrasted with what was thought to have been the purer Judaism of Palestine. But Martin Hengel and other scholars have strongly argued that such a distinction is artificial. By the Roman period Palestine and its surrounding areas were also heavily Hellenized. Caesarea Maritima, the seat of Roman government, had magnificent public buildings, including an amphitheater, theater and hippodrome. At Jericho, Herod's palace contained an ornate Roman bath, colonnaded court, mosaics and other features of a Hellenistic luxury mansion. At Jerusalem, the Temple had Greek architectural features. The cities of the Decapolis were splendidly adorned with stoas, temples, theaters and other amenities. Even in Galilee,* Sepphoris (near Nazareth) had a theater of Herodian date. Further north at Caesarea Philippi there was an ancient shrine of Pan and a temple to Augustus.

How deep did such Hellenization go? We know that Greek proper names were widely used, and it is likely that more of the population spoke Greek than was once believed. Hellenism was clearly strongest in the cities, especially the Herodian and Roman administrative centers and the Greek cities of Phoenicia and the Decapolis. How far Greek education and outlook permeated the country areas of Galilee and Judea remains uncertain (see Sevenster; Hengel).

4. Hellenism and the Gospels.

4.1. The Language of the Gospels. The clearest sign of Hellenism in the Gospels is the fact that they are written in Greek. They share this characteristic with the rest of the New Testament and with a large body of Hellenistic Jewish writings, including those of Philo, Josephus, the Jewish tragedian Ezekiel and many apocryphal and pseudepigraphical works. The reasons for this choice of language were probably threefold: (1) Greek was the most widely understood common language in the world in which the Gospels were expected to circulate; (2) it was the language conventionally used for most literary work in the Hellenized Near East; and (3) it may well have been the language with which the Evangelists themselves were most familiar (*see* Languages of Palestine).

Although all four Gospels show clear signs of an underlying Semitic tradition, including sayings of Jesus in Aramaic, it is uncertain how much Hebrew their authors knew (most of their OT quotations rely on Greek versions; *see* Old Testament in the Gospels). It has been suggested that the author of Mark may have been bilingual in Greek and Aramaic.

4.2. The Literary Form of the Gospels. The Gospels have often been compared to ancient biographies (*see* Gospel [Genre]). Thus C. H. Talbert has argued that they correspond to certain specific types, designed either to legitimate the authority of a founder or to dispel false images of him or to present a true account of him (and his successors). Luke, in particular, in his two-volume work Luke-Acts has been seen as acting in

the manner of a classical historian, with his formal dedications to Theophilus, his careful dating of Jesus' birth and the set speeches in Acts. Parallels have also been seen between the Gospels and Hellenistic aretalogies (hymns praising the virtues of gods).

But while there are general similarities, the Gospels do not correspond exactly to any ancient literary genre. Mark, almost certainly the earliest, lacks biographical interest in Jesus' ancestry, birth, education, appearance, character and achievements; his chronology is quite vague. Even Luke, with his interests in the Greek world, does not give a systematic chronology of Jesus' life, and may have been more influenced by OT and Jewish historiography than classical. The aim of all the Evangelists was to present the good news (*euangelion; see* Gospel [Good News]) of salvation* through Jesus Christ; hence, the large proportion of the Gospels devoted to Jesus' passion (*see* Passion Narrative). This is not to deny influences from the classical world in rhetorical devices (*see* Rhetorical Criticism), vocabulary, narrative form and even thought. A few of Jesus' healings* (e.g., Mk 7:31-37) are described like those of Hellenistic wonder-workers; but in most the magical element is minimal. It seems improbable that Mark was seeking to present Jesus as a Greek-style *Theios Anēr* (Divine Man*) or in contrast to one. (There has been much confused thinking about this supposed Hellenistic figure. See section 4.6.)

4.3. The World of the Gospels. With Judea, Samaria, Galilee and adjacent areas so long under Hellenistic rule one might have expected the Gospels to contain fairly frequent references to Hellenistic culture. In fact, neither the theater, amphitheater, gymnasium nor other recreational facility is mentioned, even in metaphors (contrast the epistles). There are no references to Greek literature or to the cults of the Greek gods (though some have noted Dionysiac parallels to the miracle* at Cana). But we do find allusions to the social world of Hellenism (e.g., the luxury of those who in live large houses, Mt 11:8) and to the architectural splendors of Herod's Temple (Mk 13:1). The autocratic power of the Herodian rulers is illustrated in Matthew's picture of Herod the Great (Mt 2), and in the story of Herod Antipas' execution of John the Baptist* (Mk 6:14-29; *see* Herodian Dynasty). Mention is made of the Roman emperor and of various features of the Roman administration (*see* Rome), but there is no systematic account of political conditions.

Sometimes the ways of Jesus' followers are contrasted with the Hellenistic world: in Luke 22:25 Jesus refers to the kings of the Gentiles lording it over their subjects and to those who are called "Benefactors,"* saying that it must not be like this with his followers. "Benefactor" (*Euergetēs*) is a well-attested title for Hellenistic kings such as Ptolemy III and Antiochus VII, for the emperor Augustus and other leading men. In John 18:36 Jesus contrasts his kingdom with the military kingdoms of the world. The Gospels' picture of kings and courts, including that found in Jesus' parables, seems to derive from popular perceptions of Hellenistic kings rather than the Hebrew monarchy. In Luke 19:11-27 a noble travels to a far country to receive the title of *basileus* (king): this reflects the habit of local Eastern rulers seeking vassal status from Rome, an outstanding example being that of Archelaus, son of Herod the Great, who went to Rome to obtain the title of "king," but won only that of "ethnarch." However, the general picture of life in the Gospels is not of kings and wealthy townsfolk, but of Palestinian peasants with their round of agricultural labor, herding, fishing, food production and domestic activities.

4.4. Jesus' Contacts with Hellenism. The extent of Jesus' contact with the Hellenistic cities is uncertain. Most of his ministry was in the rural areas of Galilee.* Hellenized Sepphoris, an administrative center and one-time residence of Herod Antipas, was only three or four miles from Nazareth, but there is no mention of his visiting it. The Gospels do record occasional visits to Gentile* territory: Mark 7:24-30 tells of an encounter with a Syro-Phoenician woman in the area of Tyre and possibly of a visit to Sidon (7:31). Mark also tells how Jesus traveled in the Decapolis, healing a deaf and dumb man (7:31-37) and a demoniac in the region of Gerasa (5:1-20; some versions place this event in Gadarene, or Gergesene, territory). In Mark 8:27 we find Jesus in the villages of Caesarea Philippi, but we do not know if he visited the city. He had contact with a Roman centurion at Capernaum (Mt 8:5-13; Lk 7:1-10) and with a royal official, presumably a Gentile (Jn 4:43-54—possibly a variant of the same story). In dining at the house of the wealthy tax-collector Zacchaeus in Jericho (Lk 19:1-10) he surely met with Hellenistic luxury. We have already mentioned the "Greeks" who come to see him in Jerusalem (Jn 12:20). Nonetheless, it is clear that Jesus saw his mission as primarily to the Jews and not to their Greek or Semitic neighbors (Mt 10:5-6; Mk 7:27; *see* Gentiles).

4.5. Evidence for Hellenism in the Everyday Life of the Gospels. A clear example is the use of Greek personal names (e.g., Philip, Andrew) and of Hellenized forms of Jewish names (e.g., Maria [Mary], Simon, Bartimaeus—an Aramaic-Greek hybrid). Many towns and geographical localities are called by their Greek (or Latin) rather than Semitic names (e.g., Tyre, Caesarea, Decapolis, Lake Tiberias, Galilee). There are frequent references to Greek coinage, including the valuable talent (e.g., Mt 18:24; 25:15), the *mna* (the "pound" of Lk 19:12-26), the *statēr* (Mt 17:27), the *drachma* (the coin lost by the woman in Lk 15:8) and—the smallest coin of all—the *lepton* (the widow's mite of Mk 12:42; cf. also Lk 12:59). It is not always clear where actual currency is intended and where the Evangelists are simply giving the Greek names for their Roman, Jewish or Tyrian equivalents. The Gospels also mention Greek units of measurement (e.g., the *stadion*). Sometimes we note Greek legal terms, such as the *archōn* (magistrate) and *praktōr* (jailor) of Luke 12:57-59—language derived from the Hellenistic law court rather than the Jewish scene. The name *synedrion* (Sanhedrin*) for the highest Jewish court is also Greek.

4.6. Hellenism and the Thought of the Gospels. More problematic is the question of Hellenistic influence on the thought of the Gospels. The fact that they were composed in Greek meant that Greek terms for concepts had to be used instead of Hebrew. Sometimes this presented no difficulties (e.g., when Luke uses Greek *epistatēs* [master] for Hebrew *rabbî*). At other times it may have led readers to understand important concepts in a Greek rather than a Semitic way (e.g., Son of God,* Savior* and Lord*).

Sometimes the Evangelists may have deliberately intended to evoke the connotations of the Greek terms or have used words with more than one level of meaning. An important example is John's use of *logos** for Christ as the Word (1:1, 14). While this term owes much to OT ideas of the dynamic and creative Word of God and to Jewish Wisdom traditions, it could hardly fail to suggest to educated Greeks the Stoic doctrine of the *logos* (see section 2.4.3). The sharp contrasts in John between flesh and spirit, above and below, the earthly and the heavenly, may owe something to popular Platonism (such influence might have come indirectly via Hellenistic Judaism); the question of gnostic influence on John has been much debated (*see* John, Gospel of). Greek concepts of the nature of the soul may even have influenced the Synoptic Gospels: in Matthew 10:28 the Hebrew idea of the unity of the human person seems to have been replaced by a Greek dichotomy between body and soul.

The Gospel writers belonged to a society that constituted part of the ancient world and, in spite of the uniqueness of their message, still had much in common with their contemporaries. They shared with the Greeks, Romans and other peoples of the Hellenistic world certain presuppositions, such as a stratified social structure with women subordinate to men and an economy supported by slave labor. There are similarities between some of Jesus' ethical teaching (*see* Ethics of Jesus) and that of the Greek philosophers. We note especially his emphasis on the fatherhood of God, the value of the individual and indifference to material possessions. In a fascinating work F. G. Downing has drawn attention to parallels between Jesus and the Cynics. But in spite of all this, Jesus' teaching remains distinctive for its emphasis on the kingdom of God, its radical summons to discipleship and teaching on love.*

The NT writers also shared with their contemporaries a basically pre-scientific approach to such subjects as the physical universe, sickness and miracles.* This means that Hellenistic parallels can be found to many features of the Gospels, like their understanding of demon* possession (including the idea that demons may be transferred from one home to another) and of natural phenomena (like earthquakes and eclipses). Sometimes it is hard to tell whether we are dealing with direct Hellenistic influence or a parallel development of ideas. Thus the motif of walking on water (Mk 6:47-51) is paralleled in the Argonautic saga (Apollonius Rhodius 1.179-84) but may in fact have closer links with OT ideas of Yahweh's conquest of the unruly sea.

Some of the events associated with Jesus' birth and death appear to have parallels in the so-called prestige myths of Greco-Roman folklore, including tales of astronomical portents and dreams* heralding the birth of famous people or marking their death. There are classical stories of heroes or famous men born from a mortal woman and a divinity (e.g., Perseus, Plato, Alexander). There are tales of the return of the dead to life and of a hero's ascent to heaven (cf. Dionysos and Heracles). We must stress, however, that the Greco-Roman parallels are mostly broad and general rather than precise, and that some motifs are also paralleled in the Jewish background. The Gospel stories are unique in their theological depth, doctrinal coherence, descriptive conviction and detail. The fact that important teachings are couched in the language and, sometimes, the thought forms of the Hellenistic world in no way detracts from the truth of their message.

See also JUDAISM; LANGUAGES OF PALESTINE; ROME.

BIBLIOGRAPHY. D. E. Aune, *The New Testament in Its Literary Environment* (LEC; Philadelphia: Westminster, 1987); M. Avi-Yonah and E. Stern, eds., *Encyclopedia of Archaeological Excavations in the Holy Land* (4 vols., London: Oxford University and Jerusalem: Israel Exploration Society and Massada Press, 1975-78); W. D. Davies and L. Finkelstein, eds., *The Cambridge History of Judaism* II: *The Hellenistic Age* (Cambridge: University Press, 1989); F. G. Downing, *Jesus and the Threat of Freedom* (London: SCM, 1987); P. E. Easterling and B. M. W. Knox, eds., *The Cambridge History of Classical Literature* I: *Greek Literature* (Cambridge: University Press, 1985); E. Ferguson, *Backgrounds of Early Christianity* (Grand Rapids: Eerdmans, 1987); M. Hengel, *Judaism and Hellenism* (London: SCM, 1974); idem, *Jews, Greeks and Barbarians* (Philadelphia: Fortress, 1980); idem, *The "Hellenization" of Judaea in the First Century After Christ* (Philadelphia: Trinity, 1990); H. Koester, *Introduction to the New Testament* I: *History, Culture and Religion of the Hellenistic Age* (Philadelphia: Fortress, 1982); R. H. Nash, *Christianity and the Hellenistic World* (Grand Rapids: Zondervan, 1984); J. J. Pollitt, *Art in the Hellenistic Age* (Oxford: University Press, 1986); J. N. Sevenster, *Do You Know Greek?* (NovTSup 19; Leiden: Brill, 1968); C. H. Talbert, *What Is a Gospel?* (Philadelphia: Fortress, 1978); V. Tcherikover, *Hellenistic Civilization and the Jews* (Philadelphia: Jewish Publ. Soc. of America, 1961); A. J. Toynbee, *Hellenism* (New York, Cambridge: University Press, 1959; and Westport: Greenwood Press, 1981); F. W. Walbank et al, eds., *The Cambridge Ancient History* VII, Pt. 1: *The Hellenistic World* (Cambridge: University Press, 1984); H. Windisch, "Ἕλλην κτλ," *TDNT* II.504-16.

R. B. Edwards

HERODIAN DYNASTY

The Herodian family ruled over the Palestinian area from 40 B.C. until around A.D. 100. In order to understand the political and social setting of Jesus' ministry, it is important to understand the story of the Herods up through the first four decades of the first century A.D.

1. Herod the Great (47-4 B.C.)
2. Archelaus (4 B.C.-A.D. 6)
3. Philip the Tetrarch (4 B.C.-A.D. 34)
4. Herod Antipas (4 B.C.-A.D. 39)
5. The Herodians

1. Herod the Great (47-4 B.C.).

1.1. Herod's Family Origins. The demise of the Hasmonean dynasty, the transference of Syria and Palestine to Roman rule, and the civil wars that marked the decay of the nation all created confusion which opened the way for the Herodian family to come into prominence. Upon her death Alexandra Salome's eldest son, Hyrcanus II, succeeded as king and high priest (*see* Priest, Priesthood) in 67 B.C., only to be displaced three months later by his aggressive brother Aristobulus II.

Antipater II, father of Herod the Great, was an Idumean (Josephus *J.W.* 1.6.2 §123; cf. also *Ant.* 14.1.3 §9; Justin Martyr *Dial.* 52.3; Eusebius *Hist. Eccl.* 1.6.2; 7.11; *b. B. Bat.* 3b-4a; *b. Qidd.* 70a). He realized he would not be able to be king and high priest, but he knew he could become the power behind the throne, and thus he sided with the weak Hyrcanus II. Antipater II convinced Hyrcanus II that he was unjustly deprived of his right to rule by Aristobulus II. Furthermore, Antipater II promised to help him regain that position. With the help of the Arabian king, Aretas, Aristobulus II was defeated in 65 B.C.

With the advent of Roman power in the East, each brother (Hyrcanus II and Aristobulus II) asked Pompey, the Roman general, to side with him against the other. After having some trouble with Aristobulus II, Pompey joined forces with Hyrcanus II (Josephus *Ant.* 14.3. §§46-47) and after three months in the autumn of 63 B.C. they defeated Aristobulus II. This marked the end of the Jewish independence that had first been gained in 142 B.C. Pompey entered the Holy of Holies but did not plunder it. In fact, he ordered its cleansing, the resumption of the sacrifices, and he reinstated Hyrcanus II as high priest (Josephus *Ant.* 14.4.4 §§69-73; *J.W.* 1.6.5—7.6 §133-53; Tacitus *Hist.* 5.9; Appian *Mithr. W.* 106, 114; Florus 1.40.30; Livy *Epit.* 102; Plutarch *Pomp.* 39; cf. Dio Cassius *Hist.* 37.15-17).

In 48 B.C., with the defeat of Pompey by Julius Caesar, Hyrcanus II and Antipater II attached themselves to the new ruler who in turn reconfirmed Hyrcanus II as high priest and gave him the title of Ethnarch of the Jews and recognized Antipater II as administrator of Judea (Josephus *Ant.* 14.8.1-5 §§127-55; 10.2 §191; *J.W.* 1.9.3—10.4 §§187-203). Although publicly Antipater II enjoined the people to honor Hyrcanus II, he began to show his dynastic ambitions in 47 B.C. by appointing his son, Phasael, as governor of Jerusalem and his second son, Herod, as governor of Galilee* (Josephus *Ant.* 14.9.1-2 §§156-58; *J.W.* 1.10.4 §§201-3).

1.2. Herod's Rule.

1.2.1. Herod's Governorship of Galilee (47-37 B.C.).

Although only twenty-five years of age, Herod was admired by the Galilean Jews and the Romans for the leadership he demonstrated in removing the brigand leader Ezekias and his followers (47-46 B.C.). Some in Hyrcanus' court felt that Herod was becoming too powerful, and he was brought to trial before the Sanhedrin*; however, Sextus Caesar, governor of Syria, forced Hyrcanus II to acquit him. After that Herod

joined Sextus Caesar in Damascus who appointed him governor of Coele-Syria, and thus he became involved with Roman affairs in Syria (Josephus *Ant.* 14.9.2-5 §§158-84; *J.W.* 1.10.5-9 §§204-15; *b. Qidd.* 43a). He again proved himself to Rome as an able leader in collecting taxes* and suppressing revolts (*see* Revolutionary Movements).

After Cassius and Brutus murdered Julius Caesar in 44 B.C., Cassius went to Syria and assumed the leadership there. In need of money, he reappointed Herod as governor of Coele-Syria to collect more revenue. He promised to make Herod king after he and Brutus defeated Octavius and Antony. New disturbances in Judea were quelled by Herod (43-42 B.C.), and he received praise from the people and from Hyrcanus II (Josephus *Ant.* 14.11.3—12.1 §§277-99; *J.W.* 1.11-112.3 §§220-40).

In 42 B.C. Antony defeated Cassius. About this time Herod and Phasael were accused by the Jewish leaders of usurping governmental powers and leaving Hyrcanus II with only titular honors. But Herod was acquitted (Josephus *Ant.* 14.12.2-6 §§301-23; *J.W.* 1.12.4-6 §§242-45; Plutarch *Anton.* 24; Dio Cassius 48.24; Appian *Civ. W.* 5.30-38). In 41 B.C. new accusations were made against Herod, and he was tried in Antioch with Antony present. Antony asked Hyrcanus II who would be the best-qualified ruler, and Hyrcanus II suggested Herod and Phasael. As a result, Antony appointed them as tetrarchs of Judea (Josephus *J.W.* 1.12.5 §§243-44; *Ant.* 14.13.1 §§324-26).

New troubles appeared in 40 B.C. when the Parthians arrived in Syria. The Parthians were joined by Antigonus (the son of Hyrcanus II's deposed brother Aristobulus II) who wanted to remove Hyrcanus. Jerusalem was besieged, and the Parthians asked for peace. However, Herod was suspicious of the offer. On the other hand, Phasael and Hyrcanus II met the Parthians but were betrayed by them and were put in chains. On hearing this, Herod and his family fled to Masada and then Petra. Antigonus was made king, and he mutilated his uncle Hyrcanus' ears, in order to prevent him from being restored as the high priest, and then carried him off to Parthia. Phasael died either of suicide or poisoning (Josephus *Ant.* 14.13.3-10 §§335-69; 15.2.1 §12; *J.W.* 1.13.2-11 §§250-73; Dio Cassius 48.26, 41).

Herod went to Rome,* where Antony, Octavius and the Senate designated him King of Judea (Josephus *Ant.* 14.14.6 §§381-85; *J.W.* 1.14.4 §§282-85; cf. Strabo 26.2.46; Appian *Civ. W.* 5.74; Tacitus *Hist.* 5.9). Herod returned to Palestine, recaptured Galilee and finally captured Jerusalem in the summer of 37 B.C. Just before capturing Jerusalem, he married Mariamne II, niece of Antigonus, to whom he had been betrothed for five years. Not only was this a contemptuous move against Antigonus, but also, since she was a Hasmonean, it strengthened his claim to the throne. Herod beheaded Antigonus, thus ending the Hasmonean rule and ensuring his position as king of the Jews (Josephus *Ant.* 14.15.8—16.2 §§439-80; *J.W.* 1.16.7—18.3 §§320-57; Dio Cassius 49.22; Plutarch *Anton.* 36).

1.2.2. Herod's Kingship (37-4 B.C.). The reign of Herod is divided into three periods: (1) consolidation from 37 to 25 B.C.; (2) prosperity from 25 to 12 B.C.; and (3) the period of domestic troubles from 14 to 4 B.C.

The period of consolidation lasted from his accession as king in 37 B.C. to the death of the sons of Babas, the last male representatives of the Hasmonean family in 25 B.C. The first adversaries, the people and the Pharisees,* objected both to his being an Idumean, a half-Jew, as well as his friendship with the Romans. Those who opposed him were punished, and those who took his side were rewarded with favors and honors (Josephus *Ant.* 15.1.1 §§2-3; *J.W.* 1.18.4 §358).

The second adversaries were those of the aristocracy who sided with Antigonus. Herod executed forty-five of the wealthiest and confiscated their properties and thereby replenished his own coffers (Josephus *Ant.* 15.1.2 §§5-6; cf. 14.9.4 §175; *J.W.* 1.18.4 §358).

The third group of adversaries were the Hasmonean family. His mother-in-law, Alexandra, was the main problem. She forced him, through Cleopatra's influence, to appoint her son Aristobulus as high priest even though he was only sixteen years old. After officiating at a successful Feast of Tabernacles (*see* Feasts), Aristobulus was supposedly accidentally drowned at Herod's palace in Jericho—a story never believed by Alexandra (Josephus *Ant.* 15.3.2-4 §§42-61; *J.W.* 1.22.2 §437). Alexandra told her friend Cleopatra of Herod's misdeeds, and thus Herod had to appear before Antony at Laodicea (on the coast of Syria). Not knowing what his fate might be, he ordered his uncle Joseph to kill Mariamne if he were sentenced to death. Mariamne heard of Herod's order for her execution and resented it. But through gifts and eloquence Herod was able to convince Antony that he was not guilty (Josephus *Ant.* 15.3.5-9 §§62-87; *J.W.* 1.22.4-5 §§441-44).

Herod's final adversary was Cleopatra. She had cooperated with Alexandra in the matter of Aristobulus. Next, she asked Antony to increase her territory by eliminating Herod and Malchus of Arabia in order to possess their lands. Antony did not permit this but did give her the rich district of Jericho and a part of

Arabia (Josephus *Ant.* 15.4.1-2 §§88-103). When in 32 B.C. civil war erupted between Antony and Octavius, Herod wanted to help Antony, but he was prevented by Cleopatra; she wanted Herod to make war against Malchus, who had failed to pay tribute to her. When she saw Herod winning she ordered her troops to help Malchus, hoping to weaken both parties so that she could absorb both. In the spring of 31 there was a devastating earthquake in Herod's land, killing 30,000 people, and Malchus took advantage of the situation and attacked. But in the end Herod won (Josephus *Ant.* 15.5.2-5 §§121-60; *J.W.* 1.19.3-6 §§369-85).

Soon after, on September 2, 31 B.C., Antony was defeated by Octavius in the Battle of Actium. Herod now had to ingratiate himself to Octavius and persuade him that he was the rightful ruler of Judea. In the spring of 30 B.C. he set out for Rhodes and persuaded Octavius that he had not actually fought Octavius because of his skirmish with Malchus and that he had been loyal to Rome for many years. Octavius was convinced and confirmed Herod's royal rank. When Octavius came through Palestine on his way to Egypt, Herod met him at Ptolemais and gave him 800 talents, a gesture much appreciated by Octavius (Josephus *Ant.* 15.6.6-7 §§188-201; *J.W.* 1.20.1-3 §§387-95). Following Octavius's defeat of Antony in Egypt, Herod went to Egypt to congratulate him and Octavius returned Jericho (which Cleopatra had taken) to Herod, adding to it Gadara, Hippos, Samaria, Gaza, Anthedon, Joppa and Strato's Tower (which later became Caesarea) (Josephus *Ant.* 15.7.3 §§215-17; *BJ* 1.20.3 §396).

During this time Herod continued to have domestic problems. While he was at Rhodes, his wife, Mariamne, discovered that Herod had again ordered that she be killed if he did not return. Her bitterness toward Herod was increased, and when it became evident to Herod, he placed her on trial for adultery and had her executed toward the end of 29 B.C. (Josephus *Ant.* 15.7.1-5 §§202-36). In 28 B.C. he had his mother-in-law Alexandra executed. And Herod's sister Salome, wanting to get rid of her husband, Costobarus, convinced Herod that Costobarus was concealing and protecting the influential sons of Babas who were loyal to Antigonus and who spoke ill of Herod. Herod executed Costobarus and the sons of Babas in 25 B.C., making it impossible for any of Hyrcanus' descendants to become king (Josephus *Ant.* 15.7.6-10 §§237-66).

The second period of Herod's reign was one of prosperity, which lasted from 25 to 12 B.C. The first thing Josephus mentions of this period is Herod's violations of the Jewish Law in introducing the quinquennial games in Caesar's honor as well as the fact that he built theaters, amphitheaters and hippodromes (Josephus *Ant.* 15.8.1 §§267-76; 17.10.3 §255; *J.W.* 2.3.1 §44). Herod rebuilt many fortresses in the land and temples in Gentile territories, including the rebuilding of Strato's Tower, which was renamed Caesarea. In 24 B.C. he built for himself a royal palace in Jerusalem (Josephus *Ant.* 15.8.5—9.6 §§292-341). According to Josephus the most notable achievement of Herod was the building of the Temple* in Jerusalem, which was begun in 20/19 B.C. and finished in A.D. 63, long after his death (Josephus *Ant.* 15.11.1-6 §§380-425). The rabbis said, "Whoever who has not seen the Temple of Herod has never seen a beautiful building" (*b. B. Bat.* 4a), and they saw its construction as an "atonement for having slain so many sages of Israel" (*Midr. Num. Rab.* 14:8).

Herod acquainted himself with Greek culture by surrounding himself with people accomplished in Greek literature and art (*see* Hellenism). In 22 B.C. Herod sent his sons by Mariamne I, Alexander and Aristobulus, to Rome for their education. They were personally received by Caesar. About this time Augustus (Octavius's newly acquired title) gave Herod the territories of Trachonitis, Batanea and Auranitis (Josephus *Ant.* 15.10.1-2 §§343-49; *J.W.* 1.20.4 §398). Two years later (22 B.C.) Augustus came to Syria and bestowed on Herod the former territory belonging to Zenodorus that lay between Trachonitis and Galilee (containing Ulatha and Paneas) and the adjacent area north and northeast of the lake of Gennesaret. Augustus also made the procurators of Syria responsible to Herod for all their actions (Josephus *Ant.* 15.10.3 §§354-60; *J.W.* 1.20.4 §§399-400; Dio Cassius 54.7.4-6; 9.3). In addition Herod obtained the tetrarchy of Perea for his brother Pheroras (Josephus *Ant.* 15.10.3 §§362; *J.W.* 1.24.5 §483). In a show of gratitude for Augustus' generosity, Herod built a beautiful temple for Augustus in the territory of Zenodorus, near the place called Paneion (Josephus *Ant.* 15.10.3 §§363; *J.W.* 1.21.3 §§404-6). It was around this time that Herod reduced the taxes by a third, under the pretext of a crop failure, but in reality it is more likely he did this to promote good will among those who were displeased with his emphasis on Greco-Roman culture and religion (Josephus *Ant.* 15.10.4 §§365-72). In 14 B.C. Herod again reduced taxes by one-fourth (Josephus *Ant.* 16.2.5 §§64-65). In conclusion, this period was marked by prosperity in building and success in ruling the country.

The third period of Herod's reign was characterized by domestic problems (14-4 B.C.). Many of the problems came because he had ten wives, each wanting their son(s) to succeed (Josephus *Ant.* 17.1.3 §§19-22;

J.W. 1.28.4 §§562-63). His first wife, Doris, had only one son, Antipater (Josephus *Ant.* 14.12.1 §300). In 37 B.C. Herod repudiated Doris and Antipater and married Mariamne I, permitting Doris and Antipater to visit Jerusalem only during the festivals (Josephus *J.W.* 1.22.1 §433). Mariamne was the granddaughter of Hyrcanus II and she had five children: two daughters and three sons. In late 24 B.C. Herod married his third wife, Mariamne II, by whom he had Herod (Philip). His fourth wife, Malthace, was a Samaritan who bore Archelaus and Herod Antipas. His fifth wife, Cleopatra of Jerusalem, bore Philip the tetrarch. Of the remaining five wives, only Pallas, Phaedra and Elpsis are known by name, but they play an insignificant role (Josephus *Ant.* 17.1.3 §§19-22; *J.W.* 1.28.4 §§562-63).

Of all the sons of Herod, Alexander and Aristobulus, the sons of Mariamne II, were his favorites. However, they were hated by Salome, Herod's sister, even though her daughter Bernice was married to Aristobulus. The reason for her hatred is that she wanted her son to succeed her brother, Herod the Great. Salome spread rumors that Alexander and Aristobulus had never forgiven Herod for his murder of their mother and they were seeking to avenge it by bringing charges against him before Caesar which would lead to his losing the throne (Josephus *Ant.* 16.3.1-2 §§66-77). Because of this, Herod recalled his exiled son Antipater to show Alexander and Aristobulus that there could be another heir to the throne (14 B.C.). Antipater took full advantage of the situation and used every means to acquire the coveted throne.

In 13 B.C. Herod made his second will, whereby he designated Antipater as the sole heir. Herod sent Antipater with Agrippa (a friend of Augustus) to Rome to have this will ratified. While in Rome Antipater wrote slanderous letters against Alexander and Aristobulus. Herod became more aggravated with these two sons and finally in 12 B.C. he brought them before Augustus in Aquileia (near Venice) to be tried. Rather than being executed, the two brothers were reconciled to their father.

Herod made his third will naming all three sons as successors (Josephus *Ant.* 16.3.3—4.6 §§86-135; *J.W.* 1.23.2-5 §§451-66). Shortly thereafter (c. 11 or 10 B.C.) Herod again became suspicious of Alexander and Aristobulus because the slanderous accusation that they were going to kill and succeed Herod was brought against them by Antipater and Herod's sister Salome. Herod imprisoned Alexander, but Alexander's father-in-law, the king of Cappadocia, being concerned about his daughter's welfare, interceded and was able to reconcile Herod and Alexander (Josephus *Ant.* 16.7.2—8.6 §§188-270; *J.W.* 1.24.2—25.6

§§467-512). This brought peace to the Herodian household only temporarily. A certain Eurycles from Lacedemon and other troublemakers aroused in Herod's mind new suspicions against Alexander and Aristobulus. Consequently, Herod imprisoned them and sent a report to the emperor of their involvement in treasonable plots (Josephus *Ant.* 16.10.1-5 §§300-24; *J.W.* 1.26.1—27.1 §§513-35; cf. also Pausanias 2.3.5; Strabo 8.5.1; Plutarch *Ant.* 67).

Herod had lost favor with the emperor because of the accusations of Herod's Arab neighbor, Syllaeus, that Herod had invaded his territory for no reason. However, Herod's teacher, friend and counsellor, Nicolaus of Damascus, went to Rome and convinced Augustus that Syllaeus's case was false and Herod regained the emperor's favor. Nicolaus also presented Herod's accusations against his two sons, and Herod was given permission to have them tried outside of Herod's territory. Herod had them tried at Berytus (Beirut) before a Roman court. They were found guilty and were executed by strangulation in Sebaste (Samaria) c. 7 B.C. It was there that Herod had married their mother Mariamne II thirty years earlier (Josephus *Ant.* 16.10.6—11.8 §§324-404; *J.W.* 1.27.1-6 §§536-51).

Herod made his fourth will, naming Antipater as the sole heir. But, impatient to gain the throne, Antipater attempted to poison Herod. However, this plot failed when Herod's brother, Pheroras, drank the poison by mistake. Herod imprisoned Antipater and reported this attempt on his life to the emperor (c. 5 B.C.).

After becoming very ill, Herod drew up the fifth will, in which he bypassed his oldest sons, Archelaus and Philip, because Antipater had turned Herod's mind against them, and chose his youngest son, Antipas, to succeed him as king (Josephus *Ant.* 17.1.1—6.1 §§1-146; *J.W.* 1.28.1—29.32 §§552-646).

It is against this background of palace intrigue that Matthew recounts the circumstances surrounding the birth of Jesus (*see* Birth of Jesus). Shortly before Herod's death, magi arrived in Judea looking for the newborn king of the Jews. Herod instructed them to inform him of the location of this child. But being warned in a dream they did not report back to Herod but returned to their homes via another route (Mt 2:1-8, 12). God warned Joseph (husband of Jesus' mother) to flee to Egypt because of Herod's intention to kill Jesus (Mt 2:13-15). Soon after Joseph left Bethlehem, Herod killed all the male children in Bethlehem who were two years old and under (Mt 2:16). Herod steadily grew more ill. He received permission from Rome to execute Antipater, which he promptly did.

Herod wrote his sixth will, making Archelaus king, Antipas tetrarch of Galilee and Perea, and Philip tetrarch of Gaulanitis, Trachonitis, Batanea and Paneas. Five days after Antipater's execution, Herod died at Jericho in the spring of 4 B.C. The people made Archelaus their king. Herod's reign of thirty-three or four years had been marked with violence, not unlike those of most of his contemporary rulers.

The Herodian Dynasty at the Time of Jesus

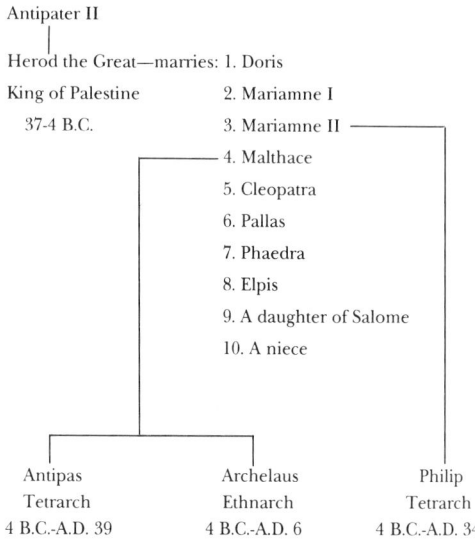

Antipater II
|
Herod the Great—marries: 1. Doris
King of Palestine   2. Mariamne I
  37-4 B.C.   3. Mariamne II
                             4. Malthace
                             5. Cleopatra
                             6. Pallas
                             7. Phaedra
                             8. Elpis
                             9. A daughter of Salome
                             10. A niece

Antipas	Archelaus	Philip
Tetrarch	Ethnarch	Tetrarch
4 B.C.-A.D. 39	4 B.C.-A.D. 6	4 B.C.-A.D. 34

1.2.3. Herod's Wills. Herod had written six wills, the sixth will being only a codicil of the fifth. Since the sixth will was made only five days before Herod's death, it did not have the ratification of the emperor. When Herod died Archelaus assumed leadership but refused to be crowned king (Josephus *Ant.* 17.8.4 §§202-3; *J.W.* 2.1.1 §3). Immediately after the Passover Archelaus and Antipas went to Rome to contest the will while Philip took care of the home front. Archelaus felt that Augustus should ratify Herod's sixth will because it expressed Herod's wish immediately preceding his death. On the other hand, Antipas argued that Herod had not been of sound mind when he wrote the sixth will. To further complicate the situation a revolt broke out in Palestine, and a Jewish delegate went to Rome asking for national autonomy and a union with the province of Syria. After much discussion, Augustus formulated a compromise whereby Archelaus was designated ethnarch of Idumea, Judea and Samaria with the promise to be made king if he proved worthy; Antipas was made tetrarch of Galilee and Perea; and Philip was tetrarch over

Gaulanitis, Trachonitis, Batanea and Paneas (Josephus *Ant.* 17.11.4 §§317-20; *J.W.* 2.6.3 §§93-100). Thus Antipas, while losing his claim to be king, did prevent Archelaus from becoming king over the entire realm.

2. Archelaus (4 B.C.-A.D. 6).

2.1. Archelaus's Rule. Archelaus (born c. 22 B.C.), the son of Herod the Great and Malthace (a Samaritan*), was made ethnarch over Idumea, Judea and Samaria with the promise to be made king if he ruled with prudence. But Archelaus got off to a bad start. Even before he left for Rome to contest Herod's final will he overreacted to an uprising in the Temple at Passover by sending in his troops and cavalry, killing about 3,000 pilgrims. While he was in Rome a revolt broke out again in Jerusalem at the feast of Pentecost, this time against Caesar's procurator, Sabinus, and spread to Judea, Galilee and Perea.

Archelaus's brutal treatment of the Jews and the Samaritans (Josephus *J.W.* 2.7.3 §111) is in keeping with what Matthew tells of Joseph, who heard that Archelaus was ruling Judea and was afraid to go there. Being warned in a dream on his return from Egypt Joseph, Mary and Jesus went to live in Nazareth in Galilee (Mt 2:20-23).

Soon after his return from Rome, Archelaus removed the high priest, Joazar, blaming him for siding with the rebels. He replaced him with Joazar's brother, Eleazar, and later replaced Eleazar with Jesus, son of See. Around this same time Archelaus divorced Mariamne and married Glaphyra, daughter of King Archelaus of Cappadocia. She was the former wife of Alexander, Herod's son and Archelaus's half-brother. This was a transgression of ancestral law (Josephus *Ant.* 17.13.1. 4-5 §§339-41, 350-53; *J.W.* 2.7.4 §§114-16). Either or both of these last two incidents may have caused the unrest that erupted. Archelaus used oppressive measures to quell the opposition.

Archelaus followed his father's example in building projects. He rebuilt the royal palace in Jericho in splendid fashion and diverted half of the water of the village of Neara into the newly planted palm trees in the plain of Jericho. He also created a village and honored himself by naming it Archelais (Josephus *Ant.* 17.13.1 §340).

2.2. Archelaus's Demise. Because of his continued oppressive rule he was finally deposed in A.D. 6. A delegation of Jews and Samaritans complained to Augustus about Archelaus's brutality and tyranny. For these two enemies to cooperate in this matter indicates the seriousness of the complaint. Also, Archelaus's brothers, Antipas and Philip, went to Rome to complain about him, presumably resenting his over-

sight of them in his role as ethnarch, or Roman representative, for Palestine. As a result, Archelaus was banished to Vienna in Gaul (modern Vienne on the Rhône, south of Lyons). Antipas and Philip retained their domains while Archelaus's territories were reduced to an imperial province under the rule of prefects (Josephus *Ant.* 17.13.1-5 §§342-55; *J.W.* 2.7.3— 8.1 §§111-18; Strabo 16.2.46; Dio Cassius 55.27.6).

3. Philip the Tetrarch (4 B.C.-A.D. 34).

Philip the tetrarch was the son of Herod the Great and Cleopatra of Jerusalem and was born around 22/21 B.C. As a result of the debate over Herod's will, Augustus made him tetrarch over the northeastern part of Herod the Great's domain, Gaulanitis, Auranitis, Batanea, Trachonitis, Paneas and Iturea (Josephus *Ant.* 17.9.4 §319; *J.W.* 2.6.3 §95; cf. Lk 3:1). His subjects were mainly Syrian and Greek (i.e., non-Jewish), and hence, he was the first and only Herodian to have the emperor's as well as his own image on his coins.

Philip built two cities (Josephus *Ant.* 18.2.1 §28; *J.W.* 2.9.1 §168). The first city was a rebuilding and enlarging of Paneas (near the source of the Jordan), which he renamed Caesarea Philippi in honor of the Roman emperor and to distinguish it from the coastal Caesarea. It was there that Peter made his confession of faith to Jesus and was given the revelation of the church (Mt 16:13-20; Mk 8:27-30). The second city was the rebuilding and enlarging of the fishing village of Bethsaida (where the Jordan flows into the Sea of Galilee). Philip gave it the status of a Greek *polis* and renamed it Julias in honor of Augustus's daughter Julia. There Jesus would heal the blind man (Mk 8:22-26), and in a nearby desert place Jesus would feed the 5,000 (Lk 9:10). Also, it may have been in the southern portion of Philip's territory that Jesus fed the 4,000.

Philip did not possess the ambitious and scheming character of his brothers. He ruled his domain with moderation and tranquility and was well liked by his subjects (Josephus *Ant.* 18.4.6 §§106-8). He married Herodias's daughter Salome, whose dance led to the beheading of John the Baptist (Mt 14:3-12; Mk 6:17-29; Lk 3:19-20; Josephus *Ant.* 18.5.2 §§116-19; *see* John the Baptist). They had no children (Josephus *Ant.* 18.5.4 §§137). When Philip died in A.D. 34 the emperor Tiberius annexed his territory to Syria, and when Caligula became emperor in A.D. 37, Philip's territory was given to Herod Agrippa I, brother of Herodias.

4. Herod Antipas (4 B.C.-A.D. 39).

4.1. Antipas's Realm. Herod Antipas, the younger brother of Archelaus, was born c. 20 B.C. He was made tetrarch of Galilee and Perea and ruled from 4

B.C. to A.D. 39. These were the territories where both Jesus and John the Baptist concentrated their ministries. On his return from Rome Antipas had to restore order and rebuild what had been destroyed at the feast of Pentecost in 4 B.C. Like his father he founded cities. He rebuilt Sepphoris (c. A.D. 8-10), the largest city in Galilee and the capital of his territories until he built Tiberias. Joseph, Mary's husband, living in Nazareth only four miles SSW of Sepphoris may well have used his skill as a carpenter (Mt 13:55; Mk 6:3) during its rebuilding. The second city Antipas rebuilt was Livias (or Julias) of Perea in honor of Augustus's wife Livia. This was completed c. A.D. 13 (Josephus *Ant.* 18.2.1 §27). Although the Herodian family had built twelve cities, Tiberias was the first city in Jewish history to be founded within the municipal pattern of the Greek *polis*. In the process of building the city an ancient cemetery was struck, and subsequently Antipas had difficulty in populating it because the Jews regarded it as an unclean area. Antipas offered free houses and lands as well as exemption from taxes for the first few years for anyone who would move into the new city. Named in honor of the emperor Tiberius, it was completed around A.D. 25 and served as Antipas's capital (Josephus *Ant.* 18.2.3 §§36-38).

4.2. Antipas's Reign. As far as Rome was concerned Herod Antipas was a good ruler who reigned over the territories of Galilee and Perea from 4 B.C. to A.D. 39.

4.2.1. Antipas and Archelaus. The only important recorded event early in Antipas's reign was the deposition of his brother Archelaus in A.D. 6. Together with his brother Philip the tetrarch and a Jewish and Samaritan delegation, he went to Rome to complain about Archelaus to Tiberius (Josephus *Ant.* 18.13.2 §§342-44; *J.W.* 2.7.3 §111). Although he hoped to receive the title of *king*, Tiberius allowed Antipas to have the dynastic title of *Herod* (cf. Josephus *J.W.* 2.9.1 §167; *Ant.* 18.2.1 §27), which was significant for both his subjects and the political and social circles of the Roman world.

4.2.2. Antipas and John the Baptist. In the Gospels Herod Antipas is most known for his imprisonment and beheading of John the Baptist (Mt 14:3-12; Mk 6:17-29; Lk 3:19-20; Josephus *Ant.* 18.5.2 §§116-19). Antipas had been married to the daughter of the Nabatean king Aretas IV, a marriage probably arranged by Augustus in order to gain peace between Jews and Arabs and provide a buffer zone between Rome and the Parthians. This marriage would have taken place before Augustus's death in A.D. 14. When Antipas travelled to Rome around A.D. 29, he visited his brother Herod (Philip), who apparently lived in one of the coastal cities of Palestine. While there he

fell in love with his niece as well as his brother's wife, Herodias. She agreed to marry Antipas when he returned from Rome, provided that he divorce* his first wife (Josephus *Ant.* 18.5.1 §§109-10). Antipas's first wife learned of the plan and fled to her father, Aretas IV, who considered the matter a personal insult and later retaliated against Antipas.

When Antipas married Herodias, John the Baptist boldly criticized him for marrying his brother's wife, and as a result he was imprisoned by Antipas. The Mosaic Law prohibited a man from marrying a brother's wife (Lev 18:16; 20:21), except in the case of levirate marriages (Deut 25:5; Mk 12:19). Since Antipas's brother had a daughter, Salome, and, more pointedly, his brother was still living, the levirate marriage did not apply.

There is a problem in identifying Herodias's first husband. The Gospels designate him as Philip (Mt 14:3; Mk 6:17), but Josephus lists him as Herod, son of Herod the Great and Mariamne II, daughter of Simon the high priest (Josephus *Ant.* 18.5 §109). Since the Herodian family line is complicated, many think that the Gospel writers confused this Herod with Philip the tetrarch who later married Herodias's daughter, Salome. However, although this may seem plausible at first, it is untenable for several reasons.

First, the Gospels would be guilty of three historical blunders, namely (1) confusing this Herod with his half-brother Philip the tetrarch, (2) making Philip the tetrarch the husband of Herodias instead of the husband of her daughter, Salome, and (3) assuming that Salome was the daughter of Philip the tetrarch who, according to Josephus, had no children. These errors would be incredible in the light of the Gospel writers' familiarity with other historical details of the era. Furthermore, the early Christian community included people like Joanna, wife of Chuza, Antipas's financial minister (Lk 8:3), and Manaen, a close friend of Antipas (Acts 13:1), who would have known the details and would have prevented such historical error.

Third, some argue that Herod the Great would not have two sons with the same name. But this is untenable because, although the two sons had the same father, they had different mothers. This is substantiated by the fact that Herod the Great did have two sons named Antipas/Antipater and two sons named Herod, all of whom had different mothers.

Fourth, it is highly probable that Herodias's first husband was called both Herod and Philip or, in other words, Herod Philip. Although some would argue that double names were not used, no one argues that Herod of Acts 12:1, 6, 11, 19-21 is the Agrippa of Josephus or that Archelaus is Herod Archelaus. Double names were used of emperors like Caesar Augustus.

Fifth, if the Evangelists intended that Herodias's former husband was actually Philip the tetrarch, why did they not call him "Philip the tetrarch" as they had called Herod Antipas first "tetrarch" and then "king" within the same pericope (cf. Mt 14:1, 9; Mk 6:14, 26)?

Therefore, it seems most reasonable to conclude that the Philip in the Gospels and the Herod in Josephus are one and the same person; otherwise it would be hopelessly confusing.

Antipas's imprisonment of John the Baptist was not enough for Herodias. At the appropriate time, probably Antipas's birthday, at Machaerus in Perea, Herodias arranged for a banquet for Antipas in order to eliminate John the Baptist. When Herodias's daughter danced before the guests, Antipas was overwhelmed and promised under oath to give her anything she wanted, up to half of his kingdom. With the advice of her mother, Salome asked for the head of John the Baptist on a platter. Although Antipas was sorry for his rash promise, he granted the request to save face before his guests. John was beheaded in A.D. 31 or 32.

4.2.3. Antipas and Jesus. Antipas's relationship to Jesus is seen in three events. First, Antipas heard of Jesus' ministry and concluded, with some irony, that Jesus was John the Baptist resurrected (Mt 14:1-2; Mk 6:14-16; Lk 9:7-9). Antipas had silenced John the Baptist's movement, and now there appeared to be a more successful people's preacher on the horizon. Hence, Antipas concluded that it was John the Baptist all over again. Antipas wanted to see Jesus, but Jesus withdrew from his territories. Antipas did not want to use force, fearing that his citizens would again resent his treatment as they had with his treatment of John the Baptist.

The second incident was Jesus' final journey to Jerusalem. While in Antipas's territories, some of the Pharisees came to warn Jesus that he should leave because Antipas wanted to kill him (Lk 13:31-33). Jesus told them to "go tell that fox" that he would continue his ministry of casting out demons and healing for a short time longer, and when he had finished he would then go to Jerusalem to die.

The third event was Jesus' trial by Antipas in A.D. 33 (Lk 23:6-12; *see* Trial of Jesus). Although some scholars think this pericope is legendary because it is not mentioned in the other Gospels, its occurrence in Luke's Gospel makes historical sense. Luke was writing to Theophilus, perhaps a Roman official, who would have been interested in the relationships between the Herods and the prefects of Judea,

especially since this pericope reports the reconciliation between Antipas and Pilate (Lk 23:12; *see* Pontius Pilate). Since the account reports no progress in the trial, it is understandable why the other Gospel writers left it out. Some scholars think the source for this incident is from the *Gospel of Peter.* But that Gospel presents no real parallel with Luke's account of Antipas's trial of Jesus. In fact, the *Gospel of Peter* holds Antipas responsible for Jesus' death, whereas there is nothing of this in Luke.

In Luke's account Pilate (*see* Pontius Pilate), knowing Antipas was in Jerusalem for the Passover and hearing that Jesus was from Antipas's territory, Galilee, sent Jesus to him. Pilate was not legally obligated to do so, but he wanted to extricate himself from an awkward situation in which the Jews wanted to crucify Jesus while Pilate felt that he was innocent. Furthermore, Pilate needed to improve his relationship with Antipas. It had been strained by his massacre of some of Antipas's subjects (Lk 13:1), and it was further aggravated when Antipas reported to Tiberius the trouble Pilate had caused the Jews when he brought the votive shields to Jerusalem. Subsequently, Tiberius had ordered their immediate removal c. A.D. 32 (Philo *Leg. Gai.* 299-304). Hence, Pilate had overstepped his bounds and needed to appease Antipas. On the other hand, Antipas did not want to give Pilate any reason to report him to the emperor, and so after mocking Jesus he sent him back to Pilate without comment, thereby paving the road for reconciliation between the two leaders from that day forward (Lk 23:12).

4.2.4. Antipas and Exile. In A.D. 36 Aretas IV attacked and defeated Antipas's army. The Jews considered this divine punishment for Antipas's execution of John the Baptist (Josephus *Ant.* 18.5.1-2 §§116-19). Tiberius commanded Vitellius, governor of Syria, to help Antipas against Aretas. However, before this could be accomplished Tiberius had died and Vitellius withheld his aid until he received orders from the new emperor Caligula.

When Caligula became emperor (A.D. 37) he gave his friend Agrippa I, brother of Herodias and nephew of Antipas, the land of Philip the tetrarch as well as the tetrarch of Lysanius with the title *king* (Josephus *Ant.* 18.6.10 §§225-39). Later, Agrippa went to Palestine (c. August of 38) to see his newly acquired domain. His presence in the land provoked Herodias's jealousy because he had obtained the much-coveted title *king* which Antipas had never received, although he had ruled well and faithfully since 4 B.C. Finally, under Herodias's persuasion, Antipas and Herodias went to Rome in A.D. 39 to seek the same honor. Agrippa heard of this and sent an envoy to Rome to bring accusations against Antipas. This action resulted in the banishment of Antipas and Herodias to Lugdunum Convenarum, now Saint-Bertrand de Comminges in southern France in the foothills of the Pyrenees. Caligula learned that Herodias was the sister of Agrippa I and excused her from the exile, but she chose to follow her husband. As a result, Agrippa I obtained Antipas's territories of Galilee and Perea (Josephus *Ant.* 18.7.1-2 §§240-55; *J.W.* 2.9.6 §§181-83).

5. The Herodians.

The Herodians were influential persons who were partisans of the Herodian dynasty. They are mentioned three times in the NT, dealing with two incidents where they joined with the Pharisees in their opposition to Jesus. The first incident took place in Galilee immediately after Jesus healed the man with the withered hand, and the Herodians and the Pharisees sought to destroy Jesus (Mk 3:6). The second episode was in Jerusalem when the Pharisees and the Herodians tried to incriminate Jesus regarding the lawfulness of paying taxes to Caesar (Mt 22:16 par. Mk 12:13). The Herodians are not mentioned in Luke or John.

The origin of the name has been debated. Some think that the ending of their name reflects the Latin suffix *-ianus* which is appended to adjectives, thus making it a substantive meaning that they were of the household of Herod, that is, domestic servants. Others think that it is a Greek suffix meaning that they were officers or agents of Herod. However, in the Gospel narratives they are not portrayed as either domestic servants or officers of Herod but as influential people whose outlook was friendly to the Herodian rule and consequently to the Roman rule upon which it rested.

The issue comes to the forefront in Mark 8:15 and Matthew 16:6 where in Mark we read of the "leaven of Herod" and the Matthean parallel refers to the "leaven of the Sadducees." This problem becomes more critical if the secondary Markan reading, "leaven of the Herodians" ($\mathfrak{P}^{45}$, $\theta f^{1, 13}$), is the correct one. The problem with this passage is not the interpretation but the question of whether the Sadducees and the Herod(ians) are the same? At first this seems impossible because Herod the Great tried to discredit the Hasmonean house. Furthermore, he and his grandson Agrippa I never selected a high priest from among the Sadducees, who were pro-Hasmonean, but rather from the house of Boethus. However, a reversal of this policy occurred between Herod's son Archelaus's deposition in A.D. 6 and Agrippa I's acquisition

of Judea in A.D. 41. At that time most of the high priests came from the Sadducean house of Annas because the province of Judea was not under Herodian rule but under direct Roman rule of the prefects. It seems probable, then, that the Boethusians, being pro-Herodian, were really the Herodians and the Sadducees were pro-Hasmonean. Actually, later rabbinic sources used the Boethusian name interchangeably with that of the Sadducees (*m. Menaḥ* 10.3). It may well be that the Sadducees and the Herodians would have been close if not identical religiously and economically. Thus, the Herodians were politically affiliated with the Herodian house, but they were religiously and economically affiliated with the Sadducees. However, the political distinctions between the Sadducees and Herodians were blurred with the marriage of Herod Antipas and Herodias (a Hasmonean on her mother's side). It could be that Herod Antipas married Herodias to gain Sadducean support. Hence, the Herodians and the Sadducees would have been on the same side politically against the Pharisees, the Herodians being pro-Herodian government while the Pharisees were both anti-Hasmonean and anti-Herodian. This is borne out in Mark 8:15 and Matthew 16:6, 12 where the Pharisees and the Sadducees/Herodians are contrary parties opposing Jesus.

In summary, the Herodians were theologically in agreement with the Sadducees and politically both of these parties would have been the opposite of the Pharisees who were anti-Hasmonean, anti-Herodian and anti-Roman. The Pharisees looked for a cataclysmic messianic kingdom to remove the rule of the Herods and Rome, whereas the Herodians wanted to preserve the Herodian rule. However, the Herodians and the Pharisees worked together to oppose Jesus, because he was introducing a new kingdom (*see* Kingdom of God) that neither wanted.

See also HELLENISM; JOSEPHUS; JUDAISM; PONTIUS PILATE; REVOLUTIONARY MOVEMENTS; ROME; TEMPLE.

BIBLIOGRAPHY. W. J. Bennett, "Herodians of Mark's Gospel," *NovT* 17 (1975) 9-14; P. M. Bernegger, "Affirmation of Herod's Death in 4 B.C.," *JTS* 34 (1983) 526-31; F. F. Bruce, "Herod Antipas, Tetrarch of Galilee and Perea," *ALOUS* 5 (1963-65) 6-23; C. Daniel, "Les 'Hérodiens' du Nouveau Testament sont-ils des Esséniens?" *RQ* 6 (1967) 31-53; J. D. M. Derrett, "Herod's Oath and the Baptist's Head," *BZ* NF 9 (1965) 49-59, 233-46; R. T. France, "Herod and the Children of Bethlehem," *NovT* 21 (1979) 98-120; H. W. Hoehner, "The Date of the Death of Herod the Great," in *Chronos, Kairos, Christos: Nativity and Chronological Studies Presented to Jack Finegan*, ed.

J. Vardaman and E. M. Yamauchi (Winona Lake, IN: Eisenbrauns, 1989) 101-11; idem, *Herod Antipas* (SNTSMS 17; Cambridge: University Press, 1972); A. H. M. Jones, *The Herods of Judea* (Oxford: University Press, 1938); M. Grant, *Herod the Great* (New York: American Heritage, 1971); A. Negoiṭa and C. Daniel, "L'énigme du levain," *NovT* 9 (1967) 306-14; P. Parker, "Herod Antipas and the Death of Jesus," in *Jesus, the Gospels, and the Church: Essays in Honor of William R. Farmer* (Macon, GA: Mercer, 1987) 197-208; S. Perowne, *The Later Herods* (London: Hodder and Stoughton, 1958); idem, *The Life and Times of Herod the Great* (London: Hodder and Stoughton, 1957); H. H. Rowley, "The Herodians in the Gospels," *JTS* 41 (1940) 14-27; S. Sandmel, *Herod: Profile of a Tyrant* (Philadelphia: J. B. Lippincott, 1987); A. Schalit, *König Herodes: Der Mann und sein Werk* (SJ 4; Berlin, 1969); E. Schürer, *The History of the Jewish People in the Age of Jesus Christ (175 B.C.-A.D. 135)*, rev. and ed. G. Vermes and F. Millar (3 vols.; Edinburgh: T. & T. Clark, 1973-79) I.287-357; M. Stern, "The Reign of Herod and the Herodian Dynasty," in *The Jewish People in the First Century*, ed. S. Safrai and M. Stern (CRINT 1:1; Philadelphia: Fortress, 1974) 216-307.

H. W. Hoehner

HIGH PRIESTS. *See* JUDAISM; PRIEST AND PRIESTHOOD.

HISTORICAL JESUS, QUEST OF

The idea of the quest of the historical Jesus gained currency through Albert Schweitzer's *The Quest of the Historical Jesus: A Critical Study of its Progress from Reimarus to Wrede* (1910). Schweitzer's original German title *Von Reimarus zu Wrede. Eine Geschichte der Leben-Jesu-Forschung* [*From Reimarus to Wrede. A History of Research into the Life of Jesus*] (1906) suggested a history of biographical research. The English title bestowed added drama to Schweitzer's narrative of the numerous efforts from the late eighteenth century down to his own day to discover the truth about Jesus as he really was. It heightened the impression that scientific research showed that the Jesus of history was different from the Christ* of Scripture, the creeds, orthodox theology and Christian piety.

The period covered by Schweitzer is commonly designated as the original quest of the historical Jesus. It is generally thought to have terminated with Schweitzer's own reconstruction of Jesus, the rise of form criticism and the growing popularity of neo-orthodoxy. In the 1950s followers of Rudolf Bultmann initiated what was called the New Quest of the historical Jesus. More recently, the term Third Quest

has been coined to describe the renewed interest in Jesus in his historical context.

1. The Original Quest (1778-1906)
2. From the History of Religions School to the New Quest
3. The Third Quest
4. Conclusion

1. The Original Quest (1778-1906).
1.1. The Initial Phase in Germany. Schweitzer dated the quest from the publication in 1778 of an anonymous article, "On the Intention of Jesus and his Disciples." The article was taken from a manuscript by the Hamburg scholar Hermann Samuel Reimarus (1694-1768), whose *Apology or Defence of the Rational Worshippers of God* had been withheld from publication on account of its dangerous ideas. Among the circle permitted to see it was the dramatist Gotthold Ephraïm Lessing (1729-81). Between 1774 and 1778 Lessing published extracts under the title *Fragments from an Unnamed Author* which he had ostensibly found in the library of the Duke of Brunswick at Wolfenbüttel. The extracts came to be known as the *Wolfenbüttel Fragments*. Although accurate guesses were made at the time, confirmation of the author's identity came long after Reimarus's death.

The *Fragments* included an attack on the historicity of the resurrection narratives. But the notoriety of this article was surpassed by the fragment "On the Intention of Jesus and his Disciples" (ET *Reimarus Fragments*, ed. C. H. Talbert, 1970). Jesus was depicted as a pious Jew, dedicated to calling Israel* to repentance in order to establish the kingdom of God on earth (*see* Kingdom of God). He did not intend to introduce new teaching or ceremonies. As time went on Jesus became more fanatical, obsessed by the idea that he could force God's hand by dying a martyr's death (*see* Death of Jesus). However, he miscalculated popular support, and his beliefs about God proved to be misguided. He died disillusioned with the God who had forsaken him.

Christianity might well have ended then but for the ingenuity and duplicity of the disciples.* When it became clear that there would be no general persecution, they emerged from hiding, proclaiming that Jesus had been raised from the dead and would return to establish the promised kingdom. Eschatology* was thus the key to understanding both Jesus and the disciples, but in both cases it is mistaken. Jesus wrongly believed that God would establish his kingdom on earth through him; the disciples were guilty of encouraging false expectations of the coming kingdom.

The *Wolfenbüttel Fragments* provoked numerous replies. The weightiest came from the leading biblical scholar of the day and founder of "liberal theology," J. S. Semler (1725-91). Semler's *Answer to the Fragments* (1791) was virtually a line-by-line refutation, written from the standpoint of a moderate orthodoxy. In the meantime, Lessing protested that, while he did not fully agree with the *Fragments*, they nevertheless raised important questions. His standpoint expressed the Age of Enlightenment's confidence in reason, and sought to detach religion from history by claiming that nothing in history could be demonstrated beyond doubt. "If no historical truth can be demonstrated, then nothing can be demonstrated by means of historical truths. That is: accidental truths of history can never become the proof of necessary truths of reason" *(On the Proof of the Spirit and of Power*, 1777, in H. Chadwick, ed., *Lessing's Theological Writings*, 1956, 53). History might exemplify rational truth, but such truth was not dependent on history. To Lessing, Jesus was one of the great educators of the human race, being "the first reliable, practical teacher of the immortality of the soul" *(The Education of the Human Race*, 1780, #58, Chadwick, 92).

1.2. German Lives of Jesus. The latter part of the eighteenth century witnessed a growing number of accounts of the life of Jesus. The more conservative accounts were meditations and paraphrases of the Gospel stories, like J. J. Hess's popular three volumes on *The History of the Three Last Years of the Life of Jesus* (1768-72). Such works were the literary counterpart to the combination of text and meditation set to music by J. S. Bach (1685-1750) in his *Passions* according to St. Matthew and St. John. A work which stressed the moral aspect of Jesus' teaching was the *Essay on the Plan Developed by the Founder of Christianity for the Benefit of Humanity* (1781) by the court preacher, F. V. Reinhard.

K. F. Bahrdt's series of letters addressed to seekers of truth on *The Execution of the Plan and Purpose of Jesus* (1784-92) introduced the genre of fictitious reconstruction. Bahrdt depicted Jesus as a tool in an Essene plot to transform Jewish society. He had acquired remedies for eye infections and nervous disorders from a mysterious Persian. The crucifixion was rigged by Nicodemus who had enlisted the aid of Luke to give Jesus pain-killing drugs. Jesus duly appeared in public to convince people that he had risen from the dead. Another work in this genre was K. H. Venturini's *Natural History of the Great Prophet of Nazareth* (1800-2).

The first professor to lecture on the life of Jesus was Friedrich D. E. Schleiermacher (1768-1834). His lectures on *The Life of Jesus* (1819-20) were subsequently repeated and published posthumously in 1864 (ET ed. J. C. Verheyden, 1975). Schleiermacher regarded John's Gospel as a historical outline into which could be inserted material from the other Gospels. He reinterpreted Jesus in the light of his own philosophical theology which was based on his analysis of religious experience. The essence of religious experience was a sense of utter dependence on God. Jesus was a man in whom this sense of dependence was uniquely developed. His consciousness of God could be said to be an existence of God in human nature *(The Christian Faith*, 2d ed. 1830-31, §94, ET 1928). It was also the source of Jesus' redemptive power. In Schleiermacher's theology Jesus' unique awareness of God replaced the traditional doctrine of Christ's divine and human natures.

While Schleiermacher sought to give a rationally credible account of Jesus' person, other scholars attempted rational explanations of his actions. In *The Life of Jesus as the Basis for a Pure History of Early Christianity* (1828) H. E. G. Paulus insisted that what was truly miraculous about Jesus was his holy disposition. Individual miracle stories (*see* Miracles and Miracle Stories) were capable of rational explanation. Jesus did not walk upon the water, but was standing on the shore. The five thousand were fed by those who had brought ample provisions. Jesus was taken down from the cross before death and revived in the cool of the tomb. Stripping off the grave clothes, he found the gardener's things, which explained the failure of Mary Magdalene to recognize him. A more restrained rationalism was adopted by K. A. von Hase in his widely used textbook on *The Life of Jesus* (1828). Like Schleiermacher he accepted John as the historical foundation of his chronology. The miracles were not violations of the laws of nature, but manifestations of the recovery of nature's original harmony. He doubted the infancy stories, but sought rational, psychological explanations for other events.

1.3. Strauss and the Question of Myth. The approaches noted so far were rejected by David Friedrich Strauss (1808-74) in *The Life of Jesus Critically Examined* (1835-36; ET 1846, repr. ed., Peter C. Hodgson, 1973). Strauss's work was prompted by reading notes based on Schleiermacher's lectures on *The Life of Jesus*. When the latter was published years later, Strauss subjected them to a bitter critique in *The Christ of Faith and the Jesus of History* (1865; ET ed. L. E. Keck, 1977). Strauss denounced Schleiermacher as a supernaturalist in his christology, but in criticism and exegesis a rationalist.

Strauss repudiated both the supernaturalism of

orthodoxy and the attempts of the rationalists to salvage the underlying historicity of events by proferring rational explanations. Both had failed to take into account the myth-making tendencies in religion which had been at work in the Gospel stories long before they were put into writing (*see* Myth).

Strauss accepted a basic historical framework for the life of Jesus: he had grown up at Nazareth; he was baptized by John the Baptist*; he collected disciples, he went about teaching, opposing Pharisaism and summoning people to the messianic kingdom; he fell victim to the hostility of the Pharisees* and died on the cross. However, this outline was overlaid by the creative imagination of the early church* which interpreted these events as the fulfillment of prophecy, and of the beliefs and institutions of the OT (*see* Old Testament in the Gospels; Typology). Messianic expectation predetermined that the Messiah should perform miracles and act like a new Moses* and a Davidic king (*see* Son of David). Once Jesus acquired the reputation of being the Messiah (*see* Christ), popular belief created myths and legends about him. The historical Jesus was thus turned into the divine Messiah by the pious, but erroneous, devotion of the church.

At the end of his work Strauss sought to rescue the underlying truth of the Christian faith by appealing to the philosophy of Hegel who had taught that reality is the manifestation of the infinite Spirit in the finite. Christianity was a symbolic representation of the general truth concerning the transformation of life by the absolute Spirit. The Incarnation was the mythological symbol of the divine manifestation in humankind in general.

Strauss's work provoked great outcry. Within five years some sixty replies appeared. A widely respected conservative response was August Neander's *Life of Jesus Christ* (1837; ET 1851). Strauss published three series of replies to his critics and made revisions to his work. But the radical character of his position cost him his academic career, and he turned to literature and politics. In 1864 Strauss published *The Life of Jesus Adapted for the German People* (ET 1865). It was prompted by the popularity of J. E. Renan's *Life of Jesus* (1863) in French. Strauss's second *Life* retained his earlier mythical explanation but dropped the appeal to Hegelian philosophy. The desupernaturalized Jesus depicted by Strauss emerged as one of the great improvers of the ideal of humanity.

Strauss's methods pioneered those of more recent times. His emphasis on the role of myth in religion anticipated the History of Religions School, and his view of the preliterary formation of Gospel material

anticipated form criticism (see 2.3. below). However, his underlying approach was if anything more rationalistic than that of the rationalists whom he repudiated. For the latter were willing to give some credence to the events for which they sought rational explanations, whereas Strauss rejected their historicity altogether. Strauss and the rationalists shared an underlying conviction that the homogeneous character of historical causes precluded special, supernatural interventions.

1.4. The Synoptics Versus John. The term "Synoptic Gospel" goes back to J. J. Griesbach's *Synopsis of the Gospels of Matthew, Mark and Luke* (1776) which set out the text of the three Gospels in parallel columns, thus facilitating comparative, critical study of the first three Gospels. Up to this date scholars had widely accepted Augustine's view that the first Gospel was the work of the apostle Matthew, and that Mark abbreviated Matthew. Griesbach himself accepted this view, with the modification that Mark had also Luke before him. Griesbach also questioned the wisdom of trying to produce a harmony of the accounts on the grounds that the Evangelists themselves were not interested in strict chronology.

The priority of Matthew was widely accepted in the early nineteenth century. Among those who did so was Ferdinand Christian Baur (1792-1860), who had been one of Strauss's teachers and who emerged as the leader of the new Tübingen School. Baur insisted upon a purely historical approach which avoided supernatural explanations. For him the key to NT study was tendency criticism, which sought to identify and evaluate sources by discovering their basic tendencies. Baur believed that Matthew was the earliest Gospel on account of its Jewish character. Luke was written by a follower of Paul with the deliberate intention of softening Matthew's Jewishness. Mark's aim was to round off the Gospel story into a harmonious whole. John reflected the conflict with Gnosticism and the church's situation in the second century. It contained a docetic tendency which stressed the Spirit at the expense of the flesh. Historically, John was remote from the time of Jesus. But since Matthew was written c. A.D. 130, it was only relatively more historically reliable. Baur's view of Jesus was akin to that of Schleiermacher. Jesus had a unique consciousness of God. As the highest emissary of God, he mediates divine knowledge.

The Tübingen School enjoyed great notoriety, but membership was limited to Baur himself and a handful of disciples. Their views were too extreme for most scholars. In the meantime, the traditional view of the priority of Matthew began to be overturned.

The year which saw the appearance of Strauss's *Life of Jesus Critically Examined* (1835) also witnessed the publication of an article by Karl Lachmann, "On the Order of Narratives in the Synoptic Gospels." Lachmann's article was the first to treat seriously the order of events as the key to understanding Synoptic relationships. Lachmann saw Mark as the middle term between Matthew and Luke. His work led to the growing popularity of the view that Matthew and Luke were dependent on Mark for their account of events. This view was supplemented by the theory of Q,* developed by H. J. Holtzmann (1832-1910). Q (German *Quelle* = "source") was the designation given to the sayings source posited behind the teaching contained in Matthew and Luke, but generally omitted by Mark who gives relatively little of Jesus' teaching (*see* Synoptic Problem).

By the end of the nineteenth century the traditional views of the apostolic authorship and priority of Matthew and the apostolic authorship of John, together with the latter's reliable chronological framework, were largely replaced by a view which discounted the historicity of John and favored a two-source theory (Mark and Q) as the substratum for recovering the historical Jesus (*see* Synoptics and John). This tendency was linked with the further tendency to discount the miraculous and supernatural. The result was a portrait of Jesus which followed Mark's general outline but focused on his moral, altruistic teaching.

1.5. French and British Lives of Jesus. Such a view of Jesus had already been developed in France by the former Catholic seminarian J. E. Renan (1823-92). In 1862 Renan was suspended from his chair at the Collège de France for describing Jesus as such an incomparable human that he would not contradict those who called him God. Renan had already completed the draft of a biography while on an archaeological expedition. Inspired by the scenery of the Holy Land, Renan resolved to write a life of Jesus. His account eschewed critical discussion of sources and method, seeking instead to retell the Gospel stories in a way that was credible to the modern French reader. Renan added imaginative splashes of local color to the scenes which he described and wrote with the calm assurance of a man who had got to the bottom of things. What made Jesus the Son of God was his realization that true worship* did not depend upon places and ritual but upon spirit (*see* Holy Spirit) and truth* (Jn 4:23). What made him unique was his dedication to the Father and to his divine mission.

Renan's work enjoyed great popularity and was translated into most European languages. In the preface to the thirteenth edition Renan explained his underlying philosophy and aims. He complained that the Christ of Strauss, Baur and the German critics was like a Gnostic Christ, an impalpable, intangible creation of their philosophy. He claimed that his own Christ was rooted in "genuine history." His method was to follow closely the original narratives, discard impossibilities, sow everywhere the seeds of doubt and put forth as conjectural different ways in which events might have happened.

The Strasbourg Protestant scholar T. Colani complained that Renan's Christ was not the Jesus of history, but that of the Fourth Gospel without a metaphysical halo. Colani set out his own views in *Jesus Christ and the Messianic Beliefs of his Time* (1864). Colani believed that there was no connection between the historical Jesus and Jewish messianic beliefs. The eschatological teaching attributed to Jesus in the Gospels (Mt 24; Mk 13; Lk 17) was not authentic. Jesus had predicted the destruction of the Temple,* and the disciples had asked when it would occur (Mt 24:3; Mk 13:4; Lk 21:7). Jesus replied that he did not know (Mt 24:36; Mk 13:32; Lk 21:33). The so-called little Apocalypse that comes between the question and answer was the work of over-zealous eschatologically minded Jewish Christians who could not accept Jesus' confession of ignorance (*see* Apocalyptic Teaching). German and French thought made an impact on the English-speaking world through the translations of Strauss and Renan and also of more conservative scholars. In comparison with the German and French scholars, British scholarship was more modest and restrained. An exception was Charles Christian Hennell's *Inquiry Concerning the Origin of Christianity* (1838), whose ideas were similar to those of Strauss, but were eclipsed by the latter. Hennell was instrumental in introducing George Eliot (Mary Ann Evans) to skeptical views and arranged for her to translate Strauss into English.

Somewhere between the skeptical products of continental criticism and the conservative, devotional works which appealed to the British Christian readership was the anonymous *Ecce Homo* (1865). The title was taken from the Latin version of Pilate's words "Behold the Man" (Jn 19:5). The author was J. R. Seeley, professor of Latin at University College, London, and later professor of modern history at Cambridge. The work was not so much a life of Jesus as an appreciation which downplayed the miraculous and the dogmatic. The power of Jesus lay in his ability to infect people with an enthusiasm for morality. Jesus stood in sharp contrast with Socrates with whom argument is everything and personal authority nothing. With Jesus personal authority was everything (*see* Authority and Power). His aim was to establish a divine society on earth, or in the language of Seeley's day, "the improvement of morality" (chap. 9).

The first major Life of Christ by a British writer was that by F. W. Farrar (1874) which set the model for the rest of the century. Like Renan's work, it was inspired by a visit to the Holy Land and was filled with imaginative descriptions of places and events. But unlike Renan, Farrar did not tamper with orthodoxy. Jesus was both the divine Son of God (*see* Son of God) and a flesh-and-blood human personality.

The most notable British "life" was Alfred Edersheim's *The Life and Times of Jesus the Messiah* (1883). Edersheim was born in Vienna of Jewish parents and studied in Berlin. He became a convert to Christianity and spent his last years in England as vicar of a country parish. Edersheim avoided critical discussion of sources and took the Gospel narratives at face value. Matthew and John were the work of the apostles* whose names they bear. Luke and Mark had access to apostolic testimony to supplement their own reminiscences. Edersheim accepted duplicate events behind duplicate traditions: there were two cleansings of the Temple (*see* Temple Cleansing), two feedings of the multitudes, numerous journeys to and from Jerusalem, and no conflict between John and the Synoptics. The value of Edersheim's work lay in its author's immense erudition. No other British (and perhaps no continental) scholar had such a grasp of the Jewish world, the Talmud (*see* Rabbinic Traditions and Writings), Philo, Josephus,* the apocryphal and pseudepigraphal literature, archeology and geography (*see* Archeology and Geography). Whereas Farrar resorted to florid prose for his effect, Edersheim was able to elucidate the details of the Gospel stories with a wealth of exact learning.

The contributions of the Cambridge trio of B. F. Westcott (1825-1901), J. B. Lightfoot (1828-89) and F. J. A. Hort (1828-92) helped to vindicate the NT against continental radicalism. However, their grand plan for a series of commentaries covering the NT was only partially realized. Wescott's commentary on John (1881) defended apostolic authorship and the historical integrity of the Gospel. The commentaries on the Synoptics remained unwritten.

The leading British NT scholars of the next generation were the brilliant but unconventional F. C. Burkitt (1864-1935) at Cambridge and William Sanday (1843-1920) at Oxford. Both were instrumental in disseminating the views of Schweitzer and modern critics. Burkitt's contributions included *The Gospel History and its Transmission* (1906) and *Christian Beginnings* (1924). Sanday never completed his projected life of Christ, but left behind a number of important studies. His seminar produced *Oxford Studies in the Synoptic Problem* (1911). His article in *Hastings' Dictionary of the Bible* was published in book form as *Outlines of the Life of Christ* (1905). Sanday gathered together various papers in *The Life of Christ in Recent Research* (1907) and developed a tentative christology in *Christologies Ancient and Modern* (1910), which was reprinted in *Christology and Personality* (1911). Drawing on William James's theories about the unconscious, Sanday suggested that the locus of divine indwelling in human beings was the "subliminal." Consciousness was the "narrow neck" through which everything comes up from the depths. While Jesus was fully human in every sense, he had a deep relationship with God in the depths of his being. It was this relationship which produced his messianic consciousness as Son of God.

1.6. The Ritschlian School. A major theological force in the second half of the nineteenth century was the school of A. B. Ritschl (1822-89). In his younger days Ritschl had followed his mentor, F. C. Baur, but came to reject the latter's account of Christian origins. Ritschl's theological outlook matched the empirical emphasis of the University of Göttingen, where he taught. The university was a center of scientific research. The focus of Ritschl's attention was the empirically observable experience of the church. The origin of the person of Jesus was not a fit subject for theological inquiry, because it transcended all inquiry. His divinity was not to be understood as a statement of fact but as an expression of the revelational value of Jesus to the church. His vocation was to be the bearer of God's ethical lordship (*see* Lord) over human beings. Ritschl's major work on *The Christian Doctrine of Justification and Reconciliation* (3 vols., 1870-74; partial ET 1900) identified two focal points in Christianity. The first was the redemption wrought by Christ, understood as freedom from guilt and freedom over the world through the realization of God's fatherhood. The second was the kingdom of God, understood ethically (*see* Ethics of Jesus) as the extension of God's ethical lordship over the world through the redeemed.

The ethical side of Christianity was stressed by the great church historian Adolf Harnack (1851-1930), who shared Ritschl's suspicion of the adverse effects of metaphysics on theology. As a historian of the development of dogma, Harnack sought to separate the kernel from the husk by extracting the essence of Christianity from the Hellenized formulations of the church. In his celebrated lectures at Berlin University on "The Essence of Christianity" (1899-1900; ET *What Is Christianity?* [1901]), Harnack argued that Jesus desired no other belief in his person than what was contained in keeping his commandments.⁺ His consciousness as Son of God was nothing but the practical consequence of knowing God as the divine Father. Jesus' teaching could be summed up under three heads: the kingdom of God and its coming; God the Father and the infinite value of the human soul; the higher righteousness (*see* Justice and Righteousness) and the commandment of love.* In *The Sayings of Jesus* (ET 1908) Harnack declared that Q expressed most clearly the teaching of Jesus and the essence of Christianity. Q provided the refutation of those who exaggerated the apocalyptic* and eschatological elements in Jesus' teaching.

Harnack's celebrated lectures prompted the comment of the French Catholic modernist Alfred Loisy, which was repeated by George Tyrrell in *Christianity at the Cross-Roads* (1909, chap. 7): "The Christ that Harnack sees, looking back through nineteen centuries of Catholic darkness, is only the reflection of a Liberal Protestant face, seen at the bottom of a deep well." However, Loisy's alternative was scarcely more acceptable to the Catholic authorities. In identifying the essence of Christianity with the "idea" of Christ in Catholic Christianity, Loisy was implicitly questioning the historical basis of that idea. Modernism was condemned by the decree *Lamentabili* and the encyclical *Pascendi* (1907), and an oath against Modernism was imposed by *Sacrorum Antistitum* (1910).

1.7. Weiss, Wrede, Schweitzer and the End of the Original Quest. Despite Harnack's prestige and popularity, signs of strain were already evident in the edifice of Ritschlian theology. In 1892 Ritschl's son-in-law, Johannes Weiss (1863-1914), published *Jesus' Proclamation of the Kingdom of God* (2d ed. 1900; ET ed. R. H. Hiers and D. L. Holland, 1971). Weiss's personal outlook was much the same as that of his father-in-law, in deference to whom he delayed publication of his findings. However, his research showed that, though it might be unacceptable to the modern mind, Jesus' teaching about the kingdom was definitely eschatological. Weiss identified six characteristics: The kingdom was transcendent and supramundane; it belonged to the future; Jesus was not the founder or inaugurator but waited for God to bring it; the kingdom was not identified with the circle of Jesus' disciples; it did not come gradually by growth or development; its ethics were negative and world-denying. Jesus was a rabbi or prophet* who believed that in God's good time he would become the Son of man (*see* Son of Man). Eventually, he came to realize

that this would occur only after his death.

A further blow to the liberal picture of the historical Jesus was delivered by William Wrede's *The Messianic Secret in the Gospels* (1901; ET 1971). Wrede challenged the prevailing assumption on which the liberal picture of the historical Jesus was based, viz., that Mark's Gospel was an unadorned account of the historical facts. Wrede saw Mark not as an objective reporter but as the theologian of the *Messiasgeheimnis* (a term which could be translated either as "messianic secret" or "messianic mystery"). According to Wrede, Jesus himself did not claim to be the Messiah. It was the church that thought of Jesus as Messiah in the light of its resurrection* faith.* The church explained the paucity of messianic claims by Jesus by devising stories that Jesus had secretly revealed his messiahship to the disciples and had forbidden them to broadcast it. On this view the Gospels were primary sources not for the life of Jesus, but for the beliefs of the Evangelists and the communities which they served.

On the same day that Wrede's book was published, Albert Schweitzer published a two-volume dissertation which put forward an alternative view. The first volume was entitled *The Problem of the Lord's Supper according to the Scholarly Research of the Nineteenth Century and the Historical Accounts* (ET 1982). The second volume dealt with *The Mystery of the Kingdom of God: The Secret of Jesus' Messiahship and Passion* (ET 1914). Although the work was published in 1901, Schweitzer had reached his conclusions as early as 1897. He later declared his "thoroughgoing eschatology" to be a consistent extension of Weiss's views and the answer to Wrede's skepticism. Whereas Weiss had made eschatology the key to Jesus' teaching, Schweitzer saw that it was also the key to the course of Jesus' life. The title *Son of man* was a designation of the Messiah coming on the clouds as judge. Jesus believed that it was his vocation to be the coming Son of man. Initially he revealed this messianic secret only to Peter, James and John. Later, Peter told it to the rest of the Twelve. Judas told the secret to the high priest (*see* Priest and Priesthood) who used it as the ground for Jesus' execution (Mk 14:61-64; cf. Dan 7:13).

Jesus had sent out the Twelve on a mission to proclaim the coming kingdom of God. He did not expect them to return. The Twelve were the "men of violence" (Mt 11:12) who would provoke the messianic tribulation that would herald the kingdom. Whereas Weiss believed that one could only wait passively for the kingdom, Schweitzer believed that the mission was designed to provoke its coming. When this did not happen, Jesus determined to give his own life as a ransom for many (Mk 10:45) and so cause the kingdom to come.

At the time that Schweitzer wrote *The Mystery of the Kingdom of God* he was an unknown instructor at Strasbourg. His work attracted little attention, and it was only after World War 1 and the collapse of liberal optimism that eschatology and the "otherworldly" gospel got a wider hearing. In the meantime, Schweitzer's celebrated *Quest of the Historical Jesus* established his reputation as a scholar. Schweitzer went on to earn doctorates in music and medicine. His medical work in Africa enhanced the impact of his writing.

The Quest of the Historical Jesus was originally intended as a supplement to the earlier, shorter book. It rapidly established the reputation of being the definitive history of research on the historical Jesus. In intent it was a massive vindication of Schweitzer's earlier conclusions which had largely been ignored and which were repeated in the final chapter. It did not show, as is often assumed, that recovery of the historical Jesus was impossible. Rather, it presented a massive critique of the views of the theological establishment, set out in such a way as to show that all paths but Schweitzer's proved to be dead ends.

Schweitzer identified three major crises in which critical study was faced with a choice between stark alternatives (238). The first was the crisis provoked by Strauss: either a purely historical approach or a purely supernatural one. The second was posed by the Tübingen school and Schweitzer's teacher, Holtzmann: either the Synoptic Gospels or John. The third was the choice between Wrede and himself: either an eschatological or a non-eschatological Jesus. In each case Schweitzer left no doubt as to the path which the reader should follow.

There were certain ironies in Schweitzer's position. Although Schweitzer was concerned with critical history, he made no attempt to deal critically with sources. He accepted the Synoptic narrative more or less at face value (though with a preference for Mark supplemented by Matthew, understood in a non-supernatural way). Consistent eschatology was the connecting theme which gave the story credibility as history, though not as something to be believed in the twentieth century. Schweitzer himself did not accept the eschatological views of Jesus and the Gospels any more than did Johannes Weiss or the liberal scholars who treated them as a husk to be discarded.

The *Quest* (403) concludes by remarking on how good it was that "the true historical Jesus should overthrow the modern Jesus." Jesus was not a teacher,* but "an imperious ruler," as can be seen from his belief in himself as the Son of man. However, titles like Messiah, Son of man, Son of God, are merely "historical parables." "We can find no designation which expresses what He is for us." Jesus comes to us "as One unknown," summoning followers and setting new tasks in each generation. Those who follow shall learn "as an ineffable mystery" in their own experience "Who He is." For Schweitzer himself, this meant life as a medical missionary in West Africa, guided by a philosophy based on "reverence for life."

If Harnack's historical Jesus was a reflection of the liberal Protestant scholar, Schweitzer's had an element of the heroic "superman" of Nietzsche, a philosopher whom Schweitzer admired. Schweitzer went on to apply his "Christ mysticism" to the apostle Paul (*Paul and His Interpreters,* 1911; ET 1912; *The Mysticism of the Apostle Paul,* 1930; ET 1931). Schweitzer's medical thesis on *The Psychiatric Study of Jesus* (1913; ET 1948) sought to vindicate Jesus against charges of paranoia. *The Kingdom of God and Christian Origins* (ET 1968) summarizes Schweitzer's final position.

1.8. Re-evaluation. The monumental character of Schweitzer's *Quest* is apt to conceal its omissions and apologetic character. It is now clear that the enterprise did not begin with Reimarus, but with the English deists on whom Reimarus had heavily drawn and whose ideas were already well known in Germany. Among the British writers cited by Reimarus in his *Apology* were Toland, Shaftesbury, Collins, Tindal, Morgan and Middleton. His personal library included most of the English deists. Hobbes, Spinoza and Hume were among the philosophers who had already raised doubts about the historical reliability of the NT picture of Jesus. Schweitzer's work took little account of the interplay between philosophy and theology, especially the influence of Kant, though Schweitzer himself had already written a dissertation on *Kant's Philosophy of Religion from the Critique of Pure Reason to Religion within the Limits of Reason Alone* (1899).

Schweitzer confined his attention largely to works in German, plus a few in French. Having adopted the methodological principle, allegedly forced upon him by Strauss, of working strictly with the "historical" which was juxtaposed to the "supernatural," the work of systematic theologians could safely be left out of account. Consequently, scant attention was paid to the Mediating School of theologians like I. A. Dorner (1809-94) whose *History of the Development of the Doctrine of the Person of Christ* (ET 5 vols., 1861-63) concluded with an attempt to restate christology drawing on contemporary philosophy. Also ignored were the confessional theologians, like J. C. K. von Hofmann (1810-77) and Gottfried Thomasius (1802-75). Hofmann sought to understand christology in the wider context of salvation history. Thomasius' doctrine of kenosis sought to show the conceivability of the divine incarnation of God, if the Son of God had in some way emptied himself of his divine glory during his earthly life (cf. Phil 2:7).

It was perhaps inevitable that not only Schweitzer but also nineteenth-century theologians in general ignored the thought of the Danish philosopher Søren Kierkegaard (1813-55) whose works remained largely inaccessible until the twentieth century. Kierkegaard's *Philosophical Fragments* (1844) provided a counterpart to the *Fragments* of Reimarus. Kierkegaard asked what conditions would have to be fulfilled if God intended to save human beings. He replied that God might communicate with human beings by becoming human and thus utterly like them. This entails the paradoxical conclusion that, in reaching out to human beings in history, God remains incognito in Christ.

In the meantime the whole enterprise of trying to get behind the church's faith and tradition was condemned by Martin Kähler (1835-1912). In *The So-Called Historical Jesus and the Historic Biblical Christ* (1896; ET ed. C. E. Braaten, 1964) Kähler repudiated the attempt to make faith dependent upon historical research. He also argued that it was impossible to separate the historical Jesus from the Christ of faith. The Christ who influenced the course of history is the Christ who is preached, the Christ of faith. Kähler's work appealed not only to conservatives who believed that their faith was grounded in history, but also to radicals like Kähler's pupil Paul Tillich, who went on to treat the Gospel stories as symbols mediating the depths of existence.

2. From the History of Religions School to the New Quest.

2.1. The History of Religions School.
The History of Religions School flourished between 1880 and 1920. In seeking to understand the Bible in the context of the broader religious and cultural setting of Egyptian, Babylonian and Hellenistic religion, it emphasized the continuity between the Bible and the ancient Near East and also the discontinuity between the Bible and the modern world. The school was anticipated by D. F. Strauss. The views of Johannes Weiss and William Wrede who were linked with the school have already been noted.

The most comprehensive application of the school's method to the historical Jesus was made by Wilhelm Bousset (1865-1920) in *Kyrios Christos* (1913; ET 1970). Bousset argued that the eschatological ideas underlying the terms Messiah and kingdom of God were derived from other religions. He traced the title Lord* (Greek *kyrios*) to Hellenistic religion, and saw the ascription of divinity to Jesus as the result of alien influences. Bousset believed that the earliest tradition of the life of Jesus was relatively free from the miraculous. People transferred to Jesus current stories about wonder workers and miracles (*see* Divine Man). Bousset made little attempt to show how such stories came to be applied to Jesus. It was enough to note alleged parallels, no matter how remote the source might be.

The methodology of the school was set out by the former Ritschlian Ernst Troeltsch (1865-1923). Troeltsch's paper "On Historical and Dogmatic Method in Theology" (1888) laid down principles for approaching history. Every tradition and interpretation must be sifted by an unending process of criticism. The principle of analogy serves as the criterion by which events are identified and their historicity assessed. Present experience and knowledge must be used to interpret the past. The historian accepts only those events which bear analogy with present experience and understanding of the world. The principle of correlation asserts that every historical event is correlated with others in the same series. Since all events are of the same order, no particular event can be final or absolute. Since Christianity belongs to the sphere of religious and human history as a whole, no absolute claims may be made on behalf of it. No absolute claims may be made on behalf of Jesus. Christianity may be the absolute religion for the Westerner, but only because there is nothing else (*The Absoluteness of Christianity and the History of Religions*, 1901; ET 1971; *Christian Thought: Its History and Application*, 1923).

2.2. Neo-Orthodoxy.
In reaction to liberalism with its emphasis on humanity, religious experience and scientific study, the neo-orthodoxy of Emil Brunner (1889-1966) and Karl Barth (1886-1968) stressed the sovereignty of the transcendent God, human need of redemption and revelation, and the centrality of Jesus Christ. Brunner's *The Mediator* (1927; ET 1934) rejected attempts to interpret Jesus as a religious hero, genius or moral personality. God must be understood biblically rather than philosophically, and known through personal encounter through Christ. Although Brunner insisted on the reality of the humanity of Christ, his lack of interest in history led to charges of docetism.

Barth's emphasis on revelation brought him into sharp conflict with his former teacher Harnack (*Revelation and Theology: An Analysis of the Barth-*

Harnack Correspondence of 1923, ed. H. M. Rumscheidt, 1972). The christocentric theology developed in Barth's *Church Dogmatics* (1932-81) elaborated the theme of God taking humanity into partnership with himself on the basis of the incarnation of God in Jesus of Nazareth. Barth stressed the historical reality of this event, but showed little interest in the historical Jesus as such.

2.3. Bultmann, Form Criticism and Demythologization. Form criticism was pioneered by K. L. Schmidt, Martin Dibelius and Rudolf Bultmann (*see* Form Criticism). Schmidt's *Der Rahmen der Geschichte Jesu* (1919) claimed that the framework of the Gospel stories was created by the Evangelists for their own purposes and was thus historically valueless. The Heidelberg scholar Martin Dibelius (1883-1947) adopted a more constructive approach in *Die Formgeschichte des Evangeliums* (1919; ET *From Tradition to Gospel*, 1934). His *Jesus* (1939; ET 1949) showed how the Gospel traditions related to the historical Jesus. However, a more skeptical view was taken by Rudolf Bultmann (1884-1976) of Marburg who was the most influential NT scholar of his generation. Bultmann's theology combined neo-orthodoxy, Neo-Kantianism, Heidegger's existentialism with the traditions of liberal criticism and the History of Religions School. His personal influence was extended through his pupils in key university chairs throughout the German-speaking world.

Bultmann's major work on *The History of the Synoptic Tradition* (1921, ET 1963) gave an analysis of the forms of the traditions behind the Gospel as shaped by the Christian communities. He concluded that the material throws more light on the *Sitz im Leben,* or life setting, of the traditions in the early church than they do on the life of Jesus. Many utterances attributed to Jesus were the deliverances of Christian prophets* speaking in his name. The Christ preached in the Hellenistic church was not the historical Jesus, but the Christ of faith and the cult. Teaching which applied to the church situation could not be attributed to the historical Jesus.

Basic to Bultmann's method was the criterion of dissimilarity as a test of authenticity. "We can only count on possessing a genuine similitude of Jesus, where, on the one hand, expression is given to the contrast between Jewish morality and piety and the distinctive eschatological temper which characterized the preaching of Jesus; and where on the other hand we find no specifically Christian features" (205). To Bultmann, as to later form critics and redaction critics (*see* Redaction Criticism), use of this criterion was the hallmark of scientific criticism. To others it was

arbitrary and absurd to assume that the historical Jesus could have nothing in common with either Judaism* or the early church. Bultmann's other test of authenticity was equally controversial. Phraseology and language serve to corroborate the origin of material (*see* Languages of Palestine). Thus, the presence of Semitisms is deemed to suggest a Palestinian origin (12). Critics of Bultmann and others who have used this criterion complain that it is equally arbitrary and useless. For the presence of Semitisms does not necessarily mean that Jesus was the original speaker. On the other hand, idiomatic translation into Greek is assumed to be a mark of inauthenticity (*see* Gospels [Historical Reliability]).

Bultmann's *Jesus* (1926, ET *Jesus and the Word*, 1935) depicted Jesus as the bearer of the word in which he assures human beings of divine forgiveness.* Bultmann understood this event existentially as a summons to decision. Bultmann's celebrated demythologization program was outlined in his paper on "New Testament and Mythology" (1941; ET in H.-W. Bartsch, ed., *Kerygma and Myth*, combined vol., 1972, 1-44). It inaugurated one of the great debates of the twentieth century. Bultmann developed his position in various writings, including *Theology of the New Testament* (2 vols.; 1948-53; ET 1952-55), *The Gospel of John* (1941; ET 1971) and *Jesus Christ and Mythology* (1958).

Bultmann contended that the thought world of the NT was essentially mythological, being shaped by myths drawn from Jewish apocalyptic and gnosticism (*see* Myth). Such myths caused Jesus to be presented as a heavenly redeemer in a cosmic struggle. Bultmann claimed that his aim was not to eliminate myth, but to interpret it so as to allow the true offense of Christianity to make its impact. The mythological eschatology of the NT with its central message of the cross and resurrection is to be seen as a summons to live existentially by faith in the cross and resurrection of Christ. Drawing on the categories of Heidegger's existentialism, Bultmann reinterpreted the life of faith as "authentic existence" in contrast with the "inauthentic existence" of life apart from faith. What God has done in Jesus Christ is not a historical fact capable of proof. The objective historian as such cannot see that a historical person is the eternal Word. Nevertheless, the NT paradoxically testifies to Jesus Christ as the eschatological event which brings liberation through the message of the cross and resurrection.

2.4. Other Approaches. Despite the claims of Schweitzer that his historical Jesus was the sole credible option, and the claims of the neo-orthodox and the Bultmann school that recovery of the historical Jesus was impossible but fortunately unnecessary, other scholars patiently pursued historical research.

In Britain T. W. Manson protested that the proper task of form criticism was the classification of the material, and that it was illegitimate to treat forms as a test of historical authenticity ("The Life of Jesus: Some Tendencies in Present-Day Research," in *The Background of the New Testament and its Eschatology. In Honour of C.H. Dodd*, eds. W. D. Davies and D. Daube, 1954, 211-21). Demythologization issues in the myth of a Heideggerian Jesus, which on closer inspection turns out to be Heideggerian robes with only a pale ghost inside them. Elsewhere he remarked that Bultmann's *History of the Synoptic Tradition* was not an account of how the life of Jesus produced the tradition, but how the tradition produced the life of Jesus. Manson's own work included *The Teaching of Jesus: Studies in its Form and Content* (1931), *The Sayings of Jesus* (1949), which first appeared in the volume Manson co-authored with H. D. A. Major and C. J. Wright, *The Mission and Message of Jesus* (1937) and *The Servant-Messiah* (1953). His "Materials for a Life of Jesus" was published posthumously in *Studies in the Gospels and Epistles* (1962).

Other British studies of form criticism drew positive results from it. Among them were William Manson's *Jesus the Messiah: The Synoptic Tradition of the Revelation of God in Christ, with Special Reference to Form-Criticism* (1943) and Vincent Taylor's *The Formation of the Gospel Tradition* (1933). Taylor's other works include *Jesus and his Sacrifice: A Study of the Passion-Sayings in the Gospels* (1937), *The Atonement in New Testament Teaching* (1940), his massive commentary on Mark (1953), *The Life and Ministry of Jesus* (1954) and *The Person of Christ in New Testament Teaching* (1958).

The challenge of form criticism and in particular of K. L. Schmidt's contention that the units of the Gospel tradition were arranged with scant regard to chronology or topography, was met by C. H. Dodd (1884-1973), who made influential studies of the early church kerygma ("The Framework of the Gospel Narrative" [1932], *NTS* [1952] 1-11; and *The Apostolic Preaching and its Developments* [1936]). Dodd argued that the early preaching of the church contained a basic outline of the ministry of Jesus which emphasized certain themes, and that this outline was used by Mark whose account is partly chronological and partly topical. Dodd's work has provoked considerable debate. It now seems clear that the early preaching was not intended to give a biography of Jesus in the modern sense (for the materials are too selective, and in any case are not full enough). Nor was it preaching designed for all occasions. Rather it was the church's answer to charges against Jesus which led to his

execution, whose purpose was to rebut the charges by appealing to teaching and incidents in the life of Jesus (see C. Brown, "The Structure and Content of the Early Kerygma," *NIDNTT* 3.57-67).

In *History and the Gospel* (1938) Dodd drew attention to the fact that different kinds of forms identified by form critics indicate a common underlying picture of God and Jesus in the tradition. Dodd's study of *The Parables of the Kingdom* (1935) developed realized eschatology in antithesis to Schweitzer. Dodd argued that the ministry of Jesus was not a prelude to the kingdom; it was the kingdom. In his later work Dodd turned to the study of John. In *The Interpretation of the Fourth Gospel* (1953) Dodd charged that the nineteenth-century quest, with its concentration on the Synoptics to the exclusion of John, "leads to an impoverished, a one-sided, and finally an incredible view of the facts—I mean, of the facts, as part of history" (446). He went on to say that the Johannine formula "the hour is coming and now is" was John's way of expressing realized eschatology. He welcomed the emendations proposed by Georges Florovsky ("inaugurated eschatology") and Joachim Jeremias ("a self-realizing eschatology") as attempts to prevent misunderstanding of the term (447). Dodd further explored John in *Historical Tradition in the Fourth Gospel* (1963). His final work was a study of *The Founder of Christianity* (1970).

In America the tradition of liberal lives of Jesus was continued by Shirley Jackson Case's *Jesus: A New Biography* (1927) and Shailer Mathews's *Jesus on Social Institutions* (1928). C. C. McCown, Frederick C. Grant, John Knox and Amos N. Wilder carried on the liberal tradition of presenting Jesus as a social prophet. Meanwhile in Europe the historical basis of the Gospel tradition continued to be investigated by distinguished scholars. Joachim Jeremias of Göttingen University sought to recover the original teaching and intentions of Jesus in *The Eucharistic Words of Jesus* (rev. ET 1966), *The Parables of Jesus* (rev. ET 1963), *The Prayers of Jesus* (ET 1967) and *New Testament Theology 1: The Proclamation of Jesus* (1971). In *Jerusalem in the Time of Jesus* (ET 1969) Jeremias investigated economic and social conditions. Ethelbert Stauffer examined rabbinic materials in his account of *Jesus and His Story* (1960). The foundation for Leonhard Goppelt's two-volume *New Testament Theology* (ET 1981-82) was "The Ministry of Jesus in its Theological Significance." Oscar Cullmann developed a functional christology which examined the connection between Jesus and the various titles applied to him in *The Christology of the New Testament* (ET 1955). Cullmann set his christology in the wider context of salvation history in *Christ and*

Time (ET 1951) and *Salvation in History* (ET 1967).

2.5. The New Quest.

2.5.1. The New Quest in Europe.
In 1959 James M. Robinson published *A New Quest of the Historical Jesus.* The book was both a history of, and an apologia for, the developments that were taking place in the Bultmann school. The starting point was a lecture given by Ernst Käsemann to a reunion of old Marburg students in 1953 on "The Problem of the Historical Jesus" (ET in Käsemann, *Essays on New Testament Themes,* 1964, 15-47). Like others engaged in the New Quest, Käsemann protested his fidelity to Bultmann's methodology and proclaimed the impossibility of writing a biography of Jesus. However, to disengage interest in the earthly Jesus would fail to grasp the earthly church's concern with the identity between the exalted and humiliated Lord, and lapse into docetism. The way forward was to discover the earthly Jesus through investigation of his preaching. Jesus did not come to proclaim general religious or moral truths, but to tell of the kingdom that had dawned and of how God had come near in grace and demand. Jesus did not preach realized eschatology; he inaugurated it.

Bultmann's successor at Marburg, Ernst Fuchs, wrote numerous articles over the years which were published in *Studies of the Historical Jesus* (1960; partial ET 1964). Fuchs drew attention to Jesus' "conduct" as the context of his preaching." Jesus' table fellowship (*see* Table Fellowship) with sinners* was the conduct of neither the prophet nor the sage, but that of a person who dared to act in God's stead, calling sinners near to him who otherwise would have to flee from God. Fuchs also introduced a psychological element by suggesting motives behind Jesus' actions. Jesus transformed the Mosaic Law* into a Law of suffering. The way of salvation* was not by works of the Law but by suffering for the faith. Fuchs suggested that, after the martyrdom of John the Baptist, Jesus began to envisage the possibility of his own suffering and death.

A further step was taken by Günther Bornkamm who wrote a full-length study of *Jesus of Nazareth* (1956; ET 1960). Bornkamm stressed the note of authority in Jesus' teaching. Whereas Bultmann had stressed the future coming of the kingdom in Jesus' teaching, Bornkamm underlined the present element: the new age was already breaking in through Jesus' words and actions. Bornkamm followed in the footsteps of his predecessor at Heidelberg, Martin Dibelius. In marked contrast with Bultmann, Bornkamm could write: "Quite clearly what the Gospels report concerning the message, the deeds and the history of Jesus is still distinguished by an authenticity, a freshness, and a distinctiveness not in any way effaced by the Church's Easter faith. These features point us directly to the earthly figure of Jesus" (24).

The methods and conclusions of the New Quest were summarized in an encyclopedia article which Hans Conzelmann wrote for *Die Religion in Geschichte und Gegenwart.* It was later published separately in expanded form as *Jesus* (ET 1973). The ethos of the New Quest was captured by Gerhard Ebeling in *Theology and Proclamation: Dialogue with Rudolf Bultmann* (1962; ET 1966). Through the person Jesus "God comes to expression in such a way that we come to know Jesus himself as the Word which brings certainty and therefore as the point where reality is radically challenged" (79). Bultmann responded to the New Quest in a paper on "The Primitive Christian Kerygma and the Historical Jesus" (ET in *The Historical Jesus and the Kerygmatic Christ,* ed. C. E. Braaten and R. A. Harrisville, 1964, 15-42). He denied that he had destroyed the continuity between the historical Jesus and the kerygma, insisting that the kerygma presupposes the historical Jesus, however much it may have mythologized him. Bultmann remonstrated with attempts to make psychological reconstructions of Jesus and to legitimate the kerygma by historical research. He concluded by accepting the charge that in his interpretation Jesus has risen in the kerygma. For it presupposes that the kerygma is an eschatological event and expresses the fact that Jesus is present in it.

2.5.2. The New Quest in the English-Speaking World.
In the English-speaking world the two leading representatives were James M. Robinson and Norman Perrin. For Robinson the key question was how did Jesus the proclaimer of the kingdom become Christ the proclaimed. He disdainfully dismissed as positivistic the methods of the original quest, claiming the old objectifying approach to historiography had been replaced by existential historiography which required openness to encounter. The quest of the historical Jesus must have meaning in terms of the human quest for meaningful existence. Inquiry into historical continuity is replaced by inquiry into its inner necessity.

Perrin sought to work within the tradition of the New Quest in *Rediscovering the Teaching of Jesus* (1967). However, to Perrin a serious weakness of the New Quest lay in the assumption of the identity of the historical Jesus with the kerygmatic Christ. The assumption ignored the variety of kerygmata in the NT, and assumed that historical research would always point to parallels between Jesus and a form of the kerygma (233). Perrin himself distinguished between "historical knowledge" (which included Jesus' acceptance of his own death as the necessary consequence of his proclamation of the kingdom, his table fellowship with tax collectors [*see* Taxes] and sinners, and belief that his death would further God's purposes), "historic knowledge" (which occurs when a historical event assumes direct significance for a future time), and "faith knowledge" (which has to do with trans-historical reality and the ascription of special significance in terms of revelation, experience and belief).

2.6. The End of the New Quest. If Harnack's Jesus had the face of a liberal Protestant, and Schweitzer's the heroic demeanor of Nietzsche's superman, the Jesus of the New Quest was an existentialist philosopher whose presence in history was barely discernible behind the kerygma. He is encountered in a kind of existential vacuum from which the historical conditions of the first century are largely excluded. The New Quest ended scarcely two decades after it started. Its demise coincided with the end of the Bultmann era and the passing of existentialist philosophy.

Despite its emphasis on scholarly rigor, its methods and assumptions were limited to those of the Bultmann school. For all its stress on history, it remained curiously indifferent to the world of first-century Judaism as known from Josephus, the Dead Sea Scrolls (*see* Dead Sea Scrolls) and rabbinic literature (*see* Rabbinic Traditions and Writings). To those engaged in the New Quest the proclamation of the cross was the pivotal event which linked existence with the historical Jesus. By positing the crucifixion of Jesus as a fact, docetism was averted. But little attention was paid to the question Why exactly was Jesus crucified? Insofar as it was answered at all, it was answered in existential terms. To exclude the close connection between religion, theology, politics, sociology and economics as interrelated factors in answering this question now looks curiously unhistorical and short-sighted.

3. The Third Quest.

3.1. The Quest Continued. It is open to question whether the term Third Quest will succeed in establishing itself to describe post-Bultmannian developments in Jesus research. There is certainly no common methodology or sense of unity of purpose beyond the conviction that more may be known about Jesus than was known or admitted in the earlier quests. If the term Third Quest is taken to embrace all scholarly investigation of the relationship between the texts of the NT and the historical figure of Jesus in the light of current

knowledge of the first-century world, we are at once confronted with a variety of conflicting views and methods. At first sight it may appear to be a case of *plus ça change, plus c'est la même chose.* For connections between current research and what has gone before appear to continue without interruption. If there is a common theme, it lies in the belief that Jesus was not the Jesus of liberal Protestantism or of the New Quest, but a historical figure whose life and actions were rooted in first-century Judaism with its particular religious, social, economic and political conditions.

3.2. Varieties of Approach. Three main lines of approach may be noted: the radical tradition, the conservative tradition and attempts to see Jesus in new perspectives.

3.2.1. The Radical Tradition. The radical redaction-critical tradition is exemplified by the Jesus Seminar in the United States which seeks to examine the layers of tradition in both the NT and extra-canonical accounts of Jesus' words and actions in order to develop a firm data base for determining who Jesus was. The Seminar meets twice yearly to discuss research papers and vote on the authenticity of the material. Using a color system of balloting, the Seminar is producing a series of Red Letter Editions. The first to be published was *The Parables of Jesus* (1988). In the text words printed in red indicate that Jesus said it or something very like it, and that it could be used for the data base. Pink indicates that Jesus probably said it. Gray indicates doubt, and black rejection of authenticity. As in all scholarship, the conclusions of the scholars involved depend on the methods employed.

Another example of the radical tradition is Burton L. Mack's *A Myth of Innocence: Mark and Christian Origins* (1988). Mack rejects Mark as a historical account of Jesus in favor of seeing the first Gospel as a complex of traditions. He suggests that Jesus' themes, topics and use of epigrammatic *chreiai* (*see* Chreia) were closer to the Cynic idiom than to characteristic Jewish piety. Jesus was not trying to reform Judaism; he was taking up a Hellenistic kind of social criticism. Similarities and differences between Jesus and the Cynics may be studied in the collection of source material compiled by F. Gerald Downing, *Christ and the Cynics* (1988).

3.2.2. The Conservative Tradition. The tradition of pre-war British scholarship is maintained by C. F. D. Moule in *The Origin of Christology* (1977). Moule rejects the idea of evolutionary process in the manner of the History of Religions School which would imply that the historical Jesus had been transformed into another species through the influence of Hellenistic savior cults. Instead he sees a developmental process taking place which relates later perceptions of Jesus to Jesus himself. Moule seeks to show how the titles Son of man, Son of God, Christ and Lord were appropriate to the historical Jesus, and how the corporate savior of Pauline theology was grounded in him.

In similar vein is Graham N. Stanton's *The Gospels and Jesus* (1989). Other examples of the conservative tradition are I. Howard Marshall's commentary on *The Gospel of Luke* (1978), Marshall's collected studies *Jesus the Saviour* (1990) and G. R. Beasley-Murray's *Jesus and the Kingdom of God* (1986). Mention may also be made of John A. T. Robinson's reappraisal of the field of Johannine scholarship and rehabilitation of the historicity of the Fourth Gospel in *The Priority of John* (ed. F. J. Coakley, 1985). At its best conservative scholarship exhibits meticulous attention to detail in careful response to previous discussion as it seeks to vindicate and refine our understanding of the history behind the text.

3.2.3. New Perspectives. Perhaps the most distinctive development in the Third Quest is the search for new approaches by way of forming general hypotheses to account for questions posed by the text. Such hypotheses seek to address questions sometimes neglected in the past and endeavor to understand Jesus in the context of the religious, social, economic and political world of Judaism. In particular, attention is focused on the questions "Why did Jesus come into conflict with the Jewish authorities?" "Why was he handed over to the Romans, and put to death in a manner normally reserved for political revolutionists?"

Among the remarkable modern phenomena is the considerable interest in Jesus on the part of Jewish scholars. In the period after World War 1 scholars like Joseph Klausner, Martin Buber and J. C. G. Montefiore pioneered Jewish studies of Jesus and Christian origins. More recently David Flusser's *Jesus* (1969) presents a picture of a religious teacher like the Pharisees. Jesus belonged to the liberal wing of the school of Hillel and sought a Judaism purified of resentment and hatred. In *Jesus the Jew* (1973) and *Jesus and the World of Judaism* (1983) Geza Vermes depicts Jesus as a Galilean charismatic miracle-worker in the mold of Honi the Circle Drawer and Hanina ben Dosa, who held loose to the stricter traditions of the Jerusalem rabbis and who ultimately came to grief. Jewish scholarship has been examined by Donald A. Hagner in *The Jewish Reclamation of Jesus* (1984).

Non-Jewish scholars are also paying much attention to the Jewish world in which Jesus lived. In this category belong John Bowker's *Jesus and the Pharisees* (1973); J. K. Riches, *Jesus and the Transformation of*

Judaism (1980); Bruce D. Chilton, *A Galilean Rabbi and His Bible* (1984); James H. Charlesworth, *Jesus within Judaism* (1988); and Sean Freyne, *Galilee, Jesus and the Gospels* (1988). In *Jesus als Lehrer* (1981) Rainer Riesner has compared Jesus' teaching methods in the Gospels with Jewish teaching methods (*see* Teacher). In *Jesus and Judaism* (1985) E. P. Sanders deviates from the traditional approach which begins with an investigation of the sayings of Jesus. Instead he focuses on the accounts of Jesus' actions. His starting point is Jesus' action in the Temple (*see* Temple Cleansing; Death of Jesus) and its significance within a contemporary eschatology which expected restoration. Sanders then works backwards, exploring the ways in which Jesus offended Judaism. He finds them in Jesus' relativizing of the present age, in his claim that sinners* would be in the kingdom and in his attack on the Temple.

A major work is Ben F. Meyer's *The Aims of Jesus* (1979). Meyer's study is significant not only for the way in which it seeks to locate Jesus within Judaism, but also for its response to previous scholarship and the challenge it makes to reconsider the question of methodology. Common features of previous scholarship were the attempt to interpret Jesus in terms of a closed view of the universe and the use of Troeltsch's principle of analogy with its reductionistic consequences. Drawing on the philosophy of Bernard Lonergan, Meyer seeks to develop a cognitional theory which enables the historian to grasp the transcendent element in history. According to Meyer the theme underlying Jesus' proclamation of the kingdom of God was the restoration of Israel. Jesus understood himself to be the unique revealer of God's will. He offered a critique and reform of Temple worship, and in his table fellowship with sinners he anticipated the messianic banquet. In private Jesus indicated to his disciples that in his mission the Scriptures were reaching their fulfillment (*see* Old Testament in the Gospels). But this would be reached only through his suffering and death. Until the definitive gathering of the saved at the end of time the aims of Jesus will be incarnated in his community, the remnant and first fruits of messianic Israel.

Another work which tries to develop an alternative methodology is Anthony Harvey's *Jesus and the Constraints of History* (1980). In any given historical situation any individual who wishes to influence others is subject to constraints imposed by culture. Jesus was no exception. Harvey endeavors to identify the constraints under which Jesus found himself and use them in his reconstruction of history. Working backwards from the crucifixion, Harvey tries to identify what led to it. Jesus died the death of an anti-

Roman revolutionary, though the historical sources do not indicate that he was. This apparent contradiction leads Harvey to think that there must have been something in Jesus' teaching and conduct that led the Jewish authorities to hand him over to the Romans. In the light of the constraints of the Law, Harvey infers that Jesus' teaching must be regarded as that of someone who claims that the urgency of the moment overrides some of the Law's provisions. The constraint of time indicates that current expectation of God's breaking into history sets the stage for Jesus' message. Other constraints are miracle, messiahship and Jewish monotheism (see God).

A major area of interest for the Third Quest is Jesus and politics (see Revolutionary Movements). S. G. F. Brandon claimed that Jesus sympathized with the ideals and aims of the Zealot movement, suggesting that these sympathies were downplayed by the Evangelists (The Fall of Jerusalem and the Christian Church, 1951; Jesus and the Zealots, 1967). This thesis has been challenged by numerous scholars, including Alan Richardson, (The Political Christ, 1973) and Martin Hengel (Victory over Violence, 1973; Christ and Power, 1974; The Zealots, 2d ed. 1976, ET 1989). Studies of numerous political issues have been collected by Ernst Bammel and C. F. D. Moule in Jesus and the Politics of His Day (1984). The importance of the Zealots in the time of Jesus has recently come under close scrutiny and has been rejected by Richard A. Horsley and John S. Hanson (Bandits, Prophets, and Messiahs, 1985; R. A. Horsley, Jesus and the Spiral of Violence, 1987). Nevertheless, Horsley allows that Jesus' actions and teaching were increasingly affected by social and political conditions.

Jesus' actions have been studied from the standpoint of sociology (see Sociological Analysis of the Gospels) by Gerd Theissen in Sociology of Early Palestinian Christianity (1978) and in an imaginative reconstructive narrative The Shadow of the Galilean (1987; see Narrative Exegesis). Horsley has responded with Sociology and the Jesus Movement (1989). Martin Hengel has compared Jesus with other types of Jewish leaders in The Charismatic Leader and his Followers (1981). Hengel's earlier studies of Crucifixion (1977) and The Atonement (1981) probe the circumstances surrounding the death of Jesus and its significance for the Christian community. The sociologist Irving M. Zeitlin sees the key to understanding Jesus in the concept of charisma, the gift which bestows authority (Jesus and the Judaism of his Time, 1988).

The links between politics and holiness have been explored by Marcus J. Borg in Conflict, Holiness, and Politics in the Teachings of Jesus (1984) and Jesus: A New Vision (1987). Borg rejects Schweitzer's eschatological interpretation of the kingdom and prefers to see the kingdom as a linguistic symbol for the power of the Spirit and the new life which it created. The image points to a life centered on God. Jesus was "an epiphany of God" and a model for human life.

Spirit christology represents an alternative way of approaching the person of Christ by way of relating the Gospel accounts of Jesus and the Spirit to the study of Jesus' identity (see Holy Spirit). In Jesus and the Spirit (1975) James D. G. Dunn examines the Gospel accounts of Jesus as the recipient of the Spirit and the testimony of the early church to Jesus as the sender of the Spirit. Dunn interprets Jesus' divinity as his relationship with the Father as son and the Spirit of God in him. The eschatological kingdom was present for Jesus only because the eschatological Spirit was present in and through him. In Christology in the Making (1980) Dunn inquires into the origins of the doctrine of the incarnation. Dunn's The Evidence for Jesus (1985) responds to negative and fanciful claims made in a TV series and the book by Ian Wilson which accompanied the series, Jesus: the Evidence (1984).

A number of studies have examined the Gospel miracle stories and their background (see Miracles and Miracle Stories). They include Gerd Theissen's The Miracle Stories of the Early Christian Tradition (ET 1983), Howard Clark Kee's Miracle in the Early Christian World (1983) and Medicine, Miracle and Magic in New Testament Times (1986), and Herman Hendrickx, The Miracle Stories of the Synoptic Gospels (1987). The most radical position was taken by Morton Smith in Jesus the Magician (1979). Smith argued that the miracle stories point to the fact that Jesus was really a magician, and that the Gospels have deliberately tried to obscure the truth.

Colin Brown has sought to respond to this view and also to earlier claims that the miracle stories belong to later layers of tradition developed under the influence of the Hellenistic world, where "divine men"* were expected to perform miracles (Miracles and the Critical Mind, 1984; "Synoptic Miracle Stories: A Jewish Religious and Social Setting," Foundations & Facets Forum 2 [1986] 55-76). The following hypothesis also seeks to take note of Jewish views of Jesus and his Jewish environment and also of Spirit christology.

The Gospels present two conflicting types of theology: that of the Evangelists and that of the Jewish authorities. According to the Evangelists' theology, Jesus was anointed and empowered by the Spirit at his baptism.* This fact determined his activity as the Christ (i.e., one who was anointed by the Spirit) who fulfilled the prophecy of John the Baptist that Jesus would baptize (i.e., consecrate) Israel with the Spirit (Mk 1:8; Mt 3:11; Lk 3:16; Jn 1:33). This ministry of consecration includes forgiving of sins, table fellowship with sinners, reinterpretation of the Law* and the Sabbath,* healing,* casting out demons,* social and political teaching, and the "baptism" of the Temple. It culminates in his sacrificial death which establishes the new covenant.

By contrast the theology of the Jewish authorities is based on the Torah, which in terms of daily life meant living in accordance with the teaching of Deuteronomy. In particular, the authorities were alarmed by the combination of teaching and wonder-working that they perceived in Jesus. Turning to the Torah for guidance, they came to the conclusion that Jesus was the kind of prophet described in Deuteronomy 13, who was performing signs and wonders in order to lead the people astray. The only recourse was to follow the prescriptions of Deuteronomy 13 and purge the evil one from the midst of the people by putting him to death.

Jesus differed from contemporaries like Hanina ben Dosa, who also had the reputation of being a "man of deed" (i.e., miracle worker, cf. Lk 24:19). Hanina disclaimed the title of prophet and put forward no new teaching. It was precisely the combination of novel teaching, actions that were perceived as threatening, and wonder working which led to Jesus' downfall. Opposition to Jesus was bound up with his miracles and exorcisms which thus belong to the earliest layers of tradition. To his opponents Jesus was an evildoer who appeared to be bent on leading the people astray and thus must be dealt with in accordance with the prescriptions of the Torah. To his followers, Jesus was the anointed one who fulfilled both the Law and the prophets. The issue became one of whether Jesus' works were wrought by someone who was possessed by Beelzebul (Mk 3:22 par.) or whether they were the work of the Holy Spirit (Mk 3:29-30 par.; Mt 12:28). In the Fourth Gospel Jesus' works are said to be the works of the Father (Jn 14:10-11), though here too his opponents see him as someone possessed who is leading the people astray (Jn 7:12; 8:48; 11:47-48). In their different ways all four Gospels develop Word and Spirit christologies.

3.3. Systematic Theology. It remains to be noted that renewed interest in the historical Jesus has made a significant impact on other areas of theology.

The issue was brought into sharp focus by the Scottish systematic theologian D. M. Baillie (1857-1954) in *God Was in Christ* (1948). Baillie agreed with the old quest in insisting that we must think of Jesus as a historical human being. Anything less would be to lapse into docetism and unreality. However, the questions raised by Schweitzer and the historical skepticism of the Bultmann school appeared to negate the possibility of knowing the historical Jesus. Moreover, neo-orthodoxy was right to stress that knowledge of God involved more than historical reconstruction. Baillie's solution drew upon the moderate form criticism of C. H. Dodd and others which saw in different layers of tradition and forms patterns of the same divine action of God reaching out to human beings in Christ. Baillie went on to suggest that the "paradox of grace" might provide the best clue for thinking about how God might be present in Christ. As God dwells in believers by grace, so he might also dwell in Christ in a more complete way. Baillie's approach seems to restate that of Schleiermacher in a more attractive way, though he seems to end with an incarnation of the Father. Nevertheless, his work draws attention to the significance of critical study for theology and raises the question of whether, if Baillie had paid more attention to the role of Word and Spirit in the NT, he might have achieved more satisfactory results.

Wolfhart Pannenberg (*Jesus—God and Man*, ET 1968) and Hans Küng (*On Being a Christian*, 1976) have urged the need to do christology "from below" as distinct from doing it "from above." To Pannenberg the idea of doing it "from above" presupposes the divinity of Christ and ignores the most important task of christology, viz., to present reasons for confessing the divinity of Christ. To take the divinity of Christ as one's starting point is to devalue the historical Jesus and his relationship with Palestinian Judaism. Moreover, human beings stand in history and do not have God's absolute perspective. Therefore, Pannenberg adopts a phenomenological approach to the Gospel accounts of Jesus' activity. However, the historical event of Jesus' resurrection removes the previous ambiguity and provides the key to understanding the meaning of history. Pannenberg's work is rich in insights, but it is open to question whether his method is successful. Nothing can be apprehended from a point of absolute neutrality. It is arbitrary to suspend judgment about God's activity until after the resurrection, at which time an approach "from above" is allowed to come into play. Judgments about Jesus did not begin with the resurrection. Rather, this event is to be seen as confirming the identity of God's personal presence in Jesus.

In the work of Jürgen Moltmann Jesus' earthly messianic activity and especially his death on the cross serve as the basis for a reinterpretation of eschatology, the church, God's character as a suffering God and the Trinity (*Theology of Hope*, 1967; *The Crucified God*, 1974; *The Church in the Power of the Spirit*, 1977; *The Trinity and the Kingdom*, 1981; *The Way of Jesus Christ*, 1990).

Latin American Liberation Theology bases its teaching and praxis on the Jesus of the Synoptic Gospels and his action among the poor and needy (*see* Liberation Hermeneutics). Important works include Leonardo Boff, *Jesus Christ Liberator* (1978) and Jon Sobrino, *Christology at the Crossroads* (1978). For a survey see Arthur F. McGovern, *Liberation Theology and its Critics* (1989). In liberation christology, social conditions and the need for liberation raise the questions that are to be asked of the text and determine the agenda. However, the methods to be used in working through the agenda and developing a christology are the critical, historical methods that are valid everywhere.

This sample review of systematic theology underlines the need for theologians to take into account the work of biblical scholars and also the need of the latter to be aware of the theological dimensions of their research.

4. Conclusion.

In retrospect it is clear that impressions of the course of the quest of the historical Jesus, and even of how many quests there have been, have been shaped by the viewpoint of the person giving the impression. It also is clear that the Jesus that was discovered in particular quests all too often reflected the image of those engaged in it. Harnack's Jesus was the reflection of a liberal Protestant face at the bottom of a well. Schweitzer's Jesus had the demeanor of Nietzsche's superman. The Jesus of the New Quest sounded like an existentialist philosopher summoning his hearers to make existential decisions. In all this the hermeneutical circle came into play: the questioner's questions and outlook helped shape the answers that were given. No single school of thought has attained absolute results and driven all rival theories from the field. As in all theorizing, all claims are open to evaluation in the light of the methods pursued. However, in the battles between rival schools of thought and in the process of successive approximation that belongs to all scholarly inquiry, positive gains have been made. It is no longer possible to have a docetic Christ. Jesus was a particular historical figure rooted in his times, but speaking to all times. The study of Jesus and the Gospels in the light of the social, economic, political and religious conditions of his times has immensely enriched our understanding

not only of history but also of theological issues embedded in history.

BIBLIOGRAPHY. G. Aulén, *Jesus in Contemporary Historical Research* (Philadelphia: Fortress, 1976); C. Brown, *Jesus in European Protestant Thought* (2d ed.; Grand Rapids: Baker, 1988); E. J. Epp and G. W. MacRae, eds., *The New Testament and its Modern Interpreters* (Atlanta: Scholars, 1989); J. A. Fitzmyer, *Scripture and Christology: A Statement of the Pontifical Biblical Commission with a Commentary* (New York/Mahwah: Paulist Press, 1986); H. Harris, *David Friedrich Strauss and His Theology* (Cambridge: University Press, 1973); idem, *The Tübingen School* (2d ed.; Grand Rapids: Baker, 1990); A. Hultgren, *New Testament Christology: A Critical Assessment and Annotated Bibliography* (New York: Greenwood, 1988); L. E. Keck, *A Future for the Historical Jesus* (Nashville: Abingdon, 1971); W. G. Kümmel, *The New Testament: The History of the Investigation of Its Problems* (Nashville: Abingdon, 1972); idem, Dreissig Jahre Jesusforschung, ed. H. Merklein (BBB 60, reprint of articles previously published in *Theologische Rundschau;* Königstein: Hanstein, 1985); A. E. McGrath, *The Making of Modern German Christology* (Oxford: Blackwell, 1986); J. Macquarrie, *Jesus Christ in Modern Thought* (Philadelphia: Trinity, 1990); I. H. Marshall, *I Believe in the Historical Jesus* (Grand Rapids: Eerdmans, 1977); J. P. Meier, *A Marginal Jew: Rethinking the Historical Jesus* (New York: Doubleday, 1991); S. C. Neill and T. Wright, *The Interpretation of the New Testament, 1861-1986* (Oxford: University Press, 1988); D. Pals, *The Victorian "Lives" of Jesus* (San Antonio: Trinity University, 1982); H. Graf Reventlow, *The Authority of the Bible and the Rise of the Modern World* (Philadelphia: Fortress, 1985); J. M. Robinson, *A New Quest of the Historical Jesus and Other Essays* (Philadelphia: Fortress, 1983); C. Rowland, *From Messianic Movement to Christian Religion* (Minneapolis: Augsburg, 1985); A. Schweitzer, *The Quest of the Historical Jesus*, Introduction by J. M. Robinson (New York: Macmillan, 1973); C. Welch, *Protestant Thought in the Nineteenth Century* (2 vols.; New Haven: Yale University, 1972, 1985). C. Brown

HOLINESS. *See* CLEAN AND UNCLEAN; PHARISEES; SINNER; TEMPLE

HOLY SPIRIT

In the Gospels the term *Holy Spirit* (along with "the Spirit," "Spirit of God," "Paraclete," etc.) is a referring expression for the power and presence of God* in action, especially as the means of God's self-revelation.

1. The Holy Spirit in Intertestamental Judaism

2. The Holy Spirit in the Synoptic Gospels

3. The Holy Spirit in John

1. The Holy Spirit in Intertestamental Judaism.

1.1. As the Spirit of Prophecy. By far the most widespread understanding of the Spirit in Judaism* is as "the Spirit of Prophecy" (a regular term for the Spirit, especially in the Targums*), in other words the Spirit acting as the organ of communication between God and a person:

(1) affording charismatic revelation and guidance (numerous examples in Rabbinic* Judaism and Targums; but see also e.g., 4 Ezra 14:22; Philo (e.g.) *Som.* II.252; *Bib. Ant.* 9.10; 31.9; Sir 48:24);

(2) affording charismatic wisdom (e.g., Targums to Ex 31:3; *Frg. Tg.* Num 11:26-27; *Tg. Onq.* Deut 34:9; *Jos. and As.* 4:9; Josephus *Ant.* 10.239; *Jub* 40:5; Philo *Jos.* 117; *Vit. Mos.* II.265; *Gig.* 24; Sir 39:6; Sus 45b (Theod); Wis 7:7; 9:17-18; and cf. 1QH 12.11-13; 13.18-19; 14.12-13);

(3) (less commonly) invasively inspiring prophetic speech (Targums to Num 11:26-27; Josephus *Ant.* 4.119; *Jub* 25:14; 31:12; Philo *Spec. Leg.* IV.49; *Vit. Mos.* I.175 and 277; *Bib. Ant.* 28.6; etc.);

(d) (rarely) invasively inspiring charismatic praise or worship* (*1 Enoch* 71:11; *Ex Rab.* 23:2; *Tg. Neb.* 1 Sam 10:6; 19:20, 23; *Bib. Ant.* 32.14; *T. Job* 48-50).

It was generally held, though not universally, that the Spirit of prophecy (*see* Prophets and Prophecy) had been withdrawn from Israel* since the last prophets (*t. Soṭa* 13:3-4) because of the nation's sin (cf. *b. Sanh.* 65b), and (especially on the basis of Joel 2:28-32 (= MT 3:1-5)) that it would be poured out on all of the restored Israel at the end (cf. *Num Rab.* 15:25; *Midr. Haggadol Gen.* 140). This would bring Israel immediate knowledge of God and of his will, and thus promote ongoing obedience fulfilling the hope of Ezekiel 36:27 (*Deut Rab.* 6:14; *Tg. Neb.* Ezek 36:25-26: cf. *b. Ber.* 31b-32a). In the meantime the Spirit had afforded the repository of wisdom and revelation in Scripture.

1.2. As the Power of Creation and Miracle. It has sometimes been held that a Judaism that thought of the Spirit as the Spirit of prophecy could not conceive of it as the power of creation and miracle.* This is at best a half-truth. While the Targums tended to translate Genesis 1:2 as "a wind from the Lord," the LXX renders *rûaḥ ʾĕlōhîm* by *pneuma theou*, a collocation which elsewhere means "the Spirit of God" (e.g., Gen 41:38; contrast Gen 8:1 etc.). *2 Baruch* 21:4 unquestionably attributes the cosmos to the work of the Spirit (cf. Is 32:15), and there is also a widespread attribution of animate creation to God's Spirit (cf. LXX

Job 33:4; Ps 103:30; 32:6 and Jdt 16:14; Philo *Op. Mund.* 29-30; *2 Apoc. Bar.* 23:5; etc.), and some rare hints of resurrection life too (Ezek 37:9-10, 14; *2 Apoc. Bar.* 23:5; *m. Soṭa* 9:15; *Pesiq. R.* 1:6; *Cant. Rab.* 1.1.§9). The LXX and the Targums also retain the tradition that the Spirit empowered Samson's exploits (Judg 14:6, 19; 15:14), might lift and/or transport prophets around (cf. 1 Kings 18:12; 2 Kings 2:16; Ezek 2:2; 3:12, 14; etc.), and, at 2 Kings 2:9-15, the power of Elisha's division of the waters is specifically traced by the Targumist to "the Spirit of prophecy" on him.

The Targums even extend the connection between Spirit and power in the Hebrew Bible by attributing to the Spirit of prophecy deeds the MT traces instead to "the hand" of the Lord (cf. Ezek 37:1). Of special interest is the tendency to trace the charismatic power of Gideon (Judg 6:34), Jephthah (Judg 11:29), Saul (1 Sam 11:6) and David (1 Sam 16:13-14) to "the Spirit of power" (as on Samson), rather than translating these passages with "Spirit of prophecy/wisdom" or "power of the Lord" which we might have expected if the relation between Spirit and miraculous "power" was thought to be problematic. Here the "Spirit of power" has become the equipment of Israel's "saviors," even the power miraculously to rout the enemy. Other examples of the Spirit understood as the power of miraculous deeds may be found outside the so-called biblical translations (e.g., *Lev. Rab.* 8:2; *Bib. Ant.* 27.9-10 and 36.2; Josephus *Ant.* 8.408 [and probably 8.346]; etc.).

1.3. As the Spirit on the Messiah. A major strand of Judaism anticipated a Messiah (*see* Christ) mightily endowed with the Spirit as both the Spirit of prophecy (affording unique wisdom and knowledge of the Lord as the basis of dynamic righteousness) and the Spirit of power. The model is first David, then more especially the Davidic figure of Isaiah 11:1-4, endowed with the Spirit of wisdom,* knowledge and power—and it is this combination, and with strong echoes of the very language of Isaiah 11:1-4, that provides the messianic portrait in *1 Enoch* 49:2-3; 62:1-2; *Psalms of Solomon* 17:37; 18:7 (cf. 1QSb 5:24-25). Other rarer strands of Jewish messianic hope also involve Spirit-endowed figures, whether the Elijah-like prophet based on Malachi 4:5 (Sir 48:10; *see* Elijah and Elishah); a Priestly Messiah (e.g., 1QS 9:10-11; *T. Levi* 18); a prophet-like-Moses based on Deuteronomy 18:15-16 (e.g., 1QS 9:10-11; *see* Moses); a Servant-Herald based on Isaiah 42:1-2 (*see* Servant of Yahweh); a Servant-Warrior derived from Isaiah 61:1-2 (e.g., 11QMelch), or some combination of these. In each case the quality of the endowment of the Spirit might be nuanced slightly differently, but would combine wisdom, revelation and some kinds of acts of power.

2. The Holy Spirit in the Synoptic Gospels.

2.1. The Spirit in the Gospel Infancy Narratives.

2.1.1. Prophecy Restored in Israel. Luke (alone) portrays a number of prophetic activities in association with Jesus' conception, birth and infancy (*see* Birth of Jesus). Elizabeth and Zechariah (*see* Zechariah's Song) experience the Spirit of prophecy in invasive prophetic speech (the invasive quality denoted here by the Lukan favorite idiom "filled with" the Holy Spirit) at 1:41-42 and 1:67, and as a result give oracles of recognition and assurance of salvation.* Simeon too receives charismatic revelation (2:26, and perhaps Anna at 2:38), guidance (2:27) and prophetic utterance (2:29-35; *see* Simeon's Song). This so closely tallies with the picture of the Spirit of prophecy in Judaism that it has been suggested Luke here creates an idealized picture of the epoch of Israel, to be succeeded by those of Jesus and the church* (so Conzelmann), and also that the deliberate likeness of the activities of the Spirit to those portrayed in Acts is intended by Luke to establish Christianity as the continuity and fulfillment of Judaism (so Chevallier). However, although even the rabbis can exceptionally speak of individuals experiencing the Spirit of prophecy (only at *t. Pesah.* 2.15; *Lev. Rab.* 21.8; *y. Šeb.* 9.1; *y. Soṭa* 1.4 and parallels?), the general belief in the full withdrawal of the Spirit until the end (see 1.1. above) and the strongly christocentric focus of the Spirit's activities in Luke 1—2 (and it is exclusively those awaiting the messianic salvation of Israel that experience the Spirit), suggest rather that Luke portrays here the dawn of the eschatological (*see* Eschatology) restoration of the Spirit to pious Israel*; not the period of Israel as such. This is further confirmed in what is said of John (*see* John the Baptist) and Jesus.

2.1.2. The Spirit on the Baptist. The eschatological quality of the Spirit restored to God's people is evidenced in the unique features within the portrayal of John the Baptist as prophet. If he is the greatest (Lk 7:26-28), that is because he fulfills the role of the awaited Elijah* to restore Israel in repentance before the eschatological visitation (Lk 7:27; Mal 3:1 [cf. Mal 4:5] denied by Conzelmann, but see Fitzmyer). Luke has carefully sculpted this understanding into the infancy narratives, not only in stepwise parallelism between John, the Prophet of the Most High (1:76), and Jesus, the Son of the Most High (1:32; *see* Son of God), who comes to effect the promised salvation, but also in the specific identification of John as the one who "will go before him in the Spirit and power of

Elijah" to prepare the Lord's people (Lk 1:17, again strongly echoing the Malachi tradition). In Judaism the collocation "Spirit and power of Elijah" (probably pre-Lukan) would normally suggest a miracle-working prophet, but in the Lukan redaction (*see* Redaction Criticism) it means rather that John preaches powerfully—according to Luke 7:21-23, miracles are what distinguish Jesus from John, and are offered to John's disciples* as evidence to their master that Jesus is indeed the "Coming One." In accordance with his eschatological stature and role, the gift of the Spirit to John is unprecedented: he is "filled with the Holy Spirit" even from his mother's womb (1:15). Hence even *in utero* he recognizes with joy the bearer of the Messiah (1:41, 44) and from birth grows and becomes strong in the Spirit (1:80 [or possibly "in spirit"]).

2.1.3. The Spirit and the Conception of the Son of God. The eschatological quality of the Spirit restored to Israel is manifest especially in connection with its role in the conception of the Messiah (1:32-35). Here Luke is almost certainly dependent on tradition, for the same motif is witnessed independently (albeit briefly) in Matthew (1:18). The child born to Mary is to be hailed Son of the Most High and given the eschatological throne of David (1:32-33; *see* Son of David), because he will be no child of ordinary wedlock (1:35). As Fitzmyer now admits, following the semi-miraculous conception of John the Baptist to his aged parents in 1:5-25, the ascending parallelism of the narrative requires that this means a virginal conception of Jesus by the creative activity of the Holy Spirit. The angelic (*see* Angel) oracle asserts that through the action of the Spirit (perceived as the new creation "power of the Most High" [cf. 1:35b]) that which is born shall be "holy, the Son of God." As G. Schneider puts it: "Jesus is not merely filled with the Spirit, like John, rather his very being is attributed to the Spirit" (Schneider, 53).

While Leisegang's attempts to explain this striking assertion in terms of pagan prophetism have been decisively overturned (see e.g., Barrett 1966), it is usually explained instead (so Brown 1977) as a late development in Christian thinking which first attributed Jesus' divine sonship by the Spirit to the resurrection*-exaltation (cf. Rom 1:4), then fed it back; first to Jesus' baptism,* then finally to his birth. It is held that the notion of creation or new creation by the Spirit (in a physical sense) was unknown in pre-Christian Judaism and could only evolve with the resurrection belief. But (1) the view is entirely conjectural: from the earliest confessions (Rom 1:3-4 and Gal 4:4-6) Jesus' birth is already a decisive christological moment, and there is no evidence Mark 1:10-11 and parallels were first understood in an adoptionistic sense; (2) an understanding of the Spirit as new creation power of miracle is already clearly attested in the tradition of Jesus' miracles (see 2.4.2. below); and (3) Judaism was not as devoid of the idea of the Spirit as the power of miracle, creation or resurrection as is alleged (see 1.2. above). Indeed, Jesus and earliest Christianity would hardly have identified the power of resurrection specifically as God's Spirit unless Judaism already invited such an identification.

The outcome of Jesus' conception by the Spirit is portrayed in Luke 2:41-52, which is understood against the background of messianic hopes for a ruler endowed with wisdom* (Is 11:2-4; *Pss. Sol.* 17:37; *1 Enoch* 49:2-3; etc.) and God's grace (cf. 2:40). Already Jesus shows a wisdom that startles the leaders of Israel; knows a duty to his Father which transcends that to his parents (2:49) and a divine "sonship" (compare *ho patēr mou* ["my Father"] here with the same expression at 10:22; 22:29 and 24:49), the depths of which Luke underscores by the redactional notice in 2:50 that Mary and Joseph did not understand the significance of what he said.

2.2. The Baptist's Promise (Mk 1:8 par. Mt 3:11 and Lk 3:16). John contrasts his own baptizing activity with that of one to come who "will baptize you with Holy Spirit-and-fire" (so the older Q version: Mark omits "and fire"). The "you" in question is all Israel (not merely the righteous), and syntactically "Holy Spirit and fire" is probably a hendiadys (i.e., one deluge consisting of Spirit and fire; not a baptism of Spirit for the righteous and one of fire for the wicked).

Speculation about whether the Baptist originally promised only judgment* in the form of a baptism of fire alone (Bultmann 1963) or of "wind and fire" (Best, taking his cue from the winnowing image which follows in Q and the fact that Heb *rûaḥ* can mean both "wind" and "spirit"—but does one "baptize" with "wind"?) is as unverifiable as it is unnecessary. The concept of an eschatological deluge of Spirit-and-fire is understandable enough within apocalyptic* Judaism. There, for example, we find an eschatological stream, deluge or flood of fire (a burning counterpart to Noah's: cf. Dan 7:10; 1QH 3:20-36; *1 Enoch* 67:13; 4 Ezra 13:10-11), destructive of the wicked, but purging the righteous (cf. *T. Isaac* 5:21-25; *T. Abr.* 13), and the connection of the Spirit with cleansing, purging, even "fiery" judgment was traditional (cf. esp. Is 4:4; 1QS 4:21-22; see Dunn 1972). This is not quite, however, a flood of *Holy Spirit*-and-fire, and in Judaism a flood of divine Spirit could only be anticipated from God himself, not from the Messiah (though 4 Ezra 13:8-11 comes close in anticipating a stream of flame and fiery

breath from the Messiah). Indeed, this is the main objection to the authenticity of the Baptist's promise as it stands: It is alleged that a promise of any human agent pouring out God's Spirit is simply inconceivable (*T. Jud.* 24:2-3 is suspect precisely as *Christian* interpolation).

But this probably misunderstands John's promise. He does not speak of the Messiah "bestowing" the gift of the Spirit. We have no need to posit that he went further than the traditional expectation of a messianic figure powerfully fulfilling Isaiah 11:1-4 (and 9:2-7— as in *1 Enoch* 49:2-3; 62:1-2; *Pss. Sol.* 17:37; 18:7; etc.). The arrival of such a figure to rule, with his decisively authoritative Spirit-imbued command, burning righteousness and dramatic acts of power, effecting both judgment and salvation, would itself be sufficient to suggest the metaphor of his unleashing a deluge of Spirit-and-fire on Israel (cf. *Tg. Neb.* Is 4:4 where the "Spirit of judgment" and "Spirit of fire" become the Messiah's powerful command of judgment and of extirpation respectively).

The imagery here was clearly capable of being applied by the Evangelists (1) to the Spirit in Jesus' ministry, (2) to the continuation of his ministry through the church in Jesus' lordship over the Spirit, and (3) to the final act of judgment and re-creation, without requiring to be applied exclusively to anyone. Yates is probably right to think Mark saw Jesus' baptismal reception of the Spirit, and powerful ministry, as fulfillment of the Baptist's promise, but wrong to restrict it to that: because a climactic new phase in the revelation of Christ and of God's reign in Mark is initiated with the Easter events. Exegetes are right to suggest Luke saw the fulfillment of John's promise in Pentecost (Acts 1:5; 11:16) and Matthew in the eschaton (cf. "fire" in Matthew), but wrong to restrict it to this if it means denying Luke thought Jesus' ministry (empowered by the Spirit, precipitating eschatological judgment-and-salvation and casting "fire" on the earth [12:49]) already began to fulfill John's logion, and if it means denying that the final act of judgment and re-creation would further fulfill it.

2.3. The Spirit Comes in the Wilderness. The Gospels portray the Baptist as preparing the way of the Lord in the wilderness (*see* Mountain and Wilderness) and appealing to Isaiah 40:3. This was to evoke an intertestamental Isaianic New Exodus ideology; that God (through a Spirit-empowered Servant [Is 61:1-2, with certain Mosaic characteristics, cf. 42:1-7]) would destroy Israel's enemies (which at the time were partly identified as the spiritual forces behind idolatry and Israel's blindness), and shepherd* her along "the way" through a transformed wilderness to a restored

Zion where he would rule. The ideology is widely reflected in Judaism (cf. 1QS 8:12b-16a; 9:17-20; 4Q176; Sir 48:24-25; *T. Moses* 10:1-8; *Pss. Sol.* 11; etc.), and is woven through the Spirit traditions.

2.3.1. Jesus "Receives" the Spirit (Mk 1:10-11 par. Mt 3:16-17 and Lk 3:21-22). Dunn (1970, chap. 3) rightly observes that for the Evangelists Jesus receives the Spirit only after he comes out of the water* (and for Luke, while he is praying); his baptism was not the first Christian sacrament. Strictly speaking, the Synoptic Gospels do not actually record an objective coming of the Spirit on Jesus at all, but a *vision* ("the heaven(s) opened" is a standard formula to denote visionary experience: cf. Acts 7:56; 10:11; etc.; Mark's "heavens rent" simply heightens the Isaianic New Exodus connections by using the language of Is 64:1). Within the structure of such visions what is seen and what is heard are mutually interpretive. Taken as a unity, the import of the vision is that from that time the Spirit will be with Jesus as the power to exercise the messianic task (thus the use of Ps 2:7 [Mk 1:11b and pars.]); particularly as the Servant-Herald of Isaiah 42:1-2 (Mk 1:11c and pars.; cf. also Is 53:7 and 61:1-2). To see the Spirit descend as a dove most probably evokes the symbolism of the dove as a herald or trustworthy messenger (so *b. Giṭ.* 45a; *b. Sanh.* 95a) and bearer of good tidings (cf. Gen 8:11), and so further interprets the Spirit on Jesus as the power to proclaim the messianic "good news."

Dunn (following a long line of exegetical tradition from Büchsel and von Baer on) attempts to explain the gift here primarily in terms of Jesus' paradigmatic experience of the Spirit in eschatological sonship, new age "life," life of the kingdom of God, etc., and only secondarily as empowering. But anyone holding the sort of messianic hopes outlined in §1.3. and §2.2. above would immediately recognize this primarily if not exclusively as messianic empowering. For Luke, Jesus already experiences a sonship to God deeper than that to which believers aspire (cf. 2:41-52), and any further dimension of sonship added by Jesus' reception of the Spirit at Jordan is of a more distinctively messianic rather than generally paradigmatic nature (see Turner 1981).

2.3.2. The Spirit and the Defeat of Satan in the Wilderness (Mk 1:12-13 par. Mt 4:1-11 and Lk 4:1-13). The Spirit who comes upon Jesus in the wilderness now leads him deeper into the wilderness into the trial with Satan (*see* Temptation of Jesus), but nothing is said of the Spirit's role in the encounter itself in Mark or Matthew. For Luke (4:1), however, the emphasis falls more on the one "full of the Spirit" now being led (by God) in the wilderness in a way that manifests the messianic empowering ("in the Spirit"). The final temptations echo Israel's in the wilderness, but while they "rebelled and grieved his Holy Spirit" there (Is 63:10), the new representative of Israel overcomes. Luke does not specify whether this is because the Spirit affords Jesus new depths of charismatic wisdom which is the basis of the hoped-for Messiah's redoubtable righteousness (*1 Enoch* 49:2-3; *Pss. Sol.* 17:37; 18:7; 1QSb 5:24-25; *Tg. Neb.* Is 11.1-2), but such is probably to be inferred. The redactional notice in Luke 4:14 that Jesus then returned "in the power of the Spirit" to Galilee* not only highlights the "power" character of the gift of the Spirit to Jesus, but may be intended to indicate that the successful encounter with Satan lies at the root of Jesus' later success in "healing all who were under the power of the devil" (Acts 10:38; *see* Demon, Devil, Satan; Healing).

2.4. The Spirit in Jesus' Ministry.

2.4.1. The Messiah-of-the-Spirit, Exorcisms and Blasphemy against the Spirit. Matthew 12:28 (a Q saying) explicitly attributes Jesus' exorcisms (*see* Demon, Devil, Satan) to his empowering with the Spirit and concludes they manifest the inbreaking of God's reign (*see* Kingdom of God). This is striking as Judaism did not connect exorcisms with the Spirit nor see them as evidence of the kingdom. The same assumption—that Jesus exorcises by the power of the Spirit—is made in the Markan tradition warning of blasphemy* against the Spirit (Mk 3:28-30 par. Mt 12:31-32). This with the saying that immediately precedes may provide a clue to the connections of thought.

The most obvious OT background to the charge of "blasphemy against the Spirit" is Isaiah 63:10 with its accusation that the perverse and blind rebellion of the wilderness generation "grieved his Holy Spirit" and turned God into their enemy. Equally, the closest OT parallel to the parable of the strong man is widely recognized to be Isaiah 49:24-26, with its New Exodus theme of the Yahweh-Warrior taking back the captives from warriors, and plunder from the fierce—i.e., releasing Israel—so that all humanity will know he is Israel's savior. By the intertestamental period these "enemies" from whom deliverance was awaited were none other than the powers of Belial, and the Messiah was the one who would act as God's agent in effecting the New Exodus release (so esp. *T. Dan* 5:10-13 and 11QMelch, but see also *T. Zeb.* 9:8 and *T. Levi* 18:12). The New Exodus hopes thus offer a plausible background to explain why the Messiah (already traditionally regarded as empowered by the Spirit to deliver Israel from her enemies) should be connected with exorcisms, and these in turn with the advent of God's reign. These hopes also provide an inviting background for labelling as "blasphemy against the Holy Spirit" the rebellious refusal to recognize such acts of redemption as *God's* work.

Luke has shifted the blasphemy against the Spirit saying to a different context (12:10-12). It probably still means obdurate and rebellious unbelief that opposes God's redemptive initiative, now in persistent antagonism to the gospel* (*see* Gospel [Good News]) preached in the power of the Spirit (so Fitzmyer)—a theme which dominates Acts. Of the alternative suggestion (Schweizer, George etc.), that "blasphemy against the Spirit" denotes failure of the Christian to confess Jesus when prompted by the Spirit in situations of trial, there is simply no trace in Luke-Acts.

Luke 11:20 has also changed the Q* saying to attribute exorcisms to "the finger of God" rather than to the Spirit. It is alleged Luke has made both these changes because he regarded the Spirit (as in Judaism) as "the Spirit of prophecy" and, for that reason, could not accept the Spirit was also the power of miracle. But this is based on a false antithesis (see 1.2. above), and Luke's changes are more readily explained in other terms. In Luke 11:20 the shift in terminology (a clear reference to Ex 8:19 [LXX Ex 8:15] is probably in the interest of Luke's prophet-like-Moses christology but still refers to the Spirit (cf. the parallel term "the hand of the Lord" which was interpreted to refer to the Spirit).

2.4.2. The Spirit and Miracles of Healing.
To the extent that illness was regarded as both directly and indirectly Satanic (e.g., Acts 10:38; Lk 13:10-15; etc.), so we might expect healings* to be regarded as part of the messianic deliverance; the acts of the Messiah endowed with the Spirit (cf. Mt 11:2) to liberate Israel from her enemies. The strong connection between healings and pronouncement of the inbreaking reign of God supports the view (notably Lk 9:2 and 10:9, 11 par. Mt 10:7-8), and the Q tradition (Mt 11:5 par. Lk 7:21-22) that Jesus responded to the Baptist's doubt by highlighting the blind seeing, the lame walking, lepers cleansed, deaf hearing and "good news" being preached to the poor, thus evoking a medley of Isaianic New Exodus texts (29:18; 35:5-7; 42:18) including the most significant, Isaiah 61:1-2 (see 2.4.3. below). Matthew specifically and redactionally traces the healings to the Spirit bestowed on the Servant-Herald of Isaiah 42:1-2 (Mt 12:15-21). The occasional Elisha or prophet-like-Moses allusions in the miracle tradition of Luke (7:11-17; 9:10b-17, 28-36; 10:1-12; 13:32-33) should not be taken as providing a competing explanation, but reflect a merging of prophetic and more traditional messianic views (anticipated in the New Exodus ideology and elsewhere).

2.4.3. The Interpretation of the Spirit in Terms of Isaiah 61:1-2.
Via the redactional bridges of 4:1 and 4:14, Luke interprets the gift of the Spirit to Jesus in 3:21-22 in terms of fulfillment of Isaiah 61:1-2 (4:18-21). The unusual text form of the citation and other non-Lukan features suggest he has received 4:16-30 from a source (Strobel, Schürmann and Tuckett differently), but Luke has given it programmatic significance.

The use of Isaiah 61:1-2 to explain the Spirit on Jesus has both christological and soteriological significance. Isaiah 61:1-2 was understood in contemporary Judaism to encapsulate the New Exodus hopes for a messianic Jubilee* and "release" of "the poor" (i.e., Israel in need of salvation; *see* Rich and Poor) from captivity to the powers of Beliar (compare 11QMelch; see Sloan). That the citation was understood this way is indicated by the intercalation of the thematic "to set the oppressed free" from Isaiah 58:6. Jesus claims to be the one empowered by the Spirit to effect the "release" of Israel from the variety of forms of Satanic oppression. That this includes healings and exorcisms is clear from Luke 7:21 (Lukan redaction) with 7:22 (Q) and Acts 10:38 (which echo the language of Lk 4:18-21: cf. also e.g., Lk 13:10-15). But that it also goes beyond these to include release from Israel's idolatrous "blindness" and "deafness" to God too (cf. 8:4-15; Acts 28:26-27) is evident from (e.g.) the way Isaiah 61:1-2 shapes the Beatitudes (Mt 5:3-6; Lk 6:20-21; *see* Sermon on the Mount).

Christologically, the use of Isaiah 61:1-2 (and 42:1-2) with a New Exodus theme probably indicates a prophet-like-Moses motif rather than the more traditional regal Messiah. But the two are complimentary, not antithetical, and whether the Messiah is Davidic or Mosaic makes only slight difference to the pneumatology: both figures are expected to experience the Spirit in acts of power and deliverance, and both experience the Spirit in charismatic wisdom. A Mosaic motif enables an emphasis on the Spirit as the source of charismatic revelation, and on the outcome in foundational and authoritative teaching, more easily than the regal. In the final analysis, however, the Synoptics are surprisingly reticent to speak of Jesus receiving revelation (contrast the paucity of such reference in Luke [only 3:21-22 (10:18?) and 10:22] with the richness in Acts), and this is never specifically attributed to the Spirit. And while Jesus is presented as the giver of foundational teaching, the authority* of the content is presented as his own ("I say to you . . ."; *see* Amen), rather than attributed to the Spirit. The Spirit has become the power that works *through* Jesus' words and deeds to affect others.

2.5. Jesus' Promise of the Spirit.
As the Synoptics

present Jesus giving minimal explicit teaching on the church,* it is hardly surprising there is little on the gift of the Spirit.

Luke 11:11-13 probably belongs to the controversy *within* Jesus' ministry about the source of the power he demonstrates. It assures the disciples who have shared in this power on Jesus (cf. 9:1; 10:17-19), that the Father does not give harmful gifts ("snake" and "scorpion" are symbols for evil powers, cf. 10:19) when good gifts are sought. Similarly he gives a *good* spirit (*pneuma agathon* 𝔓⁴⁵ L [etc.] is the reading that explains the rest), not an evil one as the opponents imply (11:14-23).

The only passage that specifically promises an activity of the Spirit in the disciples is that of Mk 13:11; Mt 10:19-20; Lk 12:11-12, where the Spirit is clearly the "Spirit of prophecy." That is, it affords charismatic revelation or wisdom to the persecuted disciple. This promise assumes the disciples will already have the Spirit promised by Joel (it is only the words of defense that are given "in that hour"; not the gift of the Spirit itself). Luke's parallel saying (21:15) derives the necessary charismatic wisdom from the heavenly Lord instead, but it is clear Luke believes the *means* by which the charisma is received is the Spirit of prophecy—for he combines the wording of both promises in his description of Stephen's preaching at Acts 6:5, 10 (which also shows he does not regard the activity as restricted to persecution contexts)—and thus 21:15 implicitly asserts Jesus' future lordship over the Spirit.

Relevant also are the two final commissioning passages: Matthew 28:18-20 and Luke 24:46-49. The former does not specify a promise of the Spirit to the disciples, but is of interest as the one substantial hint of an emerging trinitarian understanding of the Spirit. Elsewhere the ideas do not necessarily move beyond Jewish traditional conceptions, but here the one divine name is spelled out in terms of Father, Son and Spirit. (Schaberg's rejection of the apparent trinitarianism, on the grounds the Matthew passage is a midrash of Dan 7:9-27, with the Holy Spirit replacing the multitude of angels, is hardly logical, even if the tradition history—itself questionable—is right.) Luke 24:49 (strongly redactional in formulation) does not use the word *Spirit* at all, but the expression "the promise of the Father" clearly refers to Joel's promise through the verbal links Luke carefully establishes in Acts 1:8; 2:17 and 2:33. Though the activity of this gift will empower the mission to all nations (*see* Gentiles), it is not to be thought of as a second blessing. Joel's promised gift of the Spirit of prophecy will become the means by which disciples experience the presence and guidance of their heavenly Lord.*

3. The Holy Spirit in John.

In the Fourth Gospel the Spirit is to be understood primarily as a development of the Jewish understanding of the "Spirit of prophecy," redefined christologically and developed in a trinitarian direction.

3.1. The Portrait of Jesus Endowed with the Spirit (Jn 1:32-34; 3:34-36; 6:63). John's account jumps from the Prolog, which proclaims Jesus the incarnate Logos who reveals the Father (1:1-18), to the Baptist's testimony concerning Jesus' reception of the Spirit (1:32-34), with no birth or infancy scenes. Kümmel, Schweizer and others have claimed John plays down Jesus' endowment in favor of his own Logos* christology—after all, he who has descended from the Father barely needs the Spirit to supply revelation (cf. 3:12-13, 31-32). But Porsch and Burge have shown this to be misleading. The very first glimpse we see of Jesus is through the testimony of the Baptist (apparently party to Jesus' vision) that he saw the Spirit descend on the Son and "rest/remain on him" (1:32-33—a reference to Is 11:2, or a way of saying the endowment was permanent or both?), and thereby identify him as the one who baptizes with the Holy Spirit. More significant is 3:34-36. The elliptic 3:34 means "Jesus utters the words of God *because* God gives *him* the Spirit without measure" (to make *Jesus* the one who gives the Spirit without measure here breaks the logic of the "because": with Burge, against Porsch). A deliberate contrast with the prophets seems intended (cf. *Lev. Rab.* 15:2, "The Holy Spirit who rests on the prophets, rests on them only by measure"). John's point is that the immeasurable gift of the Spirit (of revelation) *to* Jesus corresponds to the perfection of revelation *through* Jesus—it provides a revelation which transcends the Law* and the Prophets. This is confirmed in 3:35b where the result of the Father's love* for the Son is that "he has given all things into his hands," that is, the totality of revelation given to the Son whereby he "utters the words of God" (3:34; cf. Mt 11:27!). John 3:36 now draws the natural conclusion: If the fullness of God's revelation is imparted through the Son, then to receive that revelation brings "life."* Correspondingly, to reject it is to reject God and so to remain under his wrath. It would seem then that John portrays the gift of the Spirit to Jesus at his baptism as the gift of full revelation and the power to impart it to others. This chimes with Jesus' claim in 6:63 that his revelatory words *are* an experience of Spirit and "life." The claim goes to the heart of John's soteriology.

3.2. Birth "from Above" and Birth of "Water and Spirit" (Jn 3). "Birth from above" (3:3; cf. 3:31 for *anōthen* as "above" not "again") is a circumlocution for birth from *God.* The explanatory "birth 'of water-

and-Spirit' " (3:5) is a hendiadys which must refer to a unitary event (so not natural birth followed by spiritual birth or John's baptism followed by reception of the Spirit, etc.), and it cannot be Christian baptism, of which Nicodemus could scarcely be expected to know. L. Belleville has shown the most probable explanation is the promise in Ezekiel 36:25-26 of eschatological cleansing and new creation in true filial obedience (which *Jub.* 1:23-25 already identifies as the gift of "sonship"). Jesus claims this essentially apocalyptic hope, and concomitant "eternal life," begins to be realized where people truly believe in the Son God has sent (3:14-18). By no means all "belief" in Jesus, however, is authentic (contrast 2:23 with 2:24; 8:31a with 8:31b-36; etc.). Even the claimed belief of the disciples (6:69) does not truly become authentic faith until after the glorification (*see* Glory) of Jesus in the cross (*see* Death of Jesus) and resurrection (cf. 16:25). The Spirit-imbued revelatory teaching of Jesus (6:63) plays a vital function in coming to true belief.

3.3. The Offer of "Living Water" (4:10, 13-14). Jesus' offer of "living (i.e., flowing) water" which truly quenches thirst and "wells up" like a spring in the believer "to eternal life" merges three kinds of symbolism: (1) the general use of flowing water as a symbol of God's eschatological salvation (e.g., Is 55:1; Zech 14:8; Ezek 47:1-12); (2) refreshing and life-giving water as a symbol for divine wisdom (Prov 13:14 ["a fountain of life"]; 18:4; Sir 24:21 ["Those who eat of me will hunger still; those who drink of me shall thirst for more"]), especially as revealed in the Law (Sir 24:23-29; CD 19:34, *Sipre Deut* 11. 22, §48) and (3) water as symbolism for the gift of the Spirit (Is 44:3; 1QS 4:21; etc.). That John intends the promise to be understood as the Spirit is evident both from 4:23 ("The Hour is coming *and now is* . . ." when true worshipers worship the Father "in Spirit and truth") and from his specific equation of the offer of living water with the Spirit in 7:37-39. But it is particularly the Spirit as the revealer of divine wisdom through Jesus' Spirit-imbued teaching (cf. 6:63b) that is meant at 4:10, 13-14. Jesus, as Wisdom* incarnate, imparts new revelatory wisdom which re-creates a person and brings "life," but he does so as the one to whom the Father has given the Spirit without measure (3:34). It is the combination of revelatory "word" and Spirit together that is the "living water" (cf. 1QS 4:21-22) which effects the "birth from above."

3.4. The Redemptive-Historical Qualification on the Gift (Jn 7:37-39). John 4:10 and 6:63b suggest the gift of life-giving Spirit-imbued revelation is available within the ministry of Jesus (cf. "the hour . . . now is" at 4:23). This would appear to be supported by 13:10; 15:3 and

17:17, which declare the disciples are already "cleansed" by Jesus' word, and by the implication of saying not *all* (who seem to) actually believe (6:64; cf. 13:11; *see* Faith)—to exclude Judas.* But while these references indicate that Jesus' revelation is already beginning to transform the disciples, John provides a strong qualification of this.

3.4.1. John 7:37-39. In a context of the ceremony of water-drawing and libation at the festival of Tabernacles (interpreted in Judaism as a promise of the rivers of salvation to pour out from the Temple [Is 12:3; Ezek 47:1-12 and Zech 14:8 were read during the festival]), Jesus invites the thirsty to drink from him instead. The invitation is supported by "Scripture" (apparently summarizing its message in the light of the fulfillment expected rather than citing; no OT passage corresponds verbally to 7:38) that "out of his/ its belly shall flow rivers of living water." Most modern exegetes (e.g., Brown 1966 and Beasley-Murray 1989, Burge) repunctuate 7:37 to make Christ (rather than the believer) the source ("If anyone thirst, let him come to me, and let him drink who believes in me"). J. B. Cortes, however, argues strongly for the traditional view that the Spirit flows from the believer (the messianic community being thus seen as the embodiment of the eschatological Temple from which the renewing waters stream (cf. Ezek 47:1-12; Zech 14:8)— with Jesus as the ultimate source. Either way, John 7:39 insists the promise relates to the gift of the Spirit (cf. *m. Sukk.* 5:55a) and affirms that this gift was not yet given, for Jesus was not yet been "glorified" (i.e., exalted through the cross, resurrection and ascension* [12:23-24; 17:5]).

3.4.2. John 20:22. According to John 20:22, when Jesus appeared to the disciples, bid them Peace and recommissioned them, "he breathed on them, and said to them, 'Receive the Holy Spirit . . .' " (RSV). The verb *enephusēsen* means "insufflated" more readily than "breathed upon," and is a direct allusion to Genesis 2:7, where God breathed the breath of life into Adam (cf. Ezek 37:9). The implication is that it is only now, beyond the cross and vindication, that the Spirit-empowered revelation to the disciples achieves what had been begun within the ministry, namely new creation transformation. Essentially the same point was anticipated at 3:14-18, where the belief in the Son, which brings life, is specifically belief in the revelation of the Son afforded by the cross and vindication. Compare also John 6, where the divine wisdom Jesus' hearers are invited to eat and drink (6:35) is first spelled out as the unity of the Father and the Son in salvation (Jesus is the life-giving counterpart to the manna God gave in the wilderness), but then narrowed down to that divine wisdom expressed in the Son's revelatory death on behalf of humanity (6:51c-58). For John the fundamental problem of humankind is alienation from God expressed in unbelief, darkness (*see* Light) and ignorance of God. What is needed to overcome it is a revealer, light and knowledge of God—which it is precisely the mission of the Son, empowered by the Spirit, to bring (8:28; 14:10; 15:22-24). His revelatory word frees (8:31-36); to "hear" it is to experience the Spirit transforming through it and to taste life (6:63b). But for John, the exaltation through the cross both deals objectively with the sin that caused the fundamental alienation (contra Bultmann and Forestell: see Turner 1990) and also provides the supreme revelation of the unity of the Father and the Son in saving love. Correspondingly, only after the Easter event can the word of Jesus be released in full transforming power through the Spirit.

3.5. Jesus Promises the Spirit as "Another Paraclete" (Jn 14-16). In three passages (14:16-26; 15:26-27; 16:7-15) John speaks of a coming gift of the Holy Spirit (14:26), or "Spirit of Truth" (14:17; 15:26; 16:13: cf. *Jub* 25:14; *T. Jud.* 20:1-5; 1QS 3:18-25), to act as a "paraclete" (*paraklētos*: 14:16, 26; 15:26; 16:7).

3.5.1. The Meaning of Paraklētos. In Greek the word is formally a passive verbal adjective, "one called alongside" (especially to offer assistance in a court), and so an "advocate" (though not with the professional legal sense of the Latin *advocatus)*, and indeed later Rabbinic Judaism came to use *p^eraqlit* (a loan word) for "advocate" (cf. *Pirqe Aboth* 4:11). Because, however, the functions actually attributed to "the Paraclete" in John are primarily teaching, revealing and interpreting Jesus to the disciples (with forensic functions only explicit at 15:26[?]; 16:8-11), other meanings of *paraklētos* have been championed. These include (1) "Comforter" (derived from *parakalein*, "to encourage" [so Davies]; but John does not use the verb, and this etymology should require an active not passive adjective); (2) "Exhorter" (so, roughly, Barrett 1950, deriving from *paraklēsis* and facing similar difficulties) and (3) "Helper" (so Bultmann 1971, by somewhat forced linguistic and conceptual association with [plural] "helpers" [arguably rather "bearers of light"] in alleged Mandean background). But none of these have forensic functions. Those that have accepted the sense "advocate" have generally found the background in the angelic intercessor-defender figures of the OT and intertestamental literature (so Mowinckel and Johansson), and Qumran (so O. Betz, who thinks John modelled the Paraclete/Spirit of Truth primarily on Qumran's cosmic dualism (Spirit of Truth v. Spirit

of Error; *see* Dead Sea Scrolls) and (e.g., for the personal traits) their Michael mythology. (For a review of the complex discussion see G. Johnston [esp. chap. 7] and G. Burge [chap. 1]. To date these background studies [esp. Betz], illuminate various traits of John's portrait of the Paraclete rather than satisfactorily explaining the redactional whole.)

3.5.2. The Paraclete is Modeled on Jesus. This point is made both in Jesus' promise of "another Paraclete of the same kind" (*allos*, and in the deliberate parallelism between Jesus and what is promised of the Spirit [e.g.]: (1) both "come forth"/are "sent"' from the Father into the world* (3:16-17; 5:43; 16:27-28; 18:37 par. 14:26; 15:26; 16:7-8, 13); (2) both are called "holy" (6:39 par. 14:26) and are characterized by "the truth" (14:6 par. 14:17; 15:26; 16:13); (3) if Jesus is the great teacher* (cf. 13:13-14), the Paraclete will "teach you . . . all things" (14:26); and (4) just as the Messiah bears witness to God and reveals all things (4:25-26; cf. 1:18; 3:34-36; etc.)—supremely himself and the Father—so too the Paraclete will witness to and reveal especially the glorified Son (15:26-27; 16:13-14). And as Jesus set out to convince and convict the world, which nevertheless did not "receive" him (1:12 etc.), so too the Paraclete's task is to convince and convict the world (Jn 16:8-12), but the world does not receive him either (14:17; 15:18-26). The *Sitz-im-Leben* of these parallels (as Müller has shown) is the usual concern of the Jewish genre "Farewell Discourses"*; namely, to establish how the decisive initiative made by the man of God will be continued beyond his death. Jesus has acted as the Paraclete so far; the Spirit is to take over that role.

3.5.3. The Paraclete Will Mediate the Presence of the Father and the Glorified Son (14:16-26). Having assured them of the gift of the Spirit in 14:16-17, in vv. 18 and 19 Jesus promises he will not leave the disciples desolate but will come to them in such a way that "the world" will not see him—he will manifest himself to any disciple who loves him (14:21). When this is pressed by Judas in 14:22, Jesus reasserts that (if a disciple love him) he and the Father will come and make their home with him. This promise cannot refer to Jesus' "Second Coming" (for then the world *shall* see); nor to resurrection appearances which were neither dependent on the love of the disciples, nor capable of being described as the coming of the Father and the Son to dwell with the disciple. As these affirmations are sandwiched by promises of the Spirit-Paraclete (14:14-17; 14:25-26), and as (in Judaism) the Spirit of prophecy was regarded as the presence of God in revelation, most exegetes infer that it is precisely the promised Spirit that will mediate the presence and self-revelation of Father and Son. Those who deny this (e.g., Beasley-Murray) do not tell us how Christ and the Father are supposed to "manifest themselves" to the disciple, nor explain why (if they can) John thinks the Spirit need be given at all. We conclude the Paraclete/Advocate is the Holy Spirit in a special role, namely as the personal presence of Jesus in the Christian while Jesus is with the Father (so Brown), though without agreeing that John significantly collapsed the delayed Parousia into his pneumatology.

3.5.4. The Paraclete as Teacher and Revealer (14:26; 16:12-14). The disciples cannot take in (16:12) or understand the significance of what Jesus has said and done until he is glorified (16:25). Consequently, the Spirit-Paraclete is given to *remind* them of Jesus' teaching (14:26) and to *interpret* it to them (e.g., 2:22). The main task of the Spirit in John is to provide a particular sort of charismatic wisdom: to bring true comprehension of the significance of the historical revelation in Christ. The truth into which he leads (16:13) is not the later doctrines of the church, but principally the truth which Jesus has incarnated and taught, and concerning which Jesus would readily explain more at the Last Supper* (if the disciples could only absorb it [16:12]); the things of Jesus and which glorify him (cf. 16:14). Even the promise of the Spirit declaring "the things that are to come" (16:13), in context of the Last Supper, refers primarily (though not exclusively) to the all-important coming events of the cross and exaltation, not the End. As Porsch put it: "Jesus brings the truth, and makes it present through his coming into the world; the Spirit-Paraclete opens up this truth and creates the entrance into it for believers" (300). The title of E. Franck's monograph on the Spirit-Paraclete—*Revelation Taught*—points to the centrality of this motif for John.

3.5.5. The Paraclete as "Advocate" and the Christian Mission. The reason why this Revealer-Teacher is called "another Paraclete" (= "advocate," 14:16) is best clarified in terms of John's presentation of Jesus' ministry under the extended metaphor of a cosmic trial. The issue contended is whether or not Jesus truly is the final manifestation of God, very Son from the Father, whom to know is "Life" transcending the possibilities offered by Judaism (cf. 20:31). As the sent one, Jesus has a mission to convince the world of God's saving truth, which he incarnates and reveals, and this mission dominates the Gospel (within 5:31-47 alone Jesus points to five "witnesses" on his side): he is the chief advocate of the case with which the disciples have become identified. The impending removal of Jesus through cross and exaltation, cannot

be allowed to leave the disciples "as orphans" (correctly NIV; RSV's "desolate" misses the point)—that is, defenseless. Nor may the case be lost because reduced to silence. Rather the disciples are now "sent" as Jesus was "sent" (Jn 20:21; cf. 17:17-18), and the Spirit from the heavenly Lord is given to them to take over the earthly Jesus' advocacy of the case (15:26-27; 16:7b-11). According to 16:8-11, the Spirit-Paraclete will prosecute the case against the world by exposing it with respect to sin (that its unbelief is the essence of sin), righteousness (that its claim to righteousness is false [?]; or—more probably—that its verdict on Jesus is reversed by the exaltation), and judgment (that the power that engineered Jesus' death, and continues to oppose Christ, stands condemned in Jesus' vindication). But the connection with 16:12-15 must be observed. The Spirit will convince the world of these things precisely by revealing the truth and by teaching its significance to the disciples. 16:8-11 does not mean the Spirit offers independent witness; John knows of no witness by the Spirit that is not witness through the church. But equally the disciples only give their witness as ones to whom the Spirit has revealed Jesus and the significance of his life, death and resurrection. It is thus as teacher and revealer that the Spirit will also be Paraclete or Advocate. This does not mean John thinks the Paraclete is given as a second blessing of revelation and wisdom for missionary empowering; but that he thinks the post-ascension gift of the Spirit is simultaneously the means by which the disciple "understands" the gospel and the means of ongoing knowledge of the presence and guidance of the Father and the Son, and this itself constitutes the witness to Christ and so is "the Spirit of mission."

3.5.6. Concluding Theological and Critical Remarks. A minor debate continues as to when John thought the Spirit was first given as the "Paraclete" (whether at 20:22 or beyond the period of the Gospel, when first the Spirit replaces Jesus). More theologically significant are the christological and trinitarian conclusions to be drawn: (1) Jesus' lordship over the Spirit expressed in his sending and commissioning of the "Paraclete" (15:26; 16:7) attest a fully divine christology; (2) the portrait of the Spirit as a replacement figure, and one which goes well beyond the frequent but incidental personifications of the Spirit in Judaism, takes the pneumatology in the direction of trinitarianism. Major differences center on the origin of the traditions about the Spirit—whether they are purely Christian creative midrash* around Jesus' minimal teaching on the Spirit as an advocate in time of persecution (2.5. above) or more substantially derive from Jesus—but a convincing tradition-history of the material would at present be very hard to establish (*see* Tradition Criticism). Nevertheless it may be observed that the Johannine Spirit teaching, with its strong wisdom accent, is evidently rooted in the Jewish conception of the Spirit as the "Spirit of prophecy," and no single formulation demonstrably moves beyond the circle of what could be expected if the Jesus we otherwise know from the Synoptics were to express his teaching in specifically pneumatological terms.

See also BAPTISM; BIRTH OF JESUS; DEMON, DEVIL, SATAN; GOD; JOHN THE BAPTIST; NEW BIRTH.

BIBLIOGRAPHY. C. K. Barrett, *The Holy Spirit and the Gospel Tradition* (2d ed., London: SPCK, 1966); idem, "The Holy Spirit in the Fourth Gospel," *JTS* 1 (1950) 1-15; G. R. Beasley-Murray, *John* (WBC 36; Waco: Word, 1989); L. Belleville " 'Born of Water and Spirit': John 3:5," *TJ* 1 (1980) 125-41; E. Best, "Spirit-Baptism," *NovT* 4 (1960) 236-43; O. Betz, *Der Paraklet* (Leiden: Brill, 1963); R. E. Brown, *The Birth of the Messiah* (New York: Doubleday, 1977); idem, *The Gospel according to John* (AB 29; Garden City, NY: Doubleday, 1966, 1970); idem, "The Paraclete in the Fourth Gospel," *NTS* 13 (1966-67) 113-32; R. Bultmann, *The Gospel of John* (Philadelphia: Westminster, 1971); idem, *The History of the Synoptic Tradition* (Oxford: Blackwell, 1963); idem, *Theology of the New Testament* (2 vols.; New York: Scribner's, 1951, 1955); G. M. Burge, *The Anointed Community: The Holy Spirit in the Johannine Community* (Grand Rapids: Eerdmans, 1987); M. A. Chevallier, "Luc et L'Esprit à la Mémoire du P. Augustin George (1915-1977)," *RSR* 56 (1982) 1-16; H. Conzelmann, *The Theology of St. Luke* (London: Faber and Faber, 1960); J. B. Cortes, "Yet Another Look at John 7:37-38," *CBQ* 29 (1967) 75-86; J. G. Davies, "The Primary Meaning of ΠΑΡΑΚΛΗΤΟΣ," *JTS* 4 (1953) 35-38; J. D. G. Dunn, *Baptism in the Holy Spirit: A Re-examination of the New Testament Teaching on the Gift of the Spirit in Relation to Pentecostalism Today* (Philadelphia: Westminster, 1970); idem, *Jesus and the Spirit* (Philadelphia: Westminster, 1975); idem, "Spirit and Fire Baptism," *NovT* 14 (1972) 81-92; J. A. Fitzmyer, *The Gospel According to Luke* (AB 28; New York: Doubleday, 1981, 1985); J. T. Forestell, *The Word of the Cross: Salvation as Revelation in the Fourth Gospel* (Rome: Pontifical Biblical Institute, 1970); E. Franck, *Revelation Taught: The Paraclete in the Gospel of John* (Lund: Gleerup, 1985); A. George, *Études sur l'Oeuvre de Luc* (Paris: Gabalda, 1978); D. E. Holwerda, *The Holy Spirit and Eschatology in the Gospel of John* (Kampen: Kok, 1959); A. Johansson, *Parakletoi* (Lund: Gleerup, 1940); G. Johnston, *The Spirit-Paraclete in the Gospel of John* (Cambridge: University Press, 1970); W. G. Kümmel, *The Theology of the New Testament*

(Nashville: Abingdon, 1973); H. Leisegang, *Pneuma Hagion* (Leipzig: Hinrichs, 1922); M. R. Mansfield, *"Spirit and Gospel" in Mark* (Peabody, MA: Hendrickson, 1987); S. Mowinckel, "Die Vorstellung des Spätjudentums vom heiligen Geist als Fürsprecher und der johanneische Paraklet," *ZNW* 52 (1933) 97-130; G. B. Müller, "Die Parakletenvorstellung im Johannesevangelium," *ZTK* 71 (1974) 31-78; F. Porsch, *Pneuma und Wort. Ein exegetischer Beitrag zur Pneumatologie des Johannesevangeliums* (Frankfurt: Knecht, 1974); J. Schaberg, *The Father, the Son and the Holy Spirit: The Triadic Phrase in Matthew 28:19b* (Chico: Scholars, 1982); G. Schneider, *Das Evangelium nach Lukas* (Gütersloh: Mohn, 1977); H. Schürmann, "Zur Traditionsgeschichte der Nazareth-Perikope Lk 4.16-30," in *Mélanges Bibliques*, ed. A. Descamps and A. de Halleux (Gembloux: Duculot, 1970) 187-205; E. Schweizer, "πνεῦμα κτλ," *TDNT* VI.389-455; R. B. Sloan, *The Favorable Year of the Lord: A Study of Jubilary Theology in the Gospel of Luke* (Austin: Schola, 1977); A. Strobel, "Die Ausrufung des Jobel-jahres in der Nazarethpredigt Jesu: zur apokalyptischen Tradition Lk. 4:16-30," in *Jesus of Nazareth*, ed. W. Eltester (Berlin: de Gruyter, 1972) 51-75; C. Tuckett, "Luke 4,16-30, Isaiah and Q," in *Logia: Les Paroles de Jésus—The Sayings of Jesus*, ed. J. Delobel (Leuven: University Press, 1982) 343-54; M. M. B. Turner, "Atonement and the Death of Jesus in John—Some Questions to Bultmann and Forestell," *EvQ* 62 (1990) 99-122; idem, "Jesus and the Spirit in Lukan Perspective," *TynB* 32 (1981) 3-42; idem, "The Significance of Receiving the Spirit in John's Gospel," *VoxEv* 10 (1977) 24-42; idem, "The Spirit and the Power of Jesus' Miracles in the Lucan Conception," *NovT* 33 (1991) 124-52; J. E. Yates, *The Spirit and the Kingdom* (London: SPCK, 1963).

M. M. B. Turner

HYPOCRITE

In contemporary English *hypocrite* denotes an insincere person, especially someone who pretends to be pious or virtuous when he or she really is not. Interpreters in recent years have expressed doubts about the adequacy of this traditional definition in connection with the NT. Alternative suggestions have been advanced on the basis of the use of the word in the Greek versions of the OT and on the basis of a fresh analysis of the "woes" in Matthew 23 (*see* Blessing and Woe).

1. Vocabulary and Historical Background
2. Usage in the Gospels

1. Vocabulary and Historical Background.

The words in question are the noun "hypocrite"

(*hypokritēs*) and its cognates, the noun "hypocrisy" (*hypokrisis*) and the verb "pretend" (*hypokrinomai*). Matthew uses words of this family almost three times as frequently as Luke (14/5) and seven times more frequently than Mark (14/2). (In addition *hypokritēs* appears in a variant reading at Mt 23:14.) The words never appear in John's Gospel. Statistics alone reveal that the charge of hypocrisy is a Matthean concern.

1.1. Classical Usage. In early Greek the active verb *hypokrinō* meant to "interrogate" and the middle verb *hypokrinomai* meant to "answer" (used both of human beings and of oracles to whom questions were put). When Attic Greek settled on *apokrinomai* for "answer," it began to use *hypokrinomai* to mean "interpret," or "explain," oracles, dreams or riddles.

The verb also came to mean "act a part in a drama," because the drama is speech in dialog with questions and answers or because the actor is an interpreter of the poet-dramatist and of the underlying myth. Later the word was used of orators in the sense of "deliver a speech" and then to "speak in exaggerated fashion." Especially under Stoic auspices the word came to be used metaphorically: all the world is a stage, and we are all actors summoned to play well our assigned parts. It was then a short step to the negative sense of "deceive" or "pretend."

Polybius notes how envoys of hostile tribes "pretended" to be humble in their words to Roman authorities but in reality were not submissive (Polybius *Hist.* 35.2.13). Epictetus declares that he is not "deceiving" or "playing a part" (used in parallel with "being silly") in explaining an ethical point (*Disc.* 1.25.1).

The history of the nouns parallels that of the verb. *Hypokrisis* once meant "reply" and then in Attic Greek came to mean "playing a part," the "delivery" (of a speech) and finally "pretense." *Hypokritēs* meant "interpreter" (of dreams or riddles), "actor," "reciter" and then "pretender" (LSJ, BAGD, *TDNT*). The Latin Vulgate simply followed a Latin tradition of transliterating the Greek by means of the noun *hypokrita* (or *hypokrites*) and *hypokrisis*. In Latin rhetoric and drama *hypokrisis* meant "mimicry," while *hypokrita* (*hypokrites*) meant a "mime" or "accompanist" who represented in gestures or dance what the actor was expressing with words (Suetonius *Nero* 24).

But is classical and secular Greek the proper trajectory within which to understand the use of these words in the NT, or should we look instead to the LXX, understanding it as representing a separate biblical Jewish-Greek trajectory?

1.2. Hellenistic-Jewish Usage. In the ancient Greek versions of the Bible the word group sometimes means simply "wickedness." The LXX uses *hypokritēs* at Job 34:30 and 36:13 to translate the Hebrew *ḥānēp*. That Hebrew word is ordinarily rendered *asebēs* ("godless," Job 8:13; 15:34; Is 33:14; Prov 11:9), *paranomos* ("transgressor," Job 17:8; 20:5) or *anomos* ("lawless," Is 9:16; 10:6; 32:6; 33:14) in the LXX. But *hypokritēs* or a cognate occurs for *ḥānēp* at these passages in the Greek versions of Theodotion, Aquila and Symmachus.

Because *hypokritēs* renders *ḥānēp* in these passages, and because Israel did not have a theater or dramatic tradition and regarded the theater as a pagan institution, Wilckens and Young deny that the modern sense of "acting a part" or "deceiving" is meant in all uses of *hypokritēs* and cognates in Jewish Greek. They suggest that "lawless, corrupt or unrighteous person" captures the essential meaning of the word.

Batey has argued that the presence of Hellenistic (*see* Hellenism) theaters in the cities of Palestine, including one at Sepphoris a few miles from Nazareth (although it cannot be dated with certainty to the first century), supports the notion that Jesus and his hearers were familiar with the vocabulary of drama, including the word *actor*.

It is simply a fact that Greek-speaking Jews both in biblical and non-biblical writings frequently used *hypokritēs* and cognates in the sense of "pretending" or "playing a part with intent to deceive." For example, the agent of Antiochus arrived in Jerusalem and "pretended" to be peaceably disposed toward the Jews, although he was looking for an opportunity to destroy them (2 Macc 5:25). Pious Eleazar, advised to "pretend" to eat swine's flesh, replied that to do so would be to "enact a part," something ill-becoming to him and inconsistent with the truth he had lived so far and with the Law* he loved (2 Macc 6:21-25; 4 Macc 6:15-23).

The *Psalms of Solomon* condemn high government officials and religious leaders who "give the impression" of piety while their hearts are far from God. They are the kind of people who commit sins at night as if no one could see them (*Pss. Sol.* 4:5-6), and by fraud they "deceive" innocent people (*Pss. Sol.* 4:22). Sirach 1:29 calls "hypocrites" those who praise God with their lips while their hearts are not fixed on God. Josephus* reports many stories of intrigue and double-cross, describing how politicians in Palestine scripted events, directed other actors and themselves played roles, pretending friendship while plotting destruction (Josephus *J. W.* 1 §§471, 516, 520; cf. *J.W.* 1 §318; 2 §587; *Ant.* 2 §160). And the same use is found often in Philo (see Wilckens).

2. Usage in the Gospels.

In the Gospels the odor of deceit and malice hovers around the words. In the pericope on paying tribute (*see* Taxes) to Caesar (Mk 12:13-17; Mt 22:15-22; Lk 20:20-26) all three Synoptic Gospels use words of the *hypokri-* family but in different places and in different ways. In his introduction to the pericope Luke (20:20) says that scribes and chief priests* watched Jesus and sent spies, "who pretended *(hypokrinomenous)* to be sincere" (RSV; cf. Lk 12:1). Mark (12:15) says that Jesus suspected the Pharisees* of "hypocrisy" *(hypokrisis)*, while Luke speaks of their "cunning" *(panourgia,* Lk 20:23) and Matthew of their "wickedness" *(ponēria,* Mt 22:18). In this same pericope, Matthew says that Jesus addressed his opponents as "hypocrites" (Mt 22:18). Thus all three Synoptic Evangelists in their varied ways render their verdict that Jesus' opponents came to him under false pretenses, flattering him and giving the impression that they sought his considered response to a difficult issue but actually seeking only to trap him.

The sense of a disastrous inconsistency is strong. The words imply some kind of fatal rift, whether between outer appearance ("lips") and inner reality ("hearts," Mk 7:6; Mt 15:7, both quoting Is 29:13; cf. Sir 1:29) or between ability in one sphere and inability in another (Lk 12:56), or between compassion in one area of life and unfeeling stubbornness in another (Lk 13:15-16), or between hypersensitivity to the failings of others and blindness to one's own shortcomings (Mt 7:5; Lk 6:42; cf. Rom 2:1-5).

Matthew frequently criticizes the discrepancy between hearts and lips (Mt 15:7), between hearing and doing (Mt 7:24-27), between telling and doing (Mt 23:3; cf. 21:28-32). And Matthew heaps scorn on people who perform acts traditionally associated with the worship* of God, doing them not as acts of worship but strutting about and performing them as attention-getters among humans (Mt 23:5; 6:2, 5, 16; cf. *Pss. Sol.* 4:6, 22).

In his Gospel Matthew ranges "hypocrisy" alongside "lawlessness" *(anomia,* Mt 7:23; 13:41; 23:28; 24:12) as opposed to the virtues of righteousness (Mt 5:6, 20; 6:1, 33; *see* Justice, Righteousness), perfection (Mt 5:48; 19:21) and wholeness (Mt 22:37-40). These latter terms speak of integrity and soundness, while "hypocrisy" describes a splintering, a division, an inconsistency between the inner and outer person, between hearts and lips, between words and deeds.

But do the passages cited so far determine the meaning of "hypocrites" in the "woes" Jesus pronounces (Mt 23:13, 14, 15, 23, 25, 27, 29; cf. 23:28; cf. Lk 11:39-52)? Albright and Mann fasten on the most ancient Greek sense of the word as involving an act of interpretation. Accordingly, Jesus is involved not in the cultivation of private virtues but in public debates about the meaning of the Law. Believing that Jesus represented the prophetic versus what they call the growing legalism of scribes,* they translate *hypokrites* as "overscrupulous" interpreter, "casuist," "pettifogging lawyer."

Garland argues for a wider range of meaning than that which the English *hypocrite* allows. He concedes that in some Matthean passages the sense of deception is present. Nevertheless, on the basis of Qumran's (*see* Dead Sea Scrolls) characterization of Pharisees as false interpreters ("seekers after smooth things"), he argues that Matthew portrays Jesus and his opponents as locked in a struggle concerning correct interpretation. The contrast in the woes, he thinks, is not between heart and lips (Mt 15:7) or between saying and doing (Mt 23:3). It is rather the contrast between the tradition of the religious teachers and the Law* of God. The teachers are guilty not of conscious pretense or sham but of nullifying God's intention by twisting the Law to their own purposes in their interpretations.

The English word *fraud* or *imposter* seems to capture the sense of *hypokrites* in Matthew 23 and in most other uses in Jewish-Greek literature and the NT. It is regularly used of teachers and leaders who are inauthentic, whether consciously or unconsciously. The sense of being false interpreters arises not from the etymology of the word (contra Albright and Mann), nor from a tradition of use like that at Qumran (pace Garland) but from the fact that the word is used in Matthew 23 of scribes, who were interpreters of the Law.

Matthew 23 contains seven woes (eight, if 23:14 is original) against the scribes and Pharisees as hypocrites. That chapter has contributed to the terrible equation: Pharisee = hypocrite. But Matthew has probably collected these sayings which condemn some habits of past religious leaders (scribes and Pharisees) not to inform readers about the character of all scribes and Pharisees, nor to wage polemic against the Pharisaic leadership of Jamnia but in order to campaign against parallel attitudes and habits he discerns in certain Christian teachers of his own religious community (see Minear, van Tilborg, Garland).

See also ANTI-SEMITISM; PHARISEES; SCRIBES.

BIBLIOGRAPHY. W. F. Albright and C. S. Mann, *The Gospel According to Matthew* (AB; Garden City: Doubleday, 1971) cvi-cxxiii; R. A. Batey, "Jesus and the Theatre," *NTS* 30 (1984) 563-74; D. E. Garland, *The Intention of Matthew 23* (NovT 52; Leiden: E. J. Brill, 1979); P. Minear, "False Prophecy and Hypocrisy in the Gospel of Matthew," in *Neues Testament und Kirche,* ed. J. Gnilka (Freiburg: Herder, 1974) 76-93; S. van Tilborg, *The Jewish Leaders in Matthew* (Leiden: E. J. Brill, 1972); U. Wilckens, "ὑποκρίνομαι κτλ," *TDNT* VIII.559-71; F. W. Young, "Hypocrisy," *IDB* 2:668-69.

R. H. Smith

I

"I AM" SAYINGS

The unique authority* and identity of Jesus are expressed particularly in the Fourth Gospel through sayings which employ the Greek formula *egō eimi* ("I am"). In some cases a simple predicate is given ("I am the bread of life"), in others an absolute usage is playing a specialized role in John's christology. The Synoptics frequently employ the so-called authoritative *egō* ("I") for Jesus, but even here the Fourth Gospel uses it more: Matthew uses *egō* 29 times, Mark 17 times, Luke 23 times and John 134 times. Likewise, *egō eimi* is used by Matthew five times (Mt 14:27; 22:32; 24:5; 26:22, 25), Mark three times (Mk 6:50; 13:6; 14:62) and Luke four times (Lk 1:19; 21:8; 22:70; 24:39), but John employs it thirty times (see below).

1. Synoptic Use
2. The Fourth Gospel
3. Background
4. The "I AM" in Johannine Christology

1. Synoptic Use.

Greek generally employs personal pronouns to express emphasis or antithesis. Thus, throughout Matthew, Mark and Luke, Jesus asserts his authority and contrasts his teaching with that of others by using such emphatic pronouns. This is especially evident in Matthew's Sermon on the Mount (see Sermon on the Mount) where Jesus teaches, "You have heard that it was said . . . but I say unto you" (*egō legō humin;* see Mt 5:22, 28, 32, 34, 39, 44 etc.). This speech form underscores Jesus' unique mission and is echoed throughout the Gospels ("all things have been given to me by my father," Lk 10:22).

There are, however, a number of Synoptic texts which may betray a more specialized meaning. In Mark 6:45-50 during the storm Jesus identifies himself saying *"egō eimi"* ("It is I") while trying to "pass by them." This parallels the theophanies given to Moses* on Mt. Sinai (Ex 33 LXX) and Elijah (1 Kings 19) where the Lord passes by (*paralambanō*) and the divine name is revealed. Is Jesus using *egō eimi* simply to identify himself, or is he too revealing a divine

name? The same question pertains to Mark 13:6 when Jesus warns about a future age when many will come in his name saying *"egō eimi."* During Jesus' trial (Mk 14:62; see Trial of Jesus), when the priest* asks if Jesus is the Christ,* he answers *"egō eimi."* And in Luke 24:39 the resurrected (see Resurrection) Christ identifies himself: "See my hands and my feet, it is I (*egō eimi*)." Are these innocent expressions of self-disclosure, or are they trying to convey something more profound?

2. The Fourth Gospel.

The repeated use of *egō* (134 times) and the highly specialized use of *egō eimi* in the Fourth Gospel shows that these terms carried a unique importance in Johannine theology (see John, Gospel of). John's use of "I Am" may be organized in the following way.

2.1. Common Identification. This use is common in John in answer to the question "Who are you?" or "What are you?" In John 1:20 the Baptist (see John the Baptist) says, "I am not the Christ." In John 18:35 Pilate asks, "Am I a Jew?" This use is evidenced throughout the Gospel and bears no theological importance.

2.2. An Explicit Predicate. In seven passages John records the well-known "I Am" sayings where Jesus describes himself using a graphic metaphor: "I am the bread* of life*" (6:35, 41, 48, 51); "I am the light* of the world" (8:12; 9:5); "I am the door of the sheep" (10:7, 9); "I am the good shepherd*" (10:11, 14); "I am the resurrection and the life" (11:25); "I am the way, the truth, and the life" (14:6); and "I am the true vine*" (15:1, 5).

These texts are often accompanied by discourses in John and serve to contrast Jesus with the Judaism* he is fulfilling. Hence, "I am the good shepherd" means that other shepherds are unnecessary and untrustworthy. These paragraphs in John serve in a way similar to the Synoptic parables* of the kingdom ("the kingdom of God is like . . ."; see Kingdom of God) where concrete images fill out the meaning of Jesus' announcement.

2.3. An Uncertain Predicate. More difficult are

passages where Jesus says "I Am" and we are left uncertain if we are to supply a predicate or if the phrase is being used for self-identification. For example, in John 6:20 the frightened disciples* are comforted when Jesus says, *"egō eimi,* do not be afraid." He may mean, "It is I" (so Barrett, who compares it with Jn 9:9). On the other hand, it may be describing a divine theophany (much like Mk 6:45-50) with some sort of divine name at its center. The same problem arises in John 18:5 during Jesus' arrest. When the soldiers announce that they are seeking Jesus of Nazareth, Jesus responds by saying *"egō eimi."* Again, this may mean "I am (the one whom you seek)." But John takes it a step further. John 18:6 reports, "When he said to them, *'egō eimi,'* they drew back and fell to the ground." The mere uttering of this name creates a powerful revelation which leaves the arresting party prostrate before God.*

2.4. An Absolute Use. There are at least four texts where the use of *egō eimi* seems incomplete and the words have assumed the form of a title: John 8:24, "For you will die in your sins unless you believe that I am"; John 8:28, "When you have lifted up the Son of man, then you will know that I am"; John 8:58, "Truly, Truly I say to you, before Abraham* was I am"; John 13:19, "I tell you this now—so that when it does take place you may believe that I am." In each case the verse seems truncated. In 8:58 before Abraham *what was Jesus?* The text gives no predicate. But as we shall see, John no doubt wishes for us to recall the sacred divine name unveiled in the OT and well known in Rabbinic Judaism (*see* Rabbinic Traditions and Writings).

3. Background.

Scholars have been divided in their explanation of this phenomenon. Many would deny a consistent theological theme running throughout John, while still others believe that John is echoing religious titles from other sources. The solution to the riddle is also tied up with the cultural milieu which we deem primary to the background of the gospel.

3.1. Non-Jewish Sources. Egō eimi enjoyed a widespread use among the religions of the ancient Near East. Parallels have been found in the magic formulas of Isis, the opening tract of the Hermetica (Poimandres) and Mandaean texts (see Bultmann, 225 note 3; Barrett, 291-93). In each case, however, it seems clear that either the predicate is supplied ("I am Poimandres," *Corp. Herm.* 1.2; "I am Isis," Ios inscription) or the form is used for self-identification ("I am the one who . . ."). But in no case have parallels been found to the Johannine absolute use in which *egō eimi*

virtually becomes a title.

3.2. The OT. The Septuagint shows abundant examples of the *egō eimi* with predicates (Gen 28:13; Ex 15:26; Ps 35:3). This is the form of God's self-disclosure when he employs a metaphor to depict himself: "The Lord appeared to Abraham and said . . . 'I am El Shaddai [God all-powerful]' " (Gen 17:1). Frequently, God affirms his exclusive relationship to Israel saying, "I am the LORD and there is no other" (Is 45:18; Hos 13:4).

The most important use is found in Exodus 3. In Exodus 3:6 God introduces himself to Moses on Mt. Sinai saying, "I am the God of your father, the God of Abrahām, the God of Isaac and the God of Jacob." Feeling that this is insufficient, Moses inquires further about God's name (Ex 3:13-14), to which God responds, "I am who I am." This becomes the truly personal name of God in Israel's faith. *YHWH* (the Hebrew consonants, used throughout the OT for the Divine Name) originated with the Hebrew verb "to be" and thus the LXX translated Exodus 3:14 *egō eimi ho ōn* ("I am the one who is"). This became the covenant name of God and was used on its own as a title (Deut 32:39). This is especially true in Isaiah where the Greek text makes *egō eimi* a consistent title for God, "I am, I am he who blots out your sins" (Is 43:25; cf. 51:12; 52:6).

3.3. Palestinian Judaism. The Septuagint is not the only source which shows a unique interest in the "I am" as a code name for Yahweh; the same appears to be true of post-biblical Judaism. *1 Enoch* (108:12), *Jubilees* (24:22) and even Philo (commentary on Exodus 3:14) all show a marked interest in the name. This flourished especially in the apocalyptic* literature and thus we find it used even in the Christian apocalypse (Rev 1:17).

4. The "I AM" in Johannine Christology.

John employs the *egō eimi* in order to echo this extensive OT background. Jesus has come to unveil the Father's name for all the world. He comes in the name of the Father (5:43; 12:13) and does all of his works in his Father's name (10:25). In 17:6 and 17:26 Jesus sums up the nature of his mission in a prayer* to the Father, "I have manifested your name to those whom you gave me out of the world." Keeping the disciples in "the name of the Father" is similarly important (17:11-12). Just as in the OT, the revelation of Yahweh always includes the disclosure of his covenant name. Jesus is carrying on this historic pattern.

John also employs this divine name to show his severe critique of Judaism and its obsolete rituals (*see*

Anti-Semitism). Jesus becomes in his person the focus of religious desire. He is bread, water,* light,* truth* and life.* In many cases Jesus can be found standing in the midst of a religious festival (Jn 6—8, 10; *see* Feasts) or personal crisis (Jn 11, 14) directing spiritual longing and need to himself. This is appropriate and justified since John is trying to make a larger theological claim about Jesus: The Son is not simply representing the Father here but in some fashion is bearing the Father's presence to the world (*see* Son of God).

This is the remarkable new step taken by the Fourth Gospel. Jesus is the Lord incarnate, and thus he himself bears this divine name. He is not simply a courier of revelation like Moses. He is revelation. Jesus' own name has power and significance (1:12; 2:23; 3:18; 14:26), and thus prayer uttered in his name will witness results (14:13; 15:16; 16:23-24, 26). But the power of prayer in Jesus' name resides in the fact that, as 14:13 shows, the Father himself is being glorified through Jesus. In fact, it is the Father himself who is present in Jesus. Thus, in the immediately preceding section (14:8-11) Philip is told that he sees the Father when he looks at Jesus. The Father and the Son share an intimate reciprocity and to glorify one is to glorify the other (*see* Glory).

The principal theological contribution of the "I AM" sayings is therefore christological. It buttresses Jesus' divine status by showing that he can work, speak and act in the Father's stead. He is no mere human. He is the Word (*see* Logos) of God dwelling in human flesh. But as such, he is also the Father's emissary— and more—and the "I AM" title he bears is simply one more of his many credentials.

This christological development linking the Father to Jesus is not unusual in the Fourth Gospel. For example, in John 5 when Jesus is accused of violating the Sabbath,* his defense turns on his connection with the Father. Since the Father works on the Sabbath giving life, so must the Son (5:19-24). Jesus' works are justified not because some day the Father will vindicate them, but because Jesus is doing the Father's work directly; and any perceptive observer should recognize this. Thus, to dishonor the Son in this situation is to offend the Father as well.

In the many "I AM" sayings Jesus is publicly applying the divine name of God—and God's authoritative presence—to himself. No prophet* or priest in Israelite history would ever have done this. For Judaism it is the most severe christological affirmation of all, leading audiences in the Gospel either to believe in Jesus or accuse him of blasphemy.*

See also AUTHORITY AND POWER; JOHN, GOSPEL OF.

BIBLIOGRAPHY.   C. K. Barrett, *The Gospel according to St. John* (2d ed.; Philadelphia: Westminster, 1978) 291-93, 341-42; G. Braumann and H.-G. Link, "I am," *NIDNTT* 2.278-283; R. E. Brown, *The Gospel according to John I-XII* (AB; Garden City, NY: Doubleday, 1966) 533-38; Buchsel, "εἰμί, ὁ ὤν," *TDNT* II.398-400; R. Bultmann, *The Gospel of John* (Philadelphia: Westminster, 1971) 225-26; D. Daube, "The I AM of the Messianic Presence," in *The New Testament and Rabbinic Judaism* (London: Athlone, 1956) 325-29; B. Harner, *The "I AM" of the Fourth Gospel* (Philadelphia: Fortress, 1970); W. Manson, "The *Ego Eimi* of the Messianic Presence in the New Testament," in *Jesus and the Christian* (London: James Clark, 1967) 174-83; L. Morris, *Jesus Is the Christ: Studies in the Theology of John* (Grand Rapids: Eerdmans, 1989) 107-125; J. H. Neyrey, *An Ideology of Revolt: John's Christology in Social Science Perspective* (Philadelphia: Fortress, 1988) 213-220; R. Schnackenburg, *The Gospel According to St. John* (New York: Crossroad, 1980) 2.79-89; E. Schweizer, *Ego Eimi* (Göttingen: Vandenhoeck, 1939); H. Zimmermann, "Das absolute *'ego eimi'* als die neutestamentliche Offenbarungs formel," *BZ* 4 (1960) 54-69, 266-76.   G. M. Burge

IMPURITY. *See* CLEAN AND UNCLEAN; SINNER.

INFANCY NARRATIVES. *See* BIRTH OF JESUS.

ISRAEL

The presence of the name "Israel" in the Gospels reminds us that Jesus lived among the people of the God* of the OT Scriptures, that these same people played an important role in the unfolding history of salvation,* and that Christ's saving work continues to possess particular relevance for them.

    1. Introduction
    2. Israel in the Gospels
    3. Jesus and Israel

1. Introduction.

The name *Israel* (Gk *Israēl*) occurs only thirty times in the four Gospels, and in no less than a third of these cases as part of another common expression, like "God of Israel" or "king of Israel." But the scarcity of the term itself is a little misleading, for the idea of Israel permeates the Gospels and comes through strongly in terms such as Jew (*Ioudaios*), Hebrew (*Hebraikos*), people (*laos*) and Israelite (*Israēlitēs*). A score of other terms and ideas (such as "feast" and "Pharisee") similarly reveal the tremendous debt of the Gospels to the concept of Israel.

For Jews of the first century the name Israel probably carried with it one or more of three basic associated ideas, all of which stemmed from their historical and religious consciousness: (1) reference to the election of Jacob (called Israel) and his progeny; (2) ongoing faithfulness to the divine covenants (notably circumcision); and (3) the theocratic ideal of Israel as it emerged in the people's history, particularly in the Davidic Golden Age. Such religious and historical associations would be largely foreign to Gentiles.* Hence the rule in the ancient world that Israel was primarily a Jewish self-designation, while Jews was the name more familiar to Gentiles. In the mouth of Gentiles the term *Jews* frequently carried a deprecatory tone, although it was used in a positive, nationalistic sense by Israelites. In fact, the latter group may have opted for this name, since out of an apparent respect for the term there seems to have been a reticence among the Jewish people to employ Israel too freely. Israel seems to have been reserved as a term of self-dignity, religious privilege or purity of the people, or to refer to biblical Israel.

There is no evidence up to this time that Israel had ever been used to define a geographic entity, even though a strong national and geographical constitution appears to have existed earlier on in biblical history. When the Gospels were written the people Israel was neither independent politically nor well-defined geographically, so the idea of a state of Israel was presently non-existent, although it had a part in certain future hopes of the people. For the time, however, the capital, Jerusalem, and in particular the Temple,* functioned as a unifying focal point. So the use of the term implied nearness to the capital and cultic center. In other words, those Jews living near Jerusalem were more commonly referred to as Israel, and in this way the term retained a certain geopolitical nuance, although this could not have been the chief sense of the word. It was primarily a socio-religious term, a self-designation of God's people.

When we come to the Gospels we see that the term likewise preserves a geopolitical nuance in some passages (Mk 15:32; Mt 2:20-21; 9:33; 10:23; Lk 4:25; 7:9; Jn 1:49; 12:13). Even these texts demonstrate, however, that the reference is primarily social (i.e., refers to a people: Lk 1:80; 2:25, 32, 34; 24:21; Jn 1:31; 3:10; cf. "sons of Israel," Mt 27:9; Lk 1:16; "God of Israel," Mt 15:31; Lk 1:68; "house of Israel," Mt 10:6; 15:24; "twelve tribes of Israel," Mt 19:28 par. Lk 22:30).

And yet the term is never simply ethnic. Israel is also a religious term. It frequently denotes a people with a particular religious identity. This religious element often takes on a negative content in the Gospels, associated with the rejection *by* Israel of the one sent *to* Israel. Yet in spite of this fact, the one

consistent feature of the usage of the word in the Gospels—in continuity with its use in the Jewish world generally—is that it retains its dignity. It continues to imply privilege associated with covenant, election and theocratic ideals. This is true even in a passage like Matthew 8:10 and its parallel Luke 7:9, where the surprise shown by Jesus (expressed in the word *oudeni/oude,* "not even") nevertheless implies a special dignity for Israel. Nor do the Gospels deviate from the traditional significance of the term as referring to the descendants of Abraham* (through Jacob). Never, for example, is the term used either of the church* or of Gentiles. While Paul can distinguish between an ethnic and a spiritual Israel (Rom 9:6), the Gospels avoid the use of the term in anything but its traditional sense (granting, however, that Pauline-type ideas may be differently expressed).

It is clear, however, that our concern goes far beyond the usage of the term, for a whole theology of Israel can be found in the Gospels. The interpretation of this theology has seen important changes throughout its history. Among the earliest Christian exegetes the Israel of the Gospels received little attention and even less sympathy. Even up to modern times the Gospels have commonly been thought to pronounce the rejection of Israel in favor of a New Israel—namely, a church consisting predominantly of Gentiles which superseded the Old Israel of the Law.* This view eventually gave way to another which recognized that it was not all of Israel which was rejected, for from that nation came a small remnant who formed the nucleus of the "True Israel." Sometimes the idea of a True Israel is used to refer to believing Jews, sometimes to Jewish and Gentile believers together, sometimes to believing Jews with a believing Gentile "addition." Simply expressed, the term "New Israel" implies some continuity with the idea of Israel, but a whole different people is intended; "True Israel," on the other hand, implies a new set of criteria for membership in the people of God (cf. "spiritual" Israel with Israel "according to the flesh," *kata sarka,* Rom 2:28-29; 9:3). In either case these terms by themselves might imply that the significance of the historic nation Israel in the divine economy has come to an abrupt and decisive end. It should be noted that the term "True Israel," like "New Israel," is not found in the Gospels.

Interest in the place of Israel in the Gospels has, until lately, chiefly been that of the redaction critics. The perspective of many of these scholars is that while the Gospels do in fact portray the rejection of Israel, this notion largely emerged during the later debate between church and synagogue* rather than in the ministry of Jesus. (With this view the form critics [*see* Form Criticism] would largely agree, with the exception that they place the same developments earlier on in the stages of oral transmission, rather than with the Evangelists as such.)

The most recent approaches to the question of Israel, however, have come from another discipline, that of historical-Jesus research (*see* Historical Jesus). These new contributions have served to place Israel not at the perimeter as earlier, but in the very center of Gospel studies. By viewing Jesus as a Jewish restorationist preacher, they have also served to accentuate the rift already discerned by redaction criticism (*see* Redaction Criticism), between the historical ministry of Jesus and the portrayal of him in the Gospels. In attempting to answer the question of Israel and its salvation, we will first consider the redaction critics' findings in the Gospels before moving on to the larger question of Israel in Jesus research.

2. Israel in the Gospels.

The view that the negative attitude toward Israel in the Gospels originates in the synagogue/church debate rather than in the ministry of Jesus itself takes its cue from passages like the parable* of the tenants (Mk 12:1-2 par. Mt 21:33-46 and Lk 20:9-19), which ends with the moral that the owner of the vineyard will "give the vineyard to others" (seemingly indicating a transferral of the kingdom [*see* Kingdom of God] from Israel to the Gentiles). This parable is felt to depend upon a highly developed christology (cf. the important place of the son and his death in the parable), a christology which could only have originated long after the ministry of Jesus and presumably, therefore, amidst the conflict between Christianity and Judaism.

But while it may seem quite a straightforward matter to discard such pericopes as later Christian expansions of the ministry of Jesus, it is nevertheless much more difficult to eliminate the still large accumulation of sayings and oracles against Israel which remain after this process. For example, the judgment* of Israel motif is present in a large proportion of the Gospel material. The "killing of the prophets" theme (a theme, incidentally, which has been thought to explain and authenticate Jesus' own use of the parable of the tenants) is also present in every layer of the Gospel tradition, including the so-called triple tradition (*see* Synoptic Problem), Mark and Q* (cf. Mt 8:11-12 par. Lk 13:28-29). Can all of this tradition be relegated to the Evangelists and their communities? This would appear to be the view of some extreme redaction critics.

2.1. Mark. While redaction critics have paid most attention to Israel's place in the other Gospels, Mark has not been ignored in this respect. The findings of Markan studies are summarized by the Jewish scholar S. Sandmel in his study of anti-Semitism* in the Gospels. Like the other Gospels, large sections of Mark develop the central plot of Jewish conspiracy against Jesus. In the process the members of Israel are portrayed as extremely stubborn and imperceptive. Even the Jewish disciples in Mark are imperceptive, an observation first given significance by W. Wrede, the father of modern Markan redaction criticism. Only a Gentile centurion clearly understands who Jesus is (15:39; cf. 8:33). Some feel that this reflects an attack by Gentile or Galilean Christianity on the establishment in Jerusalem, or on Judaizers such as Paul confronted in his ministry, while others hold that it represents a categorical rejection of all of Judaism. Some scholars find evidence for the view that Mark therefore envisages God's decisive rejection of Israel: Israel is undeserving of salvation.

But it should be noted that it is never explicitly stated in Mark's Gospel that Israel as a people is rejected. The so-called conspiracy plot, as in the other Gospels, is essential to understanding the rejection of Jesus, explaining his death and accentuating the graciousness of God in sending Jesus to die for the "many" (10:45). Furthermore, this rejection by his own people serves as one more form of opposition, along with sickness (*see* Healing) and demonic oppression (*see* Demon, Devil, Satan), over which Jesus is seen to triumph. Thus Mark has a theological-historical interest in this dramatic progression. Rather than portraying the rejection of Israel, Mark's Gospel contrasts God's saving initiative with the undeservedness, not only of Israel, but of those imperceptive Jewish disciples who will prove to be far from rejected. If Mark is guilty of theologizing in his Gospel, it is by presenting the received tradition in light of the saving event of the cross; it is not with a feeling of hostility toward Israel that he does so—such a judgment is a quite subjective one placed on Mark and on his community.

2.2. Matthew. The question of Israel in this Gospel and its sources is considerably more involved (*see* Matthew, Gospel of). While the Gospel is Pharisaic in tone, it is also highly critical of that group. Although Jesus restricts his ministry to Israel in Matthew (10:6; 15:24), according to some scholars the Gospel leads naturally and progressively to the conclusion that the Gentile mission is all that remains for its readers (cf. 28:19)—Israel is rejected and there is no future for the nation. Others see a carefully constructed salvation history at work here: Whereas Mark merely character- izes Israel as reprobate and undeserving, Matthew speaks of the transfer of salvation to the Gentiles, something deliberately orchestrated and commanded by Christ.* Matthew adjusts the wording of texts like Mark 3:7-12 (par. Mt 12:15-21) to highlight this transfer. He always emphasizes controversy and conflict. In this Gospel the blame for Jesus' death (*see* Death of Jesus) is consciously assumed by an Israel who invokes upon their race the ensuing punishment for this act (27:25, referring to A.D. 70, according to some).

W. Trilling considered such things evidence that Matthew envisaged a "True Israel" which displaced ethnic Israel, and that the Gospel came from a time when Jews and Christians were decisively split (A.D. 70-135). D. R. A. Hare, who studied Jewish persecution of Christians in this Gospel, concluded that while controversy was doubtless a part of Jesus' ministry, Matthew's situation was largely responsible for this element in his Gospel. The abundant references to Pharisees* (Matthew even seems to insert them into his sources) reflects a late date when that group was prominent. Matthew envisaged not a "New" or "True" Israel, but a "Third Race" of Christians altogether. S. H. Brooks has recently added complexity to the debate by suggesting that there is evidence of several layers of material in Matthew, ranging from times of peaceful relations between the Christian community and Judaism to times of hostile opposition.

In spite of all the relevant observations made above, much of the same rationale for including the Jesus-Israel debate applies for Matthew as well as for Mark. There is no compelling reason to doubt that the struggles witnessed in Matthew were struggles *within* Judaism and reflect the kind of interaction with his people that Jesus experienced during his ministry. A true respect for Judaism is evidenced in the Gospel, where Jesus' teaching is rooted in and emulates Jewish teaching, making Matthew the most Jewish of the Gospels. While a few have interpreted the pres- ence of extensive teaching material (the Sermon on the Mount in chapters 5—7 [*see* Sermon on the Mount]) as a competing legal system in contrast to, and in defiance of, the Law of Israel—a Christian system supplanting the Jewish one—this is only one way of interpreting the teaching material, and clearly a minority point of view.

As for the Pharisees, the little we know about this party suggests that their history extended over a much earlier period, hardly making it a controlling factor in the dating of Matthew's final redaction—a point which lately has been made by several scholars.

Pharisees appear in every Gospel, if not as frequently as in Matthew. The invective against the scribes* and Pharisees may represent nothing more than a focus- ing of blame on establishment-Judaism as Matthew knew it. More likely it reflects Matthew's characteriza- tion of Jesus' historical opponents (something we also find in John) since it was widely known that the Pharisees were notorious in their resistance to Jesus. This characterization may give us a clue to the relative dating of the Gospels but says little about their situation of writing. The theme of Israel's obduracy was taken up by Paul as early as A.D. 57 (Rom 9—11) and does not necessarily presuppose later synagogue/ church debate. As with Mark, nothing explicit is found regarding the rejection of Israel.

2.3. Luke. Luke's Gospel is of special interest because of the author's apparent concern with salvation history—God's working among Jews and Gentiles (*see* Luke, Gospel of). H. Conzelmann stressed the discontinuity between Israel and the church created by this salvation history and postulated that Luke envisaged a New Israel. But in this Gospel the continuity between Israel and Jesus' movement is also obvious. The latter appears as the valid fulfill- ment of the former. Many scholars therefore feel that the church of Luke is depicted as the "True Israel."

But others deny that any sense of continuity is intended, or else that this continuity is meant to dignify Israel in any way. What takes place in Luke's view is a gradual shifting of God's people from Jews to Gentiles (cf. the prominent location of 4:16-30, along with the story line of the companion volume Acts, the Stephen episode in Acts 7 and the conclusion of Acts at 28:23-28). R. Maddox and J. T. Sanders are the most recent exponents of this view. The church is a New Israel, and the break with the Old Israel is complete. As a sign of this Luke appears to transfer the term "people" (*laos,* a term for Israel) to the church (a view held earlier by Conzelmann). This Gospel has the entire Jewish populace united in condemning Jesus to death (23:2-5, 13-23).

It should be noted, however, that this latter passage may only reflect the perspective of Luke's source. Some feel that the Q source is itself responsible for Luke's negative view of Israel. Indeed Luke's special source (L*), or Luke himself, emphasizes the dignity and hope of Israel (1:80; 2:25, 32, 34; 24:21).

The idea that the fate of Israel comes to rest either in a New Israel or a True Israel is clearly an interpre- tation placed upon Luke. There is no need to adopt either view. Luke's interest was largely historical and apologetic. The common question of theodicy: "Why did so few from Israel respond to the Gospel?" is also dealt with by Paul in Rom 9—11 (cf. Rom 9:6, 19-20, 30; 11:1). According to Luke many in Israel did believe. We should therefore probably follow scholars like J. Jervell who see Israel divided by the ministry of Jesus, some coming to repentance, others not. But Israel never transfers its name or status to Gentiles.

2.4. John. John's Gospel is notorious for its frequent (but strangely not consistent) derogatory usage of the term "the Jews" to speak of Jesus' adversaries. Long digressions on the unbelief of the Jews and Jesus' conflict with them appear in John 5—9. The Jews as a group are treated as resisters (5:10, 15, 18; 8:48, 52, 57; 10:24, 31). In their recalcitrance they even disown the universal Jewish confession of God as king (19:12-15). This categorical distrust of the Jews is widely felt to reflect a much later situation in the life of the church when excommunication from the synagogue for confessing Christians was officially sanctioned (cf. 9:22), a view widely made known by J. L. Martyn's study of the relevant chapters and of the life setting of John's Gospel. By all appearances John's Gospel is no longer aware of the diversity of parties within early first-century Judaism.* They are all lumped together as one group: "the Jews." Jews appear to the readers of this Gospel as outsiders (e.g., "your Law," 10:34).

But Jews also believe (11:45). And they are at times divided (10:19-21). *Israel* always remains a positive term (1:31, 47), and singular respect for Judaism is evinced (4:22). Other uses of "the Jews" are neutral (e.g., 11:19; 18:20). The usage of "the Jews" seems therefore to demonstrate what has been described as a sense of remoteness rather than hatred. Considering the growing recognition among scholars of the Jewish background of the Fourth Gospel (*see* John, Gospel of), this remoteness is somewhat baffling. Perhaps the writer was a Jew, but he was writing for non-Jews. The important point is that this remoteness is also expressed in passages where Jews believe. This precludes the notion that Jews are recalcitrant because they are Jews.

While some feel that it is only the authorities who are singled out for criticism in the Gospel, the critique appears to be more widespread than that. The message seems to be that the structure of the religion of Judaism, as it was interpreted in contemporary Israel, had departed from the way of Israel historically, and this departure was reflected in the attitudes of many Jews (cf. 2:18-20). There are strong indications in the Fourth Gospel of the underlying doctrine of the remnant (cf. 10:1-18; 11:45; see 3.1. below).

2.5. Conclusions about Israel in the Gospels. Some of the tendencies noted by scholars in the individual Gospels may be significant, but these tendencies have been exaggerated. The teaching which is so often attributed to the developing tradition has a claim to go back to Jesus himself (see discussion below). The characterizations ("the Jews," "the scribes and Pharisees") often refer to a certain part of Israel which typically rejected Jesus, but the term *Israel* is never used for this group. While there are no clear statements that Israel is forever rejected by God, there nonetheless emerges through the Gospels the impression that, by the time of the Gospel writers at least, Israel had surprisingly little representation among the followers of Jesus. This needed to be explained from the events of Jesus' ministry, and the Gospels sought to fill this need. However, the theological, historical and soteriological motive—the need to explain how God brought salvation through rejection—was certainly still the dominating factor in the Gospel presentations.

3. Jesus and Israel.

3.1. Background for Jesus' Ministry to Israel. The most recent development in the study of Israel in the Gospels has come from the area of historical-Jesus research (*see* Historical Jesus). Older historically negative quests for the Jesus of history, like that of R. Bultmann, which divorced Jesus from his Jewish environment, have been abandoned in favor of a new Jewish Quest, or Third Quest, which attempts to place Jesus properly within his Jewish environment. This approach has been adopted by an impressive array of scholars both Jewish and Christian (among them: G. Vermes, B. F. Meyer, A. E. Harvey, J. Riches, G. Lohfink, E. P. Sanders and J. H. Charlesworth). Some adherents of this new school of Jesus research hold that the major presupposition for Jesus' ministry was the widespread eschatological doctrine of the restoration of Israel, and that Jesus both addressed this concern and understood his ministry in the light of the expectation.

G. Lohfink is a good example of the newly emerging restorationist perspective. He points to Jesus' deliberate choice of twelve disciples and to the significance of the miracles as evidence that Jesus intended from the beginning of his ministry to restore the nation. When his preaching failed to appeal to Israel, Jesus began to see that Israel's salvation would now only come through his own meritorious death which would result in the salvation of the "many" (Mk 10:45).

But none has been more thorough in his presentation of Jesus as an eschatological restorationist preacher than E. P. Sanders. Sanders maintains that in common with the rest of Judaism, Jesus assumed the salvation of all Israel. Jesus' preaching was in anticipation of the final restoration of Israel. This can be seen in the way Jesus predicted the destruction of the Temple (*see* Temple Cleansing) so that it could be replaced with the new eschatological Temple. In addition, the kingdom Jesus preached referred to the hope of a restored nation. Jesus' task, specifically, was gathering the sinners* and outcasts of Israel so as to assure that all Israel would be included in this blessing.

Where such a position is adopted, it could easily lead to the view that the restoration which Jesus envisaged was a failure, for Israel turned away from him and the promised gathering of Israel did not take place. The view of restoration as the salvation of all Israel and the return of the dispersed Jews does not seem to match the results of Jesus' ministry. What can be said about Jesus as a preacher of Israel's restoration, especially when the Gospels provide such clear evidence that this restoration was a failure? Are we forced to accept the pathos and tragedy of A. Schweitzer's Jesus whose goals, even at the cost of death, were scarcely acquired?

The attempt to place Jesus within Judaism is a welcome trend. But restorationism was not so prevalent a movement in Judaism as the scholars of the Jewish Quest seem to maintain, at least in the way assumed by them. We can point to many groups in Judaism who indeed looked forward to restoration in the future but also maintained that only a faithful remnant would be saved in the present.

The doctrine of the remnant consists in the idea that many, perhaps most, of Israel has abandoned the covenant in such a way as to place themselves outside salvation and in danger of judgment.* Such doctrines could be cultivated in Judaism because Israel was not a unified community at this time. It was severely divided within itself. As a result of so much intra-Jewish conflict, divisions between ethnic and religious Israel were drawn, each party claiming to be the remnant. We see the beginnings of the doctrine of segregation within Israel in Sirach (cf. 8:17; 9:16; 11:9; 12:14; 13:1, 17-18; 22:13). 1 Maccabees implies throughout that God's retribution against sinful Israel finally outweighs his concern for their election, for they have broken the covenant (1:43, 52-53; 9:23-25; 10:14). There is a clear distinction between the faithful and the apostates, and the righteous are in the minority (1:62-63; 3:15-19; 9:5-6). The rest are judged in the unfolding history (1:63-64). The apocalyptic* writings and those of Qumran (*see* Dead Sea Scrolls) take this development further and speak clearly of a remnant of the faithful, or righteous (*see* Justice,

Righteousness), in Israel (*1 Enoch* 10:16; 83:8; 94:4; 99:10; *Pss. Sol.* 12:6; 4 Ezra 7:50-61; 8:2-3; *2 Apoc. Bar.* 48:33; 77:2-6; CD 1:4-5; 2:11-12; 3:19-20; 1QM 13:8; 14:8-9; 1QH 6:7-8; 4Q181) and of the judgment of the remainder of Israel (*1 Enoch* 5:6-9; 80:2-8; 81:7-9; 90:26-27; *Jub.* 15:34; *Pss. Sol.* 8:15-20; 12:6; 13:5-10; 4 Ezra 9:8-12; *2 Apoc. Bar.* 24:1-25:2; CD 1:3-4; 1QS 4:11-14), for many in Israel, along with their leaders, have effectively broken the covenant (*1 Enoch* 94:2-5; 101:1-9; *Jub.* 23:19; 4 Ezra 7:22-24; *2 Apoc. Bar.* 41:3; CD 1:12—2:1; 1QH 15:18-21; often they are implicated in the sin of the world, e.g., 4 Ezra 8:14-18). Accordingly, ideas of national election are questioned or played down (cf. 4 Ezra 3:11-17, 36). Occasionally the community of the remnant appears to take the name Israel for itself (1 Macc 1:53; 7:9, 22; 9:27, 51; *Pss. Sol.* 10:6; 1QS 5:22; 8:4, CD(B) 2:26; 1QSa 1:6; 1QM 10:9, 1QpNah 3:2-3), although as a rule the term still refers to the nation.

In spite of their sometimes-harsh remnant theology, these works also manifest a definite respect for the promises to Israel and a hope for the eventual restoration of all Israel (*1 Enoch* 90:30-36; *Jub.* 23:27-32; *Pss. Sol.* 8:28; 17:26-46; 4 Ezra 4:26-35; 6:26b-28; 13:12-13, 39-47; *2 Apoc. Bar.* 29:3—30:3; CD 2:11-12). This restoration frequently includes the Gentiles (e.g., *1 Enoch* 10:17, 21-22; 90:33), but the remnant is consistently at the center of this restoration. Israel is not restored except by joining the remnant (cf. e.g., *1 Enoch* 90:30).

We can see therefore that a background had already been established for the kind of intra-Jewish strife recorded in the Gospels. Sociologically speaking, the most bitter battles are fought among siblings, especially when, as in the Jewish world of this time, the claims on God and salvation are mutually exclusive. It is notable that within one sectarian dispute one side was forced to adopt a negative view of the name "Judah" (cf. "Jew" in CD 4:3, 11; 8:3), suggesting a certain group which the author's community felt had corrupted the true faith* of Israel.

3.2. Jesus and the Remnant of Israel. As scholars like B. F. Meyer have insisted, the remnant theme is undeniably present in the Gospels. While it is conceivable that the Evangelists have written their contemporary controversies between church and synagogue back into their Gospels, it is difficult to remove altogether from the tradition signs that Jesus faced controversy over Israel's salvation in his day and offered comments of the type which we now find in our Gospels. Specifically, Jesus' association with John the Baptist (*see* John the Baptist) reveals that he shared the warnings about the coming judgment upon Israel.

It appears that Jesus not only warned about judgment but pronounced it (cf. Mt 11:20-24 par. Lk 10:12-15). His parables and the secrecy theme demonstrate that he shared the current practice of sheltering truth designed for the righteous from those who would misunderstand and abuse it. Sayings like that concerning Jesus' mother and brothers (an undeniably authentic tradition; Mk 3:31-35 par. Mt 12:46-50 and Lk 8:19-21) demonstrate that Jesus set his own criteria for membership in the covenant people of God. That Jesus often alluded to a "seed" in his parables may also mean that he shared the dualism of the sectarian groups who distinguished between the righteous and the unrighteous "seed" in Israel. Such a use of the concept of good and evil seed is well documented in Jewish literature (*1 Enoch* 80:2; *Jub.* 7:29; 16:26; 22:13, 27; 31:20; 4 Ezra 4:28-32; *2 Apoc. Bar.* 42:4-5; CD 2:11-12). The choice of the Twelve (*see* Disciple) who eventually assumed their role as apostles* to Israel seems also to point in this direction, although there may be something to the view that Twelve pointed more to Israel's restoration than to its reduction to a remnant. The Twelve clearly did not compose the remnant. They were just a few of the wider circle of repentant (*see* Repentance) in Israel who had committed themselves to John's baptism* and to Jesus' own preaching of the kingdom. Response to the presence of this kingdom was doubtless the criterion by which these were saved and others were not.

This brings us to one of the chief objections to the idea that Jesus called a remnant. J. Jeremias strongly influenced the view that while many groups in Judaism considered themselves to be the chosen remnant, this was far too particularist a doctrine for the liberal-minded Jesus who preached against all forms of strict Judaism. Meyer responded that Jesus could have created an "open remnant," a remnant which did not establish social boundaries and was never clearly defined. All of this discussion, however, takes us away from historical questions to dogmatic ones. The fact remains that Jesus' group from the beginning was particularistic inasmuch as Jesus required faith and response to God's message preached by him. While Jesus' remnant did not possess a legalistic base, it did have an implicit christological one. (In a sense, then, this particularism was an anti-particularism, or a particularism not based on legal requirements.) As for Meyer's view of the "open remnant," it requires that we deny any intentions by Jesus to foster community interaction—something which seems doubtful indeed (cf. e.g., Mt 18).

Then there is the persistent question whether Jesus intended, called or gathered a remnant, or whether this remnant was the unintended result of his divisive mission. It appears that there was nothing unintentional about Jesus' remnant ideas, providing we recognize the theological framework in which the idea of intention was operating. For human intention was considered subservient to divine determination in Jesus' day, and no one more than Jesus was aware of the inevitability of the working of God's word in Israel. In short, if the word of God created a remnant in Israel's past, it must be considered inevitable that such a remnant would be created by God's word to Israel through Jesus today. Such an idea would conform to the way Scripture so often appears to have molded Jesus' self-consciousness in the Gospels. It appears, therefore, not only that Jesus expected a remnant, but that he cooperated with its formation by intending, gathering and calling.

If Jesus possessed a remnant theology, what exactly did he have in mind? Was there to emerge a True Israel? Or a New Israel? A common view is that while Israel was denied salvation as an institution, individuals out of the nation might still be saved. But this is not the Jewish view of the remnant as seen in the OT or in the Judaism of Jesus' day. The remnant always relates back to Israel. There is implied in this doctrine an accountability or responsibility to Israel; the ties are not broken altogether. Through this remnant Israel is affirmed. There is certainly no New Israel, and the idea of a True Israel might falsely signify independence from ethnic Israel—a view not generally encouraged by Judaism.

3.3. Jesus and the Destiny of Israel. But what can we say about Jesus? Did he possess any hope for the restoration of Israel *kata sarka* ("according to the flesh")? Or did his view of the remnant of Israel override, or perhaps extinguish altogether, the hope for restoration? It is apparent that Paul still held the two ideas in tension in Rom 9—11. But a systematic statement such as we find there does not exist in the Gospels. In fact, there is no explicit statement to the effect that Jesus expected, either then or in the future, a restoration of Israel. Many scholars therefore argue that there is no doctrine of restoration in the Gospels. And it is difficult to disagree with this conclusion.

However, some things might be considered as less direct evidence of the restoration of Israel before the idea is dismissed out of hand. We have already mentioned the possibility that the Twelve points to the hope that Israel will be fully restored through Jesus' ministry, since twelve is manifestly the number of the tribes of Israel. And Sanders's view that the announcement of a kingdom must in its context imply restoration, also carries conviction. Then we have evidence like Matthew 23:39 (par. Lk 13:35) where Jesus announces to Jerusalem, "I tell you, you will not see me (again) until you say, 'Blessed is he who comes in the name of the Lord!' " Matthew, who places the saying after the Triumphal Entry, clearly implies the warm reception of the Son of man (*see* Son of Man) by Israel at some future date.

On any accounting the number of references to restoration in the Gospels is minimal. Can this be explained? Certainly if Jesus intended to restore Israel, all indications are that this was not expected immediately but in some indefinite future, and it was conditioned by the acceptance of his preaching— contrary to the view that Jesus was a restorationist (e.g., Sanders). In this case the most that can be said is that Jesus set in motion a (gradual?) restoration exemplified in his disciples. More likely, restoration was still a future hope. For the present, however, only a remnant would respond. In this way the judgment pronounced against Jesus' contemporaries can be taken seriously; restoration still remains valid only for those who accept the terms of salvation. In the Gospels the idea of the restoration of Israel is therefore overshadowed by the teaching about the remnant. For the relatively small group of Jesus' followers who found themselves in conflict with the rest of the Jewish world, this teaching would certainly have been the more urgent one.

Perhaps also by the time the Gospels were written, attention was turning from the hope for restoration to the influx of Gentiles into the kingdom. If Israel was not experiencing her restoration, Gentiles certainly were. In the Fourth Gospel unbelieving Jews are lumped together with the world; perhaps by analogy we can say that within the allusions to success in mission to the world, Israel herself is also to be included (cf. 17:21; 21:11). This would amount to a restoration which affects Israel as well as the Gentiles—something quite in harmony with the Jewish restoration belief.

If Jesus did teach the restoration of Israel, he probably also had some view of the role the Gentiles would play in this restoration. Both the Gospels and the Jewish background encourage this assumption. It is less clear whether Jesus intended to remove all distinctions between Jews and Gentiles, or to uphold the special privilege of Israel.

Thus the idea of a future for Israel which includes their salvation is not incongruous with the message of Jesus and may be implied in certain texts of the Gospels. Such a restoration would clearly involve the future (or possibly gradual) acceptance of the message of the kingdom by Israel based on Jesus' work on their behalf (cf. Mk 10:45).

See also ANTI-SEMITISM; CHURCH; GENTILES; JOHN, GOSPEL OF; JUDAISM; LAW; LUKE, GOSPEL OF; MATTHEW, GOSPEL OF; SINNER.

BIBLIOGRAPHY. S. H. Brooks, *Matthew's Community: The Evidence of His Special Sayings Material* (JSNTSup 16; Sheffield: JSOT, 1987); J. H. Charlesworth, *Jesus within Judaism* (New York: Doubleday, 1988); H. Conzelman, *The Theology of St. Luke* (New York: Harper & Row, 1961); D. R. A. Hare, *The Theme of Jewish Persecution of Christians in Matthew's Gospel* (SNTSMS 6; Cambridge: University Press, 1967); A. E. Harvey, *Jesus and the Constraints of History* (Philadelphia: Westminster, 1982); A. J. Hultgren, *Jesus and His Adversaries. The Form and Function of the Conflict Stories in the Synoptic Tradition* (Minneapolis: Augsburg, 1979); J. Jeremias, "Der Gedanke des heiligen Restes im Spätjudentum und in der Verkündigung Jesu," *ZNW* 42 (1949) 184-94; J. Jervell, *Luke and the People of God* (Minneapolis: Augsburg, 1972); G. Lohfink, *Jesus and Community* (Philadelphia: Fortress; New York: Paulist, 1982); R. Maddox, *The Purpose of Luke-Acts* (FRLANT 126; Göttingen: Vandenhoeck & Ruprecht, 1982); J. L. Martyn, *History and Theology in the Fourth Gospel* (New York: Harper and Row, 1968); B. F. Meyer, *The Aims of Jesus* (London: SCM, 1979); J. Riches, *Jesus and the Transformation of Judaism* (New York: Seabury, 1982); E. P. Sanders, *Jesus and Judaism* (London: SCM, 1985); J. T. Sanders, *The Jews in Luke-Acts* (London: SCM, 1987); S. Sandmel, *Anti-Semitism in the New Testament?* (Philadelphia: Fortress, 1978); K. H. Schelkle, *Israel im Neuen Testament* (Darmstadt: Wissenschaftliche Buchgesellschaft, 1985); W. Trilling, *Das wahre Israel* (3d ed.; München: Kösel, 1964); G. Vermes, *Jesus and the World of Judaism* (London: SCM, 1983).

M. A. Elliott

J

JAMES (SON OF ALPHAEUS). *See* Disciples.

JAMES (SON OF ZEBEDEE). *See* Disciples.

JERUSALEM. *See* Archeology and Geography; Destruction of Jerusalem.

JERUSALEM TALMUD. *See* Rabbinic Traditions and Writings.

JESUS IN NON-CHRISTIAN SOURCES

Traditions about Jesus appear in many literatures, Christian and non-Christian alike. The ancient non-Christian sources have value principally because they usually offer data from a non-Christian perspective, and in some instances either corroborate or clarify the Gospels.

1. Josephus
2. Roman Historians and Other Writers
3. Rabbinic Writings
4. The Qur'an

1. Josephus.

One of our most important first-century writers is Flavius Josephus* (c. A.D. 37-100). A survivor of Israel's catastrophic war with Rome (A.D. 66-70), Josephus went on to write an account of the conflict entitled the *Jewish War* (*J.W.*). He also wrote *Jewish Antiquities* (*Ant.*), an autobiography (*Life*), and a polemical treatise *Against Apion* (*Ag. Ap.*). These works were written in Greek, but were later translated into other languages, including Slavonic.

1.1. Greek. Twice in *Jewish Antiquities* Josephus refers to Jesus. "And so he [Ananus the High Priest, son of Annas; cf. Lk 3:2] convened the judges of the Sanhedrin and brought before them a man called James [cf. Acts 15:13], the brother of Jesus who was called the Christ [cf. Gal 1:19], and certain others. He accused them of having transgressed the law and delivered them up to be stoned" (20.9.1 §§200-203).

Whereas no one seriously doubts the authenticity of this passage, another passage, known as the *"Testi-monium Flavianum"* (or *"Flavium"*), is disputed: "About this time there lived Jesus, a wise man, if indeed one ought to call him a human. For he was one who wrought surprising feats and was a teacher of such people as accept the truth gladly. He won over many Jews and many of the Greeks. He was the Messiah. When Pilate, upon hearing him accused by people of the highest standing among us, had condemned him to be crucified, those who had in the first place come to love him did not give up their affection for him. On the third day he appeared to them restored to life, for the prophets of God had prophesied these and countless other marvelous things about him. And the tribe of Christians, so called after him, has still to this day not disappeared" (18.3.3 §§ 63-64). The authenticity of this passage is doubted because nowhere else does Josephus discuss Jesus, which would be very hard to explain if he believed him to be the Messiah. Moreover, Josephus regarded Vespasian as the Messiah of Judah (cf. *J.W.* 3.8.8-9 §§392-408), an interpretation probably based on Genesis 49:10, and one that cohered with the views of Tacitus (*Hist.* 5.13) and Suetonius (*Vespasian* 4) as well. Although some scholars view the *Testimonium Flavianum* in its entirety as a Christian interpolation, most regard it as a Christian embellishment of a passage that probably was originally critical of Jesus and his following. The fact that this passage was apparently unknown to most of the early fathers argues strongly for the inauthenticity of its present form. For had this form existed at the end of the first century, it is quite likely that Christian apologists would have cited it often. Although Eusebius (fourth century) knows of this passage (cf. *Hist. Eccl.* 1.11.7-8; *Dem. Ev.* 3.5), according to Origen (third century) Josephus did not regard Jesus as the Messiah (cf. *Comm. Mt.* 10.50.17; *Contra Celsum* 1.47). This suggests that the passage, as we now have it, did not exist in the third century. Moreover, the absence in the Arabic version of the very words and phrases suspected of being interpolations adds more support to the contention that the passage has been tampered with.

The Arabic version of the *Testimonium Flavianum* (taken from Agapius, *Book of the Title*) reads as follows: "Similarly Josephus the Hebrew. For he says in the treatises that he has written concerning . . . the Jews: 'At this time there was a wise man who was called Jesus. And his conduct was good, and [he] was known to be virtuous. And many people from among the Jews and the other nations became his disciples. Pilate condemned him to be crucified and to die. And those who had become his disciples did not abandon his discipleship. They reported that he had appeared to them three days after his crucifixion and that he was alive; accordingly he was perhaps the Messiah concerning whom the prophets have recounted wonders' " (Pines, 16; Klausner, 55-56, restores the passage along similar lines). The Arabic version may very well preserve a form of the passage that is closer to the original than the one we now find in the Greek manuscripts, but it too is unlikely to represent Josephus' point of view.

It is the context of the *Testimonium* that argues against any positive, or even neutral, form of the passage. The *Testimonium* falls in the middle of *Antiquities* 18.2.2-4.3 §§35-95 (from the appointment of Caiaphas to the dismissal of Caiaphas and Pilate), a section that is highly negative and critical of Roman severity and insensitivity and of the foolish and reckless behavior of various Jewish groups in Palestine. It is much more likely that the original form of the passage described Jesus and his following as yet one more "disturbance" brought on by misguided messianic aspirations.

Nevertheless, the *Testimonium Flavianum* is not without significance. Even if the original form of the passage was negative, the fact that Josephus apparently viewed Jesus as a messianic claimant is suggestive. This may tell us something about the nature of Jesus' ministry, possibly something of his self-understanding, and something about the political factors that led to his arrest and crucifixion.

1.2. Slavonic. In the Slavonic (or Old Russian) version of Josephus' *Jewish War* there appear several passages that make reference to John the Baptist,* Jesus and early Christians (passages without parallel in the Greek MSS.). A lengthy passage describes Jesus as "more than a man," yet not "an angel," one who "wrought amazing and wonderful deeds" by his "word and command" (2.9.3, between §§ 174 and 175, according to the chapter divisions of the Greek tradition). The passage goes on to say that many urged him to lead an uprising against the Romans and that out of fear that such a thing might happen the Jewish leaders bribed Pilate to have Jesus executed.

Another passage (following 5.5.4 §214) tells of the torn Temple* curtain, various signs at the time of Jesus' death* and the discovery of the empty tomb—despite the fact that it had been guarded by thirty Romans and a thousand Jews! Nevertheless, the author states that he is not sure which explanation is best: that Jesus was raised from the dead or that his friends had stolen his body.

Of interest is the passage (within 5.5.2 §195) that reports the wording of a tablet, written in Greek, Roman and Jewish characters, that hung at one of the gates leading into the Temple: "Jesus has not reigned as king. He has been crucified by the Jews because he proclaimed the destruction of the city and the laying waste of the Temple." This statement evidently reflects the charge the Jews (but apparently not the Romans) brought against Jesus when he was accused of having threatened to destroy the Temple (cf. Mk 14:58; Acts 6:14).

Scholarly opinion varies widely on the question of the authenticity and value of these additions. The lack of overt sympathy for Jesus and his followers favors authenticity, for it is hard to understand why a Christian would add so many passages that do not promote Christian views. It is equally hard to imagine why a non-Christian would add passages that concerned a figure who otherwise plays no role in *Jewish War* and for whom Jesus' life is of little or no importance. Of course, the absence of these passages in the Greek manuscripts tell against their authenticity. Even if these Slavonic passages are accepted as authentic, their historical value is another question.

2. Roman Historians and Other Writers.

Pagan writers said little about Jesus, and what they did say varies in its historical value and interest. In a letter to his son, Mara bar Serapion (c. A.D. 73) asks: "For what advantage did . . . the Jews [gain] by the death of their wise king . . . ?" Tacitus (c. A.D. 110) tells us that the name "Christian" "originates from 'Christus' who was sentenced to death by the governor, Pontius Pilate, during the reign of Tiberius" (*Ann.* 15.44). In his letter to Trajan, Pliny the Younger (A.D. 110) explains that Christians regularly assemble to recite "a hymn antiphonally to Christ as God" and to "partake of a meal" (*Epp.* 10.96).

In his *Life of Emperor Claudius*, Suetonius (c. A.D. 120) reports that "Claudius expelled the Jews from Rome [A.D. 49; cf. Acts 18:2] who, instigated by Chrestus, never ceased to cause unrest" (25.4). Apparently Suetonius has confused *"Chrestus,"* a name commonly held by slaves, with *"Christus,"* a title with which he was probably not familiar.

Celsus (c. A.D. 179), according to Origen (c. A.D. 248), claimed that Jesus was the illegitimate son of a Roman soldier (*Contra Celsum* 1.32-33), and that he performed miracles through the power of magic: "He was brought up in secret and hired himself out as a workman in Egypt, and after having tried his hand at certain magical powers he returned from there, and on account of those powers gave himself the title of God" (1.38; cf. 1.6, 68, 71).

According to Julius Africanus (c. A.D. 230), the Samaritan chronicler Thallus suggested that the darkness at the time of Jesus' death was caused by an eclipse of the sun (*Frag.* 18).

3. Rabbinic Writings.

There are relatively few references to Jesus in the Talmud (*see* Rabbinic Traditions and Writings) and Midrash*. Although the name Yeshu, or Yeshu ha Notzri ("the Nazarene"*), sometimes does occur, some of the relevant passages refer to him as "Balaam," "ben Pandira," "ben Pantera," "a certain person" and possibly "ben Stada" (although the majority of the references to Balaam and ben Stada are not to Jesus.) Most of the passages are of little historical value, representing scarcely more than secondhand acquaintance with the Gospels and later polemic with Christians. In the Middle Ages many of these traditions were compiled into a small book known as the *Toledot Yeshu* (earliest references to this writing date from the ninth century; for an edited version see Goldstein, 148-54).

3.1. On the Parents and Birth of Jesus. In what may be a reference to the Gospels' claim of Jesus' virginal conception, we are told that Mary, "who was the descendant of princes and governors, played the harlot with carpenters" (*b. Sanh.* 106a). "Princes and governors" probably allude to some of the names in Luke's genealogy,* which some Church Fathers thought was Mary's. The second part of the statement is an obvious allusion to Joseph the carpenter. "Was not . . . his mother Stada? His mother was Miriam, a women's hairdresser [*megaddela*]. As they say . . . 'Stath da [i.e., "this one strayed"] from her husband' " (*b. Šabb.* 104b; Mary "the *megaddela*" is sometimes confused with Mary Magdalene; cf. *b. ḥag.* 4b.). Elsewhere we are told that "Jesus . . . was near to kingship" (*b. Sanh.* 43a; or "near to the Kingdom," possibly as satire on Jesus' proclamation that "the kingdom of God is near"; cf. Mk 1:15). Rabbi Simeon ben Azzai (late first/early second century) claims that he "found a scroll of genealogical record in Jerusalem, in which was written: 'A certain person was illegitimately born of a married woman' " (*m. Yebam.* 4:13; cf. *b. Yebam.* 49a).

3.2. On the Life of Jesus. Stories are told of Jesus being rejected by various Rabbis: "When King Janneus [104-78 B.C.] slew our Rabbis [c. B.C. 87], Rabbi Joshua [ben Peraḥiah] and Jesus fled to Alexandria of Egypt" where Jesus was later excommunicated and condemned for worshipping an idol (*b. Sanh.* 107b; *b. Soṭa* 47a; cf. *y. ḥag.* 2:2; *y. Sanh.* 6:6). The association of Jesus with a flight to Egypt may have been suggested by Matthew 2:13-15. The chronological displacement of Jesus in this tradition is obvious, but there is good reason to identify this "Jesus" with Jesus of Nazareth.

3.3. On the Ministry of Jesus. We are told that "Jesus had five disciples: Matthai, Nakai, Nezer, Buni and Todah" (*b. Sanh.* 107b). Although the first name does resemble "Matthew" and the last possibly that of "Thaddeus," these names are only meant to serve as a basis for word-plays. This is seen in the subsequent paragraph of *Sanhedrin*, where aspersions are cast against Jesus and his disciples, and their deaths are justified. The Rabbinic view of Jesus' ministry of miracles is similar to that of Celsus already noted: "Jesus the Nazarene practiced magic and led Israel astray" (*b. Sanh.* 107b; cf. *t. Šabb.* 11:15; *b. Sanh.* 43a; *b. Šabb.* 104b; *b. Soṭa.* 47a). The charge of practicing magic parallels the accusation found in the Gospels that Jesus cast out demons by the power of Satan (cf. Mk 3:22).

3.4. On the Teaching of Jesus. The rabbis hope that they do "not have a son or a disciple who burns his food in public [i.e., teaches heresy], like Jesus the Nazarene" (*b. Sanh.* 103a; *b. Ber.* 17a-b). "One of the disciples of Jesus . . . told me, 'Thus did Jesus the Nazarene teach me: "For of the hire of a harlot has she gathered them, and to the hire of a harlot shall they return" [cf. Deut 23:18]' " (*b. 'Abod. Zar.* 16b-17a; *t. ḥul.* 2:24 ["... Jesus ben Pantera ..."]; cf. *Qoh. Rab.* 1:8 §3; *Yal. Shim.* on Mic 1 and Prov 5:8). "The disciples of Balaam the wicked shall inherit Gehenna and go down to the pit of destruction" (*m. 'Abot* 5:19). "He [a judge] said to them: 'I looked at the end of the book, in which it is written, "I am not come to take away the Law of Moses and I am not come to add to the Law of Moses" [cf. Mt 5:17], and it is written, "Where there is a son, a daughter does not inherit" [cf. Num 27:8].' She said to him: 'Let your light shine forth as a lamp' [cf. Mt 5:16]. Rabbi Gamaliel said to her: 'The ass came and kicked the lamp over' " (*b. Šabb.* 116b).

From the same tradition we find a proverbial statement that probably sums up very well the rabbinic view of Jesus' teaching: "Since the day that you were exiled from your land [i.e., the destruction of Jerusalem in A.D. 70] the Law of Moses has been abrogated, and the law of the *euangelion* [gospel] has been given" (*b. Šabb.* 116a). In fact, by playing on the Greek word *euangelion*, the rabbis sometimes referred to it as the *'awen-gillayon* ("falsehood of the scroll") or the *'awon-gillayon* ("perversion of the scroll").

Most offensive to the rabbis was Jesus' claim to be God* and Son of man* (cf. Mk 14:61-62; Jn 19:7), who would ascend to heaven (cf. Jn 20:17). Rabbi Abahu (third century) is reported to have said: "If a man says to you, 'I am God,' he is a liar; [or] 'I am the son of man,' in the end he will regret it; [or] 'I will go up to heaven'—he that says it will not perform it" (*y. Ta'an.* 2:1). Again from Abahu: "[God] says . . . 'I am the first"—I have no father; "I am the last'—I have no son' " (*Ex. Rab.* 29.5 on Ex 20:2). Similarly Rabbi Aha (fourth century) declares: "There is One that is alone, and he has not a second; indeed, he has neither son nor brother—but: 'Hear O Israel, the Lord our God, the Lord is One' " (*Deut. Rab.* 2.33 on Deut 6:4). "There was a man, the son of a woman, who would rise up and seek to make himself God, and cause the entire world to err. . . . If he says that he is God, he lies; and in the future he will cause to err—that he departs and returns in the end. He says, but will not do. . . . Alas, who shall live of that people that listens to that man who makes himself God?" (*Yal. Shim.* on Num 23:7).

Elsewhere we are told that Moses warns Israel not to expect "another Moses" who will "arise and bring another Law from heaven" (*Deut. Rab.* 8.6 on Deut 30:11-12]). The rabbis predict that "the 'servant' [i.e., Jesus] will bow down to the [real] Messiah" (*b. Sanh.* 61b). Lying behind this statement is the Christian view of Jesus as the Lord's Servant.

3.5. On the Crucifixion of Jesus. "On the eve of Passover they hanged Jesus the Nazarene. And a herald went out before him for forty days, saying: 'He is going to be stoned, because he practiced sorcery and enticed and led Israel astray. Anyone who knows anything in his favor, let him come and plead in his behalf.' But, not having found anything in his favor, they hanged him on the eve of Passover" (*b. Sanh.* 43a; cf. *t. Sanh.* 10:11; *y. Sanh.* 7:12; *Tg. Esther* 7:9). "They brought him to the Beth Din [i.e., "House of Judgment," perhaps the Sanhedrin] and stoned him . . . and they hanged him on the eve of Passover" (*b. Sanh.* 67a; *y. Sanh.* 7:16). Jesus' execution "on the eve of Passover" coheres with Johannine chronology (cf. Jn 18—19). "Balaam the lame was thirty-three years (old) when Phineas the brigand killed him" (*b. Sanh.* 106b). Although it is disputed, "Phineas the brigand" may refer to Pontius Pilate. If this is correct,

then the thirty-three-year-old "Balaam" must be Jesus. "The robber was caught and they hanged him on the gallows, and all passersby say: 'It seems that the ruler is hanged.' Thus, it is said, 'He that is hanged is a reproach to God' [cf. Deut 21:23]" (*t. Sanh.* 9:7). Excluded from the "World to Come" (*m. Sanh.* 10:2), Jesus will be boiled in filth in Gehenna (*b. Giṭ.* 56b-57a).

3.6. On the Resurrection of Jesus. "He then went and raised Jesus by incantation" (*b. Giṭ.* 57a, MS. M). "Woe to him who makes himself alive by the name of God" (*b. Sanh.* 106a). These statements probably belong to the general accusation that Jesus was a magician.

3.7. On Healing in the Name of Jesus. "It once happened that [Eliezer] ben Dama, the son of Rabbi Ishmael's sister, was bitten by a snake; and Jacob [James?], a native of Kefar Sekaniah, came to him in the name of Jesus ben Pantera. But Rabbi Ishmael did not permit him." Ishmael goes on to say that it is better to die in peace than to be healed in the name of Jesus (*t. Ḥul.* 2:22-23; cf. *y. Šabb.* 14:4; *y. 'Abod. Zar.* 2:2; *b. 'Abod. Zar.* 27b; *Qoh. Rab.* 10:5 §1).

4. The Qur'an.

Jesus, his mother Mary, and his disciples are frequently mentioned in the Qur'an (c. A.D. 620). The Arabic tradition appears to be dependent on the NT Gospels, especially Luke (cf. 3:37-41 with Lk 1:5-25, 57-79), and possibly some of the ideas that came to expression in the rabbinic writings. There is tradition that relates to the virginal conception and birth of Jesus: "And mention Mary in the Book when she drew aside from her family to an eastern place, taking a veil (to screen herself) from them. Then We sent to her Our spirit, and there appeared to her a well-made man. . . . She said: 'When shall I have a boy and no mortal has yet touched me, nor have I been unchaste? . . . So she conceived him; then withdrew herself with him to a remote place. And the throes (of childbirth) compelled her to go to the trunk of a palm tree. She said: 'Oh, would that I had died before this, and had become something utterly forgotten!' Then (the child) called out to her from beneath her: 'Grieve not . . . .' " (19:16-17, 20, 22-24; see also 66:12).

Another passage refers to the feeding of the five thousand: "When the disciples said: 'O Jesus son of Mary, will your Lord consent to send down to us food from heaven?' He said: 'Be careful of (your duty to) Allah, if you are believers.' They said: 'We desire that we should eat of it and that our hearts should be at rest, and that we may know that you have indeed spoken the truth to us that we may be of the witnesses to it.' Jesus the son of Mary said: 'O Allah, our Lord!

Send down to us food from heaven which should be to us an ever-recurring happiness, to the first of us and to the last of us, and a sign from You, and grant us means of subsistence, and You are the best of the Providers.' Allah said: 'Surely I will send it down to you, but whoever shall disbelieve afterwards from among you, surely I will chastise him with a chastisement with which I shall not chastise anyone among the nations' " (5:112-115; compare Jn 6:31-65).

Elsewhere Jesus denies divine sonship: "And when Allah will say: 'O Jesus son of Mary! Did you say to men, "Take me and my mother for two gods besides Allah?' " He will say: 'Glory be to You, it did not befit me that I should say what I had no right to (say). If I had said it, You would indeed have known it. You know what is in my mind, and I do not know what is in Your mind. Surely You are the great Knower of the unseen things' " (5:116; see also 5:71, 75; 4:171).

Finally, the Qur'an describes the death and ascension of Jesus: "Allah set a seal upon them owing to their unbelief, so they shall not believe except a few for their saying: 'Surely we have killed the Messiah, Jesus son of Mary, the apostle of Allah.' They did not kill him, nor did they crucify him, but it appeared to them (like Jesus). . . . Nay! Allah took him up to Himself" (4:155-158). A similar idea is credited to Basilides, according to Irenaeus: "He [Christ] appeared, then, on earth as a man, to the nations of these powers, and worked miracles. Wherefore he did not himself suffer death, but Simon, a certain man of Cyrene, being compelled, bore the cross in his stead; so that this latter being transfigured by him, that he might be thought to be Jesus, was crucified, through ignorance and error, while Jesus himself received the form of Simon, and, standing by, laughed at them" (*Haer.* 1.24.4).

See also GOSPELS (APOCRYPHAL); JOSEPHUS.

BIBLIOGRAPHY. J. N. Birdsall, "The Continuing Enigma of Josephus' Testimony about Jesus," *BJRL* 67 (1985) 609-22; F. F. Bruce, *Jesus and Christian Origins Outside the New Testament* (Grand Rapids: Eerdmans, 1974); J. H. Charlesworth, *Jesus within Judaism* (Garden City, NY: Doubleday, 1988); H. Conzelmann, *History of Primitive Christianity* (Nashville: Abingdon, 1973) 163-78; J. M. Creed, "The Slavonic Version of Josephus' History of the Jewish War," *HTR* 25 (1932) 277-319; G. H. Dalman and H. Laible, *Jesus Christ in the Talmud, Midrash, Zohar, and the Liturgy of the Synagogue* (Cambridge: Deighton, Bell, 1893; repr. New York: Arno, 1973); R. Dunkerley, *Beyond the Gospels* (Baltimore: Penguin, 1957); C. A. Evans, *Life of Jesus Research: An Annotated Bibliography* (NTTS 13; Leiden: Brill, 1989) 168-87; L. H. Feldman, "The Testimonium Flavianum: The State of the Question," in *Christological Perspectives,* ed. R. F. Berkey and S. A. Edwards (New York: Pilgrim, 1982) 179-99, 288-93; R. T. France, *The Evidence for Jesus* (Downers Grove: InterVarsity, 1986); M. Goldstein, *Jesus in the Jewish Tradition* (New York: Macmillan, 1950); R. T. Herford, *Christianity in Talmud and Midrash* (London: Williams & Norgate, 1903; repr. New York: Ktav, 1975); idem, "Christ in Jewish Literature," *DCG* 1.876-82; J. Klausner, *Jesus of Nazareth* (New York: Macmillan, 1925) 18-56; S. Pines, *An Arabic Version of the Testimonium Flavianum and Its Implications* (Jerusalem: Israel Academy of Sciences and Humanities, 1971).   C. A. Evans

JESUS OF HISTORY. *See* HISTORICAL JESUS, QUEST OF.

JEW(S). *See* ANTI-SEMITISM; ISRAEL; JUDAISM.

JEWISH WAR. *See* DESTRUCTION OF JERUSALEM; JUDAISM; REVOLUTIONARY MOVEMENTS.

JOHN. *See* DISCIPLES; JOHN, GOSPEL OF.

JOHN, GOSPEL OF

The Gospel of John has long been prized by Christians for its distinctive portrayal of Jesus. John characterizes Jesus as the light* of the world; way, truth* and life*; resurrection*; vine*; good shepherd*; and bread* of life. John presents extensive narrative and sayings material found in no other Gospel, and it includes some of the best-loved stories in the Gospels, such as the encounter with the woman at the well and the raising of Lazarus,* as well as some of the most familiar sayings of the NT, including Jesus' majestic "I am" statements (*see* "I Am" Sayings). And yet controversy has long swirled around problems of John's origin, historicity and theology.

1. The Origin of John
2. The Structure of John
3. The Genre and Character of John
4. The Theology of John

1. The Origin of John.

As with the other Gospels, there are questions about the purpose, intended readers, date and authorship of the Gospel of John. But with John these questions become particularly acute due to its unique content, distinctive presentation of Jesus, and the significant differences between it and the other three (Synoptic) Gospels. In this section we shall briefly take up the questions of authorship, date, place of origin and purpose of the Gospel. We shall deal with related issues, such as the nature of the tradition found only in John and John's relationship to the other three Gospels, in section 3 (The Genre and Character of John).

1.1. Authorship. The Gospel itself comes to us anonymously, as do all the Gospels and, in fact, much ancient literature. The title "According to John" (*kata Iōannēn*) is derived from the tradition that the Gospel was written by the apostle John, the son of Zebedee. This tradition has been challenged for the following reasons: (1) The evidence of the earliest sources and church fathers (external evidence) is deemed ambiguous, inadequate, wrong, legendary or polemical. (2) Those statements within the Gospel which might allude to its authorship (internal evidence) are also ambiguous and perhaps even point away from authorship by one of the Twelve. (3) The content of the Gospel suggests that it was not written by an eyewitness or by one of the twelve disciples* of Jesus. We shall look briefly at the external and internal evidence for authorship and discuss the content of the Gospel in section 3. below.

1.1.1. External Evidence. There are full discussions of the problems of assessing the external evidence in the commentaries of Barrett, Beasley-Murray, Brown and Schnackenburg. None of these scholars holds to authorship by John, the son of Zebedee. Discussion of the issue usually begins with the following statement from Irenaeus (c. A.D. 130-200): "John, the disciple of the Lord, who leaned on his breast, also published the Gospel while living at Ephesus in Asia" (*Haer.* 3.1.1; quoted in Eusebius *Hist. Eccl.* 5.8.4.). Irenaeus also writes (in a letter to a friend, Florinus) of hearing Polycarp (d. 155) recount his interaction with "John and with the others who had seen the Lord, how he remembered their words, and what were the things concerning the Lord which he had heard from them," and of which he took notes "not on paper but in my heart" (*Hist. Eccl.* 5.20.6-7; cf. 4.14.3-5). We have, then, in Irenaeus a man who claims to have traditions from John—whom Irenaeus assumes to be the apostle John, the son of Zebedee—mediated through Polycarp. But questions have been raised about the source and reliability of this information from Irenaeus, especially in light of the following facts:

(1) Other Christian literature which we know to have had its origin or destination in Ephesus, such as the Epistle of Ignatius to the Ephesians, mentions no ministry of the apostle John there, although Ignatius does stress the church's ties to the apostle Paul. Although not inexplicable, the absence of any reference to John is odd if John was known to have ministered there and if his place was firmly fixed in Ephesus.

(2) Irenaeus' testimony depends on secondhand information which he received as a young boy from the aged Polycarp. But it is possible that Irenaeus either did not remember or understand correctly Polycarp's references to "John." For Irenaeus also says that Papias was "a hearer of John and companion of Polycarp" (*Haer.* 5.33.4). But as Eusebius (*Hist. Eccl.* 3.39.33) notes, Papias—according to his own words—was not a "hearer of John" the apostle, but of John the presbyter, who was living in Papias's day (*Hist. Eccl.* 3.39.4). Perhaps this is the John meant by Polycarp as well.

(3) Other testimonies to the apostolic authorship of the Gospel seem to be either legendary or polemical, such as Clement of Alexandria's (c. A.D. 155-220) famous assertion that after the other Gospels were written, "John, perceiving that the bodily facts had been made plain in the Gospels, being urged by his friends, and inspired by the Spirit, composed a spiritual gospel" (Eusebius *Hist. Eccl.* 6.14.7). The Muratorian Canon (c. A.D. 180-200) provides a more elaborate version of the same tradition, in which the other apostles fast and pray with John and then urge him to act as their spokesperson and write a Gospel. Such stories seem to be nothing other than legends, intended, perhaps, to bolster the case for the apostolic authorship of the Fourth Gospel.

Mistakes in these testimonies, lack of corroborating evidence and fanciful narratives do not necessarily impugn the tradition of apostolic authorship, but neither do they inspire confidence in it. It will be seen that the internal evidence leaves us with similar ambiguity.

1.1.2. Internal Evidence. Evidence within the Gospel about its authorship is of two kinds: direct statements about the composition of the Gospel and statements about the "disciple whom Jesus loved" (commonly called the "Beloved Disciple"). These statements come together in 21:24, where we read that "this is the disciple who is bearing witness to these things, and who has written these things; and we know that his testimony is true" (RSV), and 21:20, where "the disciple" is identified as "the disciple whom Jesus loved, who had lain close to his breast at the supper" (RSV). Two questions arise: (1) Does 21:24 imply that "the disciple whom Jesus loved" is the author of the Gospel? (2) Does the Gospel allow us to identify the "Beloved Disciple" as John, the son of Zebedee?

The first question concerns the proper interpretation of 21:24, and several issues arise. First, what is the meaning of "these things" (*tauta*) to which the Beloved Disciple is "bearing witness" and which he "has written"? When taken in conjunction with the statements of 21:25, that "there are also many other things which Jesus did" and that "the world itself could not contain the books that would be written" about all of these, it seems most natural to interpret 21:24 as referring to the entire Gospel. And yet some scholars think that *tauta* refers only to 21:21-23 (the false interpretation of Jesus' saying that must be refuted) or to chapter 21 (which appears to be an addendum; see 2.3. below).

But even if we take "these things" (*tauta*) as referring to the entire Gospel, does John 21:24 assert that the Beloved Disciple wrote the Gospel? That depends on the understanding of the phrase "who has written these things" (*grapsas tauta*), which may be rendered "has caused these things to be written," in which case the Beloved Disciple is indirectly responsible for the Gospel. Whoever wrote 21:24-25 presumably did not write the rest of the Gospel, or at least the rest of chapter 21, since in 21:24 the author (or authors) is testifying to the veracity of the Beloved Disciple's witness. The Gospel presents the Beloved Disciple as the witness on which it is based, but not necessarily as its author.

(2) This leads us to the second question, whether the Beloved Disciple is John the son of Zebedee. "The disciple whom Jesus loved" is mentioned explicitly by that designation in 13:23, as he is in 19:26-27; 20:1-10; and 21:7, 20-24. Although 19:34-37 does not speak of "the disciple whom Jesus loved," it is generally assumed that the witness mentioned there is the Beloved Disciple. John 18:15-16 is sometimes included here and, with greater reservations, 1:35-36. We may summarize the data as follows: (a) Nowhere does the Gospel identify the Beloved Disciple by name. Moreover, the Gospel does not explicitly refer to John, the son of Zebedee, though 21:2 refers to the "sons of Zebedee." (b) It is disputed whether the Gospel presents the Beloved Disciple as one of the Twelve. If we assume that only the Twelve were present at the Last Supper (*see* Last Supper), then the Beloved Disciple must be one of the Twelve. But this assumption is neither supported nor refuted by the Gospel, which refers to those at the Supper as "his own" (13:1) and his "disciples" (13:35), a term not limited in John to the Twelve. (c) The Beloved Disciple is consistently presented as a model of faith* and discipleship,* leading some to assert that the Beloved Disciple is a purely ideal, and not historical, figure. His designation as "the disciple whom Jesus loved" puts him in a position of unique intimacy with Jesus, describing his relationship to Jesus on the same terms that Jesus' relationship to the Father is described (1:18). The suggestion that this veiled allusion is a way of preserv-

ing the author's own modesty seems strained. It would be far less presumptuous simply to name oneself than to continually speak of oneself as enjoying the most intimate of relationships to Jesus. Others would more naturally bestow such a term of honor.

A common understanding of the Beloved Disciple is that he is a person who heard and followed Jesus, although he was not one of the Twelve. That there clearly were such persons is obvious from the rest of the NT (Acts 1:21-26). He exercised a role of leadership in one group of early Christian congregations, probably gathering a circle of disciples around him. One (or more) of his disciples wrote the Gospel, but who this author is remains unknown to us. He preserved, shaped and interpreted the witness of his master, the Beloved Disciple, who had in turn interpreted the teaching of the Master himself.

1.2. Date and Place. As with all the Gospels, it is difficult to fix the date at which John was written, especially since the process of writing and editing the Gospel—whether by one person or several—seems to have occurred over some period of time. The time at which the Gospel was actually published and circulated may be somewhat later than the time of writing.

1.2.1. The Date of the Gospel. Earlier in this century it was fashionable to date the Fourth Gospel in the second century, due to its developed theology, presumed dependence on one (or more) of the Synoptic Gospels, lack of evidence of its use by early second-century writers and lack of early manuscript evidence. But the discovery of Rylands Papyrus 457 ($\mathfrak{P}^{52}$), an Egyptian codex fragment containing John 18:31-33, 37, 38 and dated by scholars to the early second century, suggests that John cannot have been published later than the end of the first century or very early part of the second. A manuscript of a similar date, Egerton Papyrus 2, may have used John. Together with re-evaluations of the theory of a linear development of NT theology, of the view that a high or developed christology must necessarily be late, and of John's use of the Synoptics, these manuscript finds have mitigated the force of the argument for a later date, although they do not solve the problem of dating. One date that has been widely accepted by scholars of all persuasions places the Gospel in the period A.D. 90-100. The earliest external witnesses date the Gospel in this period as well. However, there have always been scholars who have argued that the Gospel can easily be dated earlier, perhaps as early as A.D. 50-60, and that it ought certainly to be placed before the first Jewish-Roman war (A.D. 66-70). In recent studies, this theory has been advanced most forcefully by J. A. T. Robinson (1985). By "priority"

Robinson does not mean that John is necessarily the first of the Gospels to be written, but that it is closest to the "source" (namely, to Jesus himself). Yet, at the same time, John exhibits the deepest theological reflection of all the Gospels. In Robinson's own words, John "got it right—historically and theologically" (xiii). Robinson also argues for the reliability of the ancient tradition that the Gospel is written by John, the son of Zebedee, the Beloved Disciple, but this is not the real focus of his concern. Instead, he is primarily interested in probing the implications of his view for reconstructing the life of Jesus (*see* Historical Jesus).

While scholars typically use only the Synoptic Gospels when reconstructing the ministry and teaching of Jesus, Robinson argues that John ought to be regarded as a witness on a par with the other Gospels—and even to be preferred over them. He argues that we should no longer assume that the Synoptics provide the historical touchstone for understanding Jesus, with John regarded always as secondary and only to be fitted into the Synoptic picture. Instead, we ought to reconsider whether the Gospel story is not often illumined and clarified when we begin with John, and fit the picture of Jesus given in the Synoptic Gospels into its framework.

It is the merit of Robinson's work to point out that while many scholars no longer hold that John uses the other Gospels, and that it therefore supplements or interprets them, they have nevertheless not given up the related presumptions and presuppositions with which they approach the Gospel of John. They continue to use the Synoptics as the norm against which John is measured. But Robinson makes a strong case for reconsidering the historical witness of the Gospel of John to the ministry of Jesus.

Those who hope to find in an early dating (Robinson puts the Gospel's final form at about A.D. 65) a vindication of John's historical accuracy will not be disappointed. However, one must realize that Robinson's arguments are aimed at getting an "equal hearing" for John alongside the other Gospels, as one of four sources for understanding the historical events of Jesus' life and ministry. Its witness cannot simply be added to that of the Synoptics, but must be weighed along with theirs. Thus Robinson is not interested in harmonizing the four Gospels, but in arguing for John's priority in reconstructing our understanding of Jesus. As an example, one may take the cleansing of the Temple (*see* Temple Cleansing), which the Synoptics place toward the end of Jesus' life, and John puts quite early. Robinson does not argue for two cleansings, but rather that on historical grounds there is

good reason to prefer the Johannine dating rather than the Synoptic chronology.*

Many of Robinson's arguments carry weight even if one does not adopt all his conclusions about individual points of exegesis or historical reconstruction. While most scholars have not been persuaded to follow Robinson, he has at least reopened the question of the date of the Gospel. Most scholars continue to place the date of the Gospel post-70, and probably sometime after A.D. 85 or so. But others will ask whether John cannot comfortably be placed early in the period A.D. 70-100, rather than toward the end of that period.

1.2.2. Place. According to tradition the Gospel was published in Ephesus, but other large centers of Christian activity which also had significant Jewish populations and representatives of various Hellenistic religions, such as Alexandria and Syrian Antioch, have also been proposed. Indeed, some see the traditions of the Gospel as stemming from Palestine, but being shaped into their final form in other territory, where the influence of Diaspora Judaism* and Hellenistic religions was greater.

1.3. The Life Setting and Purpose of the Gospel.

1.3.1. The Life Setting of the Gospel. There are various clues in the Gospel from which we may make some tentative deductions about situations which shaped the traditions and material within the Gospel as we now know it. (1) The Gospel often refers to "the Jews," even when "the Jews" are distinguished from other persons who are obviously also Jewish (cf. 1:19; 2:13; 3:25; 6:42; 7:2, 11, 13, 15, passim). Indeed, throughout the Gospel the "Jews" are set over against those who believe in Jesus as Messiah; that is, "Jews" are set over against Christians, not Gentiles,* and the term is not used simply as an ethnic or racial characterization.

(2) The Gospel manifests perhaps the sharpest polemic in the NT against the "Jews"—a polemic matched in force only by passages such as Matthew 23 (e.g., Jn 8:42-47; *see* Anti-Semitism). The intensity of the polemic may be a reaction to Jewish measures, and particularly to expulsion from the synagogue* (9:22; 12:42; 16:2) of those who had become believers in Jesus. Some scholars have suggested that the reference to being expelled from the synagogue reflects the Jewish *birkat hamminîn* ("blessing against the heretics"), said to have been promulgated at Jamnia under Rabbi Gamaliel II about A.D. 85-90. In its full form this prayer invokes God's judgment* upon all heretics, including Christians and sectarian Jews. However, some scholars judge the *birkat* to have been formulated much later, perhaps as late as A.D. 135. In any case, it is questionable whether the actions

described in the Gospel mirror those dictated by the "benediction." The NT and early Christian literature testify to strained and hostile relationships between Christians and Jews at an earlier date, beginning with the confrontation between Stephen and certain Jews in Jerusalem (Acts 6—8).

(3) The Gospel is concerned for second-generation (and subsequent) believers who were not eyewitnesses (20:26-31), including Jews and Gentiles (7:35), the other "sheep not of this fold" (10:16; cf. 7:35; 11:52). The situation and role of this community's life under the guidance of the Holy Spirit (see Holy Spirit) is dealt with at length (14—16). There is reference to the need for unity and love* within the community (15:12-17; 17:20-23), continued faithfulness to Jesus (15:1-11; 17:11-12), the possibility of persecution (15:18-25; 16:1-4), anxiety and turmoil (14:1-7, 18-21, 27-31; 16:4-6; 16:16-24), the role of the Spirit's instruction (14:15-17, 25-26; 16:7-15) and the community's mission in the world (14:12-14, 23-24; 15:26-27; 17:15-19).

We may speculate that the community whose life and struggles are reflected in the Gospel was a community made up of Jewish and Gentile Christians. Prior to the composition (or at least final editing) of the Gospel, a primarily Jewish-Christian church had experienced hostile conflict with the Jews of the synagogue, to the point of ostracism and alienation. By the time the Gospel is written the hostilities between Jews and Christians are behind it, and the church includes Gentile believers. It continues to experience the pressures of existence in this world and hence needs to be reminded of the words that Jesus gave to the church about its life and mission. This leads us to a discussion of the purpose of the Gospel.

1.3.2. The Purpose of the Gospel. The Gospel presents us with a statement of its own purpose in 20:31 (RSV): "These are written that you may believe that Jesus is the Christ, the Son of God, and that believing you may have life in his name." But this broad statement leaves many details to be filled in. Some have interpreted this statement to mean that the Gospel is an evangelistic document, designed to win converts, perhaps from Diaspora Judaism. But the sharpness of the polemic against unbelieving Jews in the Gospel counts against this hypothesis. Moreover, the statement that the Gospel is written in order "that you may believe" can also be rendered, "that you may continue to believe," and much of the Gospel seems designed to encourage believers to persevere in faith.

The Gospel intends to present Jesus to second and subsequent generations of believers, those who did not "see signs" but have the Gospel's written account of them (20:30-31: "these are written"). By making clear who Jesus is and the salvation that he offers, the Gospel intends to encourage and strengthen believers in their faith in Jesus as the Messiah and Son of God. As part of its exhortative function, the Gospel endeavors to clarify the relationship of Jesus to Judaism by showing his superiority to the patriarchs of the Jewish faith (4:12; 6:32; 8:53-58), the replacement in his person of Jewish feasts* and religious institutions (2:1-11, 19-22; 6:32-41; 7:37-39), and the relationship between the Law* and Moses* on the one hand and Jesus Christ on the other (1:17; 5:39-40, 45-47; 7:19-23). Probably these traditions were shaped by disputes with the synagogue. Yet the Gospel clearly indicates the place that Gentile believers are to have in the community of faith.

Other theories, not necessarily incompatible with the broad statement of purpose outlined above, have been advanced as well. (1) An older view was that John is the Gospel in Hellenized form. While this theory has been questioned, due to a re-evaluation of the influence of Hellenism* on Judaism and of the character of the Gospel itself, there are unquestionably striking contacts with Hellenistic religion and philosophy (for example, in the Logos* doctrine). (2) The Gospel endeavors to make clear the proper relationship between John the Baptist (see John the Baptist) and Jesus (1:6-8, 15, 19-28, 30; 3:22-30; 5:33-36; 10:40-42). Although some have interpreted these statements as an anti-Baptist polemic, directed against a group claiming John to be the Messiah, such an evaluation goes too far. The Gospel presents John positively as a witness—virtually equivalent to "disciple" in John—to Jesus. (3) Similarly, the Gospel repeatedly defines the role of the Beloved Disciple vis-à-vis that of Peter (13:23-25; 20:3-8; 21:7, 20-23), which has been taken as evidence of some conflict between the churches represented by the Beloved Disciple and by Peter. The Gospel does bolster the case for the Beloved Disciple's authority and distinctive role, perhaps to show that he was in no way inferior to Peter and the Twelve. (4) Some see in those verses of John that insist on the "flesh" of Jesus (1:14; 6:51-58) an anti-docetic polemic. But the Gospel seems not so much intent on proving the true humanity or physicality of Jesus, as it does in pressing the case for the heavenly origin and identity of the incarnate Word. These statements are not directed against docetists, but against those who do not share the Christian confession of Jesus as the Word made flesh (1:14). (5) Others suggest that the Gospel contains an apologetic against or for the sacramental teaching of the church, and the material in 6:51-58 certainly has eucharistic overtones. But it is difficult to discern a theology of the sacraments from the passages on water (which seem to refer more to the Holy Spirit than to baptism) and blood.

The Gospel may have been edited over a period of years to include materials that met changing or different circumstances. Its basic purpose, to tell the story of Jesus in such a way that his identity as Messiah and Son of God is made known to later generations, shines through, regardless of the many individual polemics and situations that may also have shaped the production of the Gospel. Indeed, the very structure of the Gospel points to the purpose of the Gospel to define who Jesus is, and to do so in categories that arise out of Judaism, but speak to a broader religious milieu as well.

2. The Structure of John.

The Gospel is essentially divided into two main parts, with a prologue (1:1-18) and an epilog (chapter 21). The first main part, 1:19—12:50, was designated by C. H. Dodd as the "Book of Signs," and the second part, 13:1—20:31, as "The Book of the Passion" or "The Book of Glory" (Brown). Each "book" ends with a summary statement (12:37-50; 20:30-31). All the signs (or miracles) of Jesus are narrated in the first part, while the second part begins with the Last Supper (*see* Last Supper) and concentrates on the events leading up to and including the passion narrative and the resurrection appearances. "Book of Glory" is an apt designation for the second part of the book, since in Johannine theology Jesus' glorification occurs as he returns to the Father through his death,* resurrection and ascension.*

2.1. The Prologue (1:1-18). Parts of these verses appear to come from an early Christian hymn, or at least from creedal or confessional material of the church. And since some of the vocabulary (such as Logos and grace*) does not appear again in the Gospel, some argue that the prologue was affixed to the Gospel after it was completed. But even if the prologue has underlying sources, as it stands, it introduces the main themes, movement and chief protagonist of the Gospel. Opening with an echo of Genesis 1:1, the prologue goes on to identify its protagonist as the "Logos,"* the Word of God, and thus places the drama in a cosmic setting and against an OT background. The prologue foreshadows the division between belief and unbelief so characteristic of the rest of the Gospel (1:10-11). This division rests on one's response to and understanding of Jesus Christ (1:12-13). The prologue argues for its confession of Jesus by prohibiting false evaluations of John the

Baptist (1:6-8, 15), showing the relationship of Jesus to Moses and the Law (1:17-18) and calling for belief in Jesus Christ as the Logos of God made flesh (1:1, 14). Throughout each episode of the Gospel the drama hinted at in the prologue is replayed as the various persons that Jesus encounters endeavor to understand who Jesus is. Some (the Samaritan* woman, the man born blind, Martha, Thomas) eventually come to a confession which, if not phrased in the words of the prologue, is consonant with it, while others reject precisely the prologue's evaluation of Jesus Christ as the Word and Son of God (e.g., the disciples of 6:66; the Jewish authorities of 7:32, 35-52; 11:45-53).

2.2. The Book of Signs (1:19—12:50). The arrangement of much of the first part of the Gospel is topical and thematic. The placement of some events (e.g., Jesus' baptism) is due to chronological considerations, while that of others (the cleansing of the Temple, the raising of Lazarus) may be due to theological reasons or for dramatic effect. John thus introduces early in the Gospel the theme that Jesus replaces, in his person, the religious observances of Judaism. With the narrative of the changing of the water to wine* (2:1-11), Jesus is seen transforming the water set aside for the Jewish rites of purification into the wine symbolic of the presence of the messianic age (Amos 9:13-14; Hos 14:7; Jer 31:12).

The rest of the book of signs (2:12—12:50) refers to various feasts* of the Jewish calendar (2:13; 5:1; 6:4; 7:2; 10:22; 11:55). These references serve to move the story along chronologically, as well as to introduce imagery from the ceremonies that become the backdrop for Jesus' self-revelation in signs and discourses, which provoke his disputes with opponents. Thus, for example, the Sabbath* (the probable feast of 5:1) becomes the occasion for a Sabbath healing and subsequent disputes about Jesus' authority (*see* Authority and Power) to work on the Sabbath, to give life and to raise the dead—all privileges deemed reserved for God (chap. 5). Near Passover Jesus feeds the five thousand and gives a long discourse on being the "bread from heaven," actions and words which recall the exodus from Egypt on the original Passover and the giving of manna to provide for the people of God (chap. 6). The Feast of Tabernacles included ceremonies which featured both water and light, and it is at this feast that Jesus promises living water* (7:37-39) and proclaims that he is the light of the world (8:12; 9:5). Following the climactic deed of the raising of Lazarus from the dead, there comes a transitional chapter (chap. 12) which summarizes the results of Jesus' ministry in terms of unbelief and belief. Jesus' public ministry is over, and he will now engage in extensive private instruction to his disciples (chaps. 13—17).

2.3. Book of Glory (13:1—20:31). The Book of Glory is divided into three subsections: (1) chapter 13, the Last Supper with the disciples (*see* Last Supper); (2) chapters 14—17, the so-called Farewell Discourses of Jesus to the disciples (*see* Farewell Discourse); (3) chapters 18—20, the narratives of the passion (*see* Passion Narrative) and resurrection.* The Last Supper that Jesus eats with his disciples is apparently not a Passover meal, but occurs twenty-four hours prior to the eating of the Passover. There is no institution of the Lord's Supper, but rather the story of Jesus' washing the disciples' feet, which prefigures Jesus' sacrificial death and provides an example for the disciples to imitate in community (*see* Service). Chapters 14—17 then provide exhortations about community life, instruction about the role of the Holy Spirit in teaching and guiding the community, warnings about persecution and trouble, and encouragement to remain faithful to Jesus. Chapter 17 is a prayer* that the disciples will be kept safe and remain faithful. The passion narratives (*see* Passion Narrative) and resurrection appearances share features in common with the Synoptic Gospels, even though they have numerous incidents and scenes distinctive to John.

2.4. Epilog (chap. 21). For several reasons the last chapter of the Gospel appears to many to be an appendix of additional narratives not included in the earlier draft of the Gospel. (1) The Gospel appears to end with the summary statement at 20:30-31. (2) The additional resurrection appearance is more like a first appearance, since the disciples do not recognize Jesus (although they have previously seen and recognized the risen Lord*). (3) The narrative of Peter's restoration seems out of place, for it would have belonged more naturally prior to the giving of the Spirit and commissioning of the disciples. (4) Finally, it appears that a new problem has arisen within the church, namely, the death of the Beloved Disciple. Chapter 21 has been added to correct a rumor that circulated concerning a prophecy that Jesus had made about the death of the Beloved Disciple.

At least 21:24-25 are added later. They may reflect the fact that the Beloved Disciple has recently died, although he was alive when the first edition of the Gospel was being written (as the present tense in 19:35 suggests). His death appears to contradict Jesus' prediction that the Beloved Disciple would remain alive until he returned, but the author of the Gospel (or of these verses) notes that this is not what Jesus had said.

But most of chapter 21 deals not with the death of the Beloved Disciple, but with Peter and with Jesus' prophecy about his death. Just as Peter denied Jesus three times, so now he is asked three times whether he loves Jesus. The commands to "tend my sheep" and "feed my lambs" may be reported to show that Peter's role was understood to be that of "shepherd," whereas the Beloved Disciple is understood chiefly as a "witness." Nevertheless, Peter was commanded above all else to "follow me" (21:19), just as the Beloved Disciple is shown doing in the very next verse (21:20). Thus chapter 21 again contrasts Peter and the Beloved Disciple, includes Jesus' prediction about each disciple's death, and shows how the Beloved Disciple was ahead of Peter in recognizing and following Jesus. The chapter does not so much denigrate Peter as it shows that the role of each disciple is distinctive, but not thereby inferior to that of the other disciple.

3. The Genre and Character of John.

3.1. John and the Synoptics. The difference between John and the other Gospels is significant, and it raises the question of John's relationship to them. This question is not new, nor is it merely the product of modern biblical criticism. The assertion of the early Christian writer Clement of Alexandria that John is a "spiritual Gospel" while the others recount the "physical" or "bodily" facts (Eusebius *Hist. Eccl.* 6.14.7) was an early attempt to account for the differences between all the Gospels (*see* Synoptics and John).

3.1.1. The Johannine Difference. The particular differences between John and the other three Gospels are striking and may be set out briefly.

(1) *Material and Content.* In John we do not find: parables*; demon* exorcisms; healings of lepers (*see* Leprosy); tax* collectors; Sadducees; table fellowship with sinners* (*see* Table Fellowship); infancy narratives (*see* Birth of Jesus); the temptation of Jesus (*see* Temptation of Jesus); the Transfiguration*; the material in Matthew's Sermon on the Mount (*see* Sermon on the Mount); or the institution of the Lord's Supper (*see* Last Supper). On the other hand, the following material is in John, but not in any of the Synoptics: Jesus' baptismal ministry at the Jordan (*see* Baptism); the encounters with Nicodemus and the Samaritan woman; the "I am" sayings, coupled with long discourses; most of the material in chapters 7—11, and 14—17; the footwashing; and Jesus' conversation with Pilate (*see* Pontius Pilate). Of the Johannine miracles (*see* Miracles, Miracle Stories) only the feeding of the five thousand is found in the other Gospels.

(2) *Vocabulary.* Whereas "kingdom of God" occurs often in the Synoptics, it occurs only twice in John, and the distinctively Johannine terminology (truth, witness,* world,* abide, love,* believe, light, darkness, life, and Father and Son) occurs far less often in the other Gospels.

(3) *Chronology and Presentation of Jesus' Ministry.* While in the Synoptics Jesus goes to Jerusalem only at the end of his life (except for Luke's account of Jesus' visit to the Temple* as a boy), much of the ministry in John occurs in Jerusalem and Judea. The Temple cleansing (*see* Temple Cleansing) is placed early in the Gospel, rather than toward the end; Jesus and John the Baptist minister at the same time; the anointing* occurs prior to the triumphal entry; and the Last Supper appears to be eaten twenty-four hours earlier than in the other Gospels.

(4) *Messianic Secret.* Whereas in the Synoptics Jesus is first confessed as Messiah by Peter well into the course of the ministry, in John, Jesus is acknowledged with various messianic titles—six times in the first chapter alone (1:29, 34, 36, 41, 45, 49)!

3.1.2. The Question of John's Relationship with the Synoptics. Prior to the twentieth century most interpreters assumed that John was familiar with the other Gospels, and that his role was to supplement and interpret them. While this theory has a broad appeal, it is difficult to explain all the differences in detail and content as either supplementation or interpretation. Sometimes the theory that John wrote to interpret the other Gospels has been coupled with a denigration of its historical value (forcing a choice between John or the Synoptics in deciding historical questions), due to the problems and difficulties in reconciling the differences between John and the other Gospels. Some scholars have gone farther, suggesting that John intended to replace or supplant the other Gospels. All of these theories depend on the assumption that John knew or was familiar with the other Gospels. But in the twentieth century that theory has been challenged.

The theory that John is independent of the other Gospels was carefully argued by P. Gardner-Smith and C. H. Dodd, and it has become widely, although not unanimously, accepted. On this theory John was composed without knowledge of, or reference to, the other three written Gospels. All the similarities between them can be accounted for by shared tradition, whether written or oral, which John used without access to the Synoptics. The differences are due to variant traditions—which does not rule out eyewitness recollection—and John's highly interpretive character (*see* Tradition Criticism).

While John may have known of the other Gospels,

he did not use them as sources in the way that Matthew and Luke used Mark. Study of John ought not to proceed on the assumption that the Gospel intends to be a commentary on or elucidation of the other Gospels. Neither is it helpful to repeat older explanations that while the Synoptics are biography or history, John is doctrine or theology. At least some of the difference between John and the Synoptics is a difference of the degree to which the author's interpretation has shaped the story. This leads us to the question of the character of the Gospel of John.

3.2. The Historical Character of the Gospel of John. A recognition of the differences between John and the other Gospels and of John's intensely interpretive character raises the question of the nature of the historical tradition found only in John (*see* Gospels [Historical Reliability]). If, for example, all the other Gospels record Jesus as speaking in parables and often of the kingdom of God (*see* Kingdom of God), but never in "I am" sayings, how are we to assess the historicity of such utterances? We should note, first of all, that simply because information is found only in John is no reason to discard it as of no historical value (see esp. Robinson). Scholars consider it probable, for example, that Jesus' ministry lasted two to three years (as John implies), that he was in and out of Jerusalem (as the other Gospels hint—e.g., Lk 13:34), that some of the disciples of Jesus were first disciples of John the Baptist (1:35-37), and that Jesus and his disciples conducted a ministry of baptism (3:22).

There is also material in John which is similar or identical to that in the Synoptics, but appears in different contexts or looks like a different story. Such material includes the charges of demon possession (cf. Mk 3:22-30 and Jn 7:20; 8:48-53; 10:19-20), the unbelief of Jesus' brothers (Mk 3:31-35 and Jn 7:5), challenges to Jesus' authority (Mk 2:1—3:6; 3:22-30; 11:27-33 and Jn 5:19, 26-27, 30) and titles such as "prophet"* (Mk 6:15; 7:28 and Jn 6:14; 7:40), "Messiah" (Mk 8:29; 14:61 and Jn 1:17, 41; 7:41-42) and "Son of man" (Mk 2:28; 8:31, 38; 9:31; 10:33, 45 and Jn 1:51; 3:13-14; 5:27; 6:53, 62; 9:35; 12:34). Although most of the miracles are unique to John, they have analogies in the Synoptics.

Finally, John shows an elaboration and development of themes found in the other Gospels, such as Jesus' relationship to the Father, his messianic authority, the Holy Spirit and the meaning of Jesus' miracle-working activity.

Clearly historical traditions and reminiscences lie behind John, and information from John should not be dismissed simply because it comes from John. Nevertheless, such information must be judiciously weighed in light of what we know about the interpretative character of all the Gospels, and with awareness of the contours of Jesus' ministry as it is portrayed in the Synoptics.

Much of our understanding of the Gospel of John will depend on our prior definition and understanding of the genre of the Gospels (see Gospel [Genre]). Where the Gospels are understood to be interpretations of the life of Jesus, for specific purposes and audiences, John will be seen to fit that genre, even though it has exercised more freedom in reworking and interpreting the traditions upon which it is based. To a more marked extent than the Synoptics, John's Gospel consciously interprets the essence of Jesus' ministry and teaching in light of later theological reflection. John explicitly acknowledges the understanding gained after the resurrection (2:22; 7:39; 12:16; 13:7) and through the instruction of the Paraclete (15:26; 16:13, 14), and some of this insight is likely incorporated into the Gospel itself. In many respects, John is like one of the Pauline epistles, interpreting the meaning of Jesus' life and death in terms and categories that were not typical or characteristic of Jesus himself. As part of our canon of Scripture, the Gospel of John bears authoritative witness to Jesus, who he is, and what he means for Christians and for the world (see Canon).

4. The Theology of John.

4.1. Christology. One of the most striking features of the Gospel of John is its distinctive christology. Although John shares several important titles with the other Gospels, these are sometimes used in distinctively Johannine ways. In addition, there are other images and designations for Jesus peculiar to John. Following an overview of some of the more important titles, we will summarize the central features of John's picture of Jesus.

4.1.1. Word/Logos. The only other place in the NT that the title "Word (Gk *logos*) of God" appears is in Revelation 19:13 (see Logos). But the term was also used in Greek philosophical thought. According to Heraclitus (6th cent. B.C.), the Logos was the eternal principle of order in the universe. The Stoics saw the "word" as the mind of God, the principle of reason within the universe, controlling and directing all things. But the idea of God's word (or God's speaking) has a Jewish context as well. God created the world by speaking it into existence (Gen 1; Ps 33:6). In the prophetic books, "the word of the Lord" is nearly personified as it is described as coming to a particular prophet (Hos 1:1; Joel 1:1). The word heals (Ps 107:20), obedience to it brings life (Deut 32:46-47) and

it is a light that guides people to God (Ps 119:105, 130).

The Johannine description of the Word (*logos*) has further affinities with the Jewish concept of Wisdom* as well. In Proverbs 8, especially verses 22-31, Wisdom is said to have existed in the beginning, prior to the creation of the world; it was God's agent in creation; it brings life and light to those who accept it; and it was rejected by most human beings. According to Sirach 24:8, Wisdom made its dwelling among human beings. The verb for "made its dwelling" is a cognate of the term used of the Logos's "dwelling" (*skēnoō*) in John 1:14. The actual term "word," *logos*, is that found in the OT prophets in the Greek OT (LXX), but the characterization of that *logos* in John has striking correspondences to the biblical and apocryphal descriptions of wisdom.

The utility of the term *Logos* to speak to both the Jewish and Greek worlds is demonstrated by the Jewish writer Philo (born c. 20 B.C.), who attempted to explain Judaism in terms of Greek philosophy in order to give a rational account of the Jewish faith. Philo spoke of the Logos as an intermediary between God and his creatures, which gave meaning to the universe and was the instrument of God in creation. Like the rabbis, Philo speculated about the two "powers" of God (in the rabbinic writings, the "two measures," or *middôt*), and identified these "powers" with the names of God. In Philo these powers are frequently characterized as the creative power and ordering or ruling power of God. In commenting on Exodus 25:22, Philo describes the ark of the covenant, identifies the two cherubim with the two powers of God, in whose midst is the Logos, and goes on to say: "And from the divine Logos as from a spring, there divide and break forth two powers. One is the creative power through which the Artificer placed and ordered all things: this is named 'God.' And the other is the royal power, since through it the Creator rules over created things; this is called 'Lord' (*Quaest. in Ex.* 2.68; see *Fug.* 95-98, 100-101). In the Logos are the two powers of God, to create and to rule, and for this reason the Logos can be called "God" and "Lord" (cf. Jn 1:1; 20:28). In John the Logos is the agent of creation (1:3) and the incarnate Logos is the agent of God's judgment. And also in John's Gospel, the Logos is confessed as Lord and God, an important designation for Jesus in Johannine theology.

4.1.2. God. The opening words of the Gospel raise the problem of Johannine Christology in acute form when they say both that the Word was with God,* thereby implying a distinction between the Word and God, and that the Word was God (1:1-2). The designation of Jesus as "God" occurs once more, in John

20:28, when the risen Jesus is confessed as "Lord and God." Elsewhere, Jesus is accused of "making himself equal to God" (5:18) and "making himself God" (10:33). While the pair of titles ("Lord and God") in 20:28 may reflect the fact that the emperor Domitian (A.D. 81-96) sought to have himself addressed as "Lord and God," the absolute designation of the Word as "God" (in 1:1) requires another explanation. What the Gospel means in introducing the Word as "God" must be understood in light of the strict monotheism of Judaism that became the heritage of Christianity as well.

Here the Jewish category of *agency* sheds light. In the rabbinic writings there is reference to the figure of the *šālîaḥ*, which means literally "one who is sent" (*see* Apostle). A *šālîaḥ* was a surrogate sent on a task or mission with specific instructions and authority to carry it out. According to the Talmud, a *šālîaḥ* could, among other things, carry out business transactions, make binding treaties and arrange marriages (*b. Qidd.* 41a, 42b-43a). A common saying in the rabbis was "the one who is sent is like the one who sent him" or "a man's agent is equivalent to himself" (*m. Ber.* 5:5; *b. B. Meṣ.* 96a; *b. ḥag.* 10b; *b. Menaḥ.* 93b; *b. Nazir* 12b; *b. Qidd.* 42b, 43a). Because the *šālîaḥ* may act on behalf of the one who sent him, when one deals with the *šālîaḥ* it is as if one is dealing with the one who sent that person.

Jesus is presented in the Gospel against the backdrop of the Jewish concept of agency and, furthermore, against the understanding that there is one chief agent through whom God acts. Such chief agents were variously understood to be a principal angel* (Gabriel, Michael), an exalted patriarch (Enoch, Moses) or personified divine attributes (Wisdom, Word). Clearly the Word is understood as God's chief and exclusive agent in creation (1:3). He is shown exercising the divine prerogatives in judging (5:22, 27, 30; 8:16, 26; 9:39; 12:47-48), in raising the dead (5:21, 25-26, 28-29; 6:27, 35, 39-40, 50-51, 54-58; 10:28; 11:25-26) and in working on the Sabbath (5:9-18; 7:21-23), deeds which, according to various Jewish authors, were permitted to God alone. Because Jesus is the chief agent of God, when one confronts him, one confronts God. When the concept of agency is coupled with speculation on the names or powers of God, we see that the name of "God" for the Word is intended to show that the Word exercises the divine prerogatives. As Jesus of Nazareth, the incarnate Word continues to exercise the divine prerogatives, and exactly these actions and this claim evoke hostility from the Jewish authorities who charge Jesus with blasphemy* (10:31-38).

4.1.3. "I Am." Unique to the Gospel of John are the "I am" sayings (*see* "I Am" Sayings). In those "I am" statements with a predicate (bread of life, light of the world, vine) Jesus speaks of the salvation that he offers to human beings. The "I am" sayings without predicate (8:24, 28, 58) are more difficult to interpret. In the OT "I am" sayings are found in contexts of God's revelation to Israel. "I am" also appears, apparently, as the name of God ("I am who I am"). But note that the LXX translation of this crucial passage in Exodus 3:14 is "I am the one who is" (*egō eimi ho ōn*), thus underscoring that the essence of God's being or nature is unique, divine existence: God is.

Clearly the absolute "I am" sayings of the Gospel intend to reveal something about Jesus' person, and to do so with a formula that alludes to the OT formula of divine revelation. Yet Jesus is not simply using a familiar divine name for himself. His statement would not have been heard as "I am Yahweh." Rather, as the "I am" statements especially in chapter 8 reveal, Jesus claims to share in God's eternal existence. He has life in himself (5:26), and the power to lay down his life and to take it again (10:17-18). He also has the power to give life to those who keep his word (8:51; 17:2), thus exercising the unique life-giving prerogative of God. In chapter 8, one of the most heated disputes with his opponents, Jesus' claim "Before Abraham was, I am" (8:58) contrasts Abraham's* kind of life which "came into being" (*genesthai*) with his own, which simply "is" (*egō eimi*; present tense). These claims resonate with what is perhaps the central theme of the Gospel: that Jesus has and mediates eternal life (20:30-31; and see 3:16, 36; 4:14, 53; 5:21-26; 6:33, 35, 44, 51-58, 68; 8:12; 10:10, 17-18; 11:25; 14:6; 17:2-3).

There is, therefore, a reference to the divine OT "I am" in the claim of 8:58, but it is allusive or indirect. Jesus does not say "I am the I am." In fact, in 8:24 and 28, when Jesus uses the absolute "I am," no one reacts, except in puzzlement. It is not until he claims, in 8:48-58, to "have seen Abraham," that is, to share in eternal life, that the people react: now he is claiming to have or give what God alone has and gives. The Johannine "I am" statements link Jesus' work and person in the most intimate relationship with the divine person and work. They are, therefore, closely analogous to the predicate "Word" and "God" (see 4.1.1. and 4.1.2. above).

4.1.4. Son of God. In the Gospel and Epistles of John, Jesus is called the "Son of God" (*huios*), while Christians are called "children of God" (*tekna*) who are "born of God" (*see* Son of God). This distinction highlights the unique relationship of Jesus to the Father, which is further underscored by the Gospel's designation of Jesus as "the only Son" or "the unique Son" (*monogenēs*). (The KJV's translation of this term as "only begotten" is due to Jerome's translation of the Greek term with the Latin *unigenitus*—"only begotten"—which the KJV then echoed. Jerome was answering the Arian assertion that Jesus was "made" not "begotten.")

The frequent characterization of the Son as "sent" from the Father has a legal flavor. As Son, Jesus can function as a unique delegate (*šālîaḥ*) on his Father's behalf and, indeed, the "Father has given all things into the Son's hands" (3:35). Nevertheless, that Jesus is Son also underlines his dependence on and obedience to the Father (5:19, "The Son can do nothing of his own accord"; cf. 3:34; 7:28; 8:26, 42; 10:32, 37; 12:49). All that the Son does, he does in perfect harmony with his Father's will. Thus the Gospel speaks of reciprocal knowledge of Father and Son (10:15). Because of this intimate and reciprocal knowledge, the Son reveals the Father (1:18; 8:38; 15:15; 17:25-26). When the Gospel speaks of the unity of the Father and Son, it points especially to their unity in the work of revelation and salvation (8:16; 10:25-30; 14:10-11; 17:10). That is to say, the actions and words of Jesus were truly the actions and words of God. In the incarnate Word we are confronted by God, and the designation of Jesus as "Son" serves to underscore the intimate connection between God and Jesus.

4.1.5. Messiah. In the NT John alone presents the transliterated form of the Hebrew or Aramaic term *messias* (1:41; 4:25); "Christ" (*christos*) is used 17 times; and the compound "Jesus Christ" occurs twice (1:17; 17:3; *see* Christ). Whether or not Jesus is the Messiah becomes a topic of conversation and controversy far more often than in the Synoptics. The Baptist denies that he is the Messiah (1:20; 3:28); Jesus' disciples acclaim him as Messiah quite early in the narrative (1:41); both the Samaritans (4:29) and Jews (7:25-31, 40-43, 52; 12:49) discuss Messiahship; and the confession of Jesus as Messiah is met with expulsion from the synagogue (9:22; cf. 16:2). Yet, like the Synoptic Gospels, Jesus does not announce himself to be the Messiah, nor answer plainly when asked whether he is the Christ (10:24). There is a secret to Jesus' messiahship in John, and that secret is revealed to the eyes of faith. John's use of the term *Messiah* still maintains its meaning of the one anointed by God as vice regent in the messianic kingdom, and John emphasizes Jesus' kingly role (6:14-15; 18:33-37). In some places it appears that Messiah is virtually equivalent to "Son of God" (20:31), emphasizing again the unique relationship to God that this appointed agent has.

4.1.6. Son of Man. Few problems have vexed scholars as greatly as that of the title or phrase "Son of man" in the Gospels (*see* Son of Man). The central features of John's portrait of Jesus as "Son of man" may be sketched. (1) As the Son of man, Jesus serves as judge in the final judgment (5:27), a usage paralleling the Synoptic statements that the Son of man will return in glory (Mk 13:26). (2) Son of man is particularly linked with death, especially when it is described as Jesus being "lifted up" from the earth. (3) The Son of man reveals God by serving as the mediator between earth and heaven (1:51; 3:13; 6:27, 62). These three categories should not be kept distinct from each other, however, but are obviously closely related. Jesus' glorification and death are nearly synonymous in John, for Jesus' death is at the same time his lifting up to the Father in glory (Jn 3:14). Moreover, when he is lifted up his work is brought to its climactic fulfillment as mediator between God and all humankind.

4.1.7. Prophet. The Gospel speaks of Jesus as "prophet," but the question is whether John accepts this designation for Jesus; regards it as correct, but not ultimate or adequate; or rejects it entirely (*see* Prophet, Prophecy). A prophet was a person who spoke with divine authority and by divine inspiration. When Jesus heals the man born blind, the man acknowledges him to be "a prophet" (9:17), thus confessing him to be "from God" (9:16). Jesus' feeding of the five thousand leads people to exclaim, "Surely this is the prophet who is to come into the world!" (6:14), and some wonder whether he is "the Prophet" (7:40). These acclamations honor Jesus not just as one among the prophets, but as the Prophet who would appear in the end time, thus fulfilling the promise of Moses to the people in Deuteronomy 18:15, "The Lord your God will raise up for you a prophet like me." The expectation of a prophet-like-Moses was known among the Samaritans (cf. Jn 4:19) and the community at Qumran (4Q Testim 5-8). Thus the confession of Jesus as a prophet acknowledges Jesus' divine commissioning and authoritative message; but the confession of Jesus as the Prophet points to his unique role as the final prophet of God. Here again Jesus is portrayed as the chief and unique agent of God.

We may summarize John's portrait of Jesus by noting the importance of the category of the agent as background. Jesus is the uniquely commissioned agent of God who, in his task of bringing the salvation of God to the world, exercises a unique, mediating function between God and human beings. Because Jesus is the designated agent of God, he also represents God to human beings in such a way that the

Gospel can say that to encounter Jesus is to encounter God, to have seen him is to have seen the Father (12:45; 14:7-9), or to know and receive him is to have known and received the Father (8:19; 12:44; 13:20; 17:8; cf. 15:23). As God's agent Jesus carries out a mission which mediates God's salvation to the world, as is manifested in the signs which he does.

4.2. Signs and Faith. According to John 20:30-31 the narratives of the signs were written down in order to lead to faith. And while the signs figure prominently throughout the Gospel, there are numerous problems surrounding our interpretation of the meaning and role of signs, including such issues as the definition of a sign, the function of signs, and the relationship of signs and faith.

The term *sign* is not unique to John, although it is used differently than in the Synoptic Gospels. There a sign is either (1) an act confirming the truth of what Jesus has said, which Jesus refuses to supply (Mk 8:11-12); or (2) a portent of the end times (Mk 13:4, 22). In the Synoptics the miracles are usually called "mighty deeds" (*dynameis*). But in John the miracles are regularly called "signs" (*sēmeia*). "Sign" need not, in and of itself, mean "miracle" (*see* Miracles, Miracle Stories). In the OT prophetic acts that signalled the coming of some future act of God (such as judgment) were called "signs." Thus some scholars think that in John the signs include the healings,* feeding of the five thousand and changing of the water into wine—in short, the miracles—but possibly other acts as well, such as the Temple cleansing or even the resurrection of Jesus himself. But for the broad spectrum of Jesus' activity, the Gospel reserves the word *works*.

Whereas the Synoptics narrate several dozen miracles, John recounts but a few. They are the changing of the water to wine (2:1-11); the healing of the official's son (4:46-54); the healing of the man at the pool of Bethesda (5:1-9); the feeding of the five thousand (6:1-13); the healing of the man born blind (9:1-12); and the raising of Lazarus (11:1-44). Some also include the walking on the water (6:16-21), the resurrection and the catch of fish (21:1-8). The two healings each illustrate the truth of the statement "The hour is coming, and now is, when the dead will hear the voice of the Son of God, and those who hear will live" (5:25 RSV). These signs show Jesus' life-giving power. Even more dramatically is this power manifested in Jesus' raising of Lazarus. The two "gift" or "supply miracles" (the changing of the water to wine and the feeding) strike a note of messianic fulfillment and abundance. The extravagant provision of wine at the wedding may allude to traditions that in the messianic age the yield of the vineyards would

be enormous and spectacular (*1 Enoch* 10:19; *2 Apoc. Bar.* 29:5; Irenaeus *Haer.* 5.33.3). Similarly, the provision of bread in the wilderness calls to mind the promises of the return of the treasury of manna from on high in the age to come. Finally, the healing of the man born blind blends together favorite Johannine terms such as light and darkness, seeing and believing, judgment and guilt, in such a way that their symbolic import is obvious. But the healing on the physical level is not played down. One is to see in the magnanimous act of healing the generous grace of God and to see Jesus carrying out "the work of God."

We may define a sign as a manifestation, through the person of Jesus, of God's work in the world. Signs are not understood to prove Jesus' divinity—for, as the Synoptics make clear, miracles only raise the question of the source of one's power, whether demonic or divine—but to point to the fact that God works through him. Specifically, God works through Jesus to bring salvation to the world, a salvation not merely symbolized by the signs, but also offered through the signs inasmuch as they are tokens of the eschatological activity of God in the world (*see* Eschatology). Thus the signs are revelatory of the glory of God inasmuch as they show God's power at work through the person of Jesus. Specifically, that power is understood as life-giving power, and Jesus' signs point to the fact that he offers life. It is appropriate to his life-giving work that his deeds involve the physical universe and the elements necessary for life (bread, water, wine, healing of the human body, restoration of life). Jesus offers bread which satisfies spiritual hunger and thirst even as he also offers that which meets the physical needs of hunger and thirst, and he does so because he is the agent of the God who creates and who rules, the maker and judge of all. Through Jesus, the incarnate Word through whom the world was made, God is at work restoring health and bringing salvation.

A sign is thus properly understood when it is seen as pointing to God's work through the person of Jesus to effect salvation. To have grasped this truth is to have come to faith. Signs thus serve an indirect role in mediating faith, but by no means are they discounted. Yet some interpreters have taken texts such as 4:48 to point to a relativization of the role of miracles in John. But the statement of 2:11, that the disciples believed when they saw Jesus' glory, is programmatic for the Gospel's understanding of signs: Jesus' glory is revealed in the signs, and those who see the glory of Jesus (cf. 1:14) have grasped the secret of his person and identity.

And yet it is difficult to detect a systematic understanding of the relationship between signs and faith* in John. Sometimes those who are witnesses of a sign are also led to belief in Jesus (2:11; 4:54), so that seeing leads to believing. And yet some who see do not believe, including the Pharisees of chapter 9; perhaps the crowds of chapter 6; and, depending on how one reads the evidence, the crowds of 2:23-25, Nicodemus (cf. 3:1-2) and the man at the pool of Bethesda. The summary statement of 12:37-38, "Although Jesus had done so many signs before them, yet they did not believe," characterizes them. They did not fail to believe that a miracle had been done; rather, they did not discern the meaning of the sign. Thus they did not "see signs" as manifestations of God's work through Jesus and of God's glory in Jesus—a work and glory understood to be unique to Jesus.

On the other hand, there are those who do not see signs and yet believe. All the readers of the Gospel who were not also eyewitnesses fall into this category. Their faith is not superior to those who came to believe through Jesus' signs, but neither is it an inferior faith, and this is the point of Jesus' statement to Thomas, "Blessed are those who have not seen and yet believe" (20:29 RSV). Those who "see" the signs, "see" the secret of Jesus' person as the mediator of God's salvation to humankind.

4.3. Salvation. In Jesus' prayer there is a pithy statement that summarizes the Gospel's view of salvation*: "This is eternal life: to know God and Jesus Christ whom [God] has sent" (17:3). Here several elements of the Johannine theology of salvation come to the fore and need to be examined. First is the restatement of the Gospel message in terms of "eternal life," a term found in the Synoptic Gospels but not nearly so dominant in those Gospels as it is here in John (*see* Life). Second, this verse apparently implies this eternal life is something that one has in the present. Third, eternal life comes about through or is equated with "knowing" (rather than believing, confessing, trusting), which seems to point to a cognitive dimension of salvation. Indeed, the previous discussion of the relationship of signs and faith underscores the importance of "seeing" and "understanding" in the Gospel of John, suggesting that salvation can be characterized as the response to the revelation that one sees. These elements can be examined in turn in order to come to a fuller understanding of the Johannine view of salvation.

4.3.1. Eternal Life. It would not be amiss to summarize the Son's mission and the theme of the Gospel of John in terms of "eternal life." The Son comes so that those who believe in him may be saved or receive eternal life, and the Gospel's purpose is phrased in similar terms. But it is more difficult to explain the origin of, and impetus for, John's use of eternal life. When compared with the other Gospels, John seems to give to "eternal life" the prominence that they accord to "kingdom of God." Some scholars have suggested that John uses *eternal life* in place of *kingdom of God* in order to accent the personal and individualistic aspects of salvation. Others suggest that *eternal life* can convey the inner experience of salvation more aptly than a term like *kingdom of God*. Still other scholars have argued that John's preference for "eternal life" can be explained in terms of his historical setting: the Jewish "kingdom of God" has been reinterpreted for John's Hellenistic readership as "eternal life," perhaps emphasizing its timeless reality.

Of course the Synoptic Gospels do use the terms *life* and *eternal life* (Mt 19:16-17; Mk 10:29-30; Mt 29:29; Lk 18:29-30; cf. Mt 7:14; Lk 13:23-24; Mk 10:26; Mt 19:25; Lk 18:26). Already in the Synoptics "eternal life" and "kingdom of God" appear as virtual equivalents (Mk 9:43, 45, 47; 10:17-30; Mt 19:23-29; Lk 18:24-30). "Eternal life" translates *zōē aiōnios*, which literally means "life of the age," but was used in Jewish writings prior to, or contemporaneous with, the NT to mean "life of the age to come" (Dan 12:2; *Pss. Sol.* 3:12; 13:11; 14:10; *1 Enoch* 37:4; 58:3). The absolute "life" is used in the same way. The same situation obtains for the Gospel of John. "Life" and "eternal life" are used interchangeably, and can also be used in place of "kingdom of God" to speak of the state of blessedness that one participates in through faith in Jesus. Thus the background against which one should understand the term "eternal life" is chiefly that of the Jewish view of the "life of the age to come" that the righteous are to inherit.

This "eternal life" or "life of the age to come" is the very life that God has, God's own kind of life, divine life. We may see how the adjective "eternal" fits the noun "life," for God alone exists eternally. According to John, the Father "has life in himself" (5:26). Furthermore, the Father "has granted the Son also to have life in himself." The Son has life, then, in dependence on the Father, and as the Father has it. And believers have life insofar as they depend on the Father through the mediating work of Jesus Christ. Thus John sums up, "This is eternal life, that they know thee, the only true God, and Jesus Christ whom thou hast sent" (17:3 RSV). Here John does not state that knowing God precedes or is necessary for eternal life, but that knowing God is eternal life. Those who know God in the present have an incorruptible fellowship with God that cannot be severed or impugned by death. This understanding of eternal life shows its affinities with the Synoptic's "kingdom of God." Both "kingdom of God" and "eternal life" come from God and are mediated through the agent of divine rule, Jesus Christ.

But what makes the Johannine statements about eternal life particularly striking is that they promise eternal life in the present (5:24-26). Attempts to argue that John relegates the reception of eternal life entirely to the future have not proved convincing. And yet it seems almost a contradiction in terms to speak of having "eternal life," the life of the age to come, in the present, for eternal life is that life which does not end—and yet John clearly expects the death and resurrection of believers. "Life" and "resurrection" are not simply synonyms in John. Nor should we understand eternal life as a purely spiritual or individualized reality. John does not abandon the Jewish conception of "eternal life" as entailing the gathering of the people of God, nor does he spiritualize the hope for the resurrection of the body. Eternal life is present now insofar as through Jesus knowledge of and fellowship with God is mediated. Thus eternal life is also the appropriation by faith of unseen yet present realities that shape one's life in this world and become more fully realized in the next.

But even as salvation is present to believers through faith in Christ, so judgment is effected in the present as well (3:16-21, 36). This facet of John's theology which emphasizes the present manifestations of salvation and judgment is known as "realized eschatology." It is not unique in the NT, which stresses the present reality of salvation in Christ, but it is fair to say that in John the "realized" aspects of salvation receive greater emphasis (*see* Eschatology). John's best-known image for the presence of salvation is that of new birth, of being "born again" (*see* New Birth).

There is a play on words in the phrase "born again," for the Greek (*gennaō anōthen*) can be understood to mean either "born from above" or "born anew." Nicodemus's protest that one cannot enter into his mother's womb and be "born again" shows that he misunderstands the meaning of Jesus' assertion "you must be born from above," for Jesus refers to the importance of submitting to a new work of the Spirit in one's life. This statement is to be taken both at the individual and corporate level. On the level of the individual there is a call to pay heed to a new work of the Spirit through Jesus and the community of faith, and to be renewed by the working of the Spirit. But on the corporate level there is implicit also a statement about who the elect people of God are, for the imagery of new birth states that there is no continuous or auto-

matic movement forward from Judaism to eternal life. Although salvation is "from the Jews" in the person of the Messiah, Jesus, merely belonging to the Jewish people does not guarantee entry into life (3:36).

Not surprisingly, the Fourth Gospel also accents the role of human decision and faith, for it is through faith in Jesus that one becomes a member of the people of God, and not through descent or birth. However, faith is not to be construed as a natural human inclination, for those who come are those "drawn by God" or "taught by God" (6:44-45). John underscores both the divine sovereignty in drawing people to faith as well as the human responsibility in responding to Jesus (Carson). Similarly, there is an emphasis on God's trustworthiness in keeping believers faithful, as well as an insistent call to "abide" (or persevere) in the faith. But the Gospel does not deal philosophically with questions about predestination and free will. Its chief concern is to show that Jesus was the divinely commissioned agent, endowed with the unlimited power of the Spirit (3:34), and that those who respond to Christ in faith are enlivened by the same Spirit of God (3:5-8). Conversely, those who do not come to Christ cannot justly claim to have the Spirit of God at work within them.

4.3.2. Salvation As Revelation. The Gospel's emphasis on coming to know or believe what Jesus makes known suggests that salvation consists in accepting the revelation that Jesus brings. The image that Jesus is the light* of the world fits here as well, for "light" is frequently understood in the OT as an image for instruction and guidance. That Jesus is the light of the world (8:12; 9:5) means that he makes known the way in which people are to walk in order to have salvation. A similar statement is "I am the way, the truth, and the life" (14:6). The predicates in this statement can be read as making three distinct assertions about Jesus, or they can be subordinated, as follows: "I am the way, that leads to truth and life" (or, "I am the way and the truth that leads to life"), thus underscoring that what Jesus makes known is not a new concept about God, but the path to God. When, at times, his revelation is set over against that of the OT Scriptures or patriarchs, and especially Moses, it does not invalidate what was made known there, but rather shows that the revelation through the Son now fulfills and supersedes all other revelation. What Moses said was true, but now since the fullness of truth resides in the Son, those who claim to be "disciples of Moses" are not disciples of the truth at all, inasmuch as they reject the one who is himself truth. Salvation consists in coming to accept the embodiment of truth in the person of Jesus, not in adhering to abstract formulations of truth about Jesus.

4.3.3. The Death of Jesus.

Jesus' death as an atonement for sin does not figure prominently in John (*see* Death of Jesus). There may be an allusion to atonement when the Baptist identifies Jesus as "the Lamb of God who takes away the sin of the world" (1:36; *see* Lamb of God). But even if the atoning function of Jesus' death is not highlighted, it is clear that the mission of Jesus is brought to fulfillment with his death. While John's characterization of the effects of Jesus' death shares certain traits, both with the Synoptic Gospels and with Paul, it has distinctive features as well. (1) John particularly accents the fact that Jesus' death serves to gather together the people of God (Jn 10:1-18; 11:46-52; 12:20-33; cf. Ezek 34). The Messiah was expected to gather together those scattered throughout the diaspora, and this expectation is found fulfilled in Jesus, even though that in-gathering is not understood in literal and physical terms. Even so, the gathering together of the "children of God scattered abroad" signals God's final salvation at work in the world. (2) Jesus gives his life so that others may have life. As one who has "life in himself" he can bestow on others the gift of life, but only through his death. (3) Jesus' death shows his love for his own (13:1), as well as revealing God's love for the world (3:16-17). In its manifestation of self-giving love, it becomes an example for his disciples (13:11-17; 15:13).

4.4. The Community and the Paraclete.

4.4.1. The Paraclete.

The term "paraclete" (*paraklētos*) is unique in the NT to the Johannine literature and is ascribed once to Jesus in the Epistles (1 Jn 2:1) and to the Holy Spirit in the Gospels (*see* Holy Spirit). Scholars have debated the meaning and background of the term. The popular interpretation of the Paraclete as "one called alongside to help" is derived from analysis of the two parts of the compound Greek word: *para*, meaning "by" or "with," and *kaleō*, meaning "to call." Thus it is deduced that the Paraclete is one "called alongside (to help)." But if this is the function of the Paraclete in John, then this must be discerned from statements in the Gospel itself and not from dubious etymological arguments. Other interpreters relate the word to *paraklēsis*, which means "exhortation" or "encouragement," hence the traditional rendering "Comforter." And yet in John the Spirit's functions are not primarily to comfort or console believers.

In 1 John 2:1 "paraclete" seems closest to "intercessor" (although some take it more in a forensic sense, close to defending attorney). The Paraclete may be understood in terms of the Latin *advocatus*, who was a legal assistant or friend at court, a person of sufficient reputation to influence the king, emperor or other sovereign.

As stated above, in 1 John the Paraclete is the risen Jesus, but in the Gospel the Paraclete is the Holy Spirit (14:26), the "Spirit of Truth" (14:16; 15:26; 16:13). But Jesus also promises that upon his departure he will send "another Paraclete" (14:16). While the Greek could be construed to read "another who will be a Paraclete," most scholars prefer the translation "another Paraclete," implying that the first is Jesus. It is thus often assumed that John states that the Paraclete-Jesus comes back to the disciples in the person of the Paraclete-Spirit. But while there is continuity and overlap between the ministries of Jesus and the Paraclete, there are important distinctions as well.

The functions of the Paraclete can be divided between his relationship to the world and his relationship to the disciples. With respect to the world, the Paraclete serves as an accuser, putting the world on trial, pronouncing it guilty of sin and worthy of condemnation (16:8-11; cf. 14:17; 15:18-26). But the Paraclete's functions with respect to the disciples are described positively. Above all, the Paraclete assumes the role of teacher* (16:13), guiding the disciples into all truth by reminding them of what Jesus had said, where reminding seems to have the force not only of recollecting, but of interpreting as well. Indeed, as stated earlier, much of the Paraclete-inspired truth is found in the Gospel of John. One cannot, then, speak of the role of the Paraclete without also turning to the Gospel's vision of the community in which the Paraclete plays such a central role.

4.4.2. The Community.

Certainly the Gospel of John emphasizes the necessity of the individual appropriation of faith in God through Jesus Christ. However, the individualistic tenor of the Gospel is balanced by its stress on one's obligation within the community of faith (*see* Church). The community of which the believer becomes a part is characterized by its unity and love. Its unity is modelled on the relationship between the Father and the Son, and is thus characterized by an intimacy of love, as well as a common purpose in serving as the vehicle of bringing God's revelation and salvation to the world. We may say that the unity of which the Gospel speaks has two aspects: (1) It is contemporary, a unity among Christians of any one age or time; (2) it is historical, binding Christians to their predecessors in the faith. Both are of concern in the Gospel, as Jesus' high priestly prayer for the community demonstrates. In fact the line most often quoted in ecumenical circles, "that they may all be one," refers to the unity that exists between believers of Jesus' own day and those of second and later generations of believers. They are all, equally and together, the one people of God. A concomitant of the emphasis on unity is an accent on love, where love is understood as the peculiar bond of service and loyalty which unites Christians to their God and to each other.

The Christian fellowship is distinguished in Johannine thought from the "world"* (*kosmos*). "World" has several shades of meaning, from the positive created order, to the sphere of human beings, to human beings as they are hostile to the revelation of God in Christ. It is in the last sense that the "world" is a force opposing, rejecting or indifferent to God and the people of God. For if God's people are characterized by their trust in God, then the world is marked by its lack of similar commitment. The church's role vis-à-vis the world is to bear witness to the truth through its proclamation and example in order that the world may know its guilt, repent, and come to the light and be saved. While some scholars have painted the portrait of the Johannine church as a community alienated from its environment, hostile to unbelievers and without a sense of responsibility toward the world, the statements of the church's mission—even when the mission results in pronouncing judgment—cannot be overlooked as suggesting that the Johannine community retained its sense of mission.

See also ABIDING; BREAD; FAREWELL DISCOURSE; GLORY; "I AM" SAYINGS; LAMB OF GOD; LAZARUS; LIFE; LIGHT; LOGOS; NEW BIRTH; SHEPHERD, SHEEP; SYNOPTICS AND JOHN; VINE, FRUIT OF THE VINE; WITNESS; WORLD.

BIBLIOGRAPHY. **Commentaries:** C. K. Barrett, *The Gospel according to St. John* (2d ed.; Philadelphia: Westminster, 1978); G. R. Beasley-Murray, *John* (WBC; Waco, TX: Word, 1987); R. E. Brown, *The Gospel according to John* (AB 29, 29A; Garden City: Doubleday, 1966, 1970); F. F. Bruce, *The Gospel of John* (Grand Rapids: Eerdmans, 1983); R. Bultmann, *The Gospel of John: A Commentary* (Philadelphia: Westminster, 1971); D. A. Carson, *The Gospel according to John* (Grand Rapids: Eerdmans, 1991); E. C. Hoskyns, *The Fourth Gospel* (2d ed.; London: Faber & Faber, 1947); B. Lindars, *The Gospel of John* (NCB; Grand Rapids: Eerdmans, 1981); J. R. Michaels, *John* (San Francisco: Harper & Row, 1984); L. Morris, *The Gospel according to John* (NICNT; Grand Rapids: Eerdmans, 1970); A. Schlatter, *Der Evangelist Johannes* (4th ed.; Stuttgart: Calwer, 1975); R. Schnackenburg, *The Gospel according to St. John* (3 vols.; New York: Crossroad, 1980, 1982); B. F. Westcott, *The Gospel according to St. John* (London: J. Murray, 1881; repr. Grand Rapids: Baker, 1980). **Studies:** P. Borgen, *Philo, John and Paul: New Perspectives on Judaism and Early Christianity* (Atlanta: Schol-

ars, 1987); G. Burge, *The Anointed Community: The Holy Spirit in the Johannine Tradition* (Grand Rapids: Eerdmans, 1987); D. A. Carson, *Divine Sovereignty and Human Responsibility* (Atlanta: John Knox, 1981); O. Cullmann, *The Johannine Circle* (Philadelphia: Westminster, 1975); R. A. Culpepper, *Anatomy of the Fourth Gospel: A Study in Literary Design* (FF; Philadelphia: Fortress, 1983); C. H. Dodd, *Historical Tradition in the Fourth Gospel* (Cambridge: University Press, 1963); idem, *The Interpretation of the Fourth Gospel* (Cambridge: University Press, 1953); P. D. Duke, *Irony in the Fourth Gospel* (Atlanta: John Knox, 1985); P. Gardner-Smith, *Saint John and the Synoptic Gospels* (Cambridge: University Press, 1938); A. E. Harvey, *Jesus on Trial: A Study in the Fourth Gospel* (Atlanta: John Knox, 1976); M. Hengel, *The Johannine Question* (Philadelphia: Trinity Press International, 1989); R. Kysar, *The Fourth Evangelist and His Gospel: An Examination of Contemporary Scholarship* (Minneapolis: Augsburg, 1975); B. Lindars, *Behind the Fourth Gospel* (London: SPCK, 1971); J. L. Martyn, *History and Theology in the Fourth Gospel* (2d ed.; Nashville: Abingdon, 1979); L. Morris, *Jesus Is the Christ: Studies in the Theology of John* (Grand Rapids: Eerdmans, 1989); J. A. T. Robinson, *The Priority of John* (London: SCM, 1985); S. Smalley, *John: Evangelist and Interpreter* (Exeter: Paternoster, 1978); D. M. Smith, *Johannine Christianity* (Columbia: University of South Carolina, 1984); M. M. Thompson, *The Humanity of Jesus in the Fourth Gospel* (Philadelphia: Fortress, 1988); R. A. Whitacre, *Johannine Polemic: The Role of Tradition and Theology* (Chico, CA: Scholars, 1982).

M. M. Thompson

JOHN THE BAPTIST

1. The Importance of John the Baptist
2. John's Origins and Early Activities
3. Jewish Expectations and Practices
4. John's Eschatological Message and Ministry
5. Jesus' View of John and His Ministry
6. The Death of the Baptist
7. The Baptist Movement in the Christian Era
8. The Christian Portrayal of the Baptist

1. The Importance of John the Baptist.

Numerous lines of evidence demonstrate the importance of John the Baptist or John the Baptizer, as he is sometimes called in the NT (cf. Mk 1:4; 6:14, 24). (1) All four Gospels associate John with, or treat him as, the "beginning of the gospel" (cf. also Acts 1:22; *see* Gospel [Good News]). (2) Jesus reportedly claimed that he was more than a prophet* and, from a human point of view, the greatest human being (Mt 11:11/Lk

7:28 and Mt 11:9/Lk 7:26). (3) Unlike the case with other major NT figures (such as the apostles), only the deaths of John and Jesus are given significant treatment in the NT (cf. Mk 6:14-29 and par.). (4) The author of Luke-Acts indicates that John was such a significant figure that he still had disciples or followers long after his death (cf. Acts 18:25; 19:1-7). (5) The Synoptic Gospels state that Jesus submitted to John's baptism, and the earliest Gospel suggests that at least initially Jesus preached a message similar to John's (Mk 1:14-15). Also, the Fourth Gospel suggests that Jesus assisted John for a time or followed his example in the wilderness (see Mountain and Wilderness), collecting disciples* and supervising baptisms* (Jn 3:22-36). Indeed, during and at the end of his ministry Jesus expresses his own purpose and authority by comparing and contrasting himself with John and suggesting they are part of a single effort by God* to reach his people (cf. Mt 11:16-19/Lk 7:31-35 and Mk 11:27-33 and par.). (6) There are some traditions which suggest that Jesus saw John as the eschatological prophet Elijah* redivivus (cf. Mk 9:12-13 and par.). (7) Jesus apparently was thought by some to be John come back from the dead (cf. Mk 6:14 and par.). (8) According to the Synoptic Gospels Jesus did not begin his Galilean ministry (see Galilee) until after John died, which suggests that both John's life and death influenced how Jesus acted.

2. John's Origins and Early Activities.

Luke alone informs us that John was born into a pious and priestly family, to parents well advanced in age (Lk 1). He also informs us that John's father, Zechariah, served in Herod's Temple* and that he and his family lived in a town in the Judean hill country (Lk 1:39). Luke 1:36 tells us that his mother, Elizabeth, was a female relative of Jesus' mother, Mary. The Greek word sungenis is a general term which could refer to an aunt or a cousin (Jn 1:33 suggests that the kinship may have been rather remote). In any case, Jesus grew up in Nazareth, John apparently in Judea.

Several considerations have led some scholars to conjecture that John may have been a part of the Qumran community from an early age (see Dead Sea Scrolls). (1) The Qumran community had priestly connections, plus an interest in priestly matters and a priestly Messiah (1QS 5.2). John also had priestly connections, and John's parents may well have passed away when he was quite young. Apparently, the Qumran community frequently adopted orphans (Josephus J.W. 2.120). (2) The locale of John's ministry suggests a connection with Qumran. (3) The Gospel tradition introduces John using Isaiah 40:3 (cf. Mk

1:2), a text that was also very important at Qumran (cf. 1QS 8.14). (4) John's spartan diet and apparent ascetical behavior have analogies with Qumran (S. L. Davies). The Damascus Rule 12.13-14 in fact specifies how to eat honey and locusts. (5) John's water rite has similarities to Qumran ablution rites. (6) John's eschatological orientation and belief that the judgment* of God would soon fall on Israel* itself, with the possible exception of those who would repent,* parallel Qumran. John's apparent belief that the religious leadership of Israel was hopelessly corrupt strikes a chord with some attitudes known to have existed at Qumran.

This list, however impressive, does not prove a connection between John and Qumran for several reasons. (1) When we first meet John in the Gospels he is not, or is no longer, part of the Qumran community. Rather, he is undertaking his own ministry by calling the nation to repentance, not merely withdrawing from it as if it were hopelessly corrupt. (2) There are major differences between John's water rite and the usual lustrations at Qumran (see section 2.3), though there may have been an initiatory water rite at Qumran as well. (3) John allows both the clean and the unclean to come into contact with him (possibly even Gentiles,* cf. Lk 3:14) and apparently does not believe in an already existing "righteous remnant" of Israel, that is, one which exists prior to submitting to his baptism. (4) John was perceived by Herod Antipas (see Herodian Dynasty) to be a political threat in a way in which the Qumran community apparently was not. (5) John's diet is what would be expected of any itinerant in the wilderness. At most, it only suggests either that John was consciously taking the prophetic mantle upon himself, as his dress suggested (cf. Zech 13:4, 2 Kings 1:8), and/or assuming a Nazirite vow. In any case, fasting,* ascetic behavior and devotion to prayer* (cf. Lk 11:1; Mt 11:18 and par.) were by no means unique to the Qumran community. Indeed, Josephus* tells us of one Bannus (Life 11-12a) who ate and dressed much like John, lived in the Judean wilderness and stressed ritual ablutions. Thus, while John may have been connected with Qumran at one time, in the Gospels this is no longer the case (see Reicke).

3. Jewish Expectations and Practices.

3.1. Messianic Hope and the Baptist. In early Judaism messianic hope took on a variety of shapes (see Revolutionary Movements). Some Jews expected a particular Messianic figure in the mold of David to come and retake the promised land by force for God's people (cf. Pss. Sol. 17). Some Qumranites seem to have expected two messianic figures—a priestly one and a kingly one (cf. 1QS 9.11; also *T. Levi* 18; *T. Reuben* 6:8). Still other Jews looked for an eschatological prophet like Moses* (cf. 4QTest; 1QS 9.11; cf. also the Samaritan expectation of a *Taheb* who will be a Moses *redivivus*). There were those who looked for the coming of a messianic age in general without focusing on a particular messianic figure. Other early Jews, apparently including the Sadducees,* seem to have had no messianic hopes.

P. W. Barnett (1977) has noted a pattern that various early messianic movements took (*see* Revolutionary Movements). Whether one is talking about Theudas, or the Egyptian or the Samaritan—or a figure like Jesus—all seem to have drawn significant crowds in remote areas, whether in the Judean wilderness, near the Jordan or in remote areas of Galilee. All of them performed or promised to perform symbolic acts which had messianic overtones (i.e., divide Jordan, cause Jerusalem's walls to collapse, reveal the Temple vessels on Mt. Gerizim, provide manna in the wilderness for the 5,000). Note that John the Baptizer preached in "the wilderness," particularly at the Jordan, drew great crowds and performed an act symbolizing a change in the status of at least some of God's people—water baptism.

Given that all messianic movements in early Judaism had some social and political repercussions, even if that was not always their design, it is easy to see how John the Baptist, who so far as we know made no messianic claims, could have been viewed as some sort of messianic figure. In addition, he could have been perceived as a threat to some of the governing authorities and, in light of Jewish views about martyrdom, John could have had an ongoing group of followers long after his death. All of these messianic figures, including the Baptist, implied and in some cases articulated a belief that things were not as they ought to be among God's people. Thus, at least by implication, the existing authorities, both religious and political, both Jewish and Roman, were indicted by the very existence of these movements. It is into this sort of environment that both John and Jesus came raising messianic hopes and making various authorities uneasy, to the point that both were eventually executed.

One particular form of messianic hope which needs to be explored more fully in connection with John the Baptist is the belief that Elijah* or one like him would come, signalling the advent either of the messianic age, or of the Messiah or both. Whether there was such an expectation, or at least whether it was widespread during the lifetime of John the Baptist

and Jesus, has been disputed (cf. Faierstein; Allison; Fitzmyer).

One must consider a number of factors, however. (1) Early Christians did associate John the Baptist with Elijah as the Gospels attest. (2) It is also clear that in Mark 9:11-13 and parallels we have a tradition indicating that the teachers of the Law* taught that Elijah must come first to restore all things, but we are not told explicitly what the scribes thought he would come *before*—either the Messiah,* or the Day of the Lord or the Son of man* rising from the dead. Nevertheless, it is unlikely that early Christians would have attributed a Christian interpretation of the eschatological Elijah figure to the scribes if there was no basis for this in fact. (3) The tradition found in Malachi 3:23-24 (Mt 4:5-6) says explicitly that Elijah will come before the great and terrible Day of the Lord, which presumably refers to the Day of Judgment (this idea is also found in such texts as Sir 48 and possibly *1 Enoch* 90:31). (4) An unpublished fragment from Qumran (4QarP) reads *lkn slh l'lyh qd[m]*—"I will send Elijah before"—but unfortunately it breaks off at this point. (5) The baraita in *b. 'Erub.* 43a-b, which quotes the Malachi passage and then comments on it, provides us with the earliest *clear* extra-canonical evidence that Elijah would return before Messiah came. This tradition dates to the third century of the Common Era and may be much earlier, but since it is not associated with a particular Jewish teacher, we cannot be sure. Thus, there may have been a belief in Elijah as forerunner of Messiah in John's time, but we cannot be sure how widespread it was.

What is certain is that the Gospel tradition indicates that Jesus interpreted John the Baptist as an Elijah figure, and since this idea is found in at least two sources, it is very likely to be authentic (cf. Mk 9:12-13 and par. and Mt 11:14). It is also clear from Mark 9:12-13 that we have the sequence of first Elijah (John), then the Son of man, with both suffering similar fates. The natural way to understand Mark 9:11 is to say that the scribes were claiming Elijah would be the first in a sequence of messianic comings, an idea the early church would hardly have predicated of the scribes if the church had invented it and *also* placed it on Jesus' lips (Allison).

Thus, in the NT there are various traditions suggesting that John was viewed as an Elijah figure, and there is also evidence that Elijah was expected as a precursor of the final eschatological work of God, and perhaps also of Messiah. At least two Gospels indicate Jesus viewed John in this light.

3.2. The End of Prophecy. There are some OT and some intertestamental traditions which suggest that after Zechariah, Haggai and Malachi, OT prophecy as we know it ceased. Psalm 74:9 has been understood in this way, or one may point to 1 Maccabees 9:27 which speaks of the distress in the land since the prophets ceased to appear there (cf. 1 Macc 4:45-6; 14:41, *2 Apoc. Bar.* 85:3). Of later provenance are traditions in the Talmud that state explicitly that Haggai, Zechariah and Malachi were the last of the prophets.

Whether or not one agrees that the apocalyptic* literature that came to the fore in the intertestamental period is a form of and the sequel to OT prophecy, there is no question that the classical prophetic movement had disappeared long before the beginning of the NT era. The apocalyptic literature was by and large pseudonymous in contrast to much of classical prophecy, and furthermore it was primarily a literary rather than oral phenomenon. The rabbinic notion of the *baṭ qôl* ("daughter of a voice"), an audible echo of the heavenly voice that formerly spoke to the prophets, also attests to a difference from the period of classical prophecy. Thus, when John the Baptist arrived on the scene around A.D. 28 (cf. Lk 3:1), he was probably perceived by some as a new and different figure, unlike anyone since the OT prophets and most like such classical figures as Isaiah, Jeremiah or Elijah.

3.3. Jewish Water Rites. The discussion about what precedents there may have been for John's baptism has been a heated one among scholars (*see* Baptism). This is in part the case because it is uncertain when proselyte baptism was first practiced by early Jews. In addition to the matter of OT water rituals having to do with ceremonial uncleanness, there is also the vexed question of what, if any, connection the Baptist may have had with the Qumran community (see section 1 above). It is also possible that John's rite was something new and different, without precedent.

With regard to the matter of proselyte baptism, several considerations are relevant. (1) The Mishna (*m. Pesaḥ.* 8.8) records a dispute between the school of Hillel and Shammai concerning whether or not a newly circumcised proselyte may immerse himself and eat the Paschal meal. If this dispute goes back to Hillel and Shammai, then it pre-dates John's ministry. (2) The Babylonian Talmud (*b. Yebam.* 46a) also records a dispute between two first-century A.D. rabbis about proselyte baptism and its necessity. (3) In view of the Jewish belief that Gentiles in general were unclean, the likelihood is strong that there was some rite of initiation such as proselyte baptism for female converts to early Judaism. Thus, proselyte baptism probably did exist during John's era (but cf. Pusey, Betz, Badia and Taylor, McKnight).

However, we must note several differences between John's practice and that of Jewish proselyte baptism. (1) Apparently, John was the active immerser when he offered his rite, but Jewish proselytes immersed themselves. (2) John performed his rite primarily on *Jews* who, of course, were never subject to Jewish proselyte baptism. Thus, one may argue that John was practicing proselyte baptism on Jews, which suggests that he did not feel their heredity was an adequate safeguard from God's coming eschatological wrath. Indeed, it seems he felt Israel was *lost*, just like the Gentile world, unless they repented and received his baptism.

There are also salient differences between John's practice and both the water lustrations mentioned in the OT and those found at Qumran, including the cleansing ritual in the *mikwâ*. (1) John's rite, like proselyte baptism, was a unique and unrepeated ritual so far as we can tell. (2) There is no indication that John's rite had anything to do with purely ceremonial uncleanness caused, for instance, by touching a corpse. Apparently, it is only or at least primarily moral uncleanness that is at issue in John's rite. (3) John's baptism seems to have been an initiation rite, not a rite to continue to maintain purity or cleanliness for one who was already basically in right relationship with Yahweh. (4) There is no evidence that John required a probationary period before being immersed, nor any prior demonstration of one's earnestness to obey God other than the willingness to come forward and be baptized.

When one considers the Qumran initiatory water rite, both the probationary period and self-immersion appear to distinguish the Qumran practice from that of the Baptist. Quite possibly, the Baptist's rite was uniquely unrepeatable (cf. Badia). Note that John may have been drawing on the ancient idea of trial by water ordeal, in which case the rite is connected with his proclamation about coming wrath and is a visible symbol of preparation for that coming event. One may compare the idea of circumcision being an act invoking the oath curse on oneself, and thus of being cut off by God, if one does not go on to obey the covenant.

3.4. Geographical Considerations. John ministered "in the wilderness," but the question is "Which wilderness?" Was it Perea, as Josephus' account (*Ant.* 18.5) and John's death at the hands of Herod Antipas might suggest? Or was he ministering in the Judean wilderness adjacent to the Jordan? If full weight is given to John 1:28 and 3:23, this might suggest a ministry in the north. Riesner (cf. McCown) has even suggested a ministry in Batanaea. What is clear is that John baptized in the Jordan, and our earliest Gospel, Mark, makes clear that Jesus himself was baptized by John in the Jordan (1:9-11—*hypo Ioannou* must mean "by John," distinguishing this rite from normal proselyte baptism). John may have worked his way up and down the Jordan valley (is this what "all the environs of the Jordan" means? cf. Mt 3:5 par. Lk 3:3). Perhaps he sometimes operated adjacent to the Judean wilderness or in Perea or used some of the streams that flow into the Jordan (if Aenon near Salim is near the Salem in Samaria).

Another consideration is whether or not John fully immersed those whom he baptized. If so, presumably he would have needed a body of water of sufficient depth to do so. The Greek verb *baptizō* does not in itself indicate a particular quantity of water, but if John saw his practice as a modification of proselyte baptism, then he may have totally immersed those who came to him. In any event, there is no reason to doubt that John stayed in the remote regions adjacent to the Jordan, as various different Gospel traditions suggest. Thus the description "the voice of one crying in the wilderness" was an apt one.

4. John's Eschatological Message and Ministry

John the Baptist called his audience to repentance. One major theme of John's preaching was that Yahweh's eschatological wrath would soon fall on Israel. What is not clear is the relationship between John's preaching of repentance and his baptismal practice. Josephus (*Ant.* 18.5.2) suggests that repentance was seen as a prerequisite to receiving John's baptism. On the other hand, both Mark and Luke call John's rite a "baptism of repentance," which presumably means a baptism that expresses a willingness to repent and live a life that bears fruit corresponding to repentance (cf. Mt 3:8 par. Lk 3:8, 10-14).

That the association of repentance with John's water rite is historically authentic few would care to dispute, particularly in view of the difficulties this connection suggested for the Christian community when Jesus submitted to such a baptism. Only the First Evangelist suggests a motive for Jesus submitting to the rite—"to fulfill all righteousness" (Mt. 3:15)—which may mean to be obedient to God's plan for his life, to fully identify with the needs of God's people. Less probably it may mean he intends to fulfill all Scripture (Davies and Allison).

According to Mark, Q* and John, John the Baptist expected a successor—the Coming One. It has been suggested that John expected Yahweh to come and bring in the Day of the Lord, which is understandable in light of the prophecy in Malachi. On the other hand, the metaphor of untying the sandal (or possibly carrying the sandal), while it connotes the idea of being unworthy to be the servant of the Coming One, also suggests that John envisioned a human successor, one who would come and baptize with Spirit and fire (possibly an example of *hendiadys*—the fiery Spirit). This means that John did not see himself as the definitive revealer of God (O'Neill).

Did John see Jesus as this Coming One? John 1:29-34 seems to make this identification clear, but a likely authentic Q tradition (Mt 11:2-3 par. Lk 7:19) shows that John had doubts about such an identification even as late as the time of his imprisonment. Possibly these doubts were created by the fact that Jesus did not immediately bring down fiery judgment on Israel. Other authentic elements in John's preaching probably include: (1) an appeal to charitable and honest conduct (Lk 3:11-14), some of which Jesus also picks up in his proclamation (cf. Mt. 5:40 and par.); (2) a belief that being a descendant of Abraham* was no guarantee of avoiding the wrath to come, if it was not also accompanied by repentance and its fruit; (3) preaching against immorality, such as that exhibited by Herod Antipas and Herodias in their incestuous union (Lk 3:19) and (4) the idea that the Coming One would gather in the wheat as well as burn up the chaff (Lk 3:17). This means that John conceived of a righteous remnant being created by the Coming One—a community of the faithful who would survive the coming wrath.

These themes do not suggest that John preached the coming dominion of God (Heb. *malᶜkût Yahweh;* *see* Kingdom of God) in the same fashion as Jesus. Apparently he did not stress the aspect of good news entailed in the coming events (*see* Gospel [Good News]). The summary in Mark 1:14 does suggest that Jesus was influenced, at least in his early Galilean preaching, by John (Witherington). This continuity in preaching between John and Jesus can also be found when one compares the likely authentic parable* of the tares (cf. Mt 13:24-30 and par.) to the Johannine preaching found in Matthew 3:7-10 and parallels (Catchpole). Serious attention should also be given to the hints in John 3:22-36 that historically Jesus assisted John or had a parallel ministry involving baptizing in the Judean wilderness *prior* to John's imprisonment and Jesus' Galilean ministry (Linnemann).

Thus, in this regard, and also by virtue of the fact that Jesus' Galilean ministry begins after John baptizes Jesus (and probably after John was imprisoned), one may say that the origins of Jesus' call and ministry lie in the ministry of the Baptist, and perhaps after

John's death, in Jesus' desire to continue and to build on some of John's main emphases. John, therefore, rightly deserves the place he is given in Mark 1 as the beginning of the gospel. This raises the question of Jesus' view of John, and John's relationship to God's coming reign.

5. Jesus' View of John and His Ministry.

Jesus was not stinting in his praise of John. According to the Q tradition in Matthew 11:7-11 par. Luke 7:24-28, John is called "the greatest person ever born" and "more than just another prophet." In view of the tendency in the early church to emphasize John's role as a forerunner in relationship to Jesus, subordinating the former to the latter, it is very likely that this Q* tradition is authentic. In Matthew 11:7 we find confirmation of the setting of John's ministry—at the Jordan where there were reeds blowing in the wind. It is possible that in 11:8 we have an allusion to Herod Antipas who is contrasted with John. The way in which this Q tradition is framed suggests that Jesus saw John as *the* great eschatological prophet, hence the description "more than just another prophet." This comports with traditions which intimate that Jesus thought of John as an Elijah *redivivus* figure. The quotation of Malachi 3:1 in Matthew 11:10 also confirms Jesus' viewpoint. John is one who prepares the way for God's eschatological activity.

The saying in Matthew 11:11b might seem strange—"yet he who is least in the kingdom of heaven is greater than he [John]" (RSV). Jesus is probably not talking about John being outside the kingdom and others in it; rather, he is talking about two ways of viewing people—from a purely human perspective and from a kingdom perspective. Judged from a purely human perspective, or if one is considering human origins, Jesus thought John was the greatest. Thus Matthew 11:12 is not in conflict with 11:11, for 11:12 suggests that the beginning of the advancement of God's eschatological dominion started when John came on the scene. A similar idea is also found in Luke 16:16 (possibly a variant of the same tradition found in Matthew 11:12-13) where John is probably not said to be the last of the OT prophets, but rather the one who inaugurates the news of the Dominion of God breaking in (cf. Lk 3:18). The era of the Law and the Prophets lasted until John came on the scene. These conclusions also make sense of another difficult verse, Matthew 11:12b par. Luke 16:16b, which suggests that the violence being done to John and Jesus as proclaimers of God's new activity is in fact violence against God's reign (Schlosser).

Yet for all the praise of John and close identification with John in this new work of God, Jesus also distinguished himself from John in several ways. (1) John is seen as one who prepares the way and one who expects a successor. Jesus sees his ministry as part of that for which John prepared, and he expects no successor to follow him. (2) In their style of ministries Jesus sees a contrast between himself and John (Mt 11:19 par. Lk 7:33-34), and yet in both cases they suffered rejection by "this generation." (3) When Jesus answered John's query from prison (Mt 11:2-6 and par.) he indicated another point of distinction—that is, Jesus' ministry was characterized by miracles, and Jesus sees the Isaianic prophecies about such happenings in the messianic age to be referring to his own ministry.

Although both John and Jesus each had a ministry from God, there were points of discontinuity as well as continuity between the two men in their words, deeds and self-understanding. From a saying such as Matthew 11:19b it also appears that Jesus may have regarded himself as divine Wisdom* personified, something we have no hint of in John's case (Witherington). In any event, the measure of the continuity between the two men is perhaps shown by the fact that Mark 6:14, 16 records a likely authentic tradition suggesting that some, including Herod, thought Jesus was John raised from the dead, which they believed explained Jesus' miraculous powers.

6. The Death of the Baptist

Both Josephus and the Gospel tradition agree that John lost his life at the hands of Herod Antipas, the ruler of Galilee and Perea. If Josephus' account (*Ant.* 18.5.2) is to be believed, then it appears John was executed not long before the Nabatean War against Antipas. This likely means he died around A.D. 32 (Reicke). We also learn from Josephus that John was imprisoned in the Machaerus—a fortress in Perea east of the Dead Sea, and that he met his end there.

The Gospels do not contradict the testimony of Josephus, though it has been suggested that Mark thought the execution took place in Galilee (6:22). In fact, the text only says that the leading figures of Galilee were invited to Herod's birthday celebration, which could have been held either in Perea or Galilee. Josephus indicates that John was imprisoned and executed because Herod feared John might stir the people to insurrection. This is a believable rationale for Herod Antipas' action. Mark 6:20 (cf. Mt 14:5) also informs us that Herod was afraid of the Baptist, but Mark 6:17-29 goes on to relate that John was imprisoned because he had criticized Herod's incestuous marriage with Herodias. Further, it indicates that John was executed because Herodias nursed a grudge against the Baptist and devised a ruse to force Herod into executing the Baptist.

It may be that Josephus is only relating why John was imprisoned by Herod, not the cause of his execution, but if this is not the case then the Gospels disagree with Josephus on what actually led to the Baptist's death. It will be noted though that Josephus tends to analyze matters in terms of the political issues and forces involved, not in terms of matters of personal intrigue. Furthermore, from Josephus' account we would never have guessed the eschatological character of John's ministry or baptism, another factor Josephus downplays or eliminates in his account. Thus, it is doubtful that Josephus should be considered a more reliable authority on the matter of John's death than Mark (Scobie).

7. The Baptist Movement in the Christian Era

That John had a considerable number of disciples who followed his practices and preaching is indicated in various Gospel sources (cf. Jn 1:35; 3:25-36; Lk 11:1). Indeed, the Johannine material suggests some of Jesus' first disciples were originally John's disciples (this idea is not found in the Synoptics). That John also had a following after his death is indicated by such texts as Acts 18:25; 19:1-7. Consequently, the possibility remains that the movement not merely endured but spread after John's death.

To this day there is a small sect called the Mandaeans in parts of Iraq and Iran who claim to have kept this movement going continuously into the modern era. Modern Christendom was first made aware of their existence when Christian missionaries encountered them in the seventeenth century. It is doubtful that the Mandaean literature, which dates back only to the eighth century, can help us discern anything about the historical John the Baptist, except to witness that his ongoing impact was considerably greater than Christians have sometimes thought.

In point of fact, John the Baptist is mentioned by various early Christian writers such as Justin Martyr, Tertullian, Hippolytus and Origen. He figures in several apocryphal Christian works such as the second-century Gospel according to the Hebrews, the Protoevangelium of James, and according to Epiphanius he is mentioned in the nonextant Gospel of the Ebionites. Mention should also be made of the references to John's disciples in the Clementine Recognitions I.60, where one of John's disciples is said to claim that John was the Messiah (Farmer).

It is further witness to the ongoing fascination with John that in the twentieth century various scholars have thought they have discovered traditions in the New Testament that ultimately came from the Baptist's followers (for example, Kraeling). Few such conjectures have received widespread acceptance among scholars, though they are not totally implausible (for example, in the case of Luke 1). What is much more certain is that John the Baptist made a major impression on all the canonical Gospel writers and that each sought to present him in a particular and somewhat distinctive way.

8. The Christian Portrayal of the Baptist

It has sometimes been thought that the NT reflects an anti-Baptist polemic, based on the assumption that the Christian movement saw the Baptist movement as a competitor. However, Wink has shown that, far from polemics against the Baptist, what we find in the NT is an attempt to claim John for the Christian cause. This entails a rather full recognition of the importance of the Baptist so that his testimony about "the Coming One" may be given its full weight.

As one moves chronologically through the Gospels (Mark, Matthew, Luke, then John) one finds, with the possible exception of Luke, that John's words about Jesus become increasingly confessional. Yet even as early as Mark, John is already the beginning of the good news. Thus, it must be considered doubtful that Christians were guilty of projecting some sort of later conflict between Christians and John's followers into the Gospels. It is hard to believe that the early church would create such a notable group of traditions which grant the Baptist an important role in the Gospel, given the tendency of the church increasingly to stress the uniqueness of Jesus. Wink urges that Jesus' own positive evaluation of the Baptist led to the incorporation of these traditions in the Gospels.

8.1. John the Baptist from Four Perspectives. In terms of the editorial perspective of each evangelist several motifs are readily apparent:

8.1.1. Mark. Mark seems to portray the Baptist as Elijah incognito (paralleling the messianic secret). He also goes to some lengths to parallel the passion of John and Jesus, the only two figures whose death he gives significant attention to in his Gospel (*see* Death of Jesus). It may be that Mark 6 has been sandwiched between the sending and return of Jesus' disciples because Mark has earlier indicated that the ministry of Jesus in Galilee is precipitated by John's removal from the scene (cf. 1:14).

8.1.2. Matthew. The First Evangelist stresses that Jesus and John stand together against a hostile religious (and political) opposition to their ministries.

It is interesting however that we do not find this parallelism in the uniquely Matthean material within the birth narratives (*see* Birth of Jesus).

8.1.3. Luke. The Third Evangelist places John within his broader schema of salvation history as a notable figure in the historical chain of events initiated by God's intervention into Israel's history at the turn of the era. He also places more explicit stress than either Mark or Matthew on John's ministry involving "good news" (Lk 1:19; 3:18). In this way he stresses more than the other evangelists the continuity between Jesus and John, an emphasis seen both in the material shared in common with Matthew and Mark and in the uniquely Lukan material in the birth narratives (*see* Birth of Jesus). Luke 16:16 need not be seen as being at odds with the attempt to depict John as one who is part of the new eschatological action of God amidst his people, for in view of Luke 1:19 and 3:18, Luke 16:16 should probably be taken to mean that the period of the activity of the prophets had already ended when John came on the scene.

8.1.4. John. The Fourth Evangelist portrays John as the ideal and, indeed, almost-Christian witness to Jesus (cf. Jn 1, 3) as God's Messiah and Lamb, stressing the subordination of John to Jesus (Wink). If this element of subordination and the idea of John as a preparer for the One who is to follow actually does go back to the Baptist himself, then it is not a case of the evangelists relegating John to a position that he did not have in real life, but rather highlighting and building on John's own self-proclaimed role.

8.2. A Focus on Mark's Gospel. It is not sufficient simply to take cursory note of how the Evangelists have edited their sources about John the Baptist in service of their christological interests. It is equally important to gain a sense of the overall portrayal of the Baptist in each Gospel. Space does not allow us to develop fully the portrait of John in each of the four Gospels, thus we will focus on one such sample—the earliest, and in many ways most suggestive, portrait of the Baptist found in Mark's Gospel. Depending on how one reads Mark 1:1, it is possible that Mark intends to portray the story of the Baptist as "the beginning of the gospel of Jesus Christ, the Son of God."* If this is so, it affects not only how one reads the rest of the portrayal of the Baptist in this Gospel, but also how one understands what Mark means by "Gospel." In what sense is the story of John part of the good news about Jesus? Is it just that he was the beginning of the good news of God's climactic saving activity or is something more intended?

In terms of the structure of Mark's Gospel, one notes that all the references to John are confined to the first eleven chapters of this Gospel. In fact, John appears only periodically in these chapters. He is not an ongoing figure in the flow of the narrative nor does he link the pericopes together. In fact, after the initial paragraphs about John in 1:2-11, followed by a brief reference to John's disciples fasting in 2:18, John does not appear in the story again until chapter six. There we hear the story of two rejections—that of Jesus in Nazareth, and that of John by Herod Antipas, which led to John's demise. It is striking that this substantial narrative in chapter six is introduced by the suggestion that Jesus might be John *redivivus* (6:14), which is very close to the way in which John is introduced into the Caesarea Philippi discussion at 8:27-28. There Jesus asks his disciples, "Who do people say that I am?," to which the first reply is, "John the Baptist." Then in the following chapter, Jesus goes on to distinguish himself from John by implying that John is Elijah incognito (9:11-12), whom he says comes to restore all things. Yet in 11:27-33, in the final clear reference to John, Jesus links his authority with John and his baptism.

Thus in the Markan schema, we seem to see the following pattern emerging: (1) John linked closely with Jesus and the Gospel (Mk 1); (2) John distinguished from Jesus in his practices as noted by outsiders (Mk 2); (3) Outsiders attempt to identify Jesus with John, even considering him as possibly John come back from the dead (Mk 6 and 8); (4) Jesus distinguishes himself from John, but in the process ascribes to him a significant role in the new saving activity of God—he is Elijah, the one who restores all (Mk 9); (5) In Jerusalem before the chief priests, scribes* and elders,* Jesus publicly implies some sort of identification of John and Jesus in regard to the matter of divine authorization (Mk 11).

This suggests that Mark's intention in using the Baptist material is not *primarily* to indicate that John bore witness to Jesus (as in the Johannine material) but rather as a foil to indicate who Jesus *was not*. This is accomplished in part by distinguishing Jesus' and John's activities and correcting the false impression of outsiders about their identities, and in part by having Jesus in two key places (Mk 9 and 11) give testimony to *who John really is*, a testimony that balances that of John to Jesus in chapter one. This suggests that for Mark, John *is* the beginning of the gospel, not merely because he was seen to be Jesus' forerunner, an Elijah figure, but also because Jesus bore witness to John.

Finally, it may be important that near the end of Mark's Gospel outsiders once again misunderstand Jesus and his words, this time assuming he was calling on Elijah (15:35). But Jesus had already spoken of

"Elijah" as one who had come and gone as it was written of him (chap 9). Thus the end of the Gospel, *unlike* its beginning, is a word not about Elijah or his coming or going. Rather, it is about the going *and coming again* of Jesus. To put it another way, the conclusion of the Gospel is about the death of Jesus, about the God on whom he called, and about that unique one for whom the divine witness is given: "Do not be amazed; you seek Jesus of Nazareth, who was crucified. He has risen; he is not here" (16:6). In the end Jesus of Nazareth is *not* John *redivivus*. John's story finishes before the end of the Gospel, but as for Jesus of Nazareth, he comes back from the dead as himself—*that* is the end of the Gospel. The tension in the narrative is resolved by showing that the discontinuity between Jesus' and John's stories is more profound than the continuity.

It is no accident that in the New Quest for the historical Jesus, scholars have seen the history of John the Baptist as a rather secure foundation on which to reconstruct an historical estimate of Jesus and his ministry. A major key to understanding the historical Jesus is a proper estimation of the elements of continuity and discontinuity between the ministries and messages of the two major figures in the Gospels—Jesus and John.

See also BAPTISM; ELIJAH and ELISHA; ESCHATOLOGY; JUDGMENT; REVOLUTIONARY MOVEMENTS.

BIBLIOGRAPHY. D. C. Allison, "Elijah Must Come First," *JBL* 103 (1984) 256-58; L. F. Badia, *The Qumran Baptism and John the Baptist's Baptism* (Lanham, MD: University Press of America, 1980); P. W. Barnett, "The Jewish Sign Prophets—A.D. 40-70: Their Intentions and Origin," *NTS* 27 (1981) 679-97; O. Betz, "Die Proselytentaufe der Qumransekte und die Taufe im Neuen Testament," *RevQ* 1 (1958) 213-34; D. Catchpole, "John the Baptist, Jesus and the Parable of the Tares," *SJT* 31 (1978) 557-70; W. D. Davies and D. C. Allison, Jr., *The Gospel according to St. Matthew*, vol. 1 (ICC; Edinburgh: T. & T. Clark, 1988); S. L. Davies, "John the Baptist and the Essene Kashruth," *NTS* 29 (1983) 569-71; M. M. Faierstein, "Why Do the Scribes Say that Elijah Must Come First?" *JBL* 100 (1981) 75-86; W. R. Farmer, "John the Baptist," *IDB* (1962) 1.955-62; J. A. Fitzmyer, "More About Elijah Coming First," *JBL* 104 (1985) 295-96; C. H. Kraeling, *John the Baptist* (New York: Scribner's, 1951); E. Linnemann, "Jesus und die Täufer," in *Festschrift für E. Fuchs*, ed. G. Ebeling et al. (Tübingen: J. C. B. Mohr, 1973) 219-36; C. C. McCown, "The Scene of John's Ministry and Its Relation to the Purpose and Outcome of His Mission," *JBL* 59 (1940) 113-31; S. McKnight, *A Light among the Gentiles* (Minneapolis: Fortress, 1991); J. C. O'Neill, *Messiah. Six Lectures on the Ministry of Jesus* (Cambridge: Cochrane, 1980); K. Pusey, "Jewish Proselyte Baptism," *ExpT* 95 (1983-4) 141-45; B. Reicke, "The Historical Setting of John's Baptism," in *Jesus, the Gospels and the Church*, ed. E. P. Sanders (Macon: Mercer University Press, 1987) 209-224; R. Riesner, "Bethany beyond Jordan (John 1.28), Topography, Theology and History in the Fourth Gospel," *TynB* 38 (1987) 29-63; J. Schlosser, *Le Regne de Dieu dans les Dits de Jesus* (Paris: Gabalda, 1980); C. H. H. Scobie, *John the Baptist* (Philadelphia: Fortress, 1964); T. M. Taylor, "The Beginnings of Jewish Proselyte Baptism," *NTS* 2 (1955-56) 193-98; W. Wink, *John the Baptist in the Gospel Tradition* (Cambridge: University Press, 1968); B. Witherington, *The Christology of Jesus* (Minneapolis: Fortress, 1990).

B. Witherington III

JONAH. *See* SIGN OF JONAH.

JOSEPH. *See* BIRTH OF JESUS.

JOSEPH OF ARIMATHEA. *See* BURIAL OF JESUS.

JOSEPHUS

The first-century Jewish writer Josephus is significant for a study of Jesus for two reasons: (1) He provides the major (virtually the only) contemporary Jewish account of the history and conditions of the periods leading up to and including the New Testament era, and (2) if in one form or another they are from his pen, his references to John the Baptist,* Jesus and the death of James the Just, the relative of Jesus, are the oldest non-Christian references to Christianity.

1. Life of Josephus
2. Works of Josephus
3. The "Testimonium Flavianum"

1. Life of Josephus.

Born Joseph, son of Mattathias, he was of the priestly nobility on his father's side and from the royal Hasmonean line through his mother (*Life* 1.1-2 §§1-8). Later he called himself Flavius Josephus. The former name was that of the family of the Roman emperors who were his patrons and the latter, the Hellenized form of Joseph. Between his birth, about A.D. 37, and death, sometime after the beginning of the second century, Josephus appears as a student, sectarian, statesman, general, traitor, historian and apologist for the Jews. His writings were preserved by early Christians who recognized their contribution in establishing the historical origins of their faith.

Details of Josephus's life, often closely entwined with the crises of his nation's history, may be gleaned from his writings. He was a precocious youth. By age fourteen, Josephus claims, his learning was so widely regarded that rabbis consulted him. A couple of years later he began a study of the three primary national sects, Sadducees (*see* Judaism), Pharisees* and Essenes (*see* Dead Sea Scrolls), and lived as an ascetic in the wilderness for three years with Bannus, a hermit. He then became a Pharisee (*Life* 1.2 §§9-12). In A.D. 64 Josephus visited Rome* to seek the liberation of some priests sent by the procurator Felix for trial before Nero. He succeeded with the help of Nero's wife, Poppea, whom Josephus had met through a Jewish actor in the city (*Life* 1.3 §§13-16). In Rome Josephus was impressed with the grandeur and power of the empire.

Upon returning to Judea, Josephus found his country headed for war with Rome (*see* Revolutionary Movements). Realizing the folly of his fellow Jews, he sought to steer his nation in other directions (*Life* 1.4 §§17-19). When this failed he threw his support to the nationalistic cause and, for unknown reasons, although only twenty-nine years of age, was placed in charge of Galilee,* which would certainly be the first line of Roman attack. In *The Jewish War* (2.20.4-8 §§568-84) he implies his charge was to command in Galilee. Later, in his *Life* (1.7 §29) he implies he was supposed to pacify the region. In the fall of A.D. 67 Josephus and his forces made their last stand against the invaders at Jotapata, which fell after a forty-seven-day siege (*J.W.* 3.3.3-36 §§141-338). His soldiers preferred death with honor to surrender and servitude. Josephus proposed a plan in which each would kill his fellow and the two remaining would commit suicide (*J.W.* 3.85-86 §§361-89). However, Josephus, one of the last two, and his companion surrendered to the Romans (*J.W.* 3.8-9 §§392-408). When brought before Vespasian, Josephus predicted the general would one day become emperor. He was held as a captive (*J.W.* 3.8-9 §§392-408).

Roman military operations in Palestine were halted during A.D. 68-69 to await the outcome of the struggle for the throne following Nero's death. Eventually, Vespasian's army proclaimed him emperor (*J.W.* 4.10.3-4 §§592-604). He liberated Josephus (*J.W.* 10.7 §§623-69) who accompanied his benefactor* as far as Alexandria and returned to assist Vespasian's son, Titus, in the final siege of Jerusalem. Josephus acted as an interpreter and mediator between the combatant forces (*J.W.* 4.9.2-3 §§361-62; 5.3.2. §114; 6.4 §261; 9.1—10.1 §§361-420; 13.3 §§541-47; 6.2.1-2 §§94-111; 7.2 §365) and witnessed the overthrow of the nation

and city in A.D. 70 (*see* Destruction of Jerusalem).

After the war Josephus was taken to Rome by Titus (*Life* 76 §422), who himself eventually succeeded to the imperial throne. Under Vespasian and Titus, Josephus lived as a ward of the court, with a stipend and a villa, evidently spending much of his time in writing (*Life* 76 §423). After the death of Titus he was forced to find another patron, Epaphroditus, a grammarian (*Ant.* preface 2 §§8-9; *Life* 76 §430), and continued writing (especially after the death of Domitian in A.D. 98). Josephus outlived Herod Agrippa II, who died in A.D. 100 (*see* Herodian Dynasty).

Of his home life we know little. Josephus speaks of his four wives; the second deserted him and the third he divorced. He says he had three sons by his third wife and two by his last (*Life* 75 §§414-15; 76 §§426-28).

2. Works of Josephus.
Although Josephus mentions other works written or planned by him, only four of his writings survive (Eusebius' ascription of 4 Maccabees to Josephus [*Hist. Eccl.* 3.10] is no longer taken seriously). His first writing, *The History of the Jewish War,* is the most important. It is divided into seven books which survey the history of the Jews from the Maccabean revolt to the fall of Masada and disturbances in Syria in A.D. 73. *The Jewish War* focuses on the events of the struggle against the Romans, A.D. 66-70, in which he played a part (on both sides). The first book provides an introduction tracing those events and attitudes which Josephus thinks led to the Jewish revolt. Throughout the work the writer provides descriptions of the geography* of Palestine (including Jerusalem and its Temple,* *J.W.* 5.4.1—5.8 §§136-247) and of Jewish history, life, customs and thought which were intended to provide necessary background for Roman readers not acquainted with the region and people.

Josephus's objective is to praise his Roman patrons and to quiet anti-Jewish feelings by shifting blame for the war from the Jewish people as a whole to a minority of unwise leaders and radical parties or sects, especially the Zealots (*see* Revolutionary Movements). The book was originally written in Aramaic, then, with assistance, rewritten in Greek and presented to Vespasian before his death in 79. His primary sources of information appear to have been 1 Maccabees, Herod the Great's counselor and court historian Nicholas of Damascus, official written records, and his own experience, contacts and memory.

The Antiquities of the Jews appeared in twenty books in A.D. 93-94. The interval of almost twenty years since the appearance of *The Jewish War* was probably spent in research and writing; it was also the period of

Domitian, whose dislike of literature, and especially history, silenced other writers such as Tacitus, Pliny and Juvenal. The *Antiquities* (or "Archaeology," as he calls it) traces Jewish history from the creation of the world to his own day. For the biblical portions of history he employs the content and structure of the Greek translation of the Old Testament, the Septuagint, into which he inserts Jewish stories, legends and embellishments (Rabbinic Haggadah; *see* Rabbinic Traditions and Writings). He also is indebted to Greek historians for both form—including the speeches he places in the mouths of his characters—and content. From the end of the biblical history (in *Ag. Ap.* 1.8 §40 Josephus says biblical history was complete by the death of the Persian king Artaxerxes [Longimanus], who died about 423 B.C.) he has but scanty information. Apparently at least part of this came from the *Epistle of Aristeas* or a similar document. In *Antiquities* 11.7 §297—12.5 §264 he briefly mentions such things as inter-Jewish and Samaritan* conflicts, the arrival of Alexander the Great in Jerusalem, and eventual Ptolemaic (Egyptian) control of Palestine, the translation of the Septuagint, and conflicts over the priesthood. He then begins covering the same material found in the first and second books of *The Jewish War* up to the outbreak of the war with Rome, but often with different detail, form and emphases.

At the end of *The Jewish War* Josephus tells of charges against himself (*J.W.* 7.11.3 §448). His book *The Life of Josephus* is not so much an autobiography as a defense against continuing criticisms of his conduct and position during the war. *Against Apion,* Josephus' latest surviving writing, is a defense of Judaism against its detractors, of whom Apion, a contemporary anti-Semite, is a representative.

The accuracy of Josephus' writings has often been called into question. He is self-serving in his accounts, overly gracious and generous in his presentation of the Romans, and molds the facts of Jewish history to suit his own ends. He is notorious for his exaggeration of numbers. Parallel sections of different works have unreconcilable variants. Nevertheless, recent data such as that provided by the excavations of Masada during the 1960s, add credibility to Josephus' handling of at least the major features of his subjects. Earlier theories suggested that Luke, in both his Gospel and Acts, made use of Josephus. If true, this hypothesis would reflect negatively on Luke's accuracy. Modern studies generally support the conclusion that the two authors are independent of each other.

3. The "Testimonium Flavianum."

The Greek text of *Antiquities* makes reference to the deaths of John the Baptist (18.5 §§116-119]) and James, the relative of Jesus (20.9 §200). In the former reference Josephus says that Herod (Antipas) arrested John as a precaution against an upheaval. He also identifies the fortress Machaerus as the site of John's execution, and says that some Jews saw the defeat of Herod by the Nabatean king Aretas as "divine vengeance for his treatment of John." "James, the brother of Jesus who was called the Christ,"* says Josephus, was the victim of judicial murder by the High Priest Ananus during the inter-regnum between the death of the procurator Felix and the arrival of his successor, Festus (c. A.D. 62). Origen (*Contra Cels.* 1.47) says Josephus identified the death of James as cause for the destruction of Jerusalem and the Temple; this statement, however, is not in extant texts of the historian.

Antiquities 18.3 §63-64 contains the following statement, commonly called "The Testimonium Flavianium":

> About this time there lived Jesus, a wise man, if indeed one ought to call him a man. For he was one who wrought surprising feats and was a teacher of such people as accept the truth gladly. He won over many Jews and many of the Greeks. He was the Messiah. When Pilate, upon hearing him accused by men of the highest standing amongst us, had condemned him to be crucified, those who had in the first place come to love him did not give up their affection for him. On the third day he appeared to them restored to life, for the prophets of God had prophesied these and countless other marvelous things about him. And the tribe of Christians, so called after him, has still to this day not disappeared. (Trans. L. H. Feldman, Loeb Classical Library.)

This statement stands in all Greek manuscripts from the eleventh century onward and was known as early as the fourth century when Eusebius twice quoted it (*Hist. Eccl.* 1.11; *Dem. Ev.* 3.5, 124). Origen (c.185-c.254) knew of Josephus' allusions to John the Baptist and James but twice says Josephus did not believe Jesus to be the Christ (*Comm. Mt.* 10.17; *Contra Cels.* 1.47). However, this statement casts doubt only on Origen's knowledge of the statement "he was the Messiah," not on the "Testimonium" as a whole.

The early twentieth century witnessed the circulation and discussion of a Slavonic version of *The Jewish War,* which contains numerous additions and omissions from the traditional text. Among the additions are references to John the Baptist, Jesus and to early Christians. These are quite different from statements about the same individuals in the Greek *Antiquities.*

There is little doubt that these Slavonic additions are the work of later Christians.

In 1971 S. Pines published a study of the quotation of the "Testimonium" by Agapius, a tenth-century Christian. He quotes an Arabic text which, it could be argued, was not subject to the same Christian influences as the traditional one. It reads:

> At this time there was a wise man who was called Jesus. His conduct was good, and [he] was known to be virtuous. And many people from among the Jews and other nations became his disciples. Pilate condemned him to be crucified and to die. But those who had become his disciples did not abandon his discipleship. They reported that he had appeared to them three days after his crucifixion, and that he was alive; accordingly he was perhaps the Messiah, concerning whom the prophets have recounted wonders.

There are three views about the validity of the "Testimonium Flavianum," especially as it appears in the Greek text: (1) it is, as it stands, from the pen of Josephus; (2) it is entirely an addition by later Christian authors, and Josephus himself said nothing about Jesus; (3) the original edition of the *Antiquities* contained some statement about Jesus, but the present Greek text contains later alterations by Christian hands. Attitudes toward references to John the Baptist and James the Just in the Greek text of the *Antiquities* are similar to those about the statements about Jesus.

Nineteenth-century scholarship (including such notables as Dobschütz, Niese, Schürer and Zeitlin) rejected the "Testimonium Flavianum" as completely unauthentic. More recently, the third option has gained support. In 1929 H. St. John Thackeray (p. 148) concluded, "The paragraph in the main comes from Josephus or his secretary, but the Christian censor or copyist has, by slight omissions and alterations, so distorted it as to give it a whole different complexion." The Vermes-Millar-Black revision of Schürer's *The History of the Jewish People in the Age of Jesus Christ* (pp. 428-41) argues "Josephus mentioned Jesus. . . . Josephus wrote more about Jesus than we are able to extract from this text." The Arabic text discussed by Pines strengthens this conclusion. Pines makes no claims regarding the authenticity of the "Testimonium" in his document but notes that it contains "none of the suspicious phraseology of the 'vulgate recension' that has led many modern scholars to reject the entire passage as a Christian interpolation."

Josephus' greatest value to a study of Jesus and the Gospels lies in the background information he provides. Without his writings moderns would be left to construct a history of first-century Judaism from mere bits and pieces. In spite of his limitations, Josephus conducts us through that strange time and world which was home to Jesus and the Evangelists and so enables us better to hear and see the Word in the world in which it appeared.

See also JESUS IN NON-CHRISTIAN SOURCES; JUDAISM; HELLENISM.

BIBLIOGRAPHY. **Editions:** The major critical edition of the Greek text of Josephus is B. Niese, *Flavii Josephi Opera* (7 vols.; Berlin: Weidmann, 1955, originally 1885-95); The Loeb Classical Library edition, by H. St. J. Thackeray, R. Marcus and L. Feldman (10 vols.; Cambridge, MA: Harvard University, 1926-1965) contains both the Greek and English text. The most common edition is the single-volume English translation of W. Whiston, *Josephus: Complete Works* (rev. ed.; Grand Rapids: Kregel, 1987; originally 1736). **Studies:** H. W. Attridge, "Jewish Historiography—Josephus," in *Early Judaism and Its Modern Interpreters,* ed. R. A. Kraft and G. W. E. Nickelsburg (Atlanta: Scholars, 1986) 324-29; P. Bilde, *Flavius Josephus, between Jerusalem and Rome: His Life, His Works, and Their Importance* (JSPSup; Sheffield: JSOT, 1988); L. H. Feldman and G. Hata, eds., *Josephus, Judaism, and Christianity* (Detroit: Wayne State University, 1987); J. P. Meier, "Jesus in Josephus: A Modest Proposal," *CBQ* 52 (1990) 76-103; S. Pines, *An Arabic Version of the Testimonium Flavianum and Its Implications* (Jerusalem: Israel Academy of Science and Humanities, 1971); T. Rajak, *Josephus, The Historian and His Society* (Philadelphia: Fortress, 1983); U. Rappaport, ed., *Josephus Flavius: Historian of Eretz-Israel in the Hellenistic-Roman Period* (Jerusalem, 1982); E. Schürer, *The History of the Jewish People in the Age of Jesus Christ (175 B.C.-A.D. 135),* rev. and ed. G. Vermes, F. Millar (3 vols.; Edinburgh: T. & T. Clark, 1973); R. J. H. Shutt, *Studies in Josephus* (London: SPCK, 1961); H. St. J. Thackeray, *Josephus, The Man and the Historian* (New York: Jewish Institute of Religion, 1929; repr. New York: KTAV, 1967); G. A. Williamson, *The World of Josephus* (Boston/Toronto: Little, Brown, 1964).

J. J. Scott

JOY

The language of joy is prominent in the Gospels, being expressed by no less than seven words: *agalliaomai, agalliasis, euphrainō, skirtaō, chairō, sugchairō* and *chara. Agalliaomai* and *agalliasis,* though derived from classical use, are found only in Jewish works or writings dependent on them. *Euphrainō* and *skirtaō* are also strongly attested in the LXX and are used only by Luke in the Gospels. *Chairō* and *chara* are found only in the later books of the LXX but are dominant in the Gospels and NT generally. The following table illustrates the distribution of these words.

	Mt	Mk	Lk	Jn	Gospels Total	NT Total
agalliaomai	1	0	2	2	5	11
agalliasis	0	0	2	0	2	5
euphrainō	0	0	6	0	6	14
skirtaō	0	0	3	0	3	3
chairō	6	2	12	9	29	74
sugchairō	0	0	3	0	3	7
chara	6	1	8	9	24	59
Total	13	3	36	20	72	173

Clearly Luke merits the title "the Gospel of joy," making use of each of the words and having by far the most uses of "joy" vocabulary. Mark makes use only of *chairō* (twice) and *chara* (once). Joy is not a significant focus for Mark. Each of his three uses occurs in a negative context. In the parable* of the soils the stony ground represents those who at first receive the word with joy (Mk 4:16 par. Mt 13:20 and Lk 8:13) but fall away at the first sign of trouble. Mark (14:11 par. Lk 22:5) reports the rejoicing of the chief priests at the offer of betrayal by Judas.* Finally, Mark (15:18 par. Mt 27:29 and Jn 19:3) tells how the soldiers mocked Jesus, addressing him "Hail (*chaire*), king of the Jews." This traditional form of address using *chairein* was a wish of joy based on physical well-being and is found also in Matthew 26:49; 28:9 and Luke 1:28. In Matthew the irony that Judas betrayed Jesus with such a greeting (Mt 26:49) should not be overlooked.

Independently in both Matthew and Luke the birth of Jesus (*see* Birth of Jesus) is anticipated with joy. The wise men "rejoiced with great joy" at the sight of the star that guided them (Mt 2:10). In Luke (1:14) Zachariah is told of the joy associated with the coming birth of John (*see* John the Baptist) as the forerunner of the Messiah (cf Lk 1:58). When Mary greeted Elizabeth the baby in Elizabeth's womb leapt for joy (*eskirtēsen*, Lk 1:41, 44). The message of the angels* to the shepherds was one of "great joy" (Lk 2:10) in anticipation of the fulfillment of the promised salvation* from God.*

That Jesus taught the superficiality of attachment to earthly joys seems likely (Mk 4:16 par. Mt 13:20 and Lk 8:13). He taught those persecuted for his sake to rejoice because their reward would be great in heaven* (Mt 5:12 par. Lk 6:23 = Q). There are puzzling differences in the wording of Matthew and Luke at this point, not least Matthew's use of *agalliasthe* where Luke uses *skirtēsate*. Both of these words

are commonly used in the LXX. Perhaps Luke introduced the latter as a more vivid leaping for joy. Matthew alone (Mt 13:44) has the parable of the joy at finding the treasure hidden in the field as an analogy to the joy of the kingdom (*see* Kingdom of God), but shares with Luke the parable of joy at finding the lost sheep (Mt 18:13; Lk 15:5, 6, 7 Q?; *see* Shepherd, Sheep) where the stress on joy is much greater in Luke. Luke takes the stress further in the parables of the lost coin (Lk 15:7) and the lost son (Lk 15:23, 24, 29, 32) where the return of the lost son is celebrated with a banquet. Matthew's account of the parable of the talents includes a stress on the joy extended to the faithful servants (Mt 25:21, 23) that is absent from the Lukan version (Lk 19:17-19).

The reversal of the basis for joy is apparent in Luke's account of the return of the seventy. Jesus tells them not to rejoice because the spirits (*see* Demon, Devil, Satan) are subject to them but because their names are written in heaven (Lk 10:17, 20). Only in Luke 10:21 is Jesus said to rejoice (cf. Mt 11:25 = Q?). As a model for the correct basis of joy this shows a reversal of worldly values. Joy based on worldly values is shown to be misguided in the parable of the rich fool (Lk 12:19) and the story of the rich man (*see* Rich and Poor) and Lazarus.* The rich man had joy in this world (Lk 16:19) but torment hereafter. Zacchaeus had a sound basis for joy in receiving Jesus (Lk 19:6). Only Luke mentions that the crowd that heralded Jesus' entry into Jerusalem were disciples* and that they began to rejoice and to praise God, though the reported words are similar in Luke 19:37-38; Mark 11:9-10; Matthew 21:9 and John 12:13. Absent from Mark but important for Matthew, Luke and John is the joy at the appearance of the risen Jesus (Mt 28:8, 9; Lk 24:41, 52; Jn 20:20; *see* Resurrection).

In John the language of joy is concentrated on the lips of Jesus, though John the Baptist is the first to use it. He likens himself to the friend of the bridegroom (*see* Bride, Bridegroom) at the wedding, rejoicing at the bridegroom's voice (Jn 3:29). Here the Baptist gives voice to the Johannine theology in his role as the witness* to Jesus. In the time of eschatological fulfillment Jesus asserts that sower and reaper rejoice together (Jn 4:36). Jesus said, "Abraham rejoiced to see my day . . ." (Jn 8:56), again stressing joyful fulfillment, this time enjoyed proleptically by Abraham.* On a different level Jesus says that he was glad not to be present to heal Lazarus (Jn 11:15). The reason for his gladness was not the death of Lazarus but his resurrection through which the disciples would come to believe.

References to joy are concentrated in the farewell

discourses (*see* Farewell Discourse) and prayer* (Jn 14:28; 15:11; 16:20, 21, 22, 24; 17:13). Jesus clarifies the basis and the nature of the joy that is his gift to those who believe in him. First, though his departure leaves his disciples grieving, it is paradoxically a basis for joy because he goes to the Father. Secondly, though he leaves them grieving he will come to them again. This coming is first of all as the risen one so that they rejoice when they see him (Jn 20:20). But it is also the presence of the absent Jesus through the abiding Spirit of Truth (*see* Holy Spirit). In this way the grief of the disciples is turned to become an abiding and indestructible joy (Jn 16:20-24) which is bound to the word of Jesus spoken to prepare them for their witness and work in the world. Regardless of worldly circumstances his joy would be complete in them. In this discourse Jesus expounded more fully the reversal of values involved in the teaching of joy found in Matthew and Luke. As in Matthew and Luke the last word about joy is the rejoicing of the disciples in response to their meeting with the risen Jesus (Jn 20:20).

BIBLIOGRAPHY. R. Bultmann, "ἀγαλλιάομαι κτλ," *TDNT* I.19-21; idem, "εὐφραίνω κτλ," *TDNT* II.772-75; idem, *The Gospel of John* (Philadelphia: Westminster, 1971); H. Conzelmann and W. Zimmerli, "χαίρω κτλ," *TDNT* IX.359-415; J. Moltmann, *Theology and Joy* (London: SCM, 1971); W. G. Morrice, *Joy in the New Testament* (Grand Rapids: Eerdmans, 1985).

J. Painter

JUBILEE

The Year of Jubilee figured significantly in the theology of Jesus as it is related in the Gospel of Luke. The rejection of Jesus in Nazareth (4:16-30), an event which is programmatic for the Gospel of Luke, makes extensive use of themes related to the OT prescription of a Year of Jubilee (Ex 21:2-6; 23:10-12; Lev 25; Deut 15:1-18; 31:9-13), especially as those themes were already incorporated into Isaiah 58:6; 61:1-2, the text which was read and sermonically elaborated by Jesus (4:18-21).

The Jubilee year is best understood as an intensified Sabbath Year, announced on the Day of Atonement every fifty years as a "sabbath year of sabbath years." The Sabbath Year legislation had three basic provisions, to which a fourth was added in a Jubilee Year: (1) the freeing of all slaves; (2) the cancellation of all debts; (3) the fallowing of the land; and (4) in a Year of Jubilee, the return of all land according to the original Mosaic distribution.

The "release" of the land was the central provision of the Jubilee code. If, because of indebtedness, a Hebrew was forced to sell his property, the sale was not to be a permanent alienation of the land, but more like a lease; the price of the property was determined according to the number of harvests remaining between the time of sale and the next Year of Jubilee (Lev 25:13-17).

Corollary to this provision was the right of redemption (*gᵉ'ullâh*) attached to the sale of any land by a Hebrew. One did not have to wait for the Year of Jubilee to recover one's land; rather, it could be reclaimed at any time by the *gō'ēl* (redeemer), a kinsman of the original owner, or by the owner himself, upon payment of a sum proportionate to the number of harvests remaining from the time of repurchase to the next Jubilee Year (Lev 25:24-28). In any case, the land was to revert to its original owner at the time of the Jubilee. The primary theological basis for the "release" of slaves, debts and land was Yahweh's ownership of both the people and the land. Since he had delivered them from Egyptian servitude and given them the land, neither they nor the land could ever truly be sold (Lev 25:42, 55; Deut 15:15).

Ideas related to the Sabbath/Jubilee Year were taken up in the latter portions of Isaiah, especially chapters 58 and 61. Envisioning a day of release from Babylonian captivity, the prophet naturally described the coming redemption in terms of the well-known year of "release" (*dᵉrôr* in Hebrew, *aphesis* in Greek). Just as the Mosaic legislation had provided for the release of slaves and the recovery of land, so the prophet foresaw the release of the Babylonian captives and the recovery of their ancient patrimony.

The use of the Jubilee as a kind of eschatological motif was not, however, unique to Isaiah. A sabbatarian/jubilary messianism is attested as well in Daniel (9:24-27), the Book of Jubilees (1:21-25), Qumran (11Q Melch) and later Jewish talmudic literature (*Sanh.* 97b). The Qumran fragment known as 11Q Melchizedek is especially helpful in this regard. This brief, eschatological document weaves together Isaiah 52:7 (referring to the messianic herald of the "good news"), Isaiah 61:l-3, Leviticus 25 and Deuteronomy 15, and does so in a way that emphasizes the jubilary motifs therein. More importantly, it demonstrates the existence in the first century of an exegetical tradition which linked, from an eschatological perspective, the major Sabbath/Jubilee Year passages in the Old Testament (*see* Old Testament in the Gospels; Typology).

Luke's narration of Jesus' sermon in Nazareth represents a particular development in the eschatological use of Jubilee Year themes: Jesus himself is presented as the anointed (messianic) herald of the long-awaited Year of Jubilee. The text of Jesus' sermon (4:18-19) was:

The Spirit of the Lord is upon me,

Because he has anointed me to preach good news to the poor;

He has sent me to proclaim release (*aphesis*) to the captives

And recovery of sight to the blind,

To send away in release (*aphesis*) those who are oppressed,

To proclaim the Favorable Year of the Lord.

The dominant motifs in the text (now declared by Jesus as fulfilled) relate to the Year of Jubilee (4:21).

The term "release" (*aphesis*) represents the primary theological and verbal connection with the levitical proclamation of Jubilee. The classical Greek employment of *aphesis* was in the legal sense of a "release" from office, marriage, obligation, debt or even punishment. The word was not used, however, in religious contexts. In the LXX, of the approximately fifty instances of *aphesis*, twenty-two are in Leviticus 25 and 27, where it translates in most cases the Hebrew *yôḇel*, "Year of Jubilee"; in other cases, most notably Leviticus 25:10, it translates *dᵉrôr*, "release." *Dᵉrôr*, in fact, seems to have been the technical term of the prophets to indicate the Year of Jubilee, that is, "the year of release," or "liberty," as Jeremiah 34:8, 15, 17; Ezekiel 46:17; and Isaiah 61:1 indicate. *Aphesis* also translates the complex of Sabbath Year passages (Ex 23:11; Deut 15:1-11; 31:10) in which the Hebrew *šᵉmiṭṭāh*, or *šāmaṭ*, is used.

Thus with "liberation" or "release" as the primary meaning of *aphesis* in the LXX, and with *aphesis* highlighted as the key term holding together Jesus' conflated reading of Isaiah 61:1-2; 58:6, the Sabbath/Jubilee Year import of the Nazareth sermon would have been lost on no one in Jesus' or Luke's audience familiar with either the Mosaic traditions or the then-popular eschatological text of Isaiah 61. The "good news to the poor" is thus the happy announcement of their re-enfranchisement. It is at long last the commencement (4:21) of the eschatological Year of Jubilee, when God graciously pardons all debts and sets the oppressed and the captives free.

Given the central significance of the Nazareth pericope for Luke, there can be little doubt that further references in Luke to "preaching the gospel*" must be read with jubilary significance. This is borne out by Luke's use of the verb *euangelizō*, whereas Matthew, Mark and John show an overwhelming preference for the noun *euangelion* (a fact which argues that Luke's usage is based upon the programmatic Is 61 passage where the verb form is in evi-

dence). The same may be said for the other occurrences in Luke of the noun *aphesis*, normally translated in the NT as "forgiveness." The fact that *aphesis* occurs in the two programmatic passages of Luke's two-volume work (Lk 4:18 and Acts 2:38), as well as in the capstone passage of evangelistic commissioning in his Gospel (24:46-49), indicates, against the backdrop of its infrequent use in the NT (of only seventeen occurrences in the NT, ten are in Lk-Acts, one in Mt, two in Mk and none in Jn), not only its importance for Luke, but also that its meaning throughout must be read over against its initial jubilary use in 4:16-30.

The idea of Jubilee has also shaped other sections of the Gospel of Luke, as evidenced by Jesus' own summary of his ministry (7:22), the so-called fifth prayer of the Lukan version of the Lord's Prayer (11:4), the use of Isaiah 61:1-3 in the Lukan Beatitudes (6:20-26) and the clear use of certain Sabbath-Year motifs from Deuteronomy 15:7-11 (cf. Lev 25:35-38) in the following section of the Great Sermon in Luke 6:27-38 (*see* Sermon on the Mount).

Luke's employment of the Jubilee/Sabbath-Year themes from Isaiah 58:6; 61:1-2 (and Lev 25, Deut 15), has a distinctly eschatological application. The one-sentence summary (Lk 4:21) of Jesus' sermon is, "Today this Scripture has been fulfilled in your hearing." It was not the renewal of a purely social or economically leveling piece of Jewish legislation that concerned Jesus, though none can deny the profound social import of his teachings (*see* Liberation Hermeneutics), but the inauguration, using the eschatologically adapted language of Jubilee, of the long-awaited kingdom of God.* As such, the Jubilee-Year motif is of a piece with Jesus' apocalyptic* announcement of the reign of God, a reign which has begun with the coming of Jesus and will be finally manifested when, like the blowing of the *šôp̄ār* on the Day of Atonement to announce the Year of Jubilee, the "last trump" will herald the glorious appearance of Christ our *gōʾēl* and Kinsman Redeemer.

See also KINGDOM OF GOD; SALVATION.

BIBLIOGRAPHY. R. North, *The Sociology of the Biblical Jubilee* (Rome: The Pontifical Biblical Institute, 1954); S. H. Ringe, *Jesus Liberation, and the Biblical Jubilee* (OBT; Philadelphia: Fortress, 1985); G. K.-S. Shin, *Die Ausrufung des endgültigen Jubeljahres durch Jesus in Nazaret: Eine historisch-Kritische Studie zu Lk 4, 16-30* (EH 23: Theology 378; Bern: Peter Lang, 1989); R. B. Sloan, *The Favorable Year of the Lord: A Study of Jubilary Theology in the Gospel of Luke* (Austin: Schola Press, 1977).

R. B. Sloan

JUDAISM

In every period of its history Judaism has been rooted in the notion that Israel* is chosen. Indeed, the perennial paradox in the study of Judaism is that the notion of election is more persistent than any definition of what *Israel* might be. We might be thinking of an extended family of Aramaeans which departed from Mesopotamia in order to settle westward, of their settlement in Canaan, of the migrant group in Egypt, of those who departed from Egypt, of those who struggled for control of the land of Canaan, of the nation and its eventual monarchy (and civil war), of the dispossessed peoples in Babylonia, of the ideal Israel which the Scriptures of the Exile project, and/ or of those people both in the land and in the Diaspora who read those Scriptures as their own, for whom *Israel* was and is an identification of self.

Each of the moments of the development of Israel named above (and each of several other stages) has been the object of particular, scholarly attention. But for convenience we may categorize the history of Judaism under four stages: (1) the period from family to people; (2) the period of nationalization and monarchy; (3) the period of dispossession and the canonization of Scripture; and (4) the period of radical pluralization which is widely referred to today as "early Judaism." While a full appreciation of Judaism would call for an understanding of all of these stages, the focus of this article is set on the latter period which most directly pertains to the environment of Jesus and the Gospels.

    1. From Family to People
    2. Nationalization and Monarchy
    3. Dispossession and Canonization
    4. Radical Pluralization
    5. Early Judaism As Reflected in the Gospels

1. From Family to People.

The conviction of being divinely elect as a condition *sine qua non* of Judaism is predicated on the traditional understanding that Abraham is the father of all Jews. For Abraham is remembered as being partner to the covenant involving both God's gift of the land which would be called Israel and the sign of circumcision (Gen 15:1-21; 17:1-14). But it is Moses* who is particularly associated with the constitution of Israel as a people rather than simply a family. The transition took place in the events surrounding the liberation of Israel from Egypt and the revelation given at Sinai. The Mosaic constitution or covenant would become paradigmatic for every age of Judaism which followed. Tribal lineage, based on the assumption that the tribes were descended from the sons of Jacob/Israel,

replaced familial lineage as the operative definition of the group.

Moses is also the emblem of centralized sacrifice and judgment, both of which contribute to the understanding of Israel as an organic whole. Sacrifice within the Mosaic system is the place of meeting between God and Israel (Ex 24:1-11), such that only what is clean* may be involved (cf. Lev 11—15), and much of it passes to divine ownership (cf. Lev 3:1-17). Moreover, the declared aim of entry into the land of promise is to cleanse it of what is not acceptable to God. Everything else—people, beasts and property— is to be "devoted" (cf. Josh 6—7), in effect offered as a sacrifice for the cleansing of the land.

2. Nationalization and Monarchy.

Israel's occupation or dispossession of Canaan led to a period of leadership by judges, charismatic figures known for their success in defending tribal claims on the land or rooting out Canaanite worship. But the unsystematic convention of judges was no answer to the centralized attack of even a petty kingdom. And though the book of Judges criticizes kingship as an implicit denial of the sovereignty of Yahweh (cf. Judg 8:22—9:57), a transition to monarchy came under the leadership of Samuel, who incorporated the roles of both priest and judge. But Saul, the first king anointed by Samuel (1 Sam 10), is portrayed as persistently usurping authority not his own (1 Sam 13:8-15; 14:31-35; 15; 18—20), and is rejected by God in favor of David (1 Sam 16:1-13).

2.1. The Davidic Monarchy. The Davidic monarchy itself becomes the object of a solemn oath in 2 Samuel 7, where the prophet Nathan promises God's protection of David's progeny. It is notable that the promise is occasioned by David's undertaking to build a temple. The offer itself is accepted but deferred; it is Solomon who is to accomplish the task (2 Sam 7:12-13). But the function of the king in protecting, not leading, worship is established, and the promise to David is integrated within the covenant generally.

The centralization of the sacrificial cult in David's city, Jerusalem (2 Sam 6), had both positive and negative effects from the point of view of faithfulness to the covenant. Positive, because the new center became the focus of collecting Israel's holy traditions and presenting them at the feasts* which were primarily celebrated at Jerusalem. Negative, because with monarchy came the pressure to trade and compete with other cities: the multiplication of cults—and the de facto acceptance of their deities—being a feature of Solomon's otherwise auspicious reign (cf. 1 Kings 11).

First Kings lays the blame on Solomon's apostasy

(1 Kings 11:29-40) for the division (c. 922 B.C.) of united Israel into Israel in the north and Judah in the south. But the kings, north and south, undermined their own authority not only by their idolatry, but also by their recourse to slavery and their conspicuous consumption.

2.2. The Prophetic Movement. Prophecy (*see* Prophets, Prophecy) found its voice as a movement in its opposition to the monarchs it regarded as apostate. Prior to the crystallizing impact of that opposition, prophets appear to have been identified as those who spoke for God, often in association with worship* in particular sanctuaries. But first the association with David, and then the antagonism of kings in the north and south, made of prophecy a startlingly coherent movement.

The emergence of prophecy as a literary genre is to be dated to the eighth century and the message of Amos. Fundamentally a prophet of doom against the northern kingdom, Amos foretold judgment against Israel's apostate kings, and Hosea vividly generalized that theme to include the nation as a whole. They were quickly followed in the south by Micah and Isaiah, and an urgent appeal for social justice became a hallmark of prophecy in the south.

The announcement of doom against the north by an Amos or a Hosea must have appeared idle during periods of prosperity, but when in 722 B.C. the capital of the north was taken, and the northern kingdom was subjected to a policy of Exile, the prophetic message appeared to be vindicated.

Spurred on by the demise of Israel in the north, whose people were lost to history, the prophets in Judah attempted to purify the life of their people. Isaiah urgently argued against foreign alliances and insisted that fidelity to God alone would save Jerusalem. Jeremiah ceaselessly denounced faithlessness and was prosecuted for his trouble. Ezekiel's enactments of coming disaster won him a reputation as a crank. But in the reign of Josiah a royal reformation backed much of the critique of the prophets (cf. 2 Kings 22:1—23:30; 2 Chron 34:1—35:27). Josiah restored worship in the Temple according to covenantal norms; he centralized sacrifice, even of the Passover, in Jerusalem; he tolerated no foreign incursions. In this program he was guided by a scroll of the Law* which was found in the Temple during the restoration. Since antiquity this scroll has been associated with the present book of Deuteronomy. Like the agenda which impelled Josiah, Deuteronomy presses the issue of radical centralization and separation from foreign nations. But in 609 Josiah was killed in battle in an attempt to block the alliance between Pharaoh

Neco and the Assyrians at a place called Megiddo.

3. Dispossession and Canonization.

3.1. Exile and the Vision of Classic Israel: The Pentateuch. The end of the kingdom of Judah came quickly after the death of Josiah. In 587/6 the Babylonian Empire, having laid siege to Jerusalem and destroyed the Temple, implemented a policy of exile. Had the course of events then followed what happened to the northern kingdom, there would today be no Judaism to study. Paradoxically, however, just the forces which must have seemed sure to destroy the religion of the covenant with Yahweh instead assured its survival and nurtured its international dimension. The program of restoration which followed put a form of Israel back on the map within a generation. Even more influentially, the vision of classic Israel enshrined in the Pentateuch became a canonical standard. Sometime after the sixth century that work was combined with what many scholars have come to call the Deuteronomic History (Joshua-2 Kings), a telling of events between Moses and the Exile which explains success or failure according to the nation's adherence to the program which drove Josiah.

3.2. Restoration and New Visions for the Future: The Prophets. The dispossession of Judah to Babylon, then, set up the priestly and prophetic hegemony which made restoration possible. Just as the Pentateuch set out particular priestly concerns, the prophetic movement also brought a distinctive message to the canon. In general agreement with the priestly perspective that the land was to be possessed again, the prophetic writings found in Isaiah 40—55; Jeremiah 23:1-8; 31; and Ezekiel 40—48 constituted eloquent motivations for return to the land.

But the previous abuses of the kings and their sanctuaries made the prophetic movement insist that righteousness (*see* Justice, Righteousness) was the prior requirement of sacrifice, and that the events of the recent past were a warning. A Zechariah might be happy to set out the hope of a priestly messiah (*see* Christ) beside the Davidic king who was to rule (Zech 3, 4), but the predominant emphasis fell on the crucial necessity of loyalty to the worship of God (Zech 14). Moreover, eschatology* became characteristic of the prophetic movement. These themes are seen in the latter chapters of Isaiah and Ezekiel, as well as in fresh works such as Joel and Malachi: the contemporary governance, whether Persian, Ptolemaic or Seleucid, and the present Temple were provisional, awaiting an anointed king and an anointed priest who would rule properly. Just the image of a priestly orientation redefined by the prophets is seen in the career of Ezra as it is related in the books of Ezra and Nehemiah: prophet, priest and scribe become one in their insistence on the vision of classic Israel, centered on the restored Temple.

The Temple as restored was, however, far from anyone's ideal. Some who remembered the splendor of Solomon's edifice are reported to have wept when they saw the results of the efforts under Ezra (Ezra 3:10-13). That imperfect focus nonetheless served to attract a permanent priesthood, and the notion of a canon provided focus to the prophetic movement: now a body of literature which could be interpreted was held to provide the guidance which individual prophets formerly gave. Indeed, it is notable that Ezra's own ministry involved guiding Israel on the basis of scriptural interpretation: the scribe emerges as the dominant religious personality, as the warrant of true prophecy and the arbiter of priestly conduct (Neh 8—13).

3.3. Voices from Outside the Priestly-Prophetic Hegemony: The Writings. But the appearance that scribal leadership was settled is more superficial than representative. Battles concerning the proper conduct of the cult and the proper personnel of the priesthood raged during the period of restored Israel, and powerful movements produced literatures outside of scribal control. While the Pentateuch and what are called the Former Prophets (Joshua—2 Kings) and the Latter Prophets within Judaism may be attributed to the hegemony of priestly and prophetic interests which has been described above, the category of "Writings" (the last in the three biblical divisions of traditional Judaism), together with the "Apocrypha" and the "Pseudepigrapha" best characterize other facets of the religion.

The book of Psalms represents a cultic piety centered on just those aspects that Levitical instructions exclude: the music, dance, poetry, prayer* and praise (the term "psalms," *t'hillim*, means "songs of praise") which the Temple attracted. They speak more eloquently of the emotional effect of, and popular participation in, sacrificial worship than any other document in the Bible. Proverbs also represents a non-priestly, non-prophetic focus of piety in restored Israel defined by prudential wisdom. Job and Ecclesiastes are other examples within the canon.

Initially, wisdom* is understood to be an aspect of God which by knowing one can become familiar with God. "Wisdom" in Hebrew is a feminine noun (*hokmâ*), and came to be personified as a woman. By the time of Ecclesiasticus (or Ben Sirach; early second century B.C.) and the Wisdom of Solomon (late first century B.C. or later), she is considered a fundamental means

of access to God. The Wisdom of Solomon was composed in Greek, but the focus on Wisdom is by no means unique to what is commonly called Hellenistic Judaism: contacts with Egyptian and Babylonian inquiries into divine wisdom do probably date from the time of the Israelite and Judean kings as part of their characteristic syncretism. But unlike idolatry and polygyny, wisdom survived and prospered as a suitable and fertile means of communion with God after the notion of the unique covenant with Israel had triumphed. In the case of Philo of Alexandria, whose lifetime straddled the end of the last era and the beginning of our own, the pursuit of wisdom became a philosophical articulation of Judaism. He contributed an awareness of how Judaism and Hellenistic culture (*see* Hellenism)—whose contact is already obvious in the so-called Apocrypha and Pseudepigrapha—might be related. Philo is unusually learned in his representation of a basic development of the Judaism of his period. His simultaneously Greco-Roman and Judaic notion of the *logos* is a case in point (cf. Philo *Op. Mund.*).

3.4. Threats Against Cultic Purity and Priestly Unity. The question of the priesthood in the restored Temple, meanwhile, became increasingly fraught. The Persian regime gave way to Alexander the Great. Among the dynasties of the generals who succeeded him, first the Egyptian Ptolemies and then the Syrian Seleucids largely maintained the enlightened settlement of the Persians. The Seleucid monarch Antiochus IV (surnamed "Epiphanes") is commonly portrayed as a great exception to the policy, and he did unquestionably occupy Jerusalem and arrange for a foreign cult in the sanctuary (in 167 B.C.), which included the sacrifice of swine (a Hellenistic delicacy; 1 Macc 1:20-64; Josephus *Ant.* 12.5.4 §§248-56). But Antiochus entered the city at first as the protector of a high-priestly family, the Tobiads, who were then in dispute with the Oniad family (Josephus *J.W.* 1.1-2 §§31-35). Dispossessed, the latter group moved to Egypt, where a temple was built at Heliopolis in a form different from the restored Temple in Jerusalem (Josephus *J.W.* 1.1 §33; 7.10.2-3 §§420-32). The cult of Onias appears to have been of limited influence, but the mere existence of an alternative cult in the period of restored Israel, served by legitimate pretenders to the high priesthood in Jerusalem, is eloquent testimony of deep divisions within the sacerdotal ranks, and within Judaism generally.

4. Radical Pluralization.

Early Judaism may conveniently be dated from 167 B.C. with the entry of Antiochus's officer, named

Apollonius (2 Macc 5:24-25) into Jerusalem and his desecration of the Temple. But it is evident that the radical pluralization of Judaism prior to Jesus is rooted in the flawed unity of restored Israel during the previous period. Antiochus's campaign triggered both a fissure of interests and a reconfiguration of those interests in a way which made pluralism the order of the day. The temple of Onias at Heliopolis is only one example, but one which shows that one familial group could regard the issues of how sacrifice was offered and by whom as a better measure of acceptable worship than where sacrifice was offered.

4.1. The Rise of the Hasmoneans and the Response of the Faithful.

In Israel, however, there was another group, defined by a desire to remain faithful to sacrifice in Jerusalem by an appropriate priesthood and a resistance to the demands of Antiochus, known as "the faithful" (the famous Hasidim, Heb *ḥᵃsîḏîm*). Attempts have been made in the history of scholarship to identify the Hasidim with a particular sect of Judaism during the period of the second Temple, such as the Essenes or the Pharisees.* But the adjective "faithful" cannot usefully or legitimately be limited to any one group. In the context of reaction to Antiochus, however, the sense of the term clearly related to one's adherence to covenantal norms of sacrifice as part of a vehement resistance.

Among the resisters was Mattathias, a country priest from Modin, whose son Judas Maccabeus ("the hammer") introduced the most powerful priestly rule Judaism has ever known. This rule came to be known under the name of Hasmoneus, Mattathias's ancestor (1 Macc 2:1—9:18; Josephus *Ant.* 12.6.1 §265; 16.7.1 §187; 20.8.11 §§189; 20.10.3 §§238; 20.10.5 §247). Judas, as is well known, turned piety into disciplined revolt, including an alliance with Rome (1 Macc 8) and a willingness to break the Sabbath* for military reasons (1 Macc 2:41). This initiative saw the restoration of worship within the covenant in the Temple in 164 B.C. (1 Macc 4:36-61). After his death his brother Jonathan was named high priest (1 Macc 10:20-21), and from that time until the period of Roman rule the high priesthood was a Hasmonean prerogative.

Those events were too rapid for some and simply unacceptable in the view of others. In strictly familial terms the Hasmoneans could not claim the high priesthood as a right, and therefore competition with other families of priests was a factor. Moreover, the suspension of the Sabbath for military purposes (cf. Josephus *J.W.* 1.7.3 §146) and the arrogation of the high priesthood *and* the monarchy by the non-Davidic Hasmoneans (cf. Josephus *J.W.* 1.3.1 §70) seemed particularly vicious to many Jews in that Antiochus had sanctioned apostasy, and the regime appeared to be compounding apostasy both in its initial resistance and in its consolidation of power.

4.1.1. Apocalyptic Perspective.

The book of Daniel represents the less activist, apocalyptic* stance which many pious Jews adopted as an alternative to the nationalistic and militaristic policy of the Hasmoneans. The eschatology* of the prophets during the period of restored Israel is here transposed into a scenario of the end time in which the Temple would be restored by miraculous means, with the archangel Michael's triumph capped by the resurrection of the just and the unjust (cf. Dan 12:1-4). Folk Judaism of the period also anticipated providential interventions (cf. Tobit), but Daniel elevates and specifies that anticipation until it becomes a program of patient attention and fidelity, warranted by both heavenly vision and its ascription to the sage named Daniel of the Babylonian period (cf. Ezek 14:14).

4.1.2. Essenes.

In the case of the Essenes opposition to the Hasmoneans became overt. They pursued their own system of purity, ethics and initiation, followed their own calendar and withdrew into their own communities, either within cities or in isolated sites such as Qumran (*see* Dead Sea Scrolls). There they awaited a coming apocalyptic war when they, as "the sons of light," would triumph over "the sons of darkness": a reference not only to the Gentiles, but to anyone not of their vision (1QM; 1QS). The culmination of those efforts was to be complete control of Jerusalem and the Temple, where worship would be offered according to their revelation, the correct understanding of the Law of Moses (cf. CD 5:17—6:11). Their insistence on a doctrine of two messiahs, one of Israel and one of Aaron, would suggest that it was particularly the Hasmoneans' arrogation of priestly and royal powers which alienated the Essenes.

4.1.3. Pharisees.

Most of those who resisted the Seleucids or who sympathized with the resistance were neither of priestly families nor of Essene temperament. Nonetheless, the unchecked rule of the Hasmonean priests in the Temple was not entirely acceptable to them. For that large group the Pharisaic movement held a great attraction. The Pharisees, in their attempt to influence what the Hasmoneans did rather than to replace them definitively, appear as much more conservative than the Essenes or competing priestly families. Their focus was on the issue of purity (*see* Clean and Unclean), as defined principally in their oral tradition as well as in their interpretation of Scripture. Since issues of purity were bound to be complicated, in the Hasmonean combination of secular government and sacrificial worship, disputes were inevitable.

Josephus,* for example, implies that the Pharisees made known their displeasure at Alexander Jannaeus by inciting a crowd to pelt him with lemons (at hand for a festal procession) at the time he should have been offering sacrifice, with disastrous consequences (Josephus *Ant.* 13.13.5 §§372-373). Josephus also relates from a later period the teaching of the rabbis (probably Pharisees) who were implicated in dismantling the eagle Herod had erected over a gate of the Temple (Josephus *J.W.* 1.33.2-4 §§648-55; *Ant.* 17.6.2-4 §§149-67). This gesture was both less subversive of the established authority in the cult than what earlier Pharisees had done and more pointedly a challenge to Herod. Paradoxically, the willingness of the Pharisees to consider the Hasmoneans in their priestly function, in distinction from the Essenes, involved them not only in symbolic disputes but in vocal and bloody confrontations. Alexander Jannaeus is reported to have executed by crucifixion eight hundred opponents, either Pharisees or those with whom the Pharisees sympathized, and to have slaughtered their families; but his wife came to an accommodation with the Pharisees which guaranteed them considerable influence (Josephus *J.W.* 1.4.6-1.5.3 §§96-114).

It seems apparent that within the Hasmonean period purity was a political issue and to some extent a symbol. The acquiescence of one of the dynasty to any Pharisaic stricture implicitly acknowledged that the Hasmonean priesthood was provisional, and the Pharisaic movement probably found its original, political expression in opposition to that priesthood (cf. Josephus *Ant.* 13.10.5-6 §§288-98). The Pharisees accepted and developed the notion that with the end of the canon the age of prophecy in the classical sense had ceased (cf. 1 Macc 4:46). For that reason they plausibly saw Ezra and "the men of the great assembly" as their source and their own interpretative movement as an extension of his program of restoration (cf. *m. 'Abot* 1:1-18; 2 Esdr 14). But in two vital respects the Pharisees need to be distinguished from the reforms of Ezra. First, they identified themselves with no specific priestly or political figure: their program was its own guide and was not to be subservient to any particular family or dynasty. Second, Pharisaic interpretation was not limited to the Scriptures nor was its characteristic focus scriptural: the principal point of departure was the recollection of the earlier teaching of those called "sages."

Ultimately, after the period of the NT the ideology of the rabbis (as the Pharisees came to be called) had it that Moses conveyed two Torahs on Sinai, one written and one oral. Even before that understanding, however, the sages treated as normative the teachings of their predecessors in chains of tradition. It was not so much that oral tradition was set alongside Scripture as that oral tradition *was* Scripture until the canon itself could no longer be ignored as the functional standard of Judaism (*see* Rabbinic Traditions and Writings).

4.2. Judaism Under Roman Rule. Factionalism among the Hasmoneans, which resulted in rival claims to the high priesthood between Aristobulus and Hyrcanus (the sons of Alexandra), culminated in an appeal by both sides to the Roman general Pompey, who obliged by taking Jerusalem for Rome* and entering the sanctuary in 63 B.C. (Josephus *J.W.* 1.7.6 §§152-54).

4.2.1. Opposition and Accommodation: Pharisees, Prophets, Herodians and Revolutionaries. The *Psalms of Solomon* represents a common, pious expression of horror at the events of 63 B.C. which was probably shared by most Pharisees (whether or not the *Psalms* should be taken as specifically Pharisaic). From that period and all through the reign of Herod and his relatives, the Pharisees' attitude to the government was ambivalent. Some appear to have engaged in a principled opposition to Roman rule and its representatives as such. Today that group is known as the "Zealots," but the term is a misnomer.

The Zealots were a priestly group of revolutionaries (*see* Revolutionary Movements), not rebellious Pharisees, who were associated with Eleazar, son of Simon, during the revolt of A.D. 66-73 (Josephus *J.W.* 2.20.3 §§564-565; 4.4.1 §§224-225). The rebellious Pharisees are also to be distinguished from the movements of prophetic pretenders who claimed divine inspiration for their efforts to free the land of the Romans (Josephus *J.W.* 2.13.4-6 §§258-65; 7.11.1-2 §§437-46). Other Pharisees normally accommodated to the new regime but resisted—sometimes violently—Herodian excesses such as the erection of a golden eagle on a gate of the Temple (Josephus *J.W.* 1.33.2-4 §§648-55; *see* Herodian Dynasty). Nonetheless, an apparently Pharisaic group is called "the Herodians" (Mt 22:16; Mk 3:6; 12:13; *see* Herodian Dynasty), which presumably signals its partisanship of the interests of the royal family as the best support of their own teaching of purity. They may be associated with rabbis who enjoyed the protection of Herod and his house; the authorities referred to in rabbinic literature as the "sons of Bathyra" (cf. *b. B. Meṣ.* 85a) may have been such a group.

Others still largely cooperated with the Romans and with the priestly administration of the Temple, although they might fall out regarding such questions as whether the priestly vestments should be kept under Roman or local control (Josephus *Ant.* 18.4.3

§§90-95; 20.1.1-2 §§6-14) or the price of doves for sacrifice (*m. Ker.* 1:7; *see* Rabbinic Traditions and Writings).

4.2.2. The Fracturing of the Priesthood: Sadducees, High Priests and Priestly Nationalists. Meanwhile, the priesthood (*see* Priest, Priesthood) itself was fractured further in its response to the fact of Roman governance. Some priests, especially among the privileged families in Jerusalem, were notoriously pro-Roman. The story of sons of the high priest having the surgery called *epispasm* in order to restore the appearance of a foreskin (for gymnastic purposes) is well known (cf. 1 Macc 1:14-15; Josephus *Ant.* 12.5.1 §§240, 241). There is little doubt but that such families, the most prominent of which were the Sadducees and Boethusians, were not highly regarded by most Jews (cf. *b. Pesaḥ.* 57a). They are typically portrayed in a negative light as not teaching the resurrection* of the dead (cf. Josephus *J.W.* 2.8.14 §165; Mt 22:23; Mk 12:18; Lk 20:27; Acts 23:8), but the issue may have been one of emphasis: the Torah had stressed that correct worship in the Temple would bring with it material prosperity, and the elite priests attempted to realize that promise. The arrangement gave them such consistent control that they became known as "high priests," although there was in fact only one high priest. But Josephus indulges in the usage, as well as the Gospels, so it should not be taken as an inaccuracy: the plural is a cultic mistake, but a sociological fact.

Caiaphas held an historically long tenure as high priest during the period (Josephus *Ant.* 18.2.2 §35; 18.4.3 §95), and the frequent change of personnel reflects the collective nature of the priestly leadership as well as Roman caution regarding a post which might have produced a national leader. Herod himself understood the possibilities of the high priesthood in that regard, which is why he had his potential rivals Jonathan and Hyrcanus (albeit relatives by marriage) murdered, and why he married Mariamne (Josephus *J.W.* 1.22.1-5 §§431-44; *Ant.* 20.10.1 §§247-51). His ambition was for a new Hasmonean dynasty, and it appears that only the notorious greed of his sons, combined with his willingness to have them executed, thwarted its realization. As it was, Herod's grandson and namesake, king of Chalcis, did maintain the residual power of selecting the high priest, although as king of Chalcis he had no ordinary authority over Jerusalem (cf. Josephus *Ant.* 20.1.3 §§15-16).

Several priests were also prominent in the revolt against Rome, however, and it should not be thought that such priestly nationalists, among whom were Joseph bar Matthias, better known as Flavius Josephus, emerged only at the end of the sixties (Josephus *J.W.* 2.20.3-4 §§562-68). The precedent of the Hasmoneans was there for any priestly family to see as a possible alternative to Roman rule, direct or indirect. Indeed, some priests were not only nationalists but revolutionaries who joined with the Essenes, or with rebellious Pharisees, although any alliance of priests with a prophetic pretender is, perhaps, not a likely supposition.

4.2.3. The Growing Influence of the Pharisees. The Pharisees' mastery of the oral medium made them the most successful—in terms of popularity—of the tendencies within pluralized Judaism. In the period before written communication was standard among Jews in general, the use of memorization and recitation was far more prominent. The Pharisees were in a position to communicate guidance regarding purity, an understanding of Scripture (in the Targums,* whose development they influenced), and their own sense of the authority of the sages, without requiring general literacy. There is no reason to suppose, for example, that rabbis of the first century, such as Hillel and Hanina ben Dosa, were able to read fluently, although each was a formative member of the Pharisaic, and therefore later of the Rabbinic, movements. The Pharisees' willingness to make a living by a craft rather than by status (cf. *m. 'Abot* 2:2)—the most prominent example being Hillel's menial labor (*b. Yoma* 35b)—also meant that they could move from town to town, promulgating their views. In some respects their occasional itinerancy was comparable in Israel to that of the Greco-Roman philosophers of the Mediterranean world (Stoic, Pythagorean and/or Cynic).

The success of the Pharisees in small towns became all the more pronounced as their power was largely ceded to priestly interests in Jerusalem. Many local scribes, but not all, were likely Pharisees, and the majority would have to account for Pharisaic views. Scribes* were, strictly speaking, simply men who could read and write, a skill which in antiquity represented some social and educational attainment. In Israel, given the Roman encouragement of local government, scribes emerged in towns and villages as a focus of judicial and religious power. From the time of the writing of the Torah itself, it was accepted that both aspects of God's rule, the legal and the cultic, were articulated by Moses. The ability of the scribes to read and write made them ideal judges, adjuncts to priests, teachers* and leaders of worship.

Indeed, all those functions were probably discharged in any given village by an interactive group of scribes, people of priestly lineage, and Pharisees and other elders. It was likely in the same place in a town that cases were settled, purity or impurity declared, lessons given, and the Torah recited from the written form and from memory in Aramaic (*see* Languages of Palestine). There too disputes would take place among scribes, judges, priests, Pharisees and elders, concerning how the Torah was to be understood and applied. Later rabbinic literature tends to reduce the disputes of the period to the "houses" of Hillel and Shammai, but that is quite evidently a schematic generalization. Because they lacked any central leadership in the period before A.D. 70, Pharisees differed from movement to movement, town to town, rabbi to rabbi, and even day to day.

4.2.4. The Sanhedrin. The structure of a local council also prevailed under Roman rule in Jerusalem, the Greek term *synedrion* was applied to it, and it has become known as "the Sanhedrin,*" largely as a result of the Mishnah (*see* Rabbinic Traditions and Writings). Mishnah, a document of the second century, cannot be taken as a sure guide of events and institutions during the first century. But it does seem clear from the Gospels and Josephus, with the Mishnah, that the council in Jerusalem was largely controlled by the high priests, but that elders* or aristocrats of the city also participated, among whom were Pharisees (and, of course, some scribes who may or may not have been priests, elders or Pharisees). Whether there were actually seventy-one members of the Sanhedrin (as in rabbinic literature) cannot be known with certainty, and the extent of its capital jurisdiction is not known. But the Romans appear to have given the council the authority to execute perpetrators of blatant sacrilege (Josephus *J.W.* 2.12.2 §§228-31; 5.5.2 §194; *Ant.* 15.11.5 §417).

The authority of the council of Jerusalem outside of the city followed the prestige of the city itself and the acknowledged centrality of the Temple. But a ruling of the council in Jerusalem was not automatically binding on those in the countryside and in other major cities; acceptance of a given teaching, precept by precept, was the path of influence. Pharisees also taught in and around the Temple, which was the focus of their discussion of purity, and the Pharisees in Jerusalem were the most prestigious in the movement.

5. Early Judaism As Reflected in the Gospels.

5.1. Jesus Within Judaism. The references within the Gospels to groups and movements within Judaism become quite explicable within the context of the social history of the religion. Priests appear locally in

adjudications of purity (Mt 8:1-4; Mk 1:40-45; Lk 5:12-16; cf. Lk 10:31; 17:14, and the exceptional role of Zechariah in Lk 1:5-23), where their role is challenged by Jesus. He claims that he can declare clean in a matter which Leviticus expressly assigns to priests (cf. Lev 13; 14:1-9). Evidently, Jesus understood purity in a way which brought him into conflict with a straightforward, priestly interpretation of Scripture, and the issue of purity also set him at odds with some Pharisees. References to high priests in the Gospels portray their power as essentially circumscribed by the boundaries of Jerusalem, or they use Jerusalem as a base of power (cf. Mt 2:4; 16:21; 20:18; 21:15, 23, 45; 26:1—28:11; Mk 8:31; 10:33; 11:18, 27; 14:1—15:31; Lk 3:2; 9:22: 19:47; 20:1—24:20; Jn 1:19; 7:32, 45; 11:47, 49, 51, 57; 12:10; 18:3—19:21). Their close association with the execution of Jesus makes it plain that his activity in the Temple figured centrally in his condemnation before Pilate (*see* Trial of Jesus).

Jesus himself enters into disputes with Pharisees (Mt 9:10-13, 14-17; 12:1-8, 9-14; 15:1-20; 16:1-12; 19:3-12; 22:15-22; Mk 2:15-17, 18-22, 23-28; 3:1-6; 7:1-23; 8:11-21; 10:2-12; 12:13-17; Lk 5:29-32, 33-39; 6:1-5, 6-11; 11:37—12:1; 15:1-2) and finally teaches in the Temple itself and occupies the holy precincts (Mt 21—25; Mk 11—13; Lk 19:28—21:38). There the high priests, particularly Sadducees, find him guilty of blasphemy and denounce him to the council of Jerusalem, which in turn makes its recommendation to Pilate (Mt 26:1—27:2; Mk 14:1—15:1; Lk 22:1—23:5; *see* Pontius Pilate). Jesus' disputes with the Pharisees typically center on issues of purity (Mt 9:10-13 par. Mk 2:15-17 and Lk 5:29-32; Mt 15:1-20 par. Mk 7:1-23 and Lk 11:37-41; Mt 16:5-12 par. Mk 8:14-21 and Lk 12:1; 15:1-2), fasting* (Mt 9:14-17 par. Mk 2:18-22 and Lk 5:33-39), keeping the Sabbath (Mt 12:1-8, 9-14 par. Mk 2:23-28; 3:1-6 and Lk 6:1-5, 6-11), tithing (Mt 23:23 par. Lk 11:42; cf. Mt 17:24-27; Mt 22:15-22 par. Mk 12:13-17 and Lk 20:20-26) and the interpretation of Scripture (Mt 19:3-12 par. Mk 10:2-12 and Lk 16:18), all of which are characteristic of Pharisaic concerns.

The Pharisees engage in vigorous debate with Jesus because he is also interested in developing teaching about purity, but Jesus himself is to be understood in association with that movement precisely because purity was at the heart of his program. Moreover, he is called "rabbi" (meaning, "my master"; cf. Mt 26:25, 49; Mk 9:5; 10:51; 11:21; 14:45; Jn 1:38, 49; 3:2; 4:31; 6:25; 9:2; 11:8), has close followers, deliberately promulgates his teaching by travel and sending his disciples* to teach, and attempts to influence the conduct of worship in the Temple. (The reticence of some twentieth-century scholars to identify Jesus as a rabbi arises from their awareness of the danger of identifying Jesus with the rabbinic movement after A.D. 70, after which it became more systematized. But anxiety over an anachronistic understanding of Jesus can result in the far greater error of placing him within so-called sectarian Judaism—as if an orthodoxy existed in early, pluralized Judaism—or worse still, placing Jesus within no Judaism at all.)

In all of those aspects Jesus comports well with a recognized pattern of teaching concerning purity in early Judaism, although the substance of his teaching was distinctive (and, for many, controversial). Except perhaps for his use of Capernaum as a center, however, Jesus does appear to have been programmatically itinerant, not merely occasionally so. In this characteristic he would have been distinguished from most Pharisees. Although he may well have appeared to many observers in Jerusalem during the final conflict as one Pharisee among many, it is more plausible to see him as an itinerant rabbi, a preacher of the eschatological kingdom (see Kingdom of God) and the kingdom's holiness, whose focus upon matters related to purity brought him into conflict with the Pharisees.

Scribes appear both in a local context (Mt 5:20; 7:29; 9:3; 12:38; 15:1; 17:10; Mk 1:22; 2:6, 16; 7:5; 9:11; Lk 5:21, 30; 6:7), even as a part of Jesus' movement (Mt 8:19; 13:52; Mk 12:28, 32-34; Lk 20:39) and during the final confrontation in Jerusalem (Mt 16:21; 20:18; 21:15 [26:3]; 57; 27:41; Mk 8:31; 10:33; 11:18, 27; 12:35, 38; 14:1, 43, 53; 15:1, 31; Lk 9:22; 19:47; 20:1, 19, 46; 22:2, 66; 23:10). They are probably to be identified with references to "lawyers" in the Gospels (Mt 22:35; Lk 7:30; 10:25; 11:45, 46, 52; 14:3). The presence of "scribes" among both local and high-priestly elites reinforces the impression that the category concerns more a function than a distinctive teaching (as in the case of the Essenes or the Pharisees) or a special interest (as in the case of the Sadducees).

5.2. The Portrayal of Jesus Opposed to Judaism. The social history of Christianity itself tended to cast scribes, Pharisees and lawyers into a single category of persecutors and hypocrites,* like the "Jews" themselves, and that influence is evident in the present text of the Gospels (cf. Mt 15:1; 23:2, 13, 15, 23, 25, 27, 29; Mk 3:6, 22; 7:1, 3, 5; Lk 6:7; 11:45, 46, 53, 54; 15:2). The Matthean Jews are liars about the resurrection (Mt 28:15) and willful murderers who implicate their own children in the crucifixion (Mt 27:25; see Death of Jesus). That is the most prejudicial charge in all of the Gospels, but it is not unlike Mark's claim that "all the Jews" hold to practices of washing "cups and pots and copper vessels" (Mk 7:3, 4), or Luke's scene of Jesus' rejection at Nazareth by his own people (Lk 4:16-30), or John's note that "the Jews" excluded the followers of Jesus from synagogues* during his lifetime (Jn 9:22; 12:42; cf. 16:2). The *Gospel of Thomas* has Jesus himself ironically ask the disciples whether they have become as obtuse as the Jews in that they must ask concerning Jesus' identity when they ought simply to recognize it (*l.* 43). Within all five sources of primary importance in the study of Jesus, Judaism and the Jews appear more as a foil for Jesus than as the matrix of his movement (see Anti-Semitism). But the realities of a radically pluralized Judaism in which Jesus was a vigorous participant also shine through the texts as they may be read today.

See also ANTI-SEMITISM; CLEAN AND UNCLEAN; DEAD SEA SCROLLS; FEASTS; HELLENISM; HERODIAN DYNASTY; ISRAEL; MIDRASH; PHARISEES; RABBINIC TRADITIONS AND WRITINGS; REVOLUTIONARY MOVEMENTS; SAMARITANS; SANHEDRIN; SCRIBES; SYNAGOGUE; TARGUMS; TEMPLE.

BIBLIOGRAPHY. E. Auerbach, *Moses* (Detroit: Wayne State University, 1975), J. Bright, *A History of Israel* (3d ed.; Philadelphia: Westminster, 1981); S. J. D. Cohen, *From the Maccabees to the Mishnah* (Philadelphia: Westminster, 1987); W. D. Davies and L. Finkelstein, eds., *The Cambridge History of Judaism. Vol. One: Introduction; the Persian Period* (Cambridge: University Press, 1984); E. R. Goodenough, *An Introduction to Philo Judaeus* (BCJ; Lanham and London: University Press of America, 1986); J. H. Hayes and J. M. Miller, eds., *Israelite and Judean History* (Philadelphia: Westminster, 1977); R. A. Kraft and G. W. E. Nickelsburg, *Early Judaism and Its Modern Interpreters* (BMI 2; Atlanta: Scholars, 1986); A. R. C. Leaney, *The Jewish and Christian World 200 B.C. to A.D. 200* (CCWJCW 7; Cambridge: University Press, 1984); N. P. Lemche, *Early Israel: Anthropological and Historical Studies on the Israelite Society before the Monarchy* (VTSup; Leiden: Brill, 1985); M. McNamara, *Palestinian Judaism and the New Testament* (GNS 4; Wilmington: Glazier, 1983); G. E. Mendenhall, "The Hebrew Conquest of Palestine," in *The Biblical Archaeologist Reader* 3 (1962) 100-120; J. Neusner, "Josephus' Pharisees: A Complete Repertoire," in *Josephus, Judaism, and Christianity,* ed. L. H. Feldman and G. Hata (Detroit: Wayne State University, 1987) 274-292; idem, *The Pharisees: Rabbinic Perspectives* (SAJ; Hoboken: Ktav, 1984); E. P. Sanders, *Jesus and Judaism* (Philadelphia: Fortress, 1985); idem, *Jewish Law from Jesus to the Mishnah: Five Studies* (Philadelphia: Trinity Press International, 1990).

B. D. Chilton

JUDAS (SON OF JAMES) *See* DISCIPLES.

JUDAS ISCARIOT

One of the twelve apostles,* to be distinguished from another apostle (one of the Twelve?) who was also called Judas (Jn 14:22), he is three times identified as the son of Simon (Jn 6:71; 13:2, 26). Since Simon is also called Iscariot, and Iscariot is further explained by the addition of *apo karyōtou* in some textual witnesses of John 6:71; 12:4; 13:2, 26 and 14:22, it would appear that Iscariot identifies Judas as "a man (Heb. *'iš*) of Kerioth." Among other suggestions are: "man of Issachar" and "the assassin" (from the Gk *sikarios;* cf. Acts 21:38). Jeremiah 48:24, 41 and Amos 2:2 locate Kerioth in Moab, and it is mentioned in the Moabite Stone (1.13). Its site is uncertain, but it has sometimes been identified with Ar, a Moabite site (or possibly a region), and sometimes with Kir (probably Kir-Hareseth, about seventeen miles south of the Arnon and eleven miles east of the Dead Sea). Alternatively, it has been identified with Kerioth-Hezron, mentioned in Joshua 15:25, some twelve miles south of Hebron. On either count, Judas appears to have been the exception among the Twelve in not being a Galilean (*see* Galilee).

1. Judas's Place within the Twelve
2. Judas's Betrayal of Jesus
3. Judas's Death

1. Judas's Place within the Twelve.

The order in which the names are listed appears to reflect some sort of hierarchy within the Twelve (*see* Disciples), but the fact that Judas is consistently listed last almost certainly has more to do with subsequent events than with his place within the apostolic band during Jesus' ministry (Mt 10:4; Mk 3:19; Lk 6:16). Similarly, in John 6:70-71 the Evangelist has almost certainly transferred to this point in the narrative an element of the story of the Last Supper* (cf. 13:2, 21-30) in order to warn those who might turn back (6:66) not to join the company of Judas (Beasley-Murray, 97). Despite Judas's name appearing always at the end of the list of the apostles' names, he held an important place within their company. He was their treasurer (Jn 12:6).

2. Judas's Betrayal of Jesus.

2.1. The Plan. It is only as the Synoptic Gospels reach their climax that their silence regarding Judas's activities is broken and he emerges as Jesus' betrayer. All three Synoptics tell how Judas plotted with the Jewish leadership to have Jesus arrested. Their problem was how to have him arrested without a riot (Mt 26:5; Mk 14:2; Lk 22:2). It was that problem that Judas was able to solve for them. Within Jerusalem

itself there were few, if any, private gardens. Instead, the well-to-do had their gardens on the slopes of the Mount of Olives outside the city. Presumably, some unnamed friend had given Jesus the right to use his garden, and it was evidently Jesus' custom, when in Jerusalem, to go to that garden to pray (Lk 22:39; *see* Gethsemane). Judas knew this and he would lead Jesus' enemies to where they could find him (Jn 18:1-2). For this, he was promised (or given) money. Matthew alone specifies the amount: thirty pieces of silver (Mt 26:15), which may have been a partial payment of the agreed sum (with an implied allusion to Zech 11:12 and possibly Ex 21:32; cf. Mt 27:9).

2.2. The Motivation.

2.2.1. Mark. The enormity of Judas's proposal is highlighted in Mark by juxtaposing the story of betrayal (14:10-11) with that of the extraordinary love of the woman who anointed (*see* Anointing) Jesus at Bethany (14:3-9). To this is added the explicit comment of Jesus at the Last Supper: "The Son of man goes as it is written of him, but woe to that man by whom the Son of man is betrayed! It would have been better for that man if he had not been born" (14:21). Here is a paradox: Jesus' death was inevitable, but the betrayer was culpable. Mark makes no attempt to resolve the enigma.

2.2.2. Matthew. Matthew follows Mark in juxtaposing the anointing (26:6-13) with the betrayal (26:14-16). But by changing the conjunction from *kai* ("and") to *tote* ("then"), he links them in such a way as to present the second as the first step in the fulfillment of the prediction of death (*see* Predictions of Jesus' Death and Resurrection) in the first, thus emphasizing more than Mark the inevitability of what happened. At the same time added emphasis is given to Judas's culpability by changing the word order of Mark to draw attention to the fact that Judas was one of the Twelve. This phrase is put first in the sentence. The naming formula ("who was called . . .") is also a Matthean addition to Mark (cf. 26:3). Where the other Synoptics have the Jewish leaders only agreeing to pay him, here the money is paid to Judas (v. 15) in readiness for the story of its return (Mt 27:3-10). The announcement at the Last Supper of the woe to Jesus' betrayer (26:24) is almost identical with the report in Mark.

2.2.3. Luke. The same announcement appears in Luke 22:22. Where this Gospel differs from the other Synoptics is in omitting the story of the anointing from the passion narrative* (but cf. Lk 7:36-50) and in adding to their account of the plot an explanation of what prompted Judas to do it: "then Satan entered into Judas . . ." (22:3).

2.2.4. John. The Fourth Gospel has a similar statement that Satan (*see* Demon, Devil, Satan) entered into Judas (13:27), but here it occurs in the context of the Last Supper. In terms of vocabulary, the two statements are almost identical, but whether this coincidence is evidence of dependence is a moot point. A similar view of the motivation behind the betrayal is found earlier in this chapter: "During supper (the Last Supper), when the devil had already put it into the heart of Judas . . . to betray him, Jesus . . ." (13:2). The Greek of this verse is open to more than one reading: either the devil put it into Judas's heart to betray Jesus, or the devil resolved in his own heart that Judas should do it. On the first reading we have two verses in John agreeing with the (earlier?) Lukan view that Satan prompted Judas to act, one of them (Jn 13:2) making the same point concerning the protagonists, but locating the decisive moment of their compact at the Last Supper. On the second reading the interpretation of what happened is developed beyond Luke to the extent that Satan is presented as much more the initiator of what happened, and Judas as merely his tool. The woe pronounced on the latter in the Synoptic Gospels is not found here, unless 19:11 refers to Judas and not to the high priest: "he who delivered me to you has the greater sin." But Judas is by no means exonerated in this Gospel as the hapless tool of the devil. In John's account of the anointing at Bethany (12:1-8) Judas is singled out as the woman's critic. "Why was this ointment not sold," he asked, "and the money given to the poor?" On which the Evangelist comments: "This he said, not that he cared for the poor, but because he was a thief, and as he had the money box, he used to take (*ebastazen*) what was put into it." The verb *bastazō* means "to carry," but it is used here in the colloquial sense "to steal." The imperfect tense implies that this was Judas's practice.

This story and the story of his plot with the Jewish leaders suggest that, as far as a human motive is concerned, Judas's betrayal of Jesus was done for the money. But some find other and better motives for what he did. To understand these arguments we must recognize how completely the disciples misunderstood what Jesus meant by the kingdom (*see* Kingdom of God). Even after the resurrection* they were still thinking in terms of an earthly kingdom (Acts 1:6) and were certainly thinking in those terms before it. James and John had asked for official positions within the kingdom (Mt 20:20-24; Mk 10:35-40), and they all were still quarreling about their respective ranks and positions when they came to the Last Supper (Lk 22:24-26). Clearly they expected Jesus to contest the authority* of Rome* and were willing to die with him,

if need be, in such a glorious cause (Mt 26:33; Mk 14:29-31; Lk 22:33-34). Either, then, Judas thought to force Jesus' hand by pushing him into a confrontation with his enemies or he, better than the others, understood that Jesus was thinking not of battle with Rome but of an inglorious death at the hands of Rome and, for reasons best known to himself, saw this as a betrayal by Jesus of his disciples. On the latter view Judas was a disillusioned disciple retaliating against Jesus not so much because he loved money, but because he loved his country and thought that Jesus had failed it. But this is only speculation.

2.3. The Implementation. Whatever the reason for Judas's betrayal, the Last Supper marked the point of no return from his chosen course. During the meal Jesus declared that one of the Twelve would betray him. There was consternation at this. The disciples were perplexed and questioned Jesus about the matter. Clearly no one other than Jesus suspected Judas. Indeed, in their own ways the individual Evangelists each indicate that any one of the disciples could be the betrayer (Mt 26:22; Mk 14:19; Lk 22:23). They differ, however, in their concern to identify during the supper the betrayer as Judas, with Matthew being the most explicit and Luke the least (Mt 26:23, 25; Mk 14:20; Lk 22:21).

Of all the accounts of his betrayal, John's is by far the most developed. It seems likely from this Gospel that Judas was in the place of special honor at the Last Supper. The usual arrangement at such a meal was to have a series of couches, each accommodating three people, arranged in a U around the table. The host reclined in the center of the chief couch at the center of the curve of the U. The guests reclined on either side of him, leaning on their left elbow and eating with their right hand. The place of honor was to the left and, therefore, in a sense, behind the host. The second place was to his right, and the guest in that position would have his back to the host, "lying close to his breast." This was the position occupied by "the disciple . . . whom Jesus loved" (Jn 13:23). Peter was evidently separated from this disciple by some others, so that he had to beckon him to capture his attention. When Jesus declared that one of them would betray him, Peter asked the disciple whom Jesus loved to find out who it was. Jesus told him, "It is he to whom I shall give this morsel when I have dipped it" (Jn 13:26). So saying, he gave the morsel to Judas, telling him to do what he was going to do quickly.

On the grounds of the Evangelist's comment that "after the morsel, Satan entered into him," it is assumed by some that the action and the word of Jesus had a negative intention—that in some sense Jesus was thus severing the relationship with Judas. Such an interpretation seems highly unlikely. In normal circumstances the giving of the morsel was a mark of favor. Moreover, it would appear that Judas was in the place of honor since Jesus was able to hand him the piece of bread (Jn 13:26). We should take this portrayal of Jesus' action, then, as a sign of his friendship with Judas despite his knowledge of Judas's intentions. It was his last appeal to Judas to change his course. His words "What you are going to do, do quickly" (Jn 13:27) were in effect a demand on Judas to make up his mind either to respond to Jesus' friendship or to betray him. But with the morsel "Satan entered into him." Judas had made his choice, and in making it he had cut himself off from the light of the world (cf. Jn 8:12). John observes that when Judas left the room "it was night" (Jn 13:30). In fact the paschal moon was shining at the full, but John was using "night" symbolically. Judas had surrendered himself to the power of darkness.

The remarkable thing about this incident is that still no one at the table realized what was happening. On the other hand, Judas's departure could have been for any reason, and there was no particular reason for the other disciples to connect it with the betrayal. Some thought that Jesus had sent him to buy food for the feast* (which lasted for seven days), others that he had gone to give something to the poor (Jn 13:29; *see* Rich and Poor).

Later that evening Jesus and the disciples went to the garden called Gethsemane* on the Mount of Olives, and Judas's plan went into operation (Mt 26:36-56; Mk 14:26-50; Lk 22:39-53; Jn 18:1-14). So this became, in the words perpetuated ever since in the church's liturgy, "the night in which he was betrayed" (1 Cor 11:23). Judas was provided with a band of men and officers to carry out the arrest. Judas was clearly in charge of the proceedings. There was a full moon and enough light to see by, but to prevent any mistake, the Synoptic Evangelists write that Judas gave a sign: he would identify Jesus with a kiss, the normal mode of greeting between disciple and rabbi (Mt 26:47-50; Mk 14:43-45; Lk 22:47-48). Curiously, at the point of having identified Jesus in the garden, Judas fades from the scene.

3. Judas's Death.

The NT has two accounts of the death of Judas which, on the face of it, differ markedly. Matthew has it that Judas, overcome by remorse when he saw that an innocent man was condemned, threw the money he had received down in the Temple* and went out and hanged himself. The priests,* unwilling to put "blood

money" into the treasury, bought a potter's field with it—a worked-out clay pit—"to bury strangers in." This place came to be known as "the Field of Blood" (Mt 27:3-9; cf. Zech 11:12-13). Acts reports that Judas purchased the field himself, and "falling headlong (in the field) he burst open in the middle and all his bowels gushed out." Thus the field was known as Akeldama, "the Field of Blood" (Acts 1:18-19; cf. 2 Sam 17:23; 2 Macc 9:7-18).

As long ago as Augustine it was suggested that if Judas hanged himself in the field, perhaps sometime after his death, when his body was decomposing, the rope gave way and Luke's account describes the consequences. It might be regarded as supplementary to Matthew's account. Papias, in a fragment (Fragment 3) preserved by Apollinarius of Laodicea, relates how Judas's body swelled (this may be the meaning of *prēnēs* in Acts 1:18, see RSV note), and he died on his own land. As for the field, it could be regarded as purchased by Judas since it was his money that was used. Whatever the tradition history of these accounts, two things seem clear: Judas died a violent death, and in some way connected with him a plot of ground was bought that was called "the Field of Blood." Tradition has located this field at the confluence of the Kidron, Tyropoean and Hinnom valleys. The last word the NT gives on Judas is this: he had "turned aside" from his ministry and apostleship "to go to his own place"—a common euphemism for one's final destruction. The apostle had become an apostate and a warning to all disciples.

See also DISCIPLES; GETHSEMANE; PASSION NARRATIVE.

BIBLIOGRAPHY. J. A. Bailey, *The Traditions Common to the Gospels of Luke and John* (Leiden: E. J. Brill, 1963) 29-31; G. R. Beasley-Murray, *John* (WBC 36; Waco, TX: Word, 1987); R. B. Halas, *Judas Iscariot, A Scriptural and Theological Study of His Person, His Deeds and His Eternal Lot* (Washington: Catholic University of America, 1946); H. Ingholt, "The Surname of Judas Iscariot," in *Studia Orientalia Ioanni Pedersen* (Copenhagen: K. Munksgaard, 1953) 152-62; W. E. Sproston, " 'The Scripture' in John 17:12," in *Scripture: Meaning and Method*, ed. B. P. Thompson (Hull: University Press, 1987) 24-36. D. J. Williams

JUDGMENT

Judgment is the process whereby God calls people to account for their behavior and allots their destinies accordingly. The theme is prominent in the teaching of Jesus, which echoes many features found in the OT, apocalyptic* and rabbinic literature (*see* Rabbinic Traditions).

1. Terminology and Meaning

2. The Message of Jesus

3. Emphases of the Gospel Writers

1. Terminology and Meaning.

Like the English verb "judge," the Greek word *krinō* can mean "form an opinion" (Lk 7:43). But normally in the NT it describes the passing of a sentence—either in a law-court (Mt 5:40) or metaphorically with reference to divine judgment (Mt 7:1-2; Jn 5:22, 30). Often the focus is on the negative aspect of condemnation (Mt 7:1; Jn 3:17-18). The noun *krisis* normally refers to the act of judging (Mt 5:21-22; Lk 11:31-32), while *krima* connotes the verdict or sentence (Lk 23:40). But this distinction is sometimes blurred (e.g., *krima* in Jn 9:39). The influence of the LXX, where the word group usually translates *šp̄ṭ*, can be seen in Matthew 23:23 and Luke 11:42, where *krisis* means "justice"; and in Matthew 19:28 and Luke 22:30, where *krinō* probably means "rule." Although the noun "judge" (*kritēs*) occurs in parables* (Mt 5:25; Lk 18:2, 6), it is not used as a description of God in the direct sayings of Jesus.

Other expressions to be considered are "condemn" (*katakrinō*, Mt 12:41-42; *katadikazō*, Mt 12:37), "punishment" (*kolasis*, Mt 25:46), the *dik-* word group (*see* Justice, Righteousness), translated variously as "punishment," "retribution," "vindicate," "justice" (Lk 18:1-8; 21:22), "visitation" (*episkopē*, Lk 19:44) and references to the "day" (*hēmera)* of judgment (Mt 7:22; 12:36; Lk 21:34; *see* Eschatology). In addition there is a rich variety of parabolic images of judgment.

2. The Message of Jesus.

Jesus rejects the widespread idea that the wealth or suffering of individuals is God's reward for righteousness or punishment for sin (Mk 12:38-44; Jn 9:2-3). In Luke 13:1-5 the lesson to be learned from the sufferings of some Galileans at Pilate's hands and from the disaster in Siloam is not that the victims were especially wicked but that everyone must repent in the face of God's judgment (*see* Repentance).

2.1. Judgment on the Nation. Much of Jesus' most vivid teaching consists of warnings to his contemporaries that an unrepentant Israel* is heading for imminent historical catastrophe. According to the parable of the children in the marketplace (Mt 11:16-19), "this generation's" refusal to "play the game" with either John the Baptist* or Jesus shows its defiance of God. The phrase identifies Jesus' contemporaries with the rebellious generation of Deuteronomy 32:5, 20; Psalm 78:8 and Jeremiah 7:29. This is the last generation of a rebellious people, destined now to pay in full the accumulated debt of the nation's resistance to God (Lk 11:47-51; Mk 12:1-12). There is still time for a change of heart, but a strictly limited time (Lk 13:6-9).

Jerusalem and its religious leaders are the main target of these warnings. In the manner of an OT prophet, Jesus laments Jerusalem's failure to respond to his call and prophesies its desolation (Lk 13:34-35; 19:41-44). Judgment takes the form of God's abandonment of Israel to its enemies, as in Jeremiah 7:25-34; 12:7; 25:4-11 and Hosea 9:15-17; 10:13-15.

It has been argued, notably by C. H. Dodd and J. Jeremias, that several parables, which in the Gospels are addressed to disciples and relate to Jesus' final coming and the final judgment, were originally addressed by Jesus to his opponents or to the crowds (*see* People, Crowd), and referred to the coming catastrophe for Israel (e.g., Mt 24:45—25:30). But since Jeremias concedes that Jesus expected a final judgment, it is better to allow that some parables allude to Israel's impending crisis, others to the final judgment of all people (see Marshall). But we may of course agree with Jeremias that Jesus gave no clue that the gap between Jerusalem's destruction (*see* Destruction of Jerusalem) and the final judgment would be extended for centuries.

2.2. The Final Judgment. Jesus speaks of a judgment of all people on the "day" when the Son of man* comes to establish his kingdom in its fullness (Mt 7:22; Lk 17:30-35; *see* Kingdom of God). God is the judge (Mt 10:28). Jesus' own role at the judgment is sometimes that of witness for or against the person judged (Mt 10:32-33), but sometimes he is the judge (Mt 7:21-23; 16:27). There is some force in the argument that in the earliest Son of man sayings Jesus is witness rather than judge, and that the depiction of him as judge is therefore a later development. Yet the fact that the Son of man sits at God's right hand (Mk 14:62) shows how easily one concept could pass over into the other.

2.2.1. Judgment as Separation. The judgment involves a division between two kinds of people—"sons of the kingdom" and "sons of the evil one" (Mt 13:38), "wise" and "foolish" (Mt 7:24-27), "sheep" and "goats" (Mt 25:31-46), those who "enter into life" and those who are "thrown into hell" (Mk 9:42-48). This reflects the radical distinction between "the righteous" and "the wicked" found in much apocalyptic literature and in the Dead Sea Scrolls.*

2.2.2. The Criterion and the Outcome of Judgment. Jesus maintains the Jewish emphasis on judgment according to works (Mt 7:21-23; 12:36-37; 25:31-46). He provides examples of particular kinds of deeds which will seal a person's condemnation—e.g., causing "little ones" to sin (Mk 9:42), lack of care for the poor (Lk 16:19-31; Mt 25:31-46), failure to forgive

(Mt 18:21-35), being judgmental toward others (Mt 7:1-2). His warnings of condemnation are almost never directed at those who, for example, commit adultery (*see* Marriage and Divorce), collect taxes* dishonestly, but at the pious who would exclude such people from the community (Mt 23:33; Lk 18:9-14).

In some judgment sayings, works are bound up with relationship or response to Jesus. In Matthew 7:24-27 we read, "everyone who hears *these words of mine* and does them is like a wise man . . . ." In Matthew 25:31-46 care for the needy (or lack of it) is taken as evidence of people's reaction to Jesus. Other sayings declare that reaction to Jesus will be the key criterion at the judgment. "All who acknowledge me before other people, the Son of Man will acknowledge them before the angels of God. Those who disown me before other people will be disowned before the angels of God" (Lk 12:8-9; cf. Mk 8:38; Lk 10:8-16; 11:29-32).

Luke 12:8-9 also indicates that, just as the *criterion* of judgment is relationship to Jesus, so the *outcome* of judgment will be expressed in terms of relationship to Jesus or to God. It will involve acceptance into fellowship with God or rejection from that fellowship. Those who do not know him—who are not in genuine, obedient relationship to him—now, will not know him then. In the parables of Matthew 25 and Luke 13:25-27 the outcome of the judgment is also expressed in terms of coming into or departing from God's presence.

Apart from the language of relationship, Jesus uses other more pictorial language to depict human destiny beyond the judgment. God's family will sit at the Father's table, while others are thrown outside (Lk 13:28-29). They will see God (Mt 5:8) and experience eternal life (Mk 10:30). A negative outcome is described as unquenchable fire or Gehenna (Mk 9:43, 45, 48; Mt 5:22; Lk 12:5). Those excluded from God's kingdom will "weep and gnash their teeth" (Mt 13:42, 50; Lk 13:28). It is not clear whether such language can be taken to imply eternal torment as traditionally understood. Such imagery, together with the reference to "eternal punishment" in Matthew 25:46, may be intended not so much to describe the specific character of punishment as to underline the irreversible and negative force of separation from God's presence.

It must also be noted that, in comparison with much Jewish literature (e.g., *1 Enoch* 21-22), Jesus' references to the destiny of the wicked are remarkably allusive and unspecific; and that such references occur mostly in exhortations to the hearer to respond to Jesus' message, not in descriptions of the fate of someone else.

2.2.3. The Main Thrust: Relationship Rather Than Retribution. The evidence suggests that Jesus' understanding of judgment focuses not on a strictly retributive justice, whereby rewards and punishments are recompense for human deeds. Rather, the focus is on relationship to Jesus, or to God through him. The relationship chosen by people when confronted by the message of God's kingdom will be confirmed at the final judgment. When the language of judgment according to works is used, the character of the works is understood as evidence of a person's relationship to God, or as showing whether the basic direction of one's life is toward him or away from him.

This perspective on Jesus' message is reinforced by three other images of judgment. The motif of the Two Ways, already familiar in Judaism* (e.g., *1 Enoch* 94:1-4; 1QS 3:13—4:26), suggests that human destinies are not rewards or punishments imposed from outside, but the inherent outcome of the choices people make (Mt 7:13-14). The image of treasure in heaven (Tob 4:3-10; *Pss. Sol.* 9:9; *2 Apoc. Bar.* 14:12; 24:1) pictures people's destinies as the end-result of their desires. Those whose hearts are fixed on submission to God's rule will gain the riches of his kingdom (Mt 6:19-21; Lk 12:33-34). Finally, in the image of the banquet invitation (Lk 14:16-24), everything turns on the refusal of those invited to come to the feast. They have excluded themselves while the poor are open to the insistent gift of the host.

2.2.4. Conclusion. Jesus rejects speculation about many aspects of final judgment and its outcome. He is silent about the geography of God's kingdom or of Gehenna (*see* Heaven and Hell). Rather than speculate about the number of those saved (2 Esdr 8:1), he urges his hearers to make sure of their own entry into the kingdom (Lk 13:23-24). And he tempers stern warnings of judgment with a greater emphasis on the infinite care of God for his creatures (Lk 12:4-12). There are also hints that his own suffering and death involve taking on himself the judgment of God on behalf of others (Mk 10:45; 14:36; 15:34).

3. Emphases of the Gospel Writers.

3.1. Matthew. In comparison with Mark and Luke, Matthew heightens the emphasis on judgment, reward and punishment. He increases the number of references to Gehenna and related images (5:22; 8:12; 13:42, 50; 22:13; 23:15, 33; 24:51; 25:30), and makes more prominent use of judgment as a sanction for behavior (6:1-6, 16-18; 18:35; 25:14-30). In keeping with this is the stress on judgment according to works (16:27, different from Mk 8:38). Peculiar to Matthew is the parable of the sheep and the goats (25:31-46) in which destinies are allotted according to deeds of mercy done, or not done, toward "the least of these brothers of mine." The older view, that this refers to general humanitarian concern, has been increasingly supplanted in recent studies by the view that the "brothers" are Christians, or Christian missionaries (see France, 264). Possibly Jesus' original reference was to suffering humanity in general, but this has been narrowed down in Matthew to a reference to Christian missionaries.

Matthew's Gospel highlights God's judgment on "this generation" of Jews, in particular Jewish leaders (23:29-36). They are the object of the series of "woes" in chapter 23. Matthew alone adds to the parable of the wicked tenants the conclusion: "Therefore I tell you that the kingdom of God will be taken away from you and given to a nation producing its fruits" (21:43). Yet there are severe warnings for the church* too, lest they follow the same path of disobedience. The parable of the wedding feast ends with the ejection of the "replacement" guest who has failed to meet the condition of being properly dressed (22:1-14). The criticism of scribes* and Pharisees* becomes a warning to "you," the hearers of the Gospel, to live circumspectly (23:2-12). For even religious works will count for nothing at the judgment if they are not "the will of my Father in heaven" (7:21-23). Only at the judgment will it be clear who truly belongs to God's kingdom (13:24-30, 36-43, 47-50).

3.2. John. The Fourth Gospel refers in only two places to the final judgment. When in John 12:48 Jesus says people will be judged on the last day by the word which he has spoken, the thought seems to be close to that of Mark 8:38. John 5:26-29 offers the traditional apocalyptic description of a final general resurrection and judgment. Christ* is the judge (v. 27). He judges according to works, and there are two possible outcomes—life and condemnation (*krisis,* verse 29; for *krisis* and *krinō* denoting condemnation cf. 3:18; 12:31; 16:11). But these verses are set in relation to verses 19-25, which emphasize a process of judgment already in operation: "whoever hears my word and believes him who sent me has eternal life, and does not come under condemnation, but has crossed over from death to life." Thus the verdict of the last judgment is a ratification of the life or death which people already experience because of their reaction to Christ.

This focus on judgment as a process already at work is entirely characteristic of John. Confronted by Jesus and his revelation of God, people react either by committing themselves in trust to him, or by rejecting him (1:11-12; 3:16-21, 36; 5:24; 8:12-19; 9:39). The immediate outcome of faith* is reception of eternal life (3:16, 36; 5:24; 12:50; *see* Life), which derives its quality from relationship to Christ (17:3). The experience of eternal life reaches its goal beyond death (11:25-26) or at the last day (5:29; 6:40, 51, 54, 58). Those who do not receive Christ are out of relationship to him. God's wrath rests on them (3:36); they remain in darkness and death (12:46; 5:24). Their condition is self-imposed: They prefer darkness and that is what they get (3:19-21).

Whereas the Synoptics use colorful imagery such as kingdom and wedding, John prefers the more abstract language of love, knowing God, life, death. The overall effect of his presentation is to highlight the theme, which we have seen in the Synoptics, of judgment determined by response to the person and message of Jesus.

See also APOCALYPTIC TEACHING; ESCHATOLOGY; BLESSING AND WOE; HARDNESS OF HEART; HEAVEN AND HELL.

BIBLIOGRAPHY. J. A. Baird, *The Justice of God in the Teaching of Jesus* (Philadelphia: Westminster, 1963); C. H. Dodd, *The Parables of the Kingdom* (New York: Scribner's, 1936); A. M. Fairhurst, "The Problem Posed by the Severe Sayings Attributed to Jesus in the Synoptic Gospels," *SJT* 23 (1970) 77-91; R. T. France, *Matthew: Evangelist and Teacher* (Grand Rapids: Zondervan, 1989); J. Jeremias, *The Parables of Jesus,* 3d ed. (New York: Scribners, 1972); I. H. Marshall, *Eschatology and the Parables* (London: Tyndale, 1963); W. Strawson, *Jesus and the Future Life* (London: Epworth, 1970); S. H. Travis, *Christ and the Judgment of God* (Grand Rapids: Zondervan, 1987).

S. H. Travis

JUSTICE, RIGHTEOUSNESS

In biblical thought the idea of justice or righteousness generally expresses conformity to God's* will in all areas of life: law, government, covenant loyalty, ethical integrity or gracious actions. When humans adhere to God's will as expressed in his Law,* they are considered just or righteous. Jesus taught that those who conform their lives to his teachings are also just or righteous.

1. Terminology, Meaning and Context
2. The Message of Jesus
3. The Emphases of the Gospel Writers

1. Terminology, Meaning and Context.

English words related to justice and righteousness are usually used to translate the *dik-* word group found in the NT. The use of *dik-* in the NT reflects the LXX's usual translation of the Hebrew *ṣdq* (righteous) word-group with the Greek *dik-*. In the OT the *ṣdq* word group essentially refers to "conduct in accordance with the requirements of a particular relationship," whether that be the covenant which imposes obligations on both God and his people or the world order set up by God, with which humanity must live in accordance. Hence, though she acted sinfully in playing the harlot, Tamar is said to be "more righteous" than Judah because she acted in the interest of a social standard—Judah's obligation to provide offspring for her deceased husband (Gen 38:26). In several instances the *ṣdq* word group is translated in the LXX by other Greek terms, including *eleēmosynē* (almsgiving) and *krisis* (judgment). However, it is not just the *ṣdq* word group that conveys the idea of righteousness and justice in the Hebrew OT; the concept also embraces *mišpāṭ* (judgment,* ordinance), *ḥesed* (lovingkindness), *tôrâ* (command) and *tāmîm* (perfect, complete).

Whereas in English *justice* emphasizes conformity to a society's standards, *righteousness* usually denotes conformity to God's standards or religious norms. However, these distinctions are not helpful when *justice* and *righteousness* are used to translate biblical terms (e.g., Job 22:6-9, 23; Ezek 45:9; Amos 4:1-3). In conveying biblical thought, the two English terms are inseparable in that it is God's will to which a person conforms, whether that will is expressed in predominantly social or religious categories. In this article *justice* will be used exclusively for the social implications of God's will; *righteousness* will be used for the broader meaning of the concept. However, in many instances a clear distinction cannot and should not be made.

Throughout Jewish literature we find two dominant ideas: God is righteous and his people are to be righteous in their behavior. The righteousness of God, primarily understood as his impeccable holiness and the conformity of his actions to that holy nature, is commonplace in Jewish thought (Is 45:21; Ps 22:31; 40:10; 51:14; 71:15-24; Hos 10:12; Amos 5:21-24; Mic 6:5; 7:9; *Pss. Sol.* 2:15; 8:23; Bar 5:1-2; *Sib. Or.* 3:704; Josephus *Ant.* 2.6.4 §108; 11.3.6 §55; 1QS 1:21; 10:11, 25; 1QH 12:19; 14:15; *Sipre* Deut 307 [on 32:4]; *m. Soṭa* 1:9). In addition, as recent scholarship has shown, righteousness attributed to God's people refers to moral behavior conforming to God's will (Gen 18:19; Lev 19:36; Deut 6:25; Is 5:16; Ps 1:4-6; *Pss. Sol.* 2:34-35; 3:3-12; 15:1-13; Philo, *Leg. All.* 2.18; *Migr. Abr.* 219; 1QS 1:5, 13; 3:1; 1QH 2:13; 4:30, 31; 7:14; *Sipra Qedoshim pereq* 11:6 [on Lev 20:16]; *t. Pe'a* 4.19; *t. Sanh.* 1.3-5). These twin themes of divine and human righteousness should inform our approach to the use of righteousness in the Gospels.

Biblical statements about the necessity of righteousness sometimes seem to imply a righteous status attained by works (Gen 18:19; Mt 5:20). But in the context of biblical thought righteous behavior is generally the result of salvation* and is required of those who participate in the covenantal blessings. Throughout the OT, as well as Jewish literature from the time of Jesus, righteousness refers to behavior conforming to the will of God. Paul's doctrine of justification, an eschatological righteousness imputed to believers in view of Christ's work, is largely confined to Paul's letters and should not be read into the texts of the Gospels simply because the terminology of righteousness appears.

2. The Message of Jesus.

Jesus describes as righteous those who conform to God's will as revealed both in the OT and in his own teachings. The foundation for Jesus' teachings on righteous behavior is that the kingdom of God (*see* Kingdom of God) has been inaugurated in his own person and ministry (Lk 7:18-23; 11:20). Since God's kingdom is a righteous kingdom (Ps 97—99; Is 11:1-5; *1 Enoch* 62:1-16), when Jesus inaugurates the kingdom he brings righteousness to pass and expects righteous behavior from his followers. Participation in the kingdom of God entails an ethical obligation (Mk 1:15), just as covenantal participation required obedience in OT religion (Lev 19:36; but 24:17-8) and in later Judaism* (*see* Ethics of Jesus).

Today many scholars argue that Jesus probably did not use the vocabulary of righteousness with any frequency. Since the vocabulary is found relatively infrequently in our Gospels, this view deserves consideration. However, evidence for the presence of the concept of righteousness in Jesus' teaching should not be limited to the occurrence or frequency of the vocabulary of righteousness. From the evidence of the Gospels, Jesus' teaching stressed that his followers must conform their lives to God's will. Thus it may be argued that the idea of righteousness, if not the terminology, is found everywhere in the teachings of Jesus: in his demand for repentance, in his blessings for good works, in his practice of social mercy and in his consistent concern for personal holiness. Furthermore, the usage of the terminology of righteousness in the Gospels conforms to what we know of its usage in Judaism at the time of Jesus.

Since some of the references to righteousness in the Gospels undoubtedly come from the vocabulary of the Evangelists themselves or their tradition (e.g., Mt 3:15), we cannot always be certain that the term was used by Jesus in a particular setting. But if Matthew,

Luke or John used the term *righteousness* where Jesus did not, they are faithfully reflecting the message of Jesus, laying stress on what they considered needful for their audiences to hear.

2.1. Righteousness in the Mission of Jesus and John. Jesus and John (*see* John the Baptist) show clear continuity in their messages of righteousness. Jesus views his mission as intimately tied with John's as together they accomplish all righteousness by submitting to God—John as baptizer and Jesus as the one baptized (Mt 3:15). Furthermore, John's essential message was a call for righteous behavior (Mt 21:32; Mk 6:20) manifesting itself in repentance* (Lk 3:7-9), mercy* and the pursuit of justice (Lk 3:10-14). Jesus builds on John's message in his own call for repentance (cf. Mt 3:2 and 4:17).

2.2. Righteousness As Conformity to OT Law. Jesus is described as righteous, just or innocent in the sense that he performs all that God's will requires. We may assume that God's will in this case is that described in the OT (Lk 23:47; Mt 27:4, 19, 24). Jesus also describes as righteous those whose behavior is in conformity to God's laws found in the OT. Thus, *righteous* describes those who anticipated the Messiah (Mt 13:17) and those who were martyred (23:29, 35). In the OT (Gen 15:6; Ps 1:4-6; 11:7; 72:1; Is 1:16-17) and in Jewish literature (*Pss. Sol.* 3:3-12; Philo *Leg. All.* 2.18; Josephus *Ant.* 6.5.6 §93; 1QS 1:13, 15; CD 1:19-21; *m. Soṭa* 1:9) righteousness commonly characterizes those who adhere to God's commands in faith and obedience.

2.3. Righteousness As Conformity to Jesus' Teachings. Jesus goes beyond the OT as a standard for righteousness by describing as righteous those who obey his own teachings. In so doing Jesus redefines the term in a manner parallel to what we find in the Dead Sea Scrolls (*see* Dead Sea Scrolls), where the instruction of the Teacher of Righteousness sets a new standard for the sectarian community at Qumran (CD 4:7; 20:20-21; 1QpHab 2:2; 7:3-5).

In using his own teachings as the basis for righteousness, Jesus reveals that the OT Law and Prophets (Mt 5:17) are being fulfilled in his own teachings and that he is the Messiah (*see* Christ). Jesus fulfills the Law* and so reveals a new standard of conduct (Mt 5:20). Henceforth, the righteousness of God's people is determined by conformity to the teachings of Jesus, which in turn fulfill the OT revelation of God's will. Jesus expects his followers to be righteous in their conduct (Mt 5:6, 10), to do God's will (Mt 7:12, 13-27) and to pursue justice (Mt 23:23 [*krisis*]; 25:37; Jn 7:24). According to Jesus, only those who are righteous are finally acceptable to God (Mt 10:41; 12:37; 13:43, 49; 25:46; Lk 14:14; Jn 5:30). Again, this righteousness is not an outward conformity to the Law or an appeal to ritual observances, but the necessary fruit of commitment to Jesus as Messiah and Lord.* The link between commitment and obedience is illustrated by Jesus' words at the end of the Sermon on the Mount (*see* Sermon on the Mount): "Everyone then who hears these words of mine and does them . . ." (Mt 7:21-27). Particular manifestations of righteousness (Mt 6:1) include almsgiving (Mt 6:2-4), prayer* (Mt 6:5-15) and fasting* (Mt 6:16-18).

As for those who claim to have conformed to the standards of the Jewish legal traditions, Jesus—tongue in cheek—describes them as "righteous" (Mt 9:13; Mk 2:17). The righteousness of the Pharisees* and scribes* is not considered sufficient (cf. Lk 5:30, 32; 15:7; 18:9; 20:20; Mt 23:28) for at least two reasons: (1) their hearts are not right (Mk 7:6-7; Mt 5:28) and (2) their standard is no longer adequate since God has fulfilled the OT Law in Jesus (Mt 5:17-48). However, for the one whose heart is right and whose standard is the fulfilled Law of Jesus, their commitment to obedience is to be complete (Mt 5:48). The word *perfect* in Matthew 5:48 speaks of the response of the whole heart, a total or thorough commitment to God's will—not sinless perfection. For Jesus the pursuit of righteousness is obeying God's will in all its aspects (personal, social and communal) and is to be the first priority of his followers (Mt 6:33).

3. The Emphases of the Gospel Writers.

Among the Gospel authors only Matthew and Luke give prominent place to the vocabulary of righteousness; Mark only uses the adjective *dikaios*, and that only twice (Mk 2:17; 6:20), while John uses *dik-* terminology five times (see 3.3. below).

3.1. Matthew. There is little doubt that Matthew has reworked some important traditions and added the term *righteousness*, emphasizing behavior that conforms to the new standard revealed in Jesus (cf., e.g., Mt 5:6 with Lk 6:21; Mt 6:33 with Lk 12:31). Indeed, some scholars see Matthew's hand in each occurrence of the word. Matthew places particular emphasis on righteousness as conformity to Jesus' teachings.

3.1.1. Righteousness As Conformity to OT Law. As the wording of Matthew 3:15 indicates ("it is proper for us to fulfill all righteousness"), together John the Baptist and Jesus fulfill God's will for them in its entirety and so bring all of God's demands to a salvation-historical climax. The favored Matthean expressions, "fulfillment" and "all righteousness," set the tone for both John's work (Mt 21:32) and Jesus' life (Mt 27:19) and teachings (Mt 5:20). They do all that God has called them to do, and in so doing they fulfill all righteousness. John is later described as the one who came "in the way of righteousness," meaning he proclaimed and performed God's will (cf. Mt 21:31 and 3:1-10). Some interpreters have understood the fulfillment of righteousness in Matthew 3:15 as meaning "to bring about God's prophetic and eschatological plan of redemption." In either case the OT revelation of God's will is in view (see Old Testament in the Gospels).

In addition to John the Baptist and Jesus, Matthew describes others as righteous in their obedience to OT Law, including Joseph (Mt 1:19) and various OT saints (Mt 13:17; 23:29, 35).

3.1.2. Righteousness As Conformity to Jesus' Teachings. The Sermon on the Mount is a revelation of Jesus' teachings on righteousness, explaining what it is to do God's will and perform good works (Mt 5:6, 16, 17-20, 21-48; 6:1-18, 33; 7:12, 13-14, 16-21, 23-27). The thrust of the Sermon points to the importance of righteousness for Matthew.

For Matthew, Jesus' pre-eminent demand of his disciples* is to do God's will—to exhibit righteousness (cf. Mt 5:20, 48; 7:13-27). Accordingly, entrance into the kingdom is conditioned on moral righteousness. In light of its Jewish background and its Matthean context, the beatitude on those who hunger and thirst for righteousness should be understood as a blessing for those who desire to do God's will, who strive to conform to his standard (Mt 5:6). However, some scholars understand this as a blessing on those who are longing for eschatological (see Eschatology) vindication or salvation.* According to this interpretation, righteousness may be a gift of righteous conduct granted them in the last day or the fulfillment of their longing to see God's righteousness established on earth. But in light of the behavioral grounds for the blessings (see Blessing and Woe) in Matthew 5:3-11, it is more likely that righteousness in Matthew 5:6 refers to the habit of doing God's will. Those who have been persecuted because of righteousness (Mt 5:10) are those who suffer for obedience to God's will as revealed by Jesus. Hence, the grounds for their persecution is their loyalty to Jesus as much as it is their good works.

The righteousness expected of Jesus' disciples is a righteousness that is vastly superior to the righteousness of the scribes and Pharisees (Mt 5:20). Matthew 5:20 is often understood to mean that, whereas the Pharisees and scribes taught a righteousness that was merited by their quantity of good deeds, Jesus taught a righteousness that was given by God. Hence, Jesus' righteousness is superior. But today there is a growing consensus among scholars that the debate Jesus had

with the scribes and Pharisees was not over earning merit before God. Rather, it was about Jesus' place in God's plan for redemption. Consequently, the righteousness Jesus demands is superior, not because scribal and Pharisaic righteousness is necessarily an attempt to earn salvation, but because Jesus demands behavior that conforms to God's standard as revealed by himself. The point-counterpoints of Matthew 5:21-48 explicate the nature of the surpassing righteousness that Jesus reveals. This righteousness is messianic (Mt 5:17), deeper (Mt 5:27-30) and innovative (Mt 5:38-42). The usage of *righteousness* in Matthew 5:20 is similar to the usage of the term in the Qumran literature: it is an eschatological righteousness pertaining to a particular group of God's people. Those who are marked by the righteousness of Jesus will be approved by God and will enter the kingdom (Mt 5:6, 10; 6:33; 7:21-23; cf. 12:36-37).

For Matthew righteousness is behavioral. The "practice of piety" referred to in Matthew 6:1 is immediately related to the giving of alms in 6:2. Matthew 6:1 sets the theme for Jesus' instruction on religious behavior such as almsgiving, prayer and fasting (Mt 6:2-18). In some MSS Matthew 6:1 reads "almsgiving" (*eleēmosynēn*) instead of "practicing your piety" (*dikaiosynēn*). Interestingly, rabbinic sources show that the Hebrew and Aramaic terms for almsgiving (*ṣᵉdāqâ*) and righteousness (*ṣedeq*) are closely associated, though in this case the more general term is most likely intended, setting the stage for the specific instructions of Matthew 6:2-18 (see Przybylski).

Though some scholars have suggested that the righteousness pursued in Matthew 6:33 is a gift from God—eschatological salvation (much like Pauline usage)—many interpreters today understand it as moral behavior which includes the establishment of justice (cf. Mt 6:10 with 5:6; 6:33). The fact that pursuing righteousness is joined so closely with seeking God's kingdom—submitting to God's reign and seeking to realize it in this world—favors a behavioral sense here as well. Thus submission to God through seeking his kingdom unleashes God's provisions (Mt 6:33).

Matthew further highlights the behavioral focus of righteousness in the examples of Joseph (Mt 1:19), Abel (Mt 23:35) and other OT saints who are finally acceptable to the Father because they have lived faithfully (Mt 5:45; 12:37; 13:43, 49; 25:37, 46). On the other hand, Matthew emphasizes the absence of the proper kind of righteousness in the Pharisees and Jewish leaders, who either feign their religiosity or have not perceived the new standard set forth in Jesus' teachings (Mt 5:20; 9:13; 23:28).

It is unclear whether the "righteous person" of Matthew 10:41 refers to a special class of leaders (e.g., teachers) among Jesus' followers or to anyone who is simply obedient to his commands. Jesus' final words explicitly call for all future disciples to obey his commands (Mt 28:20) and, in keeping with Matthew's emphases, we may assume that those who do so are righteous.

3.2. Luke. Luke seems to focus less attention on whether the standard of righteousness is derived from the OT or Jesus, placing his emphasis on the pious, merciful and just behavior that is the fruit of those who are ultimately approved by God. In several passages Luke describes righteousness as conformity to God's Law (Lk 1:6; 2:25; 23:47, 50). Zechariah and Elizabeth are described as "righteous before God" because they obeyed the Lord's commandments blamelessly (Lk 1:6). The angel* tells Zechariah that John, the promised fruit of Elizabeth's womb, will turn many from disobedience to "the wisdom of the just"—a life of obedience to God's commands that conforms to God's wisdom (Lk 1:17). Simeon is described as "righteous and pious" because of his trusting hope that God would eventually save his people (Lk 2:25). Joseph from Arimathea was publicly known for his piety because he was one who lived according to God's commandments* (Lk 23:50). In Acts a similar evaluation is given of Cornelius (Acts 10:22). These people embody proper OT faith—a faith that obeys God's will, trusts in his salvation and waits for him to vindicate his purposes. Luke's concept of righteousness includes a dominant element of piety as well as social mercy and justice (Lk 14:14; cf. also Lk 12:57; 23:41). The importance of righteousness in Luke is illustrated in Luke 14:14 (cf. Acts 24:15): It is the righteous who will be raised in the last day and enjoy fellowship with the Father.

This leads to Luke's heavy emphasis on social reversal (Lk 1:53; 6:20, 24; 12:16-21; 16:19-26) and economic justice (Lk 3:11, 14; 4:18; 5:11; 7:24-25; 12:33; 14:33; 16:13; 18:22; *see* Rich and Poor). Those who finally will be declared righteous before God are humble, trusting sinners (Lk 1:6, 17; 2:25; 18:14; 23:50). On the other hand, Luke, as Matthew, emphasizes the severe condemnation that befalls the self-righteous, who in their pride desire to be noticed. These Luke ironically describes as "righteous" (Lk 5:32; 10:29; 15:7; 16:15; 18:9; 20:20).

Finally, whereas in Matthew and Mark the centurion at the cross confesses Jesus as the Son of God (*see* Son of God), in Luke he describes Jesus as *dikaios*—meaning "righteous," "just" or "innocent" (Lk 23:47; *see* Death of Jesus). This speaks indirectly of the injustice dealt Jesus by the authorities. The innocent or righteous character of Jesus is a theme Luke further emphasizes in Acts. Peter accuses the Jewish crowds (*see* People, Crowd) of denying the holy and righteous one and asking for a murderer in his place (Acts 3:14; cf. 7:52). Paul, when describing his conversion, says that Ananias told him that he was appointed by God to see the "Just One" (Acts 22:14)—referring to Jesus as vindicated and exalted in spite of his humiliating death in Jerusalem. Like the OT saints and their worthy successors in people like Zechariah, Elizabeth and Simeon, Jesus devoted his entire life to God and obeyed God's commands. Because of his obedience he was crucified.

For Luke the innocence of Jesus is more than a political or legal statement. It almost certainly connects Jesus with the Servant of Yahweh (*see* Servant of Yahweh) described in Isaiah 52:13—53:12 who both suffers and is exalted. In Acts 3:13-14 the themes of suffering and the righteous one are joined. Likewise, Luke 22:35-37, 39-46 shows traces of the theme of Jesus as the Suffering Servant. At the cross, when the centurion confesses Jesus as "righteous" (Lk 23:47), Luke is once again indicating that Jesus is the innocent, law-abiding Servant of Yahweh who brings salvation.

3.3. John. Out of the five uses of *dik-* terminology in the Fourth Gospel the adjective *righteous* is applied once to God (Jn 17:25) and twice to judgments made either by Jesus (Jn 5:30) or the crowd (Jn 7:24). John 16:8, 10 is the most notable use of *righteousness* in John, though scholars do not agree on the meaning of these verses. God has sent his Spirit (*see* Holy Spirit) into the world to convince the world* either (1) of its inadequate righteousness and consequently its need to turn to Christ or (2) of the righteous vindication of the Son in spite of his condemnation by the world. The Spirit will continue the work that Jesus performed in exposing sin (Jn 16:8, 10).

In inaugurating the kingdom of God and salvation, Jesus revealed that his followers were to be characterized by the pursuit of righteousness and justice. This is so central to Jesus' message that he states that without a righteous status/character one will not enter the kingdom of God. Though righteous character is expressed in righteous behavior, a righteous status is not obtained by good works. Rather, the person who is committed to Jesus in discipleship and has entered the kingdom of God can and should be expected to show righteousness in character and actions.

See also DISCIPLESHIP; ETHICS OF JESUS; FASTING; KINGDOM OF GOD; PRAYER; RICH AND POOR; SALVATION; SERMON ON THE MOUNT; SINNER.

BIBLIOGRAPHY. E. Achtemeier et al., "Righteousness in

the Old Testament, Jewish Literature, and the New Testament," *IDB* 4.80-99; D. Hill, *Greek Words and Hebrew Meanings: Studies in the Semantics of Soteriological Terms* (SNTSMS 5; Cambridge: University Press, 1967); B. Przybylski, *Righteousness in Matthew and His World of Thought* (SNTSMS 41; Cambridge: University Press, 1980); G. Quell and G. Schrenk, "δίκη κτλ," *TDNT* II.174-225; J. Reumann et al., *Righteousness in the New Testament* (Philadelphia: Fortress, 1982); E. P. Sanders, *Paul and Palestinian Judaism* (Philadelphia: Fortress, 1977); H. Seebass and C. Brown, "Righteousness, Justification," *NIDNTT* 3.352-77; N. Snaith, *The Distinctive Ideas of the Old Testament* (Philadelphia: Westminster, 1964); P. Stuhlmacher, *Reconciliation, Law, and Righteousness: Essays in Biblical Theology* (Philadelphia: Fortress, 1986); J. A. Ziesler, *The Meaning of Righteousness in Paul: A Linguistic and Theological Inquiry* (SNTSMS 20; Cambridge: University Press, 1972). S. McKnight

K

KINGDOM OF GOD/KINGDOM OF HEAVEN

The term "kingdom of God" or "kingdom of Heaven" signifies God's (*see* God) sovereign, dynamic and eschatological (*see* Eschatology) rule. The kingdom of God lay at the heart of Jesus' teaching. As proclaimed by Jesus the kingdom of God had continuity with the OT promise as well as with Jewish apocalyptic* thinking, but differed from them in important respects. For example, it denoted God's eternal rule rather than an earthly kingdom, its scope was universal rather than limited to the Jewish nation, and it was imminent and potentially present in him rather than a vague future hope, being inextricably connected with his own person and mission.

1. Terminology
2. Old Testament Antecedents
3. Judaism
4. Jesus and the Kingdom of God
5. The Gospels
6. The Kingdom of God and the Church Today

1. Terminology.

The Gospels use three terms to express the idea of the kingdom of God: *hē basileia tou theou* ("the kingdom of God"), *hē basileia tōn ouranōn* ("the kingdom of [the] Heaven[s]") and the absolute *hē basileia* ("the kingdom"). The equivalence of the first two expressions is indicated by their content, context and interchangeability in the Gospels. (The distinction between the kingdom of God as God's sovereignty, and the kingdom of Heaven conceived as an otherworldly, future reality, the former of which is the condition for entering the latter [Pamment], is without exegetical basis). The Greek for "the kingdom of (the) Heaven(s)" is a literal translation of the later Jewish *malᵉkût šāmayim* (e.g., *2 Apoc. Bar.* 73; *3 Apoc. Bar.* 11:2; *As. Mos.* 10; *Pss. Sol.* 17:4; 1QSb 3.5; *m. Ber.* 2.2, 5; *y. Ber.* 4a; 7b), where "Heaven" replaces "God" out of reverence, as *'ᵃdōnay* ("lord," "master") had replaced *Yahweh* ("Lord") and *mākôm* ("place") in due time replaced *šāmayim* ("Heaven") (Dalman, 91-101). The kingdom of God is also referred to by the absolute "kingdom" when the reference is obvious.

The primary meaning of the Hebrew *malᵉkût* (with synonyms), Aramaic *malkû* and Greek *basileia* is abstract and dynamic, that is, "sovereignty" or "royal rule." This is almost always the case in the OT and Jewish literature when the term is applied to God. The sense of realm—a territorial kingdom—is secondary, arising out of the necessity for a definite locus as the sphere for the exercise of sovereignty.

2. Old Testament Antecedents.

The Gospels introduce the ministries of John the Baptist (*see* John the Baptist) and of Jesus by stating that they proclaimed the nearness of the kingdom of God. No word of explanation is ever offered, and the conclusion must be that the idea of God's kingdom was well known.

In contrast to this is the total absence in the OT canonical books of the expression "kingdom of God." (The expression occurs once in Wis 10:10). Yet though the term is absent, the idea is present throughout the OT. In a number of instances Yahweh is presented as king (Deut 9:26 [LXX]; 1 Sam 12:12; Ps 24:10 [LXX 23:10]; 29:10 [LXX 28:10]; Is 6:5; 33:22; Zeph 3:15; Zech 14:16, 17). At other places he is ascribed a royal throne (Ps 9:4 [LXX 9:5]; 45:6 [LXX 44:7]; 47:8 [LXX 46:9]; Is 6:1; 66:1; Ezek 1:26; Sir 1:8) while occasionally his continuous or future reign is affirmed (Ps 10:16 [LXX 9:37]; 146:10 [LXX 145:10]; Is 24:23; Wis 3:8). In fact Psalm 22:28 (MT 22:29; LXX 21:29) says "the kingdom" (*hammᵉlûkâ;* LXX *basileia)* belongs to the Lord.

The idea is not, however, confined to these texts with explicitly royal attributes; it underlies Yahweh's whole relation to Israel.* The demand presented to Pharaoh to let Israel go is the demand of the lawful king over against the usurper. The covenant with Israel is the covenant which affirms the suzerainty of Yahweh over his people. In the conquest of Canaan Yahweh as king apportions to his people a country; a country, moreover, which he, as the creator and king of the earth, can dispose as he pleases. The rule of God over Israel is especially exemplified in the time of the Judges, who functioned as his representatives. A crisis emerged with Israel's demand for a king (1 Sam 8:4-5), a demand that was interpreted as a rejection of Yahweh's rule (1 Sam 8:6-8). With the accession of David to the throne, however, the situation was somewhat normalized and the king was understood to reign as Yahweh's representative and be under Yahweh's suzerainty. In other words, the monarchy was looked upon as the concrete manifestation of Yahweh's rule.

This explains the (authoritative) role of the prophets at the court (e.g., Nathan, Gad, Elijah). The promise to establish David's throne forever, despite the rejection of Solomon (1 Kings 11:11-14), led to the focus upon a future Messiah (see Christ) who would rule over David's kingdom in righteousness and prosperity (see Son of David). Thus the Davidic kingdom was somehow conflated with Yahweh's rule. The great ethical prophets portrayed Israel's unfaithfulness against the Creator and king (Lord) of the universe, who had been pleased to identify himself with Israel. The crisis became especially acute when the last vestiges of David's kingdom were swept away by the Babylonian captivity. The promise made to David for an everlasting kingdom was now in some circles radically reinterpreted.

No other writing of the OT has more to say about the sovereignty of God than Daniel, where the kingdom of God is the central theme. However, the conception of the kingdom of God by Daniel is transformed under the impact of the new situation. The divine sovereignty is set vis à vis human kingdoms. These are described as being under the control of the God of heaven,* who allots the sovereignty in accordance with his will. In Daniel 2 the kingdom of God is described as a direct divine intervention. Its agent, in the form of a stone cut without hands, crushes the various human kingdoms, here symbolized by various metals (and clay), and grows until it (i.e., the kingdom, king and kingdom being interchangeable in Daniel) fills the whole earth. In Daniel 7 the symbolism changes to one of wild beasts portraying the ungodly character of the human kingdoms. The agent for the kingdom of God is a figure described as "one like a son of man" (see Son of Man). This figure assumes the royal rule of the spiritual powers at work behind the earthly potentates, and his saints are given the kingly rule of the monarchs under the whole heaven (i.e., the earthly potentates).

Thus Daniel not only portrays the kingdom of God divested of its Davidic, earthly, political character, but

also depicts its agent as a heavenly, transcendental being. The new situation has brought about not only a new concept of the kingdom of God but a transformation of its agent (see Caragounis 1986, 61-80). These new ideas were of decisive importance in shaping future messianic thought and eschatology, not only in Judaism* but also in Jesus' teaching.

3. Judaism.

The concept of the kingdom of God in early Judaism was shaped principally by three factors. At the basis was the OT idea of Yahweh's eschatological epiphany in judgment* to punish the wicked (i.e., Israel's enemies) and reward the just (i.e., Israel). This was coupled with the idea of God's reign through his elect messianic king of Davidic descent, bringing in a time of untold bliss for the Jewish people. The second factor was Daniel's new understanding of the kingdom and its agent as transcendental, heavenly realities and the consequent deliverance of God's people in primarily dynamic terms. The third factor was the centuries-long Gentile rule over Palestine which intensified the longing for liberation, national identity and happiness (see Revolutionary Movements).

Although the term "kingdom of God" is rare in Judaism, the idea is almost ubiquitous, either explicitly as the kingdom of the Messiah or implicitly in descriptions of the messianic age. The two lines of messianic expectation to which Judaism was heir are reflected in the ambivalent descriptions of the messianic kingdom. This ambivalence, besides defying a strictly systematic presentation of kingdom teaching, also implies that motifs from both lines of thought are blended together to various degrees. The result is a variety of messianologies and kingdom conceptions, which are not always clearly demarcated from one another. In general, however, we may distinguish between two main tendencies in kingdom thinking: an earlier, political, this-worldly conception of a temporary, Davidic kingdom with Jerusalem as the center and the Jews as the primary beneficiaries— though sometimes encompassing the whole world— and a later, apocalyptic conception of an ultramundane, transcendental and everlasting kingdom, conceived in universalistic terms.

When the kingdom of God is considered as temporary, usually a judgment follows and a new world is posited, and a reign of God is looked for in heaven with greater bliss than that of the messianic kingdom. This view is sharply contrasted with the apocalyptic view, according to which the kingdom of God comes by a direct intervention of God and is transcendental and everlasting under a similarly transcendental and pre-existent Messiah, described as Son of man (Daniel, the so-called Parables of *1 Enoch* 37—71, 2 Ezra). In this case the Messiah takes part in the judgment, which thus precedes the messianic kingdom. This kingdom is the final kingdom of God which is to last forever.

But as is natural, even the later expectation for the most part utilizes the messianic categories of the earlier expectation, and this makes it more difficult to isolate the traits of the one from those of the other. The following is an attempt to illustrate briefly some of the main lines of thought in Jewish expectations of the kingdom of God without attempting to draw a strict demarcating line between the early and the later forms of the expectation or between the different standpoints within early Judaism.

Especially in works evincing Danielic influence, the inbreaking of the kingdom of God is preceded by a time of tribulation and upheaval both in heaven and on earth (*Sib. Or.* 3:796-808; *2 Apoc. Bar.* 70:2-8; 4 Ezra 6:24; 9:1-12; 13:29-31; 1QM 12:9; 19:1-2; cf. Mt 24:7-12 par.). In rabbinic literature this came to be called the birth pangs of the Messiah (*b. Sanh.* 98b.; Str-B I.950). The Messiah's appearance is sometimes preceded by the coming of Elijah* (Mal 3:23-24; Sir 48:10-11; cf. Mt 17:10 par.; *m. 'Ed.* 8:7; Justin *Dial. Tryph.* 8) or of the prophet-like-Moses* (Deut 18:15; 1QS 9:11; 4QTestim 5-8; Jn 1:21).

The Messiah himself is conceived variously. The traditional view of a fully human, Davidic Messiah (*Pss. Sol.* 17:5, 23; *Sib. Or.* 3:49) who conquers the wicked (*Sib. Or.* 3:652-56; *Pss. Sol.* 17:23-32) is frequent, while in works belonging to the Danielic tradition the Messiah is a pre-existent, supernatural being with powers to judge the kings and the mighty, in short, all the enemies of God, and to vindicate the righteous (*1 Enoch* 46:1-6; 48:2-6; 62:5-7; 4 Ezra 12:32). Another difference is that according to *1 Enoch* 90:16-38 the Messiah will appear after the judgment, whereas in most other works (*Sib. Or.* 3:652-6; *Pss. Sol.* 17:14-41; *1 Enoch* 46:4-6; 62:3-12; 69:27-9; 4 Ezra 13:32-8; cf. Mt 25:31-46) he actually conquers or judges his enemies.

Echoing the sentiment of Psalm 2:1-3 a number of works presuppose a final assault by the ungodly against the Messiah (*Sib. Or.* 3:663-68; *1 Enoch* 90:16; 1QM 15—19; 4 Ezra 13:33-34) in order to thwart the establishment of the messianic kingdom. These powers are annihilated sometimes by God (*T. Mos.* 10:2-7; *1 Enoch* 90:18-19) or more often by the Messiah himself (4 Ezra 12:32-33; 13:27-28, 37-39; *2 Apoc. Bar.* 39:7—40:2), who is occasionally presented as a warrior (*Tg. Isa.* 10:27; Gen 49:11), and sometimes in judicial categories (*1 Enoch* 46:4-6; 45:3; 52:4-9; 55:4;

61:8-10; cf. Mt 25:31-46).

The establishment of the Messiah's kingdom involves the gathering of the scattered Israelites (LXX Bar 4:36-37; 5:5-9; Philo *Praem. Poen.* 28; 4 Ezra 13:39-47) and the restoration of Jerusalem (*Pss. Sol.* 17:25, 33; *1 Enoch* 53:6; 90:28-29; 4 Ezra 7:26). The messianic kingdom is understood to imply the ultimate reign of God over his people (*Sib. Or.* 3:704-6, 756-59; *Pss. Sol.* 17:1-4; 1QM 19:1; *Šᵉmôneh 'Eśrēh*, 11 *bᵉrākâ*), thus fulfilling the OT idea of God being king over Israel. The kingdom is centered on Palestine, with Jerusalem being "the jewel of the world" (*Sib. Or.* 3:423), though Jubilees (mid-second century B.C.) probably presents the first instance of a temporary messianic kingdom of 1,000 years. This is brought about gradually by man's moral or spiritual development, and during this time the powers of evil are restrained (1:29; 23:26-30).

Similarly, the third book of the *Sibylline Oracles* (second century B.C.) 762-71 exhorts to righteous living as the condition for God "to raise up his kingdom for all ages over men." The Messiah is described in book 5 (c. A.D. 100) 414 as "a Blessed Man" from "the plains of heaven," perhaps reflecting Danielic influence. Under his reign there will be peace (3:702), fruitfulness and prosperity (3:744), in which even the animal world will share (3:788-95).

According to the *Testament of Moses* (first century A.D.) 10:1, God's kingdom "shall appear throughout his whole creation." However, the kingdom seems to be earthly and appears to lack a Messiah, being introduced by repentance (1:18; 9:6-7). The awaited kingdom will spell glory for Israel and punishment for the Gentiles* (10:7-10).

The *Second Apocalypse of Baruch* describes the messianic kingdom especially in three visions (considered pre-70 A.D.). In the first vision (27—30) the revelation of the Messiah will bring a time of prosperity for "those who are found in this land" and "have arrived at the consummation of time." In the second vision (36—40) the Messiah will annihilate his enemy the fourth empire (reflecting Dan 7) and reign "until the world of corruption has ended . . . and the times . . . have been fulfilled." In the third vision (53—74) prosperity and bliss follow the Messiah's annihilation of Israel's enemies. The kingdom is related to Israel's long-cherished hope, though the Messiah has supernatural status.

The two works bearing the clearest influence of the Danielic Son of man, the Parables of *1 Enoch* and the book of 4 Ezra, follow their source in associating the concepts of kingdom and Son of man. At several points in the Parables the Son of man is portrayed as exercising the functions of judge and universal ruler

(46:4-6; 62:3-12; 63:4; 69:27-29, and the book closes with a description of the messianic age (71:15-17, cf. 62:12-16) (see Caragounis 1986, 84-119).

The book of 4 Ezra conflates the earthly with the transcendental Messiah (12:32), who dies after reigning for 400 years (7:28-29, other versions have variously 1,000 and 30 years). The Davidic descent of the Messiah is perhaps his way of stressing continuity in messianic thought, though the content is that of a transcendental Messiah, as seen from (e.g.) 12:32-34; 13:26 (see Caragounis 1986, 119-31).

In the Qumran scrolls the term *mal^ekût* occurs over a dozen times, but probably only once of God's kingdom (1QM 12:7), most of the rest referring to Israel's kingdom. The idea of God's kingdom is, however, latent in the sectarians' belief that they constituted God's true people who were to fight the eschatological battle against God's enemies (see Dead Sea Scrolls; on Judaism generally, see Schürer II.492-554).

4. Jesus and the Kingdom of God.
In the teaching of Jesus the discussion of the kingdom of God revolves around two questions: (1) the character and (2) the imminence of the kingdom of God. These two questions are interrelated and have been at the center of scholarly discussion during the past hundred years.

4.1. Jesus' Dynamic View. Jesus' conception of the kingdom of God had continuity with the OT promise as well as shared certain features with apocalyptic Judaism, particularly Daniel, but went beyond them in certain important respects: (1) the kingdom of God was primarily dynamic rather than a geographical entity; (2) it was connected with the destiny of the Son of man; (3) entrance into it was not based on the covenant or confined to Jewish participation and (4) whereas in apocalypticism it was a vague future hope, in Jesus it is definite and imminent; in fact it demands immediate response.

With the apocalypticists Jesus held that the kingdom of God was no human achievement but an act of God. However, unlike them he did not expect the kingdom of God to follow on upheavals and catastrophes, but to appear in a gentle, quiet and unobtrusive manner. The catastrophic element for Jesus lay in the upheaval his call caused to his followers' relations with their family,* friends and even their own self. Jesus' followers should be willing to "hate" their own life in order to be worthy of him, worthy of the kingdom of God (see Discipleship).

4.2. The Kingdom As Present or Future—The Modern Debate. In modern discussion the kingdom of God in

the teaching of Jesus has actualized three questions: (1) What is its essence? (2) How is it related to Jesus' person and work? (3) When does it come?

In the past hundred years since the work of A. Ritschl and J. Weiss the kingdom of God has been at the center of discussion and the three questions above have received a variety of answers. Ritschl, influenced by Kant's idealistic philosophy, conceived of the kingdom of God in primarily ethical terms as the organization of redeemed humanity, whose actions are inspired by love (see Historical Jesus).

The interest generated by Ritschl's work gave rise to several interpretations of the kingdom of God, principally: (1) the individualistic, spiritual and non-eschatological interpretation (which located the kingdom of God in the experience of a person's own heart, an interpretation which was associated with the liberal school, for which the essence of Christianity lay in certain general principles taught by Jesus, as e.g., the fatherhood of God and the brotherhood of all people [e.g., A. von Harnack, 1886, and W. Herrmann, 1901]); (2) the Social Gospel movement in Germany (C. Blumhardt, c. 1900, and L. Ragaz, 1911) and especially in America with its emphasis on a present social order based on love and solidarity (S. Mathews, 1897; F. G. Peabody, 1900; and particularly W. Rauschenbusch, 1912).

But the most important interpretation for the continued scholarly discussion was given by Ritschl's own son-in-law, J. Weiss, in his epoch-making work *Die Predigt Jesu vom Reiche Gottes* (1892, ET *Jesus' Proclamation of the Kingdom of God*, 1971). Weiss reacted strongly against Ritschl's interpretation, emphasizing the future, eschatological and apocalyptic character of the kingdom of God which is opposed by the kingdom of Satan. The kingdom of God would erupt suddenly, be solely the work of God and sweep away the present order. The work of Weiss aroused a storm and with it an unprecedented interest in the theme of the kingdom of God. In the hands of A. Schweitzer the line Weiss had struck out became known as *Konsequente Eschatologie* ("consistent," "futuristic" or "thoroughgoing eschatology"). In due time this found its opposite pole in Dodd's realized eschatology. In the meantime Dalman (1898), by means of philology demonstrated the dynamic character of the kingdom of God in Judaism and the NT, which has been the basic assumption of almost all subsequent discussions. According to Dalman the idea of kingdom of God has no territorial or geographical reference but expresses dynamically the kingly rule of God which is basically eschatological. However, the theological interpretation was given by A. Schweitzer.

In his landmark works *Das Messianitäts und Leidens-geheimnis* (1901, ET *The Mystery of the Kingdom of God,* 1925) and especially in *Von Reimarus zu Wrede* (1906, ET *The Quest of the Historical Jesus,* 1910), Schweitzer interpreted not only Jesus' teaching (as Weiss had done), but also Jesus' whole ministry in consistently eschatological terms. Jesus was understood as an apocalyptic figure who expected the end to come during the mission of the Twelve (Mk 6:7-13 par.), wherefore he did not expect to see the disciples* again. In this he was, however, mistaken. The end, and with it the kingdom of God, did not come. Having staked everything on this expectation and been proved wrong in his prediction of the end, Jesus decided to cast himself headlong to death in a final, heroic attempt to force God to set up his kingdom. Schweitzer's impact, particularly in Germany, can be gauged from the fact that his futuristic eschatology became the characteristic German line.

As a reaction to the one-sidedness of this German position, a number of British scholars like A. T. Cadoux (1930) and T. W. Manson (1931) (and even Germans like E. von Dobschütz and H. D. Wendland) laid emphasis on the present element of the kingdom of God in the teaching of Jesus. Like Schweitzer, R. Bultmann thought that Jesus expected the kingdom of God to begin at his death and went up to Jerusalem to purify the Temple* in preparation for it. The kingdom of God is conceived by Bultmann as a future, eschatological, supra-historical and supernatural entity, which places a person at the position of decision. But differently from Schweitzer, in Bultmann's demythologizing interpretation the kingdom of God is ever coming and thus ceases to be a future event that is and can be hoped for. Since the decision is a continual decision, the kingdom of God is not an event in time. Thus the kingdom of God, emptied of its content, transcends time without ever entering it. In short, Bultmann sees the kingdom of God primarily in existentialist fashion as the hour for the individual's decision.

However, the scholar who gave definitive form to this reaction was C. H. Dodd. In his important little book *The Parables of the Kingdom* (1935), Dodd interpreted the *ēngiken* of (e.g.) Mark 1:15 and its parallels in light of the *ephthasen* of Matthew 12:28 (par. Lk 11:20). His claim was that LXX usage translating the Aramaic of Daniel, Modern Greek idiomatic usage and the parables* of the kingdom all lent their united support to his thesis that the kingdom of God was already a present reality during Jesus' ministry. The decisive event had occurred in the coming of Jesus. Jesus' healings,* particularly his casting out of demons

(*see* Demon, Devil, Satan), were proof that in Jesus' person and works the divine sovereignty had dealt the decisive blow to the kingdom of Satan and was indubitably a wholly present reality. In a sense Dodd identified the kingdom of God with the person of Jesus. This opened the way to viewing the kingdom of God as a timeless reality. "The absolute, the 'wholly other', has entered into time and space" (Dodd, 81). "The inconceivable had happened: history had become the vehicle of the eternal; the absolute was clothed with flesh and blood" (147). In Dodd's interpretation of the kingdom of God, "futurist eschatology disappears, and all that is left is 'the eschaton' as the Eternal" (Lundström, 121). To achieve this Dodd played down the Gospel statements which presented the kingdom of God as future.

Dodd's influence has been far-reaching, forcing significant modifications upon the futuristic interpretation. This has led in the last forty-five years to a number of mediating positions according to which the kingdom of God is conceived as both present and future (with the German side inclining more toward the future and the British more toward the present aspect), e.g., Kümmel in his important *Verheissung und Erfüllung* (1945, *Promise and Fulfilment,* 1961), G. R. Beasley-Murray (1954, 312-16; 1986, 75-80), E. Jüngel, Schnackenburg, N. Perrin, D. C. Allison (99-114). In a similar vein J. Jeremias, at the suggestion of Haenchen, speaks of the kingdom of God as *sich realisierende Eschatologie* ("an eschatology in process of realization"), a term preferred by Dodd but apparently never allowed to change his basic viewpoint. R. H. Fuller (25-27) interprets *ephthasen* as "has come," but understands it by way of the prophetic device of speaking of an event proleptically as though it had already taken place. For Fuller the powers of the kingdom of God were already making themselves felt in the deeds of Jesus by operating in advance, and his viewpoint received the label of proleptic eschatology. G. Florovsky and A. M. Hunter (94) speak of inaugurated eschatology, while G. E. Ladd argues from a rendering of *ephthasen* as "has come," for a fulfillment of the kingdom of God in history (i.e., in Jesus' ministry) as well as a full consummation at the end of history, and calls his position an eschatology of biblical realism.

Kümmel has been described as the scholar who came closest to a "genuine synthesis of realized and futurist eschatology in the teaching of our Lord" (Beasley-Murray 1954, 103). Thus, while duly recognizing the future character of sayings admitting an interval between the passion and the Parousia (Mk 2:18-20; 8:38 par. Lk 12:8-9), he understands the *ephthasen* of Matthew 12:28, with Dodd, as "has come" and as implying that the eschaton was already active in Jesus. In Jesus' person and actions the future was already realized since he who was to usher in salvation* at the end was already present. In this way the future of the kingdom of God and its coming were linked closely with the present, which had Jesus as its center. The kingdom of God was present in the person, teaching and works of Jesus. By faith in him people received the kingdom of God and the guarantee of its appearance. This guarantee implied that the kingdom of God is to be fulfilled in him. Thus promise and fulfillment are insolubly connected with each other. Ladd (123-24) criticizes Kümmel for failing to define precisely what the kingdom of God is. According to Grässer (7) what is understood as present by Kümmel is not the kingdom of God itself, but its imminence.

Morgenthaler, Schnackenburg and Beasley-Murray (1986) all take *ephthasen* as "has come" though for Morgenthaler it only implies that the kingdom of God is around here but not actually present. For Schnackenburg it means that the kingdom of God is "connected with his [Jesus'] person and his work" (109). Although he speaks of the kingdom of God as something entirely eschatological and wholly supernatural, he also conceives of it in its salvific character as present and active in Jesus. The miracles of Jesus were "the kingdom of God in action." On the other hand, it would be an overstatement to claim that the presence of the kingdom of God indicates something completed; the present kingdom functions as a precursor of the coming, perfected kingdom of God.

Beasley-Murray thinks that the meaning of "has come" for *ephthasen* in Matthew 12:28 and parallel is "unambiguously plain" and criticizes the defenders of futuristic eschatology for looking for "ways of muting its testimony" (1986, 75-76). The miracles of Jesus, especially his driving out demons, speak eloquently of the presence of the kingdom. However, the arrival of the kingdom of God spoken of in Matthew 12:28 and parallel was not the same thing as its consummation, which Beasley-Murray, like Schnackenburg, Kümmel, Ladd and others, considers as future.

A basically similar position is that of D. C. Allison. He follows the usual interpretation of *ephthasen* and thus subscribes to the present consensus that the kingdom of God is both present and future. The relation between present and future is explained by appealing to Jewish thought which "could envision the final events—the judgment of evil and the arrival of the kingdom of God—as extending over a time and as a process or series of events that could involve the present. When Jesus announced that the kingdom of

God has come and is coming, this means that the last act has begun but has not yet reached its climax; the last things have come and will come" (105-6). And again, "For Jesus, the kingdom of God, the eschatological establishment of God's kingly rule, was due to come in its fullness soon" (114).

It may then be concluded that those who emphasize the presence of the kingdom of God in Jesus' works of power also allow for a future perfection or consummation of the kingdom of God, while those who advocate the futurity of the kingdom of God allow for some kind of effect which the imminently near kingdom of God exercised in the ministry of Jesus. Both of these positions are attempts to explain important elements in the Gospel data.

Of rather different nature is the more recent work of Perrin, who has retreated from his earlier positions (1963). Receiving impulses from literary critics like P. Wheelwright (1962), P. Ricoeur (1969), A. N. Wilder (1964), R. W. Funk (1966), D. O. Via (1967) and F. D. Crossan (1973), Perrin has suggested that "kingdom of God" is not an idea or a conception, but a mythical symbol (1976, 33). He adopts Wheelwright's distinction of steno-symbol, which has fixed meaning—a one-to-one correspondence between symbol and referent as in apocalyptic language—and tensive symbol, which is open and multi-significant, having an inexhaustible set of meanings. Jesus' proclamation of the kingdom of God involved the tensive symbol, which, however, his followers turned to an apocalyptic steno-symbol, making the kingdom of God lose its rich variety of reference and instead refer to a particular event of universal experience. Perrin thinks that Jesus' whole teaching claimed "to mediate an experience of God as king, an experience of such an order that it brings world to an end" (Perrin 1976, 54). Though the symbolic and metaphorical aspects of the kingdom of God and its parables should be profitably explored, Perrin's analysis and claims can hardly be said to do justice to the biblical data or to have led to a deeper or more valid understanding of the kingdom of God. Not infrequently Perrin's position involves self-contradictions, and his categories are plainly inapplicable to the Gospel texts (see further the criticism of Beasley-Murray 1986, 338-44 and Allison, 107-12).

4.3. The Imminence of the Kingdom. From the above it must have become clear that the interpretation of *ephthasen* of Matthew 12:28 and its parallel Luke 11:20, which is normally accepted as an authentic saying of Jesus, has played a most crucial role in discussions of the kingdom of God. This is so because it is the only kingdom saying in the Synoptics that apparently describes the kingdom of God as having arrived. Dodd was so certain of this meaning that he let it determine his interpretation of the *ēngiken*-type of sayings. The claim that the kingdom of God had arrived in Jesus' person and that it consisted of, or at least was active in, his driving out demons is hardly a satisfactory answer to the three questions regarding the essence, the arrival and the relation of the kingdom of God to Jesus' person and work. If the kingdom of God had come already, say, by the time Jesus uttered the saying in Matthew 12:28 and Luke 11:20, how is the remainder of Jesus' earthly existence to be understood? And what about the Son of man's duty "to give his life a ransom for many"? What is the significance of his death? And how did Jesus relate his death to the kingdom of God? To speak of a final or full consummation at a future point of time does not satisfactorily answer these questions. And to emphasize the coming of the kingdom prior to the time of the *ephthasen* saying raises the question of whether the death of Jesus is superfluous to that coming. Any viable solution must take account of (1) the language used and (2) the relation of the kingdom of God to the Son of man (4.5. below).

4.3.1. Ephthasen (Mt 12:28/Lk 11:20). The most indubitable fact is that the Synoptics present Jesus as having spoken of the kingdom of God as imminently near (*ēngiken*), just as John did (Mt 3:2). The problem which the *ephthasen* saying raises is due to its being interpreted in a dubious way. The *ephthasen* saying makes excellent sense if understood according to a well-attested but little-known and generally misunderstood Greek idiom. The aorist tense is sometimes used to emphasize the certainty and immediacy of an action that properly belongs in the future by describing it as though it had already transpired (Caragounis 1989, 12-23). In comparison with the *ēngiken*-type of sayings the *ephthasen* logion implies an advance, but not quite the presence of the kingdom of God which, in the context of Matthew 12:28 and Luke 11:20, is still future. What Jesus is saying in effect is, "If it is by the Spirit/finger of God (rather than by Beelzebul, as you claim) that I drive out the demons (i.e., preparing for the coming of the kingdom of God by defeating the forces of evil), then the kingdom of God is about to break in upon you (and overtake you in your obstinate and unrepentant state)" (*see* Holy Spirit).

Ephthasen implies that the coming of the kingdom of God is so imminent that the kingdom of God may be considered as being virtually here. This means that the force of the saying is not purely informative, in which case the force of *eph' hymas* ("upon you") would have been lost, but one of warning, almost threat. This threatening force of *eph' hymas* shows clearly that the

kingdom of God has not yet arrived. The relation of the miracles (*see* Miracles and Miracle Stories) of Jesus to the kingdom of God is that they bear witness to the warfare of the Son of man (i.e., the agent of the kingdom of God) against the powers of evil for the establishment of the kingdom of God. But the kingdom of God does not consist of those miracles. Jesus' miracles are only the preliminaries, not the kingdom of God itself (contra Dodd). The kingdom of God is the dynamic reign of God over his people. The saying looks forward to the cross.

4.3.2. Entos Hymōn Estin (Lk 17:21). Another saying often adduced as evidence of the presence of the kingdom of God is Luke 17:21. Here Jesus is represented answering the Pharisees'* question about the time of the coming of the kingdom of God by saying, "the kingdom of God does not come with your careful observation, nor will people say, 'Here it is,' or 'There it is,' because the kingdom of God is within you" (*entos hymōn estin*) (NIV). The basic meaning of *entos* is "within," "inside," being the opposite of *ektos*, "without" (i.e., "outside"). This meaning is borne out by the entire Greek literary corpus including the papyri and Modern Greek. The attempt has sometimes been made to construe *entos hymōn* in the sense of "in your midst," "among you," "in your domain," "within your grasp," etc. in accordance with whether *hymōn* is interpreted of the Pharisees or of eventual followers of Jesus, in which case the *estin* ("is") is taken with future significance (i.e., "the kingdom of God will suddenly be among you," etc.).

An examination of the ancient Greek texts that have been appealed to for these meanings (e.g., Herodotus, Xenophon, Symmachus' translation of the OT, Papyri) shows that the meaning is regularly "within" and that the sense of "among" has been based on a few (sometimes obscure) instances in Aquila and Symmachus. On the other hand, P. Oxy 654, 16 (which is parallel to the *Gospel of Thomas*) has a saying similar to Luke's, where the meaning is unambiguously "the kingdom (of God) is within you." Luke's usage must be considered decisive. The sense of "among" occurs a good many times in Luke-Acts, but the expression is always *en (tōi) mesō hymōn*, never *entos*. The *entos hymōn* is the opposite of *meta paratēreseōs* ("with (apocalyptic?) signs that can be observed") with its amplification " 'Here it is' or 'There it is.' " Therefore any interpretation that fails to set *entos hymōn* in its intended contradistinction to *meta paratēreseōs* fails to do justice to Luke's intention. Jesus is here trying to discourage (apocalyptic) speculations and calculations based on observable signs (*see* Apocalyptic Teaching). "Within you," therefore, seems to be

Luke's way of expressing the inward nature and dynamic of the kingdom of God, rather than refer to any actual presence in or among the Pharisees.

In the Synoptics there does not seem to be a single kingdom of God saying which unequivocally demands to be taken in the present sense. The kingdom of God is presented either timelessly (notably in the parables), or as the object of proclamation, or in its demands (Mk 9 [10]x; Lk 17 [19]x; Mt 25 [31]x) or as something future from the standpoint of the utterance (Mk 5 [6]x; Lk 19 [21]x; Mt 19 [25]x; the figures in [ ] fitting either category).

4.4. The Kingdom in Jesus' Teaching. The Synoptics present Jesus from the start as charged with one message, compelling and irresistible, the message that the kingdom of God was at hand. The impression is that the eschaton has drawn near, the long-promised kingdom of God is about to appear, and the hour of decision has come. The kingdom of God is presented in two ways: (1) it forms the heart of Jesus' teaching and (2) it is confirmed by his mighty works (see e.g., Mt 4:23; 9:35). A third component is that the kingdom of God is inextricably connected with Jesus' person as Son of man (see 4.5. below).

4.4.1. The Conditions and Demands of the Kingdom. The first condition is to "repent and believe the gospel" (*see* Repentance; Mk 1:15; Mt 4:17). A childlike (*see* Children) faith is a presupposition for entering into the kingdom of God (Mt 18:3; Mk 10:14 par.). The gospel is the good news about the sovereignty of God. God's eschatological, salvific act demands an undivided heart (Mk 12:29-30 par.). Therefore, it is not lip service or even the use of Jesus' name in performing miracles, but the performance of God's will that opens the door to the kingdom of God (Mt 7:21-23). Nothing may stand in the way of the kingdom since no one who has put his hand on the plow and looks back is fit for the kingdom of God (Lk 9:62). The kingdom may demand the sacrifice of marriage and family (Mt 19:12) as well as of possessions (*see* Rich and Poor; Mk 10:21-27 par.). At the other end it holds the promise of repaying to a hundredfold (Mk 10:29-31 par.). The demand is radicalized still further when the would-be disciple is given the choice of either letting the tempting hand be cut off or the tempting eye plucked out for the kingdom of God, or keeping them and being cast into Gehenna (*see* Heaven and Hell; Mk 9:47 par.). The kingdom must be preferred to everything. All this illustrates the seriousness with which people must act with regard to the kingdom of God rather than superior moral attributes qualifying for entrance into it. In other words, they must seek to enter in by the narrow gate (Mt 7:13-14); in fact they must actively storm the kingdom (Mt 11:12).

4.4.2. The Ethics of the Kingdom. The ethics of the kingdom of God (*see* Ethics of Jesus) are the ethics that God expects from those who are set to do his will. The ethical demands are scattered throughout Jesus' teaching but occur in more concentrated form in the Sermon on the Mount (*see* Sermon on the Mount; Mt 5—7; cf. also Lk 6:17-49). Here we see a continuation with the ethical teaching of the OT, although Jesus' requirements go beyond it by penetrating behind the letter to the spirit and intent of it. In the end Jesus lifts up a performance motivated by pure love* and devotion to God and love to one's neighbor. Thus, for example, the commandments* "Do not murder," "Do not commit adultery," "Do not break your oath" are only partial and particular aspects of the greatest commandment of all, namely undivided love toward God and neighbor. Love is the fulfilling of all the commandments (cf. Mt 22:40), in fact the logical conclusion would seem to be that love makes commandments superfluous.

4.4.3. The Parables of the Kingdom. Jesus spoke about the kingdom of God also through the medium of parables (*see* Parable). After centuries of allegorical interpretation of the parables (in which every detail was given a particular significance), A. Jülicher demonstrated that the parables had one essential point, the other details being the necessary trappings of the story. (Jülicher's principle should not be applied rigidly as there are occasions when more than one point may have been intended.)

The parables of the kingdom have been regarded as the most authentic element in Jesus' teaching (*see* Form Criticism) and occur in concentrated collections in Mark 4 and Matthew 13. These parables illustrate different aspects of the kingdom of God: people's response to the message of the kingdom of God (the sower, Mk 4:3-9; Mt 13:3-9), the unobtrusive character of the kingdom of God as contrasted with the apocalyptic expectation of upheaval (the seed growing quietly, Mk 4:26-29), the immense growth of the kingdom from an insignificant beginning (the mustard-seed, Mk 4:30-32; Mt 13:31-32, and the leaven, Mt 13:33), the mixed nature of those presently involved in the kingdom of God, who will be separated at the end (the weeds, Mt 13:24-30, with its probably later allegorical interpretation, Mt 13:36-43, and in all probability the dragnet, Mt 13:47-50) and the inestimable value of the kingdom of God, for which people must be prepared to give up everything (the treasure and the pearl, Mt 13:44-46)

Jesus' use of parables raises the question of their purpose or function. Matthew has the disciples raise the question (Mt 13:10). Jesus' answer, "to you it is given to learn the mysteries of the kingdom of Heaven, but to those it is not given" (Mt 13:11), has given rise to many interpretations. The point of the explanation seems to be that, having rejected the message of Jesus when exposed to it, these "outsiders" (Mk 4:10) have willfully chosen to keep their eyes shut and their hearts hardened, that the continued message is now given in the form of half-revealing, half-concealing parables. But though the interpretation—and therewith the precise meaning—is denied to them, they still perceive their gist sufficiently well (cf. Mk 12:12 par.: "they knew he had spoken the parable against them"). It is not therefore an exaggeration to say that sometimes the parables have a polemical tone in addition to their usage to illustrate the kingdom of God.

4.5. The Kingdom of God and the Son of Man. The kingdom of God should not be dissociated from the Son of man, who in Jesus' teaching, as in Daniel, is its agent. The destiny of the Son of man is therefore directly connected with the coming of the kingdom of God. The present activity of the Son of man, especially his casting-out of demons, is an integral part of the proclamation of the kingdom of God, but they should be seen not so much as indicating the actual occurrence of the decisive event of the kingdom of God, but as the preliminary warfare of the Son of man against the evil powers in his work of making possible the entrance of the kingdom of God in human history. This warfare, the Son of man's attacks on the kingdom of evil, ought not to be construed in terms of the Hellenistic or Jewish exorcist's activity, but rather be connected with the Son of man's mission to "serve and to give his life a ransom for many" (Mk 10:45 par.), otherwise the link between the kingdom of God and the cross becomes illegitimately obscured.

We would thus submit that it was the near prospect of a violent death (*see* Death of Jesus), to which Jesus attributed atoning significance (*see* Ransom Saying), that led him to change the *ēngiken* to *ephthasen* and thus characterize the coming of the kingdom of God as unprecedentedly certain and imminent. Viewed from this perspective, though the kingdom of God had come nearer than in the *ēngiken* type of sayings, it had not arrived, as the last pre-passion occurrence(s) of kingdom of God in all three Synoptics would seem to testify.

4.6. Potential Eschatology. By way of conclusion it may be said that during Jesus' ministry the kingdom of God is spoken of always as a future event. It is expected, hoped for and prayed for. But it is never said explicitly to have arrived, not even at the Last

Supper (*see* Last Supper). What is present is the agent of the kingdom of God, Jesus. But because the agent of the kingdom of God is present and active through his teaching and mighty works, the kingdom of God may also be said to be potentially present. However, the decisive event for its coming, that is, for the release of its powers in salvific blessings, still lies ahead.

The term *potential* does not qualify the term "kingdom of God," but only the term "present in Jesus." Thus, it should not be construed as in any way implying uncertainty as to the kingdom's coming. *Potential* simply means that the kingdom of God in Jesus' ministry is not present in any absolute or independent sense but only in so far as it is represented by Jesus. Its arrival and presence in its own right is depicted as a future event. Thus if we are to speak of eschatology in connection with the kingdom of God during Jesus' earthly ministry at all, then it is more accurate to speak of *potential eschatology*. This is an eschatology that has not yet begun to unfold itself in final, catastrophic events, but the eschaton is, nevertheless, in principle present in Jesus, because he, as Son of man, is the agent of the kingdom of God. Nonetheless, the ministry of Jesus and his teaching look forward to the awful and more immediate event of the cross, the event in which the Son of man fulfills his God-given mission for the arrival of the kingdom of God.

4.7. The Consummation. But even this decisive event (the cross-resurrection complex) does not exhaust the entire content or expectation of the promise. It seems to be the key event that makes possible the arrival of the kingdom of God in time, but also in principle its full manifestation and consummation which lies at the end of history (see Ladd 1966, 307-28). In this regard the concept of the kingdom of God is parallel with the Johannine concept of eternal life (*see* Life) and the Pauline concept of salvation. Precisely as those who put their faith in the atoning work of Christ are said to possess eternal life, to be in Christ or to be saved, in spite of the fact that eternal life or salvation (*see* Salvation) are essentially eschatological concepts, so also believers may be said to have entered into the kingdom of God despite the fact that the kingdom of God, like eternal life and salvation, can be properly experienced only at the end of time.

5. The Gospels.
The Synoptic Gospels contain 76 different kingdom sayings, or 103, including the parallels:
(1) *Mark-Matthew-Luke* (Mk 4:11 par. Mt 13:11 and Lk 8:10; Mk 4:30 par. Mt 13:31 and Lk 13:18; Mk 9:1

par. Mt 16:28 and Lk 9:27; Mk 10:14 par. Mt 19:14 and Lk 18:16; Mk 10:15 par. Mt 18:3 and Lk 18:17; Mk 10:23 par. Mt 19:23 and Lk 18:24; Mk 10:25 par. Mt 19:24 and Lk 18:25; Mk 14:25 par. Mt 26:29 and Lk 22:18);

(2) *Mark-Matthew* (Mk 1:15 par. Mt 4:17);

(3) *Mark-Luke* (Mk 15:43 par. Lk 23:51);

(4) *Matthew-Luke* (Mt 5:3 par Lk 6:20; Mt 6:10 par. Lk 11:2; Mt 6:33 par. Lk 12:31; Mt 8:11 par. Lk 13:29; Mt 10:7 par. Lk 9:2; Mt 11:11 par. Lk 7:28; Mt 11:12 par. Lk 16:16; Mt 12:28 par. Lk 11:20; Mt 13:33 par. Lk 13:20);

(5) *Mark* (4:26; 9:47; 10:24; 12:34);

(6) *Matthew* (3:2; 4:23: 5:10, 19 [bis], 20; 7:21; 8:12; 9:35; 13:19, 24, 38, 41, 43, 44, 45, 47, 52; 16:19; 18:1, 4, 23; 19:12; 20:1, 21; 21:31, 43; 22:2; 23:13; 24:14; 25:1, 34);

(7) *Luke* (1:33; 4:43; 8:1; 9:11, 60, 62; 10:11; 12:32; 13:28; 14:15; 17:20-21; 18:29; 19:11; 21:31; 22:16, 29-30; 23:42);

In addition, Matthew has one more reference to "kingdom of God" (7:21) and one to "kingdom" (6:13) in part of the textual tradition. The Gospel data on the distribution of the various expressions is as follows:

	Mt	Mk	Lk	Jn
Kingdom of God	5	14	32	2
Kingdom of Heaven	32	—	—	—
Kingdom	13	—	7	3
Total	50	14	39	5

The Johannine sayings have no parallels in the Synoptics. The three expressions "Kingdom of God" (KG), "Kingdom of Heaven" (KH) and "Kingdom" (K) are distributed as follows:

time is fulfilled, and the kingdom of God is at hand; repent and believe the gospel" (1:15). The position of the statement within the structure of Mark indicates that the proclamation of the kingdom of God was at the heart of Jesus' preaching. The saying announces the fulfillment of the time for the arrival of the kingdom of God. The kingdom of God is still future, but has drawn near and already makes its demands for preparation to receive it: these are repentance and believing (*see* Faith) acceptance of the gospel. This saying does not give any clear indications whether "kingdom" refers to the national or to a more apocalyptic type of hope. The collocation of "repent" and "believe" might favor the second alternative, but even for the national hope Israel was expected to keep the Law* flawlessly for at least one day (see *b. Ta'an.* 64a).

In Mark 4 Jesus' parabolic teaching is concerned with the mystery of the kingdom of God which is given to the group of Jesus' inner disciples, while to the outsiders the kingdom of God is being conveyed in dark, unintelligible parables (4:11). The description of the kingdom of God as seed sown, shooting up and growing quietly (4:26) implies that the kingdom of God here is conceived neither in nationalistic terms of open revolt and warfare for liberation, nor in the style of apocalyptic upheavals. The emphasis in the similar idea expressed at 4:30 is on the contrast between the insignificant beginning and the immense growth of the kingdom of God.

In an isolated logion at 9:1 the kingdom of God is described as imminent, to occur within a generation or two. At 9:47 in the context of resisting various temptations, the importance of entering the kingdom of God at any price—even losing one's eye—is underlined, and entering the kingdom of God is compared to entering "life" (9:43-44).

Gospel	Total	Peculiar	Mt-Mk-Lk	Mt-Mk	Mt-Lk	Mk-Lk
Mt	50	32: 20 KH	8: 5 KH	1 KH	9: 6 KH	—
		2 KG	1 KG	—	2 KG	—
		10 K	2 K	—	1 K	—
Mk	14	4 KG	8 KG	1 KG	—	1 KG
Lk	39	21: 17 KG	8 KG	—	9: 7 KG	1 KG
		4 K	—	—	2 K	

5.1. Mark. Mark (*see* Mark, Gospel of) introduces the public ministry of Jesus with the summary statement that Jesus proclaimed the gospel of God saying, "The

According to 10:14 children should be allowed access to Jesus because the kingdom of God belongs to such as these. In fact the kingdom of God demands a childlike faith (10:15).

In the group of sayings at 10:23, 24 and 25, love of possessions is a hindrance to entering the kingdom of God, which demands the sacrifice of everything and implies being "saved" (10:26).

The scribe who recognized that the heart of Hebrew/Jewish religion lay in undivided devotion to God was told that he was not far from the kingdom of God (12:34). In the Last Supper (14:25) the kingdom of God is eschatological. In traditional Jewish imagery Jesus will feast with his own (*see* Table Fellowship). Finally, at 15:43 Joseph of Arimathea is described as awaiting the kingdom of God, presumably in the sense of the traditional hope of Israel.

5.2. Matthew. As implied above, Matthew (*see* Matthew, Gospel of) offers a richer and more nuanced picture of Jesus' teaching on the kingdom of God than Mark. For in addition to his nine Markan and his nine Q* sayings, he has another thirty-two sayings peculiar to himself.

At the very outset of his Gospel Matthew describes the preaching of John as being one of repentance in view of the nearness of the kingdom of Heaven (3:2). The wording—probably stylized by Matthew to bring out the continuity—is placed on Jesus' lips by way of a summary of his proclamation from the time of John's arrest onwards (4:17). The summary character of Jesus' preaching is repeated at 4:23 (and again at 9:35) along with the information that Jesus' preaching was accompanied by healing. The same emphasis occurs in the mission of the Twelve (10:5-8).

The kingdom of God figures at the first and last beatitude (5:3, 10), thus framing the collection of Beatitudes (an inclusio) and suggesting that they must be understood within its thought-compass (note: *autōn estin* ["theirs is"] occurs only in these two beatitudes. The beatitude of 5:11 is in different form [second person]). Humility and righteous suffering are necessary presuppositions for possessing the kingdom.

The three logia at 5:19-20 teach that even the least commandments affect people's relation to the kingdom of God and that scribal or Pharisaic (i.e., Jewish) religiosity is insufficient for entrance into it. The centrality of the kingdom of God is seen also in the Lord's Prayer (*see* Prayer), where its future coming constitutes the first petition (6:10). Some textual witnesses end the Lord's Prayer with the mention of the kingdom. If this uncertain reading were original, it would imply that here too, as in the case of the Beatitudes, the prayer occurs within the frame of the kingdom of God.

The radicalism associated with the kingdom of God is underscored at 6:33 where the interests of the kingdom of God are to go before all other interests. The Sermon on the Mount actually closes by emphasizing that entrance into the kingdom of God will depend not on mere lip-service, but on a faithful performance of God's will (7:21). Indeed, not only will there be a distinction among the Jews as far as entering into the kingdom of God is concerned, but with faith rather than descent as a condition the door to it will be opened to many Gentiles, while many of the "children of the kingdom" (i.e., physical descendants of the Patriarchs) will be excluded (8:11-12; 21:43; 22:2).

In a dispute concerning John, Jesus declares him to be the greatest of those born, but still lesser than the least in the kingdom of Heaven (11:11), the kingdom being pictured as the final eschatological reality. John's crucial role in salvation history is underscored by the statement that his day marks a new period in the realization of the kingdom. From his time on the kingdom of God is proclaimed and is being stormed by those who are eager to get in. His coming has given the signal that the kingdom of God has now drawn near and people can prepare themselves by repentance and baptism (11:12). From 21:31 we understand that those most eager to enter the kingdom of God are precisely the ones considered furthest from it. The imminence of the kingdom of God is expressed in unprecedentedly strong terms at 12:28, where Jesus' miracles, wrought by the Spirit of God, are interpreted as a sign of it.

The chapter on the parables of the kingdom contains no less than twelve kingdom logia (see 4.4.3. above). The point made in 16:19, where Peter is given the keys of the kingdom, is probably in polemic against the Jewish dispensers of God's truth, who according to 23:13 not only would not enter the kingdom themselves, but also closed the door to those who wanted to enter. The logion is often understood as the Christian counterpart to the Jewish way of speaking of authority in teaching as binding and loosing.

Matthew ascribes a kingdom to the Son of man (16:28; 20:21), which is thought of as being future. The disciples' questions as to who is greatest in the kingdom of Heaven (18:1) elicits from Jesus the statement that a condition for entering into the kingdom and being greatest in it is childlike faith and humility (18:3-4). In fact the kingdom belongs to such (19:14).

The kingdom of God illustrates God's forgiveness (*see* Forgiveness of Sins) and demands a spirit of forgiveness from those who would enter it (18:23). It may demand abstention from marriage (19:12), and it certainly demands being taken seriously and loved more than possessions (19:23-24).

The rewards of the kingdom are apportioned by different principles. Personal achievement is of little importance. In God's evaluation scheme the last can become first and the first last (20:1).

In the Olivet discourse the kingdom of God is presented in future, apocalyptic terms. Those who persevere faithfully to the end will be saved. But the end will not come until the gospel of the kingdom has been proclaimed throughout the world. The parable of the ten virgins (25:1) was intended to teach perseverance and watchfulness. This finds its fitting sequel in the great judgment, when the Son of man invites the faithful to inherit the kingdom which had been prepared for them from the time of the foundation of the world (25:34). The righteous are to go into its bliss, while the unjust are to go to everlasting torment. This picture bears the well-known features of apocalyptic thought.

The last occurrence of kingdom in Matthew is in connection with the Last Supper, when Jesus, looking forward to the eschatological feast in the Father's kingdom, promises to abstain from wine* until that day.

5.3. Luke. Luke's (*see* Luke, Gospel of) presentation of the kingdom of God is richer than Mark's but less nuanced than Matthew's, having no less than twenty-one sayings peculiar to himself.

The first mention of kingdom occurs at 1:33 and is put on the angel's lips, when he brought Mary the message of the birth of the Messiah who was to sit on the throne of his father David, reigning for ever as the definitive Messiah (*see* Birth of Jesus).

The first clear reference to kingdom in connection with Jesus' ministry occurs at 4:43, in which Jesus' mission consists of the proclamation of the kingdom of God. This gives the saying the character of a summary statement and implies that Jesus' previous ministry too was concerned with the kingdom of God. The same is repeated at 8:1.

In his Sermon on the Plain Luke has a logion similar to Matthew's first beatitude, but the saying is here directed to the poor rather than the humble (6:20). This is in line with Jesus' sermon in Nazareth (4:18) and Luke's sociological interests. Luke also has the saying on the least in the kingdom of God being greater than John (7:28). In interpreting the parable of the sower Luke too affirms that the knowledge of the mysteries of the kingdom of God are given to Jesus' disciples, but the rest must be content with unexplained parables (8:10).

Luke has both a mission of the Twelve and a mission of the Seventy-Two. The Twelve were to proclaim the kingdom of God (9:2), while the Seventy-Two were to proclaim that the kingdom had drawn near (10:9, 11). The preaching of both groups was to be accompanied by healing. And the crowds (*see* People, Crowd) that followed Jesus were instructed by him in the kingdom of God (9:11).

Luke connects the death of the Son of man with the coming of the kingdom of God and envisages the latter event as taking place within the lifetime of some who were present on the occasion (9:27). This indicates not only that the kingdom is thought of as future, but also that its coming is fairly imminent. The urgency of the kingdom makes it imperative that those who aspire to it do not let anything stand in the way—even the death of relatives (9:60)—but must devote themselves wholly to it, never looking back (9:62).

As in Matthew the coming of the kingdom figures prominently in the prayer Jesus taught his disciples (11:2). In the Beelzebul controversy Jesus' works of power accomplished through the finger (Mt: "Spirit") of God are a strong indication of the imminence of the kingdom (11:20).

The concerns of the kingdom of God are to affect all attitudes toward life. Undue worry about worldly matters is to be laid aside and the interests of the kingdom to be given priority. Then God will see to it that all legitimate needs are supplied (12:31). Trust rather than fear is to characterize Jesus' followers since God has been pleased to give them the kingdom (13:18, 20). Like Matthew, Luke too makes it clear that entrance to the kingdom of God is not based on physical acquaintance with Jesus or physical descent, but it is based on accepting the conditions of the kingdom—entering through the narrow gate. This, while leaving out many descendants of Abraham,* Isaac and Jacob, will open the door for many Gentiles* to feast with the Patriarchs in the kingdom (13:28-29).

The comment made by an outsider as to the blessed state of those who feast in the kingdom of God (14:15) leads to the parable of the great banquet, in which, with a view to the Jewish rejection of Jesus and his message, the point is made that those called first were not worthy and were replaced by the sordid mob of Gentiles. Luke does not record the incident of the man who had no wedding gown.

Luke too considers John's ministry as the beginning of a new era distinguished from that of the Law and the Prophets. It is the era of the proclamation of the kingdom of God when everyone has the chance to force their way into it (16:16). This shows that Luke does not share the apocalyptic view of the kingdom of God as being introduced suddenly following great eschatological upheavals. The subject is broached by the Pharisees. The answer is that the kingdom does not come in a way open to physical observation (17:20). No one will be able to point to it as being here or there. The kingdom of God is "within you" (17:21; see 4.3.2. above). The view of the kingdom advocated here is one in which God is at work quietly in those who have accepted his claims and faithfully take on them the yoke of his will.

The kingdom of God must be accepted in childlike trust (18:16-17). On the other hand, those who put their trust in their riches will not be able to enter into it (18:24-25). But to those who forsake everything for the kingdom of God a rich reward is promised, not only in the life to come, but even in this world (18:29-30).

By relating the parable of the pounds, Luke has Jesus correct the popular notion that the kingdom of God was about to break out in the apocalyptic way (19:11). The point is that Jesus' hearers had rather see to it that they administer faithfully what was entrusted to them and wait quietly for its full realization than speculate on the time of its full arrival. Luke generally discourages such speculation (cf. Acts 1:6-8). Even in the prediction of the destruction of Jerusalem, only general signs are given for the arrival in power of God's kingdom (21:31). It is obvious that Luke thinks of the kingdom of God as something that in a way has drawn near, so that from John's time onward people can prepare for it and be actively engaged in it, while in its full power it is something future, promised to appear after the fulfillment of certain events. Thus the apocalyptic element is not altogether absent from Luke.

That the kingdom can be spoken of as a future event is confirmed by the Last Supper, where Jesus promises to abstain from further eating and drinking until he can do so in the kingdom of God (22:16, 18).

Occasionally the kingdom is ascribed to Jesus as given to him by the Father (22:29-30). The context is again eschatological.

Finally, the thief on the cross asks to be remembered by Jesus when the latter comes in his kingdom (23:42), and Joseph of Arimathea is described as a man waiting for the kingdom of God (23:51), though it is by no means easy to decide whether his expectation was for a mundane or a transcendental kingdom.

5.4. John. The kingdom of God plays no significant role in John's Gospel (*see* John, Gospel of), its place being taken by the typically Johannine concept of "eternal life" (seventeen times) or simply "life" (nineteen times; *see* Life). The equivalence of eternal life with kingdom of God is proved from the occasional interchange of the two terms in the Synoptics (Mk

9:43-47 par.; 10:17-30 par.; Mt 25:31-46) and has its roots in rabbinic tradition (see Dalman, 116-17, 156-58). John's avoidance of the term "kingdom of God" may be owing to his desire to avoid association with current apocalyptic hopes. It may also be due to his writing for non-Jewish readers to whom a typically Jewish conception might pose communication problems, and especially because the term had been in rather rare use in the church, where the emphasis had been laid on Christ's person and work (christology and soteriology) as well as on the church (ecclesiology).

The concept kingdom of God occurs twice in the Nicodemus story and the expression "my kingdom" occurs three times in Jesus' answer to Pilate (*see* Pontius Pilate). In the Nicodemus incident no indication is given that the kingdom of God had been the main emphasis in Jesus' teaching or even a subject of discussion. But with Nathanael's confession, "Rabbi . . . you are the king of Israel!" (1:49), the reader is, however, not totally unprepared.

At John 3:3, 5 Jesus tells Nicodemus that spiritual regeneration is the condition to seeing or entering the kingdom of God. From this it becomes obvious that the idea bears no relation to the Jewish national hope. It is the sovereignty of God under which people place themselves by accepting the message of Jesus in faith and undergoing a spiritual rebirth (*see* New Birth).

In Pilate's interrogation Jesus answers the question "Are you the king of Israel?" (18:33) by explaining that "my kingdom is not of this world" (18:36, "my kingdom" being repeated three times). No clearer statement than this could be made to show that the kingdom of which Jesus thought had very little relation to Israel's national expectation. This accusation, which stemmed from the Jews as well as from the *titulus* on the cross, indicates that in John's Gospel the rejection and condemnation of Jesus depended to a large extent on the Jews' disappointment by Jesus' refusal to accept the role of the national, political messiah (cf. also 6:15, 26).

6. The Kingdom of God and the Church Today.
Does the concept of the kingdom of God have any relevance for the present proclamation of the church? Here we are confronted with the kind of dilemma that led R. Bultmann to launch his controversial demythologization program.

In his proclamation of the kingdom of God Jesus was standing firmly on OT ground. At the same time he was proclaiming a subject that made every Jewish heart throb. Yet Jesus took this concept and transformed it from a narrow-minded nationalistic hope to a universal, spiritual order in which humankind could find the fulfillment of its ultimate desires for righteousness, justice, peace, happiness, freedom from sin and guilt, and a restored relationship to God—an order in which God was king. Given the fact that the basic human problem of sin and alienation from God is as true today as it ever has been, the message of the kingdom of God ought to have as great a relevance today as it ever had.

The kingdom of God need not be demythologized (*see* Myth). But it is instructive to note that the early church, addressing primarily Gentile converts, avoided using a term loaded with Jewish national or apocalyptic connotations which might introduce confusion, seeking instead other dynamic equivalents such as "eternal life" or "salvation" as more appropriate, though "kingdom of God" did not disappear entirely from its lips. The church continued to proclaim the legacy of its Master, but in dynamic forms. Every age has to find its own appropriate forms for expressing the ever-relevant message of Jesus on the kingdom of God. The forms may change but the essence remains.

See also APOCALYPTIC; APOCALYPTIC TEACHING; CHURCH; ESCHATOLOGY; ETHICS OF JESUS; GOSPEL [GOOD NEWS]; HEALING; HOLY SPIRIT; JUBILEE; LIFE; PARABLE; REVOLUTIONARY MOVEMENTS; SERMON ON THE MOUNT.

BIBLIOGRAPHY. D. C. Allison, *The End of the Ages Has Come: An Early Interpretation of the Passion and Resurrection of Jesus* (Philadelphia: Fortress, 1987); G. R. Beasley-Murray, *Jesus and the Future* (London: Macmillan, 1954); idem, *Jesus and the Kingdom of God* (Grand Rapids: Eerdmans, 1986); C. C. Caragounis, *The Son of Man* (WUNT 38; Tübingen: J. C. B. Mohr, 1986); idem, "Kingdom of God, Son of Man and Jesus' Self-understanding," *TynB* 40 (1989) 3-23; 40.2 (1989) 223-38; G. Dalman, *The Words of Jesus* (Edinburgh: T. & T. Clark, 1902); C. H. Dodd, *The Parables of the Kingdom* (rev. ed.; London: Collins 1961); R. H. Fuller, *The Mission and Achievement of Jesus* (SBT 12; Naperville, IL: Allenson, 1954); E. Grässer, *Das Problem der Parusieverzögerung in den synoptischen Evangelien und in der Apostelgeschichte* (BZNW nr. 22; Berlin, 1957); R. H. Hiers, *The Historical Jesus and the Kingdom of God* (Gainesville, FL: University of Florida, 1973); A. M. Hunter, *The Work and Words of Jesus* (rev. ed.; London: SCM, 1973); J. Jeremias, *The Parables of Jesus* (New York: Charles Scribner's, 1963); E. Jüngel, *Paulus und Jesus* (4th ed.; HUT; Tübingen: J. C. B. Mohr, 1972); W. G. Kümmel, *Promise and Fulfilment* (2d ed.; SBT 23; Naperville: Allenson, 1961); G. E. Ladd, *The Presence of the Future* (Grand Rapids: Eerdmans, 1974); G. Lundström, *The Kingdom of God in the Teaching of Jesus* (London: Oliver and Boyd, 1963); M. Pamment, "The Kingdom of Heaven according to the First Gospel," *NTS* 27 (1981) 211-32; N. Perrin, *The Kingdom of God in the Teaching of Jesus* (Philadelphia: Westminster, 1963); idem, *Jesus and the Language of the Kingdom* (Philadelphia: Fortress, 1976); H. Ridderbos, *The Coming of the Kingdom* (Philadelphia: Presbyterian and Reformed, 1962); K. L. Schmidt et al., "Βασιλεύς κτλ," *TDNT* I.564-93; R. Schnackenburg, *God's Rule and Kingdom* (New York: Herder and Herder, 1963); E. Schürer, *The History of the Jewish People in the Age of Jesus Christ (175 B.C.-A.D. 135)*, rev. and ed. G. Vermes et al. (3 vols.; Edinburgh: T. & T. Clark, 1973-87); A. Schweitzer, *The Quest of the Historical Jesus* (London: A. & C. Black, 1910); Str-B.; W. Willis, ed., *The Kingdom of God in 20th-Century Interpretation* (Peabody, MA: Hendrickson, 1987). C. C. Caragounis

L

"L" TRADITION

"L" can be defined broadly as the unique material in the Gospel of Luke. In German scholarship it is designated "S" (*Sondergut,* "special material"). The exact extent of L is debated, but its importance is seen by noting that it accounts for between one-third to one-half of Luke's Gospel. Opinion is divided as to whether L should be thought of as a lost written document; a collected body of oral and/or written traditions; if the infancy narratives (chapters 1 and 2) are a separate entity with their own prehistory, and as to the extent of Luke's creative contribution. Much of the distinctive content and theology of the Third Gospel is found in L.

According to the two-document hypothesis (*see* Synoptic Problem), Luke in compiling his Gospel drew heavily on Mark's Gospel. He followed Mark's order, except in the passion narrative,* and included most of his material. He then added Q* and L traditions to complete his work. As the L and Q material are most commonly found together, it has been suggested that there was an earlier edition of Luke's Gospel, "proto-Luke," to which the Markan material was later added. In modified form this hypothesis continues to find some supporters, but it has not been generally endorsed because the structure of the Third Gospel is taken over from Mark, and the non-Markan material appears to have been inserted into a Markan context rather than vice versa.

The case that the L tradition reflects a written document to which Luke added the infancy narratives (*see* Birth of Jesus), which had a separate history, was popularized earlier this century by B. H. Streeter in his classic case for the four-document hypothesis. He suggested that in the two years Luke was in Caesarea with Paul he collected information and took copious notes which he then collated to form L. In more recent times E. Schweizer has also argued that the L material bears witness to a written document taken over by Luke. As evidence he points out that (1) Luke claims to be drawing on written sources (Lk 1:1); (2) in many L passages a tension between the tradition

and its interpretation can be seen; and (3) the L passages exhibit a characteristic style reflecting the LXX.

The opposing view that L was a collection of oral traditions is not widely supported today, but it is given a fresh hearing in B. Reicke's recent attempt to redirect discussion about the Synoptic problem. It has often been suggested that various prominent people in the early church, such as Mary the mother of Jesus, Philip the evangelist, Cleopas and others are the eyewitnesses to which Luke refers (Lk 1:1), and these people were his informants. Some of L may reflect diverse oral traditions, but because there are similar interests and themes in much of the L material a written collection of stories, sayings and parables* seems likely.

The infancy narratives are usually not included as part of L because in language and style they stand apart from the other special Lukan material. One widely held explanation for the differences is that in these chapters Luke has translated a Hebrew or Aramaic document. Recently Farris has provided new evidence to support this hypothesis. Others, however, maintain that here Luke has chosen simply to write in the style of the LXX, and that this explains the differences. On this view there is no reason to exclude the infancy narratives from what may be broadly called L.

But whether or not the infancy narratives are considered to be a part of L, there is today less confidence in arguing for discrete, lost sources—written or oral—than earlier. It is recognized that the special Lukan material is of a varied nature and thus possibly of varied origins. Source-critical work continues, but with the ascendancy of redaction criticism (*see* Redaction Criticism), the extent of Luke's creativity has become a major issue. It is clear that Luke felt free in editing his material to add introductions, change words and phrases and allocate contexts, and that he could compose material. Undisputed examples of composition would be the prologue (Lk 1:1-14), the historical settings (Lk 2:1-2; 3:1-3) and the summaries such as Luke 3:19-20. This can be accepted, but to argue that most if not all the distinctive Lukan material, including the birth narratives, basically represents the compositional work of Luke as Goulder does and others do in relation to particular sections of the Third Gospel, is not convincing.

It may not be possible to distinguish accurately between tradition and Lukan redaction or composition at many points in the Gospel, but a good case can be made for Luke's dependency on traditions other than Mark and Q. Several scholars (e.g., Rehkopf and Taylor) have sought to establish criteria (e.g., un-Lukan words or constructions, Semitisms etc.) to locate traditional material over against Lukan redaction for certain sections of the Third Gospel, notably the passion narrative, and Jeremias in his final published work, *Die Sprache des Lukasevangeliums*, follows this approach for the whole Gospel. He concludes that Luke extensively drew on distinctive source material; on the whole he was faithful to the traditions he received—especially when recording the words of Jesus—and in the passion narrative he had an independent, connected account in addition to Mark.

Another indicator that behind much of the L material there lies early tradition is the surprisingly large number of instances where John's Gospel and L share common stories or details, common geographical interests and common theological perspectives which are independent of the other two Gospels and sometimes stand over against them. For example, only in these two Gospels do we find mention of Lazarus,* Mary and Martha, the apostle Jude, the cutting off of the ear of the high priest's slave and certain details about Jesus' trial (*see* Trial of Jesus) and crucifixion (*see* Death of Jesus). A similar interest in Judea and Samaria is also evident and this suggests these traditions may have been first preserved in southern Palestine. If, as is generally held, John did not know Luke's Gospel and Luke did not know John's Gospel, then these parallels bear witness to the existence of independent Gospel traditions, probably in oral form, which both Evangelists drew upon (*see* Synoptics and John).

Much of the distinctive content and theology of the Third Gospel is found in L. There are fourteen unique parables including the good Samaritan (Lk 10:29-37), the prodigal son (Lk 15:11-32) and the Pharisee* and the tax collector (Lk 18:9-14; *see* Taxes); many positive stories about women,* such as Jesus' visit to the home of Mary and Martha (Lk 10:38-42), and the women at the cross who had followed Jesus from Galilee* (Lk 23:49; 8:1-3); a number of warnings about the deceit of riches (Lk 12:13-15, 16-21; 16:19-31; etc.; *see* Rich and Poor); an emphasis on prayer* (Lk 11:5-8; 18:2-8; etc.); extra teaching on the end time (Lk 12:54-56; 13:1-9; 17:20-21, 28-32; *see* Apocalyptic Teaching) and added accounts of Jesus' appearances after his resurrection* (Lk 24:13-49), the longest and most detailed being the one on the road to Emmaus (Lk 24:13-35).

See also "M" Tradition; Luke, Gospel According to; Synoptic Problem.

BIBLIOGRAPHY. S. Farris, *The Hymns of Luke's Infancy Narratives* (JSNTSup 9; Sheffield: JSOT, 1985); J. A. Fitzmyer, *The Gospel according to Luke*, 2 vols. (AB 28-28A; New York: Doubleday, 1981-85); M. Goulder, *Luke: A New Paradigm*, 2 vols. (JSNTSup 20; Sheffield: JSOT, 1989); J. Jeremias, *Die Sprache des Lukasevangeliums: Redaktion und Tradition in Nicht-Markusstoff des dritten Evangeliums* (MeyerK; Göttingen: Vandenhoeck & Ruprecht, 1980); I. H. Marshall, *Luke: Historian and Theologian* (enlarged ed.; Grand Rapids: Zondervan, 1979); F. Rehkopf, *Die Lukanische Sonderquelle: Ihr Umfang und Sprachgebrauch* (WUNT 5; Tübingen: J. C. B. Mohr, 1959); B. Reicke, *The Roots of the Synoptic Gospels* (Philadelphia: Fortress, 1986); E. Schweizer, *The Good News according to Luke* (Atlanta: John Knox, 1984); B. H. Streeter, *The Four Gospels: A Study of Origins* (London: Macmillan, 1924); V. Taylor, *Behind the Third Gospel: A Study of the Proto-Luke Hypothesis* (Oxford: Clarendon, 1926); idem, *The Passion Narrative of St. Luke* (SNTSMS 19; Cambridge: University Press, 1972).   K. Giles

LAMB OF GOD

The phrase "Lamb of God" is found in the NT only in the Gospel of John. There are two occurrences, the first in John 1:29 where John the Baptist (*see* John the Baptist) is reported as saying of Jesus: "Look, the Lamb of God (*ho amnos tou theou*), who takes away the sin of the world" and the second in John 1:36 where the first half of the saying is repeated.

The same word is used in Acts 8:32 where Jesus is compared with a sheep (*probaton*) led to the slaughter and a lamb that is silent before the shearer (citing Is 53:7; *see* Shepherd, Sheep). In 1 Peter 1:19 there is reference to redemption "with the precious blood of Christ [as of] a lamb without blemish or defect." Finally, in Revelation 5:6 Jesus is described as "a Lamb [*arnion*] looking as if it had been slain" (cf. Rev 7:14; 12:11). Scholars have had considerable difficulty in identifying the background of the ideas and hence the significance which would have been conveyed by this imagery to John's readers. We have to ask both what the statement means in the context of the Gospel in which it appears and also what it would have meant on the lips of the Baptist (assuming that it is an authentic saying). If John presents it as a saying of John the Baptist, he may well have envisaged a meaning which was credible on his lips; but it is also conceivable that John saw a fuller meaning which did not become apparent until later (cf. Jn 2:22; 11:49-52 for this kind of phenomenon).

The word *amnos* is used some seventy-five times in the LXX, mostly with reference to the lamb sacrificed in the ritual of the burnt offering, which was a daily gift offering "to make atonement" (Lev 1:4). One possibility is, therefore, that the background to John's statement was the daily offering in the Temple* (Ex 29:38-46).

A second possibility is that the reference is to the lamb associated with the Passover offering (*see* Feasts). Jesus is identified with the Passover offering in 1 Corinthians 5:7, and this concept may be present at the Last Supper (*see* Last Supper) if it is right to see Jesus there as comparing himself to the lamb (cf. also Jn 19:37). John stresses that it was at the time of the Passover that Jesus was executed (Jn 18:28; 19:14, 31). It is hardly a strong objection to this interpretation that the word used in the LXX is *arnion* rather than *amnos*. It is a more serious point that the Passover offering is said not to have been an expiatory offering (although it did have redemptive efficacy in delivering Israel from Egypt). However, L. Morris argues that all sacrifices were credited with expiatory power. He objects that the Passover animal was not known as "the lamb" but simply as "the Passover" (it could be a lamb or a goat).

A third possibility is that Jesus is being described in the language of Isaiah 57:7 (a similar but less likely allusion would be to Jer 11:19). In this chapter the lamb is used metaphorically to describe the Servant of Yahweh who bears sin (Is 53:11; *see* Servant of Yahweh), and Jesus is implicitly identified as the Servant in John 12:38 (Is 57:1). It is not a great step from the identification of the Servant as "my Servant" to the phrase "the Lamb of God."

A reference to the Servant has also been detected by scholars who argue that *amnos* here is a mistranslation of Aramaic *talyā'* which can mean both "lamb" and "servant"; in an authentic saying of John the meaning was "servant," but the church reinterpreted the word as "lamb." However, the linguistic arguments against this view seem convincing.

The lamb which was sacrificed in place of Isaac (Gen 22:8) has been adduced. In Judaism much was made of the "sacrifice" of Isaac, and it would be possible to regard the lamb as representing his sacrificial role.

Yet another possibility is that the imagery is that of the *arnion* in Revelation 5:6 which is traced back to the messianic leader of God's people who is depicted as the ram which leads the flock in *1 Enoch* 90. In *Testament of Joseph* 19:8-11 and *Testament of Benjamin* 3:8 the actual phrase "lamb of God" appears. The latter text says that there "will arise the lamb of God who will take away the sin of the world" (but the text is probably interpolated). In the time of the anointed priest (or priestly Messiah) "sin shall come to an end" (*T. Levi* 18).

With this variety of possibilities before us a certain feeling of confusion may arise. L. Morris finds it difficult to decide that any specific one of these interpretations is correct and finally concludes that the reference "awakens memories of more sacrifices than one." Probably it is best to see the origin of the idea in the concept of the strong ram as a messianic image, but to this have been linked the concepts of the Passover sacrifice and the Servant of Yahweh.

There remains the question: how is "takes away sin" to be interpreted? This phrase (which also occurs in 1 Jn 3:5 and, using *anapherō* in Heb 9:28 and in 1 Pet 2:24 of Jesus as the Servant) can be interpreted in two ways. First, "to bear sin" can mean to remove it by making expiation for it (Lev 10:17 of the sin offering; 1 Sam 15:25; 25:28). Second, it can mean to remove sin by bearing the penalty attaching to it on behalf of others (cf. Num 14:33-34; Is 53:12; Ezek 18:19-20). J. Jeremias has argued that originally the text referred to the Servant of God and hence to "the representative bearing of the punishment of sin," but that the Evangelist took it to refer to "the setting aside of sin by the expiatory power of the death of Jesus . . . by the atoning power of His blood" (*TDNT* I.186). But these two explanations may come down to the same thing in this passage. Another possibility is "to abolish sin" (cf. 1 Macc 3:29 for the verb and *T. Levi* 18:9 for the idea), a concept which C. H. Dodd finds to be credible on the lips of the Baptist.

The description of Jesus as the Lamb of God belongs to the language of sacrifice which is no longer common currency today. The concept of guilt for offenses committed remains current (although there is a tendency to confuse feelings of guilt with the objective state of guilt) and with it the consciousness that guilt can be removed only by some act of restitution or evidence of penitence or payment of a penalty. Against this background it is possible to understand the biblical concept of guilt over against God— whether in terms of disobedience to divine law or, at a more profound level, in terms of flouting and wounding his love.* In this situation reconciliation is possible only if there is a willingness on both sides to repair the relationship. This is done on God's side by his provision—in the Lamb of God—of evidence of his willingness to forgive (*see* Forgiveness of Sins), and on the human side by an appropriate offering. The wonder of the gospel* is that God himself provides the offering which humankind itself cannot provide.

See also RANSOM SAYING; SERVANT OF YAHWEH; SHEPHERD, SHEEP.

BIBLIOGRAPHY. G. R. Beasley-Murray, *John* (WBC 36; Waco, TX: Word, 1987); R. E. Brown, *The Gospel According to John (I-XII)* (AB 29A; Garden City, NY: Doubleday, 1966); C. H. Dodd, *The Interpretation of the Fourth Gospel* (Cambridge: University Press, 1953); *Historical Tradition in the Fourth Gospel* (Cambridge: University Press, 1963); J. Jeremias, "αἴρω, ἐπαίρω," *TDNT* I.185-86, 338-41; idem, "πάσχα," *TDNT* V.896-904; K. Weiss, "ἀναφέρω," *TDNT* IX.60-61; L. Morris, *The Apostolic Preaching of the Cross* (3d ed.; Grand Rapids: Eerdmans, 1965); J. C. O'Neill, "The Lamb of God in the *Testaments of the Twelve Patriarchs*," *JSNT* 2 (1979) 2-30.   I. H. Marshall

LANGUAGES OF PALESTINE

1. Introduction
2. The Languages of Palestine, 200 B.C.-A.D. 135
3. The Languages of Jesus
4. Semitic Sources for the Gospels

1. Introduction.

Which languages Jesus may have spoken, whether Semitic sources underlie portions of the Gospels and which languages were in use among Palestinian Jews in the first century—these are three related but distinct questions. It cannot simply be assumed, for example, that Jesus taught in every language which the Jews of Palestine might have used or that his teaching was written down in the same dialect, or even in the same language, in which he gave it. Thus these three questions require separate treatment. Yet an understanding of the language usage of Palestinian Jews is a prerequisite to the treatment of the other two questions; discussion of these related matters must therefore begin there. Once the evidence has been amassed, all three are best approached using a framework provided by sociolinguistic categories.

1.1. Method and Terminology. Sociolinguistics is a branch of modern linguistics which studies the interrelationships between society or social groups and language. Sociolinguistic studies have shown, for example, that it is important to differentiate between social classes in describing the language usage of a given society. Noteworthy differences often exist in

this regard between the upper and lower classes, especially in a bilingual or multilingual society such as ancient Palestine. Related work on dialect geography has focused attention on the differences and similarities which characterize various localities within a linguistic community. As ancient Palestine was subdivided into numerous geographical regions, such as Galilee* and Judea, these studies highlight the illegitimacy of simply applying the evidence derived from one such region to another.

Sociolinguistics has also led to the recognition of what is called "code switching"—the use of different levels or forms of the same language depending on certain variables within a given communicative situation. An extreme form of this phenomenon, known as "diglossia," is important for the understanding of ancient Palestine. The term refers to a situation in which a classical form of a language (designated as the "high," or H, form) exists alongside another form or forms of the same language (the "low," or L); each has a distinct role to play. The H form is not normally spoken; it derives from a highly esteemed literature written at an earlier stage of the language, is substantially different both in grammar and lexicon from the L variety, and must be learned by formal study. No one learns it at their mother's knee. In modern times Greek, the written forms of which harken back to Attic literature, and Arabic, whose speakers regard the language of the Koran as the only proper vehicle for many situations, provide excellent examples of this phenomenon.

1.2. Problems and Limitations. Unfortunately, the nature of the linguistic evidence from ancient Palestine makes a complete linguistic analysis impossible. The best one can hope for is an approximation of the facts. Many factors contribute to this difficulty. For example, in understanding a linguistic community it is essential to distinguish between spoken and written forms of language, but by definition the spoken language was rarely written down; even more rarely have any such materials survived into the present. Again, the linguistic situation in Palestine must have changed during the period of this inquiry (roughly 200 B.C. to 135 A.D.), but the evidence is not equally distributed within that period. What survives is random and spotty, and the changes are correspondingly difficult to trace. One must therefore draw appropriately tentative conclusions.

Given modern analogies, it is likely that Palestine in Jesus' day was a welter of dialects and languages, many of which have left no written record at all. Certain other languages which have left some record—for example, Latin and Nabatean—were certainly in use among small numbers of Jews (and larger numbers of Gentiles) in first-century Palestine. But as these languages are not central to the present discussion they shall be left to one side. In what follows the focus will be on evidence for the types and varieties of use of Hebrew, Aramaic and Greek.

2. The Languages of Palestine, 200 B.C.-A.D. 135

2.1. Hebrew. At the time of Jesus Hebrew was the language which had been in use among the Jews of Palestine for the longest time. Yet the Hebrew Bible never refers to the language by that name, but calls it instead either "the language of Canaan" or "Judean."

2.1.1. History of Use Prior to 200 B.C. Based on the former designation it is probable that when Israel came into existence at the end of the second millennium B.C., they spoke various Northwest Semitic dialects which they found the Canaanite inhabitants speaking. From biblical and inscriptional evidence it is clear that there were several distinct dialects in use among the Israelites, and that in particular linguistic differences existed between the south (Judah) and the north (Israel). At the time of the United Monarchy, if analogies with other areas of the ancient Near East hold true, a particular form of the language was enshrined as the official form, to be used in writing of narrative literature and court documents and to be taught as the standard to all scribes. Presumably the type of Hebrew chosen to play this role was that spoken about the year 950 B.C. in the capital, Jerusalem.

When, after the reign of Solomon, Judah and Israel formed separate polities, Jerusalemite Hebrew continued as the official language of the south. It is likely that the Hebrew of the northern capital, Samaria, came to function as its northern counterpart. Of that northern written standard, apart from relatively meager inscriptional evidence such as the Samaria ostraca, only traces may remain. These are perhaps preserved in biblical books such as Amos and Hosea. Those books, of which some form probably circulated in Israel, survived that nation's fall to Assyria in 722 B.C. only because they were borne to the south and copied in the capital of Judah, Jerusalem. At that point their language began to be assimilated to the southern dialect. Thus the southern written standard, dating from the time of David and Solomon (although with later orthographic modernization), essentially constitutes *Standard Biblical Hebrew* (SBH).

During the 350 years of pre-exilic history subsequent to the United Monarchy, the spoken forms of Hebrew in both the north and the south probably diverged more and more from the written official

languages. By the time of the destruction of Judah at the hands of Nebuchadnezzar in 587 B.C., spoken Hebrew in the south may have been substantially different from SBH. Some scholars have suggested that *Mishnaic Hebrew* (MH) represents a development from this spoken language of the late pre-exilic period.

With the return from exile following the decree of Cyrus in 538 B.C., the linguistic situation in Judah had changed. Not all of the people had gone into exile—only the elite, perhaps ten to twenty per cent of the population. These groups represented the linguistic standard-bearers, however, and in their absence SBH apparently languished; the peasants who remained in Judah during the exilic period spoke various dialects of Hebrew and, especially at the borders with the north and west, increasingly Aramaic. According to Nehemiah 13:24, Nehemiah had to contend with a situation in which, because of intermarriage with neighboring peoples, many of the Jews could not speak Hebrew—a situation he took steps to correct. Thus Hebrew began to be regarded from a nationalistic perspective; its use and survival were now connected with the survival of the Jews as a separate people.

The biblical books written during this period manifest a different form of the written language, known as *Late Biblical Hebrew* (LBH). The authors of these books varied in terms of their knowledge of their model—the earlier classical language—and in the degree to which their spoken idiom was allowed to intrude. Considerably more Aramaic influence is apparent, and so-called Mishnaisms (grammatical forms known from MH) begin to show up. The book of Ecclesiastes, for example, which reached its final form at any rate in the early Second Temple period, manifests many such linguistic peculiarities, which are most convincingly explained as examples of the L of fourth- to third-century Jerusalem. Stamp seals from this period, which read "Hezekiah the governor," show that although Imperial Aramaic was the *lingua franca* and served for many official purposes, the Jews continued to use Hebrew in connection with the government and Temple.* These stamps preferred the older paleo-Hebrew script to the Aramaic script which had generally usurped it. This fact underscores the nationalistic importance ascribed to Hebrew at a time when the Jews were no longer a sovereign nation.

2.1.2. Evidence of Use 200 B.C.-A.D. 135. Earlier scholarship used to argue that Hebrew had become a dead language after the exile, and that Aramaic was the spoken language of ordinary Jews. But this position, although still held by some scholars, is simplistic.

Moreover, as one approaches the turn of the second century B.C., it is contradicted by certain evidence. In fact, while LBH did continue as the written language for many purposes, the usual evidence for approaching language "death"—for example, vastly increased numbers of loan words, even for common expressions, and the loss of morphological integrity—is absent. On the contrary, different authors continued to shape the classical idiom to serve new needs, coining neologisms and developing a variety of types of this written language. Moreover, many of those works written in LBH contain inadvertent slips, precious evidence of the spoken language of the authors and scribes responsible for the forms in which we possess them. Not infrequently, this spoken language seems to have been Hebrew of a form different from LBH, and approaching MH.

The evidence for the Hebrew of the late-Second Temple period comes from a diversity of sources: literary, documentary, inscriptional and numismatic. Much of the literary evidence was unknown prior to the discovery in 1947-1956 of the manuscript-bearing caves near Qumran (*see* Dead Sea Scrolls). These caves contained approximately 800 manuscripts, many of them exceedingly fragmentary. The texts were inscribed in Aramaic and Greek as well as Hebrew, but the vast majority of them were in LBH of various types. Their authors varied widely in their command of written Hebrew. The person responsible for the *Songs of the Sabbath Sacrifices,* for example, wrote in what might be called a philosophical Hebrew analogous with philosophical Greek. The author of the *Temple Scroll,* on the other hand, was comparatively unimaginative and relied largely on a simplified vocabulary. The author of 4QTestimonia (or subsequent scribes) wrote a Hebrew massively affected by Aramaic, even at the level of morphology (usually the last area of a language to change through contact with another language). In addition to the Dead Sea Scrolls, literary texts originally written or preserved in LBH include Ben Sira (or Ecclesiasticus), 1 Maccabees and a substantial percentage of the apocryphal and pseudepigraphic literature produced in the three centuries between 200 B.C. and A.D. 135.

Apart from literary texts, the evidence for the use of Hebrew in this period is not substantial. At Masada finds dating from approximately the time of the First Revolt (A.D. 66-74) included jar labels attached to cultic materials, an ostracon used as a receipt reading "from Jerusalem," and numerous ostraca inscribed in the paleo-Hebrew script and serving unknown functions. From the time of the Second, or Bar Kokhba, Revolt (A.D. 132-135), in addition to the four caves of

Murabba'at, four caves in neighboring wadis yielded written materials. Among the latter, the "Cave of Letters" contained eight documents in Hebrew, consisting of three contracts from En Gedi (all by the same scribe) and five letters written to Bar Kokhba by his subordinates. Interestingly, all these were written not in LBH, but in MH. From the "Cave of Horrors" came a burial ostracon, "Saul son of Saul, peace." The other two manuscript-bearing caves of the Judean desert yielded a total of only two papyri (one a promissory note) and four ostraca used as receipts. These latter materials were so fragmentary that even the language is uncertain; they may be in either MH or Aramaic.

The finds from Murabba'at included six contracts, all in MH and all either undated or dating from the time of the revolt, and seven legible letters to Bar Kokhba in the same language (four other letters are very poorly preserved and may be, but are not certainly, written in that idiom). To these documentary finds one can add a few inscriptions from the immediate environs of Jerusalem. Two are sepulchral inscriptions: the famous Bene Ḥezir inscription on a tomb containing at least six first-century high priests of the family of Boethus, and a recently excavated find reading, "belonging to the house of David." Both are written in MH rather than LBH. Another recent discovery, the so-called Trumpet inscription, evidently comes from the southwest corner of the Herodian Temple and indicated the spot where a priest would stand to blow a trumpet to signal the beginning and end of the Sabbath.* Several Aramaic tomb inscriptions contain Hebrew titles for the deceased, such as "high priest" and "Nazirite."

Numismatic evidence consists of Hasmonean coinage, beginning apparently with John Hyrcanus I (134-104 B.C.) and running down to the time of Mattathias Antigonus (40-37 B.C.). Herod and the Romans adorned their coins only with Greek inscriptions, but at the time of both the First and Second Revolts the Jews once again minted coins with Hebrew mottos. All the Hebrew coinage of the period used the paleo-Hebrew script rather than the ordinary square script.

2.1.3. Sociolinguistic Analysis. The Hebrew materials for the time of Jesus point to a situation of diglossia. The H form of Hebrew was LBH, while the L forms were varieties of MH. In addition to contracts and letters, two texts from the Dead Sea Scrolls, 4QMMT and the *Copper Scroll,* are written in varieties of L. 4QMMT is a halakic epistle, perhaps addressed to the Temple authorities, while the *Copper Scroll* is an economic document, listing some of the treasures of the Second Temple which were cached at the time of the Roman approach to Jerusalem in about 70 A.D.

Much of the LBH material—the literary texts—ultimately or proximately derives from Jerusalem. Their authors were learned people and therefore probably members of the upper classes. The Murabba'at contracts and their subscribers all come from Judean villages and, judging from the amounts of money they involved, also relate to the upper classes, such as village elders and propertied families. The sepulchers inscribed with Hebrew belonged, of course, to the wealthy, who alone could afford such eternal monuments. One can say, then, that upper-class people in Jerusalem could often read and write the H form of Hebrew, while many in outlying villages could at least understand the L form. The linguistic competence of the lower classes is not directly evidenced, but sociolinguistic analogy suggests that in the smaller villages many would have known an L form of Hebrew. In Jerusalem, on the other hand, it is likely that the situation was linguistically less conservative, and that L forms of Hebrew were not as widely known by the lower classes.

What type of Hebrew was used for what situation? Formal written materials and virtually all literary texts would utilize LBH, the H form. An L form would be spoken, especially in smaller villages, and be used for letters and, in certain circumstances, for ephemera such as contracts. It would also be used in halakic discussions, where the topic was sacred and the vocabulary of LBH insufficient. Matters connected with the Temple and national ideology required Hebrew, ordinarily but not entirely the H form. Thus during the Bar Kokhba revolt, for example, contracts were produced in Hebrew. That there was no continuous Hebrew tradition for such materials is suggested by the fact that the contracts follow precisely the Aramaic contract formulae, for which there was a continuous tradition dating back prior to the time of Nehemiah. Indeed, sometimes Aramaic formulae appear intact in the Hebrew contracts. Thus, as noted already, the use of written Hebrew often had nationalistic overtones at the time of Jesus. Otherwise, it had specifically religious overtones, although of course these two realms were not distinct in ancient times.

All of these comments apply, however, only to Judea, whence the evidence derives. Similar evidence for Galilee is entirely lacking. Two Hebrew inscriptions are known from that region, one from Kefar Biram and one from Dabbura, but these postdate the period of this inquiry by some two centuries. By that time Jewish settlement patterns had changed substantially. As a result of the Bar Kokhba revolt in particular, Judea was depopulated, and many Jews moved north to Galilee, bringing with them (for the first

generation or two at least) their linguistic habits. Thus these inscriptions say nothing about whether Hebrew was in widespread use there in the first century. The fact that the region came under Jewish control only after some centuries of government by Aramaic and Greek-speaking rulers suggests that Hebrew was much less well known in Galilee than it would have been in Judea. Educated Jews would presumably have acquired at least some knowledge of the H form, however, and halakic discussions there, as in Judea, may have required an L form of the language.

2.2. Aramaic.

2.2.1. History of Use Prior to 200 B.C. The widespread use of Aramaic in Palestine apparently began in the late-Assyrian period (c. 720 B.C.), when the language began to function as an international language of diplomacy. As there existed numerous different dialects of Aramaic within the broad expanse of Assyrian hegemony, a standardized form intelligible to all began to develop. This process led ultimately to Imperial Aramaic, the language of government during the Persian period (c. 538-332 B.C.). The Jews of Palestine were, of course, part of the Persian Empire, and thus the upper levels of their society acquired a functional knowledge of this *lingua franca*.

Alongside this standard written language, people in Palestine spoke different dialects of Aramaic, some of which took root beginning with the exchange of populations carried out in the Assyrian period. For example, the Assyrians resettled Aramaic speakers in Gaza and Samaria. With the passage of time Aramaic became the most widely spoken language in Syria and Palestine, and, presumably, among the Jews, with the possible exception of the Jews of Judea.

Thus by the time of Jesus there had come to be a standard written language, usually called *Standard Literary Aramaic* (SLA), and various spoken dialects. The differences between them do not appear to have been as marked as those which characterize diglossia. It is more accurate to say that the switch from written to spoken language was an example of code switching. Nevertheless, while the written language was probably broadly intelligible to native speakers of Aramaic dialects, it required education to read and, especially, to write SLA. The differences between spoken and written Aramaic may have been analogous to the differences between modern spoken English and the language of the King James Bible.

2.2.2. Evidence for Use 200 B.C.-A.D. 135. Evidence for the written dialect appears in the Dead Sea Scrolls. Although these were mainly written in Hebrew, substantial Aramaic material occurs as well. These texts include the *Genesis Apocryphon*, the *Prayer of Nabonidus*, the *New Jerusalem* text, portions of Enoch literature, a "pseudo-Daniel" cycle, Tobit and the *Testament of Levi*. Akin to this material is the language of the Aramaic contracts found at Murabba'at and in the Babatha archive. While contracts in the ancient Near East were sometimes produced in the spoken tongues, the long legal tradition behind the Aramaic contracts guaranteed the use of stereotyped antique phrases dating from about the same period as the formation of SLA.

Many of the sepulchral inscriptions around Jerusalem are in Aramaic. Such inscriptions are by nature rather formal, and thus invite the use of formal language quite different from that actually spoken, as exemplified by the common use of Latin in eighteenth-century British epitaphs. Contemporary Palestinian Greek inscriptions sometimes attempt meter, a characteristic of formal language. Yet the Aramaic inscriptions near Jerusalem are often inscribed in cursive rather than formal script, perhaps suggesting that a less formal attitude toward this linguistic situation may have characterized certain circles of ancient Palestinian Jewry. Probably some of these inscriptions are evidence for spoken forms of Aramaic, while others are intended as SLA. Other than these inscriptions, the best evidence for contemporary spoken Aramaic dialects comes from two sources: the Aramaic letters of Bar Kokhba, and the words and phrases preserved in the NT.

It has often been suggested that the targums* (Aramaic translations of the Bible, made first for the Torah, then later for the whole Hebrew Bible) may preserve the spoken speech for the period. In particular, some scholars have claimed that Targum Neofiti, although its manuscript is of medieval date, instances the spoken language of Galilee at the time of Jesus. This claim outruns the evidence; the language of Targum Neofiti is most directly comparable to that of the Samaritan Targum and Christian Palestinian Aramaic, both of which postdate our era by centuries. But some discussion of the problem of the targums is warranted in the present context.

First, there is no certain evidence for the use of targums in Jesus' day. True, among the Dead Sea Scrolls a targum to Job has turned up, but Job was not a part of the liturgical reading cycle of the period as far as is known. Further, Job is a notoriously difficult Hebrew book, so that even if one knew SBH quite well, Job would remain obscure and some help might be very welcome. Such is not the case with the books of the Torah. The other so-called targum found among the Scrolls is to the book of Leviticus, but it is so fragmentary that it is entirely uncertain that it really is a targum, as opposed to a portion from some quite

different liturgical work which happened to quote Leviticus. Second, any educated Jew of Jesus' day would have been educated precisely in SBH texts, starting with the Bible, and particularly the Torah.

Thus it is unclear why a translation into Aramaic would have been necessary, unless it was to serve the needs of the uneducated. Yet an example from modern day speakers of Arabic dialects, many of whom have never learned the vastly different H form, questions even this suggestion. Such people prefer to hear the Koran and accompanying sermon in the holy language and, through long attendance at religious services, acquire a basic understanding of what they hear without formal education. Third, references to translations of the Scripture readings into Aramaic in the Mishnah and Tosephta refer to *ad hoc* oral translations, quite a different matter from the literary works which we call the targums, and date to a later time and linguistic situation. Any Aramaic translation of the Bible dating from the time of Jesus would doubtless have been composed not in the oral language but in SLA; the best claim to such status belongs to Targum Onkelos (not Targum Neofiti). The most plausible explanation for the function of Aramaic targums, if such did exist in Jesus' day, is as interpretive devices. Having heard the Hebrew of the Scriptures read aloud, the audience would be informed of its meaning and application in Aramaic. Hebrew was not used because of the desire to avoid confusion between the words of the text and its interpretation.

Thus at Jesus' time literacy would have meant for most Jews first an ability to read SBH. Only after this level had been attained would some go on to study further, presumably to acquire, among other things, literacy in Aramaic (and sometimes Greek). What then is the explanation for the existence of literary works in SLA? Three possible explanations seem worthy of consideration. First, some of these works, such as Tobit, antedate the Hasmonean Revolt, at which time some evidence suggests Hebrew acquired renewed ideological status. Among the Dead Sea Scrolls is one Hebrew translation of Tobit, apparently executed in the light of the changed attitude toward the language proper for most religious literature. Further evidence for this change found among the Scrolls includes Hebrew translations of other originally Aramaic works: the *New Jerusalem* text, the *Book of Periods,* and the *Testament of Naphtali*. Second, it is noticeable that most of the Aramaic literary materials belong to certain genres: testamentary texts, some types of interpretive texts and what might be labeled vulgar or folk genres. In this last category one might classify zodiacal texts, such as 4QZodiac, or an unpublished Aramaic brontologion or 4QChronology, which explains the divisions of time into periods. In other words, the required language for a literary work may have been genre-specific. Ready analogies exist in contemporary Greek literature—epic required archaic Homeric Greek, dramatic choral portions required Doric Greek, etc. Third, some of these Aramaic works may have originated among, or have been intended for, diasporate Jewry to the east. There Hebrew was not well known, and a standard form of Aramaic would have been the natural choice for literary composition.

2.2.3. Sociolinguistic Analysis. In terms of geography and social class it would seem that Aramaic was the best-known and most widely used language among Jews of all classes in Galilee and in Judea also, at least in the larger urban areas. Its use in Judea was confined largely to speech and to ephemeral written materials such as letters, contracts and receipts. That Aramaic was usually the language of the marketplace in both regions is shown by several economic terms found in the Gospels (e.g., *batos,* a measure [Lk 16:6], and *mna,* a unit of currency [Lk 19:23]), content-identification tags inscribed or attached to storage jars, and ostraca used as receipts found in Jerusalem and in the caves of the Judean wilderness. Literary written works would use Aramaic only for certain genres or in limited communicative situations, such as writings intended for the Diaspora (here Josephus' *Jewish Wars* is a case in point—cf. *J.W.* 1.3.6). In such cases code switching was normal and SLA rather than spoken Aramaic was the chosen vehicle of expression.

2.3. Greek.

2.3.1. History of Use Prior to 200 B.C. The advance of Greek language and culture among the Jews of Palestine began in earnest with the conquest of the region by Alexander the Great in 332 B.C. (*see* Hellenism). Even before, Greeks had been among the mercenary soldiers fighting in the region from time to time, and substantial trade between Palestinian cities and Greece or Greek-speaking regions is evident from archeological remains. Thus the Jews of Palestine had long known of the Greeks and perhaps some of them had had reason to learn some Greek, but the real advance followed upon Alexander. Upon his death his conquests were divided among his leading generals, and Palestine fell to the lot of Ptolemy of Egypt. Although he and the Seleucids of Syria fought over Palestine for the entire third century, for nearly the whole of that period it remained under Egyptian jurisdiction.

The Ptolemaic administration of Palestine was involved in every detail of life. Bureaucrats were installed in every village and hamlet and, as the Zeno papyri of c. 250 B.C. indicate, this administration was conducted in Greek. Thus the upper levels of society, as well as some lower class people such as merchants, could hardly avoid at least a minimal competence in Greek. Many of the upper classes in particular acquired considerably more than that. The Seleucids, who followed the Ptolemies in ruling Palestine at the turn of the second century, also conducted their government in Greek, and thus the die was cast. For the majority of the period of this inquiry, government affairs were conducted in that language. Even when Hebrew was advanced for ideological reasons, as on the coins of the Hasmoneans, many of the same coins also bore Greek inscriptions. It is a safe assertion that at the time of Jesus most educated Palestinian Jews of the upper classes knew at least some Greek, especially in Jerusalem and the larger cities such as Tiberias (the home of Justus, author of a history of the First Revolt written in Greek).

2.3.2. Evidence for Use 200 B.C.-A.D. 135. The earliest inscriptional evidence for Greek in Palestine subsequent to Alexander is an ostracon of the year 277 B.C. from Khirbet el-Kom, in Idumean territory. This ostracon, a bilingual Aramaic and Greek record of a loan, shows that Greek loanwords had already begun to invade Aramaic, even for mundane concepts and matters for which perfectly good words already existed in Aramaic. The Greek loanwords of Daniel 3:5 are another approximately contemporary example of this phenomenon (although the date of the Aramaic portions of Daniel is debated). How quickly and how deeply Greek language and the ideas it presented penetrated even conservative circles of Judaism is illustrated by the book of *Jubilees.* Written in Hebrew about the time of the Maccabean revolt, the author of this book made use of Greek geographic literature. To do so required an advanced knowledge of Greek language and literature, since such texts were not dealt with in the Greek *paideia* until the student had already mastered Homer and the Attic poets, as well as more prosaic skills such as the proper technique for writing a letter. Since the author of *Jubilees* would certainly not have been among those Jews most enthusiastic for Greek ways, one must assume that in those circles the knowledge of Greek was generally at least as profound as was his.

In fact Palestinian Jewish authors began to compose in Greek. For example, Eupolemus wrote an apologetic history of the Jews in Greek, of which a few fragments have survived in the form of quotations in later Greek writers. 2 Maccabees was composed in Greek, as was

1 Esdras. Semitic works were also being translated into Greek. For example, thanks to its colophon we know that Esther was translated into Greek in Jerusalem in the year 114 B.C.

Greek was well known among the upper classes even in outlying areas of Judea. One of the signatories to an Aramaic contract from Murabba'at, for example, signed in Greek, indicating that he was more comfortable in that language than in Hebrew or Aramaic. Several Bar Kokhba letters were written in Greek. Perhaps the most dramatic proof of the knowledge of Greek in outlying areas is the scroll of the Minor Prophets from Naḥal Ḥever. The Jews who fled to those caves brought it along with them, obviously because they could read it, and not improbably because at least some of them could read it better than they could a Semitic version of the Scriptures. The handwriting of the text is inelegant and its spelling nonstandard. It may therefore not be a professional copy, but a personal copy written out by the man or woman to whom it belonged.

Epigraphic evidence for the Jewish knowledge and use of Greek in this period is substantial. In particular, ninety ossuary inscriptions dating between the second century B.C. and the second century A.D. are known from the vicinity of Jerusalem. Some of these show a spectacular lack of appositional case agreement. Since such ossuaries belonged only to the upper classes, it would therefore appear that in those circles the desire to show a knowledge of Greek often outstripped the knowledge itself. If so, it would not be remarkable; Greek, as the official language of the eastern Roman Empire, was everywhere in the East regarded as a prestige language. But the attitudes toward Greek among the Jews as a whole were complex and varied during the period under discussion, as two examples may demonstrate.

Josephus,* the famous Jewish traitor of the First Revolt, and the man who through his writings is responsible for much of our knowledge of the history of the time of Jesus, described his accomplishments in Greek at the end of his *Jewish Antiquities:*

> I have also labored strenuously to partake of the realm of Greek prose and poetry, after having gained a knowledge of Greek grammar, although the habitual use of my native tongue has prevented my attaining precision in the pronunciation. For our people do not favour those persons who have mastered the speech of many nations, or who adorn their style with smoothness of diction, because they consider that not only is such a skill common to ordinary freemen but that even slaves who so choose may acquire it. But they give credit

for wisdom to those alone who have an exact knowledge of the law and who are capable of interpreting the meaning of the Holy Scriptures. Consequently, although many have laboriously undertaken this training, scarcely two or three have succeeded. . . . (*Ant.* 20.263-66; translation by L. H. Feldman, Loeb Classical Library)

This statement is self-contradictory, of course, but it nevertheless affords some insight into the attitudes toward and accomplishments in Greek learning among the upper classes of Jerusalem, to which Josephus belonged. Josephus had opportunity to study Greek at a level well beyond the elementary. The ability to speak Greek, although not the ability to write the Atticizing Greek then coming into favor with Josephus' Roman readers, was common even among the lower classes of Jerusalem; hence it was not particularly well regarded. Really advanced study of the language, of the kind that required pilgrimage to one of the literary centers of the Greco-Roman world, was not attractive to many upper-class Jews. The reason was evidently a pride in their own cultural values and a consequent devaluation of those of the broader Greco-Roman civilization. This undertone of negativity toward Greek was doubtless the flip side of the nationalistic love of Hebrew, and is more clearly seen in one of the Greek letters from the Bar Kokhba period.

This letter, 5/6ḤevEp gr 1, was sent by one of Bar Kokhba's lieutenants to the administrators of En Gedi and discusses preparations for the upcoming festival of Booths. It reads:

> Soumaios to Jonathan son of Baianos and to Masabala, greetings; I already sent Agrippa to you. Make haste to send me . . . and citrons. And he [Agrippa] will transport these things back to the headquarters of the Jews. And be sure you do so! It was written in Greek because no one was found to write it in "Hebrew." Dismiss him very speedily in view of the festival. And be sure you do so! Soumaios. Farewell. (Author's translation)

Although this letter raises problems of grammar and interpretation, one point is clear: the author would have preferred to write it in a Semitic language, and only fell back on Greek as a last resort. Probably Hebrew would have been his first choice, but the Greek word rendered "Hebrew," *hebraisti,* can mean Aramaic as well, so based on the wording of the letter alone, one cannot be sure. But clearly he had a negative attitude toward the use of Greek and expected that his readers would also. Thus he felt constrained to apologize for using it. Equally striking is the fact that among these Jews it was more difficult to find persons able to write in Hebrew or Aramaic than in Greek. Presumably this fact does not mean that more of those Jews spoke Greek than either Semitic language, but rather that Semitic speakers had not received sufficient formal education to know how properly to write letters. Certain conventions existed, and in the Greek system of education at least, one did not learn this skill unless one advanced beyond elementary formal schooling. Apparently not many of Bar Kokhba's men had, and those who had and were available were trained in the Greek language. The letter is written in good Greek, as well—another evidence of the depth of Greek penetration into even nationalist circles of the Jews.

2.4. A Sociolinguistic Model. Having reached this point in the analysis, it is fitting to attempt to construct a sociolinguistic model to describe first-century language use and attitudes in Judea (see chart below). (As has become evident in this discussion, there is simply not sufficient evidence to attempt such for Galilee, although one can say that use and attitudes differed between the two regions [and, quite possibly, within Galilee, which was divided into two distinct cultures, Upper and Lower Galilee]).

This schematic lists the languages in the order of their frequency of use. As is clear, the linguistic situation of ancient Palestine was very complex—and this schematic does not include languages of lesser relevance such as Nabatean and Latin. It is thus no simple matter, turning to the question of the language or languages which Jesus spoke, to provide a confident and straightforward answer.

3. The Languages of Jesus.

In approximately thirty instances the Gospels include Semitic loanwords in the context of reporting Jesus' interaction with his contemporaries. Some of these instances record Hebrew words or expressions, usually in connection with specifically religious ideas—for example, *geennēs*, "Gehenna," from Hebrew *gê hinnōm*, the name of the valley to the south-southwest of Jerusalem which had, through its negative associations, come even within the Hebrew Bible to connote something like the Greek *hadēs (Mt 23:15). Another example of a Hebrew expression is rabbî,* "master" (Mt 23:7-8). But such Hebrew examples are few in number. Often even specifically religious terms such as "Passover" and "Sabbath" appear in the Greek text in

Judean Villages

A. Upper Classes
High form—Standard Biblical Hebrew for most genres
Standard Literary Aramaic, Greek for contracts, receipts
Spoken Aramaic for letters
Mishnaic Hebrew dialects for letters, contracts at times of nationalistic fervor
Low form—Mishnaic Hebrew/Aramaic, Greek

B. Lower Classes
High form—Mostly illiterate
Low form—Mishnaic Hebrew/Aramaic

Jerusalem

A. Upper Classes
High form—Standard Biblical Hebrew for most genres
Standard Literary Aramaic for a few genres and ossuary inscriptions
Spoken dialects of Mishnaic Hebrew and Aramaic for letters, contracts at certain times
Mishnaic Hebrew for written halakic discussions, temple record keeping
Greek
Low form—Aramaic, Greek

B. Lower Classes
High form-Mostly illiterate
Low form-Aramaic, Greek, Mishnaic Hebrew dialects

Aramaic form (e.g., Mk 14:14 and Mt 3:4). In the overwhelming majority of instances in which Jesus' reported words contain Semitic expressions, they are Aramaic. Many of these examples, however, involve only a single noun. More meaningful are those instances in which either verbs or verbal phrases are reported, for, given the multilingual environment of Palestine in Jesus' day, isolated substantives are not necessarily indicative of the language spoken. Aramaic words might appear, for example, in the course of a conversation conducted mainly in Hebrew or *vice versa;* such phenomena are commonly observed in the speech of modern bilinguals.

For this reason scholars attach great importance to the three instances in which the Gospels record Jesus speaking a verbal sentence. The first, at Mark 5:41, involves the healing of a young girl, in which Jesus says to her in Aramaic, *ṭalyᶜṭâ, qûm,* "Little girl, arise!" Apart from the fact that this is unambiguously an Aramaic sentence, it is noteworthy that the form of the verb is grammatically nonstandard—it appears to be a masculine singular imperative rather than a feminine singular imperative. A possible explanation is that the dialect Jesus spoke had replaced certain feminine forms with their masculine equivalents (a process known as suppletion). The significance of this observation is that in attempting to reconstruct Jesus' original words, it points away from the use of those Aramaic dialects which are in fact often used, SLA and the Aramaic of Targum Neofiti. Neither of these dialects regularly suppletes the feminine imperative, especially the singular (although similar suppletion does sometimes occur in both).

The other verbal sentences recorded as Jesus' direct speech are his "*Ephphatha,*" "Open!" addressed in Mark 7:34 to a deaf man he was healing, and his cry "My God, my God, why have you forsaken me?" recorded at Mark 15:34 and Matthew 27:46, spoken as Jesus was being crucified (*see* Death of Jesus). Both are problematic as to language. The first can be understood either as Hebrew *hippaṭēaḥ* or as Aramaic *'eppaṭaḥ.* If it is Aramaic, it would again be a nonstandard (i.e., L, not H) form, of a type attested in the Bar Kokhba letters, Samaritan Aramaic and Targum Neofiti. The problem with the words from the cross is textual. Within the textual tradition of the Greek NT, the phrase as reported runs the gamut from pure Aramaic to pure Hebrew, and the traditions of each Gospel have influenced those of the other. Thus it is impossible to be certain whether on these occasions Jesus spoke Hebrew or Aramaic.

As a result, based on Mark 5:41 one can only say that Jesus certainly spoke Aramaic on occasion. This much was to be expected on the basis of our knowledge of the dominant language among the Jews of Galilee. The question whether he also knew Hebrew and Greek can only be answered on theoretical grounds. To begin with Greek, it is recorded on several occasions that Jesus held conversations with people who could not be expected to know either Semitic language: on one occasion with a Roman commander and on another with Pontius Pilate (*see* Pontius Pilate). The texts do not mention translators, but one cannot for this reason conclude with certainty that none were present. The Gospel writers were not generally interested in reporting such apparently irrelevant details of Jesus' life. Theoretically, Jesus may well have known at least some Greek, for Nazareth was in Lower Galilee, an area in which there were many Greek-speaking Gentiles and in which numerous inscriptions in Greek have been discovered—although, unfortunately, not dated to the first century.

Luke reports that on one occasion Jesus was asked to give the weekly reading from the Prophets in the synagogue.* Since he stood and did so, reading from Isaiah (a rather difficult book in Hebrew), evidently Luke understood Jesus to know the H form of Hebrew. This portion of Luke is, however, problematic as to historical application. Raised as the son of an artisan, Jesus belonged to the lower classes, who were ordinarily illiterate in the ancient world. Judaism* put such an emphasis on the study of Scripture, however, even for the lower classes, that literacy among the Jews may have been substantially higher. It is also not unlikely that Jesus knew one or more dialects of L Hebrew, MH, even though such knowledge was probably much less common in Galilee than in Judea.

The reason for this suggestion is that the Gospels commonly depict Jesus engaging in halakic arguments with the Pharisees* and scribes.* If 4QMMT and the legal portions of another Dead Sea Scroll, the Damascus Covenant (not to mention later rabbinic literature), are any indication, such discussions apparently were at least sometimes conducted in MH. Since Jesus was thus, in sociological terms, competing for honor among the peasants against a prestige group of legal interpreters, it seems unlikely that he could have had any chance of victory if he could not speak the requisite dialect of Hebrew.

Therefore, one can conclude that Jesus certainly spoke a dialect of Aramaic, one which was somewhat different from any written form that has come down to us (although the degree of difference is, of course, unknown). According to indications from the Gospels, this dialect was different from that spoken in the south. Scholars have frequently suggested that the Galilean dialect differed from the Judean dialect of Aramaic principally in that the Galileans had ceased to distinguish between certain sounds, such as those represented by *'aleḇ* and *'ayin*, or *hē* and *ḥēṭ*. The basis for this suggestion is, however, suspect. The sources quoted as supporting authorities are later Talmudic texts which describe the situation subsequent to the Bar Kokhba revolt when, as noted, the Palestinian linguistic situation had changed substantially. Further, the Dead Sea Scrolls, most of which are certainly Judean products, manifest this same phenomenon of interchange of the guttural letters. Thus it cannot easily be argued that it was characteristic of Galilean speech in contradistinction to Judean. We simply do not know precisely how to characterize the Aramaic dialect which Jesus spoke, either regarding morphology or lexicon. One may also conclude, although without such good evidence as for Aramaic, that Jesus probably knew both the H and one or more L forms of Hebrew, and that he had at least a minimal competence in Greek.

4. Semitic Sources for the Gospels.

Since the late nineteenth century and the work of G. Dalman, scholars have argued for the existence of Aramaic sources for the Gospels, and even in extreme cases for Aramaic originals for the Gospels themselves. In the twentieth century they have invested a great deal of effort attempting to reconstruct the actual words of Jesus, usually based on retrotranslation from the Greek text back into one or another dialect of Aramaic. The foremost book in English which takes this approach is M. Black's *An Aramaic Approach to the Gospels and Acts*. The two assumptions motivating this research have thus been: (1) that Jesus would have spoken in Aramaic only, and (2) that his followers preserved some sort of sayings source which then was incorporated into the Gospels, then or earlier being translated into Greek. This survey of the languages of Palestine in Jesus' day has shown that the first assumption is simplistic, and in fact the second assumption is also dubious as it has been prosecuted. Furthermore, even if these two assumptions are correct, there is the problem of deciding what material provides the best witness to the type of Aramaic which Jesus would have spoken.

To deal with the last matter first, Dalman attempted to use the type of Aramaic found in Targum Onkelos, because he regarded that Targum as the only one sufficiently ancient. He knew that it was not precisely spoken Aramaic that he was dealing with, but he felt that nevertheless Onkelos was the best source. Other scholars have suggested Christian Palestinian Aramaic and Syriac, the latter with its occasional advocates even today. Most recently, however, the two most frequently advocated types of Aramaic have been that contained in the so-called Palestinian Targums, and prominently one text of this type, Neofiti, and the Aramaic of the Qumran texts. It is possible that both claims are to some degree correct, but probable that neither is entirely so.

If an Aramaic source for the Gospels were considered by its author and readers to be a literary text, at the time of Jesus it would have been written in SLA, as noted in the previous survey. Therefore, the Aramaic of Qumran (and earlier texts in that standard) would serve as a good source for morphology, vocabulary and idioms. If, however, the text were written in an L form of Aramaic—for which the only evidence nearly contemporary to Jesus is the Aramaic Bar Kokhba letters and, perhaps, some of the Aramaic ossuary inscriptions—and if, also, it were written in a Galilean dialect, the best witness might be Neofiti, in spite of its much later date, since there is simply nothing earlier from that region. If the author wrote in a Judean L form, of course, then the letters and ossuaries would be better models for the type of Aramaic used. And this latter option is by no means out of the question, since the early church was not centered in Galilee, but in Jerusalem. Just to underline the complexities of the question, neither Syriac nor Christian Palestinian Aramaic can be entirely ruled out as sources, especially for idioms. Some of the vocabulary found in the Qumran texts, for example, was not previously known from Aramaic texts in dialects used in Palestine, but has been elucidated by Syriac usage. And at least one idiom from the Aramaic Bar Kokhba texts is unknown anywhere else except in the much later Christian Palestinian Aramaic.

As to the assumption that Jesus' disciples memorized his words and passed them on orally to their followers, this is a model based on a misunderstanding of the nature of rabbinic literature. The model assumes that rabbinic claims for memorizing the words of one's teacher found therein are both accurate and can be generalized as characteristic of all earlier Judaism. Both assumptions are questionable, especially the latter. Even if the disciples did memorize at times, they may equally well have chosen to write Jesus' words down, not simply pass them on orally. Theirs was a relatively literate culture. And if they did so, there is good reason to believe that they would have used H forms of Jesus' language, even though while speaking he, of course, used the L form (*see* Teacher).

A modern analogy may illustrate. In Egypt today, where diglossia obtains between different forms of Arabic, a newspaper reporter may interview someone with the entire interview conducted in the L form of the language. When the interview appears in the paper, however, even the quotations will be changed into the H form—such is the nature of the linguistic attitudes at the heart of code switching. Thus in ancient Palestine, Jesus' Aramaic sayings, if they were such, might well come down in writing in an H form of the language rather than the actual L form in which they were spoken.

Of course, as the previous survey has shown, most religious writings were not inscribed in Aramaic at all. The chosen linguistic vehicle for such works in first-century Palestine was ordinarily LBH. If writing for other Palestinian Jews, the early church at Jerusalem would have been likely to write the earliest descriptions of Jesus' ministry, and to voice their claims about his Messianic significance, in that form of Hebrew—not Aramaic at all.

Thus, based on a sociolinguistic appraisal of the situation, it may well be that the efforts at reconstructing an Aramaic source or sources for the Gospels have been misdirected. Again, if such a written source were to contain something akin to the Sermon on the Mount (*see* Sermon on the Mount), which is basically a halakic discussion, indications are that this genre would take as its language MH. And, given the rather widespread knowledge and use of Greek in all levels of Palestinian Jewry, it may well be that no Semitic sources ever existed. The earliest tradition may have been in Greek all along, particularly if such written materials were intended to be read by Gentiles and/or outside of Palestine. In view of all the unproven assumptions and complexities involved with the question of Semitic sources behind the Gospels, it is no exaggeration to say that even after 150 years of scholarly effort, research is still at a very early stage.

See also JUDAISM; NAZARENE; TARGUMS; TRADITION CRITICISM.

BIBLIOGRAPHY. P. Benoit, J. T. Milik and R. de Vaux, *Les Grottes de Murabba'at* (DJD 2; Oxford: Clarendon, 1961); M. Black, *An Aramaic Approach to the Gospels and Acts* (3d ed.; Oxford: Clarendon, 1967); H. Birkeland, "The Language of Jesus," *Avhandlinger det Norske Videnskaps-Akademi* (1954) 1-40; F. Britto, *Diglossia: A Study of the Theory with Application to Tamil* (Washington, D.C.: Georgetown University, 1986); G. Dalman, *The Words of Jesus* (Edinburgh: T & T Clark, 1902); J. A. Fitzmyer and D. J. Harrington, *A Manual of Palestine Aramaic Texts* (Biblica et Orientalia 34; Rome: Biblical Institute, 1978); J. A. Fitzmyer, "The Languages of Palestine in the First Century A.D.," in J. A. Fitzmyer, *A Wandering Aramean: Collected Aramaic Essays* (Missoula: Scholars, 1979) 29-56; M. Hengel, *Judaism and Hellenism* (2 vols.; Philadelphia: Fortress, 1974); B. Lifshitz, "The Greek Documents from Naḥal Ṣe'elim and Naḥal Mishmar," *IEJ* 11 (1961) 53-62; G. Mussies, "Greek in Palestine and the Diaspora," in *The Jewish People in the First Century*, ed. S. Safrai and M. Stern (CRINT, Section One, vol. 2; Philadelphia: Fortress, 1976) 1040-64; A. Myer, *Jesu Muttersprache* (Leipzig: J. C. B. Mohr, 1896); Ch. Rabin, "Hebrew and Aramaic in the First Century," in *The Jewish People in the First Century*, ed. S. Safrai and M. Stern (CRINT, Section One, vol 2; Philadelphia: Fortress, 1976) 1007-39; Y. Yadin, "Expedition D," *IEJ* 11 (1961) 36-52; Y. Yadin, "Expedition D—The Cave of the Letters," *IEJ* 12 (1962) 227-57; Y. Yadin, "The Excavation of Masada—1963/64: Preliminary Report," *IEJ* 15 (1965) 1-120.

M. O. Wise

LAST SUPPER

1. Introduction
2. Historical Background
3. The Last Supper in the Context of Passover
4. The Four Words of the Last Supper
5. The Celebration of the Supper

1. Introduction.

In the history of the Christian church a number of different terms have been associated with the Last Supper. Some of these, such as the "breaking of bread" (Acts 2:42, 46; 20:7, 11); the "eucharist" (Mt 26:27; Mk 14:23; Lk 22:17, 19; 1 Cor 11:24); the "table of the Lord" (1 Cor 10:21); "communion" (1 Cor 10:16); and the "Lord's Supper" (1 Cor 11:20) stem from the NT. Others, such as the "mass" (from the Latin ending of the Roman rite—Ite, missa est—"Go, you are dismissed") and the "Last Supper," do not.

Within the NT there are a number of references and allusions to the Last Supper (1 Cor 10:1-22; 11:20-22; Lk 24:30; Acts 27:35; Mk 6:41; 8:6; Jn 6:25-59; 19:34; Acts 2:42, 46; 20:7, 11), but the most important are the four accounts in Matthew 26:26-29; Mark 14:22-25; Luke 22:15-20 and 1 Corinthians 11:23-26, the latter being the oldest written account. In Paul's first letter to the Corinthians, written sometime during the mid-fifties, he refers to a tradition which he received from the Lord.* By this he means that ultimately the tradition of the Last Supper comes from Jesus, but by his use of the terms *received* and *delivered* it is clear that he is referring to a tradition which he was taught by the church. (*Received* and *delivered* were technical terms used to described the passing on of oral tradition. Cf. Lk 1:2; 1 Cor 15:3.) Whether this tradition was "received" from the church in Antioch (Acts 11:26) in the mid-forties or from the church in Damascus (Acts 9:19; Gal 1:17) in the mid-thirties is uncertain. The Gospel accounts date most probably from A.D. 65-90.

The four accounts of the Last Supper fall into two distinct groups representing two specific forms of the tradition. These are Matthew 26:26-29/Mark 14:22-25 and Luke 22:15-20/1 Corinthians 11:23-26. The two forms may be characterized as follows:

Matthew/Mark	Luke/1 Corinthians
"blessed" bread	"gave thanks" bread
"Take"	[lack "Take"]
"this is my body"	"this is my body + which is . . . you"
[lack "This do in my remembrance"]	"This do in my remembrance"
"this"	"this cup"
"thanks" before cup	[lack "thanks" before cup]
reference to all drinking of the cup	[lack reference to all drinking of the cup]
"my blood of the covenant"	"new covenant in my blood"
"which is poured out for many"	Luke has "which is poured out for you" [not in 1 Cor]

The Lukan account is the most unusual of the four. It alone mentions the cup before the bread* (22:17) and has the word about the future kingdom (*see* Kingdom of God) at the beginning of the Supper (22:16) rather than at the end as in the other accounts. There is also a textual problem in the Lukan account in that a few significant manuscripts, mainly Codex Bezae and several old Latin manuscripts, omit Luke 22:19b and 20, " '. . . which is given for you. This do in my remembrance.' And the cup likewise after Supper, saying, 'This cup is the new covenant in my blood which is poured out for you.'" The main arguments in favor of this shorter text are: (1) The unusual nature of the reading. It is clearly the more difficult reading, for it is unlikely that a scribe would have wanted to omit the more traditional ending. (2) It is a shorter reading, which on textual-critical principles would generally be the preferred reading. This is especially true here in the case of a Western non-interpolation (i.e., a reading not found in the Western family of manuscripts), and such shorter readings are contrary to the tendency of the Western scribal tradition (*see* Textual Criticism). Nevertheless, the overall manuscript evidence favoring the inclusion of Luke 22:19b-20 is far too strong to be ignored, and it would appear that somewhere in the manu-

script tradition a scribe was confused by the cup-bread-cup sequence in Luke and omitted the second mention of the cup.

2. Historical Background.

A number of historical issues present themselves in any proper understanding of the Last Supper. All four accounts indicate that the Supper was celebrated "on the night in which he was betrayed" (1 Cor 11:23). This is specifically stated in the Pauline version of the Last Supper, but each Gospel also indicates that on the night of the Last Supper Jesus announced his betrayal and went to Gethsemane* where he was betrayed (Mt 26:21-25, 36-56; Mk 14:18-21, 32-42; Lk 22:21-23, 39-53).

2.1. The Problem of Mark 14:12. In this verse we encounter a difficulty with regard to the dating of the Supper. Mark states, "And on the first day of Unleavened Bread when they were sacrificing the Passover lamb, his disciples say to him, 'Where do you wish that we should go and prepare in order that you might eat the Passover?' " The Passover, which was the first day of the Feast of Unleavened Bread, was celebrated on the 15th of Nisan. The sacrifice of the Passover lambs, however, took place on the 14th of Nisan when the ritual search for leaven took place. Most probably Mark is not using technical terminology here. In the more popular understanding this technical distinction was lost, for the beginning of the Feast of Unleavened Bread took place on the preceding day when preparations such as the slaughtering of the Passover lamb and the search for leaven took place. Mark, in his description, has done what individuals today do when they speak of celebrating Christmas on Christmas Eve when presents are exchanged. Mark 14:12 is best understood in a similar way as a popular, inexact designation (cf. Josephus *J.W.* 5.3.1 for a similar reference to the 14th of Nisan as the beginning of the Feast of Unleavened Bread).

2.2. Was the Last Supper Associated with a Passover Meal? It is clear in all four Gospels that the crucifixion of Jesus took place on a Friday (Mt 27:62; Mk 15:42; Lk 23:54; Jn 19:31, 42). This, of course, means before 6 P.M. Friday, for in the Jewish reckoning of time this marks the end of Friday and the start of Saturday. The cardinal question regarding the date of the Last Supper involves whether it was in fact associated with a Passover meal. This would appear to be certain from Matthew 26:17-19; Mark 14:12-16 and Luke 22:7-15. But John 13:1, 29; 18:28; 19:31 give the impression that the trial and crucifixion took place before the Passover. Thus from John it appears that the Last Supper must have taken place on or before the 14th of Nisan. There have been numerous attempts to explain this. Some of these are:

(1) The Synoptic Gospels are correct. The Last Supper was a Passover meal. The term *Passover* in John 18:28 does not refer to the Passover lamb but to later feasts and sacrifices associated with the Feast of Unleavened Bread.

(2) John is correct. Jesus did not eat the customary Passover meal with his disciples,* but anticipated it and ate it earlier because he knew he would be dead at the time of the Passover. John 18:28, however, refers to the actual Passover.

(3) Both the Synoptic Gospels and John are correct, because the Passover was celebrated that year on two separate days (*see* Chronology, Death of Jesus).

Several objections have been raised against the view that the Last Supper was associated with a Passover meal. First, no mention is made of the Passover lamb. Second, the word used for "bread" in the account is *artos*, the usual word for leavened bread, which could not be used to designate unleavened bread. Third, the four cups used in the traditional Jewish celebration of the Passover are not mentioned.

These objections are not serious, however, for the accounts of the Last Supper are abbreviated summaries of what happened, and one would expect the accounts to focus on those things which were most relevant for its celebration. Furthermore, because the early church regularly celebrated the Last Supper apart from the yearly Jewish Passover festival, those aspects of the Passover which had little or no bearing on the Last Supper were soon dropped. As for the statement that *artos* could not be used to designate the unleavened bread of the Passover, this is simply incorrect. The general term for "bread," whether the Greek *artos* or Hebrew *leḥem*, was always used in the OT, the LXX, the Mishnah and the Targums to describe the shewbread, which consisted of unleavened bread. Other objections focus on whether the trial of Jesus could have taken place on the day of the Passover (*see* Trial of Jesus).

The question of whether the Last Supper was a Passover meal needs to be clarified. The Last Supper was not a Passover meal. It was not celebrated yearly, and it involves only two elements—bread and wine. A literal Passover lamb is not involved nor are other elements of the Passover meal. Whereas Matthew 26:26; Mark 14:22 and Luke 22:15-17 envision the Last Supper taking place within the time frame of a Passover meal, it is not for them a Passover meal. This is especially clear in Luke, for none of his references to the breaking of bread in Acts is associated with the Jewish Passover. Paul furthermore appears to separate

the "cup" from the Supper itself (1 Cor 11:25). Thus, whereas the Last Supper was associated with a Passover meal, and whereas the Lord's Supper was probably associated in the early church with a meal (the "love-feast"), it was never understood as being identical with these meals.

2.3. The Last Supper Associated with a Passover Meal. There are several weighty arguments which favor the view that the Last Supper was associated with a Passover meal. Some of these are:

(1) The Passover meal had to be eaten within the walled city of Jerusalem, and the Last Supper was eaten within the city walls.

(2) The Passover night had to be spent within greater Jerusalem, which included Jerusalem and the surrounding hills facing it. That night, unlike other nights, Jesus and the disciples spent in Gethsemane, within greater Jerusalem, and not in Bethany.

(3) Jesus and the disciples reclined as they ate (Mk 14:18). It was customary to sit at ordinary meals but to recline at the Passover.

(4) People in Israel usually ate two meals a day. The first was a breakfast around 10-11 A.M., and the second was the main meal in late afternoon. The Last Supper was eaten in the evening (1 Cor 11:23; Mk 14:17) which was what the Law required for the Passover (Ex 12:8).

(5) The Last Supper ended with a hymn (Mt 26:30; Mk 14:26), and it was customary at the end of the Passover to sing the last part of the Hallel Psalms (Ps 115—118).

(6) The interpretation of the elements was a customary part of the Passover ritual (Ex 12:26-27).

(7) It was also customary at the Passover to give some money to the poor, a practice that would explain Judas' (*see* Judas Iscariot) leaving the gathering (Jn 13:29).

None of these arguments by itself is conclusive, but their overall weight argues strongly that the Last Supper was indeed associated with a Passover meal. They receive additional support from Paul's calling Jesus "Christ, our Passover" (1 Cor 5:7) and his reference to "the cup of blessing" (1 Cor 10:16), the name given to the third cup of the Passover meal. The suggestion that the Last Supper was a *qiddûš* (or some other religious meal) which was eaten on the eve of the Sabbath* and included a blessing over the bread and cup seems highly unlikely due to the numerous associations of the Last Supper with the Passover celebration. Indeed, the traditional materials which inform us about the *qiddûš* are post-Christian, and it was never celebrated twenty-four hours before the Sabbath but early on the Sabbath eve. There is even a question as to whether the *qiddûš* was an actual meal or simply a blessing pronounced at a meal. As to the Johannine dating of the Passover, it should be noted that this fits his theological emphases quite nicely, for John seeks to tie the death of Jesus closely with the Passover (cf. Jn 1:29, 35; 19:36; Ex 12:46; Num 9:12).

3. The Last Supper in the Context of Passover.

If, as has been maintained, the Last Supper took place at a Passover meal, any proper interpretation must seek to understand it in light of this particular context. The Passover was an elaborate ritual full of symbolism and redemptive history.

3.1. The Passover Elements. The meal consisted mainly of six elements.

3.1.1. The most significant was the *Passover lamb,* which had to be roasted over a fire. All the lamb had to be eaten that night. Nothing could be saved. The lamb of course reminded the participants of the first Passover in which the angel* of death was kept from visiting the first-born of Israel* because they were protected by the blood of the lamb.

3.1.2. The *unleavened bread* reminded them of the swiftness of God's* deliverance. His salvation* was so swift that the people of Israel did not have time to bake bread.

3.1.3. The bowl of *salt water* reminded them of the tears shed in their captivity and the crossing of the Red Sea.

3.1.4. The *bitter herbs* recalled the bitterness of their slavery.

3.1.5. A fruit puree called *Charosheth* reminded them of the clay which they used to make bricks in their captivity in Egypt.

3.1.6. Finally, there were four *cups of wine,* mixed three parts water to one part wine, which reminded them of the promises of Exodus 6:6-7. The third cup of blessing was probably the one Jesus used in the Last Supper (Lk 22:20; 1 Cor 10:16; 11:25). The fourth cup was followed by a benediction and singing.

3.2. The Passover Parallels. During the Passover

The Passover	The Last Supper
God remembered his covenant	A new covenant is enacted
Slavery in Egypt	[Slavery to sin?]
Deliverance from Egypt	Forgiveness of sins (Mt 26:28)
Blood of Passover lamb	Blood of Christ (our Passover, 1 Cor 5:7; the lamb of God, Jn 1:29, 35)
Interpretation of elements	Interpretation of elements
Call for continual celebration	Call for continual celebration

meal someone, usually the youngest son, was designated to ask the question "Why is this night different from other nights?" At this point the host would retell the story of Israel's deliverance out of Egypt and the meaning of the various elements of the meal. As the host of the Last Supper, Jesus would have been the one who retold the story. Later, the parallels between the Passover and the Last Supper which Jesus was establishing would be quite apparent.

4. The Four Words of the Last Supper.

Whereas some scholars have argued that the Pauline form is the most original, in general most scholars conclude that the oldest form is to be found in the Markan version. Among the more important reasons are: (1) the Markan account contains more Aramaisms than the Pauline account (e.g., "he took bread, and blessed, and broke it") and (2) it is easier to understand how the Pauline-Lukan version originated from the Markan form than vice versa. It would appear that the original form contained four elements or "words."

4.1. "This is My Body." The addition of "which is [or "is given"] for you" in Luke and 1 Corinthians may be an interpretative comment to help explain the meaning of the bread for the believer. Yet even if these are not authentic words of Jesus, this comment is certainly implied and makes explicit what was implicit in Jesus' words. It is difficult to believe that the disciples did not interpret the "is" metaphorically. If asked "Where is the body of Jesus?" they would have pointed to Jesus rather than the bread. His frequent use of metaphorical language would have provided the context for understanding "is" non-literally. This metaphorical interpretation of "is" is supported by the fact that they are still called "bread and cup" (1 Cor 11:26-28), an unlikely reference if the elements had undergone transubstantiation.

In the first word Jesus states that he has come to give his body—himself as a person—on their behalf (cf. Phil 1:20; Rom 12:1; 1 Cor 9:27). Later, the church would understand more fully what this meant and realize that the bread represents the Incarnation when the "Word* [who] became flesh" bore our sins in his body (1 Pet 2:24) in order to achieve the redemption of the world.

4.2. "This Do in My Remembrance." The authenticity of these words have been denied, primarily because they are not found in Mark and Matthew. Yet, if Jesus saw his death as sealing a [new] covenant and in the context of the continual repetition of the Passover, it would have been quite natural for him to have said that this new and more significant deliverance of the people of God by his blood should likewise be continually remembered. Furthermore, the practice of the early church in regularly celebrating the Lord's Supper, and on more than just a yearly basis like the Passover, can best be understood as due to Jesus having said something like "Do this in my remembrance." The Passover had as its purpose that "[Israel might] remember the day when [she] came out of the land of Egypt" (Deut 16:3). Similarly Jesus' vicarious death and his inauguration of a new covenant was to be remembered in like manner.

Exactly what this remembrance involves is debated. Jeremias has suggested that it involved the disciples petitioning God to remember Jesus and come to his rescue. The Last Supper thus focuses not on Jesus' mediation of humanity before God but rather on Jesus' followers seeking to intercede before God on Jesus' behalf. Another view is to understand this remembrance as a memorial in which the believer thinks back and reflects upon the death of Jesus (see Death of Jesus). A third way of understanding this term is to interpret it as meaning "to proclaim." Through the Last Supper the church proclaims the death of Jesus. This view finds support in 1 Corinthians 11:26. This tends to make the purpose of the Last Supper evangelistic in nature. The Last Supper, however, is first and foremost meant for the church. Probably the best interpretation of this command is to understand it as ordering the continual recapitulation or recounting of the passion and Parousia of Jesus Christ, even as the Passover meal recounted and represented the events of the Exodus (Ex 12:1-20).

4.3. "This Is My Blood of the Covenant Poured Out for Many." At the third cup of the Passover meal, after the traditional blessing, "Blessed be thou, Lord our God, King of the world, who has created the fruit of the vine . . ." or in lieu of it, Jesus said "this is my blood of the covenant poured out for many." The imagery recalls Exodus 24:8, where Moses seals the divine covenant by pouring half of the "blood of the covenant" upon the altar and sprinkling the other half on the people. The covenant blood of Exodus 24:8 is understood in the Targums *Pseudo-Jonathan* and *Onkelos* as being given to "atone" for the sins of the people—as being expiatory in nature. Similarly, the Matthean addition "for the forgiveness of sins" (Mt 26:28; see Forgiveness) makes explicit what is already implicit in the expression "blood of the covenant" (cf. Heb 9:20-22; 10:26-29).

Although not directly quoted, Jeremiah 31:31-34, with its reference to a "new" covenant, is also alluded to in this word. Even as the Qumran community spoke of a "new covenant" (CD 6:19; 8:21; 19:33-34; 20:1-2;

1 QpHab 2:1-4; 1 Q28b 3:25-26; 5:21-22; 1 Q34 3 ii 5-6), Jesus perceived his mission as having inaugurated a [new] covenant which would be sealed by his sacrificial death. Even if "new" was not expressly stated by Jesus, it is certainly implied. In this it recalls Jeremiah 31:34, which speaks of forgiveness of sins accompanying a new covenant. The centrality of forgiveness in this [new] covenant is also supported by the additional expression "which is poured out for many" found in the Markan and Matthean accounts. (The Lukan "for you" in 22:20 is most probably a liturgical change introduced to balance the "for you" of 22:19.) This recalls the expiatory and sacrificial self-giving of the suffering servant of Isaiah 53:12 who bears the sin of many (see Servant of Yahweh). (It is illegitimate to interpret "many" as denoting a limited atonement, for the expression here means "transgressors"; i.e., it refers to all, as the synonymous parallelism in Is 53:12b-c clearly indicates.)

This word indicates that Jesus in referring to his "blood poured out" understood his death as sacrificial (Lev 17:11-14) and sealing a [new] covenant. It is difficult not to interpret this word along the lines of Mark 10:45; 1 Corinthians 15:3; 2 Corinthians 5:21; etc., where Jesus gives his life—pours out his blood—as a vicarious atonement for sinful humanity. This and the first word indicate the voluntary nature of Jesus' self-surrender, but this word adds that this self-surrender involves a sacrificial death which establishes a [new] covenant. It also seems clear that the words "this *is* my blood" would not have been interpreted literally by any of the disciples in light of the OT prohibition against drinking blood (cf. Lev 3:17; 7:26-27; 17:14; etc.), for if one remembers the difficulty Peter encountered in Acts 10:6-16 with regard to non-kosher meat, it is difficult to conclude that the disciples would have had no qualms drinking what they thought was real blood. The fact that there is not the slightest hesitation nor reservation mentioned in any of the accounts to drinking the cup indicates that they interpreted Jesus' words metaphorically. The cup—that is, the contents of the cup—symbolizes Jesus' death, his poured-out blood, shed as a sacrifice which seals a covenant.

4.4. "Until . . . the Kingdom of God." Even as the Passover celebration involved an anticipation and longing for the final day when Israel would share in the messianic banquet (Is 25:6-9; 53:13; cf. 55:1-2), so all four accounts of the Last Supper contain a word concerning the future. Though Luke's wording varies and is exceptional in its placement before the bread, the Synoptics bear unified witness to Jesus' words: "I say to you, I shall not in any way drink any longer from the fruit of the vine until that day when I drink it new in the kingdom of God." The Pauline word about the future does not come from Jesus' lips but is a comment from the apostle in which he says that when the church celebrates the Lord's Supper they "proclaim the Lord's death until he comes." In the Synoptics this word points triumphantly to the future messianic banquet when Jesus will eat once again with the disciples.

Elsewhere Jesus on various occasions referred to the joyous participation in the consummated kingdom as a sharing in the messianic banquet (Mt 8:11 par. Lk 13:29; Mt 5:6 par. Lk 6:21; Lk 12:35-38; Mk 7:24-30; *see* Table Fellowship). The feeding of the 5,000 and the 4,000 were probably also understood by the Evangelists as proleptic participations of the Last Supper and the eschatological banquet (Mt 14:19 par. Mk 6:41 and Lk 9:16 [Jn 6:11] and Mt 15:36 par. Mk 8:6). Luke in fact heightens the allusion to this by separating the reference to the fish in 9:16. According to the Jewish tradition in *Mekilta Exodus* 12:42, Israel's future redemption would come on the night of the Passover. As a result the celebration of the Passover looked back to the greatest redemptive event of the OT and forward to the joyous anticipation of the coming of the messianic age. In a similar way Jesus in the Last Supper points his disciples to the greatest redemptive event of the NT, which is soon to be a past event, and to the arrival of the kingdom in glory* when he comes (1 Cor 11:26) and shares the messianic banquet with his followers (Mt 26:29; Mk 14:25; Lk 22:16).

Clearly, Jesus does not see his passion as a tragedy or error, but the crowning act of his ministry in which he pours out his blood as the once-for-all sacrifice which secures redemption "for many" and insures a glorious consummation in the future. Paul in his future word refers more specifically to the event which will bring about that consummation—the Parousia. Thus the Last Supper, while not itself the realization of the messianic banquet, is a proleptic experience of it, a kind of earnest, or first fruits, of that banquet.

4.5. Later Additions to the Last Supper. Within the four accounts of the Last Supper we find a number of liturgical and interpretative comments. This should not be surprising. While certainty is impossible, the following may be liturgical additions: "Take" (Mt 26:26; Mk 14:22); "eat" (Mt 26:26); "drink of it, all of you" (Mt 26:27); "and they all drank of it" (Mk 14:23); "In the same way also the cup, after Supper, saying," (1 Cor 11:25); "cup" (1 Cor 11:25; Lk 22:20); "For as often as you eat this bread and drink the cup, you are proclaiming the Lord's death until he comes" (1 Cor 11:26). Some interpretative comments which may have

been added to the account are: "which is for you" (Lk 22:19; 1 Cor 11:24); "given" (Lk 22:19); "This do in my remembrance" (Lk 22:19; 1 Cor 11:24; see 4.2 above); "new" [covenant] (Lk 22:20; 1 Cor 11:25); "for the forgiveness of sins" (Mt 26:28). In all these instances the intention of Jesus is not altered, but the additions either make explicit what is perhaps only implicit or make the format of the sacrament more liturgically serviceable.

Several additional interpretative comments are found within the NT concerning the Last Supper. In 1 Corinthians 10:3-4 Paul gives a warning against the danger of assuming that mere participation in the Lord's Supper (and in Christian baptism, 1 Cor 10:1-2) guarantees the participant a favorable standing with God (cf. also Lk 13:26). Paul clearly rejects a crass sacramental view of the Lord's Supper. As in the case of circumcision, the Lord's Supper (and baptism) is of value when accompanied by faith* and obedience (Rom 2:25). There is also a specific warning concerning the danger of partaking of the Lord's Supper "in an unworthy manner" (1 Cor 11:27-32).

5. The Celebration of the Supper.
Within Acts we find several references to the "breaking of bread" (Acts 2:42, 46; 20:7, 11; 24:30). Although it is debated whether this refers to a celebration derived from the Last Supper, it is clear that the Evangelist understood it this way. This is evident from Luke's use of the expression "breaking of bread" (Lk 22:19). It is further supported by the fact that in Acts 20:7 we find the breaking of bread taking place in the context of church worship* on the first day of the week. Thus for Luke these references to the "breaking of bread" are understood as the fulfillment of Jesus' command to "do this in remembrance of me" found in his Gospel. To interpret them as simply ordinary meals, or even as "love feasts," would contradict Luke's normal practice of showing how the church in Acts carried out Jesus' teachings. Probably the breaking of bread normally occurred in the context of a love-feast, but the similarity in wording with the Last Supper ("breaking bread") indicates that what is most important for Luke is the celebration of the Supper. (The only difficulty with this understanding is Acts 27:39, but it is not serious enough to overcome the previous facts.)

In the early church the celebration of the Supper was almost immediately separated from the Passover, for the "breaking of bread" was practiced far more frequently than once a year. There are indications that it was celebrated weekly (Acts 20:7, 11; 1 Cor 16:2) and even daily (Acts 2:46-47). No rate of frequency, however, is prescribed within the NT. In the earliest period of the church the Supper was celebrated in connection with a "love feast" (Jude 12; Acts 2:42, 46; 1 Cor 11:20-22, 33-34). It may be that Acts 2:42 should be interpreted, "They were continuing in the teaching of the apostles, and in fellowship [the love-feast], the breaking of bread [the Supper] and prayers." Likewise, Acts 2:46 might be read, "and breaking bread [the Supper] in their homes, they partook of food with glad and generous hearts [the love feast]." This practice stemmed from the fact that Jesus' Last Supper was associated with a meal (Lk 22:20; 1 Cor 11:25). Soon, however, it became completely separate due most probably to such problems as Paul mentions in 1 Corinthians 11:20-22, 33-34—where Paul refers to it as the Lord's Supper (*kyriakos deipnon*, 1 Cor 11:20)—and by the middle of the second century that separation was complete.

The Lord's Supper contains a two-dimensional focus. It recounts the passion of the Son of man (*see* Son of Man) and his sacrificial death by which he seals a new covenant for humanity. One cannot celebrate the Lord's Supper without looking backward to the cross and the suffering of Christ, our Passover. As a result a certain pathos and sadness is present at this celebration. But there is a forward-looking dimension which does not permit the Lord's Supper to become simply a morbid recalling of the passion. Believers "proclaim the Lord's death until he comes." Since the final dimension of the Supper looks forward to the messianic banquet, the Lord's Supper is not simply practiced; it is celebrated in faith. In this celebration the church believes, hopes and sings "*Marana tha*—Come, Lord Jesus" (1 Cor 16:22; Rev 22:20) and awaits the consummation when faith turns to sight at the table of the Lord.

See also DEATH OF JESUS; FEASTS; PASSION NARRATIVE; TABLE FELLOWSHIP.

BIBLIOGRAPHY. W. Barclay, *The Lord's Supper* (Nashville: Abingdon, 1967); M. Barth, *Rediscovering the Lord's Supper* (Atlanta: John Knox, 1988); G. Bornkamm, "Lord's Supper and Church in Paul," in *Early Christian Experience* (London: SCM, 1969) 123-60; J. B. Green, *The Death of Jesus* (Tübingen: J. C. B. Mohr, 1988); J. Jeremias, *The Eucharistic Words of Jesus* (London: SCM, 1966); X. Leon-Dufour, *Sharing the Eucharistic Bread* (New York: Paulist, 1987); B. Klappert, "Lord's Supper," *NIDNTT* 2.520-38; H. Lietzmann, *Mass and the Lord's Supper* (Leiden: Brill, 1979); I. H. Marshall, *Last Supper and Lord's Supper* (Grand Rapids: Eerdmans, 1980); W. Marxsen, *The Lord's Supper as a Christological Problem* (Philadelphia: Fortress, 1970); G. Ogg, "The Chronology of the Last Supper," in *Historicity and Chronology in the New Testament* (London: SPCK, 1965) 75-96; H. Patsch, *Abendmahl und Historischer Jesus* (Stuttgart: Calwer, 1972); J. Reumann, *The Supper of the Lord* (Philadelphia: Fortress, 1985); E. Schweizer, *The Lord's Supper according to the New Testament* (Philadelphia: Fortress, 1967); G. Wainwright, *Eucharist and Eschatology* (New York: Oxford University, 1981).

R. H. Stein

LAW

What impact did the coming of Jesus the Messiah (*see* Christ) and the establishment through him of the kingdom of God (*see* Kingdom of God) have on the authority and applicability of the Mosaic Law? The question is at the heart of the Gospels. It played a critical role not only in Jesus' disputes with various Jewish groups but also in the development of the early church's self-understanding as followers of Jesus sought to define the relationship between the church* and Israel.*

Jesus, living in the overlap between the old covenant and the new, is generally obedient to the Mosaic Law, but at the same time he makes clear that he has sovereign rights both to interpret and to set aside that Law. On this basis he criticizes the developing oral Law for its focus on a casuistic literalness that denied the very heart and purpose of the Law. It is in the dual command (*see* Commandment) to love* God* and neighbor that Jesus found the heart of the Law, and he used these basic demands to interpret and apply the Law in accordance with its author's intention. But Jesus was not simply a great expositor of the Law. What is most characteristic of the Gospels is Jesus' claim to be the Lord* of the Law itself. Jesus manifests this claim in his implicit abrogation of several commandments within the Law and in his independent yet authoritative proclamation of God's will for his followers. As Messiah and Son of God (*see* Son of God), Jesus stands superior to the Law. Nevertheless, Jesus never attacks the Law and, indeed, asserts its enduring validity. But it is only as taken up into Jesus' teaching, and thus fulfilled, that the Law retains its validity. The Law comes to those living on this side of the cross only through the filter of its fulfillment in Christ the Lord.

The general sketch drawn in the last paragraph is reproduced in each of the Gospels, though with considerable differences in clarity and emphasis. Mark highlights Jesus' abrogation of ritual aspects of the Law, though he shows little interest in Jesus' ethical teachings. Matthew writes his Gospel for a community deeply concerned about the relation of

Israel and church and, consequently, about the relation of the Law to Jesus' teaching. He therefore includes more of the teaching of Jesus on this issue than the other Evangelists, showing how Jesus both endorses the Law and surpasses it. Luke in his own way strikes a similar balance, commending the piety of those who follow the Law while showing that the continuing validity of the Law lies mainly in its prophetic aspects. John's stance is polemical, as he puts Jesus and his claims on a collision course with the Law and its institutions. Even here, however, the point is not so much that Jesus abrogates the Law as to show that as Son of God he replaces it.

1. Introduction
2. Jesus
3. The Gospel Writers
4. Conclusion

1. Introduction.
"Law" is the standard translation of the Greek word *nomos*. This word occurs thirty-one times in the Gospels, always in the singular, and with two possible exceptions—both in John 19:7—the word denotes the body of commandments given by God to the people of Israel through Moses.* Thus the Law can be called both "the Law of the Lord" (Lk 2:23-24, 39) as well as "the Law of Moses" (Lk 2:22; Jn 7:23; cf. Jn 1:17, "the Law came through Moses," and John 1:45, "Moses wrote in the Law"). On five occasions the Law is linked with "the prophets" (Mt. 5:17; 7:12; 11:13; 22:40; Lk 16:16; Jn 1:45—there is Jewish precedent for such a combination: cf. 4 Macc 18:10) and once with both the prophets and "the psalms" (Lk 24:44). In most of these texts *nomos* refers to the Pentateuch, and the whole phrase simply denotes "the Scriptures." The Gospel writers also refer to the Law with the words "commandment" (*entolē*) (singular: Mt 15:3 par. Mk 7:9; Mt 22:36 par. Mk 12:28; Mt 22:38 par. Mk 12:31; Mk 7:8; 10:5; Lk 23:56; plural: Mt 5:19; 19:17 par. Mk 10:19 and Lk 18:20; Mt 22:40; Lk 1:6) and "decree" (*dikaiōma*) (Lk 1:6); or with a reference simply to "Moses" (Mt 8:4 par. Mk 1:44 and Lk 5:14; Mt 19:7 par. Mk 10:3; Mt 19:8 par. Mk 10:4; Mt 22:24 par. Mk 12:19 and Lk 20:28; Mk 7:10; Jn 7:22 [*bis*]: cf. "Moses and the prophets" in Lk 16:29, 31). On the other hand, *graphē* ("Scripture") is never used to refer to the Mosaic Law alone, while the verb *graphō* ("write": e.g., "it is written") is only rarely so used (Mk 10:5; 12:19; Lk 2:23; 10:26; 20:28; Jn 1:45; 8:17; 10:34).

The virtual identification of "Law" with "Law of Moses" in the Gospels reflects OT usage and the Jewish milieu, in both of which the Law of Moses, the Torah (*tôrâ*), plays a central role. Obedience to the Law was not the means by which the people of Israel attained their covenant relationship with God. It was their response to the gracious initiative of God, a response both appropriate as a means of thanking and glorifying the God who had chosen them and necessary as the means by which the promises attached to the covenant would be actualized (see e.g., Deut 28:1-2, 9; 30:1-10, 15-16). In a development predicted in the Pentateuch (Deut 30:15-22) and identified by the prophets, Israel failed to obey the Law and so broke the terms of God's covenant. Nevertheless, God affirmed his continuing faithfulness to his people and promises, announcing that he would establish a new covenant with his people, a covenant through which God's Law would be "written on the heart" (Jer 31:31-34) and through which those very hearts would be transformed so as to make them obedient to the Lord (Ezek 36:24-28).

This pessimism about the Law did not take root in early Judaism.* While generalizations about the Jewish people as a whole are dangerous and usually misleading, it is clear that the most important Jewish groups in Jesus' day gave to the Mosaic Law a place of central importance in the life of the people and in their relationship to the Lord. Some of these groups, most notably the Pharisees,* sought to aid the Jews in their obedience to God's Law by adding to the written Law an oral tradition which would apply the written Law to the new situations faced by Jews. This development cannot be traced in detail, but it was certainly well underway in Jesus' day, as is clear from his reference to the "traditions of the elders" (Mt 15:2 par. Mk 7:3). Fueling this development were two central postulates: that the Jew must obey God, and that the complete guide for that obedience is to be found in the Torah. The growth of an authoritative tradition such as this, which could, at a latter date, be called *tôrâ* (e.g., *b. Šabb.* 31a), complicates the discussion of "Jesus and the Law." It is necessary, for instance, to determine whether Jesus' critical attitude toward certain commandments and customs embodies criticism of the written Law of Moses or of the oral traditions of the Pharisees.

2. Jesus.
From what the Gospels tell us of Jesus' behavior, he was generally obedient to the Law of Moses. He attends the major feasts* in Jerusalem, pays the half-shekel temple tax* (Mt 17:24-27), wears the prescribed tassel on his robe (Mt 9:20; cf. Num 15:38-41) and, whatever may be said about his disciples' behavior or his teaching, never clearly violates the Sabbath.* It is only in the case of Jesus' contact with unclean people

(see Clean and Unclean) in his healing* ministry (e.g., touching a leper [Mt 8:3 par. Mk 1:41 and Lk 5:13]) that he could be considered in violation of the Law of Moses. Even in this case, however, the unusual nature of Jesus' healing activities makes it difficult to identify a clear-cut violation of the Law.

The situation is certainly different with respect to the oral traditions of the Jews. Jesus deliberately associates with people considered by strict Jews to be unclean (the tax collectors and sinners*; cf. Mt 9:10-13 par. Mk 2:15-17 and Lk 5:29-32) and "works" on the Sabbath by healing people who are in no danger of losing their lives (Mk 3:1-6 par. Mt. 12:9-14 and Lk 6:6-11; Lk 13:10-17; 14:1-6; Jn 5:2-47; 9:1-41). It is not, however, that Jesus consistently flaunts the traditions, for he attends the synagogue on the Sabbath, and displays habits at mealtime and at prayer* that are consistent with the traditions. What we have, then, is a Jesus who does not go out of his way to break the traditions of his day but at the same time makes clear that he considers himself free to ignore them if need demands.

While we can conclude from Jesus' behavior that he did not endorse the "traditions of the elders" as authoritative, his general conformity to the written Law allows no clear conclusions. Did Jesus obey the Law because he considered it to be eternally valid? Or did he obey it as "old covenant" Law, valid only until his death* and resurrection* should inaugurate a new covenant? Or was there a principle that Jesus applied to determine the validity of different commandments within the Law?

2.1. Love and the Law. The principle most often cited in this regard is the love command. Jesus singled out love for God and love for neighbor as the two great commandments (Mt 22:34-40 par. Mk 12:28-34; Lk 10:25-28; cf. Jn 13:31-35), going so far as to assert that "all the Law and the prophets depend" on them (Mt 22:40). Taken with Jesus' pronouncement of the "golden rule" (Mt 7:12), his insistence that "mercy"* is more important than "sacrifice" (Mt 9:13; 12:7) and his humanitarian approach to the Sabbath (Mk 2:27; cf. Mt 12:3-4 par. Mk 2:25-26 and Lk 6:3-4; Mt 12:12 par. Mk 3:4 and Lk 6:9; Lk 13:15-16), his highlighting of the love command suggests that it plays a significant role in his understanding of the Law. But what is its role? Does love function to determine when the Law is to be obeyed? What laws are to be obeyed? And what is the meaning and intent of the Law?

Only this last role of the demand of love, that of determining the meaning and intent of the Law, has any clear basis in Jesus' teaching. Never does he suggest that he or his followers are free on the basis of love to disobey an authoritative commandment of Scripture. Nor does he dismiss the validity of commandments according to whether or not they are loving. But Jesus does appeal to love in elucidating the meaning and application of the Law. In contrast to the scribes,* who insisted on literal and scrupulous observance of the commandments, Jesus sought out the intention behind the commandments and understood their meaning and the way they were to be obeyed in light of this intention (see Westerholm). And it is to love for God and love for others that Jesus appeals in clarifying God's intention in the Law. This is what he means by claiming that "all the Law and the prophets" (i.e., the OT in its commanding aspect; cf. Mt 5:17 and 7:12) "depend" (*krematai*) on the commands of love for God (Deut 6:5) and love for neighbor (Lev 19:18). Jesus is not here teaching that love replaces the Law or that love shows how we are to obey the Law. Rather, as the greatest commandments within the Law, they are the touchstone by which the intention and meaning of all the other commandments must be understood. Several incidents reveal this role of the love commands in Jesus' interpretation of the Law.

When Jesus defends his befriending of tax collectors and sinners by appealing to Hosea 6:6 (Mt 9:13), his point is not that the moral Law ("mercy") takes precedence over the ceremonial Law ("sacrifice"), nor that being merciful to people is more important than obeying the Law, but that one has failed to understand God's intention in the Law if rigid adherence to oral tradition (i.e., prohibition of association with the "unclean") is retained at the expense of showing God's compassion on sinners.

The situation is similar in Matthew 12:7, where Jesus cites Hosea 6:6 to defend his disciples from the charge of Sabbath-breaking: they are "guiltless" (*anaitios*) because their plucking of grain is not contrary to God's intention in giving the Sabbath command. In the same incident Jesus also defends the disciples by citing the action of David and his followers in 1 Samuel 21:1-6. As they were fleeing from the wrath of Saul, David and his confederates ate the bread of the presence, "which is not Lawful for any but the priests to eat" (Mt 12:3-4 par. Mk 2:25-26 and Lk 6:3-4). Jesus, it is sometimes alleged, cites this incident to show that human need takes precedence over obedience to the Law. But only Matthew even mentions the fact that the disciples were hungry. And, in any case, their need could not have been great— surely Jesus does not encourage disobedience to the Law to meet casual wants and desires! Rather, Jesus' purpose is quite different: by comparing his disciples with David's followers, he also compares himself to David, suggesting that if, in serving David, his followers were justified in doing what was "illegal," so much the more were Jesus' own disciples justified in breaking the Sabbath halakah (see Rabbinic Traditions and Writings) in their service of the greater Son of David (see Son of David). The focus is on christology, not on the interpretation of the Sabbath command. This christological interpretation is reinforced in Matthew by the comparison that immediately follows between Jesus and the Temple* (Mt 12:5-6).

In Mark's Gospel, however, Jesus' reference to 1 Samuel 21:1-6 is followed by the strongly humanitarian statement "the Sabbath was made for humankind, not humankind for the Sabbath" (2:27). Some have found christology here also, arguing that "humankind" (anthropos) is a mistranslation of an Aramaic expression by which Jesus referred to himself as the Son of man (see Son of Man). There is no basis for this, however, and the saying fits well with similar pronouncements of Jesus such as: "it is lawful to do good on the Sabbath" (Mt 12:12; cf. Mk 3:4; Lk 6:9). Again, however, Jesus is not claiming that one can break the Sabbath command when human needs dictate, but that the Sabbath command itself must be so understood as to include this basic purpose in its promulgation. The Sabbath is truly obeyed only when its intention to aid human beings is recognized and factored into one's behavior. That is why, rather than being a violation of the Law, Jesus' Sabbath-Day healing of a woman was a true fulfillment of that Law ("it was necessary" [edei] that she be healed on the Sabbath: Lk 13:16).

For Jesus, then, love for God and for others, being basic to God's intention in giving the Law, must always be considered in interpreting the meaning of that Law.

2.2. Jesus' Use of the Law in His Ethical Teaching. The relatively few occasions on which Jesus cites the OT Law in formulating his own demands is revealing of the independent authority with which Jesus speaks. True, Jesus believes that his teaching stands in continuity with the OT demand (see, e.g., Mt 5:17 and 7:12). And he occasionally cites the OT in his own teaching (see Old Testament in the Gospels). But most of these citations come in conversation with Jewish opponents or inquirers in which the OT is appealed to because of its relevance to their situation. Jesus' teaching about the dual command of love is a case in point. He highlights these commandments in response to a question about which is the greatest commandment (Mt 22:36 par. Mk 12:28). Without minimizing the importance of these commandments,

it is significant that in John's Gospel the commandment to love one another is a new commandment, authorized by Jesus without reference to the OT (13:31-35). Jesus also appeals to the prophets to establish priorities within the Law (Hos 6:6 in Mt 9:13 and 12:7; Mic 6:8 in Mt 23:23 [cf. Lk 11:42]).

Similarly, when questioned about the legitimacy of divorce (see Marriage and Divorce), Jesus cites Genesis 1:27 and 2:24 to correct the common over-interpretation of Deuteronomy 24:1-4 (Mt 19:3-12 par. Mk 10:2-10). Some have thought that Jesus is following a rabbinic procedure by which two apparently contradictory statements within the Law could be harmonized. But rather than harmonizing the two, Jesus appeals to one over against the other. The original intention of God expressed in the Genesis texts is elevated over the Mosaic command which was given, Jesus says, because of "hardness of heart" (see Hardness of Heart). Here Jesus appeals to the OT teaching about the origin of marriage as authoritative for his followers. It is not clear, however, that this should be considered as an appeal to the Law. For Jesus' careful distinction between what God had said (in Genesis) and what Moses had said (in Deuteronomy) suggests that he cites Genesis not as part of "the Law," in the sense of the Mosaic command, but as a scriptural and hence authoritative statement of God's intention for marriage. Here Jesus makes an important distinction, one that runs counter to the tendency of Judaism in his day: the distinction between the books of Moses as Scripture, and the Law of Moses that takes up a large portion of those books.

Another polemical use of the Law appears in Jesus' debate with the Pharisees over ritual defilement. Jesus defends his disciples'* behavior in this matter by calling into question the "traditions of the elders*" generally (Mt 15:3-6 par. Mk 7:8-13). Jesus brands these traditions as contrary to the Law they purport to expound and apply. From this we can conclude that Jesus expected the Jews of his day to observe the commandments under which they lived—beyond that we cannot go.

Slightly different is Jesus' rehearsal of decalog commandments when a young man asks him how he may attain eternal life* (Mt 19:16-22 par. Mk 10:17-22 and Lk 18:18-23). Here, it could be argued, Jesus makes OT commandments basic to his own ethical demands. But such a conclusion would be too hasty. For Jesus imposes these commands not on a follower but on a seeker after eternal life. Does Jesus then view obedience to the Law as a means of salvation? This is possible, although we would then want to question whether Jesus considered it possible for any human being to render an obedience adequate to that end. For the young man, after claiming to have observed all the commandments cited by Jesus, is still seen to be short of entrance into the kingdom. But it is also possible that Jesus cites the commandments simply to initiate a discussion and to draw out this young man, and that he is not teaching that eternal life can be gained by obedience to the Law. In any case, it is significant that the climax of the narrative is Jesus' demand that the young man "follow me." This has been viewed as Jesus' further exposition of the real meaning of the commandments, but we question whether following Jesus in discipleship can be considered an exposition of any Mosaic command. Rather, whatever the role played by the commandments of the Law, it is Jesus' own demand that is crucial here. Jesus goes beyond the OT demand: it is following him, not obedience to the Law, that is the door into the kingdom of God.

It is clear, then, that Jesus' direct use of the OT in his ethical teaching is minimal (*see* Ethics of Jesus). Most of the references occur in polemical contexts where Jesus may be doing no more than assuming the reference point of his opponent. This does not necessarily mean that Jesus did not consider the OT Law to be relevant for the new age that was dawning through his ministry and work. He may simply have assumed its continuing validity. Still, what is impressive in Jesus' teaching is the way in which he taught directly, and without reference to any other authority,* what it was that God was demanding of his people. The Mosaic Law, if not discarded, is generally ignored—and this signals an important shift from both the OT and the Judaism of Jesus' day.

2.3. Abrogation of the Law? We have seen that Jesus does not generally use the Law to formulate his ethics. But does he ever go so far as to pronounce invalid the Law or commandments within the Law?

2.3.1. Clean and Unclean. When Jesus' disciples violated the scribal tradition about hand-washing, he defended them in two ways (Mt 15:1-20 par. Mk 7:1-23). First, he criticized the scribal tradition generally, branding it a "human tradition" (Mk 7:8) that interferes with true worship* of and obedience to God. He cites as an example the situation in which the scribes would insist that a person perform a vow, even if that vow were taken selfishly to avoid giving due honor to one's parents (*see* Family). Some have seen here a conflict between two parts of the written Law—the command to honor oaths and the command to honor parents—but the text makes clear that the conflict is rather between the "commandment of God" and "human tradition." This text suggests, then, that Jesus

did not endorse the developing oral Law of the Pharisees. But Jesus' second line of defense goes further. In enunciating the principle that "there is nothing outside a person which by going into a person can defile them" (Mk 7:15; cf. Mt 15:11), Jesus casts doubt on the continuing validity of the entire ritual body of laws in the OT. Certainly, this is how Mark understands him: "Thus he declared all foods to be clean" (7:19). Doubt has been cast on the authenticity of this saying of Jesus, it being argued that the debates in the early church over this matter are hard to understand if Jesus had spoken so clearly on the issue. But Jesus' almost parabolic saying would hardly have been sufficient to settle the matter, and Mark's parenthetical interpretation reflects a later, clearer perspective. The contrast in this pericope between Jesus' upholding of one commandment—to honor parents—and his effective abrogation of others—concerning unclean foods—raises the possibility that Jesus distinguished between the so-called moral and the ceremonial Law. There are hints of such a distinction in the Gospels, in Jesus' stress on the "weightier matters of the Law" (Mt 23:23) and in his picking up the prophetic focus on inner obedience. Nevertheless, the distinction was unknown in the Judaism of Jesus' day, and we would have expected him to make the distinction much clearer had it been fundamental to his assessment of the OT Law. Moreover, as we will see, Jesus' varying pronouncements about the Law cannot be fit into a neat distinction between the moral and the ceremonial.

2.3.2. The Sabbath. The centrality of the Sabbath for Jewish piety is reflected in the numerous conflicts between Jesus and the Jews over its observance: the Gospels record six separate incidents. Did Jesus abrogate the Sabbath command, as some claim? Answering this question is complicated by the need to distinguish between the Mosaic Sabbath requirements and the extensive traditional regulations developed by the scribes in an effort to regulate Sabbath observance. The OT prohibits work on the Sabbath, but gives few details about what constitutes work. It is this ambiguity that the scribal tradition seeks to clarify. Certainly Jesus and his disciples violated the scribal Sabbath regulations: by plucking grain (Mt 12:1-8 par. Mk 2:23-28 and Lk 6:1-5) and by healing people whose lives were not in danger (Mt 12:9-14 par. Mk 3:1-6 and Lk 6:6-11; Lk 13:10-17; 14:1-6; Jn 5:2-47; 9:1-41). Neither of these activities is a clear violation of the Mosaic Sabbath rules, although Jesus' healing ministry is difficult to categorize. The most that can be said is that his initiative in healing on the Sabbath, rooted in theological conviction—"it was necessary" for Jesus to heal on the Sabbath (Lk 13:16)—stretches the Sabbath commandment. But we have no evidence that Jesus ever himself violated, or approved of his disciples violating, the written Sabbath commandment.

Jesus' teaching, however, is another matter. We have already discussed (see 2.1. above) Jesus' focus on humanitarian concerns in defending his Sabbath behavior. Some think that Jesus here abrogates, or at least relativizes, the Sabbath by putting human need over observance of the command. As we have argued, this is not the case: Jesus' humanitarian emphasis is not intended to abrogate but to define the Sabbath command. More telling is Jesus' christological defense for his Sabbath activity. He justifies the disciples' grain plucking through a comparison of himself with David (Mt 12:3-4 par. Mk 2:25-26 and Lk 6:3-4) and the Temple (Mt 12:5-6). He claims the Father's own right to continue "working" on the Sabbath (Jn 5:17-18). And in a succinct and clear statement of his position vis-a-vis the Sabbath, he claims "the Son of man is Lord of the Sabbath" (Mt 12:8 par. Mk 2:28 and Lk 6:5). Here Jesus claims superiority over the Sabbath, including the right to interpret, transform or even abrogate this central Mosaic institution. Nevertheless, Jesus never actually uses this authority to abrogate the Sabbath, and whether the early church did so on the basis of Jesus' authority is another question.

2.3.3. Divorce. We have noted that Jesus responds to a question about the grounds for divorce by citing Genesis 1:27 and 2:24 (Mt 19:3-12 par. Mk 10:2-12; cf. Lk 16:18). He thereby bypasses the then-current debate about the interpretation of Deuteronomy 24:1-4 by using God's intention in creation to call into question the entire matter of an allowance for divorce. It is true that according to Matthew (19:9; cf. 5:31-32) Jesus' position is not far from that of his near-contemporary Shammai, and from Deuteronomy 24:1-4 as well. But what is important for our purposes is the logic with which Jesus arrives at his position. The Mosaic provision for divorce is simply swept aside as a concession to "hardness of heart." What is unclear is whether Jesus thinks that the inauguration of the kingdom through his redemptive work will take away that hardness of heart or whether he considers this condition to be one that will only disappear in the next life. The contrast between the creation intention of God and the Mosaic provision ("but from the beginning it was not so") favors the former. If this is so, Jesus questions the tacit approval of divorce within the Mosaic legislation.

2.3.4. The Antitheses. Matthew 5:17-48 is the most significant passage in the Gospels for determining the

relationship between Jesus and the Mosaic Law (*see* Sermon on the Mount). Verses 17-20 will be considered below (see 2.4.); here we focus on verses 21-48 in which Jesus six times compares his teaching with what had been told to "the ancients." Many scholars are convinced that Jesus abrogates Mosaic commands in at least some of these comparisons.

The introductory formulae vary, but appear to be variations of a single basic formula, seen fully in verses 21 and 33: "you have heard that it was said to the ancients (*tois archaiois*) . . . but I say to you." The dative *tois archaiois* has occasionally been understood in an ablatival sense ("by the ancients"), but is probably a pure dative (as we have translated it). Jesus' reference is probably to the generation that received the Law at Sinai, although this does not exclude the possibility that oral traditions are included in the reference: for it was taught that the "oral Law" had also been given at Sinai (cf. *m. 'Abot.* 1:1-2). Similarly, the "you have heard" refers to the hearing of the Law read in the synagogue,* a reading that often incorporated traditional interpretations (*see* Targum). The formula in itself, then, does not enable us to decide whether Jesus is citing the Mosaic Law per se or the Mosaic Law as interpreted and expanded by the scribes. Nor, while the nomenclature has become standard, is "antitheses" necessarily the best way to describe these six comparisons. The grammar allows at least three different nuances: (1) "you have heard, but I (in contrast to that) say to you"; (2) "you have heard, but I (in addition to that) say to you" or (3) "you have heard, and I (in agreement with that) say to you."

No abrogation of the Law occurs in the first two comparisons (Mt 5:21-26 and 27-30), but it is harder to know whether Jesus is expounding the true meaning of the commandments, deepening the commandments by extending them from the level of action to the level of attitude, or simply juxtaposing his own teaching with that of the Law. Against the first alternative, however, is the lack of clear evidence that the Decalog prohibitions of murder and adultery included prohibitions of, respectively, anger and lust as well. Jesus, while not necessarily going beyond the Mosaic Law and the scribal teaching (both of which prohibit anger and lust), goes beyond the actual commandments he cites.

Jesus' teaching about divorce in verses 31-32 is sometimes taken as part of the second comparison, but the abbreviated introductory formula in verse 31 suggests rather that it be considered a separate, third comparison. In our earlier discussion of Jesus' teaching on divorce (see 2.3.3. above), we noted that Matthew's exceptive clause (v. 32: "except on the ground of unchastity") has the effect of bringing Jesus' teaching fairly closely into line with the Mosaic allowance. What effect this has on the actual commandment Jesus cites—(viz.) that a person who divorces his wife give her a "bill of divorcement"—is not clear, but it is probably stretching the matter to speak of an abrogation of the commandment here. Nevertheless, Jesus' teaching that an improper remarriage constitutes adultery goes beyond the OT. Clearly, Jesus is not simply expounding the Mosaic legislation regarding divorce; nor does the idea of deepening fit the circumstances very well. He goes beyond the Law in the seriousness with which he considers improper remarriages, and his basic agreement with Deuteronomy 24:1-4 over the appropriate grounds for divorce and remarriage is, as it were, incidental to the central point.

The fourth thesis cited by Jesus as a point of departure for his own teaching is an accurate summary of the Mosaic requirements regarding oaths and vows (v. 33; see Oaths and Swearing). Oaths and vows were not carefully distinguished in the OT, both involving a pledge of truthfulness in connection with God. The rabbis reluctantly accepted the need for oaths and regulated their use, but the Essenes, who often had stricter requirements than the Pharisees (or the rabbis), apparently did prohibit most oaths (see Josephus *J.W.* 2.135). Jesus' requirement seems absolute: "do not swear at all" (v. 34). But there is considerable debate about this, for the following delineation of examples appears to reflect the casuistic debates about oaths in the scribal tradition (see *m. Šeb.*; *m. Sanh.* 3:2; *t. Ned.* 1). This background, taken with the undoubted presence of hyperbole in Matthew 5, may suggest that Jesus simply intends to encourage absolute truthfulness (see v. 37). Another possibility is that Jesus prohibits voluntary oaths. If Jesus is indeed prohibiting all oaths, then a technical abrogation of the Mosaic command requiring an oath in the court (Ex 22:10-13) occurs (Meier). But the uncertainty about Jesus' intention should make us cautious about claiming an abrogation of the Law here. In any case, we see again that Jesus is neither expounding nor deepening the Law but juxtaposing his own (perhaps more radical) demand with that of the Law.

Of the six antitheses there is most agreement among scholars that the fifth, relating to the *lex talionis*, abrogates the Mosaic Law. But this is not at all clear. The law of equivalent compensation is stated in three places in the Mosaic Law (Ex 21:23-25; Lev 24:20; Deut 19.21), and in each case it has the purpose not of justifying but of restraining private retribution

by establishing an equitable judicial guideline to which all could be held. Jesus does not question, nor does he uphold, this policy. He simply demands that his followers not use it as an excuse for retaliation. Jesus certainly goes beyond the demands of the Law, but he does not contradict it.

The final quotation in Matthew 5 differs from the others in including a clause not found in the OT—that one is to "hate one's enemy" (v. 43). It has sometimes been argued that this requirement is a fair extrapolation from the fact that the scope of the love command (Lev 19:18) is restricted to the fellow-Israelite (*rē'*) and from the frequent OT expressions of hostility to Israel's enemies. But this conclusion is not warranted, and we must consider the command to "hate your enemy" not as an OT requirement, but as a reflection of current Jewish teaching in some circles (perhaps associated with the Essenes of Qumran). Jesus does not, therefore, abrogate Mosaic Law by requiring love for one's enemy, but he does ask his followers to do something that the Mosaic Law had not asked the people of Israel to do: love one's enemy. Once more, then, Jesus' teaching transcends without clearly revoking the OT Law.

We find, then, that only one possible abrogation of the Law—that having to do with divorce and remarriage—occurs in the antitheses. In the others Jesus' teaching is juxtaposed with the Mosaic commands in a way that does not fit either of the popular categories: exposition or deepening. The dominant note, hinted at in the emphatic "I say to you" and recognized by the crowds at the end of the Sermon (7:28-29), is the independent authority of Jesus, who presumes to announce God's will for life in the kingdom without support from any other source (see Amen).

Jesus, then, abrogated some Mosaic Laws—the food Laws and possibly the divorce provisions—but this is not the dominant motif in his teaching. Jesus does not so much oppose the Law as claim to transcend it. He is the "Lord of the Sabbath" and claims the right to determine God's will without reference to the Law.

2.4. Fulfillment of the Law. The best-known statement of Jesus with respect to the Law comes in Matthew 5:17: "Do not think that I have come to abolish the Law or the prophets: I have not come to abolish, but to fulfill them." To understand this claim, we must consider its following context (Mt 5:18-19) and the partial Lukan parallel to this context (Lk 16:16-17).

In Luke 16:16 Jesus announces a fundamental shift in salvation history: "The Law and the prophets were until John: since then the good news of the kingdom of God is preached, and every one enters it violently."

Especially in light of Luke 16:17 Jesus cannot mean that the significance of the OT is terminated; he must mean that John's coming has signaled a fundamental shift in the role and importance of "the Law and the prophets." Matthew's parallel (11:13) adds an important nuance: "the Law and the prophets prophesied until John." Here Jesus claims that the entire OT has a prophetic aspect, that the Law itself has some kind of forward-looking element. This reference furnishes an important clue to the Matthean viewpoint on the Law and helps us unravel the meaning of Matthew 5:17.

Study of Matthew 5:17-19 is complicated by the complex and debated tradition-history of the verses. According to one viewpoint, for instance, each verse is to be assigned to a different stratum of the early Christian community, with none of them embodying the teaching of Jesus himself. However, while the verses may indeed come from different sources (e.g., v. 18 may be from Q; cf. Lk 16:17) and while Matthew was undoubtedly responsible for their final arrangement in his Gospel, there is no compelling reason to deny their authenticity.

The key word in this paragraph is the word "fulfill" (*pleroō*, 5:17). Its interpretation becomes the basis for, or expression of, divergent general interpretations of Jesus and the Law. We speak of *law* because in Matthean usage the expression "Law and the prophets" (cf. Mt 7:12 and 22:40) and the parallels "Law" (v. 18) and "commandments" (v. 19) refer to the commanding aspect of the OT. The clear connection with the comparisons of 5:21-48 also indicates that Jesus is focusing on the relationship between his teaching and the Law. With these qualifications in view, the following are the most important interpretations of "fulfill": (1) Jesus fulfills the Law by *confirming its validity* (presupposing that the Aramaic word *qûm* lies behind *pleroō;* Branscomb); (2) Jesus fulfills the Law by *adding to it* (based on the alleged parallel to Mt 5:17 in *b. Šabb.* 116b; Jeremias); (3) Jesus fulfills the Law by bringing out its *full, originally intended meaning* (Bahnsen); (4) Jesus fulfills the Law by *extending its demands* (Davies); (5) Jesus fulfills the Law by teaching the *eschatological will of God* which the Law anticipated (Banks, Meier).

Methodologically, we should look for the meaning of *pleroō* by referring to Matthew's usage rather than to an alleged Hebrew or Aramaic original (*see* Languages of Palestine). For there is no way of confirming what that Semitic original may have been, and there is ample evidence that Matthew himself, while reproducing Jesus' own intention, is responsible for the wording of the saying. The closest syntactical parallel

to Matthew 5:17 is 3:15, where *pleroō* is also used in the active voice and is followed by a direct object. Focusing on this parallel, Ljungman argues that "fulfilling" the Law must refer to Jesus' fulfillment of the Scripture as the means of bringing in eschatological* righteousness (*see* Justice and Righteousness). But the most distinctive use of *pleroō* in Matthew comes in the introductions to his eleven so-called formula quotations, most of which are unique to his Gospel. In these texts Matthew announces the fulfillment of a text, event or prophecy in the life of Jesus. The importance of this word in these contexts, combined with Matthew's striking reference to the Law as "prophesying" (11:13), makes this prophetic use of *pleroō* the most likely source for our interpretation of Matthew 5:17. In a way analogous to his fulfilling Israel's history in his own departure from Egypt (cf. Mt 2:15) and his fulfilling the prophets' predictions in his life, Jesus also fulfills Israel's Law in his teaching. The entire OT, in all its parts, is viewed as the promise component in a promise-fulfillment scheme of salvation history, and the Law cannot be excluded from this scheme.

We conclude, then, that the fifth alternative listed above—the eschatological will of God—is the best interpretation of Matthew 5:17. In response to rumors about his Law-negating stance, Jesus assures his listeners that his teaching stands in continuity with the OT Law. His teaching does not abolish the Law, but brings it to its intended eschatological climax. This view of Matthew 5:17 fits well with the antitheses that follow and which furnish specific examples of Jesus' fulfillment of the Law (5:21-48). For, as we have seen (2.3.4. above), what Jesus does with the Law in these six comparisons cannot all be explained by recourse to any single concept, such as exposition or deepening. What is common to each is a juxtaposition of OT teaching with Jesus' own, a teaching that transcends the OT teaching. Understanding "fulfillment" in the broad, salvation-historical sense that we have defended enables 5:17 to function as a heading to these comparisons, as indeed it was apparently intended to do.

Can this interpretation be reconciled with the context of Matthew 5:18-19? At first sight no stronger endorsement of the eternal applicability of every commandment of the Mosaic Law could be envisaged than what we have here. Agreeing with this assessment are those scholars who think that Matthew 5:19, or 5:18-19 together, is a creation of a conservative Jewish group within the early church. Matthew, they argue, has inserted this material into the present context in order to correct it. While it may well be that

Matthew has been responsible for juxtaposing verses 18-19 with verse 17, we are not so sure that we must deny these sayings to Jesus. Can these verses be read in a way compatible with Jesus' teaching about the Law elsewhere in Matthew's Gospel? Attempts to avoid the conclusion that Jesus here endorses the continuing applicability of every "jot and tittle" of the Law, and so to reconcile 5:18-19 with 5:17 and 21-48, focus on three issues: the scope of the two *heōs* ("until") clauses in 5:18, the meaning of *nomos* ("Law") in 5:18 and the antecedent of *toutōn* ("these [commandments]") in 5:19.

The first *heōs* clause in 5:18, "until heaven and earth pass away," must be compared to its counterpart in Luke 16:17: "it is easier for heaven and earth to pass away than for one dot of the Law to become void." Luke apparently uses this verse to guard against an antinomian interpretation of 16:16. Probably we are to understand the clause in Matthew in the same way; every detail of the Law remains valid until the present world order passes away. Nevertheless, this conclusion in itself does not stand in contradiction to Matthew 5:17, for the nature of this validity must be probed further.

The second *heōs* clause, which many take to be Matthew's insertion, is more difficult to interpret, for there is no clear antecedent to *panta*, "all things," and the precise force of *genētai* is not evident. One possibility is that Jesus is teaching that the Law will remain valid only until all the demands of the Law are "done" or "obeyed." We may then infer that these demands were fully met by Jesus in his obedient life and sacrificial death, and that the Law is therefore no longer valid. But *genētai* is more likely to mean "happen" in this context, while *panta* probably refers to predicted events (cf. Mt 24:34-35). These events have been identified with Jesus' death and resurrection, with those things prophesied about Jesus generally or with all the components of God's plan for history. The lack of any restriction in this context favors the last of these alternatives. This being so, the second *heōs* clause is roughly parallel to the first, both maintaining that the Law will remain valid until the end of history as we know it.

An assumption quite popular in some circles is that *nomos* in 5:18 refers only to the moral Law. But no such restriction can be entertained. Not only is there no support for such a limitation in first-century Judaism, and little in the teaching of Jesus, but the reference to "jot and tittle" in 5:18 shows that no part of the Law can be omitted from Jesus' purview.

Jesus, then, asserts in Matthew 5:18 (and in its parallel, Lk 16:17), that the whole Mosaic Law will remain valid throughout this age. But "valid" in what way? Here it is appropriate to suggest that this must be understood in light of Matthew 5:17—the continuing validity of the Law must be seen in terms of Jesus' fulfillment of it. In all its details the Law remains valid, but the manner in which people are to relate to it has now been determined by the one who brought its fulfillment. We are probably to understand Matthew 5:19 in a similar way. Indeed, some have taken *toutōn* to refer to what follows, in which case "these commandments" are the commands Jesus himself issues in 5:21-48. But there is little grammatical basis for this. "These commandments" are the detailed parts of the Law of 5:18; the teaching of these commandments must take place in conjunction with the nature of Jesus' fulfillment of the Law.

There is an undeniable tension between the stress on continuity with the Law in these two verses and the stress on discontinuity that pervades Jesus' teaching about the Law. Those who find the tension intolerable will declare these verses inauthentic. But we would argue that while some tension remains, the interpretation we have given makes credible Jesus' uttering all the statements in Matthew 5:17-19. Indeed, if tension is to be found, it is more likely to be an authentic reflection of the historical Jesus than the creation of the church or the Evangelist. Seen in this light, Matthew 5:18-19 reinforces the "I have not come to abolish" of verse 17. As Jesus proclaimed the beginning of the new era with its "new wineskins," he was aware of the danger that the newness could be pressed to the point of rupture with the OT. This he guards against by stressing, perhaps with some hyperbole, the continuing validity of the OT and its Law for the life of the kingdom.

3. The Gospel Writers.

Jesus' stance on the Law and his disputes with his Jewish contemporaries about this stance, are so integral to his mission and message that none of the Evangelists can avoid the topic. Nor is there any indication that they wanted to. However, they do differ in the degree to which they are interested in this issue and the emphases they bring to it.

3.1. Matthew. As our previous discussion would indicate, Matthew shows more interest in Jesus and the Law than do the other Evangelists. He alone records Jesus' claim to fulfill the Law (5:17). In passages paralleled in Luke's Gospel, Matthew adds references to the Law, most notably in the formulation of the so-called golden rule (Mt 7:12 par. Lk 6:31) and in the antitheses (Mt 5:21-48; cf. Lk 6:27-36; 12:57-59; 16:18). It is evident that Matthew writes to a community that is deeply concerned about the relationship between Jesus and the Law, but there is scholarly debate about the exact nature of that community and the overall force of Matthew's teaching on this matter. This is partly because Matthew presents two different—potentially conflictive—emphases: endorsement of the Law and transcendence of the Law.

3.1.1. Endorsement of the Law. In our previous discussion (see 2.4. above) we noted the strength of Jesus' endorsement of the Law as recorded in Matthew 5:18-19. But this passage is not alone. In Matthew 8:4 (with parallels in Mk 1:44 and Lk 5:14) Jesus insists that the leper (*see* Leprosy) whom he cleansed report to the priests and "offer the gift which Moses commanded, as a witness to them." In the story of the rich young man, Matthew accentuates more strongly the connection between obedience to the Law and salvation by adding the saying "If you want to enter life, keep the commandments" (19:17). In Matthew 23:23 Jesus, while scolding the religious leaders for neglecting the "weightier matters of the Law," nevertheless insists that they should continue to obey the law of tithing. Jesus in Matthew expects his disciples to bring gifts to the altar (5:23-24), to give alms (6:1-4) and to fast (6:16-18). And, in perhaps the strongest statement of its kind, Matthew presents Jesus endorsing the authority and teaching of the scribes and Pharisees (23:2-3). Here Jesus appears to endorse not only the Mosaic Law but the oral Law as well.

3.1.2. Transcendence of the Law. Along with these apparently strong endorsements of the Law come equally strong indications of Jesus' transcendence of the Law. Only Matthew records Jesus' claim to fulfill the Law (5:17) and the antitheses, with their implicit criticism of the Law (5:21-48). He, along with Mark and Luke, portrays Jesus acting with sovereign freedom on the Sabbath and records his far-reaching claim to be "Lord of the Sabbath" (12:8). In a related development that many think to be central to Matthew's view of the Law, there is a strong emphasis on love or concern for others as the embodiment of the Law (7:12; 22:40).

3.1.3. A Synthesis. With these two strands of teaching in evidence, it is no wonder that some have seen Matthew as a conservative on the Law, while others have seen him as antinomian. Others seek to do justice to both strands in Matthew by suggesting that he is fighting on two fronts—combating both Jews and/or Jewish-Christian rigorists, and Gentile-Christian antinomians (e.g., Barth). That Matthew was seeking to present a balanced teaching on the Law against opposing tendencies is possible. But it is also possible to find a theological coherence in Matthew's teaching about the Law if his salvation-historical perspective is considered.

Matthew makes clear that Jesus' death and resurrection mark a significant shift in salvation history. Prior to these events, as Jesus makes clear, his business is with "the lost sheep of the house of Israel" (15:24). After Jesus' mission is accomplished, however, the disciples are sent to "all the nations" with the good news (28:19-20). Similarly, Matthew shows that John's ministry ends the prophetic office of the OT (11:13). To some extent, then, Jesus' endorsement of the Law in Matthew reflects only its continuing validity during the period before the new era is brought in. This is almost certainly the case in Matthew 8:4; 23:23 and 5:23-24; 6:1-4 and 6:16-18. Jesus' endorsement of the teachings of the scribes and the Pharisees in 23:2-3 may also fall into this category, although we are probably to see irony here also (Jeremias).

Jesus never doubted the authority of the Mosaic Law for the time preceding the entrance of the kingdom, and his instructions to followers living in that time will naturally include admonitions to obey those Laws. Only those who think Matthew has rewritten everything in his Gospel for the consumption of the church in his day would have any difficulty with this. On the other hand, statements about Jesus transcending the Law—and these represent the dominant thrust of the Gospel—reflect the fact that a new era of salvation history is indeed breaking in. This is an era in which Jesus' own teaching will be the central authority for the people of God, and the Law will play a role only as caught up in, and re-applied by, Jesus (Mt 5:17-19).

The relationship of the Law to Jesus in Matthew is, then, only one segment of his salvation-historical, promise-fulfillment scheme. Through it Matthew integrates his stress on the continuity of the Law—for the Law looks ahead to, and is incorporated into, the teaching of Jesus—and on its discontinuity—for Jesus, not the Law, is now the locus of God's word to his people.

3.2. Mark. In comparison with Matthew, Mark seems to display little interest in the issue of the Law, as is revealed by the fact that the word never occurs in his Gospel. Nevertheless, many of those incidents that are fundamental in Matthew's presentation of Jesus and the Law are taken from Mark: the controversies over the Sabbath (2:23—3:6) and ritual defilement (7:1-23), Jesus' teaching on divorce and remarriage (10:2-10), the story of the rich young ruler (10:17-22), and Jesus' teaching about the "great commandment" (12:28-34). Indeed, in three of these incidents

Mark has important material not found in Matthew or in any other Gospel: the saying that "the Sabbath was made for humankind" (2:27), the editorial application of Jesus' teaching about defilement ("thus he made all foods clean," 7:19), and the conversation between Jesus and a scribe after Jesus' identification of the greatest commandment, in which the scribe, with Jesus' approval, asserts that loving one's neighbor is "more than all the burnt offerings and sacrifices" (12:33). This material suggests that Mark may have had a particular interest in the supersession of the ritual Law.

3.3. Luke. While Luke's perspective on the Law cannot be understood apart from Acts, the second part of his two-volume work, we will concentrate on the Gospel. Here there is evidence that Luke is conservative with respect to the Law (see Jervell), evidence that comes both from what Luke has added to and omitted from the tradition. In adding to the tradition he portrays the piety of those involved in Jesus' infancy in legal terms (1:6; 2:22-24, 27, 37, 39, 42; *see* Birth of Jesus). On the other hand, Luke omits from his Markan source the episode concerning ritual defilement, the dispute about the Law in its relation to divorce and remarriage and the teaching on the great commandment. In comparison with Matthew, Luke includes Jesus' teaching about the eternal validity of the Law (16:17), but does not have the antitheses, Jesus' claim to have fulfilled the Law or any reference to "weightier matters of the Law." But these data do not justify the conclusion that Luke, in contrast to Matthew, upholds the Mosaic Law.

First, comparisons with Matthew are difficult because we do not know whether Luke has omitted something in their common tradition or whether Matthew has himself added that which was not there. Second, Luke's omission of some of the Markan episodes suggests that he was not as interested in the Law as were Mark and Matthew, but this is not necessarily indicative of a conservative attitude. Third, almost all of the positive evidence for a Lukan endorsement of the Law comes from the infancy narrative. But his purpose in portraying the people in this narrative as obedient to the Law is simply to stress their piety and righteousness in accordance with the standards under which they lived. To conclude that Luke presents these people as exemplars of Torah piety for Christians generally is to go far beyond the evidence. Fourth, Luke adds to the tradition two Sabbath healings by Jesus (13:10-17; 14:1-6) and, while they do not present Jesus annulling the Sabbath, they share with the other Sabbath incidents an emphasis on the sovereign freedom with which Jesus treated the Sabbath.

Finally, Luke includes several sayings of Jesus that betray the same kind of salvation-historical perspective we have seen in Matthew. Luke 16:16 (with a parallel in Mt 11:12-13) is the most important: "The Law and the prophets were until John; since then the kingdom of God is being proclaimed, and everyone is entering it violently." The debate about whether John is here included in the time of the "Law and the prophets" or in the time of the kingdom is immaterial to our purposes. What is important is that Luke's Jesus affirms the cessation of the authority of the OT, in some sense, in the age of the kingdom. The important promise-fulfillment emphasis of Luke 24 (see 24:25-27, 44), while not directly applied to the Mosaic commands, contributes to this Lukan salvation-history scheme. Rather than being a "conservative," Luke in his Gospel gives many indications that he views the Law as belonging fundamentally to the past of the people of God (Blomberg).

3.4. John. True to its tendency, the Fourth Gospel follows its own course with regard to the Law. In fact there is no single teaching about the Law that is common to John and to any of the Synoptic Evangelists (*see* Synoptics and John). Like the Synoptic Evangelists, however, John records two healings of Jesus on the Sabbath (5:2-47; 9:1-41). In the first, Jesus' healing of a lame man sparks a debate about Jesus' authority to work on the Sabbath. John betrays no interest in the meaning and intent of the Sabbath command; he focuses exclusively on the christological claim: Jesus, as Son of God, has the same right to work on the Sabbath as does the Father himself. The same christological focus is evident in the second incident, the healing of the man born blind. The Pharisees deny that Jesus is from God, because he sinned in performing the miracle on the Sabbath (9:14-16). Once again, Jesus' behavior, bound up as it is with his unique status, says nothing about his attitude toward the Sabbath or the Law generally.

Jesus' references to "your Law" in disputes with the Jewish authorities (8:17; 10:34 [although note the alternative reading]) strike a much more polemical note. The use of the possessive pronoun creates some distance between Jesus and the Law, although it is not clear if this is because Jesus stands with God over against the people, because he stands with John's Gentile* readers against the Jews (as some interpret the circumstances of the Gospel) or simply because he wants to impress on the Jews their responsibility to hearken to their own Law. Probably the last of these alternatives is the best (see Jn 7:51), in which case we learn little from it about Jesus' attitude to the Law in John.

John shares with the Synoptic Evangelists an emphasis on the fulfillment of prophecy in Jesus' ministry and includes the Law as a witness to Jesus on one occasion (1:45). We should note in this regard the way John shows Jesus replacing the great feasts and institutions of Israel—Passover (1:29 [?]; 19:36 [probably]); the manna in the wilderness (chap. 6; *see* Mountain and Wilderness); Tabernacles (chaps. 7—8); Israel itself (chap. 15). Evidence that John included the Law in this replacement scheme comes from terms, commonly associated with the Law, that are applied to Jesus ("light,"* 8:12; "bread* of life," 6:35; "living water,"* 4:10), the designation of faith* in Jesus as the one "work" that disciples are to do (6:29; in contrast to the "works of the Law"?) and the Mosaic role that Jesus often assumes. It is precariously easy to read anything into John's symbolism that one wants, but there is enough evidence here to create the strong presumption that John wants to present Jesus as one who comes to fulfill for the church the role that Moses and the Law performed in Israel.

The discontinuity between the Law and Jesus seen in this replacement motif comes to clear expression in John 1:17: "the Law came through Moses, grace and truth* came through Jesus Christ." This discontinuity does not relate to the presence of grace in the OT as such, for 1:16 indicates that Christians receive grace "in place of" (*anti*) the grace found in the old covenant. The discontinuity lies rather in the suggestion that the grace available for God's people in the OT does not come through the Law, and that it is only now in Jesus Christ that such grace can be found. Moreover, in associating the Law so closely with Moses and putting Christ firmly on the other side of the salvation-historical dividing line, John implies that in Jesus the Law will no longer have the same position and significance that it had before.

4. Conclusion.

In different ways and with different emphases, all four Gospels reflect a dominant theme in the teaching of Jesus: his divine authority with reference to the Law. Jesus was quick to clarify that his authority did not negate the role of the Law in salvation history. But he also made it clear that this authority involved the right not only to exposit, add to or deepen the Law, but to make demands of his people independent of that Law. This being the case, it is quite inadequate, and potentially misleading, to think of Jesus as "the last great expositor of the Law." The Law, God's great gift to Israel, anticipated and looked forward to the eschatological teaching of God's will that Jesus brought. This teaching, not the Law, is the focus of the

Gospels, and the Law remains authoritative for the disciple of Jesus only insofar as it is taken up into his own teaching.

See also CLEAN AND UNCLEAN; COMMANDMENT; MARRIAGE AND DIVORCE; OATHS AND SWEARING; RABBINIC TRADITIONS AND WRITINGS; SERMON ON THE MOUNT.

BIBLIOGRAPHY. G. Bahnsen, *Theonomy in Christian Ethics* (Nutley, NJ: Craig, 1977); R. Banks, *Jesus and the Law in the Synoptic Tradition* (SNTSMS 28; Cambridge: University Press, 1975); G. Barth, "Matthew's Understanding of the Law," in *Tradition and Interpretation in Matthew* (Philadelphia: Westminster, 1963); K. Berger, *Die Gesetzesauslegung Jesu: Ihr historischer Hintergrund im Judentum und im Alten Testament* (WMANT 40.1: Neukirchen/Vluyn: Neukirchener, 1972); C. Blomberg, "The Law in Luke-Acts," *JSNT* 22 (1984) 53-80; B. H. Branscomb, *Jesus and the Law of Moses* (New York: Richard A. Smith, 1930); D. A. Carson, ed., *From Sabbath to Lord's Day* (Grand Rapids: Zondervan, 1982); W. D. Davies, "Matthew 5.17, 18," in *Christian Origins and Judaism* (Philadelphia: Westminster, 1962); P. Fairbairn, *The Revelation of Law in Scripture* (Grand Rapids: Zondervan, 1957 [1869]); V. P. Furnish, *The Love Command in the New Testament* (Nashville: Abingdon, 1972); W. Gutbrod, "νόμος," *TDNT* IV.1036-85; H. Hübner, *Das Gesetz in der synoptischen Tradition* (2d ed.; Göttingen: Vandenhoeck & Ruprecht, 1973); J. Jeremias, *New Testament Theology: The Proclamation of Jesus* (New York: Scribner's, 1971); J. Jervell, *Luke and the People of God* (Minneapolis: Augsburg, 1972); H. Ljungman, *Das Gesetz Erfullen: Matth. 5.17ff. und 3.15 untersucht* (LUA 50S; Lund: Gleerup, 1954); J. P. Meier, *Law and History in Matthew's Gospel* (AnBib 71; Rome: Biblical Institute, 1976); D. J. Moo, "Jesus and the Authority of the Mosaic Law," *JSNT* 20 (1984) 3-49; S. Pancaro, *The Law in the Fourth Gospel* (NovTSup 42; Leiden: Brill, 1975); A. Sand, *Das Gesetz und die Propheten* (Regensburg: Pustet, 1974); E. P. Sanders, *Jesus and Judaism* (Philadelphia: Fortress, 1985); idem, *Jewish Law from Jesus to the Mishnah: Five Studies* (Philadelphia: Trinity, 1990); H. J. Schoeps, "Jesus und das judische Gesetz," in *Aus fruhchristlicher Zeit: Religionsgeschichtliche Untersuchungen* (Tübingen: Mohr, 1950); S. Westerholm, *Jesus and Scribal Authority* (ConBNT 10: Lund: Gleerup, 1978).

D. J. Moo

LAWYER. *See* SCRIBES.

LAZARUS

The Greek name *Lazaros* is a transliteration of the contracted form of the Aramaic name, 'el 'āzār, meaning "God helps" or "God has helped." The name appears in John 11; 12:1, 10 and Luke 16:20-31. The Johannine context is the well-known raising of Lazarus, while the Lukan passage is a parable.* Whether or not there is any connection between the two has been a source of much speculation.

1. Lazarus in John
2. The Parable of Lazarus and the Rich Man

1. Lazarus in John.

The raising of Lazarus in John 11 is the climax of the series of signs which dominates the first half of the Gospel (see John, Gospel of). There can be no doubt that the resurrection* of Lazarus is also presented as *the* sign of all the signs Jesus performed and as the interpretive center of the Gospel. Lazarus' resurrection prepares the reader for the resurrection of Jesus and is the prototype for resurrection life promised all believers (11:21-27).

1.1. Critical Questions. Several critical questions arise in John 11. First is the historical question: Did the resurrection of Lazarus actually occur? The fact that the Synoptics do not know of the miracle* suggests to some that the whole miracle is contrived by John or his sources, possibly developing out of the parable of Lazarus and the rich man (Bultmann, 396 n.3). But the details of the parable and that of the Lazarus story are so different that this seems unlikely (Dunkerly, 323), and the connection of the story with Bethany (see Archeology and Geography) suggests that Lazarus was an historical figure (Schnackenburg, 2.321, 342-45). The Synoptics may have omitted the miracle either because they did not know of it (the Synoptics being more oriented to events in Galilee,* while John seems to come from Judean/Jerusalem sources) or because it was simply one of several such events (cf. the raising of the widow's son, Lk 7:11-17, and Jairus' daughter, Mk 5:21-43 and par.; see Synoptics and John). John 11 is consistent with other Johannine passages such as John 5 and John 9, where miracle stories are extended and dramatized in order to draw out the theological implications of the event.

1.2. Lazarus and the Beloved Disciple. The most interesting question raised by John 11—12 is the curious description of Lazarus as one whom "Jesus loved" (11:3, 5, 36). This has led J. N. Sanders and others to identify the anonymous authority for the Gospel, the "disciple* whom Jesus loved" (13:23; 19:26; 20:2-3, 8; 21:7, 20-24), with Lazarus. Sanders (29-34) lists the following reasons for this identification: (1) They are the only people (along with Mary and Martha) whom John designates as those that Jesus loved; (2) Lazarus' home in Bethany would explain the Jerusalem orientation of the Fourth Gospel; (3)

Lazarus' resurrection and Jesus' words to Martha (11:25-26) might explain the expectation that the beloved disciple would not die (21:23). The phrase in 12:11, "on account of him (Lazarus), many of the Jews were going away and believing in Jesus" could be seen as an implicit reference to Lazarus' role as the founder of the Johannine community. The link between Lazarus and the beloved disciple is suggestive, not only for the reasons listed above, but also because it would explain why the Gospel values so highly a miracle that the Synoptics do not record, and perhaps why the beloved disciple had more immediate insight into the meaning of the empty tomb (20:8). (For an extended presentation of these arguments in popular form, see V. Eller.)

However, this suggestion ultimately lacks compelling force. Lazarus' resurrection is not needed to explain the belief that the beloved disciple would not die: the idea is explained as rooted in Jesus' words to Peter ("If I wish for him to remain until I come, what is that to you?" 21:22). If the beloved disciple were Lazarus, the explanation of 21:22 would be superfluous. Both Lazarus and the beloved disciple are idealized figures in John. The beloved disciple exemplifies the faithful believer who has the insight given by the Holy Spirit (see Holy Spirit) to receive Jesus as the Word (see Logos). Lazarus represents the future of the disciples as those who will be given resurrection life and are given eternal life now. Neither are fictionalized characters, but idealized historical figures who serve different roles.

2. The Parable of Lazarus and the Rich Man.

The parable (Lk 16:19-31) is a curious one in its own right. It is wholly Jewish in character, and falls into two parts: the first, the reversal of rich and poor in the afterlife (16:19-25), and the second, a discussion of the refusal of some to see and receive the witness of God (16:26-31). The parable takes a new direction at 16:26, raising the issue of the chasm between the rich man in Hades (see Heaven and Hell) and the poor man, Lazarus, in the bosom of Abraham. The point in the second half is that the rich man, whose lavish lifestyle and disregard for the poor man Lazarus had led to his present misery, wishes to send Lazarus back to warn his brothers (see Rich and Poor). Abraham refuses the request, stating that even seeing a resurrected man would not convince them if they were not already responsive to Moses* and the Prophets. Thus, the first half of the parable warns the rich against their neglect of the poor, while the second half warns all people against the danger of blindness* to God's Word. This latter expansion maintains the Jewish flavor of the first part of the parable, but seems to fit a context of continued resistance to the message of Jesus' resurrection (cf. 16:30-31; 24:25, 44).

The background of John 11—12 raises intriguing questions for the interpretation of this parable. We have already rejected the idea that John 11—12 is dependent on the parable. If John 11—12 were dependent on Luke 16, we still would have no explanation for the fact that the name "Lazarus" is given to the character of the poor man. Any influence that might exist flows the other way: from the resurrection of Lazarus to the parable (so Sanders, 35; Dunkerly, 324).

This is not to say that the Lukan parable is directly dependent on the Johannine passage. Naming the poor man while the rich remains anonymous reinforces the eschatological-reversal motif of the parable: It is the poor beggar who is named and important while the rich glutton dies in nameless ignominy. However, another point of commonality emerges between the parable and the Lazarus narrative: the role of resurrection as a call to faith.* The mixed reaction to the raising of Lazarus (Jesus' enemies see the miracle as the driving reason to have Jesus executed) parallels the point of the parable, namely, that those who are closed to the work of God are also closed to seeing God's work in Jesus' miracles (Jeremias, 186-87). Something similar may be operating in passages like the parable of the pounds (Lk 19:11-27), where the story of Archelaus (Herod's son; *see* Herodian Dynasty) is woven into a parable and given a surprising application. The theory that the Lazarus story has influenced the Lukan parable remains unproven, but it provides an attractive explanation of the data.

See also PARABLES; RESURRECTION; RICH AND POOR.

BIBLIOGRAPHY. R. Bultmann, *The Gospel of John* (Philadelphia: Westminster, 1971) 392-417; R. Dunkerly, "Lazarus," *NTS* 5 (1958/1959) 321-27; V. Eller, *The Beloved Disciple* (Grand Rapids: Eerdmans, 1987); J. Jeremias, *The Parables of Jesus* (New York: Charles Scribner's, 1963) 182-87; J. N. Sanders, " 'Those Whom Jesus Loved' (John XI.5)," *NTS* 1 (1954/1955) 29-41; R. Schnackenburg, *The Gospel according to St. John* (3 vols.; New York: Crossroad, 1968, 1979, 1982) 2.316-46.

R. W. Paschal, Jr.

LECTIONARIES, JEWISH. *See* WORSHIP.

LEGION. *See* MILITARY.

LEPROSY

Modern discussion of leprosy has largely centered on the distinction between true leprosy, that is, the disease caused by Hansen's bacillus, and superficially similar diseases; on its treatment, including precautions against the infection of others; and on the avoidance of the pejorative term "leper," in referring to the patient.

Biblical concerns were almost wholly different. Hebrew ṣāraʿat, translated as *lepra* in the LXX, is explicitly used in the detailed legislation of Leviticus 13—14 to cover a variety of human diseases, carefully distinguished, together with mold on fabrics and on the wall of a house. (*Lepra* was similarly used in classical Greek of a variety of human, animal and tree diseases and also, for example, of mold on a vinegar bottle.) None of these conditions is identifiable with Hansen's disease. Whether or not Hansen's disease existed in ancient Israel is disputed. The biblical terms, where they refer to human diseases, probably cover psoriasis, lupus, ringworm and favus.

The various conditions described in Leviticus 13—14 are diagnosed, and if cured declared "clean," in analogous ways, though the procedure for human conditions is more detailed. Central to the entire process, from diagnosis to declaring clean, is the role of the priest.* Sacrifice is required to authenticate (not to effect) the cleansing of human beings and houses. The biblical references are not concerned with treatment. The possibility of spontaneous cure was presupposed, though ṣāraʿat in a house is assumed to be sent by God* (Lev 14:33-53). Nor are they specifically concerned with infection (unlike the patient in the apocryphal Gospel, Papyrus Egerton 2). The rule that the victim shall live alone "outside the camp" (Lev 13:46) appears in context to be more related to ritual impurity (*see* Clean and Unclean). The modern distinction between hygiene and cultus may however be alien to the ancient situation. Modern translations of Leviticus 14:54 use "dreaded skin diseases" (TEV), "any infectious skin disease" (NIV) and "all kinds of skin-disease" (NJB).

"To the rabbis the cure of a leper was as difficult as raising a person from the dead" (Marshall, 208, referring to Str-B IV.2.745-63). The supernatural cleansing of lepers was, however, expected as one of the signs of the messianic age (*see* Kingdom of God). It is to this, among other things, that Jesus points in reply to the question put by John the Baptist's (*see* John the Baptist) messengers: "Are you he who is to come?" (that is, the Messiah; Mt 11:3-4 par.; *see* Christ).

Synoptic occurrences of *lepra* and *lepros* (there are no others in the NT) stand firmly in the tradition of OT Law* and cultus. The major new element is the fulfillment by Jesus, and by implication the Twelve (Mt

10:8; *see* Disciples), of the expectation of miraculous healing* of this disease. As in the OT, "lepers are cleansed" (Mt 11:5) is as much a set phrase as "the deaf hear." In the account of the healing of a leper (Mk 1:40-45 par.) and of ten lepers (Lk 17:11-19), Jesus sends the healed sufferers to the priests for their cure to be confirmed. In the first case the prescribed sacrifices are to be offered (Mk 1:44 par.). In the second case the sufferers stand *porrōthen,* "outside," the village and at a distance from Jesus, in accordance with Leviticus 13:46. In the first case, Jesus' action in touching the sufferer is best understood as one of compassion (so explicitly in Mk 1:41, if *splagchnistheis* is read), by which he is symbolically welcomed back into the community. It has nothing to do with the priest's ritual smearing of parts of a healed patient's body (Lev 14:14, 17), for Jesus does not usurp the priest's functions. The force of *eis martyrion autois* in Mark 1:44 and parallels is uncertain. It may mean simply "to provide evidence of the cure," in which case *autois* will probably mean "to the priests," or the reference may be broader, as in TEV, "in order to prove to everyone that you are cured" (similarly RSV). Perhaps the most likely implication is that Jesus is telling the healed man not to speak about his cure, but rather to let it speak for itself as a messianic sign.

See also CLEAN AND UNCLEAN; HEALING.

BIBLIOGRAPHY. J. G. Anderson, "Leprosy in Translations of the Bible," *BT* 31 (1980) 107-12; E. V. Hulse, "The Nature of Biblical 'Leprosy' and the Use of Alternative Medical Terms in Modern Translations of the Bible," *PEQ* 107 (1985) 87-105; I. H. Marshall, *Commentary on Luke* (NIGTC; Grand Rapids: Eerdmans, 1978); J. Wilkinson, "Leprosy and Leviticus: The Problem of Description and Identification," *SJT* 30 (1977) 153-69; idem, "Leprosy and Leviticus: A Problem of Semantics and Translation," *SJT* 31 (1978) 153-66.
P. Ellingworth

LEVI. *See* DISCIPLES.

LIBERATION HERMENEUTICS

Liberation and feminist hermeneutics have arisen in response to the use of the Bible as a tool of oppression. Women have been excluded from ordained ministry in the church, for instance, on the basis of the male gender of Jesus or certain interpretations of the injunctions of Paul. On the other hand, the Bible has frequently been experienced by the oppressed as a source of liberation that provides the framework for identifying and transcending oppression. The purpose of liberation and feminist hermeneutics is to embrace this ambivalence toward the use of the Bible

as a source both of oppression and liberation. Several principles and interpretations unite liberation and feminist hermeneutics in general.

1. Principles of Liberation Hermeneutics
2. Discerning a Liberative Axis
3. Liberative Portraits of Jesus
4. The Challenge and Limits of Liberation Hermeneutics

1. Principles of Liberation Hermeneutics.

1.1. Principle One: A Hermeneutic of Suspicion. The awareness that the Bible can be a powerful tool of oppression results in the first principle uniting feminist and liberation hermeneutics: a hermeneutic of suspicion. Suspicion begins by observing that oppression characterizes society. All the ideologies and theologies that do not challenge such oppression are suspect. Interpretations of the Bible in particular must be suspected when they omit data that might disrupt the status quo or when they emphasize data that undergird the status quo. For example, the starting point for christology has usually been the two natures of Christ (Chalcedon), or biblical christological titles such as "Son of God"* or "Messiah," or the resurrected Christ,* etc.—none of which seems to challenge oppression directly. Therefore, Latin American liberation theologians suspect that these emphases are tools of oppression. The church can affirm, for example, the two natures of Christ while siding with the political and economic elite rather than with the poor.

Based upon their experience of oppression, feminist theologians also employ a hermeneutic of suspicion—but with one significant difference. Latin American liberation theologians suspect interpretations of the Bible. Many feminist theologians apply the hermeneutic of suspicion to the Bible itself.

The reason for this difference is that the basic conviction of liberation theology—that God* sides with the oppressed—is evident throughout the Bible, while the basic conviction of feminist theology—that God sides with oppressed women—is at times ignored or opposed by the Bible. Its injunctions to silence and subordination are well known. Therefore, E. S. Fiorenza (1984, 138-139) writes,

> . . . the critical hermeneutical task of feminist theology is more complicated [than Latin American liberation theology], since it cannot state without qualification that the "God of the Bible is the god of women," because there is considerable evidence that the Bible not only was used against women's liberation but also had no clear "option" for women's liberation.

Even an evangelical scholar such as D. M. Scholer, who gives precedence to the authority of the biblical text, asserts that evangelical feminist hermeneutics must recognize patriarchal texts and assumptions in the Bible and interpret them as limited texts and assumptions.

What feminist and liberation theologians do agree upon is that interpretations of the Bible must be held suspect. This conviction is based on the observation that society is oppressive, and that the Bible is often used to reinforce such oppression. But another reason exists for their suspicion: the recognition that no interpretation is objective. This is the second principle uniting liberation and feminist hermeneutics.

1.2. Principle Two: No Exegesis Is Objective. The social context of the interpreter inevitably determines his or her interpretation of a text. Presuppositions, prejudgments and questions all determine how a specific text is interpreted. For instance, few contemporary scholars interpret the Bible to espouse enslaving Africans, although many of their nineteenth-century predecessors did so. This difference is due to changed prejudgments about slavery rather than altered exegetical methods or linguistic analysis. That is, a changed social context leads to changed questions which result in different interpretations of the same biblical texts.

This observation is not new. A. Schweitzer in his *Quest of the Historical Jesus* illustrated how eighteenth- and nineteenth-century lives of Jesus reflected more the beliefs and ideals of their own periods than the period in which Jesus lived (e.g., the rationalist Jesus of Venturini and the romantic Jesus of Renan; *see* Historical Jesus). H. G. Gadamer and A. Thiselton provided the theoretical basis for this view of the so-called hermeneutical circle. And, of course, R. Bultmann's article, which answered "No" to the question "Is Exegesis Without Presuppositions Possible?" promulgated widely the view that objective interpretations are impossible to attain.

What is new about feminist and liberation theologies is their attempt to champion the experience of oppression as the normative social context for interpreting the Bible. For Latin American liberation theologians interpretation arises out of the experience of the oppressed. For feminist theologians interpretation arises out of the experience of women, in particular "when women become critically aware of these [patriarchally manipulated] falsifying and alienating experiences imposed upon them as women by a male-dominated culture" (Ruether, 114).

1.3. Principle Three: The Advocacy of the Interpreter. Since precommitments determine interpretations, the only appropriate precommitment in a world characterized by oppression is one which advocates justice. A precommitment to justice will result in liberative interpretations, just as precommitments to the status quo tend to result in interpretations that fossilize oppressive and patriarchal structures in church and society.

This precommitment is essentially what Marx called praxis: concrete engagement for the purpose of transformation. Liberation theologians define praxis as transforming action that transforms history. Further, the nature of that action which transforms is very specific. Praxis is action on behalf of the poor. Having this precommitment to the poor reverses theology as it is traditionally approached. Rather than beginning with theological foundations, or the Bible or tradition, liberation theologians begin with praxis among the poor. Praxis is the first step of theology.

Reading the Bible—the second step of theology—with a commitment to praxis results in two developments. On the one hand, reflecting on praxis in the light of the Bible leads to a new praxis as the Bible lends insight to the present situation. Praxis, then, is always in a state of flux. On the other hand, the vicissitudes of the social context to which the interpreter is committed lead to new interpretations of the Bible.

For liberation theologians this commitment entails emphasizing biblical texts that liberate, that demand the conversion of the powerful and wealthy and that highlight the political dimension of Jesus' life and death (*see* Death of Jesus). In particular, prophetic texts, including Gospel texts that portray Jesus as a prophetic opponent of the powerful, hold a prominent place in liberation theology. For feminists this commitment entails denouncing patriarchal biblical texts that women experience as oppressive. Conversely, it requires rediscovering biblical texts that are not androcentric and patriarchal.

This attempt to emphasize, denounce and rediscover selective texts raises the question of authority. By what criteria do feminist and liberation theologians determine which texts are liberative and which texts are oppressive or patriarchal?

1.4. Principle Four: Interpretation from Communities of the Oppressed. In the earliest Christian centuries, men—not women—wrote the texts that comprise the NT, selected those texts for canonization (*see* Canon), interpreted those texts and participated in councils that established creeds which referred to those texts. Since the Reformation biblical interpretation has been accomplished by male scholars who have been educated at major universities in Europe and North

America. The criteria for evaluating the validity of biblical interpretations came from these same few, male, educated European and North American scholars. Although these criteria were established largely without the input of women and the poor, over the centuries their criteria have become axiomatic for determining orthodox and heretical interpretations of the Bible.

In contrast, for feminist and liberation theologians interpretation and criteria of evaluation should emerge from the experience of oppressed people who have the potential to subvert society's oppressive and patriarchal social structures. In Latin America these groups have taken the form of base (poor and marginalized) communities. Base communities began to emerge in the 1960s due to the drastic shortage of priests in Latin America. At the Roman Catholic gathering of Latin American bishops in Medellín, Colombia (1968), these communities were applauded, and their numbers increased dramatically thereafter. Today there are over 80,000 in Brazil alone.

Generally, base communities consist of twelve to fifteen people who meet regularly to read Scripture and to reflect on it in light of their concrete situation. Their reflection frequently leads to further praxis (the commitment with which they have come to the meeting). Praxis may take the shape of community participation to construct a road or a well, or political involvement to effect substantive change. E. Cardenal has collected in *The Gospel in Solantiname* discussions of the Bible from a base community in a coastal village of Nicaragua.

Communities of women and men who are advocates of women in their struggle for liberation (what Fiorenza calls "women-church") have not grown as readily as base communities. This difference is due to at least two factors. First, the church has not on the whole affirmed a notion of women-church that in any way parallels the Medellin affirmation of base communities. Second, feminists hold divergent opinions about whether men can rightfully be included in such communities. Some post-Christian feminists, such as Mary Daly, prefer a total separation of men from women, while more moderate revisionist feminists, such as Fiorenza and L. M. Russell, want to include women-identified men in women-church. Such differences render a consistent feminist ecclesiology elusive.

1.5. Summary of Principles. Despite these differences in reality, liberation and feminist theologians share a common ideal that directly challenges traditional ecclesial and academic authority. Both feel that communities of the oppressed should be the interpreters of the Bible. Some of these principles are not new; feminist and liberation theologians are merely bringing to light what is true of biblical interpretation: All interpretations are suspect because they inevitably reflect the presuppositions of the interpreter who advocates, inadvertently or consciously, certain socially located ideologies. Another principle is quite new: In a world of injustice, biblical interpretation must be shifted from the educated elite to the oppressed. When this occurs, some interesting interpretations of the Bible in general and Jesus in particular result.

2. Discerning a Liberative Axis.

Liberation and feminist theologians tend to discern a unifying axis in the Bible. This axis is selected because it reflects the experience of the interpreters. For example, Latin American liberation theologians, who live in the context of poverty and call the church to side with the poor, interpret that axis as God's preference for the poor (*see* Rich and Poor). The paradigmatic event that expresses God's preference is the Exodus (Ex 2:23-25; 22:21-27), but this view of God is carried on forcibly by the prophets' demand for justice* (e.g., Amos 5:21-24; Mic 6:8; Is 58:6-7) and, quintessentially, by Jesus, the friend of outcasts and sinners, who pronounced blessings (*see* Blessing and Curse) on the poor and woes on the rich (Lk 6:20-26). Ruether, a feminist theologian who confronts patriarchy in church and society, interprets that axis as the Bible's ability to contain its own self-critique. She calls this the "prophetic-messianic" tradition, and notes that this biblical protest against itself

> parallels the critical dynamic of feminism, which likewise examines structures of injustice toward women, unmasks and denounces their cultural and religious sanctifications, and points toward an alternative humanity, an alternative society, capable of affirming the personhood of women. (Ruether, 118)

Undeniably many axes co-exist in the Bible, including God's preference for the poor and a prophetic critique included within the Bible itself. Each is chosen, however, not because it is the universal or timeless theme that unifies the Bible, but because it best reflects the advocacy stance (or praxis) of the interpreter who lives in a particular social context and works toward a specific historically and culturally bound form of liberation.

3. Liberative Portraits of Jesus.

Feminist and liberation theologians also develop portraits of Jesus on the basis of their experiences of oppression. These portraits illustrate well the interaction between text and social context that characterizes liberation and feminist hermeneutics.

Most feminists have made a precommitment to liberation that entails working toward equality with men. Of the church this requires open doors to ordained ministry. This precommitment to equality in church and society becomes the starting point for Fiorenza's reconstruction of the ministry of Jesus (1983, 99-159).

According to Fiorenza, Jesus exhibited a praxis of inclusive wholeness by measuring the Temple* and Torah (*see* Law) with the criterion of whether they engendered the wholeness of every human being. Because cult and law controlled and excluded many, especially women,* Jesus replaced the cultic meal with a festive table to which all are invited. In fact, those who gathered around this table were the poor, the sick and those so destitute as to engage in cultically dishonorable occupations: tax collectors (*see* Taxes), sinners* and prostitutes.*

These people Jesus liberated from patriarchal structures and gathered into a discipleship* of equals. His preference for the poor especially included women, for "widows and orphans" quintessentially express poverty in an androcentric world in which women and children are dependent on husbands and fathers for economic and social well-being. Jesus also unmasked patriarchy in his sayings: patriarchal marriage will cease to exist in the age to come (Mk 10:2-9; 12:18-27); Jesus brings a sword to households, setting son against father and father against son (Mt 10:34-36); the family of disciples has no father, even when disciples* have left fathers (cf. Mk 10:29; 10:30; *see* Family). Finally, Jesus rejected domination among the discipleship of equals (Mk 10:42-45). In short, "the woman-identified man, Jesus, called forth a discipleship of equals that still needs to be discovered and realized by women and men today" (154).

L. Boff portrays Jesus as a liberator who fought the three oppressions that face Latin America: economic exploitation, de-humanization of the oppressed, structural and individual sin. Jesus fought economic structures with his teaching such as the parable* of the workers who labored for different lengths of time but earned the same wage (Mt 20:1-16). This parable is a frontal attack on the view that those with more money deserve it and, concomitantly, that the poor deserve their low economic status. He fought de-humanization by placing human need above even the most sacred traditions such as Sabbath* purity (e.g., Mt 12:1-14; *see* Clean and Unclean). Jesus fought sin by denouncing everything—whether religious, political, economic or social—which alienates people from God and from their neighbors (e.g., Mt 22:34-40). In other words, the "fundamental project" of Jesus was

> to proclaim and to be the instrument of the concrete realization of the absolute meaning of the world, i.e., liberation from every stigma (including suffering, division, sin and death) and liberation for real life, for open-ended communication of love, grace, and plenitude in God." (280-281)

Both of these portraits of Jesus have as their starting point the historical Jesus. For Fiorenza this requires entering the world of Jesus behind the Gospels because the Gospels, reflecting male authors and an increasingly patriarchal church, have effaced in part the central role women had in the discipleship of equals. Now their role in Jesus' ministry must be reconstructed from subtle indicators in patriarchal texts. For liberation theologians this starting point is necessary because other christological starting points in Latin America have ignored Jesus' commitment to justice. Instead, traditional theologians have begun with questions, such as the two natures of Christ or the Trinity, which have not provided a critique of the church's historic tendency to side with the oppressors in Latin America.

Their interest in the historical Jesus, however, is different from scholars who are involved in the so-called quest of the historical Jesus. Liberation and feminist theologians are not content to establish objective data to recover precisely what Jesus said and did. Rather they want to understand the relevance of the historical Jesus for their own social contexts. Consequently, Jesus becomes the initiator of a discipleship of equals and a liberator from oppression.

4. The Challenge and Limits of Liberation Hermeneutics.

In order to fortify its role as an alternative hermeneutical approach to the Gospels, feminist and liberation hermeneutics must develop further answers to three key questions: (1) *Who* interprets? (2) *How* is interpretation accomplished? (3) *Why* is a particular feminist or liberation interpretation valid?

First, feminist and liberation hermeneutics challenges the assumption that academic training is the primary criterion for determining who is qualified to interpret the Bible. Their challenge signals a confrontation with a predominantly Caucasian, male guild whose training takes place in North American and European universities. But feminist and liberation theologians are themselves not free from the charge of elitism. The most significant Latin American liberation studies have come from males who received their doctorates from European universities (e.g., J. Sobrino from the Hochschule Sankt Georgen in Frankfurt; L. Boff from the University of Munich; J. L. Segundo from the University of Paris).

Analogously, feminist theologians, though oppressed by gender, usually are not oppressed economically. As a result, African-American women have developed an alternative to feminism, called "womanist theology," which is in part a protest against the social and economic elitism of many feminist theologians. Liberation and feminist hermeneutics, therefore, must facilitate the transition from an educated elite who speak on behalf of the oppressed to an oppressed who give voice to their own interpretations of Jesus. Cardenal's *The Gospel in Solantiname,* which transcribes conversations from base communities, should not be the notable exception; it should be supplemented by interpretations from women-churches, African-American communities, etc.

Second, liberation and feminist theologians correctly begin their christological explorations with the historical Jesus. Consequently, they must continue to develop their own historical-critical methodology. In particular, they must refine their facility in analyzing the social context of first-century Palestine (*see* Sociological Approaches to the Gospels). This refinement is essential because feminist and liberation interpretations of Jesus frequently draw social, economic and political parallels between first-century Palestine and the experience of twentieth-century oppressed peoples. Two of the most important interpretations of Jesus, Segundo's *Historical Jesus of the Gospels* and Fiorenza's *In Memory of Her,* press behind the Gospels to understand the Palestinian world of Jesus. Studies such as these, if they are to lend further insight to the enterprise of interpreting Jesus' place among the oppressed of Palestine and the contemporary world, will require greater expertise in sociological analysis.

Third, liberation and feminist theologians correctly assert that no exegesis is neutral, and that presuppositions that arise from a particular social context determine how a text is interpreted. This viewpoint challenges the assertion, often held by evangelical exegetes, that a biblical author's original intent is ascertainable and normative for today. Social context is as important for a liberation hermeneutic as is the original text. But that does not mean that all interpretations that arise out of human experience are equally valid.

The criterion normally employed by these theologians to distinguish between correct and incorrect interpretations is whether an interpretation is oppres-

sive (hence the hermeneutic of suspicion). But the notion of oppression or justice is vague and liable to countless varieties of definition. Therefore, the challenge of avoiding pure subjectivism confronts feminist and liberation hermeneutics. A cogent hermeneutic that does not allow interpretation to dissipate into pure subjectivism requires a concerted global dialog about the meaning of Jesus for today. Such an approach may be seen in the book *Conflict and Context: Hermeneutics in the Americas,* a cooperative effort of North and Latin Americans produced during a conference held in Mexico in 1983. A global dialog must broach gender, economic and racial boundaries to develop interpretations of Jesus that are not merely subjective, representing a narrow slice of human experience, but consensus christologies which come under the judgment of a variety of people in dialog.

Liberation and feminist hermeneutics, then, must develop in three key ways. First, theologians must be replaced by the oppressed as the dominant spokespersons for liberation and feminist theology in the church. Second, theologians must sharpen their scholarly approach to the NT; in particular, this requires further strides in sociological analysis of the present and past. Third, liberation and feminist theology must strive to become global in order to develop consensus criteria for evaluating the validity of liberation portraits of Jesus.

For two reasons this article represents a relatively narrow portion of liberation theologies. First, it does not address directly the most radical theologians, such as M. Daly and other post-Christian feminists, or F. Belo and other materialist interpreters of the Gospels. Second, liberation theologies are burgeoning throughout the world as the oppressed are being given voices. To North American feminists and Latin American liberation theologians can be added J. Cone (African-American), I. J. Mosala and A. Boesak (South African), A. Pieris and S. Kappen (Sri Lankan), J. Grant (North American Womanist) and many others.

See also RICH AND POOR; WOMEN.

BIBLIOGRAPHY.   D. Batstone, *From Conquest to Struggle: Jesus of Nazareth in the Liberation Christology of Latin America* (State University of New York, 1991); L. Boff, *Jesus Christ Liberator: A Critical Christology for Our Time* (Maryknoll, NY: Orbis, 1978) M. L. Branson and C. R. Padilla, eds., *Conflict and Context: Hermeneutics in the Americas* (Grand Rapids: Eerdmans, 1986); B. Brooten, "Early Christian Women in Their Cultural Context: Issues of Method in Historical Reconstruction," in *Feminist Perspectives on Biblical Scholarship,* ed. A. Y. Collins (Chico: Scholars, 1985) 65-91; S. Croatto,

Biblical Hermeneutics: Toward a Theory of Reading As the Production of Meaning (Maryknoll, NY: Orbis, 1987) 66-83; E. S. Fiorenza, Bread Not Stone: The Challenge of Feminist Biblical Interpretation (Boston: Beacon, 1984); idem, In Memory of Her: A Feminist Theological Reconstruction of Christian Origins (New York: Crossroad, 1983) 105-59; C. Osiek, "The Feminist and the Bible: Hermeneutical Alternatives," in Feminist Perspectives on Biblical Scholarship, ed. A. Y. Collins (Chico: Scholars, 1985) 93-105; R. Radford Ruether, "Feminist Interpretation: A Method of Correlation," in Feminist Interpretation of the Bible, ed. L. M. Russell (Philadelphia: Westminster, 1985) 111-24; K. D. Sakenfeld, "Feminist Uses of Biblical Materials," in Feminist Interpretation of the Bible, ed. L. M. Russell (Philadelphia: Westminster, 1985) 55-64; D. M. Scholer, "Feminist Hermeneutics and Evangelical Biblical Interpretation," JETS 30 (1987) 407-20; J. L. Segundo, The Historical Jesus of the Synoptics (Maryknoll, NY: Orbis, 1985) 3-41; J. Sobrino, Christology at the Crossroads: A Latin American Approach (Maryknoll, NY: Orbis, 1978) 1-16, 33-37; M. Tolbert, "Defining the Problem: The Bible and Feminist Hermeneutics," in Semeia: The Bible and Feminist Hermeneutics 28 (1983) 113-26.   J. R. Levison

LIFE

Three different Greek words are used in the Gospels to convey different aspects of the concept of life. Bios refers to daily life and one's resources for living. Psychē signifies the self-conscious individual self and can often be translated by a personal pronoun. Zōē usually denotes life as a gift from God* and is often modified by the adjective "eternal" (aiōnios). This article will treat the third of these three words.

1. The Synoptic Gospels
2. The Fourth Gospel
3. Theological Issues

1. The Synoptic Gospels.

Zōē occurs sixteen times in the Synoptic Gospels. Except for Luke 12:15 and 16:25 (where it refers to life in general), it always means the future life that will be given by God. It is a life that will be entered or inherited at the end of the present age (Mt 19:16-17, 29 par.). Thus it stands in chronological contrast to the present life. For example, the one who leaves all to follow Jesus will not "fail to receive a hundred times as much in this present age . . . and in the age to come eternal life," Mk 10:30 NIV). It is a life that is to be entered through the narrow gate (Mt 7:14). In fact this life is so important that disciples of Jesus must deal radically with sin in their hearts in order to avoid missing it and being cast into the hell of fire (Mt 18:8-9; see Heaven and Hell).

2. The Fourth Gospel.

Zoe occurs thirty-six times in the Gospel of John. In eleven of these occurrences it is the object of the verb "to have" (echō) and is used in the context of a promise, invitation or statement about those who believe in Jesus (Jn 3:15, 16, 36; 5:24, 40; 6:40, 47, 53, 54; 10:10; 20:31). By reading these eleven passages together, one comes to see that in the Fourth Gospel life or eternal life is not limited to a future age but can be realized in the present by the one who believes (see Faith) in Jesus. John can still speak of life as future (Jn 5:28-29; 6:27; 12:25), but it is also something that one may possess in the present (Jn 5:24).

John also makes a point of stressing the idea of life as a gift from God. The Father has life in himself and has given the Son (see Son of God) life to have in himself (Jn 5:26; cf. 1:4). The Son is the bread* of life (Jn 6:35, 48) who gives life to the world by his death (Jn 6:51) and through his Spirit (see Holy Spirit) and words (Jn 6:63, 68).

The definition of life in the Fourth Gospel has various traits. First, the life was the light of humankind (Jn 1:4). Taken out of its Johannine context, this statement might imply that the life created by the Word of God is natural human life and that this life consists of light,* that is, the human consciousness and conscience which separates humanity from the rest of the creation. But as John goes on to describe life and light in his Gospel, life in John 1:4 probably is referring to life before God or eternal life (note the Greek article which here signifies a particular kind of life). This life was in the Word (cf. Deut 30:14-15). And it was through this word of life (cf. 1 Jn 1:1) that light (revelation) came to humankind. The revelation (light) brought through the communication of this word of life brings both salvation* and judgment* (Jn 3:19-21).

Second, the words which Jesus has spoken are life (Jn 6:63). Peter, speaking for the Twelve, says to Jesus "You have the words of eternal life" (Jn 6:68). And in his final pronouncement to the nation Jesus asserts that God's commandment is eternal life (Jn 12:50). In much the same way, at the end of the Torah and in reference to it Moses says, "This is not an idle word for you; it is your life" (Deut 32:47). Thus life and the Word of God are intimately connected. But the Word is not merely the source of life; it is life itself in the sense that nourishment becomes a part of the body (thus Jesus is the bread of life, Jn 6:35, 48).

Third, Jesus himself claims to be the life (Jn 11:25; 14:6). True life traces its source to him (Jn 10:10). But he is more than its source, he is its sustaining power, apart from whom nothing can be accomplished (Jn 15:5). He is life itself.

The definition of eternal life in John is summed up in Jesus' final prayer: "This is eternal life, that they might know you, the only true God and Jesus Christ whom you have sent" (Jn 17:3). Here life is related to knowledge. This knowledge has been revealed to those the Father has given to the Son (Jn 17:2). In that sense it is objective cognitive knowledge. But the knowledge revealed is also a knowledge of persons— God the Father and God the Son. In this sense it is subjective relational knowledge. So true life consists in knowing the Word of God. Thus Christ's words are life and he himself is life. And the reason that life is bound up with Christ and his words is that he explains (*exegeomai*) the Father (Jn 1:18).

3. Theological Issues.

3.1. Life in the Fourth Gospel vis à vis the Synoptics.
Much has been made of the difference between the eschatology* of the Synoptic Gospels and of the Fourth Gospel (*see* Synoptics and John). It is asserted that the Synoptic Gospels contain a strictly futuristic eschatology. The life spoken of is something awarded at the end of the age for present activity. On the other hand, the Fourth Gospel contains the notion of an eternal life which is a present reality to the one who believes in Jesus. Hence Jesus in the Fourth Gospel says, "Truly, truly I say to you, he who hears my word and believes in the one who sent me has (present tense) eternal life and he does not come into judgment but has passed (perfect tense) out of death into eternal life" (Jn 5:24). The Synoptic eschatology is in keeping with Jewish beliefs current in early Judaism* (e.g., *T. Levi* 17—18; *1 Enoch* 91:12-17; *Pss. Sol.* 17:21-46). Johannine eschatology builds on that found in the Synoptics by asserting that the future hope is now present. A study of the use of the word *life* is used to illustrate this view (cf. Bultmann).

To deny the differences between the use of (eternal) life in the Synoptics and in John is impossible. Yet to assert that the eschatology of John is more advanced and exclusive of Synoptic eschatology is not a necessary conclusion based on the evidence.

First, it is plain that John has a futuristic eschatological viewpoint. In John 5:28 and 6:54 the resurrection is future. Bultmann recognized the difficulty of these verses in John and ascribed them to a redaction of the Fourth Gospel which attempted to bring it in line with the more traditional eschatology found in the Synoptics. But if John 5:28 and 6:54 are attributed to the Fourth Evangelist, it must be asserted that he was able

to conceive of a futuristic and a realized eschatology as not mutually exclusive.

Second, C. H. Dodd (although his point may have been overstated) has shown that in fact the Synoptic Gospels contain a realized eschatology. Dodd asserts that Jesus "used parables (which are found in the Synoptic Gospels) to enforce and illustrate the idea that the kingdom of God had come upon people there and then. The inconceivable had happened: history had become the vehicle of the eternal; the absolute was clothed in flesh and blood" (Dodd, 197).

Third, to assert that the Jewish view of "life" was future is too broad a conclusion to draw from the large bank of data available in the extant writings of early Judaism. First-century Judaism had no single eschatology, a fact now widely recognized among scholars of early Judaism and Christian origins.

3.2. The Nature of Eternal Life.
It would appear then that the eternal life spoken of in the Synoptics *vis à vis* John is a single entity with more than one facet rather than a pair of mutually exclusive concepts. Its nature can be described under four points. First, eternal life involves a personal relationship with God and all its attendant blessings. In Genesis 2—3 the tree of life was in the midst of the garden which was in Eden (Gk *paradeisos*). It was in the garden that God had fellowship with man and woman (Gen 3:8). And if man had eaten from the tree of life he would have lived forever (Gen 3:22). But because of their sin, God banished them from the garden and made it impossible for them to return to the tree of life (Gen 3:24). The life God intended for humanity was one of ideal service in an ideal location (Gen 2:15). It was a life of knowing and walking with God. It was an everlasting Sabbath* (note how the seventh day of creation has no stated end, Gen 2:1-3). This notion of life as a relationship with God carried over into the teaching of Jesus and into the Gospels.

Second, in the Gospels eternal life is intimately connected with the coming of Jesus Christ (Jn 10:10). Eternal life is the life of the future messianic age (Mt 7:14; 18:8-9), and Jesus is the Messiah (*see* Christ). Thus one's attitude toward Jesus determines one's entrance into life (Mt 25:45-46). "For God so loved the world that he gave his only Son so that whoever believes in him might not perish but have eternal life" (Jn 3:16). Only those who eat the flesh and drink the blood of Christ have eternal life. Only they will be raised to life on the last day (Jn 6:54).

Third, this life which is a relationship with God and comes through Jesus Christ is begun in the present age. In Jesus Christ one begins to know God, for he reveals his Father (Jn 1:18). By believing in Jesus one enters or has eternal life. Life is given to believers as a gift because they belong to his flock (Jn 10:27-28). Because no thief is able to snatch a believer from God's hand, no believer is able to lose the gift of life (Jn 10:29). Since eternal life is a present experience it can be said that eternity has broken into time. One does not need to wait for death. One can experience eternity now.

Finally, eternal life, which is inaugurated in the present, is fully realized only in the future. The full realization of eternal life is like receiving an inheritance (Mt 19:29). It is the opposite of punishment (Mt 25:46). Among its many blessings are the resurrection* of the body and the promise of abundant life that will never perish (Jn 3:16; 10:10).

Because of the dual nature of eternal life, on the one hand a future life but on the other hand (in the Fourth Gospel) a present experience, the issue of theological development has arisen. Is John an advance over Synoptic eschatology? Is John's understanding of eternal life a form of Platonism where life is not measured in time but is rather an ideal realm of existence parallel to earthly life? To read the Fourth Gospel platonically seems to be a misunderstanding of John. Eternal life can be experienced in the present, but it also has a future dimension as outlined above. It seems best to describe eternal life as a relationship with God. In this way there is no necessary contradiction between the Synoptics and the Gospel of John. One can begin to know God now, but will only know him fully in the eschaton.

3.3. How Eternal Life Is Entered. How is this relationship with God called eternal life entered? At this point too there seems to be a contradiction between the Synoptics and the Fourth Gospel. In Matthew 7:14 it is asserted that the way to eternal life is narrow and few find it. Disciples* must take radical measures to purify themselves or they may miss life and be cast into the eternal fires of hell (Mt 18:8-9). To a would-be disciple looking for some assurance of eternal life, Jesus said, "If you want to enter into life, keep the commandments." These commandments* he referred to came from the Decalog (Mt 19:16-19). In the same chapter Jesus told his disciples that everyone who leaves their earthly belongings and family behind will inherit eternal life (Mt 19:29). In Matthew 25:46 Jesus says that the righteous (those who care for the poor and oppressed; *see* Justice, Righteousness) will go away into eternal life.

In the Gospel of John eternal life is gained through belief or faith (Jn 3:16; 5:24; 20:31). Life is a gift from the Father that comes through the Son (Jn 5:26, 40; 6:33; 10:10, 28; 17:2). John seems to be closer to what

some consider to be the Pauline doctrine of justification by faith alone, while the Synoptic references seem to teach that eternal life is gained by works. But this conclusion arises from a misreading of all four Gospels.

First, the Synoptic Gospels do not say that life is earned by works. Matthew 7:14 places the narrow gate before the difficult way. The narrow gate might very well be a reference to faith in the sense that the way to salvation is not manifold but singular. Matthew 18:8-9 seems to be speaking primarily of the sin of pride with which faith is incompatible. In Matthew 19:16-21 the essential command is "follow me," which might be equated with faith (*see* Discipleship). The same might be said concerning Matthew 19:29. And in Matthew 25:4-6 life is not a reward for good works (note how the righteous are surprised by the Lord's response in Mt 25:37-39), but good works could be considered a consequence of being righteous (see Carson).

Second, John does not dissociate faith from its resultant works. In John 5:29 the good and the wicked are resurrected—the good to receive eternal life and the wicked to judgment. In John 12:25 we read, "He who loves his life will lose it and he who hates his life in this world will keep it unto eternal life." And only those who eat the flesh and drink the blood of Christ have eternal life and will be raised in the last day (Jn 6:54).

Thus a careful reading of both the Synoptic Gospels and the Gospel of John does not lead to soteriological disparity. Rather all four Gospels are in harmony with the rest of the NT when it comes to human responsibility for salvation. Persons cannot save themselves even by their own good works (Jn 5:39-40). They must humble themselves and trust in God who alone supplies life. But this trust is like entering a gate which heads a street of obedience and hardship (Mt 7:14). True faith inevitably yields a changed life of faithful discipleship and good works. This changed life begins in the present and continues until it is consummated at the Second Coming of Christ.

See also HEAVEN AND HELL; JUDGMENT; LIGHT; SALVATION.
BIBLIOGRAPHY. R. Bultmann et al., "ζάω κτλ," *TDNT* II.832-75; J. C. Coetzee, "Life in John's Writings and the Qumran Scrolls," *Neot* 6 (1972) 48-66; C. H. Dodd, *The Parables of the Kingdom* (New York: Scribners, 1936); D. Hill, "The Background and Biblical Usage of *zōē* and *zōē aiōnios,*" in D. Hill, *Greek Words and Hebrew Meanings* (Cambridge: University Press, 1967) 82-201; G. E. Ladd, *A Theology of the New Testament* (Grand Rapids: Eerdmans, 1974) 254-69; D. A. Carson, "Matthew," in *The Expositor's Bible Commentary*, ed. F. Gaebelein (12 vols.; Grand Rapids: Zondervan, 1979) 8.1-599. D. H. Johnson

LIGHT

The use of light in the Gospels follows, on the whole, the use of light in the OT and late Hellenistic Judaism. Hebrew thought uses light as a symbol of the divine presence and salvation (Ex 13:21; Ps 27:1; 36:9; Is 60:19), often of the future eschatological (*see* Eschatology) salvation* (Mic 7:8; Is 2:5; 9:2; 58:8, 10; 60:1-3; Bar 5:9). According to Matthew 4:16 and Luke 2:32 this expectation has been fulfilled in Jesus, who becomes the focus of the light symbolism of the Gospels. The matter appears differently in the Synoptics and John (*see* Synoptics and John). Whereas the Synoptic writers simply group together originally independent dominical sayings which contain terms for light, John has created a "rather elaborate theology of light" (Piper, 132). In the comments which follow the focus is on the symbolic use of *phōs* ("light"). The Gospels, of course, do use light in a literal sense—of the sun, of lamps and of fire (Mt 5:15; Jn 18:3; Mk 14:54; Lk 22:56). Other terms for light are also used, but do not add much to our understanding.

1. The Synoptic Gospels.

Two uses of light symbolism (not necessarily utilizing the word *phōs*) appear in all three Synoptic Gospels: (1) Matthew 17:2; Mark 9:3 and Luke 9:29 describe the brightness of Jesus' face or clothing at the Transfiguration*; and (2) the saying of the "light under a bushel" is found in Mark 4:21; Matthew 5:15; and in a doublet in Luke 8:16 and 11:33; but the meaning is different in the various contexts.

In Mark 4:21 and Luke 8:16 the saying of "light under a bushel" follows the parable of the sower and functions to warn the disciples to receive the light which comes from God. Similarly, the saying in Luke 11:33, which appears between the "sign of Jonah"* and the teaching on the "sound eye," emphasizes Jesus as the light and is addressed to those of Jesus' day who seek signs. Matthew 5:15 appears together with other sayings (about "salt" and "a city on a hill") and between two unique sayings ("you are the light of the world"; "let your light so shine"), all of which refer to the Christian community. The emphasis is no longer on the disciples receiving, but rather on spreading, the light.

Two other Q* sayings also have differing meanings in their new contexts. As we have indicated earlier, the good and bad eyes in the context of Luke 11:33-36 have to do with recognizing the Messiah.* Matthew, on the other hand, building on the Jewish associations of "a sound eye" with generosity, and "an evil eye" with stinginess (cf. Deut 15:9 [LXX]; Prov 23:6; Tob 4:7; Sir 14:10; *'Abot* 5:15), sets the "sound eye"

teaching (6:22-23) between the two sayings about treasure and serving God or mammon. Thus, in Matthew the references to light (and darkness) teach generosity as opposed to greediness. The second Q saying is part of an exhortation to fearless confession in both Matthew 10:26-33 and Luke 12:2-9. Matthew's saying, "What I tell you in the dark, utter in the light" (v. 27) suggests that the disciples' proclamation, unlike Jesus' words to them, will be public. Following closely on the warning concerning the hypocrisy of the Pharisees,* Luke 12:2 seems to warn the disciples against hypocrisy because the truth will come to light (*see* Hypocrite).

Three points need to be made about unique references to *phōs* in Matthew and Luke. First, Matthew 4:16 ("the people who sat in darkness have seen a great light") quotes Isaiah 9:2 and alludes to the nativity star (Mt 2:7) in order to emphasize the fulfillment of messianic expectations and the continuation in Jesus of the revelatory symbolism attributed to light in the OT. Second, this revelatory aspect of light has universal significance in Luke 2:32 ("a light for revelation to the Gentiles* and glory* for your people Israel*") where an Isaianic theme is evident (cf. Is 42:6; 49:6 and the conjunction of *phōs* and *doxa* ["glory"] in Is 60:1, 19 LXX; cf. also Jn 1:1-14). Third, a saying of Jesus appended to the parable of the dishonest steward, both of which are unique to Luke, contrasts "the sons of this age" with "the sons of light" (Lk 16:8b), a term not found in the OT nor in later rabbinic literature but appearing as a standard designation of the members of the community at Qumran (1QS 1:9; 2:16; 3:13, 24-25) and as a description of believers in John 12:36 (cf. 1 Thess 5:5; Eph 5:8). The frequent Qumran counterpart, "sons of darkness," is not found in the NT (cf. Jn 3:19).

2. The Fourth Gospel.

John's theology of light, which often appears in the Evangelist's redaction of the tradition (cf. Fortna), was developed in the debate with the synagogue* about the identity and significance of Jesus. John took up the symbol of light from Judaism,* where it referred variously to God's presence, God's salvation, the Law,* Wisdom* and Logos* (e.g., Philo), in order to epitomize the person and work of Jesus. By so doing, "the evangelist implies that the expectations and hopes of Judaism are fulfilled in Jesus" (Painter, 34).

Light is a primary symbol in the Fourth Gospel. "The prologue links logos [word], life, and light so powerfully that the cluster dominates the symbolic system of the entire narrative. The logos incarnate in Jesus is 'the life [that] was the light of men' (1:4) and where there is light there is life and the perception of Life" (Culpepper, 190).

John's Gospel alone has the self-predication formula, "I am the light of the world" (8:12; 9:5; cf. 12:35-36, 46). This is an exclusive claim. John the Baptist is not the light but a witness to the light (1:7-8; cf. 5:35). Moreover, all persons must receive their light from Jesus the "true light" (1:9; cf. 8:12) in order to become "the children of light" (12:36). That they do is dramatically illustrated in Jesus' restoration of sight to a blind man (Jn 9).

Light is pressed into service to express various other aspects of Johannine theology: revelation, sin, faith,* judgment* and ethics (see Ethics of Jesus).* The light invades the darkness to reveal God's salvation (1:5; 3:19; 8:12; 12:35, 46). This darkness is of two kinds: that which prevails before the light comes (1:5; 8:12; 12:46) and that which descends on those who have refused the light and have chosen to live in darkness (3:19-20). This expresses the Johannine understanding of sin. On the other hand, to believe in the light (12:36, 46) describes Christian faith. That the light exposes those who accept or reject its illumination expresses the Johannine understanding of judgment (3:19-21). Light and darkness thereby also function as indexes to human character, such as in the cases of Nicodemus (3:20), the Jews (9:40; 11:10) and Judas (13:30) (Culpepper, 192). Johannine ethics is expressed in terms of walking in the light (8:12; 12:35), which means keeping Jesus' commandment* to love* one another.

Two significant omissions may also be noted. First, there is no metaphysical nor cosmological speculation about light. As Conzelmann has put it, "Herein lies the basic distinction between Jn.'s Gospel and Gnosticism" (Conzelmann, 350). Second, unlike Matthew, John does not use light to describe the evangelistic mission of the believers.

One wonders what light as a symbol for God's revelation and salvation in Christ communicates to modern persons for whom light is just another physical phenomenon to be made and controlled and for whom light connotes little of mystery or the divine. Present-day communicators of the Gospel may wish to consider J. Macquarrie's suggestion for revivifying the biblical symbol of light: "Roughly speaking, one might say that the word 'openness' can do for the symbol of light what the word 'estrangement' has done in much of contemporary theology for the moribund word 'sin' " (Macquarrie, 209).

See also GLORY.

BIBLIOGRAPHY. E. R. Achtemeier, "Jesus Christ, the Light of the World. The Biblical Understanding of Light and Darkness," *Int* 17 (1963) 439-49; H. Conzelmann, "φῶς κτλ," *TDNT* IX.310-58; R. A. Culpepper, *Anatomy of the Fourth Gospel* (Philadelphia: Fortress, 1983); C. H. Dodd, *The Interpretation of the Fourth Gospel* (Cambridge: University Press, 1953) 201-12; H.-C. Hahn, T. McComiskey, C. Brown, "Light, Shine, Lamp," *NIDNTT* 2.484-96; R. Fortna, *The Fourth Gospel and Its Predecessors* (Philadephia: Fortress, 1988); J. Macquarrie, *God-Talk* (New York: Harper & Row, 1967); J. Painter, "Johannine Symbols: A Case Study in Epistemology," *JTSA* 27 (1979) 26-41; O. A. Piper, "Light, Light and Darkness," *IDB* 3.130-32; P. E. Wheelwright, *Metaphor and Reality* (Bloomington, IN: Indiana University Press, 1962).

G. F. Shirbroun

LITERARY CRITICISM

Literary criticism of the Gospels (see Gospel [Genre]) is concerned with literary conventions and the significance of such conventions for meaning. The rationale for such an approach is twofold: (1) the Gospels are, in part, literary; and (2) a reading or hearing of the Gospels involves literary appreciation. The Gospels are also theological, of course, and historical. Theological and historical preunderstandings of Christians will influence their use of literary criticism. Literary criticism and appreciation also impinge on theological and historical considerations.

This essay will survey the variety of literary approaches and suggest how they help in studying the Gospels, show how the history of the study of Jesus and the Gospels has intersected literary study, and delineate and illustrate major literary conventions and strategies of the Gospels and their study.

1. Literary Criticism and Its Implications for Study of the Gospels
2. Developments in Gospel Study from a Literary Perspective
3. The Gospels and Literary Conventions and Strategies

1. Literary Criticism and Its Implications for Study of the Gospels.

Christian appropriation of literary criticism does not mean the reduction of the Gospels to any one or a group of literary perspectives. The Gospels are presentations of the "good news" of Jesus Christ. But just as an understanding of the rules of Greek grammar and syntax help in reading the Gospels so does an understanding of literary rules and conventions.

1.1. The History and Theory of Criticism.

1.1.1. The History of Criticism. Literary criticism offers a variety of perspectives for the study of the Gospels, for in the history of criticism different views of the reference, role and function of literature have guided the work of criticism. An early type of criticism (mimetic criticism) views the literary work as an imitation (*mimēsis)* of the world and human life. The primary criterion is the truth of the work in relation to the object or objects it represents. This form of criticism is associated with the classical age, but it is also characteristic of contemporary theories of literary realism, and Marxist critics in particular view literature as a reflection of reality.

The criticism which was dominant from the poet Horace (first century B.C.) through the eighteenth century (pragmatic criticism) emphasizes the effect of the work on the audience, including both pleasure and instruction. Recent revival of rhetorical criticism recapitulates pragmatic criticism's emphasis on the artistic strategies used by an author in engaging and influencing the response of readers.

Another type (expressive criticism) defines the literary work in terms of the operation of the artist's imagination on his or her perception. Contemporary psychologically oriented critics retain concerns of expressive criticism, looking in the work for indications of the particular temperament and experiences of the author.

Extrinsic criticism of various sorts explains the major characteristics of a work of art in terms of external causes or influences (historical, biographical, sociological, psychological and so on). The historical and sociological approaches of conventional biblical study are examples of extrinsic criticism. Formalism and New Criticism (termed "objective" criticism) reacts to the alleged reduction of literature to external causes and approaches the work in terms of the work itself as an autonomous object, to be judged in terms of intrinsic criteria such as coherence, integrity, equilibrium, complexity and the relationships of the parts of the work to each other and to the work as a whole. Reader-oriented theories relativize the conventional view of the literary work as a structure of meaning which has been achieved and exists apart from the reader's involvement. They emphasize the role of the reader (or readership) alongside the role of the author in the "production" or "creation" of meaning and significance.

1.1.2. The Theory of Criticism.

1.1.2.1. A Compass for Criticism: Internal and External Relationships. The fact that readers of different epochs and different readers of the same epoch can read and interpret literature differently is explained in part by the nature of literature itself. Literature consists not only of a succession of words, sentences and para-

graphs; it consists also of presuppositions and perspectives taken by writers and readers.

One set of relationships in literature (syntagmatic relationships) is comparable to the syntactic relationships on the level of sentence. These relationships exist *within* discourse and enable linguistic and literary elements to have meaning as they are *combined* or chained together in a linear sequence. In Gospel narrative readers must discern relationships between words and sentences within smaller units of the Gospels such as parables* and miracle stories (*see* Miracles and Miracle Stories) in order to follow what is being said, and readers must discern relationships between these units in order to follow the plot of the Gospels as completed wholes.

Relationships outside any particular discourse are necessary for making sense of the combinations within that discourse. The topic, reference, literary category and function of the literary unit are discerned not simply from words and sentences and their combination. The topic of a sentence, for example, must be consistent with the combination of words, but the same combination can be assigned different topics. The specific topic is decided on in the context of discourse.

1.1.2.2. Interdependence and Variety of Relationships. In the episode of Jesus and the disciples* crossing the lake in Mark 8, Jesus told the disciples, "Take heed, beware of the leaven of the Pharisees and of Herod!" The disciples recognized a syntactic and semantic unity; they made sense of the sentence by judging that Jesus' statement was to be taken literally and that he was speaking about bread*—the bread which the disciples failed to bring with them. Readers know more than the disciples knew, and they know the topic is not bread—not bread in the simple literal sense in which the disciples understood it.

At the level of every literary unit some topic must be discerned. Then, at the level of the total literary work, a comprehensive organizing principle or idea must be formulated in order for the identification of topics and relationships throughout the work and, therefore, for the meaning of the work as a whole. The topic of the subordinate unit and the idea of the work as a whole must be consistent with the literary data, but the interplay of literal, figurative and often paradoxical meanings of words and other units makes the literary data susceptible to a variety of meanings. The same word, expression or entire text can signify two or more distinct references and express and elicit different attitudes or feelings.

More than topics and ideas are involved in literary appreciation. The form and content of literature do not simply convey information; they perform action. The contrast between the discernment of the readers and the intellectual and spiritual density of the disciples has an ironic function in Mark 8. This irony has an effect upon the readers and is characteristic of the Gospel of Mark. The knowing readers come to feel superior to the simple disciples as they share the point of view of the Evangelist. Readers are nudged toward the faith of the Evangelist in the literary composition. The ironic function and the discernment of topics are related. As readers discern different levels of meaning in Mark, they may see that what the disciples think is the topic is closer to the truth than readers initially realize. Readers may eventually discern that bread (at a symbolic level) is indeed the theme (or at least one of the ways that the theme of the Gospel may be expressed).

1.2. Study of Narrative. In the past literary aspects of Gospel narratives were subordinated to dogmatic and historical interests. Since the late 1960s, however, literary aspects of narrative have increasingly become the center of interest, with the subordination of dogmatic and historical concerns. As has been noted, however, dogmatic and historical preunderstandings play their appropriate part in literary study. Certainly no literary ideology will be allowed to replace Christian faith. S. McKnight rightly points out the danger of equating the poetic creativity of the Evangelists with fiction and depreciating "the importance of the real author's intent, historical reference, and background information for understanding texts" (S. McKnight, 127; *see* Gospels [Historical Reliability]).

1.2.1. Conventional Emphases. In Aristotle's mimetic poetics some aspect of reality is reconstituted by the poet through plot structures which are unified representations of human action. Readers are affected as they analyse or decompose the work into its component parts. The rules, educated insights and intelligent analysis involved in the system of Aristotle were devalued in the romantics' emphasis on aesthetic experience and the unconscious creativity of the artist. In the text-intrinsic approach of Formalism and New Criticism, both the imitated world and poetic creativity were at best secondary. With existentialism there was a return to reality—the reality of the human condition as understood by the ideology of existentialism. Modes of being and acting were not seen as determined by human nature but as possibilities for human choice, on the basis of which the human projects himself or herself.

1.2.2. Structuralist Insights. French Structuralism's desire to formulate a "morphology," or "grammar," of narrative and to establish rules that govern all forms

of narrative is best understood as a reaction to existentialism's emphasis on human choice. For structuralists the surface or superficial level of narrative was important only as a means of descending to the more fundamental or deep level where history and human choice play no part. Such an approach does not do justice to history and to the particulars of narrative, but it does provide a perspective from which to view the particulars. The multiplicity of actors and actions in the narrative may be reduced to a limited number of "character types" or spheres of action and a limited number of types of action or "functions."

Narrative may be seen as resting on profound ahistorical and general binary oppositions which are expressed in less profound and specific historical and cultural terms in the actual narrative. These oppositions must be mediated by a third category that is related to both realms in the actual narrative but which belongs to neither. Events which occur at different places in the actual narrative, then, are not seen primarily in relation to the development of the plot but in relation to each other. These events have a "paradigmatic" relationship with each other and as a bundle show the sort of solution or mediation which is taking place in the telling of the narrative. Hebrews speaks of Jesus the Son as reflecting the glory* of God* (1:1) and sharing the same flesh-and-blood nature of the children of God (2:14). Is it not possible to read the Gospels (at one level, at any rate) as portraying in narrative form this mediation presented in Hebrews in a didactic form?

Structuralist insights may help readers move beyond the view of the narrative as a one-dimensional story of events in the life of Jesus culminating with the crucifixion (*see* Death of Jesus) and resurrection.* At a certain level each of the episodes is referring beyond itself to a more central reality. The different episodes are then seen not only as a way of moving the story forward but also in relation to a theme which is illuminated by each of the episodes.

The structuralists' concern with typologies led them to discern different types of narratives, and this insight is also applicable to Gospel study. Simple narratives tell of a change of a situation (from failure to success); complex narratives relate a simple change as it is embedded within or accompanied by another sort of action—like planning and learning. In ideological narratives the different actions in the narrative are explained by a commitment, an idea or an abstract rule. There are also narratives in which the importance is the perception which readers have of the event which is narrated.

1.2.3. Poststructural Insights. Poststructuralism grows out of structuralism and uses ideas implicit in structuralism to challenge the ideology of structuralism itself. Poststructuralism recognizes the existence of codes and the value of narrative structure, grammar and logic, but it disavows the assumption that there is an ahistorical structure determining the narrative on the surface level. Disavowed also, however, is the possibility of any final synthesis of meaning. For poststructuralists the structure of the text is such that it involves the reader in a process of analysis without a *final* synthesis or end. The text is like a group of threads braided together to form a core. Some of the threads move the story along in a linear temporal pattern but narratives should not be reduced to such elements. Other threads are permutable and allow for multivalence and reversibility.

The Christian who wishes to benefit from poststructural insights must be able to accommodate a post-structural *strategy* and a firm commitment to a world which ultimately has meaning in terms of God's revelation in Jesus Christ. A poststructuralist ideology is not Christian faith.

1.3. Deconstruction.

1.3.1. Deconstruction and Poststructuralism. The term *deconstruction* results from the project of showing how the structural goal of accounting for the form and meaning of literary works is subverted by the way the texts actually work. In practice deconstruction depends on the appearance of a system of relationships which is then deconstructed by the appearance of another system of relationships which can be considered more natural with regard to the system being undone. This more natural system of relationships is substituted for the one deconstructed, but it too may be deconstructed.

1.3.2. Deconstruction in Gospel Study. The insights of deconstruction may enable us to understand and appreciate the succession of approaches in biblical studies; from dogmatic, to historical, to existential and literary approaches. We may even appreciate different levels of meaning in the early church. With the literal meaning, the things spoken about in the text were related to the real world (Gospel narratives were seen as recounting what in fact happened). Typological and allegorical meanings were gained by correlating the persons, actions and events in the Gospels with persons, actions and events in the OT and/or to the history of the church. Tropological meanings moved beyond these perspectives and sought the moral truth signified by a passage. By directing the reference of the passage to final things, yet another (anagogic) meaning was discerned.

A type of deconstruction results from the observation of the coexistence of different meanings and systems. Deconstruction may help contemporary readers/critics explain the coexistence in the Gospel of Mark of two portraits of Jesus—the divine Son of God* who reveals his power and wisdom in Galilee and the Son of man* whose passion is manifested in Jerusalem. No one portrait is able to exhaust the material of the text, and to subordinate one to the other causes a loss in both literary and religious terms.

1.4. Reader-Response Criticism. Reader-response criticism views literature in terms of readers and their values, attitudes and responses. The nature and role of the reader varies in the different forms of reader-response criticism, but in all forms there is a movement away from the view of interpretation as the determination by an autonomous reader of *the* meaning of an autonomous text. In one form (reader-reception criticism) an attempt is made to situate a literary work within the cultural context of its production and then explore the shifting relations between this context and the changing contexts of historical readers. Another form (aesthetic-response criticism) emphasizes the process by which a reader actualizes a text. A text is marked by gaps which the reader must complete and blanks which the reader must fill in. Psychological approaches to the reader emphasize the stages of development of individual readers or the role played by the "psychological set" of readers.

The community influences the attention given by the reader and the kind of "actualization" made by the reader. To some extent, then, criticism involves the determination of the perspective from which reading will proceed and becomes a matter of persuasion as well as a matter of demonstration. Interest in and appreciation of "interpretative communities" in literary study may provide appreciation for and insight into the way different religious communities read the Gospels. Evangelicals as well as Roman Catholics are inevitably constrained by histories of interpretation, traditions and contemporary communities of faith. Meaning must always have some locale.

2. Developments in Gospel Study from a Literary Perspective.

The philosophical and religious context of the early church constrained the reading of the Gospels. Nevertheless, conventions of reading in the early church allowed attention to the literal level, levels beyond the literal and the life of readers (individuals and groups). With the critical approaches warranted by the world of the Enlightenment, the reference was taken to be history, at first the history recounted in the text (to be discounted or supported by critical study) and later the historical context of the formation of the tradition or of the final composition of the Gospels. With literary approaches in the 1960s there was a return to a variety of concerns comparable to the concerns of the early church.

2.1. Developments before Modern Literary Approaches.

2.1.1. Precritical Reading of the Gospels. In the reading of the Gospels in the precritical period, no distinction was made between the world depicted and the real historical world. Indeed, the Bible as a whole was seen as referring to the whole of historical reality. Past history of the Bible and the early church was involved as early biblical stories referred directly to specific temporal events and indirectly (as figures or types) to later stories and events. But the biblical world extended to the present, to the world of the reader of any age. Readers saw their own actions and feelings and the events of their world as figures of the biblical world and so were able to fit themselves into the biblical world.

The power of a precritical realistic reading extending from the OT to the readers' day depended in part on the fact that the world depicted in the Bible and the real historical world were not the ultimate reality. OT individuals and events were types of NT individuals and events, but the deepest meaning is not the historical in any sense. The Passover lamb may be a type which is made clear in the sacrifice of Christ. But both of these refer to a heavenly sacrifice for the sins of every conceivable form of being.

2.1.2. Post-Enlightenment Reading of the Gospels. With the Enlightenment the historicity of literary and other cultural phenomena replaced the framework of the theological conceptualization of the ancient and medieval world. The realistic feature of biblical narrative was related consciously to historical reference. The role of the biblical stories was to enable readers to uncover the historical sequence of events to which they referred. Undermined was the correlation between the world of the reader and the biblical world made possible when both were seen as expressions of the pre-existing divine world. This diminished the potentiality of the narratives to allow readers to make sense of themselves in relation to the world of the narrative in a somewhat direction fashion.

2.1.3. Subordination of Literary Qualities. When literary qualities of the Gospels were noted and commented on, they were subordinated to dogmatic or historical interests, and they were not appreciated because they were not within the truth of contemporary thinking. In the period of the ancient and medieval church, Augustine noted the literary quali-

ties of the Fourth Gospel (in comparison with the Synoptics). The divine nature of the Lord was set forth by the writer "in such a way as he believed to be adequate to men's needs and notions" (*De cons.* 1.4.7). Augustine, of course, sees no tension between the dogmatic nature of the Gospel of John, the author's creative formulation of materials and the facticity of the story. The writer of the Gospel "is like one who has drunk in the secret of His divinity more richly and somehow more familiarly than others, as if he drew it from the very bosom of his Lord on which it was his wont to recline when He sat at meat" (*De cons.* 1.4.7).

2.2. Development of Literary Insights and Approaches.

2.2.1. Early Beginnings. Concern with genuine literary matters began to surface in the 1960s and 1970s and became commonplace in the 1980s. The literary turn was prepared for in the attempt of R. Bultmann and the New Hermeneutic to prolong the text hermeneutically by attention to its linguistic dimensions. Preoccupation with existential categories and the lack of interaction with genuine literary criticism hindered the task.

In his 1964 publication, *The Language of the Gospel,* A. Wilder advocated a move which takes advantage of literary insights. He expounds the NT as "language event" in terms of literary form with the conviction that "behind the particular New Testament forms lies a particular life-experience and a language-shaping faith." Wilder explicitly criticizes Bultmann's restriction of meaning to existential concepts. The view that the NT "tells us about ourselves, not about 'things' and the way they are and the way they happen," according to Wilder, results in a disparagement of "the whole story of man and salvation as the Bible presents it" (Wilder, 133). The literary criticism appropriate for NT study is not one which remains confined to forms and conventions. There is reference in the text, but the reference is not the same as that in conventional study of the Gospels. Students of the NT can learn about its literary language and reference from students of poetry: "this kind of report of reality—as in a work of art—is more subtle and complex and concrete than in the case of a discursive statement, and therefore more adequate to the matter in hand and to things of importance" (Wilder, 133).

At this point it should be re-emphasized that for the Christian, literary approaches to the Gospels must exist in relation to historical approaches and especially to the historical reality of Jesus the Christ. Concentration on the literary alone would eventually lead to the same sort of protest made by disciples of Bultmann. They refused to be left with only a mythological Lord. We cannot be satisfied with only a literary

Jesus. It should be noted, however, that the historical methods devised by scholars will never reveal the fullness of the meaning and significance of Jesus the Christ (*see* Historical Jesus). Literary approaches may assist in that task.

2.2.2. Structuralist Contributions. Wilder's work predates French Structuralism's attempt to move beneath the surface structure of a text with its historically constrained relationships to "deeper" ahistorical relationships. The structuralist turn provided impetus toward and ways of studying the relationships within the text. The structuralist interlude benefited the literary study of the Gospels, even though severely structuralist ideologies and models were not satisfying.

2.2.3. Redaction Criticism and Literary Criticism. The parables of Jesus were favorite texts for existential and structuralist exegesis, but literary study after structuralism moved beyond study of parables and other units to the literary study of the Gospels as wholes. When the Gospels were seen as forms to be correlated with their unique historical and sociological settings, redaction criticism* was born. But redaction criticism is not literary criticism. Redaction criticism seeks objectively to find *the* one correct theme, structure and historical setting. In literary study the historical setting of a text is seen as the originating circumstance and does not constitute a primary focus of study. The intention of the author to communicate certain christological, eschatological and other ideas is also relativized as literary criticism allows a variety of functions of texts and gives attention to the intention of readers (past and present).

The coordination of redactional-critical and literary-critical approaches is helpful, especially in order to guard against the ahistorical tendencies of some sorts of literary approaches. S. McKnight suggests that "a sharper profile will be obtained as one examines literary strategies in the light of the tradition-critical process, for one will be observing what the author is doing to the traditions (composition criticism)" (S. McKnight, 137).

3. The Gospels and Literary Conventions and Strategies.

The development of literary approaches to the Gospels has forced attention to the role and function of the Gospels and resulted in the recognition that the Gospels serve a variety of functions. The perception of the role and function of the Gospels influences the perception of genre and the strategies which are followed in reading and interpretation.

3.1 The Role and Function of the Gospels As Literature. A literary approach to the Gospels is not designed to reduce the Gospel text to dogma and history, but neither is it designed to reduce the text to a nexus of linguistic and literary data. What references and/or functions of Gospel texts are conceivable and satisfying in literary study? (Non-literary references and functions are not ruled out, of course.) Is there a function of Gospel texts comparable to the function of literary texts—a function which is faithful to the nature of the Gospels and which remains in a dialectical relationship to dogmatic and historical references? The Gospels may be viewed in terms of the discovery and creation of a world which sustains intellectual, spiritual and emotional vitality, a world which is a divine gift and not simply the consequence of human quest and achievement. When the reference of the text is seen as a world of grace and truth, narrow dogmatic and historical references are relativized, no longer seen as the primary goal of study. This world-creating or world-revealing function of the Gospels is comparable to the way that art and poetry function in enabling readers to create worlds, to come to know who they are and where they come from and are going, and to understand better their place in life and relation to nature and their fellows.

3.2. The Question of Genre. The question of genre cannot be avoided, for every reader reads a text in the light of its presumed purpose and nature as a representation of reality and/or a work of art, and in light of the conventions of that particular sort of writing. The question of the genre of the Gospels (*see* Gospel [Genre]) is intriguing as a historical question, and a particular Gospel may be compared formally and historically with the other canonical Gospels, non-canonical Gospels (*see* Gospels [Apocryphal]), ancient biographies and other narratives. When genre is approached as the question of how to read, the historical-critical question is transcended. Whatever hypothesis is accepted as the beginning point for reading must be tested and made precise in the process of reading, for the Gospel text will withstand attempts to reduce its potential to any a priori judgment. Every Gospel creates its own conventions of reading while it maintains relationships with other forms of ancient and modern narrative. Readers must respond to the demands of genre, but they must also actualize the genre in the process of reading. That is, in the act of reading the Gospels the determination is made as to how the Gospels are to be read.

3.3. Form and Structure. Form is sometimes used as equivalent to genre, but it is most often used to describe a work's principle of organization. Attention has been given primarily to mechanic form, the shape which is imposed externally, much as a mold imposes a shape on wet clay. (Organic form, on the contrary, is concerned with the shape which develops from within, like a growing plant.) At times the principle of organization is seen in terms of chronology. Each of the Gospels contains a passion narrative preceded by accounts of Jesus' words and deeds. In Mark and Matthew a distinction is made between an early ministry in Galilee* and a later mission and passion (*see* Passion Narrative) in Jerusalem. Luke makes this distinction, but in addition has a lengthy travel narrative connecting the two phases.

At times the different sorts of content have been the basis of structuring. Matthew has narrative and discourse material alternating in such a way that five books can be discerned, each consisting of a section of narrative and a section of discourse. This pentateuchal structuring is supported by the similarity of the conclusions of each of the five sections of discourse, something like "And when Jesus finished these sayings. . ." (7:28; 11:1; 13:53; 19:1; and 26:1). But a threefold structure is seen when 4:17 and 16:21 are taken as dividing marks. Each of these verses contains the words "from then Jesus began" with an infinitive and a summary of the content to follow. Other structures are dependent on readers observing relationships between earlier and later sections.

The threefold chronological pattern of Luke has been modified by attention to references to Jerusalem which appear at turns in the story. The conclusion of an initial section (1:5—3:38) indicates that Jerusalem is the site of Jesus' final temptation.* A second section (4:1—9:50) concludes with Jesus setting his face to go to Jerusalem. The travel narrative as a whole is movement toward Jerusalem and can be divided into 9:51—13:35 (the beginning of the journey) and 14:1—19:27 (the conclusion of the journey). The final section (19:28—24:53) tells of the reign of Jesus in Jerusalem by means of crucifixion and resurrection.

Mark can be perceived as a story of Jesus' ministry in and around Galilee followed by a journey to Jerusalem and Jesus' activities there. But it can be read as a passion narrative, prefaced by a series of controversies which lead up to the passion. It can also be read as three successive and progressively worsening stages in the story of the relations between Jesus and his disciples (1:16—8:26; 8:27—14:9; and 14:10—16:8).

The Gospel of John can be divided mechanically into prolog, book of signs and book of passion. When weight is given to organic form, the Fourth Gospel may be compared with a musical fugue, with a theme announced and developed to a point, after which other themes are introduced and interwoven with the earlier themes. The themes which appear are introduced in the prolog.

3.4. Plot. Plot or narrative unity of the Gospels is related to but is not the same as form and structure. In some measure, the concept of "story" mediates form and plot, for story normally refers to the synopsis of the temporal order of events in a narrative. In summarizing a work we say that something happened, then something else, then something else and so on. Plot goes beyond the chronological ordering and accounts for the relationships between the events and the organization of the events for the particular effect created. Luke-Acts provides directions for ordering the Gospel which are easily seen when a literary perspective is assumed. Readers are invited to read the Gospel in light of the perspective of Acts. Prologs tie the two works together, as do events in Acts which parallel those in the Gospel. Jerusalem is central in both works, with the Gospel moving toward Jerusalem and the book of Acts moving away from Jerusalem. There is a clear correlation between events predicted by characters in the Gospel and their fulfillment in Acts. Readers are prepared for this correlation between Luke and Acts by correlation within each of the writings. Jesus' declaration that a prophet is not acceptable in his own country is followed immediately by his own townspeople's rejection (Lk 4:16-30), and Agabus' prediction of Paul's suffering (Acts 21:10-14) comes true immediately (Acts 21:30-35). Just as Jesus' commission in Acts 1:8 guides the reader for the reading of the book of Acts, the prophecy of Simeon in Luke 2:34 prepares the reader for understanding the Gospel as the story of the prophet* Jesus who created a division among the people in his ministry.

The beginnings and endings of the Gospels are important from a literary perspective. The prolog of the Gospel of John prepares the reader for the entire Gospel. The infancy stories of Matthew and Luke (*see* Birth of Jesus) serve the same function for those Gospels. Mark is unique in that it lacks a full-blown prolog, contains a problematic ending and does not establish a clear and unambiguous set of connections among and between the episodes. The critical and imaginative competence and skill of readers are stretched in discerning the plot of Mark.

3.5. Character. Characters are necessary for the actions which move the story along, but actions help define characters, so there is a dialectical relationship between plot and character in the Gospels. In the Gospels characters are portrayed—their moral, emotional and volitional qualities are expressed—in what they say and do as well as in what is said of them. Of primary interest in literary study is the way that convincing portraits of Jesus, God and figures around Jesus are fashioned within the totality of the Gospel and how those portrayed persons are related to the rest of the story.

The Gospels differ widely in the way they utilize literary means to present portraits of Jesus (and other characterizations follow from the presentation of Jesus). John and Mark are at opposite poles. The Gospel of John utilizes a prolog, lengthy discourses of Jesus and a prayer to his Father, a series of signs, testimony of independent witnesses and explicit statements of the narrator to present an unambiguous picture of the messiahship and divine sonship of Jesus. In Mark there is no prolog, but the opening says that Jesus is the Christ,* the Son of God. Yet what seems to be so obvious at the beginning becomes problematic. Jesus is not Messiah in the traditional sense. What is revealed in the literary strategies is as confusing for the reader as Jesus' disclosure is to the disciples within the story.

God is a character in a literary sense in the Gospels. In the Gospel of John, God is characterized by Jesus. He is the one who sent Jesus. In Luke there is a process of deconstruction at work in the tension between revolutionary and conservative aspects of Luke's God. The purpose of God is universal salvation, and the story of Luke-Acts is a "dialogue between God and a recalcitrant humanity" (Tannehill) with God overruling as well as ruling. But Luke-Acts proclaims God's faithfulness to Israel.* The revolutionary and conservative aspects of the characterization of God creates a tension which is not clearly resolved in the story.

3.6. Narrative World and Rhetoric. The narrative worlds of the Gospels are important. The world may be considered a "poetic" (not a "fictional") world in that the writers craft a unified sequence and introduce characters and tell the readers (directly and indirectly) how those characters are to be considered and so on. But in a real sense, the world (or the values of the world) is profoundly true for the authors. So true that the Gospels are attempts to lead readers to affirm or reaffirm belief in such a world. The Gospels may then be called narrative rhetoric, and a literary approach will give attention to the means utilized in the Gospels to appeal to the reader.

3.7. Authors and Narrators. Literary criticism of the Gospels is concerned with authorship in quite a different fashion than is historical criticism. What sort of author is it who is leading readers to affirm belief? What can be discovered from the work itself? This *author* is called the "implied author" in literary criticism and is to be distinguished from the real author who can be given a name and address.

The *narrator* is also a literary figure. Literary criticism distinguishes between first- and third-person narrators and (with third-person narrators) between the omniscient and limited point of view. The omniscient narrator may be intrusive or unintrusive. The narrators of the Gospels are third person, omniscient and intrusive. Gospel narrators know what needs to be known about persons and events, even having access to the characters' feelings, motives and thoughts. The narrators not only tell the story, they introduce the story, provide explanations, translate terms, tell us what is known or not known by characters and express judgments directly and indirectly. Readers are influenced by the nature of the narrator. There is a correlation between the dependability of the narrator and the more ultimate trustworthiness and trust which are being manifested and elicited.

In conclusion, literary approaches to the Gospels complement conventional approaches. They may enable readers to rediscover value and meaning in the Gospels which have become problematic with approaches which distance texts for purposes of critical examination. The assumptions and strategies of literary criticism allow readers to interact with texts in critical and creative modes and fashions.

See also FORM CRITICISM; GOSPEL (GENRE); NARRATIVE EXEGESIS; REDACTION CRITICISM; TRADITION CRITICISM.

BIBLIOGRAPHY. R. Alter, *The Art of Biblical Narrative* (New York: Basic Books, 1981); R. A. Culpepper, *Anatomy of the Fourth Gospel: A Study in Literary Design* (Philadelphia: Fortress, 1983); H. W. Frei, *The Eclipse of Biblical Narrative: A Study in Eighteenth and Nineteenth Century Hermeneutics* (New Haven and London: Yale, 1974); C. F. H. Henry, "Narrative Theology: An Evangelical Appraisal," *TJ* 7 n.s. (1987) 3-19; J. D. Kingsbury, *Matthew As Story* (Philadelphia: Fortress, 1986); E. V. McKnight, *Postmodern Use of the Bible: The Emergence of Reader-Oriented Criticism* (Nashville: Abingdon, 1988); S. McKnight, "Literary Criticism," in *Interpreting the Synoptic Gospels* (Grand Rapids: Baker, 1988); S. D. Moore, *Literary Criticism and the Gospels* (New Haven: Yale University, 1989); N. Petersen, *Literary Criticism for New Testament Critics* (Philadelphia: Fortress, 1978); D. Rhoads and D. Michie, *Mark As Story: An Introduction to the Narrative of a Gospel* (Philadelphia: Fortress, 1982); R. A. Spencer, ed., *Orientation by Disorientation: Studies in Literary Criticism and Biblical Literary Criticism* (Pittsburg: Pickwick, 1980); M. Sternberg, *The Poetics of Biblical Narrative: Ideological Literature and the Drama of Reading* (Bloomington: Indiana University, 1985); R. C. Tannehill, *The Narrative Unity of Luke-Acts: A Literary Interpretation I:*

The Gospel According to Luke (Philadelphia: Fortress, 1986); K. J. Vanhoozer, "A Lamp in the Labyrinth: The Hermeneutics of 'Aesthetic' Theology," *TJ* 7 n.s. (1987) 25-56; D. O. Via, Jr., *The Parables: Their Literary and Existential Dimension* (Philadelphia: Fortress, 1967); A. N. Wilder, *The Language of the Gospel: Early Christian Rhetoric* (New York: Harper, 1964).

E. V. McKnight

LOGOS

Logos is the transliteration of a common Greek word that generally means "word," "speech," "account," "story" or "message." Around 500 B.C. Greek philosophers began to adopt the word and use it to signify that which gives shape, form or life to the material universe. In the NT era this special use was operative alongside the more general use.

Logos is used 128 times in the Gospels (NA[26]). The frequency of its occurrence is about the same in all four Gospels (Mt 32 x; Mk 23 x; Lk 32 x; Jn 40 x). Matthew and Mark use *logos* in a non-philosophical sense. Luke (when read in the light of Acts) begins to use *logos* in a more technical sense. The Johannine prologue uses *logos* in a particular way to refer to Jesus.

1. The Synoptic Gospels
2. The Gospel of John

1. The Synoptic Gospels.

1.1. Matthew and Mark. Matthew and Mark use *logos* fairly frequently with its general meaning of "speech" or "message." With verbs of financial accounting (*synairō; apodidōmi*) *logos* takes on the meaning of "an account" (Mt 12:36; 18:23; 25:19). Sometimes the word can bear the specific meaning of the "word of God" or the "word of Jesus" (e.g., Mk 2:2; 4:14-20 par.; Mt 15:6) where it may refer to the message of the Scriptures, of the gospel (*see* Gospel [Good News]) or of the kingdom (*see* Kingdom of God). In a very few instances *logos* describes the authoritative (*see* Authority) word of Jesus over evil (Mt 8:8, 16).

1.2. Luke. Luke uses *logos* less frequently in the general sense of "speech" and more frequently for the particular "word" of Jesus, whether it be his message or his authoritative word (e.g., Lk 4:32, 36; 6:47; 9:26; 10:39). There is even an instance where Luke equates Jesus' "word" with the "word" of God (Lk 5:1). In his prologue Luke uses *logos* to refer very pointedly to the gospel (Lk 1:2; cf. Acts 6:4). Luke (especially in material peculiar to his Gospel) seems to use *logos* more frequently than the other Synoptics to refer to the authoritative teaching of Jesus. This may be due to his desire to show continuity between the OT and the message of Jesus on the one hand, and the message of Jesus and the message of the apostles* in the book of Acts on the other hand.

2. The Gospel of John.

In the Fourth Gospel almost every occurrence of *logos* occurs in some syntactical sequence with Jesus or God,* but it is not always easy to tell if there is an exact nuance to the word or if it refers generally to Jesus' speech. In a few instances it is used in the context of a fulfillment formula (Jn 18:9, 32), that is, Jesus' prophetic (*see* Prophets, Prophecy) word about himself is fulfilled. In John 2:22 there is an equating of the predictive nature of the Scripture and Jesus' word. The word of Jesus is even equated with the word of God (Jn 14:24; 17:14). But the use of *logos* in John 1:1, 14 has been the focus of much scholarly investigation, giving rise to as much literature and debate as any other single word occurring in the Bible.

2.1. The Religious/Philosophical Background of Logos in John. The main question arising out of John's use of *logos* in John 1:1, 14 concerns the source of his language. Scholars have assumed that by determining the source of John's language the meaning of the word would become clear. Is he borrowing the term from Hellenistic (*see* Hellenism) philosophy, from a proto-gnostic source, from Jewish ideas or from a combination of two or three of these? Many have asserted that in his prologue (Jn 1:1-18) John has taken over a so-called *logos* hymn and modified it to fit his story of Jesus. The milieu in which this *logos* hymn was composed has been a matter of debate. Was it Christian, Jewish, proto-gnostic or utterly pagan? Other questions center around the structure and meaning of the prologue as a whole as it now stands in the Gospel. The ultimate question is what did the Evangelist mean by using the term *logos* in John 1:1 and 14?

2.1.1. Platonism and the Logos in the Early Church. In the early church Justin Martyr (c.100-c.165) seems to have been the earliest proponent of a developed *logos* doctrine. Justin was a converted pagan philosopher who generally followed a Platonic-type philosophy. In Platonism and the neo-Platonism of Justin's day *logos* could denote the all-pervading Reason which gives form to and governs the universe (Justin Martyr *Apol.* I.5, 46, 59; II.8, 13). Although in his extant writings Justin quotes the Fourth Gospel only once (*Apol.* I.61), much of his imagery parallels that of John. It seems likely that he interprets the *logos* of John 1:1, 14 in the Platonic or neo-Platonic sense of Reason as it was used by Plato, Heraclitus, the Stoics and Philo. But for Justin the uniqueness of the Christian *logos* lies in the Incarnation (Justin Martyr *Apol.* I.46; II.10). Justin's *logos* doctrine is paralleled or developed in Clement of

Alexandria (c.150-c.220) and especially in Augustine (354-430) (*Civ. D.* 10; *Conf.* VII.9).

2.1.2. Hellenistic Background. Since the rise of the historical-critical method the background of the *logos* concept in the Fourth Gospel has been sought out in various milieus. R. Bultmann popularized the theories of R. Reitzenstein and W. Bousset that an ancient pagan mythological speculation lay behind the Johannine idea of the *logos*. The origin of this myth* was not Jewish but was mediated to John via Jewish wisdom speculation. Bultmann, following Reitzenstein, believed that this Jewish source was an Iranian gnostic sect best exemplified in the writings of seventh-century Mandaeanism.

Others have proposed a Hellenistic-Jewish background found in Alexandrian Judaism and exemplified by the Wisdom of Solomon and in the writings of Philo. Although the Wisdom of Solomon generally uses *sophia* (wisdom) instead of *logos*, the former term is sometimes given the philosophical attributes of the latter (Wis 7:15—8:1).

Philo, the Jewish philosopher who flourished in Alexandria, Egypt, during the first Christian century, seems to combine two systems of thought in his philosophy: the divinely inspired writings of Hebrew prophets and the philosophical discussions current in his day. From the Hebrew Scriptures he gained the subject of his writings. From Platonism and stoicism he gained the hermeneutical axioms by which he interpreted this subject. For Philo, following Plato, there were two worlds, an ideal world of ideas of which God and immortality are a part and a phenomenal world which is a physical copy of the ideal. Unlike later gnostics Philo did not denigrate the physical for the sake of the ideal (*Migr. Abr.* 89-93). At times in Philo, *logos* stands for the word by which God created the world (*Op. Mund.* 20-25). At other times it refers to a mediator between the ideal and the phenomenal ("The same word both pleads with the immortal as suppliant for the afflicted mortality and acts as ambassador of the ruler to the subject." *Rer. Div. Her.* 205.)

2.1.3. Jewish Background. Still others have seen in the *logos* concept of John's prologue four more strictly Jewish ideas. First, the Jewish targums explained certain theological anthropomorphisms by attributing the activities of God on earth to his *mēmrā'*—his word. For example, in Genesis 15:1 where the Hebrew text reads, "I will be a shield for you," Targum* Onqelos reads "My word [*mēmrā'*] will be strength for you." Some have therefore thought that the background for John's use of *logos* was the Aramaic concept of *mēmrā'* as the explanation of God's relationship to creation.

Second, it could be that *logos* in John 1 is a reference to Wisdom* (*ḥokmāh*) in Proverbs 8:22-31 and other Wisdom passages (e.g., Job 28). In Proverbs 8 Lady Wisdom claims to have existed with God before the beginning of the world. In 8:30 she even claims to be the artisan (*āmôn*) at God's side by which he fashioned the world. The motifs of Proverbs 8 are further developed in Sirach 1:1-10 where wisdom is said to have been created before all else and was poured out on all God's works. In Sirach 24:23-34 Wisdom is the Law* of Moses.

A third suggested Jewish/Hebrew background to John's *logos* is the Torah. In Psalm 119:105 (LXX 118:105) the Torah is called the Word of God (LXX *ho logos sou*). This is only one of many passages of this Torah Psalm which identifies the Law with God's Word. (In fact some manuscripts of the LXX substitute *nomos* [law] for *logos* in v. 105.) Later Jewish theology identified the Torah as one of the few things which existed before the creation.

A fourth Jewish background suggested by some is the probable Hebrew translation equivalent to *logos tou theou* (the Word of God) which is *dābar YHWH* (the word of Yahweh). Like *logos*, *dābar* can mean word, thing, matter, speech, cause, promise or plan. In the OT the word of the Lord came on or to numerous people (Gen 15:1, 4; Hos 1:1 and often in the prophets). In most of these instances the word of the Lord is a prophetic promise or judgment* which is sure to come to pass. Thus the word of the Lord in many contexts becomes a dynamic concept in that it accomplishes God's work (Is 6:9-10; 24:1-3; 40:8; 45:23; 55:11). In some contexts the word of the Lord is even personified (Is 9:8; Ps 107:20; 147:15, 18). This personification became even more pronounced in Wisdom 18:15-17. John 1:1, 14 picks up this theological motif of the *dābar YHWH* which accomplishes God's work and then uses it to explain the Incarnation and to describe who Jesus is, the one sent from God to do his will.

R. Brown exemplifies the opinion of most recent scholars regarding the background to the Johannine *logos* when he says, "it seems that the Prologue's description of the Word is far closer to biblical and Jewish strains of thought than it is to anything purely Hellenistic" (1.524). (See Schnackenburg. Cf. Dunn who places the concept in the context of Alexandrian Judaism best exemplified in Philo.)

2.2. Logos within the Literary Context of the Fourth Gospel. When approaching the issue of backgrounds it is important to keep two things in mind. First, proper historical method dictates a comprehensive and reasoned evaluation of background material. Too often a supposed parallel surfaces which leads to further study in a particular corpus of literature to the neglect of other relevant bodies of literature (cf. Kysar).

Second, verbal similarities do not necessarily imply conceptual similarities. The use of similar words in seemingly similar ways can deceive us into thinking that two authors are discussing the same concept. Only when one document is understood in its own right can it be compared to another which must also be understood in its own right. This being the case, a person reading through the Philonic corpus and the Gospel of John will probably notice many verbal similarities, though they will undoubtedly come to the conclusion that John and Philo, when they use the word *logos,* are referring to different concepts which hardly overlap. For Philo the *logos* is the Reason inherent in the universe, whether that Reason be divine or human. Thus it can mediate between God and man. This neo-Platonic concept of the *logos* is foreign to Johannine thought. As the Gospel unfolds, Jesus, who is the *logos,* claims to have had a personal relationship with the Father before the Incarnation (Jn 17:5). Any real similarities that exist between Philo and the Fourth Gospel are due to the fact that both Philo and John draw on the concept of the word of the prophets as the Word of God.

The corollary to this principle is that one must seek to understand words and concepts first and foremost within the immediate literary contexts in which they occur. Therefore, it seems preferable to search for the meaning of *logos* in the Fourth Gospel itself before looking at religious or literary backgrounds outside the Gospel (cf. Carter, 37).

A careful reading of John 1:1 yields a wealth of information about the *logos.* The verse is divided into three simple clauses, each of which contains the imperfect of the verb *einai* ("to be"). In each of the clauses the verb has a different meaning. In the first clause it means "to exist." The *logos* existed in the beginning. The phrase "in the beginning" is an obvious allusion to Genesis 1:1 (LXX *en archē;* MT *bᵉrê'šît).* So John is saying that at the very beginning of creation the *logos* already existed. In the second clause the verb "to be" describes a relationship—the *logos* was with God in the sense of being in his presence. Therefore, the *logos* was distinct from God and at the same time in fellowship with God. In the third clause the verb "to be" is used in a predication in which the character or essence of the *logos* is defined—"The word was God."

The choice of words and their order is very significant in this third clause. If John had wanted to say that the word and God are the same being he could have written *ho theos ēn ho logos.* Or if he had wanted to say that the word was a god he could have written *ho logos ēn theos.* Or if he had wanted to say the word was divine he could have written *ho logos ēn theios.* As it stands, *theos ēn ho logos* could mean any of these three statements. But it could also mean the word was God in the sense that the church has explained the nature of Christ since Chalcedon. He is a part of the unity of the triune Godhead. E. C. Colwell has shown that definite predicate nouns preceding the verb do not need the article to show that they are definite. So a reference to the one God of the Bible is entirely possible in this third clause. The church has understood that Christ is deity based on this verse along with others (cf. Phil 2:6; Col 1:19; 2:9; Heb 1:3, 9). But to say that Christ is the only person in the Godhead is to neglect the second clause of the same verse. In later debates the church has interpreted the NT to say that the *logos,* with the Father and the Spirit, is one of the three eternal and co-equal persons of the Godhead.

John 1:3-4 describes the activity of the *logos.* He is the agent of creation ("all things came into being through him"), and he is the source of true life which is the light of all people. Later in the Gospel John expands on this latter activity of the word which gives life (Jn 6:35, 48, 51, 58; 11:25) and light (Jn 8:12; 9:1-12).

John 1:14 describes the Incarnation of the *logos.* Here John uses a different "to be" verb (*ginomai*) which, to this point in the prologue he has reserved for created beings: "The word became flesh." Note that John does not say the word became a man. He uses "flesh" (*sarx*) to signify the very nature of the Incarnation. Wesley captured the essence of John 1:14 in his great Christmas hymn: "Veiled in flesh the Godhead see; Hail the incarnate deity; Pleased as man with men to dwell; Jesus our Immanuel."

Finally, after saying that the incarnate *logos,* Jesus Christ, has replaced the Law given through Moses,* John identifies him as the *monogenēs theos* (the unique one of God) who reveals the unseen God. This *logos* has a personal relationship with the Father. This theme of sonship continues through the Fourth Gospel and infiltrates the rest of the NT canon (*see* Son of God).

2.3. Conclusion. The meaning of *logos* in the Johannine prologue is clear. The Word is the person of the Godhead through whom the world was created, who took on human nature in history and who is the source of life and light for humanity. But why did John use *logos* to describe this person? If John was thinking of any of the particular background discussed earlier in this article, it is not yet clear which one he had in mind. But his use of *logos* in the rest of the Gospel (which is the only evidence we have of his intentions) seems to imply that the word he is speaking of is that prophetic word which goes forth from God's mouth to accomplish creation, judgment, redemption and renewal. John uses *logos* because it is the natural word for expressing the meaning of the Hebrew word *dābar* when that word was used in the context of God's revelation. Beginning with its first sentences the Gospel asserts that Jesus is God's final Revelator (cf. Heb 1:1-2). This assertion corresponds to the evangelistic purpose of the Gospel (Carson) and fits well with recent hypotheses that the original historical context of the Fourth Gospel was a debate with first-century Judaism over the locus of revelation (cf. Carter, 47 n. 82).

See also JOHN, GOSPEL OF; WISDOM.

BIBLIOGRAPHY. J. Bergman et al., "λέγω κτλ," *TDNT* IV.84-125; R. Brown, *The Gospel According to John* (AB; Garden City, NY: Doubleday, 1966) 1.519-24; R. Bultmann, "The History of Religions Background of the Prologue to the Gospel of John," in *The Interpretation of John*, ed. J. Ashton (Philadelphia: Fortress, 1986) 18-35; D. A. Carson, "The Purpose of the Fourth Gospel: John 20:31 Reconsidered," *JBL* 106 (1987) 639-51; W. Carter, "The Prologue and John's Gospel: Function, Symbol and Definitive Word," *JSNT* 39 (1990) 35-58; E. C. Colwell, "A Definite Rule for the Use of the Article in the Greek New Testament," *JBL* 52 (1933) 12-21; J. D. G. Dunn, *Christology in the Making* (Philadelphia: Westminster, 1980); R. Kysar, "The Background of the Prologue of the Fourth Gospel: A Critique of Historical Method," *CJT* 116 (1970) 250-55; idem, *The Fourth Evangelist and His Gospel* (Minneapolis: Augsburg, 1975); R. Schnackenburg, *The Gospel According to John* (3 vols.; New York: Herder and Herder, 1968) 1.481-93. D. H. Johnson

LORD

The term *kyrios* ("Lord"), which became for the early church the central Christian confession regarding Jesus (cf. Rom 10:9; 1 Cor 12:3; Phil 2:11), had a wide variety of uses in antiquity. It is necessary to explore some of them before examining how and whether Jesus, the earliest Christians and then the Evangelists used such a term or its Aramaic equivalent to say something essential or even extraordinary about the central figure of Christian faith.

1. Greek Usage
2. Jewish Background
3. The Origin of the Christian *Kyrios* Usage
4. Jesus As *Kyrios*
5. *Kyrios* in the Gospels
6. *Kyrios* in Acts
7. Conclusion

1. Greek Usage.

The term *kyrios* was used both in religious and secular contexts in the NT era. On the one hand, both national and mystery religions, especially in the East (i.e., Egypt, Syria, Asia Minor, but also in Greece and elsewhere), frequently used the term *kyrios* or its female equivalent *kyria* to refer to gods and goddesses such as Isis, Serapis or Osiris (*see* Hellenism). For instance, we have evidence of the use of the term in countless papyri and inscriptions of Serapis (e.g., "I thank the Lord Serapis (*tō kyriō*) that when I was in peril on the sea, he saved me immediately," Letter from Apion, soldier in the Roman navy, to his father, second century A.D.). Or again in a letter from a son to his mother, Nilus, in the second century A.D. we read, "I make intercession for you day by day to the Lord Serapis" (*tō kyriō*). It is quite clear in these contexts that the term *kyrios* connotes a deity who can answer prayers and deserves thanks for divine help. This development seems to go beyond the use of *kyrios* in the period of classical Greek where the term did refer to the great power a god had over a person or group of persons but does not yet seem to have been a divine title (cf. Pindar *Isth.* 5.53; Plato *Leg.* 12.13).

Equally important for our purposes is the fact that the Roman emperor was as early as the time of Nero called *kyrios* with the sense of divinity (*see* Rome). Yet even though he was divinized, he was also known to be a human being. For instance, from an ostracon dated August 4, A.D. 63, we read, "In the year nine of Nero the Lord . . . (*tou kyriou*)." Even before this time, however, in the eastern part of the empire and in Egypt in particular the emperor was being called *kyrios* in a more-than-merely-human sense. Thus, for instance, Oxyrhynchus papyrus 1143, which dates to A.D. 1, speaks of sacrifices and libations "for the God and Lord Emperor" [Augustus]. Even in 12 B.C. we have an inscription to Augustus as *theos kai kyrios*, "God and Lord" (*BGU*, 1197, I, 15).

As A. Deissmann (349-51) long ago argued, it is quite likely that the early church deliberately and polemically ascribed to Jesus titles that had already been applied to the emperor. The meaning of the term within the Pauline communities, namely an absolute divine being to whom one belongs and owes absolute allegiance and submission, becomes all the more evident in light of the Pauline language of self-reference. Paul speaks of himself and others as *douloi*, "slaves," in order to indicate their relationship to Jesus "the Lord" (Rom 1:1; 13:4). This term may be distinguished from *misthios*, or *diakonos*, terms used for hired servants who had certain rights and privileges. The *doulos* who served a *kyrios* was not free but was the property of his or her Lord. This was the normal terminology in various oriental religions to express the relationship of the adherent to the deity. No doubt to a significant degree this usage has derived from the more ordinary usage in the institution of slavery. The term *kyrios* had a perfectly normal, nonreligious sense in both classical and *Koinē* Greek, meaning "master" or "owner" of some property (including human property).

The vocative form *kyrie* frequently was just a polite form of address like the English term "sir." This latter usage is in evidence not only in secular Greek literature but also appears at various points in the NT. For instance in Acts 9:5 (and par.) Paul addressed the heavenly Jesus with the term *kyrie*. Since he is asking who he is addressing, it is unlikely that in this case the term means anything but "sir." Again in Mark 7:28 we find the use of *kyrie*, in all probability indicating a respectful form of address, not a confession of deity. Once again, in Luke 6:46 *kyrie, kyrie* may refer to a respectful form of address, not a confession of divinity. Luke 6:46 seems to suggest that it is inconsistent to address Jesus in respectful terms as a great teacher* but not do what he commands. It is not impossible, however, that the use of *mārî*, the Aramaic equivalent of *kyrie*, was, at least in the context of Jesus' inner circle of disciples,* already taking on a deeper significance than a mere respectful form of address (see Vermes 109-115).

There may be a clear distinction between the use of the term *kyrios* and its near synonym *despotēs*. The latter term suggested arbitrariness while the term *kyrios* connoted the idea of legitimate authority (cf. Bietenhard, 510; see 6. below).

From these examples we can readily observe the scope of usage of the term *kyrios* in Greek literature. On the one hand it can have a perfectly mundane use to refer to the master or owner of slaves or some other sort of property such as a household or business. The term in the vocative could also be used as a respectful way of addressing a person, in particular a superior, who was not one's owner or employer. This second sort of usage had become so conventional that it often meant little more than our own use of the address "Dear Sir" in a letter. Yet early in the first century B.C., at least in the eastern part of the empire, the term *kyrios*, in the sense of divinity, was being applied not only to mythological gods like Serapis or Osiris, but also to one particular human being, the Roman emperor. In such a context it is understandable why Paul might say there are many so-called gods and lords, yet for Christians there is but one Lord, Jesus Christ (1 Cor 8:5-6). Because of the use of *kyrios* in these more religious senses, W. Bousset argued that it was not until Christianity reached a mainly Greek or Hellenistic environment that the title "Lord" was applied to Jesus, and then under the influence of pagan usage. This conclusion can be shown to be incorrect by a study of the Jewish usage of *kyrios* and its Aramaic cognates. To this we now turn.

2. Jewish Background.

In the Septuagint (LXX) the term *kyrios* occurs over 9,000 times and in some 6,156 occurrences it is used in place of the proper name of God,* Yahweh. This amounts not to a translation of the personal name Yahweh but a circumlocution meant to aid in avoiding saying the sacred Tetragrammaton. There are, however, some doubts as to whether the original compilers of the LXX actually in every case translated the Tetragrammaton with *kyrios*. Some older manuscripts have the Hebrew *YHWH* in the Greek text at some places, and at least one LXX manuscript from Qumran uses *IAO* for the Tetragrammaton instead of *kyrios*. The copies of the LXX which do have *kyrios* for *YHWH* date from the fourth century A.D. on and appear to be Christian copies with Christian modifications. Yet J. A. Fitzmyer has produced evidence that early Jews did use the Greek *kyrios* as well as *'ăḏôn*, or *mārē'*, of Yahweh, and thus it is not impossible that early Jewish Christians transferred such a title from Yahweh to Jesus (1979, 115-42 and 1981, 218-35). But we can no longer say with any assurance that this was done under the influence of the LXX. Examples of *kyrios* used of Yahweh can be found not only in Josephus and Philo but even as early as in the Wisdom of Solomon (some 27 times cf. Wis 1:1, 7, 9; 2:13). Of special significance is Josephus' remark that early Jews refused to call the emperor *kyrios* precisely because they regarded it as a name reserved for God (*J.W.* 7.10.1 §§418-19).

When in the LXX and other early Jewish literature *kyrios* is used to translate the Hebrew word *'ăḏôn*, it is a matter of translation and not a circumlocution. Some 190 times in the LXX *'ăḏôn* is translated *kyrios* and refers to men who were lords or commanders in some sense. In fact there is also some evidence that *'ăḏônay* was being used as a substitute for YHWH in some cases at Qumran in their Hebrew biblical manuscripts. Equally interesting is the use of *'ăḏônay* in prayers of invocation at Qumran (cf. 1QM 12:8, 18; 1Q 34).

The Aramaic use of *mārē'*, or *mārā'*, to refer to God as Lord can be traced back at least as early as Daniel 2:47 and 5:23, even though in these texts the term is not yet used in an absolute sense as a title. Evidence of a different sort comes to us from the Genesis Apocryphon (1QapGen). This Qumran document probably dates from about the turn of the era and provides us with examples of God being addressed in Aramaic as *mārî*, my Lord. This is the only known example of this usage in Aramaic. However, it is quite common to find the more mundane use of *mārî* by a wife or servant of the husband or head of the household. *Mār* is the Aramaic word for "lord," but it is almost always found with various sorts of suffixes. In 11Q Targum of Job (11QtgJob) we have *mārē'* as a rendering of the Hebrew word *šadday* (almighty). There are also some fragments from Cave 4 from the Enoch literature where *mārē'*, or *māran*, is used of God (cf. 89:31-36), and the Greek version has *ho kyrios*. Further evidence of importance comes from the temple discovered at Gaza, which was called the Marneum, where a god called *mār* was worshiped (Johnson, 151).

L. W. Hurtado has amassed material demonstrating the complex nature of early Jewish thought on such subjects as divine agents. He has shown that there is plenty of evidence that in early Judaism* the Jewish concept of the uniqueness of God could co-exist with the idea that God could give a unique place and role to a particular heavenly figure or agent. This included the idea that exalted patriarchs (e.g., Enoch or Moses) and principal angels* (e.g., Michael) could speak and act for God with divine authority and power (*see* Authority and Power). This evidence is significant because it indicates a larger context of divine agency in early Judaism by which even the first Jewish Christians could have understood Jesus.

3. The Origin of the Christian *Kyrios* Usage.

Aramaic evidence of singular importance for our study can be found in 1 Corinthians 16:22 and in what is probably the earliest of extra-canonical Christian works, the Didache (cf. *Did.* 10.6). Here Jesus is referred to as Lord by the earliest Aramaic-speaking Christians (*see* Languages of Palestine) using the phrase *maran atha*, or more likely *marana tha* (cf. Rev 22:20, which is likely a Greek translation of this phrase. This last text makes clear that it is Jesus who is in view, as is also evident in 1 Cor 16:22-23). There are basically three ways the phrase *marana tha* could be rendered: (1) "Lord come"; (2) "Our Lord has come" or (3) even as a prophetic perfect "The Lord will come." Whichever rendering one chooses, and (1)

seems most likely, especially in view of Revelation 22:20, a person who has died is being referred to as Lord. Since the first translation is the most likely, C. F. D. Moule's (41) pointed remark bears repeating: "Besides even if 'our Lord' is not the same as 'the Lord' absolutely, and even if the Aramaic *mārē* had been used mostly for humans and not for God (which we have seen reason to question) one does not call upon a mere Rabbi, after his death, to come. The entire phrase, *Maranatha*, if it meant 'Come, our Master!' would be bound to carry transcendental overtones even if the *maran* by itself did not."

It is not completely clear whether *marana tha* was used to invoke Christ's* presence in worship* or was a wish prayer* for the return of Christ from heaven.* Nevertheless, on the basis of strong evidence that the Aramaic-speaking Jewish Christians, during and likely before Paul's time (i.e., the earliest Jewish Christians), called Jesus "Lord" or at least "our Lord," we must reject Bousset's argument for the origin of the christological title *kyrios* in the Hellenistic mission of the early church.

It is striking that Paul, writing in the 50s to Greek-speaking Christians who very likely did not know Aramaic, does not bother to translate *marana tha*. This must surely mean that he assumes they understood the meaning of the phrase, which in turn suggests that it had long been a common invocation used by Christians. Consequently, the apostle sees no need to explain or translate it. The origins of the Christian use of the term *Lord* for Jesus must be traced at least back to the earliest Aramaic-speaking Jewish-Christians. Can it be traced back even further?

4. Jesus As *Kyrios*.

Several texts seem likely to go back to a historical setting during the lifetime of Jesus. They may raise the question whether and in what sense Jesus may have been called Lord during his early ministry. We have already dealt with texts where the vocative *kyrie* was used, and we will not return to them here, as they probably offer us little help. Of more importance may be a text like Mark 11:3 where Jesus tells his disciples to go and get him a colt to ride into Jerusalem and to tell whomever may question, "The Lord has need of it." The Greek reads *ho kyrios*, and presumably, if this goes back to an actual command of Jesus, it is a rendering of the Aramaic *mārē'*. There are several possible ways of looking at this text. On the one hand, even if it does go back to an utterance of Jesus, *mārē'* could here mean either the owner or the master, in which case it would imply nothing about Jesus' divine status. Some commentators have speculated either that Jesus was the owner of the animal being requested (which the text does not really suggest) or that the owner of the animal was with Jesus and was loaning the animal to Jesus. This latter view also finds no clues in the text to give it credence. It is much more probable that the meaning here is much like what we find in Mark 14:14, where Jesus is reported to have said, "The teacher says, Where is my guest room . . . ?" If so, then "Lord" here may be no more than a respectful way of referring to a master teacher, just as we might speak of a master craftsman. It does suggest one who sees himself as having authority to command or commandeer certain things of people, whether they were disciples or not. It is not clear that this particular usage of *mārē'* bears more significance than this.

Support for this suggestion can be found in several places in the Fourth Gospel. Here we find that the two terms "teacher" and "lord" are juxtaposed (Jn 13:13-16). It should also be noted that in the primitive resurrection account in John 20 we find Mary Magdalene calling her deceased teacher "my Lord" (20:13), and when she actually recognizes the voice of Jesus speaking to her we hear the cry "Rabbouni" (20:16), which is translated "Teacher." This text also seems to suggest that Jesus was called not only *rabbî*, or *rabbûnî*, during his ministry, but was probably also addressed by the term of respect *mārē'* which would have connoted that Jesus was a great teacher who exercised authority over his disciples. The disciples looked to Jesus as master in that sense. Another piece of evidence which may support this line of reasoning is the use of slave and master language (Jn 15:15, 20) in referring to the relationship between Jesus and his disciples.

A much more crucial passage for our discussion is Mark 12:35-37. Here Psalm 110:7 is quoted, "The Lord said to my lord, sit at my right hand . . . ." Jesus then asks, "David himself calls him Lord: so how is he his son?" This text should not be abruptly dismissed as reflecting the later theology of the early church, especially inasmuch as there is extensive evidence that Jesus saw himself in messianic terms and at least indirectly made messianic claims (see Witherington 1990). Indeed Mark 12:35-37 reflects precisely the sort of allusive, or indirect, manner that Jesus seems to have used in public to indicate how he viewed himself. His method was to allude to his significance in such a way as to lure his audience into careful and deep reflection on this important matter. The form of teaching here is characteristic of early Jewish teachers. Taking a puzzling text, they would raise questions about it in such a way as to challenge common misconceptions about various matters, in this case the nature of Messiah as a son of David (*see* Son of David).

Also favoring the authenticity of this tradition is the fact that it seems to suggest that Jesus challenges the idea that Messiah must be of Davidic origins, a fact which the early church went some lengths to demonstrate (e.g., Mt 1:1-20; Lk 1:27; 3:23-38). In the text as it stands Jesus is suggesting that Messiah is David's Lord, and as such he stands above and exists prior to David. This is the reason Jesus raises the question of why the scribes call Messiah "David's son." The idea of pre-existence, as Hurtado has shown (41-50), was not uncommonly predicated of God's divine agents in early Judaism.

It is then not inconceivable that Jesus here could have alluded to himself not only as Messiah but even as pre-existent Lord and been understood by his audience. V. Taylor (492-93) puts it as follows and deserves to be quoted at length:

> . . . certainly a secret of Jesus concerning Himself is implied. His question is shaped by His estimate of Messiahship embodied in Himself. His purpose, however, is not to reveal this secret, which is and remains his own, but to expose the futility of Messianic hopes which do not rise above the earthly and human plane . . . . The allusive character of the saying favours the view that it is an original utterance; it half conceals and half reveals the 'Messianic secret'. It suggests, but does not state the claim that Jesus is supernatural in dignity and origin and that His Sonship is no mere matter of human descent. It is difficult to think that the doctrinal beliefs of a community could be expressed in this allusive manner. The intention in a doctrinal statement is that it should be understood, whereas the purpose of the saying is to challenge thought and decision. This is the very idiom of Jesus Himself as his message to the Baptist shows (Lk. vii.22f.). But demonstrably, it is not the tone or the method of primitive Christianity.

This means that ultimately the proclamation of Jesus as Lord goes back to something Jesus suggested about himself, albeit obliquely, during his ministry and in public. Yet this does not explain when and at what point Jesus' followers took the hint and really began to see Jesus in this light. We have noted that the evidence is at best scant that during his ministry Jesus' disciples thought of him as *mārē'* in any sort of transcendent sense (Lk 6:46 may suggest this). What then prompted the confession of Jesus as Lord? Here we may consider clues from several sources.

First, there is the matter of the primitive confessional material Paul uses in Romans 1:3-4. This text certainly suggests that Jesus assumed new functions, authority and power as a result of his resurrection. Indeed, he was given the new title "Son of God in power" as a result of the resurrection. Another piece of evidence comes to us from what is probably a christological hymn Paul is quoting in Philippians 2:6-11. Here we are told that because of Jesus' giving up the status and prerogatives of "the being equal to God" and taking on the form not merely of a human being but of a slave, being obedient to God's plan even to the point of death, he has now been highly exalted and given the name which is above all names. Jesus moves from being a *doulos* to the *kyrios*. In the context of the hymn that name which is above all others is not Jesus, a name he already had, but the throne name he acquired when he assumed the functions of deity, ruling over all things. This name is *kyrios*. Acts 2:36, which may reflect some of the early apostolic preaching, says, "Let all the house of Israel therefore know assuredly that God has made him both Lord and Christ, this Jesus whom you crucified." In view of the fact that Luke readily calls Jesus *kyrios* in his Gospel, it is most unlikely that he would have created a text like this which suggests, if not states, that lordship is most appropriately predicated of Jesus after his death (*see* Death of Jesus). This text seems to indicate that these titles are especially apt because of what God did for Jesus after he was crucified—namely, as Acts 2:32 states, "This Jesus God raised up, and of that we are all witnesses."

Another hint comes from John 20:18 which suggests that the earliest post-Easter proclamation of faith was, "I have seen the [risen] Lord." In short the evidence suggests that the confession "Jesus is Lord" arose as a result of the earliest disciples' experiences of the risen Christ (*see* Resurrection). Indeed, Paul suggests that such a confession could not arise until after the Lord had risen and the Spirit (*see* Holy Spirit) had descended on Jesus' followers, for he says, "No one can say 'Jesus is Lord' except by the Holy Spirit" (1 Cor 12:3).

While the ultimate ground for the confession of Jesus as Lord seems to go back to something Jesus alluded to during his ministry, the formal point of departure for such a confession by the disciples was their experiences of the risen Lord on and after Easter Sunday, as well as their reception of the Holy Spirit. As best we can tell the first to so confess Jesus seems to have been the person who first claimed to have seen Jesus risen—Mary Magdalene. In view of the negative view regarding a woman's word of witness that existed in many places in the first century, but especially in Palestine (see Witherington 1984), it

is not credible that the early church invented the idea that Mary Magdalene was the first to claim, "I have seen the Lord." Indeed, the early witness list in 1 Corinthians 15:5-8 is indicative of the tendency in the early church to move in quite the opposite direction and claim the prominence of the Twelve and the apostles* as witnesses (*see* Witness) of the resurrection.

We find further evidence that the experience of the risen Lord led to the full confession of Jesus' significance in John 20:28, where the climactic confession in a Gospel full of confessions is *ho kyrios mou kai ho theos mou* ("My Lord and my God"). It may be that this material is included here because the Evangelist, writing toward the close of the first century, knew of the Emperor Domitian's (A.D. 81-96) practice of naming himself in official correspondence *dominus et deus noster* ("our Lord and God"). The Fourth Evangelist may have been countering such a claim. But even if this is so, it seems rather clear that John wishes to convey to his audience that the true confession of Jesus first came about as a result of seeing the risen Lord, both in the case of Mary Magdalene and Thomas. We conclude that Hurtado should be heeded when he says:

> Rather than trying to account for such a development as the veneration of Jesus by resort to vague suggestions of ideational borrowing from the cafeteria of heroes and demigods of the Greco-Roman world, scholars should pay more attention to this sort of religious experience of the first Christians. It is more likely that the initial and main reason that this particular chief agent (Jesus) came to share in the religious devotion of this particular Jewish group (the earliest Christians) is that they had visions and other experiences that communicated the risen and exalted Christ and that presented him in such unprecedented and superlative divine glory that they felt compelled to respond devotionally as they did (121).

Christological convictions and confessions were first generated by the experience of the risen Lord and his Spirit. This leads us to examine how the term *kyrios* came to be used by the Evangelists, who were likely composing their Gospels during the last third of the first century A.D.

5. *Kyrios* in the Gospels.

The Synoptic Gospels, and Luke in particular, include nearly the whole range of uses of the term *kyrios* as we have discussed it. There are some 717 passages where the term *kyrios* occurs in the NT, and 210 of them can be found in Luke-Acts (another 275 are found in Paul). The fact that the majority of the uses of *kyrios* are found in the writings of Luke and Paul may be explained by the fact that they were in the main addressing Gentile audiences, or at least they were writing to areas where Greek language and culture were the predominant influences. In contrast to Luke *kyrios* occurs only 18 times in Mark and 80 times in Matthew, while there are 52 instances in the Fourth Gospel.

5.1. Kyrios in the Synoptics. A sampling of the various uses not referring to Jesus can now be given. In Mark and the Q* material God is never called *kyrios* except in Mark 5:19 and Mark 13:20. Neither Matthew nor Luke follow Mark in either of these examples. In the Lukan parallel to Mark 5:19 we find *ho theos* ("God"; Lk 8:39) instead of Mark's *ho kyrios*, and Matthew does not include parallel material at all. In the Matthean parallel to Mark 13:20 the First Evangelist uses the indirect form, "and if the days had not been shortened" (Mt 24:22), instead of Mark's, "And if the Lord had not shortened the days . . . ." This difference cannot be explained by the idea that Matthew and Luke do not call God *kyrios*, for quite clearly (especially in the birth narratives) both of these Evangelists do (cf. Mt 1:20, 22, 24; 2:13, 15, 19 with Lk 1:6, 9, 11, 15, 17, 25, 28, 38, 45, 58, 66; 2:9, 15, 22, 23, 24, 26, 39). We also find *kyrios* used of God in the resurrection material at Matthew 28:2 and in two passages unique to the Third Gospel, Luke 5:17 and 20:37. *Kyrie* as a conventional address of respect is always used in the Gospels whenever a slave speaks to a master. However, it can also be found on the lips of Jews addressing Pilate (Mt 27:63; *see* Pontius Pilate), of workers speaking to the owner of a vineyard (Lk 13:8) of a son to his father when he works for him (Mt 21:30), of Mary to the gardener (Jn 20:15) and, finally, on the lips of a Syro-Phoenician woman addressing Jesus (Mk 7:28; Mt 15:27). The use of the doubled form, *kyrie kyrie*, seems to reflect Palestinian usage (cf. Mt 7:21, 22; 25:11; Lk 6:46).

Kyrios can be used to refer to the lord or owner of some property or estate, such as the owner of a vineyard (Mk 12:9 and par.). We have already noted that Mark 11:3 and parallels likely reflects the same sort of usage. The term can also be used either of the master of a (free) steward (Lk 16:3) or of an owner of slaves (almost always with a qualifier like "his" or "my"; cf. Mt 18:25; 24:45; Lk 12:37, 42; 14:23). But we do not find the Gospels using *kyrios* either for the emperor or for any pagan deities.

There are, however, some examples where *kyrios* seems to refer to ability and the right to exercise authority and power. In these cases it amounts to a non-titular use without any transcendent implications. For instance, in Mark 2:28 when Jesus says the Son of man is lord of the Sabbath,* he means he is one who exercises authority over the rules that govern the Sabbath. Of a similar nature is the non-titular use in Luke 10:2 where God is said to be the one who controls the harvest; he is "the lord of the harvest."

5.2. Kyrios in Luke. Regarding the absolute use of the noun *kyrios,* Matthew and Mark do not use the term in a transcendent sense within their narrative frameworks of the sayings of Jesus (Mk 11:3 is probably not an exception). But Luke, on the other hand, does employ such a usage. For instance, in Luke 7:13 we read, "And the Lord (*ho kyrios)* had compassion on him." Or in Luke 10:5 the Evangelist writes, "And the Lord (*ho kyrios)* appointed seventy others . . . ." Luke, as a Gentile* writing exclusively to a Gentile audience, shows no reticence in using *ho kyrios* of Jesus and thereby implying the transcendent religious sense of the term. This is not to say that Luke is being totally anachronistic, for he is usually careful not to place the term on Jesus' own lips or on the lips of his interlocutors in a sense or manner that it would not likely have been used during the ministry of Jesus. Some probable exceptions are found in Luke 1:43, where Elizabeth speaks of Mary as "the mother of my Lord"; Luke 2:11, where Jesus is identified as "Lord" to the shepherds; and Luke 1:38, where Mary is called the handmaiden of the Lord, though here it seems to refer to Yahweh (*see* Birth of Jesus).

Numerous other references in Luke's Gospel indicate the Evangelist's regular use of *kyrios* within the narrative framework of his account of Jesus' ministry (cf. 7:19; 10:1, 39, 41; 11:39; 12:42; 16:8; 17:5, 6; 18:6; 19:8a; 22:61; 24:3, 34). When he is speaking of Jesus, Luke is not reluctant to use the Christian title "Lord." The implication may be that Luke is suggesting that at least in being, if not yet fully in action or recognition, Jesus was already the *kyrios*.

Luke does not seem to introduce the title into his Markan material (22:61 might be an exception). This raises the question of whether Luke found this frequent use of the titular *kyrios* in his own source material. However, where we find *kyrios* in material drawn from Q or L, it appears to be his own addition (cf. 7:19; 10:1; 11:39; 12:42; 17:5-6). So on the whole it appears that most instances of the titular *kyrios* in the Third Gospel are a result of Luke's editorial activity (cf. I. de la Potterie). There is some justification then for H. Conzelmann's claim that for Luke, Jesus is first of all the *kyrios* who was given dominion by God and rules over the Christian community by means of the Spirit (176-79).

5.3. Kyrios in Matthew. In the First Gospel strangers,

enemies and Judas Iscariot (*see* Judas Iscariot) always greet Jesus with *didaskale* or *rabbi*, but never with *kyrie*, while the disciples and those who seek out Jesus for healing never use the former terms but always address Jesus as *kyrie*. So while J. D. Kingsbury (1975 "Kyrios") has perhaps made too much of Matthew's use of the vocative *kyrie*, there is some justification for including some of these instances in a discussion of Matthew's christology.

The First Evangelist is not shy of using *kyrios* of Jesus. For example, in Matthew 3:3 (following Mark 1:3) he quotes Isaiah 40:3 (". . . prepare the way of the Lord . . .") and implicitly applies to Jesus a title originally referring to Yahweh. This reference, however, only becomes evident from what follows in the narrative, not from the quote itself. On the other hand, within the temptation narrative (*see* Temptation of Jesus) Matthew 4:7 ("You shall not tempt the Lord your God," Deut 6:16) might at first glance seem to imply that *kyrios* refers to Jesus. But even though it is Jesus who is being tempted, two factors tell against this reading: (1) In 4:10 Jesus uses the same language (quoting Deut 6:13) and there it is rather clear that Yahweh is in view; (2) Jesus is quoting Scripture against the Devil (*see* Demon, Devil, Satan) and in both the quote that precedes and the one that follows the reference to God is a reference to someone other than Jesus the speaker (*see* Old Testament in the Gospels).

Matthew 7:21-22 is a more promising case, even though the vocative is used. Here it seems clear that it is disciples who have prophesied and done miracles in Jesus' name that call Jesus "Lord, Lord." Yet it is also clear from this text that calling Jesus "Lord" and even doing deeds and proclaiming words in his name is insufficient if one does not also hear and heed Jesus' words and do the Father's will.

There is a notable stress on the lordship of Jesus as the First Gospel works to its climax. Thus for instance in Matthew 22:44 Jesus is clearly implied to be Lord, and in 24:42 Jesus refers to himself as "your Lord" (note the parallel with Son of man in 24:39). This last example is of course not an instance of the absolute usage *ho kyrios*. But taken together with some of the other texts already cited and the fact that Jesus is speaking of this Lord in the language of the *Yôm Yahweh* (day of the Lord), we should surely understand *ho kyrios* to mean more than "master" in this instance.

Kingsbury (1975 "Kyrios") offers some helpful conclusions about the use of *kyrios* in Matthew, particularly his observation that the word is most often used in Matthew as a relational term—the master as opposed to the slave, the owner as opposed to the worker, even the father as opposed to the son (Mt

21:28-30). However, none of these examples come from passages of christological significance. Yet it is telling that in the christological passages we have examined the relational character of the term is indicated by (1) the use of the vocative "Lord, Lord" in 7:21-22; (2) the use of "*your* Lord" in 24:42; and (3) the use of "*my* Lord" in the citation of Psalm 110:1 in 22:44. Kingsbury has shown, however, that *kyrios* is not Matthew's premier title for Jesus. When it does bear christological weight it is usually explained or qualified by another title and thus at most it should be regarded as an auxiliary christological title in the First Gospel. We have also noted a certain allusive or indirect character in some of the christological passages (cf. 3:3; 22:44).

5.4. Kyrios in John. John's christological use of *kyrios* is scant compared to Luke, yet more evident than in Matthew. Basically the titles Son, Son of God (*see* Son of God) or Messiah/Christ (*see* Christ) occur in John more frequently than Lord. This may seem surprising given the likelihood that it is the latest Gospel, written well after the confession "Jesus is Lord" would have been widespread in the church. While the address of the paralytic (vocative, *kyrie*) in John 5:7 should not be counted as having christological weight, John's reference to Jesus as "the Lord" in 6:23 is a christological usage (if we do not follow the few Western manuscripts [D, 086, arm et al.] that omit the relevant phrase here).

Peter's address to Jesus, "Lord (*kyrie*), to whom shall we go?" (6:68), may be intended to be seen as more than a respectful form of address, especially in view of Peter's confession in 6:69. A christological meaning is possible but not as likely in the address of the woman caught in adultery (8:11), though the pericope was not originally part of this Gospel. More clearly, the healed blind man clearly uses *kyrie* (9:36) as a respectful form of address. The editorial comment in 11:2 provides us with a clear Christian use of *ho kyrios*. The blessing at the triumphal entry (*see* Triumphal Entry) in 12:13 (citing Ps 118:26) likely refers to God, not Jesus, as *kyrios*. John 12:38, citing Isaiah 53:1, should likely also be seen in this way.

Peter's address of "Lord" in John 13:6, 9, the narrative of Jesus' washing the disciples' feet, may have some christological implications in light of Peter's earlier use of the term in 6:68-69. But we should not discount the possibility *kyrie* is here used as a term of respect for one's teacher. The same can be said of Peter's words in 13:36-37 and Thomas's address in 14:5. It may be of some significance that (1) Jesus does not call himself *kyrios* in the Fourth Gospel; (2) the Evangelist clearly does call Jesus *kyrios* in his editorial remarks and within the narrative framework;

(3) up until John 20 whenever the term is found on a disciple's lips, it is always in the vocative, and none of these instances is clearly christological. In fact the words of Mary Magdalene in John 20:13 ("my Lord"), which is not cast in the absolute form, is the first non-vocative use of *kyrios* by a character within the narrative, and even here it may not bear christological meaning.

This means that John 20:18; 20:28; 21:7; and possibly the multiple examples of the vocative in 21:15-21, are the only clear references in this Gospel where a character in the narrative calls Jesus *kyrios* in the transcendent sense. This strongly suggests that the Fourth Evangelist is consciously trying to avoid anachronism in his use of this title and wishes to indicate that Jesus was only truly known and confessed to be Lord as a result of the disciples' encounters with the risen Lord.

6. *Kyrios* in Acts.

Not surprisingly, the use of *kyrios* in Acts reflects some of the same sort of phenomena found in Luke's Gospel. The term appears frequently and is used in a variety of ways. Since Acts reflects the period of time after the resurrection of Jesus, it is hardly surprising that the confessional use of the term is even more plainly evident here than in the Gospel. Thus, for instance, Acts 1:21 provides us with the first juxtaposition of the absolute form of Lord with the name Jesus (*ho kyrios Iēsous*), a phenomenon which occurs regularly in the Pauline epistles (cf. also Acts 15:11; 20:35). Here too at the very beginning of the book the risen Jesus is addressed in prayer as *kyrios* (cf. 1:24). We also find OT passages referring to Yahweh as Lord now being applied to Jesus (Acts 2:25 using Ps 16:8-11). We have already had occasion to refer to Acts 2:36, but note that in 2:34-35 we have yet another use of Psalm 110:1 referring to Jesus, this time by Peter. It is not impossible that Peter was following the precedent of Jesus' own use of this text. At Acts 11:16 we find an example of a saying from the period of the ministry (attributed to John in Mt 3:11; cf. Jn 1:26, 33, not to the *kyrios*). These examples are sufficient to show that the full range of early Christian uses of *kyrios* are found in Acts in a way that is not true of the Gospels, including in Luke. The use of the phrase "the Lord" continued to be Luke's favorite designation for Jesus in his narrative material (cf. e.g., Acts 11:21, 23, 24; 15:35, 40).

Mention should also be made of the use of *despotēs* in Luke-Acts. In Acts 4:24 God is addressed as *despotēs* in communal prayer, just as he is in Simeon's paean of praise in Luke 2:29 (*see* Simeon's Song). This way

of addressing God is common both in the LXX and in Josephus and reflects Hellenistic usage. Within the context of the NT it appears unlikely that this term connotes arbitrary power; more likely the one praying reflects a submission to the absolute power and authority of the *despotēs*. This would mean that while the worshippers would still see themselves as God's slaves and ascribe the appropriate antonym to God, the word no longer connotes what we mean by the English equivalent, "despot." But we must also bear in mind the likelihood that this usage in both the Gospel and Acts goes back to Luke's editorial hand, for certainly in the case of Simeon and possibly in the case of the Aramaic-speaking Christians of Acts 4, the language of prayer would not have been Greek.

7. Conclusion.

A somewhat clear development of the use of the term *kyrios* for Jesus of Nazareth can now be traced. The usage begins with indirect hints during the time of Jesus' ministry, through accounts of the experiences of the risen Lord, to the use of *marana tha* in early Palestinian Jewish-Christian contexts, to evidence of the christological use of the term in the narrative framework of Luke and John, and finally to the variegated use of the term in Acts. There it is used in combination with other names and titles, as a form of address to the exalted Christ, and in the transfer of reference from Yahweh to Jesus in quotes from the OT.

Interestingly, we do not find the use of the absolute or transcendent *kyrios* in the narrative framework of Matthew and Mark, and there is some attempt by both Luke and the Fourth Evangelist to avoid anachronism by not placing the full Christian use of the term on anyone's lips during the ministry of Jesus. It is also significant that Luke-Acts and John intimate that the confession of Jesus as Lord arose as a result of the resurrection experiences. This of course did not prevent the Evangelists from sometimes calling the Jesus of the ministry "Lord" in their narratives, for it was "this same Jesus" whom God had raised from the dead who took on the tasks of Lord in earnest when he joined God in heaven. In other words, the continuity of usage of *kyrios* from before to after the death and resurrection in the Gospels reflects the belief in the continuity of personhood between the historical Jesus (*see* Historical Jesus) and the risen Lord.

The use of the term *kyrios* in a religious sense was sure to be taken to imply Jesus' divinity, especially in the eastern part of the Roman Empire and in Gentile contexts. The evidence suggests that this remarkable mutation in the Jewish concept of monotheism took place in the earliest Palestinian Jewish-Christian community as a result of some hints from Jesus himself and especially as a result of the experiences of the risen Lord shared by some of the eyewitnesses of the life of the historical Jesus. The evidence we have studied indicates that the high christology of the early Christian church was not a new development of the late first century A.D.

See also CHRIST; GOD; "I AM" SAYINGS; LOGOS; SON OF DAVID; SON OF GOD; SON OF MAN; TEACHER; WISDOM.

BIBLIOGRAPHY. H. Bietenhard, "Lord," *NIDNTT* 2.510-20; W. Bousset, *Kyrios Christos* (Nashville: Abingdon, 1970); H. Conzelmann, *The Theology of St. Luke* (New York: Harper and Row, 1960); A. Deissmann, *Light from the Ancient East* (Grand Rapids: Baker, 1978 rpr.); J. A. Fitzmyer, "New Testament Kyrios and Maranatha and Their Aramaic Background," in *To Advance the Gospel* (New York: Crossroad, 1981) 218-35; idem, "The Semitic Background of the New Testament Kyrios-Title," in *A Wandering Aramean* (Missoula: Scholar's, 1979) 115-42; W. Foerster, "κύριος κτλ," *TDNT* III.1039-95; G. Howard, "The Tetragram and the New Testament," *JBL* 96 (1977) 63-83; L. W. Hurtado, *One God, One Lord: Early Christian Devotion and Ancient Jewish Monotheism* (Philadelphia: Fortress, 1988); S. E. Johnson, "Lord," *IDB* 3.150-51; J. D. Kingsbury, *Matthew: Structure, Christology, Kingdom* (2d ed.; Minneapolis: Fortress, 1989); idem, "The Title 'Kyrios' in Matthew's Gospel," *JBL* 94 (1975) 246-55; C. F. D. Moule, *The Origin of Christology* (Cambridge: University Press, 1977); I. de la Potterie, "Le titre KYRIOS applique a Jesus dans l'Evangile de Luc," in *Melanges Bibliques en hommage au R. P. Rigaux*, eds. A. Descamps and A. de Halleux (Gembloux: Duculot, 1970) 117-46; V. Taylor, *The Gospel according to St. Mark* (New York: St. Martin's, 1966); G. Vermes, *Jesus the Jew* (New York: Harper and Row, 1973); B. Witherington III, *The Christology of Jesus* (Minneapolis: Fortress, 1990); idem, *Women in the Ministry of Jesus* (Cambridge: University Press, 1984).

B. Witherington III

LORD'S PRAYER. *See* PRAYER.

LORD'S SUPPER. *See* LAST SUPPER.

LOVE

Jesus brought into the world* a new emphasis on love which he demonstrated in his own life and which he made clear he expected his disciples* to produce too. For him love depends on the nature of the lover rather than that of the beloved. Jesus loved because he was a loving person, not because he found attractive qualities in those he loved. His followers are to be loving people, not simply to be drawn to attractive people.

1. Terminology
2. General Use
3. Divine Love
4. Human Love

1. Terminology.

In the Gospels the usual verb for "to love" is *agapaō* (sixty-three times), *phileō* occurs twenty-one times. The noun *agapē* is found nine times; *philia* not at all; the adjective *agapētos* fifteen times. *Agapaō* was replacing *phileō* as we see also in the LXX where Hatch and Redpath have four columns of references to *agapaō* with about half a column for *phileō*. There is a clear majority of references to the *agapē* words in the Gospels, but the important thing is not so much the words chosen as the meaning and associations the Evangelists put into them. Matthew has the love words a total of seventeen times, Mark nine, Luke eighteen and John fifty-seven; John has them more than all the others put together.

2. General Use.

Jesus sometimes speaks of love in the way anyone else would, such as the words "If you love them that love you" (Mt 5:46; Lk 6:32), a reciprocal love that anybody might practice. Similarly a slave might love one master but not another (Mt 6:24), and it is not so very dissimilar with the centurion who loved the Jewish nation (Lk 7:5) or the attitude of the forgiven debtor (Lk 7:42; *see* Forgiveness of Sins). Even sinners* love those that love them (Lk 6:32). It is in this spirit that John speaks of those who love human praise (Jn 12:43). This sort of thing is the common stuff of humanity, and there is nothing remarkable about it. It is an important part of life, though the world's love may grow cold (Mt 24:12).

3. Divine Love.

More significant is the sweeping statement that God loved "the world" and loved it so much that he gave his Son (Jn 3:16). That the Father loves people is not often stated in set terms, but this love is implied throughout the Gospels. We see it, for example, in Jesus' statement that the Father cares for all creation, including the birds and the flowers, and therefore much more for people (Mt 6:25-34); he sends his sunshine and rain on all, good and bad alike (Mt 5:45). It is implied also in the address "Father," which brings the intimate language of the family, with all its overtones of love and care, into our understanding of the deity. There is no indication that any merit or attractiveness on the part of people generates this love. On the contrary, it is common to all the Gospels that people are sinners (cf. Mt 7:11; even when they do good deeds it remains that they are basically evil!). But God still loves them. The proposition "God is love" comes from 1 John 4:8, 16, but the truth it expresses runs through the Gospels.

3.1. Love within the Godhead. "The Father loves the Son" (Jn 3:35). A reason may be given for this, as when John quotes Jesus: "for this reason the Father loves me, that I lay down my life" (Jn 10:17). This does not, of course, signify that it was the death of Christ that induced the Father to love people; Jesus is saying rather that his death (see Death of Jesus) is in the loving purpose of the Father (compare how when someone does a good deed, even though there was love before the deed, there may well be the response "I love you for that!"). Jesus may take the love of the Father for him as basic and reason from it: "Just as the Father has loved me, I also have loved you" (Jn 15:9). That the Father loves him is so obvious that it does not require demonstration. Jesus simply assumes it and goes on from there. There is a similar appeal to the love of the Father as basic in the great prayer* in the upper room on the eve of the crucifixion when Jesus prays, "that the world may know that you sent me, and have loved me as I have loved them" (Jn 17:23; cf. also 17:24, 26).

In one way or another every occurrence of the word "beloved" in the Gospels refers to Jesus. When he was baptized (see Baptism) there was a voice from heaven* that greeted him as "my Son, the beloved" (Mt 3:17; Mk 1:11; Lk 3:22), an experience repeated at the Transfiguration* (Mt 17:5; Mk 9:7; Lk 9:35). Matthew makes use of the term in a quotation from Isaiah which he sees as fulfilled in Jesus (Mt 12:18), and it occurs again in a parable which surely speaks to us about God's beloved Son (Mk 12:6; Lk 20:13). The Evangelists leave us in no doubt about the love of the Father for his dear Son.

The love of the Son for the Father is not mentioned so often. In fact it comes to expression once only in the whole New Testament, namely when Jesus says, ". . . but that the world may know that I love the Father . . ." (Jn 14:31). This love is, of course, implied everywhere and very little in the Gospels makes sense apart from the truth that the Son loves the Father. The whole mission of salvation* on which Jesus was embarked was due to the divine love and the Son's part in that mission implies his love for the Father as well as the love of both for sinners. The love of the Son for the Father and of the Father for the Son is a necessary part of understanding the divine salvation

that was wrought in Christ.

3.2. The Divine Love for People. God's love is a love for all those he has created (Jn 3:16) and, of course, God loves those who love his Son (Jn 14:23). This passage brings the further thought that the Father and the Son will both make their dwelling with the person who loves Jesus. The Father's love is not to be thought of as some lofty and ethereal emotion; it has its effects here on earth in the continual presence of the divine with the believer. The followers of Jesus are "perfected into one," and this is the mark whereby the world will know that the Father has both sent the Son and loved his followers just as he loves him (Jn 17:23).

3.3. The Son's Love for People. That Jesus loved his disciples is plain in the Gospel narratives, though this does not often come to clear expression. There are references to an unnamed disciple "whom Jesus loved" (Jn 13:23; 19:26; 20:2; 21:7, 20), and who has traditionally been understood to be the apostle John (see Disciples; Farewell Discourse). For our present purpose, more important than his identity is the fact that Jesus had a warm love for this man. And his affection for Lazarus is revealed in the way people told him of his friend's illness: "Lord, look, he whom you love is sick" (Jn 11:3; cf. v. 36). John also tells us that Jesus "loved Martha and her sister and Lazarus" (Jn 11:5), where the recital of each one separately indicates that Jesus did more than love the family in a general way; it points to an affection for each individual. Elsewhere we are told explicitly that Jesus loved one young man, who nevertheless declined to follow him and went away grieving (Mk 10:21-22); Jesus' love was not confined to the disciples.

In addition to such statements about Jesus' love for individuals, there are references to his love for the disciples as a group. John prefixes his account of what happened in the upper room on the last night of Jesus' earthly life by saying that Jesus "loved his own who were in the world" and that "he loved them completely" (Jn 13:1; or "to the end"; the Jerusalem Bible has "now he showed how perfect his love was"). John goes on to recount the story of Jesus' washing of the feet of the disciples, an action that proceeded from the perfection of his love.

Later in the same chapter there is the thought that Jesus' love sets the disciples an example: they are to love one another, Jesus says, "as I have loved you" (Jn 13:34), an injunction he repeats later (Jn 15:12). Their love will show itself in keeping his commandments and then the person who loves in this way will be loved by the Father "and I will love him" (Jn 14:21). Jesus says that he has loved the little group just as the Father has loved him (Jn 15:9).

All this amounts to an impressive indication that God does not merely tolerate sinners: he loves them. It has been no part of this article to traverse the Gospel teaching on universal sinfulness, but there can be no doubt that all four Evangelists express the reality and the seriousness of sin done before a holy and all-powerful God. But God for all his ability to punish and for all his own spotless purity does not regard sinners with aversion, but with love, with the costly love that we see in the cross where Jesus died to save them. The Evangelists do not specially draw attention to the love the cross implies (apart from Jn 3:16), but the unforgettable picture they draw is that of a God of love who has done all that is necessary to bring salvation to unworthy and evil people. That is no ordinary love.

4. Human Love.

4.1. The Love of People for God. Jesus told the Pharisees* that "the first commandment" is "You shall love the Lord your God with all your heart and with all your soul and with all your mind and with all your strength" (Mk 12:29-30; cf. Mt 22:37-38; Lk 10:27). This puts love for God squarely at the heart of real religion: Nothing is more important than loving God. This love brooks no rival, and Jesus points to slavery to illustrate his point. "No one," he says, "can be a slave to two owners" (Mt 6:24; cf. Lk 16:13). It was, of course, possible for a slave to have dual ownership, but he could not give the wholehearted service that slavery demands to more than one person. It is similarly not possible to give the wholehearted love that God demands to anyone other than he. Love to God is no tepid affair, scarcely raising a ripple in life. It is wholehearted devotion, involving all of life. Love for God suffuses the whole person. This kind of love matters much more than even the most important outward ceremonies (Mk 12:33).

So it is that when Jesus is depicting a church* in decline he says "the love of the many will grow cold" (Mt. 24:12), where "love" may mean love for other people, but will surely include the love of God. Again, Jesus complains that the Pharisees, while punctilious in their tithing of herbs, neglect "justice and the love of God" (Lk 11:42), qualities that are at the heart of right religion. Similarly, John tells us that Jesus reproached those who "do not have the love of God within" themselves (Jn 5:42). Such passages are explicit, but quite apart from them the general tenor of Jesus' teaching is significant. He does not call people to face up to a stern God who is eager to punish them, a God before whom it would be important to merit rewards by good works. He depicts a

loving God, one who sent his Son to save them and to call them into an enriched life in which striving to avert punishment and merit reward is not the way. Rather, people are to trust God and respond to love with love. The whole of the Law* and the Prophets is summed up in two commandments to love (Mt 22:40).

4.2. The Love of People for People. Since Jesus emphasizes so strongly his love and that of the Father and since he calls on his followers to love God, it is not surprising that he also insists that it is important that they love other people. On the eve of the crucifixion John tells us that Jesus said to the disciples, "A new commandment I give you, that you love one another; as I have loved you, that you love one another." He goes on to say that people will know that they are his disciples if they "love one another" (Jn 13:34-35). A little later he repeats it: "This is my commandment, that you love one another even as I have loved you" (Jn 15:12). It is love that marks out the Christian from other people.

Perhaps nothing was more revolutionary in Jesus' teaching than his command that his followers love their enemies (Mt 5:44; Lk 6:27, 35). In every age it has been normal to love one's friends and hate one's enemies, and Jesus points out that words about hate have in popular understanding been added to God's command to love (Mt 5:43). The Qumran scrolls contain the explicit command to "hate all the sons of darkness," a contemporary expression of the thought. But Jesus will have none of this. To love those who love us is nothing more than the way of the world and even sinners do this (Lk 6:32). Repeatedly he insists that people must love their neighbors as they love themselves, as the commandment tells them (Mt 5:43; 19:19; 22:39; Mk 12:31). Love, not hate, is the mark of the Christian.

The importance of the love command cannot be overestimated. In Jesus' day the Jews discerned 613 commandments in the Law, and there were vigorous discussions about the relative importance of some of these (*see* Rabbinic Traditions and Writings). Jesus swept aside all such deliberations with his revolutionary insistence on the centrality of love, and for good measure he added that the teaching of the prophets is included in this command. At one stroke he did away with any understanding of the service* of God that sees it as concerned with the acquiring of merit or with an emphasis on liturgical concerns. What matters may be summed up in one word: love. The love for which Jesus looks is not, of course, a meritorious achievement. It is the response to God's prior love, a wholehearted response to all that God is and has done for us. It is a love directed first to the God from whom love comes and then overflowing in love to people. It means that love is central to the whole way of life of the follower of Jesus (*see* Discipleship).

There is a very suggestive expression toward the end of the incident in which a sinful woman anointed Jesus' feet as he reclined at table in the house of a Pharisee. Jesus said of her, "Her sins, many as they are, have been forgiven, for she loved much" (Lk 7:47). Loved whom? There is no object and the point appears to be, not that she loved any particular person, but that she had become a loving person (cf. E. Stauffer, "the person now has love, is filled with it, and is guided by it in all his actions, rather than that he is to show it to such and such people," *TDNT* I.47). Christians are loving.

See also COMMANDMENT; ETHICS OF JESUS LAW.

BIBLIOGRAPHY. M. C. D'Arcy, *The Mind and Heart of Love* (London: Collins, 1962); V. P. Furnish, *The Love Command in the New Testament* (London: SCM, 1973); W. Gunther, H.-G. Link, C. Brown, "Love," *NIDNTT* 2.538-51; C. S. Lewis, *The Four Loves* (London: Bles, 1960); L. Morris, *Testaments of Love* (Grand Rapids: Eerdmans, 1981); G. Quell, E. Stauffer, "ἀγαπάω κτλ," *TDNT* II.21-55; C. Spicq, *Agape in the New Testament* (St. Louis and London: Herder, 3 vols., 1963-66), G. Stahlin, "φιλέω κτλ," *TDNT* IX.113-171.

L. Morris

LOVE COMMAND. *See* COMMANDMENT; LOVE.

LUKE, GOSPEL OF

Luke's Gospel (*see* Gospel [Genre]) is the longest of the four Gospels. It is also the only Gospel with a sequel. By continuing his literary project into the Acts of the Apostles, Luke not only introduces us to Jesus and his ministry, but also to how that ministry relates to significant events in the early church.* This enables Luke to discuss how God* brought his salvation* in Jesus, how the church preached Jesus and how it carried out its mission to both Jew and Gentile.*

Luke's two-part work highlights God's plan. It explains how Jews and Gentiles could become equals in a community planted by God, even though that community was rooted in a promise to Israel.* More specifically, four issues would have posed problems for those who observed the church during Luke's time.

First was the question of salvation. How could Gentiles be included as God's people on an equal basis with Jews, extending even to matters like sharing table fellowship and eliminating the necessity of circumcision?

Second was the apparent paradox of the claim that God's plan was at work while Jews, the most natural recipients for the good news, were largely responding negatively. How could God's plan and God's messengers, especially Paul, meet so much hostility?

Third was the problem of explaining how the person and teaching of a crucified Jesus fit into this plan. How could Jesus continue to exercise a presence and represent the hope of God, when he was physically absent? How could the church exalt an absent and slain figure, and regard him as the center of God's work?

Fourth was the question of what it means to respond to Jesus. What is required and what can one expect for such a commitment? How should men and women live until the day Jesus returns?

Luke's Gospel and its sequel deal with all of these issues. His task is to reassure his readers of the place of Gentiles in the new community and the role of Jesus in God's plan (cf. Lk 1:4).

1. Authorship, Origin and Purpose
2. Structure and Argument of Luke
3. The Theology of Luke
4. Conclusion

1. Authorship, Origin and Purpose.

The Third Gospel and Acts do not directly identify their author. We are left to examine the internal and external evidence and draw the most plausible conclusion.

1.1. Internal Evidence for Authorship. Internal features draw our attention to two points. First, the author is not an eyewitness to most of the events in his two volumes, especially those tied to the ministry of Jesus (1:1-2). Rather, he has relied on his study of traditions derived from eyewitnesses and ministers of the Word (1:2-4). Second, he presents himself as a companion of Paul in the so-called we-sections of Acts (Acts 16:10-17; 20:5-15; 21:1-18; 27:1—28:16). This latter feature, though its significance is debated, narrows the search for possible authors.

Interpreters have debated whether the we-sections reflect the testimony of an eyewitness (Ellis) or are a literary device gauged to create the impression of an eyewitness (Haenchen and Vielhauer). Related to this issue is the question of how well the author of the Third Gospel knew Paul, since the we-sections portray its author as a travelling companion of Paul. Those who reject such a connection attempt to compare Acts' picture of Paul with the self-portrait of the Pauline epistles. They argue that the two pictures do not match in historical detail or in theological emphasis. In addition, the author fails to use the Pauline epistles to describe Paul's work and position.

Vielhauer argued that the Lukan Paul is too dissimilar from Paul as we know him from his letters for the author of the Third Gospel to have been a companion of Paul. But Fitzmyer has defended the connection, especially on the basis of the we-sections in Acts, arguing that a creative literary device cannot explain how the units appear and disappear in such an arbitrary manner (Fitzmyer 1989). He also notes that several "sailing" references, which would be candidates for such literary insertions, lack them (Acts 13:4; 13:13; 14:26; 17:14; 18:18, 21; 20:1-2). He suggests that Luke may have been only a junior companion, in contrast to Irenaeus' famous claim that Luke was "inseparable" from Paul (*Haer.* 3.14.1). In addition, Goulder has suggested that Luke may have known and alluded to Paul's letter to Corinth and, to a lesser extent, the letter to Thessalonica. Others have defended the compatibility of the portraits of Paul found in Acts and the epistles (Bruce 1975/76). From the internal evidence of Luke-Acts it appears that the writer knew Paul and was at least a second-generation Christian.

1.2. External Evidence for Authorship. The Pauline letters name some of Paul's traveling companions: Mark, Aristarchus, Demas and Luke (Philem 24; Col 4:14). To this list one could add figures such as Timothy, Titus, Silas, Epaphras and Barnabas. Yet despite the wide selection of potential candidates, early-church tradition singles out one name as the author of these volumes: Luke. By A.D. 200 this tradition had become firmly fixed without any hint of contrary opinion.

Allusions to the Gospel appear early and exist in *1 Clement* 13.2; 48.4 (late 90s) and in *2 Clement* 13.4 (c. 150). In addition a use of Jesus' teaching, similar to that found in Luke 10:7, appears in 1 Timothy 5:18. Numerous texts comment on the authorship of Luke-Acts. Justin (c. 160) in *Dialogues* 103.19 speaks of Luke having written a "memoir of Jesus" and notes the author was a follower of Paul. The Muratorian Canon (c. 170-180) attributes the Gospel to Luke, a doctor, who is Paul's companion. Irenaeus (c. 175-195; *Haer.* 3.1.1; 3.14.1) attributes the Gospel to Luke, follower of Paul, and notes how the "we sections" suggest the connection. The so-called Anti-Marcionite Canon (c. 175) describes Luke as a native of Antioch in Syria (Acts 11:19-30; 13:1-3; 15:30-35), commenting that he lived to be eighty-four, was a doctor, was unmarried, wrote in Achaia and died in Boeotia. Tertullian (early third century; *Marc.* 4.2.2; 4.5.3) calls the Gospel a digest of Paul's gospel. Finally, Eusebius (early fourth century; *Hist. Eccl.* 3.4.2) mentions that Luke was from Antioch, a companion to Paul and the author of the Gospel and Acts. The unified voice of these traditions regarding authorship enhances the identification of the Gospel with Luke, and also makes Luke's connection to Paul very likely.

1.3. Luke the Man: A Gentile or a Semite? Most scholars see Luke as a Gentile, though they debate whether he is a pure Gentile or a non-Jewish Semite. An exception is Ellis, who argues that Luke was a Hellenistic-Jewish Christian. Ellis notes that Luke's knowledge of the OT is extensive; that Colossians 4:10-11, with its reference to those "not of the circumcision," suggests merely that he is a Hellenist; and that evidences of the use of Palestinian language show Luke's Jewish roots. But Ellis's reading of Colossians 4 is not the most natural one.

Fitzmyer suggests Luke was a Semite, arguing from the evidence of the Colossians 4 text; the shortened form of Luke's name (which was a Greek form of a Latin name); and the details of the church tradition, which place him in Antioch of Syria. This view is quite plausible.

However, most scholars have argued that Luke was a non-Semitic Gentile. They too argue from Colossians 4; note the allusion of Acts 1:19, which gives the Semitic name for Judas's field and then refers to it being in "their" language; and mention the attention given to Hellenistic locales and the concern for Gentiles. These latter two arguments are not strong, since one could attribute these same concerns to a Jew like Paul. In sum, Luke was very likely a Gentile, though it is unclear whether he was a Semite.

1.4. Sources of the Gospel and Its Tie to Acts. The problem of determining Luke's sources is intimately related to the complex issue known as the Synoptic Problem.* Numerous approaches to this issue have been suggested, but in terms of Luke's Gospel alone, his preface demands a hypothesis that accounts for several sources.

1.4.1. Luke and the Synoptic Problem. While some scholars maintain the two-Gospel hypothesis, which supports the chronological priority of Matthew, followed by Luke and Mark (Farmer), today most scholars maintain some form of the two-document hypothesis (sometimes called the four-document hypothesis). This view argues for the priority of Mark and its use by Matthew and Luke, who also used a "sayings" source known as Q.* In addition Matthew has special source material (M*), while Luke has his special material (L*). Thus the two common sources are Mark and Q, while L and M constituted separate sources for Luke and Matthew respectively. Luke would have used Mark, Q and L.

In all likelihood, Luke had access to Mark. Second, he had much special material (L). Third, he had traditions which also are reflected in Matthew, though often with some (even significant) divergence. In fact the Q material is so varied in character that some speak of a Matthean and a Lukan version of Q (see Marshall 1978, who often makes this distinction). This means that Q may not have been a fixed, written tradition, so much as a pool of widely circulating traditions. Given the amount of teaching and parables shared between Matthew and Luke, we cannot rule out the possibility that L and Q might have overlapped, with Matthew using Q and Luke using L. (Though we will use the symbol "Q," we note the potential ambiguity of this source or set of sources.)

1.4.2. Markan Material. A little over 410 verses of Luke, just short of forty per cent of the whole of Luke's Gospel, corresponds to Mark. Significantly, the Markan material tends to come in blocks, especially in sections which describe Jesus' ministry. This is one of the reasons Mark is seen as a fundamental source. A few texts related to Mark also have added to them material from Q or L (Lk 3:7-14; 3:23-38; 4:2b-13; 5:1-11; 19:1-10, 11-27; 22:28-33, 35-38; 23:6-16; 23:27-31; 23:39b-43; 23:47b-49).

1.4.3. Q Material. When one turns to Q material, the picture is more complex. Problematic texts involve those sayings or parables* which one Gospel writer places in one location and the other Gospel writer includes in a very different location; those which one writer has together while another writer has separated; or those in which an account is rendered in significantly different terms.

Almost 250 verses of material not found in Mark, or slightly over twenty per cent of Luke's Gospel, might be called Q. The questionable Q texts tend to cluster in the central section of Luke's Gospel. This unit, Luke 9:51—19:44, is basically a combination of large amounts of L material with material having apparent parallels with Matthew. Given the amount of unique L material and the thematic character of some parts of this section, it is difficult to discern whether material is really from Q or from L.

Goulder has suggested a large amount of Lukan rewriting of Matthean material and has posited that little of L really comes from a source, but is actually reflective of Lukan emphases and elaboration. The problem with this approach is it means that Luke handled Markan material in a manner completely distinct from the way in which he handled Matthew (or Q), since Luke did so little to change the substance of his Markan material.

1.4.4. L Material. This unique L material is represented in about 455 verses of Luke, comprising just over forty per cent of the entire Gospel. Clearly there is much in Luke that is not found in the other Synoptics. This material not only contains a unique portrait of Jesus' infancy but also many fresh sayings and parables of Jesus.

Four miracles* are unique to Luke (7:11-17; 13:10-17; 14:1-6; 17:11-19). Several parables are indisputably unique to Luke (10:29-37; 11:5-8; 12:13-21; 15:1-10; 15:11-32; 16:1-8; 16:19-31; 18:1-8; 18:9-14). The ethical thrust of Luke's Gospel emerges in this material. An additional four parables having potential overlap with Matthew are cast in fresh light by Luke (12:39-46; 14:15-24; 15:1-7; 19:11-27). The breadth of topics in the Gospel and Luke's pastoral concern emerge in this unique or uniquely emphasized material.

1.4.5. The Third Gospel's Relationship with Acts. Luke structured his Gospel in anticipation of its sequel. This tie to Acts is seen in the repetition of the prolog (Lk 1:1-4; Acts 1:1; cf. Josephus *Ag. Ap.*). The relationship is seen also in the parallel themes which dominate the two volumes (Maddox; O'Toole). Jesus heals and so do Peter and Paul. Jesus must travel to Jerusalem, while Paul must go to Rome.* Jesus is slain by opposition and so is Stephen. The account of the ascension also links the two volumes tightly together (Lk 24:49-53; Acts 1:1-11).

Efforts to note extensive parallels between Luke and Acts have generated scholarly discussion (Talbert 1974). Some of these connections may be overdrawn and subtle, so each must be evaluated on its own merit. But there is no doubt that Luke intends to show parallels between the time of Jesus and the time of his followers. From Luke's perspective, to understand the emergence of the church one must understand Jesus and the plan of God.

1.5. Luke As Historian. One other point emerges from an examination of Luke's use of sources. Although the issue of Luke as a historian has been strongly debated, it appears that Luke was careful with his material (*see* Gospels [Historical Reliability]).

On the one hand, many scholars understand him to have handled his sources with great freedom, either for theological (Goulder, Haenchen, Dibelius) or sociological (Esler) reasons. Among the items under scrutiny are the association of Jesus' birth with a census by Quirinius (*see* Birth of Jesus), his chronological placement of the rebellion under Theudas (*see* Chronology), the authenticity of certain parables and sayings, the reality of the miracles,* his portrait of the trials of Jesus (*see* Trial of Jesus), the details of Jesus' resurrection,* the authenticity of the speeches in Acts, his portrayal of early church harmony, the uniqueness of the meeting with Cornelius, the reality of the Jerusalem council and his portrait of Paul. These details must be examined case by case, and judgments will inevitably vary. This is due not only to the complexity of the evidence but also to differences in the interpreter's philosophical world views. Nevertheless, where we can examine Luke's use of his sources, we find him trustworthy (Marshall 1970). Investigations into his descriptions of settings, customs and locales reveal a consistent concern for accuracy (Hengel, Hemer).

This does not mean Luke does not rearrange material for emphasis, summarize events in his own language or emphasize aspects of his received tradition. The Lukan speeches summarize and proclaim as well as report. Luke shows an interest in both history and theology, twin emphases evidenced not only in his attention to the time sequence of events and teachings, but in their topical and theological relationship as well. He writes as a theologian and a pastor, but is directed by the history which preceded him. To underemphasize any element in the Lukan enterprise, whether pastoral, theological or historical, is to underestimate the depth of his writing.

1.6. Purpose, Readership and Destination of Luke's Gospel. It is debated whether Theophilus (Lk 1:4) was a Christian or was thinking of becoming one. Numerous possible intentions for Luke's writing the Gospel and its sequel have been suggested (Maddox): (1) to explain why Jesus had not returned (Conzelmann), (2) to provide a defense brief for Christianity (Easton, Haenchen), (3) to defend Paul before Rome (Mattill), (4) to defend Paul before the community (Schneckenburger; Jervell), (5) to combat gnosticism (Talbert); (6) to evangelize (O'Neill), (7) to confirm the Word and the message of salvation (van Unnik, Marshall, O'Toole), (8) to present a theodicy of God's faithfulness (Tiede), (9) to provide a sociological legitimation of full fellowship for Gentiles and a defense of the new community (Esler). This plethora of credible suggestions is evidence of the complexity of the Lukan enterprise. Of all of these suggestions, those centering on God's role in salvation and the nature of the new community (views 7-9) are most likely to reflect Luke's most comprehensive agenda. An examination of the structure and theology of the Gospel will bear this out.

It is unlikely that Theophilus is only interested in becoming a Christian or is a Roman official who needs Christianity explained to him in order to accept it as a legitimate religion. Neither is Paul *per se* the object of defense. Too little of the Gospel deals with such legal, political concerns and too much focuses on issues other than evangelism. Paul's importance in the latter part of Acts is due especially to the mission and perspective he represents.

Luke 1:3-4 suggest that Theophilus had received some instruction. The amount of detail in Luke-Acts devoted to faithfulness, Jewish-Gentile relations and clinging to the hope of Jesus' return suggests a Gentile who was experiencing doubt about his association with the new community. This setting is also suggested in the controversy over table fellowship,* the issue of Gentile inclusion, the detailed examples of how rejection was faced in the early church and the amount of attention devoted to ethical exhortation. Theophilus appears to be a man of rank (Lk 1:3). Having associated himself with the church, he is undergoing doubt whether in fact he really belongs in this racially mixed and heavily persecuted community. The Gospel openly includes Theophilus in the new community, calling him to remain faithful, committed and expectant, even in the midst of intense Jewish rejection.

Given the magnitude of Luke's effort, it seems clear that he did not write for Theophilus alone but for any who shared this tension. Any Gentile who felt out of place in an originally Jewish movement would have recognized the reassurance Luke offers. Any Jew (or Jewish Christian) troubled by the lack of Jewish response to the gospel or the openness with which Gentiles were welcomed into it could see how God had given the nation multiple invitations to join in his renewed work. The Christian movement had not attempted to remove itself from Judaism,* it had been forced out. This exclusion becomes clear in Acts, but Luke carefully details the seeds of opposition being sown in the official Jewish rejection of Jesus (Lk 9—13; 22—23). For Luke the new community extends its blessings broadly, true to Jesus' preaching (Lk 4:16-30; 5:30-32; 19:10; 24:44-47) and God's direction (Acts 10:34-43; 15:1-21; 22:6-11; 26:15-20).

1.7. Date. Several possibilities have been argued, but two factors set the outside limits for a possible date. The last event in Acts takes place in 62, thus establishing the earliest possible date for the completion of the two-volume work. On the other end, Irenaeus cites texts indisputably derived from Luke, thus setting the latest possible date as c. 170 (*Haer.* 3.13.3; 3.15.1). Three possibilities present themselves:

1.7.1. Second Century. A date in the early- to mid-second century (Knox, O'Neill) has been argued on the basis of comparisons with material from Marcion, Josephus, Justin Martyr or the Pseudo-Clementines. But against this approach is the fact that the tone of Acts does not really fit that of other letters of this period such as *1 Clement* (A.D. 95) and Ignatius (A.D.

117) (Ellis). In addition, it is hard to believe that such a late work would have ignored Paul's letters as much as Acts does. Finally, possible allusions in *1 Clement* to Acts 13:22 (*1 Clem.* 18.1); 20:35 (*1 Clem.* 2.1) and 26 (*1 Clem.* 5.6-7) argue against this date. This factor also brings the upper limit for a date down to the mid nineties.

1.7.2. After the Fall of Jerusalem. The most popular view is a date sometime after the fall of Jerusalem (*see* Destruction of Jerusalem; Fitzmyer, Bovon, Kümmel, Danker, Tiede, Maddox, Talbert, Esler). The reasons set forth include: (1) the premise that Luke follows after Mark, which itself is a document of the sixties; (2) the picture of Paul as a hero figure needed time to emerge; (3) the portraits of churches like Ephesus require a period before the Domitian persecution of the mid nineties; (4) the Lukan apocalyptic discourse (*see* Apocalyptic Teaching), with its description of siege and its focus on the city, presuppose the fall of Jerusalem and require a period after A.D. 70; (5) the indications that Luke reflects a late, even "early Catholic," theology would place it toward the end of the first century.

Three of these arguments are not compelling in their force. It is not clear that (2) Paul needed time to emerge as a hero. Evidence from his epistles agrees with Acts, suggesting that he was a central figure in the church who generated some following and controversy. The portrait of the churches (3) which are not yet under Roman persecution can fit any time before Domitian or any time after Nero. The debate about early catholicism in Luke-Acts (5) continues, but it is by no means apparent that the perspective of these volumes requires a late theology (Marshall 1970).

Two arguments have more substance. The suggestion that Luke follows Mark (1) is likely. (Even if one thinks Matthew was written first, the problem remains.) But this argument creates no more difficulty for an early date than does the fact that the last event in Acts occurs in the early sixties. How long must Mark's Gospel have been in circulation before it could have served as a source for Luke?

The most weighty argument is that Luke's eschatological discourses (Lk 19:41-44; 21:20-24) assume a post-70 date. Esler has argued that the details of these discourses cannot be attributed simply to "what inevitably happens in war," because some of the features, such as building a circumvallation, the total destruction of the city or the marching off of all the captives were not the inevitable results of war. In so arguing, Esler has challenged C. H. Dodd's view that the language fits ancient military operations and parallels the LXX's descriptions of the sacking of

Solomon's temple in 587 B.C. However, Esler has missed a key point of connection with the OT. The judgment* exercised is directed toward *covenant unfaithfulness*. As such, Luke's picture of the total destruction of Jerusalem, including its siege and total defeat, is what was to be expected of an act of God. There is no need to argue that the description of the fall of Jerusalem is language shaped in light of a past event.

The prediction of Jerusalem's fall is one that Jesus would have been capable of making solely on the basis of his knowledge of how God acts to judge covenant unfaithfulness. Luke has made no effort to update this Jesus tradition, he only clarifies that in the Temple's* collapse, the city is not spared either.

1.7.3. Before the Fall of Jerusalem. The third possibility is a date during the sixties (Bruce, Hemer, Ellis, Marshall). Arguments for this date include: (1) the picture in Acts that Rome knows little about the Christian movement and is still uncertain about where it fits among the religions of the empire suggests a date in the sixties; (2) the failure to note either the death of James (A.D. 62) and especially Paul (c. late sixties) would seem to indicate an earlier date; (3) the silence about Jerusalem's destruction, even in settings where it could have been mentioned (e.g., Stephen's speech in Acts 6—7; Paul's trip to Jerusalem Acts 21—23) is odd if the work was completed after 70; and (4) the amount of uncertainty expressed about internal Gentile-Jewish relations fits a setting parallel to the Pauline epistles, which deal with similar tensions (Rom, Gal, 1 Cor 8—10).

This last argument is most significant and to date has not been thoroughly developed. Several aspects of Acts suggest that Luke was addressing the concerns of an earlier period: (1) It presupposes a racially mixed community in its attention to potentially offensive details about the Law,* table fellowship* and other practices (Acts 6:1-6, 10-11, 15); (2) its vigorous defense of the Gentile mission contrasts with the situation in the eighties when the Gentile character of the Christian movement was accepted; (3) it provides believers reassurance in the midst of intense Jewish pressure.

It is difficult to determine when in the sixties the account may have been written. Some argue that the ending of Acts indicates the date of completion. Others suggest that texts like Luke 11:49-51 presuppose the start of the struggle with Rome and suggest a date in the late sixties. The fact that Paul's death is not mentioned may be an indication that the work was completed in the early to mid sixties rather than the latter third of the sixties. On the other hand, the necessity for Luke to have received and incorporated

Mark might suggest a date in the mid sixties. Given that the Gospel would have preceded Acts, a mid sixties date is slightly more likely. Luke might have left the end of Paul's career open ended because that is where matters stood when he wrote.

2. Structure and Argument of Luke.

The Gospel may be viewed as follows, with the material devoted to Jesus' ministry being viewed geographically:

1. Introduction of John the Baptist and Jesus (1:1—2:52)

2. Preparation for Ministry: Anointed by God (3:1—4:13)

3. Galilean Ministry: The Revelation of Jesus (4:14—9:50)

4. Jerusalem Journey: Jewish Rejection and the New Way (9:51—19:44)

5. Jerusalem: The Innocent Slain and Raised (19:45—24:53)

2.1. Introduction of John the Baptist and Jesus (1:1—2:52). Following a preface in which Luke explains his task, the author launches into a comparison of John and Jesus, showing how both represent the fulfillment of promises made by God. John the Baptist* is like Elijah* (1:17), but Jesus has Davidic roles to fulfill and possesses a unique supernatural origin (1:31-35). John is forerunner, but Jesus is fulfillment. Everything in Luke 1—2 points to the superiority of Jesus.

Jesus' birth (*see* Birth of Jesus) takes place in humble circumstances, but all the figures surrounding his birth are pious and responsive to the hope of God (*see* Mary's Song; Simeon's Song; Zechariah's Song). Only the word of Simeon to Mary gives an ominous ring (2:34-35). Jesus is the salvation of God (2:30), but in the midst of hope is the reality that fulfillment comes mixed with pain. This section, dominated by OT allusions (*see* Old Testament in the Gospels), opens the Gospel with the twin themes of fulfillment and divine direction. These themes continue throughout the Gospel.

2.2. Preparation for Ministry: Anointed by God (3:1—4:13). John and Jesus remain side by side as Jesus prepares for his ministry. John is the "One who goes before" (Is 40:3-5; Lk 3:1-6), while Jesus is the "One who comes" (3:15-17). John baptizes Jesus, but the main feature of the baptism* is one of two heavenly testimonies to Jesus (3:21-22; cf. 9:28-36). The heavenly testimony calls Jesus the "beloved Son in whom I am well pleased." This fusion of Isaiah 42 and Psalm 2 marks out Jesus as a regal, prophetic figure, who as chosen servant of God brings God's revelation and salvation. The universal character of Jesus' relation-

ship to humanity is highlighted in the list of his ancestors (3:23-38; *see* Genealogy). He is "Son of Adam, Son of God.*" His first actions are to overcome temptations from Satan (*see* Temptation of Jesus), something Adam had failed to do (4:1-13). So the section shows Jesus as God's anointed, a representative of humanity and one who is faithful to God.

2.3. Galilean Ministry: The Revelation of Jesus (4:14—9:50). This section focuses primarily on the teaching of Jesus and his miraculous works. Major teaching blocks include his synagogue* declaration of the fulfillment of God's promise (4:16-30) and the Sermon on the Plain (6:17-49; *see* Sermon on the Mount). Both passages are unique to Luke. The synagogue speech represents Jesus' own understanding of his mission, while the sermon represents his fundamental ethic (*see* Ethics of Jesus) presented without the concerns related to Jewish tradition (cf. Matthew's Sermon on the Mount).

In the synagogue speech (4:16-30) Jesus raises the note of fulfillment through his appeal to Isaiah 61:1 and 58:6 (*see* Jubilee). God's promised anointing is fulfilled "today," which in the Lukan context looks back to Jesus' anointing with the Spirit in Luke 3. Here is a reminder of his regal role. He will bring salvation to all those in need: the poor, the blind and the captive.

In chapters 4—9 Luke juxtaposes Jesus' work with the gathering of disciples* and the rising opposition. Jesus' ability to bring salvation is pictured in a series of miracles (4:31-44), while disciples are called to be fishers of humankind (5:1-11). The first hints of official opposition arise with the miracles suggesting his divine-like authority*: the Son of man* claims to forgive sins (*see* Forgiveness of Sins) and heals* on the Sabbath* (5:12-26). Levi, a hated tax collector (*see* Taxes), is called (5:27-28), and four controversies emerge, one of which involves the type of company Jesus keeps, while the others center on the Sabbath (5:29—6:11). Jesus gives a mission statement: his task is to call the sick to repentance (5:32).

Subsequently, through a series of pericopae focusing on Jesus' calling of the disciples, his teaching and miracles, Luke concentrates on the question Who is Jesus? and the appropriate response to him. John the Baptist, perhaps doubtful because of Jesus' style of ministry, wonders if Jesus is the coming one. Jesus replies that his eschatological works of healing and preaching affirm his status (7:18-35; cf. Is 29:18; 35:5-6; 61:1). One is to respond to the Word, though many obstacles prevent response (8:4-15). Jesus' miraculous work over nature (8:22-25), over demons (8:26-39), and over disease and death (8:40-56) shows the extent of his authority and pictures his eschatological work. This section moves from teaching and demonstration of authority to confession and call to discipleship.* Peter confesses Jesus to be the Christ* (9:18-20). Now Jesus explains what kind of Messiah he will be; he will suffer (9:21-22). Those who follow him must have total commitment in order to survive the path of rejection that comes with following Jesus (9:23-27).

The second heavenly testimony to Jesus comes at the Transfiguration* (9:28-36). The divine voice repeats the endorsement made at the Baptism with one additional note: "listen to him" (Deut 18:15). Jesus is a second Moses* who marks out a new way.

2.4. Jerusalem Journey: Jewish Rejection and the New Way (9:51—19:44). This part of the Gospel is particularly Lukan, with over forty-four per cent consisting of material found only in Luke. There is a high concentration of teaching and parable. In fact there are seventeen parables, fifteen of which are unique to Luke. The journey to Jerusalem is not a chronological, straight line, since Jesus in 10:38-42 is near Jerusalem, while later in the section he is back in the north. Rather, it is a journey in time within the context of the necessity of God's plan. Journey notes punctuate the section (9:51; 13:22; 17:11; 18:31; 19:28, 44). Jesus travels to meet his appointed destiny in Jerusalem (13:31-35).

The thrust of this section is that Jesus initiates a new way to follow God. Its theme is "listen to him." Since his way is distinct from that promulgated by the Jewish leadership, this section discusses how Jesus' teaching relates to the Judaism of his day. The difference provokes great opposition, a theme which dominates Luke 9—13. All are invited to follow the new way, but some refuse. The seeds of discontent which will lead to Jesus' death are manifest.

The section starts with the disciples learning the basics of discipleship: mission, commitment, love for God, love for one's neighbor, devotion to Jesus and his teaching, and to prayer (9:51—11:13). In a critical section Jesus calls on the crowd to discern the nature of the times (12:49—14:24). Israel is turning away and the time for her to respond, without facing judgment, is short (13:1-9; 31-35). Nevertheless, blessing will still come.

From this point on most of the journey section concerns discipleship. In the face of such rejection disciples will need absolute commitment (14:25-35). Their mission is to seek the lost just as God does (15:1-32). God rejoices in finding lost sinners,* so Jesus' call is to pursue them. Discipleship expresses itself in service to others, so it is generous with resources (16:1-31). In fact, one is accountable to God for how they

are used. Though false teaching is a threat, it is overcome with forgiveness of the brother or sister, deep faith and service (17:1-10). The disciple is to live in hope of the king's return. Then the promise of the kingdom, already inaugurated and present, will be consummated (17:11—18:8). His coming will be a time of severe judgment but also vindication. The disciple is to live humbly, giving all and trusting all to the Father (18:9-30).

Now Jesus turns to Jerusalem, renewing the display of his authority as he predicts his suffering and heals as the Son of David (18:32-43). Zacchaeus epitomizes the transformed sinner and rich man (19:1-10). He is a picture of the mission of Jesus; he is the lost one who is sought and saved (19:10). The parable of the pounds shows the need for faithfulness and the reality that the disciple as well as the nation are accountable to the king (19:11-27). Jesus enters Jerusalem as a king, but the leadership rejects the claim (19:28-40). Jesus warns the nation that it has failed to respond to God's promise and faces judgment (19:41-44). Though opposition brings Jesus to his death, it brings far more tragic consequences on the nation of Israel.

2.5. Jerusalem: The Innocent Slain and Raised (19:45—24:53). In his concluding section Luke explains how Jesus died, why apparent defeat became victory and how God revealed who Jesus was. In addition, the task of disciples in light of God's acts becomes clear. Luke mixes fresh material with that found in the other Gospels.

The final battles in Jesus' earthly ministry occur here, recalling earlier confrontations in Luke 11—13. Jesus cleanses the Temple (*see* Temple Cleansing), thereby indicating his displeasure with official Judaism (19:45-48). The leaders fail to embarrass Jesus in various controversies concerning his authority (20:1-8, 20-26, 27-40).

In the light of the nation's refusal to accept him, Jesus predicts the fall of the Temple* and of Jerusalem, events which are a foretaste of the end (21:5-38). The fall of Jerusalem will be a terrible time for the nation, but it is not yet the End, when the Son of man returns on the clouds with authority to redeem his people (Dan 7:13-14). Disciples are to watch and be faithful.

Luke 22—23 pictures Jesus' movement toward the cross. Jesus is betrayed and yet is innocent, but his death will initiate the New Covenant and will be a sacrifice on behalf of others (22:1-20; *see* Last Supper). In his last discourse Jesus announces the betrayal, points out that greatness is in service, appoints eleven to authority, predicts Peter's denials and warns of rejection (22:21-38). Jesus is in control even as his death approaches (*see* Passion Narrative).

As Jesus prays, and thereby exemplifies for his disciples the trust they must have in the midst of rejection, he is betrayed and arrested (22:47-53; *see* Gethsemane). The trials center again on who Jesus is. The answer comes in Luke 22:69. Jesus "from now on" will be shown to be the exalted Lord who is seated with authority at the side of God. Messiahship means lordship (*see* Lord), authority over God's plan and salvation. Ironically and unwittingly, the Jewish leadership helps bring these things to pass. Jesus is on trial, or so it seems; but in fact he is the judge (22:54-71; *see* Trial of Jesus).

But it is not the leadership alone that is guilty. As Pilate* and Herod debate what to do about Jesus, the people are given the final choice (23:1-25). Despite Pilate's repeated protestations of innocence and Herod's similar reaction, the people ask for Jesus to be slain and Barabbas to be freed. Luke portrays Jesus' death with OT allusions picturing Jesus as an innocent sufferer who relies on God (23:26-56; Ps 22:8-9; 19; 69:22; 31:6; *see* Death of Jesus; Burial of Jesus).

Luke 24 presents three scenes of resurrection* and vindication. Luke 24:1-12 announces the empty tomb, but the news of the excited women is greeted with skepticism. The angelic (*see* Angel) announcement directed the women to recall the predictions of suffering (*see* Predictions of Jesus' Passion and Resurrection). The experience of the Emmaus disciples pictures the reversal the resurrection brought to the despairing disciples (24:13-36). Two disciples mourn the departure of the prophet of Israel who might have redeemed the nation. But Scripture and the revelation of Jesus himself show that God had a plan which included Jesus' death. God has indeed raised Jesus, vindicating both Jesus and the divine strategy. Despair turns to joy* when they understand the nature of God's plan and Jesus' role in it, a major note in Luke.

Just as Luke 1—2 opened with the hope of OT promises being fulfilled, so Luke 24 returns to the central theme of Jesus the Messiah as the fulfillment of God's plan and promise (24:36-53). Jesus' final Gospel appearance yields a commission, a plan and a promise. Reminding them yet again that Scripture foretold the suffering and exaltation of Messiah, Jesus tells the disciples that they are called as witnesses (*see* Witness) to preach repentance. The plan is to go to all the nations, starting from Jerusalem. The promise is the "promise of the Father," the coming of the Spirit (24:49). As the Baptist had promised (3:15-17), so it has come to pass.

The ascension* of Jesus (24:50-53) fulfills the exaltation Jesus predicted at his trial (22:69). A dead Messiah does not represent the end of God's plan. In his exaltation Jesus is vindicated and the plan to reach all nations goes on. Jesus the Messiah is Lord of all, so the message can go to all (Acts 2:14-40; 10:34-43). The Gospel closes with the disciples rejoicing that out of the ashes of apparent defeat, victory and promise have arisen. Theophilus can be reassured (1:1-4).

3. The Theology of Luke.
Our brief survey will outline the major strands and connections which show Luke's theological and pastoral concerns.

3.1. The God of Design and Concern: The Plan. At the center of Luke's concern to reassure Theophilus is the detailed discussion of God's plan. Luke emphasizes and enunciates this theme more than the other Synoptic Evangelists.

3.1.1. The Plan. A number of uniquely Lukan passages bring out this theme (1:14-17, 31-35, 46-55, 68-79; 2:9-14, 30-32, 34-35; 4:16-30; 13:31-35; 24:44-49), with one key text overlapping with the other Gospels (the inquiry of John the Baptist, 7:18-35). In addition, Luke utilizes the suffering Son of man texts, a few of which are unique to him (9:22, 44; 17:25 [L]; 18:31-33 [L]; 22:22 [L]; 24:7 [L]). Acts also highlights the details of the plan (Acts 2:23; 4:27-28; 13:32-39; 24:14-15; 26:22-23). The major elements of the plan are the career of Jesus, the hope of the spiritually humble and needy, the offer of God's blessings, the coming of the new era, along with the suffering which comes to Jesus and the division which comes to Israel.

3.1.2. The Plan's Structure: Promise and Fulfillment. Supporting the theme of God's plan is the note of promise and fulfillment running throughout the Gospel and Acts, especially as it relates to the Scriptures. The appeal to the OT concentrates on three areas: christology, Israelite rejection/Gentile inclusion and justice in the end. The latter two themes are more prominent in Acts, as "the Way" (Acts 24:14) is presented and defended from various charges, particularly as it is represented by the efforts of Paul among the Gentiles. Nonetheless, the theme of Gentiles and non-Jews responding to the gospel, while Israel stumbles, is present in numerous texts (2:34; 3:4-6; 4:25-27; 7:1-10; 10:25-37; 11:49-51; 13:7-9, 23-30, 31-35; 14:16-24; 17:12-19; 19:41-44).

3.1.3. "Today" Texts. Various themes enhance the plan. The "today" passages show the immediate availability of promise (2:11; 4:21; 5:26; 13:32-33; 19:5, 9; 19:42; 23:42-43).

3.1.4. John the Baptist. John the Baptist is the bridge stretching between the old era of promise and the new era of inauguration (Lk 1—2; esp. 1:76-79; 3:4-6; 7:24-35; 16:16). Luke 7 is instructive here. John is the forerunner of Malachi's prediction, but beyond that John represents the greatest prophet of the old era (7:27). Nonetheless, the new era is so great that the lowest member of the kingdom is higher than the greatest prophet of the old (v. 28). This passage presents the basic Lukan structure of the plan: the era of promise-expectation followed by the era of inauguration. The church's message of the gospel and Jesus' teaching on the end serve to clarify the timing and structure of the newly inaugurated era. The plan still has future elements to be realized (17:21-37; 21:5-38), but the basic turning point has come. So the second portion of the plan also has a subdivision, even though all of that era represents fulfillment. Those subdivisions are inauguration (Acts 2:14-40) and consummation (Acts 3:14-26), the "already and not yet."

3.1.5. Mission Statements. Other elements of the plan are seen in Jesus' mission statements where he outlines his task. Jesus has come to preach good news to those in need (4:18-19), to heal the sick (5:30-32) and to be heard, whether the message is communicated through him or his representatives (10:16-20). He has come to seek and save the lost (19:10). This career is reviewed in Acts 10:36-43.

3.1.6. Geographic Progression. The geographic progression also reveals the movement's growth under the plan. The basic outline of the Gospel from Galilee to Jerusalem shows this growth, as does the necessity of Paul's going to Rome in Acts (Acts 1:8; 19:21; 23:11).

3.1.7. "It Is Necessary." Many passages declare that "it is necessary" *(dei)* that something occur. In fact, 40 of 101 NT uses of *dei* occur in Luke-Acts. Jesus must be in his Father's house (2:49), he must preach the kingdom (4:43) and he must heal the woman tormented by Satan (13:16). Certain events must precede the end (17:25; 21:9). Jesus must be numbered among the transgressors (23:37). The Christ must suffer and be raised, and repentance for the forgiveness of sins must be preached. The necessity of the Son of man's suffering, already noted, is also a part of this theme. Acts continues to strike this chord (Acts 1:11; 3:21; 9:6, 16; 13:46; 14:22; 19:21; 23:11; 25:10; 27:24).

3.2. Christology and Salvation: Messiah-Lord, His Teaching and Work, and the Blessings of the Plan through Him. Jesus and deliverance stand at the center of the plan. Who is Jesus? What does he bring? How do we know he is God's chosen? These are central christological questions for Luke. In addition, there is the call to respond.

3.2.1. Christology: Messiah-Servant-Prophet to Lord.

Luke carefully develops his portrait of Jesus, though this feature is not universally recognized. Some say that Luke's christology is more of a patchwork than a unified whole; it is a collection of a variety of traditions, "the most variegated in the NT" (Evans).

It is clear from a reading of Luke 1—2 that Jesus is introduced as a regal figure. Both the announcement to Mary and the remarks of Zechariah make the Davidic connection explicit (1:31-33, 69). In addition, the anointing of Jesus at his baptism appeals to a pair of OT passages, Psalm 2 and Isaiah 42, which bring together regal-prophetic images. The images of Servant* and prophet likewise come together in Simeon's remarks (2:30-35), but the idea of a *leader-prophet* is a dominant christological theme in Luke.

Jesus' sermon at Nazareth (4:16-30) likewise joins regal and prophetic motifs. Though Elijah and Elisha are elicited as parallels to Jesus' situation (4:25-27), for Luke the anointing of Isaiah 61:1 is in the aorist tense and looks back to the baptism with its regal-prophetic motifs. Even when the people recognize that Jesus is a prophet (7:16; 9:7-9, 19), it is qualified by Peter's confession that he is the Christ (9:20) and Jesus' further explanation that his work will inevitably be that of a suffering Son of man.* In a tradition unique to his Gospel, Luke even relates Jesus' title as "Son" to Jesus' messianic role (4:41). The regal-prophetic mix reappears with the voice from heaven at the Transfiguration (9:35; cf. Ps 2:7; Is 42:1; Deut 18:15).

When Jesus is presented as a prophet he is a leader-prophet, one like Moses, so that even here the note of rule and direction is fundamental. In short, Luke regards Jesus' messianic role as pivotal for christology. Jesus' messiahship needs clarification and careful definition, and it is placed beside other expectations, but his messiahship is a category around which the other concepts revolve.

The prophetic motif plays an important role in the woes against the scribes (11:47-51), the mourning for Jerusalem (13:31-35) and the conversation on the Emmaus road (24:19, 21). Yet even in texts like Luke 13:31-35, the appeal to Psalm 118 ("Blessed is he who comes in the name of the Lord") expands in the Lukan presentation into a regal allusion (cf. the Triumphal Entry, 19:38), since "the one who comes" is for Luke fundamentally an eschatological and messianic deliverer (3:15-18; 7:22-23; 19:38). Again, on the Emmaus Road the disciples mix their perception of Jesus as a prophet with the hope that Jesus might "redeem" the nation (24:21). For Luke the deliverer-regal imagery is never very far from the prophetic.

Luke develops the elevated status of Jesus as he draws his Gospel to a close. While the authority of the

Son of man is introduced as early as 5:24, this theme and his status as Lord become the focus of dispute in 20:41-44; 21:27 and 22:69 (cf. Acts 2:30-36; 10:35). The significance of Psalm 110 and its reference to Jesus is of signal importance to Luke. Following a three-step progression that bridges both Luke and Acts, the issue is raised (20:41-44), Jesus responds (22:69) and the message of Jesus' authority as Lord is proclaimed (Acts 2:30-36; see Franklin). The Synoptics share the first two texts, but Luke's sequence, ending with the detailed exposition of Acts 2, shows the importance of this dispute. Luke 22:69 makes it clear that "from now on" Jesus—the Messiah-Servant-Prophet—will exercise his authority as Lord at the right hand of God.

This is not to say that Luke does not use other titles alongside this basic portrait of Jesus' messiahship. Jesus is savior, or one who delivers (2:11; 1:70-75; 2:30-32; Acts 5:31; 13:23-25), as well as Son of David (1:27, 32, 69; 2:4, 11; 18:38-39; Acts 2:25-31; 15:16) or King (18:38). He is the Son, who relates to God as Father, even as divine testimony declares (1:35; 2:49; 3:21; 3:38; 4:3, 9, 41; 9:35; 10:21-22). Yet he is also Son of Adam, who grows in grace (3:38; 2:40, 52; Acts 2:22). He is compared to Jonah (11:29-32, message of repentance; see Sign of Jonah) and Solomon (message of wisdom,* 11:29-32). As Son of man he not only suffers and is exalted, but he also ministers (5:24; 6:5, 22; 7:24; 9:58; 11:29-32; 12:18; 19:10). Another frequent title is Teacher* (7:40; 8:49; 9:38; 10:25; 11:45; 12:13; 18:18; 19:39; 20:21, 28, 39; 21:7; 22:11). The portrait of Jesus is variegated, but it is organized as well. Jesus bears authority as well as promise.

3.2.2. The Kingdom in Jesus' Teaching and Work. The Messiah brings the kingdom of God,* God's rule manifested on earth (4:18, 43; 7:22; 8:1; 9:6; 10:11). Here is a complex theme in Luke's Gospel. The kingdom is present now, but it comes in the future. It includes earthly hope, and yet has spiritual dimensions.

The kingdom as present reality is associated with Jesus' authority, well illustrated as he exercises his command over evil, spiritual forces. This also reveals the spiritual character of the kingdom. Jesus can speak of the kingdom as "near" (10:9). And as the seventy (-two) disciples exercise authority over demons, he sees Satan fall (10:18-19). In fact, Jesus says that if he casts out demons by the finger of God, then the kingdom has come upon those present (11:20-23; see Demon, Devil). Asked by Pharisees when the kingdom would come, he could say the kingdom is "among you" (17:21). The king, in one parable, departs "to receive a kingdom" (19:14-15). In his hearing before the council of Jewish elders,* Luke makes it clear that

from that point on Jesus will be at God's side (22:69). Finally, the appeal to Psalm 110 depicts the presence of a regal authority, ruling from the side of God.

But the kingdom is also future (see Eschatology). Luke 17:22-37 describes the judgment preceding its arrival. Here is the "not yet" aspect—the kingdom in consummation. Luke 21:5-38 also describes the "time of redemption." Here the imagery of the Day of the Lord abounds as evil is decisively judged. Within the space of a few verses (21:25-27) allusion is made to a range of OT passages suggesting the cosmic disturbance associated with the Day of the Lord (Is 13:10; Ezek 32:7; Joel 2:30-31; Ps 46:2-3; 65:7; Is 24:19 (LXX); Hag 2:6, 21; Dan 7:13). OT hope and expectation is not dead, as Acts 3:20-21 also makes clear. Jesus will return to fulfill the rest of the promise, a promise that will show itself visibly on earth to all humanity, as well as in the eternal benefits given to believers.

So the kingdom is earthly, that is, Jesus will rule as a Davidide on the earth and bring about total deliverance as he executes his sovereignty over all. Such hope is most strongly expressed in the narrative and songs of Luke 1:32-33, 46-55, 69-75. The eschatological discourses and the remarks of Acts 1:11 and 3:18-21 show that the future hope has not been absorbed in the theme of present inauguration, but remains alive, connected to its OT roots. God is faithful and brings all of his promises to fruition.

But spiritual deliverance is also his. Zechariah's Song* (1:78-79) makes this clear by speaking of Jesus as the rising sun who shines on those in darkness and leads them into the path of peace. The promise of the Spirit (3:15-18; 24:49; Acts 1:8) and the hope of forgiveness of sins (24:47) also belong to this emphasis. Jesus' authority over demons and other forces show that he is able to bring such promises to pass.

Those who are most obviously subjects of the kingdom and benefit from its presence are the disciples (18:26-30). All of salvation's benefits are theirs. But potential beneficiaries also exist. Anyone who wishes to enter in is a potential beneficiary (13:23-30; 14:16-24; see 3.3.1. below). But there are also unwilling subjects who are accountable to him now and one day will face the reality of his rule (19:27; 21:24-27; Acts 3:20-26; 10:42; 17:30-31).

3.2.3. The Spirit. The Spirit as a central figure of redemption is viewed first as the one promised (3:15-18) and then as a testifier and enabler of Jesus (3:21; 4:16-18). Later the full promise finally comes and the Spirit falls on all believers (Acts 2:1-13). Acts 2:14-21 (cf. Joel 2:28-32) explains the event as the sign that the new era has come. The Spirit is the gift of the Father through the exalted Son. He is power (or enablement) from on high (24:49; Acts 2:30-36; 10:44-47; 11:15-16; 15:8). The Spirit's presence is evidence that Jesus is raised and that Jesus directs his new community from the right hand of God. Luke reassures Theophilus that though the Messiah is dead and seemingly absent, he is present in the gift and presence of the Spirit he has sent (*see* Holy Spirit).

3.2.4. The Resurrection/Ascension. The key event at the center of God's provision of salvation is the resurrection*/ascension.* Among the Gospel writers, only Luke mentions and develops the ascension, an event which for him provides the link between Luke 24 and Acts 1 (its significance being further explained in Acts 2:23-24, 30-36; 3:14-15, 21; 4:10-12; 5:30; 17:31). A risen savior is one who can both rule and consummate his promise. He is the one who can forgive and signify forgiveness by bestowing blessings (Acts 2:21; 4:12; 10:43). Moreover, the ongoing reality of Jesus' authority is demonstrated in the activity of those who minister "in his name" (Acts 2:38; 3:6, 16; 4:6, 10; 8:11-12; 9:27-28; 10:48; 19:5). In short, the ascension shows that he is Lord* (Franklin).

3.2.5. Salvation in Jesus' Teaching and Work. Jesus brings promise and salvation.* Salvation involves sharing in hope, experiencing the kingdom, tasting forgiveness and partaking in the enabling power of the Spirit. Just as Jesus' person reveals the character and ability of the bringer of blessing, his teaching and work explain and signify the desired results. Jesus was a teacher and wonder worker (4:14-15, 31-32, 44; 6:17-19; 7:22). As we have seen, his teaching focused on the offer of the kingdom. This opportunity is pictured as the release and healing of Jubilee* (4:16-21; cf. Lev 25:10; Is 61:1-2), but it also includes a call to ethical honor reflecting the experience of blessing (6:20-49). The parables show the same dual concern. A few parables deal with God's plan (13:6-9, 23-30; 14:16-24; 20:9-18), and in some of these a meal or feast scene is employed. The feast displays not only the joy of salvation but the table fellowship of the future, a reality in which the community can now partake without racial distinction (Acts 10—11, 15). There is to be unity among the people of God.

Beyond unity stands a call to an ethical way of life. The life of relationship with God, engagement in mission and ethical honor is to be dominated by love, humility, service and righteousness—the subject of most of the other parables (10:25-37; 11:5-8; 14:1-12; 12:36-49; 15:1-32; 16:1-8, 19-31; 18:1-8; 19:11-27). Jesus did not come just to rescue people for heaven,* but to have them come to know the transforming activity of God in their life. It is to this God that they are accountable. This is why commitment is so prominent

in Jesus' teaching (9:21-26; 57-62; 14:25-34; 18:18-30).

3.2.6. The Cross. Thus far in our survey of Jesus' work and teaching, little has been said about the cross (*see* Death of Jesus). This is because Luke gives Jesus' ascension and exaltation more prominence than he does the cross. Some scholars have gone so far as to deny that Luke ascribed a saving function to Jesus' death, arguing instead that Luke portrays Jesus as an example in his death (Büchele, Glöckner). While Luke does employ exemplary elements in his narrative of Jesus' death, and thereby addresses the needs of a church under pressure, to view Jesus' death solely as an ethical example is to miss other Lukan emphases.

Though the cross is less prominent for Luke than for Paul, its significance moves beyond an ethical or historical function and occupies an important theological position in Luke's teaching. Jesus, as was noted in examining Luke 22—23, is the righteous sufferer. But two texts cast light on the meaning of his death. Luke 22:20 makes it clear that Jesus' death inaugurates the new covenant with God, while Acts 20:28 argues that the church was, in Paul's words, "purchased" with Jesus' blood. Covenant inauguration and a soteriological transaction take place in Jesus' death. Two other images reinforce this view. The substitution of Jesus for Barabbas portrays the fact that Jesus took the place of the sinner, an exchange made all the more poignant when Luke notes that the people "with one voice" shared in this unrighteous choice (23:18-25). Jesus' offer of paradise to the thief as they die together (23:43) shows that Jesus, despite his death, can offer life.

3.2.7. Miracles. Not only the resurrection, but the miracles,* in their display of the arrival of the new era, authenticate Jesus' role in the divine plan (7:22; Acts 2:22-24). In fact, the scope of Jesus' works of healing* shows the breadth of Jesus' authority. He heals the sick; exorcises evil spirits, heals those generally called "sick"; and cures a variety of specific conditions: a flow of blood, a withered hand, blindness, deafness, paralysis, epilepsy, leprosy, dropsy and fever. He resuscitates the dead and exercises power over nature. Jesus' work testifies to his person and task. The fact that Acts records the disciples continuing to perform some of these works shows that authentication continues (Acts 3:6, 16) and that Jesus' authority continues as well.

3.2.8. Jesus and Salvation. Luke's portrayal of Jesus is fundamentally concerned with his authority and then with the promise he brings. Jesus' saving work inaugurates the kingdom, delivers the sinner,* forgives sin, provides the Spirit, calls for a committed and faithful life lived in the context of hope in the future consummation, and makes all accountable to God's plan. In fact, all the covenant promises of God are inaugurated by Jesus. Luke sets forth the Abrahamic promise of blessing to the peoples of the earth as realized in Jesus (Acts 3:22-26). So is the Davidic hope (1:31-33, 69; 22:69; Acts 2:25-36) and the hope of the Spirit associated with the coming of the new era and new covenant (22:20; Acts 2:14-21). Theophilus should be reassured that Jesus can and does deliver on such promises. But who makes up the new community and what is it to be? How does christology relate to the content and task of the new community for Luke?

3.3. The New Community. Within Luke's Gospel the new community formed around Jesus is not really an organized entity. There are the Twelve and the Seventy(-Two), but beyond these basic groups there is no formal structure. Rather, those who will become the new community of Acts are called disciples. In the Gospel this group is mostly Jewish, but there are a few hints that the benefits of Jesus' program can extend to Samaritans and non-Jews (3:4-6; 4:22-30; 7:1-10; 13:23-30; 14:16-24; 17:12-19; 20:15-16; 24:47). This multiracial theme becomes prominent in Acts, but more important to the Gospel is the fact that the message goes out to those on the fringe of society.

3.3.1. The Beneficiaries of Salvation. Luke focuses on the reception of the gospel message by outcasts: the poor, sinners and tax collectors. In addition, women come in for special treatment. For Luke the poor are materially *and* spiritually impoverished. The spiritual element is clearly indicated in 1:50-53 and 6:20-23, where the poor and humble are related to God's covenant promise or to the treatment of God's prophets. The poor or rejected are mentioned in several texts (1:46-55; 4:18; 6:20-23; 7:22; 10:21-22; 14:13, 21-24; 16:19-31; 21:1-4). Sinners are also highlighted as the special objects of the gospel (5:27-32; 7:28, 30, 34, 36-50; 15:1-2; 19:7). Tax collectors, culturally understood as betrayers of their nation (*see* Taxes), are still noted as potential beneficiaries as well (5:27-32; 7:34; 18:9-14; 19:1-10).

Finally, Luke features the responsiveness of women* (7:36-50; 8:1-3; 8:48; 10:38-42; 13:10-17; 24:1-12). Often it is not just a woman but a widow who is cited, since she represented the most vulnerable status within society (2:37; 4:25-26; 7:12; 18:3, 5; 20:47; 21:2-3). Whether in parable or by example, these women show that they are sensitive to the message of Jesus. Though on the fringes of first-century society, they are in the middle of Luke's story. Often they are paired with men (2:25-28; 4:25-27; 8:40-56, 11:31-32; 13:18-21; 15:4-10; 17:34-35; Acts 21:9-10), a feature suggesting

that the gospel is for both genders, as well as all races and social strata.

In short, the makeup of the new community is to know no boundaries. The good news is available to all, but society's weak and vulnerable are often most suited to respond to its message of hope and reliance on God.

3.3.2. The Terms and Pictures of Response. Luke uses three terms to describe response to the message: "repent," "turn" and "faith" (*see* Repentance). The term translated "repent" is rooted in the OT (Lk 11:32) word *šûb*, "to turn around." The Greek term *metanoeō* has to do with a change of mind. The point is that repentance involves a reorientation of perspective, a fresh point of view. When dealing with God's plan it entails seeing that plan in a new way and orienting oneself to it. For Luke the fruit of repentance expresses itself concretely. The particular expressions of repentance are illustrated in some material unique to Luke in which the Baptist replies to those who inquire "What should we do then?" Repentance expresses itself in everyday life, especially in how men and women treat each other (Lk 3:7-14).

Four pictures of repentance stand out. Luke 5:31-32 develops the observation that those who respond to Jesus come as those seeking a physician. Just as a sick patient in need of medical attention is totally reliant on the skill of the doctor, so the one who repents comes to God as if for healing. Luke 15:17-21 portrays the repentance of the prodigal and indicates how a repentant heart makes no claims, being totally reliant on the mercy of the one entreated. Repentance involves a changed attitude toward sin, but the change primarily comes from recognizing that only God and his mercy can provide relief. Luke indicates the crucial role of repentance when, at the end of his Gospel, he summarizes the essence of the good news: "Repentance and forgiveness of sins will be preached in his name" (24:47). The parable of the tax collector who in the Temple cries out "God, have mercy on me, a sinner" (18:9-14) demonstrates the repentant response, though the term "repentance" is not used (cf. 19:1-10).

The word "turn" (Gk *epistrephō*), while rarely used in the Gospel (1:17; 17:4; 22:32), becomes prominent in Acts, where it pictures the fundamental change of direction that accompanies repentance (Acts 3:19; 19:35; 11:21; 14:15; 15:19; 26:18-20; 28:27).

"Faith"* (Gk n. *pistis*; v. *pisteuō*) also describes actions which bring credit and benefit to the bearer. Faith for Luke expresses itself concretely, whether as the faith of the paralytic's friends (5:20), the faith of the centurion (7:9) or the faith of the sinful woman who anoints Jesus (7:47-50). The Samaritan leper and the blind man also have faith that Jesus can restore them to wholeness (17:19; 18:42). Faith believes and so it acts. In Acts those who responded were sometimes called "believers" to show the centrality of faith (Acts 5:14; 15:5). In short, faith is the recognition and persuasion that God had something to offer through Jesus—forgiveness and the blessings of promise—which one must actively embrace. Such people "call on the name of the Lord" (Acts 2:21; cf. Rom 10:13).

3.3.3. The Blessings of the New Community. Luke's Gospel employs various terms for the blessings on offer: forgiveness or release (1:77 and 3:3 as tied to John the Baptist; 4:18; 24:47; Acts 2:38; 5:31; 10:43; 13:38); life (10:25; 12:16, 21; 18:29-30); peace (1:79; 2:14; 10:5-6; Acts 10:36) and, as we have seen, the kingdom and the Spirit.

3.3.4. The Opponents of Salvation. In contrast to those who respond positively to the gospel, Luke identifies spiritual and human opponents of the new community. At the transcendent level the spiritual forces of evil (*see* Demon, Devil, Satan) stand resistant though powerless before the plan (4:1-13, 33-37; 8:26-39; 9:1; 10:1-12, 18; 11:14-26; 22:3). For Luke, God's struggle not only involves reclaiming humanity's devotion, but reversing the effects of the presence of evil forces.

On a human level the opponents are primarily the scribes* and Pharisees.* When Jesus claims authority to forgive sin and challenges the Sabbath tradition (5:24; 6:1-11), their opposition becomes a regular feature of the narrative. The roots of this rejection go back to their refusal to respond to John the Baptist (7:29-30). In three instances where Jesus is seated at table with Pharisees, they are warned (7:36-50; 11:37-52; 14:1-24). In the journey section as well as in Jerusalem, it is the leaders who are at the center of Jesus' condemnation (11:37-52; 12:1; 14:1-4; 15:1-2; 16:14-15; 19:45-47; 20:45-47). While the few exceptions, such as Jairus (8:41) and Joseph of Arimathea (23:50-53), catch our attention, for the most part Luke sees the leadership standing opposed to Jesus and plotting his demise (6:11; 11:53-54; 20:19; 22:3-6, 31; 23:3-5).

The crowd's (*see* People, Crowd) reaction to Jesus is mixed. They have interest in Jesus and yet their response to him is superficial and sometimes fickle. The transition occurs in Luke 9—13. Jesus offers many warnings to them in the crucial section of Luke 12:49—14:24. In addition he rebukes "this generation" in 11:29-32, condemns various cities of Israel in 10:13-16 (*see* Blessing and Woe) and tells a few parables about the failings of the nation (13:6-9; 20:9-

19). The crowd's eventual response typifies the general response of most in Israel. Their rejection brings warnings of judgment, but such warnings do not represent Jesus' anger. They picture prophetic regret, as when Jesus weeps for those he warns (19:41-44). In the end the crowd shares in the responsibility for Jesus' death when they ask for Barabbas (23:18-25). At the final hour, on the road to the cross, Jesus delivers a prophetic message of judgment to the daughters of Jerusalem and their children (23:27-31).

The response of most of Israel is a tragic one. It was in line for blessing, but has missed its day of visitation and now awaits judgment (19:44). Now it is the "time of the Gentiles" (21:24). Israel has not lost its place in God's plan, for the faithfulness of God's promise to it cannot be denied, but it is "desolate" until it acknowledges this Messiah (13:34-35; Acts 3:14-21). In Acts the nation is warned to change its mind about Jesus and repent (Acts 2:22-24; 5:27-32).

Luke has been accused of anti-Semitism* (Sanders), but this is a harsh judgment. Luke is arguing that it was the new community which was persecuted by those who failed to respond to the message of hope. Jesus and the disciples consistently offered the gospel to the nation and suffered while making the offer. The disciples did not create the division and did not bring violence to the Jewish community. Those who responded to Jesus were forced out, as the persecution of Acts shows and as Jesus predicted (12:1-12). The new community was not anti-Jewish; it was pro-promise. Consistently in Acts the new community suffers great risk as it returns to the synagogue to offer hope to the nation. Such enemies were to be loved and prayed for, as Jesus made clear (6:27-36; 23:34; Acts 7:60).

3.3.5. A Source of Tension: The Issue of the Law. One of the primary causes of tension both in the Gospel and in Acts is the new community's relationship to the Law.* At the same time, Luke's precise understanding of this issue has been a subject of ongoing debate in Lukan scholarship.

Some have argued that Luke displays a very conservative attitude toward the Law, conservative in the sense that the new community's existence and conduct is in keeping with the Law. There is but one Israel, one covenant, one Law, and the Jewish-Christian community in particular, along with its associate Gentile Christians, are the true heirs of the OT promise (Jervell). More recently, Esler has argued that Luke maintains this position—untenable as it may be—out of the sociological motivation of legitimating the community (*see* Sociological Analysis of the Gospels).

Others (Wilson) suggest that Luke is ambivalent toward the Law. Luke sees Jewish Christians keeping the Law, while Gentiles are free from some of its demands (circumcision) and bound by others (idols, meat offered to idols, immorality).

Finally, it has been argued that Luke understands the Law to be part of the old era, but portrays the church as it slowly came to recognize that truth (Blomberg, Turner). Law was not regarded as binding, though the missionary praxis of the early church allowed its observance in matters where issues central to the new faith were not at stake. The latter view is well supported by the Gospel and Acts.

The Law or its associated traditions, especially Sabbath regulations (6:1-11, esp. v. 4), are a central source of irritation in Luke's Gospel. It is important to note that the Sabbath challenge comes after Jesus' proclamation that new wine must come in new wineskins and that those who like the old will not try the new (5:33-39). This remark was part of a dispute centered around Jesus' neglect of Jewish traditions related to cleansing (see Clean and Unclean). Jesus challenged the Law, at least in terms of its first-century Jewish interpretation, and Luke regards this challenge as the catalyst for Jewish opposition.

Acts throws further light on Luke's understanding of Law. The understanding that all foods are clean, the full table fellowship with the Gentiles and the refusal to circumcise Gentiles (Acts 10—11, 15) are vivid examples of the early church's rejection of some elements of the Law and the tradition which grew out of it. Luke's clear recounting of early Christians being charged by Jews with denying Mosaic customs, as well as his description of the early community's struggle with the issue of keeping the Law, shows an awareness of the ferment within the early community (13:10-17; 14:2-6; 23:2; Acts 6:11, 13; 15:1-5; 21:28; 25:8). Luke's understanding is that the Law pointed to the promise (16:16; 24:43-47; Acts 26:4-23; cf. Acts 3:14-26 which cites Torah texts exclusively). While he openly describes the differences within the early church, the prevailing argument is that God gave evidence of his acceptance of Gentiles by pouring out the Spirit, before they were circumcised (Acts 11:15-18) and gave a vision to Peter that commanded open table fellowship (Acts 10:1-33). Luke portrays taking vows and observing other elements of the Law as optional, sometimes necessary for unity, but not to be confused with what is necessary for salvation (Acts 15:22-29; 21:17-26).

Luke's resolution is that Jewish Christians are free to observe such customs as long as they do not force Gentiles to do so. This distinction is crucial and not unlike the solution of Paul in Romans 13—14. On this view the Law cannot be held as binding. The many texts in Acts dealing with this issue reveal some of the concerns Luke wishes to address. They also presuppose a racially mixed community struggling with its relationship to its ancient roots. Luke is honest about these differences and forthright about the complex solution and compromise which emerged out of the concern for the church's unity. Moreover, his account indicates his endorsement of the resolution.

3.3.6. The Pressure and the Plan. In the face of opposition disciples were called to a strong commitment to Jesus, for it was inevitable that with a decision for Jesus, opposition would come. Indications of division and opposition come early in the Gospel (2:34-35) and are constant throughout (8:14-15; 9:21-23, 61-62; 12:4-9, 22-34; 22:35-38). The disciples are pictured as shrinking back from responding boldly, as Peter's denial exemplifies. But in Acts the presence of the Spirit enables them to become consistently bold so that they truly exemplify the steadfastness and faithfulness that should mark a disciple.

The exhortation to steadfast discipleship surely reveals a facet of the Gospel's origin. For Theophilus and other Gentiles the pressure of conflict was the occasion for reassurance that they not only belonged in the new community but that they would partake of God's plan and blessing.

3.4. The New Community: Mission, Ethics and Accountability. The new community had not chosen to separate itself from Judaism. It had presented itself as the hope of the nation but had been forced to become distinct. On the other hand, its new experience of the Spirit set it apart from the Jewish community. The Spirit not only evidenced the presence of the ascended Lord in their midst (Acts 2:14-40; 11:15), but enabled the new community to live by the principles Jesus had laid down—a life distinct from contemporary norms of piety and current cultural standards (12:1; 14:1-14; 22:24-27).

3.4.1. Faith, Dependence and Commitment. The community was called to a fundamental reorientation toward God expressed as faith and repentance (see 3.3.2. above). This attitude of trust, so clearly indicated in Jesus' preaching, parables and encounters with individuals, not only begins the walk with God but sustains it (5:31-32; 15:17-21; with 12:22-32). Disciples are to be totally focused on their walk with God. The path is difficult and requires self-reflection, total commitment, daily dedication and cross-bearing (9:23; 9:57-62; 14:25-35).

The community was called to mission. While Acts details the early missionary activity of the community, the call to preach repentance and forgiveness to all nations, beginning at Jerusalem, is spelled out in the Gospel (24:47). The parables of Luke 15:1-32 reflect the focus on the lost, as do the clear statements of Luke 5:31-32 and 19:10. Jesus' disciples were to follow him in reaching out to others.

3.4.2. Love for God and One's Neighbor. Devotion to God is highlighted in Luke 11:1-13, a devotion expressing itself in dependent prayer. Devotion to Jesus is shown by Mary's choice to sit at Jesus' feet, absorbing his teaching and presence (10:38-42). In addition, the care of one's neighbor is also an expression of such devotion (10:25-37). In fact, what Jesus himself demonstrated, he calls his disciples to be: neighbors to all, without distinction of race or class.

3.4.3. Prayer. Jesus both models and encourages prayer* (11:1-13; 18:1-8; 18:9-14; 22:40). Prayer does not demand; it requests, humbly relying on God's mercy and will. It voices trust in God's care and provision of basic needs. It recognizes that in seeking forgiveness, men and women should be prepared to give it as well. And it looks with expectation to the eschatological consummation of God's kingdom.

3.4.4. Persistence and Watchfulness. Under the pressure of conflict and opposition, the community is to remain steadfast and faithful (8:13-15; 9:23; 18:8; 21:19; see 3.3.6. above). The church in Acts often exemplifies such persistence (Acts 4:23-31). This attitude is related in turn to patience and expectation. Disciples are to fear God, not mortals (12:1-12), recognizing that the Lord will return and that they are responsible to him (12:35-48; 19:11-27; 18:8). Like the seed on good soil, they hear the Word, cling to it and persevere to bear fruit (8:15).

It is here that eschatology makes its impact in Luke. Jesus represents both the present and the future. The promises which remain unrealized will be fulfilled (17:22-37; 21:5-38). The judgment* of Jerusalem is the guarantee and picture of the final judgment. The return will be a horrific period in which unbelieving humanity is severely judged and believers will suffer at the hands of unbelievers. Luke emphasizes that the coming of the Son of man places responsibility on disciples to be faithful and on all humanity to respond to the gospel. In Acts he will note that Jesus is the "judge of the living and the dead" (Acts 10:42; 17:31). While Luke indicates that the time of the return is unknown, it will come suddenly and the disciples must be prepared (12:35-40).

3.4.5. Overcoming Hindrances to Discipleship. The Lukan view of wealth has been a topic of recent scholarly investigation (Seccombe, Pilgrim; *see* Rich and Poor). Warnings and parables about riches abound in Luke (8:14; 12:13-21; 16:1-15, 19-31; 18:18-25). But positive examples also exist (8:1-3; 19:1-10; 21:1-4; Acts 4:36-37).

Scholars have debated whether Luke decries wealth *per se*. Zacchaeus, who generously gives half of his possessions to the poor and repays those he has wronged, hardly seems to have divested himself of every asset. His example suggests that the issue is not what a person has, but what a person does with his or her possessions. The disciples are said to have "left all" for Jesus (18:28-30), a remark that includes family as well as resources. Yet later in the Gospel, under the pressure of Jesus' arrest, they exhibit fear and denial. The issue with resources, as with the other demands of discipleship, is not the perfection of the response or the parting with one's last coin, but the fundamental orientation of the response. Disciples are called to recognize that all of life belongs to God and comes from his hand. The rich man would not even consider Jesus' request to sell all, while the disciples and Zacchaeus had entered into the process. In sum, Luke warns that the hindrances to discipleship include not only confidence in resources, but the fear of other's opinion (12:1-12) and the cares of life (8:14).

4. Conclusion.

Luke's Gospel is pastoral, theological and historical. The reality of God's plan impacts how individuals see themselves and the community to which they belong. Old barriers of race are removed. New hope abounds. The message of Jesus is one of hope and transformation. Anyone, Jew or Gentile, can belong to the new community. At the center is Jesus, the promised Messiah-Lord, who sits at God's right hand exercising authority from above. He will return one day and all are accountable to him. His life, ministry and resurrection/ascension show he is worthy of trust. Just as he has inaugurated the fulfillment of God's promises, so he will bring them to completion. In the meantime, being a disciple is not easy, but it is full of rich blessing which transcends anything else this life can offer. This is the reassurance about salvation which Luke offers to Theophilus and others like him.

See also JOHN, GOSPEL OF; MARK, GOSPEL OF; MATTHEW, GOSPEL OF.

BIBLIOGRAPHY. **Commentaries:** D. L. Bock, *Luke 1:1—9:50* (WEC; Chicago: Moody, 1992; An expanded version of this article appears as the introduction of this commentary); F. Bovon, *Das Evangelium nach Lukas* (EKK 3.1; Zurich: Benziger and Neukirchen-Vluyn: Neukirchener, 1989) vol. 1; F. Danker, *Jesus and the New Age* (rev. ed.; Philadelphia: Fortress: 1988);

E. E. Ellis, *The Gospel of Luke* (NCB; 2d ed.; Grand Rapids: Eerdmans, 1974); C. A. Evans, *Luke* (NIBC; Peabody, MA: Hendrickson, 1990); C. F. Evans, *Saint Luke* (TPINTC; Philadelphia: Trinity, 1990); J. Fitzmyer, *The Gospel According to Luke* (2 vols.; AB 28, 28a; Garden City, NY: Doubleday, 1981, 1985); W. Grundmann, *Das Evangelium nach Lukas* (THKNT; 2d ed.; Berlin: Evangelische Verlagsanstalt, 1961); I. H. Marshall, *Commentary on Luke* (NIGTC; Grand Rapids: Eerdmans, 1978); L. Morris, *Luke* (rev. ed.; TNTC; Grand Rapids: Eerdmans, 1983); J. Nolland, *Luke 1—9:20* (WBC; Dallas: Word, 1989); H. Schürmann, *Das Lukasevangelium* (HTKNT; Freiburg: Gerder, 1969); **Studies:** C. Blomberg, "The Law in Luke-Acts," *JSNT* 22 (1984) 53-80; D. L. Bock, *Proclamation from Prophecy and Pattern: Lucan Old Testament Christology* (JSNTSS 12; Sheffield: Sheffield Academic Press, 1987); F. C. Bovon, *Luke the Theologian: Thirty-Three Years of Research (1950-1983)* (PTMS 12; Allison Park: Pickwick, 1987); F. F. Bruce, "Is the Paul of Acts the Real Paul?" *BJRL* 58 (1975/76) 282-305; H. J. Cadbury, *The Making of Luke-Acts* (2d ed.; London: SPCK, 1958); R. Cassidy, *Jesus, Politics and Society: A Study of Luke's Gospel* (Maryknoll, NY: Orbis, 1978); H. Conzelmann, *The Theology of St. Luke* (New York: Harper & Row, 1960); J. Dupont, *The Salvation of the Gentiles: Essays on the Acts of the Apostles* (New York: Paulist, 1979); M. Dibelius, *Studies in the Acts of the Apostles*, ed. H. Greeven (New York: Charles Scribner's Sons, 1956); C. H. Dodd, "The Fall of Jerusalem and the Abomination of Desolation," *JRS* 37 (1947) 47-54; P. F. Esler, *Community and Gospel in Luke-Acts* (SNTMS 57; Cambridge: University Press, 1987); W. Farmer, *The Synoptic Problem* (rev. ed.; Dillsburo, NC: Western North Carolina, 1976); idem, *Luke the Theologian: Aspects of His Teaching* (London: Geoffrey Chapman, 1989); E. Franklin, *Christ the Lord: A Study in the Purpose and Theology of Luke-Acts* (London: SPCK, 1975); M. Goulder, *Luke: A New Paradigm* (JSNTSS 20; 2 vols.; Sheffield: Sheffield Academic Press, 1989); E. Haenchen, *The Acts of the Apostles: A Commentary* (Oxford: Basil Blackwell, 1971); C. J. Hemer, *The Book of Acts in the Setting of Hellenistic History*, ed. C. Gempf (WUNT 49; Tübingen: J. C. B. Mohr, 1989); M. Hengel, *Acts and the History of Earliest Christianity* (Philadelphia: Fortress, 1980); J. Jervell, *Luke and the People of God* (Minneapolis: Augsburg, 1972); R. Maddox, *The Purpose of Luke-Acts* (FRLANT 126; Göttingen: Vandenhoeck & Ruprecht, 1982); I. H. Marshall, *Luke: Historian and Theologian* (Grand Rapids: Zondervan, 1970); R. F. O'Toole, *The Unity of Luke's Theology: An Analysis of Luke-Acts* (Wilmington, DE: Michael Glazier, 1984); W. E. Pilgrim, *Good News to the Poor* (Minneapolis: Augsburg, 1981); J. T. Sanders, *The Jews in Luke-Acts* (Philadelphia: Fortress, 1987); D. P. Seccombe, *Possessions and the Poor in Luke-Acts* (SNTU, B6; Linz: Verlag F. Plöchl, 1982); C. H. Talbert, *Literary Patterns, Theological Themes and the Genre of Luke-Acts* (SBLMS 20; Missoula, MT: Scholars, 1974); R. C. Tannehill, *The Narrative Unity of Luke-Acts: A Literary Interpretation Vol 1: The Gospel According to Luke* (FFNT; Philadelphia: Fortress, 1986); D. L. Tiede, *Prophecy and History in Luke-Acts* (Philadelphia: Fortress, 1980); M. M. B. Turner, "The Sabbath, Sunday and the Law in Luke-Acts," in *From Sabbath to Lord's Day*, ed. D. A. Carson (Grand Rapids: Zondervan, 1982) 99-157; P. Vielhauer, "On the 'Paulinism' of Acts," in *Studies in Luke-Acts*, ed. L. E. Keck and J. L. Martyn (London: SPCK, 1966) 33-50; S. G. Wilson, *Luke and the Law* (SNTSMS 50; Cambridge: University Press, 1983).

D. L. Bock

M

"M" TRADITION

The M tradition generally refers to all of the material in Matthew which is unparalleled in Mark or Luke or, more narrowly, to the discourse material which is found only in Matthew. Source-critical interests related to the Synoptic problem* have dominated reconstructions of M. Source critics (Streeter, Manson, Kilpatrick) generally agreed that M was a pre-Matthean written source (c. A.D. 65) which was Jewish-Christian in nature, polemical toward the scribes* and Pharisees* and was not as reliable as the other Synoptic sources (Mark, Q* and L) for conveying authentic teachings of Jesus (see Gospels [Historical Reliability]).

1. The Nature of the M Tradition.

To source critics the kind of Christian community which produced M seemed to be a Jewish-Christian community which felt obligated to keep both the Law* and the scribal traditions (5:17-20; 23:2-3). The M community also opposed the mission to the Gentiles* (10:5b-7; cf. 28:16-20). In light of this data, it was contended that M reflected either the Jewish-Christian group at Jerusalem which had James as its leader (Streeter, 232) or, more generally, the "Jewish-Christians of Judea with their headquarters at Jerusalem" (Manson, 25). In either case M seemed to reflect a segment of Jewish Christianity which opposed the lax approach to the Law practiced by Pauline Christians in their mission to the Gentiles (cf. 5:19 and Gal 2:15-16).

Manson emphasized, however, that "M is not merely Christianized Rabbinism" since it also "shows clear traces of the influence of the teaching of John the Baptist" (p. 25). Teachings of the Baptist (e.g., 3:7 par. Luke 3:7 Q; see John the Baptist) are clearly put into Jesus' mouth in M (12:34; 23:33). Because of the Jewish-Christian polemical character of M and because of its handling of Jesus' sayings in light of John's preaching, critics have agreed that M's presentation of Jesus' teachings should be used cautiously in any reconstruction of Jesus' authentic sayings.

Although Kilpatrick also viewed M as a written

source, he can be seen as one pointing the way toward redaction-critical studies of M since he did not see any reliable means for ascertaining what material is from M and what is from the final editor. He was reluctant, therefore, in assigning to M either a life-situation in early Christianity or a clear-cut ideology.

Redaction critics (see Redaction Criticism) tend to see M as either the Evangelist's original composition or as material incorporated by him as an integral part of the entire Gospel. In particular it has been emphasized that the source critic's understanding of the development of early Christianity have caricatured their views about the nature of M. It is now generally agreed that no easy distinctions like "Jerusalem" versus "Pauline" Christianity can be made when speaking of the character of early Christian communities.

The character of the community which produced M is still the focus of research, but scholars now view M as both written material and oral traditions which have been reworked carefully by the final redactor. The "Jewish" character of M is no longer characterized by general statements about the Jerusalem Church. Rather, it is seen as reflecting several stages in the specific relationship between the Matthean community and the Judaism within its particular locale (Brooks; Levine).

2. The Christology of the M Tradition.

Since the M tradition has been seen as a Jewish-Christian "corruption" of Jesus' teachings, very little has been done with the view of Jesus in M and with the role M plays in Matthean christology as a whole. Although some general agreement about the christology of M is discernible in the history of research, the following summary must be regarded as tentative since there is still no consensus about either the content of M or the history of its transmission.

The M tradition presents Jesus as the authoritative interpreter of the Law.* This role is particularly clear in the so-called antitheses of 5:21-48, where we find the authoritative contrast of "You have heard that it was said [to the ancient ones], But I say to you. . . ." At the most, Jesus is presented in M as the giver of a New Law; at the least, he is the authoritative interpreter of the Law (Davies, 387-389). The M tradition does present Jesus' words as applicable to practical matters (e.g., 5:31-32; cf. 19:9), but this should not lead simply to the conclusion that Jesus is only a great rabbi (see Teacher).

In M Jesus is the founder of the end-time community, the church* (16:18-19; cf. 18:17), and his revelation is the standard by which God* will judge the community (5:17-20; cf. 25:31-46; see Judgment). Jesus also commissions its members for their limited mission to Israel* (10:5-7). During the short interval before the end (10:23), Jesus is the only teacher whose authority* God recognizes, as the intimate and exclusive phrases "my Father/your Father" suggest (6:1-8, 16-18; 18:19). Jesus' teaching, unlike Moses's,* is unmediated, and he is presented in M as having direct access to the Father. Thus M presents Jesus as the only authoritative interpreter of God's will. Jesus has the eschatological* authority to reinterpret what God gave to Moses at Sinai ("it was said . . . but I say"). Jesus can thus equate his eschatological teachings ("my yoke") with the final and complete will of God (11:28-30; cf. 11:25-27).

The M tradition presents Jesus in exclusive terms as the founder, the teacher and the one who commissions the end-time community under the sole authority of his heavenly Father (23:8-10). These christological themes blend well with the entire presentation of Jesus in Matthew. The M tradition, then, should probably be viewed as representing a stage in the development of the Matthean community itself (Brooks) rather than as a foreign tradition which was incorporated into the Gospel only with great difficulty. See also L TRADITION; MARK; MATTHEW, GOSPEL OF; SYNOPTIC PROBLEM; Q.

BIBLIOGRAPHY. S. H. Brooks, *Matthew's Community: The Evidence of His Special Sayings Material* (JSNTSup 16; Sheffield: JSOT, 1987); W. D. Davies, *The Setting of the Sermon on the Mount* (Cambridge: Cambridge University, 1964); G. D. Kilpatrick, *The Origins of the Gospel According to St. Matthew* (Oxford: Clarendon, 1946); A.-J. Levine, *The Social and Ethnic Dimensions of Matthean Salvation History; "Go nowhere among the Gentiles . . ."* (*Matt. 10:5b*) (Lewiston, NY: Edwin Mellen, 1988); T. W. Manson, *The Sayings of Jesus* (London: SCM, 1957); B. H. Streeter, *The Four Gospels* (London: Macmillan, 1930).   F. W. Burnett

MACCABEAN REVOLT. See REVOLUTIONARY MOVEMENTS.

MAGI. See BIRTH OF JESUS.

MAGIC. See DEMON, DEVIL, SATAN.

MAGNIFICAT. See MARY'S SONG.

MARK, GOSPEL OF

The Gospel according to Mark stands as one of the foundational documents of the Christian faith. Eclipsed for centuries as an abridged edition of the Gospels according to Matthew and Luke, this Gospel was rediscovered for its own sake in the nineteenth-century quests for the historical Jesus (see Historical Jesus) and has risen to prominence in twentieth-century Gospel studies. Indeed the number of written works on Mark over the past forty years certainly rivals and may well surpass that written on Matthew and Luke combined.

1. Introduction
2. Mark's Narrative Pattern
3. Mark's Theology
4. Mark's Ending
5. Mark's Purpose

1. Introduction.
The Gospel according to Mark has raised numerous questions about its significance, authorship, date, place, audience and genre. Some of these issues are more critical than others for a proper understanding of Mark as a Gospel. Certainly the rediscovery of Mark as a narrative text to be viewed as a whole (see Literary Criticism) rather than merely a collection of its constituent parts has done much to recapture the dynamic thrust of the thought of this Gospel.

1.1. The Significance of Mark. How does this Gospel serve as a fundamental document for the Christian faith? Two contemporary NT scholars—one in Germany and one in the USA—have attributed the very story of Jesus found in all the Gospels to the creativity of the original author of this (B. Mack, *Myth of Innocence*, 1989) or its underlying (W. Schmithals, *Das Evangelium nach Markus*, 1979) Gospel. Mack goes so far as to attribute the "origin for the Christian view of Christian origins" to the genius of the writer of Mark's Gospel (357). These extreme views stem in part from the broad consensus that Mark's Gospel was indeed the first Gospel and provided the literary basis for the Gospels of Matthew and Luke (see Synoptic Problem).

Did Mark create the story of Jesus for the church (e.g., Schmithals, Mack) or did Mark create the literary genre (see Gospel [Genre]) of the Gospel (the broad consensus of NT scholars) for the church? In other words, just how foundational was Mark's Gospel as a document in the early church?

1.1.1. "The Beginning of the Gospel." The first clue to the role of Mark's Gospel comes in the opening words: "the beginning of the gospel of Jesus Messiah [Christ], Son of God" (1:1). Taken as an independent heading, as found in most English translations, and punctuated with a period at the end, the meaning of "beginning" and "gospel" can be and has been debated. For example, does "beginning" refer to: (1) the Gospel itself as the "beginning (either as a point in time or as the rudimentary elements) of the gospel" or (2) the "beginning section" of the Gospel of Mark—that is, the opening verses? Does "gospel" then refer to: (1) the message preached by Jesus Messiah, Son of God (cf. 1:14; *see* Gospel [Good News]), (2) the message about Jesus Messiah, Son of God as understood and proclaimed by the church or (3) the story that follows as the Gospel?

The common Jewish formula for a scriptural citation, "as has been written by...," in 1:2 removes these ambiguities. This citation formula always links what has gone before to what follows. It never begins a citation by referring forward to what follows (e.g., 1:4-8). Therefore, instead of placing a period at the end of "the beginning of the gospel of Jesus Messiah, Son of God" (1:1), one must continue with "as has been written by the prophet Isaiah" (1:1-2). Accordingly, Mark opens by stating that "the beginning" (1:1) occurs "as has been written by the prophet Isaiah." References—explicit or oblique—to Isaiah in the following verses set the boundaries of "the beginning of the gospel. . . as has been written by Isaiah the prophet." Since Isaiah's promise underlies the coming of John the Baptizer (1:4-8, cf. Is 40; *see* John the Baptist), the baptism* of Jesus (1:9-11, cf. Is 42:1; 61:1), Jesus' presence in the wilderness (1:12-13, cf. Is 40; 65; *see* Mountain and Wilderness) and Jesus' proclamation of the "gospel of God" (1:14-15, cf. Is 52:7; 61:1-2), 1:1-15 represents the "beginning of the gospel about Jesus Messiah, Son of God as has been written by the prophet Isaiah . . ." (1:1-2).

If 1:1-15 represents the "beginning of the gospel . . ." in keeping with Isaiah's promise, then Mark 1:16—16:8 must be the rest of the "gospel concerning Jesus Messiah, Son of God" for which 1:1-15 is "the beginning." In other words, Mark refers to the following story about Jesus, which begins with the coming of John the Baptizer (1:4) and runs to the statement of the women's fear (16:8), as the "gospel." The story about Jesus is the "gospel."

1.1.2. Gospel Narrative before Mark. Paul's "gospel" by contrast does not focus at all on the story of the earthly ministry of Jesus. Rather it centers on statements about what God* has done through Jesus' death (*see* Death of Jesus) on the cross and subsequent resurrection.* Even the earliest Christian traditional expression of the "gospel" consists of creedal statements. "For I handed on to you [as tradition] of first importance what I in turn had received [as tradition]: 'that Christ died for our sins in accordance with the Scriptures, and that he was buried, and that he was raised on the third day in accordance with the scriptures, and that he appeared to Cephas, then to the Twelve' " (1 Cor 15:2-5). Did Mark then, in place of this propositional gospel encapsulated in pithy formulas, create what he calls "the gospel about Jesus Messiah, Son of God," a gospel in narrative form that focused more on Jesus' earthly ministry as well as his death?

The answer may well lie in Peter's sermon in Acts 10:34-43. One finds in this brief summary the *basic structure* of the narrative Gospel common to Matthew, Mark, Luke and John. It sets the beginning with John the Baptizer and runs through Jesus' ministry, death, resurrection and appearance to witnesses (*see* Witness), all accompanied by allusions to the Scriptures. In fact the reference to preaching the gospel of peace* of Isaiah 52:7 stands as the backdrop for this Gospel (cf. Acts 10:36).

If the outline of Peter's sermon in Acts 10:34-43 reflects an early Christian form of preaching the gospel, then Mark would not have been the one to create the gospel in *narrative* form in contrast to the more *propositional* statement of the gospel as found in Paul. The use of the narrative or story of Jesus as the "gospel," consisting of traditional materials about his work and words, would antedate Mark's writing of his Gospel and preclude his having created the actual form and content of his Gospel (*see* Tradition Criticism). Where does Mark's foundational contribution then lie?

1.1.3. Gospel Narrative As Literary Form. On the basis of intensive comparative studies, a scholarly consensus affirms that Mark's Gospel was the earliest of the four Gospels (*see* Synoptic Problem). Furthermore, both Matthew and Luke appear to have used Mark's Gospel as the basis for writing their own. Luke 1:1 actually notes that "many have undertaken to set down an orderly account (a "narrative") of the events that have been fulfilled among us." Whether John's Gospel was familiar with this or all three Synoptic Gospels is still debated (*see* Synoptics and John), but his narrative does follow the same broad structure of Mark and the summary in Acts 10:34-43. Therefore, Mark's foundational contribution lies in his having actually written the first of our four Gospels. He was the first to put into written or literary form a narrative of Jesus as the Gospel. Finally, Mark was the first and only Evangelist to refer to his narrative as "the gospel" (1:1; cf. Lk 1:1; Mt 1:1). By the turn of the first century, the four Gospels were known as "the Gospel according to Matthew, Mark, Luke and John" respectively. Thus Mark's opening reference to his story as "the gospel" most likely set the stage for the use of that term as a literary designation for the four distinctive literary works we now call our Gospels.

1.2. Authorship. Who was the innovative author of this foundational Gospel? Like the other three Gospels, this one is anonymous and contains neither allusions (cf. Lk 1:1-4; Jn 21:24) nor clues to authorship. Perhaps the author assumed the readers' knowledge of authorship (e.g., Lk 1:1-4; Acts 1:1). More likely the anonymity reflects the author's understanding that his Gospel was hardly a creative literary product but rather was an expression of the gospel from God promised by Isaiah (52:7; 61:1) and expressed in the teaching and stories of Jesus as preached in the early church (cf. 1:1; 1:14). Since no single author could lay personal claim to creating this Gospel, the Gospel is anonymous.

Traditionally, however, it became known as the "Gospel according to Mark." Apart from this title, which with the titles of the other Gospels may date from the end of the first century, Papias, Bishop of Hierapolis, provides the earliest documentable testimony attributing a literary work to one named Mark. But Papias, whose five-volume work *Interpretation of the Lord's Sayings* (c. A.D. 120/30) was cited by Eusebius (*Hist. Eccl.* 3.39.15), claims to have learned this from another whom he calls the Elder: "And this is what the Elder said, 'Mark, who became Peter's interpreter, accurately wrote, though not in order, as many of the things said and done by the Lord as he had noted." The subsequent extant testimony of the late second century (e.g., the anti-Marcionite prolog; Irenaeus *Haer.* 3.1.1; Clement of Alexandria as cited by Eusebius *Hist. Eccl.* 6.14; cf. 2:15) appears to be derivative of this tradition.

Who was Mark? Despite the very common occurrence of Mark (*Marcus*) as a Roman name, the association by Papias and the early church tradition of Mark with Peter has led to identifying the author as the "John Mark" known elsewhere in the NT (1 Pet 5:13; Acts 12:12, 25; 13:13; 15:37-39 and in the Pauline corpus: Philem 24; Col 4:10; 2 Tim 4:11). Some more recent scholars have sought to distinguish between the Evangelist Mark, a companion of Peter (1 Pet 5:13), and John Mark, the associate of Paul in Acts and the Pauline corpus. This distinction, however, re-

quires special pleading. Apart from the absence of any solid basis for this distinction in the tradition, the mention of both Silvanus and Mark in 1 Peter 5:12-13 makes clear that "Mark" was the "John Mark" of Acts and the Pauline corpus who with Silvanus (Silas) had also been a companion of Paul. Therefore, Mark was the companion of both Peter and Paul, a member of the primitive community in Jerusalem that met in the upper room of his mother's home (Acts 12:12) where Jesus might have celebrated the Last Supper (cf. Mk 14:14-15; Acts 1:13-14; *see* Last Supper).

In any case, the question of authorship need not have a bearing on one's reading of the Gospel. The author makes no pretense of giving either his own or another's eyewitness account of any events of the Gospel. Furthermore, his identity neither assists one's understanding nor guarantees the accuracy of the details. Consequently, his identity remains merely a historical curiosity which the author fostered by his decision to remain anonymous.

1.3. Date. When did the author write this foundational document? According to our earliest tradition (anti-Marcionite prolog; Irenaeus *Haer.* 3.1.1, c. A.D. 160/80), Mark wrote after Peter's death in Rome, assumed to be c. A.D. 64-65 during Nero's rule. Clement of Alexandria (Eusebius *Hist. Eccl.* 6.14.5-7) places the writing during Peter's time in Rome (c. A.D. 45-65). Most scholars, however, follow the earlier tradition and debate only whether he wrote before or after the fall of Jerusalem in A.D. 70 (*see* Destruction of Jerusalem).

The only relevant data in Mark may come in 13:14, when read against the historical background of the Jewish War of A.D. 67-70. The Evangelist sets the discourse in 13:3-37 in the context of the predicted fall of Jerusalem. Yet the reference to the "abomination of desolation" and the order for the Judeans to "flee to the hills" (*see* Apocalyptic Teaching) hardly makes sense after the destruction of the Temple. Not only does the "abomination" lack a personal referent in the events of the destruction of the Temple, but the summons to "flee to the hills" makes little sense after Rome completely surrounded Jerusalem with a tight military blockade in A.D. 67-69 preventing all entrance and exit. Perhaps a time c. A.D. 66-67, before the final siege of Jerusalem but when the inevitable end of Jerusalem and the Temple was in sight, corresponds more closely to the details than a date during or after the siege.

As with authorship, however, apart from 13:14 one gains little advantage in interpreting Mark's Gospel by having a precise date for its inception. The story stands without any direct connection to any current historical events. The nature of Mark's story, with its primary focus on Jesus' life and teaching as constitutive of the plot, may account for Mark's reticence to read his day and times back into the story of an earlier period. Consequently, the specific date of Mark's Gospel is more an issue of historical curiosity than a necessity or even an aid for correctly understanding Mark's text.

1.4. Place. Where did Mark write this Gospel? Various locales, including Galilee,* the Decapolis, Tyre, Sidon, Syria, the East and Rome,* have been suggested. Traditionally, the anti-Marcionite prolog places it in the "regions of Italy," with Clement of Alexandria locating it in Rome during Peter's ministry (Eusebius *Hist. Eccl.* 2.15; 6.14.6). John Chrysostom (*Hom. Mt.* 1.3) even sets it in Egypt.

The diversity of proposed locales indicates how little evidence the Gospel itself gives in helping one determine its original setting. One of the strongest arguments for Rome or Italy, apart from the traditional association of the Gospel with Peter, lies in the numerous Latinisms, several of which Mark simply transliterates into Greek. Furthermore, Mark 12:42 explains the "widow's mite," a Greek coin, as being a *quadrans* and "inside the courtyard" of 15:16 as being "the governor's headquarters." Both of the underlying Greek expressions would have needed little clarification for readers in the East, whereas they might be unfamiliar to an audience in the West and support a setting in Rome. The argument from language (*see* Languages of Palestine), however, is hardly conclusive, since many of the Latinisms do reflect semitechnical expressions common to military and trade and would be found in any area, such as the East, occupied by Roman forces.

As with date and author, the lack of explicit references supporting any one locale means that the issue of place has little to do with how one reads or understands the Gospel. Consequently, time and space locators in Mark belong strictly to the narrative rather than to the historical setting of when and where the Gospel was written.

1.5. Audience. As with place and date one cannot specify the audience and occasion for this Gospel. The frequent explanation of Aramaic expressions as well as Jewish laws and customs may well indicate an audience unfamiliar with certain forms of Judaism.* To say more goes beyond the limits of the text. Consequently, this generic quality of Mark gives it a universal character that addresses the modern disciple in much the same manner as it did its first readers. It is the "gospel concerning Jesus Messiah, Son of God" that itself summons one to "repent and believe

the gospel" that God has acted and will act again to effect his sovereign, saving rule in and through Jesus Messiah, God's Son.

1.6. Mark As Story. Because the Gospels consist of episodes focusing on Jesus' ministry and teaching, the reader often concentrates more on the individual parts than on the whole. Such a reading has marked the popular reading of the Gospels on a personal and liturgical level. At the scholarly level much of twentieth-century Markan studies has specialized in decomposing the Gospel by delineating and analyzing the underlying traditional units (*see* Form Criticism), a study that has made us aware of the rich background of the Gospels' constituent parts. Yet Mark's opening statement about the "gospel concerning Jesus Messiah, Son of God" refers to the *whole* of Mark's narrative. The Evangelist wrote a story, a narrative. Consequently, aware of this rich traditional background, one needs to step back and look at the elements involved in this Gospel as a story in order to gain a better view of its message.

1.6.1. The Narrator's Role. The narrator provides the primary point of view for this story. As one who knows all the events of the story, the narrator also knows the thoughts, feelings, emotions and intentions of the story's many characters. Yet the narrator, distinguished from the author by such omniscience, never appears as part of the story or as one of the characters of the story. The story is told by one external to its events, who clearly shares the point of view of Jesus, who in turn shares God's point of view in the story. Therefore, one is led from the outset to trust the narrator.

1.6.2. Plot and Characters. The reader discovers the plot in the opening statement. It revolves around the "good news about Jesus Messiah, Son of God" expressed in the events of the story. In other words, the plot consists in Jesus' effective proclamation in word and deed of the "gospel" from God that God's promised redemptive rule was at hand summoning people to repent (*see* Repentance) and respond in faith.* Mark wanted the reader to respond in faith, "to think the thoughts of God" (8:33). This plot is carried by the ensuing conflict motif between Jesus and the demonic (e.g., 1:12-13, 21-27; *see* Demon, Devil, Satan), between Jesus and the Jewish authorities (e.g., 2:1— 3:6; 12:13-44), between Jesus and the Roman authorities (e.g., 15:2-15), between Jesus and his family* (e.g., 3:20-21, 30-35) and even between Jesus and his disciples* (e.g., 8:14-21).

A corollary of this conflict motif is Jesus' identity. The leading character and protagonist of the story, his identity is made explicit to the reader as "Jesus Messiah, Son of God" at the outset in 1:1 with accent on the "Son of God," confirmed by God through the voice from heaven* at the baptism (1:11) and the Transfiguration* (9:7), declared by the demons (1:25; 3:11-12; 5:7), confessed by Peter (8:27-29), personally affirmed by Jesus to the high priest (14:61-62; *see* Priest and Priesthood), but declared openly without qualification for the first time at the crucifixion by the Roman centurion (15:39).

Yet apart from the demons the full significance of Jesus' identity escapes the other leading characters of the story. This failure to recognize who Jesus was comes through in the rejection of Jesus by the religious authorities (e.g., 3:22-30; 14:63-65), his parents (e.g., 3:21), his hometown (e.g., 6:1-6) and even the misunderstanding of his disciples (e.g., 4:35-41; 6:45-52; 8:31-33). Furthermore, Jesus' silencing of the demons and his disciples whenever his true identity is involved, as well as his exclusive use of the ambiguous "Son of man"* to refer to himself, enhances this "messianic secret."

The other leading role in this story is played by the disciples whose response to Jesus forms a major part of the plot. Called and privileged to be with Jesus (1:16-20; 3:7-12), privately taught by him (e.g., 4:10-20, 33-34), commissioned to participate in his ministry (e.g., 6:7-13, 30), they continually fail to understand him or accurately recognize who he really is and the implications of who he is for their discipleship* (e.g., 8:27—10:45). They waffle between having their mind on "divine things" and having their mind on "human things" (8:33).

1.6.3. Narrative Space and Time. The story covers an indefinite time span between Jesus' appearance at the Jordan to be baptized by John and his death during a Passover celebration (*see* Feasts) in Jerusalem. The tight framework constructed from the movement around Galilee (1:16—7:23), then north and east of Galilee (7:24—9:29), back to Galilee (9:30-52) and on to the Trans-Jordan (10:1-52), ending eventually in Jerusalem (11:1—16:8), suggests a period of less than one year. One must not, however, assume that the author's desire to provide a connected narrative necessarily implies a short, chronologically arranged and comprehensive account of Jesus' ministry (*see* Chronology). The narrative space and time belong primarily to the story rather than to the events themselves as a comparison with the other Gospels, especially the Fourth Gospel, indicates.

2. Mark's Narrative Pattern.

A narrative often presents difficulties for one seeking to break it into discrete parts. This Gospel is no exception, as a quick review of the numerous suggest-

ed outlines in the commentaries will indicate. The edges are fuzzy at best, but a literary pattern suggests a threefold division (1:1-15; 1:16—8:26; 8:27—16:8), with the two larger parts (1:16—8:26; 8:27—16:8) divisible into three sections respectively.

2.1. Prolog (1:1-15). The Gospel opens with a prolog, or a "beginning of the gospel," set against Isaiah's promise (1:1-2). First, the coming, baptism and preaching of John the Baptizer (1:4-8) corresponds to Isaiah's promise of a "voice in the wilderness" who "prepares the way of the Lord" as the precursor. Then Jesus' baptism accompanied by the coming of the Spirit (*see* Holy Spirit) and the voice from heaven echoes Isaiah 42:1 (cf. Is 42:1-2; 61:1) and sets the stage for his being in the wilderness for forty days (1:12-13) where he is sustained by the angels* in the company of the wild animals (cf. Is 65:17-25). Finally, in summary fashion, having been anointed by the Spirit at his baptism and led by the Spirit into the wilderness, Jesus emerges to declare the "good news of God" that the "time has been fulfilled, God's redemptive rule has come" in keeping with Isaiah 52:7 and 61:1. By introducing the ensuing story in this way, the Evangelist shows the "gospel concerning Jesus Messiah, Son of God," to be Isaiah's promised "good news" of God's salvation* (cf. Is 52:7; 61:1).

2.2. Part One (1:16—8:26). Jesus' ministry in public as the "Messiah, Son of God" runs from 1:16 to 8:26. This part consists of three smaller sections that seem to have a similar literary structure. Each begins with a story about the disciples (1:16-20; 3:13-19; 6:7-13) and each closes with an ominous story of rejection or unbelief (3:1-6; 6:1-6; and 8:10-21) followed by a summary (3:7-12; 6:6) or a story with the function of a summary (8:22-26) that is related to the theme of the respective section.

2.2.1. The first of these (1:16—3:12) might be called "new wine in old wineskins" (*see* Wine). After calling the first disciples, it moves from a day in Capernaum to a series of conflicts issuing from Jesus' authoritative ministry (2:1—3:6).

2.2.2. The second section (3:13—6:6) might be called the "mystery of the kingdom of God" as seen in Jesus' words (3:20—4:34) and deeds (4:35—5:43).

2.2.3. In the third section (6:7—8:26) Jesus' ministry extends beyond the purity (*see* Clean and Unclean) boundaries of Galilee (cf. 7:1—8:9), but the motif of misunderstanding emerges more forcefully from the public's and Herod's misconceptions about Jesus (6:14-16) to the disciples' own failure to understand (6:45-52; 8:14-21), despite the feedings of the five and four thousand. The healing of the blind man from Bethsaida (7:22-26) appears to illustrate the disciples' myopic plight (*see* Blindness and Deafness). Though seeing, they need the "second touch." Consequently, they form the primary focus of Jesus' ministry from 8:27—16:8.

2.3. Part Two (8:27—16:8). The final part of Mark's story (8:27—16:8) clearly focuses on the death of Jesus Messiah, Son of God, and it also falls into three sections.

2.3.1. The first (8:27—10:52) revolves around a threefold pattern of a Son of man passion prediction (8:31; 9:31; 10:33; *see* Predictions of Jesus' Passion and Resurrection) followed by the disciple's failure to grasp the point that sets the stage for Jesus' teaching on discipleship (8:32-38; 9:32—10:31; 10:34-45). The healing of blind Bartimaeus (10:46-52) and his enthusiastic response of joining Jesus "on the way" stands as a counterpoint to the disciples and the earlier, belabored healing* of the blind man of Bethsaida (8:22-26).

2.3.2. The second section (11:1—13:37) sets Jesus in and around the Temple* in Jerusalem where the conflict mounts from his actions (11:1-19) and teaching (11:27—12:44) in the Temple and across from the Temple (13:1-37).

2.3.3. In the third and final section (14:1—16:8) one has the Last Supper, arrest, trial (*see* Trial of Jesus), crucifixion and burial of Jesus (*see* Burial of Jesus) "Messiah, Son of God" (14:1—15:47). Clearly, one finds the climax of the Markan narrative in the ironic indictment of Jesus by the Romans as the "king of the Jews" (15:26), the taunts of the Jewish religious authorities of Jesus as "Messiah, king of Israel" (15:32) and the declaration by the Roman centurion that he indeed was the "Son of God" (15:39) after the Temple curtain had been torn in two (14:38). On Easter morning the messenger at the tomb points beyond the story to Jesus' promised meeting with his "disciples and Peter" in Galilee (cf. 14:28), despite their flight and denial (16:7-8).

Woven together from isolated units, pre-formed blocks of traditional units and an extended unit underlying the passion narrative (*see* Passion Narrative), Mark has composed a moving story full of action and pathos. Far more than a scissors-and-paste product, this narrative forms a dramatic whole that derives its power from its being the "gospel concerning Jesus Messiah, Son of God." It makes a theological statement—a statement about God—focusing on God's awaited redemptive activity in history through "Jesus Messiah, Son of God."

3. Mark's Theology.

The Evangelist wrote a story, not a theology. Conse-

quently, in describing Mark's theology one must select the leading motifs of the story and ask about their theological meaning.

3.1. Kingdom of God. Mark programmatically summarizes Jesus' message at the outset of his Gospel in terms of the kingdom of God (1:14-15; *see* Kingdom of God). One would, therefore, expect a strong emphasis on the kingdom to follow in his narrative. Yet for Mark "kingdom of God" hardly stands out in Jesus' ministry. Matthew refers to the kingdom of Heaven/God approximately fifty times, Luke forty, but Mark only fifteen. Of these references, three occur in the parables* of 4:1-34, three in the sayings about children* (10:14-15) and three in the discussion of the rich (10:23-25; *see* Rich and Poor). The usages are neither defined nor uniform.

3.1.1. Kingdom As Future Expectation. In the discussion with the disciples following the story of the rich man, Jesus refers to the kingdom as something one will enter (10:23-25; so 9:47 and 10:15). The future moment (*see* Eschatology) also appears in Jesus' promise at the Last Supper about not drinking again until the kingdom (14:25), in the description of Joseph of Arimathea as one "waiting expectantly for the kingdom of God" (15:43), in the anticipation of the seed parables (14:3-20, 26-29, 30-32) and above all in Jesus' assurance that some would "see the kingdom of God having come in power" (9:1). This future expectation correlates with the references to the coming of the Son of man in judgment* in 8:38; 13:26-32 and 14:62, and with the summons given the disciples to watch in 13:33-37. The kingdom in Mark, therefore, maintains a distinctive future significance as the time of judgment and consummation.

3.1.2. Kingdom As Present Reality. At the same time, the possibility of a present reality of God's kingdom appears in the saying about receiving "the kingdom of God as a child" (10:14-15), the prerequisite for eventually entering the kingdom (10:15). Not only does one have here a difference in time between the kingdom present and the kingdom future, but one also has a different nuance in the meaning of the kingdom of God. To receive the kingdom as a child implies a personal experience of God's sovereign rule that qualifies one to enter into at least a fuller experience of God's sovereign rule or kingdom at a time in the future. In other words, to "receive the kingdom of God as a child" in the present does not exhaust the meaning or expectation of the kingdom of God in the future, nor does the anticipation of the future kingdom of God preclude an experience or reception of the kingdom of God in the present.

3.1.3. The Mystery of the Kingdom. This dual motif of

the present and future kingdom of God correlates with Jesus' parables in Mark 4 about the "mystery of the kingdom of God" (*see* Parables). Each of the three seed parables (4:3-20, 26-29, 30-32) refers to both the present and future dimensions of the kingdom. Indeed, for Mark the "mystery of the kingdom of God" (4:11) lies precisely in this revelation to the disciples ("to you has been given") of what until then had been hidden about the kingdom of God. God's sovereign redemptive rule has come into history like a vulnerable seed (4:3-9, 13-20) that grows inexorably until the day of harvest (4:26-29) whose beginning is infinitely small but whose end is magnificently grand (4:30-32).

3.1.4. The Inauguration of God's Sovereign Reign. This dual dimension of the kingdom present and yet future may well be deliberately reflected in the programmatic summary of Jesus' proclamation of the "gospel of God" (1:14) in 1:15: "The appointed time *has been fulfilled,* the kingdom of God *has come,* repent and believe the gospel." As the parallel construction indicates, "the appointed time" and the "kingdom of God" have come to pass at a point in history. Yet the Greek verb (*ēngiken*) describing the "presence" of the kingdom usually denotes nearness rather than presence, in other words, "the kingdom of God *has come near.*" The apparent tension between the parallel construction and the lexical meaning of the verb affirms that the kingdom of God has come into history, "the appointed time has been fulfilled," even though the full appearance is yet to come ("near"). Both present and future dimensions are important for Mark. This programmatic summary at the outset of Mark's Gospel clearly indicates that the kingdom is the theme of Jesus' ministry.

For Mark, therefore, Jesus' ministry has to do with the inauguration of God's sovereign, redemptive rule, the kingdom of God, in history. The exorcisms of the demonic (e.g., 1:21-27), healing of the sick (e.g., 2:1-12; *see* Healing), fellowship with sinners* (2:13-17), feeding the hungry (e.g., 6:34-44), even the programmatic calling of the Twelve (3:13-19), all give expression in Mark's story to Jesus' preaching of the "gospel of God, the time has been fulfilled, the kingdom of God has come . . ." as found in the programmatic summary of Jesus' ministry in 1:14-15. Yet Jesus' earthly ministry does not exhaust the meaning or expectation of the kingdom of God. As seen in the declaration of the coming of the kingdom in power,* the references to the future dimension of the kingdom, the anticipation of the seed parables and the announcement of the coming judgment, Mark understood the kingdom to have a future chapter as well

when God's redemptive rule will be revealed in the consummation.

3.2. Christology. The correlation of eschatology and christology in Mark is evident in the opening statement about the "gospel concerning *Jesus Messiah, Son of God*" (1:1). Although one might render "Jesus *Messiah*" as "Jesus *Christ*"* (cf. most English translations), Mark's clear focus on Jesus as the "Messiah, Son of God" in his narrative, along with the programmatic summary of Jesus' ministry that centers on the coming of the kingdom of God, indicates that more was at stake in his use of "Christ" than simply a proper name. Mark wants to affirm that Jesus is the Messiah, the Anointed One, who inaugurated God's kingdom through his ministry.

3.2.1. Messiah. That Jesus is God's Anointed One, the Messiah (*see* Christ), is confirmed for the reader at the baptism, the first appearance of Jesus in the story (1:11-15). The voice from heaven at the baptism (1:11) calls Jesus "my son," an echo of Psalm 2:7 (cf. "You are my son, this day have I begotten you"). Since this psalm most likely was a royal psalm used at the coronation of the king in Israel,* the royal connotation of Jesus as the anointed king, the Messiah, would naturally follow. At the same time, the voice also declares Jesus to be the one with whom "I am well pleased," an echo of Isaiah 42:1. This passage introduces the Servant (*see* Servant of Yahweh) whom God equips with the Holy Spirit (Is 42:1-2), an event portrayed in Mark 1:9-11 by the coming of the Spirit at the baptism. Therefore, when Jesus appears "proclaiming the gospel of God" in 1:14, set against the promise of Isaiah (cf. Mk 1:1-2), the reader recognizes Jesus' coming not only to fulfill the promise of the coming evangel of Isaiah 52:7 who declares the good news of God's salvation and God's reign (i.e., the kingdom of God) but also to fulfill Isaiah 61:1 ("The Spirit of the Lord is upon me, because the Lord has anointed me to proclaim the good news. . ."). Jesus then is the promised Anointed One (Messiah), as seen here by his calling, equipping and message.

Jesus' public ministry, as portrayed from the calling of the four disciples in 1:16-20 to the healing of the blind man of Bethsaida in 8:22-26, also demonstrates by word and deed his coming as the Messiah to announce and inaugurate God's promised redemptive rule in history. When Jesus asks the disciples then in 8:27 who the people say he is, the answer reveals the public's awareness of God's work in him—but only as a prophet (8:28; *see* Prophet and Prophecy). When Jesus asks the disciples who they say he is, Peter responds correctly, "You are the Messiah" (8:29).

After the arrest and during the trial by the Sanhedrin,* the high priest poses the question of Jesus' identity in terms of "the Messiah, Son of the Blessed" directly to Jesus (14:61), who answers affirmatively: "I am" (14:62). This led to the Sanhedrin's deliverance of Jesus to Pilate (15:1; *see* Pontius Pilate) who posed the same question in its more political form "Are you the king of the Jews?" To which Jesus answered more cryptically, "You say so." Despite Pilate's subsequent equivocation (15:6-15), he eventually sentenced Jesus to death under the charge that he was the "king of the Jews" (15:16-20, 26). The Jewish leaders, the chief priests and the scribes then taunted the crucified Jesus as "the Messiah, king of Israel" (15:32). Yet Mark intends the reader to see the irony in Pilate's accommodating indictment and the disbelieving taunts of the religious authorities, since Jesus was indeed the "Messiah, king of the Jews." The Transfiguration (9:2-9; cf. 9:1), which comes subsequent to Peter's confession (8:27-29), Jesus' mode of entry into Jerusalem on a young donkey (11:1-11), which fulfills the promise of Zechariah 9:9 about the coming of Israel's lowly king, and especially Jesus' own affirmative response to the high priest's question confirm for the reader that Jesus was indeed the "Messiah, king of Israel," whose coming had directly to do with the inauguration of the kingdom of God in history.

For Mark's narrative, however, Jesus' identity as Messiah can only be clearly understood in the light of the cross. No sooner did Peter correctly confess Jesus to be the Messiah (8:29) than Jesus announced that the Son of man must suffer, be rejected by the elders,* chief priests and scribes, be killed, and rise again after three days (8:31). Peter's negative response (8:32) indicates the incongruity of such a possibility for the Messiah. Similarly, Jesus' instructions that Peter, James and John not disclose their experience of his transfiguration until after the resurrection (9:9) implies the necessity of his death as seen in the following dialog (cf. 9:11-13). Finally, it hardly comes as coincidental that Jesus' only explicit affirmation of his identity as "Messiah" takes place before the Sanhedrin (14:61-62 in the trial scene that leads directly to his sentence to death by Pilate under the indictment "king of the Jews," a view certainly implicit in Peter's confession (cf. 8:32) and in the glory* of the Transfiguration (cf. 9:1). Consequently, for the reader the Jewish religious leaders' unbelieving mockery of the crucified "Messiah, king of Israel" declares in fact who Jesus really is.

Mark's narrative, therefore, affirms the early Christian traditional statement of the gospel, "Christ (the Messiah) died for our sins according to the Scriptures . . ." (1 Cor 15:3; cf. Mk 10:45; 14:22-24). Yet as crucial as Jesus' death is to his identity as the Messiah for Mark, Jesus was not simply a dying Messiah, that is, a Messiah identified by his death. His earthly ministry, which led to Peter's confession "You are the Messiah," and his promised future role in the kingdom when he "will drink it (the fruit of the vine*) new in the kingdom of God" on "that day" (14:25; cf. 13:32) are also essential ingredients in Jesus' identity as Messiah. Mark's "gospel concerning Jesus Messiah" (1:1) is the "gospel from God" (1:14) relating Jesus' inauguration of God's kingdom—God's redemptive rule in history—in the present through a ministry culminating in his death and his continued role in the kingdom that is coming "in power" (9:1) in the future.

3.2.2. Son of God. Jesus is also seen as "the Son of God" (*see* Son of God) in Mark. In fact some interpreters would say that "Son of God" is Mark's particular designation for Jesus. It stands in the opening line of the Gospel alongside "Jesus Messiah" (1:1). Though omitted by some early Greek manuscripts, "Jesus Messiah, *Son of God*" represents the preferable reading and stands in tandem in Mark's narrative with the climactic concluding confession of Jesus as "Son of God" by the Roman centurion at the cross (15:39). The identification of Jesus as God's Son in 1:1 also finds its confirmation by the voice from heaven that declares at the baptism, "You are my son" (1:11). As noted above, this statement of sonship echoes Psalm 2:7, with its royal overtones consistent with the joint expression "Messiah, Son of God" in 1:1. Yet the voice also refers to Jesus as "my beloved son," a qualification foreign to Psalm 2:7 but used in Gen 22:2, 13, 16 (LXX) to refer to Isaac as Abraham's (*see* Abraham) "only" or "unique" son. Therefore, as God's "beloved Son," Jesus has a special *role* (= "anointed king," Ps 2:7) and *relationship* (= "my son, the only/beloved one," Gen 22) with God. The latter underlies the "beloved son" in the parable of the wicked vineyard keepers (12:1-12), the reference to "the Son's" lack of knowledge in 13:32, and certainly Jesus' prayer* to the "Father" (*Abba*) in Gethsemane* (14:36).

Both Jesus' role and relationship as the Son of God may explain the demons' use of "Son of God" in addressing him. In the first miracle* of Mark's Gospel, an exorcism (1:23-27), the demon addresses Jesus as "the Holy One of God," a designation suggesting a unique role and relationship of Jesus to God (1:25), though not specifically identifying Jesus as the Son of God. But in a statement summarizing the demons' response to Jesus in 3:11 they consistently address him directly as "the Son of God," and in 5:7 the Gerasene demoniac addressed Jesus as "the Son of the Most High God" (5:7). The Evangelist indirectly assures the reader of the validity of this identification by noting in 1:34 that Jesus would not permit the exorcised demons to speak "because they knew him" and by noting in 3:12 that Jesus ordered the demons, who had identified him as the Son of God, not to make him known. The exorcisms as such point for Mark to Jesus' authority as the Son of God to defeat Satan and his forces, a demonstration of the establishment of God's redemptive rule by conquering the enemy or "binding the strong man" (3:22-27).

In the Transfiguration* scene, which follows Jesus' declaration that some standing with him would not "taste death until they see that the kingdom of God has come with power" (9:1), the voice from heaven declares to Peter, James and John: "This is my beloved son . . ." (9:7). The context appears to affirm Jesus' role as the Messiah, whose revelation, along with the coming of the kingdom with power, are anticipated by Jesus' Transfiguration and the disciples' experience on the mountain (*see* Mountain and Wilderness). Yet, as was the case with the demons, Jesus orders the disciples not to reveal what they had experienced, including his identity as God's Son, until after the resurrection (9:9).

In the high priest's question—"Are you the Messiah, the Son of the Blessed?" (14:61)—the two designations of "Messiah" and "Son of God" explicitly come together again. Since "Son of the Blessed" represents a Jewish circumlocution for "Son of God," one has here an echo of the opening statement about "Jesus Messiah, Son of God" (1:1). Obviously the high priest's question reflects the royal motif of sonship present in Psalm 2:7, whose roots extend back to Nathan's promise to David that his son would know God as "father" and God would know him as "son" (2 Sam 7:14).

After affirming that he was indeed the "Messiah, Son of the Blessed" (14:62), Jesus immediately warns the Sanhedrin that they would see "the Son of man seated on the right hand of power and coming with the clouds of heaven" (14:62). At that the high priest tore his clothes and charged Jesus with blasphemy (14:63-64). The basis for this charge has been disputed. It most likely has more to do with Jesus' follow-up response when he appears to lay claim to God's role of judge (cf. the similar charge in 2:7 for usurping God's right to forgive sins) than with his affirmative response to the question of his being the "Messiah, Son of the Blessed."

Finally, the passion narrative reaches a climax with Jesus' death, the rending of the Temple curtain, and the response by the Roman centurion in 15:37-39. In contrast to the *Jewish* religious authorities who stood at the cross mocking Jesus as the "Messiah, king of Israel" (15:32), the *Roman* centurion publicly declares, "Truly, this man was God's Son!" (15:39). In this way the two designations, "Messiah" and "Son of God," come together once again, both qualified and clarified by the cross. Mark's opening statement about the gospel concerning "Jesus Messiah, Son of God" has now come full circle in these words from the final scenes at the cross.

Jesus for Mark, then, is the "Son of God" in his role as "Messiah, Son of God" (1:1; 14:61-62; 15:32, 39). At the same time, as God's Son, Jesus has a special relationship with God that sets him apart (cf. 1:11 and 9:7, "my *beloved* son"; the Father and the Son, 13:32 and 14:36; and the "beloved son" of the vineyard owner, 12:6). Nevertheless, the Roman centurion's climactic confession of Jesus as God's Son at the end of the passion narrative affirms for Mark and his readers that Jesus as "Son of God," like Jesus as "Messiah," takes on special coloring in the light of the cross.

3.2.3. Son of Man. Mark opens and concludes his narrative by identifying Jesus as the "Messiah, Son of God" (1:1; 15:32, 39; cf. 1:11; 8:29; 9:9; 14:61-62), but the designation that occurs most frequently is "Son of man" (*see* Son of Man). Appearing only twice and in close proximity in the first half of the Gospel (2:10, 28), the expression appears thirteen times from 8:31 through 14:62. Contrary to "Christ" and "Son of God," "Son of man" is used exclusively by Jesus and always with reference to himself in Mark's narrative and never with the accompanying qualifications or reticence that mark the use of the other designations.

Twice Jesus uses "Son of man" to refer to his authoritative earthly ministry—"to forgive sins on earth" (2:10) and as "Lord of the Sabbath" (2:28). Each of these references in the first half of Mark's narrative do, however, carry an ominous tone. The former comes in the context of the charge of blasphemy, a capital crime (2:7). The latter comes in the context of Sabbath* conflicts that culminate in a conspiracy to have him killed (cf. 3:6). Three times Jesus uses Son of man to refer to the future coming of the Son of man as judge at the consummation (8:28; 13:26; 14:62). And two of these references appear in the larger context of Jesus' impending death—8:38 follows the passion prediction of 8:31 and the reference to taking up one's cross (8:34), while 14:62 comes in the trial before the Sanhedrin and evokes the charge of the capital crime of blasphemy and its consequent death sentence (14:64).

It follows, therefore, that the bulk of the Son of man references in Mark have to do specifically with Jesus' impending suffering and death. Three occur within explicit passion predictions about the suffering and death of the Son of man (8:31; 9:31; 10:33). Five other usages echo motifs found in these passion predictions (9:9, 12; 14:21 [2x], 41). And 10:45 explains the significance of the coming passion by declaring that the "Son of man came not to be served but to serve and to give his life a ransom for many." Therefore, like "Messiah" and "Son of God," "Son of man" also stands under the shadow of the cross in the multiple, direct references to his coming death, a shadow that hangs over even the references to the Son of man's authoritative earthly ministry and his coming role as judge at the consummation.

However, in contrast to the use of "Messiah" and "Son of God" in Mark, Jesus publicly and without qualification refers to himself as the "Son of man" before friend and foe—the disciples (8:31, 38; 9:9, 12, 31; 10:33, 45; 13:26; 14:21, 41), the scribes* (2:10), the Pharisees (3:28) and the Sanhedrin (14:62). Furthermore, Jesus never cautions against the use of this designation as he does with the use of "Messiah" and "Son of God." Nor does he qualify it by the use of another clarifying designation or statement as he consistently does with "Messiah" and "Son of God." Yet the reader never doubts from the first to the last occurrence that "Son of man" refers to anyone but Jesus. Consequently, for Mark "Son of man" functions simply as a self-designation by Jesus, a way of referring to himself without any inherent christological overtones, as with "Messiah" or "Son of God."

If Son of man has so little christological weight, why then does Mark have Jesus refer to himself as the "Son of man"? One can only hazard a suggestion. First, Mark's use most likely has its roots in Jesus' own ministry and choice of "Son of man" as a self-designation. Thus, Mark would simply have been faithfully reflecting the tradition stemming from Jesus' practice of using "Son of man" as a self-designation. Second, the extensive scholarly discussion of the background and meaning of "Son of man" indicates at least the ambiguity surrounding its meaning and use. It hardly seems to have given a clear messianic signal to the hearer, certainly not in Mark's Gospel. This ambiguity was appropriate not only to the hiddenness that marked Jesus' christological identity during his earthly ministry but was especially appropriate to the "messianic secret" in Mark which the nuanced uses of "Messiah" and "Son of God" reflected. Therefore, "Son of man" denoted a self-designation by Jesus but carried little of the christological or messianic overtones of "Messiah" and "Son of God" for Mark.

3.3. The Messianic Secret. Since W. Wrede's epoch-making work *The Messianic Secret* (*Das Messiasgeheimnis in den Evangelien,* 1901), Mark's emphasis on the "messianic secret" has highlighted the discussion of Mark's theology. Without doubt this motif stands out in Mark's Gospel when compared to the other Gospels. A closer look shows that it correlates with Mark's christology as seen above.

3.3.1. Silencing the Demons. We find this motif first in Jesus' response to the demons. In the first miracle, an exorcism, the demon addresses Jesus as "Jesus from Nazareth . . . the Holy One of God" (1:25). Jesus then rebukes the demon by silencing and exorcising him (1:26). On the surface Jesus' command of silence offers little out of the ordinary for an exorcism, since the use of a name and the counter by a silence command represent the common ingredients of the power struggle between a demon and a first-century exorcist. The use of the name was a common attempt by either the demon or the exorcist to gain power or control and the silence command was a move to overcome that attempt in the exorcism.

Yet in Mark the use of the name by the demon and the silence command hardly have their typical exorcistic function. First, the demons or the demon possessed in Mark's Gospel are never in a power position with Jesus. The exorcisms are marked by a total absence of the demons' struggle or resistance to Jesus. Furthermore, their immediate reaction to Jesus betrays the recognition of their subjugation or defeat from the outset (cf. "You have come to destroy *us,*" 1:24; their prostration before Jesus, 3:10; 5:6; 9:20). Second, Mark reveals his own understanding of the silence command to be a secrecy command in the summary statements of 1:34 and 3:11 where Jesus prohibits the exorcised demons from speaking "because they knew him" (1:34) to be the "Son of God" (3:10). Third, Mark's understanding that the silence command is a secrecy command rather than a part of the exorcistic pattern is further supported by the absence of any silence command in contexts where Jesus' identity was not an issue (cf. 5:1-20; 7:24-30; 9:14-29). Consequently, Mark clearly qualifies the demons' correct identification of Jesus as the Son of God by having Jesus silence them, commanding them to keep it a secret.

3.3.2. Silencing the Disciples. Similarly, Jesus gives a silence command to his disciples who know who he is. In 8:30 Jesus prohibits the disciples from making public that he is the Messiah, as correctly confessed by Peter (8:29) in contrast to the public's view of him as a prophet (8:27-28; cf. 6:14-16). In 9:9 he prohibits Peter, James and John from making known what they had experienced at the Transfiguration, including the voice from heaven that identified Jesus as "my beloved son." But here we learn the temporal limits of this silence command. They were only to keep this a secret "until after the Son of man had risen from the dead." Consequently, Jesus' identity as the Messiah and Son of God could not be revealed publicly until after the cross and resurrection, a motif commensurate with Jesus' qualification of Peter's confession (8:29) by his announcement of the coming suffering, death and resurrection of the Son of man (8:31).

In other words Mark's messianic secret corresponds to his portrait of Jesus as Messiah, Son of God whose true significance could only be grasped in the light of the cross. Mark's portrait consistently identifies Jesus as Messiah, Son of God both in the light of his ministry on earth (cf. 1:25; 3:10; 8:29) and his future glory (9:7; cf. 9:1). But he qualifies this identity by Jesus' death as the Messiah, Son of God (8:30-31; 9:9; 14:61-64; 15:25-32, 39). In so doing, the Evangelist accents Jesus' death as part of the significance of Jesus' identity as Messiah, Son of God without denying the corresponding aspects of his earthly ministry or his future role. Therefore, Mark's messianic secret qualifies Jesus' identity as Messiah, Son of God without attempting in any way to conceal who Jesus really is until a later time.

3.3.3. Broken Silences. But what about the times when the silence command is broken? In the healing of the leper (1:40-45; *see* Leprosy) and the deaf stutterer (7:31-37), Jesus' silence command is explicitly broken (cf. 5:20-21). And one can only assume the silence command to Jairus' family would be broken in view of the public awareness of the girl's death (5:21-43).

Yet in none of these instances is Jesus' identity *per se* at stake, only his actions. Furthermore, these actions involve a healing. Silence commands were also characteristic of healing stories in the ancient world. They intended to keep the means or healing formulas a secret. Obviously, for Mark these silence commands no longer applied to Jesus' healing technique, since none is given in the cleansing of the leper (1:40-45) and the formulas (*Talitha cum* and *Ephphata*) are actually translated for the reader (5:41; 7:34). Rather in these instances Jesus' silence command seems to evoke the opposite response in 1:44-45 and 3:37. When the opposite response is noted (cf. 5:21-43), however, the contrary behavior results in large crowds (1:45; 8:1-8) and sets the stage for Jesus' next move in the story line (cf. 6:1-6).

Therefore, these silence commands, once functioning as a part of the healing narrative, have little to do with the healing secret or the messianic secret in Mark

and have more to do now with the story line of Mark's Gospel. These commands and their contrary behavior function as literary devices to set the stage by providing crowds for the next event in Jesus' ministry, a role not played by the other silence commands directed at the demons and the disciples.

3.4. Discipleship. Mark's emphasis on discipleship becomes quite evident from the place he gives the disciples in the structure of his narrative (*see* Disciple; Discipleship). Not only does the story of Jesus' ministry open with the calling of Peter, Andrew, James and John (1:16-20), but pericopes involving the disciples begin each of the three constituent sections (1:16-20 in 1:16—3:12; 3:13-19 in 3:13—6:6; 6:7-13 in 6:7—8:26) of the second part of the Gospel. In the third part (8:27—16:8) the disciples form Jesus' primary audience within the section (8:27—10:52). They accompany Jesus to Jerusalem as his constant companions in the second section (11:1—13:37) and remain on the scene in the final section (14:1—16:8) until their flight highlighted by Peter's denial (14:50, 66-72). Despite their failure, the story ends as it begins, with a final reference to the disciples. The messenger at the tomb gives the women a message of hope for "the disciples and Peter" (16:7).

3.4.1. Who Are the Disciples in Mark? Actually, one finds both a narrower circle comprised of the Twelve who are called to be "with him" and specially commissioned to share in his ministry of teaching, healing and exorcism (3:13-14; cf. 5:18; 6:7-13, 30) and a larger circle who also are called (e.g., Levi 2:13), commissioned (e.g., 5:19-20) "followers" (e.g., 2:15-17). Both groups are beneficiaries of Jesus' miraculous works (e.g., 1:40-45; 6:45-52), teaching (e.g., 3:20, 31-35; 4:10-20) and company (e.g., 2:15-17; 3:13-14; 3:20, 31-35). Yet most of the references to the disciples appear to denote the narrower circle and its members who are accorded special privileges (e.g., 5:21-43; 9:2-8; 14:12-25) and given special teaching (e.g., 7:17-23; 10:10-12; 13:3-37; 14:22-25).

3.4.2. The Failure of the Disciples. Nevertheless, Mark portrays the disciples in a less-than-positive light. They fail to understand Jesus' teaching in parables (e.g., 4:13, cf. 4:34; 7:18), on divorce* (10:10-12) and especially about his coming death (8:32-33; 9:9-13, 32). They fail to understand what he does when he calms the storm (4:35-41) and walks on the water (6:45-52). Indeed, they fail to understand fully who he is, as seen by Peter's response to the passion prediction in 8:31-33, a failure that constantly reappears throughout the section of 8:27—10:52, as well as in their behavior at his arrest and trial.

3.4.3. The Leaven of the Pharisees and Herod. One

pericope in particular portrays their halting relationship with Jesus, the warning against the leaven of the Pharisees* and Herod* (8:14-21). The warning comes at the end of the first half of the Gospel, which has focused on Jesus' public ministry (1:16—8:26), and follows the two feeding miracles (6:34-44; 8:1-9). And it is enclosed by a reference to Herod's question about Jesus (6:14-17) and the Pharisee's request for a sign (8:11-13). Within this context Mark points out the weakness in the disciples' faith relationship to Jesus.

First, recognizing their concern about having failed to bring sufficient provisions with them (8:14, 16), Jesus warns the disciples about the "leaven of the Pharisees and Herod" (8:15). Within the Markan context this can only refer to their failure like Herod (6:16) and the Pharisees (8:10-12) to comprehend who Jesus really was. Second, Jesus specifically asks if they do not "perceive and understand" or if their "hearts are hardened" (8:17; cf. 6:52), a trait ascribed earlier to the Pharisees for their failure to recognize Jesus for who he was (3:5). Third, citing the words of Jeremiah 5:21, Jesus asks if having eyes they do not see and ears they do not hear (8:18). These words echo the motif first sounded in the earlier citation of Isaiah 6:9 to describe "those outside" (4:12). Jesus' response to the disciples' concern about lack of sufficient provisions betrays a lack of faith (cf. 4:35-41; 6:45-52) dangerously comparable to the response of Herod, the Pharisees and the outsiders, despite their having been "given the mystery of the kingdom of God" (4:11). Finally, Jesus asks the disciples specifically about the amount of leftovers from the feedings of the five and four thousand respectively (8:19-20) before concluding once again with the question "Do you not yet understand?" (8:21).

Although the disciples seem precariously close to the leaven of Herod and the Pharisees as they respond to Jesus in the hour of their own need (cf. 4:35-41; 6:45-52), their special role, privilege and response in the previous Markan narrative has shown them to be different. Yet, as the next story about the blind man (8:22-26) indicates, their sight is at best partial. Their response to Jesus' teaching and his coming death in 8:27—14:63 demonstrates even more clearly their need for the second touch.

3.4.4. The Cost of Discipleship. Indeed their response and behavior following the three Son of man passion predictions in 8:27—10:52 become the basis for Jesus' teaching on discipleship in 8:27—10:52. Their failure to recognize his coming death in 8:31-33; 9:31-32; 10:33 leads to Jesus' teaching about the cost of discipleship and the way of the cross (8:34-38), about status and kingdom conduct (9:33—10:31), and about

the inverse nature of greatness illustrated ultimately by Jesus coming to serve as the Son of man (10:34-45). In this way Mark uses the disciples as a means of addressing what discipleship really means when lived in the already/not yet of God's redemptive activity in Christ. Just as the way of Jesus Messiah, Son of God had to be set in the light of the cross, so those who would follow Jesus must see discipleship, with all its privilege and promise, set on "the way" of Jesus Messiah, Son of God.

4. Mark's Ending.

As it now stands, 16:8 offers the best attested ending of Mark's Gospel: "They went out and fled from the tomb, for they were trembling and astonished. They said nothing to anyone. For they were afraid." The abruptness of this ending and the resurrection appearances in the Gospels of Matthew, Luke and John (implied by the promise of Mark 14:7) have led to the conclusion that a more complete ending has been lost. The so-called shorter and longer endings (vv. 9-20) to Mark's Gospel represent attempts to provide an appropriate ending. Yet both the external evidence drawn from the witness of the ancient manuscript traditions and the internal evidence based on vocabulary and style rule against the authenticity of any extant ending other than Mark 16:8 as it stands. The evidence, however, obviously cannot prove that 16:8 was the original ending, since a longer ending could have been lost prior to the earliest manuscript evidence we possess.

Indeed, Mark hardly intended for his readers to think that his story of "the gospel concerning Jesus Messiah, Son of God" (1:1) ended with the women's failure. The evidence for this is varied: the Transfiguration, followed by the command that the disciples not reveal it until after the resurrection (9:2-9), the promise of the coming of the Son of man in 13:26 following a mission period entailing much suffering (cf. 13:9-13), the warning to the Sanhedrin about the coming Son of man (14:62). All of these elements correspond to the anticipation of the future found in the parables of the kingdom of 4:1-34 and make clear that Mark's story, the "gospel," does not end with 16:8. The cross and the empty tomb are not the end. Jesus' role as Messiah, Son of God, has a future chapter. Furthermore, Mark's readers certainly knew of the resurrection appearances and the mission of the church. The conviction that the story continued on doubtless led to the so-called shorter ending: "They promptly announced to Peter all they had been told. After these things Jesus himself sent the holy and imperishable proclamation of the eternal salvation from East to West through them."

Yet when one looks at Mark's narrative from the standpoint of a literary text, the present ending fits his literary pattern quite well. The ultimate climax of Mark's story comes at the crucifixion and death of Jesus with the ironic taunts of the Jewish leaders and the declaration by the Roman centurion that show Jesus to indeed be the "Messiah, Son of God," as introduced in the opening statement (15:32-39; cf. 1:1). Furthermore, the disciples have repeatedly failed throughout the narrative to grasp the total import of Jesus and his teaching. Their failure never altered Jesus' course as the "Messiah, Son of God" (cf. 4:35-41; 6:45-52; 8:14-21; 8:27—14:63). Nor did this failure, as dangerous as it may have been for the disciples (cf. 8:14-21), lead to Jesus' giving up on the disciples. In fact their most glaring failure comes in their flight at his arrest (14:50) and Peter's denial (14:66-72). Yet the message of 16:7 is addressed to "the disciples and Peter."

The women, who enter the scene at the cross (15:40-41), note Jesus' place of burial (15:47) and come to the tomb to anoint him (16:1), pick up where the disciples left off. But they too "are afraid" (cf. 4:41; 6:50). With a final touch of irony, one of Mark's favorite literary devices, the women fail to disclose (they "tell no one") Jesus' resurrection, even though commanded to do so (16:7). But the leper at the beginning of the Gospel proclaims what he has been commanded to "tell no one" (1:44-45; cf. 8:36). On the one hand the present ending corresponds with Mark's portrait of the disciples, and on the other hand it leaves open both the future fulfillment of Jesus' promise to meet the disciples in Galilee (cf. Mk 14:28) and the glorious future of the Parousia (13:26-37).

5. Mark's Purpose.

Despite numerous attempts to find Mark's purpose in the theological struggles (e.g., christology) or social circumstances of the early church (e.g., the fall of Jerusalem), the rather generic character of the story (lacking specific clues about place and date of authorship) and the narrative integrity of the Gospel makes such historical or theological reconstructions at best speculative. Taken on its own terms, the leading characters—Jesus and the disciples—and the nature of the conflict motif provide the best clues for understanding the author's design in writing this Gospel.

Once again we appeal to 1:1 as a statement of what the author intended to do, namely, write the "gospel concerning Jesus Messiah, Son of God." For the Evangelist this Gospel clearly shows Jesus as coming to inaugurate God's sovereign rule, the kingdom, as seen in the programmatic summary of Jesus' ministry in 1:14-15. At the same time God's sovereign rule, the kingdom, has a future component that will appear "in power" (9:1) when the Son of man comes to bring God's salvation to its consummation (13:26-37). But why did the Evangelist write this Gospel?

This "gospel" according to Mark corresponds to Isaiah's promised good news of God's rule and salvation (Is 52:7) as proclaimed by Jesus (1:14), but it contains within it the question of how God's promised sovereign rule could be both present and future. In what sense was Jesus "Messiah, Son of God," since he was crucified rather than crowned in Jerusalem?

The confusion was no less intense in Mark's day than in Jesus' own experience. Drawing on the disciples, who doubtless reflect the confusion of Jesus' followers, Mark uses them to illustrate the standpoint of his own privileged and perplexed community. By focusing on who Jesus was in his repeated reminders throughout the narrative (e.g., 1:11; 1:25; 1:34; 3:11; 5:7; 8:27-29; 9:7; 14:61-62; 15:39), the Evangelist reassured his readers that Jesus was indeed the "Messiah, Son of God." This was seen not only in his authoritative defeat of Satan, his forgiveness of sinners, his healing the sick, his feeding the hungry and his raising the dead, but above all in his death (e.g., 8:27-31; 14:61-62; 15:39).

By emphasizing in the seed parables (4:1-20, 26-29, 30-32) that the kingdom is present but vulnerable, warning about troubling times (13:3-37), issuing silence commands, hinting of a mortal conflict, making explicit statements of coming death, the rejection of family, friends and the religious establishment, and, finally, setting the centurion's climactic confession in the light of the cross, the Evangelist warns his readers against any triumphalist reading of the Gospel. Mark's own readers needed to know that God had indeed acted decisively, "the time has been fulfilled" (1:15) in Jesus Messiah, Son of God, but the way of discipleship was also the way of the cross (8:34-38). Right thinking and right faith must issue in right living. Right living was the way of the cross.

We conclude that pastoral concern was foremost in Mark's mind as he wrote the "gospel concerning Jesus Messiah, Son of God." He wanted to address a community under duress, a duress that may well have given rise to questions about who Jesus really was and the nature of the kingdom he had come to inaugurate. This Gospel offered a renewed basis for their faith, made clear the trials and tribulations along the journey of that faith, and offered the hope of the kingdom future when the harvest, the full-grown mustard tree, the resurrection and the consummation of God's salvation would make all things right.

See also JOHN, GOSPEL OF; LUKE, GOSPEL OF; MATTHEW, GOSPEL OF.

BIBLIOGRAPHY. **Commentaries:** H. Anderson, *The Gospel of Mark* (NCB; Grand Rapids: Eerdmans, 1981); C. E. B. Cranfield, *The Gospel according to St. Mark* (CGTC; Cambridge: University Press, 1963); J. Gnilka, *Das Evangelium nach Markus* (EKK 2; 2 vols.; Zürich: Benziger/Neukirchen-Vluyn: Neukirchener, 1978, 1979); R. A. Guelich, *Mark 1-8:26* (WBC 34a; Waco: Word, 1989); L. Hurtado, *Mark* (NIBC; Peabody, MA: Hendrickson, 1983); W. L. Lane, *The Gospel according to Mark* (NICNT; Grand Rapids: Eerdmans, 1974); D. Lührmann, *Das Markusevangelium* (HNT 3; Tübingen: J. C. B. Mohr, 1987); D. E. Nineham, *The Gospel of St. Mark* (New York: Penguin, 1963); R. Pesch, *Das Markusevangelium* (HTKNT 2; 2 vols.; Freiburg: Herder, 1976, 1980); E. Schweizer, *The Good News According to Mark* (Richmond: John Knox, 1970); V. Taylor, *The Gospel according to St Mark* (2d ed; New York: St Martin's, 1966); **Studies:** E. Best, *Following Jesus: Discipleship in the Gospel of Mark* (JSNTS 4; Sheffield: JSOT, 1981); idem, *Mark: The Gospel As Story* (Philadelphia: Fortress, 1983); M. Hengel, *Studies in the Gospel of Mark* (Minneapolis: Fortress, 1985); H. C. Kee, *Community of the New Age: Studies in the Gospel of Mark* (Philadelphia: Westminster, 1977); W. Kelber, *The Kingdom in Mark: A New Place and a New Time* (Philadelphia: Fortress, 1974); J. D. Kingsbury, *Conflict in Mark* (Minneapolis: Fortress, 1989); idem, *The Christology of Mark's Gospel* (Philadelphia: Fortress, 1989); A. T. Lincoln, "The Promise and the Failure—Mark 16:7, 8," *JBL* 108 (1989) 283-300; R. P. Martin, *Mark: Evangelist and Theologian* (Grand Rapids: Zondervan, 1973); W. Marxsen, *Mark the Evangelist: Studies on the Redaction History of the Gospel* (Nashville: Abingdon, 1969); R. P. Meye, *Jesus and the Twelve: Discipleship and Revelation in Mark's Gospel* (Grand Rapids: Eerdmans, 1968); C. Myers, *Binding the Strong Man: A Political Reading of Mark's Story of Jesus* (Maryknoll, NY: Orbis, 1988); E. J. Pryke, *Redactional Style in the Marcan Gospel* (SNTSMS 33; Cambridge: University Press, 1978); D. Rhodes and D. Miche, *Mark As Story* (Philadelphia: Fortress, 1982); C. M. Tuckett, ed., *The Messianic Secret* (IRT 1; Philadelphia: Fortress, 1983); T. J. Weeden, *Mark: Traditions in Conflict* (Philadelphia: Fortress, 1971).

R. A. Guelich

MARRIAGE. *See* DIVORCE; ETHICS OF JESUS.

MARY. *See* BIRTH OF JESUS; MARY'S SONG; WOMEN.

MARY'S SONG

The traditional name for Mary's hymn of praise in Luke 1:46-55 is the *Magnificat,* a translation of Luke 1:46 in Jerome's Latin text, which begins: *Magnificat anima mea Dominum* ("my soul magnifies the Lord"). Perhaps the best known and loved of the four lyrical psalms in the Lukan infancy narrative (see also the *Benedictus,* Lk 1:68-79; the *Gloria in Excelsis,* Lk 2:14; the *Nunc Dimittis,* Lk 2:29-32; *see* Birth of Jesus), Mary's Song has for centuries been incorporated into the liturgies, hymnody and art of many Christian traditions.

Some early textual traditions and patristic writers proposed that the hymn was originally attributed to Elizabeth, but the consensus of authoritative textual traditions, witnesses of the church and critical scholarship favors the traditional view in attributing the hymn to Mary. Attempts to identify the life setting of the Song have yielded proposals of an early Greek-speaking Jewish Christian community, and a Jewish-Christian circle of the poor ones, or *'ānāwîm* (a remnant of Israel's economically poor who lived in pious dependence on God*; *see* Rich and Poor). Certainly the Song's predominant dependence on the Septuagint (LXX) or Greek OT is indicated by the Greek forms of the OT verses involved.

Mary's Song echoes OT traditions in which men and women sang hymns of praise in response to God's mighty deeds in the life of the people Israel* (Moses, Ex 15:1-18; Miriam, Ex 15:19-21; Deborah, Judg 5:1-31; *see* Worship). The close literary, stylistic and thematic parallels between Mary's Song and the Song of Hannah in 1 Samuel 2:1-10 has led many interpreters to conclude that the Song of Hannah served as the model for Mary's sonorous poem. Mary, like Hannah, extols God's greatness (Lk 1:46-49; 1 Sam 2:1-10). Both Mary and Hannah are called God's "handmaiden," or "maidservant," underscoring their availability to God (Lk 1:48; 1 Sam 1:11). Both women acknowledge that God's purposes will be accomplished through the birth of their respective child (Lk 1:32-35, 46-50; 1 Sam 1:11, 21-28). Striking points of comparison have also been noted between Mary's Song and the Song of Moses (Ex 15:1-18), the Song of Asaph (1 Chron 16:7-36) and hymns of praise in the canonical psalms (Ps 33; 47; 136).

Structurally, this beautiful hymn of praise begins with an introduction (Lk 1:46b-47) in which Mary proclaims Yahweh's greatness and recognizes Yahweh as her Savior.* The theme of salvation is thus sounded at the very outset of the poem. Verses 48-50 reveal Mary's motives for praising God. Mary was a mere Palestinian peasant girl, but God chose her as an agent through whom the divine promises would be fulfilled in the person of Jesus, the Son of God (Lk 1:31-34; *see* Son of God). She is blessed, not because she is pregnant, or because of any intrinsic holiness or merit but because God's salvific purposes are being accomplished through her. Mary thus becomes one in a long line of recipients of God's grace and mercy* in salvation history (Lk 1:50).

Verses 51-53 set forth Yahweh's great deeds. The six verbs in the aorist tense (the simple past tense) in this section have been interpreted as referring to God's past redemptive actions toward Israel (e.g., the Exodus event, Deut 5:15). As Luke is also interpreting in retrospect the significance of the life, death (*see* Death of Jesus) and resurrection* of Jesus (post-resurrection soteriology), the celebration of Yahweh's mighty acts in the career of Jesus may also be in view. The carefully constructed climax of this section betrays creative literary artistry with a concluding chiasm: mighty/humble: hungry/rich. Yahweh "puts down the mighty from their thrones" and "exalts those of low degree" (RSV). This reversal motif (cf. 1 Sam 2:7-8; Job 5:8-11; Is 2:11; 5:15-16; Ezek 17:24; 21:25-26; Mt 23:11-12; Jas 1:9) suggests a new order of life and hope wherein God is at work in both the lives of individuals and in the whole social order. This emphasis forecasts a theme that Luke will develop in his succeeding Gospel narrative: God is not only mighty, holy and merciful toward all of those who fear God (Lk 1:49-50, 54), but the dawning of the messianic age reveals God's continued deep regard for the widow, the orphan, the lowly, the hungry and the poor (Deut 15:7-11; Lev 19:9-18; Is 1:12-17; Amos 2:6-7). Jesus' programmatic statement in the Temple* affirms this concern about those on the social and economic margins of society (Lk 4:18-19), as do the Lukan Beatitudes and Woes (Lk 6:20-26; *see* Sermon on the Mount).

The poem concludes in verses 54-55 with a rehearsal of the availability of God's mercy in every generation, and that particularly through God's servant Israel. It is through the covenant that God made with Abraham* and his posterity that God's promises and mercy will extend to all peoples in all generations.

Mary's Song resonates with grateful and expectant joy. Mary as mother of the Son of the Most High (*see* Son of God) and the King in the line of David (Lk 1:31-33; *see* Son of David) is presented as both lowly handmaiden and active (believing) agent in Christian salvation. This canticle of grace foreshadows several recurrent themes which will unfold in Luke's two-volume work Luke-Acts, including the use of speeches and citations to provide advance summaries of the

Christian kerygma (Lk 3:3-6; 4:16-20; Acts 2:17-21); the accent on the fulfillment of God's promises (Lk 7:20-27; Acts 13:16-40); the grateful celebration of salvation (Lk 2:13, 20; 13:17; Acts 2:43-47; 3:1-16; 5:40-42); and the favor which Jesus showed toward women* (Lk 7:12-17; 8:1-3; 10:38-42; 11:27-28; 13:10-17). The central theme of the Song, the celebration of God's fulfillment of the promises of old through the birth of Jesus the Christ, represents the heart of the enduring message and the empowering legacy of Mary's Song for generations of Christian believers.

See also BIRTH OF JESUS; SIMEON'S SONG; WORSHIP; ZECHARIAH'S SONG.

BIBLIOGRAPHY. P. Bemile, *The Magnificat within the Context and Framework of Lukan Theology* (RST 34; New York: Peter Lang, 1986); R. E. Brown, "The Annunciation to Mary, the Visitation, and the Magnificat (Luke 1:26-56)," *Worship* 62 (1988) 249-59; idem, *The Birth of the Messiah: A Commentary on the Infancy Narratives in Matthew and Luke* (New York: Doubleday, 1977); S. Farris, *The Hymns of Luke's Infancy Narratives: Their Origin, Meaning and Significance* (JSNTSup 9; Sheffield: JSOT, 1985); J. A. Fitzmyer, *The Gospel according to Luke I-IX* (AB 28; New York: Doubleday, 1981); P. S. Minear, "Luke's Use of the Birth Stories," in *Studies in Luke-Acts*, ed. L. E. Keck and J. L. Martyn (Philadelphia: Fortress, 1966); R. Reuther, "She's a Sign of God's Liberating Power," *The Other Side* 104 (1980) 17-21; R. C. Tannehill, *The Narrative Unity of Luke-Acts: A Literary Interpretation* (2 vols.; Philadelphia: Fortress, 1986) 1.26-32; D. M. Scholer, "The Magnificat (Luke 1:46-55): Reflections on Its Hermeneutical History," in *Conflict and Context: Hermeneutics in the Americas*, ed. M. Lau Branson and C. R. Padilla (Grand Rapids: Eerdmans, 1986) 210-19.   C. J. Martin

MASTER. *See* TEACHER.

MATTHEW. *See* DISCIPLES.

MATTHEW, GOSPEL OF

1. The Origin of Matthew
2. The Structure of Matthew
3. The Theology of Matthew

1. The Origin of Matthew.

In order to find an adequate solution to the question of the origin of Matthew's Gospel, a series of interrelated questions must be answered: Who is the author or who are the authors? What is the date of its composition(s)? What is its relationship to the other Gospel traditions and Gospels? Satisfactory answers to each of these questions, however intertwined they may be, will yield the most probable solution to the mystery of Matthew's origin.

1.1. The Papias Logion. A strategic place to begin is with the traditional view that the apostle Matthew wrote a Gospel in Hebrew or Aramaic (*see* Languages of Palestine). This tradition stems from the testimony of Papias, bishop of Hierapolis in Phrygia (died c. A.D. 130). The record of Papias's statement about Matthew survives only in Eusebius (*Hist. Eccl.* 3.39.16). It reads, "Matthew collected *(synetaxato)* the oracles *(ta logia)* in the Hebrew language *(Hebraidi dialektō)*, and each interpreted *(hērmēneusen)* them as best he could." On first analysis the tradition of Papias appears to say that the apostle Matthew wrote a Gospel in Hebrew or Aramaic, and various translations were made of his work. So it was apparently understood, with minor modifications, in the early churches (for texts see Orchard and Riley, 111-226).

Irenaeus confirms this analysis, adding that the First Gospel was composed while Peter and Paul were founding the church in Rome (*Haer.* 3.1.1; from Eusebius, *Hist. Eccl.* 5.8.2). Eusebius corroborates the Semitic origin in a legend concerning Pantaenus, who reportedly discovered a Semitic Matthew, supposedly brought to India (or Arabia) by Bartholomew (*Hist. Eccl.* 5.10.3). Origen affirms this tradition, adding only that the First Gospel was written for Jewish believers (*Hist. Eccl.* 6.25.4). In addition to passing on these traditions, Eusebius himself states that the occasion for the First Gospel was Matthew's departure from Palestine (*Hist. Eccl.* 3.24.6). Further support for this traditional understanding of the origin of Matthew can be found in Cyril of Jerusalem (*Cat.* 14), Epiphanius (*Haer.* 30.3) and Jerome (*Prol. in Matt.; Praef. in Quat. Ev.; Vir.* 3).

In more recent times, however, this tradition has been given several interpretations. First, some scholars have argued that the apostle Matthew penned an original Aramaic Gospel which was later translated into Greek by an unknown Christian (though some have contended that Matthew himself also translated the work). This Greek Gospel, it is argued, is substantially the same as the Aramaic Gospel (see the NT introductions of D. Guthrie, T. Zahn and the commentaries of Lagrange, Tasker, Maier; see also Wenham).

Second, others have argued that Matthew himself composed an original Aramaic collection of the sayings of Jesus (sometimes clearly identified with Q*), and this was later translated and augmented with Markan traditions, probably after A.D. 70 (see, with variations, the commentaries of Meyer, Hill, Allen, Plummer; see also Martin, Manson, Moule).

Third, some scholars have challenged this interpretation of the early Christian evidence. In effect these scholars contend that an original Aramaic Gospel is a faulty inference from the evidence and this contention is buttressed with the arguments that (at least) substantial portions of Matthew were not penned by Matthew and that the linguistic evidence suggests that the Gospel was originally composed in Greek (Nepper-Christensen, Bacon, Strecker, Meier; the commentaries of Beare, Green, Grundmann, Schniewind; the introductions of Kümmel, Marxsen).

This variety of interpretations compels us to look again at Papias, the apparent source of most of the early church traditions.

First, in light of Eusebius's previous reference to Mark as an "arrangement of the Lord's oracles" (*Hist. Eccl.* 3.39.15), wherein the same word *oracles (logia)* is used as in the Matthean reference, it is most probable that *logia* in "Matthew collected the oracles *(logia)*" refers to the entire Gospel, rendering the second interpretation discussed above unlikely. Second, although a majority of scholars have inferred that "in the Hebrew language *(Hebraidi dialektō)*" means a Gospel written either in Hebrew or Aramaic, recent scholarship has virtually overturned this interpretation.

It has been argued (1) that Matthew betrays no evidence of being a translated Gospel; (2) that the Greek expression *Hebraidi dialektō*, when investigated carefully in its Asia Minor context, means not "in the Hebrew *language*" but "in a Hebrew rhetorical style" (Kürzinger, 9-32; Gundry, 619-20); (3) that the context shows that Papias is comparing Matthew's *style* ("orderly" and "in a Hebrew style") with Mark's style ("chreia* form" [*pros tas chreias*], "not, indeed, in order"; 3.39.15), and (4) that "interpreted" *(hērmēneusen)* in Papias's statement (3.39.16) most probably refers to the explanation and communication of Matthew's style by others rather than its translation (Kürzinger, 15-19; Gundry, 619). Prior to this statement about Matthew, Papias, according to Eusebius, had said that Mark was Peter's interpreter *(hērmēneutes)*. This most likely refers not to Mark's translation of Peter's words but to his interpretation and composition of Peter's words into the form of a Gospel.

In conclusion, the most recent scholarship on the Papias logion suggests that the traditional rendering is insufficient and should be understood now in the following manner: In contrast to Mark's unordered, chreia-style Gospel, Papias contends, Matthew composed a more Jewish, orderly styled Gospel. The original language, then, is of no concern to Papias. This suggests that the first interpretation is unlikely. In all likelihood our Gospel of Matthew was composed originally in Greek and in a Jewish style. But was the First Gospel composed by an apostle?

1.2. Was the Author the Apostle? Although there is an impressive list of scholars who argue that the First Gospel was apostolic (the commentators: Zahn, Lagrange, Schlatter, Tasker, Albright and Mann, Maier, Gundry, Carson), there are several arguments that have been used to argue that the First Gospel was not penned by the apostle Matthew.

Foremost, it is argued that if the First Gospel used Mark as its primary source, it is most unlikely that an apostle (Matthew) would need to borrow from a non-apostolic source (Mark) (e.g., the commentators Allen, Schniewind, Grundmann, Beare; see also Bacon, Martin). This observation appears most penetrating when one observes that, assuming Matthew used Mark, the supposed apostolic author largely copied Mark's account of his own call (Mt 9:9-13 par. Mk 2:13-17). However significant this objection may seem, and however many esteemed scholars rely on this source-critical argument, it is not finally persuasive. If one simply grants that Peter somehow stands behind Mark—and early Christian evidence supports this view (Eusebius *Hist. Eccl.* 3.39.15)—thereby lending it some level of apostolic authority, then Matthew's use of Mark is hardly beneath apostolic dignity.

Second, it is argued that the author did not write the Gospel in Aramaic or Hebrew but wrote in Greek, and that therefore the author could not have been the apostle Matthew (esp. Strecker). This argument has some important features: To be sure, it is now clear that our present Gospel is most likely not originally an Aramaic or Hebrew Gospel. In fact, it often betrays its Greek origin in Greek word plays (e.g., 6:16; 21:41; 24:30) and its dependence on the Septuagint (1:23; 11:10; 12:21; 13:14-15; 21:16). However, evidence clearly pointing toward a Greek original is not proof of a Gentile (or non-apostolic) author. Matthew, having been a tax collector (*see* Taxes), would very likely have been quite versatile in several languages. The argument over language proves little.

Third, various scholars (e.g., Abel, Strecker) have pointed to features that suggest to them a Gentile author. These features include: (1) the universalism of the First Gospel (2:1-12; 4:14-16; 12:21; 28:19) when coupled with the condemnation of the Jewish nation (20:1-16; 21:28-32, 43; 27:25); (2) the torture of 18:34, which was not a Jewish practice (Jeremias 1972, 210-14); (3) the so-called misunderstood Hebrew parallelism of 21:5-7; and (4) various other non-Jewish features (5:43; 12:11-12; 27:5). For these scholars, this data points away from a Jewish (apostolic) author and toward a Gentile author. Without going into details

regarding each of these pieces of evidence (and each of those listed in 2-4 is not easy to explain), it must be said that neither universalism nor a clear stance against unbelieving Judaism* (see McKnight, forthcoming) is evidence for non-Jewish authorship. There is nothing ideological in the First Gospel that is not also found in either the OT prophets or in the letters of Paul, sources which are clearly Jewish in origin.

A final argument lodged against apostolic authorship pertains to the *date* of the First Gospel. If we assume (as the majority of scholarship does) that Matthew used Mark (*see* Synoptic Problem), and if Mark was written in the late 60s, say 68-70 (but before the destruction of Jerusalem in A.D. 70 [*see* Destruction of Jerusalem]; see Hengel, 1-30), then it follows that the First Gospel was written sometime after A.D. 70. Making allowance for enough time for Mark to circulate and gain authority, most scholars estimate that Matthew would have been written a decade later. If we grant that Mark could have been written as early as the mid-60s, we have the earliest possible date for Matthew between A.D. 75-80, with a date between A.D. 75-85 being widely held (the commentators Bonnard, Grundmann, Davies and Allison). Could the apostle Matthew have penned the Gospel that late? Perhaps so. Earliest Christian evidence does not suggest that Matthew died before A.D. 70 and so traditional authorship is not excluded even with a date as late as A.D. 85.

It follows from the preceding arguments that the traditional view that the First Gospel was authored by the apostle Matthew is a reasonable position. However, this conclusion is not without problems. Several issues caution against regarding the authorship of the First Gospel a settled matter. (1) The later one dates Matthew after the destruction the less likely it becomes that its author was the apostle. Furthermore (2) its probable use of Mark and (3) its evidently Greek origin should give one pause. Further (4) the several problems with respect to Jewish customs make one hesitate in coming to a firm conclusion regarding authorship. (5) If Matthew used Mark, it is at best peculiar that Matthew would have recorded his own conversion by copying Mark (cf. Mt 9:9-13 with Mk 2:13-17). Finally (6) it needs to be noted that textual critics are agreed that the original copy of the First Gospel did not contain an ascription of authorship to Matthew. This means that the matter of authorship has nothing to do with canon or with interpretation of the original; it is simply an intriguing historical issue on which scholars have cast some illuminating, but not yet definitive, light.

2. The Structure of Matthew.

Over the last twenty years Matthean scholars have engaged in an important discussion centered on the structure of Matthew's Gospel (see Bauer, 21-55). A summary of this discussion will permit the reader to gain a glimpse of the First Gospel in its entirety. Four major models for understanding the structure of Matthew have been proposed. Following an overview of these models, a synthetic proposal will be presented.

2.1. Geographical-Biographical. The oldest, and perhaps simplest, is the *geographical-biographical* model. This proposal organizes Matthew according to a suggested outline of the life of Jesus as he moves through his Galilean and Jerusalem ministries. In his commentary on Matthew (1912) W. C. Allen proposed the following:

1. The Birth and Infancy of the Messiah (1:1—2:23)
2. Preparation for Ministry (3:1—4:11)
3. Public Ministry in Galilee (4:12—15:20)
4. Ministry in the Neighborhood of Galilee (15:21—18:35)
5. Journey to Jerusalem (19:1—20:34)
6. Last Days of the Messiah's Life (21:1—28:20)

Several features dominate this perspective on Matthew: (1) The view is harmonious with nineteenth- and early twentieth-century views of the life of Jesus; (2) the life of Jesus so predominates that a feature from Luke (the so-called travel narrative) finds its way into Matthew, though Matthew gives no serious attention to the travel at all (e.g., Mt 19:1—20:34); (3) the progress of Gospel studies in the last two centuries has drawn more and more attention to the various presentations of the Evangelists, and this aspect of Matthew has been completely neglected. Consequently, although many of the older commentaries used this essential outline (e.g., Zahn, Plummer, McNeile, Lagrange, Schlatter), few would follow it today. Rather, it is recognized that this approach reflects a preoccupation of the nineteenth-century Gospel studies: how to compose a life of Jesus (*see* Historical Jesus).

2.2. Fivefold Discourse. Matthean scholarship changed when B. W. Bacon proposed his *fivefold topical model* (1918 and 1930). Bacon presented an entirely new outline, one based on Matthew's clear alternation between narrative and discourse. Departing from the life-of-Jesus approach, he took a literary perspective. Moreover, Bacon argued, Matthew's use of five major discourses reveals a christological tendency: Jesus is a new Moses* who gives a new Law* for the church. Bacon's proposal follows:

Preamble (1:1—2:23)

1. Book 1: Concerning Discipleship (3:1—7:29)
2. Book 2: Concerning Apostleship (8:1—11:1)
3. Book 3: Concerning Hiding Revelation (11:2—13:53)
4. Book 4: Concerning Church Administration (13:54—19:1a)
5. Book 5: Concerning the Judgment (19:1b—26:2)
Epilog (26:3—28:20)

Apart from relegating the passion (*see* Passion Narrative) and resurrection* narratives (26:2—28:20) only to an epilog, Bacon made a great advance for Matthean studies by paying attention to Matthew's own structuring devices. Accordingly, we are indebted to Bacon when we call attention to Matthew's major structural marker for the discourses (7:28; 11:1; 13:53; 19:1; 26:1: "And when Jesus had finished these things . . ."). We must also credit Bacon with transforming the obvious alternation between narrative and discourse in Matthew from a banal observation to a significant key to Matthew's structural plan. However, Bacon's suggestion of a Pentateuchal pattern behind Matthew's five discourses was not accepted and further modifications were made to his view (see esp. Farrer, Barr, Bauer).

2.3. Chiastic/Concentric. Anticipating the trend of literary analysis, C. H. Lohr proposed that Matthew's Gospel was arranged chiastically (or concentrically). That is, each earlier section of the Gospel is related to a later section, which are in turn arranged in reverse order from the center ("F" below):

1. Narrative: Birth and Beginnings (1—4) A
2. Sermon: Blessings, Entering the Kingdom (5—7) B
3. Narrative: Authority and Invitation (8—9) C
4. Sermon: Mission (10) D
5. Narrative: Rejection by this Generation (11—12) E
6. Sermon: Parables of the Kingdom (13) F
7. Narrative: Acknowledgment by the Disciples (14—17) E'
8. Sermon: Community Discourse (18) D'
9. Narrative: Authority and Invitation (19—22) C'
10. Sermon: Woes, Coming of the Kingdom (23—25) B'
11. Narrative: Death and Rebirth (26—28) A'

Lohr's theory (and those who have modified his essential view; see Bauer, Fenton, Gooding, Combrink, Rolland, Gaechter) has several important features. Besides recognizing Matthew's structural alternation between narrative and discourse, the proposal observes the connections between various sections of Matthew as well as the various topics that Matthew develops. However, Lohr's approach has been widely criticized for its failure to heed chronological features inherent to the text itself as well as its fancifulness in connecting various sections. One example will suffice: it may be structurally pleasing to say that chapters 1—4 are birth and beginnings and chapters 26—28 are death and rebirth, but this does not represent the theological and literary content of these important sections of Matthew. Any skilled literary artist (or homiletician) can find connections of this sort at the abstract level, but such constructions fail at the level of exegesis and details.

2.4. Biographical and Theological. The fourth proposal, a *biographical and theological model*, has commanded the most discussion as well as consent. This model, originally developed by N. B. Stonehouse and then improved by E. Krentz, has been fully worked out by J. D. Kingsbury and D. R. Bauer. In essence this model recognizes an essential biographical aspect to the drama of Matthew's Gospel but sees it as subservient to an overall theological program. Matthew leaves clues to this structure through a superscription device: namely, at 4:17 and 16:21 Matthew uses an expression ("From that time on Jesus began . . .") that signals the outset of a new division. This provides a neat and useful threefold division to the Gospel.

1. The Person of Jesus Messiah (1:1—4:16)

2. The Proclamation of Jesus Messiah (4:17—16:20)

3. The Suffering, Death and Resurrection of Jesus Messiah (16:21—28:20)

The alternatives are clear: either the structural devices of alternating narratives and discourses, or the repetition of the formula at 4:17 and 16:21 are to be given the structural priority. Scholars have argued that (1) the additional use of the superscription formula at 26:16 as well as (2) the essential use of Mark 8:31 at Matthew 16:21 (rather than a unique signal in Matthew) suggest that Kingsbury has gone too far in making Matthew 4:17 and 16:21 structurally determinative. In fact, it can be said that though 16:21 may have been a major turning point in Jesus' actual life, it is not a necessary turning point in Matthew's structural plot. Kingsbury has elevated to the level of a structuring device a Markan comment on the life of Jesus that Matthew has incorporated into his Gospel. In neither Gospel was it intended to play such a role.

2.5. Considerations for Determining Matthew's Structure. In light of the above survey several features must be incorporated into any adequate proposal for understanding Matthew's structure.

First, it must determine the *genre* of the Synoptic Gospels and, in particular, the *genre* of Matthew (*see* Gospel [Genre]). P. L. Shuler has investigated this matter recently with respect to Matthew and has concluded that Matthew is essentially encomium, or laudatory, biography (see Shuler, Aune).

Second, the structure needs to reckon with the clear theological tendencies of the author. Both redaction critics (*see* Redaction Criticism) and literary critics (Literary Criticism) have expanded our knowledge of the nature of a Synoptic Gospel in highlighting the Evangelist's contributions and literary strategies. The implication of these approaches for structure is a recognition that the Gospels, however biographical, are directed by an author's theological and literary designs. The authors of the Synoptics are more than historians.

Third, at times the structure of sections of Matthew may well be determined by the traditions and sources Matthew inherited. Thus, while we see major innovation on the part of Matthew in chapters 4—13 when compared to Mark, from Matthew 14 on we see very few deviations from the essential Markan structure. One gains the impression that church tradition had grown accustomed to what we now see in Mark and this tradition, rather than the Evangelist's own designs, controlled the direction of Matthew's pen.

Fourth, at times sections in Matthew may be controlled more by theme than by chronology and historical succession. Hence Matthew, in the interest of a more thematic arrangement, may at times reorder and relocate traditions found elsewhere in Mark or Luke. When we look at Matthew's discourses and compare their material with the same material found in either Mark or Luke, we often find that Matthew's arrangement differs and that Matthew's pattern seems to be thematic. For example, the material Luke relates in the context of two different missions (Lk 9:1-6 [cf. Mk 6:6-13]; 10:1-12) Matthew records as only one mission (Mt 9:36—11:1). It is apparent that Matthew has thematically grouped material around "missionary instructions" rather than paying strict attention to chronology. (In the same discourse of Matthew, compare Mt 10:17-25 with Mk 13:9-13; Mt 10:26-33 with Lk 12:2-9; Mt 10:34-36 with Lk 12:51-53; Mt 10:37-39 with Lk 14:26-27 and 17:33.)

Fifth, for a structural proposal to be complete it must pay special attention to Matthew's redactional alterations and arrangements. Hence, in reading a "red letter" edition of Matthew, it may at times be very important to give special attention to the black letters to observe Matthew's authorial angle. Whether that redaction of Matthew pertains to smaller (cf. Mt 11:2 and 11:19 with Lk 7:18 and 7:35; cf. Mt 8:1—9:35 to 10:8 and Mk 6:7 or Lk 9:1-2) or larger (cf. the structural importance of Mt 4:23 and 9:35) units, painstaking observations of details distinct to Matthew are significant for determining Matthew's overall structure.

2.6. A Proposed Structure. As Bacon and Lohr have observed, the most important literary and redactional feature of Matthew's Gospel is an alternation between narrative and discourse. Furthermore, five discourses stand out in relief on the Matthean landscape. These two features are crucial to Matthew's ordering of his material. The following outline organizing these two structural features under an essential biographical or chronological plot:

Prologue (1:1—2:23)
Introduction (3:1—4:11)

1. The Messiah Confronts Israel in His Galilean Ministry (4:12—11:1)
    1.1. Narrative: Introduction (4:12-22)
        Summary (4:23-25)
    1.2. Discourse: The Messiah's Call to Righteousness (5:1—7:29)
    1.3. Narrative: The Messiah's Ministry (8:1—9:34)
        Summary (9:35; cf. 4:23-25)
    1.4. Discourse: The Messiah Extends His Ministry (9:36—11:1)

2. The Responses to the Messiah: Rejection and Acceptance from Galilee to Jerusalem (11:2—20:34)
    2.1. Narrative: The Messiah Is Rejected by Jewish Leaders but Accepted by the Disciples (11:2—12:50)
    2.2. Discourse: The Messiah Teaches about the Kingdom (13:1-53)
    2.3. Narrative: The Messiah Is Rejected by Jewish Leaders but Accepted by the Disciples: Responses Intensify (13:54—17:27)
    2.4. Discourse: The Messiah Instructs on Community Life (18:1—19:1)
    2.5. Narrative: The Messiah Instructs on the Way to Jerusalem (19:2—20:34)

3. The Messiah Inaugurates the Kingdom of Heaven through Rejection and Vindication: Jesus the Messiah Confronts Jerusalem (21:1—28:20)
    3.1. Narrative: The Messiah Confronts Israel in Jerusalem (21:1—22:46)
    3.2. Discourse: The Messiah Predicts the Judgment of Unbelieving Israel (23:1—26:2)
    3.3. Narrative: The Messiah Is Rejected in Jerusalem but Vindicated by God through Resurrection (26:3—28:20)

This outline utilizes the guiding themes (see 3. below) of Matthew for its main points: Jesus as Messiah, kingdom, confrontation, etc. In addition, we make the following observations. First, it needs to be observed that Matthew has essentially two introductions, a prologue (1:1—2:23) and an introduction to the public ministry of Jesus (3:1—4:11). These two introductions stem from two essential traditions: the prologue is derived from Matthew's special material ("M"; *see* M Tradition) and the second introduction is a conflation of Mark's introduction with Q traditions on John the Baptist (*see* John the Baptist) and the temptation of Jesus (*see* Temptation of Jesus). Thus the problem of two introductions is essentially a source-critical matter (*see* Synoptic Problem); Matthew had at his disposal two different ways to begin his Gospel and he chose to use both.

Second, Matthew 4:23 and 9:35 are virtually identical in wording and form an inclusio around the material between them. In fact 4:23 is an outline of 5:1—9:34: Jesus is described in 4:23 as one who teaches and preaches (5:1—7:29) and one who heals all diseases (8:1—9:34; *see* Healing). It appears that 4:23 and 9:35 are a literary device used by Matthew to announce to the reader what is coming (4:23) in 5:1—9:34 and what has transpired (9:35). This device of beginning and ending a section with the same literary form is called an *inclusio*. Furthermore, the essential unity of the first major section, 4:12—11:1, is seen in that the last element of 4:23 and 9:35 is then used for describing what the disciples* are to do—heal every disease and sickness (cf. 10:1). In addition, Jesus' ministry of healing and casting out demons (*see* Demon, Devil, Satan) in 8:1—9:34 is then commanded of the disciples in 10:8. What needs to be noted here is that the missionary commands of Matthew (10:8) are much more complete than those of either Mark (6:7) or Luke (9:1-2), and the commands of Matthew are clearly a repetition of what Jesus has done previously.

Third, in light of these observations it follows that Matthew 4:12—11:1 is essentially a programmatic description of the ministry of Jesus directed toward those who wish to follow him as disciples. Put differently, in 4:12—11:1 Matthew presents Jesus in the fullness of his ministry, thereby enabling readers to decide how they will respond to him. It is therefore of no surprise that the section following 4:12—11:1 is primarily wrapped around various responses to Jesus (11:2—20:34).

Fourth, there are two sections in 11:2—20:34 that are organized around the twin response to Jesus: rejection by leaders and acceptance by the disciples. These sections are 11:2—12:50 and 13:54—17:27, the latter section revealing both deeper acceptance by the disciples (cf. 16:21—17:27) and more radical rejection of Jesus by the leaders (cf. 14:1-12; 15:1-20; 16:1-12). Between these two sections falls the third discourse (13:1-53). To entitle this the "Discourse on Parables*" gives too much attention to form rather than content.

Instead, chapter 13 is concerned with Jesus' parabolic teaching about the nature of the "kingdom of the heavens" (Matthew's literal rendering of a Jewish equivalent to "kingdom of God," hereafter translated "kingdom of heaven"; *see* Kingdom of God). Here we see that the kingdom (1) effects various responses (13:1-9, 18-23), (2) comes silently and nonviolently (13:24-30, 31-32, 33, 36-43), (3) calls for drastic commitment (13:44, 45-46) and (4) has an ethical call that is rooted in God's* final judgment* (13:47-50). Buttressing these teachings are comments by Jesus on the privileged knowledge of the disciples (13:10-17) and the dawn of fulfillment in Jesus' parabolic teaching itself (13:34-35). Those who can understand Jesus' teachings about the kingdom of heaven are compared to scribes who understand all things (13:51-52).

Fifth, perhaps because of Christian familiarity with the final week of Jesus, several comments need to be made about how to read 21:1—28:20. To begin with, in light of Matthew's theology (and NT theology in general), readers need to bear in mind that this section is not just a rehearsal of the last week of Jesus for the convenience of historians or for the liturgical needs of church calendars. Rather, this section tells of the passion and vindication of Jesus that together bring about salvation* for the world. From the Matthean perspective these climactic events inaugurated the kingdom of heaven more fully than had any other event or set of events since the advent of John the Baptist (3:2). Furthermore, there is an essential unity to 21:1—25:46: (1) Jesus enters Jerusalem as Messiah (*see* Christ) to display who he is (21:1-22), (2) he enters into a contest with the Jerusalem authorities to demonstrate his wisdom and calling by God (21:23—22:46), and (3) he then warns the nation that judgment is coming because it has rejected God's appointed Messiah (23:1—25:46).

Due to a keen interest in end-time eschatology,* modern-day evangelicals have frequently separated 23:1-39 from 24:1—25:46. This separation usually leads to major interpretive errors. It is important to recognize that 23:1-39 leads into 24:1-36; the rejection of Jesus Messiah by the leaders prompts Jesus to predict the destruction of Jerusalem (*see* Destruction of Jerusalem). Jesus predicts not the destruction of Judaism but the destruction of Jerusalem, thereby making it clear that he sees God's judgment directed primarily against the Jewish establishment centralized in Jerusalem (see Levine). It follows from this contextual tie (cf. 23:36 and 23:37-39 with 24:1-3, 8, 33, 34 in their uses of "all these things") that the dominant concern of 24:1-36 is the destruction of Jerusalem in

A.D. 70 and not a final tribulation at the end of history. Indeed, it is difficult to interpret 24:29 ("immediately . . .") and 24:34 in any other way than as a primary (if not total) reference to the destruction of Jerusalem in A.D. 70 (see France, 333-48).

3. The Theology of Matthew.

By discussing Matthew's theology we do not imply that the evidence is sufficient for us to infer an entire systematic theology. Rather, what we find in the Gospel of Matthew is a record of the life of Jesus which has been shaped by Matthew in such a way that we can detect emphases and patterns of thought that are the author's. It is these patterns and themes that we describe when we outline Matthew's theology. Matthew certainly believed a great deal more than what we are able to infer, but these themes contribute to our understanding of biblical theology.

When scholars today discuss Matthew's theology as distinct from that of Mark, Luke or John, a subtle but significant difference is being made between the theology of the Evangelist and the teachings of Jesus. Whereas the expression "teachings of Jesus" describes all that Jesus taught as it is found in the four canonical Gospels and elsewhere (with little appreciable being added by sources outside the canonical Gospels), an analysis of Matthew's theology studies the particular contributions and shaping of tradition observable in this particular Gospel. Accordingly, in describing Matthew's theology the scholar looks for the Evangelist's beliefs as they are embedded in the First Gospel and considers what his beliefs meant in their cultural and religious contexts.

There are four major themes in the First Gospel: (1) Christology, or what the Evangelist believed about Jesus Christ, who is the center of Matthew's theology; (2) the kingdom of heaven, which often reveals what he believed about God himself; (3) salvation-history, the conceptual and hermeneutical grid through which Matthew reads and interprets the past, present and future; and (4) discipleship,* the expectation laid upon humans in light of the dawn of the kingdom in Jesus Christ.

3.1. Christology. There have been three major approaches to Matthew's christology. First, many scholars have found in the titles Matthew ascribes to Jesus the decisive clues for constructing Matthew's christology. This approach usually revolves around the centrality of "Son of God" (Kingsbury; *see* Son of God). This approach has the advantage of a clear organizational method for categorizing the evidence. But this method can neglect the fact that the titles ascribed to a person reveal only certain aspects of that person.

Second, others (esp. Hill, Verseput, France, Suggs) have argued that while Son of God is a central title, it must be supplemented by additional ideas in order to achieve a comprehensive and accurate portrayal of Matthew's christology.

Third, in essential support of traditional interpretation of Matthew, B. M. Nolan has argued that Matthew develops a "royal christology" with the predominant category for Jesus being "Messianic King and Son of God."

The first two approaches emphasize an aspect or title of Matthew's portrayal of Christ that is clearly present in the Gospel. But in each case the emphasis is reductionistic, whether or not the title is then augmented with other ideas. In what follows we propose that a larger synthesis, using both titles and functions, describes more comprehensively and accurately the christology of Matthew.

We may summarize Matthew's christology as follows: Jesus is God's Messiah who fulfills OT promise, reveals God's will and inaugurates the kingdom of heaven through his public ministry, passion and resurrection, and consequently, reigns over the new people of God.

3.1.1. Messiah. Even apart from the number of times the title occurs in the First Gospel (1:1, 16, 17, 18; 2:4; 11:2; 16:16, 20; 22:42; 23:10; 26:63, 68; 27:17, 22), for Matthew Jesus is pre-eminently the *Messiah.* The use of the term *Messiah* for Jesus implies a confession that in Jesus the OT promises of restoration and salvation are coming to pass (cf. 2:4; 26:63). For Matthew the term *Messiah* seems inherently to bear some concept of preexistence (2:4; 22:41-46). But primarily the Messiah fulfills the OT in his person and ministry (1:1—2:23; 5:17-48). Thus, according to Matthew's typological exegesis (*see* Typology), Jesus is a sort of new Moses, he brings a new Exodus, and he is a kind of new Israel (1:18—2:23; 3:3; see the commentary of Davies and Allison; France, 185-91). Further, he brings the fulfillment of the Law* and prophets (3:15; 5:17-48; 12:17-21; 13:35; 21:5, 16, 42; 22:44; 23:39; 26:31; 27:9, 35, 46) and has become the suffering and rejected Servant of Yahweh (3:17; 8:17; 10:35; 12:17-21; 13:14-15; 21:5, 42; 23:39; 26:31, 38; 27:9, 35, 46; *see* Servant of Yahweh).

As Messiah, Jesus is described at several crucial junctures in the Gospel as "Son of God." In fact J. D. Kingsbury has contended in numerous writings that Matthew regards *Son of God* as the central and most theologically laden term used for Jesus (see Kingsbury). Thus at 3:17 the Father announces publicly "this is my Son" (cf. with Mk 1:11 and Lk 3:22: "you are my Son"); at 4:3, 6 the devil addresses Jesus as

God's Son; at 11:27 Jesus refers to his special relationship to God as that of a son to a father; at 14:33 the men in the boat, on seeing a marvel beyond description, confess Jesus as God's Son; at 16:16 Matthew apparently glosses Peter's confession of Jesus as God's Messiah with "Son of the living God"; at 17:5 the Father again announces to the inner circle that Jesus is the Son of God; at 24:36 Jesus reveals that, in spite of his privileged knowledge of God's will, not even he, the Son of God, knows the date of the Parousia; at 26:63 the high priest explains the term *Messiah* with "Son of God"; at 27:40, 43 the passersby appeal to Jesus as Son of God to tempt him to come down from his ignominious crucifixion; and at 27:54 the Gentile centurion confesses Jesus, in what is taken by many to be the climax of human perception in the First Gospel, to be the Son of God.

In light of the preceding survey, it is not surprising that many scholars have argued that "Son of God" is the most important title in Matthew. While one cannot doubt its crucial or central role as a title, the issue is not so much which title is more important, but what does the First Gospel assert about Jesus in light of what he says, does and is called. Thus a more functional (and less titular) approach gives us a more comprehensive and accurate picture. And, while it may be true that Son of God is highly important, it remains the case that two of the instances of "Son of God" are explained by the concept of Jesus as God's servant (3:17—4:11; 16:16 and 16:21).

As Messiah, Jesus is also the destined king of Israel, in spite of his crucifixion. To be Messiah is to be the king of Israel (2:2; 21:5; 27:11, 29, 37, 42). But even though Jesus is Messiah, king of Israel, he is a unique king because he is God's unique Son and he reigns through his suffering (27:11, 29, 37, 42; cf. also the rejection inherent at 2:2 and 2:1-12; see Hill, Gerhardsson 1974).

3.1.2. Teacher and Preacher. For Matthew, Jesus Messiah *reveals God's will.* Jesus Messiah teaches and reveals God's will in his public ministry, but his teaching and preaching are largely ignored or rejected. Although the terms have fallen out of favor with Matthean scholars, *teacher** and *preacher* are important categories for understanding the Jesus of Matthew. Even if it is clear that *teacher* (i.e., rabbi) is inadequate for fully comprehending the nature of Jesus' person and mission, Matthew evidently regarded this category as nonetheless vital for understanding him. Thus, the very structure of Matthew, punctuated as it is by five major discourses (nine chapters), leads the reader to think of Jesus as a great teacher, a special rabbi, a revealer of wisdom* (esp. chaps. 5—7; 13; 18). In scholarship's tendency to go beyond "teacher" for describing Jesus, it has bypassed this important category. To be sure, it is non-disciples in Matthew who describe Jesus as teacher (cf. 8:19; 9:11; 12:38; 17:24; 19:16; 22:16, 24, 36), while the disciples of Jesus never call him "teacher." On the other hand, Jesus does describe himself as teacher (10:24, 25; 23:8; 26:18), and his ministry, according to Matthew, revolves around teaching God's will as revealed in the new age (3:15; 5:17-48; 11:27; 13:10-17; 23:8). As teacher, Jesus will suffer (10:24-25).

One of Jesus' messianic tasks is to *preach* the gospel of the kingdom of heaven (4:17, 23; 9:35), a message requiring repentance and obedience to God's will (4:17). Interestingly, as the preacher of the gospel Jesus falls in line with the rejected prophets of Israel (5:10-12; 23:34-39; 24:14) and John the Baptist (3:1-2; 14:1-13). A motif running through Matthew's presentation of Jesus as revealer of God's will is the rejection of his teaching and preaching (cf. 11:1—12:50).

3.1.3. Inaugurator of the Kingdom. Another important feature of Matthew's christology is that Jesus Messiah *inaugurates the kingdom of heaven,* apparently in three moments or phases: in his public ministry, in his passion and in his vindicating resurrection. Each of these moments is important to the story line of Matthew and each is associated with the inauguration of the kingdom. Hence, we have chosen to speak of three "moments" or "phases" of the inauguration of the kingdom of heaven in Matthew. In the First Gospel it is absolutely critical to recognize that Jesus' primary calling is to inaugurate the kingdom of heaven.

In his *public ministry* Jesus anticipates the kingdom's inauguration (4:17; *engiken* means "has drawn near but is not yet here"), but that kingdom begins to demonstrate its presence especially through Jesus' mighty deeds of wonder (*see* Kingdom of God). Thus Jesus points to his powerful miracles as evidence of the inauguration of the kingdom (11:2-6; 12:28; see Gerhardsson 1979; Held). As Son of David (*see* Son of David), Jesus is healer (9:32-34; 12:24), but it is also important to observe that Matthew connects Jesus' mighty works with his ministry as servant and his atoning sacrifice (8:16-17; 12:15-21; 27:51-53; cf. Allison, 40-50). In Jesus' public ministry we must also observe that Jesus' revelatory teaching and preaching is an integral aspect of the beginning of the inauguration of the kingdom of heaven as Jesus teaches the "ethic of the New Era" or, as others have put it, "kingdom ethics." These teachings (e.g., 5:17-20) are an integral aspect of the dawning of the kingdom (also Guelich, 134-74; Giesen; *see* Ethics of Jesus).

In his *passion* Jesus accomplishes the second phase of the inauguration of the kingdom of heaven (*see* Death of Jesus). Even if it is a commonplace to observe that the Gospels have given much attention to the passion story of Jesus—and so we point to the cruciform nature of the earliest Christian story about Jesus—it is nonetheless important to incorporate this very structure into our understanding of Matthew's theology. If it is true that Matthew anticipates to some degree the kingdom of God being inaugurated (cf. 4:17; 20:28), it is reasonable to expect that the passion itself, the story of Jesus' rejection and death, will be an important phase in its inauguration.

We can observe the importance of the passion for Matthew's telling of the story of Jesus in the fourfold prediction of Jesus' death and rejection (16:21; 17:22-23; 20:18-19; 26:2). As mentioned above, even the mighty miracles of Jesus are seen as proleptic realizations of the kingdom on the basis of the passion ministry of Jesus (8:16-17). For Matthew, Jesus is the one who forgives sins (9:6) and the Son of man (*see* Son of Man) who will ransom many through his self-sacrifice (20:28). This latter passage clearly suggests an integral connection between the death of Jesus (*see* Death of Jesus), the forgiveness of sins (*see* Forgiveness of Sins) and the kingdom of God. And in the Last Supper Matthew again makes similar connections: Jesus' blood, forgiveness, anticipation of the consummation of the kingdom (26:29).

When it comes to describing the passion itself, the Gospel writers are notoriously silent in their reflection on its soteriological significance. However, in Matthew we find several indications that Matthew, among other things, sees the kingdom of God being inaugurated through Jesus' passion and rejection (Allison, 40-50). First, the connection of Jesus' death (27:50) with the resurrection of the holy ones (27:51-53), with its clear allusion to Zechariah 14:4-5 (LXX), indicates for Matthew that Jesus' death breaks the bonds of death and inaugurates the general resurrection (a clear end-time, or kingdom, expectation). Second, the confession of the Gentile* centurion (27:54) may well be a sign of the commencement of Gentile salvation that was to occur at the end of history (universalism; cf. 2:1-12; 4:12-17; 8:5-13, 28-34; 12:38-42; 15:21-28; 21:33-46; 22:1-14; 24:14; 28:16-20). And Matthew tightens the connection between Jesus' death, the resurrection of the saints and the confession of the Gentile centurion (and others with him) by adding "When . . . they saw the earthquake and what took place . . ." (27:54 RSV). Finally, the connection of the themes of 26:64 with their partial realization in 28:16-20 suggests another instance wherein the passion and rejection of Jesus is described as the inauguration of the kingdom of heaven. Thus Matthew's treatment of his traditions, as well as his addition of new ones, indicates that he sees the death of Jesus as an important phase in the inauguration of the kingdom of heaven.

In his *resurrection* Jesus is vindicated, and this too is a phase in the inauguration of the kingdom. Matthew's narrative of the resurrection (27:62—28:20) gives indications of his seeing the resurrection of Jesus as the inauguration of a new epoch in history. The descriptive language of 28:2-4, with its report of the earthquake, the descent of the angel* and the fear of the guards borrows heavily from language shared by texts rooted in Jewish eschatological speculation. As Allison has put it, "Matthew 28:2-4 appears to recount the events of Easter morning as though they were events of the last times" (48).

Matthew's eschatological orientation becomes particularly apparent when we examine the Great Commission (28:16-20). There we observe massive reorientations in history, revealing quite clearly that a new epoch has dawned as a result of Jesus' resurrection. First, although it is true that prior to his resurrection the Father has given Jesus personal authority* (5:17-48; 7:29; 21:23, 24, 27) and authority over sickness and demons (9:6, 8; 10:1), that authority is only fully granted after his resurrection (28:18: "all authority"). Christologically, Jesus has moved from one acting with authority within the narrow confines of Palestine to one who possesses universal sovereign authority.

Second, as with Mark and Luke, throughout Matthew's Gospel Jesus is regularly vindicated in the face of opposition. Thus, in line with the essence of a pronouncement story (*see* Form Criticism), Jesus is victoriously vindicated as God's special messenger (e.g., 12:1-8). It follows that the resurrection of Jesus is God's unique and final vindication of his Son following a momentary victory by his opponents (cf. 27:39-44 and 28:1-10; Osborne, 73-98).

Third, Matthew's heavy emphasis on universalism (see 3.1.6. above) reaches its consummation in Jesus' command to disciple the entire world (28:19). The people of Jesus includes those of all nations, all social levels and both genders (Levine, 165-92). What was previously prohibited (10:5-6, "Do not go among the Gentiles") is now the culminating command (28:19); those who were previously exceptions (8:5-13; 15:21-28) are now the focus. And, in continuity with the old era, the new era does not erase Israel from God's plan of salvation. On the contrary, the term *nations* includes Jews alongside Gentiles (see Levine, 185-92). A subtle reminder of Matthew's attempt to evangelize

Jews may be observed in Matthew's narrative of the guards at the tomb, the appearance of the angel and the women's encounter with Jesus (27:62-66; 28:5-7, 9-10). The manner in which this material speaks about Jews and addresses Jewish concerns demonstrates a clear apologetic tendency. The rescinding of the previous prohibition against evangelizing the Gentiles and the proclamation of a new duty of evangelizing the nations reveals that Matthew sees the resurrection of Jesus as inaugurating a new age.

Finally, it is no overstatement to say that the Great Commission envisions the formation of a new people of God, founded no doubt on the disciples of Jesus. This new people of God Matthew calls "the church*" (16:18; 18:17). The commission to form this new people reveals that something new is happening as a result of Jesus' resurrection. Thus the final scenes of Matthew show Jesus now vindicated by God as Messiah, invested with all authority, and commissioning the disciples to disciple the world.

Although the three phases of the inauguration of the kingdom sketched above are only different (chronologically distinct) aspects of the ministry of Jesus, they each contribute to the inauguration of that kingdom. In general, through Jesus God inaugurated the kingdom of heaven; in particular, God has done this through Jesus' public ministry, his passion and most climactically through his resurrection. But what is the kingdom of heaven?

3.2. The Kingdom of Heaven. In general, we can say the kingdom of heaven is God's reign through Jesus Christ over all people, and that those who repent (*see* Repentance) and believe (*see* Faith) in Jesus enter into God's reign in the present. The experience of God's sovereign reign brings with it righteousness* and joy* as well as the hope of its future consummation in glory* at the Parousia of the Son of man (*see* Apocalyptic Teaching). An inevitable consequence of the conviction that the kingdom of heaven has come through Jesus Messiah is the judgment against any who do not respond properly to Jesus Messiah.

For Matthew the *kingdom of heaven* (literally, "kingdom of heavens"; *see* Kingdom of God) is both present (6:33; 11:12; 12:28; 13:24-30, 36-43; 16:19; 23:13) and future (4:17; 5:19; 8:12; 16:28; 25:1-13; 26:29). This teaching both of the kingdom's presence and its futurity has led a vast number of interpreters to speak of "inaugurated eschatology" in the teachings of Jesus and the Evangelists (see Kingsbury, 128-60; Ladd; Jeremias). This article operates from this understanding and maintains that the essential orientation of Jesus himself did not revolve exclusively around the presence of the kingdom of God but around its potentiality or futurity and the impact that its nearness was to make on the present. Interpreters disagree on the time of its full realization. The following presentation works from a view that sees the kingdom being inaugurated in three phases (public ministry, passion and resurrection, to which Luke adds Pentecost). We also assume that the kingdom of God has a future finality to it that can be described as the consummation of the kingdom.

In its *present* aspects the kingdom (1) demonstrates itself in God's strength and power (10:7-8; 12:28; 16:28; *see* Authority and Power); (2) is opposed by cosmic powers and their human allies (11:12; 13:24-30; 23:13); (3) demands responsible, righteous behavior (4:17; 5:20; 6:33; 7:21; 13:44-45; 18:3, 23; 19:12, 23-24; 21:31-32; 24:14); (4) is presently (for Jesus) Jewish but includes the unlikely or the marginal and will in the future be universal (5:3, 10; 8:11-12; 13:31-32; 19:14; 21:31, 43; 22:1-14; 23:13; 24:14); and (5) warns of judgment on those who do not respond appropriately (16:19; 21:43).

In its *future* aspects the kingdom of heaven (1) will be brought to consummation at the Parousia of the Son of man (13:24-30, 36-43, 47-50; 16:28; 25:1-13); (2) will begin with a judgment by God (8:12; 18:3; 19:23-24; 20:1-16; 22:1-14; 25:1-13); and (3) will be characterized by God's final approbation of his people (5:19; 8:12; 11:11; 13:43; 18:1, 3, 4; 20:1-16; 25:31-46; 26:29). In spite of the importance of the kingdom of heaven for Matthew's theology, there has been very little scholarly discussion on the particular nuances of Matthew's view of the kingdom.

3.3. Salvation History. Salvation history is an expression scholars use to describe the manner in which God acts in the past, present and future in redeeming people from sin and calling them to become his own. In another sense, salvation-history refers to the development of God's salvific purposes in history. In this latter sense the expression is used for tracing the history of God's actions for the salvation of persons. In Gospel studies the expression *salvation history* is used similarly to the second sense: it refers to how each Evangelist conceives of God's history of redemption.

3.3.1. Proposals for Understanding Matthew's View of Salvation History. The history of the discussion of Matthew's view of salvation history was initially shaped by H. Conzelmann's important study, *The Theology of St. Luke* (1960), which explored Luke's concept of salvation-history. Conzelmann concluded that Luke saw salvation history as divided into three periods: (1) Israel*; (2) Jesus, the "Center of Time"; and (3) the church. Conzelmann's work on Luke has

led Matthean scholars to debate whether or not Matthew saw history in two periods (Israel and church/Jesus) or three (Israel, Jesus, church). There have been four major approaches to Matthew's view of salvation history. R. Walker has argued that Matthew's scheme of salvation history is oriented around *mission*. Three major periods emerge: (1) The pre-history of the Messiah; (2) the calling of Israel through John the Baptist, Jesus and the resurrected Lord; and (3) the Gentile mission beginning at A.D. 70. Essentially, Walker sees the history of salvation in terms of the mission to the world. A.-J. Levine also observes a mission pattern in Matthew, though she differs radically on how Matthew sees the future of Israel. Levine sees two axes in Matthew's salvation-history, one temporal and the other social. The temporal axis moves through two periods, from Israelite privilege to universalism, and the social axis represents the incorporation of the marginal elements of a patriarchal society into the new people of God. Unlike Walker, Levine sees the major shift coming at the Great Commission, not at A.D. 70.

Second, an *ecclesiastical* orientation has been articulated by W. G. Thompson. Emphasizing the present situation of Matthew's church, Thompson's detailed analysis of 24:4b-14 has rendered three periods: (1) Abraham* and Israel, (2) Jesus' offer to Israel and its Jewish opposition, and (3) the church's offer to the Gentiles and its Gentile opposition. Thompson concludes that Matthew views the third period as largely future.

Third, J. D. Kingsbury has expounded a *christological* orientation to Matthew's salvation-history, demonstrating the importance of integrating the various motifs in Matthew's theology. Kingsbury sees two periods: (1) the time of Israel (ending with 3:1) and (2) the time of Jesus Messiah (beginning with 3:1 and ending with the Parousia). In the latter period there are three sub-periods: (a) John to Jesus, (b) post-Easter times and (c) the consummation of history at the end. Kingsbury bases his view on Matthew's non-distinction between Israel and the church, the "transparency of the disciples" (i.e., they are typological equivalents to the church of Matthew and not just historical figures) and the absence of time references related to the church. Although Kingsbury's analysis has thrown fresh light on Matthew's views, his neglect of significant events in Matthew's description of history and the future (including John the Baptist in 11:11-12; the destruction of Jerusalem; the Gentile mission as seen from 10:5-6 and 28:16-20) call for a modification of his schema.

Fourth, an *apocalyptic* orientation has been utilized

by J. P. Meier to explain the data in Matthew. Meier approaches Matthew from the perspective of Jewish apocalyptic* which sees major acts of God altering the course of history. Meier sees three periods: (1) Israel, (2) Jesus until the cross and resurrection, and (3) the consummation, which includes the Gentile mission.

3.3.2. A New Synthesis. In presenting a modification and synthesis of the above views, several introductory remarks need to be made. First, the issue of whether there are two or three periods in Matthew's scheme of salvation-history is a subordinate point to which the Evangelist seems oblivious. Second, Kingsbury is surely right in pleading for an integration of Matthew's view of history with his christology, particularly because the latter is the most important aspect of Matthew's theology. Third, one's view of the function of the canon as it relates to systematic theology or hermeneutics will undoubtedly influence how one perceives Matthew's view of salvation-history. For example, among evangelicals covenant theologians will tend to stress the continuities in Matthew's scheme, and dispensationalists will emphasize the discontinuities. Finally, one's view must derive from careful consideration of texts that speak in salvation-historical terms, texts that include 1:1-17; 3:1-12; 5:17-20; 9:14-17; 11:2-19; 16:13-28; 21:33—22:14; 23:1—25:46; 27:51-53; 28:1-10; 28:16-20.

The following outline of Matthew's concept of salvation-history attempts to synthesize both the data and the scholarly positions sketched above. There are basically six periods in Matthew's scheme: (1) The time of anticipatory revelation and promise, (2) the time of transition with John the Baptist, (3) the time of the Messiah's inauguration of the kingdom of heaven, (4) the time of Israel's decision, (5) the time of all nations and (6) the time of the consummation.

(1) *The Time of Anticipatory Revelation and Promise.* In Matthew's perspective the past, particularly the period from Abraham to David and then from David until the birth of Jesus Messiah (1:1-17), was a time of God's salvation but more especially the time of anticipatory promise. This period from Abraham onward pointed to, prefigured and awaited with promises the inauguration of the kingdom through God's Son. Thus the fulfillment of the OT in Jesus' ministry is an indication that the past is a time of promise and anticipation (1:23; 2:6, 15, 18, 23; 4:12-16; 12:15-21; 13:35). This past was a time in which revelation was restricted to one nation, Israel (4:12-16), and a time when God's Law was incompletely revealed (5:17-48).

(2) *The Time of Transition with John the Baptist.* Although scholars have debated whether 11:11-12 implies that John's ministry was prior to the inaugu-

ration of the kingdom or post-inauguration, it may be said with fairness that John was the transitional prophet* from anticipation to inauguration. Thus it is John who first announces the dawning of the kingdom and the call to the kingdom's righteousness (3:2; 21:28-32), who first announces the end of nationalism (3:7-10), who points to the kingdom's Messiah (3:11-12) and who, along with Jesus, "fulfills all righteousness" (3:15; *see* Justice, Righteousness; John the Baptist). Indeed, Jesus refers to John's transitional status by saying that he was greater than all humans prior to him but less than the "least" (*mikroteros)* in the kingdom of heaven (11:11). John marks a decisive turning point in God's redemptive plan (3:15; 11:12).

(3) *The Time of the Messiah's Inauguration of the Kingdom of Heaven and His Revelation of Its Ethical Standards.* Jesus, however, is the one through whom the kingdom of heaven comes and this stage in history must be seen as the center of history in Matthew's scheme. It is Jesus who receives the Holy Spirit (3:16; *see* Holy Spirit); who is the object of Satan's attacks against the dawning of the kingdom of heaven (4:1-11; 11:12); who not only announces the dawning of the kingdom (4:17) but who also effects its powers (4:23; 9:14-17, 35; 11:2-6; 12:28, 43-45); who reveals God's radical will (5:1-7:29; 11:25 27; 13:10-17; 18:1—19:1; 23:1—25:46); who, on the basis of revealing God's will, forms a new people of God around him (4:18-22; 5:3-12; 6:9-13; 7:15-23; 12:46-50; 16:17-19; 18:1—19:1); and who inaugurates the world mission (8:5-13; 10:18; 13:31-33; 15:21-28; 21:33-46; 22:1-14; 24:14; 28:16-20). Most especially, as we have already noted (see 3.1.5—3.1.7 above), it is Jesus who inaugurates the kingdom of heaven through his public ministry, passion and resurrection.

The following two points, the "time of Israel's decision" and "time of all nations," may not in fact be separate periods for Matthew's view of salvation history. Instead, they may simply be two complementary aspects of the inauguration of the kingdom of heaven, one emphasizing the dilemma of Israel and the other the dilemma of the Gentiles.

(4) *The Time of Israel's Decision.* It is clear that Matthew's Gospel no longer distinguishes humans along ethnic lines, as in Jew versus Gentile (see esp. Levine), but it is also clear that the Evangelist and probably his early Christian community were struggling with the place of Israel in salvation history. Matthew's approach is to demonstrate that the true people of God are those who believe and obey Jesus (12:46-50), those who are righteous according to Jesus' new standards (7:21-23). In asserting this the First Gospel reveals that the privileged position of Israel as

a nation (as seen in the time of anticipatory revelation) has been forfeited (21:43). This is not to say that all Jews are condemned (that would be a racial comment, bordering on anti-Semitism*; see McKnight forthcoming), but that non-messianic Judaism is condemned. Further, it is to say that the former privileged position of the nation of Israel has been annulled and that all nations are now just as privileged as Israel formerly was (22:1-14).

The evidence of Matthew suggests that this privilege began to be lifted during the ministry of Jesus (10:13-15; 11:20-24) but was not completely lifted until the destruction of Jerusalem. For Matthew the destruction of Jerusalem is the highly important and visible demonstration of God's judgment on unbelieving Judaism and its leaders. The destruction of Jerusalem highlights the tearing down of the centralized power in Jerusalem, emphasizing of course a judgment on the leaders and elite within Judaism. We may perhaps be justified in seeing the period from Jesus until the destruction as the one generation for decision regarding Jesus as Messiah.

Three pieces of evidence point to the conclusion that the destruction of Jerusalem renders a finality to Israel's mission. First, Matthew emphasizes the exclusive nature of the missions of John the Baptist, Jesus and the Twelve to Israel (10:5; 11:16-19, 20-24; 15:24), showing that the time of the past, and of John, Jesus and the Twelve, was a time of mission directed almost exclusively toward Israel. Second, it is Matthew who highlights the significance of the destruction of Jerusalem in salvation history. The structure of Matthew's last chapters draws attention to the destruction as a judgment by God on unbelieving Judaism and its leaders (21:1—25:46; esp. 23:34-39; 24:1-2, 34). We catch a glimpse of this position in two parables: 21:33-46 and 22:1-14. In the former the lifting of the privilege is asserted (21:43) and in the latter that lifting, graphically symbolized in the burning of the city, seems to be followed by a universal mission (22:7-10). Third, the Gentile mission, or all-nations mission (since it is not limited to Gentiles only), is portrayed as something crucial but future. The mission to all nations is yet future for the Twelve (10:18), since it is associated with end-time events (24:14), and Jesus will only later command its commencement (28:16-20).

Interestingly, Matthew gives no indication that the all-nations mission will take a central role prior to the time associated with the destruction of Jerusalem. While Jesus commands the mission after he is resurrected, the description of events between the resurrection and the destruction shows no traces of the importance of the all-nations mission. Rather, this is apparently the time for Israel's decision regarding Jesus.

(5) *The Time of All Nations.* Again, the lines are not drawn clearly: as in the Abrahamic promise (Gen 12:1-3) and in periodic episodes in the OT (see Mt 1:1-17), so in the ministry of Jesus there are occasional receptions of Gentiles* into the blessings of the covenant (perhaps 2:1-12; 8:5-13; 15:21-28). Furthermore, the passion itself arouses a significant response of faith on the part of a Gentile (27:54). And Jesus' final commission commands a mission to all nations (28:16-20; see Levine, 165-92). However, even that commission is given special impetus by the destruction of Jerusalem, an event which turns the focus from Israel's decision to universal mission (21:33—22:14). Inasmuch as it was customary for Judaism at the time of Jesus to associate the fulfillment of the Abrahamic promise of universal salvation with the end times, it is perhaps not surprising that Matthew's Gospel makes the same connection.

At any rate, the inauguration of the kingdom of heaven in Jesus forces decisions on the part of both Jews and Gentiles, with Jesus' program emphasizing the non-ethnic character of the future subjects of God's kingdom. In light of Matthew's probable Palestinian origin and the time it took for the early church to incorporate Gentiles, we should not wonder at the ambivalence the First Gospel portrays with respect to the time of the all-nations mission and the place of Israel in God's new period of history.

(6) *The Time of the Consummation.* As with many early Christian writers, the end of history focuses on the return of Jesus (sometimes as the Son of man), the final judgment and the glorious salvation that God's people will inherit. For Matthew, Jesus, the Son of man, will return and bring all ordinary history to a close (25:31-46). This end brings with it a universal and eternal judgment (8:11-12; 13:43; 16:27-28; 19:27-30; 24:37—25:46). This judgment is based upon a person's works (16:27-28) and that person's association with Jesus (10:32-33; 25:31-46). The salvation described in the First Gospel is characterized by endless table fellowship (*see* Table Fellowship) with the Father and Son (8:11-12; 26:29), the glory of God's new people (13:43) and the reign of the Twelve (19:27-30).

3.4. Discipleship. With the exception perhaps of Exodus or Deuteronomy, no other book of Christian Scripture is devoted as much to ethics as the First Gospel. The keynote of Matthew's view of discipleship is radical obedience to the teachings of Jesus, summarized at times with the term *righteousness* (5:17-20) and at others with *love** (22:37-40). Disciples, or adherents (see Wilkins), are those who have radically conformed their lives to the teachings of Jesus. However, it must not be thought that Jesus expects perfection; indeed, in the pages of Matthew the disciples fail frequently. But a pattern is established in Matthew that has comforted countless followers of Jesus since then: failure is met by Jesus' stern rebuke; Jesus' rebuke gives way to instruction for future improvement; Jesus restores the repentant disciple (see 14:15-21).

The importance of discipleship to Matthew can be seen in the final command of Jesus: "Go, make disciples in all the nations . . ." (28:19; see McKnight 1988, 111). A disciple is here defined as one who is baptized (see Baptism) and has been taught to obey all the teachings of Jesus (28:19-20). The essence of discipleship for Matthew is to form a new people of God that conforms to the entirety of the ethical demands of Jesus. For Matthew orthopraxis has as much importance as orthodoxy. Being a disciple is equivalent to being a Christian and to being in a position of final approval by God. The distinction between Jesus as "Savior" and Jesus as "Lord" is a modern one and wholly foreign to the message of Jesus and the Gospels.

3.4.1. Called by Jesus. A disciple is one who has been called by Jesus. Whereas in Judaism (as we have come to know it) the prospective rabbinical student would seek out his teacher and volunteer to be his student, Jesus himself sought out his own followers. These calls of Jesus are depicted by Matthew in an authoritative way (4:18-22; 9:9-13). At times he called disciples and others to deeper commitment (11:28-30; 15:13; 19:21). Because being a follower of Jesus meant adherence to Jesus, both as a person and as a teacher, Jesus spoke harshly about superficial following (8:18-22; 19:16-22). Those who are called by Jesus share certain characteristics in their relationship to Jesus: first, they exercise faith in Jesus, whether understood as faith in Jesus' person as Messiah or in his ability to effect miracles* (8:10, 13, 23-27; 9:2, 22, 28-29; 13:58; 15:28; 17:20; 21:21-22, 32); second, they seek, receive and dispense the forgiveness of sins (6:12; 9:2-8; 9:10-13; 18:23-35); third, they are privileged to receive the revelations of Jesus that pertain to the inauguration of the kingdom of heaven (11:25-27; 13:1-52; 16:12, 17-21; 17:1-13, 22-23; 20:17-19; 26:2); fourth, those called by Jesus are commissioned in various ways, including evangelism (4:18-22; 10:5-8; 28:16-20), service to others (20:24-28; 23:11), and teaching (5:19; 13:51-52; 23:8-10; 28:20).

3.4.2. Radically Committed. Disciples of Jesus are marked by a radical commitment to the demands of Jesus. At times (apparently not always), the demand of Jesus challenged one's pattern of life and so called a person away from that pattern into the sphere of obedience to Jesus (see Commandment). For Matthew, there is no higher priority in life than obedience to Jesus, commitment to his righteousness and God's kingdom (6:25-34; 8:21-22; 10:21-22). At times this implies rejection (5:10-12) and relative loneliness (7:13-14).

In light of the prior demand of righteousness, following Jesus may involve great costs, including perhaps job (9:9), family* (10:34-39), economic security (19:16-30), physical comforts (8:18-22; 23:34-36) and social acceptance (10:24-25). Ultimately, the real cost of following Jesus involves the self, which must be offered to the Lord (16:24-28). All other "costs" are but consequences of this central cost.

3.4.3. Ethically Committed. Disciples of Jesus have an ethical commitment to the teachings of Jesus. Matthew uses a host of images and terms for proper behavior, including humility (5:3; 16:24-27; 18:1-5), peacefulness (5:9, 38-42; 17:24-27; 22:15-22; see Peace), honesty (5:33-37), economic and material contentment (6:19-34), fearless obedience (10:26-33) and perseverance (24:36—25:46). The virtuous life for Matthew may be categorized under two central terms: (1) love and (2) righteousness.

(1) *Love.* God loves all persons and so Jesus' disciples are expected to be kind to all; they are not to observe ethnic and political lines in their treatment of others (5:44-45; see Love). God's non-parochial love is seen in his choice of certain women as part of the Messiah's heritage (1:1-17), in his prompting of the Gentile Magi to be the first worshippers of the Messiah (2:1-12), in his choice of "Galilee of the Gentiles" as the arena of the Messiah's ministry (4:12-16) and in his generating faith in the heart of the centurion (8:5-13) and the Syro-Phonoecian woman (15:21-28). God's universal love becomes the capstone of the entire Gospel as Jesus commands the eleven to disciple all nations (28:16-20). Not only does God love all, he also responds to humans in mercy* and forgives their sins against him (6:12; 9:1-8, 13; 12:7).

God's love, accordingly, becomes the paradigm for true human existence. The disciples of Jesus are to be loving toward all others. Jesus, according to Matthew, states that the greatest demand of the Law is love (22:37-40) and sums up the ethical dimension of life with the Golden Rule (7:12). Consequently, the final judgment of God will be based on whether humans have been loving, acting mercifully to those in need (25:31-46), and whether or not they have been forgiving of others (18:23-35). Love for the disciple is the love of God which manifests itself through the concrete behavior shown to others. Whereas in Matthew the term *love* primarily relates to one's relationship to others, the next term primarily relates to one's relationship to God and his will.

(2) *Righteousness.* Although Matthew does use the term *righteousness* for conformity to OT Law (e.g., 1:19), his primary interest is in Christian righteousness, that is, conformity to God's will as revealed by Jesus (*see* Justice, Righteousness). The term, accordingly, is one that nicely bridges the transition now taking place in salvation history and one that surely provides a touchstone with Judaism (see Przybylski).

Righteousness is a requirement for entrance into the kingdom of heaven. It outstrips the righteousness of the scribes and Pharisees because it is behavior that conforms to the standard of the new salvation-historical era that Jesus inaugurates (5:17-20). Thus righteousness is a virtue that Jesus praises (5:6, 10). Furthermore, the disciples of Jesus are not to do their righteous deeds (works done in obedience to God's will) in order to be seen (6:1-18). If righteousness is required for entrance into the kingdom, it must be pursued in the here and now (6:33). As examples of righteousness, Matthew presents Joseph (1:19), Abel (23:35), those who respond properly to the Son of man (13:43) and those who perform deeds of mercy (25:37, 46). The Great Commission, in essence, exhorts the eleven to raise up disciples of Jesus who are righteous; that is, disciples who live out the teachings of Jesus (28:20).

3.4.4. Recipients of God's Promises. Disciples of Jesus are recipients of God's rich promises. To those who follow Jesus in discipleship come the added blessings of receiving God's present and final promises. For the present the disciple of Jesus is promised physical provisions (6:33; 19:29), rest for the soul (11:29) and Jesus' continual presence (28:20). For the future the disciple is promised God's approval (6:1; 10:40-42; 16:27; 20:1-16), eternal life (19:29) and table fellowship with the Father and the Son (26:27-29).

See also LUKE, GOSPEL OF; M TRADITION; MARK, GOSPEL OF; JOHN, GOSPEL OF; Q; SERMON ON THE MOUNT.

BIBLIOGRAPHY. **Commentaries:** W. F. Albright and C. S. Mann, *Matthew* (AB; Garden City, NY: Doubleday, 1971); W. C. Allen, *The Gospel according to St. Matthew* (ICC; 3d ed; Edinburgh: T. & T. Clark, 1912); F. W. Beare, *The Gospel According to Matthew: A Commentary* (New York: Harper and Row, 1982); D. A. Carson, "Matthew," in *The Expositor's Bible Commentary* (Grand Rapids: Zondervan, 1984) vol. 8; W. D. Davies and D. C. Allison, Jr., *A Critical and Exegetical Commentary on the Gospel According to Saint Matthew: Vol. 1, Introduction and Commentary on Matthew I-VII* (ICC; Edinburgh: T. & T. Clark, 1988); R. T. France, *Matthew* (TNTC; Grand Rapids: Eerdmans, 1986); W. Grundmann, *Das Evangelium nach Matthäus* (THKNT; 3d ed; Berlin: Evangelische Verlagsanstalt, 1972); R. H. Gundry, *Matthew: A Commentary on His Literary and Theological Art* (Grand Rapids: Eerdmans, 1982); D. Hill, *The Gospel of Matthew* (NCB; Grand Rapids: Eerdmans, 1981) M.-J. Lagrange, *Évangile selon St. Matthieu* (EB; 8th ed.; Paris: J. Gabalda, 1948); U. Luz, *Matthew 1-7* (Minneapolis: Augsburg, 1989); A. H. McNeile, *The Gospel According to St. Matthew: The Greek Text with Introduction and Notes* (London: Macmillan, 1915); G. Maier, *Matthäus-Evangelium* (2 vols.; Neuhasen, Stuttgart: Hänssler, 1979); J. P. Meier, *Matthew* (Wilmington, DE: Michael Glazier, 1980); H. A. W. Meyer, *Critical and Exegetical Hand-Book to the Gospel of Matthew* (New York: Funk and Wagnalls, 1884); A. Plummer, *An Exegetical Commentary on the Gospel of Matthew* (London: Clarke, 1909); L. Sabourin, *The Gospel according to St. Matthew* (2 vols.; Bombay: St. Paul, 1982); A. Schlatter, *Der Evangelist Matthäus* (Stuttgart: Calwer, 1959); J. Schniewind, *Das Evangelium nach Matthäus* (NTD; 12th ed.; Göttingen: Vandenhoeck & Ruprecht, 1968); E. Schweizer, *The Good News According to Matthew* (Atlanta: John Knox, 1975); R. V. G. Tasker, *The Gospel According to St. Matthew* (TNTC; Grand Rapids: Eerdmans, 1961); T. Zahn, *Das Evangelium des Matthäus* (KNT; 4th ed; Wuppertal: R. Brockhaus, repr. 1984). **Studies:** E. L. Abel, "Who Wrote Matthew?" *NTS* 17 (1971) 138-52; D. C. Allison, Jr., *The End of the Ages Has Come* (Philadelphia: Fortress, 1985); D. E. Aune, *The New Testament in Its Literary Environment* (Philadelphia: Westminster, 1987); B. W. Bacon, "The 'Five Books' of Matthew against the Jews," *The Expositor* 15 (1918) 56-66; idem, *Studies in Matthew* (New York: Henry Holt, 1930); idem, "Why 'According to Matthew'?" *Expositor* 20 (1920) 289-310; D. L. Barr, "The Drama of Matthew's Gospel: A Reconsideration of Its Structure and Purpose," *TD* 24 (1976) 349-59; D. R. Bauer, *The Structure of Matthew's Gospel* (Sheffield: Almond, 1988); H. J. B. Combrink, "The Structure of the Gospel of Matthew As Narrative," *TynB* 34 (1983) 61-90; A. M. Farrer, *St. Matthew and St. Mark* (London: Dacre, 1954); J. C. Fenton, "Inclusio and Chiasmus in Matthew," *Studia Evangelica* (Berlin: Akademie, 1959), 174-79; R. T. France, *Matthew: Evangelist and Teacher* (Grand Rapids: Zondervan, 1989); P. Gaechter, *Die literarische Kunst im Matthäus-Evangelium* (Innsbruck: Tyrolia, 1963); B. Gerhardsson, *The Mighty Acts of Jesus according to Matthew* (Lund: Gleerup, 1979); idem, "Sacrificial Service and Atonement in the Gospel of Matthew," in *Reconciliation and Hope: New Testament Essays on Atonement and Eschatology Presented to L. L.*

Morris on his 60th Birthday, ed. R. Banks (Grand Rapids: Eerdmans, 1974) 25-35; H. Giesen, Christliches Handeln (Frankfurt am Main: Peter Lang, 1982); D. W. Gooding, "Structure littéraire de Matthieu, XIII, 53 à XVIII, 35," RB 85 (1978) 227-52; R. A. Guelich, The Sermon on the Mount (Waco, TX: Word, 1982); H. J. Held, "Matthew As Interpreter of the Miracle Stories," in Tradition and Interpretation in Matthew, ed. G. Bornkamm (Philadelphia: Westminster, 1963) 165-99; M. Hengel, Studies in the Gospel of Mark (Philadelphia: Fortress, 1985); D. Hill, "Son and Servant: An Essay in Matthean Christology," JSNT 6 (1980) 2-16; J. Jeremias, New Testament Theology: The Proclamation of Jesus (New York: C. Scribner's, 1971); idem, The Parables of Jesus (2d ed.; New York: Scribner's, 1972); J. D. Kingsbury, Matthew: Structure, Christology, Kingdom (2d ed.; Minneapolis: Fortress, 1989); E. Krentz, "The Extent of Matthew's Prologue: Toward the Structure of the First Gospel," JBL 83 (1964) 409-15; J. Kürzinger, Papias von Hierapolis und die Evangelien des Neuen Testaments (Regensburg: F. Pustet, 1983); G. E. Ladd, A Theology of the New Testament (Grand Rapids: Eerdmans, 1974); A.-J. Levine, The Social and Ethnic Dimensions of Matthean Salvation History (Lewiston/Queenston, Lampeter: Edwin Mellen, 1988); C. H. Lohr, "Oral Techniques in the Gospel of Matthew," CBQ 23 (1961) 403-35; T. W. Manson, "The Gospel according to St. Matthew," in Studies in the Gospels and Epistles, ed. M. Black (Philadelphia: Westminster, 1962) 68-104; R. P. Martin, New Testament Foundations (2 vols.; Grand Rapids: Eerdmans, 1975, 1978); S. McKnight, Interpreting the Synoptic Gospels (Grand Rapids: Baker, 1988); idem, "A Loyal Critic: Matthew's Polemic with Judaism in Theological Perspective," in The New Testament and Anti-Semitism, ed. C. A. Evans and D. A. Hagner (Minneapolis: Fortress, forthcoming); J. P. Meier, The Vision of Matthew (New York: Paulist, 1979); C. F. D. Moule, "St. Matthew's Gospel: Some Neglected Features," in Essays in New Testament Interpretation (Cambridge: University Press, 1982) 67-74; P. Nepper-Christensen, Das Matthäusevangelium: Ein juden-christliches Evangelium? (Aarhus: Universitetsforlaget, 1958); B. M. Nolan, The Royal Son of God (Göttingen: Vandenhoeck & Ruprecht, 1979); B. Orchard and H. Riley, The Order of the Synoptics: Why Three Synoptic Gospels? (Macon, GA: Mercer University, 1987); G. R. Osborne, The Resurrection Narratives (Grand Rapids: Baker, 1984); B. Przybylski, Righteousness in Matthew and His World of Thought (SNTSMS 41; Cambridge: University Press, 1980); P. Rolland, "From the Genesis to the End of the World: The Plan of Matthew's Gospel," BTB 2 (1972) 155-76; P. L. Shuler, A Genre for the Gospels: The Biographical Character of Matthew (Philadelphia: Fortress, 1982); N. B. Stonehouse, The Witness of the Synoptic Gospels to Christ (Grand Rapids: Baker, 1979); G. Strecker, Der Weg der Gerechtigkeit (3d ed.; Göttingen: Vandenhoeck & Ruprecht, 1971); M. J. Suggs, Wisdom, Christology and Law in Matthew's Gospel (Cambridge: Harvard University, 1970); W. G. Thompson, "An Historical Perspective in the Gospel of Matthew," JBL 93 (1974) 243-62; D. Verseput, "The Role and Meaning of the 'Son of God' Title in Matthew's Gospel," NTS 33 (1987) 532-56; R. Walker, Die Heilsgeschichte im ersten Evangelium (Göttingen: Vandenhoeck & Ruprecht, 1967); J. W. Wenham, "Gospel Origins," TJ 7 (1978) 112-29; 2 NS (1981) 37-39; M. J. Wilkins, The Concept of Disciple in Matthew's Gospel (Leiden: E. J. Brill, 1988).

S. McKnight

MERCY

In discussing the concept of mercy we face the common difficulty of such studies that there is more than one English word that expresses the idea (e.g., compassion, pity), that the one English word might be used to render a number of Greek and Hebrew roots, each with its own shade of meaning, and that the one Hebrew or Greek root might be translated by more than one word in English. In short, we have a number of overlapping concepts, between which it is not always easy to know where to draw the line. As far as the Gospels are concerned, the Greek root most commonly translated into English by "mercy" is elee- and we shall concentrate our attention on that, but not exclusively. Some reference will be made to other words of kindred meaning.

1. OT Usage
2. NT Usage

1. OT Usage.

In the LXX the noun eleos is normally used for the Hebrew ḥesed which has to do with the attitude of a human or of God arising out of a mutual relationship. Bultmann defines it as "the attitude which one expects of the other in this relationship, and to which he is pledged in relation to him," but Andersen finds that "the formal, legal side of ḥesed as obligation and duty has been exaggerated. It is incidental and marginal. The heart of the matter is generous and beneficial action, not at all required." ḥesed is used sometimes in a purely human context, as that between David and Jonathan and his house (1 Sam 20:14-16), but chiefly the term is used of God's relationship with his people, and in this context the notion of grace rather than obligation comes to the fore. Indeed, contrary to the popular view that his ḥesed issued from his covenant with Israel,* it may be closer to the truth to turn that equation around and to speak of his *ḥeseḏ* as issuing in covenant. And, when Israel broke covenant with God, what might otherwise have been described as the latter's faithfulness to the relationship becomes again his uncovenanted mercy, that is, the "steady, persistent refusal of God to wash his hands" of his faithless and erring people becomes "the essential meaning of the Hebrew word" (Snaith). Thus *ḥeseḏ* is not something prescribed, it is "an expression of love and generosity," it is often "surprising, ingenious" and always "meritorious—the performer could not have been blamed for its omission" (Andersen). And yet the covenantal association remains. God shows his *ḥeseḏ* especially to Israel, despite its persistent failure (Ex 33:19; Is 63:9).

God's mercy consistently manifests itself in his saving (*see* Salvation) acts: in *forgiveness,** whereby the individual or the nation is restored to a relationship with him (Deut 13:17; 2 Sam 24:14; 2 Kings 13:23; Ps 25:6; 40:11; 51:1; 79:8; 103:4; Is 54:8; 55:7; Lam 3:32; Dan 9:9, 18; Hos 1:6-7; Joel 2:18; Mic 7:19; Hab 3:2; Zech 1:12, 16); in his *deliverance* of Israel from their enemies (Neh 9:27-28; Ps 25:6; 40:11; 69:16; 79:8; Is 30:18; Jer 42:12); in the *restoration* of the exiles (Deut 30:3; Is 14:1; 49:10, 13; Jer 12:15; Ezek 39:25). And his mercy has an eschatological dimension. From God's *ḥeseḏ* flows the final forgiveness and redemption of his people (Deut 13:17; Is 54:8; 55:3; Jer 33:26; Mic 7:20).

Less frequently (six times), *eleos* is used in the LXX for the Hebrew *raḥ⁴amim* (as is *oiktirmoi*, etc.), which appears to derive from the same root as *reḥem*, "womb," and thus denotes the feeling of kinship between those born from the same womb or the motherly feeling of the one who has given birth (*BDB*). In more general terms it expresses familial love,* and God's mercy is sometimes defined in these terms. In Isaiah 49:15 God is a "mother" to Israel; in Isaiah 54:4-8, a "husband"; and in a number of references a "father" (Ps 103:13; Is 63:15-16; Jer 31:20; cf. Hos 11:1-4). Thus, if *ḥeseḏ* expresses the idea of covenant love, that is the kindness that issues in and from a relationship (though it may well exceed the bounds of any obligations of that tie), *raḥ⁴mim* expresses the affective side of love, its compassion or pity. When used of God it expresses the thought, in Barth's phrase, that "the personal God has a heart." It denotes the seat of a feeling that is felt physically. The nearest approach in English to the sense of this word is "emotion," but the application of the word is not restricted to the emotions. It often expresses the outworking of the feeling in action: one demonstrates *raḥ⁴mim* (Zech 7:9), one asks for it (Ps 69:16) and looks

for it in others (1 Kings 8:50; Ps 106:46). In effect, then, the meaning of this word is not unlike that of *ḥeseḏ*, and in the language of later Judaism* the two are barely distinguishable (Bultmann). The sense of "faithfulness" can still be found in *ḥeseḏ*, but for the most part both *ḥeseḏ* and *raḥ⁴mim* express the idea of compassion (outworking in action) for the needy and the distressed.

2. NT Usage.

Some of the OT background outlined above is taken into the NT by other words, such as *charis*, "grace," and the words for forgiveness. But something of what the *elee-* root signifies in the LXX can still be found in the NT.

2.1. God's Mercy.

2.1.1. As Faithfulness. This sense of *eleos* is found especially in the canticles of Luke 1. Thus in Luke 1:72, "to perform the mercy promised to our fathers" is the same as "remembering his holy covenant," and this thought of covenant and of God's covenant faithfulness similarly colors the other occurrences of *eleos* in this chapter (Lk 1:50, 54, 58, 72, 78). However, it should be said again that with God mercy is never simply faithfulness, but goes beyond that obligation to grace. Israel had long since forfeited any claim on God, but still he showed mercy in visiting and redeeming his people (Lk 1:68). This note of God's (merciful) visitation sounds particularly loudly in Luke (cf. 7:16; Acts 15:14), to which is added the thought of his compassion. In Luke 1:78 he employs the striking phrase *splagchna eleous*, "bowels of mercy." *Splagchna* expresses the idea of "feelings" (see 2.1.2. below); the genitive *eleous* is one of kind: the kind of feelings God has are merciful. The thought has moved from *ḥeseḏ* (in so far as there is a distinction of meaning) to *raḥ⁴mim*.

2.1.2. As Compassion in Action. God's visitation was in the person of Jesus and, in accordance with the note sounded in the opening chapters of Luke (see 2.2.1. above), those who came to him for help asked for it in terms of mercy (the verb *eleeō*, Mt 9:27; 15:22; 17:15; 20:30-31; Mk 10:47; Lk 17:13; 18:38-39; cf. also Mk 5:19; Lk 16:24 where the mercy is attributed to God). His response is twofold: inward and active.

Inwardly, "he [Jesus] had compassion for them because they were . . . helpless." In such expressions (Mt 9:36; 14:14; 15:32; 20:34; Mk 1:41; 6:34; 8:2; 9:22; Lk 7:13. Cf. also Mt 18:27; Lk 10:33; 15:30 which portray such compassion in parables*), the Greek verb is *splagchnizomai* (cf. the noun *splagchna* above) which, like the Hebrew *raḥ⁴mim* (which the noun once translates in Prov 12:10), denotes a feeling that is felt physically, an emotion. Literally, *splagchnizomai* means "to be moved in one's bowels." The Greeks regarded the bowels as the seat of violent passion such as anger and love; the Jews regarded them as the center of the more tender affections, especially kindness and pity. The "bowels" were for them what we mean by "the heart." When Jesus was confronted with human need, the Gospels say that he was moved in his bowels, as we might say, "his heart went out to these people" or "they broke his heart," that is, he had compassion on them. This portrait of the divine visitor appears especially in Luke. Not that the words are more frequent there than elsewhere, but Menken has shown that where they do occur (*splagchna* in 1:78 and *splagchnizomai* in 7:13; 10:33; 15:20), in each case they constitute the turning point of the pericope, demonstrating that compassion is "the most important element" in the passage. This, of course, fits with the generally accepted view that this Gospel is especially concerned to show God's love for the needy, the poor (*see* Rich and Poor), the sinner and that this love manifests itself in Jesus.

But what he felt inwardly led to action: to the giving of sight to the blind (Mt 20:34); to cleansing the leper (Mk 1:41; *see* Leprosy); to teaching the ignorant (Mk 6:34); to feeding the hungry (Mt 15:32; Mk 8:2); to raising the dead (Lk 7:13). Thus, for Jesus to have mercy was to help the needy and the helpless. His desire was that men and women might be whole.

2.1.3. As Eschatological. The greatest need of humanity, from the biblical perspective, lies not only in the physical and temporal sphere but also in the spiritual and eternal. We are sinners,* separated from God, and in that sense already dead and liable to remain so for ever. Our problem is separation and our need is reconciliation, and God's mercy is, accordingly, directed especially to that end. This has been the goal of all his dealings with humanity, and it was reached with the advent of Christ.* In Christ God's mercy in its final, fullest sense, was made manifest. By the same token, God's covenant faithfulness was fully realized. What had still been future for the prophets—God's final forgiveness and redemption of his people—had now come about. "God's *eleos* is his eschatological act in salvation history in Christ" (Bultmann; *see* Eschatology).

This theme is dealt with more explicitly in the epistles (e.g., Eph 2:4-10; Tit 3:3-7) and, to that extent, lies beyond the scope of this article. Nevertheless, we may be sure that Jesus lived his life in the constant sense of God's saving mercy, giving expression to it in his own words and actions: "Be merciful, *even as your Father is merciful*" (Lk 6:36); "love one another as I have loved you" (Jn 15:12). He embodied the mercy of God; he was God's compassion in action: "I lay down my life (for the sheep) . . . this charge I have received from my Father" (Jn 10:17-18; cf. 1 Pet 1:3). On this basis, believers are said to have received mercy (2 Cor 4:1; 1 Tim 1:13, 16; 1 Pet 2:10).

2.2. The Mercy of One to Another. God's mercy to us is made necessary by our need and especially our sinfulness, and it has this objective: "That you might be children of your Father who is in heaven" (Mt 5:45). The parable of the unmerciful servant (Mt 18:23-35) expresses this objective negatively. Other teaching of Jesus, such as his commandment* that we love one another (Jn 13:34-35; 15:12-13; cf. 1 Jn 2:5; 4:12, 17), sets it forth in positive terms.

This is Jesus' teaching in the parables of the good Samaritan (Lk 10:30-37) and the sheep and the goats (Mt 25:31-46). Mercy should be manifested in giving help to the needy and the helpless (Mt 18:27; Lk 10:37; 16:24). Beyond this, there are hints in the teaching of Jesus of the old idea of mercy as a communal obligation. Thus Jesus demanded of the Pharisees "mercy and not sacrifice" with respect to those whom they despised (Mt 9:13; 12:7; cf. Hos 6:6). Again, he accused the scribes* and Pharisees* of neglecting "the weightier matters of the Law," which included mercy (Mt 23:23). "These you ought to have done," he said, emphasizing their practice, "without neglecting the other."

See also GOD; LOVE.

BIBLIOGRAPHY. F. I. Andersen, "Yahweh, the Kind and Sensitive God," in *God Who Is Rich in Mercy*, ed. P. T. O'Brien and D. G. Peterson (Sydney: Lancer, 1986) 41-48; K. Barth, *CD* II, 1, Section 30; R. Bultmann, "ἔλεος κτλ," *TNDT* II.477-87; C. H. Dodd, *The Bible and the Greeks* (London: Hodder and Stoughton, 1935); W. Eichrodt, *Theology of the Old Testament* (2 vols.; Philadelphia: Westminster, 1961) I.232-39; N. Glueck, *Das Wort ḥesed im alttestamentlichen Sprachgebrauche als menschliche und gottliche gemeinschaftgemasse Verhaltungsweise* (Geissen: Alfred Topelmann, 1927); M. J. J. Menken, "The Position of *Splanchnizomai* and *Splanchna* in the Gospel of Luke," *NT* 30 (1988) 107-14; N. H. Snaith, *The Distinctive Ideas of the Old Testament* (London: Epworth, 1944); H. J. Stoebe, "Die Bedeutung des Wortes Häsäd im Alten Testament," *VT* 2 (1952) 244-54.
D. J. Williams

MESSIAH. *See* CHRIST.

MESSIANIC SECRET. *See* CHRIST; MARK, GOSPEL OF.

MESSIANISM. *See* CHRIST; REVOLUTIONARY MOVEMENTS.

MIDRASH

The Hebrew noun *midrash* (*midrāš* pl., *midrāšim*) is derived from the verb *dāraš*, which means to "search (for an answer)." Midrash accordingly means "inquiry," "examination" or "commentary." The word often refers to rabbinic exegesis, both with respect to method as well as to form. Scholars therefore refer to "midrashic" interpretation and rabbinic "midrashim." However, in recent years midrash has been discussed against the broader background of ancient biblical interpretation and textual transmission in general. It has become increasingly apparent that portions of the NT itself reflect aspects of midrash. Indeed, there has been considerable interest recently in the question to what extent Jesus and the Evangelists may have employed midrashic exegesis.

1. Semantic Development
2. Rabbinic Midrash
3. Midrash in Jesus and the Gospels
4. The Gospels as Midrash

1. Semantic Development.

The verb *dāraš* occurs in a variety of contexts in the OT, meaning "to seek," "to inquire" or "to investigate." Scripture speaks of seeking God's will (2 Chron 17:4; 22:9; 30:19; Ps 119:10), making inquiry of God through prophetic oracle (1 Sam 9:9; 1 Kings 22:8; 2 Kings 3:11; Jer 21:2) or investigating a matter (Deut 13:14; 19:18; Judg 6:29; cf. 1QS 6:24; 8:26). The nominal form, *midrāš*, occurs in the OT twice, meaning "story," "book" and possibly "commentary" (2 Chron 13:22; 24:27 cf. RSV).

In later usage there is a shift from seeking God's will through prophetic oracle to seeking God's will through study of Scripture. In later traditions we are told that Ezra the scribe "set his heart to search the Law of the Lord" (Ezra 7:10). Other texts convey similar meanings: "Great are the works of the Lord, studied by all who have pleasure in them" (Ps 111.2); "I have sought your precepts" (Ps 119:45; cf. 119:94, 155); "Observe and seek out all the commandments of the Lord" (1 Chron 28:8). Although this "searching" of God's Law should not in these passages be understood as exegesis in a strict sense, it is only a small step to the later explicit exegetical reference of midrash: "This is the study [*midrāš*] of the Law" (1QS 8:15); "The interpretation [*midrāš*] of 'Blessed is the man . . .' [cf. Ps 1:1]" (4QFlor 1:14). Indeed, the Teacher of Righteousness is called the "searcher of the Law" (CD 6:7). Philo urges his readers to join him in searching

(*ereunan* = *dāraš*) Scripture (*Det. Pot. Ins.* 17 §57; 39 §141; *Cher.* 5 §14). In rabbinic writings midrash becomes standard and its practice as an exegetical method was consciously considered.

2. Rabbinic Midrash.

In the writings of the rabbis midrash attains its most sophisticated and self-conscious form. In searching the sacred text the rabbis attempted to update scriptural teaching to make it relevant to new circumstances and issues. This approach was felt to be legitimate because Scripture was understood as divine in character and therefore could yield many meanings and many applications: " 'Is not my word like a hammer that breaks the rock in pieces?' [Jer 23:29]. As the hammer causes numerous sparks to flash forth, so is a verse of Scripture capable of many interpretations" (*b. Sanh.* 34a; cf. *m. 'Abot* 5:22).

2.1. Rules of Midrash. According to early rabbinic tradition midrash could be practiced following seven rules (or *middôt*) of Hillel the Elder (cf. *t. Sanh.* 7.11; *'Abot R. Nat.* [A] §37). All of these rules are utilized in the Gospels:

(1) *Qal wāḥômer.* ("Light and heavy.") According to this rule, what is true or applicable in a "light" (or less important) instance is surely true or applicable in a "heavy" (or more important) instance. This rule is plainly in evidence when Jesus assures his disciples (cf. Mt 6:26; Lk 12:24) that because God cares for the birds (light), they can be sure that he cares for them (heavy).

(2) *Gizērâ šāwâ.* ("An equivalent regulation.") According to this rule one passage may be explained by another if similar words or phrases are present. Comparing himself to David, who on one occasion violated the Law* in eating consecrated bread (1 Sam 21:6), Jesus justifies his apparent violation of the Sabbath* (Mk 2:23-28).

(3) *Binyan 'āb mikkāṭûb 'eḥād.* ("Constructing a father [i.e., principal rule] from one [passage].") Since God is not the God of the dead but of the living, the revelation at the burning bush, "I am the God of Abraham . . ." (Ex 3:14-15), implies that Abraham* is to be resurrected. From this one text and its inference one may further infer, as Jesus did (Mk 12:26), the truth of the general resurrection.*

(4) *Binyan 'āb miššᵉnê kᵉtûbîm.* ("Constructing a father [i.e., principal rule] from two writings [or passages].") From the commands to unmuzzle the ox (Deut 25:4) and share sacrifices with the priests (Deut 18:1-8) it is inferred that those who preach are entitled to support (Mt 10:10; Lk 10:7; 1 Cor 9.9, 13; 1 Tim 5:18).

(5) *Kᵉlāl ûp̄ᵉrāṭ ûp̄ᵉrāṭ ûk̄ᵉlāl.* ("General and partic-

ular, and particular and general.") When Jesus replies that the greatest commandment (the "general") is to love* the Lord with all one's heart (Deut 6:4-5) and to love one's neighbor as one's self (Lev 19:18), he has summed up all of the "particular" commandments* (Mk 12:28-34).

(6) *Kayyôṣē' bô bᵉmāqôm 'aḥēr.* ("Like something in another place [or passage].") If the Son of man* (or Messiah; *see* Christ) is to sit on one of the thrones set up before the Ancient of Days (Dan 7:9, which is how Rabbi Aqiba interprets Daniel's plural reference to "thrones," cf. *b. ḥag. 14a; b. Sanh.* 38b), and if Messiah is to sit at God's right hand (Ps 110:1), it may be inferred that when the Son of man comes with the clouds (Dan 7:13-14), he will be seated at the right hand of God and will judge his enemies. This is evidently what Jesus implied in his reply to Caiaphas (Mk 14:62).

(7) *Dābār halāmēd mēʿinyānô.* ("Word of instruction from its context.") This rule is exemplified in Jesus' teaching against divorce (Mt 19:4-8). Although it is true that Moses* allowed divorce (Deut 24:1-4), it is also true that God never intended the marriage union to be broken, as implied in Genesis 1:27 and 2:24 (*see* Marriage and Divorce).

Tradition holds that these rules were expanded to thirteen by Ishmael, a rabbi of the second century (cf. *Bar. de Rabbi Ishmael* §1 in Prologue to *Sipra*). Rabbi Eliezer ben Yose the Galilean is credited with further expanding these rules, particularly as they relate to the interpretation of narrative. He is probably the author of the tractate *Thirty-Two Rules for Interpreting the Torah* (also called the *Baraita of Thirty-Two Rules;* cf. beginning of *Midrash Mishnat R. Eliezer* and beginning of *Midrash ha-Gadol* on Genesis). Unlike the seven *middôt* of Hillel the Elder, many of these later rules are contrived and atomistic (e.g., finding significance in the numerical value of the letters themselves) and have little or nothing to do with the literary or historical context of the scriptural passage under consideration. Most of these thirty-two rules, rules which made it possible to enjoy the "savory dishes of wisdom" (*m. 'Abot* 3:18), were applied to homiletical, not legal, midrash.

2.2. Halakah and Haggadah. Rabbinic midrash falls into two basic categories. These categories are distinguished not by method but by objectives. Halakah (*hᵃlākâ* from *hālak,* "to walk") refers to a legal ruling (plural: *hᵃlākôt*). Hence, halakic midrash is in reference to legal interpretation. The purpose of halakoth was to build an oral "fence" around written Torah, making violation of it (written Torah) less likely (*m. 'Abot* 1:1; 3:13). Haggadah (*haggadâ,* lit. "telling,"

from the root *nāgad,* "to draw") refers to the interpretation of narrative and is usually understood as homiletical or non-legal interpretation (plural: *haggadôt*). Best-known is the Passover Haggadah (cf. *b. Pesaḥ.* 115b, 116b). Haggadic midrash was much more imaginative in its attempts to fill in the gaps in Scripture and to explain away apparent discrepancies, difficulties and unanswered questions. Legal rulings were not to be derived from haggadic interpretation (cf. *y. Pe'a* 2.6).

2.3. Rabbinic Periods. The rabbis of the pre-Mishnaic period (50 B.C.-A.D.200) are referred to as the Tannaim (i.e., the "repeaters"), while the rabbis of the later period ("early": A.D. 200-500; "late": A.D. 500-1500) are called the Amoraim (i.e., the "speakers" from *'ᵃmôrā', "interpreter"*). Obviously the tannaitic traditions are of the greatest value for NT interpretation.

2.4. Rabbinic Literature. The legal corpus in which halakic concerns predominate is made up of Mishnah (lit. "repetition" or "[memorizable] paragraph"; c. A.D. 200), Tosefta (lit. "supplement [to Mishnah]"; c. A.D. 300) and Talmud (lit. "learning"; Palestinian [or Jerusalem]: c. A.D. 500; Babylonian: c. A.D. 600; note that the word for "disciple" is *talmîd,* i.e., "one who learns"; *see* Rabbinic Traditions and Writings). Many of the halakoth found in the Mishnah date back in one form or another to the time of Jesus (e.g., cf. Mk 2:16 and *m. Dem.* 2:3 concerning being the guest of a non-observant Jew; Mk 3:1-6 and *m. Šabb.* 14:3-4; 22:6 concerning healing on the Sabbath; Mk 7:3-13 and *m. Ned.* 1:3 concerning *qorban*). It was believed that the oral Law ultimately derives from Moses: "Many rulings were transmitted to Moses on Sinai [and] . . . all of them are embodied in Mishnah" (*y. Pesaḥ* 2.6).

Many of the non-legal works are called *midrashim* ("commentaries"). From the tannaitic period we have *Mekilta de Rabbi Ishmael* (on Exodus), *Sipre Numbers, Sipre Deuteronomy,* and *Sipra Leviticus.* From the early Amoraic period we have *Midrash Rabbah* (on the Pentateuch and the Five Scrolls), *Midrash on the Psalms; Pesiqta Rabbati, Pesiqta de Rab Kahana, Seder Elijah Rabbah* and *Midrash Tanhuma.* Tannaitic tradition is often found in these writings as well (and when it is, it is called *baraita*).

2.5. Forms of Midrash. J. Neusner (1987) classifies midrash as three types: (1) paraphrase (e.g., the LXX and Targums*), midrash of the synagogue and of Diaspora Judaism; (2) prophecy (e.g., Qumran and Matthew), midrash of eschatologically oriented Judaism* and (3) parable* (e.g., Philo and the rabbis), midrash of the academies. Midrash operates at two levels: obvious and subtle. M. Gertner (268) describes these levels as "overt" and "covert" midrash. To be preferred, however, is E. E. Ellis's use of the words *explicit* and *implicit* (1988, 703-709). Interpretive paraphrase, as in the LXX, the Targum or even echoing older scriptural traditions in later scriptural texts, is covert or implicit, while citing Scripture (i.e., the lemma) and then interpreting it (i.e., the midrash or pesher) is overt or explicit. The rabbinic writings, the pesharim of Qumran and many passages of the NT (as seen particularly in Matthew, John and Paul) afford examples of explicit interpretation. The retelling of biblical history as seen in *Jubilees*, 1QapGen (*Genesis Apocryphon*), Pseudo-Philo's *Biblical Antiquities*, Josephus' *Jewish Antiquities* and the Targums, represents implicit interpretation. The very manner in which the biblical narrative is retold in these writings brings to light new insights and new teachings. Its purpose is, in effect, to update Scripture. Matthean and Lukan rewriting of Mark may at places parallel this kind of midrashic paraphrase (see 4. below).

3. Midrash in Jesus and the Gospels.

Some of the biblical exegesis found in the Gospels reflects midrashic principles. As were the students of the rabbis, the followers of Jesus were called "disciples"* (*mathetes*, i.e., "learner" = *talmîd*). B. Gerhardsson and R. Riesner have argued that Jesus' teaching has been carefully preserved by his disciples, who had been taught according to rabbinic practices (*see* Teacher). Such comments as "you search the Scriptures" (Jn 5:39; 7:52; cf. Philo *Det. Pot. Ins.* 5 §13; *m. Ber.* 1:15; *b. Ta'an.* 5b), "go and learn" (Mt 9:13; cf. *S. Elijah Rab.* §18 [94]; *Num. Rab.* 8:4 [on 5:6]), "take my yoke upon you" (Mt 11:29-30; cf. *'Abot* 3:5; *m. Ber.* 2:2, 5) and "hear" (Mt 21:33; cf. *m. Ber.* 2:2; *b. Šabb.* 13b), found throughout the Gospels, echo the language of midrash and exegetical dispute (see Jn 3:25: "a dispute [*zētēsis*] arose between some disciples of Jesus with a Jew concerning purification"; cf. Acts 6:9; 9:29; 15:7). Surely the comment "You search the Scriptures because you suppose that you find life in them" (Jn 5:39) has in mind the widespread rabbinic conviction that "more Torah means more life" (credited to Hillel, cf. *'Abot* 2:8; cf. 2:7) and that "Torah is for eternal life" (credited to Ishmael, cf. *Mek. Pisḥa'* §16 [on Ex 13:3]). Specific exegeses preserved in the Gospels closely parallel, and at times are apparently part of, midrashic interpretations of the first century.

3.1. Matthew. The Matthean infancy narrative (*see* Birth of Jesus) is rich with scriptural allusions and themes that to some extent reflect midrashic principles and practice. When the Evangelist presented the genealogy* of Jesus in three clusters of fourteen

generations each (Mt 1:2-17), he probably was hinting at the numerical value of the Hebrew name "David" (*dwd*, i.e., 4 + 6 + 4 = 14), the messianic father of Jesus (Mt 1:1). The "star" in Matthew 2:7 very likely reflects Numbers 24:17 ("a star shall come forth out of Jacob, and a scepter shall arise out of Israel"), as its interpretation in Midrash and Targum would seem to indicate (e.g., ". . . a mighty king of the house of Jacob shall reign, and shall be anointed Messiah, wielding the mighty scepter of Israel," *Tg. Ps.-J.*). Evidently both Philo (*Praem. Poen.* 16 §95) and Josephus (*J.W.* 6.5.4 §§312-13) understood Numbers 24:17 as messianic. When the Evangelist tells us that Jesus' return from Egypt fulfilled Hosea 11:1 ("Out of Egypt have I called my son"; Mt 2:15), he has likely interpreted Hosea in light of the similar passage in LXX Numbers 24:7-8 ("There shall come a man out of his seed, and he shall rule over many nations . . . God led him out of Egypt"). Dwelling in "Nazareth" fulfills the prophets (Mt 2:23) probably because the three root consonants of "Nazareth" (*nṣr*) are common to the word "branch" (*nēṣer*), a word which has messianic overtones (cf. Is 11:1 [*nēṣer*]; Is 4:2; 49:6 [*nṣyry*]; Jer 23:5; 33:15; Zech 3:8; 6:12 ["sprout," *ṣemaḥ*]; cf. also Judg 13:5-7 ["nazarite," *nᶜzîr*]).

3.2. Mark. In several places Mark's Gospel gives evidence that Jesus was acquainted with Israel's Scriptures as they were interpreted in the synagogue of his day (Chilton, 1984). When Jesus paraphrased Isaiah 6:10, ". . . lest they repent and it be forgiven them" (Mk 4:12), he has followed the Targum ("and it be forgiven them"), not the Hebrew ("and I heal them"). When Jesus cited Isaiah 66:24 ("where their worm does not die and the fire is not quenched") as descriptive of Gehenna (Mk 9:47-48), it is again clear that he had in mind not the Hebrew, which does not mention Gehenna, but the Targum: "for their spirits will not die, and their fire will not be quenched, and the wicked will be judged in Gehenna." Jesus' reworking of Isaiah's Song of the Vineyard (Is 5:1-7) into a parable directed against Jerusalem's religious leaders (Mk 12:1-11), instead of the nation as a whole (as it is in Isaiah), likely reflected the Targum's insertion of "sanctuary" (*Tg. Isa.* 5:2), and the rabbinic interpretation that Isaiah 5:1-7 specifically predicted the destruction of the Temple and its altar (cf. *t. Me'il.* 1:16; *t. Sukk.* 3:15; *Tg. Isa.* 5:5).

3.3. Luke. One of the Lukan Evangelist's most remarkable accomplishments is the framing and enrichment of the infancy narrative in terms of the stories and language of the OT. Most impressive are the echoes of the infancy narrative of the prophet Samuel (1 Sam 1—2). Mary's *Magnificat* (1:46-55; *see*

Mary's Song) is modeled after Hannah's song of thanksgiving following the birth of Samuel (1 Sam 2:1-10). In fact the *Magnificat* is replete with scriptural allusions (e.g., cf. Lk 1:48 with LXX 1 Sam 1:11; Lk 1:50 with Ps 103:17). When Luke wrote that "Jesus increased in wisdom* and in stature, and in favor with God and people" (2:52), he undoubtedly had in mind the similar progress report concerning Samuel: "Now the boy Samuel continued to grow both in stature and in favor with the Lord and with people" (1 Sam 2:26). Borrowing from older scriptural traditions to tell the biblical story, as undoubtedly Luke regarded the story of Jesus, was very much part of the biblical retelling that is seen in books such as *Jubilees*, Pseudo-Philo's *Biblical Antiquities* and the Targums.

3.4. John. The opening verses of the Johannine prolog reflect midrashic interpretation at many points. We are told that the Word [*logos**] existed with God from the beginning, that all things were made through the Word and that the Word was the source of light and illumination (esp. Jn 1:1, 4-5, 9). All of these ideas are found in the midrashim and Targums: "You find that at the very beginning of the creation of the world, the King Messiah had already come into being" (*Pesiq. R.* 33:6); "By my Word [*memra*] I have perfected the heavens" (*Tg. Isa.* 48:13; cf. 45:12); "And the Word of the Lord said, 'Let there be light' " (*Frg. Tg. Gen.* 1:3); "The earth was void and empty and darkness was spread over the face of the abyss. And the Word of the Lord was the light and it shone . . ." (*Tg. Neof.* Exod. 12:42; cf. *Gen. Rab.* 1:6 [on Gen 1:1]).

The Fourth Gospel presents us with an interesting comparison between Jesus and Jacob. When Jesus tells the astonished Nathanael, "You will see heaven opened and the angels* of God ascending and descending on the Son of Man" (Jn 1:51), he has alluded to Genesis 28:12 where the Patriarch Jacob saw the staircase of angels in a dream. According to midrashic traditions the angels came down to gaze upon Jacob, because his image was on God's throne in heaven* (*Frg. Tg. Gen.* 28:12; cf. *Gen. Rab.* 68.12 [on 28:12]). Indeed, one interpretation understands that the angels ascended and descended *on Jacob,* and not simply on the staircase (*Gen. Rab.* 69.3 [on 28:12]). The Fourth Evangelist probably would like his readers to view Jesus as superior to the patriarch, for Jesus, not Jacob, is the true image of God, and it is Jesus the Son of man, not Jacob, upon whom the angels ascend and descend. A similar concern likely underlies Jesus' encounter with the woman at the well (Jn 4:10-26). "When our father Jacob lifted up the stone from upon the mouth of the well, the well surged up, and continued to surge up for twenty years" (*Frg. Tg. Gen.*

28:10). In contrast Jesus offers water that will "surge up" not for twenty years but for an eternity (Jn 4:14).

4. The Gospels As Midrash.

Recently some have argued that the Gospels themselves, in their entirety, represent instances of midrashim. J. Drury suggests that the variations in the Synoptic parallels may represent midrashic embellishment and creation. M. D. Goulder has argued that the Gospels are midrashim whose contents have followed primitive Jewish-Christian lectionaries. One scholar has suggested that Mark's Gospel constitutes a "gigantic midrash" on the Hexateuch and Lamentations (Derrett 1.38; see also D. Miller). Another scholar (Maynard) has argued that the Fourth Gospel is a midrash of the three Synoptic Gospels. But these conclusions are problematic.

Has Mark really produced a midrash on various OT books? On the contrary, he has not given us an interpretation of the Hexateuch; he has given us an interpretation of Jesus. It is true that this interpretation of Jesus has been influenced by OT themes, and perhaps a few specific passages, but it is surely inaccurate to describe Mark as a whole as a midrash on parts of the OT. B. D. Chilton (1986) has offered a more accurate assessment. According to him, the Gospels share certain affinities with midrashic paraphrase (as in 2. above) and probably should be regarded in places as "midrashic" but not "midrash," as "targumic" but not "targum." Reaching a conclusion that is compatible to Chilton's findings, F. G. Downing has compared the Evangelist's use of sources, particularly Luke's use of Mark, to Josephus' use of the LXX. It is probably best to conclude, therefore, that the Evangelists' interpretation of the OT and their respective presentations of the story of Jesus are to an extent midrashic in character, but not midrashim.

See also OLD TESTAMENT IN THE GOSPELS; RABBINIC TRADITIONS AND WRITINGS; TARGUM; TYPOLOGY.

BIBLIOGRAPHY. D. A. Carson and H. G. M. Williamson, eds., *It Is Written: Scripture Citing Scripture* (Cambridge: University Press, 1988) 99-140; B. D. Chilton, *A Galilean Rabbi and His Bible* (Wilmington: Glazier, 1984); idem, *Targumic Approaches to the Gospels* (Studies in Judaism; Lanham and New York: University Press of America, 1986); R. le Deaut, "Apropos a Definition of Midrash," *Int* 25 (1971) 259-82; J. D. M. Derrett, *The Making of Mark: The Scriptural Bases of the Earliest Gospel* (2 vols.; Shipston-on-Stour: Drinkwater, 1985); F. G. Downing, "Redaction Criticism: Josephus' *Antiquities* and the Synoptic Gospels," *JSNT* 8 (1980) 46-65; 9 (1980) 29-48; J. Drury, "Midrash and Gospel," *Theology*

77 (1974) 291-96; E. E. Ellis, "Biblical Interpretation in the New Testament Church," in *Mikra*, ed. J. Mulder (Philadelphia: Fortress, 1988) 691-725; idem, "Midrash, Targum and New Testament Quotations," in *Neotestamentica et Semitica*, eds. E. E. Ellis and M. Wilcox (Edinburgh: T & T Clark, 1969) 61-69; R. T. France and D. Wenham, eds., *Gospel Perspectives 3: Studies in Midrash and Historiography* (Sheffield: JSOT, 1983); B. Gerhardsson, *The Origins of the Gospel Traditions* (Philadelphia: Fortress, 1979); M. Gertner, "Midrashim in the New Testament," *JSS* 7 (1962) 267-92; M. D. Goulder, *Midrash and Lection in Matthew* (London: SPCK, 1974); J. Kugel and R. Greer, *Early Biblical Interpretation* (Philadelphia: Westminster, 1986); B. McNeil, "Midrash in Luke?" *HeyJ* 19 (1978) 399-404; D. Miller, *The Gospel of Mark as Midrash on Earlier Jewish and NT Literature* (Lewiston and Queenston: Mellen, 1990); M. P. Miller, "Targum, Midrash, and the Use of the OT in the NT," *JSJ* 2 (1971) 29-82; J. Neusner, *Midrash in Context: Exegesis in Formative Judaism* (Philadelphia: Fortress, 1983); idem, *What Is Midrash?* (Guides to Biblical Scholarship; Philadelphia: Fortress, 1987); D. Patte, *Early Jewish Hermeneutic in Palestine* (SBLDS 22; Missoula: Scholars, 1975); G. Porton, "Defining Midrash," in *The Study of Ancient Judaism*, ed. J. Neusner (New York: Ktav, 1981); idem, *Understanding Rabbinic Midrash* (Hoboken: Ktav, 1985); R. Riesner, *Jesus als Lehrer. Ein Untersuchung zum Ursprung der Evangelien-Überlieferung* (3d ed.; Tübingen: Mohr-Siebeck, 1988); G. Vermes, "Bible and Midrash: Early OT Exegesis," in *The Cambridge History of the Bible*, ed. P. R. Ackroyd and C. F. Evans (3 vols.; Cambridge: University Press, 1970) 1.199-231; A. G. Wright, *The Literary Genre Midrash* (Staten Island: Alba House, 1967).   C. A. Evans

MILITARY

During the lifetime of Jesus military establishments were maintained in Judea for policing, customs (*see* Taxes) and defensive duties, and some of Jesus' teaching reflects this situation (Mt 5:41; 22:7; Lk 21:20). Care must be taken to distinguish between the situation in Judea proper (with Samaria), which was under direct Roman jurisdiction (*see* Rome) throughout the ministry of Jesus, and in the separate tetrarchies of Herod Antipas (Galilee* and Perea) and Herod Philip (the northeastern areas; *see* Herodian Dynasty); these rulers each had their own military establishments (e.g., Lk 23:11) modelled on the Roman pattern.

The imperial Roman army was a professional organization raised by recruiting rather than by conscription. Its major units were called legions (about twenty-five in number at this time), each of about 6,000 men, subdivided into ten cohorts (nominally 600 men); each cohort was divided into three maniples, and each maniple into two centuries. Alongside these infantry formations were groups of "auxiliary troops," including infantry and cavalry formations (for the latter see Acts 23:23). Most of the legionaries and nearly all of the auxiliaries were natives of the various Roman provinces, and the former group became Roman citizens if they did not already have this status when they enlisted. Jews were exempted from Roman military service. The legionaries took an annual direct oath of allegiance to the emperor. Legionaries normally served for twenty years, and auxiliaries for twenty-five years, and on retirement they generally settled in the provinces where they had been stationed. Some were settled into "colonies," towns founded or extended to provide retirement homes for such veterans.

Syria, as a major province under a high-ranking military governor, had four legions to defend the eastern Roman frontier. Judea was administered as a separate area, or *provincia*, under a governor of lower rank (a *praefectus*) with much more limited forces. Pilate's troops were auxiliaries estimated at about 3,000 men. Antipas and Philip had armies that probably consisted of Jews and non-Jews and may have had some officers and men drawn from the Roman army. Soldiers were among the audience of John the Baptist (Lk 3:14; *see* John the Baptist); these would have been forces serving Herod Antipas in Perea. They acted to some extent as a peace-keeping and police force (and could be used to carry out a death penalty, Mk 6:27). John did not condemn their profession but urged them to avoid acting unjustly in carrying out their duties and to be satisfied with their admittedly low wages rather than to rob and steal to supplement them.

A story common to Matthew (8:5-13) and Luke (7:1-10) tells of a centurion who sought healing from Jesus for his servant. Where Mark refers to centurions by their Latin name, *kentyriōn*, Matthew and Luke have the Greek equivalent *hekatontarchēs*. Since there was no Roman military presence in Galilee before A.D. 44, the reference will again be to one of Herod Antipas's troops, which could nevertheless have included Roman soldiers. This man was well disposed to the Jews and enjoyed their esteem because he had built a synagogue.* This implies that he gave a substantial donation toward the building costs. We do not know at what level a centurion was paid, but he corresponded to a lower-ranking officer in a modern army. He is a significant figure in the Gospels because he showed faith* in Jesus and took the initiative in approaching him; he thus prefigures later soldiers like Cornelius (Acts 10) who were attracted to the Jewish religion and responded to the gospel (see Gospel [Good News]).

According to the first three Gospels the people who arrested Jesus were a crowd (see People, Crowd) armed with swords and clubs sent by the Sanhedrin.* This group included the Jewish Temple* guards (Lk 22:4, 52). In the Fourth Gospel the arresting party included "a detachment of soldiers" (Jn 18:3); the word used could refer to a "cohort" of 600 soldiers, but this is most unlikely, and it is more probable that a "maniple" of no more than 200 men is meant. Although some scholars have argued that John has here unhistorically involved the Gentiles* along with the Jews in the arrest of Jesus, there is nothing improbable about the Jewish authorities seeking the help of a Roman police force in arresting a person who could well be represented as a possible leader of violent revolution (see Revolutionary Movements).

Jesus himself responded to his arrest in a peaceable and nonviolent manner (see Peace). Although he predicted that his coming would bring division and "the sword" rather than peace (Mt 10:34), he rejected violence: the saying in Luke 22:36 is grimly ironic and was never meant to be taken literally, as verse 38 shows.

The crucifixion itself was carried out under the orders of Pilate, the Roman governor (see Death of Jesus). Although his headquarters were in Caesarea on the seacoast, he maintained a military presence in Jerusalem at the Fortress of Antonia, adjacent to the Temple. It was a detachment of his soldiers who mocked Jesus (Mk 15:16-20) and who then carried out the crucifixion under the command of a centurion (Mk 15:39, 44-45). Later, according to Matthew (Mt 27:62-66; 28:4, 11-15), a Roman guard watched over his tomb to prevent any attempt at removing the body of Jesus. Again, it is noteworthy how the (presumably non-Jewish) centurion is impressed by the manner of Jesus' death. He comments that Jesus was "the Son of god" (so NIV, but the Gk could equally mean "a son of God," i.e., a person of more than ordinary human character; see Son of God), or, as Luke has it, "a righteous man" (Lk 23:47). The centurion may have meant little more than that Jesus was an innocent victim whose manner of dying showed his extraordinary character; the Evangelists saw that his words could have a deeper significance than he may have intended.

See also DESTRUCTION OF JERUSALEM; PEACE; ROME.
BIBLIOGRAPHY. T. R. S. Broughton, "Note XXXIII. The

Roman Army," in *The Beginnings of Christianity*, ed. F. J. Foakes-Jackson and K. Lake (London: Macmillan, 1933) 5.427-45; R. W. Davies, *Service in the Roman Army* (Edinburgh: University Press, 1989); B. Reicke, *The New Testament Era. The World of the Bible from 500 B.C. to A.D. 100* (London: A. & C. Black, 1969); E. Schürer, *The History of the Jewish People in the Age of Jesus Christ (175 B.C.-A.D. 135)*, rev. and ed. G. Vermes, F. Millar (3 vols.; Edinburgh: T. & T. Clark, 1973-79) I.362-27 passim.   I. H. Marshall

MIRACLES AND MIRACLE STORIES

In biblical scholarship the English word *miracle* normally denotes a supernatural event, that is, an event which so transcends ordinary happenings that it is viewed as a direct result of supernatural power. In the Gospels such events are due to the exercise of God's* power (see Authority and Power)—whether directly or through human or superhuman agents— and reveal and/or effect his saving or judging purposes. Though some writers use *miracle* with enough latitude to include (predictive) prophecy (see Prophets, Prophecy), it is more common to restrict it to supernatural events in the space-time world. In contrast to *miracle, miracle stories* denotes relatively self-contained narratives in which an individual miraculous happening constitutes the, or at least a, major focus of the account. Unless one regards narratives describing angelophanies (see Angels) as miracle stories, Jesus is the subject of all such Gospel stories. Various summaries of Jesus' healings* and exorcisms (e.g., Mk 1:32-34, 39) are not ranked as miracle stories since they do not relate individual miracles. Such texts will be subsumed under the broad category "miracle traditions."

1. Miracle Traditions According to the Gospels
2. Tradition History and Historicity
3. Significance of the Miracles

1. Miracle Traditions According to the Gospels.

In a sense the Gospels testify to the truth of Goethe's description of miracle as "faith's favorite child." For example, they narrate or refer to no less than thirty-four specific miracles (exclusive of parallels) performed by Jesus during his earthly ministry. In addition there are fifteen texts (again, exclusive of parallels) that narrate or refer to Jesus' miraculous activity (almost always healings and exorcisms) in summary fashion. Beyond this, there are miracles in which Jesus is the object of the miraculous action (including the virginal conception [see Birth of Jesus], baptism,* Transfiguration,* resurrection* and ascension*) and several (at least seven) epiphanies of the risen Christ. When one includes the angelophanies, portents and texts which refer to the disciples'* miracles, the degree to which miracles dominate the Gospels becomes apparent.

1.1. The Synoptic Gospels Compared with the Fourth Gospel. The miracle traditions of the Synoptic Gospels evince several affinities. It is especially noticeable that the triple tradition contains eleven accounts of miraculous deeds performed by Jesus (excluding the baptism and Transfiguration pericopae), whereas only two (possibly three) Johannine miracles (feeding of the five thousand; walking on the sea; healing of official's son[?]) have Synoptic parallels. (Of these, only the feeding of the five thousand appears in all four Gospels.) For the Synoptic Evangelists Jesus' miracles are *dynameis*, "deeds of power." *Sēmeia*, "signs," used consistently in the Fourth Gospel, never denotes Jesus' miracles in the Synoptics (*see* John, Gospel of). Conversely, Jesus' antagonists demand a sign (Mk 8:11 par.), and future false Christs/prophets will perform "signs and wonders" (Mk 13:22; Mt 24:24). In Luke, however, this avoidance of "sign/s" for Jesus' miracles is insignificant; after all, the Evangelist repeatedly describes miracles of Jesus and the apostles as "signs and wonders" in Acts (e.g., Acts 2:22, 43). Matthew's convictions are more difficult to determine, though it seems clear that he regarded Jesus' resurrection as a sign—perhaps the only sign— of Jesus (Mt 12:39-40). Mark's Gospel never brings "sign/s" into positive connection with Jesus' ministry, but twice devalues it (Mk 8:11-12; 13:22). Perhaps Mark regarded the use of "sign/s" for Jesus' miracles as a flagrant contradiction of Jesus' refusal to furnish any sign (Mk 8:12). Furthermore, *dynameis* accords better with Mark's emphasis on Jesus as the strong and Spirit-filled Son of God (e.g., Mk 1:7-8, 10; 3:27; 5:1-8; *see* Holy Spirit; Son of God).

In the Synoptics Jesus' miracles are closely related to his proclamation of the advent of the kingdom of God (*see* Kingdom of God). Especially in summaries and in pericopae describing the mission efforts of the disciples, the preaching of the kingdom and the performance of healings and exorcisms (*see* Demon, Devil, Satan) are carefully coordinated (e.g., Mk 1:39 par.; 3:14-15 par.; 6:12-13 par.). In one saying of Jesus transmitted in Matthew and Luke this relationship is defined: ". . . if it is by the finger [Mt: "Spirit"] of God that I cast out the demons, then the kingdom of God has come to you" (Lk 11:20; Mt 12:28 NRSV). Thus the Synoptists regarded Jesus' miracles, perhaps especially his exorcisms (never mentioned in the Fourth Gospel), as one mode of God's assertion of his royal power, so that while the kingdom in its fullness still

lies in the future, it has already become a reality in Jesus' words and works. Of course, the Synoptists' linkage between Jesus' miracles and the assertion of God's power against evil, demonic forces closely coheres with their use of *dynameis*, "deeds of power," for Jesus' miracles.

The noun *pistis* "faith,"* or the verb *pisteuein*, "to believe," plays a fairly dominant role in the Synoptic miracle stories. However, unlike the Fourth Gospel, where miracles ideally result in *pistis*, the Synoptic narratives regularly present *pistis* on the part of the suppliants (or their representatives) as a prerequisite for receiving miraculous help (cf. e.g., Mk 2:5 par.; 6:5-6 par.). This is not to say, however, that the Synoptic Evangelists failed to appreciate the ability of the miracles to engender faith. This is particularly true of Luke, as can clearly be seen in Acts (e.g., 2:22; 13:6-12; 14:3; see Achtemeier).

Finally, the Synoptics agree in emphasizing the miracle-working of the disciples. Various texts note or imply that the disciples, commissioned and empowered by Jesus, effected exorcisms and healings as they helped Jesus proclaim the coming of the kingdom (e.g., Mk 3:14-15; 6:7, 12-13).

1.1.1. Mark. Mark can truly be called a Gospel of miracles, for the amount of narrative relating miraculous events in proportion to the entire Gospel is the highest among the canonical Gospels. The vast majority of these miracles are directly related to Jesus. In three cases (baptism, Transfiguration, resurrection) Jesus is, as it were, the object of the miracle. In most cases, however, he is the subject, performing eighteen specific miracles. Also, as in the other Gospels, there are summaries of Jesus' miracle-working activities (Mk 1:32-34, 39; 3:10-12; 6:5, 54-56).

In the history of Markan interpretation scholars have often grappled with two interrelated issues: the so-called messianic secret and the function of Jesus' miracles within the Gospel as a whole (*see* Mark, Gospel of). Long ago W. Wrede argued that the injunctions to secrecy following some of Jesus' miracles (Mk 1:44; 5:43; 7:36; 8:26) were part and parcel of an early Christian effort to harmonize the contradiction between the original Christian belief that Jesus became Messiah upon his resurrection and a growing conviction that Jesus must have also been the Messiah during his earthly life. This tension is resolved if Jesus revealed himself to his disciples as the Messiah during his ministry but kept it a secret until his resurrection (cf. Mk 9:9).

Bultmann agreed with Wrede's analysis of the secrecy motif and further argued that within Mark, Jesus' miracles function positively as proofs that Jesus

The Miracles of Jesus

Markan Miracles	Mark	Matthew	Luke	John
Possessed Man in Synagogue	1:23-26		4:33-35	
Peter's Mother-in-Law	1:30-31	8:14-15	4:38-39	
Man with Leprosy	1:40-42	8:2-4	5:12-13	
Paralyzed Man	2:3-12	9:2-7	5:18-25	
Man with Shriveled Hand	3:1-5	12:10-13	6:6-10	
Calming the Storm	4:37-41	8:23-27	8:22-25	
Gadarene Demoniac(s)	5:1-15	8:28-34	8:27-35	
Raising Jairus's Daughter	5:22-24, 38-42	9:18-19, 23-25	8:41-42, 49-56	
Hemorrhaging Woman	5:25-29	9:20-22	8:43-48	
Feeding of Five Thousand	6:35-44	14:15-21	9:12-17	6:5-13
Walking on Water	6:48-51	14:25		6:19-21
Canaanite Woman's Daughter	7:24-30	15:21-28		
Deaf Mute	7:31-37			
Feeding of Four Thousand	8:1-9	15:32-38		
Blind Man at Bethsaida	8:22-26			
Demon-Possessed Boy	9:17-19	17:14-18	9:38-43	
Two Blind Men	10:46-52	20:29-34	18:35-43	
Fig Tree Withered	11:12-14, 20-25	21:18-22		

Miracles Found Only in Matthew and Luke

	Mark	Matthew	Luke	John
Roman Centurion's Servant		8:5-13	7:1-10	
Blind, Mute and Possessed Man		12:22	11:14	

Miracles Found Only in Matthew

	Mark	Matthew	Luke	John
Two Blind Men		9:27-31		
Mute and Possessed Man		9:32-33		
Coin in Fish's Mouth		17:24-27		

Miracles Found Only in Luke

	Mark	Matthew	Luke	John
First Catch of Fish			5:1-11	
Raising Widow's Son at Nain			7:11-15	
Exorcism of Mary Magdalene			8:2	
Crippled Woman			13:11-13	
Man with Dropsy			14:1-4	
Ten Men with Leprosy			17:11-19	
High Priest's Servant			22:50-51	

Miracles Found Only in John

	Mark	Matthew	Luke	John
Wine Miracle at Cana				2:1-11
Official's Son at Capernaum				4:46-54
Sick Man at Pool of Bethesda				5:1-9
Healing of the Blind Man				9:1-41
Raising Lazarus				11:1-44
Second Catch of Fish				21:1-11

is the Messiah. And in Mark, he argued, the title denotes a mythological figure: the Son of God, whose being is permeated by the Spirit of God and whose divinity is revealed by stunning miracles.

While Bultmann's understanding remained dominant for a time, the 1960s and 1970s saw a spate of works which argued that Mark employed the messianic secret as a theological means of subordinating the significance of Jesus' miracles to the proclamation of his death (*see* Death of Jesus) and resurrection. T. Weeden, for example, argued that Mark intended to attack heretical Christians whose christology is best subsumed under the rubric *theios aner,* or *divine man* (*see* Divine Man/*Theios Anēr*). "In such a perspective Jesus is characterized as the epiphany of God . . . , who intervenes in human affairs to work miracles . . . . He is embued with the power and authority of God, and possesses supernatural knowledge and wisdom . . ." (55). Correspondingly, these heretics practiced a type of discipleship* whose primary criterion of success was "the quantity, magnitude, and spectacular character of their miraculous acts and pneumatic experiences" (60). True, in the first half of the Gospel Jesus behaves as a *theios anēr,* but this "*theios anēr* position is set up only to be discredited by Jesus once the disciples confess to that position" (164). Weeden, however, is unconvincing. The essential arguments against this type of interpretation are assembled, among others, by Theissen. He asks the obvious question: "Can Mark really have told sixteen miracle stories in order to warn against belief in miracles?" (294). In addition, the Transfiguration (Mk 9:2-8) and three other miracles (Mk 9:12-29; 10:46-52; 11:12-14, 20-21) occur after the first passion prediction. Even the passion narrative contains miracles (Mk 15:33-38; *see* Passion Narrative).

In view of these and other objections it has become more acceptable to interpret Jesus' miracle-working in Mark more positively. It is doubtful that the command to secrecy following the miracles is cut from the same cloth as the command to keep Jesus' divine sonship/messiahship secret. Jesus, for example, frequently performs miracles in public (in synagogues,* packed houses, etc.). Mark 1:43-45, which contains the first command to keep a miracle secret, in conjunction with Mark 1:38 shows that the leper's disobedience resulted in a frustration of Jesus' plans, namely, to preach in other towns (cf. also Mk 7:24 with 7:36). Thus Mark may well have understood the four prohibitions in practical-strategic terms.

Jesus' miracles portray him as he is described by the Baptist: the mighty one—mightier than John—who acts in the power of the Spirit (Mk 1:7-8). As such he silences and expels demons (Mk 1:21-27; 5:1-20; 7:24-30; 9:14-29) since he has overpowered and bound the strong man, Satan (Mk 3:22-27). Wind and sea obey him (Mk 4:41), and power proceeds from him and immediately cures a woman beyond the help of physicians (Mk 5:29-30). Little wonder then that in Mark his miracles are called *dynameis,* "deeds of power." And yet this powerful Son of God treads the path to horrible suffering and death in Jerusalem. This juxtaposition naturally heightens the narrative tension and serves to underscore the enormity and humiliation of the self-offering of the Son of man as a ransom for many (Mk 10:45; *see* Ransom Saying).

Jesus' miracles are also closely connected to the proclamation of the coming kingdom of God and the related presentation of Jesus as a teacher.* A comparison of Mark 1:21-27 with 1:14-15 and 1:39 reveals a Jesus who repeatedly proclaimed/taught concerning the kingdom of God in various synagogues and who exorcised demons. Similarly, Mark 3:20-29 implies that Jesus' exorcisms are to be construed as successful attacks of the reign of God against the kingdom of Satan. In the context of miraculous activity Jesus is addressed as "teacher" (Mk 4:38; 5:35; 9:17), and the teaching of Jesus and his apostles* is closely linked to miracle-working (Mk 6:2, 30, 34-44). Thus Mark—as well as Matthew and Luke—viewed these miracles as episodic manifestations of the advent of the kingdom of God.

Bultmann was therefore correct in his assessment of the positive function of the Markan miracles. However, in light of Jesus' refusal to provide a sign to skeptics (Mk 8:11-13), it is perhaps more accurate to view them not as proofs of Jesus' messiahship (*see* Christ) but as means of re-presenting the messianic Son of God, through whose miraculous ministry, death and resurrection God had inaugurated his long-awaited rule.

To Bultmann's view of the Markan miracles as proofs for the divinity of Jesus belongs the later attempt to classify Mark as an aretalogy, a Hellenistic biographical narrative aiming to glorify and propagandize for a *theios anēr.* Although this hypothesis has become less popular, G. Theissen has argued that the structure of ancient miracle stories, pressing forward as they do toward wonder/acclamation, has heavily contributed to the overall structure of Mark's Gospel. Thus Mark, Theissen surmises, purposefully suppressed titles in the acclamations of the miracle stories in order to create a powerful tension only released in the centurion's confession: "Truly this man was God's Son" (Mk 15:39 NRSV). One should observe, however, that most ancient miracle stories do not conclude with titular acclamations. Moreover, Theissen unfortunately viewed the centurion's confession as enabled by miraculous cosmic signs (Mk 15:33, 38), rather than by Jesus' loud cry (Mk 15:37, 39). A titular confession prompted by the resurrection would have made his theory more plausible.

Mark, like the other Synoptists, presents *pistis* ("faith") as a precondition for the reception of a miracle. Mark's contribution, however, is to forge a close link between faith and struggle: *pistis* is concretely demonstrated when the one(s) seeking a miracle encounter(s) a barrier which is subsequently overcome through determined struggle (Mk 2:4-5; 5:27-34, 35-36; 7:27-29; 9:22-24; 10:47-52).

1.1.2. Matthew. Matthew, according to the two-source hypothesis (*see* Synoptic Problem), has taken over almost all of the Markan miracle traditions, although he has abbreviated the miracle stories. On the other hand, Matthew contains additions. The infancy story contains angelophanies and the account of the star, but most importantly the account of the virginal conception (Mt 1:18-25; *see* Birth of Jesus). Matthew lacks three Markan miracles from the period of Jesus' ministry (Mk 1:23-28; 7:31-37; 8:22-26), but contains six additional ones: Matthew 8:5-13; 9:32-33; and 12:22 belong to or have parallels in Q; Matthew 9:27-31 is very similar to Mark 10:46-52; Matthew 14:28-33 and 17:24-27 are unique to Matthew. In the passion narrative Matthew adds that when Jesus died an earthquake shattered the rocks and many saints emerged from their tombs (Mt 27:51-53). Likewise, only Matthew describes a later earthquake occurring when an angel descended and rolled the stone from Jesus' tomb (Mt 28:2). The Evangelist concludes his Gospel with a christophany in Galilee,* another account peculiar to this Gospel.

When one examines Matthew's miracle traditions along with those of Mark and Luke, several Matthean predilections surface. Two such are the phrases, "according to your faith be it done to you" (Mt 8:13; 9:29; 15:28) and "x was healed from that hour" (Mt 8:13; 9:22; 15:28; 17:18). Matthew is also fond of repetition (Mt 9:32-34/12:22-24; 9:27-31/20:29-34; 12:38-39/16:1-4). Is this also related to the doubling of Markan characters in Matthew 8:28 and 20:30?

Three Matthean changes *vis-à-vis* Mark result in a heightening of Jesus' dignity. Thus characters in Matthean miracle traditions are much more apt to address Jesus as "Lord" (*kyrie:* Mt 8:2, 6, 8, 25; 9:28; 15:22, 25; 17:4; 20:31, 33). Likewise, suppliants or witnesses "worship" Jesus (*proskynein:* Mt 8:2; 9:18; 14:33; 15:25). Finally, Matthew insists that Jesus performed a miracle for *all* who needed it, or that *all*

the sick were brought to him (Mt 4:23-24; 8:16; 12:15; 14:35; 15:37).

Scholars have long noted that Matthew is a Gospel of fulfilled Scripture, and this concern has influenced its miracle traditions (*see* Old Testament in the Gospels; Typology). The virginal conception fulfilled Isaiah 7:14 (Mt 1:22-23); Jesus' exorcisms and healings fulfilled Isaiah 53:4 (Mt 8:17); and Jesus' miracles described in Matthew 11:5 correspond to Isaianic prophecies. Furthermore, Matthew rewrites a Markan summary (Mk 3:7-12) so that Jesus no longer prohibits demons from revealing his identity but rather forbids the healed to make him known (Mt 12:15-21). This in turn is interpreted as a fulfillment of the unobtrusive and gentle ways of God's servant (Is 42:1-4; *see* Servant of Yahweh). The desire to show fulfilled prophecy may also explain the tendency to underscore Jesus' healing ministry (cf. Mt 4:23; 10:1, 7-8; 12:15-16 with their Markan counterparts; see also Mt 9:35; 14:14; 15:30; 19:2; 21:14-15). For this activity Matthew could adduce OT prophecies (Mt 8:17; 11:5; 12:18-21). Twice Matthew notes the accusation that Jesus performed his miracles by Beelzebul's power (Mt 9:34; 12:24; cf. 13:56). He also knows that false prophets will try to legitimate themselves by miracles (Mt 7:15-23; 24:24). It is therefore very important for this author, perhaps a Jewish-Christian "scribe"* (Mt 13:52) and certainly one vitally concerned about the fulfillment of the Law* and Prophets (Mt 5:17-20), to show that Jesus' miracles were in accord with the Torah and thus were of divine origin. This subordination of miracle to Torah, rooted in Deuteronomy 13:1-5, has possibly influenced Matthew's decision to present the Sermon on the Mount (cf. esp. Mt 5:17-20; *see* Sermon on the Mount) prior to any individual miracle stories.

Held, observing Matthew's abbreviations and expansions of Mark, concluded that the Evangelist intended primarily to provide instruction to the church* concerning christology, faith and discipleship. Christological themes have already been noted: Jesus' fulfillment of OT prophecy and his status as the Lord* who is to be worshiped (*see* Worship). Instruction on faith is also important to Matthew, though Theissen has noted that Matthew's dropping of *pistis* from three Markan stories retold in Matthew 9:18-26; 17:14-21; and 20:29-34 militates against "Held's view that the motif of faith is Matthew's critical principle of selection for including Markan miracle stories" (137). On the other hand, rebuke of the disciples for little faith does play a more prominent role in Matthew than in Mark (cf. Mt 14:31; 17:20). Finally, Held identified Matthean changes that evince an interest in the nature and demands of discipleship (e.g., Mt 9:8; 14:28-33).

Matthew made a noticeable change in the way his miracle stories are ordered within the overall story of Jesus' ministry. After a brief summary of Jesus' message and ministry (Mt 4:23-25), he initiates his account of Jesus' work with an extensive account of his teaching, the Sermon on the Mount (Mt 5—7). Only then does he narrate a series of miracle stories (Mt 8—9). Moreover, the Sermon and the narratives of the following two chapters appear to constitute one major unit in Matthew's structure, judging from the similar summaries (Jesus taught, preached and healed) which form an *inclusio* (Mt 4:23-25; 9:35-38). On the other hand, Kingsbury, noting the mention of Jesus' teaching and preaching in Matthew 11:1, envisions chapters 8—9 as part of a section comprising Matthew 4:17—11:1 in which Jesus conducts a Galilean ministry of teaching, preaching and healing. In turn, this section would constitute the first major subdivision of Matthew 4:17—16:20, over which he places the rubric "The Proclamation of Jesus Messiah" (17).

But what is the function of the miracles within this unit? There are ten miracles in chapters 8—9, but the presence of pericopae that do not narrate miracles and the merciful nature of Jesus' miracles make it unlikely either that these chapters intend to present the Messiah of deed (alongside the Messiah of word) or that Jesus is being portrayed as the new Moses.* The themes of faith and discipleship surface several times, but it is difficult to subsume every pericope in chapters 8—9 under either heading. Gnilka has suggested that the principal message concerns Jesus the Son of God and the Son of David (*see* Son of David), who acts with grace toward his people and who is to be encountered in faith and in willing discipleship. Luz has recently proposed that chapters 8—9 recapitulate the history of the Matthean church. The attempt to comprehend the precise import of these two chapters will no doubt continue.

1.1.3. Luke. The contours of the miraculous in Jesus' life, according to Luke's Gospel, are interesting to trace. Like Matthew, Luke commences with birth narratives which relate angelophanies and the virginal conception. Gabriel, in fact, draws a direct link between this generation by the Holy Spirit and Jesus' identity as "Son of God" (Lk 1:35). Between Matthew's five and Luke's three angelophanies there is no overlap.

Luke's presentation of Jesus' miracles largely corresponds to those of Mark and Matthew, yet there are interesting modifications. All of the Markan miracles appear in sequence in Luke save the cursing of the fig tree (cf. Lk 13:6-9) and the five miracle stories within Luke's so-called great omission (Mk 6:45—8:26). Luke also included a healing (Lk 7:1-10) and an exorcism (Lk 11:14) belonging to the Q* material. And finally, Luke contains seven specific miracles unique to this Gospel, including the notice concerning the exorcism of seven demons from Mary Magdalene (Lk 8:2) and a report of the healing of the ear of the high priest's servant (Lk 22:51; cf. also 5:1-11; 7:11-17; 13:10-17; 14:1-6; 17:11-19).

Luke, of course, concludes with the Easter story. However, in his story the women* received the Easter news from two men wearing dazzling clothes (Lk 24:4). Subsequently, Luke narrates two christophanies and refers to a third, all of which occurred on Easter Sunday: an appearance to the Emmaus disciples (Lk 24:13-35), a reference to an epiphany before Simon (Lk 24:34) and an evening appearance before the eleven and others (Lk 24:36-49). At this point Luke shows more affinity with the Fourth Gospel than with the other Synoptics. Mark contains no resurrection appearances, and Matthew's only one is situated in Galilee. On the other hand, John knows a christophany to the disciples on Easter evening (Lk 20:19-23), and Magdalene had an encounter with two angels in white (Lk 20:11-13). Finally, Luke concludes his Gospel by narrating the ascension more fully described in Acts 1:1-11.

In various ways Luke left his stamp on the traditions passed on by him. For example, certain vocabulary preferences are evident. To convey the immediate occurrence of the miracles he prefers the literary term *parachrēma* (Lk 4:39; 5:25; 8:44, 47, 55; 13:13; 18:43) to *euthus* (Mk) or *eutheōs* (Mt). Like Matthew, he expands Mark's use of *kyrios,* "Lord," both in direct address (Lk 5:12) and as an appellation in the third person (Lk 7:13; 13:15), but his frequent use of *epistata,* "master," is unique (Lk 5:5; 8:24, 45; 9:33; 17:13). Luke also prefers the verb *iaomai,* "to heal" (Lk 5:17; 6:18-19; 7:7; 8:47; 9:2, 11, 42; 14:4; 17:15; 22:51) more than do his Synoptic counterparts.

Comparison with the other Synoptics also reveals characteristic emphases in the Lukan miracle traditions. For all the Synoptists the miracles of Jesus are *dynameis,* "powerful deeds," but Luke stresses that they are the result of the *dynamis,* "power," which is at Jesus' disposal (Lk 4:36; 5:17; 6:19; 8:46), which he shares with his disciples (Lk 9:1), and which therefore enables them to crush the enemy's *dynamis* (Lk 10:19). Perhaps this emphasis is related to Luke's inclination to describe illness as *astheneia,* a bodily "weakness" (Lk 4:40; 5:15; 8:2; 13:11-12). Busse, on the basis of such texts as Luke 4:39 and 13:11, 16, argued that for Luke all sickness was caused by demons. Perhaps, but Luke never expressly affirms it, and some healings are narrated without explicit mention of demons or exorcistic motifs.

It has long been recognized that Luke redacted his sources to emphasize the praying of Jesus (*see* Prayer), and twice this motif appears in Luke's miracle stories (Lk 5:16; 9:29; cf. 3:21). Theissen observed that Luke on three occasions records that Jesus prayed shortly before divine power was manifested through or in him (Lk 5:16-17; 6:12-19; 9:29). This shows, according to Theissen, that Luke viewed Jesus' *dynamis* as a dynamic, not a static, phenomenon and accords with a Lukan tendency to emphasize the work of God behind and above Jesus' ministry. Accordingly, in several miracle story endings the suppliant and/or the witnessing crowd (*see* People, Crowd) "give glory to God" or in some other way acknowledge God's activity (Lk 5:25; 7:16; 9:43; 13:13; 17:15, 18; 18:43; 19:37).

One may deduce from Acts 3:22-23 and 7:37 (cf. Lk 9:35) that Luke viewed Jesus as the Mosaic prophet predicted in Deuteronomy 18:15, 18. This prophet christology also makes itself felt in the Gospel, especially in those passages which relate Jesus' prophetic status to miracle-working (Lk 7:16; 24:19). Luke seemingly borrowed hues from the Elijah-Elisha narratives (*see* Elijah and Elisha) to paint his portrait of Jesus (Lk 4:25-27; 7:11-17; 9:62), but it is unlikely that he presents him, even in a qualified sense, as Elijah *redivivus* (cf. Mal 4:5-6). It is the Baptist who comes in the "spirit and power of Elijah" (Lk 1:17), and Jesus declares John to be the coming messenger of Malachi 3:1 (a figure probably generally identified as the returning Elijah of Mal 4:5-6; *see* John the Baptist).

Finally, Theissen has called attention to how Luke's salvation-history schema has influenced his retelling of the miracle stories. Just as God's plan of salvation, anticipated in the OT, reached its denouement in the "today" of Jesus' ministry (Lk 4:21), so those who witnessed the forgiving (*see* Forgiveness of Sins) and healing of the paralytic declare, "We have seen strange things *today*" (Lk 5:26 NRSV [my emphasis]). Likewise, those who are confronted with Jesus' raising of the widow's son exclaim that now at last in Jesus, "God has looked favorably on his people" (Lk 7:16 NRSV).

1.2. The Fourth Gospel. Miracle plays a dominant role in the Fourth Gospel, and especially in this domain the distinctive Johannine perspective becomes evident. Jesus' miracles, for example, are set within the context of the one grand miracle, the incarnation of the Logos* (Jn 1:14). Thus the Fourth Gospel contains no birth narratives, but in its prologue directs the reader all the way back to the preincarnate Son.

As in the Synoptics, Jesus receives the Spirit at his baptism (Jn 1:32-34). The Fourth Gospel also agrees that Jesus performed many miracles during his ministry, but it narrates only seven—far fewer than in the Synoptics. The feeding of the five thousand (Jn 6:1-15), Jesus walking on the sea (Jn 6:16-21) and probably the healing of the nobleman's son (Jn 4:46-54) have Synoptic parallels, but the other four, including the raising of Lazarus* (Jn 11:1-44), are unique. Alongside these seven "signs" and predictive prophecy (attested in all the Gospels), the Johannine Jesus displays supernatural knowledge of hidden realities (Jn 1:47-49; 2:24-25; 4:16-19; 5:6?; 6:64, 70-71; 13:1; 21:6). While not entirely absent from the Synoptics, this feature is more pronounced in John.

The premier miracle of the last half of the Fourth Gospel is Jesus' resurrection/return to the Father. As noted above, John's resurrection narratives have interesting points of contact with Luke's: the two figures who convey the Easter message to Mary/the women, a resurrection appearance to the disciples on Easter and explicit mention of Jesus' ascension (though apparently understood differently). Nevertheless, the following miraculous elements are unique to John: a christophany to Mary Magdalene (Jn 20:14-18), Jesus' bestowal of the Holy Spirit on his disciples on Easter evening (Jn 20:21-22), a christophany to his disciples a week later (Jn 20:26-29) and, yet later, an early morning christophany to seven disciples (Jn 21:1-23).

On one level the miracle stories of the Fourth Gospel are similar to those of the Synoptic tradition. Three have Synoptic parallels, and of the remaining four, two are healings (from lameness, blindness), one a "gift" miracle (the production of wine from water) and one a resuscitation (Lazarus)—three types which have Synoptic parallels. Nevertheless, the Johannine presentation is distinctive.

In the first place, while in the Synoptics Jesus' miracles are normally called *dynameis*, "mighty deeds," the Fourth Evangelist repeatedly calls them *sēmeia*, "signs." He emphasizes that Jesus performed many signs, but scholars generally agree that he chose to narrate only seven. Since these appear within the first twelve chapters, R. Brown chose to label these chapters the "Book of Signs." Also, Burge has noted that most of the twenty-seven instances of *ergon*, "work," in the Fourth Gospel refer to Jesus' signs, although "work/s" includes more than signs (Jn 14:10; 17:4).

Whereas in the Synoptics the *dynameis* are closely correlated with the kingdom of God, proclaimed and proleptically established in Jesus' words and deeds, the Johannine *sēmeia* are said to evoke faith in Jesus as the Christ, the Son of God (Jn 20:30-31). The framework of the Johannine signs (especially the "I am" sayings; *see* "I Am" Sayings) shows that the Evangelist has by no means simply adopted a traditional linguistic usage (cf. e.g., Acts 2:22; Rom 15:19). "Signs" are precisely what the Johannine miracles are, for in very concrete, physical ways they point to the deep and crucial truth about Jesus (and God), namely, that he is the absolutely unique Son of God who descended from heaven to reveal the Father and through whose "lifting up" on the cross, resurrection and return to the Father believers receive the Holy Spirit and thus eternal life.* The signs, in other words, point to the present glory* of the exclusive mediator of eschatological salvation and also portend the salvation* to be enjoyed by the beneficiaries of the completion of his messianic work (cf. Jn 7:37-39).

Secondly, among the Johannine signs there are no exorcisms. In fact, Jesus' exorcisms are not even mentioned in John. In the Fourth Gospel it is in the "hour" of Jesus that the devil, the ruler of this world, makes his supreme assault against Jesus (Jn 13:2, 27; 14:30), but through Jesus' "lifting up" he is "cast out" (Jn 12:31-32).

Thirdly, while the Fourth Gospel knows that faith is a prerequisite for miracles (Jn 4:50; 11:40), its emphasis is on the hope that retelling the signs will engender faith (Jn 20:30-31). Thus in the Fourth Gospel Jesus takes the initiative in performing signs, in fact, many signs (Jn 7:31; 11:47; 12:37; 20:30) "which no one else did" (Jn 15:24). The Fourth Gospel does not devalue faith based upon witnessing or hearing about signs unless such faith is less than a commitment to Jesus as (what the Evangelist understands by) the Christ, the Son of God. On the other hand, the Fourth Gospel does critique the demand to see signs before coming to faith (Jn 4:48; 6:30; 20:24-29).

2. Tradition History and Historicity.

2.1. Miracles of the Birth Narratives. In the Matthean infancy narratives appear five angelophanies, the story of the star and the account of the virginal conception. This last-mentioned miracle is also presented in Luke, along with three angelophanies. Strictly speaking there are no parallels between these two sets of angelophanies, though it is true that both Gospels contain an angelic announcement of Jesus' birth (Matthew's to Joseph; Luke's to Mary). Because there is such little overlap between these birth narratives (cf. Fitzmyer, 1.307), it is difficult to trace their tradition history (*see* Tradition Criticism). Alongside appeal to the Evangelists' own creativity, a bewildering assortment of oral and written sources

have been postulated, but no consensus has emerged. At any rate one thing is clear: Assuming that Matthew and Luke independently composed their birth narratives, both were relying on older tradition containing the virginal conception and probably an angelic announcement of Jesus' birth. The tradition of the virginal conception, therefore, predates Matthew and Luke, but by how long? Some conclude that it is a late creation since no other NT author—including the earliest, Paul—betrays knowledge of it (except perhaps the author of the Fourth Gospel [Jn 8:41; cf. Mk 6:3]). But can one show the probability that a given author would have mentioned it had he known about it? Moreover, some explain this silence by appeal to a "birth secret" (cf. Lk 2:19, 51) which was not divulged until considerably later (*see* Birth of Jesus).

There have been a variety of efforts to explain the origin of belief in the virginal conception without recourse to the supernatural, but each is beset with difficulties. It is not clear that Isaiah 7:14, either in the MT or LXX, speaks of a virginal conception, and a messianic interpretation of this text in pre-Christian times is not forthcoming. In an allegorical exegesis of the birth of Isaac, Philo (*Cher.* 43-52) employs the pagan notion that a woman might become pregnant through the spirit, power or breath of a god (Aeschylus *Suppl.* 17-19; Plutarch *Ser. Num. Pun.* 4; *Mor.* 9.114-19). Yet Philo only uses this notion to explain the generation of virtue in the soul; there is no evidence that he or any other Jew believed that Isaac or anyone else had been fathered by God's Spirit apart from a human father. That the tradition of Jesus' virginal conception arose from a direct assimilation to pagan stories of gods copulating with mortal women is virtually excluded by the intensely Jewish ambience of the birth narratives. In sum, historical analysis of the tradition that Jesus had no biological father can yield neither proof nor refutation.

2.2. Miracles Performed by Jesus. Among NT scholars there is almost universal agreement that Jesus performed what he and his contemporaries regarded as miraculous healings and exorcisms. This judgment is based primarily on several sayings of Jesus which, when evaluated against widely recognized criteria of authenticity (*see* Form Criticism), prove to be utterances of Jesus (Mt 12:28 par. Lk 11:20; Mk 3:23; Lk 13:32; Mt 11:4-6 par. Lk 7:22-23; Mt 13:16-17 par. Lk 10:23-24). To this evidence one may add the fact that Jesus' exorcistic and/or healing activity is attested in every stratum of Gospel material (Q,* Mark, M,* L,* John) and in a variety of literary forms (sayings, miracle stories, summaries, controversy stories, the so-called legends and the passion narratives [Mk 15:31

par.]). Outside of early Christianity Jesus was also known as an exorcist/healer in the magical papyri (PGM 4.3019-30) and within later Jewish circles (e.g., *t. Ḥul.* 2:22-23). Despite the recent, highly speculative reconstruction of Christian origins by B. Mack, who argues that Jesus was not a miracle worker, sober historical analysis will continue to affirm the high probability that Jesus performed healings and exorcisms.

Evidence that Jesus raised the dead and performed so-called nature miracles is less pervasive. Only Jesus' revivification of the dead is attested in a saying (from Q) which scholars have frequently judged authentic (Mt 11:4-6 par. Lk 7:22-23). However, since Matthew, Luke and John contain at least one revivification and/or nature miracle not found in Mark, it is highly improbable that all such stories in Mark are Markan creations. We can, therefore, safely say that revivification and nature miracles were attributed to Jesus at some point prior to Mark. Of course, those who deny in principle the possibility of supernatural events reject such miracles (with the exception perhaps of revivifications which could be explained on naturalistic grounds). On the other hand, those who believe that Jesus was raised from the dead are naturally open to the possibility that some such miracles actually occurred.

While most scholars agree that Jesus performed exorcisms and healings (and possibly deeds regarded as revivifications), many would be wary about claiming that any one of the miracle stories of the Gospels is based on actual reminiscence. This obviously raises questions concerning the source(s) employed by the Evangelists. To the degree that one is sure of the traditional link between Mark and Peter, or that John Zebedee was the ultimate authority for the Johannine signs, one will be very open to the historicity of these stories. These two hypotheses, however, have been—perhaps unwisely—widely abandoned. At the very least, it is virtually certain, as we have seen, that some if not all of the Gospel stories antedate Mark. Among the traditions designated as Q there are two miracle stories (Mt 8:5-13 par. Lk 7:1-10 [Jn 4:46-54 is possibly a variant]; Mt 12:22-23 par. Lk 11:14). Various scholars have also attempted to delineate prior oral or written catenae, or chains, of miracles which were incorporated into the Gospels. Achtemeier (1970, 1972), for example, argues that two such catenae lie behind the Markan miracle stories appearing in Mark 4:35—6:44 and 6:45—8:26. Many Johannine scholars have appealed to a signs source to explain the composition of the Fourth Gospel. Recently Mack has endeavored to find at the root of all these catenae a Christian

effort to transform Jesus into a miracle worker.

In reality, however, these source theories involve a high degree of speculation (cf. Koch), and Mack's reconstruction in particular is not likely to inspire confidence. Source analysis may help to show that the miracle stories had an existence prior to their inclusion in the Gospels, but this fact does not in itself yield a verdict on historicity (*see* Gospels [Historical Reliability]).

Skepticism concerning the probable historicity of any particular miracle story has also been fueled by the conviction that those who formulated these accounts assimilated Jesus to the typical miracle-working divine man (*theios anēr*) familiar to the Hellenistic world (*see* Hellenism). Nevertheless, the *theios anēr* hypothesis and its implications for the tradition history of the miracle stories is much weaker than its advocates realize. As its weaknesses are exposed elsewhere (*see* Divine Man/*Theios Anēr*), it will suffice here to note that (1) one can posit several reasons why the earliest Aramaic-speaking church would have narrated Jesus' miracles (see 3.2 below), and that (2) in fact a significant number of respected Gospel scholars have argued that at least a few of the miracle stories circulated in the earliest church.

Though one would be hard pressed to prove that some of the miracle stories did not originate among Hellenized Christians, one can with confidence exclude few if any from the early Aramaic-speaking church. Such early circulation would not in itself prove historicity, but with all other things equal this fact would enhance the case for historical verity. R. Pesch has thoughtfully pointed to elements within healing and exorcism stories that argue for their historicity, though some may hesitate to agree that some narratives contain elements which make historicity improbable.

2.3. Resurrection/Discovery of the Empty Tomb. Whether Jesus rose from the dead is a complex philosophical, theological and historical problem. This complexity is demonstrated in the work of W. Pannenberg, the theologian who more than anyone else in this half century has pressed for recognition of the historicity and centrality of Jesus' resurrection. Of this fact, however, all historians are confident: that very shortly after Jesus was crucified, his disciples became convinced by multiple visionary appearances of Jesus (1 Cor 15:5-8) that God had restored his life and ushered him into the heavenly world. Thus the resurrection belongs to the bedrock of Christian belief (*see* Resurrection).

Many, however, would refrain from saying the same about the story of the discovery of the empty tomb.

Bultmann argued that it was not part of the early passion narrative, but late apologetic (*see* Passion Narrative). Some scholars have since credited Mark with its origin. Pesch (1974), on the other hand, has argued cogently that it formed the conclusion of the old Jerusalem passion narrative. Yet he maintains that it was not based on a historical report, but was freely constructed after a pattern attested in the Jewish as well as in the Greco-Roman world: the unsuccessful search for the translated or resurrected person.

It is true that difficult questions face the defender of the substantial historicity of the empty tomb story. Why, for example, does the empty tomb tradition not surface in the early confessional statement quoted by Paul in 1 Corinthians 15:3-7, in his own words, or in the sermons of Acts? Yet an impressive list of exegetes have concluded that jettisoning a historical core for the empty tomb story presents even more formidable problems. When Jesus' resurrection was first proclaimed, why did the authorities not exhume the corpse? Even if it had decayed beyond recognition, its presence in Joseph's tomb—a detail with strong historical credentials—would have been damning. And if the authorities themselves had discovered it empty, would they have revealed it? And had they done so, would Christians have not heavily exploited that fact? Morever, if the empty tomb narrative had been freely constructed, would a few women have been chosen as witnesses of the opened and empty tomb? Why not some or all of the eleven disciples? Finally, as Craig has argued, the discovery of the empty tomb on Easter Sunday following Good Friday offers the only really satisfying explanation of the creedal affirmation, "He was raised on the third day." While belief in Jesus' resurrection does not necessarily hinge on the historicity of the empty tomb story, a variety of historical considerations make the latter plausible.

3. Significance of the Miracles.

3.1. Miracles of the Birth Narratives. As different as they are, the Matthean and Lukan birth narratives converge in situating Jesus' nativity in a matrix of miracles. In general the angelophanies underscore the importance of Jesus' birth for salvation history. Matthew's five dream-angelophanies reveal God's ability to uphold his divine plan, prophesied in Scripture, over against historical ambiguities and Herod's machinations. Specifically, the angelic annunciation of Jesus' birth (to Joseph [Mt] and Mary [Lk]) is appropriate for the messianic scion of David, just as angels heralded important figures of the past. Isaac, Moses (e.g., Josephus *Ant.* 2.210-16) and Samson.

Matthew's star, connected to the oracle of Numbers 24:17, portends the birth of "King David's greater Son" (cf. e.g., 4QTestim 12-13). According to Kee, Matthew's portents at Jesus' birth and death are to be interpreted in light of Roman historical tradition, in which such portents demonstrate the divine governance of history in the rise and fall of emperors. Thus the perceptive will see in the star a disclosure of God's purpose in history, centered upon Jesus the king.

The virginal conception, like the angelophanies and the star, exalts Jesus and links him to OT history and expectation. Several key Israelite figures (e.g., Isaac, Joseph, Samson, Samuel) were born to barren women blessed by God. On the other hand, none was born to a virgin. R. Brown has called attention to this same "step-parallelism" between the birth accounts of John and Jesus in Luke. Such a unique origin was fitting for God's eschatological plenipotentiary, to whom worship would be the appropriate response. At some point this miraculous conception was regarded as the fulfillment of Isaiah 7:14 (Mt 1:22-23; allusion in Lk 1:26-31)—a promise given to the "house of David"—and associated with the title Son of God (Lk 1:35).

3.2. Miracles Occurring in Jesus' Ministry. Almost all scholars believe that Jesus saw a direct connection between the miracles he performed and his proclamation of the coming of God's kingdom (*see* Kingdom of God). In the opinion of advocates of *consistent eschatology*, Jesus viewed his miracles as signs that the kingdom of God was on the verge of bringing the present age to an end. C. H. Dodd, the principal voice of *realized eschatology*, argued on the basis of his interpretation of Matthew 12:28 and Luke 11:20 that Jesus saw his miracles as actual expressions of God's reign, already fully present in his ministry. According to others, however, Jesus performed his miracles knowing that in his ministry the reign of God was being inaugurated, yet also intending his miracles to portend the cosmic renewal that the future consummation of the kingdom would entail.

This connection between Jesus' miracles and his message about the advent of the kingdom accounts for most if not all of the miracles attributed to him in the Gospels. According to Isaiah, in the future era of salvation—the "kingdom of God" in apocalyptic thought—the deaf will hear, the blind will see, the lame will walk and the mute will sing (29:18-19; 35:5-6; 61:1). Beyond that, both the OT and intertestamental apocalyptic* know that the "age to come" will mean resurrection for the dead (Is 26:19; Dan 12:1-3). Although the OT has little to say about demons or exorcism, several noncanonical apocalyptic authors expected the advent of the kingdom to spell doom for Satan and his demonic minions (*1 Enoch* 10:11-15; 54-55; 11QMelch; *T. Levi* 18:12; *T. Mos.* 10:1-2; cf. Mt 12:28; Lk 11:20).

One can even posit an eschatological/apocalyptic background for the so-called nature miracles (*see* Eschatology). All three gift or provision miracles (feedings of five thousand and four thousand; Cana wine miracle) actualize and foreshadow the messianic feast (Is 25:6-9; *2 Apoc. Bar.* 29:4; Mt 8:11 par.), characterized by an abundance of bread*—the eschatological equivalent of the manna miracle (*2 Apoc. Bar.* 29:7-8; cf. Jn 6:4, 14, 30-31; Rev. 2:17)—and wine* (*2 Apoc. Bar.* 29:5-6). The two rescue miracles, Jesus' calming of and walking on the sea, are meaningful against the horizon of Yahweh's assertion of his sovereignty over the sea in creation (Job 26:12-13; Ps 74:12-15), the Exodus (Ps 77:16-20) and the eschaton (Is 27:1; cf. Rev 21:1). As apocalyptic also looked for divine judgment* on God's enemies, it is tempting to see in Jesus' cursing of the fig tree an acted parable* threatening the Jewish nation with disaster in the absence of repentance* (cf. Mk 11:13; Mic 7:1-6; Jer 8:13). Even the visionary experiences of Jesus' baptism and Transfiguration fall within the orbit of apocalyptic eschatology insofar as (1) literature of the latter type often employed vision as a revelatory medium, and (2) the two visions in question have eschatological content.

The miracles of Jesus are, however, not only integrally related to the coming of the kingdom, but also support and promote the identity of Jesus as God's eschatological agent, the Messiah (*see* Christ). It is admittedly difficult to produce pre-Christian texts in which the expected Messiah appears as a miracle worker, but considerable evidence suggests that by the first Christian century at least some Jews saw Moses and the saving events of the Exodus period as prototypical of the Messiah and the liberating events of his reign. This typology probably lies behind the sign prophets of Josephus (*see* Revolutionary Movements), the reaction of the crowd in John 6:14-15, the behavior of the false christs of Mark 13:21-22 and parallels, and the description of the miracle working of the Davidic Messiah of 4 Ezra 13:32, 50. One thing is certain: at least as early as Luke-Acts—and probably much earlier—Jesus was regarded as the predicted mosaic prophet of Deuteronomy 18:15, 18 (Acts 3:22-23; 7:37), and thus his miracles appear as "signs and wonders" standing in a typological relation to those that Moses performed (Acts 2:22; *see* Prophets, Prophecy).

Other factors also contributed to the christological significance of Jesus' miracles: (1) they document qualities expected in the shepherd-Messiah (*see* Shepherd, Sheep)—compassion and mercy* (esp. emphasized in Mt); (2) they demonstrate God's approbation of Jesus and his ministry, on the basis of the deeply rooted scriptural principle that miracles (performed within the framework of divine revelation) legitimate divinely authorized agents; and (3), aside from pre-Christian messianic expectations, their transmission and repetition are inevitable, given the desire of early Christians to glorify and exalt their Messiah.

3.3. Resurrection/Discovery of the Empty Tomb. In the historical-theological context in which belief in Jesus' resurrection originated, certain implications of this divine action were present from the beginning: Jesus was truly God's Messiah, and his resurrection marked the inauguration of the eschatological resurrection, though an interval of time would separate Jesus' resurrection from that of believers (1 Cor 15:20-28).

The Gospels proclaim the resurrection by narrating both the story of the empty tomb and—collectively—at least seven epiphanies of the risen Christ. The empty tomb story is narrated first, but the significance of the vacant tomb does not emerge until Jesus' continued existence is revealed by angelic mediation and/or a christophany. In light of these divine revelations, however, the mystery (or misinterpretation) of the empty tomb is clarified, for the dominant Jewish notion of resurrection would have required that the earthly body of Jesus be transformed into the glorified body, hence resulting in an empty tomb.

In conclusion, taken as a whole the Gospels testify that Jesus performed many miracles and in addition that breathtaking wonders marked both the beginning and end of his earthly life. While this composite picture does not admit of scientific proof, the evidence at hand is sufficient to challenge the honest inquirer to consider seriously the Christian conviction about the identity of Jesus, and to perceive in him and his ministry the inauguration of the reign of God expected in Jewish apocalyptic. For believers these expressions of God's royal and benevolent power constitute a continual reminder of the divine power available in weakness for the church militant and in unveiled glory for the church triumphant.

See also AUTHORITY AND POWER; BIRTH OF JESUS; DEMON, DEVIL, SATAN; DIVINE MAN/THEIOS ANĒR; GOSPELS (HISTORICAL RELIABILITY); HEALING; KINGDOM OF GOD; RESURRECTION.

BIBLIOGRAPHY. P. Achtemeier, "Toward the Isolation of Pre-Markan Miracle Catenae," *JBL* 89 (1970) 265-91; idem, "The Origin and Function of the Pre-Marcan Miracle Catenae," *JBL* 91 (1972) 198-221; idem, "The

Lucan Perspective on the Miracles of Jesus: A Preliminary Sketch," *JBL* 94 (1975) 547-62; O. Betz and W. Grimm, *Wesen und Wirklichkeit der Wunder Jesu* (ANTJ 2; Frankfurt: Peter Lang, 1977); B. Blackburn, *Theios Anēr and the Markan Miracle Traditions* (WUNT 2.40; Tübingen: J. C. B. Mohr, 1991); C. Brown, *Miracles and the Critical Mind* (Grand Rapids: Eerdmans, 1984); R. Brown, *The Gospel according to John* (AB 29, 29A; Garden City, NY: Doubleday, 1966, 1970); idem, *The Birth of the Messiah* (Garden City, NY: Doubleday, 1979); R. Bultmann, *History of the Synoptic Tradition* (rev. ed.; New York: Harper and Row, 1963); G. Burge, *The Anointed Community: The Holy Spirit in the Johannine Tradition* (Grand Rapids: Eerdmans, 1987); U. Busse, *Die Wunder des Propheten Jesu: Rezeption, Komposition und Interpretation der Wundertradition im Evangelium des Lukas* (FB 24; Stuttgart: Katholisches Bibelwerk, 1977); W. Craig, "The Historicity of the Empty Tomb of Jesus," *NTS* 31 (1985) 39-67; J. A. Fitzmyer, *The Gospel according to Luke* (AB 28, 28A; Garden City, NY: Doubleday, 1981, 1985); R. Fortna, *The Gospel of Signs* (SNTSMS 11; Cambridge: University Press, 1970); J. Gnilka, *Das Matthäusevangelium* (HTKNT 1; Freiburg: Herder, 1986); H. J. Held, "Matthew As Interpreter of the Miracle Stories," in *Tradition and Interpretation in Matthew*, G. Bornkamm, G. Barth, H. J. Held (Philadelphia: Westminster, 1963); H. C. Kee, *Miracle in the Early Christian World* (New Haven: Yale University, 1983); K. Kertelge, *Die Wunder Jesu im Markusevangelium* (SANT 13; Munich: Kösel-Verlag, 1970); D.-A. Koch, *Die Bedeutung der Wundererzählungen für die Christologie des Markusevangeliums* (BZNW 42; Berlin: W. de Gruyter, 1975); U. Luz, "Die Wundergeschichten von Mt 8-9," in *Tradition and Interpretation in the New Testament: Essays in Honor of E. Earle Ellis*, ed. G. Hawthorne and O. Betz (Grand Rapids: Eerdmans, 1987); B. Mack, *A Myth of Innocence: Mark and Christian Origins* (Philadelphia: Fortress, 1988); W. Pannenberg, *Jesus—God and Man* (Philadelphia: Westminster, 1977); R. Pesch, *Jesu ureigene Taten?* (QD 52; Freiburg: Herder, 1970); idem, "Der Schluss der vormarkinischen Passionsgeschichte und des Markusevangeliums: Mk 15,42-16,8," in *L'Évangile selon Marc: Tradition et Rédaction*, ed. M. Sabbe (Leuven: Leuven University, 1974) 365-409; G. Theissen, *The Miracle Stories of the Early Christian Tradition* (Philadelphia: Fortress, 1983); T. Weeden, *Mark—Traditions in Conflict* (Philadelphia: Fortress, 1971); D. Wenham and C. Blomberg, eds., *Gospel Perspectives 6: The Miracles of Jesus* (Sheffield: JSOT, 1986); W. Wrede, *The Messianic Secret* (Cambridge: James Clarke, 1971). B. L. Blackburn

MISHNAH. *See* RABBINIC TRADITIONS AND WRITINGS.

MISSION. *See* APOSTLE; GENTILES; RESURRECTION.

MISSION OF JESUS. *See* DEATH OF JESUS; HISTORICAL JESUS, QUEST OF; KINGDOM OF GOD/HEAVEN.

MONEY. *See* RICH AND POOR; TAXES.

MORAL TEACHING. *See* ETHICS OF JESUS.

MOSES

The Gospels present Moses as the mediator of the Law* and more significantly as one who foretold and foreshadowed Jesus' coming. Jesus is presented as a prophet* like Moses (Deut 18:15-19) and as a lawgiver like Moses (not as merely an interpreter of Moses).

1. Moses As Mediator of the Law
2. A Prophet/Lawgiver Like Moses
3. Conclusion

1. Moses As Mediator of the Law.
In the Synoptics the expressions "the Law/book of Moses" (Mk 12:26; Lk 2:22; 24:44) or simply "Moses" (Lk 16:29, 31; 24:27) appear to denote the Pentateuch. Most references tie Moses to specific laws, such as those concerning circumcision (Lk 2:22; cf. Lev 12:2-8; Ex 13:2, 12), the offering after the cleansing of a leper (Mt 8:4 par. Mk 1:44 and Lk 5:14; cf. Lev 13:49; 14:2-32; *see* Leprosy), honoring parents (Mk 7:10; cf. Ex 20:12; 21:17; Lev 20:9), divorce* (Mt 19:7-8 par. Mk 10:3-5; cf. Deut 24:1-4) and levirate marriage (Mt 22:24 par. Mk 12:19 and Lk 20:28; cf. Deut 25:5). Only one passage refers to narrative, namely the dialog at the burning bush (Mk 12:26 par. Lk 20:37; cf. Ex 3:6). In the above passages Jesus, the Pharisees,* the Sadducees, and in one instance the Evangelist Luke, regard Moses as the mediator of the Law. Matthew 23:2 refers to "Moses' seat" (cf. Ex 18:13), an office in which the scribes* and Pharisees claim to carry on the exposition of the Law.

In the Fourth Gospel Jesus acknowledges that Moses gave the Law (Jn 7:19 [8:5]) and—with qualification—circumcision (Jn 7:22-23), while the Pharisees profess that God* spoke to Moses (Jn 9:28-29). John 1:17 implies a comparison and contrast in both the content and means of revelation: "For the Law was given (*edothē*) through Moses; grace and truth came into being (*egeneto*) through Jesus Christ."

2. A Prophet/Lawgiver Like Moses.
2.1. The Transfiguration. In the Synoptics the Transfiguration* is the key passage drawing parallels between Moses and Jesus. There Moses and Elijah* appear together with Jesus (Mt 17:1-9 par. Mk 9:2-10

and Lk 9:28-36). Various conjectures can be made as to why these OT characters appear. They, like Jesus, fasted for forty days (Ex 24:18; 34:28; 1 Kings 19:8), saw a theophany on "the mountain" (Sinai/Horeb, Ex 19—24; 32—34; 1 Kings 19:8-18) and experienced a remarkable departure from this life (Deut 34:1-6; 2 Kings 2:1-12). Moses and Elijah are also mentioned together in the closing verses of Malachi (Mal 4:4-6). In view of the coming "day of the Lord" Malachi enjoins the people to "remember the Law of Moses my servant, which I commanded him at Horeb" and are promised that the Lord "will send you Elijah the prophet before the coming of the day of the *Lord.*"

In connection with this appearance of Moses the Synoptics note several parallels between Moses and Jesus. The Transfiguration occurred "after six days" (cf. Ex 24:16, although Luke reads "about eight days"). Jesus ascended a mountain ("a high mountain" in Matthew and Mark, "the mountain" in Luke; cf. Ex 19:3, 20; 24:9-18; 34:2-4), bringing three disciples* with him (cf. Ex 24:1, 9). We read that Jesus was "transfigured" (Matthew, Mark and Luke), that "the appearance of his face was altered" (Luke) and "his face shone" (Mark; cf. Ex 34:29-35). Moreover, Peter's suggestion to "make three booths" is reminiscent of the booths in the wilderness. The visual and auditory elements also evoke the memory of Moses: "A cloud came and overshadowed them" (cf. Ex 19:9, 16; 24:15-18; 34:5); "A voice came out of the cloud" (cf. Ex 24:16); "This is my son; listen to him." Here the heavenly voice identifies Jesus as the prophet-like-Moses promised in Deuteronomy 18:14-19, a passage in which "listening" is the leitmotif throughout (Deut 18:14, 15, 16, 19). The additional words of Matthew ("with whom I am pleased") and Luke ("my chosen") allude to the suffering servant of Isaiah 42:1: "my chosen one in whom I delight" (*see* Servant of Yahweh).

Luke notes two other Mosaic parallels. He alone informs us of the subject of Jesus' conversation with Moses and Elijah, who "appeared in glory and spoke of his departure *[exodos]*." As Moses had led an exodus of liberation, so Jesus would lead his. In addition, Luke tells us that the disciples "were afraid as they entered the cloud" (9:34; cf. Ex 19:16; 20:18-21).

The mere fact that Moses and Elijah appear and converse with Jesus shows that they authenticate his mission. Moreover, the convergence of these parallels indicates that Jesus is being portrayed as a new Moses with a new revelation of God as significant as the Mosaic Law. In view of Jesus' recent revelation that he would suffer rejection (Mt 16:21 par. Mk 8:31 and Lk 9:22), the Transfiguration of Jesus in the company of two OT witnesses affirms him as God's spokesperson

nonetheless. The sudden disappearance of Moses and Elijah after the pronouncement of the Father may suggest that Jesus alone will fulfill what they had begun.

2.2. Mountain Typology. Mark and especially Matthew feature the symbol of the mountain, which serves as a place of revelation for Jesus as it had for Moses (*see* Mountain and Wilderness). In the Sermon on the Mount (Mt 5:1; 8:1; cf. esp. Ex 19:3; *see* Sermon on the Mount) and in the antitheses "you have heard that it was said . . . , but I tell you" (Mt 5:21-48), Jesus adopts the role of lawgiver-like-Moses. Likewise, the eschatological discourse is given "on the Mount of Olives" (Mt 24:3 par. Mk 13:3; contrast Lk 21:1, 5, 37-38 but note 22:39; *see* Apocalyptic Teaching). After feeding the five thousand in a "deserted place" (*erēmos*, the LXX and NT term for the "wilderness/desert" where Israel had wandered and Moses provided manna, Ex 16:1, 3, 10, 14, 32; cf. Deut 8:2; Jn 3:14; 6:31; Acts 7:36), Jesus "went up on the mountain to pray" (Mt 14:13, 15, 23 par. Mk 6:32, 35, 46). Matthew reinforces the parallel to Moses' being alone on Sinai by adding the words "by himself" and "he was there alone." Finally, the Great Commission was given from "the mountain where Jesus had told them to go" in Galilee (Mt 28:16; *see* Resurrection).

The Synoptics also note that it was on a mountain that Jesus appointed his twelve disciples (Mk 3:13-14 par. Lk 6:12-13). Of these disciples it is later said that they "will sit on twelve thrones, judging the twelve tribes of Israel" (Mt 19:28 par. Lk 22:29-30). The Twelve may be reminiscent of the twelve tribes and especially of the twelve tribal leaders (Num 1:4).

2.3. Events in Moses' Life Foreshadowing Jesus' Life. Matthew's telling of Jesus' infancy (Mt 2) is similar to that of Moses (*see* Birth of Jesus). The lives of both are threatened by the political leader of the region, who slaughters many innocent children, and both enjoy a narrow escape. Both return to the land of their birth at a divine command, whose wording is very similar (Ex 4:19; Mt 2:20).

John notes two events in Moses' life that foreshadow Jesus' life and work. Moses and the bronze snake (Num 21:8-9) parallels Jesus on the cross in that both are "lifted up" and both yield life from death when looked upon—the difference being that gazing on Jesus produces *eternal* life (Jn 3:14-15). While Moses gave manna to the people, who later died, the Father gives "the true bread from heaven," which is Jesus and which yields life* *eternal* (Jn 6:32-35, 49-51, 58; *see* Bread).

Other key Mosaic motifs, such as the Passover lamb whose bones are not to be broken (Ex 12:46; Num

9:12; cf. Jn 19:36) and "the blood of the covenant" (Ex 24:8; cf. Mt 26:28 par. Mk 14:24 and Lk 22:20), foreshadow Jesus' sacrificial death, although explicit reference to the person of Moses is lacking.

2.4. Moses Foretells Christ. Both Luke and John claim that Moses foretold the Christ. According to Luke 24:25, 27, Moses may be classified among the prophets. The claim that Moses foretold Christ's sufferings (Lk 24:26-27, 44-46) seems remarkable since the Pentateuch contains no such explicit prophecy. The answer to this problem may be found in the other half of Luke-Acts, where in Stephen's speech the Deuteronomic promise of a "prophet like Moses" (Deut 18:15) appears in the context of the people's rejection of Moses (Acts 7:35-39; cf. Peter's sermon in Acts 3:18, 22-23). As Moses the prophet was rejected by his own people, so was Jesus. It is, in fact, a distinctive emphasis of Deuteronomy that Moses suffered Yahweh's anger (vicariously?) solely on account of the people (Deut 1:37; 3:26; 4:21; 34:4; contrast Num 20:12). Luke's account of the Transfiguration may also imply a connection between the prophet-like-Moses and experience of suffering rejection. Only Luke records that Moses spoke with Jesus of his impending "exodus" in Jerusalem (Lk 9:31). Both before and after this announcement of Jesus as the Deuteronomic Moses-like prophet (Lk 9:35; see 2.1. above), Jesus reveals that he will be rejected in Jerusalem (Lk 9:22, 43-45).

Equally remarkable in Luke 24:26-27, 44-46 is the claim that Moses foretold that Christ* should "enter into his glory" and "rise (*anastēnai*) from the dead." A closer investigation of Yahweh's promise to Moses that "I will *raise up* for them a prophet like you" (Deut 18:15, 18) shows that the LXX translates the Hebrew verb *qûm* (Hiphil, "to raise up") with *anastēsō/ei* ("to raise up"), which is also used of Jesus' resurrection* in the NT. Elsewhere in Luke, Jesus claims that Moses spoke of resurrection in the book of Exodus: "That the dead are raised, even Moses showed" (Lk 20:37 referring to Ex 3:6; cf. Mk 12:26; Mt 22:31-32; also note Lk 16:29-31).

In the Fourth Gospel Jesus' disciples claim that Moses foretold his coming (Jn 1:45). While the Jews assert a clear either/or distinction between being a disciple of Moses or of Jesus (Jn 9:28-29), Jesus asserts that Moses in fact wrote about him and that Moses will thus be their accuser (Jn 5:45-46). (Similarly, in Mt 23:2-3 Jesus faults the Pharisees not with propagating the authority of Moses, which Jesus apparently endorses, but with their failing to "practice what they preach.") That the priests and Levites expected "*the* Prophet" to come is evident from the question they pose John the Baptist (Jn 1:21, 25; *see* John the

Baptist). (Note that these verses distinguish the Messiah, Elijah and the Prophet as separate figures: cf. Jn 7:40-41; and note Mt 16:14-16 par. Mk 8:28-29 and Lk 9:19-20.) In fact, some of the people, after seeing Jesus' miracles* (Jn 6:14) and hearing his words (Jn 7:40), confess that he is "*the* Prophet."

3. Conclusion.

With Jeremias we must affirm that "Moses is for later Judaism the most important figure in salvation history thus far," but at the same time "the Moses/Christ typology did not exercise a central or controlling influence on NT Christology" (Jeremias 849, 873; see further 849-64 for the development of the Moses tradition in Judaism*—esp. the Messiah as a second Moses, along with contrasts and comparisons with the NT). The points of contact between Moses and Jesus noted in the Gospels are points of continuity. Each figure endorses the other, but Jesus is presented as one greater than Moses. In the Synoptics this is especially clarified in the Transfiguration, where both Moses and the heavenly voice endorse *Jesus'* work and where Jesus alone remains to fulfill God's work. In John's Gospel, while Moses' work is recognized as providing life out of death, Jesus' provides eternal life (note also the implied contrast in Jn 1:17).

Both Matthew and Luke move beyond Mark in amplifying Moses' foreshadowing of Jesus. Matthew alone draws parallels between their birth narratives and highlights the mountain motif as the place where both mediated between God and the people. In the Synoptic account of the Transfiguration Luke alone notes that Jesus' death and resurrection should be seen as a kind of Mosaic Exodus. And only Luke indicates that much of Jesus' post-resurrection teaching consisted of explaining how Moses' teaching prophetically spoke of the Christ's sufferings and glory.*

John's Gospel is also clear that Moses foretold Jesus' coming. John makes explicit what is only implicit in the Synoptic account of Jesus' feeding of the five thousand; his Gospel presents the event as a parallel to Moses' providing manna. He also uniquely parallels Moses' lifting up the bronze snake and Jesus' being lifted up on the cross.

See also ELIJAH AND ELISHA; MOUNTAIN AND WILDERNESS; PROPHETS, PROPHECY; TYPOLOGY.

BIBLIOGRAPHY. J. Jeremias, "Μωσῆς," *TDNT* IV.848-73; R. N. Longenecker, *The Christology of Early Jewish Christianity* (SBT 2/17; Naperville, IL: Allenson, 1970) 32-41; W. A. Meeks, *The Prophet-King: Moses Traditions and the Johannine Christology* (NovTSup 14; Leiden: Brill, 1967).   C. C. Broyles

MOUNT OF OLIVES. *See* Apocalyptic Teaching; Gethsemane; Mountain and Wilderness.

MOUNTAIN AND WILDERNESS

In the Gospels geographical facts are the vehicles of literary and theological ideas. What matters primarily is not on which mountain or in what part of the wilderness any particular event occurred but the typological or symbolic significance of a given location.

1. Mountain
2. Wilderness

1. Mountain.

Most of the mountains in the Gospels carry theological meaning because they can be related to (1) Sinai; (2) speculation about Zion; or (3) the eschatological prophecy in Zechariah 14:4 about the Mount of Olives.

1.1. Terminology. In the LXX and Josephus* *to oros* can mean not only "(the) mountain" but also "mountainous area" or "(the) hill country." But "(the) mountain" is the more common meaning of the Greek expression, and as there were other words available for "mountainous area" and "(the) hill country," and as in several Gospel texts *to oros* must mean "(the) mountain" (e.g., Mt 5:14; 17:1), it seems best to render *to oros* consistently by "(the) mountain."

1.2. Jewish Background. In Jewish literature mountains are associated with numerous themes, including power (Jer 51:25; Dan 2:45), revelation (*Jub.* 1:2-4; *2 Apoc. Bar.* 13:1), antiquity (Prov 8:25; Job 15:7), eternity (Gen 49:26; Ps 125:1) and pagan religion (Is 14:13; 16:12). But the most important fact is that several mountains were the scenes of theophanies and/or played crucial roles in salvation-history, as the names Moriah, Nebo/Pisgah, Carmel and especially Sinai and Zion attest. Around the latter two there gathered relatively well-defined clusters of motifs (Sinai: Moses,* wilderness, Law*-giving; Zion: kingship, Jerusalem,* Temple,* inviolability).

While Sinai only occasionally appears in material about the latter days (e.g., in *1 Enoch* 1:4 it is the place of future judgment and in *Liv. Proph. Jer.* 11—19 the ark and the saints will be gathered to Sinai, where they shall be protected), Zion is prominent in Jewish eschatology.* In the OT and elsewhere Zion is to be the place of Israel's congregating (Jer 31:1-25; Tob 14:5-7), the goal of the Gentiles' pilgrimage (Is 2:2-3; Zech 2:6-12), the site from which the eschatological Torah will be promulgated (Is 2:2-3; Mic 4:2), the location of the enthronement of God or his representative (Mic 4:6-7; *Pss. Sol.* 17:21-46) and the home of

the new temple (*Jub.* 1:29).

1.3. Jesus' Ministry. The following Gospel texts place Jesus on a mountain: Matthew 4:8; 5:1; 14:23 par. Mark 6:46; Matthew 15:29; 17:1 par. Mark 9:2 and Luke 9:28; Matthew 21:1 par. Mark 11:1; Matthew 24:3 par. Mark 13:3; Matthew 26:30 par. Mark 14:26 and Luke 22:39; Matthew 28:16; Mark 3:13 par. Luke 6:12; Mark 5:5, 11 par. Luke 8:32; Luke 4:29; 21:37; John 6:3, 15; 8:1. Christian tradition has repeatedly sought to identify the several unnamed mountains in these texts (e.g., Tabor has been thought the site of the Transfiguration*). It is not possible, however, to link more than a very few events with known mountains, at least with any degree of probability. The Gospels explicitly identify only three mountains: the Mount of Olives (Mk 11:1; 13:3; 14:26), the hill on which Nazareth was situated (Lk 4:29) and Mount Gerizim (Jn 4:20-21; *see* Archeology and Geography).

Given the regularity with which the Gospel tradition, in all its strands (Mk, Q,* M,* L,* Jn), has Jesus on a mountain, the association may be accepted as historical. Perhaps Jesus sometimes retired to mountains for solitude. It is also just possible that mountains held some symbolic or theological significance in his own thinking; but no specifics can be credibly hazarded.

1.4. Parallels with Sinai. In accordance with the conviction that Jesus fulfilled the oracle of Deuteronomy 18:15, 18 (cf. Acts 3:22-23), the Gospel writers and those who passed on the tradition before them drew parallels between Jesus and Moses. In this way Sinai made its presence felt. For instance, in Matthew 17, Mark 9 and Luke 9, Jesus is transfigured on a "high mountain." This recalls Sinai. Sinai was thought to have been "high" (Philo *Vit. Mos.* 2.70; Josephus *Ant.* 3.76), and there are numerous parallels between Mark 9:2-9 par. and traditions about Moses on Sinai (see especially Ex 24 and 34). Both Jesus and Moses were transfigured by light; both were accompanied by a select group of three and both went up on the seventh day. In addition, both transfigurations were associated with a descending cloud; in both incidents a voice came forth from that cloud and in both cases those who saw the radiant figure became afraid. Furthermore, Moses and Elijah,* who appeared and conversed with the transfigured Jesus (*see* Transfiguration), are the only OT figures of whom it is related that they spoke with God on Sinai. Clearly the Gospel story was told in such a fashion as to call to mind the theophany on Sinai. (This holds for all three Synoptic accounts.)

Matthew 5:1 ("and going up on a mountain he sat down") and 8:1 ("coming down from the mountain") are also illuminated by Sinai. Not only does the wording of the Greek sentences resemble OT texts about Moses (e.g., Ex 19:3; 32:1; 34:29; Deut 9:9 LXX), but the Sermon on the Mount* follows a series of events which is closely paralleled in the story of Moses as it is known from Scripture, Josephus* and other sources (e.g., prophecy of Israel's savior, a father's uncertainty about his wife's pregnancy, the slaughter of Jewish infants by a wicked Gentile king, a return from exile after those seeking the savior's life have died, crossing of the waters/baptism* [cf. 1 Cor 10:1-5], temptation* in the wilderness for forty years/days); and in some Jewish texts Moses sits on Sinai (Ezekiel the Tragedian, *Exagōgē* 67-82; *b. Meg.* 21a-b; *b. Soṭa* 49a; the notion is based on a possible translation of Deut 9:9 MT: "and I sat on the mountain forty days and forty nights"). The Sermon on the Mount is obviously some sort of counterpart to the giving of the Law on Sinai.

John 6:3 reads: "Jesus went up to the mountain and sat down there with his disciples" (cf. 6:15, where Jesus is alone on the mountain; this is reminiscent of Ex 24:2; 34:3 LXX). This verse, which so closely resembles Matthew 5:1-2 and its OT parallels, heads a chapter filled with explicit correlations between Jesus and Moses. Here too, then, Jesus on the mountain is like Moses on Sinai. In this way it is plain that Jesus fulfilled the eschatological expectations of Judaism,* according to which the last redeemer (Messiah*) will be like the first redeemer (Moses; cf. also Mk 3:13?).

1.5. Zion Typology. In Matthew 15:29 Jesus goes up and sits on a mountain (cf. 5:1-2). This mountain is a place of gathering, healing* and feeding. Also, 15:30-31 may well allude to Isaiah 35:5-6, part of an eschatological prophecy concerning Zion (cf. Origen *Comm. Mt.* 11:18). All this suggests a Mount Zion typology (see Donaldson). In Jewish expectation Zion is the eschatological gathering site of Israel (see section 1.2), a place of healing (Is 35:5-6; cf. Mic 4:6-7) and the location of the messianic feast (Is 25:6-10; *Pesiq. R.* 41.5). Matthew 15:29-38 seemingly interprets the ministry of Jesus as the fulfillment of the Jewish hopes surrounding Zion.

How does this relate to the fact that elsewhere in Matthew the mountain motif is so clearly linked to Sinai (see section 1.4)? Already in the OT Sinai and Zion are closely associated, as in Psalm 68, and this is true also in later Jewish tradition (e.g., *Liv. Proph. Jer.* 11—19; *Tg. Neof.* Ex 4:27; *Midr. Bab.* Ps 68:9). A key text in this regard is Isaiah 2:2-3: "Torah shall go forth out of Zion." Here Mount Zion functions as the eschatological Sinai, the mountain of the Law. In view of this, the Sinai and Zion parallels should not be set over against each other. The two go hand in hand. Both make Jesus the eschatological counterpart of Moses.

It is sometimes suggested that Matthew 5:14 ("a city set on a mountain cannot be hid") has in view eschatological Zion or the New Jerusalem. It was expected that Zion would be raised to a great height and shed its light throughout the whole world (Is 2:2-4; 60:1-22; *Sib. Or.* 5:420-23). But the reference is uncertain. The verse is perfectly understandable without it referring to any particular city, and the wording lacks a definite article ("a city"). Furthermore, the parallel in 5:15 (one does not hide a lamp under a lampstand) speaks against the proposal: any lamp would fit the bill.

1.6. The Mount of Olives. Zechariah 14:4 reads: "In that day his feet will stand on the Mount of Olives . . . and the Mount of Olives will be split in two from east to west . . . ." This eschatological prophecy makes Jesus' choice of the Mount of Olives as the site for his eschatological discourse (Mk 13 par.) appropriate (note also Acts 1:11, which links the Parousia and the Mount of Olives). But there may also be an allusion to Zechariah's prophecy in Mark 11:23 (true belief can cast "this mountain" into the sea). In its context 11:23 could allude to the Mount of Olives (cf. Mk 11:1) and so to Zechariah 14:4, which foresees the splitting of that mountain. One additionally wonders whether Matthew 27:51-53 does not draw on Zechariah 14:4 (interpreted, as in the Targum,* as a prophecy of the resurrection*). In both texts there is a resurrection of the dead immediately outside Jerusalem, an earthquake occurs, the same verb is used (*schizō*, "to split," in the passive) and the resurrected ones are called *hoi hagioi* ("the holy ones").

1.7. A Literary Function in Matthew. The mountain in Matthew 4:8 (the Lukan parallel, presumably following Q, has no mountain) serves a literary function. It relates a scene near the beginning of the Gospel to the Gospel's conclusion. In 4:8 the devil (*see* Demon, Devil, Satan), on a mountain, offers Jesus, who has yet to suffer and die, all the kingdoms of the world. But in 28:16-20, again on a mountain, Jesus, who has been crucified,* declares himself to have all authority* in heaven and earth. The lesson, made plain by Matthew's redactional insertion of a mountain into the two scenes, is that only after the passion,* and only from God, can Jesus accept legitimate authority.

2. Wilderness.

The wilderness is significant primarily because of its association with New Exodus themes.

2.1. Terminology. In the Gospels *hē erēmos* refers to

an abandoned or uncultivated place, not necessarily a desert. In the LXX the word translates several Hebrew equivalents, including *midbār, ʿᵃrābâ* and *negeḇ*—words with different shades of meaning.

2.2. Jewish Background. The Law was handed down in the wilderness of Sinai, and the entry into the promised land was preceded by Israel's desert wanderings. Thus, despite the tradition of disobedience and murmuring in the desert and the fact that there is no nomadic or desert ideal in the OT, the time in the wilderness was sometimes described in glowing terms (e.g., Is 63:11-14). Moreover, it came to be held that a return to the wilderness and a Second Exodus would herald the messianic age, and the blessings of the new age were moved to the period of the wandering and vice versa—not unnatural developments given that the desert had been a place of revelation and Israel's constitution. Pertinent texts include Isaiah 35:1-2; 40:3-5; Hosea 2:14-23; Ezekiel 20:33-44; 1QS 8:12-16; Revelation 12:6, 13-14.

That the expectation of a return to the desert could be taken literally is shown by the activity of the Jews at Qumran (they chose to dwell in the desert in fulfillment of Is 40:3-4; *see* Dead Sea Scrolls), by the behavior of certain so-called prophets (Josephus, *J.W.* 2.259, 261; 6.351; 7.438) and by the warning in Matthew 24:26.

2.3. Jesus' Ministry. Jesus, like John the Baptist* (Mt 11:7; Lk 7:24; Mk 1:3-4; Jn 1:23), spent time in the wilderness (Mt 4:1 par. Mk 1:12 and Lk 4:1; Mt 14:13, 15 par. Mk 6:31-32, 35 and Lk 9:12; Mk 1:35 par. Lk 4:42; Mk 1:45 par. Lk 5:16; Jn 11:54). The motivation for withdrawal was probably not to enact a New Exodus (although this is a possible explanation of John's behavior) but simply a desire to escape on occasion the crowds and the demands of ministry. This would concur with the tradition stating that Jesus' retreats to the wilderness were occasions for prayer* (Mk 1:35; Lk 5:16).

2.4. New Exodus. The theme of returning to the wilderness in fulfillment of eschatological expectation dominates Mark 1:1-13. John dwells in the wilderness and calls Israel thence to be baptized. He is the fulfillment of Isaiah 40:3 LXX (a voice crying in the wilderness). Jesus himself first appears in the wilderness and there undergoes temptation.* In addition, two of the three OT texts combined in verses 2-3 (Ex 23:20; Mal 3:1; Is 40:3) have to do with the wilderness tradition (Ex 23:20 is about an angelic guardian [*see* Angels] and guide for the desert, and Is 40:3 explicitly refers to the desert). The concentrated focus on the wilderness means that the story of Jesus begins as a Second Exodus. Beginning and end mirror one another (cf. 1 Cor 10:1-5).

The theme would seem to be continued in Mark 6:30-44, where Jesus in the wilderness gives rest (cf. Deut 3:20; 12:9-10) and feeds the people (cf. Ex 16; Num 11). There are several other parallels here between Jesus and Moses (e.g., Mk 6:34 recalls Num 27:17), and one suspects that Mark intended 6:30-44 to call to mind Exodus 16 and Numbers 11: like Moses Jesus fed Israel in the wilderness. (That Jesus himself had similar thoughts has sometimes been suggested but cannot be affirmed or denied: the data are quite insufficient.)

Whether Matthew and Luke saw a New Exodus theme in the feeding of the five thousand is not so clear. But in John 6:31 and 49, in a discourse following the miraculous feeding, reference is made to Israel eating manna "in the desert" (cf. 3:14). It is true that the Fourth Evangelist places the feeding near a mountain (6:3), not "in the wilderness." But John 6:3 alludes to Sinai (see section 1.4. above), and Sinai and the wilderness were firmly linked ("the wilderness of Sinai" being a fixed expression) and in some contexts "the mountain(s)" and "the wilderness" were almost interchangeable (note Mt 18:12 par. Lk 15:4). So the story in John 6 apparently takes place in the wilderness, and the explicit reference to the desert in verses 31 and 49 means that the theme of the eschatological return to the wilderness is present.

We have already observed (see section 1.4) that Matthew 1—8 draws extensive correlations between the story of Moses and the Exodus and the story of Jesus. Here we may note that Israel's time in the wilderness has its parallel in Matthew 3—4, where Jesus in the wilderness passes through the waters of baptism and then enters the desert to undergo temptation. Once again the wilderness setting is at the service of the New Exodus motif.

2.5. The Wilderness and Demons. In the temptation narratives Jesus confronts Satan in the wilderness. In Luke 8:29 we are told that the Gerasene demoniac was driven into the desert by a demon. And in Matthew 12:43-45 and its parallel Luke 11:24-26 the unclean spirit who has been cast out "passes through waterless places." These texts are illumined by the Jewish belief that the wilderness, being beyond the bounds of society, is the haunt of evil spirits (see Lev 16:10; Is 13:21; *1 Enoch* 10:4-5; Tob 8:3; 4 Macc 18:8; *2 Apoc. Bar.* 10:8; *see* Demon, Devil, Satan). The idea dominated later Christian monasticism.

See also ARCHEOLOGY AND GEOGRAPHY; JOHN THE BAPTIST; MOSES; SERMON ON THE MOUNT; TEMPTATION OF JESUS; TRANSFIGURATION.

BIBLIOGRAPHY. D. C. Allison, Jr., "Jesus and Moses (Mt 5:1-2)," *ExpT* 98 (1987) 203-205; T. L. Donaldson,

Jesus on the Mountain: A Study in Matthean Theology (JSNTS 8; Sheffield: JSOT Press, 1985); E. S. Malbon, *Narrative Space and Mythic Meaning in Mark* (San Francisco: Harper & Row, 1986); U. Mauser, *Christ in the Wilderness* (SBT 39; London: SCM Press, 1963); S. Talmon, "The 'Desert Motif' in the Bible and in Qumran Literature," in *Biblical Motifs*, ed. A. Altmann (Cambridge, MA: Harvard University, 1963) 31-63.

D. C. Allison, Jr.

MURDER. *See* ETHICS OF JESUS.

MYTH

Myth is a term of at best doubtful relevance to the study of Jesus and the Gospels. The basic problem lies in defining the word itself, since the definition used will determine not only its relevance but also point to the solution of the further problems its use poses.

1. Defining "Myth"
2. D. F. Strauss
3. R. Bultmann
4. Myth and Miracle
5. Myth and Midrash

1. Defining "Myth."

In current study of religion the usage of "myth" tends to be restricted to the following sense: a narrative of origins, a study of the beginning of all things, a story of primordial time. If that is taken to be the primary meaning it obviously will have little or no relevance to the study of Jesus and the Gospels.

However, that primary meaning leads at once into secondary meanings. For a myth is also a story of beginnings, of fundamental events, told to explain current beliefs and practices. It narrates the origin of the world in order to inform as to what is (still) basic to the world. Moreover, a myth tells a story of a time before all history, of a time beyond the reach of recordable history. Not only so, but a myth typically speaks of gods and superhuman beings and is an attempt to express the human sense of the sacred in words.

With these attenuated meanings the possibility of "myth" becoming a relevant category increases. For the Gospels are about beginnings, events which remain fundamental for Christianity. They narrate events—virginal conception, miracles,* resurrection* —which can properly be said to transcend history. And some of the stories involve angels* and demons (*see* Demon, Devil, Satan), and all are about one whom Christians recognize as God* incarnate.

Such a use of "myth" carries an immediate corollary: "myth" is something other than "history," and is

defined in large part by that contrast. Thus the definition of myth depends on the definition of history. And history from its earliest usage (the Greek word, *historia*) has denoted knowledge or information obtained by systematic observation. It follows that the more positive the weight given to "history," the more negative the sense of "myth." Consequently, myth may mean anything from an untrue or unbelievable story (history as the measure of what is believable), through the sense of a narrative embodying unverifiable claims (history as the study of the verifiable), to the sense of that which expresses truths beyond the reach of history (history as limited to analysis of the observable).

If "myth" is to be used as a category in the study of Jesus and the Gospels, therefore, two preliminary points must always be made: (1) The term is not being used in its (current) primary sense; and (2) its precise force depends on the meaning and scope attributed to "history."

The fact that "myth" even appears here as a subject related to the study of Jesus and the Gospels can be attributed almost entirely to the use made of the term by two NT scholars.

2. D. F. Strauss.

In the nineteenth century "myth" came into prominence as a category to describe the miraculous in the Gospels, first with regard to the virginal conception and resurrection of Jesus. Since "myth" was used as a category to describe the foundational stories of other religions, including miraculous births and the like, why should it be withheld from the equivalent stories about Jesus? So the reasoning ran. This attitude was the corollary to a growing confidence in history as able to ascertain "what really happened."

D. F. Strauss (1808-1874) extended the use of "myth" to cover all the miraculous in the Gospels. He also shifted the focus of myth from the story of a *miraculous occurrence* to the *story* of a miraculous occurrence. For him myth was the expression or embodiment of an *idea*—not in a historical event (history cannot observe a miracle, only claims to a miracle) but in a narrative. In the case of the Gospels the idea or conviction was the messiahship of Jesus. The stories were the vehicles by which that idea was expressed. Their unhistorical character (the burden of Strauss's exegesis) should simply focus attention the more firmly on their principal function: to express Christian belief in the messiahship of Jesus.

With Strauss the category of *miracle* in the Gospels was thus completely transformed from something positive (a proof of Jesus' messiahship) to something problematic (the claim to miracle more disconcerting to the historian's critical scrutiny than the claim to messiahship). In previous centuries such accounts had raised few questions for those who took for granted a continuous traffic between heaven and earth, between the spiritual and the natural, between God, spiritual powers and creation. But now the realm of the observable had begun to determine the scope of the reasonable. For a history concerned with the (in principle) observable trail of cause-and-effect events, the suggestion that observable events might be caused by the intervention of forces from outside the historian's range of observation had to be treated as an explanation of last resort. In reality such an explanation was unnecessary in virtually every case, since other explanations from within observable history could be found which were quite sufficient to account for the facts. So in Strauss's case the theory of myth became a way of explaining the stories of miracles in the Gospels without recourse to miraculous events.

Strauss's contribution was fundamentally flawed therefore in that his critique depended both on the older concept of miracle (divine *intervention* in human affairs) and on the then-young historical method confident of its ability to determine facts in a wholly objective way. On the more positive side, his focusing on the narrative rather than on the historical events behind the narrative gave a greater priority to the text itself than to the work of historical reconstruction. And in so doing, he brought firmly into play the recognition that factors other than an unvarnished desire to record bare facts will have come into play. Of lasting value is his still valid insight that a claim to miracle may simply divert attention from the purpose intended by the story of the miracle, leading to a focus on the problem of the claimed miracle itself.

3. R. Bultmann.

A century after Strauss, R. Bultmann (1884-1976) revived the category of myth as a tool in interpreting the NT. His definition of the concept, however, was very imprecise and his use of it rather idiosyncratic. Nevertheless, his 1941 essay was exceedingly influential in the post-war hermeneutical debate and poses issues of continuing significance.

For Bultmann myth is not simply about miracle or a story of miracle. It is rather about the way in which reality as a whole is conceived. In specific terms, myth is a primitive, pre-scientific way of conceptualizing reality. The pejorative note is clear ("primitive"). The ancients conceived of the cosmos as a three-storied structure, with events on earth attributable to spiritual powers from above (or below) and mental disorders attributable to the activity of demons. That world view has been long superseded and is no longer even possible for the products of a modern scientific education. "It is impossible to use electric light and the wireless and to avail ourselves of modern medical and surgical discoveries, and at the same time to believe in the New Testament world of demons and spirits" (Bultmann, 5).

It is important to grasp at once that Bultmann's concern here was primarily apologetic. It is obvious that he shared in an uncritical way the presumption of pre-Einsteinian physics that the cosmos was a closed continuum of cause and effect which would sooner or later yield up all its secrets to the all-conquering march of scientific inquiry. But his designation of the ancient world view as mythical was not simply a reflection of the modern disparaging the primitive. It was also a way of removing the mythical from the realm of the scientific and objective. If the Gospel miracles are not scientific descriptions of maladies or cures, then they are about something else, a something else *not* vulnerable to objective analysis or scientific reductionism. Bultmann's endeavor was therefore aimed at expounding this "something else."

Here the further dimension of Bultmann's understanding of myth becomes crucial. For him myth was not simply the ancients' way of *conceptualizing* the world. It was their way of expressing their *experience* of reality. The early Christians' understanding of the death and resurrection of Jesus, in particular, was their way of expressing the gospel,* that is, their experience of the gospel. This is the "something else" which comes to mythical expression in the miraculous accounts of the Gospels—namely, the kerygma, the gospel proclaimed and realized in the experience of faith.*

This understanding of myth leads immediately into Bultmann's program of demythologizing. For Bultmann this is *not* to be understood as stripping away the mythical expression of the gospel, as though an objective gospel or objective facts would thereby be left exposed to view. For that would leave the gospel once again vulnerable to scientific scrutiny and verification. Worse still, it would miss the character of myth as expressing the initial experience of the gospel. Demythologizing is rather a matter of experiencing again the gospel and of re-expressing that encounter in the conceptuality of today, though never in such a way that the gospel becomes a mere object. For Bultmann that was only possible in a Christian form of existentialist philosophy. But his apologetic concern retains validity even though his particular solution has not provided a lasting answer.

Strauss and Bultmann were children of their time, both in posing myth as a problem and in the solutions they offered. But the issues they highlighted have to be dealt with in our own terms.

4. Myth and Miracle.

A common feature in the previous sections is the contrast between myth and history—myth as doing something which history does not and cannot do. Traditionally that contrast has given myth a negative connotation, because history was presented as very positive. To say a Gospel miracle is "unhistorical" is generally reckoned, understandably, a very negative judgment. But if history is a more limited discipline, confined in scope to the observable and ascertainable, then language is needed to describe a more penetrating analysis which goes beyond these limits. In which case it becomes possible to retain myth in a positive sense to describe what goes beyond history, even when it speaks of events which are also historical. All this becomes important in a day when history is no longer seen as simply delivering objective information, but as depending on subjective judgment and as involving some kind of two-way encounter between historians and their sources. Here myth can retain a place of considerable importance, even if as a shorthand for the historian's ideological presuppositions, world view, assumptions regarding the beginnings and stuff of reality. In the particular case of miracle, the greater humility of modern physical scientists is also an important factor. For if the cosmos as a system is not closed, even if only at the edges, new possibilities are opened up for conceptualizing influences acting within and upon that system. And if a unified field theory is achievable only at the level of the cosmos in its totality, the Christian may be forgiven for suggesting that God seems to provide the missing factor to complete the equation. In which case "miracle" becomes a category once again by which such influences within and from "beyond" the system can be described, with "angels" and "demons" simply older conceptualizations of such influences appropriate to an earlier stage of human understanding.

A further weakness of the historical method is that it cannot cope with the wholly unique. Historical judgment depends so much on comparing like with like and on analogy ("this is how people generally react in such circumstances") that the tendency is always to discount any unusual or unique features. But Christian claims for Jesus major precisely on his uniqueness. And the whole point of Christianity's central claim, that Jesus was raised from the dead, is that he alone has so conquered death. Myth here

could be an appropriate category, not simply because history cannot reach beyond death, but also because in this case it is dealing with a primary event. By which I mean (the account of) a happening which explains other events but which is not explained by them. The very (historical) fact that it was the category of eschatological (*see* Eschatology) *resurrection* which was used from the beginning, rather than, say, visions of the dead Jesus, or translation to heaven or even survival of the soul, points in this direction.

Bultmann's program of demythologizing also retains some validity, at least to the extent that it highlights the problem of translating from one culture and world of meaning to another. Translation of the Gospels is not simply a matter of finding the English (or whatever) words and idioms most nearly equivalent to the original Greek. It is also a matter (in pulpit and study group and classroom) of translating what was not simply expressed but also experienced within one way of conceptualizing reality into the expressions of contemporary experience (including religious experience). And that may not be as straightforward as it sounds. The classic example here is the ascension* of Jesus. The very word *ascension* ("going up") is an expression of an assumption that heaven is "up there." To demythologize the ascension is not to deny that Jesus "went to heaven"; it is simply to find a way of expressing this in language which takes it out of the realm of current or future space research.

5. Myth and Midrash.

Finally, it is important to remember that the word *myth* is most properly used when it means a story or account, whether of supernatural agents or of miraculous events. And a story which embodies and expresses claims *which cannot be expressed in any other way*. Here the closeness of myth's likeness to history has been misleading. Myth in fact is the equivalent in *words* of the sacred place and sacred ritual in religion, and so is closer to poetry, say, than to history (bearing in mind, of course, that poetry can also serve a historical function).

Here we recall the lasting value of Strauss's otherwise destructive contribution. To say the Gospel miracle stories are myth is to recognize that they are *more* than history. To reduce them to a record of historical facts, then, is to lose their point and, as Bultmann saw so clearly, to make the gospel they express vulnerable to scientific dispute. That there is something important here has been confirmed by the fuller exegetical recognition of what may simply be called "midrashic" features in the various Gospel accounts (*see* Midrash). That is, accounts which function in at least some degree as expositions of OT Scriptures, as drawing their significance from these Scriptures and as told in such a way as to make this significance clear to the readers who know their Scriptures.

The clearest example is probably Matthew's account of the temptations of Jesus (*see* Temptation of Jesus), which may properly be described as a sort of midrash on Deuteronomy 6—8 (Mt 4:1-11). But the birth narratives (*see* Birth of Jesus) seem also to be modelled in part at least on such OT figures as Abraham* and Sarah and the parents of Samuel, and the story of the magi is in some measure built around Numbers 24:17. To take one other example, the echoes of the story of Jonah in the account of the stilling of the storm can hardly be denied (Mk 4:35-41). In each case stories are being told not solely, or perhaps even primarily, to convey historical information. They are being told to evoke this response: Here is the one who triumphed where Israel failed, who fulfilled ancient prophecy, who is greater than Jonah. Likewise, the different conclusions to the story of the walking on the water in Matthew and Mark serve as clear indications that the narrators have their own (and different) points to make (Mt 14:33 par. Mk 6:51-2). In the Fourth Gospel such notes as John 2:11, the potent use made of such symbols as water* and light,* and the intermeshing of miracle and discourse, are even clearer indicators that John tells his stories of Jesus' miracles not so much as proof, but more as demonstration ("signs") of Jesus' status and of the significance of his ministry.

In all this the power of such stories is the power of poetry and symbol. And "myth" remains a possible way of indicating that potency. This is not to say that myth and history are outright and mutually exclusive opposites. On the contrary, as poetry and symbol speak to rational mind as well as to emotion and spirit, so myth can also communicate history; or, perhaps better, a story can contain both myth and history. The point of recognizing mythical elements in a Gospel story, however, is to insist that its full significance can neither be found solely at the straightforward historical level nor, therefore, be disputed by purely historical analysis. In other words, to say "myth" is not to say "untrue." As prose history is not the only way to express historical truth, so there are other ways of expressing the truth of Jesus than through the medium of historical narrative. If "myth" helps to express this important insight, then perhaps it has some continuing relevance for the study of Jesus and the Gospels after all.

See also GOSPELS (HISTORICAL RELIABILITY); MIRACLES, MIRACLE STORIES.

BIBLIOGRAPHY. K. W. Bolle and P. Ricoeur, "Myth," in *The Encyclopedia of Religion*, ed. M. Eliade (New York: Macmillan, 1987) 10.261-82; R. Bultmann, "The New Testament and Mythology" (1941), in *Kerygma and Myth*, ed. H. W. Bartsch (London: SPCK, 1953) 1-44; J. D. G. Dunn, "Demythologizing—The Problem of Myth in the New Testament," in *New Testament Interpretation*, ed. I. H. Marshall (Grand Rapids: Eerdmans, 1977) 285-307; R. A. Johnson, *The Origins of Demythologizing: Philosophy and Historiography in the Theology of Rudolf Bultmann* (Leiden: Brill, 1974); J. Macquarrie, *The Scope of Demythologizing* (London: SCM, 1960); R. Morgan and J. Barton, *Biblical Interpretation* (Oxford University, 1988); S. M. Ogden, *Christ without Myth* (New York: Harper and Row, 1961); W. Pannenberg, "The Later Dimensions of Myth in Biblical and Christian Tradition," in *Basic Questions in Theology* (3 vols.; London: SCM, 1973) vol. 3; D. F. Strauss, *The Life of Jesus Critically Examined* (London: SCM, 1973); A. C. Thiselton, *The Two Horizons* (Grand Rapids: Eerdmans, 1980) 252-92.   J. D. G. Dunn

N

NAG HAMMADI. *See* CANON; GOSPELS (APOCRY-PHAL).

NARRATIVE CRITICISM. *See* LITERARY CRITICISM; NARRATIVE EXEGESIS.

NARRATIVE EXEGESIS

Exegesis is the art and science of interpreting biblical texts. Normally exegesis takes the form of an exposition of the text: linguistic, historical, literary, theological and—nowadays—sociological, psychological or political. Narrative exegesis contains similar elements but takes the form of a story instead of an exposition. Though the story is in some respects a fiction, it is constructed on the basis of many small pieces of evidence. To do justice to narrative exegesis it is necessary to consider influences upon it, examples of it and characteristics it possesses.

    1. Influences on Narrative Exegesis
    2. Examples of Narrative Exegesis
    3. Characteristics of Narrative Exegesis

1. Influences on Narrative Exegesis.

What has influenced biblical scholars to adopt this mode of presenting their findings? While indirectly the growing interest in sociological* and literary* approaches to the NT set the scene for the development of narrative exegesis, of themselves these have not been sufficient to produce it.

1.1. Sociological Analysis. Sociological enquiry into the NT has produced a thicker description of the broader, everyday first-century context of the Gospels and which the Gospels themselves reflect. We now know more about, and can more accurately interpret, the setting of Jesus and his first followers. This lays the basis for a fuller description of the way in which both Jesus and the early Christians interacted with, and were shaped by, their social and cultural environment. As a result we are in a better position to see what it was like to walk and talk in the first century.

1.2. Literary Analysis. The renewed interest in a literary approach to the NT includes a stronger appreciation of the role, intention and character of stories and storytelling. The Gospels have provided a focus for much of this work, not just individual pericopes or particular features of Jesus' teaching such as parables* or miracles,* but also the Gospels as a whole, read as integrated narratives. This contemporary interest in narrative elements in the Bible, in structural analysis of texts and in reader-response theories opens up the possibility of interpreting the Bible in a way that resonates with its form as well as its content.

2. Examples of Narrative Exegesis.

Although sociological and literary investigations have provided a background for the development of narrative exegesis, the key motivation among those engaged in it seems to have been the desire to communicate the results of their research more effectively.

In recent years several disciplines have stressed the fundamental role of story in human understanding, both for the individual and community. This emphasis can be found in anthropological, psychological and philosophical studies. While interest in stories has always been part of pedagogy and homiletics, mostly it has been their secondary illustrative character that has been discussed, rather than their integral or elemental character.

Again, while various experiments in biblical fiction writing have been conducted (e.g., the unashamedly popular writings of Lloyd Douglas, the more literary works of Howard Fast, the philosophical novels of Nikos Kazantzakis), these have not been designed chiefly for historical instruction and have generally contained a considerable amount of fabrication. (Cinematic reconstructions along similar lines, viz., so-called biblical epics and other films, could also be discussed.) Mention should also be made here of the imaginative reconstructions of biblical passages for devotional purposes, a tradition that stretches back to Thomas à Kempis and is carried on today by M. Kelsey and others.

However, these approaches to learning theory or story-telling do not appear to have directly stimulated those who have carried out narrative exegesis. Their decision to do so seems to have arisen from more practical considerations, such as the desire to communicate the results of scholarly investigation in a more graphic way, for a broader lay audience, in a more holistic fashion or to engage hearers more personally with the text. Some of these examples of narrative exegesis first came to expression in workshops or addresses before taking written form.

Beginning in the late 1970s, the main experiments in narrative exegesis have been carried out independently of one another in various countries and with different constituencies in view. Alongside a few representations of OT exegesis, the first examples concentrating on the NT focussed chiefly on class tensions (W. Hollenweger) and churchgoing generally (R. Banks). Attention to the Gospels concentrated first on miracle-stories (W. Hollenweger) and attitudes to children (H.-R. Weber) but has since, in the most extended exercise in narrative exegesis yet to appear, concerned itself with the impact of Jesus on his contemporaries (G. Theissen).

3. Characteristics of Narrative Exegesis.

According to G. Theissen, "The basic structure of narrative exegesis consists of historical reconstructions of patterns of behavior, conflicts and tensions, and its superstructure consists of fictitious events in which historical source material is worked over in a poetic way" (19). These two aspects of the enterprise require further elaboration.

In the first instance the narrative exegete approaches the task no differently from any other scholarly investigation of biblical texts. Traditional textual, linguistic and historico-critical methods are all utilized, though more attention may be accorded to sociological—and increasingly anthropological and psychological—approaches as well. It is especially this second group which provides a fuller understanding of the ethos and context of the original situation described in the Gospels, and also shapes perceptions of divergences between the first-century cultural world and our own.

Instead of presenting this material as an ordered discussion of evidence and its interpretation, narrative exegetes weave their findings into a story. While this contains a partially fictional element, if responsibly conducted, it will have its basis in first-century materials. At this stage various devices may be employed, such as third-person description, memories of a participant, eyewitness reports of an outsider. The stories may also contain other compositional devices such as the building of tension, a climatic confrontation, the resolution of differences. At this level there is always the danger of artificial characterization, inadequate plotting or propagandist writing. But where these are largely avoided there are also substantial gains in vividness of presentation and reader involvement. Importantly, narrative exegesis is accessible to the broadest range of people, sometimes even children, yet allows each to engage with the material at the level most appropriate to them.

BIBLIOGRAPHY. R. J. Banks, *Going to Church in the First Century; An Eyewitness Account* (2d ed.; Auburn, ME: Christian, 1990); W. J. Hollenweger, "Intercultural Theology," *Theological Renewal* 10 (1978) 2-14; idem, *Konflikt in Korinth und Memoiren Eines Alten Mannes: Zwei Narrativen Exegesen zu 1 Korinther 12-14 und Ezechiel 37* (Münich: Kaiser, 1978); idem, *Erfahrungen in Ephesus; Darstellung eines Davongekommen d.n.e. zu 1 Mose 8, 15-22; Joh 6, 1-15 und Offb. 21, 1-6* (Münich: Kaiser, 1979); G. Theissen, *The Shadow of the Galilean: The Quest of the Historical Jesus in Narrative Form* (Philadelphia: Fortress, 1987): H.-R. Weber, "A Child? A Story for Adults—A Bible Study of the Word and Actions of Jesus Recorded in Mk. 9:33-37 and Mk. 10:13-16," *Biblical Studies* (Redhill, Surrey: WCC, 1979).

R. J. Banks

NATIVITY. *See* BIRTH OF JESUS.

NAZARENE

1. The Problem
2. The Gospel Data
3. Proposed Solutions
4. A Linguistic Solution

1. The Problem.

The English term *Nazarene* renders two Greek words, *nazarēnos* and *nazōraios*. Grammatically speaking, both are apparently gentilic adjectives, that is, adjectives derived from a proper noun. The first form is a type of gentilic almost unknown from earlier Greek, although it is represented in the Gospels by several examples—such as "Magdalene"—and in approximately contemporary Greek documents found near the Dead Sea. By virtue of its unexplained development it is somewhat problematic, but any problems related to this form pale in comparison with those touching *nazōraios*.

In both cases the central problem concerns the relationship of the Greek form to a putative underlying Aramaic gentilic meaning "the man from Nazareth." Given the Semitic name for Nazareth, *Noṣ^eraṭ* or

Naṣṣeret—known only from postbiblical texts—the expected Aramaic form would be *nāṣᵉrāyā/nāṣᵉrā'ā*. From either possibility we would anticipate Greek renderings of *nasarēnos* and *nasaraios*. What then is the explanation and significance of the aberrant forms we actually encounter, in which *z* replaces *s*, and *ō* appears where we should expect only a very short semi-vowel (*shwa mobile,* usually understood to be of indifferent vocalic quality)? Scholars have offered both linguistic and theological explanations.

2. The Gospel Data.

It is important to notice that the Greek terms do not occur haphazardly, but rather they appear in more or less complementary distribution according to Gospel author. Numerous scholars have suspected that this distribution may be theologically meaningful. The chart illustrates the data:

	Nazōraios	*Nazarēnos*
Matthew	*3x*	*0*
Mark	*0*	*4x*
Luke	*1x*	*2x*
John	*3x*	*0*

As shown, *nazōraios* appears seven times in the Gospels, and *nazarēnos* occurs six times. Although an exact count is complicated by the fact that in five instances there are textual variants (with both options supported by significant textual witnesses), the only really uncertain case is Luke 24:19. In that verse it is impossible to decide which is the original reading. Accordingly, Matthew and John use only *nazōraios,* Mark uses only *nazarēnos,* and Luke uses now one, now the other. The three instances of Lukan usage constitute a paradigm of the redactional difficulties (*see* Redaction Criticism) involved with these terms, for the Gospel once follows Mark (Lk 4:34 par. Mk 1:24), once changes Mark's *nazarēnos* to *nazōraios* (Lk 18:37 par. Mk 10:47—although some witnesses to Luke give *nazarēnos*), and once, in the instance referred to above (material peculiar to Luke's Gospel) it is uncertain whether it followed Mark or not (*see* Synoptic Problem). In the NT as a whole *nazōraios* easily predominates over *nazarēnos,* but neither form occurs outside the Gospels and Acts. Early in the history of the church *nazōraios* apparently took on a new connotation, for according to Acts 24:5 the Christians were called by its plural *nazōraioi.*

3. Proposed Solutions.

3.1. "A Man from Nazareth." Linguistic explanations

for the original significance of *nazōraios* focus on whether it is possible to construe it as a gentilic from the name Nazareth. Scholars are divided, but the majority believe it is possible. Unfortunately, they have lacked the means to explain rigorously and precisely how the word acquired the problematic *ō*. The question of the *z* is less difficult, for in Greek texts of the OT there are numerous instances of this equation of Semitic *ṣ* with Greek *z*. For example, in several uncials at Judges 1:5 Greek *adōnizedek* corresponds to the Hebrew name *'ᵃdōnî ṣedeq*. Similarly, Hebrew *mibṣār* at Genesis 36:42 is rendered *mazar* by the most important manuscript of the Greek OT, Codex Alexandrinus.

But in the view of many scholars, attempts to use these same LXX manuscripts to explain the *ō* have not been as successful. The proponents of this approach have not appreciated the fact that, in contrast to the *z*, here we are dealing with a vowel. The difference is that unlike the consonantal text of the MT, the vowels often represent a late—perhaps fourth- to ninth-century A.D.—traditional reading of the text. Hence, in comparing LXX manuscripts with the MT, it is incorrect to assume, as have these proponents, that the ancient translators rendering the Hebrew into Greek necessarily vocalized any given word as it is now found in the MT. Indeed, it is precisely the differences between the vocalization systems underlying the LXX and the MT which provide insight into pre-Masoretic Hebrew. Unconvinced, then, by such methodologically problematic explanations of the *ō*, a significant minority of scholars have argued that the word *nazōraios* cannot be connected with the town of Nazareth. In their view, *nazōraios* originally arose from another Aramaic word, and was only later and secondarily attached, by folk etymology or punning, to the town name.

3.2. "One Taking a Vow." Those who reject the derivation of *nazōraios* from Nazareth attempt to derive it from various other Aramaic words. The best suggestion connects it to the root *nzr*, meaning "to vow," "to abstain." The argument here invokes a reasonably well-attested Aramaic deverbal nominal pattern, the *nomen agentis qātōl* (originally *qātûl*). This pattern is known from Imperial Aramaic and the Hebrew Bible portions dealing with Balaam, and was still productive in Syriac and Samaritan Aramaic—and thus, perhaps, in Palestinian Aramaic of Jesus' day. In Syriac, for example, any verb in the simple stem can form a *nomen agentis* by means of this pattern. The hypothetical form *nāzōrā'* would mean "the one taking a vow," especially a Nazirite vow. This Aramaic word would indeed then come into Greek as *nazōraios*. Advocates of this suggestion suppose that the Aramaic term originally attached to the adherents of an ascetic

Jewish sect in first-century Palestine. Religio-political sects of that period, such as the Pharisees* and Sadducees (*see* Judaism), regularly took names which stressed their devotion to God. Thus *Pharisees* means "the separated ones," ostensibly referring to the group's higher standards of ritual purity (*see* Clean and Unclean). *Nāzōrā'* would fit this pattern, and according to this view Jesus belonged to such a group. Seeking to anchor the group historically, it is common to suggest that John the Baptist (*see* John the Baptist) was its founder or leader, and that Jesus was originally his follower. Hints of such can be found in the Gospels and Acts according to a certain reading of the text.

Commonly, advocates turn to the so-called Mandaic connection to flesh out the picture further. The Mandaeans, an Aramaic-speaking group of obscure origins who lived in southern Babylonia, also called themselves "Nasoraeans." They had forgotten the significance of the term, but some scholars have found evidence of a connection to first-century Palestine in elements of their liturgy. Yet their literary works and written liturgy date some six to eight centuries after the time of Jesus; using them to explain the term *nazōraios* is a case of explaining an obscurity by appealing to something obscure. Less questionable evidence linking Jesus to a group of "vowers" may perhaps appear in Matthew 2:23, and here theological explanations enter the picture.

Matthew 2:23 says that Jesus and his family returned from Egypt to live in Nazareth "so that what was spoken through the prophets might be fulfilled, 'He shall be called a *nazōraios*.' " The text is a famous crux because no OT passage straightforwardly connects a messianic figure with Nazareth. How, then, could Jesus' return to that town relate to a prophetic declaration? An answer may be found in the Greek text of Judges 13:5, 7, if one agrees that *nazōraios* does not mean "man from Nazareth" but rather refers to an ascetic baptistic sect. The Greek text of Alexandrinus reads, "so that the child shall be sanctified to God as a Nazirite from the womb." If the Matthean tradition referred to this text (Judges was a book of the "prophets" in Jewish parlance), then here may be additional support for the view connecting *nazōraios* with the hypothetical Aramaic *nāzōrā'*.

On this reading of Matthew 2:23, the original denotation has been lost, and the term *nazōraios* has been reinterpreted to cement a connection between Jesus and Nazareth which was never in view in the OT passage. Understood in this way, this text and a few other tenuous bits of evidence combine in favor of divorcing *nazōraios* from the town name. But it is important to realize how much conjecture and how

little hard evidence goes to support the derivation from the hypothetical *nāzōrā'*. It should be emphasized that this *nomen agentis* is unattested even in those Aramaic dialects wherein the pattern was widely productive. Further, the advocates of this solution do not explain why the early traditions did not simply use the common form "Nazir" (i.e., "Nazirite") if they wanted to denominate Jesus as one who had taken such a vow. And it is further significant that some Gospel texts seem baldly to assert that *nazōraios/nazarēnos* means "man from Nazareth" (e.g., Mt 26:69 compared with Mt 26:71; Mt 21:11; Jn 1:45). These traditions cannot easily be explained away, and certainly deserve the benefit of any doubt.

4. A Linguistic Solution.

As we noted above, the reason some scholars rejected the meaning "man from Nazareth" in the first place was the lack of a persuasive explanation for the *ō* of *nazōraios*. It now appears that such an explanation is possible, based on Hebrew and Aramaic documents roughly coeval with the NT, the Dead Sea Scrolls (*see* Dead Sea Scrolls). The clearest evidence actually occurs in a Hebrew text, 1QIsaᵃ, but since Hebrew and Aramaic had entered into an *adstratum* linguistic relationship already in the Persian period, the careful use of such evidence is legitimate. In comparing 1QIsaᵃ with the MT, it is striking that its scribe sometimes wrote the *schwa mobile* (the semi-vowel we would expect in a putative *nāṣērāyā*) with the grapheme for an *o/u* vowel. He did not make this substitution in every case, but only when the *schwa mobile* was followed by the bilabial *b* or an *r* (which in Aramaic generally patterns with the gutturals, but which in the Hebrew of the MT is reconstructed as a trilled letter), and even then not always. Thus for MT *pĕrî*, "fruit," at Isaiah 10:12 of 1QIsaᵃ the text reads *pwry*, probably vocalized as *pᵒrî*, or perhaps even *pôrî*. In the same way, at Isaiah 37:38 one encounters *hwrrṭ* (=*hᵒrārāṭ* or *hôrārāṭ*) for MT *'ᵃrārāṭ*, "Ararat."

It is not necessary to multiply examples, although there are a fair number of other instances of the phenomenon; the import of this observation for the problem of *nazōraios* is by now clear. In at least some spoken Hebrew and Aramaic dialects of the time of Jesus (the probable provenance of 1QIsaᵃ is Jerusalem), *r* could influence a preceding reduced vowel, causing it to be pronounced further back in the mouth. It could then assume an *o* tone. This pronunciation was previously unknown to scholars, for it was not ordinarily represented in standard written speech. It was an oral phenomenon. In the case of *nāṣᵉrāyā*, application of the principle leads to *nāṣᵒrāyā* or *nāṣôrāyā'*. Either Aramaic possibility could lead to Greek *nazōraios*, while not applying the shift could yield *nazarēnos*.

It must be admitted that this solution is based on relatively meager data; that, however, is by no means a count against it. All the solutions to the problem at hand similarly work with few hard facts. Antiquity simply did not provide any more; thus any solution must be considered tentative. But if the present solution be correct, the *ō* is accounted for, and exotic derivations are ruled out. If it is correct, then nothing precludes the straightforward understanding of both Greek terms as "the man from Nazareth." And, if it is correct, then the tradition of *nazōraios* may well stem from Jerusalem, where 1QIsa[a] probably originated, rather than from Galilee.* Based on the fact that the early church was centered in Jerusalem, and considering the dialect affinities of the remnants of Aramaic contained in the Gospels, that connection is only to be expected.

See also LANGUAGES OF PALESTINE.

BIBLIOGRAPHY. L. Abramowski, "Die Entstehung die dreigliedrigen Taufformel—ein Versuch; mit einem Exkurs, Jesus der Naziräer," *ZTK* 81 (1984) 416-40; W. F. Albright, "The Names 'Nazareth' and 'Nazoraean,' " *JBL* 65 (1946) 397-401; *BDF* §39.4; M. Black, *An Aramaic Approach to the Gospels and Acts* (3rd ed.; Oxford: Clarendon Press, 1967). G. Dalman, *Grammatic des Jüdisch-Palästinischen Aramäisch* (Darmstadt: Wissenschaftliche Buchgesellschaft, 1981); B. Gärtner, *Die rätselhaften Termini Nazoräer und Iskariot* (Horae Soederblomianae 4; Uppsala: C. W. K. Gleerup, 1957). E. Y. Kutscher, *The Language and Linguistic Background of the Isaiah Scroll (1QIsa[a])* (Leiden: Brill, 1974); H. Schaeder, "Ναζαρηνός, Ναζωραῖος" *TDNT* IV.874-79.   M. O. Wise

NAZARETH. *See* ARCHEOLOGY AND GEOGRAPHY.

NEW BIRTH

The term "new birth" embraces two Greek expressions found in the Gospels: *palingenesia* (Mt 19:28; variously translated as "the renewal of all things" [NIV], "the world that is to be" [NEB], "the new world" [RSV]) and *gennēthēnai anōthen* (Jn 3:3, 7; "to be born again" or "to be born from above"). These two expressions point to the saving activity of God* in imparting spiritual life to his people and in restoring all of creation. This activity has both present and eschatological* dimensions, reflecting Jesus' teaching of the presence and future coming of the kingdom of God (*see* Kingdom of God).

1. Cosmic New Birth

2. Personal New Birth
3. New Birth and the Kingdom of God

1. Cosmic New Birth.

In Matthew 19:28 Jesus promises his disciples* who have left everything to follow him that in the *palingenesia*, when the Son of man (*see* Son of Man) sits upon his glorious throne, they too will occupy positions of glory.* This saying roughly parallels Luke 22:30 in which Jesus locates this exaltation simply, "in my kingdom." The redaction history of this logion is disputed, but the comparative rarity and difficulty of the term found in Matthew's account supports the view that he found it in his sources.

Palingenesia is found elsewhere in the NT only once (Tit 3:5) and there in a very different context, but it had a long history in Hellenism,* especially in Stoic circles where it was used to depict the rebirth of the universe, including human souls, after the cosmic conflagration (cf. Chrysippus *Stoic* 2.191; Boethus Sidonius *Stoic* 3.265). Philo used the term both for the restoration to life of individuals (e.g., *Cher.* 114; *Poster. C.* 124) as well as of the reconstitution of the world after the Flood (*Vit. Mos.* 2.65), while Josephus* used *palingenesia* to refer to the re-establishment of Israel* after the Exile (*Ant.* 11.66).

Though the term itself is distinctively Greek, the concept of cosmic rebirth is very much at home in Jewish thought. In the OT language of restoration and renewal, and explicitly in Isaiah 65:17 and 66:22 which express the hope of a new heaven and a new earth, we encounter a notion found widely in Jewish apocalyptic* (cf. *1 Enoch* 45:4-5; 72:1; 91:16; *2 Apoc. Bar.* 32:6; 44:12; 57:2; *Jub.* 1:29; *4 Ezra* 7:31), at Qumran (cf. 1QH 13:11-12; 1QS 4:25) and in the targums (cf. *Tg. Onq.* Deut 32:12; *b. Sanh.* 92b, 97b; also, the Kaddish Prayer: "Magnified and sanctified be His Great Name in the world that is to be created anew . . ."). The birth of this new age is often associated with the pouring forth of God's Spirit (e.g., Is 32:15; Joel 2:28-29; *Jub.* 1:23; 1QS 4:19-21; *see* Holy Spirit). The NT also looks forward to the eschatological new birth, as Jesus answers the disciples' question about the end of the age by warning of wars, famines and earthquakes as "the beginning of birth pains" (Mt 24:8) which point to the time of the coming of the Son of man. This ushers in "the age to come" (cf. Mt 12:32), which elsewhere in the NT is also pictured as the new heaven and new earth (cf. 2 Pet 3:13; Rev 21:1, 5).

The cosmic new birth represents a moral transformation of the world order accomplished by the power of God. At the end of this present age, "the Son of

Man will send out his angels to weed out of his kingdom everything that causes sin and all who do evil. . . . Then the righteous will shine like the sun in the kingdom of their Father" (Mt 13:41, 43 NIV). Those who have served Jesus in lowliness will be exalted to his right hand in exaltation (Mt 19:28).

2. Personal New Birth.

The imagery of personal or individual new birth is found in the teaching of Jesus only in the Fourth Gospel. In his dialog with Nicodemus, Jesus asserts, "Truly, truly, I say to you, unless one is born again, one cannot see the kingdom of God" (Jn 3:3). The Greek word translated "again" or "anew" (anōthen) can also be rendered "from above" (cf. Jn 3:31; 19:11, 23). In this case both senses contain truth, but the former translation is slightly better-suited to the context. Nicodemus's response, "Surely one cannot go into the mother's womb a second time and be born!" (3:4), suggests that he understood "again," and this makes his baffled reaction more understandable. On the other hand, "from above" would give emphasis to the divine origin of this new birth—it is of God (cf. 1:13) through the mysterious work of the Spirit (3:5-6, 8). To be born of God by the Spirit is not the natural state of men and women, implying that it must be a second birth (cf. 3:6).

2.1. Born of Water and Spirit. In response to Nicodemus's incredulity Jesus repeats his initial assertion, now describing this new birth as one "of water and spirit" (3:5). The meaning of this phrase has been much debated with several major lines of interpretation claiming adherents.

First are those who contend that "water"* in this context must refer to baptism. It is argued that in the context of the Gospel narrative John's (see John the Baptist) baptism* would be assumed, signifying Nicodemus's need for repentance as a prerequisite for the Spirit's work in his life. In the context of the early church, however, "water" would suggest Christian baptism, which was both the prerequisite and the occasion for the bestowing of the Spirit. But a mysterious work of divine power, not an external rite, is at issue here. From this view the role and response of Nicodemus is intelligible.

A second approach attempts a physiological interpretation of "water," either as a reference to the waters of birth associated with the rupture of the fetal water sac, or to the rabbinic use of "water" (*may* as well as *tipah*, "drop," cf. *Pirqe 'Abot* 3.1) to denote the male semen. Both literal and figurative uses of this birth imagery have been suggested, understanding the phrase to refer in turn to physical and spiritual birth,

or understanding the phrase as a hendiadys denoting a spiritual birth alone. The paucity of references to these uses of the term "water" and the difference in the contexts of those references from that in the Gospel diminish the strength of these interpretations.

A third view, going back at least to the time of Origen, understands "water and spirit" as a figurative expression referring to the cleansing and purifying work of God's Spirit. In the OT both water and spirit are symbols of God's renewing, life*-giving activity (cf. Is 55:1-3; Jer 2:13; 17:13; Ezek 37:1-14; 47:9; Zech 14:8; cf. also *Jub.* 1:23-25), and both are sometimes used in the same contexts: "I will sprinkle clean water on you, and you will be clean; . . . I will give you a new heart and put a new spirit in you" (Ezek 36:25-26 NIV; cf. Is 32:15-17; 44:3-5; also 1QS 4:19-21; Jn 7:37-39).

This imagery was something that "a teacher of the Jews" (Jn 3:10) ought to have recognized. The fact that both nouns are governed by a single preposition (*ek*) and that both are anarthrous suggests that they should be understood together as a conceptual unit describing the nature of this new birth rather than the agents or instruments of it. It is a "water-spirit" birth as opposed to the birth which is "of flesh" (3:6). In this birth one shares in the nature of God as "spirit" (cf. Jn 4:23) through the life-giving activity of the Holy Spirit (cf. Jn 5:21; 6:63). Just as natural life is a result of God's breathing spirit into the first human (cf. Gen 2:7; 6:3; Job 34:14-15; Eccles 12:7), so eternal life is a consequence of God's giving his Holy Spirit to human life through a new birth. Moreover, it is the birth of the new age which was to come, the age of the Spirit.

2.2. New Birth and Discontinuity. Integral to the teaching of the new birth is the notion that natural growth and development will not suffice. A radical discontinuity with the past and a fundamental internal change is required if one is to enter the kingdom of God. This element of newness featured prominently in Jesus' ministry. Though he claimed to fulfill the Law* and the Prophets (Mt 5:17), and in that sense stood in continuity with the OT, he also instituted a "new covenant" (Lk 22:20; see Last Supper). The least in this new dispensation is greater than the greatest of those of the old (Mt 11:11); the new wine* requires new wineskins (Mk 2:21-22).

Jesus also taught the need for a radical change of life. Unless a person changes and becomes like a child,* they will never enter the kingdom of heaven* (Mt 18:3). In John's Gospel this transformation is put in the starkest terms: "I tell you the truth, whoever hears my word and believes him who sent me has eternal life and will not be condemned; he has crossed over from death to life" (Jn 5:24 NIV). But this momentous change was also ascribed in Luke's Gospel to the repentant (*see* Repentance) prodigal son who "was dead and is alive again" (Lk 15:24).

2.3. New Birth and Divine Life. The new birth not only speaks of a fundamental internal change but more specifically of a new origin and source of life. Though Israel is called the Lord's "firstborn son" (Ex 4:22; Deut 32:6; Jer 31:9; Hos 11:1), this relationship is more properly ascribed to divine election than to divine procreation (even Ps 2:7, referring to the begetting of the king, is set within the context of the Lord's covenant with Israel). But with the prominence of the title "Son of God" (*see* Son of God) given to Jesus and perhaps the interest in the role of the Spirit in his birth (Mt 1:18-25; Lk 1:26-38; cf. Jn 8:41-42), the theme of divine sonship is broadened in the NT, particularly in the Johannine literature.

John opens his Gospel prolog with a statement that all who believe in the name of Jesus are born of God (1:13). This divine begetting is referred to five times in the Nicodemus pericope of John 3. In addition John's First Epistle speaks eight times of being born of God (2:29; 3:9 [twice]; 4:7; 5:1, 4, 18 [twice]). Being a child of God is not simply a covenant relationship. It involves a change in the heart, as the Spirit who gives new life (Jn 5:21; 6:63) is imparted to the believer. In this sense the Johannine teaching goes far beyond the rabbinic notion that "the proselyte is like a new-born child" (*b. Yebam.* 22a).

Moral transformation is the expected consequence of this new birth, resulting in righteousness (*see* Justice, Righteousness) and love* (1 Jn 3:9; 4:7; 5:18). Jesus, the Son of man (*see* Son of Man) who has his origin in heaven* (cf. Jn 3:13), now allows the believer to share in his own source of life. The Spirit, mediated by Jesus, is the agent of regeneration, and apart from his mysterious work one cannot see the kingdom of God (cf. Jn 3:5-8).

3. New Birth and the Kingdom of God.

The OT prophets had spoken of a future day of restoration and glorification of Israel when the Lord would pour out his Spirit on his people and manifest his rule in righteousness among the nations (e.g., Joel 2:28—3:2; Is 2:1-4; 65:17-25; Ezek 37:15-28). Jesus' reference to the *palingenesia,* or "restoration of all things," reflects this view (Mt 19:28). The reign of God will one day come to earth (*see* World) through a cosmic rebirth when the Son of man sits on his throne of glory.

However, Jesus also spoke of the kingdom of God as a present reality to be entered in this present age (Mt 12:28). In his ministry the life of the future had come near, and his teaching concerning the personal new birth points to that invasion of the future into the present.

The future age of restoration would be characterized by the work of the Spirit transforming the hearts of God's people (Jer 31:33; Ezek 36:26), and this transformation is just what Jesus promised and required in his words concerning the new birth. The coming kingdom could be entered now by the work of the life-giving Spirit who was at work in Jesus' ministry. Moreover, in the promise of eternal life to those who believe in him (Jn 3:15), Jesus linked the kingdom of God with eternal life, also a feature of the eschatological age, and drew them both into the present experience of his hearers. In Jesus the coming kingdom had drawn near, but one could enter only through new birth by the Spirit.

See also HOLY SPIRIT; LIFE; WATER.

BIBLIOGRAPHY. C. K. Barrett, *The Gospel according to St. John* (2d. ed.; New York: Macmillan, 1978); G. R. Beasley-Murray, *John* (WBC 36; Waco, TX: Word, 1987); L. L. Belleville, " 'Born of Water and Spirit': John 3:5," *Trinity Journal* n.s. 1 (1980) 125-41; R. E. Brown, *The Gospel according to John (I-XII)* (AB 29; Garden City, NJ: Doubleday, 1966); F. Büchsel, "γεννάω κτλ," *TDNT* I.665-75; C. H. Dodd, *The Interpretation of the Fourth Gospel* (Cambridge: University Press, 1953); G. E. Ladd, *A Theology of the New Testament* (Grand Rapids: Eerdmans, 1974); R. Schnackenburg, *The Gospel according to St. John* (3 vols.; New York: Crossroad, 1980, 1982); P. Toon, *Born Again: A Biblical and Theological Study of Regeneration* (Grand Rapids: Baker, 1987).   W. L. Kynes

NEW COMMANDMENT. *See* COMMANDMENT.

NEW COVENANT. *See* LAST SUPPER.

NEW EXODUS. *See* MOSES; MOUNTAIN AND WILDERNESS; TYPOLOGY.

NONVIOLENCE. *See* PEACE.

NUNC DIMITTIS. *See* SIMEON'S SONG.

O

OATHS AND SWEARING

Oath taking was a prevalent practice that was much abused in the time of Jesus. In the OT one was enjoined to swear by the name of God* (Deut 6:13; 10:20) as a sign of allegiance to the Lord rather than idols. Not only do pillars of the OT swear oaths (Gen 14:22; 21:24; 47:31; Josh 2:12), God does as well (Gen 22:16; 26:3; Is 45:23; Ezek 17:19; Amos 6:8; 8:7; Sir 44:21; Wis 12:21). False oaths or violations of oaths were considered to be a profanation of the name of God, something that God would severely punish (Ex 20:7; 1 Kings 8:31-32; Wis 14:30-31). Jesus' reference to oaths and vows in the fourth antithesis of the Sermon on the Mount* (Mt 5:33) has no exact parallel in the OT but reflects a combination of texts (Lev 19:12; Num 30:2; Deut 23:21-23; Ps 50:14; Zech 8:17) that were intended to safeguard their sanctity and to ensure that they were kept. In keeping with his demand for a greater righteousness* (Mt 5:20), Jesus prohibits all swearing (Mt 5:34). The plain sense of *holōs* ("at all") allows no exception.

1. Oaths in Contemporary Judaism
2. Jesus' Rejection of Oaths

1. Oaths in Contemporary Judaism.

Jesus was not alone in his opposition to oaths. Josephus* says of the Essenes: "Any word of theirs has more force than an oath; swearing they avoid, regarding it as worse than perjury for they say that one who is not believed without an appeal to God stands condemned already" (*J.W.* 2.8.6 §135). This stance was rooted in a pious abhorrence of using the name of God in an oath (CD 15:1-5; 1QS 6:27), and Philo viewed it as a testimony of their love* for God (*Quod. Omn.* 84). On entrance into their society, however, new members were "made to swear tremendous oaths" regarding the practice of piety and secrets of the sect (*J.W.* 2.8.6-7 §§139-42; see CD 15:5-6; 1QS 5:7-8). The Essenes also permitted swearing a judicial oath (CD 9:9-12), but one could only swear by the curses of the covenant and thereby not become liable to death for profaning the name by breaking the oath (CD 15:1-5).

Philo also looked askance at oaths, but his reasoning has a Hellenistic (*see* Hellenism) tint: not swearing best suits "a rational life which has been taught to speak the truth so well on each occasion that its words are regarded as oaths." To swear truly is only second best, he wrote, "because the mere fact of swearing casts suspicion on the trustworthiness of the man." (*Dec.* 84; see *Spec. Leg.* 2:1-8). For Philo, "the good man's word should be an oath, firm, unswerving, free from falsehood, planted in truth" (*Spec. Leg.* 2:2). He roundly condemned taking oaths to disguise the truth because it is the height of profanity to implicate God in knavery, and he criticized the habit of many to fill up the gaps in their talk with oaths (*Dec.* 92; see also *Spec. Leg.* 2:6; and Sir 23:9-10). He was by no means as radical as Jesus, because he advised that one should swear an oath only after examining whether a matter is important enough to warrant it, whether one knows all the facts, and whether one is pure from lawlessness, bodily pollution and evil-speaking (*Dec.* 93; see *Spec. Leg.* 2:6).

When Herod (*see* Herodian Dynasty) demanded oaths of loyalty from his subjects, the Essenes were excused; but Josephus reports that Pollion the Pharisee* and Samaias and his disciples also refused to take the oath and were not punished (*Ant.* 15.10.4 §§368-72). This suggests that others were sensitive about oaths; and, according to the Mishna, one who wants to become an associate "may not be profuse in vows" (*m. Dem.* 2:3). Rabbinic literature (*see* Rabbinic Traditions and Writings), however, devotes significant attention to oaths and vows. The Mishna tractate Šebu'ot addresses the issue of what constitutes valid oaths, and *Nedarim* does the same with vows and their annulment.

The rabbis carefully distinguished between oaths and vows. In a vow a person pledges before God that some item or act is forbidden to him or another. Oaths are of two kinds (*m. Šebu.* 1:1; 3:1, 5). In assertive oaths, persons swear that they have or have not done something, usually in a judicial context to substantiate or reject testimony. Voluntary oaths are similar to vows in that persons swear that they will or will not do something. This kind of oath was a prominent element of everyday life.

The development of divine circumlocutions and ersatz oaths, the subject of Matthew 5:34b-36 and 23:16-22, probably arose from a desire to avoid profaning the holy name (Ex 20:7). Because of a pious fear of real oaths (see Deut 23:23; Eccles 5:4; *Sipre* Deut 265 [on 23:23]), substitute oaths were in vogue among the populace. Lieberman argued that the rabbis sought to correct the abuse of vows and oaths. Unschooled in the fine points, the masses tended to confuse the distinctions between oaths and vows, to regard substitute oaths as valid, and to use them on all occasions. Some rabbis acquiesced to the widespread practice of the masses, but others protested against the use of invalid oaths. The latter stressed that valid oaths were sacred and not to be transgressed but taught that some oaths were not binding. The rabbis were no less concerned than Jesus to make clear that an oath was no substitute for habitual veracity, and it is not legitimate to infer from Jesus' attack in Matthew 23:16-22 that the scribes* and Pharisees employed oaths for dishonest advantage. They were concerned about the legal niceties of oaths and vows.

2. Jesus' Rejection of Oaths.

While many may have lamented the abuse of oaths, Jesus differed from all others by rejecting them entirely. In Matthew 5:34-36, he scorns the pious effort to skirt around the name of God in oaths by using such terms as "heaven"* and "earth" (see *m. Šebu.* 4:13; Philo *Spec. Leg.* 2:1), and "Jerusalem" (see *m. Ned.* 1:3; *t. Ned.* 1:2, 3). He demonstrates from the OT that each circumlocution directly involves God and is therefore a valid oath. He condemns swearing by one's head (or life) because it usurps God's jurisdiction over one's life. Consequently, Jesus not only prohibits valid oaths, he prohibits even so-called substitute oaths. An oath is an oath regardless of how oblique the reference to God.

Some have mistakenly taken Jesus' statement in 5:37, "Let your 'yes' [be] 'yes' and your 'no,' 'no,' " to be simply another version of a substitute oath (see *b. Šebu.* 36a; *2 Enoch* 49:1-2), but this would controvert what Jesus just said forbidding all oaths. The doubling of the words intensifies the "yes" into a real "yes" and the "no" into a real "no" (see Jas 5:12; *b. B. Meş.* 49a). Some scholars also argue that what Jesus says in Matthew 23:16-22 contradicts 5:34. Jesus is not endorsing oaths "by the temple," etc.; he is indicting Pharisaic logic about what makes a valid oath. To think that one who swears by the Temple, altar or heaven

has not sworn by the living God is nonsense. God cannot be evaded through word games. This woe (*see* Blessing and Woe) does not sanction swearing but lampoons a disingenuous casuistry that Jesus considered to be a symptom of the blindness of his opponents.

In Matthew 26:63 the high priest abjures Jesus by the living God to speak under oath (see *m. Šebu.* 4:13). Some conclude that Jesus' response in Matthew 26:64 accepts the oath demanded. Others consider Jesus' answer to be simply an assertion or an evasion that reflects his refusal to swear, and this would stand in stark contrast to Peter's swearing that he was not a disciple (Mt 26:74). Peter's oath and Herod's frivolous vow that led to the death of John the Baptist* (Mk 6:23) are two illustrations of the truth of Jesus' statement in Matthew 5:37 that anything more than "yes" or "no" is from "evil" or from "the evil one," the father of lies (Jn 8:44).

In some respects Jesus accords with Jewish tradition that one way to avoid violating oaths is to avoid them altogether. While others advocated total honesty, Jesus demands it and insists that honesty needs nothing to prop it up. Disciples are to speak the truth as a matter of course because they are inwardly pure in heart, not because it has been imposed by external necessity. Jesus rejects substitute oaths because they are a legal mirage. He rejects valid oaths because they diminish the demand for absolute truthfulness at all times. Their use either implies that one is normally untruthful or that one need only be truthful when swearing an oath. He also assumes that humans are bound to God in all of life, not just when they call upon God as a witness, since they will be accountable for every idle word (Mt 12:34-37).

Another reason Jesus rejects oaths is that they guarantee the veracity of a human statement by calling God as a corroborating witness. It is probable that Jesus viewed this to be an infringement on God's majesty, since it requires God to bear witness to fallible human statements and, in effect, reduces God to an object of human manipulation. In forbidding oaths, Jesus ignores the practical problems this would create for his disciples in society since oaths were required in all manner of disputes. With the advent of the kingdom of God* all such concerns are superseded.

BIBLIOGRAPHY. R. A. Guelich, *The Sermon on the Mount* (Waco: Word, 1982); S. Lieberman, *Greek in Jewish Palestine* (New York: The Jewish Theological Seminary of America, 1942); H.-G. Link, "Swear, Oath," *NIDNTT* 3.737-43; J. Schneider, "ὀμνύω κτλ," *TDNT* V.176-85; Idem, "ὅρκος κτλ," *TDNT* V.457-67.

D. E. Garland

OBEDIENCE. *See* COMMANDMENT; DISCIPLESHIP; LAW; SON OF GOD.

OIL. *See* ANOINTING.

OLD TESTAMENT IN THE GOSPELS

It is difficult to overemphasize the importance of the function of the OT in the Gospels. It is readily apparent that the Jewish Scriptures were foundational to many of Jesus' teachings and probably to his self-understanding as well. Specific OT passages and themes lie behind many of the parables* and often lie at the center of debate between Jesus and his opponents. The relationship of Jesus to the OT was not lost on the Evangelists. They sought in various ways to show how Jesus understood Scripture, fulfilled Scripture and was clarified by Scripture. In fact there is no significant idea developed in the Gospels that does not in some way reflect or depend on the OT.

    1. Text Types
    2. Phenomena
    3. Jesus' Use of the OT
    4. The OT in Mark
    5. The OT in Matthew
    6. The OT in Luke
    7. The OT in John

1. Text Types.

Citations of the OT in the Gospels reflect the Hebrew (Mt 11:10, 29; Mk 10:19; 12:30; Lk 22:37), the Greek (Mt 18:16; 21:16; Mk 7:6-7; 10:8; Lk 4:18; 23:46; Jn 12:38), and the Aramaic (Mt 4:10; Mk 4:12; 9:48). Given the nature and origin of the material, the respective contexts of the Evangelists and the fact that they wrote their Gospels in Greek, such diversity is hardly surprising. But citations attributed to Jesus also reflect the same diversity. Since Jesus likely did not speak much Greek, he probably did not quote the Greek version (LXX; *see* Languages of Palestine). But the Greek citations are not necessarily inauthentic, that is, deriving from the Greek-speaking church rather than from Jesus. In many cases Jesus' citations of Scripture have been assimilated to the wording of the Greek, especially when the point that he had made was not lost in such assimilation.

2. Phenomena.

In the Gospels the OT is quoted with introductory formulae (e.g., "in order that it be fulfilled"), and sometimes without; it is often paraphrased and many times alluded to through the use of a few key words or phrases. At other times the Gospels reflect OT themes and structures. With regard to exegetical style, scholars

have pointed to parallels with *pesher* as practiced at Qumran (esp. Matthew) and parallels with rabbinic *midrash** (esp. John). In Jesus and the Gospels the OT has three principal functions: (1) legal, (2) prophetic and (3) analogical. *Legal* interpretation has to do with determining what is required of the one that has faith* in God. *Prophetic* interpretation has to do with what has been fulfilled in Jesus' advent and what is expected to be fulfilled in the future. *Analogical* interpretation has to do with comparisons. Typology is a familiar form of analogical interpretation. Several examples of these principal functions are considered in the following sections.

3. Jesus' Use of the OT.

Every attempt to evaluate the role that the OT played in the ministry of Jesus involves the question of authenticity (*see* Form Criticism). According to the criterion of dissimilarity the presence of the OT in the dominical tradition might be owing to pre-Christian Jewish usage, or to later Christian interpretation and not to Jesus himself. Strict application of this criterion, however, is unwarranted and uncritical. One should expect that a Palestinian Jew who preached in Israel's synagogues* and taught disciples* who regarded him as Israel's Messiah (*see* Christ), the fulfillment of prophetic expectation, would surely make frequent appeal to the Scriptures. And this Jesus does. He quotes, alludes to and interprets Scripture to advance legal opinions, to prophesy or to make comparisons between himself and/or his ministry and the OT. Each of these aspects contributes significantly to our understanding of the historical Jesus. And it is ultimately Jesus' use of Scripture that lies behind the function and interpretation of the OT in the Gospels.

3.1. Legal. According to Matthew 5:17-20 Jesus held the Jewish Law* in high regard. Not only has he come to fulfill the Law (and the prophets), "not an iota, not a dot, will pass from the Law until all is accomplished. Whoever then relaxes one of the least of these commandments . . ." (Mt 5:18). This assessment of the complete and permanent value of the Law was shared by Jesus' contemporaries: "Be heedful of the light [i.e., least] commandment as of a grave one, for you do not know the grant of reward for each commandment" (*m. 'Abot* 2:1; 4:2: "Run to do a light command"; cf. *b. Sanh.* 107a).

Matthew 5:21-48, probably a selected and edited compilation of Jesus' legal interpretation of Scripture, provides several important examples. Six times Jesus says, "You heard that it was said," then quotes from the Mosaic Code (Mt 5:21 [Ex 20:13; Deut 5:17]; Mt 5:27 [Ex 20:14; Deut 5:18]; Mt 5:31 [Deut 24:1]; Mt 5:33 [Lev

19:12; Num 30:2]; Mt 5:38 [Ex 21:24]; Mt 5:43 [Lev 19:18]) and offers a rejoinder: "But I say to you." (This mode of speaking was not unknown among the rabbis; cf. *b. Yebam.* 65a, where Rabbi Ammi [3rd to 4th century A.D.] began his challenge to biblical interpretation that supported polygamy with the words "But I say.") Jesus is not controverting Scripture (see Mt 5:17-20), but its popular interpretation (for this reason Jesus' statements are often referred to as "antitheses"). Jesus' interpretations, nevertheless, do not always necessarily contradict those of his contemporaries. For example, when Jesus said, "Love* your enemies" (Mt 5:44), he was not saying anything new. Not only did the Law teach this (see Ex 23:4-5), the rabbis taught the same thing also. Commenting on Leviticus 19:18 ("Love your neighbor as yourself"), a verse which Jesus also cites (see Mk 10:19), Rabbis Aqiba, Ben Azzai and Tanḥuma find in this command "a great principle of Torah," one that requires the faithful not to curse those who curse them (*Gen. Rab.* 24.7 [on Gen 5:1]; *Sipra Lev.* on 19:18; see also *m. 'Abot* 4:24; *b. Meg.* 28a; cf. Mt 5:11).

But Jesus' interpretations do bring to light implications of the Law that might have gone unrecognized by many of his contemporaries: One might not actually commit murder, but one might hate his neighbor (or people outside of one's community; cf. 1QS 1.10); one might not actually commit adultery, but one might lust for another person; and one might take revenge thinking that the Law allowed for it, etc. Jesus' interpretations, however, are not unparalleled, for there are several sayings of the rabbis that approximate them (on hatred see *b. B. Meṣ.* 58b; on lust and divorce see *b. Yoma* 29a; on swearing see Sir 23:9-11; on revenge see *b. Yoma* 23a; on love of one's enemies see *b. Ber.* 10a).

In most respects Jesus' view of the legal portions of Scripture was essentially that of his Palestinian contemporaries. When tempted (*see* Temptation) by the Devil (Mt 4:1-11; Lk 4:1-13), Jesus responded with appropriate citations from Deuteronomy 8:3 ("One does not live by bread alone"); 6:16 ("You shall not tempt the Lord your God") and 6:13 ("You shall worship the Lord your God"). When asked what the greatest commandment was, Jesus cited Deuteronomy 6:4-5 ("Hear O Israel . . . love the Lord your God with your whole heart . . ."; cf. Mk 12:29-30) and Leviticus 19:18 ("You shall love your neighbor as yourself"; cf. Mk 12:31).

Deuteronomy 6:4-5 was part of the Shema that an observant Jew was to recite twice a day (cf. *m. Ber.* 1:1-4). The idea of loving one's neighbor as oneself and so fulfilling the whole Law is found in Jewish sources: "This [Lev 19:18] is a great principle in the Torah"

(*Sipra Lev.* on Lev 19:18; cf. *Gen. Rab.* 24.7 [on Gen 5:1]). The two commandments in combination are probably alluded to in the *Testaments of the Twelve Patriarchs:* "Each of you speak the truth clearly to his neighbor. . . . Throughout all your life love the Lord and one another with a true heart" (*T. Dan* 5:2-3); "Love the Lord and the neighbor" (*T. Iss.* 7:6); and are probably what Philo referred to: "Among the great number of particular propositions and principles, two, as it were, stand as preeminent topics: one of duty toward God in piety and holiness, one of duty toward people in generosity and justice" (*Spec. Leg.* 2.15 §63). When the young man asked Jesus what he must do to inherit eternal life, Jesus responded, "You know the commandments . . . ," and then cited approximately half of the Decalog (Mk 10:19; cf. Ex 20:12-16 [Deut 5:16-20]).

In condemning legalism and hypocrisy (Mk 7:1-23; *see* Hypocrite), Jesus argued that the Pharisaic *qorban* tradition (cf. *m. B. Qam.* 9:10; *m. Ned.* 1:1; 9:1) controverted God's commands: " 'Honor your father and mother'; and 'He who speaks evil of father or mother, let him surely die' " (Mk 7:10; cf. Ex 20:12 [Deut 5:16] LXX Ex 21:17). Herein we find an important difference between Jesus and the Pharisees.*

On another occasion Jesus cites Hosea 6:6, "I desire mercy, not sacrifice" (Mt 9:13; 12:7), to defend his habit of fellowshipping with "tax collectors and sinners" (Mt 9:10). According to the rabbis, one was to avoid the company of sinners* (*t. Dem.* 3:6-7; *b. Ber.* 43b). But the citation of Hosea did not imply that Jesus was opposed to the cultus, as is seen when he urged his followers to be reconciled before offering something upon the altar (Mt 5:23-24). Moreover, implicit in Jesus' command not to take oaths (*see* Oaths and Swearing) is a profound respect for Jerusalem and the Temple* (Mt 5:34-35; cf. Is 66:1). Indeed, Jesus' action in the Temple (Mk 11:15-17) was likely a call for greater respect for Temple worship.*

The Gospels, however, do provide several episodes where the activity of Jesus and his disciples was thought to break the Law. Perhaps best-known was the frequent charge that Jesus violated Sabbath* laws, even when he healed (*see* Healing) someone (cf. Mk 2:23-28; 3:1-6; Lk 13:10-17; 14:1-6; Jn 5:1-18; 9:1-34). To be sure, the rabbis taught that the "saving of life overrides the sabbath" (*Mek. Šabbata* §1 [on Ex 31:12]), after all, "the Sabbath was given to [people], not [people] to the Sabbath" (*Mek. Šabbata* §1 [on Ex 31:14]). This reasoning obviously parallels Jesus' claim that "the Sabbath was made for humanity, not humanity for the Sabbath" (Mk 2:27). (It is possible, of course, that the tradition in *Mekilta* is dependent on Jesus.) But in cases where a person's life was not in immediate danger, some rabbis felt that healing activity was unnecessary and so constituted a violation of the Sabbath. Indeed, the Essenes were even more strict in their interpretation of Sabbath laws (CD 11:13-14: "If a [beast] fall into a cistern or into a pit, let it not be lifted out on the Sabbath"; cf. Mt 12:11: "Who among you, having a sheep that falls into a pit on the Sabbath, will not lay hold of it and lift it out?"). Obviously the difference between Jesus and his opponents lay in the interpretation and application of the Sabbath laws; they did not dispute their validity.

Jesus applied Mosaic Law to settling disputes among his disciples, enjoining that "every word be confirmed by the evidence of two or three witnesses" (Mt 18:16; cf. LXX Deut 19:15). On the permanence of the marriage* union, Jesus cited texts from Genesis: "God made them male and female" (Mk 10:6; cf. LXX Gen 1:27; 5:2); and "For this reason a man shall leave his father and mother and be joined to his wife, and the two shall become one flesh" (Mk 10:7-8; cf. LXX Gen 2:24). Jesus' legislation is clearly at variance with some of the more permissive interpretations of Deuteronomy 24:1: "The School of Hillel says, '[Divorce is permitted] if she spoils the cooking'. . . Rabbi Aqiba says '[Divorce is permitted] if he has found another more beautiful than she, as it is said . . .' " (cf. m. Gîṭ. 9:10). In this case the Essenes apparently held to Jesus' view (cf. 11QTemple 57:17-18: "And he must not select in addition to her another woman because she, and she alone, will remain with him all the days of her life"; cf. CD 4:20-21, where Gen 1:27 is cited).

It is clear from his interpretation of the legal portions of Scripture that Jesus was committed to the essentials of the Jewish faith, even if some of his interpretations apparently were at variance with, at times even stricter than, those of his contemporaries. The chief difference between Jesus' interpretation of Scripture and that of many of his contemporaries is seen in the relationship between the Law and people. When it came to morals (e.g., divorce) Jesus' interpretation was stricter than most of his contemporaries. When it came to cultic laws (e.g., the Sabbath) Jesus' interpretation was comparatively lenient. Jesus' emphasis seems to have fallen on *compassion* as over against *holiness (see* Law).

3.2. Prophetic. Jesus cites Isaiah 61:1-2 as fulfilled in, and perhaps the occasion for, his public ministry: "The Spirit of the Lord is upon me, because he has anointed me to preach good news to the poor . . ." (Lk 4:18-19; cf. Lk 7:22 par. Mt 11:5). Jesus' interpretation of Micah 7:6 ("For I have come to set a man against his father, and a daughter against her mother . . ." [Mt 10:35-36])

is similar to the messianic interpretation of this text in Jewish sources (cf. *Jub.* 23:16, 19; *m. Soṭa* 9:15; cf. *b. Soṭa* 49b; *b. Sanh.* 97a).

Apparently the rabbis also believed that division within families (*see* Family) would take place in the time of the Messiah. The theme of division is reflected in the allusion to Psalm 6:8 ("Depart from me, you evildoers") in the sayings concerning false prophets (Mt 7:23; *see* Prophets and Prophecy). The early Christian understanding of John the Baptist* as the fulfillment of Malachi 3:1 ("Behold, I am sending my messenger to prepare the way before me") apparently derives from Jesus (Mt 11:10).

Jesus explains the incomprehension and unbelief of his contemporaries in terms of Isaiah's strange commission from God: "in order that they may indeed see but not perceive, and may indeed hear but not understand; lest they should turn again, and be forgiven" (Mk 4:12, alluding to *Tg. Isa.* 6:9-10; cf. Mt 13:14-15, which cites LXX Is 6:9-10). But even Jesus' disciples are rebuked in similar terms: "Having eyes do you not see, and having ears do you not hear?" (Mk 8:18; cf. Jer 5:21; Ezek 12:2; Is 6:9-10). Jesus castigates Israel's religious leaders: "This people honors me with their lips, but their heart is far from me; in vain do they worship me, teaching human precepts as doctrines" (Mk 7:6-7, citing LXX Is 29:13; *see* Hardness of Heart).

Many of Jesus' prophetic statements looked to fulfillment in the future. In alluding to Isaiah's oracle against Babylon ("will you be exalted to heaven? You shall be brought down to Hades" [Is 14:13, 15]) Jesus offered the cities that have rejected him a grim warning of coming judgment* (Mt 11:23). Jerusalem itself received a warning no less foreboding in language borrowed from Jeremiah 22:5 ("Behold, your house is forsaken and desolate" [cf. Mt 23:38]). The thought is completed in the reference to Psalm 118:26: "Blessed is he who comes in the name of the Lord" (Mt 23:39). The prophetic implication is that Jerusalem will be in a state of spiritual desolation until Jesus returns at the Parousia and is properly received.

Jesus predicted Jerusalem's impending fate (*see* Destruction of Jerusalem) in terms of Daniel's "abomination of desolation" (Mk 13:14; cf. Dan 11:31; 12:11). The eschatological day will approach ". . . suddenly like a snare; for it will come upon all who dwell upon the face of the whole earth" (Lk 21:34-35; cf. Is 24:17). When these things happen, "they will begin to say to the mountains, 'Fall on us,' and to the hills, 'Cover us' " (Lk 23:30; cf. Hos 10:8; *see* Apocalyptic Teaching).

Jesus described his impending arrest and crucifixion in the words of Zechariah 13:7: "I will strike the shepherd and the sheep will be scattered" (Mk 14:27).

Jesus told his troubled disciples: "And then they will see the Son of man coming in clouds with great power and glory" (Mk 13:26; cf. Dan 7:13). Before the high priest, Jesus similarly predicted: "You will see the Son of man seated at the right hand of Power, and coming with the clouds of heaven" (Mk 14:62; cf. Ps 110:1 + Dan 7:13; cf. *b. Sanh.* 96b-97a where Messiah is called *bar naphle*, that is, "son of the fallen (tent of David)" [MT Amos 9:11] or "son of the cloud" [LXX Dan 7:13]; *see* Son of Man).

Jesus apparently understood himself in terms of Daniel's "son of man," to whom the kingdom* would be given (cf. Dan 7:14; *1 Enoch* 69:29; *Pss. Sol.* 17:44), and his disciples as the "saints" to whom judgment would some day be given (cf. Dan 7:22). This is likely what lies behind Jesus' saying, "Truly, I say to you, in the new world, when the Son of man shall sit on his glorious throne, you who have followed me will also sit on twelve thrones, judging the twelve tribes of Israel" (Mt 19:28; cf. Lk 22:28-30: ". . . I assign to you, as my Father assigned to me, a kingdom . . . that you may . . . sit on thrones judging . . ."). It is likely that Psalm 122:3-5 ("Jerusalem . . . to which the tribes go up . . . There thrones for judgment were set, the thrones of the house of David") has also contributed to this eschatological saying. Both passages, Daniel 7 and Psalm 122, are cited side by side in a rabbinic exegesis that anticipates the day when God and Israel's elders will sit in judgment on the peoples of the world (cf. *Tanḥuma, Qedoshim* 1.1). Elsewhere, Rabbi Aqiba interpreted the plural "thrones" of Daniel 7:9 as implying that the Messiah would take his seat next to God himself (*b. Sanh.* 38b; *b. ḥag.* 14a). Finally, Jesus warns his followers of the judgment of Gehenna: "where their worm does not die, and the fire is not quenched" (Mk 9:48; cf. *Tg. Isa.* 66:24). According to Jesus, when the Son of man comes, "he will repay everyone for what he has done" (Mt 16:27; cf. LXX Ps 61:13).

3.3. Analogical. This category includes typology and other points of comparison. Jesus explicitly compared his ministry to the ministries of Elijah and Elisha (Lk 4:25-27; cf. 1 Kings 17:1-16; 2 Kings 5:1-14; *see* Elijah and Elisha). Later deeds resemble the exploits of these prophets of old (compare Lk 7:11-17 with 1 Kings 17-24 and 2 Kings 4:32-37; Lk 9:51-56 with 2 Kings 1:9-16; Lk 9:61-62 with 1 Kings 19:19-21). The kingdom is compared to the crop that grows of its own accord and then is harvested (Mk 4:29; cf. LXX Joel 3:13). Jesus enjoined his listeners to take his yoke upon them and "find rest for [their] souls" (Mt 11:29; cf. Jer 6:16). Jesus may have presented himself here as the personification of Wisdom* (compare Sir 51:23-27; cf. Mt 11:19,

where Jesus apparently did identify himself with Wisdom). The rabbis spoke variously of taking upon oneself the yoke of the kingdom, the Law or repentance (*b. Ber.* 10b; *m. 'Abot* 3:5; *b. 'Abod. Zar.* 5a).

The comparison with Jonah (*see* Sign of Jonah) is one of the most significant and one of the most debated: "For as Jonah was three days and three nights in the belly of the whale, so will the Son of man be three days and three nights in the heart of the earth" (Mt 12:40; cf. Jon 1:17). In Matthew (12:38-39) the "sign of Jonah" has something to do with Jesus' resurrection* (cf. 3 Macc 6:8). In Luke (11:31-32) it appears to be no more than Jesus' preaching. In a late rabbinic work Jonah's remarkable deliverance is described as a sign to the heathen (*Pirqe R. El.* §10). Not only is Jesus greater than Jonah, he is also greater than Solomon, who was visited by the "queen of the South" (Mt 12:41-42; cf. 1 Kings 10:1-10).

When he took action in the Temple, Jesus said: " 'My house shall be called a house of prayer* for all the nations.' But you have made it a 'den of robbers' " (Mk 11:17; cf. Is 56:7 + Jer 7:11). Isaiah 56 anticipates the day when all peoples will gather at Jerusalem to worship the Lord. By crowding the Temple's "court of the Gentiles" with sacrificial animals, the ruling priests made it difficult to pray and so showed callous disregard for Gentile* worshippers. Jeremiah 7 is a prophetic indictment of a violent and avaricious priesthood (*see* Priest and Priesthood), one destined to come under divine judgment. In alluding to this passage Jesus implied that the ruling priests were corrupt and possibly violent. Other Jewish sources reflecting upon the pre-70 A.D. ruling priesthood paint a similar picture (cf. Josephus, *Ant.* 20.8.8 §181; 20.9.2 §§206-207; *2 Apoc. Bar* 10:18; *m. Ker.* 1:7; *t. Yoma* 1:6-7; *t. Menaḥ* 13:18-22; *b. Pesaḥ.* 57a). As a rejoinder to the chief priests' indignation over the children's (*see* Child, Children) shouts of acclamation (which hark back to the triumphal entry; *see* Triumphal Entry) and the citation of Ps 118:26, cf. Mt 21:9), Jesus replied: "Out of the mouth of babes and sucklings you have brought perfect praise" (Mt 21:16; cf. LXX Ps 8:3, one of the Hallel Psalms that small children were taught; *t. Soṭa* 6:2-3).

Jesus' parable of the wicked vineyard tenants begins with an important allusion to Isaiah's Song of the Vineyard (*see* Vine): "A man planted a vineyard, and set a hedge around it, and dug a pit for the wine press, and built a tower" (Mk 12:1; cf. Is 5:1-2). Whereas Isaiah's original song indicted all of Judah (cf. Is 5:3, 7), Jesus' parable limits the indictment to the Jewish religious leaders (cf. Mk 12:12). His application likely reflects exegetical traditions current in his time (cf. *Tg. Isa.* 5:1-

7; *t. Me'il.* 1:16; *t. Sukk.* 3:15, where the song's "tower" is explicitly identified as the Temple, and the "wine vat" the altar). At the conclusion of the parable Jesus quotes Psalm 118:22-23: "The very stone which the builders rejected has become the head of the corner; this was the Lord's doing, and it is marvelous in our eyes" (Mk 12:10-11). The rejected stone of Psalm 118 is to be understood as further explanation of the significance of the rejected son of the parable. The Targum's* paraphrase "the son which the builders rejected" (based upon a play on the words "son" [*ben*] and "stone" [*eben*]), and the rabbis' custom of referring to themselves as the "builders" (cf. *b. Šabb.* 114a; *b. Ber.* 64a [in a positive sense]; CD 4:19; 8:12, 18 [in a negative sense]; cf. 1 Cor 3:10), likely facilitated Jesus' comparison.

Many of Jesus' parables either reflect or are based on the OT. The parable of the sower (Mk 4:3-9) may illustrate the truth of Isaiah 55:10-11 that God's Word is always fruitful, giving bread* to the sower (see also Jer 4:3 ["sow not among thorns"]; Is 6:13 ["the holy seed"]). The parable of the mustard seed (Mk 4:30-32) alludes to passages that speak of worldwide kingdoms (cf. Ezek 31:5-6; Dan 4:9, 18). The parable of the good Samaritan (Lk 10:30-37) is surely based on the story of the merciful Samaritans* in 2 Chronicles 28:8-15 (see v. 15, where the naked and wounded Judeans are clothed, provided with food and drink, anointed, carried on donkeys and taken to Jericho by Samaritans).

The parable of humility (Lk 14:7-14), in which Jesus urged his hearers to recline at the lower positions around the table, is based on the advice given in Proverbs 25:6-7: "Do not put yourself forward in the king's presence or stand in the place of the great; for it is better to be told, 'Come up here,' than to be put lower in the presence of the prince" (cf. Sir 3:17-20).The excuses proffered by the invited guests of the parable of the great banquet (Lk 14:15-24; cf. *m. 'Abot* 4:16: "[Prepare to] enter the banqueting hall") approximate those found in Deuteronomy 20:5-7.

The parable of the prodigal son (Lk 15:11-32) is probably commentary on the Deuteronomistic legislation concerned with the rights of inheritance of the first-born son and of the punishment for a rebellious son (cf. Deut 21:15-17, 18-21). Similarly, the parable of the lost sheep (Lk 15:3-7; cf. Mt 18:12-14) may reflect the command to restore a lost sheep or ox to its owner (Deut 22:1-4; cf. Jer 31:10-14, parts of which read: " 'He who scattered Israel will gather him, and will keep him as a shepherd keeps his flock.' . . . Then shall maidens rejoice . . . and the young men and the old shall be merry").

Legislation concerning displaced or runaway servants (Deut 23:15-16) and the charging of interest (Deut 23:19-20) may underlie the parable of the dishonest manager (Lk 16:1-8). The parable of the rich fool may echo the words of the Preacher (Eccles 8:15: "to eat and drink, and enjoy himself"). The saying about salt (Mk 9:50; Mt 5:13) may reflect Job 6:6 ("Can that which is tasteless be eaten without salt?"). The parable of the dishonest judge (Lk 18:1-8) likely reflects Sirach 35:12-20. Jesus' statement "All who exalt themselves will be humbled; and all who humble themselves will be exalted," found sometimes appended to his parables (Lk 14:11; 18:9-14; cf. Mt 23:12), derives from Ezekiel 21:26 (cf. Job 22:29; Prov 29:23). When in the parable of the fig tree (Mk 13:28-31) Jesus says, "Heaven and earth will pass away, but my words will not pass away" (v. 31), he not only echoes various OT passages that speak of the abiding permanence of God's Word (cf. Is 40:8; 55:11; Ps 119:89), he has implied that his words equal the very words of God.

In defending the hope of the resurrection, Jesus cites the words spoken from the burning bush: "I am the God of Abraham,* and the God of Isaac and the God of Jacob" (Mk 12:26; cf. Ex 3:6, 15). His point here is that God would not identify himself with the names of the dead, but with the living. With the citation "The Lord said to my Lord, Sit at my right hand till I put your enemies under your feet" (Mk 12:36; cf. LXX Ps 109:1), Jesus startled his hearers by suggesting that the Son of David (i.e., the Messiah; *see* Christ; Son of David) is in fact greater than King David (not lesser as might be implied by his identification as the *Son* of David). Jesus' interpretation of this verse provides important evidence that Jesus understood his messiahship in terms very different from those of his contemporaries.

When Jesus asked God to forgive his executioners "for they know not what they do" (Lk 23:34), he alluded to Numbers 15:25-31 in which forgiveness is allowed for those who sin ignorantly. In quoting Psalm 22:1, "My God, my God, why have you forsaken me?" (Mk 15:34), Jesus identified himself with the righteous sufferer who endures insult and injury but anticipates divine vindication. At the moment of his death Jesus again identified with the righteous person who has been ill, tormented and abandoned by friends: "Father, into your hands I commit my spirit!" (Lk 23:46; cf. Ps 31:5; *see* Death of Jesus). This particular verse was sometimes cited by observant Jews before going to sleep (cf. *b. Ber.* 5a).

4. The OT in Mark.

Virtually all uses of the OT references in the Gospel of Mark are derived from the tradition. Although some have found extensive OT typology underlying this writing (usually based on the hexateuch), while others have concluded that the Markan Evangelist had little or no interest in the OT, it is likely that a mediating position is most accurate. When the Markan Jesus cries out, "Let the Scriptures be fulfilled" (14:49), he probably has given expression to a viewpoint not too different from that of the Evangelist's.

4.1. Legal. In a dispute with the Pharisees and scribes* concerning eating with ceremonially unclean hands (7:1-23; *see* Clean and Unclean), the Evangelist Mark (or possibly the tradition before him) comments: "Thus he declared all foods clean" (7:19). Evidently this is a traditional extension of Jesus' interpretation of the Mosaic dietary laws. (See also Mark's description of the Pharisaic "tradition of the elders"* in 7:3-4.) In light of this example, and judging by the way the laws of the Pentateuch are regularly presented in Mark in a favorable light (7:10; 10:4, 19; 12:19, 29-30), it is evident that the Markan Evangelist understood Jesus as upholding the Law, but possessing a power that transcends it.

4.2. Prophetic. Mark apparently defines the good news (*see* Gospel [Good News]) of Jesus Messiah in terms of the fulfillment of Isaiah's oracle of salvation* and deliverance: "Behold, I send my messenger before your face, who shall prepare your way; the voice of one crying in the wilderness: Prepare the way of the Lord, make his paths straight" (1:2-3; cf. Mal 3:1 + LXX Is 40:3). In other words, the good news of the Christian message is the fulfillment of that for which Israel had for many years longed. Qumran (1QS 8:12-14; 9:19-20; *see* Dead Sea Scrolls), as well as others (Bar 5:7; *T. Moses* 10:1-5), also understood Isaiah 40:3 as a prophetic text that spoke of restoration. At Jesus' baptism the heavenly voice echoed the words of Psalm 2:7: "You are my beloved Son; with you I am well pleased" (1:11; cf. Gen 22:2; Ex 4:22-23; Is 42:1). With this utterance Jesus' identity is made clear. Such recognition will not come forth from a human being until Jesus' death on the cross (cf. Mk 15:39). At the Mount of Transfiguration (*see* Transfiguration), where Jesus conversed with Moses, the heavenly voice once again spoke, only this time addressing the disciples: "This is my beloved Son; listen to him" (9:7; cf. Ps 2:7; Gen 22:2; Deut 18:15). The injunction to listen is probably an allusion to Deuteronomy 18:15 ("The Lord your God will raise up for you a prophet like me [Moses] . . . listen to him"). These citations and allusions strongly suggest that Mark understood Jesus as the fulfillment of Jewish messianic expectation. As God's beloved Son and as the prophet who was to come (see 8:28), Jesus was the long-awaited Messiah of Israel.*

The function of Scripture in the passion narrative (*see* Passion Narrative) would also suggest that Jesus was understood in terms of the righteous sufferer. There are three principal allusions or citations: the dividing and casting lots for Jesus' clothing (15:24; cf. Ps 22:18); the cry of abandonment (15:34; cf. Ps 22:1); and the giving of vinegar to drink (15:36; cf. Ps 69:21). Although it is possible that these allusions are not to be understood as fulfillments of Scripture, since after all not one is introduced as a fulfillment (compare Matthew and John), the earlier declaration, "Let the Scriptures be fulfilled" (14:49), uttered at the moment of the arrest, probably requires that they be so understood.

4.3. Analogical. When Mark tells the reader that Jesus "had compassion on [the people], because they were like sheep without a shepherd" (6:34; *see* Shepherd and Sheep), he has alluded to Moses* and his successor, Joshua, who had together functioned as Israel's shepherds: "Moses said to the Lord, '. . . appoint a man over the congregation . . . that the congregation of the Lord may not be as sheep which have no shepherd.' And the Lord said to Moses, 'Take Joshua [LXX: Jesus] the son of Nun, a man in whom is the spirit . . .' " (Num 27:17-18). The Mount of Transfiguration (9:2-8) contains numerous allusions to the theophanic traditions associated with the giving of the Law at Sinai: "after six days" (9:2; Ex 24:16); Moses/Jesus accompanied by three companions (9:2; Ex 24:9); mountain setting (9:2; Ex 24:12); Jesus and Moses together (9:4; Ex 24:1-18: "Jesus" in LXX); transfigured appearance (9:3; Ex 34:29-30); divine presence attended by cloud (9:7; Ex 24:15-16); heavenly voice (9:7; Ex 24:16); fear (9:6; Ex 34:30); "Hear him" (9:7; Deut 18:15). When the enthusiastic crowd (*see* People, Crowd) cries out, "Hosanna! Blessed is he who comes in the name of the Lord! Blessed is the kingdom of our father David that is coming!" (Mk 11:9-10; cf. Ps 118:25-26), they have messianically interpreted this Hallel Psalm, one often cited as a greeting for pilgrims approaching Jerusalem for a religious festival.

Larger portions of Mark may reflect biblical themes. For example, the miracle stories (*see* Miracles and Miracle Stories) of Mark 4—8 parallel several of the elements found in Psalm 107: Deliverance from hunger and thirst in the wilderness (Mk 6:30-44; 8:1-10, 14-21; cf. Ps 107:4-9; *see* Mountain and Wilderness); deliverance from imprisonment (Mk 5:1-20; 6:13; 7:24-30; cf. Ps 107:10-16); deliverance from sickness (Mk 5:21—6:5, 13, 53-56; 7:31-37; 8:22-26; cf. Ps 107:17-22; *see* Healing); and deliverance from peril at sea (Mk 4:35-41; 6:45-52; cf. Ps 107:23-32). The citation of Ps 118:22-23 ("The very stone which the builders rejected has become the head of the corner . . ."), the apparent conclusion and explication of the parable of the wicked vineyard tenants (12:10-11), seems to lie at the heart of Mark's polemic against the Temple establishment of Jesus' day. Jesus found the Temple buzzing with religious activity, but it was as fruitless as the barren fig tree (11:11-21; *see* Cleansing of the Temple). The parable of the wicked vineyard tenants (12:1-12) implies that the religious leaders will lose their stewardship. The scribes are described as those who devour the estates of widows (12:38-40), while the widow who gave her last penny (12:41-44) is probably to be understood as a tragic example of the oppression that the Temple establishment inflicted upon the poor.

The magnificence of the Temple (13:1), as implied by the context, only testifies to its oppression. But the Temple will be destroyed (13:2). After his arrest Jesus is accused of threatening to destroy the Temple (14:58). Literally such an accusation is false, but theologically it is actually quite true. When Jesus died, the veil of the Temple was torn (15:38), the meaning of which is probably that Jesus' prophecy of the Temple's destruction has begun to be fulfilled. It was at the moment of his death and the tearing of the veil that the centurion confessed Jesus to be "Son of God"* (15:39). Mark's point in all of this is probably to show that Jesus, the rejected stone (or "son," as in the parable of the wicked vineyard tenants), has replaced the Temple, which at the time of his writing probably had been destroyed. The Temple that was "made with hands" has given way to the Temple "not made with hands," a Temple founded upon the rejected stone.

5. The OT in Matthew.

The extensive use of the OT in the Gospel of Matthew is well known. The Matthean Evangelist was keenly interested in showing how Jesus fulfilled every aspect of Scripture. All three components of the Hebrew Bible—legal, prophetic and wisdom/praise—have been fulfilled in Jesus. Not only has he personally fulfilled the requirements of the Law, but he is the Law's master interpreter. He not only fulfilled messianic prophecies, he is Israel's greatest prophet. Finally, he is the incarnation of Wisdom* itself, a master teacher who was unparalleled.

5.1. Legal. Matthew's interest in Jesus' *halakah* is plainly evident. Jesus is not only the fulfillment of the prophetic Scriptures, but the legal Scriptures as well (cf. 3:15: "to fulfill all righteousness"). The arrangement of the Sermon on the Mount* (chaps. 5—7) is the clearest example of this interest. In chapter 5 Jesus makes it clear that his intention was not to break the Law, not even the smallest commandments (5:17-20). Indeed, as

the antitheses illustrate (5:21-48), Jesus' ethical requirements are more stringent. In chapter 6 Matthew underscores Jesus' demands for religious purity and sincerity. Hypocrisy, whether Gentile or Jewish, is roundly condemned. It is Matthew who records Jesus' command to do what the scribes and Pharisees teach when they "sit on Moses' seat," that is, when they teach the Law of Moses (23:1-3). It is their hypocrisy that the Matthean Jesus condemns (23:3-12).

From time to time Matthew qualifies Mark's presentation of Jesus' interpretation of the Law. Whereas in Mark 10:11-12 Jesus states that divorce and remarriage (*see* Marriage and Divorce) constitute adultery, Matthew (19:9) states that remarriage constitutes adultery "except for unchastity." Matthew goes on to add a saying of Jesus on men who make themselves eunuchs for the kingdom (19:10-12).

5.2. Prophetic. At many points in his narrative Matthew describes such-and-such event as something that happened "in order that" a certain Scripture "be fulfilled." Five times in the infancy narrative various Scriptures are introduced this way: 1:23 (cf. LXX Is 7:14); 2:6 (cf. Mic 5:2); 2:15 (cf. Hos 11:1); 2:18 (cf. Jer 31:15) and 2:23 (probably alluding to the *nēzer* ["branch"] of Is 11:1; cf. Is 4:2; Jer 23:5; Judg 13:5). Jesus' ministry in Galilee is said to fulfill Scripture (4:15-16; cf. Is 9:1-2). Jesus' ministry of healing is said to fulfill the task of the Suffering Servant (*see* Servant of Yahweh): "He took our infirmities and bore our diseases" (8:17; cf. Is 53:4). Jesus' peaceful style of ministry is said to fulfill yet another aspect of the role of the Servant: "Behold, my servant whom I have chosen . . . He will not wrangle or cry aloud . . . ." (12:17-21; cf. Is 42:1-3 + LXX 42:4). Moreover, Jesus' habit of teaching by means of parables fulfilled Scripture: "I will open my mouth in parables, I will utter what has been hidden since the foundation of the world" (13:35; cf. Ps 78:2). Jesus' entry into Jerusalem, mounted on a donkey, also fulfilled Scripture (21:4-5; cf. Is 62:11 + Zech 9:9). (Note how many messianic passages from Isaiah have been quoted or alluded to.) Judas' (*see* Judas Iscariot) betrayal of Jesus for thirty pieces of silver, and the subsequent purchase of the potter's field, also fulfilled Scripture (26:15; 27:9-10; cf. Zech 11:12-13 + Jer 18—19, 36). Finally, Jesus' arrest fulfilled Scripture (26:54, 56).

5.3. Analogical. Scriptural themes and echoes may be heard in Matthew's infancy narrative (*see* Birth of Jesus). Jesus' brush with death and flight to Egypt to escape Herod likely mirror the similar experience of the infant Moses, who was threatened by Pharaoh. Matthew's grouping of OT citations is also noteworthy: Five times in the infancy narrative Scripture is cited as "fulfilled." Five scriptural topics are discussed in the Sermon on the Mount (5:21-48). This parallelism may suggest that Matthew is trying to show how Jesus is the fulfillment of both *prophetic* and *legal* portions of Scripture. Matthew presents Jesus' teaching in five major discourses (chaps. 5—7, 10, 13, 18 and 23—25), ending each with something like "when Jesus finished these sayings" (cf. 7:28; 11:1; 13:53; 19:1; 26:1).

Matthew's arrangement may have been an attempt to present Jesus' teaching (*see* Teacher) in a way that parallels that of Moses, whose Law is presented in five major books, and whose discourses sometimes close with words like "when he finished speaking all these words" (cf. Num 16:31; Deut 32:45). The resurrected Jesus standing before his disciples on the mountain (28:16-20) once again is presented as the new Moses. But Jesus is greater than Moses, for "all authority* in heaven and on earth has been given to" him (28:18).

6. The OT in Luke.

Because Luke is usually viewed as the Gospel for Gentiles,* and because it does not regularly cite Scripture with the formula "in order that it be fulfilled," as do Matthew and John, the significance of this Evangelist's use of the OT is often underrated. The OT (i.e., the LXX) plays a very important role in this Gospel. The Evangelist not only cites specific passages and alludes to many others, he borrows its vocabulary and imitates its style. It is probable that the Evangelist understood the story of Jesus (the Gospel) and the early church* (the book of Acts) as the continuation of the biblical story. This may be implied, at least in part, when the risen Jesus told his disciples that "everything written about me in the Law of Moses and the Prophets and the Psalms must be fulfilled" (24:44-47; cf. 24:26-27).

6.1. Legal. Although Luke is not nearly as concerned with the legal aspects of the Scriptures, there are indications that the Evangelist wished to portray Jesus and his parents as pious, observant Jews (*see* Birth of Jesus). At the end of eight days the infant Jesus was circumcised (2:21) in compliance with the Law (Gen 17:12; Lev 12:3; *m. Šab.* 18:3). The Evangelist is then careful to note that in observing the Mosaic laws of purification, Joseph and Mary brought the infant Jesus to Jerusalem (2:22). This they did in compliance with the laws concerning the firstborn (2:23; cf. Ex 13:2, 12, 15) and purification of the mother (2:24; cf. Lev 12:8). Although the Evangelist concedes that there are sins from which people "could not be freed by the Law of Moses" (Acts 13:39), he felt that it was important to record Paul telling Governor Felix that he believed "everything laid down by the Law" (Acts 24:14). Luke

has not denigrated the Law; he believed that only through faith in Jesus could one overcome the problems of sin and unbelief.

6.2. Prophetic. Luke's prophetic perspective is clearly seen in his summarizing statements. Five times Jesus spoke of scriptural fulfillment (4:21; 18:31; 21:22; 24:25-27, 44-47; cf. 22:16). In Acts the Lukan Paul told the synagogue of Antioch: "And when they had fulfilled all that was written of him, they took him down from the tree . . ." (Acts 13:29). But there are several specific prophetic fulfillments that are distinctive to Luke. The angel* Gabriel told Zechariah that he was soon to have a son who "will go before [the Lord] in the spirit and power of Elijah,* to turn the hearts of the fathers to the children" (1:17; cf. Mal 4:5-6; Sir 48:10; the passage is alluded to in Mk 9:11-12 par.). After John's birth, Zechariah again alludes to the prophecy of Malachi: "And you, child, will be called the prophet of the Most High; for you will go before the Lord to prepare his ways" (1:76; cf. Mal 3:1). In the same canticle Zechariah proclaims that God's salvation will "give light to those who sit in darkness and in the shadow of death" (1:79; cf. Is 9:2; portions of this passage are cited in Mt 4:15-16). One of the most significant citations is found in Luke's extension of the quotation from Isaiah 40: "The voice of one crying in the wilderness . . . and all flesh shall see the salvation of God" (3:4-6; cf. LXX Is 40:3-5). By extending this traditional prooftext to include Isaiah 40:5, the Evangelist has underscored the universal mission of the Christian message. The preaching of John was not simply to bring about Israel's repentance and salvation, but the repentance and salvation of "all flesh."

The prophetic use of Scripture is also seen in Jesus' oracles predicting the doom of Jerusalem. When Jesus wept over the city and described the coming disaster (19:41-44), he borrowed vocabulary and imagery from the prophets who had spoken of the first destruction of Jerusalem (cf. Is 29:3; Jer 6:6; Ezek 4:2; *see* Destruction of Jerusalem). This tragedy will befall the holy city, "because [it] did not know the time of [its] visitation" (19:44; cf. LXX Jer 6:15: "in the time of their visitation they will perish"; Wis 3:7; 1 Pet 2:12). In his eschatological discourse (*see* Apocalyptic Teaching) the Lukan Jesus repeats his dire prediction concerning Jerusalem's fate (21:20-24). The inhabitants of the city should flee the coming wrath, "for these are days of vengeance, to fulfill all that is written" (21:22; cf. LXX Hos 9:11: "the days of vengeance have come"). According to Luke 21:24 the people of Jerusalem "will fall by the edge of the sword" (cf. Sir 28:18) and will "be led captive among all nations" (cf. LXX Deut 28:64); Jerusalem itself "will be trodden down by the Gentiles" (cf. LXX Zech 12:3), "until the times of the Gentiles are fulfilled" (cf. Tob 14:5; Rom 11:25). When led away to crucifixion (23:26-31), the Lukan Jesus one last time warns of Jerusalem's coming destruction: "Then they will begin to say to the mountains, 'Fall on us,' and to the hills, 'Cover us' " (23:30; cf. Hos 10:8).

6.3. Analogical. At several points and in a variety of ways the Evangelist draws comparisons between Jesus and great figures of Israel's biblical history. The story of Jesus' birth is told with the story of Samuel in mind. Mary's *Magnificat* (1:46-55; *see* Mary's Song) is modeled after Hannah's song of thanksgiving following the birth of Samuel (1 Sam 2:1-10). In fact, the *Magnificat* is replete with scriptural allusions (e.g., compare 1:48 with LXX 1 Sam 1:11; 1:50 with Ps 103:17). When Luke wrote that "Jesus increased in wisdom and in stature, and in divine and human favor" (2:52), he undoubtedly had in mind the similar progress report concerning Samuel: "Now the boy Samuel continued to grow both in stature and in divine and human favor" (1 Sam 2:26). The Evangelist apparently exploited comparison between Jesus and the prophets Elijah and Elisha. When the disciples recommend that fire be called down from heaven to destroy the Samaritans (9:54), the reader is reminded of the fire that Elijah called down from heaven (2 Kings 1:10, 12). (For further examples see 3.3. above.) Luke's Gospel also compares Jesus with the Suffering Servant (*see* Servant of Yahweh) who would be "reckoned with transgressors" (22:37; cf. Is 53:12) and who, "as a sheep led to the slaughter," would not "open his mouth" (Acts 8:32-33; cf. Is 53:7-8).

Perhaps the most ambitious comparison that Luke has produced is between Jesus and Moses.* Not only has Luke explicitly cited parts of Deuteronomy 18:15-19 as fulfilled in Jesus (cf. Acts 3:22-23; 7:37), he apparently has arranged the contents of his so-called central section (9:51—19:27) to correspond to the contents and order of Deuteronomy 1—26. But Luke's point in doing this was not simply to underscore the conviction that Jesus was indeed the prophet-like-Moses, rather, Luke wished some of the main concepts of Deuteronomy to be refracted through the dominical tradition. He apparently wanted his readers to study the materials of the central section in the light of the parallel passages and themes from Deuteronomy. Thus, the central section and Deuteronomy, by being set side by side, are mutually illuminating. This feature is readily seen in numerous examples.

When the legist acknowledged that it was the Samaritan, the one who "showed mercy," that fulfilled the Great Commandment (10:37; *see* Commandment), he thereby alluded to Deuteronomy's command that

Israel in occupying Canaan not show mercy to the resident nations (cf. Deut 7:2, 16). This command was given lest foreigners cause Israel to break its covenant with God. Ironically, it was the foreigner, the Samaritan, who in showing mercy fulfilled the covenant. The Mary and Martha episode in Luke 10:38-42, in which Martha is busy preparing food while Mary sits listening to Jesus, illustrates the truth of Deuteronomy 8:3 that "one does not live by bread alone, but by every word that proceeds out of the mouth of the Lord." The excuses of those invited in the parable of the great banquet (Lk 14:15-24) approximate the excuses for not participating in holy war (Deut 20:5-7). The parable of the lost sheep (Lk 15:3-7) falls opposite legislation requiring lost sheep and oxen to be returned to their owners (Deut 22:1-4). The parable of the prodigal son (Lk 15:11-32) contrasts with Deuteronomy's legislation upholding the rights of inheritance for the oldest son (Deut 21:15-17) and that concerning the punishment of a disobedient and drunken son (Deut 21:18-21). The parable of the dishonest steward (Lk 16:1-8) is set over against laws concerned with the treatment of unemployed slaves (Deut 23:15-16).

7. The OT in John.
The formal usage of Scripture in the Fourth Gospel underscores the movement from Jesus' ministry of signs (chaps. 2—12) to his passion (chaps. 13—20). In the first half of the Gospel Scripture is introduced in a variety of ways, usually with the word *written* (1:23; 2:17; 6:31, 45; 7:38, 42; 8:17; 10:34; 12:14). In the second half Scripture is invariably introduced "in order that it be fulfilled" (12:38, 39-40; 13:18; 15:25; 19:24, 28, 36, 37). What is the meaning of this pattern? Whereas Jesus' ministry of signs was in keeping with scriptural requirements and expectations, his rejection (first formally acknowledged at 12:37 in reference to his ministry of signs) was in fulfillment of scriptural prophecy. Herein lies the Fourth Evangelist's apologetic: Rejection and crucifixion did not disprove Jesus' claim to messiahship (a position likely held in the late first-century synagogue); on the contrary, they proved it, as seen in the numerous fulfillments of Scripture. Consequently, we should not be surprised that the fundamental function of the OT in the Fourth Gospel is christological.

7.1. Legal. The Fourth Gospel provides few examples of the legal use of Scripture. In 7:14-24 Jesus complained that Jewish interpretation of the laws of Sabbath* (Ex 20:8-11) and circumcision (Lev 12:3) were inconsistent and unjust. This argument to some extent parallels that of Rabbi Eliezer (*c.* A.D. 90): "If one supersedes the Sabbath on account of one of his members, should he not supersede the Sabbath for his whole body [if in danger of death]?" (*t. Šab.* 15:16). The question that Nicodemus put to the Pharisees ("Our law does not judge people without first giving them a hearing to find out what they are doing, does it?" [Jn 7:51 NRSV]) may have in mind the provisions of Deut 1:16-17; 17:6. The closest parallel, however, comes from the "oral law": "People pass judgment on a person if they hear his words; if they do not hear his words they cannot establish judgment on him" (*Exod. Rab.* 21.3 [on Ex 14:15]).

In a textually uncertain passage Jesus was asked what should be done with the woman caught in the act of adultery, in light of the Law's command that such an offender be stoned (Jn 8:5; cf. Lev 20:10). Jesus' gesture of writing on the ground may very well have been a deliberate allusion to Jeremiah 17:13 ("all who forsake thee [God] shall be put to shame; those who turn away from thee shall be written in the earth"), which would imply that the woman's accusers were unqualified to pass judgment on her.

In 8:17 Jesus alluded to Deuteronomy 19:15: "In your Law it is written that the testimony of two people is true." But even here the point is christological: not only does Jesus bear witness to himself; so does his Father (cf. 8:18). Other examples of legal interpretation also reflect christological interests. After Jesus was arrested and interrogated, Pilate told the Jews: "Take him yourselves and judge him by your own Law" (Jn 18:31). Jesus was judged by the "Law," and was found deserving of death: "We have a law, and by that law he ought to die, because he has made himself the Son of God" (Jn 19:7). The law that was being referred to here is probably the command not to follow a prophet who introduces other gods (Deut 13:1-11) or the command against blasphemy (Lev 24:16), since Jesus' claim to be God's Son was considered by Caiaphas to be blasphemous (Mk 14:61-64). This same idea may lie behind the Talmudic tradition: "[Jesus] is going to be stoned because he . . . led Israel astray" (*b. Sanh.* 43a; cf. 107b; *b. Šab.* 104b; *b. Soṭa* 47a).

7.2. Prophetic. In the Fourth Gospel it is John the Baptist* himself who said: "I am the voice of one crying in the wilderness, 'Make straight the way of the Lord' " (Jn 1:23; cf. LXX Is 40:3). The prophetic interpretation, however, is essentially the same as that found in the Synoptics. Similarly, Micah 5:2 is alluded to in the question about Jesus' origin: "Does not the Scripture say that the Christ is descended from David, and comes from Bethlehem?" (Jn 7:41-42). Jewish rejection and unbelief not only fulfilled prophecy: "Lord, who has believed our report, and to whom has the arm of the Lord been revealed?" (12:38; cf. LXX Is 53:1); it was God's will: "He has blinded their eyes and hardened their heart, lest they should see with their eyes and perceive with their heart, and turn for me to heal them" (12:40; cf. Is 6:10; *see* Blindness and Deafness; Hardness of Heart). Judas's betrayal also fulfilled Scripture: "The one who ate my bread has lifted his heel against me" (13:18 NRSV; cf. Ps 41:9). Many of the elements of the passion fulfilled details of prophetic Scripture: "They hated me without a cause" (15:25; cf. Ps 69:4); "They parted my garments among them, and for my clothing they cast lots" (19:24; cf. LXX Ps 21:19); " 'I thirst'. . . vinegar" (19:28-29; cf. Ps 69:21); "Not a bone of him shall be broken" (19:36; cf. Ex 12:46); and "They shall look on him whom they have pierced" (19:37; cf. Zech 12:10; *see* Death of Jesus).

7.3. Analogical. At several points in the Fourth Gospel comparison is made between Jesus (as well as other characters) and OT figures and themes. In these examples Scripture is explicitly cited. When Jesus told the impressed Nathanael, "You will see heaven opened, and the angels of God ascending and descending upon the Son of man" (1:51; cf. Gen 28:12), he compared himself implicitly with the patriarch Jacob. According to rabbinic tradition (*see* Rabbinic Traditions and Writings) the angels descended in order to look at Jacob (cf. *Gen. Rab.* 70.12 [on Gen 29:10]; *Frg. Tg.* Gen 12:28). The point seems to be that now it is Jesus who is the gateway between heaven and earth (cf. Jn 14:6). The zeal that Jesus showed for the Temple, the house of God, is comparable to David's zeal: "Zeal for your house will consume me" (2:17; cf. Ps 69:9). Of those who believe in Jesus it is said: "And they all shall be taught of God" (6:45; cf. LXX Is 54:13). In "consuming" Jesus, who is the "bread of life" which "came down from heaven" (cf. 6:35-65), Christians absorb God's teaching (much as the rabbis believed that in consuming the manna, the wandering Israelites absorbed Torah; cf. Philo, *Mut. Nom.* §§253-263; *Mek. Bešallaḥ* §1 [on Ex 13:17]). In justifying his divine sonship, Jesus reminded his opponents of what Scripture has said to them: "I said, 'You are gods' " (10:34; cf. Ps 82:6). If regarded as "gods, sons of the Most High," for receiving the Law at Sinai (cf. *b. 'Abod. Zar.* 5a), then how can Jesus be justly accused of blasphemy when, as the Word of God sanctified and sent from heaven, he rightly has claimed to be the "Son of God" (Jn 10:35-36)?

In John the cry of the crowd, "Hosanna! Blessed is he who comes in the name of the Lord" (12:13; cf. Ps 118:25-26), takes on added meaning that extends significantly beyond what is present in the Synoptic tradition (cf. Mt 21:9). The Fourth Gospel, mindful of the importance of the name of God (*see* Name, Naming), points out that Jesus has come in the Father's name, has worked in the Father's name, and has declared the Father's name (cf. 5:43; 10:25; 17:6, 11, 12, 26). The citation from Psalm 118 is therefore particularly appropriate in the Johannine context. Finally, comparison is made between Jesus and the gentle King Messiah of whom it is said: "Fear not, daughter of Zion; behold, your king is coming, sitting on an ass's colt!" (12:15; cf. Is 40:9 + Zech 9:9).

There are many significant allusions to scriptural passages and themes. The Johannine Prolog (1:1-18) echoes biblical wisdom traditions at many points: "From the beginning with wisdom the Word of the Lord perfected the heavens and the earth" (*Tg. Neof.* Gen 1:1; cf. Jn 1:1); "In the beginning [*archē*] he created me [Wisdom]" (Sir 24:9; cf. Jn 1:1); "He established me in the beginning [*archē*]" (LXX Prov 8:23; cf. Jn 1:1); "Before the mountains were shaped, before all the hills, he begets [*genna*] me" (LXX Prov 8:25); "I am the word which was spoken by the Most High" (Sir 24:3; cf. Jn 1:1); "He gave authority [*exousia*] in Jerusalem" (Sir 24:11; cf. Jn 1:12); "Your all-powerful word [*logos*] leaped from heaven, from the royal throne, into the midst of the land" (Wis 18:15; cf. Jn 1:1, 14); "My Creator . . . said, 'Dwell [*kataskēnoun*] in Jacob' " (Sir 24:8; cf. Jn 1:14); "Who has seen [*heoraken*] him [God] and can describe [*ekdiēgēsetai*] him?" (Sir 43:31; cf. Jn 1:18).

The final paragraph of the Prolog (Jn 1:14-18) deliberately contrasts Jesus with Moses. Jesus is the incarnate Word of God (*see* Logos), "full of grace and truth" (Jn 1:14), the very virtues with which God himself abounds (Ex 34:6). In Jesus is seen the glory* that Moses had hoped to see in God (Jn 1:14; Ex 33:18). In Jesus people "have received (new) grace* in place of (old) grace" (Jn 1:16). Whereas the Law was given through Moses, grace and truth* were realized through Jesus the Messiah (Jn 1:17). And finally, although no one can see God (Jn 1:18)—not even Moses ("no one can see my face and live" [Ex 33:20]), who was permitted no more than a fleeting glance of God's retreating back (Ex 33:20-23), Jesus existed with God face to face ("in his bosom" [Jn 1:18]; cf. "with [*pros*] God" [Jn 1:1]) for all eternity.

Comparisons between Jesus and Moses are seen in many places in the Fourth Gospel. Some are explicit: "Of whom Moses wrote in the Law we have found" (Jn 1:45, probably alluding to the promise of Deut 18:15-18); "Just as Moses lifted up the serpent in the wilderness, so must the Son of man be lifted up" (Jn 3:14; cf. Num 21:9); "If you had believed Moses, you would have believed in me, for that one wrote concerning me" (Jn 5:46); "Moses has not given to you the bread* from heaven, but my Father gives you the true bread from heaven" (Jn 6:32; cf. 6:31-35, citing LXX Ps 77[78]:24, which in turn is alluding to Ex 16:15; Num 11:7-9); "If a man receives circumcision on the Sabbath lest the Law of Moses be broken, are you angry with me because I made a whole man well on the Sabbath?" (Jn 7:23); " 'You are a disciple of [Jesus]; we are disciples of Moses' " (Jn 9:28). Other comparisons involve no more than important verbal parallels (as, in these cases, seen clearly in the LXX): "This is indeed the prophet who is to come" (Jn 6:14; cf. Deut 18:18); "I who speak to you am he" (Jn 4:26; cf. Deut 18:18); "though he had done so many signs before them, yet they did not believe in him" (Jn 12:37; cf. Num 14:11; Ex 4:30-31); "For God sent the Son into the world" (Jn 3:17; cf. Num 16:28); "I speak as the Father taught me" (Jn 8:28; cf. Exod 4:12); "I do as the Father has commanded me" (Jn 14:31; cf. Lev 16:34; Num 27:22); "and he will enter and he will go out and he will find pasture" (Jn 10:9; cf. Num 27:21); "The Good Shepherd lays down his life for his sheep" (Jn 10:11; cf. Num 27:17).

See also MIDRASH; TYPOLOGY; TARGUMS.

BIBLIOGRAPHY. R. Banks, *Jesus and the Law in the Synoptic Tradition* (Cambridge: University Press, 1975); G. Barth, "Matthew's Understanding of the Law," in G. Bornkamm et al., *Tradition and Interpretation in Matthew* (Philadelphia: Westminster, 1963) 58-164; D. L. Bock, *Proclamation from Prophecy and Pattern: Lucan Old Testament Christology* (Sheffield: JSOT, 1987); R. P. Booth, *Jesus and the Laws of Purity* (Sheffield: JSOT, 1986); B. H. Branscomb, *Jesus and the Law of Moses* (New York: R. R. Smith, 1930); D. A. Carson and H. G. M. Williamson, eds., *It Is Written: Scripture Citing Scripture: Essays in Honour of Barnabas Lindars* (Cambridge: University Press, 1988) 205-64; R. H. Charles, *The Decalogue* (Edinburgh: T. & T. Clark, 1923); B. D. Chilton, *A Galilean Rabbi and His Bible* (Wilmington: Glazier, 1984); D. Daube, *The New Testament and Rabbinic Judaism* (London: Athlone, 1956); W. D. Davies, *The Setting of the Sermon on the Mount* (Cambridge: University Press, 1964); C. H. Dodd, *According to the Scriptures* (New York: Scribner's, 1952); R. A. Edwards, *The Sign of Jonah* (London: SCM, 1971); R. T. France, *Jesus and the Old Testament* (Downers Grove: InterVarsity, 1971); E. D. Freed, *Old Testament Quotations in the Gospel of John* (Leiden: Brill, 1965); M. Hilton and G. Marshall, *The Gospels and Rabbinic Judaism* (Hoboken: Ktav, 1988); T. Holtz, *Untersuchungen über die alttestamentlichen Zitate bei Lukas* (Berlin: Akademie, 1968); R. H. Gundry, *The Use of the Old Testament in St. Matthew's Gospel* (Leiden: Brill, 1967); S. T. Lachs, *A Rabbinic Commentary on the New Testament* (Hoboken:

Ktav, 1987); B. Lindars, *New Testament Apologetic* (Philadelphia: Westminster, 1961); R. N. Longenecker, *Biblical Exegesis in the Apostolic Period* (Grand Rapids: Eerdmans, 1975); T. W. Manson, "The Old Testament in the Teaching of Jesus," *BJRL* 34 (1951-52) 312-32; R. S. McConnell, *Law and Prophecy in Matthew's Gospel* (Basel: Reinhardt, 1969); R. P. Meye, "Psalm 107 as 'Horizon' for Interpreting the Miracle Stories of Mark 4:35—8:26," in R. A. Guelich, ed., *Unity and Diversity in New Testament Theology* (Grand Rapids: Eerdmans, 1978) 1-13; D. Moo, *The Old Testament in the Gospel Passion Narratives* (Sheffield: Almond, 1983); idem, "Jesus and the Authority of the Mosaic Law," *JSNT* 20 (1984) 3-49; S. Pancaro, *The Law in the Fourth Gospel* (Leiden: Brill, 1975); G. Reim, *Studien zum alttestamentlichen Hintergrund des Johannesevangelium* (Cambridge: University Press, 1974); J. A. Sanders, "From Isaiah 61 to Luke 4," in J. Neusner, ed., *Christianity, Judaism and Other Greco-Roman Cults* (Leiden: Brill, 1975) 75-106; idem, "Isaiah in Luke," *Int* 36 (1982) 144-55; P. Sigal, *The Halakah of Jesus of Nazareth according to the Gospel of Matthew* (Lanham: University Press of America, 1986); K. Stendahl, *The School of St. Matthew and Its Use of the Old Testament* (Philadelphia: Fortress, 1968); A. Suhl, *Die Funktion der alttestamentlichen Zitate und Anspielungen im Markusevangelium* (Gütersloh: Gütersloher Verlagshaus, 1965); G. Van Groningen, *Messianic Revelation in the Old Testament* (Grand Rapids: Eerdmans, 1990); J. W. Wenham, *Christ and the Bible* (Downers Grove: InterVarsity, 1973). C. A. Evans

OLIVET DISCOURSE. *See* APOCALYPTIC TEACHING.

ORAL TRADITION. *See* FORM CRITICISM; SYNOPTIC PROBLEM; TEACHER; TRADITION CRITICISM.

OUTCASTS. *See* SINNER; TABLE FELLOWSHIP.

P

PACIFISM. *See* PEACE.

PALESTINIAN TARGUM. *See* TARGUM.

PARABLE

The English word *parable* refers to a short narrative with two levels of meaning. The Greek and Hebrew words for "parable" are much broader. Jesus' parables are both works of art and the weapons he used in the conflict with his opponents. They were the teaching method he chose most frequently to explain the kingdom of God (*see* Kingdom of God) and to show the character of God* and the expectations God has for people. Despite the tradition that argues Jesus' parables have only one point, many parables convey two or three truths, and there may be several correspondences between a specific parable and the reality it portrays.

    1. History of Interpretation
    2. Definition of *Parabolē* and Related Terms
    3. Characteristics of the Parables
    4. The Use of Parables Prior to Jesus
    5. Distribution of the Parables in the Gospels
    6. The Authenticity of the Parables
    7. The Purpose of the Parables
    8. Guidelines for Interpretation
    9. The Teaching of the Parables

1. History of Interpretation.

A history of interpretation is virtually a prerequisite for studying Jesus' parables. That history must be framed in relation to the work of A. Jülicher, a German NT scholar whose two-volume work on the parables (1888, 1889) has dominated parable studies, even though it has never been translated.

1.1. Before Jülicher. Throughout most of the church's history Jesus' parables have been allegorized instead of interpreted. That is, people read into the parables elements of the church's theology that had nothing to do with Jesus' intention. The best-known example of this is Augustine's interpretation of the parable of the good Samaritan (Lk 10:30-37) in which virtually every item was given theological significance: the man is Adam; Jerusalem is the heavenly city; Jericho is the moon, which stands for our mortality; the robbers are the devil (*see* Demon, Devil, Satan) and his angels* who strip the man of his immortality and beat him by persuading him to sin; the priest and Levite are the priesthood (*see* Priest and Priesthood) and the ministry of the OT; the good Samaritan* is Christ*; the binding of the wounds is the restraint of sin; the oil and wine are the comfort of hope and the encouragement to work; the animal is the Incarnation; the inn is the church; the next day is after the resurrection of Christ; the innkeeper is the apostle Paul; and the two denarii are the two commandments* of love* or the promise of this life and that which is to come (*Quaest. Evan.* 2.19). Similarly, Gregory the Great allegorized the parable of the barren fig tree (Lk 13:6-9) so that the three times the owner came looking for fruit represent God's coming before the Law* was given, his coming at the time the Law was written, and his coming in grace and mercy in Christ. The vinedresser (*see* Vine) represents those who rule the church, and the digging and dung refer to the rebuking of unfruitful people and the remembrance of sins (*Hom.* 31). Some, such as John Chrysostom of the school of Antioch and John Calvin did not allegorize the parables, but until the end of the nineteenth century allegorizing was the dominant means of interpretation.

1.2. Jülicher. Although others before him had argued against allegorizing, Jülicher's two-volume work on the parables sounded the death knell on this interpretive procedure. Jülicher denied that Jesus used allegory (a series of related metaphors) or allegorical traits (where a point in the story stands for something else in reality). Where allegory or allegorical traits occur, such as in the parable of the sower and the parable of the wicked tenants, the Evangelists are to blame. Jülicher viewed Jesus' parables as simple and straightforward comparisons that do not require interpretation. They have only one point of comparison: between the image and the idea being expressed. That one point is usually a general religious maxim. The parables are extended similes, whereas allegories are extended metaphors. Like metaphors, allegories are inauthentic speech and must be decoded. Jesus' purpose was not to obscure, therefore his parables cannot be viewed as allegories.

1.3. After Jülicher. All subsequent studies of the parables have had to deal with Jülicher's views. There were early attacks on Jülicher's arguments, particularly by P. Fiebig (beginning in 1904), who argued that Jülicher derived his understandings of parables from Greek rhetoric rather than from the Hebrew world where allegorical parables are common. Others recognized that Jülicher had thrown out allegory, a literary form, while the problem was *allegorizing*, the interpretive procedure of reading into the parables a theology that Jesus did not intend. Few today would accept Jülicher's descriptions of metaphor or his argument that the parables give general religious maxims. There have been devastating critiques of his description of allegory, but even so, people often still speak of one point for parables and are suspicious of any parts of Jesus' parables that have allegorical significance. In addition, there have been several stages through which parable interpretation has gone.

1.3.1. C. H. Dodd and J. Jeremias. The Dodd and Jeremias era of parable studies extends from 1935 to roughly 1970, although Jeremias' book on the parables is still influential. Jeremias' work was an extension of Dodd's and both were influenced by Jülicher. Both Dodd and Jeremias tried to understand the parables of Jesus in their historical and eschatological context (*see* Eschatology). Both attempted to remove allegorical elements from the parables. Dodd understood Jesus' message as realized eschatology: the kingdom had already arrived. Parables about harvest are not about a coming end time but about the time of Jesus' earthly ministry.

Jeremias sought to provide historical and cultural evidence for understanding the parables and, under the influence of form criticism, to ascertain a given parable's original form by stripping away allegorical features or other additions supplied by the early church. Typically this led to a reconstruction of the supposedly original form of a given parable. Almost invariably the context in the Gospels, the introductions, the conclusions, and any interpretive comments were considered secondary. Such shortened, de-allegorized forms are close to the versions of the parables in the *Gospel of Thomas*, a collection of sayings of Jesus dating probably from the second century (*see* Gospels [Apocryphal]). The relation of the *Gospel of Thomas* to the canonical Gospels, its date and

its character are all debated. The fact that Jeremias and others had suggested shorter forms of the parables before the discovery of *Thomas* was made known has erroneously led some to argue that *Thomas* preserves the original form of some of the parables.

While granting the presence of the kingdom in Jesus' ministry, Jeremias described Jesus' message as an eschatology in the process of realization. In his parables Jesus presented people with a crisis of decision and invited them to respond to God's mercy.* Jeremias' influence has been so strong that N. Perrin argued that future interpretation of the parables should be interpretation of the parables as Jeremias has analyzed them (101).

1.3.2. Existentialist, Structuralist and Literary Approaches. Several modern approaches to parables have grown out of philosophical currents and partly out of dissatisfaction with the focus of Dodd and Jeremias on a historical approach. While seeking something more than the merely historical, however, these approaches still follow Jeremias in stripping off allegorical and interpretive additions. The new hermeneutic of E. Fuchs and E. Jüngel focused on the power of Jesus' parables to bring to expression the reality to which they point. The parables are viewed as "language events" (*Sprachereignisse*). In the parables Jesus expresses his understanding of his own existence in such a way that this existence is available to his hearers. The parables are a summons to this existence.

Similarly, G. V. Jones, A. N. Wilder and D. Via all have focused on the artistic and existential character of the parables. Especially for Via the parables are not bound by the author's intention. They are aesthetic works which address the present because in their patterns is an understanding of existence that calls for decision.

K. Bailey's work on the parables is noteworthy because of his detailed focus on the rhetorical structure of the parables as well as his interpretation in light of the Palestinian mindset, a mindset he encountered as a missionary in Lebanon.

In the decade between 1970 and 1980 structuralist approaches dominated parable studies. Structuralists were not concerned for historical meaning or the author's intention. Rather they sought to compare both surface and deep structures of various texts; that is, they sought to compare the movements, motives, functions, oppositions and resolutions within texts. At times structuralist analyses have been helpful, such as J. D. Crossan's identification of the categories of advent, reversal and action as basic to understanding the parables. The kingdom of God comes as advent as a gift of God, as a reversal of a person's world, and as an empowering for action. For the most part, however, structuralist studies have been dominated by technical jargon and have not provided much additional insight.

The 1980s witnessed several discernible shifts in parable studies, largely because of the influence of literary criticism (*see* Literary Criticism). Although a concern for redactional emphases of the Gospel writers has been a focus since the 1950s, literary concerns have led to much more attention on the technique and purposes of the Evangelists in the composition of their works. Literary criticism has also tended to emphasize a reader-response approach in which a text's meaning is determined by the interaction of the reader with the text. This approach is highly subjective and yields a variety of meanings, all of which are considered correct. Such a polyvalent understanding of texts invites the interpreter to be a "trained player" and read texts with as many different associations as desired. For example, the parable of the prodigal son can be read in light of Freudian psychology in which the prodigal, the elder brother and the father reflect the id, the super-ego and the ego. It can be read just as legitimately in other contexts with this method. However, such subjective readings of the parables are not interpretations at all; they are retellings of the stories in new contexts. To understand the message of Jesus one will have to do justice to the historical context in which the parables were told.

1.4. Interpretations Based on Comparisons with Jewish Parables. An alternative trend in recent parable studies focuses on insights gained by studying early rabbinic parables (*see* Rabbinic Traditions and Writings). Comparing Jewish parables to Jesus' parables is not new. P. Fiebig had already done this in combating Jülicher's approach, and about the same time A. Feldman had collected Jewish parables that made such comparison easier. Now approximately 2,000 rabbinic parables have been collected. In recent years several works have appeared that discuss parable theory in light of rabbinic parables and rethink previous theories and interpretations. Most important of these is the research of D. Flusser, a Jewish NT scholar whose primary work has not yet been translated into English. Flusser's work, and that of other scholars focusing on Judaism, challenges the conclusions not only of Jülicher, but also of Jeremias, of the reader-response approaches and of much of NT scholarship. Flusser acknowledges a thoroughgoing editing of the parables by the Evangelists, but he is optimistic about the reliability of the Gospel material. He argues that the contexts of the parables are usually correct and that the introductions and conclusions to the parables

are necessary and usually derive from Jesus. He views the *Gospel of Thomas* as dependent on the Synoptic Gospels and as unimportant for researching the words of Jesus.

The distance some recent studies have moved from the works of Jülicher and Jeremias is evidenced in C. Blomberg's treatment of the parables. Blomberg argues that the parables of Jesus, like the rabbinic parables, are allegories and usually have two or three points to make, depending on the number of main characters the parable has.

2. Definition of *Parabolē* and Related Terms.

The Greek word *parabolē* has a much broader meaning in the Gospels than the English word *parable*. It can be used of a proverb (Lk 4:23), a riddle (Mk 3:23), a comparison (Mt 13:33), a contrast (Lk 18:1-8) and both simple stories (Lk 13:6-9) and complex stories (Mt 22:1-14). This range of meaning derives from the Hebrew word *māšal* which is usually translated by *parabolē* in the LXX (28 of 39 occurrences). In addition *māšal* can be used of a taunt, a prophetic oracle or a byword. A *māšal* is any dark saying intended to stimulate thought.

The concept of a parable needs to be clarified beyond distinguishing the wide meanings of the words *parabolē* and *māšal*. Four forms of parables are often distinguished: similitude, example story, parable and allegory. A *similitude* is an extended simile (an explicit comparison using "like" or "as"). It is a comparison relating a typical or recurring event in real life and is often expressed in the present tense. The parable of the leaven (Mt 13:31-32) is a similitude. An *example story* presents a positive or negative character (or both) who serves as an example to be imitated or whose traits and actions are to be avoided. Either explicitly or implicitly the example story says, "Go and do [or do not do] likewise" (cf. Lk 10:37). Usually only four Gospel parables, all in Luke, are identified as example stories: the good Samaritan, the rich fool, the rich man and Lazarus, and the pharisee and the tax collector. A *parable* is an extended metaphor (an implied comparison) referring to a fictional event or events narrated in past time to express a moral or spiritual truth. The parable of the banquet (Lk 14:15-24) would fit this definition. In this classification system an *allegory* is a series of related metaphors, and the parable of the sower would be an example of an allegory.

Although this fourfold classification is popular, many scholars find it unworkable. Some object to the category "example story," but as long as one does not overlook that more may be involved in these stories than merely providing an example, this is a helpful classification. Clearly these stories are different from other parables in some respects. More troublesome is the supposed distinction between *parable* and *allegory*, which is among the most debated issues in NT studies. For some, such as M. Boucher, allegory is not a literary form at all, but a device of meaning; therefore, all parables are allegorical either as wholes or in their parts. Parables rarely have only one correspondence between the story and the reality being reflected, even though one should not view interpretation of the parables as the process of deciphering points. Parables are best defined as stories with two levels of meaning; the story level provides a mirror by which reality is perceived and understood. In effect, parables are imaginary gardens with real toads in them.

3. Characteristics of the Parables.

Parables tend to be brief and symmetrical. They often make use of balanced structures involving two or three movements. They typically omit unnecessary descriptions and frequently leave motives unexplained and implied questions unanswered. They usually are taken from everyday life, but they are not necessarily realistic. Because of hyperbole or elements of improbability they often are pseudo-realistic and have elements that shock. For example, it is unlikely that anyone in first-century Palestine would owe a 10,000-talent debt (several million dollars) as in the parable of the unforgiving servant (Mt 18:23-35). In addition, parables elicit thought. Twenty-two parables start with a question such as "Who from you . . . ?" or "What do you think . . . ?" Parables frequently cause a hearer to pass judgment on the events in the story and then require a similar judgment about religious matters. Often the parables require a reversal in one's thinking. The despised Samaritan is a neighbor; the tax collector (*see* Taxes), not the Pharisee,* is righteous (*see* Justice, Righteousness). The crucial matter is placed at the end of the parables, and correspondingly, "the rule of end stress" requires that the interpretation focus on the end of the parable. Although the parable of the wicked tenants has christological implications, most parables are theocentric in that they focus on God, his kingdom and his expectations for humans. Consequently, the parables are often invitations to changed behavior and discipleship.* The degree to which the theological referent is transparent varies from parable to parable.

4. The Use of Parables Prior to Jesus.

Jesus was not the first person to teach by parables and stories. There are both Greek and Semitic antecedents, but there is no evidence of anyone prior to Jesus using parables as consistently, creatively and effectively as he did. There are so many rabbinic parables similar to the ones Jesus told that some scholars argue Jesus drew from a fund of popular stories or at least that he drew his themes and structures from such a fund. As always with the rabbinic evidence, the problem is that these writings are later than the time of the NT. Because there is so little actual evidence of teaching in parables prior to Jesus, some scholars argue that Jesus' use of parables was entirely new. There are no parables so far from Qumran and none in the Apocrypha and Pseudepigrapha (excluding the so-called Similitudes of Enoch, which are apparently later in origin). Virtually none of the rabbinic parables is from as early as the first half of the first century. In addition to the problem of date, rabbinic parables, all of which are in Hebrew rather than Aramaic, primarily are used as a means to interpret Scripture, whereas Jesus did not use parables this way.

The OT does provide seven parables which are antecedents to Jesus' parables: Nathan's parable to David about the poor man and his lamb (2 Sam 12:1-10); the woman from Tekoa's story about her two sons (2 Sam 14:5-20); the prophet's acted parable condemning Ahab (1 Kings 20:35-40); the song of the vineyard (Is 5:1- 7); the eagles and the vine (Ezek 17:2-10); the lioness and her cubs (Ezek 19:2-9); and the vine (Ezek 19:10-14). (Only Ezek 17:2-10 is explicitly called a *māšal*. In addition, Judg 9:7-15 and 2 Kings 14:9 contain fables.) Of these OT parables only Nathan's parable of the poor man and his lamb is a true parallel to the parables of Jesus.

5. Distribution of the Parables in the Gospels.

Approximately one-third of Jesus' teaching is in parables. The Greek word *parabolē* occurs fifty times in the NT, and except for Hebrews 9:9 and 11:19 all the occurrences are in the Synoptic Gospels. Parables appear in all strata of the Synoptics. If one accepts the four-source hypothesis of Gospel origins, parables make up about sixteen per cent of Mark, about twenty-nine per cent of Q,* about forty-three per cent of M* and about fifty-two per cent of L.* John does not have story parables, but does have forms that would fit the broad sense of *māšal* such as the good shepherd (Jn 10; *see* Shepherd and Sheep) and the true vine (Jn 15). (John uses the word *paroimia* four times. This word is similar in some respects to *parabolē*.)

An exact number of the parables cannot be given since there is no agreement among scholars as to

The Parables of Jesus

Markan Parables	Mark	Matthew	Luke
Bridegroom's Guests	2:19-20	9:15	5:33-39
Unshrunk Cloth	2:21	9:16	5:36
New Wine	2:22	9:17	5:37-39
Strong Man Bound	3:22-27	12:29-30	11:21-23
Sower	4:1-9, 13-20	13:1-9, 18-23	8:4-8, 11-15
Lamp and Measure	4:21-25		8:16-18
Seed Growing Secretly	4:26-29		
Mustard Seed	4:30-32	13:31-32	13:18-19
Wicked Tenants	12:1-12	21:33-46	20:9-19
Budding Fig Tree	13:28-32	24:32-36	21:29-33
Watchman	13:34-36		12:35-38

Parables Shared by Matthew and Luke (Q)

	Matthew	Luke
Wise and Foolish Builders	7:24-27	6:47-49
Father and Children's Requests	7:9-11	11:11-13
Two Ways/Doors	7:13-14	13:23-27
Leaven	13:31-32	13:20-21
Lost Sheep	18:12-14	15:1-7
Wedding Banquet	22:1-14	14:15-24
Thief in the Night	24:42-44	12:39-40
Faithful and Unfaithful Steward	24:45-51	12:42-46
Talents and Pounds	25:14-30	19:11-27

Parables Found Only in Matthew

	Matthew
Good and Bad Trees	7:16-20
Fishnet	13:47-50
Wheat and Tares	13:24-30, 36-43
Treasure	13:44
Pearl	13:45-46
Unmerciful Servant	18:23-35
Laborers in the Vineyard	20:1-16
Two Sons	21:28-32
Wise and Foolish Maidens	25:1-13
Sheep and Goats	25:31-46

Parables Found Only in Luke

	Luke
Two Debtors	7:41-50
Good Samaritan	10:25-37
Friend at Midnight	11:5-8
Rich Fool	12:13-21
Barren Fig Tree	13:6-9
Tower Builder	14:28-30
Warring King	14:31-33
Lost Sheep	15:1-7
Lost Coin	15:8-10
Prodigal Son	15:11-32
Unjust Steward	16:1-8
Rich Man and Lazarus	16:19-31
Humble Servant	17:7-10
Unjust Judge	18:1-8
Pharisee and Tax Collector	18:9-14

Parables Found Only in John
Good Shepherd (10:1-18; cf. Mt 18:12-14; Lk 15:1-7)
True Vine (15:1-8)

which forms should be classified as a parable. There are thirty forms explicitly labeled *parabolē*, but this includes proverbs (Lk 4:23); riddles (Mk 3:23); short sayings (Mk 7:15) and questions (Lk 6:39). There are at least forty parables on a more restricted definition, but as many as sixty-five if one includes such items as Jesus' saying about a person with a beam in his or her eye trying to get a speck out of the eye of another (Mt 7:3-5).

The parables are thematically arranged in the Synoptics. Mark has only four story parables: in chapter four the sower, the mustard seed, the seed growing secretly; and in chapter twelve the wicked tenants. Except for the seed growing secretly, Matthew and Luke have Mark's story parables and both of them have the parables of the leaven and of the lost sheep. Both Matthew and Luke have parables about guests who reject invitations to a feast (Mt 22:1-14; Lk 14:16-26) and about servants who are entrusted with money to invest (Mt 25:14-30; Lk 19:11-27). However, the wording is not close in either of these parallels, and whether Matthew and Luke are reporting the same parables or only similar parables is debated. Jesus, no doubt, told some of the parables more than once and offered several variations on the same basic structure. Matthew has arranged most of his parables in chapters 12—13, 18 and 20—25. He has at least twelve parables that are unique to him. Luke has placed most of his parables in chapters 10—19 of his so-called travel narrative. Luke has at least fifteen parables that are unique to him.

Fourteen parables occur among the sayings of the *Gospel of Thomas,* three of which are not recorded in the canonical Gospels. The *Apocryphon of James* also has three parables not recorded in the canonical Gospels.

6. The Authenticity of the Parables.

Even scholars who are persuaded that the Gospel parables include additions by the early church still view the parables as providing some of the most authentic and reliable teaching from Jesus (*see* Form Criticism). Supporting evidence for this confidence is strong:

(1) The parables reflect the clarity and eschatology of Jesus' preaching and his conflict with Jewish authorities.

(2) They reflect daily life in Palestine.

(3) Little evidence exists that parables were used frequently prior to Jesus.

(4) In view of the fact that parables do not appear in the NT outside the Gospels and rarely in other early Christian literature, the early church shows no propensity for creating parables.

At the same time critical scholarship has gone to great lengths debating the authenticity of both the parts and the whole of specific parables. The so-called Jesus Seminar has even produced a Red Letter edition of the parables of Jesus which prints the wording of the parables in red, pink, gray or black reflecting the opinions respectively that Jesus said those words, said something like those words, did not say those words but expressed similar ideas, or did not say those words and the ideas are from a later time. Only three parables represented in the canonical tradition are printed entirely in black (the tower builder and the warring king, both in Lk 14:28-32, and the fishnet, Mt 13:47-50), and only four more in which all accounts are printed entirely in gray. (However, in these cases preference is often for the version of the parable in the *Gospel of Thomas.*)

While this underscores the confidence expressed in the parable tradition, the assumptions and procedures adopted by the Jesus Seminar and many other scholars are unacceptable. The Jesus Seminar, like so many earlier scholars, has succumbed to the tendency to find a Jesus who is amenable with modern expectations. Far too much preference is given to the *Gospel of Thomas,* which appears to derive from a second stage of the oral tradition. Furthermore, the rejection of the introductions and conclusions of the parables and of any allegorical significance is unjustified in light of recent research on Jewish parables. The oral tradition no doubt shaped the parables, and the Evangelists have clearly edited them in keeping with their stylistic tendencies and theological purposes. We can and should identify many such changes. However, any attempt to identify the *ipsissima verba* (the exact words) of Jesus is naive at best. The Gospels present the *ipsissima vox* (the very voice) of Jesus, and nowhere is that voice so clearly heard as in the parables.

7. The Purpose of the Parables.

Often it has been said that the parables of Jesus are not merely illustrations of Jesus' preaching but are themselves the preaching. Clearly the parables are to engage and instruct, but it is not fair to say that the parables are themselves the preaching. Parables demand interpretation; they point to something else. They are not merely stories to enjoy. They hold up one reality to serve as a mirror of another, the kingdom of God. They are avenues to understanding, handles by which one can grasp the kingdom. Jesus told parables to confront people with the character of God's kingdom and to invite them to participate in it and to live in accordance with it.

Mark 4:10-12, however, seems to say the exact opposite. On the surface these verses argue that Jesus gives the secret of the kingdom only to his disciples. "To those outside all things are in parables in order that seeing they may see and not see, and hearing they may hear and not understand, lest they turn and it be forgiven them" (Mk 4:11-12). The latter part of this saying is from Isaiah 6:9-10.

An understanding of Mark requires attention to his technique, structure and theological emphases. Mark uses the technique of *bracketing* to provide insight into the individual sections of his Gospel. For example, the cleansing of the Temple (11:15-19; *see* Temple Cleansing) is bracketed by the cursing of the fig tree (11:12-14) and the lesson drawn from the withered fig tree (11:20-25). Furthermore, the material in 4:1-34 has been carefully arranged:

4:1-2—Narrative introduction telling that Jesus taught parables from a boat

4:3-9—The parable of the sower

4:10-12—Jesus alone with disciples with whom he contrasts those who are *outside*

4:13-20—Interpretation of the parable of the sower

4:21-25—Parabolic sayings about hearing

4:26-32—Parables of the seed growing secretly and the mustard seed

4:33-34—Narrative conclusion summarizing the intent of this section

Some argue that this structure is chiastic, with the center of the chiasmus being the interpretation of the parable of the sower. (Chiasmus is a poetic a b b' a' pattern.) Note that in 4:35-41 Jesus and his disciples are back in the boat. This section picks up chronologically where 4:9 seems to have left off. Therefore, 4:10-34 comprise a thematic arrangement by the author. Note also that 3:31-34, with its focus on Jesus' family standing *outside* seeking him and 4:10-12 with its focus on those *outside* bracket the parable of the sower just as the parable of the sower and its interpretation bracket 4:10-12.

The dominant theme in the whole chapter is "hearing," which is mentioned thirteen times. Isaiah 6:9-10, which is quoted in a version similar to the targum* on Isaiah, was a classic text on the hardness of people's hearts as they refused to hear God's prophetic word. Hardness of heart (*see* Hardness of Heart) is an important theme for Mark and is even possible of Jesus' disciples. (Note Mk 8:16-21, which uses words similar to Is 6:9-10, but this time drawn from Jer 5:21 or Ezek 12:2.)

Several scholars have tried to soften the impact of Mark 4:12 by interpreting *hina* ("in order that") as expressing something less than purpose. T. W. Man-

son suggested *hina* was a mistranslation of the Aramaic *de* which can mean "who." Accordingly, he would translate, ". . . all things come in parables to those outside who see indeed, but do not know . . ." (76-78). J. Jeremias argued *hina* was shorthand for *hina plerothē* ("in order that it might be fulfilled"). Others suggest *hina* should be interpreted as "because" as in Revelation 14:13, especially since the parallel in Matthew 13:13 has *hoti* ("because"). Jeremias' suggestion is helpful, but these explanations are unnecessary. They only mark the difficulty people have with the possibility that Jesus told parables to prevent understanding. Scholars have often attributed this to "Mark's parable theory," rather than to Jesus. Mark, however, does not have a theory that parables prevent understanding (cf. Mk 12:12).

The intent of Mark 4:10-12 is clear if one pays attention to the context. The kingdom is a kingdom of the word, and the issue is how people hear and respond to the word. The parable of the sower is a parable about hearing. In Mark 4:10-12 the Evangelist shows what typically happened in Jesus' ministry. (Note the use of the Grk imperfect tenses in Mk 4:10-11 indicating what happened *customarily*.) Jesus taught the crowds, but his teaching called for response. Where people responded, additional teaching was given. The pattern of public teaching followed by further private teaching to a circle of disciples* is used elsewhere by Mark (7:17; 10:10). The strong words in Isaiah 6:9-10 were not an indication that God did not want to forgive people. They were a blunt statement expressing the inevitable. People would hear, but not really understand.

The hardness of heart and lack of receptivity that Isaiah encountered were mirrored in the ministry of Jesus. The issue is whether one's heart will be hardened or whether one will hear and respond obediently. Even receiving the message with joy is not sufficient (4:16). What is required is hearing that leads to productive living. That this is Mark's intent is clear from the summary in 4:33: "With many such parables he was expressing the word to them, even as they were able to hear." The saying in 4:22 is also an important guide to understanding Mark's intent: "Nothing is hidden except that it should be revealed." This saying seems to be Mark's understanding of the parables. Parables hide in order to reveal. Even though some would respond with hardness of heart and lack of hearing, Jesus taught in parables to elicit hearing and obedient response.

8. Guidelines for Interpretation.

The interpretation of the parables is not a scientific

procedure, but guidelines can be offered to enhance understanding and prevent abuse of the parables.

(1) Analyze the sequence, structure and wording of the parable, including any parallels in the other Gospels. Plot the movement of the parable, and note any specific structure such as parallelism or chiasmus. For example, there are significant parallels between the prodigal and the elder son in Luke's parable of the prodigal son (Lk 15:11-32). Significant changes in wording between the various accounts need to be understood in light of the redactional purposes of the Evangelists (*see* Redaction Criticism). One should not assume any particular Gospel always gives the earliest version of a specific parable. Certainly one should not excise the introductions and conclusions to the parables.

(2) Note cultural or historical features in the parable that provide insight. Most of the parables contain such features that require investigation. For example, the impact of the parable of the pharisee and the tax collector (Lk 18:9-14) is strengthened if one is aware that these two men probably went to the Temple* to pray* at the time of the morning or evening atoning sacrifice. In effect, the tax collector prayed, "Let the sacrifice result in mercy for me."

(3) Listen to the parables in the context of the ministry of Jesus. Modern readers are often so familiar with the parables that they miss the shock that Jesus' hearers would have felt. We tend to have negative views of Pharisees and are not surprised to hear Jesus say that the tax collector was declared righteous instead of the Pharisee. Jesus' hearers would have assumed that the Pharisee was a righteous man and that the tax collector was a cheat. We are not surprised that a Samaritan helps a victim (Lk 10:30-37), but Jesus' hearers, like the scribe to whom he spoke, could hardly say "Samaritan" and "neighbor" in the same breath. Parables often force such reversals in our thinking.

(4) Look for help in the context, but know that the context of many of the parables has not been preserved. The parable of the wicked tenants (Mt 21:33-44 and pars.) must be seen in light of the question about the authority* by which Jesus does his acts (Mt 21:23-27). On the other hand, Matthew 13 provides a thematic grouping of eight parables on the kingdom, the contexts of which have not been preserved.

(5) Note how the parable and its redactional shaping fit into the plan and purposes of the Gospel in which it appears. Most of the parables have been arranged thematically by the Evangelists to highlight Jesus' message. With such arrangements the Evangelists show their own theological tendencies. For example, Luke's parables appear primarily in his travel narrative (9:51—19:48), which is chiastic in its structure. Luke is concerned

about prayer, wealth and the outcasts. Not surprisingly, Luke has arranged parables on prayer in 11:5-13 and 18:1-14, on wealth in 12:13-21 and 16:1-31, on invitations to a feast (particularly invitations to outcasts; *see* Table Fellowship) as reflective of the kingdom in 14:7-24, and on the joy of recovering that which was lost in 15:1-32. In addition to the kingdom parables in chapter 13, Matthew has placed two parables in the context of his "ecclesiastical discourse" in 18:10-14, 21-35 and has also grouped three parables on Israel's rejection of God's invitation in 21:28—22:14 and seven more on eschatology in 24:32—25:46. Matthew and Luke differ on the placement of some of the parables as well. For example, Luke has the parable of the lost sheep (15:1-7) in a context dealing with the repentance of sinners, but Matthew has this parable in a context dealing with an erring disciple. Jesus surely told some of the parables more than once, but such variations may result from intentional editorial activity.

(6) Determine the function of the story as a whole in the teaching of Jesus and for the Evangelists. There may be more than one truth to the parable and several correspondences between the parable and the reality that it reflects. This is not, however, a license to allegorize. Some parables even have two climaxes. (Note the parable of the prodigal, or more aptly titled the parable of the father and his two sons, in Lk 15:11-32 and the parable of the wedding feast in Mt 22:1-14, although the latter could be a joining of two parables.) Any correspondence between the parable and the reality it reflects will probably be limited to the main characters in the story. Details should not be allegorized and parables should not be pushed beyond their purpose. The goal is to hear the intention of Jesus as conveyed by the Evangelists. A helpful way to determine the function of a parable is to ask what question it seeks to answer. Sometimes the question is explicit, such as in the parable of the good Samaritan (Lk 10:25-37) which addresses the question "Who is my neighbor?" At other times the question is implicit, such as in the parables of the warring king and the tower builder, which address the question "Is it easy to be a disciple?"

(7) Determine the theological significance of the story. What the parable teaches about God and his kingdom should be reflected elsewhere in the teaching of Jesus. There is no suggestion that we are to reduce the parable to theological propositions, but the parables do express theology. Again, the details of parables should not be pushed. For example, while Matthew 18:34 may underscore the seriousness of God's judgment, it does not mean that God has tormentors!

(8) Pay special attention to the end of the parable. The rule of end stress recognizes that the most important part of the parable is the conclusion where the parable often requires a decision or forces the hearer to reverse his or her way of thinking. The end of the parable of the wicked tenants (Mt 21:33-44) is a quotation from Psalm 118:22 which via a wordplay forces the religious authorities to realize that they, the "builders" of the Jewish nation, have rejected God's Son (*see* Son of God). Whatever else may be true in the parable of the lost sheep, the focus is on the joy* at recovering that which was lost.

9. The Teaching of the Parables.

The primary focus of the parables is the coming of the kingdom of God and the resulting discipleship that is required. When Jesus proclaimed the kingdom he meant that God was exercising his power and rule to bring forgiveness,* defeat evil and establish righteousness in fulfillment of the OT promises. In Jesus' own person and ministry these acts were happening, and the kingdom was made available to people. The kingdom comes with limitless grace, but with it comes limitless demand. That is why it is impossible to speak of the kingdom without at the same time speaking of discipleship. While a number of Jesus' parables anticipate a future aspect of God's kingdom, much of the focus is on the kingdom as present and available to Jesus' hearers. The kingdom is both present and still awaits consummation in the future. With the focus on the kingdom as present comes an invitation to enter the kingdom and live according to its standards. Prayer and the use of wealth are two areas of kingdom living that are treated specifically in the parables.

9.1. The Kingdom As Present. A short parable in Matthew 12:29 is one of the strongest statements about the presence of the kingdom, and this parable also has christological implications. In response to the charge that he cast out demons by the power of Beelzebub (Mt 12:24), Jesus pointed to the activity of the Spirit (*see* Holy Spirit) in his ministry as proof that the kingdom was present (Mt 12:28). The parable in Matthew 12:29 argues that no one can enter and plunder the house of the strong man unless he first binds the strong man. Clearly Jesus viewed his ministry as binding Satan and plundering his house.

While all the parables are kingdom parables in one sense, the parables in Matthew 13 are grouped specifically to provide insight into the kingdom. The Parable of the Sower indicates that the kingdom involves the presentation of a message and the necessity of a response that leads to productive living. Several parables in this section seem designed to answer questions from Jesus' hearers about his claims that the kingdom was present. The Parable of the Wheat and the Tares seems designed to answer the question "How can the kingdom have come if evil is still present?" The kingdom is present and growing even in the midst of evil, and judgment will take place in the future. Therefore, the kingdom invites both involvement and patience. The twin Parables of the Mustard Seed and the Leaven both address the question "How can the kingdom be present if the results seem so small?" The beginning may be small, but the effect will be large and extensive. The twin Parables of the Treasure and of the Pearl both underscore that the kingdom is of ultimate value and is to be chosen above all else. In his section on kingdom parables Mark includes the Parable of the Growing Seed (Mk 4:26-29) which stresses that the kingdom is God's work and not the result of human action.

Other parables also emphasize the present aspect of the kingdom. The parables of the banquet (Lk 14:15-24) and of the wedding (Mt 22:1-14) affirm that all is ready and people should come now (Lk 14:17; Mt 22:4). The banquet theme is used to express other points as well. These parables and several others point to the refusal of many of the Jewish people to respond to Jesus' message. With parables like that of the barren fig tree (Lk 13:6-9) they mark a crisis of decision which should lead to repentance. Furthermore, the banquet parables and parables like that of the prodigal son (Lk 15:11-32) in effect proclaim that God is having a celebration and ask people why they are not joining in.

The kingdom is revealed as an amazing expression of God's grace. The Gospels do not record that Jesus taught about grace, but no other word summarizes so well the effect of the kingdom. The invitation to outcasts in the banquet parables is obviously an expression of grace. The parables of the two debtors (Lk 7:41-43), of the lost sheep, lost coin and prodigal son (Lk 15), of the unmerciful servant (Mt 18:23-35) and of the laborers in the vineyard (Mt 20:1-16) all point to God's eagerness to benefit people by seeking them, forgiving them and accepting them. The parable of the laborers in the vineyard also offers a critique of those who think God's grace should be given out based on merit.

9.2. The Kingdom As Future. Jesus' teaching on the future aspect of the kingdom is seen most clearly in those parables that speak of judgment* or of a master who returns to settle accounts. The parables of growth also point to the future as a time of harvest. Particularly in Matthew parables of judgment point to a separation between those who were obedient, faithful, prepared or merciful, and those who were not. The first group enters the kingdom and experiences praise and joy. The other group suffers punishment or destruction. Either explicitly or implicitly, judgment is based on whether one has shown mercy. Not all judgment parables are about the future. Some speak of judgment that is more immediate, such as the parable of the rich man and Lazarus (Lk 16:19-31) or the parables that express the crisis facing the Jewish people (Lk 13:6-9). Even so, future judgment is a major theme in Jesus' parables.

Parables about the future are not intended to satisfy curiosity. They are intended to alter life in the present. By focusing on judgment and the Master's return, the focus of these parables is to encourage faithfulness, wisdom and preparation. These themes are expressed in the parable of the faithful and unfaithful servants (Mt 24:45-51 and Lk 12:41-48), the parable of the ten maidens (Mt 25:1-13) and the parable of the talents (Mt 25:14-30 with a possible parallel in Lk 19:11-27). These themes are also stressed in parables about the present. (Note especially Lk 16:1-13.) Both present and future eschatology have as their goal right living in the present.

9.3. Discipleship. Since discipleship is the main purpose of Jesus' teaching, the parables focus on this theme frequently. In many cases discipleship is the assumed subject. Elsewhere the concern for discipleship is explicit. In the twin parables of the tower builder and the warring king (Lk 14:28-32), people are warned to consider the cost, for being a disciple is no easy task. The parable of the owner and his servant (Lk 17:7-10) views obedience as an expectation, something people should do, rather than something noteworthy. (Contrast the parable in 12:37 which tells of a master serving his servants because they were faithful!) The parable of the two builders describes the wise person as the one who hears and does Jesus' teachings. As elsewhere, the wise person is the one who understands the eschatological realities and lives accordingly. Likewise, the parable of the two sons (Mt 21:28-32) stresses the importance of obedience over against the *intent* to do the Father's will. Where obedience is made specific, the focus is on the necessity of doing acts of mercy. (Note especially Mt 18:33; 25:32-46 and Lk 10:25-37.) One cannot experience the grace of the kingdom without extending that grace to others.

9.3.1. The Right Use of Wealth. While the use of money is a frequent subject in the teaching of Jesus, Luke has a particular focus on the right use of wealth (*see* Rich and Poor). Several of the parables unique to

him discuss this theme. The rich fool (Lk 12:16-21) thought only of his own enjoyment in the use of his wealth. He failed to consider the source of his wealth or the fact that life consists of much more than possessions. Verse 20 suggests that life is on loan from God and that we are accountable to him for it. The parables and sayings in Luke 16 provide some of the most direct teaching on wealth. The parable of the dishonest steward is debated because there is uncertainty whether his reduction of the amounts owed was a reduction of his own commission, the reduction of the illegal usurious portion that would go to his owner, or merely a rash act counting on the master's mercy. The intent of the parable is still clear. Jesus' point in Luke 16:8-9 is that people in this world understand the shrewd use of resources better than his disciples understand the economics of the kingdom. Jesus' disciples should make friends for themselves by the right use of "unrighteous mammon," money that tends to lead to unrighteousness. By the right use of wealth in acts of mercy, they make friendships with eternal benefits (cf. 12:33). The parable of the rich man and Lazarus poignantly makes the same point. This parable is not intended to provide a description of judgment so much as it is to underscore the eternal consequences of failing to show mercy. To be a disciple of the kingdom is to have one's priorities reorganized with regard to finances.

9.3.2. Prayer. Another redactional concern which Luke conveys through parables is his focus on prayer.* Two of these parables, that of the friend at midnight (Lk 11:5-8) and the wicked judge (Lk 18:1-8), are *contrasts* between human responses to requests and the way God responds to prayer. The friend at midnight is not about persistence. The word *anaideia* in 11:8, which is sometimes translated "persistence," actually means "shamelessness" and almost certainly refers to the boldness of the man knocking. The point of the parable is that if a human responds to such knocking, how much more will God respond to the prayers of his people (cf. Lk 11:13). Similarly, the unjust judge acts on behalf of the widow so that she will not keep pestering him. But the parable indicates that God is not like the unjust judge; rather, he will adjudicate the cause of his people quickly. Luke gives his readers confidence that God hears and responds to prayer. The remaining parable on prayer, that of the pharisee and the tax collector, emphasizes the humility and repentance with which one should approach God.

See also FORM CRITICISM; HARDNESS OF HEART; KINGDOM OF GOD; LITERARY CRITICISM.

BIBLIOGRAPHY. K. E. Bailey, *Poet and Peasant: A*

Literary Cultural Approach to the Parables in Luke (Grand Rapids: Eerdmans, 1976); idem, *Through Peasant Eyes: More Lucan Parables, Their Culture and Style* (Grand Rapids: Eerdmans, 1980); C. L. Blomberg, *Interpreting the Parables* (Downers Grove: InterVarsity, 1990); M. Boucher, *The Mysterious Parable* (Washington, D.C.: The Catholic Biblical Association of America, 1977); J. D. Crossan, *In Parables* (New York: Harper and Row, 1973); J. D. M. Derrett, *Law in the New Testament* (London: Darton, Longman, and Todd, 1976); C. H. Dodd, *The Parables of the Kingdom* (London: Nisbet, 1936); D. Flusser, *Die rabbinischen Gleichnisse und der Gleichniserzähler Jesus; 1 Teil: Das Wesen der Gleichnisse* (Bern: Peter Lang, 1981); R. W. Funk et al., *The Parables of Jesus: Red Letter Edition* (Sonoma, CA: Polebridge, 1988); J. Jeremias, *The Parables of Jesus* (New York: Charles Scribner's, 1963); G. V. Jones, *The Art and Truth of the Parables* (London: SPCK, 1964); P. R. Jones, *The Teaching of the Parables* (Nashville: Broadman, 1982); A. Jülicher, *Die Gleichnisreden Jesu* (2 vols.; Tübingen: J. C. B. Mohr [Paul Siebeck], 1888-89); J. D. Kingsbury, *The Parables of Jesus In Matthew 13* (Richmond: John Knox, 1969); W. S. Kissinger, *The Parables of Jesus* (Metuchen, NJ: Scarecrow, 1979); H. K. McArthur and R. M. Johnston, *They Also Taught in Parables* (Grand Rapids: Zondervan, 1990); T. W. Manson, *The Teaching of Jesus* (Cambridge: University Press, 1935); N. Perrin, *Jesus and the Language of the Kingdom* (Philadelphia: Fortress, 1976); B. B. Scott, *Hear Then the Parable* (Minneapolis: Fortress, 1989); K. Snodgrass, *The Parable of the Wicked Tenants* (Tübingen: J. C. B. Mohr [Paul Siebeck], 1983); R. H. Stein, *An Introduction to the Parables of Jesus* (Philadelphia: Westminster, 1981); D. O. Via, Jr., *The Parables* (Philadelphia: Fortress, 1967); C. Westermann, *The Parables of Jesus in the Light of the Old Testament* (Minneapolis: Fortress, 1990); B. H. Young, *Jesus and His Jewish Parables* (New York: Paulist, 1989).

K. R. Snodgrass

PARACLETE. *See* HOLY SPIRIT; JOHN, GOSPEL OF.

PARADISE. *See* HEAVEN AND HELL.

PAROUSIA. *See* APOCALYPTIC TEACHING; ESCHATOLOGY; SON OF MAN.

PASSION NARRATIVE

The dramatic story portraying and interpreting the events of Jesus' suffering and death (*see* Death of Jesus). In the Synoptic Gospels the account of the Jewish plot against Jesus' life during the Feast of Unleavened Bread (*see* Feasts) is usually regarded as the beginning point of the passion narrative; its finale is marked by Jesus' burial (*see* Burial of Jesus). Thus the passion narrative in the Synoptics is found in Matthew 26—27, Mark 14—15 and Luke 22—23. The parameters of the Johannine account are less easily determined, for material otherwise found in the Synoptic passion narrative is scattered throughout John 10—19. The extant remains of the apocryphal *Gospel of Peter* (c. A.D. 125) constitute a narrative of Jesus' passion and resurrection, beginning with the story of Jesus before Pilate (*see* Pontius Pilate). According to long-standing and widely held views, the story of Jesus' suffering and death was the first among the developing Gospel traditions to achieve written form (*see* Tradition Criticism).

1. The Formation of the Passion Narrative
2. The Role of the OT in the Passion Narrative
3. The Genre of the Passion Narrative

1. The Formation of the Passion Narrative.

The origins of the passion narrative have been widely debated (see Green, 9-14). Early in this century the form critics observed the passion narrative's relative self-sufficiency and coherence, its chronological and topographical cohesion, and the fundamental correspondence of narrative sequence among the four Gospel accounts (*see* Form Criticism). They found that, unlike other Gospel segments, this one did not dissolve easily into component parts. On this basis they insisted on the existence of a connected story of Jesus' passion long before the composition of the Gospels. From this consensus arose widely divergent opinions regarding the narrative's sources, content and purpose. One particularly widespread thesis postulated an evolutionary, multi-stage process of growth, from a primitive outline (such as Mk 10:33-34; Acts 13:27-29; or 1 Cor 15:3-5) to a short account beginning with Jesus' arrest. Additional materials were thought to have been appended to this brief story to achieve the expanded narratives of our four Gospels. A number of multi-source theories have also been championed.

During the 1960s, however, the whole notion of a primitive narrative of Jesus' passion was called into question. A few independent passion traditions might have existed from earliest times, it was alleged, but Mark composed the first passion account from beginning to end. W. H. Kelber developed this view further, arguing that Mark constructed the first passion narrative largely from OT texts and reflection on the OT against the backdrop of Jesus' execution (*see* Old Testament in the Gospels; Typology). This basic thesis claims a growing number of adherents, especially in North America.

This is not to say, however, that study of the early formation of the passion narrative has ceased. Some recent proposals have taken up a number of earlier, form-critical observations and argued them with a greater degree of sophistication. Combining this line of study with additional support from new source- and redaction-critical studies, research on the literary forms of antiquity, and observations regarding the enigma of Jesus' death in its milieu, these scholars support with renewed vigor the probability of an early, written, self-contained passion narrative. These studies focus on the formation of the passion story within the context of early Christian worship*—the commemoration of the death of Jesus by Christians during the Jewish Passover celebration (Trocmé) or the regular celebration of the Lord's Supper* (Green). D. Crossan also supports the idea of a primitive, self-contained narrative of Jesus' passion. His point of departure, however, is the apocryphal *Gospel of Peter*, which he regards as best embodying this primitive passion account. For him, the first passion story was practically devoid of historical reminiscence, but was created under the influence of passion prophecy.

With the influx of newer literary-based methods into Gospels research, the question of the origins and development of the passion narrative is being eclipsed (e.g., Karris; *see* Literary Criticism). This has led to a healthy emphasis on understanding the theology of the passion narratives within their larger Gospel contexts. Unfortunately, however, some redactional and literary studies of the passion accounts have been carried out under the assumption of a high level of creative license on the part of the Gospel writers. Thus, the relatively late development of the passion tradition is not argued but presupposed.

In any case, the crucial importance of understanding how the earliest Christians came to terms with the suffering and death of the one they proclaimed as Messiah (*see* Christ) is reason enough to continue raising the question of the formation of the passion narrative.

2. The Role of the OT in the Passion Narrative.

In order to understand the passion narratives, we must come to terms with the use of the OT in these accounts. Not only does a widely held thesis maintain that the substance of the passion story derives from Christian reflection on the OT, but OT references play a crucial interpretive role in the story of Jesus' death.

2.1. The OT: Creative Agent? Kelber and Crossan are only two among many voices arguing that the passion story was either largely or entirely created out of OT texts. According to this thesis, early Christians knew almost nothing of the events of Jesus' suffering and death, so they turned to the OT (prophecy of his passion) for information and inspiration.

The initial query that might be raised against this theory is, In the context of hermeneutics in late Judaism, was it a matter of course that narratives were worked up from OT texts? Was the procedure posited by Kelber and Crossan commonplace in the interpretive milieu of late Judaism and early Christianity? In fact, recent research on this question points to a negative verdict (Moo). Indeed, studies of the use of the OT at Qumran (*see* Dead Sea Scrolls), among apocalyptists (*see* Apocalyptic) and in post-biblical historiography indicate that the direction of influence was primarily from event to Scripture rather than vice versa. Biblical texts were adapted to fit events more readily than were events created to fit biblical texts.

Those who regard the passion narrative as a midrash* on selected OT texts must overcome the additional obstacle presented by the narrative itself. Biblical references abound in the passion narrative, but follow no discernible pattern as might have been determined by an OT passage or passages. Although some OT texts reappear in the passion story (e.g., Ps 22 and Is 53), ". . . the biblical allusions in the passion narrative have almost no continuity and seldom concern the same book twice in succession, while the themes vary from one allusion to the next" (Trocmé, 58).

Still further, we should note that not every aspect of the passion story can be accounted for by an appeal to the creative role of the OT. A list of such elements in Mark might include the anointing* at Bethany (14:3-9), the singing of a hymn after the Last Supper (14:26), the sword incident at the arrest (14:47), the reference to the fire at the courtyard (14:54), the mention of Simon of Cyrene and his two sons (15:21), the hour-scheme at the cross (15:25, 33), and the tearing of the temple veil (15:38). Clearly, factors beyond the influence of the OT were at work in the formation of the passion narrative.

Finally, evidence from the Gospel passion narratives themselves supports the conclusion that passion events were primarily interpreted by, not created from, the OT. For example, just as Psalm 41:9 explains the problem raised by Judas Iscariot* (cf. Mk 14:18; Jn 13:18), so Zechariah 13:7 justifies the flight of the disciples (Mk 14:27, 50; Mt 26:31, 56). For this reason, some have judged that the citation was placed on Jesus' lips by the early church. Even if this were true, however, it remains evident that the reason for doing so would have been to downplay the scandalous character of the disciples' flight at Jesus' arrest. If Jesus' suffering and death were God's will, why did the disciples flee? According to Zechariah 13:7, this, too, was foretold as part of the divine plan. That is, an historical event, the flight of the disciples, gave rise to a riddle which was solved with recourse to the OT. The OT interpreted, but did not create, this problematic event.

To give an example of a different sort, a number of canonical and extra-canonical texts demonstrate that it was understood that Jesus was *nailed* to the cross (Jn 20:25; Acts 2:23; Col 2:14; *Gos. Pet.* 6.21; Justin, *Dial.* 97; and perhaps Lk 24:39; *see* Death of Jesus). Aside from the fact that this detail has a good claim to being historically accurate, it is remarkable that, in not mentioning this detail in the crucifixion story itself, early Christians bypassed an excellent opportunity to show one more substantial intersection between the fate of the Suffering Righteous in Psalm 22 and Jesus. In Psalm 22:16 (21:17 LXX) we read: "they pierced my hands and feet." It is true that the reading of the (possibly corrupt) MT would not have suggested this correspondence ("as a lion my hands and feet"), but elsewhere in the passion story references to Psalm 22 employ the Greek version. If the passion narrative depended heavily on the creative role of the OT, we would have expected "passion prophecy" to have rendered this connection explicit.

If the best way to describe the relationship of the OT to the passion narrative is not with reference to its creative role, what is a more appropriate explanation?

2.2. The OT: Interpretive Agent. One way of grappling with the crucial role of the OT in the passion narrative is to begin by recognizing the enigma of Jesus' death. Jesus' public humiliation and execution on a cross ran counter to practically every strand of first-century messianic expectation. The cross of Christ constituted a scandal of no mean proportions. How could it be explained? The answer could only be cast in terms of God's will, his redemptive plan, and it was to the OT that early Christians went in search of ways of making sense of the death of their Messiah.

In the process of working out the significance of Jesus' death in a narrative context, early Christians employed the OT at a number of levels. In some cases they incorporated *direct citations* of OT materials into the passion story (e.g., Lk 22:37, citing Is 53:12; Mk 15:34, citing Ps 22:1). In other instances *allusions* to OT texts were woven into the narrative material. Thus, for example, language from Isaiah 50:6 has been borrowed in the account of Jesus' mockery in Mark 15:19; Matthew 27:30 and John 19:1, 3. In this way, Jesus is identified typologically as the Isaianic Servant of Yahweh.*

The framers of the passion tradition were not interested in specific OT texts only. These Christians were convinced that, whatever God's plans for redemption were, they were all fulfilled in Jesus. Hence, in the passion narrative we read that "the Son of Man* will go just as it is written about him" (Mk 14:21) or "the Son of Man will go as it has been decreed" (Lk 22:22). These are probably not allusions to specific OT texts, but rather intentionally *general references* to the divine will.

Moreover, throughout the passion narratives there are evidences of the interpretation of Jesus' suffering and death along larger, *typological* lines (*see* Typology). For example, in many ways the passion accounts portray Jesus against the interpretive framework of the Suffering Servant of the Lord. "Like the Servant, Jesus (1) is God's chosen one who will complete his mission through suffering; (2) willingly submits to his divine mission; (3) is innocent; (4) maintains his silence; (5) dies 'for many'; (6) is 'handed over'; (7) is abused; (8) is 'numbered with transgressors'; (9) anticipates his vindication; and (10) is vindicated after maltreatment" (Green, 317-318). Similarly, especially in the Markan and Matthean passion accounts, Jesus is the Suffering Righteous One.

By these means we are instructed that, far from being a contradiction of the divine will, far from being an inexplicable puzzle in redemptive history, Jesus' suffering and death was actually willed by God. Whether by slightest allusion or explicit citation, the use of the OT in the passion story underscores the necessity of Jesus' death in God's salvific plan.

3. The Genre of the Passion Narrative.

The centrality of the passion of Jesus to redemptive history is suggested not only by the use of the OT in its interpretation, but also by the genre within which it is related. In fact, the genre, or literary form, of this story is a significant indicator of the passion narrative's meaning and antiquity.

Recent studies in genre have isolated the traditional literary schema known to some as the genre of "court conflict," to others as the "story of the vindication of the innocent sufferer" (see Crossan, 297-334; Green, 169-173). Set against a legal or royal setting, the protagonists in these stories are recognized for their outstanding qualities; their lives are endangered, usually through evil schemes; though innocent, they are persecuted; and finally, they are vindicated. In the earlier examples of this genre (e.g., the story of Joseph, Gen 37—42), the protagonist is rescued from death; however, with time, the genre was transformed so that vindication comes after death (e.g., 2 Macc 7; Wis 2, 4—5). Significantly, within the development of this genre, Isaiah 52:13—53:12, which combines the twin motifs of vindicated innocence and vicarious death, comes to play a pivotal role.

The parallels between this genre and the passion narratives of our Gospels are remarkable. They demonstrate further the possibility of an early, self-contained passion narrative constructed along the lines of this readily available literary convention. Moreover, they underscore the intimate relation of Jesus' passion with God's redemptive activity, and especially with the interpretation of innocent death found in Is 52:13—53:12.

See also BURIAL OF JESUS; DEATH OF JESUS; GETHSEMANE; LAST SUPPER; SERVANT OF YAHWEH; TRIAL OF JESUS.

BIBLIOGRAPHY. J. D. Crossan, *The Cross That Spoke: The Origins of the Passion Narrative* (San Francisco: Harper & Row, 1988); J. R. Donahue, "From Passion Traditions to Passion Narrative," in *The Passion in Mark: Studies on Mark 14-16*, ed. W. H. Kelber (Philadelphia: Fortress, 1976) 1-20; J. B. Green, *The Death of Jesus: Tradition and Interpretation in the Passion Narrative* (WUNT 2:33; Tübingen: J.C.B. Mohr [Paul Siebeck], 1988); R. Karris, *Luke: Artist and Theologian. Luke's Passion Account as Literature* (New York/Mahwah: Paulist, 1985); W. H. Kelber, *The Oral and the Written Gospel* (Philadelphia: Fortress, 1983); D. J. Moo, *The Old Testament in the Gospel Passion Narratives* (Sheffield: Almond, 1983); R. Pesch, "Die Überlieferung der Passion Jesu," in *Rückfrage nach Jesu: Zur Methodik und Bedeutung der Frage nach den historischen Jesus*, ed. K. Kertelge (Freiburg: Herder, 1974) 148-173; E. Trocmé, *The Passion as Liturgy: A Study in the Origin of the Passion Narratives in the Four Gospels* (London: SCM, 1983); H.-R. Weber, *The Cross: Tradition and Interpretation* (London: S.P.C.K., 1979).

J. B. Green

PASSOVER. *See* FEASTS; LAST SUPPER.

PEACE

References to peace (usually *eirēnē*) in the teaching of Jesus and the Gospel writers can be fully appreciated only in the light of the Hebrew concept of *šālôm*, Jewish expectations concerning the coming kingdom of peace and the violence of first-century life in Israel.

1. Šālôm
2. Kingdom of Peace
3. Peace and Violence
4. Conclusion

1. Šālôm

The Hebrew term for peace means "well-being" (e.g., Num 25:12; Ps 38:3; 73:3; Jer 14:13; cf. P. B. Yoder). It covers health, prosperity, security, friendship and salvation.* It is the desired experience of individuals, families and Israel* as a nation. It is present because of God's own presence and his favor toward his people. The Greek term *eirēnē* in classical Greek literature means little more than absence of war. In the NT, however, it incorporates the breadth of meaning conveyed by the Hebrew *šālôm*.

This can be sensed in passages like Mark 5:24-34. Verse 29 reports the physical healing* of a socially and religiously unclean woman (*see* Clean and Unclean). Jesus, not content to provide mere physical relief, exposes the woman's secrecy, publicly discloses her faith* and her healing, and thus effectively restores her to community and wholeness. Jesus "saves" her (5:34). His final "Go in peace" is more than a parting blessing. It is the bestowal of *šālôm*, the gift Jesus gives whenever he ministers to needy people.

2. Kingdom of Peace.

Peace was central to the eschatological (*see* Eschatology) expectations of the OT prophets. The messianic child would be a "Prince of Peace" (Is 9:6). He was expected to come in peace, to end warfare and to proclaim peace throughout the land (Zech 9:9-12). He would reunite families (Mal 4:6); he would decimate Israel's enemies in order to bring lasting peace to Jerusalem (meaning "city of peace") (cf. Is 66:10-16). With his first coming, Jesus fulfilled some of these expectations.

Through his caring ministry, his miraculous works (*see* Miracles and Miracle Stories), his gift of salvation, his offer of acceptance and community to outsiders, Jesus gave a foretaste of that eschatological well-being. Yet, instead of reuniting families, he divided them (Lk 12:51-53). Instead of destroying Israel's national enemies, he rejected the revolutionary option, preached non-violence (Mt 5:38-48) and suffered a violent death at the hands of enemies he loved and forgave (Lk 23:34). Jesus planted the seeds of the "Kingdom of Peace." Its harvest awaits his Second Coming.

In John's Gospel "Peace be with you" (20:19, 21, 26) is Jesus' post-resurrection greeting to his followers. It is, however, more than a greeting. It is the bestowal of eschatological peace on those who join his victory over death. It is the fulfillment of Jesus' earlier promise that his followers will have tranquility, harmony and security in Jesus while still living in a troubled world (14:27; 16:33).

In Matthew and Mark peace is a gift from God that must be experienced and shared in human relationships. Jesus called his followers to live at peace with each other (Mk 9:50), and he empowered them to bestow peace on those who are worthy (Mt 10:13). "Blessed are the peacemakers," said Jesus, "for they will be called God's children" (Mt 5:9). Peacemaking will sometimes be unsuccessful (Mt 10:34-37). Moreover, peacemaking is costly. It involved a cross for Jesus, and it involves a cross for his followers (Mt 10:37-39). According to Jesus and the Evangelists, no cost is too great for the privilege of receiving, experiencing and sharing God's peace.

Luke's Gospel develops the idea that peace comes to those who prove worthy. The shepherds hear the angels* proclaiming that with the arrival of the savior, peace is available "on earth" to people "on whom God's favor rests" (2:14; *see* Birth of Jesus). But on whom does God's favor rest? Throughout Luke's gospel, "peace on earth" comes to outcasts, disciples, foreigners, any who will receive God's grace and respond with faith. But peace on earth does not come to Jerusalem, the city of peace (a play on words Luke may have intended to be understood as irony). On the contrary, Jerusalem (through its leaders) rejects Jesus and therefore proves unworthy (19:42). God's favor cannot rest there.

The Jerusalem crowd ironically praises the "King of Peace" by shouting "Peace in heaven!" (19:28-38). There can be no "peace on earth" for Jerusalem. The city missed its chance to receive God's eschatological *šālôm*. Jerusalem is not even destined for a minimal peace defined as absence of war, for foreign enemies will serve as instruments of God's judgment* on the city that failed to recognize and accept God's offer of peace (19:42-44). Yet God's favor still rests on the faithful in Israel. Those who have accepted Jesus receive God's *šālôm*. To them the risen Christ announces, "Peace be unto you" (24:36).

3. Peace and Violence.
Jesus promised his followers the blessing of being in God's family if they would be "peacemakers" (Mt 5:9), respond non-violently to aggressors (5:38-42) and even love their enemies (5:43-48).

Luke's Gospel has been the center of pacifistic interpretations of the Gospels. J. H. Yoder argues persuasively that both Jesus and Luke are self-consciously instructing Christian hearers/readers to adopt the pacifistic model of Jesus in contrast to the violent political options available to Jesus, his followers, the early church and modern Christians. Chris-

tians are called to be peacemakers in situations of interpersonal, national and international conflict.

Jesus' words to his disciples to "buy swords" (22:35-38) has been variously judged as ironic, symbolic and unhistorical. Given the time designations marking Jesus' passion as the turning point ("then . . . but now"), however, it probably signifies the hostility with which Jesus' disciples will be confronted (cf. Mt 10:34-36/Lk 12:51-53; cf. Lampe). On any reading it is clear from 22:49-51 that Jesus did *not* endorse his disciples' use of their swords. Armed conflict—so to speak—is permitted only with demonic enemies (11:21-22). Only in relation to Satan's kingdom does Jesus come as a divine warrior, leading his followers into battle (10:17-19; cf. Rom 16:20).

4. Conclusion.
Jesus proclaims and brings God's *šālôm*. Eschatological peace on earth comes only to those on whom God's favor rests. Jesus' followers join him in combatting demonic evil, while loving human enemies. Like the kingdom of God, the eschatological peace Jesus and his followers proclaim and practice is already but not yet. The church's task is to bring about God's peace "on earth as it is in heaven."

See also ETHICS OF JESUS; KINGDOM OF GOD.

BIBLIOGRAPHY. W. Brueggemann, *Living Toward a Vision: Biblical Reflections on Shalom* (Philadelphia: United Church, 1976); J. Dewey, "Peace," in *HBD* 766-67; W. Foerster and G. von Rad, "εἰρήνη κτλ," *TDNT* II.400-20; J. M. Ford, *My Enemy Is My Guest* (Maryknoll: Orbis, 1984); P. L. Hammer, *Shalom in the New Testament* (Philadelphia: United Church, 1973); D. J. Harris, *Shalom! The Biblical Concept of Peace* (Grand Rapids: Baker, 1970); M. Hengel, *Victory Over Violence* (Philadelphia: Fortress, 1973); W. Klassen, *Love of Enemies: The Way to Peace* (Philadelphia: Fortress, 1984); G. W. H. Lampe, "The Two Swords (Luke 22:35-38)," in *Jesus and the Politics of His Day*, ed. E. Bammel and C. F. D. Moule (Cambridge: University Press, 1984) 335-51; J. H. Yoder, *The Politics of Jesus* (Grand Rapids: Eerdmans, 1972); P. B. Yoder, *Shalom: The Bible's Word for Salvation, Justice, and Peace* (Newton, KS: Faith and Life, 1982).   T. J. Geddert

PEOPLE, CROWD
The crowd is the gathering of the nameless common people of Palestine who provided an audience for Jesus' public ministry. The crowd is the recipient of his teachings (*see* Teacher) and beneficiary of his healings.* The portrayal of the crowd in each Gospel not only helps set the scene for a teaching or healing of Jesus, but is a significant part of

the theology of the Gospel as a whole.

1. Terminology
2. General Portrayal
3. Specific Portrayals

1. Terminology.

Several Greek terms make up the topic people/crowd: *ochlos* ("crowd" or "throng"), *laos* ("people"), *plēthos* ("multitude" or "number") and *polloi* ("many"). These terms are almost completely limited to the Gospels and Acts. *Ochlos, laos* and *plēthos* are synonyms (Mt 27:24-25; Mk 3:7-10; Lk 6:17; 7:24, 29; 8:42, 47). They are often contrasted with the authorities, Pharisees* and scribes* (Mt 14:5; Mk 11:32 par. Mt 21:26 and Lk 20:6; Mk 12:12 par. Mt 21:46 and Lk 20:19). *Plēthos,* absent in Matthew and not used of the crowd in John, is used in Mark and Luke to describe the wide appeal of Jesus and his message with the populace (Lk 6:17 par. Mk 3:7-8; Lk 8:37; 23:27).

2. General Portrayal.

Jesus is most frequently portrayed encountering crowds during his extensive ministry in Galilee.* It was composed of day laborers, farmers and fishermen of both Gentile* and Jewish background from Galilee and the surrounding regions. These regions included Judea, Galilee, Decapolis, Trans-Jordan, Tyre and Sidon (Mt 4:25; Mk 3:7-8; Lk 6:17-18; *see* Archeology and Geography). During his stays in Jerusalem at the close of his ministry, Jesus encountered a crowd composed mainly of Jews drawn from all over the Hellenistic world (*see* Hellenism) who had come to the city to celebrate the Passover (*see* Feasts).

The crowd was originally drawn to John the Baptist's* proclamation (Lk 3:7, 10, 15, 18), but was subsequently attracted to Jesus throughout his public ministry. His teaching and miracles* drew them, especially his healings (Mk 1:32-34 par. Lk 4:40-41; Mt 15:29-31), but they also came simply to be fed (Jn 6:26). The crowd was comprised of thousands (Mk 6:44 par. Mt 14:21; Mk 8:9 par. Mt 15:38 and Lk 12:1), a feature reflected in the Johannine hyperbole "the whole world has gone after him" (Jn 12:19). The crowd is often referred to as following Jesus (Mt 4:25; 8:1; Mk 3:7; Lk 7:9; Jn 6:2, 5). It presses intensely around him (Mk 5:31 par. Lk 8:45), once even necessitating that a ship take him away (Mk 3:9). The people were partially spurred by messianic hopes (*see* Revolutionary Movements), for at the feeding of the five thousand they almost proclaimed him king (Jn 6:15).

The crowd was astonished by Jesus' teaching, particularly because he did not teach like the rabbis* by quoting other authorities, but taught with his own

authority* (Mt 7:28-29; 22:33; Mk 1:22, 27 par. Lk 4:32, 36; Mk 6:2 par. Mt 13:54; Mk 11:18; Lk 4:22). As expected, the crowd also marveled at his miracles (Mk 2:12 par. Mt 9:8 and Lk 5:26; Mt 9:33; Mk 7:37 par. Mt 15:31; Lk 7:16) and exorcisms (Lk 9:43; 11:14; *see* Demon, Devil, Satan). Even so, the crowd was divided in its opinion of Jesus, thinking him to be John the Baptist, Elijah,* a prophet* (Mk 8:27-29 par. Mt 16:13-16 and Lk 9:18-20), the Messiah (Jn 7:40-43; *see* Christ), an agent of Satan (Lk 11:15-16) or simply someone leading the people astray (Jn 7:12).

The governing authorities disdained the crowd, thinking it could easily be led astray (Jn 7:45-49; cf. 7:12). However, the authorities often considered the power of the crowd when formulating policy. Herod Antipas (*see* Herodian Dynasty) hesitated to kill John the Baptist for fear of the crowd which thought that John was a prophet (Mt 14:5). Josephus* (*Ant.* 18.118) records that John so inspired the crowd that Herod feared rebellion. The leadership of Israel* was afraid of affronting the crowd's opinion that John the Baptist was a prophet (Mk 11:32 par. Mt 21:26 and Lk 20:6; Mt 21:46). The crowd's belief that Jesus was the Christ motivated the leadership to arrest Jesus before even more people could become his followers (Jn 7:31-32, 45-49; 11:47-53). However, they carefully plotted strategy for the arrest because of the potential for rioting (Mk 11:18 par. Lk 19:47-48; Mk 12:12 par. Mt 21:46 and Lk 20:19; Mk 14:1-2 par. Mt 26:3-5 and Lk 22:2), hiring Judas* to betray Jesus in the absence of the crowd (Lk 22:6).

In turn the crowds also feared the leadership and could be influenced by it (Jn 7:12-13). An armed crowd was present at the arrest of Jesus (Mk 14:43 par. Mt 26:47 and Lk 22:47). Once arrested, the crowd was easily swayed to turn on Jesus (Mk 15:11 par. Mt 27:20; Jn 19:15; cf. Lk 23:18). Pilate condemned Jesus against his will and under the pressure of the crowd, which in turn had been swayed by the leadership (Mk 15:15 par. Lk 23:24). The crowd did, however, repent once it witnessed the crucifixion (Lk 23:48; *see* Death of Jesus).

Jesus' reaction to the crowd was typified by compassion (Mt 9:36; Mk 6:34 par. Mt 14:14; Mk 8:2 par. Mt 15:32). It is noteworthy that in Luke Jesus is portrayed as having compassion for the individual rather than the crowd (7:13; 30:33; cf. 15:20). Jesus taught the crowd (Mt 5:1-2; 7:28-29; Mk 7:14 par. Mt 15:10), usually with parables* (Mk 4:33-34 par. Mt 13:34-35). He healed many of its number (Mt 14:14 par. Lk 9:11), fed them (Mk 6:41 par. Mt 14:19 and Lk 9:16; Mk 8:6 par. Mt 15:36; Jn 6:11) and prayed for them (Jn 11:42). He even considered them closer than his own relatives (Mk 3:31-35; *see* Family). He often withdrew from the crowd for prayer* and rest after teaching them and/or performing miracles (Mt 8:18; 13:36; Mk 4:36; Mk 6:45-46 par. Mt 14:22-23; Jn 5:13; 6:15). Because of its diverse opinions of him, its lack of understanding and the ease with which it was swayed, Jesus did not place great confidence in the profession of the crowd (Mt 13:10-17; Mk 8:27-29 par. Mt 16:13-16 and Lk 9:18-20).

As an actor within Gospel narrative, the crowd is a "chorus which confirms Jesus' words and acts by joy, admiration, astonishment and fear . . ." (Meyer and Katz, 586). Rhetorically, the crowd functions as an artificial proof, that is, a proof not manufactured by the Gospel writers. The crowds provide an implicit eyewitness testimony to verify the narrative of the Gospels.

3. Specific Portrayals.
The Synoptists in particular were very careful to identify the particular audience of virtually every facet of Jesus' ministry. Interpretation of the Synoptics as a whole and in part must account for the audience of each pericope. We are particularly indebted to Minear's groundbreaking studies of the crowd for each of the Synoptic Gospels.

3.1. Mark. Mark carefully differentiates between audiences composed of *laos* ("people"), *ochlos* ("crowd") and disciples.* In Mark "people" is never Jesus' immediate audience, except in 7:6 where he attacks the scribes and Pharisees described as "people." In 11:32 and 14:2, the only two other Markan occurrences of "people," it is used of the crowd as the source of fear for the authorities. With one exception (10:1) Mark always uses the singular of "crowd" (*ho ochlos*), indicating that he is thinking of the crowd as a unified group. Matthew and Luke use a mixture of singular and plural. In Mark the specific designation "disciple" is limited to the Twelve.

In his study of discipleship* in Mark, Best concludes that ". . . the crowd possesses no unitary role in the gospel" and "the crowd is a vague amorphous mass of men" (392). He argues that the crowd does not function as disciples in working for Jesus or receiving private instruction. Rather, the disciples are merely drawn from the crowd. However, Malbon compares the activities of the disciples and the crowd in relation to Jesus and proves just the opposite is the case in Mark. The crowd (*ochlos*) is not merely a mixed group of onlookers, but disciples. The crowd and the disciples are portrayed both in their strength and their weakness to serve as realistic models of Christian discipleship for the reader.

Jesus calls both the disciples and the crowd to follow him and teaches them the price that following him requires (8:34—9:1). As he did with the disciples, Jesus calls the crowd as a group to follow him (8:34) and calls out individuals from the crowd to follow him (2:13-14; 10:46-52). Also, as did the disciples, the crowd does follow Jesus (2:15; 3:7; 5:24), including specifically named individuals (2:14; 10:52; 15:40-41).

Both the disciples and the crowd are taught by Jesus. Jesus is often portrayed teaching the crowd without the subject being specified (2:13; 4:1-2; 6:34; 7:14; 10:1). He often withdrew from the crowd to give the disciples more detailed instruction on what he had already taught them in the presence of the crowd (4:10-34; 7:17-23; 9:28; 10:10-12). In particular, in private Jesus instructed the disciples about the passion and resurrection* of which the crowd was not informed (8:31; 9:31). Jesus commands both the crowd (4:3, 9; 7:14) and the disciples to hear (4:23; 8:18) and both the crowd (3:8; 4:12; 6:2; 12:37) and the disciples heard (8:18; 11:14).

Both the disciples and the crowd share in amazement at Jesus. The crowds are amazed at his teaching (1:22, 27; 6:2; 11:18), healings (2:12; 5:33; 7:37; 9:15) and exorcisms. The disciples are amazed at his teaching (10:24, 26), his power over the sea (4:41; 6:51), at the Transfiguration* (9:6) and his prediction of the passion and resurrection (9:32; *see* Predictions of Jesus' Death and Resurrection). However, the disciples' amazement is never at healing (except perhaps 5:42), the usual object of the crowd's amazement.

The crowd is the chief beneficiary of Jesus' ministry of teaching and healing, whereas the disciples are Jesus' assistants in these activities. Jesus healed (1:34; 3:10), taught (2:2, 13; 4:1-2; 7:14; 10:1) and fed the crowd (6:41-42; 8:7-8). Unlike the crowd, the disciples assist Jesus in feeding (6:41; 8:6), teaching (3:14; 6:12, 30) and healing (3:15; 6:7, 13). At the end of Jesus' life, both disciples and crowds abandon him (15:8, 11, 15).

Through the disciples and the crowd, Mark presents a composite picture of fallible followers to show that discipleship is demanding, inclusive and difficult. Through the disciples and the crowd the demand to follow is extended to the larger group of hearer/readers. This extension comes in Jesus' statements of the "whoever" type addressed to both groups, and in Jesus' statements about "many" and "all" which usually refer to crowds but are spoken to the disciples (4:23; 8:34, 35; 9:35, 41, 42; 10:15; 11:23). An example is, "If any want to become my followers, let them deny themselves and take up their cross and follow me" (Mk 8:34 NRSV).

3.2. Matthew. Matthew is careful to distinguish *laos*

("people") and *ochlos* ("crowd"). *People* is used in Matthew in the LXX sense of the nation of Israel (2:4; 21:23). Only in one place do *crowd* and *people* describe the same group (27:24-25). Matthew refers to the "crowd" (*ochlos*) more than the other Synoptists, often adding it to tradition borrowed from the Markan account (4:25; 7:28; 8:1; 13:34, 36; 14:5; 21:8-11; 22:33). Whereas Mark prefers the singular, Matthew prefers the plural "crowds" (*ochloi*). When Matthew uses the singular it is usually incorporated from Mark (Mt 13:2b par. Mk 4:1b).

Overall, the crowds are presented positively in Matthew, responding to Jesus' message from the start of his ministry. The crowds do not press or jostle Jesus as in Mark and Luke (cf. 9:1-2 with Mk 2:3-4 par. Lk 5:18-19; 9:22 with Lk 8:45-48). As in Mark, the crowds follow Jesus, usually expressed with the verb "to follow" (*akoloutheō*) signifying qualitative allegiance (4:25; 8:1; 14:13) and discipleship (4:20, 22; 8:22-23; 9:9; 19:27-28). The crowds hear Jesus' teaching, particularly as the designated audience of two of the five sermons in Matthew (5:1-2; 13:1-2). The crowd is astonished at his authoritative teaching (7:28; 22:33) and healing (9:8, 33; 12:23; 15:31). They accept Jesus as a prophet (21:11, 26, 46) and proclaim him to be the Son of David* (12:23; 21:9).

However, a clear distinction between the crowd and the disciples is maintained. In contrast to the crowds who are followers of Jesus, the disciples are a more limited group of chosen trainees and successors of Jesus in healing and teaching (10:1—11:1; 28:16-20). Unlike the crowds, the disciples share Jesus' ministry of teaching (11:1) and healing (10:1, 8). Like the disciples, the crowds abandon Jesus in the end (26:55; 27:20).

Doyle has noted that the first reference to the crowd in a passage is plural; those that follow singular (13:2a, 2b; 21:8-11 is the exception in the reverse). The singular is used where the crowd is portrayed in a non-following role: the mourners for a little girl (9:23, 25), those that fear the authorities (14:5; 21:26); the crowd as mere background (8:18; 17:14) and the arresting mob (26:47). The crowd at Jesus' trial is singular when set against Jesus (26:47; 27:15, 24) and plural when for him (26:55; 27:20). Two exceptions to this pattern are 15:10 and 20:29 where the singular is used, but the crowd is positively related to Jesus.

3.3. Luke. Luke's conception of the audience of Jesus varies from the very similar portrayals of Mark and Matthew. In Luke *laos* ("people") takes a wider role. *Laos* with the article retains its specific LXX connotation of Israel as the covenant people (1:10, 17, 21, 68, 77; 2:32; 7:16; 20:1; 23:2, 13; 24:19), but can also

be used more generally of crowds (9:12-13).

Unlike Matthew and Mark, in Luke the people are less guilty of Jesus' death. They did not turn against Jesus and demand his crucifixion (cf. 23:18-25). There is only a passing reference to God's wrath on the people (21:23). Instead "people" is associated with the women* who faithfully follow Jesus to his execution (23:27, 35). The cry "Let his blood be on us and on our children!" (Mt 27:25) is not found on the lips of the people, nor are the Isaianic denunciations of Mark 7:6-7 par. Matthew 15:7-9 (Is 29:13) or Matthew 13:14-15 (Is 6:9-10; *see* Hardness of Heart) preserved by Luke. The rulers of the people are clearly more responsible for Jesus' death.

In Luke the crowd (*ochlos*) refers either to potential believers who become disciples or to enemies of Jesus who turn against him through the influence of the leadership. The crowd primarily wants to hear Jesus' teaching and see or personally experience the miracles (5:15). They misunderstand the mission of Jesus and are criticized by him (12:54-56). The crowd (*ochlos*) is distinguished from the people (*laos*) and the disciples. It is a group drawn from and representing the people (3:7-22; 8:47), and consists of potential disciples (9:10-11, 18-19; 12:1). Unlike Mark and Matthew where the crowd is composed of followers of Jesus, in Luke the crowd must respond to Jesus' proclamation to become followers. In Luke the crowds "constitute a neutral, anonymous, undifferentiated entity, a necessary but indistinct part of the stage setting . . ." (Minear, *NovT* 1974, 87). Like the people (*laos*), the crowd (*ochlos*) is less guilty of Jesus' death in Luke than in Matthew and Mark. They are associated with the betrayal and execution of Jesus, but not as directly (cf. 22:47; 23:4).

3.4. John. As in Luke, the two uses of *laos* ("people") in John refer to the Jews as a theocratic people. However, in John the word refers to the people of God incorporating more than the Jewish nation, for now it is the new people of God formed by the death of Jesus (11:50; 18:14). When John refers to numbers of people in other contexts he uses *ochlos*. The only use of *laos* for the multitude (8:2) is found in the interpolation of 7:53—8:11. In John "crowd" (*ochlos*) is used almost exclusively in the sense of the *'am hā'āreṣ*, "people of the land" (Jn 7:31-49).

See also DISCIPLE; DISCIPLESHIP.

BIBLIOGRAPHY. J. A. Baird, *Audience Criticism and the Historical Jesus* (Philadelphia: Westminster, 1969); E. Best, "The Role of the Disciples in Mark," *NTS* 23 (1977) 377-401; B. Citron, "The Multitude in the Synoptic Gospels," *SJT* 7 (1954) 408-18; B. R. Doyle, " 'Crowds' in Matthew: Texts and Theology," *CTR* 6

(1984) 28-33; E. S. Malbon, "Disciples/Crowds/
Whoever: Markan Characters and Readers," *NovT* 28
(1986) 104-130; R. Meyer and H. Strathmann, "λαός,"
TDNT IV.29-57; R. Meyer and P. Katz, "ὄχλος," *TDNT*
V.582-90; P. S. Minear, "Audience Criticism and
Markan Ecclesiology," in *Neues Testament und Ge-
schichte,* eds. H. Baltensweiler and B. Reicke (Zürich:
Theologischer Verlag; Tübingen: J. C. B. Mohr [Paul
Siebeck], 1972) 79-89; idem, "The Disciples and the
Crowds in the Gospel of Matthew," *ATR* Supp. Ser. 3
(1974) 28-44; idem, "Jesus' Audiences, According to
Luke," *NovT* 16 (1974) 81-109; A. W. Mosley, "Jesus'
Audiences in the Gospels of St Mark and St Luke,"
NTS 10 (1963/64) 139-49.   D. F. Watson

PEOPLE OF THE LAND. *See* RICH AND POOR.

PESHER. *See* MIDRASH.

PETER. *See* DISCIPLES; DISCIPLESHIP.

PHARISEES

The Pharisees appear in our sources as a distinct party
in Judaism of the late Second Temple period, with
their own vision of what Israel's* standing as God's
covenant people entailed. Characteristic of the
Pharisaic position was their adherence to a body of
traditional material (Gk *paradosis)* handed down
"from the fathers," which defined correct behavior in
a number of ways and which represented both an
interpretation of and a supplement to Pentateuchal
Law.* In the Gospels Pharisees are generally (though
not quite universally) depicted as opponents of Jesus,
critical of his behavior, hostile in their questions,
malicious in their deliberations. In turn, their piety is
attacked as hypocritical, their spiritual leadership is
declared bankrupt, and they are charged with leading
the nation to its doom. Through all the polemic the
significant role played by the Pharisees in Jewish life
in first-century Palestine is apparent.

1. Sources
2. Name and History
3. The Tradition of the Pharisees
4. Pharisees in the Gospels
5. Conclusion

1. Sources.
Historical reconstruction must begin with an awareness of the problems posed by the nature of our
sources. The Gospels will be treated in a later section.
Here we focus on Josephus* and rabbinic literature
(*see* Rabbinic Traditions and Writings).

1.1. Josephus. In his autobiographical *Life* Josephus

claims that he acquired firsthand knowledge of
various Jewish schools of thought, then chose to
govern his life according to the norms of the Pharisees (*Life* 10-12 §2). This suggests that Josephus, as a
Pharisee, can be counted on to provide an informed
and sympathetic picture of the party. Unfortunately,
matters are not so simple.

First, to a surprising extent what Josephus actually
writes about the Pharisees is negative, at times sharply
so. Such passages are commonly thought to have been
uncritically reproduced from sources harboring ill will
for the Pharisees (see Schwartz). An alternative explanation questions Josephus's claim to be a Pharisee,
noting that his writings betray little evidence of
support for peculiarly Pharisaic beliefs and practices.
The problem remains unresolved (see Mason).

Second, Josephus describes the various Jewish
parties (which he calls *haireseis,* or philosophical
schools) in terms familiar to his Gentile readers. The
Pharisees he compares with the Stoics (*Life* 12 §2). He
notes their belief in the immortality of the soul (*Ant.*
18.1.3 §14), in the resurrection* of the righteous (*J.W.*
2.8.14 §163) and in a fate which determines some, but
not all, human actions (so *Ant.* 13.5.9 §172; cf. 18.1.3
§13; *J.W.* 2.8.14 §162-163). Their simplicity of life and
deference to elders are also noted (*Ant.* 18.1.3 §12).
While Pharisaic belief in resurrection was certainly
characteristic, Josephus's depiction misleads by focusing on matters readily comprehensible to his readers
while omitting issues of legal observance which in fact
marked the dividing lines between parties.

Third, some scholars (e.g., J. Neusner) have suggested that Josephus in his *Antiquities* (which, in this
respect, is contrasted with his *Jewish War)* produced
propaganda for the Pharisees, exaggerating their
influence on the people in order to convince the
Roman authorities that any government installed in
Palestine needed Pharisaic support to survive. The
suggestion, while a healthy reminder that Josephus's
intentions must be taken into account, seems ill-
founded. The evidence for considerable Pharisaic
influence is not restricted to the *Antiquities.* Moreover,
references to Pharisaic influence in the *Antiquities* are,
considering the bulk of the work, few and confined to
its later sections. Negative assessments of the Pharisees are also found (especially 17.2.4 §41-45). Had
Josephus been motivated by the propagandistic
purpose ascribed to him, he was singularly optimistic
in hoping that the proper Roman officials would read
the twenty books of his history with unflagging
attention, ignore negative depictions of the Pharisees,
link in their minds the few scattered references to
Pharisaic influence in Books 13 and 18, and draw the

correct conclusions—without authorial prodding.

1.2. Rabbinic Literature. The use of rabbinic materials for our purposes is also problematic. Josephus's writings at least come from the first century; rabbinic literature from centuries later. Some of the references it contains to the $p^c r \hat{u} \check{s} \hat{i} m$ clearly intend a party (rival to the Sadducees) in the years before A.D. 70, though the historical value of even these traditions is not assured. Other references to $p^c r \hat{u} \check{s} \hat{i} m$ do not relate to the Pharisees.

Most vexed is the broad question of the relation between the Pharisees and subsequent rabbinic Judaism (*see* Judaism). A longstanding tradition interprets the post-70 period in Judaism as marking the triumph of Pharisaism over its rivals. The rabbis are seen as successors to the Pharisees, and rabbinic materials (often cited as the "Pharisaic-rabbinic tradition") are used to reconstruct Pharisaic positions. There are, to be sure, good reasons for positing substantial continuity between the Pharisees and the rabbis of the later period. Men called Pharisees in the NT and Josephus are recognized as authorities in rabbinic literature (Gamaliel; Simeon, son of Gamaliel). Pharisaic adherence to an extrabiblical "tradition from the fathers" corresponds nicely with rabbinic insistence on the validity of the oral as well as the written Torah. Belief in the resurrection is championed by both Pharisees and rabbis against opponents who deny it. When rabbinic literature juxtaposes positions of the Pharisees with those of the Sadducees (or others), the rabbis align themselves with the former. Nonetheless, it is an oversimplification to speak of the "Pharisaic-rabbinic tradition," nor can rabbinic literature be used uncritically as evidence for Pharisaic positions. In part, the question must be put to each tradition in the rabbinic texts whether it in fact preserves memories from the pre-70 period. If this is granted, we must still ask whether it is Pharisaic positions which are represented. Rabbinic Judaism was open to many influences not specifically Pharisaic, and it is perhaps significant that the rabbis did not choose to see themselves as Pharisees. According to Cohen the post-70 period marks not the triumph of Pharisaism but the end of sectarianism as it was known in the period prior to the destruction of Jerusalem (*see* Destruction of Jerusalem).

2. Name and History.

The derivation, force and use of the name "Pharisee" are all disputed. Commonly the name is traced to the Hebrew $p^c r \hat{u} \check{s} \hat{i} m$ and taken to mean "separatist." It is then debated whether the term's connotations were good or bad, and whether it was first used by Phari-

sees of themselves or of Pharisees by opponents. Recently, Baumgarten, noting that an evident claim of the Pharisees was to be the party of *akribeia*, of scrupulous exactness in their observance of God's laws, has suggested that behind the name "Pharisee" may lie the Hebrew $p \bar{a} r \hat{o} \check{s} \hat{i} m$, "specifiers" (i.e., of the correct understanding of the divine requirements).

Typically, the circumstances surrounding the origin of the Pharisaic party are lost to the historian's view. Many scholars see them as spiritual descendants of the Hasidim, a group of pious Jews who attached themselves to the Maccabean opposition to the Seleucid King, Antiochus IV Epiphanes (see Kampen). In the narrative of Josephus, Pharisees first appear in connection with the reign of John Hyrcanus. They are presented as a group with a defined set of laws and views of punishment which are alternately espoused and abrogated by Hasmonean monarchs. Herod's wrath is said to have been roused by the Pharisees, many of whom he is purported to have killed.

The character of the Pharisaic movement after the time of Herod is, again, in dispute. Neusner, granting that the Pharisees were a political force until Herod's time, claims that they then evolved into a non-political group concerned primarily with the preservation of ritual purity for the eating of ordinary meals: a political party became a table-fellowship sect. Not unrelated is the observation, noted above, that Neusner believes Josephus in his *Antiquities* has grossly exaggerated the power of the Pharisees in the pre-70 period. In fact they did not, Neusner insists, control the religious or political institutions of pre-destruction Judaism. But the distinction between political party and table-fellowship (*see* Table Fellowship) sect is a false one. Pharisees committed themselves to the scrupulous observance of a particular understanding of Israel's Law (cf. Phil 3:5). Since requirements of tithing and ritual purity (*see* Clean and Unclean) form a part of Israel's sacred tradition, it is likely that Pharisees of all periods followed a distinctive view of these requirements and, in order to ensure their observance at mealtimes, were restrictive in the company they kept (a "separateness" reflected in the usual understanding of the name *Pharisee*). In all periods, then, Pharisaism would have functioned in part as a table-fellowship sect.

But a party acknowledged to be the most accurate interpreters of Israel's Law could hardly have confined its attention—in any period—to tithing and ritual purity. A more comprehensive agenda is both inherently likely and attested by the sources. Were the Pharisees, then, a political party? Again, the designation misleads. Pharisees were drawn from all classes and professions of Jewish society; many would not have been involved in politics at all. On the other hand, since Pharisaism was based on a view of what Israel's responsibilities under the covenant entailed, those Pharisees who occupied positions of influence and power naturally did what they could to promote the acceptance of Pharisaic norms. In this sense Pharisees were involved in politics from Hasmonean times until the destruction of Jerusalem, though undoubtedly the effectiveness of their involvement underwent shifts.

In any case, given the diversity of first-century Jewish Palestine, Pharisees of necessity competed with rival groups for influence and power. Whereas they might at times succeed in influencing the proceedings of particular religious and political institutions, they controlled none. It is hard to believe, for example, that Sadducean priests would have taken directions from Pharisees in conducting Temple* worship. Nor should Pharisaic dominance of the Sanhedrin* or even the synagogues* be assumed. That the Sadducees could count on support from the priestly aristocracy underlines a further dilemma facing the Pharisees: with no certain power base, they needed to be aggressive both in attracting members and in promoting their views.

The evidence suggests that they achieved considerable success. Josephus describes the Pharisees as the leading sect (*J.W.* 2.8.14 §162). Both the rabbinic and Gospel materials appear to support the view that Pharisaic influence with the masses exceeded that of their rivals. Pharisaic claims of scrupulous piety and the preservation of ancestral laws were accorded wider circulation and support than any slogans the Sadducees or Essenes could devise (*Life* 191 §38; *J.W.* 1.5.2 §110; 2.8.14 §162; Acts 26:5). Indeed, the latter groups may have suffered in public estimation by their association, in the case of the Sadducees, with the Roman occupiers of the land (*see* Rome), and, in that of (some) Essenes, with none but themselves. Popular support was undoubtedly the main base of what influence the Pharisees possessed.

The Pharisees emerge then as an organized party of members committed to a particular understanding of Israel's Law, maintaining its practice themselves and advocating its adoption by others. Where rulers could be influenced, Pharisees lobbied for their views. Moreover, Pharisees were sufficiently schooled in the ways of the world to participate in councils and coalitions with rivals when the situation required it and common goals could be established (e.g., *J.W.* 2.17.3 §411; *Life* 20-23 §5). In this respect they functioned as a "political interest group" (Saldarini).

On the other hand, competition with rival groups was fierce and, fueled by the fervor of religious conviction, mutual denunciations were harsh. The tone of the pre-70 party debates found in rabbinic literature, the polemic against opponents found in the Dead Sea Scrolls (the Pharisees are apparently reproached as "seekers of smooth things"; *see* Dead Sea Scrolls), and the controversies and condemnations which fill the pages of the Gospels all attest to the bitter divisiveness which marked and (according to rabbinic literature) marred pre-destruction Judaism.

As far as we can tell, Pharisaism was a phenomenon of the pre-70 period. To depict the post-70 situation as the triumph of the Pharisees is oversimplistic and misleading. It was not until years later that the rabbis established effective leadership of the people; when they did so, they did not appear as Pharisees.

3. The Tradition of the Pharisees.
The adoption by Pharisees (and by later rabbis) of non-biblical prescriptions as binding law was on their part programmatic; for opponents, it served as an easy target for attack (*Ant.* 13.10.6 §297; Mk 7:6-13; perhaps 1QH 4:10). Much work remains to be done to define (where possible) the precise content of the Pharisaic tradition.

Particular attention was clearly given to matters of ritual purity and tithing, since the failure of the general populace to observe these laws according to Pharisaic norms compelled the Pharisees to regulate their own affairs in such a way as would ensure that their food was properly prepared. Many of the rulings preserved in rabbinic literature which can be traced with some confidence back to the Pharisees of the pre-70 era are in fact "party law" of this kind: not prescriptions thought to represent God's will for all Israel but necessary adaptations and applications of Pharisaic ideals to a situation in which the majority of Jews (the so-called people of the land) were, by Pharisaic standards, insufficiently observant. Rabbinic literature attests to distinctions drawn between the "people of the land," the "reliable" (i.e., people who could be trusted to observe certain requirements of purity and tithing), and full-fledged "associates" who had pledged to conform with defined standards, including the attempt to maintain ritual purity while eating ordinary meals. Relations between ordinary people and such associates inevitably required some definition. For example, the associate could not eat with outsiders. To some extent tithes had to be paid on what was purchased from a non-member, while foodstuff that was wet (and hence specially susceptible to impurity) could not be purchased from outsiders.

The state of the rules for associates in the time of Jesus is not known, nor can we be sure that all Pharisees were associates. But these rules do seem to reflect Pharisaic ideals and illustrate the Pharisaic goal of maintaining higher standards of ritual purity than were observed by ordinary Jews.

Generally, NT references are insufficiently specific to be of much help in defining Pharisaic legal positions. As exceptions we may note the use made of Mark 7:10-12 by A. I. Baumgarten and of Matthew 23:16-22 by S. Lieberman.

4. Pharisees in the Gospels.

In proclaiming to Israel the dawning reign of God, Jesus demanded a response quite different from that sought by the Pharisees, who summoned the nation to adhere to Torah's laws as interpreted by Pharisaic scribes. Since both were competing for the allegiance of the masses, conflict and mutual attempts to discredit might seem inevitable. Any perceived departure from Torah on the part of Jesus or his disciples was liable to be attacked by Pharisees. Disputes arising from apparent violations of Sabbath laws are especially frequent in the Gospels. Pharisees could be counted on to cite Deuteronomy 24 against Jesus' (widely attested) condemnation of divorce (Mk 10:2-9). Again, Jesus' open association (even at mealtimes) with notorious sinners could hardly have passed uncontested, providing as it did a stark contrast with Pharisaic efforts to cultivate careful adherence to the laws and Pharisaic scruples about mealtime company. In each of these cases, the Pharisees appear in the Gospels appropriately enough as the party advocating precision (*akribeia*) in the interpretation and performance of the Mosaic code.

The seriousness with which Pharisees would have regarded Jesus' departures from their norms is a matter of some debate. In a lengthy review of the issue E. P. Sanders (1990) has suggested that even if the conflict stories in the Gospels are historically reliable (and Sanders regards this as dubious), no significant conflict was involved. Disputes between groups within the Pharisaic movement, he suggests, were at least as substantial as were Pharisaic differences from the Sadducees. Yet the Pharisees had learned to tolerate those who did not share their views, worshiped with them at the Temple, and certainly did not regard those whose opinions on details of observance differed from their own as "sinners"* outside the pale of true Israel.* The latter category was restricted to those who lived in flagrant transgression of the fundamental laws of Israel's covenant. J. D. G. Dunn, responding to an earlier form of Sanders's position

(1985), thinks such a "quietistic" portrayal of Pharisees, absorbed in their own affairs and uncritical of others, highly unrealistic. And that Pharisees would have labelled outsiders to their ranks as "sinners" he finds plausible, given the evidence for contemporary usage of the term to disparage outsiders to one's faction.

On the latter point, and as far as the Gospel evidence is concerned, Sanders's position is to be favored. The "sinners" whose company Jesus kept were not so merely from a factional, Pharisaic viewpoint: It is not simply Pharisees, but "this generation," which reproaches his behavior (Mt 11:16-19). Furthermore, the use of the term for tax collectors (*see* Taxes) and prostitutes* (Mk 2:16; Lk 7:37; 19:7; etc.) and Jesus' acceptance of it as a designation of his companions (Mk 2:17; cf. Lk 7:47; Mt 21:31) make it clear that the notoriously wicked are intended.

On the other hand, there seems little point in attempting to establish how Pharisees would have responded to Jesus, or how accurately the Gospels portray their response, on the basis of the degree to which he departed from their norms. That would be a pressing issue only if deviation from Pharisaic standards constituted a crime for which Jesus was formally charged, but the Gospels do not suggest this happened. They do depict Jesus as rousing Pharisaic hostility by his actions, a claim which is not easy to dismiss. After all, the passion with which a person responds when their convictions are ignored and their sensibilities offended often says more about their personality, and even about other aspects of their relations with the offender, than about the seriousness of the offense. Moreover, the tolerance which Sanders finds characteristic of the Pharisees as a group (a tolerance which, incidentally, he believes they had only recently learned, and which he maintains without considering the behavior of Paul the Pharisee) can hardly be guaranteed of all its members.

Finally, tolerance, even if a part, is not the whole explanation for Pharisaic worship with Sadducees and others at the Temple: Their own commitment to the institution, combined with the impossibility of dictating its procedures, must surely be taken into account. The broad picture of Pharisees in conflict with Jesus seems well rooted in the Gospel tradition. It also seems consistent with, and inevitable in the light of, their different understandings of the divine will.

For Jesus' part the "old wineskins" could not contain "new wine" (Mk 2:22; *see* Wine). Believing that a new divine initiative had begun, the Jesus of the Gospels is exasperated by Pharisaic failure to discern and respond to the significance of the moment (Mk

2:19; 8:11-12; cf. Mt 21:28-32; 23:13). In the well-known parable* of the prodigal son (Lk 15:11-32) Jesus defends his association with "sinners" by arguing in effect that God is even now demonstrating his love to the most profligate of his people. Those of the Pharisaic ilk are represented in the figure of the sulking older brother, whose offended sensibilities keep him from partaking of the family feast.

The criticisms directed in the Gospels against the Pharisees go beyond their failure to respond to the message of the kingdom. Pharisaic claims of meticulous observance are depicted as leading both to pride (Mt 23:5-7; Lk 11:43; cf. *Ant.* 17.2.4 §41) and to contempt for the less observant—an unwarranted contempt, since the latter in turn are portrayed as more sensitive to their failings, more open to Jesus' proclamation of God's sovereignty and love* (Lk 7:37-50; 15:1-32; 18:9-14; 19:1-10). Again, the attention to the minutiae of tithing and ritual purity required by Pharisaic scruples would inevitably appear to an opponent with a different focus as evidence of distorted perspectives; hence the attack on those who tithe mint, dill and cummin while neglecting the essentials of the Law; the charge that cleansing cups is combined by Pharisees with inner corruption (Mt 23:23, 25-26; cf. the charge of corruption in *Ant.* 17.2.4 §41-45). Jesus' penchant for the striking picture and his attacks on expressions of Pharisaic piety are both to be recognized in the caricature of people who strain out gnats and swallow camels (Mt 23:24), or who turn the appointed hour of prayer* into a recitation of their merits (Lk 18:9-12).

Charges of this sort are rooted in different views of Israel's task and opportunity, and were certainly raised already in the lifetime of Jesus. That confrontation continued in the post-resurrection period can be seen in the attempts of the Pharisee Paul to show his "zeal" for his ancestral faith by persecuting the church (Phil 3:5-6; cf. Gal 1:13-14). The Gospels' depictions of Pharisees reflect both memories from the career of Jesus and subsequent developments in the Christian communities.

4.1. Mark. Mark's community was scarcely one which experienced Pharisaic opposition at firsthand; indeed, the Evangelist must explain Jewish customs for his readers (7:1-4). Part of the reason Pharisees are remembered may well be that some account had to be given, in a Gospel of the crucified Son of God (*see* Son of God), of how his appearance roused hostility. Conflicts arise over Jesus' association with sinners (2:16) and the failure of Jesus or his disciples to conform to norms of fasting* (2:18), Sabbath observance (2:24; 3:2) and purity (7:5). The propriety of divorce* is also disputed (10:2-9). The confrontations are said to lead Pharisees to plot against Jesus (3:6). Further inquiries, with malicious intent, are brought to Jesus (8:11; 12:13). The Markan Jesus responds, sometimes sharply (cf. 7:6-13), to such queries, but otherwise he devotes no attention to Pharisees.

Clearly the teaching of the Pharisees represented no attraction for Mark's readers. On the contrary, the old order has passed for Mark (2:22). Its food laws, the subject of considerable controversy in parts of the early church, are perceived in Mark as irrelevant and unproblematic (7:19). Consequently, the Pharisaic endeavor can only be seen as serving no purpose. But the hostility which the Pharisees showed toward Jesus remains a part of the tradition and determines their portrayal as hypocrites, unfaithful to God's Word in the past (7:6-13) and insensitive to his dealings in the present (8:11-12). Worth noting, however, is Mark 12:28-34. Since the scribe who admired Jesus' reply to the Sadducees was probably a Pharisee, the passage suggests that there were Pharisees whose views of what is fundamental overlapped substantially with those of Jesus. But Mark himself makes no mention of the scribe's party affiliation.

4.2. Matthew. Matthew's community, which includes both Jewish and Gentile* Christians, clearly lives in an environment with a noticeable Jewish presence. Relations are tense, and the Matthean community perceives itself to be the object of persecution (cf. 5:10-12; 10:17-18; 23:34). Much in the Gospel is intended to support Matthew's claim, maintained in the teeth of Jewish counter-claims, that the appearance of Jesus represents the climax of Israel's sacred history (most emphatically, 5:17) and that followers of Jesus—Jews and Gentiles alike—have displaced the unbelieving and disobedient "sons of the kingdom" as the people of God (8:10-12; 21:43). Great emphasis is placed on the differences to be observed between the piety of those who follow Jesus and that of Jews who do not: The latter is portrayed as superficial, hypocritical (*see* Hypocrite) and ostentatious (5:20; 6:1-18). Pharisees, the epitome of such religiosity (23:4-7), are always hostile to Jesus in Matthew's Gospel, and the attention paid to their teaching witnesses to its relevance for Matthew's readers (especially chap. 23).

Though some would see in Matthew a Christian response to Pharisaic hegemony within Judaism of the post-70 period, it is unlikely that contemporaries perceived Judaism in those terms. The roots of the anti-Pharisaic polemic are better seen in the factiousness prevailing before the war. On the other hand, Garland has shown the Evangelist's intention in assembling the "woes" of Matthew 23 (*see* Blessing and

Woe): The chapter reaches its climax in verses 35-39 (see v. 38) and is deliberately juxtaposed with prophecies of Jerusalem's destruction in chapter 24. Thus the Evangelist is attributing Jerusalem's devastation to divine judgment* on the sins of the "scribes and Pharisees" as false leaders of the people.

4.3. Luke. Luke's Pharisees present a more complex picture. In part this is because they appear in Acts as well, where they are at times comparatively sympathetic to the Christian movement (Acts 5:33-39; 23:9; cf. 15:5). Paul's own Pharisaic ties are exploited and never explicitly renounced (23:6; 26:5; cf. 22:3). In Luke Jesus eats in the homes of Pharisees (7:36; 11:37; 14:1) and is warned by Pharisees of Herod's plots (13:31). On the other hand, conflicts remain (5:21, 30-35; 6:1-11; 15:2), as do the familiar charges of hypocrisy (11:38-41; 12:1), distorted perspectives (11:42), ostentation (11:43-44) and self-righteousness (18:9-14). To these, new accusations (16:14) and instances of ill-will (19:39) have been added. It is unlikely that Pharisaism had a contemporary relevance for Luke. The negative depiction which had become established in the tradition is preserved. Indeed, Pharisees serve Luke's purposes in providing a foil for Jesus' attitude toward sinners (cf. particularly the parable of the prodigal son, peculiar to Luke [15:11-32]). Still, the negative note is tempered somewhat by Luke's desire to show continuity between the Christian movement and its Jewish heritage (Lk 24:25-27; Acts 23:6; 25:14-15; 26:6-7, 22-23; 28:20).

4.4. John. As a rule, John paints Judaism with a broad brush. Jesus' opponents appear often simply as "Jews" without more specific identification (*see* John, Gospel of). Where Pharisees do figure, they are often represented as holding positions of power and acting in collaboration with other authorities (3:1; 7:32, 45; 11:47, 57; 12:42; 18:3). One at least is sympathetic toward Jesus (3:1; 7:50-51), but hostility predominates. The opposition of Pharisees is perceptively motivated in their own terms in 9:16; elsewhere it is attributed to spiritual obstinacy (9:39-41).

5. Conclusion.

Gospel texts depicting certain Pharisees, when detached from their historical context and seen as portraying Jewish piety as a whole, have prevented Christians from arriving at a sympathetic understanding of Judaism. The concern of much contemporary scholarship to portray Judaism (and Pharisaism) in its own terms represents an important corrective. But it must be combined with an insistence on reading the Gospels in their historical setting. Pharisees and the earliest followers of Jesus—all Jews—stood for alter-native visions of the destiny and responsibilities of Israel. Doubtless there lie at the root of some of the mutual denunciations instances of abuse and the failure of behavior to match ideals, At a deeper level, however, lay the conflict of convictions deeply held about the course which Israel must pursue, and that from which they must turn, if they were to fulfill their divine calling (cf. Rom 10:2; the career of Paul saw him fervently maintain both sides of the dispute). First-century Judaism was the setting for many such disputes, the result of common convictions about Israel's past combined with different readings of what Israel's God now demanded of his people.

See also JUDAISM; LAW; RABBINIC TRADITIONS AND WRITINGS; SCRIBES.

BIBLIOGRAPHY. A. I. Baumgarten, "*Korban* and the Pharisaic Paradosis," *JANES* 16-17 (1984-85) 5-17; idem, "The Name of the Pharisees," *JBL* 102 (1983) 411-28; idem, "The Pharisaic Paradosis," *HTR* 80 (1987) 63-77; R. L. Brawley, *Luke-Acts and the Jews: Conflict, Apology, and Conciliation* (Atlanta: Scholars, 1987); S. J. D. Cohen, "The Significance of Yavneh: Pharisees, Rabbis, and the End of Jewish Sectarianism," *HUCA* 55 (1984) 27-53; D. E. Cook, "A Gospel Portrait of the Pharisees," *RevExp* 84 (1987) 221-33; J. D. G. Dunn, *Jesus, Paul and the Law* (Louisville: Westminster/John Knox, 1990) 61-88; D. E. Garland, *The Intention of Matthew 23* (Leiden: Brill, 1979); J. Kampen, *The Hasideans and the Origin of Pharisaism* (Atlanta: Scholars, 1988); S. Lieberman, *Greek in Jewish Palestine* (New York: P. Feldheim, 1965) 115-43; S. N. Mason, "Was Josephus a Pharisee? A Re-Examination of Life 10-12," *JJS* 40 (1989) 31-45; J. Neusner, *From Politics to Piety* (Englewood Cliffs, NJ: Prentice-Hall, 1973); E. Rivkin, *A Hidden Revolution: The Pharisees' Search for the Kingdom Within* (Nashville: Abingdon, 1978); A. J. Saldarini, *Pharisees, Scribes and Sadducees in Palestinian Society* (Wilmington, DE: Michael Glazier, 1988); E. P. Sanders, *Jesus and Judaism* (Philadelphia: Fortress, 1985); idem, *Jewish Law from Jesus to the Mishnah* (Philadelphia: Trinity Press International, 1990); D. R. Schwartz, "Josephus and Nicolaus on the Pharisees," *JSJ* 14 (1983) 157-71; S. Westerholm, *Jesus and Scribal Authority* (Lund: CWK Gleerup, 1978).

S. Westerholm

PHILIP. *See* DISCIPLES.

PHILIP THE TETRARCH. *See* HERODIAN DYNASTY.

PIETY. *See* BENEFACTOR; JUSTICE, RIGHTEOUSNESS; PRAYER.

PONTIUS PILATE

Roman governor of Judea A.D. 26-36/37 (*see* Rome) who was involved in the trial of Jesus in A.D. 33.

1. Sources for Pilate
2. Reign of Pilate
3. Trial of Jesus
4. Recall of Pilate

1. Sources for Pilate.

The little that is known of Pilate is from the account of his governorship of Judea in Josephus* (*Ant* 18.2.2 §35; 3.1-2 §§55-62; 4.1-2 §§85-89; *J.W.* 2.9.2-4 §§169-77), from an episode given in Philo (*Leg. Gai.* 299-305), from his participation in the trial of Jesus (*see* Trial of Jesus) recorded in the four Gospels, and from a brief mention by Tacitus that the execution of "Christus" was by Pilate in the reign of Tiberius (*Ann.* 15.44.4). Also, in 1961 an incomplete inscription was found in Caesarea which gives the correct technical title of his position as *praefectus Iudaeae*, a military title of a commander of auxiliary troops (500-1,000 soldiers) rather than *procurator,* a financial officer of a province, or *governor,* a general term for leader which is consistently used in the NT.

2. Reign of Pilate.

According to Philo it seems that Pilate obtained his position via his mentor Sejanus, the commander of the Praetorian Guard (Philo *Leg. Gai.* 159). Pilate is described by his contemporary Philo, and later by Josephus, as being one who was greedy, inflexible, cruel, and who resorted to robbery and oppression (Philo *Leg. Gai.* 301-2; Josephus *Ant.* 18.3.1 §§55-59; *J.W.* 2.9.2-4 §§169-77).

Pilate is known to have treated Jewish customs with contempt (*see* Judaism). Almost immediately upon his arrival in Palestine in A.D. 26, he was at odds with the Jews. His first act of provocation against the Jews was the introduction into Jerusalem of Roman standards with embossed figures of the emperor. Previous prefects had been careful not to offend Jewish religious views by not allowing any sign of emperor worship when the troops entered Jerusalem. This act of Pilate aroused great indignation on the part of the Jews, and as a result they sent a delegation to Caesarea who pled for five days for removal of the standards. Pilate on the sixth day ordered a detachment of soldiers among the crowd, and at a given signal they would draw their swords. When this occurred, all the Jews bared their necks and stated that they would rather die than transgress their laws. Pilate, realizing that this might lead to a national revolution, removed the offensive images from Jerusalem (Josephus *J.W.*

2.9.2-3 §§169-74; *Ant.* 18.3.1 §§55-59; *see* Revolutionary Movements).

Josephus's second recorded conflict was when Pilate seized funds from the sacred treasury known as the *Corbonas* in order to construct an aqueduct. Later, when Pilate visited Jerusalem, the Jews besieged him with angry clamor and he, seeing the possibility of an uprising, ordered his soldiers to mingle among the crowd dressed as civilians armed with hidden clubs. When the protest became more pronounced, the soldiers, on a prearranged signal, drew the clubs from under their tunics and began to beat the protestors, killing many (Josephus *J.W.* 2.9.3 §§172-74; *Ant.* 18.3.2 §§60-62).

The final conflict recorded by Josephus is one that caused Pilate's dismissal. In A.D. 36 a Samaritan* false prophet promised his followers that he would show them the sacred vessels which, according to tradition, Moses had buried on Mount Gerizim. Many believed him and gathered with arms at a village at the foot of the mountain, but Pilate blocked the projected route with a detachment of cavalry and heavily armed infantry. Some of the followers were killed in battle, others were imprisoned, still others fled. The more prominent prisoners were later executed. The Samaritans complained to Vitellius, prefect of Syria, who shortly afterwards sent Marcellus to take temporary charge of Judea, ordering Pilate to report to Tiberius (Josephus *Ant.* 18.4.1-2 §§85-89).

Philo, who extols Tiberius's liberal policy toward the Jews, records the episode when Pilate had set up gilded votive shields bearing the name, though not the image, of the emperor in the former palace of Herod in Jerusalem (an incident to be distinguished from his earlier placement in Jerusalem of standards bearing the embossed figure of the emperor). Prominent Jews, including the four sons of Herod, appealed to Pilate to remove the shields. But when he refused to hear their request, they wrote to the Emperor Tiberius. Upon receiving the letter, Tiberius was enraged and immediately replied, ordering Pilate to remove the shields from Jerusalem and place them in the temple of Augustus at Caesarea (*Leg. Gai.* 299-305). Unlike the previous incident of the standards, prominent Jews and Herod's sons were able now to write directly to Tiberius, an event made possible by Sejanus's execution by Tiberius on October 18, A.D. 31. Tiberius was now trying to reverse Sejanus's anti-Semitic policies and hence gave a quick response to the Jews' request.

But why would Pilate have done such a thing when he had already been defeated in the incident of the standards? It seems that with the removal of his mentor Sejanus, whose anti-Semitic policies he had followed, Pilate wanted to dissociate himself from Sejanus and ingratiate himself with Tiberius. Consequently, he brought into Jerusalem shields that had no image but bore the name of the emperor. But the plan backfired and Tiberius was sorely displeased. The most likely time for this incident to have occurred is at a Jewish festival when the sons of Herod would have been in Jerusalem, possibly the Feast of Tabernacles in A.D. 32,

The NT mentions a little-known incident of Pilate mixing the blood of the Galileans with their sacrifices (Lk 13:1). The interpretation of this incident seems to intimate that Pilate had killed some Galileans when they were offering sacrifices at Jerusalem. Although nothing else is known of this event, it fits the assessment of Josephus and Philo regarding Pilate's brutal character.

3. Trial of Jesus.

The Jewish leaders brought Jesus to Pilate early on Friday morning of passion week, accusing Jesus of setting himself up as king (Mt 27:1-2, 11-14; Mk 15:1-5; Lk 23:1-5; John 18:28-38). When Pilate found no wrong in Jesus, and when the Jewish leaders suggested that Jesus had caused trouble both in Judea and Galilee, Pilate sent Jesus to Herod Antipas who was ruler over Galilee (Lk 23:6-12). Herod took no action and sent him back to Pilate, who then wanted to release him. However, Pilate finally gave in to the pressure of the Jewish leaders when they threatened him with the accusation of not being a friend of Caesar (Mt 27:15-26; Mk 15:6-15; Lk 23:13-25; Jn 18:39—19:15). Hence the Gospels portray Pilate in the trial of Jesus as one who was weak and willing to comply with the wishes of the Jewish leaders against his own desires.

This profile of Pilate's character is quite different from that given by Philo and Josephus. Historical explanations vary according to the dating of the crucifixion. If Jesus was crucified in A.D. 30, Pilate may have been trying to be conciliatory toward Herod Antipas (see Herodian Dynasty) because of the little-known episode of Pilate mixing the blood of the Galileans—Antipas' citizens—with their sacrifices (Lk 13:1). If Jesus was crucified in A.D. 33, the removal of Pilate's mentor Sejanus, and his failure to ingratiate himself with the emperor, may have broken Pilate's backbone and left him fighting for political survival. He might then have handed Jesus over to Herod Antipas in order to prevent Herod from making another unfavorable report to Tiberius as he had done within the last few months (as one of the sons

of Herod). In this event, Herod Antipas took no action and handed Jesus back to Pilate so that Pilate could gain no advantage, for Herod also had been a friend of Sejanus.

One further problem needs to be addressed. Luke states that Pilate and Herod became friends from that day forward (Lk 23:12). If this took place in A.D. 30 (see Chronology), it would imply that the settlement between Pilate and Antipas regarding Pilate's slaying of the Galileans accounts for the enmity that was overcome (Lk 23:12). But there was a fierce battle after Sejanus's death in A.D. 31, and thus some would conclude that if Jesus was executed in A.D. 30, Luke is in error regarding the relationship between Pilate and Herod. Another criticism from scholars holding to A.D. 30 crucifixion is that the portrayal of an anemic Pilate in the Gospels (compared with the Pilate of Josephus and Philo) betrays the anti-Semitic bias of the Evangelists (see Anti-Semitism). Pilate is absolved from blame and the Jewish people are held responsible for Jesus' death (see Death of Jesus).

However, if Jesus was crucified in A.D. 33, the reconciliation of the enmity between Pilate and Herod Antipas becomes more historically realistic. The Jews, having only recently received the news of Sejanus's death (possibly during the winter of 32/33 or early 33), threatened Pilate that if he did not release Jesus, he was not a friend of Caesar (Jn 19:12). Pilate realized the reverse of this was that the Jews would regard him as still being a friend of Sejanus and/or friendly toward his policies which Tiberius had now repudiated. Hence Pilate's compliance with the Jews during the trial of Jesus would be fully understandable in light of recent events that made him more cautious.

4. Recall of Pilate.

Because of the Samaritan complaint to Vitellius, prefect of Syria, Pilate was deposed at the end of A.D. 36 or at the beginning of 37. He arrived in Rome after Tiberius's death (March 16, 37). There are no records of his life after his travel to Rome, and he may well have been exiled to the southern part of France. The Christian tradition reported by Eusebius is that Pilate committed suicide after his trial of Jesus (Eusebius *Hist. Eccl.* 2.7).

See also HERODIAN DYNASTY; ROME; TRIAL OF JESUS.

BIBLIOGRAPHY. E. Bammel, "The Trial before Pilate," in *Jesus and the Politics of His Day*, ed. E. Bammel and C. F. D. Moule (Cambridge: University Press, 1984) 415-51; H. W. Hoehner, *Herod Antipas* (SNTSMS 17; Cambridge: University Press, 1972) 172-83; idem, "Why Did Pilate Hand Jesus over to Pilate?" in *The Trial of Jesus: Cambridge Studies in Honour of C. F. D.*

Moule, ed. E. Bammel (SBT 13; London: SCM, 1970) 84-90; E. Schürer, *The History of the Jewish People in the Age of Jesus Christ (175 B.C.-A.D. 135)*, rev. and ed. G. Vermes, F. Millar (3 vols.; Edinburgh: T. & T. Clark, 1973-79) I.383-88; E. M. Smallwood, *Jews under Roman Rule* (Leiden: E. J. Brill, 1976) 160-74; idem, "Philo and Josephus as Historians of the Same Events," in *Josephus, Judaism, and Christianity*, ed. by L. H. Feldman and G. Hata (Detroit: Wayne State University, 1987) 114-29; M. Stern, "The Province of Judea," in *The Jewish People in the First Century*, ed. S. Safrai and M. Stern (CRINT 1:1; Philadelphia: Fortress, 1974) 308-76.   H. W. Hoehner

POOR. *See* RICH AND POOR.

POSSESSIONS. *See* RICH AND POOR.

POVERTY. *See* RICH AND POOR.

POWER. *See* AUTHORITY AND POWER.

PRAYER

1. Jewish Prayer at the Time of Jesus
2. Jesus' Practice of Prayer
3. Jesus' *Abba* Prayer
4. Jesus' Teaching on Prayer: The Lord's Prayer
5. Jesus' Teaching on Prayer: The Main Emphases

1. Jewish Prayer at the Time of Jesus.

The Jews (*see* Judaism) were a praying people. Their sacred writings contain many prayers which no doubt were regularly used as such, and the Qumran Scrolls (*see* Dead Sea Scrolls) and Jewish apocrypha and pseudepigrapha attest a continuing creativity in Jewish formulation and practice of prayer. The Temple* was called a "house of prayer" (Is 56:7), and the sacrifices were accompanied by prayers (Sir 50:19; Josephus *Ag. Ap.* 2.196; Lk 1:10), so that the hour of sacrifice (morning and evening) could be called simply "the hour of prayer" (Acts 3:1; see Cohen). The Jewish meeting places (synagogues*) were also distinctive in the ancient world precisely as places of prayer and could be represented simply by the word *prayer*, given an extended meaning to signify "prayer-house" or "place of prayer" (Josephus *Life* 277; *Ag. Ap.* 2.10; see LSJ and BAGD, *proseuchē*). The synagogue prayers were probably not said in unison but by the person called on by the ruler of the synagogue to lead in prayer, with the congregation responding, "Amen" (cf. Neh 8:6; 1 Chron 16:36; Tob 8:8; 1QS 1:20; 1 Cor 14:16; *m. Ber.* 8:8; *m. Ta'an.* 2:5). Every adult member was entitled to exercise this privilege (cf. *m. Meg.* 4:6).

Prayer would be offered standing (cf. Mt 6:5; Mk 11:25; Lk 18:11; *m. Ber.* 5:1).

The prayer of prayers for the Jews subsequently, but probably at the time of Jesus too, was the *Shemoneh Esreh*, the Eighteen Benedictions. It was probably given this form in the period A.D. 70-100, but several at least of the more elaborate eighteenfold form would certainly have been known to and used by Jesus. Characteristic of each is the final response or blessing (hence the title): "Blessed are you, Lord . . ."—"shield of Abraham," "who makes the dead alive," "who delights in repentance," "rich in forgiveness," "who humbles the insolent," "who builds Jerusalem," "who hears prayer."

Another ancient Jewish prayer whose earliest form probably goes back to the time of Jesus, the *Qaddish*, is of particular interest to Christians, since it may well have been used by Jesus in formulating the Lord's Prayer. The earliest form known to us begins thus:

> Exalted and hallowed be his great name in the world, which he created according to his will.
> May he establish his kingdom in your lifetime and in your days, and in the lifetime of the whole household of Israel, speedily and at a near time.

The fact that these prayers were already so well established does not signify a high degree of formalism in Jewish prayer at the time of Jesus. On the contrary, the different forms of these prayers shows that they are part of a developing tradition. The innovativeness of Jewish practice is clearly indicated also by the continuing composition of psalms and prayers (as again at Qumran and in the Hellenistic synagogal prayers preserved in the Christian *Apostolic Constitutions*). And we should also note the rabbinic rulings preserved in Mishnah, *Berakot* 4:3-4, to the effect that it is necessary to pray only the substance of the Eighteen Benedictions unless the pray-er's prayer "is fluent in his mouth," and that a mechanical repetition of prayer is no (real) supplication.

The tradition of every Jew praying twice a day, at sunrise and sunset, at the third and ninth hours, the hours of sacrifice, is very old (Ezra 9:5; Dan 9:21; Jdt 9:1; *Pss. Sol.* 6:4); it is attributed to Moses* by Josephus* (*Ant.* 4.212), was certainly the practice of the Essenes (as can now be seen particularly from the fragmentary 4Q 503), and was regularized in the Mishnah as an accompaniment to the saying of the *Shema* (*m. Ber.* 1:1-4). But there is also the old tradition of prayer at mid-day (the sixth hour), giving three hours of prayer (Ps 55:17; Dan 6:10; *m. Ber.* 4:1; implied also by *2 Enoch* 51:4; Acts 10:9; *Did.* 8.3).

Also to be noted is the established tradition of

giving thanks to God* before a meal (Deut 8:10), carefully regulated at Qumran (Josephus *J.W.* 2.131; 1QS 6:4-5) and in the Mishnah (*m. Ber.* 6-8), and followed both by Jesus (Mk 6:41 par.; 8:6-7 par.; 14:22-23 par.) and by the first Christians (Rom 14:6; 1 Cor 10:30; 1 Tim 4:4). The typical thanksgiving over the bread would be: "Blessed are you, Lord, who brings forth bread from the earth."

2. Jesus' Practice of Prayer.

We do not know for certain but may assume that Jesus was brought up to say the *Shema* and the Eighteen Benedictions twice a day (cf. Mk 12:29). The fact that he regarded the Temple pre-eminently (?) as "a house of prayer" (Mk 11:17 par.; cf. Is 56:7), or is so remembered, suggests that prayer was central for Jesus within the much larger ritual and sacrificial ritual focussed on the Temple (contrast Mt 17:24-6). And it was evidently his regular practice to attend the synagogue on the Sabbath* (Lk 4:16), when he would no doubt join with the rest in the prayers; although the particular occasions recalled by the Evangelists speak only of his teaching and preaching (Mk 1:21-29 par.; 1:39 par.; 3:1 par.; 6:2 par.; Mt 9:35; Lk 4:15-16; 13:10).

However, Jesus' own practice of prayer is vividly recalled in all the Gospels. Mark 1:35 recalls an occasion when Jesus had gone off "a great while before day" to "a lonely place" to pray. And again in 6:46 he went off again alone, up the mountainside (*see* Mountain and Wilderness) to pray, evidently through the evening and into the night. Mark's third account finds Jesus in the Garden of Gethsemane* (14:35-42), when again Jesus is recounted as praying well into the night. Two points are worthy of note. (1) Although his praying covered the usual times of prayer, morning and evening, his need of prayer, at least on these occasions, went far beyond the formal saying of prayers. (2) Each of the occasions recalled by Mark seems to have been a time of decision and temptation (*see* Temptation of Jesus) regarding the character and emphases of his vocation. This would explain the longer time spent in prayer on these occasions. Consequently, the Markan account should not be regarded as indicating Jesus' normal practice of prayer.

Matthew follows Mark's second account (Mt 14:23), and both Matthew and Luke record the Gethsemane prayer (Mt 26:36-46; Lk 22:40-46). Matthew and Luke (Q*) also share the record of Jesus' prayer in Matthew 11:25-26 and Luke 10:21. But in addition Luke records a further eight occasions when Jesus prayed—following his baptism* (3:21), following his early success (5:16; equivalent to Mk 1:35), prior to his choosing the

Twelve (6:12-13; *see* Disciple), prior to Peter's confession (9:18), on the mountain of Transfiguration* (9:28-29; closely parallel to 3:21), prior to his teaching the Lord's Prayer (11:1) and twice on the cross (23:34 and 46; *see* Death of Jesus). Why Luke contains so many extra recollections of Jesus at prayer is not clear, but it certainly matches the emphasis he also gives to Jesus' teaching on prayer (see 5. below). Evidently, only Luke wants to present Jesus as a model of prayerful piety (Lk 11:1-4; cf. Lk 3:21-22 with Acts 1:14 and 2:1-4; Lk 6:12-13 with Acts 13:2-3; and Lk 23:34 with Acts 7:60). But we need not doubt that he was able to draw on a substantial living memory of Jesus as a man of prayer.

The instances recorded by the Fourth Evangelist, on the other hand, are curiously stylized and artificial: in 11:41-42, he prays not for his own benefit, but "on account of the people standing by"; in 12:27-28, he denies the sort of distress and petition the Synoptics attribute to him in Gethsemane; in 17:1-26, without parallel in the other Gospels. John's purpose is clearly very different from Luke's on this topic: to portray Jesus as the incarnate (Son of) God rather than as the Jewish Messiah (Son of God*) dependent on prayer (*see* Christ).

In short, even when the Evangelists' pastoral and apologetic motivations are discounted, the evidence is still clear and consistent: that Jesus was a man of prayer whose natural response particularly to situations of crisis and decision was to seek God alone in prayer.

3. Jesus' *Abba* Prayer.

A great deal has been made during the past forty years of Jesus' style of address to God and its significance. Jeremias made the case for Jesus having regularly addressed God by the Aramaic word *'abbā'* (*see* Languages of Palestine); and he also noted that *'abbā'* was "a child's word"; and this led too quickly to the conclusion that *'abbā'* meant "Daddy"—an early conclusion which Jeremias soon qualified, but which has come back to haunt the study of the Gospel traditions ever since.

The basic evidence is clear and Jeremias's initial conclusion probably sound. The key evidence is the appearance of *abba* itself in Mark 14:36. Added to that is the clear attestation that the same form was used by the early Christians (Rom 8:15; Gal 4:6). Two points of significance are to be noted in the last two passages. (1) The Aramaic word was retained in the worship* of the Greek-speaking churches. This must mean both that this particular prayer address had become so established among the earliest Palestinian believers and so precious for them that it was carried over into Greek-speaking worship. That is to say, its continuing value lay not in its meaningfulness to Greek speakers but in the meaningfulness of the living tradition of prayer which it expressed. (2) It is remembered as a word particularly associated with Jesus: to say *abba* is to share in a common sonship and a common inheritance with Jesus (Rom 8:16-17; Gal 4:6-7; cf. 8:29). This must mean that the word was recalled as a word particularly and peculiarly associated with Jesus' own sonship to God (*see* Son of God). Were it a common prayer idiom of (some) Jews at the time of Jesus (as some have suggested, without supporting evidence), it would not have had this significance of linking the one who said *abba* so distinctively and directly with the sonship of Jesus.

It is true that *abba* occurs nowhere else in the Gospels, including the traditions of Jesus' prayers. But in each stratum of the Gospel tradition Jesus is recalled as praying, and on each occasion the address is *patēr/pater* ("Father"; Mk 14:36; Mt 11:25-6 par. Lk 10:21; Lk 23:34, 46; Mt 26:42; Jn 11:41; 12:27-28; 17:1, 5, 11, 21, 24-25). In the light of Romans 8:15-17 and Galatians 4:6-7 Jeremias's conclusion must be judged fair: that underlying the Greek *patēr,* or "Father," was the Aramaic *'abbā'*. In this case the further conclusion is sound: that *'abbā'* was Jesus' regular and characteristic address to God. The only recorded prayer of Jesus which does not address God as "Father" is Mark 15:34 (par. Mt 27:46)—"My God, my God, why have you forsaken me?" But here the words are those of Psalm 22:1, and the very sense of forsakenness which they express may well be sufficient explanation of why the more familiar *'abbā'* did not come so naturally to Jesus' lips on that occasion.

Jeremias made the further claim that this form of prayer address was without parallel in Palestinian piety. This was overstating the case, since there are records of individuals addressing God as "Father" with a degree of intimacy which could have been expressed in the Aramaic *'abbā'* (Wis 14:3; Sir 23:1, 4; 51:10; 3 Macc 6:3, 8; *m. Ta'an.* 3:8). Nevertheless, the typical address to God, as in the Eighteen Benedictions, is a good deal more formal and had the practice been widespread among the Jews it could hardly have been regarded as distinctive of Jesus and his disciples, as a distinctive hallmark of the Spirit of the Son, in the way that Romans 8:15-17 and Galatians 4:6-7 clearly imply. So the likelihood remains that Jesus was marked out among his fellow Jews at least in the fact that *'abbā'* was his characteristic and regular form of address to God in prayer.

The reason why *'abbā'* would be so little used is presumably because it was typically a family word, or expressive of a degree of intimacy with reverence which would be characteristic of children (but not just little children) within the family circle, or of disciples of a loved and revered teacher.* This more qualified statement of the case can probably be defended quite adequately even in the face of the criticisms brought against the more simplistic equating of *'abbā'* with "Daddy." If so, we may still deduce that the reason why Jesus used the word so regularly in prayer was that he experienced his relationship with God through prayer as such a relation of intimacy and reverence. The earliest disciples likewise retained the usage because they too experienced prayer thus prompted by the Spirit as a relationship of sonship—but not of a sonship independent of Jesus' sonship. Rather, their relationship was dependent on his *abba* sonship and shared in his inheritance as God's Son.

The importance of this conclusion for the larger concerns of Christian theology can hardly be underestimated. (1) The subsequent classic Christian understanding of Jesus as God's Son is firmly rooted in Jesus' own sense of intimate sonship to God. It is not that a unique category was thrust upon Jesus (the Son of God) to give him a status he had not claimed. It is rather that a less specific term of relationship (God's son), shared by angel,* king, righteous individual or charismatic rabbi, and indicating God's approval and evident favor, became filled and absorbed by the distinctive character of Jesus' sonship, and thus came to be seen as uniquely applicable to him (*see* Son of God). (2) This Christian assertion did not begin as a theological assertion but in Jesus' own experience of intimate sonship and specifically in his experience of prayer. So too it was confirmed in the earliest days of Christianity by the first Christians' shared experience of sonship, in the shared experience of prayer, as a participation in his sonship or, alternatively expressed, as an access to God as Father in prayer through and by virtue of Jesus' own sonship. This integration of christology, soteriology and spirituality, of doctrine and experience, is thus at the heart of Christianity.

4. Jesus' Teaching on Prayer: The Lord's Prayer.

Jesus not only lived out the practice of prayer, but prayer was also one of the most consistent themes in his teaching. Moreover, the teaching reflects the practice—another integration fundamental to Christianity. This is evident at once in the opening of the Lord's Prayer. Since it is the single most important part of Jesus' teaching on prayer and the most characteristic prayer of Christians from then on, it will be given particular attention.

4.1. The Form of the Prayer. The Lord's Prayer is preserved in two forms: Matthew 6:9-13 and Luke 11:2-4 (*Did.* 8:2 is virtually the same as Matthew).

Matthew 6:9-13	Luke 11:2-4
1. Our Father who is in the heavens.	Father,
2. May your name be sanctified.	May your name be sanctified.
3. May your kingdom come.	May your kingdom come.
4. May your will be done,	
5. as in heaven, so on earth.	
6. Give us today the bread we need;	Give us each day the bread we need;
7. And forgive us our debts.	And forgive us our sins,
8. as we also have forgiven those in debt to us.	for we ourselves forgive everyone who is indebted to us.
9. And do not bring us to the test,	And do not bring us to the test.
10. but deliver us from evil.	

While it is possible that Jesus taught the twofold form on different occasions, it is more likely that Luke's form is nearer the original length and that Matthew reflects a process of liturgical elaboration. There are a number of reasons for this conclusion.

(1) It is highly unlikely that the teaching of Jesus was preserved and passed on in rigid, unchanging forms, either in Aramaic or in Greek (*see* Tradition Criticism). The clear testimony of the Synoptic traditions is that the words and deeds of Jesus were recalled in varied form and patterns (*see* Form Criticism), with particular wording adapted or recast as between Gospels. Otherwise we would have three Gospels saying precisely the same things in precisely the same words, which is manifestly not the case.

(2) Teaching of Jesus which was *used* in worship would be particularly subject to liturgical elaboration—that is, to a development of form shaped by the character of the worship or to make it more usable in worship. Here the clearest signs are the fuller form of Matthew's first line (more sonorous and easier for a congregation to say than Luke's abrupt "Father"), the

elaborations of lines 4-5 and 10 (coming, as we might expect, at the end of each of the two halves of the prayer), and the subsequent addition of the familiar conclusion "For yours is the kingdom . . ." (clearly a later addition, as all modern translations indicate, and evidence that liturgical development continued after the Gospels had been written, with *Did.* 8.2 as an early stage in the process—"For yours is the power and the glory for ever"). The different forms of "the words of institution" at the Last Supper (*see* Last Supper) attest the same process (Mk 14:22-24 par.).

(3) The prayer itself seems to be a development from or (in part at least) an adaptation of a contemporary Jewish prayer (see 1. above). The process reflected in the different versions of Matthew and Luke and subsequently is thus of a piece with evolving patterns of prayer in the Judaism* of Jesus' day (see 1. above).

(4) Luke presents the prayer precisely as a badge which was designed to mark out the disciples of Jesus from those of John the Baptist (Lk 11:1-2; *see* John the Baptist). This suggests that the Lukan form is closer to what Jesus taught as the prayer peculiar to his disciples.

(5) Luke's use of "Father" (line 1) probably presupposes the Aramaic *'abbā'*, and provides the undergirding for Romans 8:15-16 and Galatians 4:6-7 with their implication that the disciples' *abba* prayer was a conscious echo of Jesus' own prayer style (see 3. above).

At the same time it would be widely accepted that Matthew's wording is closer to an underlying Aramaic original (particularly lines 6-7), while Luke reflects a certain degree of adaptation (lines 6, 8) to take account of the longer time span envisaged by the churches of his day (as also in, e.g., Lk 19:11).

However, these issues are not of great importance so far as the significance of the prayer itself is concerned. What does matter is (1) that Jesus thought it of sufficient importance to teach his disciples a model prayer; (2) that it was a prayer which both drew on Jesus' and the first disciples' Jewish heritage and marked out those who used it as identified with Jesus; and (3) that, whether taught by Jesus in two forms or used by the first Christians in two forms, it is both the same prayer and yet a living and adaptable form. To be noted is the fact that the different forms of the Lord's Prayer in modern liturgies express the same sense of the living vehicle of communication with God and not a petrified formula or talisman whose virtue lies in precise reproduction of a set pattern. The fact that the Lord's Prayer has thus provided a vehicle of living prayer for nearly two millennia says much for the spiritual power of these words and for the spiritual insight of the one who taught them.

4.2. The Content of the Prayer. The opening of the prayer at once marks out its character as the prayer of Jesus and the attitude it expresses. This is clearer in the Lukan form ("Father"), which almost certainly reflects Jesus' own style of addressing God and which therefore also indicates Jesus' intention that his disciples should share in his own sense of intimate sonship to God as Father (see 3. above). The point is obscured in Matthew's version, whose more stately formulation ("Our Father who is in the heavens") is more like the language used in several of the Eighteen Benedictions (see 1. above). Matthew's form thus underscores the extent to which the spirituality of the Lord's Prayer is consonant with and grows out from that of Jewish prayer as attested both in the OT and for the time of Jesus. But Luke's brings out more the intimate boldness of the Jesus prayer and underscores the directness of the link between Jesus' prayer style and that of the first Christians (Rom 8:15; Gal 4:6). However, the two versions (of Matthew and Luke) are not at all at odds with each other. In both cases the first note struck is that of the dependence and trust of the pray-er on God. In fact all three Evangelists emphasize the need for the disciples to recognize their littleness before God if they are to enter the kingdom of God (Mt 18:3; Mk 10:15; Lk 18:17); and the Q tradition elsewhere takes pains to inculcate an attitude of trust (see Faith) in God as Father (Mt 7:7-11 par. Lk 11:9-13; Mt 6:25-34 par. Lk 12:22-31; see 5.1. below). The strength and outworking of this basic conviction was and remains a distinctive feature of Christianity.

4.2.1. First Petition. The first petition reflects the significance of a person's name in the ancient world. To act in the name of someone was to exercise that person's power and authority. To call on the name of someone was to put oneself under that person's protection and command. That is to say, the name of the person used in such formulae indicated the perceived significance of that person or, as we might say, that person's effective reputation (effective in that others could act confidently on the basis of that reputation; so in modern formulations like "His name carries weight" or "His name is mud"). The request here, then, is that God might be known for who he is, that people might recognize and acknowledge the power and authority (see Authority and Power) of God as God.

Of central importance, however, is the fact that the name of God is the name as evoked or used by human creatures. The possibility that God's name might not be set apart, that God's holy otherness might not be recognized, arises from the fact that humankind uses that name and abuses that name. Almost certainly there is an allusion here to the complaint of the prophets (as in Is 52:5 and Ezek 36:17-23) that Israel by its conduct and disloyalty had *dishonored* God's name, caused God's reputation (that which he was known as) to be despised and profaned. The point is that God had committed his name to his chosen people ("the God of Israel"), so that their failure redounded to his discredit. As Ezekiel goes on to show, God would vindicate his name precisely by restoring and renewing his scattered people (Ezek 36:24-36). All this indicates that the prayer for God's name to be made holy is a prayer that God may so act in his creation, and particularly through his people, that the rest of humankind may in turn come to honor him as God. In this again the petition taught by Jesus grows out of Jewish self-consciousness and hope (see 1. above on the *Qaddish*).

4.2.2. Second Petition. Like the opening words, the second petition both reflects contemporary Jewish prayer (the *Qaddish*), and brings to focus one of the most characteristic features of Jesus' preaching (the kingdom of God; *see* Kingdom of God). As is now generally recognized, "the kingdom of God" denotes God's kingly rule, God himself in the exercise of his royal power or authority. The request, then, is that this rule might be manifest and effective throughout the world* (cf. Dan 2:44). Whether this means the end of the world (or simply of the present world order), and how the request fits into the other emphases in Jesus' kingdom teaching must be dealt with elsewhere. What is notable here is that it is the future emphasis which Jesus enshrined in the prayer he taught his disciples as their distinctive prayer. Here again the attitude of dependency and trust in God for the future is underscored.

In some manuscripts the second petition in Luke reads, "May your Holy Spirit come upon us and cleanse us." It is undoubtedly late, and presumably reflects a concern lest Christian aspiration be too much oriented to the (still distant?) future. But as a replacement for the kingdom petition, it recognizes that the kingly rule of God is exercised through the Spirit (cf. Mt 12:28; *see* Holy Spirit); and as a petition made regularly, it expresses recognition of the pray-er's repeated need of enabling and cleansing (*see* Clean and Unclean) by the Spirit of God.

4.2.3. Third Petition. The third petition is in effect an expansion of the second: Where God's rule is acknowledged, God's will is done. Implicit is the confession that God's will is not done on earth, and that there will always be a tension between the divine will and the actuality of human structures and relationships until the kingdom comes. As (probably) an elaboration of the second petition, it is likely to be characteristic of other interpretive additions to the Jesus tradition—that is, not a wholly new element, but an explanation of an established element, spelling out its implications.

In the transition from the first to the second half of the prayer two important features need to be noted. (1) The fact that the first two/three petitions are prayers for God, for his name, kingly rule (and will). Only in the second half does the prayer turn to human needs. The priority is clear and matches Jesus' prioritizing of the Law elsewhere: "The first (commandment*) is . . . You shall love the Lord your God with all your heart . . . . The second is this, You shall love your neighbor as yourself" (Mk 12:29-31 par.). The implication is the same as in Luke 12:31 and Matthew 6:33: "Seek (first) his kingdom and . . . these things shall be yours as well"; the life which sees its first priority as its right ordering before God can put its needs confidently before God. (2) The transition from second person singular ("your name," "your kingdom," "your will") to first person plural ("our bread," "our debts," "us"). The pray-er prays to God alone, but not for the pray-er alone. There is no selfish self-seeking or attempt to steal advantage over another. The pray-er prays as part of and on behalf of the whole community of those dependent on God. The one is benefitted only by that which benefits all.

4.2.4. Fourth Petition. The precise force of the fourth petition has always been a matter of some unclarity, principally because the word usually translated "daily" (*epiousios*) occurs only here (and *Did.* 8:2) in ancient literature. Since the word is unknown elsewhere, most attempts to translate it are derived from the Greek form of the word itself. This allows three main alternatives: (1) from the noun meaning "substance, being, essence"—so "bread* for subsistence, necessary for existence"; (2) from the verb "to be"—so "bread for the present (day), for today"; (3) from the future tense of the verb "to come"—so "bread for the coming (day), for the future" (see Fitzmyer). It is not possible to choose between these with any confidence, and perhaps at least a degree of ambiguity was intended. (1) is favored by Fitzmyer. It focuses on the actual needs of the pray-ers (cf. Prov 30:8). (2) seems to have been favored by Luke since he renders the verb in the present tense ("keep on giving us") and since he reads "each day" instead of "today." It emphasizes the continuous and repeated, day-by-day, dependence of the pray-ers on God's provision. (3) is favored by Jeremias and Brown. It

may be implied by the positioning of "today" in a place of emphasis: "give us today the bread of the future." And it ties in with the eschatological (*see* Eschatology) emphasis of the second petition and possibly also the final petition: "give us the bread of the kingdom, the bread of salvation." In this case it would accord with the tension evident elsewhere in the Gospels and Paul between a salvation already begun and in process but not yet complete. What sustains the disciple now are resources from beyond the constraints of the present, from the future which God will bring about and has already achieved in raising Christ from the dead (*see* Resurrection).

However, whatever the precise emphasis, the petition is a powerful expression of trust and dependence: Give us what we need, not what we want, or even what we think we need, but what God sees our need actually to be. The more material needs are in view, the clearer the implication that God is concerned for the provisions of these needs. The modern interpreter should certainly hesitate long before reading any kind of dichotomy between spiritual and material needs here. Note also the implication that a concern to satisfy material wants rather than needs falls outside the scope of this prayer, and so also outside the primary concerns of the God to whom this prayer is addressed.

4.2.5. Fifth Petition. The fifth petition is one of the most frightening requests that can ever be put to God—that he should forgive us just as we forgive others, that God should measure his forgiveness in accordance with the forgiveness we have actually extended to others (*see* Forgiveness of Sins). As Jeremias notes, this is the one condition that Jesus sets for the one who would pray this prayer—readiness to forgive. Thus is underlined the importance for community of a giving and receiving of forgiveness, and the interdependence of divine forgiveness with human forgiveness (cf. Sir. 28:2). No wonder Jesus made this one of the most important emphases of his teaching on prayer (see 5.2. below)—a fact underlined by the way Matthew has appended to the Lord's Prayer one of the most important words of Jesus on the subject, introducing it as an explanation ("for") of that prayer, and thus implying that it is the element of the prayer most needing reinforcement. To be noted is the fact that the prayer does not envisage a forgiveness restricted to those within the community of discipleship*—"as we forgive those in debt to us/everyone who is indebted to us," not "as we forgive one another in our mutual indebtedness." The refusal to extend forgiveness beyond the church is a barrier to divine forgiveness for the church.

4.2.6. Sixth Petition. The final petition reflects the ambiguity in Jewish talk of "testing." It can have both the negative sense of "temptation" and the positive sense of "proving"—reflecting the common experience of trying situations, which, depending on the response of the person being thus tested, can be either negative (destructive of relationship) or positive (maturing of character). That God provides such tests is a common thought in the Jewish Scriptures (Gen 22:1; Ex 15:25; 16:4; 20:20; Num 14:22; Deut 8:2; 13:3; etc.); faith/faithfulness is demonstrated by such trials (Ps 26:2-3; Jdt 8:25-26; Sir 2:1; Wis 3:5-6; 1 Macc 2:52). The ambiguity is reflected elsewhere in the NT, particularly in James (1:12 and 13-14). The petition here shows full awareness of this ambiguity. It does not hesitate to attribute testing to God, while at the same time expressing an understandable anxiety lest the outcome of the testing be negative. It is a prayer of conscious and confessed human weakness; it makes no pretense of confidence in its own strength and commitment; rather it expresses an unconditional abandonment to the will and grace of God. The closest parallel is thus Jesus' own prayer in Gethsemane (Mk 14:36; cf. Mt 26:42 and Lk 22:42, both of which closely parallel the petition of Mt 6:10). The expanded Matthean form expresses the implied awareness that the real threat is not the trial itself, but of succumbing under trial to the destructive power of evil (or the evil one; *see* Demon, Devil, Satan). It is the fear of how one will fare in one's own unaided human strength which inspires the petition. But the confession of such fear, without pretense or excuse, is itself a confession of faith. Whether the thought is of all trials throughout the life of discipleship or of the final eschatological trial, the final tribulation which will usher in a new age (as in Rev 3:10, and probably by implication in Mk 14:36, 38) or both, is unclear. The distinction may not be important since any and every trial can be decisive in the growth (or destruction) of faith.

The prayer is amazingly comprehensive despite its brevity. It sets human need within a heavenly perspective and in accord with divine priorities. It prays for "us" without being narrowly or exclusively introspective. And it covers the needs of present (bread sufficient), past (healing of memories and relationships) and future (preservation within a threatening environment). Words with such timeless relevance, and yet able to express specific and occasional needs, make the prayer truly unique, constantly repeatable without degenerating into vain repetition because expressive of all human condition of whatever time or place.

5. Jesus' Teaching on Prayer: The Main Emphases.
The chief notes of the Lord's Prayer are emphasized elsewhere in Jesus' other teaching on the subject.

5.1. Trust. Matthew prefaces the Lord's Prayer with the word of Jesus assuring disciples that God knows their needs before they ask (Mt 6:8), a point beautifully elaborated in the second half of the chapter (6:25-33 par. Lk 12:22-31). The same attitude is encouraged in the equally beautiful exposition of God as the Father to whom requests should be made known in full confidence (Mt 7:7-11 par. Lk 11:9-13). Common experience indicates that a human father delights to give good things to his children; how much more the heavenly Father. (Luke's version expresses the belief that the Holy Spirit is the best "good thing" that anyone can receive from God.)

Note well that the teaching here does not assure askers that they will get whatever they ask for. Rather the assurance is given that whatever they receive from God will be good. It is such confidence in the goodness of God which Jesus inculcates here rather than any presumption that the pray-er knows best. It is prayer with this confidence, rather than insisting on our own way, which Jesus thus encourages. The teaching occasioned by the cursing of the fig tree seems, on the other hand, to encourage a boldness of faith in asking for specific things (Mk 11:22-24 par. Mt 21:21-22; cf. Mk 9:29). But the conditional clause "without doubting" may reflect Jesus' own experience on specific occasions of a God-given conviction which was itself God's means to achieve the desired end. Faith "without doubting" is an open channel of God's power such as is given to few humans to experience and express.

It should also be noted here that in Matthew's Gospel the teaching of 6:8 is contrasted with a praying which is public, pretentious and empty repetition (Mt 6:5-8). A similar contrast is implicit in the parable* of the Pharisee* and the tax collector (Lk 18:11, 13; *see* Taxes), the latter being heard for his simple honesty and refusal to make excuse or offer justification for his conduct (Lk 18:13). (Compare Mk 12:40 par. Lk 20:47 which speak dismissively of long prayers which are a cloak for greed.) The implication is clear: not the amount of praying makes the difference (Jesus and his disciples were criticized for not praying enough, Lk 5:33), but the attitude of humble, unpretentious, unconditional trust is what matters.

5.2. Forgiveness. As already noted, Matthew appends a further word about forgiveness to the Lord's Prayer (Mt 6:14-15 par. Mk 11:25-26). The point is strikingly reinforced in the parable of the unmerciful servant—forgiven much and yet unwilling to forgive little (Mt

18:23-35; note the moral at the end: v. 35)—appended by Matthew to the teaching on the need to be ready to forgive a fellow disciple not just seven times but seventy times seven (Mt 18:21-22 par. Lk 17:4). It is also implicit in the parable of the Pharisee and the tax collector, where the Pharisee's dismissive disregard for the tax collector is an important part of the story (Lk 18:11; cf. the attitude of the older brother in the parable of the prodigal son, Lk 15:28-30). As indeed it is also in Jesus' instruction that his disciples should pray for those who persecute them (Mt 5:44 par. Lk 6:28). The point can be put in different ways, each emphasizing the interrelatedness of divine and human forgiveness. Refusal to grant forgiveness demonstrates that forgiveness has not been received. Where there is no human forgiveness offered or received, God's forgiveness is absent. Genuinely to forgive is to open oneself to divine forgiveness, is indeed to become in some measure a channel of divine forgiveness. It is recognition of the need for divine forgiveness which opens the eyes to the need for human forgiveness; it is the experience of God's forgiveness which enables forgiveness to be offered and received on the human level. As with the interdependence of love* of God and love of neighbor, so with the interdependence of divine and human forgiveness (cf. Lk 6:37). Since the church* can be defined as that community which prays the Lord's Prayer, so it can be defined as the community in which forgiveness (acceptance) is genuinely given and received as expressive of and enabled by the forgiveness/acceptance of God.

5.3. Persistence. The implication that the Lord's Prayer is a daily prayer, the Christian equivalent of the *Shema* and the Eighteen Benedictions, is matched by a striking emphasis in Luke's account of Jesus' teaching on the need to persist in prayer. Thus, Luke has appended to his version of the Lord's Prayer the parable of the friend at midnight (Lk 11:5-8), where the point seems to be the shamelessness of the petitioner knocking on his friend's door at midnight, persisting in his request despite the lateness of the hour. The point would be lost if the shamelessness referred to the sleeping neighbor (Bailey, Brandon), but the "him," "his" throughout the verse refers to the petitioner, and Luke follows it with the encouragement to persistence in asking, seeking, knocking (present tenses: "go on asking . . ."; Lk 11:9-13 par. Mt 7:7-11). It is also Luke who records the parable of the unjust judge and Luke who says that Jesus told the parable with a view to emphasizing the need to pray and never give up; and the parable ends with talk of God's chosen ones crying to him day and night (Lk

18:1-8). The point in both parables, of course, is one of contrast: if a sleeping neighbor and dishonest judge will act in response to persistent request, how much more God.

Here too the meaning should not be wrested so as to imply, for instance, that persistence will always get its way with God, even if the petition is contrary to God's will. In one case the petitioner had the sacred obligation of hospitality as his spur; and in the other the implication is that the widow (a disadvantaged and often oppressed status) had right on her side over against the dishonesty of the judge. The point is rather the refusal to look elsewhere for the help that only God can give, and the need for constancy of reliance upon and openness to his provision, in the confidence that it will be both fair and generous. The need for a prayerful watchfulness in the face of threatening trial (Mk 13:33, some manuscripts; Mk 14:38 and par.; Lk 21:36) underscores the same point in terms similar to that of the final petition of the Lord's Prayer.

5.4. Communal. Finally, we should note Matthew 18:19, a reminder that the Lord's Prayer speaks always of "us" and never of "me." It is a reminder too that the will of God will rarely be wholly clear to an individual alone and that God usually works through a community of like-motivated, mutually interdependent and mutually supportive people. It is such a community which is the more likely to be able to pray in confidence regarding God's will, to pray, and praying also to act, in the name of Jesus.

See also DISCIPLESHIP; FASTING; FORGIVENESS OF SINS; GETHSEMANE; GOD; JUSTICE, RIGHTEOUSNESS; KINGDOM OF GOD; SON OF GOD; WORSHIP.

BIBLIOGRAPHY. K. E. Bailey, *Poet and Peasant/Through Peasant Eyes* (Grand Rapids: Eerdmans; two vols., 1976, 1980, in one, 1983); R. E. Brown, "The Pater Noster as an Eschatological Prayer," in *New Testament Essays* (Garden City, NY: Doubleday, 1967) 217-53; J. H. Charlesworth, ed., *The Old Testament Pseudepigrapha* (2 vols.; Garden City, NY: Doubleday, 1985) 2.607-97; S. J. D. Cohen, *From the Maccabees to the Mishnah* (Philadelphia: Westminster, 1987) 62-73; J. D. G. Dunn, *Jesus and the Spirit* (Philadelphia: Westminster, 1979) 15-40; idem, *Christology in the Making* (Philadelphia: Westminster, 1980, 1989) 22-33; P. Edmonds, "The Lucan Our Father: A Summary of Luke's Teaching on Prayer?" *ExpT* 91 (1979-80) 140-43; J. A. Fitzmyer, *The Gospel according to Luke (X-XXIV)* (AB 28B; Garden City, NY: Doubleday, 1985); J. Jeremias, *The Parables of Jesus* (New York: Charles Scribner's, 1963); idem, *The Prayers of Jesus* (Naperville, IL: Allenson, 1967); idem, *New Testament Theology: The*

Proclamation of Jesus (New York: Charles Scribner's, 1971) 178-203; E. Lohmeyer, *The Lord's Prayer* (London: Collins, 1965); C. F. D. Moule, " '. . . As we forgive . . .': a Note on the Distinction between Deserts and Capacity in the Understanding of Forgiveness," in *Donum Gentilicum: New Testament Studies in honour of David Daube*, ed. C. K. Barrett et al. (Oxford: Clarendon, 1978) 68-77, reprinted in C. F. D. Moule, *Essays in New Testament Interpretation* (Cambridge: University Press, 1982) 278-86; J. J. Petuchowski and M. Brocke, eds., *The Lord's Prayer and Jewish Liturgy* (London: Burns and Oates, 1978); E. Schürer, *The History of the Jewish People in the Age of Jesus Christ (175 B.C.-A.D. 135)*, rev. and ed. G. Vermes and F. Millar (3 vols.; Edinburgh: T. & T. Clark, 1973-79) vol. II. 448-50, 454-63, 481-83; B. B. Scott, *Hear Then the Parables. A Commentary on the Parables of Jesus* (Minneapolis: Fortress, 1989); G. Vermes, *The Dead Sea Scrolls in English* (3d ed; London: Penguin, 1987) 165-238.

J. D. G. Dunn

PREACHING FROM THE GOSPELS

Since the Gospels are a unique genre (*see* Gospel [Genre]) of biblical literature, preaching from the Gospels presents a distinct set of challenges. On the one hand, the Gospel genre is a form of preaching, and therefore contemporary preaching from the Gospels conforms well with the nature of this genre. On the other hand, in the Gospels contemporary preachers are faced with the complexities of various homiletical horizons (e.g., that of Jesus and of the Gospel writers), four different Gospels (*see* Canon) about the same historical Jesus, and numerous human characters who threaten to upstage Jesus in the sermon. The challenge is to preach sermons that do justice to the complexities of the Gospels while they speak relevantly to the church here and now.

1. The Gospels As Preaching
2. Various Homiletical Horizons
3. The Homiletical Significance of Four Gospels
4. Christocentric Messages
5. Preparing Gospel Sermons
6. The Relevance for Today

1. The Gospels As Preaching.

The Gospels communicate "the good news" (*to euangelion*) about "Jesus Christ, the Son of God" (Mk 1:1; *see* Gospel [Good News]). As good news addressed to the church, the written Gospels themselves are a form of preaching (*kerygma*). Moreover, the Gospels are rooted in the preaching of Jesus and the apostles: "Jesus came into Galilee, preaching the gospel of God,* and saying, 'The time is fulfilled, and the kingdom of God is at hand; repent, and believe the gospel' " (Mk 1:14-15 RSV; cf. Mt 10:7; 28:18-20). Since the Gospels are formed out of early Christian preaching and are themselves a form of preaching, contemporary preaching from the Gospels is not contrary to their nature but is a natural extension of the Gospel genre. This affinity of the Gospels and preaching facilitates contemporary preaching of Gospel passages, for the message and its objective are given in the Gospel itself. Other characteristics of the Gospels, however, complicate their preaching today and require careful reflection.

2. Various Homiletical Horizons.

In preaching from the Gospels one of the first issues confronting preachers is which homiletical horizon is the proper level for interpretation and preaching. Redaction criticism (*see* Redaction Criticism) distinguishes various life settings in the Gospels. For preaching purposes, two life settings other than the contemporary horizon are important: (1) the life setting of the historical Jesus (*see* Historical Jesus) as he preached to the disciples,* the Jewish leaders and the crowds (*Sitz im Leben Jesu*) and (2) the life setting of the Gospel writers as they used the oral and written traditions about Jesus to write the Gospels for their churches (*Sitz im Leben des Verfassers*).

2.1. The Horizon of Jesus. Many preachers almost automatically opt for the horizon of the historical Jesus, preaching sermons on Jesus calling his disciples, Jesus healing* the sick, Jesus challenging the Pharisees,* etc., and applying the message from that original horizon to the church today. The question may be raised, however, if this approach does full justice to the written text. To be sure, this method uses the written text, but only as a transparent windowpane through which to view the historical Jesus and his words and actions. The Gospels, however, as a comparison of the four will show, are not transparent windowpanes but distinctly colored presentations of the historical Jesus. To look right through the written text to Jesus' historical horizon is to miss the kerygmatic point made by the Gospel writer in a later horizon. This method fails to do full justice to the inspired Gospels.

2.2. The Horizon of the Evangelist. Other preachers seek to preach the Gospels from the homiletical horizon of the Gospel writers. They try to detect the message Matthew proclaimed to the Jewish Christian church or the message Luke formulated for the church of Theophilus, and then transfer that message to the church today. For support, this approach can appeal to the fact that the church received as God's inspired Word the written Gospels and not our reconstructions of the historical Jesus. As well, it can appeal to Jesus' promise to his disciples, "When the Spirit of truth comes, he will guide you into all the truth" (Jn 16:13 RSV). Only after Jesus' resurrection* and the outpouring of the Holy Spirit (*see* Holy Spirit) did the apostles* begin to understand what had taken place in Jesus (see Lk 24:25-27; Jn 14:25-26; 16:12-15). By itself, however, this method of focussing on the horizon of the Gospel writer also fails to do full justice to the Gospels as we have them. For it tends to slight the historical referents in the Gospels; it tends to overlook the very reason for which the Gospels were written, namely to convey the meaning of the life, death* and resurrection of the historical Jesus.

2.3. Working with Both Horizons. A more thorough approach than either of the above seeks to work with both ancient horizons. This procedure naturally gives rise to the question, Which horizon has priority, that of the historical Jesus or that of the Gospel writer? Although the horizon of Jesus is chronologically prior, one learns about the historical Jesus only through the later Gospel writer. Hence one's interpretation needs to begin with the horizon of the Gospel writer.

By studying the composition of a Gospel in its own historical context and by comparing it with the other three Gospels, one becomes aware of the differences among the Gospels: They offer not four identical photographs of Jesus but four unique portraits. These distinct views of what Jesus did and taught are not, as is often supposed, a liability for contemporary preaching but an advantage. They are a liability only when one allows a naturalistic or immanentistic historical-critical method to use the variations in the Gospels to undermine their fundamental historicity (see Greidanus, 24-47, 268-77). But for contemporary preachers who assume the Gospels' basic historicity (*see* Gospels [Historical Reliability]), these distinct views of the Gospel writers are an advantage. For the portrait each Gospel writer paints of Jesus reveals the homiletical use to which he put the received traditions (*see* Tradition Criticism). Each unique slant may reveal the relevant point for a particular early Christian church. That homiletical point, it should be emphasized, is made by proclaiming "all that Jesus began to do and to teach" (Acts 1:1). In spite of the variations, therefore, the horizon of the Gospel writer in the early church is firmly linked to that of the historical Jesus.

This connection between the two ancient horizons enables contemporary preachers to use the Gospels for exploring the horizon of the historical Jesus. They can probe for the point Jesus made as he taught his disciples or the crowds (*see* People, Crowd) with sayings, parables* or miracles (*see* Miracles and Miracle Stories). Next they can investigate how Matthew, Mark, Luke or John, in a later setting, used that original message or event to bring the same or a revised message for a different time and place. And finally they can reflect on the significance of this point for the church today.

In the sermon itself one need not necessarily begin with the horizon of the Gospel writer but can frequently start with the point made by Jesus in his historical horizon, next show how the Gospel writer applies this to the church in his day, and finally show the implications of this point for the church today.

For example, if one preaches on the conclusion of Matthew's Gospel (28:16-20), one can begin at the level of Jesus commissioning his eleven disciples, "to make disciples of all nations" and promising them for this awesome task his abiding presence. Next one can show how Matthew in his later horizon introduces this mandate with a reference to "the mountain" (v. 16; *see* Mountain and Wilderness), thus reminding his Jewish readers once again that Jesus is indeed the new Moses,* the new mediator between God and his people, the Law* giver of the new covenant (cf. Ex 19:20; Mt 5:1; 17:1). Matthew further notes that the disciples "worshiped him" (v. 17) as Jews would worship* only God. This sets the stage for Jesus' astounding statement "All authority* in heaven and on earth has been given to me" (v. 18). The King of kings himself commands not only the original disciples but through them the early Christian church to go and "make disciples of all nations" (v. 19). Along with this mandate the early church receives also the empowering promise "I am with you always, to the close of the age" (v. 20). Matthew makes this promise (which forms an "inclusion" with the Immanuel of 1:23) the grand finale of his Gospel. Once the message has been understood in both of these horizons, its implications for the church today will be evident: The Lord* of the church commands and empowers also his church today to make disciples of all nations (*see* Gentiles) because he is Lord of all.

3. The Homiletical Significance of Four Gospels.
The validity of this double-horizon approach is borne out by the fact that the Bible contains four different Gospels about the historical Jesus. This biblical given can be made homiletically fruitful by discovering the specific objective or goal of each Gospel writer and by comparing their parallel passages.

3.1. The Objective of Each Gospel. Luke and John explicitly state their homiletical objectives. Luke writes

Theophilus, "It seemed good to me also, having followed all things closely for some time past, to write an orderly account for you, most excellent Theophilus, that you may know the truth concerning the things of which you have been informed" (Lk 1:3-4 RSV). Even more precisely, John writes his audience that "Jesus did many other signs in the presence of the disciples, which are not written in this book; but these are written that you may believe that Jesus is the Christ, the Son of God, and that believing you may have life in his name" (Jn 20:30-31 RSV). Although Matthew and Mark do not mention their objectives explicitly, redaction criticism, or more precisely, composition criticism can help bring them to light. One of Matthew's objectives, clearly, is to persuade his audience that Jesus of Nazareth was indeed the promised Messiah (*see* Christ), the long-awaited King of Israel.* One of Mark's objectives, by contrast, is to demonstrate to his audience that Jesus Christ had freely chosen the road of suffering and that his followers should be prepared to do the same (cf. Mk 8:31-38). These homiletical objectives—"that you may know the truth," "that you may believe that Jesus is the Christ," etc.—are beacons lighting the way to understanding the specifics of each Gospel.

3.2. Comparing Parallel Passages. The specifics of each Gospel can be discerned even more exactly when, because of double or triple traditions, one has opportunity to compare parallel Gospel passages (*see* Synoptic Problem). Most biblical scholars hold that Mark was the first Gospel and that Matthew and Luke used Mark (or his source Urmark) and other sources in writing their Gospels. Consequently, any variations from a Markan passage might indicate the specific interests of Matthew or Luke. Although this procedure frequently works, there are too many variables to accept it as foolproof. Since preachers are primarily interested in discerning the specific emphases in each Gospel and each passage (rather than who changed what), the most dependable method for them is carefully to compare the parallel Gospel passages in the light of the different objectives of each writer (see Fee, 39-40, 103-116). Such a comparison will reveal the kind of material each Gospel writer selected for transmission and how they rearranged and/or modified it. This information, in turn, will lead to understanding the homiletical interests and purposes of each writer and provide insight into the point of the preaching text (Greidanus, 271-73).

For example, if one preaches on Luke 18:15-17, the story of people bringing their children (*see* Child, Children) to Jesus, a comparison with Mark (10:13-16) and Matthew (19:13-15) will enable one to discern

Luke's homiletical interests. First, in contrast to Mark and Matthew, Luke precedes this story with the parable* of the pharisee and the tax collector (*see* Taxes). Thus Luke sets this story about children in the context of proper humility: "he who humbles himself will be exalted." Second, in contrast to Mark and Matthew, Luke changes the Greek word for children in verse 15 to a word denoting infants or babies. Thus Luke sharpens Jesus' point for his particular audience: "Whoever does not receive the kingdom of God like a child [the way a helpless baby receives its nourishment] shall not enter it" (v. 17 RSV). A sermon on Luke 18:15-17, therefore, would seek to emphasize our utter inability to contribute anything toward receiving the kingdom of God and encourage us to place our full trust in our heavenly Father who provides this wonderful gift for his children free of charge.

4. Christocentric Messages.
All four Gospel writers intend to preach Jesus Christ. For example, in his second volume Luke writes, "In the first book, O Theophilus, I have dealt with all that Jesus began to do and teach, until the day when he was taken up" (Acts 1:1-2 RSV). The new literary criticism (or narrative criticism; *see* Literary Criticism) confirms that Jesus is central in the Gospels: he is described as "the central figure," "the subject around which every narrative turns" (Achtemeier, 53), "the major character," "the protagonist," "the supreme exponent of God's evaluative point of view" (Kingsbury 1988, 10-13, 36). In sermons that would be true to the Gospels, this centrality of Jesus may not be subverted.

4.1. The Peril of Anthropocentrism. Unfortunately, in contemporary "biographic" and "character preaching," Jesus is frequently upstaged by the other characters in the Gospels: Mary or Peter or Thomas receive center stage. Often this switch is made for the sake of relevance: the characters are sketched as warning examples whose attitudes and actions the hearers ought to avoid, or as good examples the hearers ought to emulate. In spite of good intentions, however, this kind of example or moralistic preaching cannot be recommended, for it turns the christocentric Gospel message into an anthropocentric sermon and in the process loses the real relevance of the Gospel. One important question preachers need to ask is, Was this the intention of the Gospel writer? Did he intend to portray these characters as moral examples for the early Christians?

4.2. The Role of Gospel Characters. One must grant, of course, that these human characters play their parts in the Gospels and may not simply be ignored in preaching. The question is, If they may not upstage Jesus, what is the place of Mary, Peter or Thomas in the sermon? Genuine biblical preaching, it seems fair to suggest, should seek to give the same place and function to these persons in the sermon as they have in the Gospels. In other words, preachers need to ask how the Gospel writer has used these characters in presenting his Gospel.

Narrative criticism has shown that some characters function simply as catalysts for other characters to exhibit their traits or to move along the action in a scene. Other characters, however, function as foils to contrast and highlight certain traits of Israel or of the disciples. For example, Matthew contrasts the magi's faith in Jesus and later that of the Roman centurion with Israel's unbelief (Mt 2:1-12; 8:5-13), and he contrasts the faith of the leper and that of the father of an epileptic with the disciples' "little faith" (Mt 8:2, 26; 17:14-21; see Kingsbury 1988, 25-27). When we realize that Matthew's Jewish audience would tend to recognize itself in Israel and more particularly in the disciples, his polemical as well as his homiletical point comes into view.

4.3. The Story of Jesus the Christ. Further, it is clear that the characters in the Gospels function not independently but as parts of an overall plot. This fact would also argue against the practice of isolating characters for the sake of presenting them as moral examples for the congregation. For the narrative structure entails that these characters ought to be understood and preached in the context of the whole story. That whole story, of course, is the story about Jesus Christ. Thus every character in the Gospels stands in relation to Jesus, and every Gospel sermon, also when dealing with these characters, can be genuinely christocentric.

Contemporary preachers need only follow the lead of the Gospel writer. For example, when Matthew (11:2-6) uses John the Baptist's* doubt to emphasize that the very miracles that made John doubt are proof that Jesus is the promised Messiah, contemporary preachers can follow suit. When Luke (19:1-10) uses the wealthy, chief tax collector Zacchaeus to proclaim that Jesus is able to save even rich sinners (*see* Rich and Poor; Sinner), contemporary preachers can make the same use of Zacchaeus. By thus following the lead of the Gospel writers, contemporary preachers can pay appropriate attention to the various human characters while retaining center stage for Jesus and his teachings.

4.4. Christocentric Preaching and Theocentric Preaching. The Gospels themselves, of course, are not independent stories either but now form an integral part

of the Bible and its all-encompassing story. This unity of the Gospels and the Bible elucidates how christocentric preaching is related to theocentric preaching. The one story the Bible relates is the history of God's kingdom (*see* Kingdom of God) which began with God's good creation (Gen 1), continued its up-and-down course despite the fall into sin (Gen 3:15), and will come to completion with the new creation (Rev 21—22). The Gospels proclaim that the coming of Jesus is God's mightiest act in this history of God's coming kingdom. The Word that was with God in the beginning "became flesh and dwelt among us," proclaims John (1:1, 14). In the coming of Jesus, God's promised King has come, preaches Matthew, for Jesus is the Messiah, the great Son of David (*see* Son of David), "God with us" (1:1-23). Consequently, christocentric preaching is theocentric preaching.

Jesus himself preached "the gospel of the kingdom" (Mt 4:23), defeated Satan, the pretender to the throne, and established a major beachhead for God's kingdom on earth (Mt 12:28). Jesus in turn commanded his disciples and church to spread the gospel of the kingdom and "make disciples of all nations" (Mt 10:7; 28:19). The Gospel writers responded to this mandate by writing their Gospels, thus spreading into the world the good news of the kingdom of God that has come in Jesus Christ. By preaching these Gospels today, contemporary preachers can transmit the same good news of Jesus Christ and his kingdom. With the Gospels they can challenge their hearers with the broad vision of the kingdom of God that has come on earth and is still coming.

5. Preparing Gospel Sermons.
The Gospels, it was observed above, are formed out of early Christian preaching and are themselves a form of preaching. By their very nature, therefore, the Gospels are well suited to be sources for contemporary preaching.

5.1. Selecting Preaching Texts. In order to conform to the Gospels as preaching, contemporary preachers should select as preaching texts not isolated fragments of the Gospels but complete literary units. Form criticism (*see* Form Criticism) has shown that the basic preaching units underlying the written Gospels are the pericopes—roughly corresponding to paragraphs in our English Bibles. These pericopes will frequently make excellent preaching texts. "When the pericopes of the Gospels are taken as texts for preaching, one is in close touch with their original intent and purpose" (Smith, 20). Naturally, these literary units, whatever their size, must now be interpreted in the light of the whole written Gospel and ultimately in the light of the whole Bible.

Sometimes, for the sake of congregational retention, one may wish to select as preaching text a very brief text, perhaps the heart of a pericope. At other times, especially with scenic narrative, it may be advisable to select several consecutive pericopes. Whether short or long, preaching texts must be literary units. Frequently, rhetorical criticism (*see* Rhetorical Criticism) can help discover ideal preaching texts in the Gospels by identifying rhetorical structures such as repetition, inclusion and chiasm which mark the limits of literary units.

Since these pericopes now proclaim their message in the context of a particular written Gospel, it is not advisable to create one's own preaching text by combining verses from different Gospels. Such a hybrid preaching text mixes decidedly different literary and historical contexts and makes it extremely difficult if not impossible to do justice to the intention of each Gospel writer.

The Gospels lend themselves well to series of sermons on consecutive pericopes. Scenic narratives in particular, as well as composite discourses (e.g., Matt 5—7, 10, 13, 18, 24—25), are excellent sources for consecutive treatment. By preaching a series of sermons on similar Gospel pericopes, preachers can take advantage of the similarity by sketching the background material only once and concentrating in subsequent sermons on reinforcing and expanding the main point. For the sake of retaining interest, however, a series should seldom extend beyond five or six sermons on the same material or topic.

5.2. Stating the Theme and Objective. Once the preaching text has been tentatively selected, one should formulate its theme and objective. The theme is the main thought of the text: a brief assertion (subject and predicate) of what the text is saying. The objective or goal is what the Gospel writer is trying to accomplish with this theme. The sermon theme functions as a magnet for attracting and selecting only appropriate ideas for the sermon. The objective functions as a compass for setting the direction and focus of the sermon for the desired congregational response. Although the textual theme needs to be reviewed in the context of the whole Gospel and the Bible before it can be used to construct the sermon, as a rule Gospel themes can serve directly as sermon themes.

5.3. Choosing the Sermonic Form. The preacher also needs to choose an appropriate form for the sermon. The form of a Gospel sermon can be either narrative or didactic (teaching), or a combination of these forms. Ideally, the form of a specific sermon should do justice to the form of the preaching text and its objective. In general a narrative text from the Gospels would be best served by a narrative sermon form (*see* Narrative Exegesis), while a didactic text from the sayings would be best served by a logical, didactic form.

In addition to choosing the appropriate sermon form, preachers need to decide whether to develop this form deductively or inductively. Deductive development states the theme at the beginning and leads (deduces) from this theme the particular points. Inductive development, by contrast, begins with the particulars and leads them (induces) into the theme. Deductive development is effective in a didactic sermon, for it enables one to state the theme at the beginning of the sermon and to explain, expand and reinforce it throughout the sermon. Inductive development, by contrast, is especially effective in a narrative sermon, for it creates suspense regarding the outcome of the sermon and may stimulate greater congregational involvement in discovering the point of the narrative.

Various combinations of deductive and inductive development are possible, such as inductive-deductive (also known as the "plain style sermon") and deductive-inductive (see Greidanus, 141-56). Preachers should choose a sermon form which, on the one hand, shows respect for the preaching-text and, on the other hand, pays attention to congregational interest and involvement. In addition preachers need to be aware of their own strengths since different forms require different skills.

6. The Relevance for Today.

Without relevance there is no sermon, for a sermon is God's relevant word for his church today. This definition of a sermon makes relevance a crucial issue for preaching. How does one preach relevant sermons from the Gospels?

6.1. Discovering the Original Relevance. The first requirement for relevant preaching of the Gospels is the recognition that they were extremely relevant in their own historical horizons. The Gospels were God's astonishing, comforting, imploring good news to various early Christian churches. This original relevance implies that the Gospels need not be *made* relevant, least of all by questionable methods such as moralizing or spiritualizing. Instead of trying to make the Gospels relevant for today, preachers need only discover that past relevance and seek to transfer it from the early church to the church today.

To discover that past relevance, contemporary preachers should ask, What was the Gospel writer's objective with this passage? What response did he seek from his hearers with this particular message? Was he aiming at the response of faith? or repentance? or trust? or obedience? or thanksgiving? The particular response sought reveals the specific relevance of this message for an early Christian church. The remaining problem for contemporary preachers is how to transfer this past relevance from the early church to the church today.

6.2. Transferring the Original Relevance to Today. For transferring relevant preaching from the past to the present one needs to appreciate the continuity that obtains in the one kingdom-history. Although this kingdom history forges forward, resulting in discontinuities between different historical horizons, these discontinuities occur within the one kingdom history which is characterized by the overarching continuities of the constancy of God (Yahweh), his covenant faithfulness to his people, as well as the similarity of his people throughout the ages. These overarching continuities enable one to observe analogies between the early Christian church and the church today and between the situation they faced and the situation we face today. As a result, preachers can draw parallels between the early church and its historical circumstances and the contemporary church and its circumstances. These parallels form a bridge across the historical-cultural gap—a bridge for transferring God's relevant message from the horizon of the early Christian church to the church today.

By making use of these analogies to extend the Gospel message from the past to the present, preachers will be under less pressure to make the text relevant by questionable means. Given the obvious analogies between the church then and the church today, there is no reason to seek relevance in spiritualizing the original Gospel message or in presenting certain Gospel characters as moral examples for today's congregations (see further Greidanus, 175-81).

When the relevance of a passage for one's congregation has been clearly discerned, the preacher is ready to start writing the sermon with that relevance in mind. This procedure ensures that relevance will not be confined to an application at the end of a lengthy exposition, but that it will permeate the sermon from its introduction to its conclusion.

BIBLIOGRAPHY. P. J. Achtemeier, *Mark* (2d ed.; Philadelphia: Fortress, 1986); F. B. Craddock, *The Gospels* (Nashville: Abingdon, 1981); G. D. Fee, *New Testament Exegesis: A Handbook for Students and Pastors* (Philadelphia: Westminster, 1983); S. Greidanus, *The Modern Preacher and the Ancient Text: Interpreting and Preaching Biblical Literature* (Grand Rapids: Eerdmans, 1988); W. E. Hull, "Preaching on the Synoptic Gospels," in *Biblical Preaching: An Expositor's Treasury,* ed. J. W. Cox (Philadelphia: Westminster, 1983) 169-194; L. E. Keck, *The Bible in the Pulpit: The Renewal of Biblical Preaching* (Nashville: Abingdon, 1978); J. D. Kingsbury, "The Gospel in Four Editions," *Int* 33 (1979) 363-375; idem, *Matthew as Story* (Philadelphia: Fortress, 1988); W. L. Liefeld, *New Testament Exposition: From Text to Sermon* (Grand Rapids: Zondervan, 1984); T. G. Long, *Preaching and the Literary Forms of the Bible* (Philadelphia: Fortress, 1989); I. H. Marshall, ed., *New Testament Interpretation: Essays on Principles and Methods* (Grand Rapids: Eerdmans, 1977); G. R. Osborne, "Preaching the Gospels: Methodology and Contextualization," *JETS* 27 (1984) 27-42; D. Rhoads, "Narrative Criticism and the Gospel of Mark," *JAAR* 50 (1982) 411-434; D. M. Smith, *Interpreting the Gospels for Preaching* (Philadelphia: Fortress, 1979).   S. Greidanus

PREDICTIONS OF JESUS' PASSION AND RESURRECTION

Acts 3:22 and 7:37 identify Jesus as a prophet*-like-Moses* (quoting Deut 18:15). Jesus is thus viewed by the early church as the proclaimer and interpreter of God's past, present and future counsel. According to the Gospels Jesus' prophetic ministry ranges from his proclaiming the nearness of the kingdom of God (Mk 1:14-15; *see* Kingdom of God), the prediction of the destruction of Jerusalem (*see* Destruction of Jerusalem) and the Temple* (Mk 13:2; Lk 13:33-35) to the prediction of his Parousia as the Son of man* (Lk 17:24). Of particular interest, however, are those predictions of Jesus which focus on his own immediate future. They testify to an inescapable crisis in the earthly life of Jesus. These latter predictions will be explored, paying particular attention to the relationship between implicit and explicit predictions of Jesus' death* and resurrection.*

1. The Account of the Gospels
2. Implicit Predictions of Jesus
3. Explicit Predictions of Jesus
4. Jesus As Proclaimer and Interpreter of His Destiny
5. Conclusion

1. The Account of the Gospels.

The Synoptic Gospels in particular contain repeated predictions of the passion* and resurrection of Jesus. In the second half of each of the Synoptics three major passion and resurrection predictions serve as significant landmarks in the unfolding narratives. Like birth pangs signalling a delivery, they point to Jesus' inescapable mission awaiting him in Jerusalem.

Each of the Synoptic Gospels reports the predictions within the same thematic context. The first prediction follows Peter's confession, the second prediction follows the narrative of the Transfiguration and the healing* of the epileptic boy, the third prediction essentially follows the discourse with the rich young man (note Mt's insertion in 20:1-16). Except for Luke 18:35-43, all three predictions in each of the Synoptic accounts are followed by a discipleship* theme stressing the common future of rejection and vindication that will be shared by Jesus and his disciples.*

1.1. The Predictions in Mark. The three major Markan predictions (8:31; 9:31; 10:32-34) are most conspicuously placed within their narrative context. Mark 8:27-32 denotes a clear change of focus from chronicling the demonstration of Jesus' *exousia* ("power") to the final test of his *exousia*. Furthermore, Mark 8:27-32 leads to the first instruction of the disciples that the Son of man must die and rise after three days. Mark 10:32-34, on the other hand, is placed immediately prior to the entry into Jerusalem via Jericho. Mark clearly presents a climactic development beginning with the first prediction focusing on rejection, to the theme of being delivered into the human hands and finally to humiliation and death in the third prediction.

1.2. The Predictions in Luke. While Luke displays great similarities to the arrangement of the Markan narrative, the passion and resurrection predictions (9:18-22; 9:44 and 18:31-33) take a subordinate place within the overriding theme of the necessity to hasten to—and suffer in—Jerusalem (see Lk 9:51; 13:33).

1.3. The Predictions in Matthew. Matthew appears to be least concerned among the Synoptic Evangelists to emphasize these predictions (Mt 16:13-23; 17:22b-23 and 20:17-19). Nevertheless, in Matthew's section prior to the passion narrative we may notice a certain significance attributed to these predictions as well.

1.4. The Predictions in John. John refers to the impending crisis in terms of the "lifting up" (*hypsoō*) of the Son of man. By means of this verb both crucifixion and exaltation may be implied (Jn 3:14; 8:28; 12:32, 34). The latter concept is closely related to the glorification (*doxazō;* see Glory) of the Son of man (Jn 12:23; 13:31; 17:5; 21:19). The most explicit statement recorded in John is the Temple* saying in 2:19-22 (cf. Mk 14:58 par. Mt 26:61; Mk 15:29 par. Mt 27:39). Jesus predicts the tearing down and raising up of his body within three days.

2. Implicit Predictions of Jesus.
Certain redactional (*see* Redaction Criticism) and form-critical (*see* Form Criticism) analyses of these explicit predictions have led exegetes like G. Strecker to the conclusion that historically there is little authentic data to be derived from these sayings. According to these exegetes they more or less appear to bear the mark of predictions after the event. Especially the third major passion and resurrection prediction seems to betray post-Easter knowledge (see 3.1. below). To arrive at a historically convincing view regarding Jesus' predictions of his immediate future, it is crucial to consider implicit predictions alluding to a crisis-event of rejection and vindication.

2.1. References to Rejection and Vindication. The Gospels transmit a rich cluster of rejection-vindication sayings. It includes the eschatological prospect (Mk 14:25 par. Mt 26:29 and Lk 22:16, 18), the cup metaphor (Mk 10:38-39 par. Mt 20:22-23; Mk 14:36 par. Mt 26:39 and Lk 22:42; John 18:11), the metaphor of baptism* (Mk 10:38-39 par. Mt 20:22-23; Lk 12:50), the metaphor of the hour (Mk 14:35, 41 par. Mt 26:39, 45; Lk 22:53), the parable of the wicked tenants (Mk 12:1-12 par. Mt 21:33-46 and Luke 20:9-19) as well as the sign of Jonah* saying (Mt 12:38-40; 16:1-2; Lk 11:29-32). What do these veiled predictions signify in detail?

2.1.1. The Eschatological Prospect. The matrix of the eschatological (*see* Eschatology) prospect spans a great arch between the death of Jesus and the consummation of the kingdom in the Messianic banquet (*see* Table Fellowship). Jesus views his death not as a cul-de-sac but rather as a necessary passage leading eventually to the consummation of the kingdom of God.

2.1.2. The Metaphors of the Cup, Baptism and the Hour. The metaphors of the cup and baptism in particular refer to the impending crisis in terms of a severe yet temporary outpouring of divine judgment.* Against the background of the OT (For cup see e.g., Is 51:17-23; Jer 25:15-29. For flood/baptism: Job 9:31; Ps 18:17; 32:6; 42:8; 69:2, 14-15; 124:4-5; 144:7; Is 8:7-8; 43:2; Jon 2:4) these metaphors refer to internal (cup) and external (baptism) inundation in the wrath of God. Luke 12:49-50 clearly establishes the fact that this event of divine judgment is temporary and not permanent. Jesus' inundation in judgment is followed by the outpouring of the fire of division upon the earth as well as suffering for the disciples (see Mk 10:38-39).

2.1.3. The Parable of the Wicked Tenants. The authentic citation of Ps 118:22 at the end of this parable (1) confirms the eschatological prospect by stating the fact of rejection and vindication and (2) proclaims the establishment of the messianic foundation stone. By indirectly identifying himself as the rejected stone (i.e., son of the vineyard owner), Jesus views his impending rejection as a step toward the establishment of a new messianic rule. Despite (and we might add "through") rejection God will establish his Messiah (*see* Christ).

2.1.4. The "Sign of Jonah" Saying. The Sign of Jonah (*see* Sign of Jonah) is the vindication of the preacher (Jonah/Jesus) as an eschatological warning to repentance.* While refusing to give a heavenly and visible sign demanded by the Pharisees,* Jesus promises the sign of the invisible yet consequential divine vindication of the mortally endangered preacher.

3. Explicit Predictions of Jesus.

Only against the background of these diverse intimations of rejection and vindication can a historical and material investigation of the explicit predictions of death and resurrection promise to be convincing. The segregated investigation of Jesus' implicit predictions and his explicit intimations has been the Achilles heel of modern exegesis. If Jesus, however, spoke about his impending rejection and vindication in the terms outlined above, the question of the historical authenticity of death and resurrection predictions appears in a considerably different light. In addition, arguments adduced against the authenticity of death and resurrection predictions are frequently based on uncertain source-critical and form-critical grounds.

3.1. Explicit References to Passion and Resurrection. Detailed investigation of the three major Synoptic passion and resurrection predictions (see references cited in 1.1. to 1.3. above) yields the observation that each of them possesses its own linguistic and contextual integrity. Each prediction functions within a plausible historical setting (note especially the first prediction at the beginning of the journey toward Jerusalem, the third prediction immediately prior to entry into Jerusalem). Multiple attestation and Semitic coloring (see especially the first and second predictions) further support that which the Synoptic Evangelists claim to transmit, namely genuine predictions of the historical Jesus.

Some exegetes, such as F. Hahn, argue that the available form of the predictions reflects post-Easter redaction, while a core goes back to Jesus' vague prediction of a crisis event. Most notably, the detailed descriptions contained in the third prediction appear to support this argument. Jesus predicts his being delivered up to the chief priests, being condemned to death, being delivered up to the Gentiles,* being mocked, insulted, spat upon and scourged, being killed and raised after three days. Detailed comparison, however, between the third Markan passion and resurrection prediction (Mk 10:33b-34) and the

Markan passion narrative (see especially Mk 14:43-44; 14:64; 15:1; 15:20, 31; 14:65; 15:19; 15:15; 15:24 and 16:6) shows that both in terms of the sequence of events and in word usage the third passion prediction precedes the very old Markan passion narrative. J. Jeremias adds the observation that this most detailed prediction contains no features which would not be generally known in capital proceedings in Palestine at the time of Christ. Further detailed study discloses the weakness of arguing that these predictions were composed in part or in total after the event.

3.2. The Relationship to Passion-Parousia Sayings. C. H. Dodd and more recently K. Berger (among others) have suggested that Jesus' words about his impending crisis may have been sufficiently ambiguous to have been the source for both resurrection and early Parousia sayings. Matthew 10:23; Mark 9:1 (par. Mt 16:28 and Lk 9:27); Mark 13:30 (par. Mt 24:34 and Lk 21:32) as well as Luke 17:24-25 and Mk 14:62 (par. Mt 26:64) seem to suggest the imminent occurrence of the Parousia. It is indeed true that we do not possess any saying of Jesus which directly relates the events of death-resurrection and Parousia to each another. However, three factors distinguish the vindication/resurrection sayings from the early Parousia sayings, and thus call into question the argument that they were originally interchangeable.

First, there is a difference regarding time references. While the vindication/resurrection event occurs immediately following rejection and death, the Parousia event is merely an imminent event (compare the specific three-day reference to speedy recovery with vague time frames in Mt 10:23 and in Mk 9:1 and 13:30).

Second, the vindication/resurrection sayings convey a degree of urgency absent in the early Parousia sayings (compare *dei*, "one must," in Mk 8:31 and *mellei*, "one will have to" in Mk 9:31 with the general anticipation of fulfillment regarding the Parousia sayings). While the vindication/resurrection occurs in the paradoxical context of the judgment of the righteous, the Parousia marks the triumph of the Son of man (Mt 10:23).

Third, the references to vindication/resurrection display a different relationship to the event of rejection and death. While references to vindication/resurrection following rejection and death function as complementary contrasts, death-Parousia sayings merely display a loose connection to one another (see Mk 14:25; Lk 13:35 and Lk 17:24-25; the inverted order of Parousia-death in the latter example illustrates the loose connection between the two events). It is therefore most convincing to argue that Jesus predicted his immediate vindication/resurrection from rejection/ death side by side with his imminent Parousia.

4. Jesus As Proclaimer and Interpreter of His Destiny.
Historiographical research frequently separates the facts of history from their interpretation by following generations. On the basis of the preceding observations we conclude that *Jesus functions as the divine interpreter of his own history.* The disciples are being given interpretive keys by which they may eventually understand the events of the death and resurrection of the Messiah. The following specific points may be noted:

4.1. The Anticipation of Death. Schürmann and others have emphasized the fact that Jesus' message inherently carried an element of danger. Jesus' claim to *exousia* (Mt 5:17-48), his controversial inclusion of sinners in the offer of entry into the kingdom and his opposition to the ruling clergy of his day (cf. Mk 6:1-6 par. Lk 1:14-30; Mk 12:1-12 par. Mt 21:33-46 and Lk 20:9-19) suggest that Jesus must have been facing the possibility of death. This prospect would have been all the more likely in light of the execution of John the Baptist and the rejection of Jesus' own message by the religious authorities. The predictions of rejection and death (e.g., Lk 17:25; Jn 10:11; 12:7) thus operate in a realistic historical setting.

4.2. The Resurrection Assurance. Jesus' predictions of vindication and resurrection (see also Mk 9:9 par. Mt 17:9; Mk 14:28 par. Mt 26:32) mark the first step toward interpreting the event of his death as a God-intended, universally significant event. Far from being a fateful and tragic end of Jesus' ministry, the cursed event has a particular meaning before God.

4.3. The Ransom Saying. Jesus reportedly interpreted his death as a ransom (*see* Ransom Saying) for many, thus alluding to Isaiah 53:11b, 12b. This Son of man saying, which stands up as authentic under critical scrutiny (Page), marks the interpretive teaching of Jesus as the foundation of early Christian belief in the sacrificial death and justifying resurrection of Jesus.

5. Conclusion.
Mark 9:10 reports that prior to Easter the disciples were unable to understand Jesus' teaching regarding his resurrection. This suggests that resurrection predictions were not as explicit in the ears of the disciples as they now appear in the light of 1 Corinthians 15:4. Hearing them as predictions of a Messiah, whose eternal reign rather than death was expected (Dan 7:13-14), the consternation on the part of the disciples is understandable. Furthermore, from the perspective of the disciples resurrection was to occur at the end of the age to all people (Dan 12:2). Their lack of understanding Jesus' reference to his individual resurrection is therefore all the more plausible. In the minds of the disciples both rejection/vindication and death/resurrection predictions were, before the Easter event, opaque and offensive teachings of Jesus as Messiah. After the resurrection, however, Jesus' predictions took on a new dimension and provided the disciples with a framework for interpreting these wholly unparalleled events which had taken place before their eyes according to the divine will.

See also DEATH OF JESUS; RANSOM SAYING; RESURRECTION; SON OF MAN.

BIBLIOGRAPHY. H. F. Bayer, *Jesus' Predictions of Vindication and Resurrection* (WUNT 2/20; Tübingen: J. C. B. Mohr, 1986); K. Berger, *Die Auferstehung des Propheten und die Erhöhung des Menschensohnes* (Göttingen: Vandenhoeck & Ruprecht, 1976); J. Blank, "Der eschatologische Ausblick Mk 14, 25 und seine Bedeutung," in *Kontinuität und Einheit,* ed. P.-G. Müller and W. Stenger (Freiburg: Herder, 1981) 508-18; C. H. Dodd, *Historical Tradition in the Fourth Gospel* (2d ed., Cambridge: University Press, 1979); F. Hahn, *The Titles of Jesus in Christology: Their History in Early Christianity* (London: Lutterworth, 1969); J. Jeremias, *The Servant of God* (2d ed., London: SCM, 1965); S. H. T. Page, "The Authenticity of the Ransom Logion (Mark 10:45b)," in *Gospel Perspectives 1: Studies of History and Tradition in the Four Gospels,* ed. R. T. France and D. Wenham (Sheffield: JSOT Press, 1980) 137-61; H. Schürmann, *Gottes Reich—Jesu Geschick. Jesu ureigener Tod im Lichte seiner Basileia—Verkündigung* (Freiburg: Herder, 1983); K. R. Snodgrass, *The Parable of the Wicked Tenants* (Tübingen: J. C. B. Mohr, 1983); G. Strecker, "Die Leidens- und Auferstehungsvoraussagen im Markusevangelium," in *Eschaton und Historie* (Göttingen: Vandenhoeck & Ruprecht, 1979) 52-75; V. Taylor, "The Origin of the Markan Passion Sayings," in *New Testament Essays* (Grand Rapids: Eerdmans, 1972) 60-71. H. F. Bayer

PRIEST, PRIESTHOOD

1. Introduction
2. Priesthood in the NT Period
3. Individual Priests in the Gospels
4. Chief Priests

1. Introduction.
Israel itself was to be a "kingdom of priests" (Ex 19:4-6); however, early on in the nation's history a priestly order was constituted within Israel* and charged with representing the people before God* through the cultic affairs of the tabernacle/temple and perform-

ing sacrifices. After the Exile priests played a primary role in the reorganization of the people (*see* Judaism). While their political power waxed and waned in the centuries leading up to the NT era, among the people of God their positions of influence continued to receive divine legitimation until the final destruction of the Temple* by Rome (*see* Destruction of Jerusalem); after all, theirs was the exclusive right to perform sacrifices (cf. Ex 28—29; Lev 8—10) on behalf of God's people. Moreover, following the Exile, the Temple and its priesthood became the destination of an increasing flow of tithes and taxes,* adding to the centrality of the priesthood on the sociopolitical stage of Palestine at the turn of the era (see Schürer, 2.257-74). This portrait of priestly power and privilege concerns especially those priests residing in Jerusalem, and not so much those priests of lower status, such as Zechariah (mentioned in Lk 1), from villages and more rural areas.

The functions of priests were many, primary among which was the offering of sacrifices. Duties of ordinary priests included pronouncing blessings (*see* Blessing and Woe), providing Temple music (vocal and instrumental), policing the boundaries of the Temple area, blowing trumpets on various festive occasions, inspecting and repairing the grounds and buildings of the Temple, fixing the sacrificial limits of worshippers according to their ability to pay, collecting tithes and maintaining the Temple treasury, inspecting diseases and performing purification rites (cf. Mk 1:44), and evaluating problems resulting from contact with dead bodies and bodily emissions (*see* Clean and Unclean).

Up to and during the time of Jesus, the high priest served both political and cultic roles; he was the only priest who could perform the great sin offering on the Day of Atonement, involving entry into the Holy of Holies.

2. Priesthood in the NT Period.

In the first half of the first century A.D. the basis of priesthood continued to be genealogical, involving Levites (a member of the tribe of Levi) and priests (a Levite descended from Aaron). A third group, the Zadokites (those who traced their ancestry back to Zadok, priest during the time of David and Solomon), probably served priestly functions during this period as well. In the Qumran community the Zadokite priests were especially revered (*see* Dead Sea Scrolls).

The zenith of priestly influence was attained during the Hasmonean era (c. 165-63 B.C.), and at least one ruler (John Hyrcanus, who ruled 135-104 B.C.) was able to combine kingship and priesthood. The *Testament of Levi*, with its anticipation of a "new priest"

whose star "will rise in heaven like that of a king" (*T. Levi* 18:2-6) may also date from this period (cf. Ps 100:4; Zech 6:12-13). Later rulers, however, were less successful in perpetuating the union of king and priest, and with the arrival of Herod the Great (36-4 B.C.) the situation changed dramatically (*see* Herodian Dynasty).

Under Herod the high priesthood lost much of the power it had previously enjoyed. Like the earlier Hellenists, Herod usurped the right to appoint the high priest. Moreover, he kept in his own quarters the high priest's sacred vestments.

Following the death of Herod, the Romans (*see* Rome) ruled Palestine more directly, and during this period the high priests worked closely with the Roman procurators and prefects. This in itself is evidence that high priests typically arose from the party of the Sadducees (*see* Judaism), since other Jews would not have been so quick to embrace as political partners these alien overlords. Sadducees, however, were more concerned with the continuing status of the Temple and its cult among the people of God than they were fearful of religious compromises in the context of first-century political exigencies.

From the point of view of the common folk, resentment toward Roman occupation combined with the divine legitimation of the Temple and its priesthood to grant the high priest far-reaching power and lofty status within the nation. This perception was bolstered by the high priest's role as president of the Sanhedrin.* With the Roman government moved to Caesarea, the high priest had no rival except when the procurator journeyed to Jerusalem.

The immense power of the high priest before and after Herod is crucial to an understanding of the NT period. The high priest had the power to collect taxes, supervise both the Temple and the Sanhedrin, and represent the Jews in all their dealings with Rome.

3. Individual Priests in the Gospels.

Within the Gospels three individuals stand out in connection with the priesthood: Zechariah, Annas and Caiaphas.

3.1. Zechariah. Luke alone mentions Zechariah, naming him as the father of John the Baptist (3:2; *see* John the Baptist) and relating the story of John's extraordinary birth (1:5-80). According to Luke, Zechariah is a priest in the order of Abijah—a designation reflecting the division of the priests into groups due to their excessive numbers (cf. 1 Chron 24:10; Neh 12:4, 17; Josephus *Ant.* 7.14.7 §§ 363-67). Each group served in the Temple twice each year for one week. During their Temple service, duties were divided among the priests by lot, with the greatest honor falling to the one chosen to enter the Temple and burn incense. Luke narrates that Zechariah was chosen for this exceptional duty, which could be performed by a priest only once in his lifetime.

In the opening of his story, Luke is primarily concerned with the tragedy of Zechariah and Elizabeth's life. She also comes from a priestly family (Lk 1:5); hence, their marriage protected the purity and dignity of the priesthood. Their tragedy consists in this: They are blameless before God, yet childless, and beyond the age of childbearing (Lk 1:6-7). Undoubtedly, Luke is drawing a parallel between these two and such OT precedents as Abraham* and Sarah (Gen 18:11) and Hannah (1 Sam 1:1-2). Given these OT stories of divine intervention in cases of childlessness, we are not surprised to discover that God has heard their prayers* (Lk 1:13) and will provide a son. Zechariah receives the message with unbelief, seeking a sign (Lk 1:18; cf. Lk 11:16, 29-30), with the result that he loses his speech until the moment when Gabriel's words are fulfilled. After John's birth and naming, in which Zechariah shows his obedience, his voice returns to him and he is enabled by the Spirit to prophesy concerning the coming redemption and the role of his son in God's salvific work (Lk 1:64, 67-69; *see* Zechariah's Song).

3.2. Annas. Annas, high priest from A.D. 6-15 (Josephus *Ant.* 18.2.1-2 §§26-34), is mentioned twice each by both Luke (Lk 3:2; Acts 4:6) and John (Jn 18:13, 24). Luke's apparently anachronistic reference to Annas as "high priest" (Lk 3:2: "the high priesthood of Annas and Caiaphas") may reflect Luke's dependence on a group who refused to acknowledge Annas's deposition (cf. Acts 4:6; Schürmann, 151). It is more likely that this language reflects the continued use of the title for Annas after his departure from the office and, even more so, his continued power and influence, underscored by the fact that five of his sons (as well as his son-in-law, Caiaphas [see 3.3]), were appointed to the office of high priest.

John's introduction of Annas in the narrative of Jesus' trial (*see* Trial of Jesus) is puzzling from both literary and historical points of view. Thus, after Jesus' arrest he is taken to Annas (Jn 18:13), even though Caiaphas is clearly high priest during this time (Jn 18:13b-14). Then, in John 18:19, "the high priest questioned Jesus," but the name of this "high priest" is not given, so we are left to assume from John 18:24 that it was in fact *Annas* who interviewed Jesus about "his disciples and his teaching." Hence, in spite of the fact that John knows of the role of Caiaphas and the Jewish leadership in Jesus' trial (Jn 11:47-53; 18:3, 12,

24, 28), he narrates no trial before the Sanhedrin.

In relating the story along these lines, John is almost certainly drawing on early tradition about the trial of Jesus, and it seems to be a tradition with some contacts with the pre-Lukan material. This is suggested not only by the narrative seams in this account, but also by John's apparent lack of interest in Annas elsewhere in his Gospel (see Dauer, 62-99; Green, 272-75). On the other hand, the Fourth Evangelist is clearly aware of material like that found in the Synoptic versions of the hearing of Jesus before the Sanhedrin (cf. Jn 2:9; 10:24-26, 33, 36; 18:24, 28). In refocusing the trial scene first on Annas' participation, then on the hearing before Pilate (*see* Pontius Pilate), John may be motivated by his interest in sharpening the role of the Romans in the whole process of the arrest and trial (Rensberger).

3.3. Caiaphas. Joseph Caiaphas, son-in-law of Annas, is mentioned in Matthew 26:3, 57; Luke 3:2; John 11:49; 18:13-14, 24, 28. He was high priest from A.D. 18-36/37 (Josephus *Ant.* 18.2.1-2 §§ 26-34). As both Matthew and John note, he was high priest during the time of Jesus' arrest, trial and execution.

His portrayal in the Gospel of John is that of a champion of political expediency. Speaking to the Jewish council, he remarks, "You do not recognize that it is expedient that one person die for the people, rather than the whole nation perish" (Jn 11:50). Ironically, Caiaphas thus unwittingly prophecies the sacrificial nature of Jesus' death for all people (Jn 11:51-52; cf. Jn 18:14). The political savvy of the high priest shown in this context is fully consonant with the fact that, apparently through diplomatic finesse, Caiaphas was able to remain in office for such a long period of time.

John's repeated reference to Caiaphas as high priest "in that year" (Jn 11:51; 18:13) has sometimes been taken as evidence of the Evangelist's lack of understanding of the high priest's office, as though John thought the high priesthood rotated on an annual basis. Today, however, there is widespread agreement that "that year" refers to "this particularly memorable year"—namely, the year of Jesus' redemptive death (*see* Death of Jesus).

4. Chief Priests.

Found more than sixty times in the Gospels and Acts, *archiereis* is typically translated "chief priests." In the Gospels, they appear as a group in opposition to Jesus (Lk 19:47; 20:19; 22:2, 4, 52; 23:4-5, 10, 13; 24:20). Josephus* also speaks of "chief priests" (e.g., *J.W.* 2.16.2 §336), but neither the Gospels nor Josephus provide much information more specific about their identity. Schrenk, followed by many others, holds that they are "an established college with oversight of the cultus, control of the temple, administration of the temple treasury, and supervision of priestly discipline" (Schrenk, 270-71). According to the Gospels, they were members of the Sanhedrin (cf. Mk 14:53; Lk 22:66). The chief priests were centered in Jerusalem, the socioreligious and economic center of Palestine, and the Gospels consistently refer to them in this locale (e.g., Mt 2:4; 16:21; 20:18; 21:15, 23, 45; passim). Together with the high priest, they would have been the bearers of significant power and privilege within the Judaism of Jesus' day.

See also JUDAISM; SANHEDRIN; TEMPLE; TRIAL OF JESUS.

BIBLIOGRAPHY. A. A. Cody, *A History of the Old Testament Priesthood* (Rome: Pontifical Biblical Institute, 1969); A. Dauer, *Die Passionsgeschichte im Johannesevangelium: Eine traditionsgeschichtliche und theologische Untersuchung zu Joh 18.1-19, 30* (München: Kösel, 1972); R. de Vaux, *Ancient Israel: Its Life and Institutions* (2 vols.; New York: McGraw-Hill, 1961) vol. 2; J. B. Green, *The Death of Jesus: Tradition and Interpretation in the Passion Narrative* (WUNT 2:33; Tübingen: J. C. B. Mohr, 1988); D. Rensberger, "The Politics of John: The Trial of Jesus in the Fourth Gospel," *JBL* 103 (1984) 395-411; G. Schrenk, "ἀρχιερεύς," *TDNT* III.265-83; E. Schürer, *The History of the Jewish People in the Age of Jesus Christ (175 B.C.-A.D. 135)*, rev. and ed. G. Vermes, F. Millar and M. Black (3 vols.; Edinburgh: T. & T. Clark, 1973-79) vol. 2; H. Schürmann, *Das Lukasevangelium* (HTKNT; 3d ed; Freiburg: Herder, 1984); E. M. Smallwood, "High Priests and Politics in Roman Palestine," *JTS* n.s. 13 (1962) 14-34.

L. D. Hurst and J. B. Green

PRONOUNCEMENT STORY. *See* FORM CRITICISM.

PROPHETS, PROPHECY
1. OT Background
2. Terminology of the Gospels
3. General Remarks about Prophets
4. People Identified as Prophets
5. Jesus as Prophet
6. Early Christian Prophets
7. Prophets and the Gospel Tradition

1. OT Background.
The Gospel writers say much about prophets and prophecy. Their understanding of who these people were and the nature of the phenomenon is primarily informed by the OT. Hence, a brief survey of the nature and contribution of the OT prophets is necessary.

1.1. Terminology. The Hebrew term most commonly translated "prophet" is *nābī'*. Etymologically it means "one called [of God]," but it was also used to refer to a speaker, a preacher or a spokesperson [for God]. Older OT terms for prophet were *rō'eh* or *ḥōzeh*, and referred to "seers," people who had the ability to see what others could not, especially things concerning the divine will.

1.2. The Work of a Prophet. OT prophets were people who had a special encounter with God* and who, as a result, received a message directly from God (cf. Num 22:8-9; 1 Kings 22:14). This message came to them in many different ways—dreams, visions, moments of ecstasy, external voices, internal voices, etc. (cf. Num 12:6; 1 Sam 3:3-9; 1 Kings 13:18-22; Is 1:1; Ezek 3:14)—but the word was always God's and never the prophet's. The prophets' message—or the word of the Lord through the prophet—took many forms: proclamations of divine judgment (2 Kings 1:6), divine salvation (2 Kings 20:6) or judgment and salvation (Is 65:7-8); oracles of woe (Is 5:8-23) or assurance (Jer 30:10-11); admonitions to the people to do what they were failing to do (Amos 4:4-5); judicial speeches (Hos 4:1-3); and symbolic dramatic acts in which the prophet acted out the content of the message to impress it on the minds of the people (Is 20:2-4; Jer 28:10). Sometimes prophets predicted what was yet to come (cf. Ezek 20:45-48), but the verb "to prophesy" does not in itself mean "to predict [the future]." Its primary meaning is simply "to do the work of a prophet," which was to be God's spokesperson.

The prophets themselves were of various kinds and from different walks of life. Some of them were itinerants like Elijah* and Elisha, holy men and miracle workers. Some were ecstatics (cf. 1 Kings 19:19-24). Some gathered around a prominent person to form groups or schools of prophets (2 Kings 2:3-7). Some were localized, attached even to the Temple in Jerusalem and closely associated with the priesthood (cf. Jer 1:1). Others stood outside the social structures of their day, acting as reformers who called Israel back to the covenant God had made with them and from which they had departed.

1.3. Prophetic Inspiration. But the hallmark of a prophet, that which enabled these men and women to speak for God, was their inspiration by the Holy Spirit. They were a "Spirit-bearing people" (Hos 9:7 LXX). The prophet was the one who could say, "I am filled with power, with the Spirit of the Lord" (Mic 3:8) or "The Spirit of the Lord speaks by me; his word is upon my tongue" (2 Sam 23:2). Thus when prophets spoke with the Spirit on them or in them (cf. Ezek 2:2), they spoke with the authority* of God. It was this that gave weight and significance to their message. And so it is that the phrase "Thus says the Lord" runs throughout the writings of the prophets (Is 7:7, passim). It was the Spirit catching away the prophets and lifting them up into communion with God (cf. Ezek 3:12-14) that gave them superhuman understanding. It was the Spirit that gave them their prophetic immediacy of insight into the will of God so that their hearers recognized in their message an authority unlike that of their merely human advisers or teachers—a message that in reality was the revelation of the mind of God to their minds by persons especially endowed with the Spirit.

1.4. The Cessation of Prophecy. Theologically speaking, it may be argued that God would never leave himself without a witness. And among historians of the period "it has become increasingly recognized that prophecy did not disappear in Judaism* during the Hellenistic and Roman periods" (Aune). Nevertheless, the popular opinion at the beginning of the NT era, fed no doubt by important OT texts, some authoritative teachers, as well as other Jewish literature, seems to have been that God's prophets were no more, and prophecy was a thing of the past.

The Talmud illustrates this opinion: "When Haggai, Zechariah and Malachi, the latter prophets, were dead, the Holy Spirit departed from Israel" (*b. Soṭa* 48b). Josephus also maintains, ". . . From Artaxerxes to our time our history is also depicted, but it does not deserve the same credibility as the earlier work, since the prophets have no true successors" (Josephus, *Ag. Ap.* 1.8; cf. Ps 74:9; Dan 9:24; Zech 13:2-6; 1 Macc 4:46; 9:27; 2 *Apoc. Bar.* 85:3; see Friedrich, 816-819).

But whatever the popular opinion concerning prophets and prophecy may have been, at the very beginning of the Gospel narratives there is not only renewed interest in the Spirit of God, but this Spirit is said to be once again at work in the lives of humans. It is as though the writers of these Gospels wished to awaken within the minds of their readers an awareness of the present reality of the Spirit and to create within them a new spiritual excitement. Not only do the Gospel writers say that the Spirit was active at Jesus' birth (Mt 1:18; Lk 1:35), baptism (Mt 3:16; Mk 1:10; Lk 3:22; Jn 1:33) and temptation (Mt 4:1; Mk 1:12; Lk 4:1), but indications run throughout the Gospels that the Spirit was at work in others as well. This is especially true of the early chapters of Luke where several individuals experience the working of the Spirit: John the Baptist* (1:15); Elizabeth (1:41); Zechariah (1:67; *see* Zechariah's Song); and Simeon (2:25, 26; *see* Simeon's Song). Luke in particular (though the other Gospel writers concur) seems to be

saying that the longed-for universal age of the Spirit (cf. Joel 2:28, 29) had at last arrived (Lk 4:18, 19; cf. Is 61:1-3) and that the age of prophets and prophecy, if it had indeed died out, was now being re-born.

2. Terminology of the Gospels.
That the Evangelists believed a new era of prophecy had arrived can be seen from the number of times they refer to prophets and prophecy in their writings, and from the varied terms they use.

The most frequently used term, *prophētēs*, means "one who speaks forth," being derived from the two Greek words *pro* ("before") and *phēmi* ("speak"). From ancient times this word was used of one who speaks for a god and interprets that god's will to people. In the Gospels it means, as did the Hebrew *nābî'* which it translated in the LXX, a person who expounds the will of the one true God, one who speaks forth the words of God under the influence of the Holy Spirit* (Lk 1:67), one who speaks for God. *Prophētēs* is used thirty-seven times in Matthew, only six times in Mark, twenty-nine times in Luke and fourteen times in John. The Gospels account for 86 of its 144 occurrences in the NT.

The verb *prophēteuō* shows up much less frequently, appearing only nine times in the Gospels. It essentially means "to do the work of a prophet," which more narrowly means "to proclaim a divine revelation" (cf. Mt 7:22), "to reveal prophetically what is hidden" (cf. Mt 26:68) or "to foretell the future" (cf. Jn 11:51). Only once does the noun *prophēteia* occur and then, as would be expected, it refers to the prophetic word uttered by a prophet, which in reality is the word of the Lord spoken through the prophet to the people (Mt 13:14).

Prophētis ("prophetess"), a related word, also appears in the Gospels, though only once (Lk 2:36). Yet its single occurrence is sufficient to indicate that women, too, played an important role in expounding the word of the Lord to his people, of seeing into and giving expression to the will of God (cf. Acts 2:17-18; 21:9).

But wherever there is the true prophet or prophetess, there is also the threat of counterfeits. Hence, the word *pseudoprophētēs* also shows up in the Gospels—three times in Matthew and once in both Mark and Luke. With this word Jesus warns that there will be those who will come falsely claiming to speak for God and, if possible, will lead God's people away from the truth (Mt 7:15; 24:11, 24; Mk 13:22; Lk 6:26).

3. General Remarks about Prophets.
3.1. References to the OT. In some instances the

Gospels link "the prophets" with other terms to create phrases such as "the Law and the Prophets," "the Prophets and the Law," "Moses and the Prophets" or "the Law of Moses and the Prophets and the Psalms" (Mt 5:17; 7:12; 11:13; 22:40; Lk 16:16, 29, 31; 24:27, 44; Jn 1:46). In these cases the word "prophets" is used in a most general way, referring not to any specific prophet or group of prophets, or even to individual writing prophets such as Isaiah or Jeremiah. Rather, expressions such as "the Law and the Prophets" were commonly used by Jews of Jesus' day and by Jesus himself to refer to the OT in its entirety.

3.2. Proverbial Sayings. The stories of God's prophets had often ended in disappointment and even tragedy. Their faithful and truthful proclamation of the word of the Lord to God's people often led to the prophet's rejection and ostracization by those same people. Against this background proverbial sayings about prophets sprang up and were readily understood in Palestine: "A prophet has no honor in his own country or among his own relatives or in his own household [though he might have it elsewhere]"; "It is not possible for a prophet to perish outside of Jerusalem" (Mt 13:57; Mk 6:4; Lk 13:33; Jn 4:44).

3.3. General References. There are still other general remarks about prophets in the Gospels. These do not identify the prophets. They do not set them completely apart from others. They occasionally include people one would not usually consider to be a prophet. Nevertheless, these general remarks continue to emphasize the role of prophets—probing, seeking, eagerly desiring to perceive and understand the mysteries of God, and then suffering for their efforts. Jesus is recorded as having said to his disciples,* "Truly, I say to you that many prophets and just people longed to see what you see and they did not see, and to hear what you hear and did not hear" (Mt 13:17). Luke reports that Jesus spoke of the blood of all the prophets which had been spilled from the foundation of the world to the present generation (Lk 11:50).

4. People Identified as Prophets.

4.1. OT Prophets. All of the Gospel writers make reference to OT prophets, but Matthew does so more frequently than the rest. He seems especially concerned to show that the presence of Jesus in the world, the events of his life, the things that he did and said, even his betrayal and death, were in fact the fulfillment of the words of the ancient prophets (Mt 1:22; 2:15, 17, 23; 4:14; 8:17; 12:17; 13:35; 21:4; 26:56; 27:9).

Whatever initial meaning their words may have had, for Matthew their ultimate meaning was realized in Jesus. Hence, over and over, almost like a refrain, he writes, "[This all happened to Jesus] in order that the word of the prophet might be fulfilled." This "word" predicted his virgin birth, where he was to be born, his descent into and return from Egypt, the killing of the innocent children precipitated by his birth, the fact that he would be called a Nazarene and many other events (Mt 1:23; 2:5-6, 15, 17-18, 23, etc.; cf. Lk 18:31-34). For the Evangelists, and Matthew in particular, the message of the prophets concerned Jesus. But lest anyone should think this message came from the prophets themselves, Matthew is careful to remind his readers that the word was in fact spoken by the Lord through the prophet (cf. Mt 1:22; 2:15). The prophet is always the channel through whom God's message comes.

4.1.1. Anonymous Old Testament Prophets. When the word "prophet" is used in the Gospels it most often refers to the OT prophet. Many times, however, these OT prophets are not identified, a fact that again underscores the idea that in and of themselves the prophets were of little importance in comparison to the message they proclaimed—it was the message of the Lord that was of supreme significance (Mt 1:22; 2:5, 15, 23; 21:4; Lk 1:70; 18:31; 24:25; Jn 6:45). Although not named, these special people, nevertheless, faithfully proclaimed the word of the Lord (cf. Mt 1:22), were persecuted by those to whom they proclaimed this word (Mt 5:12; Lk 6:23) and were murdered for their faithfulness (Mt 23:30-31, 37; Lk 11:47-48; 13:34). But God did not abandon them, and Jesus affirms that they all are in the kingdom of God along with Abraham, Isaac and Jacob (Lk 13:28).

4.1.2. Specific Old Testament Prophets. On the other hand, a few OT prophets are singled out and identified by name: Isaiah is the prophet most often referred to (Mt 3:3; 4:14; 8:17; 12:17; 13:35; Mk 1:2; Lk 3:4; 4:17; Jn 1:23; 12:38) and then Jeremiah (Mt 2:17; 16:14; 27:9). Only two other so-called writing prophets are mentioned by name—Jonah (Mt 12:39; *see* Sign of Jonah) and Daniel (Mt 24:15). The only additional OT figures that are designated as prophets by the Gospel writers are Elijah (Mt 16:14) and Elisha (Lk 4:27).

4.1.3. The Abiding Message of the Prophets. Whether the prophets were named or unnamed, it was their message that was all-important. But it is worth noticing that their message, though spoken centuries before the Gospels, was nevertheless to be understood as having abiding significance and to be applied to contemporary events. Jesus chides his disciples for having failed to do this: "O foolish people, and people slow of heart to believe all that the prophets spoke. Was it not necessary for the Christ to suffer and to enter into his glory?" Then he began with Moses and continued on through the prophets to interpret for them from all their writings those things they had written about himself (Lk 24:25-27).

4.2. Instances of Prophets and Prophesying in the Gospel Story.

4.2.1. Zechariah. The Gospel writers do not restrict their comments about prophecy and prophesying to the OT prophets. Zechariah, the father of John the Baptist, though not explicitly referred to as a prophet by the Evangelists, has the marks and performs the work of a prophet. Luke says that he was filled with the Holy Spirit and only as he was thus inspired did he prophesy. As Luke tells the story, it is clear that Zechariah had been granted special divine insight into the nature and calling of his own son and was thereby enabled to predict John's ministry of going before the Lord to prepare his way (Lk 1:67-76).

4.2.2. Elizabeth. Elizabeth also spoke prophetically. She is not called a prophetess, nor is the verb *prophēteuō* ("to prophesy") used to describe her words when she cried out with a loud voice and blessed Mary, the mother of Jesus, who had come to visit her (*see* Mary's Song). But it is said of her as it was said of Zechariah: she "was filled with the Holy Spirit . . ." (Lk 1:41). "Having the prophetic Spirit, she is able to know the past and see what is hidden without anyone telling her. She thus greets Mary as the mother of the Messiah." (Friedrich, 835).

4.2.3. Simeon. Though a mere man (*anthrōpos*, Lk 2:35), Simeon, like the prophets of old, experienced the Holy Spirit coming upon him and revealing to him something that he could not otherwise have known— that he would not die until he had seen the Lord's Christ (Lk 2:25-27). Furthermore, the Spirit directed his movements so that he came into the Temple at the precise moment the parents of Jesus brought him into the Temple court.

4.2.4. Anna. Though Luke knows and records Anna's lineage, he mentions her solely because she was a prophetess, a person of the Spirit who was enabled to see what others could not see of things divine. Coming suddenly upon the infant Jesus in the Temple as his parents were presenting him to the Lord, she saw in him something that made her break out in praise to God and speak knowingly of him to all those around her who were looking for the redemption of Jerusalem (Lk 2:36-38).

4.2.5. Caiaphas. Most surprising is the remark that Caiaphas, who certainly was no friend of Jesus, prophesied about Jesus that he would die in behalf of the nation and thus spare the nation. Caiaphas was not a prophet, yet apparently he was, if only for a moment, granted the powers of a prophet by the Spirit of God. As a result he predicted correctly the course of Jesus' life (Jn 11:49-51).

4.2.6. John the Baptist. The Gospel writers all indicate that John the Baptist was a genuine prophet who stood in the tradition of the OT prophets. Luke records that Zechariah, his father, was the first to designate him as such (Lk 1:76). The crowds of common people held him in high esteem as a prophet (Mt 14:5; 21:26; Lk 20:6). Even a delegation sent to him from the Jews—apparently the Jewish elite—in Jerusalem was forced to ask whether or not he was "the prophet" (Jn 1:21, 25). Jesus is recorded as having affirmed that John was indeed a prophet, though more than a prophet, or perhaps even the greatest of all prophets (Mt 11:9-10; Lk 7:26-28).

Like the OT prophets "the word of the Lord came to John" and started him on his prophetic ministry (Lk 3:2; cf. Jer 1:1-2; Hos 1:1). Like them he confronted those in high places, in his case openly denouncing Herod's evil ways (Mk 6:18; cf. 2 Sam 12:1-14; 1 Kings 21:17-26). As with many prophets before him, he lost his life for his temerity (Mk 6:18-28). Like them he thundered against the sin of the people and called them to return to God and his ways which they had forsaken (Lk 3:7-14). In this regard his baptism* played a large part in his ministry. It was not proselyte baptism, intended to initiate Gentiles* into the Jewish community, nor was it like that practiced at Qumran, for all were invited to come. Rather, as his preaching was a prophetic call to the people to repent, so his baptism was a dramatic prophet-like act which sealed their repentance.

John the Baptist was such a powerful figure, and was held in such high esteem as a prophet by the masses, that it was only natural for some to begin to think that he was "*the* prophet" (cf. Jn 1:21, 25; 7:52 𝔓[66]). They presumably had in mind the prophet like Moses, whom God would raise up from among the people and to whom the people would listen (Deut 18:15). This eschatological prophet would inaugurate the age of salvation. There are hints that a sect later arose from among the followers of John the Baptist, claiming that the Baptist was the Messiah (*see* Christ). It may be that certain NT writers, and the Fourth Evangelist in particular, were at pains to counter and correct these claims (cf. Jn 6:1-9, 21, 26, 32-33, 35; 3:27-30). Although the Gospel tradition regards John as a great prophet (cf. Mt 11:8-9), it nevertheless refuses him the title of Messiah. He is the eschatological forerunner of the Messiah, who would prepare the way for the Messiah's coming (Mt 3:1-3; Mk 1:2-6; Lk 3:3-6).

5. Jesus As Prophet.

5.1. Jesus' Popular Acclaim As Prophet. The Gospels make it clear that the masses saw in the words and actions of Jesus convincing evidence that he was a prophet. For example, like the OT prophets he pronounced on the people threats of judgment to come (cf. Mt 11:21-24; 23:13-29; Lk 6:24-26) and offered them promises of blessings from God (Mt 5:3-11; 13:16-17; Mk 10:29-30). He, too, had an ability to see what ordinary people could not see. He surprised people with what can only be called supernatural knowledge or insight by the Spirit (cf. Mk 2:5, 8; Lk 9:47; Jn 2:24-25). He, too, had visions (Mk 3:10), heard the voice of God (Mk 3:11) and was caught up in moments of ecstasy (Lk 10:21). He, too, performed miracles* and did mighty works—even raising the dead to life—that made the people marvel and fear (Lk 7:11-16; cf.1 Kings 17:17-23). He, too, acted out his message in dramatic form (Mk 11:13-14, 21; 11:15-17). When the thousands were fed by Jesus from a very small supply of food, they concluded that he was the long-expected prophet (Jn 6:17). When the crowds at the Feast of Tabernacles listened to Jesus teach and heard his claims, they were certain that he was the prophet (Jn 7:40).

Both individuals and the masses saw in Jesus a prophet like the classical OT prophets. The Samaritan* woman called Jesus a prophet (Jn 4:19). The blind man to whom Jesus restored sight said, "He is a prophet" (Jn 9:17). Two of Jesus' own disciples spoke of him "as a prophet mighty in deed and word in the sight of God and all the people" (Lk 24:19). The demand of the guards given to Jesus as he was on trial, "Prophesy!" (Mk 14:65; Mt 26:68; Lk 22:64), which was not part of the usual games played by the Roman soldiers with the condemned prisoner (Jeremias, 78), makes it certain that they too were aware that Jesus was perceived as a prophet (*see* Trial of Jesus).

5.2. Jesus' Prophetic Self-Understanding. The Gospel writers record that Jesus regarded himself as a prophet.

5.2.1. The Nazareth Episode. The story that Luke tells of Jesus' return to his own home town of Nazareth (Lk 4:16-30), where he read and expounded Isaiah 61:1, confirms this (*see* Jubilee). It is true that many have understood Luke to be presenting Jesus here as one who viewed himself as the Servant of the Lord (*see* Servant of Yahweh) or, because of the reference to the anointing in Isaiah 61, as the kingly or priestly Messiah. But several factors make this unlikely.

First, the Isaiah 61 passage is not part of the Song of the Servant. To conclude that it speaks of the Servant is to import that idea into the text.

Second, kings and priests (*see* Priest and Priesthood) were not the only OT figures who were anointed (cf. 1 Kings 19:16; 2 Kings 2:9, 15). Therefore, the simple mention of an "anointing" should not be taken as proof that a kingly or priestly Messiah was intended, especially when the Lukan context of the quotation from Isaiah makes no mention of a royal or priestly function belonging to Jesus.

Third, the OT designated prophets as the anointed of the Lord (Ps 105:15; 1 Chron 16:22). Interestingly, the Targum* on Isaiah 61 is introduced with the words "the prophet said," implying that the very prophet who sketched for Israel the summit of its glory in chapter 60 is now in chapter 61 himself expressing gratitude to the Lord for having given him such an exalted commission.

Fourth, the idea of prophets as anointed servants of the Lord is clearly found in later pre-Christian Judaism (cf. CD 2:12; 6:1; 6QD 3:4), and the "herald of good news" in Isaiah 52:7 shows up in 11QMelch 18 as one "anointed with the Spirit" (Fitzmyer, 530).

Fifth, Jesus, in the immediate context of this synagogue sermon, places himself among the prophets. His sermon was given with such power and authority that those who heard it, even though they had known him from childhood and were familiar with his humble origins, were both astonished at his words and angry with him because he of all people dared to teach them (Lk 4:22; Mk 6:2; Mt 13:54). Hence, instead of welcoming him and accepting his message they were repelled by him, rejecting him and his message (Lk 4:29; Mk 6:3; Mt 13:57). Jesus' response to them came in the form of a familiar proverb: "No prophet is welcome in his own country" (Lk 4:24; cf. Mk 6:4; Mt 13:57). By quoting a proverbial saying and applying it to himself he accepted the popular estimation of who he was and of what he was doing (cf. Mt 16:14; 21:11, 46; Mk 6:15). He did not hesitate to identify himself with the prophets (cf. also Lk 13:31-33).

Finally, as Fitzmyer has pointed out, to so understand the Isaianic anointing as applied by Jesus to himself "makes it intelligible why Jesus is compared to Elijah and Elisha in the verses toward the end of the episode. Elisha in particular is introduced as 'the prophet'; implicitly, Jesus is suggested to be such too" (Fitzmyer, 530).

5.2.2. The Amen Formula. Still another example, strengthening the presumption that Jesus thought of himself as a prophet, is the extraordinary formula "Amen, I say to you" (*see* Amen). Several astonishing features of this formula emerge: (1) no exact Hebrew equivalent to this phrase has yet been discovered; (2)

it is found only in the Gospels, yet in all four Gospels; and (3) it was always and only spoken by Jesus as an introduction to and an endorsement of his own words—never (as in its closest OT equivalent) as a response affirming the words of someone else. Hence, it is a completely new way of speaking, "a highly characteristic mode of speech for which there is no parallel" (Manson, 107). But what did Jesus intend by this new way of speaking? What was the significance of this formula? Luke, who retains "amen" as the only foreign word in either his Gospel or Acts, and who uses the amen-formula most sparingly of all the Evangelists (only 6 times), may provide a clue to the answers of these questions. It is instructive to note where Luke places the very first instance of Jesus speaking these extraordinary words, "Amen, I say to you." He places them in the context of the Nazareth synagogue sermon (discussed above), where Jesus consciously identifies himself, his words and his works with the prophets (Lk 4:24; cf. Mt 13:57; Mk 6:4). Thus, by using the amen-formula initially as an introduction to Jesus' saying that "no prophet is ever welcome in his native place"—a saying by which Jesus set himself among those prophets who were rejected by their own people—Luke seems to understand the formula as a pattern of speech characteristic of the prophets. This is to say, that Jesus' introductory expression, "Truly (*amēn*), I say to you," although recognizably different in form, may nevertheless have been viewed by Luke as similar in meaning to that introductory formula of the OT prophets—"Thus says the Lord"—by which the word of the Lord came to the people.

Such an understanding seems to be confirmed by Mark. The amen-formula first appears in Mark at the end of a section where Jesus repeatedly laid claim to being a person who possessed the Spirit. In the Judaism of Jesus' time to possess the Spirit was almost always a mark of prophetic inspiration: " 'Truly (*amēn*), I say to you, people will be forgiven for their sins . . . but whosoever blasphemes against the Holy Spirit never has forgiveness'—for they had said, 'He has an unclean spirit' " (Mk 3:28-29; Mt 12:31-32; Lk 11:14-15, 17-23; 12:10). Hence, although the amen-sayings are unique and point to the uniqueness of Jesus, at the same time they are in harmony with the "Thus says the Lord" of the OT prophets and point to his unity with them. Long ago the prophet Micaiah had defined perfectly the scope of prophetic authority when he stated: "What the Lord says to me that will I speak" (1 Kings 22:14). Thus, Jesus' "Amen, I say to you" should not be understood to mean "I say this," that is, "I alone, I on my own initiative, I by virtue of my own divine authority say to you!" Rather, he

means, "I, as God's unique messenger, with God's authority and power, say this to you!"

The point is substantiated in the Fourth Gospel when Jesus is himself quoted as saying, almost in the words of Micaiah, "My teaching is not mine, but his who sent me" (Jn 7:16) and again, "The words that I speak to you, I do not speak on my own authority [or on my own initiative]" (Jn 14:10). Without doubt Jesus' "Amen, I say to you" exceeded anything spoken by the OT prophets, if for no other reason than that he, unlike them, had been given the Spirit without measure (Jn 3:34). And yet with this formula he was in essence saying the same thing they had said before him, but with a sharper point: "You must listen to what I have to say, because the words I speak are not mine; they are the very words of God" (Jn 3:34).

5.2.3. More Than a Prophet. It would be incorrect, or at least inadequate, simply to conclude that Jesus viewed himself as a prophet and no more than a prophet, or that the Evangelists did the same. The Evangelists are careful to avoid that conclusion. For example, they record that when certain people came to Jesus and asked for a sign, he would only give them the sign of Jonah (*see* Sign of Jonah) saying, "As Jonah was three days and three nights in the belly of the great fish, so the Son of Man will be three days and three nights in the heart of the earth. The people of Nineveh will rise up against this generation at the judgment and condemn it, for when Jonah preached they repented, and here is one greater than Jonah" (Mt 12:38-41; Lk 11:29-32). In effect the Evangelists claim that Jesus was saying that the Ninevites, strangers to Israel, had been able and willing to admit that the authority and presence of the true God was with the prophet Jonah. But in his own person Jesus stood as one significantly greater than Jonah, and yet his own people could not recognize him and give him that respect and belief which must be offered to him.

We conclude, then, that though Jesus did understand himself as a prophet—a Spirit-inspired and Spirit-empowered person—and his ministry as a prophetic ministry, yet neither Jesus nor the Evangelists would have stopped there. For both Jesus himself and the Evangelists he was "a prophet, yes, but more than a prophet" (cf. Mt 11:9; Lk 7:26); he was the unique Son of the Father (Mt 11:26-27), the Son of God* (Mk 1:1).

6. Early Christian Prophets.

Not only was Jesus considered to be a prophet in the new era that was dawning, but Jesus spoke of prophets yet to come. As he sent his disciples out to minister he instructed them that those of them who would receive a prophet in the name of a prophet would share with that prophet in the prophet's reward (Mt 10:41). From this statement we conclude that Jesus was aware of the presence of genuine prophets in his time, or in a day soon to come, who would need assistance from his followers and protection. He promises that whatever his followers might do for the benefit of these prophets simply because they were prophets, with no ulterior motive in mind, would be remembered [by God] and rewarded [by him] in the day of judgment.*

Furthermore, the Evangelists record the following words of Jesus: "Look! I [or "the wisdom of God"] will send prophets to you, and wise ones and scribes [apostles]. Some of them you will kill and crucify; some of them you will beat up in your synagogues*; some of them you will persecute from city to city" (Mt 23:34; Lk 11:49). Although one may not be able to ascertain precisely the words of Jesus lying behind this particular saying, nevertheless, it is clear that whatever the exact words may have been, they predicted prophets yet to come. These were prophets that the Wisdom of God or Jesus himself (as the Wisdom of God?; see Wisdom) would send out into the world with a message just as authoritative as any proclaimed by Isaiah, Jeremiah or any other classical OT prophet. Here, then, is at least a hint of the early Christian prophets who were to play so prominent a role in the church in the years following the death,* resurrection* and exaltation of Jesus.

7. Prophets and the Gospel Tradition.

It is clear from the letters of Paul that this word came true. There were in the early church* people filled with the Spirit, endowed by the Spirit with the gift of prophecy, who ranked in importance with the apostles* (1 Cor 12:28; Eph 4:11) and together with the apostles formed the foundation on which the church is built (Eph 2:20). Their principal work was to build up, exhort and encourage believers in Christ (1 Cor 14:3). But that was not the whole of their work. They, like their OT counterparts, were empowered to see by the Holy Spirit what others could not see—divine mysteries—and to know what others could not know (cf. 1 Cor 13:2). They were gifted to receive revelations from God or from the risen exalted Christ (1 Cor 14:30; Rev 1:1, 4-5), and were commissioned to communicate that revelation to the Christian community.

A particular line of reasoning has emerged in NT scholarship, linking the role of early Christian prophets with certain sayings of Jesus in the Gospel tradition. Christian prophets are known to have played an important part in the early days of the church, being people of the Spirit whose words and actions were especially prompted by the Spirit (Acts 11:27-28; 13:2) and whose revelations came from the exalted Christ (cf. Rev 1:10 with 4:1-2). These revelations were regarded as originating not with the prophet's will, but with the Lord, being occasioned by the prophetic Spirit resting on them and filling them (2 Pet 1:20-21). It has been suggested that some of the Gospel sayings attributed to the Jesus of history were actually spoken by the resurrected, exalted Christ and communicated to his church through his prophets—only later to find their way back into the Gospel tradition.

A considerable amount of evidence has been accumulated to support this conclusion (see Hawthorne), and strong arguments have been mounted against its possibility (Aune, 233-45; Hill, 174-185). If the possibility should be granted that words of the exalted Lord spoken through his prophets existed side by side with those of the earthly Jesus, and as a consequence the two were mingled together, it would not mean that the sayings originating with Christian prophets are in any way inferior to the so-called genuine sayings of Jesus. As E. E. Ellis has concluded, "Granting the prophets' credentials, [their] saying is as genuine a word of the Lord as a verbatim saying from the pre-resurrection ministry. For 'authenticity' has to do with the authority by which a word of Jesus comes to us, not with the ability of scientific historians to give the word a certain ratio of historical probability" (Ellis, 172).

See also AMEN; AUTHORITY AND POWER; ELIJAH, ELISHA; HOLY SPIRIT; JOHN THE BAPTIST.

BIBLIOGRAPHY. D. E. Aune, *Prophecy in Early Christianity* (Grand Rapids: Eerdmans, 1983); J. D. G. Dunn, "Prophetic 'I'-Sayings and the Jesus Traditon: The Importance of Testing Prophetic Utterances within Early Christianity," *NTS* 24 (1978) 175-198; idem, "Rediscovering the Spirit," *ExpT* 94 (1982) 10; E. E. Ellis, *The Gospel of Luke* (NCB; Grand Rapids: Eerdmans, 1981); J. A. Fitzmyer, *The Gospel according to Luke, I-IX* (AB 28; New York: Doubleday, 1981); G. Friedrich, "προφήτης κτλ," *TDNT* VI.781-861; esp. 828-61; G. F. Hawthorne, "The Role of Christian Prophets in the Gospel Tradition," in *Tradition and Interpretation in the New Testament: Essays in Honor of E. Earle Ellis*, ed. G. F. Hawthorne with O. Betz (Grand Rapids: Eerdmans, 1987; Tübingen: J. C. B. Mohr, 1988) 119-33; idem, *The Presence and the Power: The Significance of the Holy Spirit in the Life and Ministry of Jesus* (Dallas: Word, 1991); A. Heschel, *The Prophets* (2 vols.; New York: Harper, 1962); D. Hill, *New Testament Prophecy* (Atlanta: John Knox, 1979), J. Jeremias, *New Testament Theology, Part I: The Proclamation of Jesus* (New York: Scribners, 1971); T. W. Manson, *The Teaching of Jesus* (Cambridge: University Press, 1951). G. F. Hawthorne

PROSTITUTE

Although the term "prostitute" (*pornē*) occurs rarely in the four canonical Gospels, it has long been assumed that Jesus gathered around himself various outcasts of Greco-Roman society, particularly prostitutes. The roots of this image of Jesus stem from the tradition that Jesus was known for eating (*see* Table Fellowship) with "tax collectors and sinners" (*see* Taxes; Sinner), which is the more common phrase found in the Gospels. This tradition is early, as it occurs in Q* as well as in Mark (2:15-16) and is taken over by the later Evangelists (Lk 5:27-30; 7:34; 15:1-2; Mt 9:10-11; 11:19). Moreover, the frequent identification of the central woman disciple* of Jesus, Mary Magdalene, as a reformed prostitute, as well as Gospel depictions of Jesus' sympathy for other women, such as the "sinner" who anoints Jesus at a meal (Lk 7), the Samaritan* woman (Jn 4), and the woman taken in adultery (now following Jn 7) have also contributed to the idea that actual prostitutes numbered among the followers of Jesus and that Jesus was unusually compassionate toward such women (*see* Women).

Nowhere in the Gospels is it explicitly stated that Jesus dined with prostitutes. Although Matthew also uses the phrase "tax collectors and prostitutes" (Mt 21:31-32), this phrase is not actually used to describe Jesus' dining company, but is rather a comment by Jesus to his opponents that "tax collectors and prostitutes" will get into the kingdom (*see* Kingdom of God) before they do, as even these social outcasts have a greater faith* than do the Pharisees.* However, although Jesus is only accused of eating with "tax collectors and sinners," there is still reason to include prostitutes in this image as well. Connected to this tradition is that of Jesus being a "wine* bibber" and a "glutton" (Q), which adds to the association of Jesus with banquet revelry.

Given the context and setting of banquets (*symposion*) as we know them from both pagan and Jewish literature of the Greco-Roman period, the image created by such an accusation would still include prostitutes of various sorts; courtesans, flute girls and the like were part and parcel to the banquet scene, and as a banquet *topos* prevailed in the art and literature of the Greek and Roman periods. Moreover, tax collectors, as a stereotype of despicable people, were rhetorically connected in Greco-Roman literature with those who trafficked in prostitution, particularly the "brothel-keepers" (*pornoboskoi*). One could therefore argue that although the term "sinners" would not necessarily be equated with "prostitutes" or even include them, in the context of banquet imagery the accusation of eating with "tax collectors and sinners" would at least evoke an image of men who ate and drank with courtesans.

For example, in Luke 15, after the Pharisees chide Jesus for the fact that tax collectors and sinners come to hear his teaching, Jesus tells the story of the prodigal son who wastes his father's money on "loose living" (Lk 15:13 RSV), which includes squandering it on prostitutes (Lk 15:30). It is also likely that Luke intends to portray the "sinner" of Luke 7 as a prostitute or at least as one guilty of sexual sin. Matthew's shift to "tax collectors and prostitutes" (Mt 21:31) is therefore understandable. In the context of banquet imagery the "flute players" found in Matthew 9:23 might also be considered as another possible reference to prostitutes in the Gospels.

Although the historical veracity of the image created by the accusation that Jesus ate with "tax collectors and sinners" has been disputed, it is clear that the early church grasped this image as being central both to their portraits of Jesus and to their own self-understanding as a Christian community.

A related term in the Gospels is *porneia*, which is usually translated "fornication," "adultery" or simply "unchastity." This term occurs primarily in the context of Matthew's exception to the divorce prohibition (Mt 5:32; 19:9; *see* Marriage and Divorce), but it is also that which defiles a person from within (Mk 7:21; Mt 15:19). This usage is not unexpected, as the paradigmatic moral failure in much of Greco-Roman literature involved sexual immorality, especially on the part of women, who were often first accused of unchastity whenever they failed morally or overstepped their ideal womanly roles.

See also TABLE FELLOWSHIP; SINNER; WOMEN.

BIBLIOGRAPHY. V. and B. Bullough, *Prostitution: An Illustrated Social History* (New York: Crown, 1978); K. E. Corley, "Were the Women Around Jesus Really Prostitutes? Women in the Context of Greco-Roman Meals," *SBL 1989 Seminar Papers,* ed. D. Lull (Atlanta: Scholars, 1989) 487-521; F. Hauck and S. Schulz, "πόρνη κτλ," *TDNT* VI.579-95; D. Smith, "The Historical Jesus at Table,' " *SBL 1989 Seminar Papers,* ed. D. Lull (Atlanta: Scholars, 1989) 466-86; idem, "Social Obligation in the Context of Communal Meals: A Study of the Christian Meal in 1 Corinthians in Comparision with Greco-Roman Communal Meals" (Th.D. diss. Harvard Divinity School, 1980); M. Vickers, *Greek Symposia* (London: Joint Association of Classical Teachers, n.d.).

K. E. Corley

PURITY. *See* CLEAN AND UNCLEAN.

Q

Q

For over a century "Q" has been used to refer to the 230 or so sayings of Jesus which Matthew and Luke share, but which are not found in Mark (*see* Synoptic Problem). In 1861 H. J. Holtzmann built on earlier discussion of the sources of the Gospels and claimed that Matthew and Luke had drawn on two main sources: Mark's Gospel and a collection of the sayings of Jesus. The latter soon came to be referred to by German scholars as *Quelle* ("source"). In 1890 J. Weiss abbreviated *Quelle* to Q; this quickly gained wide acceptance.

In the twentieth century the Q hypothesis has been the basis of nearly all serious study of the origin and development of the Gospel traditions. This article sets out the main reasons why Q has been accepted so widely. It also includes discussion of the two most influential rival hypotheses. The final section sketches the very different ways the theological perspective of Q has been understood.

1. Terminology and Importance of the Q Hypothesis
2. The Case for the Q Hypothesis
3. The Nature and Extent of Q
4. The Case against the Q Hypothesis
5. The Theology and Purpose of Q

1. Terminology and Importance of the Q Hypothesis.

1.1. Terminology. The term *Q* has been used in several ways, with resulting confusion. (1) For some scholars *Q* is simply a shorthand way of referring to non-Markan traditions shared by Matthew and Luke: Q traditions may have existed in a number of short written documents or collections of oral traditions. (2) Some scholars see Q as a cycle of oral tradition which circulated in the early church with a fairly fixed order. (3) Most recent writers assume that Q existed as a written document which disappeared shortly after it was incorporated by Matthew and Luke into their Gospels. They accept that with few exceptions Luke has preserved the original order of the Q traditions, though not necessarily the original wording. Hence it has recently become customary to refer to Q passages

with the Lukan chapter and verse numbers. For example, Q 7:22 is a reference to the Q tradition which lies behind Luke 7:22.

1.2. Importance. The Q hypothesis is important in current study of the Gospels for two quite different reasons.

1.1.1. Q As Authentic Jesus Tradition. Q traditions are often considered to be particularly important in attempts to reconstruct the teaching of the historical Jesus (*see* Historical Jesus). Many early supporters of the Q hypothesis believed that Q provided direct access to the authentic teaching of Jesus (*see* Gospels [Historical Reliability]). More recently, the criterion of "multiple attestation" has attracted wide support in discussions of the authenticity of the Gospel traditions: traditions found in several strands of the Gospel tradition (Mark, Q, traditions found only in Matthew [M*] or only in Luke [L*], traditions behind the Fourth Gospel) are more likely to be authentic than traditions less widely attested.

1.1.2. Q As Representative of Diversity in Early Christianity. In recent years some have claimed that the existence of Q underlines the diversity of earliest Christianity. Since Q did not contain passion (*see* Passion Narrative) or resurrection* traditions, the Q community's understanding of the Christian faith differed markedly from Paul's or Mark's strong emphasis on the centrality of the cross (*see* Death of Jesus) and resurrection. Q is alleged to represent a very early form of Christianity in which (for example) Jesus was understood to be God's* Wisdom,* or Wisdom's representative, or in which expectations of the imminent return of Jesus as an apocalyptic* "Son of man"* figure were dominant.

2. The Case for the Q Hypothesis.

Five main arguments have been advanced in support of the view that both Matthew and Luke used Q as a primary source as well as Mark. Although some are stronger than others, taken cumulatively these arguments confirm that there are good grounds for accepting that both Matthew and Luke used Q.

2.1. Verbal Agreement. There is often very close verbal agreement between Matthew and Luke which extends over several verses. As examples, the following passages should be compared carefully:

Matthew 3:7-12 par. Luke 3:7-9, 16-17

Matthew 4:1-11 par. Luke 4:1-13

Matthew 11:2-11, 16-19 par. Luke 7:18-28, 31-35

Matthew 23:37-39 par. Luke 13:34-35

In line after line of the Greek text (and even in an English translation) there is such close verbal correspondence that it is probable that Matthew and Luke are drawing on traditions from the same source. If both Evangelists drew on independent traditions (i.e., oral traditions which had not been collected into a source), very much greater divergence in wording would be expected. This observation is supplemented by an appeal to Markan priority: even though Matthew and Luke are two very different Gospels, they have both used Mark. Thus it is likely (so the argument runs) that where they agree closely in non-Markan sections, they are both using a common source.

Although in many of the non-Markan passages which Matthew and Luke share the verbal agreement is striking, in the following three passages (and in many others) it is not. Both Matthew and Luke include the parable* of the man who built his house on the rock (Mt 7:21, 24-27 par. Lk 6:46-49), but the wording differs considerably. In Matthew 23:4, 6-7, 13, 23, 25-27, 29-32, 34-36 par. Luke 11:39-52 a large number of similar sayings are found in the same order; in some sayings the wording is very close, but in others there is striking variation. Matthew and Luke both include what is clearly the same parable of the pounds, but their versions of the lengthy parable differ in numerous details (Mt 25:14-30 par. Lk 19:11-27).

Supporters of Q account for the differences in the wording of non-Markan traditions in two main ways. Since both Matthew and Luke often revise the wording of Mark quite extensively, we should not be surprised to find that they have also done so with the second main source which they have utilized. This is a plausible argument, and in some passages the Evangelists' redaction of Q can be discerned with little difficulty (*see* Redaction Criticism). But why have the Evangelists revised some Q traditions quite considerably but not others? Many scholars suggest that the variations in some passages are so great that it is likely that Matthew and Luke drew on two different editions of Q. In other words, Q was revised and even extended (perhaps more than once); it was utilized at different stages in its evolution by Matthew and by Luke. Some writers use the abbreviation Q^{Mt} and Q^{Lk} to refer to the versions of Q used by Matthew and Luke. Some such explanation seems necessary to account for the close verbal similarity in some passages but differences in others.

2.2. The Phenomena of Order. Although Matthew weaves his sources together (especially in the five large discourses) and Luke places them in "strips" or blocks, there are some significant agreements in the order in which the non-Markan traditions are found in Matthew and Luke. These agreements in order cannot be coincidental and strongly suggest the use of a common source. For example, the following individual sayings or small units appear in Matthew in the same order: Luke 3:7-9, 16-17; 4:1-13; 6:20b-21, 22-23, 29, 30, 32-35, 36, 37-38, 41-42, 43-44, 46, 47-49; 7:1-10, 18-23, 24-26, 27, 28, 31-34, 35. In at least 85 per cent of the Q traditions it is possible to ascertain the common order or to determine which Evangelist disturbed the common order (Kloppenborg, 80).

The phenomena seem to rule out the possibility that both Evangelists were drawing on independent oral traditions. Why should so many traditions appear in both Gospels in the same order, especially when there is often no obvious reason for their juxtaposition? At the very least, Matthew and Luke seem to have drawn on a cycle of oral traditions with a fairly fixed order. The phenomena of order are so striking that they strongly suggest that Q was a written document.

2.3. Doublets. In several passages in Matthew and Luke we find that essentially the same tradition is repeated; these repetitions are known as doublets. They occur where Matthew and Luke both use the Markan form of a saying, but elsewhere they also both include a non-Markan or Q form of essentially the same saying. The following two doublets are particularly striking (though there are many more):

(1) "The one who has, to that one will more be given . . . ," Mark 4:25 par. Matthew 13:12 and Luke 8:18; a similar saying is found at Matthew 25:29 par. Luke 19:26.

(2) "If anyone wants to follow me, they must deny themselves . . . ," Mark 8:34-35 par. Matthew 16:24-25 and Luke 9:23-24, with a similar saying at Matthew 10:38-39 par. Luke 14:27; 17:33.

The presence of so many doublets is taken by many scholars to suggest or even confirm that Q was a written document rather than a set of oral traditions. If Matthew and Luke drew on oral traditions (so the argument runs), we might have expected that an oral Q tradition would have been conflated with the similar Markan saying.

2.4. Q As a Coherent Entity. The Q material hangs

together as an entity. With one exception, the narrative of the healing of the centurion's son (Mt 8:5-13 par. Lk 7:1-10), the Q traditions are all sayings of Jesus. Many supporters of the Q hypothesis go further and claim that the non-Markan traditions shared by Matthew and Luke betray a similar theological outlook and belong to a similar literary genre (see 4. below). Q did not survive beyond its incorporation into Matthew and Luke, but the *Gospel of Thomas,* which was discovered in 1945, does consist of a collection of sayings of Jesus. This suggests that other collections of the sayings of Jesus may have been made in the early church.

This general line of argument is obviously less compelling than the preceding three, but its force should not be underestimated. Both in terms of content and literary genre, traditions which are found only in Matthew (M traditions) or only in Luke (L traditions) are much more disparate than Q traditions.

2.5. Other Explanations Are Less Satisfactory. On close inspection rival explanations of the non-Markan material shared by Matthew and Luke are much less plausible than the Q hypothesis. Downing (*NTS* 37 [1991]) has added fresh considerations in support of this conclusion. He has shown that the redactional methods involved in the two-Gospel (Griesbach) hypothesis and in the claim that Luke used Matthew are quite unlike the ways ancient writers handled their sources. On the other hand, Matthew and Luke use Mark and Q in ways which do bear comparison with well-established conventions in antiquity. This important observation strengthens still further the conclusion that the case for Markan priority and Q is far stronger than the case for any of the rival solutions of the Synoptic problem.

The cumulative force of the five preceding arguments is very impressive, but the case for Q falls short of absolute proof. Even the strongest supporters of Q accept that the hypothesis is less securely established than Markan priority. However, Q remains a valid working hypothesis for serious study of the Gospels.

3. The Nature and Extent of Q.

The evidence is marginally stronger for concluding that Q was a written document rather than a collection of oral traditions which were transmitted with a fairly fixed order. However, comparative studies of the transmission, revision and expansion of oral and of written traditions in antiquity urgently need to be undertaken.

Although most of the early supporters of Q believed that it was a collection of sayings in Aramaic (and therefore earlier and more reliable than traditions which circulated in Greek), this view is not now widely accepted. It was based partly on one interpretation of the comments of Papias (early second century) which were quoted by Eusebius (at the beginning of the fourth century): "Matthew collected the sayings [*ta logia*] in the Hebrew language [i.e., perhaps Aramaic] and each one interpreted [or translated] them as he was able." However, since Papias also uses *ta logia* to include Mark's *narratives,* as well as sayings of Jesus, most scholars now conclude that Papias was referring to canonical Matthew and not Q. If so, Papias's phrase "in the Hebrew language" may either be a reference to the Jewish features of Matthew's Gospel or a mistake.

Several scholars have claimed that some Q traditions which differ considerably in Matthew and in Luke rest on the Evangelists' differing, or even in some cases mistaken, translations of underlying Aramaic traditions. However, the linguistic evidence is not clear-cut, and Matthew's and Luke's knowledge of Aramaic is not demonstrable (*see* Languages of Palestine). On the other hand, there is some linguistic evidence which supports the conclusion that Q was composed originally in Greek. Since there is often close verbal correspondence in Matthew's and Luke's Q traditions, it is probable that they were both drawing on traditions in the same language, that is, Greek.

Q was probably originally a little larger than the 230 or so verses shared by Matthew and Luke. Since both Matthew and Luke omit some Markan material, why should we suppose that they have both incorporated Q in full? Hence some of the traditions found only in Matthew or in Luke (M or L) may have belonged originally to Q, though the precise extent of such additional Q traditions is far from clear. Two examples will show just how difficult it is to be sure. Matthew 11:28-30 follows immediately after a Q block and (according to some) even though these verses are not found in Luke, they may have belonged to Q. However, if they did belong to Q, why did Luke omit traditions which he surely would have included if he had known them? Luke 4:16-30 is at least partly independent of Mark. Did Luke include some Q traditions in this important passage, even though there is no trace of non-Markan material in the equivalent passage in Matthew? Since some of the non-Markan traditions in Luke 4:16-30 cohere well with a number of Q traditions, several scholars accept this suggestion.

4. The Case against the Q Hypothesis.

Until two decades or so ago the two-document hypothesis (i.e., Markan priority and Q) was accepted widely by scholars from very different backgrounds. Earlier objectors to the Q hypothesis had made little headway. Some claimed that the alleged contents of Q are so heterogeneous that it is unlikely to have existed as a distinct source; this point will be discussed below. Others noted that no other writing quite like Q seems to have existed in the early church—though the discovery of the *Gospel of Thomas* (*see* Gospels [Apocryphal]) partly undermined this point. Other objectors claimed that the considerable variations in the proposed reconstructions of Q eroded confidence in the hypothesis. More recently, however, reconstructions have shown that there is broad agreement about the contents of Q.

Since 1965, however, there have been several fresh attempts to undermine the Q hypothesis by offering alternative explanations of the evidence. Two rival hypotheses have been vigorously supported and must be considered seriously, even though they have not attracted wide support. On the two-Gospel hypothesis (to be distinguished from the two-document hypothesis), which was first set out in 1789 by J. J. Griesbach and which has recently been defended vigorously by W. R. Farmer and others, Luke has used Matthew, and Mark has used both the earlier Gospels. Other scholars (most notably A. M. Farrer and his pupil M. D. Goulder) retain Markan priority and dispense with Q by claiming that Luke has used Matthew. Both solutions of the Synoptic problem eliminate the need for any form of the Q hypothesis by claiming that Luke used Matthew.

4.1. Did Luke Use Matthew? If this claim is accepted, there are major implications for our understanding of the origin, transmission and development of the Gospel traditions. On this view the earliest form of the traditions must always lie behind Matthew's Gospel, not Luke's; hence, Matthew is particularly important in historical reconstruction. If Luke has used Matthew, then he has used this major source extremely freely indeed: He is the first "interpreter" of Matthew, which he has dismantled in order to write his own very different Gospel. For the following reasons, this alternative to the Q hypothesis is most unlikely.

4.1.1. The Matthean Discourses. If Luke has used Matthew, what has happened to Matthew's five impressive discourses? On this view a small part of Matthew's Sermon on the Mount in chapters 5—7 reappears in Luke 6:20-49 (*see* Sermon on the Mount), but the rest of the material is either scattered (apparently haphazardly) right through Luke's Gospel and set in very different contexts, or it is omitted completely. Why would Luke wish to do this? Matthew's other discourses have been treated similarly. For example,

Matthew's second discourse in chapter 10 reappears in no fewer than seven different chapters in Luke!

While attempts have been made to account for Luke's rather odd treatment of the Matthean discourses, they have convinced few. M. D. Goulder (1989) recognizes that Matthew's fifth discourse poses particular difficulties for his hypothesis. He has to concede that Luke has carefully separated the Markan and non-Markan parts of Matthew 24—25. The former are included in Luke 21, the latter are isolated (by marking a copy of Matthew with a pen!) and included in Luke chapters 12—13, 17 and, we may add, 19. This is a tortuous explanation of Luke's methods, to say the least.

4.1.2. The Matthean Expansions of Mark. If Luke has used Matthew, we would expect him to have adopted some of the expansions and modifications Matthew makes to Mark. But hardly a trace of them can be found in Luke. Where Matthew and Mark have the same tradition, Luke opts for Mark's version and ignores Matthew's; at the same time he rearranges Matthew very considerably. Why did Luke find Matthew so unattractive, when in almost all other parts of early Christianity it became the favorite Gospel?

Peter's confession at Caesarea Philippi provides a good example. At Luke 9:18-21 Mark's account (Mk 8:27-30) has been used, but there is not a sign in Luke of the major addition Matthew makes to Mark at 16:16-19. Here several sayings of Jesus addressed to Peter, including the words "On this rock I will build my church" have not been used.

Why, then, does Luke omit so many of Matthew's numerous expansions of Markan material? This point has often been pressed by those who deny that Luke has used Matthew. Goulder replies as follows. Luke has a "block policy": "when he (Luke) is treating Marcan matter he has Mark in front of him, and he has made it his policy not to keep turning up Matthew to see what he has added. . . . Luke does not include the additions because he had decided on a policy which involved letting them go" (Goulder, 1.44). This leads Goulder to suggest that once a Markan block has been dealt with, Luke sometimes comes back to Matthew's additions to Mark: some of the additions are transferred to other contexts, some are ignored unintentionally, some are rewritten.

4.1.3. Agreements of Matthew and Luke against Mark. There is a further phenomenon which seriously erodes the plausibility of Goulder's hypothesis: the minor agreements of Matthew and Luke against Mark. Goulder appeals (as have other scholars) to the minor agreements in order to undermine the Q hypothesis and also to offer clear-cut support for Luke's use of

Matthew. The minor agreements, however, can be turned against his own hypothesis.

On Goulder's explanation of the minor agreements, in Markan contexts Luke sometimes prefers Matthean words or phrases. But Goulder also insists that in Markan contexts Luke makes it his policy *not* to keep turning up Matthew to see what he has added. There is clearly an important flaw in his case against Q. The claim that the minor agreements undermine the Q hypothesis must either be abandoned, or we must accept that in passage after passage Luke has had Matthew in front of him and has redacted Matthew quite perversely. For on Goulder's view Luke has repeatedly retained quite tiny modifications Matthew has made to Mark (the minor agreements); at the same time Luke has ignored numerous *major* Matthean additions or modifications to Mark which would have suited his purposes, and transferred or rewritten only some of them.

4.1.4. Variations in Similar Non-Markan Traditions. Where Matthew and Luke contain similar non-Markan traditions, most scholars accept that it is very difficult to decide which Evangelist has the earlier form of the tradition. But scholars who claim that Luke has used Matthew must accept that it is *always* Luke who has changed Matthew's earlier form of the tradition. Their attempts to defend this view often look like special pleading.

For example, if Luke has used Matthew, then he has *abbreviated* Matthew's earlier and fuller version both of the Beatitudes (Mt 5:1-12; *see* Sermon on the Mount) and of the Lord's Prayer (Mt 6:9-13; *see* Prayer). Why should Luke wish to do this? In both cases it is difficult to discover plausible reasons; it is much less difficult to suppose that while Luke has retained Q traditions with few changes, Matthew has expanded them.

4.1.5. Variations in Placing Q Sayings Relative to Markan Contexts. After the temptations of Jesus (Mt 4:1-11 par. Lk 4:1-13), Luke and Matthew never use the Q sayings they share in the same Markan context. If Luke has used Matthew, then he has carefully removed every non-Markan (Q) saying from the Markan context it has in Matthew and placed it in a different context!

4.1.6. Implied Differences between Luke's Treatment of Mark and Matthew. One final point sums up several of the above observations. If we accept that Luke has used Mark, then with the help of a synopsis we can readily discover the changes of various kinds which he has made to Mark. On the whole he has retained the order of Mark's traditions and has considerable respect for their content, especially when he is quoting sayings of Jesus. If Luke has also used

Matthew, we would expect him to have modified his second source in broadly similar ways. But this is by no means the case.

4.2. Conclusions. Enough has been said to show that it is by no means easy to suppose that Luke has used Matthew. However, it is as difficult to falsify this hypothesis as it is to establish conclusively that Matthew and Luke both used Q. At the end of the day we are left to balance probabilities. Redaction criticism (*see* Redaction Criticism) does in fact offer a way forward, for the results which rival theories offer at the redactional level can be compared. For example, if for the sake of argument we were to assume that Matthew's main source was Luke's Gospel, it would be possible to examine the modifications made by Matthew and then to consider whether this hypothesis offers a more coherent explanation of Matthean redaction than the assumption that Matthew's sources were Mark and Q.

The two-Gospel (Griesbach) solution of the Synoptic problem can be tested along these lines, as can the proposal that Luke has used Matthew. While it is possible to offer some explanation of Lukan and Markan redaction of Matthew on the Griesbach hypothesis, Markan priority offers a much more plausible and coherent account of the origin and distinctive purpose of Matthew and Luke. So too with the claim that Luke has used Matthew. This hypothesis is not, as is sometimes claimed, the simplest solution of the Synoptic problem. On this view Luke has used his sources in an extremely complex set of ways. His redaction of Matthew and of Mark cannot readily be explained as the result of his own literary or theological preferences.

On the other hand, the success of redaction criticism in clarifying the literary methods and distinctive theological emphases of Matthew and Luke on the assumption of dependence on Mark and Q is an important argument in favor of the two-source hypothesis. While some of the arguments which were used in the past to support this solution of the Synoptic problem have now been shown to be reversible or, in one or two cases, untenable, no more satisfactory account of the phenomena presented to us by the text of the three Synoptic Gospels has yet been produced.

5. The Theology and Purpose of Q.

Were Q traditions brought together simply as an anthology or summary of the sayings of Jesus? How coherent are they? Do they contain one primary theological perspective? Were Q traditions selected, arranged and modified for particular theological or pastoral reasons? Discussion of these questions has been approached from three quite different angles.

5.1. The Relationship of Q to the Earliest Kerygma. At the turn of the century several writers on the purpose of Q accepted that it must have contained an account of the death and resurrection of Jesus as well as a collection of his sayings. However, since in their passion and resurrection narratives Luke and Matthew share no more than a few phrases which are not found in Mark, it is impossible to sustain this view.

In his influential study of Q (1907) Harnack insisted that Q was a source of unparalleled value. It had been compiled without any discernible bias, "whether apologetic, didactic, ecclesiastical, national or anti-national" (171). Mark had exaggerated apocalypticism and subordinated the "purely religious and moral element" of Jesus' message (250-51). Q, on the other hand, was a relatively complete account of "the message of Jesus" which expressed clearly the very essence of Christianity for twentieth-century men and women.

Harnack's theological presuppositions were challenged by Barth and Bultmann who insisted that proclamation of the cross and the resurrection, not the teaching of the historical Jesus, was at the heart of the earliest Christian preaching. Harnack's confidence in Q as "the message of Jesus" was also challenged by the work of the first form critics (*see* Form Criticism). They insisted that since all the Gospel traditions have been shaped by the faith and the needs of the post-Easter communities, not even Q provides *direct* access to the teaching of Jesus.

So what was the relationship of Q to the kerygma or proclamation of the earliest post-Easter communities? M. Dibelius (1919), B. H. Streeter (1924) and T. W. Manson (1937) all saw Q as a supplement to the early kerygma of the cross and resurrection of Jesus. Q traditions were used as ethical guidance and encouragement for those who had accepted the kerygma.

Although this general view held sway for some time, it was strongly challenged by H. E. Tödt (1956). Tödt noted that many Q traditions are not hortatory and argued that the purpose of Q can be uncovered by elucidating the Q community's use and development of Son of man sayings. The community did not develop a passion kerygma, but was convinced that Jesus, who had re-established fellowship with his followers as the risen one, is also the one who, as the coming Son of man, will be the eschatological guarantor of that fellowship.

Tödt's proposals depended heavily on an unlikely view of the Son of man traditions in Q, but other scholars followed his lead and showed that Q traditions had been arranged and shaped in the light of christological concerns. Stanton (1973) drew attention to the importance of the accounts of the baptism* and temptations of Jesus (*see* Temptation of Jesus) which stood at the beginning of Q; together with Matthew 11:2-6 par. Luke 7:18-23 (and related passages) they confirm that for the Q community the prophetic eschatological (*see* Eschatology) promises were being fulfilled in the actions and words of Jesus. The past of Jesus (including his rejection by those to whom he was sent), as well as his soon-expected Parousia, was important to the Q community (*see* Apocalyptic Teaching).

5.2. Redaction-Critical Studies. In the 1950s the ways the four Evangelists reshaped and arranged the traditions at their disposal were studied intensively. It soon became possible to show that "redaction" of earlier traditions had been carried out in accordance with particular theological emphases. Discussion of Q from this perspective was pioneered by D. Lührmann (1969) and has been continued by a number of scholars. Attention is focused on the ways originally separate traditions have been linked together in Q and on sayings which have been "created" by the Q community in order to clarify or interpret earlier traditions. Separation of original tradition and later redaction is obviously much more difficult and hypothetical than it is in the case of Matthew's and Luke's redaction of their sources, but that has not deterred scholars from trying to discern the primary purposes of the compiler(s) of Q.

It is possible to demonstrate that several blocks of Q traditions share strikingly similar literary features or theological emphases. For example, R. A. Piper (1989) has shown that Q traditions include a number of *collections* of proverbs, or aphorisms, which develop an argument in similar ways. D. R. Catchpole (1992) argues that many Q traditions reflect the call of Jesus to Israel*: a radical commitment to God's will in light of the imminent end-times is expected; some traditions reflect concern over the delay of the Parousia.

But it is not easy to discern the overriding concern of the final redactor of Q. Hence it is no surprise to discover that some have suggested that Q traditions underwent two or more major redactions. Reconstructions of possible stages in the development of Q traditions are likely to be influenced strongly by the investigator's presuppositions concerning the transmission and development of Gospel traditions, and even by views on the development of earliest Christianity.

5.3. The Literary Genre of Q. Since an appreciation

of the literary genre of a writing is a crucial first step in interpretation, it is surprising that earlier writers on Q paid so little attention to its literary genre. J. M. Robinson (1964) remedied this in a bold claim that Q was part of a "trajectory" of sayings genres which extended from Proverbs to Gnostic writings (especially the *Gospel of Thomas*) and the rabbinic tractate *m. 'Abot*. On this view the wisdom sayings in Q are dominant, and Jesus is portrayed primarily as the representative of the heavenly Sophia (Wisdom).

Robinson's proposals have been refined and extended in J. Kloppenborg's major study (1987). Kloppenborg notes that the writings with which Robinson associates the literary genre of Q are much more homogeneous than Q itself. He argues that the formative component of Q consisted of a group of six "wisdom speeches" which were hortatory in nature and in their mode of argumentation similar to other wisdom writings. This stratum was subsequently expanded by the addition of groups of sayings which adopted a critical and polemical stance with respect to Israel; the temptation story (Mt 4:1-11 par. Lk 4:1-13), which was the final addition to Q, gave it a more biographical cast.

M. Sato (1988) argues that the literary genre of Q is comparable with OT prophetic writings. In all three of the main stages of Q's composition, many individual Q traditions are prophetic in form and in emphasis. Whereas for Kloppenborg prophetic traditions in Q are subsidiary to wisdom traditions, for Sato precisely the reverse is the case. Debate on the genre of Q is likely to continue for some time.

We may now be reasonably certain that Q existed as a written document; its 230 or so sayings of Jesus were used and partly reinterpreted by both Matthew and Luke. But we can be less certain about Q's earlier history, literary genre, overall theological perspective and purpose. Although clusters of traditions with related themes can be identified, Q contained such varied material that it is unwise to claim that it had *one* primary theological perspective or that it was used in the early church in any *one* specific way. The Q hypothesis will continue to be prominent not only in nearly all serious study of the Gospels, but also in discussion of the origin and nature of the earliest expressions of Christian faith.

See also L TRADITION; M TRADITION; SYNOPTIC PROBLEM.

BIBLIOGRAPHY. **Synopses:** J. Kloppenborg, *Q Parallels: Synopsis, Critical Notes and Concordance* (Sonoma, CA: Polebridge, 1988); F. Neirynck, *Q-Synopsis: The Double Tradition Passages in Greek* (Leuven: Peeters, 1988); A. Polag, *Fragmenta Q: Textheft zur Logienquelle* (Neukirchen-Vluyn: Neukirchener Verlag, 1979). **Studies:** D. R. Catchpole, *Studies in Q* (Edinburgh: T. & T. Clark, 1992); M. Dibelius, *From Tradition to Gospel* (New York: Charles Scribner's Sons, 1935); M. D. Goulder, *Luke: A New Paradigm* (2 vols.; JSNTSup 20; Sheffield: JSOT, 1989); A. Harnack, *The Sayings of Jesus* (London: Williams & Norgate, 1907); J. Kloppenborg, *The Formation of Q* (Philadelphia: Fortress, 1987); H. Koester, *Ancient Christian Gospels: Their History and Development* (Philadelphia: Trinity Press International, 1990); D. Lührmann, *Die Redaktion der Logienquelle* (Neukirchen-Vluyn: Neukirchener, 1969); T. W. Manson, *The Sayings of Jesus* (London: SCM, 1949); R. A. Piper, *Wisdom in the Q Tradition: The Aphoristic Teaching of Jesus* (Cambridge: University Press, 1989); J. M. Robinson, "LOGOI SOPHON: On the *Gattung* of Q," in *Trajectories through Early Christianity*, eds. J. M. Robinson and H. Koester (Philadelphia: Fortress, 1964) 71-113; M. Sato, *Q und Prophetie* (Tübingen: J. C. B. Mohr, 1988); S. Schulz, *Q. Die Spruchquelle der Evangelisten* (Zürich: Theologischer, 1972); G. N. Stanton, "On the Christology of Q," in *Christ and Spirit in the New Testament*, eds. B. Lindars and S. S. Smalley (Cambridge: University Press, 1973) 27-42; B. H. Streeter, *The Four Gospels: A Study of Origins* (London: Macmillan, 1924); H. E. Tödt, *The Son of Man in the Synoptic Tradition* (Philadelphia: Westminster, 1965).

G. N. Stanton

QUEST OF HISTORICAL JESUS. *See* HISTORICAL JESUS, QUEST OF.

QUIRINIUS. *See* BIRTH OF JESUS: CHRONOLOGY.

QUMRAN. *See* DEAD SEA SCROLLS.

R

RABBI. *See* TEACHER; RABBINIC TRADITONS AND WRITINGS; SCRIBES.

RABBINIC TRADITIONS AND WRITINGS

1. The Roots of the Rabbinic Movement
2. The Transition to Rabbinic Judaism
3. The Emergence of Rabbinic Literature
4. The Use of Rabbinica in Understanding Jesus and the Gospels

1. The Roots of the Rabbinic Movement.

In its earliest phase the rabbinic movement may be identified with Pharisaism. The Pharisees* are portraycd by Josephus* as being critical of the Hasmonean priesthood. Their expression was at first political (Josephus *Ant.* 13.10.5-6 §§288-98) and could extend to violent action, as in the demand that the counselors who advised Alexander Jannaeus to kill some of their sympathizers should themselves be executed (Josephus *J.W.* 1.5.2-3 §§110-14). At base, however, the orientation of the Pharisees was toward the achievement and maintenance of purity (*see* Clean and Unclean). The purity they strived for had to do fundamentally with making offerings, people and priests (*see* Priest, Priesthood) fit for the cult of sacrifice in the Temple.* For that reason the issues of the personnel of the priesthood, the sorts of animals and goods that might be brought, and their permissible proximity to all sources of uncleanness were vitally important.

1.1. Hillel. By the dawn of the present era the Pharisees found a distinguished teacher in Jerusalem in the person of Hillel. Hillel is justly famous for the dictum, uttered some twenty years before Jesus, "That which you hate, do not do to your fellow; that is the whole Torah, while all the rest is commentary thereon" (*b. Šabb.* 31a). The saying is striking, but it can also be misleading. In context Hillel is talking to an impatient proselyte who wishes to learn the Torah while he stands on one foot; his impatience has just won him a cuff with a measuring rod from Shammai,

the rabbi with whom Hillel is programmatically contrasted in Mishnah. Obviously, Hillel has no overt desire to reduce the Torah on the grounds of principle, and he goes to tell the proselyte, "Go and learn it." In other words, the Gentile* is told that the revelation to Moses is the expression of the best ethics, and for that reason the whole should be mastered.

In any case, Hillel was understood among the Pharisees as having come to prominence for adjudicating quite a distinct issue: whether the Passover could be offered on the Sabbath.* Hillel first offers a scriptural argument for accepting the practice: since other forms of priestly service are permitted, so is the slaying of the lamb. His hearers are unimpressed until he simply states that he learned the position in Babylon, from Shemaiah and Abtalion, distinguished predecessors in the movement. Their authority is sufficient to displace the current leaders of Pharisaic opinion, the sons of Bathyra (cf. *t. Pesaḥ.* 4.13-14; *y. Pesaḥ.* 6.1; *y. Šabb.* 19.1; *b. Pesaḥ.* 66a).

The latter story may appear the more arcane, but it is also more redolent of Pharisaic culture. Hillel consistently involved himself in cultic questions and disputes in Jerusalem. His position also is said to have convinced another teacher,* Baba ben Buṭa, to provide cultically correct beasts in great numbers for slaughter, with the stipulation (against the school of Shammai) that the offerer lay hands on the victim immediately prior to the killing (cf. *t. ḥag.* 2.11; *y. ḥag.* 2.3; *y. Beṣa* 2.4; *b. Beṣa* 20a, b; see 4.3. below).

Moreover, the basis of Hillel's authority was not so much—as has been seen above—any scriptural expertise as his mastery of what he had been taught by previous masters. Hillel embodies the Pharisaic principle that the "chains" of their tradition were normative for purity. Such chains were understood to have been developed from Moses to the Prophets, after that by Ezra and "the men of the great congregation," and then by teachers who were generally invoked as "pairs" (*m. 'Abot* 1:1-18). The last "pair" was Hillel and Shammai, from which point the Pharisees acknowledged that division increased in Israel (*b. Soṭa* 47b; *b. Sanh.* 88b; *t. Soṭa* 14.9; *t. ḥag.* 2.9; *t. Sanh.* 7.1; *y. ḥag.* 2.2; *y. Sanh.* 1.4). The notion of primeval unity disturbed by recent faction is probably mythical, but it is plain that the Pharisees developed their oral tradition by means of a structured understanding of the past as well as by mnemonic techniques.

1.2. Pharisees. The term *Pharisee* is probably an outsiders' name for the movement, and may mean "separatist" or "purist"; participants in the movement appear to have referred to their ancient predecessors (after Ezra) as "the sages" or "the wise," and to their more recent predecessors and contemporaries as "teachers" (cf. *rab* in *m. 'Aboth* 1:6, 16; *sophistēs* in Josephus). The normal, respectful address of a teacher was "my great one" or "my master," *rabbi.* In the Gospels people address Jesus as "rabbi" more frequently than by any other title. Moreover, Jesus had a characteristic interest in purity, and a dispute concerning appropriate sacrifice in the Temple cost him his life.

The Gospels as they stand allow the straightforward deduction that Jesus' followers called him "rabbi" (Mt 26:25, 49; Mk 9:5; 10:51; 11:21; 14:45; Jn 1:38, 49; 3:2; 4:31; 6:25; 9:2; 11:8); they likewise allow the straightforward inference that he is most naturally to be associated with the Pharisees of his period. But in the course of the twentieth century scholars have expressed reservations regarding this finding, bearing in mind the danger of identifying Jesus with the rabbinic movement after A.D. 70. The latter movement was more systematized than the Pharisees before A.D. 70, amounting to the established power within Judaism.* Unfortunately, anxiety with respect to the danger of anachronism can result in the far greater error of locating Jesus within sectarian Judaism (as if orthodoxy existed in early, pluralized Judaism). Worse still, Jesus might be placed within no Judaism at all.

During the time of Hillel and Shammai, and until A.D. 70, Pharisaic teaching was targeted at the conduct of the cult in the Temple, but its influence was limited. Nonetheless, Pharisees appeared to have succeeded reasonably well in towns and villages. Even in Galilee* they urged local populations to maintain the sort of purity which would permit them to participate rightly in the cult. Josephus' fellow in the armed resistance against Rome* and his arch-rival, John of Gischala, may well have been representing Pharisaic interests when he arranged for Jews in Syria to purchase oil exclusively from Galilean sources (Josephus *J.W.* 2.21.2 §§591-93). In any case, it does appear plain that some Pharisees supported the revolt of A.D. 66-70 while others did not (*see* Revolutionary Move-

ments). But while many priests and Essenes perished in the internecine strife of the revolt and in the war with the Romans, and while the aristocracy of scribes* and elders* in Jerusalem was discredited and decimated, the Pharisees survived the war better than any other single group. They were well accepted locally, had long ago accommodated to some marginality, and survived with their personnel and their traditions comparatively in tact.

Rabbinic literature itself personifies the survival of the movement in a story concerning Rabbi Yoḥanan ben Zakkai. According to the story Yoḥanan had himself borne out of Jerusalem on the pretense that he was dead, only to hail Vespasian as king. On his ascent to power Vespasian granted Yoḥanan his wish of settlement in the town of Yavneh, the group of Rabbi Gamaliel, and medical attention for Rabbi Zadok (cf. *b. Giṭ.* 56a, b). In that Josephus claims similarly to have flattered Vespasian (*J.W.* 3.8.9 §§399-408) and to have seen in his coming the fulfillment of messianic prophecy (*J.W.* 6.5.4 §§310-15), the tale is to be used with caution. But it remains expressive of the rabbinic ethos.

2. The Transition to Rabbinic Judaism.

With the foundation of academies such as the one at Yavneh after A.D. 70, one may speak of the transition of Pharisaism to rabbinic Judaism. The rabbis, those who directly contributed to rabbinic literature and to the Judaism which is framed by that literature, belonged to a movement much changed from the popular puritanism of the Pharisees. Initially this was for reasons not of their own making.

2.1. The Wider Application of Tradition. The sort of leadership which a Yoḥanan ben Zakkai might offer became suddenly attractive in the absence of priestly, Essene or scribal alternatives. The target of the tradition's application became correspondingly wider. The Pharisaic/rabbinic program was applied not simply to issues of purity and sacrifice, but to worship generally, to ethics and to daily living.

Yoḥanan is explicitly attributed with the view that the world, which had been sustained by the Law,* the Temple and deeds of faithful love,* now was to be supported only by the last two of the three (*'Abot R. Nat.* 4). Moreover, on the basis of his tradition he specifically adjudicated how feasts might be kept in the gathering for reading, prayer and discussion which was called a "congregation," or "synagogue"* (*kᵉnēseṯ*, also applied to buildings erected for the purpose of such gatherings; cf. *m. Sukk.* 3:12; *m. Roš Haš.* 4:1, 3, 4). The development of that sort of worship as a replacement for activity within the

Temple was not without analogy during the period prior to A.D. 70. Mishnah (*m. Ta'an.* 4:2) envisages a system in which priests, Levites and lay people alike gathered in local synagogues while their representatives were in Jerusalem.

The germ of such piety perhaps lay in the priestly system of courses of service which allowed for a substantial population of priests, divided into twenty-four courses. During the course of the week a given course was appointed to cover, a few priests were chosen to officiate in Jerusalem. Meanwhile, the remainder may have gathered and read the appropriate lections in the villages of Judea and Galilee where they normally lived (1 Chron 24:1-19; Josephus *Ant.* 7.14.7 §365-67). The inclusion of the faithful in Israel in such meetings was a natural development under the rabbis, and general meetings for prayer and instruction had long been a customary feature of Judaism in the Diaspora. It was therefore natural that worship in synagogues should develop as something of a replacement for worship in the Temple.

2.2. The Consolidation of Power.

However, the transition from Pharisaism to rabbinic Judaism was not accomplished immediately after A.D. 70, nor was it simply a matter of the same movement with the same personnel carrying on in a totally new environment. The environment was new, of course, and uniquely favored the emerging authority of rabbis. But the Pharisees of the period were sufficiently flexible to accommodate an influx of priests and scribes into their ranks after the destruction of the Temple. The priestly interest of the Pharisaic movement, of course, was historically organic, and the references to priests in stories and teachings from the time of Yoḥanan (cf. Rabbi Yosi the Priest, *m. 'Abot* 2:8) and well into the second century is striking. Moreover, the consolidation of the rabbis' power after A.D. 70, predicated as it was on local influence, could only be assured by means of the control of local adjudication, as well as worship and study. The tendency of scribes to align themselves with the Pharisees, together with priestly adherents and sympathizers with the movement, assured the emergence and the success of the rabbis.

The triumph of rabbinic authority assured the continuing influence of the priests in decisions regarding purity, in blessings and in receipts of payment of redemption and of tithe. At the same time, scribal influence in the production of written materials and the convocation of formal courts is also striking. Nonetheless, the functional consolidation of the power of the old groups and factions was only achieved during the time of Rabbi Judah (toward the end of the second century) with the emergence of a patriarchate recognized and supported by the Romans.

2.3. The Priority of Learned Consensus.

In the wake of A.D. 70 and the Roman confiscation of the tax formerly paid for the Temple, neither Jerusalem nor its environs was amenable to the maintenance of a hub of the movement. During the second century centers in prosperous Galilee, such as Usha and Beth She'arim would eclipse even Yavneh. Later yet, metropolitan cities such as Sepphoris and Tiberias were the foci of leadership. There was at first nothing like a central leadership or even a common policy, but rabbinic Judaism was constituted in the Pharisaic, priestly and scribal quest for the purity of the nation. The health of the movement required a shift from the highly personal authority of the Pharisees to some notion of learned consensus.

Just that shift is reflected in a Talmudic story concerning a great teacher, Rabbi Eliezer ben Hyrcanus. The story has it that, against a majority of his colleagues, Eliezer held that a ceramic stove, once polluted, might be reassembled, provided the tiles were separated by sand. The majority taught that the result would be unclean; such materials should never be used again. Eliezer's correctness was demonstrated by a tree which was uprooted at his behest, by a stream which ran backwards at his command, by a building he similarly demolished, and by a voice from heaven. Despite all that, the majority held that its decision was binding (*b. B. Meṣ.* 59a, b). As the rudiments of an institution emerged, Eliezer's personal authority clearly diminished; the rabbis of the second century were to stress a rational, consensual achievement of purity, and by the time of the Talmud that was held to be a greater purity than charismatic authority could achieve.

2.4. The Failure of Popular Messianism.

The historic concern for the Temple as the actual focus of purity nonetheless resulted in a final and nearly disastrous attempt—encouraged by some rabbis—to free and restore the holy site. The most prominent rabbinic supporter of that attempt was Aqiba, a student of Eliezer's renowned for his expertise in the tradition. Aqiba supported the claims of one Simeon bar Kosibah to be the new prince of Israel, acting in conjunction with a priest named Eleazar. Simeon's supporters referred to him as Bar Kokhba, "son of a star," projecting onto him the messianic expectations of Numbers 24:17, while his detractors came to know him as Bar Koziba, "son of a lie" (*see* Revolutionary Movements). His initial success and military acumen is attested in letters he sent his commanders during his revolt and regime, which lasted from A.D. 132 until

135. This time the response of the empire was even more definitive than it had been in A.D. 70. The emperor Hadrian ordered the remnants of the Temple taken apart and new shrines built in the city. Jerusalem itself was now called Aelia Capitolina, Jews were denied entry, and Judea became Syria Palaestina.

The rabbis survived by disowning the aspirations embodied by Aqiba, but keeping much of his teaching. "Aqiba, grass will grow out of your jaw, before the son of David comes" (*y. Ta'an.* 4.7; cf. *Lam. Rab.* 2.2.4); that is to say, the Messiah is to be of David (*see* Son of David), not of popular choosing, and his time cannot be pressed. But the greatness of the rabbinic response to national defeat and their consequent redefinition of Judaism consisted less in their formulation of a particular teaching regarding messianism (which emerges in any case from time to time in many forms of Judaism) than in their textual constitution of a form of thought, discipline and life—the Mishnah.

3. The Emergence of Rabbinic Literature.

3.1. Mishnah. Rabbis such as Aqiba had taught their own norms, which came to be known as halakoth (*hᵃlākôt,* pl. of *hᵃlākâ,* "the way"), and had their disciples learn them by heart. A disciple (*talmîd*) might himself internalize what he learned (his teacher's *mišnâ,* or "repetition"; pl. *mišnâyôt*), and proceed to promulgate both it and his own halakoth. But after the failure of Bar Kokhba, the rabbis engaged in an extraordinary synthetic effort under Rabbi Judah ha-Nasi (or "the Prince," in stark contrast to Bar Kokhba's aspirations) to assemble the mishnayoth commonly held to be worthy.

Certain features of the work are both striking and of paradigmatic importance for rabbinic Judaism. First and foremost, the Mishnah represents earlier traditions forced into a dialectical relationship; argument exists in an eternal present between positions which earlier had been separated by time and/or geography. The principal contribution of Mishnah is precisely this invitation to dialectical reasoning concerning purity, unconstrained by history or chronology. However, it must be said that the often uneven synthesis is presented in a definite plan of tractates which typically address the topic of their title, arranged within orders (*sᵉdārîm*). Each order presupposes the agricultural activity the rabbis came to see as normal for Israel. As rabbis, they implied, we speak of the purity we may achieve for a Temple which should always have been, but we do so in the knowledge that the Israel we address and which supports us is more a collection of farms than a nation. Paradoxically, however, Rabbi Judah's move from Beth She'arim to

Sepphoris signalled the emergence of rabbinic authority within cities, and in close association with Roman power. In reading the Mishnah, anachronism must be taken into account at several levels.

Among formative events in the history of Judaism the radical centralization accomplished under Rabbi Judah ranks with Ezra's reform. But where Ezra's program was located in a particular city (which could only be Jerusalem), Judah's was headquartered in one (whether Beth She'arim or Sepphoris) but located in the mind. The Mishnah which emerged was a pattern of reflection which enabled any rabbi anywhere to join in the reflection and the discipline of keeping or making Israel pure. Sanctity in that sense could become the project of the learned in any place. The emergence of Mishnah, of course, called into question its status as compared to Scripture, and the revolt under Bar Kokhba radically raised the issue of the status of those works which had promised the speedy rebuilding of the Temple after A.D. 70 (cf. 2 Esdras and the Targum of Isaiah).

The priestly canon, represented (although oddly counted) by Josephus (*Ag. Ap.* 1.8 §39), had already called for the recognition of twenty-four books. The rabbis could both invoke the support of that group and control messianic yearnings by insisting that those who read books outside that canon would have no part in the world to come (*m. Sanh.* 10:1). Nonetheless, the issue of messianism was more accidental than systemic; it needed to be addressed by the rabbis—and it was definitively addressed—but the crucial matter was the relationship between Scripture and Mishnah. That relationship required several centuries to resolve.

3.2. Midrash. Midrash* may be said to be a category of thought and literature which seeks the resolution of Scripture with the teaching of the rabbis. It is true—as is frequently reported—that the noun derives from the verb *dāraš,* meaning "to inquire," but that fact is largely beside the point. Formally, any midrash will cite the scriptural locus under consideration, somewhat in the manner of the pesherim of Qumran (*see* Dead Sea Scrolls), but typically exegesis is not the point of the exercise. Rather, the citation becomes an occasion to invoke the rabbinic teaching which may be associated with Scripture at that juncture. The relative autonomy of that teaching from any text is usually apparent in what are called the tannaitic or halakic midrashim. "Tannaitic" refers to the Tannaim ("the repeaters," the rabbis of the mishnaic period, although the ascription is traditional, derived from the Aramaic *tᵉnā',* "repeat"), while "halakic" refers to the substance of their teaching. Such documents include

Orders and Tractates of the Mishnah, Tosepta and Talmud

Zera'im "Seeds"
Berakot "Benedictions"
Pe'a "Gleanings"
Demai "Produce not certainly tithed"
Kil'ayim "Diverse Kinds"
Šebi'it "Seventh Year"
Terumot "Heave Offerings"
Ma'aśerot "Tithes"
Ma'aśer Šeni "Second Tithe"
Ḥalla "Dough Offering"
'Orla "Fruit of Young Trees"
Bikkurim "First-fruits"

Mo'ed "Set Feasts"
Šabbat "Sabbath"
'Erubin "Sabbath Limits"
Pesaḥim "Passover"
Šeqalim "Shekel Dues"
Yoma (= *Kippurim*) "Day of Atonement"
Sukka "Tabernacles"
Beṣa (= *Yom Ṭob*) "Festivals"
Roš Haššana "New Year"
Ta'anit "Days of Fasting"
Megilla "Scroll of Esther"
Mo'ed Qaṭan "Mid-Festival Days"
Ḥagiga "Festival Offering"

Našim "Women"
Yebamot "Sisters-in-Law"
Ketubot "Marriage Deeds"
Nedarim "Vows"
Nazir "Nazirite Vow"
Soṭa "Suspected Adulteress"
Giṭṭin "Bills of Divorce"
Qiddušin "Betrothals"

Neziqin "Damages"
Baba Qamma "The First Gate"
Baba Meṣi'a "The Middle Gate"
Baba Batra "The Last Gate"
Sanhedrin "Sanhedrin"
Makkot "Stripes"
Šebu'ot "Oaths"
'Eduyyot "Testimonies"
'Aboda Zara "Idolatry"
'Abot "Fathers"
Horayot "Instructions"

Qodašin "Hallowed Things"
Zebaḥim "Animal Offerings"
Menaḥot "Meal Offerings"
Ḥullin "Animals killed for food"
Bekorot "Firstlings"
'Arakin "Vows of Valuation"
Temura "Substituted Offering"
Keritot "Extirpation"
Me'ila "Sacrilege"
Tamid "Daily Whole Offering"
Middot "Measurements"
Qinnim "Bird Offerings"

Ṭoharot "Cleannesses"
Kelim "Vessels"
Oholot "Tents"
Nega'im "Leprosy Signs"
Para "Red Heifer"
Ṭoharot "Cleannesses"
Miqwa'ot "Immersion Pools"
Niddah "The Menstruant"
Makširin (= *Mašqin*) "The Predisposers"
Zabim "They that suffer a flux"
Ṭebul Yom "He that immersed himself that day"
Yadayim "Hands"
'Uqṣin "Stalks"

two midrashim on Exodus, each called the *Mekilta* (which means "measure"); one is ascribed to Rabbi Ishmael and another (although it is clearly to be dated to a later period) to Rabbi Simeon ben Yoḥai, both of whom lived during the second century. Leviticus receives similar treatment in *Sifra* (or Sipra, meaning "book"), and Numbers and Deuteronomy in *Sifre* (or Sipre, meaning "books").

The influence of Rabbi Ishmael is apparent in the attribution to him (as to Hillel earlier) of rules (*middôt*) of interpretation. The rules by no means govern what

rabbis may teach, but they do represent the evolving grammar of the association of that teaching with Scripture. Formally, the *middôt* set out the patterns of similarity, analogy and logical categorization which might permit scriptural patterns to be adduced in support of a given teaching or assertion. Their application may be observed within rabbinic discussion, but they more aptly describe the sort of inference involved in interpretation than provide the program by which that association was effected. The clear impression conveyed by *Mekilta* (in both traditions), *Sifra* and *Sifre* is that the biblical text is an occasion for the exposition of fundamentally rabbinic ideas and modes of thought.

3.3. Tosefta. Despite the triumph of Rabbi Judah's experiment, the third century saw a crisis in the understanding of what might be done with Mishnah. The crisis is visible in two dilemmas. The first dilemma concerned Scripture, as discussed above. The second was even more basic, in that it involved how the discussion occasioned by Mishnah was to be handled. If the question of Scripture turned on the issue of the rabbis' authority in respect of the past as embodied in the canon, the latter question turned on the issue of their authority in respect of that of their successors. Mishnah considered a dialectic of eternal purity, but how was that dialectic, once it was consigned to writing, to be related to rabbinic discussion in the present? Both dilemmas receive a tentative treatment in the Tosefta (or Tosepta). The term means "addition," in that the corpus was seen as an addendum to the Mishnah in later centuries.

In fact, however, the Tosefta is to some extent a fresh Mishnah which incorporates the work of later rabbis and brings their views into a pattern of discussion with those of the Tannaim. Nonetheless, the Tosefta is essentially conservative in its reliance on the materials and the structure of Mishnah, and it does not promulgate the radical notion—adumbrated in *'Abot,* a tractate appended to the Mishnah around A.D. 250—that, alongside the Torah written in Scripture, Moses received an oral Torah which was passed on through the prophets and sages, and finally to the rabbis. Tosefta represents a greater comprehensiveness in its supplementation of the Mishnah. But it points to the necessity of the daring it lacks: To elevate rabbis not merely by including their teaching, but by permitting them to engage directly in dialog with their illustrious predecessors in Scripture and memory.

3.4. Talmud. The relative comprehensiveness of the Tosefta did not assure its triumph. Mishnah was not superseded by it, nor by any subsequent work within the rabbinic tradition. Moreover, even the rabbis accorded Scripture privilege, in that the capacity to cite a text in order to demonstrate or illustrate a point was privileged. The problem of how to address the present with the eternal truth of the tradition (and vice versa) was met by means of an innovation.

The rabbis as expositors (Amoraim, from *'ᵃmôrā'* "interpreter," as distinct from Tannaim, "repeaters") undertook to treat Mishnah as Scripture. That is, they generated a commentary on Mishnah, which became known as Talmud (*talmûd,* a noun meaning "learning"). The commentary (as in the case of midrash) is

more a matter of using a text as an occasion on which to associate teaching than it is an exposition or exegesis. But the Amoraim triumphantly accomplished what the rabbis of the Tosefta did not: Mishnah was preserved, and at the same time its generative activity and logic was perpetuated in the present. The ideological advance which allowed that accomplishment was the doctrine that Torah was known orally, not only in writing.

3.4.1. The Jerusalem Talmud (c. A.D. 400). The Talmud of Jerusalem, or the *Yerushalmi,* was the last great product of rabbinic Judaism in Palestine (as it came to be called in the Roman period). Sociologically, it was difficult to maintain the sort of discipline of purity the rabbis practiced—and wished others to practice—in a territory recently vanquished by the Romans. The Hadrianic prohibition of circumcision may or may not have been a great impediment (depending upon time and place within the history of the empire), but the incursion of Roman institutions and culture, even at a local level, was a reality from the second century in a way it was not earlier.

Toward the end of the period of the Palestinian Amoraim, the very patriarchate which had sealed the victory of the rabbis in the redaction of Mishnah, appears to have become more aligned with the local aristocracy. Progressive urbanization was not congenial to the maintenance of rabbinic power in Palestine. Moreover, Babylonia during the third century saw the rise of the Sassanids and their form of Zoroastrianism, whose policy toward the practice of Judaism was relatively tolerant. The economic life of the Jews in Babylon, located in largely autonomous towns and villages and supported by agriculture, was better suited to the rabbinic ethos than the increasing syncretism of the Roman Empire from the second century. Particularly, the Sassanids encouraged or tolerated (in varying degrees over time) the formation of the academies in places such as Sura, Pumbeditha and Nehardea, which were the *dynamos* of rabbinic discussion.

3.4.2. The Babylonian Talmud (c. 6th cent.). The rabbis of Babylon gave Judaism its distinctive character, at least until the modern period. This character was and is conveyed in their monument (probably completed during the sixth century), the Babylonian Talmud, or the *Babli.* It is a more comprehensive and subtle treatment of the Mishnah than the *Yerushalmi,* often employing rich, narrative means which permit the contemporization of the rabbinic ethos. Each rabbi is here to some extent a Moses* of his own, as when Moses himself is said to visit the academy of Aqiba and to observe to God that the discussion is so complex, his own unworthiness is obvious (*b. Menaḥ.* 29b). But the rabbis are also respectful tradents, as when Rab Joseph of Pumbeditha, the blind master, acknowledges that without the Targum he would not understand Scripture (*b. Sanh.* 94b). Their knowledge and expertise is functionally infinite: a rabbi can be consulted regarding the vision of God's chariot, how to make love or to relieve constipation. Although the Talmud (and *Babli* for practical purposes is the Talmud) is vast, its very range is a succinct statement of its intent: To transform the whole of life with the light of the Torah as interpreted by the rabbis.

3.5. Targums and Midrash Rabbah. Their energy and their resources enabled the rabbis of Babylon to see to the completion of the standard recension of the targums (*see* Targum) and to the publication of as definitive a form of the midrash as was ever produced. *Midrash Rabbah* presents not only the biblical books used for festal and commemorative occasions (Esther, Ruth, Song of Songs, Ecclesiastes, Lamentations) but also the Pentateuch. The confidence of the rabbis of Babylonia in their own ethos was so great that the comment upon Scripture might include explicit narrative concerning rabbis, as well as exposition and discourse. *Midrash Rabbah* was likely completed during the eighth century, and it represents the confidence that Torah, whether in Scripture or Talmud, is fundamentally one. The interweaving of Scripture and rabbinic teaching is also represented in the homiletic midrashim of a later period: The *Pesiqta Rabbati*, the *Pesiqta de-Rab Kahana* and *Tanḥuma*.

3.6. The Sefer Yesirah. The rabbinic period closes with the rise of Islam and the subsequent reaction of the Geonim, the successors of the rabbis who maintained and extended rabbinic Judaism with a distinctively academic, and sometimes rationalistic, bent. Increasingly, their work is of a literary nature and takes the rabbinic canon as a fact which is to be acknowledged, rather than achieved. Moreover, a tendency toward philosophy and esoterism becomes manifest.

The *Sefer Yesirah*, or "book of formation," is a good representative of a work which is transitional between the Amoraim and the Geonim, and was perhaps composed during the seventh century. It builds on a mystical tradition reaching back at least until Yohanan ben Zakkai, according to which it is possible to see the chariot (the *Merkabah)* of Ezekiel 1, and to know the structure of the creation. But where the rabbis held that such experiments were a matter for private exposition (and then under tight controls, cf. *b. Šabb.* 80b; *b. ḥag.* 11b, 13a, 14b), the *Sefer Yesirah* commences a tradition of literary and rational esoter-

ism which is more typical of the Qabbala of the Middle Ages than of the Judaism of the rabbis. The dialectic of the rabbis was rooted in the oral argument which produced their literature and which their literature was designed to serve. When the logic of literary discourse takes over, the constitution of the Judaism which is reflected is no longer, strictly speaking, rabbinic.

4. The Use of Rabbinica in Understanding Jesus and the Gospels.
Rabbinic literature plainly developed in a way which makes it unlike the Gospels; in social and religious terms, the writings of rabbinic Judaism and early Christianity are not directly comparable. For that reason the existence of an alleged parallel in rabbinica to a passage in the Gospels is not to be taken by itself as proof that Judaism was the origin of the motif at issue. (Sometimes, the term *parallel* is only useful when it is borne in mind that the adjective describes lines which do not in fact meet.) Moreover, the very program of the rabbis, of taking up a perennial discussion of purity and promulgating that as Torah caused words or sayings to be ascribed anachronistically to their predecessors. The attribution of positions to any rabbi, particularly of the Tannaitic period or earlier, is to be used only with caution.

4.1. Anachronisms. The earlier reference (see 1.1. above) to Hillel's teaching concerning love is a case in point. Hillel was revered as the progenitor of the patriarchate and was even—over the course of time—endowed with Davidic ancestry (*Gen. Rab.* 98), which reinforced the claim to authority of any patriarch descended from him. By the time of the Amoraim a rabbi was understood to render with his own halakah the functional equivalent of Torah, and that is precisely what Hillel does in the story. In a single stroke he defeats the glib request of the proselyte and the rude exclusivism of Shammai. Hillel becomes what any Amoraim wanted to be: a hero for the Torah who succeeded because he understood the force of the Torah. In that this story of Hillel is consistent with the ethos of the Amoraim and appears only at this stage of the *Babli* (*b. Šabb.* 31a), its emphasis on learning the whole of Torah should not necessarily be ascribed to Hillel himself.

4.2. Analogies. On the other hand, the ubiquity of a form of what is commonly known as the Golden Rule makes it unwise to deny Hillel may have said something such as ascribed to him in the *Babli.* The story as it stands may reflect the ethos of the Amoraim, but a statement of Hillel's may lie at its point of origin. Negatively formulated as an imperative against doing what one finds loathsome, the maxim appears to have circulated generally during the ancient period (cf. Confucius *Analecta* 15.23; Tob 4:15; *Ep. Arist.* 207; Eusebius *Praep. Ev.* 8.7 [for its citation of Philo]; *T. Naph.* [Hebrew] 1:6; *2 Enoch* 61:1, 2; Sextus *Sententiae* 89 [and 210b]). It has also influenced the form of the Golden Rule in the *Didache* (1:2; cf. Acts 15:20, 29 in Bezae; Rom 13:10): Whatever you wish not to be done to you, do not do to another.

Given that the proverbial form of the Rule (i.e., in the negative) is the form that predominates in Christian antiquity, there is no question of attempting to argue that Hillel's version specifically influenced Jesus' saying. Further, the negative form of the Rule is as common in the Christian tradition as in many others; there is no need or reason to posit some specific source (such as Hillel's dictum) for a conventional statement.

Indeed, the feature which may be significantly distinctive in the maxim as attributed to Jesus in Matthew 7:12 and Luke 6:31 is that its form is positive. Although the substance of the teaching is proverbial, and far from unique, there is unquestionably an unusual element in the application of its principle. The active desire to do to others the good one wants for oneself is evidently a more aggressive version of the imperative not to inflict the harm one would avoid. The significance of what is attributed to Hillel in the *Babli* is not that it can be established to provide a parallel to Jesus' teaching from the first century, but that it establishes by contrast that, in rabbinic Judaism and probably in the Pharisaic circles of early Judaism, the proverbial, negative form of the maxim was current. Even that marginal insight is only obtainable when *Babli* is read within the terms of reference of earlier documents. There is no question of a critically acceptable, direct comparison between Jesus and Hillel on the basis of the Gospels and the *Babli* alone.

4.3. Milieu. As has already been mentioned (see 1.1. above), Hillel is reported to have taught that offerings should be brought to the Temple, where the owners would lay hands on them and then give them over to priests for slaughter (cf. *t. ḥag.* 2.11; *y. ḥag.* 2.3; *y. Beṣa* 2.4; *b. Beṣa* 20a, b). His perennial and stereotypical disputants, the house of Shammai, resist, insisting that the animals might be handed over directly. One of the house of Shammai (named Baba ben Buṭa in the *Babli* and Tosefta), however, was so struck by the rectitude of Hillel's position that he had some 3,000 animals (a number specified only in the *Yerushalmi*) brought to the Temple and gave them to those who were willing to lay hands on them in advance of sacrifice.

Generally speaking, the haggadah (*haggaddâ*, "nar-

ration, instruction") concerning Hillel, Baba ben Buṭa and the sheep is more characteristic of the Pharisaic/rabbinic program than is the vignette containing the Golden Rule. Moreover, the broader attestation of the story within the two Talmuds and its appearance in the Tosefta indicate that it may reflect an actual dispute. Finally, although Hillel's disputants are stereotypical, it is striking that in *Beṣa* 20a (cf. *t. ḥag.* 2.11) Hillel pretends the animal is a female for a shared sacrifice (*zibḥê šᵉlāmîm*) in order to get it by the disciples of Shammai. That is, the Babli's version of the story assumes that the followers of Shammai are in actual control of what worshipers do in the Temple. The haggadah is a far cry from the sort of tale in which Hillel is portrayed as the prototypical patriarch of rabbinic Judaism.

In one sense the tradition concerning Hillel envisages a movement opposite from that of Jesus in the Temple (Mt 21:12-13; Mk 11:15-17; Lk 19:45-46; Jn 2:13-17; *see* Temple Cleansing): Animals are introduced, rather than their traders expelled. But the purpose of the action by Hillel's partisan is to enforce a certain understanding of correct worship, and that is also the motivation attributed to Jesus in the Gospels. Hillel's halakah, in effect, insists on the participation of the offerer by virtue of his ownership of what is offered, an ownership of which the laying on of hands is a definitive gesture (cf. *b. Pesaḥ.* 66b). The house of Shammai is portrayed as sanctioning sacrifice, without mandating that sort of emphatic participation on the part of the offerer. Although nothing like the violence of Jesus is attributed to Baba ben Buṭa, he does offer an analogy for a forcible attempt to insist on correct worship in the Temple on the part of a Pharisee.

Mishnah itself reflects a concern to control commercial arrangements connected with the Temple, and such concern is also somewhat analogous to Jesus' action in the exterior court. The following story is told concerning one of the successors of Hillel (*m. Ker.* 1:7):

> Once in Jerusalem a pair of doves cost a golden denar. Rabban Simeon ben Gamaliel said: By this Place I will not rest this night before they cost but a [silver] denar. He went into the court and taught: If a woman suffered five miscarriages that were not in doubt or five issues that were not in doubt, she need bring but one offering, and she may then eat of the sacrifices; and the rest is not required of her. And the same day the price of a pair of doves stood at a quarter denar each.

Although the story requires more effort to understand than the one concerning Hillel, it rewards the attention required. The assumption of the whole tale is that a pair of doves might be offered by a woman as both a burnt offering and a sacrifice for sin in order to be purified after childbirth; the second of the two would be offered normally, while the first—in the case of poverty—might take the place of a yearling lamb (Lev 12:6-8). The story also assumes that from the point of view of purity miscarriages and unusual issues of blood akin to miscarriages should be treated under the category of childbirth. That association is characteristically Pharisaic, as is the issue of when the woman might be considered entitled to eat of offerings. The Pharisees defined purity as fitness to take part in sacrifice and in meals which—in their teaching—were extensions of the holiness of the Temple.

Simeon's anger, which causes him to swear by the Temple (cf. Mt 23:16-22), is therefore motivated to some extent by economic considerations. His response is, like that of Jesus, to teach in the court of the Temple, where such offerings would be brought. But his action there is far less direct than that of Hillel or Jesus. Instead of importing more birds or releasing those bought at an extortionate price, he promulgates a halakah designed to reduce the trade in doves, no matter what their price.

If a woman may await several (up to five) miscarriages or flows of blood and then offer a single pair of doves and be considered pure enough to eat of the animal offering, the potential revenue from sales of doves would obviously decline. In effect, Simeon counters inflationary prices with sacrificial monetarism. The political lesson was quickly appreciated (on the very day, if we believe the story), and prices went even lower than Simeon had intended. Presumably there was no reason for him to continue promulgating his view in the court of the Temple, and both he and the traders were content with the settlement.

The date of the Mishnah, as compared to the Tosefta, the *Yerushalmi* and the *Babli*, makes its material, when in any way comparable to the Gospels, of immediate interest to the student of Jesus' life and teaching. For all its complexity the haggadah in the mishnaic tractate *Keritot* is vitally important for appreciating the sort of Pharisaic intervention in the operation of the Temple which was considered possible during the first century. (Perhaps the story concerning Simeon is more complicated precisely because it is closer to particulars of Pharisaic concern than the later haggadah concerning Hillel and Baba ben Buṭa.) Hillel, Simeon and Jesus are all portrayed as interested in the animals offered in the Temple to the extent that they intervene (or, in the case of Hillel, a surrogate intervenes) in the exterior court in order

to influence the ordinary course of worship. To that extent we may say that rabbinic traditions and writings provide a context within which it is possible to interpret a well-attested action of Jesus.

4.4. Summary. The usefulness of the documents of rabbinic Judaism for interpreting Jesus and the Gospels is qualified by three critical considerations, each of which we have observed in the examples provided above. First, the relatively late date of the literature must be taken into account, although the continuities between rabbinic Judaism and Pharisaism of the first century suggest some analogies between the Gospels and rabbinica. Second, a recognition of the social and religious transformations involved in the emergence of rabbinic Judaism must alert the reader to the possibility of anachronistic attributions or to the presentation of early teachers as spokesmen of later theologies. And finally, we must understand that the initial target of inquiry is the recovery of the milieu of early Judaism. That is, we should seek not so much particular events and sayings paralleled in the Gospels but to recapture the matrix of the Christian faith, as it is reflected indirectly both in the Gospels and in rabbinica.

See also JUDAISM; MIDRASH; PHARISEES; TARGUMS; TEACHER.

BIBLIOGRAPHY. W. G. Braude, *Pesikta Rabbati: Discourses for Feasts, Fasts, and Special Sabbaths* (New Haven: Yale University, 1968); W. G. Braude and I. J. Epstein, *Pesikta de-Rab Kahana: R. Kahana's Compilation of Discourses for Sabbaths and Special Days* (Philadelphia: Jewish Publication Society, 1975); W. D. Davies and D. C. Allison, Jr., *A Critical and Exegetical Commentary on the Gospel according to Saint Matthew* (ICC; Edinburgh: T. & T. Clark, 1988); I. Epstein, ed., *The Babylonian Talmud . . . Translated with Notes, Glossary, and Indices* (London: Soncino, 1936-1948); A. Finkel, *The Pharisees and the Teacher of Nazareth* (AGSU 4; Leiden: Brill, 1964); J. A. Fitzmyer, "The Bar Cochba Period," in *Essays on the Semitic Background of the New Testament* (SBLSBS 5; Missoula: Scholars, 1974) 305-54; H. Freedman and M. Simon, *Midrash Rabbah, Translated into English with Notes, Glossary and Indices* (London: Soncino, 1983); J. Goldin, *The Fathers according to Rabbi Nathan* (New York: Schocken, 1974); J. Z. Lauterbach, *Mekilta de-Rabbi Ishmael* (Philadelphia: Jewish Publication Society, 1976); L. I. Levine, *The Rabbinic Class of Roman Palestine in Late Antiquity* (New York: The Jewish Theological Seminary, 1989); J. N. Neusner, *The Mishnah. A New Translation* (New Haven: Yale University, 1988); idem, *The Pharisees: Rabbinic Perspectives* (Hoboken: Ktav, 1973); idem, *The Peripatetic Saying: The Problem of the Thrice-Told Tale in Talmudic*

Literature (BJS 89; Chico: Scholars, 1985); idem, *Sifre.
An Analytic Translation* (BJS 138; Atlanta: Scholars,
1988-); idem, *Talmud of the Land of Israel* (Chicago:
University of Chicago, 1982-); idem, *Torah: From Scroll
to Symbol in Formative Judaism* (FJ; Philadelphia:
Fortress, 1985); E. Schürer, *The History of the Jewish
People in the Age of Jesus Christ (175 B.C.-A.D. 135)*, rev.
and ed. G. Vermes and F. Millar (3 vols.; Edinburgh:
T. & T. Clark, 1973-87).   B. D. Chilton

RANSOM SAYING

The ransom saying consists of the second half of
Mark 10:45 (par. Mt 20:28) where Jesus says: "For even
the Son of Man* did not come to be served, but to
serve, and to give his life as a ransom for many." It
is extremely important because it purports to show the
significance Jesus attached to his death (*see* Death of
Jesus). Any attempt to determine how Jesus understood his mission or to trace the development of the
christology of the early church* must take this saying
into account.

    1. Context
    2. Background
    3. Authenticity
    4. Meaning

1. Context.

The saying appears at the climax of a dispute about
greatness precipitated by the request that James and
John receive positions of honor in the coming
kingdom. In his response to the sons of Zebedee (Mt
20:22-23 par. Mk 10:38-40) Jesus asks them whether
they can drink the cup he drinks or (Mk only) be
baptized with the baptism* he is baptized with. Then
he calls the disciples* together and proceeds to teach
them that true greatness consists in service* (Mt 20:25-
28 par. Mk 10:42-45). This teaching culminates in the
ransom saying. In it Jesus sets himself forth as an
example of selfless service and at the same time
clarifies what he meant by the reference to the cup
and baptism.

    The saying plays a vital role in its broader as well
as its immediate context. It provides a climax to the
section of the Gospel narratives which begins with
Peter's confession at Caesarea Philippi. The confession has a pivotal function in the Synoptic Gospels.
From that point on the narratives focus on the passion
(*see* Passion Narrative), and Jesus begins to give
explicit teaching about the necessity of his death. In
addition to more veiled references there are three
major passion predictions attributed to Jesus (Mt 16:21
par. Mk 8:31 and Lk 9:22; Mt 17:22-23 par. Mk 9:31
and Lk 9:44; Mt 20:18-19 par. Mk 10:33-34 and Lk

18:31-33; *see* Predictions of Jesus' Passion and Resurrection). Each of these is followed by some indication
of the failure of the Twelve to comprehend what Jesus
meant and by instruction concerning discipleship.
The third of these prophecies is given while Jesus and
his disciples are on their last journey to Jerusalem and
precedes the selfish request of James and John. All
three Gospels portray Jesus as being preoccupied with
his death from the time of Peter's confession onwards,
and the ransom saying reveals how he understood it.
Coming just before the arrival in Jerusalem, it helps
explain the reason for the journey to the holy city and
the suffering that awaits Jesus there.

2. Background.

There used to be a virtual consensus that the ransom
saying was based on the description of the Suffering
Servant in Isaiah 52:13—53:12 (*see* Servant of Yahweh), but an essay by C. K. Barrett has convinced
many scholars to look elsewhere for the background
to the saying. His study shows that there is little verbal
similarity between the saying and the Septuagintal
version of Isaiah 53. Nevertheless, Barrett may be
faulted for treating linguistic parallels separately from
conceptual parallels, concentrating too narrowly on
parallels to Isaiah 53:12 and underestimating the
cumulative significance of the parallels. Though
Barrett disputes this, it remains likely that the ransom
saying was formed on the basis of Isaiah 53. Both
combine the ideas of servanthood and atoning death
and speak of the servant voluntarily "giving his life."
The Greek *lytron* ("ransom") in Matthew 20:28 and
Mark 10:45 corresponds to the Hebrew *'āšām* ("guilt
offering") in Isaiah 53:10, despite the fact that it is not
used to translate it elsewhere. Most importantly, both
use the phrase "for many" to indicate who benefits
from the servant's death.

    There are two major alternatives to the view that the
ransom saying alludes to Isaiah 53. The first is that it
draws on the general conception in late Judaism that
the suffering of martyrs has atoning efficacy. This
idea comes to expression in 4 Maccabees 6:28-29
where Eleazer prays, "Be merciful to your people and
let our punishment be a satisfaction on their behalf.
Make my blood their purification and take my life as
a ransom for theirs" (cf. 2 Macc 7:37-38; 4 Macc 17:21-
22). This, however, fails to account for the emphasis
in the Gospels on the death of Jesus as a scriptural
necessity. The other option is that the ransom saying
is based on a corporate interpretation of the "one like
a son of man" in Daniel 7. The "Son of man" title
probably was derived from Daniel 7, but although that
chapter speaks of the sufferings of the "saints of the

Most High," it does not associate suffering directly with the "son of man," and it is unlikely that it was interpreted as doing so in the first century (*see* Son of Man). Isaiah 53 is much more credible as the background for the saying than either of these alternatives.

3. Authenticity.

There is considerable disagreement over whether the ransom saying should be accepted as an authentic saying of Jesus. Four arguments have been advanced against its genuineness. First, it has been said that the idea of death as ransom is foreign to the preceding context and destroys the analogy between the behavior of the Son of man and that expected of the disciples. This argument wrongly assumes that the transition from the thought of a life of exemplary service to that of a unique, atoning death is awkward. Having introduced himself as a servant, it was only natural that Jesus should go on to speak of the supreme demonstration of his servanthood in his death. A similar combination of ideas can be found in John 12:23-27; Philippians 2:5-8; 1 Peter 2:21-25; and 1 John 3:16.

Second, it has been alleged that the tense of the main verb, "did . . . come" (*ēlthen*), looks back on the life of Jesus as being in the past. This allegation is unwarranted. The verb simply expresses a consciousness of having been divinely commissioned for a special task. There are many sayings in which Jesus speaks of "coming" or "being sent." Some of these—for instance Luke 12:49, "I have come to bring fire on the earth, and how I wish it were already kindled!"—clearly originated during the lifetime of Jesus. This motif is deeply imbedded in the Gospel tradition and must go back to the historical Jesus.

Third, the saying has been assailed on the grounds that it presents an interpretation of Jesus' death not otherwise attested in his teaching. Older critics thought it had been influenced by Pauline conceptions of the atonement, though this hypothesis has largely been abandoned. In opposition to those who suggest that the saying is without parallel in Jesus' teaching, it must be noted that it is not at all out of character with what Jesus taught about his death. There is abundant evidence that Jesus anticipated that his life would end violently and that he believed this had been prophesied in Scripture. It is inherently probable that he would have reflected on the meaning of this. If, as Luke 22:37 suggests, he did so in the light of Isaiah 53, the authenticity of the ransom saying is perfectly credible. That it expresses the mind of Jesus is confirmed by the presence of similar ideas in the words over the cup at the Last Supper* (Mt

26:28 par. Mk 14:24 and Lk 22:20).

The final and most substantial argument against the genuineness of the saying is based on its absence from Luke 22:25-27, which otherwise parallels Matthew 20:25-28 and Mark 10:42-45 quite closely. Luke presents the same main thoughts in the same sequence, and many believe that he is relating the same conversation, with his version being closer to what Jesus actually said. In response to this the following observations are in order. (1) The semitic character of the version in the first two Gospels suggests that it is more primitive than that in Luke. (2) It is unwarranted to assume that the version with the richest theology must be secondary. (3) It appears that Luke drew Luke 22:24-27 from his special source(s) rather than from either Matthew or Mark, and there is no reason to think that he intended to suppress the theology of the saying. (4) Luke places his account in a different historical setting than the other Evangelists, and it is not at all certain that he is describing the same incident. (5) Even if the placing of the saying in its present location was editorial, the saying itself could be genuine.

All things considered, it is more probable that the saying originated in the mind of Jesus than in the early church. It coheres well with Jesus' preoccupation with his death toward the end of his life, especially if he saw himself in the role of the Suffering Servant of Isaiah 53. In addition, its simplicity suggests that it was the fountainhead of the Christian understanding of redemption. The evidence of early and widespread belief in the redeeming efficacy of Jesus' death (cf. 1 Cor 15:3; 1 Pet 1:18-19) is most easily explained if it goes back to something Jesus himself said.

4. Meaning.

"Son of man" is an exalted title and implies that Jesus has the right to be served (cf. Dan 7:13-14), but according to Matthew 20:28 and its parallel Mark 10:45, the purpose of his coming to earth was to serve others. This service included giving his life for them after the pattern of the Suffering Servant in Isaiah 53.

Jesus characterizes his death as a "ransom" (*lytron*), employing a word that does not appear elsewhere in the NT (a related word *antilytron*, also translated "ransom," is used in 1 Tim 2:6). In extrabiblical sources *lytron* denotes the price paid to free slaves, and it is likely that it has this meaning here, though obviously it is used in a metaphorical sense. Some scholars think that, when used with reference to God, the term refers to deliverance in a general way, without implying anything about cost. It appears that the related verb *lytroō* can describe an act of deliverance which does not involve payment, but it is doubtful that *lytron* is ever used in this way. It specifically designates the means of deliverance and always seems to include the notion of cost. When used metaphorically, however, it need not imply that payment is given to a particular individual, and the NT references to redemption never specify to whom the ransom is paid. In this case the term stresses that the emancipation of the many was accomplished at great cost, namely the death of the Son of man.

If the idea of cost attaches to *lytron*, the use of this word suggests that the death of Jesus had a substitutionary significance. The presence of the idea of substitution receives further support, if, as argued above, the ransom saying is indebted to Isaiah 53, where the servant is pictured as suffering vicariously. In any case there can be little doubt that the Evangelists thought in terms of substitution, since the saying calls to mind the question "What can a man give in exchange for his soul?" (Mt 16:26 par. Mk 8:37), which Jesus addressed to the disciples in the teaching he gave on discipleship* after the first passion prediction. This passage, which echoes Psalm 49:7-9, indicates that those who forfeit eternal life* cannot buy it back. With the ransom saying Jesus claims that he can do for others what they cannot do for themselves.

The idea of substitution is reinforced by the use of the preposition *anti* after *lytron*. This preposition normally indicates a relationship of equivalence or exchange. It is most often rendered "instead of" or "in place of." This is the only place in the NT where it is used with reference to those who benefit from the death of Christ, and some have suggested that in this instance it means "on behalf of" and has no substitutionary implications. In view of the context, however, it is preferable to understand the preposition as having its customary sense.

The far-reaching effects of the substitutionary death of Jesus are indicated by the phrase "for many." Some scholars believe that the term "many" (*pollōn*) was intended to have an inclusive rather than exclusive sense, and that it may be seen as synonymous with "all." Others think, largely on the basis of the way the term "many" (*rabbîm*) is used in the Qumran literature, that it refers to the elect community. Certainly "many" stands in contrast to "one" not "all," and the basic idea is that the death of Jesus brings benefit to a great number of persons.

See also DEATH OF JESUS; PREDICTIONS OF JESUS' PASSION AND RESURRECTION.

BIBLIOGRAPHY. C. K. Barrett, "The Background of Mark 10:45," in *New Testament Essays: Studies in Memory of T. W. Manson,* ed. A. J. B. Higgins (Manchester: University Press, 1959) 1-18; C. Brown, "λύτρον," *NIDNTT* 3.189-200; F. Büchsel, "λύτρον," *TDNT* IV.340-49; R. T. France, "The Servant of the Lord in the Teaching of Jesus," *TynB* 19 (1968) 26-52; D. Hill, *Greek Words and Hebrew Meanings: Studies in the Semantics of Soteriological Terms* (SNTSMS 5: Cambridge: University Press, 1967) 49-81; B. Lindars, "Mark 10:45: A Ransom for Many," *ExpT* 93 (1982) 292-95; I. H. Marshall, "The Development of the Concept of Redemption in the New Testament," in *Reconciliation and Hope: New Testament Essays on Atonement and Eschatology presented to L. L. Morris,* ed. R. Banks (Exeter: Paternoster, 1974) 153-69; L. Morris, *The Apostolic Preaching of the Cross* (Grand Rapids: Eerdmans, 1956) 9-59; W. J. Moulder, "The Old Testament Background and the Interpretation of Mark x.45," *NTS* 24 (1978) 120-27; S. Page, "The Authenticity of the Ransom Logion (Mark 10:45b)," in *Gospel Perspectives 1: Studies of History and Tradition in the Four Gospels,* ed. R. T. France and D. Wenham (Sheffield: JSOT, 1980) 137-61; P. Stuhlmacher, "Vicariously Giving His Life for Many, Mark 10:45 (Matt. 20:28)," in *Reconciliation, Law, and Righteousness: Essays in Biblical Theology* (Philadelphia: Fortress, 1986) 16-29.   S. Page

READER-RESPONSE CRITICISM. *See* LITERARY CRITICISM.

REDACTION CRITICISM

Redaction criticism is a historical and literary discipline which studies both the ways the redactors/editors/authors changed their sources and the seams or transitions they utilized to link those traditions into a unified whole. The purpose of this approach is to recover the author's theology and setting. Redaction criticism is the third of four "schools" of criticism developed in this century to study the Gospels and other biblical narratives: *Form criticism,** which seeks the original or authentic tradition behind the final form found in the Gospels but tends to assume that the Evangelists were mere scissors-and-paste editors who artificially strung together the traditions they inherited; *tradition criticism,** a stepchild of form criticism, which tries to reconstruct the history or development of the Gospel traditions from the earliest to the final form in the Gospels but often ignores the contribution of the Evangelists; and *literary criticism,** which bypasses the historical dimension and studies only the final form of the text, assuming that the value of the Gospels is to be found apart from considerations of originating event or author. Redaction criticism originally developed as a corrective to areas of neglect in form and tradition criticism, but it functions also as a corrective to excesses in literary criticism.

1. The Process of Redactional Inquiry
2. The Origins of Redaction Criticism
3. The Methodology of Redaction Criticism
4. The Weaknesses of Redaction Criticism
5. The Place and Value of Redaction Criticism

1. The Process of Redactional Inquiry.
Redaction criticism must build upon the results of source criticism, for the final results are determined in part by one's choice of Markan or Matthean priority (*see* Synoptic Problem). The most widely held hypothesis remains the Oxford, or four-document, hypothesis of B. H. Streeter, who taught that Matthew and Luke utilized two primary sources, Mark and Q,* along with their own secondary sources (M* and L*). Redaction critics begin with this assumption and study the alterations which the Evangelists made to their sources. This means that redactional study is most relevant for Matthew and Luke, less so for Mark (we don't know what sources he may have used) or John (independent for the most part from the Synoptics; *see* Synoptics and John).

Redaction critics work also with the results of form and tradition criticism, assuming the process of tradition development but studying primarily the final stage, the changes wrought by the Evangelists themselves. When examining Luke's redaction of the crucifixion narrative (*see* Death of Jesus), these scholars ask which of the three "last sayings" peculiar to Luke (23:34, 43, 46) may have been added earlier by the community and which were added by the Evangelist. They believe that these changes to the tradition provide a clue to the Evangelist's theological intentions and the life-situation (*Sitz im Leben*) of his community.

This is accomplished by asking *why* the changes were made and by seeking consistent patterns in the alterations made by the redactor. Such modifications denote redactional interests or theological tendencies on the part of the Evangelist who introduced them. In Luke's crucifixion narrative two such tendencies might be noted: a christological stress on Jesus as the innocent righteous martyr (exemplified also in Lk 23:47, "Surely this man was righteous [*dikaios*]") and an emphasis on the crucifixion as a scene of worship (seen in the absence of negative aspects like the earthquake, in the redaction of the taunts which in Luke are contrasted with Jesus' prayer* for forgiveness,* and in the fact that two of the sayings are prayers).

Finally, the setting or situation of the Lukan church is reconstructed by asking what led to these changes.

This is of course a speculative enterprise, but most critics believe that sociological factors hinted at in the text were behind the pastoral concerns which determined the final form. Thus redaction criticism is interested in both the theological interests and the ecclesiastical situation behind the Gospel texts.

2. The Origins of Redaction Criticism.
There were several precursors to this movement, such as W. Wrede's "messianic secret"; N. B. Stonehouse's study of christological emphases in the Synoptic Gospels; R. H. Lightfoot's Bampton lectures of 1934, which studied Mark's theological treatment of his sources; or K. L. Schmidt's form-critical treatment of the Markan seams. Like the origins of form criticism via three German scholars working independently in post-World-War-1 Germany (Schmidt, Dibelius, Bultmann), redaction criticism began in post-World-War-2 Germany with three independent works—those of Bornkamm, Conzelmann and Marxsen.

G. Bornkamm launched the movement with his 1948 article, "The Stilling of the Storm in Matthew," later combined with articles by two of his students in *Tradition and Interpretation in Matthew*. He argued that Matthew not only changed but reinterpreted Mark's miracle story (*see* Miracles, Miracle Stories) into a paradigm of discipleship* centering on the "little faith" of the disciples as a metaphor for the difficult journey of the "little ship of the church." In a 1954 article, "Matthew As Interpreter of the Words of the Lord" (expanded to "End-Expectation and Church in Matthew" and included in the volume mentioned above) Bornkamm considered Matthew's Gospel as a whole, stating that for Matthew eschatology* is the basis for ecclesiology: the church* defines itself and its mission in terms of the coming judgment.*

N. Perrin states, "If Günther Bornkamm is the first of the true redaction critics, Hans Conzelmann is certainly the most important" (28). Conzelmann's study of Luke began with a 1952 article, "Zur Lukasanalyse," later expanded into *The Theology of St. Luke* (1954). He challenged the prevalent view by arguing that Luke was a theologian rather than a historian; the delay of the Parousia led Luke to replace the imminent eschatology of Mark with a salvation-historical perspective having three stages—the time of Israel, ending with John the Baptist; the time of Jesus (the "center of time," the original German book title); and the time of the church (*see* Luke, Gospel of). According to Conzelmann the kingdom (*see* Kingdom of God) in Luke has become virtually a timeless entity, with the Parousia no longer the focus. Mark's brief interim has become an indefinite period, and the church is prepared for prolonged conflict in the lengthy period before the final judgment.

W. Marxsen in his *Mark the Evangelist* (1956) was the first to use the term *Redaktionsgeschichte,* and the first and most influential portion of his work described the differences between form and redaction criticism, asserting that form-critical research has missed the third *Sitz im Leben* (after the situations of Jesus and the early church), namely that of the Evangelist. His method is called "backwards exegesis," which interprets each pericope from the perspective of those preceding it. By this theory Mark used the John the Baptist (*see* John the Baptist) story not to tell what happened but rather to provide a base for what came after, the story of Jesus. Marxsen's actual theory regarding Mark was much less influential; he stated that Mark wrote to tell the church to flee the terrible persecution during the Jewish War of A.D. 66 and to proceed to Galilee* where the imminent return of the Son of man (Parousia) would take place.

3. The Methodology of Redaction Criticism.

The difficulty in redactional research is determining with some degree of probability that a redactional nuance is present in the text. The discipline is prone to highly speculative theories because the methodology as well as the thoroughness of the search completely determines the results. Marxsen, on the one hand, makes Mark a Jewish-Christian work centering on an imminent Parousia, while Weeden, on the other hand, turns Mark into a Hellenistic work countering a "divine man" heresy (*see* Divine Man/Theios Aner) by recasting Mark's battle with his opponents in the form of a dramatic conflict between Jesus (= Mark) and his disciples (= Mark's opponents). Few interpreters have followed either theory because both failed to consider all the evidence. The key to redactional study is a good synopsis of the Gospels, which becomes the basis for the research. A scholar compares the Gospel accounts, compiles the differences and then studies the resultant data by means of the following stages of analysis.

3.1. Tradition-Critical Analysis. The historical development of the pericope from Jesus through the early church to the Evangelist is determined by applying the criteria of authenticity to the passage: (1) *Dissimilarity* (the tradition is authentic if it exhibits no ties to Judaism* or the church); (2) *multiple attestation* (the pericope is repeated in several of the primary sources like Mark, Q, M, L or in more than one form); (3) *divergent patterns* (it is contrary to emphases in the early church); (4) *unintended evidence of historicity* (details which suggest an eyewitness report); (5)

Aramaic or Palestinian features (Semitic constructions [*see* Languages of Palestine] or Palestinian customs which point to a early origin); and (6) *coherence* (it is consistent with other passages proven reliable on the basis of other criteria). These in and of themselves do not prove authenticity, of course, but they can demonstrate that the tradition goes back to the earliest stages and they do shift the burden of proof to the skeptic.

These criteria were originally developed under a so-called hermeneutic of suspicion which assumed that the stories were "guilty unless proven innocent," that is, they were nonhistorical unless shown otherwise. However, it has repeatedly been shown that the criteria when used in this manner have proved inconclusive, and most today use them more positively to trace the text's development. In this way tradition criticism provides the data for the form-critical and redaction-critical stages which follow. Nevertheless, demonstrating the text's reliability (the positive side) is an important step in itself since it grounds the interpreters in history and forces them to realize that they are not just tracing the ideas of Mark or Matthew (a danger of redactional study) but also the very life and teachings of the historical Jesus (*see* Historical Jesus).

Tradition criticism used in this way is an important step prior to carrying out redactional study. Its primary value lies in the area of historical verification, for it links redactional study with the quest for the historical Jesus and anchors the results in history. One danger of redaction criticism is the tendency of many critics today to take an ahistorical approach—to study the Gospels as purely literary creations rather than as books which trace the life of Jesus. Tradition criticism provides a control against such tendencies. Moreover, the study of the history of the development of the text, though admittedly speculative at times, leads to greater accuracy in identifying redactional tendencies. By tracing with greater precision how an author is using the sources and how the sources have developed, the results of redactional criticism will be established on a stronger data base.

3.2. Form-Critical Analysis. Before beginning the detailed study of a pericope it is crucial to determine the form it takes, since the interpreter will apply a different set of hermeneutical principles to each subgenre in the Gospels. A pericope can take the form of a *pronouncement story* (the setting and details lead up to a climactic saying of Jesus); *miracle story* (some emphasizing the miracle or exorcism, others discipleship,* christology, cosmic conflict or the presence of the kingdom); *dominical saying* (further classified by Bultmann as wisdom logia, prophetic or apocalyptic* sayings, legal sayings or church rules, "I" sayings and similitudes); *parable* (further subdivided into similitudes, example stories, and one-, two- or three-point parables depending on the number of characters involved); *event or historical story* (episodes in Jesus' life like the baptism* or Transfiguration*—often labeled "legends" because of their supernatural nature); and *passion story* (considered a separate type even though the passion narrative contains several actual "forms"; *see* Passion Narrative). In the final analysis the formal features help more in the stage of composition criticism than in redactional study, but these are two aspects of a larger whole and therefore form-critical analysis is an important part of the redactional process.

3.3. Redaction-Critical Analysis. The interpreter examines the pericope and notes each time the source (Mark or Q) has been changed in order to determine whether the alteration is redactional or stylistic; that is, whether it has a theological purpose or is cosmetic, part of the Evangelist's normal style. While this process is obviously more conducive for Matthew and Luke, since sources in Mark are so difficult to detect and John is so independent, most scholars believe that a nuanced redaction criticism may still be applied to Mark and John (though without many of the source-critical techniques). The principles which follow are intended to guide the student through the process as it applies to all four Gospels. There are two stages—the individual analysis of a single pericope, and holistic analysis which studies redactional strata that appear throughout the Gospel. These aspects work together, as the data emerge from the individual studies and are evaluated on the basis of recurring themes in the whole.

3.3.1. Individual Analysis. The text of the synopsis should first be underlined with different colors to denote which readings are unique to a Gospel, which are paralleled in Mark and Matthew, Mark and Luke or Matthew and Luke (Q), and which are found in all three. The next step is to evaluate the data. S. McKnight (85-87) notes seven ways the Evangelists redact their sources: (1) They can *conserve* them (important because this also has theological significance for the Evangelist); (2) *conflate two traditions* (as in the use of both Mark and Q in the temptation story of Matthew and Luke); (3) *expand the source* (e.g., Matthew's added material in the walking-on-the-water miracle, Mt 14:22-33; cf. Mk 6:45-52); (4) *transpose the settings* (as in the different settings for Jesus' compassion for Jerusalem in Mt 23:37-39 and Lk 13:34-35); (5) *omit portions* of the tradition (e.g., the missing descriptions of demonic activity in the healing* of the demon-

possessed child, Mt 17:14-21; cf. Mk 9:14-29; *see* Demon, Devil, Satan); (6) *explain details* in the source (e.g., Mark's lengthy explanation of washing the hands, Mk 7:3-4; or Matthew changing "Son of man"* to "I," 10:32; cf. Lk 12:8); or (7) *alter a tradition to avoid misunderstandings* (as when Matthew alters Mark's "Why do you call me good?" [Mk 10:18] to "Why do you ask me about what is good?" [Mt 19:17]).

By grouping the changes the student can detect patterns which point to certain theological nuances within the larger matrix of the story as a whole. Each change is evaluated in terms of potential meaning; that is, does it possess theological significance as it affects the development of the story? For instance, Matthew changes the endings of both Mark 6:52 ("Their heart was hardened," cf. Mt 14:33, "Surely you are the Son of God") and 8:21 ("Don't you understand yet?" cf. Mt 16:12, "Then they understood . . ."). In both Gospels these two sets of endings conclude the group of stories centered on the feedings of the five thousand and four thousand. It is likely that the differences are due to Mark's stress on the reality of discipleship failure and Matthew's emphasis on the difference that the presence of Jesus makes in overcoming failure.

3.3.2. Holistic Analysis. The individual analysis is now expanded to note the development of themes as the narrative of the whole Gospel unfolds. Decisions regarding single accounts are somewhat preliminary until they are corroborated by the presence of similar themes elsewhere. Also, these steps enable one to discover redactional emphases in Mark and John, for which the interpreter has difficulty noting sources.

The "seams" in a Gospel are the introductions, conclusions and transitions which connect the episodes and provide important clues to the theological purpose of the author. They often contain a high proportion of the author's own language and point to an Evangelist's particular reasons for including the pericope. For instance, the two seams in Mark 1:21 and 3:1 provide a synagogue* setting for the christological emphasis on Jesus' authority in word and deed as he confronts the Jewish leaders. Also, the summaries in a Gospel are redactional indicators of theological overtones. An example of this would be Matthew 4:23 and 9:35 (introducing the Sermon on the Mount [*see* Sermon on the Mount] and missionary discourse, respectively), which contain similar wording and summarize Jesus' itinerant missionary activity. The threefold emphasis on teaching, preaching and healing are major theological emphases in Matthew.

Editorial asides and insertions are key indicators of the theological direction a narrative is taking. John has long been known for his tendency to add explanatory comments to describe the significance more fully, as in his famous commentary (3:16-21) on the soteriological significance of the Nicodemus dialog (3:1-15). In similar fashion, repeated or favorite terms show particular interests. Again, John is the master of this technique; nearly every theological stress is highlighted by terms which appear nearly as often in his Gospel as in the rest of the NT together (e.g., *alētheia* [85 of the 163 NT uses; *see* Truth], *zōē* [66 of the 135 NT uses; *see* Life], or *kosmos* [105 of the 185 NT uses; *see* World]) and by word groups of synonymous terms (e.g., the two terms for "know," two for "love"* or five for "see").

Finally, theme studies (McKnight calls this "motif analysis") trace the development of theological emphases within the Gospel as a whole. Here one reads through the Gospel, noting the theological threads which are woven together into the fabric of the whole. For instance, one of Mark's primary themes is discipleship failure, introduced in Mk 4:38, 40 and then emerging as a major emphasis in the "hardened heart" passages of Mk 6:52 and 8:17 (*see* Hardness of Heart). The passion predictions are contrasted with the disciples' failure (Mk 8:31-33; 9:31-34; 10:32-40). Chapter 14 contains several scenes of failure (Mk 14:4-5, 10-11, 17-20, 27-31, 37-40, 50-51, 66-72), and the Gospel ends on a note of discipleship failure (Mk 16:8).

Mark is a special test case for holistic analysis and for redaction criticism as a whole. If one accepts the prevalent theory of Markan priority, then there are no obvious sources (Matthew and Luke have Mark and Q) with which to compare Mark in order to determine redactional peculiarities. The traditions behind Mark are very difficult to detect, and no scholarly consensus has yet emerged as to their identity. As a result there is a bewildering array of theories regarding the redactional nature of the Second Gospel. In order to overcome these problems, R. Stein (positive regarding the possibilities) and M. Black (skeptical about the possibilities) have proposed several criteria for redactional research: (1) Study the seams, insertions and summaries; (2) determine whether Mark has created (a controversial criterion) or modified traditional material; (3) note Mark's process of selecting and arranging material; (4) ask whether Mark has omitted material (also controversial because the question always arises whether Mark has omitted an emphasis or been unaware of it, e.g., the famous Matthean addendum to the divorce* passage, "except for adultery"); (5) study Mark's introduction and conclusion; and (6) elucidate Mark's vocabulary, style

and christological titles. When all these tools are used together, the Gospels of Mark or John open themselves to redactional study.

3.4. Composition-Critical Analysis. The task is incomplete so long as one focuses only on the redactional changes, so most recent redaction critics wish to study the traditions included as well as the redactional modifications. Obviously, each Evangelist unified tradition and redaction into a larger whole in producing a Gospel. It is erroneous to examine only the redaction.

3.4.1. The Structure. The way the Evangelist arranges material tells a great deal about the meaning of the whole. At both the micro and macro levels the rearrangement of the inherited tradition is significant. In the temptation narrative Matthew and Luke reverse the last two temptations (*see* Temptation of Jesus). Most believe that Matthew contains the original order and that Luke concludes with the Temple* temptation due to his special interest in Jerusalem and the Temple (Lk 4:9-12). But it is also possible that Matthew concludes with a mountain scene for thematic reasons (Mt 4:8-10; cf. 5:1; 8:1; 14:23; 15:29; 17:1). At the macro level, one could note the quite different things which Mark and Luke do with Jesus' early Capernaum-based ministry, with Mark placing the call to the disciples first, due to his discipleship emphasis (Mk 1:16-20), and reserving the rejection at Nazareth for later (Mk 6:1-6), while Luke begins with Jesus' inaugural address and rejection at Nazareth (Lk 4:16-30) in order to center upon christology, reserving the call of the disciples for later (Lk 5:1-11).

3.4.2. Intertextual Development. Each Evangelist arranges pericopes in such a way that their interaction with one another yields the intended message. Intertextuality at the macro level is the literary counterpart to redaction criticism at the micro level, for the Evangelist uses the same techniques of selection, omission and structure in both. This is exemplified in Mark's strategic placing of the two-stage healing of the blind man in Mark 8:22-26 (found only in Mark). On one level it forms an inclusion with the healing of the deaf man in Mark 7:31-37, stressing the need for healing on the part of the disciples (note the failure of Mk 8:14-21, in which the disciples are accused of being both blind and deaf!; *see* Blindness and Deafness). On another level it metaphorically anticipates the two-stage surmounting of the disciples' misunderstanding via Peter's confession (Mk 8:27-33, only a partial understanding) and the Transfiguration (Mk 9:1-10, at which time they glimpse the true nature of Jesus, cf. esp. Mk 9:9).

3.4.3. Plot. Plot refers to the interconnected sequence of events which follows a cause-effect pattern and centers upon conflict. The student examines how the characters interact and how the lines of causality develop to a climax. For redaction criticism this means especially the individual emphases of the Evangelists. The differences are often striking, as in the resurrection narratives. Mark follows a linear pattern, tracing the failure of the disciples and concluding with the women's inability to witness (Mk 16:8). This is countered by the enigmatic promise of Jesus to meet them in Galilee (Mk 16:7; cf. 14:28), apparently the place of reinstatement (note Mk 14:28 following 14:27). Matthew constructs a double-edged conflict in which the supernatural intervention of God (Mt 28:2-4) and the universal authority of Jesus (Mt 28:18-20) overcome the twofold attempt of the priests (see Priest, Priesthood) to thwart the divine plan (Mt 27:62-66; 28:11-15).

3.4.4. Setting and Style. When the Evangelists place a saying or event in different settings, they often produce a new theological thrust. For instance, Matthew places the parable of the lost sheep (Mt 18:12-14) in the context of the disciples and the church, with the result that it refers to straying members, while in Luke 15:3-7 Jesus addresses the same parable to the Pharisees* and scribes,* so that it refers to those outside the kingdom.

Style refers to the individual way that a saying or story is phrased and arranged so as to produce the effect that the author wishes. There can be gaps, chiasm, repetition, omissions and highly paraphrased renditions in order to highlight some nuance which Jesus gave his teaching but which is of particular interest to the Evangelist. Here it is important to remember that the Evangelists' concern was not the *ipsissima verba* (exact words) but the *ipsissima vox* (the very voice) of Jesus. They were free to give highly paraphrastic renditions to stress one certain aspect. One example is the Matthean and Lukan forms of the Beatitudes, which most scholars take to be derived from the same occasion (Luke's "plain" can also mean a mountain plateau in Greek). In Matthew the central stress is on ethical qualities ("blessed are the poor in spirit," Mt 5:3), while in Luke the emphasis is on economic deprivation ("blessed are you poor," Mt 5:20; cf. "woe to you rich," Mt 5:24). Both were undoubtedly intended by Jesus, while the two Evangelists highlighted different aspects.

4. The Weaknesses of Redaction Criticism.

Many have discounted the value of redaction criticism due to the excesses of some of its practitioners. Primarily, it has been the application of redaction criti-

cism along with historical skepticism that has led some to reject the approach. As a result of the influence of form and tradition criticism in the past and of narrative criticism in the present, the historical reliability of Gospel stories has been called into question (see Gospels [Historical Reliability]). Certainly some critics have begun with the premise that redaction entails the creation of Gospel material which is unhistorical, but this is by no means a necessary conclusion.

Techniques like omission, expansion or rearrangement are attributes of style and are not criteria for historicity. Another problem is redaction criticism's dependence on the four-document hypothesis. It is true that the results would look quite different if one were to assume the Griesbach hypothesis (the priority of Matthew). However, one must make a conclusion of some sort regarding the interrelationship of the Gospels before redactional study can begin, and most scholars have judged the four-document hypothesis to be clearly superior to the others (see Synoptic Problem).

As in form criticism, redactional studies tend to fragment the pericopes when they study only the additions to the traditions. Theology is to be found in the combined tradition and redaction—not in the redaction alone. The movement to *composition criticism* has provided a healthy corrective. The Evangelists' alterations are the major source of evidence, but the theology comes from the whole. Similarly, there has been a problem with overstatement. Scholars have often seen significance in every "jot and tittle" and have forgotten that many changes are stylistic rather than theological. Once again, composition criticism helps avoid excesses by looking for patterns rather than seeing theology in every possible instance.

Subjectivism is another major danger. Studies utilizing the same data frequently produce different results, and thus some argue that no assured results can ever come from redaction-critical studies. The only solution is a judicious use of *all* the hermeneutical tools along with cross-pollination between the studies. Interaction between theories can demonstrate where the weaknesses are in each. Subjectivism is especially seen in speculations regarding *Sitz im Leben*, which are too often based on the assumption that every theological point is addressed to some problem in the community behind the Gospel. This ignores the fact that many of the emphases are due to christological, liturgical, historical or evangelistic interests. The proper life-situation study is not so much concerned with the detailed reconstruction of the church behind a Gospel as in the delineation of the Evangelists' message to that church.

5. The Place and Value of Redaction Criticism.

A careful use of proper methodology can reduce the problems inherent in redaction criticism, and the values far outweigh the dangers. In fact, any study of the Gospels will be enhanced by redaction-critical techniques. A true understanding of the doctrine of inspiration demands it, for each Evangelist was led by God to utilize sources in the production of a Gospel. Moreover, they were given the freedom by God to omit, expand and highlight these traditions in order to bring out individual nuances peculiar to their own Gospel. Nothing else can explain the differing messages of the same stories as told in the various Gospels. There is no necessity to theorize wholesale creation of stories, nor to assert that these nuances were not in keeping with the original Gospels. Here a judicious harmonizing approach like that espoused by C. Blomberg is valuable. In short, redaction criticism has enabled us to rediscover the Evangelists as inspired authors and to understand their books for the first time as truly Gospels; not just biographical accounts but history with a message. They did not merely chronicle events but interpreted them and produced historical sermons.

Until redaction criticism arose, Christians tended to turn to the epistles for theology. Now we know that the Gospels are not only theological but in some ways communicate a theology even more relevant than the epistles, because these truths are presented not through didactic literature but by means of the living relationships reflected in narrative. The Gospels are "case-study" workbooks for theological truth, yielding not just theology taught but theology lived and modelled. Redactional study enables us to reconstruct with some precision the theology of each of the Evangelists by noting how they utilized their sources and then by discovering patterns in the changes which exemplify themes developed through the Gospels. The whole (tradition, redaction and compositional development) interact together to produce the inspired message of each Evangelist.

In this way the reader understands the twofold purpose of the Gospels: to present the life and teachings of the historical Jesus (the historical component) in such a way as to address the church and the world (the kerygmatic component). History and theology are valid aspects of Gospel analysis, and we dare not neglect either without destroying the God-ordained purpose of the Gospels. While redaction criticism as a discipline centers on the theological aspect, it does not ignore the historical nature of the Gospels.

Finally, redaction criticism is a preaching and not just an academic tool. The Gospels were originally contextualizations of the life and teaching of Jesus for the reading and listening audiences of the Evangelists' time. They were biographical sermons (one aspect of the meaning of the term "Gospel") applying Jesus' impact on his disciples, the crowds (see People, Crowd) and the Jewish leaders to first-century readers and listeners. This is perhaps the best use of life-situation approaches, for they show how Matthew or Luke addressed problems in their communities and demonstrate how they can address similar problems in our churches.

See also FORM CRITICISM; GOSPELS (GENRE); GOSPELS (HISTORICAL RELIABILITY); JOHN, GOSPEL OF; LITERARY CRITICISM; LUKE, GOSPEL OF; MARK, GOSPEL OF; MATTHEW, GOSPEL OF; SYNOPTIC PROBLEM; TRADITION CRITICISM.

BIBLIOGRAPHY. C. C. Black, *The Disciples according to Mark: Markan Redaction in Current Debate* (Sheffield: JSOT, 1989); G. Bornkamm, G. Barth and H. J. Held, *Tradition and Interpretation in Matthew* (Philadelphia: Westminster, 1963); D. A. Carson, "Redaction Criticism: On the Legitimacy and Illegitimacy of a Literary Tool," in *Scripture and Truth*, ed. D. A. Carson and J. Woodbridge (Grand Rapids: Zondervan, 1983) 119-42; H. Conzelmann, *The Theology of St. Luke* (New York: Harper and Row, 1960); W. Kelber, "Redaction Criticism: On the Nature and Exposition of the Gospels," *PRS* 6 (1979) 4-16; W. Marxsen, *Mark the Evangelist: Studies on the Redaction History of the Gospel* (New York: Abingdon, 1969); S. McKnight, *Interpreting the Synoptic Gospels* (GNTE 2; Grand Rapids: Baker, 1988) 83-95; E. V. McKnight, "Form and Redaction Criticism," in *The New Testament and Its Modern Interpreters*, ed. E. J. Epp and G. W. MacRae (Philadelphia: Fortress, 1989) 149-74; G. R. Osborne, "The Evangelical and Redaction Criticism: Critique and Methodology," *JETS* 22 (1979) 305-22; idem, "Redaction Criticism," in *New Testament Criticism and Interpretation*, ed. D. A. Black and D. Dockery (Grand Rapids: Zondervan, 1991); N. Perrin, *What Is Redaction Criticism?* (Philadelphia: Fortress, 1969); E. J. Pryke, *Redactional Style in the Marcan Gospel: A Study of Syntax and Vocabulary As Guides to Redaction in Mark* (SNTSMS 33; Cambridge: University Press, 1978); J. Rohde, *Rediscovering the Teaching of the Evangelists* (Philadelphia: Westminster, 1968); E. P. Sanders and M. Davies, *Studying the Synoptic Gospels* (Philadelphia: Trinity Press International, 1989); S. Smalley, "Redaction Criticism," in *New Testament Interpretation: Essays on Principles and Methods*, ed. I. H. Marshall (Grand Rapids: Eerdmans, 1977) 181-95; R. H. Stein, "What Is Redaktionsgeschichte?" *JBL* 88 (1969) 45-56; idem, "The

Proper Methodology for Ascertaining a Markan Redaction History," *NovT* 13 (1971) 181-98; idem, *The Synoptic Problem: An Introduction* (Grand Rapids: Baker, 1987) 231-72.   G. R. Osborne

REDEMPTION. *See* JUBILEE; RANSOM RSAYING.

RENEWAL MOVEMENTS, JEWISH. *See* DEAD SEA SCROLLS; PHARISEES; REVOLUTIONARY MOVEMENTS.

REPENTANCE

Repentance in the Gospels refers to the radical "turning away" from anything which hinders one's wholehearted trust in God.* As such, the notion of "turning to" God in love* and obedience is most often included.

1. Jewish Conceptual Background
2. Repentance in John the Baptist and Jesus
3. The Emphases of the Gospel Writers

1. Jewish Conceptual Background.

The English words *repentance* and *repent* are used mainly to translate the Greek words *metanoia* and *metanoeō* in the NT. Etymology suggests the meaning "a change of mind or thinking," a sense which is encountered frequently in the LXX. In the Gospels, however, the force of the concept goes far beyond the etymological suggestion.

1.1. OT Background. The concept finds its roots in the OT, expressed especially by the verb *šûb*. Though *šûb* is frequently used in more literal senses, it often implies a metaphorical "turning," describing the actions of both God and people. For example, in Exodus 32:12 Moses beseeches God to "turn from" his anger against his people (cf. Josh 7:26; 2 Kings 23:26) and consequently from the disciplinary actions which would have ensued. More relevant to the Gospel usage are those instances when it is used to describe the "turning" of people away from sin. Thus, Solomon prays to God that he will respond in forgiveness* and graciousness when the people "turn" from their sin and pray (1 Kings 8:35). Conversely, Jeremiah pronounces God's judgment on Judah because they did not "turn from" their sinful ways (Jer 15:7; cf. 18:8; Is 59:20; Ezek 3:19; 13:22: 1 Kings 13:33). Implicit within this prophetic call to "turn from" sin is a corresponding "turning to" God. Accordingly, Hosea exhorts the people to "return" to the Lord after acknowledging their guilt (Hos 6:1; cf. 7:10; Is 10:21; Jer 3:7; Amos 4:6; 1 Kings 8:33, 48). Such a "turning to" assumes a vital trust in God (cf. Jer 3:22-23; Hos 14:4-5; Is 30:15 *šûbâ*), as well as renewed obedience to him (Jer 26:3-5).

1.2. Septuagint. While *šûb* is translated in the LXX mainly by the Greek *epistrephō* and *apostrephō*, *metanoeō* is employed by the translators almost exclusively to express the niphal Hebrew verb *niham*. The noun *metanoia* does not occur except in Proverbs 14:15, which is neither a translation of the extant Hebrew text nor relevant to Gospel usage. Among other meanings, *niham* often merely expresses the notion of "relenting" from one's actions, whether that be action not yet taken or already in process. Thus, in Jonah 3:9 the king of Nineveh calls for a fast in the hope that God would "relent" from the fierce judgment which he had threatened to bring upon the city (cf. also Jon 4:2; Jer 4:28; 18:8, 10; Joel 2:14; Amos 7:3, 5; Zech 8:14). More important are those few instances where *niham* approaches a meaning synonymous with *šûb* in expressing the "turning away" of people from their sin. Thus, the Lord indicts the people of Judah for not "turning away" from their wickedness (Jer 8:6). In Jeremiah 38:19 (MT 31:19) God describes the coming restoration of his people who then will have "repented" in shame after being chastised by God. Once again, the idea is a renouncing of the sinful past and an inevitable renewal of a relationship with God.

1.3. Other Jewish Literature. Throughout Jewish literature the predominant sense of "repentance" is this narrower, ethical and spiritual sense of "turning." In Sirach 17:24 God is said to give "a return" to those who repent, which is filled out in 17:25-26 as a "turning from" sin and a "returning to" God (cf. also Sir 48:15; Wis 11:23; 12:10, 19; Pr Man 13-15; *T. Zeb.* 9:7). The results of repentance are forgiveness and salvation* (e.g., *Sib. Or.* 1:128; Pr Man 7; *T. Gad* 5:7; 7:5; *1 Enoch* 40:9; *b. Sanh.* 97b), as well as a renewed obedience to God and love for one's neighbor (e.g., *T. Sim.* 2:13; *T. Gad* 5:7; 6:3; *T. Asher* 1:6; *2 Apoc. Bar.* 84:1-10; cf. also 1QS 5:8; 10:20; 1QH 2:9). God is often understood to be the giver of repentance (Wis 12:19; *b. Sanh.* 107b; *Sib. Or.* 4:168), or at least providing the opportunity for it (Wis 11:23; 12:10; Sir 48:14-15; *Ep. Arist.* 188). It is also occasionally perceived to be the achievement of humans (*Midr.* Ps. 32), often taking the form of ritualistic fasting and lamentation (e.g., *T. Reub.* 1:9; *T. Jud.* 15:4; *b. Sanh.* 37a). Though many sins are atoned for by means of repentance alone (cf. *b. Qidd.* 40b; *b. Sanh.* 7a; *b. Šabb.* 32a), some require an accompanying sacrifice (e.g., *m. Yoma* 8:8-9; *b. Hor.* 2a; *b. Šebu.* 12b). Throughout, the universality of its demand is acknowledged (cf. *b. Šabb.* 153a; Sir 44:16; Wis 11:23; *Sib. Or.* 1:128).

2. Repentance in John the Baptist and Jesus.

This same, narrower conception of repentance is

carried into the Gospels, where it is used by John the Baptist (*see* John the Baptist), Jesus and the Gospel writers to express the "turning away" of people from their sinful ways, along with the corresponding "turning to" God.

2.1. The Message of John the Baptist. John's call to repentance derives from his conviction that the kingdom of God (*see* Kingdom of God) had drawn near (Mt 3:2). Therefore, the time of fulfillment had arrived (Mt 3:3 par. Lk 3:4-6), bringing with it the certain expectation of divine judgment* (Mt 3:7, 10 par. Lk 3:7, 9). This perspective is not surprising, given the wealth of similar expectations in antecedent and contemporary Jewish literature (e.g., *2 Apoc. Bar.* 30:1-5; 54:21; 72:1-6; *4 Ezra* 7:113-15; *1 Enoch* 53:1—54:6; 60:5-6; 62:1-12; 91:7-9; 100:4; *Apoc. Abr.* 31:1-8). Accordingly, John fulfilled his prophetic (*see* Elijah and Elisha) and preparatory role by calling Israel* out to the wilderness (*see* Mountain and Wilderness) to repent, reminiscent of the beginning of the nation's relationship with God. For only by radical repentance, sealed and symbolized graphically by baptism,* would Israel be prepared to meet its judge (see Meyer 115-22). Thus, John summoned Israel to what Goppelt terms "eschatological repentance." Only those who respond in this way obtain forgiveness of sins (Mk 1:4 par. Lk 3:3) and can anticipate being "harvested" by the "one coming after him" (Mt 3:12 par. Lk 3:17). Those who reject his message are left only with the gloomy expectation of imminent divine reprisal (Mt 3:7, 10-12 par. Lk 3:7, 9, 16-17).

Significantly, John's summons is universal, ignoring both societal and religious status. Accordingly, the religious elite (Mt 3:7-10 par. Lk 3:7-9), "the crowds" (Lk 3:10-11; *see* People, Crowd) and even such blatant "sinners"* as the tax collectors (Lk 3:13; *see* Taxes) are addressed with the same, sweeping demand. For each, repentance involves the acknowledgment of one's sinfulness (Mk 1:5 par. Mt 3:6) as well as a new and holy pattern of daily behavior in relation to others (Mt 3:8 par. Lk 3:8; Lk 3:10-14). Thus it is clear that repentance for John does not simply consist in a "change of mind," but in a transformation of the entire person (Mt 3:10 par. Lk 3:9). It is in this sense that one can speak of repentance with the language of conversion.

2.2. The Message of Jesus.

2.2.1. Terminology and Importance. The full meaning of Jesus' use of the concept cannot be exhausted by means of a word study. Actually, the words are found on the lips of Jesus in a limited number of Gospel texts (cf. Mk 1:15 par. Mt 4:17; Mt 11:21 par. Lk 10:13; Mt 12:41 par. Lk 11:32; Lk 5:32; 13:3, 5; 15:7, 10; 16:30;

17:3-4; 24:47), some of which are clearly redactional (e.g., Lk 5:32; cf. Mk 2:17 par. Mt 9:13; cf. also Mt 11:20; Mk 6:12). The words are completely absent from the Fourth Gospel, although the concept is present.

It is this apparent paucity of evidence that has led E. P. Sanders to argue that Jesus' preaching did not call for a national repentance in view of the coming kingdom. Sanders supports this by questioning the authenticity of virtually all of the passages in the Gospels in which the actual words *metanoia/metanoeō* are used in reference to Jesus' preaching. Rather, the presence of such elements are the result of redaction, motivated by a perceived lack of emphasis on "repentance" in Jesus' message. Though Sanders admits that Jesus did "believe in" repentance and turning to God, this was only on an individual basis, and even this is largely muted in Sanders's construal. In addition he maintains that the primary offense of Jesus' actions stemmed from his variant conception of repentance which did not provide for sacrifice and restitution. Indeed, it was this very thing which precipitated the condemnation of Jesus as the "friend of sinners"; in his opponents' evaluation, several of Jesus' friends remained "sinners" even after Jesus accepted them in the name of the kingdom. If Sanders is correct, not only is the relative importance of repentance in Jesus' proclamation greatly reduced, but the meaning of repentance for Jesus becomes innovative rather than rooted in his Jewish heritage.

Several points must be raised in opposition to Sanders. In the first place Chilton observes that such a parable* as the "lost sheep" (Mt 18:12-14 par. Lk 15:4-7) presents a corporate image of Israel in the form of the "flock" and God as its "shepherd" (*see* Shepherd, Sheep). Given the collective image, to distinguish here between "national" and "individual" repentance is illegitimate. Moreover, other passages directly imply a universal and national summons (e.g., Mt 11:20-24 par. Lk 10:12-15; Lk 13:1-5; Mt 12:39-42 par. Lk 11:29-32), although Sanders questions their authenticity. Furthermore, though the words themselves may not often appear in the text, radical renunciation (e.g., Mt 13:44-46) and transformation (e.g., Mk 10:15 par. Mt 18:3 and Lk 18:17) are repeatedly called for by Jesus in those who will enter the kingdom. Jesus' words are most often occasional in that they were addressed to particular hearers rather than to the nation as a whole. But the fact that Jesus expected individuals from several societal groups to respond in repentance strongly implies that his call was intended to be universal. Such is also evidenced indirectly by the centrality of repentance in the message of the commissioned disciples* (Mk 6:12).

To reject this and other editorial summary statements (e.g., Mk 1:15; Mt 4:17) demands the assumption that everything interpretive in the Gospels is hopelessly biased according to the Gospel writers rather than indicative of Jesus' influence on them (see Chilton). Finally, Jesus' emphasis on repentance, without the corresponding emphasis on the cultic expression, finds precedence in the great preachers of the OT (e.g., Mt 9:13; 12:7; cf. Hos 6:6; Mic 6:6-8). To imply that Jesus' conception of repentance was in some way innovative does not take this motif seriously.

Thus, in spite of the relative paucity of explicit repentance-language in Jesus' teachings, it is accurately understood by the Evangelists as a collective term summarizing what Jesus wanted people to do (Mk 1:15 par. Mt 4:17). Accordingly, such concepts as "being poor" (Mt 5:3; see Rich and Poor), "becoming as a little child" (e.g., Mk 10:14-15 par. Lk 18:16-17 and Mt 19:4; 18:3; see Children), "following in discipleship*" (e.g., Mk 8:34 par. Mt 16:24 and Lk 9:23) and simply "believing" (Mk 1:15; Mt 21:32; see Faith) are closely aligned with it.

2.2.2. Repentance As Demand. Consistent with John, Jesus perceived repentance to be a complete "turning away" from one's sinful way of life. In addition to blatant sins (e.g., Lk 7:47; 19:8-10), this includes anything or any attitude which prevents an appropriate posture before God. The urgency and totality of this demand is demonstrated most clearly in the drastic images he uses (e.g., Mk 9:43-48 par. Mt 5:29-30; 18:8-9; cf. Mt 7:13-4). Thus, anything that offends or hinders one's relationship with the Father is to be parted with.

Jesus' demand for repentance is frequently directed toward one's love of wealth and possessions (cf. Lk 14:33; Mt 6:24 par. Lk 16:13). In Luke 6:24 Jesus pronounces judgment on those who have received "their comfort"; those whose sole desire is to enjoy the comforts that wealth brings. Such is also the point of the condemnation against the rich man who languished in hades (Lk 16:25); again, he had received his "good things," thinking that by them he could live. Even the "righteous" wealthy are indicted (Mk 10:17-22 par. Mt 19:16-22 and Lk 18:18-23), who, in spite of their relatively righteous lives, treasure their wealth above God. For the rich and anyone who seeks to establish life's security apart from trust in God this is ultimately a call to repentance, for it involves a "turning away" and a "letting go" of former supports to existence. Rather than presumption on God, the rich are to allow themselves to become "poor" and to be granted entrance into the kingdom (Lk 12:32;

cf. Mk 10:27; see Goppelt).

As did the Baptist before him, Jesus did not spare the apparently "righteous." Having established their righteousness in relation to the Law,* they were impugned by means of the Law. With great vigor they applied themselves to the observance of legal minutiae, but in the process they had both neglected and transgressed the very Law they revered (e.g., Mt 23:23 par. Lk 11:42; Mt 23:16-22; Mk 7:1-13 par. Mt 15:1-9). Moreover, their conscientious observance is revealed ultimately to be in their own self-interest (Mk 12:38-40 par. Mt 23:5-7, 14 and Lk 20:46-47; cf. Mt 6:1-6, 16-18; Lk 15:28-30). Thus, Jesus' condemnation is a call to repent and to return to the Lord of the Law.

In the OT repentance always implied a renewal of one's relationship to God. Now, because God's kingdom is present in Jesus, discipleship naturally becomes the positive counterpart to repentance. Therefore, in favor of a wholehearted devotion to himself, Jesus calls for a renunciation of the primary importance of all other relationships (Mt 10:34-39 par. Lk 12:51-53 and 14:25-27; cf. Mk 3:31-5 par. Mt 12:46-50 and Lk 8:19-21). This extends ultimately to the love of one's own life (Mk 8:34-37 par. Mt 16:24-26 and Lk 9:23-25; cf. Jn 12:25). Anyone who would deny Jesus before the world is therefore not worthy of him (Mt 10:32-33 par. Lk 12:8-9).

2.2.3. Repentance As Response to the Kingdom. Again, like John the Baptist Jesus indissolubly unites his call for repentance with the nearness of the kingdom of God (Mk 1:15 par. Mt 4:17; cf. Mt 3:2). They differ, however, in the emphases they give to the kingdom's coming. While John highlights judgment, Jesus heralds the salvific opportunity, perceiving it to be the "day of salvation." Though judgment is retained in Jesus' proclamation (e.g., Lk 13:1-5; cf. Mt 11:22-24 par. Lk 10:14-15; Mt 12:36, 41-42 par. Lk 11:31-32; Mt 24:40-41 par. Lk 17:34-35), it is no longer foremost as it is in John's. This not only gives rise to a major difference in their conduct (Mt 11:18-19 par. Lk 7:33-34), it also alters the primary motivation that each gives for the repentance that is sought; for John, it is the fear of impending judgment, while for Jesus it is the gracious goodness of God.

Crucial to this discussion is the understanding that with Jesus, the kingdom had not only "drawn near" (*engiken*), it had in some sense arrived (*ephthasen;* cf. Mt 12:28 par. Lk 11:20), albeit in an "inaugurated manner" (cf. Mk 4:26-29; Mk 4:30-32 par. Mt 13:31-32 and Lk 13:18-19; Mt 13:24-30; Mt 13:33 par. Lk 13:20-21). Therefore, the entire public ministry of Jesus reveals the kingdom, giving rise to his emphasis on its salvific character. Until the time of the judgment the

671

power (*see* Authority and Power) of the kingdom is present and efficacious to liberate people (Mk 3:27 par. Mt 12:29 and Lk 11:21-22). Thus, though the demand for repentance is unchanged, the divine initiative is understood to be antecedent to its realization. Those who remain unrepentant place themselves under the judgment of God (Mt 12:39-42; Mt 11:20-24 par. Lk 10:12-15; Lk 13:1-5). Conversely, forgiveness and salvation* come (e.g., Lk 7:36-50; 19:9) to those who repent and thereby enter the kingdom (e.g., Mk 9:45).

The focus on the divine initiative is evident most of all in Jesus' ministry among "the sinners," a group comprised of at least the tax collectors (Mk 2:14-17 par. Mt 9:9-11 and Lk 5:27-30; Mt 5:46 par. Lk 6:32; Lk 18:13; 19:7; Mt 11:19 par. Lk 7:34), the harlots (Lk 7:37, 39; *see* Prostitute) and possibly the Gentiles* (Lk 6:32-34 [cf. Mt 5:47]; Mk 14:41 par. Mt 26:45). Considering the manifest contempt for such individuals in that society, it is striking to find Jesus frequently in their company (Lk 19:1-10; Mk 2:13-17 par. Mt 9:9-13 and Lk 5:27-32; Lk 7:37-50) so often that he is despised as a "friend of sinners" (Mt 11:19 par. Lk 7:34; cf. Lk 15:1-2). Clearly, this activity greatly disturbed the religious leaders, though scholars are presently in much disagreement over the exact nature of the offense (e.g., Mk 2:16 par. Mt 9:11 and Lk 5:30; Lk 19:7; see Sanders, Jeremias, Goppelt, Chilton). What is understood, and most relevant to the topic at hand, is that by means of this shocking and yet parabolic action (Mt 8:11 par. Lk 13:29; Mt 22:1-14 par. Lk 14:15-24; Mt 18:12-14 par. Lk 15:1-7; Lk 15:8-10, 11-32; 19:9) Jesus declared what he was about; he had come to seek out the lost (Lk 19:10; 15:4-32) and to heal the sick (Mk 2:17 par. Mt 9:12 and Lk 5:31; *see* Healing).

There was nothing inherent in this group that caused them to be singled out by Jesus except for their obvious need. By reaching out to them in this way, Jesus dramatized the free grace of God which confronts humanity precisely in its bankrupt predicament. In this way he confronts every person with this reality, not just the notorious "sinner," and thereby moves them toward repentance. Those who recoil in contempt demonstrate by their actions that they do not see how needy they are (Lk 7:39-47; 15:25-30; cf. Mt 21:31), thereby disqualifying themselves from the kingdom (Mt 8:12). Those who respond in repentance are "found" (Lk 15:5-7, 9-10, 32). It is for this reason that repentance in Jesus' ministry can be understood as a response to God's goodness. The paradigm of the one who enters the kingdom is the dependent child who freely receives (Mt 18:3-4; Mk 10:14-15 par. Mt 19:14 and Lk 18:16-17; cf Jn 3:3, 5). Understood in this

way, the event of repentance is often characterized by rejoicing and celebration (e.g., Mt 13:44; 22:1-10; Mk 2:14-15 par. Mt 9:9-10 and Lk 5:27-29; 19:6, 8; cf. also God's joy* expressed in Lk 15:6-7, 10, 22-24, 32), though connotations of mourning and regret are appropriately still found (cf. Lk 7:37-50; 15:17-20; 18:13-14; see Meyer, Jeremias).

3. The Emphases of the Gospel Writers.

3.1. Mark. Mark explicitly mentions *repentance* only three times, but he does so in passages which serve to centralize the concept in the messages of the primary figures in the Gospel. In Mark 1:4 repentance is linked with John's baptism for the forgiveness of sins. Jesus picks up this theme of repentance in Mark 1:15, uniting it with faith as the appropriate responses to the nearness of the kingdom. Finally, in Mark 6:12 repentance is mentioned as the content of the disciples' message. Thus, repentance can describe the entire conversion process, but Mark 1:15 reminds us that its positive counterpart is faith.

3.2. Matthew. Matthew, too, centralizes the concept, redacting the tradition at Matthew 4:17 to make the summary of Jesus' preaching identical to that of the Baptist, whose ministry reflects the prophetic tradition (*see* Prophets, Prophecy) that summoned Israel to repentance (cf. Mt 3:2). This is further buttressed by the comparison Jesus makes between himself and Jonah, the great preacher of repentance (Mt 12:38-41; *see* Sign of Jonah). As does Luke, Matthew identifies repentance as the goal of Jesus' ministry (Mt 11:20-24). He is the only Evangelist who employs the verb *metamelomai* as a synonym for *metanoeō* to describe the response of the tax collectors and harlots to the preaching of John the Baptist (Mt 21:29, 32). However, the use of the same word in Matthew 27:3, in reference to Judas' regret following his betrayal of Jesus, does not carry the same spiritual/ethical force.

3.3. Luke. Luke places greater stress on repentance (*metanoeō* 9 x; *metanoia* 5 x) than the other Evangelists, though the meaning remains the same throughout. He alone provides the ethical teachings that flesh out John's summons to repentance (Lk 3:10-14; *see* Ethics of Jesus). In Luke 5:32, he makes the call to the sinners explicitly one unto repentance (cf. Mk 2:17; Mt 9:13), making it possible that the explanatory notes concluding the parables of the lost sheep (Lk 15:7) and the lost coin (Lk 15:10) are also Lukan explanatory redaction. He alone preserves the record of events which Jesus employs as an occasion to call for national repentance (Lk 13:3, 5), as well as other explicit references to the need for repentance (Lk 16:30; 17:3-4). Finally, he highlights the place of repentance in the message of the commissioned disciples (Lk 24:47; this is continued on in Acts; e.g., 2:37-39; 3:19; 5:31; 11:18; 17:30; 20:21; 26:20).

Fitzmyer maintains that Luke conceives of repentance, *metanoeō*, as the negative counterpart to the positive *epistrephō*, the latter expressing the "turning to God" aspect of conversion (cf. esp. Acts 9:35; 11:21; 14:15; 15:19; 26:18; 28:27). But in the Gospel alone *epistrephō* is used only three or four times with this spiritual sense (i.e., Lk 1:16-17; 22:32; and possibly 17:4), and it appears with *metanoeō* only at Luke 17:4 where it relates to human relations. Conversely, Luke frequently employs *metanoia/metanoeō* to summarize the conversion event, which implies the establishment of a relationship to God (cf. Lk 5:32; 10:13; 11:32; 13:3, 5; 15:7, 10; 16:30; 24:47). Thus, *epistrephō* can function as a synonym for *metanoeō* (Lk 1:16-17), or it can emphasize the notion of "turning to God" (e.g., Acts 26:18-20). But, similar to the Hebrew *šûḇ*, which often carries the sense of "return," *metanoeō* can and does express the latter notion by itself.

See also FAITH; FORGIVENESS OF SINS; SINNERS.

BIBLIOGRAPHY. U. Becker et al., "Conversion etc.," *NIDNTT* 1.353-62; J. Behm and E. Wurthwein, "μετανοέω, μετάνοια," *TDNT* IV.975-1008; B. Chilton, "Jesus and the Repentance of E. P. Sanders," *TynB* 39 (1988) 1-18; J. Fitzmyer, *The Gospel According to Luke (I-IX)* (AB 28; Garden City, NY: Doubleday, 1981) 237-39; L. Goppelt, *Theology of the New Testament* (2 vols.; Grand Rapids: Eerdmans, 1981) 1.77-138; W. G. Kümmel, *The Theology of the New Testament* (Nashville: Abingdon, 1973); J. Jeremias, *New Testament Theology, Vol. 1: The Proclamation of Jesus* (New York: Macmillan, 1971); I. H. Marshall, *Luke: Historian and Theologian* (rev. and enlarged; Grand Rapids: Zondervan, 1989); B. Meyer, *The Aims of Jesus* (London: SCM, 1979); E. P. Sanders, *Jesus and Judaism* (Philadelphia: Fortress, 1985).												J. Lunde

RESURRECTION

Jesus assumed and taught an eschatological (*see* Eschatology) doctrine of the resurrection of the dead, an event whereby the ungodly would be delivered to judgment* and the godly receive eternal life.* Moreover, Jesus performed miracles* of resuscitation and, as he predicted, was himself raised from the dead. Both categories of events are regarded by the Gospel writers as eschatologically significant. But whereas the individuals Jesus raised from the dead were, technically speaking, resuscitated and would once again face death, the resurrection of Jesus from the dead was an event of cosmic consequence. Each of the Gospel writers portrays this event in a distinctive way, each

developing their own themes and yet together affirming the reality of the empty tomb and risen Christ, and the eschatological significance of this unique event in the mission of Jesus.

1. Pre-Christian Antecedents
2. Resurrection and Afterlife in the Sayings of Jesus
3. Miracles of Raising the Dead
4. Jesus' Resurrection in the Four Gospels

1. Pre-Christian Antecedents.

1.1. Resurrection in the OT. Evidence from the Hebrew Scriptures indicates that Israel* did not dwell on the question of the afterlife until late in the OT period. Rather, they stressed the involvement of Yahweh in this life. The blessing of the righteous and punishment of the wicked were seen as taking place in the present age. Life and death were also related primarily to this life.

This does not mean that Israelites believed in annihilation after death. The OT maintains that in one sense death is the cessation of life—at death a person returns to the "dust" (Gen 3:19; Ps 90:3). In another sense it is not the absolute end of life, for existence continues—at death the person descends to Sheol (*šᵉʾôl*), a term at times synonymous with "death" (Gen 42:38; Ps 89:48), the "grave" (Gen 37:35; Is 14:11) or the "netherworld" (Ezek 32:21; perhaps Ps 86:13). In some cases the dead are said to dwell in Sheol as *repāîm*, or "shades" (Job 26:5; Ps 88:10; Prov 9:18; Is 26:14)—possibly either a shadowy, wraith-like existence or a synonym for "the dead" (Ugaritic parallels favor the former). These references to *repāîm* and Sheol suggest a burgeoning view of the afterlife.

But while the OT does not give explicit witness to an early belief in existence after death, neither does it deny it. Moreover, two figures were "taken up" to be with God and do not experience death—Enoch (Gen 5:24) and Elijah (2 Kings 2:9-11; *see* Elijah and Elisha). While these narratives do not theologically reflect on the implications of these events (we read that Enoch "was no more, for God took him"), later Judaism* (cf. Heb 11:5) interpreted this as an "assumption" to eternal life. The incident in 1 Samuel 28:1-25, where Saul attempts to consult Samuel through the medium of Endor, provides further evidence for popular belief that death was not the end of existence.

Several OT statements affirm resurrection in the sense of a corporate preservation rather than individual afterlife. For instance, Hosea 6:1-3 states, "After two days he will revive us; on the third day he will restore us, that we may live in his presence." Similarly, Hosea 13:14 promises, "I will ransom them from the power of the grave; I will redeem them from death" (cf. RSV). In both cases the redemption of Israel from exile is envisaged in terms of deliverance from death (exile) to life (national restoration). In the same way Ezekiel's famous vision of the dry bones coming to life (37:1-14) depicts the national reconstitution of Israel. Other passages are often used as evidence of a resurrection hope but seem to refer to rescue from life-threatening situations (Deut 32:39; 1 Sam 2:6).

The basic question is stated in Job 14:14, "If mortals die, will they live again?" A tentative answer is given in Job's response to Bildad in 19:25-27, "I know that my Redeemer *(gô'ēl)* lives, and that in the end he will stand upon the earth. And after my skin has been destroyed, yet in my flesh I will see God." It is likely that the "redeemer" is God and that the time of deliverance is after death, thereby constituting a confession of belief in life after death.

The Psalms contain many similar statements. In Psalm 49:15 clearly and in Psalms 16:10 and 73:24 implicitly, a belief in resurrection is apparent, though without any speculation regarding the form the afterlife will take. As G. E. Ladd put it,

> the hope is based on confidence in God's power over death, not on a view of something immortal in man. The Psalmists do not reflect on what *part* of man survives death—his soul or spirit; nor is there any reflection on the nature of life after death. There is merely the confidence that even death cannot destroy the reality of fellowship with the living God. (Ladd, 47)

The prophets provide additional testimony to a resurrection faith. In the so-called Isaiah Apocalypse (24:1—27:13) there are two statements, 25:8 and 26:19. The former says that Yahweh will "swallow up death forever" and is used by Paul of the resurrection (1 Cor 15:54). This leads to the affirmation of 26:19, "But your dead will live, their bodies will rise. You who dwell in the dust, wake up and shout for joy." However, this resurrection is restricted to God's people. The next two verses (26:20-21) speak of God's wrath upon "the people of the earth" but mention no resurrection to judgment. Less certain is Isaiah 53:10, which asserts that the Servant of Yahweh (*see* Servant of Yahweh), after being "assigned a grave with the wicked" (53:9), will "see his offspring and prolong his days." Most agree that "prolong his days" refers to eternal life, but there is disagreement as to whether the song refers to an individual or corporate figure, the nation or the remnant.

The resurrection faith attested in the prophets climaxes in Daniel 12:1-3, 13. Here the first complete statement of a resurrection of the just and the unjust appears: "Multitudes who sleep in the dust of the earth will awake; some to everlasting life, others to shame and everlasting contempt" (12:2). There is some question whether "many" is restricted to Israel or the righteous remnant ("many *among* those who sleep") or refers to a general resurrection ("many, *namely* those who sleep"). Verse 13 adds the promise that "at the end of your days you will rise to receive your allotted inheritance."

In conclusion, the OT stresses the presence of God in the daily affairs of this life and tends thereby to ignore the larger issue of life after death. Nevertheless, it is not entirely silent, and several passages demonstrate that at a later period in Israel's history a belief in resurrection became more explicit. Two emphases emerge: (1) a close connection between the corporate and individual aspect of resurrection (i.e., national restoration and individual resurrection) and (2) a link between ethics and eschatology (i.e., resurrection is associated with reward and punishment).

1.2. Intertestamental Developments. While intertestamental Jewish literature witnesses to a great deal more speculation regarding the afterlife, there is clearly no uniformity in the views expressed. Ladd explains that this was due in part to the emphasis in Judaism upon Torah and orthopraxy (correct practice) rather than orthodoxy (correct doctrine) (Ladd, 52).

Indeed, like the Sadducees of Jesus' day (see Josephus *Ant.* 18.1.4 §16 as well as Acts 4:1-2; 23:8), some Jews did not believe in a resurrection. Jesus ben Sirach wrote in his first book that at death the person abides in Sheol, a place of unending sleep (Sir 30:17; 46:19) and silence (Sir 17:27-28); and immortality is restricted to the nation and the person's good name (Sir 37:26; 39:9; 44:8-15).

Other texts show the influence of Hellenism,* speaking of the afterlife in terms of immortality without linking it to a physical resurrection. 4 Maccabees, in describing the same seven martyrs mentioned in 2 Maccabees, seemingly substitutes an immortality of the soul where 2 Maccabees spoke of a physical resurrection (cf. 4 Macc 10:15 with 2 Macc 7:14; cf. also 4 Macc 9:22; 16:13; 18:23). Likewise, Wisdom of Solomon speaks of the righteous finding peace* (3:1-4) and an incorruptible existence (2:23-24; cf. 5:5; 6:19; and Philo *Op. Mund.* 135; *Gig.* 14). In the last book of Enoch (*1 Enoch* 91—104; notice that the five books contain quite variant views on this topic) there is language that at first glance seems to suggest a physical resurrection (e.g., *1 Enoch* 92:3-5; 104:2, 4), but in 103:4 we learn that it is their "spirits" that will "live and rejoice" and will "not perish."

Of those texts which do speak of a resurrection,

some restrict it to Israel or "the saints" (*1 Enoch* 22:13; 46:6; 51:1-2; *Pss. Sol.* 3:11-16; 13:9-11; 14:4-10; 15:12-15), while several from the first century and later attest to belief in the resurrection of the righteous and the wicked (4 Ezra 4:41-43; 7:32-38 cf. *T. Benj.* 10:6-9; *2 Apoc. Bar.* 49:2—51:12; 85:13). While the possibility of some Christian influence and interpolation cannot be discounted, the resurrection of the righteous and the wicked is itself essentially Jewish, reflecting the eschatology of Daniel 12:2-3. Finally, an extremely literalistic concept of bodily resurrection can be found in 2 Maccabees, which speaks not only of the raising of the body but even the restoration of missing limbs or other body parts (7:10-11; 14:46). Similarly, the *Sibylline Oracles* states that the resurrection body will be fashioned exactly after the earthly body (4:176-82).

Clearly, intertestamental Judaism showed a much greater interest than does the Hebrew Bible in the question of the afterlife, with interest centering on the theme of God vindicating his people. In addition, a variety of viewpoints emerged. This variety is reflected in the beliefs of the various parties or sects within the Judaism of Jesus' time. The Sadducees rejected any idea of an afterlife (Acts 23:8; 26:8; Josephus *Ant.* 18.14; *b. Sanh.* 90b). The Pharisees* taught a resurrection and eternal reward for Israel in the age to come, excluding only apostates (Acts 23:6-8; *b. Sanh.* 90b; *b. Ketub.* 111b). The Essene view on the matter was not clear, as exemplified in the Qumran scrolls (*see* Dead Sea Scrolls). Josephus* asserts that they held to the immortality of the soul (Josephus *J.W.* 8.1.2 §11), but many scholars maintain that statements referring to the habitation of the faithful with the angels* (1QS 2:25; 1QH 3:19-23; 11:10-14) should be understood as the sectarians' experience in this life rather than an eschatological hope.

2. Resurrection and Afterlife in the Sayings of Jesus.

Jesus followed in the tradition extending from Daniel to the Pharisees, teaching that there would be a twofold resurrection: the righteous to reward and the wicked to judgment. While a full tradition-critical study (*see* Tradition Criticism) is beyond the scope of this article, it is helpful to view the relevant teaching of Jesus from a source-critical perspective (*see* Synoptic Problem).

2.1. Sayings of the Triple Tradition. The clearest discussion of resurrection in Jesus' teaching can be found in the triple-tradition story of his controversy with the Sadducees (Mk 12:18-27 par. Mt 22:23-33 and Lk 20:27-38). Even those who maintain that the final form is a later catechetical elaboration accept the first pronouncement ("become like angels") as authentic.

Luke in particular stresses the contrast between the "people of this age" and those "worthy of taking part in that age and in the resurrection from the dead" (Lk 20:34-35), a distinct reference to eschatological views of an afterlife. Yet the major question is the significance of the phrase "like the angels in heaven." Some conclude from this that Jesus believed in a spiritual rather than physical resurrection or that he had a view, like some within Judaism, that in heaven there would be no consciousness of prior existence. However, this reads more into the passage than is intended, since the phrase is contrasting marriage on earth with marriage in heaven rather than teaching the state of the resurrection body.

Sayings on reward and judgment also appear in the triple tradition. The query of the wealthy young man in Mark 10:17 (par. Mt 19:16 and Lk 18:18), "What must I do to inherit eternal life?" is often understood as a desire to "enter the kingdom" in its realized presence (*see* Kingdom of God). While this is certainly part of the meaning, it does not exhaust its thrust. Jesus' final statement in Mark 10:30 (par. Mt 19:29 and Lk 18:30), "and in the age to come eternal life," forms an inclusio with the young man's question and clearly refers to the afterlife. There is both a present and future connotation in "eternal life" in 10:17, 30 and parallels. The other side, resurrection to judgment, is found in the Gehenna warning of Mark 9:43, 45, 47 (par. Mt 18:8-9; omitted in Luke). Using successive metaphors of the hand, foot and eye, Jesus exhorts the disciples* to disciplined resistance against temptation, lest one (Mark and Matthew both stress the singular "you") be cast into "hell, where the fire never goes out" (9:43; cf. Matthew's "eternal fire," 18:8).

2.2. The Passion Predictions. The best-known tradition is the threefold passion prediction of Mark 8:31; 9:31; 10:33-34 and parallels (*see* Predictions of Jesus' Passion and Resurrection). Many interpreters have understood these as *vaticinium ex eventu* (prophecies written after the event), but the absence of the type of theological elaboration found in the creeds (e.g., "for our sins," "according to the scriptures" and the exaltation theme) makes it more likely that these are indeed historical reminiscences. The one constant in all three accounts is Jesus' prediction that "three days after" his death he would be vindicated by resurrection. The third-day theme (cf. 1 Cor 15:4) may reflect Hosea 6:2 ("on the third day he will raise us"), a more general allusion to the OT theme of the third day as a day of deliverance (cf. Gen 22:4; 42:17-18; Is 2:16; Jon 2:1), or more simply a reference on Jesus' part to a brief period of time.

Added to these direct predictions are the numerous

parallel passages where Jesus presumes his future resurrection, such as: Mark 9:9 (tell no one of the Transfiguration* "until the Son of Man has risen from the dead"); Mark 12:10-11 ("the stone the builders rejected has become the capstone"); Mark 13:26 ("the Son of man coming in clouds with great power and glory"); Mark 14:25 ("when I drink it [the eschatological cup] anew in the kingdom of God"); Mark 14:28 ("after I have arisen I will go before you into Galilee") and Mark 14:62 ("you will see the Son of man sitting at the right hand of the Mighty One and coming on the clouds of heaven" [see Son of Man]).

One of the most remarkable prophecies of Jesus is not found in Luke but is recorded indirectly in Mark (14:58; 15:29) and a Matthean parallel (26:61; 27:40) and directly in John 2:19: "Destroy this temple, and I will raise it again in three days." John 2:21-22 explains that this direct prophecy of physical resurrection was not understood by the disciples until after the resurrection itself (ironically, the chief priests and Pharisees, according to Mt 27:63, correctly interpreted this saying before the disciples did). In summation, according to the Gospels Jesus clearly expected to be vindicated by resurrection.

2.3. The Q Tradition. The Q* tradition contains similar teaching. The "sign of Jonah"* (Mt 12:39-42 par. Lk 11:29-32) is problematic because only Matthew spells out the sign as a cryptic reference to the resurrection ("the Son of man will be three days and three nights in the heart of the earth," 12:40). But it is just as likely that Luke has omitted the Q statement on resurrection (due to the difficulty of "three days and three nights" for his readers) as Matthew has added it.

There are also several Q passages on final reward and punishment, such as those found at the end of Matthew's Olivet Discourse (see Apocalyptic Teaching). At the end of the exhortation to watchfulness (Mt 24:40-44 par. Lk 17:34-37) we have three successive short parables* (men in the field, women grinding, two in a bed) demonstrating that "one will be taken, the other left." These form a severe warning regarding the sudden, unexpected separation at the Parousia (cf. Mt 24:44; cf. Lk 12:40) between those receiving salvation* and those doomed for judgment. This contrast is further emphasized in the parable of the good and wicked servants (Mt 24:45-51 par. Lk 12:41-46), in which the faithful servant is given a share in Jesus' future authority while the wicked servant will be "dismembered" (Lk 12:46) and placed with the unfaithful. Finally, Matthew 10:28 and Luke 12:5 add a further saying on Gehenna, that the disciple should fear not those who can kill the body but the one who

"can destroy both soul and body in hell." These passages show that Jesus followed Daniel 12:2 regarding the resurrection of good and evil alike, one to vindication and the other to judgment.

2.4. The M and L Traditions. The source material peculiar to Matthew (M*) and Luke (L*) adds further data. In the M tradition judgment will be universal; both good and evil people will be accountable "on the day of judgment for every careless word they have spoken" (Mt 12:35-37). While evil or "careless" speech is stressed, the "acquittal" or "condemnation" (Mt 12:37) of all speech is in mind. Two further parables address the radical separation of believer from unbeliever at the last judgment. The parable of the weeds in Matthew 13:24-30, 36-43 teaches that only at "the end of the age" (Mt 13:43) will the wicked finally be separated from the good, the former headed for "the fiery furnace" and the latter for glory* (Mt 13:42-43). The parable of the sheep and the goats (also called "the judgment of the nations") has a similar theme but adds that the judgment will be determined also by the way the nations have treated God's people (the "least of these" of Mt 13:40, 45). The reward for the merciful will be "your inheritance, the kingdom prepared for you since the creation of the world" (Mt 13:34); the punishment for the merciless will be "the eternal fire prepared for the devil and his angels" (Mt 13:41; see Demon, Devil, Satan).

Several L passages demonstrate the Lukan theme of the reversal of roles at the final resurrection. At the conclusion of the sayings on proper conduct at banquets (Lk 14:7-14), Jesus says that those who invite the poor (see Rich and Poor) and the crippled "will be repaid at the resurrection of the righteous" (Lk 14:14). While there may be no thanks in this life, God will vindicate good deeds at the eschaton. The key is a life of servanthood which seeks the lesser rather than the greater place (Lk 14:8-11) and is oriented to the dispossessed rather than the wealthy (Lk 14:12-14).

This theme is taken further in the parable of the rich man and Lazarus* in Luke 16:19-31. The rich man, who undoubtedly had a lavish earthly funeral, is described in terse clauses: "died and was buried and in Hades." The poor man, who seemingly is not buried at all, has exactly the opposite afterlife: "angels carried him to Abraham's side." There are two concurrent emphases in this parable: the reversal of roles at the final resurrection and the radical faith* demands of the kingdom message. Similar warnings of final judgment are addressed to the rich and to all disciples in Luke 3:7-14; 6:24-26 (cf. 1:51-53); 12:16-21, 32-34, 42-48; 16:8-9. The implications of this parable for a doctrine of the afterlife cannot be pressed too far. The picture of a compartmentalized "Hades" does not describe "the way it is" but is a feature of the parable probably derived from a popular Jewish conception of Sheol (see Heaven and Hell).

2.5. The Johannine Tradition. The Johannine tradition contains a few sayings which relate to the resurrection theology of Jesus and the early church. While the Fourth Gospel primarily sets forth a realized eschatology, a growing consensus of scholarship has detected a future eschatology within this characteristic Johannine matrix (see John, Gospel of). In John 5:28-29 Jesus speaks of the "coming time" when the dead will hear his voice and "come out— those who have done good will rise to live, and those who have done evil will rise to be condemned." The context centers on Jesus as the eschatological Judge in the present (Jn 5:19-24) and the future (Jn 5:25-30). Then in John 6:40, 44, 54—within a context emphasizing the united sovereignty of the Father and Son in the salvation process (cf. "will never die" in 11:25-26)—Jesus thrice repeats that he will "raise" the faithful "at the last day."

The other side is found in John 12:48, in which the unbeliever is warned that Jesus' words will "condemn him at the last day." Finally, Jesus promises in John 14:2-3 that he is "preparing a place" for his disciples and "will come back" to bring them to his side. Some have interpreted this of the Paraclete/Holy Spirit (see Holy Spirit) "coming back" as Jesus' representative, but the consensus is that this is a reference to the Parousia. Bultmann and others have long argued that these futuristic passages were added by a later redactor (see Redaction Criticism), and that realized passages like John 12:31 and 16:11 (the judgment "*now*" of the "prince of this world") are original. Yet there is no reason why the two cannot stand side-by-side, with present salvation and future promise interrelated.

Jesus' teaching fits into the ongoing tradition from Daniel through the Pharisees, attesting to the physical resurrection of God's people to reward and of the resurrection of the ungodly to final judgment.

3. Miracles of Raising the Dead.

Jesus affirmed his belief in resurrection not only by his words but also by his deeds. In one sense these are not true resurrections but miracles of resuscitation, for the recipients would still face death at a later date. However, in the Gospels they are treated as harbingers of Jesus' coming resurrection, proof of God's (and Jesus') control over the power of death.

3.1. Jairus's Daughter. The most fully attested miracle of resuscitation is the raising of Jairus'

daughter. Found in the triple tradition (Mk 5:21-24, 35-43 par. Mt 9:18-19, 23-26 and Lk 8:40-42, 49-56), it is intertwined in all three accounts with the healing* of the woman with a hemorrhage. The movement from healing to resuscitation shows Jesus as lord over both chronic illness and death. The overriding concern is christological, seeking to demonstrate Jesus' lordship. That Jairus—a ruler or president of a synagogue and a man with great social and religious prestige—would prostrate himself before Jesus would be astonishing to a first-century reader and point to Jesus as a God-ordained prophet.

On the basis of Jesus' statement "She is not dead, but asleep," many interpreters have argued that this is a healing miracle. However, the details regarding the mourning of the relatives and professional mourners all point to the reality of the girl's death. Instead, Jesus' comment is a theological pointer to the miracle as an "awakening" from the dead. In all three Gospels this story is part of a complex of miracles (the stilling of the storm, the Gerasene demoniac) demonstrating the messianic authority* of Jesus over all earthly and heavenly powers. Even the ultimate power of death is conquered by him.

3.2. The Widow's Son. A second account is the Lukan tradition of Jesus raising the son of a widow of Nain (Lk 7:11-17). Recalling the similar raising of the widow's son by Elijah (1 Kings 17:8-24), this is also part of a section dealing with Jesus' prophetic ministry (note the healing of the centurion's son that precedes and the dialog regarding the Baptist that follows). The miracle concludes with expressions of awe and wonder which are anchored in the "rising" of a "great prophet" (see Prophet, Prophecy) and especially in the statement that "God has visited his people" (Lk 7:16), the latter echoing the language of Zechariah's Song (Lk 1:68, 78; see Zechariah's Song) and the Lukan theme of salvific deliverance. Jesus' power over life and death is vividly portrayed.

3.3. Lazarus. The raising of Lazarus* (Jn 11:1-44) is the concluding and most astounding sign-miracle of John's so-called Book of Signs (1:19—12:50). It also functions as a transition to the Book of Glory (13:1—20:31), with the plot of the Jewish leaders being clearly tied to this event (cf. 11:53; 12:17-19).

Of the so-called resurrection miracles the raising of Lazarus is most clearly connected with the question of the afterlife. This becomes evident in the dialog with Martha (11:20-26) and its connection to the Johannine theme of eternal life as resurrection (cf. 5:19-30). In John 11:21, 25, 28-29 Jesus demonstrates the presence of resurrection both now (the *spiritual* dead hear his voice and live, Jn 11:25) and in the future (those in the grave come forth, Jn 11:28-29). This is actualized in Lazarus—Jesus raises him as a clear foretaste of the final resurrection—and emphasized in the juxtaposition of Martha's confession ("I know he will rise again in the resurrection at the last day," Jn 11:24) and Jesus' bold claim ("I am the resurrection and the life," Jn 11:25). In fact, John 11:25 is the theological culmination of 5:21, "For just as the Father raises the dead and gives them life, even so the Son gives life to whom he is pleased to give it." Jesus is equated with the Father as the one who gives "resurrection and life," so uniting the Johannine themes of realized (raising the spiritually dead to life) and final (the resurrection at the last day) eschatology.

3.4. The Saints. Finally, the enigmatic raising of the saints in Matthew 27:51-53 provides a theological bridge from the cross to the empty tomb. In what is likely an allusion to Ezekiel's vision of the valley of dry bones (37:1-14, esp. 13-14, "When I open your graves and bring you up from them . . . and you will live"), the brief story summarizes the effects of Jesus' death (judgment and the defeat of the powers of death; *see* Death of Jesus) and resurrection (the raising of the dead saints and their appearance in the holy city). Thus Jesus' passion and resurrection are inextricably linked as a single event in salvation-history, and the effect upon the raising and uniting of the true "saints" of God, both past and future, is guaranteed by this supernatural deed.

The question of the historicity of these miracles is beyond the purview of this study (for arguments pro see Harris 1990; con see Perkins; *see* Gospels [Historical Reliability]). But the claim that Jesus raised the dead on the basis of his prophetic and messianic (*see* Christ) office and as a harbinger of his own resurrection can at least tentatively be affirmed (*see* Miracles, Miracle Stories). Miracles of raising the dead permeate all the traditions behind the Gospels (Mark, M, L, John, possibly Q), and their historicity can be argued on the basis of the criterion of multiple attestation (*see* Form Criticism).

4. Jesus' Resurrection in the Four Gospels.

4.1. The Resurrection in Mark. With the growing consensus among Gospel scholars that Mark's Gospel concludes at 16:8 with the words *ephobounta gar* ("for they were afraid"), Mark 16:1-8 has come to be regarded as a literary masterpiece (*see* Mark, Gospel of). Moreover, Mark 16:1-8 may be seen as a brilliant conclusion to the Gospel as a whole, bringing Mark's two major themes to culmination: the hidden epiphany of Jesus as Messiah and Son of God (*see* Son of God); and discipleship,* particularly the

problem of discipleship failure.

The first unit (Mk 16:1-4) combines tradition and Markan redaction. Pre-Markan tradition can be found in the names of the women* and the trip to the tomb at dawn. Yet the whole narrative is tied together in Markan fashion and presents some basic Markan themes, particularly in the misunderstanding of the women. The chronological notes provide an important transition from the passion to the resurrection. The action proceeds from the terrible events on "the day before the Sabbath" (Mk 15:42) to the decision to bring spices "when the Sabbath was over" and then depicts the trip itself.

Continuity is also provided by the names. There are three in Mark's passion narrative (15:40, 47; 16:1), with Mary Magdalene, Mary and Salome in 15:40 and 16:1 and the two Marys in 15:47. Luke adds Joanna (24:10), while Matthew only has the two Marys (28:1; though 27:56 par. Mk 15:40 adds "the mother of the sons of Zebedee"). It is likely that tradition and redaction are again combined. The key to Mark's purpose is found in his use of *theorein* with each name list, thereby making the women official witnesses of the crucifixion events (15:40), the burial (15:47; *see* Burial of Jesus) and the empty tomb (15:47).

The purchase of the spices for anointing Jesus' corpse parallels both Joseph's purchase in Mark 15:46 and the anointing (pointing to his death) of Mark 14:3-9. It is ironic in this context, for the messianic connotations of the earlier anointings, signifying Jesus' death as the assumption of his office as royal Messiah, make this anointing unnecessary. Jesus has not only become Messiah but has already risen, so there will be no further anointing. Irony and misunderstanding continue not only in the women's desire to anoint Jesus' body but in their perplexity as to how they can find help to "roll away the stone" (16:3) which was "very large" (16:4). A narrative gap occurs in the passive "had been rolled away" of 16:4, anticipating the supernatural intervention of the angel (Mt 28:2 explicitly names the angel as the agent) in 16:5. In short, Mark 16:1-4 centers on the misunderstanding of the women (who play a role in Mark's discipleship theme) and directs the reader forward to the divine intervention which alone can solve the dilemma.

The angelic message (16:5-7) also contains both tradition (the angelophany, the exhortation not to fear, the implied rebuke, the basic proclamation of the resurrection and empty tomb) and redaction (their "amazement," *Nazarenos*, the command to go to Galilee). The "messianic secret," partially lifted in the centurion's cry of 15:39 ("Surely this man was the Son of God"), is now completely disclosed. The women's astonishment and the angel's command not to fear belong to the genre of epiphany, and the message is a kerygmatic formula which completely removes any doubt as to who this "Nazarene" is, confirming the significance of the threefold passion predictions centering on the "Son of man" (see above). There is again a tension introduced into the contrast between the women's pious but ignorant purpose ("seeking" to anoint one who "is not here") and the stupendous significance of the reality of resurrection as announced.

The promise of Mark 16:7—that the disciples will see Jesus in Galilee*—is the key to Mark's narrative and is intimately connected to the promise of 14:28 (cf. also 9:9) that the disciples' misunderstanding and failure would be reversed in a Galilee experience. Some (e.g., W. Marxsen) have argued that this refers to a Parousia expectation rather than a resurrection appearance, but the absence of a glory motif and the fact that both Galilee and the promise "you will see him" (opsesthe) are connected in Mark with the resurrection rather than Parousia make such an assumption unlikely. "Galilee" occurs thirteen times in Mark, usually in the context of Jesus' mission and its success (cf. 1:14, 28, 39; 3:7; 15:40). Therefore, it implicitly promises the overcoming of their failure and the passing of the baton, thus launching the church's mission. This is exemplified further in the pre-Markan tradition (cf. Lk 24:34, 1 Cor 15:5) "tell the disciples and Peter" which may well indicate the reinstatement of the disciples.

This makes the Markan ending all the more startling. The reader would expect the fear to have ceased in 16:6, yet here the fear overpowers the women and forces them to disobey the angel's mandate. However, the stress is not on an act of disobedience but on the numbing effect of the overwhelming awe. In every sense 16:8 concludes Mark's theme of discipleship failure, for the women parallel the many scenes of similar awe, silence and misunderstanding on the part of the disciples (e.g., 6:52; 8:14-21; 9:6, 32; 10:32). If 16:8 were to be considered alone, it would make an incredibly negative conclusion; we would be left only with the warning that believers today not repeat the failure of the disciples and the women. However, Mark's actual message is to be found in the interaction between 16:7 and 8. The resurrection appearances are not related in the narrative because Mark's emphasis is on the presence of the Risen One in our Galilee. Awe and failure are very real experiences for every disciple, but Jesus is at all times waiting to remove that fear and to guarantee success in mission.

4.2. The Resurrection in Matthew. Matthew follows Mark's basic outline but adds a great deal of his own material, primarily the narrative of the guards at the tomb (Mt 27:62-66; 28:4, 11-15) and the story of Jesus' appearance in Galilee (Mt 28:16-20). In so doing he has fashioned an episode employing two sets of contrasting scenes, thereby demonstrating the intervention of God* against all attempts to obstruct his salvific plan. This plan follows the similar structure of both the infancy and passion narratives, which for Matthew center apologetically on the power of God to overcome all obstacles. Matthew's resurrection narrative also emphasizes the twin themes of authority and mission/commission, utilizing the theme of recognition or coming-to-understanding. All of this summarizes major themes which have occurred throughout Matthew's Gospel (see Matthew, Gospel of). Whereas Mark focuses on the failure of the disciples, Matthew in every episode (e.g., Mt 14:27-32; cf. Mk 6:52; Mt 16:12; cf. Mk 8:21) shows how the presence of Jesus allows the disciples to overcome their failure and attain understanding. The resurrection scene culminates this development in discipleship (see Discipleship).

The first set of contrasting scenes (Mt 27:62—28:10) contrasts the priests' complex plot to post the guards and seal the tomb with the sovereign act of God in raising Jesus from the dead. There are certainly strong redactional overtones in the guard narrative of 27:62-66 as well as in the related episodes of 28:4, 11-15. Yet this does not mean that there was no tradition behind the story. This is suggested by the non-Matthean vocabulary such as *epaurion, paraskeuē, planos* and *asphalizō*. Moreover, historical problems such as the likelihood of the priests going to Pilate on the Sabbath* are not as problematic as they first appear. Research into Sabbath exceptions at the time of Jesus shows that such an incident would have been allowed, so long as the individuals did not travel more than a Sabbath day's journey or enter the palace (cf. Jn 18:28). It seems likely that Matthew has developed tradition regarding the priests' request for a setting of the guard in order to answer contemporary Jewish charges that the body had been stolen and to emphasize the sovereign power of God in the resurrection despite all such plots. Matthew has also removed Mark's stress on the women's misguided purpose to anoint the body of Jesus, emphasizing instead the theme of witness* (cf. 27:56, 61). In the Matthean setting the women's simple act of reverence is set in contrast with the priestly intrigue.

The supernatural intervention of God in the two scenes of Matthew 28:2-4 and 5-10 is remarkable.

Matthew favors such eschatological scenes (see the earthquake [*seismos*] scenes of Mt 8:24 and 27:51 as well as angel scenes in Mt 1:20, 24; 2:13, 19) to emphasize the inbreaking of the messianic age by direct acts of God. The earthquake establishes continuity with the crucifixion (Mt 27:51); as in Acts 16:26 and Revelation 6:12; 8:5; 16:18 it is not so much a symbol of judgment as a positive sign of divine deliverance. The angel's act in rolling back the stone and sitting upon it also has apocalyptic* overtones (cf. also his description in Mt 28:3, paralleling Dan 7:9; 10:6; *1 Enoch* 71:1; Rev 1:14-15; 10:1), depicting the dawn of a new age. The tomb has been opened, allowing all to witness the triumph of God.

Matthew has clearly departed from the simple portrait of Mark; yet his restraint can be seen by comparing Matthew 28:2-4 with the elaborate narration in the *Gospel of Peter* (9:35-45; *see* Gospels [Apocryphal]), in which two angels help the risen Lord* from the tomb, "and the heads of the two reaching to heaven, but that of him who was led of them by the hand surpassing the heavens." Matthew has deliberately avoided describing the resurrection itself. The reaction of the guards, who faint and "become like dead men," provides a negative "witness" (that of opponents to God's plan) to the theophanic overtones of the scene. This is not the fear of reverence (like that of the women in 28:9) but the terror that God's enemies alone will feel.

The angel's message (Mt 28:5-7) is more closely aligned with Mark. Yet there are significant redactional alterations. Matthew replaces Mark's "do not be alarmed" with "do not be afraid," probably to strengthen the contrast with the guards' terror. He also connects the announcement of Jesus' resurrection directly with the passion predictions by adding "as he said." Mark uses this phrase after the reference to Jesus preceding them to Galilee, but Matthew at this point has the angel conclude his pronouncement with "Now I have told you," stressing the authority of the divinely commissioned messenger. The meeting in Galilee thus becomes more directly the result of the angel's proclamation than of Jesus' previous promise (as in Mark). Mark's startling ending is radically altered by Matthew, who in 28:8-10 has the women go forth "afraid yet filled with joy" and "run to tell his disciples." The appearance of Jesus to the women is attested independently in John 20:11-18 and stems from tradition. But Matthean elements may be observed in the stress on "joy"* (cf. 2:10; 13:20, 44; 25:21, 23), "worship"* (2:2, 11; 4:9-10; 8:1; 9:18; 14:33; 15:25) and "my brothers," which indicates in a single word the forgiveness* and reinstatement of the fallen

disciples (cf. Jn 15:11-17; 20:17 for a similar emphasis). The repetition of the command to go to Galilee prepares for the climactic scene in Matthew 28:16-20.

The second set of contrasts is between the evil plot to spread lies in Matthew 28:11-15 and the great commission of divine truth* in 28:16-20. The irony of the priestly deception in 28:11-15 is obvious; the very thing they had sought to prevent in 27:62-66 (i.e., the possibility that Jesus' body might be stolen) they are now forced to proclaim. Matthew's apologetic against this Jewish polemic (note "to this very day," 28:15) is now made explicit.

The aptly named "great commission" of Matthew 28:16-20 belongs to the genre of commissioning narratives seen often in the OT and Jewish literature. It consists of two parts, a narrative introduction (16-18a) and a threefold saying composed of a statement of authority (18b), a commission (19-20a) and reassurance of the Risen One's continued presence (20b). It is very likely that the episode is based on tradition, since it parallels similar commissionings in Luke 24:47-49 and John 20:21-23, and contains elements pointing to a source in the tradition: "the mountain* where Jesus had told them to go" (no such command occurs in Matthew); "but some doubted" (a major resurrection tradition but apparently out of place here); and "in heaven and on earth" (not found elsewhere in Matthew). However, the language and themes are so Matthean that it is impossible to separate redaction from tradition (nor would we wish to limit historical trustworthiness to one but not the other).

Matthew has carefully crafted the whole to summarize many of the major themes in his Gospel. Some interesting points occur in the introduction, such as the meeting on a mountain, so important in Matthew as a place of revelation (cf. 4:8; 5:1; 8:1; 14:23; 15:29; 17:1; 21:1); and the presence of doubt in the midst of the disciples' worship. This latter element probably continues the Matthean theme of the "little-faithed ones." *Distazō* occurs in the NT only here and in Matthew 14:31, where Jesus chides his disciples, "O you of little faith, why did you doubt?" But they respond (14:32), "Truly you are the Son of God." It is likely that the doubt means uncertainty rather than unbelief and that this is part of the message throughout the First Gospel: Spiritual hesitation in the midst of worship is the constant struggle of every disciple. The answer can only be found when one applies the promise inherent in Matthew 28:18-20.

The key term in the commission itself is "all"—"all authority," "all nations," "all things," "always." In many ways this short homily could be labelled the

"Allness of Yahweh" passed on to the mission of the disciples through the presence of the Risen One among them. The "authority in heaven and on earth given" to Jesus is a reflection of Daniel 7:14, and therefore the Risen Jesus is depicted as the exalted Son of man who now has universal authority over all of God's kingdom. The authority of Jesus in Matthew's Gospel is now extended to all of God's kingdom, heavenly as well as earthly. The mission to disciple "all the nations" (possibly also connected to Dan 7:14) echoes the church's participation in the God-given mission of Jesus, which was limited to Israel* (10:5-6; 15:24) but is now extended to all people. There is considerable debate as to whether *ethnē* ("nations," "peoples") refers only to the Gentile* mission (due to the common restriction of the term to Gentiles) or whether the addition of *pas* ("all") extends the reference to include Israel as well as the nations. Several recent studies on the scope of the universal mission in Matthew find the latter interpretation more likely. Moreover, in Matthew 24:9, 14 and 25:32 (the other three places where the full expression "all nations" occurs) it refers to "all people," including Jew and Gentile (*see* Matthew, Gospel of).

There are two concomitant aspects to the discipling process, baptism and instruction. Jesus' resurrection command becomes the basis of Christian baptism,* which is here seen as an entrance "into" (*eis*, as Matthew normally observes the distinction between *eis* and *en*) the lordship and fellowship of the triune godhead. There is Matthean background in the trinitarian formula, summarizing the Father-Son (Mt 3:17; 11:27) and Son-Spirit (Mt 3:11, 16; 12:32) relationships. The second aspect, teaching, also concludes a major theme. Matthew's Gospel is organized around the five great discourse units of chapters 5—7, 10, 13, 18 and 23—25, and discipleship itself is defined as an ethical response to Jesus' demands. As in 5:17-20 and 24:35, Jesus' teaching is presented as the authoritative words of Yahweh and as the fulfillment of the Torah (*see* Law). The Torah of the Messiah has come, and in this new age the disciple will obey "all the commands" of Jesus.

The disciple's obedient response to Jesus' teaching is paralleled by the promise of Jesus' continued presence, building upon earlier promises of Jesus as the *Immanuel*, or "God with us" (1:23) and as the one present whenever "two or three are gathered" (18:20). Here we see the solution to the "little faith" of Matthew 28:17; namely, the powerful presence of the Risen One would sustain them in their weakness. Moreover, that presence is constant "to the very end of the age." Many have called this a "proleptic parousia," due to the apocalyptic overtones (again building upon Dan 7:14) in which Jesus' future or final coming is mediated to the church now.

4.3. The Resurrection in Luke. In Luke and John the basic approach to the resurrection changes, with the appearances centered in Jerusalem rather than Galilee. For Luke this lends the account a geographical focus in which Jerusalem becomes both an ending (for the life and ministry of Jesus) and a beginning (for the ongoing mission of the church). Luke's presentation prepares for the book of Acts, so the resurrection provides a transition from the ministry of Jesus to that of the early church. As many have noted, there is a salvation-historical perspective throughout. Moreover, there is a strong creedal emphasis, with constant commentary elucidating the significance of the events from the perspective of prophetic fulfillment (Lk 24:5-7, 25-27, 44-47). Finally, there is a strong polemic focusing on doubt and the reality of the resurrection. An emphasis on witness, including proofs for the resurrection, is evident, but this is constantly met by perplexity and unbelief. Luke presents these themes in linear fashion, with all the events occurring on the same day in four stages: the empty tomb (24:1-12), the road to Emmaus (24:13-35), the appearance to and commissioning of the disciples at the meal (24:36-49) and the ascension* into heaven (24:50-52).

Luke's empty-tomb narrative (24:1-12) follows Mark's general order but introduces some interesting redactional twists. It is debated whether Luke utilizes Mark and adds L material (the women entering the tomb, the two angels, the appearance to Peter in 24:12, 34) or has followed a non-Markan source and inserted some Markan details. Whichever is the case, Lukan redaction is evident. He has an extensive discussion of the women's preparation and rest on the Sabbath (23:54-56), with four time notes (23:54a, 54b, 56; 24:1) which unite the burial and tomb event into a salvation-historical whole. The emphasis is not so much on the women's misunderstanding (as in Mark) as on God's work behind the scenes. The action leads to the direct pronouncement in 24:3 that the women "did not find the body" in the tomb. The role of the women as witnesses is expanded; they "saw" not only the tomb but "how his body was laid" (23:55) and then were witnesses to the empty tomb. The significance is seen in the added note that it was "the body of the Lord Jesus" (though this is a "western non-interpolation," missing in the normally adventuresome Western family of manuscripts, most scholars agree that the phrase "of the Lord Jesus" is original to the text; *see* Textual Criticism). This introduces Luke's characteristic theology of glory at the very outset of the resurrection narrative.

The women's perplexity in Luke 24:3 turns into fearful awe (24:4) as there are now two angels in dazzling apparel (pre-Lukan tradition, cf. Jn. 20:12). The message itself (24:5-7) departs from the Markan form. There is no alleviation of their fear but rather a direct challenge and proclamation of the critical reality of the resurrection. "Galilee" in this pronouncement is not the place where Jesus will meet them but the place where Jesus had formerly predicted his passion and resurrection. In Luke Galilee is the place of authoritative witness; the women themselves are from Galilee (8:1-3), and Galilean disciples attest to the Jerusalem appearances in Acts 1:11 and 13:31. In other words, the focus changes from the future to the past, and the repetition of the passion prediction in Luke 24:7, being derived from 9:22, 44; 18:31-33, adds a promise-fulfillment thrust. In 24:8 the women "remember," a Lukan emphasis pointing to an awakening faith (contra Dillon) in the salvific plan of God (especially in its connection with the divine "must" [dei] of 24:7; cf. Lk 1:54, 72; Acts 11:16). Their understanding leads them to report "all these things" (including not only the angel's message but their own witness to the empty tomb). Unlike Matthew and Mark, this is not in response to an angelic commission (omitted by Luke) but is the direct result of their burgeoning faith (seen in the and . . . and [kai . . . kai] pattern of 24:8-9). Luke reserves the list of names (even adding "the other women with them") for this point (24:10) in order to give greater stress to the women's function as witnesses to the reality of the resurrection. Yet the result is startling; the "apostles"* (Luke uses this title six times in his Gospel [as opposed to once in Matthew and twice in Mark] to stress the point of continuity between the disciples and the apostolic band of Acts) not only doubt but "disbelieve," considering the women's testimony to be "nonsense."

This unbelief is a major emphasis in Luke's empty-tomb narrative, preparing for the overcoming of doubt via the direct presence of the Risen One in the next episode. To give added stress to this motif Luke incorporates (another Western non-interpolation which most today accept as authentic) a further episode from the tradition (the language shows similarities with Jn 20:3-10) regarding Peter's trip to the tomb (24:12). Peter's "perplexed" departure from the tomb mutes somewhat the disbelief of the disciples, but conclusively, for he provides continuity from the confusion of the women in 24:4 to the "amazement" of the travellers in 24:22. Full-fledged faith

comes only after the sovereign intervention of the Risen One himself (24:16, 31).

This struggle of faith continues in the Emmaus Road journey of 24:13-35. The interplay of tradition and redaction is difficult to detect since this story only occurs in Luke. However, while there is a great deal of Lukan redaction, there are few scholars who would identify this as a free composition. It is likely that a pre-Lukan form of this story formed the basis for a portion of the later Markan appendix (Mk 16:12-13), and the names "Emmaus" and "Cleopas" would have been unlikely in a story freely created. Most critical scholars accept the pre-Lukan origin of at least 24:13, 16, 28-31, and many would accept a historical nucleus behind the whole.

Viewed within its larger context, several themes emerge. As so often in Luke, geography dominates the structure. In this case the journey "from" Jerusalem is characterized by defeat, the return "to" Jerusalem by witness and victory. The turn-about through Jesus' instruction takes place "on the way." The reality of the resurrection is the goal of the story, with 24:28-32 climaxing not only this episode but the empty-tomb narrative as well. This reality is particularly stressed in the proof-from-prophecy (24:25-27) as Jesus shows that he is more than a powerful prophet (the travelers' belief in 24:19) but is indeed the fulfillment of the prophetic vision of a suffering and glorified Messiah.

The movement toward understanding is accomplished utilizing a non-recognition/recognition motif. During the first half of the story the travellers are "kept from recognizing" Jesus, a feature recalling the disciples' need for divine disclosure in order to understand the passion predictions (9:45; 18:34). This is undoubtedly intended to lead the reader to the opening of blind eyes (see Blindness and Deafness) via the proclamation of the Word (24:25-27, 32) and the breaking of the bread (24:30-31, 35). The spoken word controls the narrative of 24:17-27 and includes a summary of the tomb events, thereby elaborating on the confession that Jesus was "the prophet powerful in word and deed" (24:19; cf. 24:20-24), and on the scriptural fulfillment motif (24:25-27).

Many see a parallel here with the Ethiopian eunuch story of Acts 8:26-39, each story following a similar pattern: a stranger opens up the Word for the traveller, leading to conversion. Yet the instruction in Luke 24 is actually "pre-evangelism," for while their hearts did "burn" as Jesus opened the Scriptures (24:32), the breaking of bread is the turning point of the Emmaus episode. It is here that God sovereignly opens their blind eyes (note the divine passive "were opened" in 24:31, the counterpart to "were kept from recognizing him" in 24:16).

It is debated whether this implies a eucharistic celebration. "Breaking of bread" is seen by some as a technical phrase for the eucharist (Acts 2:42; 20:7; 1 Cor 11:20), and the order of events in 24:30 (taking, giving thanks, breaking, distributing) might be reminiscent of the Last Supper (cf. 22:19; *see* Last Supper). However, the motif could also be more general, alluding to the Lukan meal or table-fellowship scenes (*see* Table Fellowship) which feature Jesus' instruction (5:29; 7:36; 11:37; 12:37; 13:29; 14:1, 8-9; 22:14; cf. esp. 9:10-17 [the feeding of the five thousand] which also has parallels to this passage). On the whole, it is possible that both aspects are found here, especially when one realizes that the eucharist was a meal scene in the Gospels. Yet one cannot be dogmatic, and it may be table fellowship rather than eucharist which is intended. The final emphasis is on witness and culminates this theme, from the incredulity of 24:11 to the faith response of 24:34. Interestingly, the witness of the two disciples does not produce faith; rather, it confirms the faith which resulted from the report of the appearance to Simon. In other words, the reality of the resurrection is confirmed by a double witness, that of Peter and of the two disciples.

In Luke's Gospel Jesus' appearance occurs in Jerusalem rather than Galilee. Scholars have discussed at length the significance of the Galilee versus Jerusalem appearance traditions, especially since they do not occur together in any single Gospel account (John 21 is an appendix added later—see below). Many believe that the Galilee tradition is prior, since it is found in the oldest tradition (Mk 14:28; 16:7). However, this is not a necessary conclusion, for even in Matthew—where the Galilee appearance takes center stage—there is a "Jerusalem" appearance to the women (Mt 28:8-10). The redactional interests of the Evangelists may have been reason enough for them to center on one tradition. C. F. D. Moule (1957-58) presents a quite plausible thesis that as festival pilgrims (*see* Feasts) the disciples would have remained in Jerusalem for the feast of unleavened bread (thus the appearances of Mt 28:9-10; Lk 24:13-49; Jn 20:11-29), gone back to Galilee for the interim between the feasts (Mt 28:16-20; Jn 21) and finally returned to Jerusalem for Pentecost (the ascension in Lk 24:50-53; Acts 1:6-11).

The appearance recorded in 24:36-43 centers on the physical reality of the resurrection. Structurally, it is closely connected to 24:13-35, for Jesus appears while the eleven are discussing the report of the two travellers. Again, a pre-Lukan tradition lies behind the story. This is evidenced in the appearance itself (witnessed by three other disparate sources—1 Cor

15:5; Mk 16:14-15; Jn 20:19-21); the charges by the Risen One of "Peace be with you" (cf. Jn 20:19, 21, 26) and "Touch me and see" (cf. Jn 20:27); the doubt motif; and the apologetic proof.

The "peace" greeting (24:36) has theological overtones, paralleling the "peace" given by the seventy-two in their own mission (10:5-6) and possibly including the same type of messianic promise as the "peace is yours" of John 20. This is followed by a strong emphasis on the disciples' doubt, seen in the successive verbs of 24:37-38: startled; frightened; thinking they had seen a ghost; troubled; doubting. This is a surprising development following the faith they evidenced in 24:31-35, but it prepares for Jesus startling proof of his resurrection in 24:39-43. The movement from sight to touch to actually sharing a meal with them gives great stress to the continuity between the crucified and risen Christ (showing his nail-scarred hands and feet) as well as to the corporeality of the resurrection ("a ghost does not have flesh and bones, as you see I have," 24:39; eating the fish in 24:43). Some have interpreted this as Luke's interest in refuting a docetic heresy in his church, but the emphasis is on the nature of the Risen Christ ("I am he," 24:39) rather than on false teaching.

The commission scene of 24:44-49 blends a liturgical tradition of 24:44 (paralleling the sermons of Acts), a commission tradition of 24:47 (like Mt 28:19; Jn 20:21) and a Spirit tradition of 24:49 (like Jn 20:22). The fulfillment theme recapitulates Luke 24:6-7, 25-27, but adds the Psalms to the Law and the Prophets; the Psalms are used frequently in Acts (cf. 2:25-26, 34-35; 4:11, 25-26; 13:33-35) to anchor the creedal stress on humiliation-vindication. The commission deepens mission preaching with soteriological themes. In fact, as Marshall notes, the terms "repentance"* (cf. 5:32; 13:3-4; 15:7-8; 16:30; 17:3-4), "forgiveness of sins" (cf. 1:77; 3:3; 5:17-18; Acts 2:38; 5:31; 10:43) and "preach" (3:3; 4:18-19, 43-44; 8:39; 9:2; 12:3) virtually sum up the Lukan doctrine of salvation.* This mission is to be done "in his name" (a Lukan phrase denoting power and authority in mission) "to all nations" (the universal mission) "beginning at Jerusalem" (the origin of the mission, looking forward to Acts 1—5). Each phrase prepares for the launching of the church's mission in Acts (note that the concatenation of "Jerusalem," "witnesses" and "power" occurs again in Acts 1:8, the table of contents for that book).

The powerful witness* probably includes not only the eleven, but the 120 (including women, cf. Lk 8:1-3; 24:9-10; Acts 1:14-15). Both Luke and John (Jn 20:21-23) anchor this witness in the bestowal of the Spirit. In John this occurs on the first day of the resurrection, but Luke does not have this in mind; here Jesus points to the coming of the Spirit in Acts 2 ("Stay in the city until you have been clothed with power from on high"). In Luke-Acts the Holy Spirit is the means of continuity from the time of Jesus to that of the church.

The ascension in Luke furnishes a structural transition from Luke's Gospel to Acts. In fact, a good argument can be made that the ascension has been the goal ever since Luke 9:31, in which Jesus, Moses* and Elijah spoke of his "departure" (*exodos*) which would be "fulfilled at Jerusalem," an event which would come most naturally at the ascension (cf. Lk 9:51). In Luke 24:50-53 the ascension takes on a doxological tone, with Jesus imparting a priestly blessing; in Acts 1:6-11 it has ecclesiastical implications, with the Risen Lord empowering and launching the church's mission. In Luke it provides an ending, and in Acts 1 it becomes a beginning. Thus ends the theme of Jesus' glory in Luke 24. The Risen Lord now becomes the Exalted One and like Elijah is taken up to heaven. A further transition to Acts is seen in the disciples, who "worship" and "with great joy" return to Jerusalem, remaining "continually in the Temple" (24:52-53). Each of these—worship, joy and Temple*—are major themes both in the Gospel and Acts. The disciples and the church continue the ministry of Jesus in these areas.

4.4. The Resurrection in John. The resurrection in the Synoptic Gospels functions as the culmination of Jesus' life; it is both vindication and exaltation, and the Gospel accounts in one sense anticipate it. John, however, takes the opposite tack. His entire Gospel is told from a post-resurrection point of view. The resurrection is not so much the time when Jesus assumes his *doxa;* rather, his entire life and ministry comprise *doxa.* The disciples are not depicted as having "hardened hearts" (cf. Mk 6:52; 8:17; *see* Hardness of Hearts); instead, they "believe" because they perceive his revealed glory (2:11). John replaces the Synoptic passion predictions with three sayings on the "Son of man lifted up" (3:14; 8:28; 12:31-32), which looks at the passion as exaltation. Jesus' life and death are pictured as resurrection events. The resurrection itself then becomes the final moment in this drama of glory, and as such it culminates the major emphases of the Fourth Gospel: christology and soteriology in chapter 20; mission and discipleship in chapter 21.

4.4.1. John 20. Each of the four episodes in chapter twenty exhibits a crisis of faith, as the participants struggle with the reality of the resurrection. In each the level of faith drops to a lower level, from the beloved disciple with his natural faith (20:8-9) to Mary's sorrow (20:11) to the disciples' fear (20:19) to Thomas' cynical demand (20:25). Yet with each crisis Jesus meets the need, and the results become increasingly greater, culminating in Thomas' faith-cry, "My Lord and my God" (20:28), which climaxes the christology of John. As in Luke, the four episodes occur on the same day, two in the morning (20:1-18) and two in the evening (20:19-29).

There are actually three scenes in John 20:1-18, as the race to the tomb (20:3-10) separates Mary's discovery of the empty tomb (20:1-2) from Jesus' appearance to her (20:11-18). Several clues point to a tradition lying behind the passage. Mary's "we" in 20:2 is a relic of a Synoptic-like tradition where several women are present. There are also connections with Luke 24:12, 34 and the Peter-tradition. Most scholars believe that each part—the trips to the tomb by the women and the disciples as well as the appearance to Mary—stem from tradition. In 20:1-10 there is a subtle shift from Matthew's polemical use of the belief that Jesus' body had been stolen. In this case it is not an apologetic but part of the motif of misunderstanding among Jesus followers; it is Mary, not the chief priests (Mt 27:62-66) who fears this, and she sets the scene for the race to the tomb. This motif is heightened by John's comment that it occurred "while it was still dark" (20:1). Darkness belongs to the Johannine light*-darkness dualism (cf. Jn 3:2; 11:10; 13:30) and here symbolizes a time of misunderstanding (cf. 20:9).

Yet misunderstanding is restricted primarily to 20:1-2. In the trip to the tomb (20:3-10) John goes even further than Luke in giving the empty tomb an apologetic function. He does this in several ways. The so-called rivalry between Peter and the Beloved Disciple make both witnesses (cf. Deut 19:15) of the import of the empty tomb. Scholars have debated the significance of this rivalry: both race to the tomb, but the Beloved Disciple arrives first; the Beloved Disciple delays entering, but Peter goes directly into the tomb. Upon entering, the Beloved Disciple simply "sees and believes" while Peter by implication does not.

Some see the two disciples as symbolic of conflict within the Johannine community, but the consistently positive portrait of Peter throughout the Fourth Gospel makes this doubtful. In the scenes where the two are juxtaposed (13:23-25; 18:15-16; 20:3-10; 21:7-8), there is a certain rivalry, but not at the expense of Peter. Peter typifies the dilemma of all disciples in coming to grips with the significance of Jesus. He is filled with questions (13:23-24), uncomprehending (20:6-7) and lacking vision (21:7-8). Yet Christians of every age have identified with him. The Beloved

Disciple is the archetypal disciple, the one whose authentic witness (cf. 19:35; 21:24) and belief (20:8-9) provide a model for successful discipleship.

The extensive description of the graveclothes (20:6-7) first of all proves that the body would not have been stolen. No thief would have taken the time to roll up the grave cloths so neatly. Moreover, the presence of the wrappings is proof that Jesus had indeed risen from the dead (cf. Jn 11:44, with Lazarus "coming forth" still wrapped in the linens). Finally, the Beloved Disciple believes even without benefit of the witness of "the Scriptures" (20:9). Faith response is one of the primary themes in John and is consistently linked with seeing and knowing (note "see" in 20:6, 8, 14, 18 and "know" in 20:2, 9, 13-14; 21:4, 12, 15-17). The tension between seeing and knowing typifies the resurrection narratives of both chapters 20 and 21. Commitment to Christ is deepened when vision leads faith to knowledge. Here is the first step: vision leading to faith.

The dramatic scene in which the distraught Mary comes to understanding (20:11-18) takes us more deeply into this encounter with the significance of the resurrection. Here the angels do not play a revelatory role as in the Synoptics. They encounter her grief (note the centrality of "weeping" in 20:11, 13, 15) and prepare for the presence of the Risen One. The repetition of question and response in the two scenes with the angels and Jesus (20:13, 15) produce a narrative tension. The reader would expect one of the two (the presence of angels or of the Risen Lord himself) to suffice. But her grief is too deep. This prepares for the marvelous removal of blindness from her eyes in 20:16. The good shepherd (10:1-18) calls her by name (cf. "calls his sheep by name," 10:3), and she recognizes him (cf. "his sheep follow him because they know his voice," 10:4). The results are notably different from 20:10, where the disciples simply return home in an anti-climactic conclusion to their trip to the tomb. Here Jesus commissions Mary as the first herald of the resurrection tidings.

However, the wording is difficult. First Jesus says, "Stop clinging to me," which could reflect a situation like Matthew 28:9 where the women "grasp" Jesus' feet. Yet John might have a deeper meaning in mind, with Jesus asking her not to "cling" to the old relationships (note she has just called him "my teacher"). The seeming contradiction between "I have not yet returned" and "I am (in the process of) returning" explains the tension. Jesus is no longer to relate to them as their teacher, for in the course of his appearances he is finishing his work and is on the verge of fulfilling the promise of the Farewell Discourse (*see* Farewell Discourse): To return to the Father so the

promised Paraclete can come (13:1, 3; 14:4, 25-26, 28; 15:26; 16:5, 7, 17, 28; 17:13; *see* Paraclete). All previous relationships have been transformed and so the disciples are now "brothers" (cf. Mt 28:10; cf. Jn 15:15); in this one word the forgiveness and reinstatement of the disciples is assured.

Yet Mary's message (20:18), as in the other Gospels, apparently has little effect. In the following scene the disciples are still cowering "for fear of the Jews" (20:19). There are quite a few similarities to Luke 24: "the first day of the week," "stood in the midst," "peace be with you," "showed them his hands and side," the commission to mission, the gift of the Spirit and the stress on forgiveness of sins. This is filled out with Johannine redactional emphases and is a unique, well-balanced story. Jesus, as he did with Mary, meets their fearful lack of faith head on. Mary needed to hear the voice of the good shepherd (*see* Shepherd, Sheep), but they need more—to recognize that he is indeed the same Jesus raised from the dead. Jesus not only supplies that need but promises them messianic peace; the threefold "peace is yours" (20:19, 21, 26) controls the second unit of the chapter and fulfills the promise of 14:1, 27 and 16:23. It is more than the basic greeting *"shalom";* it culminates the significance of the resurrection as bringing the peace of God to the believer. As the disciples see Jesus' hands and side (pointing, as in Luke, to the reality of the physical resurrection) they experience not only peace but joy in fulfillment of Jesus' promise in John 16:20-22.

The commission of John 20:21-23 is especially rich theologically. After the repeated "peace is yours," Jesus in a sense graduates the disciples and gives them the degree of "sent ones" (fulfilling 17:18). One of the pre-eminent concepts in Johannine christology is that of Jesus as "sent" by the Father. Based on the Jewish institution of a *šāliah,* a messenger or envoy authorized to carry out functions on behalf of another (*see* Apostle), Jesus as the sent one is presented as the living representative who reveals the Father to the world. In the Farewell Discourse the Spirit/Paraclete is "sent" by the Father (14:16, 26) and the Son (15:26; 16:7). Yet this chain of revelation is not complete, for now in a sense the entire godhead is involved in "sending" the disciples. The place of the Spirit is seen in the "Johannine Pentecost" of 20:22.

In fulfillment of John 7:39; 15:26 and 16:7, Jesus now "breathes" the Spirit into the disciples, enabling them to bear witness to the sin-sick world (cf. 14:16-17; 15:26-27; 16:7-11). In comparison with Acts 2, this is a private in-filling of the disciples while the later event at Pentecost is a public empowering which launches the church's mission (see Benoit). The mission is primary also in 20:23, a statement which, like its counterpart in Matthew 16:19, has occasioned great debate. The power to bind/retain and loose/forgive sins is a legal authority and depicts the disciples as full-fledged ambassadors of the new age, dispensing judgment or salvation, depending on people's acceptance or rejection of their message (cf. Jesus' authority as judge in 5:22, 27; 8:15-16; 9:39). In Matthew this saying deals with church discipline, while here it centers on mission evangelism.

The final episode (20:24-29) centers on the cynical doubt of Thomas and presents this doubt in even stronger fashion than does Luke 24:10-11. Thomas's declaration that he would not believe unless he could not only see but touch the wounds in Jesus' hands and side is an extension of John 20:20 in which Jesus showed the disciples his wounds in order to allay their fear. In the Fourth Gospel Thomas is a hardheaded realist who exemplifies the disciples' lack of understanding (11:16) and their confusion (14:5). Here he sums up their doubts as well.

As in the other episodes of chapter 20, Jesus acquiesces to his need, and Thomas's response is astonishing, culminating the high christology of John's Gospel with his confession "(You are) my Lord and my God." This goes beyond affirming the reality of the resurrection to interpreting its significance. The resurrection proves the validity of the emphasis throughout—that Jesus is one with the Father and therefore divine (cf. 1:1, 14; 3:18; 8:58; 10:30, 34-38; 12:45; 14:9; 17:11). Jesus' concluding statement in 20:29 is at one and the same time an admonition (against the demand for empirical proof) and a recognition (that Thomas had now come to faith). Yet the focus, as in John 10:16 and 17:20, is on the beatitude regarding future believers who will come to faith without benefit of such signs. It is they who are truly "blessed" (by God).

In John 20:30-31 the centrality of faith will conclude not only the resurrection narrative but the Gospel as a whole. Many have debated (partly on the basis of textual evidence for both a present and aorist verb) whether "believe" here is primarily evangelistic (thus the Gospel would be intended more for non-believers) or didactic (thus intended for believers). But the Fourth Gospel as a whole is clearly meant both to strengthen the faithful and to call non-believers to faith.

4.4.2. John 21. Most scholars assert that this is an appendix written some time after the completion of the Fourth Gospel, perhaps because of a crisis in the church as eyewitnesses were passing from the scene (cf. 21:18-23). The debate is whether it was penned by the Evangelist or by someone else. The latter is suggested by 21:24-25, which seems to be the imprimatur of a church official attesting to the validity of the Beloved Disciple's witness. Yet the chapter's language, style and emphases parallel the rest of the Gospel (see Osborne), and one can tentatively equate the authors of chapters 20 and 21. Much like John 20, the chapter divides into four episodes (21:1-14, 15-17, 18-19, 20-23) followed by a conclusion (21:24-25).

Many scholars find two separate traditions (an appearance and a meal story) in the account of the miraculous catch of fish (21:1-14). Others (e.g., Bultmann) have argued for a unified tradition. In either case the author has once again combined tradition and redaction into a theological whole. The primary thrust is the power of the Risen One which is made available to the church. While there is no overt mention of mission, the symbolism as well as general thrust of the chapter has led most scholars to apply this to the church in mission, both in terms of evangelism (21:1-8) and fellowship (21:9-13). Jesus' appearance by the Sea of Galilee is often linked with the similar miracle at the call of the disciples in Luke 5:1-11, which is thought to be a displaced miracle story. However, as Marshall points out, the differences outweigh the similarities, and it is better to see them as separate episodes. Nevertheless, the themes are similar, with Jesus asking for radical obedience and then granting an astounding catch of fish to demonstrate the new call to "catch" people.

The first theological element of the story (recalling the Emmaus journey of Lk 24) concerns a recognition scene. The disciples, after fishing all night and catching nothing, encounter a man whom they fail to recognize. Interestingly (unlike the calling of the disciples in Lk 5 or the story of the road to Emmaus in Lk 24), they fail to recognize Jesus even as they obey him (21:6). Only after the overwhelming catch does the Beloved Disciple recognize that it is the Risen Lord. As in John 20:8, the Beloved Disciple represents the quintessential disciple whose love gives him greater insight into spiritual truth. The order of events points the reader toward the significance of the Risen Lord for the success of all Christian endeavors.

The next aspect is the promised success of Christian mission under the power of the Risen Lord. This theme is premised on the great size of the catch—153 large fish (21:6, 11). Many ingenious solutions have been propounded for the significance of the 153 fish, but the majority today interpret it as a more general reference to the universally great results of the mission.

The final aspect is the meal scene, which many see

as a eucharistic celebration. While there are similarities to the feeding of the 5,000 (cf. Jn 21:13 and 6:11), there is no clear textual hint that this involves eucharistic connotations (while fish are used in second-century eucharistic services, there is no evidence that was used in the first century). The one thing that can be said with probability is that the emphasis is on a new level of fellowship (built upon a table-fellowship theme similar to that of Luke) between Jesus and his followers. This is seen in the strange statement that "none of the disciples dared to ask him, 'Who are you?' They knew it was the Lord" (21:12). On one level the old doubt is experienced (they "dared not ask"), but on a deeper level a new certitude has appeared (they "knew").

The reinstatement (or rehabilitation) of Peter (Jn 21:15-17) is certainly one of the better-known resurrection stories. Many a minister has preached from this text, distinguishing between the two levels of love* (*philos* and *agapē*), but this is a misjudgment. In reality four sets of synonyms are used in the passage (two terms for "love" and "know," three terms for "feed" and "sheep"). And it can be demonstrated that in the Fourth Gospel both *philos* and *agapē* are used for the love between Father and Son, both for the love between Father/Son and disciples, and both for the love which characterizes the community. In other words, the terms in all four cases are meant to be understood synonymously, and the purpose is to show the theological richness of the terms and the breadth of love between Jesus and his followers. The basic message of this episode deals with pastoral responsibility: Love for Jesus can only be complete when the leader tends his flock. This may also be the rehabilitation of Peter because the question "Do you love me more than these?" may recall Peter's promise to surrender his very life for Jesus if necessary (Jn 13:37), and the threefold repetition parallels Peter's threefold denial.

The final two sections concern the martyrdom of Peter (21:18-19) and the fate of the Beloved Disciple (21:20-23). The two are linked by the discipleship command "follow me" (21:19, 22), and this may indeed be the primary thrust of 21:18-23: whether one's life is cut short or one is given a long life in which to minister for the Lord, "What is that to you? You must follow me" (21:22).

Most scholars have accepted Bultmann's hypothesis that the prophecy of Peter's martyrdom adapts an alleged proverb regarding old age; like the elderly, Peter at the end of his life would be bound and led where he does not wish to go. This was a prophecy predicting "the kind of death (i.e., martyrdom) by which Peter would glorify God" (21:19). There has

been extensive debate over whether "stretch out your hands" is a reference to crucifixion (tradition tells us Peter was crucified upside-down). Those who doubt such a reference argue that the order (stretching the hands followed by being bound and led) does not fit crucifixion. However, if the language is understood to depict the bearing of the crossbeam to the place of crucifixion, the objection disappears. As such, this fulfills not only Peter's promise to follow Jesus to the death (Jn 13:36-38; cf. 12:23-24, 31-33; 17:1 on the connection between death and glorifying God) but the Johannine emphasis on Jesus carrying his own cross (19:17). The command "follow me" thereby has two meanings, referring both to Peter's present pastoral duties (21:15-17) and to his death as an act of discipleship in which he follows even Jesus' martyrdom via crucifixion.

Peter's query regarding the destiny of the Beloved Disciple (21:20-21) would be natural under the circumstances. The note that the Beloved Disciple "was following them" (21:20) ties the two sections together and supports the thesis that the main idea is discipleship. Jesus' reply to Peter's query is surprisingly harsh in tone ("What is that to you?"). In other words, Peter should not worry about someone else's calling and fate; his responsibility is to his own path of obedience. Yet from another perspective Peter's is the greater privilege—that of "following" his Lord in martyrdom. Many scholars interpret 20:23 (in light of 20:24) as indicating that the whole of 20:20-23 was written in light of the fact that the Beloved Disciple had died and the prophecy that he would live until the Parousia was unfulfilled. Yet this goes beyond the passage, which stresses, "*if* I want him to remain" (21:22-23). The message would be just as meaningful if the Beloved Disciple were approaching death and the church was concerned about the prophecy. Either way, the broader point remains the same: the key to the meaning of the resurrection for discipleship is a willingness to follow Jesus no matter what a person's God-ordained destiny might be.

See also BURIAL OF JESUS; DEATH OF JESUS; ESCHATOLOGY; HEAVEN AND HELL; LIFE; MIRACLES, MIRACLE STORIES; PREDICTIONS OF JESUS' PASSION AND RESURRECTION.

BIBLIOGRAPHY. J. E. Alsup, *The Post-Resurrection Appearance Stories of the Gospel Tradition: A History-of-Tradition Analysis* (Stuttgart: Calwer, 1975); P. Benoit, *The Passion and Resurrection of Jesus Christ* (New York: Sheed and Ward, 1969); E. L. Bode, *The First Easter Morning: The Gospel Accounts of the Women's Visit to the Tomb of Jesus* (Rome: Biblical Institute, 1970); R. E. Brown, *The Virginal Conception and Bodily Resurrection of Jesus* (New York: Paulist, 1973); W. L. Craig, "The

Empty Tomb of Jesus," in *Gospel Perspectives* 2: *Studies of History and Tradition in the Four Gospels*, ed. R. T. France and D. Wenham (Sheffield: JSOT, 1981); R. J. Dillon, *From Eye-Witnesses to Ministers of the Word: Tradition and Composition in Luke 24* (Rome: Biblical Institute, 1978); C. F. Evans, *Resurrection and the New Testament* (SBT 12; London: SCM, 1970); D. P. Fuller, *Easter Faith and History* (Grand Rapids: Eerdmans, 1965); R. H. Fuller, *The Formation of the Resurrection Narratives* (New York: Macmillan, 1971); P. Gardner-Smith, *The Narratives of the Resurrection* (London, 1926); G. R. Habermas, *Resurrection of Jesus: An Apologetic* (Grand Rapids: Baker, 1980); M. J. Harris, *Raised Immortal: Resurrection and Immortality in the New Testament* (Grand Rapids: Eerdmans, 1985); idem., *From Grave to Glory: Resurrection in the New Testament* (Grand Rapids: Zondervan, 1990); S. H. Hooke, *The Resurrection of Christ As History and Experience* (London: Darton, 1967); B. J. Hubbard, *The Matthean Redaction of a Primitive Apostolic Commissioning: An Exegesis of Matthew 28:16-20* (Missoula, MT: Scholars, 1974); J. Kremer, *Die Osterbotschaft der vier Evangelien* (Stuttgart: Katholisches Bibelwerk, 1968); G. E. Ladd, *I Believe in the Resurrection of Jesus* (Grand Rapids: Eerdmans, 1975); K. Lake, *The Historical Evidence for the Resurrection of Jesus* (New York: Putnam's, 1907); P. Lapide, *The Resurrection of Jesus: A Jewish Perspective* (Minneapolis: Augsburg, 1983); X. Leon-Dufour, *Resurrection and the Message of Easter* (London: Chapman, 1974); R. Mahoney, *Two Disciples at the Tomb. The Background and Message of Jn 20. 1-10* (Frankfurt: Peter Lang, 1974); I. H. Marshall, "The Resurrection of Jesus in Luke," *TynB* 24 (1974) 55-98; R. Martin-Achard, *From Death to Life* (Edinburgh: Oliver & Boyd, 1960); W. Marxsen, *The Resurrection of Jesus of Nazareth* (Philadelphia: Fortress, 1970); C. F. D. Moule, ed., *The Significance of the Message of the Resurrection for Faith in Jesus Christ* (London: SCM, 1968); idem., "The Post-Resurrection Appearances in the Light of Festival Pilgrimages," *NTS* 4 (1957-58) 58-61; G. W. E. Nickelsburg, *Resurrection, Immortality, and Eternal Life in Intertestamental Judaism* (HTS 26; Cambridge: Harvard University, 1972); G. O'Collins, *The Easter Jesus* (London: Darton, 1973); idem, *What Are They Saying about the Resurrection?* (New York: Paulist, 1978); idem, *Jesus Risen* (New York: Paulist, 1987); G. R. Osborne, *The Resurrection Narratives: A Redactional Study* (Grand Rapids: Baker, 1984); P. Perkins, *Resurrection: New Testament Witness and Contemporary Reflection* (New York: Doubleday, 1984); R. H. Smith, *Easter Gospels* (Minneapolis: Augsburg, 1983); K. Stendahl, ed., *Immortality and Resurrection* (New York: Macmillan, 1965); E. Sutcliffe, *The Old Testament and the Future Life* (London: Barnes, Oates & Washborn, 1964); N. J. Tromp, *Primitive Conceptions of Death and the Nether World in the Old Testament* (Rome: Pontifical Biblical Institute, 1969); J. Wenham, *Easter Enigma: Are the Resurrection Accounts in Conflict?* (Grand Rapids: Zondervan, 1984); U. Wilckens, *Resurrection* (Atlanta: John Knox, 1978).

G. R. Osborne

REVOLUTIONARY MOVEMENTS

Revolutionary movements were a response of some Jews to the injustice of Israel's* oppressors, particularly the Roman Empire (see Rome). The first century was one of the most violent epochs of Jewish history, with the cauldron of unrest reaching its apex in the destruction of Jerusalem (see Destruction of Jerusalem) by the Romans in A.D. 70. This in turn was punctuated by the mass suicide of Jewish rebel forces at Masada in 74. Sixty years later the smoldering embers from this war were fanned into flame by the Jewish leader Simon Bar Kokhba (or Kosiba), who led the second revolt against the Romans in 132-35.

The causes of this unrest were many and varied, but the following factors contributed to a milieu ripe for revolution: foreign military occupation, class conflicts, misconduct of Jewish and Roman officials, Hellenization (see Hellenism), burdensome taxation (see Taxes) and the Samaritan* situation. When the Roman army occupied a land, it was accompanied by thousands of civilians (wives, children, doctors, merchants, etc.). The army lived off the occupied country, pilfering its natural resources, enslaving members of its population, raping women and generally terrorizing the populace. The gentry of Palestine collaborated with the occupying forces and, in exchange for personal safety and affluence, aided Israel's oppressors. This collusion led to class conflict between the rich and the poor (see Rich and Poor), the faithful and the unfaithful, the rulers and the people (see Horsley and Hanson).

With conditions so difficult for the average Palestinian Jew, a good deal of revolutionary activity arose among them. This took a variety of forms.

1. Social Bandits
2. Messianic Pretenders
3. Revolutionary Prophets
4. Apocalypticists
5. The Fourth Philosophy and the Martyr Tradition
6. The Sicarii
7. The Zealots
8. Conclusion

1. Social Bandits.

Generally speaking, social banditry arises in agrarian

societies where peasants are exploited by the government or ruling class. Social bandits are the "Robin Hoods" of the land and usually increase during times of economic crisis, famine, high taxation and social disruption. The people of the land usually side with the bandits since they are champions of justice for the common people. These brigands usually symbolize the country's fundamental sense of justice and its basic religious loyalties.

In 57 B.C. Gabinius, proconsul in Syria, gave increased power to the nobility, thereby putting extreme pressure on the peasantry. In response the peasantry rebelled and not until a decade later was Palestine able to govern itself effectively again. It is therefore not surprising to find social banditry on the rise during and after this period of civil war and economic hardship. In fact, Josephus* reports that a certain Hezekiah led a band of social bandits who raided the Syrian border (*J.W.* 1.10.5-7 §§204-11; *Ant.* 14.9.2-4 §§159-74). Herod (*see* Herodian Dynasty), when he was governing Galilee,* caught and killed Hezekiah and many of his cohorts. These deaths, however, did not mark the end of social banditry. Years later Herod was still trying to exterminate the brigands (*J.W.* 1.16.2 §304). In 39-38 B.C. Herod assembled an army to track down these social bandits in order to consolidate his power as Rome's client king. Josephus notes that there was a "large force of brigands" (*J.W.* 1.16.1-2 §§303-4). Undoubtedly these social bandits were attacking the gentry who were in league with Herod.

The brigands retreated to the caves near Arbela, but were strong enough to continue to harass the gentry and challenge Herod's complete control of the land. Herod, not to be defied, formulated a strategy which Josephus narrates:

> With ropes he lowered [over the cliffs] the toughest of his men in large baskets until they reached the mouths of the caves; they then slaughtered the brigands and their families, and threw firebrands at those who resisted. . . . Not a one of them voluntarily surrendered and of those brought out forcibly many preferred death to captivity (*J.W.* 1.16.4 §311).

> An old man who had been caught inside one of the caves with his wife and seven children . . . stood at the entrance and cut down each of his sons as they came to the mouth of the cave, and then his wife. After throwing their dead bodies down the steep slope, he threw himself down too, thus submitting to death rather than slavery (*Ant.* 14.15.5 §§429-30).

Since subsequent sources from Herod's reign contain no references to social bandits, this attack may have extinguished them, but it is an argument from silence. Indeed, until the end of the reign of Agrippa I (A.D. 44), there is very little evidence for active resistance through social banditry. In Mark 15:27, however, two "bandits" are mentioned. Josephus also mentions a certain Tholomaus as a bandit leader (*Ant.* 20.1.1 §5). Tholomaus was likely not the only one because we read that Fadus (A.D. 44-46) set out to purge the "whole of Judea" of brigands (*Ant.* 20.1.1 §5). It seems that around the middle of the first century, probably as a result of a severe famine, social banditry sharply increased. Eleazar was one of these brigands and he enjoyed a twenty-year career (*J.W.* 2.13.2 §253). Actions taken by the authorities seem to have only proliferated Palestinian banditry. Cumanus (A.D. 48-52) took aggressive military action against the brigands, but they merely retreated into their strongholds and "from then on the whole of Judea was infested with brigands" (*Ant.* 20.6.1 §124).

Just before the Jewish revolt the rich and the poor were sharply polarized, taxation was very high, Roman oppression was grievous, justice was perverted and poverty was widespread. Consequently, Jewish banditry swelled to epidemic proportions so that a sizable number of the population were outlaws. This situation obviously took its toll on the gentry and contributed to the spiraling social unrest. Without doubt, social banditry is a major factor to be considered in any study of the First Jewish Revolt.

As the revolt broke out the bandits played an important role in resisting the Roman army's forays into Judea and Galilee, with brigand groups dominating the region of Galilee. The effectiveness of the brigands against Rome was due not only to their impressive military strength, but also to their favorable relationship with the peasants and their ability to build alliances with other rebel forces. The most important contribution made by these social bandits was their highly effective use of guerrilla warfare, which they demonstrated in routing the army of Cestius Gallus in A.D. 66. Ultimately, however, the brigands failed in their attempt to free Palestine from Roman rule.

2. Messianic Pretenders.

In Judaism prior to the first century there was no single, messianic expectation held by Jews (see Christ). Furthermore, *Messiah*, as a title, does not appear frequently in pre-Christian literature. Only after the destruction of Jerusalem in A.D. 70, when rabbinic theological reflection (see Rabbinic Traditions and Writings) standardized and popularized the term, does *Messiah* appear frequently, with essentially the

Jewish Revolutionary Movements and Conflict with Rome

c. 4 B.C.	Archelaus massacres Passover pilgrims in Jerusalem.
c. 36 A.D.	The Samaritan leads followers to Mt. Gerizim.
40	Caligula attempts to set up his statue in the Temple.
44	Herod Agrippa, the last Jewish king, dies.
45	Theudas persuades followers to accompany him to Jordan.
50s	The Egyptian leads followers to Mt. of Olives to experience fall of Jerusalem's walls.
c. 60-62	Unnamed prophet leads people into wilderness to receive salvation.
66	Florus, procurator, antagonizes Jews by taking from Temple treasury.
66-68	Simon bar Giora is popularly acclaimed king and later will play a leadership role in Jerusalem.
66 August	Jewish insurgents capture Antonia; Cestius, Syrian legate, attacks Jerusalem and retreats.
67 Spring-Fall	Roman army under Vespasian subdues Galilee.
67-68 Winter	Zealot party formed under Eleazar controls Jerusalem.
69 Spring	Turmoil divides Jerusalem with three parties vying for power.
70 Spring-Fall	Titus conquers and destroys Temple and Jerusalem.
74	Jewish rebels at Masada commit mass suicide.
132-135	Bar Kokhba leads second revolt against Rome.

same meaning in each usage. The scarcity of the term, however, *does not* suggest that there were no expectations of an anointed royal Jewish leader. The OT had begun to shape an expectation with its promises of a "branch" God would raise for David (see Son of David). This notion can be seen in Jeremiah 23:5-6 and Isaiah 11:2-9 where the "shoot from the stump of Jesse" shall "judge the poor with righteousness." Micah also contributed to the expectation by identifying Bethlehem as the home town of Messiah (Mic 5:2). But it is inappropriate to speak of a widespread OT expectation of Messiah.

During the period of Persian and Hellenistic domination, there is also little evidence of a Messianic hope. The promises to David and the prophecies of a future Davidic king were known during these periods (cf. Sir 47:11, 22; 1 Macc 2:57), but the fulfillment was postponed to the distant future. This is also probably the case during the persecution by Antiochus Epiphanes, although a few references may

be interpreted otherwise (cf. *1 Enoch* 90:9, 37-38; 1 Macc. 3:4). During the Hasmonean period, however, the hope of an anointed royal figure who would deliver Israel became more prominent. At Qumran (see Dead Sea Scrolls) there were apparently two anointed figures: a high priestly Messiah and the Prince of the Congregation, a lay head of the eschatological community. And in other Jewish literature of the period an anointed royal figure begins to emerge (*Pss. Sol.* 17). But among extant writings, only those coming from the period following the death of Herod (4 B.C.) refer unambiguously to a promised anointed figure.

After the death of Herod in 4 B.C. the Jews pressed Herod's son and heir apparent, Archelaus, for a number of reforms. During the Passover, when the demands reached a feverish pitch, Archelaus sent his armies into Jerusalem and massacred thousands of worshipping pilgrims. This action catalyzed revolt in every major area of Herod's kingdom, and some of these revolts took the form of messianic movements. Josephus identifies several leaders of these movements: Judas, the son of Ezekias (*Ant.* 17.10.5 §§271-72; *J.W.* 2.4.1 §56); Simon, servant of King Herod (*Ant.* 17.10.6 §§273-76); and Athronges (*Ant.* 17.7 §§278-85). Josephus clearly indicates that they aspired to be Israel's king (*J.W.* 2.4.1 §55; *Ant.* 17.10.8 §285). All of these messianic figures were of humble origins, and their followers were primarily peasants (see Barnett).

The principal goal of these revolutionaries was to overthrow Herodian and Roman domination of Palestine. In addition to fighting the Romans, these revolutionaries attacked the mansions of the aristocracy and the royal residences. This undoubtedly reveals the frustration of years of social inequality. In response, Varus, legate of Syria, dispatched two legions (6,000 troops each) and four regiments of cavalry (500 each). This was in addition to the troops already in Judea and the auxiliary troops provided by the city states and client kings in the area. In spite of this military might these messianic movements were difficult to subdue.

Because of the lack of sources it is difficult to identify any messianic movements between the above-mentioned revolts and those surrounding the First Jewish Revolt (except, of course, the followers of Jesus). With regard to the First Jewish Revolt, Josephus notes two messianic movements that bear mentioning. The first was led by Menahem, son of Judas, the Galilean, who

> took his followers and marched off to Masada. There he broke open king Herod's arsenal and armed other brigands, in addition to his own group. With these men as his bodyguards, he returned to Jerusalem as a king, and becoming a leader of the insurrection, he organized the siege of the palace (*J.W.* 2.17.8 §§433-34; cf. 2.17.5 §§422-42).

The second messianic movement mentioned by Josephus was built around Simon bar Giora (i.e., "Simon son of a proselyte"). In A.D. 66, at the outbreak of the war, Simon helped aid the Jews against Cestius by attacking the Roman rear guard. Simon's messianic movement was also motivated by the social oppression exerted by Israel's aristocracy. When Simon had gained control of the Judean and Idumean countryside, the citizens of Jerusalem invited him to lead the defense against Rome. After a power struggle in which he forced the Zealots and John of Gischala aside, Simon took control of Jerusalem. Simon was a strict disciplinarian and did well in his struggle against the Romans, but the Roman army was overwhelmingly powerful. Adorned in a white tunic and a purple cape

as the king of the Jews, Simon surrendered and was taken to Rome. There he was ritually executed. The messianic movement led by Simon was the largest of all the movements described by Josephus, lasting nearly two years. It may have been fueled by eschatological hopes.

The final messianic movement in recorded Jewish antiquity (A.D. 132-35) was led by Simeon bar Kokhba. Rabbi Akiba proclaimed that Simeon was indeed the Messiah, and a large portion of the Judean peasantry responded to the claim. Simeon had three years of independence and even minted coins (inscribed "Year 1 of the liberation of Israel"). When Rome sent in a massive army, Simeon resorted to guerrilla warfare and forced the Romans into a prolonged war of attrition. Nevertheless, the Romans finally did "annihilate, exterminate and eradicate" them from the land (*Dio Cassius* 59.13.3).

3. Revolutionary Prophets.

Despite the amount of prophetic activity prior to the first century, there is virtually no evidence for a Jewish expectation of the imminent return of the promised eschatological prophet (see Prophet, Prophecy). Nor were there vivid expectations for the appearance of the prophet-like-Moses* mentioned in Deuteronomy 18:18. There may have been some expectations for the return of Elijah (see Elijah and Elisha), but a claimant to this identity never materialized. Thus the appearance of any popular prophet of reputed eschatological significance was more than just the fulfillment of a popular expectation.

R. A. Horsley has helpfully distinguished between "popular prophetic movements" and "oracular prophets." The latter group was similar in character to classical oracular prophets such as Hosea or Jeremiah; they prophesied either judgment* or deliverance. Oracular prophets proclaiming deliverance appeared just prior to and during the First Jewish Revolt. Typically, those oracular prophets who pronounced judgment were not well received, being perceived by the establishment as a threat and consequently silenced.

3.1. Popular Prophets. Popular prophetic movements, on the other hand, had leaders who led sizable movements of peasants. The political authorities generally viewed this activity as insurrectionist and therefore forced a military confrontation. These prophets and their followers generally arose in anticipation of the appearance of God's eschatological liberation. This liberation was perceived as imminent, and when it arrived the Jews would be freed from their political bondage and would again govern

Palestine, the land God had given to them as their own possession. The leaders of these popular prophetic movements are described by Josephus in general terms:

> Impostors and demagogues, under the guise of divine inspiration, provoked revolutionary actions and impelled the masses to act like madmen. They led them out into the wilderness so that there God would show them signs of imminent liberation. (*J.W.* 2.13.4 §259; cf. *Ant.* 20.8.6 §168)

These popular prophets, preying upon social conditions, apparently taught that God was about to transform their society—characterized by oppression and social injustice—into a society marked by peace,* prosperity and righteousness (see Justice, Righteousness). Responding to the call, large numbers of peasants left their homes, their work and their communities to follow these charismatic leaders into the desert. There in the wilderness (see Mountain and Wilderness) they awaited God to manifest his presence through signs and wonders (see Miracles and Miracle Stories), purify his people (see Clean and Unclean) and unveil the eschatological plan of redemption which he had previously revealed to his prophet. At this juncture God himself would act and defeat Israel's enemies.

3.1.1. The Samaritan. The first of these prophets appeared when Pontius Pilate was procurator. Interestingly, this first movement appeared among the Samaritans. The Samaritans, like the Jews, revered Moses as the prophet and cultivated hopes for a future Mosaic prophet who was discussed in terms of "the restorer" (*taheb*). The *Taheb* would appear and restore Solomon's Temple on Mount Gerizim. Josephus has described one such Samaritan prophetic movement:

> Nor was the Samaritan nation free from disturbance. For a man who had no qualms about deceit, and freely used it to sway the crowd, commanded them to go up with him as a group to Mount Gerizim, which is for them the most sacred mountain. He promised to show them, when they got there, the holy vessels buried at the spot where Moses had put them. Those who thought his speech convincing came with arms and stationed themselves at a village called Tirathana. There they welcomed late-comers so that they might make the climb up the mountain in a great throng. But Pilate was quick to prevent their ascent with a contingent of cavalry and armed infantry. They attacked those who had assembled beforehand in the village, killed some, routed others, and took many into captivity. From this group Pilate executed the ringleaders as well as the most able among

the fugitives. (*Ant.* 18.4.1 §§85-87)

3.1.2. Theudas. Perhaps ten years later, about A.D. 45, a second major prophetic movement began. A certain Theudas (probably not the Theudas mentioned in Acts 5:36) organized one of these prophetic movements during the reign of Fadus (A.D. 44-46). Josephus also describes this prophet's ministry:

> When Fadus was governor of Judea, a charlatan named Theudas persuaded most of the common people to take their possessions and follow him to the Jordan River. He said he was a prophet, and that at his command the river would be divided and allow them an easy crossing. Through such words he deceived many. But Fadus hardly let them consummate such foolishness. He sent out a cavalry unit against them, which killed many in a surprise attack, though they also took many alive. Having captured Theudas himself, they cut off his head and carried it off to Jerusalem. (*Ant.* 20.5.1 §§97-98)

Obviously Theudas' movement attracted large numbers of Jews, so much so that Josephus hyperbolically states that Theudas deceived "most of the common people." Perhaps Theudas, in some sort of reverse Exodus, saw himself as the new Moses leading the people out of bondage (like Egypt) and across the Jordan (like the Red Sea) into the wilderness to be divinely prepared for the new conquest. Fadus, not taking any chances, acted decisively, thus showing his fear of such movements. The movement's swift annihilation almost certainly indicates that, unlike the messianic movements, this prophetic band was unarmed. Theudas' posthumous public humiliation by the ceremonial parading of his severed head was intended to send a stern warning to any would-be leaders of similar prophetic movements.

3.1.3. The Egyptian. Another movement, about ten years later, involved a Jewish prophet who originated from Egypt (*Ant.* 20.8.6 §§169-71; *J.W.* 2.13.5 §§261-63; cf. Acts 21:38). Josephus records that this prophet had a following of 30,000 who were to march from the wilderness to the Mount of Olives and then into Jerusalem. Felix sent Roman troops to slaughter all those involved in the movement. The Roman army easily defeated this prophetic band, even though the Egyptian himself escaped.

It seems fairly clear that these prophetic movements saw themselves in some sort of continuity with Israel's past great historical deliverances. They also had an eschatological dimension in their claim that God was about to deliver Israel and grant their autonomy in the promised land.

3.2. Oracular Prophets. The second category of

prophets, the oracular prophets, pronounced imminent divine deliverance; these prophets were concentrated around the First Jewish Revolt. Josephus (*J.W.*
6.5.3 §§300-309) recalls with considerable detail a
prophet named Jesus, son of Hananiah. This Jesus
appeared four years before the First Revolt, during a
time when Jerusalem "was enjoying great peace and
prosperity," and prophesied against Jerusalem for
seven years and five months. In the end he was struck
by a stone from one of the "missile engines" and
killed. As the war began and the number of prophets
increased, the Jews were urged to await help from God
(*J.W.* 6.5.2 §§286-87). Even at the end of the war, when
the Temple had already been sacked and set on fire,
a prophet pronounced to 6,000 refugees that they
would receive "tokens of their deliverance" and "help
from God." Every one of those 6,000 (*J.W.* 6.5.2 §§283-
84).

4. Apocalypticists.

The apocalypticists do not seem to have been a party
per se, but many of the Jews in the period 200 B.C.-
A.D. 100, including some of the oracular prophets,
apparently became persuaded of apocalyptic* eschatology.* For the apocalypticists Israel's situation
looked funereal. It was a depressing period of unfulfilled hopes, shattered eschatological dreams,
conflict with the ruling class, no authorized prophetic
spokesperson and, above all, periods of persecution
for the righteous who remained faithful to the Torah.
At the same time the Hellenized and severely compromised Jewish aristocracy was prospering. This
situation, perceived as a crisis by some within Israel,
forced a search for creative solutions. This gave rise
to an apocalyptic eschatology which represented a
new interpretation of human history and destiny with
new emphases and insights. While maintaining continuity with the prophetic eschatology of the
past, it developed in a direction that was at once
dualistic, cosmic, universalistic, transcendental and
individualistic.

Apocalyptic eschatology led to an emphasis on
other-worldliness and a disinterest in temporal affairs.
With its stress on cosmic dualism, the apocalypticists
understood the real battle to be in the heavenlies
between the powers. They were called upon therefore
to participate with Michael and the heavenly host in
the battle against evil (*see* Angels). The primary
weapon of this warfare was prayer, but it also included
personal holiness and faithfulness to the Torah, even
if that meant severe trial. In this way the apocalypticists could defeat Israel's oppressor and rightly be
classified a "revolutionary movement."

5. The Fourth Philosophy and the Martyr Tradition.

Josephus mentions, in addition to the Pharisees,*
Sadducees and Essenes, a "Fourth Philosophy."
Although many have linked this Fourth Philosophy
with the Zealots and the sicarii, recently Horsley has
persuasively argued that this identification is not
correct. Horsley notes that, on the one hand, Judas
the Galilean was a teacher with his own party (*J.W.*
2.3.3 §118), but on the other, Judas, as part of the
Fourth Philosophy "agreed with the views of the
Pharisees in everything except their unconquerable
passion for freedom since they take God as their only
leader and master" (*Ant.* 18.1.6 §23). At least prima
facie this Fourth Philosophy was a branch of Pharisaism in which certain teachers (e.g., Judas, Saddok,
etc.) advocated a strongly proactive stance against
Roman rule. Horsley suggests that the advocacy of
resistance against Rome was rooted in four interrelated concepts.

The first concept was related to taxes: to pay tax was
equivalent to slavery. Moreover, it was argued that
Scripture prohibited it (2 Sam 24). Taxes therefore
should not be paid to Rome. Second, Israel was a
theocracy and to be ruled solely by God. To submit to
foreign rule was no less than idolatry and a violation
of the first commandment: "Thou shalt have no other
gods before me." Third, God would work synergistical-
ly through his faithful people if they would stand firm
and actively resist their oppressors. Fourth, if Israel
would demonstrate their resistance, God would work
through them to establish his kingdom on earth. If the
worst case occurred, and they ended in ruin, they
would "at least have honor and glory for their high
ideals" (*Ant.* 18.1.1 §§5-7).

This resistance, Horsley notes, is never stated by
Josephus as armed rebellion. In fact they seem instead
to be willing sufferers: "They shrug off submitting to
unusual forms of death and stand firm in the face of
torture of relatives and friends, all for refusing to call
any person master" (*Ant.* 18.1.6 §23). Instead of armed
resistance, proponents of the Fourth Philosophy felt
that if they remained firm and resisted Rome through
obedience to the Torah, "God would eagerly join in
promoting the success of their plans, especially if they
did not shrink from the slaughter that might come
upon them" (*Ant.* 18.1.1 §5). If this understanding of
the Fourth Philosophy is correct, this group traced its
lineage to the martyrs under Antiochus Epiphanes IV.

The martyrological tradition, though it had antecedents, largely developed in the second century B.C.
when Israel was experiencing severe persecution. The
aristocracy had compromised its faith and was coop-
erating with the oppressing nation while those faithful

to Torah were experiencing severe persecution. The suffering of the righteous, however, was interpreted as "warfare." Part of the world view of these pious Jews was the belief that their innocent suffering would be so heinous that it would almost in a reflex action force God to act. This notion is most obvious in the *Testament of Moses:*

> If we . . . die, our blood will be avenged before the Lord and then his kingdom shall appear throughout all his creation. . . . he shall . . . avenge them of their enemies. . . . he will go forth from his holy habitation with indignation and wrath on account of his sons. (*T. Mos.* 9:7—10:3)

Underlying Taxo's speech to his sons is the belief that God is the *kinsman redeemer* (*gōʾēl*) of the righteous. This doctrine of divine vengeance taught that God protects and avenges the innocent and the vulnerable when they are victimized by social injustice (Ps 9:21; Is 5:4-5; 16:1-6; Jer 11:20; 15:15) or the spilling of blood (Gen 4:9; Deut 32:43; 2 Kings 9:7-10; Ps 9:11-12; Ezek 24:7-11; Joel 3:19-20). God is portrayed as not responding to the crime itself but to the prayers of the oppressed and the cry emanating from the slain victim's blood. "You shall not afflict any widow or orphan. If you afflict him at all, and if he does cry out to me, I will surely hear his cry . . . and I will kill you with the sword" (Ex 22:22-23). It is clear, therefore, that the martyrdom of the innocent Taxo and his sons was portrayed by the author of the *Testament of Moses* to provoke God to action because of the cry of innocent blood. God's response would be no less than the complete annihilation of Israel's enemies and the appearance of the eschatological kingdom (see Kingdom of God). This perspective also appears in literature from this period, especially 4 Maccabees.

Fourth Maccabees was written sometime just before the First Jewish Revolt as an encomium to the martyrs under Antiochus IV. The purpose of the book was not only to apotheosize the martyrs, but also to encourage those who were facing similar trials to stand firm and fight against the opposition with the weapons of obedience and suffering. In 4 Maccabees 9 the eldest brother, after enduring a series of appalling acts of cruelty, encourages his compatriots: "Fight the sacred and noble battle for religion. Thereby the just Providence of our ancestors may become merciful to our nation and take vengeance on the accursed tyrant" (4 Macc 9:24 NRSV).

In this verse the brother is exhorting the others not to compromise or to fight with illicit means. Rather, they are to hold fast and endure righteous suffering. In so doing they will defeat the king, because God will take vengeance upon the despot. This is equally as clear in the fourth brother's response to his torture and torments:

> Even if you remove my organ of speech, God hears also those who are mute. See, here is my tongue; cut it off, for in spite of this you will not make our reason speechless. Gladly, for the sake of God, we let our bodily members be mutilated. God will visit you swiftly, for you are cutting out a tongue that has been melodious with divine hymns. (4 Macc 10:18-21 NRSV; cf. 9:9)

Again, it is the innocent suffering which elicits God's response, and therefore his judgment is precipitated upon Israel's persecutors.

Atrocities against the innocent accumulate, and the cries for vengeance rise to heaven. Thus, as each martyr dies, he knows that the testimony against the tyrant is strengthened, and judgment upon the king has been brought nearer. We also see this clearly in 4 Maccabees 11:3, the fifth brother's speech, "I have come of my own accord, so that by murdering me you will incur punishment from the heavenly justice for even more crimes" (NRSV). This martyr believed that by his righteous suffering the perpetrator of the grave evil, Antiochus, would increase his guilt which would soon reach the level whereupon the divine Judge would necessarily act on behalf of justice. We can see this same theological construct operating in the sixth brother's poignant speech: "I also, equipped with nobility, will die with my brothers, and I myself will bring a great avenger upon you, you inventor of tortures and enemy of those who are truly devout" (4 Macc 11:22-23 NRSV; cf. 9:32).

The strength of this avenger is found in his armor, namely, his virtue. The *innocent* death of the martyrs promptly precipitates the avenging wrath of God; the righteous victims need not wait indefinitely—judgment is at hand. This fact obviously had motivated the fourth brother as he endured the agony: "Gladly, for the sake of God, we let our bodily members be mutilated. God will visit you swiftly" (4 Macc 10:20-21 NRSV; cf. 12:20). Vengeance has even been personified as one in pursuit of the archvillain. The author intimates that it does not take long for vengeance to stalk its prey and administer justice. "The tyrant Antiochus was both punished on earth and is being chastised after his death" (4 Macc 18:5 NRSV). And again in the same chapter we read, "For these crimes divine justice pursued and will pursue the accursed tyrant" (4 Macc 18:22 NRSV).

The author clearly perceives the martyrs' struggle as nothing less than war. It is a conflict of good against evil, God against Satan. This is again made clear from his comment after recounting the martyrs' eulogy:

Indeed it would be proper to inscribe on their tomb these words as a reminder to the people of our nation: "Here lie buried an aged priest and an aged woman and seven sons, because of the violence of the tyrant who wished to destroy the way of life of the Hebrews. They vindicated their nation, looking to God and enduring torture even to death. Truly the contest in which they were engaged was divine. (4 Macc 17:8-11 NRSV)

The mother of the seven sons has earned the complete respect of the author as an assailant in the battle against Antiochus. He gives her the title *warrior*, and remarks in amazement at her spirited combat. The writer goes so far as to credit her with the victory in the national struggle against the despot:

O mother, soldier of God in the cause of religion, elder and woman! By steadfastness you have conquered even a tyrant . . . you stood and watched Eleazar being tortured, and said to your sons in the Hebrew language, "My sons, noble is the contest to which you are called to bear witness for the nation. Fight zealously for our ancestral law. (4 Macc 16:14-16 NRSV)

In the battle against Antiochus the martyrs' role is to endure suffering and die; they are not to compromise or take up arms. The martyrs are merely to acquiesce to the tyrant's torture and sword. In performing this function they provide the key element in the battle which will defeat the enemies' forces and deliver the nation from their oppressors. This is a consistent theme throughout the book. Note these representative texts:

[the martyrs are] the cause of the downfall of tyranny over their nation, they conquered the tyrant. (4 Macc 1:11 NRSV)

O mother, who with your seven sons nullified the violence of the tyrant, frustrated his evil designs. (4 Macc 17:2 NRSV; cf. 9:30)

In most of the passages commenting on the effect of the martyrs' deaths, the martyrs themselves are the agents of victory. Thus, the contribution of the martyrs is the cardinal contribution in the war effort. It justifies the amount of time devoted in 4 Maccabees to the martyrs' heroics. Without them victory would have been impossible. In the author's opinion the martyrs single-handedly defeat Antiochus and his evil forces. They accomplish his downfall by clinging to their Law, not compromising and giving clear testimony to their faith. Righteousness is the lethal weapon in their struggle. They fight by persevering in their righteousness and patiently enduring torture and martyrdom; these are the martyrs' only weapons. Their foe is Antiochus, to be sure, but only insofar as he is in league with evil. The martyrs' real enemy is Satan, and their souls are at stake in the war. The heavenly host aids their effort, and by dying the martyrs are assured of victory. The picture is nearly identical to that contained in the martyrological literature written earlier.

This evidence suggests that the martyrs, by their innocent suffering, participated in the war against Antiochus and were the principal agents of victory. Their suffering was the decisive factor in the war effort. If Horsley is indeed correct in his identification of the Fourth Philosophy, these martyrs with their theology of martyrdom are likely to have been its antecedents, and the Fourth Philosophy held many, if not all, of the above-mentioned theological constructs. Although this was principally a theology of suffering, the outcome was victory over Israel's enemies and therefore no less a revolutionary movement than any other.

6. The Sicarii.

The name *sicarii* was derived from the weapon that they employed, a curved dagger like the Roman *sicae* (*Ant.* 20.8.10 §186). Josephus describes them thus:

A different type of bandit, known as *sicarii*, sprang up in Jerusalem. This group murdered people in broad daylight right in the middle of the city. Mixing with the crowds, especially during the festivals, they would conceal small daggers beneath their garments and stealthily stab their opponents. Then, when their victims fell, the murderers simply melted into the outraged crowds, undetected because of the naturalness of their presence. The first to have his throat cut was Jonathan the High Priest, and after him many were murdered daily (*J.W.* 2.13.3 §§254-56).

Some have identified these sicarii with the Zealots, others with social bandits, but as Horsley points out, these sicarii are a "different type" of bandit. As noted earlier, ordinary banditry is a rural activity in which the bandits pillage the wealthy. Because of their notoriety they normally congregate in hideouts and are always on the move. The sicarii, however, were urban assassins (not rural robbers) who, because of their secrecy, could live apparently normal lives (without fleeing to a hideout).

Obviously these violent tactics are not those of the Fourth Philosophy. Josephus, however, seems to suggest a connection in the leadership: "Menahem, leader of the sicarii at the outbreak of the revolt, was Judas of Galilee's grandson or perhaps son" (*J.W.* 7.8.1 §§253-54). If this conclusion is correct, it means that there must be some degree of correspondence between the religio-political orientation of these two groups. The assassination strategy is, however, a new development.

The tactics of assassinations first appeared during the reign of Felix in the fifties (cf. *J.W.* 2.13.3 §§254-57; 2.13.6 §§264-65; *Ant.* 20.8.5 §§163-65; 20.8.10 §§187-88). Unlike the social bandits who preyed on Roman petty officials and supply trains, the sicarii apparently attacked the Jewish aristocracy. These attacks took one of three forms. First, there were the selective assassinations of the ruling elite. The assassination of the high priest Jonathan is an example. Second, the sicarii slaughtered selected pro-Roman members of the Jewish aristocracy who lived in the countryside. These attacks also included plundering and burning selected aristocratic estates (*J.W.* 2.13.6 §§264-66; *Ant.* 20.8.6 §172). Third, the sicarii practiced terrorist hostage-taking.

These attacks of the sicarii helped precipitate a revolutionary situation. They led to distrust among the ruling elite, fear among the aristocracy and catalyzed the fragmentation of the social order. That which normally provided the upper class with security began to erode and vague feelings of anxiety and insecurity came in their place; anyone could be next. The fragmentation of the ruling class was inevitable; individual personal safety became society's most important value. Thus, instead of cooperative efforts to protect their interests, the ecclesiastical aristocracy and ruling class began hiring personal armies to protect their interests (*Ant.* 20.9.2 §§206-7). By responding with force and violence the ruling class further contributed to the breakdown of the social fiber and helped set the stage for the First Jewish Revolt.

The sicarii's role in the revolt itself seems quite limited. Apparently, at first they were not in the midst of the fray, but before long they entered the action. They helped in the siege of the Upper City and its aristocratic inhabitants (*J.W.* 2.17.6 §425); they also helped raze the royal palaces and the residence of the high priest Ananias. Shortly thereafter conflict broke out between the sicarii and the rest of the revolutionary forces. Within weeks the main body of the sicarii either had been executed, had retreated to Masada or had fled into hiding. The sicarii who occupied Masada sat out the rest of the war and preyed upon the surrounding countryside for their food supplies. In A.D. 73 the Romans attacked Masada, one of the last holdouts, only to discover that all of its occupants had committed suicide (*J.W.* 7.8.6-9.1 §§320-401).

7. The Zealots.

Although Luke mentions a certain Simon "the zealot"

(Lk 6:15; Acts 1:13) this is probably a characterizing name (namely, Simon was zealous), rather than a technical term identifying his affiliation with a revolutionary party (*see* Disciples). The Zealot party per se was not formed until the winter of A.D. 67-68. The party's origins can be traced back to the clash between the Roman procurator Florus (A.D. 64-66) and the Jerusalem citizenry. During his term Florus had pilfered the Temple* treasure, allowed his army to loot the city and attempted to capture and control the Temple. With such abuses left without redress and the city in a rebellious mood, the lower priests began to agitate for war. The Temple captain, Eleazar, son of Ananias, provided leadership and, together with the lower priests and the revolutionary leaders of the populace, decided to terminate the sacrifices offered twice each day on behalf of Rome and the Roman emperor (*J.W.* 2.17.2 §§409-10). Previously, the offering of this sacrifice had been negotiated as a satisfactory substitute for emperor worship and therefore was a tangible sign of Jewish loyalty to Rome. Thus the refusal to offer sacrifices was tantamount to a declaration of war; it broke the peace treaty, and Israel was now regarded outside the Roman Empire (*J.W.* 2.17.3 §415). The Temple was subsequently cleansed and Israel began again to show its absolute fidelity to the Torah. God was about to shower the nation with blessing.

The chief priests and leading Pharisees, however, resisted the changes, and civil war soon broke out. Eleazar was joined by the sicarii (*J.W.* 2.17.5 §423) and together they defeated their rivals. But a power struggle ensued, with the sicarii battling Eleazar and his faithful; the sicarii were defeated and took refuge in Masada. Eleazar was now in control in Jerusalem. In August of 66, however, Cestius, the governor of Syria, bolstered with Roman forces, attacked Jerusalem. Through an unexpected turn of events Cestius abandoned the siege of Jerusalem and, in the process of retreat, lost a good number of troops. Buoyed by their success, most of Jerusalem and Judea rallied around the revolutionary cause. Now basically unified, the nation named Ananus, the high priest, as its head. The traditional high priests resumed their positions, and Eleazar joined them as general to Idumea (*J.W.* 2.20.4 §566).

The Romans then began their reconquest. During the summer and fall of A.D. 67 they had subdued Galilee and were marching through Judea. The brigands and revolutionary forces in these areas were retreating. As these fugitives, as well as those from Idumea and Perea, took refuge in the city, their own views seemed to resonate with those lower priests who had started the revolt with the cessation of the sacrifices on behalf of Rome. This new coalition is the group Josephus calls "zealots." The Zealots agitated against the ecclesiastical aristocracy and soon decided to assert themselves. First, they attacked some Herodian nobles against whom they still had some "ancient quarrel" and who also were accused of treason (*J.W.* 4.3.4-5 §§140-146). These "ancient quarrels" almost certainly were focused on those members of the nobility who were wealthy landowners with a large number of peasants indebted to them. The Zealots, regardless of the Roman threat, were also fighting a class war against the Jewish aristocracy.

Obviously, this activity against the Herodian nobility would give rise to anxiety throughout the rest of Israel's upper class. If this discriminate violence were not enough, the Zealots elected by lot their own people to priestly offices—even installing an uneducated lay person in the office of high priest. Without doubt the Zealots were conspiring for political control. Given the inflammatory nature of this Zealot activity, it is no surprise that the Jewish aristocracy immediately turned on the Zealots and viciously attacked them (*J.W.* 4.3.6-8 §§147-57). Incited by Ananus and Jesus son of Gamala, both high priests, the people of Jerusalem forced the Zealots into the inner court (*J.W.* 4.3.12 §§197-204). Trapped in the Temple, the Zealots contacted sympathizers outside of Jerusalem to free them (*J.W.* 4.4.1 §§224-32). The Idumeans responded, freed the Zealots and slaughtered Ananus and Jesus, son of Gamala. While they were at it, a number of other nobles also were assassinated (*J.W.* 4.4.2-3 §§233-53). There was yet another purge of Jerusalem's nobility, and this one also included many who were formerly in power, as well as the wealthy.

Within the Zealot ranks, however, all was not well. Many of the Zealots were not responsive to the dictatorial ways of John of Gischala. Since John could not gain absolute authority among the Zealots, he broke away to form his own revolutionary faction (*J.W.* 4.7.1 §§389-96). John's independence, however, was short-lived. The messianic movement by Simon bar Giora was a threat to the Zealot regime in Jerusalem, and a good part of John's army deserted so that John and the Zealots again formed an alliance. This alliance, however, did not prevent Simon bar Giora from attempting to liberate the city from the Zealots and John of Gischala (*J.W.* 4.9.11 §§571-76). Simon was able to force the Zealots back into the Temple (*J.W.* 4.9.12 §§577-84). The faction-prone Zealots split over the leadership of John. Josephus records that for a time there was even a three-way

battle raging. Simon bar Giora, in control of Jerusalem, pressed in upon John of Gischala who was fighting to control the Temple courtyard and was caught between Simon and the rest of the Zealot party who were in the inner court above the Temple (*J.W.* 5.1.1-3 §§1-12). Shortly thereafter, John was able to reconcile himself to the rest of the Zealot party, although he was only able to accomplish it by way of trickery. John of Gischala was now the Zealot leader again (*J.W.* 5.2.3-3.2 §§67-106).

By this time the Romans were at Jerusalem's gates; this threat galvanized the rival factions to form a united front. The Jews, however, were no match for the Romans. During the siege the Zealots were the smallest of the rival groups and therefore had the least significant role to play (2,400 Zealots, 6,000 others under John of Gischala, 15,000 under Simon bar Giora). Nevertheless, the Zealots, in spite of their less significant role did fight courageously to the end in cooperation with their Jewish rivals against the overwhelming military strength of the Romans (*J.W.* 5.6.1-9.3 §§248-374).

The Zealots should be remembered primarily for their thwarting of the nobility's plan to negotiate a settlement with the Romans. Moreover, the Zealots were not the Fourth Philosophy mentioned by Josephus; indeed, they were not a sect or philosophy at all. Furthermore, the Zealots were not in the vanguard among those who were agitating for rebellion, but once the revolt was underway and the only choice was to fight or to flee, they stayed and fought to the death.

8. Conclusion.

The centuries leading up to the First and Second Jewish Revolts were very painful for the Jewish nation. The political subjugation by foreign nations was extremely difficult, as well as the erosion of religious, cultural and socioeconomic structures. Israel's general response to the unrest was revolt, but not always via armed rebellion. The social bandits, Zealots, sicarii and messianic pretenders generally advocated armed rebellion and agitated for a military solution. These groups, however, often fought among themselves, significantly weakening their impact. The other response, generally advocated by the apocalypticists, prophets and martyrs, believed in waiting upon God who, they believed, was about to intervene and personally defeat the enemy. The Fourth Philosophy, generally identifiable as having a genealogical link with the Maccabean martyrs, advocated suffering and martyrdom in order to move God to deliver Israel. None of these responses, however, was adequate to deal with the Roman threat. After the Second Jewish

Revolt (A.D. 132-35) Israel lost its political identity for almost two millennia.

See also APOCALYPTIC; DESTRUCTION OF JERUSALEM; JUDAISM; ROME; TAXES.

BIBLIOGRAPHY. S. A. Applebaum, "The Zealots: The Case for Reevaluation," *JRS* 61 (1971) 165; E. Bammel and C. F. D. Moule, eds., *Jesus and the Politics of His Day* (Cambridge: University Press, 1984); P. W. Barnett, "The Jewish Sign Prophets—A.D. 40-70—Their Intentions and Origin," *NTS* 27 (1981) 679-97; S. G. F. Brandon, *Jesus and the Zealots* (Manchester: University Press, 1967); O. Cullmann, *Jesus and the Revolutionaries* (New York: Harper and Row, 1970); W. R. Farmer, *Maccabees, Zealots and Josephus* (New York: Columbia University, 1956); W. J. Heard, "The Maccabean Martyrs' Contribution to Holy War," *EvQ* 58 (1986) 291-318; D. Hellholm, ed., *Apocalypticism in the Mediterranean World and the Near East* (Tübingen: J. C. B. Mohr, 1983); M. Hengel, *Was Jesus a Revolutionist?* (Philadelphia: Fortress, 1971); idem, *The Zealots* (Edinburgh: T. & T. Clark, 1988); R. A. Horsley and J. S. Hanson, *Bandits, Prophets and Messiahs* (New York: Winston, 1985); P. Kingdon, "Who Were the Zealots and Their Leaders in A.D. 66?" *NTS* 17 (1970) 60-75; J. Neusner, *Messiah in Context* (Philadelphia: Fortress, 1984); D. M. Rhoads, *Israel in Revolution: 6-74 C.E.* (Philadelphia: Fortress, 1976); D. S. Russell, *The Message and Method of Jewish Apocalyptic* (Philadelphia: Fortress, 1974); S. Safrai and M. Stern, *The Jewish People in the First Century* (2 vols.; Philadelphia: Fortress, 1976); E. Schürer, *The History of the Jewish People in the Age of Jesus Christ* (175 B.C.—A.D. 135), rev. and ed. G. Vermes and F. Millar (3 vols.; Edinburgh: T. & T. Clark, 1973-79) vol. II; M. Smith, "Zealots and Sicarii, Their Origins and Relations," *HTR* 64 (1971) 1-19.

W. J. Heard

REWARDS. *See* ETHICS OF JESUS.

RHETORICAL CRITICISM

Rhetorical criticism is the analysis of portions of the Gospels or an entire Gospel according to Greco-Roman and modern rhetorical and literary conventions and theories. It is the effort to understand the Gospel writer's message, its structure and persuasive techniques, how individual passages as well as the Gospel as a whole were intended to influence an audience, and how various audiences actually would respond.

1. Introduction
2. The Muilenburg Approach
3. The Greco-Roman Approach
4. The Distinctive Role of the Chreia
5. The Literary-Critical Approach

1. Introduction.

Rhetorical criticism is one of several tools for interpreting the Gospels. It is best used in conjunction with the traditional methods of source (*see* Synoptic Problem), form* and redaction* criticisms. The insights of each informs the others. For example, the findings of source criticism provide the working assumption that Mark and Q* are literary sources for Matthew and Luke. Redaction criticism clarifies how the writer of Matthew and Luke adapted the material of Mark and Q to suit their rhetorical needs. Form criticism partially explains how Gospel tradition received its current shape as a result of the rhetorical needs of worship,* teaching and preaching.

Rhetorical criticism of the Gospels has precursors in studies at the turn of this century. However, these dealt mostly with stylistics, neglecting the important matters of the formation of argumentation (invention) and the placement of these in a persuasive order (arrangement). Rhetorical criticism, which today uses a more comprehensive system encompassing invention, arrangement and style, is still in its infancy. It exhibits many exciting trends that are not yet fully evaluated, developed or integrated. The following approaches are those currently definable within published literature.

2. The Muilenburg Approach.

J. Muilenburg originated a proposal and methodology for the use of rhetorical criticism in biblical studies in general. In his presidential address to the Society of Biblical Literature in 1968, Muilenburg pointed out the deficiency of form criticism in that it emphasizes the conventional elements of literary genre and composition to the neglect of the individual and unique features of a given pericope—its artistry. He proposed supplementing form criticism with an examination of the linguistic patterns of a pericope in order to discover the author's thoughts and the process by which the author put his or her thoughts into written language.

The methodology Muilenburg offered delimits the literary unit and observes major motifs, points of climax and inclusio. This is followed by discovering the structure of the unit (macro-structure) and the configuration of its component parts (micro-structure). Clues to these are found in features such as rhetorical questions, parallelism, repetitions, antitheses, strophes and chiasm. The interrelationship of the structure and its parts gives insight into the meaning of the text as a whole.

Muilenburg's methodology has been utilized in Gospel studies. One significant work is J. Dewey's study of Mark 2:1—3:6. Dewey first identifies literary devices such as insertion, intercalation and concentric structures, then describes how each device functions in the text, and finally sees what rhetorical stress shows us about the theological intentions and emphases of the narrative. She concludes that concentric literary patterns are a key feature organizing Mark's Gospel.

3. The Greco-Roman Approach.

Rhetorical criticism is also conducted using the principles of persuasion that were current within the era of the Gospels themselves. The primary materials are the rhetorical handbooks of the Greco-Roman age, particularly those of Aristotle, Cicero and Quintilian. These handbooks contain discussions of how to speak persuasively, and thereby provide modern-day scholars with tools to evaluate the rhetorical features of the Gospels.

Very early in the development of this approach W. Kurz demonstrated that Luke's christological proofs that Jesus was the prophesied Christ are the rhetorical *enthymeme* as understood by Aristotle. *Enthymemes* are arguments constructed from a premise and conclusion with one premise unstated. In light of other rhetorical conventions evident in Luke-Acts, he argued for the likelihood that Luke was trained in rhetoric as part of his secondary education.

The classicist G. Kennedy has proposed a five-step methodology for rhetorical criticism using Greco-Roman rhetorical handbooks.

(1) Determine the *rhetorical unit*.

(2) Analyze the rhetorical situation's three components of *exigence* (the reason the author wrote), the *audience* and the *constraints* brought to bear on the exigence by the rhetor.

(3) Determine the *species of rhetoric*, the *question* and the *stasis*. The three species are *judicial* (the rhetoric of accusation and defense), *deliberative* (persuasion and dissuasion) and *epideictic* (praise and blame). The question is any subject on which two or more opinions can be offered. The four stases, or bases for a cause, are fact, definition, quality and legal.

(4) Analyze *invention, arrangement* and *style*. Invention is the mustering of evidence to support a position. Arrangement is the positioning of this supporting material into *exordium* (introduction), *narratio* (exposition of facts), *partitio* (listing of the propositions), *probatio* (support for the propositions), *refutatio* (refutation of the opposition) and *peroratio* (summary and emotional appeal). Style is choosing the language and figures of speech and thought to best convey position.

(5) Evaluate the *rhetorical effectiveness* of the material.

Kennedy has provided several cursory rhetorical analyses of select portions of the Gospels. Regarding the Sermon on the Mount* (Mt 5—7), the rhetorical situation as presented by Matthew is an outdoor address on a hill to the disciples and the crowds who are attracted to him as a healer (4:24-25). The healing miracles, fulfillment of OT prophecies, and the disciples and eyewitnesses provide external proof. The exigence is provided by Jesus' understanding of his mission and his anticipation of its effect. The species of rhetoric is deliberative, for it gives advice on a course of action advantageous to the audience regarding the future (5:29-30; 7:24). The focus is what should be done and by whom, so the stasis is one of fact. The arrangement is an *exordium* (The Beatitudes 5:3-16) followed by a *propositio* (5:17-20) with two propositions: the Law* and prophets are fulfilled (5:17) and the righteousness of the audience must exceed that of the Pharisees* and scribes* (5:20). These propositions are developed in the *probatio* in 5:21-48 and 6:1-18 and 6:19—7:20 respectively. The first unit is supported mainly by ethos (authority) and pathos (appeal to emotion), and the second by logos or enthymemes. The epilog (7:21-27) contains both summary (7:21-23) and appeal to pathos (7:24-27).

The Sermon on the Plain (Lk 6:17-49) does not have the clear structure of the Sermon on the Mount. Kennedy suggests that the *exordium* is 6:20-26, the *propositio* 6:27-31, the *probatio* 6:32-45, and the *peroratio* 6:46-49. The species seems to be deliberative overall, but contains much epideictic.

Kennedy sees the Sermon on the Mount as Matthew's collection of material representative of Jesus' speeches to the crowds and not a verbatim account of a sermon delivered at one particular time. Luke's Sermon on the Plain may simply be a condensed version of what was typical of Jesus' preaching.

Kennedy also analyzes the Farewell Discourse* of John 13—17. It is classified as epideictic rhetoric, particularly the subspecies of consolation. The entire discourse is a rhetorical unit. The rhetorical situation is the Last Supper,* and the exigence is the distress of the disciples as Jesus' death draws near and their deficient understanding of his mission.

The *exordium* is 13:1 which introduces the topics of the remainder of the discourse. The *narratio* follows in 13:2-30 and the *propositio* in 13:31-35, restating the topics of the *exordium*. The consolation proper is the *probatio* of 14:1—16:28. The epilog is 16:29-33, with a larger epilog being composed of all of chapter 17.

On the rhetoric of the Gospels in general, Kennedy, like Kurz, states that Luke may have had some formal rhetorical training. All the Gospels, however have rhetorical features, especially those common to encomiastic biography (*see* Gospel [Genre]). Matthew most widely uses the elements of rhetoric, particularly in his interest to provide the audience with logical proof that Jesus was the Messiah (*see* Christ). Mark is an example of radical Christian rhetoric, rhetoric characterized by absolute claims of authority* devoid of logical proof. Luke is noted for his prosopopoeia, recreating speech and dialog for characters as they are likely to have occurred on an occasion (e.g., Magnificat; *see* Mary's Song). Of the Gospel writers Luke is the closest to a classical biographer. John is noted for its elevated style or *hypsos* created by great thoughts, strong emotion, elevation in the use of figures, choice of diction and arrangement of words.

4. The Distinctive Role of the Chreia.

Central to rhetorical criticism of the Gospels is the ancient chreia (pl. chreiai; *see* Chreia/Aphorism). A *chreia* is a concise saying or action that is attributed to a person and useful for daily living. The chreia was common to both oral and written expression in the Greco-Roman world, and was particularly a feature of ancient biography. The chreiai are the literary form of the sayings and actions of Jesus which are recounted in the Gospels, particularly the Synoptics. An example would be: "Now after John was arrested, Jesus came into Galilee, preaching the gospel of God, and saying, 'The time is fulfilled, and the kingdom of God is at hand; repent and believe in the gospel' " (Mk 1:14-15 RSV). Discussions of the chreiai are found in the school-book exercises of Greece and Rome called *Progymnasmata*.

An understanding of the chreiai gives us new insights into the formation, oral transmission and literary composition of the Gospel tradition. The sayings and actions of Jesus circulated as chreiai, both orally and as written collections. The Synoptic Gospel writers used them in conventional ways to produce rhetorically effective biographies. Since the chreia was a major part of the curriculum in the ancient grammar school, the Synoptic Gospel writers' knowledge of the chreia and their ability to use it makes it most probable that they had at least a grammar-school education. The discovery of the use of chreiai by the Synoptics has reshaped and reintroduced old issues. The study of ancient chreiai indicates that the practice of manipulating a chreia in a variety of ways (particularly recitation and expansion) introduced minor or major modifications in the wording of the chreia, though the meaning remained essentially the same. These findings illumine the issue of the relation of

the words and deeds of Jesus related in the Gospels to those of the historical Jesus. The sayings and actions of Jesus were placed in chreiai form, thus providing some parameters for their faithful transmission in tradition. However, we must account for some elaboration of the wording of the sayings and actions of Jesus in the formation and transmission of the chreiai, as well as in their incorporation into the Gospel framework. Those who passed on the Jesus tradition and the Gospel writers themselves edited the chreiai. It was customary to embellish internal description, expand brief dialogs and align the point of the *chreia* with the needs of the discourse, although without change in meaning.

5. The Literary-Critical Approach.

Rhetorical criticism is also performed using modern literary criticism. In literary criticism a distinction is often made between the content of the narrative (the story) and the form of the narrative (the rhetoric). The content of the narrative involves narrator, characters, settings, narrative patterns and plot. The form of the narrative includes how rhetorical devices are used to create the desired impact of the narrative on the reader. Thus there is a great deal of overlap between rhetorical and literary criticism. One particularly notable work by R. Tannehill studies the rhetorical form of Jesus' sayings in the Synoptics and how their form and content challenge the audience to accept new insight and action.

The Gospels of Mark and John have received careful scrutiny from this perspective. These studies try to determine how the rhetoric of the Gospel narrative establishes authority with and has its impact on the reader. It does so through a study of narrator, style and narrative patterns. In one prominent study Rhoads and Michie conclude that Mark is an omniscient narrator unbound by time or space, speaking from an ideological point of view, who can give the inside view of the characters' minds. Mark's style is terse, lively, direct, with rapid movement of action and characters. Episodes in series of three, two-step progressions, concentric patterns, repetition, questions and framing are characteristic narrative patterns in Mark.

5.1. Socio-Rhetorical Criticism. Another promising approach using literary criticism, first espoused by V. Robbins, is that of *Socio-Rhetorical Criticism*. Using the literary criticism of K. Burke, Robbins stresses that an author persuades an audience by using forms which cause the audience to identify with the author's interests. From the identification of interests the author establishes rapport with the audience. Robbins analyzes and compares the intermingling of social, cultural, religious and literary traditions and forms of Mark and the ancient Mediterranean world. Mark is found to be a biography depicting the career of a disciple-gathering teacher* who enacted a system of thought and action. Mark portrays Jesus as a composite of the biblical prophets* and the Greco-Roman philosopher-teachers. In so doing he makes Jesus understandable and identifiable to first-century Mediterranean society.

5.2. Reader-Response Criticism. Another subcategory of literary criticism, Reader-Response Criticism, seeks to investigate how the reader responds to a text. It seeks to understand how an author controls and directs the reader and how a reader creates meaning from interaction with the text. It attempts to gauge the rhetorical impact of a manuscript on its various types of readers. J. Staley has analyzed the implied reader in the Fourth Gospel, that is, the reader that the author has invited us to become as we read. He discovers that the author of the Gospel used the rhetorical strategy of "reader victimization" in which the implied reader is led to assume he or she understands and is an insider, only to be forced to be a misunderstanding outsider. After each instance of victimization the implied reader is made an insider again through irony and inside information.

Rhetorical criticism is clearly an interdisciplinary approach to the Gospels which has already yielded many new insights into the message of the Gospels. It will continue to be a major tool in Gospel interpretation.

See also CHREIA; LITERARY CRITICISM.

BIBLIOGRAPHY. J. R. Butts, "The Chreia in the Synoptic Gospels," *BTB* 16 (1986) 132-38; J. Dewey, *Markan Public Debate: Literary Technique, Concentric Structure, and Theology in Mark 2:1-3:6* (SBLDS 48; Ann Arbor: Scholars, 1980); G. A. Kennedy, *New Testament Interpretation through Rhetorical Criticism* (Chapel Hill: University of North Carolina, 1984); W. S. Kurz, "Hellenistic Rhetoric in the Christological Proof of Luke-Acts," *CBQ* 42 (1980) 171-95; B. L. Mack, *Rhetoric and the New Testament* (Minneapolis: Augsburg Fortress, 1989); B. L. Mack and V. K. Robbins, *Patterns of Persuasion in the Gospels* (Sonoma, CA: Polebridge, 1989); J. Muilenburg, "Form Criticism and Beyond," *JBL* 88 (1969) 1-18; J. L. Resseguie, "Reader-Response Criticism and the Synoptic Gospels," *JAAR* 52 (1984) 307-24; D. Rhoads and D. Michie, *Mark As Story: An Introduction to the Narrative of a Gospel* (Philadelphia: Fortress, 1982); V. Robbins, *Jesus the Teacher: A Socio-Rhetorical Interpretation of Mark* (Philadelphia: Fortress, 1984); J. L. Staley, *The Print's First Kiss: A Rhetorical Investigation of the Implied Reader in the Fourth Gospel* (SBLDS 82; Atlanta: Scholars, 1988); R. C. Tannehill, *The Sword of His Mouth* (SBLSS 1; Missoula: Scholars; Philadelphia: Fortress, 1975). D. F. Watson

RICH AND POOR

In the first-century Palestinian world the main classes were a relatively small wealthy class and a large poor, peasant and artisan class, in some contexts referred to as "the people of the land." Judaism* dealt with this social disparity by accepting it and encouraging the wealthy to give alms to the poorest of the poor. Jesus, however, saw wealth as a hindrance to entering the kingdom of God (*see* Kingdom of God) and pronounced a blessing on those poor who were seeking God. He taught his followers a radical ethic (*see* Ethics of Jesus) of giving based on trust in God* and the coming of the kingdom (i.e., an eschatological perspective) and lived out in the context of the new community of disciples.* The texts indicate that Jesus is to be understood from within this eschatological perspective as a Jewish sage, not as a lawgiver or a teacher* of an unattainable ideal.

1. Rich and Poor in First-Century Judaism
2. Rich and Poor in the Teaching of Jesus
3. Eschatology and the Ethic of Jesus

1. Rich and Poor in First-Century Judaism.
The material in the Gospels on rich and poor is set against a background of the social world of Jesus' day and the response that Judaism was making to that world. It was not without reason that Jesus has more to say on this topic than on almost any other he chose to address.

1.1. The Social World of First-Century Judaism. In the first-century Palestinian world there were essentially two major groups of people, the rich and the poor. The rich included especially the wealthy high-priestly clans (*see* Priest and Priesthood). Consisting of four extended families, they must be distinguished from the lower clergy (e.g., Zachariah of Luke's birth narrative) who were in general poor and felt oppressed by the high-priestly group. It was the chief priests who not only profited from the sacrifices offered in the Temple* (the lower clergy officiated for only two weeks a year, while the high-priestly clans were always present) but also controlled the considerable commerce associated with that sacrifice and other religious activities (e.g., the activity noted in Mk 11:15-19).

Another wealthy group was the Herodian* family and retinue, whose political power was easily translated into wealth. It has been estimated that Herod and later his family may have owned more than half the land in his dominions. Gifts of land to faithful followers were not unusual.

The third group of wealthy people were the remnants of the older Jewish aristocracy (although much of their land was confiscated by Herod and his sons) and individuals who had become rich through trade, tax* farming or the like. To be considered truly rich one had to own land, so a person would purchase landholdings as he became wealthy, but such a person would not farm his own land. Instead, he rented it to tenant farmers and spent much of his time on civic and religious affairs in the city (principally, Jerusalem). This system led to the abuse of tenants and hired laborers, which mistreatment was seen by the wealthy as perfectly legal, but was viewed by the poor as totally unjust (cf. Jas 5:1-6).

A final group of wealthy people were the prosperous merchants who had not yet joined the land-owning aristocracy, although like them they controlled much of the economic life of the country. Both the land-owning and non-land-owning groups were deeply resented by the people of the land. It was no accident that during the Jewish revolt of A.D. 66-70, when the common people got the upper hand in Jerusalem, one of their first acts was the burning of the debt records and the slaughter of many of the aristocrats.

Religiously and socially then, the four groups of wealthy people could be split into two groups: (1) observant Jewish leaders and (2) those wealthy persons associated with the Herodians and Romans, whose power gained them a certain acceptance, but who were considered to be moral outcasts (i.e., "Jews who have made themselves Gentiles"), although obviously one dared not despise them too openly. Both groups at times used their power to oppress the lower classes. The less religious group did it through sheer abuse of power. The observant group justified their oppression through legal interpretation, which in the eyes of Jesus was viewed as more culpable, for it appeared to put God on the side of injustice.

Although there was a small middle class of some of the skilled artisans, land-owning medium-sized farmers and merchants (and socially, although not economically, the lower clergy), the second major social group was the poor, the peasants, the "people of the land" ('am hā-'āreṣ, although the Hebrew term was also used with a broader meaning, as will be seen below). This group included several sub-groups.

The best-off were the small landowners, who tended to lead a precarious life which depended on the harvest. A bad year or two could spell the loss of their

land to the wealthy neighbor who lent them seed after the first crop failure. It could also mean the starvation of their family.* The tenant farmers were next best-off, although they had to pay their landlord his due before providing for their own families. Worst off were those without land (and without the skills of artisans), the hired laborers and the beggars. They were the truly poor. Their hand-to-mouth existence was considered hardly worth living. Mixed in among these various levels of poorer people were such trades as fishermen and carpenters, whose social level depended on their relative prosperity, even though they were landless. Zebedee, for example, appears to have been relatively prosperous, for he had hired workers on his boats, not simply family. Jesus' family, on the other hand, offered the sacrifice of the poor when he was born (Lk 2:24), but it is possible that when established back in Galilee they may have had a higher (if still modest) standard of living, which skilled work could at times command.

Cultural differences existed among the "people of the land" in that some (perhaps eight per cent of the population) were urban-dwellers and thus closer to the life and values of the urban elite, while the rest (i.e., ninety per cent of the people) were villagers, a step removed from the urban centers. A village carpenter, for example, would probably have been viewed by his urban fellow-carpenter as a "rustic," for his values would have been more those of the small landowner than those of the urban elite.

There were other minor classes in Jewish society. There were some slaves, although in Palestine hired laborers were preferred since slaves had to be cared for in bad years and Jewish ones then released in the Sabbath* year. Furthermore, Gentile slaves might convert to Judaism and receive all the rights of Jewish slaves. Slaves tended to be house-servants in the city. There were also Jews who were forced (or chose) to drop out of respectable society and become outcasts ("Jews who had made themselves Gentiles"): tax collectors, hired shepherds, tanners, prostitutes.* All except the tax collectors were among the poor, but the tax collectors, even if financially well-off, were never counted among the higher classes.

The poor in Judaism, then, included first of all those who owned no land (a definition based on the OT categories of poor, principally the Levite, the foreigner, the widow and the orphan). But because some non-landowners were wealthy, there was in the NT period also a secondary definition of poor in financial terms (reflected in *m. Pe'a.* 8:7-8, which was recorded by A.D. 250). However defined, the poor lived on the edge of existence even in the best of times, for to be in an agricultural economy without owning sufficient productive land to provide security is to be economically marginal. Yet the first century was not the best of times. Even if they managed to scrape by in normal years, the first century included years of famine, especially in the 40s (Josephus *Ant.* 20.2.5 records one incidence). This threat could never be far from any of the poorer people. Then there were Roman (or Herodian) taxes to pay and on top of that the Law prescribed a tithe (which could amount to from seventeen to twenty-three per cent of one's gross income). It is no wonder that the "people of the land" in general were looked down on by the religious as lax in their observance of the Law.

This laxness was not universal in that many of the later rabbis and even the great Pharisaic teachers of Jesus' day appear to have been poor, at least during their time of study and in some cases throughout their life (teachers did not charge for their teaching). Yet most of the Pharisees were urban-dwellers, while most peasants in the village lacked the zeal and discipline of the rabbis or their closeness to the high culture. Their legal observance (and knowledge of the Law) was minimal and based on village tradition. On the one hand, the choice for them often appeared to be between the piety proclaimed by city-dwellers and starvation. On the other hand, even if they had a desire to follow the Law exactly, their hand-to-mouth existence left little time for study and meditation or for being sure all food was kosher and the tithe (in its Pharisaic sense) meticulously paid.

Thus, virtually all poor peasants were considered among "the masses" or the "people of the land" (*'am hā-'āreṣ*), which was for the Pharisees more a religious than a socioeconomic classification. In the OT it indicates either those who are not aristocrats (the earlier OT material) or non-Jews living within the traditional Jewish land (Ezra-Nehemiah). In rabbinic literature (thus beginning in the NT period) it frequently refers to those who are not observant of the Law as opposed to the Pharisees (and later rabbis). Virtually all rural peasants were included within this category, for, as we have noted, the Pharisees were predominantly town-dwellers. As a result, this pejorative term could include not simply the economically poor, but also somewhat better-off individuals (including the tiny middle class) and even the wealthy, unless they made the effort to follow the Pharisaic concept of purity (*see* Clean and Unclean). In general practice, however, it usually designated the semi-observant masses, the peasant population.

1.2. The Response of Judaism to Social Inequality. Judaism in general did not have any problem with

wealth. Possessions were not viewed as evil. Indeed, because of the OT stories of Abraham, Solomon and Job, there was a tendency to connect wealth with the blessing of God (the piety-prosperity equation), but while for the most part this attitude continued in the first century, it was modified in two directions. On the one hand, the empirical observation was made that wealth tended to beget greed and the abuse of power. And in a society in which the supply of wealth was believed to be limited, any gathering of wealth which was not clearly from God was suspected of being done through such abuse (cf. Malina 1981, 75-78). In fact, in the light of the experience of the righteous (*see* Justice, Righteousness) under the Seleucid rulers and later the Hasmoneans and Herods, it even appeared that most wealth was gained by injustice and that righteousness tended to make one poor. Some intertestamental writers questioned if there were any wealthy people who were righteous (Sir 31:3-10). On the other hand, the same authors made it clear that a wealthy person could be righteous or honorable (especially if the wealth had been inherited) and the way that he or she could demonstrate this righteousness was through charity. Thus in Jewish tradition Abraham and Job were singled out as being wealthy persons who were righteous because they excelled in generosity (see *Jub.* or *T. Job*).

The real problem in first-century Judaism was that of poverty, especially the poverty of the righteous. Some anthropologically oriented scholars argue that the poverty that was a problem was that caused by the loss of one's inherited position, whether that position was economically rich or poor. This resulted in the OT categories of poor as noted above (cf. Malina 1981, 84). However, although this may have been true for the OT period, it does not completely fit that of the NT. A number of rabbinic sayings note the economic misery of the life of the poorer peasant (e.g., *Lev Rab.* 34:6 on Lev 25:25; b. *B. Bat.* 116a; b. *Sanh.* 151b). As it was later expressed, "There is nothing in the world more grievous than poverty—the most terrible of all sufferings. Our Teachers said: all sufferings are on one side and poverty is on the other" (*Ex R.* 31:12 on Ex 22:24). Furthermore, the Jesus tradition (e.g., Lk 6) contrasts the poor, not with the greedy or the wicked (as in the OT), but with the rich, showing that economic issues had become more important. James also exhibits this pattern. Economic lack was a problem, even if inherited social status was not ignored.

The first response of Judaism to the poor was to encourage the voluntary sharing of wealth, for outside of assistance from a person's extended family, charity or almsgiving was the only form of social assistance available. Governments of that day only intervened, if at all, when mass starvation was threatened (and in those cases the motives were to preserve future tax revenues and prevent social unrest). Almsgiving included (1) private charitable actions (e.g., giving to a beggar, forgiving a debt, providing for the proper burial of an impoverished person), which in the case of the wealthy could include significant aid to large areas (Queen Helena of Adiabene, for example, sent major food aid to Jerusalem in the 40s); (2) group charitable actions (i.e., those organized through a village council of elders* or a synagogue*); (3) religious charity (e.g., the charitable fund collected and distributed through the Temple). Later Judaism would develop a highly organized system of collection and distribution of charity. In the first century, however, individual initiative in almsgiving was the primary force.

The giving of alms was therefore viewed by Judaism in general as a very important righteous work in the eyes of God. In fact, in rabbinic Judaism only meditation on Torah could have outranked charity as a righteous deed. Deeds of charity were seen as greater than all the commandments (b. B. Bat. 9a, b) and defended the giver before God whenever Satan tried to accuse him (Ex Rab. 31:1). In other words, almsgiving was so significant that the term "righteousness" became synonymous with the giving of alms. Because of this, "The poor do more for the wealthy than do the wealthy for the poor," for the poor provide the righteous with a means of gaining merit with God (b. Šabb. 151b). On the negative side, evil comes upon Israel because of the neglect of obedience to the OT laws of giving to the poor (m. 'Abot 5:9). One does not know exactly how much of this attitude can be attributed to the time of Jesus, but charity was certainly highly ranked: "Upon three things the world stands: the Law, worship [i.e., the service of God, including obedience], and deeds of loving-kindness [i.e., almsgiving and other charitable acts]" (m. 'Abot. 1:2); in fact, charity is equivalent to sacrifice and atones for sins (Sir 35:1-2; 3:3-4).

At the same time, at least in rabbinic circles, the giving of alms was not viewed as a means of changing a person's social status, but as a means of rescuing him or her from the misfortune into which they had fallen and restoring them to their former station in life. Differing social status itself was not viewed as a problem. Thus a peasant who needed alms would not be supported at the same level as an impoverished aristocrat. For example, there is the (possibly apocryphal) story about Hillel, a contemporary of Jesus, who upon discovering that an impoverished member of a noble family was travelling, arranged that he be provided with a horse. But there was no servant to run in front of the man, so the rabbi himself took the role so the man could travel in the style appropriate to his rank (b. Ketub. 67b). This is certainly charity, but it is a charity which took social rank into account. Thus, while almsgiving was not to raise persons above their normal social rank, it might restore a noble person to his or her rank and fortune (e.g., an appropriately generous dowry might be provided so that a woman might marry at her accustomed status level).

Yet at the same time, there was, as noted above, a social status below which life was miserable. Thus, we find that people who fall below a certain level (defined in m. Pe'a 8, some discussions of which are first century) are always subjects of charity, whether it is their inherited status or not. In other words, once people were separated from inherited land the traditional social distinctions began to break down and economic ones started to take their place.

Charity was covered by a number of areas of Jewish Law, not simply the encouragements to almsgiving. Observant Jews not only gave the poor tithe in the third year and alms throughout the year, but also allowed the poor to glean in their fields and left their fields fallow one year in seven with the poor being allowed to gather what grew of itself. The repeated OT theme of caring for the poor was not lost in later Judaism, even if it was regulated.

At the same time, there was a recognition that even with plenty of charity the rich and powerful would tend to oppress the righteous. In other words, in this world righteousness tended to make one poor. This led to two final responses. First, the community of the righteous was in all likelihood the community of the poor (this identification is made explicitly in the Dead Sea Scrolls* and in the Pharisaic Psalms of Solomon). It is this community that must exercise generosity. Second, wealth will come to the righteous, but not in this age. God will redress all wrongs in the age to come, when the righteous poor of this age will reap the reward of their charitable deeds. This eschatological piety-prosperity equation is also important in considering the teaching of Jesus.

2. Rich and Poor in the Teaching of Jesus.

Jesus fits into the social situation of first-century Palestine as we have come to know it. He himself belonged to the people of the land as the son of a carpenter who owned neither inherited land nor land he had acquired himself (Mt 8:20; Lk 9:58). He was not an officially recognized teacher, but a charismatic leader with a ragtag group of followers (which explains the negative response to him in Nazareth, where his class origins were well known, Mk 6:3). He accepted the outcasts of society and was frequently found associating with the poor. This provides the immediate context for his teaching.

That teaching is reported in the Synoptic Gospels (the Fourth Gospel having relatively little to say on this topic). While Mark has some significant narratives and sayings on the issue, the vast majority of the teaching is found in Q* material, blocks of which occur in Matthew 6 and in Luke 6, 12 and 16. Of the two Gospels Luke has both more material than Matthew and a stronger form of the material which both include. For example, Luke includes woes along with his Beatitudes (Lk 6:20-26; *see* Blessing and Woe), which sharpen the teaching by explicitly stating the obverse. Therefore it can be said fairly that Luke has a special interest in the topic (which is the reason that most of the studies on Jesus' economic teaching focus on Luke), although the same general attitude is shared by Matthew and perhaps also by Mark. The three Evangelists give a consistent picture of Jesus' attitude toward wealth and poverty. Furthermore, the viewpoint they share is consistent with the ancient Mediterranean view that goods are limited and that collection of wealth by some implies the loss of basic subsistence for others. Yet Jesus does not accept inherited wealth to the same degree that his contemporaries did.

2.1. The Danger of Wealth. While Jesus never looks on possessions *per se* as evil (he was not a dualist), for him wealth was not something safe, but a dangerous substance. In many of his sayings it is personified as Mammon (which in the Aramaic of Jesus' day meant simply "possessions" and could be viewed as evil or neutral, depending on its modifiers) and functions exactly as the idols did in the eyes of ancient Hebrew prophets in that it seductively draws people away from total allegiance to God. For example, in the parable of the sower (Mk 4:18-19) it is "the deceit of wealth and the desires for other things" that come in and choke the word, making it unfruitful, just as if it had been snatched by Satan (*see* Devil, Demons, Satan) or burned out by persecution. Here wealth is personified and acts with effects similar to that of personal evil (i.e., Satan), although in a slower, less dramatic way. It draws the person away from God.

The issue is not simply a matter of giving both possessions and God their proper place. Both God and possessions (i.e., Mammon) claim a person's service. Mammon's claim is evident: Wealth must be preserved; daily bread must be earned. Yet Jesus categorically rejects that there is a proper service of Mammon: It is impossible to serve both money and God (Mt 6:24).

This impossibility is underlined by his next point, for, far from being a mark of divine favor, wealth makes it impossible to enter the kingdom (*see* Kingdom of God). This constitutes a total denial (at least in the terms of this world) of the piety-prosperity equation. This idea is presented in a number of ways. The Markan story of the rich young man ends in all three Synoptics with the comment, "It is easier for a camel to go through the eye of a needle than for a rich man to enter the kingdom of God" (Mk 10:25). This clearly means that the salvation of the rich is an impossibility. Can such folk never be saved? "All things are possible with God," responds Jesus to the shocked question of his disciples. Luke follows his version of this story with the Zacchaeus narrative (Lk 19:1-10), which shows the impossible taking place. But this does not leave Zacchaeus rich (i.e., his possession of riches is not neutral), for in the process Zacchaeus gives up his wealth. It is only when he announces this intention that Jesus responds, "Salvation has come to this house today."

Jesus also emphasizes the impossibility of serving both God and money in his parable of the rich man and Lazarus (Lk 16:19-31). Abraham says to the rich man in Hades, "In your lifetime you received your good things . . . but now . . . you are in agony." This fits with the woe of Luke 6:24, "Woe to you who are rich, for you have already received your comfort." In the parable the woe receives a literal pictorial presentation, showing that to hold on to one's comfort today is to risk damnation tomorrow.

Finally, the parable of the rich fool (Lk 12:16-21) emphasizes once again that one cannot serve both God and Mammon. The rich man in the story, who simply has the good fortune of a bumper crop, prudently takes the excess of the present and stores it for the future, rejoicing that his future will be free from financial worry. That worldly prudence qualifies him in Jesus' eyes as a fool. The mere possession of this windfall condemns him. He has stored up for himself instead of giving to the poor (and thereby becoming "rich towards God").

2.2. The Only Healthy Use of Wealth Is in the Care of the Poor. In both of the parables cited above there are implied alternatives to the behavior of the rich. The first man could have cared for Lazarus, having both the means (the parable notes that he had plenty) and opportunity (Lazarus lay at his gate and was known to the rich man, cf. Lk 16:23-24). As for the rich fool, Luke defines what is meant by being "rich towards God" when a dozen verses later he concludes the section on the topic of wealth with, "Sell your possessions and give to the poor" (Lk 12:33). This interpretation of what one is to do with surplus is a consistent theme in the teaching of Jesus (and of the rest of the NT). If one has more than enough, the best thing to do with it is to give it to those who have less than enough and so invest in heaven.

Another example of this teaching is found in Luke 16:9 in which Jesus states, "Make friends for yourselves by means of unrighteous Mammon ["worldly wealth" NIV], so that when it is gone, they will welcome you into eternal dwellings." In context this probably means that one should care for the poor with one's wealth ("make friends for yourselves") so that when one dies ("when it is gone," left behind at death) those poor welcome their benefactor into heaven ("eternal dwellings").

This teaching, of course, is in line with the Judaism of the period. Wealthier persons demonstrated their righteousness by caring for the poor, just as Job and Abraham (or, for Christians, perhaps Joseph of Arimathea or Barnabas) had done before them. Within their Mediterranean culture this both demonstrated the virtue of their class and showed that their wealth was not gained by injustice. Jesus differed from the Judaism of his day not in the high value he placed on charity, but in the extent of the charity he required and the basis on which he founded his demand.

2.3. God Has a Special Interest in the Poor. Jesus was no ascetic. There is no glorification of poverty for its own sake nor a masochistic enjoyment of want. Indeed, Jesus consistently pictured the consummation of the kingdom as a time of plenty, and he was known as a person who enjoyed a party (e.g., Mt 11:19, not to mention Luke's well-known banquet theme; *see* Table Fellowship), so he was certainly not against good food and drink, even if he might be a guest who could make a host uncomfortable.

At the same time Jesus clearly stated that God has a special interest in the poor, a teaching that builds on God's care of the poor in the OT. For example, in both Luke and Matthew one finds him describing his mission in terms of Isaiah 61:1-2 with specific reference to the poor having good news announced to them (Mt 11:5; Lk 4:18-21). These poor are surely the "people of the land" (*'am hā 'āreṣ*) to whom he sends his disciples in Matthew 10:6-7. And it is on these poor that he pronounces, "Blessed are you poor, for yours is the kingdom of God" (Lk 6:20). While Matthew 5:3 has a different version of the saying, "Blessed are the poor in spirit," the sense is similar once one realizes that in Luke Jesus is addressing the poor who are following him and in Matthew he is speaking of the

poor who display the (OT) spirit of the poor, that is, those who are seeking and depending on God (cf. 1QM 14:7, where the Hebrew equivalent of this phrase occurs).

Some scholars, however, question whether these are the materially poor or the metaphorically poor. Is not the phrase "I am poor and oppressed" used in the Psalms by individuals who are materially well-off? Has not the term "poor" become by the time of Jesus simply a synonym for Israel* as an oppressed and helpless people? Certainly, as noted above, there is a spiritual qualification of the poor being addressed. It is also clear that in such intertestamental works as the *Psalms of Solomon* and the Dead Sea Scrolls the term "poor" had come to designate the Pharisaic and Dead Sea communities respectively as the pious remnant of Israel. Finally, it is clear that some among Jesus' band of disciples were not poor to the extent of being destitute, even if they were not necessarily well-off (e.g., Peter and Andrew owned a house; James and John came from a reasonably prosperous family; Matthew/Levi, while not necessarily a wealthy tax collector, is reported to have afforded a feast for Jesus).

Yet, taking all of this into account, the term "poor" always carries with it a sense of the experience of oppression and helplessness or, as Malina put it, the inability to maintain inherited status. A person who was comfortable and secure would not be termed "poor." The disciples had left their relative security to identify with the insecurity of Jesus. The sects who referred to Israel as "the poor" were in fact experiencing oppression by the ruling classes. Even in the Psalms the term is used only if the psalmist feels helpless; he may in fact have money, but it is of no use to him in his need. In his helplessness he calls upon God to look on him with the special concern that God in the Law and Prophets proclaims that he has for the poor. Thus the so-called metaphorical use of "poor" is not entirely metaphorical; it always contains an element of real suffering and insecurity, even if the suffering is not necessarily economic, but is instead a physical threat.

In the case of the two Beatitudes, groups experiencing real impoverishment are blessed. While one could be materially poor without receiving this blessing because of not following Christ/having the right spirit, there is no intention in either these or any similar passages that one can hold onto wealth or other security and yet claim such blessings because one's spirit is "poor." It is significant that the blessings are never pronounced on the rich, either in this passage or elsewhere. And in Luke this distinction is underlined by a curse on the rich three verses later (because "you have already received your comfort;" i.e., because they have maintained their wealth, not because of any other injustice). Again, it is "the poor, the maimed, the blind and the lame" whom God is inviting to his messianic banquet, while the wealthier people (who can afford to purchase fields and oxen) are excluded (Lk 14:21).

If people have their own security, they have no need for the "good news" Jesus preaches to the poor. Jesus not only quotes from Isaiah 61:1-2, with its theme of good news to the poor, release for prisoners, sight for the blind and release for the oppressed, he enacts it in his ministry. He gives sight to the blind and releases those who are bound and oppressed (which in Luke refers to his casting out demons [*see* Devil, Demon, Satan], although the freedom of his new community of disciples was surely experienced as another form of release). And while there are wealthy people who receive the kingdom, the only ones mentioned in the Gospels are those like Zacchaeus, who are engaged in acts of generosity (and thus identify with the suffering). Those who refuse to so humble themselves are turned away.

Is Jesus then proclaiming a time of Jubilee* (Lev 25:8-56) when he proclaims "the year of the Lord's acceptance"? Does this mean a time of economic redistribution of wealth? While this possibility is attractive and while Luke certainly sees the ideals of Sabbath* and Jubilee years realized in the early church (Acts 4:34; cf. Deut 15:4), this is unlikely. Such an interpretation hangs on too narrow a linguistic base and focuses Jesus' concerns too exclusively on economic and class issues. There is a realization of the Jubilee ideal, but in terms much broader than those envisioned in the OT literature and without its specific regulations.

The language of Jesus is not class language, which would include all materially poor Israelites within it and exclude all materially rich Israelites. If that were the case, he would surely have had to define how poor one had to be to qualify. But at the same time it is not spiritual language which speaks only of an inner condition without reference to outer circumstances. Rather, it refers to those actually experiencing oppression and helplessness in one form or another, or those identifying with this group by giving up their own security and generously sharing what they have.

2.4. Caring for the Poor Earns Eternal Reward. If God has a special concern for the poor (which is clear even in the OT where God proclaims himself the special protector of the classic Israelite poor—the widow, the orphan and the alien), one would expect that his

followers would also display this concern. Jesus argues for such a conclusion by noting that it is treasure in heaven that is lasting (Mt 6:20; Lk 12:32-34; Luke makes it clear that people put treasure in heaven by "sell[ing] your possession and giv[ing] to the poor," while Matthew is content to simply use the phrase which was well known to his Jewish audience). The reason given for such radical action is that the heart naturally follows the treasure, so treasure in heaven means a heart fixed on heaven, while treasure on earth equally means a heart fixed on earth. Jesus' own practice must have followed his advice, for John 13:29 indicates that almsgiving ordered by Jesus was what the disciples suspected Judas was about when he left them. It was apparently a customary action, for it is presented as a natural assumption on the part of the disciples.

Charity, however, is not simply a matter of making sure that one's heart is in the right place or getting rid of a dangerous substance. It earns a reward. Just as the rich man is condemned for not practicing charity toward Lazarus and the rich fool for not putting treasure in heaven, so in the context of a banquet the promise is held out to those who invite the poor to their feasts: "You will be repaid at the resurrection of the just" (Lk 14:14). It is likely that Jesus is here applying Proverbs 19:17, "He who is kind to the poor lends to the Lord, and he will reward him for what he has done."

2.5. Radical Trust in God Is the Basis for the Ability to Give Up Wealth. The call of Jesus is radical with its point-counterpoint of "do not invest on earth—do invest in heaven," but it is based in an equally radical promise, "Seek first his kingdom and his righteousness, and all these [material] things shall be yours as well" (Mt 6:33). Likewise, the promise "Fear not, little flock, for it is your Father's good pleasure to give you the kingdom" precedes "Sell your possessions" in Luke 12:32-33. Those who are convinced that their heavenly Father will indeed care for them are also those who are able to give freely. Conversely, the lack of trust in the Father (including doubting the goodness of his will) leads to the need to provide for one's own security, to serve Mammon.

Jesus suggests that even on the level of natural theology people ought to realize that they can trust God, for if God cares for the birds without their providing for their own security and if he clothes the lilies with beauty, surely he is more concerned about his human children (Lk 12:22-31). Furthermore, human anxiety and attempts at providing for security are useless anyway (Mt 6:27). Instead, what counts is the assurance that "your heavenly Father knows that you need them all" (Mt 6:32; Lk 12:30). Renunciation flows out of security, not out of demand. But security is rooted in the knowledge of the Father, not in what is physically present.

It is at this level that the Fourth Gospel supports the teaching on rich and poor found in the Synoptics. While the language of wealth and poverty is almost entirely absent (occurring only in two passages in Jn 12—13), the language of radical trust in God is not. For example, John's Jesus argues that after the resurrection "my Father will give you whatever you ask in my name." This asking and receiving is so that "your joy will be complete" (Jn 16:23-24). Such joyful dependence on the Father, underlined multiple times in the surrounding chapters along with the insistence that the Father loves them, is the foundation on which the carefree generosity of the Synoptics is based.

2.6. The Primary Context of Renunciation Is in the New Community. Jesus' whole life and teaching took place within the context of the social world of first-century Judaism in which a person was embedded in a social matrix, a community. Within the modern Western individualism, much of what he taught on wealth and poverty appears to be nonsense. But given that his followers assumed that Jesus was correct in his teaching that the kingdom of God had come, it made good sense. As the Pharisees, the Dead Sea community and even the Zealots invited people to join a supportive community which pointed to the new order that was coming, so Jesus invited those who accepted his message into a new social world. They were to become his followers, part of the renewed community. The disciples left what they had, but they did so to follow Jesus, to be part of his band. The rich young ruler is not called simply to sell what he has and give to the poor, but to do that and then "follow me." In other words, the call of Jesus to radical generosity is at one level an individual decision, but its context is that of a call to community in line with the function of voluntary communities within his society.

Much of the teaching of Jesus can only be understood within this context. For example, the parable of the sheep and goats (Mt 25:31-46) is entirely related to community. People are certainly judged according to their charitable acts (all of the acts mentioned would have been viewed in Judaism as varieties of almsgiving), but the focus is on their acts of charity toward "one of the least of these brothers of mine" and not toward the poor in general. While it is clear that the charitable actions of Jesus and his followers (especially their healings and other miracles) extended beyond their own group, most of the concrete actions named have to do with actions toward his

followers. This is true even for the offering of the proverbial "cup of cold water."

Likewise, the promises of Jesus are primarily addressed to his followers. The "you poor" of Luke 6 is put into the context of his "looking at his disciples." The Beatitudes of the Sermon on the Mount* are spoken when "his disciples came to him." There is no blessing spoken to poor who are not disciples, although there is some type of blessing for anyone, rich or poor, who, though they are not his disciple, comes to the aid of a disciple (Mk 9:41; Mt 10:40-42).

Finally, the blessings pronounced by Jesus are primarily received within the context of the eschatological community (i.e., the band of disciples). When Peter notes that, unlike the rich man, "we have left everything to follow you," Jesus responds that he and the other disciples will receive "a hundred times as much in this present age" and "in the age to come, eternal life" (Mk 10:28-30). The reception of "one hundred times as much" (with persecutions added) refers not to an individual's personal reward, but to their sharing in the wealth of the community. In anthropological terms, they receive a new network of dyadic relationships. It is as the disciples form a new extended family* that each receives a larger family than they left behind. It is as the discipled community shares among itself that each member has access to much more than they gave up. Conceivably, this could also be said about heavenly reward. Certainly, at least on the level of temporal reward, without this community emphasis the teaching of Jesus easily degenerates into an ethic of personal fulfillment.

3. Eschatology and the Ethic of Jesus.

It is well known that Jesus' teaching was set within a context of expectation of the kingdom. Jesus came announcing that the time of fulfillment had come and that the kingdom of God was at hand. Each of the promises about the provision of the Father as well as the blessings of the Beatitudes, contains the command to seek the kingdom or the promise of the kingdom. God had broken into history in a decisive way; now was the time for radical change.

Given this context it is possible to read the ethic of Jesus in four different ways. First, following A. Schweitzer and others, we might view it as an interim ethic established in the face of the soon-to-appear kingdom. This perspective views Jesus' teaching about rich and poor as totally conditioned by his end-time expectation, an expectation that was not fulfilled. Thus the ethic was irrelevant to later generations in the church. Yet it does not appear that this was the position taken by the first interpreters of Jesus, for the

Gospels were certainly written a generation into the Christian movement and such works as the Epistle of James demonstrate a relatively literal application of the teaching of Jesus.

Second, we can view it as an ideal ethic designed either to force Jesus' contemporaries to confront their own inability and their need for grace (so in part, R. Guelich) or to take effect when the kingdom would be consummated. The test of this position is to observe whether or not Jesus' disciples practiced his teaching literally or whether Jesus himself accepted it as an unattainable ideal for them. Furthermore, one can ask whether the early church so understood Jesus (recognizing that the Gospels were their books and that they were responsible for shaping the tradition).

Third, is to see Jesus as giving a literal guideline to a particular group of followers. For communal Anabaptists this was a literal rule binding on all Christians who wish to walk in the way of full discipleship.* For monastic orders this "gospel perfection" was only incumbent on the religious who wished to forsake the world and live the fullness of Christian life. In either case there is the implication that those who do not divest themselves of wealth and give to the poor are at best second-class followers of Jesus.

Fourth, we might understand his teaching as an ethic to be lived in the light of eschatology. The premises for this reading are: (1) the kingdom is in fact the wave of the future in the sense that, although it is unseen (except in the various signs of its coming) it is actual and the present observable features of this age are going to pass; (2) the Father in fact does love and care for his own; and (3) the Holy Spirit* (promised in the Gospels) frees the follower of Jesus to respond to his demand. In light of these factors the application of Jesus' teaching on rich and poor to life in Christian community makes sense.

Related to the consideration of any of these positions is the fact that it is unlikely that Jesus is giving a new Law. In fact, only the third of these positions would suggest something like that. In the Gospels one discovers that Peter still owned a house (Mk 1:29) and that women of means continued supporting Jesus, apparently not ridding themselves of wealth in one act (Lk 8:3). They evidently understood Jesus to be speaking in the black-white hyperbole of a Jewish sage (as in Proverbs) or storyteller, rather than in the stark literalism of a lawgiver.

In fact, these and other examples show two things. First, while the disciples "left all" and followed Jesus, they did not necessarily renounce their possessions totally, although their decision did involve considerable economic loss and risk as well as trust in Jesus.

Second, their joyful and generous giving was precisely that. It was not a rule enforced on them. For example, the narrative of the anointing at Bethany (Mk 14:1-9; it is found in all Gospels except Luke, who at best has it in quite a different form) shows quite a different type of generosity. The anointing of Jesus "for burial" was certainly a radical act of giving (even an act of charity, if the burial idea was in any way conscious in the woman's mind, which is unlikely), but it was enacted toward Jesus, not toward the poor (which offended the disciples, and in John's Gospel especially offended Judas). There is certainly no suggestion that it would have been good for the woman to have kept the ointment for her own security. The issue for the Evangelists is the proper direction of the extravagant act. Jesus suggests that he took precedence over the poor; the eschatological moment took priority over all other demands. This is hardly the word of a lawgiver in any conventional sense.

The test of these positions, then, is threefold. First, we must look within the Gospels and ask how Jesus' contemporaries could have interpreted his message, a task which has been attempted in part above. Second, we must look at the Gospels (and perhaps along with them Acts as being of one perspective with Luke) and, realizing that they were foundation documents for Christian communities, ask if there is anything in them or in the NT epistolary literature that might direct us toward understanding this teaching as anything other than a command of the Founder to be practiced. Third, we must look at the early interpretations of the Christian tradition (e.g., Paul in 2 Cor 8—9; 1 Tim 6; James) and see if they agree with the perspective of Jesus or in some way mitigate the sharp edges of his teaching.

None of these considerations will remove the aspect of eschatology from Jesus' teaching on rich and poor. But they will show how eschatology (and, in Paul and others, the gift of the Spirit as the down payment on the eschatological future) was related to ethics in the early Christian tradition. We will then be better able to interpret that tradition for today.

See also ETHICS OF JESUS; JUSTICE; RIGHTEOUSNESS; TAXES.

BIBLIOGRAPHY. E. Bammel, "πτωχός κτλ," *TDNT*, VI.885-915; R. A. Cassidy, *Jesus, Politics, and Society* (Maryknoll, NY: Orbis Books, 1978); B. Chilton and J. I. H. McDonald, *Jesus and the Ethics of the Kingdom* (Grand Rapids: Eerdmans, 1987); P. H. Davids, "New Testament Foundations for Living More Simply," in *Living More Simply*, ed. R. J. Sider (Downers Grove, IL: InterVarsity, 1980) 40-58; J. R. Donahue, "Two Decades of Research on the Rich and Poor in Luke-Acts," in *Justice and the Holy: Essays in Honor of Walter*

Harrelson, ed. D. A. Knight and P. J. Paris (Atlanta: Scholars, 1989) 129-44; J. Eichler et al., "Possessions, Treasure, Mammon, Wealth," *NIDNTT* 3.829-47, 852-53; H.-H. Esser and C. Brown, "Poor," *NIDNTT* 3.820-29; R. T. France, "God and Mammon," *EvQ* 51 (1979) 3-21; R. A. Guelich, *The Sermon on the Mount* (Waco: Word Books, 1982); M. Hengel, *Poverty and Riches in the Early Church* (London: SCM, 1974); L. J. Hopps, *Being Poor: A Biblical Study* (GNS 20; Wilmington: Michael Glazier, 1987); J. Jeremias, *Jerusalem in the Times of Jesus* (London: SCM, 1969); L. T. Johnson, *Sharing Possessions: Mandate and Symbol of Faith* (Philadelphia: Fortress, 1981); D. B. Kraybill, *The Upside-Down Kingdom* (Scottdale, PA: Herald, 1978); H. Kvalbein, "Jesus and the Poor," *Themelios* 12 (1987) 80-87; B. J. Malina, *Christian Origins and Cultural Anthropology* (Atlanta: John Knox, 1986); idem, *The New Testament World: Insights from Cultural Anthropology* (Atlanta: John Knox, 1981); idem, "Wealth and Poverty in the New Testament and Its World," *Int* 41 (1987) 354-67; W. E. Pilgrim, *Good News for the Poor* (Minneapolis: Augsburg, 1981); J. S. Pobee, *Who Are the Poor? The Beatitudes As a Call to Community* (RBS 32; Geneva: WCC, 1987); D. P. Seccombe, *Possessions and the Poor in Luke-Acts* (Linz: Studien zum Neuen Testament und seiner Umwelt, 1982); T. E. Schmidt, *Hostility to Wealth in the Synoptic Gospels* (JSNTSup 15; Sheffield: JSOT, 1987); L. Schotroff and W. Stegemann, *Jesus and the Hope of the Poor* (Maryknoll, N.Y.: Orbis, 1980); E. Schürer, *The History of the Jewish People in the Age of Jesus Christ* (Edinburgh: T. & T. Clark, 1979); A. Verhey, *The Great Reversal: Ethics and the New Testament* (Grand Rapids: Eerdmans, 1984); J. H. Yoder, *The Politics of Jesus* (Grand Rapids: Eerdmans, 1972).

P. H. Davids

RICH AND YOUNG RULER. *See* COMMANDMENT.

RIGHTEOUS SUFFERER. *See* DEATH OF JESUS; SERVANT OF YAHWEH; TYPOLOGY.

RIGHTEOUSNESS. *See* JUSTICE, RIGHTEOUSNESS.

RITUAL PURITY AND IMPURITY. *See* CLEAN AND UNCLEAN.

ROME

In NT times Rome was the chief city in Italy and the capital of the Roman Empire. Because of its prestige and importance its name is used both for the city itself and for Roman civilization as a whole. This article deals with Rome in its broadest sense and its impact on the Gospels.*

1. Historical and Cultural Background
2. The Romans in Palestine
3. Rome and the Gospels

1. Historical and Cultural Background.

1.1. The Roman Republic. Rome began as a small settlement on the east bank of the Tiber. Traditionally founded by Romulus by about 753 B.C. and ruled by kings, Rome became a republic in 509 B.C., governed by a Senate under two consuls. It rapidly expanded, conquering its neighbors and establishing the dominance of its language, Latin. In the third to second centuries B.C. Rome became a naval power, defeating its rival Carthage in two Punic Wars. The Romans also gained ascendancy in the East with the defeat of Antiochus III of Syria and the conquest of Macedon and Greece (Corinth was sacked in 146 B.C.). By this time Rome had a highly efficient and well-disciplined professional army.

After class struggles, political rivalries and civil wars, the Republic came to an end in a contest for power, initially between Pompey, Crassus and Julius Caesar (assassinated 44 B.C.), and then between Mark Antony and Octavian, who emerged victor at Actium (31 B.C.). In 27 B.C. Octavian "restored the Republic," taking the surname "Augustus," or "venerable" (cf. Lk 2:1). This was the beginning of an empire which was to last for many centuries.

1.2. The Early Empire. Our concern here is with only the first phase of the Roman Empire, notably the Julio-Claudian and Flavian dynasties. For our knowledge of this period we are indebted especially to Tacitus, *Annals* and *Histories;* Suetonius, *Lives of the Caesars;* Cassius Dio, *Histories;* Josephus, *Jewish War* and *Antiquities;* and to inscriptions, papyri and data derived from coins and other material remains (see Balsdon; Jones and Milns; Avi-Yonah).

Augustus (27 B.C.-A.D. 14) is rightly famous for establishing and maintaining peace; for his efficient administration, including legal and financial reforms; his upholding of traditional Roman values and morality; and his patronage of the arts. Modest in his lifestyle, he preferred to be known as *princeps*, "first citizen," rather than *imperator*, "emperor." The principate of his stepson Tiberius (A.D. 14-37) proved more tyrannical and ended in a reign of terror. The evils of autocratic power became still more evident under Gaius ("Caligula," A.D. 37-41), who may have been insane. He offended the Jews by ordering his statue to be placed in the Temple* at Jerusalem (the Syrian legate Petronius only averted a confrontation by delaying tactics). After Gaius' assassination,

Claudius' reign (A.D. 41-54) provided stability with the development of the civil service, the strengthening of empire and the generous extension of Roman citizenship. He continued Augustus' policy of allowing the Jews freedom of worship* and was a friend of Herod Agrippa I (*see* Herodian Dynasty), whom he set up as king (see 2.2. below). In the later part of his reign he expelled the Jews from Rome, an event which suetonius (*Claudius* 25.4) claims was precipitated by disturbances caused by "Chrestus" (perhaps a distortion of "Christ"; see stern, 113-17). Nero's eccentric and extravagant reign (A.D. 54-68) was marked by a great fire at Rome, probably accidental but attributed to Christians. It led to the first persecutions.

Roman Emperors 31 B.C.—A.D. 117

Augustus (27 B.C.-A.D. 14)

Tiberius (14-37)

Gaius Caligula (37-41)

Claudius (41-54)

Nero (54-68)

Civil War (68/69)

Galba (68)

Otho (69)

Vitellius (69)

Vespasian (69-79)

Titus (79-81)

Domitian (81-96)

Nerva (96-98)

Trajan (98-117)

On Nero's death different military factions fought over the succession (A.D. 68-69, "the Year of the Four Emperors"), until Vespasian, a plebeian and commander of the army in the East, emerged victorious (reigned A.D. 69-79). This period saw the Jewish revolt of A.D. 66-70 with the brutal sack of Jerusalem by Vespasian's son Titus (who commemorated the event by his Arch in Rome). After this Judea became an imperial Roman province. Titus himself reigned only two years (A.D. 79-81) and was followed by his brother Domitian (A.D. 81-96), an efficient administrator who carried out a public building program. But his rule, like that of Tiberius, ended in a reign of terror. He claimed the title "lord and god" (Suetonius *Domitian* 13) and was responsible for a major persecution of Christians. In contrast, the reigns of Nerva (A.D. 96-98) and Trajan (A.D. 98-117) brought peace* and stability.

It is against this political background that the Gospels were written, probably in the 60s to 90s (though some place the Gospel of John as late as the reign of Trajan).

1.3. The Roman Religion and Character. Roman religion was originally animistic, involving the spirits of the woods, springs, mountains, etc. The Romans also worshipped anthropomorphic gods such as Jupiter, Juno, Mars and Minerva, whom they identified with their Greek counterparts (Zeus, Hera, etc.). Tolerant of other religions, they came successively under the influence of the Etruscans, the Greeks and various oriental peoples, and imported foreign cults, including those of Cybele, Isis and Mithras. Emperor worship seems to have originated in the East, where Hellenistic monarchs had long been recognized as divine "saviors." In the Empire it became a focus and test of loyalty (cf. Pliny, *Epp.* 10.96-97), but at Rome it was restricted either to the deceased emperor (cf. the earlier worship of ancestors) or his "genius" (guardian spirit). In the provinces (later at Rome also) the emperor often shared his cult with the goddess Roma, personification of the power and spirit of Rome.

The Romans are famous for their military and administrative genius, their law and their skills in architecture, engineering and road building. Deeply indebted to Greece (*see* Hellenism) in the world of literature, philosophy and the creative arts, they nevertheless had their own gift of the lucid expression of ideas in precise and elegant language (see further Howatson; Bandinelli). Traditionally, the Romans valued family life and the virtues of *gravitas* ("dignity") and *pietas* ("devotion" or "dutifulness"). But like all peoples they had their darker side, and many instances are recorded of corruption, sexual immorality, brutality and murder. One should be wary of either idealizing or denigrating them as a people.

1.4. Roman Provincial Administration. The first provinces, in the West, were acquired already in the third century B.C. After Rome's expansion into the East, Asia (i.e., western Turkey), Cilicia and Bithynia were added, followed by Syria and Egypt. Augustus annexed several more provinces, and Claudius added Britain (A.D. 43).

Under the Empire provinces were of two kinds: (1) "public" or "consular," governed by *proconsuls* under the authority of the Senate (these were generally the richer and more settled provinces); or (2) "imperial," governed by *legates*, appointed by the Emperor (mostly frontier provinces, such as Syria, where legions were stationed). Both these types of governor were of senatorial rank. There was a third class of governors, known as *prefects* or *procurators*, of lower "equestrian" rank, who were in charge of smaller provinces (e.g., Judea). These were often experts in financial administration. All governors had judicial and military powers. The number of troops available might be quite small (e.g., one cohort, consisting of 300-600 men), but in frontier provinces could rise to three or four legions (a legion consisting of some 3,000-6,000 infantry and 100-200 cavalry). Governors could not be prosecuted for mismanagement until after their term of office.

Roman provincial government has been described as "supervisory rather than executive" (Sherwin-White, *ISBE* 3.1027), which meant that few Roman officials were involved, detailed administration being in the hands of municipal authorities or, in the case of Judea, councils of elders grouped into "toparchies." Revenue was raised by a system of tax farming (*see* Taxes). Local laws and religious customs were respected as long as they did not interfere with smooth government. Roman citizens came under Roman law. Citizenship could be granted both to whole communities and to individuals (e.g., to men with long service in auxiliary units of the army), and was passed down from father to son. In the Eastern provinces it was often acquired by members of the wealthy upper classes through influence.

2. The Romans in Palestine.

2.1. Down to Herod the Great.
The history of the Roman government of Palestine is complex. In 66-63 B.C. Pompey conducted his celebrated Eastern campaign, during which he was called into Palestine by the two sons of Salome Alexandra in their dispute over the succession. He captured Jerusalem and entered the Temple. But he ordered its cleansing and reinstated Hyrcanus as High Priest. After this Syria became a Roman imperial province, with the Decapolis and Samaria (now freed from Jewish rule) under its wing. Judea, Galilee, Idumea and Perea were retained by the Jews as client kingdoms, dependent on Rome. Julius Caesar appointed Antipater procurator of Judea. His son Herod, who had been governor of Galilee,* won from Rome the title "King of the Jews," a title which he had to make a reality by force of arms. Herod reigned from 37 to 4 B.C., extending his territories and restoring the Jerusalem Temple on a lavish scale (including Greco-Roman architectural features). Herod was both a lover of Hellenism and an admirer of Roman culture. He encouraged Hellenistic education and social mores; he built theaters, amphitheaters and other civic amenities such as aqueducts. Under his rule Judea was materially prosperous. But he was also violent and cruel. The massacre of the innocents at Bethlehem (Mt 2), though not confirmed by external sources, is consistent with his character.

2.2. After Herod the Great.
On Herod's death his kingdom was split into three with Herod Antipas as "tetrarch" of Galilee and Perea (4 B.C.-A.D. 39); Philip, "tetrarch" of Trachonitis and Iturea (4 B.C.-A.D. 34); and Archelaus "ethnarch" in Judea, Idumea and Samaria (4 B.C.-A.D. 6; cf. Mt 2:22; Lk 3:1; *see* Herodian Dynasty). Archelaus' rule ended in riots, and he was banished. Judea now came under the control of Roman governors.

Pontius Pilate* was governor of Judea from A.D. 26/27-36. Tacitus (*Ann.* 15.44) refers to him as "procurator" and mentions that "Christus" was put to death by him when Tiberius was emperor. However, an inscription from Caesarea (the Roman capital of Judea) shows that his title was more correctly "prefect." He was of equestrian rank, presumably a former military tribune, and had five cohorts of infantry and a cavalry regiment under his command. He had absolute authority in his own province but was responsible to the legate in Syria. We know from Josephus* and

---

Roman Rule in Palestine 63 B.C.-39 A.D.

Pompey captures Jerusalem (63 B.C.)

Hyrcanus appointed ethnarch and reinstated high priest (63 B.C.)

Antipater procurator of Judea (55-43 B.C.)

Herod the Great (37-4 B.C.)

Archelaus, ethnarch (4 B.C.-A.D. 6)

Judea made a Roman province (A.D. 6)

Quirinius governor of Syria (A.D. 6-9)

Philip, tetrarch (4 B.C.-A.D. 34)

Herod Antipas, tetrarch (4 B.C.-A.D. 39)

Pontius Pilate governor of Judea (A.D. 26/27-36)

Herod Agrippa I rules as "King of the Jews" (A.D. 41-44)

Palestine's rule returns to Roman governors (A.D. 44)

Philo that his governorship was marred by bloodshed, including a massacre of some Galileans (possibly alluded to in Lk 13:1) and the slaughter of many Samaritans* in an ugly incident which resulted in protests to the legate Vitellius in Syria and Pilate's recall to Rome. According to Eusebius he later committed suicide.

In A.D. 41 Herod Agrippa I, who had previously governed northern Palestine and Galilee, was made "King of the Jews" (cf. Acts 12), but in A.D. 44 Palestine reverted to Roman governors. In A.D. 66-70 occurred the tragic Jewish War, with the siege and fall of Jerusalem (A.D. 70); the Jewish patriots held out at Masada until A.D. 73 and committed suicide rather than submit to Rome. In A.D. 132-35 the Bar Kokhba revolt finally sealed the fate of Judea, and Jerusalem became a Roman colony (Aelia Capitolina) inhabited by non-Jews.

The Jewish leaders and people varied immensely in their attitudes to the Romans. The Herodian rulers and their party were naturally pro-Roman. The High Priests also generally favored cooperation, as did the Sadducees. The Essenes (*see* Dead Sea Scrolls) withdrew to the desert, while the Zealots worked for armed rebellion (*see* Revolutionary Movements). The Pharisees* saw as their first loyalty absolute adherence to the Mosaic Law* and traditions (*see* Rabbinic Writings and Traditions). They refused to take an oath of loyalty to Herod (Josephus *Ant.* 17.42); some actively resisted Roman rule, but others were more acquiescent. The common people must have simply scraped a living in a society where there was great inequality between rich and poor and much scope for oppression (*see* Rich and Poor).

3. Rome and the Gospels.

3.1. The General Situation.
The city of Rome is not mentioned by name in the Gospels. The Roman people are mentioned just once, when the chief priests and Pharisees warn the Sanhedrin* of the danger that the Romans will come and destroy the Temple and the Jewish nation (Jn 11:47-48). The Latin language is also mentioned only once (Jn 19:20), where the *titulus* on the cross is said to have been written in Hebrew, Latin (*Rōmaïsti)* and Greek. Latin was not much used in Palestine except for military purposes, the chief language of the administrators being Greek. The ordinary people spoke Aramaic (though Greek was also in use among the better educated; *see* Languages of Palestine). The Gospels contain Latin loanwords for such things as coins, notably the *dēnarion*, or "penny," the *assarion* and *kodrantēs* (= Latin *quadrans)*, the *kēnsos* (in the sense of tribute money), and other technical or military terms, including *kenturiōn, koustōdia, legiōn, praitōrion, spekoulatōr* (in the sense "executioner") and the verb *phragelloō* for scourging (cf. Latin *flagellare)*. There are also a number of Latin linguistic constructions, especially in Mark, and a possible reference to Roman marriage law whereby a woman may divorce* her husband (Mk 10:12). Taking these points together some have seen confirmation of an early church tradition that Mark's Gospel was written in Rome, either in association with Peter or shortly after his

death (cf. 1 Pet 5:13). But Latin loanwords occur in all four Gospels and were surely part of the general currency of Roman imperial administration. Some have seen in texts like Mark 10:30 and 13:9-11 allusions to Nero's persecution of Christians (cf. 1.2. above), but the evidence is insufficient to prove this.

3.2. Rome and the Birth Narratives.
Luke (2:1-2) dates Jesus' birth by a Roman census, ordered by "Caesar Augustus," which took place "when Quirinius was governor of Syria." There are problems over both the date and nature of this census: we know from external sources that Quirinius was governor A.D. 6-9, but Herod the Great, in whose reign Jesus was born (Mt 2:1; cf. Lk 1:5), died in 4 B.C. (*see* Birth of Jesus). The important point is that Luke saw the very birth of Jesus at Bethlehem as occasioned by a Roman census, which required Joseph to register at his native city.

3.3. The Romans and Jesus' Public Ministry.
Luke (3:1) dates John the Baptist's* preaching, and hence the beginning of Jesus' public ministry, from Roman sources, saying that this took place in the fifteenth year of the Emperor Tiberius' reign (probably A.D. 27/28 or 28/29), when Pontius Pilate was governor of Judea, and when Herod (Antipas) was tetrarch of Galilee (cf. "that fox" in Lk 13:32). The Greek word *hēgemōn* "governor" (cf. Lk 20:20; Mt 27:2; etc.) is used loosely for Pilate's official title of Prefect (cf. 2.2. above).

Although the Romans are rarely mentioned by name, their presence pervades the Gospels. Cities and localities are called after them (e.g., Caesarea Philippi; Lake Tiberias, i.e., Galilee). We have references to Roman time-reckoning, Roman coinage and the hated tax collectors (*see* Taxes), who may have been wealthy men like Zacchaeus (described in Lk 19:2 as an *architelōnēs*, or "chief tax collector"), but were probably mostly minor officials such as local customs officers (cf. Levi/Matthew in Mk 2:14; Lk 5:27; Mt 9:9). All three Synoptics record the trap question over the Roman *kēnsos*, or tribute (Mk 12:13-17; Mt 22:15-22; Lk 20:20-26). This tax was especially hated because it had to be paid in Roman currency. It is probable that the coin shown to Jesus was a *denarius* of the reigning emperor Tiberius (see Hart, 241-48, and on Jesus' reply, Bruce, 249-63, both in Bammel and Moule). Matthew (17:24-27) records a second trap question about the *didrachma*, or Temple Tax. This was a Jewish religious due of one half-shekel (half-stater), later taken over by the Romans and applied to the temple of Jupiter Capitolinus (Josephus *J.W.* 6.218; Suetonius *Domitian* 12; Cassius Dio 46.7). Many scholars have assumed that Matthew here refers to a post-A.D. 70 Roman tax (cf. the term *kēnsos* in Jesus' reply), but W. Horbury has convincingly argued that the pericope dates to Jesus' own lifetime and concerns a controversy over the interpretation of Jewish Law (see Bammel and Moule, 265-86).

The Sermon on the Mount* alludes to the forced carrying of the Roman soldiers' baggage (Mt 5:41; note the Latin loanword *milion*, "mile" and the technical term *angareuō*, "press into service"). Jesus praises the faith of a centurion, whose servant he heals (Mt 8:5-13). Luke mentions the love of this centurion for the Jewish people and the fact that he had built a synagogue* for them (7:5). The centurion who supervised the crucifixion is also sympathetically portrayed (cf. 3.4. below). Jesus predicts the destruction of the Temple and the fall of Jerusalem (Mk 13 par.; *see* Destruction of Jerusalem). Some have seen in the phrase "abomination of desolation" (Mk 13:14; Mt 24:15) an allusion to Caligula's attempt to set up his statue in the Temple (A.D. 40), but others see the Danielic allusion as purely eschatological (*see* Apocalyptic Teaching). It has further been suggested, with greater probability, that some details of Luke's version (e.g., the allusion to the "army camps" in 21:20) are *post-eventum* prophecy, being colored by Jewish experience of the Roman siege and destruction (see Fitzmyer).

It should be noted that Jesus nowhere denounces the Romans or explicitly says anything politically subversive (cf. his masterly—and ambiguous—reply to the question over the tribute). He never calls for military or political action, and he flees to the hills when the crowd, excited by a feeding miracle,* seeks to take him by force to make him king (Jn 6:15). In the Sermon on the Mount he preaches non-violence and love* of one's enemies. At his arrest he rebukes the disciple* who takes up his sword (Mt 26:52; cf. Jn 18:11). The conjecture sometimes put forward that Jesus was a zealot or military revolutionary cannot be maintained without doing violence to all this evidence.

3.4. The Trial and Death of Jesus. The Romans were directly concerned with the trial (*see* Trial of Jesus) and execution of Jesus (*see* Death of Jesus). John's Gospel suggests that Roman soldiers were involved in Jesus' arrest (cf. the technical terms *speira*, "cohort," and *chiliarchos*, "tribune," in 18:3, 12); but the Synoptic accounts imply otherwise. After his Jewish trial Jesus was brought before Pontius Pilate as governor. The Gospels differ in their details, but it seems probable that Jesus was charged with the political offense of sedition or treason (i.e., *maiestas minuta*) rather than the religious offense of blasphemy. Luke (23:2) has a general charge of stirring up the people and specific

charges of forbidding to give tribute to Caesar and claiming to be "Christ a king." The other Gospels also suggest a political charge by Pilate's opening question, "Are you the King of the Jews?" and John's account (19:20) of the wording of the *titulus* on the cross argues the same.

John gives a dramatic dialog between Pilate, Jesus, the Jewish leaders and the crowd (*see* People, Crowd); but there is no explicit charge nor condemnation. The crowd, as in the Synoptics, choose to have the insurrectionist Barabbas released rather than Jesus. Then Pilate has Jesus scourged (this severe beating was required by Roman law during the crucifixion process). Some have seen Pilate's presentation of the bleeding Jesus to the crowd ("Behold the man," Jn 19:5) as an attempt to win sympathy for him; others as a further mockery. All four Gospels represent Pilate as eager to release Jesus (cf. esp. Jn 19:6). Many scholars have suggested that there has been some whitewashing of his character, possibly in order to heighten the responsibility of the Jewish leaders. External sources (e.g., Philo *Leg. Gai.* 302) portray Pilate as a harsh and inflexible governor who had difficulty in coping with his intractable province (cf. 3.3. above; see further Sherwin-White 1978, chap. 2; Bammel and Moule, 403-51).

The Gospels narrate that the Roman soldiers mocked Jesus before taking him to be crucified (Mk 15:16-20; Mt 27:27-31; cf. Jn 19:2-3). Luke is unique in mentioning a "trial" before Herod Antipas and a mocking by his soldiers (23:6-12). Jesus is crucified between two *lēstai*, or insurrectionists (Mk 15:27 par.), under the eye of a centurion who exclaims as Jesus dies, "Truly, this man was the Son of God" (Mk 15:39; cf. Lk 23:47, "Indeed, this man was innocent"). From the Gospel accounts one would assume that Jesus' execution, like that of the two *lēstai*, was carried out by Roman soldiers, but E. Bammel has recently marshalled evidence for the view that Jesus was executed by Jews (Bammel and Moule, 440-43). All four Evangelists mention Joseph of Arimathea's request to Pilate for the body of Jesus for burial (*see* Burial of Jesus). Matthew (27:65) alone records a request for Roman guards to watch the tomb (it is not clear whether he envisages those who were placed as Roman or Jewish). Thus there remain many problems concerning the precise roles of the Romans and the Jews during the trial and execution of Jesus. It is likely that apologetic, theological and other factors have helped shape the narratives.

The restrained way in which the Romans are described throughout the Gospels is quite remarkable in view of the Jewish suffering during their rule, the

Roman part in Jesus' death and the later persecutions of Christians at their hands.

See also HELLENISM; HERODIAN DYNASTY.

BIBLIOGRAPHY. M. Avi-Yonah, *Gazetteer of Roman Palestine* (*Qedem* 5, Jerusalem: Hebrew University, 1976); J. P. V. D. Balsdon, *Rome: The Story of an Empire* (London: Weidenfeld and Nicolson, 1970); E. Bammel and C. F. D. Moule, eds., *Jesus and the Politics of His Day* (Cambridge: University Press, 1984); R. B. Bandinelli, *Rome, The Centre of Power* (London: Thames and Hudson, 1970); S. Freyne, *Galilee from Alexander the Great to Hadrian* (Wilmington/Notre Dame: Glazier/ University of Notre Dame, 1980); M. C. Howatson, ed., *The Oxford Companion to Classical Literature* (2d ed., Oxford: University Press, 1989); B. W. Jones and R. D. Milns, *The Use of Documentary Evidence in the Study of Roman Imperial History* (Sydney: University Press, 1984); E. Lohse, *The New Testament Environment* (Nashville: Abingdon, 1976); A. N. Sherwin-White, "Provinces, Roman, " *ISBE* 3.1026-28; idem, *Roman Society and Roman Law in the New Testament* (2d ed.; Grand Rapids: Baker 1978); M. Stern, ed., *Greek and Latin Authors on Jews and Judaism* II (Jerusalem: Israel Academy of Sciences and Humanities, 1980).

R. B. Edwards

S

SABBATH

The English *Sabbath*, like the Greek *sabbaton*, is a transliteration of the Hebrew *šabbāt*. The term designates the seventh day of the Jewish week, a day marked by the cessation of work and by religious and ceremonial observances. All four Gospels depict Jesus in conflict with his contemporaries on matters of Sabbath observance. The traditions, rooted in Jesus' ministry, are used to accentuate themes central to each Evangelist.

1. Sabbath Law
2. The Sabbath in the Gospels
3. Conclusion

1. Sabbath Law.

A prohibition of work on the Sabbath is found in the Decalog (Ex 20:8-11; Deut 5:12-15) and several other OT texts (e.g., Ex 31:12-17; 35:2), and its transgression is treated in the Law codes as a capital offense (Ex 31:14-15; 35:2; cf. Num 15:32-36). Different motivations for the interruption of normal activities on the seventh day are given. The Israelite community was to be allowed to rest (the emphasis of Deut 5:12-15; cf. Ex 23:12); but the day was also to be considered holy (Ex 20:8; Deut 5:12), a portion of the Israelites' time which was consecrated to Yahweh (Ex 20:10; 35:2) just as the tithe of their produce was to be reserved for him. Israel's observance of the Sabbath was to be a sign of its special covenantal relationship with Yahweh (Ex 31:12-17; Ezek 20:12, 20), an imitation of God's* own rest after the completion of his creative work (Gen 2:2-3; Ex 20:11) and a reminder of the relief God granted his people in delivering them from slavery in Egypt (Deut 5:15). Those whose vision failed to extend beyond their pursuit of business naturally found the interruption an irritation to be evaded (Amos 8:5; cf. Jer 17:19-27; Neh 13:15-22). For Yahweh's faithful, however, the day's observance was a delight (Is 58:13-14).

In the Second Temple period (515 B.C.-A.D. 70) the words of Scripture became the object of interpretation by legal experts (*see* Scribes). Their goal was to spell out the duties of God's people by defining the terms and limits of God's revealed commands. The Sabbath provided a significant challenge since, from this point of view, the faithful needed to know precisely what constituted the "work" which was to be avoided if the command was not to be transgressed. Lists were drawn up (*Jub.* 2:29-30; 50:6-13; CD 10:14-11:18). Scripture itself provided some guidelines. Fires were not to be lit (Ex 35:3). Burdens were not to be carried (Jer 17:21-22), though from this point of view the term "burden" now needed legal definition. Similarly, a general prohibition of travel could be derived from Isaiah 58:13 (and see Ex 16:29). When such a prohibition took on the force of a legal statute, it became necessary to define the limits of a legitimate journey (cf. a "sabbath day's journey," Acts 1:12). That sowing and reaping are forbidden could be based on Exodus 34:21 (cf. 16:25-30).

Further problems arose when the prohibition of work on the Sabbath was perceived to conflict with other commands or with considerations of practicality or prudence. The principle that the prohibition may be disregarded when human life is in danger became well established (see 1 Macc 2:29-41). The service of the Temple* was conceded to take precedence over the Sabbath (cf. Num 28:9-10; 1 Chron 23:31), as was circumcision. The extent to which considerations of practicality were allowed to influence Sabbath regulations varied considerably with different interpreters.

Jewish observance of the Sabbath was well known and distinctive in the ancient world. It called forth both admiration (Josephus *Ag. Ap.* 2.39 §282; Philo *Vit. Mos.* 2.21) and scorn (Josephus *Ag. Ap.* 2.2 §§20-21) from outsiders and led, for example, to the excusal of Jews from service in foreign military forces (Jews would neither march forbidden lengths nor carry arms on the Sabbath; see Josephus *Ant.* 14.10.12 §§226-227). With laws whose scriptural background seemed clear, and with customs long and widely established, many Jews could be expected to comply. It can also be seen, however, that questions of proper observance were often a matter of interpretation. The various religious parties of Jesus' day not infrequently differed in their practice. And though each group doubtlessly pressed on others the claims of its interpretation to represent the will of heaven, such claims in our period were terrestrially unenforceable.

Positively, Jews met in synagogues* on the Sabbath Day for prayer, Scripture readings and edifying discourses. The welter of prohibitions may strike the outsider, and surely struck the half-hearted, as a burden grievous to be borne; still, it should not be doubted that faithful Jews continued to find in their Sabbath observance an occasion for joy.

2. The Sabbath in the Gospels.

2.1. Mark. Jesus is said to have participated in synagogue services on the Sabbath in Mark 1:21; 3:1 and 6:2. Instances of Sabbath observance may be noted in 1:32 (the people wait until Sabbath is over to carry the sick to Jesus) and 16:1 (the women* wait until Sabbath has passed before attending to the body of Jesus; *see* Burial of Jesus). Interestingly, Mark connects no queries with the Sabbath healings* reported in 1:21-28 and 29-31. In the latter case, Jesus is depicted among friends; in the former, he is in the synagogue. That not every record of a Sabbath healing is linked with a dispute suggests that Jesus' activities were not in flagrant transgression of existing formulations of Sabbath law and that, perhaps in the initial stages of his career, public enthusiasm may have silenced whatever private compunctions may have been felt. That objections are recorded on other occasions suggests that healing was liable to be construed as work, and that in the absence of a life-threatening situation the scrupulous might well find cause for offense.

The issue in Mark 2:23-28 appears more clear-cut. Though gleaning in the fields of another was expressly permitted by pentateuchal Law* (Lev 19:9-10; 23:22), such activity on the Sabbath breached the prohibition on Sabbath reaping. Since the prohibition has a scriptural base (Ex 34:21; cf. 16:25-29), it is hazardous to apply the claim here that Jesus merely challenges scribal additions while conforming to scriptural commands. Nor does the defense of the disciples'* activity in 2:25-28 follow that tack (David's transgression, cited as a precedent, was clearly of pentateuchal Law). Rather a precedent is cited from Scripture (1 Sam 21:1-6) for activity which, on the strict application of scriptural commands, was "not lawful" (*see* Abiathar).

The force of the illustration has been differently construed. (1) Some see the point of the comparison in the hunger felt by both Jesus' followers and those of David. The point would then be that, though the Sabbath prohibitions insisted on by Jesus' opponents are valid in principle, they must yield to the higher claims of human need. But Mark makes no mention of the disciples' hunger, as he would surely have done if hunger had been the crux of the defense. Nothing suggests that their need was so extreme as to legitimate the transgression of the Law. And indeed the unlawfulness of what David did is explicitly mentioned (2:26) in the defense of the disciples' activity. The point can hardly be that when the extenuating circumstances are taken into account, nothing unlawful has been done.

(2) Others note that the illustration records the behavior of David, and suggest that Jesus is tacitly claiming a similar right as David's son (*see* Son of David), the Messiah (*see* Christ), to somehow transcend the Law. But the necessary implication of this view is that David was entitled by his calling or office to transgress divine commands applicable to other people, a point which neither scriptural Law nor its later interpreters would concede.

(3) Most likely is the view that the example illustrates how Scripture itself countenances the breaking of the Law strictly construed, and thus calls in question the facile identification of God's will with a rigid interpretation of the terms of the Law. Verse 27 (perhaps an independent logion introduced here because it was felt appropriate; so at least the new introduction and the absence of the logion from the parallels in Matthew and Luke may suggest) can be construed as advancing the previous argument on either the first or third reading given above. The divine origin of the Sabbath is granted on either reading. Following interpretation (1) above, the logion represents a fresh insistence that humanitarian concerns must take priority over Sabbath commands. In the case of the third interpretation proposed above, the point would now be that God's design in giving the Sabbath for his people's good is overthrown when human behavior is subjected to rules developed in the casuistic interpretation of the Law.

Finally, 2:28 clearly and remarkably insists on Jesus' superiority as Son of Man* over the Sabbath law. It is not evident whether the verse is intended to represent a claim on Jesus' own lips or one added by the Christian community as a commentary on the preceding episode.

According to Mark 3:1-6 a healing performed by Jesus on the Sabbath was found objectionable and occasioned the plotting of Pharisees* and Herodians (*see* Herodian Dynasty) against his life. For his part Jesus is said to be grieved by the attitude of those more concerned with the niceties of the Law than with the well-being of a person (3:5). The defense of Jesus' activity given in 3:4 is striking. No attempt is made to show that the healing does not overstep the command prohibiting "work." The interpretation of the terms of the command (*see* Commandment), by which the legal experts of contemporary Judaism* defined the divine will, is not here an issue. Rather, the Markan Jesus insists that God can hardly be offended or his will transgressed by the doing of good and the restoring of health on the Sabbath (regardless, apparently, of whether or not the deed may be construed as "work"). God's will is rather disobeyed when evil is done or life "killed." It is debated whether the "evil" intended is that of leaving unperformed the miracle* of healing or the active plotting against Jesus' life in which, according to the pericope, his opponents were involved on the Sabbath.

It seems unlikely that Sabbath observance was a significant issue for the Second Evangelist or the community for which he wrote. The two relevant episodes do not appear to focus on the community's need of either guidance or a defense for its Sabbath behavior. Rather, the first incident celebrates the authority* of the community's Lord over the institutions of Israel's Law; the second is clearly meant to account for the hostility which Jesus' ministry aroused.

2.2. Matthew. For Matthew and his community, on the other hand, proper Sabbath observance may well have remained an issue. Admittedly, the prayer* in Matthew 24:20 (that the community's flight might not occur on the Sabbath) does not point unambiguously in that direction. Even a Christian congregation not observing the Sabbath would be exposed to hardship and danger if its people attempted to flee on that day in a Jewish environment. Nor does Matthew's Gospel preserve instances of Sabbath conflict or discussions of proper Sabbath behavior not found in Mark. But the parallels to Mark 2:23-28 and 3:1-6 in Matthew 12:1-14 show differences designed apparently to show that the Sabbath command, when properly interpreted, had not been transgressed. Its continuing relevance may therefore be implied.

Perhaps the explicit reference to the hunger of Jesus' disciples (12:1) is intended to provide a humanitarian legitimation for their behavior. Matthew 12:5 adds an illustration from the Torah (cf. Num 28:9-10) by which priests violate the Sabbath law without incurring guilt. Verse 6 then at least claims that the coming of the kingdom ("something greater than the Temple") in the person of Jesus causes the Sabbath laws to pale in significance. But perhaps the legal argument is implied that the activity of those in the

service of the kingdom, like that of priests* in the Temple, takes precedence over Sabbath laws. In verse 7 a favorite Matthean OT citation (Hos 6:6) is repeated, indicating that Sabbath laws are to be interpreted in such a way that divine mercy* is emphasized rather than strict conformity with ritual prescriptions.

In the second pericope (12:9-14) verse 12 preserves but a fragment of the argument of Mark 3:4. The main emphasis in the Matthean account falls rather on a logion shared with Luke (14:5) which Matthew introduces here. Though the stricter construction of the Law forbade the drawing up on the Sabbath of an animal from a pit (CD 11:13-14; *t. Šabb.* 14.3), the logion assumes that in ordinary practice compassion prevailed and assistance was given. This being the case, no objection should be raised when a human being (who is, after all, worth far more than a sheep) is healed on the holy day. Proper Sabbath observance does seem here to be a concern, but priority is given to claims of compassion over strict adherence to Sabbath rules.

2.3. Luke. In the two conflict pericopes common to the three Synoptic Gospels, Luke (6:1-5, 6-11) follows Mark quite closely without the Matthean additions. But two new instances of controversy arising from Sabbath healings are recorded. In Luke 13:10-17 the ruler of the synagogue objects to the healing of a woman with a chronic deformity. Work is allowed, he says, on six days of the week, and healings are then in order. There is therefore no need to desecrate the Sabbath with such activity. The Lukan Jesus finds the objection hypocritical, noting that domestic animals are commonly "unbound" and led to water on the Sabbath. Far more justified, surely, is the "unbinding" of a daughter of Abraham* from a satanic affliction (*see* Demon, Devil, Satan). Jesus' opponents are said to have been shamed by the response and the crowd delighted by the whole episode. In Luke 14:1-6 a variant of the argument presented in Matthew 12:11-12 is presented and leaves potential objectors speechless. The Sabbath discussions in Luke seem designed to show compassion on the part of Jesus, the ready acceptance it meets from the crowds (*see* People, Crowd) and the speechless shame to which opponents are reduced.

2.4. John. Johannine irony is undoubtedly to be seen in 19:31 (cf. 18:28), where punctilious Sabbath observance is grimly juxtaposed with the crucifixion (*see* Death of Jesus) of God's Son (*see* Son of God). Sabbath healings lead to disputes in chapters 5 and 9; the former is recalled in 7:22-23. In no case does the Evangelist evince a concern for guiding the Sabbath behavior of his readers. In John 5 offense is first raised when, at Jesus' command, a pallet is carried on the Sabbath (5:10) and exacerbated when it is learned that Jesus has healed on that day (5:15-16). Remarkably, the Johannine Jesus concedes that he "works" on the Sabbath (5:17)—precisely what the Law prohibits—but claims that he is merely acting as God his father does. The charge that Jesus breaks the Sabbath is thus conceded (5:18), but the interest of the Evangelist is rather on the christological claim to which it leads. In John 7:22-23 the unreasonableness of Jesus' opponents seems the point: they permit Sabbath circumcision but object to the restoration of a man's health. Similarly, in John 9 the Sabbath healing gives the Evangelist the opportunity to show Jesus' opponents as blind to the manifest workings of God in their midst (9:30-33), a blindness* induced by their insistence that a divine representative must conform to the niceties of the old code (9:16). The memory of Sabbath disputes aroused by Jesus is preserved in John, but it becomes the starting-point for the pursuit of favorite Johannine themes: the divine sonship of Jesus and the necessity of faith* in him.

3. Conclusion.

As we have seen, Sabbath controversies are found in Mark (2:23-28; 3:1-6), in material common to Matthew and Luke (Mt 12:11-12a par. Lk 14:5), in material unique to Matthew (12:5-7) and Luke (13:10-17; the incident of 14:1-6), and in John (5; 7:22-23; 9). Furthermore, the authenticity of crucial logia (Mk 2:27; 3:4; etc.) is widely conceded. At the roots of the Gospel tradition, then, are memories of opposition to Jesus' Sabbath behavior aroused among his contemporaries.

Opponents saw the divine will as requiring conformity with the terms of Torah's statutes as interpreted by legal authorities. Hence activities which could be construed as the "work" which Torah forbade were to be avoided unless extenuating circumstances (as defined by the legal experts) could be found to legitimate the activity. Jesus' behavior (and, according to one story, that of his disciples) was found to violate this stricture. The basic line of Jesus' defense as portrayed in the Gospels shows a different approach to the understanding of the divine will. No more than Jesus allows the terminology of Deuteronomy 24:1-4 to define the propriety of divorce* (Mk 10:1-12) or the terminology of scriptural Law to define norms for oaths* (Mt 5:33-36), does he allow that the divine will for the Sabbath rests in the proper interpretation of the word "work." When opposed he does not reply by arguing that, counter to his opponents' claims, "work" has not been done nor the command transgressed.

He insists that doing "good" can never be wrong on the Sabbath (Mk 3:4—a criterion quite different from the question whether or not "work" has been done), that compassion is a better guide to proper behavior than rules defined by legal experts (Mt 12:10-11a), that God's intentions with the Sabbath are distorted when humans are subjected to a rigid code (Mk 2:27). Implicit in each case, and explicit at various points in the Gospel narrative, is the claim that Jesus has authority to interpret the divine will.

Only for Matthew is it likely that proper Sabbath observance remained an issue. Only in this Gospel is it likely that the relevant pericopes were intended to provide guidance in the matter. In the other Gospels the traditional material serves other ends. Sabbath discussions provide the opportunity to highlight Jesus' authority, his compassion and the nature of his opposition.

See also LAW.

BIBLIOGRAPHY. S. Bacchiocchi, *From Sabbath to Sunday: A Historical Investigation of the Rise of Sunday Observance in Early Christianity* (Rome: Pontifical Gregorian University, 1977); R. Banks, *Jesus and the Law in the Synoptic Tradition* (Cambridge: Cambridge University, 1975) 113-31; D. A. Carson, "Jesus and the Sabbath in the Four Gospels," in *From Sabbath to Lord's Day: A Biblical, Historical, and Theological Investigation,* ed. D. A. Carson (Grand Rapids: Zondervan, 1982) 57-97; D. M. Cohn-Sherbok, "An Analysis of Jesus' Arguments Concerning the Plucking of Grain on the Sabbath," *JSNT* 2 (1979) 31-41; F. Neirynck, "Jesus and the Sabbath: Some Observations on Mark II, 27," in *Jésus aux origines de la christologie,* ed. J. Dupont (Louvain: Leuven University, 1975) 227-270; H. Riesenfeld, "The Sabbath and the Lord's Day in Judaism, the Preaching of Jesus and Early Christianity," in *The Gospel Tradition* (Philadelphia: Fortress, 1970) 111-37; L. H. Schiffman, *The Halakhah at Qumran* (SJLA 16; Leiden: E. J. Brill, 1975) 77-133; P. Sigal, *The Halakah of Jesus of Nazareth according to the Gospel of Matthew* (Lanham, MD: University Press of America, 1986); S. Westerholm, *Jesus and Scribal Authority* (ConBNT 10; Lund: CWK Gleerup, 1978) 92-103.

S. Westerholm

SABBATH YEAR. *See* JUBILEE.

SACRIFICE. *See* DEATH OF JESUS.

SADDUCEES. *See* HERODIAN DYNASTY; JUDAISM.

SALVATION

The term *salvation* (with its associated word group)

has become widely used in Christian theology to express the provision of God* for our human situation of need and sin. The word group has a less prominent theological role in the Gospels but nevertheless is important in expressing the effects of the ministry of Jesus. The present article is largely confined to the use of the word group and does not develop the broader concept of salvation at length.

    1. Overview of Linguistic Usage
    2. Background to the Usage in the Gospels
    3. Salvation in the Individual Gospels
    4. The Understanding of Salvation in the Gospels

1. Overview of Linguistic Usage.

1.1. The Verb Sōzō. According to Louw and Nida the verb *to save* (*sōzō*) has three meanings in the NT: (1) "To rescue from danger and to restore to a former state of safety and well being"; (2) "to cause someone to become well again after having been sick"; (3) "to cause someone to experience divine salvation—'to save.' "

The verb is found frequently in the Gospels (Mt 15 x; Mk 14 x + Mk 16:16; Lk 17 x; Jn 6 x; the sayings in Mt 18:11 and Lk 9:56 are not found in the oldest MSS; Mk 16:16 is part of a later addition to the Gospel). It has various senses.

1.1.1. The Synoptics. (1) The verb means "to deliver" from danger. So in Matthew 8:25 and 14:30 it is used of rescue from the danger of drowning. In Matthew 27:40 (par. Mk 15:30); 27:42b (par. Mk 15:31b and Lk 23:35b); 27:49; Luke 23:37, 39 it is used of Jesus being delivered from dying on the cross (presumably by miraculous means or by Elijah* coming to help him). It is probably in this same general sense that reference is made to Jesus "saving" others (Mt 27:42a par. Mk 15:31 and Lk 23:35a).

In the passive the verb can mean "to come" or to be brought safely through a period of danger to life (Mt 10:22 and 24:13 par. Mk 13:13; cf. Mt 24:22 par. Mk 13:20).

A more metaphorical use is found in Luke 19:10, where Jesus is like a shepherd who seeks out and saves the lost [sheep] from danger of death (*see* Shepherd, Sheep).

(2) The verb often has the meaning "to heal" (namely, from disease; *see* Healing). It is so used in Matthew 9:21 (par. Mk 5:28); 9:22a (par. Mk 5:34 and Lk 8:48); 9:22b; Mark 5:23; 6:56 (par. Mt 14:36, Gk *diasōzō*); 10:52 (par. Lk 18:42); Luke 7:50; 8:36, 50; 17:19 (note also Lk 7:3, Gk *diasōzō*). In some of these cases the reference is to deliverance from the power of evil spirits by exorcism (*see* Demon, Devil, Satan) or to the raising of the dead (*see* Resurrection). In Mark

3:4 (par. Lk 6:9) "to save a life" (Gk *psychē* may have the sense "person" here) is contrasted with killing. The phrase is used in the context of healing in a broad sense of doing whatever is needed to promote life and health, and the thought is probably of physical life.

(3) In the story of the conversation between Jesus, the rich young man and the disciples* the phrases "to inherit eternal life" (*see* Life), "to enter the kingdom of God" (*see* Kingdom of God) and "to be saved" appear to be used synonymously (Mk 10:17, 23-25, 26; cf. Mt 19:16, 23-24, 25; Lk 18:18, 24-25, 26). What might be regarded as a technical usage of spiritual salvation is found in Luke 13:23 ("are 'the saved' few?") and in Luke 8:12 ("so that they may not believe and be saved"). Jesus is so named according to the angel of the Lord in Matthew 1:21 because "he will save his people from their sins."

In a paradoxical saying Jesus talks about people who want to save their lives and lose them (Mt 16:25 par. Mk 8:35a and Lk 9:24a) in contrast to those who lose their lives and (thus) save them (Mk 8:35b par. Lk 9:24b).

(4) In some passages the language is ambiguous, and it is not clear whether the reference is purely to physical and mental health and well-being or also to spiritual salvation (e.g., Lk 7:50, "Your faith has saved you"; note that this phrase is used elsewhere of physical healing: Mk 5:34 par. Lk 8:48; Mk 10:52 par. Lk 18:42; cf. Lk 8:50; 17:19).

1.1.2. John. The usage in John is similar to that of the Synoptics.

(1) In John 12:27 Jesus prays about the possibility of being delivered from having to undergo the cross. In John 10:9 he refers to people being like sheep who enter the sheepfold and live in safety.

(2) In John 11:12 Lazarus is thought to be asleep (i.e., in a coma) and therefore capable of being healed.

(3) Jesus is said to have come to save the world* (Jn 3:17), and he refers to this as his purpose in 12:47. He speaks of his hearers being saved in 5:34.

1.2. The Verb Rhyomai. Meaning "to rescue, deliver," *rhyomai* is used much less frequently, generally with reference to deliverance from extreme danger, such as death or falling into the hands of enemies. In Matthew 27:43 it is found in the satirical quotation of Psalm 22:8 by the Jewish leaders to Jesus on the cross. In Luke 1:74 deliverance from enemies is part of the salvation awaited by Zechariah. In Matthew 6:13 the disciples are encouraged to pray (*see* Prayer) for deliverance from the evil one (or from evil).

1.3. The Noun Sōtēr. Sōtēr, meaning "savior," is used

by Mary with reference to God in Luke 1:47, and Jesus is so designated at his birth by the angel* of the Lord to the shepherds (Lk 2:11). In John 4:42 the Samaritan* people who have responded to Jesus declare that he is "the Savior of the world" (Jn 4:42).

1.4. The Noun Sōtēria. *Sōtēria,* a noun meaning "salvation," can refer to the process of saving or to the result. It is found in Luke 1:69 where Zechariah declares that God has raised up "a horn of salvation," and then defines God's gift more closely as "salvation [deliverance] from our enemies." Later, in the same hymn the task of his son John (*see* John the Baptist) is defined as giving to his people "the knowledge of salvation through the forgiveness of their sins." Jesus comments that his visit to Zacchaeus has brought "salvation" to his household (Lk 19:9). And Jesus tells the woman of Samaria that "salvation is from the Jews" (Jn 4:22).

1.5. The Noun Sōtērion. Another word meaning "salvation," *sōtērion,* is found in Luke 2:30 where Simeon says that his eyes have seen God's salvation, and in Luke 3:6 where the Evangelist himself quotes Isaiah 40:5, "And all humanity will see God's salvation." According to Louw and Nida this word signifies rather "the means by which people experience divine salvation."

1.6. Salvation in a Spiritual Sense. This survey demonstrates that the spiritual sense is clearly present in Matthew (1:21) and Mark (10:26), but that it is most prominent in Luke, who alone of the Synoptic Evangelists develops the use of the nouns alongside the verb. One interesting fact which emerges is that the "literal" meaning of the word can be either broadly to "rescue" or to "heal," and both of these meanings can underlie the "spiritual" usage of the terminology. Louw and Nida (1.241 n. 4) comment that on the whole Bible translators have used words reflecting the former meaning, but that there has been a shift to using words reflecting the latter meaning or to using words that signify more "to restore, recreate." Thus, the accent has shifted from the action of God or the newness of what he creates to the restoration of what has been lost or marred.

2. Background to the Usage in the Gospels.

The Gospels were written at a time when the church had already developed a special vocabulary to refer to Christian experience. We may envisage a two-way process whereby the vocabulary of the Christians will have been influenced by that of Jesus and conversely the diction of the Gospels may have been influenced by that of the church. The modes of expression of Jesus and his followers will also have been influenced

by their heritage in the OT and Judaism,* and to some extent also by the need to speak in terms that would be readily understood in the wider world.

The extensive and readable survey by E. M. B. Green considers the background to the NT use of the concept. There is a considerable amount of material in the OT where the corresponding Hebrew words are often used of deliverance in times of conflict, especially war. But the idea of deliverance is much wider and refers to being set free from all kinds of perils and dangers to life and even more generally to the state of well-being which God desires for his people. The Israelites naturally looked to God as their supreme and ultimate deliverer from all kinds of trouble and distress. He is the Savior *par excellence* (cf. Ps 27:1 and frequently).

The term *savior* was well known in the Greco-Roman world as an epithet for gods in their roles as helpers of humanity and particular communities; the god Asclepius was particularly important as the healer of the sick at various shrines. It was also used of statesmen, and when a religious cult of rulers developed, *savior* was one of the honorific titles used in this connection.

3. Salvation in the Individual Gospels.

3.1. Matthew.

3.1.1. Salvation from Sin. Right at the outset Matthew's Gospel announces that "Jesus" is to be so-called because he will save his people from their sins (*see* Forgiveness of Sins). In this context the "people" is a designation for Israel which is regarded as a sinful nation. Deliverance from sin is associated with the response of the people to John the Baptist (Mt 3:6) and with the sovereign declarations of Jesus as the Son of man (Mt 9:2, 5, 6; *see* Son of Man). At the Last Supper (*see* Last Supper) Jesus declares that his blood is to be poured out for the forgiveness of sins (Mt 26:28). He also states that he has come with a mission to sinful people (Mt 9:10-13; cf. 11:19). The significance of "saving" is not spelled out in detail, but the three references to forgiveness indicate clearly enough what is probably in mind. One would naturally think of delivering people from the effects of their sins, but at the same time enabling them not to sin is in mind. In the ironic summary on the lips of the Jewish leaders at the crucifixion: "He saved others" (Mt 27:42a), the verb is used in a broad sense and is not to be limited to the sense of saving a person from death (Mt 27:42b). However, it is unlikely that we are to find a spiritual significance on the level of the original speakers.

3.1.2. Salvation As Physical and Spiritual. The references to deliverance from impending death at sea and to the cure of physical ailments need not necessarily imply anything further than this. However, a number of factors may suggest a different understanding.

First, there is the fact that stories in the Gospels about physical "salvation" may well have been used in the church with a symbolic significance; thus the story of the disciples in the boat during a storm has been taken to symbolize the church in the world suffering tribulation. In this case it is the followers of Jesus who cry out to the Lord to "save" them in the difficulties of life, and the answer to their prayers may lie in the removing or mitigating of their trials, or their being brought safely through them, or their being brought to final salvation despite even death itself. The collocation of healing a paralyzed man and forgiving his sins may equally have led to seeing healing as symbolic of spiritual forgiveness and salvation.

Second, there is the fact that the formula translated elsewhere in the Gospels as "your faith* has healed you" is used once in Luke (7:50) of a sinful woman who had experienced forgiveness. Here the formula is naturally translated as "your faith has saved you" (so NIV), which is essentially the same as Ephesians 2:8 (cf. Acts 15:11 [if translated with F. F. Bruce, "we believe (so as) to be saved"]; 16:31; Rom 10:9; Jas 2:14; in the longer addition to Mark [16:16] the same church terminology is to be found). In view of the ambiguity of the formula when taken out of a healing context, it is quite probable that early Christians were led to see healing as symbolic of salvation and to draw the parallel between healing by faith and salvation by faith.

Third, no hard and fast line was drawn between the physical and the spiritual in the ancient world. In fact, the same is often true today. If Christians pray for God to "bless" somebody, it is often hard to say whether they are thinking of successfully carrying through some piece of business or aspect of daily life or enjoying some kind of sense of divine favor or doing some aspect of Christian ministry and service successfully. It would, therefore, be hard to distinguish between a physical healing and the healing of the "inner person" (cf. Lk 17:19, where it is not clear whether the statement refers purely to the cure of the leprosy).

It is therefore likely that the healing stories in the Gospels were understood as accounts of a process that involved the whole person and not merely a physical or mental healing.

3.1.3. Salvation Despite Persecution. Matthew 10:22 and parallels could refer to being brought through persecution in physical safety; however, the reference to possible death in verse 21 suggests that the verse is about standing firm in loyalty to Jesus despite persecution and that standing firm leads to "final salvation." However, in Matthew 24:22 (par. Mk 13:20) the force could be that if persecution went on too long, nobody would survive alive, and therefore there would be nobody left alive to welcome the Son of man at his coming. The saying cannot mean that nobody would stand firm to the point of martyrdom. Here, then, we have two different uses of the word quite close to each other.

3.1.4. Final Salvation. Similarly, Matthew 19:25 and parallels must refer to "final salvation." It is about a future state of being saved as opposed to being lost, and in the imagery of the Gospels signifies entry to the heavenly banquet instead of exclusion, a welcome by the Son of man and entry to the heavenly kingdom instead of rejection and consignment to eternal fire (*see* Judgment). This raises the question whether "being saved" refers exclusively to a future state in the next world, or whether it can also refer to those who are already sure of entry to the kingdom.

3.1.5. Saving and Losing One's Life. In Matthew 16:25 and parallels there is an important set of sayings about saving and losing one's life. The difficulty here is partly caused by the ambiguity and uncertainty of the word *life* (Gk *psychē*) which can refer to the "soul" as distinct from the body (and hence signify an individual person), or to "life" or to one's "real life." Jesus appears to be saying that those who try to "save" (i.e., preserve) their lives, either in the sense of avoiding martyrdom or by holding fast to the things that give them pleasure and satisfaction in this world, will in the end "lose" their lives, either by finding that death cannot be kept at bay or that attachment to earthly things leads to loss at the final judgment and hence in the next world. On the other hand, those who are prepared to say "no" to their self, possibly even by dying, for the sake of Jesus (Mark adds "and the gospel"), find that they will "save" their lives in the sense that they will attain to the kingdom of God and enjoy the blessings that are really worth having (cf. the parallel in somewhat different wording in Mt 10:39 par. Lk 17:33).

3.2. Mark. The picture in Mark's Gospel is simpler than in Matthew. The one significant reference not paralleled in Matthew is Mark 3:4, where Jesus comments on the lawfulness of doing good and "saving life" on the Sabbath* in the broad sense of healing a sick man. The phrase stands in contrast to "killing" and is pointedly directed against what Jesus implies to be the secret intentions of his critics who attacked him for healing on the Sabbath. Otherwise, Mark lacks the programmatic text found in Matthew 1:21, and only in Mark 10:26 is there an explicitly theological use of the term.

3.3. Luke. The case is different with Luke. He has the same broad pattern of usage as the other two Gospels, but there is a special emphasis on salvation which is not found in them.

3.3.1. The Overture to the Story of Salvation. This is clear above all from the birth stories (*see* Birth of Jesus), which function like an overture, setting out the main themes of the following drama, but doing so with their own distinctive music. One of the most characteristic tones here is that of salvation, with six significant references.

The note is first struck in Luke 1:47 where Mary, as the mother-to-be of the Messiah aligns herself with the people of God and rejoices in God her savior (*see* Mary's Song). The development of her song makes it clear that he is savior both of her and of the people. God's action is depicted in terms of powerful action against the mighty and the proud and on behalf of the poor and humble. These sets of terms connote respectively those who are opposed to God and those who trust him to provide for their needs. Further, God's action is seen as forming part of a long history of merciful concern for the people of his choice.

In the second song, that of Zechariah (*see* Zechariah's Song), the nature of salvation is brought out more clearly. Again, the note of powerful intervention is struck—"a horn of salvation" (1:69)—and it is associated with the coming of the Messiah (*see* Christ). Again we hear of God's action against the powerful wicked people making it possible for his people to serve him righteously without fear of attack (1:71). But above all Zechariah speaks of an experience (Gk *gnōsis*, "knowledge") of salvation which is closely associated with the forgiveness of sins (1:77). What Matthew 1:21 said with the utmost brevity Luke expresses on a broader canvas. It is not surprising after all this that when Jesus is born, the lofty language used to describe him refers not only to his Davidic links, to his messiahship and his position as Lord,* but also to his being a savior (2:11). And the whole drama is summed up in the comment of Simeon (*see* Simeon's Song) that he has seen the salvation which the Lord has prepared—a salvation which is for all peoples (NIV "for all people" [singular] is not sufficiently literal), including the Gentiles* (Lk 2:30-32).

3.3.2. Salvation As the Mission of the Son of Man. The notes of this overture are intended to stay in our ears as we continue to listen to Luke's Gospel, and other uses of the "salvation" terminology should resonate with what we have already heard. Luke repeats a good deal of what we have already found in Matthew and Mark. We may note that in recounting material parallel to that in Mark he has added a reference in 8:12 to the way in which the devil snatches away the word from some hearers "so they may not believe and be saved" (Lk 8:12). Here the language of the early church is echoed, and Luke is clearly referring to the experience of spiritual salvation which comes through hearing the word of God. The same is true in Luke 13:23 where Jesus is asked whether "the saved" are few. This question should be interpreted in the light of Matthew 7:13-14, which speaks of the many people who tread the road to destruction and the few who find the way to life, and of the equating of terms which we saw in Mark 10. This is confirmed by the context which refers to the coming feast in the kingdom of God.

Luke's theology of salvation is summed up in Luke 19:10 where the Son of man's mission is to seek and to save the lost. The language is that of shepherding and refers to the rescue of sheep from death in various possible ways. The metaphorical usage of such language to refer to God's care of his people was well established and is echoed here. In consequence of the coming of Jesus to him, it can be said that salvation has come to Zacchaeus's house there and then (Lk 19:9). It is thus a present experience involving the table fellowship (*see* Table Fellowship) between Jesus and Zacchaeus and the commencement of a new way of life in which the latter abandons the sinful habits of the past. Jesus emphasizes that even though Zacchaeus is a sinner,* yet he is one of the lost sheep of the house of Israel and therefore a rightful object of his mission.

3.4. John. In the Gospel of John salvation is associated with the mission of the Son of God (*see* Son of God) and is placed in direct contrast with the possibility of condemnation and perishing. To be saved is thus the opposite of being judged and destroyed. It is the same as to gain eternal life (Jn 3:16-17; cf. 12:47). Salvation is not confined to the Jewish people. It is for the world, and this includes the Samaritans,* whom Jewish orthodoxy regarded as excluded from God's favor; it is they who confess that Jesus is the "savior of the world" (Jn 4:42), even if it is true that salvation comes to the world "from the Jews." It follows that testimony to Jesus is what can lead people to experience salvation (Jn 5:34). The shepherding metaphor (*see* Shepherd, Sheep) is also used to express the role of Jesus in this Gospel, but here Jesus functions as the door through which the sheep enter into the safety of the fold and so are free from the dangers outside. (The metaphor is not to be pressed; the sheep can go freely in and out in safety; the implication is that those who "belong" to the sheepfold are assured of the protection of the shepherd wherever they are.)

4. The Understanding of Salvation in the Gospels.

Sufficient has been said to show that salvation is not a dominant word group in the Gospels in the same way as, say, the kingdom of God is. This is particularly obvious in Mark. Matthew associates the coming of Jesus with his role as a savior, but does not develop the terminology significantly. Luke makes much of the theme in the birth narratives, and never altogether loses sight of it thereafter, but the terminology can scarcely be said to be prominent. In John the word group occupies a minor but significant role, alongside other word groups that receive much greater attention.

It is obvious that the Evangelists are here reflecting the historical realities of the situation, that this was not a word group used greatly by Jesus, especially in its full theological sense. Nevertheless, it is arguable that the Evangelists have correctly represented the situation in that they recognized that the mission of Jesus was ultimately concerned with salvation. Jesus announced the kingdom of God with its attendant blessings; the language of salvation spells out what this means in terms of the benefits for humankind.

Several themes emerge from the Gospels:

(1) Salvation is closely related to Jesus and his mission. It is a comprehensive term for the benefits brought by the sovereign action of God through the Messiah.

(2) It is thought of as a future experience, identical with entry into the kingdom of God and gaining eternal life, but it is also a present experience resulting from personal encounter with Jesus.

(3) God brings salvation through Jesus for his people Israel. The implication is that, although they are God's people, they are not enjoying the fullness of life which he wishes for them. This is due both to the effects of evil in the world at large (e.g., the action of enemies) and the workings of illness and death.

(4) Individuals are not by their sinfulness cut off from the possibility of gaining the salvation intended for God's people. On the contrary, this fact establishes their need. Nor in fact is salvation in principle limited to the Jews. There are hints that it is for all peoples, although within the ministry of Jesus there are only occasional contacts with Samaritans and other non-Jews.

(5) The linking of healing with faith and the wider

use of the "your faith has saved you" formula indicate that the reception of salvation was associated with faith, understood in a broad sense as recognition of Jesus as God's sovereign and powerful agent and a commitment to him.

(6) Turning aside from evil is part of the process of salvation. Zacchaeus in fact not only abandons his former dishonest practices but pledges himself to a new way of life which involves giving to the poor.

(7) In presenting Jesus as the savior the Evangelists are assigning to him a role which Judaism reserved for Yahweh. Although the term could be applied to earthly leaders (the judges), it was used predominantly of Yahweh, and the echoes of OT passages about Yahweh's saving activity indicate that his role is now assigned to Jesus. The term *savior* was not previously applied to the Messiah in Judaism. At the same time, it is implied that Jesus stands over against other human figures (such as the Roman emperor) who were regarded as saviors.

See also FAITH; FORGIVENESS OF SINS; GENTILE; HEALING; KINGDOM OF GOD; LIFE; LUKE, GOSPEL OF.

BIBLIOGRAPHY. W. Foerster and G. Fohrer, "σῴζω κτλ," *TDNT* VII.965-1024; A George, *Etudes sur l'oeuvre de Luc* (Paris: Gabalda, 1978) 307-20 (= "L'emploi chez Luc du vocabulaire de salut," *NTS* 23 [1977] 308-20); E. M. B. Green, *The Meaning of Salvation* (London: Hodder and Stoughton, 1965); J. P. Louw and E. A. Nida, *Greek-English Lexicon of the New Testament Based on Semantic Domains* (New York: United Bible Societies, 1988); I. H. Marshall, *Luke: Historian and Theologian* (3d ed; Grand Rapids: Zondervan, 1989); J. Schneider and C. Brown, "Redemption etc.," *NIDNTT* 3.205-21; W. C. van Unnik, "L'usage de *sozein* 'sauver' et de ses dérivés dans les Evangiles synoptiques," in J. Coppens, ed., *La formation des Evangiles* (Bruges: Desclée de Brouwer, 1957) 178-94 (= W. C. van Unnik, *Sparsa Collecta* [Leiden: Brill, 1973] 16-34).

I. H. Marshall

SAMARIA. *See* ARCHEOLOGY AND GEOGRAPHY; SAMARITANS.

SAMARITAN WOMAN. *See* SAMARITANS; WOMEN.

SAMARITANS

In NT times the Samaritans were a substantial religious group inhabiting parts of the central hill country of Samaria between Galilee* to the north and Judea to the south, but with Diaspora communities in addition (*see* Archeology and Geography). Physically, they focused on Mount Gerizim, close to the ancient town of Shechem, while religiously the focus of their faith was on a form of the Law* of Moses,* the Pentateuch, which differed only slightly, but in one or two respects crucially, from the form of the Pentateuch familiar to us from its Masoretic recension.

1. Sources and Their Difficulties
2. Origins and Early History
3. Varieties of Samaritanism and Principal Beliefs
4. Samaritans in the Gospels

1. Sources and Their Difficulties.

Despite the explosion in recent years in the publication of Samaritan texts and secondary discussions based upon them, considerable problems still confront us regarding most questions relating to the Samaritans in the first half of the first century A.D.

1.1. Samaritan Sources. Apart from the Samaritan Pentateuch itself, all Samaritan sources date from periods considerably later than the NT. Moreover, many of these sources, whether historical, doctrinal or liturgical, are known only from manuscripts of far more recent date still. In addition, it must be remembered that the Samaritan community has survived in unbroken continuity to this very day, and that during its history it has both developed internally and, being usually a minority group, has inevitably been influenced by external pressures in its quest for survival. Scholars thus disagree, often quite widely, over the extent to which these sources can help in reconstructing early Samaritan history and belief.

Among the more important texts which incorporate valuable earlier traditions are: (1) the *Memar Marqah,* a fourth-century composition but also including later material; it is an expansive retelling of the biblical account of Moses, incorporating many midrashic supplements (*see* Midrash); (2) the *Kitāb al-Ta'rīkh* ("annals") of *Abu 'l-Fath,* composed in A.D. 1355, and now generally recognized as the most valuable of the various Samaritan "Chronicles"; and (3) the Samaritan Targum (*see* Targums). Of course, even though the greatest caution has to be exercised before historical conclusions can be drawn from these and other such Samaritan sources, they have considerable significance on their own account in terms of heightening our appreciation of the Samaritans' sense of self-awareness.

1.2. Jewish Sources. Pride of place here belongs to Josephus,* who both recounts a version of the origin of the Samaritans and includes frequent references to them in his *Antiquities* and *Jewish War.* This material has to be evaluated in the light of Josephus' evident anti-Samaritan stance and his historical confusion (which can be independently verified) surrounding

especially the last part of the Persian period and the start of the Hellenistic period, precisely the time in which he locates the most important step in the development of the Samaritan community.

There are also references of varied significance in the inter-testamental literature and in the later Mishnah and Talmud (*see* Rabbinic Traditions and Writings). Though generally negative, scholars have frequently remarked on the fact that several of these are a good deal more ambivalent than might at first have been supposed, reflecting, no doubt, the fact that the status of the Samaritans was extremely problematic from a Jewish point of view.

1.3. Other Sources. The NT itself contains important material from an historical point of view. In the context of our present discussion, we need therefore to be particularly aware of the dangers of circular argumentation. Some of the early church fathers also include potentially relevant material. Finally, archeology is a particularly important source of information in an area where the textual data are so uncertain. Shechem has been extensively excavated, and work is currently in progress unearthing the remains of a substantial Hellenistic town on Mount Gerizim itself, so that we may hope for further advances in our understanding in the coming years.

A full survey of all these sources is now available in *The Samaritans,* a magisterial compendium by a number of leading experts, edited by A. D. Crown (1989).

2. Origins and Early History.

Several views of Samaritan origins are attested in antiquity. Though each contains problems from a modern perspective, they retain their importance as evidence for how the situation was perceived in the first century. The following survey represents a heavy simplification for the sake of clarity.

2.1. Samaritan Views. The Samaritans have always believed that they are the direct descendants of a faithful nucleus of ancient Israel. From their perspective, Israel's apostasy began as early as the time of Eli (eleventh century B.C.), when the nation's cultic center was removed from Gerizim to Shiloh (and thence eventually to Jerusalem); they would thus not have regarded themselves as the remnant of the old northern kingdom of Israel, but as a separate group alongside them. This helps explain their acceptance of the Pentateuch alone as authoritative. For them, therefore, the question of origins should be directed more toward Judaism* than to themselves.

2.2. Jewish Traditions. The origins of the Samaritans are linked with the account in 2 Kings 17:24-41 about how, following their conquest of the northern kingdom, the Assyrians colonized the area by settling it with people from a number of Mesopotamian towns, including Cuthah. These colonists adopted the Israelite faith alongside their own religion (v. 41), and their descendants, often called "Cuthaeans" in Jewish polemical sources, are the Samaritans of later times. The hostilities between Judah and her northern neighbor recorded in the books of Ezra and Nehemiah demonstrate the antiquity of the division between the two groups.

2.3. Josephus. While sharing the previous opinion, Josephus adds a further significant ingredient, namely that at the end of the Persian period the priest Manasseh was expelled from Jerusalem, and that a sanctuary was built for him shortly after at the start of the Hellenistic period by Sanballat, his father-in-law, on Mount Gerizim. Over the course of time other priests from Jerusalem joined him there. Josephus thus recognizes a certain degree of Samaritan priestly legitimacy (at least in terms of descent), and his account helps him explain the Jewish character of much Samaritan practice.

2.4. Critical Reconstruction. After decades of discussion (which cannot be surveyed here), as new pieces of evidence have come to light, scholars are now agreed that none of these positions can be maintained as an accurate reflection of the situation. While disagreement inevitably remains, there is a widespread measure of agreement on some of the salient issues, the upshot of which for our present purposes is that the situation as reflected in the NT developed far more recently than had previously been thought and that the division was by no means as clear-cut as the earlier views might be thought to imply. The following points deserve notice.

2.4.1. The account in 2 Kings 17 should be discounted in discussions of Samaritan origins. (1) The word *haššōmrōnîm* in verse 29, often translated "the Samaritans," seems merely to mean "inhabitants of (the city or province of) Samaria," and this fits the context best. (2) There is no evidence to link the later Samaritans with Samaria. The earliest certain references to them all point clearly to their residence at Shechem, as we should expect on the basis of their theology (Sir 50:26; 2 Macc 5:22-23; 6:2), and one of Josephus' sources refers to them as "Shechemites" (*Ant.* 11.340-47; 12.10). Shechem was rebuilt only in the early Hellenistic period, following an interruption in settlement of some 150 years. (3) Despite earlier mistaken suggestions, it is now clear that nothing of later Samaritan religion and practice owes anything to the proposed pagan influence of 2 Kings 17 or Ezra 4.

2.4.2. It is not known for certain precisely who resettled Shechem (and Mount Gerizim itself?) at the start of the Hellenistic period. Most probably, an important element comprised a group of religious purists who were descendants of the original Israelite population in the north who had not been exiled by the Assyrians (that there were some is recognized by the OT itself; cf., for instance, 2 Chron 30; 34:6; Jer 40:5). Following the severe suppression of a revolt in Samaria in the time of Alexander the Great and the complete hellenization of this city, the ancient site of Shechem would have been an obvious place to settle. "It often happened that when a Greek colony was established, native villages under its control formed a union around an ancestral sanctuary" (E. Bickerman, 43-44). The discovery of over 200 skeletons in a cave in the *Wâdi ed-Dâliyeh* is generally thought to reflect part of this same upheaval.

Less certain, but in the present writer's view very attractive, is the suggestion that they were joined, or even preceded, by a group of priests from Jerusalem who had been forced to leave the Temple* service there because of the rigorous policies of those who succeeded Ezra and Nehemiah. Josephus' account may include some memory of this; there is strong circumstantial evidence in the OT for a major reorganization of the Jerusalem priesthood at about this time; it would help account for Samaritan claims to a legitimate priesthood, their close association with a number of inner-Jewish developments (e.g., in halachah), and the apparently continuing inner-Samaritan tensions between the priesthood and the laity (see below). The later establishment of the Qumran community (*see* Dead Sea Scrolls), this time by a more strict group of priests and their followers, forms an interesting parallel development.

2.4.3. The formation of this community and the building of a temple soon after would not of themselves have caused a decisive breach or schism. Purvis (1986), however, notes four possible reasons for a steadily deteriorating situation during the third and second centuries B.C.: (1) political tensions because of different alliances with the Ptolemies and the Seleucids; (2) Jewish resentment because of Samaritan acceptance of a greater degree of hellenization and their consequent failure to join in the resistance to Antiochus Epiphanes; (3) tensions between their respective Diaspora communities; and (4) Hasmonean expansion.

This last element was probably decisive, for in 128 B.C. John Hyrcanus captured Shechem and destroyed the sanctuary on Mount Gerizim. Apart from natural resentment, this drove the Samaritans to a closer religious rationale of their situation (compare the effect of the destruction of the Jerusalem Temple in A.D. 70; *see* Destruction of Jerusalem). As Purvis (1968) has shown, it was at this period that the Samaritan Pentateuch began its own separate history in terms of script, orthography and, crucially, textual tradition and recension. From this point on, therefore, though one should certainly continue to regard Samaritanism as a form of Judaism ("sect" would be an anachronistic term to use), it became crystallized as by far the most distinct by virtue of its wholesale rejection of the Jerusalem-centered salvation history, something which cannot be said of any other variety of Judaism in antiquity.

2.4.4. Not surprisingly, relations continued thereafter at a low ebb, and isolated events that are recorded from the first century A.D. may be regarded as symptomatic, though told from a Jewish standpoint. For instance, between A.D. 6 and 7, some Samaritans scattered bones in the Jerusalem Temple during Passover (*Ant.* 18. 29-30), while in A.D. 52 Samaritans massacred a group of Galilean pilgrims at *En-gannîm* (*Ant.* 20.118).

3. Varieties of Samaritanism and Principal Beliefs.

Just as it is clearly mistaken to speak of normative Judaism in the first century in view of the number of groups which often differed quite sharply from one another, so recent research has suggested that the same was probably true of the Samaritans (cf. Kippenberg and Isser).

3.1. The Dositheans. Because of the fragmentary nature and late date of all our relevant sources, it is not possible to go beyond informed conjecture, but Isser has made out a strong case for the view that "Dositheus was an early first century A.D. eschatological figure among the Samaritans, who applied the 'Prophet like Moses' passage of Dt. 18 to himself" (163). He further argues that he became prominent within a Samaritan sect which had already been formed during the previous century and which, as a synagogue*-based lay movement, was somewhat akin to the Pharisaic movement within Judaism, in contradistinction to the more Sadducee-like orthodox Samaritans, who were no doubt predominantly priestly and centered on Gerizim.

Such distinctions need to be borne in mind when evaluating references to contacts between the Samaritans and Jesus or the first Christians as well as between Jews and Samaritans, for the degrees of affinity between different groups across the divide may have varied far more than our severely fragmented knowledge allows us to recognize.

3.2. Principal Beliefs. The previous remarks also mean that it is difficult to speak in general terms about Samaritan beliefs. However, from the Samaritan Pentateuch, whose primary recension should be dated, as we have seen, earlier than the first century, a few comments may be made. From the text-type of the Pentateuch which they elected to adopt for themselves, it is probable that already the passage in Deuteronomy 18:18-22 about a future "prophet like Moses" had been joined to the Exodus version of the Sinai account (following Ex 20:21). They will themselves, however, have added to the Decalogue the commandment, based on Deuteronomy 27, to build an altar on Gerizim.

Thus we can be reasonably certain that the following elements of their later creed were already established in early times: belief in one God, in Moses the prophet, in the Law and in Mount Gerizim as the place appointed by God for sacrifice. The other two elements of the creed are less certain: the day of judgment and recompense, and the return of Moses as *Taheb* (the "restorer" or "returning one"). The latter is of particular interest in view of what we have seen about Dositheus, while in addition we may note the unrelated report of Josephus (*Ant.* 18. 85-87) that in A.D. 36 a Samaritan fanatic assembled a crowd on Gerizim, promising to reveal the sacred vessels thought to have been hidden there by Moses. These indications, coupled with the Samaritan Pentateuch, suggest that from early times an important element of Samaritan belief, especially amongst the laity, was the coming of the "prophet like Moses," but that only later did this develop into the more crystallized concept of the *Taheb* (cf. Dexinger in Crown); beyond that it would be hazardous to speculate.

4. Samaritans in the Gospels.

Although we have sought not to go beyond the available evidence in our treatment of Samaritan history and belief, we probably now have enough data to do justice to the references to the Samaritans in the Gospels.

4.1. The Synoptic Gospels. In the first three Gospels there are references to the Samaritans at Matthew 10:5; Luke 9:52; 10:33 and 17:16. These can all be understood against the background described above, once it is additionally borne in mind that they are told from a predominantly Jewish standpoint. Thus, in order to make a point similar to that in Luke 7:1-10, the foreignness of the grateful Samaritan is emphasized in Luke 17:11-19, even though he is instructed according to Jewish Law along with the other nine lepers in v. 14. Similarly, Jesus' instruction to his disciples* to go only to "the lost sheep of the house of Israel" (Mt 10:6) is contrasted not only with the negative command concerning the Gentiles but also, as in a separate and distinctive category, "any city of the Samaritans" (v. 5). The incident in Luke 9:51-56 reflects typical Jewish-Samaritan personal antipathies of the time, though it is of interest to note both here and elsewhere that Jesus did not always bypass Samaritan territory (by taking a circuitous route through Transjordan) as many Galilean pilgrims to Jerusalem did. At the same popular level, the selection of a Samaritan for the positive role in the parable told in answer to the question "Who is my neighbor?" (Lk 10:25-37) is telling, and in a veiled manner anticipates the Jewish acknowledgement (recorded much later) that the Samaritans were often more punctilious in their observance of the Law than the Jews (b. Qidd. 76a).

4.2. John. It is John 4 which gives the most extended account of an encounter of Jesus with the Samaritans (the only other reference in this Gospel being Jn 8:48). Despite its popularity, the title "woman of Samaria" is misleading. The incident takes place at Sychar (v. 5), clearly identified as being close to Shechem and Mount Gerizim (cf. vv. 5-6 and 20; Gen 48:22 LXX). The parenthetical comment in verse 9 about Jewish-Samaritan relations following the woman's expression of surprise that Jesus should ask her for a drink is probably not a general statement, but reflects a halakhic ruling (mid-first century?) that "the daughters of the Samaritans are menstruants from their cradle" (b. Nid. 31b) and hence that the vessels which they handle are unclean. If so, the comment may reflect more the time of the Evangelist than of Jesus himself, and the woman's surprise may not have been so specifically motivated. The woman's question about the right place to worship* (v. 20) is, as we have seen, entirely appropriate as reflecting the issue that stood at the heart of Samaritan identity and is just the kind of easily grasped popular polemic which someone of her status might have been expected to raise. Her response to Jesus' reply (v. 25), however, is more problematic; talk of a "Messiah" would probably have been foreign to a Samaritan (though our earlier caveat about diversity in this particular area of eschatology must be borne in mind). If historical tradition lies behind the saying, its present expression must be regarded as a Johannine paraphrase for his more Jewish-orientated readership. A reference to the prophet like Moses* in the context of a discussion of the right place and mode of worship would have fitted well here, as is clear from our earlier discussion.

See also JUDAISM.

BIBLIOGRAPHY. E. Bickerman, *From Ezra to the Last of the Maccabees* (New York: Shocken, 1962); A. D. Crown, *A Bibliography of the Samaritans* (ATLA Bibliography Series 10; Metuchen: American Theological Library Association and Scarecrow Press, 1984); idem, ed., *The Samaritans* (Tübingen: J. C. B. Mohr [Paul Siebeck], 1989); F. Dexinger, "Limits of Tolerance in Judaism: The Samaritan Example," in *Jewish and Christian Self-Definition*, Vol. 2: *Aspects of Judaism in the Graeco-Roman Period*, ed. E. P. Sanders (Philadelphia: Fortress, 1981) 88-114; K. Haacker, "Samaritan, Samaria," *NIDNTT* 3.449-67; S. J. Isser, *The Dositheans: A Samaritan Sect in Late Antiquity* (SJLA 17; Leiden: E. J. Brill, 1976); H. G. Kippenberg, *Garizim und Synagoge: Traditionsgeschichtliche Untersuchungen zur samaritanischen Religion der aramäischen Periode* (RVV 30; Berlin: W. de Gruyter, 1971); A. Montgomery, *The Samaritans: The Earliest Jewish Sect* (Philadelphia: J. C. Winston, 1907); R. Pummer, "The Present State of Samaritan Studies," *JSS* 21 (1976) 39-61; and 22 (1977) 27-47; J. D. Purvis, *The Samaritan Pentateuch and the Origin of the Samaritan Sect* (HSM 2; Cambridge, MA: Harvard University, 1968); idem, "The Samaritans and Judaism," in *Early Judaism and its Modern Interpreters*, ed. R. A. Kraft and G. W. E. Nickelsburg (Philadelphia: Fortress; Atlanta: Scholars, 1986) 81-98.

H. G. M. Williamson

SANCTUARY. *See* TEMPLE.

SANHEDRIN

The supreme Jewish religious, political and legal council in Jerusalem in NT times. The term was also used of the smaller courts governing the affairs of the Jewish communities throughout Palestine and the Diaspora.

    1. Terminology
    2. Theories
    3. Origin and History
    4. Membership
    5. Powers and Functions
    6. Times and Procedures

1. Terminology.

1.1. Synedrion. In the LXX *synedrion* (*syn*, "together" and *hedra*, "a seat") had no fixed meaning and translated a variety of Hebrew words (*ma* Ps 25:4 [Mt 26:4]; *sôd-*, Prov 11:13; *dîn*, Prov 22:10; *qāhāl*, 26:26). By the end of the Maccabean period *synedrion* is widespread in the Greek literature for the supreme Jerusalem council. The Hebrew word *sanhēdrîn*, a transliteration of *synedrion*, is also used in the Mishnah for the Jerusalem court (*m. Soṭa* 9:11).

In the Gospels *synedrion* refers to the Jerusalem council (Mt 26:59; Mk 15:1; Jn 11:47; cf. Acts 5:27). In Matthew 5:22 and 10:17 (par. Mk 13:9) any judicial body may be in mind, such as the Sanhedrin, a local Jewish council or a group in the Christian community. In Luke 22:66 *synedrion* probably refers to the assembly room.

Josephus also uses the term for the Jerusalem council (*Ant.* 14.167-80; *Life* 62) and for the five districts and councils created in Palestine by Gabinius (*Ant.* 14.89-91). In other Greek literature of the period a "sanhedrin" was often a council of representatives from various constituencies (e.g., Diodorus 16.41).

1.2. Gerousia. Generally translated as "senate" or "council," *gerousia* was a word used mainly for the Greek and Roman non-democratic senates (Aristotle *Pol.* 2.6.15) and was an older term than *synedrion* for the Jerusalem council from the end of the Persian period and the beginning of the Hellenistic period (Josephus *Ant.* 12.138 and especially the apocrypha, Jdt 4:8; 2 Macc 11:27). Only in a puzzling verse in Acts 5:21 is the term used in the NT where the high priest (*see* Priest and Priesthood) "called together the council (*synedrion*) and all the senate (*gerousia*) of the sons of Israel." Luke may have thought there were two supreme bodies in Jerusalem, though it is more likely that, for the sake of his Greek readers, he means to say "the Sanhedrin, that is, all the senate."

1.3. Presbyterion. In Luke 22:66 *presbyterion* ("council of elders"; also Acts 22:5 and 1 Tim 4:14) may refer to the group of elders,* one of the constituents of the Sanhedrin, but probably refers to the supreme Jerusalem council.

1.4. Boulē. Josephus often uses *boulē* ("council") for the Senate in Rome (*J.W.* 1.284; 13.164), local Roman city councils (*Ant.* 14.230), local Jewish city councils (*Life* 64), the Jerusalem Sanhedrin (*J.W.* 5.532) and its meeting place (*bouleutērion, J.W.* 5.144). However, the NT does not use the word in this way (cf. Lk 7:30; 23:51).

2. Theories.

According to the Greek literature (apocrypha, NT and Josephus) there was a single body in Jerusalem. However, the Mishnah says that there were two major courts in Jerusalem: "The greater Sanhedrin was made up of one and seventy [judges] and the lesser [Sanhedrin] of three and twenty" (*m. Sanh.* 1:6). The conflicting sources and multitude of terms has resulted in a number of theories about the Sanhedrin. A. Büchler proposed that before A.D. 70 there was a political body (*boulē*), a college of mostly priests (*synedrion*) and the Great Sanhedrin which oversaw Jewish religious life. M. Wolff argued that the high priest presided over a little Sanhedrin, and there was also a Great Sanhedrin (*gerousia*) of scribes* which condemned Jesus. S. B. Hoenig's theory was that there were three Sanhedrins: a political as well as a priestly and also a scribal one which was the Great Sanhedrin. However, it is difficult to determine how far the Mishnah has preserved reliable traditions on the Sanhedrin, for it is now generally agreed that it is reflecting the entirely different situation at Jamnia, not that in Jerusalem before A.D. 70. On the other hand the Greek sources are more contemporaneous to the time of Jesus and are therefore to be favored in reconstructing the history of the Sanhedrin before A.D. 70.

3. Origin and History.

The rabbis at Jamnia legitimized their governing body by tracing it back to Moses* and his seventy elders (Deut 27:1; *m. Sanh.* 1:6). However, apart from a supreme law court in Jerusalem (Deut 17:8-13; 19:15-21) and the occasional mention of "elders" (Ex 3:16; Deut 5:23), there is no hint of the existence of such an institution as the Sanhedrin in this period.

The actual seeds of the Jerusalem Sanhedrin in the time of Jesus were planted in the time of Ezra and Nehemiah. Joshua the high priest and the Davidic governor of Jerusalem, Zerubbabel, ruled the community together (Hag 1:1; Zech 4:14). The community was headed by a priestly nobility which formed an aristocratic council (Neh 2:16; 5:7) representing the people in negotiations with the Persian provincial governor Tattenai in the reconstruction of the Temple (Ezra 5:5, 9; 6:7-8, 14). With the death of Zerubbabel the house of David came to an end and the high priest emerged as the head of the *gerousia* and Jewish state (1 Macc 12:6).

From Hecataeus of Abdera, a contemporary of Alexander the Great, we learn that the council was dominated by the priests: "He (Moses) picked out the men of most refinement and with the greatest ability to head the entire nation, and appointed them priests. . . . These same men he appointed to be judges in all major disputes, and entrusted to them the guardianship of the laws and customs. For this reason the Jews have never had a king, and authority over the people is regularly vested in whichever priest is regarded as superior to his colleagues in wisdom and virtue. They call this man the high priest" (Diodorus 40.3.4-5).

Under the relative freedom provided by the Hellenistic kings, the influence of the Jerusalem court increased. The Seleucid king, Antiochus III (223-187 B.C.), said that it was his will that the Jewish nation "shall have a form of government in accordance with the laws of their country, and the senate (*gerousia*), the priests, the scribes of the temple and the temple-singers shall be relieved from poll-tax" (Josephus *Ant.* 12.142).

From the beginning of the Maccabean Revolt (167 B.C.) the power of the high priest increased (1 Macc 12:6) and with Simon being established as high priest, military chief and ethnarch (140 B.C.), the power of the Sanhedrin was reduced (1 Macc 14:24-49). With the reign of Queen Alexandra (76-67 B.C.) the Sanhedrin's power increased and the domination of the priests and nobility was exchanged for that of the Pharisees.* Alexandra permitted "the Pharisees to do as they liked in all matters, and also commanded the people to obey them; and whatever regulations, introduced by the Pharisees in accordance with the traditions of their fathers, had been abolished by her father-in-law Hyrcanus, these she again restored" (Josephus *Ant.* 13.408).

Gabinius (57-55 B.C.), the Roman governor in Syria, divided the nation into five districts with councils (*synedria*) in Jerusalem, Gadara, Amathus, Jericho and Sepphoris (Josephus *Ant.* 14.91). In 47 B.C. Caesar overturned this arrangement so that the high priest and the Jerusalem council were responsible for the affairs of the whole nation even though these local councils survived (Josephus *Ant.* 14.192-95). The Sanhedrin became sufficiently confident in its authority that the high priest and ethnarch Hyrcanus II (63-40 B.C.) summoned Herod to stand trial on capital sentences he had passed without the Sanhedrin's authority (Josephus *J.W.* 1.204-15). When Herod took Jerusalem in 37 B.C. he retaliated by killing the entire membership of the Sanhedrin (Josephus *Ant.* 14.174, though *Ant.* 15.6 says only forty-five leading men were killed). Herod abolished the privilege of serving as high priest for life and appointed high priests with ceremonial duties and no political power.

Under the Roman procurators (A.D. 6-41) the Sanhedrin's power increased again (Josephus *Ant.* 20.200, 251). So, in the NT the Sanhedrin is represented as the supreme court of justice (Mk 14:55).

After the destruction of Jerusalem and the Temple in A.D. 70 (*see* Destruction of Jerusalem), the Sanhedrin was recreated at Jamnia (Yavneh in the OT; 2 Chron 26:6) in the Northwest of Judea (*m. Soṭa* 9:11; *m. Sanh.* 11:4) before moving to Galilee in A.D. 118.

4. Membership.

The Mishnah is probably correct in saying that prior to A.D. 70 the Sanhedrin in Jerusalem had seventy-one members (cf. Num 11:16; Josephus *J.W.* 2.482; *Ep.*

Arist. 46-50; *m. Sanh.* 1:6).

After the exile the Jerusalem council was composed of Levites, priests and heads of families (2 Chron 19:5-11). In the Maccabean period the Sanhedrin consisted of lay aristocracy and priests of Sadducean sympathy (1 Macc 7:33; 11:23; 14:28). In the time of Queen Alexandra Pharisaic scribes belonged to the assembly.

Both the NT and Josephus agree that in the first century the chief priests (*archiereis*) were the key figures in the Sanhedrin (Mt 27:41; Mk 14:53; Josephus *J.W.* 2.301, 316-42). These were probably the former high priests and members of the priestly aristocracy from which the high priests were chosen and belonged to the party of the Sadducees (Acts 4:1; 5:17; Josephus *Ant.* 20.199). The scribes (*grammateis*) were the second major component of the Sanhedrin and dominated the body (Acts 5:34; 23:6; Josephus *Ant.* 18.17; *J.W.* 2.411). In the Persian period all the members of the Sanhedrin (*gerousia*) were called "elders" (*presbyteroi*, 1 Macc 14:20; 2 Macc 4:44). By NT times the term "elders" was used for a third group consisting of priests and lay members of the nobility (Mt 26:3; 27:1; 28:11-12) within the Sanhedrin. From observing the synonyms for these elders we learn that they are leading men of the people (Lk 19:47; Josephus *Life* 194), the leading men of Jerusalem, the powerful and the dignitaries (Josephus *J.W.* 2.316, 410; *Life* 9).

Josephus says that, along with Ishmael the high priest and Helcias the treasurer, ten leading men were sent on a delegation to Nero (*Ant.* 20:194). Also, as Greek cities had a committee of ten leading men, there may have been a group of the ten foremost members within the Sanhedrin.

The high priest was always the president of the Sanhedrin (1 Macc 14:44; Mt 26:57; Acts 5:17; 24:1; Josephus *Ag. Ap.* 2.194; *Ant.* 20.200, 251). From the time of Herod the Great the high priest was often appointed arbitrarily and out of political considerations. Otherwise, the office was hereditary (Num 3:32; 25:11-13; 35:25, 28; Neh 12:10-11) and the Palestinian Talmud says that the high priest would not be elected high priest if he had not first been captain of the Temple (*y. Yoma* 3:8; 41a. 5; cf. Josephus *J.W.* 2.409).

Second in rank to the high priest was the captain of the Temple (Hebrew, *sāgān* or *segen*, Aramaic *sᵉgan*, Greek, *stratēgos*; Josephus *Ant.* 20.131; Lk 22:4, 52; Acts 4:1, 24, 26; *m. Yoma* 3:1). Josephus also mentions a secretary of the Sanhedrin (*J.W.* 5.532).

We know little of how people were appointed to the Sanhedrin, though they may have been co-opted (*m. Sanh.* 4:4) from among those of legitimate Israelite descent (*m. Qidd.* 4:5). Actual admission was through the laying on of hands (*m. Sanh.* 4:4; cf. Num 27:18-23; Deut 34:9).

5. Powers and Functions.

At least theoretically, the Jerusalem Sanhedrin's sphere of authority extended over the spiritual, political and legal affairs of all Jews (*m. Ta'an.* 3:6). Thus, the Mishnah says that where members of a local court disagreed on a point of law the matter was referred to the Jerusalem court which sat at the gate of the Temple Mount. If the dispute could not be resolved, it went to the court which sat at the gate of the Temple Court. If a resolution was still not found, the Sanhedrin heard the dispute. Thereafter, on pain of death local judges were to follow the decision (*m. Sanh.* 11:2; cf. Josephus *Ant.* 4.214-18; *J.W.* 2.570-71). However, the sphere of authority and geographical area over which the Jerusalem Sanhedrin exercised jurisdiction varied greatly over time according to the relative freedom of the Jews in relation to the succession of foreign oppressors.

In the time of the Hasmonean rulers the whole of Palestine was a single political unit over which the Sanhedrin exercised oversight. When Gabinius (57-55 B.C.) divided Jewish territory into five areas the authority of the Jerusalem Sanhedrin may have covered only one-third of Judea (Josephus *Ant.* 14.91; *J.W.* 1.170). From the death of Herod the Great, Galilee and Perea were separate administrative regions so that the civil jurisdiction of the Jerusalem Sanhedrin did not extend beyond Judea. Thus while Jesus remained in Galilee, the Sanhedrin had no judicial authority over him. Even so, Luke says that the Sanhedrin authorized Paul to arrest Christians in Damascus (Acts 9:1-2; 22:5). Then Josephus says that in a peaceful period after the first stages of the Jewish War in A.D. 60, magistrates and members of the Sanhedrin dispersed from Jerusalem and collected the Roman taxes from the whole of Judea (*J.W.* 2.405).

In A.D. 6 Augustus appointed a procurator for Judea "with full powers, including the affliction of capital punishment" (Josephus *J.W.* 2.117). That the Sanhedrin could no longer order and execute a capital sentence is reflected in John 18:31 and in the rabbinic literature (*y. Sanh.* 18a; 24b; *b. Sanh.* 41a; *b. 'Abod. Zar.* 8b). On the other hand, Josephus says (*J.W.* 5.193-94) that the second court of the Temple was surrounded by a stone balustrade on which at regular intervals stood slabs giving warning in Greek and Latin: "No foreigner is to enter within the forecourt and the balustrade around the sanctuary. Whoever is caught will have himself to blame for his subsequent death" (*CII*, 1400 n. 85) This could be a special case granted

to the Jews. In any case it is more likely to be a warning against being lynched (cf. Acts 6:8—8:2; Jn 10:31).

Also, Josephus says that the Sanhedrin condemned James, the brother of Jesus, to be stoned. In this case the procurator, Porcius Festus, had died, and Ananus took the opportunity of convening the Sanhedrin before Albinus, the new procurator, had arrived (*Ant.* 20.197-203). Further, the Mishnah relates the burning of a priest's daughter convicted of adultery (*m. Sanh.* 7:2). Those who argue that the Sanhedrin did not have the power of death under the Roman procurators suggest that this took place during the brief reign of Agrippa I (A.D. 41-44) when the Jews had their own independent state. Whether or not the Sanhedrin was able to execute capital punishment, the Romans maintained the right to intervene when a political crime was suspected (Acts 22:30; 23:15, 20, 28).

6. Times and Procedures.

The Sanhedrin probably met on the western boundary of the Temple Mount (Josephus *J.W.* 5.144; 6.354) in the "Hall of Hewn Stone" (*lishkaṭ ha-gaziṭ*), indicating that it was next to the gymnasium, or Xystus (*gaziṭ* = *xystos*, 1 Chron 22:2; Amos 5:11).

The night meeting in Mark 14:53 (par. Mt 26:57; Lk 22:54) was probably to be considered a preliminary meeting in the high priest's palace because trials could only be held in the hours of daylight (cf. Mk 15:1; *m. Sanh.* 4:1).

No record remains of the proceedings of the Jerusalem Sanhedrin. However, the Mishnah gives details of the judicial procedure of the lesser Sanhedrin of Twenty-Three which may reflect procedure of the Jerusalem Sanhedrin before A.D. 70. Members sat in a half-circle so they could see each other. Before them stood two scribes, one writing down what was said in favor and the other what was said against the accused. Before them sat three rows of students who could participate in non-capital trials (*m. Sanh.* 4:1-4).

Non-capital trials began with either case, but capital trials were to begin with the case for acquittal. A majority of one was sufficient in non-capital trials to acquit the accused of a capital charge. A majority of two was required for a guilty verdict on a capital charge. Verdicts could be reversed but not from an acquittal to a conviction in a capital trial. Those participating in the case could speak for and against the accused in non-capital trials. In capital trials a speaker in favor of conviction could only change and argue in favor of the accused, not the reverse. In non-capital cases the daytime trial could be followed by reaching a verdict that same night. In capital cases the verdict for an acquittal could be reached that night but a verdict of conviction had to wait until the following day (*m. Sanh.* 4:1). In that way members of the Sanhedrin could go off in pairs to eat a little (no wine was permitted) and discuss the matter all night before meeting in court early next morning (*m. Sanh.* 5:5). Therefore, trials were not to be held on the days before a Sabbath* or festival (*m. Sanh.* 4:1). In capital cases voting began with the most junior members standing, each giving their verdict (*m. Sanh.* 5:5).

See also PRIESTS, PRIESTHOOD; SCRIBES; TRIAL OF JESUS.

BIBLIOGRAPHY. E. Bammel, ed., *The Trial of Jesus* (London; SCM, 1970); J. Blinzler, *The Trial of Jesus* (Cork, U.K.; Mercer, 1959); D. R. Catchpole, *The Trial of Jesus* (Leiden; E. J. Brill, 1971); H. Danby, "The Bearing of the Rabbinical Criminal Code on the Jewish Trial Narratives in the Gospels," *JTS* 21 (1919-20) 51-76; S. B. Hoenig, *The Great Sanhedrin* (Philadelphia: Dropsie College, 1953); E. Lohse, "συνέδριον," *TDNT* VII. 860-71; H. Mantel, *Studies in the History of the Sanhedrin* (Cambridge: Harvard University, 1961); E. Schürer, *The History of the Jewish People in the Age of Jesus Christ (175 B.C.-A.D. 135)*, rev. and ed. G. Vermes, F. Millar (3 vols.; Edinburgh; T. & T. Clark, 1973-79) 2.199-226; P. Winter, *On the Trial of Jesus* (Berlin: Walter de Gruyter, 1974).   G. H. Twelftree

SATAN. *See* DEMON, DEVIL, SATAN; TEMPTATION OF JESUS.

SAVIOR. *See* SALVATION.

SAYINGS OF JESUS. *See* FORM CRITICISM.

SCRIBES

In the NT era the scribes (*grammateis*) were a class of professional exponents and teachers of the Law.*

1. Background
2. Scribes and Pharisees
3. Work of the Scribes
4. Scribes in the Gospels
5. Jesus and the Scribes

1. Background.

In ancient Near Eastern civilizations the highly prized skill of writing made the scribes significant members of the community, especially as political advisors, diplomats and experts in the ancient sciences and mysteries, including astrology.

Scribes began as recorders and copyists of official data (2 Kings 12:10) and formed themselves into guilds (1 Chron 2:55). They came to hold high political office (1 Kings 4:3; 2 Kings 18:18; 25:19; 1 Chron

27:32; 2 Chron 26:11; Is 22:15) and became the heirs of the priests (*see* Priest and Priesthood) and Levites as interpreters of the Law (2 Chron 34:13; Ezra 7:12) because of their familiarity with and understanding of the Scriptures (1 Chron 27:32).

In exilic times the scribes emerged as wise men of understanding (see Proverbs) as the Jews in a foreign land depended on them for interpreting the Torah in a new situation. Baruch was a scribe taking down Jeremiah's dictation (Jer 36:4, 18), collecting the prophet's sayings (36:32) and acting as his representative (36:6-15).

From the fourth century B.C. Ezra, the priest and scribe, embodied all that was expected of a scribe in that period (Ezra 7:6-26; Neh 8:1-9). By about 180 B.C., when Jesus ben Sirach the scribe who probably had a school in Jerusalem (Sir 51:23) assembled his book, the scribes were a well-developed and distinct class of high social status alongside the priesthood (Sir 38:24-39:11; *Jub.* 4:17-25). In the crisis perpetuated by Antiochus Epiphanes the reputation of lay scribes rose as they were zealous for the Law to the point of martyrdom (2 Macc 6:18-31), while the priestly scribes succumbed to Hellenism.*

After the fall of Jerusalem the most respected scribes settled at Jamnia as well as Lydda (*m. Roš. Haš.* 1:6; 4:1-2). In Judaism* the learned were also known as elders,* experts, sages and scholars. The Mishnah says that they were to be "deliberate in judgment; raise up many disciples; and make a fence around the Torah" (*m. 'Abot* 1:1).

1.1. Leading Scribes. Little of historical value is known about individual scribes before A.D. 70, the most famous pair being Hillel and Shammai (*m. 'Abot* 1:1-18). Hillel came to Palestine from Babylon and, because of his poverty, hired himself out as a day laborer. His kindness and gentleness characterized his school and the leniency of his decisions (*b. Šabb.* 30b-31a; *b. Soṭa* 48b). He drew up seven hermeneutical principles in order to establish the harmony between Scripture and tradition (*t. Sanh.* 7:11; *see* Old Testament in the Gospels).

Shammai, a native of Judea, is said to have been more stringent than Hillel in his interpretation of the Law. Even though both agreed on the need to fulfill the letter of the Law, the two schools met to discuss their differences (*m. Šabb.* 1:4-11).

As the regulations of the scribes were intended to be applicable throughout the Jewish community, the most respected authorities lived and worked in one place to reach common conclusions.

After the fall of Jerusalem (*see* Destruction of Jerusalem) Rabban Yohanan ben Zakkai, who lived mainly in Jamnia, was the most distinguished scribe. Another celebrated scribe, well known in the NT, was Gamaliel I who, according to Acts 5:34-39 and 22:3, taught Paul.

1.2. Lifestyle. Some scribes came from the priestly aristocracy (*m. 'Abot* 3:2; *m. Šeqal.* 8:5). Others were ordinary priests (*m. 'Abot* 2:8) or members of the lower orders of clergy (*b. 'Arak.* 11b). The vast majority of scribes came from every other section of society, some supporting themselves by carrying on a trade. The literature gives evidence of a commander of the Temple fortress, a wine merchant, a carpenter, a leather worker, a flax comber and a day laborer being scribes. For economic reasons even the most respected rabbis undertook writing and copying of Scripture (*b. Giṭ.* 67a).

With the need to spend time studying the Law and with no set fee for giving instruction, even the most respected of these scribes could be poor and depended on gifts from their students, funds from the distribution to the poor and the Temple treasury (*b. Yoma* 35b; *b. Ned.* 49b-50a). Also, it was meritorious to show hospitality to a scribe, to give him a share of one's property or to run his business for him (*b. Ber.* 34b). Scribes were also exempt from taxes (*m. 'Abot* 3:5). On the other hand, some scribes were overzealous in receiving this kindness (Josephus *J.W.* 1.571). Others, with many pupils, were very wealthy (*b. Ketub.* 67b).

2. Scribes and Pharisees.

Along with the chief priests these two groups are often associated in the Gospels. Some have denied that there is any relationship between them. Others have understood the scribes to be the Pharisees learned in the Law or an elite amongst them. The phrase "scribes of the Pharisees" (Mk 2:16; Acts 23:9) indicates the probability that scribes were associated with various sects and associations within first-century Judaism.

3. Work of the Scribes.

In relation to their knowledge of the Scriptures the scribes occupied themselves with a number of tasks (Sir 38:24—39:11).

3.1. Interpretation and Preservation of the Law. On the basis of existing regulations and by recourse to ancient customs which had become binding as common law (Mk 7:5-8), the scribes applied the general instructions of the Torah to daily living and even extended the Law to theoretical situations to build a safety fence against inadvertent breaches (*m. Hor.* 1:5). In turn, the findings of the scribes, related mainly

to festivals, prayers,* cleanness* and uncleanness and the Temple, became common law (*m. Šabb.* 1:1-24:5; *m. ḥag.* 1:8; *m. Ned.* 4:3). In some places writing down the tradition of the scribes is forbidden (*b. Šabb.* 115b; *b. Giṭ* 60b), so continuous study was required to maintain a working knowledge of the traditions.

3.2. Teaching the Law. Instruction usually began at an early age (Josephus *Life* 9; *b. Giṭ.* 58a). A student was expected to give allegiance to his teacher* above that of his parents and, certainly after the NT period, teachers were generally addressed as "my lord" or "master" (*rabbi*). A student was expected to reproduce every word and expression of his teacher. In NT times teaching took place "in the Temple," probably in rooms associated with the main building (cf. Mk 14:49). In other centers instruction took place in "houses of instruction" (Sir 51:23; *m. Ber.* 4:2; *m. Ter.* 11:10) which sometimes may have been the home of the scribe (*m. 'Abot* 1:4). The scribe sat on a raised area and the pupils on rows of benches or on the floor (Acts 22:3). The scribe posed questions for the students to answer. The teacher repeated his material over and over so it could be memorized. When the student had mastered the material and was competent to make his own decisions, he was a non-ordained student. When he came of age (*b. Soṭa* 22b says forty years of age) he could be received into the company of scribes as an ordained scholar.

3.3. Scribes As Lawyers. Any Jew could be asked to judge a case by a community (*b. Sanh.* 3a). But where there was a scribe he would invariably be chosen for a judicial office (Sir 38:33) and some were members of the Sanhedrin.* Aside from these major functions the scribes also attended to the following tasks.

3.4. Scribes As Theologians. Some scribes gave more attention to studying and elaborating the doctrine in the text of Scripture rather than its legal elements. While preaching was not restricted to specific people, these scribes were well qualified to speak in the synagogues.*

3.5. Scribes As Guardians of Tradition. The significance of the scribes in Jewish society was also associated with their being guardians of an esoteric tradition (Lk 11:52). They considered secrecy necessary because Scripture was silent on the reasons for many laws (*b. Sanh.* 21b); because of the offense of some stories (*m. Meg.* 4:10); because the teaching might be misused (e.g., amelioration of purity laws, *b. Ber.* 22a) and because genealogical traditions might discredit public figures (*b. Qidd.* 70b). According to the Mishnah this secret knowledge also included the story of creation and the vision of the chariot (*m. Ḥag.* 2:1). From the description of such things in the apocalyptic writings (*1 Enoch* 69:16-25; *2 Esdr* 6:38-56) as well as direct evidence (*2 Esdr* 14:45-48; *As. Mos.* 1:17-18), it seems that these writings contain the theological constructions and teachings of the scribes.

3.6. Scribes As Curators of the Text. Copying Scripture was considered divine work (*b. Soṭa* 20a), and Temple funds may have been used to pay for corrections in scrolls (*b. Ketub.* 106a). Even though the sacred text was known by heart, a written edition had to be before the copyist (*b. Meg.* 18b) who would read aloud the text as he worked (*m. Meg.* 2:2). The Qumran scriptorium may have been modelled on something similar in the Jerusalem Temple (*see* Dead Sea Scrolls).

4. Scribes in the Gospels.

Scribe occurs fifty-seven times in the Synoptic Gospels (and Jn 8:3 in some MSS). Twenty-one times they are mentioned with the chief priests and eighteen times with the Pharisees. The scribes are depicted as scholars and teachers of Scripture, the custodians of Jewish traditions, the major opponents of Jesus and heavily involved in his trial.

4.1. Mark. The scribes, mentioned twenty-one times, are the chief opponents of Jesus in this earliest Gospel and appear throughout the Gospel. In the first report of Jesus' teaching, his teaching with authority* is contrasted with that of the scribes (2:22). Unlike the scribes, Jesus did not appeal to tradition but acted as having an authority direct from God.

Mark depicts the scribes as opposing Jesus in a number of ways. When the Pharisees are mentioned with the scribes they are questioning Jesus' understanding of the Law. They ask why he contaminates himself by eating with sinners* and tax collectors (2:16; *see* Taxes) and why he eats with defiled hands (7:5). The scribes also question the identity and credentials of Jesus (2:6; 3:22; 11:27) and so provide a foil over against which Mark highlights the identity, teaching and powerful authority of Jesus. On learning of Jesus cleansing the Temple they seek to destroy him (11:18; 14:1, 43) and are involved in his condemnation (15:1). While on the cross the scribes mock Jesus (15:31). Indeed, in predicting his death, Jesus twice mentions the scribes as some who will be involved (8:31; 10:33). One scribe, however, who questions and approves Jesus' answer is said not to be far from the kingdom of God (12:28-34).

Part of Jesus' teaching is his criticism of the scribes (12:35-40) and his highlighting the new understanding of Scripture in the light of his coming (9:11-13). He says they do not understand who he is (12:35-37). The scribe is the antithesis of a disciple* (3:15; 6:7; 8:29; 9:35; 10:31, 43-44) in that scribes like to go about

in splendid clothes (*stolai*, cf. 16:5) and, even though they do not have authority (1:22), they desire recognition and positions of honor in the synagogue and at feasts* (12:38-39). They also exploit the poor (*see* Rich and Poor) to support their religion (12:40; see 11:17-18). In showing the scribes also in conflict with the disciples (9:14), Mark may be conveying to his readers the message that they will continue to face opposition in the same areas as Jesus.

4.2. Matthew. The scribes play a more important role in Matthew than in the other Gospels. The Pharisees, chief priests, elders of the people and the scribes are brought together to represent Jewish opposition to Jesus and, in leading the people astray, they carry responsibility for the fate of Jesus (2:4; 23:1-39; 26:57; 27:19-26, 41).

One aspect of Matthew's complex presentation of the scribes is the desire to rehabilitate them, apparent in his omission of material where his sources have portrayed them negatively (e.g., Mt 12:24 par. Mk 3:22). Also, when the scribes are depicted negatively they are always associated with another group, especially with the Pharisees (e.g., Mt 5:20; 23:2-29), but also with the chief priests (e.g., Mt 16:21; 27:41) and elders (Mt 16:21). However, Matthew's antagonism is probably only toward the scribes of the Pharisees. For he makes a distinction between the scribes of the Pharisees and other scribes (Mt 7:29 par. Mk 1:22). And, in chapter 23, where Matthew is most vicious in his attack on the scribes and Pharisees, he reverts to calling them Pharisees in verse 26 (see also Mt 12:24 par. Mk 9:34; Mt 22:34-36 par. Mk 12:28; Mt 22:40 par. Mk 12:32-34; Mt 9:11 par. Mk 2:16).

Matthew also treats scribes positively (23:2) and the terms *scribe* and *disciple* of Jesus are interchangeable (cf. 8:19 and 21), though disciples are not to use the title "rabbi" (23:8; *see* Teacher). Like the students of the traditional scribe, a disciple of Jesus is to leave his family (8:21-22), follow Jesus wherever he goes (8:19-20) and have a righteousness (*see* Justice, Righteousness)—set out in the Sermon on the Mount* (cf. 7:29)—that exceeds the Pharisaic scribe (5:20). Such a Christian scribe will gain new understanding of the secrets of the kingdom of heaven (*see* Kingdom of God) as well as treasuring "old things" through the teaching of Jesus (13:11, 52) which he is to do and teach (5:19). In 23:34 Matthew seems to be warning the Christian scribe of the impending dangers of being a disciple of Jesus (cf. 5:10-12).

4.3. Luke. Luke also uses *nomikoi* ("lawyers," 7:30; 10:25; 11:45-46, 52; 14:3) and *nomodidaskaloi* ("teachers of the law," 5:17; Acts 5:34) for the scribes. In 11:37-54, the first of two series of criticisms, Luke softens the criticism by omitting (cf. Mt 23:23-36) references to the scribes until 11:45. The second series of criticisms of the scribes, following an attack on their theology (20:41-44), is in the form of a warning to the disciples to beware of the cruelly selfish lifestyle of the scribes (20:45-47). Also, following his tradition, Luke shows the scribes antagonistic to Jesus' ministry (Lk 5:21 par. Mk 2:6; Lk 5:30 par. Mk 2:16; Lk 14:1-6; Lk 20:1 par. Mk 11:27). Furthermore, Luke shows the scribes among those attempting to destroy Jesus (Lk 19:47 par. Mk 11:18; Lk 22:2 par. Mk 14:1; Lk 22:66 par. Mk 15:1) and into the hands of whom Jesus expected to be delivered (Lk 9:22 par. Mk 8:31).

There are a number of passages where Luke removes criticism of the scribes (e.g., Lk 20:47 par. Mt 23:15; Lk 4:32 par. Mk 1:22) or softens an attack by using the term *ruler* (Lk 23:35 par. Mk 15:31), "someone" (Lk 9:57 par. Mt 8:19) or by including the Pharisees in criticism (Lk 5:21 par. Mk 2:6; Lk 5:30 par. Mk 2:16). In fact Luke only once mentions the scribes alone in a criticism of their lifestyle (20:46). This probably means that Luke does not single out the scribes as being especially antagonistic to Jesus, nor any more worthy of Jesus' censure than any of the other Jewish rulers. On the other hand, Luke has Jesus compliment a lawyer on his knowledge of the Law (10:25).

5. Jesus and the Scribes.
Embedded in the traditions about Jesus generally held to be reliable is a contrast between the teaching and lifestyle of Jesus and the scribes. In his teaching Jesus is not only critical of the Jewish traditions (Mk 7:1-23), but also in his teaching he places himself above, not under, the Torah (Mk 2:23-28; 10:9; cf. Deut 24:1-4). So while Jesus was addressed as a rabbi or teacher, his teaching was recognized to be authoritative in that it was charismatic rather than dependent on tradition or the Scriptures (cf. Mk 1:22). In contrast to pupils of scribes choosing their own teachers, Jesus selected his own students (Mk 1:17; cf. Jn 15:16). As with a student of a scribe, Jesus' disciples were expected to place their relationship with Jesus above all other relationships. As with some scribes Jesus is depicted as being poor and dependent on others for his support (Mt 8:20 par. Lk 9:58; Lk 8:1-3).

Numbered among the opponents of Jesus are the scribes. One reason for the scribes' disapproval of Jesus was his claim to speak and act for God (Mk 2:7). This not only provoked jealousy among the scribes but, among those including Sadducean scribes in the Sanhedrin, concern for the delicate peace with Rome

being disturbed by the popular excitement Jesus caused (Mk 11:15-19). Jesus further discredited himself in the eyes of the Pharisaic scribes because of his frequent association with less desirable elements of society (Mk 2:15-17).

In turn Jesus criticizes the Pharisaic scribes in particular for their hypocrisy (*see* Hypocrite) in knowing the Scriptures and how to enter the kingdom of God yet, by placing insurmountable legal burdens on people, preventing them from entering it. They also live a lifestyle which the disciples are warned not to follow (cf. Mt 23:1-36 par. Lk 20:45-47). At least those scribes who were members of the Sanhedrin shared the guilt of handing Jesus over to be crucified. Yet there is evidence that Jesus found some of the teaching of the scribes acceptable (Mk 9:11-13), and it is reported that on one occasion Jesus complimented a scribe for his understanding of Scripture (Mk 12:34).
See also Judaism; Pharisees; Sadducees; Sanhedrin; Teacher.
Bibliography. M. J. Cook, *Mark's Treatment of the Jewish Leaders* (Leiden: E. J. Brill, 1978); B. Gerhardsson, *Memory and Manuscript* (Lund: C. W. K. Gleerup, 1961); N. Hillyer, "Scribe," *NIDNTT* 3.477-82; J. Jeremias, "γραμματεύς," *TDNT* I.740-42; G. F. Moore, *Judaism in the First Centuries of the Christian Era* (3 vols.; Cambridge: Harvard, 1927-1930) I:37-47; D. E. Orton, *The Understanding Scribe* (Sheffield: Sheffield Academic Press, 1989); E. Schürer, *The History of the Jewish People in the Age of Jesus Christ (175 B.C.-A.D. 135)*, rev. and ed. G. Vermes, F. Millar (3 vols.; Edinburgh: T. & T. Clark, 1973-79) vol. 2; S. Westerholm, *Jesus and Scribal Authority* (ConBNT 10; Lund: C. W. K. Gleerup, 1978).   G. H. Twelftree

SCRIPTURES. *See* Old Testament in the Gospels.

SENDING. *See* Apostle.

SERMON ON THE MOUNT/PLAIN
No other short section of the Bible has been more prominent in theological discussion and in the general life of the church. Even in our modern secular societies the Sermon's influence continues. Though they may have given the matter little careful thought, many men and women who have little or no contact with the church believe that the Sermon contains clear ethical teaching for all people of good will.

The Sermon is well known to Christians today, but few appreciate the richness of these sayings of Jesus: their radical promises and demands have often been blunted either through familiarity or as a result of a precipitate quest for immediate relevance. Interpretation of this influential and apparently simple passage is far from easy, but the scholar, preacher or lay person who perseveres will be amply rewarded, for the Sermon sets out powerfully both the gift and demand of the Gospel.

There are two versions of the Sermon: the Sermon on the Mount (Mt 5:3—7:27) which contains 106 verses, and the Sermon on the Plain (Lk 6:20b-49) which contains 29 verses. The term "the Sermon on the Mount" goes back to the title Augustine gave to his important commentary on Matthew 5—7, *De Sermone Domini in Monte*, which was probably written between 392 and 396. In spite of Augustine's enormous influence on many later Christian writers, Matthew 5—7 was not generally referred to as "the Sermon on the Mount" until the sixteenth century. The term "Sermon on the Plain" is modern; it is used primarily to distinguish Luke's much shorter Sermon from Matthew's.

The two Sermons may be interpreted either as integral parts of Matthew's and Luke's Gospels, or as collections of sayings of the historical Jesus. In the former case scholars who accept Markan priority and some form of the Q* hypothesis conclude that Matthew has composed chapters 5—7 as the first of his five carefully constructed discourses. Matthew's Sermon is a considerably expanded version of the Q "sermon" on which Luke drew, with few changes, in the Sermon on the Plain (see 2.1. below). By his arrangement and, in some cases, adaptation of earlier traditions, Matthew has sought to meet the needs of Christians in his own day. Matthew's first discourse contains many of his own distinctive emphases. Luke's Sermon is also related to his overall purposes, though less clearly.

If the sayings of Jesus in Matthew 5—7 or Luke 6:20-49 are used to reconstruct the teaching of the historical Jesus, it is important to recognize that they have been modified by the Evangelists (*see* Redaction Criticism) and probably also at earlier stages in the transmission of the Gospel traditions (*see* Tradition Criticism). They can be appreciated fully only when they are interpreted alongside related sayings from other parts of the Gospels. Although Matthew's Sermon on the Mount is often assumed to be a summary of the ethical teaching of Jesus, this is mistaken: there are important ethical sayings of Jesus which are not included in Matthew's Sermon, and not all the traditions in these chapters are ethical (*see* Ethics of Jesus).

1. The Sermon on the Plain in Luke
2. The Sermon on the Mount in Matthew

1. The Sermon on the Plain in Luke.

The term "Sermon on the Plain" comes from Luke's

introduction to his version of the Sermon. Luke notes that Jesus went out into the hills to pray and continued in prayer* to God* all night; when day came he called his disciples* and came down with them and stood *on a level place* (Lk 6:12, 17). In the presence of a large crowd, Jesus addressed his disciples with the words of the Sermon (Lk 6:20b-49). Although Luke's Sermon is much closer to the earlier version in Q than to Matthew's, it has attracted less attention down through the centuries than the Sermon on the Mount.

1.1. The Sermon in Q. Almost the whole of Luke's Sermon is also found in Matthew 5—7. Where the two Gospels overlap in content, there is often close agreement in the wording of the traditions. However, a number of verses which are similar in content differ considerably in wording. It is probable that Matthew and Luke drew on different versions of the Q Sermon.

The chart below, which is based on Luke's order, shows that in spite of their great disparity in size, the two versions agree strikingly in the order of the traditions.

	Luke 6	Matthew 5—7
Introduction	20a	5:1-2
Beatitudes	20b-23	5:3-12
Woes	24-26	
Love of enemy	27-36	5:38-47
Golden Rule	31	7:12
Judge not	37-38	7:1-2
The blind guide	39	
Teacher and disciple	40	
Speck and log	41-42	7:3-5
The tree and its fruit	43-45	7:16-20
Lord, Lord	46	7:21
House on the rock	47-49	7:24-27

Matthew differs from Luke's order at only one significant point: The Golden Rule does not appear, as we might have expected, as part of the "love your enemy" traditions (Mt 5:38-47; *see* Love), but as the climax of Matthew's Sermon in 7:12. With only three exceptions, the whole of the Sermon on the Plain is found in Matthew 5—7: Matthew does not have woes to counterbalance the Beatitudes, as Luke does (*see* Blessing and Woe); the saying about the blind guide appears at Matthew 15:14, and the saying on the disciple-teacher* relationship is found in Matthew 10:24.

This close agreement in order and in content has led most scholars to conclude that Q contained an earlier form of the Sermon. Luke has retained the order of the traditions in Q. Although Luke has modified some Q traditions, and has perhaps omitted a few verses from Q and added a few others which were not part of Q, his version of the Sermon is usually considered to be very close to the original version in Q.

An alternative explanation has been defended by a small number of scholars. They argue that for his own purposes Luke drastically abbreviated Matthew's Sermon and included many of the omitted traditions at other points in his Gospel. Luke is thus seen as the first interpreter of Matthew's Sermon. Opponents of this view claim, surely correctly, that if Luke did use Matthew, he acted in a quite arbitrary way. He has included only just over a quarter of Matthew 5—7; he has failed to include numerous sayings at any point in his Gospel (Mt 5:17, 19-20, 21-24, 27-28, 33-39a, 43; 6:1-8, 16-18; 7:6, 15); he has placed the remainder in six different places with little regard for Matthew's order. Although attempts have been made to explain why Luke might have revised Matthew's Sermon so radically, they have not been persuasive. At least in this case, the Q hypothesis offers a much simpler and more plausible explanation of the evidence.

In most reconstructions of Q the traditions behind Luke 6:20b-49 form the initial collection of the sayings of Jesus: these verses were already an "inaugural sermon" in Q, preceded only by John's preaching of the Coming One (Lk 3:7-9, 16-17; see John the Baptist) and the Temptation traditions (Lk 4:1-13; see Temptation of Jesus). The opening Beatitudes in Q pronounce God's blessing on those in dire need: the poor, those who hunger, sorrow and suffer persecution (Lk 6:20b-23). These sayings declare that the coming of God's kingdom (see Kingdom of God) brings about radical transformation: They proclaim good news (see Gospel [Good News]).

Matthew has followed Q's lead and used the Beatitudes as the opening section of his Sermon. Luke places the Sermon on the Plain at a later point in his Gospel, but he may nonetheless have been strongly influenced by the position of the Beatitudes as the opening of an "inaugural sermon" in Q. If, as is likely, the Q Beatitudes are to be understood as the fulfillment of Isaiah 61:1-3, it is significant that this very passage is quoted in Luke's dramatic and programmatic account of the opening of the ministry of Jesus in the synagogue* at Nazareth (Lk 4:16-30). Quite independently, both Matthew and Luke may have been influenced by Q's insistence that the signifi-

cance of Jesus is to be seen in terms of Isaiah 61:1-3, a claim which goes back to Jesus himself.

1.2. Luke's Emphases. Luke has not reshaped the Q Sermon in the way that Matthew has, but two emphases are clear and important. In four places Luke has added "now" to the traditions: to the beatitude and corresponding woe on hunger (Lk 6:21a and 25a) and to the beatitude and woe on mourning and laughing (Lk 6:21c and 25c). These additions reveal the Evangelist's concern for Christian life here and now. A similar emphasis is found in numerous passages in Luke. For example, Luke 9:23 stresses that taking up one's cross and following Jesus is to be carried out *daily* (cf. Mk 8:34).

In Luke, but not in Matthew, there are four woes which correspond precisely to his four beatitudes (cf. Lk 6:20-21 and 24-26). Most scholars accept that Luke has added the woes to the Q Sermon, either from independent tradition or on his own initiative. In this way Luke underlines the contrast between, on the one hand, people who are in desperate circumstances (the poor, the hungry, those who mourn and those who are persecuted) and, on the other hand, people who are self-satisfied and complacent. In numerous passages in his Gospel Luke attacks complacency and stresses the particular concern of Jesus for the poor, for those in need and for those on the margins of society (see Mary's Song; Rich and Poor).

2. The Sermon on the Mount in Matthew.
A brief survey of the history of interpretation of the Sermon confirms just how influential these chapters have been and how many major theological issues they raise.

2.1. History of Interpretation. The first commentary on the Sermon was probably written by Origen in the middle of the third century, but only a short fragment of it has survived. The two most important expositions of the Sermon in the early church were written by Chrysostom and Augustine at the end of the fourth century, both of whom insisted that the Sermon was the perfect pattern for the life of all Christians. In his homilies on the Sermon Chrysostom attacked the heretical views of Gnostics and Manicheans. He rejected their view that the body is evil and only the mind and spirit are good; he insisted that Matthew 5:29 teaches that it is the "evil mind" which is accursed, not bodily organs such as the eye and hand. Chrysostom also refuted "those heretics who say that the old covenant is of the devil"; the sayings of Jesus do not repeal the old Law, they "draw out and fill up its commands."

Augustine also grappled with the relationship of the

Sermon to the Law of Moses. The Manichean Faustus had claimed that Matthew 5:17 was a saying neither of Jesus nor of Matthew: someone else had written it under Matthew's name! In his *Reply to Faustus* Augustine stressed the continuity of the "old Law" and the "new" more strongly than was usually the case in the early church. In his own exposition of the Sermon, however, the more common line of interpretation is prominent. Augustine drew attention to the sharp discontinuity between the "old Law" and the "new" by distinguishing between the "lesser precepts given by God through his holy prophets and servants to a people who still needed to be bound by fear" (i.e., to Israel before the coming of Christ) and "the greater precepts given through his Son to a people now ready to be freed by love."

Augustine is not the only interpreter who interpreted Matthew 5:17-48 in different ways either in different contexts or at different points in his life. Augustine may have been inconsistent, but the issue is still with us today. To what extent and in what ways is the ethical teaching of the OT still important today? How "new" is the teaching of Jesus, and does it have priority over Scripture? Do we retain the parts of Scripture to which Jesus refers, and ignore or reject the rest?

In the thirteenth century Thomas Aquinas also stressed the discontinuity between the old Law ("the Law of bondage") and the new Law ("the Law of liberty") but without conceding that the latter contradicted or abrogated the former. In his interpretation of the Sermon he used the analogy of the tree (the new Law) which is in a sense contained in the seed. Aquinas also introduced a distinction which was to become very influential in Catholic thought. In addition to the *commandments* of the new Law, which are necessary in order to gain salvation, there are also optional *counsels* which "render the gaining of eternal bliss more assured and expeditious." The latter are intended for those who strive for perfection; they are based on poverty, chastity and obedience and are therefore primarily for those who join the religious life. This distinction is hardly hinted at in interpretation of the Sermon in the early church, though it may be implied by the harsh saying of Jesus concerning the renunciation of marriage: "Let those accept it who can" (Mt 19:11-12). Luther, Zwingli and Calvin wrote extensively on the Sermon. They all insisted that Matthew 5—7 represents the true interpretation of the Law of Moses,* which had been obscured in Judaism. On the whole they emphasized the continuity between the "Law of Christ" and the "Law of Moses" more than their Catholic opponents. They rejected the use made of the Sermon by radical Anabaptist groups who claimed that the ethical teaching of Christ was a clear development beyond the Law of Moses, parts of which have been abrogated. Anabaptists claimed that the Sermon should be interpreted literally and that Christians should therefore never use violence (Mt 5:39; *see* Peace), never swear oaths (Mt 5:34; *see* Oaths and Swearing) and never hold office as a judge or ruler (Mt 7:1). Their literal interpretation of the Sermon led them to opt out of secular government completely.

In a series of sermons on Matthew 5—7 (and in other writings) Luther developed his well-known doctrine of the two realms—the secular and the spiritual. The Christian lives in both spheres. In the spiritual sphere (i.e., within the life of the church) the Christian must obey all the commands of the Sermon; in the secular sphere, natural law or "common sense" must prevail. In his remarks on Matthew 5:38-42 (the use of violence and compulsion), for example, Luther claimed that most interpreters failed to distinguish properly between the kingdom of Christ and the kingdom of the world. In these verses

> Christ is not tampering with the responsibility and authority of the government, but he is teaching individual Christians how to live personally, apart from their official position and authority . . . A Christian should not (use violence to) resist evil; but within the limits of his office, a secular person should oppose firmly every evil.

For Luther a "secular person" included Christians participating in the secular realm.

Luther also discussed the Sermon in terms of "Law" and "gospel." In some of his writings he emphasized that the Sermon is the "law of Christ" that makes people aware of the gospel of God's grace through Christ: "we are not able properly to fulfil one tittle out of our own strength . . . but must always crawl to Christ." But in other passages Luther stated that the Sermon is not just the accusing Law that points to sin: it is also "gospel." This is especially true of the Beatitudes (Mt 5:3-12). Christ "does not press, but in a friendly way entices and speaks: 'Blessed are the poor.' "

By referring in different passages in his writings to the Sermon both as Law and as gospel, Luther confused some of his later followers. Many Lutheran theologians have stressed that the Sermon is the Law that awakens knowledge of sin. But some (notably J. Jeremias 1961) have claimed that the demands of Jesus in the Sermon are preceded by gospel, that is, by his proclamation of the kingdom and by his encouragement to his disciples to share his own sense of sonship.

In his comments on Matthew 5:21 Calvin noted that "we must not imagine Christ to be a new legislator, who adds anything to the eternal righteousness of his Father. We must listen to him as a faithful expounder. . . ." Calvin partially anticipated eighteenth- and nineteenth-century discussion of the sources of the Sermon in his recognition that Matthew 5—7 is "a brief summary of the doctrine of Christ . . . collected out of his many and various discourses."

All the various approaches just sketched can be found in modern discussion of the Sermon. Twentieth-century scholarship, however, has added two new issues: the extent to which the Sermon reflects the views of Jesus (or of Matthew) concerning the end-times (eschatology*) and the extent to which Matthew the Evangelist has shaped the traditions he has incorporated into chapters 5—7.

In 1892 J. Weiss published a short but influential discussion of Jesus' proclamation of the kingdom of God. He claimed that Jesus expected that the kingdom would shortly be ushered in through a cataclysmic divine intervention. In 1901 A. Schweitzer developed this approach even more vigorously. Both writers believed that the ethical teaching of Jesus was intended as a preparation for the short period before the end ("interim ethics"). The sayings of Jesus were not intended to be used by later generations, as most readers of the Sermon down through the centuries had simply assumed. Thus most of the issues with which earlier interpreters of the Sermon had grappled were declared to be irrelevant. Weiss and Schweitzer raised in an acute form the relationship between the ethical teaching of Jesus and his proclamation of the coming kingdom. Discussion of this issue has to range far beyond Matthew 5—7 and consider all the relevant sayings of Jesus.

B. W. Bacon (1902) was one of the first writers in English to attempt to reconstruct the earliest attainable form of the Sermon. He concluded that in its original form Jesus spoke as a prophetic (*see* Prophets, Prophecy) interpreter of a new Law; Jesus did not lay down rules, but opened up principles. These conclusions were hardly novel, but in his isolation of the "intrusive additions" of Matthew, Bacon paved the way for later redaction-critical studies. Bacon claimed that Matthew has supplied "neo-legalistic touches" in verses such as 5:16 ("good works"); 5:18-19; 5:32 (the exception to "no divorce*"); 7:12b. The original Sermon of Jesus is not legislative (as Matthew seems to have regarded it) but prophetic.

Since 1945 interpretation of the Sermon and of Matthew's Gospel as a whole has been dominated by redaction criticism. This approach explores the ways in which the Evangelist has reshaped the traditions at his disposal in the light of the needs of his first readers. Redaction criticism has confirmed that Matthew is more than a compiler. Matthew's five discourses have been composed in the same way: in all five the Evangelist has rearranged and reinterpreted the sayings on which he drew. He often elucidates earlier traditions with extra phrases or even (on occasion) with whole verses which he himself has composed. The following may be noted as possible examples: 5:10, 13a, 14a, 16, 20; 6:10b and c, 13b; 7:12c, 19, 20, 21. In many places in the Sermon Matthew's own distinctive vocabulary and emphases are evident. For example, the five important references to "righteousness" (Mt 5:6, 10, 20; 6:1, 33; *see* Justice, Righteousness) are all redactional additions made by the Evangelist himself.

In recent decades numerous studies of the Sermon and several detailed commentaries have been published. In nearly every case the Sermon has been isolated from the rest of Matthew's Gospel and treated as a separate entity simply for convenience. There has been no suggestion that Matthew 5—7 have a quite distinctive origin or purpose which sets them apart from the rest of Matthew's Gospel, and also from Mark and Luke.

There are, however, two notable exceptions. In his influential study of the Sermon (1964) W. D. Davies suggests that "one fruitful way of dealing with the Sermon on the Mount is to regard it as the Christian answer to Jamnia. Using terms very loosely, the Sermon is a kind of Christian, mishnaic counter-part to the formulation taking place there" (315). Davies sets out at length a cumulative case which rests on a large number of observations. He himself recognizes that some of his points are stronger than others. Davies appeals both to the Sermon and to other parts of Matthew's Gospel. Some of the latter passages are undoubtedly significant. For example, Davies is able to show that the Evangelist's community was at odds with contemporary Judaism.*

But the evidence from the Sermon itself is not compelling. None of the *direct* links proposed between the Sermon and the reconstruction taking place within Judaism during the Jamnian period is entirely satisfactory. It is the whole of Matthew's Gospel, not the Sermon in isolation, which can plausibly be related (though only indirectly) to the Jamnian period. Although Davies suggests that "there was an outside stimulus for the Evangelist to shape the Sermon" (315), he does not claim that Matthew 5—7 contains theological emphases which are quite distinct from the rest of the Gospel. Davies seems to accept that the

Sermon and the rest of Matthew come from the same social setting, though he does not discuss this point.

H. D. Betz's hypothesis, however, is not compelling. The links with the epitomes of the Greco-Roman rhetorical tradition are not strong, and the claim that the theological perspective of the Sermon is said to be at odds with Matthew's own theology is difficult to defend. Betz overlooks the extent to which in chapters 5—7 the Evangelist Matthew has shaped and reinterpreted the traditions at his disposal in ways which are completely consistent with the methods and themes developed elsewhere in his Gospel.

The latter point is one of the pillars of redaction-critical study of the Sermon. From a quite different angle narrative critics (led by J. D. Kingsbury) have recently underlined the ways in which the Sermon is part and parcel of the Evangelist's overall presentation of the story of Jesus.

2.2. Questions for Current Interpretation. The above survey of the history of interpretation confirms that careful study of these chapters involves a large number of issues, some of which are theological, some ethical, some historical and some exegetical. For convenience they may be divided into five sets of overlapping questions, some of which are discussed further in later sections of this article.

(1) Does Jesus simply interpret or clarify the Law* of Moses*? Or does he present radically new teaching? Is Jesus portrayed as the "new Moses" who "goes up on the mountain*" (Mt 5:1) in order to present on a "new Mt. Sinai" a "new Law" for a "new people"?

(2) What is the relationship between Matthew 5—7 and Paul's gospel of grace? Is the Sermon (as Law) intended to make the readers or listeners aware of their need of grace? Or does the Sermon *presuppose* God's forgiveness and acceptance of the sinner* and therefore set out demands for true discipleship*?

(3) To whom is the Sermon addressed? To men and women in general, or to those committed to the way of Jesus? The text itself is ambiguous at this point. The introduction and conclusion (Mt 5:1 and 7:28) imply that the Sermon was addressed to the crowds, but 5:2 notes that "when the disciples had gathered around him Jesus began to address them." While many parts of the Sermon seem to set out an "ethic of Christian discipleship," the final verses of the whole Gospel imply that the teaching of Jesus is to be part of the message taken to "all nations" (Mt 28:18-20).

(4) Are all parts of the Sermon to be interpreted literally, as some have claimed? Or do some sayings (such as Mt 5:22, 39, 43) contain hyperbole? Does the Sermon set out a *code* of ethics, or principles or attitudes appropriate for "members of the kingdom"?

These questions arise whether the intention of Matthew or of Jesus is in view.

(5) To what extent are individual sayings dominated by the expectation (either of Jesus or of Matthew) of the approach of the end-times (i.e., eschatology)? For example, does Jesus commend a casual attitude to food and clothing in Matthew 6:25-34 because of the approach of the end-times, or simply because this is the right attitude regardless of when the end-times come? Is every petition of the Lord's Prayer (Mt 6:9-13) to be interpreted eschatologically? If so, when we pray "Give us this day our daily bread" we are not asking for the basic necessities of everyday life, but requesting a partial anticipation now of the "feast of heaven"—the "bread* of heaven." Does the petition "lead us not into temptation" concern the time of testing expected in the end-times or everyday temptations?

The modern interpreter will quickly find that interpretation of individual sayings or groups of sayings will be determined by the answers given to all five sets of questions. These questions have been discussed for nearly two thousand years, though some have been more prominent than others in different periods of church history.

2.3. The Structure of the Sermon and Key Sections.

2.3.1. Structure. In recent years several proposals concerning the structure of the Sermon have been made. The overall structure of the Sermon is clear. The Beatitudes (5:3-12) are an introduction to the Sermon as a whole; the similarly structured "salt" and "light"* sayings in 5:13-16 form the second part of the introduction. The central section of the Sermon extends from 5:17 to 7:12; it opens and closes with references to the Law and the Prophets: 5:17-20 and 7:12. The Sermon is rounded off by an epilog, 7:13-27, in which, as we shall see, there is considerable coherence.

It is not difficult to set out the structure of the first half of the Sermon, from Matthew 5:3 to 6:18. Following the general introduction in 5:1-16, the important sayings on the continuing significance of the Law and the Prophets in 5:17-20 are clarified and expounded, as it were, by the six antitheses in 5:21-47. Matthew 5:48 is probably intended to round off all the antitheses. Matthew 6:1 introduces three paragraphs on almsgiving, prayer and fasting* (6:2-18), all of which have exactly the same structure; the Lord's Prayer and two related sayings (6:9-15) partly breaks the very impressive symmetry in this part of the Sermon.

But what about the structure of the second half of the Sermon? Matthew 6:19 to 7:11 has long puzzled interpreters. This part of the Sermon seems to be a rag-bag of sayings, only some of which are loosely related to others. G. Bornkamm has offered a novel solution: the second half of the Sermon is a commentary on the Lord's Prayer. Matthew 6:19-24 expounds the first three petitions, 6:9-10; 6:25-34, then works out the implications of the bread petition, 6:11; 7:1-5 is an exposition of the forgiveness* petition and, finally, 7:6 takes up the theme of 6:13. Bornkamm's ingenious explanation has not convinced other scholars, but he has shown just how strongly the whole section from Matthew 6:5 to 7:11 is dominated by the theme of prayer.

U. Luz claims that the Sermon has been built symmetrically around its centerpiece, the Lord's Prayer (Mt 6:7-15). The first section, 5:3-16, corresponds to the last section, 7:13-27; the second section, 5:17-20, corresponds to 7:12; 5:21-48 corresponds to 6:19—7:11 (these two passages are identical in length); and 6:1-6 corresponds to 6:16-18. Although the theory is not completely convincing (the correspondence between 5:21-48 and 6:19—7:11 is forced), there is little doubt that Matthew does intend 5:17-20 to introduce the central section of the Sermon, and 7:12 to conclude it.

2.3.2. The Prologue: The Beatitudes (Mt 5:3-12). In Matthew there are nine Beatitudes, only four of which are found in Luke. The word *makarios* at the beginning of all the Beatitudes has long teased translators. *Makarios* echoes LXX usage, where it expresses the happiness which is the result of God-given salvation. The English phrase "Happy are those who . . ." hardly catches this rich meaning. "Blessed" is perhaps preferable, but in some colloquial English usage "blessed" can mean "cursed." "God's gift of salvation is given to those who . . ." is accurate but clumsy, especially if repeated nine times.

Matthew and Luke have taken over the four Beatitudes found in Q which referred to the poor, the hungry, those who weep and those who are persecuted. Matthew has added (in part from earlier oral traditions) five further Beatitudes which are found in his Gospel alone: the blessings on the meek (Mt 5:5), the merciful, the pure in heart, the peacemakers and a second saying concerning persecution (Mt 5:7-10). These additional Beatitudes and the changes made by Matthew to the Q sayings confirm that he is particularly concerned with ethical conduct. In Luke those in desperate need—those who are literally poor, hungry, weeping and persecuted (Lk 6:20-23)—are promised that their position will be reversed by God. In Matthew the dominant theme is very different. Those addressed, that is, the disciples and also the followers of Jesus in the Evangelist's own day, are promised that

their positive qualities—their meekness, mercy, purity of heart, and abilities as peacemakers—will be rewarded by God.

This general observation may be illustrated by the two references to righteousness which Matthew adds to Q Beatitudes. The saying at Luke 6:21 which corresponds to Matthew's fourth Beatitude (Mt 5:6) refers to those who are literally hungry: In their rather desperate state they will be blessed by God and their hunger satisfied. In Luke (but not in Matthew) there is a corresponding "woe" on the rich (Lk 6:24). In Matthew, however, God's blessing is promised to a rather different group: to those who "hunger and thirst *after righteousness*" (Mt 5:6), that is, to disciples who are "hungry" to do God's will.

In Matthew 5:10 those who are "persecuted for righteousness' sake" are promised that the kingdom of heaven is theirs. This saying (like Mt 5:20) contains so many of Matthew's favorite words that the Evangelist may have created it himself. As in several other similar cases, Matthew develops themes already present in the sources he is using. The second half of Matthew 5:10, "for theirs is the kingdom of heaven," echoes 5:3 (Q); the first half of Matthew 5:10 underlines the importance of the Q Beatitude which follows in 5:11, where disciples are encouraged in the face of persecution. Whereas Luke explains that the fierce opposition being experienced is "on account of the Son of man" (Lk 6:22), in 5:10 Matthew gives a different explanation: Followers of Jesus are being pilloried on account of their righteous conduct. A few verses later a more positive note is struck: "Let your light so shine before others, that they may see your good works and give glory to your Father in heaven" (Mt 5:16). Here "good works" seems to be synonymous with the "righteousness" or "righteous conduct" stressed so strongly in Matthew's Beatitudes.

2.3.3. The Law and the Prophets (Mt 5:17-20). Matthew 5:17 is often taken as the preface to the central section of the Sermon which runs from Matthew 5:17 to 7:12. But what is meant by, "Think not that I have come to abolish the Law and the Prophets; I have not come to abolish them but to fulfill them" (Mt 5:17)? In the Evangelist's day some Jewish opponents may well have claimed that followers of Jesus had abandoned the Law completely; in Matthew 5:17 words of Jesus may have been shaped as a response: Jesus did *not*, as some were claiming, come to destroy the Law and the Prophets. But what is meant by "fulfilling" them? From Matthew's perspective does Jesus set forth the real intention of the Law? Or does he confirm or establish the Law? The latter suggestion is often supported by linguistic arguments based on the force of the Aramaic word which Jesus may have used and by an appeal to Matthew 5:18 and 19. These two verses seem to underline the continuing importance of the Law: "not a letter, not a dot will disappear from the law" (5:18b REB).

However, this strong emphasis on the Law may be modified in the last phrase of Matthew 5:18, "until all things come to pass." "The law remains valid only *until all things come to pass* in Jesus' coming and ministry" (Guelich, 148). If this is the correct interpretation of Matthew 5:18, the warning in 5:19 not to relax "one of the least of these commandments" may refer to the sayings of Jesus rather than (as in the more usual interpretation) the Law. If, however, Matthew 5:19 does refer to strict and complete retention of the Law (without a hint of modification), then this verse must be seen as a very conservative saying which is somewhat out of character with Matthew 5:17, 18 and 20, and with Matthew's emphases elsewhere. In Matthew 5:20 disciples of Jesus are urged to carry out the will of God in their ethical conduct to an even greater degree than the scribes* and Pharisees.*

2.3.4. The Antitheses (Mt 5:21-48). In Matthew 5:21-48 six paragraphs of sayings of Jesus all have the same structure: "You have heard that it was said (by God) to those of ancient times (i.e., in Scripture) . . . but I say to you. . . ." The full formula just quoted introduces the first and fourth paragraphs and thus divides the six into two groups of three; in the other paragraphs the formula is abbreviated. Although three of the six paragraphs have partial parallels in Luke and belonged originally to Q (Mt 5:21-22, 27-28, 33-37), Matthew himself has added the other three groups of sayings which he has drawn from oral tradition.

The phrase "but I say to you" occurs in all six passages and *seems* to set sayings of Jesus in opposition to Scripture; hence Matthew 5:21-48 is usually referred to as the "antitheses." Matthew is responsible for the striking antithetical structure of all six passages. But, as is frequently the case elsewhere, the Evangelist develops considerably an earlier tradition: the antithetical structure is already found in embryonic form in Luke 6:27a (Q), "but I say to you who hear. . . ."

The term *antitheses* is something of a misnomer, for it can hardly be claimed that in all six paragraphs the teaching of Jesus is intended to be in direct contrast to, or opposition to (i.e., is "antithetical" to), the Law of Moses. Matthew has ruled out that possibility in 5:17 by stressing that Jesus has not come to destroy the Law and the Prophets. In addition the six uses of the passive verb "it was said" almost certainly imply "it was said *by God* in Scripture"; Jesus could hardly be understood to be contradicting what God had said.

Although it has sometimes been claimed that in at least some of these passages Jesus is contrasting his own teaching with Jewish interpretations of the Law current in his own day, rather than the Law itself, this explanation is unconvincing. Matthew 5:17-20, which is clearly intended to be an introduction to the antitheses, prepares the reader for discussion of the relationship of the teaching of Jesus to the Law, and not merely for learned scribal discussion about the *interpretation* of the Law.

So what is the primary thrust of the antitheses? Is there a consistent theme, or do they point in two (or more) directions? Many scholars have claimed that in some cases Jesus seems to strengthen the teaching of the Law (Mt 5:22, 28, 34); in others he seems to overturn the teaching of Moses (Mt 5:39, 44 and perhaps 32). Given that Matthew 5:21-48 is no mere anthology of sayings of Jesus but has been very carefully constructed by the Evangelist himself, we should expect a consistent pattern unless the text forces us to conclude otherwise.

On the one hand, the antithetical pattern implies that Jesus is not simply confirming the teaching of the Law which is quoted. On the other hand, as we have seen, Matthew does not set out sayings of Jesus as a contradiction of God-given Scripture. So how are the antitheses to be understood? Davies and Allison (1.509-10) correctly suggest that their primary function is twofold:

> to show through six concrete examples, (i) what sort of attitude and behavior Jesus requires and (ii) how his demands surpass those of the Torah without contradicting the Torah. . . . The letter of the law does not give life. All things lawful may not be helpful. One may refrain from murder and still hate, refrain from committing adultery and still lust in the heart, and it is possible to follow the OT's provisions with regard to divorce and oaths and yet be found in sin. . . . Purely legal norms, such as those cited in Mt. 5.21, 27, 31, 33, 38, and 43, can never convey how life is to be lived by those who are genuinely poor in spirit, pure in heart, and full of mercy (5.3, 7, 8).

Matthew 5:20 and 48, which act as a frame for the six antitheses in 5:21-47, confirm that this is the Evangelist's intention. (Mt 5:48, like 7:12, opens with *oun*, "so," "therefore"; both verses are intended to act as a summary and conclusion to the preceding block.) Matthew 5:20 insists that the righteousness which followers of Jesus are to carry out must exceed that of the scribes and Pharisees; that righteousness is not to be construed as obedience to legislation, but as perfect conformity to God's will (Mt 5:48).

The same fundamental point is illustrated further with three carefully constructed examples in Matthew 6:1-18. In each case the same pattern recurs: "when you give alms (pray, fast), do not do it as the hypocrites do, but when you give alms (fast, pray), do it in secret, and your Father who sees in secret will reward you." The "greater righteousness" of Matthew 5:20 is once again purity of motive rather than mere outward observance.

2.3.5. The Golden Rule (Mt 7:12). "Whatever you wish that others would do to you, do so to them" has been known as the Golden Rule since the eighteenth century. There are numerous parallels to this saying in Greco-Roman, oriental and Jewish writings. There is a particularly close rabbinic tradition in *b. Sabb.* 31a: "What is hateful to you, do not do to your fellow creatures." Although a negative formulation along these lines is much more common than the positive formulation of Matthew 7:12, the latter is found in some Jewish writings (*Ep. Arist.* 207; *T. Naph.* 1; *2 Enoch* 61:1); hence it is a mistake to claim that the positive form of the Golden Rule is distinctively Christian.

Matthew 7:12 opens with *oun,* "so," "therefore." This word has often been ignored by translators (e.g., NIV; REB). If *oun* is translated, the saying is often placed (as in the RSV) as the conclusion of the preceding block of sayings on "asking, seeking, finding" (Mt 7:8-11). This is equally mistaken, for Matthew 7:12 does not round off these sayings. Matthew intends *oun* to indicate to the reader that 7:12 is a summary and conclusion to all the material in the central section of the Sermon which starts at Matthew 5:17. The Evangelist has removed the Golden Rule from the conclusion of the "Love your enemies" sayings in Luke (and Q) 6:27-30 and given it an even more important role. This is confirmed by the dramatic words "for this is the Law and the Prophets" which Matthew adds to the Golden Rule. This additional phrase recalls Matthew 5:17 in which the coming of Jesus is the fulfillment of the Law and the Prophets.

Matthew makes the same point in the explanatory addition he makes to Mark 12:28-34, the teaching of Jesus on the two greatest commandments: "love God, and love your neighbor as yourself." In Matthew 22:40 the Evangelist adds, "On these two commandments depend all the Law and the Prophets." Hence for Matthew the Golden Rule and the love commandments express the very essence of Scripture. These sayings of Jesus (and his whole coming) are a lens through which his followers now read the Law and the Prophets.

2.3.6. The Epilog: Two Ways (Mt 7:13-27). The epilog of the Sermon contains a series of contrasts. It opens with the contrast between the gate and the way which lead to destruction and the gate and the way which lead to life* (Mt 7:13-14). A similar contrast between "two ways" is found in Deuteronomy 11:26; 30:15; Jeremiah 21:8, and in numerous Jewish and early Christian writings.

Matthew continues the general theme in the warnings about false prophets. "Good fruit" and "evil fruit" are contrasted (Mt 7:15-20), as are those who do the will of the Father and those who do not (Mt 7:21-23). In both cases there is a clear warning about a "way that leads to destruction."

Both Matthew and Luke conclude their Sermons, as did Q, with the parable* of the two houses. The general point of the parable is the same in both versions: A sharp contrast is drawn between those who hear and obey the words of Jesus and those who do not. U. Luz notes that the books of Leviticus (chap. 26) and Deuteronomy (30:15-20), and also several later Jewish writings, end similarly: two alternatives are placed squarely before the reader. Whereas similar Jewish traditions focus on study and practice of the Law, hearing and obeying the words of Jesus are central here. Matthew uses eschatological parables as the climax of two of his other discourses, Matthew 18:23-35 and 25:31-46; in both "two ways" are once again contrasted.

The wording of the parables in Matthew and in Luke differs considerably. The Evangelists have probably drawn on different versions of the Q parable. Luke's version emphasizes the care taken to dig deeply in order to place the foundations of the house on rock; a river which bursts its banks is unable to dislodge it.

Matthew's version is much more carefully structured and rhythmical. The threefold description of the storm is memorable: the rain came down, the floods rose, and the winds beat upon that house . . . (Mt 7:25 and 27). Matthew adds (or perhaps retains from Q) two references to the last judgment* (Mt 7:24 and 26) which are not present in Luke. The words of Jesus are referred to in a rather general way in Luke (6:47), but by adding "these" to "my words" twice over (Mt 5:24 and 26), Matthew refers specifically to the words of Jesus in the Sermon on the Mount (cf. Mt 28:20).

2.4. Matthew's Purposes. For Matthew the Sermon is but one part of his attempt to set out the significance of the story and teaching of Jesus for the life of his own community. The Sermon is the largest and most impressive of his five discourses, but it must not be separated from the rest of the Gospel.

Some of the themes Matthew emphasizes in the first of his five discourses are also prominent elsewhere in the Gospel. For example, in Matthew 5:20, one of the key verses which Matthew himself has almost certainly composed, disciples are told that their ethical conduct must exceed that of the scribes and Pharisees. In Matthew 5:48, a related verse, they are told to be perfect or wholehearted. In Matthew 6:1-18 their conduct is contrasted starkly with that of the "hypocrites"* (Mt 6:2, 5, 16), whom the reader naturally assumes to be none other than the scribes and Pharisees of Matthew 5:20.

These same points are developed in Matthew 23. The crowds (see People, Crowd) and disciples are urged not to follow the example of the scribes and Pharisees (Mt 23:2-3) who are then referred to explicitly as "hypocrites" six times. There is even some verbal correspondence between Matthew 6:1, 5 and 16 on the one hand, and Matthew 23:5 and 28 on the other. Both in chapters 5 and 6 of the Sermon, and in chapter 23, the Evangelist uses the scribes and Pharisees as a foil: disciples of Jesus are called to superior ethical conduct.

In the verses immediately preceding the Sermon, Matthew provides the interpreter with an important theological clue. Jesus announces the "good news of the kingdom" (Mt 4:17, 23) and calls Peter, Andrew, James and John into radical discipleship which involves renunciation of their occupation and of their family* ties (Mt 4:18-22). As in the Sermon which follows, and as in Matthew's Gospel as a whole, grace and demand are linked inextricably. The Jesus of Matthew's Sermon is the Son of God (Mt 3:17, the baptism* of Jesus; and Mt 4:1-11, the temptations; see Son of God) through whom God is acting for humankind: It is his demanding teaching which is to be central in the life of the community and in its discipling of the nations (Mt 28:20; see Gentiles).

In the past the Sermon has often been removed from its present setting in Matthew and treated as a convenient summary of the teaching of Jesus. By reading the Sermon as part of Matthew's Gospel we are able to see how the Evangelist intended his first readers to approach these chapters. But this important principle of interpretation does not resolve all the difficulties. Many verses in the Sermon still puzzle us. Can any man claim to have avoided committing adultery "in his heart" by not looking on a woman* with a lustful eye (Mt 5:28)? What are the pearls which are not to be thrown to the pigs (Mt 7:6)? Difficult parts of the Bible often provoke us to think about issues we might otherwise have avoided.

It is a mistake to suppose that we cannot understand the Sermon without the assistance of an expert. We do not need to be musicians to be profoundly moved by a piece of music; nor do we need to be art historians in order to appreciate a work of art. At the very heart of the Sermon we find one of the most radical and demanding of the sayings of Jesus, a saying which sums up the ethos of the Sermon as a whole and is as relevant today as it was in the first century. "You have learned (from Scripture), 'Love your neighbor, hate your enemy.' But what I tell you is this: Love your enemies and pray for your persecutors" (Mt 5:43-44).

See also BLESSING AND WOE; COMMANDMENT; DIVORCE; ETHICS OF JESUS; LAW; LOVE; MATTHEW, GOSPEL ACCORDING TO; Q.

BIBLIOGRAPHY. H. D. Betz, *Essays on the Sermon on the Mount* (Philadelphia: Fortress, 1985); G. Bornkamm, "Der Aufbau der Bergpredigt," *NTS* 24 (1977-78) 419-32; W. D. Davies, *The Setting of the Sermon on the Mount* (Cambridge: University Press, 1964); W. D. Davies and D. C. Allison, Jr., *Matthew* (ICC; Edinburgh: T. & T. Clark 1988) vol. 1; J. Dupont, *Les Béatitudes* (Paris: Gabalda, vol. I, 2d ed., 1969; vol. II, 1969; vol. III, 2d ed., 1973); R. A. Guelich, *The Sermon on the Mount: A Foundation for Understanding* (Waco: Word, 1982); R. H. Gundry, *Matthew: A Commentary on His Literary and Theological Art* (Eerdmans: Grand Rapids, 1982); H. Hendrickx, *The Sermon on the Mount* (London: Chapman, 1984); J. Jeremias, *The Sermon on the Mount* (FB; Philadelphia: Fortress, 1963); W. S. Kissinger, *The Sermon on the Mount: A History of Interpretation and Bibliography* (ATLABibS 3; Metuchen: Scarecrow, 1975); J. Lambrecht, *The Sermon on the Mount* (Wilmington, DE: Glazier, 1985); U. Luz, *Matthew 1—7: A Commentary* (Minneapolis: Augsburg Fortress, 1989); G. N. Stanton, "The Origin and Purpose of Matthew's Sermon on the Mount," in *Tradition and Interpretation in the New Testament: Essays in Honor of E. Earle Ellis,* ed. G. F. Hawthorne with O. Betz (Grand Rapids: Eerdmans; Tübingen: J. C. B. Mohr, 1987) 181-94; G. Strecker, *The Sermon on the Mount: An Exegetical Commentary* (Nashville: Abingdon, 1988).

G. N. Stanton

SERVANT OF YAHWEH

Four passages in Isaiah 40—55 are conventionally designated as the "Servant Songs" on the understanding that they together present a distinctive vision of a particular "Servant of Yahweh" or "Suffering Servant" to whom is entrusted a special mission on behalf of his people. This figure was one of those used by NT writers to illuminate the mission of Jesus (see Typology).

1. The Servant of Yahweh in the Book of Isaiah
2. Jesus As the Servant in the Gospels

1. The Servant of Yahweh in the Book of Isaiah.

B. Duhm in 1892 isolated Isaiah 42:1-4; 49:1-6; 50:4-9 and 52:13—53:12 as the "Servant Songs." Others have wished to extend their limits or even add part of Isaiah 61 as a fifth Song. Many earlier scholars assumed that these passages had an origin independent of their present context in the book of Isaiah, but more recent scholarship has generally agreed that they belong integrally to the text of Isaiah 40—55 and must not be interpreted independently of that context. The idea of Israel* as God's* Servant is not confined to these passages, but in them, and especially in Isaiah 53, there is a new and striking concept of a Servant whose role of vicarious suffering brings healing* and deliverance to the people.

It is explicitly Israel who is here described as God's Servant (Is 49:3), as in much of the surrounding context (Is 41:8-9; 43:10; 44:1-2; etc). But in some parts of the Songs, notably in Isaiah 53:4-6, 10-12, the Servant is portrayed as an individual over against Israel and as suffering on their behalf.

This ambiguity as to the identity of the Servant, and whether he is intended to be understood as a corporate or an individual figure (or indeed whether there is a unified "Servant figure" in Isaiah at all), has led to intense debate among interpreters ancient and modern.

Any statement about Jewish interpretation around the first century A.D. must be tentative, as the documentary evidence for Jewish thought at that period is minimal, and need not be typical of common belief. But while Jewish writers could apply phrases from these passages to various historical figures as well as to Israel corporately, there is also evidence that by NT times they were understood by some to refer to a future individual who would act as God's agent for his people's restoration—in other words, a messianic figure. (Jeremias, *TDNT* V.682-700, presents sufficient evidence for this, though his survey has rightly been criticized as one-sided.)

This is particularly clear in the Targum on Isaiah 53, which explicitly identifies the Servant as "the Messiah" even though its author is so hostile to the idea of messianic suffering that each reference to suffering is carefully reinterpreted or transferred to the people or to some other subject; the messianic identification is apparently too firmly entrenched to allow the targumist the easy option of an alternative identification as Israel or as some historical figure. NT references especially to Isaiah 53 presuppose such a messianic interpretation.

2. Jesus As the Servant in the Gospels.

Christian devotion has always found in Isaiah 53 an unrivalled portrayal of the vicarious and redemptive suffering of Jesus, which offers perhaps a clearer presentation of the classic Christian doctrine of the atonement than any single passage in the NT.

A number of scholars have questioned, however, whether the figure of the Servant of Yahweh did in fact play any significant role in the development of Christian understanding of the mission of Jesus in the NT period. This has been argued by C. K. Barrett and C. F. D. Moule, and most fully by M. D. Hooker. Hooker has shown that some alleged references to the Servant passages are at least questionable and has rightly emphasized that even where such reference is undeniable, the focus is not so one-sidedly on the Servant's role of vicarious redemption as later Christian usage might expect. But she has not convinced most scholars that the Servant figure was not an important factor in the earliest christology. In particular no equally plausible source has yet been suggested for Jesus' conviction that it was his mission to suffer and die because this was "written" (*see* Death of Jesus).

The direct use of the title "Servant" *(pais)* [of God] for Jesus does not occur in the NT outside the early chapters of Acts (Acts 3:13, 26; 4:27, 30). But the Servant passages of Isaiah are quoted several times, and their language and ideas underlie some of the most central statements about Jesus' mission.

2.1. The Synoptic Tradition in General. Each of the Synoptic Gospels identifies Jesus at his baptism* by means of a direct pronouncement by God, subsequently repeated at the Transfiguration,* "You are [this is] my beloved Son, with whom I am pleased" (Mk 1:11; 9:7). While the term *servant* is not used, almost all commentators agree that the words are a deliberate echo of the introduction to the first Servant Song (Is 42:1). Jesus' mission is thus marked out at the outset, and in the most authoritative way possible, as that of the Servant.

More specific allusions to Isaiah 53 occur in two key sayings about the redemptive significance of Jesus' coming death (*see* Death of Jesus). Mark 10:43-44 defines greatness for Jesus' disciples in terms of accepting the role of a servant, and Mark 10:45 goes on to reinforce this demand by Jesus' own example: "The Son of man came not to be served but to serve, and to give his life as a ransom for many" (*see* Ransom Saying). Here it is not only the language of *service* which recalls the Isaiah passages but more specifically the idea of vicarious death, of ransom and the phrase "for many" which echoes the language of Isaiah 53:11-12. And at the Last Supper (*see* Last Supper)

Jesus' words over the cup use similar terminology about his blood being poured out "for many" (Mk 14:24). (For a detailed analysis of the verbal and conceptual links between these passages and the Servant Songs see France 116-23.)

Other verbal allusions have been claimed with much less plausibility, but more important than any verbal echo is the frequently repeated concept of the mission of the Son of man (*see* Son of Man) as one which fulfills the will of God by means of his rejection, suffering and death because these things are "written" about him (Mk 8:31; 9:12, 31; 10:32-34; 14:21, etc.). While some have argued that Daniel 7 supplies an adequate background for this concept (in the oppression of the saints which precedes their vindication, symbolized in the figure of "one like a son of man"), Jewish understanding of the human figure of Daniel 7:13-14 was in fact consistently of a majestic, victorious figure. That this "Son of man" should suffer and be killed was a striking paradox, and no more probable source for this innovative theology can be suggested than the suffering of the Isaianic Servant. A suffering Messiah might have been derived from some of the psalms of the righteous sufferer or from the pierced and rejected shepherd of Zechariah 11—13, but no passage in the OT offers so clear a prediction of messianic suffering as Isaiah 53, and we have seen above that this passage is clearly echoed in some key pronouncements of Jesus on his mission.

It is on such grounds that many believe that Isaiah's Servant figure was a major factor in Jesus' understanding of his own mission and the crucial basis on which his followers found it possible to make sense of his death as the fulfillment of Scripture. The main Markan texts for this belief have already been cited, but each of the other Evangelists in his own way develops the theme of Jesus as the Servant of Yahweh.

2.2. Matthew. Two of Matthew's eleven formula quotations are drawn from Isaiah's Servant Songs. In Matthew 8:17 Jesus' healing ministry is seen as fulfilling Isaiah 53:4, "He took our weaknesses and carried our diseases," while in Matthew 12:15-21 Jesus' withdrawal from public attention is understood in the light of the first Servant Song, Isaiah 42:1-4, which is quoted in full. There is no doubt then that it is important for Matthew that Jesus fulfills the role of the Isaianic Servant of Yahweh. Yet it is remarkable that neither of these passages refers to the distinctive role of redemptive suffering, either in the specific words cited or in the aspect of Jesus' ministry to which they are applied. Jesus' earthly ministry of healing and deliverance, and his non-confrontational demeanor, are no less a fulfillment of the Servant's mission than his vicarious death.

Another possible allusion to Isaiah 53 has been seen in Matthew 3:15, where the divine designation of Jesus in terms drawn from Isaiah 42:1 is preceded by the justification of his baptism as "fulfilling all righteousness." This notoriously obscure pronouncement may be understood not only as referring to the Servant's representative role, thus leading Jesus to identify himself with repentant (*see* Repentance) sinners,* but also as a rather cryptic allusion to Isaiah 53:11, "The righteous one shall make many to be accounted righteous." The same idea of identification may also lie behind Matthew's mention that Joseph of Arimathea was a "rich" man (27:57), thus recalling Isaiah 53:9, "They made his grave . . . with a rich man in his death" (*see* Burial of Jesus).

2.3. Luke. In the canticles of Luke 1 the designation "Servant of God" is applied not to Jesus but to Israel (Lk 1:54) and to David (Lk 1:69). And while Matthew has almost exact parallels to Mark 10:45 and 14:24, the Lukan equivalents do not share the same clear allusions to the language of Isaiah 53 (though the language of "service" is still emphasized in Lk 22:26-27). This might suggest that Luke is less interested than Mark and Matthew in the Isaianic Servant as a model for Jesus' ministry. But we should not forget that it is the same Luke who subsequently records the actual title "Servant of God" used for Jesus (Acts 3:13, 26; note, however, that David is also described as God's *pais* in 4:25). (Cf. the verbal parallels between Acts 3 and Is 52:13—53:12 [LXX]: Acts 3:13/Is 52:13; 3:13/53:6, 12; 3:14/53:11.) And it is Luke also who presents the only formal citation from Isaiah 53 in the Synoptic Gospels: the clause "And he was numbered among the lawless" (from Is 53:12) is introduced by the formula, "This which is written must be fulfilled in me," and followed by the further affirmation, "For what is [written] about me has its fulfillment" (Lk 22:37). There is no doubt, then, that for Luke the mission of the Servant in Isaiah 53 is a blueprint for that of Jesus; the Servant is Jesus.

The OT passage which in Luke's Gospel most prominently defines Jesus' ministry is Isaiah 61:1-2, the text of Jesus' Nazareth sermon in Luke 4:16-27 (*see* Jubilee). This Scripture, Jesus declares, is now being fulfilled in his ministry (Lk 4:21). Isaiah 61 is not, of course, one of Duhm's Servant Songs. But it shares with Isaiah 42:1-4 several important themes concerning the ministry of the one anointed by God for the work of delivering his people, and many commentators have understood the passages as related in their essential content, even if not in a formal literary sense. It is not unlikely that Luke, in recording Jesus' sermon on Isaiah 61, was thinking of his mission as the Servant of Yahweh.

2.4. John. John also has a formal citation from Isaiah 53. In John 12:38 the unbelief of the Jews is explained by the text, "Who has believed our report? And to whom has the arm of the Lord been revealed?" (Is 53:1). Inasmuch as this unbelief in Isaiah is a mark of the paradoxical nature of the Servant's appearance and experience, and Jesus' ministry was similarly open to misunderstanding and rejection, a parallel is here drawn between Jesus and the Servant which in the light of other Christian references to the Servant seems entirely appropriate. But it must be admitted that the focus at this point in John is not on the redemptive mission of the Servant or of Jesus, but rather on the mere fact of Jewish unbelief.

Another possible allusion to Isaiah 53 may be found in John the Baptist's description of Jesus as "the lamb of God who takes away the sin of the world" (1:29, 36; *see* Lamb of God). The Servant is compared in Isaiah 53:7 to a lamb led to the slaughter, and the whole tenor of the chapter is on the taking away of the sins of the people through his suffering and death. The phrase "the lamb of God" can be related to several different lambs in OT and later Jewish thought, but most of these (e.g., the Passover lamb, the lamb of the daily offering or the messianic lamb of later apocalyptic*) do not directly support the idea of taking away sin, so that it is reasonable to see the Servant figure as making a major contribution to this image.

2.5. Conclusion. The above evidence suggests that while the figure of the Servant of Yahweh was not necessarily the most prominent in the christological thinking of all the Evangelists, they all accepted it as an appropriate and illuminating model for Jesus' mission of vicarious suffering and death for the sins of his people, and also (at least for Matthew) in his wider ministry of healing and deliverance. It was Jesus' own consciousness that he had come to fulfil the role of the Servant which gave scriptural backing to his revolutionary new conception of the Messiah's role as one of rejection, suffering and death rather than of earthly victory and glory.* And it was this model which eventually enabled his disciples to come to terms with his death as not defeat but achievement, the basis of the salvation of the people of God.

See also CHRIST; DEATH OF JESUS; OLD TESTAMENT IN THE GOSPELS; RANSOM SAYING.

BIBLIOGRAPHY. C. K. Barrett, "The Background of Mark 10:45," in *New Testament Essays*, ed. A. J. B. Higgins (Manchester: University Press, 1959) 1-18; O. Cullmann, *The Christology of the New Testament* (rev. ed.; Philadelphia: Westminster, 1963) 51-82; R. T. France, *Jesus and the Old Testament* (London: Tyndale,

1971) 110-35; B. Gerhardsson, "Sacrificial Service and Atonement in the Gospel of Matthew," in *Reconciliation and Hope*, ed. R. Banks (Grand Rapids: Eerdmans, 1974) 25-35; J. B. Green, "The Death of Jesus, God's Servant," in *Reimaging the Death of the Lukan Jesus*, ed. D. D. Sylva (BBB 73; Frankfurt am Main: Anton Hain, 1990) 1-28, 170-73; M. D. Hooker, *Jesus and the Servant* (London: SPCK, 1959); J. Jeremias, *New Testament Theology, Vol. 1: The Proclamation of Jesus* (New York: Scribner's, 1971) 286-99; D. Juel, *Messianic Exegesis: Christological Interpretation of the Old Testament in Early Christianity* (Philadelphia: Fortress, 1988); O. Michel, I. H. Marshall, "παῖς θεοῦ κτλ," *NIDNTT* 3.607-13; C. F. D. Moule, *The Phenomenon of the New Testament* (London: SCM, 1967) 82-99; C. R. North, *The Suffering Servant in Deutero-Isaiah* (2d ed.; Oxford: University Press, 1956); W. Zimmerli, J. Jeremias, "παῖς θεοῦ," *TDNT* V.654-717.   R. T. France

SERVICE

For Jesus and the Evangelists service can characterize the essence of Jesus' ministry and the nature of discipleship.* Jesus' ultimate service is seen in his obedience to God* and death for others. His disciples* are likewise to serve God with undivided loyalty and, on the social level, serve one another—especially the helpless—rather than themselves.

1. Vocabulary
2. Cultural and Religious Background
3. Service in the Synoptic Gospels
4. The Footwashing (Jn 13:1-17)
5. Conclusion

1. Vocabulary.

The primary Greek word used in the Gospels meaning "to serve" is *diakoneō* and its noun counterparts *diakonos* ("servant") and *diakonia* ("service"). Closely related to this, however, is the word group *doulos/douleuō*, meaning "slave/to serve as a slave." Technically, *diakonia* deals more with table service done in the employment of a master, while *doulos* means "slave" and reflects a condition of bonded servitude. However, the distinction is not rigidly maintained in the Gospels. Indeed, the *diakonia/diakoneō* group is not used at all in the Greek OT. Instead, the Hebrew word *'ebed*, which we would translate "service/servant," is translated by *doulos*. In the NT the close link between the two word groups is seen in Matthew 20:25-27/Mark 10:42-44 where the two words are used parallel to one another.

Greek had specialized words indicating service to God or to community, *latreuō/latreia* and *leitourgeō/leitourgia*. The latter is found only in Luke 1:23, and the former is found in the context of the temptation of Christ (Mt 4:10 par. Lk 4:8, "you shall serve God alone"), and in other contexts reflecting people serving God (Lk 1:74; 2:37). In John 16:2 *latreia* is used ironically: People will seek to kill Christians, thinking that to do so is service to God. However, the use of these words is fairly rare in the Gospels. Instead, it is the symbol of the humble household servant or slave which Jesus uses to describe the nature of discipleship.

2. Cultural and Religious Background.

In general neither Greeks nor Jews thought very much of their servants. The Greeks looked down on the common table servant. The Jewish attitude was somewhat better, providing some protection for slaves/servants in the Law* (see Lev 25:42-55; Deut 5:15; 15:15 et al.), but the overall attitude was still negative. The harsh words of Sirach 33:26-28 (RSV) suggest the skeptical attitude of the public, "Yoke and thong will bow the neck, and for a wicked servant there are racks and tortures. Put him to work, that he may not be idle, for idleness teaches much evil. Set him to work, as is fitting for him, and if he does not obey, make his fetters heavy." The call to service and servanthood which we find in the Gospels is all the more remarkable against this background. When Jesus tells the disciples "You know that those who are supposed to rule over the Gentiles lord it over them, and their great men exercise authority over them" (Mk 10:42 RSV) he is saying the obvious: The mark of greatness in both the Gentile* and the Jewish world was authority.* Those who served did so out of need.

This does not mean that the Jewish world was without ideas of charity and caring. Giving of alms to the poor was a critical act of piety (see Prov 19:17; Tob 1:17). Rabbinic writings detail an elaborate system of caring for the poor and raising alms (Moore, II.169). There is no reason to doubt that similar systems existed in Jesus' day, and we may see some evidence of this in the way the disciples were themselves fed (Mk 2:23-28; 6:7-11). However, this in no way indicates a positive view of the poor or of service. Numerous episodes in Jesus' ministry confirm this (e.g., the rich young ruler, Mk 10:17-22; and Jesus' criticism of the scribes,* Mk 12:38-44). The desire to be served instead of serving was as common in the Judea of Jesus' day as in any other day or place.

3. Service in the Synoptic Tradition.

The Synoptics understand "service" in the customary sense of "table service" as the parables of Jesus (Mt 13:27-30; 18:23-34; 21:34-41; 22:3-13 and par.) and the stories of Mary and Martha (Lk 10:40 and par.; Jn 12:2) make clear. The words of the centurion in Matthew 8:9 and parallel passages confirm the normal view of service and servants in the Greco-Roman and Judean world: "I say to my servant, 'Do this' and he does it." In short, "service" meant menial service to meet the needs of a master.

3.1. The Two Masters Saying. It is all the more significant that Jesus chooses the image of the servant to describe his idea of discipleship. The servant is an appropriate image for the relationship of the believer with God because of the exclusive nature of the demand the master makes on the servant. We see this in the Q* saying of Matthew 6:24/Luke 16:13, "No one is able to serve two masters. . . . You cannot serve God and mammon." The concept is familiar in proverbial statements outside the NT (Manson, 133), but there is no reason to think that we are not dealing with an authentic saying of Jesus here (contra R. Bultmann, 1972, 85). The point is not that one cannot serve two masters; indeed, servants are not usually free to choose their masters. But the servant who tries to divide loyalty between two masters inevitably favors one or the other. "Mammon" represents all forms of wealth and power which tempt the disciple (as indeed they figure prominently in the temptations of Jesus, Mt 4:7-10 par. Lk 4:5-8; *see* Temptation of Jesus) to compromise his or her commitment. The God of the NT is no less jealous than the God of Sinai. Anything less than total commitment of the person to God leads ultimately to the rejection of God. The choice is between seeking salvation through what we control or salvation* through God.

3.2. Greatness in Service. Alongside this Jesus builds a picture of service which is in radical distinction from the cultural norm. The Synoptic Gospels picture the disciples in disputes over rank and pre-eminence (Mk 9:35 par. Lk 9:48; Mk 10:41-45 par. Mt 20:25-28; Lk 22:25-27; Mt 23:11). Jesus rejects this all-too-human wrangling for status: "You know that those who are supposed to rule over the Gentiles lord it over them, and their great men exercise authority over them. But, it shall not be so among you; but whoever would be great among you must be your servant, and whoever would be first among you must be slave of all" (Mk 10:42-44). Exhortations to humility and warnings against pride were well known in Judaism* (Manson, 233), but these sayings go beyond pious humility. Jesus is suggesting a transformation of society into a culture without rank or privilege (Horsley, 243-45). Obviously, Jesus is talking in the first sense only to those who accept his claims on their lives and is not offering this as a general social program. But the distinctive mark of those who belong to the dawning kingdom of God (*see* Ethics of Jesus) will be the rejection of power in favor of service to one another.

Luke 22:24-27 is closely related to Mark 10:42-44, but reflects what is probably an independent tradition (Marshall, 811; Fitzmyer, 1412). J. Roloff argues that Luke 22:27 originally connects with verses 15-20 in the pre-Lukan version of the Last Supper (*see* Last Supper), so that the concept of service here flows as an interpretation of the self-giving of Jesus symbolized in the Last Supper (Roloff, 54-58). These verses suggest that even in its pre-Lukan form the Last Supper was presented as a Farewell Discourse of Jesus (*see* Farewell Discourse). Farewell discourses typically include warnings and exhortations to the followers of the leader (*Adam and Eve* 30:1; *2 Apoc. Bar.* 44:2-15; 77:6; *1 Enoch* 82; 93—101; *2 Enoch* 44—46; *4 Ezra* 14:34-36), and frequently contain the appointment of a successor (*Adam and Eve* 50:1; *2 Apoc. Bar.* 45:2; *1 Enoch* 82:1-2; 104:11-13; *2 Enoch* 54:1; *4 Ezra* 14:26). What is significant here is that Jesus appoints no successor in the normal sense of that word. Instead, Jesus' last words and instructions interpret his own life and death as an act of sacrificial service, and this is held up as his heritage for the disciples.

3.3. The Eschatological Parables. This concept of service implies both risk and commitment for the disciple who follows in Jesus' path. The parable* of the faithful and the unfaithful servants (Mt 24:45-51 par. Lk 12:42-46) extols the virtue of the servant who is doing the Master's will even when the Master is away, and warns against the servant who exploits others in the Master's absence. We need not assume here that the emphasis on the delay of the Master is interjected into the parable by the church in order to deal with the problem of Jesus' delayed return (Jeremias, 55-59; for a contrary view see Marshall, 533-34). Jesus undoubtedly anticipated some interim period before his return when the disciples would have to operate on their own. The emphasis on faithful service in this interim and resisting the temptation to turn to selfish goals is consistent with the earlier teaching on service.

The parable of the pounds/talents supplements this picture. The Matthean version of the parable occurs in the context of the eschatological discourses (Mt 24—25; *see* Apocalyptic Teaching), a setting implying an emphasis on faithful witness* in the context of distress and uncertainty. The Lukan version of the parable, the parable of the pounds, occurs in a different context (prior to the entrance into Jerusalem, Lk 19:11-27) from that of Matthew's. But the addition of the details about the master—now a

nobleman who goes to receive a kingdom, followed by a hostile delegation of citizens who oppose him—adds political tension to the story and thus matches the eschatological (*see* Eschatology) context of Matthew. In both cases faithful service is carried out in the context of opposition and uncertainty. Service to Jesus is not without risk, and is itself an act of faith.*

At the same time it is significant that Matthew closes the eschatological section with a parable of the Last Judgment (sheep and the goats) that emphasizes the treatment of the poor and dispossessed as the true measure of faith and commitment (Mt 25:31-46). J. R. Donahue argues that the scene assumes the fulfillment of the Great Commission of Matthew 28:16-20 (*see* Gentiles), so that it depicts the judgment* at the end of the age after the gospel* has been taken to every nation. In this sense the "oppressed" and the "least of these" represent the disciples who have taken the gospel to others. The parable in this sense could be of comfort to the disciples: you will be mistreated, but the nations will be judged by the way they treat you (cf. Mt 10:42). However, the disciples themselves are not excluded from the message of the parable. Within the Matthean context these last parables focus on the faithfulness and readiness of the disciples. Discipleship inevitably issues in concrete actions (5:16), especially acts of service and mercy.* Those who are drawn to this and identify with the ministry of Jesus and the disciples are those who are welcomed into the kingdom and named "blessed." Those who respond in indifference are those who are cast out (Donahue, 109-25). True service is best measured by acts toward those who are utterly helpless and unable to repay.

4. The Footwashing (Jn 13:1-17).
The footwashing scene of John 13 has enjoyed a long and lively discussion among scholars. In general, the critical arguments have centered around the two interpretations given the footwashing within the chapter: (1) a soteriological/christological interpretation in 13:6-10 and (2) a moral interpretation in 13:12-17. A persistent question has been whether the former (so Brown, 559-72) or latter (Boismard) interpretation was the earlier and more original of the two, or whether the Evangelist found both interpretations in his sources and wove the two together (Onuki; Bultmann, 1971).

The evidence suggesting a two-stage history of the passage is found in 13:7, "What I am doing you do not know now, but afterward you will understand." A similar statement in John suggests a type of knowledge and insight into the meaning of Jesus' ministry that only comes after the resurrection (cf. 2:21-22). The second interpretation (13:12-17), however, seems to explain clearly what Jesus means by the footwashing and so is at odds with 13:7. On the other hand, Onuki points out that the inclusio structure of the chapter is a hallmark of the Evangelist (cf. 13:11, 18, 21-24 with 14:15, 21, 23-24; Onuki, 162-63). It is also open to question whether 13:7 precludes any further explanation of the footwashing. The theme of "understanding afterwards" is carried out throughout the first part of the Farewell Discourse (13:36; 14:20, 25-26, 29) in the midst of ongoing discussions of the meaning of Jesus' departure (14:1-6, 21-24, 30-31). The tension between 13:7 and 13:12-17 may be more apparent than real.

It is not clear that a simple distinction between two interpretations—one christological and the other moral—is justified. On the one hand, the sayings of Jesus in John 13:12-20 can themselves be understood on two levels: (1) the obvious example of practical service focused on the menial needs of others and (2) the deeper type of service and personal sacrifice that Jesus models when the footwashing is viewed in light of the cross and Easter. The servant sayings of Jesus in John 13:12-17 have christological implications that we should not miss: the Lord* of the disciples is also the obedient son and servant of the Father (cf. Jn 14:10-12; 17:1-5).

Neither is there a total absence of the horizontal dimension in the first so-called christological interpretation. Jesus words, "If I do not wash you, you will have no part in me" (13:8), point not only to the meaning of Jesus' obedient death on the cross, but also to a humble acceptance by faith of the gift of Christ's sacrifice. The footwashing is a drama of Jesus' act of sacrifice on the cross, and Peter's response represents the reaction of believers. The disciples are made "clean" (13:10) by their acceptance of Jesus and his death for them. Where we find the vertical dimension of the gracious act of service of Christ in his death for us, we also tend to find an emphasis on loving and caring for the community (e.g., Mk 10:41-45; Phil 2:1-11; 1 Pet 2:21-25). Indeed, Jesus' rebuke of Peter's attempt to resist the gift offered in the footwashing (13:8), and then his overreaction to it (13:9), is difficult to understand unless we see that Jesus is rejecting Peter's attempt to draw distinctions between himself and the community. The humility that Jesus is pressing on Peter is both to accept the gracious gift of service from the Master and to accept a common human need for the same gift.

In this sense the link made between the betrayer and the footwashing is not accidental (13:11, 18-19, 21-24). The stories of Peter and Judas (see Judas Iscariot) are deliberately interwoven (note the similar tech-

nique in Jn 18:12-27 and Peter's role in the trial of Jesus). As Peter represents the community of faith, Judas represents those who reject Jesus' sacrificial gift and its concomitant demand for service to others. Not to accept Jesus' death for us is to betray him, to leave the community of faith and embrace the darkness (13:30).

The example Jesus gives the disciples in washing their feet (13:12-20) is the pattern of sacrificial and costly service. The key word for this service is *agapē*, given in the command that disciples should "love* one another" (13:34-35) and thereby witness to the world. The Johannine writings are not concerned with specific ethical actions and make no reference to the care of the poor and the outcast. This is in part because John writes to a community which is itself being cast out of the synagogue* and is already dispossessed (cf. 9:22; 12:42-43; 16:1-2). But it is also because John is content to paint the big picture and only imply the details. Christ served his disciples and others in utter humility—even at the cost of the cross—so his disciples' lesser deeds of love and sacrifice for those in need are fitting witnesses to the Master (13:35).

5. Conclusion.

Service in the Gospels and in the ministry of Jesus takes its starting point from the example of Jesus on the cross (*see* Death of Jesus). Considering the price he paid, his followers should be willing to serve humbly and care for one another. Properly understood, this is a revolutionary concept. The call to service in love overshadows normal human desires for rank and preference and calls individuals to lay all these aside for the sake of Christ and the needs of others. There can be no doubt that Jesus intended the community of faith to be radically distinct from the world in this regard. Indeed, selfless service and concern for the weak and powerless would prove to be the distinguishing mark of the Christian community and the most tangible and attractive witness to its character and faith.

See also AUTHORITY AND POWER; DEATH OF JESUS; DISCIPLESHIP; LORD; SERVANT OF YAHWEH.

BIBLIOGRAPHY. M. E. Boismard, "Le Lavement des Pieds (Jn XIII, 1-17)" *RB* 71 (1964) 5-24; R. Bultmann, *The Gospel of John: A Commentary* (Oxford: Basil Blackwell, 1971); idem, *The History of the Synoptic Tradition* (Oxford: Basil Blackwell, 1972); J. R. Donahue, *The Gospel in Parable: Metaphor, Narrative, and Theology in the Synoptic Gospels* (Philadelphia: Fortress, 1988); J. A. Fitzmyer, *The Gospel According to Luke, X-XXIV* (AB 28a; Garden City, NY: Doubleday, 1985);

K. Hess, "Serve, Deacon, Worship," *NIDNTT* 3.544-53; R. A. Horsley, *Jesus and the Spiral of Violence* (San Francisco: Harper and Row, 1987); T. W. Manson, *The Sayings of Jesus* (London: SCM, 1949); I. H. Marshall, *The Gospel of Luke* (NIGTC; Grand Rapids: Eerdmans, 1978); G. F. Moore, *Judaism in the First Centuries of the Christian Era* (2 vols.; New York: Schocken, 1958); T. Onuki, "Die johanneische Abscheidsreden und die synoptische Tradition," *AJBI* 3 (1977) 157-268; J. Roloff, "Anfänge der Soteriologischen Deutung des Todes Jesu (Mk X.45 und Lk. XXII.27)," *NTS* 19 (1972-1973) 38-64.   R. W. Paschal, Jr.

SEVENTY-(TWO). *See* APOSTLE.

SHEPHERD, SHEEP

The pastoral setting of a large portion of Ancient Near Eastern culture made motifs of sheep and shepherding apt descriptions of human and divine roles and relationships. The primary background for the Gospel references to shepherd and sheep lies in the OT where Israel* is the lost sheep and the king or promised future ruler is the shepherd. The Gospels also develop the notion of the apostles as shepherds, again reflecting the OT context wherein Israel's leaders were sometimes referred to as shepherds. The motif of sheep and goats is also used in the Gospels to illustrate eschatological judgment.*

1. The Lost Sheep
2. Jesus the Shepherd
3. The Apostles As Shepherds
4. The Sheep and the Goats
5. Miscellaneous Occurrences

1. The Lost Sheep.

The lost sheep of Israel represent people who have been abandoned by their leaders and/or have wandered away from God* (for a similar use of the motif of Israel as sheep see *1 Enoch* 89—90). A number of OT passages form the background for this imagery, especially Ezekiel 34.

Matthew and Mark describe the multitude for whom Jesus felt compassion as sheep without a shepherd. Mark tells us that as a result of his compassion Jesus began to teach them many things (Mk 6:34). Matthew says Jesus' compassion motivated him to challenge his disciples to pray (*see* Prayer) for more workers to go into the harvest (Mt 9:36). The OT language behind the saying about sheep without a shepherd is clear (Num 27:17; 1 Kings 22:17 par. 2 Chron 18:16; Ezek 34:5). Mark follows the saying with the story of the feeding of five thousand in the wilderness (*see* Mountain and Wilderness), thereby

possibly alluding to Psalm 23, "The Lord is my shepherd, I shall not want."

Jesus also gives instructions to the Twelve not to go to Gentiles* or Samaritans* but only to the lost sheep of the house of Israel (Mt 10:6). This may be an allusion to Ezekiel 34:6 which describes Israel as God's sheep scattered over the face of the earth with no one to look for them. As the disciples* carry out their mission they will fulfill Jeremiah 23:4, " 'I will appoint shepherds over them and they will shepherd them and they will no longer fear nor be terrified nor missing' says the Lord." Thus their mission "heralds the messianic age of salvation" (Gundry, 185).

In response to the petition of a Canaanite woman to exorcise a demon* from her daughter, Jesus remains silent (Mt 15:21-28). When his disciples urge him to send her away, he responds, "I have been sent only to the lost sheep of the house of Israel" (Mt 15:24). The combination of the woman's address of Jesus as "Son of David"* and Jesus' response again recalls Ezekiel 34 (vv. 23-24). If Ezekiel 34 is rightly considered as background for this imagery, the lostness of Israel referred to in these passages is a result of both God's judgment and the unwillingness of her leaders to fulfill their role as the shepherds of Israel.

A lost sheep also plays a part in a parable* found in both Matthew 18:12-14 and Luke 15:3-7. Although the basic plot of both accounts is the same, the discrepancy in wording has led interpreters to debate whether they were derived from a common source. It is possible that Jesus could have told such a short parable more than once using different words or that the single parable could have been translated from an Aramaic tradition in different ways. In Matthew the parable is addressed to believers (cf. Mt 18:6) and points out the Father's pastoral concern as motivation for not causing sheep to stumble. The parable in Luke is addressed to Pharisees* and scribes* (Lk 15:1-3) and points to their lack of compassion for "sinners."* The faithful shepherd stands in contrast to the wicked shepherds of Ezekiel 34:7-8 who refused to go into the wilderness to look for the lost sheep of Israel. Luke also includes the detail that the shepherd, when he found the lost sheep, placed it on his shoulders to take it home (Lk 15:5). This emphasizes the price paid by the shepherd to restore lost sheep to the fold (Bailey, 144-56). The future tense in Luke 15:7 gives the parable eschatological force (Jeremias, 135-36).

2. Jesus the Shepherd.

Since the people of God were like sheep without a shepherd, God provided a shepherd in the person of his Son. There are a number of OT passages in which a Davidic ruler is referred to as a shepherd. One which plays a significant role in the Gospel tradition is Micah 5:2-4 [MT 5:1-3]: "... from you [Bethlehem] will come a ruler in Israel ... who will shepherd in the strength of Yahweh." In the First Gospel the Jewish leaders refer to this passage when asked about the birthplace of the king of the Jews (Mt 2:1-6; see Birth of Jesus).

In the OT shepherding the people was a common metaphor for leadership (2 Sam 7:7), but in 2 Samuel 5:2 the shepherding metaphor was used specifically in an oracle concerning David (cf. 1 Chron 11:2). This oracle also stands behind the prophecy of Micah 5:2-4. In fact, since Matthew 2:6 is not a verbatim citation, it may have resulted from a procedure common in early Judaism whereby 2 Samuel 5:2b would have been attached to the Micah oracle in order to interpret it. Micah 5:2 predicts a leader who is later called a shepherd (v. 4; see Old Testament in the Gospels). By adding 2 Samuel 5:2b "you (David) will shepherd my people Israel," the Jews in Matthew are represented as having interpreted Micah's prophecy as referring specifically to the Davidic Messiah (see Christ; Son of David). Similarly, the targum explicitly identifies the promised ruler as the Messiah, though it drops this metaphorical use of "shepherding" in favor of a reference to "ruling in strength" (*Tg. Neb.* Mic 5:1-3). Jeremiah (23:1-6) and Ezekiel (34:23-24; 37:22-24) both promised a Davidic ruler who would shepherd God's people (cf. also *Pss. Sol.* 17:40; CD 19:5-9).

The motif of the Messiah as shepherd also stands behind the citation of Zechariah 13:7 in both Matthew 26:31 and Mark 14:27 (cf. Jn 16:32): "Strike the shepherd and the sheep will be scattered." The citation is a variation of the MT and may be from a different textual tradition found in certain manuscripts of the LXX (although these mss may have been copied by Christian scribes to bring them in line with the Gospels). It is also possible that the variation is an interpretation by Jesus or the tradition, which has taken over the first person singular later in the verse and changed the imperative accordingly. Thus Matthew and Mark read, "I will strike the shepherd and the sheep ('of the flock' in Mt) will be scattered."

The tradition history (see Tradition Criticism) behind this citation continues to be debated, but it should be noted that it is of a piece with the widely attested identification of Jesus as a shepherd in the Gospels, and with the otherwise frequent use of Zechariah 9—14 in the passion material (see France, 107-110; see Passion Narrative). In Zechariah 13:7 the shepherd is God's agent, a royal figure, whose death

provides a decisive turning point in redemptive history. In the Markan and Matthean contexts similar overtones are transparent. "Striking the shepherd" clearly finds its fulfillment in Jesus' arrest (and the fleeing of the disciples; cf. Mk 14:50; Mt 26:56) and execution. Although Zechariah 13:8-9 is not explicitly quoted in either Gospel context, it should not be overlooked that the covenant promise to the remnant of God's people contained therein has its obvious parallel in Jesus' subsequent prediction: "After I have arisen I will go before you to Galilee."

The idea of Messiah as shepherd is most fully developed in John 10:1-18. This passage follows a section dealing with the spiritual blindness (see Blindness and Deafness) of the Jewish leaders (Jn 9:35-41). Immediately Jesus tells a "parable" comparing a good shepherd to a thief, robber or stranger (Jn 10:1-6). The thief does not enter the sheepfold through the gate (Jn 10:1). The good shepherd enters through the gate, and when he calls each of his sheep by name they follow him because they recognize his voice (Jn 10:2-4). But when the stranger calls, the sheep flee because they do not recognize his voice (Jn 10:5). In its present context the sheepfold is the nation of Israel (Ps 95:7; 100:3). The thief represents the Jewish leadership of Jesus' day. The explanation of this parable is found in John 10:7-18. Tragan divides this exposition into three parts: verses 7-10; verses 11-13 and verses 14-18. His outline seems correct although his hypothesis that each part represents a different redactional layer is not a necessary conclusion. In John 10:7-10 Jesus presents himself as the door to the sheepfold. (Tragan follows 𝔓[75] in v. 7 and thinks *thura*, "door" should actually read *poimēn* "shepherd." The papyri disagree with one another here, but the internal evidence for *poimēn*, "shepherd," as set forth by Tragan, is not as decisive as he thinks. Cf. most of the major commentaries.) He is the door in many respects. The Law* came through Moses, grace and truth* came through Jesus Christ (Jn 1:17). Thus Jesus is the fulfillment of the Law and the replacement of Moses* who wrote of him (Jn 1:45; 5:46). He replaces the Temple* as the place of worship* (Jn 2:19-22). He is the light* of the world (Jn 8:12). He is the way to the Father, and no one can enter God's presence except through him (Jn 14:6).

In the second exposition of the parable (Jn 10:11-13), Jesus presents himself as the good shepherd. The main thrust of this exposition is soteriological and ecclesiastical, highlighting the sacrifice of Jesus for his sheep. Again there is a contrast between the good shepherd and the one who watches the sheep only in exchange for wages. The good shepherd lays down his life for the sheep, but when danger comes the hireling runs away. There is a lesson in this exposition, not only about the sacrifice of the Savior but also the true nature of ministry. Adversity tests the true motivation of the shepherds of the church* (cf 1 Tim 6:5; 1 Pet 5:2).

The third exposition (Jn 10:14-18) adds a christological theme to what has already been said. The antithesis between true and false shepherds disappears. The sacrifice of the good shepherd is repeated (Jn 10:15). And an ecclesiastical concern about sheep from another fold belonging to the good shepherd is noted. This is probably a reference to the Gentile mission of the early church. The christological theme comes out in John 10:17-18. The sacrifice of the shepherd is his sovereign choice based on his relationship with the Father.

The good shepherd is mentioned later in the chapter (Jn 10:26-30) with specific reference to the sheep recognizing his voice. The image painted is that of a shepherd entering a fold containing more than his own sheep. He calls to his sheep and those who recognize his voice follow him. Thus Jesus came to the Jewish nation and those who recognized him followed him and received eternal life,* and no one could snatch them from him. They became his little flock to whom the Father would give the kingdom (cf. Lk 12:32; see Kingdom of God).

Derrett is probably correct in seeing the metaphor of the good shepherd and its explications as a midrash on the OT, but the particular OT background he cites (Ex 21:1; Num 27; Is 56—57; Mic 2:12-13) should include Ezekiel 34. Ezekiel castigates the shepherds of Israel because they do not care for the flock of God. He threatens to remove them from their role as shepherds. Then he promises to raise up one shepherd to shepherd them, "namely, my servant David" (Ezek 34:23). This shepherd will be the means by which God blesses his people (Jn 10:10) and protects them from the wild beasts (Jn 10:12).

3. The Apostles As Shepherds.

The notion of Jesus as the shepherd over the people of God shifts to his disciples as shepherds. This idea is already present in the commissioning of the disciples in Matthew 10:6: "Go to the lost sheep of the house of Israel." But the theme comes out most clearly in the epilog to the Fourth Gospel (Jn 21:15-17). Peter is three times asked by Jesus, "Peter do you love me?" Each time Peter responds positively. After each of Peter's responses Jesus gives a command related to apostolic duty: "Feed my lambs"; "Shepherd my sheep"; "Feed my sheep" (Jn 21:15, 16, 17). The role

of the good shepherd in the church is carried out through his appointed under-shepherds (see Apostle).

The question of the nature of this ministry entrusted to Peter in John 21 has divided the church for centuries. Is this ministry a ruling one, limited to Peter, and making him the first in a line of prime ministers of the church? Or is this pericope more general and a type-scene for the designation of shepherds (pastors) of God's flock wherever they might be? G. R. Beasley-Murray points out that those who hold to the primacy of Peter are surprisingly neglectful of the relevance of other NT pastoral passages for interpreting this passage (e.g., Acts 20:28; 1 Pet 5:3; Beasley-Murray, 406-407). These pastoral passages are addressed to the elders of individual churches and seem to bear no thought of one person presiding over the whole church.

Matthew 7:15 also uses shepherd/sheep terminology to discuss leadership. "Beware of false prophets who come to you in sheep's clothing but inside are ravenous wolves." The identity of these false prophets has engendered much discussion regarding Matthew's audience—without yielding any firm conclusions. Some have thought that Matthew created the statement with reference to false prophets* in the church and anachronistically put it on the lips of Jesus. But this seems to assume that Jesus gave no thought to a community of followers that would perpetuate his teachings and face deceivers (cf. Mk 13:22; see Church). The notion of false prophets was a common theme in Jesus' Bible (Jer 6:13-15; 8:8-12; Ezek 13; 22:27; 34; Mic 3; Zech 11:16). There is no reason to doubt that he appropriated this theme and borrowed the imagery with the intent of warning his present and future followers about wolves in sheep's clothing who would claim to follow Jesus but in the end devour the people of God.

4. The Sheep and the Goats.

In Matthew 25:31-46 the shepherd/sheep imagery is used in describing eschatological judgment. The Son of man (see Son of Man) sits on his throne before the gathering of the nations and separates them from one another as a shepherd separates the sheep from the goats (cf. Ezek 34:17). The sheep on his right hand represent those who serve him in this life. The goats on his left are those who refuse to serve him. But their destinies are not directly determined by their works. Rather, their works are determined by their nature as sheep or goats. The key to the interpretation of the passage lies in the interpretation of Jesus' brothers as his disciples (Mt 25:40; see Gray). The judgment is thus based on one's reception and identification with

Christian missionaries and their message (Carson, 520). Acceptance brings inclusion in the flock of the good shepherd. Rejection brings banishment to the eternal fire (Mt 25:41; *see* Heaven and Hell).

5. Miscellaneous Occurrences.

Luke highlights the role of shepherds at the coming of the Savior (Lk 2:8-20). It was to them that the angel* of the Lord* announced the good news of the birth of the Messiah. The literary significance of the shepherds may lie in their humble estate. Although rejected by the world, the Savior (*see* Salvation) is revealed to the lowly. This theme continues throughout the Third Gospel.

Jesus, in justifying his own healing of a man on the Sabbath,* used the example of saving a sheep from a pit on the Sabbath. The value of a man is greater than that of a sheep (Mt 12:11-12; cf. CD 11.13-14). And in Luke 17:7 he describes the work of a servant as possibly encompassing that of a shepherd.

In Matthew 10:16 Jesus sends his disciples out as sheep in the midst of wolves. Here the imagery pictures the dangers of the world into which Jesus sends his followers (Lk 10:3 renders Jesus' saying as "lambs in the midst of wolves"—thus heightening the danger). Wolves here are not false prophets within the church but members of the world. The saying in Matthew may have been a common figure of speech and thus would have had very general referents.

See also APOSTLE; ISRAEL; LAMB OF GOD.

BIBLIOGRAPHY. K. Bailey, *Poet and Peasant* (Grand Rapids: Eerdmans, 1976); G. R. Beasley-Murray, *John* (WBC; Waco: Word, 1987); F. F. Bruce, *The New Testament Development of Old Testament Themes* (Grand Rapids: Eerdmans, 1968); D. A. Carson, "Matthew," in *The Expositor's Bible Commentary*, ed. F. Gaebelein (vol. 8; Grand Rapids: Zondervan, 1979); J. D. M. Derrett, "The Good Shepherd: St John's Use of Jewish Halakah and Haggadah," in *Studies in the New Testament* (2 vols.; Leiden: Brill, 1978) 2.121-47; R. T. France, *Jesus and the Old Testament* (Downers Grove, IL: InterVarsity, 1972); S. W. Gray, *The Least of My Brothers. Matthew 25:31-46: A History of Interpretation* (Atlanta: Scholars, 1989); R. Gundry, *Matthew: A Commentary on His Literary and Theological Art* (Grand Rapids: Eerdmans, 1982); J. Jeremias, "ποιμήν κτλ," *TDNT* VI.485-502; idem, *The Parables of Jesus* (New York: Scribners, 1975); P.-R. Tragan, *La Parabole du "Pasteur" et ses Explications: Jean, 10, 1-18* (Rome: Anselmiana, 1980).

D. H. Johnson

SIGN OF JONAH

When asked to offer a sign in support of his provoc-

ative deeds and claims, Jesus on more than one occasion is said to have responded that the only sign to be offered to that generation would be the "sign of Jonah." Was he referring to his ministry, his proclamation, his death* and resurrection,* or his future advent? Did Jesus really make such a statement? Matthew and Luke both report that Jesus spoke of the "sign of Jonah," but they disagree in their interpretations of it.

1. The Data
2. The Meaning of "Sign"
3. Interpretations by the Evangelists
4. In the Ministry of Jesus

1. The Data.

Jesus' critics came seeking "a sign" (Mt 12:38) or "a sign from heaven" (Mk 8:11; Mt 16:1; Lk 11:16). The call for a sign occurs also in other contexts (Lk 23:8; cf. 9:7-9; Jn 2:18; 6:30) and in other language elsewhere in the Synoptic Gospels (Mk 11:28; Mt 21:12; Lk 20:2).

Mark's Gospel offers one form of Jesus' response: "Certainly no sign will be given to this generation" (Mk 8:12). However, the parallel passage in Matthew has the added phrase "except the sign of Jonah" (Mt 16:4). Matthew has once previously referred to "the sign of Jonah," also in response to a request for Jesus to perform a sign, in a passage shared by Matthew and Luke but not found in Mark (i.e., Q*; Mt 12:39; Lk 11:29). Perhaps Mark omitted reference to Jonah, regarding the miracles* as sufficient demonstration (Perrin) or in criticism of the notion that proofs of any sort might smooth the way of faith in the crucified.

Matthew reproduced the Q form of Jesus' response (12:39) at 16:4 where, apparently coming to Mark 8:11 in his sources, he read it as a second request for a sign. It should further be noted that Matthew is alone among the Synoptic Evangelists in designating Jonah as "the prophet" (12:39).

Matthew and Luke further agree, again apparently on the basis of Q as their common source, in following the saying about "the sign of Jonah" (Mt 12:39; Lk 11:29) with Jesus' sayings about "something greater than Solomon" and "something greater than Jonah" (Mt 12:41-42; Lk 11:31-32).

In sum, Mark speaks only of a request for a sign, with a flat denial from Jesus that any will be offered, while Matthew has two "sign of Jonah" sayings (including one designating Jonah as "the prophet"), and Luke has one. Both Matthew and Luke immediately follow the (first) "sign of Jonah" saying with sayings about Solomon and Jonah.

2. The Meaning of "Sign."

The saying about the sign of Jonah is Jesus' response to the request that he offer "a sign" (*sēmeion*) or "a sign from heaven." That the sign is described as "from heaven" indicates that the questioners seek proof that Jesus in his mission really does enjoy the backing of God which Jesus implicitly or explicitly claims.

The public work of Jesus provoked antagonism as well as faith (cf. "a sign to be spoken against" in Lk 2:34). Even (or especially) the miracles of Jesus were susceptible of divergent interpretations. Does he do them by the power (*see* Authority and Power) of God as a prophet* of God, or is he in league with Satan (*see* Demon, Devil, Satan)? Therefore, when some people asked for a sign (always in the singular), they were seeking not an additional miracle or miracles but some other irrefutable confirmation that he acted with God's approval.

Furthermore, the word *sign* in the Synoptic Gospels (unlike John) is not the usual word for a "miracle." The Synoptics have other language for miracles (e.g., *dynameis*, "mighty deeds"), although the word *signs* does appear in combination with "wonders" (*terata*), which has the meaning "miracles" (Mk 13:22; Mt 24:24). In Acts *sign* or *signs* is used both alone (4:16, 22; 8:6) and in combination with "mighty deeds" (8:13) and with "wonders" (2:43 and eight more times) to mean miracles.

In the Synoptic Gospels "sign" by itself usually means a unique signal: the manger as crib (Lk 2:12), Judas's kiss (Mt 26:48), or awesome portents in the skies, like those signalling the nearness of the last days (e.g., Mk 13:4; Mt 24:3; Lk 21:7; cf. Lk 21:11, 25). Matthew speaks of the climactic "sign of the Son of man*" (Mt 24:30), where the other Synoptists speak of "the Son of man" without calling his appearing a sign (Mk 13:26; Lk 21:27).

3. Interpretations by the Evangelists.

Matthew and Luke have different sentences linking the "sign of Jonah" saying with the sayings about Solomon and Jonah. These intermediate sentences offer each Evangelist's interpretation of the sign of Jonah.

Matthew understands the resurrection of Jesus as the fulfillment of the "sign of Jonah" (12:40): "Just as Jonah was in the belly of the sea monster for three days and three nights, so will the Son of Man be in the heart of the earth for three days and three nights [only this limited time]." Matthew's use of the phrase "after three days" in 27:63 (cf. "on the third day" in 16:21; 17:23; 20:19 par.) is an echo of the Jonah tradition and confirmation that Matthew understands

Jesus' resurrection as the sign of Jonah.

Luke 11:30 (unlike Mt 12:40) does not point to the resurrection of Jesus. But what exactly Luke understood as constituting "the sign of Jonah" is disputed by interpreters.

(1) Some stress the future tense of the verb "will be given" (*dothēsetai*, Lk 11:29), and say that the sign of Jonah is the future coming of Jesus as Judge: Just as Jonah came from a distant country as a preacher of judgment* to the Ninevites, so the Son of man will come as the judge from heaven to this generation (Bultmann; Perrin).

(2) Others interpret the analogy as follows: As Jonah preached repentance to Nineveh before its judgment, so Jesus preaches repentance to this generation before its judgment. Therefore, the sign of Jonah is either Jesus himself as preacher of judgment (Kümmel, Rengstorf) or the actual preaching of Jesus (Tödt, Lindars). The Ninevites made the appropriate response to the preaching of Jonah, but now, says Jesus, "something greater," namely his own wisdom* and proclamation, is here.

(3) Perhaps Luke, in speaking of "this generation," reflects not only on the response of Jesus' contemporaries but on the response of his own contemporaries (as late as the eighties of the first century). Luke focuses on his present and declares that Jesus was and is the great preacher of repentance* (Kloppenborg). His work continues in the preaching of the community. Like Jonah, Jesus has been vindicated by being lifted up to new life, and he and the word about him will continue to be vindicated (Edwards).

(4) Reference to the resurrection of Jesus is not obvious in Luke as it is in Matthew, but it may not be entirely absent. The parable of the rich man and Lazarus in Luke 16:19-31 concludes with conversation between the rich man and Abraham* concerning the possible effects of the resurrection of Lazarus on the rich man's brothers. That conclusion sounds like a Lukan echo of an understanding of the resurrection as a sign. And the book of Acts concludes with the recital of the great storm and the shipwreck of Paul. That report (Acts 27—28) not only echoes the book of Jonah but appears in that section of Acts often described as the narrative of "Paul's passion and resurrection." The parable of the rich man seems to deny that the resurrection would serve as any kind of effective sign, while the narrative of the sea voyage seems to affirm that it may yet be.

4. In the Ministry of Jesus.

It is widely asserted that the saying at first (during the ministry of Jesus) had no connection with the resurrection of Jesus. This assertion is argued on several grounds: (1) Jesus could not have known that he would be raised after three days in the grave (*see* Predictions of Jesus' Passion and Resurrection); (2) even if Jesus had declared that he would rise, his audience would have found such a declaration meaningless; (3) the Q document, which is the reputed source of the saying for Matthew and Luke, never speaks of the resurrection of Jesus.

All of these critical assertions are themselves denied by many scholars. No consensus exists concerning the path from the texts to the historical Jesus (*see* Historical Jesus). But in spite of all difficulties, some continue to think that Jesus (and not just Matthew) meant that his death and subsequent resurrection would be the sign of Jonah.

Jeremias concludes that the sign of Jonah, both in the ministry of Jesus and in the Gospel of Luke, refers to the miraculous deliverance of Jonah from the belly of the fish rather than to the preaching of Jonah. Jeremias understands Luke to be saying that Jesus declared that he would be displayed to his generation as Jonah had been manifested long ago—as one raised from the dead. Jonah and Jesus were divine messengers authorized or certified as genuine by their deliverance from death.

Ancient Jewish tradition can be cited in support of the notion that Jesus and his contemporaries might understand a dramatic rescue from death as the sign of Jonah. In 3 Maccabees 6:7 the pious priest Eleazar called on God for a rescue just like that which God had accomplished for Daniel and Jonah. Daniel was thrown as food to the lions dwelling underground, but God brought him up again to the light unscathed. Jonah was lifted up from the belly of the monster of the deep and was restored uninjured to all his family. Another tradition identifies Jonah as that son of the widow of Zarephath whom Elijah raised from the dead (*The Lives of the Prophets* 10:1-6; see Jeremias for further references). Josephus retells the story of Jonah (*Ant.* 9.208-14), stressing not the preaching of repentance but the casting of the prophet into the sea, his being swallowed by a great fish and his subsequent deliverance onto the shore.

Perrin speaks for many who think that Jesus pointed by means of the Jonah saying not to his resurrection but to his proclamation. Jesus meant that his mission and message would be vindicated and bear fruit in the future in ways beyond the wildest imaginings of his own generation.

BIBLIOGRAPHY. R. Bultmann, *The History of the Synoptic Tradition* (Oxford: Blackwell, 1963); R. A. Edwards, *The Sign of Jonah in the Theology of the Evangelists and* Q (London: SCM, 1971); idem, *A Theology of Q* (Philadelphia: Fortress, 1976). J. A. Fitzmyer, *The Gospel according to Luke X-XXXIV* (AB; Garden City, NY: Doubleday, 1985); J. Jeremias, " Ἰωνᾶς," *TDNT* III.406-10; J. S. Kloppenborg, *The Formation of Q* (Philadelphia: Fortress, 1987); W. G. Kümmel, *Promise and Fullfilment* (London: SCM, 1957); B. Lindars, *Jesus Son of Man* (Grand Rapids: Eerdmans, 1983); N. Perrin, *Rediscovering the Teaching of Jesus* (New York: Harper & Row, 1967); K. H. Rengstorf, "σημεῖον," *TDNT* VII.229-59; H. Tödt, *The Son of Man in the Synoptic Tradition* (Philadelphia: Westminster, 1965).

R. H. Smith

SIGNS. *See* JOHN, GOSPEL OF; MIRACLES AND MIRACLE STORIES; SIGN OF JONAH.

SIMEON'S SONG

Also known as the *Nunc Dimittis,* Simeon's Song (Lk 2:29-32) is a particularly beautiful and moving poetic feature of Luke's overture to the Gospel and Acts.

It has been argued that Luke himself, following the known practice of the Greek historians who were to some degree his models, composed this and the other hymns of Luke 1—2 to enrich his narrative. It has also been suggested that the hymn comes to us from the worship* of a particular community, either Jewish, adherents of John the Baptist* or early Jewish Christian. The last option appears to be the most frequently advanced at present. Some scholars argue that the hymn was originally composed in Greek; others advance linguistic arguments which tend to show that the psalm was translated from a Semitic, probably Hebrew, original (*see* Languages of Palestine). Still others continue to maintain that the hymn was indeed composed by the aged Simeon himself.

Simeon's Song bears many of the essential characteristics of Hebrew praise. It rejoices, albeit in a somewhat unusual form, in the goodness of God, states the reason for that rejoicing and expands poetically on that statement. It displays the parallelism characteristic of Hebrew poetry (v. 32). The hymn is a mosaic of OT allusions, chiefly to so-called Deutero-Isaiah (Is 40—55).

The Song's meaning cannot be considered apart from consideration of its place in Luke's narrative. The narrative features a parallelism between stories about John the Baptist and stories about the infant Christ. In this parallelism Simeon's Song plays a key role. Just as an ancient Israelite of great holiness, Zechariah, offers praise to God over the young John, so an ancient and holy Israelite, Simeon, offers praise over the infant Jesus. One may also compare Zechariah's prophecy concerning John (Lk 1:76-79) with the prophecy concerning Jesus, also spoken by Simeon (Lk 2:34-35).

The narrative as a whole contains the *promise* that Simeon would see the Lord's Messiah; *fulfillment* when Simeon sees the infant Jesus; followed by the *praise* of the hymn itself. The order of promise—fulfillment—praise is also found in connection with the other hymns of Luke's infancy narratives. The theological theme of promise and fulfillment, also manifest within the Song (v. 29), reappears frequently in Luke-Acts.

So great is Simeon's rejoicing over the presence of God's "salvation," a play on the Hebrew root of Jesus' name, that he is ready now to depart into death (cf. the words of the aged Jacob-Israel, Gen 45:30, *Jub.* 45:3-4). This salvation is both glory to the people Israel and the means by which God will reach out to enlighten the Gentiles. As such the hymn is a foretaste of Luke-Acts as a whole.

See also BIRTH OF JESUS; MARY'S SONG; ZECHARIAH'S SONG.
BIBLIOGRAPHY. R. E. Brown, *The Birth of the Messiah* (Garden City, NY: Doubleday, 1977); idem, "Gospel Infancy Narrative Research from 1976 to 1986: Part II (Luke)," *CBQ* 48 (1986) 660-80; S. C. Farris, *The Hymns of Luke's Infancy Narratives: Their Origin, Meaning and Significance* (JSNTSup 9; Sheffield: JSOT Press, 1985).

S. C. Farris

SIMON PETER. *See* DISCIPLES; DISCIPLESHIP.

SIMON THE CANANAEAN. *See* DISCIPLES.

SIMON THE ZEALOT. *See* DISCIPLES.

SINNER

In the Gospels the term *sinner* is used in two ways—to describe the individual who is opposed to God and his will, and by Jesus' opponents to describe those outside of their group to whom Jesus offers the gospel* of salvation.*

1. Terminology and Meaning
2. Usage in the Gospels
3. Jesus and Sinners
4. Conclusion

1. Terminology and Meaning.
Sinner is the English word most frequently used to translate the Greek term *hamartōlos,* an adjective related to the verb *hamartanō,* "to sin," and the nouns for *sin, hamartēma* and *hamartia.*

Within the LXX the Greek term *hamartōlos* occurs approximately ninety-four times, corresponding to

five roots in the MT: *ḥṭ'* (15x: e.g., Num 32:14), *ḥnp* (1x: Prov 11:9), *ḥrš* (1x: Ps 128:3), *r'* (1x: Prov 12:13) and *ršʿ* (74x: e.g., 2 Chron 19:2). In the Aramaic Targums* there is evidence that a broader term, *ḥwb',* meaning "debtor" or "sinner," is the natural counterpart of *hamartōlos* in the LXX. In the *Tg. Isa* "debtors, sinners" are punished by Messiah (11:4) and destroyed by the Lord (14:4-5), but are also capable of repentance (28:24-25). *Hamartōlos* corresponds most frequently in the LXX with the Hebrew *rāšāʿ,* "wicked one." Especially in the Psalms, *rāšāʿ* is used in parallel with almost every Hebrew word for sin, evil and iniquity, and functions also as an adjective to designate the actions and conduct of a type of person (cf. Ps 10:4, 7; 36:1; 49:6, 13; 50:16-17). The *rāšāʿ,* "wicked one," is usually placed in antithetic parallelism to the *ṣaddîq,* "righteous one" (cf. Ps 1:6). This is the common meaning of the term in the early writings within Judaism* as well (e.g., Sir, *1 Enoch* [Gᵃ] 22:10-14).

The word *sinner* also occurs in what we may call factional contexts to designate those who are outside the boundary of the group who use the term. In these cases wickedness, by definition, is conduct outside the boundary, conduct which is unacceptable to those inside. *Sinner* could thereby be used more or less as a synonym for *Gentile*ering* (Ps 9:17; Tob 13:8; *Jub.* 23:23-24). But as Judaism developed, those boundaries could also be drawn *within* the people of Israel* as well, with "sinner" used to designate those for whom a particular faction showed disapproval. Thus "sinners" could be apostate Jews (1 Macc 1:34; 2:44, 48), Jews who wrongly reckoned the months and the feasts* and the years (*1 Enoch* 82:4-7), Jews who did not hold to the sectarian interpretation of the Qumran community (CD 4:8; 1QS 5:7-11; 1QH 7:12; *see* Dead Sea Scrolls), Jewish opponents of the "devout" (*Pss. Sol.* 1:8; 2:3; 7:2; 8:12-13; 17:5-8; 23) or Jews with different interpretations of ritual purity requirements (*As. Mos.* 7:3, 9-10; *see* Clean and Unclean).

2. Usage in the Gospels.
Hamartōlos occurs forty-seven times in the NT; thirty-three times in the Gospels; never in Acts; fourteen times in the epistles; and never in Revelation. Although the term occurs thirty-three times in the Gospels, those occurrences are clustered in thirteen pericopes, ten of which have the substantive form and three of which have the adjectival form. For the most part the term appears to be enmeshed in traditional materials which the Evangelists have adopted. Of the thirteen Gospel accounts in which the term occurs, one appears in all three Synoptic Gospels (*see* Synoptic

Problem), a so-called triple tradition (the table-fellowship* dispute: Mt 9:10; 11, 13 par. Mk 2:15, 16 [twice] and Lk 5:30, 32), one is shared between Mark and Matthew (the arrest in the Garden: Mt 26:45 par. Mk 14:41) and one is a passage shared between Matthew and Luke, being thereby designated as Q* material (the contrast between John the Baptist and Jesus: Mt 11:19 par. Lk 7:34).

Matthew refers to "sinners" on only three occasions: the triple tradition (Mt 9:10, 11, 13 par. Mk 2:15, 16 [twice] and Lk 5:30, 32), the passage shared with Mark (Mt 26:45 par. Mk 14:41) and the passage shared with Luke/Q (Mt 11:19 par. Lk 7:34). Similarly, Mark refers to sinners on only three occasions: the triple tradition (Mk 2:15, 16 [twice] par. Mt 9:10; 11, 13 and Lk 5:30, 32), the passage shared with Matthew (Mk 14:41 par. Mt 26:45) and one triple-tradition incident in which only Mark uses the adjectival form of term ("this sinful generation": Mk 8:38 par. Mt 16:26-27 and Lk 9:26). John does not share with the Synoptics any references to sinners, and he refers to sinners in only one pericope (the healed blind man interacts with the Pharisees*: Jn 9:16, 24, 25, 31).

Luke has the most extensive references to "sinners." He refers to them on ten occasions: the triple tradition (Lk 5:30, 32 par. Mk 2:15, 16 [twice] and Mt 9:10, 11, 13), the passage shared with Matthew/Q (Lk 7:34 par. Mt 11:19) and eight incidents found only in Luke. Of those eight, one incident is triple-tradition material in which only Luke has included the term (the angels' testimony, Lk 24:7), and two incidents have material similar to Matthew (not Q material), but only Luke uses the term (love of one's enemies, Lk 6:32, 33, 34 [2x]; parables* about the lost ones, Lk 15:7, 10). In five of the eight incidents the term occurs in material unique to Luke's Gospel (Peter's confession, Lk 5:8; Simon the Pharisee and the woman* called a "sinner," Lk 7:37, 39; Galilean martyrs, Lk 13:2; parable of the Pharisee and the tax collector, Lk 18:13; Zacchaeus' calling, Lk 19:7; see Taxes).

3. Jesus and Sinners.

One of the most distinctive features of Jesus' message and ministry is the promise of salvation to sinners. Not only is there much material which includes that message, but it is found in diverse forms—ranging from sayings and parables to reports of Jesus' activity and accusations against him. Jesus is said to have associated with sinners (Mk 2:15, 16 par.) and to have sought out the sinner as one who was lost (e.g., Lk 15:7, 10). Jesus flatly declares that one aspect of his ministry was "not to call the righteous, but sinners" (Mk 2:17 par.). One encounters no difficulty under-standing the general use of "sinner" in the Gospels to designate the person who commits acts of sin defined by Law,* as is likely the case of the sinful woman in Lk 7:36-50. But in the Gospel accounts the term "sinner" also designates a narrow segment of the people. A well known combination, "tax collectors and sinners," appears to specify an identifiable segment of the people called "sinners" as being linked with "tax collectors" (Mt 9:10,11, 13 par.; Mt 11:19 par.; Lk 15:7). On several occasions the Pharisees are placed in contrast with "sinners," apparently an identifiable segment of the people held up for special criticism by the Pharisees (cf. Mt 9:10, 11, 13 par.; Lk 7:37, 39; 15:1, 2; 18:13; Jn 9:16, 24, 25). Recent scholarly investigation has attempted to identify the segment of people called "sinners."

3.1. Sinners Are Those Who Do Not Observe Sectarian Rituals. J. Jeremias is representative of a widely held interpretation which identifies the sinners as the common people, the *'ammê hā'āreṣ*, who are disapproved by the Pharisees (*see* Rich and Poor). This interpretation suggests that the people known as "sinners" are viewed from a double perspective in the Gospels. From the perspective of Jesus' opponents the term *sinner* was coined to express contempt for Jesus' following. Jesus' opponents were primarily Pharisees, whom Jeremias makes virtually co-extensive with the *ḥaberîm*, the brotherhood which insisted on ritual purity for table fellowship. They considered Jesus' following to consist primarily of the disreputable, the *'ammê hā'āreṣ*, the uneducated, whose religious ignorance and moral behavior stood in the way of their access to salvation. Other derogatory names used by these opponents to refer to Jesus' followers included: "the little ones" (e.g., Mk 9:42); "the simple ones"; "babes" (e.g., Mt 11:25).

Hence, *sinners* are those who have offended the exclusivism of the Pharisees' purity laws (especially table fellowship) and/or their rigorous observance of the Law. Although from the perspective of Jesus' opponents the followers of Jesus are called sinners, from Jesus' perspective they are called "the poor" or "those who labor and are heavy laden" (e.g., Mt 11:5, 28)—those disenfranchised from the religious, social and political life of Israel.

3.2. Sinners Are Those Wicked Ones Who Are Outside the Law. E. P. Sanders is representative of a challenge to Jeremias' view. Sanders argues that the OT equivalent for *hamartōloi is rᵉša'îm* (or the Aramaic equivalent), and that it is virtually a technical term. He suggests that it is best translated "the wicked," and it refers to those who sinned willfully and heinously and did not repent. When placed with "tax collectors," the two names stand for "traitors": the tax collectors are those who collaborated with Rome, and the sinners are the wicked who betrayed the God who redeemed Israel and gave them his Law.

Sanders further argues that the Pharisees were not primarily a table-fellowship group who were offended by Jesus' offering salvation to those outside their fellowship. Rather, they were a party devoted to the Torah in its oral explication. The sinners were not simply impure common people ('ammê hā'āreṣ) but the wicked who were offered inclusion in Jesus' company without being required to undergo the normal repentance required by the Law. Jesus allowed them to become his followers and remain "wicked ones." This put Jesus into conflict with all of the leaders of Israel, who focused on the Law as the center of religious and social life.

The strength of Sanders's argument is that it replaces a simplistic caricature of Judaism. Jeremias' view paints the Pharisees as hopelessly formalistic, to the degree that they were so incensed at Jesus' offer of salvation to the common people that they were willing to put him to death (see Trial of Jesus). But Sanders's alternative, that Jesus offered sinners salvation without any thought of them changing their behavior, is not true to the Gospel portrait of Jesus.

3.3. Sinners Are Those Opposed to God's Will. A number of passages in the Gospels indicate a broad use of the term sinner to indicate a person opposed to the will of God. An important perspective is found in Mark 14:41 par. Matthew 26:45, where Jesus, announcing his impending arrest, says "the Son of Man* is betrayed into the hands of sinners." This is ultimately directed at the chief priests* and scribes* and elders* who had arranged the arrest (Mk 14:43 par. Mt 26:47). What makes the leaders of Israel sinners is that they are opposing the will of God as worked out in Jesus' ministry. Luke's story of the angels* at the tomb echoes these words with the adjectival use of hamartōlos (Lk 24:7).

In Mark 8:38 Jesus' words about "this adulterous and sinful generation" are not addressed to any particular segment of the people, but to the people of Israel as a whole who have rejected him. In Luke 5:8 Simon Peter's reaction to Jesus' miraculous catch of fish is to confess that he is a sinful man. His confession comes in the presence of one whom he calls "Lord,"* indicating, at least, that Peter recognizes his own humility in the presence of the activity of God in Jesus.

Luke 13:1-2 tells the story of Galilean pilgrims put to death by Pilate while in Jerusalem to make sacrifices in the Temple. Jesus, using the term sinner,

counters the common Jewish belief that calamity in life was the result of past sin. This is a general sense of the term sinner, since the expectation is that the judgment would ultimately have been from God and, hence, punishment for a sin against God. This is especially borne out in verse 4, where the parallel term is opheiletai, used in the sense of a debtor or sinner against God.

These Synoptic passages demonstrate a use of the term in non-factional contexts, and point to a broad use of the term to designate a person opposed to the will of God. This understanding of "sinner" is corroborated in the Fourth Gospel. In the story of the controversy with the Pharisees, the man who has been healed of blindness says, "We know that God does not listen to sinners, but if any one is a worshiper of God and does his will, God listens to him" (Jn 9:31). Here the implication is that the sinner is one who does not worship* God and does not do God's will. Although in the preceding context the Pharisees have emphasized Sabbath observance (Jn 9:16, 24, 25), the healed man implies a broader use of the term, not just specifying the unobservant person.

4. Conclusion.
The use of *sinner* in the LXX and early Jewish literature is helpful for understanding the divergent usage of the term in the Gospels. The common use of the term was to indicate a "wicked one," often placed in antithetic parallelism with the "righteous one." But the term was also used in factional contexts, both to speak of Gentiles *outside* the boundaries of Israel, and within the context of factional rivalry *within* Judaism. These two emphases accord with the use of sinner in the Gospels. There are a significant number of passages which have a broad use of *sinner* to designate "one opposed to the will of God." There are a number of other passages which are factionally oriented.

Jeremias focuses primarily on the group of passages which pit the Pharisees against the sinners. Despite Sanders's objections, the strength of Jeremias' argument is that it gives proper attention to the factional use of the term in Judaism. In a recent analysis, J. D. G. Dunn suggests that the Pharisees were a sect with clear ideas of the character of life and conduct required to maintain the covenant righteousness* of the people of God. As such they were highly likely to regard as sinners those who disagreed with them and who lived in open disregard of this righteousness—as had the groups behind the apocalyptic Enoch traditions, the *Psalms of Solomon* and the Dead Sea Scrolls. The Pharisees firmly believed in the authority of their developing oral traditions, and those who were opposed to their practices were considered to be opposed to God.

Sanders tends to rely most heavily on those passages which align the tax collectors with the sinners. He has criticized Jeremias for downplaying the strength of the term and for making it simply an equivalent term for non-Pharisees. The Pharisees were not as rigid on matters of purity as were the Essenes. They did not necessarily regard all non-Pharisees as sinners—perhaps only those who made light of Pharisaic concerns. Nevertheless, the more members of the Jewish community moved away from Pharisaic standards, the more likely the Pharisees would dub them *sinners.*

While Sanders goes too far in pressing the term always to mean blatant lawbreakers, when the Pharisees used the term *sinners* they meant one who was opposed to the will of God as reflected in their understanding of *halakah,* the rabbinic laws governing life. Behind the objections and charges leveled against Jesus was the central fact that he was ignoring and abolishing boundaries which more sectarian attitudes had erected *within* Israel. Hence, from the standpoint of Jesus' opponents a person was a sinner as long as he or she did not conform to the expectations of the sect. From the standpoint of Jesus, a person was a sinner as long as he or she remained opposed to the will of God. Once a person accepted the offer of forgiveness and made a commitment of faith* to follow Jesus, he or she became a disciple of Jesus. Jesus' offer of salvation to sinners apart from factional observance was a threat to the very foundation and way of life of sectarian Jews, yet it was at the heart of the gospel he came announcing.

See also CLEAN AND UNCLEAN; DISCIPLE; DISCIPLESHIP; ISRAEL; PHARISEES; SALVATION; TABLE FELLOWSHIP.

BIBLIOGRAPHY. I. Abrahams, "Publicans and Sinners," *Studies in Pharisaism and the Gospels,* First Series (1917, 1924; New York: KTAV, 1967); R. G. Bratcher, "Unusual Sinners," *BT: Technical Papers* 39 (1988) 335-37; B. D. Chilton, "Jesus and the Repentance of E. P. Sanders," *TynB* 39 (1988) 1-18; J. D. G. Dunn, "Pharisees, Sinners, and Jesus," in *Jesus, Paul and the Law: Studies in Mark and Galatians* (Louisville: Westminster/John Knox, 1990) 61-88; W. Günther, "Sin," *NIDNTT* 3.573-587; J. Jeremias, *New Testament Theology: The Proclamation of Jesus* (New York: Charles Scribner's Sons, 1971); G. H. Livingston, "רָשָׁע (rashāʻ)," *TWOT* 2.863-4; A. Oppenheimer, *The 'Am Ha-Aretz: A Study in the Social History of the Jewish People in the Hellenistic-Roman Period* (ALGHJ VIII; Leiden: E. J. Brill, 1977); K. H. Rengstorf, "ἁμαρτωλός," *TDNT* I:317-335; A. J. Saldarini, *Pharisees, Scribes and Sadducees* *in Palestinian Society: A Sociological Approach* (Wilmington, DE: Michael Glazier, 1988); E. P. Sanders, *Jesus and Judaism* (Philadelphia: Fortress, 1985); N. H. Young, " 'Jesus and the Sinners': Some Queries," *JSNT* 24 (1985) 73-75. M. J. Wilkins

SOCIOLOGICAL APPROACHES TO THE GOSPELS

Since 1970 the use of the social sciences has played an increasingly prominent role in Gospel studies. Early efforts concentrated on applying specific sociological theories to biblical studies, but more recent research has drawn from a wider range of social-scientific disciplines and sub-disciplines, including anthropology, peasant studies, political science, economics and Mediterranean sociology. Assessing this movement requires tracing its evolution and identifying its relationship to the disciplines of the historical-critical method before analyzing two pioneering works illustrating its use on a Gospel text and evaluating its contributions.

1. The History and Evolution of an Interdisciplinary Approach
2. Relationship to the Historical-Critical Method
3. An Analysis of Two Pioneering Works
4. Social-Scientific Criticism in Use
5. Evaluation

1. The History and Evolution of an Interdisciplinary Approach.

The origins of the current interest in applying the social sciences to biblical texts cannot be defined precisely, but it is possible to place the movement in some historical perspective. During the 1920s and 1930s the Chicago School, especially in the works of S. J. Case and S. Mathews, devoted its attention to the social setting of early Christianity and the "social mind" that formed theology. But the work of Case and Mathews was informed by a philosophical idealism that largely ignored the material conditions of life reflected in the texts. Being indebted to disciplines like the sociology of religion and the history of religions, it emphasized the functional aspect of religion and religious texts. Understanding the Gospels, therefore, mainly involved learning what needs they were intended to meet.

In spite of its achievements, the Chicago School did not set the agenda for future Gospel studies largely because the middle decades of the twentieth century were consumed by the debate between R. Bultmann's existential reading of the NT and his neo-orthodox adversaries, typified by a figure like O. Cullmann, who argued for the salvation-history character of the documents. This meant that issues central to the social sciences, from the political and economic to the social, were relegated to the periphery on both sides of the discussion, while questions of human existence and salvation history occupied the center. The extent of the neglect can be gauged by scanning the twentieth-century quests for the historical Jesus (*see* Historical Jesus). As little as they otherwise had in common, *The Quest of the Historical Jesus,* recounted by A. Schweitzer (1906, ET 1910), Bultmann's *Jesus and the Word* (ET 1926, ET 1934), and the new quest of the historical Jesus, conducted by such post-Bultmannians as E. Fuchs, G. Bornkamm, H. Conzelmann and J. M. Robinson, shared one conviction, namely that Jesus and the Gospels were unrelated to social, political or economic questions. A reading of Cullmann's *Christ and Time* (1946, ET 1950) or *Salvation in History* (1965, ET 1967) would yield a similar result for the other side of the debate.

Occasionally minority reports were registered in the form of specific issues or projects. During the 1960s, for instance, S. G. F. Brandon published *Jesus and the Zealots* (1967) and so initiated a debate about Jesus' relationship to the Zealots (and revolutionary movements in general; *see* Revolutionary Movements). O. Cullmann responded three years later with *Jesus and the Revolutionaries* (1970), and the debate widened as it continued. J. H. Yoder's *The Politics of Jesus* (1972), essentially a recap of A. Trocmé's *Jesus and the Non-violent Revolution* (1961, ET 1973), argued that one could discern in the Lukan portrayal of Jesus' ministry both a coherent political strategy and "a messianic ethic."

During the late 1960s the Philadelphia Seminar on Christian Origins devoted its attention to a study of imperial Rome as the background for Christianity and published its results in a collection of essays edited by S. Benko and J. J. O'Rourke, *The Catacombs and the Colosseum: The Roman Empire As the Setting of Primitive Christianity* (1971). Such projects continued a strand of scholarship that could claim antecedents like F. C. Grant, *The Economic Background of the Gospels* (1926) and A. N. Sherwin-White, *Roman Society and Roman Law in the New Testament* (1963). But such work remained a distinctly minority voice.

By 1970 the debates spawned by form criticism,* redaction criticism,* salvation history, existentialism and the quests were challenged from an unexpected quarter. The rise of Latin-American liberation theology (*see* Liberation Hermeneutics) placed social analysis at the heart of the theological task, a synthesis clearly found in G. Gutierrez, *A Theology of Liberation* (1972) and developed in subsequent works by J. So-

brino, *Christology at the Crossroads* (1978), L. Boff, *Jesus Christ Liberator* (1978) and J. L. Segundo, *The Historical Jesus of the Synoptics* (1985). The efforts of these liberation theologians to integrate discussions of Jesus and the Gospels into their work, however, exposed a deficiency. Although they had developed an adequate methodological basis for their theological reflection and its relationship to the social sciences, they were handicapped when discussing Jesus or the Gospels because they were forced to use forms of biblical scholarship essentially unrelated to their project. This created a dilemma. Either they could use biblical materials in a pre-critical way (speaking of the "Galilean crisis" in Jesus' ministry, for example) or they could try to integrate historical-critical scholarship, usually in a Bultmannian vein, into their endeavors. In either case, the results were unsatisfactory. Eventually Segundo turned his attention to the problem of Jesus and the Gospels in an attempt to rectify the shortcoming. But the emergence of Latin American theology had revealed the basic failure of biblical scholarship to incorporate social analysis into its horizon of possibilities.

In 1973 a study group sponsored jointly by the American Academy of Religion (AAR) and the Society of Biblical Literature (SBL) was convened to explore "The Social World of Early Christianity." J. Z. Smith outlined the four tasks facing the group: (1) "a description of social facts given in early Christian materials"; (2) "the achievement of a genuine social history of early Christianity"; (3) determining "the social organization of early Christianity," especially the social forces that gave rise to its institutions; and (4) defining the social world created by the early Christians, their symbolic universe and plausibility structure (Smith). Of these four tasks the first three are essentially descriptive or reconstructive while the fourth is analytical and requires the use of models.

As its first project, the group attempted a description of the social world of early Christianity in Antioch-on-the-Orontes from its beginnings to the fourth century and published the results of its work in 1978 (W. A. Meeks and R. L. Wilken, *Jews and Christians in Antioch in the First Four Centuries of the Common Era*). As both its research agenda and initial project indicated, the pursuits of this group were essentially descriptive and data gathering in nature. Although the group did not produce another Chicago School, it did encourage a continuing discussion of issues related to the social world of the early church. Characteristic examples of the work produced by scholars following the methods of social description are: H. C. Kee, *Miracle in the Early Christian World: A Study in Socio-Historical Method*

(1983) and J. Stambaugh and D. Balch, *The New Testament in Its Social Environment* (1986).

In 1980 members of the Catholic Biblical Association (CBA) formed a working group to investigate the social sciences and biblical interpretation. This group concentrated its attention on the use of crosscultural models derived from anthropology. The consistent procedure of the CBA group, and the similar SBL section that was formed in 1983, was to select anthropological models and apply them either to NT texts or to social and cultural realities found in them. Each year the group identified a specific focus (the notion of limited good, honor and shame, or the Mediterranean personality, for instance) and used selected readings from anthropology as a lens through which to read NT texts. Characteristic of the work produced by this group are: B. Malina, *The New Testament World: Insights from Cultural Anthropology* (1981) and *Christian Origins and Cultural Anthropology* (1986); and J. H. Elliott, ed., *Semeia 35: Social-Scientific Criticism of the New Testament and Its Social World* (1986).

2. Relationship to the Historical-Critical Method.
It could be argued that the body of scholarship concerned with the social sciences emerged to address a task identified but neglected by early proponents of the historical-critical method. Form critics had proposed the need to place each Gospel pericope (unit of tradition) in its life setting. Although that job would appear to require the use of the social sciences, form critics did not employ them. Rather, following a history of religions approach, they tended to locate texts in the life and cult of the church (its preaching and worship) or define their use in terms of the needs of the nascent church for apologia and self-definition. Attempts to contextualize sayings or narratives in this way did not ask how the texts reflected the social and cultural or political and economic systems of the Mediterranean world.

Nor did the situation change substantially when, in the mid-1950s, form criticism yielded to redaction criticism which tried to deduce the theology of the Evangelists by observing the way in which they either worked with traditional materials or created their own. Interest in the Gospels was confined to understanding how their theology was relevant for the issues facing the Gospel writer and his community. In this procedure the search for the life setting of the oral forms behind the Gospel text was replaced by a search for the life setting of the Evangelist, and efforts to determine the nature of the communities to which the Evangelists were writing were generally conducted without reference to the social sciences or the kinds of information they could provide. Community conflict tended to be seen as a function of ideological differences. Yet, like their form-critical predecessors, redaction critics were raising issues their methods were not equipped to answer. Whether seeking a life setting behind the text or of the text required forms of knowledge beyond the horizon of historical-critical inquiry.

Form criticism dominated NT studies roughly from 1920 to 1955, and redaction criticism from about 1955 to 1975. It was during the ferment of the 1970s that social-scientific criticism of the Gospels emerged to address some of the issues overlooked by both form criticism and redaction criticism as well as to open up new areas of scholarly inquiry.

3. An Analysis of Two Pioneering Works.
By any account J. Gager's *Kingdom and Community* (1975) and G. Theissen's *Sociology of Early Palestinian Christianity* (ET 1978, but based on essays written as early as 1974) were two of the more important early attempts to employ sociology. Equally important for this review is the fact that they combine all four of the programmatic elements described in J. Z. Smith's working paper but in different ways and with varying emphases.

Gager's work was inspired by his discovery that the scholarly methods used to study other religions had not been applied to the study of early Christianity. Accordingly, in an effort to understand the rise of earliest Christianity, Gager drew on two works devoted to the study of millenarian cults, P. Worsley's *The Trumpet Shall Sound* (1968) and K. Burridge's *New Heaven, New Earth* (1969). Burridge traces the evolution of millenarian movements through three stages: alienation (old rules); crystallization (no rules); and reintegration (new rules). Social alienation provides the environment in which "premillenial murmurings" begin, usually among the disinherited and politically marginalized. But prepolitical unrest would never crystallize into a movement without the figure of the millenarian prophet who gives voice to the voiceless and interprets their situation in a way they find compelling. This charismatic figure shapes the free-floating disgruntlement into a movement promising social and moral transformation of the world order. During this phase, which Burridge calls "no rules," the movement may develop ideal communal mores, such as abolishing the distinction between the sexes and kinship obligations. In *The Ritual Process* (1969), V. Turner described this phase as the time of liminality when all members of the group experience social unity (*communitas*). However, since such movements are inherently unstable and short lived, they eventually settle down into reformist movements after forging an uncertain truce with the corrupt world that gave them birth.

Using this theoretical framework, Gager interprets the early church as a millenarian cult that arose out of the widespread social and political alienation of the Roman world. Jesus functioned as the prophet of the movement around whose promises the early church formed its vision of a new heaven and new earth. The failure of the Parousia led to the inevitable adjustment and reintegration of the millennial cult into the social structure of the Roman Empire.

But prior to its reintegration the cult passed through a severe internal crisis when the expected Parousia did not occur. To interpret this critical period in the life of the early church, Gager turns to the work of L. Festinger, especially his study of a modern group that predicted the end of the world, *When Prophecy Fails* (1956). Festinger found that the group he studied was not at all disheartened by the failure of its prediction. It did, however, respond to the "cognitive dissonance" created by falsification of its prediction by renewing its efforts at proselytizing. Its renewed missionary activity, he conjectured, attempted to minimize the group's cognitive dissonance by recruiting new members. Their influx would reinforce the group's identity and sense of being right even though its prediction had failed to materialize.

Once again, Gager applies the theoretical framework to interpret the relationship between the delay of the Parousia and the beginning of the church's missionary activity. The cognitive dissonance created by Jesus' death was intensified by the delay of the expected Parousia. In response to the felt crisis, the early church initiated its missionary movement into the Roman world.

The aim and scope of Theissen's work was quite different. He focussed his efforts on delineating the sociology of the early Jesus movement in Palestine whose ethos was embodied by wandering charismatics. Like their Cynic counterparts, these figures travelled as mendicants, without home or family ties or claims to protection. They were supported by a network of local sympathizers who provided them with food and shelter in exchange for protection from the coming judgment. When correlated with the Son of man (*see* Son of Man) statements, the sayings of the wandering charismatics reveal congruence, thereby placing the itinerant figures in the same situation as the "bearer of revelation," the risen Son of man.

The issues so prominent in the sayings of Jesus preserved by the wandering preachers (homelessness,

lack of family* ties, lack of possessions and lack of protection, in essence the so-called hard sayings of Jesus) indicate sources of social and political alienation in Palestine. These conditions influenced the form and ideology of the Jesus movement which was "to renew this society from within . . . [by] experimenting with a vision of love and reconciliation." In turn the Jesus movement effected its society by compensating for aggression (e.g., the antitheses of the Sermon on the Mount, forgiving another seventy times seven; *see* Sermon on the Mount), transferring aggression (visualized judgment, exorcisms), and internalizing or introjecting aggression (call for repentance).

The function of the Jesus movement was to relieve the pressure caused by the oppressive social and exploitative economic situation. It was a renewal movement whose volatile origins were transmuted into a socially useful purpose.

In apparent contrast to Gager, Theissen seemingly began with a social description of Palestine, sketching its economic, ecological, political and cultural conditions, before reconstructing the role of the Jesus movement and its itinerant charismatics in that environment. How did they constitute a response to the social forces at work in Palestine? What organizations were required to sustain their lifestyle? What effect did they have on the institutional structures of their world? However, when Theissen comes to evaluate the role of the Jesus movement in the violent and oppressive world of Palestine, he interprets it very much like Gager interpreted the role of a millenarian movement. The reason is rather clear. Both figures worked out of a larger shared sociological framework which emphasized the structural-functional role of renewal movements as contributors to a stable public order. Their value was assessed in terms of how they were able to reduce social tensions and thereby preserve the pre-existing social order. So, in spite of their divergent methods and scope, they reached similar conclusions.

Like all pioneering efforts, their work reveals hidden contradictions and unexamined assumptions that others would disclose and discuss, but it also proved to be fruitful for generating subsequent discussion. In this sense the works of Gager and Theissen served a useful purpose.

4. Social-Scientific Criticism in Use.

Perhaps the most effective way to evaluate approaches to the Gospels using the social sciences is to compare their results with those gained through other methods. The test case chosen for this article is the interpretation of the Markan version of the so-called cleansing of the Temple (Mk 11:15-19; *see* Temple Cleansing).

Form-critical interpretation has tried to establish the original episode/oral pericope before it was redacted by Mark or pre-Markan redactors, and in this case some consensus exists that Mark 11:15b, 17 form such a core. Of course, detaching the pericope from Mark's narrative also detaches the event from the Markan chronology and raises questions about when it occurred in the context of Jesus' ministry. Although Mark has framed the incident by placing it late in Jesus' ministry, V. Taylor (*The Gospel according to St. Mark*, 2d ed., 1966) believed that it occurred much earlier and reflected Jesus' "reforming zeal." To Taylor, Jesus was expressing his opposition to conducting trade in the Temple* precincts. His action was "a spirited protest" against the fleecing of pilgrims by unscrupulous businessmen.

Other scholars searching for a pre-Markan meaning add Mark 11:16 to the core because they read it as an act of hope and judgment.* Jesus was trying to restore the Temple to its proper role, "the house of God" it was supposed to be in the last days. If this were his intent, then Jesus resembled the sectarians at Qumran (*see* Dead Sea Scrolls) in his attitude toward the Temple; he did not repudiate the Temple but judged it defiled and in need of purification. In this case Mark 11:16 expresses Jesus' desire that no unconsecrated vessels be brought to the Temple for cultic use or even carried through the outer court of the Temple by thoughtless Jerusalemites taking a short cut through its precincts. In a variation of this position R. H. Lightfoot (*The Gospel Message of St. Mark*, 1950) argued that the cleansing was an attempt to reclaim the outer courtyard for pious Gentiles* so they could pray in peace undisturbed by the clamor of commercial transactions. Jesus saw the buying and selling as infringing on the "rights and privileges" of the Gentiles. This is why the cleansing was limited to the so-called Court of the Gentiles. By avoiding the inner courts of the Temple, Jesus signalled his approval of the sacrificial system.

Redaction critics focus on the setting of the passage in Mark as well as on the additions to the original core of the pericope. Using this approach, E. Schweizer (*The Good News according to Mark*, 1970) thinks that Mark 11:16 came from the hand of a pre-Markan redactor concerned to make the incident appear like an attempt at reform. But as the Markan framing of the episode makes clear (cf. Mk 11:12-14, 20-26), the withered fig tree is a symbolic counterpart of the Temple. In Mark's Gospel Jesus was performing a symbolic destruction of the Temple. But why? Be-

cause, argues Schweizer, it was an institution restricted exclusively to Jews, and Jesus' mission was to all peoples. So the Temple episode reflects an intimation of the Gentile mission.

Kelber (*The Kingdom in Mark: A New Place and A New Time*, 1973) also finds the same message. Jesus' initial scrutiny of the Temple (Mk 11:11, the verb *periblepsamenos*) communicates disapproval, and Mark 11:16 indicates that Jesus interfered with the transport of cultic vessels. So his protest is aimed at the whole Temple system, commercial and cultic. The withered fig tree "strikes at the eschatological prestige" of the Temple. The eschatological crisis (*see* Eschatology) brought by Jesus takes precedence over the Temple and relativizes its value. These readings then arrive at a conclusion strikingly different from the inferences derived from form-critical readings of the text.

Yet after the differences have been noted, one notable similarity exists. Both form critics and redaction critics view the conflict as essentially religious or symbolizing the conflict between religion and commerce. This consensus is not shared by critics using the social sciences, who specify the conflict more in political and economic terms. C. Myers interprets the entry episodes (into Jerusalem and into the Temple) as launching "the second direct action campaign" of Jesus' ministry, whose purpose is to force a showdown with the Jerusalem elites. The entry into Jerusalem and the Temple can be seen as "political street theatre." The Temple cleansing refers back to the strong man parable* (3:27) as the use of *skeuos* (translated "goods" in 3:37 and "vessels" in 11:16) in each passage suggests. But for Myers the Temple is primarily an economic institution, the center of ruling-class interests in Jerusalem. The money changers are simply the street-level representatives of the Temple's banking interests, and the dove sellers dispense the basic commodity used by the poor (*see* Rich and Poor) to participate in the Temple system of sacrifices and purity (*see* Clean and Unclean) requirements, both of which Jesus has repudiated. By singling out these two groups, Jesus has assaulted the visible representatives of oppression "within a political economy that doubly exploited the poor." In agreement with Myers, Belo noted the use of the verb *ekballein* (to drive out) to describe Jesus' actions. Prior to this episode it had been used to describe the expulsion of demons (*see* Demon, Devil, Satan). Its use in this context, Belo argues, equates the monetary system of the Temple and its functionaries with the demonic.

H. Waetjen, who basically shares Myers' view, argues that Jesus intends to shut down the Temple, which is nothing less than the center of power regulating the economic, political and social life of the people. Through its demand for tithes, the Temple participated in a tributary mode of production that oppressed peasants while maintaining its own power and prestige. At the same time, the Temple propagated and legitimized the dehumanizing purity/pollution system which rendered the people of the land (the *'am hā'āreṣ*) unclean and degraded.

The differences between the social-scientific interpreters and their historical-critical counterparts are obvious, and they reflect the consequences of methodological choices as well as ideological investments. The nature of the Temple is clearly an important issue. So is the intent, character and scope of Jesus' actions. Is he a reformer, a prophetic critic or a destroyer? Why is he perceived to be fulfilling the role assigned to him by various interpreters?

5. Evaluation.

The use of methods and models derived from the social sciences and their application to Jesus and the Gospels have not been without their critics. Generally speaking, this approach remains subject to the withering criticisms levelled against a "bankrupt" historical-critical method by W. Wink (*The Bible in Human Transformation*, 1973). Taking stock of the assets and liabilities of "the biblical critical paradigm," Wink listed five deficits: (1) the method was incommensurate with the intention of the texts; (2) it reflected the "ideology of objectivism" and (3) it "fell prey" to a technologism that limited the kinds of questions asked of a text to those which its method could answer; (4) it removed itself from the community of faith for whom its results were intended and, finally, (5) it failed to change with a changing historical context so that its polemical origins became increasingly anachronistic. Wink's bill of particulars could equally well be applied to forms of social-scientific criticism. In fact the specific concerns noted below repeat them in varied ways.

Other criticisms and questions relate more specifically to the distinctive approaches used by the social sciences. The first concerns the models used. How can models created by moderns interpret an ancient culture? The danger of anachronism is always present. A related issue is transferability. How transferable—not just from the present to the past but from culture to culture—are models developed by anthropologists or sociologists? A second concerns the incommensurability of the methods and the texts. The biblical texts were not written to yield the kind of information sought by the social sciences. How can social-scientific models extract knowledge not within

the purview of the biblical writer?

A third criticism concerns reductionism. Some think that the social sciences tend to reduce all theology to sociology or anthropology in disguise. Social forces either determine or cause specific theologies to arise. The accusation of reductionism was filed against N. Gottwald (*The Tribes of Yahweh: A Sociology of the Religion of Liberated Israel*, 1979); once he had explored the sociology of Israel's religion, he had defined a sufficient cause for its emergence. Such an approach may ignore or minimize the truth claims of theological statements or religious expressions.

Finally, while objectivity may be desirable, it also distances the interpreter from the text and renders it a subject for investigation but not a Scripture that scrutinizes and searches the interpreter.

While acknowledging the validity of many of these criticisms, other considerations must also be kept in mind. While models run the risk of introducing anachronism, they also supply controls to a study. The more self-conscious scholars are about research models and methods, the more completely they can define the limits of an investigation and avoid making extravagant claims for its results or implications. The alternative is to use implicit methods and models (for all interpreters operate with some methods and models) drawn from one's current culture and unconsciously impose them on the ancient texts. This procedure effectively muzzles the ancient texts although it gives the appearance of showing their relevance because they speak to the contemporary situation. The strangeness of the Gospels as first-century documents is lost. The concern that modern methods and models may not apply to ancient texts is, therefore, somewhat misleading since every modern interpreter uses contemporary models to understand the ancient texts. The question is how self-conscious the interpreter is about the models and methods being employed.

The related question of incommensurability between texts and models does suggest the need for prudence. But candor requires the acknowledgment that all theological, ecclesial and scholarly inquiries confront the same issue. If the use of the social sciences highlights the importance of this issue for all academic study of the Gospels, it will have served an invaluable purpose.

Reductionism is indeed a danger of any form of biblical criticism, and no less so for those forms using the social sciences. But the social sciences can also be seen as restoring perspective to the development of the early church and the formation of Scripture. As G. Casalis noted, "correct ideas don't fall from the skies," and the capacity to understand the human and social dimensions of these developments can reduce the mystification that all too often reinforces unwarranted claims and authoritarian appeals. Put in another but related perspective, the use of the social sciences can contribute to our understanding of the inspiration of Scripture. Any view of the inspiration of Scripture must respect the way God chose to give Scripture to the church, and for whatever reasons, God chose to provide Scriptures that are simultaneously ancient documents (e.g., first-century Gospels) and contemporary "Word of God." Therefore, any path of interpreting the Scripture must pass through the ancient world to speak to the modern world. The social sciences provide many useful tools (though not the only ones) for conducting that difficult task precisely because they can elucidate that first-century Mediterranean world.

Gaining perspective on the ancient world is not the same thing as being objective, and the social sciences can deliver objectivity no more than any other method, particularly for those who study the Gospels as documents of faith. But any method that makes one aware of the relativity of one's own culture and, therefore, of the need to use crosscultural models as part of the study of the Gospels has made a significant contribution.

See also FORM CRITICISM; LIBERATION HERMENEUTICS; REDACTION CRITICISM; REVOLUTIONARY MOVEMENTS; RICH AND POOR.

BIBLIOGRAPHY. E. Bammel and C. F. D. Moule, eds., *Jesus and the Politics of His Day* (Cambridge: University Press, 1984); F. Belo, *A Materialist Reading of the Gospel of Mark* (Maryknoll, NY: Orbis, 1981); E. Cardenal, ed., *The Gospel in Solentiname* (5 vols.; Maryknoll, NY: Orbis, 1975-1982); R. Cassidy, *Jesus, Politics and Society: A Study of Luke's Gospel* (Maryknoll, NY: Orbis, 1978); M. Clevenot, *Materialist Approaches to the Bible* (Maryknoll, NY: Orbis, 1985); M. Crosby, *House of Disciples: Church, Economics and Justice in Matthew* (Maryknoll, NY: Orbis, 1988); J. H. Elliott, ed., *Semeia 35: Social-Scientific Criticism of the New Testament and Its Social World* (1986); J. G. Gager, "Shall We Marry Our Enemies? Sociology and the New Testament," *Int* 36 (1982) 256-65; D. Harrington, "Sociological Concepts and the Early Church: A Decade of Research," *TS* 41 (1980) 181-90; idem, *Kingdom and Community* (Englewood Cliffs, NJ: Prentice Hall, 1975); P. W. Hollenbach, "Recent Historical Jesus Studies and the Social Sciences," in *SBLASP* (1983) 61-78; B. Holmberg, *Sociology and the New Testament: An Appraisal* (Minneapolis: Fortress, 1990); R. Horsley, *Jesus and the Spiral of Violence: Popular Jewish Resistance in Roman Palestine* (San Francisco: Harper and Row, 1987); idem, *Sociology and the Jesus Movement* (New York: Crossroad, 1989); R. Horsley and J. Hanson, *Bandits, Prophets and Messiahs: Popular Movements at the Time of Jesus* (Minneapolis: Winston, 1985); H. C. Kee, *Miracle in the Early Christian World: A Study in Socio-Historical Method* (New Haven: Yale University, 1983); B. Malina, *Christian Origins and Cultural Anthropology* (Atlanta: John Knox, 1986); idem, "Jesus as Charismatic Leader?" *BTB* 14 (1984) 55-62; idem, *The New Testament World: Insights from Cultural Anthropology* (Atlanta: John Knox, 1981); B. Malina and J. Neyrey, *Calling Jesus Names: The Social Value of Labels in Matthew* (Sonoma, CA: Polebridge, 1988); H. Moxnes, *The Economy of the Kingdom: Social Conflict and Economic Relations in Luke's Gospel* (Minneapolis: Fortress, 1988); C. Myers, *Binding the Strong Man: A Political Reading of Mark's Story of Jesus* (Maryknoll, NY: Orbis, 1988); J. Neyrey, *An Ideology of Revolt: John's Christology in Social-Scientific Perspective* (Philadelphia: Fortress, 1988); J. K. Riches, "The Sociology of Matthew: Some Basic Questions Concerning Its Relation to the Theology of the New Testament," *SBLASP* (1983) 259-71; P. J. Richter, "Recent Sociological Approaches to the Study of the New Testament," *Religion* 14 (1984) 77-90; R. Rohrbaugh, *The Biblical Interpreter: An Agrarian Bible in an Industrial Age* (Philadelphia: Fortress, 1978); J. Z. Smith, "The Social Description of Early Christianity," *RelSRev* 1,1 (September 1975) 19-25; W. Schottroff and W. Stegemann, *God of the Lowly: Socio-Historical Interpretations of the Bible* (Maryknoll, NY: Orbis, 1984); J. Stambaugh and D. Balch, *The New Testament in Its Social Environment* (Philadelphia: Westminster, 1988); G. Theissen, *Sociology of Early Palestinian Christianity* (Philadelphia: Fortress, 1978); D. Tidball, *The Social Context of the New Testament* (Grand Rapids: Zondervan, 1984); H. Waetjen, *A Reordering of Power: A Socio-Political Reading of Mark's Gospel* (Minneapolis: Fortress, 1989).

W. R. Herzog II

SOLDIER. See MILITARY.

SON OF DAVID

When used as a christological title, Son of David points to Jesus as the royal Messiah (see Christ) in the line of David. As such he fulfills the promises God* made to David regarding the eternal reign of David's "offspring" (e.g., 2 Sam 7:12-16), and he acts as the unique agent in bringing the rule of God (see Kingdom of God) to the earth, a rule that is characterized by salvation* and blessing.* In contrast to major streams of popular messianic expectation, Jesus refused to establish his kingly rule through political ascendancy or military conquest (*see* Revolutionary Movements). Rather, this Davidic king wielded his royal power by attending to the needs of the poor and oppressed, and by suffering and dying in order to bring salvation to his people.

In comparison with christological titles such as Son of God* and Son of Man,* Son of David plays a relatively minor role in the NT. It seems to be used always with reference to Jesus' earthly existence, never of his heavenly or exalted state. Moreover, it appears in just eleven passages, all of them within the Synoptic Gospels. Nevertheless, the idea of Davidic sonship is often present even when the phrase itself does not occur, as when Jesus is described as "King." The concept of Son of David contributed to the early development of the church's christology, and within the Synoptic tradition it provided specific content for the more general christological categories of Christ and Son of God.

1. The OT and Judaic Background
2. The Son of David and the Historical Jesus
3. The Son of David in the Christology of the Gospels

1. The OT and Judaic Background.

The expectation of a Davidic Messiah had its beginnings during the Exile, for central to the notion of such a Messiah is the re-establishment of the throne of David and the deliverance of Israel from its (foreign) oppressors. This expectation resulted from a combination of disappointment and confidence: Disappointment at the destruction of Jerusalem and the suspension of the Davidic dynasty, and confidence in the faithfulness of God who had made an everlasting covenant with David to establish David's kingdom forever through his offspring (2 Sam 7:10-16; cf. Ps 89:1-4, 19-37; 132:11-12). Prophets such as Jeremiah, Ezekiel, Haggai and Zechariah spoke of the Davidic "righteous Branch" who would soon appear to reconcile the people to their God, re-establish Israel in the land, cleanse the land of foreign oppressors as well as unrighteous Israelites, and cause peoples from all over the earth to flock to Jerusalem where they would behold the glory of Yahweh (Jer 23:5-8; 30:21-22; Ezek 37:21-23; Zech 3:8-10; 6:12-15; Hag 2:21-22). These prophets thought of an entirely earthly figure, a mortal man, who would inaugurate a dynasty which would continue forever through his descendants (Ps 89:3-4; Jer 17:25; 33:15-18).

Although there was much diversity in messianic speculation among individual Jewish groups, a general consensus emerged within later Judaism* that the Messiah would be Davidic along the lines set out by the exilic prophets. A representative statement of Jewish messianic expectations is Psalms of Solomon 17—18 (a Pharisaic composition written around 50 B.C.). According to this description the "Son of David" (the title appears here for the first time) will (1) violently cast out the foreign nations occupying Jerusalem (17:15, 24-25, 33); (2) judge all the nations of the earth (17:4, 31, 38-39, 47) and cause these nations to "serve him under his yoke" (17:32); (3) reign over Israel in wisdom* (17:23, 31, 42) and righteousness* (17:23, 28, 31, 35, 41; 18:8), which involves removing all foreigners from the land (17:31) and purging the land of unrighteous Israelites (17:29, 33, 41) in order to eliminate all oppression (17:46) and gather to himself a holy people (17:28, 36; 18:9).

Although the Davidic Messiah is still pictured as an earthly figure, his rule obviously takes on eschatological and universal dimensions not found in the prophets. Essentially the same description of the Davidic Messiah appears at Qumran (1QM 11:1-18; 4QFlor 1:11-14; 4QPBless 1-7; 4QTestim 9-13; *see* Dead Sea Scrolls) and in the Pseudepigrapha (4 Ezra 12:31-32; *T. Jud.* 24:1-5).

2. The Son of David and the Historical Jesus.

The Gospels reveal that Davidic expectations along the lines of Psalms of Solomon were very much alive in Jesus' milieu. Jesus was executed on the charge that he claimed to be the king of the Jews (or of Israel; *see* Death of Jesus), thus inciting political and military rebellion against Rome (Mk 15:2, 26; cf. 10:46—11:10). The request from James and John for seats on the right and left of Jesus suggest that the disciples viewed Jesus' kingdom in terms of political authority* and social supremacy (Mk 10:35-45). Moreover, the question posed by the disciples* in Acts 1:6 indicates a nationalistic understanding of the kingdom. Jesus himself was aware of the popular expectations surrounding the Davidic Messiah and seems to have struggled with them (Mk 8:32-33; Mt 4:1-11; 27:32-44; Jn 6:15).

On only one occasion did Jesus specifically raise the issue of Davidic sonship: Mark 12:35-37 and its parallels. There is general scholarly consensus that Jesus did not wish, in this passage, to deny the Davidic sonship of the Messiah. Certainly the Evangelists who included this pericope in their Gospels did not understand it in that sense. Rather, Jesus engaged here in the rabbinic form of argument known as *haggadah*, according to which an apparent contradiction between two passages is presented and discussed in such a way that the truth of each is affirmed. Here

Jesus (implicitly) sets all those passages which teach the Davidic sonship of the Messiah over against Psalm 110:1, which on the surface seems to contradict this teaching. In this way Jesus indicated that (1) the Messiah is the Son of David and (2) the Messiah is a transcendent being, whose glory* and authority far surpass that of David. "Son of David," therefore, is an accurate but not fully adequate description of the Messiah.

Although Jesus accepted the Davidic sonship of the Messiah, he rejected the nationalistic and militaristic conceptions of the Son of David which were so much a part of Jewish expectations. As far as Jesus was concerned, the kingdom does not come by violence (Mt 11:12), nor is it characterized by oppressive, authoritarian rule (Mk 10:42-44). On the contrary, Jesus as Son of David is presented as he who acted mercifully to blind Bartimaeus (Mk 10:46-52). He seems to have viewed himself as one who dies on behalf of his people (Mk 8:31; 9:30-31; 10:32-34; 15:1-32; *see* Predictions of Jesus' Passion and Resurrection), and indeed on behalf of all peoples ("the many," Mk 10:45; *see* Ransom Saying). Those who participate in his kingdom follow him in the way of submission and sacrificial service* (Mk 8:34-38).

This new understanding of the Son of David explains the reticence of Jesus concerning his Messianic and Davidic status. At no time did he claim to be the Son of David. As Cullmann points out, even Jesus' answer to the question Pontius Pilate* put to him regarding his kingship was, in the Aramaic original, equivocal and ambiguous (Mk 15:2; *see* Trial of Jesus). The most natural interpretation of Jesus' reserve on this point is that he wished to avoid any tendency on the part of the people to view him as a nationalistic and military leader (Lk 22:47-53; Jn 6:15; 18:33-38).

3. The Son of David in the Christology of the Gospels. Matthew gives greater prominence to "Son of David" than do the other Gospel writers. The title appears four times each in Mark and Luke, but ten times in Matthew. The phrase does not occur at all in the Fourth Gospel (but cf. Jn 7:42).

3.1. Mark. The reader is introduced to Jesus as Son of David in the story of Bartimaeus (10:46-52). Twice this blind beggar cries out, "Son of David, have mercy upon me" (vv. 47-48); and in response to his pleas Jesus heals him (v. 52). The fact that Jesus fulfills Bartimaeus' request to the letter suggests that the Markan Jesus accepts this title. This story indicates that (1) Jesus is in the lineage of David; (2) he fulfills Jewish expectations that the Son of David would bring wholeness to the oppressed; and (3) he wields his

royal power by humbly submitting to those in need rather than by "exercising authority," like the rulers of the Gentiles* (10:35-45).

Mark employs the healing of Bartimaeus as an introduction to the triumphal entry (11:1-11; cf. 10:52). As such, Jesus enters Jerusalem as the Son of David. By presenting Jesus as one who enters upon his kingship riding a colt (Zech 9:9; cf. 2 Kings 9:13; *see* Triumphal Entry), Mark indicates that Jesus is the type of Davidic king described by Zechariah: a humble savior who brings peace* and blessing to the nations. Although the people properly hail Jesus as the Davidic prince who brings God's kingdom of salvation to them (11:9-10), subsequent events indicate that the people have an entirely different understanding of this kingdom and of the Son of David who introduces this kingdom than does Jesus. In the passion narrative (*see* Passion Narrative) the crowds reject Jesus' conception of a suffering and dying king who saves others by refusing to save himself (15:6-15, 25-39).

This section of Mark comes to a climax in the question regarding "David's son" (Mk 12:35-37). Mark has indicated that Jesus is the Son of David. Now he suggests that Jesus is much more than Son of David. Given Mark's accent on Jesus as Son of God (1:1, 11; 9:7; 15:39), he is probably contending here that Jesus should be viewed primarily as Son of God, and in only an ancillary way as Son of David. Mark employs "Son of David" in such a way that it might contribute its own specific content to the broader conception of Jesus' divine sonship, a christological category which (in Mark) emphasizes the suffering and death of Jesus.

3.2. Matthew. Matthew has appropriated the four references to Son of David which he found in his Markan source, and he has introduced an additional six, presumably from his own hand. An examination of Matthew's use of this title indicates that he employs it with deliberation and consistency.

For Matthew, Jesus can function as Son of David because he is of the lineage of David (1:1-17; *see* Genealogy). But Matthew immediately encounters a problem with this assertion; for he attempts to trace Jesus' Davidic ancestry through Joseph, while maintaining that Jesus was not, in fact, the biological son of Joseph. Jesus has been conceived, not by Joseph, but by the Holy Spirit* (1:16, 18-25; *see* Birth of Jesus). The reader is thus confronted with a question: How can Jesus be the Son of David through Joseph if he is not the natural son of Joseph? The answer: Joseph, son of David, adopts Jesus by giving him his name (1:20-25). The fact that Jesus is adopted by Joseph in no way makes Jesus' Davidic lineage questionable. In Jewish circles a child became a man's son not so much by physical procreation itself as by acknowledgment on the part of the man. Nevertheless, Jesus is Son of David by adoption, but Son of God by conception (2:15; 3.17).

But Jesus is not simply a son of David; he is *the* Son of David. As Son of David, Jesus is the Messiah-king in the line of David who has been sent by God specifically to the people of Israel,* not in order to exercise oppressive rule over them (20:20—21:17) but to bring them salvation and deliverance by healing* them of their diseases. Three times persons in need of healing cry out to him, "Have mercy upon me [us], Son of David" (9:27; 15:22; 20:31). In all instances Jesus grants the healing they seek. Moreover, on two other occasions Jesus' healings induce persons to speak about him in terms of "Son of David" (12:23; 21:15).

These passages have a double function. On the one hand, they make a positive statement about Jesus, demonstrating that Jesus fulfills the messianic expectation that the Son of David would bring wholeness to the oppressed, and that those who have faith to confess that Jesus is the Jewish Messiah will experience the blessings of the eschatological age. On the other hand, they make a negative statement about Israel. As J. D. Kingsbury has observed, only the "no-accounts" of Jewish society, and on one occasion a Gentile, appeal to Jesus as Son of David and are thereby healed. The crowds, however, generally respond to these healings with doubt (12:23), and the religious authorities respond with anger (21:15) and blasphemy (12:22-32). Matthew thus uses "Son of David" to point to Israel's rejection of its Messiah and to highlight the blindness* and guilt (*see* Hardness of Heart) that attended this rejection on the part of Israel as a whole.

The fact that Matthew gives more attention to "Son of David" than do the other Evangelists has led some scholars, such as Bornkamm and Burger, to argue that Son of David is the chief christological category in Matthew. Yet in the question regarding David's son Matthew suggests that Jesus' Davidic sonship is secondary to another type of sonship (22:41-46; cf. Mk 12:35-37). No doubt Matthew has in mind that Jesus' divine sonship takes precedence over his Davidic sonship. In Matthew's Gospel Jesus is presented primarily as Son of God, the eschatological figure in whom God has drawn near to dwell with his people (1:18-25; 3:17; 16:16; 27:54), and in only a secondary and supportive way as Son of David.

3.3. Luke. Luke records the birth of Jesus in Bethlehem, "the city of David" (2:4, 11), to a woman betrothed to Joseph, "of the house and lineage of David" (2:4). Yet Luke gives relatively little attention to the title "Son of David." It appears only in passages which he takes over from Mark. In one of these passages (the question regarding David's son, 20:41-47) Luke suggests that although Jesus is the Son of David, his Davidic sonship is subordinate to another christological category, probably that of Son of God (1:26-35; 3:23-38).

Nevertheless, the concept of Davidic sonship does appear in Luke's Gospel. As Son of David, Jesus is the royal heir to the throne of David (1:32-33). In him the promises which God made regarding the establishment of David's kingdom and the consequent salvation of Israel find fulfillment (1:54, 68-75; 4:16-30; 19:28-40).

Jesus' Son of David is the one whom God has designated to usher in his kingdom, and the one through whom God exercises his will over his people Israel (including those Gentiles who by faith become part of the true Israel of God, 1:30-32; cf. Acts). Luke emphasizes, even more than Mark and Matthew, that this Davidic king and the kingdom he inaugurates are not characterized by military revolt or political aspirations, but involve rather the salvation of God's people from demonic oppression (4:16-19; 11:14-23; 18:35-43; *see* Demon, Devil, Satan) and the establishment of a community which fulfills the will of God (23:1-15, 32-49).

See also CHRIST; SON OF GOD.

BIBLIOGRAPHY. G. Bornkamm, "End Expectation and Church in Matthew," in *Tradition and Interpretation in Matthew*, ed. G. Bornkamm et al. (Philadelphia: Westminster, 1963) 15-51; R. E. Brown, *The Birth of the Messiah* (Garden City, NY: Doubleday, 1977); C. Burger, *Jesus als Davidssohn* (FRLANT 98; Göttingen: Vandenhoeck & Ruprecht, 1967); O. Cullmann, *The Christology of the New Testament* (Philadelphia: Westminster, 1963); J. M. Gibbs, "Purpose and Pattern in Matthew's Use of the Title 'Son of David,' " *NTS* 10 (1963-64) 446-464; F. Hahn, *The Titles of Jesus in Christology* (London: Lutterworth, 1969); J. D. Kingsbury, *Jesus Christ in Matthew, Mark, and Luke* (PC; Philadelphia: Fortress, 1981); idem, "The Title 'Son of David' in Matthew's Gospel," *JBL* 95 (1976) 591-602; E. Lohse, "υἱός Δαυίδ," *TDNT* VIII.478-88; S. Mowinckel, *He That Cometh* (New York: Abingdon, 1955).

D. R. Bauer

SON OF GOD

This is arguably the most significant christological title in the NT. "Son of God" or its equivalents ("the Son," "my Son," etc.) occur more than 124 times in the NT, and may be the foremost christological category in each of the Gospels. The NT characteristically describes Jesus' relationship to God in terms of divine sonship. The concept itself carries a variety of meanings, including commissioning to special work, obedience, intimate fellowship, knowledge, likeness and the receiving of blessings and gifts.

1. Divine Sonship in the OT, Judaism and Hellenism
2. Divine Sonship in the Life and Ministry of the Historical Jesus
3. Divine Sonship in the Christology of the Gospels

1. Divine Sonship in the OT, Judaism and Hellenism.
The notion of divine sonship appears in the OT with regard to three persons or groups of persons: *angels** (Gen 6:2; Job 1:6; Dan 3:25), *Israel** (Ex 4:22-23; Hos 11:1; Mal 2:10) and the *king* (2 Sam 7:14; Ps 2:7; 89:26-27). When used of Israel and the king sonship emphasizes belonging in a special way to God,* election to perform the service of God (i.e., to obey God) and the experience of God's love,* mercy,* protection and gifts.

Although there are relatively few OT references to the king as son of God, this usage stands closer to the meaning of the title in the NT than do references to angels or even to the people as a whole. There are two emphases in the divine sonship of the king which set it apart from the sonship of the people. First, the king in his capacity as son of God exercises authority over both the people of Israel and the nations (see esp. Ps 2). Second, the divine sonship of the king has its basis in the covenant God made with David in 2 Samuel 7:4-17 (cf. Ps 89:19-45), thereby (1) restricting royal divine sonship to descendants of David, (2) laying the foundation for relating the concepts of Son of David and Son of God, and (3) infusing the notion of royal Son of God with the ideas of immutable divine promise, decree and covenant.

It is clear that the OT does not speak explicitly of the Messiah or of a specifically messianic figure as Son of God. This seems generally to be the case in post-biblical Palestinian Judaism* as well. The expression refers to angels (*1 Enoch* 69:4-5; 71:1; *Jub* 1:24-25) and miracle workers (esp. Honi the circle-drawer [*b. Ta'an.* 24b; *b. Ber.* 17b; *b. ḥul.* 86a] and Ḥanina ben Dosa [*m. Ta'an.* 3:8]; see Vermes), but many passages that once were cited as evidence for the messianic use of Son of God have been discounted as later interpolations or mistranslations of the word for "servant."

There are three passages in the literature from Qumran (*see* Dead Sea Scrolls), however, which may connect the idea of Son of God to the Messiah: 4QFlor 1:10-14 applies 2 Samuel 7:11-14 to the Messiah; 1QSa 2:11-12 could be read in terms of God begetting the Messiah; and 4QpsDan A^a (4Q246) is reported to read "he shall be hailed as the Son of God, and they shall call him Son of the most High" (Fitzmyer). In spite of the sparsity of references which relate the Messiah to divine sonship, the observations that (1) messianic hope in the period was almost always linked to an ideal Davidic king (who in the OT is described as Son of God) and (2) some NT statements seem to assume a connection between Messiah and Son of God (e.g., Mk 14:61; Mt 16:16) suggest that the Messiah as Son of God was not totally foreign to Palestinian Judaism. Yet the Messiah was not understood primarily in terms of Son of God.

The consideration that Son of God was not a typical messianic designation in Palestinian Judaism and that Hellenism was acquainted with descriptions of heroes, philosophers, rulers and miracle workers who were designated sons of god has led many historians to argue for the Hellenistic origin of the title as applied to Jesus. These historians claim that Hellenistic Christians were responsible for the confession of Jesus' divine sonship, and that they understood Jesus to be Son of God along the lines of the "divine man" (*theios anēr; see* Divine Man/Theios Aner), a heroic miracle-worker. This understanding of the origin of the title in christology is today generally rejected, since (1) the Hellenistic concept stands in tension with the NT emphasis on the uniqueness of Jesus' divine sonship as well as with the NT insistence that the divine sonship of Jesus involves primarily suffering and death (*see* Death of Jesus) rather than the performance of miracles (*see* Miracles, Miracle Stories); (2) the notion of "divine man" was not as pervasive or uniform as once thought; and (3) there is no explicit connection in Hellenistic sources between "divine man" and persons held to be "sons of the gods." It is thus preferable to look to the OT and Palestinian Judaism for the religious background to the divine sonship of Jesus.

2. Divine Sonship in the Life and Ministry of the Historical Jesus.
The issue of divine sonship in the thinking and ministry of the historical Jesus revolves around two questions: Did Jesus consider himself to be the Son of God; and if so, how did he understand this role?

2.1. Did Jesus Consider Himself to Be the Son of God?
According to the Synoptic Gospels, Jesus understood himself and his mission according to divine sonship and clearly implied that he was the Son of God. Yet there are two sets of data that may challenge the historicity of the Gospel accounts at this point.

The first challenge comes from the almost total absence in literature from Palestinian Judaism of a connection between messianic expectations and the title Son of God. This observation has led to the conclusion that neither Jesus nor his contemporaries would have thought of the Messiah in terms of Son of God, and that the christological confession of divine sonship must have arisen with the Hellenistic church, which was responsible for introducing its confession into the traditions of Jesus' earthly ministry. But we noted above that although specific references are few, there is reason to believe that the Messiah was in fact sometimes understood in terms of divine sonship.

The second challenge involves statements in the NT which may be understood as linking the divine sonship of Jesus to his resurrection*/exaltation, thereby suggesting that Jesus became Son of God at that point (esp. Acts 13:33; Rom 1:3-4). Many scholars have argued that this was the original understanding of the divine sonship of Jesus and that the early church gradually pushed the inauguration of Jesus' status as Son of God back to the Transfiguration,* then to the baptism* and finally to either virginal conception (*see* Birth of Jesus) or pre-existence (*see* Logos).

Virtually everyone agrees that Romans 1:3-4 reflects an early creed that Paul has included in order to establish a point of theological contact between himself and his Roman readers. It is often claimed, furthermore, that the pre-Pauline formula lacked the phrase "in power," and thus signified that Jesus became Son of God at the resurrection. By adding this phrase Paul has transformed the meaning of the statement so as to imply that Jesus had been Son of God all along, and that at the resurrection he became Son in a new sense. But some scholars (e.g., Dunn) have argued that "in power" may have been part of the pre-Pauline formula. Moreover, even if the original formula lacked this phrase, it is possible to construe *oristhentos* of verse 4 as "designated" (so RSV) rather than "appointed," thus indicating that in the resurrection God declared Jesus to be what he had been during his earthly ministry. But ultimately the interpretation of this verse turns on prior decisions regarding the connection of Messiah with the Son title in earliest Christianity. Those who deny such a connection see a dichotomy between the earthly Jesus as Son of David and his post-resurrection status as Son of God, while those who affirm the connection between Son and Messiah argue that Davidic sonship implies divine sonship.

Acts 13:33 represents a similarly ambiguous case. On the surface this quotation from Psalm 2:7 seems to intimate that Jesus was "begotten" as Son of God at the resurrection. But it is possible to maintain with Marshall that both the flow of thought in Paul's sermon and the analogy with Wisdom 2:13-18 indicate that Psalm 2:7 was employed not to establish Jesus' divine sonship on the basis of his resurrection, but rather to prove that in the resurrection God confirmed the righteousness (*see* Justice, Righteousness) of his obedient Son. Thus, the passage links sonship to the obedience of the earthly Jesus and not to the event of the resurrection. We conclude, then, that there is no firm evidence in the NT for the view that Jesus entered into his role as Son of God at the resurrection.

Virtually all critics agree that Jesus addressed God* as *Abba*, "Father," and typically referred to God by this designation when teaching his disciples. These phenomena are firmly embedded in the earliest strata of Gospel tradition, and throughout the Synoptic Gospels it is almost exclusively the way Jesus speaks of God and his relationship to God. This does not necessarily imply, however, that every reference to "Father" in our Gospels was spoken by the historical Jesus; the wide disparity in the number of occurrences in the four Gospels suggests that at points the Evangelists may have inserted the designation into traditions they inherited.

Scholarly debate has focused on those passages in which Jesus refers to himself as the Son. A strong claim for authenticity can be made especially for Mark 13:32; 12:6; and Matthew 11:27/Luke 10:22. In the case of Mark 13:32 it is unlikely that the early church would have created a saying which asserted the ignorance of Jesus. The objections raised to the authenticity of the parable* of the tenants (Mk 12:1-12) are not convincing. The fact that the parable contains some allegorical elements does not necessarily exclude it as coming from Jesus; and the argument that it contradicts Jesus' reticence to speak publicly about his sonship fails to take seriously the oblique nature of this reference to the "son." The reference to the "sending" of the son in this passage does not suggest pre-existence (as in Paul), but points rather to the calling, mission and eschatological significance of Jesus. A more difficult passage is Matthew 11:27/Luke 10:22 (*see* Wisdom). In the face of claims that this statement reflects a relatively late—even Johannine—christology, Jeremias has successively argued that its language, style and structure reflect Semitic usage and that the relationship between Father and Son found here accords with Jesus' statements regarding the Father encountered throughout the Synoptic Gospels.

A focus on these three statements does not imply that other passages in which Jesus speaks of himself as the Son have no historical validity. Bauckham has argued for the historical value of many of the Son sayings in the Fourth Gospel, following Cullmann's hypothesis that behind much of the sayings material in this Gospel stands independent tradition passed on by the "beloved disciple" and preserved by the Johannine circle. Nevertheless, the task of assessing the historical character of Johannine material is extremely complicated, and it is therefore preferable to concentrate on the earliest strands of the Synoptic tradition.

2.2. How Did Jesus Understand His Divine Sonship? An examination of the authentic sayings of Jesus regarding the "Father" and the "Son" reveals the following emphases.

2.2.1. Personal Intimacy with the Father. It points to intimate personal fellowship between Jesus and God. Jesus experienced this intimate fellowship especially through prayer, and consequently addressed God in prayer* almost exclusively as "Father" (Aramaic *'Abba;* Mk 14:36; cf. Rom 8:15; Gal 4:6). Jeremias has argued that Jesus was apparently the first Jew to address God in prayer as *'Abba* (Jewish prayers typically used the obsolete and formalized Hebrew term *'Abi*), and that *'Abba* was a term of familiarity and intimacy, having originally developed from the speech of children ("daddy"). Subsequent scholarship has been unable to contradict the claim that this prayer language of *'Abba* was original with Jesus. Although Jeremias' employment of etymological considerations is questionable (Barr), his distinction between formal prayer speech, which suggests distance, and the more colloquial expression used to address earthly fathers bears the weight of critical scrutiny.

Jesus' use of *'Abba* prompts the question as to how and when Jesus came to understand himself and his messianic role in terms of this intimate filial relationship with God. The attempt to reconstruct Jesus' messianic self-consciousness is notoriously difficult. Nevertheless, the tradition itself suggests that Jesus may have become conscious of his divine sonship at the point of his baptism. In the earliest form of the baptism account the divine voice addresses Jesus directly in the second person: "You are my beloved Son" (Mk 1:11). If this experience did not initiate Jesus' Son-consciousness, it confirmed and informed it.

2.2.2. Obedience to the Will of God. This reference to the baptism leads to a second emphasis: Absolute obedience to the will of God understood in terms of the Suffering Servant (*see* Servant of Yahweh). The divine speech at the baptism accentuates obedience: "With you I am well pleased." Moreover, the heavenly voice alludes to Psalm 2:7 and Isaiah 42:1, thereby bringing together the concepts of divine sonship and the Servant of Yahweh. Thus, divine sonship is defined in terms of obedience, and obedience is described in terms of the image of the Servant. Although intertestamental Judaism sometimes connected the Messiah with the Servant of Yahweh, it failed to link vicarious suffering of the Servant to the Messiah. But there is no doubt that Jesus made this connection, and he seems to have based the connection on his understanding of his role as Son of God. Jesus' construal of his divine sonship in terms of obedient submission to suffering and death emerges also in his prayer in Gethsemane* (Mk 14:32-42).

2.2.3. The Unique Son of God. The foregoing implies a further emphasis in Jesus' speech involving his divine sonship: it is exclusive. Jesus is Son of God in a unique sense. In his capacity as Son of God Jesus has the power to bring his followers into an experience of divine sonship, but Jesus consistently distinguishes between the sonship of disciples and his own sonship. He speaks of "my Father" and "your Father," but never "our Father" (the "our" of the Lord's Prayer [Mt 6:9] is what the disciples are to say).

It is clear that in the authentic statements from the Synoptic Gospels Jesus did not speak of his divine sonship in terms of pre-existence or focus on ontological realities (such as his divine "nature"). Rather, Jesus emphasized the elements of personal relationship and active function.

3. Divine Sonship in the Christology of the Gospels.

Although there is wide disparity in the number of occurrences of "Son (of God)" and "Father" in the four Gospels, each of the Gospels gives significant attention to Jesus' divine sonship, and may in fact present "Son of God" as the pre-eminent christological title.

3.1. Mark. "Son (of God)" appears in Mark's Gospel only eight times and "Father" (referring to God) only four. Yet these titles surface at crucial points in Mark and play a role in the christology of the Gospel that surpasses their few occurrences (*see* Mark, Gospel of).

Scholars have generally recognized the importance of this title for Mark's christology, but they have assessed its function differently. Many authorities have linked the title to the concept of divine man, described above, arguing that in this Gospel Jesus became Son of God at his baptism when the Spirit descended upon him, thus providing him with divine power according to which he performed miracles and exorcisms. There is, however, a division among scholars who hold this divine man theory: some maintain that the Evangelist himself espoused such a christology, while others contend that Mark presented this portrait of Jesus as divine man only to correct it by presenting Jesus above all as the suffering Son of man. Indeed, scholars such as Perrin have argued that because the title Son of God could be linked to the divine man concept which Mark himself rejects, Mark has subordinated this title to that of Son of man (see Son of Man), which unambiguously points to Jesus' suffering and death.

The difficulties of employing the concept of divine man in NT christology were discussed above. In addition to these problems it should be observed that Mark gives unqualified approval to the title Son of God, and understands this title primarily in terms of Jesus' obedient suffering and death. There is no evidence that Mark holds Son of God and Son of man in tension, nor that he gives prominence to the latter over the former.

Mark indicates the importance of this title for his christology by placing it within the general heading to the Gospel (Mk 1:1). The specific meaning of Jesus' divine sonship begins to come to expression in the account of the baptism (Mk 1:9-11), where the heavenly voice declares, "You are my beloved Son, with you I am well pleased." This pericope indicates that God views Jesus primarily in terms of divine sonship and that Jesus' role as Son of God involves especially obedience to his Father. As mentioned above, the heavenly declaration alludes to Isaiah 42:1 and thus links the divine sonship of Jesus to his role as the Suffering Servant of Yahweh.

God makes this announcement to Jesus alone; at this point in the narrative only God and Jesus are aware that Jesus is Son of God. In Mark 3:11 and 5:7 the demons address Jesus as "Son of (the Most High) God" (cf. Mk 1:24, 34), which seems to indicate they were privy to the divine communication at the baptism. Nevertheless, Jesus does not wish his divine sonship to be publicly announced and consequently commands the demons to be silent. The observation that Jesus also commands silence from those who were healed (Mk 1:43-44; 5:43; cf. 7:24) suggests the reason for this messianic secret. The Markan Jesus does not wish to be proclaimed as Son of God until it is clear his divine sonship involves not spectacular miracles but suffering and death. Hence, the secret of Jesus' divine sonship is revealed only gradually.

In Mark 9:7 the divine communication originally voiced at the baptism is repeated in the presence of the inner circle of the disciples,* but they will not understand what it means until after the resurrection (Mk 9:9-13). In Mark 12:6, in the course of the parable of the tenants, Jesus speaks of the sending of a "son";

the religious authorities apparently understood Jesus to be referring to himself, since at the trial before the Sanhedrin* they accuse him with the question "Are you the Christ, the Son of the Blessed?" (Mk 15:39; cf. 12:12). Yet they remain ignorant of Jesus' identity as Son of God, for they reject the very idea as a blasphemous claim (see Trial of Jesus).

It is only in Mark 15:39 that the secret of Jesus' status as Son of God is fully revealed to humans. As the centurion faces the cross he declares, "Truly this man was the Son of God." By bringing his Gospel to a climax with this christological confession at the cross, Mark indicates that Jesus is first and foremost Son of God, and that Jesus is Son of God as one who suffers and dies in obedience to God (cf. Mk 14:36). Yet this title relates not only to Jesus' earthly mission, but also to his resurrection (Mk 12:10-11; cf. 9:9) and Second Coming (Mk 8:38; 13:32); for Mark emphasizes that it is precisely Jesus crucified as Son of God who is raised (Mk 16:6) and will return in glory* (Mk 14:61-62).

3.2. Matthew. Although various scholars have seen Matthew's focus in different titles, many today would argue that Son of God is the pre-eminent christological title in Matthew (see Matthew, Gospel of). The First Evangelist retains virtually all of Mark's statements regarding the sonship of Jesus and the fatherhood of God, while adding ten references to Jesus as Son (of God) and forty references to God as Father. According to Matthew's Gospel, Son of God is the only adequate christological confession, and one can come to this understanding of Jesus solely through divine revelation (Mt 16:13-17; cf. 27:51-54).

Although Matthew begins by connecting Jesus' divine sonship to his virginal conception (Mt 1:18-25), he does not develop the notion of the divine nature of Jesus, but focuses instead on more functional aspects of Jesus' sonship. In this Gospel Jesus is Son of God primarily in the sense that he perfectly obeys the will of his Father, especially the will of God that the Messiah must suffer and die.

The emphasis on obedience to the will of the Father appears already in the baptism narrative (Mt 3:13-17). As in Mark, the heavenly voice expresses divine approval. But Matthew goes beyond Mark in stressing the obedience of Jesus: Jesus submits to baptism "to fulfill all righteousness" (Mt 3:15; see Justice, Righteousness); and immediately after the baptism Jesus is tempted in his capacity as Son of God, and as Son of God he refuses to yield to Satan's temptations (Mt 4:1-11; see Temptation of Jesus). Here Jesus is tempted to manifest his divine sonship through the performance of spectacular signs, but chooses instead to demonstrate his sonship through submission to the Father's will.

This reference to temptation indicates that the Matthean Jesus struggles with the will of God regarding the nature of his messianic role. In Matthew 16:22-23 Peter assumes the role of Satan in that he, like Satan in the wilderness temptations, would turn Jesus aside from obedience to the Father's will for the Messiah and would encourage Jesus to construe his sonship in ways other than obedient suffering and death. In Gethsemane Jesus voices his desire to avoid the "cup" of suffering, but as Son of God he yields to the will of his Father (Mt 26:39, 42; *see* Gethsemane). Indeed, Matthew presents the event of the crucifixion as the ultimate temptation for Jesus as well as the climactic expression of his sonship. Jesus is condemned to death on the charge that he claimed to be the Son of God (Mt 26:63). Twice the passers-by tempt Jesus to demonstrate his divine sonship by the sign of coming down from the cross (Mt 27:40, 43). But, as in his earlier temptations, Jesus refuses to yield to such appeals and dies as the righteous one who places his trust in God (Mt 27:43). In response to the obedience of Jesus his Son, God himself provides the signs (Mt 27:51-53), which prompt the centurion to declare, "Truly this was the Son of God" (Mt 27:54).

In addition to this focus on obedience to the will of God, there are three related dimensions to Jesus' divine sonship in Matthew: (1) As Son of God, Jesus knows the Father and his will and has unique authority* to interpret that will (Mt 5:17-48; 7:28-29; 11:25-27). (2) Because Jesus is Son of God his disciples also become sons of God who address God as "Father." Their sonship, like his, is characterized above all by obedience to God's will (Mt 12:50). (3) Because Jesus remained the obedient Son until the end, his Father has given him "all authority in heaven and on earth" (Mt 28:18); he now reigns as Son (Mt 28:19; 24:36) and will return in that capacity (Mt 10:32; 16:27; 25:31-46).

3.3. Luke. The divine sonship of Jesus receives relatively less attention in Luke than in the other Gospels. Luke's allusions to Jesus as Son of God are for the most part taken over from tradition, and in fact Luke omits some references to Jesus' divine sonship found in Mark (Mk 13:32; 15:39). Still, the concept plays a significant role in Luke's Gospel. In fact, some scholars argue that it is the foremost christological title in this Gospel (e.g., Kingsbury).

Luke establishes the basic contours of Jesus' divine sonship in three passages at the beginning of the Gospel. The annunciation to Mary highlights several dimensions of Jesus' divine sonship (Lk 1:32-35). First, Jesus is Son of God as one who has been conceived by the Holy Spirit. Although Luke is moving toward understanding divine sonship in ontological terms (i.e., the divine nature of Jesus), he does little to develop his christology along these lines. Rather, Luke suggests that the conception of Jesus by the Spirit (*see* Holy Spirit) forms the basis of Jesus' intimate personal relationship with God, a theme that stands at the center of the presentation of divine sonship throughout the Gospel (Lk 2:49; 10:21-22). Indeed, by having Jesus address God as "Father" on the cross, Luke indicates that even at that point in Jesus' life his intimate fellowship with God continues unabated (Lk 23:34, 46). Second, as Son of God Jesus inherits the kingdom (*see* Kingdom of God) which God promised to the Son of David, thus pointing to transcendent rule and authority (cf. Lk 22:28-30). Third, as Son of God Jesus is holy, set apart for the special service of bringing salvation* to the people of God (Lk 1:68-69; 2:11; 19:9-10).

The second key passage for understanding Jesus' divine sonship is the genealogy* (3:23-38). The genealogy begins by describing Jesus as the "supposed" son of Joseph, suggesting that he was not actually the son of Joseph, but Son of God through divine conception (Lk 1:32-35). But this statement also points to the mystery of Jesus' divine sonship: God (Lk 3:22; 9:35), the devil (Lk 4:3, 9) and demons (Lk 4:41; 8:28; *see* Demon, Devil, Satan) address Jesus as Son of God, but humans do not. They suppose him to be son of Joseph (Lk 4:22), that is, he is explicable in purely human terms. Consequently, they tend to remain blind to his transcendent power and authority. Moreover, Luke traces the genealogy of Jesus through Adam to God (Lk 3:38), thus indicating that as God's Son Jesus has power to bring all humanity to its destiny as sons of God.

The temptation narrative (Lk 4:1-13) demonstrates that Jesus' divine sonship involves perfect obedience to the will of the Father (Lk 2:49; 23:47) and the exercise of authority over Satan and the forces of evil (Lk 10:17-19; 11:17-23; 13:11-17).

3.4. John. The Fourth Gospel places the divine sonship of Jesus at the center of its christology (*see* John, Gospel of). The Gospel speaks of "Son (of God)" twenty-nine times and refers to God as "Father" over a hundred times. Moreover, John expressly states that the purpose of his Gospel is to confirm his readers in the belief that "Jesus is the Christ, the Son of God" (Jn 20:31). Although John incorporates most of the main elements in the Synoptic presentation of Son of God, his portrait of Jesus' divine sonship is distinct from that found in the Synoptic Gospels.

One of the points of distinction between the Syn-

888888888888

optic portrayal of Jesus as Son of God and that of the Fourth Gospel involves the pre-existence of the Son. While the Synoptics nowhere describe Jesus' sonship in terms of pre-existence, John begins his Gospel by linking the "Word" (logos*), operative at creation, to the Son (Jn 1:1-18); and at subsequent points in the Gospel Jesus Son of God speaks of his pre-incarnate existence (Jn 8:56-58; 17:5, 24). Yet John relates Jesus' divine sonship primarily to his earthly functioning. This Gospel emphasizes that God sent his Son into the world (Jn 3:17; 10:36; 17:18), and that he has come from the Father (Jn 3:31; 6:33-42) and is about to return to the Father (Jn 13:1-3; 14:28; 16:28; 20:17). He thus reflects God's person and glory (Jn 1:14; 14:6-11).

Jesus' role as Son of God is characterized by the following elements. First, Jesus Son of God perfectly obeys the will of his Father (Jn 4:34; 5:30; 6:38; 7:28; 8:29); even his coming into the world reflects his obedience to the Father's will (Jn 8:42). Second, as Son of God Jesus shares the work of the Father (Jn 5:19; 9:4; 10:37), including those tasks belonging uniquely to God: giving life to the dead (Jn 5:21, 24; 6:40) and performing judgment (Jn 5:22, 27-29; 8:16). Indeed, Jesus says nothing except what he has heard from the Father (Jn 3:32-34; 12:49-50; 15:15) and does nothing except what he has seen the Father do (Jn 5:20; 8:38). The works he does are actually the Father's works performed through him (Jn 5:17; 9:4; 10:32). Third, as Son of God Jesus enjoys intimate fellowship with the Father. John describes this intimacy in spatial terms: "in the bosom of the Father" (Jn 1:18). Specifically, this relationship involves (1) "knowing" the Father and his will (Jn 4:22-23; 6:45-47; 8:55; 15:15); (2) sharing in all that the Father has (Jn 16:15); and (3) enjoying special access and influence with the Father (Jn 14:13-16). Fourth, the relationship between the Father and the Son is characterized by love: The Father loves the Son (Jn 3:35; 5:20; 10:17; 17:23) and the Son loves the Father (Jn 14:31). The Father expresses his love for the Son by giving to the Son all things (Jn 3:35; 13:3), especially those who come to the Son (Jn 6:37, 44, 65; 10:29; 17:2).

All of this implies that the divine sonship of Jesus is unique; he is Son of God in a sense not true of anyone else, even believers. John calls attention to this uniqueness by designating Jesus the "only" (monogenēs) Son (Jn 1:14, 18; 3:16) and by constantly employing the absolute forms "the Father" and "the Son." In John's Gospel the disciples are never called "sons," nor do they address God as "Father." Only once is God described as the "Father" of disciples (Jn 20:17), and there the distinction between "my Father" and "your Father" is emphasized.

The proclamation that Jesus is Son of God forces the decision of faith. Persons are called to believe that Jesus is the Son whom God has sent into the world, and the decision they make regarding this call to belief will determine the quality of their present existence as well as their eternal destiny (Jn 3:17-21, 36; 5:24; 11:26). Believing in the Son is the "work" which God requires. This belief involves, specifically, obeying the Son (Jn 3:36), coming to the Son (Jn 14:6) and honoring the Son (Jn 5:23). Such belief will result in salvation (Jn 5:34) and life* (Jn 6:40, 47; 20:31).

See also CHRIST; DIVINE MAN/THEIOS ANER; GOD; SON OF DAVID; SON OF MAN.

BIBLIOGRAPHY. J. Barr, " 'Abba' Isn't 'Daddy,' " *JTS* 39 (1988) 28-47; R. Bauckham, "The Sonship of the Historical Jesus in Christology," *SJT* 31 (1978) 245-60; O. Cullmann, *The Christology of the New Testament* (Philadelphia: Westminster, 1963); J. D. G. Dunn, *Christology in the Making* (Philadelphia: Westminster, 1980); J. Fitzmyer, "The Contribution of Qumran Aramaic to the Study of the New Testament," *NTS* 20 (1973-74) 382-407; F. Hahn, *The Titles of Jesus in Christology* (London: Lutterworth, 1969); J. Jeremias, *The Prayers of Jesus* (Philadelphia: Fortress, 1978); M. de Jonge, *Christology in Context* (Philadelphia: Westminster, 1988); J. D. Kingsbury, *Jesus Christ in Matthew, Mark, and Luke* (Philadelphia: Fortress, 1981); idem, *The Christology of Mark's Gospel* (Philadelphia: Fortress, 1983); I. H. Marshall, *The Origins of New Testament Christology* (rev. ed.; Downers Grove, IL: InterVarsity, 1990); W. von Martitz, "υἱός, υἱοθεσία," *TDNT* VIII.334-40; N. Perrin, *A Modern Pilgrimage in New Testament Christology* (Philadelphia: Fortress, 1974); R. Schnackenburg, *The Gospel according to St. John* (New York: Crossroad, 1987); G. Vermes, *Jesus the Jew* (Philadelphia: Fortress, 1973); B. Witherington, *The Christology of Jesus* (Minneapolis: Fortress, 1990).

D. R. Bauer

SON OF MAN

The person whose name was Jesus (perhaps more closely defined as "Jesus of Nazareth" or as "Jesus the son of Joseph" [Jn 1:46; 6:42] to make clear which holder of the name was meant) is known by various forms of words in the Gospels and the NT generally. To some extent these forms of words are interchangeable, but clearly some of them are used with specific functions and in specific contexts.

The phrase "the Son of man" (*ho huios tou anthropou*) is such a form of words. It is the phrase used more frequently than any other (except "Jesus" itself) to refer to Jesus in the Gospels. It occurs in all four Gospels and only once outside them (Acts 7:56; Heb

2:6 [quoting Ps 8:5] and Rev 1:13; 14:14 [alluding to Dan 7:13] have "a son of man"). Within the Gospels it is found only in sayings ascribed to Jesus; the only clear exception is John 12:34a,b where the people quote Jesus' phrase back at him and ask to whom he is referring.

This evidence shows that "the Son of man" functions as a self-designation of some kind; it never became a way for other people to refer to Jesus, and it thus played no part in the confessional and doctrinal statements of the early church, unlike "Christ,"* "Lord"* and "Son of God."*

1. Usage in the Gospels
2. Jesus and the Son of Man
3. Conclusion

1. Usage in the Gospels.
In what kind of situation is the phrase used? Why does Jesus sometimes say "I" and sometimes "the Son of man"? There is manifestly some flexibility in usage, as is seen by comparing:

Luke 6:22 with Matthew 5:11
Matthew 16:13 with Mark 8:27
Luke 12:8 with Matthew 10:32

1.1. The Gospel of Mark. Broadly speaking, we can trace a pattern in the Gospel of Mark, where the phrase occurs fourteen times (Mk 2:10, 28; 8:31, 38; 9:9, 12, 31; 10:33, 45; 13:26; 14:21a, b, 41, 62).

1.1.1. The Present Authority of Jesus. Jesus speaks of his authority to forgive sins (Mk 2:10) and of his lordship of the Sabbath* (Mk 2:28). In both cases the context makes it clear that it is the authority* of Jesus which is at issue; he exercises it there and then; and it is an authority which would normally belong to God or to somebody authorized by him. It is possible that the phrase might signify "human" in a generic sense (i.e., any particular member of the species; see further below), but it is doubtful whether a Greek reader would take this sense from the phrase.

1.1.2. The Suffering and Resurrection of Jesus. Jesus speaks of the impending suffering, death and resurrection of the Son of man in a series of predictions which emphasize that this must happen in accordance with the Scriptures; he speaks of the mission of the Son of man as being to serve others and to give his life as a ransom for many, and he speaks of himself as the Son of man in references to his impending betrayal and arrest (Mk 8:31; 9:9, 12, 31; 10:33, 45; 14:21a, b, 41; *see* Predictions of Jesus' Passion and Resurrection). The threefold repetition of the prediction in Mark is particularly impressive. The sufferings of Jesus are clearly linked to his role as the Son of man; they are not mentioned explicitly without some

reference to him as the Son of man.

1.1.3. The Future Coming of Jesus. There are three references to a future coming of the Son of man "in clouds with great power and glory" to gather his chosen people and reject (literally "be ashamed of") those who were ashamed of Jesus (*see* Apocalyptic Teaching); this coming is associated with his being seated on the right hand of God (Mk 8:38; 13:26; 14:62). Mark 13:26 and 14:62 are clearly reminiscent of Daniel 7:13-14 where a figure "like a son of man" comes with the clouds of heaven,* appears before God and is given everlasting sovereign power and dominion (*see* Kingdom of God).

Allusions are also made to Psalm 11:1 and possibly to Zechariah 12:10. What is said in other passages in the OT about a future coming of God* himself in judgment* (Zech 14:5) is here attributed to the Son of man as his agent.

1.1.4. The Suffering, Vindicated and Authoritative Son of Man. With this background now coming into focus, it is possible to argue that for Mark the teaching which he attributes to Jesus identifies him as the figure prophesied by Daniel who will come as God's agent to gather his people and act as judge. But already as a human figure Jesus acts with the authority which is inherent in this role. If we ask how the suffering and rejection of the Son of man fit into this picture, two (not necessarily exclusive) answers may be given. The first is that in Daniel 7 the Son of man is seen as the representative of "the saints of the Most High" who suffer defeat and oppression at the hands of their enemies (Dan 7:21, 25). The second is that the language used in Mark 9:12 and 10:45 and in the crucifixion narrative suggests that the Son of man undergoes the experiences of the "righteous sufferer" and the "rejected stone" in the Psalms (Ps 22; 69; 118:22) and the Servant of Yahweh (Is 52:13—53:12; *see* Servant of Yahweh) who suffers but is vindicated by God (*see* Death of Jesus). Thus, not surprisingly, motifs from several OT passages which were regarded as providing the pattern for the destiny of Jesus are coalesced to give a picture of him as the suffering, vindicated and authoritative Son of man.

It also emerges that in Mark, Jesus prefers this way of describing himself to other possibilities. It is notable that, when Jesus is identified as the "Christ" (Mk 8:29-30; 14:61-62; and implicitly in 13:21-22; 9:41 is an exception), he responds by speaking of what "the Son of man" will do. This curious fact suggests that Jesus almost wishes to replace the concept of Messiah (or Christ) by that of the Son of man. The reasons for this are not clear (*see* Mark, Gospel of).

1.2. The Gospel of Matthew. The picture in the other

two Synoptic Gospels is not markedly dissimilar. The phrase is used thirty times by Matthew.

Matthew takes over thirteen of the usages in Mark (Mt 9:6; 12:8; 16:27; 17:9, 12, 22; 20:18, 28, 24:30b; 26:24a, b, 45, 64) and adds it editorially four times (Mt 16:13; 16:28; 24:30a (?); 26:2). He shares it with Luke eight times (Mt 8:20 par. Lk 9:58; Mt 11:19 par. Lk 7:34; Mt 12:32 par. Lk 12:10); Mt 12:40 par. Lk 11:30; Mt 24:27, 37, 39, 44 par. Lk 17:24, 26, 30; 12:40), and it is found in passages peculiar to Matthew five times (Mt 10:23; 13:37, 41; 19:28; 25:31).

Matthew's new uses of the phrase fall into the same general pattern as in Mark. In a series of sayings which he shares with Luke the Son of man is an object of derision for associating with sinners (Mt 11:19) and invites his followers to share his homeless situation (Mt 8:20). There is more detailed teaching on the future coming of the Son of man which will be unexpected and catastrophic for those who are not ready for him (Mt 24:27, 37, 39, 44). The saying, which compares the way in which people treat Jesus now with the way in which they will be treated at the judgment (Mk 8:38 par. Mt 16:27), appears a second time in an expanded form in Luke 12:8-9; but in the corresponding saying in Matthew (10:32-33) the verbal contrast between Jesus and the Son of man is dropped and Jesus speaks of himself in the first person throughout. (Similarly, Mt 5:11 speaks of persecution for the sake of "me," whereas Lk 6:22 has "the Son of man.") Another interesting fact is that a saying which in Mark 3:28 speaks of forgiveness* being extended to the sons of men for their sins and blasphemies except against the Holy Spirit, appears in Luke 12:10 in the form that if a person speaks against the Son of man he will be forgiven but not if he speaks against the Spirit (see Holy Spirit). Matthew 12:31-32 combines these two sayings (by substituting "men" for "the sons of men" in the Markan saying). The way in which the Evangelists understood this saying is debated, but it seems probable that they saw a contrast between speaking against Jesus on earth, when people might be forgiven for not recognizing who he really was, and opposition to the Holy Spirit by people (possibly disciples) when there should be no doubt that to do so was to take sides against God.

In the teaching peculiar to Matthew the Son of man is especially understood as the coming savior (see Salvation) and judge (Mt 13:41; 19:28). In Matthew 10:23 Jesus tells his disciples* that they will not finish the cities of Israel* until the Son of man comes. Matthew may have seen this as a reference to the fall of Jerusalem (see Destruction of Jerusalem) understood as the coming of the Son of man in judgment.

The general tendency in Matthew is thus to emphasize the identity of Jesus as the coming Son of man and as a figure who is rejected on earth.

1.3. The Gospel of Luke. Luke uses the phrase twenty-five times. He has equivalents to nine of the texts in Mark (Lk 5:24; 6:5; 9:22, 26, 44; 18:31; 21:27; 22:22, 69). He has the ten texts from Q* which he shares with Matthew (the eight texts listed above with Lk 6:22 and 12:8). This leaves six occurrences peculiar to Luke (Lk 17:22; 18:8; 19:10; 21:36; 22:48; 24:7). In these fresh sayings we hear of the Son of man's mission to save the lost (Lk 19:10), his betrayal by Judas* (Lk 22:48; cf. Mk 14:21b) and his sufferings and resurrection* (Lk 24:7—a report of what Jesus had said earlier by the two angels* at the tomb), and of his future coming (Lk 17:22; 18:8; 21:36). It is evident that the picture in Luke is very similar to that in the other Gospels. A notable omission by Luke is the ransom saying in Mark 10:45 (see Ransom Saying). There is a similar saying about "service" in Luke 22:27, but it does not use "the Son of man" nor the idea of ransom. Again there is no essential difference from the general picture given in Mark.

1.4. The Gospel of John. When we turn to the Gospel of John we get a picture with similarities and differences. The phrase is used thirteen times. We can readily find references that correspond to those of the passion and resurrection of Jesus in the other Gospels. But in John the reference is to the "lifting up" of the Son of man (*hypsoō*). The verb is ambiguous and can refer to "being lifted up" on a cross or to "being exalted" (Jn 3:14; 8:28; 12:34a, b). Jesus can thus refer to the final events in his life as the glorification (see Glory) of the Son of man (Jn 12:23; 13:31). Jesus also speaks of the authority to judge which has been committed to him as the Son of man (Jn 5:27), and of the power (see Authority and Power) of the Son of man to grant life (Jn 6:27). These functions are summed up in his appeal to the blind man who had been healed (see Healing) to believe in the Son of man (Jn 9:35). And the life-giving function also appears in the reference to eating the flesh of the Son of man (Jn 6:53), a phrase which doubtless reflects the language of the Last Supper (see Last Supper) but stresses the need for a spiritual partaking. Finally, there is the concept of the Son of man coming down from heaven (Jn 3:13) and ascending to where he formerly was (Jn 8:28); linked to this is the difficult saying about the angels ascending and descending on the Son of man (Jn 1:51).

2. Jesus and the Son of Man.

It is clear that the expression is used in much the same

way in each of the Synoptic Gospels but that in John it is used in a wider manner. The crucial question is to what extent this usage corresponds with that of Jesus himself. We have already seen that the Evangelists can add the expression to their sources or subtract it from them. But much more far-reaching questions have been raised by modern scholarship concerning the origin of the phrase.

2.1. Son of Man and Messiah? Some scholars dispute whether Jesus expressed verbally any consciousness of being the Messiah or a messianic type of figure. It would follow that he could not have used "the Son of man" as a messianic self-designation. Or, it is claimed, Messiah and Son of man represent two different types of figure and, if Jesus identified himself as the former, he could not have identified himself also with the latter (*see* Christ).

Both of these claims are very doubtful. The evidence that Jesus acted in messianic ways is convincing: why otherwise did his followers recognize him as the Messiah? This makes the view that he could not have referred to himself in a messianic fashion most improbable. Further, while it is true that the traditional Jewish Messiah is an earthly figure, whereas the Son of man has transcendent features, the role assigned to the latter is messianic in that he is given dominion and authority as the representative of God's people. This indicates, incidentally, that the claim that the Son of man is not associated with the kingdom of God in Judaism* is without foundation.

2.2. Present and/or Future Son of Man? It has been observed that in those sayings where Jesus talks about the future activity of the Son of man, he is not necessarily talking about himself, and that in one or two sayings (Mk 8:38 par. Lk 12:8-9; Mk 14:62) there appears to be a distinction drawn between Jesus, presently active on earth, and the Son of man, active in the future at the last judgment. On the assumption that the early church would not have created such a distinction, it is argued that such sayings have strong claims to authenticity. It is then further argued that originally Jesus envisaged the Son of man as a figure distinct from himself. It then follows that sayings which identify Jesus as the Son of man must either be compositions by the early church or have had the phrase added to them at a later stage. If this argument is valid, it fits in with the view that Jesus did not refer to himself in messianic terms.

Despite the wide popularity of this view among scholars influenced by R. Bultmann, it cannot be upheld. Essentially, the claim is being made that the future Son of man sayings have been reinterpreted by the early church to refer to Jesus. But there are various arguments against this view.

The crucial sayings (Mk 8:38 par. Lk 12:8-9; Mk 14:62) can be interpreted much more naturally as sayings in which Jesus draws a contrast between himself as a figure whose authority is not recognized and the Son of man as a figure whose authority cannot be gainsaid. The apparently odd switch from the first person to the third person is to be explained by the incorporation of an allusion to Daniel 7:13-14.

The theory requires that the authenticity of a very large number of occurrences of the expression as self-designations of Jesus be surrendered for no better reason than that they stand in conflict with a couple of texts whose interpretation in terms of another coming figure is highly uncertain. The fact that in so many other texts "Son of man" cannot be other than a self-designation must seriously damage the claim that the "future" texts originally spoke of a figure other than Jesus.

2.3. Son of Man As a Self-Designation of Jesus. Two lines of argument raise the question whether Jesus could have used "the Son of man" as a title to refer to himself.

2.3.1. The Interpretation of Daniel 7. In the vision of Daniel there appear four great beasts like various animals and a figure "like a son of man." This last phrase should undoubtedly be translated "like a man" (so NEB). The Aramaic phrase is used to designate a particular member of a species, and (as in Hebrew) "man" and "son of man" can be used interchangeably to refer to an individual. The force of *like* is that the figure is not a man but is like a man, just as the beasts are "like" different animals. In the interpretation of Daniel's vision the beasts represent four kingdoms and (implicitly) the manlike figure stands for "the saints of the Most High," the (faithful) people of Israel. It can therefore be argued that the manlike figure is a symbol for a collective entity. On the other hand, it is equally plausible that the manlike figure stands for the ruler of God's people, just as the beasts appear to represent both kingdoms and their rulers. There is no doubt that in subsequent interpretation the manlike figure was regarded as a messianic individual. This is true of *1 Enoch* 37—71 and also of 4 Ezra 13 (where the actual phrase is not used, but the dependence on Dan 7 is clear). Nevertheless, it can be argued that in no sense is "a (son of) man" a title in Daniel 7.

2.3.2. Son of Man As an Aramaic Idiom of Self-Reference. There is a further idiom involving the use of the phrase "son of man." It occurs in a number of Aramaic texts with the sense of "an individual man" but with some kind of reference to the speaker (*see*

Languages of Jesus). The precise way in which this happens is debated.

(1) It has been argued that the phrase is used to make statements that are true of people in general and therefore of the speaker in particular (M. Casey). It is thus a kind of self-designation, but what is said is not true exclusively of the speaker. (For example, in the Palestinian Targum* Cain says: "Behold thou hast cast me forth this day on the face of the ground, and from before you, Lord, it is not possible for the son of man [*bar nāš*] to hide.")

(2) It has also been claimed that a speaker could use this expression to make statements that were true of himself in particular (G. Vermes). Against this interpretation it is argued that in every case cited a general or generic reference is possible. The idiom in fact seems to have arisen out of the use of the phrase to mean "a man" and hence "any man" to refer to the speaker, inasmuch as he is a man.

(3) However, there are cases where the reference is manifestly not to "everybody" but to people in a particular class, and therefore it is more accurate to say that it refers to such people, a group to which the speaker belongs (B. Lindars). (Thus: "When E. Hiyya ben Adda died . . . R. Levi received his valuables. This was because his teacher used to say: 'The disciple of *bar nāšâ* is as dear to him as his son.' " Here the expression plainly refers to the group of teachers.) It is suggested that the idiom was used as a form of self-reference in cases where the speaker wished to show modesty or to speak of matters (such as his own death) which were distasteful—in any case in sayings where he wished to avoid speaking directly in the first person.

2.4. Evaluating the Options. The current opinion seems to favor view (3) as the appropriate explanation of the idiom. Those who hold this view then argue that there are a number of sayings in the Gospels which can be understood as examples of this usage. Jesus says something which is true of himself inasmuch as it is true of a group of people to whom he belongs.

2.4.1. Analyzing the statements as idiomatic self-references, Casey, Lindars and Vermes (the three major scholars who have done work in this area) have each determined which Son of man sayings are authentic. Their results may be compared in the following table.

Vermes has the largest number of authentic sayings because he includes sayings that are true only of the speaker (Jesus). His selection, as with that of Casey and Lindars, is reached by rejecting the sayings which reflect the influence of Daniel 7. Casey and Lindars

		Casey	Lindars	Vermes	Comments
Mark	2:10	*	*	*	
	2:28	*		*	
	8:31			*	(Mark only)
	8:38	*			
	9:9			*	
	9:12	*		*	
	9:31		*	*	(Lindars: core only)
	10:33			*	
	10:45	*	*	*	(Lindars: v.45b)
	14:21a,b	*	*	*	(Lindars: v. 21a)
	14:41			*	
Matthew	8:20	*	*	*	(par. Lk 9:58 Q)
	11:19	*	*	*	(par. Lk 7:34 Q)
	16:13			*	(diff. Mk 8:31)
	26:22			*	
Luke	11:30		*	*	(par. Mt 12:40 Q)
	12:8	*	*		(diff. Mt 10:32 Q)
	12:10	*	*	*	(diff. Mt 12:32 Q)
	19:10			*	
	22:48	*			
	24:7			*	

agree substantially in their more limited selection.

There are instances where the Casey/Lindars approach to the sayings is plausible. Mark 2:10 could mean that there is a class of people with authority to forgive, including Jesus. (But the people comment with surprise that no human can forgive sins; only God can do so.) In Mark 2:28 the Sabbath is made for humanity, and therefore people in general, including Jesus, have authority over it. In Matthew 11:18 Casey finds a group of people, including Jesus, who eat and drink with tax collectors (*see* Taxes) and sinners* and who are attacked by the Pharisees.* (But the text seems to be comparing two individuals.) In Matthew 8:20 Jesus says that there is a group of people, including his disciples and himself, who have no homes, and therefore a prospective disciple must expect the same situation. This is the most cogent example, but it must be observed that Jesus could be saying that, if he himself as a messianic figure is rejected, so too will his disciples be (cf. the identical argument in Mt 10:25b; Jn 15:18, 20b). The other examples lack all cogency.

2.4.2. The effect of the approach in question is to deny that Jesus thought of himself in terms of the Son of man of Daniel 7. According to Lindars, "it carried no christological meaning as such" (Lindars, 170). Jesus remains a figure possessed of some authority, totally committed to his vocation, a prophet who believes that to speak against him is to speak against God, and by their response to him people will stand or fall at the last judgment.

However, the fact that the Lindars/Casey theory simply fails to work, in that it can credibly explain such a tiny handful of sayings, must raise serious doubts about it. There is more to be said for Vermes's understanding of the sayings, according to which Jesus used the idiom to speak of himself with modesty or to avoid a direct reference to his own death.

2.5. According to C. Colpe some of the sayings are generic. That is, Mark 2:10 comments on the fact that Jesus, as a human, can forgive; in Matthew 11:18-19 John is contrasted with "a human," namely Jesus. And in Matthew 8:20 Jesus says that even animals have dens but a human such as he, Jesus, has nowhere to lay his head (Colpe, 430-33). What appears to be essentially the same view is upheld by R. Bauckham who thinks that the phrase is used indefinitely rather than generically to mean "somebody, a person," and that it could then be used as an oblique self-reference.

We are left with a problem in that the Aramaic usage remains unclear. But it is arguable that the sayings in the Gospels are evidence that the underlying Aramaic phrase could have been used on occasion to refer to the speaker only.

This leaves us with a number of sayings where the allusion to Daniel 7 is clear. J. Dunn has suggested that Jesus began by using the Aramaic idiom to refer to himself and then recognized in the use of the same phrase in Daniel 7 an allusion to the vindication which he expected from God. This led to the use of Daniel 7 on a broader scale in his sayings, and to the development of the term as a means of referring to himself as the authoritative messianic figure. Thus, in some sayings Jesus will simply have used a self-designation, but in others he was making a conscious allusion to Daniel 7. No doubt early Christians would have understood most if not all of his sayings as references to himself as the figure of Daniel 7. The point is that not all uses of the term would necessarily have conveyed the same sense on the lips of Jesus.

To adopt this position is not necessarily to claim that all occurrences of the phrase or all the texts in which it occurs are authentic sayings of Jesus as they stand. We have to reckon with the activity of the Evangelists in adding the phrase (and also in replacing it by a personal pronoun or other equivalent; see the examples cited above). It is also possible that

similar activity took place even before the writing of the Gospels.

One particular problem is raised by Mark 3:28-29 and its parallels (Mt 12:31-33; Lk 12:10). It seems certain that we have two variant forms of the same basic saying. The hypothetical original said that there was forgiveness available for sins and blasphemies for/against "the son of man." Mark's tradition took this to mean forgiveness for humankind (collective use), but the Q tradition took it to refer to blasphemies against the man (Jesus). On this view, the Markan tradition understood the Aramaic phrase in a way that was probably not the meaning as originally intended, but, although the reference to blasphemy against Jesus dropped out, it was implicitly included in that the saying promised forgiveness of all blasphemies except those against the Spirit. In its Aramaic form, the saying probably did not refer to Jesus as "the [Danielic] Son of man," and therefore the problem detected by modern readers as to what is the difference between speaking against the Son of man and against the Holy Spirit disappears. It is one thing to speak against Jesus under the humble appearance of a man, but it is another thing to speak against the manifest work of the Spirit (in Jesus or in anybody else).

3. Conclusion.

It emerges that two things happen in the Son of man texts.

3.1. Son of Man As Divine and Human. On the one hand, there is the phrase itself and the associations it would have for hearers and readers. In the Gospels as we have them, it points the reader to the figure in Daniel 7 who is a person with sovereign authority, a messianic figure, identified in *1 Enoch* and 4 Ezra with the Messiah, God's Son and Elect One. Such a figure would be seen as in some sense divine in that he comes from heaven, and the description of him in Daniel 7 could be taken as an apotheosis, or "deification." He would be associated with the people of God, and in that sense the Son of man can be regarded as a corporate figure. (But the view that "Son of man" is a symbol for a corporate group which then becomes individualized in Jesus is to be rejected.) His associates are bound up with his destiny. But it must be emphasized that it is doubtful whether all of these associations would be present for the original hearers of Jesus and would have been intended by him every time he used the phrase. It is because of this dual origin of the phrase that it can be used to refer both to the humanity of Jesus and also to his divine origin. Jesus can use the term to refer to himself as a human over against God (Mk 2:10, 28), but also to indicate his divine origin. In the latter case "Son of man" is a veiled way of expressing his relationship to God (Kim).

3.2. The Son of Man's Mission. On the other hand, this self-designation becomes the vehicle for teaching about the activity and fate of Jesus. He appears in the Synoptic Gospels as a figure of authority on earth who is not accepted by many people. He has a divinely ordained destiny, expressed in the Scriptures, which involves betrayal, rejection, suffering, death and resurrection. He has a future role in which he "comes" and brings salvation and judgment. In the Gospel of John there is greater stress laid on the fact that he comes from God and returns to be with him.

3.3. Son of Man As Jesus' Self-Designation. When Jesus refers to his own role, he adopts this term rather than "Messiah" or "Son of God." After the resurrection it never entered into Christian usage as a way of referring to Jesus or as a confessional term (not even in Jn 9:35-36 is it actually used by a believer; Acts 7:56 is a unique usage, probably a deliberate echo of Jesus' own words). It was recognized as a self-designation, and it was replaced by other terms which expressed its significance with greater clarity. It was in any case a term which would not have been meaningful for non-Jews. Since modern readers on the whole do not pick up the original nuances of the term (whether as a self-designation or as an allusion to Dan 7), the example of the early church in not using it remains valid for today. There is indeed a grave danger of using "Son of man" as a means of referring to the humanity of Jesus, as opposed to his divinity (expressed by "Son of God"), whereas in fact the Danielic background suggests a figure closely associated with the Ancient of Days.

We may conclude that in Aramaic "Son of man" was not a title but a self-designation used in certain specific contexts. Jesus used it in this way. However, in Daniel 7 the phrase was used nontechnically to refer to somebody "like a man," and hence the phrase came to be a means of reference to the person so described. Jesus took over this sense of the phrase, and thus identified his role with that of the figure in Daniel 7. Consequently, the phrase came to be used as a title of dignity for Jesus, although the memory of the fact that the idiom was used as a self-designation prevented it from being taken over by his followers.

See also CHRIST; KINGDOM OF GOD; LORD; SERVANT OF YAHWEH; SON OF DAVID; SON OF GOD.

BIBLIOGRAPHY. R. J. Bauckham, "The Son of Man: 'A Man in my Position' or 'Someone,' " *JSNT* 2 (1985) 23-33 (with a reply by B. Lindars, ibid. 35-41); C. C. Caragounis, *The Son of Man* (WUNT 38; Tübingen:

J. C. B. Mohr, 1986); M. Casey, *Son of Man* (London: SPCK, 1979); idem, "General, Generic and Indefinite: The Use of the Term 'Son of Man' in Aramaic Sources and in the Teaching of Jesus," *JSNT* 29 (1987) 21-56; C. Colpe, "ὁ υἱός τοῦ ἀνθρώπου," *TDNT* VIII.400-77; J. D. G. Dunn, *Christology in the Making* (Philadelphia: Westminster, 1980); S. Kim, *The Son of Man As the Son of God* (Grand Rapids: Eerdmans, 1983); B. Lindars, *Jesus Son of Man* (Grand Rapids: Eerdmans, 1983); H. E. Tödt, *The Son of Man in the Synoptic Tradition* (Philadelphia: Westminster, 1965); G. Vermes, *Jesus the Jew* (New York: Harper, 1973).

I. H. Marshall

SONSHIP. *See* SON OF GOD.

SOURCE CRITICISM. *See* SYNOPTIC PROBLEM.

SPIRIT. *See* HOLY SPIRIT.

SPIRITS. *See* DEMON, DEVIL, SATAN.

SUFFERING. *See* DEATH OF JESUS.

SUFFERING SERVANT. *See* SERVANT OF YAHWEH.

SWEARING. *See* OATHS AND SWEARING.

SWORD. *See* PEACE.

SYMPOSIUM. *See* TABLE FELLOWSHIP.

SYNAGOGUE

The regular Jewish assembly for prayer* and worship.* Jesus is depicted as teaching and performing miracles* in synagogues in Galilee* (Mt 4:23; Lk 4:15), especially in Nazareth (Mt 13:54; Mk 6:2; Lk 4:16) and in Capernaum (Mk 1:21; Lk 7:5; Jn 6:59). The synagogue in the latter city was probably built by the centurion (Lk 7:5), whose servant Jesus healed (*see* Healing).

1. Names and Origin
2. Offices
3. Services and Other Activities
4. Remains of Buildings
5. Interior

1. Names and Origin.

"Synagogue" is a word derived from the Greek *synagōgē*, which meant originally an assembly such as of the Jews meeting for worship. In the Septuagint it is used, for example, in Exodus 12:3 of the whole congregation of Israel. It came to mean local gatherings of Jews and then the building where Jewish congregations met. Especially after the destruction of the Temple* in Jerusalem in A.D. 70, synagogues became the centers of both religious and communal activity wherever there was a *minyan*, or quorum, of ten Jewish men. The Talmud claimed that there were 480 synagogues in Jerusalem before A.D. 70. The Pilgrim of Bordeaux (fourth cent. A.D.) reported but seven left in his day.

The Greek word *proseuchē*, literally "prayer," was also used as a synonym for synagogues in inscriptions, papyri, Philo and Josephus.* Whether the occurrence of this word in Acts 16:13 designates a synagogue or a prayer meeting at Philippi is a matter of dispute. Another Greek word used in one papyrus for a Jewish place of prayer is the term *eucheion*. In one passage Josephus (*Ant.* 16.6.2 §164) quotes the term *sabbateion* to mean "synagogue." In later Hebrew tradition the synagogue was called variously *bêṭ tᵉp̄illâ*, "house of prayer"; *bêṭ midrāš*, "house of study"; and *bêṭ kᵉnēsseṭ*, "house of assembly."

Though a few scholars (e.g., J. Weingreen) have stressed the pre-exilic roots of the synagogue, most would ascribe its rise to the postexilic period. Many would place this development in the Jewish exilic community in Mesopotamia.

The earliest possible inscriptional evidences are references to *proseuchē* in inscriptions and papyri from Ptolemaic Egypt (E. Schürer), the earliest of which dates to the reign of Ptolemy III Euergetes (246-221 B.C.). This text refers to the foundation of a *proseuchē* at Schedia some twenty miles from Alexandria. Another text from the same reign refers to a *proseuchē* at Arsinoë-Crocodilopolis in the Fayum. The existence of a synagogue at this town is also confirmed by a land survey (P. Tebt. 86). An inscription from Ptolemy VII (145-17 B.C.) refers to the dedication of "the pylon," the monumental gate, of a synagogue (Griffiths, 10).

Some scholars who dispute the interpretation of references to these *proseuchai* in Egypt as synagogues, maintain that the synagogues as an institution developed in Palestine in the second century B.C. with the rise of the Pharisees* (J. Gutmann).

2. Offices.
Jairus, whose daughter Jesus healed (Mk 5:22, 35, 36, 38; Lk 8:49), was the head of the synagogue (Gk *archisynagōgos*). Luke 8:41 has Jairus listed as one of the *archōn tēs synagōgēs*, "leaders of the synagogue"; Matthew 9:23 refers to him simply as an *archōn*. From Luke 13:10-17 and from passages in Acts (18:1-17), we

can infer that such an officer was responsible for keeping the congregation faithful to the Torah.

The relative esteem in which the "head of the synagogue" was held in Jewish society is revealed in a passage from the Talmud (*b. Pesaḥ* 49b): "Our rabbis taught: Let a man always sell all he has and marry the daughter of a scholar. If he does not find the daughter of a scholar, let him marry the daughter of [one of] the great men of the generation. If he does not find the daughter of [one of] the great men of the generation, let him marry the daughter of a head of a synagogue. If he does not find the daughter of a head of a synagogue, let him marry the daughter of a charity treasurer. If he does not find the daughter of a charity treasurer, let him marry the daughter of an elementary school teacher, but let him not marry the daughter of an 'am hāʾāreṣ ("people of the land") because they are detestable and of their daughters it is said, 'Cursed be the one who lies with any manner of beast' (Deut 27:21)."

The word *archisynagōgos* appears in thirty Greek and Latin inscriptions. In three cases from Smyrna and Myndos in western Turkey and from Gortyn on Crete the term is used of women. B. Brooten has argued that these and other titles (*presbytera*, "elder," *hiereia*, "priestess") were not just honorific but referred to women leaders. One inscription to an infant as an *archisynagōgos* was certainly honorific.

A group of elders* would direct the activities of the synagogue. The *archisynagōgos* was probably chosen from among them. An almoner would collect and distribute alms. The *ḥazzān*, or "attendant," was the one who took care of the Scripture scrolls. Jesus gave back the Isaiah scroll to such an attendant (Gk *hypēretē*, Lk 4:20). The *ḥazzān* also announced the beginning and the end of the Sabbath by blowing the *šôp̄ār*, or ram's horn. In later practice the *ḥazzān* was paid and lodged at the synagogue as a caretaker.

3. Services and Other Activities.
We know that the later synagogue services included such features as the recitation of the Šᵉmaʿ ("Hear O hear," Deut 6:4-9; 11:13-21; Num 15:37-41), prayer facing Jerusalem, the "Amen" response from the congregation, the reading of excerpts from the scrolls of the Torah (Acts 15:21) and of the Prophets, translation of the Scriptures into Aramaic paraphrases, a sermon and a benediction (cf. Neh 8).

It became customary to recite while standing the Šᵉmoneh 'Eśrēh, or "Eighteen Benedictions," as a prayer. Toward the end of the first century A.D. a nineteenth was added, which was actually a curse against the *mînîm*, or heretics, namely the Christians.

Any male could be called upon to pray or to read the portions from the Torah or the Prophets (*haptārôt*). On one occasion Jesus read from the scroll of the prophet Isaiah (61:1-2) in the synagogue at Nazareth. Any competent individual could also be called upon to give the sermon (cf. Acts 13:15, 42; 14:1; 17:2).

Jesus refers to the custom of the teachers of the Law* and the Pharisees* sitting in Moses'* seat (Mt 23:2). Such a seat of honor has been found at Chorazin. Stone benches along the walls were reserved for dignitaries. The general congregation may have sat on mats or carpets.

Though synagogues in the Middle Ages had segregated galleries for women,* there is no evidence for such segregation in ancient synagogues. In the NT the presence of women in the congregation is attested inasmuch as Jesus healed a crippled woman as he was teaching in a synagogue (Lk 13:10-17).

As the major community building, the synagogues were not only used for services on the Sabbath,* Mondays, Thursdays and festival days, but also for various community functions. Children would be taught there by the *hazzān*. Funds could be kept in a communal treasury at the synagogue.

Offenders could be judged before the elders in the synagogues and flogged forty stripes save one by the *hazzān* (Mk 13:9; 2 Cor 11:24). Apostates could be excommunicated (Jn 9:22; 12:42; 16:2).

4. Remains of Buildings.

It is estimated that we have archeological remains for over one hundred synagogue sites from Palestine and for about twenty from the Diaspora. There are relatively few archeological evidences for synagogues in Palestine from either the first or the second century A.D. An inscription of Theodotus from Jerusalem, which has usually been dated prior to A.D. 70, refers to the establishment of a hostel for pilgrims and may possibly be related to the synagogue of the Freedmen (i.e., former slaves, Acts 6:9). It reads as follows: "Theodotus, son of Vettenos, the priest and *archisynagōgos*, son of a *archisynagōgos* and grandson of a *archisynagōgos*, who built the synagogue for purposes of reciting the law and studying the commandments, and the hostel, chambers and water installations to provide for the needs of itinerants from abroad, and whose father, with the elders, and Simonides, founded the synagogue."

A building (12 x 15 m.) at the Herodian fortress of Masada has been identified as a first-century synagogue by Y. Yadin. It is equipped with benches and two rows of columns. The building's entrance was oriented toward Jerusalem. Yadin found an ostracon

with the inscription "priestly tithe" at the site. He argues that Herod had originally constructed the building as a synagogue for his Jewish followers. The Herodian building was later reused by the Zealots until the fall of Masada in 73 A.D. to the Romans. Pits in this building served as a *genîzâ*, or storage, for discarded Scriptural scrolls (Deuteronomy and Ezekiel). Nearby were *miqwā'ōt*, or stepped pools, for ritual purification.

A *triclinium* (dining room) at Herodium was transformed into a synagogue by the Zealots. The building measures 10.5 x 15 m. with benches along the walls. A *miqwâ* is near the entrance. This building is similar in appearance to that at Masada. S. Guttman believes that a building at Gamla in the Golan heights, which he uncovered in 1976, is also a first century A.D. synagogue.

But the alleged synagogue uncovered at Magdala in 1975 by V. Corbo and S. Loffreda has turned out to be part of a villa. No remains are visible from a first-century building excavated at Chorazin and identified by some scholars as a synagogue. The basalt synagogue which is visible at Chorazin is from a much later period. (In the Diaspora a building on the Aegean island of Delos has been identified as a synagogue dating from pre-Christian times.)

The most splendid synagogue remains in Palestine are those of the white limestone structure at Capernaum. On the basis of coins the Franciscan excavators have dated this building to the fourth or fifth century A.D.; Israeli scholars still prefer to date it to the second or third century. In 1981 V. Corbo uncovered dark basalt walls underneath this synagogue, which he has identified as the remains of an earlier synagogue. He dug a trench within the nave and exposed a basalt wall for a length of 24 m. (78 ft.). The walls are nearly four feet thick. The floor was a cobbled pavement made up of black basalt. Pottery associated with the floor establishes its date as the first century A.D. Corbo has identified this structure as the synagogue, built by the centurion, which Jesus attended (Lk 7:1-5). (See J. F. Strange and H. Shanks.)

No certain synagogue remains from the second century have been identified except for those at Nabratein, though Catholic excavators have claimed to have discovered a synagogue of "Jewish Christians" (third-fourth cent.) at the site of the Church of the Annunciation in Nazareth. They also identify several architectural fragments from the Franciscan monastery in Nazareth as derived from a synagogue (second-third cent.).

Most synagogue remains are from the Late Roman and Byzantine eras (A.D. 300-600), including about fifteen from Galilee and a similar number from the Golan Heights. The synagogues are of three architectural types: (1) Broad House, with the bema, or platform, on the southern long wall such as at Khirbet Shema; (2) the Basilica type, as at Capernaum and Chorazin; (3) the Basilica with an apse at Beth Alpha.

5. Interior.

These later synagogues were elaborately decorated with symbols such as the lampstand (*m^e nôrâ*), palm frond and citron. They were provided with a bema, or platform, for the reading of the Scriptures, and a niche for the display of the ark or chest (*'ᵃrôn*) for the biblical scrolls. In 1980 E. and C. Meyers discovered the fragment of such an ark niche from Nabratein. This pediment is decorated with reliefs of rampant lions, and a scallop shell with a hole for the chain of a perpetual lamp.

Many of the Byzantine synagogues were lavishly decorated with mosaics, including four mosaics of the zodiac at Hammath Tiberias, Beth Alpha, Na'aran and Husifa. The mosaic at Hammath Tiberias has a central panel with *Helios* (sun) on his chariot and figures reflecting the four seasons at the corners.

We also have three examples of lists of the twenty-four priestly courses (*mišmārôṭ*), which hung in synagogues. Most synagogue inscriptions are of donors. The third-century A.D. synagogue at Dura Europos on the Euphrates River even had paintings on its walls depicting biblical narratives.

Because of the scant remains of synagogues from first-century A.D. Palestine, some scholars have argued that Luke-Acts is anachronistic when it refers to synagogue buildings. But this is to underestimate the fragmentary nature of the archeological evidence and to disregard not only the testimony of the New Testament but also of Josephus (*Life* 277, 280), who speaks of a *proseuchē* which was a large building at Tiberia (cf. also Jos. *J.W.* 2.14.4 § 285; *Ant.* 14.10.23 § 258; 19.6.3 § 300). Philo's report of the anti-Semitic mob's attacks on *proseuchas* in Alexandria in A.D. 38 (*Leg. Gai.* 132) clearly refers to synagogue buildings.

See also JUDAISM; TEMPLE; WORSHIP.

BIBLIOGRAPHY. B. Brooten, *Women Leaders in the Ancient Synagogue* (Chico: Scholars, 1982); M. J. S. Chiat, *Handbook of Synagogue Architecture* (Chico: Scholars, 1982); L. L. Grabbe, "Synagogues in Pre-70 Palestine," *JTS* n.s. 39 (1988) 401-10; J. G. Griffiths, "Egypt and the Rise of the Synagogue," *JTS* n.s. 38 (1987) 1-15; J. Gutmann, ed., *Ancient Synagogues: The State of Research* (Chico: Scholars, 1981); idem, ed., *The Synagogue: Studies in Origins, Archaeology and Architecture* (New York: KTAV, 1975); M. Hengel, "Proseuche und Synagoge," in *Tradition und Glaube: Festgabe für Karl Georg Kuhn,* ed. G. Jeremias, H. W. Kuhn, and H. Stegemann (Güttingen: Vandenhoeck & Ruprecht, 1971) 157-84; F. Huttenmeister and G. Reeg, *Die antiken Synagogen in Israel* (2 vols.; Wiesbaden: L. Reichert, 1977); L. Levine, ed., *Ancient Synagogues Revealed* (Jerusalem: Israel Exploration Society, 1981); idem, *The Synagogue in Late Antiquity* (Philadelphia: American Schools of Oriental Research, 1987); I. Levinskaya, "A Jewish or Gentile Prayer House? The Meaning of ΠΡΟΣΕΥΞΗ," *TynB* 41 (1990) 154-59; E. M. Meyers, "Synagogues of Galilee," *Archaeology* 35.3 (1985) 51-58; E. Schürer, *The History of the Jewish People in the Age of Jesus,* rev. and ed. G. Vermes et al. (Edinburgh: T. & T. Cark, 1979) II.423-54; H. Shanks, *Judaism in Stone: The Archaeology of Ancient Synagogues* (New York: Harper & Row, 1979); J. F. Strange and H. Shanks, "Synagogue Where Jesus Preached Found at Capernaum," *BAR* 9.6 (1983) 24-31; J. Weingreen, "The Origin of the Synagogue," *Hermathena* 98 (1964) 68-84; Y. Yadin, *Masada* (New York: Random House, 1966).

E. Yamauchi

SYNOPTIC PROBLEM

In reading the four Gospels it is apparent that three of them resemble one another and one does not. A brief time spent in any synopsis of the Gospels will indicate that Matthew, Mark and Luke share a number of striking similarities. The "Synoptic Problem" is the name that has been given to the problem of why the Gospels of Matthew, Mark and Luke look so much alike. Why are they so similar in content, in wording and in the order of events found within them?

1. The Similarity of the Synoptic Gospels
2. The Existence of a Literary Relationship
3. Various Literary Explanations
4. The Griesbach Hypothesis
5. The Two-Document Hypothesis
6. Problems with the Two-Document Hypothesis
7. The Value of the Solution of the Synoptic Problem

1. The Similarity of the Synoptic Gospels.

1.1 Similarity in Wording.

The similarity of wording can easily be seen by comparing various parallel accounts found in these Gospels. This is best done by the use of a synopsis. Some helpful passages to compare are:

Matthew 19:13-15	Mark 10:13-16	Luke 18:15-17
Matthew 22:23-33	Mark 12:18-27	Luke 20:27-40
Matthew 24:4-8	Mark 13:5-8	Luke 21:8-11

1.2. Similarity in Order. Another area of similarity can be found when one compares the order of the various accounts (pericopes). Note:

Matthew 16:13—20:34	Mark 8:27—10:52	Luke 9:18-51/18:15-43
Matthew 12:46—13:58	Mark 3:31—6:6a	Luke 8:19-56

1.3. Similarity in Parenthetical Material. There also exists common parenthetical material. Note for example: "let the reader understand" in Matthew 24:15 and Mark 13:14; "he then said to the paralytic" in Matthew 9:6/Mark 2:10/Luke 5:24; "For he had said . . ." in Mark 5:8/Luke 8:29.

1.4. Similarity in Biblical Quotations. At times we find the exact same form of an OT quotation (*see* Old Testament in the Gospels). This would not be unusual if that form was identical either with the Hebrew OT or the Greek translation of the OT known as the Septuagint, but when we find an identical quotation of the OT which is different from both the Hebrew OT and the Greek OT, this similarity requires some sort of explanation (cf. Mk 1:2 par. Mt 3:3 and Lk 3:4; Mk 7:7 par. Mt 15:9).

2. The Existence of a Literary Relationship.

There have been various ways in which people have sought to explain the similarities mentioned above. One attempt has been to explain their similarity as due to the inspiration of the Gospels. The similarity is due to the Holy Spirit* (*see* Holy Spirit) having guided Matthew, Mark and Luke. Such an explanation, however, does not really solve the problem, for those who posit this explanation usually maintain that the Gospel of John was also inspired. Yet John does not look like the Synoptics. If all four Gospels were written under the superintendence of the Holy Spirit, this superintendence cannot at the same time explain why some Gospels look alike and why another does not.

A second attempt to explain this similarity involves the argument from history. Matthew, Mark and Luke look alike because they are accurate historical records of what Jesus said and did. Without denying that the Synoptic Gospels do provide an accurate account of what Jesus said and did, it must be pointed out that at times we find a different ordering of the events and a different wording. In these instances are we to assume that the sayings and incidents are not historical? An incident in Jesus' ministry could be recounted correctly in different ways and in association with various events. Furthermore, a saying of Jesus in his native tongue, which was Aramaic, could be translated into Greek in several different ways (*see* Languages of Palestine).

These two explanations do not explain adequately the kind of similarities we find in the Synoptic Gospels. Some other explanation must be sought. As early as 1796 J. G. von Herder sought to explain the Synoptic Problem by positing a common oral tradition used by Matthew, Mark and Luke. This explanation was developed more fully by J. K. L. Gieseler in 1818. According to this explanation the disciples* created this oral tradition which soon became fixed in form. Some time after it was translated into Greek, this common tradition was used by the Synoptic writers. Thus Matthew, Mark and Luke look alike because they all follow the exact same oral tradition.

There is little doubt that there was a period when the Gospel traditions circulated orally. Whether there ever was a period in which these traditions circulated only orally, how long that period lasted, the extent to which Matthew, Mark and Luke were influenced by the oral tradition, etc., have not been and may never be resolved. But can this explanation elucidate adequately the degree of similarity found in the Synoptic Gospels? This does not appear to be the case. At times the degree of similarity seems to require more than just a common oral tradition. More importantly, a common oral tradition is not able to explain the similar editorial comments which we find. Why do we find in the exact same location a word from the writer to his audience— "let the reader understand" (Mt 24:15/Mk 13:14)? Even more difficult for this explanation is the extensive agreement in the order of the material. Thus, although one does not want to minimize the influence of a common oral tradition upon the writers of the Gospels, it would appear that the similarities we encounter require the existence of some sort of a literary relationship.

3. Various Literary Explanations.

If a literary relationship exists between the Synoptic Gospels, then the next question that must be investigated is the nature of that literary relationship. One explanation, originating with F. Schleiermacher (1817), suggested that the disciples had taken notes (memorabilia) of Jesus' words and deeds. These eventually were collected and arranged topically. From these collected memorabilia the Synoptic Gospels arose. This "fragmentary hypothesis" never received much support, for like the oral hypothesis it was not able to explain the extensive agreements in order.

Another theory is that of a so-called Ur-Gospel ("primitive" or "original" Gospel). According to G. E. Lessing (1776) and J. G. Eichhorn (1796), there existed an early written Gospel in Aramaic. This was translated into Greek and went through several revisions. The similarities we find in the Synoptic Gospels are due to the common use of a Greek translation of this "Ur-Gospel." The differences are explained by their use of different Greek recensions. The main problem with this argument is that as one sought to reconstruct what this Ur-Gospel looked like, it began to look more and more like an Ur-Markus, that is, an earlier non-canonical form of the Gospel of Mark. This in turn began to look more and more like the canonical Gospel of Mark.

A more likely literary explanation is to see some sort of interdependence between the Synoptic Gospels themselves. The three most common explanations involving interdependence are:

Matthew wrote first, Mark used Matthew, Luke used Mark (Augustine).

Matthew wrote first, Luke used Matthew, Mark used Matthew and Luke (J. J. Griesbach, 1783 and 1789; W. R. Farmer, 1964).

Mark wrote first, Matthew used Mark, Luke used Mark. Matthew and Luke also used another common source—"Q" (H. J. Holtzmann, 1863; B. H. Streeter, 1924).

Of these three theories the most viable are the latter two: the Griesbach hypothesis and the two-document hypothesis.

4. The Griesbach Hypothesis.

This hypothesis, which argues that Matthew was the first Gospel written, that Luke used Matthew and that Mark used both Matthew and Luke, was first proposed by H. Owen in 1764. It received its name due to its advocacy by J. J. Griesbach. It has been revived and received considerable impetus recently as the two-Gospel hypothesis through the work of W. R. Farmer, J. B. Orchard and H.-H. Stoldt. Its early popularity and demise were associated with the rise and fall of the Tübingen Hypothesis (i.e., Matthew, Thesis; Luke, Antithesis; Mark, Synthesis). The strength of the Griesbach Hypothesis is that it appears to explain several aspects of the Synoptic Problem.

4.1. The Strengths of the Griesbach Hypothesis.

4.1.1. It Agrees with the Church Tradition. The early church tradition is quite unanimous in claiming that Matthew was the first Gospel written (Irenaeus, Eusebius, Augustine). Clement of Alexandria stated that the Gospels with genealogies* were written first. Augustine furthermore called Mark an abridgment of Matthew. Whereas the priority of Mark was unknown in the early church, the priority of Matthew was assumed. It is clear that the Griesbach hypothesis fits this early tradition concerning the Synoptic Gospels better than the two-document hypothesis. It also fits the order of the Gospels in the NT canon* better.

4.1.2. It Can Explain All the Gospel Agreements. In comparing the various agreements between the triple tradition (parallel passages in Matthew, Mark and Luke) we find that frequently we have Matthew-Mark agreements against Luke, Mark-Luke agreements against Matthew and even Matthew-Luke agreements against Mark. The Griesbach hypothesis can explain these quite simply: the Matthew-Mark agreements against Luke result when Luke deviates from his Matthean source but Mark does not; the Mark-Luke agreements against Matthew result when Luke deviates from his Matthean source and Mark follows Luke rather than Matthew; the Matthew-Luke agreements against Mark result when Luke follows Matthew and Mark deviates from both his sources. With regard to the latter the Griesbach hypothesis is strong where the two-document hypothesis is weak. It can easily explain the Matthew-Luke agreements against Mark, whereas the two-document hypothesis struggles with how Matthew and Luke can agree independently against their Markan source when they did not know each other, that is, when one did not use the other.

4.1.3. It Explains the Markan Redundancies. Within Mark we find at least 213 cases of redundancy such as: 1:32 ("When evening came, as the sun was setting"); 1:42 ("And immediately the leprosy left him and he was cleansed"); 4:21 ("Is a lamp brought in order to be placed under a bushel basket or under a bed?"); etc. The Griesbach hypothesis suggests that this can best be explained by understanding that Mark tended to act with respect to his sources in the same way as the early scribes and copyists of the NT. When they found two different readings in their sources, they tended to harmonize them by including both. Mark's redundancies are therefore due to his having conflated his two sources when he came across different readings. Thus Matthew 8:16, "When evening came," and Luke 4:40, "While the sun was setting," become in Mark 1:32, "When evening came, as the sun was setting"; Matthew 5:14, "They do not set under a bushel basket," and Luke 8:16, "Nor set it under a bed," become in Mark 4:21, "Is a lamp brought in order to be placed under a bushel basket or under a bed?"

Other evidence for the Griesbach hypothesis, such as there being no need for the postulation of an additional hypothetical source such as "Q,"* could also be mentioned.

4.2. Problems for the Griesbach Hypothesis. A number of problems encountered by the Griesbach hypothesis have led many scholars to consider the two-document hypothesis a more viable option for explaining the Synoptic Problem. Two of these, the arguments in favor of the priority of Mark and the difficulty of claiming that Luke used Matthew, will be discussed at length below (see 5.1. and 5.2.1.). There are several additional weaknesses.

4.2.1. The Griesbach Hypothesis Also Conflicts with the Church Tradition. Whereas the church tradition is unanimous in stating that Matthew was written before Mark and Luke, that tradition in the same breath also argues that Matthew was written in Aramaic (or Hebrew). Yet it is clear that our present Matthew is not a simple translation from Aramaic (or Hebrew) into Greek. Thus the Matthew of church tradition does not fit the Greek Matthew of the Synoptic Problem. If therefore the tradition at this point is either incorrect or speaking of a predecessor (or source) of our Greek Matthew, this greatly weakens the value of the church tradition for solving the Synoptic Problem (*see* Matthew, Gospel of).

Other aspects of the church tradition also cause difficulty for the Griesbach hypothesis. These include Papias' statement that Mark had as his main source the "memoirs" of Peter and wrote his Gospel independently of Matthew, and the views of Origen, the Anti-Marcionite Prologues and Augustine that Luke was written last.

4.2.2. Certain Gospel Agreements Are Best Explained by the Priority of Mark. Whereas the Griesbach hypothesis can explain all the Gospel agreements, in numerous instances the particular explanation of why two Gospels agree against the other is not persuasive. This is particularly true with regard to Matthew-Mark agreements against Luke, and Mark-Luke agreements against Matthew. In the abstract the Griesbach hypothesis can explain such agreements easily, but when one seeks to explain why Mark and Luke agree against Matthew and why Mark and Matthew agree against Luke, the explanations are often quite unconvincing (see 5.1.6. below). In general the attempts on the basis of the Griesbach hypothesis to explain Luke's use of Matthew and Mark's use of Matthew and/or Luke are less convincing than the explanations of how Matthew and Luke used Mark according to the two-document hypothesis. Clearly the vast majority of redaction-critical investigation in the Synoptic Gospels has been based on the view that Matthew and Luke used Mark. Attempts to do redaction-critical work on the basis of a Matthean priority are meager and less convincing.

4.2.3. The Markan Redundancies Can Be Explained by the Two-Document Hypothesis. At first glance the argument that the 213 examples of Markan redundancy are due to his conflation of Matthew and Luke appears convincing, but on closer examination it is clear that out of these 213 examples only 17 are clear cases of redundancy in which Matthew has only one half of the redundancy and Luke has the other. (In 39 instances Matthew and Luke have the same parallel redundancy and lack the other; in 37 instances they possess neither redundant parallel; in 60 instances Matthew has one or both parallels and Luke has neither; in 26 instances Luke has one or both parallels and Matthew has neither; in 11 instances Luke has both parallels and Matthew has one; in 17 instances Matthew has both parallels and Luke has one; and in 6 instances Matthew and Luke have both parallels.) Thus we are essentially speaking of only 17 possible examples of conflation and not 213.

The attempt of the Griesbach hypothesis to see the Gospel of Mark as being typified by conflation is furthermore compromised when it at the same time speaks of Mark as an abridgment of Matthew and Luke. These supposed tendencies are essentially contradictory. The harmony of Tatian called the *Diatesseron* (c. 150) is an early example of conflation at work. But when one compares the portions of the *Diatesseron* derived from the Synoptic Gospels, they are considerably longer than any of the Synoptic Gospels. Mark, on the other hand, is considerably shorter than either Matthew or Luke. It is therefore quite unlike this early example of conflation. The Markan redundancies are therefore not a convincing argument in favor of the Griesbach hypothesis. It may even be that they can be better explained by the two-document hypothesis (See 5.1.2. below).

5. The Two-Document Hypothesis.
The explanation which has come to dominate Synoptic studies during the last century and a half has been the two-document hypothesis. This theory argues that Mark was the first Gospel written and that it was used independently by Matthew and Luke. It also argues that along with Mark, Matthew and Luke used another common source which has been called "Q." Evidence for the priority of Mark and the existence of "Q" follow.

5.1. The Priority of Mark.
5.1.1. Mark Is the Shortest Gospel. Of the three Synoptic Gospels, Mark is the shortest in length: It contains 661 verses; Matthew contains 1,068; Luke contains 1,149. When their content is compared, 97.2 per cent of Mark is paralleled in Matthew and 88.4 per cent is paralleled in Luke. It is easier to understand Matthew and Luke using Mark, and choosing to add additional materials to it, than to think of Mark using Matthew, Luke or both, and deciding to omit so much material. Why would he have omitted the birth accounts (*see* Birth of Jesus), the Sermon on the Mount

(*see* Sermon on the Mount), the Lord's Prayer (*see* Prayer), various resurrection* appearances, etc. It is easier to understand Matthew and Luke choosing to add this material to their Markan source than Mark choosing to omit so much material. The suggestion that Mark may have desired to produce a shorter, more abridged account stumbles over the fact that the common accounts in the Synoptic Gospels are generally longer in Mark. If Mark wanted to write an abbreviated account of Matthew and/or Luke, why would he choose to make the stories in his abridged account longer? These are contrary tendencies. When one seeks to abridge a work, one generally does so not only by eliminating certain materials but by abridging what one decides to keep.

5.1.2. Mark Has the Poorest Greek. There is a consensus that the Greek of Mark is poorer than that of either Matthew or Luke. It is easier to understand Matthew and Luke using Mark and improving on his Greek than to think of Mark copying the better Greek of Matthew and/or Luke and making it worse. There are numerous examples of peculiar Markan expressions.

(1) Mark contains various colloquialisms (Mk 10:20, "I have observed," aorist middle; 2:4, "bed" as *krabatton)* and grammatical problems (Mk 4:41, "hears" as a singular verb; 16:6, "see" as a singular verb; 5:9-10, "he begged" for the plural "we").

(2) Mark has Aramaic expressions (Mk 3:17; 5:41; 7:11, 34; 14:36; 15:22, 34) which are not found in Matthew or Luke. It is much easier to see Matthew and Luke omitting these Aramaic expressions and giving their Greek counterparts than to see Mark choosing to abridge Matthew and/or Luke but adding Aramaic expressions which his Greek readers did not understand.

(3) Mark is frequently redundant. On numerous occasions (there are 213 examples), Mark has a redundant expression such as "When evening came, as the sun was setting" (1:32) (cf. also Mk 1:42; 2:25-26; 4:21; 15:24). It is easier to understand why Matthew and/or Luke would seek to eliminate such redundancies than to understand why, in abridging Matthew and/or Luke, Mark would have added them.

5.1.3. Mark Has Harder Readings. At times we find in Mark a saying which creates a theological difficulty but do not find this difficulty in Matthew and/or Luke. In Mark, for example, we find apparent limitations of Jesus' power (cf. Mk 1:32-34; 3:9-10; 6:5-6 with par.). At other times we find theological difficulties in Mark but not in Matthew or Luke (cf. Mk 10:17-18; 3:4-5; 2:25-26). In Mark 10:17-18 we have Jesus saying, "Why do you call me good? No one is good but God alone." It is easy to see why Matthew would want to change this

to "Why do you ask me about what is good? One there is who is good." The changing (or explaining) of Mark's harder readings by Matthew and/or Luke is much easier to understand than Mark choosing to make the easier reading in Matthew and/or Luke more difficult.

5.1.4. The Lack of Matthew-Luke Verbal Agreements against Mark. If one observes the various kinds of agreements in the Synoptic Gospels, it is clear that, whereas we have numerous Matthew-Mark agreements against Luke and Mark-Luke agreements against Matthew, there is a paucity of Matthew-Luke agreements against Mark. Assuming the simplest kind of interdependence in which one Gospel writer used one other Gospel writer, we have the following possibilities.

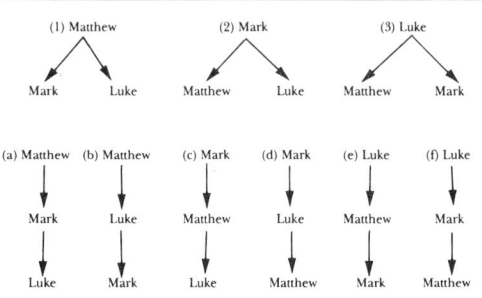

All other possible combinations of interdependence require that either Matthew "knew" (in the sense of "used") Luke or that Luke "knew" Matthew. As we shall see, this is most unlikely (see 5.2.1. below).

Given the fact that accounts of the triple tradition seldom show Matthew and Luke agreeing against Mark in their wording, explanations (1) and (3) cannot explain this. Furthermore (1), (c) and (e) cannot account for the Mark-Luke agreements and (3), (b) and (d) cannot explain the Matthew-Mark agreements. Only explanations (2), (a) and (f) can explain the abundance of Matthew-Mark and Mark-Luke agreements and the lack of Matthew-Luke agreements. However, the arguments given earlier argue against (a) and (f).

5.1.5. The Lack of Matthew-Luke Agreements in Order against Mark. Similar to the preceding argument but involving the order of the materials is the observation that when Matthew differs from the order of the accounts found in Mark, Luke never agrees with Matthew. Likewise, when Luke differs from the order which we find in Mark, Matthew never agrees with Luke against Mark. This observation by K. Lachmann (1835) has sometimes been thought to be an absolute proof for the priority of Mark. This, however, is not a proof of Markan priority, for with the Griesbach hypothesis in which Matthew was written first, Luke used Matthew, and Mark used both Matthew and Luke, we can explain such agreements in order. Lachmann, however, added to this observation the fact that, whereas Matthew's deviation from Mark and Luke's deviation from Mark are understandable, a Markan deviation from the order of Matthew and Luke is much less so. In light of this observation, there is no reason to refer to this as the "Lachmann Fallacy."

5.1.6. Certain Literary Agreements Are Best Explained by a Markan Priority. There exist in the Synoptic Gospels certain literary agreements which are best explained on the basis of Matthew and Luke having used Mark. For instance, in Matthew 9:1-2/Mark 2:1-5/Luke 5:17-20 Matthew has, as he does frequently elsewhere (cf. Mt 8:5-13; 9:18-26), abbreviated the Markan account and omitted the reason why Jesus saw the faith* of the paralytic and his friends. In Matthew 27:15-22/Mark 15:6-13/Luke 23:18-21, Luke has abbreviated the account and omitted the explanation of the Barabbas episode by not referring to the custom of releasing a prisoner at the time of the Passover. In Matthew 3:13-16/Mark 1:9-10/Luke 3:21-22 Matthew has sought to change the wording of Mark and has, by changing the verb *baptized* to the participle "having been baptized," mistakenly placed the word *immediately* with the verb "went up" (*see* Baptism). The result, although understandable, has Jesus immediately coming up out of the water rather than immediately seeing the heavens* opened. In Matthew 19:16-17/Mark 10:17-18/Luke 18:18-19 Matthew has sought to eliminate the difficulty created by Mark's "Why do you call me good? No one is good but God alone." Instead he has "Why do you ask me about what is good?" However, his next verse indicates that his source spoke about God being good—not "good" in an abstract sense, for he adds, "One there is who is good."

These and other literary agreements are more understandable on the basis of Matthew and Luke having used Mark than on the basis of any other theory of interdependence.

5.1.7. The Argument from Redaction. Probably the most significant argument today in favor of the priority of Mark involves redactional studies. It is undeniable that the great majority of redactional investigations of the Synoptic Gospels proceed on the basis of the priority of Mark. It is easier, for example, to understand why Matthew added his emphasis on Jesus as the "Son of David" to the Markan account than to understand why Luke and Mark would have chosen to omit this reference (cf. Mt 12:23; 15:22; 21:9, 15). Similarly, it is easier to understand Matthew having added his

famous "this was to fulfill . . ." in 1:22; 2:15, 17; 4:14; 8:17; 12:17; 13:14, 35; 21:4; 27:9 to his Markan source than to understand why Mark and Luke would have chosen to omit them. Five of the last six references reveal this clearly, for the parallels in Mark and Luke lack this reference. To assume that Mark and Luke used Matthew and chose to omit these references is most difficult to comprehend. On the other hand Matthew's having added them to his Markan source is easily understandable.

We also discover that certain Markan stylistic features, when found in Matthew, appear almost exclusively in the material which Matthew has in common with Mark. The famous Markan use of "immediately" occurs forty-one times within his Gospel. In Matthew it occurs eighteen times. Of these eighteen times, fourteen occur in the material he shares with Mark. The other four occur in his M* (Matthew's special material) and Q material. However, of the 18,293 words which are in Matthew, 10,901 have parallels in Mark. A total of 7,392 do not have a parallel. This means that there is one "immediately" for every 778 words in the material Matthew has in common with Mark, but there is only one "immediately" for every 1,848 words in the non-Markan material (M* and Q*). The more frequent appearance of the word *immediately* in the material Matthew has in common with Mark is more easily explained by his use of Mark, where this word is found in abundance, than by any other explanation.

Another Markan stylistic feature is his use of an editorial "for (*gar*)" clause to explain something to his reader (see Mk 1:16, 22; 5:28; 6:17-18 etc.). Within Mark we find thirty-four such clauses; within Matthew we find ten, but all ten appear in the material he shares with Mark. Not one is found in the remaining material. If Matthew used Mark, the presence of these editorial "for" clauses is understandable. But why would they be only in one area of the Matthean material, the material he shares with Mark, if Matthew did not use Mark?

5.1.8. Mark's Theology Is Less Developed. When one compares the common material in Matthew, Mark and Luke, it is obvious time and time again that the materials in Matthew and Luke are theologically more developed. Mark, for example, uses the term "Lord" (*kyrios*) for Jesus six times, but in Matthew we find it used not only in the same six instances, but in an additional twenty-four. Fifteen of these instances are found in material where Mark lacks this term. The same can be said of Luke, who uses this title even more frequently. It is easier to understand how Matthew and Luke would have added this title to their Markan source than to understand why Mark would have chosen to eliminate it if he were using Matthew and/or Luke. The same can be said for the title "Christ."

5.1.9. Conclusion. The reason why most scholars maintain the priority of Mark is not based on any one argument listed above. Rather, the priority of Mark is based on the entire collection of arguments. The weight of any one argument may not be convincing, but together they are quite convincing, and the best available hypothesis for explaining the Synoptic Problem is that Matthew and Luke used Mark in the composition of their Gospels. Being a "hypothesis," absolute proof is by definition lacking, and the Synoptic Problem must always remain open to a better hypothesis if one should become available.

5.2. The Existence of "Q." Once the priority of Mark has been accepted, we are faced with another problem. This involves the common material found in Matthew and Luke which we do not find in Mark, the so-called Q material. Some examples of this are: Matthew 6:24/Luke 16:13; Matthew 7:7-11/Luke 11:9-13; Matthew 11:25-27/Luke 10:21-22; Matthew 23:37-39/Luke 13:34-35. How is this common material to be explained? We shall discuss below the suggestion that Matthew and Luke obtained this material from various oral traditions, but the simplest explanation is that either Matthew used Luke or that Luke used Matthew to obtain this material. There are a number of reasons, however, why it is unlikely that Luke used Matthew. (The theory that Matthew used Luke is held by few, and most of the arguments given below also demonstrate that Matthew did not use Luke.)

5.2.1. Matthew and Luke Did Not Know Each Other. This is evident from several lines of evidence.

(1) *Luke lacks the Matthean additions to the triple tradition.* When we find an account in the triple tradition and Matthew has something in the account not found in Mark, we never find that Matthean addition in Luke (cf. Mt 8:17; 12:5-7; 13:14-15 etc.). If Luke used Matthew, why do we never find any of these additions in Luke? The easiest explanation is that Luke did not use Matthew. (The same can be said about Lukan additions to the triple tradition. They are never found in Matthew.)

(2) *The "Q" material is found in a different context in Luke.* The Q material is arranged in Matthew into five blocks of teachings surrounded by six blocks of narrative. As a result we find: Narrative (1—4); Teaching (5—7); N (8—9); T (10); N (11—12); T (13); N (14—17); T (18); N (19—22); T (23—25); N (26—28). It should also be noted that each of these five teaching sections end similarly with "and when Jesus finished these sayings" (7:28; 11:1; 13:53; 19:1; 26:1). Luke, however, has lumped the Q material into two

sections: 6:20—8:3; 9:51—18:14. It is difficult to understand why, if Luke used Matthew, he would have wanted to destroy the framework of the Q material in Matthew for his arrangement.

(3) *At times the Q material is less developed in Luke.* If Luke had used Matthew, one would expect that the form of the material in Luke would generally be more theologically developed than the corresponding material in Matthew. We do not find this, however. At times the Q material in Luke is clearly less developed. (Cf. Lk 6:20, "poor"; 21, "hunger now"; 31, no reference to "Law and the prophets"; 11:2, "Father"; 14:26, "hate.")

(4) *The lack of Matthew-Luke agreements in order and wording against Mark.* If Luke used Matthew, it is difficult to understand why his order never agrees with Matthew against Mark and why there are so few verbal agreements in Matthew-Luke against Mark.

(5) *The lack of M material in Luke.* By definition the M material consists of the material in Matthew not found in either Mark or Luke. If Luke used Matthew it is difficult to explain why he did not include some of this material. Such an argument from silence is always questionable. Nevertheless, knowing some of the theological interests of Luke, it is difficult to understand why, if he used Matthew, he did not include such material as the coming of the wise men (Mt 2:1-12). To have Gentiles present at the birth of Jesus would have fit his universal emphasis quite well. Likewise, the exclusion of such stories as the flight to Egypt and the return to Nazareth (Mt 2:13-23); the story of the guards at the tomb (Mt 27:62-66) and their report (Mt 28:11-15); and the unique Matthean material concerning the resurrection (Mt 28:9-10, 16-20) is inexplicable.

On the basis of the above arguments it seems reasonable to conclude that Luke did not know Matthew (and Matthew did not know Luke). As a result, some other common source has been posited. The origin of "Q" as a symbol for this common material found only in Matthew and Luke is debated, but most probably it comes from the first letter of the German word *Quelle*, which means source.

5.2.2. Was Q a Written Source? If we assume that Matthew and Luke used a common source alongside Mark, was this source written or oral? The main arguments in favor of a written Q involve the exactness in wording of some of the Q parallels. The exactness in wording is at times quite impressive (cf. Mt 6:24 par. Lk 16:13 where twenty-seven of twenty-eight words are exactly the same; Mt 7:7-8 par. Lk 11:9-10 where all twenty-four words are exactly the same). Is this exactness better explained on the basis of a common written source? On the other hand, at times some of the Q material is not very exact.

Another argument frequently put forward for a written Q involves an agreement in order. At times one can observe a certain degree of order between the Q material in Matthew and Luke, but these agreements in order are not sufficient to require a common written source. Some have also sought to find a common order between the Q material in Luke and the Q material in each of the five Q sections in Matthew, that is, the order of Q in Luke is compared to Matthew 5—7, then to Matthew 10, to Matthew 13 etc. The argument from order has been convincing to some scholars but not to most.

A third argument for Q being a written source is the presence of doublets (double accounts of the same incident) in Matthew and Luke. This supposedly demonstrates that they used two separate written sources—Mark and Q. At best, however, if such doublets exist, they prove the use of a second common source, but this could have been oral or fragmentary written sources. A further attempt to prove that Q was a written source has been the effort to demonstrate that there is a common vocabulary and style in the Q material which reveals that it comes from a common written source. This attempt, however, has not been convincing.

5.2.3. Summary. The Q hypothesis is not without its problems, but it possesses fewer difficulties than alternative hypotheses. As to its form, it is difficult to determine if the Q material came to Matthew and Luke as a single written source, as several written sources or from a common oral tradition. That Matthew and Luke did not know each other seems fairly certain. This, along with the argument for Markan priority, favors some sort of a two-document hypothesis in which Matthew and Luke used Mark and probably a written Q. A related version of this is the four-document hypothesis which assumes that the unique material found in Matthew (the M material) and Luke (the L material) came from two additional written sources.

The Two- (or Four-) Document Hypothesis

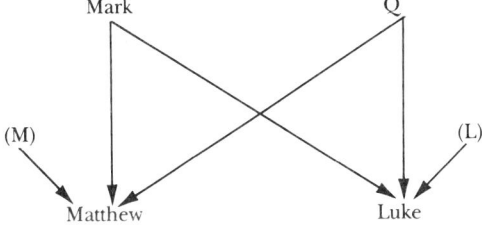

6. Problems with the Two-Document Hypothesis.

The major alternative to the two- (or four-) document hypothesis is the Griesbach hypothesis (see 4. above). This hypothesis explains well the major problem facing the two-document hypothesis—the existence of Matthew-Luke agreements against Mark. Along with various agreements in omission created by their abbreviation of Mark, and the agreements which came about by their improvement of Mark's grammar, there are several significant Matthew-Luke agreements against Mark (cf. Mk 1:7-8; 2:12; 3:24, 26-29; 5:27; 6:33; 8:35; 9:2-4, 18-19; 10:29; 14:65, 72 and the Matthew-Luke parallels).

Although the Griesbach hypothesis can explain these agreements better than the two-document hypothesis, we must not forget that the reverse is true concerning all the arguments for Markan priority and against Matthew and Luke knowing each other. These arguments are far more numerous and weighty. As to the Matthew-Luke agreements against Mark, several explanations can be offered.

6.1. Overlapping Traditions. The Q material and Mark must have overlapped in certain places. At times Matthew and Luke may have preferred the Q readings over Mark and thus created a Matthew-Luke agreement.

6.2. Textual Corruption. We know that the early scribes had a tendency to make parallel accounts in the Gospels conform to one another, and since Matthew was the best-known and most frequently used Synoptic Gospel, it may be that some early scribe copying Luke may have changed his Lukan text to conform to the reading in Matthew. In such instances, the result would be a Matthew-Luke agreement.

6.3. Overlapping Oral Tradition. It may also be possible that at times Matthew and Luke knew a form of the oral tradition which was more familiar to them than the wording in their Markan source and so chose, quite independently of each other, to word their accounts according to the oral tradition. Again, a Matthew-Luke agreement would have resulted.

Among the several other possible reasons for a Matthew-Luke agreement are: coincidental modifications of Mark's grammar; coincidental omissions of Markan material; the common use of a different Mark and coincidental modifications of difficult passages in Mark.

7. The Value of the Solution of the Synoptic Problem.
The solution of the Synoptic Problem proves to be of value in several ways.

7.1. Historical Criticism. In seeking the solution to this problem great impetus was provided by the desire to find the oldest and, it was assumed, best historical source for investigating the life of Jesus. It was hoped that once the basic source of the Synoptic Gospels was discovered, scholars would possess an historical source uncluttered with the theology of the early church which would then be the basis for the quest for the historical Jesus (see Historical Jesus). Mark, it was thought, provided this source. Today we realize that Mark, like the other Gospels, is not an objective biography of the life of Jesus (see Gospel [Genre]). What biography would omit the first thirty years of a person's life? And what Gospel writer is "objective"? It is evident, therefore, that this quest for a completely objective biography of the life of Jesus was doomed from the start.

The solution of the Synoptic Problem, however, has provided certain tools which are useful for historical investigation. The criterion of multiple attestation is based on the premise that several witnesses are better than one, and if a teaching of Jesus is witnessed to in Mark, Q,* M,* L* and John, then we have five different sources which witness to its historicity (see Gospels [Historical Reliability]). Another useful tool is the criterion of divergent patterns from the redaction. Because of the application of the two-document hypothesis, Synoptic scholarship today is better acquainted with the literary style and theological emphases of the different Evangelists. It is quite apparent that if an Evangelist included something in his Gospel which seemed to conflict with his own emphasis, he witnessed to that tradition being very old and well-known.

7.2. Redactional Investigation of the Gospels. By observing how Matthew and Luke used Mark and Q, we are better able to understand their theological emphases. Thus we are better able to comprehend the meaning of their works. One only needs to compare the following examples with their parallels to see how they help reveal the theological emphases of the Gospel writer: Luke 5:17; 6:27-28; 11:13; Matthew 8:15; 13:35; 15:22.

7.3. Hermeneutical Insights. It is frequently helpful to observe how one Evangelist interpreted his source, for the Evangelists were closer in time, situation, language and thought-world to their contemporaries than we. As a result, we can at times find help in interpreting a difficult text by observing how they interpreted this text. For example, it is evident from Matthew 10:37-38 that Luke's command to "hate one's parents" (14:26) means that his disciples must love Jesus more. One can also gain insight on how particular teachings of Jesus can be applied by observing how the Evangelists seek to apply them to their situation. A good example of this

is the parable* of the lost sheep (Lk 15:3-7 par. Mt 18:10-14).

See also FORM CRITICISM; GOSPEL (GENRE); L; M; Q; REDACTION CRITICISM; SYNOPTICS AND JOHN; TRADITION CRITICISM.

BIBLIOGRAPHY. A. J. Bellinzoni, Jr., et al., *The Two-Source Hypothesis: A Critical Appraisal* (Macon: Mercer, 1985); W. R. Farmer, *The Synoptic Problem: A Critical Analysis* (New York: Macmillan, 1964); A. M. Farrer, "On Dispensing with Q," in *Studies in the Gospels* (Oxford; Blackwell, 1955) 55-88; J. A. Fitzmyer, "The Priority of Mark and the 'Q' Source in Luke," in *Jesus and Man's Hope* (Pittsburgh: Pittsburgh Theological Seminary, 1970) 131-170; J. C. Hawkins, *Horae Synopticae* (Oxford: Clarendon, 1909); J. S. Kloppenborg, *The Formation of Q: Trajectories in Ancient Wisdom Collections* (Philadelphia: Fortress, 1987); T. R. W. Longstaff and P. A. Thomas, *The Synoptic Problem: A Bibliography 1716-1988* (Macon: Mercer, 1988); F. Neirynck, *The Minor Agreements of Matthew and Luke Against Mark with a Cumulative List* (Leuven: University Press, 1974); B. Reicke, *The Roots of the Synoptic Gospels* (Philadelphia: Fortress, 1986); R. H. Stein, *The Synoptic Problem* (Grand Rapids: Baker, 1987); B. H. Streeter, *The Four Gospels* (London: Macmillan, 1951); H.-H. Stoldt, *History and Criticism of the Markan Hypothesis* (Macon: Mercer, 1980); G. M. Styler, "The Priority of Mark," in C. F. D. Moule, *The Birth of the New Testament* (3d ed., New York: Harper & Row) 285-316; C. M. Tuckett, "The Argument from Order and the Synoptic Problem," *TZ* 36 (1980) 338-54; idem, *The Revival of the Griesbach Hypothesis: An Analysis and Appraisal* (Cambridge: University Press, 1983).

R. H. Stein

SYNOPTICS AND JOHN

The differences between the Gospel of John and the Synoptic Gospels have been remarked on through the centuries, certainly since the second century of our era. One solution to account for the differences was to assume that (1) John was the last Gospel (see Gospel [Genre]) to be written and (2) it was written to complement the others. Clement of Alexandria came near to this in his famous assertion: "Last of all John, perceiving that the bodily facts had been made plain in the Gospel, being urged by his friends and inspired by the Spirit, composed a spiritual Gospel" (Eusebius, *Hist. Eccl.* 4.14.7). The Muratorian Canon, following that tradition, observed, "Although various points are taught in the several books of the Gospels, yet it makes no difference to the faith of the believers, since all things in all of them are declared by one supreme Spirit." That sounds as though John's Gospel may have been questioned in light of its differences from the Synoptics, and assurance was given that the Holy Spirit* was behind all four Gospels (*see* Canon).

In reality there is no hint in the Fourth Gospel that the Evangelist was either complementing or correcting the other three. What is indisputable is that the Synoptic Gospels are clearly linked with each other and can be set alongside each other for easy comparison, but the Fourth Gospel does not readily permit such treatment. It is our task to consider the nature of the differences and the possible relations between the first three Gospels and the Gospel of John.

1. Relations As to Content.
2. The Teaching of Jesus
3. Literary Relations

1. Relations As to Content.

1.1. Topography. The first three Gospels recount the ministry of Jesus in Galilee. His only ministry in Jerusalem was in the week leading to the Passover (*see* Feasts), at which time he was opposed by the Jewish rulers, arrested, tried and put to death by the Romans. In the Fourth Gospel the scene of Jesus' ministry is almost entirely set in Jerusalem and Judea; the only description of ministry in Galilee* is of three signs in John 2:1-11; 4:43-54; and chapter 6. Apart from chapter 4, which tells of the encounter of Jesus with Samaritans,* the rest of the Gospel is devoted to his work in Judea (*see* Archeology and Geography).

This feature is emphasized by the prominence given to the presence of Jesus at the Jewish festivals in the Temple.* We read of Jesus attending the festivals of Pentecost (Jn 5), Tabernacles (Jn 7—8), Dedication (Jn 10) and Passover (2:13; 12—19). These festivals in varied ways set forth the dealings of God with his people in the past, their faith* in God in the present, and their hope of the kingdom of God* for the future. Jesus is presented in these episodes as the fulfillment of all that these festivals represented of God's revelation and promised salvation.*

The frequent presence of Jesus in Jerusalem and the increasingly intense opposition to him from the Pharisees* and Jewish authorities described by John, shed light on the Synoptic references to the early hostility to Jesus of the scribes* and Pharisees, as well as his frequent mention of the destiny that awaited him in Jerusalem (see e.g., Mk 8:31 par.; Lk 13:33). The same applies to the weeping of Jesus over Jerusalem because the people did not know the season of its visitation (Lk 19:41-42), and his desire time after time to gather Jerusalem under his care ("How often did I wish to gather your children . . . but you were unwilling," Mt 23:37-38).

There are hints that a primary source of John's Gospel is of a person living in Judea during the ministry of Jesus and of the story being written from the viewpoint of one dwelling in Jerusalem. Note the reference to the disciple who was a friend of the High Priest (*see* Priest) and who was able to use his influence to bring Peter into the High Priest's court at the trial of Jesus (18:15-16; *see* Trial of Jesus). The account of the Triumphal Entry (*see* Triumphal Entry) of Jesus into Jerusalem is told from the viewpoint of one in the city (12:9-18) in contrast to the Synoptics, which describe the event from the viewpoint of the Galileans entering the city (Mk 11:1-11 par.). This probably explains the fuller information in John about the trial of Jesus than that of the Synoptics, particularly of the trial before Pilate (*see* Pontius Pilate).

1.2. Chronology.

1.2.1. Beginning of Jesus' Ministry. Whereas in the Synoptic Gospels the ministry of Jesus and the call of the first disciples is set after the imprisonment of John the Baptist* (Mk 1:14-20), in John's Gospel Jesus commences his ministry in Judea during the period of John's work, and his earliest disciples appear to be disciples of the Baptist (Jn 1:35-51). From John 2—3 it is evident that Jesus not only labored in Judea at the same time as John, but he is reported to have baptized more disciples than John himself. It is in this context that the most specific witness of John the Baptist to Jesus in the Gospels is given (1:29, 35; 3:27-30).

1.2.2. Length of Ministry of Jesus. The length of the ministry of Jesus according to the Synoptic Gospels is difficult to determine, but the mention of one solitary visit of Jesus to Jerusalem for the celebration of the Passover gives the impression that it could have been limited to a year. In the Gospel of John, by contrast, three Passovers are mentioned by the Evangelist (2:13; 6:4; 12:1), implying that the ministry of Jesus could have extended over two to three years (*see* Chronology).

1.2.3. Time of Cleansing of the Temple. The so-called cleansing of the Temple (*see* Temple Cleansing) in the Synoptic Gospels occurs in the only place where it could happen in their representation of the ministry of Jesus, namely on his visit to Jerusalem at the Passover season (Mk 11:15-18). In John, however, it is set at the beginning of the public ministry of Jesus, immediately following the record of the turning of the water* into wine* at Cana (2:13-22). This has led many to assume that Jesus cleansed the Temple twice. Others have championed the Synoptics over against John, or John over against the Synoptics.

It is now commonly believed that the Synoptic dating is correct, and that the Fourth Evangelist has placed the event at the beginning of his account to emphasize its significance for understanding the ministry of Jesus. Chapter 2 is a kind of program chapter for the Gospel: Whoever understands the turning of the water into wine (cf. Is 25:6-9) and the cleansing of the Temple has the key to grasping the meaning of our Lord's words and work, above all his redeeming action for the kingdom of God and the new worship* thereby opened for humankind.

1.2.4. The Date of the Last Supper. The Synoptic Gospels indicate that the last meal of Jesus with his disciples was a Passover celebration (cf. Mk 14:12; Lk 22:15; *see* Last Supper). John states that the meal took place on the eve of the Passover (Jn 13:1; 18:28), and that Jesus died immediately prior to the Passover (19:31). How to deal with this clash of evidence has taxed the minds of scholars for generations. Many hold that the Synoptics are right, and that John changed the date to emphasize that Jesus died as God's Passover Lamb (cf. 1:29; 19:31-37). Such a suggestion is to be repudiated.

A Jewish tradition (*baraita*) preserved in the Talmud states that Jesus was stoned and hanged on the eve of the Passover because he practiced magic and enticed and led Israel astray (*Sanh.* 43a). It has been suggested that the Passover was observed on two different dates, one on the basis of a solar calendar, followed by the Essenes, the other a lunar calendar, observed by the Jewish authorities. If Jesus followed the former, he celebrated the Passover with his disciples on the Tuesday evening, whereas the official calendar, known to John in Jerusalem, set the observance on the Friday evening, and the days between Tuesday and Friday would have been taken up with the trial proceedings (Jaubert). The suggestion is disputed. Other solutions include the belief that the Synoptics record an anticipated Passover, a meal replete with Passover associations. Further investigation of this problem is required. The chief point made by all four Gospels is the fulfillment of the Passover in the death of Jesus (*see* Passion Narrative).

2. The Teaching of Jesus.

2.1. Johannine Style. The mode of the teaching of Jesus is recognizable in each of the Synoptic Gospels, despite the individual style of the Evangelists, notably his aphorisms (*see* Chreia; Form Criticism) and parables.* These are represented in John's Gospel, but much less frequently, and that for a simple reason: the Fourth Evangelist mediates the teaching of Jesus in his own language. The contrast of the collections of sayings in the Synoptics with the longer discourses in John is a matter of degree; the five Matthean

discourses are all compilations of sayings according to subject, and so are those in John. (An examination of the Discourses of chapters 13—17 will show that the same applies even to them.)

2.2. Thematic Contrast and Similarity. The supreme theme of the teaching of Jesus in the Synoptic Gospels is summarized in Mark 1:15: It was God's good news that the time of waiting for the fulfillment of his promise was over; his kingdom was upon people and all must repent to receive it. John's Gospel contains one saying about the kingdom, 3:3, expanded for clarification in 3:5, together with an oblique reference in the trial before Pilate (18:36-37). Yet every line in this Gospel is informed by it. John's reproduction of the teaching of Jesus in his own language, however, has entailed a translation: his key term is one found in the Synoptics, namely "life"* or "eternal life," which is life in the kingdom of God (see Mk 10:17, 23). The purpose of John's Gospel, declared by the Evangelist, was precisely that its readers might receive and be established in the life of the kingdom of God (20:31).

3. Literary Relations.

3.1. Dependence of John. The early Christian belief that John knew the Synoptic Gospels and supplemented them gave place in modern times to a conviction that John used those Gospels in composing his own—certainly Mark, probably Luke, less certainly Matthew. It was urged that as the use of Mark by Matthew and Luke was grasped through their reproducing Mark's material in Mark's order and language, so the like is observable in John's treatment of the Synoptics (for a recent statement of this argument see Barrett 1978, 42-46). It is often admitted that John used the Synoptics differently from their use of each other. None of them became the basis of John's Gospel. They supplied but a fraction of his material, and he probably used them from memory (see Kümmel, 145). Some recent writers, however, advance beyond this position and claim that John frequently composed passages through adaptation of Synoptic material (see, e.g., Neirynck, 95-106, who attempts to demonstrate that Jn 20:1-18 was constructed on the basis of Lk 24:1-12 and Mt 28:9-10).

3.2. Independence of John. The thesis that the Fourth Evangelist used the Synoptic Gospels in writing his Gospel was challenged by P. Gardner-Smith on two grounds: (1) the critics have overlooked the influence of the continued existence of oral tradition at the time when John was written; (2) they have concentrated too much on the similarities between John and the Synoptics and underestimated the differences between them. Features like John's lengthy description of John the Baptist's ministry, Peter's confession, the trial of Jesus by Annas and not by Caiaphas, the trial by Pilate, the insufflation of the Spirit in the resurrection narrative etc., show the use of independent tradition(s), not adaptation of Synoptic traditions.

The effect of this work was to change the majority opinion on this subject. The contacts between John and the Synoptics came to be explained in terms of contacts between the sources of the Synoptic writers and those available to the Fourth Evangelist, rather than between the Gospels themselves. This was the thesis of C. H. Dodd in his monumental work *Historical Tradition in the Fourth Gospel*, and it has been adopted by many recent commentators and writers on John, including R. Bultmann, R. E. Brown, B. Lindars, L. Morris, J. N. Sanders and B. N. Mastin, and R. Schnackenburg.

3.3. Mediating Views. In face of a revival among some scholars of the belief that the Fourth Evangelist was dependent on the Synoptists, a mediating view is being advanced by some writers. This was anticipated by Sanders and Mastin (1968). On examining evidence advanced for the use of Mark by John they remained unconvinced that Mark was a source for John but felt that John must have known Mark. They added, "But knowing Mark and using it as a source are two different things" (10). This conviction was shared by D. M. Smith in a review of current thought on this issue. He recognized the possibility that in due time, after the traditions of the Gospel had become familiar in John's church through preaching and controversy, the Synoptic Gospels became known, without being fully absorbed. John's concerns were different from those of the Synoptics, so he did not employ them in the manner that Matthew and Luke used Mark.

Nevertheless, even though the Fourth Evangelist did not use the Synoptics as his sources, neither did his Gospel take shape in isolation from them. Accordingly, we should not ignore the Synoptics in interpreting John. "This means . . . that the question of the mode of the relationship should remain open in principle" (Smith, 443-44). Therein lies an indication that our minds also should remain open in this matter.

See also GOSPELS (HISTORICAL RELIABILITY); JOHN, GOSPEL OF; SYNOPTIC PROBLEM.

BIBLIOGRAPHY. C. K. Barrett, *The Gospel According to St. John*, 2d ed. (Philadelphia: Westminster, 1978); idem, "John and the Synoptic Gospels," *ExpT* 85 (1973-74) 228-33; C. H. Dodd, *Historical Tradition in the Fourth Gospel* (Cambridge: University Press) 1963; H. J. Flowers, "Mark as a Source for the Fourth Gospel," *JBL* 46 (1927) 207-36; P. Gardner-Smith, *Saint John and the Synoptic Gospels* (Cambridge: University Press) 1938; A. Jaubert, *The Date of the Last Supper* (Staten Island, NY: Alba, 1965); W. G. Kümmel, *Introduction to the New Testament*, rev. ed. (Nashville: Abingdon, 1975); R. Kysar, *The Fourth Evangelist and His Gospel* (Minneapolis: Augsburg, 1975); F. Neirynck, "John and the Synoptics," in *L'évangile de Jean, sources, rédactions, théologie*, ed. M. de Jonge (Leuven: Leuven University and Gembloux: Duculot, 1977) 73-106; J. N. Sanders and B. A. Mastin, *The Gospel according to St. John* (New York: Harper and Row, 1969); D. M. Smith, "The Sources of the Gospel of John: An Assessment of the Present State of the Question," *NTS* 10 (1963-64) 336-51; H. M. Teeple, *The Literary Origin of the Gospel of John* (Evanston, IL: Religion and Ethics Institute, 1974). G. R. Beasley-Murray

T

TABERNACLES, FEAST OF. *See* FEASTS.

TABLE FELLOWSHIP

One distinctive feature of Jesus' ministry was his practice of a radically inclusive and non-hierarchical table fellowship as a central strategy in his announcement and redefinition of the inbreaking rule of God. In so doing, Jesus challenged the inherent exclusivism and status consciousness of accepted social and religious custom and presented a living parable of a renewed Israel.

1. The Significance of Shared Meals
2. The Historical Jesus and Table Fellowship
3. Jesus' Table Praxis according to Mark
4. Jesus' Open "Symposia" according to Luke
5. Conclusion

1. The Significance of Shared Meals.

It would be difficult to overestimate the importance of table fellowship for the cultures of the Mediterranean basin in the first century of our era. Mealtimes were far more than occasions for individuals to consume nourishment. Being welcomed at a table for the purpose of eating food with another person had become a ceremony richly symbolic of friendship, intimacy and unity. Thus betrayal or unfaithfulness toward anyone with whom one had shared the table was viewed as particularly reprehensible. On the other hand, when persons were estranged, a meal invitation opened the way to reconciliation. Even everyday mealtimes were highly complex events in which social values, boundaries, statuses and hierarchies were reinforced. Anyone who challenged these rankings and boundaries would be judged to have acted dishonorably, a serious charge in cultures based on the values of honor and shame. Transgressing these customs consistently would make a person an enemy of social stability.

The extended family was the usual context in which meals were consumed. Coming together to eat became the occasion for sensing again that one was an integral, accepted part of a group. Beyond the household, people generally preferred to eat with persons from their own social class. Such meals of like with like reinforced the systems of social stratification, with the seating arrangements further signaling the relative status of each guest. People invited their social, religious and economic equals, that is, those who were in a position to return the favor in a relationship of balanced reciprocity.

In Israel a very salient social division had been created by the existence of a priestly class (*see* Priest, Priesthood) obliged by Torah (Lev 17—26) to live in a special state of ritual purity (*see* Clean and Unclean) for at least six weeks a year while preparing to serve and then serving in the Temple.* Keeping this obligation led to a certain physical and social distance between priestly families and all other Israelites, whom the priests regarded as more or less unclean.

During the heavy-handed Hellenization (*see* Hellenism) that led to the Maccabean revolt (167-164 B.C.), many Jews, including an alarming number of leading priests, compromised both their purity and their identity by sacrificing to pagan gods and adopting Greek customs. In reaction, those who came to be known as Pharisees,* remembering the call to separation from pagan ways that characterized the restoration of Israel* after the Exile (cf. Ezra 10:11; *see* Judaism), exhorted all Jews to intensify their holiness and sense of unique identity by voluntarily living according to the priestly laws of ritual purity every day of the year. Although they did not reject the priesthood or the Temple cult, in light of the priests' and the Temple's vulnerability to impurity, the Pharisees sought to renew Israel by shifting the locus of holiness to their homes. This resulted in a special focus on the purity of one's everyday food and of one's companions at every meal.

The Pharisees regarded their tables at home as surrogates for the Lord's altar in the Temple in Jerusalem and therefore strove to maintain in their households and among their eating companions the state of ritual purity required of priests in Temple service (Neusner). The food had to be properly tithed, prepared and served but in itself did not symbolize any event (Passover was an exception). Pharisees prescribed no special prayers or unusual foods for their meals. But they did insist on eating only with companions who had "undefiled hands" (Mk 7:2-4), that is, with persons in a state of ritual purity (cf. Ex 30:19-21). The Pharisees longed for the time when all of Israel would live in such a state of holiness. They believed that Israel's identity and blessed future depended on it.

This is the context in which Jesus' practice of a radically open table fellowship is remembered in the NT. The exclusive and hierarchical meal practices of other Jewish groups, such as the Essenes, play no explicit role in any early Christian document. The Synoptic Gospels are consistent in specifically presenting Jesus in sharp contrast to Pharisaic practice as a teacher* and healer (see Healing) who in God's* name welcomed at table an astonishing variety of both reputable and disreputable persons. This strongly suggests that Jesus' open table fellowship was a strategy used to challenge social and religious exclusivism wherever it was accepted as normal or officially sanctioned (Koenig, 20).

2. The Historical Jesus and Table Fellowship.
There is a high level of scholarly agreement that Jesus practiced a radically inclusive table fellowship as a central strategy in his announcement and redefinition of the in-breaking rule of God (see Kingdom of God). Although a few writers have challenged the historicity of Jesus actually eating with "toll collectors (see Taxes) and sinners*" (Smith 1989), the evidence for such an intentionally and symbolically open table is quite strong, being found in multiple sources and in various traditional forms. The sources include Mark, the Synoptic sayings source (Q*), Luke's unique material and probably the Gospel of Thomas (see Gospels [Apocryphal]). The forms include controversy stories (Mk 2:15-17 par. Mt 9:9-13 and Lk 5:29-32), kingdom parables* (Lk 14:15-24 par. Mt 22:1-13; Gos. Thom. 64), pronouncement stories (Lk 7:36-50; 19:1-10), brief sayings (Mt 8:11-12 par. Lk 13:28-29; 14:12-14), opponents' criticisms (Mt 11:18-19 par. Lk 7:33-34) and a summary (Lk 15:1-2).

Scholars have called particular attention to the odd saying of Jesus found in the Synoptic Sayings Source (Q), Matthew 11:16-19 and its parallel Luke 7:31-35. The presentations of this saying reveal little if any post-resurrection idealization of Jesus; thus they seem to offer an authentic glimpse into Jesus' own milieu by noting the people's criticism of John the Baptizer (see John the Baptist) as one who "has a demon" and of

Jesus as "a glutton and a drunkard, a friend of toll collectors and sinners." The charge against John is unique in the NT and seems strange in light of the early Christians' memory of the claim that Jesus was possessed by a demon* (Mk 3:22 and par.). The charge against Jesus is also unique and must have been an embarrassment for the early church, especially since the insult is not rebutted in this passage.

In no other Christian tradition is Jesus' open table fellowship denounced so sharply, and here the memory may be of Jesus' own caricature of the responses to John and him from their Galilean contemporaries. By expressing the spirit of their responses in pointed self-insults, Jesus may have intended to take the wind out of his critics' sails (Koenig, 23). In any case, the circumstances of the historical Jesus, rather than those of the post-resurrection Christian communities, provide the most plausible context for this sort of serious word-play. Supporting this judgment is the unique use of friend (philos) in this saying. The term appears nowhere else on Jesus' lips as a self-designation, nor is it used in any other charge against him. To be reproached as a "friend of toll collectors" places Jesus plausibly in a Galilean context, where Herod's toll collectors were shunned by most people not so much because of their ritual impurity as because of their reputation for dishonest gouging of both rich and poor (see Rich and Poor).

It is thus highly probable that Jesus did associate frequently with such immoral people, at table and elsewhere. And as one who claimed to speak for God, his indiscriminate behavior greatly offended a wide spectrum of people who had been injured by the likes of Levi (Mk 2:13-17). In his message and table praxis, eating with anyone who would eat with him, Jesus challenged the central role played by table fellowship in reinforcing boundaries and statuses widely believed to be sanctioned by God. His use of table fellowship as a divine tool for undermining boundaries and hierarchies made him an enemy of social stability in the eyes of leading contemporaries.

Furthermore, a strong case may be made for the historicity of Jesus' criticism of hierarchical human relationships, found in Mark, Luke's unique material and Matthew's unique material, and remembered in the form of pronouncement stories (Mk 9:33-37 par. Lk 9:46-48; Mk 10:42-45 par. Mt 20:25-28 and Lk 22:24-30), parables (Lk 14:7-11; 18:9-14), brief sayings (Mt 23:11-12) and symbolic narrative and comment (Jn 13:3-16). Such status differences were reinforced at social meals, so that the meal settings for Jesus' challenge of this social practice, which are emphasized by Luke 14:7-11; 22:24-30 and by John 13:3-16, would have rung true for their readers in the ancient world.

Of the Evangelists, Mark and Luke seem particularly concerned about the role of meals in the congregations of their readers. They express this concern by presenting the traditions regarding Jesus' criticism of traditional rankings at meals and his offensively inclusive table fellowship with unique and striking emphases.

3. Jesus' Table Praxis in Mark.

Mark presents Jesus' table praxis as a metaphor for Christian discipleship* in general; the disciples' growing inability to comprehend the significance of Jesus' meal strategy is symbolic of their failure to understand the nature of Jesus' entire mission (Klosinski). For Mark the Last Supper is the climactic last meal at which discipleship collapses completely. Mark emphasizes the rule of God and Christian discipleship together as the basis for an alternative community that practiced a social ethic undermining boundaries and subverting traditional categories of status and hierarchy. For this community the primary social virtue was serving (slave's work), symbolized by serving each other at an inclusive table, with Jesus himself as the prime example (Mk 10:43-45; see Jn 13).

Mark dramatizes Jesus' strategy in his story about the celebration following Levi's positive response to Jesus' call to discipleship (Mk 2:15-17; see Mt 9:10-13 and Lk 5:29-32). At this banquet (Mark's Greek implies that they were reclining at a formal meal) Jesus and his "many followers" crossed significant social boundaries by eating with "many toll collectors and sinners," provoking sharp criticism from the scribes of the Pharisees (were they also invited?). This sets up Jesus' general observation that "those who are well do not need a physician but those who are sick do. I didn't come to call the righteous, but sinners."

In Mark 7:1-23 Pharisees accuse some of Jesus' disciples of eating with "defiled hands" and presumably of not caring if the hands of their table companions were unwashed, that is, of practicing open table fellowship and ignoring the boundaries set by the traditions of the elders.* Jesus defends their praxis by arguing that the ritual purity of one's body or one's food is irrelevant to God. The important matter is how one treats others. Yet the disciples are presented as resistant and missing the point, requiring special instruction (Mk 7:17-19).

Thematically related to these passages is the feeding of the five thousand (Mk 6:30-44; Mt 14:13-21; Lk 9:11-17; Jn 6:5-13), which is the only miracle tradition attributed to Jesus present in all four Gospels (see also the feeding of the four thousand in Mk 8:1-9 par. Mt 15:32-39). Common to all four writers was a meal tradition made extraordinary by the very large number who shared in an unexpected abundance for which Jesus was the host. The food was shared with all who were present, without any boundaries or tests of purity. Unique to Mark is his apparent intention to link the feedings of the five thousand and the four thousand to Jesus' final meal with his disciples, suggested by Jesus' "blessing, breaking and giving" of bread in all three passages.

In Mark's presentation of the Last Supper (Mk 14:18-25) the disciples' increasing inability to understand Jesus and his mission climaxes in betrayal. At this last occasion of table fellowship before his crucifixion, Jesus continued to practice the forgiveness (see Forgiveness of Sins) which had characterized his earlier table praxis. Mark stresses that Jesus and his betrayer dipped their bread in the common bowl together; Judas (see Judas Iscariot), not Jesus, withdrew his hand from the table (Bartchy, 56). At the only meal in the narrative which Jesus and the Twelve celebrate together by themselves, all followed Judas in turning the bread of forgiveness into the bread of abandonment. Only the women, including the unnamed disciple who anointed Jesus for his burial while he reclined at table in the home of Simon the Leper (see Leprosy), remained faithful (Mk 14:3-11; 15:40-41). For Mark and his community faithful discipleship is based on understanding what Jesus was about when he shared bread at his table and then living according to his serving praxis.

4. Jesus' Open "Symposia" in Luke.

Luke gives more attention to table etiquette, table fellowship and the households in which these meals were eaten than any other NT writer (see Luke, Gospel of). He highlights offering hospitality and sharing food as occasions which display the sharp contrast between the radical inclusiveness of Jesus' mission and the various degrees of exclusiveness demanded by his competitors for renewing Israel, the Pharisees and scribes,* who repeatedly charged Jesus with "receiving sinners and eating with them" (Lk 15:1-2).

Among scholars of meals in the ancient world, a consensus has begun to develop that Luke's unique presentation of Jesus as a teacher in the context of meals was influenced by his awareness of the symposium tradition that was popular in Greco-Roman literature (Smith 1987). According to that tradition, with the *Symposia* of Plato and Xenophon as archetypes, the symposium was the drinking and talking party that followed a formal banquet. It provided not only for eating with one's peers but also for exchanges of wit and discussion of serious subjects of mutual interest. Many of Luke's readers would have experienced symposia as the central social activity of such groups as the popular funeral clubs, trade associations and philosophical schools. At these formal meals the diners reclined around a central table on couches most commonly arranged in a U-shape called a "triclinium." Since one's position at the table displayed one's rank relative to the other guests, the host used special care in assigning positions of honor, beginning at the right of the entrance.

Luke 14:7-11 presents Jesus reclining (Luke's Greek implies a formal banquet setting) and teaching at the table of a Pharisee whose many guests had sought out the positions of honor. In this parable unique to Luke, Jesus urges the guests not to seek honor but to defer to others, "for everyone who exalts himself will be humbled, and he who humbles himself will be exalted" (Lk 14:11), a saying which both Matthew 23:12 and Luke 18:4 present in settings without meals. The structure of Luke 14 suggests further influence of the symposium genre, not only in the ambiance of a dialog (Lk 14:7, 12, 15), but also in the specific mention of the host, the guest of honor and main speaker (Jesus), the invited guests and the uninvited guests (Lk 14:13, 23, 25; 15:1).

Perhaps the most striking evidence for Luke's interest in the symposium format is the meal setting provided in Luke 22:24-27 for the anti-hierarchical tradition found in Mark 10:35-45. While reclining at the Last Supper with his disciples, Jesus speaks strong words to them about who among them was to be regarded as the greatest, then asks: "For which is greater, one who reclines at table, or one who serves? Is it not the one reclining? But I am among you as one who serves!" With such words Luke must have hoped to motivate his readers to modify their own traditional meal praxis (see Service).

Luke 7:36-50 and 11:37-52 provide further evidence for this Hellenistic emphasis on meals as the context for Jesus' teaching, describing two more occasions at which Jesus reclined at table and taught in a Pharisee's house. Luke uses these settings to dramatize the sharp contrast between Jesus' radically inclusive message, reinforced by his table praxis, and the exclusive boundaries of purity set by the Pharisees and scribes that circumscribed their own meals.

Unique to the tension-filled meal setting of the special tradition in Luke 7:36-50 (but see also Mk 14:3-9) is the presentation of a woman described as a "sinner" who intruded into the meal hosted by Simon the Pharisee. Jesus and Simon are shown disagreeing

strongly about the appropriateness of her presence. She clearly felt at home in the company of Jesus, who had forgiven her many sins; and she lavished attention on him in ways that highlighted Simon's failure to show the customary marks of hospitality. In view of the immediately following and unique listing of Mary called Magdalene, Joanna, Susanna and "many" other women, both as supporters of Jesus' itinerant ministry in Galilee* and as traveling companions (Lk 8:1-3), it is likely that Luke intended here to emphasize that Jesus welcomed all kinds of women at his table (see Women; Prostitute). Note also Luke's unique presenting of Jesus' welcoming Mary as his student in the context of a meal about to be served (Lk 10:38-42).

The order of the symposium pattern seems to be reversed in Jesus' post-resurrection meal with two disciples in Emmaus (Lk 24:13-35). For although the meal is described formally as one at which they reclined, the discourse came first, while they were on the road. And although the two had invited Jesus, he quickly became the host. Luke drew on both Mark and the Synoptic sayings source (Q) for traditions about Jesus' eating with "toll collectors and sinners" and developed this theme by characterizing Jesus' entire ministry as a special mission to the poor, the captives, the blind, the oppressed and society's outcasts.

Luke especially uses meal imagery as a major means of conveying Jesus' good news. Central elements of this theme are recalled in Luke's unique story of Jesus' eating with Zacchaeus, described as both a chief "toll collector" and a "sinner" (Lk 19:1-9) in a scenario probably intended to remind the reader of Jesus' remarkably inclusive meal at Levi's house (Lk 5:27-32). And in Luke's presentation of the great banquet (Lk 14:15-24), a parable from the sayings source, Jesus' table companions under the rule of God include "the poor and maimed and blind and lame" (Matthew's version in Mt 22:10 mentions "both bad and good" guests). Luke's emphasis was probably "hard bread" for the elite Christians among his readers. For participation in such a socially inclusive community might well have cut them off from their prior social networks on which their status depended. From the perspective of Luke and Acts together, God intends this new community to offer reconciliation and solidarity among Jews and Gentiles,* men and women, rich and poor.

5. Conclusion.

Apparently, one goal of Jesus' strategy of inclusive table fellowship was presenting himself and his followers as a living parable of how a renewed Israel could indeed live together from God's abundance

(Koenig 28). He presented the rule of God, using images of food, drink (*see* Wine) and home as a roving banquet hall by which God sought Israelites to be guests and then hosts. At this table they were offered reconciliation with God, a true home, and a spiritual and material abundance, as the basis for offering all these good things to each other, to others yet to come and even to enemies. A saying of Jesus, probably preserved in the Synoptic sayings source, linked the practice of inclusive table fellowship with the final consummation: "Many will come from east and west and recline at table with Abraham, Isaac and Jacob in the kingdom of Heaven" (Mt 8:11 par. Lk 13:29; see Is 25:6-8).

See also BREAD; LAST SUPPER; PROSTITUTE; RICH AND POOR; SINNER; TAXES.

BIBLIOGRAPHY. S. S. Bartchy, "Table Fellowship with Jesus and the 'Lord's Meal' at Corinth," in *Increase in Learning: Essays in Honor of James G. Van Buren*, ed. R. Owens and B. Hamm (Manhattan, KS: Manhattan Christian College, 1979) 45-61; M. J. Borg, *Conflict, Holiness and Politics in the Teachings of Jesus* (New York: Edwin Mellen, 1984) 71-143; J. Jeremias, *The Eucharistic Words of Jesus* (rev. ed.; New York: Scribner's, 1966; repr. Philadelphia: Fortress, 1977); L. E. Klosinski, "The Meals in Mark" (Ph.D. Diss., Claremont Graduate School, 1988); J. Koenig, *New Testament Hospitality* (Philadelphia: Fortress, 1985); H. Moxnes, "Meals and the new community in Luke," *SEA* 51 (1986) 158-67; J. Neusner, 1982. "Two Pictures of the Pharisees: Philosophical Circle or Eating Club?" *ATR* 64 (1982) 525-38; J. H. Neyrey, "Ceremonies in Luke-Acts: The Case of Meals and Table-Fellowship," in *The Social World of Luke-Acts: Models for Interpretation*, ed. J. H. Neyrey (Peabody, MA: Hendrickson, 1991) 361-87; D. E. Smith, "Table Fellowship as a Literary Motif in the Gospel of Luke," *JBL* 106 (1987) 613-38; idem, "The Historical Jesus at Table," *Society of Biblical Literature 1989 Seminar Papers*, ed. D. J. Lull (Atlanta: Scholars, 1989) 466-89.   S. S. Bartchy

TALMUD. *See* RABBINIC TRADITIONS AND WRITINGS.

TARGUMS

Interpretive renderings of the Hebrew Bible in Aramaic for use in synagogue* worship* are called by the Aramaic term *targûm* (pl. *targûmîm*), meaning simply "translation." But the type and purpose of the rendering involved in Judaism* was distinctive. The general phenomenon of targum needs to be appreciated, and the specific documents involved need to be described before the question of targumic influence on Jesus and the Gospels may be taken up.

1. Language and Character of Targums
2. Classifications of Targums
3. The Relevance of the Targums for Jesus and Gospels Studies
4. Summary

1. Language and Character of Targums.

1.1. The Aramaic Language. Aramaic survived the demise of the Persian Empire as a lingua franca in the Near East. It was embraced enthusiastically by Jews (as by other peoples, such as Nabateans and Palmyrenes), and the Aramaic portions of the Hebrew Bible (in Ezra and Daniel) testify to a significant change in the linguistic constitution of Judaism.* Conceivably, one reason for Jewish enthusiasm in embracing Aramaic was a distant memory of its affiliation with Hebrew, but it should be borne in mind that Hebrew is a different language from Aramaic (*see* Languages of Palestine). By the time of Jesus, Aramaic appears to have been the common language of Judea, Samaria and Galilee* (although distinctive dialects were spoken); Hebrew was understood by an educated stratum of the population, and some familiarity with Greek was a commercial and bureaucratic necessity.

1.2. The Character of the Targums. The linguistic situation in Judea and Galilee demanded translation of the Hebrew Bible for the purpose of popular study and worship. Although the fragments of Leviticus and Job in Aramaic which have been discovered at Qumran (*see* Dead Sea Scrolls) are technically targums, they do not represent the literary genre targum. They are reasonably literal renderings; that is, there is some attempt at formal correspondence between the Hebrew rendered and the Aramaic which is presented. The targums which are extant, as documents deliberately guarded within rabbinic Judaism, are of an altogether different character.

The aim of producing targums was to give the sense of the Hebrew Scriptures. Hence, paraphrase is characteristic of the targums. Theoretically, in the synagogue a passage of Scripture was to be rendered orally by an interpreter *(meturgeman)*, after the reading in Hebrew. The meturgeman was not to be confused with the reader, lest the congregation mistake the interpretation for the original text (cf. *m. Meg.* 4:4-10 and *b. Meg.* 23b-25b). (Regulations which specify the number of verses which may be read prior to the delivery of a targum probably date from well after the period of the NT.) Although the renderings so delivered were oral in principle, over the course of time traditions in important centers of learning became fixed, and coalescence became possible. Moreover, the emergence of the rabbis as the dominant leaders within Judaism after A.D. 70 provided a centralizing tendency without which literary targums could never have been produced (see Rabbinic Traditions and Writings).

The targums preserved by the rabbis are notoriously difficult to describe. They are paraphrases, but the theological programs conveyed are not always consistent, even within a given targum. Although the rabbis attempted to control targumic activity, the extant targums themselves sometimes contradict rabbinic proscriptions. For example, *Mishnah Megillah* 4:9 insists that Leviticus 18:21 ("You must not give of your seed, to deliver it to Moloch") should *not* be interpreted with respect to sexual intercourse with Gentiles.* On the other hand, the Targum Pseudo-Jonathan—a late work produced long after rabbinic authority had been established—takes just that line. The targums evince such oddities because they are the products of a dialectical interaction between folk practice and rabbinic supervision, a dynamic tension which continued over centuries. Each of the extant targums crystallizes that relationship for a given moment, and toward the end of the process—as Arabic replaced Aramaic as the vernacular—the targums came to be the preserve of a learned few.

2. Classifications of Targums.

The targums may conveniently be classified as those of the Torah (the Pentateuch); those of the Prophets (both "Former Prophets," or the so-called historical works; and the "Latter Prophets," or the Prophets as commonly designated in English); and those of the Writings (or Hagiographa), following the conventional designations of the Hebrew Bible in Judaism. We should stress at the outset, however, that although the Hebrew Bible is almost entirely rendered by the targums in aggregate, there was no single moment, and no particular movement, which produced a comprehensive Bible in Aramaic. The targums are essentially complex in their purposes, places of origin and dialects of Aramaic.

2.1. The Pentateuch. Among the targums to the Pentateuch, Targum Onqelos is a suitable point of departure. Among all the targums, Onqelos appears to correspond best to rabbinic ideals of translation. Although paraphrase is evident, especially in order to describe God and his revelation in suitably reverent terms, the high degree of correspondence with the Hebrew of the Masoretic Text (and, presumably, with the Hebrew text current in antiquity) is striking. The dialect of Onqelos is "Middle Aramaic," which would place the targum between the first century B.C. and the third century A.D. The targum should probably be

dated toward the end of that period, in the wake of similar efforts to produce a literal Greek rendering during the second century, and well after any strict construal of the principle that targums were to be oral. By contrast with the rabbinic ethos which permitted the creation and preservation of Onqelos, one might recall the story of Rabbi Gamaliel, who is said during the first century to have immured a targum of Job in a wall of the Temple (b. Šabb. 115a). The Targum Neophyti I was discovered in 1949 by Alejandro Díez Macho in the Library of the Neophytes in Rome. The paraphrases of Neophyti are substantially different from those of Onqelos. Entire paragraphs are added (as when Cain and Abel argue in the field prior to the first case of murder, Gen 4:8), the rendering is looser, and it is impossible to predict when remarkable freedom is to be indulged. The dialect of Neophyti is known as Palestinian Aramaic, to distinguish it from the Babylonian Aramaic of Onqelos. But the chronology of the two targums is about the same; the differences between them are a function more of program than dating. The rabbis of Babylonia, who called Onqelos "our targum," exerted greater influence there than did their colleagues in the west. In order to avoid confusion, it is probably wiser to designate non-Babylonian targums as Tiberean, rather than Palestinian.

The latest representative of the type of expansive rendering found in Neophyti is Targum Pseudo-Jonathan. Its reference to the names of Mohammed's wife and daughter in Genesis 21:21 put its final composition sometime after the seventh century A.D. (This oddly designated targum is so called in that the name "Jonathan" was attributed to it during the Middle Ages because its name was abbreviated with the Hebrew letter *yod*. But the letter probably stood for "Jerusalem," although that designation is not established critically. "Pseudo-Jonathan" is therefore an admission of uncertainty.) Neophyti and Pseudo-Jonathan are together known as Palestinian targums, to distinguish their dialects and their style of interpretation from those of Onqelos, but the designation Tiberean is (once again) to be preferred.

Neophyti and Pseudo-Jonathan are to be associated with two other targums, or to be more precise, groups of targums. The first group, in chronological order, consists of the fragments of the Cairo Geniza. They were originally part of more complete works, dating between the seventh and the eleventh centuries, which were deposited in the Geniza of the Old Synagogue in Cairo. In the type and substance of interpretation, these fragments are comparable to the other targums of the Tiberean type. The same may be said of the Fragments Targum which was collected as a miscellany of targumic readings during the Middle Ages. An interesting feature of the targums of the Tiberean type is that their relationship might be described as synoptic, in some ways comparable to the relationship among the Gospels. All four of the Palestinian targums, for example, convey a debate between Cain and Abel, and they do so with those variations of order and wording which are well known to students of the Synoptic Gospels (*see* Synoptic Problem).

2.2. The Prophets. Both the Former and the Latter Prophets are extant in Aramaic in a single collection, although the date and character of each targum within the collection needs to be studied individually. The entire corpus, however, is ascribed by rabbinic tradition (*b. Meg.* 3a) to Jonathan ben Uzziel (hence the designation as Targum Jonathan), a disciple of Hillel, the famous contemporary of Jesus. On the other hand, there are passages of the Targum of the Prophets which accord precisely with renderings given in the name of Joseph bar Ḥiyya, a rabbi of the fourth century (cf. *Tg.Isa* 5:17b and *b. Pesaḥ.* 68a). As it happens, the Targum of Isaiah (which has been subjected to more study than any of the Targums of the Prophets) shows signs of a nationalistic eschatology* which was current just after the destruction of the Temple in A.D. 70 (*see* Destruction of Jerusalem), and of the more settled perspective of the rabbis in Babylon some three hundred years later. It appears that Targum Jonathan as a whole is the result of two major periods of collecting and editing interpretations by the rabbis, the first period being Tannaitic (from Hillel to the completion of the Mishnah, c. A.D. 20-200), and the second Amoraic (from the completion of the Mishnah until the completion of the Babylonian and Jerusalem Talmuds, c. A.D. 200-400/500). After Targum Jonathan was composed, probably near the time the Fragments Targum was assembled, targumic addenda were appended in certain of its manuscripts. They are represented in the Codex Reuchlinianus (which is dated A.D. 1105).

2.3. The Writings. Of the three categories of targums, that of the Writings is without question the most diverse. Although the Targum to Psalms is formally a translation, substantially it is better described as a midrash, while the Targum of Proverbs appears to be a fairly straightforward rendition of the Peshitta, and the Targum of Esther seems designed for use within a celebration of the liturgy of Purim. The Targums of the Writings are the most problematic within modern study. In view of their late date (in most cases medieval), of the three general categories of targums

they are also of the least interest for students of the New Testament.

3. The Relevance of the Targums for Jesus and Gospels Studies.
The significance of the targums for appreciating Jesus and the Gospels follows naturally from assessing their purpose and provenience. Fundamentally, the targums constitute evidence of the first class for the way in which the Hebrew Scriptures were understood, not simply among rabbis, but more commonly by the congregations for whom the targums were intended.

3.1. Obstacles in Utilizing the Targums. Insofar as what is reflected in a targum is representative of the reception of Scripture in the first century, that targumic material is of crucial importance for any student of the New Testament. But care must also be taken lest the perspective of *later materials* be accepted uncritically as representative of an *earlier period,* thus resulting in anachronistic exegeses. There are clearly readings in the targums which presuppose events long after the death of Jesus. One example of such a reading is Targum of Isaiah 53, which clearly anticipates that the reader takes the destruction of the Temple as given. The "Suffering Servant" as presented in the Targum simply cannot be assumed to be a model of the Messiah in the time of Jesus, and in any case the targumic Messiah is triumphant rather than a man of sorrows (*see* Servant of Yahweh).

A particular problem is posed for modern study by the persistent notion that there is somewhere extant today a single "Palestinian Targum," which substantially represents the understanding of the Hebrew Bible in the time of Jesus. There was a time when that was a comprehensible position, because it was taken that "Palestinian Aramaic" was more ancient than "Babylonian Aramaic." Today, however, the discoveries at Qumran have cast a dazzling new light upon Targum Onqelos and Targum Jonathan for the Prophets, which makes them appear more ancient than was supposed some fifty years ago, and more similar to Aramaic as spoken in Palestine (*see* Languages of Palestine). Targum Pseudo-Jonathan appears to represent a more recent tendency, not only in language, but also in its historical allusions and its form. Moreover, the present understanding of early Judaism is that it was too variegated to allow for the formation of a single, authoritative tradition of rendering, such as the designation "Palestinian Targum" would suggest.

The difficulty of assessing the precise form of targumic tradition(s) within the first century should also make us wary of any claim that we know the dialect(s) of Aramaic which were current in that period. The literary remains of the language are sporadic, dialectical variation was great and there sometimes appears to have been a significant difference between the language as spoken and the language as written. For all these reasons, attempts to retranslate the Greek Gospels into Jesus' own language are extremely speculative. When the Tiberean targums are appealed to by way of antecedent, speculation is piled upon speculation.

3.2. The Proper Use of the Targums for Gospels Studies. The composite nature of the targums is, nonetheless, such that on occasion one may discern in them the survival of materials which did circulate in the time of Jesus and which therefore influenced his teaching and/or the memory of that teaching among those disciples who were familiar with such traditions. An example of such a survival might be Leviticus 22:28 in Pseudo-Jonathan, "My people, children of Israel, since our father is merciful in heaven, so should you be merciful upon the earth." The expansion in the targum is unquestionably innovative, as compared to what may be read in the Masoretic Text, so that the possible echo in Luke 6:36, within the address known conventionally as "the sermon on the plain" (*see* Sermon on the Mount), is with the Targum or with nothing at all.

It is, of course, theoretically possible that the saying originated with Jesus, and was then anonymously taken up within the Targum. Without doubt, the statement is rhetorically more at home within Luke than in Pseudo-Jonathan, where it appears unmotivated. But it seems inherently unlikely that Pseudo-Jonathan, which of all the Pentateuchal targums is perhaps the most influenced by a concern to guard and articulate Judaic integrity, would inadvertently convey a saying of Jesus. More probably, both Pseudo-Jonathan and Luke's Jesus are here independently passing on the wisdom of a proverbial statement. The targumic echo is therefore most certainly not the source of Jesus' statement, but it may help us to describe the nature of Jesus' statement.

Examples such as Leviticus 22:28 demonstrate that the targums might have a heuristic value in illustrating the sort of Judaism which Jesus and his followers took for granted. Recent study has greatly increased the catalog of such instances. But there are also cases in which Jesus appears to have cited a form of the book of Isaiah which is closer to the Targum Jonathan than to any other extant source. In such cases, an awareness of the fact helps us better to understand his preaching.

Targum Isaiah 6:9-10 is an especially famous exam-

ple, and it helps to explain Mark 4:12. The statement in Mark could be taken to mean that Jesus told parables *with the purpose that* (Gk *hina*) people might see and not perceive, hear and not understand, lest they turn and be forgiven. But the Targum also (unlike the Masoretic Text and the Septuagint) refers to people not being forgiven (rather than not being healed), and that suggests that the Targum may give the key to the meaning supposed in Mark. The relevant clause in the targum refers to people who behave in such a way *so that* (*d* in Aramaic) they see and do not perceive, hear and do not understand, lest they repent and be forgiven. It appears that Jesus was characterizing people in the targumic manner, as he characterizes himself similarly in Mark with a clause employing *hina* (cf. 9:12), not acting in order to be misunderstood (*see* Hardness of Heart). In much the same way, Jesus in Mark 9:48 links a phrase from Isaiah (66:24) to the idea of punishment in Gehenna, a linkage also attested in the Targum.

Time and again the targums present a synoptic relationship amongst their materials, be it in the instance of the dispute between Cain and Abel (as already mentioned), the *Aqedah* (the "binding" of Isaac: Gen 22 in the Tiberean Targums and Is 33:7 in the margin of Reuchlinianus), or the Poem of the Four Nights (Ex 12:42 in the Tiberean Targums). Because the synoptic phenomenon of the targums involves four documents, not three (as in the case of the relationship among the Gospels), it is even more complicated to trace a purely documentary, rigidly literary relationship among the texts. The study of the synoptic aspect of the targums remains in its infancy, but it appears possible that once it is better understood we will also conceive of the literary relationship among the Gospels in a different way.

4. Summary.

The targums are a rich source of that form of early Judaism and rabbinic Judaism where the folk and the expert aspects of the religion met. For that reason, serious students of the New Testament might well read them, as helping them to comprehend the context within which Jesus taught and his movement first developed, before the transition to a Hellenistic* compass and to the Greek language. In particular cases the targums uniquely present material which helps to illuminate Jesus' teaching. In other instances they may support what we know from other sources. It might be that a targum just happens to preserve proverbial material which Jesus cites, or alludes to. But there are also cases in which Jesus seems to have been influenced by a specifically targumic understanding of the Bible. Finally, quite apart from what they may tell us of particular passages in the Gospels, the targums give us an example of how composite documents evolved within Judaism, and to that extent they may provide an analogy for understanding the Gospels themselves.

See also JUDAISM; LANGUAGES OF PALESTINE; RABBINIC TRADITIONS AND WRITINGS.

BIBLIOGRAPHY. **Texts:** A critical English edition of the targums is being published in 19 vols.: M. McNamara, ed., The Aramaic Bible (The Targums) (Wilmington: Michael Glazier, 1987—). **Studies:** J. Bowker, *The Targums and Rabbinic Literature: An Introduction to Jewish Interpretation of Scripture* (Cambridge: University Press, 1969); A. N. Chester, *Divine Revelation and Divine Titles in the Pentateuchal Targumim* (TSAF; Tübingen: J. C. B. Mohr, 1986); B. D. Chilton, *A Galilean Rabbi and His Bible: Jesus' Use of the Interpreted Scripture of His Time* (GNS 8; Wilmington: Glazier, 1984); idem, *The Glory of Israel: The Theology and Provenience of the Isaiah Targum* (JSOTSup 23; Sheffield: JSOT, 1982); J. A. Fitzmyer, *Essays on the Semitic Background of the New Testament* (SBLSBS 5; Missoula: Scholars, 1974); idem, *A Wandering Aramean: Collected Aramaic Essays* (SBLMS 25; Missoula: Scholars, 1979); M. McNamara, *The New Testament and the Palestinian Targum to the Pentateuch* (AnBib 27; Rome: Pontifical Biblical Institute, 1966); idem, *Targum and Testament. Aramaic Paraphrases of the Hebrew Bible: A Light on the New Testament* (Grand Rapids: Eerdmans, 1972); A. D. York, "The Dating of Targumic Literature," *JSJ* 5 (1974) 49-62; idem, "The Targum in the Synagogue and the School," *JSJ* 10 (1979) 74-86.   B. D. Chilton

TAX COLLECTOR. *See* TAXES; SINNER.

TAXES

Jews in the time of Jesus were subject to a complex system of religious and secular taxation, the extent and burden of which is difficult to determine. The Gospels reveal the scorn directed toward those who participated especially in the Roman customs system because they were presumed to be dishonest.

1. Roman Taxation
2. Tax Collector
3. Temple Tax

1. Roman Taxation.

When Rome* annexed Judea in 63 B.C., the High Priest Hyrcanus (*see* Priest and Priesthood) was given responsibility to pay tribute to Rome. Julius reduced the tribute in 47 B.C. from an uncertain amount (perhaps 33 per cent of the harvest, as under the

Seleucids) to 12.5 per cent of the harvest, and he remitted taxes in the sabbatical year (*Ant.* 14.202). Herod was required initially to pay tribute for Idumea and Samaria, but this was remitted in 30 B.C., leaving him to raise his own revenues after the Roman fashion and presumably on a Roman scale (although he did occasionally reduce taxes during crises: *Ant.* 15.365; 16.64). After Herod's death Rome allowed Antipas to raise tribute for Rome in Galilee* and Perea, while Judea (after the deposition of Archelaus in A.D. 6) came under direct Roman control in the form of procurators, who probably made the Sanhedrin* responsible for the collection of Roman dues (*J.W.* 2.405).

According to the larger of Josephus' two estimates, the total revenue of Herod's territories distributed after his death was 800 talents (*J.W.* 2.92-97; in *Ant.* 17.318-20 it is 600 talents), which is the equivalent of 4.8 million drachmae, or day-wages, per annum. Population estimates vary, but if we estimate 250,000 working males, we can calculate that the average man worked abou t three weeks per year for the state. For those who lived close to the edge of poverty—and the majority of scholars think that there were many who did—this amount would be felt as a heavy burden.

1.1. Kinds of Taxes. There were three principal kinds of duties: the land tax, or *tributum soli;* the head tax, or *tributum capitis;* and the customs system. These must be distinguished in terms of liability and quantity.

1.1.1. Land Tax. The bulk of the tribute due to Rome was collected in the form of a tax on the produce of the land. This exempted those who did not own land, although tenant farmers certainly paid indirectly in the form of rent. Owners of small plots may also have been exempt. Itinerant laborers and others such as fishermen were by definition exempt, but there may have been other taxes which served to distribute liability to the nonagricultural sector. Residents of Jerusalem, for example, were subject to a house tax and a city sales tax (*Ant.* 18.90; 19.299). The amount (usually payable in grain) required for the land tax was probably fixed by landlords or other authorities based on estimates of a percentage of the likely yield: probably about one-tenth. Since these amounts were determined in advance, the obligation for revenues lost due to bad crops or individual bankruptcy had to be absorbed by distribution within the tax district.

So little information is available concerning crop yield, population, rents and taxes, that it may never be possible to calculate the burden on the average farmer. General statements in the ancient sources are not conclusive. Josephus complains about Herod's high revenues, but he specifies the charge by reference to direct appropriation of the property of nobles (*Ant.* 17.307). In another place Josephus describes prewar Galilee as thriving (*J.W.* 3.42-50). He makes no reference to economic causes for the war, unless this is to be deduced from his accounts of the increase in banditry (presumably due to bankruptcy) in the decade before the war. Tacitus records a request (probably granted) for reduction of taxes in A.D. 17 (*Ann.* 2.42), but he describes the region as peaceful during the reign of Tiberius (*Hist.* 5.9). Neither the amount nor the impact of the land tax, therefore, can be determined with precision from the extant sources. It is likely, however, that most of those in the agricultural sector lived close enough to minimal subsistence to feel almost any amount of tribute as a threatened or real burden.

Currency and Sums of Money in the Gospels

Name	Metal	Equivalent and Comment
Lepton (Greek)	bronze	coin of least value circulating at time of Jesus (the "widow's mite" of Mk 12:42) and worth an eighth of a Roman asarion
Quadrans (Roman)	bronze	equal to one-fourth an asarion (*kodrantēs*, Mt 5:26; Mk 12:42)
As/Asarion (Roman)	bronze	equal to one-sixteenth of a denarius (Mt 10:29)
Denarius (Roman)	silver	one denarius was average pay for a day laborer (cf. Mt 20:1-15) and equal to 16 asses
Drachma (Greek)	silver	roughly equal to a Roman denarius; four equal to a shekel
Didrachmon (Greek)	silver	two drachmae, equivalent to half-shekel Temple tax (Mt 17:27)
Shekel (Jewish)	silver	equal to four drachmas
Stater (Greek)	silver	roughly equal to four drachmae (Mt 17:27)
Mina (Greek)	silver	a sum of money, not a coin, equal to 100 drachmae (cf. Lk 15:8)
Talent	silver	a sum of money, not a coin, equal to 6,000 drachmae (cf. Mt 25:14-28)

1.1.2. Head Tax. Another significant portion of tribute due to Rome was collected by means of the head tax. This tax involved a periodic census (Lk 2:1-5; Acts 5:37). The amount was probably one denarius, or one day's wage, per annum (Mt 22:19-21). Liability is more difficult to assess. That males aged fourteen to sixty-five paid seems consistent with Gospel accounts, but this does not preclude the possibility that men were assessed for their wives. It is also possible that, as in other parts of the empire, those who paid the land tax were exempted from the head tax.

1.1.3. Customs System. The Romans appropriated a long-standing system of tolls and duties collected at ports and at tax offices near city gates (Mk 2:11). Rates varied from two to five per cent of value, but goods were subject to multiple taxation on long journeys. Rates and commissions were regulated by law, and from the time of Nero these were posted for inspection. But the complexity of the system and the assessor's power to determine value allowed for injustice. Still, given the prevalence of a village-based subsistence economy, liability was limited to those few who engaged in commercial travel through towns and cities. In these locations of large-scale exchange, tax collectors gathered—and were esteemed—like flies.

1.2. Tax Collection. The direct taxes (the land tax and the head tax) were collected by councils of Jewish leaders and their representatives on an annual basis. The indirect taxes of the customs system were "farmed": the highest bidder paid in advance to collect taxes from a district. These were Jews, not "publicans" (a technical term for members of tax collection organizations abolished by Julius Caesar in 30 B.C.). In this tax-farming system Rome received its money in advance, and the tax farmer made his living from commissions on tolls and customs. These were the "tax collectors" (*telōnai*) of the Gospels. A "chief tax collector," such as Zacchaeus (Lk 19:1-10), was a tax farmer who supervised other collectors.

2. Tax Collector.

It is evident in the Gospels that the title itself is a term of abuse (Mt 5:46; 18:17) or a foil to the hypocrites* (Lk 3:12; 7:29; 8:10-14). Elsewhere it is joined in vituperative apposition to "prostitutes"* (Mt 21:31-32), and most commonly, "sinners"* (e.g., Mk 2:15; Lk 15:1). This attitude was universal: the rabbis* joined tax collectors with "robbers" (*m. B. Qam.* 10:2), and Roman writers joined them with brothel-keepers (Dio Chrysostom, *Disc.* 14.14). The reasons for this scorn vary according to time, place and tax type.

2.1. Tax Farmers and Dishonesty. Some distinction was made between those who collected direct taxes and the tax farmers. The latter were constantly visible and clearly made a living from commissions. To stop people on the road and demand a portion of their goods certainly appeared to be institutionalized robbery, and the only apparent beneficiary was the tax farmer himself. Although the commission system was regulated, the power of the assessor to determine the value of some goods encouraged dishonesty. The instructions of John the Baptist* to tax collectors (Lk 3:12-13) and the restitution pledge of Zacchaeus (Lk 19:8) are consistent with this tendency toward fraud.

Indeed, the practice of selling the office built into the system disregard for the taxpayer: the highest bid translated into the most inflated assessments and the highest commissions. The fact that the tax farmer advanced the money meant that he had excessive wealth to begin with, and in an agrarian subsistence economy, usury was the most common source of such portable wealth. On this assumption, the rabbis regarded as unclean (see Clean and Unclean) any house entered by a tax farmer (m. ohar. 7:6). A corollary to all of this is the practical observation that an occupation which depends for success on suspicion, intrusion, harassment and force tends not to attract the most pleasant personalities. These factors combine to suggest that one did not need to be victimized to share the general view of the tax farmer as an embodiment of dishonesty.

2.2. Tax Collectors and Rome. While tax farmers were scorned primarily for their dishonesty, collectors of direct taxes were despised for their collusion with Rome. This hatred was particularly intense in Judea, which was under direct Roman control. A visiting Galilean with a reputation for association with tax collectors (Lk 7:34; 19:1-10) might well have been suspected of disloyalty, in some minds even for paying the head tax (Mk 12:13-17). It is significant that the question posed to Jesus pertains to the lawfulness, not the amount, of the tax. Its evil was not in its quantity but in its quality: to a fiercely independent people who did not understand or acknowledge the military and economic security afforded by the Roman presence, taxation was a painful symbol of conquest. Jewish labor enriched a distant idolater and his local military representatives. Jesus' answer is not intended to give sanction to Roman taxation but to expose the hypocrisy of the Pharisees,* who ask the question only to force him to choose between popularity with the people and liability to secular law.

3. Temple Tax.

The half-shekel Temple* tax was derived from the one-third shekel Temple tax of Nehemiah 10:32-33 and was raised to a half-shekel possibly under the influence of the half-shekel atonement price of Exodus 30:11-16 (cf. 2 Chron 24:6). The fund was used for Temple maintenance and sacrifices.

3.1. Liability for the Temple Tax. Jewish males over the age of twenty (excepting priests: m. Šeqal. 1:3-4), including the Diaspora (J.W. 7.281), were subject to the Temple tax. The half-shekel was the approximate equivalent of one day's wage, and it was assessed annually. None of the ancient sources, however, state that all Jews paid, and even the inference (e.g., from Ant. 14.110 or m. Šeqal. 1:4) may represent ideology rather than history. The Essenes, for example, interpreted Exodus 30:11-16 to require only one half-shekel per lifetime (4Q159 2:6-7). It is likely that, as in the case of tithes, the Temple tax was voluntary and was paid almost exclusively by Pharisees.

After the war, Vespasian used the Temple tax as a pretense for what amounted to a war indemnity, the didrachmon. Liability for this tax was expanded to women,* children* and slaves. The tax was now compulsory, and the proceeds went to the Temple of Jupiter in Rome (J.W. 7.218). The fact that the Jews had used their own Temple fund for the war (J.W. 6.335) contributed to this connection and perhaps to a limitation (at least initially) of the tax to Pharisees throughout the Empire (possibly implied in Dio Cassius Epit. 65.7.2). Such a situation would have exacerbated tensions between the Pharisees and other Jewish groups, including Christians.

3.2. Jesus and the Temple Tax. Matthew 17:24-27 uses the term didrachma. This may be an anachronistic reference to the Temple tax, an attempt to speak to an issue in Matthew's community, or both. The passage does not imply that all Jews paid the tax, only that Jesus chose to do so. Indeed, the statement of Jesus that "the sons (of the king) are free" stresses voluntarism. If the passage is intended to speak to Matthew's community, it is understandable that questions of solidarity with the Jews would arise before the war, and more poignantly after the war if Pharisees were the focus of the didrachmon. It is less likely but also possible that by "sons of the king" Jesus is referring only to himself (and therefore only to exemption from the Temple tax). But to the extent that the passage has implications for practice, it represents a conciliatory position motivated by love for the Jews.

See also RICH AND POOR; ROME.

BIBLIOGRAPHY. G. Alon, The Jews in Their Land in the Talmudic Age (Jerusalem, 1980); S. Freyne, Galilee from Alexander the Great to Hadrian (Notre Dame: University of Notre Dame, 1980); D. E. Garland, "Matthew's Understanding of the Temple Tax (Matt 17:24-27)," SBLASP 26 (1987) 190-209; F. M. Heichelheim, "Roman Syria," in An Economic Survey of Ancient Rome, ed.

T. Frank (Paterson, NJ: Pagenat Books, 1959); S. Mandell, "Who Paid the Temple Tax When the Jews Were Under Roman Rule?" *HTR* 77 (April 1984) 223-32; O. Michel, "τελώνης," *TDNT* VIII.88-105; P. Perkins, "Taxes in the New Testament," *JRE* 12 (1984) 182-200; E. M. Smallwood, *The Jews Under Roman Rule* (Leiden: E. J. Brill, 1976); M. Stern, "The Province of Judea," in *The Jewish People in the First Century,* ed. S. Safrai and M. Stern (2 vols.; Amsterdam: Van Gorcum, 1974-76) 1.308-76.   T. E. Schmidt

TEACHER

1. "Teacher" As a Form of Address for Jesus
2. "Teacher" As Jesus' Self-Designation
3. "Teacher"—a Christological Title of Exaltation?
4. The Teaching Authority of Jesus
5. Settings for Teaching
6. Forms of Teaching
7. Jesus As Teacher and the Tradition of the Gospels

1. "Teacher" As a Form of Address for Jesus.

1.1. The Forms of Address Used. In all four Gospels Jesus is addressed as *didaskalos.* The parallelism in Matthew 23:8 shows that the vocative *didaskale* normally translates the Hebrew/Aramaic *rabbî* ("my great one"). John 1:38 makes this equation explicit, and it is further supported by some epigraphic evidence from Jerusalem in NT times (*CII* II.1266, 1268-69). In the first century *rabbî* was not yet a fixed title for academically schooled, ordained scribes* as was later the case; it was, however, the form of address most of all for teachers. The Gospels reflect the usage of the word at this earlier stage in its development. *Rabbûnî* is a more exalted-sounding Aramaic variant of *rabbî.* The title *ribbôn* is reserved for God* except in the targums.*

1.2. Luke. The Evangelist who wrote for non-Jews omitted the term *rabbi,* which would have been meaningless to his readers. *Didaskale* also never appears as the form of address used by the disciples for Jesus. Here Luke prefers his own word, *epistatēs,* a more general term for a supervisory or official person. Luke uses it once instead of *rabbi* (Lk 9:33) and twice in place of *didaskale* (Lk 8:24; 9:49), which occur in the parallel incidents found in the other two Synoptics. This word is also used as a term of address (*epistata*) twice by disciples* (Lk 5:5; 8:45) and once by those seeking help (Lk 17:13). It has been assumed that with this special expression Luke sought to heighten Jesus' authority.* Since *epistatēs,* however, occurs not only in material unique to Luke (Lk 5:5; 17:13) but also in pericopes showing strong influence of non-Markan

textual variants (Lk 8:24, 45; 9:33, 49), it could just as well be due to the usage in Luke's sources. Luke has also preserved the use of *didaskale* as a term of address for Jesus by outsiders (Lk 7:40; [8:49]; 9:38; 10:25; 11:45; 12:13; 18:18; 19:39; 20:21, 28, 39; 21:7). The Third Evangelist thus makes it clear that while Jesus appeared to be a teacher, this function did not exhaust the significance he held for his disciples.

1.3. Matthew. In Matthew, as in Luke, *didaskale* is never used by the disciples to address Jesus. Twice Matthew, in contrast to Mark, has replaced the term with the more exalted *kyrie* (Mt 8:25; 17:15; *see* Lord). Where Mark uses the *rabbi* title twice, Matthew omits it in one instance (Mt 21:20) and replaces it with *kyrie* in another (Mt 17:4). Perhaps one cannot fully exclude the possibility that Matthew found *mârî* once in a Semitic source where other exemplars read *rabbî.* It is more likely, however, that intentional replacement is going on. According to Matthew Jesus is more than simply a teacher for his followers; he is the Lord. This is confirmed by the apparent exception in the choice of titles of address: It is a disciple of Jesus, but also the betrayer Judas, who greets Jesus with the normal designation for a teacher, *"rabbi"* (Mt 26:25, 49). In Matthew it is also outsiders who use *didaskale* (Mt 19:16; 22:16, 24, 36), occasionally more so than in the Lukan parallels (see also Mt 8:19; 12:38).

1.4. Mark. In Mark *rabbi* is used only by disciples (Mk 9:5; 11:21; 14:45); in lieu of this a blind beggar calls Jesus *rabbouni* (Mk 10:51). Both Jesus' disciples (Mk 4:38; 9:38; 10:35; 13:1) and outsiders (Mk 9:17; 10:17, 20; 12:14, 19, 32) say *didaskale.*

1.5. John. The Fourth Evangelist, like Mark, presents an unredacted picture of the terms of address for "teacher." *Didaskale* is used by followers (Jn 1:38; 20:16). Disciples say *rabbi* (Jn 1:38, 49; 4:31; 9:2; 11:8), as do outsiders (Jn 3:2; 6:25). One female follower uses *rabbouni* (Jn 20:16).

2. "Teacher" As Jesus' Self-Designation.

In the pericope of the preparation for the Last Supper, which Luke knew both in a Markan and in an additional, strongly semiticized tradition, Jesus speaks of himself in the third person as *ho didaskalos* (Mt 26:18; Mk 14:14; Lk 22:13). The proverb*-like logion of Matthew 10:24-25 and Luke 6:40 implies a teacher-pupil relationship of Jesus to his followers. In contrast to the assumption that Matthew 23:10 is a Hellenized variant of Matthew 23:8-9, formal analysis suggests the division of Matthew 23:8 into a three-part logion and Matthew 23:9-10 into a four-part logion. Probably in conjunction with the pre-Easter sending out of the disciples (cf. Mk 6:30), Jesus forbade his disciples to let themselves be called *rabbi*, because he is their only authoritative teacher (*didaskalos*, Mt 23:8). Matthew 23:9-10 forbids the disciples to submit themselves to other teaching authorities ("fathers") or to assume such a position themselves. Perhaps the Semitic equivalent to *kathegetēs* in Matthew 23:10 is the term *môreh* found in the Qumran writings (*see* Dead Sea Scrolls).

3. "Teacher"—a Christological Title of Exaltation?

The total absence of "teacher" as a title for Jesus outside the Gospels speaks against seeing in it an early Christian title of exaltation. Prior to Justin only Ignatius of Antioch (*Eph.* 15.1; *Magn.* 9.1) uses the designation *didaskalos*. Both the frequency of the titles for teacher and their apparent christological suppression in Matthew and Luke show that we are dealing with an authentic feature of the life of Jesus. Josephus, too, called Jesus a *didaskalos* (*Ant.* 18.3.3 §63). The Hebrew/Aramaic *rabbî* points most overtly to ancient tradition; outside of Palestine there are hardly any epigraphic instances of it. Furthermore, aside from the canonical Gospels, in the entire corpus of early Christian literature the concept is attested only in one apocryphon (*PBerol.* 11710). The designation of Jesus as teacher in the Gospels serves not to express his exalted status, but to describe the outward form of his ministry.

4. The Teaching Authority of Jesus.

If the respectful title *rabbi* placed Jesus on a level with other scribes, his own claim went much farther. This was sensed by his own contemporaries (Mk 1:21-22 par.). Jesus laid claim not merely to prophetic (*see* Prophets and Prophecy) but to messianic (*see* Christ) authority, first in a hidden fashion and then quite openly within the inner circle of his disciples (Mk 8:27-30). Various Jewish groups expected that the Messiah would teach in the fullness of God's wisdom.* This is borne out both in the targums (*Tg. Gen.* 49:10-11; *Tg. Isa.* 53:5, 11) and in apocalyptic* (*1 Enoch* 46:3; 49:3-4; 51:3), Essene (CD 6:11, 7:18; 4QFlor 1:11; 4QMess ar; 4QAhA; 11QMelch 18-20, cf. *T. Jud.* [A] 21:1-4; *T. Levi* 18:2-6), Samaritan* (*Memar Marqa* 4:12, cf. Jn 4:25) and rabbinic (e.g., *Midr. Ps* 21:90a) writings (*see* Rabbinic Traditions and Writings). Such a claim becomes clear also in various words of Jesus (Mt 11:16-19, 25-26; 12:42; 23:37-39 par.; Mt 11:28-30). Thus he did not view his words on the same level as those of other Jewish teachers but rather ascribed to them eschatological validity (Mt 7:26-29; 24:35; Mk 8:38 par.). This was an inducement for Jesus' followers, already at the pre-Easter stage, to take the most important of his statements deeply into their minds.

5. Settings for Teaching.

5.1. Teaching in the Synagogues. The establishment of synagogues* facilitated the instruction of broader masses of the people in the Law. It also furnished a setting for them to be involved in Sabbath* worship (*GBL* III.1507-12). In Jesus' day every adult Jewish male could take part in the worship service by leading in prayer* and Scripture reading as well as by giving an interpretation of the Scripture. Training for this was provided by an elementary school system, unique for its time (*GBL* III.1410-14), in which youth were taught reading and writing from the holy Scriptures, usually by the person who oversaw synagogue activities (*m. Sabb.* 1:3-4; cf. Lk 4:20). In the synagogues adult males had access to at least the most important scrolls of Scripture (Pentateuch, Isaiah, Psalms) for making preparations for the worship* service. It was natural for Jesus to teach in the framework of the synagogue, both through the interpretation of Sabbath readings from the Law* and Prophets (Lk 4:16-21) and in conjunction with preparation for the worship service.

5.2. Scribal Debates. Although he had received no formal academic training, Jesus was accepted as a discussion partner by other scribes, who at the time were by no means all members of the sect of the Pharisees* (e.g., Mk 12:13-34 par.). While the everyday language in Galilee and probably also in Jerusalem was Aramaic, it is possible that scribal debates were conducted in the so-called holy language of Hebrew. There were also pious Jews living in Jerusalem who spoke Greek (Acts 9:29, *hellēnistai*). It is accordingly possible that Jesus himself debated and taught in Greek. In any case, translating his teaching presented no particular problem in a Palestine that was strongly bilingual, if not indeed trilingual (*see* Languages of Palestine).

5.3. Proclamation to the Masses. While the leading rabbis taught in fixed locations and as a rule devoted themselves only to a chosen circle of pupils, Jesus resembled John the Baptist (*see* John the Baptist) and other prophetic preachers in directing his proclamation to the general populace (e.g., Mk 3:7-8 par.). In order to address people Jesus also taught in the open air in heavily traveled locations such as the northwest shore of the Sea of Galilee.* Nevertheless, that does not exclude temporary stays in Capernaum and making a building belonging to Peter's family estate into a sort of educational center (Mt 4:13; 9:1; Mk 1:29; 2:1-2). Jesus distinguished himself fundamentally from the Zealot preachers of revolution (*see* Revolutionary Movements) by directing his call for repentance and discipleship* not to the masses but to individuals from among the masses (Mk 1:16-20; Lk 9:57-62 par.). Chief among the themes of Jesus' public proclamation was the message of God's love* and the imminent manifestation of his sovereign reign (*see* Kingdom of God).

5.4. The Instruction of the Disciples. From among a larger number of followers Jesus called a circle of men who accompanied him constantly and learned from him by both word and example (Mk 3:13-19 par.). For this reason these followers were designated "disciples" (Heb. *talmîdîm,* Gk. *mathētai).* In contrast to early forms of rabbinic schools, the initiative for membership lay entirely with Jesus himself. The bond to him was so absolute that connection with another teacher was out of the question (Mt 23:9-10). Jesus instilled in his disciples rules for their common life and for dealing with those outside their circle (*see* Discipleship). He also sent them out on their own preaching mission, preparing them for this with special instruction (Mt 10; Mk 6:6-11; Lk 9:1-5; cf. Lk 10:1-12). Those who listened to Jesus' messengers (Heb. *šᵉlûḥîm,* Gk. *apostoloi;* Mk 3:14 [א, B], Lk 6:13; cf. Mt 10:16; Lk 10:3) expected them to be capable of passing on the basic features of their master's teaching in his own words. After rejection of his call to repentance in Galilee, Jesus (reminiscent of Is 8:16-17) withdrew into the inner circle of the Twelve (Jn 6:66-69.). He disclosed to them his messiahship and the way of substitutionary suffering for sin (Mk 8:27-32 par.; 10:35-45 par.; *see* Ransom Saying). In this manner the Twelve came to be especially qualified transmitters of Jesus' teaching in the aftermath of the first Easter (cf. Acts 1:21-26; 2:42; 6:4). If one asks which ancient didactic school Jesus' band of disciples most closely resembles, the best answer is probably those circles of followers attached to the OT prophets. There are also similarities with the early rabbinic schools. On the other hand, only remote comparisons are possible with the circles that formed around the peripatetic Cynic philosophers. On the whole, however, Jesus' band of followers in its entirely distinctive orientation must be traced back to Jesus' messianic authority.

6. Forms of Teaching.

6.1. Interpretation of Scripture. Apart from the abbreviated account of a synagogue sermon in Luke 4:21-27, the Synoptics preserve no extended examples of Jesus' interpretations of Scripture. Entire sermons were not well suited for polished oral reproduction, and the Synoptic writers declined to create any on their own. Nevertheless, quite apart from direct citations, Jesus' words are pervaded by allusions to Scripture (*see* Old Testament in the Gospels; Typology). Through school and synagogue he must have learned large sections of the OT by heart. This was a virtual necessity in part because the vowelless Hebrew texts could be recited error-free and with the right emphasis only through memorization. Occasionally one encounters interpretive methods (like the inference from the lesser to the greater, e.g., Mt 10:29-31) found in rabbinic exegesis as well.

6.2. Summaries of Teaching. In order to impress the basic tenets of his teaching on both outsiders and his disciples, Jesus made use of another technique already developed by the OT prophets. He summarized pithy sayings in short, poetically constructed utterances (Heb. *māšāl,* Gk. *parabolē).* In so doing he made use of parallelism (*parallelismus membrorum)* or chiasm. But translating his sayings back into Aramaic indicates that he also took advantage of such mnemonic helps as rhythm and rhyme. Jesus often called attention to the importance of such summaries through the introductory "amen"* formula typical of him or through admonitions to "listen." Jesus' words were also easily remembered because of their vividness and his frequent use of rhetorical devices such as paradox, hyperbole, riddles, contrast, irony or emphasis.

6.3. Parables. While Jesus formulated many utterances as summaries of a sermon or debate, he set others before his hearers for their contemplation (cf. Mt 13:24, 31). Most worthy of mention here are those pericopes commonly known as parables.* Even these were not blurted out ad hoc but show every indication, like other forms above, of being very deliberate and condensed formations. The boundless allegorization of Jesus' parables by previous generations of interpreters was without doubt a mistake. Comparison with Jewish parables shows, however, that graphic depictions of spiritual matters enjoyed wide circulation. It presented no difficulties in a religious context (e.g.) to relate the mention of servants to prophets (Mk 12:1-11 par.). Jesus' parables are such densely formulated oral texts that it is legitimate to interpret them by paying close attention to each individual detail. Sayings of Jesus that we call parables are normally longer than the summaries of teaching mentioned in the previous section (6.2.). This helps explain why there is rather more divergence in wording in the transmission of these parables.

6.4. Parabolic Acts. Following prophetic precedent, Jesus also often taught in this memorable manner. An example would be the Temple cleansing (Mk 11:13-17 par.) or the cursing of the fig tree (Mk 11:12-14). A number of miracles need to be seen not only as merciful acts of assistance but also as acted out parables. When they were sent out the disciples are sure to have told of such deeds, as well as incidents illustrative of Jesus' exemplary deportment. It is therefore highly likely that prior to the first Easter not only words of Jesus but also the beginnings of a historical tradition were already being passed on. Instruction through exemplary stories was an established custom both in Hellenistic schools in the form of *chreiae** and later with the rabbis (*ma'ᵃśîm*).

6.5. Final Form of Oral and Written Tradition. The summaries of teaching and parables were forms deliberately shaped to preserve memoirs; they were easily remembered oral texts. About eighty per cent of Jesus' sayings take the form of *parallelismus membrorum*. As an itinerant preacher, Jesus repeated them many times. They would have quite naturally embedded themselves in the hearers' minds. In addition, as the example of the Lord's Prayer shows (Lk 11:1-4), one may even assume that Jesus' disciples learned some material from him by heart in rather direct fashion. Learning through memorization was a basic pedagogical method in first-century Judaism* (Philo *Som.* 1.105; Josephus *Ant.* 4.8.12 §210; *Ag. Ap.* 2.19 §178) as well as in antiquity as a whole, whether at the elementary or advanced academic level. Most of Jesus' devotees maintained their residence where they heard him, not traveling with him. For them the need was all the more pressing for a body of teaching that could be easily remembered in the absence of the master. In the circle of resident sympathizers it is possible that words of Jesus were already fixed in written form prior to Easter (Ellis, 242-47).

7. Jesus As Teacher and the Tradition of the Gospels. Classic form criticism (M. Dibelius, R. Bultmann) assessed the Synoptic tradition using the analogy of uncontrolled folk traditions (*see* Tradition Criticism). At the beginning of the Gospel tradition, however, stood Jesus as the teacher of his disciples. In other respects as well there is every indication that the Jesus tradition will not admit of being treated as a fluctuating tradition of folklore. It was passed on within the early church in the form of a school tradition, a body of information taught and learned (1 Cor 11:23-26; 15:1-8). In both the popular and scientific mind today there is a widespread romantic notion that regards Jesus and his disciples as uneducated country folk. This appraisal overlooks the role that teaching and learning played among pious Jews already at that time. Acts 4:13 expresses the haughty point of view of the Jerusalem ruling class. It says nothing about the

competence of Jesus' disciples—some of whom had already been pupils of John the Baptist (Jn 1:35-39; cf. Acts 1:21-22)—to pass on tradition. From the contemporary standpoint early Christianity, like Judaism, functioned rather more like a philosophy than a religion. For this reason teachers played an important role in the early church (Acts 13:1; 1 Cor 12:28-29; Eph 4:11; Jas 3:1). This holds especially true for the passing along of traditions. Perhaps Matthew had such teachers in mind when he recorded words of Jesus like those found in Matthew 13:52; 23:8-10, 34-36.

Attempts have been made to minimize the significance of teaching and learning by referring to the prophetic-eschatological consciousness that reigned among Jesus' disciples and the early church (*see* Prophets and Prophecy). But the example of Qumran shows how little an end-times orientation excludes methodical handling of Scripture and regimented transmission of texts (Betz). Oral tradition can accomplish a great deal when it is passed along (1) by a group of limited size using (2) mnemonically effective techniques. Both of these qualifications were fulfilled by the Gospel tradition through the form of Jesus' words and the existence of the circle of disciples.

See also AMEN; CHREIAI; FORM CRITICISM; GOSPELS (HISTORICAL RELIABILITY); PARABLE; OLD TESTAMENT IN THE GOSPELS; PROPHETS, PROPHECY; SCRIBE; TRADITION CRITICISM.

BIBLIOGRAPHY. O. Betz, *Offenbarung und Schriftforschung in der Qumransekte* (Tübingen: J. C. B. Mohr, 1960); G. Dalman, *The Words of Jesus* (Edinburgh: T. & T. Clark, 1902); C. H. Dodd, "Jesus als Lehrer und Prophet," in *Mysterium Christi*, ed. G. K. A. Bell (Berlin, 1931) 67-86; E. E. Ellis, *Prophecy and Hermeneutic* (Grand Rapids: Eerdmans, 1979); E. Fascher, "Jesus der Lehrer," *TLZ* 79 (1954) 325-42; B. Gerhardsson, *The Origins of the Gospel Tradition* (Philadelphia: Fortress, 1979); J. A. Grassi, *Teaching the Way* (Washington: University Press of America, 1982); M. Hengel, *The Charismatic Leader and His Followers* (New York: Crossroad, 1981); J. P. Kealy, *Jesus the Teacher* (Denville, NJ: Dimension Books, 1978); G. Mussies, "Jesus' idiolect," *TD* 26 (1978) 254-58; F. Normann, *Christos Didaskalos* (MBTh 32; Münster: Aschendorff, 1967); K. H. Rengstorff, "διδάσκω κτλ," *TDNT* II.135-65; idem, "μανθάνω κτλ," *TDNT* IV.390-461; R. Riesner, "Der Ursprung der Jesus-Überlieferung," *TZ* 38 (1982) 493-513; idem, *Jesus als Lehrer* (WUNT II/7; 3d ed; Tübingen: J. C. B. Mohr, 1988); H. Schürmann, *Traditionsgeschichtliche Untersuchungen* (Düsseldorf: Patmos, 1968) 39-65; idem, "Lehrende in den neutestamentlichen Schriften," in W. Baier, *Weisheit Gottes* (St. Ottilien: Eos, 1987) I.419-40; K. Wegenast and D. Fürst, "Teach," *NIDNTT* 3.759-81; H. F. Weiss, "διδάσκω κτλ," *EDNT* I.316-20; A. Zimmerman, *Die urchristlichen Lehrer* (WUNT II/12; 2d ed.: Tübingen: J. C. B. Mohr, 1988). R. Riesner

TEACHER OF RIGHTEOUSNESS. *See* DEAD SEA SCROLLS.

TEACHER OF THE LAW. *See* SCRIBES; TEACHER.

TEACHINGS OF JESUS. *See* EHICS OF JESUS; GOD; HISTORICAL JESUS, QUEST OF; PARABLES; PRAYER; SERMON ON THE MOUNT/PLAIN; KINGDOM OF GOD; TEACHER.

TEMPLE

The Jerusalem Temple was a significant element in the religious, social and political setting of Jesus' life and ministry. It comes to the forefront most prominently in Jesus' cleansing of the Temple (*see* Temple Cleansing) and his words about its coming destruction (*see* Destruction of Jerusalem), but its presence and significance is assumed in many other Gospel contexts. In order to comprehend the meaning of the Temple for Jesus and the Gospels, one must understand the history of the Temple and particularly the attitudes represented in Judaism of approximately the first century A.D.

1. The Temple Structures
2. Attitudes Toward the Temple
3. The Temple in the Gospels

1. The Temple Structures.

Before Solomon built the Temple at Jerusalem, the tribes of Israel had worshipped in a number of sanctuaries, most prominently Shiloh. Shiloh was destroyed around 1050 B.C., evidently by the Philistines as a result of the battle recorded in 1 Samuel 4, when they also took from Israel the Ark of the Covenant. Eventually, however, the Ark returned to rest in Jerusalem, and Solomon (or perhaps better, David, his father—note the difference in emphasis between 1 Kings 5:17-19; 8:15-21 and 1 Chron 22:8-10; 28:3) determined to build a Temple in which it might be housed. A description of the Solomonic Temple appears in 1 Kings 6—7 and again, with a few variations, in the summarizing 2 Chronicles 3—4.

The description in Kings is very difficult to interpret for a number of reasons. First, the account utilizes a large number of technical terms not known elsewhere in Hebrew, some of which were distorted during scribal transmission. Second, the editor of Kings either did not have or chose to omit many details which, from an architectural perspective, are absolutely essential for any reconstruction—for example, the layout of various structures and the thickness of walls. And archeology is no help with this matter, as virtually nothing has survived from the First Temple. Thus scholars attempting to visualize Solomon's work make do with the texts as best they can, and have recourse where applicable to comparisons with other Semitic sanctuaries, especially those of Syro-Phoenicia. Not surprisingly, reconstructions differ markedly from one another, and the following discussion attempts merely to highlight those points on which there is a measure of agreement.

The Solomonic Temple was a long, narrow structure oriented toward the east. It was divided into three parts: an outer vestibule (*'ûlām*), a large interior for worship (*hêkāl*) and a rear compartment known in Hebrew as *dᵉbîr* or *qōdeš qᵉdāšîm*, "the holy of holies." Excluding the walls, whose thickness is not given, the whole was 70 cubits long and 20 cubits wide. The interior paneling consisted of cedar imported from Lebanon. In front of the vestibule stood two bronze pillars, approximately 27 feet high; their function is uncertain, but apparently they did not support the lintel of the vestibule. Some scholars liken them to the traditional steles (*maṣṣēbôt*) which are well known from Canaanite and Phoenician sanctuaries. The Temple stood within a courtyard or inner court; later, by the mid-seventh century at the latest, there were two courts (2 Kings 21:5; Jer 36:10).

The furnishings of the Temple included at first the Ark, which however was lost very early in the history of the First Temple. This stood in the *dᵉbîr*, surmounted by the cherubim. Outside the rear compartment, in the *hêkāl*, stood the golden altar of incense, the table of shewbread and ten candlesticks. Outside the Temple building was the altar of bronze upon which the sacrifices took place. To the southeast of the Temple stood the "Sea" of bronze, which contained water used by the priests for their ablutions. On either side of the Temple entrance were located ten bronze basins, five to each side. Here the priests would cleanse the sacrificial victims. All of these basic cultic elements, with certain modifications, were later to be found in the Herodian Temple.

It was essentially the Temple of Solomon that Nebuchadnezzar destroyed in 587 B.C. when Jerusalem fell to the Babylonians. With the return from Exile beginning in 538 B.C., the Temple was rebuilt; apparently it was structurally very similar to the earlier version, though lacking that Temple's rich adornment. Completed in 515 B.C., it is known as the Temple of Zerubbabel, the governor of the period. Over the centuries that followed this Temple was damaged or, perhaps, even destroyed on various occasions; of the details little is known. In the period 200 B.C.—150 B.C. we know that it suffered substantial damage at least twice. Still, it was rebuilt, and when Herod (see Herodian Dynasty) came to build the structure whose beauty was proverbial throughout the Roman world, practically speaking it was the Temple of Zerubbabel that he tore down and replaced.

For the reconstruction of Herod's Temple, we are somewhat better informed than is the case with the earlier Temples. Detailed descriptions have come down in tractate *Middot* of the Mishnah and in the two major works of Josephus,* the *Jewish War* and the *Antiquities*. Tradition assigns the mishnaic tractate to Rabbi Eliezer ben Jacob, who was a young boy at the time of the First Revolt. Although his description (if it really is his) is perhaps idealizing at points, it is still useful for the task of reconstruction. Josephus's descriptions (*Ant.* 15.11.1-3 §§380-402; *J.W.* 5.5.1-6 §§184-227) do not always agree with each other or with that of the Mishnah, but by and large these disagreements do not affect major elements of the Temple structures.

Herod's work began in 20/19 B.C., and except for matters of detail and added adornment was completed within a decade. Those additional matters, however, occupied the Jews for almost all of the years between c. 10 B.C. and the outbreak of the revolt in A.D. 66, in part by design: Such labor provided jobs for many who would otherwise have been unemployed.

Herod was a man of grand ambitions, and his reconstruction of the Temple of the Jews reflected that aggrandizing character. He essentially doubled the foundation, or Temple Mount, that had existed from Solomon's day. To do so he lengthened the eastern wall at both ends and added new walls on the other three sides. In the process, he found it necessary to reshape the topography of Jerusalem. The middle or Tyropoean Valley, bordering the Temple on the west, he filled in. He did the same to a small valley lying to the north of the old mount, and to the upper slope of the Kidron Valley to the south. According to the Ritmyers' recent study of the archeological remains, the Temple Mount retaining wall measured 1,590 feet on the west, 1,035 feet on the north, 1,536 feet on the east and 912 feet on the south; it thus approximated a rhomboid equivalent in area to thirty-five football fields.

If a Jewish man and woman at the time of Jesus

were to enter the Temple complex from the south, they would emerge from a large plaza to ascend a broad stairway. Off to their right they would see a ritual bathhouse (it was forbidden to enter the precincts without such immersion) and the council house where the Sanhedrin* sat in session. Straight ahead would be the Double Gate and further to the right the Triple Gate. Entering through the Double Gate, they would pass directly beneath the royal stoa that surmounted the wall of the outer court. In the outer court, or Court of the Gentiles, they would now be standing in the place where the blind and lame came to Jesus (Mt 21:14), where the children greeted him (Mt 21:15) and where he drove out the merchants (Mt 21:12; cf. Mk 11:15; Lk 19:45; Jn 2:14). Surrounding this court were the pillared halls where Jesus and later the disciples* taught (Mk 14:49 etc.).

Their eyes would now light upon the Temple structure, rising high above them and separated by yet another stairway, a barricade and the walls of the inner courts. Entering from the outside, the first inner court would be the Court of the Women (*'ezrat hannašîm*), where all Jews including women could advance, but which was off-limits to Gentiles* on pain of death. Here Anna prayed (Lk 2:37), Jesus watched the widow offer the last of her money (Mk 12:44 and par.) and, probably, the encounter with the adulterous woman has its setting (Jn 8:2-3).

The man alone could continue to advance toward the sanctuary itself, entering the Court of the Israelites. This court was open to all ritually pure (see Clean and Unclean) Jewish men, but none others. The sacrificial altar stood here. This inner court is the narrative setting for the Pharisee* praying (Lk 18:11), for the disciples praying (Lk 24:53) and, of course, for Jesus standing before the altar (Mk 11:11). No one but priests could continue on to enter the Temple building itself.

If the man were to look beyond the Temple to the northwest corner of the complex, he could see the fortress called Antonia. This fortress connected to the Temple's outer court by means of a stairway, so that Roman soldiers could very quickly cross if needed. They did just that, for example, at the time of the riot associated with the apostle Paul's last visit to Jerusalem (Acts 21:31-32).

Josephus relates that the entire façade of the Temple was covered with gold plates. When the sun rose the reflection was nearly blinding. On a clear day the brilliance of the Temple was visible from a considerable distance outside Jerusalem. And this brilliance was not due to gold alone; the upper parts of the Temple were pure white, probably marble. Once a year the priests applied whitewash to this upper section. At the very top gold spikes lined the roof. Approaching the Temple, twelve steps led up to the entrance of the vestibule (*'ûlām*). The inner walls of this vestibule, like the façade, were gilded. Carved oak beams comprised the lintel of the portal. The vestibule rose to the full height of the inner portions of the Temple, but exceeded these in width by twenty-six feet on each side. This space formed two rooms wherein were housed sacrificial implements.

At the entrance to the sanctuary (*hêkāl*) hung a veil woven in Babylon, embroidered in four colors: scarlet, light brown, blue and purple. According to Josephus the veil symbolized "a panorama of the heavens, excluding the signs of the zodiac" (*J.W.* 5.5.4 §§212-14). In front of the veil was a golden lamp given by Queen Helena of Adiabene, a convert to Judaism.* Two tables also stood at the entrance before the veil, one of marble and the other of gold. At the weekly changing of the priestly courses, the marble table received the new shewbread introduced into the Temple, while the golden one held the old bread. Standing outside the Temple and looking into the entrance, one could see into the vestibule as far as the veil and the tables holding the shewbread, but it was impossible to see further into the sanctuary.

The sanctuary and the Holy of Holies comprised one long room, 103 feet long, 35 feet wide and 69 feet high and demarcated by curtains. These curtains were beautifully embroidered with lions and eagles. Entirely overlaid with gold panels, the interior of the sanctuary housed the lampstand, the shewbread table (distinct from the two tables already described that stood outside the entrance), and the altar of incense. All were made of gold. The seven branches of the lampstand symbolized the seven planets, while the twelve loaves of the shewbread, which had originally stood for the twelve tribes of Israel, had been reinterpreted so that they now represented the signs of the zodiac as well.

Only the high priest could enter the Holy of Holies, and that only on the Day of Atonement. In the Second Temple period the interior was devoid of all furnishings save for a small rock upon which the high priest made his annual offerings of incense. The artisans who maintained the Temple did "enter" the inner sanctum, but only in a way that was interpreted as not entering. Lowered from the roof in cages closed on the sides, they were unable to see their surroundings. Thus they worked blind and, technically, did not enter the room since they did not come through the entrance and saw and touched nothing.

A great deal of the intellectual and spiritual life of the city took place in the courtyards of the Temple, the outermost of which, as indicated, was extremely capacious. There scholars wrote, read and instructed their students, and there political debate occurred. Surrounded by the splendors of the Temple, it was only natural to feel a sort of numinous awe. That, however, was not the only or, perhaps, the most important emotion to which the Temple built by Herod gave rise.

2. Attitudes Toward the Temple.
Attitudes toward the Temple at Jerusalem varied considerably from time to time and from group to group within intertestamental Judaism. In many respects the theology of the Temple within this period continued along the lines already developed in the First Temple period. Thus, the Temple was considered to be the very dwelling place of God,* in a way shared by no other place on earth. Even the prophets who had grave reservations about the cultic practices going on in their own time believed that the Temple was nevertheless God's dwelling among humankind. Ezekiel, for example, who says that he saw the glory of God depart the Temple because of defiling practices (Ezek 8—10), also says that God will return to live forever in a new Temple (Ezek 43:1-12).

The Temple was considered a sign of Israel's election from among the peoples of the earth. It stood on a site chosen by theophany (2 Sam 24:16) long before its construction; Zion was the mountain of God (Ps 68:17) and was even identified with the original location of the Garden of Eden (cf. Ezek 34). Even the destruction of 587 B.C. did not disprove Israel's election; rather, God would return and once more make Jerusalem his choice (Zech 1:17). The peoples of the earth would one day stream to Jerusalem to worship,* and Israel would stand at the head of the nations (cf. Is 2:1-4).

These ideas and other positive assessments of the Temple continued to be believed and elaborated in the intertestamental period. But another strain of thought, also having its roots in the OT, is noticeably more prominent now: the tradition of hostility toward the Temple. This tradition particularly characterizes apocalyptic* thought, and—as is becoming more and more recognized—apocalypticism was the popular religion of Second Temple Judaism. This tradition of hostility toward the Temple is worthy of extended consideration, since it sheds light on the Gospel tradition.

The apocalyptic tradition of aversion toward the Temple at Jerusalem takes a great deal of its inspiration from the book of Ezekiel. Ezekiel 40—48 constitutes the prophet's famous vision of a new Temple, a new Jerusalem and a new theocratic state. He is given a vision of a Temple in heaven, whence it will be manifest in the end of days. Then the heavenly Temple will descend on Zion, and God will once more take up permanent residence there. Different streams of Judaism understood this vision in different ways. As noted above, Zechariah, for example, believed that the promise was fulfilled in the Temple rebuilt in his own day. But for some groups the Temple of Zerubbabel was not the one promised.

This rejection of the Second Temple probably had its basis in several related perceptions. First was the fact that the Temple rebuilt under Haggai and Zechariah was singularly unimpressive compared with the Solomonic version it attempted to re-create. Surely the God of all the earth would not be content to reside in such a pathetic edifice, which dimmed in comparison not only with Solomon's structure, but much the more so when compared with visions of the heavenly Temple (cf. *1 Enoch* 90:28-29). Even a foremost proponent of this Temple, Haggai, had to recognize this problem. He did his best to blunt the criticisms of those unimpressed with the Temple of Zerubbabel (Hag 2:9; cf. Zech 14:8-11), but he was unable to silence all the critics.

A second significant reason for the rejection of the Second Temple by certain elements of the Jewish people centered on cultic practices. Already in the latter portions of Isaiah and in Ezekiel one can recognize hints of such disputes. These disagreements concerned the proper structures and procedures for the sacrificial cultus, and even the proper times for festivals and assemblies (*see* Feasts). Note, for example, the words of Isaiah 66:3, "Whoever kills an ox is like one who slays a man; whoever sacrifices a lamb is like one who breaks a dog's neck; whoever offers a grain offering is like one who offers swine's blood. . . . They have chosen their own ways, and their soul delights in their abominations" (NASB, modified). This passage is hyperbolic, of course; no one was really offering dogs or pigs. But in the author's view the priests of the Temple in Jerusalem were not practicing the proper methods, and the result was the same: an illegitimate cultus. The disagreements could hardly have been more fundamental.

It would appear that during the fourth and third centuries B.C.—a period for which we have virtually no written evidence—these disagreements were to some extent resolved. Some sort of *modus vivendi* did emerge. But the problems did not simply go away. Those whose ideas were defeated naturally felt disenfranchised, and it is probably among such groups

that apocalyptic ideas found their most fertile soil. In the view of these disenfranchised elements the groups regnant in the Temple practiced the wrong halakah (*see* Law); consequently, both the priesthood and the Temple were defiled.

Again and again in the apocalyptic literature these notions recur. Thus in *1 Enoch* 83—90 (c. 150 B.C.) the writer portrays the Temple of Zerubbabel as ritually impure; he says the priests tried to offer bread on the altar "but all the bread on it was polluted and impure" (*1 Enoch* 89:72-73). The Apocalypse of Weeks (now found in portions of *1 Enoch* 91 and 93; c. 200 B.C. or earlier) claims that every generation since the exile has been apostate because no one was able to discern the true cultus or "things of heaven" (*1 Enoch* 93:9). The *Testament of Levi* (first century B.C./first century A.D.) calls the priests of the former Temple impure. In the last days, however, when a new priest would arise, "The heavens shall be opened, and from the glorious Temple sanctification shall come upon him" (*T. Levi* 17:10). Along with many others, the author of Jubilees (c. 170 B.C.) despairs that the only remedy is the replacement of the sullied present structure by the eschatological version (23:21).

But perhaps the strongest reason for the rejection of the present Temple stemmed from a belief that it was not built to the specifications that God had provided. This belief in turn derived from a straightforward reading of the biblical accounts. The Temple of Solomon, after all, was built to specifications given to him by his father David. Where had David gotten those plans? The account in Kings does not specify. This was a bothersome problem for some Second Temple Jews. The Chronicler had already offered his solution in 1 Chronicles 28:19, saying that David gave Solomon, "Everything (the whole plan detailed in 1 Chron 28:11-18) in a book from the hand of God. . . ." Thus the Chronicler believed that David must have received his Temple plans from God himself, and could not have relied on human artifice for so important a structure. But many Jews did not agree with the Chronicler's solution. It must be recalled that the portion of Hebrew Scripture called the Writings, among which Chronicles is numbered, were not everywhere accorded the authority given the Torah and the Prophets.

Instead, apocalyptic visionaries found another scriptural portion where God had revealed the divine plan for an earthly Temple. This portion was the description of the building of the Tabernacle contained in the latter chapters of the book of Exodus. Prima facie, it was inconceivable that God would have instructed Moses* about every matter of the Law while neglecting to describe the perfect Temple. Warrant for the view that Moses had indeed seen the plan for the Temple—or even the heavenly Temple itself—was found in verses such as Exodus 25:9, "According to all that I am showing you, the plan of the dwelling place and the plan of all its implements, thus shall you do." For such intertestamental exegetes, the equation of "dwelling place" (*miškān;* conventionally translated "tabernacle") with the Temple was self-evident. Indeed, Exodus 25:8 explicitly connected the plans which Moses was seeing with the "Temple" (*miqdāš*). Accordingly, any proper Temple would have to be constructed not along the lines of the Davidic/Solomonic model, but according to the plans which God had delivered once for all to his pre-eminent prophet, Moses. It further followed that the Davidic/Solomonic Temple, the Temple of Zerubbabel and the Herodian Temple were all illegitimate. For the proponents of such views (which continued even after the destruction of A.D. 70—cf. *2 Apoc. Bar.* 4:2-6), the proper Temple had yet to be built. The present, improper one was unacceptable to God and, accordingly, to all true worshippers.

Of course, those who held that the Temple should be built according to the plans God had shown Moses faced a certain difficulty: what had happened to those plans? They were not recorded in the OT. The answer that Second Temple authors devised to handle that problem was twofold: First, they said, the plans had been kept hidden until the end and were to be known only to the elect; and second, some details would require additional revelation. In accordance with such an approach several writings from the intertestamental period make claims for new Temple visions.

The Qumranic text (*see* Dead Sea Scrolls) known as the *New Jerusalem* (5Q15) is one such writing. An angel appears to the anonymous seer (perhaps Ezekiel?) and takes him on a tour of the city and Temple of the last days. The New Jerusalem takes up where Ezekiel 40—48 leaves off, providing exact dimensions for buildings associated with the sacrificial cultus. It also describes the city of that new Temple, making interesting modifications on the ideas found in Ezekiel. Evidently the prophet's vision was not felt to be the last word.

The *Temple Scroll* (11QT), another text from Qumran, goes somewhat further. This text implicitly claims to be a new revelation to a Mosaic figure who, like that prophet, speaks with God face to face. Many details of the Temple buildings appear in this text, often in the language of the tabernacle description from Exodus. That was only to be expected, since the allusions to Moses' vision of the heavenly Temple occur in those portions of Exodus dealing with the tabernacle. Neither the *New Jerusalem* nor the *Temple Scroll*

describe a Temple precisely like that of Solomon; some of the details are decidedly different. Presumably the authors of these and similar texts must have regarded the actual Temple in Jerusalem as a sort of imposter.

Still, despite all their rhetoric and even with these fundamental reasons for rejecting the Second Temple structures, one must be cautious about concluding that any groups among the Jews boycotted the Temple altogether. Claims that the so-called Qumran community, for example, had deserted the Temple and that its members considered themselves a new, spiritual Temple, are problematic. These claims mainly depend on certain passages in the *Manual of Discipline* (the view that 4QFlor, with its reference to a *miqdaš 'ādām,* means a spiritual rather than physical Temple must be rejected).

The difficulties with this particular conclusion properly require a separate exposition, but perhaps several points should be made. First, we really do not know how the authors of the *Manual of Discipline* regarded that work; some of the imagery which it uses, such as the mustering of "Israel" by hundreds and by thousands, suggests that the text describes an idealized future. If so, then the passages which many understand as rejecting the sacrificial cultus (esp. col. 9) should not automatically be taken as evidence that the group avoided the Temple in the present age. Second, the *Manual of Discipline* stands in some sort of relation with the *Damascus Covenant* (CD), although scholars do not agree on precisely how to define that relationship. The *Damascus Covenant* certainly envisions a circumscribed participation in the Temple cultus (col. 6). This fact has to be borne in mind before reaching any conclusions about the *Manual of Discipline,* especially since the latter work does not explicitly declare the Temple obsolete. Third, at least one unpublished copy of the *Manual* (from cave 4) contains a passage describing the comings and goings of the priestly courses. Such a description may imply that the authors recognized the Temple's fundamental importance and could not simply reject it. Fourth, a point related to this last—the *Manual* apparently existed in various recensions. If so, it is arbitrary to decide that the cave 1 manuscript (the only one fully published) was necessarily the one being followed at any one time—if indeed any of the versions were "followed" or were intended as anything more than idealizing literature.

Even though the present cultus be flawed, sacrifices and festivals were divinely ordained after all. Might one really entirely cease to observe them? A more prudent approach is to suggest that such groups limited their involvement with the Temple to the bare necessities, while working to change the situation and to force the acceptance of their own viewpoints.

3. The Temple in the Gospels.

In addition to the various Gospel portions which take the Temple structures for their narrative setting (some of which have been noted in the Temple description above), the Temple plays a critical role in three particular pericopes. These are (1) the cleansing of the Temple (Mk 11:15-17; Mt 21:12-13; Lk 19:45-46; Jn 2:14-17; *see* Temple Cleansing); (2) the saying attributed to Jesus concerning the destruction and rebuilding of the Temple (Mk 14:57-58; 15:29-30; Mt 26:61; 27:40; Jn 2:18-22; cf. Acts 6:14; see Destruction of Jerusalem); and (3) the prophecy of the Temple's destruction contained in the Little Apocalypse and related texts (Mk 13:2-3; Mt 24:1; Lk 21:5-6; cf. Mk 13:14; Mt 24:15; Lk 21:20; *see* Apocalyptic Teaching). All of these passages have in common a negative attitude toward the Temple. In order to gain a balanced perspective, before examining them it is important to take notice of positive attitudes toward the Temple implicit within the Gospels.

These positive attitudes continue one line of Temple theology alluded to above. Prominently, the Gospels view the Temple as the special place of God's presence (Mt 12:4; Lk 6:4). This dogma underlies the saying about swearing by the Temple (Mt 23:31; cf. Mt 23:16, with a similar rationale). Jesus is depicted as saying that the Temple should be a house of prayer,* not of thieves—a strong affirmation of the sanctity connected with God's presence. Matthew also portrays Jesus as paying the Temple tax (*see* Taxes), if only out of tolerance rather than conviction (Mt 17:24-27).

The three negative pericopes are all problematic, and their interpretation is often a function of a particular scholar's model for understanding the historical Jesus. Furthermore, all three are currently at the vortex of Gospel scholarship. The following discussion is therefore intended as representative and suggestive rather than exhaustive.

Jesus' cleansing of the Temple was an extremely dramatic, if not apocalyptic, act. At its heart is the attitude that the present cultus is corrupt—on that all agree. But is this merely the response of a prophet (*see* Prophets, Prophecy) who acts from the righteous anger of an Isaiah or a Jeremiah in the face of improper worship, or is it more—a messianic claim? Although the cleansing plays no part in the narratives of the trial of Jesus, some (most recently and notably E. P. Sanders) have claimed that the act was that of a revolutionary, and was perceived as such by the

Temple authorities and the Romans (*see* Rome). Sanders can find no other reason for Jesus' arrest, trial (*see* Trial of Jesus) and crucifixion (*see* Death of Jesus). In the context of what we know about apocalyptic thinking it is undeniable that contemporaries might well have believed that Jesus was seeking to inaugurate the eschaton by his actions. In apocalyptic writings renewal of the Temple is often a messianic act, or is at least connected with the rise of the messiah (*see* Christ). And even if it were not so intended, one suspects that Jesus' act was sufficiently militant to arouse zealot feelings and thus discomfit the Romans (*see* Revolutionary Movements). The saying about the destruction and rebuilding of the Temple is, if anything, even more problematic. It is convenient to consider the so-called Little Apocalypse prediction of the Temple's destruction at the same time, as the two appear to be interrelated in the Gospel traditions. According to the latter (Mk 13:1-4 and par.) Jesus predicted the destruction of A.D. 70 many years before it happened. This prediction is strikingly reminiscent of the charge made against Jesus in the trial before the Sanhedrin. There witnesses declare that they have heard Jesus say that he will destroy the Temple "made with hands" and in three days raise up another "made without hands." As usually understood, Mark seems to say that this charge was false and did not stand because the witnesses contradicted each other. They were, in other words, false witnesses. But it should be noted that Mark does not necessarily mean that the charge was substantively false—he says only that the witnesses disagreed in their accounts of Jesus' declaration in some unspecified manner (*houtōs*). Then in Mark 15:29 bystanders taunt Jesus with the same charge as he hangs on the cross. Were these people aware of the proceedings before the court, wanting only to repeat the false charges? Or did they perhaps believe (whether from the earlier testimony or for other reasons) that Jesus had in fact made some such statement?

The Markan account apparently wants the reader to conclude that Jesus never said that he would destroy the Temple. In and of itself that conclusion would not be problematic. But on comparison with John 2:19-22 a tension arises. John places the saying in the context of the cleansing of the Temple rather than in his account of Jesus' trial. The Jews ask Jesus what warrant he has for his actions, and he replies, "Destroy this Temple, and in three days I will raise it up." The Johannine interpretation then follows, "But he spoke of his body." John seems to admit that Jesus did say something about destroying the Temple, either advocating it or predicting it. John then seeks to deflect or at least avoid the straightforward interpretation of this tradition. If he did not have a tradition according to which Jesus said something about the Temple being destroyed, his allegorical interpretation could not have arisen.

John therefore attributes a crucial saying to Jesus while Mark, as often understood, may deny that Jesus said it. Scholars have wrestled with this (apparent) contradiction without producing a consensus. If one finds some truth in a zealot model for understanding Jesus, it is felicitous to see here a messianic declaration in which Jesus clears the way for the Temple of the eschaton. Such a declaration would be in keeping with the negative attitudes toward the Temple, and would look forward to a new Temple and, presumably, a new Jerusalem. Even if one rejects this alternative, it seems clear that the Gospel narrators, writing many years after Jesus spoke these words, found them somewhat embarrassing and in need of explanation. Perhaps that is understandable in the face of the First Revolt and the desire to distance nascent Christianity from the parent Judaism. In any event, the place of the Temple traditions within the Gospels will continue to merit study.

See also DESTRUCTION OF JERUSALEM; JUDAISM; TEMPLE CLEANSING.

BIBLIOGRAPHY. T. A. Busink, *Der Tempel von Jerusalem von Salamo bis Herodes* (2 vols; Leiden: E. J. Brill, 1979-80); R. G. Hamerton-Kelly, "The Temple and the Origins of Jewish Apocalyptic," *VT* 20 (1970) 1-15; J. Maier, "The Architectural History of the Temple in Jerusalem in the Light of the Temple Scroll," in *Temple Scroll Studies*, ed. G. Brooke (JSPSup 7; Sheffield: Sheffield Academic, 1989) 23-62; J. Patrich, "Reconstructing the Magnificent Temple Herod Built," *BRev* 4, 5 (1988) 16-29; K. and L. Ritmeyer, "Reconstructing Herod's Temple Mount in Jerusalem," *BAR* 15, 6 (1989) 23-43; E. P. Sanders, "The Synoptic Jesus and the Law," in *Jewish Law from Jesus to the Mishnah* (Philadelphia: Fortress, 1990) 1-96; M. Stone, "Lists of Revealed Things in the Apocalyptic Literature," in *Magnalia Dei: The Mighty Acts of God*, ed. F. M. Cross (Garden City, NY: Doubleday, 1976) 414-52; G. Schrenk, "ἱερός κτλ," *TDNT* III.221-47; R. de Vaux, *Ancient Israel. Volume 2: Religious Institutions* (New York: McGraw-Hill, 1965); M. O. Wise, *A Critical Study of the Temple Scroll from Qumran Cave 11* (Studies in Ancient Oriental Civilization 49; Chicago: Oriental Institute, 1990). M. O. Wise

TEMPLE CLEANSING

The incident in the Temple* is recorded in all four Gospels (Mt 21:10-17; Mk 11:11, 15-17; Lk 19:45-46; Jn 2:13-17), although each Gospel writer has interpreted the event in a distinctive way. Precisely because it is attested in all four Gospels, many believe that the incident traces to an event in Jesus' ministry although there is considerable debate about its meaning.

This article will first examine the incident as interpreted by each of the Evangelists before suggesting what the incident might have meant in the context of Jesus' ministry.

1. The Temple Incident in the Four Gospels
2. The Temple Incident in the Ministry of Jesus

1. The Temple Incident in the Four Gospels.

Assuming that Mark is the earliest of the Gospels and that both Matthew and Luke used Mark, we will examine Mark first and then compare it with the Matthean and Lukan versions of the incident (*see* Synoptic Problem). While John's version of the incident has obvious affinities with the Synoptic accounts and may have grown out of a common tradition, it most likely was not drawn from Mark (*see* Synoptics and John).

1.1. Mark: The Symbolic Destruction of the Temple. The following table will set the Temple incident in its Markan context:

(1) Entry, 11:11
(2) Framing A (fig tree), 11:12-14
(3) Incident in Temple, 11:15-17
(4) Outcome, 11:18-19
(5) Framing B (fig tree), 11:20-26

Mark frames the incident in the Temple with the cursing of the fig tree so that the two episodes comment on each other. Seen in light of the fig tree episode, the Temple incident is not so much a cleansing as a symbolic destruction (*see* Destruction of Jerusalem). Because it has been unfruitful like the fig tree, the Temple itself will be withered away to its very roots.

Peculiar to Mark is the separation of the entry from the Temple incident by a full day. Jesus first enters Jerusalem, and coming to the Temple "scrutinizes (*periblepsamenos*) everything" before returning to Bethany for the night. The verb is distinctively Markan (six of its seven NT uses occur in Mark) and, when used in reference to Jesus, connotes casting a critical or discerning eye. (3:5, 34; 5:32; 10:23). The first visit prepares the reader for Jesus' return. By depicting two visits to the Temple, Mark creates a place for the first portion of the fig tree episode which otherwise would have interrupted the triumphal entry (11:1-10; *see* Triumphal Entry).

When, on the following day, Jesus enters the Temple he "throws out" (*ekballein*) the buyers and the dealers and "throws over" (*katestrepsen*) the tables of money-changers and the chairs of the dove sellers (11:15). His actions seem directed against all dealers in sacrifices as well as their customers who include, no doubt, pilgrims visiting Jerusalem in fulfillment of their Torah obligation. In particular, Jesus singles out both the money-changers who convert the varied currencies brought by pilgrims into the Tyrian coinage required by Temple authorities for payment of the Temple tax (*see* Taxes) and the dove dealers who provide sacrifices for the poor.

Many have interpreted these actions as a cleansing of the Temple, although the nature of the cleansing has been disputed. Was Jesus preserving the spiritual nature of the Temple by purging it of commercial transactions? Or was he objecting to the abuse of the merchants who took advantage of the pilgrims through overcharging? Or was Jesus protesting the involvement of the priesthood (*see* Priest and Priesthood) in the commerce of the outer court?

Read in this framework, 11:16 has been taken to mean either that Jesus forbade people from taking short cuts through the Temple's outer court or that he prevented anyone from bringing an unconsecrated vessel into that courtyard. In either case, Jesus would be expressing a desire to restore the holiness of the Temple because he believed in its sanctity (*see* Clean and Unclean).

Problems with these readings of 11:15-16 abound. The dealers and money-changers were performing an essential service for pilgrims and other worshippers (*see* Feasts). Indeed, without their infrastructure of services, it would be difficult to see how the Temple sacrifices could have continued. Moreover, the money-changers charged a modest commission to convert currency into the Tyrian coinage required by the Temple, and the dealers in sacrifices provided unblemished and ritually acceptable victims. It is hard to interpret Jesus' assault on them as cleansing the Temple of crass commercialism. Nowhere does Jesus exhibit the zealous loyalty toward the Temple ascribed to him by those who read the passage in this way. Finally, all such readings conflict with the Markan framing.

What reading then respects the framing and accounts for Jesus' action? The incident makes good sense as a symbolic prophetic action (*see* Prophets and Prophecy) in which Jesus dramatizes the rejection of both the Temple authorities and the economic systems that supported and enhanced their control over its functions. "Throwing out" and "throwing over" represent a rejection not a cleansing. If *skeuos* in verse 16 refers to sacred cult vessels (Jesus would

not permit anyone to carry a sacred vessel through the courtyard), then Jesus' actions are complementary. He would permit no business as usual, either in the subsystems that support the Temple or in the cultic activities themselves.

Jesus' pronouncement, drawn allusively from Isaiah 56:7 and Jeremiah 7:11, reinforces this reading. It declares God's will in making the Temple a source of access to Yahweh for all peoples and denounces the perversion of that purpose by those who have made it "a cave of social bandits" (*spēlaion lēston*). The use of Isaiah 56:7 probably reflects Mark's concern for the Gentiles,* while the allusion to Jeremiah's Temple sermon constitutes a prophetic oracle of doom. The reason for the destruction of the Temple is made clear.

When the incident is understood as a prophetic act signalling the rejection and destruction of the Temple, then the reaction of the chief priests and scribes is understandable. They seek a way to destroy Jesus.

1.2. Matthew: Cleansing the Temple. The following table indicates how Matthew places the incident in his narrative:

(1) Entry, 21:10-11
(2) Incident, 21:12-13
(3) Outcomes:
   (i) 21:14-17
   (ii) 21:18-22
   (iii) 21:23-27

Matthew removes the cursing of the fig tree as a framework for the incident in the Temple. This allows him to elaborate on the entry itself. When Jesus enters Jerusalem, "the whole city was shaken" (*eseisthē*, 21:10). The language is seismic and thereby casts his entry in the imagery of a theophany. This is no demonstration limited to Jesus' followers as in Mark. The entire city takes note, though its citizens are puzzled, asking "Who is this?" But what Jerusalem does not know, the crowd does: This is "the prophet Jesus from Nazareth of Galilee." The implicit opposition of the crowd to Jerusalem indicates that this is a positive affirmation not a deficient christology. "The prophet Jesus" may identify Jesus as the fulfillment of the promise made in Deuteronomy 18:15.

Matthew follows Mark in describing the initial actions of Jesus in the Temple. Jesus "threw out" the sellers and buyers and "threw over" the tables of money-changers and dove sellers. However, he omits Mark 11:16 altogether, perhaps because its meaning was unclear. The pronouncement of Jesus is likewise streamlined. The phrase "for all nations" is omitted from the compound quotation, thereby intensifying the accusation against the Temple authorities whose leadership has led the Temple away from its divine purpose (see Gundry, 412-13).

The justification for the indictment is illustrated in the special Matthean material that follows (21:14-16). Having denounced the perversion of the Temple, Jesus restores its purpose by healing the broken and the outcast. His miraculous powers are hailed by the children in the Temple in fulfillment of Scripture (Ps 8:2; see Old Testament in the Gospels) but draw a predictably negative response from the Temple leaders.

Taken together, the healings and the controversy they generate reflect a typical Matthean pattern: Jesus acts—his opponents protest—Jesus quotes Scripture. They also depict the fulfillment of the purpose for which the Temple was given, a purpose frustrated by the very chief priests and scribes* who object indignantly to what Jesus says and does. The blind, the lame and the children (see Child, Children) on the Temple Mount parallel the crowds at the entry just as the puzzled city parallels the Temple authorities. Matthew portrays a great reversal: the insiders are either ignorant or indignantly obstinate, while the outsiders respond graciously to God's Messiah (see Christ) as he restores the Temple.

Two other outcomes follow rapidly from the incident and its aftermath. The fig tree episode (21:18-22) confirms the reversal of insider and outsider, especially the judgment on the Temple insiders, while the dispute over authority* must now be read in the light of the entire Temple incident. The episode of the question about authority (21:23-27) hearkens back to the healings as well as the disruptions in the Temple's outer court.

1.3. Luke: Preparing the Temple. Again, it will be helpful to study the Temple incident in its Lukan narrative context.

(1) Frame: weeping over the city, 19:41-44
(2) Incident, 19:45-46
(3) Outcomes:
   (i) 19:47-48
   (ii) 20:1-8
   (iii) 20:9-19

Most strikingly, Luke has muted the entire incident. Jesus "began to throw out the dealers." Missing are the references to buyers, money-changers and dove sellers. Moreover, the pronouncement is directed to them alone in such a way that it appears as though Jesus is objecting to their commercial activity, presumably because it detracts from the divine purpose of the Temple as a house of prayer.*

The immediate outcome is that Jesus "was teaching daily in the Temple courtyard" to the enthusiastic people (*laos*, not *ochlos* "crowd") who listen to his every word. Luke portrays Jesus clearing away the activity of the buyers, preparing the Temple so that he can restore the Temple courtyard as a place of teaching (see Teacher). The twin themes of that teaching are spelled out in the two pericopes that follow, the question about authority (20:1-8) and the parable of the wicked tenants along with its associated sayings (20:9-19). The former pericope establishes Jesus' authority for teaching on the Temple, while the latter specifies the indictment against the current authorities.

The entire episode is introduced by Jesus' prophetic lament over Jerusalem (19:41-44) which concludes by revealing the reason for the turmoil and devastation that awaits city and Temple alike. "You did not grasp the critical moment (*kairon*) of your visitation." The contrast between the deadly visitation of siege armies in 19:43, 44a and the gracious visitation of Jesus is stark. The failure to understand one leads to the fatal outcome of the other.

For what then does Jesus prepare the Temple? In light of its subsequent destruction, prophetically glimpsed in the lament, was Jesus preparing the Temple for its destruction? No. Understood in the context of Luke-Acts, the incident was preparing the Temple for its role as the starting point of a new movement away from Jerusalem announced in the pattern of witness found in Luke 24:47 and elaborated in Acts 1:8. Jerusalem and the Temple would no longer be the goal of pilgrimage but the launching pad of a new mission.

1.4. John: The Cleansing and Replacement of the Temple. The incident in John occurs at the beginning of Jesus' ministry during his first trip to Jerusalem.

(1) Entry, 2:13
(2) Incident, 2:14-17
(3) Challenge, 2:18-22

The entire episode is self-contained, being separated from the miracle at Cana by 2:12 and from subsequent events in Jerusalem by 2:23-25.

Significant differences exist between the Johannine and the Synoptic versions. Jesus' actions are more extreme in John. He makes a whip to drive out the sellers of sheep and oxen, along with the money-changers whose coins he pours out onto the Temple courtyard. But he treats the dove sellers more leniently, simply ordering them to leave with their wares.

The pronouncement itself contrasts "the house of my Father" with "a house of trade," and the scriptural allusion is to Zechariah 14:21. The allusion to Zechariah certainly helps one to interpret the consequent challenge and call for a sign as well as Jesus' response

(2:18-19). The prophecy of Zechariah refers to the eschatological Day of the Lord (*see* Apocalyptic Teaching; Eschatology) when the Temple would become the center of worship* for all peoples. On that day, "there shall be [no] trader in the house of the Lord of hosts" (14:21). So Jesus' actions appear to be informed by a purifying zeal (cf. Ps 69:9) to convert God's house into its eschatological form. In this context 2:19 is a promise to perform such an act. It carries the sense "even if you were to destroy the Temple, in just three days I would raise a better one in its place."

But John intrudes by reinterpreting the saying of Jesus to refer to his resurrection (2:21-22), and with the narrator's reading of the saying the purification theme becomes a replacement motif. For John's community Jesus' body is the Temple that has replaced the Temple of former times.

2. The Temple Incident in the Ministry of Jesus.

Given the diversity among the Gospel writers, it is not surprising that scholars have argued over both the meaning and the details of the incident in Jesus' ministry. Consensus does seem to place the incident at the end of Jesus' ministry rather than at the beginning, thereby favoring the Synoptics over John, but beyond this point, agreement ends.

Although varied, the interpretations of the incident do fall into four basic categories: (1) it is a *religious* event intended to cleanse the Temple of impurities, whether commercial or sacerdotal; (2) it is a *messianic* event intended to include the Gentiles in the scope of the Temple's activities; (3) it is a *prophetic* event intended to announce the destruction of the Temple and its eschatological restoration; (4) it is a *political* event intended to disrupt the commercial and sacerdotal activities of the Temple because they had become oppressive and exploitative. Whatever approach or combination of approaches interpreters may take, however, they must resolve some basic questions about the scope, purpose and content of the event. These can best be examined by looking at its two component parts, Jesus' actions and his pronouncement.

2.1 The Actions of Jesus in the Temple. For some scholars the incident recounts Jesus cleansing the Temple and reclaiming it for its spiritual purpose as a house of prayer. For others, the event is an assault on and attempted political take-over of the Temple. Between these extremes, scholars like R. A. Horsley and E. P. Sanders read the event as a symbolic prophetic action, limited in scope, but condemning the Temple.

Sanders concludes that Jesus either prophesied or threatened the destruction of the Temple as a prelude to its eschatological restoration. Horsley sees the action as an attack on the oppressive political and economic system that found its center in the Temple. More than a symbolic action, it involved violence against the exploiters of the people. Both agree that the demonstration was sufficiently limited in scope so that it would not attract the attention of the Temple police or the Roman troops stationed in the Antonia fortress, yet noteworthy enough to elicit concerted action against Jesus.

2.2 Jesus' Pronouncement in the Temple. The saying is highly debated, most scholars judging it to be Markan or pre-Markan but not traceable to Jesus. G. W. Buchanan, for instance, argues a Markan setting by identifying the *lēstai* of the saying with the "brigands" who seized the Temple during the revolt against Rome.* Others argue that the saying in John 2:19 may reflect Jesus' words more closely than the Markan saying.

If the prophetic-political readings of the passage are correct, however, they suggest a possible reading of the saying recorded in Mark that could place it in the context of Jesus' ministry. If this were the case, then Jesus would be declaring that the true social bandits were not the deviants operating out of caves in the Judean wilderness but the prominent officials of the Temple built over the sacred cave on the Temple Mount. Their exploitative and oppressive domination of the people through taxation and tribute represent the real social banditry of the time, even though it was masked as piety and religious obligation. Understood in this way, the saying fits the action, and both delineate Jesus' prophetic judgment of the Temple that would set the authorities against him and lead to his crucifixion.

BIBLIOGRAPHY. C. K. Barrett, "The House of Prayer and the Den of Thieves," in *Jesus und Paulus: Festschrift für Werner Georg Kümmel,* eds. E. E. Ellis and E. Grasser (Göttingen: Vandenhoeck & Ruprecht, 1975) 13-20; G. W. Buchanan, "Mark 11:15-19: Brigands in the Temple," *HUCA* 30 (1959) 169-77; J. D. M. Derrett, "The Zeal of the House and the Cleansing of the Temple," *DRev* 95 (1977) 79-94; V. Eppstein, "The Historicity of the Gospel Account of the Cleansing of the Temple," *ZNW* (1964) 42-58; C. A. Evans, "Jesus' Action in the Temple: Cleansing or Portent of Destruction?" *CBQ* 51 (1989) 237-70; R. H. Gundry, *Matthew: A Commentary on His Literary and Theological Art* (Grand Rapids: Eerdmans, 1982); N. Q. Hamilton, "Temple Cleansing and Temple Bank," *JBL* 83 (1964) 365-72; R. H. Hiers, "Purification of the Temple:

Preparation for the Kingdom of God," *JBL* 90 (1971) 82-90; R. A. Horsley, *Jesus and the Spiral of Violence: Popular Jewish Resistance in Roman Palestine* (San Francisco: Harper & Row, 1987); C. Roth, "The Cleansing of the Temple and Zechariah," *NovT* 4 (1960) 174-181; E. P. Sanders, *Jesus and Judaism* (Philadelphia: Fortress, 1985).

W. R. Herzog II

TEMPLE TAX. *See* Taxes.

TEMPTATION OF JESUS

In biblical thought "to tempt" means to test something or someone in order to determine or demonstrate worth or faithfulness. Temptation also refers to an attempt, often by Satan (*see* Demon, Devil, Satan), to incite a person to sin. The Gospels depict Jesus experiencing a range of temptations.

1. Terminology and Background
2. The Temptation in the Wilderness
3. Temptation in the Gospels

1. Terminology and Background.
The Greek verb for "tempt" is *peirazō* (Mt 4:1, 3; 16:1; 19:3; 22:18, 35; Mk 1:13; 8:11; 10:2; 12:15; Lk 4:2; 11:16; [Jn 8:6?]). It can be used in a positive sense, as when Jesus tests his disciples* (Jn 6:6), as well as in a negative sense, as when the Pharisees* try to entangle Jesus in his conversation (Mt 22:15-22). In Acts 15:10 and 1 Corinthians 10:9 *peirazō* is used of challenging God. The word is best known for its use of the devil tempting in order to cause sin (Mt 4:1 par. Mk 1:13 and Lk 4:2; see 2. below) so that the devil can be called "the tempter" (*ho peirazōn*, only in Mt 4:3 and 1 Thess 3:5). The noun "temptation" (*peirasmos)* is used of trials sent by God* or encountered while serving him (Lk 22:28; Acts 20:9). It is also used of trials or tests that do or may lead to sin (Mt 6:13 par. Lk 11:4; Mt 26:41 par. Mk 14:38 and Lk 22:46; cf. Lk 22:40) as well as the temptation of Jesus by the devil (Lk 4:13). The word is also used to describe a trial or test which causes a follower of Jesus to fall away or apostatize (Lk 8:13).

The Greek verb *dokimazō* ("prove" or "examine") can be used interchangeably with *peirazō* (2 Cor 13:5; 1 Pet 1:6-7). However, while *dokimazō* generally implies that the testing will have positive results (1 Thess 2:4; 1 Tim 3:10), *peirazō* came to signify the testing for good or evil (Mt 16:1; 19:3; 22:18), and even the hope or expectation of failure (Mt 4:1; 1 Cor 7:5; Rev 2:10).

In the LXX *peirazō* translates the strong active form of the verb *nasāh* (Gen 22:1; Ex 15:25; Num 14:22) and

the Greek *peirasmos* is used to translate the Hebrew noun *massāh* (Ex 17:7; Deut 4:34; 9:22; Ps 95 [94]:8). A sword and armor could be tried or tested (1 Sam 17:39), though almost always the testing has a personal object. People can test each other's reputation (1 Kings 10:1 par 2 Chron 9:1), they can "make a test of pleasure" (Eccles 2:1) and test another's beliefs (Dan 1:12, 14), or simply attempt or try to do something difficult (Deut 4:34; 28:56; cf. 7:19; 29:3). Daniel 12:10 uses *peirazesthai* of the eschatological tribulations which will act as a means of purification before the end (*see* Eschatology). Most often in the OT it is God who is depicted as testing the faithfulness and obedience of his own people to know whether or not they are true to him (Gen 22:1-19; [Heb 11:17-20]; Ex 15:25; Deut 8:2; 33:8; 1 Kings 22:21-23; 2 Chron 32:31). On the other hand, God is not said to test heathen people. None of the *peir*-group of words occurs in LXX of Job for "testing" (cf. 4:2; 9:23), but the theme of God permitting the testing of the faithfulness of his servant, here through Satan, is evident (Job 1—2). To pass the test is to remain obedient to God despite profound and incomprehensible suffering. In 2 Samuel 24:1, 10 the Lord is said to incite David to sin. However, the later rewriting of this story introduces Satan as the one enticing to sin (1 Chron 21:1). Similarly, the tendency to say that someone is tempted or is in temptation, avoiding the idea that God tempts directly, is a development in post-exilic thought (Jub 17:15-18).

Also frequent in the OT are references to God's people wrongfully putting him to the test, notably by questioning his care as at Massah (Ex 17:2, 7; Deut 6:16; 9:22; 33:8), by refusing to recognize and remember his obvious power (Num 14:22; Ps 78:40-43; 106:14), by asking him to prove himself (Is 7:12) or by disobeying him (Mal 3:15). To test God was the antithesis of trusting him and thus a very serious violation of God's honor.

In Hellenistic times *peirazō* was used to reflect God educating his people (Wis 3:5-6) and testing the obedience of his servants, of which Abraham* was a model of faithfulness (1 Macc 2:51-52) as he was in the rabbinic literature (*m. 'Abot* 5:3). The experience of testing also highlighted God's care in times of trial (Sir 33:1).

In the Dead Sea Scrolls* God's people are depicted as continually facing afflictions which may deflect them from faithfulness (CD 1:15; 1Q14 11:1; 1QH 4:12, 16; 1QS 3:24; 5:4-5; 4QpHos 2:5; 6QD 3:3).

In the rabbinic literature the theme is maintained that God tests and disciplines those whom he loves (Ps 11:5; Prov 3:12; *2 Apoc. Bar.* 79:2; *b. Ber.* 5a). Further, the homonymous verbs *nāsāh* ("test" or "tempt") and *nāsā'* ("exalt") give rise to the often used rabbinic pun: "God tempts the righteousness, implies that the Holy One, blessed be He, never exalts a man without first having tested and tempted him; if that man withstands the temptation, then he exalts him" (*Num. Rab.* 15:12; cf. *Gen. Rab.* 32:3; 34:2; 55:2-3; *Exod. Rab.* 2:2-3; *Cant. Rab.* II:16:2).

2. The Temptation in the Wilderness.

Mark's very brief account gives no details of the temptation (Mk 1:12-13), while Matthew's and Luke's stories are in the form of a longer, three-part conversation not unlike the debates of the scribes* which utilize proof-texts from Scripture (Mt 4:1-11 par. Lk 4:1-13; cf. the secondary *Gos. Heb.* [Origen, *Comm. Joh.* II:12:87]).

It has been suggested that Mark's version is an abbreviation of the tradition known to Matthew and Luke. However, in view of the importance of the conflict between Jesus and Satan in Mark, it is unlikely he would undertake such an abbreviation. Also, the paradisal motif inherent in the mention of Jesus being with the wild beasts is to be contrasted with the Exodus theme recurrent in Matthew and Luke. Thus, it is more likely that Mark's tradition is independent of that shared by Matthew and Luke, the latter being derived most probably from Q.* However, it is possible that the narrative is a late addition to Q, for the temptation story is anomalous in what is generally thought to be a collection of sayings and speeches.

In all three Synoptic Gospels the importance of the account of the temptation of Jesus is seen from its position in the Gospels: after his baptism* and immediately prior to and introducing his public ministry.

The Fourth Gospel has no account of the temptation in the wilderness (*see* Mountain and Wilderness). However, in a scene reminiscent of the Synoptic temptation narrative, the people who saw the miracle of the loaves and fishes (6:1-14) want a sign similar to the gift of the manna in the wilderness so that they can believe in Jesus as the second Moses* (6:30; cf. *Rab. Eccl.* 1:9). Jesus' reply in John 6:32-33 echoes both Deuteronomy 8:3 and his reply in the first temptation in the wilderness (Mt 4:4 par. Lk 4:4).

2.1. The Origin of the Temptations. It is difficult to establish definitely the origin of the temptation narrative as being in the life of Jesus. But the history-of-religion parallels from the stories of Buddha and Zarathustra, for more distant examples, at least indicate that holy men were thought to experience times of testing.

The first three Evangelists agree that the Spirit (*see* Holy Spirit) led Jesus into the wilderness and that he was tempted by Satan (Mk 1:13) or the devil (Mt 4:1 par. Lk 4:2). The sharp saying "Get behind me Satan" directed at Peter (Mk 8:33), which is hardly likely to have been invented by the early church, also depicts Jesus being tempted by Satan. The Fourth Gospel also reflects the idea of Jesus being tempted (Jn 6:15, 26-34; 7:1-4).

It can be stated with some certainty that the temptations are so distinctive that they are hardly likely to have been created in the light of later Christian experience of temptation, even though Jesus and his followers later may have shared other trials (cf. Lk 22:28). Also, if the temptations revolve around the sonship of Jesus (see 2.3. below), then the early church would have been unlikely to create material showing Jesus' inner struggle with his obedience and trust in God and the responsibilities of his relationship with his Father. Further, the difficulty early Christians had with the idea of the Messiah (*see* Christ) being tempted is probably suggested by the affirmations of the writer of the letter to the Hebrews that Jesus suffered being tempted, though without sin (Heb 2:18; 4:15-16; cf. 5:7-9).

That the scenes comprising the temptation narrative in Q resemble a scribal haggadic midrash* does not in itself tell against their historicity, but that a Palestinian origin for them is likely, even though the OT quotations from the LXX show the tradition has passed through the hands of a Greek-speaking community (*see* Tradition Criticism).

The temptation story is told as a visionary experience. There are two other reported visionary experiences of Jesus in relation to his dealing with Satan, each of them handed down in the first person. In Luke 10:18 Jesus says that he has seen Satan falling from heaven in relation to his disciples' exorcisms. In Luke 22:31-32, reminiscent of the heavenly court scenes in Job 1:6-12 and 2:1-6, Jesus says he has prayed for Simon because he and the other disciples are going to be sifted like wheat. It is possible then that Jesus could have related to his disciples his experiences now reflected in the temptation narratives. Furthermore, it is quite probable that, anticipating the nature of his ministry, Jesus had to face just such issues as conveyed in the temptation narratives. Therefore, there is no need to suppose that Jesus' desert experience was invented. Rather, it is quite probable that the temptation narratives have their origin in the initial stage of the ministry of the historical Jesus, who later reported his visionary experiences to his disciples, perhaps in the context of later teaching about trials and temptations (see 3. below).

2.2. *The Order of the Temptations.* Given the historicity of both stories, the association of the temptation with the baptism is to be expected for, as Sirach 2:1 says in reflecting human experience, "My son, if you come forward to serve the Lord, prepare yourself for temptation." The same pattern is found in the story of the Israelites who, after passing through the waters of the Red Sea, spend time being tested in the wilderness (Deut 8:2-5; cf. 1 Cor 10:1-22).

Matthew and Luke agree that the devil (Matthew has "tempter") first tempts Jesus to demonstrate that he is the Son of God (*see* Son of God) by turning stones into loaves of bread.* But while Matthew says Jesus was then taken to the pinnacle of the Temple* and thirdly to a high mountain, Luke has these in reverse order. If Luke's order is original then Matthew has made the last temptation correspond to the climax of his Gospel (Mt 28:18). On the other hand, Luke's interest in Jerusalem and the Temple (Lk 24:49; Acts 1:4; 6:8—7:60; 21:17—22:21) means that he is likely to have wanted the temptations to reach a climax there (Lk 4:9). Alternatively, it has been suggested that Luke may have relied on Psalm 106 to reorder the scenes. For in this psalm there is reference to the manna (v. 14), worship of the golden calf (v. 19-20) and the testing of God in the wilderness (vv. 32-33), all in the order they appear in the Lukan temptation story. However, this explanation is probably too subtle, even though the same order of themes is evident in 1 Corinthians 10.

Nevertheless, it is generally agreed that Matthew has maintained the order of the temptations in Q and that Luke has changed the order of the last two. For there is a progression in Matthew's order from desert to Temple pinnacle to a mountain. Also, Matthew has a tidy reverse order of the quotation of Scripture from Deuteronomy (8:3; 6:16, 13), and the two temptations concerning Jesus' sonship come together in Matthew.

2.3. *Jesus and the Temptations.* The opening words of the temptation story in all three Synoptic Gospels are remarkably similar to Deuteronomy 8:2. Therefore, the importance of Deuteronomy and the Exodus theme in understanding the narrative is suggested from the beginning.

That Jesus should have been especially conscious of the presence and direction of the Holy Spirit in his desert experience of temptation (Mk 1:12 par. Mt 4:1 and Lk 4:1) is not surprising, for the OT speaks of the presence and leading of the Spirit (Neh 9:20; cf. Is 63:7-10) during Israel's desert wandering, as does later Jewish literature (e.g., *Rab. Exod.* 23:2).

That Satan tempts Jesus here is probably due to an increasing desire in the period to preserve the transcendence and loving goodness of God by not depicting God as directly involved in being tempted (see 1. above). The role of Satan also recalls that in Job where the faithfulness of God's servant is being tested in Satan's attempt to cause failure.

2.3.1. *The First Temptation (Mt 4:3-4 par. Lk 4:3-4).* In calling on Jesus to satisfy his hunger by turning stones into bread the devil appeals to Jesus' power as Son of God. This could be seen as a temptation to repeat the miracle (*see* Miracles and Miracle Stories) of the provision of manna in the wilderness (Ex 16:13-21; 2 *Apoc. Bar.* 29:1—30:1; Josephus *Ant.* 20.8.6 §§167-68; *J.W.* 7.11.1 §438), or to perform a sign expected of the messianic age in order to win over people (cf. Jn 6:1-40) or perhaps, depending on the conditional "if" for this interpretation, the devil is to be seen attempting to raise doubt about Jesus' miraculous powers and, hence, his divine sonship.

However, the text of Jesus' reply, "Not on bread alone shall a person live . . . ," is almost exactly that of Deuteronomy 8:3, where allusion is made to the Israelites being disciplined in the wilderness as a man disciplines his son. For this reason Jesus is probably being tempted to assert his independence from God by performing a miracle for his own benefit, rather than trusting God as a son for all his needs (cf. Deut 28:1-14; Ps 33:18-19; 34:10). The Israelites failed their test; they grumbled against their leaders and God, craving different food from what God was providing (Deut 2:7; Neh 9:21; Ps 23:1; 78:18-22). But in the first scene of the temptations the Son of God rejected the devil's temptation and remained obedient to his Father, being satisfied with his Father's nourishment and care.

2.3.2. *The Second Temptation (Mt 4:5-7 par. Lk 4:9-12).* In this scene the devil is said to take Jesus to the "pinnacle" (*pterugion*) of the Temple. *Pterugion* ("winglet") was used figuratively of the edge or extremity of something and first used here of some high and visible part of the Temple (Josephus *Ant.* 15.11.5 §412; Eusebius *Hist. Eccl.* 2.23.11). In asking Jesus to throw himself down from the Temple, the devil may be tempting Jesus to display his messiahship, for a rabbinical saying in the *Pesiqta Rabbati* says that "when the King, the Messiah, reveals himself, he will come and stand on the roof of the temple" (36). However, we cannot be certain that this saying reflects expectations of Jesus' time.

In any case, in light of Jesus' reply that "you shall not tempt the Lord your God" (cf. Deut 6:16), the devil is more likely to be understood as tempting God by challenging God to keep his promise of protection for his children (Ex 19:4-5; Deut 28:1-14; 32:10-11), particularly in the Temple (Ps 36:7-9; 91). This interpretation is further supported by noting that the devil has already quoted Psalm 91:11-12 about God's protection (Mt 4:6 par. Lk 4:10). Furthermore, the Fourth Gospel depicts Jesus' brothers suggesting a dangerous course of action, that he go to Jerusalem in order to display his works and identity. Jesus connects their suggestion with the evil world, Satan's domain, and rejects it on the grounds that his hour has not completely come (7:1-13).

2.3.3. The Third Temptation (Mt 4:8-10 par. Lk 4:5-8). In Matthew's order the temptation narrative climaxes with the devil taking Jesus to a very high mountain to show him all the kingdoms of the world and their glory,* as an ancient land seller might take a prospective buyer to a vantage point to see the land (Cicero *Pro Tullio;* cf. Gen 13:14-15; Deut 34:1). Perhaps recognizing that no actual mountain could give such a vantage point, and emphasizing the visionary nature of Jesus' experience, Luke does not mention the mountain, but only says that the devil led Jesus up (4:5, *anagō*). This temptation appears to break the pattern of the narrative. Satan does not mention Jesus' sonship, but says, "All these I will give you if you will fall down and worship me." However, the echo of Psalm 2 maintains the issue of Jesus' sonship in these scenes.

It has been suggested that the temptation is of a political nature. That is, this temptation explains that Jesus rejected zealotism and the role of a miraculous political Messiah as a satanic option. But the meaning of the temptation, again governed by OT background, is probably quite different. In the story of the baptism which immediately precedes the temptations there is an echo of Psalm 2:7, "The Lord said to me, 'You are my Son....'" The psalm goes on to say, "Ask me, and I will give you the nations for your inheritance" (2:8). So clearly is this part of the background to the third temptation that the devil is thereby seen to be offering Jesus what is not his to give in return for the worship of the devil.

That the essence of this temptation is for Jesus to receive his rightful inheritance without obedience to God is confirmed in Jesus' reply, which is a quotation from Moses warning the Israelites against idolatry as they enter the promised land (Deut 6:10-15). In the OT idolatry and demon worship are closely associated (Deut 32:17; Ps 106:37-38; cf. *1 Enoch* 99:7). So, in being tempted to idolatry or to acknowledge the devil rather than God being in control of the world, Jesus answers the devil with the command of God "You

shall worship the Lord your God, and him only shall you serve" (Deut 6:13; Mt 4:10 par. Lk 4:8). This final temptation is, then, the most devilish of all; the call to Jesus to receive his proper inheritance without obedient worship of God.

Each of the temptation scenes recalls aspects in the Exodus story when the Israelites failed to remain faithful to God. By contrast, Jesus remains the obedient Son. As the Exodus through the wilderness confirmed that the Israelites were God's chosen, so in his experience in the desert Jesus is confirmed to be God's Son. The three scenes of Jesus' visionary experience show him triumphing in his battle with Satan to remain obedient to his Father without recourse to cheap displays of power.

2.4. The Emphases of the Gospel Writers. For all the Synoptic Evangelists the background to the temptation of Jesus is God leading the Israelites for forty years in the wilderness to humble them and test what was in their hearts, whether or not they would keep the commandments (Deut 8:2). Thus through the instrument of Satan, God tests the obedience of his Son Jesus.

2.4.1. Matthew. The first Evangelist has maintained the Q association between the baptism and temptation stories of Jesus. The climax of the baptism story is the voice from heaven, "This is my beloved Son, with whom I am well pleased" (3:17), so that the theme of sonship overshadows the story of the temptation in the wilderness. Matthew maintains the theme of Jesus' sonship in the first two temptations (4:3, 6) and highlights the idea that the temptations in the wilderness are God testing his Son (cf. Deut 1:31; 8:5; 32:5) through an attempt by Satan to cause Jesus to displease God through being a disobedient Son (cf. Mt 3:17; 4:3, 6).

In saying that Jesus was "led up" (*anēchthē*) into the wilderness, Matthew may be showing a knowledge of the Judean desert plateau above the Jordan.

Matthew has associated the forty days and forty nights in the wilderness with Jesus' fasting so that the story conforms to Moses fasting for the same period. Matthew has already drawn parallels between Jesus and Moses in 2:13, 16, 20-21. In the temptation story the parallels continue. Jesus was led into the wilderness just as Moses went to Mount Sinai in the wilderness (Deut 9:9); Jesus was not only forty days but also forty nights (Mt 4:2; cf. Lk 4:2) in the wilderness, as was Moses in the wilderness forty days and forty nights. During this time Jesus fasted (*nēsteuō*), just as Moses neither ate nor drank in the story in Exodus 34:28 (cf. Deut 9:9-18, 25). It is most likely that Matthew sees Jesus' fasting as an example, for he is the only Evangelist to give the followers of Jesus directions for fasting* (16:16-18; cf. 9:14-15). Finally, Jesus is shown all the kingdoms of the world from a mountain as Moses saw the promised land from a mountain (Deut 3:27; 34:1-4).

After the first temptation to turn stones into loaves of bread, it is probably Matthew who extends Jesus' reply in light of his interest in enhancing the wisdom* motif to include the words from the LXX, "but by every word that comes from the mouth of God" (4:4; cf. Deut 8:3). In this way Matthew is able not only to affirm the view that Jesus was victorious in being obedient to God (contrast Israel in Ex 16; Num 11) but also to begin to establish the view that Jesus is the new wise teacher* of Israel (cf. Prov 9:1-5).

Matthew is probably responsible for calling Jerusalem the holy city (4:5 par. Lk 4:9), for the only other place it occurs in the Gospels is in Matthew 27:53 where the Evangelist relates a story of events surrounding the crucifixion. If Matthew intended his readers to associate this story with that of the temptation, it is possible that Matthew is saying that while Jesus refused to tempt God by throwing himself down from the highest point of the holy city, when he was "thrown down" on the cross (*see* Death of Jesus), in the resurrection* he was shown to be the Son of God (cf. 4:6 and 27:54) and to be cared for by God (cf. 27:53).

In retaining the temptation to worship Satan as the climax of the story, Matthew highlights the ensuing battle in his Gospel between the kingdom of Heaven and the kingdom of Satan (cf. 12:24-29). In resisting this temptation Matthew has Jesus say, "Go, Satan!" (*hypage satana*), just as he has Jesus say later in his ministry to the demons (Mt 8:32; cf. Mk 5:13 par. Lk 8:32) as well as to Peter as he represents Satan (16:23 par. Mk 8:33).

In this temptation Jesus is shown not only to win the battle here, but later Matthew depicts Jesus again on a mountain, having his sonship affirmed in a visionary experience (17:1-13). Finally, Matthew's Gospel affirms Jesus' victory by ending with Jesus on a mountain, as ruler of the world, declaring to his disciples: "All authority in heaven and on earth has been given to me" (28:18).

For Matthew Jesus' victory over Satan in the temptations is complete. However, Jesus will go on doing battle with Satan in other areas. Thus the devil is said to leave (*aphiēsin*, historic present) Jesus, so that Matthew may be intending to give the impression that the departure is only temporary (cf. Lk 4:13). Further, God is seen to be faithful, providing Jesus' needs. Following Mark, Matthew says that angels* ministered to him, which would imply the provision of food (cf. 1 Kings 19:5-8).

2.4.2. Mark. As in the Q tradition, Mark has the story of the temptation tied directly to Jesus' baptism and the voice from heaven declaring, "You are my son . . ." (1:11). Thus for Mark the temptation is to be seen as a test of Jesus in relation to his sonship. Also, as Satan is the archdemon in Mark, Jesus is depicted as being involved in a spiritual and cosmic battle of the highest order.

The temptation narrative in Mark consists of four simple statements, each linked by "and" (*kai*). The brevity of the account, along with Jesus' frequent conflict with Satan through his exorcisms (3:22-27; cf. 1:21-28, 39; 3:11; 5:1-20; 7:24-29; 9:14-29), through encounters with the Pharisees (see 3. below), as well as through his disciples (8:33), gives the impression that Jesus' ministry was an almost-uninterrupted confrontation with Satan.

Perhaps to indicate that the whole of Jesus' life and ministry was directed by the Spirit, Mark says that the Spirit drove or compelled (*ekballō*) Jesus into the wilderness, though not to temptation (1:12). There is an emphasis on the place of temptation being in the wilderness (*erēmos*), probably not because it is a place of prayer* (cf. Lk 5:16), but because Israel had been tested in the wilderness (Ps 78:17-20), because the age of salvation* was expected to begin in the wilderness (Mk 1:3; cf. Is 40:3; Josephus *J.W.* 2.13.5 §261; 7.11.1 §438) and because the wilderness was the habitat of the demons (1QM 1).

"Forty" is a common round number in the OT, and it is often used in stories of fasting and God's sustenance (Gen 7:4, 12; Ex 34:28; 1 Kings 19:4-8; cf. *Adam and Eve* 6:1-2), a motif reinforced in Mark's temptation story with his reference to the angels ministering to Jesus (Mk 1:13 par. Mt 4:11). Although Mark does not mention Jesus' fasting, he may intend it to be implied here.

Jesus said to be with the wild beasts (*thēria*) and the angels ministering to him does not emphasize the loneliness of the temptation but recalls the OT eschatological expectation of harmony in the animal kingdom and between people and animals (Is 11:6-9; 32:14-20; 65:25; Hos 2:18) as it was in Genesis 1:26-28. As early as Justin a paradisal background to Mark's story of the temptation has been suggested (*Dial. Tryph.* 103). And there was a Jewish tradition that Adam and Eve were being ministered to by the angels (*Adam and Eve* 4; *b. Sanh.* 59b) and associated demons, wild beasts and angels (Ps 91:11-13; *T. Iss.* 7:7; *T. Benj.* 5:2; *T. Naph.* 8:4). This probably means that, for Mark, whereas Adam failed to resist temptation, Jesus overcame Satan and was able to live at peace with the wild beasts and receive the ministration of the angels.

It is generally accepted that Mark gives no hint of the nature nor the outcome of the temptation. However, the association of the temptation with the declaration of Jesus' sonship (1:11) and the reference to ministering angels (1:13) recalls the second temptation in Q (Mt 4:5-7 par. Lk 4:9-12). Thus Mark may have in mind that Jesus was being tempted to doubt his sonship and put God to the test. It is more likely that the nature of the temptation can be gleaned from noting that in Mark Satan's role is to attempt to deflect Jesus from his mission (3:23, 26; 4:15; 8:33). That in Mark's temptation story Satan attempts to deflect Jesus and that Jesus emerges victorious, can also be seen by the fact that immediately following the temptation, Mark has Jesus embarking on his mission (1:14-15). Jesus' victory is also suggested in the mention of the angels who, in the OT, ensured the safe passage of God's chosen servant through a difficult period (Ex 23:20, 23; 32:34; 33:2; 1 Kings 19:5-7). Further, Jesus being with the wild beasts also suggests a victory to be contrasted with Adam's failure (see above). There is no suggestion in the Markan temptation story that Satan was completely or finally overthrown or bound.

2.4.3. Luke. In view of the temptations immediately following the baptism in Mark and Matthew, it is most probable that Luke has inserted the genealogy* (3:23-38) between the two narratives. The genealogy allows Luke to support the declaration at the conclusion of the baptism—that Jesus is the Son of God—by a genealogy which traces Jesus back through Adam to God. In turn, the temptations maintain a focus on the sonship of Jesus being at stake. As a faithful Son Jesus is bringing to an end the human disobedience typified in Adam and the Israelites during the Exodus.

In Luke, not only is it emphasized that Jesus is being led (*ēgeto*, imperfect passive) by the Spirit, but he is filled (*plērēs*) with the Holy Spirit. This, along with his precise echo of Deuteronomy 8:2 (*en tē erēmō*, "in the wilderness"), shows that Luke understands that it is God who is leading Jesus in the temptations, to test what was in his heart and his faithfulness to God (Deut 8:2). Matthew (4:2) gives the impression that the tempter came to Jesus after he had fasted forty days in the desert. For Luke, Jesus was being tempted by the devil for the whole forty days (4:1-2). The most significant alteration Luke has made to the temptation narrative is the order of the scenes, transposing the last two so that the order is bread, kingdoms of the world and pinnacle of the Temple. It is probably too subtle to expect Luke's order to reflect the reverse order of the first three petitions of the Lord's Prayer. It is more reasonable to suppose that Luke wanted the temptations to reach their climax at the Temple in

Jerusalem. Luke's order also maintains the theme of the testing of the Son of God (4:9).

In the first scene of the temptations the devil's challenge "If you are the Son of God . . ." recalls the declaration of Jesus' sonship at his baptism. For Luke, Jesus' sonship is not in doubt, but the way Jesus will use his power. The singular "bread" and "stone" (cf. Mt 4:3) emphasize that the devil is testing to see if Jesus will use his powers for his selfish ends rather than depend on what God supplies (Lk 4:4).

In the second scene Jesus is not taken to a high mountain, not only perhaps because no mountain could afford such an advantage (see 2.3.3. above), but because for Luke a mountain is primarily a place of prayer and revelation (6:12; 9:28; 22:39). The awkwardness of verse 6 and Luke's interest in "authority" (*exousia; see* Authority and Power) means that he has probably added it here and it has a political meaning as in 12:11; 20:20; 23:7. That is, Jesus is being tempted to take up political authority and its associated glory. This offer Jesus rejects.

Luke sums up the temptations by saying that the devil finished "every temptation" (4:13). That is, in these three scenes Luke sees portrayed the whole range of temptations Jesus will face in his ministry. In turn this means that while Jesus' victory over temptation may have been an encouraging model for Luke's readers, Jesus' experience was unique to his sonship and mission. In fact, every other time Luke uses the word *temptation* of followers of Jesus, it does not have a positive outcome (8:13; 11:4; 22:28, 40, 46). From his unique ending of the story—that the devil left him until an opportune time—it is obvious that Luke does not intend to convey the idea that Satan was finally defeated, or that this marks the absolute end of temptation for Jesus. Rather, he anticipates the conflicts between Jesus and Satan (10:18; 11:18; 13:16).

3. Temptation in the Gospels.

Outside the temptation narrative the Synoptic Gospels depict Jesus as continuing to be tempted, principally by the Pharisees.

In Mark 8:11 (par. Mt 16:1) the Pharisees are said to test Jesus by seeking from him a sign from heaven* (cf. Lk 11:16). As this request comes in the context of a series of miracle stories and as the Synoptic Gospels never use "sign" (*sēmeion*) to refer to a miracle, the Pharisees are being portrayed as seeking more than a miracle or a display of power from Jesus. In the tradition of the OT (Deut 13:1-2; 1 Sam 2:30-33; Is 7:10-14) they sought some obvious, compelling authentication of Jesus' divine ministry beyond the healings (see Healing) which they may have seen in others of their holy men. They may have expected some apocalyptic sign in the heavens of cosmic proportions (cf. Ezra 5:4; 7:39) or, as with the prophets* (Deut 13:2-6; 18:18-22; 2 Kings 20:1-11; Is 7:10-14), they may have expected God to confirm Jesus' status. Such testing recalls the Q temptations testing the sonship of Jesus. Mark says that Jesus refused to offer a sign (8:12), probably because such lack of insight could never be satisfied, for it sets human conditions for faith,* and those with an eye of trust already knew who Jesus was. In light of the temptation story this aligns the Pharisees with Satan.

Jesus is also depicted as being tempted in the sense of the Pharisees trying to trap him (Mk 10:2 par. Mt 19:3; cf. Mt 22:35 par. Lk 10:25, ekpeirazō). In just one instance Jesus speaks of himself being trapped or tempted by the Herodians (see Herodian Dynasty) and Pharisees (Mk 12:15 par. Mt 22:18).

In Luke 22:28 the whole of Jesus' ministry is described as temptations, that is, being confronted continually by Satan in the trials and tribulations of his ministry. In that the disciples are paradigms of discipleship* for Luke, this verse also shows that being a follower of Jesus includes sharing in his temptations or trials. However, in the use of peirasmos in the story of the Garden of Gethsemane (see Gethsemane), Luke and the other Synoptic Evangelists show they see the climax of Jesus' trial and battle with Satan to be in the Easter story. In the Garden the disciples are said to be encouraged not to enter or succumb to temptation, that is, fall away. In view of the absence of the definite article with "temptation" in this story (Mk 14:38 par. Mt 26:41 and Lk 22:46; cf. Lk 22:40), it is unlikely that the eschatological tribulation is in mind. Luke also sees temptation causing those who hear and receive the word with joy,* to fall away (8:13).

In John's Gospel peirazō is used of Jesus "testing" Philip's understanding of and trust in Jesus' ability to meet the needs of those who come to him for food (6:6). In light of 6:32 and the great number of people requiring feeding (6:7), John probably intends to convey the message that on a spiritual level Jesus is able to meet the profound needs of those who come to him.

In the temptation stories Jesus is not portrayed as being tempted to satisfy people's material needs, nor to display his wonder-working power for all to see but to test whether or not he would remain obedient and loyal as the Son of God. The faithfulness of Jesus is highlighted against the background of the disobedience of the children of Israel in their wanderings in the desert. While the temptation narratives are primarily christological in intent, they are also a source of encouragement for the followers of Jesus in their trials and sufferings. There is no suggestion in any of the Synoptic Evangelists that Satan was completely destroyed in the temptations. Throughout the Gospels Jesus is depicted as continuing to face temptation from the evil one who was bound principally through Jesus' ministry of exorcism.

See also DEMON, DEVIL, SATAN; MOUNTAIN AND WILDERNESS; SON OF GOD.

BIBLIOGRAPHY. E. Best, *Temptation and Passion: The Markan Soteriology* (Cambridge: University Press, 1965); P. Doble, "The Temptations," *ExpT* 72 (1960-61) 91-93; J. Dupont, *Die Versuchung Jesu in der Wüste* (Stuttgart: Katholisches Bibelwerk, 1969); R. Funk, "The Wilderness," *JBL* 78 (1959) 205-214; B. Gerhardsson, *The Testing of God's Son* (Lund: CWK Gleerup, 1966); E. Graham, "The Temptation in the Wilderness," *CQR* 162 (1961) 17-32; H. A. Kelly, "The Devil and the Desert," *CBQ* 26 (1964) 190-220; J. S. Kloppenborg, *The Formation of Q* (Philadelphia: Fortress, 1987); U. W. Mauser, *Christ in the Wilderness* (London: SCM, 1963); P. Pokorny, "The Temptation Stories and their Intention," *NTS* 20 (1973-74) 115-127; J. A. T. Robinson, "The Temptations," in *Twelve New Testament Studies* (London: SCM, 1962) 53-60; H. Seesmann, "πεῖρα κτλ," *TDNT* VI.23-26; H. Swanston, "The Lucan Temptation Narrative," *JTS* 17 (1966) 71; A. B. Taylor, "Decision in the Desert: The Temptation of Jesus, in the Light of Deuteronomy," *Int* 14 (1960) 300-309; G. H. P. Thompson, "Called-Proved-Obedient: A Study in the Baptism and Temptation Narratives of Matthew and Luke," *JTS* 11 (1960) 1-12.

G. H. Twelftree

TEN COMMANDMENTS. *See* COMMANDMENT; LAW.

TESTIMONIUM FLAVIANUM. *See* JOSEPHUS.

TESTIMONY. *See* WITNESS.

TEXTUAL CRITICISM

Textual criticism is the science that compares all known copies (manuscripts, abbrev. MSS [pl.] MS [sg.]) of a given document in an effort to trace the history of variations in the copying process so as to discover the original form of the text. Although generally established procedures have led to a widespread consensus about the nature of the original text of the Gospels, that it looks very much like that in our best critical edition (United Bible Societies, *The Greek*

New Testament, 3d ed. [abbrev. UBS³], and Nestle-Aland, *Novum Testamentum Graece,* 26th ed. [abbrev. NA²⁶]), there are some unique features about the text of the Gospels that require special consideration.

1. The Need
2. The Method
3. The Problem of Harmonization
4. Hort's "Western Non-Interpolations"
5. Textual Criticism and the Synoptic Problem

1. The Need.
The need for textual criticism of any NT document is the result of three combined factors: (1) The originals, probably written on papyrus, have all perished. (2) For over 1,400 years the NT was copied by hand, and the copyists (scribes) made every conceivable error, as well as at times intentionally altered the text (probably with the idea of correcting it). (3) There are now extant, in whole or in part, about 5,400 Greek MSS for the whole NT (any one of the Gospels has about 2,325), as well as hundreds of copies of ancient translations, plus the evidence from the quotations of the NT in the writings of the early church fathers—and no two MSS anywhere in existence are exactly alike.

- The task of textual criticism is to sift through all this material, carefully collating (comparing) each MS with all the others, in order to detect the errors and changes in the text, and thus to decide which variant reading at any given point is more likely to be the original.

2. The Method.
The method which most textual critics use to work through this mass of material and large number of variations is called eclecticism. This means that all the variants in any given unit of variation are evaluated individually on the basis of all the kinds of evidence that are available for such an evaluation.

The evidence is primarily of three kinds, having to do respectively with the MSS and the quotations from the fathers (external evidence), with the errors made by the scribes (transcriptional probability) and with the author's style and vocabulary (intrinsic probability).

2.1. External evidence. At any given unit of variation, the textual critic must first take note of the external evidence supporting each variant, although with few exceptions scholars are agreed that knowledge of this evidence alone does not guarantee one's finding the original text. The following matters must be noted: how old are the witnesses supporting each variant or how old is the text they represent; how good is the

general quality of the MSS involved in each case; and how widely distributed geographically are the witnesses, especially the early ones. This latter question is especially important, because early and widespread geographical distribution of a reading points to an original parent much further back before the document in question (in this case one of the Gospels) was widely scattered throughout the early church.

Thus, for example, the fact that no early evidence East or West, either from the MSS or the church fathers, contains the account of the adulterous woman in John 7:53—8:11 (the earliest certain evidence being two fifth-century Latin MSS), argues strongly, along with transcriptional and intrinsic probabilities, against this story as a part of the original text of John's Gospel.

2.2. Transcriptional probability. This has to do with scribal errors and is based on certain inductively derived criteria about scribes and their copying habits. For example, it is usually true that the more difficult reading is probably original, because it is the demonstrated tendency of scribes to have made the text easier to read (by improving grammar, substituting synonyms, adding the subject when unexpressed, etc.). Thus it is far more likely that in 7:8 John wrote "I am not *[ouk]* going up to the Feast," rather than "I am not yet *[oude]* going up to the Feast," since in verse 10 Jesus does in fact go up to the Feast. (This is probably a play on the word for "going up": his brothers meant "go up" to the Feast; Jesus answered that not at this Feast would he "go up" in the ultimate sense.)

It is also true that scribes often elaborated or added words to the text for the sake of clarity, so that more often than not the shorter reading represents the original—although this criterion must be used with some caution. With the Gospels in particular, scribes often harmonized the text of one Gospel to another, so that the least harmonized reading most often represents the original (see below). The scribal conformations over many years of Luke's version of the Lord's Prayer to that of Matthew is a good illustration of both of these criteria.

2.3. Intrinsic Probability. This is the most subjective kind of evidence and must be used with great caution. It has to do with an author's vocabulary and style, his ideas as they are expressed elsewhere and the probabilities based on the immediate context. When all other things are equal, this is something of a matter of last resort, although it also frequently plays a role in determining transcriptional probability.

2.4. The Overarching Criterion. The single most important criterion, involving both transcriptional and intrinsic probabilities, is sometimes called "Bengel's first rule": That reading is to be preferred as the original which best explains the origin of all the others. When this criterion, in conjunction with the others, is applied to the variants in the text of the Gospels, in the vast majority of cases the variant that emerges as the original text is that which also has the best supporting external evidence. Thus NT textual critics have a high degree of confidence that for the most part the best critical text very closely represents the original text of the Gospels.

3. The Problem of Harmonization.

Although harmonization has sometimes occurred elsewhere in the NT (e.g., between Colossians and Ephesians), this is a problem of special import for arriving at the original text of the Gospels. The problem here is especially complex, for we are dealing both with authors who used the text of one (or two) of the others in varying degrees of exactness and with scribes who in a variety of ways made parallel passages conform but who also, by intent or otherwise, could disharmonize passages. Thus, in making textual decisions in the Gospels, textual critics must broaden their perspective to include the following considerations.

First, in the Gospels harmonization can be of four kinds: (1) between or among the Gospels, (2) within a single Gospel, (3) to the LXX or (4) to a well-known phrase or idea quite apart from any immediate parallel. The addition of "for bread, will give him a stone; or if" in Luke 11:11 (from Mt 7:9) illustrates the first; the addition of "where their worm does not die and the fire is not quenched" in Mark 9:44 and 46 (under the influence of v. 48) illustrates the second; the addition of "lamentation and" (from Jer 31:15 LXX) in Matthew 2:18 illustrates the third; and the addition (probably) of "of God" to the phrase "Seek first the kingdom" in Matthew 6:33 illustrates the fourth. This problem is especially complex when two or three of these kinds of harmonization can be active at any variation unit. However, the second and fourth, because they are more immediate to the scribe, are more likely to have occurred in "minor harmonizations" (see below) than the first type.

Second, one must not automatically presuppose what an author or scribe would have done. The problem with authors here is probably greater than with the scribes. For example, Synoptic relationships (*see* Synoptic Problem) are sometimes extremely close, such as in the standard text of the Matthew/Luke account of John's preaching of repentance (Mt 3:7-10; Lk 3:7-9). Luke has sixty-four words and Matthew sixty-three; they have sixty-two words in common, without a single change of word order, and only one

difference between a singular and a plural. Although this level of agreement occurs infrequently and is almost exclusively limited to the double tradition between Matthew and Luke, it is evidence that such high-level agreement can occur. For the most part, however, the writers tend to rewrite with varying degrees of exactness.

Copyists, on the other hand, show extremely strong tendencies to make passages conform to one another. Yet not every possible harmonization must be adjudged to be so. For example, assimilation is far more likely to have occurred in the sayings of Jesus than in the Evangelists' narratives. Similarly, harmonization is far more likely to have occurred in major additions/omissions or with significant words (so-called major harmonizations) than with the addition/omission of pronouns, conjunctions, articles and such items or with word order (so-called minor harmonizations). These latter especially may be due to all kinds of other factors. Modern scholars who work with synopses are almost certainly more aware of alleged harmonizations than was likely to have been the case for scribes, whose memories cannot be assumed to have been so keen as to have recalled all the jots and tittles from parallel passages.

Third, by the very historical fact that the early church used Matthew to a greater extent than it did Mark and Luke (especially the former), the manuscript traditions of the latter two have far more variants that could be attributed to harmonization than does Matthew; and between them Mark has far more than Luke. It is almost inevitable that this factor will weigh heavily in making textual choices in Matthew and Mark.

Fourth, similarly, although no manuscript or manuscript tradition has escaped some degree of harmonizing corruption to its text, this phenomenon is a hallmark of the Western and later Byzantine traditions, whereas the earlier Alexandrians are relatively pure at this point. Again, this factor must be taken into account when making textual decisions.

Fifth, there can be little question that a given scholar's resolution of the Synoptic Problem will sometimes affect textual decisions, a matter that needs further discussion (see below).

4. Hort's "Western Non-Interpolations."

Another area of special concern for the textual criticism of the Synoptic Gospels is a phenomenon related to the so-called Western text (codex D and its Old Latin and Old Syriac allies). This text is especially noteworthy for its large number of harmonizations and interpolations (including the interesting saying in

Luke 6:5: "On the same day when Jesus saw a certain man working on the Sabbath,* he said to him, 'Man, if you know what you are doing, blessed are you; but if you do not know, you are cursed and a transgressor of the Law' "). However, there are several passages in the Gospel of Luke which turn up missing in much of this tradition, including such significant texts as Luke 22:19b-20 (the so-called second cup); 24:12 (Peter's run to the tomb) and 24:51c-52 (the ascension*). (See also Mt 27:49; Lk 24:3, 6, 36, 40.)

This series of variants has had a checkered history in the textual criticism of the Gospels from the time of Westcott and Hort, who in their monumental edition of 1881 rejected them all. Their reasoning was simple: In every case they are not found in the very early evidence in the West; but since this evidence most commonly interpolates into the text, it seemed highly unlikely that these variants were original. Otherwise they would have been found in the Western text that tends to be "full." On the other hand, in the introduction to their text, Hort could not bring himself to label them "neutral interpolations," since that was contrary to his view of his "neutral" (= original) text. Since in his view they were not "omissions" in the Western text, but interpolations into the other text, he chose the strange designation of "Western non-interpolation."

Since the time of Westcott-Hort, these readings have gradually been making their way back into the critical editions, having been judged to be Western "omissions." Various reasons, mostly theological, have been offered for the omissions. Thus these are judged as peculiarities of the Western text of a different kind, but quite in keeping with the idiosyncratic nature of that textual tradition.

5. Textual Criticism and the Synoptic Problem.
In the Synoptic Gospels textual criticism both affects and is affected by the Synoptic Problem.* On the one hand, one's solution to the Synoptic Problem will necessarily affect one's textual decisions. In the area of harmonization, for example, if one believes with W. R. Farmer and others in the priority of Matthew, then one should also tend to see the alleged harmonizations in Mark as original to Mark himself, since he should be suspected to have used Matthew more closely in such cases. The problem with this solution is that it runs full face into the external evidence, which leads to the opposite conclusion, that the Markan harmonizations to Matthew are chiefly the work of later scribes.

In the same vein one might also compare the solutions offered by B. H. Streeter (pp. 325-28), G. D.

Kilpatrick (pp. 29-30) and W. R. Farmer (pp. 148-51) to the well-known "minor agreement" between Matthew 26:67-68 and Luke 22:64 (par. Mark 14:65). Following the command "Prophesy," Mark has "and the guards took him and beat him" (NIV), whereas Matthew and Luke have "to us, Christ* (Mt only), who hit you?" The textual problems lie with Mark, where some significant but later MSS have added the words from Matthew. Streeter, holding to Markan priority, takes the radical step of alleging early (before our extant MSS) interpolations into both Mark and Matthew; Farmer, holding to Matthean priority and Luke's use of Matthew, accepts the text of our critical editions as supporting his revival of the Griesbach hypothesis; Kilpatrick, holding both to Markan priority and a more radical form of textual eclecticism, opted for the "harmonization" in the Western and Caesarean texts as original to Mark.

On the other hand, textual criticism also teaches one to ask the right kinds of questions in the resolution of the Synoptic Problem. Although there is an obvious difference between the Evangelists as redactors and copyists, in both cases the crucial criterion is the textual one: That reading (version) is to be preferred as original which best explains the existence of all the others. In the case of our Gospels that must include both the arrangement of the materials (order, form, etc.) and the close study of the parallels between/among the Gospels. It is this criterion above all others that leads the majority of scholars to continue to hold to the solution of Markan priority. Both in the general arrangement and in the details, when this ultimate textual question is posed, over and again Mark's Gospel seems clearly to be the one that best explains the order and wording of the others.
See also CANON; SYNOPTIC PROBLEM.

BIBLIOGRAPHY. K. and B. Aland, *The Text of the New Testament* (2d ed., rev.; Grand Rapids: Eerdmans, 1989); W. R. Farmer, *The Synoptic Problem* (New York: Macmillan, 1964); G. D. Fee, "Modern Textual Criticism and the Synoptic Problem," in *Synoptic and Textual Studies in Honour of J. J. Griesbach: 1776-1976* (SNTSMS 40; Cambridge: University Press, 1979) 154-169; idem, "A Text-critical Look at the Synoptic Problem," *NovT* 20 (1980) 12-28; G. D. Kilpatrick, "Western Text and Original Text in the Gospels and Acts," *JTS* 44 (1943) 24-36; B. M. Metzger, *The Text of the New Testament: Its Transmission, Corruption, and Restoration* (rev. ed.; New York: Oxford University, 1968); idem, *A Textual Commentary on the Greek New Testament: A Companion Volume to the United Bible Societies' Greek New Testament* (3d ed.) (London/New York: United Bible Societies, 1971); K. Snodgrass, "The Western

Non-Interpolations," *JBL* 91 (1972) 369-379; B. H. Streeter, *The Four Gospels* (London: Macmillan, 1924); B. F. Westcott and F. J. A. Hort, *The New Testament in the Original Greek, with Introduction and Appendix* (2 vols.; London: Macmillan, 1881-82).

G. D. Fee

THADDAEUS. *See* Disciples.

THEIOS ANĒR. *See* Divine Man/Theios Anēr; Hellenism.

THOMAS. *See* Disciples.

TOMB. *See* Burial of Jesus; Resurrection.

TOSEPTA. *See* Rabbinic Traditions and Writings.

TRADITION CRITICISM

Tradition criticism or tradition history (both translations of the German technical term *Traditionsgeschichte*) refer to the study of the development of traditions, especially those about Jesus, until they were fixed in their final written form. Because of this interest in historical development, a secondary concern of this discipline has been that of determining the authenticity of a given saying or narrative, the criteria for determining such authenticity and the stages of historical development through which the tradition passed. Yet these issues have been tempered with more recent evidence of an interest, even before the passion* and resurrection,* to transmit carefully the traditions about Jesus.

1. Defining Tradition Criticism
2. Criteria of Authenticity
3. Historical Development of Tradition
4. Issues in Tradition Criticism

1. Defining Tradition Criticism.

The German term *Traditionsgeschichte*—and the occasionally used *Überlieferungsgeschichte* (although technically this should have a different translation)—refer to the historical development of a tradition. They are normally translated "tradition criticism," but "tradition history" (or perhaps the more awkward "traditio-historical criticism") would be a more accurate translation. The first translation has become common currency among English-speaking NT scholars due to its parallelism with form criticism* and redaction criticism.*

As a discipline tradition criticism was developed in OT studies by G. von Rad, M. Noth, S. Mowinckel and I. Engnell, but as an attitude it was already practiced

in New Testament studies by W. Wrede, whose argument it was that the community created the tradition, not the tradition the community. The methodology has been focused on Gospel studies, and in particular on the Gospel tradition in the pre-Pauline period (A.D. 30-50).

1.1. Assumptions. The basic assumption of tradition criticism is that the stories about and sayings of Jesus circulated as oral tradition for a period of some three decades or longer before they were written down. During this period they were shaped by the historical situation (*Sitz im Leben*) of the communities within which they circulated. By studying the differences in the various traditions one can determine: (1) which traditions actually go back to the historical Jesus (*see* Historical Jesus); (2) at which point in the oral period a given tradition actually arose; and (3) what the historical situation of the Christian community actually was.

1.2. Differentiation from Form and Redaction Criticism. Two other disciplines overlap with tradition criticism. The first is form criticism, which in theory focuses on the form in which various types of traditions circulated, but in practice has included the study of how such forms may have changed over time and at which period of oral transmission a given form may have arisen. When it moves from categorization to historical analysis, form criticism means the same as tradition criticism. It is because of this overlap that one cannot say when the methodology was first used in modern NT studies, for many of the form critics were in fact doing tradition criticism.

The second discipline is redaction criticism, which focuses on how the Gospel writers edited their sources (e.g., Mark). In theory such editorial work is part of the changing of the tradition and thus could be included under the heading of tradition criticism, but in practice tradition criticism has been concerned with the period of oral transmission. Therefore, as soon as scholars speak of written sources, they have moved beyond the scope of tradition criticism and into redaction criticism. But the distinction is not always so clear-cut, for at times the Evangelists may have been working with oral sources ("M" Tradition, "L" Tradition and Q may all have been oral) or their communities (e.g., the Johannine community) may have shaped the materials they were using.

2. Criteria of Authenticity

If in fact the traditions about and from Jesus were shaped over time by the life situations and needs of the communities in which they circulated, then there must be some means of determining which parts of

831

the tradition actually stem from the period of Jesus. Three major criteria have been proposed, no one of which should be used in isolation, but which together build a case for genuineness.

2.1. Criterion of Multiple Attestation. Any tradition that is found in more than one independent strand of the Gospel tradition is likely to be genuine. While in and of itself this does not prove genuineness, for different communities facing similar situations (e.g., persecution) could shape the tradition in a similar way, it is certainly a pointer in that direction. The major issue is whether the tradition is found in truly independent strands rather than in strands which borrowed from each other. And of course this does not rule out independent shaping within each strand.

2.2. Criterion of Coherence. Any tradition that coheres or is similar to traditions about Jesus known to be genuine is likely to be genuine itself. Obviously this requires that some tradition be known to be genuine first before one can know that others cohere with it. A series of sayings in a given strand of tradition might cohere, but that could simply indicate a common theme or interest (*Tendenz*) of a given period of development. Of course, the coherence does not have to be among sayings, for a saying could cohere with a narrative that pictured Jesus acting in a manner consistent with the saying. Furthermore, the fact that a tradition does not cohere with any other does not indicate that it is not genuine. It may simply be unique. Finally, even if a tradition appears to conflict with others, one must be cautious before arguing for incoherence and therefore inauthenticity. It may be a case of paradox, although there is always a danger that paradox will be invoked when incoherence is the more reasonable explanation.

2.3. Criterion of Dissimilarity. Any tradition that is dissimilar to (1) Jewish tradition (including apocalyptic* and Rabbinic tradition*) and (2) the traditions of the post-Easter church (including their faith, practice and life situation) is likely to be a genuine tradition of or about Jesus. For some scholars this criterion may be used along with others as a way of establishing authentic traditions. But for many scholars (e.g., Fuller or Perrin) this is not simply a way of proving some traditions are genuine, but *the* criterion of authenticity. All traditions not established by it are rejected.

The criterion of dissimilarity, however, cannot bear the weight of being the sole guarantor of authenticity. First, it is certain that Jesus was a Jew, and to excise from his teaching all that agreed with previous Jewish tradition is certainly to remove some genuine material. In other words, while this criterion can discover what was unique about Jesus, it does so by destroying

the context in which that uniqueness was set. And without that context does one really have the authentic Jesus?

Second, when used exclusively this criterion assumes that there was no continuity between the post-Easter church and Jesus, and this assumption is highly doubtful. Were there no traditions of Jesus which inspired that church* and which it therefore wanted to preserve? Why were the authentic traditions not totally forgotten rather than passed on if they were not important to the church (for even those which meet this criterion were handed down by the church)?

Third, the assumptions underlying this criterion contain a built-in self-contradiction. On the one hand, it is assumed that communities passed on tradition because it fit the life situation of the community. On the other hand, this criterion is looking for traditions which were passed on but which did not fit the life situation of any Christian community. Therefore, while this criterion can indeed point out genuine Jesus tradition, it can only point to those traditions of such uniqueness that they indicate where Jesus stood apart from Judaism* and yet (in the perception of scholars) was not followed by the early church, which blindly transmitted the tradition. Traditions of such a unique quality are rare indeed.

2.4. Other Criteria. At times other criteria have been proposed from what have been assumed to be the laws of the development of tradition. Following the lead of textual criticism it has been argued that the longer, more developed tradition is less likely to be genuine and that the theologically more difficult tradition is more likely to be genuine. However, the problem with such assumptions is that they are just that—assumptions.

While some traditions may be elaborated over time, others may be truncated because the details had no meaning to the tradent. This can be observed on a written level in the use made of Mark. For example, neither Matthew 14:19 nor Luke 9:15 pick up the detail in Mark 6:39 that the grass was green. Mark in this case has the more detailed tradition, but is probably the source of the other two. Yet one could also find examples in which the reverse is true.

When it comes to the issue of theological difficulty, the problem is the standard by which difficulty is measured. Certainly a later tradent, or writer, will tend to hear and repeat a tradition in terms which are consonant with his or her own beliefs. But one must ask whether modern New Testament scholars know enough about the beliefs of even the writers of Scripture, let alone the tradents of the oral period, to be sure that a given saying would have been theologically difficult for them. And given the inconsistency observed in our modern thinking, the perception of difficulty could well be a perception of what a given ancient should have felt, not what he or she did in fact feel.

A further issue needs to be raised at this point. These criteria are often used with the assumption that a tradition is the product of the post-Easter church unless proven otherwise. But given the research cited below in the closing paragraphs of this article, this is an unwarranted assumption. Skeptical assumptions will lead to minimal results, not necessarily results which accurately reflect the historical situation of the early church and its interest in Jesus. On the other hand, one must not therefore leap into a fideism which ignores evidence of the shaping of the tradition by the Evangelists or their predecessors.

3. Historical Development of Tradition.
When describing the historical development of a tradition, it is necessary to bear in mind a general schema of development through which this tradition may have passed.

3.1. A Developmental Scheme. A large number of scholars assume the following developmental scheme:

3.1.1. Palestinian Jewish-Christian Church. The earliest post-Easter church was the Aramaic-speaking church made up of Palestinian Jews. It is assumed that this church had the most primitive christology and traditions enshrining such terms as "servant" (*see* Servant of Yahweh), "Messiah" (*see* Christ), "Son of God"* and "Son of man."*

3.1.2. Hellenistic Jewish-Christian Church. The church soon expanded into the Diaspora as Greek-speaking Jews were converted. These believers are assumed to have been interested in making the gospel relevant to their environment as can be seen in such titles as "Christ" and "Lord"* as well as a shift in the meaning of "Son of God."

3.1.3. Hellenistic Gentile Church. Finally, of course, Gentiles became a major influence in the church, carrying the Hellenistic terminology into a fully Gentile realm.

3.2. Problems with Historical Development. The main problem with this developmental scheme is that it is too neat. Even if one were not to accept the data of Acts 6 that Hellenistic Jewish-Christians were part of the Jerusalem church within at most a few years of the resurrection, there is plenty of evidence that Hellenism* was an active force in Jerusalem well before the first century A.D. There is no reason to believe that the so-called more Hellenistic titles would not have been meaningful and therefore popular virtually from the beginning, although it is true that some titles (e.g., Son of David*) were so Jewish that they were never popular in the Gentile world. But once the assumptions about historical development (and the use of titles for Jesus or other theological content as markers) are relativized, it becomes most difficult to construct a firm developmental history of tradition.

Furthermore, historical material about the development of the church is so scarce (even Paul moved in a rather limited and largely Gentile sphere) that there is a great danger of falling into a circular argument. After constructing from a Gospel a hypothesis regarding the historical situation of the community within which it arose, tradition critics have too frequently used this hypotheses to determine the authenticity of the various traditions within that Gospel.

4. Issues in Tradition Criticism.
We can be sure that the Jesus tradition did undergo development as the more significant items were selected out of the mass of data available to the post-Easter church. In turn this material was shaped by the needs of the community, including the exigencies of translation into new cultures and languages. A study of parallel narratives in the Gospels will demonstrate as much, for not all of the differences can be attributed to the Evangelists. But tradition criticism is now beyond its early decades of self-assurance and must proceed with more caution.

A number of scholars (see Ellis) have demonstrated (1) the keen interest of the post-Easter church in Jesus' teaching, including his deeds (Stanton); (2) the fact that Jesus was viewed as a teacher* and thus his teachings were learned and passed on (Riesner); (3) the probability of not only the deliberate transmission of Jesus' teaching but also of its written form even before Jesus' death (Schürmann); and (4) the availability in Judaism of models for the accurate transmission of tradition (Gerhardsson). All of these factors severely limit tradition criticism's basic assumption that there was a long period of oral transmission. On the one hand, Gospel interpreters must objectively reckon with the shaping and adapting of the Jesus tradition that did take place (as can be demonstrated from Gospel narratives of words and events which are unlikely to have been spoken or to have taken place more than once, but which are recorded differently). On the other hand, there is no firm historical basis for assuming that traditions about Jesus were not carefully transmitted even before his death or that there was a clear developmental track along which traditions evolved.

See also FORM CRITICISM; LITERARY CRITICISM; REDACTION

CRITICISM; RHETORICAL CRITICISM; SYNOPTIC PROBLEM; TEACHER.

BIBLIOGRAPHY. R. S. Barbour, *Traditio-Historical Criticism of the Gospels* (London: SPCK, 1972); D. R. Catchpole, "Tradition History," in *New Testament Interpretation*, ed. I. H. Marshall (Grand Rapids: Eerdmans, 1977) 165-80; E. E. Ellis, "New Directions in Form Criticism," in *Prophecy and Hermeneutic in Early Christianity* (Grand Rapids: Eerdmans, 1978) 237-53; R. H. Fuller, *The Foundations of New Testament Christology* (Glasgow: William Collins and Sons, 1965); B. Gerhardsson, *Memory and Manuscript: Oral Tradition and Written Transmission in Rabbinic Judaism and Early Christianity*, 2d ed. (Uppsala and Lund: Gleerup, 1964); I. H. Marshall, *I Believe in the Historical Jesus* (Grand Rapids: Eerdmans, 1977); R. P. Martin, *New Testament Foundations: A Guide for Christian Students*, Vol. 1, *The Four Gospels* (Grand Rapids: Eerdmans, 1975) 119-38; N. Perrin, *Rediscovering the Teaching of Jesus* (New York: Harper and Row, 1976); R. Riesner, *Jesus als Lehrer* (Tübingen: J. C. B. Mohr, 1980); H. Schürmann, *Traditionsgeschichtliche Untersuchungen zu den Synoptischen Evangelien* (Düsseldorf: Patmos, 1968); G. Stanton, *Jesus of Nazareth in New Testament Preaching* (Cambridge: University Press, 1974).

P. H. Davids

TRANSFIGURATION

The word *transfiguration* (from the Latin *transfiguratio*) signifies in biblical studies the remarkable transformation that once took place in the appearance of Jesus. Matthew 17:2 and Mark 9:2, though not Luke, use the equivalent Greek verb *metamorphoō* (cf. metamorphosis) to describe that change. It affected his face, which shone, and his clothing, which glistened.

The narrative itself occurs in three of the four Gospels, Matthew 17:1-9; Mark 9:2-10; Luke 9:28-36. A further description of the Transfiguration occurs in 2 Peter 1:16-18. The setting of the Transfiguration in the narrative and argument respectively of these passages, as well as its setting historically and geographically, must be determined as closely as possible. The reason for its omission from John cannot be determined with certainty, but some reflection on the possibilities will be in order. The similarities and differences between these passages (contextual, structural and verbal) all require careful attention. Certain motifs or themes occur within these accounts which must be interpreted and evaluated as to their implications. The significance of the Transfiguration in its various biblical settings and finally its significance christologically need to be determined from a study of the previous points.

1. The Narratives in Matthew 17:1-9; Mark 9:2-10; Luke 9:28-36
2. The Transfiguration in 2 Peter 1:16-18
3. The Omission of the Transfiguration Narrative from John
4. The Immediate Context
5. Structure
6. Verbal Similarities and Differences Between the Synoptics
7. Motifs
8. Conclusion

1. The Narratives in Matthew 17:1-9; Mark 9:2-10; Luke 9:28-36.

1.1. Setting. Each of the Synoptic Gospels has the following sequence: (1) Peter's confession that Jesus is the Messiah (*see* Christ); (2) Jesus' charge not to divulge this to others; (3) Jesus' prediction of his coming suffering, death and resurrection (*see* Predictions of Jesus' Passion and Resurrection); (4) his call to those who want to be his disciples* to follow him in self-sacrifice (*see* Discipleship); (5) the Transfiguration; (6) Jesus' command not to tell others about this until after his resurrection*; (7) a discussion (except in Luke) on the coming of Elijah*; (8) the healing* of a boy; and (9) a second prediction of Jesus' passion.

Every one of these short sections of narrative and dialog pertains in some way to who Jesus is and why he came. The discussion about Elijah (7) may at first seem out of place, but it was triggered by the appearance of Elijah at Jesus' Transfiguration, and it explains the congruence of the coming of Jesus with predictions about the coming of Elijah and of John the Baptist (*see* John the Baptist). The healing story serves, among other things, to contrast Jesus' healing power in dependence on God* with the lack of believing prayer* on the part of the disciples. The relevance of the other conversations and events is more easily seen.

The Transfiguration occurs in a particularly significant setting in Luke. The Messianic confession by Peter (Lk 9:20) is part of a sequence that Luke has featured by drawing three events more closely together than they are in the accounts of Matthew and Mark: (1) Jesus calms the sea, which evokes the disciples' words "Who is this? He commands even the winds and the water and they obey him" (Lk 8:25); (2) Herod Antipas hears of Jesus' miracles* and says, "Who, then, is this about whom I hear such things?" (Lk 9:9); (3) Jesus asks the disciples who they say he is, to which Peter replies, "The Christ (Messiah) of God" (Lk 9:20). The question of the identity of Jesus is thus emphasized.

Luke arranges the significant events and dialog introduced by Peter's confession in a chiastic order, that is, by means of a stylistic reversal of sequence:

(A) Jesus' *identity* is stated by Peter in Luke 9:20.

(B) Jesus' *death* is stated in verse 22.

(C) His future coming in *glory* is stated in verse 26.

(C′) His *glory* is visibly demonstrated in the Transfiguration in verse 29.

(B′) His *departure* (= *death?*—see later discussion) is discussed by Moses and Elijah in verse 31.

(A′) His *identity* is affirmed by the voice from heaven ("This is my Son") in verse 35.

1.2. Historical Situation. As noted, the Transfiguration occurs in the same narrative context in all of the Synoptic Gospels. The assumption is clearly that the event described actually took place at this juncture in the life and ministry of Jesus. In spite of this, some scholars do not consider it historically authentic. For a time the theory promoted by Bultmann that it was a misplaced story of a post-resurrection appearance of Jesus gained prominence.

While the brilliance of Jesus' appearance and his identification as the Son of God (*see* Son of God) may seem to give plausibility to this suggestion, several aspects of the narrative militate against the theory. Among these are (1) the uniformity, just mentioned, of the contextual placement within the lifetime of Jesus in each of the Synoptic Gospels; (2) the appropriateness of the event in that context; (3) the fact that the narrative is integral with that context; (4) the command from heaven to "hear him," which would be superfluous after the resurrection; and (5) the fact that there is no specific mention of resurrection in the narrative (even if this is assumed in the word *departure* in Lk 9:31).

Other alternatives to a historical event that have been offered range from a blend of epiphany (appearance) stories such as were recited in ancient times, or a literary adaptation of some OT narrative (such as Ex 24) to a fresh literary construction of one of the Evangelists or some other early Christian writer. If such a supernatural transformation as the Transfiguration is considered unbelievable at the outset (as with Bultmann), some alternative to historicity must be found. But since, as noted, the narrative is embedded in each Synoptic Gospel in a tight, flowing narrative sequence, there is little objective reason to question its authenticity. The story is certainly compatible with the assumption prevailing throughout the Bible of the possibility of immanent supernatural activity and appearance.

As it stands, the Transfiguration takes place at a crucial time in Jesus' ministry. For some time Jesus had been preaching and healing, enjoying popularity among many and yet becoming increasingly detested by others, especially those in the religious power structure. The issue of his identity and mission was escalating. In each of the Synoptic Gospels the confession of Jesus' messiahship (and, in the longer Matthean narrative of the confession, also his deity) comes at a crucial stage and introduces a new phase of Jesus' ministry. From this point on he faces his city of ultimate destiny, Jerusalem, with its climactic events (especially noted in Lk 9:51, just fifteen verses after the conclusion of the Transfiguration narrative).

The location of the Transfiguration has never been established with certainty (*see* Archeology and Geography). A long-standing tradition places it at Mt. Tabor. Since isolation would have been difficult here (there is evidence that a Roman fortress existed at the summit around the time of Christ; Josephus *J.W.* 2.20.6; 4.1.8), and since it is at a considerable distance from Caesarea Philippi, which is the location of the immediately preceding event in the Gospels, it seems wise to seek another site. Mt. Hermon, near Caesarea Philippi, offers a possibility. Problems attend this theory also, however, including the height of 2,813 meters or 9,232 feet (difficult to reach if the group went to or near the top) and the improbability (though not impossibility) that upon his descent from a mountain some 30 miles north of the Sea of Galilee* Jesus would have met a crowd that even included scribes (Mk 9:14). Also, Mark notes immediately after this that they "left that place and passed through Galilee" (Mk 9:30). This could be interpreted to mean that they left a place *outside* of Galilee (such as Mt. Hermon), went *to* Galilee and then travelled *through* it, but it could also imply that they left a place *in* or *near* Galilee and immediately proceeded *through* it. The latter understanding would suggest a site other than Mt. Hermon.

There is another mountain site that was more isolated than Mt. Tabor and more accessible than Mt. Hermon. That is Mount Meiron, located in Galilee some eight or so miles northwest of the Sea of Galilee. It is, in fact, within Galilee itself and boasts the highest peak within Palestine proper. Meiron later became a center of Jewish mysticism, and some stories developed there about the future coming of the Messiah in company with Elijah. It would have been natural for crowds, including scribes,* to have been near its base, and on leaving the mountain one would already be in Galilee. None of this is conclusive evidence, but at least a possible site exists that can satisfy the geographical requirements for an historically plausible Transfiguration.

2. The Transfiguration in 2 Peter 1:16-18.

The author of this passage refers to the Transfiguration to validate his teaching regarding the "power and coming" of Christ. The description of the Transfiguration lacks much of the detail found in the Synoptic accounts, focussing almost entirely on the voice from the "majestic glory." The reality of the Transfiguration is assumed rather than argued. In using the word *eyewitnesses* and in saying "we heard his voice" (where the first-person-plural personal pronoun has an emphatic effect), the author communicates that the event was observed and is not mere legend. The certainty of the expectation of the Parousia of Christ receives further support in the fulfillment of the "word of the prophets" (v. 19).

3. The Omission of the Transfiguration Narrative from John.

Since the Gospel of John is intended to prove the messiahship and divine sonship of Jesus, one might expect that he would employ the Transfiguration narrative as part of his demonstration. On the other hand, this Gospel seems to portray the glory* of Jesus throughout the narrative rather than mainly at one point (*see* John, Gospel of). There is one place, at least, where there may be a deliberately veiled allusion to the Transfiguration. That is the testimony "We have seen his glory, the glory of the one and only, who came from the Father, full of grace and truth" (Jn 1:14). Also, in John 12:27-33 God's voice comes from heaven saying that he had glorified his name and would do it again. There is a prediction of Jesus' death in this passage. The way of death and the way of glory are connected here as well as in the Caesarea Philippi conversation and in Luke's account of the Transfiguration. John may have considered the event of 12:27-33, along with the fact of 1:14, sufficient without recording the Transfiguration as well.

4. The Immediate Context.

All three of the Synoptics precede the Transfiguration account with an enigmatic saying of Jesus that some who were standing with him at the time would not "taste death" until they had seen (and here the Gospels differ) "the Son of man coming in his kingdom" (Mt 16:28), "the kingdom of God come with power" (Mk 9:1) or simply "the kingdom of God" (Lk 9:27; *see* Kingdom of God).

The meaning of this saying is debated, but one possibility certainly is that Jesus refers to the Transfiguration. There are several reasons that can be offered for this option: (1) The term Son of man (*see* Son of Man), which occurs in the Matthean version, has just

been used in connection with Jesus' *glory*, and 2 Peter 1:17 says that at the Transfiguration Jesus "received honor and glory" from God. (2) Mark's version has the word *power* (*see* Authority and Power) which occurs in 2 Peter 1:16, where the Transfiguration is described as the "power and coming" of Jesus. (3) Likewise, similar terms, *come* and *coming*, occur in Mark 9:1 and 2 Peter 1:16 respectively. It can be argued that the Transfiguration was indeed a visible demonstration of the future glorious coming of the Lord* Jesus in his kingdom. (4) Only "some" of the disciples would see the event described before they died. This accords with the Transfiguration narrative in which only three, Peter, James and John, accompanied Jesus up the mountain. (5) Immediately after this saying each of the Synoptics provides a reference to the short span of time—about a week—between that statement and the Transfiguration. If the saying did refer to the Transfiguration, such a time reference is easily understood. At the same time it must be observed that the words "shall not taste death" could be understood to imply a vaguely distant fulfillment. Luke's reference to the time period (Lk 9:28) differs from the others in that the word *after* is followed immediately by "these words," which could well include the whole teaching of Jesus following Peter's confession. This knits together the whole chiasm observed above. But whether the connection is mainly viewed with the "taste of death" saying or with the whole passion prediction, the time reference in each (Mt 17:1; Mk 9:2; Lk 9:28) is undoubtedly important.

5. Structure.

The narrative in each account begins with the choice of Peter, James and John (Luke: Peter, John and James) and the ascent up the mountain (Luke adds "to pray"), and immediately proceeds to describe the change in Jesus' appearance. Next, the focus broadens to include Moses and Elijah and quickly (in Matthew and Mark) shifts to Peter and his proposal to construct three booths. Between the introduction of Moses and Elijah, and Peter's suggestion, Luke has a section of several narrative elements (Lk 9:31-33a) that do not occur in the other Gospels. All three Gospels follow Peter's words with a reference to the cloud and then to the voice. Matthew alone mentions the prostration of the disciples before Jesus but is joined by the other two Evangelists in a concluding observation that only Jesus was visible as the incident drew to a close.

An obvious question is why Luke has material not found in Matthew or Mark. This includes: (1) the observation that the appearance of Moses and Elijah was "in glory"; (2) the conversation of Moses and

Elijah about Jesus' "departure, which he was about to bring to fulfillment at Jerusalem"; (3) the note that Peter and the other disciples were "very sleepy" and then that they became "fully awake"; (4) the statement that they saw Jesus' glory and the two "men" who stood with him; and (5) the comment that Peter made his proposal "as the men were leaving."

The reason that those who hold to the priority of Mark (and the derivation of much of Matthew's and Luke's material from that Gospel) might offer is that Luke has chosen to insert these elements which were at his disposal (*see* Synoptic Problem). This would accord with the fact that even where similar phrases occur in the three accounts, the wording in Luke departs frequently from that of Mark and Matthew. Yet the account in Luke coheres together well as it is, and it could be argued that Luke's account could have stood without data from Mark. It could be theorized that Luke began not with Mark but with an earlier source (cf. Lk 1:1-4; *see* "L" Tradition). In this case Mark may not have been the basic narrative with which Luke worked, but rather: (1) Mark used the early source of Luke, along with whatever other traditions he may have had, such as Peter's reminiscences; (2) Mark kept the essence of this material and modified it to bring out certain features when he produced the canonical account; (3) Luke used that same early source as a basis of his historical reconstruction and wove together some material from Mark's completed work (see Reid).

As an example of such a possibility, Luke's description of the Last Supper (*see* Last Supper) has elements that are closer to Paul's account in 1 Corinthians 11 than to Mark's. Paul probably wrote his Epistle before the Gospels were committed to writing, and one could conclude that in this case Luke has followed a tradition of the Last Supper even closer to the event itself than Mark. Similarly, it could well be that Luke has an earlier tradition of the Transfiguration. This would strengthen the connection with the actual event and, at least as some would see it, would in consequence strengthen the case for its accuracy. This reconstruction is hypothetical but may be useful as a possible explanation of Luke's individualistic account.

6. Verbal Similarities and Differences Between the Synoptics.

As with any passage in the Synoptic Gospels, the authors had freedom to utilize vocabulary and idioms they considered appropriate to convey the facts and their implications. In some cases such differences are merely stylistic, in others they bring out different significant aspects of the narrative or dialog. For example, Matthew and Mark specify a six-day interlude between Jesus' saying about those who would witness the coming of the kingdom (Mt 17:1; Mk 9:2) and the Transfiguration, whereas Luke has a more general "about eight days" (Lk 9:28). Usually Luke is specific about time references. The two chronologies are certainly compatible (see 7. below).

In each narrative Jesus takes Peter, James and John, but Luke does not specify that the mountain they ascended was "high." Luke does say they went up to pray. This is in accord with Luke's habit of stressing prayer and is an addition to, not a contradiction of, the others.

A significant difference is that whereas Matthew and Mark say that Jesus was "transfigured" (the passive form of *metamorphoō* which, as noted above, signifies a remarkable transformation), Luke omits this verb and has instead "the appearance of his face changed" (Lk 9:29). The most probable reason for this is that he wished to avoid any specialized terminology that might call to mind the stories in pagan mythologies of divine epiphanies (appearances). Luke's own background was more Hellenistic than that of Matthew and Mark, so such sensitivity can easily be understood. Mark has the shortest description, confining himself to the word *transfigured*, and Matthew adds to that word, "His face shone like the sun."

The description of the changed appearance of Jesus' clothing also differs among the three Gospels. Matthew compares them with white light, Mark says they "became dazzling white, whiter than anyone in the world could bleach them," and Luke writes that they "became as bright as a flash of lightning" (Mt 17:2; Mk 9:3; Lk 9:29). Each author reached for words that would convey something of the extraordinary unearthly brilliance of the Transformation. Together they elicit from the reader a reverent amazement before the glory of Jesus Christ. In their mention of Moses and Elijah, although Matthew and Mark call them by name, Luke twice refers to them only as "two men" not only before but also after naming them (Lk 9:30, 32). It is unusual for Luke to revert to the generic term after having mentioned someone's name. However, in contrast to Matthew he, as well as Mark, describes the angelic (*see* Angels) presence at the empty tomb of Jesus in human terms: "men" in Luke 24:4 and the singular "young man" in Mark 16:5. It is possible that he is emphasizing the fact that these figures are indeed in human form.

Luke observes that the two men appear with Jesus "in glory," and says in verse 32 that they saw Jesus' glory. Although Matthew has the word *glory* seven times in the course of his Gospel, and Mark only three times, Luke uses it thirteen times, far out of proportion to the others. Likewise, he has *glorify* nine times, in comparison with Matthew's four times and Mark's once (together, the figures are Matthew 11 x, Mark 4 x but Luke 22 x). Even if Luke had not directly chosen the terminology for his narration but found it in his source(s), it was his decision to keep it. The way he uses these terms shows that he is especially sensitive to God's glory and to what brings him glory.

The word *departure* translates the Greek form of the word we know in transliteration as *exodus (exodos)*. It certainly brings to mind the escape of the people of Israel from Egypt, and it may signify a redemptive theme in Luke as well as alluding to the experience of Moses, with whose person and experience Jesus stands in superior comparison. The word appears only twice elsewhere in the NT. In Hebrews it refers to the Exodus from Egypt. In 2 Peter 1:15 it stands in parallel to the writer's reference in the preceding verse to the putting off of his "tabernacle" (i.e., his death). Here in Luke there is no such clear indication, but it may well refer either to Jesus' impending death or to the whole culmination of his earthly life. The phrase "which he was about to bring to fulfillment at Jerusalem" echoes Luke's strong theme of Jesus' intentional fulfillment of the divine will (cf. Luke's frequent use of *dei*, "it is necessary" [Lk 2:49; 4:43; 9:22; 11:42; 12:12; 13:14, 16, 33; 15:32; 17:25; 18:1; 19:5; 21:9; 22:7, 37; 24:7, 26, 44) and of *pleroō*, "fulfill" [Lk 1:20; 4:21; 21:24; 22:16; 24:44, as well as here]). Whether Jesus' resurrection is intended to be understood as part of his "departure" is not clear. One could also argue for inclusion of the ascension, since Luke is the only Gospel to describe that final departure (Lk 24:50-53; cf. Acts 1:1-11). Also, shortly after the Transfiguration episode Luke has an allusion to the ascension in the expression "received up" (Lk 9:51). The root of the Greek word for that *(analēmpsis)* is the same as the root for the word used for the ascension* *(analambanō)* in Acts 1:2.

Whatever meaning may be found in the expression, it is a remarkable subject of conversation between Moses and Elijah. It could be taken as an indication that inhabitants of heaven* were aware of and concerned with the destiny of Jesus at the cross. The two men, while not angels, do bring a heavenly interpretation of an event, as do angels at the resurrection and ascension in Luke. The conversation also provides a strong contrast to the glory he was at that very time experiencing. Further, it suggests that the Transfiguration was in part providing assurance for Jesus in preparation for his suffering. The use of another remarkable word, *accomplish*, adds to the force of the

prediction. Jesus is not described as an involuntary victim but as the one who himself brings about the departure.

The scene of the departure was to be Jerusalem. The importance of that place reference here is seen in the fact that Matthew uses the two Greek terms for Jerusalem thirteen times, Mark ten times, but Luke thirty-one times. It is the city of destiny for Jesus in Luke, as seen especially in Luke 13:33, "I must keep on going . . . for surely no prophet can die outside of Jerusalem." One might have expected Matthew, the more Jewish Gospel, to emphasize Jerusalem, and indeed Matthew contains the only reference to that city in the passion predictions that Jesus gave immediately before and after the Transfiguration (Mt 16:21). By the time of Jesus' third passion prediction, however, all three Gospels include one or two specific references to Jerusalem (Mt 20:17-18; Mk 10:32-33; Lk 18:31). Thus each of the Evangelists in one place or another emphasizes the place of Jesus' passion, but Luke includes it in other contexts and, remarkably, here in the Transfiguration narrative. Luke also is the only writer to include a reference to the sleepiness of the disciples on the mountain (Lk 9:32), perhaps a psychological reaction due to their difficulty in coping with the happening, so the vocabulary is unique here as well. Likewise, he is the only one to mention that it was as the men were *leaving* that Peter made his proposal about the booths (Lk 9:33). In the same verse Luke has the word *Master*, where Matthew and Mark have *Rabbi* (*see* Teacher). All seven occurrences of this word are in Luke, most of them in his editorial comments rather than in material derived from other sources.

One striking difference between the three Gospels is the place where they mention the disciples' fear. Matthew 17:6 says they "fell to the ground terrified" on hearing the voice. Mark 9:6 attributes the proposal of Peter regarding booths to their fright (cf. Mk 4:40 where fear is associated with unbelief). Luke 9:34 mentions their fear as they were entering the cloud. One could postulate reasons why each of the three Gospels thus locates the fear or simply assume that fear gripped the disciples in waves at successive stages of the event. There are other verbal differences, the significance of which is variously assessed, but the most clearly important ones that remain are in the words spoken by the voice from heaven, which topic is reserved for discussion below. In addition the vocabulary in Matthew's section immediately following the voice (Mt 17:6-7) recalls some of the vocabulary in the vision narrative in Daniel 10, especially verses 9-12.

7. Motifs.

There are several distinct motifs and features in the Transfiguration narrative that allude to one or more biblical circumstances. The first motif is the brief lapse of time between Jesus' words about seeing the power of the kingdom and the Transfiguration. All three Synoptic Gospels make a point of mentioning the time, but, as noted above, they vary slightly. Against the possibility that this is no more than a narrative time marker is the striking similarity with the six days of Exodus 24:16 during which Moses, with Aaron, Nadab and Abihu, experienced the glory of God on Mount Sinai. The variation between the six days of Matthew and Mark and "about eight days" in Luke could well be due to the fact that Exodus 24:16 specifies a waiting period of six days but also mentions a seventh day when the Lord calls to Moses plus an unspecified time for approach and descent. A period of six days is a common literary pattern in Semitic literature (McCurley) and "after six days" may mean on the seventh day, just as "on the third day" explains "after two days" in Hosea 6:2. A parallel with Exodus 24:16 seems very likely.

The second feature is the mountain itself (*see* Mountain and Wilderness). This also is reminiscent of Mount Sinai, although the mountain as a place of revelation is known elsewhere in Scripture (e.g., Ezek 40:2; Rev 21:10). In Isaiah 40:9 those who "bring good tidings to Zion go up on a high mountain." These last two words in the LXX (*oros hupsēlon*) are identical to "high mountain" in Matthew and Mark. *Mountain* occurs sixteen times in Matthew, where it seems to have special significance, eleven times in Mark and twelve times in Luke.

The third motif is the cloud. Once more the Exodus event provides a referent. The cloud led them on their journey, showed the glory of the Lord prior to the giving of manna, marked the induction of seventy elders and appeared at the entrance to the tabernacle (Ex 13:21-22; 16:10; 24:16; 40:34-38). Above all, the cloud symbolized the presence of the Lord at Sinai (Ex 19:16-19), notably also when Moses and the three companions were there (Ex 24:15-18). In that account the LXX uses a synonym (*kalyptō;* cf. use in Ex 40:34) for the Greek word for "overshadow" (*episkiazō*) that is used in each account of the Transfiguration. Of perhaps even more significance, this word (*episkiazō*) is used by the LXX to translate the Hebrew word describing the dwelling or glorious *shekinah* presence of God at the tabernacle (Ex 40:35). On the other hand, Isaiah 4:5 refers to the cloud not with reference to past time but rather in the context of the future. So does the familiar Daniel 7:13 describing the coming

of the Son of man with the clouds of heaven. Jesus took up this prophecy (Mk 13:26; 14:62), and it also appears in Revelation 1:7. The cloud motif therefore could refer either to the past (the Exodus) or to the future (the Parousia).

The fourth motif is the appearance of Moses and Elijah. It can be considered a "motif" because it has symbolic meaning, and its significance must be appraised along with that of the other elements in the narrative. Since the time of Origen it has been common to think of the two as representing the Law and the Prophets respectively. This does not, however, express their significance in first-century Judaism.* There are other reasons why these, rather than other OT figures, appear. In addition to their prominence and importance as spiritual leaders, they have in common an unusual conclusion to life. Although Moses' death seems to have been normal, he was apparently buried by God unseen (Deut 34:5-6). Elijah was taken to heaven by a whirlwind in the chariot scene (2 Kings 2:11). Later Jewish legend had Moses mysteriously brought to heaven. Moses was connected in Jewish thought with the future as well as with the past, since he was the paradigm for the eschatological prophet* mentioned in Deuteronomy 18:18. Elijah* was arguably an eschatological figure in Jewish reflection (cf. Mal 4:5-6). Both are surpassed by Jesus not only in the significance of their persons and ministries, but also in that Jesus was not merely translated to heaven but died, rose again and ascended.

Elijah seems to be more prominent than Moses in Mark's Gospel than he is in either Matthew or Luke. His name appears first ("Elijah with Moses"); there is no reference to Jesus' face shining, thus omitting a possible point of comparison with Moses; and there is no allusion to an "exodus" as in Luke.

Whether Peter's proposal to build three huts or "tabernacles" is considered a motif, it is a constant element in each account. Mark seems to make the most of it, explaining why Peter said it, as though it were a horrendous error. One culpable aspect of the proposal is that it puts Jesus on the same level with the two heavenly visitors. Another may be that Peter was building on a concept of the Feast* of Tabernacles as a symbol not only of the past but a future time of rest for Israel, thinking that the day of Jesus' future glorification had come. In this case he would have again missed the place of the cross (cf. Mt 16:22).

The voice from heaven is not only a motif but the climax of the experience. In Exodus 24 and in the chapters that follow, the words from heaven are words of the Law; in the Transfiguration the voice speaks of Christ. The words reflect the essence of several OT passages. One is Psalm 2:7, "You are my Son" (*see* Son of God). The heavenly voice had spoken these words at Jesus' baptism* (where Matthew has "This is . . ." and the others "You are . . ."; Mt 3:17; Mk 1:11; Lk 3:22). In the context of Psalm 2 it not only states the relationship of the Son to the Father but does so in a context of future vindication, victory and earthly rule. (A comprehensive interpretation of the Transfiguration must consider its relationship to Jesus' baptism.) The additional designation, "the chosen [One]," appears in Luke's version, a slight verbal modification of the LXX of Isaiah 42:1. This is one of Isaiah's "Servant songs" and describes the Servant as one who ultimately brings justice to the nations (*see* Servant of Yahweh). The context of the two christological designations is thus related to eschatology,* specifically to the future rule of Christ.

It is difficult to know whether there is any one OT passage to which the words "my son, my beloved" allude. Various proposals have been made. It may be that there is no other allusion than to Psalm 2:7. However, there is another possibility, namely Genesis 22:2 where God says to Abraham,* "Take your son, your only son, Isaac, whom you love" (cf. vv. 12, 16). The LXX reads *ton huion sou ton agapēton,* and Matthew and Mark have *ho huios mou ho agapētos,* the only differences being the case and the substitution of pronouns for the article. It is striking that in the LXX *agapētos,* "beloved," is used instead of *monogenēs,* "one and only" or "only begotten," where focus is on mourning for an only child (Jer 6:26; Amos 8:10; Zech 12:10), as is the case in Genesis 22:2, 12, 16. In both OT and NT, narratives about an only child involve mortal danger or death (e.g., Jephthah's daugher, Judg 11:34; the widow's son, Lk 7:12; Jairus's daughter, Lk 9:42; see De Kruijf, 112-16). The voice seems to be comparing Jesus to Isaac, the only and beloved son, who embodied the hope of the covenant (cf. Acts 3:25; Heb 6:13-15). Isaac willingly went to the place of sacrifice and "figuratively speaking" (Heb 11:19) was received back from death. Moreover, an allusion to Isaac brings into focus the father who offered him (for which act of faith he is cited in Heb 11:17-19; cf. Jas 2:21), whose willingness to sacrifice his son forms a background for Romans 8:32 ("He who did not spare his own Son . . ."). God, in speaking of his beloved Son, may also indirectly speak of himself.

8. Conclusion.

Theories about the meaning and significance of the Transfiguration narrative have abounded. Lohmeyer at first thought it was influenced by ancient epiphany stories, then changed his mind. Gerber proposed

Jewish parallels. Sabbe found parallels with Daniel 10. Boobyer viewed it as a foreshadowing of the Parousia. Bultmann saw it as a transposed resurrection account. Kee gave the final blow to Hellenistic parallels. Riesenfeld proposed an enthronement context, following a trend in OT studies. Baltensweiler (unlike many others) held that it was a historical event, a crisis experience in Jesus' life. H.-P. Müller saw in it a synthesis of the figures of the Messiah and the Son of man. For Mauser it embodied an Exodus motif. Thrall emphasized the contrast with Moses and Elijah who had gone to heaven without resurrection. Trites called it "the gospel in microcosm." More recent works have tended to interpret the Transfiguration by means of a redactional or literary methodology. In such studies the important benefit of emphasizing the theology of the individual Gospels must be weighed against the possible loss of comprehending the Transfiguration as a historical event with its own integrity and message. Each of the foregoing interpretations needs to be challenged by the insights of the others as well as by a continuing vigorous study of the texts themselves.

The following synthesis may be proposed: Two clusters of events form the conceptual framework for the Transfiguration. The first is the Exodus event, the revelation of God's glory at the tabernacle and especially as focused in the experience of God's presence in the mountain scene in Exodus 24. That scene is recalled in the Transfiguration by the reference to six days, and is expanded by the circumstances of the mountain, the three men, the discussion about Jesus' "exodus" and the manifestation of the presence of God through the cloud. The second circumstance or cluster of events is the anticipated exaltation of Christ, the glory of the Son of man. This may be at his resurrection (then still future) or at some kind of enthronement, but much more likely at his future Parousia when he comes with the clouds of heaven. It may be suggested that Moses represents the first conceptual framework and Elijah the second.

One might propose in conclusion that, first of all, the three Gospels uniformly present Jesus as the Son of God. In addition Matthew seems to draw mainly on the Moses analogy, Luke on that of a redemptive "exodus" and on the prediction of the chosen Servant, while Mark focusses on Elijah. If there is an allusion in the voice from heaven to Abraham's offering of his "beloved son," a sacrificial motif is present in Matthew and Mark. In each Gospel the Transfiguration affirms (1) the confession of Peter and (2) the statements of Jesus about himself, his mission (the cross must be endured) and his glorious destiny. But further, (3) in the heavenly voice God himself provides the final affirmation concerning his Son and his Son's mission. All three Gospels then conclude with God's command to erring Peter, to all the disciples and to the reader, "Listen to him."

See also ELIJAH AND ELISHA; GLORY; MOSES

BIBLIOGRAPHY. P. R. Baldacci, *The Significance of the Transfiguration Narrative in the Gospel of Luke: A Redactional Investigation* (Ann Arbor: University Microfilms International, 1974); H. Baltensweiler, *Die Verklärung Jesu: Historisches Ereignis und synoptische Berichte* (Zurich: Zwingli, 1959); G. H. Boobyer, *St Mark and the Transfiguration Story* (Edinburgh: T. & T. Clark, 1942); R. Bultmann, *History of the Synoptic Tradition* (New York: Harper, 1968) 259-61, 309, 423-33; G. B. Caird, "The Transfiguration," *ExpT 67* (1955) 291-94; C. E. Carlston, "Transfiguration and Resurrection," *JBL* 80 (1961) 233-40; Th. C. De Kruijf, "The Glory of the Only Son (John 1:14)," in *Studies in John Presented to Prof. Dr. J. N. Sevenster* (NovTSup 24; Leiden: E. J. Brill, 1970) 111-123; W. Gerber, "Die Metamorphose Jesu, Mark 9,2f. par," *TZ 23* (1967) 385-95; D. F. Harry, *The Transfiguration (Mark 9:2-13 and Parallels). A Redaction Critical and Traditio-Historical Study* (Ann Arbor: University Microfilms International, 1976); M. D. Hooker, " 'What Doest Thou Here, Elijah?': A Look at St. Mark's Account of the Transfiguration," in *The Glory of Christ in the New Testament: Studies in Christology*, ed. L. D. Hurst and N. T. Wright (Oxford, Clarendon, 1987) 59-70; H. C. Kee, "The Transfiguration in Mark: Epiphany or Apocalyptic Vision?," in *Understanding the Sacred Text*, ed. J. Reumann (Valley Forge: Judson, 1972) 137-52; A. Kenny, "The Transfiguration and the Agony in the Garden" *CBQ* 19 (1957) 444-52; W. L. Liefeld, "Theological Motifs in the Transfiguration Narrative," in *New Dimensions in New Testament Study*, ed. R. N. Longenecker and M. C. Tenney (Grand Rapids: Zondervan, 1974) 162-79; E. Lohmeyer, "Die Verklärung Jesu nach dem Markus-Evangelium," *ZNW* 21 (1922) 185-215; E. Lohmeyer and W. Schmauch, *Das Evangelium des Matthäus* (3d ed.; Göttingen: Vandenhoek & Ruprecht, 1939); U. Mauser, *Christ in the Wilderness* (SBT 39; Naperville, Il: Allenson, 1963) 111-18; F. R. McCurley, Jr., " 'And After Six Days' (Mk 9:2): A Semitic Literary Device," *JBL* 93 (1974) 67-81; J. A. McGuckin, *The Transfiguration of Christ in Scripture and Tradition* (SBEC 9; Lewiston/Queenston: Edwin Mellen, 1986); H.-P. Müller, "Die Verklärung Jesu," *ZNW* 51 (1960) 56-64; J. Murphy-O'Connor, "What Really Happened at the Transfiguration?" *BRev* 3,3 (1987) 8-21; A. M. Ramsay, *The Glory of God and the Transfiguration of Christ* (London: Longmans, Green, 1949) 101-47; B. O. Reid, "Voices and Angels: What Were They Talking About at the Transfiguration? A Redactional Critical Study of Luke 9:28-36," *BR* 34 (1989) 19-31; H. Riesenfeld, *Jesus Transfigure. L'arrière-plan du récit évangélique de la Transfiguration de Notre-Seigneur* (ASNU 16: Copenhagen: Munksgaard, 1947); M. Sabbe, "Le rédaction du recit de la transfiguration," in *La Venue du Messie, Messianisme et Eschatologie* (Paris-Brugge: 1962) 65-100; R. Stein, "Is the Transfiguration (Mark 9:2-8) a Misplaced Resurrection-Account?" *JBL* 95 (1976) 76-96; M. E. Thrall, "Elijah and Moses in Mark's Account of the Transfiguration," *NTS* 16 (1970) 305-17; A. A. Trites, "The Transfiguration of Jesus: The Gospel in Microcosm," *EvQ* 51 (1979) 67-79; idem, "The Transfiguration in the Theology of Luke: Some Redactional Links," in *The Glory of Christ in the New Testament: Studies in Christology*, ed. L. D. Hurst and N. T. Wright (Oxford: Clarendon, 1987) 71-81.

W. L. Liefeld

TRIAL OF JESUS

The trial and death* of Jesus, in addition to being a celebrated problem of jurisprudence, is the focal point of the gospel story and thus assumes paramount importance as a historical and theological issue. Opinions are sharply divided over a wide range of historical, literary and legal aspects of the trial. However, the Jewish and Roman background supports a traditional approach to these questions, namely: after a religious trial before the Sanhedrin* which found Jesus guilty of blasphemy,* the Jewish leaders brought a charge of sedition before Pilate who conducted a political trial and had Jesus crucified.

1. Roman and Jewish Sources
2. NT Witnesses
3. Passion Narratives
4. Legal Issues
5. Theological Significance

1. Roman and Jewish Sources.

As a fact of history the trial and death of Jesus of Nazareth is a matter beyond dispute. It is better attested and supported with a wider array of evidence than any other comparable event known to us from the ancient world (Harvey, 11). This datum, so prominent in the apostolic preaching and in the written Gospels,* is featured in reports of the historical Jesus in non-Christian sources (see Jesus in Non-Christian Sources); these notices, meager though they are, confirm the historical character of the NT's witness to Christ crucified. They furnish no details of the trial itself which are of independent value but, much in the manner of some NT references, make summary statements of what happened.

An official Roman record of the trial of Jesus was probably made at the time and subsequently lost. Imperial Rome received dispatches from the provinces at regular intervals which included reports of major events. Among the *acta* entered in these official registers (Cassius Dio *Hist.* 57.21.5; 67.11.3) were trials and executions ordered by Roman governors. Such archives of Jesus' trial were reported to exist in the middle of the second Christian century: "That these things happened you may learn from the 'Acts' which were recorded under Pontius Pilate" (Justin Martyr *Apol.* 1.35.9; cf. 1.48.3; and Tertullian *Marc.* 4.17.19; Eusebius *Hist. Eccl.* 2.2.1-4). The later *Acts of Pilate* (fourth century A.D.) is a cycle of pious legends which probably appeared when the archives were no longer available.

On the Jewish side the situation is less certain. The rabbinic law directing two court clerks to write down the speeches pleading for acquittal and conviction (*m. Sanh.* 4:3; *see* Sanhedrin) may reflect first-century procedures, but there are no allusions to such recordings in the case of Jesus. The Jewish folklore about the last days of Jesus called *Toledoth Jeshu* is medieval in origin and has no historical value. A number of rabbinic and historical texts, however, lay fair claim to be worthy of credence and have been studied intensively.

1.1. Talmud. A common theme runs through all the Talmudic (*see* Rabbinic Traditions and Writings) references to Jesus: He was executed as a dangerous teacher, a seducer, or *mēsîṯ*, who led Israel astray. A notable text from the Babylonian Talmud (*b. Sanh.* 43a) preserves a saying handed down from the earliest period (a *baraita* from the Tannaim, A.D. 70-200): "Jesus was hanged on Passover Eve. For forty days before the execution took place, a herald went forth and cried, 'He is going forth to be stoned because he has practiced sorcery and enticed Israel to apostasy. Anyone who can say anything in his favor, let him come forward and plead on his behalf.' But since nothing was brought forward in his favor he was hanged on Passover Eve." The emphatic point is that the trial and execution, carried out under Jewish not Roman procedures, were absolutely fair. Putting aside the questionable details in the account, the attempt to justify Jewish involvement in the death of Jesus is remarkable and stands in contrast to modern Jewish research on the trial. Other Talmudic statements are similar: "Jesus the Nazarene practiced magic and led Israel astray" (*b. Sanh.* 107b; cf. *b. Soṭa* 47a; *y. ḥag.* 2.2). Also, a series of disputed passages which refer to an executed heretic, a certain Ben Stada (*b. Sanh.* 67a; *t. Sanh.* 10.11; *b. Šabb.* 104b; *y. Sanh.* 7.16; *y. Yebam.*

16.6; *y. Šabb.* 12.4; *t. Šabb.* 11.15), in all likelihood is linked to the false-prophet tradition about Jesus (Catchpole, 64).

1.2. Josephus. The well-known passages about Jesus, the so-called *Testimonium Flavianum*, are widely regarded to be genuine, with some obvious Christian interpolations (*see* Josephus). The authentic text (cf. *Ant.* 20.9.1 §200) underscores the leading role of Pilate and the complicity of the Jewish leaders in the trial of Jesus: "On the accusation of our leading men, Pilate condemned him to the cross, but those who were attracted to him from the first did not cease to love him" (*Ant.* 18.3.3 §64). The Slavonic version of Josephus has fuelled much speculation, but its embellished accounts of Jesus' life and death are legendary expansions of the Greek originals.

1.3. Tacitus. The information provided by Tacitus, who wrote between A.D. 115 and 117, is very sketchy and may be derived from Josephus: "They got their name from Christ, who was executed by sentence of the procurator Pontius Pilate in the reign of Tiberius" (*Ann.* 15.44.2). For Roman readers the pertinent information about the Christians, whom Nero had blamed for the fire in Rome (A.D. 64), was the identity and death of their namesake. Another allusion to Roman knowledge of the crucifixion appears in the Christian writer of the early third century, Julius Africanus; he cites (*PG* 10.89) one Thallus, a freedman of Tiberius who wrote a history (c. A.D. 50) now lost, for the opinion that the darkness and earthquake attending the cross were to be explained as an eclipse, inferring that Thallus mentioned the crucifixion in book three of his history.

1.4. Mara bar Serapion. A Syriac letter written from prison by Mara bar Serapion to his son cautions that misfortune overtakes those who persecute wise men, such as Socrates, Pythagoras and Jesus: "What advantage did the Jews gain from executing their wise King? It was just after that that their kingdom was abolished. . . . Nor did the wise King die altogether; he lived on in the teaching he had given." The date of Mara bar Serapion is uncertain; the only extant copy of the letter is seventh century, but historical clues place its origin in the first three centuries, perhaps as early as A.D. 73 (Blinzler, 36). The author was probably a pagan and, if first century, provides independent testimony to Jewish responsibility for the execution of Jesus.

In summary, the literary evidence confirms three facts: (1) Jesus was crucified by Roman authority under the sentence of Pontius Pilate (Josephus, Tacitus); (2) the Jewish leaders made a formal accusation against Jesus and participated decisively in the events leading to his execution (Josephus, Mara) and (3) Jewish involvement in the trial was explained as a proper undertaking against a heretic or seducer who led Israel astray (Talmud).

2. NT Witnesses.

The centrality of the cross in apostolic preaching gave rise to trial summaries which are found outside the passion narratives (*see* Passion Narrative), primarily in sermons and creedal formulas. They were part of the earliest Gospel tradition proclaimed by the apostles* and handed down to their converts (Acts 1:3; 1 Cor 15:3); these kerygmatic summaries disclose the contours of a written passion narrative in its earliest stages of formation.

2.1. Letters of Paul. The language of "handing over" (*paradidōmi*) describes Jesus' voluntary death as a divine necessity (Rom 4:25; 8:32; 1 Cor 11:32; Gal 2:20; Eph 5:2). The proximate agents of the crucifixion can be the "rulers of this age" (1 Cor 2:8; Col 2:15) or, from another point of view, the "Jews, who killed both the Lord Jesus and the prophets" (1 Thess 2:14-15). Paul alludes directly to the trial when he says that Christ Jesus "witnessed the good confession before Pontius Pilate" (1 Tim 6:13). Other epistolary texts emphasize the innocence of Jesus and the plight of those who caused him to suffer (1 Pet 2:22-24; Heb 6:6; 10:26-29; Rev 1:7).

2.2. Acts of the Apostles. Speeches in Acts provide eleven passages which relate to the trial. (1) The events in Jerusalem were part of a divine plan fulfilling the prophetic Scriptures (2:22-23; 3:17-19; 4:10-11, 25-28; 13:27-29). (2) Being ignorant of who Jesus was, the Jews in Jerusalem and their leaders delivered up and disowned him in the presence of Pilate (3:13, 17; 13:27). (3) The crucifixion was carried out by the Romans, but the Jews, specifically the leaders of the Sanhedrin, were chiefly responsible: "You killed him, having him crucified by the hand of godless men" (2:23; cf. 2:36; 3:15, 17; 4:10; 5:28, 30; 7:52; 10:39; 13:27-28). (4) In a prayer of the church the circle of conspiracy is widened to "both Herod and Pontius Pilate along with the Gentiles and the peoples of Israel" (4:27).

The writings and sermons preserved in the Letters and Acts concur in the assertion that the handing over of Jesus to death was taken at the initiative of the Jews in Jerusalem and their leaders; moreover, the Gentile* authorities bear equal responsibility whenever they are addressed. Whatever else may be said, the human actors played out a divine drama, doing what God's hand and purpose had predetermined to happen (Acts 4:28; cf. 2:23; 3:18; Rom 8:32; 1 Cor 2:7).

2.3. Gospel Predictions. What were hints earlier in the ministry of Jesus (e.g., Mk 2:18-22; Jn 7:6-8) become explicit predictions of impending death on the last journey to Jerusalem (Mk 8:31; 9:31; 10:33-34; cf. Mt 16:21; 17:22-23; 20:18-19; Lk 9:22, 44; 18:31-33; *see* Predictions of Jesus' Passion and Resurrection). The three Synoptic predictions in the triple tradition converge with the apostolic proclamation on the basic points of importance: (1) the trial and death of Jesus is ordained of God*; "the Son of man must suffer many things" (Mk 8:31) is a "must" (*dei*) of divine necessity (cf. Lk 17:25; 24:6-7) issuing from the will of the Father (Mk 9:11; 12:10; Mt 12:39; Lk 9:31; 24:26, 44); (2) the "handing over" of Jesus is a betrayal to the Sanhedrin in Jerusalem (the chief priests,* scribes* and elders*), which condemns him to death (Mk 8:31; 10:33; cf. 12:1-12; Lk 24:20, chief priests and rulers deliver him up to the sentence of death); and (3) the ultimate suffering, that is, his mockery, being spit upon, scourging and death, comes at the hands of Gentiles, namely, the Roman authorities (Mk 10:34; Lk 18:32).

Lack of explicit details in the Markan predictions (e.g., no mention of Pilate or the cross) counts against the view that these sayings are prophecies (*see* Prophets and Prophecy) after the fact created by the early church. They are better explained as seminal utterances which were elaborated in apostolic preaching. The impetus to proclaim the scandal of a crucified Messiah lies in the memory of Jesus' own words (Lk 24:44-49; 1 Cor 11:23-26).

3. Passion Narratives.

Our best sources of information are the accounts of the passion story in the four Gospels (Mt 26—27; Mk 14—15; Lk 22—23; Jn 13; 18—19), where the documents exhibit their highest degree of similarity. How is their striking relationship to be explained? The evidence tips in favor of the answer, vigorously contested in some quarters, that a connected passion narrative of some length circulated before the writing of the Gospels and underlies the work of the Evangelists (*see* Passion Narrative). The further inference that Luke and John are independent witnesses to this earlier tradition, seen in their departures from the Markan-Matthean scheme, is less certain but can be strongly supported (Jeremias, Green).

This approach to the formation of the four passion narratives is based on the following observations: (1) the four Gospels narrate a unified story of some twenty pericopes, with minor transpositions, beginning with a plot which converges on the arrest of Jesus; (2) OT motifs of the Servant of the Lord (Isaiah;

see Servant of Yahweh), stricken shepherd (Zechariah; *see* Shepherd and Sheep) and righteous sufferer (Psalms; *see* Death of Jesus) link Jesus' death to the fulfillment of the Scriptures (cf. Mk 14:49; *see* Old Testament in the Gospels) in a pattern distinctive of earliest Christian preaching; (3) the "handing over" theme found in kerygmatic summaries and dominical sayings emerges in the betrayal and trial scenes (Mt 26:2, 46; 27:2; Mk 14:10; 15:1, 15; Lk 23:25; Jn 19:16); (4) the shared vocabulary of Luke with Mark decreases from fifty per cent to twenty-seven per cent in the passion narratives; and (5) Luke and John agree together on numerous details which are absent from Mark and Matthew (e.g., Pilate's three verdicts of not guilty, Lk 23:4, 14, 22 par. Jn 18:38; 19:4, 6). On these grounds we will proceed to consider key episodes in the passion story, giving full weight to the testimony of each Evangelist.

3.1. Plot to Destroy Jesus. The enemies of Jesus hatched their plot during the earliest controversies in Galilee* and Jerusalem (Mk 3:6; Jn 5:18), but their intention was forestalled until the final week when Jesus' triumphal entry (*see* Triumphal Entry), the cleansing of the Temple (*see* Temple Cleansing), and head-on disputes prodded them into action (Mk 11:18; 12:12; 14:1). John records that Jesus lived under a constant death threat (7:1, 19, 25; 8:37; 11:16) and escaped a series of attempted arrests and stonings (7:30, 32, 44; 8:20, 59; 10:31, 39; cf. Lk 4:29-30). The popularity of Jesus with the crowds (Mt 7:28-29; Jn 4:1; *see* People, Crowd) precluded an open arrest by the religious leaders for fear of a riot but spurred their resolve to delay no longer: "See, this is getting us nowhere. Look how the whole world has gone after him" (Jn 12:19 NIV).

3.1.1. Proscription and Warrant. A crucial decision had been made weeks before, recounted in John 11:47-57. After the stir caused by the raising of Lazarus,* "the chief priests and the Pharisees convened a meeting of the Sanhedrin" (11:47) in order to deal with Jesus. The high priest Caiaphas (*see* Priest and Priesthood), an unwitting prophet, persuaded them that Jesus must die on behalf of the nation, thus keeping peace in the homeland and restoring the scattered people of God. The council, having formally decided to kill Jesus (11:52), issued a warrant for his arrest and solicited informers to come forward (11:57). This distinctive passage, filled with semitechnical terms, marks the beginning of the legal process and, in effect, makes Jesus a fugitive from Jewish law (Bammel 1971, 33-35). An ongoing prosecution instigated by the Jews and led by Caiaphas helps to explain what appears to be a precipitous rush to judgment in the Synoptic account of Passover (*see* Feasts) night.

3.1.2. Passover Treachery. The Synoptic time note, "after two days was the feast of Passover" (Mk 14:1 par. Mt 26:2 and Lk 22:1), appears to refer to a subsequent meeting of the council at the palace of Caiaphas. Here the discussion centered on a covert plan, as Luke puts it, "the how" (*to pōs*, 22:2) of getting rid of Jesus without causing an uproar during the feast (cf. Mt 26:4; Mk 14:2). The question was how to implement the resolution already passed (Jn 11:52, 57). An unexpected visitor brought what they hoped for: Judas Iscariot (*see* Judas Iscariot), one of Jesus' disciples,* agreed to collaborate for a sum of money. In turn he would "look for an opportunity to hand Jesus over to them without drawing a crowd" (Lk 22:6; cf. Mt 26:14-16; Mk 14:10-11).

Matthew and Mark tell the story of the anointing in Bethany (Mt 26:6-13; Mk 14:3-9) before the conspiracy visit by Judas with no hint of connection. John may well give the link: the indignation expressed among the disciples at the expensive waste of perfume (Mt 26:8; Mk 14:4) was voiced by Judas himself (Jn 12:4). The act of devotion by the woman contrasts to and leads to the act of treachery by the man. A sinister motive lies underneath the monetary concerns in the priests' contract and the anointing episode; Luke and John concur that Satan (*see* Demon, Devil, Satan) had entered the heart of Judas (Lk 22:3; Jn 13:2, 27).

3.2. Arrest in Gethsemane. The fateful Thursday evening begins with the intimacy of the Last Supper shattered by the talk of betrayal and the exit of Judas into the "night" (Jn 13:30). The scene is dominated by Jesus' knowledge that what will happen is God's plan: "The Son of man now goes as it has been decreed, but woe to that person by whom he is betrayed" (Lk 22:22; cf. Mt 26:24; Mk 14:21, "as it has been written about him"; *see* Son of Man). The predictive element heightens when Jesus leaves the table. The Synoptics focus on the scattering of the disciples and the approaching defection of Peter (Mt 26:31-35; Mk 14:27-31; Lk 22:24-38), while John relates the farewell discourses (14:1—17:26; *see* Farewell Discourse). As he frequently had done (Lk 22:39; Jn 18:1-2), Jesus walked with the disciples across the brook Kidron into a garden, a place on the Mount of Olives named Gethsemane* (Mt 26:36 par. Mk 14:32). The calm of the upper room here gives way to burdened prayer* as the cup of death looms before Jesus, an agony made all the greater by the sleeping disciples. The hour had come; the betrayer was at hand.

3.2.1. Judas's Betrayal. The actual arrest happened quickly. After Judas identified Jesus by a prearranged signal, a customary kiss of greeting (Mt 26:48-49; Mk 14:44-45; Lk 22:47-48), the armed crowd from the Temple Mount laid hands on him. Since the authorities knew Jesus by face ("I was daily with you," Mk 14:49 par.), the approach with a kiss was more than simple identification; it was calculated to allay suspicion and to point out Jesus in the surrounding darkness. Theories suggesting that Judas betrayed who Jesus was or something he said have little support in the texts; more likely, he divulged the whereabouts of Jesus at a time and place when a quiet seizure was possible (cf. Mk 14:11; Jn 11:57) and guided the arrest party to the spot (Lk 22:47; Acts 1:16, "guide"). John's language, "Judas having received [*labōn*] the cohort and the officers of the chief priests and the Pharisees" (18:3), does not imply that Judas took charge but rather that he procured and escorted the band.

3.2.2. Flight of the Disciples. A flurry of resistance was offered by a sword-wielding disciple who cut off the ear ("right ear," Lk 22:50; Jn 18:10) of the high priest's servant—according to John it was Simon Peter who attacked Malchus. Jesus intervened, commanding Peter to stop ("Put your sword back in its place," Mt 26:52 par. Jn 18:11), and healing the servant's ear (Lk 22:51). Matthew alone records the sayings on perishing by the sword and the twelve legions of angels standing ready to help (Mt 26:52-54). The ironical question "Have you come out to arrest me, as you would a robber, with swords and clubs?" (Synoptics), a reply of peaceful surrender, exhausted the courage of the disciples. They deserted Jesus and fled. All four Gospels understand these events in the light of prophecy, as fulfillment of the Scriptures (Mt 26:54, 56; Mk 14:49), the hour of darkness (Lk 22:53) and the word of Jesus (Jn 18:9). The unique tradition in Mark of a young man who fled naked (14:51-52) may be the Evangelist's own modest signature.

3.2.3. Company and Commander. The Synoptics describe the personnel who arrested Jesus as a crowd sent from the Sanhedrin (chief priests, elders and scribes; Mk 14:43; Mt 26:47; "a large crowd"), and Luke puts the chief priests and elders at the scene along with the Temple police (*stratēgoi*, constables or court officers, Lk 22:52). The impression of a solely Jewish initiative, however, diminishes in John who twice distinguishes "the company" (*speira*, 18:3, 12) of soldiers and its "commander" (*chiliarchos*, 18:12) from the Jewish detachment. These are the regular terms for the cohort and tribune of the Roman army (cf. Mt 27:27; Mk 15:16; Acts 10:1; 21:31; 27:1 NASB) and strongly suggest Roman participation in the arrest (*pace* Blinzler, Bammel, Catchpole). Objections to this view are not convincing: (1) the definite article with

speira denotes the garrison regularly stationed at the Antonia fortress during festivals (cf. Josephus *J.W.* 2.12.1 §224; *Ant.* 20.5.3 §106; Acts 21:31); (2) the phrase does not demand that the entire cohort of 600 soldiers came to the garden; (3) pursuit of a "robber" (*lēstēs,* bandit, freedom fighter, revolutionary) by a heavily armed force was a matter for Roman jurisdiction (cf. Mk 15:7, 27; Jn 18:40) and (4) remanding a prisoner in Roman custody to a Jewish court is paralleled in the case of Paul (Acts 22:30). The first action against Jesus, instigated by agents of the Jewish court, was in collaboration with the Roman authorities.

3.3. The Jewish Proceedings. The Gospels report that swiftly following the arrest, probably before midnight, the Jewish leaders began an interrogation and trial of Jesus, arguing the case throughout the night and returning a death verdict at daybreak. The sequence and relationship of these blocks of narrative material are the most complex in the passion story. Alleged discrepancies have prompted some scholars to be dubious of the entire account of the Jewish trial, even to the point of denying that a formal trial before the Sanhedrin ever happened (Lietzmann, Winter). A composite version of the proceedings must bring together four graphic scenes: (1) an initial examination by Annas in John, (2) Peter's denials of Jesus in all four Gospels, (3) a nighttime trial before Caiaphas in Matthew and Mark and (4) a Sanhedrin trial at dawn in Luke.

3.3.1. Preliminary Hearing before Annas. John writes that Jesus was led "first" (implying knowledge of a second hearing, 18:13) to Annas, where he was briefly questioned about "his disciples and his teaching" (18:19) and struck in the face by a displeased captor (18:20-23). The atmosphere is not that of a trial but of a roughshod interrogation by a notable examiner to get incriminating evidence. Based on a straightforward reading of verse 24, "Annas then sent him, still bound, to Caiaphas the high priest," the examiner must have been Annas, a former high priest (A.D. 6-15) and father-in-law to his successor, Joseph Caiaphas (A.D. 18-36). The preceding passage twice then calls Annas the "high priest" (18:19, 22) and locates the denial scene at his residence (18:15). The Synoptics, on the other hand, place Jesus and Peter in the house and courtyard of Caiaphas (Mt 26:57-58 par. Mk 14:53-54 and Lk 22:54-55). A few minuscules and versions (225 1195 syrs, h, p Cyril of Alexandria) solve the problem by rearrangement of verse 24 after verse 13 in John's account, thereby making Caiaphas the unnamed high priest in verses 15-23. A similar effect is gained by translating the aorist *apesteilen* (v. 24) with a pluperfect force, "Now Annas *had sent* him bound . . ." (KJV, NIV mg). Neither expedient, however, is necessary: (1) Annas, as other high priests, would have kept the dignity and title of the office for life (Josephus *Ant.* 18.2.2 §34; *m. Hor.* 3:4), (2) that Caiaphas should defer to the elderly father-in-law is fully in keeping with the influence and power of Annas (cf. Lk 3:2; Acts 4:6) and (3) as for location, a more feasible conjecture is that Annas and Caiaphas were in wings of the same residence somewhere in the upper city (cf. Josephus *J.W.* 2.17.6 §426).

3.3.2. Peter's Denials. While Jesus was inside the high priest's residence until about 3 A.M. (the time of cockcrow for Jerusalem in April), Peter was outside (Mt 26:69; Jn 18:16) in the courtyard below where Jesus was being held (Mk 14:66). The four Gospels show this coincidence emphatically but in differing ways: Mark and Matthew intercalate the night session led by Caiaphas before the denial scene (Mk 14:55-65 par. Mt 26:59-68); John breaks up the scene itself, placing the Annas interrogation after the first denial (Jn 18:19-24); Luke tells Peter's story without interruption (Lk 22:55-62) but places him within sight of Jesus' withering gaze when the cock crowed. "And the Lord, having turned, looked straight at Peter" (22:61). By intertwining the two scenes the Gospels stress not only simultaneity (the connectives may be rendered "meanwhile," cf. NEB) but the gravity of Peter's act. While Jesus faced his accusers and denied nothing he truly was, Peter cringed before his accusers and denied everything.

3.3.3. Nighttime Trial before Caiaphas. Was then Jesus formally tried during the night? This has been the crucial question in trial research. John, who mentions delivery to Caiaphas (18:24), and Luke, who describes only a mockery and beating at night (22:63-65), are silent on the issue. Luke does however report a morning session of the Sanhedrin, probably in the council chamber (*eis to synedrion*, Lk 22:66), where Jesus was questioned by the entire body (22:67-71). Matthew and Mark are quite definite that Caiaphas, in the company of "the chief priests and the whole council," held a nocturnal interrogation with all the earmarks of a formal trial (Mt 26:59-68 par. Mk 14:55-65).

First, the required evidence ("false testimony," Mt 26:59) was sought in order to prosecute Jesus on a capital charge. From among several false witnesses who failed to agree at all, two eventually contrived the charge that Jesus had threatened to destroy the Temple and rebuild it in three days (Mt 26:61; Mk 14:58; cf. Jn 2:19). Then the high priest himself, driven by Jesus' unwillingness to answer the charge, pressed

for an admission of guilt, "Are you the Christ, the Son of the Blessed?" (Mk 14:61 par. Mt 26:63, "Son of God"). In Mark the explicit reply "I am" (implicitly in Matthew and Luke), followed by the future Son of man saying (Mk 14:62; cf. Mt 26:64; Lk 22:69) linked Jesus' identity to three elevated titles, Messiah (*see* Christ), Son of God (*see* Son of God) and Son of man (*see* Son of Man). This claim constituted blasphemy in the eyes of the court, and "they all condemned him to be worthy of death" (Mk 14:64; Mt 26:66).

Although specific time notices are lacking, it is difficult to dislodge the timing of the trial in Matthew and Mark. They both report a summation of the proceedings in "early morning" (*prōi,* Mt 27:1; Mk 15:1), thus a time frame is fixed unless one treats the passage as an awkward insertion or a curious doublet. Again, the quaint detail of lighting a charcoal fire in the courtyard indicates a commotion that kept people awake during the night (Sherwin-White, Bruce) and puts Jesus before Caiaphas while Peter warmed himself (Mk 14:54, 66; Lk 22:55, 61; Jn 18:18, 24-25).

3.3.4. Morning Decision of the Sanhedrin. Luke's record of the morning session ("as day was dawning," 22:66) strikingly echoes most of the nighttime dialog found in Matthew and Mark, except the questions are put by the entire body (plural subject throughout) and no witnesses are called, although Luke 22:71, "Why do we still need testimony?" implies their presence. The morning assembly described by Mark and Matthew is not so much another trial as a culmination of the preceding events during the night. The descriptive phrases mean "to take counsel, reach a decision" (*symboulion + poiein,* Mk 15:1; *lambanein,* Mt 27:1; cf. 12:14; 22:15; 27:7; 28:12) and refer to the legal formulation of charges against Jesus, not to a second council meeting (Sherwin-White, 44).

Has one or the other of the Synoptics dislocated a single Jewish trial in the narrative sequence, or were there two sessions of the Sanhedrin, one at night and a second in the morning? Among those who defend the historicity of the Sanhedrin trial, the former option of a single trial is widely accepted, but its timing is debated: (1) a single morning session, according to Luke, the night setting being a Markan literary technique (Catchpole, Black, Robinson); or (2) a single nighttime session extending to dawn, following Mark and Matthew, with Luke telescoping the trial summary to the morning (Blinzler, Smalley, Sherwin-White). Luke's narrative does not fill the night with trial activity but does retain a nocturnal mocking and abuse by those guarding Jesus (Lk 22:63-65). A minor agreement here with Matthew, the tag line in blind man's bluff, "Who is the one who hit you?" (Lk 22:64

par. Mt 26:68; omitted in Mk 14:65), hints at Luke's knowledge of the nighttime trial. Since the morning assembly went to Pilate with expanded allegations (Lk 23:2), the entire Sanhedrin may well have rehearsed the previous night's dialog (22:66-71) in order to devise the sedition charge. Luke's arrangement shows that these political accusations were obtained by a legally convened Sanhedrin in a religious prosecution.

The probable order of events surrounding the Jewish trial can be tabulated as follows:

Gospels feature a Roman interrogation, condemnation and mockery of Jesus, but there are fundamental differences at each stage: (1) the questioning centers on the issue of kingship; (2) when Pilate proposes to release Jesus their king, the crowds shout for Barabbas instead, and under increasing pressure Pilate hands Jesus over to be crucified; and (3) Roman soldiers also mock and abuse Jesus, as did the Jewish constables, but in contempt of his kingship. Three independent stories accentuate the officials: Luke prefaces the Barabbas scene with an account of the

	Matthew	Mark	Luke	John
1. Jesus led to the high priest's house	26:57	14:53	22:54	18:13-14
2. Peter follows into the courtyard	26:58	14:54	22:55	18:15
3. Peter's denials begin	26:69-71a	14:66-68	22:56-57	18:16-18
4. Jesus interrogated by Annas				18:19-23
5. Jesus tried before Caiaphas at night	26:59-66	14:55-64	[22:67-71]	18:24
6. Peter's final denial at cockcrow	26:71b-75	14:69-72	22:58-62	18:25-27
7. Jesus abused and mocked by captors	26:67-68	14:65	22:63-65	
8. Jesus before the Sanhedrin at dawn	27:1	15:1a	22:66-71	18:28b
9. Jesus led to Pilate	27:2	15:1b	23:1	18:28a

The Gospels present events 3 and 6 as occurring simultaneously with 4 and 5; in Matthew and Mark the trial and mockery scenes (5 and 7 conflated) are the erratic blocks of material in the narrative order, whereas Luke (placing 7 at night) and John have the sequence intact.

3.4. The Roman Proceedings. The narratives of the trial before Pilate depict a separate prosecution aimed to secure a death sentence under terms of Roman law. The Sanhedrin, knowing well that blasphemy was not a capital offense in the eyes of Rome, urged the governor that Jesus had committed treason against the state. Like the structure of the Jewish trial, the four

examination by Herod Antipas (Lk 23:8-12), while in Matthew's interludes we see Pilate warned by a troubled wife and washing his hands (Mt 27:19, 24-25).

The trial in John's account is extended with great dramatic effect. Whereas Jesus remains silent in the Synoptics (Mt 27:14; Mk 15:5; Lk 23:9), most of John is a private dialog between Jesus and Pilate on kingship. The scene shifts in seven episodes between frontstage, the outside court where "the Jews" waited, and backstage, the inner Praetorium where Jesus was held. Pilate's shuffling back and forth (cf. Jn 18:29, 33, 38b; 19:1, 4, 9, 13) gives the impression of a vacillating judge who finally condemns an innocent "King of the

Jews." A tragic irony emerges in John as well as the Synoptics: the "pretender" who went to the cross actually was the king, the crucified Messiah (cf. Jn 19:15; Mk 15:12-13; 1 Cor 2:8).

3.4.1. Accusation before Pilate. The reason why the Jews came to the Roman authority is made clear by John: "It is not lawful for us to put anyone to death" (Jn 18:31). The Synoptics also assume that only Pilate was able to authorize the execution demanded by the Sanhedrin; moreover, he did not simply ratify the Jewish decision but made a new investigation of the case, asking for the charges against Jesus, "What accusation are you bringing against this man?" (Jn 18:29; cf. Mt 27:12; Mk 15:3; Lk 23:2). Luke gives the precise wording in a threefold form: leading astray the nation, forbidding payment of taxes* to Caesar and claiming to be the Messiah, a king (Lk 23:2; cf. 23:5, stirring up the people; 23:14, inciting the people to rebel). The obvious political overtones of this accusation explain Pilate's first and uppermost question, "Are you the King of the Jews?" (Mt 27:11; Mk 15:2; Lk 23:3; Jn 18:33). The force of Jesus' reply "The words are yours" eases some of the procurator's anxiety about sedition and revolution.

3.4.2. Transfer to Herod Antipas. The crowd protested Pilate's first attempt to dismiss the charge with the complaint that Jesus began his seditious activity in Galilee, the tetrarchy of Herod Antipas (*see* Herodian Dynasty). Having learned that Jesus was a Galilean under Herod's jurisdiction, Pilate made a hasty arrangement ("Herod and Pilate became friends with one another that very day," Lk 23:12) to put Jesus before his old adversary (Lk 23:6-12; cf. 9:7-9; 13:31-32). The examination, carried on with a circus-like barrage of questions from Herod and "full-pitched accusations" (Lk 23:10) from the chief priests and scribes, stalled when Jesus would not answer; the sham ended in a staged ridicule of Jesus' kingship, by sending him back to Pilate dressed in a regal, shining robe (Lk 23:11). What Pilate had hoped to gain is not clear, but he interpreted Jesus' return as an acquittal (Lk 23:15).

The whole affair, plausible enough in itself, fully accords with what we know of the situation at the time: (1) the tetrarch's father, Herod the Great, had exercised unusual privileges of extradition (Josephus *J.W.* 1.24.2 §474), and Antipas himself had the ear of the emperor Tiberius (*Ant.* 18.2.3 §36; 18.4.5 §104); (2) procurators often used a *consilium,* a body of legal advisors or friends, to reach a verdict (Acts 25:12, 26; Justinian *Digest* 4.8.3; *SIG* 3 780.25; cf. Bickerman, 110); (3) advice or judgment sought in Jerusalem from a Herodian official would have been advantageous for

Pilate whose relations with Antipas and Galilee needed repair (Lk 23:12b, "previously they had been enemies"; cf. 13:1) and (4) although not required to do so, Pilate likely wanted a transfer to Herod's jurisdiction (available in the legal custom of home venue, or *forum domicilii*) to rid himself of a troublesome case (Sherwin-White, 28-31).

3.4.3. Release of Barabbas. The second stage of Pilate's trial in all four Gospels is an attempt to free Jesus by means of a Passover amnesty, the so-called *privilegium paschale* (Passover privilege), which failed and led to the release of Barabbas instead (Mt 27:15-26; Mk 15:6-15; Lk 23:13-25; Jn 18:39-40). Matthew and Mark introduce Barabbas at the beginning of the incident, building up the intervention of the crowd on his behalf. With the Jewish leaders stirring the people (Mt 27:20; Mk 15:11) to ask for Barabbas, Pilate's appeal for Jesus, "Do you wish that I release to you the King of the Jews?" (Mk 15:9) was futile. Luke and John stress Pilate's resolve to set Jesus free (Lk 23:20; Jn 19:12) because he had found "no basis for a charge against him" (Jn 18:38; cf. 19:4, 6; Lk 23:14, 22). The governor intended, after Jesus was punished by flogging (Lk 23:16, 22; Jn 19:1), to invoke the amnesty custom for his release; however, the crowd wanted Jesus crucified. The crescendo of shouts, "Crucify him! Crucify him!" depicted by all four Evangelists in two distinct phases (Mt 27:22-23; Mk 15:13-14; Lk 23:21-23; Jn 19:6, 15), was decisive for Pilate.

The Gospels contain all we know about Barabbas, a revolutionary (*lēstēs,* Jn 18:40; "robber" KJV, RSV) who had committed murder in a Jerusalem insurrection (Lk 23:19, 25; Mk 15:7) and likely had followers in the Praetorium crowd (*see* Revolutionary Movements). His name, the Greek form of an Aramaic surname *Bar-'Abbā',* means "son of Abba" (or literally, "son of the father"); it occurs in Aramaic texts from the fifth century B.C. down to rabbis of the Amoraic period (e.g., *ḥiyya bar 'Abbā', Lev. Rab.* 3.1). The form *'Abbāh* is attested as a personal name on a funerary inscription near Jerusalem dated about the time of Jesus (*MPAT* §68); if the man had a son, he would have been called *Barabbas* in Greek. The variant *Barrabbas* (with two r's meaning "son of the teacher") read by Origen and Jerome is improbable. A better case has been made for the Caesarean text of Matthew 27:16-17 (Θ 700* *f*¹syr^{s, pal} geo² Origen^{pt}) which supplies a first name, "Jesus Barabbas" (cf. NEB). Some commentators who adopt this reading suggest that Pilate mistook shouts for Jesus Barabbas as a plea for Jesus of Nazareth and eventually had to ask which one the crowd preferred (Mt 27:21). The variant, however, is weakly supported and probably arose from conjecture about the two names, still an irrepressible desire in some modern critics (e.g., Winter, 142-43).

The Barabbas incident and the paschal amnesty in particular are often dismissed as nonhistorical, "nothing but a figment of the imagination" (Winter, 134). The objections to the episode, based on the lack of evidence for such a custom in antiquity, do not carry sufficient weight. In the provincial cities, acclamation of the people (*acclamatio populi*) played a significant role in Roman legal administration (Strobel, 126-27); there are numerous examples of Roman magistrates who heeded a crowd's wishes at the tribunal (e.g., Tacitus *Ann.* 1.44.4; Justinian *Digest* 49.1.12; 48.8.16; see Bickerman, 103, 133-34). This custom is well illustrated by an incident in Egypt (A.D. 85) where the Roman governor released the accused, saying, "You deserve to be scourged [*mastigōthēnai*] . . . , but I will deal more humanely with you and will release you to the crowds" [*ochlois*] (Papyrus Florentinus 61.59-65; cf. Blinzler, 207]). The political situation for Pilate was acutely unstable because of a series of clashes with the Jews (cf. Philo *Leg. Gai.* 38 §301-302), so he would have been inclined to placate them on this occasion. He did not want a bad report in Rome, and the Jews traded on his insecurity as a "friend of Caesar" (Jn 19:12), a title weighted with political intrigue during the last stages of Tiberius' reign (cf. Tacitus *Ann.* 6.8; Philo *Flacc.* 6 §40; *NewDocs* 1978, 75). No clear evidence has yet come to light for a regular amnesty at a feast, but a provision stated in the Mishnah may be relevant: "They may slaughter the Passover . . . for one whom they have promised to bring out of prison" (*m. Pesaḥ.* 8:6). This much-discussed text may refer to an evening release from a Jewish prison (Jeremias, 73), but it must have occurred with regularity to become a topic of rabbinic legislation, and a Roman detention cannot be ruled out (Blinzler, 218-21; Robinson, 261). These analogies favor the historical plausibility of the Gospel account much more than the explanations which try to derive the story in purely theological terms.

3.4.4. Scourging, Mockery and Death Sentence. The Barabbas scene closes in the Synoptics with Jesus sentenced to death by crucifixion (Mt 27:26; Mk 15:15; Lk 23:24-25). Matthew and Mark add the temporal participle, "having scourged [Jesus]," so that this punishment precedes the final sentence; then both relate the mockery by Roman soldiers in the Praetorium, where Jesus wore a crown of thorns and purple robe (Mt 27:27-31; Mk 15:16-20). Once again John sketches in the details which the Synoptics have summarized. Following the scourging and mockery in the Fourth Gospel, Jesus is brought before the Jews by a frustrated Pilate, who attempts to shift responsibility from himself ("You take him yourselves and crucify him," Jn 19:6). Amidst the insistent cries of "Crucify! Crucify!" a clear theological gravamen against Jesus finally emerges: "We have a law, and by that law he ought to die, because he made himself the Son of God" (Jn 19:7). Pilate retires in fear and in another exchange warns Jesus that he has power even at this stage in the proceedings to free him or to crucify him, but the governor's good intentions quickly turn to appeasement once the Jews question his loyalty to the Emperor ("after he heard these words," Jn 19:13). Then, at a place called the *Lithostrōton* ("stone pavement"), the formal sentence of death is spoken from the judgment seat (*bēma*) where Pilate sits (the intransitive sense of *ekathisen* in v. 13, "Pilate sat down," is preferred over the idea that Pilate "set Jesus down" as a jest). Roman law required the magistrate to pronounce a capital sentence from the judgment seat (Mommsen, 447). John, in agreement with the other Evangelists, marks this point in the trial narrative with a judicial use of *paredōken;* Pilate "handed over" Jesus to the condemnation of the cross (Jn 19:16 par. Mt 27:26; Mk 15:15 and Lk 23:25).

John's order of events—scourging, mockery, sentence—leaves little reason to question its correctness. The placement of the mockery after the sentence in Matthew and Mark has a dual function. It summarizes Pilate's decision and emphasizes the role of the Roman soldiers who carried out the order: "Then the soldiers of the governor took Jesus into the Praetorium . . . and they led him away to crucify him" (Mt 27:27, 31 par. Mk 15:16, 20; note the ambiguous "they" in Lk 23:25-26 and Jn 19:16, where the NIV supplies "soldiers"). That Pilate attempted to end the trial by having Jesus flogged conforms to Roman practice. Scourging could be inflicted as the first stage of capital punishment (Josephus *J.W.* 2.14.9 §306; 7.6.4 §200; Livy *Hist.* 1.26; 33.36) or, as it is in the Gospels (Lk 23:16, 22; Jn 19:10), an independent penalty followed by release or imprisonment (cf. Acts 16:23; 22:24; Josephus *J.W.* 2.13.7 § 269; Philo *Flacc.* 10 §75; Justinian *Digest* 48.2.6). A notable parallel is the case of Jesus bar Ananias, a strange prophet of doom who spoke against Jerusalem and the Temple; after a trial and flogging by the Jewish authorities, he was charged before the procurator Albinus (A.D. 62), who released him as a madman, only when he had him "flayed to the bone with scourges" (*J.W.* 6.5.3 §304). The details of the Gospel narratives are, on the whole, in remarkable accord and are fully intelligible in light of the legal situation in Roman Palestine.

4. Legal Issues.

The modern history of trial research, both the Jewish and Christian contributions, entails a legal debate which has largely run its course (Catchpole, 221-60). Interest has shifted to literary (*see* Literary Criticism) and redactional (*see* Redaction Criticism) questions, sometimes with negative results (e.g., continued dissection of the Gospel narratives will yield no reliable details because of the "conflicting evidence and the unpersuasive accounts," Sanders, 300). The major work of this kind by P. Winter categorizes the trial pericopes in three redactional levels (190-93): primary tradition, secondary tradition and editorial accretion. The upshot of Winter's analysis, indeed his thesis, eliminates the bulk of the Jewish trial, allowing only a brief, morning deliberation of the Sanhedrin as primary tradition, and posits a Roman trial and sentence on political grounds. While elaborated as redactional insights, these literary judgments revert to the historical premises shared by Winter with earlier studies of J. Juster and H. Lietzmann. Their assumptions of pro-Roman bias in the Gospels advance the argument only slightly and, in net effect, still turn on legal issues which can be summarized as follows:

1. Since the Sanhedrin retained the power of capital punishment, Jesus would have been executed by stoning if the Jewish court had in fact found him guilty of blasphemy and pronounced sentence.

2. A nocturnal session of the Sanhedrin, convened in the high priest's residence on a feast day, violates Jewish legal procedure and was contrived by Mark to shift blame away from the Roman government.

3. The crucifixion of Jesus, a penalty never used by the Jews, indicates a political crime, that a Roman court found him guilty of sedition and excludes the possibility that religious charges were also preferred.

Each of these assertions has faced spirited challenge from both the literary and historical points of view (see Strobel, 21-61; cf. Sherwin-White, Kilpatrick, Blinzler, Catchpole, Betz). The crucial points of discussion pertain to the judicial competence of the Sanhedrin, the relevance of the Mishnaic law code and the procedures of the Roman provincial court.

4.1. Judicial Powers of the Sanhedrin. Did the Sanhedrin in the time of Jesus retain the right to sentence and execute criminals? Much hangs on this question which admits no easy solution. The standard view, that the "Roman government retained for itself the right of life and death" (Mommsen, 240), implies a curtailment of the Sanhedrin's powers as John 18:31 precisely states: The Jews might pass a death sentence but the power to execute lay in the hands of the Roman procurator alone (Lohse, 865). Few had disputed

this assessment of matters, notably the Jewish scholar J. Salvador (1838) and the Christian J. J. I. von Döllinger (1860), until the influential work of Juster (1914), who carefully assembled the pertinent evidence demonstrating that the Sanhedrin could and did execute capital offenders (2:127-45). Prominent endorsement of Juster's interpretation (Lietzmann, 258-60; Winter, 12-26; 110-30; Burkill, 80-96) initiated a critical debate which has yet to subside ("neither theory can be effectively proved," Schürer, 2:222). However, in the items of evidence cited below, the balance of interpretation leans toward Mommsen and the traditional view.

4.1.1. Roman Sanctions. While still competent to try religious cases, the prerogatives of the Sanhedrin changed with the beginning of direct Roman rule in Judea: (1) Coponius, the first governor (A.D. 6), was sent out by Augustus with full powers "extending to capital punishment" (Josephus *J.W.* 2.8.1 §117; cf. *Ant.* 18.1.1 §2); (2) Tannaitic tradition confirms that "the right to try capital cases was taken from Israel forty years before the destruction of the Temple" (*y. Sanh.* 1.1; 7.2; cf. *b. Sanh.* 41a; *b. 'Abod. Zar.* 8b); (3) the Jewish death penalty was reinstated a week after the Romans lifted the siege of Jerusalem in September A.D. 66: "On the twenty-second of the month [Elul] the execution of malefactors began again" (*Meg. Ta'an.* 6).

4.1.2. Religious Concessions. Among concessions granted the Jews, violations of religious law were investigated and punished by the Sanhedrin (cf. Acts 4:5-23; 5:21-40; 26:10-11), but it cannot be shown that stipulations involving the death penalty were independent of Roman authority: (1) the warning inscription on Herod's Temple (*CII* §1400; Josephus *J.W.* 5.5.2 §194; *Ant.* 15.11.5 §417; Philo *Leg. Gai.* 31 §212; *m. Kelim* 1.8), indicating that a Gentile, even a Roman citizen, caught trespassing in the inner Temple court would be put to death, had Roman approval (Josephus *J.W.* 6.2.4 §126); (2) the same can be said of the death penalty prescribed for unlawful entry of a Jew, even the high priest, into the Holy of Holies (Philo *Leg. Gai.* 39 §307); (3) the Jewish authorities surely brought Jesus bar Ananias before Albinus (Josephus *J.W.* 6.5.3 §§300-305) to get an execution, since they had already scourged him; (4) reiterated attempts by the Sanhedrin to extradite Paul point to an illegal murder plot, not to legal competence (Acts 23:15, 20-21; 24:6-8; 25:3, 7-11), and even if capital charges were pressed in Jerusalem, it would have been before the Roman procurator Festus (Acts 25:9, 20).

4.1.3. Jewish Executions. During the period A.D. 6-66 executions carried out on orders of the Sanhedrin, prima facie testimony for the court's competence, turn out to be disruptions of normal legal process: (1) burning of a priest's daughter convicted of adultery (*m. Sanh.* 7:2) happened during the reign of Agrippa I (A.D. 41-44), as did the execution of James, brother of John (Acts 12:2), when Judea had independent status; (2) during the interval between Festus and his successor, Albinus (A.D. 62), the high priest Ananus convened the Sanhedrin and had James, the Lord's brother, stoned to death (*Ant.* 20.9.1 §200-3), an illegal undertaking for which Ananus was deposed from office; (3) the episode of the woman taken in adultery (Jn 7:53—8:11), a scene of mob violence, hardly qualifies as due process and proper sentence; (4) the stoning of Stephen, admittedly the strongest piece of evidence for the Juster-Lietzmann thesis, follows a Jewish trial (Acts 6:11-14) and exhibits required procedures (7:57-58); however, the trial was interrupted and ended without proper sentence—an act of lynch law—suggested by the death lament for Stephen (8:2), a custom forbidden in the case of legally executed offenders (*m. Sanh.* 6:6; Josephus *Ant.* 4.8.6 §202).

The theory of two (or three) Sanhedrins, a political one named in Greek sources and a religious one, the esteemed Great Sanhedrin (*Beth Din*) in rabbinic writings, offers a tidy solution to the legal problem: the political institution of the Gospels (*synedrion*), a court of priests responsible for Jesus' condemnation, is distinct from the Great Sanhedrin whose interests lay only in religious matters. The sources, however, seem to be unaware of multiple institutions, and the theory creates more difficulties than it resolves (Schürer, 2:207-8; Lohse, 863). It is more probable that a single institution, the Sanhedrin, was allowed a limited criminal jurisdiction, both to police the Temple area and to maintain Jewish Law,* whereby death sentences could be pronounced, but execution was kept strictly in Roman hands (cf. Blinzler, 165; Sherwin-White, 41-42; Catchpole, 254). The legal situation then offers little reason to doubt a Sanhedrin prosecution of Jesus which eventually led to a Roman court.

4.2. Violations of Mishnaic Law.

Hints of illegality in the Gospel narratives (Mt 26:59; Mk 14:59) have been fully exploited in modern inquiries where no less than twenty-seven breaches of the Jewish legal code have been alleged. How many of the procedural rules in the Mishnah tractate *Sanhedrin* (see Schürer, 2:225-26) applied before A.D. 70 is difficult to say; some at least are purported to be independently attested in the time of Jesus. Recent discussion has accordingly limited itself to five violations of the Mishnaic code in the trial of Jesus: (1) it was improperly convened in the high priest's house (*m. Sanh.* 11:2); (2) met during the night (*m. Sanh.* 4:1); (3) on a Sabbath* eve or feast day (*m. Sanh.* 4:1); and (4) reached a guilty verdict on the same day (*m. Sanh.* 4:1; 5:5) (5) based on inadequate grounds for blasphemy (*m. Sanh.* 7:5). Whether one argues that a Sadducean code was current in the days of Jesus (Blinzler) or that some aspects of the later Mishnaic law were operative (Lohse), it is unwarranted to assume that an illegal trial could not have happened; justice does not always outweigh expedience (cf. Jn 11:50).

4.2.1. Time and Place of the Sessions. Our sources disagree about the precise location of the Sanhedrin's regular assembly, but it is clearly distinct from the courtyard and palace of the high priest (Mt 26:3). The Mishnah locates it, the Hall of Hewn Stone, inside the inner forecourt of the Temple (*m. Sanh.* 11:2; *m. Mid.* 5.4; cf. *b. Yoma* 25a), whereas according to Josephus, the *boulē* ("council chamber") stood outside the upper city on the western slope of the Temple Mount (Josephus *J.W.* 2.16.3 §344; 5.4.2 §144; 6.6.3 §354). Certainly by the time of Paul's trial, the Sanhedrin met outside the Temple because Roman soldiers, who were forbidden to enter the inner court, appear in the council chamber (Acts 22:30; 23:10). The rabbinic tradition is that the chamber was moved "forty years before the destruction of the Temple" (*b. Sanh.* 41a; *b. 'Abod. Zar.* 8b). If the Sanhedrin still met within the Temple area during the time of Jesus, access may have been delayed by the fact that the gates of the Temple, only on the night of Passover, were opened at midnight (Josephus *Ant.* 18.2.2 §29; cf. *m. Mid.* 1:1, normally locked all night). This would have dictated the initial choice of the high priest's residence and explain the impression of movement and double session in the trial accounts (Jn 18:13, 24; Mk 15:1; Mt 27:1). In any event Luke 22:66 reports the morning session in the council chamber as a new location (cf. 22:54) and corresponds to the framework of the other narratives (*pace* Winter, 27-30).

The rule that no trials could be held on a Sabbath (Josephus *Ant.* 16.6.2 §163; Philo *Migr. Abr.* 16 §91; CD 10.18) probably also applied to festival days in Jesus' time (*m. Beṣa* 4.4; 5.2); further stipulations that "in capital cases they hold the trial during the daytime . . . but a verdict of conviction not until the following day" (*m. Sanh.* 4:1) meant also that no trial could begin on the eve of a Sabbath or of a festival day. These latter regulations, however, may date from the Tannaitic period when the Pharisees were keen to prevent miscarriages of justice (Blinzler, Catchpole). Their date notwithstanding, an exception is made for the convicted *mēsît*, a seducer to idolatry or false prophet (Deut 13:1-11). In such a case the verdict was passed on the day of the trial (*t. Sanh.* 10.11), and based on Deuteronomy 17:13, the execution took place in Jerusalem on a feast day: " . . . bring them to the Sanhedrin in Jerusalem and keep them in custody until the feast and carry out the sentence on the feast" (*t. Sanh.* 11.7; cf. *m. Sanh.* 11:4). This procedure may explain the haste with which the Sanhedrin acted to have Jesus crucified on 15 Nisan (a Synoptic chronology; cf. Jeremias, 78-79); be this as it may, a strong caution should at least be entered against the notion of wholesale illegality.

4.2.2. Charge of Blasphemy. However obscure the particulars may be, the Sanhedrin eventually convicted Jesus of a specific crime: blasphemy (Mk 14:64 par. Mt 26:65). The blasphemer, "one who curses God" (Lev 24:15), was liable to death by stoning under OT Law, but again to provide a legal safeguard the rabbis formulated a rather narrow definition: "The blasphemer is only guilty if he pronounces the name of God distinctly" (*m. Sanh.* 7:5). Nothing uttered by Jesus in the trial records fits this strict requirement, but the term on the lips of Caiaphas had wider significance in the NT period (cf. Philo *Vit. Mos.* 2.37-38 §§204-6; Josephus *Ant.* 4.8.6 §202). Blasphemy referred to acts or words which violate God's power and majesty, a claiming of prerogatives which belong to God alone (Kilpatrick, 10-11; Juel, 103-7). The Evangelists clearly use the word with this meaning (Mk 2:7; Jn 10:33-36), and parallels occur in pagan Greek and the rabbis (*t. Sanh.* 1.2; *b. Sanh.* 38b; cf. Bickerman, 86-88). Since the blasphemy charge was broad enough to encompass several wrongs, what offense lay behind the conviction of Jesus? No single proposal put forward has won a consensus (see Catchpole, 126-48), but it seems that discrete items are linked together. We suggest that the blasphemy charge had three components: christological claims, threats against the Temple, and false prophecy, any one of which could carry a death warrant.

First, the utterances of Jesus in the trial itself were decisive: (1) an open avowal of messiahship ("I am," Mk 14:62), a claim without precedent in Judaism until Simon bar Kochba (A.D. 132-35) provoked immediate outrage; (2) Jewish messianism had embraced the concept of sonship (4QFlor 1.10-11; *Pss. Sol.* 17:27, 36; 18:6, 8; *see* Son of God), but when unified in the person of Jesus with the glorious Son of man, enthroned at God's right hand (cf. Dan 7:13; Ps 110:1; *Midr. Pss.* 1.40 §9 [Ps. 2:7]), the titles Messiah and Son of God gave him an exalted status the Sanhedrin found intolerable. In John 19:7 the overriding com-

plaint even to Pilate was that Jesus claimed divine sonship.

Second, blasphemous overtones were heard in the accusation that Jesus threatened to destroy and rebuild the Temple: (1) Stephen was charged with blasphemy for "speaking against this holy place," having also reportedly said that "this Jesus of Nazareth will destroy this place" (Acts 6:11, 13-14), so that a threat to the Temple was tantamount to blasphemy; (2) Jesus' Temple prophecy (Mk 13:2, 14; Lk 19:43-44) was probably misconstrued (Mk 14:57-59; 15:29) along the same lines of confusion reported in John 2:19-21; (3) talk of restoring the Temple also invited the messianic question (see Sanders, 77-90; Green, 276-81; Juel, 198) since in Jewish eschatology the Messiah builds a new Temple (4QFlor 1.1-7; *1 Enoch* 90:28-29; 4 Ezra 9:38-10:28; *Tg. Neb.* Is 53:5; *Tg. Neb.* Zech 6:12-13).

Finally, some elements of the Gospel narratives may be traced to a false-prophet tradition: (1) two marks of a false prophet—he leads others astray (Deut 13:2-6), and he presumes to speak in the Lord's name a message which does not come true (Deut 18:22)—fit the two queries by Annas about Jesus' disciples and teaching (Jn 18:19); (2) the mockery of Jesus after the trial, "Prophesy!" (Mk 14:65), is the horseplay of guards who no longer fear his words (cf. Deut 18:22); (3) the subversion charge put before Pilate, leading the people astray (Lk 23:2, 5, 14), is stated in terms of Roman politics, but on the religious side it echoes Jewish claims that Jesus was a deceiver (Mt 27:63; Jn 7:12, 47) betraying his people with misleading words (cf. Deut 13:5-8, 13; *m. Sanh.* 7:4; 11:1).

4.3. Roman Trial and Penal Law. A further point of dispute stresses the nature of the penalty stemming from the charge in the Roman trial. Death by crucifixion, it is objected, was exclusively a Roman mode of execution reserved for political offenders. Therefore, the sentence carried out against Jesus was not based on religious charges from the Jews. We are asked to conclude that the Gospel portrayal of a religious accusation before Pilate was impossible, indeed that the account of a previous Jewish trial was "contrived to conceal that Jesus had been condemned and executed on a charge of sedition" (Winter, 34; cf. 79, 90; Lietzmann, 258-60; Lohse, 869). The evidence of Roman trial procedures in the first century shows this to be an unwarranted deduction, and the basic premise of the argument regarding crucifixion in the province of Judea has been brought into question.

4.3.1. Trials in the Provinces. We have no formal descriptions of capital trials in the Roman provinces between Cicero's *Verrines* (70 B.C.) and the *Letters* of

Pliny (c. A.D. 110). The standard exposition depends on scattered excerpts from classical jurists of the second and third centuries of the empire compiled in the *Digest* of Roman law (Mommsen, 234-45). Under Augustus, in order to expedite the legal process, capital trials were usually conducted by provincial governors who could grade the penalty (cf. Justinian *Digest* 48.19.16). This procedure, named *cognitio extra ordinem* or *extraordinaria,* by and large replaced the jury court (Sherwin-White, 13-23) which had operated within the procedures and penalties stipulated by the fixed order of law (*ordo*). By contrast, the governor himself heard the formal accusation so that he could investigate the case by personal inquiry (*cognitio*), and he was free to choose any procedure he thought fit— determine the issue, hear the evidence and prescribe the penalty—without legal restriction (*extra ordinem*). The earliest evidence for trial by *cognitio* is the fourth edict of Augustus to the province of Cyrene (7/6 B.C.) which requires that in capital cases ". . . the one who governs the province has the duty of conducting the investigation and rendering judgments himself . . ." (*SEG* 9.8; *FIRA* 1.68 [ET: *TDGR* 6:27]).

The governor Pliny provides a good example: after the famous orator Dio Chrysostom placed a statue of the Emperor Trajan near his family burial plot, he was accused by an enemy of a treasonable act. The accuser, one Flavius Archippus, petitioned Pliny for a *cognitio* before the judgment seat (*Epp.* 10.81.3); Trajan dismissed the case when Pliny, faced with a *cognitio* of such magnitude, wrote to ask for direction in the matter (10.82). Such trials follow a regular pattern, clearly attested in the case of Paul as well as Jesus: (1) the charges were drawn up and a formal accusation was brought by *delatores,* "accusers" (Mk 15:1; Lk 23:2; Jn 18:29); (2) the governor heard the case *pro tribunali,* "before the judgment seat" (Mt 27:19; Jn 19:13); (3) in the absence of a defense (Mt 27:14; Mk 15:5; Jn 19:10) a *condemno,* or "guilty," verdict was certain, and some form of punishment had to be prescribed (Lk 23:15-16, 22; Jn 19:6).

4.3.2. Charge of Sedition. The first question Pilate asked Jesus in the Roman trial, "Are you the King of the Jews?" indicates a shift of charge from the religious to the political. The issue of kingship in Pilate's court would raise the alarm of sedition (Jn 19:12; cf. Josephus *Ant.*17.10.8 §285, on bandit "kings"), an act deserving crucifixion (Justinian *Digest* 48.8.3.4; 48.19.38.2). Sedition, or inciting people to rebel, came under the treason crimes headed "offense against majesty" (*laesa maiestatis),* which were applied to all sorts of "misconduct." During the principate, especially under Tiberius, trials for lese-majesty were exploit-

ed as a convenient means to dispose of enemies, and many far-fetched examples are found (Suetonius *Tiberius* 61.3; Tacitus *Ann.* 1.72-74; 3.49, 70; Cassius Dio *Hist.* 59.3.6; Pliny *Epp.* 10.82; *Digest* 48.4.5). The nature of the alleged crime and its penalty would have been obvious to Pilate, even while he harbored doubts about the guilt of Jesus. The placard which he inscribed and refused to change, "The King of the Jews" (Jn 19:19-22), shows both the fixed reason for the condemnation (a *titulus* normally hung on the victim or was carried before him; cf. Suetonius *Caligula* 32.2; *Domitian* 10.1; Cassius Dio *Hist.* 54.3.7; Eusebius *Hist. Eccl.* 5.1.44; Josephus *Ant.* 14.3.1 §36), and a mocking affirmation of Jesus' claims to the chief priests.

Suggestions that Jesus was involved with a Zealot plot to overthrow the Romans are groundless (see Bammel-Moule). The Sanhedrin would also have known that a sedition charge was "a surer way of securing the death of Christ" (Smalley, 1054), and the morning session was likely occupied with recasting the indictment in acceptable terms for Pilate. The Lukan account of multiple charges, common in trials of the Flavian period (cf. Sherwin-White, 35), amounts to a political version of the blasphemy findings. The connection avowed is that Jesus held the kingly pretensions of the Jewish messiah, "saying that he himself is Christ a king" (Lk 23:2). This phrase is the crucial link between the religious and political charges and explains much of Pilate's dilemma. Even the ambiguous "Son of God" phrase to a Roman ear, when voiced by a crowd demanding that its law be respected (Jn 19:7), has fearful political implications for a governor already embroiled in the violation of Jewish customs. There is every reason to believe that the sedition alternative carried the day only because of the religious fervor behind it.

4.3.3. Penalty of Crucifixion. It is a commonplace in trial research, even to opposing sides of the debate (cf. Blinzler, 247; Winter, 96), that the Jews never practiced crucifixion as a mode of execution. The episode when Alexander Jannaeus "hung up alive" 800 Pharisees, abhorred as that "never done in Israel before" (4QpNah 1.7-8; cf. Josephus *J.W.* 1.4.6 §97) is taken as the exception which proves the point. This consensus ought now to be revised in light of the Qumran Temple Scroll which interprets Deuteronomy 21:22-23 as crucifixion: "You shall hang him on the wood so that he dies" (11QT 64.8, 10-11). The OT ruled that after a capital offender had been executed by stoning, the cursed body was to be publicly exhibited by hanging on a tree (cf. *m. Sanh.* 6:4; 7:4; 9:3), but in the Scroll text hanging is clearly the cause of death. Those liable to this penalty are described in six phrases: (1) one who informs against his people, (2) betrays his people to a foreign nation, (3) does evil to his people, (4) one who commits a capital offense, (5) flees away to the Gentiles and (6) curses his people Israel (11QT 64.7, 9b-10a). Such accusations are reminiscent of those made against Jesus (Bammel 1984, 442), and although the regulation is sectarian in character, we must reckon with the wider possibility that other Jews in the first century had equated the practice of crucifixion with the law of Deuteronomy 21:23, viz., to bury the body before sunset (cf. Josephus *J.W.* 4.5.2 §317; *t. Sanh.* 9.7; Acts 5:30; 10:39). The Mishnaic criminal code excludes crucifixion (four methods in *m. Sanh.* 7:1: stoning, burning, beheading and strangling), but a thesis based on the assertion that no Jews in Jesus' time would have sought his death on the cross strains the evidence (see Betz, 603-12).

5. Theological Significance.

A lamentable feature of Christian reaction to the trial of Jesus across the centuries has been an odious persecution of the Jews for putting Jesus to death. It has been maintained above that the Evangelists did not invent the fact of Jewish involvement, but the NT never says that the Jews alone, least of all every succeeding generation, were responsible for the cross. The perennial instinct to kindle anti-Semitism* by the findings of historical scholarship is deplorable in all its forms. The theological stance of the Gospels indicts us all, Jew and Gentile alike: "He was numbered with the transgressors" (Lk 22:37), yet "this man has done nothing wrong" (Lk 23:41).

See also DEATH OF JESUS; GETHSEMANE; PASSION NARRATIVE.

BIBLIOGRAPHY. E. Bammel, ed., *The Trial of Jesus* (SBT, 2d ser., 13; 2d ed.; London: SCM, 1971); E. Bammel and C. F. D. Moule, eds., *Jesus and the Politics of His Day* (Cambridge: University Press, 1984); O. Betz, "Probleme des Prozesses Jesu," *ANRW* II.25.1 (New York: De Gruyter, 1982) 565-647; E. J. Bickerman, "Utilitas crucis," in *Studies in Jewish and Christian History* (AGJU 9; Leiden: E. J. Brill, 1986) pt. 3.82-138; M. Black, "The Arrest and Trial of Jesus and the Date of the Last Supper," in *New Testament Essays* (Manchester: University Press, 1959) 19-33; J. Blinzler, *The Trial of Jesus* (3d ed.; Cork: Mercier, 1961); F. F. Bruce, "The Trial of Jesus in the Fourth Gospel," in *Gospel Perspectives 1: Studies of History and Tradition in the Four Gospels* (Sheffield: JSOT, 1980) 7-20; T. A. Burkill, "The Competence of the Sanhedrin," *VC* 10 (1956) 80-96; D. R. Catchpole, *The Trial of Jesus* (SPB 18; Leiden: Brill, 1971); J. B. Green, *The Death of Jesus* (WUNT, 2d ser., 33; Tübingen: J. C. B. Mohr, 1988); A. E. Harvey, *Jesus and the Constraints of History* (London: Duckworth, 1982); J. Jeremias, *The Eucharistic Words of Jesus* (New York: Scribner's, 1966); D. Juel, *Messiah and Temple* (SBLDS 31; Missoula: Scholar's, 1977); J. Juster, *Les Juifs dans l'Empire Romain* (2 vols.; Paris: Geuthner, 1914); G. D. Kilpatrick, *The Trial of Jesus* (London: Oxford University, 1953); H. Lietzmann, "Der Prozess Jesu," *Kleine Schriften II* (TU 68; Berlin: Akademie, 1958; repr. of 1931) 251-63; E. Lohse, "συνέδιον," *TDNT* VII.860-71; T. Mommsen, *Römisches Strafrecht* (vol. 1, pt. 4; Leipzig: Duncker & Humblot, 1899); J. A. T. Robinson, *The Priority of John* (London: SCM, 1985); E. P. Sanders, *Jesus and Judaism* (Philadelphia: Fortress, 1985); E. Schürer, *The History of the Jewish People in the Age of Jesus Christ (175 B.C.-A.D. 135)*, rev. and ed. G. Vermes, F. Millar (3 vols.; Edinburgh: T. & T. Clark, 1973-86); A. N. Sherwin-White, *Roman Law and Roman Society in the New Testament* (Oxford: University Press, 1963); S. Smalley, "Arrest and Trial of Jesus Christ," *ISBE* 2.1049-55; A. Strobel, *Die Stunde der Wahrheit* (WUNT 21; Tübingen: J. C. B. Mohr, 1980); P. Winter, *On the Trial of Jesus* (SJ 1; 2d rev. ed.; New York: De Gruyter, 1974) B. Corley

TRIUMPHAL ENTRY

The formal entry of Jesus into Jerusalem at a climactic point in his life is recorded by all four Evangelists (Mt 21:1-11; Mk 11:1-11; Lk 19:28-40; Jn 12:12-19). Accordingly, the essential historicity of the portrayal of Jesus coming into Jerusalem at a time of festal celebration (perhaps on an animal) has not usually been doubted by critical scholars. But questions have been raised concerning how much those who handed on the tradition shaped the story in order to make it a vehicle for expressing the allegedly later belief of the early church that Jesus was the fulfillment of the Jewish hope for a messianic deliverer in the form of a Davidic king (*see* Christ; Son of David). R. Bultmann, for example, while not denying that the story has a historical core, labelled it "a Messianic legend under the influence of Zech. 9⁹" (262), noting that the prophecy mentions the donkey, the entry and the acclamation.

1. The Form of the Triumphal Entry Accounts
2. The Triumphal Entry in the Four Gospels
3. The Historicity of the Triumphal Entry

1. The Form of the Triumphal Entry Accounts.

D. R. Catchpole has argued that the story fits the pattern of accounts in Jewish literature of "the celebratory entry to a city by a hero figure who has previously achieved his triumph" (319): (1) the achievement of victory and its corresponding status, (2) a formal entry into the city, (3) a welcome with greetings and/or acclamations as well as invocations to God, (4) entry into the Temple (if there is one) and (5) cultic activity which can be positive (sacrifice) or negative (cleansing—although this negative activity is better attested as part of [1]). Finding the basis of this pattern in the Israelite kingship ritual (1 Kings 1:32-40; Zech 9:9), Catchpole cites as evidence of its existence the stories of the victorious entries of Alexander the Great (Josephus *Ant.* 11.8.4-5 §§325-39; 11.8.6 §§342-45), Apollonius (2 Macc 4:21-22), Judas Maccabeus (1 Macc 4:19-25; 5:45-54; Josephus *Ant.* 12.7.4 §312; 12.8.5 §§348-49), Jonathan (1 Macc 10:86), Simon (1 Macc 13:43-51), Antigonus (Josephus *J.W.* 1.3.2 §§73-74; *Ant.* 13.11.1 §§304-6), Marcus Agrippa (Josephus *Ant.* 16.2.1 §§12-15), Archelaus (Josephus *Ant.* 17.8.2—9.5 §§194-239) and an imposter of Herod's son Alexander (Josephus *J.W.* 2.7.1-2 §§101-10; *Ant.* 17.12.1 §§324-28). The presence of this pattern in the story of Jesus' entry into Jerusalem, Catchpole concludes, means that the account should not be interpreted as an opening gambit in which Jesus challenges the power structure of the nation, but instead should be understood as an acknowledgment of the status Jesus has already achieved.

Catchpole's form-critical work disputes the proposal of S. G. F. Brandon that Jesus' action was "obviously calculated to cause the authorities, both Jewish and Roman, to view him and his movement as subversive" (324), revealing Jesus' sympathies with the revolutionary cause of the Zealots (*see* Revolutionary Movements). The historical question, rather, is whether this event indeed celebrated the "triumph" of Jesus' ministry in recognition of the kingship he had previously won, or whether this interpretive framework has been superimposed on the story at a later time after the experience of victory at Easter (*see* Resurrection).

2. The Triumphal Entry in the Four Gospels.
The historical question can be better addressed after a survey of the presentations of Jesus' entry into Jerusalem in each of the Gospels.

2.1. Mark. As has recently been confirmed by J. D. Kingsbury, it is clear to the reader of Mark's Gospel that Jesus enters Jerusalem as the anointed victor (Messiah) ready to lay claim to the Davidic kingship over Israel.* In Mark's account of "Jesus, Messiah, Son of God" (Mk 1:1; *see* Christ; Son of God), Jesus receives his divine anointing at his baptism* by John, where the heavens are torn apart and the Spirit descends upon him like a dove (Mk 1:10; cf. Is 61:1;

64:1; *see* Holy Spirit). With multiform allusions, the voice from heaven, "you are my Son, the Beloved; with you I am well pleased" (Mk 1:11), proclaims Jesus to be God's "anointed [Messiah]," his "king on Zion," about whom God declares, "You are my son; today I have begotten you" (Ps 2:2, 6-7); God's "only son . . . whom [he] loves" (Gen 22:2); and God's "servant, . . . [his] chosen, in whom [his] soul delights" (Is 42:1).

From this investiture Jesus proceeds to demonstrate the authority* of his messianic status. He does battle with Satan (*see* Temptation of Jesus) in the wilderness (*see* Mountain and Wilderness) and emerges victorious (Mk 1:12-13; cf. Is 11:1-9), having bound the "strong man" (Mk 3:27; *see* Demon, Devil, Satan). Coming to Galilee,* he then launches into a ministry of preaching, calling disciples,* teaching, and performing mighty works of healing* and exorcism, all of which testify to his authority (Mk 1:22, 27; 2:10; 3:15; 6:7; cf. Mk 11:27-33; Is 61:1-3). Although the people who encounter Jesus only gradually become aware of who he is, a process highlighted by the secrecy motif (*see* Mark, Gospel of), the revelations coming from the heavenly realm (Mk 1:24-25, 34; 3:11-12; 5:7) confirm that Jesus is acting as the anointed Son of God, contending for his position of regency in God's kingdom (*see* Kingdom of God). Peter's confession "You are the Messiah" (Mk 8:29), in response to Jesus' query about his identity, is therefore an appropriate, if not exhaustive, evaluation of Jesus' significance, reinforced by the subsequent revelation on the mountain of the Transfiguration* (Mk 9:2-8). After Jesus' extended journey "on the way" to his passion in Jerusalem (Mk 8:27—10:52), with its sobering teaching on the cost of discipleship* and the necessity for the Son of man (*see* Son of Man) to suffer (Mk 8:31; 9:31; 10:33-34, 45), Jesus' messianic dignity is reiterated, as blind Bartimaeus cries out, "Son of David, have mercy on me!" (Mk 10:47-48; cf. *Pss. Sol.* 17:21).

It is as a messianic claimant to the throne of David, then, that Jesus enters Jerusalem, and Mark's account of this event is replete with allusions that evoke images of the celebration of a royal triumph (Mk 11:1-11). From a location near the Mount of Olives (Mk 11:1), the scene of the Lord's eschatological advent (Zech 14:4; cf. Josephus *J.W.* 2.13.5 §262; *Ant.* 20.8.6 §169; *see* Apocalyptic Teaching), Jesus exercises kingly authority by requisitioning an animal for transport with the claim "its master has need" (Mk 11:1-3; cf. 1 Sam 8:10-11, 17). The animal is identified as a "colt" (Mk 11:2, 4-5, 7), using the same term found in the LXX to identify the donkey's foal of the entering king of Jerusalem in Zechariah 9:9 (cf. *Gen. Rab.* 75 [48c]; 98 [62a]; *b. Sanh.* 98a; 99a; *b. Ber.* 56b; cf. 1 Kings 1:35) and of the coming one who holds the scepter of Judah in Genesis 49:10-11 (where the foal is "bound" to a vine; cf. 4QPBless; Justin *Apol.* 32.6). This animal is also one "on which no one has ever sat" (Mk 11:2), symbolizing its sacredness for royal use (*m. Sanh.* 2:5; cf. 1 Sam 6:7; or perhaps a reference to the "new colt" of Zech 9:9 LXX).

As Jesus mounts the animal and begins his entry into the city, many who accompany him pay homage by their actions and by their words. Reminiscent of the respect shown to King Jehu, the people spread their cloaks on the road (Mk 11:8; cf. 2 Kings 9:13; Josephus *Ant.* 9.6.2 §111; cf. *Yal.* Exod 2:15 [1.168]; *Acts Pil.* 2), as well as leafy branches cut from the field (cf. *Tg. Esth* 8:15; the term is hapax legomenon and may refer to mattresses as padding for the steep descent [POxy 3.520.10] or to the festal *lulab* of Tabernacles [*m. Sukk.* 3:8-9, 11-15; 4:1-2, 4] also used during Hanukkah [1 Macc 13:51; 2 Macc 10:6-7]; *see* Feasts).

As the procession (Mk 11:9a; cf. Josephus *J.W.* 1.33.9 §673; *Ant.* 7.1.6 §40) continues, the people shout antiphonally in acclamation: "Hosanna! Blessed is the one who comes in the name of the Lord! Blessed is the coming kingdom of our father David! Hosanna in the highest!" (Mk 11:9b-10). In the first half of this chiastically balanced strophe, Jesus is greeted as a pilgrim entering the city in a familiar chant from the festal Hallel psalms (Ps 118:25-26 [117:25-26 LXX]; cf. *Midr.* Ps 118 §22; *m. Sukk.* 3:9; 4:1, 5, 8; *b. Sukk.* 27b; *b. Pesaḥ.* 119a; *Tg.* Ps 118:22-29). This is the welcome, moreover, that would also be given to the eschatological deliverer, as is attested in a saying of Jesus from Q* (Mt 23:39 par. Lk 13:35). In the second half of the strophe, Jesus' messianic status is again brought into focus as he is hailed as the one who will establish the Davidic kingship over Israel, even though the phrase "kingdom of our father David" has no direct Jewish parallels (cf. Acts 4:25; 14th of the Eighteen Benedictions in the Palestinian rescension).

Jesus' entry into the city in Mark's account, however, does not fulfill any Jewish nationalistic hopes "to destroy the unrighteous rulers, to purge Jerusalem from Gentiles" (*Pss. Sol.* 17:21-46). Jesus, rather, brings judgment* upon unfruitful Israel (Mk 11:12-14, 20-21; cf. Hos 9:10-17) which has turned God's "house of prayer for all nations" into a "den of brigands" (Mk 11:15-19; cf. Is 56:7; Jer 7:11; *see* Temple Cleansing). As Mark concludes his story, Jesus maintains his claim to kingship (Mk 14:61-62; 15:2), but over the universal realm of the "Son of God" (Mk 15:39; cf. Mk 12:6, 35-37).

2.2. Matthew. Matthew's account of Jesus' entry into Jerusalem follows Mark, enhancing the theme of the royal entry of the Davidic king and heightening the impact of the event upon the city. Mark's allusion to Zechariah 9:9 in his reference to the "colt" is made explicit in Matthew through an editorial comment that introduces a quotation of this prophecy (combined with Is 62:11) with a fulfillment formula (Mt 21:4-5), and in the words of the prophecy the reader is advised that "the king" of "Zion" has come to claim his city (cf. Mt 5:35). The people who take part in the event, moreover, have a greater awareness of Jesus' link to the Davidic line than the bystanders in Mark, as they shout "Hosanna to the son of David!" (Mt 21:9; cf. Mk 11:10). And the city is set in an uproar as "a very large crowd" spreads their cloaks and cuts branches from the trees, shouting their acclamation and literally shaking the city like an earthquake (Mt 21:8-10).

The theme of triumph, however, is muted in Matthew's version of the story. In his citation of Zechariah 9:9, Matthew omits the phrase "righteous and delivered [or victorious; LXX: saving] is he," allowing the accent to fall on the phrase "humble and mounted upon a donkey and upon a colt, the foal of a pack animal" (Mt 21:5). He seems also to have a special interest in demonstrating that the animal is indeed a donkey and not a beast of conquest (cf. *Pss. Sol.* 17:33), in that at the critical point in the citation he switches from quoting the LXX ("humble and mounted upon a pack animal and a new colt") to quoting the MT ("humble and riding upon a [male] donkey and upon a [male] donkey, the foal of [female] donkeys"). Matthew also, for emphasis, refers to the "donkey" at three points in the narrative (Mt 21:2, 5, 7). In a possible allusion to Jesus' future passion (cf. Mt 23:37-39), Matthew adds that as Jesus enters the city he is acknowledged as "the prophet" (Mt 21:11; *see* Prophets, Prophecy), as well as the "son of David."

This stress on the humble arrival of the Davidic king is reinforced by the context, in which the "Son of David" performs acts of mercy. The "Son of David," for Matthew, is one who heals (Mt 9:27-34; 12:22-30; 15:21-28; 20:29-34) and who upon entering Jerusalem clears (rather than judges) the Temple so that the outcasts, the blind and the lame (cf. 2 Kgdms 5:8 LXX; *m. Ḥag.* 1:1; 1QSa 2:3-10; 11QTemp 45:12-14), can be welcomed and cured of their infirmities (Mt 21:12-17; *see* Temple Cleansing). Matthew's "Son of David" is thus the "servant" (Mt 12:15-21; cf. Is 42:1-4; *see* Servant of Yahweh) and the "coming one" (Mt 11:2-6; cf. Is 29:18-19; 35:5-6; 61:1) who practices the divine injunction "I desire mercy and not sacrifice" (Hos 6:6; cf. Mt 9:10-13; 12:5-7; cf. '*Abot R. Nat.* 4). The contrast with the pharisaic "son of David," who exhibits "strength" to "destroy" and "smash," is obvious (*Pss. Sol.* 17:21-46).

One curious feature of Matthew's narrative has puzzled interpreters—the introduction of two animals, upon which the disciples spread their cloaks and Jesus apparently rides (Mt 21:2-3, 5, 7). It seems unlikely that Matthew, whose knowledge of Hebrew is evident, has misunderstood the parallelism in Zechariah 9:9 and forced a literal fulfillment upon the story, and the suggestion that this is an instance of Matthew's interest in the validity of two witnesses (Mt 8:28; 9:27; 18:16, 19; 20:30; 21:1; 26:60) seems far-fetched (pace Num 22:28-30). Since Matthew tailors his OT citations to fit his narrative tradition (see Old Testament in the Gospels), rather than vice versa, a better proposal is that he had an independent tradition of two animals—a donkey's foal and its mother (cf. Jn 12:14; Gen 49:11; b. B. Bat. 5:3)—which may also explain his omission of the Markan reference to a colt "on which no one has ever sat" (Mk 11:2). Matthew's statement that Jesus sat "on [or over] them" (Mt 21:7) may refer to the cloaks on the animals (the immediate antecedent), with the implication that Jesus sits on the cloaks of one animal (Origen), or it may be a textual error (some MSS have the singular "on it"), but less likely is the suggestion that it is a reference to an oriental throne supported by the two animals (Clement of Alexandria).

2.3. Luke. As in the case of Matthew, Luke's account of the entry follows Mark, bringing greater prominence to Jesus' royal dignity and the nature of his triumph. After a lengthy journey in which Jesus has "set his face to go to Jerusalem" (Lk 9:51—18:34), which is his destiny as the "coming one" (Lk 13:31-35, the center of the chiastically constructed travel narrative), Jesus approaches the city via Jericho, where, as in Mark, he encounters a blind man who entreats him with the messianic title "Son of David" (Lk 18:35-43). Before Jesus begins his entry into the city, however, Luke inserts two pericopes to reinforce the theme that Jesus is indeed the Davidic "Savior, who is the Messiah, the Lord" (Lk 2:11): a story of the salvation* of Zacchaeus, a lost son of Abraham* (Lk 19:1-10; cf. Ezek 34:16), and an allegorical parable* of a nobleman who is summoned to a distant country to receive royal power and returns to judge the wicked citizens of his own country who refuse to accept his kingship (Lk 19:11-28; cf. Acts 1:11; 3:20-21; 17:31). With this theme established, Jesus makes his way to the Mount of Olives, a location repeated twice for emphasis (Lk 19:29, 37; cf. Zech 14:4), from which he will make his royal "descent" on the colt into the city and the Temple. As he approaches the place of descent on the colt, the whole multitude of disciples openly acknowledges his triumph, praising God

"joyfully with a loud voice for all the deeds of power that they had seen" (Lk 19:37). In Luke's version of the subsequent acclamation, Jesus' kingship is explicitly recognized, as the disciples alter the pilgrim welcome of Psalm 118:26 and shout, "Blessed is the king who comes in the name of the Lord!" (Lk 19:38; cf. Jn 12:13), and the Hebrew cry for help in Mark ("Hosanna!") is replaced by the exclamation "Peace in heaven, and glory in the highest!" (Lk 19:38; contrast Lk 2:14). The jubilation of the occasion cannot be contained, for "if these were silent, the stones would shout out" (Lk 19:40).

According to Luke the purpose of Jesus' entry into Jerusalem is to lay claim on his Temple (cf. Lk 2:49), cleansing it to prepare it as a place for his teaching (Lk 19:45-48; 20:1; 21:37-38; see Temple Cleansing). His coming, therefore, is not as an earthly king, but is, in fact, no less than a divine visitation (Lk 19:44; cf. Lk 1:68, 78; 7:16) of the Lord (Lk 19:31, 34, but cf. 19:33; Mal 3:1). And even when the significance of this event goes unrecognized and Jesus suffers the fate of the prophets (Lk 19:41-44), his claim on the Temple remains in force, as the Temple, after his resurrection,* becomes the place for the proclamation of the power of the "name of Jesus" (Acts 3:1—4:22; cf. 1 Kings 8:27-30), a name which ultimately can transcend the limitations of this particular location (cf. Acts 7:39-50; 8:12; 10:48; 16:18). The realm of Jesus' kingship in Luke, accordingly, is beyond the sphere of earthly kingdoms (cf. Acts 1:6-8), and hence is not a political threat to the reigning powers (cf. Lk 23:3-4, 47; cf. Acts 25:8, 25). The peace that Jesus as king establishes is "peace in heaven" (Lk 19:38, 42), which will be poured out through his Holy Spirit upon those who call upon his name (cf. Acts 2:1-42; 10:34-43).

2.4. John. The account of Jesus' entry into Jerusalem in the Fourth Gospel is strikingly similar to the accounts in the Synoptic tradition. A crowd greets Jesus with branches of palm trees (Jn 12:13; cf. Mk 11:8; Mt 21:8) and shouts the festal welcome of Psalm 118:25-26, retaining the Hebrew cry "Hosanna!" but following the LXX for the rest of the refrain, "Blessed is the one who comes in the name of the Lord!" (Jn 12:13; cf. Mk 11:10). Jesus is then acclaimed as "the King of Israel" (Jn 12:13-14; cf. Lk 19:38), and sits on a "young donkey" (Jn 12:14; cf. Mk 11:7; Mt 21:7; Lk 19:35), which is interpreted through an editorial remark as the fulfillment of Zechariah 9:9 (Jn 12:14-15; cf. Mt 21:4-5).

Significant differences in the Johannine account, however, indicate an independent tradition of the same event. Jesus is not escorted by a procession of disciples and well-wishers who erupt into spontaneous celebration along the way (Mk 11:8-10; Mt 21:8-9; Lk 19:36-38), but is greeted by a reception party from Jerusalem that has come prepared for an ovation (Jn 12:12-13). These greeters, moreover, bring the branches of palm trees with them from the city and presumably hold them in their hands (Jn 12:13), instead of strewing them along the pathway as Jesus descends into the city (Mk 11:8; Mt 21:8). In further divergence from the Synoptic tradition, the animal upon which Jesus rides is labelled a "young donkey" (Jn 12:14), rather than a "colt" (Mk 11:2, 4-5, 7; Lk 19:30, 33, 35) or simply a "donkey" (Mt 21:2, 5, 7), and Jesus does not requisition the animal in a provocative act that initiates the celebration (Mk 11:1-7; Mt 21:1-7; Lk 19:28-35) but finds it and sits on it in response to the welcome of the crowd from the city (Jn 12:14). Finally, the text of Zechariah 9:9, as quoted in the Johannine account (Jn 12:15), follows neither the LXX nor the form of the text in Matthew (Mt 21:4-5), and may be conflated with another OT text (e.g., Zeph 3:16).

On the surface of John's narrative the story of the entry is a celebration of the triumph of the messianic "King of Israel" (Jn 12:13; cf. Jn 1:49). Jesus has just performed a sign (Jn 12:18) that is the culmination of his mighty deeds on earth (Jn 11:47)—the raising of Lazarus* of Bethany from the dead (Jn 11:1-44)—and this has caused a flurry of enthusiasm as well as catalyzed the opposition among the Jews (Jn 11:45-54). As the festival of the Passover approaches, bringing crowds to Jerusalem (Jn 11:55-57), Jesus returns to Bethany, the scene of his great victory, to visit the home of Lazarus (Jn 12:1-8), and the news soon spreads to Jerusalem (Jn 12:9-11). Hearing that Jesus is coming to Jerusalem, a delegation sets out to greet him, carrying branches of palm trees in a manner evocative of the celebration of the Maccabaean triumph over Antiochus IV Epiphanes (Jn 12:12-13; cf. 1 Macc 13:51; 2 Macc 10:7; cf. Suetonius *Gaius Caligula* 32). To the acclamation that he is the "King of Israel" (Jn 12:13), Jesus responds by finding and sitting on a "young donkey," which the Johannine author interprets as a fulfillment of a prophecy concerning the coming king of Zion (Jn 12:15-16; Zech 9:9). As the crowd continues to exult in the miracle* at Bethany, the opposition grumbles, "Look, the world has gone after him!" (Jn 12:17-19).

The framework of the entry narrative, however, indicates that the Fourth Evangelist intends this event to have a deeper significance than this surface reading would suggest. Hints earlier in the Gospel indicate that Jesus' claim to kingship is not to be interpreted politically (Jn 1:49-51; 6:14-15), and if the

phrase "Do not be afraid, daughter of Zion" in the citation of Zechariah 9:9 with which the Johannine Evangelist interprets the entry (Jn 12:15) is an allusion to Zephaniah 3:14-16, the implication is that the "King of Israel" is no earthly leader, but indeed "the Lord ... in your midst" (cf. Jn 8:24, 28, 58). This is consistent with an editorial remark (an external prolepsis; cf. Jn 2:22; 20:9) appended to the entry, in which the acclamation of Jesus' kingship confirmed by prophecy is linked to his glorification (Jn 12:16; *see* Glory), a reference to his coming sacrificial death (*see* Death of Jesus) and resurrection (cf. Jn 7:39; 12:23, 28; 13:31-32; 17:1, 4-5) when he will be lifted up to draw all people to himself (cf. Jn 3:14; 8:28; 12:32, 34). As the account of the entry concludes with a reference to the crowd "that had been with him when he called Lazarus out of the tomb and raised him from the dead" (Jn 12:17-18; cf. Jn 11:1-53; 12:1-2, 9-11), the theme of Jesus' future conquest over death is further reinforced. In the midst of all of these contextual clues, therefore, Jesus' triumphal entry into Jerusalem, following upon his anointing* for burial (*see* Burial of Jesus) in the home of Lazarus (Jn 12:1-8), becomes a proleptic celebration of the victory of Easter. And thus the stage is set for the irony of Jesus' trial, when rejected "King of the Jews" (Jn 18:33-39; 19:3-22) establishes a kingdom which is "not of this world" (Jn 18:36).

3. The Historicity of the Triumphal Entry.

The survey of the presentations of Jesus' entry into Jerusalem in each of the Gospels demonstrates that the significance of the event has been amplified through subsequent interpretation by the early church (*see* Tradition Criticism). The observation of this phenomenon has led some critical scholars to question, in particular, the historicity of the messianic features of the story. Noting that the account falls into two parts, the acquisition of the animal (Mk 11:1-7; cf. Jn 12:14) and the festal entry into the city (Mk 11:8-10; cf. Jn 12:12-13), these critics have proposed that the story has grown from a simple narrative about Jesus' entry into Jerusalem during festival time (probably on foot) to a messianic legend that includes a royal animal (through the influence of Zech 9:9) procured by supernatural means (cf. Mk 14:12-16; 1 Sam 10:2-10; 1 Kings 17:8-16). Since there allegedly is no evidence that the original event attracted the attention of the authorities or that Jesus' followers at this time had recognized him as a Messiah who had achieved a triumph, it is said that the messianic interpretation of the event must reflect the confession of the early church after the victory of Easter.

Such skepticism, however, is unwarranted. The story of the acquisition of the animal, as J. D. M. Derrett has shown, exhibits the common procedure of a ruler (or rabbi) procuring transportation, using the royal right of impressment (*angaria;* cf. 1 Sam 8:16) and also follows the Jewish law on borrowing (Ex 22:14-15); thus it should not be categorized as a legend. Jesus' decision to ride into the city on an animal, moreover, is a "startling and ostentatious reversal of the normal constraint which would have obliged him to enter on foot" (Harvey 129; cf. *m. Ḥag.* 1:1; *b. Ḥag.* ba; *m. Ber.* 9.5), and since the messianic interpretation of Zechariah 9:9 is not attested in Judaism* until the fourth century A.D., it seems likely that the memory of this provocative act has its origin in the historical event. The activities of the bystanders, spreading (or waving) branches along the way and shouting an acclamation from Psalm 118:25-26, also have a historical ring, reflecting the practices of the festivals of Passover (*m. Pesaḥ.* 5:7; 10:5-7), Tabernacles (*m. Sukk.* 3-4) and Hanukkah (1 Macc 13:51; 2 Macc 10:6-7; *see* Feasts). Furthermore, the Hebrew cry "Hosanna!" (which is not transliterated in the LXX of Ps 117:25), although preserved in the eucharistic liturgy of the early church (*Did.* 10:6), may be a historical reminiscence.

It is also reasonable to suggest that the original event indeed celebrated the arrival of a triumphant king. Although the accounts of the entry do not mention a reaction to this event by the authorities, the charge "King of the Jews" brought against Jesus at his trial (Mk 15:2, 26; *see* Trial of Jesus) may indicate that this event raised suspicions about his activities (Sanders). This would not be unusual, since R. A. Horsley and J. S. Hanson have demonstrated that charismatic leaders among the Jewish peasants of the first century A.D., even without a direct claim to Davidic or royal lineage, received the appellation of "king" from time to time in the hope that they might be the one who would liberate the people from foreign oppression (cf. Josephus *Ant.* 17.10.5-8 §§271-85). Jesus' activity of proclaiming the kingdom of God, teaching (*see* Teacher) with authority, performing mighty works and calling disciples would certainly have raised the expectation that he might be such a liberator (cf. Mt 11:2-6 par. Lk 7:18-23). But by entering Jerusalem on a donkey, Jesus met this expectation in a way that was consistent with the tenor of his ministry—his kingship would be one of humility and service* rather than political conquest (Zech 9:9; cf. Mt 20:28 par. Mk 10:45 and Lk 22:27).

See also CHRIST; SON OF DAVID; SON OF GOD; TEMPLE; TEMPLE CLEANSING.

BIBLIOGRAPHY. S. G. F. Brandon, *Jesus and the Zealots* (New York: Scribner's, 1967); R. Bultmann, *The History of the Synoptic Tradition* (rev. ed.; New York: Harper & Row, 1968); D. R. Catchpole, "The 'Triumphal' Entry," in *Jesus and the Politics of His Day,* ed. E. Bammel and C. F. D. Moule (Cambridge: University Press, 1984); J. D. M. Derrett, "Law in the New Testament: The Palm Sunday Colt," in *Studies in the New Testament* (2 vols.; Leiden: E. J. Brill, 1978), 2.165-77; C. H. Dodd, *The Interpretation of the Fourth Gospel* (Cambridge: University Press, 1965); J. A. Fitzmyer, *The Gospel according to Luke (X-XXIV)* (AB 28A; Garden City, NY; Doubleday, 1985); R. H. Gundry, *The Use of the Old Testament in St. Matthew's Gospel* (NovTSup 18; Leiden: E. J. Brill, 1967); A. E. Harvey, *Jesus and the Constraints of History* (Philadelphia: Westminster, 1982); M. Hengel, *Was Jesus a Revolutionist?* (Philadelphia: Fortress, 1971); R. A. Horsley and J. S. Hanson, *Bandits, Prophets, and Messiahs* (Minneapolis: Winston, 1985); J. D. Kingsbury, *The Christology of Mark's Gospel* (Philadelphia: Fortress, 1983); C.-P. März, *"Siehe, dein König kommt zu dir . . ." : Eine Traditionsgeschichtlich Untersuchung zur Einzugsperikope* (ETS 43; Leipzig: St. Benno, 1980); J. A. T. Robinson, *The Priority of John* (London: SCM, 1985); E. P. Sanders, *Jesus and Judaism* (Philadelphia: Fortress, 1985).

L. A. Losie

TRUTH

Truth vocabulary plays a small role in the Synoptic Gospels, though the language and the concept of truth are certainly present. The Gospel of John most frequently uses the language of truth, and there it undergoes significant theological development. John uses truth vocabulary in its conventional sense of veracity/genuineness/opposite of falsehood; but he also develops his own particular meaning, where truth refers to the reality of God* the Father revealed in Jesus the Son (*see* Son of God). This truth can only be apprehended by disciples* through faith.* Revelation is at the heart of John's usage—revelation, not as the unveiling of knowledge, but as the unveiling of Christ,* who is both the messenger *and* the message. Consequently, since truth is personal, acquiring truth is personal. It is not learned as much as it is accepted, with all its life-transforming implications, when one comes into a relationship with Jesus.

1. Synoptic Gospels
2. The Gospel of John

1. Synoptic Gospels.

Truth vocabulary occurs eighteen times in the Synoptic Gospels: (1) truth (*alētheia;* Mt 22:16; Mk 5:33; 12:14,

32; Lk 4:25; 20:21; 22:59); (2) true/truthful (alēthēs; Mt 22:16; Mk 12:14); (3) truly (alēthōs; Mt 14:33; 26:73; 27:54; Mk 14:70; 15:39; Lk 9:27; 12:44; 21:3); (4) true/genuine (alēthinos; Lk 16:11). The language is used in a straightforward manner to refer to honesty as opposed to falsehood, such as when the woman with the issue of blood comes forward to speak "the whole truth" (Mk 5:33) or the Pharisees* admit that Jesus "honestly teaches the way of God" (Mt 2:16; Mk 12:14; Lk 20:21). The adverb alēthōs (truly) is used as the Greek equivalent of the Semitic 'āmēn, asserting the validity or authority of a statement.

Only Luke's Gospel places truth language on the lips of Jesus (as either alēthōs or ep' alētheias; 4:25; 9:27; 12:44; 21:3), although in each instance it is merely Luke's rendition of an amēn saying (cf. Mk 8:9; Mt 24:47; Mk 12:43; see Amen). This absence of truth vocabulary in Jesus' teaching does not mean that the Synoptic Jesus is disinterested in the value of truthfulness. The concept is present even when the words are absent. Jesus' criticism of the Jewish leaders' hypocrisy (Mt 23:2-3, 23-24; Lk 11:46; see Hypocrite), as well as the personal consistency between his own words and actions—eventually culminating in the cross—makes Jesus' concern in the Synoptics for honesty and integrity clear.

2. The Gospel of John.
John's usage is much more complex. Both his frequent and peculiar use of the language provide ample opportunity for John to construct his own context for meaning. Thus the interpreter must sort through those instances where words are used with their conventional sense, and occurrences where John imports his own sense for truth. The challenge of understanding such multiple meanings of words (polyseme) requires that the reader exercise discipline in reading neither more nor less into the passage than is warranted by the context.

2.1. Alēthōs. The word generally translated "truly" in the NT occurs seven times in John (1:47; 4:42; 6:14; 7:26, 40; 8:31; 17:8). In all but one instance it means "indeed" or "really." It is generally used as a simple adverb, and in this way differs from its common Synoptic usage. One exception is found in John 1:47 where it used as a synonym for alēthinos, identifying Nathanael as a "true" or "genuine" Israelite.

2.2. Alēthinos. This adjective occurs nine times in John (1:9; 4:23, 37; 6:32; 7:28; 8:16; 15:1; 17:3; 19:35) and is used with two different senses. First, it refers to something which is "authentic" or "genuine." Thus Jesus is the "true light" (1:9); the Father is looking for "real worshippers" (4:23); and eternal life* is found by

knowing the "only true God" (17:3). Two other instances fit this category, but with a distinctly metaphorical significance, when Jesus describes himself as the "true bread*" and the "true vine*" (6:32; 15:1).

Second, alēthinos is used as a synonym for the adjective alēthēs ("true"; 4:37; 7:28; 8:16; 19:35). Fundamentally, these are assertions that something or someone is "valid," "reliable" or "is not being false." But at this point we also begin to make contact with the additional significance attached to this vocabulary by John. Because the Father is both "true" and the one who sent Jesus into the world (7:28), and because Jesus comes only to reveal the Father, Jesus' teaching is "true" (8:16). The sense of this language begins to move beyond the borders of mere opposition to falsehood and unfolds as expanded meaning where truth refers to the eternal, heavenly reality of God now brought to the world in the incarnate Jesus.

2.3. Alēthēs. This adjective, usually translated as "true," occurs thirteen times in John's Gospel (3:33; 4:18; 5:31, 32; 6:55; 7:18; 8:13, 14, 17, 26; 10:41; 19:35; 21:24) and is used with three distinct senses. First, in the majority of cases John uses this word to refer to something which is "valid" or "reliable" (4:18; 5:31, 32; 8:13, 14, 17; 10:41; 19:35; 21:24). Second, in one instance alēthēs appears as a synonym for alēthinos (6:55). This is another metaphorical usage where Jesus' flesh is called "real" bread (see 2.2. above). Third, in three instances alēthēs contributes to the Johannine theology of divine truth. Briefly, all those who receive Christ's revelation (3:3) acknowledge through their faith that he is the true revealer (7:18) of the true God (8:26). This concept comes into its own with John's use of alētheia discussed below.

2.4. Alētheia. The noun alētheia ("truth") occurs twenty-one times in John (1:14, 17; 3:21; 4:23, 24; 5:33; 8:32, 30, 44, 45, 46; 14:6, 17; 15:26; 16:7, 13; 17:17, 19; 18:37 [twice], 38). Within the Johannine context the word has been so thoroughly infused with John's view of heavenly reality revealed in Christ, that even in those few instances where its primary reference is to truth, as opposed to falsehood (5:33; 8:44; 16:7), it nevertheless evokes clear implications of the deeper significance of truth's revelation in Christ.

To understand John's usage one should look to the beginning of the Gospel where Jesus is said to be "full of grace and truth" (1:14). Exodus 34:6 is clearly the relevant OT background, not because of the linguistic arguments linking charitos kai alētheias ("grace and truth") with ḥesed ûᵉ'met ("steadfast love and faithfulness"), but because of the context which compares the incarnation of the Logos* with God's revelation to Moses* on Mt. Sinai (Jn 1:17-18). The vocabulary differences between Exodus 34 and John 1 (the LXX of Ex 34:6 translates *ḥesed weʾmet* as *polueleos kai alēthinos* ("compassionate and true"), not *charitos kai alētheias;* but cf. Dodd) indicate that we should allow John's usage to determine the meaning of each word. This explains why attempts to equate *alētheia* with the OT concept of "faithfulness" (*ʾemet,* commonly translated "truth") do not work in John. This conclusion is based on the observation of John's own context and usage and has nothing to do with preconceptions about Hebrew versus Greek concepts of truth. J. Barr and A. Thiselton have shown that the common distinction made between Greek and Hebrew meanings for truth simply does not work linguistically. John's usage is not "Greek," it is "Johannine," and as we shall see it is not incompatible with an OT/Hebrew background.

What, then, is the point of John's connection with Exodus 34? *Revelation.* The incarnation of God in the Logos is presented as the supreme disclosure of the Lord who revealed himself to Moses in the giving of the Law at Sinai (1:17). Jesus shows us God as he really is. This assertion sets the stage for John's use of "truth." Contrary to Greek background, truth is personal, not merely intellectual; truth is acquired through the revelation of God, not through mental application; truth is not abstract, but has been individually revealed in history. It is also reminiscent of the Jewish view of both Torah and Wisdom.*

2.4.1. God Is Truth. As the revealer of truth, Jesus only teaches what the Father has given to him (3:33; 8:40; 18:37). The Father *is* the truth. His eternal reality is ultimate reality. There are no external standards to evaluate his reality; according to John, his truth can only be accepted through faith in Jesus as the one who comes down from heaven. Thus "the time has now come" when true worshippers will worship* the Father only as revealed by Christ (4:23-24). However, as ultimate reality, God the Father is the only standard by which all truth or falsehood, light or darkness are measured in this world* (5:33; 8:31-32, 42-47).

2.4.2. Jesus Is Both the Messenger and the Message of Truth. No one but Jesus can reveal truth because only he has been personally sent into the world by God. His authority* is rooted in his commission (3:17; 4:34; 5:24, 30; 6:29; 8:25; 17:18; 20:21). But Jesus is more than a mere courier. By perfectly testifying to the Father, he also testifies to himself (8:18), because he and his Father are one (10:30). To know Jesus is to know the Father (14:9). Consequently, Jesus can say that he, too, *is* the truth (14:6). Of course, this is commensurate with the prologue's claim that the Logos is God (1:1, 18). John presents Jesus as the final

revelation of God, who is himself God; the one against whom all claims to meaning and reality are to be evaluated.

2.4.3. The Spirit of Truth. For the Spirit (*see* Holy Spirit) to be called the Spirit of truth is basically to assert three things. First, like Jesus, the Spirit is sent from the Father (who is the truth, 15:26)—the "Spirit of truth" is the "Spirit of God." Second, the Spirit continues the mission of Jesus (14:17), revealing to the world both the Father and the Son (who is also the truth). Third, the Spirit will lead disciples into the truth by further instructing them in the knowledge of the Father and the Son (16:13). The Spirit becomes the "advocate" (an alternative for the "counselor") of heavenly reality in this world, advancing God's case, as it were, and exposing, or at least condemning, all counterfeit claims to truth (16:5-11).

2.4.4. Doing the Truth. At times John may seem to imply that certain individuals have an innate affinity for the truth, that those who listen to Jesus do so because they were *already* "on the side of truth" (18:37). While on the surface this may appear to credit humankind with an inherent sympathy for heavenly reality, it actually reveals John's strong views on divine election and underscores the fact that truth is only apprehended through revelation. God's sheep have been marked from eternity so that they always "hear his voice" and come to him (10:14, 27); yet because of God's election they are considered to be his people long before they ever hear the words of Jesus (10:16; 11:52). In this way the revelation of truth becomes key to the cosmic dualism (above/below, heaven/earth, light/darkness) so characteristic of John's Gospel. By virtue of their election, disciples have received this revelation through faith in Jesus. Consequently, they become "sanctified by the truth" and set apart from the world (17:15-19), children of light who have nothing to do with the present system of darkness ruled by the father of lies (3:21; 8:42-47; *see* Demon, Devil, Satan).

This sovereign, divine transformation is the root of Johannine ethics. As children of God, disciples "live by the truth" (3:21), which is the same as "remaining in Jesus' teaching" (8:32). Genuinely knowing divine reality will inevitably be reflected in the way disciples live; they will obey everything that Jesus has taught them (14:15, 23; 15:10, 14; *see* Teacher). The disciple's life of obedience is the only true life because it is aligned with God (*see* Discipleship).

For example, disciples now worship the Father in Spirit and in truth (4:23-24). This does not direct disciples inwardly to examine motivations or sincerity; rather, it orients them outwardly, directing them to offer worship that is commensurate with who God truly is: The divine Spirit approached only through the incarnate Christ.

See also AMEN; LIGHT; LOGOS; TEACHER; WISDOM.

BIBLIOGRAPHY. S. Aalen, "Truth, A Key Word in St. John's Gospel," *SE* 2 (1964) 3-24; J. Barr, *The Semantics of Biblical Language* (Oxford: University Press, 1961) 187-205; R. E. Brown, *The Gospel according to John* (AB; Garden City, NY: Doubleday, 1966) 1.499-501; R. Bultmann et al., "ἀλήθεια κτλ," *TDNT* I.232-50; C. H. Dodd, *The Interpretation of the Fourth Gospel* (Cambridge: University Press, 1953) 170-78; J. Giblet, "Aspects of the Truth in the New Testament," *Concilium* 83 (1973) 35-42; D. J. Hawkin, "The Johannine Concept of Truth and Its Implications for a Technological Society," *EvQ* 59 (1987) 3-13; L. J. Kuyper, "Grace and Truth: An Old Testament Description of God and Its Use in the Fourth Gospel," *Int* 18 (1964) 3-19; I. de la Potterie, *La Verité dans Saint Jean* (2 vols.; Rome: Biblical Institute, 1977); A. Thiselton, "Truth," *NIDNTT* 3.874-902. D. M. Crump

TWELVE, THE. *See* APOSTLE; DISCIPLE; ISRAEL.

TWO-DOCUMENT HYPOTHESIS. *See* SYNOPTIC PROBLEM.

TYPOLOGY

The NT makes several comparisons between various OT and NT events, individuals and institutions. These comparisons are often expressed, sometimes explicitly, in terms of typology and constitute major components of christology and ecclesiology. But typology offers more than comparisons between specific events and details; it establishes important links between and within the testaments themselves. Typology therefore has played a significant role in the very formation of the biblical canon.* By means of typology, as well as by means of prophetic fulfillment, the NT writers present Jesus and the church* as the continuation and completion of the OT.

   1. Terminology, Meaning and Context
   2. Typology and First-Century Exegesis
   3. Jesus
   4. Jesus' Disciples

1. Terminology, Meaning and Context.

The biblical concept of typology is based upon the word *typos,* which literally means "impression," "mark" (Jn 20:25) or "image" (Acts 7:43), and metaphorically usually means "example" or "model" (Phil 3:17; 1 Thess 1:7; 2 Thess 3:9; 1 Tim 4:12; Tit 2:7; cf. *hypotypōsis* in 1 Tim 1:16; 2 Tim 1:13) or even "warn-

ing" (1 Cor 10:6, cf. *typikos* in 1 Cor 10:11). In hermeneutical contexts this word means something like "pattern" or "figure" (Heb 8:5). Although the hermeneutical usage of this word, and the related word *antitypos* ("copy" or "counterpart"; Heb 9:24; 1 Pet 3:21), is found only in the Pauline and General Epistles, important typologies are also present in the Gospels.

Typology is not unique to the NT. Within the OT itself typological comparisons are made. The Exodus story becomes a type of salvation* in Isaiah (Is 40:3-5; 43:16-24; 49:8-13), the wilderness rebellion (Ex 17:1-7; Num 20:1-13) is presented in Psalm 95:7-11 as an example of hardness of heart (*see* Hardness of Heart) that Israel* is to avoid, and Melchizedek, priest of Salem (Gen 14:18), is cited in Psalm 110:4 as a biblical example of the priestly role of the king.

Typology is not to be confused with allegory. Allegorical interpretation assigns, usually rather arbitrarily, so-called deeper meanings to biblical stories and their various details. The actual history of the biblical story is unimportant to this method of interpretation. But in typological interpretation history is essential. It is believed that the original historical event is the "type" and the later corresponding event is the "antitype" that parallels, perhaps fulfills and sometimes even transcends it.

2. Typology and First-Century Exegesis.

Because biblical exegesis in the early Jewish and Christian period was founded on the belief that Scripture contained the ever-relevant will of God, every effort was made to bring its teaching to bear upon the contemporary world and the concerns of the believing community. This effort lies behind all interpretive methods: allegorization, midrash,* pesher and typology. *Allegorization* discovers morals and theological symbols and truths from various details of Scripture; *pesher* seeks to unlock the prophetic mysteries hidden in Scripture and *midrash* seeks to update Torah and clarify obscurities and problems in Scripture. But *typology* represents the effort to coordinate the past and present (and future) according to the major events, persons and institutions of Scripture.

Despite their differences, there is significant overlap between these methods of interpretation. For example, to some extent all four involve a searching of Scripture (midrash); all four find symbolic meaning that transcends the letter of the text (allegory); all four recognize the presence of mystery and hidden truth within the text (pesher); and all four believe that to some extent the present and future are foreshadowed by biblical history (typology). To paraphrase B. D.

Chilton (138), the real difference among these methods is less a matter of method than what Scripture is essentially taken to be.

Emphasis on the unity of Scripture and history is the distinctive of typological interpretation. What God has done in the past (as presented in Scripture), he continues to do in the present (or will do in the future). Recent events or future events that are interpreted as salvific are frequently compared to major OT events of salvation. Such comparison does at least two things: (1) It lends credibility to the belief that the newer events are indeed part of the divine plan; and (2) it enables the interpreter to grasp more fully the theological significance of the newer events. Typological interpretation makes it possible for later communities of faith to discern the continuing activity of God in history. It is likely that these ideas lay behind the typologies that Jesus developed.

Typological interpretation is not limited to the NT; it is also found in rabbinical writings (*see* Rabbinic Traditions and Writings). Just as Israel prevailed over Amalek, as long as Moses was able to hold his hands high, so Israel has prospered when it has obeyed the Law* of Moses (*Mek. Amalek* §1 [on Ex 17:11]). The messianic age is often compared with the Exodus, a comparison frequently developed by typological interpretation. For example, when Messiah comes manna will once again be provided in the wilderness (*Mek., Vayassa* §4 [on Ex 16:13] and §6 [on Ex 16:33]).

3. Jesus.

Most christological typologies apparently derive from Jesus himself, though the Evangelists themselves sought in various ways to extend the typologies or develop new ones.

3.1. The Prophet. At the Transfiguration* the voice from heaven* enjoins the disciples,* "Hear him" (Mk 9:7 par.), an injunction that echoes Deuteronomy 18:15-18 and the promise that some day God would raise up a prophet* like Moses.* The point of the passage is that Jesus is this anticipated prophet (cf. Mk 8:28 par.; Lk 7:16). Unlike prophetic fulfillment, however, typology looks for broader points of comparison. Consequently, it comes as no surprise that the Transfiguration episode at many points parallels the Sinai theophany ("six days," Mk 9:2; Ex 24:16; presence of Moses, Mk 9:4; Ex 24:1-18; mountain setting, Mk 9:2; Ex 24:12 [*see* Mountain and Wilderness]; three companions, Mk 9:2; Ex 24:9 [cf. Deut 19:15]; changed face, Mk 9:3 [cf. Mt 17:2; Lk 9:29]; Ex 34:29-30; cloud, Mk 9:7; Ex 24:15-16 [cf. 2 Macc 2:8]; heavenly voice, Mk 9:7; Ex 24:16; fear, Mk 9:6; Ex 34:30). The point of these parallels is that once again

a major act of salvation is being revealed.

Elsewhere in the NT Jesus is explicitly identified as the awaited prophet-like-Moses (Acts 3:22-23; 7:37; cf. Jn 6:14-15; 7:40). Moses typology lies behind the infancy narrative in Matthew (2:13-20; cf. Ex 1:15—2:10; *see* Birth of Jesus), the Sermon on the Mount* (esp. Mt 5:1-48), the Fourth Evangelist's portrait of Jesus (1:14-17; 2:1-10; 3:14-15; 4:7-26; 6:25-65; 7:37-39; 10:1-18) and various miracles, notably the feeding of the five and four thousand (Mk 6:35-44; 8:1-9 par.).

The prophet typology is also supplemented by parallels with and allusions to the Elijah-Elisha tradition (*see* Elijah and Elisha). Jesus is the prophet whose requirements for discipleship* are more demanding than those of Elijah (Lk 9:61-62; 1 Kings 19:19-21), but who is also more compassionate and long-suffering (Lk 4:25-27; 9:52-56; 2 Kings 1:9-12). The Lukan portrait of the ascension* also reflects Elijah typology (Lk 24:51; Acts 1:9; 3:21; 2 Kings 2:1, 11). In reference to prophetic tradition in general, Jesus' anticipation of death in Jerusalem (Mt 23:37 par.) reflects typological thinking.

3.2. Son of David. Throughout the Gospels Jesus is called "Son of David."* Although typology is clearly at work, literal descent from David is claimed (Mt 1:20; Lk 1:27; 2:4; Rom 1:3). Matthew's infancy narrative emphasizes Jesus' Davidic kingship. This is seen especially in the genealogy* (Mt 1:1, 6, 17); the citation of Isaiah 7:14 (Mt 1:23), an oracle originally addressed to King Ahaz; the visit of the Magi (Mt 2:2, "Where is he who was born king of the Jews?"); the citation of Micah 5:2, part of a larger oracle (Mic 5:2-6) that promised a king like David; and King Herod's interest and fear (Mt 2:3-18). The Davidic typology is also seen in Jesus' ministry. The blind man cries out to Jesus as "Son of David" (Mk 10:47-48). Jesus justifies his action and the action of his disciples by appeal to the action of David and his men (Mk 2:25-26; *see* Abiathar). If David can violate a cultic law (1 Sam 21:1-6), then surely can Jesus, who is greater than David (indeed, is "Lord of the Sabbath," Mk 2:28). Finally, Jesus was hailed as Son of David when he entered Jerusalem (Mt 21:9; *see* Triumphal Entry).

The most significant comparison with David is that drawn by Jesus himself. Jesus' quotation of Psalm 110:1 and the point that he makes about David's son was meant to draw a comparison between himself and Israel's famous king (Mk 12:35-37 par.) and not simply to pose an exegetical riddle. It is likely that Jesus implied that, although he is like David, in that he is "David's son," he is superior to David, in that he is "David's Lord" (cf. Mt 12:42 par. where Jesus declares that one [i.e., he himself] "greater than Solomon is here"). Jesus is not only David's son; he is his Lord. Behind this claim lies typological thinking. David is the type (of Messiah), Jesus the antitype.

3.3. Son of Man. It is commonly asserted that the "Son of man"* sayings in the Gospels fall into two disparate categories: the Son of man who identifies with and suffers for humanity, and the Son of man who comes in judgment* (with the latter possibly authentic and the former probably not). It is more likely, however, that these sayings form a typological unity founded on Daniel 7 (and not *1 Enoch* 37-71 and *4 Ezra* 13 as is often assumed) and that they do indeed derive from Jesus. (There is little evidence that these sayings or the title "Son of man" were of special interest to the early church. Hence the likelihood that they derive from Jesus.) Jesus probably saw himself as the fulfillment of the prophesied Son of man of Daniel 7, who stands with the saints and, after initial opposition and defeat, overcomes and receives the kingdom. Jesus' sayings about rejection, suffering and death (Mk 8:31; 9:31; 10:33; 14:21; *see* Predictions of Jesus' Passion and Resurrection) reflect the first aspect (an aspect enriched by allusions to the Suffering Servant; see 3.4. below), while the sayings that speak of vindication (Mk 9:9; 13:26; 14:62) reflect the second.

3.4. Servant of the Lord. Four times in Acts, where Isaianic and Davidic themes are combined, Jesus is called the "Servant" (*pais*; cf. Acts 3:13, 26; 4:27, 30; *see* Servant of Yahweh). Although in the Gospels Jesus is never so designated, Servant typology nevertheless appears to be present. Four times Second Isaiah's Servant Songs are quoted and applied to Jesus. Jesus' healing ministry fulfills Isaiah 53:4 (Mt 8:14-17). Jesus' injunctions to silence fulfill Isaiah 42:1-4 (Mt 12:15-21; cf. Is 53:7-8 in Acts 8:32-33). His impending arrest fulfills Isaiah 53:12 (Lk 22:37). Finally, the unbelief of the people fulfills Isaiah 53:1 (Jn 12:37-38). It is noteworthy that in every instance these Isaianic passages are cited as "fulfilled." There are also important allusions to the Servant Songs. The righteous sufferer predicts his rejection and death (Mk 9:12; Is 53:3). When accused he remains silent (Mk 14:60-61; Is 53:7; cf. Acts 8:32-33). He is beaten (Mk 14:65; Is 50:6). He intercedes for sinners* (Is 53:11-12; Lk 23:34, 42-43). He dies in the company of criminals (Mk 15:27; Is 53:9). His death is on behalf of many (Mk 10:45; 14:24; Is 53:11-12), and he is buried in a rich man's tomb (Mt 27:57-60; Is 53:9; *see* Burial of Jesus).

3.5. Second Adam. Luke's arrangement of Jesus' genealogy* (Lk 3:23-38; cf. Mt 1:2-16) and its juxtaposition with the temptation narrative (Lk 4:1-13; *see* Temptation of Jesus) constitute an Adam-Christ

typology. Unlike Paul's similar typology (Rom 5:12-21), with which the Evangelist may or may not have been familiar, the point of comparison is not so much between the first and second *Adam*, but the First and Second *Son of God*. According to Luke, Adam and Jesus were "sons of God" by virtue of their being directly created by God's Spirit (Gen 2:7; Lk 1:35; *see* Holy Spirit). In order to heighten the comparison, Luke has his genealogy conclude (not begin) with "Adam, the Son of God" (Lk 3:38). This conclusion contrasts deliberately with the opening question of the temptation narrative, "If you are the Son of God" (Lk 4:3). Unlike the first Son of God who fell when tempted by Satan (*see* Demon, Devil, Satan), Jesus, the second Son of God, does not. Here again Jesus is presented in typological fashion as the antitype that parallels and in this case clearly transcends the type.

3.6. Righteous Sufferer. The function of the psalms of lament in the Gospels, especially in the passion narratives, reflects a righteous sufferer typology. Jesus is betrayed by his friends (Mk 14:18; Ps 41:9; 55:12-14). He is sorrowful (Mk 14:34; Ps 43:5). He is falsely accused (Mk 14:56 par.; Ps 27:12). Pilate (*see* Pontius Pilate) washes his hands of Jesus' death (Mt 27:24; Ps 26:6). Jesus' clothes are divided among his enemies (Mk 15:24; Ps 22:18). He is mocked (Mk 15:29-31; Ps 22:7-8; 109:25). He thirsts (Jn 19:28; Ps 69:21). He is given vinegar to drink (Mk 15:36; Ps 69:21). He is abandoned by God (Mk 15:34; Ps 22:1). His friends do not stand by him (Lk 23:49; Ps 38:11), and in death he commits his soul to God (Lk 23:46; Ps 31:5). Allusions to the Servant Songs of Second Isaiah add further details to this typology (see 3.4. above; Death of Jesus).

3.7. Jonah. According to Matthew 12:39-41 (cf. Lk 11:16, 29-32), the only sign that was to be given to Jesus' generation was the "sign of Jonah"*: "For just as Jonah was in the belly of the great fish three days and three nights, so shall the Son of man be in the heart of the earth three days and three nights" (v 40; cf. Jon 1:17). The sign to which Jesus alludes is his death, burial and resurrection* "on the third day" (1 Cor 15:4; cf. Mk 9:32; 10:34). There are two parts to this typological interpretation: (1) Jesus' death, burial and resurrection correspond to the experience of Jonah; and (2) Jesus, like Jonah (Jon 3:4-5), calls for repentance. Again, Jesus understands himself not simply like Jonah but as "something greater than Jonah" (Mt 12:41). Because the people of Nineveh responded to Jonah's preaching, whose only sign was his remarkable deliverance from the great fish, the people of Jesus' generation are without excuse, for Jesus himself is greater than Jonah, and his attesting sign, his resurrection from the dead, is also greater.

3.8. Rejected Stone. Before the time of Jesus the stone idea had already taken on typological meaning. The "stone," laid by God, could be a stone of stumbling (Is 8:14) or a stone of faith (Is 28:16). The rejected stone of Psalm 118:22-23 was understood to be Israel, who, although rejected by the nations, would some day enjoy a favored place. Finally, Daniel 2:45, where the stone has a messianic nuance, describes the destruction of Israel's enemies. At the conclusion of his parable* of the wicked vineyard tenants (Mk 12:1-9) Jesus quotes Psalm 118:22-23 ("The stone which the builders rejected has become the cornerstone") and applies it to himself (Mk 12:10-11). Assuming that the charge later brought against Jesus ("We heard him say, 'I shall destroy this Temple made with hands and in three days I shall build another without hands' " [Mk 14:58]) approximates something Jesus actually said (cf. Jn 2:19), it is quite possible that Jesus thought of himself as the foundation of a new community of faith* and worship.* Luke's version of the rejected stone saying is unique ("Everyone who falls upon that stone will be broken; upon whomever it should fall, he will be crushed" [Lk 20:18]), probably reflecting parts of Daniel 2:45 and Isaiah 8:14, and adds an element of judgment. This typology is foundational to the early community's self-understanding (see 4. below).

3.9. High Priest. Although by no means certain, the high priest (see Priest and Priesthood) typology of Hebrews (cf. Heb 4—7) may derive in part from certain priestly prerogatives that Jesus had assumed. The most significant of these were his declarations of the forgiveness* of sins (Mk 2:5-10; Lk 7:48). Perhaps his cleansing pronouncements (Mk 1:41; see Clean and Unclean), his action in the Temple (Mk 11:15-17; see Cleansing of the Temple) and his intercessory prayers* (Lk 22:32, "Peter, I have prayed for you"; 23:34, "Father, forgive them"), including the so-called high-priestly prayer (Jn 17:9, 20), also contributed to this later typology of Jesus as the ultimate high priest.

3.10. Sacrifice. The sacrifice typology in Hebrews (cf. Heb 7—10) may have its roots in an early interpretation of the significance of Jesus' death, possibly an interpretation that derives from Jesus' anticipation and understanding of his death. If authentic, the statements found in Mark 10:45 and 14:24 would support this notion (see Ransom Saying). It has also been suggested that John 1:29 ("Behold, the Lamb of God, who takes away the sin of the world") may reflect Jewish tradition of the ᵃqēdaṭ yiṣḥāq ("the binding of Isaac") and the promise given to Abraham* that God will provide a lamb (see Lamb of God). Such a typology understands Jesus' death as the ultimate sacrifice

which need never be repeated (see Church).

4. Jesus' Disciples.
The earliest ecclesiology also derives from Jesus and in large measure is expressed with significant typologies (see Church).

4.1. The "Twelve." Jesus' appointment of twelve apostles* (Mk 3:14), clearly an allusion to the twelve tribes of Israel, in all probability symbolized reconstituted Israel. The twelve apostles will also function as Israel's rulers in the kingdom (perhaps as new tribal patriarchs), "sitting on twelve thrones, judging the twelve tribes of Israel" (Mt 19:28; cf. Lk 22:28-30; Ps 122:3-5; Dan 7:9). Recognizing the importance of this symbolism, Luke does not neglect to tell us of the replacement of the betrayer (Acts 1:15-26). The Twelve also function as emissaries of their king in carrying out their mission of evangelism (Mt 10:1-42; 28:18-20; Lk 24:45-49; Acts 1:6-8; see Kingdom of God).

4.2. The People of the New Covenant. The new covenant idea in the Gospels reflects Passover traditions and the promise of the "new covenant" of Jeremiah 31:31-34. The new covenant is explicitly alluded to in the words of the Lord's Supper*: "This is my blood of the [new] covenant which is poured out for many" (Mk 14:24 and par.). Jewish haggadic tradition believed that the blood shed at the first Passover was the blood that established the covenant later proclaimed at Sinai (*Tg. Zech* 9:11; *Mek. Pish* §5 [on Ex 12:6]). Just as the blood of the lambs at the first Passover delivered Israel from judgment and made the old covenant possible, so too will the shed blood of Jesus deliver the people of God and establish the new covenant.

4.3. The Spiritual Temple. Jesus' prophetic demonstration in the Temple* (Mk 11:15-17 par.), his implicit criticism of and threat against the ruling priests (Mk 12:1-11; cf. *Tg. Isa* 5:1-7), his explicit pronouncement of the Temple's impending destruction (Mk 13:2: "not one stone will be left upon another"), the accusation brought against Jesus at his trial before the Sanhedrin* (Mk 14:58: "I shall destroy this Temple made with hands and in three days I shall build another without hands") and his personal comparison with the Temple (Mt 12:6: "Something greater than the Temple is here"; cf. Jn 2:19-21) form part of a spiritual Temple typology. In these various statements one is given the impression that Jesus has replaced Jerusalem's Temple with himself and the community of those who believe in him. This idea, however, may not have been unique to Jesus, for the people of Qumran may have held to a similar idea (4QFlor 1:6: "a sanctuary of men"). 1 Peter 2:4-8 reflects a later and more explicit expression of this typology.

See also MIDRASH; OLD TESTAMENT IN THE GOSPELS.

BIBLIOGRAPHY. B. D. Chilton, "Commenting on the Old Testament," in *It Is Written: Scripture Citing Scripture: Essays in Honour of Barnabas Lindars,* ed. D. A. Carson and H. G. M. Williamson (Cambridge: University Press, 1988) 122-40; R. M. Davidson, *Typology in Scripture: A Study of Hermeneutical ΤΥΠΟΣ Structures* (Berrien Springs, MI: Andrews University, 1981); J. W. Drane, "Typology," *EvQ* 50 (1978) 195-210; R. A. Edwards, *The Sign of Jonah* (SBT, 2d series, 18; London: SCM, 1971); L. Goppelt, *Typos: The Typological Interpretation of the Old Testament in the New* (Grand Rapids: Eerdmans, 1982); idem, "Τύπος κτλ," *TDNT* VIII.246-59; R. N. Longenecker, *The Christology of Early Jewish Christianity* (SBT, 2d series, 17; London: SCM, 1970); G. R. Osborne, "Type," *ISBE* 4.930-32; D. Patte, *Early Jewish Hermeneutic in Palestine* (SBLDS 22; Missoula: Scholars, 1975) 159-67.

C. A. Evans

V

VENGEANCE. *See* GENTILES; JUDGMENT.

VINE, FRUIT OF THE VINE

The word "vine" (*ampelos*) is used six times in the Gospels. In the Synoptics it occurs at the Last Supper* in Jesus' reference to wine* as "the fruit of the vine" (*to genēmatos tēs ampelou*, lit., "the produce of the vine," Mt 26:29; Mk 14:25; Lk 22:18). In John it appears three times in Jesus' description of himself as the true vine (*hē ampelos hē alēthinē*, 15:1, 4-5). In the accounts of the Last Supper the phrase "the fruit of the vine" is only used once in each Synoptic Gospel. The more usual reference is to "the cup (of blessing)" (Mt 26:27; Mk 14:23; Lk 22:17, 20; cf. 1 Cor 10:16; 11:25). The common word for wine (*oinos*) is not used at all.

1. Background.

It is sometimes suggested on the basis of texts such as Numbers 6:4; Deuteronomy 22:9; Isaiah 32:12 and Habakkuk 3:17 that the phrase "the fruit of the vine" is an expression used for wine in the Old Testament. In none of these passages, however, does the exact phrase "the fruit of the vine" occur, nor is there explicit reference to wine. The LXX of Numbers 6:4 interprets the unusual Hebrew *miggepen hayyayin* (lit., "from the vine of the wine") as referring explicitly to wine but the use of this same expression in Judges 13:14 shows that it refers to something other than wine. The LXX of Isaiah 32:12 comes the closest (*ampelou genēmatos*) but should be translated "fruitful vine" (cf MT: *gepen pôriyâ*).

While our phrase is not in the OT, it was very familiar in Jesus' day, due to its frequent liturgical usage. It occurs in the Mishnah in a section concerning the appropriate blessings for various forms of fruit: "What Benediction do they say over fruits? Over the fruit of trees a man says, '[Blessed art thou . . .] who createst the fruit of the tree,' except over wine, for over wine a man says '. . . who createst the fruit of the vine' [*pᵉrî haggepen*]" (*m. Ber.* 6:1, Danby). There was debate over whether this blessing was only for drinking-wine (i.e., wine that had been mixed with

water) or all wine (*m. Ber.* 7:5; *t. Ber.* 4:3). If this debate goes back to the time of Jesus, it would raise the question of whether he mixed the water before the blessing, but not which blessing he used; the phrase "fruit of the vine" indicates he used the blessing for wine. Later, *pᵉrî haggepen* is the way of referring to the blessing over the cup (*b. Pesah.* 103a). It can even be considered as the Great *Qiddûš* (consecration), "for all blessings [of *Qiddûš*] we first say '. . . who createst the fruit of the vine' " (*b. Pesah.* 106a). This phrase in the Gospels confirms that the language in these later Jewish sources is itself early.

Thus, when Jesus refers to wine as "the fruit of the vine" he uses language associated with prayer.* Such language is especially fitting for the vow he is taking since wine is a sign of God's blessing (e.g., Gen 27:28, 37; Joel 2:24) and gift of joy (Ps 104:15), and he will now abstain until the coming of the kingdom, God's ultimate blessing and gift of joy (*see* Kingdom of God).

2. Gospel of John.

John's use of *ampelos* also occurs in the context of the Last Supper. Indeed, the passage on the vine in John 15 serves as a meditation on "the fruit of the vine" and the associated cup in the Synoptics since they are each concerned with the common eucharistic theme of sharing in Christ (Barrett, Brown).

The symbols in John's Gospel, including vine, "are drawn from everyday life, but derive their significance from the rich associations they have acquired in the OT and apocalyptic* literature" (Culpepper). Vine (*gepen*) is used many times in the OT to represent Israel* (Ps 80:8, 14; Jer 2:21; 6:9; 8:13; Ezek 15:1-8; 17:6-8; 19:10-14; Hos 10:1; 14:7; cf. 2 Esdr 5:23, *vinea*), as is the associated image of the vineyard (*kerem*, Is 3:14; 5:1-7; Jer 12:10). The vine/vineyard is the people of God, planted and cultivated by God for his delight and the produce it should yield.

Most of these texts include the theme of God's judgment* against Israel; the vine has not proved fruitful in that Israel has been unfaithful. The same use of these images is continued in the Synoptic

Gospels (Mt 20:1-16; 21:28-46; Mk 12:1-12; Lk 20:9-19; 13:6-9). The image of the vine is thus almost always associated with the contrast between God's ideal for his people and their falling short of it.

With such associations attaching to this image, Jesus' claim to be the "true" vine is very dramatic. This image, as with all of the symbols in John, is used for the "exploration of Jesus' identity and the responses to him" (Culpepper). Jesus is the "real" vine, the vine that is the fullness of that which is only partial or even false in other vines. Jesus, the completely obedient Son, embodies what Israel was meant to be. This image expresses Jesus' own perfect sonship and contrasts it with the faithlessness of the Jews who were rejecting him, a theme clearly present in the context (Jn 15:18—16:4a).

As the image is developed in John 15:1-17 emphasis is placed on the relation between Jesus and his disciples,* some of whom remain and others of whom are cast out. Jesus does not call himself the stalk but rather the vine, that is, the whole plant. Since the disciples are a part of the plant only as they remain in him, this image contributes to a key theme in John that believers are one with God in Christ (17:20-23, cf. the image of the body in Paul and texts such as Acts 9:5 and Eph 1:23). As the image is developed in 15:1-17, it is clear that as the disciples remain in Jesus, the true vine, they are that faithful, fruitful vine/vineyard that God was looking for in Israel.

The vine image is used in 15:1-17 to develop such important aspects of discipleship* as love,* faith,* remaining (*see* Abiding) and obedience, topics further developed in 1 John. Indeed, the parallels with 1 John

are strong enough to convince some scholars that it is "absolutely necessary" to assign 15:1-17 to the same life situation as 1 John (Segovia).

Thus the thought conveyed through this image in John is very rich, adding dimensions to an already well-used Old Testament image. In turn it seems to have influenced not only Christian thought but also other traditions, in particular the Mandaean religion (Behm).

See also LAST SUPPER; WINE.

BIBLIOGRAPHY. C. K. Barrett, *The Gospel According to St John: An Introduction with Commentary and Notes on the Greek Text* (2d ed.; Philadelphia: Westminster, 1978); J. Behm, "ἄμπελος" *TDNT* I.342-3; C. Brown, "Vine, Wine," *NIDNTT* 3.918-23; R. E. Brown, *The Gospel According to John (xiii-xxi)* (AB 29A; Garden City, NY: Doubleday, 1970); R. A. Culpepper, *Anatomy of the Fourth Gospel: A Study in Literary Design* (Philadelphia: Fortress, 1983); C. H. Dodd, *The Interpretation of the Fourth Gospel* (Cambridge: University Press, 1953); R. Hentschke, "gelpen," *TDOT* III.53-61; J. Jeremias, *The Eucharistic Words of Jesus* (New York: Scribners, 1966); F. F. Segovia, *Love Relationships in the Johannine Tradition: Agapē/Agapan in I John and the Fourth Gospel* (SBLDS 58; Atlanta: Scholars Press, 1982).

R. A. Whitacre

VIOLENCE. *See* PEACE.

VIRGIN BIRTH. *See* BIRTH OF JESUS.

VOWS. *See* OATHS AND SWEARING.

W

WAR. *See* Destruction of Jerusalem; Military; Peace; Revolutionary Movements.

WASHING. *See* Clean and Unclean

WATCHFULNESS. *See* Apocalyptic Teaching; Gethsemane.

WATER

The arid climate of Palestine and the absence of major rivers for agriculture gave a unique value to water in its culture. When Moses* described this land to the Israelites he had to explain that it did not have a river like Egypt's Nile, but that it "drinks water from heaven" (Deut 11:11). The Jordan River has a constant flow but is inaccessible to the central mountains. And it has only been recently that Israeli engineers have succeeded in pumping water from the Sea of Galilee (*see* Galilee) into the rest of the country.

In antiquity all life in Israel depended on rainfall which fell sporadically from mid-October through mid-March. Even though the coastal plain could boast 15-20 inches of rain per year—and the mountains around Jerusalem even more (20-25 inches)—drought was a constant threat (Gen 26:1; Acts 11:28). Thus, springs and wells were a commonplace feature of life (Gen 21:30; Jn 4:11-12). Water could even be stored in open pools (Jn 5:2-7) or cisterns (Jer 2:13). But despite these systems, everyone knew the quality of "living water" or running water which brimmed with refreshment.

In the Gospels "water" (*hydōr*) occurs thirty-nine times. These include references to the Sea of Galilee where Peter walks on the water (Mt 14:28), swine who rush headlong into the lake (Mt 8:32) and the disciples'* boat which fills in the storm before Jesus exerts his authority (Lk 8:23-25). In the Middle East water is also the primary means of refreshment. Feet were washed as a sign of hospitality (Lk 7:44; Jn 13:5). Jesus even illustrates generosity by describing the offer of a cup of cold water to a stranger (Mt 10:42; Mk 9:41).

This interest and respect for water led to its symbol-

ic and ritual use. Hand washing was observed before and after meals (Mk 7:2-23). Ritual bathing was well known in Judaism,* as was baptism,* which washed not just the body, but symbolically cleansed the soul (*see* Clean and Unclean). This is illustrated well at the Dead Sea Community of Qumran (*see* Dead Sea Scrolls) which constructed an elaborate system of ritual baths. These have also been found at Masada and in the south wall excavations of the Jerusalem Temple.* Worshippers in Jerusalem would no doubt bathe as they approached the Temple staircase. John the Baptist's (*see* John the Baptist) call "repent and be baptized" could thus be translated "repent and immerse yourself." Jesus is thus baptized in water (Mt 3:11; Mk 1:8; Lk 3:16; Jn 1:26) to hallmark the righteousness (*see* Justice, Righteousness) and purity which the kingdom of God will demand (*see* Kingdom of God).

If water symbolized life,* cleansing, refreshment and renewal, it comes as no surprise to learn that it symbolized the Holy Spirit* (Is 44:3-4; Ezek 36:25-26). This is why the Bible describes the Spirit as "poured out" (Joel 2:28-29; Acts 2:17; 10:45) and believers as being "filled" (Lk 1:15, 41). In the eschatological vision described by Zechariah 14, Jerusalem itself would give birth to a mighty spring of water which would create two rivers, one flowing west to the Mediterranean, the other flowing east to the Dead Sea. In the NT era rabbinic interpreters viewed this effluence as a symbol of the Spirit which would flow in abundance in the messianic age (*see* Eschatology).

The Fourth Gospel knows this theological symbolism well and uses it fully to express the new gift of life brought by Christ. John employs *hydōr* twenty-one times (compared with Matthew seven times, Mark five times and Luke six times). In addition to John's account of Jesus' baptism (1:26-34), seven other passages introduce unique uses of water: Jesus' miracle* of water and wine* at Cana (2:1-11), the challenge to Nicodemus (3:1-15), Jesus' offer of living water to the Samaritan* woman* (4:7-42), the lame man at the pool of Bethesda (5:1-18), Jesus' announcement at Tabernacles (7:37-39; *see* Feasts), the washing of the disciples' feet (13:1-20), and the blood and water from Jesus' side (19:34).

In John water sometimes represents the old institutions of Judaism which require complete transformation (Samaria, Cana, Bethesda). These cannot be ignored (i.e., Nicodemus must be reborn "in water and Spirit"), but in each instance they must be changed. Ritual water becomes wine, well water becomes living or running water. Above all, for John water is a frequent metaphor for the Spirit (see 7:39). It symbolizes the spiritual renewal promised in the OT prophets and offered in Christ. This living water is flowing within Christ (7:37-38) who becomes a renewing spring from whom we are invited to drink (4:13-14). At his death (*see* Death of Jesus), his Spirit is released—this water is poured forth (19:34)—and the fulfillment of Jewish eschatological hope begins. No doubt within the theology of the Fourth Gospel, Jesus' Tabernacles discourse is at the heart of this water imagery. Here in a season of threatening drought when the prayer for autumn rain is heard and the eschatological rivers of Zechariah 14 are symbolized, Jesus announces that he is the source of the promise and its fulfillment. He is the fountain from which the Holy Spirit may be obtained.

BIBLIOGRAPHY. D. Baly, *Basic Biblical Geography* (Philadelphia: Fortress 1987) 19-26; O. Bocher, "Water," *NIDNTT* 3.982-93; G. Burge, *The Anointed Community* (Grand Rapids: Eerdmans, 1987); J. Dunn, *Baptism in the Holy Spirit* (Philadelphia: Westminster, 1977); idem, *Jesus and the Spirit* (Philadelphia: Westminster, 1979); L. Goppelt, "ὕδωρ," *TDNT* VIII.314-33; R. K. Harrison, "Water," *ISBE* 4.1024-26; G. A. Smith, *The Historical Geography of the Holy Land* (rev. ed.; London: Hodder and Stoughton, 1931).

G. M. Burge

WEALTH. *See* RICH AND POOR.

WEDDING. *See* BRIDE; BRIDEGROOM.

WEDDING AT CANA. *See* WINE.

WEEKS, FEAST OF. *See* FEASTS.

WICKED. *See* SINNER.

WILDERNESS. *See* MOUNTAIN AND WILDERNESS.

WILL OF GOD. *See* COMMANDMENT; JUSTICE, RIGHTEOUSNESS; LAW.

WINE

The fermented juice of the grape and other fruits. Wine was an important drink in the ancient world, and it figures significantly in the imagery of Jesus' parables* and proclamation in the Gospels.

1. Terminology and Types
2. Production
3. Use of Wine
4. The Biblical Attitude toward Wine
5. Drunkenness
6. The Wedding at Cana

1. Terminology and Types.

The main words for wine are the Hebrew *yayin*, the Aramaic *ḥᵃmar* (6 times: Ezra 6:9; 7:22; Dan 5:1-2, 4, 23), and Greek *oinos*. Other Hebrew terms include *sobe'* (Is 1:22; Hos 4:18; Nahum 1:10) and *ḥemer* (Deut 32:14; Is 27:2). The main words for new wine are Hebrew *tîrôš* (Is 65:8; Hos 9:2; Joel 2:24; Mic 6:15; Hab 1:11; Zech 9:17) and Greek *oinos* (LXX), *oinos neos* (Mt 9:17; Mk 2:22; Lk 5:37-39) and *gleukos* (Acts 2:13). A poetic synonym of *tîrôš* is *'āsîs* (Song 8:2; Joel 1:5; 3[4]:18; Amos 9:13). All wine mentioned in the Bible is fermented grape juice with an alcohol content. No non-fermented drink was called wine.

New wine is wine from the most recent harvest, while old wine is wine of a previous year's harvest (*m. B. Bat.* 6.3). Of the two, old wine was preferred because it was sweeter and stronger (Sir 9:10; Lk 5:39). At Qumran new wine (*tîrôš*) was their normal drink (1QS 6:4-6; 1QSa 2:17-18, 20; 1QH 10:24). New wine was fermented, as references to its ability to cause intoxication indicate (Is 49:26; Hos 4:11; Acts 2:13; cf. Judg 9:13), but it was not fermented as long as other wine (Joel 2:24), or barely more than grape juice (Is 65:8; Mic 6:15). The LXX usually translates *tîrôš* as *oinos*, and the latter was definitely fermented.

Strong drink (Heb *šēkār*, Gk *sikera*) was a fermented beverage not made from the grapes but from barley and was more akin to beer (Prov 20:1; Is 24:9). The word is related to *šākar*, "to be or become drunk" (Gen 9:21; Is 29:9; Jer 25:27). Strong drink was definitely intoxicating (Is 28:7-8; 29:9; cf. 1 Sam 1:15). With the exception of Numbers 28:7, where it is used as an older term for wine, strong drink is always coupled with wine. The pair "wine and strong drink" occurs in contexts that warn against, forbid or denigrate their use (Lev 10:9; Num 6:3; Deut 29:6; Judg 13:4, 7, 14; 1 Sam 1:15; Prov 20:1; 31:4, 6; Is 5:11, 22; 24:9; 28:7; 29:9; 56:12; Mic 2:11; Lk 1:15; cf. Deut 14:26).

Synonyms for wine are the blood of the grape (Gen 49:11; Deut 32:14; Sir 39:26; 50:15), fruit of the vine* (Mk 14:25 par.; cf. Is 32:12) or the cup (Mk 14:22-23 par.; 1 Cor 11:25). Wine is explicitly attested to be typically red (Prov 23:31). Other indications of color are the red discoloring of the clothing of winetreaders (Is 63:2-3; cf. Rev 14:20), the poetic synonym for wine as "the blood of grapes" (cf. Gen 49:11-12) and the analogy of wine as blood at the Lord's Supper (cf. Mk 14:23-24 par; 1 Cor 11:25).

Wine could also be made from pomegranates (Song 8:2), raisins (*b. B. Bat.* 97b), apples, dates, honey, herbs and figs. However, wine from grapes predominated. Wine was also often classified by its color or age, or by the region of its origin. The wine of Helbon (Ezek 27:18) and the wine of Lebanon (Hos 14:7[8]) were well known.

Wine could also be mixed with spices (Song 8:2; cf. Ps 75:8 [9]; Prov 9:2, 5; 23:30), balsam, honey and pepper, or oil and garum (*b. 'Abod. Zar.* 30a). Jesus was offered wine mixed with myrrh while dying on the cross (Mt 27:34 par. Mk 15:23).

2. Production.

To produce wine the grapes were usually stomped in winepresses (Num 18:27; Judg 6:11; 7:25; Job 24:11; Is 16:10; 63:3; Joel 3[4]:13; Zech 14:10). These presses were usually stone (cf. Is 5:2), but could also be constructed of a pit in the ground coated with plaster and covered with pitch (cf. Mt 21:33; Mk 12:1) or of wood or pottery coated with pitch. The stone press usually consisted of two rectangular rock-hewn pits, one higher than the other and connected with a channel. Presses with three or four pits have also been discovered. As the juice was expressed in the upper, wider, shallower pit (Job 24:11; Is 16:10; 63:1-3; Jer 25:30; 48:33; Joel 3[4]:13; Mic 6:15), it flowed through a channel into the lower, smaller, deeper fermenting compartment(s), leaving the lees or dregs of the grapes in the upper pit.

After four to six days the expressed juice was drawn off and placed in stone jars lined with pitch (called *amphorae* in Greece) (Jer 13:12; 48:11) or in whole tanned goatskins in which the apertures where the legs and tail were cut off had been sealed (1 Sam 1:24; 10:3; 16:20; 25:18; 2 Sam 16:1; Job 32:18-19; Mk 2:22 par.). Once the wine was in the skin the neck was tied off. As the wine fermented and released CO_2, the skin expanded (cf. Job 32:19). Fermentation begun in the press continued in the containers for two to four months.

Old wineskins could not be reused to store new wine because they had already expanded to their limit, and the expansion required in the fermentation of new wine would burst them. This is the source of the imagery in Jesus' saying about the wineskins (Mt 9:17 par. Mk 2:22 par. Lk 5:37-39).

The lees left in the upper pit were also pressed of whatever juice remained, thus creating a second-quality wine. This could be achieved by piling stones or planks on the husks, anchoring a press beam in the wall on one end, weighting it on the other and pressing out the remaining juice. Wine on the lees (Heb *š°mārîm*, Is 25:6; cf. Ps 75:8[9]; Jer 48:11; cf. Zeph 1:12) was wine that had matured in the container into which it had been poured and was thus resting on the particles of foreign matter that had settled out of the wine and fallen to the bottom of the container. Before drinking, wine was often strained through a linen cloth in order to remove lees, insects and other foreign matter (cf. Is 25:6; *m. Šabb.* 20.1-2). This practice lay behind Jesus' rebuke of the Pharisees* that they strained out a gnat but let a camel remain in the wine (Mt 23:24).

3. Use of Wine.

Wine was consumed at daily meals (Gen 14:18; Judg 19:19; 1 Sam 16:20; 2 Chron 11:11; Is 55:1; Dan 1:5; Lk 7:33-34). It was customary in Greek, Roman, Jewish and early Christian cultures to mix wine (2 Macc 15:39; *m. Ber.* 7:5; 8:2; *m. 'Abod. Zar.* 5:5; *b. Šabb.* 77a), usually with water (Is 1:22; cf. Ps 75:8[9]; Prov 9:2, 5; Is 65:11). The ratio of water to wine varied anywhere from twenty to one, averaging three to one as noted in ancient references (see Stein). Wine mixed with water acted as a purifier and made the water safe to drink (2 Macc 15:39; cf. 1 Tim 5:23).

Wine used at the Last Supper was probably mixed three parts water to one part wine. Wine began to be used in the Passover celebration in Hellenistic times (*Jub.* 49:6), was mixed three to one (*b. Pesah* 108b) and, as indicated in the Synoptic Gospels, the Last Supper* was a Passover meal. According to the church fathers, wine then used in the Lord's Supper was mixed (Justin Martyr *Apol.* 1.67; Hippolytus *Apos. Trad.* 23.1; Clement of Alexandria *Paed.* 2.2), and was so even in the original (Cyprian *Ep.* 62.2.11.13).

Jesus appropriated wine as an element of the Lord's Supper (Mt 26:27-29 par. Mk 14:23-25 par. Lk 22:20). As the "blood of the grape" wine symbolized his blood poured out as the blood of the Pascal lamb slaughtered for the redemption of humankind. Wine was the table drink used in fellowship meals to affirm Jesus' continued presence, anticipating the messianic banquet (Lk 22:17-18; *see* Table Fellowship).

Wine could also be used for medicinal purposes. Wine mixed with myrrh or gall was a drug. By offering this to Jesus the soldiers were trying to ease his pain (Mt 27:34; Mk 15:23; cf. Prov 31:6; *b. Sanh.* 43a). Wine and oil were used by the Good Samaritan to dress the wounds of the beaten man (Lk 10:34). Paul advises Timothy to take a little wine to help his digestion (1 Tim 5:23). The Talmud states that wine is the greatest of all medicines (b. B. Bat. 58b).

The ancients thought that wine was especially appreciated by the gods (Deut 32:37-38; Judg 9:13) and so wine was often a part of offerings to the gods (Deut 32:37-38; Is 57:6; 65:11; Jer 7:18; 19:13). In the Israelite cult, wine was poured out as a libation in the sacrifices of petition, thanksgiving and expiation (Ex 29:38-42; Num 15:2-19; 28:14; Lev 23:13; Hos 9:4; cf. Gen 35:14; Num 28:7). In ancient Israel priests were not to drink wine when ministering in the Temple* (Lev 10:9; Ezek 44:21).

Wine is usually associated with feasting and celebration (Esther 1:7-9; Is 25:6; Dan 5:1; Sir 31:31; cf. Is 22:13). It was used at coronations (1 Chron 12:39-40) and at weddings (Jn 2:1-11). In Hebrew the word for feasting or banquet (mišteh) derives from the word for drinking (šātāh) (Gen 21:8; Judg 14:10; 1 Sam 25:36; 2 Sam 3:20).

A great feast celebrated in the presence of God is common to the prophetic and apocalyptic imagery of later Judaism (Is 25:6; 1 Enoch 62:14; 2 Enoch 42:5) and anticipates the messianic heavenly banquet mentioned in Jesus' teaching (Mk 8:11; Mt 26:29 par. Mk 14:25; Lk 13:29-30). This feast is anticipated in the parables of the marriage feast (Mt 22:1-14; Lk 14:16-24) and the great banquet (Lk 14:7-14). Wine was a natural element in such feasts (Is 25:6).

Wine is used metaphorically in both testaments, particularly in the prophets. Commonplace are the metaphors of God as the vinedresser and Israel as the vine* (Ps 80[79]:8-13; Is 5:1-7; Jer 2:21; Hos 10:1) or Jesus as the vine (Jn 15:1-11). God, or an agent of God, treading the winepress is a metaphor for divine judgment (Is 63:2-3; Lam 1:15; Joel 3[4]:13; Rev 14:19-20; 19:15). God's cup of judgment is also a metaphor of judgment (Ps 75:8[9]; Is 51:17, 22; Jer 25:15-16, 27-28; 49:12; Lam 4:21; Ezek 23:31-35; Hab 2:16; Rev 14:10; 16:19). In Rev 14:8 wine is a metaphor for worldly passion.

4. The Biblical Attitude toward Wine.
Both OT and NT view wine drinking favorably. Abundant wine was considered a sign of blessing and prosperity from God (Gen 27:28, 37; 49:11-12; Deut 7:13; Ps 104:15; Prov 31:6; Eccles 9:7; Joel 2:24; 3:18; Amos 9:13-14; Is 55:1; Zech 10:7) as was a season of good wine production (Jer 13:12; Joel 3:18; Amos 9:13-14). Wine was also considered a source of joy* (Judg 9:13; 2 Sam 13:28; Esther 1:10; Ps 104:15; Eccles 2:3;

9:7; 10:19; Is 24:11; Zech 10:7; Sir 31:27-28), one of the good things created for people (Sir 39:25-26). Conversely the lack of wine was a symbol of judgment* and calamity (Deut 28:30; Is 16:10; 24:11; 65:21; Jer 48:33; Joel 1:5; Amos 5:11; Mic 6:15; Zeph 1:13). In the Judeo-Christian tradition, complete abstinence from drinking was not the norm but the exception for reasons of strict religious purity. Daniel and his friends abstained from the king's wine, probably because it was somehow involved in the pagan cult and/or drinking it would be in violation of Jewish dietary laws (Dan 1:8-16). The Rechabites (Jer 35:1-19) also abstained from wine as part of their rejection of the urban culture for the more ancient desert nomad lifestyle that originally characterized Israel. Abstinence from wine, strong drink or any produce of the vine was the norm for the Nazirites as part of their vows (Num 6:1-4; Judg 13:4-5, 7, 14; cf. Amos 2:11-12). John the Baptist* abstained from drinking wine and may have been a Nazirite (Mt 11:18 par. Lk 7:33). This is strongly implied by the angel's announcement to his father, Zechariah, "he shall drink no wine nor strong drink" (Lk 1:15).

Jesus upheld the popular attitude toward wine. He drank wine (Mt 11:18-19 par. Lk 7:33-34; Mt 26:29; Lk 22:18) and permitted its use in festivities like the wedding of Cana (Jn 2:1-11). Jesus even used the imagery of wine to describe his teaching as "new wine" (Mt 9:17 par. Mk 2:22 par. Lk 5:37-39). The case for abstinence cannot be built from what the NT says of wine. Abstinence was not an issue in the early church, and there is no direct prohibition of the use of wine in the NT. However, as in the OT, drunkenness and excessive use of wine is forbidden. Moderation is the watchword (cf. Sir 31:25-30). The use of wine is dependent upon the conscience and the sensitivities of others. It is not to be indulged in if it will lead others to drink against their conscience (Rom 14:19-21; cf. Rom 15:1-3; 1 Cor 8:1-12; 10:23-11:1; Phil 2:4).

5. Drunkenness.
Drunkenness (Heb šikārôn [Jer 13:13; Ezek 23:33]; Gk methē [Lk 21:34; Rom 13:13; Gal 5:21], oinophlygia [1 Pet 4:3]) was a widespread vice in the Ancient Near East. Drunkenness is portrayed negatively in the OT and Jewish tradition, particularly in the prophets. Such characteristics as staggering, reeling, vomiting, loss of mental control, and the resulting addiction and poverty are commonly mentioned characteristics of drunkenness (Job 12:25; Ps 107:27; Prov 20:1; 21:17; 23:20-21, 29-35; 31:4-7; Is 5:11-12, 22; 19:14; 24:20; 28:7-8; 29:9; Jer 25:27; 48:26; 51:39, 57; Hos 4:11; Sir

19:1; 31:29-30; 1 Esdr 3:17b-24). Often a connection is drawn between drunkenness and sexual perversion, prostitution or immorality (Gen 9:20-27 [Noah]; Gen 19:30-38 [Lot]; Amos 2:8; Hab 2:15).

In the Law of Moses drunkenness is one of the characteristics of a hopelessly rebellious son who is subject to death (Deut 21:20-21). Drunkenness was clearly not to characterize those in a leadership position. The OT admonishes kings to stay away from strong drink (Prov 31:4-5), and leaders are chastised for being drunk (Is 56:11-12; Hos 7:5). Priests and prophets are judged for drunkenness, which prevents them from performing their duties (Is 28:7). In the NT no bishop, deacon or older woman who teaches younger women Christian ways (Titus 2:3-5) can be a drunkard (1 Tim 3:2-3, 8; Tit 1:7; 2:2-5). The understanding that no leader was to be a drunkard underlies the charge of the Pharisees that Jesus was a drunkard, the implication being that he should not be leading the people (Mt 11:18-19 par. Lk 7:33-34).

Jesus explicitly addresses drunkenness only once: "But take heed to yourselves lest your hearts be weighed down with dissipation and drunkenness and cares of this life, and that day come upon you suddenly like a snare . . ." (Lk 7:33-34 RSV). Here drunkenness is a part of the carnal life that poses a threat to salvation.* In addition to this explicit reference, the parables of Jesus contain the image of the drunken servant excluded from heaven* (Mt 24:45-51 par. Lk 12:42-48).

6. The Wedding at Cana.

In the Gospel of John, Jesus' first miracle is the changing of water into wine at the wedding of Cana. The account presents a host of challenges to interpretation, one of which is the role of wine. Jesus ordered that six stone jars be filled with water, each jar holding two or three measures. A measure is approximately eight gallons, so each jar held between sixteen and twenty-four gallons for a total capacity of 96 to 144 gallons. It is often asked why Jesus made wine at all and particularly such a large quantity.

It must be noted that both wine and its quantity are important symbols. In the Old Testament and Judaism abundant wine (and oil or milk) is a sign of the age of salvation (Jer 31:12; Joel 3[4]:18; Amos 9:13-14; 2 Apoc. Bar. 29:5; Sib. Or. 2.317-18; 3.620-23, 744-49). The image of abundant wine is associated with the blessing to accompany the arrival of the Messiah of Judah (Gen 49:11-12). The image of a banquet describes the coming time of messianic blessing (Is 25:6-8; 65:13; 1 Enoch 62:14; 2 Enoch 42:5; 2 Apoc. Bar. 29:8). In Jesus' parables the kingdom of God* is portrayed as a wed-

ding feast (Mt 9:14-15 par. Mk 2:18-20 and Lk 5:33-35; Mt 22:1-14 par. Lk 14:15-24; Mt 25:1-13; cf. Lk 12:36; Jn 3:29-30; Rev 19:7-9) or simply a feast (Mt 8:11-12). Jesus himself portrays the disciples in his presence as guests at a wedding (Mt 9:15; Mk 2:19; Lk 5:34).

John's account of Jesus' conversion of such a large quantity of water into wine at a wedding feast is one way of announcing that the kingdom of God, the eschatological time of salvation, had arrived in the presence of the long-awaited Messiah. Jesus shows himself to be the Son of God come down from heaven bringing the blessing of the eschatological age symbolized by abundant wine. The miracle of Cana allowed Jesus to manifest his glory* to his disciples and evoke their belief (Jn 2:11; cf. 1:14). It is also very likely that Jesus was fulfilling his obligations as a wedding guest. As invited guests Jesus and his disciples were expected to provide wedding gifts. Their presence at the festivities may have contributed to the wine shortage. Jesus' provision of wine saved the bridegroom the embarrassment of a shortage. Not only that, he relieved the bridegroom of the obligation to compensate for his lack of provision should any of his guests invite him to their weddings. Moreover, since the gift of wine was non-reciprocal, the bridegroom would not be obligated to reciprocate at the weddings of the disciples (see Derrett).

See also VINE, FRUIT OF THE VINE.

BIBLIOGRAPHY. C. Brown, "Vine, Wine," *NIDNTT* 3.918-23; J. P. Brown, "The Mediterranean Vocabulary of the Vine," *VT* 19 (1969) 146-70; A. Demsky, " 'Dark Wine' from Judah," *IEJ* 22 (1972) 233-34; D. M. Derrett, "Water into Wine," in *Law in the New Testament* (London: Darton, Longman & Todd, 1970) 228-46; J. Doller, "Der Wein in Bibel und Talmud," *Bib* 4 (1923) 143-67, 267-99; R. J. Forbes, *Studies in Ancient Technology* (Vol. 3, 2d ed. Leiden: Brill, 1965) 72-80; M. Jastrow, Jr., "Wine in the Pentateuchal Codes," *JAOS* 33 (1913) 180-92; H. F. Lutz, *Viticulture and Brewing in the Ancient Orient* (New York, 1922); S. M. Paul, "Classifications of Wine in Mesopotamian and Rabbinic Sources," *IEJ* 25 (1975) 42-44; I. W. Raymond, *The Teaching of the Early Church on the Use of Wine and Strong Drink* (Studies in History, Economics and Public Law 286; New York: Columbia University, 1927; rept. ed. New York: A M S Press, 1970); H. Seesemann, "οἶνος," *TDNT* V.162-66; R. H. Stein, "Wine-Drinking in New Testament Times," *CT* 19 (June 20, 1975) 9-11; V. Zapletal, "Der Wein in der Bibel," *BibS* (F) 21 (1920) 103-6.   D. F. Watson

WISDOM

In biblical thought wisdom has a wide range of

meaning. Wisdom can mean simply the practical skills and qualities which humans can acquire in order to live successfully, or wisdom can refer to God's knowledge and creative power which transcend human scrutiny. Given this range of meaning, it is extremely difficult to give a comprehensive definition of wisdom.

There are certain lines of development about wisdom, however, which can be traced from the OT through later Judaism* and, finally, to the Gospels. Two traditions are of particular importance: the relationship of wisdom and Law* (the rabbinic tradition*), and speculation about the end of history and the transcendent world (apocalypticism*). The Gospels utilize these traditions with varying emphases in their presentations of Jesus.

1. The Double Tradition (Q)
2. Matthew
3. The Fourth Gospel

1. The Double Tradition (Q).

Most of Jesus' wisdom sayings and the wisdom motifs which are applied to him in the Synoptic Gospels occur in the material shared by Matthew and Luke (the so-called double tradition, or Q*; *see* Synoptic Problem). It is now generally agreed that the shift from the presentation of Jesus as a wisdom teacher* to the presentation of Jesus as the final and most important messenger for the Wisdom of God had already been made in the double tradition. According to this view, a further development in the Synoptic tradition to an explicit wisdom christology occurs in Matthew, where Jesus is identified in some sense with divine Wisdom itself (Suggs, Robinson, Dunn, Burnett). Although Luke and Mark present wisdom sayings of Jesus, they show no interest in a wisdom christology, that is, in presenting the significance of Jesus and his status as the Christ* in terms of divine *Sophia* ("Wisdom").

1.1. Wisdom Material in the Double Tradition. The double tradition contains many aphoristic wisdom sayings of Jesus which do not necessarily distinguish him from any other Jewish wisdom teacher (e.g., Mt 12:33b par. Lk 6:44). Furthermore, it is not crucial in Judaism that such aphorisms be attached to any particular context, person or message. For Gospel studies, therefore, the contexts of such aphorisms in the double tradition become the crucial concern since they alone indicate how early Christians related Jesus to wisdom emphases. There are at least five crucial wisdom passages in the double tradition.

1.1.1. The Wisdom of Solomon (Mt 12:42; Lk 11:31). In this saying there is a direct reference to "the wisdom of Solomon," and an ambiguous assertion that

"behold, here is something greater than Solomon." The emphasis in both Matthew and Luke is on the judgment of "this generation" in connection with the preaching (*kērygma*) of Jonah (Mt 12:41 par. Lk 11:32; *see* Sign of Jonah) and the wisdom of Solomon. The "something greater" than the preaching of Jonah and the wisdom of Solomon, then, seems to be Jesus' message. In this context Jesus is a messenger who proclaims God's wisdom with eschatological urgency to "this generation."

1.1.2. Wisdom Vindicated (Mt 11:16-19; Lk 7:31-35). This passage is also concerned with "this generation," but it emphasizes that John the Baptist* and Jesus (= the Son of man*) have come to it as messengers of Wisdom (*sophia*). The ending of the pericope in Luke is usually considered earlier than Matthew's ending: "And wisdom (*sophia*) is vindicated by all her children." Sophia is personified as having children who come proclaiming her message.

Wisdom was personified already in the Hebrew Bible. She calls out and pleads with humans to heed her message (Prov 8:1—9:2). Wisdom also sends out messengers to issue her call (Prov 9:3-6). As this tradition developed in Judaism, it could finally be claimed that "in every generation she [Wisdom] passes into holy souls and makes them friends of God and prophets" (Wis 7:27 RSV).

If the word "all," which is only in Luke 7:35 (Mt 11:19), was present in the double tradition which Luke adopted, then the implication would be that all who respond to Wisdom's call are her children. "All," however, seems to be a Lukan addition (cf. Lk 7:29). The focus of the double tradition, then, is on John and Jesus as the culmination of all of Wisdom's messengers (cf. Mt 11:12-15; Lk 16:16).

1.1.3. Wisdom's Envoys (Mt 23:34-36; Lk 11:49-51). Luke 11:49 is regarded as the earlier form of this saying ("Therefore also the Wisdom of God said, 'I will send them prophets and apostles, some of whom they will kill and persecute . . .' " RSV; see 2.2 below). The saying seems to be a quotation attributed to personified Wisdom. The emphasis on Wisdom sending messengers ("prophets and apostles") is present again, but the motif of their rejection is strongly emphasized. The implication of this double-tradition passage is clear: God's judgment for the rejection of the entire line of Sophia's envoys culminates with Jesus' message to "this generation."

1.1.4. Wisdom's Spokesperson (Mt 23:37-39; Lk 13:34-35). In this case Matthew has Jesus' lament over Jerusalem linked with the emphasis on the fate of all the messengers sent to Israel* (Mt 23:34-36 par. Lk 11:49-51), while Luke has the lament linked explicitly to Jesus' death as another of the rejected prophets* (13:33). It is difficult to know, then, whether Matthew or Luke has preserved the order of the double tradition. Has Matthew combined the sayings (Mt 23:34-36 par. 23:37-39) or has Luke separated them (par. Lk 11:49-51 and 13:34-35)? An understanding of the context would help us determine the identity of the speaker, whether it be Wisdom, Jesus on behalf of Wisdom or Jesus as Wisdom itself.

In this double-tradition passage the emphasis seems to be on the rejection of Wisdom's messengers (Mt 23:37a par. Lk 13:34a) and on Jesus as the final messenger of Wisdom ("you will surely not see me until . . . the one who comes in the name of the Lord," Mt 23:39 par. Lk 13:35). Since no explicit identification is made between Jesus' person and the figure of Sophia, it seems reasonable to conclude that the same emphasis already seen in other double-tradition passages is found also in this one: Jesus is the final spokesperson who has attempted to reveal Wisdom's message to humanity.

1.1.5. Wisdom's Revealer (Mt 11:25-27; Lk 10:21-22). This passage from the double tradition seems to emphasize wisdom motifs different from the passages examined so far. First, Jesus as God's Son seems to be the only recipient and mediator of God's wisdom (e.g., "All things have been delivered to me by my Father . . ." RSV). Second, it is implied that either God has hidden his Wisdom from Israel because of their unbelief or that Wisdom is unattainable by Israel without the Son's mediation (e.g., "Thou hast hidden these things from the wise and understanding . . ." RSV).

Although this is a difficult passage to interpret, it is clear that stress is placed on the filial relationship between God and Jesus, and the passage implies that the wisdom which only God knows fully is revealed as a gift (cf. Job 28:12-28; Bar 3:15—4:1; Sir 1:10; Wis 8:21). At the very least, this passage seems to focus on (1) the recipients of God's wisdom (i.e., Jesus and those to whom he reveals it) rather than on those who have rejected wisdom, and on (2) Jesus' function as the revealer of God's wisdom. These emphases are not incompatible with the other double-tradition passages, though admittedly they are enhanced only here (see 2.3. below).

1.1.6. Summary of the Double Tradition. The wisdom passages of the double tradition place emphasis on Jesus' message rather than on the relation of Jesus' person to divine Wisdom. Jesus is presented as the culmination of a long line of messengers to Israel whose message of God's wisdom has been rejected. The christological aspects of the double tradition emphasize both Jesus as the final but rejected spokesperson for Wisdom and his filial relationship to God (*see* Abba; Son of God) in fulfilling this function. Jesus is not yet identified with Wisdom itself. This christological step is taken by Matthew.

2. Matthew.

Matthew's presentation of Jesus in relation to wisdom motifs is to be seen primarily in the redaction of wisdom material from the double tradition. The most important passages are: 11:2-19; 23:34-39; and 11:25-30.

2.1. Jesus as Wisdom (Mt 11:2-19 par. Lk 7:18-35). The setting of this passage is John the Baptist's question concerning Jesus and Jesus' testimony regarding John. Matthew introduces this section with a phrase that seems to be his: "the works of the Christ" (Mt. 11:2; cf. Lk 7:18). As we have seen (1.1.2. above), most interpreters of the double tradition regard Luke's version of the wisdom saying at the conclusion of this section ("wisdom is justified by all her *children*," Lk 7:35) as earlier than Matthew's ("wisdom is justified by her *works*," Mt 11:19b). It appears that Matthew has framed the passage to equate "the works of the Christ" (11:2) with "wisdom is vindicated by her works" (11:19b). This change virtually identifies Jesus, "the Christ" (cf. Mt 1:1, 16-17), with God's divine Wisdom. If this is the case, then in Matthew Jesus is no longer just Wisdom's messenger; Jesus is *Sophia* incarnate (Suggs).

2.2. Wisdom Speaks (Mt 23:34-39 par. Lk 11:49-51; 13:34-35). Matthew's redaction of the double tradition in order to equate Jesus with Wisdom is consistent also with the differences between Matthew and Luke in this passage. We have already discussed Jesus' lament for Jerusalem in 23:37-39 (1.1.4.), a passage following on Matthew's larger context of Jesus' woes on the Scribes* and Pharisees* and, finally in 23:34-36, the sending of prophets, the wise and scribes who are killed and persecuted by Israel's leaders.

If the parallel passage of Luke 11:49-51 (par. Mt 23:34-36) represents the earlier form of the double tradition, as most interpreters believe, then Matthew has made several significant modifications. First, the phrase "the Wisdom of God said" (past tense) becomes in Matthew an emphatic first-person saying of Jesus in the present tense ("Behold! I am sending you prophets . . ."). A saying of Wisdom has become a saying of Jesus.

Second, although it is unclear that Matthew is responsible for joining the tradition found in 23:37-39 (par. Lk 13:34-35) with that of 23:34-36 (par. Lk 11:49-51), a strong contextual argument can be made that he did. Matthew 23:37-39 in the double tradition is a lament of Jesus about Jerusalem's rejection of his message. In order to express his pathos, Jesus uses the image of Wisdom-Shekinah ("God's presence") as a mother bird gathering its brood. In Matthew, however, Jesus has just been identified with Wisdom (23:34 par. Lk 11:49) so that the lament over Jerusalem now reads as their rejection of Jesus as God's incarnate Wisdom.

The rejection theme fits both the overall context of the woes (*see* Blessing and Woe) against the Scribes* and Pharisees* (Mt 23) and Jesus' subsequent departure from the Temple* (24:1). Matthew has also omitted the story of the widow's mite (cf. Mk 12:41-44 par. Lk 21:1-4). This omission links Jerusalem's rejection of Jesus as Wisdom with Jesus' emphatic departure from the Temple. In this way the theme of rejection is enhanced in Matthew. Jerusalem's "house" (i.e., the Temple) is "forsaken and desolate" (23:38 par. Lk 13:35) because Jerusalem has rejected the very incarnation of Wisdom itself.

In so doing Matthew seems to be building on the motifs present in the Jewish wisdom tradition. In Sirach, Sophia sought a dwelling place among all peoples, but God assigned her to dwell in the Temple at Jerusalem (Sir 24:1-12). Elsewhere we find the emphasis that Wisdom was rejected and left desolate because of God's judgment* of Jerusalem (Bar 4:12), or that she could find no place to dwell at all and returned to heaven* (*1 Enoch* 42:1-2; cf. 4 Ezra 5:9-10). While we cannot establish Matthew's direct literary dependence on these traditions, given Matthew's evident redaction of the double tradition it seems reasonable to suggest that Jesus is presented as Wisdom incarnate who is rejected by Israel, pronounces judgment on her (23:35-36, 38) and then withdraws his presence (23:39—24:1).

2.3. Wisdom Beckons (Mt 11:25-30). The double tradition has emphasized already that Jesus' function as the Son is to reveal God's wisdom (Mt 11:25-27 par. Lk 10:21-22; see 1.1.5.). Matthew now links 11:25-27 with 11:28-30, so that Jesus not only reveals God's wisdom but issues an invitation to take his yoke and learn from him. The language certainly alludes to the yoke of the Law, but because Wisdom and Torah had already been identified in some traditions (Sir 24:23; Bar 3:37-4:1), Wisdom could also invite any who would do so to take her yoke and experience her rest (e.g., Sir 51:26-27).

In Matthew Jesus no longer only reveals Wisdom; his teaching is the total expression of God's revelation because he is Wisdom-Torah. The community of Jesus studies his words as God's revelation (cf. 5:18; 24:35),

and he, as the very presence of God's revelation (1:21-23), guides them (18:20; cf. *'Abot* 3.3, 7; 6.10). Righteousness now consists of knowing and doing Jesus' teachings rather than the yoke of Torah (*see* Law; Justice, Righteousness).

2.4. Summary. In the Synoptic tradition Matthew goes beyond both Judaism (in which wisdom is never incarnate as a human) and the double tradition (in which Jesus and John are both Wisdom's final messengers) by moving to a wisdom christology in which Jesus is Wisdom incarnate. The Fourth Gospel takes a similar step but by different means and with different emphases.

3. The Fourth Gospel.
John 1:1-18 presents Jesus as the cosmic *logos** ("Word"). Logos and Wisdom were virtually interchangeable concepts in both Philo (Dodd) and The Wisdom of Solomon (9:1-2; 18:15). Knowledge of this background has led interpreters to note the emphasis on wisdom in John's prologue.

In the wisdom tradition Wisdom is depicted as participating with God's Word in creation (Prov 8:27-31; Wis 9:1-2, 9). John goes beyond this tradition by emphasizing not only that God created Wisdom before anything else and that Wisdom assisted with creation (Prov 8:22-26; Sir 1:4, 9; 24:3-5), but that the Logos was pre-existent with God (1:1; cf. Sir 24:9).

Wisdom and life are also associated in the wisdom tradition (e.g., Prov 4:1-13; Wis 8:13, 17), and John emphasizes that life* is in the Logos (1:4). The theme that Wisdom is the perfect reflection of God's light* (e.g., Wis 7:26) is also in John (1:4-5). The emphasis in John, however, is on the Logos who came to his own with God's revelation but was rejected (1:9-11). The scheme of the appearance of the Logos, his rejection and his departure (Jn 14-17) is like Sophia's rejection and departure (cf. 1 Enoch 42:1-2; 4 Ezra 5:9-10).

If the wisdom emphases in John's prologue are intended to apply to the entire Gospel's presentation of Jesus, then some very important christological points have been made. John has already gone beyond the traditions which relate Wisdom and Logos with his statement that they are incarnate in Jesus (1:14). Furthermore, in contrast to gnostic traditions, for John Wisdom and Logos do not stay with Jesus only temporarily, but they are given a particular narrative history in the life of Jesus. Jesus is thus presented materially and essentially as the unique Wisdom-Word of God. This means, for example, that in the "I Am"* statements (6:35; 8:12; 10:9; 11:25-26; 14:6; 15:1; cf. 8:58; 10:36) Jesus himself is the message of salvation.* The person, so to speak, is the kerygma.

If this is true, then of all the NT wisdom traditions John's presentation of Jesus as Wisdom is the strongest christological development.

See also JOHN, GOSPEL OF; LAW; LOGOS; MATTHEW, GOSPEL OF.

BIBLIOGRAPHY. F. W. Burnett, *The Testament of Jesus-Sophia: A Redaction-Critical Study of the Eschatological Discourse in Matthew* (Lanham, MD: University Press of America, 1981); C. E. Carlston, "Proverbs, Maxims, and the Historical Jesus," *JBL* 99 (1980) 87-105; H. Conzelmann, "Wisdom in the NT," *IDBSup* 956-960; C. H. Dodd, *The Interpretation of the Fourth Gospel* (Cambridge: University Press, 1953); J. D. G. Dunn, *Christology in the Making* (Philadelphia: Westminster, 1980); R. A. Piper, *Wisdom in the Q-Tradition: The Aphoristic Teaching of Jesus* (SNTSMS 61; Cambridge: University Press, 1989); J. M. Robinson, "Jesus as Sophos and Sophia: Wisdom Tradition and the Gospels," in *Aspects of Wisdom in Judaism and Early Christianity*, ed. R. L. Wilken (Notre Dame: University of Notre Dame, 1975) 1-15; M. J. Suggs, *Wisdom, Christology, and Law in Matthew's Gospel* (Cambridge, MA: Harvard, 1970).

F. W. Burnett

WISE MEN. *See* BIRTH OF JESUS.

WITNESS

The witness theme occupies a place of considerable importance in the Bible. Witness (*martys*) is a forensic term employed by writers in ancient Israel and the early church. A witness is a person who knows the truth and can testify before a court of law, declaring what has been seen or heard. Witness terminology is also employed in connection with Israel* and the church* as God's* witnesses.

    1. Introduction
    2. Witness in Mark
    3. Witness in Matthew
    4. Witness in Luke
    5. Witness in John

1. Introduction.

Witnesses throughout the Bible can certify facts (Jer 32:10, 12; Ruth 4:9-11; Is 8:2; Acts 10:39). Unfortunately, they can also prove to be false or malicious witnesses; these are frequently condemned in biblical literature (Ex 23:1; Prov 19:5, 9; Acts 7:58). False witnesses are mentioned in the NT in the trials of Jesus and Stephen (Mt 26:60; Mk 14:57-59; Acts 6:13).

The Jewish law of multiple witness was important throughout biblical times. The law of Moses demanded the evidence of several witnesses to convict a person of a capital crime (Deut 17:6-7; Num 35:30).

The principle of multiple witness is honored in the NT (Jn 5:31-32; Heb 10:28) and features prominently in cases of church discipline (Mt 18:16; 2 Cor 13:1; 1 Tim 5:19).

Thus witness language is used in a juridical manner throughout the Bible. However, the most significant use of witness terminology is in connection with Israel and the church as God's witnesses (Is 43:10, 12; 44:8; Lk 24:48; Jn 15:27; Acts 1:8, 22; 2:32; 5:32; 10:39, 41).

In the NT the witness theme is prominent in John's Gospel (1:7, 19; 3:11, 32-33; 4:39; 5:31-39; 8:13-14, 18), Acts (3:15; 13:31; 22:15, 20; 26:16) and Revelation (1:5; 2:13; 3:14; 6:9; 11:3; 17:6). The idea of witness also appears frequently elsewhere (e.g., Lk 22:71; Rom 1:9; 1 Cor 1:6; 2 Cor 1:23; Phil 1:8; 1 Thess 2:5, 10; 1 Tim 6:12-13; 2 Tim 2:2; 1 Pet 5:1; 2 Pet 1:16; 1 Jn 5:6-11).

2. Witness in Mark.

Mark recognizes the importance of valid evidence (Mk 1:44) and accepts the Jewish law of multiple witness (14:56, 59). He knows of demoniac "confessions" of Jesus (1:24; 3:11; 5:7; cf. Lk 4:34; Mt 8:29; *see* Demon, Devil, Satan), but he believes that Christ* is to be confessed by disciples.* The demonic forces are opposed to God's purposes; for this reason, their testimony is unacceptable (Mk 1:25; 3:12; cf. Lk 4:35, 41).

When the Twelve are sent forth they are told to shake off the dust from their feet if their message meets with rejection, "for a testimony unto them" (Mk 6:11 RV). Witness has been given to God, but if that witness does not lead to repentance and faith,* it will provide evidence which will be brought forth against that community on the day of judgment.* This ominous note is even stronger in Luke, where the action is viewed as a threat ("testimony against them," Lk 9:5 NIV).

The themes of testimony and confession appear in Mark 13:9-13 and its parallels. Here witness is offered against a background of persecution (Mk 13:12-13; Lk 21:16-17; Mt 24:9). Christians will be hauled before local councils, flogged in the synagogues* (Mk 13:9; Mt 10:17; Lk 21:12) and delivered to the custody of the police or courts (Mk 13:9, 11-12; Lk 21:16). In such circumstances the Holy Spirit* will tell them what to say (Mk 13:11; Mt 10:19-20). Their task is to remain alert and be faithful (Mk 13:37). Those who are ashamed of Christ will be put to shame on the Last Day before the Son of man, "when he comes in the glory of his Father with the holy angels" (Mk 8:38 RSV; *see* Son of Man).

3. Witness in Matthew.

Matthew contributes to an understanding of courtroom procedure. Both Matthew and Luke use the proper terms to describe the "accuser" and the "judge" (Mt 5:25-26; Lk 12:58-59). A final "day of judgment" is mentioned when an "account" must be given (Mt 12:36-37). This evidence will provide the basis for a verdict of acquittal or condemnation. No witnesses will be called, for the evidence will be furnished by their own "words" (cf. Job 15:6; Lk 19:22; 22:71; *see* Apocalyptic Teaching).

A striking use of witness imagery occurs in Christ's reference to the people of Nineveh and the Queen of the South (*see* Sign of Jonah). They are cited as accusing witnesses who will "condemn this generation" (Mt 12:41-42; cf. Lk 11:31-32). They will provide the evidence which will secure the conviction of Jesus' unbelieving contemporaries (cf. Mt 12:27; Lk 11:19).

Matthew recognizes that witnesses can testify against themselves (Mt 23:29-36; Lk 11:47-51). Unless there is genuine repentance, the recalcitrant will be charged with the blood of all the martyrs from the time of Abel onwards (Mt 23:35; cf. Lk 11:50-51). In repeatedly opposing God's "prophets and sages and scribes" (Mt 23:34), they are providing incriminating evidence that they are ethically the children of those who killed the prophets* (Mt 23:30-31). Thus they witness "against" themselves (Mt 23:31; cf. Lk 11:48).

One of Matthew's most gripping scenes is that of the Last Judgment (25:31-46). The judge is the Son of man. With him are the angels* who function as court officials. There is a judgment seat or throne on which the judge sits to judge (25:31). The nations are gathered and a process of judgment takes place in which the sheep (*see* Sheep and Shepherd) and the goats are separated. Verdicts are formally pronounced on the two classes (25:34-36, 41-43). Christ is here described as the judge at the Last Day while in similar passages he is depicted as a witness (Mt 10:32-33; cf. Lk 12:8-9).

4. Witness in Luke.

Luke is acquainted with some of the main terms of witness and makes use of them in his Gospel. The nouns "witness" (11:48; 24:48) and "testimony" (*martyria*, 22:71) are used, and reference is made to legally admissible evidence (*martyrion*, 5:14; 9:5). The normal verb for "bearing witness" is used once (*martyreō*, 4:22), as is the verb for "bearing false witness" (*pseudo-martyreō*, 18:20). The compound verb for "bearing solemn witness" is used once in a context of warning (*diamartyromai*, 16:28).

Luke begins by giving special recognition to the primary witnesses, the apostles. They are qualified to attest the basic facts of Jesus' life, death (*see* Death of

Jesus) and resurrection* because they were "eyewitnesses" (*autoptai*, Lk 1:2) as well as servants of the word.

Luke views witness as a live metaphor against a background of strife, contention and debate. This leads him to draw attention to Jesus' exhortation to fearless confession (12:1-12): "I tell you, everyone who acknowledges me before others, the Son of man also will acknowledge before the angels of God, but whoever denies me before others will be denied before the angels of God" (Lk 12:8-9 NRSV; cf. Mt 10:32-33). As in the other Gospels, Peter fails when he denies his Lord (Lk 22:57, 61; cf. Mk 14:68, 70-71; Mt 26:70, 72, 74). Luke sees Jesus preparing his followers for witnessing in difficult circumstances: "When you are brought before synagogues, rulers and authorities, do not worry about how you will defend yourselves or what you will say, for the Holy Spirit will teach you at that time what you should say" (12:11-12 NIV). Similarly, in Luke 21 there is a warning of hard times, but the crisis situation is seen as an opportunity for bearing witness: "This will result in your being witnesses to them" (21:13 NIV). The fulfillment of these predictions is amply illustrated in Acts, where Paul appears before governors, kings and the house of Israel on numerous occasions (Acts 22:1-22; 25:1-27; 28:23-31). Witnessing was to be a joyful, but precarious, activity of the church, fraught by the possibility of arrest, imprisonment and death. The death of Stephen is a case in point (7:54-60). Luke describes him as a "witness" who paid the supreme price of martyrdom (22:20).

Luke's witness theme assumes even greater importance in Acts, where "witness" and six related terms occur a total of thirty-nine times. Jesus had prepared his disciples for their future role as witnesses (Lk 24:44-49). He had told them: "You will receive power when the Holy Spirit comes on you; and you will be my witnesses in Jerusalem, and in all Judea and Samaria, and to the ends of the earth" (Acts 1:8 NIV). This verse summarizes the thrust of Acts. The witness theme is explained further when Ananias is divinely instructed: "Go! This man is my chosen instrument to carry my name before the Gentiles and their kings and before the people of Israel" (9:15 NIV). The remainder of Acts is largely the unfolding of Paul's faithful witness, with occasional attention to the work of Peter and other Christian leaders. It is, as F. Stagg has often observed, the story of an "unhindered" gospel (28:31).

With the coming of the Holy Spirit the disciples are empowered for witness (2:4; cf. 1:5). Luke notes: "With great power the apostles continued to testify to the resurrection of the Lord Jesus" (4:33 NIV). As this text implies, Luke regards as particularly central to the role of the apostles* their service* as witnesses to the resurrection of Jesus (e.g., Acts 1:22; 2:32; 3:15; et al.). In times of persecution the church prayed for boldness in witness, and asked for divine signs and wonders to be performed in the name of Jesus (4:29-30).

This remarkable "boldness" (parrēsia) is a striking feature of apostolic witness, and it is clearly in evidence in church leaders such as Peter, John, Stephen, Philip, Barnabas and Apollos (2:29; 4:9-10, 13; 7:2-53; 8:30-35; 14:3; 18:26). It is most prominent in the case of Paul (9:27-28; 19:8; 28:31), whose speeches in Jerusalem, Rome and before Felix, Festus and Agrippa are remarkably bold and fearless (22:3-21; 23:1-6; 24:10-21; 25:8-11; 26:2-29; 28:16-20, 23-31; cf. 13:9-11; 14:14-18; 17:30-31). This outspoken quality is given by the Holy Spirit, who energizes the witness and directs the entire mission of the church (8:29; 10:19-20; 11:12; 16:6-7).

To summarize, Luke in both his Gospel and Acts highlights the witness motif. The apostles have a special role as the original eyewitnesses of the whole public ministry of Jesus from the baptism* to the ascension* (Acts 1:21-22). Jesus tells them: "You are witnesses of these things" (Lk 24:48 NIV). But they do not stand alone. Other Christians are summoned to take Christ's side, plead his case and urge all to accept his claims as Messiah and Lord.* This loyal witness will frequently entail persecution and suffering, for the witness is messianic and religious and often takes Christians into the lawcourts. However, these stressful situations will be opportunities for bearing testimony. Witnesses are empowered by the Spirit, who enables them to speak boldly for their Lord and to do signs and wonders in the name of Jesus. Thus the Jewish principle of multiple witness is honored, that every matter be established on the evidence of two or three witnesses (Deut 19:15; cf. 17:6). The witness of the apostles and other Christians is corroborated by the Holy Spirit (Acts 5:32), and also by the OT Scriptures (Lk 24:25-27, 44-49; Acts 10:43), presenting a cohesive case for the claims of Jesus as Savior* and Lord.

5. Witness in John.

In the Fourth Gospel witness is a central issue. John follows rather closely the formal pattern of the covenant lawsuit which is worked out in detail in Isaiah 43—48. There God has a lawsuit with his people and takes them to court, calling witnesses and laying charges against them. In John, God incarnate in Jesus has a controversy with the world* as it is incarnate in "the Jews," the Jewish leaders who epitomize the world in its opposition to the Gospel (Jn 5:16, 18; 6:41; 7:1; 10:31; 11:8). Each side presents witnesses, offers evidence and pleads its case. Witnesses such as John the Baptist (5:33-35; see John the Baptist), the disciples (15:27), the Scriptures (5:39), the mighty works of Christ (5:36; cf. 10:25) and the Father (5:32, 37) are called to offer testimony on behalf of Christ. This evidence fails to convince opponents, however, unless it is accompanied by the inward witness of the Holy Spirit (15:26; cf. 14:16-17, 26). When the Spirit comes, he drives home the truth,* convicting the world of sin, of righteousness and of judgment (16:8-11). Christ won his case on the cross, and as the victor will judge all people on the Last Day (16:33; 5:27-30).

The witness theme assumes major importance in the first twelve chapters of John. This is particularly evident in "the great controversy" of John 5—12. This controversy, or covenant lawsuit, revolves around three miracles performed by Jesus, namely, the healing of the man at the pool (Jn 5), the feeding of the 5,000 (Jn 6) and the healing of the man born blind (Jn 9). In each case a common pattern is observed. The miracle takes place, followed by a debate with opponents in which the claims of Jesus are asserted, objections are handled and further development of the argument takes place. This results in a division of opinion, some coming to faith in Christ, and others taking offense at his teaching (6:60-69; 7:43; 9:16; 10:19). The argument wages fast and furious, some charging Jesus with demon-possession (7:20; 8:48) or deception of the people (7:12), while others acknowledge him as "a good man" (7:12), "a prophet" (9:17), "the Christ" (7:41) or "Lord" (9:38). A decisive judgment follows (Jn 11 and 12).

The situation changes following the glorification (see Glory) of Jesus and his return to the Father. While he was on earth, Jesus bore witness to the truth and served as the chief advocate for God in the world (18:37; 10:34-38; 14:10-11; 18:23). Now his juridical functions are taken over by "another Paraclete" (see Holy Spirit), the Holy Spirit promised by Jesus (14:16-18). The Spirit acts as "the advocate," taking charge of Christ's case and calling on the disciples to support it. Christ now serves as "advocate" in heaven* (1 Jn 2:1 KJV). As in Acts, the apostles have a twofold role to play. First, they are eyewitnesses and can attest the basic facts of Jesus' life, death and resurrection (Jn 15:27). Second, they serve as witnesses to convictions, for they believe that they have been called to attest the great redemptive act of God. Thus they serve as advocates, taking Christ's side and pleading his cause in a hostile world (15:18-20; 16:1-4).

The Holy Spirit bears witness in two ways. First, he reminds the disciples of the things which Jesus had communicated to them (14:26). Then he explains to them how the scriptural promises find their proper fulfillment in the long-awaited Christ (2:17; cf. Ps 69:9; Jn 19:23-24; cf. Ps 22:18). The Spirit functions both as a witness and an advocate of Christ.

One other element in John's Gospel is the lawsuit of the Last Day (Jn 5:28-29). Christ will exercise a judicial role, for the Father "has given him authority to judge because he is the Son of Man" (5:27 NIV; cf. Dan 7:13-14; Lk 21:36). The final judgment will be closely related to what has preceded it. Those who have rejected the claims of Christ will find his words standing as accusing witnesses against them in the Last Day (Jn 12:48; cf. Mt 12:41-42; Lk 11:31-32). For the believer the judgment of the Last Day has already been met, and the divine sentence of acquittal has been pronounced (Jn 5:24).

See also APOCALYPTIC TEACHING; JUDGMENT.

BIBLIOGRAPHY. J. M. Boice, *Witness and Revelation in the Gospel of John* (Grand Rapids: Zondervan, 1970); S. de Dietrich, " 'You are My Witnesses'—A Study of the Church's Witness," *Int* 8 (1954) 273-79; J. C. Hindley, "Witnesses in the Fourth Gospel," *SJT* 18 (1965) 319-37; H. Strathmann, "μάρτυς κτλ," *TDNT* IV.474-514; M. C. Tenney, "The Meaning of Witness in John," *BSac* 132 (1975) 229-41; A. A. Trites, *The New Testament Concept of Witness* (SNTSMS 31; Cambridge: University Press, 1977); idem, *New Testament Witness in Today's World* (Valley Forge: Judson, 1983); idem, "The Idea of Witness in the Synoptic Gospels—Some Juridical Considerations," *Themelios* 5 (1968) 18-26; A. A. Trites and L. Coenen, "Witness," *NIDNTT* 3.1038-51.   A. A. Trites

WOE. *See* BLESSING AND WOE.

WOMEN

All four Gospels contain information on Jesus' relationship to women and the involvement of women in Jesus' life and ministry. Jesus accepted and affirmed as persons of worth various women who were neglected or rejected within his society. Jesus taught women and included them among his disciples.* Women also participated in the proclamation of the gospel.* Many women associated with Jesus are known by name. Among the four Gospels Luke evidences the greatest interest in Jesus' relationship with women and their involvement in his life and ministry. The contacts and involvements between Jesus and women need to be set within the social and cultural contexts of the first

century A.D. The Gospel data on Jesus and women lead also to discussions about the significance of this data for women in ministry, leadership and authority* within the church.*

1. Women in the Social-Cultural Contexts of the First Century A.D.
2. Women As Persons of Dignity and Worth
3. Women As Disciples
4. Women As Proclaimers
5. Women Specifically Named
6. Women in the Perspective of Each Gospel
7. Conclusions and Significance

1. Women in the Social-Cultural Contexts of the First Century A.D.

In very general terms Jesus lived in social-cultural contexts (the Jewish context and the larger Greco-Roman society) in which the male view of women was usually negative and the place of women was understood to be limited for the most part to the domestic roles of wife and mother. Women were perceived by extant male writers to be responsible for most (all?) sin, and especially for sexual temptation and sin. There are, on the other hand, clear indications both from literary and non-literary sources that there were positive roles for women as well.

The extant male literary sources of ancient Judaism,* which reflect both a class and gender perspective, present a fairly consistent pattern of a negative view toward women (see Swidler 1976). For example, Josephus,* the first-century A.D. Jewish historian, states that the Law* holds women to be inferior in all matters and that, therefore, women should be submissive (*Ag. Ap.* 2.25 §201). Philo, the first-century A.D. Alexandrian Jewish philosopher and biblical commentator, refers throughout his writings to women and female traits as examples of weakness (e.g., *Op. Mund.* 151-52; *Quaest. in Gen.* 1.33). Philo argues that women ought to stay at home, desiring a life of seclusion (*Spec. Leg.* 3.169-77; *Flacc.* 89). Sirach, a proto-Pharisaic work from about 180 B.C., presents women either as good wives or as problems. It even states that "better is the wickedness of a man than a woman who does good; it is woman who brings shame and disgrace" (Sir 42:14 NRSV). According to the rabbinic Tosefta, which may well in this case reflect first-century A.D. tradition, a Jewish man prayed three benedictions each day, including one in which he thanked God* that he was not made a woman (*t. Ber.* 7.18).

Such texts reflect social reality to some extent and set a framework of societal expectation for the behavior and relationships of men and women.

This negative picture within Judaism was greatly shaped and influenced by Greek and Greco-Roman androcentrism and misogynism. However, as some have argued (e.g., Meyers), women's place in Israel began to decline with the emergence of a bureaucratic monarchy, prior to Greek influence.

However, there are, in spite of the lack of literary evidence from women, substantial indications that positive roles did exist for women within Judaism, even if limited. Especially important is the evidence that some women held the office of ruler or president of synagogues* in ancient Judaism (see Kraemer). Significant religious roles for women are also indicated by the portrayal of Job's three daughters as those who speak the language of angels* in the *Testament of Job* and in the traditions about Beruriah, a second century A.D. rabbi (see Swidler 1976). Women as strong leaders are portrayed in the Hellenistic Jewish story of Judith and in the rule of Salome Alexandra as Queen in Judea (approximately 76-67 B.C.). There is also substantial non-literary evidence which shows that Jewish women often took initiative for their lives and activities in spite of the male orientation and domination prevalent in the culture (see Kraemer). These positive roles and opportunities constitute Jewish evidence for the significance of women in ancient Judaism.

Thus, it is important for Christians not to set a "Christian" Jesus over against his Judaism and Jewish context as the deliverer of women and thus engage in a subtle form of anti-Judaism. Christians can hardly deny that the history of the church shows that it, as much as any human social reality, has neglected and oppressed women over many centuries.

Yet, as a Jewish male in an androcentric, patriarchal society, Jesus' respect for women as persons of dignity and worth and his inclusion of them as disciples and proclaimers in his life and ministry was very significant in its own first-century context for women and their place and activity in ministry in the earliest churches and is important as a heritage for both Jewish and Christian people today.

2. Women As Persons of Dignity and Worth.
According to the Gospels Jesus clearly regarded women as persons of dignity and worth by his many healings* of women, by his acceptance and forgiveness* of undesirable and ritually unclean (*see* Clean and Unclean) women, and by his implicit challenges to male sexual devaluation of women.

2.1. Women Healed by Jesus. Jesus healed various unnamed women: Peter's mother-in-law (Mt 8:14-15; Mk 1:29-31; Lk 4:38-39); the daughter of Jairus and the woman with the twelve-year flow of blood (Mt 9:18-26; Mk 5:21-43; Lk 8:40-56); and the eighteen-year crippled woman (Lk 13:11-17) whom Jesus called a "daughter of Abraham,*" probably an important status marker for a woman (see further the discussion of Lk 8:1-3 in 3.1. below). In addition, Jesus raised the son of the widow of Nain (Lk 7:11-17). In most of these stories Jesus touched or was touched by the woman involved. This is particularly important in terms of the woman with the twelve-year flow of blood, since she would have been considered ritually unclean according to levitical law (Lev 18).

2.2. Women's Sexual Integrity Affirmed by Jesus. According to two Gospel stories Jesus accepted and forgave two women understood to be guilty of sexual sins. In Luke 7:36-50 a woman, called a sinner,* anoints (*see* Anointing) and kisses Jesus' feet in the home of a Pharisee.* Jesus accepted her actions as those of love* and declared: "Your faith has saved you; go in peace" (7:50). In the story of the woman caught in adultery (Jn 7:53—8:11; although not found in any of the oldest Greek manuscripts of the NT, most scholars regard this as an authentic story about Jesus) Jesus said: "Neither do I condemn you; go, and sin no longer" (Jn 8:11). This Jesus did in the presence of male critics who had brought only the woman, of the two involved, to Jesus.

Also to be noted in this connection is Jesus' encounter with the Samaritan* woman (see 4.2. below), who is presented as one living in adultery. The male disciples are offended that Jesus is talking with a woman but dare not ask him why (Jn 4:27), indicating their negative sexual assumptions.

In fact, one saying of Jesus makes the general statement that "tax collectors and sexually immoral women (*hai pornai;* often translated "prostitutes"*) will enter before you [religious leaders] into the kingdom of God" (Mt 21:31; *see* Kingdom of God). Jesus notes that such persons had already responded to the preaching of John the Baptist (Mt 21:32; *see* John the Baptist).

In one saying of Jesus in the Sermon on the Mount (Mt 5:27-30; *see* Sermon on the Mount) concerning adultery, Jesus places the blame for lust on men, something rather unusual in ancient Mediterranean cultures.

In the Matthean account of Jesus' debate with the Pharisees on divorce* (Mt 19:3-9), reference appears to be made to the dominant position that men could divorce their wives for virtually any reason (see "for any cause" in Mt 19:3; see Josephus *Ant.* 4.8.23 §253; *Life* 76 §426; *m. Giṭ.* 9:10). Jesus responds by placing Deuteronomy 24:1-4 in a secondary position to

Genesis 2:24 (Mt 19:5-6) which affirms the concept of "one flesh," giving sexual equality to both women and men.

2.3. Women As Positive Examples in Jesus' Teaching. Jesus often used women as positive examples in stories and events for those who have responded to God with appropriate faith.* Such regard prepares the way for women as disciples and proclaimers (as described in 3. and 4. below).

Women are used, sometimes in parallel with men, to describe the faithful and faithless at the time of the arrival of the future kingdom (Mt 24:41; Lk 17:35; Mt 25:1-13). A woman and her leaven are central in a parable* about God's kingdom (Mt 13:33; Lk 13:20-21).

More important are the instances in which women portray persons of faith: the widow of Zarephath (Lk 4:26; see 1 Kings 17—18); the Syrophoenician (or Canaanite) woman (Mt 15:21-28; Mk 7:24-30); and the persistent widow (Lk 18:1-8). Faith is also an explicit feature of the women in the stories noted above (2.1. and 2.2.), of the woman who anoints Jesus' feet (Lk 7:50) and of the woman with the twelve-year flow of blood (Mt 9:22; Mk 5:34; Lk 8:48). The story of the "widow's mite" (Mk 12:41-44; Lk 21:1-4) presents a woman as one who fulfills Jesus' requirements, made especially clear in Luke, of discipleship with reference to material possessions.

The parable of the lost coin (Lk 15:8-10) presents a woman as the finder who rejoices with a party, the same role portrayed by the shepherd and the father in Luke 15. In all three cases this person images God who rejoices over repentant (*see* Repentance) sinners (see also Mt 23:37; Lk 13:34 in which Jesus likens his concern for Jerusalem to that of a mother hen for her chicks).

3. Women As Disciples.

The Gospels indicate that women were among the followers (= disciples) of Jesus and were taught by him with the understanding that they could respond with obedience and commitment to the word of God.

3.1. The Women Who Followed Jesus. All four Gospels attest to the fact that a group of women followed Jesus in Galilee and to Jerusalem where they were present as faithful and active at the crucifixion (*see* Death of Jesus), burial* and resurrection* of Jesus (Mt 27:55-56; 27:61—28:1; Mk 15:40-41; 15:47—16:1; Lk 23:49; 23:55—24:1; Jn 19:25-27; 20:1).

The verb used to designate their following of Jesus is *akoloutheō* (or its compounds), a term which occurs over seventy-five times in the Gospels and normally means following Jesus in the sense of being a disciple.

This lexical evidence confirms the narrative presentation of women as disciples of Jesus, although some would argue that when this term is used of women it does not designate discipleship.*

Luke describes these female disciples in the Galilean context (Lk 8:1-3). Luke notes that the women were traveling with Jesus and the Twelve and that they were providing for them as well, which is probably an indication of their upper-class status and comparative wealth. These women apparently became disciples of Jesus as a result of the healing they had received from him. Luke mentions three by name, Mary Magdalene, Joanna and Susanna, and notes that there were also many others.

The mention of these women in the Jerusalem context repeats the name of Mary Magdalene and adds the names of Mary the mother of James the younger and Joses (Joseph), Salome and Mary the wife of Clopas (Jn 19:25), who may be the same person as Mary the mother of James and Joseph. Also noted are the mother of Jesus (Jn 2:5 and 19:26-27 also attest to her discipleship), her sister and the mother of the sons of Zebedee (who may be the same person as Salome).

Luke, whose Gospel alone mentions these women in both the Galilean and Jerusalem contexts, also notes in Acts 1:14 that certain women, presumably those he has described in Luke 8:1-3 and in the passion narrative, are present in the upper room in Jerusalem, along with Mary the mother of Jesus. Presumably, then, these female disciples were among the one hundred twenty followers of Jesus (Acts 1:15) who waited for and received the Holy Spirit (*see* Holy Spirit) on the day of Pentecost, fulfilling the prophecy of Joel that ". . . in the last days . . . I will pour out my Spirit upon all flesh, and your sons and your daughters shall prophesy . . ." (Acts 2:17; see Joel 2:28-29). The mention by Luke of Tabitha (Acts 9:36), also known as Dorcas, designated as a disciple (*mathetria*), and Mary the mother of John Mark (Acts 12:12) as the one (leader?) in whose home believers were meeting, may indicate additional women by name who were followers of Jesus.

3.2. Mary of Bethany As a Disciple. According to Luke 10:38-42 Mary assumed the posture of a disciple by sitting at Jesus' feet (see Acts 22:3; *m. 'Abot* 1:4), listening to Jesus' word (*logos*). In spite of the objections of Mary's sister Martha, based on the traditional female obligation to prepare the meal, Jesus affirmed Mary's choice: "Mary has chosen the better part which will not be taken from her" (Lk 10:42). Presumably, the "better part" refers to Jesus' teaching on the kingdom which characterizes Luke's central section of the

Gospel (Lk 9:51—19:28) in which this story occurs.

Some interpreters have understood the story to present an image of women as silent learners rather than as active participants or speakers in the life of the church, indicating a redactional stage which reflects an alleged retreat from a more positive, egalitarian role for women in the very earliest years of the church. However, it is more likely that the story of Mary presents the image of women as disciples in equal partnership with men.

The presentation of Mary in John 11:28-33, 45; 12:1-8 may also point to her role as a disciple of Jesus, although it is certainly not as clear as it is in the Lukan story. Martha's confession in John 11:27, parallel to Peter's confession in John 6:69 and in the Synoptic tradition (see Mt 16:16), indicates her discipleship as well.

3.3. Motherhood and Obedience. Two Gospel pericopes contain a similar saying of Jesus in which response and obedience to God's word (discipleship) appears to be placed above motherhood, the traditional role for women (Mt 12:46-50 par. Mk 3:31-35 and Lk 8:19-21; Lk 11:27-28). In the common Synoptic story Jesus says: "My mother and my brothers and sisters are those who hear the word (*logos*) of God and do it" (Lk 8:21; *see* Family). In the incident reported only in Luke, Jesus says in response to a woman's affirmation of his mother: "Blessed rather are the ones who hear and keep the word (*logos*) of God" (Lk 11:28).

4. Women As Proclaimers.

The Gospels present three occasions in which women were proclaimers of Jesus, the Lukan infancy narrative (Lk 1—2), the story of the Samaritan woman (Jn 4:4-42) and the accounts of the women at the tomb in the resurrection narratives.

4.1. The Women Who Interpreted Jesus' Birth. In the Lukan infancy narrative (Lk 1:5—2:40) there are five persons, three of whom are women (Elizabeth; Mary, the mother of Jesus; and Anna; Zechariah and Simeon are also named), who speak by the power of the Holy Spirit or as a prophet* in order to provide a divine interpretation of the meaning of Jesus' birth for the history of God's salvation (*see* Birth of Jesus).

Elizabeth (Lk 1:41-45) is filled with the Holy Spirit and pronounces a blessing* on Mary, including designating her as "the mother of my Lord." Mary (Lk 1:26-38, 46-56), assuming her to be the speaker of the *Magnificat* (Lk 1:46-55; *see* Mary's Song), declares the saving work of God in language and structure similar to Hannah's prayer in 1 Samuel 2:1-10. Anna (Lk 2:36-38) is a prophet who praises God and speaks about

Jesus to all who were waiting for the redemption of Jerusalem. In the structure of Luke's Gospel these three women, along with Zechariah, Simeon, the angel Gabriel (Lk 1:26-38) and the angels who speak to the shepherds (Lk 2:8-15), proclaim Jesus' place in God's salvation,* giving theological understanding and perspective to the event of his birth.

4.2. The Samaritan Woman. After Jesus' discourse with the Samaritan woman (Jn 4:7-26) she returns to her city and recounts her experience with Jesus: "Many of the Samaritans from that city believed in him, because of the word (*logos*) of the woman that he told me all that I did" (Jn 4:39). The Johannine account does go on to note that the Samaritans then have a direct encounter with Jesus' word (*logos*), which they understand as the basis for their faith (Jn 4:40-42).

4.3. The Women As Witnesses to Jesus' Resurrection. All four Gospels report that the female disciples of Jesus were the first ones to receive the angelic account of Jesus' resurrection* and commission to go and tell the male disciples of this event (Mt 28:1-8; Mk 16:1-8; Lk 24:1-12; see Jn 20:1-13). According to Luke (Lk 24:10-11, 22-24) the men did not believe the report of the women (see also Mk 16:11 in the long addition to Mark).

Further, the Gospels of Matthew and John and the long ending of Mark report that Jesus appeared first to Mary Magdalene (Jn 20:14-18; Mk 16:9-11; in Mt 28:9-10 the other Mary [see Mt 27:61; 28:1] is with Mary Magdalene; this other Mary is presumably Mary the mother of James the younger and Joseph, mentioned in Mt 27:56). In the Matthean and Johannine accounts Mary Magdalene is commissioned by Jesus to tell the male disciples what she has seen and heard.

It has often been noted that Paul, who provides the earliest written account of resurrection appearances of Jesus (1 Cor 15:3-8), does not mention the role of the women. It is often assumed that this is due to a Jewish understanding of the inadmissibility of the testimony of women in legal contexts (see Josephus *Ant.* 4.8.15 §219) and the argument Paul wishes to establish.

The first known pagan written critique of Christianity, that of the middle Platonist Celsus entitled *The True Word* (c. A.D. 175), builds on the Gospels' report of women as the first witnesses and proclaimers of Jesus' resurrection. Celsus, citing his alleged source, says that a hysterical female (and perhaps someone else) was the witness to Jesus' resurrection, which Celsus then discounts (*apud* Origen *Contra Celsum* 2.55). Origen responds (c. A.D. 225) to Celsus by saying that there were other witnesses in addition to the woman and that the Gospels do not say that she was hysterical (Origen *Contra Celsum* 2.59-60). Celsus' attack on Christianity shows how clearly and firmly the role of the women as the first witnesses of Jesus' resurrection was in the Gospel tradition and early church. It may be worth noting how important this theme is to the history of the discussion of the significance of Jesus' relationship to women for the church. In what may be the first book published in English in defense of women's preaching, Margaret Fell refers to the role of Mary Magdalene in the title of her book: *Womens Speaking Justified, Proved and Allowed of by the Scriptures, . . . And how Women were the first that preached the Tidings of the Resurrection of Jesus, and were sent by Christ's Own Command, before He ascended to the Father, John 20.17* (London, 1666).

4.4. Women in Non-Canonical Gospel Traditions. Women are frequently presented as disciples and leaders, especially in resurrection narratives, in various non-canonical apocryphal (*see* Gospels [Apocryphal]) and gnostic Gospels (e.g., *Gos. Thom.* 21, 61, 114; *Dial. Sav.*; see the comments on Mary Magdalene in 5.6. below).

This data is a witness to the strength of the Gospel tradition of the involvement of women as disciples and proclaimers of Jesus. It may also suggest, according to some scholars, that in some second-century A.D. circles women had more options for involvement among gnostic groups than in the "orthodox" church, which was increasingly excluding women from leadership. This understanding is, however, debatable and fraught with problems of social-historical analysis.

5. Women Specifically Named.

In the Gospels seventeen women are specifically named (some of them may, however, actually be the same person; see especially 5.7, 5.10 and 5.11). The amount and character of information concerning them varies as does their relationship to Jesus. What follows is an alphabetical list of these women with the Gospel references and basic information provided.

5.1. Anna. Anna was a prophet mentioned only in Luke 2:36-38. She spoke in the Temple* of the infant Jesus to all who were waiting for the redemption of Jerusalem. She was the daughter of Phanuel of the tribe of Asher and a widow who spent most of her time in the Temple. It is not clear whether she was eighty-four at the time of the story or whether she had been a widow for eighty-four years (probably fourteen at marriage, plus seven years of marriage plus eighty-four years as a widow = one hundred five years of age, the age reached by Judith, a hero in Israel [Jdt 16:23]).

5.2. Elizabeth. Elizabeth, mentioned only in Luke 1,

was of priestly descent (*see* Priest and Priesthood) and the wife of the priest Zechariah, mother of John the Baptist and a relative of Mary the mother of Jesus. Elizabeth was filled with the Holy Spirit and greeted Mary as the mother of her Lord.*

5.3. Herodias. Herodias, noted in Mark 6:17-29; Matthew 14:3-12 and Luke 3:19-20, was the granddaughter of Herod the Great (*see* Herodian Dynasty), the daughter of Aristobulus, the wife of Herod (called Philip in the Gospels), the mother of Salome and the mother-in-law of Philip the tetrarch (Josephus *Ant.* 18.5.1 §§110-11, 136). She conspired to have Herod Antipas kill John the Baptist (Josephus *Ant.* 18.5.2 §§116-19).

5.4. Joanna. Joanna is mentioned in Luke 8:3 and 24:10 as one of the female disciples of Jesus who followed him in Galilee and to Jerusalem, where she is mentioned as one of the women who first received the message of Jesus' resurrection. She is identified as the wife of Chuza, a steward of Herod (Antipas), about whom nothing else is known.

5.5. Martha. Martha lived in Bethany and was the sister of Mary and Lazarus.* She is described in Luke 10:38-42 and in John 11:1-44 and 12:2. Martha, in contrast to Mary in both stories, was the one who prepared the meals for Jesus as a guest in their home. In the Lukan story Martha objects to Mary's involvement as a disciple of Jesus. In the Johannine story Martha makes a disciple's confession of Jesus as the Messiah, the Son of God (Jn 11:27; *see* Christ; Son of God).

5.6. Mary Magdalene. Mary Magdalene (from the Galilean town of Magdala; *see* Archeology and Geography) was a prominent disciple of Jesus who followed him in Galilee and to Jerusalem. She is always listed first in groups of named female disciples and was the first person to whom the resurrected Jesus made an appearance (Mt 27:56, 61; 28:1; Mk 15:40, 47; 16:1 [16:9]; Lk 8:2; 24:10; Jn 19:25; 20:1, 11, 16, 18). Her status is attested by the numerous references to her in early apocryphal and gnostic Christian literature (see Grassi; e.g., the Nag Hammadi *Gos. Phil.* 59, 6-9).

5.7. Mary the Mother of James [the Younger] and Joseph [Joses]. This Mary is mentioned as one of the female disciples of Jesus (Mt 27:56; Mk 15:40, 47; 16:1; Lk 24:10) who was among those who received the first message of Jesus' resurrection. She is probably to be identified with the "other Mary" of Matthew 27:61 and 28:1, based on the Markan and Lukan parallel texts (see 5.11. and also 5.10. below).

5.8. Mary the Mother of Jesus. Jesus' mother is mentioned by name in the Synoptic Gospels (Mt 1—2; 13:55; Mk 6:3; Lk 1—2). John refers to her as Jesus' mother without ever noting her name (Jn 2:1, 3, 5, 12; 6:42; 19:25-27). Mary is prominent in the birth narratives and functions as God's obedient servant (see Lk 1:42 "Blessed are you among women . . .") and as an interpreter of God's saving work (the *Magnificat* in Lk 1:46-55; *see* Mary's Song). Jesus' conversation with her in John 2 does not indicate disrespect, but rather shows John's emphasis on Jesus' own authority and responsibility for his mission and implies Mary's discipleship. Mary is understood as a disciple (see Jn 19:25-27; Acts 1:14).

5.9. Mary of Bethany. Mary was the sister of Martha and Lazarus and lived in Bethany (Lk 10:38-42; Jn 11:11-45; 12:1-8). She was a disciple of Jesus, commended by him for choosing the "better part" (see 3.2. above). She, according to the Johannine story, anointed Jesus' feet with costly perfume (the parallel stories in Mt 26:6-13 and Mk 14:3-9 do not name the woman; the story in Lk 7:36-50 is set in a different time and place). Jesus defends her act of devotion as an act of discipleship.

5.10. Mary the Wife of Clopas. This disciple of Jesus is mentioned only in John (Jn 19:25), along with Mary the mother of Jesus, her sister and Mary Magdalene at the cross of Jesus (*see* Death of Jesus). Due to the names in the parallel texts in Matthew 27:56 and Mark 15:40, there is some possibility that this Mary is to be identified with the Mary the mother of James and Joseph (see 5.7. above; see also 5.11. below).

5.11. The Other Mary. The "other Mary" is a designation which appears only in Matthew 27:61 and 28:1. She is one of Jesus' disciples at the cross and the resurrection. The parallel texts in Mark 15:47 and 16:1 and the data of Matthew 27:56 and Luke 24:10 suggest that the "other Mary" is probably to be identified with Mary the mother of James and Joseph (see 5.7. and also 5.10. above).

5.12. Rahab. Rahab is mentioned in the Matthean genealogy* of Jesus (1:5; see Josh 2 and 6). She was considered an important woman in the Jewish and early church traditions, as suggested here and attested in Hebrews 11:31 and James 2:25. She is one of four women mentioned in Matthew's genealogy (see 5.13., 5.16. and 5.17. below). All of these women are Gentiles; their mention here may signify God's mercy and point to the Gentile mission (cf. Mt 28:18-20). They may also point to Mary as indicative of God's choice of unexpected women in the history of salvation.

5.13. Ruth. Ruth is mentioned in the Matthean genealogy of Jesus (Mt 1:5; see 5.12. above).

5.14. Salome. Salome is mentioned in Mark 15:40 and 16:1 as one of Jesus' disciples at the cross and the resurrection. Due to the parallel to Mark 15:40 in

Matthew 27:56, it is possible that Salome is the wife of Zebedee and, thus, the mother of James and John, two of Jesus' twelve disciples.

5.15. Susanna. Susanna is one of Jesus' disciples mentioned only in Luke 8:3. Nothing else is known of her.

5.16. Tamar. Tamar is mentioned in the Matthean genealogy of Jesus (Mt 1:3; see Gen 38; Ruth 4; 1 Chron 2:4; see 5.12. above).

5.17. The Wife of Uriah. Uriah's wife, Bathsheba, is mentioned in the Matthean genealogy of Jesus (Mt 1:6; see 2 Sam 11; 12:24; 1 Chron 3:5; see 5.12. above).

6. Women in the Perspective of Each Gospel.

Another way of viewing the data on Jesus and women is to look at the individual approach of each of the four Gospels. Among the four, Luke evidences the greatest interest in material that relates to women in the life and ministry of Jesus.

6.1. Matthew. The Gospel of Matthew contains stories about the healing (Mt 8:14-15; 9:18-26) and faith (Mt 9:22; 15:21-22) of women, as well as stories in which women are involved which define the kingdom (Mt 13:33; 24:41; 25:1-13). Four Gentile women are included in the genealogy of Jesus (Mt 1:3, 5-6). The sexual integrity of women is upheld in the discussions of lust (Mt 5:27-30) and divorce (Mt 19:3-9), and the inclusion of sexually immoral women in the kingdom is noted for the preaching of both John the Baptist and Jesus (Mt 21:31-32).

The discipleship of women, including their involvement in proclamation, is noted both in a general saying of Jesus (Mt 12:49-50) and in the passion (*see* Death of Jesus) and resurrection narratives (Mt 27:55-56; 27:61—28:10).

Matthew is the only Gospel which tells the story (Mt 27:19) of Pilate's wife who, because of a dream, attempts to dissuade Pilate from being involved with Jesus (*see* Pontius Pilate).

6.2. Mark. The Gospel of Mark probably has the least amount of data about Jesus and women, yet Mark, with the rest of the Gospels, presents women as among the disciples of Jesus. Mark contains stories about the healing (Mk 1:29-31; 5:21-43) and faith (Mk 5:34; 7:24-30) of women.

The discipleship of women is noted in a general saying of Jesus (Mk 3:31-35), in the story of the widow who gave all her money (Mk 12:41-44) and in the passion and resurrection narratives (Mk 15:40-41; 15:47—16:8; see also 16:9-11).

6.3. Luke. The Gospel of Luke shows the greatest interest in women in the life and ministry of Jesus, including numerous accounts and stories about women unique to its presentation. Luke also gives the specific names of more women in Jesus' life than do the other Gospels. This interest is continued in Acts (for Jesus' female disciples see Acts 1:14).

Luke relates stories about the healing (Lk 4:38-39; 8:1-3, 40-56; 13:11-17; 17:11-17) and faith (Lk 4:26; 7:36-50; 8:48; 18:1-8; 21:1-4) of women, many of which are unique to Luke. Women are important in two parables unique to Luke (Lk 15:8-10; 18:1-8) and are mentioned in two stories about the kingdom of God (Lk 13:20-21; 17:35).

The place of women in discipleship is particularly stressed by Luke, both in general statements (Lk 8:19-21; 11:27-28), in the story of Mary and Martha (Lk 10:38-42) and in the reports of the female disciples who traveled with Jesus (Lk 8:1-3) and are described in the passion and resurrection narratives (Lk 23:49; 23:55—28:12). Again, some of these accounts are unique to Luke (Lk 8:1-3; 10:38-42; 11:27-28).

Woman are prominent as proclaimers in the infancy narratives (Elizabeth, Mary the mother of Jesus, Anna; Lk 1—2) and in the resurrection narratives (Lk 24:10-11, 22-24).

6.4. John. The Gospel of John portrays in particular the discipleship of the mother of Jesus (Jn 2:1-12; 19:25-27), the Samaritan woman (Jn 4:7-42), Mary and Martha (Jn 11:1-45; 12:1-8) and Mary Magdalene (Jn 19:25; 20:1-18). Both the Samaritan woman and Mary Magdalene are proclaimers of Jesus in John, and both receive extended attention in the Johannine narratives.

7. Conclusions and Significance.

Jesus' respect for and inclusion of women as disciples and proclaimers provided the foundation for the positive place of women in the earliest churches and their ministry.

In fact the baptismal formula reflected in Galatians 3:28 and its statement that in Christ "there is neither . . . male nor female" is probably rooted in the traditions of Jesus (see MacDonald). This indicates the formative role of Jesus in Paul's theological vision for the church's inclusive character.

The fact that there were no women among the Twelve is often cited as evidence that Jesus did not intend women to exercise leadership or authority in the church. However, it would not have been culturally possible to have included women in that most intimate group of Jesus' followers. It is remarkable and significant enough that many women, at least eight of whom are known by name and often with as much or more data as some of the Twelve, were included as disciples and proclaimers during Jesus'

ministry (not to mention Elizabeth and Anna in Luke 1—2). It has often been observed that all of the Twelve were Jews, yet the early church, as it developed in other social contexts, included Gentiles in leadership. Thus, the precise composition of the Twelve should not be pressed too far.

More significant is the fact that the Twelve did not constitute or provide the model or framework for leadership or authority in the early church, apart from the very earliest days in the Jerusalem church. Rather, what was significant for the character of leadership in the early church was Jesus' call to discipleship and its definition in terms of service and the fact that both men and women were among Jesus' followers as disciples and proclaimers.

It sometimes is noted that Jesus did not appoint any women to office. Neither did Jesus appoint any men to office (apart from the case of Peter, and that did not determine church structure apart from initial leadership in the Jerusalem church). The structures of leadership and authority in the early churches, especially those of Paul, for which the best evidence is available, were somewhat fluid and unstructured. In such contexts women did exercise leadership and authority (twelve women are known by name among Paul's coworkers in ministry; see Rom 16:1-16; Phil 4:2-3; 1 Cor 1:11; Col 4:15; Acts 16:14-15, 40).

See also Birth of Jesus; Divorce; Mary's Song; Prostitute; Resurrection.

Bibliography. S. S. Bartchy, "Jesus, Power and Gender Roles," *TSFBul* 7.3 (1984) 2-4; R. E. Brown, "Roles of Women in the Fourth Gospel," *TS* 36 (1975) 688-99 [reprinted in *The Community of the Beloved Disciple* (New York: Paulist, 1979) 183-98]; E. S. Fiorenza, *In Memory of Her: A Feminist Theological Reconstruction of Christian Origins* (New York: Crossroad, 1983); K. Giles, "Jesus and Women," *Interchange* 19 (1976) 131-36; A. Gill, "Women Ministers in the Gospel of Mark," *AusBR* 35 (1987) 14-21; C. M. Grassi and J. A. Grassi, *Mary Magdalene and the Women in Jesus' Life* (Kansas City: Sheed & Ward, 1986); J. B. Hurley, *Man and Woman in Biblical Perspective* (Grand Rapids: Zondervan, 1981); W. Klassen, "The Role of Jesus in the Transformation of Feminine Consciousness," *JCSR* 7 (1980) 182-210; J. Kopas, "Jesus and Women: Luke's Gospel," *TToday* 43 (1986) 192-202; R. S. Kraemer, *Maenads, Martyrs, Matrons, Monastics: A Sourcebook on Women's Religions in the Greco-Roman World* (Philadelphia: Fortress, 1988); D. R. MacDonald, *There Is No Male and Female: The Fate of a Dominical Saying in Paul and Gnosticism* (HDR 20; Philadelphia: Fortress, 1987); C. Meyers, *Discovering Eve: Ancient Israelite Women in Context* (New York: Oxford University, 1988); G. R. Osborne, "Women in

Jesus' Ministry," *WTJ* 51 (1989) 259-91; L. Swidler, *Biblical Affirmations of Woman* (Philadelphia: Westminster, 1979); idem, *Women in Judaism: The Status of Women in Formative Judaism* (Metuchen: Scarecrow, 1976); R. A. Tucker and W. Liefeld, *Daughters of the Church: Women and Ministry from New Testament Times to the Present* (Grand Rapids: Zondervan, 1987); B. Witherington III, *Women in the Ministry of Jesus: A Study of Jesus' Attitudes to Women and Their Roles As Reflected in His Earthly Life* (SNTSMS 51; Cambridge: University Press, 1984).   D. M. Scholer

WORD. *See* LOGOS; WISDOM.

WORLD

The language of the Gospels provides us with no exact precedent for what we mean by "world," though *kosmos* comes close to doing this. The distinctiveness of the modern perception of the world constitutes a difficulty in the task of reconstructing ancient understandings of the world. Difficulty also arises because the Gospel writers did not give detailed accounts of their understandings of the world, though John comes closer to doing this than the Synoptics. When writing about the "world" in the Gospels gaps must be filled in on the basis of what we suppose the authors would have known. It is frequently suggested that the writers of the NT thought of the earth as a disk upon which the heavens rest like a dome and under which the waters of the deep also formed the sea. But from the time of Aristotle the Greeks understood the world to be a sphere (*Cael.* II:2.285a.32) and perceptive attempts were made to calculate the circumference of the earth. It is not safe to assume that knowledge of this sort was foreign to the Gospel writers. It could also be a mistake to interpret biblical imagery as scientific description rather than as poetic portrayal.

1. Terminology and Usage
2. Age
3. Earth
4. Inhabited World
5. World

1. Terminology and Usage.

The Gospel writers build on both Jewish- and Greek-language traditions when writing of the world. The Greeks provided the word *kosmos*, which has become a technical term in Western tradition. By the first century this word was used to convey a complex range of meaning. The dominant sense of an ordered system had applications to areas other than cosmology. They do not concern us here. The *kosmos* is sometimes understood as planet earth but also, in a wider sense, as the universe. In this latter sense it has the same meaning as the OT "heaven and earth" (Hebrew, *haššāmayim wᵉhā'areṣ*) meaning the creation. Writers closely dependent on the OT used this language instinctively even though *kosmos* had become part of the vocabulary of Greek-speaking Jews. But the translators of the Greek version of the OT (LXX) had no cause to use the term *kosmos* because the natural translation for the Hebrew of "heaven and earth" is *ouranos kai gē* and the OT has no single word which covers the same semantic area as *kosmos*. Consequently, it is only in the later books composed in Greek, such as Wisdom of Solomon (19 x), 2 Maccabees (5 x) and 4 Maccabees (4 x) that *kosmos* is used. The Synoptic Gospels show a preference for the use of *gē* rather than *kosmos*. Matthew uses *gē* forty-three times, Mark nineteen times and Luke twenty-five times compared with the use of *kosmos* eight times, three times and three times respectively. The reverse tendency is seen in John, where *kosmos* is used seventy-eight times and *gē* eleven times.

Two other expressions relate to what we mean by "world" and overlap the Greek use of *kosmos*. The first of these is *oikoumenē*, which is short for *oikoumenē gē* and was used in the LXX to translate the Hebrew *ṭēbēl*. In the poetic works of the OT *ṭēbēl* is frequently used in parallel with *ereṣ* ("earth"). By the time the Gospels were written *oikoumenē* had come to mean "the inhabited world," which was sometimes considered to be coterminus with the Roman Empire (*see* Rome). The second word is *aiōn*, which was used to translate the Hebrew *'ôlām*. Both the Hebrew and the Greek words have a reference to time but when used in the expression "this age" have substantially the same meaning as "this world."

2. Age (Gk *aiōn;* Heb *'ôlām*).

In the Synoptics the world is conceived as a temporal reality with beginning and end. Beyond that it is also a new world (a notion found also in Stoicism) which finds expression in the terms "this age" and "the age to come," expressions which are found on the lips of Jesus.

2.1. Mark. Jesus speaks of what awaits his disciples* in this and the coming age (Mk 10:30 par. Lk 18:30; cf Mt 19:29). In the phrase "this age" the word used is *kairos* while in "the coming age" it is *aiōn* (*see* Kingdom of God). Strangely (see 2.2. below), Matthew omits this reference to the two ages. Reference to "the cares of the age" (Mk 4:19 par. Mt 13:22; Luke has "cares") is to be understood in terms of "this age."

2.2. Matthew. Matthew has increased the references to the two ages by introducing these terms into a

Markan context from which they were absent (Mt 12:32 par. Mk 3:29 and Lk 3:10); by transforming the wording of "all things to be fulfilled" (*synteleisthai panta*, Mk 13:4, cf. Lk 21:7) to "the fulfillment (end) of the age" (*synteleias tou aiōnos*, Mt 24:3) and by introducing frequent references to "the end of the age" (Mt 13:39-40, 49; 28:20).

2.3. Luke. Jesus speaks of "the sons of this age" (*hoi huioi tou aiōnos toutou*), contrasting them with "the sons of light" (*see* Light) who also exist in the present time. The contrast suggests that "the sons of this age" are "the sons of darkness" and "the sons of light" are "the sons of the age to come" (16:8). In Luke 20:34-35 "the sons of this age" are contrasted with "those who are accounted worthy to attain to that age and the resurrection* from the dead." The two ages appear to be in sequence, present and future. Apparently, "the sons of light" (16:8) are those thought worthy to attain to "that age."

The language of the two ages, a feature of Jewish apocalyptic,* was probably characteristic of the teaching of Jesus, being found in Mark and the traditions peculiar to Matthew and Luke. Matthew, influenced by Jewish apocalyptic, has increased the use of this language. It is altogether absent from Q* and from John, though John's use of "this world" (*kosmos*) is formally similar but on closer inspection differs in meaning.

3. Earth (Gk *Gē;* Heb *'eres*).

Each of the four Gospels uses the word *earth* to mean "soil," a particular "land" and planet "earth," though the latter sense is rarely found in John. It is evident in the phrase "heaven and earth," in which the OT spoke of creation, an idiom familiar to Jesus and found in each of the Synoptics but not in John. Sayings which have reference only to the earth can be ambiguous because the word can mean "soil" and "land" as well as "planet earth."

3.1. Mark. Jesus asserts, "heaven and earth will pass away" (Mk 13:31 par. Mt 24:35 and Lk 21:33), a notion consistent with the language of the two ages. Jesus claims, "the Son of man has authority to forgive sins on earth" (Mk 2:10; Mt 9:6; Lk 5:24; *see* Forgiveness). The authenticity of this saying, along with the other Son of man sayings (*see* Son of Man), has been hotly debated. It asserts the universal authority of the Son of man on earth. Two other uses of "earth" by Mark (4:31; 9:3) are omitted by Matthew and Luke, though they make use of the parable* of the mustard seed and the narrative of the Transfiguration* from Mark. The mustard seed is described as the smallest of seeds on earth, and Jesus' clothing is described as whiter

than any fuller on earth could achieve. Both could be considered as Markan editorial comments. In Mark the finite character of the creation and the universal nature of Jesus' authority* are affirmed.

3.2. Q Material. Jesus asserts "heaven and earth shall pass away" (Mt 5:18 par. Lk 16:17). He says, "I thank you, Father, Lord of heaven and earth" (Mt 11:25 par. Lk 10:21), affirming God's* lordship over all creation. Referring to his own mission Jesus says, "Do not suppose that I came to bring peace on earth" (Mt 10:34 par. Lk 12:51); and contrasting the response to his word he tells his hearers that "the queen of the South came from the ends of the earth to hear the wisdom of Solomon" (Mt 12:42 par. Lk 11:31). Matthew appears to have added reference to "the heart of the earth" in a Q context (Mt 12:40 par. Lk 11:30) and may have omitted it from another (Mt 16:3 par. Lk 12:56), though it is more likely that Luke has added it along with the reference to "hypocrites," which Matthew is not likely to have omitted. As in Mark the finite character of the creation is clear. God's lordship over creation is affirmed and Jesus' mission is further clarified in terms of conflict with the world.

3.3. Matthew. Jesus promised the meek that they would inherit the earth (Mt 5:5), meaning either the promised land or the world (*see* Sermon on the Mount). He tells the disciples, "You are the salt of the earth" (Mt 5:13), a Matthean saying combined with Markan material (Mk 9:50). He forbids swearing by heaven or earth (5:34-35) and teaches the disciples to pray, "Let your will be done, as in heaven so on earth" (6:10), which may be a Matthean interpretation of the petition (found also in Lk 11:2), "Let your kingdom come." He admonishes, "Do not store up treasures on earth" (Mt 6:19). The relative value of earthly possessions is a dominant theme in Luke. Distinctive to Matthew are the sayings to Peter (16:19) and the disciples (18:18) about binding and loosing on earth with apparent consequent effects in heaven. The closest parallel in meaning—though not in language—is found in John 20:23, which is expressed in terms of forgiving sins. The thought of the influence of earth on heaven* is continued where Jesus says that the agreed request of two disciples on earth will be granted by "my Father in heaven" (18:19). In the idiom of apocalyptic Jesus speaks of "the kings of the earth" (17:25) and "the tribes of the earth" (24:5), which appears to be Matthean redaction introduced into a Markan context (Mk 13:2 par. Lk 21:27). Finally, Jesus asserts, "All authority in heaven and earth has been given to me" (28:18) and commissions his disciples to continue his mission, promising to be with them until the end of the age (28:20). While the relative value of the created order is maintained, salvation* is increasingly interpreted in terms of this world. The lordship ascribed by Jesus to his Father in Q is claimed by him in Matthew, and indeed his authority is extended to his disciples as they carry on his mission to the world.

3.4. Luke. At the birth of Jesus the angels announce "peace on earth" (2:14; *see* Birth of Jesus), a view of Jesus' mission apparently in conflict with the Q saying of Jesus, "Do not suppose that I came to bring peace on earth" (Mt 10:34 par. Lk 12:51). Consistent with the Q saying, Luke's "I came to cast fire on earth" (Lk 12:49) could be a part of Q not used by Matthew. Jesus asks, "When the Son of man comes, will he find faith on earth?" (18:8), and in the Markan context of the apocalyptic discourse Jesus in Luke refers to distress (*anagkē*) on earth (Lk 21:23; see Mk 13:19) and anxiety (*synochē*) of the nations on earth (Lk 21:25; see Mk 13:25) and warns that "that day will come suddenly upon all who dwell on the face of all the earth" (Lk 21:35; see Mk 13:33-34 and Lk 21:36; *see* Apocalyptic Teaching). Luke may reduce the political scandal of Jesus' life, but the crisis of his mission remains clear, and the apocalyptic expectation of the end of the age is undiminished.

3.5. John. References to planet earth are few because John has favored the use of *kosmos*. In John 3:31 there are three references to being "of the earth" (*ek tēs gēs*), the equivalent of being "from below" (*katō*) as opposed to "from above" (*anō*). In John 12:32 "lifted up from the ground" (cf. Jn 3:14) is intended to have overtones of leaving the world (cf. Jn 3:13). Jesus, the Son of man, is exalted from earth to heaven by way of the cross upon which he is lifted up from the earth. Finally, Jesus asserts, "I glorified you (the Father) upon earth" (17:4). While the antithesis between heaven and earth is strong in John, the mission of the heavenly emissary is carried out on earth for the sake of those on earth.

4. Inhabited World (Gk *oikoumenē;* Heb *ṭēbēl*).

Oikoumenē is used only fifteen times in the NT of which Luke is responsible for eight (five in Acts and three in the Gospel). It is used once in Matthew 24:14 in the context of the Markan apocalyptic discourse to assert that before the end comes this gospel of the kingdom must first be preached in the whole inhabited world. Here Matthew's use of *oikoumenē* is an interpretation of Mark's "all the nations" (*ta ethnē*, Mk 13:10). In the Q account of the temptation narrative (*see* Temptation of Jesus), where Jesus is shown all the kingdoms of the world, Luke's use of *oikoumenē* (4:5) is probably redactional, being more appropriate to the

political sense than Matthew's *kosmos* (4:8). Luke 2:1 refers to the decree to tax "the whole world," in other words, "the entire Roman empire." Luke has also probably introduced *oikoumenē* into the Markan apocalyptic discourse when Jesus warns of people fainting with fear and foreboding of what is coming on the inhabited world (Lk 21:26). Thus this and the other use of *oikoumenē* by Jesus (Mt 24:14) are probably due to the redaction of Matthew and Luke.

5. World (Gk *kosmos*).

Thus far there has been little discussion of John's view of the world. This now changes because the Gospel and first letter of John provide more than half of the uses of *kosmos* in the NT. Only Paul in 1 Corinthians comes even close to this frequency of use. Paul uses *kosmos* forty-seven times, of which twenty-one uses occur in 1 Corinthians.

Jesus asks the value of gaining the whole world and losing life* itself (Mk 8:36 par. Mt 16:26 and Lk 9:25). This relative value of possessions was an important emphasis in the teaching of Jesus (*see* Rich and Poor). Jesus says that wherever the gospel* is preached in the whole world the details of his anointing* will be spoken of (Mk 14:9 par. Mt 26:13). This notion of the gospel being preached universally was introduced by Mark or the tradition that came to him as is suggested by the use of the word *gospel* (*euangelion*). In the longer ending of Mark (16:15) Jesus commissioned the disciples to "go into all world (*kosmos*) and proclaim the gospel to the whole creation" (*ktisis*). This text has no strong claim to contain authentic Markan tradition, let alone genuine sayings of Jesus.

5.1. Foundation of the World (*katabolēs tou kosmou*); ***Beginning of the World*** (*archē tou kosmou*). Jesus spoke of "the blood of all the prophets shed from the foundation of the world" (Lk 11:50; cf. Mt 23:35). Into the Markan framework of the explanation of parables (Mk 4:33-34), Matthew has inserted as his commentary Psalm 78:2, "I will open my mouth in parables, I will utter what has been hidden since the foundation of the world." John's christology is expressed when Jesus asserts the Father's love for him "before the foundation of the world" (Jn 17:24 and cf. Jn 17:5). In the parable of the great judgment* the king tells those on his right hand, "inherit the kingdom prepared for you from the foundation of the world" (Mt 25:34). The beginning of the world (*archē tou kosmou*) has the same meaning (Mt 24:21). The Markan parallel has "from the beginning of the creation" (*ap' archēs ktiseōs*, 13:19). The same phrase is used by Jesus in his discussion of marriage and divorce (*see* Marriage and Divorce), arguing that "from the beginning of creation

God made them male and female" (Mk 10:6). In this way the idea of the creation by God was clearly expressed in the teaching of Jesus and finds expression in each of the Gospels.

5.2. The World of Humanity. The nations of the world (*ta ethnē tou kosmou*, Lk 12:30; *see* Gentiles) and the kingdoms of the world (*hai basileiai tou kosmou*, Mt 4:8), like the references to the kings of the earth and the tribes of the earth (Mt 17:25; 24:30), refer to the world of humanity and might have used the term *oikoumenē*. The disciples are told by Jesus, "You are the salt of the earth" (Mt 5:13), a saying which stands beside "You are the light of the world" (Mt 5:14). In Hebrew this parallelism might have been expressed using *ereṣ* and *ṭēbēl*. John may have developed the discipleship* saying in a christological direction when Jesus claims, "I am the light of the world (*kosmou*)" (Jn 8:12; 9:5). In the parable of the tares it is explained that the field is the world (Mt 13:38). Woe is pronounced on the world of humanity (Mt 18:7). This reminds us that this world, though the creation of God, is dominated by the demonic (*see* Demon, Devil, Satan). That the world is under the power of evil and needs to be liberated by God is part of the apocalyptic world-view which dominates the Synoptics, especially Mark. Jesus' role in inaugurating the kingdom of God is expressed in exorcisms. They are evidence that the present world ruler has been overthrown and that the kingdom of God is already dawning (Mk 3:20-30; Mt 12:2 par. Lk 11:20).

5.3. John. John's prolog (Jn 1:1-18) provides a detailed reinterpretation of the Genesis creation story. A Jewish understanding of creation is daringly reinterpreted in the light of faith in Jesus as the savior of the world. Here the *kosmos* is first the universe, the totality of the creation. The word is used four times in the prolog, but the most emphatic statement occurs in verse 3, "All things (*panta*) were made (*egeneto*) by him and without him was not anything made that was made." Speaking of the creation in terms of "the all" may owe something to the influence of Platonism, though precedent can also be found in Jewish tradition. What is distinctive about the prolog is that the mediating role of the *logos** in creation is identified with the figure of Jesus.

The form and content of the prolog raise questions about its milieu. R. Bultmann argued that this is to be found in the syncretistic Jewish baptist movement influenced by gnosis. Certainly, the view of the world in John's Gospel, amongst other matters, sets it apart from the Synoptics (*see* Synoptics and John). Like the writings of Philo, John shares a concentrated use of *kosmos*, which signals a form of Hellenistic influence

scarcely to be found in the Synoptics. Concentrated use of *kosmos* is matched by the distinctly dualistic framework in which it is set with references to "this world" (planet earth) and "the judgment of the prince of this world" (12:31; 14:30; 16:11). This world is not contrasted with some future world. Rather, the world below is contrasted with the world above, the world of darkness with the world of light. This world, though created by the *logos*, is ruled by the prince of this world. In John only Jesus is accused of demon possession; there are no exorcisms. Nevertheless, Jesus' struggle with the prince of this world is a central feature, further accentuated by the antithesis of light and darkness dominating the Gospel.

Jesus, the emissary from above, has come into this world (1:9-10; 3:16-17, 19; 6:14; 10:36; 11:27; 12:46; 16:28; 17:18, 21, 23; 18:37). His mission was an expression of God's love* for the world (3:16). This world is dominated by darkness and the prince of this world. The world in view is humanity. The coming of the emissary was to save, not to condemn the world (3:17; 4:42; 6:33, 51; 12:47), but condemnation is inevitable where the saving mission is rejected (9:39). The coming of the emissary is expressed in terms of the coming of the light into the world as the light of the world (3:19; 8:12; 9:5; 12:46). The light does not belong to the world (8:23; 17:16; 18:36) but has come to reveal the Father and his love for the world (14:31; 17:21, 23-24). His coming was to bring life to the world (6:33) by giving his life for the world (1:29; 6:51). Having entered the world and completed his mission, the emissary departs from it (13:1; 14:19; 16:28), having commissioned his disciples to continue his mission to the world (17:21, 23). Those who are called out from the world (by the emissary) and no longer belong to it (15:19; 17:6, 11, 14, 16) are consequently hated by it, as the emissary himself was hated (15:18-19; 17:14). The mission was made possible by the coming of the Paraclete/Spirit of Truth (*see* Holy Spirit) to expose the world to the truth revealed by the light (3:19-21; 16:8). Yet the world does not recognize the Spirit just as it did not recognize the emissary. It knows only the mission of Jesus and those who continue his mission. Only those who believe perceive the light of the world which has the power to transform those who belong to the world so that their lives are shaped by the light from above.

In John the focus moves from the world perceived as creation to the world of humanity dominated by the darkness of false loves, false values, false knowledge and to the mission to save the world. Much of this interpretation of the world is given in the words of the narrator (1:9-10; 3:16-17, 19) or other characters such as John the Baptist* (1:29), the Samaritans* (4:42) and the crowd (6:14; *see* People, Crowd) in addition to Jesus himself. Jesus, narrator and believing witnesses (*see* Witness) present a consistent view of the world, its predicament and its salvation.

See also HEAVEN.

BIBLIOGRAPHY. R. Bultmann, *Theology of the New Testament,* (London: SCM, 1951, 1955); idem, "The Understanding of Man and the World in the New Testament and in the Greek World," in *Essays Philosophical and Theological* (London: SCM, 1955) 67-89; C. H. Dodd, *The Interpretation of the Fourth Gospel* (Cambridge: University Press, 1953); G. Gloege, "Welt"; J. Klein, "Weltanschauung"; E. Dinkler and H.-H. Schrey, "Weltbild," RGG³ VI.1595-1629; G. Johnston, "*Oikoumene* and *kosmos* in the New Testament," *NTS* 10 (1963-64) 352ff.; O. Michel, "ἡ οἰκουμένη," *TDNT* V.157-59; R. Schnackenburg, *Christian Existence in the New Testament* (Notre Dame: University Press) I (1968) 190-228 and II (1969) 184-229; H. Sasse, "αἰων, αἰώνιος," *TDNT* I.197-209; idem, "γῆ, ἐπίγειος," *TDNT* I.677-81; idem, "κόσμος," *TDNT* III.868-95.

J. Painter

WORSHIP

The Gospels do not speak often of worship. The various Greek terms which might be considered its equivalents (*latreia, leitourgia, proskynēsis,* etc.) and the many technical terms connected with worship do not frequently appear in them. Moreover, many references to worship occur almost in passing; the time and place of a healing* miracle,* the Sabbath* in a synagogue,* for example, might be given. While the references to worship are often incidental, however, worship itself is by no means peripheral. It is there in the Gospels in much the same way as the air that Jesus and the disciples* breathed. It is so omnipresent that it is more assumed than mentioned.

One may speak of worship in the Gospels in two ways, of the worship practices of Jesus and the disciples and what one may infer about the worship practices of the early Christian churches in which the Gospels themselves were composed. The Gospels are not as directly informative about these last matters as the Acts of the Apostles or the various epistles, but can nevertheless make a useful contribution to our knowledge of Christian worship in the NT era. This article will discuss those two areas and also the theory that the Gospels were shaped according to the lectionary of OT readings in use in that period.

1. The Worship of Jesus and the Disciples
2. The Worship of the Early Church
3. The Gospels and Jewish Lectionaries

1. The Worship of Jesus and the Disciples.

Jesus and his disciples were, of course, Jewish. As such he (and they) took part in the religious life of the Jewish people (*see* Judaism). It is a reasonable assumption that the religious practices of his people were acceptable to Jesus except for those cases in which the Gospels record an attack against them.

There were three great foci of Jewish worship in the period, the home, the synagogue and the Temple.* Of the first the Gospels speak very little. We know it was Jesus' custom, as with all pious Jews, to bless God* before sharing bread* (God rather than "bread" should be supplied as the object of the verb "bless" in such cases). The Synoptic Gospels also describe the Last Supper* as a Passover meal (*see* Feasts), implying that Jesus shared the practices of the Jewish home in this respect also. It was also his custom to pray, usually in private. He also commended to his disciples the practice of private prayer* (Mt 6:6). It is especially noteworthy that in his prayers all four Gospels report that Jesus addressed God as "Father" (probably the Aramaic '*Abbā'*). Sometimes the simple address "Father" appears; sometimes a qualifying term expressing the transcendence of God is linked with it. Beyond this, little can be said.

It is also clear that Jesus shared in the corporate worship life of Israel in the synagogues of Galilee.* Jesus' word concerning private prayer (Mt 6:6) should not be interpreted as criticism of corporate worship; the focus is on hypocrisy (*see* Hypocrite) and ostentation. It is in the synagogue that Jesus habitually teaches and preaches. He is apparently a welcome guest at the assemblies of his native province. Only in Luke 4:16-30, Luke's account of the rejection at Nazareth, is there any description, even in passing, of the synagogue service itself. There Jesus is invited to read the lesson, apparently a perfectly normal procedure, in itself not at all surprising. Only the subsequent interpretation of the reading of Isaiah 61 provokes outrage.

During the time of Jesus synagogue services were held three or perhaps four times on the Sabbath. The normal pattern of the synagogue service appears to have included the recital of the *Shema,* a combination of Deuteronomy 6:4-9; 11:13-21 and Numbers 15:37-41, the *Tephillah,* also known as the *Amidah,* or the *Shemoneh Esreh,* a lengthy and elaborate corporate prayer, and the reading and interpretation of Scripture, perhaps on the basis of a lectionary. There is no comment about these matters in any of the Gospels. The worship of the early church tended to carry on the worship practices of the synagogue. While that affinity is chiefly the result of factors other than Jesus' own precept and example, it is hard to imagine the early church carrying on a form of worship so reminiscent of the synagogue if Jesus himself had condemned such worship. In this instance the argument from silence seems compelling.

With respect to the Temple the picture is more complex. The Temple is held in esteem by the Synoptic Gospels, especially by Luke, who places much of his infancy narratives (see Birth of Jesus) and much of the early portions of Acts within its precincts. It is rightly a house of prayer (Mk 11:17 and par.) and, inasmuch as prayer was indeed a regular part of the Temple liturgy, it could rightly be considered of value. It is worthy of note that Acts represents early Christians such as Peter and John (Acts 3:1-3) frequenting the Temple for prayer. Paul, at the urging of James, even involves himself indirectly with the sacrificial cult (Acts 22:17-26). Jesus is willing to pay the tax* which maintains it, although the willingness springs mainly from a desire to avoid unnecessary offense (Mt 17:24-27). In John also much of the action of the Gospel takes place within the Temple. It is the spiritual center of Judaism and "salvation* is of the Jews" (Jn 4:22). Yet it is not truly necessary for right worship. John asserts most vigorously that in the new age inaugurated by Jesus right worship is "in spirit and in truth" (Jn 4:23). Moreover, it will, after all, be destroyed with not one stone standing upon another (Lk 21:6). The clear implication is that the Temple is no longer essential (see Destruction of Jerusalem).

The chief difficulty here lies, it seems, in the Temple's reason for being, the sacrificial system itself. A consideration of a key pericope, the cleansing of the Temple, may be useful here (Mt 21:1-11; Mk 11:15-19; Lk 19:45-48; Jn 2:13-22; see Temple Cleansing). This heavily symbolic action may be more than a reaction to the excesses and the corruption involved in the system. The moneychangers, the animal sellers and of course the animals themselves are necessary if the system is to function at all. Driving them out may therefore symbolize a rejection of not only the corruption associated with the sale of sacrificial animals but also the sacrificial system itself. The Temple functions rightly not as place of sacrifice but as a "house of prayer" (Mk 11:17 and par.). The Temple is a convenient and appropriate place for worship but, inasmuch as the sacrificial system is no longer valid in the new age inaugurated by the life, death (see Death of Jesus) and resurrection* of Jesus Christ, it is not an essential place for worship of the God of Israel.*

Perhaps this last point is best symbolized by the rending of the veil of the Temple at the moment of Jesus' death on the cross (Mt 27:31; Mk 15:38; Lk 23:45). The old system with its limited and carefully regulated means of access to God has died. The Gospels and indeed the NT as a whole have a new and utterly different world view with respect to the relationship between God and humanity. The distinction between the sacred and the common is radically altered, not by the decrease of the realm of the holy as in modern secularization, but in the sacralization of that which had formerly been considered common (cf. Acts 10 and the Letter to the Hebrews). All human religious practices are diminished in significance because the new age is breaking into the world in Jesus Christ. Old practices are therefore necessary no longer; old ways of speaking about the worship of God no longer suffice (see Kingdom of God).

One's estimate of the accuracy of these various reports concerning the worship attitudes and practices of Jesus will be very much influenced by one's general attitude with respect to the historical reliability of the Gospels (see Gospels [Historical Reliability]). There is a considerable consistency between the reports about the attitudes and practices of Jesus on the one hand and those of the early church on the other. This would render these reports suspect in the eyes of a critic devoted to the criterion of dissimilarity (the principle that suggests one may safely accept as historical primarily those sayings or reports that are dissimilar from both the Jewish background of Jesus' time and from the teaching or practices of the later church; see Form Criticism). The application of the criterion seems out of place in this instance, however. While one may doubt the historicity of specific pericopes, there seems no reason to doubt the accuracy of the general picture of Jesus' practices and attitudes with respect to worship presented by the Gospels.

2. The Worship of the Early Church.
The Gospels also provide us with information concerning the worship of the early church or, to put it more precisely, with the early churches known by the Evangelists. It is important not to speak with excessive precision regarding the worship of the early church. The NT era is marked by a very considerable diversity in many areas of Christian life, including worship. Moreover, one may not safely read back into the first century practices and attitudes typical of the third century, an era concerning which our knowledge of worship practices is more extensive. Generalizations concerning worship in this period are both difficult and dangerous.

It is also reasonably clear that early Christian

worship owes much to Jewish worship, especially that of the synagogue. Recent scholarship is not, however, willing to speak about Jewish liturgical forms and practices in the NT era as precisely as did a previous generation.

With some caution, however, a few observations may be made with respect to early Christian worship. Some passages in the Gospels may come from the worship of the early church. The Gospels may, for example, provide several examples of early Christian praise. In the infancy narratives of the Gospel of Luke we find three magnificent psalms of praise, the songs of Mary (Lk 1:46-55; *see* Mary's Song), of Zechariah (1:68-79; *see* Zechariah's Song) and of Simeon (Lk 2:29-32; *see* Simeon's Song). These are identified by many scholars as hymns of the early Jewish-Christian church inserted by Luke to enrich his narrative. These hymns are so Jewish in their vocabulary and form that it is difficult to prove beyond reasonable doubt that they are in fact Christian. The Jewishness of these psalms suggests, as one might expect, that Jewish Christians, at least, continued to offer praise in much the same manner as they had always done.

One may recall at this point the manner in which the Evangelists speak so acceptingly of synagogues with little of the ambivalence one notices with respect to the Temple. The word *synagogue* is sometimes actually used to describe the assemblies of Christians (cf. Jas 2:2 and various extra-canonical sources). All this may tend to support, though it cannot prove, the contention that early Christian worship was in many ways a continuation of Jewish worship.

Luke's hymns are not the only examples of praise in the Gospel. The angelic (*see* Angels) acclamation of Luke 2:14 and the various forms of the human acclamation at Jesus' entry into Jerusalem (Mt 21:9 and par.; *see* Triumphal Entry) are other examples of the explosion of praise that seems to have accompanied the early years of Christianity. These ejaculations of praise, perhaps best labelled "victory shouts," are not dissimilar to certain fragments of praise in the Book of Revelation. Perhaps all these materials are clues to the kind of praise offered in the first years of Christianity.

The prolog to the Fourth Gospel (Jn 1:1-18) probably contains another early hymn. Scholars differ as to the exact extent of the original hymn embedded in these verses (at least the references to John the Baptist are interpolated by the Evangelist) but widely agree that a hymn is actually present. In this case praise overlaps with confession of faith. Communities define themselves by means of the praise they offer as well as by the doctrines they profess. This impressive hymn

may have functioned in precisely that manner for the community of the Beloved Disciple (*see* John, Gospel of).

With respect to prayer there also appears to be a continuity between material in the Gospels and the practice of the early church. The Lord's Prayer (*see* Prayer) was certainly used by early Christians. The *Didache,* an early Christian manual of instruction, provides a version of the Prayer almost identical to Matthew's, and enjoins repetition of the Prayer three times a day. This appears to be a continuation of the practice of pious Jews who recited the *Tephillah* three times daily. We know, likewise, that early Christians followed Jesus' example in addressing God as *"Abba,"* Father (Rom 8:15; Gal 4:6).

The accounts of the Last Supper (Mt 26:26-30; Mk 14:22-26; Lk 22:14-23; cf. 1 Cor 11:23-25; *see* Last Supper) reflect in their variety not only the events of the night before the crucifixion but also the eucharistic practices of the Evangelists' churches. For example, Mark and Matthew have separate prayers over both bread and cup, whereas in Luke and in Paul the two prayers were apparently combined into one prayer of thanksgiving, the pattern that has endured in the liturgies of later centuries. It also appears that the actual words of interpretation, "This is my body . . . ," were not part of the prayers themselves, as in many later liturgies, but were associated with the sharing of the elements themselves. The words are addressed to the disciples rather than to God (note the second-person-plural verb forms). Moreover, in each case the words for prayer (either *eucharisteō,* "to give thanks," or *eulogeō,* "to bless"; the two appear to be synonymous in this context) are aorist participles. This form, which normally indicates the action of the participle, precedes the action of the main verbs of the sentence.

3. The Gospels and Jewish Lectionaries.

Various scholars have advanced in different forms a remarkable theory that the Gospels were shaped and some of their pericopes created to meet the needs of Christian worship. The theory begins with the unchallenged observation that Christian churches appear to have continued the synagogue practice of reading and interpreting the Torah and the Prophets. It is then argued that the churches also observed the Jewish sacred calendar and followed a fixed Jewish lectionary. The Evangelists, it is affirmed, ordered the various pericopes of the Gospels not according to the life of the historical Jesus nor according to their own theological programs but according to the texts of the Law and Prophets of the hypothetical lectionary. So, to give but one example, the Emmaus road story of

Luke 24, in which the risen Christ eats with two unknowing disciples, corresponds to the hypothetical reading of Genesis 18—22 on the fourth Sabbath of the month of Nisan, chapters which include accounts of the Lord, under the form of three men, eating with both Abraham and the unknowing Lot. In some cases, it is alleged, the Evangelists created pericopes of the Gospels according to the rather elastic rules of midrash,* a Jewish method of interpretation of Scripture, to provide correspondences in the life of Christ to the prescribed readings of the day (*see* Old Testament in the Gospels).

The hypothesis is daring and far-ranging. In some cases most of the NT and large sections of the OT are explained according to this principle. The hypothesis has not met with wide approval, however. The exact shape of Jewish lectionaries of the period and the degree to which they were fixed is uncertain. The reconstructions employed are therefore highly speculative. When one comes to examine particular Gospel passages OT texts other than the supposed lectionary readings often seem to be more clearly connected with the passages in question. Some proponents ignore evidence accumulated over decades of pains-taking scholarship of sources underlying our Gospels and grant a degree of creativity to the Evangelists that few have found likely (*see* Form Criticism). In short the hypothesis is more ingenious than it is persuasive.

See also MARY'S SONG; PRAYER; SIMEON'S SONG; SYNAGOGUE; ZECHARIAH'S SONG.

BIBLIOGRAPHY. R. T. Beckwith, "The Daily and Weekly Worship of the Primitive Church in Relation to Its Jewish Antecedents," *EvQ* 56 (1984) 65-80, 139-58; P. F. Bradshaw, "The Search for the Origins of Christian Liturgy: Some Methodological Reflections," *StudLit* 17 (1987) 26-34; J. D. G. Dunn, *Unity and Diversity in the New Testament* (Philadelphia: Westminster, 1977) 124-49; idem, *Jesus and the Spirit* (Philadelphia: Westminster, 1979); M. D. Goulder, *The Evangelists' Calendar* (London: SPCK, 1978); F. Hahn, *The Worship of the Early Church* (Philadelphia: Fortress, 1973); I. H. Marshall, *Last Supper and Lord's Supper* (Grand Rapids: Eerdmanns, 1981); R. P. Martin, *Worship in the Early Church* (rev. ed.; Grand Rapids: Eerdmans, 1974); A. Millgram, *Jewish Worship* (Philadelphia: Jewish Publication Society of America, 1971); L. Morris, *The New Testament and the Jewish Lectionaries* (London: Tyndale, 1964). S. C. Farris

Z

ZACCHAEUS. *See* TAXES.

ZEALOTS. *See* REVOLUTIONARY MOVEMENTS.

ZECHARIAH'S SONG

The first two chapters of Luke's Gospel set forth the circumstances surrounding the birth of both Jesus (*see* Birth of Jesus) and John the Baptist (*see* John the Baptist). The account is carefully crafted in the form of a diptych to display both a parallelism between the two figures and the subordination of John to Jesus. Zechariah's song (Lk 1:68-79), also known as the *Benedictus,* is one of the most striking features of those segments of the infancy narratives which deal with John the Baptist.

The hymn functions in two ways, as a hymn praising God* (vv. 68-75 and perhaps 78-79) and as a prophecy (*see* Prophet and Prophecy) concerning the destiny and task of the infant John the Baptist (vv. 76-77). As such it parallels very closely Simeon's Song (Lk 2:29-32; *see* Simeon's Song) and Simeon's prophecy concerning the infant Jesus (Lk 2:34-35). In both cases pious aged men, representative of the best in Israel,* praise God upon the fulfillment of a promise and declare the future work of the special child in question. The pattern of Luke's concern is clear—promise, sign of fulfillment and praise—a pattern repeated with respect to both Mary's Song (*see* Mary's Song) and Simeon's Song.

The origin of the hymn is disputed. Some conservative scholars maintain that this and the other hymns of the infancy narratives were composed by the persons named in the narrative, in this case Zechariah. Others credit the hymn to Luke himself, believing that the Evangelist, like his Greek historian models, felt free to place appropriate speeches in the mouths of his characters. Still others believe that this hymn and the John the Baptist sections of the narrative originated in circles of disciples* who venerated John as the Messiah. The purpose of this part of the Gospel, according to this theory, would be to persuade those people to recognize Jesus as the true Messiah (*see*

Christ). Others believe that the hymn originated in an early Jewish-Christian community and was inserted by the Evangelist to enrich his narrative.

It does appear that the hymn praises God for the advent of a Messiah of David's line (*see* Son of David), "He has raised up a horn of salvation in the house of David his servant" (v. 69). Moreover, the *anatolē,* or "dayspring," of verse 78, a difficult word which contains within its range of meaning reference both to the sprouting up of a plant and the rising of a star, seems to refer to the "sprout" or "root" of David (Jer 23:5; cf. Zech 3:8; 6:12). The images are combined in Revelation 22:16 in which the exalted Christ declares, "I am the root and offspring of David, the bright morning star." The hymn seems an answer to those hopes later formalized in the fifteenth benediction of the great synagogue* prayer,* the eighteen benedictions (*šᵉmōneh 'eśrēh),* "Let the shoot of David speedily spring up and raise his horn in Your Salvation. . . . May you be blessed, O Lord, who lets the horn of salvation flourish." A reference to the coming of Jesus seems clearly indicated, making a Baptist origin unlikely.

The question of the original language of the hymn is also disputed. The favored options at present are Greek, whether by the Evangelist himself or a Jewish-Christian community or, on the other hand, Hebrew (*see* Languages of Palestine). There is likewise a dispute over the form and extent of the hymn. Among scholars one can find support for the position that the hymn is a unity as it stands at present, that the hymn concludes at verse 75, with verses 76-79 added at a later point, and that verses 76 and 77 are insertions by Luke into a freestanding hymn comprising the present verses 68-75 and 78-79.

In form the hymn resembles those hymns of praise that thank God for salvation accomplished. The introductory word of praise, "Blessed is . . . ," is a particularly common Jewish prayer and praise of the period. A striking parallel is the "Hymn of the Return" from Qumran (1QM 14), the hymn to be sung when God has given the faithful community its decisive victory over the power of evil. Perhaps those who first loved and used this hymn believed that the coming of Jesus Christ represented the ultimate victory of God in the long struggle against evil. The hymnic portions of this psalm, verses 68-75 and 78-79, are heavily influenced by the language of the OT, so much so as almost to be a mosaic of allusions (*see* Old Testament in the Gospels). The similarities in the prophecy concerning John the Baptist, verses 76-77, are, on the other hand, to the Synoptic description of the Baptist.

Zechariah's Song proclaims a vision of a God who has never forgotten the people, who has promised to Abraham* and to all the forebears a consummation of a worship-filled peace, untroubled by enemies and without fear. This people is apparently Israel; there is at this point no distinction between Christian and Jew. This long-promised time now has drawn near in the miraculous birth of the infant John and, still more definitively, in the advent of the one whose coming it will be the task of the adult John to proclaim. The hymn praises with an overflowing heart the "tender mercies of our God" (v. 78; *see* Mercy), whose will it is to "guide our feet into the way of peace" (v. 79; *see* Peace). As such the hymn is one of the most magnificent examples of the explosion of praise of God that surrounded the coming of Jesus Christ and is testimony to Luke's theology of the significance of the coming of Jesus Christ.

See also BIRTH OF JESUS; MARY'S SONG; SIMEON'S SONG.

BIBLIOGRAPHY. R. E. Brown, *The Birth of the Messiah* (Garden City, NY: Doubleday, 1977); idem, "Gospel Infancy Narrative Research from 1976 to 1986, Part II (Luke)," *CBQ* 48 (1986) 660-80; S. C. Farris, *The Hymns of Luke's Infancy Narratives* (JSNTSup 9; Sheffield: JSOT, 1985); W. Carter, "Zechariah and the Benedictus (Luke 1.68-79), Practising What He Preaches," *Bib* 69 (1988) 239-47; D. R. Jones, "The Background and Character of the Lukan Psalms," *JTS* 19 n.s. (1968) 19-50.   S. C. Farris

ZION. *See* MOUNTAIN WILDERNESS.

Gospel Reference Index

7:15 *637, 753*
7:15-23 *537, 553*
7:16-20 *215*
7:16-21 *414*
7:17-20 *220*
7:19 *214, 311*
7:20 *214*
7:21 *271, 308, 426, 427, 489, 536*
7:21-22 *211, 490*
7:21-23 *15, 52, 306, 409, 411, 414, 424, 537, 699, 743*
7:21-27 *413, 699*
7:22 *409, 489, 637*
7:23 *353, 581*
7:23-27 *414*
7:24 *699, 743*
7:24-27 *220, 353, 409, 410, 699*
7:26-29 *808*
7:28 *177, 479, 529, 586, 740, 790*
7:28-29 *53, 155, 183, 456, 774, 844*
7:29 *405, 535, 734*
8:1 *561, 666, 680*
8:1-4 *404*
8:1—9:34 *531*
8:1—9:35 *530*
8:1—11:1 *529*
8:1-13 *5*
8:2 *271, 303, 628*
8:3 *823*
8:4 *459*
8:5-12 *264*
8:5-13 *260, 262, 300, 316, 535, 537, 539, 548, 557, 628, 646, 789*
8:8 *481*
8:8-10 *201, 223*
8:8-12 *311*
8:10 *5, 7, 8, 201, 223, 357, 539*
8:10-11 *5, 301*
8:10-13 *224*
8:11 *4, 5, 308, 309, 426, 449, 559, 672, 800*
8:11-12 *45, 261, 262, 358, 427, 536, 538, 797, 873*
8:12 *5, 311, 410, 535, 536, 672*
8:13 *201, 223, 539, 553*
8:14-15 *881, 885*
8:14-17 *864*
8:15 *300, 792*
8:16 *300, 481, 553, 786*
8:16-17 *534*
8:17 *157, 303, 306, 553, 585, 638, 746, 790*
8:18-21 *177, 183, 187*
8:18-22 *187, 213, 539*
8:18-27 *227*
8:19 *178, 405, 534, 734, 735, 807*
8:19-20 *734*
8:20 *44, 243, 308, 704, 735, 777, 779, 780*
8:21 *178, 182, 734*
8:21-22 *249, 539, 734*

8:22-26 *553*
8:23 *182, 459*
8:23-27 *539*
8:24 *37, 680*
8:25 *182, 720, 807*
8:26 *224, 295, 628*
8:28 *45, 164, 296, 553, 857*
8:28-34 *40, 302*
8:29 *169, 272, 311*
8:31 *164*
8:32 *825, 869*
9:1 *39, 808*
9:1-2 *789*
9:1-8 *302, 303, 539*
9:1-17 *262*
9:2 *539, 721*
9:2-8 *539*
9:3 *405*
9:5 *721*
9:6 *535, 721, 777*
9:8 *269, 535, 553*
9:9 *32, 187*
9:9-10 *672*
9:9-11 *672*
9:9-13 *187, 528, 529, 539, 672, 797*
9:10 *580, 758*
9:10-11 *124*
9:10-13 *404, 452, 539, 798, 856*
9:11 *534, 672, 734, 758*
9:12 *672*
9:12-13 *385*
9:13 *130, 413, 414, 452, 453, 539, 543, 580, 670, 671, 672, 758*
9:13-41 *304*
9:14 *233*
9:14-15 *825, 873*
9:14-17 *404, 537*
9:15 *87, 88, 234*
9:17 *870, 871*
9:18 *680*
9:18-19 *677*
9:18-26 *295, 553, 789, 881, 885*
9:19 *182*
9:20 *451*
9:21 *720*
9:22 *539, 553, 882, 885*
9:23 *643, 782*
9:23-25 *177*
9:23-26 *677*
9:27 *182, 255, 542, 769, 857*
9:27-31 *39, 45, 300, 303, 553*
9:27-34 *856*
9:28-29 *539*
9:29 *553*
9:32 *33, 306*
9:32-34 *165, 168, 169, 534, 553*
9:33 *357*
9:34 *164, 166, 553*
9:35 *253, 283, 286, 301, 303, 424, 531, 534, 537*
9:35—10:15 *183*
9:35-38 *177, 183, 554*
9:36 *542, 751*

9:36—11:1 *530, 531*
10:1 *52, 182, 535*
10:1-2 *187*
10:1-4 *32*
10:1-10 *305*
10:1-15 *178*
10:1-42 *31, 865*
10:5 *538, 681*
10:5-6 *31, 44, 45, 260, 262, 303, 316, 535*
10:5-7 *511, 512*
10:5-8 *32, 427, 539*
10:5-15 *185, 188*
10:6 *357, 358, 681*
10:6-7 *706*
10:7 *628*
10:7-8 *31, 52, 346, 536*
10:9-10 *83*
10:10 *544*
10:11 *204*
10:13-15 *262, 538*
10:15 *8*
10:16 *32, 754, 809*
10:16-25 *188*
10:17 *183*
10:17-25 *530*
10:18 *262, 537, 538*
10:19-20 *347, 877*
10:20 *129*
10:21 *101*
10:21-22 *539*
10:21-23 *227*
10:22 *720, 722*
10:23 *7, 357, 512, 632, 777*
10:24 *534*
10:24-25 *178, 188, 227, 534, 539, 807*
10:25 *164, 534, 779*
10:26-33 *472, 530, 539*
10:28 *51, 214, 310, 311, 316, 409, 676*
10:29-31 *809*
10:29-32 *273*
10:32 *308, 665, 774, 776, 779*
10:32-33 *10, 309, 409, 538, 777, 878*
10:34 *549, 888, 889*
10:34-36 *467, 530*
10:34-39 *227, 539, 671*
10:35 *86*
10:37 *101, 295*
10:37-38 *792*
10:37-39 *188, 530*
10:38-39 *645*
10:40 *29, 30, 31*
10:40-42 *540*
10:41 *413, 415, 642*
10:42 *7, 109, 178, 182, 749*
11:1 *479, 529, 586, 790*
11:1-4 *82*
11:1-6 *305*
11:1—12:50 *534*
11:1-19 *155*
11:2 *533*
11:2-3 *36, 387*
11:2-6 *29, 30, 168, 286, 388, 534, 537, 628, 649, 856, 859*
11:2—12:50 *531*

11:2—13:53 *529*
11:2-19 *875*
11:2—20:34 *531*
11:3-4 *463*
11:4-5 *303*
11:4-6 *301, 556, 557*
11:5 *286, 553, 758*
11:7-11 *388*
11:7-19 *262*
11:8-9 *639*
11:9 *639*
11:10 *8, 388, 528, 579, 581, 639*
11:11 *309, 384, 388, 426, 427, 536, 537, 575*
11:11-12 *536, 537*
11:12 *24, 388, 424, 426, 427, 535, 536, 537, 768*
11:12-13 *153, 388, 460, 585*
11:13 *451, 457*
11:14 *35, 204*
11:15 *82*
11:16 *78*
11:16-19 *101, 384, 409, 538, 797, 808, 874*
11:18 *384, 779, 822*
11:18-19 *671, 780, 797*
11:19 *124, 131, 388, 582, 672, 706, 758, 777, 874, 875*
11:20 *670*
11:20-24 *19, 39, 44, 52, 262, 300, 311, 362, 538, 670, 672*
11:21 *39, 670*
11:21-22 *80*
11:21-24 *253*
11:22 *80*
11:22-24 *671*
11:23 *310, 311, 581*
11:24 *80*
11:25 *301, 308, 395, 758, 888*
11:25-26 *808*
11:25-27 *273, 512, 537, 539, 774, 790, 875, 876*
11:25-30 *876*
11:27 *249, 347, 534, 681, 771*
11:28 *219, 758*
11:28-30 *512, 539, 646, 808*
11:29 *102, 540, 579, 582*
11:29-30 *546*
12:1-8 *188, 404, 454, 535*
12:1-14 *262, 303, 467, 718*
12:3-4 *452, 455*
12:5-6 *453*
12:5-7 *218, 719, 790, 856*
12:7 *130, 452, 539, 543, 580, 671*
12:8 *777*
12:9-14 *404, 452, 454, 718*
12:10-11 *719*

12:11 *581*
12:11-12 *131, 528, 718, 754*
12:12 *452, 453*
12:13 *298*
12:14 *846*
12:15 *182, 553*
12:15-21 *52, 262, 346, 359, 534, 537, 553, 746, 856, 864*
12:17 *638*
12:17-21 *157, 533, 585*
12:18 *57, 493*
12:18-21 *553*
12:21 *528*
12:22-24 *306, 553*
12:22-30 *171, 856*
12:22-45 *262*
12:23 *255, 769, 789*
12:24 *51, 164, 169, 534, 553*
12:24-29 *825*
12:26 *164, 169*
12:27 *51, 164, 165, 878*
12:27-28 *243*
12:28 *24, 30, 51, 166, 168, 169, 212, 249, 301, 340, 345, 421, 422, 423, 426, 534, 535, 536, 537, 550, 556, 558, 559, 576, 628, 671*
12:29 *166, 168, 169, 672*
12:31 *8, 777*
12:31-32 *75, 345, 641*
12:31-33 *780*
12:32 *75, 574, 777, 779, 888*
12:33 *874*
12:34 *511*
12:34-37 *578*
12:35-37 *676*
12:36 *409, 481, 671*
12:36-37 *409, 414, 878*
12:37 *409, 413, 414, 676*
12:38 *405, 534, 754, 807*
12:38-39 *553, 582*
12:38-40 *631*
12:38-41 *641, 672*
12:38-42 *262, 304, 306*
12:39 *8, 638, 754, 843*
12:39-41 *44, 99, 864*
12:39-42 *14, 672, 676*
12:40 *120, 582, 755, 777, 779, 888*
12:41 *409, 670, 864, 874*
12:41-42 *52, 582, 671, 754, 878, 880*
12:42 *409, 808, 864, 874, 888*
12:43-45 *167, 537, 565*
12:45 *164*
12:46—13:58 *785*
12:46-49 *188*
12:46-50 *187, 227, 228, 362, 537, 671, 883*
12:49 *182*
12:49-50 *885*
12:50 *271, 272, 273, 309, 774*
13:1 *45*
13:1-9 *532*

587, 799, 882, 884, 885, 886
10:39 *481, 489*
10:40 *748*
10:41 *489*
10:42 *882*
11:1 *184, 185*
11:1-4 *810*
11:1-13 *509*
11:2-4 *267*
11:4 *170, 826*
11:5-8 *432, 497, 505, 624*
11:9-10 *790*
11:9-13 *273, 624, 790*
11:11 *85, 829*
11:11-13 *347*
11:13 *85*
11:14 *165, 169, 170, 557*
11:14-23 *168, 170, 171, 769*
11:14-26 *507*
11:15 *164, 166*
11:15-19 *170*
11:16 *635, 754, 821, 826, 864*
11:17-23 *774*
11:18 *164, 826*
11:19 *164, 165, 878*
11:20 *19, 24, 51, 57, 166, 168, 207, 212, 218, 346, 412, 421, 422, 423, 426, 550, 556, 558, 559, 671, 890*
11:20-23 *504*
11:21-22 *166, 168, 672*
11:22 *207*
11:24-26 *167, 565*
11:26 *164*
11:27-28 *185, 883, 886*
11:28 *79, 82, 883*
11:29 *8, 754, 755*
11:29-30 *635*
11:29-32 *14, 261, 410, 504, 507, 631, 641, 670, 676, 864*
11:30 *755, 777, 779, 888*
11:31 *874, 888*
11:31-32 *207, 409, 506, 582, 671, 754, 878, 880*
11:32 *506, 670, 874*
11:33 *34, 472*
11:33-36 *472*
11:34-36 *82*
11:37 *683*
11:37—12:1 *404*
11:37-38 *130*
11:37-41 *404*
11:37-52 *220, 507*
11:39 *489*
11:39-52 *15, 353*
11:41 *130*
11:42 *219, 220, 404, 409, 453, 494, 838*
11:42-44 *80*
11:42-54 *80*
11:43 *80*
11:44 *220, 266*
11:45 *405, 504, 734*
11:46 *80, 220, 405, 860*

11:46-53 *80*
11:47-51 *159, 409, 503, 878*
11:48 *878*
11:49 *28, 94, 642, 874, 876*
11:49-51 *499, 502, 874, 875*
11:50 *94, 638*
11:50-51 *878*
11:51 *8, 94*
11:52 *405, 733*
11:53 *405*
11:53-54 *507*
11:54 *405*
12:1 *404, 507*
12:1-12 *507, 509, 878*
12:2-9 *472, 530*
12:3 *683*
12:4-5 *311*
12:4-9 *508*
12:4-12 *410*
12:5 *310*
12:6-8 *273*
12:8-9 *9, 10, 207, 309, 410, 421, 671, 777, 778, 878*
12:8-12 *76, 185*
12:10 *75, 777, 780*
12:10-12 *346*
12:11-12 *347, 878*
12:12 *838*
12:13 *504*
12:13-15 *432*
12:13-21 *185, 497, 509*
12:15 *469*
12:16 *507*
12:16-21 *244, 415, 432, 705*
12:18 *504*
12:19 *395*
12:20-22 *264*
12:21 *507*
12:22-23 *251*
12:22-31 *623, 707*
12:22-32 *273, 508*
12:22-34 *508*
12:23 *85, 264*
12:24 *273, 309, 544*
12:27 *269*
12:28 *224*
12:30 *309, 708, 890*
12:31 *413, 426, 428*
12:31-32 *213*
12:32 *123, 213, 216, 426, 671, 753*
12:32-33 *707*
12:32-34 *707*
12:33 *308, 415, 706*
12:33-34 *410*
12:35-40 *509*
12:35-48 *509*
12:36 *873*
12:36-49 *505*
12:37 *161, 489, 683*
12:39-46 *497*
12:40 *676, 777*
12:41-46 *311, 676*
12:42 *489*
12:42-46 *749*
12:43-44 *308*
12:44 *8, 860*

12:45 *209*
12:46 *224, 676*
12:49 *204, 661, 889*
12:49—14:24 *501, 507*
12:49-50 *631*
12:49-53 *19, 153, 207*
12:50 *58, 631*
12:51 *888, 889*
12:51-53 *228, 530, 671*
12:53 *86*
12:54-56 *243, 432*
12:56 *308, 353, 888*
12:57 *415*
12:57-59 *316, 458*
12:58-59 *878*
12:59 *8, 316*
13:1-2 *759*
13:1-3 *240, 253*
13:1-5 *260, 409, 670, 672*
13:1-9 *432, 501*
13:3 *50, 670*
13:5 *670*
13:5-37 *111*
13:6-9 *44, 207, 209, 263, 409, 505, 507, 554, 868*
13:7-9 *502*
13:10-12 *251*
13:10-15 *346*
13:10-17 *5, 6, 159, 171, 218, 300, 301, 306, 454, 460, 497, 506, 508, 554, 580, 719, 782, 783*
13:11 *170*
13:11-12 *303, 554*
13:11-17 *774, 881, 886*
13:13 *269, 274, 554, 555*
13:14 *838*
13:15 *554*
13:15-16 *353, 452*
13:16 *4, 5, 123, 164, 170, 218, 453, 455, 503, 826, 838*
13:17 *526*
13:18 *309, 426, 428*
13:18-21 *506*
13:19 *308*
13:20 *426, 428*
13:20-21 *882, 886*
13:22 *501*
13:22-30 *5, 185*
13:23 *723*
13:23-24 *380, 410*
13:23-30 *502, 504, 505, 506*
13:24 *44*
13:25-27 *410*
13:26 *449*
13:27-28 *5*
13:28 *4, 5, 311, 410, 426, 428, 638*
13:28-29 *5, 263, 264, 308, 358, 410, 797*
13:28-30 *6, 261*
13:29 *5, 6, 309, 426, 428, 449, 672, 683, 800*
13:29-30 *872*
13:31 *90*
13:31-32 *848*

13:31-33 *37, 253, 324, 640*
13:31-35 *15, 501, 502, 503, 857*
13:32 *166, 170, 556*
13:32-33 *502*
13:33 *44, 793, 838*
13:33-34 *159*
13:33-35 *630, 683*
13:34 *375, 875, 882*
13:34-35 *15, 44, 175, 409, 507, 790, 874, 875*
13:35 *363, 856, 876*
14:1 *683*
14:1-4 *507*
14:1-6 *218, 301, 454, 460, 497, 554, 580, 718, 735*
14:1-12 *505*
14:1-24 *244, 507*
14:2-6 *508*
14:3 *405*
14:4 *554*
14:7 *799*
14:7-11 *797, 799*
14:7-14 *583, 676, 872*
14:8-9 *683*
14:8-11 *676*
14:10 *269*
14:11 *583, 799*
14:12 *799*
14:12-14 *215, 676, 797*
14:13 *311, 506, 799*
14:14 *79, 215, 413, 415, 676, 707*
14:15 *78, 85, 426, 428, 799*
14:15-24 *228, 263, 497, 583, 587, 672, 797, 799, 873*
14:16-24 *308, 410, 502, 504, 505, 506, 872*
14:21 *311, 707*
14:21-24 *506*
14:23 *489, 799*
14:23-24 *185*
14:25 *799*
14:25-34 *505*
14:25-28 *187*
14:25-33 *185, 187*
14:25-35 *228, 501, 508*
14:26 *101, 184, 185, 249, 295, 792*
14:26-27 *103*
14:27 *185*
14:33 *185, 415, 671*
14:50-52 *267*
15:1 *404, 758, 799*
15:1-2 *506, 507, 672, 797, 798*
15:1-3 *751*
15:1-7 *497, 672*
15:1-10 *497*
15:1-32 *501, 505, 509*
15:2 *404, 405, 758*
15:2-32 *131*
15:3-7 *583, 587, 667, 751, 792*
15:4-7 *670*
15:4-10 *506*
15:4-32 *672*

15:5 *395*
15:5-7 *672*
15:6 *395*
15:6-7 *672*
15:7 *11, 50, 395, 413, 415, 670, 758*
15:8-10 *882, 886*
15:9-10 *672*
15:10 *11, 670, 672, 758*
15:11-32 *103, 243, 263, 432, 497, 583, 587*
15:13 *643*
15:17 *85*
15:17-20 *672*
15:17-21 *506, 508*
15:18 *308*
15:21 *308*
15:22-24 *672*
15:23 *395*
15:24 *395, 576*
15:25-30 *672*
15:28-30 *624*
15:29 *132, 395*
15:30 *195, 542, 643*
15:32 *395, 672, 838*
16:1-8 *497, 505, 583, 587*
16:1-9 *213*
16:1-15 *509*
16:1-31 *501*
16:8 *489*
16:10-13 *185*
16:11 *860*
16:13 *415, 494, 748, 790*
16:14 *198*
16:14-15 *507*
16:14-16 *185*
16:14-17 *198*
16:15 *415*
16:16 *198, 212, 283, 284, 286, 388, 390, 426, 451, 456, 458, 460, 503, 508, 638, 874*
16:16-17 *456*
16:16-18 *217*
16:17 *8, 218, 308, 457, 458, 460, 888*
16:18 *192, 193, 194, 196, 197, 198, 404, 455, 458*
16:19 *395*
16:19-25 *462*
16:19-26 *415*
16:19-31 *185, 245, 263, 307, 308, 311, 312, 410, 462, 497, 505, 506, 509, 676, 705, 755*
16:20-31 *462*
16:22 *11, 310*
16:22-30 *4*
16:23 *310*
16:23-24 *311*
16:24 *6, 55, 543*
16:25 *6*
16:25-26 *6*
16:26 *6*
16:26-31 *462*
16:27 *6*
16:27-31 *311*
16:29 *93, 451, 560, 638*

Subject Index

Abba *30, 156, 227, 265, 266, 268, 273, 275, 276, 299, 519, 617-620, 771, 772, 775, 848, 875, 893*

Abiathar *1, 717, 863*

Abide, abiding *2, 3, 57, 136, 186, 198, 225, 231, 297, 375, 381, 383, 396, 415, 583, 626, 638, 868*

Abomination of desolation *20-23, 26, 175, 510, 514, 581, 714*

Abraham *3-7, 5, 18, 65, 77, 96, 112, 123, 155, 165, 167, 168, 171, 204, 218, 228, 239, 254-256, 262, 266, 306, 355, 357, 377, 387, 395, 398, 428, 462, 506, 519, 526-538, 544, 569, 583, 617, 635, 638, 676, 703, 705, 706, 718, 755, 800, 821, 840, 857, 865, 881, 894, 896*

Abyss *311, 547*

Adam *4, 65, 66, 141, 230, 256, 291, 348, 500, 504, 591, 749, 774, 825, 826, 864*

Adultery *133, 155, 192-198, 219, 243, 256, 293, 319, 410, 424, 455, 456, 490, 580, 585, 588, 643, 666, 731, 742, 744, 759, 812, 828, 851, 881*

Advocate *238, 349, 350, 422, 861, 879, 880*

Aenon *35, 36, 387*

Agony *178, 694, 705, 841, 844*

Alexander (Herod's son) *320-322*

Alexander Jannaeus *141, 239, 402, 651, 853*

Alexander the Great *253, 312-314, 317, 393, 400, 439, 715, 726, 729, 806, 855*

Allegory *52, 87, 88, 126, 132, 244, 424, 476, 556, 591-594, 596, 598, 771, 817, 857, 862*

Alms, almsgiving *130, 202, 412-414, 459, 701, 703, 704, 707, 708, 740, 743, 748, 782*

Altar *23, 38, 41, 212, 239, 314, 448, 459, 546, 578, 580, 583, 727, 796, 811-814*

Amen *7, 8, 52, 75, 76, 346, 617, 640-642, 782, 809, 810, 860, 862*

Amoraic period *545, 848*

Andrew *97, 115, 166, 177-180, 253, 316, 522, 706, 744*

Angel of the Lord *8-11, 200, 273, 720*

Angels *4, 6, 8-11, 23, 25, 41, 49, 63, 68, 71, 102, 113, 141, 143, 164, 200, 256, 263, 266, 271, 273, 283, 288, 307, 308, 311, 343, 347, 365, 377, 395, 410, 415, 428, 447, 486, 502, 516, 535, 547, 549, 553, 554, 558, 566, 568, 575, 586, 588, 591, 605, 619, 675, 676, 678-682, 685, 693, 720, 721, 754, 758, 759, 770, 777, 815, 825, 826, 837, 838, 841, 845, 872, 877, 878, 881, 883, 889, 893*

Anger *241, 301, 302, 455, 507, 543, 562, 659, 669, 769, 816*

Anna *61-63, 90, 233, 290, 343, 639, 812, 883, 884, 886*

Annunciation *36, 64, 71, 290, 526, 558, 774, 783*

Anoint *11-13, 29, 53, 57, 89, 106, 107, 155, 159, 169, 184, 201, 302, 308, 375, 406, 407, 495, 500, 503, 524, 581, 583, 602, 640, 678, 679, 709, 798, 844, 855, 858, 885, 889*

Anointed, the *16, 26, 51, 66, 77, 106, 107, 117, 152, 213, 285, 339, 340, 378, 396-399, 433, 500, 518, 519, 546, 690, 746, 855*

Anthropology *59, 60, 148, 229, 234, 248, 251, 405, 570, 571, 708, 710, 760, 762, 765, 766*

Antigonus *202, 318, 319, 436, 855*

Antiochus *19, 23, 143, 238, 312, 314, 316, 352, 400, 401, 610, 690, 693-695, 710, 726, 729, 732, 858*

Antipas *35-37, 39, 121, 180, 196, 252, 253, 315-317, 320-326, 384, 386-388, 390, 393, 548, 606, 616, 712-714, 804, 834, 847, 848, 884*

Antipater *318, 320, 321, 323, 712*

Anti-Semitism *13, 14, 17, 264, 288, 353, 356, 358, 363, 371, 405, 507, 538, 541, 615, 616, 784, 854*

Antitheses *215, 217, 219, 455-460, 511, 561, 580, 585, 698, 740, 742, 763*

Antonia *42, 172, 174, 549, 812, 820, 845*

Anxiety *85, 228, 251, 313, 372, 405, 623, 652, 696, 697, 707, 848, 889*

Aphorisms *104-106, 217,*

246, 296, 649, 650, 700, 794, 874, 877

Apocalypse *6, 17-21, 25, 171, 208, 291, 329, 355, 419, 674, 814, 816*

Apocalyptic *10, 11, 15, 17-26, 43, 48, 75, 79, 94, 122, 143, 175, 178, 187, 200, 203, 206, 207, 209-211, 229, 243, 246, 248, 251, 254, 269, 291, 294, 307, 311, 329, 331, 334, 344, 348, 355, 361, 386, 397, 401, 408, 409, 411, 417, 418, 420-424, 426, 428-430, 432, 499, 514, 535-537, 558, 559, 561, 574, 581, 586, 602, 644, 649, 664, 676, 680, 681, 693, 698, 714, 733, 747, 749, 759, 776, 808, 813, 814, 816, 817, 820, 827, 832, 841, 855, 867, 872, 878, 880, 888-890*

Apocalypticism *17, 19, 20, 26, 420, 649, 698, 874*

Apocrypha *36, 41, 73-75, 88, 98, 100, 101, 104, 127, 132, 137, 138, 142, 246, 278, 282, 286, 289, 291, 293, 304, 309, 310, 315, 330, 368, 376, 389, 400, 436, 463, 594, 601, 602, 617, 704, 729, 884*

Apocryphal Gospels *74, 88, 98, 286, 291, 293, 463, 601, 602*

Apophthegms *244, 248*

Apostasy *76, 259, 398, 401, 725, 842*

Apostle *7, 27-33, 46, 48-50, 91, 95-98, 113, 123, 125, 177-181, 187, 188, 227, 247, 249, 259, 261, 263, 296, 306, 328, 330, 332, 362, 368, 369, 377, 384, 406, 408, 432, 449, 450, 481, 486, 488, 493, 495, 510, 527, 528, 550, 552, 591, 625, 626, 642, 682, 685, 751, 753, 812, 843, 865, 874, 878, 879, 891*

Aqedah (see Binding of Isaac) *803*

Aramaic *18, 28, 36, 38, 42, 43, 75, 76, 85, 115, 123, 124, 140, 142-144, 150, 168, 181, 191, 210, 237, 247, 253, 265, 273, 275, 276, 285, 289, 307, 310, 312, 315, 316, 378, 392, 404, 414, 417, 421, 431, 433, 435-444, 453, 457, 461, 482, 484-486, 491, 492, 515, 527, 528, 557, 579, 571-574, 594, 597, 618-620, 646, 654, 664,*

705, 713, 730, 742, 751, 757, 758, 768, 772, 775, 778, 780-782, 785, 787, 788, 800-804, 807-809, 833, 848, 870, 891

Archangel *141, 401*

Archelaus *118, 316, 317, 320-325, 463, 690, 712, 804, 855*

Aretalogy *190, 294, 552*

Aretas *318, 323, 324, 393*

Aristobulus *252, 318-321, 402, 884*

Arrest of Jesus *11, 17, 77, 91, 105, 120, 121, 148, 153, 154, 156, 160, 162, 177, 265, 268, 303, 355, 365, 393, 406, 408, 502, 509, 517, 518, 522, 524, 549, 581, 584, 585, 588, 601-603, 606, 635, 714, 731, 752, 758, 759, 776, 793, 816, 843-845, 854, 864, 878*

Ascension *4, 35, 44, 46-50, 97, 122, 181, 228, 263, 286, 288, 289, 291, 348, 350, 368, 373, 395, 497, 502, 505, 509, 549, 554, 555, 568, 681, 683, 684, 830, 838, 863, 879*

Asceticism *226, 233, 234, 313, 384, 392, 572, 573, 706*

Astral phenomena *66, 68, 72*

Atonement *44, 141, 143, 152, 158, 160, 162, 163, 233, 235, 237, 243, 306, 320, 335, 339, 351, 382, 396, 397, 425, 433, 448, 534, 540, 598, 634, 660, 661, 662, 745, 747, 806, 813*

Authority *1, 7, 8, 28, 31, 33, 50-53, 68, 73, 76, 93-100, 105, 109, 123, 125, 132, 136, 147, 148, 154, 156, 166, 168, 170, 173, 183, 190, 191, 201, 202, 209, 212, 214, 218, 221, 223, 224, 226-228, 230, 231, 241, 243, 247, 248, 250, 270, 272, 273, 279, 287, 289, 297, 301, 302, 305, 315, 329, 330, 336, 339, 341, 346, 354, 356, 372, 373, 375, 377, 378, 384, 389, 390, 398, 399, 402-404, 407, 427, 429, 450, 453-456, 459-462, 465, 466, 481, 485-489, 491, 500-505, 507, 509, 512, 520, 528, 529, 535, 536, 549, 552, 557, 559, 562, 564, 586, 589, 590, 598, 606, 614, 621, 626, 636, 637, 640-642, 651, 653, 654, 656, 657, 665, 667, 672, 676, 677, 679-681, 683, 686,*

Articles Index